THE NORTON ANTHOLOGY OF

ENGLISH

LITERATURE

THE MAJOR AUTHORS
NINTH EDITION

VOLUME 2

THE NORTON ANTHOLOGY OF

ENGLISH

LITERATURE

THE MAJOR AUTHORS
NINTH EDITION

Stephen Greenblatt, *General Editor*

COGAN UNIVERSITY PROFESSOR OF THE HUMANITIES

HARVARD UNIVERSITY

VOLUME 2

W · W · NORTON & COMPANY

NEW YORK · LONDON

W. W. Norton & Company has been independent since its founding in 1923, when William Warder Norton and Mary D. Herter Norton first published lectures delivered at the People's Institute, the adult education division of New York City's Cooper Union. The firm soon expanded its program beyond the Institute, publishing books by celebrated academics from America and abroad. By midcentury, the two major pillars of Norton's publishing program—trade books and college texts—were firmly established. In the 1950s, the Norton family transferred control of the company to its employees, and today—with a staff of four hundred and a comparable number of trade, college, and professional titles published each year—W. W. Norton & Company stands as the largest and oldest publishing house owned wholly by its employees.

Editor: Julia Reidhead
Associate Editor: Carly Fraser Doria
Managing Editor, College: Marian Johnson
Manuscript Editors: Susan Joseph, Jennifer Harris, Katharine Ings, Pam Lawson, and Jack Borrebach
Project Editor: Rachel Mayer
Electronic Media Editor: Eileen Connell
Editorial Assistant(s): Hannah Blaisdell, Jennifer Barnhardt
Marketing Manager, Literature: Kimberly Bowers
Production Manager: Sean Mintus
Photo Editor: Michael Fodera
Permissions Manager: Megan Jackson
Permissions Clearing: Nancy J. Rodwan
Text Design: Jo Anne Metsch
Art Director: Rubina Yeh
Composition: The Westchester Book Group
Manufacturing: R. R. Donnelley & Sons—Crawfordsville, IN

The text of this book is composed in Fairfield Medium with the display set in Aperto.

Since this page cannot legibly accommodate all the copyright notices, the Permissions Acknowledgments constitute an extension of the copyright page.

Library of Congress Cataloging-in-Publication Data has been applied for.

ISBN 978-0-393-91965-3

W. W. Norton & Company, Inc., 500 Fifth Avenue, New York, NY 10110-0017
wwnorton.com

W. W. Norton & Company Ltd., Castle House, 75/76 Wells Street, London W1T 3QT

5 6 7 8 9 0

Contents*

The Romantic Period (1785–1832)

* To explore the table of contents of the supplemental ebook, visit wwnorton.com/nael.

DOROTHY WORDSWORTH (1771–1855) 234

SAMUEL TAYLOR COLERIDGE (1772–1834) 250

GEORGE GORDON, LORD BYRON (1788–1824) 312

The Victorian Age (1830–1901)

The Twentieth Century and After

Preface to the Ninth Edition

A great anthology of English literature is a compact library for life. Its goal is to bring together works of enduring value and to make them accessible, comprehensible, and pleasurable to a wide range of readers. Its success depends on earning the reader's trust: trust in the wisdom of the choices, the accuracy of the texts, and the usefulness and good sense of the apparatus. It is not a place for the display of pedantry, the pushing of cherished theories, or the promotion of a narrow ideological agenda. If it succeeds, if it manages to give its readers access to many of the most remarkable works written in English during centuries of restless creative effort, then it furthers a worthwhile democratic cause, that of openness. What might have been a closed pleasure ground, jealously guarded as the preserve of a privileged elite, becomes open to all. Over fifty years and nine editions, *The Norton Anthology of English Literature* has served this important goal.

The works anthologized here generally form the core of courses that are designed to introduce students to English literature. The selections reach back to the earliest moments of literary creativity in English, when the language itself was still molten, and extend to some of the most recent experiments, when, once again, English seems remarkably fluid and open. That openness—a recurrent characteristic of a language that has never been officially regulated and that has constantly renewed itself—helps to account for the sense of freshness that characterizes the works brought together here.

One of the joys of literature in English is its spectacular abundance. Even within the geographical confines of England, Scotland, Wales, and Ireland, where the majority of texts in this collection originated, one can find more than enough distinguished and exciting works to fill the pages of this anthology many times over. But English literature is not confined to the British Isles; it is a global phenomenon. This border-crossing is not a consequence of modernity alone. It is fitting that among the first works here is *Beowulf*, a powerful epic written in the Germanic language known as Old English about a singularly restless Scandinavian hero. *Beowulf*'s remarkable translator in *The Norton Anthology of English Literature*, Seamus Heaney, was one of the great contemporary masters of English literature—he was awarded the Nobel Prize for Literature in 1995—but it would be potentially misleading to call him an "English poet" for he was born in Northern Ireland and was not in fact English. It would be still more misleading to call him a "British poet," as if the British Empire were the most salient fact about the language he spoke and wrote in or the culture by which he was shaped. What matters is that the language in which Heaney wrote is English, and this fact links him powerfully with the authors assembled in this edition, a linguistic community that stubbornly refuses to fit comfortably within any firm geographical or ethnic or national boundaries. So too, to glance at other authors and writings in the anthology, in the twelfth century, the noblewoman Marie de France wrote her short stories in an Anglo-Norman dialect at home on both sides of the channel; in the sixteenth century William Tyndale, in exile in the Low Countries and inspired by German religious reformers, translated the New Testament from Greek and thereby changed the course of the English language; in the seventeenth century Aphra Behn touched readers with a story that moves from Africa, where its hero is born, to South America, where Behn herself may have witnessed some of the tragic events she describes; and early in the twentieth century Joseph Conrad, born in Ukraine of Polish parents, wrote in eloquent English a celebrated novella whose ironic vision of European empire gave way by the century's end to the voices of those over whom the empire, now in ruins, had once hoped to rule: the Caribbean-born Derek Walcott; the African-born Chinua Achebe and J. M. Coetzee; and the Indian-born Salman Rushdie.

A vital literary culture is always on the move. This principle was the watchword of M. H. Abrams, the distinguished literary critic who first conceived *The Norton Anthology of English Literature,* brought together the original team of editors, and, with characteristic insight, diplomacy, and humor, oversaw seven editions and has graciously offered counsel on subsequent editions. Abrams wisely understood that new scholarly discoveries and the shifting interests of readers constantly alter the landscape of literary history. To stay vital, the anthology, therefore, would need to undergo a process of periodic revision, guided by advice from teachers, as well as students, who view the anthology with a loyal but critical eye. As with past editions, we have benefited from detailed information on the works actually assigned and suggestions for improvements from 133 reviewers. Their participation has been crucial as the editors grapple with the task of strengthening the selection of more traditional texts while adding texts that reflect the expansion of the field of English studies.

The great challenge (and therefore the interest) of the task is inevitably linked to space constraints. The virtually limitless resources of the Web make some of the difficult choices less vexing: in addition to the print anthology, we have created for our readers a supplemental ebook, with more than one thousand texts from the Middle Ages to the turn of the twentieth century. The expansion of the anthology's range by means of this ebook is breathtaking: at no additional cost, readers have access to remarkable works, edited, glossed, and annotated with the sensitivity to classroom use for which the Norton Anthology is renowned. Hence teachers who wish to extend the selections from major authors included in the print anthology will find hundreds of further readings—Milton's *Comus* and *Samson Agonistes,* for example, or Conrad's *Youth*—in the supplemental ebook. At the same time, the ebook contains marvelous works that might otherwise be lost from view: among them, to cite several of my personal favorites, Gascoigne's "Woodmanship," Wycherley's *The Country Wife,* Mary Robinson's "The Camp," and Edward Lear's "The Jumblies." In addition, there are many fascinating topical clusters—"The First Crusade: Sanctifying War," "Genius," "Romantic Literature and Wartime," "Victorian Issues: Education," "Imagining Ireland," to name only a few—all designed to draw readers into larger cultural contexts and to expose them to a wide spectrum of voices.

With each edition, *The Norton Anthology of English Literature* has offered a broadened canon without sacrificing major writers and a selection of complete longer texts in which readers can immerse themselves. Perhaps the most emblematic of these great texts is the epic *Beowulf*. Among the many other complete longer works in the Major Authors Edition are four new selections—*Sir Gawain and the Green Knight* (new in Simon Armitage's spectacular translation) and, much requested by instructors, William Shakespeare's *Othello*, Virginia Woolf's *Mrs. Dalloway,* and Samuel Beckett's *Waiting for Godot*—as well as Aphra Behn's *Oroonoko*, Robert Louis Stevenson's *The Strange Case of Dr. Jekyll and Mr. Hyde*, Rudyard Kipling's *The Man Who Would Be King*, and Joseph Conrad's *Heart of Darkness*. To augment the number of complete longer works instructors can assign, and—a special concern—better to represent the achievements of novelists, the publisher is making available the full list of Norton Critical Editions, more than 220 titles, including such frequently assigned novels as Jane Austen's *Pride and Prejudice*, Mary Shelley's *Frankenstein*, Charles Dickens's *Hard Times*, and Chinua Achebe's *Things Fall Apart*. A Norton Critical Edition may be packaged with the one-volume version, two-splits package, or either individual paperback-split volume for free.

In The Major Authors, Ninth Edition, we have continued to expand the selection of writing by women in several historical periods. The sustained work of scholars in recent years has recovered dozens of significant authors who had been marginalized or neglected by a male-dominated literary tradition and has deepened our understanding of those women writers who had managed, against considerable odds, to claim a place in that tradition. The First Edition of the Major Authors *Norton Anthology* included no women writers; this Ninth Edition includes twenty-seven, of whom two are newly added and four are reselected or expanded. Poets and dramatists whose names were scarcely mentioned even in the specialized literary histories of earlier generations—Aemilia Lanyer, Lady Mary Wroth, Margaret Cavendish, Anna Letitia Barbauld, Charlotte Smith, and many others—now appear in the company of their male contemporaries. There are in addition two complete long prose works by women—Aphra Behn's *Oroonoko* and Virginia Woolf's *Mrs. Dalloway*—along with new selections from such celebrated fiction writers as Jean Rhys, Katherine Mansfield, Margaret Atwood, and Zadie Smith.

Now, as in the past, cultures define themselves by the songs they sing and the stories they tell. But the central importance of visual media in contemporary culture has heightened our awareness of the ways in which songs and stories have always been closely linked to the images that societies have fashioned and viewed. The Major Authors Edition features sixty pages of color plates and more than 90 black-and-white illustrations throughout this edition. In selecting visual material—from the Sutton Hoo treasure of the seventh century to Yinka Shonibare's *Nelson's Ship in a Bottle* in the twenty-first century—the editors sought to provide images that conjure up, whether directly or indirectly, the individual writers in each section; that relate specifically to individual works in the anthology; and that shape and illuminate the culture of a particular literary period. We have tried to choose visually striking images that will interest students and provoke discussion, and our captions draw attention to important details and cross-reference related texts in the anthology.

Period-by-Period Revisions

The Middle Ages, edited by James Simpson and Alfred David, has taken on a striking new look, with a major revision and expansion of its selections. The heart of the Anglo-Saxon portion is the great epic *Beowulf,* in an acclaimed translation, specially commissioned for *The Norton Anthology of English Literature,* by Seamus Heaney. The array of Anglo-Saxon texts includes Alfred David's new verse translations of the poignant, visionary *Dream of the Rood* and the elegiac *Wanderer,* and *The Wife's Lament.* A new Irish Literature selection features a tale from *The Tain* and a group of vivid ninth-century lyrics. The Anglo-Norman section—a key bridge between the Anglo-Saxon period and the time of Chaucer—includes a story by Marie de France. The Middle English section centers, as always, on Chaucer, with a generous selection of texts carefully glossed and annotated so as to heighten their accessibility. New to the Major Authors Edition is a brilliant, specially revised verse translation of *Sir Gawain and the Green Knight* by Simon Armitage, one of the foremost poets and translators of our time. Among the highlights of the revised and expanded medieval section of the ebook—too extensive to enumerate here—is a new, fully annotated edition of the great fifteenth-century morality play, *Mankind.*

The Sixteenth Century, edited by Stephen Greenblatt and George Logan, features two complete longer texts: Marlowe's *Doctor Faustus* and Shakespeare's *Othello,* the latter included for the first time in the Major Authors Edition. New to the ebook are the originals (in Italian and modern English translation) of key Petrarchan poems by Wyatt and Surrey, Skelton's brooding, paranoidal vision of life in the orbit of Henry VIII, "The Bowge of Court," and a greatly expanded cluster of texts of exploration and discovery in "The Wider World."

The Early Seventeenth Century. At the heart of this section, edited by Katharine Eisaman Maus and Barbara Lewalski, is the substantial selection from John Milton's *Paradise Lost.* Complete longer works include John Donne's soul-searching *Satire 3;* Aemilia Lanyer's country-house poem "The Description of Cookham"; and Milton's "Lycidas." Significant additions have been made to the works of Donne, Ben Jonson, George Herbert, and Robert Herrick. Headnotes, introductions, and bibliographies have all been revised. And among the highlights of the ebook are a selection from Donne's startling defense of suicide, the *Biathanatos;* Ben Jonson's *Masque of Blackness;* and the complete text of the first tragedy in English from the pen of a woman, Elizabeth Cary's *The Tragedy of Mariam.*

The Restoration and the Eighteenth Century. The impressive array of complete longer texts in this section, edited by James Noggle and Lawrence Lipking, includes Dryden's satires *Absalom and Achitophel* and *Mac Flecknoe;* Aphra Behn's novel *Oroonoko;* Pope's *Essay on Criticism, The Rape of the Lock,* and *Epistle to Dr. Arbuthnot;* Hogarth's graphic satire "Marriage A-la-Mode"; Johnson's *Vanity of Human Wishes;* and Gray's "Elegy Written in a Country Churchyard." There are new texts by Samuel Johnson, and Christopher Smart is represented for the first time. The Major Authors Edition continues to include such distinguished women writers as Aphra Behn, Lady Mary Wortley Montagu (with a new selection of Turkish Embassy letters), and Frances Burney. Among the many features of the corresponding ebook section are extensive readings in eighteenth-century aesthetics (with texts on grace, on the general and the particular, and on genius); topical clusters on daily life in London, slavery and the slave trade, the plurality of worlds, and travel, trade, and the expansion of empire; and the complete text of William Wycherley's scandalous Restoration comedy *The Country Wife*.

The Romantic Period, edited by Deidre Shauna Lynch and Jack Stillinger, has been extensively revised; every text, headnote, and annotation has been reconsidered. The result is a dramatic reimagining of the entire period. There are new works in this edition for almost every author, including Felicia Hemans's ambitious and exciting dramatic monologue "Properzia Rossi." But the revision of this period in the anthology is not only a matter of strong additions. The facing-page comparison in the new section on "Versions of *The Prelude*" allows readers to see Wordsworth as a reviser and to gauge the significance of the changes he wrought. By replacing the 1850 *Prelude* with the 1805 *Prelude*, the Norton Anthology provides a text that shows Wordsworth immediately engaged with his Romantic contemporaries. This sense of engagement—as if windows in an ornate room had been thrown open to the world outside—extends to the new ebook topic, "Reviewer vs. Poet in the Romantic Period," conveys the rough-and-tumble of literary battles, while another new ebook topic, "Romantic Literature and Wartime," documents Romantic writers' pointed efforts to make literature do justice to the wider world.

The Victorian Age, edited by Catherine Robson and Carol Christ, opens with a revised introduction that features expanded discussions of fiction and the cultural role of poetry. Among the many complete longer works included here are major poems by Elizabeth Barrett Browning, Alfred, Lord Tennyson, Robert Browning, Christina Rossetti, and Gerard Manley Hopkins. The distinguished array of complete prose works, includes Oscar Wilde's *The Importance of Being Earnest*, Elizabeth Gaskell's *The Old Nurse's Story*, Robert Louis Stevenson's *The Strange Case of Dr. Jekyll and Mr. Hyde*, and Rudyard Kipling's *The Man Who Would Be King*. The extensive ebook section includes a new topic on Victorian education that brings together powerful reflections by Newman, Mill, and others with key passages from such works as *Hard Times*, *Alice's Adventures in Wonderland*, and *Jude the Obscure*.

The Twentieth Century and After. The editors, Jahan Ramazani and Jon Stallworthy, have undertaken a root-and-branch reconsideration, leading to a dramatic revision of the entire section. Its spine, as it were, consists of two modernist masterpieces: Virginia Woolf's *Mrs. Dalloway*, and Samuel Beckett's *Waiting for Godot*. These complete works are surrounded by a dazzling choice of other fiction and drama, including, among others, Joseph Conrad's *Heart of Darkness* and powerful stories by D. H. Lawrence, Katherine Mansfield, Jean Rhys, and Nadine Gordimer. A generous representation of poetry centers on a substantial selection of key works by Thomas Hardy, William Butler Yeats, and T. S. Eliot, and extends out to a wide array of other poets, from W. H. Auden and Dylan Thomas to Philip Larkin, Derek Walcott, and Seamus Heaney. Other new fiction includes works by Jean Rhys, Chinua Achebe, Margaret Atwood, Ian McEwan, and Zadie Smith. There are also new images and new nonfiction selections, including a text by Salman Rushdie.

Editorial Procedures and Format

The Major Authors, Ninth Edition, adheres to the principles that have always characterized *The Norton Anthology of English Literature.* Period introductions, headnotes, and annotations are designed to enhance students' reading and, without imposing an interpretation, to give students the information they need to understand each text. The aim of these editorial materials is to make the anthology self-sufficient, so that it can be read anywhere—in a coffee shop, on a bus, under a tree.

The Norton Anthology of English Literature prides itself on both the scholarly accuracy and the readability of its texts. To ease students' encounter with some works, we have normalized spelling and capitalization in texts up to and including the Romantic period—for the most part they now follow the conventions of modern English. We leave unaltered, however, texts in which such modernizing would change semantic or metrical qualities. From the Victorian period onward, we have used the original spelling and punctuation. We continue other editorial procedures that have proved useful in the past. After each work, we cite the date of first publication on the right; in some instances, this date is followed by the date of a revised edition for which the author was responsible. Dates of composition, when they differ from those of publication and when they are known, are provided on the left. We have used square brackets to indicate titles supplied by the editors for the convenience of readers. Whenever a portion of a text has been omitted, we have indicated that omission with three asterisks. If the omitted portion is important for following the plot or argument, we have provided a brief summary within the text or in a footnote. Finally, we have reconsidered annotations throughout and increased the number of marginal glosses for archaic, dialect, or unfamiliar words.

Thanks to the thorough work of James Simpson, with help from Lara Bovilsky of the University of Oregon, The Major Authors, Ninth Edition, provides a more useful "Literary Terminology" appendix, recast as a quick-reference alphabetical glossary with examples from works in the anthology. We have also overhauled and updated the General Bibliography that appears in the print edition, as well as the period and author bibliographies, which now appear in the supplemental ebook, where they can be more easily searched and updated.

Additional Resources from the Publisher

For students using *The Norton Anthology of English Literature,* the publisher provides a wealth of resources on the free StudySpace website (wwnorton. com/nael). Students who activate the free password included in each new copy of the anthology gain access both to the supplemental ebook and to StudySpace, where they will find approximately fifty multiple-choice reading-comprehension quizzes on widely taught individual works with extensive feedback; summaries of the period introductions; period review quizzes with feedback; a new "Literary Places" feature that uses images, maps, and Google Tours tools to offer students a practical way to (virtually) visit the Lake District, Dover Beach, Canterbury, and other literary places; art galleries—one per period—including author portraits, interactive time-lines, and over three hours of spoken-word and musical recordings. The rich gathering of content on StudySpace is designed to help students understand individual works and appreciate the places, sounds, and sights of literature.

The publisher also provides extensive instructor-support materials. Designed to enhance large or small lecture environments, the Instructor Resource Disc, expanded for the Ninth Edition, features more than 300 images with explanatory captions; PowerPoint slides for each period intro-duction and for most topic clusters; and audio recordings (MP3). Much praised by both new and experienced instructors, *Teaching with* The Nor-ton Anthology of English Literature: *A Guide for Instructors* by Sondra Archimedes (University of California–Santa Cruz), Laura Runge (Univer-sity of South Florida), Philip Schwyzer (University of Exeter), Leslie Ritchie (Queen's University), and Scott-Morgan Straker (Queen's University) pro-vides extensive help, from planning a course and developing a syllabus and course objectives to preparing exams. Guide entries provide a "hook" to start class discussion; a Quick Read section to refresh instructors on essen-tial information about a text or author; Teaching Suggestions that call out interesting textual or contextual features; Teaching Clusters of suggested groups or pairs of texts; and Discussion Questions. To help instructors inte-grate the anthology's rich supplemental ebook, the Guide features new entries for online texts and clusters. The Guide also offers revised material on using technology in the classroom, with suggestions for teaching the anthology's multimedia with the texts and for incorporating the media into traditional or distance-learning courses. For the first time, the Guide will also be made available in a searchable online format. Finally, Norton Coursepacks bring high-quality Norton digital media into a new or existing online course. The coursepacks include all content from the StudySpace website, short-answer questions with suggested answers, and a bank of dis-cussion questions adapted from the Guide. Norton's Coursepacks are avail-able in a variety of formats, including Blackboard/WebCT, Desire2Learn, Angel, and Moodle at no cost to instructors or students.

The editors are deeply grateful to the hundreds of teachers worldwide who have helped us to improve the Major Edition of *The Norton Anthology of English Literature*. A list of the instructors who replied to a detailed ques-tionnaire follows, under Acknowledgments. The editors would like to express appreciation for their assistance to Elizabeth Anker (University of Virginia), Paul B. Armstrong (Brown University), Derek Attridge (University of York, UK), Homi Bhabha (Harvard University), Glenn Black (Oriel College, Oxford), Gordon Braden (University of Virginia), Mary Ellen Brown (Indi-ana University), Sandie Byrne (Oxford University), Sarita Cargas (Univer-sity of New Mexico), Joseph W. Childers (University of California, Riverside), Jason Coats (University of Virginia), Kathleen Coleman (Har-vard University), Daniel Cook (University of California, Davis), Guy

Cuthbertson (University of St. Andrews), Pamela Dalziel (University of British Columbia, Vancouver), Linda David, Roy Davids (Oxford University), Jed Esty (University of Pennsylvania), Christopher Fanning (Queen's University), Laura Farwell Blake (Harvard University Library, who provided invaluable and expert help with the General Bibliography), Jamie H. Ferguson (University of Houston), Anne Fernald (Fordham University), William Flesch (Brandeis University), Robert Folkenflik (University of California, Irvine), Ryan Fong (University of California, Davis), Robert D. Fulk (Indiana University), Hans Walter Gabler (University of Munich), Kevis Goodman (University of California, Berkeley), Susannah Gottlieb (Northwestern University), Omaar Hena (University of Virginia), Heather Jackson (University of Toronto), Anuj Kapoor (University of Virginia), Tom Keirstead (University of Toronto), Theresa Kelley (University of Wisconsin, Madison), Tim Kendall (University of Exeter), Shayna Kessel (University of Southern California), Scott Klein (Wake Forest University), Cara Lewis (University of Virginia), Joanna Lipking (Northwestern University), Ian Little (Liverpool University), Tricia Lootens (University of Georgia), Lynne Magnusson (University of Toronto), Laura Mandell (Texas A & M University), Steven Matthews (Oxford Brookes University), Peter McDonald (Oxford University), Tara McDonald (University of Toronto), Edward Mendelson (Columbia University), Erin Minear (Harvard University), Andrew Motion, Elaine Musgrave (University of California, Davis), J. Morgan Myers (University of Virginia), Kate Nash (University of Virginia), Bernard O'Donoghue (Oxford University), Paul O'Prey (Roehampton University), Daniel O'Quinn (University of Guelph), Ruth Perry (M.I.T.), Emily Peterson (Harvard University), Kate Pilson (Harvard University), Adela Pinch (University of Michigan), Jane Potter (Oxford Brookes University), Leah Price (Harvard University), Mark Rankin (James Madison University), Angelique Richardson (Exeter University), Ronald Schuchard (Emory University), Philip Schwyzer (Exeter University), John W. Sider (Westmont College), Claire Marie Stancek (University of California, Berkeley), Paul Stevens (University of Toronto), Ramie Targoff (Brandeis University), Elisa Tersigni (University of Toronto), and Daniel White (University of Toronto). We also thank the many people at Norton who contributed to the Ninth Edition: Julia Reidhead, who served not only as the inhouse supervisor but also as an unfailingly wise and effective collaborator in every aspect of planning and accomplishing this Ninth Edition; Marian Johnson, managing editor for college books; Carly Fraser, associate editor and Course Guide editor; Eileen Connell, electronic media editor; Rachel Mayer, Susan Joseph, Jennifer Harris, Pam Lawson, Jack Borrebach, and Katharine Ings, manuscript editors; Ben Reynolds, senior production manager; Sean Mintus, production manager; Nancy Rodwan, permissions; Jo Anne Metsch, designer; Mike Fodera, photo editor; and Hannah Blaisdell and Jennifer Barnhardt, editorial assistants. All these friends provided the editors with indispensable help in meeting the challenge of representing the unparalleled range and variety of English literature.

STEPHEN GREENBLATT

Acknowledgments

The editors would like to express appreciation and thanks to the hundreds of teachers who provided reviews:

John Achorn (New England College); Robert Aguirre (Wayne State University); Maureen Amos (Keiser University); Rhonda Armstrong (Paris Junior College); Edmondson O. Asgill (Bethune-Cookman University); Brenda Ayres (Liberty University); George H. Bailey (Northern Essex Community College); Eric Ball (Langara College); John Baxter (Dalhousie University); John Black (Moravian College); Deborah Blacklock (Langara College); Elizabeth Bobo (University of Louisiana at Lafayette); Alan Brown (University of West Alabama); Douglas Bruster (University of Texas at Austin); Karen Budra (Langara College); Sarah Burns (Virginia Western Community College); Eric R. Carlson (University of South Carolina, Aiken); Glynis Carr (Bucknell University); Elvira Casal (Middle Tennessee State University); Youngjeen Choe (Chung-Ang University); Lynn Childress (Clemson University); Tim Conley (Brock University); Carl Curtis (Liberty University); Phillip Dale Davis (Northwest Mississippi Community College); Wayne G. Deahl (Eastern Wyoming College); Mary J. Dengler (Dordt College); Michael John DiSanto (Algoma University); Elizabeth Evans (Penn State University-DuBois); Joshua Everett (Central Texas College); Paula R. Feldman (University of South Carolina); John Flood (University of Groningen); James Flynn (Western Kentucky University); Beverly Forsyth (Odessa College); Pamela J. Francis (Northwestern State University); Joel Fredell (Southeastern Louisiana University); Anne Frey (Texas Christian University); LaDonna Friesen (Central Bible College); David Galef (Montclair State University); David Gay (University of Alberta); Stephen Geller (Savannah College of Art and Design); Michael Gilmour (Providence College); Sunithi Gnanadoss (Germanna Community College); Eva Gold (English Southeastern Louisiana University); Richard J. Grande (Penn State University, Abington College); David A. Grant (Columbus State Community College); Elissa S. Guralnick (University of Colorado at Boulder); Corrinne Harol (University of Alberta); Licia Hendriks (The Citadel); Teshie Herbert (Keiser University); David Ingham (St. Thomas University); Randy R. James (Florida Memorial University); Suzanne James (University of British Columbia); Yvonne Jocks (Tarrant County College South East); John Kerrigan (Rockhurst University); Mark Knockemus (Northeastern Technical College); Seunghyeok Kweon (Seoul Women's University); Sean Lawrence (University of British Columbia, Okanagan); Anne Lockwood (Limestone College); Paul Lumsden (Grant MacEwan University); Kim Manganelli

(Clemson University); Ami Massengill (Nashville State Community College); Jeannine McDevitt (Pennsylvania Highlands Community College); Howard Gene Melton II (North Carolina State University); L. Adam Mekler (Morgan State University); Terry L. Meyers (College of William and Mary); Gregg Neikirk (Westfield State University); Meg Pearson (University of West Georgia); John Pekins (Tallahassee Community College); Jenny Perkins (Tallahassee Community College); Curtis Perry (University of Illinois); Kate Pilhuj (The Citadel); Kendrick Prewitt (University of West Alabama); Helaine Razovsky (Northwestern State University of Louisiana); Wayne A. Rebhorn (University of Texas); Joseph Register (Harrisburg Area Community College); Stephen R. Reimer (University of Alberta); Chris Roark (John Carroll University); Catherine Ross (University of Texas at Tyler); Marilyn Sandidge (Westfield State University); Lisa Schnell (University of Vermont); Dr. M.P.A. Sheaffer (Millersville University); Paul Sheneman (Warner University); Lisa Shoemaker (State Fair Community College); Mary Simpson (Central Texas College); Stephen Slimp (University of West Alabama); Isabel Stanley (East Tennessee State University); Claire Strasbaugh (Bethany University); Kathryn Strong (The Citadel); Kim Trainor (University of British Columbia); Martin Trapp (Northwestern Michigan College); Michael E. Travers (The College at Southeastern, Southeastern Baptist Theological Seminary); J.K. Van Dover (Lincoln University); Lisa Vargo (University of Saskatchewan); Jennifer Vaught (University of Louisiana at Lafayette); Deborah Vause (York College of Pennsylvania); Preston L. Waller (McLennan Community College); Ellen Weir (Belmont Abbey College); Steve Werkmeister (Johnson County Community College); Mary Kathleen Whitaker (East Georgia College); Gwen Whitehead (Lamar State College-Orange); Lance Wilder (University of Georgia); Ed Wiltse (Nazareth College); Rita Wisdom (Tarrant County College-Northeast); Stefanie Wortman (University of Missouri); James F. Wurtz (Indiana State University)

Congratulations to Shelton J. Handy (University of Maryland Eastern Shore), Elizabeth Scoville (Bradley University), and Jakia Propst (St. Stephens High School), winners of the 2012 Norton Anthology Student Recitation Contest.

THE NORTON ANTHOLOGY OF

ENGLISH

LITERATURE

THE MAJOR AUTHORS
NINTH EDITION

VOLUME 2

The Romantic Period
1785–1832

1787:	Establishment of the Society for Effecting the Abolition of the Trade in Slaves
1789–1815:	Revolutionary and Napoleonic period in France.—1789: Revolution begins with the assembly of the Estates General in May and the storming of the Bastille on July 14.—1793: King Louis XVI executed; England joins the alliance against France.—1793–94: Reign of Terror under Robespierre. 1804: Napoleon crowned emperor.—1815: Napoleon defeated at Waterloo
1807:	British slave trade outlawed (slavery abolished throughout the empire, the West Indies included, twenty-six years later)
1811–20:	The Regency—George, Prince of Wales, acts as regent for George III, who has been declared incurably insane
1819:	Peterloo Massacre
1820:	Accession of George IV
1830:	Accession of William IV
1832:	Passage of the Reform Act in Parliament

The Romantic period, though by far the shortest, is at least as complex and diverse as any other period in British literary history, and it is, tellingly, demarcated differently than any of the other eras that literary historians and anthologists include in their timelines. By convention, the boundaries delimiting those other epochs are either set by the reigns of monarchs (so that we have the "Elizabethan" and "Victorian" ages named for two long-reigning queens) or conceptualized as coinciding with the openings and closings of centuries (as with the section of this Norton Anthology titled "The Twentieth Century and After"). The date usually serving as the terminus

Sir Brooke Boothby, by Joseph Wright. For more information about this image, see the color insert in this volume.

of the Romantic age, 1832, represents a contrast to this pattern, strongly associated as it is with a signal political event, the first major reform of the British Parliament. A diverse range of dates have been identified as marking off the beginning of the Romantic period, but, almost always, each of these, too, is associated with an event of tremendous political and social impact. As some scholars tell it, the new era began in 1776, the year Americans declared their independence; others single out 1783, when shattering military defeat at the hands of those Americans dealt a blow to the credibility of Britain's ruling elites; and many settle on 1789, the year that launched democratic revolution in France, ushered in decades of fierce political unrest in Britain in its turn, and laid the ground for a war between the British and French Empires and their allies that would envelop an entire generation and take almost the whole of the globe as its theater.

Although politics has often provided a framework for the Romantic period, as such arrangements for periodization suggest, the fascination and provocation that this moment of cultural watershed presents for students of literary history have equally to do with another peculiarity in its construction: the Romantic is also the sole period that is named after a literary form, the romance. A great scholarly achievement of the later eighteenth century had been the recovery from obscurity of the medieval romances, previously ignored by literary historians more concerned with classical influences, and the Romantic period witnessed a re-evaluation of those wild verse-tales of adventure, chivalry, and love. Exactly the traits—their barbarous deviations from probability and rationality, their unabashed fictionality, the fantasies they induced in their readers—that once justified medieval romances' fall into oblivion were seen anew, as commentators moved from lauding the room for idealization and visionary imagination that romance had afforded premodern writers to proposing that *modern* literature should follow suit and become, in one sense, more romantic, too. At a moment when real political events themselves seemed to entail improbabilities and impossibilities (for example the common people proclaiming independence from their rulers), that rehabilitation of romance was, in addition, spurred by the period's probing of the relation between what William Godwin in a subtitle to his 1794 novel *Caleb Williams* called "Things as They Are" and the alternative worlds that imagination could summon into being. "What is now proved was once, only imagin'd," William Blake declared in *The Marriage of Heaven and Hell* in 1790. His declaration is imbued with the new sense of power that poets, those professional imaginers, were inclined to claim at this moment, when the literary imagination appeared in new ways both to speak to and to guide historical change, and when political philosophy gained a new authority in and through poetry and fiction.

About a hundred years ago, the *Cambridge History of English Literature* segmented the era that this section of the *Norton Anthology* covers into two parts, tidily divvying off the "Period of the French Revolution" (1789–1815) from a subsequent period of "Romance Revival" that filled in the years between the defeat of Napoleonic France and the ascent of Queen Victoria. The messier option of treating the era as a single entity equips us better to do justice to its complex multiplicity. In refraining from the attempt to disentangle romance from history and literary from political change, we can better see how this period, in confronting their entanglement, originated the questions about the relations of art and activism, aesthetics and politics, that trouble us still. We can better see, too, how the notions of poetic autonomy that were involved in the rehabilitation of romance's extravagant, untrammelled fictionality were likewise forged under the pressure of political events, and how the reconception of the relation of the present to the past at stake in this recovery of a lost literary tradition often entailed as well imagining a new political future.

Since the days of the old *Cambridge History*, we have likewise begun to engage with a greater range of literary accomplishments, thereby recognizing the centrifugal energies and the eclecticism distinguishing this era, even as its authors firmly believed themselves to be participating in a common temporal period. Recent scholarship has expanded, or re-expanded, a canon formerly centered on introspective lyric poems inspired by poets' encounters with objects in or features of the natural world. Abolitionist songs, ballads and ballad imitations, Turkish tales (favorite forms of Byron's), versified fairy tales (Letitia Landon's "Fairy of the Fountains"), poems in which nature does not prompt a human speaker's meditation but rather speaks itself (John Clare's "Swordy Well"; Anna Barbauld's "Mouse's Petition"), and, in prose, travelogues, "table talk," Gothic novels, and historical romances—all now get numbered among the forms of Romantic literature, a more capacious category than it was in the past. And whereas earlier criticism, especially during the third quarter of the twentieth century, developed accounts of a unified Romanticism by extrapolating from the writings of the six male poets that it had singled out for attention (Blake, Wordsworth, and Coleridge in the first generation, and Byron, Shelley, and Keats in the second), we are readier to stress the friction among these figures, whose poetic and social aspirations divided as well as united them. We are also readier to accept that the work of women writers helped make this exciting period what it was. The conspicuous presence on the literary scene of a new "female literature" and the "poetesses" producing it (to use the quaint phraseology of the male reviewers)—and the fact, more generally, that this was the most prolific age of literary production ever seen in European history—attracted much commentary and some lament. The learned lady or Bluestocking, one critic complained in 1823, "is a creature of modern growth, and capable of existing only in such times as the present."

REVOLUTION AND REACTION

During these times, England was experiencing the ordeal of change from a primarily agricultural society, where wealth and power had been concentrated in the landholding aristocracy, to a modern industrial nation. And this change occurred, as mentioned above, in a context of revolution—in America, then France, then Haiti—of counterrevolution, of war, of economic cycles of inflation and depression, and of the constant threat to the social structure from imported revolutionary ideologies to which the ruling classes responded by the repression of traditional liberties.

The early period of the French Revolution, marked by the Declaration of the Rights of Man and the storming of the Bastille, evoked enthusiastic support from English liberals and radicals alike. Three important books epitomize the radical social thinking stimulated by the Revolution. Mary Wollstonecraft's *A Vindication of the Rights of Men* (1790) justified the Revolution against Edmund Burke's attack in his *Reflections on the Revolution in France* (1790). Thomas Paine's *Rights of Man* (1791–92) also advocated for England a democratic republic that was to be achieved, if lesser pressures failed, by popular revolution. More important as an influence on Wordsworth and Percy Shelley was Godwin's *Enquiry Concerning Political Justice* (1793), which foretold an inevitable but peaceful evolution of society to a final stage in which property would be equally distributed and government would wither away. But English sympathizers dropped off as the Revolution followed its increasingly grim course: the accession to power by Jacobin extremists, intent on purifying their new republic by purging it of its enemies; the "September Massacres" of the imprisoned nobility in 1792, followed by the execution of the king and queen; the new French Republic's invasion of the Rhineland and the Netherlands, which brought England into the war against France; the guillotining of thousands in the Reign of Terror under Robespierre; and, after the execution in their turn of the men who had directed the Terror, the emergence of Napoleon, first as dictator then as emperor of France. As Wordsworth wrote in *The Prelude*,

> become Oppressors in their turn,
> Frenchmen had changed a war of self-defence
> For one of Conquest, losing sight of all
> Which they had struggled for. . . . (11.206–09)

Napoleon, the brilliant tactician whose rise through the ranks of the army had seemed to epitomize the egalitarian principles of the Revolution, had become an arch-aggressor, a despot, and would-be founder of a new imperial dynasty. By 1800 liberals found they had no side they could wholeheartedly espouse. Napoleon's defeat at Waterloo in 1815 proved to be the triumph, not of progress and reform, but of reactionary despotisms throughout continental Europe. In this year, accordingly, the debates about the legitimacy of the ruling class and about patrician degeneracy that figures such as Godwin, Paine, and Wollstonecraft had launched in the early 1790s returned with a vengeance.

From start to finish, this was a period of harsh, repressive measures. Public meetings were prohibited in 1795, the right of habeas corpus (the legal principle protecting individuals from arbitrary imprisonment) was suspended for the first time in over a hundred years, and advocates of even moderate political change were charged with treason. Efforts during these war years to repeal the laws that barred Protestants who did not conform to the Anglican Church from the universities and government came to nothing: in the new climate of counterrevolutionary alarm, it was easy to portray even a slight abridgement of the privileges of the established Church as a measure that, validating the Jacobins' campaigns to de-Christianize France, would aid the enemy cause. Another early casualty of this counterrevolution was the movement to abolish the slave trade, a cause supported initially by a wide cross-section of English society. In the 1780s and 1790s numerous writers, both white (Anna Letitia Barbauld, Coleridge, and Hannah More) and black (Ottobah Cugoano and Olaudah Equiano), attacked the greed of the owners of the West Indian sugar plantations and detailed the horrors of the traffic in African flesh that provided them with their labor power. But the bloodshed that accompanied political change in France strengthened the hand of apologists for slavery, by making any manner of reform seem the prelude to violent insurrection. Parliament rejected a bill abolishing the trade in 1791, and sixteen years—marked by slave rebellions and by the planters' brutal reprisals—elapsed before it passed a new version of the bill.

The frustration of the abolitionist cause is an emblematic chapter in the larger story of how a reactionary government sacrificed hopes of reform while it mobilized the nation's resources for war. Yet this was the very time when economic and social changes were creating a desperate need for corresponding changes in political arrangements. For one thing, new classes inside England—manufacturing rather than agricultural—were beginning to demand a voice in government proportionate to their wealth. The "Industrial Revolution"—the shift in manufacturing that resulted from the invention of power-driven machinery to replace hand labor—had begun in the mid-eighteenth century with improvements in machines for processing textiles, and was given immense impetus when James Watt perfected the steam engine in 1765. In the succeeding decades steam replaced wind and water as the primary source of power for all sorts of manufacturing processes, beginning that dynamic of ever-accelerating economic expansion and technological development that we still identify as the hallmark of the modern age. A new laboring population massed in sprawling mill towns such as Manchester, whose population increased by a factor of five in fifty years. In agricultural communities the destruction of home industry was accompanied by the acceleration of the process of enclosing open fields and wastelands (usually, in fact, "commons" that had provided the means of subsistence for entire communities) and incorporating them into larger, privately owned holdings. Enclosure was by and large necessary for the more efficient methods of agriculture required to feed the nation's growing population (although some of the land that the wealthy acquired through parliamentary acts of enclosure they in fact incorporated into their private estates). But enclosure was socially destructive, breaking up villages, creating a landless class who either migrated to the industrial towns or remained as farm laborers, subsisting on starvation wages and the little they could obtain from parish charity. The landscape of England began to take on its modern appearance—the hitherto open rural areas subdivided into a checkerboard of fields enclosed by hedges and stone walls, with the factories of the cities casting a pall of smoke over vast areas of cheaply built houses and slum tenements. Meanwhile, the population was increasingly polarized into what Benjamin Disraeli later called the "Two Nations"—the two classes of capital and labor, the rich and the poor.

No attempt was made to regulate this shift from the old economic world to the new, since even liberal reformers were committed to the philosophy of laissez-faire. This theory of "let alone," set out in Adam Smith's *The Wealth of Nations* in 1776, holds that the general welfare can be ensured only by the free operation of economic laws; the government should maintain a policy of strict noninterference and leave people to pursue, unfettered, their private interests. On the one hand, laissez-faire thinking might have helped pave the way for the long-postponed emancipation of the slave population of the West Indies; by 1833, when Parliament finally ended slavery, the anomaly that their unfree labor represented for the new economic and social orthodoxies evidently had become intolerable. But for the great majority of the laboring class at home, the results of laissez-faire and the "freedom" of contract it secured were inadequate wages and long hours of work under harsh discipline and in sordid conditions. Investigators' reports on the coal mines, where male and female children of ten or even five years of age were harnessed to heavy coal-sledges that they dragged by crawling on their hands and knees, read like scenes from Dante's *Inferno*. With the end of the war in 1815, the nation's workforce was enlarged by demobilized troops at the very moment when demand for manufactured goods, until now augmented by the needs of the military, fell dramatically. The result was an unemployment crisis that persisted through the 1820s. Since the workers had no vote and were prevented by law from unionizing, their only recourses were petitions, protest meetings, and riots, to which the ruling class responded with even more repressive measures. The introduction of new machinery into the mills resulted in further loss of jobs, provoking sporadic attempts by the displaced workers to destroy the machines. After one such outbreak of "Luddite" machine-breaking, the House of Lords—despite Byron's eloquent protest—passed a bill (1812) making death the penalty for destroying the frames used for weaving in the stocking industry. In 1819 hundreds of thousands of workers organized meetings to demand parliamentary reform. In August of that year, a huge but orderly assembly at St. Peter's Fields, Manchester, was charged by saber-wielding troops, who killed nine and injured hundreds more; this was the notorious "Peterloo Massacre," so named with sardonic reference to the Battle of Waterloo.

Suffering was largely confined to the poor, however, while the landed classes and industrialists prospered. So did many merchants, who profited from the new markets opened up as the British Empire expanded aggressively, compensating with victories against the French for the traumatic loss of America in 1783. England's merchants profited, too, thanks to the marketing successes that, over time, converted once-exotic imports from these colonies into everyday fare for the English. In the eighteenth century tea and sugar had been transformed in this way, and in the nineteenth century other commodities followed suit: the Indian muslin, for instance, that was the fabric of choice for gentlemen's cravats and fashionable ladies' gowns, and the laudanum (Indian opium dissolved in alcohol) that so many ailing writers of the period appear to have found irresistible. The West End of London and new seaside resorts like Brighton became in the early nineteenth century consumers' paradises, sites where West Indian planters and nabobs (a Hindi word that entered English as a name for those who owed their fortunes to Indian gain) could be glimpsed displaying their purchasing power in a manner that made them moralists' favorite examples of nouveau riche vulgarity. The word *shopping* came into English usage in this era. Luxury villas sprang up in London, and the prince regent, who in 1820 became George IV, built himself palaces and pleasure domes, retreats from his not very onerous public responsibilities.

But even, or especially, in private life at home, the prosperous could not escape being touched by the great events of this period. French revolutionary principles were feared by English conservatives almost as much for their challenge to the "proper" ordering of the relations between men and women as for their challenge to traditional political arrangements. Yet the account of what it meant to be English that developed in reaction to this challenge—an account emphasizing the special virtues of the English sense of home and family—was in its way equally revolutionary. In an unprecedented way, the war that the English waged almost without intermission between 1793 and 1815 had a "home front." The menaced sanctuary of the domestic fireside became the symbol of what the nation's military might was safeguarding. What popularity the monarchy held on to during this turbulent period was thus a function not of the two King Georges' traditional exercise of a monarch's sovereign powers but instead of the publicity, tailored to suit this nationalist rhetoric, that emphasized each one's domestic bliss within a "royal family." Conceptions of proper femininity altered as well under the influence of this new idealization and nationalization of the home, this project (as Burke put it) of "binding up the constitution of our country with our dearest domestic ties."

And that alteration both put new pressures on women and granted them new opportunities. As in earlier English history, women in the Romantic period were provided only limited schooling, were subjected to a rigid code of sexual behavior, and (especially after marriage) were bereft of legal rights. In this period women began, as well, to be deluged by books, sermons, and magazine articles that insisted vehemently on the physical and mental differences between the sexes and instructed women that, because of these differences, they should accept that their roles in life involved child rearing, housekeeping, and nothing more. (Of course, in tendering this advice promoters of female domesticity conveniently ignored the definitions of duty that industrialists imposed on the poor women who worked in their mills.) Yet a paradoxical byproduct of the connections that the new nationalist rhetoric forged between the well-being of the state and domestic life was that the identity of the patriot became one a woman might attempt, with some legitimacy, to claim. Within the framework created by the new accounts of English national identity, a woman's private virtues now had a public relevance. They had to be seen as crucial to the nation's welfare. Those virtues might well be manifested in the work of raising patriotic sons, but, as the thousands of women in this period who made their ostensibly natural feminine feelings of pity their alibi for participation in abolitionism demonstrated, they could be turned to nontraditional uses as well.

The new idea that, as the historian Linda Colley has put it, a woman's place was not simply in the home but also in the nation could also justify or at least extenuate the affront to proper feminine modesty represented by publication—by a woman's entry into the public sphere of authorship. "Bluestockings"—educated women—remained targets of masculine scorn, as we have seen. This became, nonetheless, the first era in literary history in which women writers began to compete with men in their numbers, sales, and literary reputations. These female authors had to tread carefully, to be sure, to avoid suggesting that (as one male critic fulminated) they wished the nation's "affectionate wives, kind mothers, and lovely daughters" to be metamorphosed into "studious philosophers" and "busy politicians." And figures like Wollstonecraft, who in the *Vindication of the Rights of Woman* grafted a radical proposal about gender equality onto a more orthodox argument about the education women needed to be proper mothers, remained exceptional. Later women writers tended cautiously to either ignore her example or define themselves against it.

Only in the Victorian period would Wollstonecraft's cause of women's rights rally enough support for substantial legal reform to begin, and that process would not be completed until the twentieth century. In the early nineteenth century the pressures for political reform focused on the rights of men, as distinct from women. From 1785 on, the year in which Prime Minister William Pitt (who would soon shift his political allegiances) proposed in vain a bill for parliamentary reform, middle-class and working-class men, entering into strategic and short-lived alliances, made the restructuring of the British electoral system their common cause. Finally, at a time of acute economic distress, the first Reform Bill was passed in 1832. It did away with the rotten boroughs (depopulated areas whose seats in the House of Commons were at the disposal of a few noblemen), redistributed parliamentary representation to include the industrial cities, and extended the franchise. Although about half the middle class, almost all the working class, and all women remained without a vote, the principle of the peaceful adjustment of conflicting interests by parliamentary majority had been firmly established. Reform was to go on, by stages, until Britain acquired universal adult suffrage in 1928.

THE NEW POETRIES: THEORY AND PRACTICE

Writers working in this period 1785–1832 did not think of themselves as constituting a group of "Romantic" authors. It was Victorian critics who first wrote of the previous generation as the Romantics and promoted the term as a description for a period of recent, modern rather than premodern, history. Contemporaries, by contrast, treated these writers as independent individuals or else grouped them (usually maliciously, but with some basis in fact) into a number of separate "schools" or "sects": the "Lake School" of Wordsworth, Coleridge, and Robert Southey (a "sect of poets," the critic Francis Jeffrey sniped, determined to be "*dissenters* from the established systems in poetry and criticism" and valuing themselves highly "for having broken loose from the bondage of ancient authority"); the "Cockney School," a derogatory term for vulgar Londoners Leigh Hunt, William Hazlitt, and associated writers who had pretensions beyond their station, including Keats; and the impious "Satanic School" of Leigh Hunt (again), Percy Shelley, and Byron. At the start of the period, the satirist Richard Polwhele also practiced this name-calling as he catalogued the sphere of "female literature": the aim of his 1797 *The Unsex'd Females* was, by naming and shaming, to firmly distinguish the virtuous lady writers of his moment from the "Amazonian band" formed by Wollstonecraft and her followers, a group who, so Polwhele complained, had sacrificed their feminine charms for lead roles in revolutionary polemicizing.

The proliferation of "schools" and "sects" suggests the fault lines running through this fractious literary world. Where agreement could be found was around the proposition that this was a watershed moment in literary history. "Literature, well or ill conducted," the satirist Thomas James Mathias proclaimed in the book that inspired Polwhele's, "is the great engine by which . . . all civilized states must ultimately be supported or overthrown." Radicals concurred with conservatives like Mathias in this conviction that literature was where the action was—that literature in effect *was* action—even as they disagreed on the meaning to be ascribed to that very term (a term formerly synonymous with learning in general, only in this period did *literature* begin to settle down into that modern meaning that confines it exclusively to artistic expression, works of the imagination particularly). Introducing the *New Cambridge History of the English Romantic Period*, James Chandler has recently highlighted, as a defining characteristic of the Romantic age, how often this era's most talented men gravitated to poetry in particular. They confirmed poetry's elevated cultural status by abandoning other careers, the ministry in Coleridge's case, the law in Sir Walter Scott's, medicine in Keats's. Even George Canning, Tory leader of Britain's House of Commons, published in 1823 a *Collected Poems.* In his 1802 Preface to *Lyrical Ballads* Wordsworth unfavorably contrasted what the "Man of Science" could do as a benefactor of humanity with what the "Poet" could, whose vocation it was to "bind together by passion and knowledge the vast empire of human society, as it is spread over the whole earth and over all time." "The most unfailing herald, companion, and follower of the awakening of a great people to work a beneficial change in opinion or institution, is Poetry," Percy Shelley declared.

The "most eccentric feature of this entire culture," literary historian Stuart Curran suggests, was that it was "simply mad for poetry." To a degree inconceivable in the twenty-first century, poetry back then penetrated everyday life, as something appearing in daily papers alongside news stories and notices of bankruptcies, deaths, and marriages, and as something to be memorized, sung, transcribed into commonplace books, and made the basis of parlor games on long winters' evenings. The calling of poet beckoned to many: among those hordes of devoted readers, many were eager—too eager, their reviewers complained—to become authors in turn, imagining that verse might provide their springboard to fame. If those enthusiasms laid the ground for confident declarations like Shelley's and Wordsworth's, they also, inevitably, generated a backlash, the more so as the new poetries of the Romantic period rode to this cultural prominence on the back of a media culture that at this moment was reaching increasing numbers of readers more quickly than ever before. Indeed, as Mathias's word "engine" suggests, with the expansion of modern publishing, it had begun to appear as though modern writing, too, had started to conform to the accelerated production rhythms of the Industrial Revolution. (The nervousness aroused by these developments, anticipations of the twentieth century's mass culture, is also registered in Wordsworth's Preface, which proposes as one cause of the "almost savage torpor" found among Wordsworth's countrymen and women, city-dwellers especially, the "rapid communication of intelligence" provided by the new popular press.) The spectacle of new sorts of people enlisting as authors and the multiplication of new venues for their writings generated gloomy warnings about overproduction and an accompanying debasement of artistic standards.

The genius poet was therefore shadowed throughout the Romantic period's literary discussion by a less admirable double, the Grub Street hack. *Poet* could in this era designate the visionary and universal benefactor profiled in Wordsworth's Preface and Shelley's *Defence of Poetry*, but it also evoked an impoverished and pretentious truant from a more honest trade, a misguided *romantic scribbler*. (That last phrase, often bandied about in this era, reminds us that even as the term *romantic* became synonymous with an admirable responsiveness to the promptings of imagination, it never completely shed its association with a deplorable and impractical deviation from common sense.) As Mary Robinson mischievously pointed out, it was a mistake to equate "the airy throne/ Of bold imagination, rapture fraught/ Above the herds of mortals" with a desolate mountaintop or isolated green dell, even though the period's poetic speakers tended to image themselves in such sublime settings. The poet's haunt was in mundane reality likely to be a shabby, low-rent attic. Many motives drove the poets who in this era tried to make poetry new by reviving what was old and who thereby contrived to bypass the eighteenth-century

poets whose heirs they were supposed to be: their medievalisms and primtiv-
isms were, for a start, reactions against the neoclassical canons of good taste,
as well as expressions of a new nationalism. But certainly ideas about the
literary past's exemption from the commercial pressures of the present also
helped make the outmoded old romances a radically new source of inspiration for this period, precisely because of rather than despite their historical
distance. The energy invested at this moment in the scholarly investigation
and poetic imitation of the ballads being sung or chanted by common people
in the streets and fields suggests something similar. It registers the fascination that the participants in literate culture who listened in on these performances were inclined to ascribe to a cultural form whose origins predated
the invention of the printing press and the advent of a print market. The
ballad was transmitted by word of mouth and not by commercial exchange.

The double image of the poet—product of an era that both idealized poetry
and fretted over its standing in modern, commercial society—is an important
context for the questions centering Wordsworth's 1802 Preface, his retroactive statement of the principles guiding him in the poems he contributed to
Lyrical Ballads. "What is meant by the word Poet? What is a Poet?" The questions were the more urgent because in a fractious period, there was increased
pressure on the aesthetic sphere to act as a site in which human beings could
rediscover the commonalities linking them as humans, as Wordsworth's definition of the poet as a figure of unification, "bind[ing] together . . . the vast
empire of human society," suggests. One way to approach the period's new
poetries and isolate some of the distinctive trends that were precipitated out
of a welter of reforms and radical innovations is to start by tracing the shifting conceptions of poet and poetry that emerged then. If by taking this

Contrasting views of the Romantic poet. On the left, Henry Fuseli, "The Poet's Vision,"
unused design for frontispiece to William Cowper's *Poems* (1807). On the right, Henry
Heath, "Fine Arts, Pt. 1: Poetry," published August 8, 1826.

approach we take our cue from Wordsworth's Preface, we should also acknowledge that his manifesto for a new poetics can be deemed representative only to a limited extent. Wordsworth would have wished it otherwise, but during this era of revolution definitions of good poetry, like definitions of the good society, were sure to create as much contention as consensus.

Concepts of the Poet and the Poem

Seeking a stable foundation on which social institutions might be constructed, eighteenth-century British philosophers had devoted much energy to demonstrating that human nature must be everywhere the same, because it everywhere derived from individuals' shared sensory experience of an external world that could be objectively represented. As the century went on, however, philosophers began emphasizing—and poets began developing a new language for—individual variations in perception and the capacity the receptive consciousness has to filter and to re-create reality. This was a shift Wordsworth registered when in his Preface he located the source of a poem not in outer nature but in the psychology of the individual poet. What distinguished the poems of *Lyrical Ballads* from the popular poetry of the day Wordsworth declared, vindicating his own departures from those norms, is that "[t]he feeling therein developed gives importance to the action and situation, and not the action and situation to the feeling." Wordsworth maintained, in continuation, that "[A]ll good poetry," was, at the moment of composition, "the spontaneous overflow of powerful feelings." Other contemporary discussions of poetry concurred with this account by referring likewise to the mind, emotions, and imagination of the poet for the origin, content, and defining attributes of a poem. "The poet, the man of strong feelings, gives us only an image of his mind, . . . marking the impression which nature had made on his own heart," Wollstonecraft wrote in an essay that appeared in the *Monthly Magazine* the year before the first edition of *Lyrical Ballads*. Though Romantic poetry is interchangeable for many modern readers with "nature poetry" (an equation that William Godwin, her widower, endorsed when he reprinted Wollstonecraft's essay under a new title, "On Poetry, and Our Relish for the Beauties of Nature"), this characterization of Romantic poetics risks downplaying the poets' emphatic attention to the operations of consciousness. Certainly, many poets participated enthusiastically in the touring of picturesque scenery that was a new leisure activity of their age. Wordsworth, Coleridge, and Southey, the "Lake School," even set up their households in the midst of that scenery, announcing in their residential arrangements as well as their works their antipathy to "the increasing accumulation of men in cities" and faith in the restorative powers of a benevolent Nature. Even so, it is fair to say that when the great Romantic lyrics—Smith's *Beachy Head*, Wordsworth's "Tintern Abbey," Coleridge's "Frost at Midnight," Keats's "Nightingale"—remark on an aspect in the natural scene, this attention to the external world serves only as stimulus to the most characteristic human activity, that of thinking.

Infused with this emphasis, the lyric poem written in the first person, which for much of literary history was regarded as a minor kind, thus became for many among the Romantics a major form and was often described as the most essentially poetic of all the genres. And in most Romantic lyrics the "I" is no longer a conventionally typical lyric speaker, such as the Petrarchan lover or Cavalier gallant of Elizabethan and seventeenth-century love poems, but one who shares recognizable traits with the poet. The experiences and states of mind expressed by the lyric speaker often accord closely with the known facts of the poet's life.

This reinvention of the lyric complicated established understandings of the gender of authorship. It may not be an accident, some critics suggest, that Wordsworth in his Preface defines poetry as "the real language of men" and the Poet as a "man speaking to men": Wordsworth, who began to publish when women such as Robinson and Charlotte Smith occupied the vanguard of the new personal poetry, might have decided that to establish the distinctiveness of his project he needed to counterbalance his emphasis on his feelings with an emphasis on those feelings' "manly" dignity. This is not to say that women writers' relationship to the new ideas about poetry was straightforward either. In one of her prefaces Smith says that she anticipates being criticized for "bringing forward 'with querulous egotism,' the mention of myself." For many female poets the other challenge those ideas about poetry posed might have consisted in their potential to reinforce the old, prejudicial idea that their sex—traditionally seen as creatures of feeling rather than intellect—wrote about their own experiences because they were capable of nothing else. For male poets the risks of poetic self-revelation were different—and in some measure they were actively seized by those who, like Coleridge and Percy Shelley, intimated darkly that the introspective tendency and emotional sensitivity that made someone a poetic genius could also lead him to melancholy and madness.

It was not only the lyric that registered these new accounts of the poet. Byron confounded his contemporaries' expectations about which poetic genre was best suited to self-revelation by inviting his audience to equate the heroes of *Childe Harold, Manfred*, and *Don Juan* with their author, and to see these fictional protagonists' experiences as disclosing the deep truths of his secret self. Wordsworth's *Prelude* represents an extreme instance of this tendency to self-reference. Though the poem, half a century in the making, is of epic length and seriousness, its subject is not, as is customary in an epic, history on a world-changing scale but the growth of the poet's mind: "a thing unprecedented in Literary history that a man should talk so much about himself," Wordsworth admitted.

Spontaneity and the Impulses of Feeling

In traditional poetics, poetry had been regarded as supremely an art—an art that in modern times was practiced by poets who had assimilated classical precedents, were aware of the "rules" governing the kind of poem they are writing, and (except for the happy touches that, as Alexander Pope said, are "beyond the reach of art") deliberately employed tested means to achieve premeditated effects on an audience. But in her 1797 *Monthly Magazine* essay, Wollstonecraft foretold a shift in aesthetic doctrine when she wrote that "[t]he silken wings of fancy are shrivelled by rules," and that "a desire of attaining elegance of diction occasions an attention to words, incompatible with sublime, impassioned thoughts." In Wordsworth's account in the Preface, although the composition of a poem originates from "emotion recollected in tranquillity" and may be preceded and followed by reflection, the immediate act of composition must be spontaneous—impulsive, artless, and free from rules. Keats listed as an "axiom" a similar proposition—that "if poetry comes not as naturally as the leaves to a tree it had better not come at all."

On occasion in this period's discussions of poetics, this interest in a poetry that came naturally could act in concert with that nostalgia, already discussed, which abandoned the prosaic here-and-now for the more romantic possibilities housed in a remote, preliterate past. For instance, for many poets of the period, the ancient bard, a composite figure resembling at once the biblical prophets, Homer, Milton, and the harp-playing patriots whom eighteenth-century antiquarians had located in a legendary Dark Ages Britain, was a charismatic role model. Imagining the songs a bard might have sung in long-ago times made it easier to conceive an alternative to the mundane language of modernity—a natural, oral poetry, blissfully unconscious of modern decorums and artificial conventions and sublimely irreducible to rule or measure. (Though they chafed against this expectation, writers from the rural working class—Robert Burns and later John Clare—could be expected, by virtue of their perceived distance from the restraint and refinement of civilized discourse, to play a comparable role inside modern culture, that of peasant poet or natural genius.) When, after the end of the Napoleonic war, writers like Byron and Percy and Mary Shelley traveled to Italy, taking these bardic ideals with them, they became enthralled with the arts of the improvisatore and improvisatrice, men and women whose electrifying oral

The Bard. Frontispiece by Thomas Rowlandson for Edward Jones, *The Bardic Museum of Primitive British Literature* (1802), a collection of traditional Welsh melodies. Rowlandson pictures the bard as a figure unifying his community.

performances of poetry involved no texts but those of immediate inspiration. One writer who praised and emulated that rhapsodic spontaneity, Percy Shelley, thought it "an error to assert that the finest passages of poetry are produced by labour and study." He suggested instead that these were the products of an unconscious creativity: "A great statue or picture grows under the power of the artist as a child in the mother's womb."

The emphasis in this period on unlabored art and on the spontaneous activity of the imagination producing it, and the premium placed on the immediacy of the relationship between author and poem, are linked to a belief in the essential role of passion. According to this view (which connects the literary productions of the Romantic period to the poetry and fiction of sensibility written earlier in the eighteenth century), the intuitive feelings of "the heart" had to supplement the judgments of the purely logical faculty, "the head." "Deep thinking," Coleridge wrote, "is attainable only by a man of deep feeling"; hence, "a metaphysical solution that does not tell you something in the heart is grievously to be suspected as apocryphal."

Glorification of the Ordinary

In the lecture he gave "On the Living Poets" in 1818 Hazlitt declared the poetry of the Lake school, with Wordsworth at its head, to be the literary equivalent of the French Revolution, a translation of political change into poetical experiment. "Kings and queens were dethroned from their rank and station in legitimate tragedy or epic poetry, as they were decapitated elsewhere. . . . The paradox [these poets] set out with was that all things are by nature, equally fit subjects for poetry; or that if there is any preference to give, those that are the meanest [i.e., most humble] and most unpromising are the best." Furthermore, as Hazlitt pointed out, the Lake School had done more than take the subjects of serious poems from the lives of humble country folk; it overtly elicited a genteel audience's sympathies for the disgraced, outcast, and delinquent—"convicts, female vagrants, gypsies . . . idiot boys and mad mothers," in Hazlitt's list. To some extent Hazlitt's analogizing between poetic and political experiments suggests more about him than the living poets he discusses: an avid youthful reader of Jean-Jacques Rousseau, he sounds as though he took to heart the Swiss-French philosopher's advocacy of a simplicity of manners against aristocratic corruption. Still, Hazlitt would have found support for his characterization of the Lake School from Wordsworth's statement in the Preface that his aim in *Lyrical Ballads* was "to choose incidents and situations from common life." For Wordsworth's polemical purposes, it was in "humble and rustic life" that a natural language—"a language really spoken by men" and "incorporated with the beautiful and permanent forms of nature"—was to be found, and the speech of rustics was in the Preface promoted as a cure for the ailments of the overcivilized.

Hazlitt would have known as well that later-eighteenth-century writers had already experimented with the simple treatment of simple subjects. Burns had with great success represented "the rural scenes and rural pleasures of [his] natal Soil," and in a language aiming to be true to the rhythms of the Scots language. Women poets, too—Barbauld, Robinson, Joanna Baillie—assimilated to their poems the subject matter of everyday life. Many later-eighteenth-century writers had taken their cue from the stark simplicity of the popular ballad: the ballad's appeal for an up-market, metropolitan readership, capitalized on by eighteenth-century collections like Percy's *Reliques of Ancient English Poetry*, was in a part a function of the contrast between primitive plainness and outright crudity of these song traditions and the tame, elaborate poetic diction defining poetry's modern milieu.

Once it had arrived on this scene Wordsworth's Preface of 1802 underwrote such poetic practice with a theory that inverted the traditional hierarchy of poetic genres, subjects, and styles. It elevated humble life and the plain style, which in earlier theory were appropriate only for the pastoral, the genre at the bottom of the traditional hierarchy, into the principal subject and medium for poetry in general. Byron reacted with scorn to this poetic program and facetiously summoned ghosts from the eighteenth century to help him protest against what *he* perceived as Wordsworth's bathos:

> "Peddlers," and "Boats," and "Wagons"! Oh! ye shades
> Of Pope and Dryden, are we come to this?

Yet Wordsworth's project was not simply to represent the world as it is but, as he explained in his Preface, to throw over "situations from common life . . . a certain coloring of imagination, whereby ordinary things should be presented to the mind in an unusual aspect." No one can read his poems without noticing the reverence with which he invests words that for earlier writers had been derogatory—words such as "common," "ordinary," "everyday," "humble." Wordsworth's aim was to shatter the lethargy of custom so as to refresh our sense, of wonder in the everyday and the lowly.

In the eighteenth century Samuel Johnson had said that "wonder is a pause of reason"—"the effect of novelty upon ignorance." But for many Romantics, to arouse in the sophisticated mind that sense of wonder presumed to be felt by the ignorant and the innocent—to renew the universe, Percy Shelley wrote, "after it has been blunted by reiteration"—was a major function of poetry. Commenting on the imaginative quality of Wordsworth's early verse, Coleridge remarked in *Biographia Literaria*: "To combine the child's sense of wonder and novelty with the appearances, which every day for perhaps forty years had rendered familiar . . . this is the character and privilege of genius." Contributing to this poetry of the child's-eye view, Baillie and Barbauld wrote poems centered on an observer's effort to imagine the unknowable perspective of beings for whom thought and sensation are new or not begun—in Baillie's case, a "waking infant," in Barbauld's, a "little invisible being who is expected soon to become visible" but is still in its mother's womb.

The Supernatural, the Romance, and Psychological Extremes

There was a counterpoint to this poetry devoted to reviving the wonder of the familiar—"characters and incidents such as will be found in every village and its vicinity"—and proposing the authenticity of that local knowledge that long familiarity brings: a poetry that instead was founded on frank violation of natural laws and the ordinary course of events and that thereby cultivated the romantic in the understanding of that term that was to the forefront during the Romantic period itself. Coleridge contrasts these two sorts of poem when in *Biographia Literaria* he describes the division of labor organizing his collaboration with Wordsworth on *Lyrical Ballads*: his responsibility was poetry in which "the incidents and agents were to be, in part at least, supernatural, or at least romantic." Stories of bewitchings, hauntings, and possession—shaped by antiquated treatises on demonology, folklore, and Gothic novels—supplied Coleridge in poems such as *Rime of the Ancient Mariner, Christabel*, and "Kubla Khan" with the means of impressing upon readers a sense of occult powers and unknown modes of being.

Poems like these, as Coleridge's epithet "romantic" suggests, were often grouped together by contemporaries under the medievalizing rubric "romance." On the one hand romances were writings that turned, in their quest for settings conducive to supernatural happenings, to distant pasts, faraway, exotic places, or both—Keats's "perilous seas, in faery lands forlorn" or the China of "Kubla Khan." On the other hand romance also named a homegrown, native tradition of literature, made unfamiliar and alien by the passage of time. For many authors, starting with Horace Walpole, whose *Castle of Otranto* (1764) began the tradition of Gothic fiction, writing under the banner of romance meant reclaiming their national birthright: a literature of imagination—associated, above all, with Spenser and the Shakespeare of fairy magic and witchcraft—that had been forced underground by the Enlightenment's emphasis on reason. Byron negotiated between romance's two sets of associations in *Childe Harold*, having his hero travel in far-off Albania and become entranced by the inhabitants' savage songs, but also giving the poem the subtitle "A Romaunt" (an archaic spelling of romance) and writing it in Spenserian stanzas. This was the same stanzaic form, neglected for much of the eighteenth century, that Keats drew on for *The Eve of St. Agnes*, the poem in which he proved himself a master of that Romantic mode that establishes a medieval setting for events violating our sense of realistic probability. The Romantic period's "medieval revival" was also promoted by women: Robinson, for instance (author of "Old English," "Monkish," and "Gothic" Tales), as well as Letitia Landon, Felicia Hemans, and others, women who often matched the arch-medievalist Sir Walter Scott in the historical learning they brought to their compositions.

The "addition of strangeness to beauty" that Walter Pater near the end of the nineteenth century would identify as a key Romantic tendency is seen not only in this concern with the exotic and archaic landscapes of romance, but also in an interest in the mysteries of mental life and determination to investigate psychological extremes. Coleridge and Thomas De Quincey shared an interest in dreams and nightmares and in the altered consciousness they experienced under their addiction to opium. In his odes, as in the quasi-medieval "ballad" "La Belle Dame sans Merci," Keats recorded strange mixtures of pleasure and pain with extraordinary sensitivity, pondering the destructive aspects of sexuality and the erotic quality of the longing for death. And Byron made repeated use of the fascination of the forbidden and the appeal of the terrifying yet seductive Satanic hero.

There were, of course, writers who resisted these poetic engagements with fantasized landscapes and strange passions. Significant dissent came from some women writers, who, given accounts of their sex as especially susceptible to the delusions or romantic love, had particular reason to continue the Enlightenment program and promote the rational regulation of emotion. Barbauld wrote a poem gently advising the young Coleridge not to prolong his stay in the "fairy bower" of romance but to engage actively with the world as it is. Often satirical when she assesses characters who imagine themselves the pitiable victims of their own powerful feelings, Jane Austen had her heroine in *Persuasion*, while conversing with a melancholy, Byron-reading young man, caution him against overindulgence in Byron's "impassioned descriptions of hopeless agony" and "prescribe" to him a "larger allowance of prose in his daily study." And yet this heroine, having "been forced into prudence in her youth," has "learned romance as she grew older." The reversal of the sequence that usually orders the story line of female socialization suggests a receptivity to romance's allure—the allure of the improbable—that links Austen to the spirit of the age.

Individualism and Alienation

Another feature of Byron's poetry that attracted notice and, in some quarters, censure was its insistence on his or his hero's self-sufficiency. Hazlitt, for instance, borrowed lines from Shakespeare's *Coriolanus* to object to Byron's habit of spurning human connection "[a]s if a man were author of. himself, / And owned no other kin." The audacious individualism that Hazlitt questions in this passage from *The Spirit of the Age* was, however, central to the celebrations of creativity occupying many Romantic-period writers. Indeed, in the Preface, Wordsworth had already characterized his poetic experimentation in *Lyrical Ballads* as an exercise in artistic self-sufficiency. The Preface has been read as a document in which Wordsworth, proving himself a self-made man, arranges for his disinheritance—arranges to cut himself off, he says, "from a large portion of the phrases and figures of speech which from father to son have long been regarded as the common inheritance of Poets." The German philosophers who generated many of the characteristic ideas of European Romanticism had likewise developed an account of how individuals might author and create themselves. In the work of Immanuel Kant and others, the human mind was described as creating the universe it perceived and so creating its own experience. Mind is "not passive," Kant's admirer Coleridge wrote, but "made in God's image, and that too in the sublimest sense—the Image of the *Creator*." And Wordsworth declared in *The Prelude* that the individual mind "Even as an agent of the one great mind, / creates, creator and receiver both." The Romantic period, the epoch of free enterprise, imperial expansion, and boundless revolutionary hope, was also an epoch of individualism in which philosophers and poets alike put an extraordinarily high estimate on human potentialities.

In representing this expanded scope for individual initiative, much poetry of the period redefined heroism and made a ceaseless striving for the unattainable its crucial element. Viewed by moralists of previous ages as sin or lamentable error, longings that can never be satisfied—in Percy Shelley's phrase, "the desire of the moth for a star"—came to be revalued as the glory of human nature. "Less than everything," Blake announced, "cannot satisfy man." Discussions of the nature of art developed similarly. The German philosopher Friedrich Schlegel's proposal that poetry "should forever be becoming and never be perfected" supplied a way to understand the unfinished, "fragment" poems of the period ("Kubla Khan" most famously) not as failures but instead as confirmations that the most poetic poetry was defined as much by what was absent as by what was present: the poem, in this understanding, was a fragmentary trace of an original conception that was too grand ever to be fully realized. This defiant attitude toward limits also made many writers impatient with the conceptions of literary genre they inherited from the past. The result was that, creating new genres from old, they produced an astonishing variety of hybrid forms constructed on fresh principles of organization and style: "elegiac sonnets," "lyrical ballads," the poetic auto-biography of *The Prelude*, Percy Shelley's "lyric drama" of cosmic reach, *Prometheus Unbound*, and (in the field of prose) the "historical novels" of Scott and the complex interweaving of letters, reported oral confessions, and interpolated tales that is Mary Shelley's *Frankenstein*.

In this context many writers' choice to portray poetry as a product of solitude and poets as loners might be understood as a means of reinforcing the individuality of their vision. (The sociability of the extroverted narrator of *Don Juan*, who is forever buttonholing "the gentle reader," is exceptional—Byron's way of harkening back to the satire of the eighteenth century.) And the appeal that nature poetry had for many writers of the period can be attributed to a determination to idealize the natural scene as a site where the individual could find freedom from social laws, an idealization that was easier to sustain when nature was, as often in the era, represented not as cultivated fields but as uninhabitable wild wastes, unploughed uplands, caves, and chasms. Rural *community*, threatened by the enclosures that were breaking up village life, was a tenuous presence in poetry as well.

Wordsworth's imagination is typically released, for instance, by the sudden apparition of a single figure, stark and solitary against a natural background; the words "solitary," "by one self," "alone" sound through his poems. In the poetry of Coleridge, Shelley, and Byron (before *Don Juan* launched Byron's own satire on Byronism), the desolate landscapes are often the haunts of disillusioned visionaries and accursed outlaws, figures whose thwarted ambitions and torments connect them, variously, to Cain, the Wandering Jew, Satan, and even Napoleon. A variant of this figure is Prometheus, the hero of classical mythology, who is Satan-like in setting himself in opposition to God, but who, unlike Satan, is the champion rather than the enemy of the human race. Mary Shelley subjected this hero, central to her husband's mythmaking, to ironic rewriting in *Frankenstein:* Victor Frankenstein, a "Modern Prometheus," is far from championing humankind. For other women writers of the period, and for Shelley in her later novels, the equivalent to these half-charismatic, half-condemnable figures of alienation is the woman of "genius." In a world in which—as Wollstonecraft complained in the *Rights of Woman*—"all women are to be levelled by meekness and docility, into one character of . . . gentle compliance," the woman who in "unfeminine" fashion claimed a distinctive individuality did not gain authority but risked ostracism. As for the woman of genius, in writings by Robinson, Hemans, and Landon particularly, her story was often told as a modern variation on ancient legends of the Greek Sappho, the ill-fated female poet who had triumphed in poetry but died of love. Pressured by the emergent Victorianism of the 1820s and playing it safe, Hemans especially was careful to associate genius with self-inflicted sorrow and happiness with a woman's embrace of her domestic calling.

WRITING IN THE MARKETPLACE AND THE LAW COURTS

Even Romantics who wished to associate literature with isolated poets holding mute converse with their souls had to acknowledge that in real life the writer did not dwell in solitude but confronted, and was accountable to, a crowd. For many commentators the most revolutionary aspect of the age

Printing Press. George Cruikshank's image of a printing press in human form, superhero and harbinger of modern liberty, opens William Hone's satiric pamphlet *The Political Showman—At Home!* (1821).

was the spread of literacy and the dramatic expansion of the potential audience for literature. This revolution, like the Revolution in France, occasioned a conservative reaction: the worry, frequently expressed as books ceased to be written exclusively for an elite, that this bigger audience (by 1830, about half England's population of fourteen million) would be less qualified to judge or understand what it read. Beginning in the 1780s, more members of the working classes had learned to read as a result of lessons provided in Sunday schools (informal sites for the education of the poor that long antedated state-supported schools). At the same time reading matter became more plentiful and cheaper, thanks to innovations in retailing—the cut-rate sales of remaindered books and the spread of circulating libraries where volumes could be "rented"—and thanks to technological developments. By the end of the period, printing presses were driven by steam engines, and the manufacture of paper had been mechanized; publishers had mastered publicity, the art (as it was called) of "the puff." Surveying the consequences of these changes, Coleridge muttered darkly about that "misgrowth," "a Reading Public," making it sound like something freakish and pathological. Books had become a big business, one enrolling increasing numbers of individuals who found it possible to do without the assistance of wealthy patrons and who, accordingly, looked to this public for their hopes of survival. A few writers became celebrities, invested with a glamour that formerly had been reserved for royalty and that we nowadays save for movie stars. This was the case for the best-selling Byron, particularly, whose enthusiastic public could by the

1830s purchase dinner services imprinted with illustrations from his life and works.

How such popular acclaim was to be understood and how the new reading public that bestowed it (and took it away) could possibly be reformed or monitored when, as Coleridge's term "misgrowth" suggests, its limits and composition seemed unknowable: these were pressing questions for the age. Opponents of the French Revolution and political reform at home pondered a frightening possibility: if "events . . . [had] made us a world of readers" (as Coleridge put it, thinking of how newspapers had proliferated in response to the political upheavals), it might also be true that readers could *make* events in turn, that the new members of the audience for print would demand a part in the drama of national politics. Conservatives were well aware of arguments conjecturing that the Revolution had been the result of the invention of the printing press three centuries before. They certainly could not forget that Paine's *Rights of Man*—not the reading matter for the poor the Sunday-school movement had envisioned—had sold an astonishing two hundred thousand copies in a year.

However, the British state had lacked legal provisions for the prepublication censorship of books since 1695, which was when the last Licensing Act had lapsed. Throughout the Romantic period therefore the Crown tried out other methods for policing reading and criminalizing certain practices of authoring and publishing. Paine was in absentia found guilty of sedition, for instance, and in 1817 the radical publisher William Hone narrowly escaped conviction for blasphemy. Another government strategy was to use taxes to inflate the prices of printed matter and so keep political information out of the hands of the poor without exactly violating the freedom of the press. In the meantime worries about how the nation would fare now that "the people" read were matched by worries about how to regulate the reading done by women. In 1807 the bowdlerized edition was born, as the Reverend Thomas Bowdler and his sister Henrietta produced *The Family Shakespeare*, concocting a Bard who, his indelicacies expurgated, could be sanctioned family fare.

Commentators who condemned the publishing industry as a scene of criminality also cited the frequency with which, during this chaotic time, best-selling books ended up republished in unauthorized, "pirated" editions. Novels were the pirates' favorite targets. But the radical underground of London's printing industry also appropriated one of the most politically daring works of Percy Shelley, *Queen Mab*, and by keeping it in print, and accessible in cheap editions, thwarted attempts to posthumously sanitize the poet's reputation. And in 1817 Southey, by then a Tory and the Kingdom's Poet Laureate, was embarrassed to find his insurrectionary drama of 1794, *Wat Tyler*, published without his permission. There was no chance, Southey learned, that the publishers who had filched his play and put this souvenir of his youthful radicalism into circulation would be punished. The court refused to grant an injunction, citing the precedent that there could be no protection for publications deemed injurious to the public.

OTHER LITERARY FORMS

Prose

Although we now know the Romantic period as an age of poetry, centered on works of imagination, nonfiction prose forms—essays, reviews, political pamphlets—flourished during the epoch, as writers seized the opportunity to speak to and for the era's new audiences. In eighteenth-century England, prose, particularly in the urbane, accessible style that writers such as Joseph Addison and David Hume cultivated in their essays, had been valued as the medium of sociable exchange that could integrate different points of view and unify the public space known as the "republic of letters." That ideal of civil discussion came under pressure in the Romantic period, however, since by then many intellectuals were uncertain whether a republic of letters could survive the arrival of those new readers, "the people," and whether in this age of class awareness such a thing as a unified public culture was even possible. Those uncertainties are never far from the surface in the master-pieces of Romantic prose—a category that ranges from the pamphleteering that drew Burke, Wollstonecraft, and Paine into the Revolution controversy of the 1790s, to the periodical essays, with suggestive titles like *The Watchman* and *The Friend*, in which Coleridge turned controversialist, to the magazine writing of Hazlitt, Charles Lamb, and De Quincey in the 1820s.

The issue of how the writer should relate to audience—as watchman or friend?—was especially tricky, because this period, when so many more people defined themselves as readers, saw the emergence of a new species of specialist reader. This was the critic, who, perhaps problematically, was empowered to tell all the others what to read. Following the establishment in 1802 of the *Edinburgh Review* and in 1809 of the *Quarterly Review*, a new professionalized breed of book reviewer claimed a degree of cultural authority to which eighteenth-century critics had never aspired. Whereas later-eighteenth-century periodicals such as the *Monthly Review* and *Critical Review* had aimed to notice almost everything in print, the *Edinburgh* and *Quarterly* limited themselves to about fifteen books per issue. The selectivity enabled them to make decisive statements about what would count as culture and what would fall beyond the pale. They also conceptu-alized criticism as a space of discipline, in which the reputations of the writers under review were as likely to be marred as they were to be made. The stern Latin motto of the *Edinburgh* (founded by lawyers) translates as "the judge is condemned when the guilty go free." The continuing tension in the relations between criticism and literature and doubt about whether critical prose can be literature—whether it can have artistic value as well as social utility—are legacies from the Romantic era. Hazlitt wondered self-consciously in an essay on criticism whether his was not in fact a critical rather than a poetical age and whether "no great works of genius appear, because so much is said and written about them."

Hazlitt participated importantly in another development. In 1820 the founding editor of the *London Magazine* gathered a group of writers, Hazlitt, Lamb, and De Quincey, who in the *London*'s pages collectively developed the Romantic form known as the familiar essay: intimate-feeling commen-taries, often presented as if prompted by incidents in the authors' private lives, on an eclectic range of topics, from pork to prize-fighting. In some of his essays, Hazlitt modeled an account of the individual's response to works of art as most important not for how, for instance, it prepares that person for public citizenship, but for what it helps him discover about his personality. For their essays Lamb and De Quincey developed a style that harkened back to writers who flourished before the republic of letters and who had more idiosyncratic eccentricities than eighteenth-century decorum would have allowed. Though these essayists were very differently circumstanced from the Romantic poets who were their friends—paid by the page and writing to a deadline, for a start—their works thus parallel the poets' in also turning toward the subjective. One consequence of the essayists' cultivation of intimacy and preference for the impressionistic over the systematic is that, when we track the history of prose to the 1820s, we see it end up in a place very different from the one it occupies at the start of the Romantic period. Participants in the Revolution controversy of the 1790s had claimed to speak for all England. By the close of the period the achievement of the familiar essay was to have brought the medium of prose within the category of "the literary"—but by distancing it from public life.

Drama

Whether the plays composed during the Romantic period can qualify as literature has been, by contrast, more of a puzzle. England throughout this period had a vibrant theatrical culture. Theater criticism, practiced with flair by Hazlitt and Lamb, emerged as a new prose genre; actors like Sarah Siddons and Edmund Kean numbered the poets among their admirers and found their way into Romantic poetry; Mary Robinson was known as an actor before she was known as an author. But there were many restrictions limiting what could be staged in England and many calls for reform. As places where crowds gathered, theaters were always closely watched by suspicious government officials. The English had habitually extolled their theater as a site of social mixing—a mirror to the political order in that it supplied all the classes in the nation (those who, depending on how their tickets were priced, frequented the box, the pit, or the gallery) with another sort of representative assembly. But during this era *dis*order seemed the rule: riots broke out at Covent Garden in 1792 and 1809. The link between drama and disorder was one reason that new dramas had to meet the approval of a censor before they could be performed, a rule in place since 1737. Another restriction was that only the Theaters Royal (in London, Drury Lane and Covent Garden) had the legal right to produce "legitimate" (spoken word) drama, leaving the other stages limited to entertainments—pantomimes and melodramas mainly—in which dialogue was by regulation always combined with music. An evening's entertainment focused on legitimate drama would not have been so different. The stages and auditoriums of the two theaters royal were huge spaces, which encouraged their managers to favor grandiose spectacles or, more precisely, multimedia experiences, involving musicians, dancers, and artists who designed scenery, besides players and playwrights.

This theatrical culture's demotion of *words* might explain why the poets of the era, however stage-struck, found drama uncongenial. Nonetheless, almost all tried their hands at the form, tempted by the knowledge that the plays of certain of their (now less esteemed) contemporaries—Hannah Cowley and Charles Maturin, for example—had met with immense acclaim. Some of the poets' plays were composed to be read rather than performed: "closet dramas," such as Byron's *Manfred*, Percy Shelley's *Prometheus Unbound*, and most of Joanna Baillie's *Plays on the Passions*, permitted experimentation with topic and form. Others were written expressly for the stage, but their authors were hampered by their inexperience and tendency, exacerbated by the censorship that encouraged them to seek safe subject matter in the past, to imitate the style of Elizabethan and Jacobean drama. There were exceptions to this discouraging record. Coleridge's tragedy *Remorse*, for instance, was a minor hit and ran for twenty nights in 1813. The most capable dramatist among the poets was, surprisingly, Percy Shelley. His powerful tragedy *The Cenci* (1820), the story of a monstrous father who rapes his daughter and is murdered by her in turn, was deemed unstageable on political rather than artistic or technical grounds. It had no chance of getting by the Examiner of Plays; indeed, by thematizing the unspeakable topic of incest, Shelley predicted his own censoring.

The Novel

Novels at the start of the Romantic period were immensely popular but—as far as critics and some of the form's half-ashamed practitioners were concerned—not quite respectable. Loose in structure, they seemed to require fewer skills than other literary genres. This genre lacked the classic pedigree claimed by poetry and drama. It attracted (or so detractors declared) an undue proportion of readers who were women, and who, by consuming its escapist stories of romantic love, risked developing false ideas of life. It likewise attracted (so some of these same critics complained) too many *writers* who were women. (By the 1780s women were publishing as many novels as men.) Because of its popularity, the form also focused commentators' anxieties about the expansion of the book market and commercialization of literature: hence late-eighteenth-century reviewers of new novels often sarcastically described them as mass-produced commodities, not authored exactly, but instead stamped out automatically in "novel-mills." Matters changed decisively, however, starting around 1814. Reviews of Scott's *Waverley* series of historical novels and then a review that Scott wrote of Austen's *Emma* declared a renaissance—"a new style of novel." By this time, too, the genre had its historians, who delineated the novel's origins and rise and in this manner established its particularity against the more reputable literary forms. It was having a canon created for it, too; figures like Barbauld and Scott compiled and introduced collections of the best novels. So equipped, the novel began to endanger poetry's long-held monopoly on literary prestige.

There had in fact been earlier signs of these new ambitions for the genre, although reviewers did not then know what to make of them. The last decade of the eighteenth century saw bold experiments with novels' form and subject matter—in particular, new ways of linking fiction with philosophy and history. Rather than, as one reviewer put it, contentedly remaining in a "region of their own," some novels showed signs of having designs on the real world. The writers now known as the Jacobin novelists used the form to test political theories and represent the political upheavals of the age. Thus in *Caleb Williams, or, Things as They Are*, William Godwin (husband of Mary Wollstonecraft, father of Mary Shelley) set out, he said, to "write a tale, that shall constitute an epoch in the mind of the reader, that no one, after he had read it, shall ever be exactly the same": the result was a chilling novel of surveillance and entrapment in which a servant recounts the persecutions he suffers at the hands of the master whose secret past he has detected. (The disturbing cat-and-mouse game between the two gets rewritten two decades later as the conclusion to *Frankenstein*, a novel that, among many other things, represents Shelley's tribute to the philosophical fictions of her parents.) Loyalists attacked the Jacobins with their own weapons and, in making novels their ammunition, contributed in turn to enhancing the genre's cultural presence.

The Novel. Illustration from 1787 by James Northcote of a scene in William Hayley's didactic poem *The Triumphs of Temper* (1781): the heroine's maiden aunt has just caught her in possession of a novel and seized the book as "filthy trash"—while secretly intending to keep it for herself.

Another innovation in novel-writing took shape, strangely enough, as a recovery of what was old. Writers whom we now describe as the Gothic novelists revisited the romance, the genre identified as the primitive fore-runner of the modern novel, looking to a medieval (i.e., "Gothic") Europe that they pictured as a place of gloomy castles, devious Catholic monks, and stealthy ghosts. These authors—first Walpole, followed by Clara Reeve, Sophia Lee, Matthew Lewis, and the hugely popular Ann Radcliffe—developed for the novel a repertory of settings and story lines meant to purvey to readers the pleasurable terror of regression to a premodern, pre-rational state. This Gothic turn was another instance of the period's "romance revival," another variation on the effort to renew the literature of the present by reworking the past. Gothic fiction was thus promoted in terms running parallel to those in accounts of the powers of poetry: when novels break with humdrum reality, Barbauld explained, "our imagination, darting forth, explores with rapture the new world which is laid open to its view, and rejoices in the expansion of its powers."

Possibly this "new world" was meant to supply Romantic-period readers with an escape route from the present and from what Godwin called "things as they are." Certainly, the pasts that Gothic novelists conjure up are con-ceived of in fanciful, freewheeling ways; it is comical just how often a Rad-cliffe heroine who is supposed to inhabit sixteenth-century France can act like a proper English girl on the marriage market in the 1790s. But even that example of anachronism might suggest that some Gothic novelists were invit-ing readers to assess their stories as engaging the questions of the day. Gothic horrors gave many writers a language in which to examine the nature of power—the elements of sadism and masochism in the relations between men and women, for instance. And frequently the Gothic novelists probe the very ideas of historical accuracy and legitimacy that critics use against them, and meditate on who is authorized to tell the story of the past and who is not.

The ascendancy of the novel in the early nineteenth century is in many ways a function of fiction writers' new self-consciousness about their relation to works of history. By 1814 the novelist and historian encroached on each other's territory more than ever. This was not exactly because nineteenth century novelists were renewing their commitment to probability and realism (although, defining themselves against the critically reviled Gothic novelists, many were), but rather because the nature of things historical was also being reinvented. In light of the Revolution, history's traditional emphasis on public affairs and great men had begun to give way to an emphasis on beliefs, customs, everyday habits—the approach we now identify with social history. Novelists pursued similar interests: in works like *Castle Rackrent*, Maria Edgeworth, for instance, provides an almost anthropological account of the way of life of a bygone Ireland. The only novelist before Scott whom the influential *Edinburgh Review* took seriously, Edgeworth builds into her "national tales" details about local practices that demonstrate how people's ways of seeing are rooted in the particularities of their native places. Scott learned from her, incorporating her regionalism into his new style of historical novels, in which, with deeply moving results, he also portrayed the past as a place of adventure, pageantry, and grandeur.

Scott and Edgeworth establish the master theme of the early-nineteenth-century novel: the question of how the individual consciousness intermeshes with larger social structures, of how far character is the product of history and how far it is not. Jane Austen's brilliance as a satirist of the English leisure class often prompts literary historians to compare her works to witty Restoration and eighteenth-century comedies. But she too helped bring this theme to the forefront of novel-writing, devising new ways of articulating the relationship between the psychological history of the individual and the history of society, and, with unsurpassed psychological insight, creating unforgettable heroines who live in time and change. As with other Romantics, Austen's topic is revolution—revolutions of the mind. The momentous event in her fictions, which resemble Wordsworth's poetry in finding out the extraordinary in the everyday, is the change of mind that creates the possibility of love. Contrasting his own "big bow-wow strain" with Austen's nuance, Scott wrote that Austen "had a talent for describing the involvements and feelings and characters of ordinary life, which is to me the most wonderful I ever met with." Nineteenth-century reviewers of his triumphant *Waverley* series were certain that Scott's example foretold the future of novel-writing. He, however, recognized the extent to which Austen had also changed the genre in which she worked, by developing a new novelistic language for the workings of the mind in flux.

The Romantic Period

TEXTS	CONTEXTS
1773 Anna Letitia Aikin (later Barbauld), *Poems*	
1774 J. W. von Goethe, *The Sorrows of Young Werther*	
	1775 American War of Independence (1775–83)
1776 Adam Smith, *The Wealth of Nations*	
1778 Frances Burney, *Evelina*	
1779 Samuel Johnson, *Lives of the English Poets* (1779–81)	
	1780 Gordon Riots in London
1781 Immanuel Kant, *Critique of Pure Reason*. Jean-Jacques Rousseau, *Confessions*. J. C. Friedrich Schiller, *The Robbers*	
	1783 William Pitt becomes prime minister (serving until 1801 and again in 1804–6)
1784 Charlotte Smith, *Elegiac Sonnets*	1784 Death of Samuel Johnson
1785 William Cowper, *The Task*	
1786 William Beckford, *Vathek*. Robert Burns, *Poems, Chiefly in the Scottish Dialect*	
	1787 W. A. Mozart, *Don Giovanni*. Society for the Abolition of the Slave Trade founded
1789 Jeremy Bentham, *Principles of Morals and Legislation*. William Blake, *Songs of Innocence*	1789 Fall of the Bastille (beginning of the French Revolution)
1790 Joanna Baillie, *Poems*. Blake, *The Marriage of Heaven and Hell*. Edmund Burke, *Reflections on the Revolution in France*	1790 J. M. W. Turner first exhibits at the Royal Academy
1791 William Gilpin, *Observations on the River Wye*. Thomas Paine, *Rights of Man*. Ann Radcliffe, *The Romance of the Forest*	1791 Revolution in Santo Domingo (modern Haiti)
1792 Mary Wollstonecraft, *A Vindication of the Rights of Woman*	1792 September Massacres in Paris. First gas lights in Britain
1793 William Godwin, *Political Justice*	1793 Execution of Louis XVI and Marie Antoinette. France declares war against Britain (and then Britain against France). The Reign of Terror
1794 Blake, *Songs of Experience*. Godwin, *Caleb Williams*. Radcliffe, *The Mysteries of Udolpho*	1794 The fall of Robespierre. Trials for high treason of members of the London Corresponding Society
	1795 Pitt's Gagging Acts suppress freedom of speech and assembly in Britain
1796 Matthew Gregory Lewis, *The Monk*	
	1797 Mary Wollstonecraft dies from complications of childbirth

TEXTS	CONTEXTS
1798 Joanna Baillie, *Plays on the Passions,* volume 1. Bentham, *Political Economy.* Thomas Malthus, *An Essay on the Principle of Population.* William Wordsworth and Samuel Taylor Coleridge, *Lyrical Ballads*	**1798** Rebellion in Ireland
1800 Maria Edgeworth, *Castle Rackrent.* Mary Robinson, *Lyrical Tales*	
	1801 Parliamentary Union of Ireland and Great Britain
1802–3 Walter Scott, *Minstrelsy of the Scottish Border*	**1802** Treaty of Amiens. *Edinburgh Review* founded. John Constable first exhibits at the Royal Academy
	1804 Napoleon crowned emperor. Founding of the republic of Haiti
1805 Scott, *The Lay of the Last Minstrel*	**1805** The French fleet defeated by the British at Trafalgar
1807 Wordsworth, *Poems in Two Volumes* Charlotte Smith, *Beachy Head*	**1807** Abolition of the slave trade
1808 Goethe, *Faust,* part I	**1808** Ludwig van Beethoven, *Symphonies* 5 and 6
	1809 *Quarterly Review* founded
1811 Jane Austen, *Sense and Sensibility*	**1811** The Prince of Wales becomes regent for George III, who is declared incurably insane
1812 Lord Byron, *Childe Harold's Pilgrimage,* cantos 1 and 2. Felicia Hemans, *The Domestic Affections*	**1812** War between Britain and the United States (1812–15)
1813 Austen, *Pride and Prejudice*	
1814 Scott, *Waverley.* Wordsworth, *The Excursion*	
	1815 Napoleon defeated at Waterloo. Corn Laws passed, protecting economic interests of the landed aristocracy
1816 Byron, *Childe Harold,* cantos 3 and 4. Coleridge, *Christabel,* "Kubla Khan." Percy Shelley, *Alastor*	
1817 Byron, *Manfred.* Coleridge, *Biographia Literaria* and *Sibylline Leaves.* John Keats, *Poems*	**1817** *Blackwood's Edinburgh Magazine* founded. Death of Princess Charlotte. Death of Jane Austen
1818 Austen, *Persuasion* and *Northanger Abbey.* Keats, *Endymion.* Thomas Love Peacock, *Nightmare Abbey.* Mary Shelley, *Frankenstein*	
1819 Byron, *Don Juan,* cantos 1 and 2. Percy Shelley, *The Mask of Anarchy*	**1819** "Peterloo Massacre" in Manchester
1820 John Clare, *Poems Descriptive of Rural Life.* Keats, *Lamia, Isabella, The Eve of St. Agnes, and Other Poems.* Percy Shelley, *Prometheus Unbound*	**1820** Death of George III; accession of George IV. *London Magazine* founded

TEXTS	CONTEXTS
1821 Thomas De Quincey, *Confessions of an English Opium-Eater*. Percy Shelley, *Adonais*	**1821** Deaths of Keats in Rome and Napoleon at St. Helena
	1822 Franz Schubert, *Unfinished Symphony*. Death of Percy Shelley in the Bay of Spezia, near Lerici, Italy
1823 Charles Lamb, *Essays of Elia*	
1824 Letitia Landon, *The Improvisatrice*	**1824** Death of Byron in Missolonghi
1826 Mary Shelley, *The Last Man*	
1827 Clare, *The Shepherd's Calendar*	
1828 Hemans, *Records of Woman*	**1828** Parliamentary repeal of the Test and Corporation Acts excluding Dissenters from state offices
	1829 Catholic Emancipation
1830 Charles Lyell, *Principles of Geology* (1830–33). Alfred Tennyson, *Poems, Chiefly Lyrical*	**1830** Death of George IV; accession of William IV. Revolution in France
	1832 First Reform Bill

ANNA LETITIA BARBAULD
1743–1825

Anna Barbauld, born Anna Letitia Aikin, received an unusual education from her father, who was a minister and a teacher at the Warrington Academy in Lancashire, the great educational center for the Nonconformist community, whose religion barred them from admission to the universities of Oxford and Cambridge. During the eighteenth century Dissenting academies such as Warrington had developed a modern curriculum in the natural sciences, as well as in modern languages and English literature. This progressive educational program deviated significantly from the curriculum, scarcely altered since the sixteenth century, that was supplied by the old universities. The benefits Barbauld received from her exposure to an educational system that the Dissenters had designed with their sons in mind are suggested by the astounding versatility of her literary career.

She made her literary debut in 1773 with *Poems* and *Miscellaneous Pieces in Prose*, the latter cowritten with her brother John. The books immediately established her as a leading author. Her marriage the next year to Rochemont Barbauld, a Dissenting minister like her father, and their decision to set up a boys' school together therefore struck the critic Samuel Johnson as squandering this woman's own unusual education: "Miss [Aikin] was an instance of early cultivation, but in what did it terminate?" Thereafter, until Rochemont Barbauld's increasing mental instability necessitated the closing of their school, Barbauld divided her time between writing and teaching the younger boys. Because of the popularity of Barbauld's *Lessons for Children* (1778–79) and *Hymns in Prose for Children* (1781), William Hazlitt was recording a common experience when he recalled that he read her books "before those of any other author . . . , when I was learning to spell words of one syllable." This writing for child audiences registered Barbauld's Enlightenment faith in human potential.

Her fame continued to grow in the 1790s, and in 1797 the up-and-coming poet Samuel Taylor Coleridge walked forty miles to meet her. During this decade Barbauld contributed poetry to her brother John's *Monthly Magazine*, published her "Epistle to William Wilberforce" attacking British involvement in the slave trade, and wrote pamphlets that opposed the war with France and campaigned for the repeal of the Test Acts that had barred participation in the public life of the nation to Nonconformists (those men who would not subscribe, as "tests" of their loyalty, to the thirty-nine Articles of the Established Church). She accompanied this writing with editing, producing editions of William Collins's poems (1797) and the novelist Samuel Richardson's letters (1804). Her fifty-volume compilation *The British Novelists* (1810) was the first attempt to establish a national canon in fiction and thereby do for the novel what Samuel Johnson's *Works of the English Poets* (1779–81) had done for poetry. Its introductory essay, "On the Origin and Progress of Novel-Writing," makes a pioneering argument for the educational and artistic value of the still disreputable genre.

Barbauld's last major work was *Eighteen Hundred and Eleven* (1812), a long poem that despairs over the war with France (then in its seventeenth year) and the corruption of English consumer society. (An excerpt from *Eighteen Hundred and Eleven* may be found in "Romantic Literature and Wartime," in the supplemental ebook.) Critics were unnerved, even disgusted, by the poem's apocalyptic vision of a future in which England, its pride humbled, would lie in ruins—the more so because of its author's gender. The Tory critic John Wilson Croker thus warned Barbauld "to desist from satire": it was not up to a "lady-author" to sally forth from her knitting and say how "the empire might . . . be saved." After this lambasting, Barbauld fell publicly silent and published no more. She did not stop writing, however: the collection of her aunt's *Works* that her niece Lucy Aikin brought out in 1825 after her aunt's death contained several previously unpublished pieces.

The Mouse's Petition[1]

Found in the trap where he had been confined all night by Dr. Priestley, for the sake of making experiments with different kinds of air

"Parcere subjectis, et debellare superbos."
—Virgil

Oh hear a pensive prisoner's prayer,
For liberty that sighs;
And never let thine heart be shut
Against the wretch's cries.

5 For here forlorn and sad I sit,
Within the wiry gate;
And tremble at th' approaching morn,
Which brings impending fate.

If e'er thy breast with freedom glow'd,
10 And spurn'd a tyrant's chain,
Let not thy strong oppressive force
A free-born mouse detain.

Oh do not stain with guiltless blood
Thy hospitable hearth;
15 Nor triumph that thy wiles betray'd
A prize so little worth.

The scatter'd gleanings of a feast
My frugal meals supply;
But if thine unrelenting heart
20 That slender boon deny,

The cheerful light, the vital air,
Are blessings widely given;
Let nature's commoners enjoy
The common gifts of heaven.

25 The well-taught philosophic mind
To all compassion gives;

1. Addressed to the clergyman, political theorist, and scientist Joseph Priestley (1733–1804), who at this time was the most distinguished teacher at the Nonconformist Protestant Warrington Academy, where Barbauld's father was also a member of the faculty. The imagined speaker (the petitioning mouse) is destined to participate in just the sort of experiment that led Priestley, a few years later, to the discovery of "phlogiston"— what we now call oxygen. Tradition has it that when Barbauld showed him the lines, Priestley set the mouse free. According to Barbauld's modern editors, the poem was many times reprinted and was a favorite to assign students for memorizing. The Latin epigraph is from *The Aeneid* 6.853, "To spare the humbled, and to tame in war the proud."

Casts round the world an equal eye,
And feels for all that lives.

If mind, as ancient sages taught,[2]
30 A never dying flame,
Still shifts through matter's varying forms,
In every form the same,

Beware, lest in the worm you crush
A brother's soul you find;
35 And tremble lest thy luckless hand
Dislodge a kindred mind.

Or, if this transient gleam of day
Be *all* of life we share,
Let pity plead within thy breast
40 That little *all* to spare.

So may thy hospitable board
With health and peace be crown'd;
And every charm of heartfelt ease
Beneath thy roof be found.

45 So, when destruction lurks unseen,
Which men, like mice, may share,
May some kind angel clear thy path,
And break the hidden snare.

ca. 1771   1773

A Summer Evening's Meditation[1]

'Tis past! The sultry tyrant of the south
Has spent his short-lived rage; more grateful° hours   *pleasing*
Move silent on; the skies no more repel
The dazzled sight, but with mild maiden beams
5   Of tempered lustre court the cherished eye
To wander o'er their sphere; where, hung aloft,
Dian's bright crescent, like a silver bow
New strung in heaven, lifts high its beamy horns
Impatient for the night, and seems to push
10 Her brother° down the sky. Fair Venus shines   *Apollo*
Even in the eye of day; with sweetest beam
Propitious shines, and shakes a trembling flood
Of softened radiance from her dewy locks.

2. Lines 29–36 play on the idea of transmigra-
tion of souls, a doctrine that Priestley believed
until the early 1770s.
1. This poem looks backward to poems such as
William Collins's "Ode to Evening" (1748), Anne
Finch's "A Nocturnal Reverie" (1713), and even
to Milton's description in book 2 of *Paradise Lost*
of Satan's daring navigation of the realm of

Chaos. At the same time Barbauld's excursion-
and-return structure anticipates the high flights
(and returns) of later lyrics by Coleridge, Percy
Shelley, and Keats. But her account of the journey, with its references to Diana's crescent (line
7) and Venus's sweetest beams (10 and 11) is *differently* gendered: this soul that launches "into
the trackless deeps" (82) is clearly female.

The shadows spread apace; while meekened² Eve,
15 Her cheek yet warm with blushes, slow retires
Through the Hesperian gardens of the west,
And shuts the gates of day. 'Tis now the hour
When Contemplation from her sunless haunts,
The cool damp grotto, or the lonely depth
20 Of unpierced woods, where wrapt in solid shade
She mused away the gaudy hours of noon,
And fed on thoughts unripened by the sun,
Moves forward; and with radiant finger points
To yon blue concave swelled by breath divine,
25 Where, one by one, the living eyes of heaven
Awake, quick kindling o'er the face of ether
One boundless blaze; ten thousand trembling fires,
And dancing lustres, where the unsteady eye,
Restless and dazzled, wanders unconfined
30 O'er all this field of glories; spacious field,
And worthy of the Master: he, whose hand
With hieroglyphics elder than the Nile
Inscribed the mystic tablet, hung on high
To public gaze, and said, "Adore, O man!
35 The finger of thy God." From what pure wells
Of milky light, what soft o'erflowing urn,
Are all these lamps so fill'd? these friendly lamps,
For ever streaming o'er the azure deep
To point our path, and light us to our home.
40 How soft they slide along their lucid spheres!
And silent as the foot of Time, fulfill
Their destined courses: Nature's self is hushed,
And, but° a scattered leaf, which rustles through   *except for*
The thick-wove foliage, not a sound is heard
45 To break the midnight air; though the raised ear,
Intensely listening, drinks in every breath.
How deep the silence, yet how loud the praise!
But are they silent all? or is there not
A tongue in every star, that talks with man,
50 And woos him to be wise? nor woos in vain:
This dead of midnight is the noon of thought,
And Wisdom mounts her zenith with the stars.
At this still hour the self-collected soul
Turns inward, and beholds a stranger there
55 Of high descent, and more than mortal rank;
An embryo God; a spark of fire divine,
Which must burn on for ages, when the sun,—
Fair transitory creature of a day!—
Has closed his golden eye, and wrapt in shades
60 Forgets his wonted journey through the east.

Ye citadels of light, and seats of Gods!
Perhaps my future home, from whence the soul,
Revolving° periods past, may oft look back   *Meditating on*
With recollected tenderness on all

---

2. Softened, made meek.

65 The various busy scenes she left below,
Its deep-laid projects and its strange events,
As on some fond and doting tale that soothed
Her infant hours—O be it lawful now
To tread the hallowed circle of your courts,
70 And with mute wonder and delighted awe
Approach your burning confines. Seized in thought,
On Fancy's wild and roving wing I sail,
From the green borders of the peopled Earth,
And the pale Moon, her duteous fair attendant;
75 From solitary Mars; from the vast orb
Of Jupiter, whose huge gigantic bulk
Dances in ether like the lightest leaf;
To the dim verge, the suburbs of the system,
Where cheerless Saturn 'midst his watery moons[3]
80 Girt with a lucid zone,° in gloomy pomp,   belt
Sits like an exiled monarch: fearless thence
I launch into the trackless deeps of space,
Where, burning round, ten thousand suns appear,
Of elder beam, which ask no leave to shine
85 Of our terrestrial star, nor borrow light
From the proud regent of our scanty day;
Sons of the morning, first-born of creation,
And only less than Him who marks their track,
And guides their fiery wheels. Here must I stop,
90 Or is there aught beyond? What hand unseen
Impels me onward through the glowing orbs
Of habitable nature, far remote,
To the dread confines of eternal night,
To solitudes of vast unpeopled space,
95 The deserts of creation, wide and wild;
Where embryo systems and unkindled suns
Sleep in the womb of chaos? fancy droops,
And thought astonished stops her bold career.
But O thou mighty mind! whose powerful word
100 Said, thus let all things be, and thus they were,[4]
Where shall I seek thy presence? how unblamed
Invoke thy dread perfection?
Have the broad eyelids of the morn beheld thee?
Or does the beamy shoulder of Orion
105 Support thy throne? O look with pity down
On erring, guilty man! not in thy names
Of terror clad; not with those thunders armed
That conscious Sinai felt, when fear appalled
The scattered tribes;[5]—thou hast a gentler voice,
110 That whispers comfort to the swelling heart,
Abashed, yet longing to behold her Maker.

But now my soul, unused to stretch her powers
In flight so daring, drops her weary wing,

---

3. Saturn marked the outmost bounds of the solar system until the discovery of Uranus in 1781.
4. An echo of Genesis 1.3.
5. When God came down to deliver the Ten Commandments "there were thunders and lightnings . . . so that all the people . . . trembled" (Exodus 19.16).

And seeks again the known accustomed spot,
115 Drest up with sun, and shade, and lawns, and streams,
A mansion fair, and spacious for its guest,
And full replete with wonders. Let me here,
Content and grateful, wait the appointed time,
And ripen for the skies: the hour will come
120 When all these splendours bursting on my sight
Shall stand unveiled, and to my ravished sense
Unlock the glories of the world unknown.

1773

The Rights of Woman[1]

Yes, injured Woman! rise, assert thy right!
Woman! too long degraded, scorned, opprest;
O born to rule in partial° Law's despite,   biased
Resume thy native empire o'er the breast!

5 Go forth arrayed in panoply° divine;   suit of armor
That angel pureness which admits no stain;
Go, bid proud Man his boasted rule resign,
And kiss the golden sceptre of thy reign.

Go, gird thyself with grace; collect thy store
10 Of bright artillery glancing from afar;
Soft melting tones thy thundering cannon's roar,
Blushes and fears thy magazine° of war.   storehouse of arms

Thy rights are empire: urge no meaner claim,—
Felt, not defined, and if debated, lost;
15 Like sacred mysteries, which withheld from fame,
Shunning discussion, are revered the most.

Try all that wit and art suggest to bend
Of thy imperial foe the stubborn knee;
Make treacherous Man thy subject, not thy friend;
20 Thou mayst command, but never canst be free.

Awe the licentious, and restrain the rude;
Soften the sullen, clear the cloudy brow:
Be, more than princes' gifts, thy favours sued;—
She hazards all, who will the least allow.

25 But hope not, courted idol of mankind,
On this proud eminence secure to stay;
Subduing and subdued, thou soon shalt find
Thy coldness soften, and thy pride give way.

1. A response—seemingly favorable until the last two stanzas—to Mary Wollstonecraft's *A Vindication of the Rights of Woman* (1792). In chapter 4 of *Vindication*, Wollstonecraft had singled out Barbauld's poem "To a Lady with Some Painted Flowers" as evidence that even women of sense were capable of adopting the masculine-centered gender code that identified the feminine with the ornamental and the frivolous.

Then, then, abandon each ambitious thought,
30   Conquest or rule thy heart shall feebly move,
In Nature's school, by her soft maxims taught,
That separate rights are lost in mutual love.

ca. 1792–95   1825

To a Little Invisible Being
Who Is Expected Soon to Become Visible

Germ of new life, whose powers expanding slow
For many a moon their full perfection wait,—
Haste, precious pledge of happy love, to go
Auspicious borne through life's mysterious gate.

5   What powers lie folded in thy curious frame,—
Senses from objects locked, and mind from thought!
How little canst thou guess thy lofty claim
To grasp at all the worlds the Almighty wrought!

And see, the genial season's warmth to share,
10   Fresh younglings° shoot, and opening roses glow!   *young plants*
Swarms of new life exulting fill the air,—
Haste, infant bud of being, haste to blow!°   *bloom*

For thee the nurse prepares her lulling songs,
The eager matrons count the lingering day;
15   But far the most thy anxious parent longs
On thy soft cheek a mother's kiss to lay.

She only asks to lay her burden down,
That her glad arms that burden may resume;
And nature's sharpest pangs her wishes crown,
20   That free thee living from thy living tomb.

She longs to fold to her maternal breast
Part of herself, yet to herself unknown;
To see and to salute the stranger guest,
Fed with her life through many a tedious moon.

25   Come, reap thy rich inheritance of love!
Bask in the fondness of a Mother's eye!
Nor wit nor eloquence her heart shall move
Like the first accents of thy feeble cry.

Haste, little captive, burst thy prison doors!
30   Launch on the living world, and spring to light!
Nature for thee displays her various stores,
Opens her thousand inlets of delight.

If charmed verse or muttered prayers had power,
With favouring spells to speed thee on thy way,

35   Anxious I'd bid my beads° each passing hour,   *offer a prayer*
      Till thy wished smile thy mother's pangs o'erpay.°   *more than compensate*

ca. 1795?   1825

Washing-Day

> *. . . and their voice,*
> *Turning again towards childish treble, pipes*
> *And whistles in its sound.*[1]

    The Muses are turned gossips; they have lost
    The buskined° step, and clear high-sounding phrase,   *tragic, elevated*
    Language of gods. Come then, domestic Muse,
    In slipshod measure loosely prattling on
5   Of farm or orchard, pleasant curds and cream,
    Or drowning flies, or shoe lost in the mire
    By little whimpering boy, with rueful face;
    Come, Muse; and sing the dreaded Washing-Day.
    Ye who beneath the yoke of wedlock bend,
10 With bowed soul, full well ye ken° the day   *know*
    Which week, smooth sliding after week, brings on
    Too soon;—for to that day nor peace belongs
    Nor comfort;—ere the first gray streak of dawn,
    The red-armed washers come and chase repose.
15 Nor pleasant smile, nor quaint device of mirth,
    E'er visited that day: the very cat,
    From the wet kitchen scared, and reeking hearth,
    Visits the parlour,—an unwonted° guest.   *unaccustomed*
    The silent breakfast-meal is soon dispatched;
20 Uninterrupted, save by anxious looks
    Cast at the lowering sky, if sky should lower.
    From that last evil, O preserve us, heavens!
    For should the skies pour down, adieu to all
    Remains of quiet: then expect to hear
25 Of sad disasters,—dirt and gravel stains
    Hard to efface, and loaded lines at once
    Snapped short,—and linen-horse° by dog thrown down, *drying rack*
    And all the petty miseries of life.
    Saints have been calm while stretched upon the rack,
30 And Guatimozin[2] smiled on burning coals;
    But never yet did housewife notable
    Greet with a smile a rainy washing-day.
    —But grant the welkin° fair, require not thou   *sky*
    Who call'st thyself perchance the master there,
35 Or study swept or nicely dusted coat,
    Or usual 'tendance;—ask not, indiscreet,
    Thy stockings mended, though the yawning rents
    Gape wide as Erebus;° nor hope to find   *the underworld*

---

1. Loosely quoted from Shakespeare's *As You Like It* 2.7.160–62.
2. The last Aztec emperor (Cuanhtémoc, d. 1525), who was tortured and executed by the Spanish conquistadors.

Some snug recess impervious: shouldst thou try
40   The 'customed garden walks, thine eye shall rue
The budding fragrance of thy tender shrubs,
Myrtle or rose, all crushed beneath the weight
Of coarse checked apron,—with impatient hand
Twitched off when showers impend: or crossing lines
45   Shall mar thy musings, as the wet cold sheet
Flaps in thy face abrupt. Woe to the friend
Whose evil stars have urged him forth to claim
On such a day the hospitable rites!
Looks, blank at best, and stinted courtesy,
50   Shall he receive. Vainly he feeds his hopes
With dinner of roast chicken, savoury pie,
Or tart or pudding:—pudding he nor tart
That day shall eat; nor, though the husband try,
Mending what can't be helped, to kindle mirth
55   From cheer deficient, shall his consort's brow
Clear up propitious:—the unlucky guest
In silence dines, and early slinks away.
I well remember, when a child, the awe
This day struck into me; for then the maids,
60   I scarce knew why, looked cross, and drove me from them;
Nor soft caress could I obtain, nor hope
Usual indulgencies; jelly or creams,
Relic of costly suppers, and set by
For me, their petted one; or buttered toast,
65   When butter was forbid; or thrilling tale
Of ghost or witch, or murder—so I went
And sheltered me beside the parlour fire:
There my dear grandmother, eldest of forms,
Tended the little ones, and watched from harm,
70   Anxiously fond, though oft her spectacles
With elfin cunning hid, and oft the pins
Drawn from her ravelled stocking, might have soured
One less indulgent.—
At intervals my mother's voice was heard,
75   Urging dispatch: briskly the work went on,
All hands employed to wash, to rinse, to wring,
To fold, and starch, and clap,° and iron, and plait.   *flatten*
Then would I sit me down, and ponder much
Why washings were. Sometimes through hollow bowl
80   Of pipe amused we blew, and sent aloft
The floating bubbles; little dreaming then
To see, Montgolfier,[3] thy silken ball
Ride buoyant through the clouds—so near approach
The sports of children and the toils of men.
85   Earth, air, and sky, and ocean, hath its bubbles,[4]
And verse is one of them—this most of all.

1797

3. Brothers Joseph-Michel and Jacques-Étienne
Montgolfier successfully launched the first hot-
air balloon, at Annonay, France, in 1783.

4. Cf. Shakespeare's *Macbeth* 1.3.77: "The earth
hath bubbles, as the water has."

CHARLOTTE SMITH
1749–1806

The melancholy of Charlotte Smith's poems was no mere literary posture. After her father married for the second time, she herself was married off, at the age of fifteen, and bore a dozen children (three of whom died in infancy or childhood), before permanently separating from her husband, Benjamin Smith, because of his abusive temper, infidelities, and financial irresponsibility. She began writing to make money when her husband was imprisoned for debt in 1783. Her first book, *Elegiac Sonnets, and Other Essays by Charlotte Smith of Bignor Park, Sussex,* came out in 1784 and went through nine expanding editions in the following sixteen years.

Beginning with the 1788 publication of *Emmeline,* Smith also enjoyed considerable success as a novelist, rapidly producing nine more novels within the decade, including *Desmond* (1792), *The Old Manor House* (1793), *The Banished Man* (1794), and *The Young Philosopher* (1798). She also wrote books for children and, once, for the stage. The liberal political views espoused in her novels made the books key contributions to the Revolution Controversy in Britain. This was also the case with her eight-hundred-line blank verse poem *The Emigrants* (1793), which both evokes the suffering endured by political refugees from France and links their plight to that of the poet herself, who as a woman has discovered the emptiness of her native land's "boast / Of equal law." Such views earned Smith a place of dishonor, alongside Mary Wollstonecraft and Anna Letitia Barbauld, in Richard Polwhele's conservative satire *The Unsex'd Females* (1797), which scolds her for having suffered "her mind to be infected with the Gallic mania."

The sonnet as a form, after its great flourishing in the Renaissance in the hands of Sidney, Spenser, Shakespeare, Donne, and Milton, dropped out of fashion in the eighteenth century. It was, Samuel Johnson declared in his *Dictionary* (1755), "not very suitable to the English language." Its revival toward the end of that century—by Coleridge in the 1790s; Wordsworth (who wrote some five hundred sonnets beginning in 1802); and in the next generation, Shelley and Keats—was largely the result of Smith's influential refashioning of the sonnet as a medium of mournful feeling. In the introduction to his privately printed "sheet of sonnets" in 1796, Coleridge noted that "Charlotte Smith and [William Lisle] Bowles are they who first made the Sonnet popular among the present English," but in fact, in his *Fourteen Sonnets* of 1789 Bowles was simply following in Smith's footsteps.

In that commentary on the sonnet Coleridge made Smith his principal example when he remarked that "those Sonnets appear to me the most exquisite, in which moral Sentiments, Affections, or Feelings, are deduced from, and associated with, the scenery of Nature." Subsequently, of course, the connecting of feelings and nature became recognized as a central theme and strategy in Romantic literature, especially in the lyric poetry we associate with Coleridge and Wordsworth. But Smith's engagement with nature differs in illuminating ways from theirs. This is in part because of its quasi-scientific insistence on the faithful rendering of detail (one of Smith's sonnets is addressed to the "goddess of botany") and because of the otherness and multitudinousness in the natural world which that detail discloses. This carefully realized close-up view of nature is central to her masterpiece, the posthumously published *Beachy Head* (1807).

FROM ELEGIAC SONNETS

Written at the Close of Spring

The garlands fade that Spring so lately wove,
    Each simple flower, which she had nursed in dew,
Anemonies,[1] that spangled every grove,
    The primrose wan, and hare-bell mildly blue.
5 No more shall violets linger in the dell,
    Or purple orchis variegate the plain,
Till Spring again shall call forth every bell,
    And dress with humid hands her wreaths again.—
Ah! poor humanity! so frail, so fair,
10 Are the fond visions of thy early day,
Till tyrant passion, and corrosive care,
    Bid all thy fairy colors fade away!
Another May new buds and flowers shall bring;
Ah! why has happiness—no second Spring?

1784

To Sleep

Come, balmy Sleep! tired nature's soft resort!
    On these sad temples all thy poppies shed;
And bid gay dreams, from Morpheus'° airy court,   *Greek god of dreams*
    Float in light vision round my aching head!
5 Secure of all thy blessings, partial° Power!   *friendly*
    On his hard bed the peasant throws him down;
And the poor sea boy, in the rudest hour,
    Enjoys thee more than he who wears a crown.[1]
Clasp'd in her faithful shepherd's guardian arms,
10 Well may the village girl sweet slumbers prove
And they, O gentle Sleep! still taste thy charms,
    Who wake to labor, liberty, and love.
But still thy opiate aid dost thou deny
To calm the anxious breast; to close the streaming eye.

1784

To Night

I love thee, mournful, sober-suited Night!
    When the faint moon, yet lingering in her wane,

---

1. Anemonies. *Anemony Nemeroso.* The wood Anemony [Smith's note].
1. "Wilt thou upon the high and giddy mast / seal up the ship boy's eyes, and rock his brains / In cradle of the rude impetuous surge?" Shakespeare's *Henry IV* [Smith's note; "imperious surge" in the original].

And veil'd in clouds, with pale uncertain light
Hangs o'er the waters of the restless main.
5   In deep depression sunk, the enfeebled mind
Will to the deaf cold elements complain,
And tell the embosom'd grief, however vain,
To sullen surges and the viewless wind.
Though no repose on thy dark breast I find,
10   I still enjoy thee—cheerless as thou art;
For in thy quiet gloom the exhausted heart
Is calm, though wretched; hopeless, yet resign'd.
While to the winds and waves its sorrows given,
May reach—though lost on earth—the ear of Heaven!

1788

Written in the Church-Yard at Middleton in Sussex[1]

Press'd by the Moon, mute arbitress of tides,
While the loud equinox its power combines,
The sea no more its swelling surge confines,
But o'er the shrinking land sublimely rides.
5   The wild blast, rising from the Western cave,
Drives the huge billows from their heaving bed;
Tears from their grassy tombs the village dead,
And breaks the silent sabbath of the grave!
With shells and sea-weed mingled, on the shore
10   Lo! their bones whiten in the frequent wave;
But vain to them the winds and waters rave;
They hear the warring elements no more:
While I am doom'd—by life's long storm opprest,
To gaze with envy on their gloomy rest.

1789

On Being Cautioned against Walking on an Headland Overlooking the Sea, Because It Was Frequented by a Lunatic

Is there a solitary wretch who hies
To the tall cliff, with starting pace or slow,
And, measuring, views with wild and hollow eyes
Its distance from the waves that chide below;
5   Who, as the sea-born gale with frequent sighs

1. Middleton is a village on the margin of the sea, in Sussex, containing only two or three houses. There were formerly several acres of ground between its small church and the sea, which now, by its continual encroachments, approaches within a few feet of this half ruined and humble edifice. The wall, which once surrounded the churchyard, is entirely swept away, many of the graves broken up, and the remains of bodies interred washed into the sea: whence human bones are found among the sand and shingles on the shore [Smith's note].

Chills his cold bed upon the mountain turf,
With hoarse, half-utter'd lamentation, lies
   Murmuring responses to the dashing surf?
In moody sadness, on the giddy brink,
10   I see him more with envy than with fear;
He has no *nice felicities* that shrink[1]
   From giant horrors; wildly wandering here,
He seems (uncursed with reason) not to know
The depth or the duration of his woe.

1797

---

1. "'Tis delicate felicity that shrinks / when rocking winds are loud." Walpole [Smith's note; citing Horace Walpole's 1768 tragedy *The Mysterious Mother* I.70].

WILLIAM BLAKE
1757–1827

What William Blake called his "Spiritual Life" was as varied, free, and dramatic as his "Corporeal Life" was simple, limited, and unadventurous. His father was a London tradesman. His only formal education was in art: at the age of ten he entered a drawing school, and later he studied for a time at the school of the Royal Academy of Arts. At fourteen he entered an apprenticeship for seven years to a well-known engraver, James Basire, and began reading widely in his free time and trying his hand at poetry. At twenty-four he married Catherine Boucher, daughter of a market gardener. She was then illiterate, but Blake taught her to read and to help him in his engraving and printing. In the early and somewhat sentimentalized biographies, Catherine is represented as an ideal wife for an unorthodox and impecunious genius. Blake, however, must have been a trying domestic partner, and his vehement attacks on the torment caused by a possessive, jealous female will, which reached their height in 1793 and remained prominent in his writings for another decade, probably reflect a troubled period at home. The couple was childless.

The Blakes for a time enjoyed a moderate prosperity while Blake gave drawing lessons, illustrated books, and engraved designs made by other artists. When the demand for his work slackened, Blake in 1800 moved to a cottage at Felpham, on the Sussex seacoast, to take advantage of the patronage of the wealthy amateur of the arts and biographer William Hayley (also a supporter of Charlotte Smith), who with the best of narrow intentions tried to transform Blake into a conventional artist and breadwinner. But the caged eagle soon rebelled. Hayley, Blake wrote, "is the Enemy of my Spiritual Life while he pretends to be the Friend of my Corporeal."

At Felpham in 1803 occurred an event that left a permanent mark on Blake's mind and art—an altercation with one John Schofield, a private in the Royal Dragoons. Blake ordered the soldier out of his garden and, when Schofield replied with threats and curses against Blake and his wife, pushed him the fifty yards to the inn where he was quartered. Schofield brought charges that Blake had uttered seditious statements about king and country. Since England was at war with France, sedition was a hanging offense. Blake was acquitted—an event, according to a newspaper account, "which so gratified the auditory that the court was . . . thrown into an uproar by their

noisy exultations." Nevertheless Schofield, his fellow soldier Cock, and other participants in the trial haunted Blake's imagination and were enlarged to demonic characters who play a sinister role in *Jerusalem*. The event exacerbated Blake's sense that
ominous forces were at work in the contemporary world and led him to complicate
the symbolic and allusive style by which he veiled the radical religious, moral, and
political opinions that he expressed in his poems.

The dominant literary and artistic fashion of Blake's youth involved the notion
that the future of British culture would involve the recovery, through archaeology as
well as literary history, of an all but lost past. As an apprentice engraver who learned
to draw by sketching the medieval monuments of London churches, Blake began his
artistic career in the thick of that antiquarianism. It also informs his early lyric
poetry. *Poetical Sketches*, published when he was twenty-six, suggests Blake's affinities with a group of later-eighteenth-century writers that includes Thomas Warton,
poet and student of Middle English romance and Elizabethan verse; Thomas Gray,
translator from Old Icelandic and Welsh and author, in 1757, of "The Bard," a poem
about the English conquest of Wales; Thomas Percy, the editor of the ballad collection
Reliques of Ancient English Poetry (1765); and James Macpherson, who came before
the public in the 1760s claiming to be the translator of the epic verse of a third-
century Gaelic bard named Ossian. Like these figures, Blake located the sources of
poetic inspiration in an archaic native tradition that, according to the prevailing
view of national history, had ended up eclipsed after the seventeenth century, when
French court culture, manners, and morals began their cultural ascendancy. Even in
their orientation to a visionary culture, the bards of Blake's later Prophetic Books
retain an association with this imagined version of a primitive past.

Poetical Sketches was the only book of Blake's to be set in type according to customary methods. In 1788 he began to experiment with relief etching, a method that
he called "illuminated printing" (a term associating his works with the illuminated
manuscripts of the Middle Ages) and used to produce most of his books of poems.
Working directly on a copper plate with pens, brushes, and an acid-resistant medium,
he wrote the text in reverse (so that it would print in the normal order) and also drew
the illustration; he then etched the plate in acid to eat away the untreated copper and
leave the design standing in relief. The pages printed from such plates were colored
by hand in watercolors, often by Catherine Blake, and stitched together to make up a
volume. This process was laborious and time-consuming, and Blake printed very few
copies of his books; for example, of *Songs of Innocence and of Experience* only twenty-
eight copies (some of them incomplete) are known to exist; of *The Book of Thel*, sixteen; of *The Marriage of Heaven and Hell*, nine; and of *Jerusalem*, five.

To read a Blake poem without the pictures is to miss something important: Blake
places words and images in a relationship that is sometimes mutually enlightening
and sometimes turbulent, and that relationship is an aspect of the poem's argument.
In this mode of relief etching, he published *Songs of Innocence* (1789), then added
supplementary poems and printed *Songs of Innocence and of Experience* (1794). The
two groups of poems represent the world as it is envisioned by what he calls "two
contrary states of the human soul."

Gradually Blake's thinking about human history and his experience of life and
suffering articulated themselves in the "Giant Forms" and their actions, which came
to constitute a complete mythology. As Blake's mythical character Los said, speaking
for all imaginative artists, "I must Create a System or be enslaved by another Man's."
This coherent but constantly altering and enlarging system composed the subject
matter first of Blake's "minor prophecies," completed by 1795, and then of the major
prophetic books on which he continued working until about 1820: *The Four Zoas*,
Milton, and *Jerusalem*.

In his sixties Blake gave up poetry to devote himself to pictorial art. In the course of
his life, he produced hundreds of paintings and engravings, many of them illustrations
for the work of other poets, including a representation of Chaucer's Canterbury pilgrims, a superb set of designs for the Book of Job, and a series of illustrations of Dante,

on which he was still hard at work when he died. At the time of his death, Blake was little known as an artist and almost entirely unknown as a poet. In the mid-nineteenth century he acquired a group of admirers among the Pre-Raphaelites, who regarded him as a precursor. Since the mid-1920s Blake has finally come into his own, both in poetry and in painting, as one of the most dedicated, intellectually challenging, and astonishingly original artists. His marked influence ranges from William Butler Yeats, who edited Blake's writings and modeled his own system of mythology on Blake's, to Allen Ginsberg and other Beat writers, Philip Pullman's *His Dark Materials* trilogy, and the graphic novels of the present day.

The explication of Blake's cryptic prophetic books has been the preoccupation of many scholars. Blake wrote them in the persona, or "voice," of "the Bard! / Who Present, Past, & Future sees"—that is, as a British poet who follows Spenser, and especially Milton, in a lineage going back to the prophets of the Bible. "The Nature of my Work," he said, "is Visionary or Imaginative." What Blake meant by the key terms *vision* and *imagination,* however, is often misinterpreted by taking literally what he, speaking the traditional language of his great predecessors, intended in a figurative sense. "That which can be made Explicit to the Idiot," he declared, "is not worth my care." Blake was a born ironist who enjoyed mystifying his well-meaning but literal-minded friends and who took a defiant pleasure in shocking the dull and complacent "angels" of his day by being deliberately outrageous in representing his work and opinions.

Blake declared that "all he knew was in the Bible" and that "The Old & New Testaments are the Great Code of Art." This is an exaggeration of the truth that all his prophetic writings deal, in various formulations, with some aspects of the overall biblical plot of the creation and the Fall, the history of the generations of humanity in the fallen world, redemption, and the promise of a recovery of Eden and of a New Jerusalem. These events, however, Blake interprets in what he calls "the spiritual sense." For such a procedure he had considerable precedent, not in the neoplatonic and occult thinkers with whom some modern commentators align him, but in the "spiritual" interpreters of the Bible among the radical Protestant sects in seventeenth- and eighteenth-century England. In *The French Revolution, America: A Prophecy, Europe: A Prophecy,* and the trenchant prophetic satire *The Marriage of Heaven and Hell*—all of which Blake wrote in the early 1790s while he was an ardent supporter of the French Revolution—he, like Wordsworth, Coleridge, Southey, and a number of radical English theologians, represented the contemporary Revolution as the purifying violence that, according to biblical prophecy, portended the imminent redemption of humanity and the world. (For discussion of these apocalyptic expectations, see "The French Revolution" in the supplemental ebook.) In Blake's later poems Orc, the fiery spirit of violent revolution, gives way as a central personage to Los, the type of the visionary imagination in the fallen world.

BLAKE'S MYTHMAKING

Blake's first attempt to articulate his full myth of humanity's present, past, and future was *The Four Zoas,* begun in 1796 or 1797. A passage from the opening statement of its theme exemplifies the long verse line (what Blake called "the march of long resounding strong heroic verse") in which he wrote his Prophetic Books and will serve also to outline the Books' vision:

> Four Mighty Ones are in every Man; a Perfect Unity
> Cannot Exist, but from the Universal Brotherhood of Eden,
> The Universal Man. To Whom be Glory Evermore, Amen. . . .
> Los was the fourth immortal starry one, & in the Earth
> Of a bright Universe Empery attended day & night
> Days & nights of revolving joy, Urthona was his name
> In Eden; in the Auricular Nerves of Human life

> Which is the Earth of Eden, he his Emanations propagated. . . .
> Daughter of Beulah, Sing
> His fall into Division & his Resurrection to Unity.

Blake's mythical premise, or starting point, is not a transcendent God but the "Universal Man" who is God and who incorporates the cosmos as well. (Blake elsewhere describes this founding image as "the Human Form Divine" and names him "Albion.") The Fall, in this myth, is not the fall of humanity away from God but a falling apart of primal people, a "fall into Division." In this event the original sin is what Blake calls "Selfhood," the attempt of an isolated part to be self-sufficient. The breakup of the all-inclusive Universal Man in Eden into exiled parts, it is evident, serves to identify the Fall with the creation—the creation not only of man and of nature as we ordinarily know them but also of a separate sky god who is alien from humanity. Universal Man divides first into the "Four Mighty Ones" who are the Zoas, or chief powers and component aspects of humanity, and these in turn divide sexually into male Spectres and female Emanations. (Thus in the quoted passage the Zoa known in the unfallen state of Eden as Urthona, the imaginative power, separates into the form of Los in the fallen world.) In addition to Eden there are three successively lower "states" of being in the fallen world, which Blake calls Beulah (a pastoral condition of easy and relaxed innocence, without clash of "contraries"), Generation (the realm of common human experience, suffering, and conflicting contraries), and Ulro (Blake's hell, the lowest state, or limit, of bleak rationality, tyranny, static negation, and isolated Selfhood). The fallen world moves through the cycles of its history, successively approaching and falling away from redemption, until, by the agency of the Redeemer (who is equated with the human imagination and is most potently operative in the prophetic poet), it will culminate in an apocalypse. In terms of his controlling image of the Universal Man, Blake describes this apocalypse as a return to the original, undivided condition, "his Resurrection to Unity."

What is confusing to many readers is that Blake alternates this representation of the Fall (as a fragmentation of the one Primal Man into separate parts) with a different kind of representation, in terms of two sharply opposed ways of seeing the universe. In this latter mode the Fall is a catastrophic change from imaginative insight (which sees the cosmos as unified and humanized) to sight by the physical eye (which sees the cosmos as a multitude of isolated individuals in an inhuman and alien nature). In terms of this distinction, the apocalypse toward which Blake as imaginative artist strives unceasingly will enable men and women once again to envision all beings as participant in the individual life that he calls "the Universal Brotherhood of Eden"—that is, a humanized world in which all individuals, in familial union, can feel at home.

The text for Blake's writings is that of *The Complete Poetry and Prose of William Blake*, edited by David V. Erdman and Harold Bloom (rev. ed., Berkeley, 1982). Blake's erratic spelling and punctuation have been altered when the original form might mislead the reader. The editors are grateful for the expert advice of Joseph Viscomi and Robert Essick in editing the selections from Blake.

There Is No Natural Religion[1]

[a]

The Argument. Man has no notion of moral fitness but from Education. Naturally he is only a natural organ subject to Sense.

---

1. In this selection Blake presents his version of English empiricism, which derives all mental content (including the evidences from which, in "natural religion," reason is held to prove the existence of God) from perceptions by the physical senses.

I. Man cannot naturally Percieve but through his natural or bodily organs.

II. Man by his reasoning power can only compare & judge of what he has already perciev'd.

III. From a perception of only 3 senses or 3 elements none could deduce a fourth or fifth.

IV. None could have other than natural or organic thoughts if he had none but organic perceptions.

V. Man's desires are limited by his perceptions; none can desire what he has not perciev'd.

VI. The desires & perceptions of man, untaught by any thing but organs of sense, must be limited to objects of sense.

Conclusion. If it were not for the Poetic or Prophetic character the Philosophic & Experimental would soon be at the ratio of all things, & stand still unable to do other than repeat the same dull round over again.

1788

There Is No Natural Religion[1]

[b]

I. Man's perceptions are not bounded by organs of perception; he percieves more than sense (tho' ever so acute) can discover.

II. Reason, or the ratio[2] of all we have already known, is not the same that it shall be when we know more.

[III lacking]

IV. The bounded is loathed by its possessor. The same dull round even of a universe would soon become a mill with complicated wheels.

V. If the many become the same as the few when possess'd, More! More! is the cry of a mistaken soul. Less than All cannot satisfy Man.

VI. If any could desire what he is incapable of possessing, despair must be his eternal lot.

VII. The desire of Man being Infinite, the possession is Infinite & himself Infinite.

Application. He who sees the Infinite in all things sees God. He who sees the Ratio only sees himself only.

Therefore God becomes as we are, that we may be as he is.

1788

---

1. In this third document Blake presents his assertions (in opposition to those in the preceding tract) that knowledge is not limited to the physical senses, but is as unbounded as the infinite desires of humankind and its godlike capacity for infinite vision.

2. In Latin *ratio* signifies both "reason" and "calculation." Blake applies the term derogatorily to the 18th-century concept of reason as a calculating faculty whose operations are limited to sense perceptions.

Separate title page for *Songs of Innocence* (1789),
Songs of Innocence and of Experience, plate 3,
copy C, ca. 1801.

FROM SONGS OF INNOCENCE AND OF EXPERIENCE[1]

SHEWING THE TWO CONTRARY STATES OF THE HUMAN SOUL

FROM SONGS OF INNOCENCE

Introduction

Piping down the valleys wild
Piping songs of pleasant glee
On a cloud I saw a child,
And he laughing said to me,

1. *Songs of Innocence* was etched in 1789, and in 1794 was combined with additional poems under the title *Songs of Innocence and of Experience;* this collection was reprinted at various later times with varying arrangements of the poems. In his songs of innocence Blake assumes the stance that he is writing "happy songs / Every child may joy to hear," but they do not all depict an innocent and happy world; many of them incorporate injustice, evil, and suffering. These aspects of the fallen world, however, are represented as they appear to a "state" of the human soul that Blake calls "innocence" and that he expresses in a simple pastoral language, in the tradition both of Isaac Watts's widely read *Divine Songs for Children* (1715) and of the picture-books for child readers pioneered by mid-18th-century booksellers such as John Newbery. The vision of the same world, as it appears to the "contrary" state of the soul that Blake calls "experience," is an ugly and terrifying one of poverty, disease, prostitution, war, and social, institutional, and sexual repression, epitomized in the ghastly representation of modern London. Though each stands as an independent poem, a number of the songs of innocence have a matched counterpart, or "contrary," in the songs of experience. Thus "Infant Joy" is paired with "Infant Sorrow," and the meek "Lamb" reveals its other aspect of divinity in the flaming, wrathful "Tyger."

5 Pipe a song about a Lamb;
So I piped with merry chear;
Piper pipe that song again—
So I piped, he wept to hear.

Drop thy pipe thy happy pipe
10 Sing thy songs of happy chear;
So I sung the same again
While he wept with joy to hear.

Piper sit thee down and write
In a book that all may read—
15 So he vanish'd from my sight.
And I pluck'd a hollow reed,

And I made a rural pen,
And I stain'd the water clear,
And I wrote my happy songs
20 Every child may joy to hear.

1789

The Ecchoing Green

The Sun does arise,
And make happy the skies.
The merry bells ring
To welcome the Spring.
5 The sky-lark and thrush,
The birds of the bush,
Sing louder around,
To the bells' chearful sound.
While our sports shall be seen
10 On the Ecchoing Green.

Old John with white hair
Does laugh away care,
Sitting under the oak,
Among the old folk.
15 They laugh at our play,
And soon they all say:
Such, such were the joys.
When we all, girls & boys,
In our youth-time were seen,
20 On the Ecchoing Green.

Till the little ones weary
No more can be merry
The sun does descend,
And our sports have an end:
25 Round the laps of their mothers,
Many sisters and brothers,
Like birds in their nest,

Are ready for rest;
And sport no more seen,
30 On the darkening Green.

1789

The Lamb[1]

Little Lamb, who made thee?
Dost thou know who made thee?
Gave thee life & bid thee feed,
By the stream & o'er the mead;
5 Gave thee clothing of delight,
Softest clothing wooly bright;
Gave thee such a tender voice,
Making all the vales rejoice!
Little Lamb who made thee?
10 Dost thou know who made thee?

Little Lamb I'll tell thee,
Little Lamb I'll tell thee!
He is callèd by thy name,
For he calls himself a Lamb;
15 He is meek & he is mild,
He became a little child;
I a child & thou a lamb,
We are callèd by his name.
Little Lamb God bless thee.
20 Little Lamb God bless thee.

1789

The Little Black Boy

My mother bore me in the southern wild,
And I am black, but O! my soul is white;
White as an angel is the English child,
But I am black as if bereav'd of light.

5 My mother taught me underneath a tree,
And sitting down before the heat of day,
She took me on her lap and kissèd me,
And pointing to the east, began to say:

Look on the rising sun: there God does live
10 And gives his light, and gives his heat away;
And flowers and trees and beasts and men receive
Comfort in morning, joy in the noon day.

And we are put on earth a little space,
That we may learn to bear the beams of love,

---

1. The opening of this poem mimes the form of the catechistic questions and answers customarily used for children's religious instruction.

15 And these black bodies and this sun-burnt face
Is but a cloud, and like a shady grove.

For when our souls have learn'd the heat to bear,
The cloud will vanish; we shall hear his voice,
Saying: Come out from the grove, my love & care,
20 And round my golden tent like lambs rejoice.

Thus did my mother say, and kissèd me;
And thus I say to little English boy:
When I from black and he from white cloud free,
And round the tent of God like lambs we joy,

25 I'll shade him from the heat till he can bear
To lean in joy upon our father's knee.
And then I'll stand and stroke his silver hair,
And be like him, and he will then love me.

1789

The Chimney Sweeper

When my mother died I was very young,
And my father sold me while yet my tongue
Could scarcely cry 'weep! 'weep! 'weep! 'weep![1]
So your chimneys I sweep & in soot I sleep.

5 There's little Tom Dacre, who cried when his head
That curl'd like a lamb's back, was shav'd, so I said,
Hush, Tom! never mind it, for when your head's bare,
You know that the soot cannot spoil your white hair.

And so he was quiet, & that very night,
10 As Tom was a-sleeping he had such a sight!
That thousands of sweepers, Dick, Joe, Ned, & Jack,
Were all of them lock'd up in coffins of black;

And by came an Angel who had a bright key,
And he open'd the coffins & set them all free;
15 Then down a green plain, leaping, laughing they run,
And wash in a river and shine in the Sun.

Then naked & white, all their bags left behind,
They rise upon clouds, and sport in the wind.
And the Angel told Tom, if he'd be a good boy,
20 He'd have God for his father & never want joy.

And so Tom awoke; and we rose in the dark
And got with our bags & our brushes to work.
Tho' the morning was cold, Tom was happy & warm;
So if all do their duty, they need not fear harm.

1789

1. The child's lisping attempt at the chimney sweeper's street cry, "Sweep! Sweep!"

The Divine Image

To Mercy, Pity, Peace, and Love,
All pray in their distress,
And to these virtues of delight
Return their thankfulness.

5   For Mercy, Pity, Peace, and Love,
Is God, our father dear:
And Mercy, Pity, Peace, and Love,
Is Man, his child and care.

For Mercy has a human heart,
10   Pity, a human face,
And Love, the human form divine,
And Peace, the human dress.

Then every man of every clime,
That prays in his distress,
15   Prays to the human form divine,
Love, Mercy, Pity, Peace.

And all must love the human form,
In heathen, Turk, or Jew.
Where Mercy, Love, & Pity dwell,
20   There God is dwelling too.

1789

Holy Thursday[1]

'Twas on a Holy Thursday, their innocent faces clean,
The children walking two & two, in red & blue & green;
Grey headed beadles[2] walkd before with wands as white as snow,
Till into the high dome of Paul's they like Thames' waters flow.

5   O what a multitude they seemd, these flowers of London town!
Seated in companies they sit with radiance all their own.
The hum of multitudes was there, but multitudes of lambs,
Thousands of little boys & girls raising their innocent hands.

Now like a mighty wind they raise to heaven the voice of song,
10   Or like harmonious thunderings the seats of heaven among.
Beneath them sit the agèd men, wise guardians of the poor;
Then cherish pity, lest you drive an angel from your door.[3]

ca. 1784

1789

---

1. A special day during the Easter season when the poor (frequently orphaned) children of the charity schools of London—sometimes as many as 6,000—marched in a procession to a service at St. Paul's Cathedral.

2. Lower church officers, one of whose duties is to keep order.

3. Cf. Hebrews 13.2: "Be not forgetful to entertain strangers: for thereby some have entertained angels unawares."

Nurse's Song

When the voices of children are heard on the green
And laughing is heard on the hill,
My heart is at rest within my breast
And everything else is still.

5   Then come home my children, the sun is gone down
And the dews of night arise;
Come, come, leave off play, and let us away
Till the morning appears in the skies.

No, no, let us play, for it is yet day
10   And we cannot go to sleep;
Besides, in the sky, the little birds fly
And the hills are all coverd with sheep.

Well, well, go & play till the light fades away
And then go home to bed.
15   The little ones leaped & shouted & laugh'd
And all the hills ecchoèd.

ca. 1784   1789

Infant Joy

I have no name,
I am but two days old.
What shall I call thee?
I happy am,
5   Joy is my name.
Sweet joy befall thee!

Pretty joy!
Sweet joy but two days old,
Sweet joy I call thee;
10   Thou dost smile,
I sing the while—
Sweet joy befall thee.

                                                                                     1789

FROM SONGS OF EXPERIENCE

Introduction

Hear the voice of the Bard!
Who Present, Past, & Future sees;
Whose ears have heard

Separate title page for *Songs of Experience* (1794), *Songs of Innocence and of Experience,* plate 29, copy Z, ca. 1801.

The Holy Word
5   That walk'd among the ancient trees;[1]

Calling the lapsèd Soul[2]
And weeping in the evening dew,
That might controll[3]
The starry pole,
10   And fallen, fallen light renew!

O Earth, O Earth, return!
Arise from out the dewy grass;
Night is worn,
And the morn
15   Rises from the slumberous mass.

Turn away no more;
Why wilt thou turn away?
The starry floor

1. Genesis 3.8: "And [Adam and Eve] heard the voice of the Lord God walking in the garden in the cool of the day." The Bard, or poet-prophet, whose imagination is not bound by time, has heard the voice of the Lord in Eden.
2. The syntax leaves it ambiguous whether it is "the Bard" or "the Holy Word" who calls to the fallen ("lapsèd") soul and to the fallen earth to stop the natural cycle of light and darkness.
3. The likely syntax is that "Soul" is the subject of "might controll."

The watry shore[4]
20 Is giv'n thee till the break of day.

1794

Earth's Answer[1]

Earth rais'd up her head,
From the darkness dread & drear.
Her light fled:
Stony dread!
5 And her locks cover'd with grey despair.

Prison'd on watry shore
Starry Jealousy does keep my den,
Cold and hoar
Weeping o'er
10 I hear the Father of the ancient men.[2]

Selfish father of men,
Cruel, jealous, selfish fear!
Can delight
Chain'd in night
15 The virgins of youth and morning bear?

Does spring hide its joy
When buds and blossoms grow?
Does the sower
Sow by night,
20 Or the plowman in darkness plow?

Break this heavy chain
That does freeze my bones around;
Selfish! vain!
Eternal bane!
25 That free Love with bondage bound.

1794

The Clod & the Pebble

Love seeketh not Itself to please,
Nor for itself hath any care;
But for another gives its ease,
And builds a Heaven in Hell's despair.

5 So sang a little Clod of Clay,
Trodden with the cattle's feet;
But a Pebble of the brook,
Warbled out these metres meet:

4. In Blake's recurrent symbolism the starry sky ("floor") signifies rigid rational order, and the sea signifies chaos.
1. The Earth explains why she, the natural world, cannot by her unaided endeavors renew the fallen light.

2. This is the character that Blake later named "Urizen" in his prophetic works. He is the tyrant who binds the mind to the natural world and also imposes a moral bondage on sexual desire and other modes of human energy.

Love seeketh only Self to please,
10 To bind another to its delight;
Joys in another's loss of ease,
And builds a Hell in Heaven's despite.

1794

Holy Thursday

Is this a holy thing to see,
In a rich and fruitful land,
Babes reduced to misery,
Fed with cold and usurous hand?

5   Is that trembling cry a song?
Can it be a song of joy?
And so many children poor?
It is a land of poverty!

And their sun does never shine,
10 And their fields are bleak & bare,
And their ways are fill'd with thorns;
It is eternal winter there.

For where-e'er the sun does shine,
And where-e'er the rain does fall,
15 Babe can never hunger there,
Nor poverty the mind appall.

1794

The Chimney Sweeper

A little black thing among the snow
Crying 'weep, 'weep, in notes of woe!
Where are thy father & mother? say?
They are both gone up to the church to pray.

5   Because I was happy upon the heath,
And smil'd among the winter's snow;
They clothed me in the clothes of death,
And taught me to sing the notes of woe.

And because I am happy, & dance & sing,
10 They think they have done me no injury,
And are gone to praise God & his Priest & King,
Who make up a heaven of our misery.

1790–92   1794

Nurse's Song

When the voices of children are heard on the green
And whisperings are in the dale,
The days of my youth rise fresh in my mind,
My face turns green and pale.

5 Then come home my children, the sun is gone down
And the dews of night arise;
Your spring & your day are wasted in play,
And your winter and night in disguise.

1794

The Sick Rose

O Rose, thou art sick.
The invisible worm
That flies in the night
In the howling storm

5 Has found out thy bed
Of crimson joy,
And his dark secret love
Does thy life destroy.

1794

The Tyger[1]

Tyger! Tyger! burning bright
In the forests of the night,
What immortal hand or eye
Could frame thy fearful symmetry?

5 In what distant deeps or skies
Burnt the fire of thine eyes?
On what wings dare he aspire?
What the hand dare seize the fire?

 And what shoulder, & what art,
10 Could twist the sinews of thy heart?
And when thy heart began to beat,
What dread hand? & what dread feet?

 What the hammer? what the chain?
In what furnace was thy brain?
15 What the anvil? what dread grasp
Dare its deadly terrors clasp?

---

1. For the author's revisions while composing "The Tyger," see "Poems in Process," in the supplemental ebook.

"The Tyger," *Songs of Innocence and of Experience*, plate 52, copy C, ca. 1801.

When the stars threw down their spears[2]
And water'd heaven with their tears,
Did he smile his work to see?
20　Did he who made the Lamb make thee?

Tyger! Tyger! burning bright
In the forests of the night,
What immortal hand or eye
Dare frame thy fearful symmetry?

1790–92　　　　　　　　　　　　　　　　　　　　　　　1794

My Pretty Rose Tree

A flower was offerd to me;
Such a flower as May never bore,
But I said, I've a Pretty Rose-tree,
And I passed the sweet flower o'er.

2. "Threw down" is ambiguous and may signify that the stars either "surrendered" or "hurled down" their spears.

5 Then I went to my Pretty Rose-tree,
   To tend her by day and by night.
   But my Rose turnd away with jealousy,
   And her thorns were my only delight.

1794

Ah! Sun-flower

Ah Sun-flower! weary of time,
Who countest the steps of the Sun,
Seeking after that sweet golden clime
Where the traveller's journey is done;

5 Where the Youth pined away with desire,
   And the pale Virgin shrouded in snow,
   Arise from their graves and aspire,
   Where my Sun-flower wishes to go.

1794

The Garden of Love

I went to the Garden of Love,
And saw what I never had seen:
A Chapel was built in the midst,
Where I used to play on the green.

5 And the gates of this Chapel were shut,
   And Thou shalt not writ over the door;
   So I turn'd to the Garden of Love,
   That so many sweet flowers bore,

   And I saw it was filled with graves,
10 And tomb-stones where flowers should be;
   And Priests in black gowns were walking their rounds,
   And binding with briars my joys & desires.

1794

London

I wander thro' each charter'd[1] street,
Near where the charter'd Thames does flow,
And mark in every face I meet
Marks of weakness, marks of woe.

5 In every cry of every Man,
   In every Infant's cry of fear,

---

1. "Given liberty," but also, ironically, "preempted as private property, and rented out."

"London," *Songs of Innocence and of Experience*, plate 51, copy C, ca. 1801.

In every voice, in every ban,[2]
The mind-forg'd manacles I hear:

How the Chimney-sweeper's cry
10 Every blackning Church appalls,
And the hapless Soldier's sigh
Runs in blood down Palace walls.

But most thro' midnight streets I hear
How the youthful Harlot's curse
15 Blasts the new-born Infant's tear,[3]
And blights with plagues the Marriage hearse.[4]

1794

The Human Abstract[1]

Pity would be no more,
If we did not make somebody Poor;

---

2. The various meanings of *ban* are relevant (political and legal prohibition, curse, public condemnation) as well as "banns" (marriage proclamation).
3. Most critics read this line as implying prenatal blindness, resulting from a parent's venereal disease (the "plagues" of line 16) by earlier infection from the harlot.
4. In the older sense: "converts the marriage bed into a bier." Or possibly, because the current sense of the word had also come into use in Blake's day, "converts the marriage coach into a funeral hearse."
1. The matched contrary to "The Divine Image" in *Songs of Innocence*. The virtues of the earlier poem, "Mercy, Pity, Peace, and Love," are now represented as possible marks for exploitation, cruelty, conflict, and hypocritical humility.

And Mercy no more could be,
If all were as happy as we;

5 And mutual fear brings peace,
Till the selfish loves increase;
Then Cruelty knits a snare,
And spreads his baits with care.

He sits down with holy fears,
10 And waters the ground with tears;
Then Humility takes its root
Underneath his foot.

Soon spreads the dismal shade
Of Mystery over his head;
15 And the Catterpiller and Fly
Feed on the Mystery.

And it bears the fruit of Deceit,
Ruddy and sweet to eat;
And the Raven his nest has made
20 In its thickest shade.

The Gods of the earth and sea,
Sought thro' Nature to find this Tree,
But their search was all in vain:
There grows one in the Human Brain.

1790–92   1794

Infant Sorrow

My mother groand! my father wept.
Into the dangerous world I leapt,
Helpless, naked, piping loud;
Like a fiend hid in a cloud.

5 Struggling in my father's hands,
Striving against my swadling bands;
Bound and weary I thought best
To sulk upon my mother's breast.

1794

A Poison Tree

I was angry with my friend:
I told my wrath, my wrath did end.
I was angry with my foe:
I told it not, my wrath did grow.

5 And I waterd it in fears,
Night & morning with my tears;

And I sunnèd it with smiles,
And with soft deceitful wiles.

And it grew both day and night,
10 Till it bore an apple bright.
And my foe beheld it shine,
And he knew that it was mine,

And into my garden stole,
When the night had veild the pole;
15 In the morning glad I see
My foe outstretchd beneath the tree.

1794

To Tirzah[1]

Whate'er is Born of Mortal Birth
Must be consumèd with the Earth
To rise from Generation free;
Then what have I to do with thee?[2]

5 The Sexes sprung from Shame & Pride,
Blow'd° in the morn, in evening died;   *blossomed*
But Mercy changd Death into Sleep;
The Sexes rose to work & weep.

Thou, Mother of my Mortal part,
10 With cruelty didst mould my Heart,
And with false self-deceiving tears
Didst bind my Nostrils, Eyes, & Ears.

Didst close my Tongue in senseless clay
And me to Mortal Life betray.
15 The Death of Jesus set me free;
Then what have I to do with thee?

ca. 1805

A Divine Image[1]

Cruelty has a Human Heart
And Jealousy a Human Face,
Terror, the Human Form Divine,
And Secrecy, the Human Dress.

1. Tirzah was the capital of the northern kingdom of Israel and is conceived by Blake in opposition to Jerusalem, capital of the southern kingdom
of Judah, whose tribes had been redeemed from
captivity. In this poem, which was added to late
versions of *Songs of Experience*, Tirzah is represented as the mother—in the realm of material
nature and "Generation"—of the mortal body,
with its restrictive senses.

2. Echoing the words of Christ to his mother at
the marriage in Cana, John 2.4: "Woman, what
have I to do with thee? mine hour is not yet come."
1. Blake omitted this poem from all but one copy
of *Songs of Experience*, probably because "The
Human Abstract" served as a more comprehensive and subtle contrary to "The Divine Image" in
Songs of Innocence.

5   The Human Dress is forgèd Iron,
    The Human Form, a fiery Forge,
    The Human Face, a Furnace seal'd,
    The Human Heart, its hungry Gorge.°   *maw, stomach*

1790–91

The Book of Thel

The Book of Thel   Although Blake dated the etched poem 1789, its composition probably extended to 1791, so that he was working on it at the time he was writing the *Songs of Innocence* and some of the *Songs of Experience*. The Book of Thel treats the same two "states"; now, however, Blake employs the narrative instead of the lyrical mode and embodies aspects of the developing myth that was fully enacted in his later prophetic books. And like the major prophecies, this poem is written in the fourteener, a long line of seven stresses.

The name *Thel* possibly derives from the Greek word for "wish" or "will" and may be intended to suggest the failure of desire, because of timidity, to fulfill itself. Thel is represented as a virgin dwelling in the Vales of Har, which seems equivalent to the sheltered state of pastoral peace and innocence in Blake's *Songs of Innocence*. Here, however, Thel feels useless and unfulfilled, and appeals for comfort, unavailingly, to various beings who are contented with their roles in Har. Finally, the Clay invites Thel to try the experiment of assuming embodied life. Part 4 (plate 6) expresses the brutal shock of the revelation to Thel of the experience of sexual desire—a revelation from which she flees in terror back to her sheltered, if unsatisfying, existence in Har.

Some commentators propose that Thel is an unborn soul who rejects the ordeal of an embodied life in the material world. Others propose that Thel is a human virgin who shrinks from experiencing a life of adult sexuality. It is possible, however, to read Blake's little myth as comprehending both these areas of significance. The reader does not need to know Blake's mythology inside and out to recognize the broad symbolic reach of this poem in ordinary human experience—the elemental failure of nerve to meet the challenge of life as it is, the timid incapacity to risk the conflict, physicality, pain, and loss without which there is no possibility either of growth or of creativity.

The Book of Thel

PLATE i[1]

Thel's Motto

Does the Eagle know what is in the pit?
Or wilt thou go ask the Mole?
Can Wisdom be put in a silver rod?
Or Love in a golden bowl?[2]

PLATE 1

1

The daughters of Mne[3] Seraphim led round their sunny flocks,
All but the youngest; she in paleness sought the secret air,

1. The plate numbers identify the page, each with its own pictorial design, as originally printed by Blake. These numbers are reproduced here because they are frequently used in references to Blake's writings.
2. Ecclesiastes 12.5–6 describes a time when "fears shall be in the way . . . and desire shall fail: because man goeth to his long home, and the mourners go about the streets: Or ever the silver cord be loosed, or the golden bowl be broken." Perhaps Blake changed the silver cord to a rod to make it, with the golden bowl, a sexual symbol.
3. There has been much speculation about this curious term. It may be an abbreviation for the name "Mnetha," the goddess of the Vales of Har in Blake's earlier poem *Tiriel*.

To fade away like morning beauty from her mortal day;
Down by the river of Adona her soft voice is heard,
5 And thus her gentle lamentation falls like morning dew:

"O life of this our spring! why fades the lotus of the water?
Why fade these children of the spring? born but to smile & fall.
Ah! Thel is like a watry bow, and like a parting cloud,
Like a reflection in a glass, like shadows in the water,
10 Like dreams of infants, like a smile upon an infant's face,
Like the dove's voice, like transient day, like music in the air.
Ah! gentle may I lay me down, and gentle rest my head,
And gentle sleep the sleep of death, and gentle hear the voice
Of him that walketh in the garden in the evening time."[4]

———————————

15 The Lilly of the valley breathing in the humble grass
Answer'd the lovely maid and said: "I am a watry weed,
And I am very small, and love to dwell in lowly vales;
So weak, the gilded butterfly scarce perches on my head;
Yet I am visited from heaven, and he that smiles on all
20 Walks in the valley and each morn over me spreads his hand,
Saying: 'Rejoice, thou humble grass, thou new-born lilly flower,
Thou gentle maid of silent valleys and of modest brooks;
For thou shalt be clothed in light, and fed with morning manna,
Till summer's heat melts thee beside the fountains and the springs
25 To flourish in eternal vales.' Then why should Thel complain?

PLATE 2

Why should the mistress of the vales of Har utter a sigh?"

She ceasd & smild in tears, then sat down in her silver shrine.

Thel answer'd: "O thou little virgin of the peaceful valley,
Giving to those that cannot crave, the voiceless, the o'ertired;
5 Thy breath doth nourish the innocent lamb, he smells thy milky
         garments,
He crops thy flowers, while thou sittest smiling in his face,
Wiping his mild and meekin° mouth from all contagious taints.   *humble*
Thy wine doth purify the golden honey; thy perfume,
Which thou dost scatter on every little blade of grass that springs,
10 Revives the milkèd cow, & tames the fire-breathing steed.
But Thel is like a faint cloud kindled at the rising sun:
I vanish from my pearly throne, and who shall find my place?"

"Queen of the vales," the Lilly answered, "ask the tender cloud,
And it shall tell thee why it glitters in the morning sky,
15 And why it scatters its bright beauty thro' the humid air.
Descend, O little cloud, & hover before the eyes of Thel."
The Cloud descended, and the Lilly bowd her modest head,
And went to mind her numerous charge among the verdant grass.

———————————

4. Genesis 3.8: "And they heard the voice of the Lord God walking in the garden in the cool of the day."

Title page of *The Book of Thel*
(1789), plate ii, copy N, ca. 1815

PLATE 3

2

"O little Cloud," the virgin said, "I charge thee tell to me,
Why thou complainest not when in one hour thou fade away:
Then we shall seek thee but not find; ah, Thel is like to Thee.
I pass away, yet I complain, and no one hears my voice."

5   The Cloud then shew'd his golden head & his bright form emerg'd,
Hovering and glittering on the air before the face of Thel.

"O virgin, know'st thou not our steeds drink of the golden springs
Where Luvah[5] doth renew his horses? Look'st thou on my youth,
And fearest thou because I vanish and am seen no more,
10   Nothing remains? O maid, I tell thee, when I pass away,
It is to tenfold life, to love, to peace, and raptures holy:
Unseen descending, weigh my light wings upon balmy flowers,
And court the fair eyed dew, to take me to her shining tent;
The weeping virgin trembling kneels before the risen sun,
15   Till we arise link'd in a golden band, and never part,
But walk united, bearing food to all our tender flowers."

"Dost thou O little Cloud? I fear that I am not like thee;
For I walk through the vales of Har and smell the sweetest flowers,

5. The earliest mention in Blake's work of one of his "Giant Forms," the Zoas. Luvah is the mythical embodiment of the passional and sexual aspect of humankind. He is represented here, like the Greek Phoebus Apollo, as the driver of the chariot of the sun; he repairs to the Vales of Har simply to rest and water his horses. The cloud in this passage describes the cycle of water, from cloud to rain and (by the vaporizing action of the sun on water) back to the cloud.

But I feed not the little flowers; I hear the warbling birds,
20 But I feed not the warbling birds; they fly and seek their food;
But Thel delights in these no more, because I fade away,
And all shall say, 'Without a use this shining woman liv'd,
Or did she only live to be at death the food of worms?'"

The Cloud reclind upon his airy throne and answer'd thus:

25 "Then if thou art the food of worms, O virgin of the skies,
How great thy use, how great thy blessing! Every thing that lives
Lives not alone, nor for itself; fear not, and I will call
The weak worm from its lowly bed, and thou shalt hear its voice.
Come forth, worm of the silent valley, to thy pensive queen."

———————————

30 The helpless worm arose, and sat upon the Lilly's leaf,
And the bright Cloud saild on, to find his partner in the vale.

PLATE 4

3

Then Thel astonish'd view'd the Worm upon its dewy bed.

"Art thou a Worm? Image of weakness, art thou but a Worm?
I see thee like an infant wrapped in the Lilly's leaf;
Ah, weep not, little voice, thou can'st not speak, but thou can'st weep.
5 Is this a Worm? I see thee lay helpless & naked, weeping,
And none to answer, none to cherish thee with mother's smiles."

The Clod of Clay heard the Worm's voice, & raisd her pitying head;
She bow'd over the weeping infant, and her life exhal'd
In milky fondness; then on Thel she fix'd her humble eyes.

10 "O beauty of the vales of Har! we live not for ourselves;
Thou seest me the meanest thing, and so I am indeed;
My bosom of itself is cold, and of itself is dark,

PLATE 5

But he that loves the lowly, pours his oil upon my head,
And kisses me, and binds his nuptial bands around my breast,
And says: 'Thou mother of my children, I have lovèd thee,
And I have given thee a crown that none can take away.'
5 But how this is, sweet maid, I know not, and I cannot know;
I ponder, and I cannot ponder; yet I live and love."

The daughter of beauty wip'd her pitying tears with her white veil,
And said: "Alas! I knew not this, and therefore did I weep.
That God would love a Worm, I knew, and punish the evil foot
10 That, wilful, bruis'd its helpless form; but that he cherish'd it
With milk and oil I never knew; and therefore did I weep,
And I complain in the mild air, because I fade away,
And lay me down in thy cold bed, and leave my shining lot."

"Queen of the vales," the matron Clay answered, "I heard thy sighs,
15   And all thy moans flew o'er my roof, but I have call'd them down.
Wilt thou, O Queen, enter my house? 'tis given thee to enter
And to return; fear nothing, enter with thy virgin feet."

PLATE 6

4

The eternal gates' terrific porter lifted the northern bar:[6]
Thel enter'd in & saw the secrets of the land unknown.
She saw the couches of the dead, & where the fibrous roots
Of every heart on earth infixes deep its restless twists:
5   A land of sorrows & of tears where never smile was seen.

She wanderd in the land of clouds thro' valleys dark, listning
Dolours & lamentations; waiting oft beside a dewy grave,
She stood in silence, listning to the voices of the ground,
Till to her own grave plot she came, & there she sat down,
10   And heard this voice of sorrow breathed from the hollow pit:

"Why cannot the Ear be closed to its own destruction?
Or the glistning Eye to the poison of a smile?
Why are Eyelids stord with arrows ready drawn,
Where a thousand fighting men in ambush lie?
15   Or an Eye of gifts & graces, show'ring fruits & coinèd gold?
Why a Tongue impress'd with honey from every wind?
Why an Ear, a whirlpool fierce to draw creations in?
Why a Nostril wide inhaling terror, trembling, & affright?
Why a tender curb upon the youthful burning boy?
20   Why a little curtain of flesh on the bed of our desire?"

The Virgin started from her seat, & with a shriek
Fled back unhinderd till she came into the vales of Har.

1789–91

The Marriage of Heaven and Hell   This, the most immediately accessible of Blake's longer works, is a vigorous, deliberately outrageous, and at times comic onslaught against timidly conventional and self-righteous members of society as well as against stock opinions of orthodox Christian piety and morality. The seeming simplicity of Blake's satiric attitude, however, is deceptive.

Initially, Blake accepts the terminology of standard Christian morality ("what the religious call Good & Evil") but reverses its values. In this conventional use Evil, which is manifested by the class of beings called Devils and which consigns wrong-doers to the orthodox Hell, is everything associated with the body and its desires and consists essentially of energy, abundance, actions, and freedom. Conventional Good, which is manifested by Angels and guarantees its adherents a place in the orthodox Heaven, is associated with the Soul (regarded as entirely separate from the body) and consists of the contrary qualities of reason, restraint, passivity, and prohibition. Blandly adopting these conventional oppositions, Blake elects to assume the diabolic persona—what he calls "the voice of the Devil"—and to utter "Proverbs of Hell."

6. Homer, in *Odyssey* 13, described the Cave of the Naiades, of which the northern gate is for mortals and the southern gate for gods. The Neo- platonist Porphyry had allegorized it as an account of the descent of the soul into matter and then its return.

But this stance is only a first stage in Blake's complex irony, designed to startle the reader into recognizing the inadequacy of conventional moral categories. As he also says in the opening summary, "Without Contraries is no progression," and "Reason and Energy" are both "necessary to Human existence." It turns out that Blake subordinates his reversal of conventional values under a more inclusive point of view, according to which the real Good, as distinguished from the merely ironic Good, is not abandonment of all restraints but a "marriage," or union of the contraries, of desire and restraint, energy and reason, the promptings of Hell and the denials of Heaven—or as Blake calls these contraries in plate 16, "the Prolific" and "the Devouring." These two classes, he adds, "should be enemies," and "whoever tries to reconcile them seeks to destroy existence." Implicit in Blake's satire is the view that the good and abundant life consists in the sustained tension, without victory or suppression, of co-present oppositions.

When Blake composed this unique work in the early 1790s, his city of London was teeming with religious mystics, astrologers, and sometimes bawdy freethinkers who were determined to challenge the Established Church's monopoly on spirituality and who were reviving the link, created in the seventeenth century, between enthusiasm in religion and political revolution. The work is also a response to the writings of the visionary Swedish theologian Emanuel Swedenborg, whom Blake had at first admired but then had come to recognize as a conventional Angel in the disguise of a radical Devil. In plate 3 the writings of Swedenborg are described as the winding clothes Blake discards as he is resurrected from the tomb of his past self, as a poet-prophet who heralds the apocalyptic promise of his age. Blake shared the expectations of a number of radical English writers, including the young poets Wordsworth, Coleridge, and Southey, that the French Revolution was the violent stage that, as the biblical prophets foresaw, immediately preceded the millennium. The double role of *The Marriage* as both satire and revolutionary prophecy is made explicit in *A Song of Liberty*, which Blake etched in 1792 and added as a coda.

The Marriage of Heaven and Hell

PLATE 2

The Argument

Rintrah[1] roars & shakes his fires in the burdend air;
Hungry clouds swag on the deep.
Once meek, and in a perilous path,
The just man kept his course along
5 The vale of death.
Roses are planted where thorns grow,
And on the barren heath
Sing the honey bees.

Then the perilous path was planted,
10 And a river, and a spring,
On every cliff and tomb;

---

1. Rintrah plays the role of the angry Old Testament prophet Elijah as well as of John the Baptist, the voice "crying in the wilderness" (Matthew 3), preparing the way for Christ the Messiah. It has been plausibly suggested that stanzas 2–5 summarize the course of biblical history to the present time. "Once" (line 3) refers to Old Testament history after the Fall; "Then" (line 9) is the time of the birth of Christ. "Till" (line 14) iden-tifies the era when Christianity was perverted into an institutional religion. "Now" (line 17) is the time of the wrathful portent of the French Revolution. In this final era the hypocritical serpent represents the priest of the "angels" in the poem, while "the just man" is embodied in Blake, a raging poet and prophet in the guise of a devil. "Swag" (line 2): sag, hang down.

And on the bleached bones
Red clay[2] brought forth;

Till the villain left the paths of ease,
15 To walk in perilous paths, and drive
The just man into barren climes.

Now the sneaking serpent walks
In mild humility,
And the just man rages in the wilds
20 Where lions roam.

Rintrah roars & shakes his fires in the burdend air;
Hungry clouds swag on the deep.

PLATE 3

As a new heaven is begun, and it is now thirty-three years since its advent, the Eternal Hell revives. And lo! Swedenborg[3] is the Angel sitting at the tomb; his writings are the linen clothes folded up. Now is the dominion of Edom, & the return of Adam into Paradise; see Isaiah xxxiv & XXXV Chap.[4]

Without Contraries is no progression. Attraction and Repulsion, Reason and Energy, Love and Hate, are necessary to Human existence.

From these contraries spring what the religious call Good & Evil. Good is the passive that obeys Reason. Evil is the active springing from Energy.

Good is Heaven. Evil is Hell.

PLATE 4

The Voice of the Devil

All Bibles or sacred codes have been the causes of the following Errors:

1. That Man has two real existing principles; Viz: a Body & a Soul.

2. That Energy, calld Evil, is alone from the Body, & that Reason, calld Good, is alone from the Soul.

3. That God will torment Man in Eternity for following his Energies.

But the following Contraries to these are True:

1. Man has no Body distinct from his Soul; for that calld Body is a portion of Soul discernd by the five Senses, the chief inlets of Soul in this age.

2. In Hebrew the literal meaning of "Adam," or created man. The probable reference is to the birth of the Redeemer, the new Adam.
3. Emanuel Swedenborg (1688–1772), Swedish scientist and religious philosopher, had predicted, on the basis of his visions, that the Last Judgment and the coming of the Kingdom of Heaven would occur in 1757. This was precisely the year of Blake's birth. Now, in 1790, Blake is thirty-three, the age at which Christ had been resurrected from the tomb; correspondingly, Blake rises from the tomb of his past life in his new role as imaginative artist who will redeem his age. But, Blake ironically comments, the works he will engrave in his resurrection will constitute the Eternal Hell, the contrary brought into simultaneous being by Swedenborg's limited New Heaven.
4. Isaiah 34 prophesies "the day of the Lord's

vengeance," a time of violent destruction and bloodshed; Isaiah 35 prophesies the redemption to follow, in which "the desert shall . . . blossom as the rose," "in the wilderness shall waters break out, and streams in the desert," and "no lion shall be there," but "an highway shall be there . . . and it shall be called The way of holiness" (cf. "The Argument," lines 3–11, 20). Blake combines with these chapters Isaiah 63, in which "Edom" is the place from which comes the man whose garments are red with the blood he has spilled; for as he says, "the day of vengeance is in mine heart, and the year of my redeemed is come." Blake interprets this last phrase as predicting the time when Adam would regain his lost Paradise. Also relevant is Genesis 36.1, where the Edomites are identified as the descendants of the disinherited Esau, cheated out of his father's blessing by Jacob.

2. Energy is the only life, and is from the Body; and Reason is the bound or outward circumference of Energy.

3. Energy is Eternal Delight.

_____

PLATE 5

Those who restrain desire, do so because theirs is weak enough to be restrained; and the restrainer or reason usurps its place & governs the unwilling.

And being restraind, it by degrees becomes passive, till it is only the shadow of desire.

The history of this is written in *Paradise Lost*,[5] & the Governor or Reason is call'd Messiah.

And the original Archangel, or possessor of the command of the heavenly host, is calld the Devil or Satan, and his children are call'd Sin & Death.[6]

But in the Book of Job, Milton's Messiah is call'd Satan.[7]

For this history has been adopted by both parties.

It indeed appear'd to Reason as if Desire was cast out; but the Devil's account is, that the Messi[PLATE 6]ah fell, & formed a heaven of what he stole from the Abyss.

This is shewn in the Gospel, where he prays to the Father to send the comforter or Desire that Reason may have Ideas to build on;[8] the Jehovah of the Bible being no other than he who dwells in flaming fire. Know that after Christ's death, he became Jehovah.

But in Milton, the Father is Destiny, the Son, a Ratio[9] of the five senses, & the Holy-ghost, Vacuum!

Note. The reason Milton wrote in fetters when he wrote of Angels & God, and at liberty when of Devils & Hell, is because he was a true Poet and of the Devil's party without knowing it.

A Memorable Fancy[1]

As I was walking among the fires of hell, delighted with the enjoyments of Genius, which to Angels look like torment and insanity, I collected some of their Proverbs; thinking that as the sayings used in a nation mark its character, so the Proverbs of Hell shew the nature of Infernal wisdom better than any description of buildings or garments.

When I came home, on the abyss of the five senses, where a flat sided steep frowns over the present world, I saw a mighty Devil folded in black clouds, hovering on the sides of the rock; with cor[PLATE 7]roding fires he wrote the

5. What follows, to the end of this section, is Blake's "diabolical" reading of Milton's *Paradise Lost*. For other Romantic comments on the magnificence of Milton's Satan see "The Satanic and Byronic Hero" in the supplemental ebook.

6. Satan's giving birth to Sin and then incestuously begetting Death upon her is described in *Paradise Lost* 2.745ff.; the war in heaven, referred to three lines below, in which the Messiah defeated Satan and drove him out of heaven, is described in 6.824ff.

7. In the Book of Job, Satan plays the role of Job's moral accuser and physical tormentor.

8. Possibly John 14.16–17, where Christ says he "will pray the Father, and he shall give you another Comforter . . . Even the Spirit of truth."

9. The Latin *ratio* means both "reason" and "sum." Blake applies the term to the 18th-century view, following the empiricist philosophy of John Locke, that the content of the mind, on which the faculty of reason operates, is limited to the sum of the experience acquired by the five senses.

1. Blake parodies Swedenborg's accounts, in his *Memorable Relations*, of his conversations with the inhabitants during his spiritual trips to heaven.

following sentence[2] now perceived by the minds of men, & read by them on earth:

> How do you know but ev'ry Bird that cuts the airy way,
> Is an immense world of delight, clos'd by your senses five?

Proverbs of Hell[3]

In seed time learn, in harvest teach, in winter enjoy.
Drive your cart and your plow over the bones of the dead.
The road of excess leads to the palace of wisdom.
Prudence is a rich ugly old maid courted by Incapacity.
5   He who desires but acts not, breeds pestilence.
The cut worm forgives the plow.
Dip him in the river who loves water.
A fool sees not the same tree that a wise man sees.
He whose face gives no light, shall never become a star.
10   Eternity is in love with the productions of time.
The busy bee has no time for sorrow.
The hours of folly are measur'd by the clock; but of wisdom, no clock can
      measure.
All wholsom food is caught without a net or a trap.
Bring out number, weight, & measure in a year of dearth.
15   No bird soars too high, if he soars with his own wings.
A dead body revenges not injuries.
The most sublime act is to set another before you.
If the fool would persist in his folly he would become wise.
Folly is the cloke of knavery.
20   Shame is Pride's cloke.

PLATE 8

Prisons are built with stones of Law, Brothels with bricks of Religion.
The pride of the peacock is the glory of God.
The lust of the goat is the bounty of God.
The wrath of the lion is the wisdom of God.
5   The nakedness of woman is the work of God.
Excess of sorrow laughs. Excess of joy weeps.
The roaring of lions, the howling of wolves, the raging of the stormy sea,
      and the destructive sword, are portions of eternity too great for the
      eye of man.
The fox condemns the trap, not himself.
Joys impregnate. Sorrows bring forth.
10   Let man wear the fell of the lion, woman the fleece of the sheep.
The bird a nest, the spider a web, man friendship.
The selfish smiling fool & the sullen frowning fool shall be both thought
      wise, that they may be a rod.
What is now proved was once only imagin'd.
The rat, the mouse, the fox, the rabbit watch the roots; the lion, the tyger,
      the horse, the elephant, watch the fruits,

2. The "mighty Devil" is Blake, as he sees himself reflected in the shiny plate on which he is etching this very passage with "corroding fires," i.e., the acid used in the etching process. See also the third from last sentence in plate 14.

3. A "diabolic" version of the Book of Proverbs in the Old Testament, which also incorporates sly allusions to 18th-century books of piety such as Isaac Watts's *Divine Songs*.

15 The cistern contains; the fountain overflows.
One thought fills immensity.
Always be ready to speak your mind, and a base man will avoid you.
Every thing possible to be believ'd is an image of truth.
The eagle never lost so much time as when he submitted to learn of the crow.

PLATE 9

The fox provides for himself, but God provides for the lion.
Think in the morning, Act in the noon, Eat in the evening, Sleep in the
   night.
He who has sufferd you to impose on him knows you.
As the plow follows words, so God rewards prayers.
5 The tygers of wrath are wiser than the horses of instruction.
Expect poison from the standing water.
You never know what is enough unless you know what is more than enough.
Listen to the fool's reproach! it is a kingly title!
The eyes of fire, the nostrils of air, the mouth of water, the beard of earth.
10 The weak in courage is strong in cunning.
The apple tree never asks the beech how he shall grow, nor the lion the
   horse, how he shall take his prey.
The thankful reciever bears a plentiful harvest.
If others had not been foolish, we should be so.
The soul of sweet delight can never be defil'd.
15 When thou seest an Eagle, thou seest a portion of Genius; lift up thy head!
As the catterpiller chooses the fairest leaves to lay her eggs on, so the priest
   lays his curse on the fairest joys.
To create a little flower is the labour of ages.
Damn braces; Bless relaxes.
The best wine is the oldest, the best water the newest.
20 Prayers plow not! Praises reap not!
Joys laugh not! Sorrows weep not!

PLATE 10

The head Sublime, the heart Pathos, the genitals Beauty, the hands & feet
   Proportion.
As the air to a bird or the sea to a fish, so is contempt to the contemptible.
The crow wish'd every thing was black, the owl that every thing was white.
Exuberance is Beauty.
5 If the lion was advised by the fox, he would be cunning.
Improvement makes strait roads, but the crooked roads without
   Improvement are roads of Genius.
Sooner murder an infant in its cradle than nurse unacted desires.
Where man is not, nature is barren.
Truth can never be told so as to be understood, and not be believ'd.
10   Enough! or Too much.
                   ——————————

PLATE 11

   The ancient Poets animated all sensible objects with Gods or Geniuses,
calling them by the names and adorning them with the properties of woods,

rivers, mountains, lakes, cities, nations, and whatever their enlarged & numerous senses could perceive.

And particularly they studied the genius of each city & country, placing it under its mental deity.

Till a system was formed, which some took advantage of & enslav'd the vulgar by attempting to realize or abstract the mental deities from their objects; thus began Priesthood,

Choosing forms of worship from poetic tales.

And at length they pronounced that the Gods had ordered such things.

Thus men forgot that All deities reside in the human breast.

PLATE 12

A Memorable Fancy

The Prophets Isaiah and Ezekiel dined with me, and I asked them how they dared so roundly to assert that God spake to them; and whether they did not think at the time that they would be misunderstood, & so be the cause of imposition.

Isaiah answer'd: "I saw no God, nor heard any, in a finite organical perception; but my senses discover'd the infinite in every thing, and as I was then perswaded, & remain confirm'd, that the voice of honest indignation is the voice of God, I cared not for consequences, but wrote."

Then I asked: "Does a firm perswasion that a thing is so, make it so?"

He replied: "All poets believe that it does, & in ages of imagination this firm perswasion removed mountains; but many are not capable of a firm perswasion of any thing."

Then Ezekiel said: "The philosophy of the East taught the first principles of human perception. Some nations held one principle for the origin & some another; we of Israel taught that the Poetic Genius (as you now call it) was the first principle and all the others merely derivative, which was the cause of our despising the Priests & Philosophers of other countries, and prophecying that all Gods [PLATE 13] would at last be proved to originate in ours & to be the tributaries of the Poetic Genius; it was this that our great poet, King David, desired so fervently & invokes so pathetically, saying by this he conquers enemies & governs kingdoms; and we so loved our God, that we cursed in his name all the deities of surrounding nations, and asserted that they had rebelled; from these opinions the vulgar came to think that all nations would at last be subject to the Jews."

"This," said he, "like all firm perswasions, is come to pass, for all nations believe the Jews' code and worship the Jews' god, and what greater subjection can be?"

I heard this with some wonder, & must confess my own conviction. After dinner I ask'd Isaiah to favour the world with his lost works; he said none of equal value was lost. Ezekiel said the same of his.

I also asked Isaiah what made him go naked and barefoot three years? He answered, "the same that made our friend Diogenes,[4] the Grecian."

4. Greek Cynic (4th century), whose extreme repudiation of civilized customs gave rise to anecdotes that he had renounced clothing. In Isaiah 20.2–3 the prophet, at the Lord's command, walked "naked and barefoot" for three years.

I then asked Ezekiel why he eat dung, & lay so long on his right & left side?[5] He answered, "the desire of raising other men into a perception of the infinite; this the North American tribes practise, & is he honest who resists his genius or conscience only for the sake of present ease or gratification?"

PLATE 14

The ancient tradition that the world will be consumed in fire at the end of six thousand years is true, as I have heard from Hell.

For the cherub with his flaming sword is hereby commanded to leave his guard at the tree of life;[6] and when he does, the whole creation will be consumed, and appear infinite and holy, whereas it now appears finite & corrupt.

This will come to pass by an improvement of sensual enjoyment.

But first the notion that man has a body distinct from his soul is to be expunged; this I shall do, by printing in the infernal method, by corrosives, which in Hell are salutary and medicinal, melting apparent surfaces away, and displaying the infinite which was hid.[7]

If the doors of perception were cleansed every thing would appear to man as it is, infinite.

For man has closed himself up, till he sees all things thro' narrow chinks of his cavern.

PLATE 15

A Memorable Fancy

I was in a Printing house[8] in Hell & saw the method in which knowledge is transmitted from generation to generation.

In the first chamber was a Dragon-Man, clearing away the rubbish from a cave's mouth; within, a number of Dragons were hollowing the cave.

In the second chamber was a Viper folding round the rock & the cave, and others adorning it with gold, silver, and precious stones.

In the third chamber was an Eagle with wings and feathers of air; he caused the inside of the cave to be infinite; around were numbers of Eagle-like men, who built palaces in the immense cliffs.

In the fourth chamber were Lions of flaming fire, raging around & melting the metals into living fluids.

In the fifth chamber were Unnam'd forms, which cast the metals into the expanse.

There they were receiv'd by Men who occupied the sixth chamber, and took the forms of books & were arranged in libraries.[9]

PLATE 16

The Giants[1] who formed this world into its sensual existence, and now seem to live in it in chains, are in truth the causes of its life & the sources of

---

5. The Lord gave these instructions to the prophet Ezekiel (4.4–6).
6. In Genesis 3.24, when the Lord drove Adam and Eve from the Garden of Eden, he had placed Cherubim and a flaming sword at the eastern end "to keep the way of the tree of life."
7. See n. 2, p. 71.
8. A covert pun runs through this section: workers, ink-blackened, who did the dirty work in the printing houses of the period were humorously known as "printer's devils."
9. In this "Memorable Fancy" Blake allegorizes his procedure in designing, etching, printing, and binding his works of imaginative genius.
1. In this section human creative energies, called "the Prolific," in their relation to their indispensable contrary, "the Devourer."

all activity; but the chains are the cunning of weak and tame minds which have power to resist energy; according to the proverb, the weak in courage is strong in cunning.

Thus one portion of being is the Prolific, the other, the Devouring; to the Devourer it seems as if the producer was in his chains, but it is not so; he only takes portions of existence and fancies that the whole.

But the Prolific would cease to be Prolific unless the Devourer as a sea received the excess of his delights.

Some will say, "Is not God alone the Prolific?" I answer, "God only Acts & Is, in existing beings or Men."

These two classes of men are always upon earth, & they should be enemies; whoever tries [PLATE 17] to reconcile them seeks to destroy existence.

Religion is an endeavour to reconcile the two.

Note. Jesus Christ did not wish to unite but to separate them, as in the Parable of sheep and goats! & he says, "I came not to send Peace but a Sword."[2]

Messiah or Satan or Tempter was formerly thought to be one of the Antediluvians[3] who are our Energies.

A Memorable Fancy

An Angel came to me and said: "O pitiable foolish young man! O horrible! O dreadful state! consider the hot burning dungeon thou art preparing for thyself to all eternity, to which thou art going in such career."

I said: "Perhaps you will be willing to shew me my eternal lot, & we will contemplate together upon it and see whether your lot or mine is most desirable."

So he took me thro' a stable & thro' a church & down into the church vault at the end of which was a mill; thro' the mill we went, and came to a cave; down the winding cavern we groped our tedious way till a void boundless as a nether sky appeared beneath us, & we held by the roots of trees and hung over this immensity, but I said: "If you please, we will commit ourselves to this void, and see whether Providence is here also, if you will not I will." But he answered: "Do not presume, O young man, but as we here remain, behold thy lot which will soon appear when the darkness passes away."[4]

So I remain with him sitting in the twisted [PLATE 18] root of an oak; he was suspended in a fungus which hung with the head downward into the deep.

By degrees we beheld the infinite Abyss, fiery as the smoke of a burning city; beneath us at an immense distance was the sun, black but shining; round it were fiery tracks on which revolv'd vast spiders, crawling after their prey, which flew, or rather swum in the infinite deep, in the most terrific shapes of animals sprung from corruption; & the air was full of them, & seemed composed of them; these are Devils, and are called Powers of the air. I now asked my companion which was my eternal lot? He said, "Between the black & white spiders."

2. Matthew 10.34. The parable of the sheep and the goats is in Matthew 25.32–33.
3. Those who lived before Noah's Flood.
4. The "stable" is that where Jesus was born, which, allegorically, leads to the "church" founded in his name and to the "vault" where this institution effectually buried him. The "mill" in Blake is a symbol of mechanical and analytic philosophy; through this the pilgrims pass into the twisting cave of rationalistic theology and descend to an underworld that is an empty abyss. The point of this Blakean equivalent of a carnival funhouse is that only after you have thoroughly confused yourself by this tortuous approach, and only if you then (as in the next two paragraphs) stare at this topsyturvy emptiness long enough, will the void gradually assume the semblance of the comic horrors of the fantasized Hell of religious orthodoxy.

But now, from between the black & white spiders a cloud and fire burst and rolled thro the deep, blackning all beneath, so that the nether deep grew black as a sea & rolled with a terrible noise. Beneath us was nothing now to be seen but a black tempest, till looking east between the clouds & the waves, we saw a cataract of blood mixed with fire, and not many stones' throw from us appeared and sunk again the scaly fold of a monstrous serpent. At last to the east, distant about three degrees, appeared a fiery crest above the waves. Slowly it reared like a ridge of golden rocks till we discovered two globes of crimson fire, from which the sea fled away in clouds of smoke. And now we saw it was the head of Leviathan;[5] his forehead was divided into streaks of green & purple like those on a tyger's forehead; soon we saw his mouth & red gills hang just above the raging foam, tinging the black deep with beams of blood, advancing toward [PLATE 19] us with all the fury of a spiritual existence.

My friend the Angel climb'd up from his station into the mill. I remain'd alone, & then this appearance was no more, but I found myself sitting on a pleasant bank beside a river by moon light, hearing a harper who sung to the harp, & his theme was: "The man who never alters his opinion is like standing water, & breeds reptiles of the mind."

But I arose, and sought for the mill, & there I found my Angel, who surprised asked me how I escaped?

I answered: "All that we saw was owing to your metaphysics: for when you ran away, I found myself on a bank by moonlight hearing a harper. But now we have seen my eternal lot, shall I shew you yours? He laughd at my proposal; but I by force suddenly caught him in my arms, & flew westerly thro' the night, til we were elevated above the earth's shadow; then I flung myself with him directly into the body of the sun. Here I clothed myself in white, & taking in my hand Swedenborg's volumes, sunk from the glorious clime, and passed all the planets till we came to Saturn. Here I staid to rest & then leap'd into the void between Saturn & the fixed stars.[6]

"Here," said I, "is your lot, in this space, if space it may be calld." Soon we saw the stable and the church, & I took him to the altar and open'd the Bible, and lo! it was a deep pit, into which I descended, driving the Angel before me. Soon we saw seven houses of brick;[7] one we enterd; in it were a [PLATE 20] number of monkeys, baboons, & all of that species, chaind by the middle, grinning and snatching at one another, but withheld by the shortness of their chains. However, I saw that they sometimes grew numerous, and then the weak were caught by the strong, and with a grinning aspect, first coupled with & then devourd, by plucking off first one limb and then another till the body was left a helpless trunk. This, after grinning & kissing it with seeming fondness, they devourd too; and here & there I saw one savourily picking the flesh off of his own tail. As the stench terribly annoyd us both, we went into the mill, & I in my hand brought the skeleton of a body, which in the mill was Aristotle's Analytics.[8]

So the Angel said: "Thy phantasy has imposed upon me, & thou oughtest to be ashamed."

I answered: "We impose on one another, & it is but lost time to converse with you whose works are only Analytics."

5. The biblical sea monster.
6. In the Ptolemaic world picture, Saturn was in the outermost planetary sphere; beyond it was the sphere of the fixed stars.
7. The "seven churches which are in Asia," to which John addresses the Book of Revelation 1.4. Blake now forces on the angel his own diabolic view of angelic biblical exegesis, theological speculation and disputation, and Hell.
8. Aristotle's treatises on logic.

Opposition is true Friendship.

PLATE 21

I have always found that Angels have the vanity to speak of themselves as the only wise; this they do with a confident insolence sprouting from systematic reasoning.

Thus Swedenborg boasts that what he writes is new; tho' it is only the Contents or Index of already publish'd books.

A man carried a monkey about for a shew, & because he was a little wiser than the monkey, grew vain, and conceiv'd himself as much wiser than seven men. It is so with Swedenborg; he shews the folly of churches & exposes hypocrites, till he imagines that all are religious, & himself the single [PLATE 22] one on earth that ever broke a net.

Now hear a plain fact: Swedenborg has not written one new truth. Now hear another: he has written all the old falsehoods.

And now hear the reason: He conversed with Angels who are all religious, & conversed not with Devils, who all hate religion, for he was incapable thro' his conceited notions.

Thus Swedenborg's writings are a recapitulation of all superficial opinions, and an analysis of the more sublime, but no further.

Have now another plain fact: Any man of mechanical talents may from the writings of Paracelsus or Jacob Behmen[9] produce ten thousand volumes of equal value with Swedenborg's, and from those of Dante or Shakespear, an infinite number.

But when he has done this, let him not say that he knows better than his master, for he only holds a candle in sunshine.

A Memorable Fancy

Once I saw a Devil in a flame of fire, who arose before an Angel that sat on a cloud, and the Devil utterd these words:

"The worship of God is, Honouring his gifts in other men, each according to his genius, and loving the [PLATE 23] greatest men best. Those who envy or calumniate great men hate God, for there is no other God."

The Angel hearing this became almost blue; but mastering himself, he grew yellow, & at last white, pink, & smiling, and then replied:

"Thou Idolater, is not God One? & is not he visible in Jesus Christ? and has not Jesus Christ given his sanction to the law of ten commandments, and are not all other men fools, sinners, & nothings?"

The Devil answer'd; "Bray a fool in a mortar with wheat, yet shall not his folly be beaten out of him.[1] If Jesus Christ is the greatest man, you ought to love him in the greatest degree. Now hear how he has given his sanction to the law of ten commandments: did he not mock at the sabbath, and so mock the sabbath's God?[2] murder those who were murderd because of him? turn away the law from the woman taken in adultery?[3] steal the labor of others to

---

9. Jakob Boehme (1575–1624), a German shoemaker who developed a theosophical system that has had persisting influence on both theological and metaphysical speculation. Paracelsus (1493–1541), a Swiss physician and a pioneer in empirical medicine, was also a prominent theorist of the occult.

1. Proverbs 27.22: "Though thou shouldst bray a fool in a mortar among wheat with a pestle, yet will not his foolishness depart from him." "Bray": pound into small pieces.
2. Mark 2.27: "The sabbath was made for man."
3. Cf. John 8.2–11.

support him? bear false witness when he omitted making a defence before Pilate?[4] covet when he pray'd for his disciples, and when he bid them shake off the dust of their feet against such as refused to lodge them?[5] I tell you, no virtue can exist without breaking these ten commandments. Jesus was all virtue, and acted from im[PLATE 24]pulse, not from rules."

When he had so spoken, I beheld the Angel, who stretched out his arms embracing the flame of fire, & he was consumed and arose as Elijah.[6]

Note. This Angel, who is now become a Devil, is my particular friend; we often read the Bible together in its infernal or diabolical sense, which the world shall have if they behave well.

I have also The Bible of Hell,[7] which the world shall have whether they will or no.

One Law for the Lion & Ox is Oppression.

1790–93   1790–93

---

4. Cf. Matthew 27.13–14.
5. Matthew 10.14: "Whosoever shall not receive you . . . when ye depart . . . shake off the dust of your feet."

6. In 2 Kings 2.11 the prophet Elijah "went up by a whirlwind into heaven," borne by "a chariot of fire."
7. I.e., the poems and designs that Blake is working on.

ROBERT BURNS
1759–1796

When Robert Burns published *Poems, Chiefly in the Scottish Dialect* in 1786, he was immediately hailed by the Edinburgh establishment as an instance of the natural genius, a "Heaven-taught ploughman" whose poems owed nothing to literary study, but instead represented the spontaneous overflow of his native feelings. Burns took care to call attention to those qualities in his verse—the undisciplined energy and rustic simplicity—that suited the temper of an age worried that modern refinement and propriety had undermined the vigor of poetry. But even though he cast himself (in the half-modest, half-defiant words of his Preface to *Poems*) as someone "unacquainted with the necessary requisites for commencing Poet by rule," Burns was in fact a widely read (although largely self-educated) man and a careful craftsman who turned to two earlier traditions for his poetic models. One of these was an oral tradition of folklore and popular balladry. The other was the highly developed literary tradition of poetry written in Scots or Lallans—the distinct English of Lowland Scotland.

His father—William Burnes, as he spelled his name—was a God-fearing and hardworking farmer of Ayrshire, a county in southwestern Scotland, who, unable to make a go of it in a period of hard times and high rents, died in 1784 broken in body and spirit. Robert, with his brother Gilbert, was forced to do the heavy work of a man while still a boy and began to show signs of the heart trouble of which he was to die when only thirty-seven. Although his father had the Scottish esteem for education and saw to it that his sons attended school whenever they could, Burns's education in literature, theology, politics, and philosophy came mainly from his own reading. At the age of fifteen, he fell in love and was inspired by that event to write his first song. "Thus," he said, "with me began Love and Poesy." After he reached maturity, he practiced at both. He began a series of love affairs, fathering in 1785 the first of a number of illegitimate children. He also extended greatly the range and quantity of his attempts at poetry. So rapid was his development that by the time he published the Kilmarnock edition, at the age of twenty-seven, he had written all but a few of his greatest long poems.

The Kilmarnock volume (so named from the town in which it was published) is one of the most remarkable first volumes by any British poet, and it had a great and immediate success. Burns was acclaimed "Caledonia's Bard" and championed by intellectuals and gentlefolk when he visited the city of Edinburgh soon after his book came out. The peasant-poet demonstrated that he could more than hold his own as an urbane conversationalist and debater. But he was also wise enough to realize that once the novelty wore off, his eminence in this society would not endure. He had a fierce pride that was quick to resent any hint of contempt or condescension toward himself as a man of low degree. His sympathies were democratic, and even in 1793 and 1794, when partisans of parliamentary reform were being prosecuted for sedition in Edinburgh and Glasgow, he remained (like William Blake in London) an outspoken admirer of the republican revolutions in America and France. In religion, too, he was a radical. Against the strict Calvinism of the Presbyterian kirk (church) in which he had been raised, Burns was known to profess "the Religion of Sentiment and Reason." A letter of December 1789, in which he seizes the chance to play a free-thinking Son "of Satan," merrily proclaims his intention to take up a theme that will, he says, be "pregnant with all the stores of Learning, from Moses & Confucius to [Benjamin] Franklin & [Joseph] Priestl[e]y—in short . . . I intend to write Baudy." Burns's satires on the kirk and taste for bawdy vulgarity could offend. Furthermore, his promiscuity gained him considerable notoriety, less because womanizing was out of the common order for the time than because he flaunted it. Many of the friendships that he made in high society fell apart, and Burns's later visits to Edinburgh were less successful than the first.

In 1788 Burns was given a commission as excise officer, or tax inspector, and he settled down with Jean Armour, a former lover, now his wife, at Ellisland, near Dumfries, combining his official duties with farming. This was the fourth farm on which Burns had worked; and when it, like the others, failed, he moved his family to the lively country town of Dumfries. Here he was fairly happy, despite recurrent illness and a chronic shortage of money. He performed his official duties efficiently and was respected by his fellow townspeople and esteemed by his superiors; he was a devoted family man and father; and he accumulated a circle of intimates to whom he could repair for conversation and conviviality. In 1787 James Johnson, an engraver, had enlisted Burns's aid in collecting Scottish ballads for an anthology called *The Scots Musical Museum*. Burns soon became the real editor for several volumes of this work, devoting all of his free time to collecting, editing, restoring, and imitating traditional songs, and to writing verses of his own to traditional dance tunes. Almost all of his creative work during the last twelve years of his life went into the writing of songs for the *Musical Museum* and for George Thomson's *Select Collection of Original Scottish Airs*. This was for Burns a devoted labor of love and patriotism, done anonymously, for which he refused to accept any pay, although badly in need of money; and he continued the work when he was literally on his deathbed.

Because of its use of Scots, the language spoken by most eighteenth-century Scottish people (lower and upper class alike), and because, in addition, of its lyricism and engagement with folk culture, Burns's verse is often said to anticipate William Wordsworth's idea of a poetry founded on "a selection of language really used by men." This account is based primarily on his songs. By far the major portion of the poems that he published under his own name are concerned with men and manners and are written in the literary forms that had been favored by earlier eighteenth-century poets. They include brilliant satire in a variety of modes, a number of fine verse epistles to friends and fellow poets, and one masterpiece of mock-heroic (or at any rate seriocomic) narrative, "Tam o' Shanter." It can be argued that, next to Pope, Burns is the greatest eighteenth-century master of these literary types. (Byron would later claim those forms for his own generation.) Yet Burns's writings in satire, epistle, and mock-heroic are remote from Pope's in their heartiness and verve, no less than in their dialect and intricate stanza forms. The reason for the difference is that Burns turned for his models not to Horace and the English neoclassic tradition but to the native tradition that had been established in the golden age of Scots poetry by Robert Henryson, William Dunbar, Gavin Douglas, and other Scottish Chaucerians of the fifteenth and sixteenth centuries. He knew this literature through his eighteenth-century Scottish predecessors, especially Allan Ramsay and Robert Fergusson, who had collected some of the old poems and written new ones based on the old models. Burns improved greatly on these predecessors, but he derived from them much that is characteristic in his literary forms, subjects, diction, and stanzas.

Burns's songs, which number more than three hundred, have, however, in them-selves been enough to sustain his poetic reputation. They made him, for a start, a central figure for his contemporaries' discussions of how music, valued by them for awakening sympathies that reason could not rouse, might serve as the foundation of a national identity. (William Wordsworth would explore this new notion of "national music"—of ethnically marked melody—in his 1805 poem "The Solitary Reaper.") But beyond being the bard of Scots nationalism, Burns is a songwriter for all English-speaking people. Evidence of that standing is supplied each New Year's Eve, when, moved once again to acknowledge their common bondage to time, men and women join hands and sing "Auld Lang Syne," to an old tune that Burns refitted with his new words.

Holy Willie's Prayer[1]

> And send the Godly in a pet to pray—
> POPE

Argument

Holy Willie was a rather oldish batchelor Elder in the parish of Mauchline, and much and justly famed for that polemical chattering which ends in tip-pling Orthodoxy, and for that Spiritualized Bawdry which refines to Liquor-ish Devotion.—In a Sessional process with a gentleman in Mauchline, a Mr. Gavin Hamilton, Holy Willie, and his priest, Father Auld, after full hearing in the Presbytry of Ayr, came off but second best; owing partly to the ora-torical powers of Mr. Robt. Aiken, Mr. Hamilton's Counsel; but chiefly to Mr. Hamilton's being one of the most irreproachable and truly respectable characters in the country.—On losing his Process, the Muse overheard him at his devotions as follows—

> O thou that in the heavens does dwell!
> Wha, as it pleases best thysel,
> Sends ane to heaven and ten to h-ll,
>   A' for thy glory!
> 5 And no for ony gude or ill
>   They've done before thee.[2]

1. This satire, in the form of a dramatic mono-logue, was inspired by William Fisher, a self-righteous elder in the same Ayrshire parish that in 1785 had forced Burns and Betty Paton to do public penance in church for "fornication," and is directed against a basic Calvinist tenet of the old Scottish kirk. Holy Willie assumes that he is one of a small minority, God's "elect"—in other words that he has been predestined for grace, no matter what deeds he does in this world. The sessional processes were court proceedings carried on under the auspices of the Kirk. The epigraph is from *The Rape of the Lock*.
2. Here as elsewhere Burns uses the virtuosic

stanza form known as the "standard Habbie" (named for "The Life and Death of Habbie Simp-son" a ballad in this form by Robert Sempill, a 17th-century poet who, also hailing from the west of Scotland, was a countryman of Burns's). In each sestet three lines of iambic tetrameter that rhyme *aaa* are followed by a dimeter rhyming *b*, another line of tetrameter rhyming *a*, and a final dimeter rhyming *b*. Associated at its origins with the troubadour poetry of Europe, the form came to Scotland during the Renaissance and had been revived in the 18th century by Ramsay and Fer-gusson as a distinctively national Scots measure.

I bless and praise thy matchless might,
When thousands thou has left in night,
That I am here before thy sight,
10   For gifts and grace,
A burning and a shining light
     To a' this place.

What was I, or my generation,
That I should get such exaltation?
15 I, wha deserv'd most just damnation,
     For broken laws
Sax° thousand years ere my creation,   *six*
     Thro' Adam's cause!

When from my mother's womb I fell,
20 Thou might hae plunged me deep in hell,
To gnash my gooms, and weep, and wail,[3]
     In burning lakes,
Where damned devils roar and yell
     Chain'd to their stakes.

25 Yet I am here, a chosen sample,
To shew thy grace is great and ample:
I'm here, a pillar o' thy temple
     Strong as a rock,
A guide, a ruler and example
30   To a' thy flock.

O Lord thou kens what zeal I bear,
When drinkers drink, and swearers swear,
And singin' there, and dancin' here,
     Wi' great an' sma';
35 For I am keepet by thy fear,
     Free frae them a'.

But yet—O Lord—confess I must—
At times I'm fash'd° wi' fleshly lust;   *troubled*
And sometimes too, in warldly trust
40   Vile Self gets in;
But thou remembers we are dust,
     Defil'd wi' sin.

O Lord—yestreen°—thou kens°—wi' Meg—   *yesterday / knowest*
Thy pardon I sincerely beg!
45 O may't ne'er be a living plague,
     To my dishonor!
And I'll ne'er lift a lawless leg
     Again upon her.

Besides, I farther maun° avow,   *must*
50 Wi' Leezie's lass, three times—I trow°—   *believe*
But Lord, that Friday I was fou°   *drunk*

---

3. An echo of Matthew 8.12, "the children of the kingdom shall be cast out into outer darkness: there shall be weeping and gnashing of teeth."

When I cam near her;
Or else, thou kens, thy servant true
   Wad never steer° her.   *molest*

55 Maybe thou lets this fleshly thorn
Buffet thy servant e'en and morn,[4]
Lest he o'er proud and high should turn,
   That he's sae gifted;
If sae, thy hand maun e'en be borne
60   Untill thou lift it.

Lord bless thy Chosen in this place,
For here thou has a chosen race:
But God, confound their stubborn face,
   And blast their name,
65 Wha bring thy rulers to disgrace
   And open shame.

Lord mind Gaun Hamilton's[5] deserts!
He drinks, and swears, and plays at cartes,°   *cards*
Yet has sae mony taking arts
70   Wi' Great and Sma',
Frae God's ain priest the people's hearts
   He steals awa.

And when we chasten'd him therefore,
Thou kens how he bred sic a splore,°   *disturbance*
75 And set the warld in a roar
   O' laughin at us:
Curse thou his basket and his store,
   Kail° and potatoes.   *broth*

Lord hear my earnest cry and prayer
80 Against that Presbytry of Ayr!
Thy strong right hand, Lord, make it bare
   Upon their heads!
Lord visit them, and dinna spare,
   For their misdeeds!

85 O Lord my God, that glib-tongu'd Aiken!
My very heart and flesh are quaking
To think how I sat, sweating, shaking,
   And piss'd wi' dread,
While Auld wi' hingin° lip gaed sneaking   *hanging*
90   And hid his head!

Lord, in thy day o'vengeance try him!
Lord visit him that did employ him!
And pass not in thy mercy by them,

4. An echo of 2 Corinthians 12.7, "there was given to me a thorn in the flesh, the messenger of Satan to buffet me, lest I should be exalted above measure."
5. Burns's friend Gavin Hamilton, whom Holy Willie had brought up on moral charges before the Kirk Session of the Presbytery of Ayr. As Burns explains in the Argument, Hamilton was successfully defended by his counsel, Robert Aiken (referred to in line 85).

Nor hear their prayer;
95   But for thy people's sake destroy them,
And dinna spare!

But Lord, remember me and mine
Wi' mercies temporal and divine!
That I for grace and gear° may shine,   *wealth*
100   Excell'd by nane!
And a' the glory shall be thine!
Amen! Amen!

1789   1789

To a Mouse

On Turning Her up in Her Nest with the Plough,
November, 1785[1]

Wee, sleeket,° cowran, tim'rous beastie,   *sleek*
O, what a panic's in thy breastie!
Thou need na start awa sae hasty,
        Wi' bickering brattle![2]
5   I wad be laith° to rin an' chase thee   *loath*
        Wi' murd'ring pattle!°   *plowstaff*

I'm truly sorry Man's dominion
Has broken Nature's social union,
An' justifies that ill opinion,
10   Which makes thee startle,
At me, thy poor, earth-born companion,
        An' fellow mortal!

I doubt na, whyles,° but thou may thieve;   *sometimes*
What then? poor beastie, thou maun° live!   *must*
15 A daimen-icker in a thrave[3]
        'S a sma' request:
I'll get a blessin wi' the lave,°   *remainder*
        An' never miss 't!

Thy wee-bit housie, too, in ruin!
20 It's silly wa's° the win's are strewin!   *frail walls*
An' naething, now, to big° a new ane,   *build*
        O' foggage° green!   *coarse grass*
An' bleak December's winds ensuin,
        Baith snell° an' keen!   *bitter*

25 Thou saw the fields laid bare an' waste,
An' weary Winter comin fast,
An' cozie here, beneath the blast,
        Thou thought to dwell,

---

1. Burns's brother claimed that this poem was
composed while the poet was actually holding
the plow.

2. With headlong scamper.
3. An occasional ear in twenty-four sheaves.

Till crash! the cruel coulter° past   *cutter blade*
30   Out thro' thy cell.

That wee-bit heap o' leaves an' stibble°   *stubble*
Has cost thee monie a weary nibble!
Now thou 's turn'd out, for a' thy trouble,
      But° house or hald,[4]   *without*
35 To thole° the Winter's sleety dribble,   *endure*
      An' cranreuch° cauld!   *hoarfrost*

But Mousie, thou art no thy-lane,°   *not alone*
In proving foresight may be vain:
The best laid schemes o' Mice an' Men
40   Gang aft agley,[5]
An' lea'e us nought but grief an' pain,
      For promis'd joy!

Still, thou art blest, compar'd wi' me!
The present only toucheth thee:
45 But Och! I backward cast my e'e,
      On prospects drear!
An' forward tho' I canna see,
      I guess an' fear!

1785   1786

To a Louse

On Seeing One on a Lady's Bonnet at Church

Ha! whare ye gaun, ye crowlan° ferlie!°   *crawling / wonder*
Your impudence protects you sairly:°   *sorely*
I canna say but ye strunt° rarely,   *strut*
      Owre gawze and lace;
5 Tho' faith, I fear ye dine but sparely,
      On sic a place.

Ye ugly, creepan, blastet wonner,°   *wonder*
Detested, shunn'd, by saunt an' sinner,
How daur ye set your fit° upon her,   *foot*
10   Sae fine a Lady!
Gae somewhere else and seek your dinner,
      On some poor body.

Swith,° in some beggar's haffet° squattle;°   *swift / locks / sprawl*
There ye may creep, and sprawl, and sprattle,°   *struggle*
15 Wi' ither kindred, jumping cattle,
      In shoals and nations;
Whare horn nor bane[1] ne'er daur unsettle,
      Your thick plantations.

---

4. Hold, holding (i.e., land).
5. Go oft awry.

1. I.e., fine-tooth comb made of horn or bone ("bane").

Now haud you there, ye're out o' sight,
20 Below the fatt'rels,° snug and tight,   *ribbon ends*
Na faith ye yet![2] ye'll no be right,
    Till ye've got on it,
The vera tapmost, towrin height
    O' Miss's bonnet.

25 My sooth! right bauld ye set your nose out,
As plump an' gray as onie grozet:°   *gooseberry*
O for some rank, mercurial rozet,°   *rosin*
    Or fell,° red smeddum,°   *sharp / powder*
I'd gie you sic a hearty dose o't,
30   Wad dress your droddum!°   *buttocks*

I wad na been surpriz'd to spy
You on an auld wife's flainen toy,°   *flannel cap*
Or aiblins° some bit duddie° boy,   *perhaps / ragged*
    On 's wylecoat;°   *undershirt*
35 But Miss's fine Lunardi,[3] fye!
    How daur ye do 't?

O Jenny dinna toss your head,
An' set your beauties a' abread!°   *abroad*
Ye little ken what cursed speed
40   The blastie's° makin!   *creature's*
Thae° winks and finger-ends, I dread,   *those*
    Are notice takin!

O wad some Pow'r the giftie gie us
To see oursels as others see us!
45 It wad frae monie a blunder free us
    An' foolish notion:
What airs in dress an' gait wad lea'e us,
    And ev'n Devotion![4]

1785   1786

Auld Lang Syne[1]

Should auld acquaintance be forgot
    And never brought to mind?
Should auld acquaintance be forgot,
    And auld lang syne!

Chorus

5   For auld lang syne, my jo,
    For auld lang syne,
We'll tak a cup o' kindness yet
    For auld lang syne.

2. Confound you!
3. A balloon-shaped bonnet, named after Vin-
cenzo Lunardi, who made a number of balloon
flights in the mid-1780s.
4. I.e., even pretended piety.
1. Long ago.

And surely ye'll be° your pint stowp!°   *pay for / pint cup*
10 And surely I'll be mine!
And we'll tak a cup o' kindness yet,
For auld lang syne.
Chorus

We twa hae run about the braes°   *slopes*
And pou'd° the gowans° fine;   *pulled / daisies*
15 But we've wander'd many a weary fitt,
Sin° auld lang syne.   *since*
Chorus

We twa hae paidl'd in the burn°   *stream*
Frae morning sun till dine;°   *dinner, noon*
But seas between us braid° hae roar'd,   *broad*
20 Sin auld lang syne.
Chorus

And there's a hand, my trusty fiere!°   *friend*
And gie's a hand o' thine!
And we'll tak a right gude-willie-waught,°   *cordial drink*
For auld lang syne.
Chorus

1788   1796

Tam o' Shanter: A Tale[1]

Of Brownyis and of Bogillis full is this buke.
GAWIN DOUGLAS

When chapman billies[2] leave the street,
And drouthy° neebors neebors meet,   *thirsty*
As market-days are wearing late,
An' folk begin to tak the gate;°   *road*
5 While we sit bousing at the nappy,°   *strong ale*
And getting fou° and unco° happy,   *drunk / very*
We think na on the lang Scots miles,
The mosses, waters, slaps,° and styles,   *gaps (in walls)*
That lie between us and our hame,
10 Whare sits our sulky sullen dame,
Gathering her brows like gathering storm,
Nursing her wrath to keep it warm.

1. This poem, written to order for a book on Scottish antiquities, is based on a witch story told about Alloway Kirk, an old ruin near Burns's house in Ayr. As a mock-heroic rendering of folk material, "Tam o' Shanter" is comparable to *The Nun's Priest's Tale* of Chaucer. Burns recognized that the poem was his most sustained and finished artistic performance; it discovers "a spice of roguish waggery" but also shows "a force of genius and a finishing polish that I despair of ever excelling." The verve and seriocomic sympathy with which Burns manages this misadventure of a confirmed tippler won Wordsworth, a teetotaler, to passionate advocacy against the moralists who objected to Burns's ribaldry: "Who, but some impenetrable dunce or narrow-minded puritan in works of art, ever read without delight the picture which he has drawn of the convivial exaltation of the rustic adventurer, Tam o' Shanter?" ("Letter to a Friend of Burns," 1816). The epigraph is from the prologue to book 6 of Gavin Douglas's 16th-century Scots translation of Virgil's *Aeneid*. In this book the epic hero Aeneas, soon to be the founder of Rome, descends into the world of the dead. See the StudySpace for a sound recording of "Tam o' Shanter."
2. Peddler fellows.

This truth fand° honest Tam o' Shanter,   *found*
As he frae Ayr ae night did canter,
15 (Auld Ayr, wham ne'er a town surpasses,
For honest men and bonny lasses).

O Tam! hadst thou but been sae wise,
As ta'en thy ain wife Kate's advice!
She tauld thee weel thou was a skellum,°   *good-for-nothing*
20 A blethering,° blustering, drunken blellum;°   *chattering / babbler*
That frae November till October,
Ae market-day thou was nae sober;
That ilka° melder,³ wi' the miller,   *every*
Thou sat as lang as thou had siller;°   *silver, money*
25 That every naig° was ca'd° a shoe on,   *nag / driven*
The smith and thee gat roaring fou on;
That at the Lord's house, even on Sunday,
Thou drank wi' Kirkton Jean till Monday.
She prophesied that late or soon,
30 Thou would be found deep drown'd in Doon;
Or catch'd wi' warlocks in the mirk,°   *night*
By Alloway's auld haunted kirk.

Ah, gentle dames! it gars° me greet°   *makes / weep*
To think how mony counsels sweet,
35 How mony lengthen'd sage advices,
The husband frae the wife despises!

But to our tale: Ae market-night,
Tam had got planted unco right;
Fast by an ingle,° bleezing° finely,   *fireplace / blazing*
40 Wi' reaming swats,° that drank divinely;   *foaming new ale*
And at his elbow, Souter° Johnny,   *shoemaker*
His ancient, trusty, drouthy crony;
Tam lo'ed him like a vera brither;
They had been fou for weeks thegither.
45 The night drave on wi' sangs and clatter;
And ay the ale was growing better:
The landlady and Tam grew gracious,
Wi' favours secret, sweet, and precious:
The Souter tauld his queerest stories;
50 The landlord's laugh was ready chorus:
The storm without might rair° and rustle,   *roar*
Tam did na mind the storm a whistle.

Care, mad to see a man sae happy,
E'en drown'd himsel amang the nappy:
55 As bees flee hame wi' lades o' treasure,
The minutes wing'd their way wi' pleasure:
Kings may be blest, but Tam was glorious,
O'er a' the ills o' life victorious!

3. The amount of corn processed at a single grinding.

But pleasures are like poppies spread,
60 You seize the flower, its bloom is shed;
Or like the snow falls in the river,
A moment white—then melts for ever;
Or like the borealis race,
That flit ere you can point their place;
65 Or like the rainbow's lovely form
Evanishing amid the storm.—
Nae man can tether time or tide;
The hour approaches Tam maun° ride;   must
That hour, o' night's black arch the key-stane,
70 That dreary hour, he mounts his beast in;
And sic a night he taks the road in,
As ne'er poor sinner was abroad in.

The wind blew as 'twad blawn its last;
The rattling showers rose on the blast;
75 The speedy gleams the darkness swallow'd;
Loud, deep, and lang, the thunder bellow'd:
That night, a child might understand,
The Deil had business on his hand.

Weel mounted on his gray mare, Meg,
80 A better never lifted leg,[4]
Tam skelpit° on thro' dub° and mire,   slapped / puddle
Despising wind, and rain, and fire;
Whiles holding fast his gude blue bonnet;
Whiles crooning o'er some auld Scots sonnet;
85 Whiles glowring° round wi' prudent cares,   staring
Lest bogles° catch him unawares.   hobgoblins
Kirk-Alloway was drawing nigh,
Whare ghaists° and houlets° nightly cry.—   ghosts / owls

By this time he was cross the ford,
90 Whare in the snaw, the chapman smoor'd;[5]
And past the birks° and meikle stane,°   birches / big stone
Whare drunken Charlie brak's neck-bane;
And thro' the whins, and by the cairn,[6]
Whare hunters fand the murder'd bairn;
95 And near the thorn, aboon the well,
Where Mungo's mither hang'd hersel.—
Before him Doon pours all his floods;
The doubling storm roars thro' the woods;
The lightnings flash from pole to pole;
100 Near and more near the thunders roll:
When, glimmering thro' the groaning trees,
Kirk-Alloway seemed in a bleeze;°   blaze
Thro' ilka bore° the beams were glancing;   hole
And loud resounded mirth and dancing.—

4. Compare this "lifted leg" to Willie's use of the
term about himself in line 47 of "Holy Willie's
Prayer." Tam's horse, Meg (also called Maggie),
occasions the poem's bawdiest wordplay.

5. The peddler smothered.
6. Stones heaped up as a memorial. "Whins":
furze (an evergreen shrub).

105   Inspiring bold John Barleycorn!
      What dangers thou canst make us scorn!
      Wi' tippeny,[7] we fear nae evil;
      Wi' usquabae,° we'll face the devil!—   *whiskey*
      The swats sae ream'd in Tammie's noddle,
110   Fair play, he car'd na deils a boddle.[8]
      But Maggie stood right sair astonish'd,
      Till, by the heel and hand admonish'd,
      She ventured forward on the light;
      And, vow! Tam saw an unco° sight!   *strange*
115   Warlocks and witches in a dance;
      Nae cotillion brent° new frae France,   *brand*
      But hornpipes, jigs, strathspeys,[9] and reels,
      Put life and mettle in their heels.
      A winnock-bunker° in the east,   *window seat*
120   There sat auld Nick, in shape o' beast;
      A touzie tyke,° black, grim, and large,   *shaggy dog*
      To gie them music was his charge:
      He screw'd the pipes and gart° them skirl,°   *made / screech*
      Till roof and rafters a' did dirl.°—   *rattle*
125   Coffins stood round, like open presses,
      That shaw'd the dead in their last dresses;
      And by some devilish cantraip° slight   *charm, trick*
      Each in its cauld hand held a light.—
      By which heroic Tam was able
130   To note upon the haly° table,   *holy*
      A murderer's banes in gibbet airns;°   *irons*
      Twa span-lang,[1] wee, unchristened bairns;
      A thief, new-cutted frae a rape,°   *rope*
      Wi' his last gasp his gab° did gape;   *mouth*
135   Five tomahawks, wi' blude red-rusted;
      Five scymitars, wi' murder crusted;
      A garter, which a babe had strangled;
      A knife, a father's throat had mangled,
      Whom his ain son o' life bereft,
140   The grey hairs yet stack° to the heft;   *stuck*
      Wi' mair o' horrible and awefu',
      Which even to name wad be unlawfu'.

      As Tammie glowr'd, amaz'd, and curious,
      The mirth and fun grew fast and furious:
145   The piper loud and louder blew;
      The dancers quick and quicker flew;
      They reel'd, they set, they cross'd, they cleekit,°   *joined hands*
      Till ilka carlin° swat and reekit,   *old woman*
      And coost her duddies to the wark,[2]
150   And linket° at it in her sark![3]   *tripped lightly*

      Now, Tam, O Tam! had thae been queans,°   *girls*
      A' plump and strapping in their teens,

7. Twopenny (usually of weak beer).
8. I.e., he didn't care a farthing about devils (a "boddle" is a very small copper coin).
9. Slow Highland dance.

1. Two spans long (a span is the distance from outstretched thumb to little finger).
2. Cast off her clothes for the work.
3. Shirt (underclothes).

Their sarks, instead o' creeshie flannen,°   *greasy flannel*
Been snaw-white seventeen hunder linnen!⁴
155 Thir° breeks o' mine, my only pair,   *these*
That ance were plush, o' gude blue hair,
I wad hae gi'en them off my hurdies,°   *buttocks*
For ae blink o' the bonie burdies!°   *bonny (pretty) girls*

But wither'd beldams,° auld and droll,   *hags*
160 Rigwoodie° hags wad spean° a foal,   *bony / wean*
Lowping° and flinging on a crummock,°   *leaping / staff*
I wonder didna turn thy stomach.

But Tam kend what was what fu' brawlie,°   *finely*
There was ae winsome wench and wawlie°   *strapping*
165 That night enlisted in the core,°   *corps*
(Lang after kend on Carrick shore;
For mony a beast to dead she shot,
And perish'd mony a bony boat,
And shook baith meikle corn and bear,°   *barley*
170 And kept the country-side in fear:)
Her cutty° sark, o' Paisley harn,°   *short / yarn*
That while a lassie she had worn,
In longitude tho' sorely scanty,
It was her best, and she was vauntie.°—   *proud*
175 Ah! little kend thy reverend grannie,
That sark she coft° for her wee Nannie,   *bought*
Wi' twa pund Scots ('twas a' her riches),
Wad ever grac'd a dance of witches!

But here my Muse her wing maun cour;°   *lower*
180 Sic flights are far beyond her pow'r;
To sing how Nannie lap and flang,
(A souple jade° she was, and strang),   *disreputable woman*
And how Tam stood, like ane bewitch'd,
And thought his very een° enrich'd;   *eyes*
185 Even Satan glowr'd, and fidg'd fu' fain,⁵
And hotch'd° and blew wi' might and main: *jerked*
Till first ae caper, syne° anither,   *then*
Tam tint° his reason a' thegither,   *lost*
And roars out, 'Weel done, Cutty-sark!'
190 And in an instant all was dark:
And scarcely had he Maggie rallied,
When out the hellish legion sallied.

As bees bizz out wi' angry fyke,°   *fuss*
When plundering herds° assail their byke;°   *herdsmen / hive*
195 As open° pussie's mortal foes,   *begin to bark*
When, pop! she starts before their nose;
As eager runs the market-crowd,
When 'Catch the thief!' resounds aloud;

4. Very fine linen, woven on a loom with seven-   5. Fidgeted with pleasure.
teen hundred strips.

So Maggie runs the witches follow,
200 Wi' mony an eldritch° skreech and hollow.   *unearthly*

Ah, Tam! Ah, Tam! thou'll get thy fairin'!°   *deserts*
In hell they'll roast thee like a herrin!
In vain thy Kate awaits thy comin!
Kate soon will be a woefu' woman!
205 Now, do thy speedy utmost, Meg,
And win the key-stane of the brig;[6]
There at them thou thy tail may toss,
A running stream they dare na cross.
But ere the key-stane she could make,
210 The fient a tail she had to shake!
For Nannie, far before the rest,
Hard upon noble Maggie prest,
And flew at Tam wi' furious ettle;°   *intent*
But little wist she Maggie's mettle—
215 Ae spring brought off her master hale,°   *whole*
But left behind her ain gray tail:
The carlin claught° her by the rump,   *clutched*
And left poor Maggie scarce a stump.[7]

Now, wha this tale o' truth shall read,
220 Ilk man and mother's son, take heed:
Whene'er to drink you are inclin'd,
Or cutty-sarks run in your mind,
Think, ye may buy the joys o'er dear,
Remember Tam o' Shanter's mare.

1790   1791

A Red, Red Rose[1]

O my Luve's like a red, red rose,
    That's newly sprung in June;
O my Luve's like the melodie
    That's sweetly played in tune.

5   As fair art thou, my bonie lass,
        So deep in luve am I;
    And I will love thee still, my Dear,
        Till a' the seas gang dry.

    Till a' the seas gang dry, my Dear,
10   And the rocks melt wi' the sun:
    O I will love thee still, my Dear,
        While the sands o' life shall run.

6. It is a well known fact that witches, or any evil spirits, have no power to follow a poor wight any farther than the middle of the next running stream.—It may be proper likewise to mention to the benighted traveler, that when he falls in with *bogles*, whatever danger may be in his going forward, there is much more hazard in turning back [Burns's note]. "Brig": bridge.
7. I.e., she had no tail left at all.
1. Like many of Burns's lyrics, this one incorporates elements from several current ballads.

And fare thee weel, my only Luve!
And fare thee weel, a while!
15   And I will come again, my Luve,
Tho' it were ten thousand mile!

1794   1796

Song: For a' that and a' that[1]

Is there, for honest Poverty
That hangs his head, and a' that;
The coward-slave, we pass him by,
We dare be poor for a' that!
5   For a' that, and a' that,
Our toils obscure, and a' that,
The rank is but the guinea's stamp,°   *inscription on a coin*
The Man's the gowd° for a' that.   *gold*

What though on hamely fare we dine,
10   Wear hodden grey,[2] and a' that.
Gie fools their silks, and knaves their wine,
A Man's a Man for a' that.
For a' that, and a' that,
Their tinsel show, and a' that;
15   The honest man, though e'er sae poor,
Is king o' men for a' that.

Ye see yon birkie° ca'd a lord,   *fellow*
Wha struts, and stares, and a' that,
Though hundreds worship at his word,
20   He's but a coof° for a' that.   *dolt*
For a' that, and a' that,
His ribband, star and a' that,
The man of independant mind,
He looks and laughs at a' that.

25 A prince can mak a belted knight,
A marquis, duke, and a' that;
But an honest man's aboon° his might,   *above*
Guid faith he mauna fa' that![3]

For a' that, and a' that,
30   Their dignities, and a' that,
The pith o' Sense, and pride o' Worth,
Are higher rank than a' that.

Then let us pray that come it may,
As come it will for a' that,
35   That Sense and Worth, o'er a' the earth
Shall bear the gree,° and a' that.   *win the prize*

1. This song was set to a dance tune, known as   2. A coarse cloth of undyed wool.
Lady Macintosh's Reel, that Burns had drawn on   3. Must not claim that.
for previous songs.

> For a' that, and a' that,
>   It's coming yet for a' that,
>   That Man to Man the warld o'er,
> 40   Shall brothers be for a' that.

1795   1795

MARY WOLLSTONECRAFT
1759–1797

Mary Wollstonecraft's father inherited a substantial fortune and set himself up as a gentleman farmer. He was, however, both extravagant and incompetent, and as one farm after another failed, he became moody and violent and sought solace in heavy bouts of drinking and in tyrannizing his submissive wife. Mary was the second of five children and the oldest daughter. She later told her husband, William Godwin, that she used to throw herself in front of her mother to protect her from her husband's blows, and that she sometimes slept outside the door of her parents' bedroom to intervene if her father should break out in a drunken rage. The solace of Mary's early life was her fervent attachment to Fanny Blood, an accomplished girl two years her senior; their friendship, which began when Mary was sixteen, endured and deepened until Fanny's death.

At the age of nineteen, Mary Wollstonecraft left home to take a position as companion to a well-to-do widow living in Bath, where for the first time she had the opportunity to observe—and scorn—the social life of the upper classes at the most fashionable of English resort cities. Having left her job in 1780 to nurse her dying mother through a long and harrowing illness, Wollstonecraft next went to live with the Bloods, where her work helped sustain the struggling family. Her sister Eliza meanwhile had married and, in 1784, after the birth of a daughter, suffered a nervous breakdown. Convinced that her sister's collapse was the result of her husband's cruelty and abuse, Wollstonecraft persuaded her to abandon husband and child and flee to London. Because a divorce at that time was not commonly available, and a fugitive wife could be forced to return to her husband, the two women hid in secret quarters while awaiting the grant of a legal separation. The infant, automatically given into the father's custody, died before she was a year old.

The penniless women, together with Fanny Blood and Wollstonecraft's other sister, Everina, established a girls' school at Newington Green, near London. The project flourished at first, and at Newington, Wollstonecraft was befriended by the Reverend Richard Price, the radical author who was soon to play a leading role in the British debates about the Revolution in France, and whose kindly guidance helped shape her social and political opinions. Blood, although already ill with tuberculosis, went to Lisbon to marry her longtime suitor, Hugh Skeys, and quickly became pregnant. Wollstonecraft rushed to Lisbon to attend her friend's childbirth, only to have Fanny die in her arms; the infant died soon afterward. The loss threw Wollstonecraft (already subject to bouts of depression) into black despair, which was heightened when she found that the school at Newington was in bad financial straits and had to be closed. Tormented by creditors, she rallied her energies to write her first book, *Thoughts on the Education of Daughters* (1786), a conventional and pious series of essays, and took up a position as governess for several daughters in the Anglo-Irish family of Viscount Kingsborough, a man of great wealth whose seat was in County Cork, Ireland.

The Kingsboroughs were well intentioned and did their best to introduce Wollstonecraft into the busy trivialities of their social life. But the ambiguity of her position as governess, halfway between a servant and a member of the family, was galling. An antagonism developed between Wollstonecraft and Lady Kingsborough, in part because the children feared their mother and adored their governess. Wollstonecraft was dismissed. She returned to London, where Joseph Johnson in 1788 published *Mary, a Fiction*, a novel, as Wollstonecraft described it, about "the mind of a woman who has thinking powers." Johnson also published her book for children, *Original Stories from Real Life*, a considerable success that was translated into German and quickly achieved a second English edition illustrated with engravings by William Blake. Wollstonecraft was befriended and subsidized by Johnson, the major publisher in England of radical and reformist books, and she took a prominent place among the writers (including notables such as Barbauld and Coleridge) whom he regularly entertained at his rooms in St. Paul's Churchyard. She published translations from French and German (she had taught herself both languages) and began reviewing books for Johnson's newly founded journal, the *Analytical Review*. Though still in straitened circumstances, she helped support her two sisters and her improvident and importunate father, and was also generous with funds—and with advice—to one of her brothers and to the indigent family of Fanny Blood.

In 1790 Edmund Burke's *Reflections on the Revolution in France*—an eloquent and powerful attack on the French Revolution and its English sympathizers—quickly evoked Wollstonecraft's response, *A Vindication of the Rights of Men*. This was a formidable piece of argumentation; its most potent passages represent the disabilities and sufferings of the English lower classes and impugn the motives and sentiments of Burke. This work, the first book-length reply to Burke, scored an immediate success, although it was soon submerged in the flood of other replies, most notably Thomas Paine's classic *Rights of Man* (1791–92). In 1792 Wollstonecraft focused her defense of the underprivileged on her own sex and wrote, in six weeks of intense effort, *A Vindication of the Rights of Woman*.

Earlier writers in both France and England had proposed that, given equivalent educations, women would equal men in achievement. Wollstonecraft was particularly indebted to the historian Catharine Macaulay, whose *Letters on Education* (1790) she had reviewed enthusiastically. At the same time Wollstonecraft was contributing to a long-running discussion of human rights that in Britain dated back to John Locke's publication of the *Second Treatise of Civil Government* (1690). Prefaced with a letter addressed to the French politician Bishop Talleyrand, the *Vindication* was in part her rejoinder to the inconsistent actions of France's National Assembly, which in 1791 had formally denied to all Frenchwomen the rights of citizens, even as, ironically enough, it set about celebrating the "universal rights of man."

Her book was also unprecedented in its firsthand observations of the disabilities and indignities suffered by women and in the articulateness and passion with which it exposed and decried this injustice. Wollstonecraft's views were conspicuously radical at a time when women had no political rights; were limited to a few lowly vocations as servants, nurses, governesses, and petty shopkeepers; and were legally nonpersons who lost their property to their husbands at marriage and were incapable of instituting an action in the courts of law. An impressive feature of her book, for all its vehemence, is the clear-sightedness and balance of her analysis of the social conditions of the time, as they affect men as well as women. She perceives that women constitute an oppressed class that cuts across the standard hierarchy of social classes; she shows that women, because they are denied their rights as human beings, have been forced to seek their ends by means of coquetry and cunning, the weapons of the weak; and, having demonstrated that it is contrary to reason to expect virtue from those who are not free, she also recognizes that men, no less than women, inherit their roles, and that the wielding of irresponsible power corrupts the oppressor no less than it distorts the oppressed. Hence her surprising and telling comparisons between women on the one hand and men of the nobility and military on the other as classes whose values and behavior have been distorted because their social roles prevent them from becoming fully human. In writing this pioneering work, Wollstonecraft found the cause that she was to pursue the rest of her life.

In December 1792 Wollstonecraft went to Paris to observe the Revolution at firsthand. During the years that she lived in France, 1793–94, the early period of moderation was succeeded by extremism and violence. In Paris she joined a group of English, American, and European expatriates sympathetic to the Revolution and fell in love with Gilbert Imlay, a personable American who had briefly been an officer in the American Revolutionary Army and was the author of a widely read book on the Kentucky backwoods, where he had been an explorer. He played the role in Paris of an American frontiersman and child of nature, but was in fact an adventurer who had left America to avoid prosecution for debt and for freewheeling speculations in Kentucky land. He was also unscrupulous in his relations with women. The two became lovers, and their daughter, Fanny Imlay, was born in May 1794. Imlay, who was often absent on mysterious business deals, left mother and daughter for a visit to London that he kept protracting. After the publication of her book *An Historical and Moral View of the Origin and Progress of the French Revolution* (1794), Wollstonecraft followed Imlay to London, where, convinced that he no longer loved her, she tried to commit suicide. The attempt, however, was discovered and prevented by Imlay. To get her out of the way, he persuaded her to take a trip as his business envoy to the Scandinavian countries. Although this was then a region of poor or impassible roads and primitive accommodations, the intrepid Wollstonecraft traveled there for four months, sometimes in the wilds, accompanied by the year-old Fanny and a French nursemaid.

Back in London, Wollstonecraft discovered that Imlay was living with a new mistress, an actress. Finally convinced he was lost to her, she hurled herself from a bridge into the Thames but was rescued by a passerby. Imlay departed with his actress to Paris. Wollstonecraft, resourceful as always, used the letters she had written to Imlay to compose a book, *Letters Written during a Short Residence in Sweden, Norway, and Denmark* (1796), full of sharp observations of politics, the lives of Scandinavian women, and the austere northern landscape.

In the same year Wollstonecraft renewed an earlier acquaintance with the philosopher William Godwin. His *Inquiry Concerning Political Justice* (1793), the most drastic proposal for restructuring the political and social order yet published in England, together with his novel of terror, *Caleb Williams* (1794), which embodies his social views, had made him the most famed radical writer of his time. The austerely rationalistic philosopher, then forty years of age, had an unexpected capacity for deep feeling, and what began as a flirtation soon ripened into affection and (as their letters show) passionate physical love. She wrote Godwin, with what was for the time remarkable outspokenness on the part of a woman: "Now by these presents [i.e., this document] let me assure you that you are not only in my heart, but my veins, this morning. I turn from you half abashed—yet you haunt me, and some look, word or touch thrills through my whole frame. . . . When the heart and reason accord there is no flying from voluptuous sensations, do what a woman can." Wollstonecraft was soon pregnant once more, and Godwin (who had in his *Inquiry* attacked the institution of marriage as a base form of property rights in human beings) braved the ridicule of his radical friends and conservative enemies by marrying her.

They set up a household together, but Godwin also kept separate quarters in which to do his writing, and they further salvaged their principles by agreeing to live separate social lives. Wollstonecraft was able to enjoy this arrangement for only six months. She began writing *The Wrongs of Woman*, a novel about marriage and motherhood that uses its Gothic setting inside a dilapidated madhouse to explore how women are confined both by unjust marriage laws and by their own romantic illusions. On August 30, 1797, she gave birth to a daughter, Mary Wollstonecraft Godwin, later the author of *Frankenstein* and wife of Percy Shelley. The delivery was not difficult, but resulted in massive blood poisoning. After ten days of agony, she lapsed into a coma and died. Her last whispered words were about her husband: "He is the kindest, best man in the world." Godwin wrote to a friend, announcing her death: "I firmly believe that there does not exist her equal in the world. I know from experience we were formed to make each other happy."

To distract himself in his grief, Godwin published in 1798 *Memoirs of the Author of "A Vindication of the Rights of Woman,"* in which he told, with the total candor on which he prided himself, of her affairs with Imlay and himself, her attempts at suicide, and her freethinking in matters of religion and sexual relationships. In four companion volumes of her *Posthumous Works*, he indiscreetly included her love letters to Imlay along with the unfinished *Wrongs of Woman*. The reaction to these revelations was immediate and ugly. The conservative satirist the Reverend Richard Polwhele, for instance, remarked gloatingly on how it appeared to him providential that as a proponent of sexual equality Wollstonecraft should have died in childbirth—"a death that strongly marked the distinction of the sexes, by pointing out the destiny of women, and the diseases to which they are liable." The unintended consequence of Godwin's candor was that Wollstonecraft came to be saddled with a scandalous reputation so enduring that through the Victorian era advocates of the equality of women circumspectly avoided explicit reference to her *Vindication*. Even John Stuart Mill, in his *Subjection of Women* (1869), neglected to mention the work. It was only in the twentieth century, and especially in the later decades, that Wollstonecraft's *Vindication* gained recognition as a classic in the literature not only of women's rights but of social analysis as well.

From A Vindication of the Rights of Woman

Introduction

After considering the historic page, and viewing the living world with anxious solicitude, the most melancholy emotions of sorrowful indignation have depressed my spirits, and I have sighed when obliged to confess, that either nature has made a great difference between man and man, or that the civilization which has hitherto taken place in the world has been very partial. I have turned over various books written on the subject of education, and patiently observed the conduct of parents and the management of schools; but what has been the result?—a profound conviction that the neglected education of my fellow-creatures is the grand source of the misery I deplore; and that women, in particular, are rendered weak and wretched by a variety of concurring causes, originating from one hasty conclusion. The conduct and manners of women, in fact, evidently prove that their minds are not in a healthy state; for, like the flowers which are planted in too rich a soil, strength and usefulness are sacrificed to beauty; and the flaunting leaves, after having pleased a fastidious eye, fade, disregarded on the stalk, long before the season when they ought to have arrived at maturity.—One cause of this barren blooming[1] I attribute to a false system of education, gathered from the books written on this subject by men who, considering females rather as women than human creatures, have been more anxious to make them alluring mistresses than affectionate wives and rational mothers; and the understanding of the sex has been so bubbled[2] by this specious homage, that the civilized women of the present century, with a few exceptions, are

1. Wollstonecraft compares women to "luxuriants," botanical science's technical term for those plants that late 18th century gardeners, drawing on the latest techniques, cultivated for their showy blooms and at the expense of their seeds.
2. Deluded, cheated (archaic).

only anxious to inspire love, when they ought to cherish a nobler ambition, and by their abilities and virtues exact respect.

In a treatise, therefore, on female rights and manners, the works which have been particularly written for their improvement must not be overlooked; especially when it is asserted, in direct terms, that the minds of women are enfeebled by false refinement; that the books of instruction, written by men of genius, have had the same tendency as more frivolous productions; and that, in the true style of Mahometanism, they are treated as a kind of subordinate beings,[3] and not as a part of the human species, when improveable reason is allowed to be the dignified distinction which raises men above the brute creation, and puts a natural sceptre in a feeble hand.

Yet, because I am a woman, I would not lead my readers to suppose that I mean violently to agitate the contested question respecting the equality or inferiority of the sex; but as the subject lies in my way, and I cannot pass it over without subjecting the main tendency of my reasoning to misconstruction, I shall stop a moment to deliver, in a few words, my opinion.—In the government of the physical world it is observable that the female in point of strength is, in general, inferior to the male. This is the law of nature; and it does not appear to be suspended or abrogated in favour of woman. A degree of physical superiority cannot, therefore, be denied—and it is a noble prerogative! But not content with this natural pre-eminence, men endeavour to sink us still lower, merely to render us alluring objects for a moment; and women, intoxicated by the adoration which men, under the influence of their senses, pay them, do not seek to obtain a durable interest in their hearts, or to become the friends of the fellow creatures who find amusement in their society.

I am aware of an obvious inference:—from every quarter have I heard exclamations against masculine women; but where are they to be found? If by this appellation men mean to inveigh against their ardour in hunting, shooting, and gaming, I shall most cordially join in the cry; but if it be against the imitation of manly virtues, or, more properly speaking, the attainment of those talents and virtues, the exercise of which ennobles the human character, and which raise females in the scale of animal being, when they are comprehensively termed mankind;—all those who view them with a philosophic eye must, I should think, wish with me, that they may every day grow more and more masculine.

This discussion naturally divides the subject. I shall first consider women in the grand light of human creatures, who, in common with men, are placed on this earth to unfold their faculties; and afterwards I shall more particularly point out their peculiar designation.

I wish also to steer clear of an error which many respectable writers have fallen into; for the instruction which has hitherto been addressed to women, has rather been applicable to *ladies*, if the little indirect advice, that is scattered through Sandford and Merton,[4] be excepted; but, addressing my sex in a firmer tone, I pay particular attention to those in the middle class, because they appear to be in the most natural state.[5] Perhaps the seeds of

3. It was a common but mistaken opinion among Europeans that in the Koran, the sacred text of Islam, the Prophet Mohammed taught that women have no souls and would not be permitted an afterlife.
4. *Sandford and Merton*, a children's book by Thomas Day (1786–89), is the story of Tommy

Merton, a spoiled wealthy child who is befriended by Harry Sandford, a poor but principled lad.
5. Wollstonecraft considers the middle classes to be more "natural" and also more educable than the aristocracy—"the great"—because they are as yet uncorrupted by the artificiality of leisure-class life.

false-refinement, immorality, and vanity, have ever been shed by the great. Weak, artificial beings, raised above the common wants and affections of their race, in a premature unnatural manner, undermine the very foundation of virtue, and spread corruption through the whole mass of society! As a class of mankind they have the strongest claim to pity; the education of the rich tends to render them vain and helpless, and the unfolding mind is not strengthened by the practice of those duties which dignify the human character.— They only live to amuse themselves, and by the same law which in nature invariably produces certain effects, they soon only afford barren amusement.

But as I purpose taking a separate view of the different ranks of society, and of the moral character of women, in each, this hint is, for the present, sufficient; and I have only alluded to the subject, because it appears to me to be the very essence of an introduction to give a cursory account of the contents of the work it introduces.

My own sex, I hope, will excuse me, if I treat them like rational creatures, instead of flattering their *fascinating* graces, and viewing them as if they were in a state of perpetual childhood, unable to stand alone. I earnestly wish to point out in what true dignity and human happiness consists—I wish to persuade women to endeavour to acquire strength, both of mind and body, and to convince them that the soft phrases, susceptibility of heart, delicacy of sentiment, and refinement of taste, are almost synonymous with epithets of weakness, and that those beings who are only the objects of pity and that kind of love, which has been termed its sister, will soon become objects of contempt.

Dismissing then those pretty feminine phrases, which the men condescendingly use to soften our slavish dependence, and despising that weak elegancy of mind, exquisite sensibility, and sweet docility of manners, supposed to be the sexual characteristics of the weaker vessel, I wish to shew that elegance is inferior to virtue, that the first object of laudable ambition is to obtain a character as a human being, regardless of the distinction of sex; and that secondary views should be brought to this simple touchstone.

This is a rough sketch of my plan; and should I express my conviction with the energetic emotions that I feel whenever I think of the subject, the dictates of experience and reflection will be felt by some of my readers. Animated by this important object, I shall disdain to cull my phrases or polish my style;—I aim at being useful, and sincerity will render me unaffected; for, wishing rather to persuade by the force of my arguments, than dazzle by the elegance of my language, I shall not waste my time in rounding periods,[6] or in fabricating the turgid bombast of artificial feelings, which, coming from the head, never reach the heart.—I shall be employed about things, not words!—and, anxious to render my sex more respectable members of society, I shall try to avoid that flowery diction which has slided from essays into novels, and from novels into familiar letters and conversation.

These pretty superlatives, dropping glibly from the tongue, vitiate the taste, and create a kind of sickly delicacy that turns away from simple unadorned truth; and a deluge of false sentiments and overstretched feelings, stifling the natural emotions of the heart, render the domestic pleasures insipid, that ought to sweeten the exercise of those severe duties, which educate a rational and immortal being for a nobler field of action.

6. Formulating balanced sentences.

The education of women has, of late, been more attended to than formerly; yet they are still reckoned a frivolous sex, and ridiculed or pitied by the writers who endeavour by satire or instruction to improve them. It is acknowledged that they spend many of the first years of their lives in acquiring a smattering of accomplishments;[7] meanwhile strength of body and mind are sacrificed to libertine notions of beauty, to the desire of establishing themselves,—the only way women can rise in the world,—by marriage. And this desire making mere animals of them, when they marry they act as such children may be expected to act:—they dress; they paint, and nickname God's creatures.[8] Surely these weak beings are only fit for a seraglio![9]— Can they be expected to govern a family with judgment, or take care of the poor babes whom they bring into the world?

If then it can be fairly deduced from the present conduct of the sex, from the prevalent fondness for pleasure which takes place of ambition and those nobler passions that open and enlarge the soul; that the instruction which women have hitherto received has only tended, with the constitution of civil society, to render them insignificant objects of desire—mere propagators of fools!—if it can be proved that in aiming to accomplish them, without cultivating their understandings, they are taken out of their sphere of duties, and made ridiculous and useless when the short-lived bloom of beauty is over,[1] I presume that *rational* men will excuse me for endeavouring to persuade them to become more masculine and respectable.

Indeed the word masculine is only a bugbear: there is little reason to fear that women will acquire too much courage or fortitude; for their apparent inferiority with respect to bodily strength, must render them, in some degree, dependent on men in the various relations of life; but why should it be increased by prejudices that give a sex to virtue, and confound simple truths with sensual reveries?

Women are, in fact, so much degraded by mistaken notions of female excellence, that I do not mean to add a paradox when I assert, that this artificial weakness produces a propensity to tyrannize, and gives birth to cunning, the natural opponent of strength, which leads them to play off those contemptible infantine airs that undermine esteem even whilst they excite desire. Let men become more chaste and modest, and if women do not grow wiser in the same ratio, it will be clear that they have weaker understandings. It seems scarcely necessary to say, that I now speak of the sex in general. Many individuals have more sense than their male relatives; and, as nothing preponderates where there is a constant struggle for an equilibrium, without it has naturally more gravity, some women govern their husbands without degrading themselves, because intellect will always govern.

*　*　*

---

7. I.e., the lessons in music, dancing, art, and needlework that were central elements in the education provided for genteel young women and that were supposed to enhance their value on the marriage market.

8. Shakespeare's Hamlet, charging Ophelia with the faults characteristic of women, says, "you jig, you amble, and you lisp and nickname God's creatures" (*Hamlet* 3.1.143–44).

9. Harem, the women's quarters in a Muslim household.

1. A lively writer, I cannot recollect his name, asks what business women turned of forty have to do in the world? [Wollstonecraft's note]. Perhaps Wollstonecraft is referring to a passage in Frances Burney's popular novel *Evelina* spoken by the licentious Lord Merton: "I don't know what the devil a woman lives for after thirty: she is only in other folks' way."

Chapter 2. The Prevailing Opinion of a Sexual Character Discussed

To account for, and excuse the tyranny of man, many ingenious arguments have been brought forward to prove, that the two sexes, in the acquirement of virtue, ought to aim at attaining a very different character: or, to speak explicitly, women are not allowed to have sufficient strength of mind to acquire what really deserves the name of virtue. Yet it should seem, allowing them to have souls, that there is but one way appointed by Providence to lead *mankind* to either virtue or happiness.

If then women are not a swarm of ephemeron triflers, why should they be kept in ignorance under the specious name of innocence? Men complain, and with reason, of the follies and caprices of our sex, when they do not keenly satirize our headstrong passions and groveling vices.—Behold, I should answer, the natural effect of ignorance! The mind will ever be unstable that has only prejudices to rest on, and the current will run with destructive fury when there are no barriers to break its force. Women are told from their infancy, and taught by the example of their mothers, that a little knowledge of human weakness, justly termed cunning, softness of temper, *outward* obedience, and a scrupulous attention to a puerile kind of propriety, will obtain for them the protection of man; and should they be beautiful, every thing else is needless, for, at least, twenty years of their lives.

Thus Milton describes our first frail mother; though when he tells us that women are formed for softness and sweet attractive grace,[2] I cannot comprehend his meaning, unless, in the true Mahometan strain, he meant to deprive us of souls, and insinuate that we were beings only designed by sweet attractive grace, and docile blind obedience, to gratify the senses of man when he can no longer soar on the wing of contemplation.

How grossly do they insult us who thus advise us only to render ourselves gentle, domestic brutes! For instance, the winning softness so warmly, and frequently, recommended, that governs by obeying. What childish expressions, and how insignificant is the being—can it be an immortal one? who will condescend to govern by such sinister methods! 'Certainly,' says Lord Bacon, 'man is of kin to the beasts by his body; and if he be not of kin to God by his spirit, he is a base and ignoble creature!'[3] Men, indeed, appear to me to act in a very unphilosophical manner when they try to secure the good conduct of women by attempting to keep them always in a state of childhood. Rousseau[4] was more consistent when he wished to stop the progress of reason in both sexes, for if men eat of the tree of knowledge, women will come in for a taste; but, from the imperfect cultivation which their understandings now receive, they only attain a knowledge of evil.[5]

Children, I grant, should be innocent; but when the epithet is applied to men, or women, it is but a civil term for weakness. For if it be allowed that women were destined by Providence to acquire human virtues, and by the exercise of their understandings, that stability of character which is the firm-

---

2. Milton asserts the authority of man over woman on the grounds that "For contemplation he and valor formed, / For softness she and sweet attractive grace; / He for God only, she for God in him" (*Paradise Lost* 4.298ff).
3. Francis Bacon, Essay XVI, "Of Atheism."
4. Throughout his writings Jean-Jacques Rousseau (1712–1778) argued against the notion that civilization and rationality brought moral perfec-

tion, proposing that virtuous societies were instead the primitive ones that remained closest to nature.
5. Both Adam and Eve ate the fruit from the tree of knowledge of good and evil in the garden of Eden. In the fallen state both men and women need to work at virtue, but according to Wollstonecraft, women have been denied the education, and thus the means, to attain it.

est ground to rest our future hopes upon, they must be permitted to turn to the fountain of light, and not forced to shape their course by the twinkling of a mere satellite. Milton, I grant, was of a very different opinion; for he only bends to the indefeasible right of beauty, though it would be difficult to render two passages which I now mean to contrast, consistent. But into similar inconsistencies are great men often led by their senses.

> To whom thus Eve with *perfect beauty* adorn'd.
> My Author and Disposer, what thou bidst
> *Unargued* I obey; So God ordains;
> God is *thy law, thou mine:* to know no more
> Is Woman's *happiest* knowledge and her *praise.*[6]

These are exactly the arguments that I have used to children; but I have added, your reason is now gaining strength, and, till it arrives at some degree of maturity, you must look up to me for advice—then you ought to *think*, and only rely on God.

Yet in the following lines Milton seems to coincide with me; when he makes Adam thus expostulate with his Maker.

> Hast thou not made me here thy substitute,
> And these inferior far beneath me set?
> Among *unequals* what society
> Can sort, what harmony or true delight?
> Which must be mutual, in proportion due
> Giv'n and receiv'd; but in *disparity*
> The one intense, the other still remiss
> Cannot well suit with either, but soon prove
> Tedious alike: of *fellowship* I speak
> Such as I seek, fit to participate
> All rational delight—[7]

In treating, therefore, of the manners of women, let us, disregarding sensual arguments, trace what we should endeavour to make them in order to co-operate, if the expression be not too bold, with the supreme Being.

By individual education, I mean, for the sense of the word is not precisely defined, such an attention to a child as will slowly sharpen the senses, form the temper,[8] regulate the passions as they begin to ferment, and set the understanding to work before the body arrives at maturity; so that the man may only have to proceed, not to begin, the important task of learning to think and reason.

To prevent any misconstruction, I must add, that I do not believe that a private education[9] can work the wonders which some sanguine writers have attributed to it. Men and women must be educated, in a great degree, by the opinions and manners of the society they live in. In every age there has been a stream of popular opinion that has carried all before it, and given a family character, as it were, to the century. It may then fairly be inferred, that, till society be differently constituted, much cannot be expected from education. It is, however, sufficient for my present purpose to assert, that, whatever effect circumstances have on the abilities, every being may become virtuous

---

6. *Paradise Lost* IV.634–38. The italics are Wollstonecraft's.
7. *Paradise Lost* VIII.381–92. The italics are Wollstonecraft's.
8. Temperament, character.
9. Education at home.

by the exercise of its own reason; for if but one being was created with vicious inclinations, that is positively bad, what can save us from atheism? or if we worship a God, is not that God a devil?

Consequently, the most perfect education, in my opinion, is such an exercise of the understanding as is best calculated to strengthen the body and form the heart. Or, in other words, to enable the individual to attain such habits of virtue as will render it independent. In fact, it is a farce to call any being virtuous whose virtues do not result from the exercise of its own reason. This was Rousseau's opinion respecting men: I extend it to women, and confidently assert that they have been drawn out of their sphere by false refinement, and not by an endeavour to acquire masculine qualities. Still the regal homage which they receive is so intoxicating, that till the manners of the times are changed, and formed on more reasonable principles, it may be impossible to convince them that the illegitimate power, which they obtain, by degrading themselves, is a curse, and that they must return to nature and equality if they wish to secure the placid satisfaction that unsophisticated affections impart. But for this epoch we must wait—wait, perhaps, till kings and nobles, enlightened by reason, and, preferring the real dignity of man to childish state, throw off their gaudy hereditary trappings: and if then women do not resign the arbitrary power of beauty—they will prove that they have *less* mind than man.

I may be accused of arrogance; still I must declare what I firmly believe, that all the writers who have written on the subject of female education and manners from Rousseau to Dr. Gregory,[1] have contributed to render women more artificial, weak characters, than they would otherwise have been; and, consequently, more useless members of society. I might have expressed this conviction in a lower key; but I am afraid it would have been the whine of affectation, and not the faithful expression of my feelings, of the clear result, which experience and reflection have led me to draw. When I come to that division of the subject, I shall advert to the passages that I more particularly disapprove of, in the works of the authors I have just alluded to; but it is first necessary to observe, that my objection extends to the whole purport of those books, which tend, in my opinion, to degrade one half of the human species, and render women pleasing at the expense of every solid virtue.

Though, to reason on Rousseau's ground, if man did attain a degree of perfection of mind when his body arrived at maturity, it might be proper, in order to make a man and his wife *one*, that she should rely entirely on his understanding; and the graceful ivy, clasping the oak that supported it, would form a whole in which strength and beauty would be equally conspicuous. But, alas! husbands, as well as their helpmates, are often only overgrown children; nay, thanks to early debauchery, scarcely men in their outward form— and if the blind lead the blind, one need not come from heaven to tell us the consequence.[2]

Many are the causes that, in the present corrupt state of society, contribute to enslave women by cramping their understandings and sharpening their

---

1. John Gregory (1724–1773), Scottish physician, philosopher, and professor at the University of Edinburgh. In her edited anthology *The Female Reader* (1789) Wollstonecraft had quoted extensively from Gregory's widely read advice book, *A*

Father's Legacy to His Daughters (1774). Here she returns to that work in a more critical spirit.
2. Matthew 15.14: "And if the blind lead the blind, both shall fall into the ditch." "One . . . from heaven": Jesus.

senses. One, perhaps, that silently does more mischief than all the rest, is their disregard of order.

To do every thing in an orderly manner, is a most important precept, which women, who, generally speaking, receive only a disorderly kind of education, seldom attend to with that degree of exactness that men, who from their infancy are broken into method, observe. This negligent kind of guess-work, for what other epithet can be used to point out the random exertions of a sort of instinctive common sense, never brought to the test of reason? prevents their generalizing matters of fact—so they do to-day, what they did yesterday, merely because they did it yesterday.

This contempt of the understanding in early life has more baneful consequences than is commonly supposed; for the little knowledge which women of strong minds attain, is, from various circumstances, of a more desultory kind than the knowledge of men, and it is acquired more by sheer observations on real life, than from comparing what has been individually observed with the results of experience generalized by speculation. Led by their dependent situation and domestic employments more into society, what they learn is rather by snatches; and as learning is with them, in general, only a secondary thing, they do not pursue any one branch with that persevering ardour necessary to give vigour to the faculties, and clearness to the judgment. In the present state of society, a little learning is required to support the character of a gentleman; and boys are obliged to submit to a few years of discipline. But in the education of women, the cultivation of the understanding is always subordinate to the acquirement of some corporeal accomplishment; even while enervated by confinement and false notions of modesty, the body is prevented from attaining that grace and beauty which relaxed half-formed limbs never exhibit. Besides, in youth their faculties are not brought forward by emulation; and having no serious scientific study, if they have natural sagacity it is turned too soon on life and manners. They dwell on effects, and modifications, without tracing them back to causes; and complicated rules to adjust behaviour are a weak substitute for simple principles.

As a proof that education gives this appearance of weakness to females, we may instance the example of military men, who are, like them, sent into the world before their minds have been stored with knowledge or fortified by principles. The consequences are similar; soldiers acquire a little superficial knowledge, snatched from the muddy current of conversation, and, from continually mixing with society, they gain, what is termed a knowledge of the world; and this acquaintance with manners and customs has frequently been confounded with a knowledge of the human heart. But can the crude fruit of casual observation, never brought to the test of judgment, formed by comparing speculation and experience, deserve such a distinction? Soldiers, as well as women, practice the minor virtues with punctilious politeness. Where is then the sexual difference, when the education has been the same? All the difference that I can discern, arises from the superior advantage of liberty, which enables the former to see more of life.

It is wandering from my present subject, perhaps, to make a political remark; but, as it was produced naturally by the train of my reflections, I shall not pass it silently over.

Standing armies can never consist of resolute, robust men; they may be well disciplined machines, but they will seldom contain men under the influence of strong passions, or with very vigorous faculties. And as for any depth of understanding, I will venture to affirm, that it is as rarely to be found in the army as amongst women; and the cause, I maintain, is the same. It may be further observed, that officers are also particularly attentive to their persons, fond of dancing, crowded rooms, adventures, and ridicule.[3] Like the *fair* sex,[4] the business of their lives is gallantry.—They were taught to please, and they only live to please. Yet they do not lose their rank in the distinction of sexes, for they are still reckoned superior to women, though in what their superiority consists, beyond what I have just mentioned, it is difficult to discover.

The great misfortune is this, that they both acquire manners before morals, and a knowledge of life before they have, from reflection, any acquaintance with the grand ideal outline of human nature. The consequence is natural; satisfied with common nature, they become a prey to prejudices, and taking all their opinions on credit, they blindly submit to authority. So that, if they have any sense, it is a kind of instinctive glance, that catches proportions, and decides with respect to manners; but fails when arguments are to be pursued below the surface, or opinions analyzed.

May not the same remark be applied to women? Nay, the argument may be carried still further, for they are both thrown out of a useful station by the unnatural distinctions established in civilized life. Riches and hereditary honours have made cyphers of women to give consequence to the numerical figure;[5] and idleness has produced a mixture of gallantry and despotism into society, which leads the very men who are the slaves of their mistresses to tyrannize over their sisters, wives, and daughters. This is only keeping them in rank and file, it is true. Strengthen the female mind by enlarging it, and there will be an end to blind obedience; but, as blind obedience is ever sought for by power, tyrants and sensualists are in the right when they endeavour to keep women in the dark, because the former only want slaves, and the latter a play-thing. The sensualist, indeed, has been the most dangerous of tyrants, and women have been duped by their lovers, as princes by their ministers, whilst dreaming that they reigned over them.

I now principally allude to Rousseau, for his character of Sophia[6] is, undoubtedly, a captivating one, though it appears to me grossly unnatural; however it is not the superstructure, but the foundation of her character, the principles on which her education was built, that I mean to attack; nay, warmly as I admire the genius of that able writer, whose opinions I shall often have occasion to cite, indignation always takes place of admiration, and the rigid frown of insulted virtue effaces the smile of complacency, which his eloquent periods are wont to raise, when I read his voluptuous reveries. Is this the man, who, in his ardour for virtue, would banish all the soft arts of peace, and almost carry us back to Spartan discipline? Is this the man who delights to paint the useful struggles of passion, the triumphs of good dispositions, and the heroic flights which carry the glowing soul out of itself?—How are

---

3. Why should women be censured with petulant acrimony, because they seem to have a passion for a scarlet coat? Has not education placed them more on a level with soldiers than any other class of men? [Wollstonecraft's note].
4. Women.
5. As a zero added to a number multiplies its value by a factor of ten, in a hierarchical society women magnify the status of the men with

whom they are allied.
6. "*Sophie ou la Femme*" is the title of Book v of *Émile*, Rousseau's blend of educational treatise and novel. Having tracked the development of Émile, his imaginary pupil, up to age twenty, Rousseau invents the character of Sophie (Sophia in the 1762 English translation) to supply his hero with a wife and to address, belatedly, the topic of female education.

these mighty sentiments lowered when he describes the pretty foot and enticing airs of his little favourite! But, for the present, I wave[7] the subject, and,
instead of severely reprehending the transient effusions of overweening sensibility, I shall only observe, that whoever has cast a benevolent eye on society,
must often have been gratified by the sight of a humble mutual love, not dignified by sentiment, or strengthened by a union in intellectual pursuits. The
domestic trifles of the day have afforded matters for cheerful converse, and
innocent caresses have softened toils which did not require great exercise of
mind or stretch of thought: yet, has not the sight of this moderate felicity
excited more tenderness than respect? An emotion similar to what we feel
when children are playing, or animals sporting,[8] whilst the contemplation
of the noble struggles of suffering merit has raised admiration, and carried
our thoughts to that world where sensation will give place to reason.

Women are, therefore, to be considered either as moral beings, or so weak
that they must be entirely subjected to the superior faculties of men.

Let us examine this question. Rousseau declares that a woman should
never, for a moment, feel herself independent, that she should be governed
by fear to exercise her natural cunning, and made a coquetish slave in order
to render her a more alluring object of desire, a *sweeter* companion to man,
whenever he chooses to relax himself. He carries the arguments, which he
pretends to draw from the indications of nature, still further, and insinuates
that truth and fortitude, the corner stones of all human virtue, should be
cultivated with certain restrictions, because, with respect to the female character, obedience is the grand lesson which ought to be impressed with unrelenting rigour.[9]

What nonsense! when will a great man arise with sufficient strength of
mind to puff away the fumes which pride and sensuality have thus spread over
the subject! If women are by nature inferior to men, their virtues must be the
same in quality, if not in degree, or virtue is a relative idea; consequently, their
conduct should be founded on the same principles, and have the same aim.

Connected with man as daughters, wives, and mothers, their moral
character may be estimated by their manner of fulfilling those simple
duties; but the end, the grand end of their exertions should be to unfold
their own faculties and acquire the dignity of conscious virtue. They may
try to render their road pleasant; but ought never to forget, in common
with man, that life yields not the felicity which can satisfy an immortal
soul. I do not mean to insinuate, that either sex should be so lost in
abstract reflections or distant views, as to forget the affections and duties
that lie before them, and are, in truth, the means appointed to produce the
fruit of life; on the contrary, I would warmly recommend them, even while

---

7. A common spelling for "waive" in the eighteenth century.
8. Similar feelings has Milton's pleasing picture
of paradisiacal happiness ever raised in my mind;
yet, instead of envying the lovely pair, I have, with
conscious dignity, or Satanic pride, turned to hell
for sublimer objects. In the same style, when
viewing some noble monument of human art, I
have traced the emanation of the Deity in the
order I admired, till, descending from that giddy
height, I have caught myself contemplating the
grandest of all human sights;—for fancy quickly
placed, in some solitary recess, an outcast of fortune, rising superior to passion and discontent

[Wollstonecraft's note]. Wollstonecraft is referring to the portrait of Adam and Eve in book IV of
Milton's *Paradise Lost* and stating what has since
become critical commonplace, that Milton's
Eden, for all its bliss, is not as compelling as his
suffering Satan.
9. *Émile:* "The first and most important qualification in a woman is good nature or sweetness of
temper: formed to obey a being so imperfect as
man, often full of vices, and always full of faults,
she ought to learn betimes even to suffer injustice, and to bear the insults of a husband without
complaint: it is not for his sake, but her own, that
she should be of a mild disposition."

I assert, that they afford most satisfaction when they are considered in their true, sober light.

Probably the prevailing opinion, that woman was created for man, may have taken its rise from Moses's poetical story;[1] yet, as very few, it is presumed, who have bestowed any serious thought on the subject, ever supposed that Eve was, literally speaking, one of Adam's ribs, the deduction must be allowed to fall to the ground; or, only be so far admitted as it proves that man, from the remotest antiquity, found it convenient to exert his strength to subjugate his companion, and his invention to shew that she ought to have her neck bent under the yoke, because the whole creation was only created for his convenience or pleasure.

Let it not be concluded that I wish to invert the order of things; I have already granted, that, from the constitution of their bodies, men seem to be designed by Providence to attain a greater degree of virtue. I speak collectively of the whole sex; but I see not the shadow of a reason to conclude that their virtues should differ in respect to their nature. In fact, how can they, if virtue has only one eternal standard? I must therefore, if I reason consequentially, as strenuously maintain that they have the same simple direction, as that there is a God.

It follows then that cunning should not be opposed to wisdom, little cares to great exertions, or insipid softness, varnished over with the name of gentleness, to that fortitude which grand views alone can inspire.

I shall be told that woman would then lose many of her peculiar graces, and the opinion of a well known poet might be quoted to refute my unqualified assertion. For Pope has said, in the name of the whole male sex,

> Yet ne'er so sure our passion to create,
> As when she touch'd the brink of all we hate.[2]

In what light this sally places men and women, I shall leave to the judicious to determine; meanwhile I shall content myself with observing, that I cannot discover why, unless they are mortal, females should always be degraded by being made subservient to love or lust.

To speak disrespectfully of love is, I know, high treason against sentiment and fine feelings; but I wish to speak the simple language of truth, and rather to address the head than the heart. To endeavour to reason love out of the world, would be to out Quixote Cervantes,[3] and equally offend against common sense; but an endeavour to restrain this tumultuous passion, and to prove that it should not be allowed to dethrone superior powers, or to usurp the sceptre which the understanding should ever coolly wield, appears less wild.

Youth is the season for love in both sexes; but in those days of thoughtless enjoyment provision should be made for the more important years of life, when reflection takes place of sensation. But Rousseau, and most of the male writers who have followed his steps, have warmly inculcated that the whole tendency of female education ought to be directed to one point:—to render them pleasing.

1. See Genesis 2.21–23 for one account of the creation of woman. Moses was thought to be the author of the first five books of the Old Testament (the Pentateuch).
2. Alexander Pope, "Of the Characters of Women," Epistle 2, lines 51–52, of his *Moral Essays* (1735).
3. I.e., to outdo the idealistic but ineffectual hero of Miguel de Cervantes' *Don Quixote* (1605) in trying to accomplish the impossible.

Let me reason with the supporters of this opinion who have any knowledge of human nature, do they imagine that marriage can eradicate the habitude of life? The woman who has only been taught to please will soon find that her charms are oblique sunbeams, and that they cannot have much effect on her husband's heart when they are seen every day, when the summer is passed and gone. Will she then have sufficient native energy to look into herself for comfort, and cultivate her dormant faculties? or, is it not more rational to expect that she will try to please other men; and, in the emotions raised by the expectation of new conquests, endeavour to forget the mortification her love or pride has received? When the husband ceases to be a lover—and the time will inevitably come, her desire of pleasing will then grow languid, or become a spring of bitterness; and love, perhaps, the most evanescent of all passions, gives place to jealousy or vanity.

I now speak of women who are restrained by principle or prejudice; such women, though they would shrink from an intrigue with real abhorrence, yet, nevertheless, wish to be convinced by the homage of gallantry that they are cruelly neglected by their husbands; or, days and weeks are spent in dreaming of the happiness enjoyed by congenial souls till their health is undermined and their spirits broken by discontent. How then can the great art of pleasing be such a necessary study? it is only useful to a mistress; the chaste wife, and serious mother, should only consider her power to please as the polish of her virtues, and the affection of her husband as one of the comforts that render her task less difficult and her life happier.—But, whether she be loved or neglected, her first wish should be to make herself respectable, and not to rely for all her happiness on a being subject to like infirmities with herself.

The worthy Dr. Gregory fell into a similar error. I respect his heart; but entirely disapprove of his celebrated Legacy to his Daughters.

He advises them to cultivate a fondness for dress, because a fondness for dress, he asserts, is natural to them.[4] I am unable to comprehend what either he or Rousseau mean, when they frequently use this indefinite term.[5] If they told us that in a pre-existent state the soul was fond of dress, and brought this inclination with it into a new body, I should listen to them with a half smile, as I often do when I hear a rant about innate elegance.—But if he only meant to say that the exercise of the faculties will produce this fondness—I deny it.—It is not natural; but arises, like false ambition in men, from a love of power.

Dr. Gregory goes much further; he actually recommends dissimulation, and advises an innocent girl to give the lie to her feelings, and not dance with spirit, when gaiety of heart would make her feel eloquent without making her gestures immodest. In the name of truth and common sense, why should not one woman acknowledge that she can take more exercise than another? or, in other words, that she has a sound constitution; and why, to damp innocent vivacity, is she darkly to be told that men will draw conclusions which she little thinks of?[6]—Let the libertine draw what inference he pleases; but, I hope, that no sensible mother will restrain the natural

---

4. "The love of dress is natural to you, and therefore it is proper and reasonable." John Gregory, *A Father's Legacy to His Daughters*, 2nd ed. [London, 1775].
5. I.e., "natural."
6. For this and the previous sentence see Greg-

ory: "I would have you to dance with spirit; but never allow yourselves to be so far transported with mirth, as to forget the delicacy of your sex.—Many a girl dancing in the gaiety and innocence of her heart, is thought to discover a spirit she little dreams of."

frankness of youth by instilling such indecent cautions. Out of the abundance of the heart the mouth speaketh;[7] and a wiser than Solomon hath said, that the heart should be made clean,[8] and not trivial ceremonies observed, which it is not very difficult to fulfill with scrupulous exactness when vice reigns in the heart.

Women ought to endeavour to purify their heart; but can they do so when their uncultivated understandings make them entirely dependent on their senses for employment and amusement, when no noble pursuit sets them above the little vanities of the day, or enables them to curb the wild emotions that agitate a reed over which every passing breeze has power? To gain the affections of a virtuous man is affectation necessary? Nature has given woman a weaker frame than man; but, to ensure her husband's affections, must a wife, who by the exercise of her mind and body whilst she was discharging the duties of a daughter, wife, and mother, has allowed her constitution to retain its natural strength, and her nerves a healthy tone, is she, I say, to condescend to use art and feign a sickly delicacy in order to secure her husband's affection? Weakness may excite tenderness, and gratify the arrogant pride of man; but the lordly caresses of a protector will not gratify a noble mind that pants for, and deserves to be respected. Fondness is a poor substitute for friendship!

In a seraglio, I grant, that all these arts are necessary; the epicure must have his palate tickled, or he will sink into apathy; but have women so little ambition as to be satisfied with such a condition? Can they supinely dream life away in the lap of pleasure, or the languor of weariness, rather than assert their claim to pursue reasonable pleasures and render themselves conspicuous by practising the virtues which dignify mankind? Surely she has not an immortal soul who can loiter life away merely employed to adorn her person, that she may amuse the languid hours, and soften the cares of a fellow-creature who is willing to be enlivened by her smiles and tricks, when the serious business of life is over.

Besides, the woman who strengthens her body and exercises her mind will, by managing her family and practising various virtues, become the friend, and not the humble dependent of her husband; and if she, by possessing such substantial qualities, merit his regard, she will not find it necessary to conceal her affection, nor to pretend to an unnatural coldness of constitution to excite her husband's passions. In fact, if we revert to history, we shall find that the women who have distinguished themselves have neither been the most beautiful nor the most gentle of their sex.

Nature, or, to speak with strict propriety, God, has made all things right; but man has sought him out many inventions to mar the work. I now allude to that part of Dr. Gregory's treatise, where he advises a wife never to let her husband know the extent of her sensibility or affection.[9] Voluptuous precaution, and as ineffectual as absurd.—Love, from its very nature, must be transitory. To seek for a secret that would render it constant, would be as wild a search as for the philosopher's stone, or the grand panacea:[1] and the

---

7. Matthew 12.34.
8. "Wiser than Solomon": Jesus (who describes himself in comparable terms in Luke 11.31). In Luke 11.39–44 and Matthew 23.25–28, Jesus speaks of purifying the inner self and denounces the Pharisees' self-righteous observance of the letter of the law.

9. Gregory: "If you love him, let me advise you never to discover to him the full extent of your love, no, not although you marry him."
1. A medicine reputed to cure all diseases. "Philosopher's stone": sought by alchemists because it was supposed to have the power to transmute base metals into gold.

discovery would be equally useless, or rather pernicious to mankind. The most holy band of society is friendship. It has been well said, by a shrewd satirist, "that rare as true love is, true friendship is still rarer."[2]

This is an obvious truth, and the cause not lying deep, will not elude a slight glance of inquiry.

Love, the common passion, in which chance and sensation take place of choice and reason, is, in some degree, felt by the mass of mankind; for it is not necessary to speak, at present, of the emotions that rise above or sink below love. This passion, naturally increased by suspense and difficulties, draws the mind out of its accustomed state, and exalts the affections; but the security of marriage, allowing the fever of love to subside, a healthy temperature is thought insipid, only by those who have not sufficient intellect to substitute the calm tenderness of friendship, the confidence of respect, instead of blind admiration, and the sensual emotions of fondness.

This is, must be, the course of nature.—Friendship or indifference inevitably succeeds love.—And this constitution seems perfectly to harmonize with the system of government which prevails in the moral world. Passions are spurs to action, and open the mind; but they sink into mere appetites, become a personal and momentary gratification, when the object is gained, and the satisfied mind rests in enjoyment. The man who had some virtue whilst he was struggling for a crown, often becomes a voluptuous tyrant when it graces his brow; and, when the lover is not lost in the husband, the dotard, a prey to childish caprices, and fond jealousies, neglects the serious duties of life, and the caresses which should excite confidence in his children are lavished on the overgrown child, his wife.

In order to fulfil the duties of life, and to be able to pursue with vigour the various employments which form the moral character, a master and mistress of a family ought not to continue to love each other with passion. I mean to say, that they ought not to indulge those emotions which disturb the order of society, and engross the thoughts that should be otherwise employed. The mind that has never been engrossed by one object wants vigour—if it can long be so, it is weak.

A mistaken education, a narrow, uncultivated mind, and many sexual prejudices, tend to make women more constant than men; but, for the present, I shall not touch on this branch of the subject. I will go still further, and advance, without dreaming of a paradox, that an unhappy marriage is often very advantageous to a family, and that the neglected wife is, in general, the best mother.[3] And this would almost always be the consequence if the female mind were more enlarged: for, it seems to be the common dispensation of Providence, that what we gain in present enjoyment should be deducted from the treasure of life, experience; and that when we are gathering the flowers of the day and revelling in pleasure, the solid fruit of toil and wisdom should not be caught at the same time. The way lies before us, we must turn to the right or left; and he who will pass life away in bounding from one pleasure to another, must not complain if he acquire neither wisdom nor respectability of character.

2. La Rochefoucauld (1613–1680, French noble), *Les Maximes*, No. 473.
3. Wollstonecraft's point is that a woman who is not preoccupied with her husband (and his attentions to her) has more time and energy for her children.

Supposing, for a moment, that the soul is not immortal, and that man was only created for the present scene,—I think we should have reason to complain that love, infantine fondness, ever grew insipid and palled upon the sense. Let us eat, drink, and love, for tomorrow we die, would be, in fact, the language of reason, the morality of life; and who but a fool would part with a reality for a fleeting shadow? But, if awed by observing the improbable[4] powers of the mind, we disdain to confine our wishes or thoughts to such a comparatively mean field of action, that only appears grand and important, as it is connected with a boundless prospect and sublime hopes, what necessity is there for falsehood in conduct, and why must the sacred majesty of truth be violated to detain a deceitful good that saps the very foundation of virtue? Why must the female mind be tainted by coquetish arts to gratify the sensualist, and prevent love from subsiding into friendship, or compassionate tenderness, when there are not qualities on which friendship can be built? Let the honest heart shew itself, and *reason* teach passion to submit to necessity; or, let the dignified pursuit of virtue and knowledge raise the mind above those emotions which rather imbitter than sweeten the cup of life, when they are not restrained within due bounds.

I do not mean to allude to the romantic passion, which is the concomitant of genius.—Who can clip its wing? But that grand passion not proportioned to the puny enjoyments of life, is only true to the sentiment, and feeds on itself. The passions which have been celebrated for their durability have always been unfortunate. They have acquired strength by absence and constitutional melancholy.—The fancy has hovered round a form of beauty dimly seen[5]—but familiarity might have turned admiration into disgust; or, at least, into indifference, and allowed the imagination leisure to start fresh game. With perfect propriety, according to this view of things, does Rousseau make the mistress of his soul, Eloisa, love St. Preux, when life was fading before her;[6] but this is no proof of the immortality of the passion.

Of the same complexion is Dr. Gregory's advice respecting delicacy of sentiment, which he advises a woman not to acquire, if she have determined to marry.[7] This determination, however, perfectly consistent with his former advice, he calls *indelicate*, and earnestly persuades his daughters to conceal it, though it may govern their conduct;—as if it were indelicate to have the common appetites of human nature.

Noble morality! and consistent with the cautious prudence of a little soul that cannot extend its views beyond the present minute division of existence. If all the faculties of woman's mind are only to be cultivated as they respect her dependence on man; if, when a husband be obtained, she have arrived at her goal, and meanly proud rests satisfied with such a paltry crown, let her grovel contentedly, scarcely raised by her employments above the animal kingdom; but, if, struggling for the prize of her high calling,[8] she look beyond the present scene, let her cultivate her understanding without stopping to

---

4. The first edition reads "improvable" here, which makes more sense in context.
5. "Fancy": Imagination.
6. In Rousseau's *Julie; ou la Nouvelle Héloïse* (1761), the heroine, Julie, reveals her long-held passionate love for St. Preux as she is dying, even though she has been a faithful wife to Wolmar since her marriage.
7. Gregory: "But if you find that marriage is absolutely essential to your happiness ... shun ...

reading and conversation that warms the imagination, which engages and softens the heart, and raises the taste above the level of common life ... [otherwise] you may be tired with insipidity and dullness; shocked with indelicacy, or mortified by indifference."
8. An echo of Philippians 3.14, where Saint Paul writes, "I press toward the mark for the prize of the high calling of God in Christ Jesus."

consider what character the husband may have whom she is destined to marry. Let her only determine, without being too anxious about present happiness, to acquire the qualities that ennoble a rational being, and a rough inelegant husband may shock her taste without destroying her peace of mind. She will not model her soul to suit the frailties of her companion, but to bear with them: his character may be a trial, but not an impediment to virtue.

If Dr. Gregory confined his remark to romantic expectations of constant love and congenial feelings, he should have recollected that experience will banish what advice can never make us cease to wish for, when the imagination is kept alive at the expence of reason.

I own it frequently happens that women who have fostered a romantic unnatural delicacy of feeling, waste their[9] lives in *imagining* how happy they should have been with a husband who could love them with a fervid increasing affection every day, and all day. But they might as well pine married as single—and would not be a jot more unhappy with a bad husband than longing for a good one. That a proper education; or, to speak with more precision, a well stored mind, would enable a woman to support a single life with dignity, I grant; but that she should avoid cultivating her taste, lest her husband should occasionally shock it, is quitting a substance for a shadow. To say the truth, I do not know of what use is an improved taste, if the individual be not rendered more independent of the casualties of life; if new sources of enjoyment, only dependent on the solitary operations of the mind, are not opened. People of taste, married or single, without distinction, will ever be disgusted by various things that touch not less observing minds. On this conclusion the argument must not be allowed to hinge; but in the whole sum of enjoyment is taste to be denominated a blessing?

The question is, whether it procures most pain or pleasure? The answer will decide the propriety of Dr. Gregory's advice, and shew how absurd and tyrannic it is thus to lay down a system of slavery; or to attempt to educate moral beings by any other rules than those deduced from pure reason, which apply to the whole species.

Gentleness of manners, forbearance and long-suffering, are such amiable Godlike qualities, that in sublime poetic strains the Deity has been invested with them; and, perhaps, no representation of his goodness so strongly fastens on the human affections as those that represent him abundant in mercy and willing to pardon.[1] Gentleness, considered in this point of view, bears on its front all the characteristics of grandeur, combined with the winning graces of condescension; but what a different aspect it assumes when it is the submissive demeanour of dependence, the support of weakness that loves, because it wants protection; and is forbearing, because it must silently endure injuries; smiling under the lash at which it dare not snarl. Abject as this picture appears, it is the portrait of an accomplished woman, according to the received opinion of female excellence separated by specious reasoners from human excellence. Or, they[2] kindly restore the rib, and make one moral being of a man and woman; not forgetting to give her all the 'submissive charms.'[3]

9. For example, the herd of Novelists [Wollstonecraft's note].
1. Isaiah 55.7: "And he will have mercy upon him; and to our God, for he will abundantly pardon."
2. Vide Rousseau, and Swedenborg [Wollstonecraft's note]. The Swedish mystic Emanuel Swedenborg (1688–1772) believed that in the afterlife each married couple would form a single angel, with the wife contributing her capacity for love and the husband his wisdom.
3. *Paradise Lost* IV.497–99: "he in delight / Both of her Beauty and submissive charms / Smil'd with superior love."

How women are to exist in that state where there is to be neither marrying nor giving in marriage, we are not told.[4] For though moralists have agreed that the tenor of life seems to prove that *man* is prepared by various circumstances for a future state, they constantly concur in advising *woman* only to provide for the present. Gentleness, docility, and a spaniel-like affection are, on this ground, consistently recommended as the cardinal virtues of the sex; and, disregarding the arbitrary economy of nature, one writer has declared that it is masculine for a woman to be melancholy.[5] She was created to be the toy of man, his rattle, and it must jingle in his ears whenever, dismissing reason, he chooses to be amused.

To recommend gentleness, indeed, on a broad basis is strictly philosophical. A frail being should labour to be gentle. But when forbearance confounds right and wrong, it ceases to be a virtue; and, however convenient it may be found in a companion—that companion will ever be considered as an inferior, and only inspire a vapid tenderness, which easily degenerates into contempt. Still, if advice could really make a being gentle, whose natural disposition admitted not of such a fine polish, something towards the advancement of order would be attained; but if, as might quickly be demonstrated, only affectation be produced by this indiscriminate counsel, which throws a stumbling-block in the way of gradual improvement, and true melioration of temper, the sex is not much benefited by sacrificing solid virtues to the attainment of superficial graces, though for a few years they may procure the individuals regal sway.

As a philosopher, I read with indignation the plausible epithets which men use to soften their insults; and, as a moralist, I ask what is meant by such heterogeneous associations, as fair defects, amiable weaknesses, &c.?[6] If there be but one criterion of morals, but one archetype for man, women appear to be suspended by destiny, according to the vulgar tale of Mahomet's coffin;[7] they have neither the unerring instinct of brutes, nor are allowed to fix the eye of reason on a perfect model. They were made to be loved, and must not aim at respect, lest they should be hunted out of society as masculine.

But to view the subject in another point of view. Do passive indolent women make the best wives? Confining our discussion to the present moment of existence, let us see how such weak creatures perform their part? Do the women who, by the attainment of a few superficial accomplishments, have strengthened the prevailing prejudice, merely contribute to the happiness of their husbands? Do they display their charms merely to amuse them? And have women, who have early imbibed notions of passive obedience, sufficient character to manage a family or educate children? So far from it, that, after surveying the history of woman, I cannot help, agreeing with the severest satirist, considering the sex as the weakest as well as the most oppressed half of the species. What does history disclose but marks of inferiority, and how few women have emancipated themselves from the galling

4. An echo of Jesus' account of the resurrection in Matthew 22.30.
5. Perhaps a recollection of Edmund Burke's *Philosophical Enquiry into the Origins of Our Ideas of the Sublime and the Beautiful* (1757). In attempting to distinguish the aesthetic category of "the beautiful" from the aesthetic category of "the sublime," Burke resorts frequently to analogy and so devotes many pages to outlining his notions of the distinctions that separate femininity from masculinity.
6. *Paradise Lost* X.891–92: "This fair defect / Of nature"; and Pope, "Of the Characters of Women," line 44: "Fine by defect, and delicately weak."
7. Wollstonecraft refers to a discredited European legend maintaining that at Mohammed's tomb in Medina giant magnets were used to suspend his coffin in midair.

yoke of sovereign man?—So few, that the exceptions remind me of an ingenious conjecture respecting Newton: that he was probably a being of a superior order, accidentally caged in a human body.[8] Following the same train of
thinking, I have been led to imagine that the few extraordinary women who
have rushed in eccentrical directions out of the orbit prescribed to their sex,
were *male* spirits, confined by mistake in female frames. But if it be not
philosophical to think of sex when the soul is mentioned, the inferiority must
depend on the organs; or the heavenly fire, which is to ferment the clay, is not
given in equal portions.

But avoiding, as I have hitherto done, any direct comparison of the two
sexes collectively, or frankly acknowledging the inferiority of woman, according to the present appearance of things, I shall only insist that men have
increased that inferiority till women are almost sunk below the standard of
rational creatures. Let their faculties have room to unfold, and their virtues
to gain strength, and then determine where the whole sex must stand in the
intellectual scale. Yet let it be remembered, that for a small number of distinguished women I do not ask a place.

It is difficult for us purblind mortals to say to what height human discoveries and improvements may arrive when the gloom of despotism subsides,
which makes us stumble at every step; but, when morality shall be settled
on a more solid basis, then, without being gifted with a prophetic spirit, I will
venture to predict that woman will be either the friend or slave of man. We
shall not, as at present, doubt whether she is a moral agent, or the link which
unites man with brutes. But, should it then appear, that like the brutes they
were principally created for the use of man, he will let them patiently bite the
bridle, and not mock them with empty praise; or, should their rationality be
proved, he will not impede their improvement merely to gratify his sensual
appetites. He will not, with all the graces of rhetoric, advise them to submit
implicitly their understanding to the guidance of man. He will not, when he
treats of the education of women, assert that they ought never to have the
free use of reason, nor would he recommend cunning and dissimulation to
beings who are acquiring, in like manner as himself, the virtues of humanity.

Surely there can be but one rule of right, if morality has an eternal foundation, and whoever sacrifices virtue, strictly so called, to present convenience, or whose *duty* it is to act in such a manner, lives only for the passing
day, and cannot be an accountable creature.

The poet then should have dropped his sneer when he says,

> If weak women go astray,
> The stars are more in fault than they.[9]

For that they are bound by the adamantine chain of destiny is most certain, if it be proved that they are never to exercise their own reason, never
to be independent, never to rise above opinion, or to feel the dignity of a
rational will that only bows to God, and often forgets that the universe
contains any being but itself and the model of perfection to which
its ardent gaze is turned, to adore attributes that, softened into virtues,

8. Possibly a reference to Pope's 1733–34 *Essay
on Man*, Epistle II, lines 31–34: "Superior beings,
when of late they saw / A mortal Man unfold all
Nature's law, / Admir'd such wisdom in an earthly
shape, / And shew'd a NEWTON as we shew an
Ape." Isaac Newton (1643–1727) was revered
across Europe for his foundational work of physics, the *Principia* (1687), in which he formulated
the laws of gravitation and motion.
9. Matthew Prior, "Hans Carvel" (1700), lines
11–12.

may be imitated in kind, though the degree overwhelms the enraptured mind.

If I say, for I would not impress by declamation when Reason offers her sober light, if they be really capable of acting like rational creatures, let them not be treated like slaves; or, like the brutes who are dependent on the reason of man, when they associate with him; but cultivate their minds, give them the salutary, sublime curb of principle, and let them attain conscious dignity by feeling themselves only dependent on God. Teach them, in common with man, to submit to necessity, instead of giving, to render them more pleasing, a sex to morals.

Further, should experience prove that they cannot attain the same degree of strength of mind, perseverance, and fortitude, let their virtues be the same in kind, though they may vainly struggle for the same degree; and the superiority of man will be equally clear, if not clearer; and truth, as it is a simple principle, which admits of no modification, would be common to both. Nay, the order of society as it is at present regulated would not be inverted, for woman would then only have the rank that reason assigned her, and arts could not be practised to bring the balance even, much less to turn it.

These may be termed Utopian dreams.—Thanks to that Being who impressed them on my soul, and gave me sufficient strength of mind to dare to exert my own reason, till, becoming dependent only on him for the support of my virtue, I view, with indignation, the mistaken notions that enslave my sex.

I love man as my fellow; but his scepter, real, or usurped, extends not to me, unless the reason of an individual demands my homage; and even then the submission is to reason, and not to man. In fact, the conduct of an accountable being must be regulated by the operations of its own reason; or on what foundation rests the throne of God?

It appears to me necessary to dwell on these obvious truths, because females have been insulated, as it were; and, while they have been stripped of the virtues that should clothe humanity, they have been decked with artificial graces that enable them to exercise a short-lived tyranny. Love, in their bosoms, taking place of every nobler passion, their sole ambition is to be fair, to raise emotion instead of inspiring respect; and this ignoble desire, like the servility in absolute monarchies, destroys all strength of character. Liberty is the mother of virtue, and if women be, by their very constitution, slaves, and not allowed to breathe the sharp invigorating air of freedom, they must ever languish like exotics,[1] and be reckoned beautiful flaws in nature.

As to the argument respecting the subjection in which the sex has ever been held, it retorts on man. The many have always been enthralled by the few; and monsters, who scarcely have shewn any discernment of human excellence, have tyrannized over thousands of their fellow-creatures. Why have men of superiour endowments submitted to such degradation? For, is it not universally acknowledged that kings, viewed collectively, have ever been inferior, in abilities and virtue, to the same number of men taken from

1. Hothouse plants, which do not thrive in the English climate. Wollstonecraft also echoes here the language of the *Mansfield Judgment* of 1772, the legal decision that prohibited slavery within England by declaring "the air of England . . . too pure for slaves to breathe in."

the common mass of mankind—yet, have they not, and are they not still treated with a degree of reverence that is an insult to reason? China is not the only country where a living man has been made a God.[2] *Men* have submitted to superior strength to enjoy with impunity the pleasure of the moment— *women* have only done the same, and therefore till it is proved that the courtier, who servilely resigns the birthright of a man, is not a moral agent, it cannot be demonstrated that woman is essentially inferior to man because she has always been subjugated.

Brutal force has hitherto governed the world, and that the science of politics is in its infancy, is evident from philosophers scrupling to give the knowledge most useful to man that determinate distinction.

I shall not pursue this argument any further than to establish an obvious inference, that as sound politics diffuse liberty, mankind, including woman, will become more wise and virtuous.

•　•　•　•　•

From *Chapter 4. Observations on the State of Degradation to Which Woman is Reduced by Various Causes.*

*　*　*

In the middle rank of life, to continue the comparison,[3] men, in their youth, are prepared for professions, and marriage is not considered as the grand feature in their lives; whilst women, on the contrary, have no other scheme to sharpen their faculties. It is not business, extensive plans, or any of the excursive flights of ambition, that engross their attention; no, their thoughts are not employed in rearing such noble structures. To rise in the world, and have the liberty of running from pleasure to pleasure, they must marry advantageously, and to this object their time is sacrificed, and their persons often legally prostituted. A man when he enters any profession has his eye steadily fixed on some future advantage (and the mind gains great strength by having all its efforts directed to one point), and, full of his business, pleasure is considered as mere relaxation; whilst women seek for pleasure as the main purpose of existence. In fact, from the education, which they receive from society, the love of pleasure may be said to govern them all; but does this prove that there is a sex in souls? It would be just as rational to declare that the courtiers in France, when a destructive system of despotism had formed their character, were not men, because liberty, virtue, and humanity, were sacrificed to pleasure and vanity.—Fatal passions, which have ever domineered over the *whole* race!

The same love of pleasure, fostered by the whole tendency of their education, gives a trifling turn to the conduct of women in most circumstances: for instance, they are ever anxious about secondary things; and on the watch for adventures, instead of being occupied by duties.

A man, when he undertakes a journey, has, in general, the end in view; a woman thinks more of the incidental occurrences, the strange things that may possibly occur on the road; the impression that she may make on her fellow-travellers; and, above all, she is anxiously intent on the care of the fin-

2. The emperors of China were known as the "sons of heaven."
3. I.e., her comparison between the social expec-
tations that shape men and those that shape women and lead them to "degradation."

ery that she carries with her, which is more than ever a part of herself, when going to figure on a new scene; when, to use an apt French turn of expression, she is going to produce a sensation.—Can dignity of mind exist with such trivial cares?

In short, women, in general, as well as the rich of both sexes, have acquired all the follies and vices of civilization, and missed the useful fruit. It is not necessary for me always to premise, that I speak of the condition of the whole sex, leaving exceptions out of the question. Their senses are inflamed, and their understandings neglected, consequently they become the prey of their senses, delicately termed sensibility, and are blown about by every momentary gust of feeling. Civilized women are, therefore, so weakened by false refinement, that, respecting morals, their condition is much below what it would be were they left in a state nearer to nature. Ever restless and anxious, their over exercised sensibility not only renders them uncomfortable themselves, but troublesome, to use a soft phrase, to others. All their thoughts turn on things calculated to excite emotion; and feeling, when they should reason, their conduct is unstable, and their opinions are wavering—not the wavering produced by deliberation or progressive views, but by contradictory emotions. By fits and starts they are warm in many pursuits; yet this warmth, never concentrated into perseverance, soon exhausts itself; exhaled by its own heat, or meeting with some other fleeting passion, to which reason has never given any specific gravity, neutrality ensues. Miserable, indeed, must be that being whose cultivation of mind has only tended to inflame its passions! A distinction should be made between inflaming and strengthening them. The passions thus pampered, whilst the judgment is left unformed, what can be expected to ensue?—Undoubtedly, a mixture of madness and folly!

This observation should not be confined to the *fair* sex; however, at present, I only mean to apply it to them.

Novels, music, poetry, and gallantry, all tend to make women the creatures of sensation, and their character is thus formed in the mould of folly during the time they are acquiring accomplishments, the only improvement they are excited, by their station in society, to acquire. This overstretched sensibility naturally relaxes the other powers of the mind, and prevents intellect from attaining that sovereignty which it ought to attain to render a rational creature useful to others, and content with its own station: for the exercise of the understanding, as life advances, is the only method pointed out by nature to calm the passions.

Satiety has a very different effect, and I have often been forcibly struck by an emphatical description of damnation:—when the spirit is represented as continually hovering with abortive eagerness round the defied body, unable to enjoy any thing without the organs of sense. Yet, to their senses, are women made slaves, because it is by their sensibility that they obtain present power.

And will moralists pretend to assert, that this is the condition in which one half of the human race should be encouraged to remain with listless inactivity and stupid acquiescence? Kind instructors! what were we created for? To remain, it may be said, innocent; they mean in a state of childhood.—We might as well never have been born, unless it were necessary that we should be created to enable man to acquire the noble privilege of reason, the power of discerning good from evil, whilst we lie down in the dust from whence we were taken, never to rise again.—

It would be an endless task to trace the variety of meannesses, cares, and sorrows, into which women are plunged by the prevailing opinion, that they were created rather to feel than reason, and that all the power they obtain, must be obtained by their charms and weakness:

Fine by defect, and amiably weak![4]

And, made by this amiable weakness entirely dependent, excepting what they gain by illicit sway, on man, not only for protection, but advice, is it surprising that, neglecting the duties that reason alone points out, and shrinking from trials calculated to strengthen their minds, they only exert themselves to give their defects a graceful covering, which may serve to heighten their charms in the eye of the voluptuary, though it sink them below the scale of moral excellence?

Fragile in every sense of the word, they are obliged to look up to man for every comfort. In the most trifling dangers they cling to their support, with parasitical tenacity, piteously demanding succour; and their *natural* protector extends his arm, or lifts up his voice, to guard the lovely trembler—from what? Perhaps the frown of an old cow, or the jump of a mouse; a rat, would be a serious danger. In the name of reason, and even common sense, what can save such beings from contempt; even though they be soft and fair?

These fears, when not affected, may produce some pretty attitudes; but they shew a degree of imbecility which degrades a rational creature in a way women are not aware of—for love and esteem are very distinct things.

I am fully persuaded that we should hear of none of these infantine airs, if girls were allowed to take sufficient exercise, and not confined in close rooms till their muscles are relaxed, and their powers of digestion destroyed. To carry the remark still further, if fear in girls, instead of being cherished, perhaps, created, were treated in the same manner as cowardice in boys, we should quickly see women with more dignified aspects. It is true, they could not then with equal propriety be termed the sweet flowers that smile in the walk of man; but they would be more respectable members of society, and discharge the important duties of life by the light of their own reason. 'Educate women like men,' says Rousseau, 'and the more they resemble our sex the less power will they have over us.'[5] This is the very point I aim at. I do not wish them to have power over men; but over themselves.

In the same strain have I heard men argue against instructing the poor; for many are the forms that aristocracy assumes. 'Teach them to read and write,' say they, 'and you take them out of the station assigned them by nature.' An eloquent Frenchman has answered them, I will borrow his sentiments. But they know not, when they make man a brute, that they may expect every instant to see him transformed into a ferocious beast.[6] Without knowledge there can be no morality!

4. A misquotation of Pope, "Of the Characters of Women," line 44: "Fine by defect, and delicately weak."
5. The passage continues: "and when once they become like ourselves, we shall then be truly their masters" (*Émile*).
6. Wollstonecraft might be remembering a remark made in 1790 by the statesman Mirabeau, responding to the aggressive tone of the debates in revolutionary France's new Constituent Assembly and reflecting, more generally, on the power the common people had come to exercise in the nation's political arguments: "you have loosed the bull: do you expect he will not use his horns?"

Ignorance is a frail base for virtue! Yet, that it is the condition for which woman was organized, has been insisted upon by the writers who have most vehemently argued in, favour of the superiority of man; a superiority not in degree, but essence; though, to soften the argument, they have laboured to prove, with chivalrous generosity, that the sexes ought not to be compared; man was made to reason, woman to feel: and that together, flesh and spirit, they make the most perfect whole, by blending happily reason and sensibility into one character.

And what is sensibility? 'Quickness of sensation; quickness of perception; delicacy.' Thus is it defined by Dr. Johnson;[7] and the definition gives me no other idea than of the most exquisitely polished instinct. I discern not a trace of the image of God in either sensation or matter. Refined seventy times seven,[8] they are still material; intellect dwells not there; nor will fire ever make lead gold!

I come round to my old argument; if woman be allowed to have an immortal soul, she must have, as the employment of life, an understanding to improve. And when, to render the present state more complete, though every thing proves it to be but a fraction of a mighty sum, she is incited by present gratification to forget her grand destination, nature is counteracted, or she was born only to procreate and rot. Or, granting brutes, of every description, a soul, though not a reasonable one, the exercise of instinct and sensibility may be the step, which they are to take, in this life, towards the attainment of reason in the next; so that through all eternity they will lag behind man, who, why we cannot tell, had the power given him of attaining reason in his first mode of existence.

When I treat of the peculiar duties of women, as I should treat of the peculiar duties of a citizen or father, it will be found that I do not mean to insinuate that they should be taken out of their families, speaking of the majority. 'He that hath wife and children,' says Lord Bacon, 'hath given hostages to fortune; for they are impediments to great enterprises, either of virtue or mischief. Certainly the best works, and of greatest merit for the public, have proceeded from the unmarried or childless men.'[9] I say the same of women. But, the welfare of society is not built on extraordinary exertions; and were it more reasonably organized, there would be still less need of great abilities, or heroic virtues.

In the regulation of a family, in the education of children, understanding, in an unsophisticated sense, is particularly required: strength both of body and mind; yet the men who, by their writings, have most earnestly laboured to domesticate women, have endeavoured, by arguments dictated by a gross appetite, which satiety had rendered fastidious, to weaken their bodies and cramp their minds. But, if even by these sinister methods they really *persuaded* women, by working on their feelings, to stay at home, and fulfil the duties of a mother and mistress of a family, I should cautiously oppose opinions that led women to right conduct, by prevailing on them to make the discharge of such important duties the main business of life, though reason were insulted. Yet, and I appeal to experience, if by neglecting the under-

7. Wollstonecraft cites the emended definition Johnson included in the fourth (1773) edition of his *Dictionary*.
8. Matthew 18.22: "Jesus saith unto him, I say not unto thee, Until seven times: but, Until seventy times seven."
9. Francis Bacon, Essay VIII, "Of Marriage and the Single Life."

standing they be as much, nay, more detached from these domestic employ-ments, than they could be by the most serious intellectual pursuit, though it may be observed, that the mass of mankind will never vigorously pursue an intellectual object,[1] I may be allowed to infer that reason is absolutely neces-sary to enable a woman to perform any duty properly, and I must again repeat, that sensibility is not reason.

The comparison with the rich still occurs to me; for, when men neglect the duties of humanity, women will follow their example; a common stream hurries them both along with thoughtless celerity. Riches and honours pre-vent a man from enlarging his understanding, and enervate all his powers by reversing the order of nature, which has ever made true pleasure the reward of labour. Pleasure—enervating pleasure is, likewise, within women's reach without earning it. But, till hereditary possessions are spread abroad, how can we expect men to be proud of virtue? And, till they are, women will gov-ern them by the most direct means, neglecting their dull domestic duties to catch the pleasure that sits lightly on the wing of time.

'The power of the woman,' says some author, 'is her sensibility';[2] and men, not aware of the consequence, do all they can to make this power swallow up every other. Those who constantly employ their sensibility will have most: for example; poets, painters, and composers.[3] Yet, when the sensibility is thus increased at the expence of reason, and even the imagination, why do philosophical men complain of their fickleness? The sexual attention of man particularly acts on female sensibility, and this sympathy has been exercised from their youth up. A husband cannot long pay those attentions with the passion necessary to excite lively emotions, and the heart, accustomed to lively emotions, turns to a new lover, or pines in secret, the prey of virtue or prudence. I mean when the heart has really been rendered susceptible, and the taste formed; for I am apt to conclude, from what I have seen in fashion-able life, that vanity is oftener fostered than sensibility by the mode of edu-cation, and the intercourse between the sexes, which I have reprobated; and that coquetry more frequently proceeds from vanity than from that incon-stancy, which overstrained sensibility naturally produces.

Another argument that has had great weight with me, must, I think, have some force with every considerate benevolent heart. Girls who have been thus weakly educated, are often cruelly left by their parents without any pro-vision; and, of course, are dependent on, not only the reason, but the bounty of their brothers. These brothers are, to view the fairest side of the question, good sort of men, and give as a favour, what children of the same parents had an equal right to. In this equivocal humiliating situation, a docile female may remain some time, with a tolerable degree of comfort. But, when the brother marries, a probable circumstance, from being considered as the mistress of the family, she is viewed with averted looks as an intruder, an unnecessary burden on the benevolence of the master of the house, and his new partner.

1. The mass of mankind are rather the slaves of their appetites than of their passions [Wollstone-craft's note].
2. Possibly a recollection of *A Father's Legacy to His Daughters*, in which Gregory, discussing women's blushing, asserts "That extreme sensibil-ity which it indicates, may be a weakness and incumbrance in our sex . . . but in yours it is pecu-liarly engaging."
3. Men of these descriptions pour it into their compositions, to amalgamate the gross materials; and, moulding them with passion, give to the inert body a soul; but, in woman's imagination, love alone concentrates these ethereal beams [Wollstonecraft's note].

Who can recount the misery, which many unfortunate beings, whose minds and bodies are equally weak, suffer in such situations—unable to work, and ashamed to beg? The wife, a cold-hearted, narrow-minded, woman, and this is not an unfair supposition; for the present mode of education does not tend to enlarge the heart any more than the understanding, is jealous of the little kindness which her husband shews to his relations; and her sensibility not rising to humanity, she is displeased at seeing the property of *her* children lavished on an helpless sister.

These are matters of fact, which have come under my eye again and again. The consequence is obvious, the wife has recourse to cunning to undermine the habitual affection, which she is afraid openly to oppose; and neither tears nor caresses are spared till the spy is worked out of her home, and thrown on the world, unprepared for its difficulties; or sent, as a great effort of generosity, or from some regard to propriety, with a small stipend, and an uncultivated mind, into joyless solitude.

These two women may be much upon a par, with respect to reason and humanity; and changing situations, might have acted just the same selfish part; but had they been differently educated, the case would also have been very different. The wife would not have had that sensibility, of which self is the centre, and reason might have taught her not to expect, and not even to be flattered by, the affection of her husband, if it led him to violate prior duties. She would wish not to love him merely because he loved her, but on account of his virtues; and the sister might have been able to struggle for herself instead of eating the bitter bread of dependence.

I am, indeed, persuaded that the heart, as well as the understanding, is opened by cultivation; and by, which may not appear so clear, strengthening the organs; I am not now talking of momentary flashes of sensibility, but of affections. And, perhaps, in the education of both sexes, the most difficult task is so to adjust instruction as not to narrow the understanding, whilst the heart is warmed by the generous juices of spring, just raised by the electric fermentation of the season; nor to dry up the feelings by employing the mind in investigations remote from life.

With respect to women, when they receive a careful education, they are either made fine ladies, brimful of sensibility, and teeming with capricious fancies; or mere notable women.[4] The latter are often friendly, honest creatures, and have a shrewd kind of good sense joined with worldly prudence, that often render them more useful members of society than the fine sentimental lady, though they possess neither greatness of mind nor taste. The intellectual world is shut against them; take them out of their family or neighbourhood, and they stand still; the mind finding no employment, for literature affords a fund of amusement which they have never sought to relish, but frequently to despise. The sentiments and taste of more cultivated minds appear ridiculous, even in those whom chance and family connections have led them to love; but in mere acquaintance they think it all affectation.

A man of sense can only love such a woman on account of her sex, and respect her, because she is a trusty servant. He lets her, to preserve his own peace, scold the servants, and go to church in clothes made of the

---

4. I.e., industrious and energetic housewives.

very best materials. A man of her own size of understanding would, prob-ably, not agree so well with her; for he might wish to encroach on her pre-rogative, and manage some domestic concerns himself. Yet women, whose minds are not enlarged by cultivation, or the natural selfishness of sensi-bility expanded by reflection, are very unfit to manage a family; for, by an undue stretch of power, they are always tyrannizing to support a superior-ity that only rests on the arbitrary distinction of fortune. The evil is some-times more serious, and domestics are deprived of innocent indulgences, and made to work beyond their strength, in order to enable the notable woman to keep a better table, and outshine her neighbours in finery and parade. If she attend to her children, it is, in general, to dress them in a costly manner—and, whether this attention arise from vanity or fondness, it is equally pernicious.

Besides, how many women of this description pass their days; or, at least, their evenings, discontentedly. Their husbands acknowledge that they are good managers, and chaste wives; but leave home to seek for more agreeable, may I be allowed to use a significant French word, *piquant*[5] society; and the patient drudge, who fulfils her task, like a blind horse in a mill, is defrauded of her just reward; for the wages due to her are the caresses of her husband; and women who have so few resources in themselves, do not very patiently bear this privation of a natural right.

A fine lady, on the contrary, has been taught to look down with contempt on the vulgar employments of life; though she has only been incited to acquire accomplishments that rise a degree above sense; for even corporeal accomplishments cannot be acquired with any degree of precision unless the understanding has been strengthened by exercise. Without a foundation of principles taste is superficial, grace must arise from something deeper than imitation. The imagination, however, is heated, and the feelings ren-dered fastidious, if not sophisticated; or, a counterpoise of judgment is not acquired, when the heart still remains artless, though it becomes too tender.

These women are often amiable; and their hearts are really more sensible to general benevolence, more alive to the sentiments that civilize life, than the square-elbowed family drudge; but, wanting a due proportion of reflection and self-government, they only inspire love; and are the mistresses of their husbands, whilst they have any hold on their affections; and the platonic friends of his male acquaintance. These are the fair defects in nature; the women who appear to be created not to enjoy the fellowship of man, but to save him from sinking into absolute brutality, by rubbing off the rough angles of his character; and by playful dalliance to give some dignity to the appetite that draws him to them.—Gracious Creator of the whole human race! hast thou created such a being as woman, who can trace thy wisdom in thy works, and feel that thou alone art by thy nature exalted above her,—for no better purpose?—Can she believe that she was only made to submit to man, her equal, a being, who, like her, was sent into the world to acquire virtue?—Can she consent to be occupied merely to please him; merely to adorn the earth, when her soul is capable of rising to thee?—And can she rest

5. Stimulating.

supinely dependent on man for reason, when she ought to mount with him the arduous steeps of knowledge?—

Yet, if love be the supreme good, let women be only educated to inspire it, and let every charm be polished to intoxicate the senses; but, if they be moral beings, let them have a chance to become intelligent; and let love to man be only a part of that glowing flame of universal love, which, after encircling humanity, mounts in grateful incense to God.

* * *

WILLIAM WORDSWORTH
1770–1850

William Wordsworth was born in Cockermouth in West Cumberland, just on the northern fringe of the English Lake District. When his mother died, the eight-year-old boy was sent to school at Hawkshead, near Esthwaite Lake, in the heart of that sparsely populated region that he and Coleridge were to transform into one of the poetic centers of England. William and his three brothers boarded in the cottage of Ann Tyson, who gave the boys simple comfort, ample affection, and freedom to roam the countryside at will. A vigorous, unruly, and sometimes moody boy, William spent his free days and occasionally "half the night" in the sports and rambles described in the first two books of *The Prelude*, "drinking in" (to use one of his favorite metaphors) the natural sights and sounds, and getting to know the cottagers, shepherds, and solitary wanderers who moved through his imagination into his later poetry.

John Wordsworth, the poet's father, died suddenly when William was thirteen, leaving to his five children mainly the substantial sum owed him by Lord Lonsdale, whom he had served as attorney and as steward of the huge Lonsdale estate. This harsh nobleman had yet to pay the debt when he died in 1802. Wordsworth was nevertheless able in 1787 to enter St. John's College, Cambridge University, where four years later he took his degree without distinction.

During the summer vacation of his third year at Cambridge (1790), Wordsworth and his closest college friend, the Welshman Robert Jones, journeyed on foot through France and the Alps (described in *The Prelude* 6) at the time when the French were joyously celebrating the first anniversary of the fall of the Bastille. Upon completing his course at Cambridge, Wordsworth spent four months in London, set off on another walking tour with Robert Jones through Wales (the time of the memorable ascent of Mount Snowdon in *The Prelude* 13), and then went back alone to France to master the language and qualify as a traveling tutor.

During his year in France (November 1791 to December 1792), Wordsworth became a fervent supporter of the French Revolution—which seemed to him and many others to promise a "glorious renovation" of society—and he fell in love with Annette Vallon, the daughter of a French surgeon at Blois. The two planned to marry, despite their differences in religion and political inclinations (Annette belonged to an old Catholic family whose sympathies were Royalist). But almost immediately after their daughter, Caroline, was born, lack of money forced Wordsworth to return to England. The outbreak of war made it impossible for him to rejoin Annette and Caroline. Wordsworth's guilt over this abandonment, his divided loyalties between England and France, and his gradual disillusion with the course of the Revolution brought him—according to his account in *The Prelude* 10 and 11—to the verge of an emotional breakdown, when "sick, wearied out with contrarieties," he "yielded up moral questions in despair." His suffering, his near-collapse, and the successful effort, after his break with his past, to reestablish "a saving intercourse with my true self," are the experiences that underlie many of his greatest poems.

At this critical point, a friend died and left Wordsworth a sum of money just sufficient to enable him to live by his poetry. In 1795 he settled in a rent-free house at Racedown, Dorsetshire, with his beloved sister, Dorothy, who now began her long career as confidante, inspirer, and secretary. At that same time Wordsworth met Samuel Taylor Coleridge. Two years later he moved to Alfoxden House, Somersetshire, to be near Coleridge, who lived four miles away at Nether Stowey. Here he entered at the age of twenty-seven on the delayed springtime of his poetic career.

Even while he had been an undergraduate at Cambridge, Coleridge claimed that he had detected signs of genius in Wordsworth's rather conventional poem about his tour in the Alps, *Descriptive Sketches*, published in 1793. Now he hailed Wordsworth unreservedly as "the best poet of the age." The two men met almost daily, talked for hours about poetry, and wrote prolifically. This close partnership, along with the hospitality the two households offered to another young radical writer, John Thelwall, aroused the paranoia of people in the neighborhood. Already fearful of a military invasion by France, they became convinced that Wordsworth and Coleridge were political plotters, not poets. The government sent spies to investigate, and the Wordsworths lost their lease.

Although brought to this abrupt end, that short period of collaboration resulted in one of the most important books of the era, *Lyrical Ballads, with a Few Other Poems,* published anonymously in 1798. This short volume opened with Coleridge's *Ancient Mariner* and included three other poems by Coleridge, some lyrics in which Wordsworth celebrated the experience of nature, and a number of verse anecdotes drawn from the lives of the rural poor. The book closed with Wordsworth's great descriptive and meditative poem in blank verse, "Tintern Abbey."

William Hazlitt said that when he heard Coleridge read some of the newly written poems of *Lyrical Ballads* aloud, "the sense of a new style and a new spirit in poetry came over me," with something of the effect "that arises from the turning up of the fresh soil, or of the first welcome breath of spring." The reviewers were less enthusiastic, warning that, because of their simple language and subject matter, poems such as "Simon Lee" risked "vulgarity" or silliness. (For a sampling of these reactions, see "'Self-constituted judge of poesy': Reviewer vs. Poet in the Romantic Period" in the supplemental ebook.) Nevertheless *Lyrical Ballads* sold out in two years, and Wordsworth published under his own name a new edition, dated 1800, to which he added a second volume of poems. In his famous Preface to this edition, planned in close consultation with Coleridge, Wordsworth outlined a critical program that provided a retroactive rationale for the "experiments" the poems represented.

Late in 1799 William and Dorothy moved back permanently to their native lakes, settling at Grasmere in the little house later named Dove Cottage. Coleridge, following them, rented at Keswick, thirteen miles away. In 1802 Wordsworth finally came into his father's inheritance and, after an amicable settlement with Annette Vallon, married Mary Hutchinson, whom he had known since childhood. His life after that time had many sorrows: the drowning in 1805 of his favorite brother, John, a sea captain; the death in 1812 of two of his and Mary's five children; a growing rift with Coleridge; and, from the 1830s on, Dorothy's physical and mental illness. Over these years Wordsworth became, nonetheless, increasingly prosperous and famous. He also displayed a political and religious conservatism that disappointed readers who, like Hazlitt, had interpreted his early work as the expression of a "levelling Muse" that promoted democratic change. In 1813 a government sinecure, the position of stamp distributor (that is, revenue collector) for Westmorland, was bestowed on him—concrete evidence of his recognition as a national poet and of the alteration in the government's perception of his politics. By 1843 he was poet laureate of Great Britain. He died in 1850 at the age of eighty. Only then did his executors publish his masterpiece, *The Prelude, or Growth of a Poet's Mind*, the autobiographical poem that he had written in two parts in 1799, expanded to its full length in 1805, and then continued to revise almost to the last decade of his long life.

Most of Wordsworth's greatest poetry had been written by 1807, when he published *Poems, in Two Volumes*. After *The Excursion* (1814) and the first collected edition of his poems (1815), although he continued to write prolifically and to work on the revisions for additional collected editions, his powers appeared to decline. The causes of that decline have been much debated. One seems to be inherent in the very nature of his writing. Wordsworth is above all the poet of the remembrance— also the reinterpretation—of things past. But the memory of one's early emotional experience is not an inexhaustible resource for poetry, as Wordsworth recognized almost from the start of his career. In book 11 of *The 1805 Prelude* he already seems to be entertaining a premonition of future loss, in the lines that describe the recurrence of "spots of time" from his memories of childhood:

> The days gone by
> Come back upon me from the dawn almost
> Of life: the hiding places of my power
> Seem open; I approach and then they close.
> I see by glimpses now; when age comes on,
> May scarcely see at all.

The simple (maybe even prosy) lines, on the perplexities of memory, on the mystery that the self poses for the self, and on the sorrows and losses brought by time, announce an imminent imaginative failure. At the same time, contrariwise, they also suggest the reason Hazlitt would declare Wordsworth's poetry pre-eminent among that of the living poets: "he has communicated interest and dignity to the primal movements of the heart of man."

FROM LYRICAL BALLADS

We Are Seven[1]

————A simple Child,
That lightly draws its breath,
And feels its life in every limb,
What should it know of death?

5   I met a little cottage Girl:
She was eight years old, she said;
Her hair was thick with many a curl
That clustered round her head.

---

1. Written at Alfoxden in the spring of 1798. . . . The little girl who is the heroine I met within the area of Goodrich Castle [in the Wye Valley north of Tintern Abbey] in the year 1793 [Wordsworth's note, 1843]. Wordsworth also tells us that, "while walking to and fro," he composed the last stanza first, beginning with the last line, and that Coleridge contributed the first stanza.

She had a rustic, woodland air,
10 And she was wildly clad:
Her eyes were fair, and very fair;
—Her beauty made me glad.

"Sisters and brothers, little Maid,
How many may you be?"
15 "How many? Seven in all," she said,
And wondering looked at me.

"And where are they? I pray you tell."
She answered, "Seven are we;
And two of us at Conway[2] dwell,
20 And two are gone to sea.

"Two of us in the church-yard lie,
My sister and my brother;
And, in the church-yard cottage, I
Dwell near them with my mother."

25 "You say that two at Conway dwell,
And two are gone to sea,
Yet ye are seven! I pray you tell,
Sweet Maid, how this may be."

Then did the little Maid reply,
30 "Seven boys and girls are we;
Two of us in the church-yard lie,
Beneath the church-yard tree."

"You run about, my little Maid,
Your limbs they are alive;
35 If two are in the church-yard laid,
Then ye are only five."

"Their graves are green, they may be seen,"
The little Maid replied,
"Twelve steps or more from my mother's door,
40 And they are side by side.

"My stockings there I often knit,
My kerchief there I hem;
And there upon the ground I sit,
And sing a song to them.

45 "And often after sun-set, Sir,
When it is light and fair,
I take my little porringer,[3]
And eat my supper there.

2. A seaport town in north Wales.
3. Bowl for porridge.

"The first that died was sister Jane;
50 In bed she moaning lay,
Till God released her of her pain;
And then she went away.

"So in the church-yard she was laid;
And, when the grass was dry,
55 Together round her grave we played,
My brother John and I.

"And when the ground was white with snow,
And I could run and slide,
My brother John was forced to go,
60 And he lies by her side."

"How many are you, then," said I,
"If they two are in heaven?"
Quick was the little Maid's reply,
"O Master! we are seven."

65 "But they are dead; those two are dead!
Their spirits are in heaven!"
'Twas throwing words away; for still
The little Maid would have her will,
And said, "Nay, we are seven!"

1798   1798

Lines Written in Early Spring

I heard a thousand blended notes,
While in a grove I sate reclined,
In that sweet mood when pleasant thoughts
Bring sad thoughts to the mind.

5 To her fair works did Nature link
The human soul that through me ran;
And much it grieved my heart to think
What man has made of man.

Through primrose tufts, in that green bower,
10 The periwinkle¹ trailed its wreaths,
And 'tis my faith that every flower
Enjoys the air it breathes.

The birds around me hopped and played,
Their thoughts I cannot measure:—
15 But the least motion which they made,
It seemed a thrill of pleasure.

---

1. A trailing evergreen plant with small blue flowers (U.S. myrtle).

The budding twigs spread out their fan,
To catch the breezy air;
And I must think, do all I can,
20   That there was pleasure there.

If this belief from heaven be sent,
If such be Nature's holy plan,
Have I not reason to lament
What man has made of man?

1798   1798

Expostulation and Reply[1]

"Why, William, on that old grey stone,
Thus for the length of half a day,
Why, William, sit you thus alone,
And dream your time away?

5   "Where are your books?—that light bequeathed
To Beings else forlorn and blind!
Up! up! and drink the spirit breathed
From dead men to their kind.

"You look round on your Mother Earth,
10   As if she for no purpose bore you;
As if you were her first-born birth,
And none had lived before you!"

One morning thus, by Esthwaite lake,
When life was sweet, I knew not why,
15   To me my good friend Matthew spake,
And thus I made reply.

"The eye—it cannot choose but see;
We cannot bid the ear be still;
Our bodies feel, where'er they be,
20   Against or with our will.

"Nor less I deem that there are Powers
Which of themselves our minds impress;
That we can feed this mind of ours
In a wise passiveness.

25   "Think you, 'mid all this mighty sum
Of things for ever speaking,
That nothing of itself will come,
But we must still be seeking?

1. This and the following companion poem have often been attacked—and defended—as Wordsworth's own statement about the comparative merits of nature and of books. But they are a dialogue between two friends who rally one another by the usual device of overstating parts of a whole truth.

"—Then ask not wherefore, here, alone,
30   Conversing² as I may,
I sit upon this old grey stone,
And dream my time away."

Spring 1798   1798

The Tables Turned

An Evening Scene on the Same Subject

Up! up! my Friend, and quit your books;
Or surely you'll grow double:°   *double over*
Up! up! my Friend, and clear your looks;
Why all this toil and trouble?

5   The sun, above the mountain's head,
A freshening lustre mellow
Through all the long green fields has spread,
His first sweet evening yellow.

Books! 'tis a dull and endless strife:
10   Come, hear the woodland linnet,°   *small finch*
How sweet his music! on my life,
There's more of wisdom in it.

And hark! how blithe the throstle° sings!   *song thrush*
He, too, is no mean preacher:
15   Come forth into the light of things,
Let Nature be your Teacher.

She has a world of ready wealth,
Our minds and hearts to bless—
Spontaneous wisdom breathed by health,
20   Truth breathed by cheerfulness.

One impulse from a vernal wood
May teach you more of man,
Of moral evil and of good,
Than all the sages can.

25   Sweet is the lore which Nature brings;
Our meddling intellect
Mis-shapes the beauteous forms of things:—
We murder to dissect.

Enough of Science and of Art;
30   Close up those barren leaves;°   *pages*
Come forth, and bring with you a heart
That watches and receives.

1798   1798

2. In the old sense of "communing" (with the "things for ever speaking").

Lines[1]

Composed a Few Miles above Tintern Abbey, on Revisiting the Banks of the Wye during a Tour, July 13, 1798

Five years have past; five summers, with the length
Of five long winters! and again I hear
These waters, rolling from their mountain-springs
With a soft inland murmur.[2]—Once again
5 Do I behold these steep and lofty cliffs,
That on a wild secluded scene impress
Thoughts of more deep seclusion; and connect
The landscape with the quiet of the sky.
The day is come when I again repose
10 Here, under this dark sycamore, and view
These plots of cottage-ground, these orchard-tufts,
Which at this season, with their unripe fruits,
Are clad in one green hue, and lose themselves
'Mid groves and copses. Once again I see
15 These hedge-rows, hardly hedge-rows, little lines
Of sportive wood run wild: these pastoral farms,
Green to the very door; and wreaths of smoke
Sent up, in silence, from among the trees!
With some uncertain notice, as might seem
20 Of vagrant dwellers in the houseless woods,
Or of some Hermit's cave, where by his fire
The Hermit sits alone.

           These beauteous forms,
Through a long absence, have not been to me
As is a landscape to a blind man's eye:
25 But oft, in lonely rooms, and 'mid the din
Of towns and cities, I have owed to them
In hours of weariness, sensations sweet,
Felt in the blood, and felt along the heart;
And passing even into my purer mind,
30 With tranquil restoration:—feelings too
Of unremembered pleasure: such, perhaps,
As have no slight or trivial influence
On that best portion of a good man's life,
His little, nameless, unremembered, acts
35 Of kindness and of love. Nor less, I trust,
To them I may have owed another gift,
Of aspect more sublime; that blessed mood,
In which the burthen° of the mystery,   *burden*

---

1. No poem of mine was composed under circumstances more pleasant for me to remember than this. I began it upon leaving Tintern, after crossing the Wye, and concluded it just as I was entering Bristol in the evening, after a ramble of 4 or 5 days, with my sister. Not a line of it was altered, and not any part of it written down till I reached Bristol [Wordsworth's note, 1843]. Wordsworth had first visited the Wye valley and the ruins of Tintern Abbey, in Monmouthshire, while on a solitary walking tour in August 1793, when he was twenty-three years old. (See *"Tintern Abbey*, Tourism, and Romantic Landscape" in the supplemental ebook.)

2. The river is not affected by the tides a few miles above Tintern [Wordsworth's note, 1798 ff.]. Until 1845 the text had "sweet" for "soft," meaning fresh, not salty.

In which the heavy and the weary weight
40　Of all this unintelligible world,
Is lightened:—that serene and blessed mood,
In which the affections gently lead us on,—
Until, the breath of this corporeal frame
And even the motion of our human blood
45　Almost suspended, we are laid asleep
In body, and become a living soul:
While with an eye made quiet by the power
Of harmony, and the deep power of joy,
We see into the life of things.

If this
50　Be but a vain belief, yet, oh! how oft—
In darkness and amid the many shapes
Of joyless daylight; when the fretful stir
Unprofitable, and the fever of the world,
Have hung upon the beatings of my heart—
55　How oft, in spirit, have I turned to thee,
O sylvan Wye! thou wanderer thro' the woods,
How often has my spirit turned to thee!

    And now, with gleams of half-extinguished thought,
With many recognitions dim and faint,
60　And somewhat of a sad perplexity,
The picture of the mind revives again:
While here I stand, not only with the sense
Of present pleasure, but with pleasing thoughts
That in this moment there is life and food
65　For future years. And so I dare to hope,
Though changed, no doubt, from what I was when first
I came among these hills; when like a roe°   deer
I bounded o'er the mountains, by the sides
Of the deep rivers, and the lonely streams,
70　Wherever nature led: more like a man
Flying from something that he dreads, than one
Who sought the thing he loved. For nature then
(The coarser pleasures of my boyish days,
And their glad animal movements all gone by)
75　To me was all in all.—I cannot paint
What then I was. The sounding cataract
Haunted me like a passion: the tall rock,
The mountain, and the deep and gloomy wood,
Their colours and their forms, were then to me
80　An appetite; a feeling and a love,
That had no need of a remoter charm,
By thought supplied, nor any interest
Unborrowed from the eye.—That time is past,
And all its aching joys are now no more,
85　And all its dizzy raptures.[3] Not for this
Faint° I, nor mourn nor murmur; other gifts   lose heart
Have followed; for such loss, I would believe,

3. Lines 66ff. contain Wordsworth's famed description of the three stages of his growing up, defined in terms of his evolving relations to the natural scene.

Abundant recompense. For I have learned
To look on nature, not as in the hour
90 Of thoughtless youth; but hearing oftentimes
The still, sad music of humanity,
Nor harsh nor grating, though of ample power
To chasten and subdue. And I have felt
A presence that disturbs me with the joy
95 Of elevated thoughts; a sense sublime
Of something far more deeply interfused,
Whose dwelling is the light of setting suns,
And the round ocean and the living air,
And the blue sky, and in the mind of man:
100 A motion and a spirit, that impels
All thinking things, all objects of all thought,
And rolls through all things. Therefore am I still
A lover of the meadows and the woods,
And mountains; and of all that we behold
105 From this green earth; of all the mighty world
Of eye, and ear,—both what they half create,[4]
And what perceive; well pleased to recognise
In nature and the language of the sense,
The anchor of my purest thoughts, the nurse,
110 The guide, the guardian of my heart, and soul
Of all my moral being.

                    Nor perchance,
If I were not thus taught, should I the more
Suffer my genial spirits[5] to decay:
For thou art with me here upon the banks
115 Of this fair river; thou my dearest Friend,[6]
My dear, dear Friend; and in thy voice I catch
The language of my former heart, and read
My former pleasures in the shooting lights
Of thy wild eyes. Oh! yet a little while
120 May I behold in thee what I was once,
My dear, dear Sister! and this prayer I make,
Knowing that Nature never did betray
The heart that loved her; 'tis her privilege,
Through all the years of this our life, to lead
125 From joy to joy: for she can so inform
The mind that is within us, so impress
With quietness and beauty, and so feed
With lofty thoughts, that neither evil tongues,[7]
Rash judgments, nor the sneers of selfish men,
130 Nor greetings where no kindness is, nor all
The dreary intercourse of daily life,
Shall e'er prevail against us, or disturb
Our cheerful faith, that all which we behold

4. This line has a close resemblance to an admirable line of Young, the exact expression of which I cannot recollect [Wordsworth's note, 1798 ff.]. Edward Young in *Night Thoughts* (1744) says that the human senses "half create the wondrous world they see."
5. Creative powers. ("Genial" is here the adjectival form of the noun *genius*.)
6. His sister, Dorothy.
7. In the opening of *Paradise Lost* 7, Milton describes himself as fallen on "evil days" and "evil tongues" and with "dangers compassed round" (lines 26–27).

Is full of blessings. Therefore let the moon
135 Shine on thee in thy solitary walk;
And let the misty mountain-winds be free
To blow against thee: and, in after years,
When these wild ecstasies shall be matured
Into a sober pleasure; when thy mind
140 Shall be a mansion for all lovely forms,
Thy memory be as a dwelling-place
For all sweet sounds and harmonies; oh! then,
If solitude, or fear, or pain, or grief,
Should be thy portion,° with what healing thoughts   *inheritance, dowry*
145 Of tender joy wilt thou remember me,
And these my exhortations! Nor, perchance—
If I should be where I no more can hear
Thy voice, nor catch from thy wild eyes these gleams
Of past existence[8]—wilt thou then forget
150 That on the banks of this delightful stream
We stood together; and that I, so long
A worshipper of Nature, hither came
Unwearied in that service; rather say
With warmer love—oh! with far deeper zeal
155 Of holier love. Nor wilt thou then forget,
That after many wanderings, many years
Of absence, these steep woods and lofty cliffs,
And this green pastoral landscape, were to me
More dear, both for themselves and for thy sake!

July 1798   1798

Preface to *Lyrical Ballads* (1802)   To the first edition of *Lyrical Ballads*, published jointly with Coleridge in 1798, Wordsworth prefixed an "Advertisement" asserting that the majority of the poems were "to be considered as experiments" to determine "how far the language of conversation in the middle and lower classes of society is adapted to the purposes of poetic pleasure." In the second, two-volume edition of 1800, Wordsworth, aided by frequent conversations with Coleridge, expanded the Advertisement into a preface that justified the poems not as experiments, but as exemplifying the principles of all good poetry. The Preface was enlarged for the third edition of *Lyrical Ballads*, published two years later. This last version of 1802 is reprinted here.

    Although some of its ideas had antecedents in the later eighteenth century, the Preface as a whole deserves its reputation as a revolutionary manifesto about the nature of poetry. Like many radical statements, however, it claims to go back to the implicit principles that governed the great poetry of the past but have been perverted in recent practice. Most discussions of the Preface, following the lead of Coleridge in chapters 14 and 17 of his *Biographia Literaria*, have focused on Wordsworth's assertions about the valid language of poetry, on which he bases his attack on the "poetic diction" of eighteenth-century poets. As Coleridge pointed out, Wordsworth's argument about this issue is far from clear. However, Wordsworth's questioning of the underlying premises of neoclassical poetry went even further. His Preface implicitly denies the traditional assumption that the poetic genres constitute a hierarchy, from epic and tragedy at the top down through comedy, satire, pasto-

___
8. I.e., reminders of his own "past existence" five years earlier (see lines 116–19).

ral, to the short lyric at the lowest reaches of the poetic scale; he also rejects the traditional principle of "decorum," which required the poet to arrange matters so that the poem's subject (especially the social class of its protagonists) and its level of diction conformed to the status of the literary kind on the poetic scale.

When Wordsworth asserted in the Preface that he deliberately chose to represent "incidents and situations from common life," he translated his democratic sympathies into critical terms, justifying his use of peasants, children, outcasts, criminals, and madwomen as serious subjects of poetic and even tragic concern. He also undertook to write in "a selection of language really used by men," on the grounds that there can be no "essential difference between the language of prose and metrical composition."

Wordsworth's assertions about the materials and diction of poetry have been greatly influential in expanding the range of serious literature to include the common people and ordinary things and events, as well as in justifying a poetry of sincerity rather than of artifice, expressed in the ordinary language of its time. But in the long view other aspects of his Preface have been no less significant in establishing its importance, not only as a turning point in English criticism but also as a central document in modern culture. Wordsworth feared that a new urban, industrial society's mass media and mass culture (glimpsed in the Preface when he refers derisively to contemporary Gothic novels and German melodramas) were threatening to blunt the human mind's "discriminatory powers" and to "reduce it to a state of almost savage torpor." He attributed to imaginative literature the primary role in keeping the human beings who live in such societies emotionally alive and morally sensitive.

From Preface to *Lyrical Ballads, with Pastoral and Other Poems* (1802)

[THE SUBJECT AND LANGUAGE OF POETRY]

The first volume of these poems has already been submitted to general perusal. It was published, as an experiment, which, I hoped, might be of some use to ascertain, how far, by fitting to metrical arrangement a selection of the real language of men in a state of vivid sensation, that sort of pleasure and that quantity of pleasure may be imparted, which a poet may rationally endeavour to impart.

I had formed no very inaccurate estimate of the probable effect of those poems: I flattered myself that they who should be pleased with them would read them with more than common pleasure: and, on the other hand, I was well aware, that by those who should dislike them they would be read with more than common dislike. The result has differed from my expectation in this only, that I have pleased a greater number than I ventured to hope I should please.

For the sake of variety, and from a consciousness of my own weakness, I was induced to request the assistance of a friend, who furnished me with the poems of the *Ancient Mariner*, the *Foster-Mother's Tale*, the *Nightingale*, and the poem entitled *Love*. I should not, however, have requested this assistance, had I not believed that the poems of my friend[1] would in a great measure have the same tendency as my own, and that, though there would be found a difference, there would be found no discordance in the colours of our style; as our opinions on the subject of poetry do almost entirely coincide.

---

1. The "friend" of course is Coleridge.

Several of my friends are anxious for the success of these poems from a belief, that, if the views with which they were composed were indeed realized, a class of poetry would be produced, well adapted to interest mankind permanently, and not unimportant in the multiplicity, and in the quality of its moral relations: and on this account they have advised me to prefix a systematic defence of the theory upon which the poems were written. But I was unwilling to undertake the task, because I knew that on this occasion the reader would look coldly upon my arguments, since I might be suspected of having been principally influenced by the selfish and foolish hope of *reasoning* him into an approbation of these particular poems: and I was still more unwilling to undertake the task, because, adequately to display my opinions, and fully to enforce my arguments, would require a space wholly disproportionate to the nature of a preface. For to treat the subject with the clearness and coherence of which I believe it susceptible, it would be necessary to give a full account of the present state of the public taste in this country, and to determine how far this taste is healthy or depraved; which, again, could not be determined, without pointing out, in what manner language and the human mind act and re-act on each other, and without retracing the revolutions, not of literature alone, but likewise of society itself. I have therefore altogether declined to enter regularly upon this defence; yet I am sensible, that there would be some impropriety in abruptly obtruding upon the public, without a few words of introduction, poems so materially different from those upon which general approbation is at present bestowed.

It is supposed, that by the act of writing in verse an author makes a formal engagement that he will gratify certain known habits of association; that he not only thus apprizes the reader that certain classes of ideas and expressions will be found in his book, but that others will be carefully excluded. This exponent or symbol held forth by metrical language must in different eras of literature have excited very different expectations: for example, in the age of Catullus, Terence, and Lucretius and that of Statius or Claudian,[2] and in our own country, in the age of Shakespeare and Beaumont and Fletcher, and that of Donne and Cowley, or Dryden, or Pope. I will not take upon me to determine the exact import of the promise which by the act of writing in verse an author, in the present day, makes to his reader; but I am certain, it will appear to many persons that I have not fulfilled the terms of an engagement thus voluntarily contracted. They who have been accustomed to the gaudiness and inane phraseology of many modern writers, if they persist in reading this book to its conclusion, will, no doubt, frequently have to struggle with feelings of strangeness and awkwardness: they will look round for poetry, and will be induced to inquire by what species of courtesy these attempts can be permitted to assume that title. I hope therefore the reader will not censure me, if I attempt to state what I have proposed to myself to perform; and also (as far as the limits of a preface will permit) to explain some of the chief reasons which have determined me in the choice of my purpose: that at least he may be spared any unpleasant feeling of disappointment, and that I myself may be protected from the most dishonorable accusation which can be brought against an author, namely, that of an indolence which prevents him from endeavouring to ascertain what is his duty, or, when this duty is ascertained, prevents him from performing it.

---

2. Wordsworth's implied contrast is between the naturalness and simplicity of the first three Roman poets (who wrote in the last two centuries B.C.E.) and the elaborate artifice of the last two Roman poets (Statius wrote in the 1st and Claudian in the 4th century C.E.).

The principal object, then, which I proposed to myself in these poems was to choose incidents and situations from common life, and to relate or describe them, throughout, as far as was possible, in a selection of language really used by men; and, at the same time, to throw over them a certain colouring of imagination, whereby ordinary things should be presented to the mind in an unusual way; and, further, and above all, to make these incidents and situations interesting by tracing in them, truly though not ostentatiously, the primary laws of our nature: chiefly, as far as regards the manner in which we associate ideas in a state of excitement. Low and rustic life was generally chosen, because in that condition, the essential passions of the heart find a better soil in which they can attain their maturity, are less under restraint, and speak a plainer and more emphatic language; because in that condition of life our elementary feelings co-exist in a state of greater simplicity, and, consequently, may be more accurately contemplated, and more forcibly communicated; because the manners of rural life germinate from those elementary feelings; and, from the necessary character of rural occupations, are more easily comprehended; and are more durable; and lastly, because in that condition the passions of men are incorporated with the beautiful and permanent forms of nature. The language, too, of these men is adopted (purified indeed from what appear to be its real defects, from all lasting and rational causes of dislike or disgust) because such men hourly communicate with the best objects from which the best part of language is originally derived; and because, from their rank in society and the sameness and narrow circle of their intercourse, being less under the influence of social vanity they convey their feelings and notions in simple and unelaborated expressions. Accordingly, such a language, arising out of repeated experience and regular feelings, is a more permanent, and a far more philosophical language, than that which is frequently substituted for it by poets, who think that they are conferring honour upon themselves and their art, in proportion as they separate themselves from the sympathies of men, and indulge in arbitrary and capricious habits of expression, in order to furnish food for fickle tastes, and fickle appetites, of their own creation.[3]

I cannot, however, be insensible of the present outcry against the triviality and meanness both of thought and language, which some of my contemporaries have occasionally introduced into their metrical compositions; and I acknowledge, that this defect, where it exists, is more dishonorable to the writer's own character than false refinement or arbitrary innovation, though I should contend at the same time that it is far less pernicious in the sum of its consequences. From such verses the poems in these volumes will be found distinguished at least by one mark of difference, that each of them has a worthy *purpose*. Not that I mean to say, that I always began to write with a distinct purpose formally conceived; but I believe that my habits of meditation have so formed my feelings, as that my descriptions of such objects as strongly excite those feelings, will be found to carry along with them a *purpose*. If in this opinion I am mistaken, I can have little right to the name of a poet. For all good poetry is the spontaneous overflow of powerful feelings: but though this be true, poems to which any value can be attached, were never produced on any variety of subjects but by a man who, being possessed of more than usual organic sensibility, had also thought long

3. It is worthwhile here to observe that the affecting parts of Chaucer are almost always expressed in language pure and universally intelligible even to this day [Wordsworth's note].

and deeply. For our continued influxes of feeling are modified and directed by our thoughts, which are indeed the representatives of all our past feelings; and, as by contemplating the relation of these general representatives to each other we discover what is really important to men, so, by the repetition and continuance of this act, our feelings will be connected with important subjects, till at length, if we be originally possessed of much sensibility, such habits of mind will be produced, that, by obeying blindly and mechanically the impulses of those habits, we shall describe objects, and utter sentiments, of such a nature and in such connection with each other, that the understanding of the being to whom we address ourselves, if he be in a healthful state of association, must necessarily be in some degree enlightened, and his affections ameliorated.

I have said that each of these poems has a purpose. I have also informed my reader what this purpose will be found principally to be: namely, to illustrate the manner in which our feelings and ideas are associated in a state of excitement. But, speaking in language somewhat more appropriate, it is to follow the fluxes and refluxes of the mind when agitated by the great and simple affections of our nature. This object I have endeavored in these short essays to attain by various means; by tracing the maternal passion through many of its more subtile[4] windings, as in the poems of the *Idiot Boy* and the *Mad Mother*; by accompanying the last struggles of a human being, at the approach of death, cleaving in solitude to life and society, as in the poem of the *Forsaken Indian*; by shewing, as in the stanzas entitled *We Are Seven*, the perplexity and obscurity which in childhood attend our notion of death, or rather our utter inability to admit that notion; or by displaying the strength of fraternal, or to speak more philosophically, of moral attachment when early associated with the great and beautiful objects of nature, as in *The Brothers*; or, as in the Incident of *Simon Lee*, by placing my reader in the way of receiving from ordinary moral sensations another and more salutary impression than we are accustomed to receive from them. It has also been part of my general purpose to attempt to sketch characters under the influence of less impassioned feelings, as in the *Two April Mornings, The Fountain, The Old Man Travelling, The Two Thieves*, &c., characters of which the elements are simple, belonging rather to nature than to manners,[5] such as exist now, and will probably always exist, and which from their constitution may be distinctly and profitably contemplated. I will not abuse the indulgence of my reader by dwelling longer upon this subject; but it is proper that I should mention one other circumstance which distinguishes these poems from the popular poetry of the day; it is this, that the feeling therein developed gives importance to the action and situation, and not the action and situation to the feeling. My meaning will be rendered perfectly intelligible by referring my reader to the poems entitled *Poor Susan* and the *Childless Father*, particularly to the last stanza of the latter poem.

I will not suffer a sense of false modesty to prevent me from asserting, that I point my reader's attention to this mark of distinction, far less for the sake of these particular poems than from the general importance of the subject. The subject is indeed important! For the human mind is capable of being excited without the application of gross[6] and violent stimulants; and he must have a very faint perception of its beauty and dignity who does not

4. Subtle.
5. Social custom.

6. Coarse.

know this, and who does not further know, that one being is elevated above another, in proportion as he possesses this capability. It has therefore appeared to me, that to endeavour to produce or enlarge this capability is one of the best services in which, at any period, a writer can be engaged; but this service, excellent at all times, is especially so at the present day. For a multitude of causes, unknown to former times, are now acting with a combined force to blunt the discriminating powers of the mind, and, unfitting it for all voluntary exertion, to reduce it to a state of almost savage torpor. The most effective of these causes are the great national events which are daily taking place, and the increasing accumulation of men in cities, where the uniformity of their occupations produces a craving for extraordinary incident, which the rapid communication of intelligence hourly gratifies.[7] To this tendency of life and manners the literature and theatrical exhibitions of the country have conformed themselves. The invaluable works of our elder writers, I had almost said the works of Shakespeare and Milton, are driven into neglect by frantic novels, sickly and stupid German tragedies,[8] and deluges of idle and extravagant stories in verse.—When I think upon this degrading thirst after outrageous stimulation, I am almost ashamed to have spoken of the feeble effort with which I have endeavoured to counteract it; and, reflecting upon the magnitude of the general evil, I should be oppressed with no dishonorable melancholy, had I not a deep impression of certain inherent and indestructible qualities of the human mind, and likewise of certain powers in the great and permanent objects that act upon it which are equally inherent and indestructible; and did I not further add to this impression a belief, that the time is approaching when the evil will be systematically opposed, by men of greater powers, and with far more distinguished success.

Having dwelt thus long on the subjects and aim of these poems, I shall request the reader's permission to apprize him of a few circumstances relating to their *style*, in order, among other reasons, that I may not be censured for not having performed what I never attempted. The reader will find that personifications of abstract ideas[9] rarely occur in these volumes; and, I hope, are utterly rejected as an ordinary device to elevate the style, and raise it above prose. I have proposed to myself to imitate, and, as far as is possible, to adopt the very language of men; and assuredly such personifications do not make any natural or regular part of that language. They are, indeed, a figure of speech occasionally prompted by passion, and I have made use of them as such; but I have endeavoured utterly to reject them as a mechanical device of style, or as a family language which writers in metre seem to lay claim to by prescription. I have wished to keep my reader in the company of flesh and blood, persuaded that by so doing I shall interest him. I am, however, well aware that others who pursue a different track may interest him likewise; I do not interfere with their claim, I only wish to prefer a different claim of my own. There will also be found in these volumes little of what is usually called poetic diction;[1] I have taken as much pains to avoid it as others ordinarily take to produce it; this I have done for the reason already alleged,

7. This was the period of the wars against France, of industrial urbanization, and of the rapid proliferation in England of daily newspapers.
8. Wordsworth had in mind the "Gothic" terror novels by writers such as Ann Radcliffe and Matthew Gregory Lewis and the sentimental melodrama, then immensely popular in England, of August von Kotzebue and his German

contemporaries.
9. This practice was common in 18th-century poetry.
1. In the sense of words, phrases, and figures of speech not commonly used in conversation or prose that are regarded as especially appropriate to poetry.

to bring my language near to the language of men, and further, because the pleasure which I have proposed to myself to impart is of a kind very different from that which is supposed by many persons to be the proper object of poetry. I do not know how, without being culpably particular, I can give my reader a more exact notion of the style in which I wished these poems to be written than by informing him that I have at all times endeavoured to look steadily at my subject, consequently, I hope that there is in these poems little falsehood of description, and that my ideas are expressed in language fitted to their respective importance. Something I must have gained by this practice, as it is friendly to one property of all good poetry, namely, good sense; but it has necessarily cut me off from a large portion of phrases and figures of speech which from father to son have long been regarded as the common inheritance of poets. I have also thought it expedient to restrict myself still further, having abstained from the use of many expressions, in themselves proper and beautiful, but which have been foolishly repeated by bad poets, till such feelings of disgust are connected with them as it is scarcely possible by any art of association to overpower.

If in a poem there should be found a series of lines, or even a single line, in which the language, though naturally arranged and according to the strict laws of metre, does not differ from that of prose, there is a numerous class of critics, who, when they stumble upon these prosaisms as they call them, imagine that they have made a notable discovery, and exult over the poet as over a man ignorant of his own profession. Now these men would establish a canon of criticism which the reader will conclude he must utterly reject, if he wishes to be pleased with these volumes. And it would be a most easy task to prove to him, that not only the language of a large portion of every good poem, even of the most elevated character, must necessarily, except with reference to the metre, in no respect differ from that of good prose, but likewise that some of the most interesting parts of the best poems will be found to be strictly the language of prose, when prose is well written. The truth of this assertion might be demonstrated by innumerable passages from almost all the poetical writings, even of Milton himself. I have not space for much quotation; but, to illustrate the subject in a general manner, I will here adduce a short composition of Gray, who was at the head of those who by their reasonings have attempted to widen the space of separation betwixt prose and metrical composition, and was more than any other man curiously elaborate in the structure of his own poetic diction.[2]

> In vain to me the smiling mornings shine,
> And reddening Phoebus lifts his golden fire:
> The birds in vain their amorous descant join,
> Or cheerful fields resume their green attire:
> These ears, alas! for other notes repine;
> *A different object do these eyes require;*
> *My lonely anguish melts no heart but mine;*
> *And in my breast the imperfect joys expire;*
> Yet Morning smiles the busy race to cheer,
> And new-born pleasure brings to happier men;

2. Thomas Gray (author in 1751 of the "Elegy Written in a Country Churchyard") had written, in a letter to Richard West, that "the language of the age is never the language of poetry." The poem that follows is Gray's "Sonnet on the Death of Richard West."

The fields to all their wonted tribute bear;
To warm their little loves the birds complain.
I fruitless mourn to him that cannot hear
And weep the more because I weep in vain.

It will easily be perceived that the only part of this sonnet which is of any value is the lines printed in italics: it is equally obvious, that, except in the rhyme, and in the use of the single word "fruitless" for fruitlessly, which is so far a defect, the language of these lines does in no respect differ from that of prose.

By the foregoing quotation I have shewn that the language of prose may yet be well adapted to poetry; and I have previously asserted that a large portion of the language of every good poem can in no respect differ from that of good prose. I will go further. I do not doubt that it may be safely affirmed, that there neither is, nor can be, any essential difference between the language of prose and metrical composition. We are fond of tracing the resemblance between poetry and painting, and, accordingly, we call them sisters: but where shall we find bonds of connection sufficiently strict to typify the affinity betwixt metrical and prose composition? They both speak by and to the same organs; the bodies in which both of them are clothed may be said to be of the same substance, their affections are kindred and almost identical, not necessarily differing even in degree; poetry[3] sheds no tears "such as Angels weep,"[4] but natural and human tears; she can boast of no celestial ichor[5] that distinguishes her vital juices from those of prose; the same human blood circulates through the veins of them both.

* * *

["WHAT IS A POET?"]

Taking up the subject, then, upon general grounds, I ask what is meant by the word "poet"? What is a poet? To whom does he address himself? And what language is to be expected from him? He is a man speaking to men: a man, it is true, endued with more lively sensibility, more enthusiasm and tenderness, who has a greater knowledge of human nature, and a more comprehensive soul, than are supposed to be common among mankind; a man pleased with his own passions and volitions, and who rejoices more than other men in the spirit of life that is in him; delighting to contemplate similar volitions and passions as manifested in the goings-on of the universe, and habitually impelled to create them where he does not find them. To these qualities he has added a disposition to be affected more than other men by absent things as if they were present; an ability of conjuring up in himself passions, which are indeed far from being the same as those produced by real events, yet (especially in those parts of the general sympathy which are pleasing and delightful) do more nearly resemble the passions produced by real events, than any thing which, from the motions of their

---

3. I here use the word "poetry" (though against my own judgment) as opposed to the word "prose," and synonymous with metrical composition. But much confusion has been introduced into criticism by this contradistinction of poetry and prose, instead of the more philosophical one of poetry and matter of fact, or science. The only strict antithesis to prose is metre; nor is this, in truth, a *strict* antithesis; because lines and passages of metre so naturally occur in writing prose, that it would be scarcely possible to avoid them, even were it desirable [Wordsworth's note].
4. Milton's *Paradise Lost* 1.620.
5. In Greek mythology the fluid in the veins of the gods.

own minds merely, other men are accustomed to feel in themselves; whence, and from practice, he has acquired a greater readiness and power in expressing what he thinks and feels, and especially those thoughts and feelings which, by his own choice, or from the structure of his own mind, arise in him without immediate external excitement.

But, whatever portion of this faculty we may suppose even the greatest poet to possess, there cannot be a doubt but that the language which it will suggest to him, must, in liveliness and truth, fall far short of that which is uttered by men in real life, under the actual pressure of those passions, certain shadows of which the poet thus produces, or feels to be produced, in himself. However exalted a notion we would wish to cherish of the character of a poet, it is obvious, that, while he describes and imitates passions, his situation is altogether slavish and mechanical, compared with the freedom and power of real and substantial action and suffering. So that it will be the wish of the poet to bring his feelings near to those of the persons whose feelings he describes, nay, for short spaces of time perhaps, to let himself slip into an entire delusion, and even confound and identify his own feelings with theirs; modifying only the language which is thus suggested to him, by a consideration that he describes for a particular purpose, that of giving pleasure. Here, then, he will apply the principle on which I have so much insisted, namely, that of selection; on this he will depend for removing what would otherwise be painful or disgusting in the passion; he will feel that there is no necessity to trick out[6] or to elevate nature: and, the more industriously he applies this principle, the deeper will be his faith that no words, which his fancy or imagination can suggest, will be to be compared with those which are the emanations of reality and truth.

But it may be said by those who do not object to the general spirit of these remarks, that, as it is impossible for the poet to produce upon all occasions language as exquisitely fitted for the passion as that which the real passion itself suggests, it is proper that he should consider himself as in the situation of a translator, who deems himself justified when he substitutes excellences of another kind for those which are unattainable by him; and endeavours occasionally to surpass his original, in order to make some amends for the general inferiority to which he feels that he must submit. But this would be to encourage idleness and unmanly despair. Further, it is the language of men who speak of what they do not understand; who talk of poetry as a matter of amusement and idle pleasure; who will converse with us as gravely about a *taste* for poetry, as they express it, as if it were a thing as indifferent as a taste for rope-dancing, or Frontiniac[7] or sherry. Aristotle, I have been told, hath said, that poetry is the most philosophic of all writing;[8] it is so: its object is truth, not individual and local, but general, and operative; not standing upon external testimony, but carried alive into the heart by passion; truth which is its own testimony, which gives strength and divinity to the tribunal to which it appeals, and receives them from the same tribunal. Poetry is the image of man and nature. The obstacles which stand in the way of the fidelity of the biographer and historian, and of their consequent utility, are incalculably greater than those which are to be encountered by the poet who has an adequate notion of the dignity of his art. The poet writes under one restriction only, namely, that of the necessity of giving

6. Dress up.
7. A sweet wine made from muscat grapes.
8. Aristotle in fact said that "poetry is more philosophic than history, since its statements are of the nature of universals, whereas those of history are singulars" (*Poetics* 1451b).

immediate pleasure to a human being possessed of that information which may be expected from him, not as a lawyer, a physician, a mariner, an astronomer or a natural philosopher, but as a man. Except this one restriction, there is no object standing between the poet and the image of things; between this, and the biographer and historian there are a thousand.

Nor let this necessity of producing immediate pleasure be considered as a degradation of the poet's art. It is far otherwise. It is an acknowledgment of the beauty of the universe, an acknowledgment the more sincere because it is not formal, but indirect; it is a task light and easy to him who looks at the world in the spirit of love: further, it is a homage paid to the native and naked dignity of man, to the grand elementary principle of pleasure, by which he knows, and feels, and lives, and moves.[9] We have no sympathy but what is propagated by pleasure: I would not be misunderstood; but wherever we sympathize with pain it will be found that the sympathy is produced and carried on by subtle combinations with pleasure. We have no knowledge, that is, no general principles drawn from the contemplation of particular facts, but what has been built up by pleasure, and exists in us by pleasure alone. The man of science, the chemist and mathematician, whatever difficulties and disgusts they may have had to struggle with, know and feel this. However painful may be the objects with which the anatomist's knowledge is connected, he feels that his knowledge is pleasure; and where he has no pleasure he has no knowledge. What then does the poet? He considers man and the objects that surround him as acting and re-acting upon each other, so as to produce an infinite complexity of pain and pleasure; he considers man in his own nature and in his ordinary life as contemplating this with a certain quantity of immediate knowledge, with certain convictions, intuitions, and deductions which by habit become of the nature of intuitions; he considers him as looking upon this complex scene of ideas and sensations, and finding every where objects that immediately excite in him sympathies which, from the necessities of his nature, are accompanied by an overbalance of enjoyment.

To this knowledge which all men carry about with them, and to these sympathies in which without any other discipline than that of our daily life we are fitted to take delight, the poet principally directs his attention. He considers man and nature as essentially adapted to each other, and the mind of man as naturally the mirror of the fairest and most interesting qualities of nature. And thus the poet, prompted by this feeling of pleasure which accompanies him through the whole course of his studies, converses with general nature with affections akin to those, which, through labour and length of time, the man of science has raised up in himself, by conversing with those particular parts of nature which are the objects of his studies. The knowledge both of the poet and the man of science is pleasure; but the knowledge of the one cleaves to us as a necessary part of our existence, our natural and unalienable inheritance; the other is a personal and individual acquisition, slow to come to us, and by no habitual and direct sympathy connecting us with our fellow-beings. The man of science seeks truth as a remote and unknown benefactor; he cherishes and loves it in his solitude: the poet, singing a song in which all human beings join with him, rejoices in the presence of truth as our visible friend and hourly companion. Poetry is the breath and finer spirit of all knowledge; it is the impassioned expression which is in the countenance of all science. Emphatically may it be said

9. A bold echo of the words of St. Paul, that in God "we live, and move, and have our being" (Acts 17.28).

of the poet, as Shakespeare hath said of man, "that he looks before and after."[1] He is the rock of defence of human nature; an upholder and preserver, carrying everywhere with him relationship and love. In spite of difference of soil and climate, of language and manners, of laws and customs, in spite of things silently gone out of mind and things violently destroyed, the poet binds together by passion and knowledge the vast empire of human society, as it is spread over the whole earth, and over all time. The objects of the poet's thoughts are every where; though the eyes and senses of man are, it is true, his favorite guides, yet he will follow wheresoever he can find an atmosphere of sensation in which to move his wings. Poetry is the first and last of all knowledge—it is as immortal as the heart of man. If the labours of men of science should ever create any material revolution, direct or indirect, in our condition, and in the impressions which we habitually receive, the poet will sleep then no more than at present, but he will be ready to follow the steps of the man of science, not only in those general indirect effects, but he will be at his side, carrying sensation into the midst of the objects of the science itself. The remotest discoveries of the chemist, the botanist, or mineralogist, will be as proper objects of the poet's art as any upon which it can be employed, if the time should ever come when these things shall be familiar to us, and the relations under which they are contemplated by the followers of these respective sciences shall be manifestly and palpably material to us as enjoying and suffering beings. If the time should ever come when what is now called science, thus familiarized to men, shall be ready to put on, as it were, a form of flesh and blood, the poet will lend his divine spirit to aid the transfiguration, and will welcome the being thus produced, as a dear and genuine inmate of the household of man.—It is not, then, to be supposed that any one, who holds that sublime notion of poetry which I have attempted to convey, will break in upon the sanctity and truth of his pictures by transitory and accidental ornaments, and endeavour to excite admiration of himself by arts, the necessity of which must manifestly depend upon the assumed meanness of his subject.

What I have thus far said applies to poetry in general; but especially to those parts of composition where the poet speaks through the mouth of his characters; and upon this point it appears to have such weight that I will conclude, there are few persons, of good sense, who would not allow that the dramatic parts of composition are defective, in proportion as they deviate from the real language of nature, and are coloured by a diction of the poet's own, either peculiar to him as an individual poet, or belonging simply to poets in general, to a body of men who, from the circumstance of their compositions being in metre, it is expected will employ a particular language.

It is not, then, in the dramatic parts of composition that we look for this distinction of language; but still it may be proper and necessary where the poet speaks to us in his own person and character. To this I answer by referring my reader to the description which I have before given of a poet. Among the qualities which I have enumerated as principally conducing to form a poet, is implied nothing differing in kind from other men, but only in degree. The sum of what I have there said is, that the poet is chiefly distinguished from other men by a greater promptness to think and feel without immediate external excitement, and a greater power in expressing such thoughts and feelings as are produced in him in that manner. But these passions and

1. Cf. Shakespeare's *Hamlet* 4.4.9.27.

thoughts and feelings are the general passions and thoughts and feelings of men. And with what are they connected? Undoubtedly with our moral senti-ments and animal sensations, and with the causes which excite these; with the operations of the elements and the appearances of the visible universe; with storm and sunshine, with the revolutions[2] of the seasons, with cold and heat, with loss of friends and kindred, with injuries and resentments, grati-tude and hope, with fear and sorrow. These, and the like, are the sensations and objects which the poet describes, as they are the sensations of other men, and the objects which interest them. The poet thinks and feels in the spirit of the passions of men. How, then, can his language differ in any material degree from that of all other men who feel vividly and see clearly? It might be *proved* that it is impossible. But supposing that this were not the case, the poet might then be allowed to use a peculiar language, when expressing his feelings for his own gratification, or that of men like himself. But poets do not write for poets alone, but for men. Unless therefore we are advocates for that admiration which depends upon ignorance, and that pleasure which arises from hearing what we do not understand, the poet must descend from this supposed height, and, in order to excite rational sympathy, he must express himself as other men express themselves. * * *

["EMOTION RECOLLECTED IN TRANQUILLITY"]

I have said that poetry is the spontaneous overflow of powerful feelings: it takes its origin from emotion recollected in tranquillity: the emotion is con-templated till by a species of reaction the tranquillity gradually disappears, and an emotion, kindred to that which was before the subject of contempla-tion, is gradually produced, and does itself actually exist in the mind. In this mood successful composition generally begins, and in a mood similar to this it is carried on; but the emotion, of whatever kind and in whatever degree, from various causes is qualified by various pleasures, so that in describing any passions whatsoever, which are voluntarily described, the mind will upon the whole be in a state of enjoyment. Now, if nature be thus cautious in preserving in a state of enjoyment a being thus employed, the poet ought to profit by the lesson thus held forth to him, and ought especially to take care, that whatever passions he communicates to his reader, those passions, if his reader's mind be sound and vigorous, should always be accom-panied with an overbalance of pleasure. Now the music of harmonious metrical language, the sense of difficulty overcome, and the blind association of pleasure which has been previously received from works of rhyme or metre of the same or similar construction, an indistinct perception perpet-ually renewed of language closely resembling that of real life, and yet, in the circumstance of metre, differing from it so widely, all these impercepti-bly make up a complex feeling of delight, which is of the most important use in tempering the painful feeling which will always be found intermin-gled with powerful descriptions of the deeper passions. This effect is always produced in pathetic and impassioned poetry; while, in lighter composi-tions, the ease and gracefulness with which the poet manages his numbers are themselves confessedly a principal source of the gratification of the reader. I might perhaps include all which it is *necessary* to say upon this sub-ject by affirming, what few persons will deny, that, of two descriptions, either of passions, manners, or characters, each of them equally well executed, the

2. Recurrence.

one in prose and the other in verse, the verse will be read a hundred times where the prose is read once. * * *

I know that nothing would have so effectually contributed to further the end which I have in view, as to have shewn of what kind the pleasure is, and how the pleasure is produced, which is confessedly produced by metrical composition essentially different from that which I have here endeavoured to recommend: for the reader will say that he has been pleased by such composition; and what can I do more for him? The power of any art is limited; and he will suspect, that, if I propose to furnish him with new friends, it is only upon condition of his abandoning his old friends. Besides, as I have said, the reader is himself conscious of the pleasure which he has received from such composition, composition to which he has peculiarly attached the endearing name of poetry; and all men feel an habitual gratitude, and something of an honorable bigotry for the objects which have long continued to please them: we not only wish to be pleased, but to be pleased in that particular way in which we have been accustomed to be pleased. There is a host of arguments in these feelings; and I should be the less able to combat them successfully, as I am willing to allow, that, in order entirely to enjoy the poetry which I am recommending, it would be necessary to give up much of what is ordinarily enjoyed. But, would my limits have permitted me to point out how this pleasure is produced, I might have removed many obstacles, and assisted my reader in perceiving that the powers of language are not so limited as he may suppose; and that it is possible that poetry may give other enjoyments, of a purer, more lasting, and more exquisite nature. This part of my subject I have not altogether neglected; but it has been less my present aim to prove, that the interest excited by some other kinds of poetry is less vivid, and less worthy of the nobler powers of the mind, than to offer reasons for presuming, that, if the object which I have proposed to myself were adequately attained, a species of poetry would be produced, which is genuine poetry; in its nature well adapted to interest mankind permanently, and likewise important in the multiplicity and quality of its moral relations.

From what has been said, and from a perusal of the poems, the reader will be able clearly to perceive the object which I have proposed to myself: he will determine how far I have attained this object; and, what is a much more important question, whether it be worth attaining; and upon the decision of these two questions will rest my claim to the approbation of the public.

1800, 1802

Strange fits of passion have I known[1]

Strange fits of passion have I known:
And I will dare to tell,
But in the Lover's ear alone,
What once to me befel.

---

1. This and the four following pieces are often grouped by editors as the "Lucy poems," even though "A slumber did my spirit seal" does not identify the "she" who is the subject of that poem. All but the last were written in 1799, while Wordsworth and his sister were in Germany and homesick.

5 When she I loved looked every day
 Fresh as a rose in June,
 I to her cottage bent my way,
 Beneath an evening moon.

 Upon the moon I fixed my eye,
10 All over the wide lea;
 With quickening pace my horse drew nigh
 Those paths so dear to me.

 And now we reached the orchard-plot;
 And, as we climbed the hill,
15 The sinking moon to Lucy's cot
 Came near, and nearer still.

 In one of those sweet dreams I slept,
 Kind Nature's gentlest boon!
 And all the while my eyes I kept
20 On the descending moon.

 My horse moved on; hoof after hoof
 He raised, and never stopped:
 When down behind the cottage roof,
 At once, the bright moon dropped.

25 What fond and wayward thoughts will slide
 Into a Lover's head!
 "O mercy!" to myself I cried,
 "If Lucy should be dead!"[2]

1799   1800

She dwelt among the untrodden ways[1]

 She dwelt among the untrodden ways
  Beside the springs of Dove,[2]
 A Maid whom there were none to praise
  And very few to love:

5 A violet by a mossy stone
  Half hidden from the eye!
 —Fair as a star, when only one
  Is shining in the sky.

 She lived unknown, and few could know
10 When Lucy ceased to be;

---

2. An additional stanza in an earlier manuscript version demonstrates how a poem can be improved by omission of a passage that is, in itself, excellent poetry: "I told her this: her laughter light / Is ringing in my ears; / And when I think upon that night / My eyes are dim with tears."

1. For the author's revisions while composing this poem, see "Poems in Process," in the supplemental ebook.
2. There are several rivers by this name in England, including one in the Lake District.

But she is in her grave, and, oh,
The difference to me!

1799   1800

Three years she grew

Three years she grew in sun and shower,
Then Nature said, "A lovelier flower
On earth was never sown;
This Child I to myself will take;
5   She shall be mine, and I will make
A Lady of my own.[1]

"Myself will to my darling be
Both law and impulse: and with me
The Girl, in rock and plain,
10   In earth and heaven, in glade and bower,
Shall feel an overseeing power
To kindle or restrain.

"She shall be sportive as the fawn
That wild with glee across the lawn
15   Or up the mountain springs;
And hers shall be the breathing balm,
And hers the silence and the calm
Of mute insensate things.

"The floating clouds their state shall lend
20   To her; for her the willow bend;
Nor shall she fail to see
Even in the motions of the Storm
Grace that shall mould the Maiden's form
By silent sympathy.

25   "The stars of midnight shall be dear
To her; and she shall lean her ear
In many a secret place
Where rivulets dance their wayward round,
And beauty born of murmuring sound
30   Shall pass into her face.

"And vital feelings of delight
Shall rear her form to stately height,
Her virgin bosom swell;
Such thoughts to Lucy I will give
35   While she and I together live
Here in this happy dell."

Thus Nature spake—the work was done—
How soon my Lucy's race was run!

---

1. I.e., Lucy was three years old when Nature made this promise; line 37 makes clear that Lucy had reached the maturity foretold in the sixth stanza when she died.

She died, and left to me
40 This heath, this calm, and quiet scene;
The memory of what has been,
And never more will be.

1799   1800

A slumber did my spirit seal

A slumber did my spirit seal;
  I had no human fears:
She seemed a thing that could not feel
  The touch of earthly years.

5 No motion has she now, no force;
  She neither hears nor sees;
Rolled round in earth's diurnal° course,   *daily*
  With rocks, and stones, and trees.

1799   1800

I travelled among unknown men

I travelled among unknown men,
  In lands beyond the sea;
Nor, England! did I know till then
  What love I bore to thee.

5 'Tis past, that melancholy dream!
  Nor will I quit thy shore
A second time; for still I seem
  To love thee more and more.

Among thy mountains did I feel
10   The joy of my desire;
And she I cherished turned her wheel
  Beside an English fire.

Thy mornings showed, thy nights concealed
  The bowers where Lucy played;
15 And thine too is the last green field
  That Lucy's eyes surveyed.

ca. 1801   1807

Nutting[1]

——————————It seems a day
(I speak of one from many singled out)

---

1. Wordsworth said in 1843 that these lines, written in Germany in 1798, were "intended as part of a poem on my own life [*The Prelude*], but struck out as not being wanted there." He published them in the second edition of *Lyrical Ballads*, 1800.

One of those heavenly days that cannot die;
When, in the eagerness of boyish hope,
5   I left our cottage-threshold, sallying forth
With a huge wallet° o'er my shoulder slung,   bag, knapsack
A nutting-crook in hand; and turned my steps
Tow'rd some far-distant wood, a Figure quaint,
Tricked out in proud disguise of cast-off weeds°   clothes
10   Which for that service had been husbanded,
By exhortation of my frugal Dame[2]—
Motley accoutrement, of power to smile
At thorns, and brakes,° and brambles,—and, in truth,   thickets of ferns
More ragged than need was! O'er pathless rocks,
15   Through beds of matted fern, and tangled thickets,
Forcing my way, I came to one dear nook
Unvisited, where not a broken bough
Drooped with its withered leaves, ungracious sign
Of devastation; but the hazels rose
20   Tall and erect, with tempting clusters hung,
A virgin scene!—A little while I stood,
Breathing with such suppression of the heart
As joy delights in; and, with wise restraint
Voluptuous, fearless of a rival, eyed
25   The banquet;—or beneath the trees I sate
Among the flowers, and with the flowers I played;
A temper known to those, who, after long
And weary expectation, have been blest
With sudden happiness beyond all hope.
30   Perhaps it was a bower beneath whose leaves
The violets of five seasons re-appear
And fade, unseen by any human eye;
Where fairy water-breaks[3] do murmur on
For ever; and I saw the sparkling foam,
35   And—with my cheek on one of those green stones
That, fleeced with moss, under the shady trees,
Lay round me, scattered like a flock of sheep—
I heard the murmur and the murmuring sound,
In that sweet mood when pleasure loves to pay
40   Tribute to ease; and, of its joy secure,
The heart luxuriates with indifferent things,
Wasting its kindliness on stocks[4] and stones,
And on the vacant air. Then up I rose,
And dragged to earth both branch and bough, with crash
45   And merciless ravage: and the shady nook
Of hazels, and the green and mossy bower,
Deformed and sullied, patiently gave up
Their quiet being: and, unless I now
Confound my present feelings with the past,
50   Ere from the mutilated bower I turned
Exulting, rich beyond the wealth of kings,

2. Ann Tyson, with whom Wordsworth lodged
while at Hawkshead grammar school.
3. Places where the flow of a stream is broken by
rocks.
4. Tree stumps. ("Stocks and stones" is a conventional expression for "inanimate things.")

I felt a sense of pain when I beheld
The silent trees, and saw the intruding sky.—
Then, dearest Maiden,[5] move along these shades
55   In gentleness of heart; with gentle hand
Touch—for there is a spirit in the woods.

1798   1800

The Ruined Cottage[1]

First Part

'Twas summer and the sun was mounted high.
Along the south the uplands feebly glared
Through a pale steam, and all the northern downs
In clearer air ascending shewed far off
5   Their surfaces with shadows dappled o'er
Of deep embattled clouds: far as the sight
Could reach those many shadows lay in spots
Determined and unmoved, with steady beams
Of clear and pleasant sunshine interposed;
10   Pleasant to him who on the soft cool moss
Extends his careless limbs beside the root
Of some huge oak whose aged branches make
A twilight of their own, a dewy shade
Where the wren warbles while the dreaming man,
15   Half-conscious of that soothing melody,
With side-long eye looks out upon the scene,
By those impending branches made more soft,
More soft and distant. Other lot was mine.
Across a bare wide Common I had toiled
20   With languid feet which by the slipp'ry ground
Were baffled still, and when I stretched myself
On the brown earth my limbs from very heat
Could find no rest nor my weak arm disperse
The insect host which gathered round my face
25   And joined their murmurs to the tedious noise
Of seeds of bursting gorse that crackled round.
I rose and turned towards a group of trees
Which midway in that level stood alone,
And thither come at length, beneath a shade
30   Of clustering elms that sprang from the same root
I found a ruined house, four naked walls
That stared upon each other. I looked round
And near the door I saw an aged Man,
Alone, and stretched upon the cottage bench;

5. In a manuscript passage originally intended to lead up to "Nutting," the maiden is called Lucy.
1. Wordsworth wrote *The Ruined Cottage* in 1797–98, then revised it several times before he finally published an expanded version of the story as book 1 of *The Excursion*, in 1814. *The Ruined Cottage* was not published as an independent poem until 1949, when it appeared in the fifth volume of *The Poetical Works of William Wordsworth*, edited by Ernest de Selincourt and Helen Darbishire, who printed a version known as "MS. B." The text reprinted here is from "MS. D," dated 1799, as transcribed by James Butler in the Cornell Wordsworth volume, *"The Ruined Cottage" and "The Pedlar"* (1979).

35 An iron-pointed staff lay at his side.
With instantaneous joy I recognized
That pride of nature and of lowly life,
The venerable Armytage, a friend
As dear to me as is the setting sun.
40   Two days before
We had been fellow-travellers. I knew
That he was in this neighbourhood and now
Delighted found him here in the cool shade.
He lay, his pack of rustic merchandize
45 Pillowing his head—I guess he had no thought
Of his way-wandering life. His eyes were shut;
The shadows of the breezy elms above
Dappled his face. With thirsty heat oppress'd
At length I hailed him, glad to see his hat
50 Bedewed with water-drops, as if the brim
Had newly scoop'd a running stream. He rose
And pointing to a sun-flower bade me climb
The [   ]² wall where that same gaudy flower
Looked out upon the road. It was a plot
55 Of garden-ground, now wild, its matted weeds
Marked with the steps of those whom as they pass'd,
The goose-berry trees that shot in long lank slips,
Or currants hanging from their leafless stems
In scanty strings, had tempted to o'erleap
60 The broken wall. Within that cheerless spot,
Where two tall hedgerows of thick willow boughs
Joined in a damp cold nook, I found a well
Half-choked [with willow flowers and weeds.]³
I slaked my thirst and to the shady bench
65 Returned, and while I stood unbonneted
To catch the motion of the cooler air
The old Man said, "I see around me here
Things which you cannot see: we die, my Friend,
Nor we alone, but that which each man loved
70 And prized in his peculiar nook of earth
Dies with him or is changed, and very soon
Even of the good is no memorial left.
The Poets in their elegies and songs
Lamenting the departed call the groves,
75 They call upon the hills and streams to mourn,
And senseless⁴ rocks, nor idly; for they speak
In these their invocations with a voice
Obedient to the strong creative power
Of human passion. Sympathies there are
80 More tranquil, yet perhaps of kindred birth,
That steal upon the meditative mind
And grow with thought. Beside yon spring I stood
And eyed its waters till we seemed to feel
One sadness, they and I. For them a bond
85 Of brotherhood is broken: time has been

2. The brackets here and in later lines mark
blank spaces left unfilled in the manuscript.
3. Wordsworth penciled the bracketed phrase
into a gap left in the manuscript.
4. Incapable of sensation or perception.

When every day the touch of human hand
Disturbed their stillness, and they ministered
To human comfort. When I stooped to drink,
A spider's web hung to the water's edge,
90   And on the wet and slimy foot-stone lay
The useless fragment of a wooden bowl;
It moved my very heart. The day has been
When I could never pass this road but she
Who lived within these walls, when I appeared,
95   A daughter's welcome gave me, and I loved her
As my own child. O Sir! the good die first,
And they whose hearts are dry as summer dust
Burn to the socket. Many a passenger°   *passerby, traveler*
Has blessed poor Margaret for her gentle looks
100   When she upheld the cool refreshment drawn
From that forsaken spring, and no one came
But he was welcome, no one went away
But that it seemed she loved him. She is dead,
The worm is on her cheek, and this poor hut,
105   Stripp'd of its outward garb of household flowers,
Of rose and sweet-briar, offers to the wind
A cold bare wall whose earthy top is tricked
With weeds and the rank spear-grass. She is dead,
And nettles rot and adders sun themselves
110   Where we have sate together while she nurs'd
Her infant at her breast. The unshod Colt,
The wandring heifer and the Potter's ass,
Find shelter now within the chimney-wall
Where I have seen her evening hearth-stone blaze
115   And through the window spread upon the road
Its chearful light.—You will forgive me, Sir,
But often on this cottage do I muse
As on a picture, till my wiser mind
Sinks, yielding to the foolishness of grief.
120   She had a husband, an industrious man,
Sober and steady; I have heard her say
That he was up and busy at his loom
In summer ere the mower's scythe had swept
The dewy grass, and in the early spring
125   Ere the last star had vanished. They who pass'd
At evening, from behind the garden-fence
Might hear his busy spade, which he would ply
After his daily work till the day-light
Was gone and every leaf and flower were lost
130   In the dark hedges. So they pass'd their days
In peace and comfort, and two pretty babes
Were their best hope next to the God in Heaven.
—You may remember, now some ten years gone,
Two blighting seasons when the fields were left
135   With half a harvest.⁵ It pleased heaven to add

5. As James Butler points out in his introduction, Wordsworth is purposely distancing his
story in time. The "two blighting seasons" in fact
occurred in 1794–95, only a few years before
Wordsworth wrote *The Ruined Cottage*, when a
bad harvest was followed by one of the worst
winters on record.

A worse affliction in the plague of war:
A happy land was stricken to the heart;
'Twas a sad time of sorrow and distress:
A wanderer among the cottages,
140 I with my pack of winter raiment saw
The hardships of that season: many rich
Sunk down as in a dream among the poor,
And of the poor did many cease to be,
And their place knew them not. Meanwhile, abridg'd°   *deprived*
145 Of daily comforts, gladly reconciled
To numerous self-denials, Margaret
Went struggling on through those calamitous years
With chearful hope: but ere the second autumn
A fever seized her husband. In disease
150 He lingered long, and when his strength returned
He found the little he had stored to meet
The hour of accident or crippling age
Was all consumed. As I have said, 'twas now
A time of trouble; shoals of artisans
155 Were from their daily labour turned away
To hang for bread on parish charity,[6]
They and their wives and children—happier far
Could they have lived as do the little birds
That peck along the hedges or the kite
160 That makes her dwelling in the mountain rocks.
Ill fared it now with Robert, he who dwelt
In this poor cottage; at his door he stood
And whistled many a snatch of merry tunes
That had no mirth in them, or with his knife
165 Carved uncouth figures on the heads of sticks,
Then idly sought about through every nook
Of house or garden any casual task
Of use or ornament, and with a strange,
Amusing but uneasy novelty
170 He blended where he might the various tasks
Of summer, autumn, winter, and of spring.
But this endured not; his good-humour soon
Became a weight in which no pleasure was,
And poverty brought on a petted° mood   *ill-tempered*
175 And a sore temper: day by day he drooped,
And he would leave his home, and to the town
Without an errand would he turn his steps
Or wander here and there among the fields.
One while he would speak lightly of his babes
180 And with a cruel tongue: at other times
He played with them wild freaks of merriment:
And 'twas a piteous thing to see the looks
Of the poor innocent children. 'Every smile,'
Said Margaret to me here beneath these trees,
185 'Made my heart bleed.'" At this the old Man paus'd

---

6. The so-called able-bodied poor were entitled to receive from the parish in which they were settled the food, the clothing, and sometimes the cash that would help them over a crisis.

And looking up to those enormous elms
He said, "'Tis now the hour of deepest noon,
At this still season of repose and peace,
This hour when all things which are not at rest
190   Are chearful, while this multitude of flies
Fills all the air with happy melody,
Why should a tear be in an old man's eye?
Why should we thus with an untoward mind
And in the weakness of humanity
195   From natural wisdom turn our hearts away,
To natural comfort shut our eyes and ears,
And feeding on disquiet thus disturb
The calm of Nature with our restless thoughts?"

END OF THE FIRST PART

Second Part

He spake with somewhat of a solemn tone:
200   But when he ended there was in his face
Such easy chearfulness, a look so mild
That for a little time it stole away
All recollection, and that simple tale
Passed from my mind like a forgotten sound.
205   A while on trivial things we held discourse,
To me soon tasteless. In my own despite
I thought of that poor woman as of one
Whom I had known and loved. He had rehearsed
Her homely tale with such familiar power,
210   With such a[n active][7] countenance, an eye
So busy, that the things of which he spake
Seemed present, and, attention now relaxed,
There was a heartfelt chillness in my veins.
I rose, and turning from that breezy shade
215   Went out into the open air and stood
To drink the comfort of the warmer sun.
Long time I had not stayed ere, looking round
Upon that tranquil ruin, I returned
And begged of the old man that for my sake
220   He would resume his story. He replied,
"It were a wantonness° and would demand   *reckless ill-doing*
Severe reproof, if we were men whose hearts
Could hold vain dalliance with the misery
Even of the dead, contented thence to draw
225   A momentary pleasure never marked
By reason, barren of all future good.
But we have known that there is often found
In mournful thoughts, and always might be found,
A power to virtue friendly; were't not so,
230   I am a dreamer among men, indeed
An idle dreamer. 'Tis a common tale,

---

7. Wordsworth penciled the bracketed phrase into a gap left in the manuscript.

By moving accidents[8] uncharactered,
A tale of silent suffering, hardly clothed
In bodily form, and to the grosser sense
235 But ill adapted, scarcely palpable
To him who does not think. But at your bidding
I will proceed.
                              While thus it fared with them
To whom this cottage till that hapless year
Had been a blessed home, it was my chance
240 To travel in a country far remote,
And glad I was when, halting by yon gate
That leads from the green lane, again I saw
These lofty elm-trees. Long I did not rest:
With many pleasant thoughts I cheer'd my way
245 O'er the flat common. At the door arrived,
I knocked, and when I entered with the hope
Of usual greeting, Margaret looked at me
A little while, then turned her head away
Speechless, and sitting down upon a chair
250 Wept bitterly. I wist not what to do
Or how to speak to her. Poor wretch! at last
She rose from off her seat—and then, oh Sir!
I cannot tell how she pronounced my name:
With fervent love, and with a face of grief
255 Unutterably helpless, and a look
That seem'd to cling upon me, she enquir'd
If I had seen her husband. As she spake
A strange surprize and fear came to my heart,
Nor had I power to answer ere she told
260 That he had disappeared—just two months gone.
He left his house; two wretched days had passed,
And on the third by the first break of light,
Within her casement full in view she saw
A purse of gold.[9] 'I trembled at the sight,'
265 Said Margaret, 'for I knew it was his hand
That placed it there, and on that very day
By one, a stranger, from my husband sent,
The tidings came that he had joined a troop
Of soldiers going to a distant land.
270 He left me thus—Poor Man! he had not heart
To take a farewell of me, and he feared
That I should follow with my babes, and sink
Beneath the misery of a soldier's life.'
This tale did Margaret tell with many tears:
275 And when she ended I had little power
To give her comfort, and was glad to take
Such words of hope from her own mouth as serv'd
To cheer us both: but long we had not talked
Ere we built up a pile of better thoughts,

---

8. Othello speaks "of most disastrous chances, / Of moving accidents by flood and field, / Of hair- breadth 'scapes" (Shakespeare, *Othello* 1.3. 133–35).

9. The "bounty" that her husband had been paid for enlisting in the militia.

280 And with a brighter eye she looked around
As if she had been shedding tears of joy.
We parted. It was then the early spring;
I left her busy with her garden tools;
And well remember, o'er that fence she looked,
285 And while I paced along the foot-way path
Called out, and sent a blessing after me
With tender chearfulness and with a voice
That seemed the very sound of happy thoughts.
    I roved o'er many a hill and many a dale
290 With this my weary load, in heat and cold,
Through many a wood, and many an open ground,
In sunshine or in shade, in wet or fair,
Now blithe, now drooping, as it might befal,
My best companions now the driving winds
295 And now the 'trotting brooks'[1] and whispering trees
And now the music of my own sad steps,
With many a short-lived thought that pass'd between
And disappeared. I came this way again
Towards the wane of summer, when the wheat
300 Was yellow, and the soft and bladed grass
Sprang up afresh and o'er the hay-field spread
Its tender green. When I had reached the door
I found that she was absent. In the shade
Where now we sit I waited her return.
305 Her cottage in its outward look appeared
As chearful as before; in any shew
Of neatness little changed, but that I thought
The honeysuckle crowded round the door
And from the wall hung down in heavier wreathes,
310 And knots of worthless stone-crop[2] started out
Along the window's edge, and grew like weeds
Against the lower panes. I turned aside
And stroll'd into her garden.—It was chang'd:
The unprofitable bindweed spread his bells
315 From side to side and with unwieldy wreaths
Had dragg'd the rose from its sustaining wall
And bent it down to earth; the border-tufts—
Daisy and thrift and lowly camomile
And thyme—had straggled out into the paths
320 Which they were used° to deck. Ere this an hour   *accustomed*
Was wasted. Back I turned my restless steps,
And as I walked before the door it chanced
A stranger passed, and guessing whom I sought
He said that she was used to ramble far.
325 The sun was sinking in the west, and now
I sate with sad impatience. From within
Her solitary infant cried aloud.
The spot though fair seemed very desolate,
The longer I remained more desolate.

1. From Robert Burns ("To William Simpson," line 87).

2. A plant with yellow flowers that grows on walls and rocks.

330 And, looking round, I saw the corner-stones,
Till then unmark'd, on either side the door
With dull red stains discoloured and stuck o'er
With tufts and hairs of wool, as if the sheep
That feed upon the commons[3] thither came
335 Familiarly and found a couching-place
Even at her threshold.—The house-clock struck eight;
I turned and saw her distant a few steps.
Her face was pale and thin, her figure too
Was chang'd. As she unlocked the door she said,
340 'It grieves me you have waited here so long,
But in good truth I've wandered much of late
And sometimes, to my shame I speak, have need
Of my best prayers to bring me back again.'
While on the board she spread our evening meal
345 She told me she had lost her elder child,
That he for months had been a serving-boy
Apprenticed by the parish. 'I perceive
You look at me, and you have cause. Today
I have been travelling far, and many days
350 About the fields I wander, knowing this
Only, that what I seek I cannot find.
And so I waste my time: for I am changed;
And to myself,' said she, 'have done much wrong,
And to this helpless infant. I have slept
355 Weeping, and weeping I have waked; my tears
Have flow'd as if my body were not such
As others are, and I could never die.
But I am now in mind and in my heart
More easy, and I hope,' said she, 'that heaven
360 Will give me patience to endure the things
Which I behold at home.' It would have grieved
Your very heart to see her. Sir, I feel
The story linger in my heart. I fear
'Tis long and tedious, but my spirit clings
365 To that poor woman: so familiarly
Do I perceive her manner, and her look
And presence, and so deeply do I feel
Her goodness, that not seldom in my walks
A momentary trance comes over me;
370 And to myself I seem to muse on one
By sorrow laid asleep or borne away,
A human being destined to awake
To human life, or something very near
To human life, when he shall come again
375 For whom she suffered. Sir, it would have griev'd
Your very soul to see her: evermore
Her eye-lids droop'd, her eyes were downward cast;
And when she at her table gave me food
She did not look at me. Her voice was low,
380 Her body was subdued. In every act
Pertaining to her house-affairs appeared

3. Land belonging to the local community as a whole.

The careless stillness which a thinking mind
Gives to an idle matter—still she sighed,
But yet no motion of the breast was seen,
385 No heaving of the heart. While by the fire
We sate together, sighs came on my ear;
I knew not how, and hardly whence they came.
I took my staff, and when I kissed her babe
The tears stood in her eyes. I left her then
390 With the best hope and comfort I could give;
She thanked me for my will, but for my hope
It seemed she did not thank me.
                          I returned
And took my rounds along this road again
Ere on its sunny bank the primrose flower
395 Had chronicled the earliest day of spring.
I found her sad and drooping; she had learn'd
No tidings of her husband: if he lived
She knew not that he lived; if he were dead
She knew not he was dead. She seemed the same
400 In person [or][4] appearance, but her house
Bespoke a sleepy hand of negligence;
The floor was neither dry nor neat, the hearth
Was comfortless [   ],
The windows too were dim, and her few books,
405 Which, one upon the other, heretofore
Had been piled up against the corner-panes
In seemly order, now with straggling leaves
Lay scattered here and there, open or shut
As they had chanced to fall. Her infant babe
410 Had from its mother caught the trick of grief
And sighed among its playthings. Once again
I turned towards the garden-gate and saw
More plainly still that poverty and grief
Were now come nearer to her: the earth was hard,
415 With weeds defaced and knots of withered grass;
No ridges there appeared of clear black mould,
No winter greenness; of her herbs and flowers
It seemed the better part were gnawed away
Or trampled on the earth; a chain of straw
420 Which had been twisted round the tender stem
Of a young apple-tree lay at its root;
The bark was nibbled round by truant sheep.
Margaret stood near, her infant in her arms,
And seeing that my eye was on the tree
425 She said, 'I fear it will be dead and gone
Ere Robert come again.' Towards the house
Together we returned, and she inquired
If I had any hope. But for her Babe
And for her little friendless Boy, she said,
430 She had no wish to live, that she must die
Of sorrow. Yet I saw the idle loom
Still in its place. His Sunday garments hung

4. The word *or* was erased here; later manuscripts read "and."

Upon the self-same nail, his very staff
Stood undisturbed behind the door. And when
435 I passed this way beaten by Autumn winds
She told me that her little babe was dead
And she was left alone. That very time,
I yet remember, through the miry lane
She walked with me a mile, when the bare trees
440 Trickled with foggy damps, and in such sort
That any heart had ached to hear her begg'd
That wheresoe'er I went I still would ask
For him whom she had lost. We parted then,
Our final parting, for from that time forth
445 Did many seasons pass ere I returned
Into this tract again.
                              Five tedious years
She lingered in unquiet widowhood,
A wife and widow. Needs must it have been
A sore heart-wasting. I have heard, my friend,
450 That in that broken arbour she would sit
The idle length of half a sabbath day—
There, where you see the toadstool's lazy head—
And when a dog passed by she still would quit
The shade and look abroad. On this old Bench
455 For hours she sate, and evermore her eye
Was busy in the distance, shaping things
Which made her heart beat quick. Seest thou that path?
(The green-sward now has broken its grey line)
There to and fro she paced through many a day
460 Of the warm summer, from a belt of flax
That girt her waist spinning the long-drawn thread
With backward steps.—Yet ever as there passed
A man whose garments shewed the Soldier's red,
Or crippled Mendicant in Sailor's garb,
465 The little child who sate to turn the wheel
Ceased from his toil, and she with faltering voice,
Expecting still to learn her husband's fate,
Made many a fond inquiry; and when they
Whose presence gave no comfort were gone by,
470 Her heart was still more sad. And by yon gate
Which bars the traveller's road she often stood
And when a stranger horseman came, the latch
Would lift, and in his face look wistfully,
Most happy if from aught discovered there
475 Of tender feeling she might dare repeat
The same sad question. Meanwhile her poor hut
Sunk to decay, for he was gone whose hand
At the first nippings of October frost
Closed up each chink and with fresh bands of straw
480 Chequered the green-grown thatch. And so she lived
Through the long winter, reckless and alone,
Till this reft house by frost, and thaw, and rain
Was sapped; and when she slept the nightly damps
Did chill her breast, and in the stormy day

485 Her tattered clothes were ruffled by the wind
Even at the side of her own fire. Yet still
She loved this wretched spot, nor would for worlds
Have parted hence; and still that length of road
And this rude bench one torturing hope endeared,
490 Fast rooted at her heart, and here, my friend,
In sickness she remained, and here she died,
Last human tenant of these ruined walls."
    The old Man ceased: he saw that I was mov'd;
From that low Bench, rising instinctively,
495 I turned aside in weakness, nor had power
To thank him for the tale which he had told.
I stood, and leaning o'er the garden-gate
Reviewed that Woman's suff'rings, and it seemed
To comfort me while with a brother's love
500 I blessed her in the impotence of grief.
At length [towards] the [Cottage I returned]5
Fondly, and traced with milder interest
That secret spirit of humanity
Which, 'mid the calm oblivious tendencies
505 Of nature, 'mid her plants, her weeds, and flowers,
And silent overgrowings, still survived.
The old man, seeing this, resumed and said,
"My Friend, enough to sorrow have you given,
The purposes of wisdom ask no more;
510 Be wise and chearful, and no longer read
The forms of things with an unworthy eye.
She sleeps in the calm earth, and peace is here.
I well remember that those very plumes,
Those weeds, and the high spear-grass on that wall,
515 By mist and silent rain-drops silver'd o'er,
As once I passed did to my heart convey
So still an image of tranquillity,
So calm and still, and looked so beautiful
Amid the uneasy thoughts which filled my mind,
520 That what we feel of sorrow and despair
From ruin and from change, and all the grief
The passing shews of being leave behind,
Appeared an idle dream that could not live
Where meditation was. I turned away
525 And walked along my road in happiness."
    He ceased. By this the sun declining shot
A slant and mellow radiance which began
To fall upon us where beneath the trees
We sate on that low bench, and now we felt,
530 Admonished thus, the sweet hour coming on.
A linnet warbled from those lofty elms,
A thrush sang loud, and other melodies,
At distance heard, peopled the milder air.
The old man rose and hoisted up his load.
535 Together casting then a farewell look

5. The words inside the brackets were added in MS. E.

Upon those silent walls, we left the shade
And ere the stars were visible attained
A rustic inn, our evening resting-place.

THE END

1797–ca.1799   1949

Michael[1]

A Pastoral Poem

If from the public way you turn your steps
Up the tumultuous brook of Green-head Ghyll,[2]
You will suppose that with an upright path
Your feet must struggle; in such bold ascent
5   The pastoral mountains front you, face to face.
But, courage! for around that boisterous brook
The mountains have all opened out themselves,
And made a hidden valley of their own.
No habitation can be seen; but they
10   Who journey thither find themselves alone
With a few sheep, with rocks and stones, and kites°   hawks
That overhead are sailing in the sky.
It is in truth an utter solitude;
Nor should I have made mention of this Dell
15   But for one object which you might pass by,
Might see and notice not. Beside the brook
Appears a straggling heap of unhewn stones!
And to that simple object appertains
A story—unenriched with strange events,
20   Yet not unfit, I deem, for the fireside,
Or for the summer shade. It was the first
Of those domestic tales that spake to me
Of Shepherds, dwellers in the valleys, men
Whom I already loved;—not verily
25   For their own sakes, but for the fields and hills
Where was their occupation and abode.
And hence this Tale, while I was yet a Boy
Careless of books, yet having felt the power
Of Nature, by the gentle agency
30   Of natural objects, led me on to feel
For passions that were not my own, and think
(At random and imperfectly indeed)
On man, the heart of man, and human life.
Therefore, although it be a history

1. This poem is founded on the actual misfortunes of a family at Grasmere. For the account of the sheepfold, see Dorothy Wordsworth's *Grasmere Journals*, October 11, 1800 (p. 238). Wordsworth wrote to Thomas Poole, on April 9, 1801, that he had attempted to picture a man "agitated by two of the most powerful affections of the human heart; the parental affection, and the love of property, *landed* property, including the feelings of inheritance, home, and personal and family independence."
2. A ravine forming the bed of a stream. Greenhead Ghyll is not far from Wordsworth's cottage at Grasmere. The other places named in the poem are also in that vicinity.

35 Homely and rude, I will relate the same
For the delight of a few natural hearts;
And, with yet fonder feeling, for the sake
Of youthful Poets, who among these hills
Will be my second self when I am gone.

40   Upon the forest-side in Grasmere Vale
There dwelt a Shepherd, Michael was his name;
An old man, stout of heart, and strong of limb.
His bodily frame had been from youth to age
Of an unusual strength: his mind was keen,
45 Intense, and frugal, apt for all affairs,
And in his shepherd's calling he was prompt
And watchful more than ordinary men.
Hence had he learned the meaning of all winds,
Of blasts of every tone; and, oftentimes,
50 When others heeded not, he heard the South°   *south wind*
Make subterraneous music, like the noise
Of bagpipers on distant Highland hills.
The Shepherd, at such warning, of his flock
Bethought him, and he to himself would say,
55 "The winds are now devising work for me!"
And, truly, at all times, the storm, that drives
The traveller to a shelter, summoned him
Up to the mountains: he had been alone
Amid the heart of many thousand mists,
60 That came to him, and left him, on the heights.
So lived he till his eightieth year was past.
And grossly that man errs, who should suppose
That the green valleys, and the streams and rocks,
Were things indifferent to the Shepherd's thoughts.
65 Fields, where with cheerful spirits he had breathed
The common air; hills, which with vigorous step
He had so often climbed; which had impressed
So many incidents upon his mind
Of hardship, skill or courage, joy or fear;
70 Which, like a book, preserved the memory
Of the dumb animals, whom he had saved,
Had fed or sheltered, linking to such acts
The certainty of honourable gain;
Those fields, those hills—what could they less? had laid
75 Strong hold on his affections, were to him
A pleasurable feeling of blind love,
The pleasure which there is in life itself.

      His days had not been passed in singleness.
His Helpmate was a comely matron, old—
80 Though younger than himself full twenty years.
She was a woman of a stirring life,
Whose heart was in her house: two wheels she had
Of antique form; this large, for spinning wool;
That small, for flax; and if one wheel had rest,

85   It was because the other was at work.
     The Pair had but one inmate in their house,
     An only Child, who had been born to them
     When Michael, telling° o'er his years, began   *counting*
     To deem that he was old,—in shepherd's phrase,
90   With one foot in the grave. This only Son,
     With two brave sheep-dogs tried° in many a storm,   *tested*
     The one of an inestimable worth,
     Made all their household. I may truly say,
     That they were as a proverb in the vale
95   For endless industry. When day was gone,
     And from their occupations out of doors
     The Son and Father were come home, even then,
     Their labour did not cease; unless when all
     Turned to the cleanly supper-board, and there,
100 Each with a mess of pottage and skimmed milk,
     Sat round the basket piled with oaten cakes,
     And their plain home-made cheese. Yet when the meal
     Was ended, Luke (for so the Son was named)
     And his old Father both betook themselves
105 To such convenient work as might employ
     Their hands by the fire-side; perhaps to card
     Wool for the Housewife's spindle, or repair
     Some injury done to sickle, flail, or scythe,
     Or other implement of house or field.

110   Down from the ceiling, by the chimney's edge,
     That in our ancient uncouth country style
     With huge and black projection overbrowed
     Large space beneath, as duly as the light
     Of day grew dim the Housewife hung a lamp;
115 An aged utensil, which had performed
     Service beyond all others of its kind.
     Early at evening did it burn—and late,
     Surviving comrade of uncounted hours,
     Which, going by from year to year, had found,
120 And left the couple neither gay perhaps
     Nor cheerful, yet with objects and with hopes,
     Living a life of eager industry.
     And now, when Luke had reached his eighteenth year,
     There by the light of his old lamp they sate,
125 Father and Son, while far into the night
     The Housewife plied her own peculiar work,
     Making the cottage through the silent hours
     Murmur as with the sound of summer flies.
     This light was famous in its neighbourhood,
130 And was a public symbol of the life
     That thrifty Pair had lived. For, as it chanced,
     Their cottage on a plot of rising ground
     Stood single, with large prospect, north and south,
     High into Easedale, up to Dunmail-Raise,
135 And westward to the village near the lake;
     And from this constant light, so regular

And so far seen, the House itself, by all
Who dwelt within the limits of the vale,
Both old and young, was named THE EVENING STAR.

140   Thus living on through such a length of years,
The Shepherd, if he loved himself, must needs
Have loved his Helpmate; but to Michael's heart
This son of his old age was yet more dear—
Less from instinctive tenderness, the same
145 Fond spirit that blindly works in the blood of all—
Than that a child, more than all other gifts
That earth can offer to declining man,
Brings hope with it, and forward-looking thoughts,
And stirrings of inquietude, when they
150 By tendency of nature needs must fail.
Exceeding was the love he bare to him,
His heart and his heart's joy! For oftentimes
Old Michael, while he was a babe in arms,
Had done him female service, not alone
155 For pastime and delight, as is the use
Of fathers, but with patient mind enforced
To acts of tenderness; and he had rocked
His cradle, as with a woman's gentle hand.

      And, in a later time, ere yet the Boy
160 Had put on boy's attire, did Michael love,
Albeit of a stern unbending mind,
To have the Young-one in his sight, when he
Wrought in the field, or on his shepherd's stool
Sate with a fettered sheep before him stretched
165 Under the large old oak, that near his door
Stood single, and, from matchless depth of shade,
Chosen for the Shearer's covert from the sun,
Thence in our rustic dialect was called
The CLIPPING TREE, a name which yet it bears.
170 There, while they two were sitting in the shade,
With others round them, earnest all and blithe,
Would Michael exercise his heart with looks
Of fond correction and reproof bestowed
Upon the Child, if he disturbed the sheep
175 By catching at their legs, or with his shouts
Scared them, while they lay still beneath the shears.

      And when by Heaven's good grace the boy grew up
A healthy Lad, and carried in his cheek
Two steady roses that were five years old;
180 Then Michael from a winter coppice[3] cut
With his own hand a sapling, which he hooped
With iron, making it throughout in all
Due requisites a perfect shepherd's staff,

---

3. Grove of small trees.

And gave it to the Boy; wherewith equipt
185   He as a watchman oftentimes was placed
At gate or gap, to stem or turn the flock;
And, to his office prematurely called,
There stood the urchin, as you will divine,
Something between a hindrance and a help;
190   And for this cause not always, I believe,
Receiving from his Father hire° of praise;   *wages*
Though nought was left undone which staff, or voice,
Or looks, or threatening gestures, could perform.

But soon as Luke, full ten years old, could stand
195   Against the mountain blasts; and to the heights,
Not fearing toil, nor length of weary ways,
He with his Father daily went, and they
Were as companions, why should I relate
That objects which the Shepherd loved before
200   Were dearer now? that from the Boy there came
Feelings and emanations—things which were
Light to the sun and music to the wind;
And that the old Man's heart seemed born again?

Thus in his father's sight the Boy grew up:
205   And now, when he had reached his eighteenth year,
He was his comfort and his daily hope.

While in this sort the simple household lived
From day to day, to Michael's ear there came
Distressful tidings. Long before the time
210   Of which I speak, the Shepherd had been bound
In surety for his brother's son, a man
Of an industrious life, and ample means;
But unforeseen misfortunes suddenly
Had prest upon him; and old Michael now
215   Was summoned to discharge the forfeiture,
A grievous penalty, but little less
Than half his substance.[4] This unlooked-for claim,
At the first hearing, for a moment took
More hope out of his life than he supposed
220   That any old man ever could have lost.
As soon as he had armed himself with strength
To look his trouble in the face, it seemed
The Shepherd's sole resource to sell at once
A portion of his patrimonial fields.
225   Such was his first resolve; he thought again,
And his heart failed him. "Isabel," said he,
Two evenings after he had heard the news,
"I have been toiling more than seventy years,
And in the open sunshine of God's love
230   Have we all lived; yet if these fields of ours
Should pass into a stranger's hand, I think

4. Michael has guaranteed a loan for his nephew and now has lost the collateral, which amounts to half
his financial worth.

That I could not lie quiet in my grave.
Our lot is a hard lot; the sun himself
Has scarcely been more diligent than I;
235 And I have lived to be a fool at last
To my own family. An evil man
That was, and made an evil choice, if he
Were false to us; and if he were not false,
There are ten thousand to whom loss like this
240 Had been no sorrow. I forgive him;—but
'Twere better to be dumb than to talk thus.

"When I began, my purpose was to speak
Of remedies and of a cheerful hope.
Our Luke shall leave us, Isabel; the land
245 Shall not go from us, and it shall be free;°   unmortgaged
He shall possess it, free as is the wind
That passes over it. We have, thou know'st,
Another kinsman—he will be our friend
In this distress. He is a prosperous man,
250 Thriving in trade—and Luke to him shall go,
And with his kinsman's help and his own thrift
He quickly will repair this loss, and then
He may return to us. If here he stay,
What can be done? Where every one is poor,
What can be gained?"
255   At this the old Man paused,
And Isabel sat silent, for her mind
Was busy, looking back into past times.
There's Richard Bateman,[5] thought she to herself,
He was a parish-boy[6]—at the church-door
260 They made a gathering for him, shillings, pence
And halfpennies, wherewith the neighbours bought
A basket, which they filled with pedlar's wares;
And, with this basket on his arm, the lad
Went up to London, found a master° there,   employer
265 Who, out of many, chose the trusty boy
To go and overlook his merchandise
Beyond the seas; where he grew wondrous rich,
And left estates and monies to the poor,
And, at his birth-place, built a chapel floored
270 With marble, which he sent from foreign lands.
These thoughts, and many others of like sort,
Passed quickly through the mind of Isabel,
And her face brightened. The old Man was glad,
And thus resumed:—"Well, Isabel! this scheme
275 These two days, has been meat and drink to me.
Far more than we have lost is left us yet.
—We have enough—I wish indeed that I
Were younger;—but this hope is a good hope.
Make ready Luke's best garments, of the best

5. The story alluded to here is well known in the country. The chapel is called Ings Chapel and is on the road leading from Kendal to Ambleside [Wordsworth's note, 1802–5].

6. A poor boy supported financially by the poor rates (taxes) paid out by the wealthier members of his parish.

280 Buy for him more, and let us send him forth
To-morrow, or the next day, or to-night:
—If he *could* go, the Boy should go to-night."

Here Michael ceased, and to the fields went forth
With a light heart. The Housewife for five days
285 Was restless morn and night, and all day long
Wrought on with her best fingers to prepare
Things needful for the journey of her son.
But Isabel was glad when Sunday came
To stop her in her work: for, when she lay
290 By Michael's side, she through the last two nights
Heard him, how he was troubled in his sleep:
And when they rose at morning she could see
That all his hopes were gone. That day at noon
She said to Luke, while they two by themselves
295 Were sitting at the door, "Thou must not go:
We have no other Child but thee to lose,
None to remember—do not go away,
For if thou leave thy Father he will die."
The Youth made answer with a jocund voice;
300 And Isabel, when she had told her fears,
Recovered heart. That evening her best fare
Did she bring forth, and all together sat
Like happy people round a Christmas fire.

With daylight Isabel resumed her work;
305 And all the ensuing week the house appeared
As cheerful as a grove in Spring: at length
The expected letter from their kinsman came,
With kind assurances that he would do
His utmost for the welfare of the Boy;
310 To which, requests were added, that forthwith
He might be sent to him. Ten times or more
The letter was read over; Isabel
Went forth to show it to the neighbours round;
Nor was there at that time on English land
315 A prouder heart than Luke's. When Isabel
Had to her house returned, the old Man said,
"He shall depart to-morrow." To this word
The Housewife answered, talking much of things
Which, if at such short notice he should go,
320 Would surely be forgotten. But at length
She gave consent, and Michael was at ease.

Near the tumultuous brook of Green-head Ghyll,
In that deep valley, Michael had designed
To build a Sheep-fold;[7] and, before he heard
325 The tidings of his melancholy loss,
For this same purpose he had gathered up

---

7. A sheepfold [pen for sheep] in these mountains is an unroofed building of stone walls, with different divisions [Wordsworth's note, 1802–5].

A heap of stones, which by the streamlet's edge
Lay thrown together, ready for the work.
With Luke that evening thitherward he walked:
330 And soon as they had reached the place he stopped,
And thus the old Man spake to him:—"My Son,
To-morrow thou wilt leave me: with full heart
I look upon thee, for thou art the same
That wert a promise to me ere thy birth,
335 And all thy life hast been my daily joy.
I will relate to thee some little part
Of our two histories; 'twill do thee good
When thou art from me, even if I should touch
On things thou canst not know of.——After thou
340 First cam'st into the world—as oft befals
To new-born infants—thou didst sleep away
Two days, and blessings from thy Father's tongue
Then fell upon thee. Day by day passed on,
And still I loved thee with increasing love.
345 Never to living ear came sweeter sounds
Than when I heard thee by our own fire-side
First uttering, without words, a natural tune;
While thou, a feeding babe, didst in thy joy
Sing at thy Mother's breast. Month followed month,
350 And in the open fields my life was passed
And on the mountains; else I think that thou
Hadst been brought up upon thy Father's knees.
But we were playmates, Luke: among these hills,
As well thou knowest, in us the old and young
355 Have played together, nor with me didst thou
Lack any pleasure which a boy can know."
Luke had a manly heart; but at these words
He sobbed aloud. The old Man grasped his hand,
And said, "Nay, do not take it so—I see
360 That these are things of which I need not speak.
—Even to the utmost I have been to thee
A kind and a good Father: and herein
I but repay a gift which I myself
Received at others' hands; for, though now old
365 Beyond the common life of man, I still
Remember them who loved me in my youth.
Both of them sleep together: here they lived,
As all their Forefathers had done; and when
At length their time was come, they were not loth
370 To give their bodies to the family mould.°   *grave plot*
I wished that thou should'st live the life they lived:
But, 'tis a long time to look back, my Son,
And see so little gain from threescore years.
These fields were burthened° when they came to me;   *mortgaged*
375 Till I was forty years of age, not more
Than half of my inheritance was mine.
I toiled and toiled; God blessed me in my work,
And till these three weeks past the land was free.
—It looks as if it never could endure

380   Another Master. Heaven forgive me, Luke,
      If I judge ill for thee, but it seems good
      That thou should'st go."
                       At this the old Man paused;
      Then, pointing to the stones near which they stood,
      Thus, after a short silence, he resumed:
385   "This was a work for us; and now, my Son,
      It is a work for me. But, lay one stone—
      Here, lay it for me, Luke, with thine own hands.
      Nay, Boy, be of good hope;—we both may live
      To see a better day. At eighty-four
390   I still am strong and hale;—do thou thy part;
      I will do mine.—I will begin again
      With many tasks that were resigned to thee:
      Up to the heights, and in among the storms,
      Will I without thee go again, and do
395   All works which I was wont to do alone,
      Before I knew thy face.—Heaven bless thee, Boy!
      Thy heart these two weeks has been beating fast
      With many hopes; it should be so—yes—yes—
      I knew that thou could'st never have a wish
400   To leave me, Luke: thou hast been bound to me
      Only by links of love: when thou art gone,
      What will be left to us!—But, I forget
      My purposes. Lay now the corner-stone,
      As I requested; and hereafter, Luke,
405   When thou art gone away, should evil men
      Be thy companions, think of me, my Son,
      And of this moment; hither turn thy thoughts,
      And God will strengthen thee: amid all fear
      And all temptation, Luke, I pray that thou
410   May'st bear in mind the life thy Fathers lived,
      Who, being innocent, did for that cause
      Bestir them in good deeds. Now, fare thee well—
      When thou return'st, thou in this place wilt see
      A work which is not here: a covenant
415   'Twill be between us; but, whatever fate
      Befal thee, I shall love thee to the last,
      And bear thy memory with me to the grave."

      The Shepherd ended here; and Luke stooped down,
      And, as his Father had requested, laid
420   The first stone of the Sheep-fold. At the sight
      The old Man's grief broke from him; to his heart
      He pressed his Son, he kissèd him and wept;
      And to the house together they returned.
      —Hushed was that House in peace, or seeming peace,
425   Ere the night fell:—with morrow's dawn the Boy
      Began his journey, and when he had reached
      The public way, he put on a bold face;
      And all the neighbours, as he passed their doors,
      Came forth with wishes and with farewell prayers,
430   That followed him till he was out of sight.

A good report did from their Kinsman come,
Of Luke and his well-doing: and the Boy
Wrote loving letters, full of wondrous news,
Which, as the Housewife phrased it, were throughout
435 "The prettiest letters that were ever seen."
Both parents read them with rejoicing hearts.
So, many months passed on: and once again
The Shepherd went about his daily work
With confident and cheerful thoughts; and now
440 Sometimes when he could find a leisure hour
He to that valley took his way, and there
Wrought at the Sheep-fold. Meantime Luke began
To slacken in his duty; and, at length,
He in the dissolute city gave himself
445 To evil courses: ignominy and shame
Fell on him, so that he was driven at last
To seek a hiding-place beyond the seas.

There is a comfort in the strength of love;
'Twill make a thing endurable, which else
450 Would overset the brain, or break the heart:
I have conversed with more than one who well
Remember the old Man, and what he was
Years after he had heard this heavy news.
His bodily frame had been from youth to age
455 Of an unusual strength. Among the rocks
He went, and still looked up to sun and cloud,
And listened to the wind; and, as before
Performed all kinds of labour for his sheep,
And for the land, his small inheritance.
460 And to that hollow dell from time to time
Did he repair, to build the Fold of which
His flock had need. 'Tis not forgotten yet
The pity which was then in every heart
For the old Man—and 'tis believed by all
465 That many and many a day he thither went,
And never lifted up a single stone.

There, by the Sheep-fold, sometimes was he seen
Sitting alone, or with his faithful Dog,
Then old, beside him, lying at his feet.
470 The length of full seven years, from time to time,
He at the building of this Sheep-fold wrought,
And left the work unfinished when he died.
Three years, or little more, did Isabel
Survive her Husband: at her death the estate
475 Was sold, and went into a stranger's hand.
The Cottage which was named the Evening Star
Is gone—the ploughshare has been through the ground
On which it stood;[8] great changes have been wrought
In all the neighbourhood:—yet the oak is left

---

8. The land on which Michael's sheep had grazed has been turned over to cultivation.

480   That grew beside their door; and the remains
      Of the unfinished Sheep-fold may be seen
      Beside the boisterous brook of Green-head Ghyll.

Oct. 11–Dec. 9, 1800   1800

Resolution and Independence[1]

1

    There was a roaring in the wind all night;
    The rain came heavily and fell in floods;
    But now the sun is rising calm and bright;
    The birds are singing in the distant woods;
5   Over his own sweet voice the Stock-dove broods;
    The Jay makes answer as the Magpie chatters;
    And all the air is filled with pleasant noise of waters.

2

    All things that love the sun are out of doors;
    The sky rejoices in the morning's birth;
10   The grass is bright with rain-drops;—on the moors
    The hare is running races in her mirth;
    And with her feet she from the plashy earth
    Raises a mist; that, glittering in the sun,
    Runs with her all the way, wherever she doth run.

3

15   I was a Traveller then upon the moor;
    I saw the hare that raced about with joy;
    I heard the woods and distant waters roar;
    Or heard them not, as happy as a boy:
    The pleasant season did my heart employ:
20   My old remembrances went from me wholly;
    And all the ways of men, so vain and melancholy.

4

    But, as it sometimes chanceth, from the might
    Of joy in minds that can no further go,
    As high as we have mounted in delight
25   In our dejection do we sink as low;
    To me that morning did it happen so;
    And fears and fancies thick upon me came;
    Dim sadness—and blind thoughts, I knew not, nor could name.

1. "This old man I met a few hundred yards from my cottage," Wordsworth told Isabella Fenwick in 1843, and "the account of him is taken from his own mouth." He wrote the poem eighteen months after the meeting. For the account of the meeting and the writing of the poem, which had the working title "The Leech Gatherer," see Dorothy Wordsworth's *Grasmere Journals*, October 3, 1800, p. 238, and May 4 and 7, 1802, pp. 243 and 244.

5

I heard the sky-lark warbling in the sky;
30 And I bethought me of the playful hare:
Even such a happy Child of earth am I;
Even as these blissful creatures do I fare;
Far from the world I walk, and from all care;
But there may come another day to me—
35 Solitude, pain of heart, distress, and poverty.

6

My whole life I have lived in pleasant thought,
As if life's business were a summer mood;
As if all needful things would come unsought
To genial° faith, still rich in genial good;   *creative*
40 But how can He expect that others should
Build for him, sow for him, and at his call
Love him, who for himself will take no heed at all?

7

I thought of Chatterton,[2] the marvellous Boy,
The sleepless Soul that perished in his pride;
45 Of Him[3] who walked in glory and in joy
Following his plough, along the mountain-side:
By our own spirits are we deified:
We Poets in our youth begin in gladness;
But thereof come in the end despondency and madness.

8

50 Now, whether it were by peculiar grace,
A leading from above, a something given,
Yet it befel, that, in this lonely place,
When I with these untoward thoughts had striven,
Beside a pool bare to the eye of heaven
55 I saw a Man before me unawares:
The oldest man he seemed that ever wore grey hairs.

9

As a huge stone is sometimes seen to lie
Couched on the bald top of an eminence;
Wonder to all who do the same espy,
60 By what means it could thither come, and whence;
So that it seems a thing endued with sense:
Like a sea-beast crawled forth, that on a shelf
Of rock or sand reposeth, there to sun itself;

---

2. After his early death through drug overdose, a
death believed by many to have been a suicide,
the poet Thomas Chatterton (1752–1770) became
a prime symbol of neglected boy genius for the
Romantics.

3. Robert Burns, here considered, as Chatterton
is, a natural poet who died young and poor, without adequate recognition, and who seemed to
have hastened his death through dissipation.

10

Such seemed this Man,[4] not all alive nor dead,
65 Nor all asleep—in his extreme old age:
His body was bent double, feet and head
Coming together in life's pilgrimage;
As if some dire constraint of pain, or rage
Of sickness felt by him in times long past,
70 A more than human weight upon his frame had cast.

11

Himself he propped, limbs, body, and pale face,
Upon a long grey staff of shaven wood:
And, still as I drew near with gentle pace,
Upon the margin of that moorish flood
75 Motionless as a cloud the old Man stood,
That heareth not the loud winds when they call;
And moveth all together, if it move at all.

12

At length, himself unsettling, he the pond
Stirred with his staff, and fixedly did look
80 Upon the muddy water, which he conned,°   studied
As if he had been reading in a book:
And now a stranger's privilege I took;
And, drawing to his side, to him did say,
"This morning gives us promise of a glorious day."

13

85 A gentle answer did the old Man make,
In courteous speech which forth he slowly drew:
And him with further words I thus bespake,
"What occupation do you there pursue?
This is a lonesome place for one like you."
90 Ere he replied, a flash of mild surprise
Broke from the sable orbs of his yet-vivid eyes.

14

His words came feebly, from a feeble chest,
But each in solemn order followed each,
With something of a lofty utterance drest—
95 Choice word and measured phrase, above the reach
Of ordinary men; a stately speech;
Such as grave Livers[5] do in Scotland use,
Religious men, who give to God and man their dues.

4. To outline his theory of the imagination, Wordsworth himself commented on lines 57–65 and 75–77, pointing out how the stone "is endowed with something of the power of life to approximate it to the sea-beast," the sea-beast is "stripped of some of its vital qualities to assimilate it to the stone," and the old man is divested of enough life and motion to make "the two objects unite and coalesce in just comparison." In this manner, he stated, "the conferring, the abstracting, and the modifying powers of the Imagination" were "all brought into conjunction" (Preface to the *Poems* of 1815).
5. Those who live gravely (as opposed to "loose livers," those who live for a life of pleasure).

15

He told, that to these waters he had come
100   To gather leeches,[6] being old and poor:
Employment hazardous and wearisome!
And he had many hardships to endure:
From pond to pond he roamed, from moor to moor;
Housing, with God's good help, by choice or chance;
105   And in this way he gained an honest maintenance.

16

The old Man still stood talking by my side;
But now his voice to me was like a stream
Scarce heard; nor word from word could I divide;
And the whole body of the Man did seem
110   Like one whom I had met with in a dream;
Or like a man from some far region sent,
To give me human strength, by apt admonishment.

17

My former thoughts returned: the fear that kills;
And hope that is unwilling to be fed;
115   Cold, pain, and labour, and all fleshly ills;
And mighty Poets in their misery dead.
—Perplexed, and longing to be comforted,
My question eagerly did I renew,
"How is it that you live, and what is it you do?"

18

120   He with a smile did then his words repeat;
And said, that, gathering leeches, far and wide
He travelled; stirring thus about his feet
The waters of the pools where they abide.
"Once I could meet with them on every side;
125   But they have dwindled long by slow decay;
Yet still I persevere, and find them where I may."

19

While he was talking thus, the lonely place,
The old Man's shape, and speech—all troubled me:
In my mind's eye I seemed to see him pace
130   About the weary moors continually,
Wandering about alone and silently.
While I these thoughts within myself pursued,
He, having made a pause, the same discourse renewed.

6. Used by medical attendants to draw their patients' blood for curative purposes. A leech gatherer, bare legged in shallow water, stirred the water to attract them and, when they fastened themselves to his legs, picked them off.

20

And soon with this he other matter blended,
135 Cheerfully uttered, with demeanour kind,
But stately in the main; and when he ended,
I could have laughed myself to scorn to find
In that decrepit Man so firm a mind.
"God," said I, "be my help and stay[7] secure;
140 I'll think of the Leech-gatherer on the lonely moor!"

May 3–July 4, 1802   1807

I wandered lonely as a cloud[1]

I wandered lonely as a cloud
That floats on high o'er vales and hills,
When all at once I saw a crowd,
A host, of golden daffodils;
5 Beside the lake, beneath the trees,
Fluttering and dancing in the breeze.

Continuous as the stars that shine
And twinkle on the milky way,
They stretched in never-ending line
10 Along the margin of a bay:
Ten thousand saw I at a glance,
Tossing their heads in sprightly dance.

The waves beside them danced; but they
Out-did the sparkling waves in glee:
15 A poet could not but be gay,
In such a jocund company:
I gazed—and gazed—but little thought
What wealth the show to me had brought:

For oft, when on my couch I lie
20 In vacant or in pensive mood,
They flash upon that inward eye
Which is the bliss of solitude;
And then my heart with pleasure fills,
And dances with the daffodils.

1804   1807

My heart leaps up

My heart leaps up when I behold
A rainbow in the sky:
So was it when my life began;
So is it now I am a man;

---

7. Support (a noun).
1. For the original experience, two years earlier,
see Dorothy Wordsworth's *Grasmere Journals*,
April 15, 1802 (p. 241).

5   So be it when I shall grow old,
       Or let me die!
  The Child is father of the Man;
  And I could wish my days to be
  Bound each to each by natural piety.[1]

Mar. 26, 1802   1807

Ode: Intimations of Immortality

In 1843 in a long note on this poem dictated to Isabella Fenwick, Wordsworth said:

> To that dreamlike vividness and splendor which invest objects of sight in childhood, everyone, I believe, if he would look back, could bear testimony * * * but having in the Poem regarded it as presumptive evidence of a prior state of existence, I think it right to protest against a conclusion, which has given pain to some good and pious persons, that I meant to inculcate such a belief. It is far too shadowy a notion to be recommended to faith, as more than an element in our instincts of immortality.

Wordsworth was troubled by objections that his apparent claim for the preexistence of the soul violated the Christian belief that the soul, although it survives after death, does not exist before the birth of an individual. His claim is that he refers to the preexistence of the soul not in order to set out a religious doctrine but only so as to deal "as a Poet" with a common human experience: that the passing of youth involves the loss of a freshness and radiance investing everything one sees.

Ode

Intimations of Immortality from Recollections of Early Childhood

        The Child is Father of the Man:
        And I could wish my days to be
        Bound each to each by natural piety.[1]

I

There was a time when meadow, grove, and stream,
The earth, and every common sight,
    To me did seem
    Apparelled in celestial light,
5 The glory and the freshness of a dream.
It is not now as it hath been of yore;—
    Turn wheresoe'er I may,
      By night or day,
The things which I have seen I now can see no more.

2

10   The Rainbow comes and goes,
      And lovely is the Rose,

---

1. Perhaps as distinguished from piety based on the Bible, in which the rainbow is the token of God's promise to Noah and his descendants never again to send a flood to destroy the earth.

1. The concluding lines of Wordsworth's "My heart leaps up."

The Moon doth with delight
Look round her when the heavens are bare,
   Waters on a starry night
15   Are beautiful and fair;
The sunshine is a glorious birth;
But yet I know, where'er I go,
That there hath past away a glory from the earth.

3

Now, while the birds thus sing a joyous song,
20   And while the young lambs bound
      As to the tabor's[2] sound,
To me alone there came a thought of grief:
A timely utterance[3] gave that thought relief,
And I again am strong:
25 The cataracts blow their trumpets from the steep;
No more shall grief of mine the season wrong;
I hear the Echoes through the mountains throng,
The Winds come to me from the fields of sleep,[4]
    And all the earth is gay;
30   Land and sea
Give themselves up to jollity,
    And with the heart of May
Doth every Beast keep holiday;—
Thou Child of Joy,
35 Shout round me, let me hear thy shouts, thou happy
    Shepherd-boy!

4

Ye blessed Creatures, I have heard the call
    Ye to each other make; I see
The heavens laugh with you in your jubilee;
    My heart is at your festival,
40   My head hath its coronal,[5]
The fulness of your bliss, I feel—I feel it all.
    Oh evil day! if I were sullen
    While Earth herself is adorning,
    This sweet May-morning,
45   And the Children are culling
      On every side,
In a thousand valleys far and wide,
Fresh flowers; while the sun shines warm,
And the Babe leaps up on his Mother's arm:—
50   I hear, I hear, with joy I hear!
      —But there's a Tree, of many, one,

2. A small drum often used to beat time for dancing.
3. Perhaps "My heart leaps up," perhaps "Resolution and Independence," perhaps not a poem at all.
4. Of the many suggested interpretations, the simplest is "from the fields where they were sleeping." Wordsworth often associated a rising wind with the revival of spirit and of poetic inspiration (see, e.g., the opening passage of *The Prelude*, p. 194).
5. Circlet of wildflowers, with which the shepherd boys trimmed their hats in May.

A single Field which I have looked upon,
Both of them speak of something that is gone:
    The Pansy at my feet
55   Doth the same tale repeat:
Whither is fled the visionary gleam?
Where is it now, the glory and the dream?

5

Our birth is but a sleep and a forgetting:
The Soul that rises with us, our life's Star,[6]
60   Hath had elsewhere its setting,
        And cometh from afar:
    Not in entire forgetfulness,
    And not in utter nakedness,
But trailing clouds of glory do we come
65   From God, who is our home:
Heaven lies about us in our infancy!
Shades of the prison-house begin to close
      Upon the growing Boy,
But He beholds the light, and whence it flows,
70   He sees it in his joy;
The Youth, who daily farther from the east
      Must travel, still is Nature's Priest,
      And by the vision splendid
      Is on his way attended;
75 At length the Man perceives it die away,
And fade into the light of common day.

6

Earth fills her lap with pleasures of her own;
Yearnings she hath in her own natural kind,
And, even with something of a Mother's mind,
80   And no unworthy aim,
      The homely[7] Nurse doth all she can
To make her Foster-child, her Inmate Man,
      Forget the glories he hath known,
And that imperial palace whence he came.

7

85 Behold the Child among his new-born blisses,
A six years' Darling of a pigmy size!
See, where mid work of his own hand he lies,
Fretted[8] by sallies of his mother's kisses,
With light upon him from his father's eyes!
90 See, at his feet, some little plan or chart,
Some fragment from his dream of human life,
Shaped by himself with newly-learnèd art;
      A wedding or a festival,
      A mourning or a funeral;

6. The sun, as metaphor for the soul.
7. In the old sense: simple and friendly.

8. Irritated; or possibly in the old sense: checkered over.

95   And this hath now his heart,
         And unto this he frames his song:
           Then will he fit his tongue
   To dialogues of business, love, or strife;
           But it will not be long
100   Ere this be thrown aside,
           And with new joy and pride
The little Actor cons° another part;   *studies*
Filling from time to time his "humorous stage"[9]
With all the Persons, down to palsied Age,
105 That Life brings with her in her equipage;
          As if his whole vocation
          Were endless imitation.

8

   Thou, whose exterior semblance doth belie
         Thy Soul's immensity;
110 Thou best Philosopher, who yet dost keep
Thy heritage, thou Eye among the blind,
That, deaf and silent, read'st the eternal deep,
Haunted for ever by the eternal mind,—
         Mighty Prophet! Seer blest!
115   On whom those truths do rest,
Which we are toiling all our lives to find,
In darkness lost, the darkness of the grave;
Thou, over whom thy Immortality
Broods like the Day, a Master o'er a Slave,
120 A Presence which is not to be put by;
Thou little Child, yet glorious in the might
Of heaven-born freedom on thy being's height,
Why with such earnest pains dost thou provoke
The years to bring the inevitable yoke,
125 Thus blindly with thy blessedness at strife?
Full soon thy Soul shall have her earthly freight,
And custom lie upon thee with a weight,
Heavy as frost, and deep almost as life!

9

        O joy! that in our embers
130   Is something that doth live,
        That nature yet remembers
        What was so fugitive!°   *fleeting*
The thought of our past years in me doth breed
Perpetual benediction: not indeed
135 For that which is most worthy to be blest;
Delight and liberty, the simple creed
Of Childhood, whether busy or at rest,
With new-fledged hope still fluttering in his breast:—
        Not for these I raise

9. From a sonnet by the Elizabethan poet Samuel Daniel. In Daniel's era *humorous* meant "capricious" and also referred to the various characters and temperaments ("humors") represented in drama.

140   The song of thanks and praise;
   But for those obstinate questionings
   Of sense and outward things,
   Fallings from us, vanishings;
   Blank misgivings of a Creature
145 Moving about in worlds not realised,[1]
High instincts before which our mortal Nature
Did tremble like a guilty Thing surprised:
   But for those first affections,
   Those shadowy recollections,
150   Which, be they what they may,
Are yet the fountain light of all our day,
Are yet a master light of all our seeing;
   Uphold us, cherish, and have power to make
Our noisy years seem moments in the being
155 Of the eternal Silence: truths that wake,
   To perish never;
Which neither listlessness, nor mad endeavour,
   Nor Man nor Boy,
Nor all that is at enmity with joy,
160 Can utterly abolish or destroy!
  Hence in a season of calm weather
   Though inland far we be,
Our Souls have sight of that immortal sea
   Which brought us hither,
165 Can in a moment travel thither,
And see the Children sport upon the shore,
And Hear the mighty waters rolling evermore.

      10

Then sing, ye Birds, sing, sing a joyous song!
   And let the young Lambs bound
170   As to the tabor's sound!
We in thought will join your throng,
   Ye that pipe and ye that play,
   Ye that through your hearts to-day
   Feel the gladness of the May!
175 What though the radiance which was once so bright
Be now for ever taken from my sight,
Though nothing can bring back the hour
Of splendour in the grass, of glory in the flower;
   We will grieve not, rather find
180   Strength in what remains behind;
   In the primal sympathy
   Which having been must ever be;
   In the soothing thoughts that spring
   Out of human suffering;
185   In the faith that looks through death,
In years that bring the philosophic mind.

1. Not seeming real.

11

And O, ye Fountains, Meadows, Hills, and Groves,
Forebode° not any severing of our loves!   *predict, portend*
Yet in my heart of hearts I feel your might;
190 I only have relinquished one delight
To live beneath your more habitual sway.
I love the Brooks which down their channels fret,
Even more than when I tripped lightly as they;
The innocent brightness of a new-born Day
195   Is lovely yet;
The Clouds that gather round the setting sun
Do take a sober colouring from an eye
That hath kept watch o'er man's mortality;
Another race hath been, and other palms are won.[2]
200 Thanks to the human heart by which we live,
Thanks to its tenderness, its joys, and fears,
To me the meanest° flower that blows° can give   *lowliest / blooms*
Thoughts that do often lie too deep for tears.

1802–4   1807

Ode to Duty[1]

*Jam non consilio bonus, sed more eo perductus, ut non tantum recte
facere possim, sed nisi recte facere non possim.*[2]

Stern Daughter of the Voice of God![3]
O Duty! if that name thou love
Who art a light to guide, a rod
To check the erring, and reprove;
5 Thou, who art victory and law
When empty terrors overawe;
From vain temptations dost set free;
And calm'st the weary strife of frail humanity!

There are who ask not if thine eye
10 Be on them; who, in love and truth,
Where no misgiving is, rely
Upon the genial sense[4] of youth:
Glad Hearts! without reproach or blot;
Who do thy work, and know it not:

2. In Greece foot races were often run for the prize of a branch or wreath of palm. Wordsworth's line echoes Paul, 1 Corinthians 9.24, who uses such races as a metaphor for life: "Know ye not that they which run in a race run all, but one receiveth the prize?"
1. This Ode . . . is on the model of Gray's "Ode to Adversity" which is copied from Horace's "Ode to Fortune." Many and many a time have I been twitted by my wife and sister for having forgotten this dedication of myself to the stern lawgiver [Wordsworth's note, 1843].
2. Now I am not good by conscious intent, but

have been so trained by habit that I not only can act rightly but am unable to act other than rightly (Latin). Added in 1837, this epigraph is an adaption from *Moral Epistles* 120.10 by Seneca (4 B.C.E.–65 C.E.) Stoic philosopher and writer of tragedies.
3. Cf. Milton's *Paradise Lost* 9.652–54. Eve for a moment resists the serpent's recommendation of the forbidden fruit by stating, "God so commanded, and left that Command / Sole Daughter of his voice; the rest, we live / Law to ourselves, our Reason is our Law."
4. Innate vitality.

15 Oh! if through confidence misplaced
   They fail, thy saving arms, dread Power! around them cast.

   Serene will be our days and bright,
   And happy will our nature be,
   When love is an unerring light,
20 And joy its own security.
   And they a blissful course may hold
   Even now, who, not unwisely bold,
   Live in the spirit of this creed;
   Yet seek thy firm support, according to their need.

25 I, loving freedom, and untried;
   No sport of every random gust,
   Yet being to myself a guide,
   Too blindly have reposed my trust:
   And oft, when in my heart was heard
30 Thy timely mandate, I deferred
   The task, in smoother walks to stray;
   But thee I now would serve more strictly, if I may.

   Through no disturbance of my soul,
   Or strong compunction[5] in me wrought,
35 I supplicate for thy control;
   But in the quietness of thought:
   Me this unchartered freedom tires;
   I feel the weight of chance-desires:
   My hopes no more must change their name,
40 I long for a repose that ever is the same.

   Stern Lawgiver! yet thou dost wear
   The Godhead's most benignant grace;
   Nor know we any thing so fair
   As is the smile upon thy face:
45 Flowers laugh before thee on their beds
   And fragrance in thy footing treads;
   Thou dost preserve the stars from wrong;
   And the most ancient heavens, through Thee, are fresh and strong.

   To humbler functions, awful Power!
50 I call thee: I myself commend
   Unto thy guidance from this hour;
   Oh, let my weakness have an end!
   Give unto me, made lowly wise,[6]
   The spirit of self-sacrifice;
55 The confidence of reason give;
   And in the light of truth thy Bondman[7] let me live!

1804   1807

---

5. In the older sense: sting of conscience, or remorse.
6. Another echo from Milton. The angel Raphael had advised Adam (*Paradise Lost* 8.173–74), "Be

lowly wise: / Think only what concerns thee and thy being."
7. Man in bondage, serf or slave.

The Solitary Reaper[1]

Behold her, single in the field,
Yon solitary Highland Lass!
Reaping and singing by herself;
Stop here, or gently pass!
5   Alone she cuts and binds the grain,
And sings a melancholy strain;
O listen! for the Vale profound
Is overflowing with the sound.

No Nightingale did ever chaunt
10   More welcome notes to weary bands
Of travellers in some shady haunt,
Among Arabian sands:
A voice so thrilling ne'er was heard
In spring-time from the Cuckoo-bird,
15   Breaking the silence of the seas
Among the farthest Hebrides.[2]

Will no one tell me what she sings?[3]
Perhaps the plaintive numbers° flow   *verses*
For old, unhappy, far-off things,
20   And battles long ago:
Or is it some more humble lay,
Familiar matter of to-day?
Some natural sorrow, loss, or pain,
That has been, and may be again?

25   Whate'er the theme, the Maiden sang
As if her song could have no ending;
I saw her singing at her work,
And o'er the sickle bending;—
I listened, motionless and still;
30   And, as I mounted up the hill,
The music in my heart I bore,
Long after it was heard no more.

Nov. 5, 1805   1807

1. One of the rare poems not based on Wordsworth's own experience. In a note published with
the poem in 1807, Wordsworth says that it was
suggested by a passage in Thomas Wilkinson's
Tours to the British Mountains (1824), which he
had seen in manuscript: "Passed a female who was
reaping alone: she sung in Erse [the Gaelic language of Scotland] as she bended over her sickle;
the sweetest human voice I ever heard: her strains
were tenderly melancholy, and felt delicious, long
after they were heard no more."
2. Islands off the west coast of Scotland.
3. The poet does not understand Erse, the language in which she sings.

Elegiac Stanzas

*Suggested by a Picture of Peele Castle, in a Storm,
Painted by Sir George Beaumont*[1]

I was thy neighbour once, thou rugged Pile!°   *building*
Four summer weeks I dwelt in sight of thee:
I saw thee every day; and all the while
Thy Form was sleeping on a glassy sea.

5   So pure the sky, so quiet was the air!
So like, so very like, was day to day!
Whene'er I looked, thy Image still was there;
It trembled, but it never passed away.

How perfect was the calm! it seemed no sleep;
10   No mood, which season takes away, or brings:
I could have fancied that the mighty Deep
Was even the gentlest of all gentle Things.

Ah! THEN, if mine had been the Painter's hand,
To express what then I saw; and add the gleam,
15   The light that never was, on sea or land,
The consecration, and the Poet's dream;

I would have planted thee, thou hoary Pile
Amid a world how different from this!
Beside a sea that could not cease to smile;
20   On tranquil land, beneath a sky of bliss.

Thou shouldst have seemed a treasure-house divine
Of peaceful years; a chronicle of heaven;
—Of all the sunbeams that did ever shine
The very sweetest had to thee been given.

25   A Picture had it been of lasting ease,
Elysian[2] quiet, without toil or strife;
No motion but the moving tide, a breeze,
Or merely silent Nature's breathing life.

Such, in the fond illusion of my heart,
30   Such Picture would I at that time have made:
And seen the soul of truth in every part,
A stedfast peace that might not be betrayed.

So once it would have been,—'tis so no more;
I have submitted to a new control:
35   A power is gone, which nothing can restore;
A deep distress hath humanised my Soul.[3]

1. A wealthy landscape painter who was Wordsworth's patron and close friend. Peele Castle is on an island opposite Rampside, Lancashire, where Wordsworth had spent a month in 1794, twelve years before he saw Beaumont's painting.
2. Referring to Elysium, in classical mythology the peaceful place where those favored by the gods dwelled after death.
3. Captain John Wordsworth, William's brother, had been drowned in a shipwreck on February 5, 1805. He is referred to in lines 41–42.

Not for a moment could I now behold
A smiling sea, and be what I have been:
The feeling of my loss will ne'er be old;
40 This, which I know, I speak with mind serene.

Then, Beaumont, Friend! who would have been the Friend,
If he had lived, of Him whom I deplore,°   mourn
This work of thine I blame not, but commend;
This sea in anger, and that dismal shore.

45 O 'tis a passionate Work!—yet wise and well,
Well chosen is the spirit that is here;
That Hulk° which labours in the deadly swell,   ship
This rueful sky, this pageantry of fear!

And this huge Castle, standing here sublime,
50 I love to see the look with which it braves,
Cased in the unfeeling armour of old time,
The lightning, the fierce wind, and trampling waves.

Farewell, farewell the heart that lives alone,
Housed in a dream, at distance from the Kind!°   humankind
55 Such happiness, wherever it be known,
Is to be pitied; for 'tis surely blind.

But welcome fortitude, and patient cheer,
And frequent sights of what is to be borne!
Such sights, or worse, as are before me here.—
60 Not without hope we suffer and we mourn.

Summer 1806   1807

SONNETS

Composed upon Westminster Bridge, September 3, 1802[1]

Earth has not any thing to show more fair:
Dull would he be of soul who could pass by
A sight so touching in its majesty:
This City now doth, like a garment, wear
5 The beauty of the morning; silent, bare,
Ships, towers, domes, theatres, and temples lie
Open unto the fields, and to the sky;
All bright and glittering in the smokeless air.
Never did sun more beautifully steep
10 In his first splendour, valley, rock, or hill;
Ne'er saw I, never felt, a calm so deep!

---

1. The date of this experience was not September 3, but July 31, 1802. Its occasion was a trip to France, made possible by a brief truce in the war (see Dorothy Wordsworth's *Grasmere Journals*, July 1802, p. 244).

The river glideth at his own sweet will:
Dear God! the very houses seem asleep;
And all that mighty heart is lying still!

1802   1807

It is a beauteous evening

It is a beauteous evening, calm and free,
The holy time is quiet as a Nun
Breathless with adoration; the broad sun
Is sinking down in its tranquillity;
5   The gentleness of heaven broods o'er the Sea:
Listen! the mighty Being is awake,
And doth with his eternal motion make
A sound like thunder—everlastingly.
Dear Child! dear Girl! that walkest with me here,[2]
10   If thou appear untouched by solemn thought,
Thy nature is not therefore less divine:
Thou liest in Abraham's bosom[3] all the year;
And worshipp'st at the Temple's inner shrine,
God being with thee when we know it not.

Aug. 1802   1807

London, 1802[4]

Milton! thou should'st be living at this hour:
England hath need of thee: she is a fen
Of stagnant waters: altar, sword, and pen,
Fireside, the heroic wealth of hall and bower,
5   Have forfeited their ancient English dower°   *endowment, gift*
Of inward happiness. We are selfish men;
Oh! raise us up, return to us again;
And give us manners, virtue, freedom, power.
Thy soul was like a Star, and dwelt apart:
10   Thou hadst a voice whose sound was like the sea:
Pure as the naked heavens, majestic, free,
So didst thou travel on life's common way,
In cheerful godliness; and yet thy heart
The lowliest duties on herself did lay.

Sept. 1802   1807

---

2. The girl walking with Wordsworth is Caroline, his daughter by Annette Vallon. For the event described see Dorothy Wordsworth's *Grasmere Journals*, July 1802 (p. 244).
3. Where the souls destined for heaven rest after death. Luke 16.22: "And it came to pass, that the beggar died, and was carried by the angels into Abraham's bosom."
4. One of a series "written immediately after my return from France to London, when I could not but be struck, as here described, with the vanity and parade of our own country . . . as contrasted with the quiet, and I may say the desolation, that the revolution had produced in France. This must be borne in mind, or else the reader may think that in this and the succeeding sonnets I have exaggerated the mischief engendered and fostered among us by undisturbed wealth" [Wordsworth's note, 1843].

The world is too much with us

The world is too much with us; late and soon,
Getting and spending, we lay waste our powers:
Little we see in Nature that is ours;
We have given our hearts away, a sordid boon![5]
5   This Sea that bares her bosom to the moon;
The winds that will be howling at all hours,
And are up-gathered now like sleeping flowers;
For this, for every thing, we are out of tune;
It moves us not.—Great God! I'd rather be
10   A Pagan suckled in a creed outworn;
So might I, standing on this pleasant lea,
Have glimpses that would make me less forlorn;
Have sight of Proteus rising from the sea;
Or hear old Triton[6] blow his wreathèd horn.

1802–4   1807

Surprised by joy[7]

Surprised by joy—impatient as the Wind
I turned to share the transport—Oh! with whom
But Thee, deep buried in the silent tomb,
That spot which no vicissitude can find?
5   Love, faithful love, recalled thee to my mind—
But how could I forget thee? Through what power,
Even for the least division of an hour,
Have I been so beguiled as to be blind
To my most grievous loss!—That thought's return
10   Was the worst pang that sorrow ever bore,
Save one, one only, when I stood forlorn,
Knowing my heart's best treasure was no more;
That neither present time, nor years unborn
Could to my sight that heavenly face restore.

1813–14   1815

Mutability[8]

From low to high doth dissolution climb,
And sink from high to low, along a scale
Of awful° notes, whose concord shall not fail;   *awe-inspiring*
A musical but melancholy chime,

---

5. Gift. It is the act of giving the heart away that is sordid.
6. A sea deity, usually represented as blowing on a conch shell. Proteus was an old man of the sea who (in the *Odyssey*) could assume a variety of shapes.
7. This was in fact suggested by my daughter

Catherine, long after her death [Wordsworth's note]. Catherine Wordsworth died June 4, 1812, at the age of four.
8. This late sonnet was included in an otherwise rather uninspired sequence, *Ecclesiastical Sonnets,* dealing with the history and ceremonies of the Church of England.

5   Which they can hear who meddle not with crime,
    Nor avarice, nor over-anxious care.
    Truth fails not; but her outward forms that bear
    The longest date do melt like frosty rime,
    That in the morning whitened hill and plain
10   And is no more; drop like the tower sublime
    Of yesterday, which royally did wear
    His crown of weeds, but could not even sustain
    Some casual shout that broke the silent air,
    Or the unimaginable touch of Time.

1821   1822

Steamboats, Viaducts, and Railways

    Motions and Means, on land and sea at war
    With old poetic feeling, not for this,
    Shall ye, by Poets even, be judged amiss!
    Nor shall your presence, howsoe'er it mar
5   The loveliness of Nature, prove a bar
    To the Mind's gaining that prophetic sense
    Of future change, that point of vision, whence
    May be discovered what in soul ye are.
    In spite of all that beauty may disown
10   In your harsh features, Nature doth embrace
    Her lawful offspring in Man's art; and Time,
    Pleased with your triumphs o'er his brother Space,
    Accepts from your bold hands the proffered crown
    Of hope, and smiles on you with cheer sublime.

1833   1835

The 1805 Prelude

We cannot be sure what William Wordsworth would have thought of the title by which readers now know his major work, *The Prelude, or Growth of a Poet's Mind*. The poet's widow gave the poem that title when her husband's literary executors published it in July 1850, three months after his death. Wordsworth himself had referred to it, variously, as "the poem to Coleridge," or "the poem on the growth of my own mind." Wordsworth's readership had known of the existence of this autobiographical poem since his 1814 publication of *The Excursion*, which had the subtitle "Being a portion of *The Recluse*." In the preface to that poem, which explained that *The Excursion* was part of a philosophical poem, still in preparation, titled *The Recluse*, Wordsworth revealed further that *The Recluse* would appear with a supplement: a poem, "long finished," he stated, that traced how Nature and Education had prepared the poet for executing the "arduous labour" which that philosophical poem would entail. This other poem—which is the one we now know as *The Prelude*—scrutinized his qualifications for that task. The "two Works have the same kind of relation to each other," he explained, as an ante-chapel has to a nave or "body of a gothic church."

Where *The Recluse* was never really begun, despite what that 1814 subtitle and preface indicated, *The Prelude*, by contrast, appears to have been a poem that Wordsworth could never really declare finished. He completed it, and then, rather than declaring it ready for the press, he completed it again. Revision occupied him for a half-century, claiming the time he had aimed to devote to *The Recluse*. Because he held it back from publication, this poem of self-scrutiny became a kind of lifetime companion to the poet, its account of his past altered to keep pace with the changes that age brought to its creator. The resulting gap between its dates of composition and date of publication is obliquely acknowledged in the title Mary Wordsworth devised. *The Prelude* was a good title, one of Wordsworth's executors observed, precisely because it would discourage readers from supposing that "it was his final production, instead of being, as it really is, one of his *earlier* works." Wordsworth had so arranged things, however, that when at last in 1850 it appeared as a book, this "earlier" work did double duty (in the words of Wordsworth scholar Mary Jacobus) as "a self-authored epitaph."

In 1926 Ernest de Selincourt, working from manuscripts, printed the version of the poem that Wordsworth completed in 1805, and which for many readers since then has become the preferred version. Other scholars later established the existence of a still earlier and shorter version that Wordsworth composed in 1798–99. The process that produced these three principal versions of *The Prelude*—1798–99; 1805; 1850—seems to have unfolded as follows.

1. While living in Germany during the autumn and winter of 1798–99 Wordsworth composed a number of blank verse passages about his formative experiences with nature, meaning thus to begin the philosophical poem Coleridge had urged him to write. Then, after settling with his sister, Dorothy, at Grasmere, what had first been intended as part of *The Recluse* evolved further, becoming a poem of almost a thousand lines, in two parts, that described his life up to the end of his school days. This poem corresponds to books 1 and 2 of later versions of *The Prelude*.

2. In 1801 Wordsworth began to expand this poem, adding the material that would ultimately form the beginning of book 3. He renewed this work in earnest at the start of 1804, with a new plan for a poem in five books. Scholars disagree as to whether this version, whose concluding book would have begun with the poet's vision on Mount Snowdon (later transposed to the poem's conclusion) and moved to the discussion of "spots of time" (later transposed to book 11), ever materialized. However, it is clear that by March 1804, Wordsworth had determined that the poem would require further enlarging. It would have to represent some of his experiences in France during the 1790s and the failure of his hopes for the French Revolution, dramatizing the interaction of the imagination and historical forces, as well as the interaction of the imagination and nature. Adding books 6, then 9, and 10, and 8, he completed this new version in thirteen books in May 1805 and had Dorothy and his wife copy it out. This is the version printed in this volume, which reproduces the edition of the 1805 text that Jonathan Wordsworth, Stephen Gill, and M. H. Abrams prepared in 1979 for the Norton Critical Edition of *The Prelude*.

3. For the next thirty-five years, without altering in any essential way the *Prelude*'s subject matter or design, Wordsworth revised. Our section on "The Versions of *The Prelude*" aims, through comparison of two sets of passages, to illustrate some of the characteristic effects, on tone and mood, of those revisions. This period also saw some parts of the poem published separately. "There was a boy" (from book 5) and "Simplon Pass" (from book 6), for example, appeared in Wordsworth's *Poems* of 1815. Coleridge (the first outside Wordsworth's family to encounter the 1805 text) had earlier published sections from books 1 and 6 in *The Friend*. The version of the whole poem his executors ushered into print in 1850 was in fourteen books, Wordsworth having split book 10 into two parts in 1832. The printer's copy was the transcript the poet's daughter and a friend had prepared in 1838 of the 1832 text, and into which Wordsworth and his clerk had later inserted corrections.

As this summary of the *Prelude*'s multiple recastings suggests, Wordsworth's vision of his poem—his view of himself, too—altered substantially over the years, at the start of the process especially. When he decided to enlarge the two-part *Prelude* of 1799, he committed himself to expanding lyric introspection to epic dimensions. It was "a thing unprecedented in Literary history," he observed in an 1805 letter that hints at this experiment with genre, "that a man should talk so much about himself." Between 1801 and 1805 he heightened his poem's style and incorporated allusions to earlier epics, self-consciously measuring his achievement as a poet-prophet against Milton's in *Paradise Lost*. Another prototype for his poem can be found in the tradition of spiritual autobiography that Saint Augustine had founded with his *Confessions* in the fourth century and that the scandalous Frenchman Jean-Jacques Rousseau had revived in the 1780s. Rousseau's *Confessions* made big, bold claims for the fascination of the author's subjectivity in all its unique intricacies, and Wordsworth's *Prelude* in some measure follows suit, as it personalizes epic and makes a literary form devoted to the public life of great collectivities (the fall of Troy or of Man) absorb representations of childhood anxieties and guilt that we might nowadays think of as belonging to a psychological case history. But as narrator, rather than narrated subject, Wordsworth insists on the wider import of this singular story. *The Prelude* thus asks to be read as the representative testimony of someone who (along with Coleridge, to whom the poem is addressed as a kind of letter, and along with an entire generation, in fact) has grappled with the traumatic experience of revolutionary optimism followed by defeat.

THE VERSIONS OF *THE PRELUDE*

This section pairs excerpts from the 1805 and 1850 *Prelude*—from book 6, the celebration of the imagination's powers, and, from the final book, the meditation on Mount Snowdon—to suggest the impact of Wordsworth's revisions. *1850* is shaped by Wordsworth's reviewing, with an eye to its posthumous publication, a poem that, addressed to a friend, occasionally read as the transcript of frank talk held in private. *1850* is a more formal poem therefore, its diction weightier. Its poet explains more, elaborating to achieve precision. The sense of spontaneity that informs the passages in *1805* in which the poet seems to think aloud (as in the phrase "the sea, the real sea" in *1805* 13.49) is harder to locate in *1850*. Wordsworth in *1850* also supplements lines announcing his faith in the mind of man with more conventional expressions of piety (e.g., the reference in *1850* 14.77 to "soul of more than mortal privilege"). Since Coleridge in *Biographia Literaria*, readers have been debating where in his poetry Wordsworth is most authentically himself. These texts, which may be read in conjunction with the lengthier excerpts from *1850* available in the supplemental ebook, suggest the stakes of those debates.

The Crossing of the Alps

From 1805. Book Sixth

525 Imagination!—lifting up itself
Before the eye and progress of my song
Like an unfathered vapour, here that power,
In all the might of its endowments, came
Athwart me. I was lost as in a cloud,
530 Halted without a struggle to break through,
And now, recovering, to my soul I say
'I recognise thy glory'. In such strength
Of usurpation, in such visitings
Of awful promise, when the light of sense
535 Goes out in flashes that have shewn to us
The invisible world, doth greatness make abode,
There harbours whether we be young or old.
Our destiny, our nature, and our home,
Is with infinitude—and only there;
540 With hope it is, hope that can never die,
Effort, and expectation, and desire,
And something evermore about to be.
The mind beneath such banners militant
Thinks not of spoils or trophies, nor of aught
545 That may attest its prowess, blest in thoughts
That are their own perfection and reward—
Strong in itself, and in the access of joy
Which hides it like the overflowing Nile.

From 1850. Book Sixth

Imagination—here the Power so called
Through sad incompetence of human speech,
That awful Power rose from the mind's abyss
595 Like an unfathered vapour that enwraps,
At once, some lonely traveller. I was lost;
Halted without an effort to break through;
But to my conscious soul I now can say—
'I recognise thy glory': in such strength
600 Of usurpation, when the light of sense
Goes out, but with a flash that has revealed
The invisible world, doth greatness make abode,
There harbours, whether we be young or old.
Our destiny, our being's heart and home,
605 Is with infinitude, and only there;
With hope it is, hope that can never die,
Effort, and expectation, and desire,
And something evermore about to be.
Under such banners militant, the soul
610 Seeks for no trophies, struggles for no spoils
That may attest her prowess, blest in thoughts
That are their own perfection and reward,
Strong in herself and in beatitude
That hides her, like the mighty flood of Nile
615 Poured from his fount of Abyssinian clouds
To fertilise the whole Egyptian plain.

The Climbing of Snowdon

From 1805. Book Thirteen

The moon stood naked in the heavens at height
Immense above my head, and on the shore
I found myself of a huge sea of mist,
Which meek and silent rested at my feet.
45 A hundred hills their dusky backs upheaved
All over this still ocean, and beyond,
Far, far beyond, the vapours shot themselves
In headlands, tongues, and promontory shapes,
Into the sea, the real sea, that seemed
50 To dwindle and give up its majesty,
Usurped upon as far as sight could reach.
Meanwhile, the moon looked down upon this shew
In single glory, and we stood, the mist
Touching our very feet; and from the shore
55 At distance not the third part of a mile
Was a blue chasm, a fracture in the vapour,
A deep and gloomy breathing-place, through which
Mounted the roar of waters, torrents, streams
Innumerable, roaring with one voice.
60 The universal spectacle throughout
Was shaped for admiration and delight,
Grand in itself alone, but in that breach
Through which the homeless voice of waters rose,
That dark deep thoroughfare, had Nature lodged
65 The soul, the imagination of the whole.

A meditation rose in me that night
Upon the lonely mountain when the scene
Had passed away, and it appeared to me
The perfect image of a mighty mind,
70 Of one that feeds upon infinity,
That is exalted by an under-presence
The sense of God, or whatsoe'er is dim
Or vast in its own being.

From 1850. Book Fourteenth

40 The Moon hung naked in a firmament
    Of azure without cloud, and at my feet
    Rested a silent sea of hoary° mist.   *white*
    A hundred hills their dusky backs upheaved
    All over this still ocean, and beyond,
45 Far, far beyond, the solid vapours stretched,
    In headlands, tongues, and promontory shapes,
    Into the main Atlantic, that appeared
    To dwindle, and give up his majesty,
    Usurped upon far as the sight could reach.
50 Not so the ethereal vault; encroachment none
    Was there, nor loss; only the inferior stars
    Had disappeared, or shed a fainter light
    In the clear presence of the full-orbed Moon,
    Who, from her sovereign elevation, gazed
55 Upon the billowy ocean, as it lay
    All meek and silent, save that through a rift—
    Not distant from the shore whereon we stood,
    A fixed, abysmal, gloomy, breathing-place—
    Mounted the roar of waters, torrents, streams
60 Innumerable, roaring with one voice
    Heard over earth and sea, and, in that hour,
    For so it seems, felt by the starry heavens.

        When into air had partially dissolved
    That vision, given to spirits of the night
65 And three chance human wanderers, in calm thought
    Reflected, it appeared to me the type
    Of a majestic intellect, its acts
    And its possessions, what it has and craves,
    What in itself it is, and would become.
70 There I beheld the emblem of a mind
    That feeds upon infinity, that broods
    Over the dark abyss, intent to hear
    Its voices issuing forth to silent light
    In one continuous stream; a mind sustained
75 By recognitions of transcendent power,
    In sense conducting to ideal form,
    In soul of more than mortal privilege.

The 1805 Prelude

Book First.

Introduction: Childhood and School-time

Oh there is blessing in this gentle breeze,
That blows from the green fields and from the clouds
And from the sky; it beats against my cheek,
And seems half conscious of the joy it gives.
5   O welcome messenger! O welcome friend!
A captive greets thee, coming from a house
Of bondage, from yon city's° walls set free,   *London's*
A prison where he hath been long immured.
Now I am free, enfranchised and at large,
10   May fix my habitation where I will.
What dwelling shall receive me, in what vale
Shall be my harbour, underneath what grove
Shall I take up my home, and what sweet stream
Shall with its murmurs lull me to my rest?
15   The earth is all before me[1]—with a heart
Joyous, nor scared at its own liberty,
I look about, and should the guide I chuse
Be nothing better than a wandering cloud
I cannot miss my way. I breathe again—
20   Trances of thought and mountings of the mind
Come fast upon me. It is shaken off,
As by miraculous gift 'tis shaken off,
That burthen of my own unnatural self,
The heavy weight of many a weary day
25   Not mine, and such as were not made for me.
Long months of peace—if such bold word accord
With any promises of human life—
Long months of ease and undisturbed delight
Are mine in prospect.° Whither shall I turn,   *anticipation*
30   By road or pathway, or through open field,
Or shall a twig or any floating thing
Upon the river point me out my course?

    Enough that I am free, for months to come
May dedicate myself to chosen tasks,
35   May quit the tiresome sea and dwell on shore—
If not a settler on the soil, at least
To drink wild water, and to pluck green herbs,
And gather fruits fresh from their native bough.
Nay more, if I may trust myself, this hour
40   Hath brought a gift that consecrates my joy;
For I, methought, while the sweet breath of heaven
Was blowing on my body, felt within

---

1. One of many echoes from *Paradise Lost*, where the line is applied to Adam and Eve as they begin their new life after the fall and their expulsion from Eden: "The world was all before them" (12.646).

A corresponding mild creative breeze,
A vital breeze which travelled gently on
45 O'er things which it had made, and is become
A tempest, a redundant° energy,   *abundant*
Vexing its own creation. 'Tis a power
That does not come unrecognised, a storm
Which, breaking up a long-continued frost,
50 Brings with it vernal° promises, the hope   *springtime*
Of active days, of dignity and thought,
Of prowess in an honorable field,
Pure passions, virtue, knowledge, and delight,
The holy life of music and of verse.[2]

55   Thus far, O friend,[3] did I, not used to make
A present joy the matter of my song,[4]
Pour out that day my soul in measured strains,
Even in the very words which I have here
Recorded. To the open fields I told
60 A prophesy; poetic numbers° came   *verses*
Spontaneously, and clothed in priestly robe
My spirit, thus singled out, as it might seem,
For holy services. Great hopes were mine:
My own voice cheared me, and, far more, the mind's
65 Internal echo of the imperfect sound—
To both I listened, drawing from them both
A chearful confidence in things to come.

     Whereat, being not unwilling now to give
A respite to this passion[5] paced on
70 Gently, with careless steps, and came erelong
To a green shady place where down I sate
Beneath a tree, slackening my thoughts by choice
And settling into gentler happiness.
'Twas autumn, and a calm and placid day
75 With warmth as much as needed from a sun
Two hours declined towards the west, a day
With silver clouds and sunshine on the grass,
And, in the sheltered grove where I was couched,
A perfect stillness. On the ground I lay
80 Passing through many thoughts, yet mainly such
As to myself pertained. I made a choice
Of one sweet vale[6] whither my steps should turn,
And saw, methought, the very house and fields
85 Present before my eyes; nor did I fail

---

2. This opening passage (lines 1–54), which Wordsworth wrote in 1799, and which in book 7, line 4 he will call his "glad preamble," replaces a traditional epic's opening prayer to the Muse for inspiration. To be "inspired" is literally to be breathed or blown into by a divinity (in Latin *spirare* means both "to breathe" and "to blow"). The "breath of heaven" that blows on the poet's body in lines 41–42, answered by a breeze within (lines 42–43), fills that role here.
3. Samuel Taylor Coleridge, to whom Wordsworth addresses the whole of the *Prelude*. For Coleridge's response, see "To William Wordsworth" (p. 297).
4. In the Preface to *Lyrical Ballads*, Wordsworth says that his poetry usually originates in "emotion recollected in tranquillity"; hence not, as in the preamble of lines 1–54, during the experience that it records.
5. I.e., "willing to prolong the passion."
6. Grasmere, where Wordsworth settled with his sister, Dorothy, in December 1799.

To add meanwhile assurance of some work
Of glory there forthwith to be begun—
Perhaps too there performed.[7] Thus long I lay
Cheared by the genial pillow of the earth
Beneath my head, soothed by a sense of touch
90 From the warm ground, that balanced me, else lost
Entirely, seeing nought, nought hearing, save
When here and there about the grove of oaks
Where was my bed, an acorn from the trees
Fell audibly, and with a startling sound.

95   Thus occupied in mind I lingered here
Contented, nor rose up until the sun
Had almost touched the horizon; bidding then
A farewell to the city left behind,
Even with the chance equipment of that hour
100 I journeyed towards the vale which I had chosen.
It was a splendid evening, and my soul
Did once again make trial of the strength
Restored to her afresh; nor did she want
Eolian visitations[8]—but the harp
105 Was soon defrauded, and the banded host
Of harmony dispersed in straggling sounds,
And lastly utter silence. 'Be it so,
It is an injury', said I, 'to this day
To think of any thing but present joy.'
110 So, like a peasant, I pursued my road
Beneath the evening sun, nor had one wish
Again to bend the sabbath of that time[9]
To a servile yoke. What need of many words?—
A pleasant loitering journey, through two days
115 Continued, brought me to my hermitage.°   secluded dwelling

    I spare to speak, my friend, of what ensued—
The admiration and the love, the life
In common things, the endless store of things
Rare, or at least so seeming, every day
120 Found all about me in one neighbourhood,
The self-congratulation,° the complete   rejoicing
Composure, and the happiness entire.
But speedily a longing in me rose
To brace myself to some determined aim,
125 Reading or thinking, either to lay up
New stores, or rescue from decay the old
By timely interference. I had hopes
Still higher, that with a frame of outward life
I might endue,° might fix in a visible home,   invest
130 Some portion of those phantoms of conceit,°   mental images

---

7. The work is *The Recluse*, which Wordsworth planned as his major poetic work but never finished.
8. Influences to which his soul responded as an Eolian harp, placed in an open window, responds with music to gusts of a breeze. For a description of this instrument, named for Aeolus, the classical god of the winds, see Coleridge's *The Eolian Harp*, n. 1, p. 252.
9. That time of rest.

That had been floating loose about so long,
And to such beings temperately deal forth
The many feelings that oppressed my heart.
But I have been discouraged: gleams of light
135　Flash often from the east, then disappear,
And mock me with a sky that ripens not
Into a steady morning. If my mind,
Remembering the sweet promise of the past,
Would gladly grapple with some noble theme,
140　Vain is her wish—where'er she turns she finds
Impediments from day to day renewed.

　　And now it would content me to yield up
Those lofty hopes awhile for present gifts
Of humbler industry. But, O dear friend,
145　The poet, gentle creature as he is,
Hath like the lover his unruly times—
His fits when he is neither sick nor well,
Though no distress be near him but his own
Unmanageable thoughts. The mind itself,
150　The meditative mind, best pleased perhaps
While she as duteous as the mother dove
Sits brooding,[1] lives not always to that end,
But hath less quiet instincts—goadings on
That drive her as in trouble through the groves.
155　With me is now such passion, which I blame
No otherwise than as it lasts too long.

　　When, as becomes a man who would prepare
For such a glorious work, I through myself
Make rigorous inquisition, the report
160　Is often chearing; for I neither seem
To lack that first great gift, the vital soul,
Nor general truths which are themselves a sort
Of elements and agents, under-powers,
Subordinate helpers of the living mind.
165　Nor am I naked in external things,
Forms, images, nor numerous other aids
Of less regard, though won perhaps with toil,
And needful to build up a poet's praise.
Time, place, and manners,° these I seek, and these　　　*customs*
170　I find in plenteous store, but nowhere such
As may be singled out with steady choice—
No little band of yet remembered names
Whom I, in perfect confidence, might hope
To summon back from lonesome banishment
175　And make them inmates in the hearts of men
Now living, or to live in times to come.
Sometimes, mistaking vainly, as I fear,

---

1. An echo of Milton's description in *Paradise Lost* of the original act of creation: the Holy Spirit, whom Milton calls on for inspiration, "Dovelike satst brooding on the vast Abyss / And mad'st it pregnant (1.21–22).

Proud spring-tide swellings for a regular sea,
I settle on some British theme, some old
180 Romantic tale by Milton left unsung;[2]
More often resting at some gentle place
Within the groves of chivalry I pipe
Among the shepherds, with reposing knights
Sit by a fountain-side and hear their tales.
185 Sometimes, more sternly moved, I would relate
How vanquished Mithridates northward passed
And, hidden in the cloud of years, became
That Odin, father of a race by whom
Perished the Roman Empire;[3] how the friends
190 And followers of Sertorius, out of Spain
Flying, found shelter in the Fortunate Isles,
And left their usages, their arts and laws,
To disappear by a slow gradual death,
To dwindle and to perish one by one,
195 Starved in those narrow bounds—but not the soul
Of liberty, which fifteen hundred years
Survived, and, when the European came
With skill and power that could not be withstood,
Did like a pestilence maintain its hold,
200 And wasted down by glorious death that race
Of natural heroes.[4] Or I would record
How in tyrannic times, some unknown man,
Unheard of in the chronicles of kings,
Suffered in silence for the love of truth;
205 How that one Frenchman, through continued force
Of meditation on the inhuman deeds
Of the first conquerors of the Indian Isles,
Went single in his ministry across
The ocean, not to comfort the oppressed,
210 But like a thirsty wind to roam about
Withering the oppressor;[5] how Gustavus found
Help at his need in Dalecarlia's mines;[6]
How Wallace fought for Scotland, left the name
Of Wallace to be found like a wild flower
215 All over his dear country, left the deeds

2. In *Paradise Lost* 9.24–41 Milton relates that, in seeking a subject for his epic poem, he considered then rejected the "fabled Knights" of medieval romance.
3. Mithridates VI, king of Pontus in Asia Minor, was defeated by the Roman general Pompey in 66 B.C.E. Wordsworth finds epic potential in the legend that, following this defeat, he (in some versions, one of his chieftains) led his people in migration from Asia, north to Scandinavia; there he so impressed the inhabitants with his power that he was able to make them take him for a god, becoming the real-life prototype for the Norse god of war, Odin. In 1796 Coleridge and Robert Southey cowrote an essay for Coleridge's journal *The Watchman* that retold this story, emphasizing Odin's choice of a dangerous freedom over Roman subjugation. This account of Odin links him to other figures whom Wordsworth here considers as potential subjects for his poem, all of them victims of and fighters against tyranny.
4. Sertorius, a Roman general temporarily allied with Mithridates, sought to establish an independent Roman republic in Spain. Following his assassination in 72 B.C.E. the republic was crushed, but there is a legend that his followers fled to the Canary Islands (known then as the "Fortunate Islands," line 191), where their descendants flourished until the arrival of Spanish conquistadors late in the 15th century.
5. "Dominique de Gourges, a French gentleman who went in 1568 to Florida to avenge the massacre of the French by the Spaniards there" [Wordsworth's note in 1850 *Prelude*].
6. Gustavus Vassa (1496–1530) worked to advance Sweden's liberation from Danish rule while concealing himself in his country's Dalecarlia mines.

Of Wallace like a family of ghosts
To people the steep rocks and river-banks,
Her natural sanctuaries, with a local soul
Of independence and stern liberty.[7]
220 Sometimes it suits me better to shape out
Some tale from my own heart, more near akin
To my own passions and habitual thoughts,
Some variegated story, in the main
Lofty, with interchange of gentler things.
225 But deadening admonitions will succeed,
And the whole beauteous fabric seems to lack
Foundation, and withal appears throughout
Shadowy and unsubstantial.

                          Then, last wish—
My last and favorite aspiration—then
230 I yearn towards some philosophic song
Of truth[8] that cherishes° our daily life,   *fosters tenderly*
With meditations passionate from deep
Recesses in man's heart, immortal verse
Thoughtfully fitted to the Orphean lyre;[9]
235 But from this awful° burthen I full soon   *solemn*
Take refuge, and beguile myself with trust
That mellower years will bring a riper mind
And clearer insight. Thus from day to day
I live a mockery of the brotherhood
240 Of vice and virtue, with no skill to part°   *distinguish*
Vague longing that is bred by want° of power,   *lack*
From paramount impulse not to be withstood;
A timorous capacity, from prudence;
From circumspection,° infinite delay.   *carefulness*
245 Humility and modest awe themselves
Betray me, serving often for a cloak
To a more subtle selfishness, that now
Doth lock my functions up in blank reserve,°   *total inaction*
Now dupes me by an over-anxious eye
250 That with a false activity beats off
Simplicity and self-presented truth.
Ah, better far than this to stray about
Voluptuously° through fields and rural walks   *luxuriously*
And ask no record of the hours given up
225 To vacant musing, unreproved neglect
Of all things, and deliberate holiday.
Far better never to have heard the name
Of zeal and just ambition than to live
Thus baffled by a mind that every hour
260 Turns recreant° to her task, takes heart again,   *unfaithful*
Then feels immediately some hollow thought

7. William Wallace, Scottish patriot, fought
against the English until captured and executed
in 1304.
8. I.e., *The Recluse.*

9. The lyre of Orpheus. In Greek myth the singing and playing of Orpheus, a traditional figure
for the powers of poetry, enchanted both humans
and the natural world.

Hang like an interdict° upon her hopes.   *prohibition*
This is my lot; for either still I find
Some imperfection in the chosen theme,
265 Or see of absolute accomplishment
Much wanting—so much wanting—in myself
That I recoil and droop, and seek repose
In indolence from vain perplexity,
Unprofitably travelling towards the grave,
270 Like a false steward who hath much received
And renders nothing back.[1]

                Was it for this[2]
That one, the fairest of all rivers, loved
To blend his murmurs with my nurse's song,
And from his alder shades and rocky falls,
270 And from his fords and shallows, sent a voice
That flowed along my dreams? For this didst thou,
O Derwent, travelling over the green plains
Near my 'sweet birthplace',[3] didst thou, beauteous stream,
Make ceaseless music through the night and day,
280 Which with its steady cadence tempering
Our human waywardness, composed my thoughts
To more than infant softness, giving me
Among the fretful dwellings of mankind,
A knowledge, a dim earnest,° of the calm   *foretaste*
285 Which Nature breathes among the hills and groves?
When, having left his mountains, to the towers
Of Cockermouth that beauteous river came,
Behind my father's house he passed, close by,
Along the margin of our terrace walk.[4]
290 He was a playmate whom we dearly loved:
Oh, many a time have I, a five years' child,
A naked boy, in one delightful rill,
A little mill-race[5] severed from his stream,
Made one long bathing of a summer's day,
295 Basked in the sun, and plunged, and basked again,
Alternate, all a summer's day, or coursed
Over the sandy fields, leaping through groves
Of yellow grunsel;[6] or, when crag and hill,
The woods, and distant Skiddaw's lofty height,[7]
300 Were bronzed with a deep radiance, stood alone
Beneath the sky, as if I had been born
On Indian plains,[8] and from my mother's hut
Had run abroad in wantonness to sport,
A naked savage, in the thunder-shower.

---

1. The reference is to Christ's parable of the steward who fails to use his talents (literally, the coins his master has entrusted to him and, figuratively, his God-given abilities) in Matthew 25.14–30.
2. The two-part *Prelude* that Wordsworth wrote in 1798–99 begins with this abrupt question.
3. Quoting Coleridge's "Frost at Midnight," line 28.
4. The Derwent River flows by Cockermouth

Castle and then past the garden terrace behind Wordsworth's childhood residence in Cockermouth, Cumbria.
5. The current that drives a mill wheel.
6. Or groundsel, a common European weed.
7. Skiddaw: one of the highest peaks in the Lake District, nine miles east of Cockermouth.
8. I.e., in America.

305 Fair seed-time had my soul, and I grew up
  Fostered alike by beauty and by fear,
  Much favored in my birthplace, and no less
  In that beloved vale[9] to which erelong
  I was transplanted. Well I call to mind—
  'Twas at an early age, ere I had seen
310 Nine summers—when upon the mountain slope
  The frost and breath of frosty wind had snapped
  The last autumnal crocus, 'twas my joy
  To wander half the night among the cliffs
  And the smooth hollows where the woodcocks ran
315 Along the open turf. In thought and wish
  That time, my shoulder all with springes° hung,   *bird snares*
  I was a fell destroyer. On the heights
  Scudding away from snare to snare, I plied
320 My anxious visitation, hurrying on,
  Still hurrying, hurrying onward. Moon and stars
  Were shining o'er my head; I was alone,
  And seemed to be a trouble to the peace
  That was among them. Sometimes it befel
325 In these night-wanderings, that a strong desire
  O'erpowered my better reason, and the bird
  Which was the captive of another's toils[1]
  Became my prey; and when the deed was done
  I heard among the solitary hills
330 Low breathings coming after me, and sounds
  Of undistinguishable motion, steps
  Almost as silent as the turf they trod.

   Nor less in springtime, when on southern banks
  The shining sun had from her knot of leaves
335 Decoyed the primrose flower, and when the vales
  And woods were warm, was I a plunderer then
  In the high places, on the lonesome peaks,
  Where'er among the mountains and the winds
  The mother-bird had built her lodge. Though mean°   *petty*
340 My object and inglorious, yet the end°   *result*
  Was not ignoble. Oh, when I have hung
  Above the raven's nest, by knots of grass
  And half-inch fissures in the slippery rock
  But ill sustained, and almost, as it seemed,
345 Suspended by the blast which blew amain,
  Shouldering the naked crag, oh, at that time
  While on the perilous ridge I hung alone,
  With what strange utterance did the loud dry wind
  Blow through my ears; the sky seemed not a sky
350 Of earth, and with what motion moved the clouds!

   The mind of man is framed even like the breath
  And harmony of music. There is a dark
  Invisible workmanship that reconciles

---

9. The valley of Esthwaite, 35 miles from Cockermouth, where Wordsworth went to school

after 1779.
1. "Toils" can mean snares or labors.

Discordant elements, and makes them move
355 In one society. Ah me, that all
The terrors, all the early miseries,
Regrets, vexations, lassitudes, that all
The thoughts and feelings which have been infused
Into my mind, should ever have made up
360 The calm existence that is mine when I
Am worthy of myself. Praise to the end,
Thanks likewise for the means! But I believe
That Nature, oftentimes, when she would frame
A favored being, from his earliest dawn
365 Of infancy doth open out the clouds
As at the touch of lightning, seeking him
With gentlest visitation; not the less,
Though haply° aiming at the self-same end,   *perhaps*
Does it delight her sometimes to employ
370 Severer interventions, ministry
More palpable—and so she dealt with me.

One evening—surely I was led by her—
I went alone into a shepherd's boat,
A skiff that to a willow-tree was tied
375 Within a rocky cove, its usual home.
'Twas by the shores of Patterdale, a vale
Wherein I was a stranger, thither come
A schoolboy traveller at the holidays.
Forth rambled from the village inn alone,
380 No sooner had I sight of this small skiff,
Discovered thus by unexpected chance,
Than I unloosed her tether and embarked.
The moon was up, the lake was shining clear
Among the hoary mountains; from the shore
385 I pushed, and struck the oars, and struck again
In cadence, and my little boat moved on
Even like a man who moves with stately step
Though bent on speed. It was an act of stealth
And troubled pleasure. Nor without the voice
390 Of mountain-echoes did my boat move on,
Leaving behind her still on either side
Small circles glittering idly in the moon,
Until they melted all into one track
Of sparkling light. A rocky steep uprose
395 Above the cavern of the willow-tree,
And now, as suited one who proudly rowed
With his best skill, I fixed a steady view
Upon the top of that same craggy ridge,
The bound of the horizon—for behind
400 Was nothing but the stars and the grey sky.[2]
She was an elfin pinnace;° lustily   *small boat*
I dipped my oars into the silent lake,
And as I rose upon the stroke my boat

---

2. To direct his boat in a straight line, the rower (sitting facing the stern of the boat) has fixed his eye on a point on the ridge above the nearby shore, which blocks out the landscape behind.

Went heaving through the water like a swan—
405　When from behind that craggy steep, till then
The bound of the horizon, a huge cliff,
As if with voluntary power instinct,°　　　　　　　　　　　*endowed*
Upreared its head. I struck, and struck again,
And, growing still in stature, the huge cliff
410　Rose up between me and the stars, and still
With measured motion, like a living thing
Strode after me. With trembling hands I turned
And through the silent water stole my way
Back to the cavern of the willow-tree.
415　There, in her mooring-place, I left my bark
And through the meadows homeward went with grave
And serious thoughts; and after I had seen
That spectacle, for many days my brain
Worked with a dim and undetermined sense
420　Of unknown modes of being. In my thoughts
There was a darkness—call it solitude
Or blank desertion—no familiar shapes
Of hourly objects, images of trees,
Of sea or sky, no colours of green fields,
But huge and mighty forms that do not live
425　Like living men moved slowly through my mind
By day, and were the trouble of my dreams.

　　　Wisdom and spirit of the universe,
Thou soul that art the eternity of thought,
430　That giv'st to forms and images a breath
And everlasting motion—not in vain,
By day or star-light, thus from my first dawn
Of childhood didst thou intertwine for me
The passions that build up our human soul,
435　Not with the mean and vulgar° works of man,　　　*lowly, commonplace*
But with high objects, with enduring things,
With life and Nature, purifying thus
The elements of feeling and of thought,
And sanctifying by such discipline
440　Both pain and fear, until we recognise
A grandeur in the beatings of the heart.
Nor was this fellowship vouchsafed to me
With stinted kindness. In November days,
When vapours rolling down the valleys made
445　A lonely scene more lonesome, among woods
At noon, and 'mid the calm of summer nights
When by the margin of the trembling lake
Beneath the gloomy hills I homeward went
In solitude, such intercourse was mine—
450　'Twas mine among the fields both day and night,
And by the waters all the summer long.

　　　And in the frosty season, when the sun
Was set, and visible for many a mile
The cottage windows through the twilight blazed,
455　I heeded not the summons; happy time

It was indeed for all of us, to me
It was a time of rapture. Clear and loud
The village clock tolled six; I wheeled about
Proud and exulting, like an untired horse
460   That cares not for its home. All shod with steel°   *i.e., on skates*
We hissed along the polished ice in games
Confederate, imitative of the chace
And woodland pleasures, the resounding horn,
The pack loud bellowing, and the hunted hare.
465   So through the darkness and the cold we flew,
And not a voice was idle. With the din,
Meanwhile, the precipices rang aloud;
The leafless trees and every icy crag
Tinkled like iron; while the distant hills
470   Into the tumult sent an alien sound
Of melancholy, not unnoticed; while the stars,
Eastward, were sparkling clear, and in the west
The orange sky of evening died away.

    Not seldom from the uproar I retired
475   Into a silent bay, or sportively
Glanced sideway[3] leaving the tumultuous throng,
To cut across the image of a star
That gleamed upon the ice. And oftentimes
When we had given our bodies to the wind,
480   And all the shadowy banks on either side
Came sweeping through the darkness, spinning still
The rapid line of motion, then at once
Have I, reclining back upon my heels,
Stopped short—yet still the solitary cliffs
485   Wheeled by me, even as if the earth had rolled
With visible motion her diurnal° round.   *daily*
Behind me did they stretch in solemn train,°   *succession*
Feebler and feebler, and I stood and watched
Till all was tranquil as a dreamless sleep.

490   Ye presences of Nature, in the sky
Or on the earth, ye visions of the hills
And souls of lonely places, can I think
A vulgar hope was yours when ye employed
Such ministry—when ye through many a year
495   Haunting me thus among my boyish sports,
On caves and trees, upon the woods and hills,
Impressed upon all forms the characters°   *signs*
Of danger or desire, and thus did make
The surface of the universal earth
500   With triumph, and delight, and hope, and fear,
Work° like a sea?   *seethe*

    Not uselessly employed,
I might pursue this theme through every change
Of exercise and play to which the year

3. Moved off obliquely.

Did summon us in its delightful round.
505 We were a noisy crew; the sun in heaven
Beheld not vales more beautiful than ours,
Nor saw a race in happiness and joy
More worthy of the fields where they were sown.
I would record with no reluctant voice
510 The woods of autumn, and their hazel bowers
With milk-white clusters hung, the rod and line—
True symbol of the foolishness of hope—
Which with its strong enchantment led us on
By rocks and pools, shut out from every star
515 All the green summer, to forlorn cascades
Among the windings of the mountain brooks.
Unfading recollections—at this hour
The heart is almost mine with which I felt
From some hill-top on sunny afternoons
520 The kite, high up among the fleecy clouds,
Pull at its rein like an impatient courser,°   *racehorse*
Or, from the meadows sent on gusty days,
Beheld her breast the wind, then suddenly
Dashed headlong and rejected by the storm.

525   Ye lowly cottages in which we dwelt,
A ministration of your own was yours,
A sanctity, a safeguard, and a love.
Can I forget you, being as ye were
So beautiful among the pleasant fields
530 In which ye stood? Or can I here forget
The plain and seemly countenance with which
Ye dealt out your plain comforts? Yet had ye
Delights and exultations of your own:
Eager and never weary we pursued
535 Our home amusements by the warm peat fire
At evening, when with pencil and with slate,
In square divisions parcelled out, and all
With crosses and with cyphers scribbled o'er,°   *tic-tac-toe*
We schemed and puzzled, head opposed to head,
540 In strife too humble to be named in verse;
Or round the naked table, snow-white deal,°   *pine or fir*
Cherry, or maple, sate in close array,
And to the combat—lu or whist—led on
A thick-ribbed army, not as in the world
545 Neglected and ungratefully thrown by
Even for the very service they had wrought,
But husbanded through many a long campaign.
Uncouth assemblage was it, where no few
Had changed their functions—some, plebean cards
550 Which fate beyond the promise of their birth
Had glorified, and called to represent
The persons of departed potentates.[4]

---

4. The cards for these games of loo and whist have changed their functions in ways that remind us that *The Prelude* was begun soon after the downfall of the French monarchy during the Revolution. The "potentate" cards—the kings, queens, and jacks—have over time been lost from the pack and so selected "plebean," or commoner, cards have come to be used in their place.

Oh, with what echoes on the board they fell!
Ironic diamonds—clubs, hearts, diamonds, spades,
555 A congregation piteously akin.
Cheap matter did they give to boyish wit,
Those sooty knaves, precipitated down
With scoffs and taunts like Vulcan out of heaven;[5]
The paramount ace, a moon in her eclipse;
560 Queens, gleaming through their splendour's last decay;
And monarchs, surly at the wrongs sustained
By royal visages. Meanwhile abroad
The heavy rain was falling, or the frost
Raged bitterly with keen and silent tooth;
565 And, interrupting the impassioned game,
From Esthwaite's neighbouring lake the splitting ice,
While it sank down towards the water, sent
Among the meadows and the hills its long
And dismal yellings, like the noise of wolves
570 When they are howling round the Bothnic main.°   *Baltic Sea*

        Nor, sedulous° as I have been to trace   *diligent*
How Nature by extrinsic passion first
Peopled my mind with beauteous forms or grand
And made me love them, may I well forget
575 How other pleasures have been mine, and joys
Of subtler origin—how I have felt,
Not seldom, even in that tempestuous time,
Those hallowed and pure motions of the sense
Which seem in their simplicity to own
580 An intellectual° charm, that calm delight   *spiritual*
Which, if I err not, surely must belong
To those first-born° affinities that fit   *innate*
Our new existence to existing things,
And, in our dawn of being, constitute
585 The bond of union betwixt life and joy.

        Yes, I remember when the changeful earth
And twice five seasons on my mind had stamped
The faces of the moving year, even then,
A child, I held unconscious intercourse
590 With the eternal beauty, drinking in
A pure organic pleasure from the lines
Of curling mist, or from the level plain
Of waters coloured by the steady clouds.
The sands of Westmoreland, the creeks and bays
595 Of Cumbria's° rocky limits, they can tell   *Cumberland's*
How when the sea threw off his evening shade
And to the shepherd's huts beneath the crags
Did send sweet notice of the rising moon,
How I have stood, to fancies such as these,
600 Engrafted in the tenderness of thought,

---

5. Roman god of fire and the forge. His mother, Juno, when he was born lame, threw him down from Olympus, home of the gods.

A stranger, linking with the spectacle
No conscious memory of a kindred sight,
And bringing with me no peculiar sense
Of quietness or peace—yet I have stood
605 Even while mine eye has moved o'er three long leagues°   *about 9 miles*
Of shining water, gathering, as it seemed,
Through every hair-breadth of that field of light
New pleasure, like a bee among the flowers.

    Thus often in those fits of vulgar° joy   *ordinary*
610 Which through all seasons on a child's pursuits
Are prompt attendants, 'mid that giddy bliss
Which like a tempest works along the blood
And is forgotten, even then I felt
Gleams like the flashing of a shield. The earth
615 And common face of Nature spake to me
Rememberable things; sometimes, 'tis true,
By chance collisions and quaint accidents—
Like those ill-sorted unions, work supposed
Of evil-minded fairies—yet not vain
620 Nor profitless, if haply they impressed
Collateral° objects and appearances,   *secondary*
Albeit lifeless then, and doomed to sleep
Until maturer seasons called them forth
To impregnate and to elevate the mind.
625 And if the vulgar joy by its own weight
Wearied itself out of the memory,
The scenes which were a witness of that joy
Remained, in their substantial lineaments
Depicted on the brain, and to the eye
630 Were visible, a daily sight. And thus
By the impressive discipline of fear,
By pleasure and repeated happiness—
So frequently repeated—and by force
Of obscure feelings representative
635 Of joys that were forgotten, these same scenes,
So beauteous and majestic in themselves,
Though yet the day was distant, did at length
Become habitually dear, and all
Their hues and forms were by invisible links
640 Allied to the affections.

                I began
My story early, feeling, as I fear,
The weakness of a human love for days
Disowned by memory—ere the birth of spring
Planting my snowdrops among winter snows.[6]
645 Nor will it seem to thee, my friend, so prompt
In sympathy, that I have lengthened out
With fond and feeble tongue a tedious tale.

6. I.e., he fears that he may have mistakenly attributed his later thoughts to a time of life he can no longer remember.

Meanwhile my hope has been that I might fetch
Invigorating thoughts from former years,
650 Might fix the wavering balance of my mind,
And haply meet reproaches too, whose power
May spur me on, in manhood now mature,
To honorable toil. Yet should these hopes
Be vain, and thus should neither I be taught
655 To understand myself, nor thou to know
With better knowledge how the heart was framed
Of him thou lovest, need I dread from thee
Harsh judgments if I am so loth to quit
Those recollected hours that have the charm
660 Of visionary things,[7] and lovely forms
And sweet sensations, that throw back our life
And almost make our infancy itself
A visible scene on which the sun is shining?

One end hereby at least hath been attained—
665 My mind hath been revived—and if this mood
Desert me not, I will forthwith bring down
Through later years the story of my life.
The road lies plain before me. 'Tis a theme
Single and of determined bounds, and hence
670 I chuse it rather at this time than work
Of ampler or more varied argument,
Where I might be discomfited and lost,
And certain hopes are with me that to thee
This labour will be welcome, honoured friend.

From Book Second.

School-time (Continued)

[BOYHOOD ADVENTURES; "BLEST THE INFANT BABE"]

Thus far, O friend, have we, though leaving much
Unvisited, endeavoured to retrace
My life through its first years, and measured back
The way I travelled when I first began
5 To love the woods and fields. The passion yet
Was in its birth, sustained, as might befal,
By nourishment that came unsought—for still
From week to week, from month to month, we lived
A round of tumult. Duly° were our games   *appropriately*
10 Prolonged in summer till the daylight failed:
No chair remained before the doors, the bench
And threshold steps were empty, fast asleep
The labourer and the old man who had sate
A later lingerer, yet the revelry
15 Continued and the loud uproar. At last,

7. Things seen in a vision.

When all the ground was dark and the huge clouds
Were edged with twinkling stars, to bed we went
With weary joints and with a beating mind.
Ah, is there one who ever has been young
20   And needs a monitory voice to tame
The pride of virtue and of intellect?
And is there one, the wisest and the best
Of all mankind, who does not sometimes wish
For things which cannot be, who would not give,
25   If so he might, to duty and to truth
The eagerness of infantine desire?
A tranquillizing spirit presses now
On my corporeal frame, so wide appears
The vacancy between me and those days,
30   Which yet have such self-presence in my mind
That sometimes when I think of them I seem
Two consciousnesses—conscious of myself,
And of some other being. A grey stone
Of native rock, left midway in the square
35   Of our small market-village, was the home
And centre of these joys; and when, returned
After long absence, thither I repaired,
I found that it was split and gone to build
A smart assembly-room that perked and flared
40   With wash and rough-cast, elbowing the ground
Which had been ours.[1] But let the fiddle scream,
And be ye happy! Yet, my friends,[2] I know
That more than one of you will think with me
Of those soft starry nights, and that old dame
45   From whom the stone was named, who there had sate
And watched her table with its huxter's wares,°   *peddlar's goods*
Assiduous through the length of sixty years.

     We ran a boisterous race, the year span round
With giddy motion; but the time approached
50   That brought with it a regular desire
For calmer pleasures—when the beauteous forms
Of Nature were collaterally attached[3]
To every scheme of holiday delight,
And every boyish sport, less grateful° else   *pleasing*
55   And languidly pursued. When summer came
It was the pastime of our afternoons
To beat along the plain of Windermere
With rival oars; and the selected bourne°   *destination*
Was now an island musical with birds
60   That sang for ever, now a sister isle
Beneath the oak's umbrageous° covert, sown   *shady*
With lilies-of-the-valley like a field,
And now a third small island where remained

1. The Hawkshead Town Hall, built in 1790.
2. Coleridge and John Wordsworth (William's brother), who had visited Hawkshead together with William in November 1799.
3. Associated as an accompaniment.

An old stone table and a mouldered cave—
65 A hermit's history.[4] In such a race,
So ended, disappointment could be none,
Uneasiness, or pain, or jealousy;
We rested in the shade, all pleased alike,
Conquered and conqueror. Thus the pride of strength
70 And the vainglory of superior skill
Were interfused with objects which subdued
And tempered them, and gradually produced
A quiet independence of the heart.
And to my friend who knows me I may add,
75 Unapprehensive of reproof, that hence
Ensued a diffidence and modesty,
And I was taught to feel—perhaps too much—
The self-sufficing power of solitude.

No delicate viands sapped our bodily strength:
80 More than we wished we knew the blessing then
Of vigorous hunger, for our daily meals
Were frugal, Sabine fare[5]—and then, exclude
A little weekly stipend,[6] and we lived
Through three divisions of the quartered year
85 In pennyless poverty. But now, to school
Returned from the half-yearly holidays,
We came with purses more profusely filled,
Allowance which abundantly sufficed
To gratify the palate with repasts
90 More costly than the dame of whom I spake,
That ancient woman, and her board, supplied.
Hence inroads into distant vales, and long
Excursions far away among the hills,
Hence rustic dinners on the cool green ground—
95 Or in the woods, or near a river-side,
Or by some shady fountain°—while soft airs   *spring or stream*
Among the leaves were stirring, and the sun,
Unfelt, shone sweetly round us in our joy.

* * *

Those incidental charms which first attached
My heart to rural objects, day by day
205 Grew weaker, and I hasten on to tell
How Nature, intervenient[7] still this time
And secondary, now at length was sought
For her own sake. But who shall[8] parcel out
His intellect by geometric rules,
210 Split like a province into round and square?
Who knows the individual hour in which
His habits were first sown even as a seed,

---

4. The 1850 *Prelude* clarifies that this is the island of Lady Holm, former site of a chapel dedicated to the Virgin Mary, by then a ruin.
5. Like the meals of the Roman poet Horace on his Sabine farm.
6. In his last year at school, Wordsworth had an allowance of sixpence a week; his younger brother Christopher, threepence. After the Midsummer and Christmas holidays (line 86), the boys received larger sums.
7. I.e., entering only incidentally into his other concerns.
8. I.e., who is able to.

Who that shall point as with a wand, and say
'This portion of the river of my mind
215   Came from yon fountain'? Thou, my friend, art one
More deeply read in thy own thoughts; to thee
Science[9] appears but what in truth she is,
Not as our glory and our absolute boast,
But as a succedaneum,[1] and a prop
220   To our infirmity. Thou art no slave
Of that false secondary power by which
In weakness we create distinctions, then
Deem that our puny boundaries are things
Which we perceive, and not which we have made.
225   To thee, unblinded by these outward shows,
The unity of all has been revealed;
And thou wilt doubt with me, less aptly skilled
Than many are to class the cabinet
Of their sensations,[2] and in voluble phrase°   *fluent words*
230   Run through the history and birth of each
As of a single independent thing.
Hard task to analyse a soul, in which
Not only general habits and desires,
But each most obvious and particular thought—
Not in a mystical and idle sense,
235   But in the words of reason deeply weighed—
Hath no beginning.

                   Blessed the infant babe—
For with my best conjectures I would trace
The progress of our being—blest the babe
240   Nursed in his mother's arms, the babe who sleeps
Upon his mother's breast, who, when his soul
Claims manifest kindred with an earthly soul,
Doth gather passion from his mother's eye.[3]
Such feelings pass into his torpid life
245   Like an awakening breeze, and hence his mind,
Even in the first trial of its powers,
Is prompt and watchful, eager to combine
In one appearance all the elements
And parts of the same object, else detached
250   And loth to coalesce. Thus day by day
Subjected to the discipline of love,
His organs and recipient faculties
Are quickened, are more vigorous; his mind spreads,
Tenacious of° the forms which it receives   *holding fast to*
255   In one beloved presence—nay and more,
In that most apprehensive habitude[4]
And those sensations which have been derived
From this beloved presence—there exists

9. In the older sense: learning.
1. In medicine a drug substituted for a different drug. Wordsworth, however, uses the term to signify a remedy.
2. To classify feelings as if they were exhibits in a display case.

3. Like modern psychologists, Wordsworth recognized the importance of earliest infancy in the development of the individual mind.
4. Relationship ("habitude") most suited to the apprehension of the world.

A virtue which irradiates and exalts
260   All objects through all intercourse of sense.
No outcast he, bewildered and depressed;
Along his infant veins are interfused
The gravitation and the filial bond
Of Nature that connect him with the world.[5]
265   Emphatically such a being lives,
An inmate of° this *active* universe.   *dweller in*
From Nature largely he receives, nor so
Is satisfied, but largely gives again;
For feeling has to him imparted strength,
270   And—powerful in all sentiments of grief,
Of exultation, fear and joy—his mind,
Even as an agent of the one great mind,
Creates, creator and receiver both,
Working but in alliance with the works
275   Which it beholds.[6] Such, verily, is the first
Poetic spirit of our human life—
By uniform controul of after years
In most abated and suppressed, in some
Through every change of growth or of decay
280   Preeminent till death.

                      From early days,
Beginning not long after that first time
In which, a babe, by intercourse of touch
I held mute dialogues with my mother's heart,[7]
I have endeavoured to display the means
285   Whereby the infant sensibility,
Great birthright of our being, was in me
Augmented and sustained. Yet is a path
More difficult before me, and I fear
That in its broken windings we shall need
290   The chamois'° sinews and the eagle's wing.   *mountain antelope's*
For now a trouble came into my mind
From unknown causes. I was left alone
Seeking the visible world, nor knowing why.
The props of my affections were removed,[8]
295   And yet the building stood, as if sustained
By its own spirit. All that I beheld
Was dear to me, and from this cause it came
That now to Nature's finer influxes°   *influences*
My mind lay open—to that more exact
300   And intimate communion which our hearts
Maintain with the minuter properties
Of objects which already are beloved,
And of those only.

5. The infant, in the sense of security and love that is shed by his mother's presence, perceives what would otherwise be an alien world as a place to which he is connected, in a "filial bond" (line 263).
6. The mind partially creates, by altering, the world it seems simply to perceive.
7. I.e., both infant and mother feel the pulse of the other's heart.
8. Wordsworth's mother died the month before his eighth birthday.

             Many are the joys
      Of youth, but, oh, what happiness to live
305   When every hour brings palpable access
      Of knowledge, when all knowledge is delight,
      And sorrow is not there. The seasons came,
      And every season to my notice brought
      A store of transitory qualities
310   Which but for this most watchful power of love
      Had been neglected, left a register
      Of permanent relations else unknown.[9]
      Hence, life, and change, and beauty, solitude
      More active even than 'best society',[1]
315   Society made sweet as solitude
      By silent inobtrusive sympathies,
      And gentle agitations of the mind
      From manifold distinctions, difference
      Perceived in things where to the common eye
320   No difference is, and hence, from the same source,
      Sublimer joy. For I would walk alone
      In storm and tempest, or in starlight nights
      Beneath the quiet heavens, and at that time
      Have felt whate'er there is of power in sound
325   To breathe an elevated mood, by form
      Or image unprofaned; and I would stand
      Beneath some rock, listening to sounds that are
      The ghostly° language of the ancient earth,   *disembodied*
      Or make their dim abode in distant winds.
330   Thence did I drink the visionary power.
      I deem not profitless those fleeting moods
      Of shadowy exultation; not for this,
      That they are kindred to our purer mind
      And intellectual life,[2] but that the soul—
335   Remembering how she felt, but what she felt
      Remembering not—retains an obscure sense
      Of possible sublimity, to which
      With growing faculties she doth aspire,
      With faculties still growing, feeling still
340   That whatsoever point they gain they still
      Have something to pursue.

                        *   *   *

               [ADDRESS TO COLERIDGE]

                  Thou, my friend, wert reared
      In the great city, 'mid far other scenes,[3]
      But we by different roads at length have gained

9. I.e., had it not been for the "watchful power of love" (line 310), the "transitory qualities" (line 309) would have been neglected, and the "permanent relations" now recorded in his memory would have been unknown.
1. A partial quotation of a line spoken by Adam to Eve in *Paradise Lost* 9.249: "For solitude sometimes is best society."

2. I.e., not because they are related to the non-sensuous ("intellectual") aspect of life.
3. A reminiscence of Coleridge's "Frost at Midnight," lines 51–52: "For I was reared / In the great city, pent 'mid cloisters dim." The two-part *Prelude* Wordsworth completed in 1799 ended with the address to Coleridge in lines 467–84.

The self-same bourne.° And for this cause to thee   *destination*
470   I speak unapprehensive of contempt,
The insinuated scoff of coward tongues,
And all that silent language which so oft
In conversation betwixt man and man
Blots from the human countenance all trace
475   Of beauty and of love. For thou hast sought
The truth in solitude, and thou art one
The most intense of Nature's worshippers,
In many things my brother, chiefly here
In this my deep devotion. Fare thee well.
480   Health and the quiet of a healthful mind
Attend thee, seeking oft the haunts of men—
And yet more often living with thyself,
And for thyself—so haply shall thy days
Be many, and a blessing to mankind.

From Book Fifth.

Books

[THE DREAM OF THE ARAB]

*   *   *

Thou also, man, hast wrought,
For commerce of thy nature with itself,[1]
Things worthy of unconquerable life;
20   And yet we feel—we cannot chuse but feel—
That these must perish. Tremblings of the heart
It gives, to think that the immortal being
No more shall need such garments;[2] and yet man,
As long as he shall be the child of earth,
25   Might almost 'weep to have' what he may lose[3]—
Nor be himself extinguished, but survive
Abject, depressed, forlorn, disconsolate.
A thought is with me sometimes, and I say,
Should earth by inward throes be wrenched throughout,
30   Or fire be sent from far to wither all
Her pleasant habitations, and dry up
Old Ocean in his bed, left singed and bare,
Yet would the living presence still subsist
Victorious; and composure would ensue,
35   And kindlings like the morning—presage sure,
Though slow perhaps, of a returning day.

1. From the works of God's creation, Nature, Wordsworth turns at this point in *The Prelude* to human creations. Man, as well as God, has created works by which to communicate with man ("commerce of thy nature with itself"): those creations are books, and the title of book 5 underlines their importance to Wordsworth's account of himself.

2. Wordsworth draws on the traditional image of the body as the garment of the soul, no longer needed at death and so discarded.
3. The quotation is from Shakespeare's sonnet 64, in which the thought that Time might come and take his love away is for the speaker "as a death, which cannot choose / But weep to have that which it fears to lose."

But all the meditations of mankind,
Yea, all the adamantine holds° of truth   *indestructible fortresses*
By reason built, or passion (which itself
40 Is highest reason in a soul sublime),
The consecrated works of bard and sage,
Sensuous or intellectual, wrought by men,
Twin labourers and heirs of the same hopes—
Where would they be? Oh, why hath not the mind
45 Some element to stamp her image on
In nature somewhat nearer to her own?
Why, gifted with such powers to send abroad
Her spirit, must it lodge in shrines so frail?

 One day, when in the hearing of a friend
50 I had given utterance to thoughts like these,
He answered with a smile that in plain truth
'Twas going far to seek disquietude—
But on the front of his reproof confessed
That he at sundry seasons had himself
55 Yielded to kindred hauntings, and, forthwith,
Added that once upon a summer's noon
While he was sitting in a rocky cave
By the seaside, perusing as it chanced,
The famous history of the errant knight
60 Recorded by Cervantes,[4] these same thoughts
Came to him, and to height unusual rose
While listlessly he sate, and, having closed
The book, had turned his eyes towards the sea.
On poetry and geometric truth
65 (The knowledge that endures) upon these two,
And their high privilege of lasting life
Exempt from all internal injury,
He mused—upon these chiefly—and at length,
His senses yielding to the sultry air,
70 Sleep seized him and he passed into a dream.
He saw before him an Arabian waste,
A desart, and he fancied that himself
Was sitting there in the wide wilderness
Alone upon the sands. Distress of mind
75 Was growing in him when, behold, at once
To his great joy a man was at his side,
Upon a dromedary° mounted high.   *camel*
He seemed an arab of the Bedouin tribes;[5]
A lance he bore, and underneath one arm
80 A stone, and in the opposite hand a shell
Of a surpassing brightness. Much rejoiced
The dreaming man that he should have a guide
To lead him through the desert; and he thought,
While questioning himself what this strange freight

4. I.e., *Don Quixote*, the 17th-century novel about a man unable to distinguish between reality and books' romantic fictions.

5. Mathematics had flourished in Arabic culture—hence the Arab rider.

85   Which the newcomer carried through the waste
Could mean, the arab told him that the stone—
To give it in the language of the dream—
Was *Euclid's Elements*.[6] 'And this', said he,
'This other', pointing to the shell, 'this book
90   Is something of more worth.' 'And, at the word,
The stranger', said my friend continuing,
'Stretched forth the shell towards me, with command
That I should hold it to my ear. I did so
And heard that instant in an unknown tongue,
95   Which yet I understood, articulate sounds,
A loud prophetic blast of harmony,
An ode in passion uttered, which foretold
Destruction to the children of the earth
By deluge now at hand. No sooner ceased
100   The song, but with calm look the arab said
That all was true, that it was even so
As had been spoken, and that he himself
Was going then to bury those two books—
The one that held acquaintance with the stars,
105   And wedded man to man by purest bond
Of nature, undisturbed by space or time;
Th' other that was a god, yea many gods,
Had voices more than all the winds, and was
A joy, a consolation, and a hope.'
110   My friend continued, 'Strange as it may seem
I wondered not, although I plainly saw
The one to be a stone, th' other a shell,
Nor doubted once but that they both were books,
Having a perfect faith in all that passed.
115   A wish was now engendered in my fear
To cleave unto this man, and I begged leave
To share his errand with him. On he passed
Not heeding me; I followed, and took note
That he looked often backward with wild look,
120   Grasping his twofold treasure to his side.
Upon a dromedary, lance in rest,
He rode, I keeping pace with him; and now
I fancied that he was the very knight
Whose tale Cervantes tells, yet not the knight,
125   But was an arab of the desert too,
Of these was neither, and was both at once.
His countenance meanwhile grew more disturbed,
And looking backwards when he looked I saw
A glittering light, and asked him whence it came.
130   "It is", said he, "the waters of the deep
Gathering upon us." Quickening then his pace
He left me; I called after him aloud;
He heeded not, but with his twofold charge

---

6. Celebrated book on geometry and the theory of numbers by the Greek mathematician Euclid (3rd century B.C.E.); it continued to be used as a textbook into the 19th century.

Beneath his arm—before me full in view—
135 I saw him riding o'er the desart sands
With the fleet waters of the drowning world
In chace of him; whereat I waked in terror,
And saw the sea before me, and the book
In which I had been reading at my side.'[7]
140   Full often, taking from the world of sleep
This arab phantom which my friend beheld,
This semi-Quixote, I to him have given
A substance, fancied him a living man—
A gentle dweller in the desart, crazed
145 By love, and feeling, and internal thought
Protracted among endless solitudes—
Have shaped him, in the oppression of his brain,
Wandering upon this quest and thus equipped.
And I have scarcely pitied him, have felt
150 A reverence for a being thus employed,
And thought that in the blind and awful lair
Of such a madness reason did lie couched.
Enow° there are on earth to take in charge   *enough*
Their wives, their children, and their virgin loves,
155 Or whatsoever else the heart holds dear—
Enow to think of these—yea, will I say,
In sober contemplation of the approach
Of such great overthrow, made manifest
By certain evidence, that I methinks
160 Could share that maniac's anxiousness, could go
Upon like errand. Oftentimes at least
Me hath such deep entrancement half-possessed
When I have held a volume in my hand—
Poor earthly casket of immortal verse—
165 Shakespeare or Milton, labourers divine.

*   *   *

[THE BOY OF WINANDER; THE DROWNED MAN]

    There was a boy[8]—ye knew him well, ye cliffs
390 And islands of Winander—many a time
At evening, when the stars had just begun
To move along the edges of the hills,
Rising or setting, would he stand alone
Beneath the trees or by the glimmering lake,

7. A late-17th-century biography reported that on a single night in 1619 three dreams troubled René Descartes, who believed them to be a supernatural visitation foretelling his future vocation as a philosopher. The third dream, which has had many interpreters, involved two books that appeared mysteriously to the dreamer and then vanished again, a dictionary and an anthology of poetry. Coleridge is usually thought to have told the story of that dream to Wordsworth, who in lines 56–139 reworks it brilliantly.
8. In an early manuscript version of lines 389–

413, Wordsworth uses the first-person pronoun, suggesting the boy's experience was his own. Under the title "There was a Boy," the lines were published as a separate poem in Wordsworth's 1815 *Poems*. In the preface to that volume Wordsworth describes how the account of the boy's listening dramatizes a moment when internal feelings cooperate with external accidents and "plant, for immortality, images of sound and sight, in the celestial soil of the Imagination."

395 And there, with fingers interwoven, both hands
Pressed closely palm to palm, and to his mouth
Uplifted, he as through an instrument
Blew mimic hootings to the silent owls
That they might answer him. And they would shout
400 Across the wat'ry vale, and shout again,
Responsive to his call, with quivering peals
And long halloos, and screams, and echoes loud,
Redoubled and redoubled—concourse wild
Of mirth and jocund din. And when it chanced
405 That pauses of deep silence mocked his skill,
Then sometimes in that silence, while he hung
Listening, a gentle shock of mild surprize
Has carried far into his heart[9] the voice
Of mountain torrents; or the visible scene
410 Would enter unawares into his mind
With all its solemn imagery, its rocks,
Its woods, and that uncertain heaven, received
Into the bosom of the steady lake.
         This boy was taken from his mates, and died
415 In childhood ere he was full ten years old.
Fair are the woods, and beauteous is the spot,
The vale where he was born; the churchyard hangs
Upon a slope above the village school,
And there, along that bank, when I have passed
420 At evening, I believe that oftentimes
A full half-hour together I have stood
Mute, looking at the grave in which he lies.
Even now methinks I have before my sight
That self-same village church: I see her sit—
425 The thronèd lady spoken of erewhile—
On her green hill, forgetful of this boy
Who slumbers at her feet, forgetful too
Of all her silent neighbourhood of graves,
And listening only to the gladsome sounds
430 That, from the rural school ascending, play
Beneath her and about her. May she long
Behold a race of young ones like to those
With whom I herded—easily, indeed,
We might have fed upon a fatter soil
435 Of Arts and Letters, but be that forgiven—
A race of real children, not too wise,
Too learned, or too good, but wanton, fresh,
And bandied up and down by love and hate;
Fierce, moody, patient, venturous, modest, shy,
440 Mad at their sports like withered leaves in winds;
Though doing wrong and suffering, and full oft
Bending beneath our life's mysterious weight

9. Thomas De Quincey responded to this line in
Recollections of the Lakes and the Lake Poets:
"This very expression, 'far,' by which space and its
infinities are attributed to the human heart, and
to its capacities of re-echoing the sublimities of
nature, has always struck me as with a flash of
sublime revelation."

Of pain and fear, yet still in happiness
Not yielding to the happiest upon earth.
445   Simplicity in habit, truth in speech,
Be these the daily strengtheners of their minds!
May books and Nature be their early joy,
And knowledge, rightly honored with that name—
Knowledge not purchased with the loss of power!

450   Well do I call to mind the very week
When I was first entrusted to the care
Of that sweet valley[1]—when its paths, its shores
And brooks, were like a dream of novelty
To my half-infant thoughts—that very week,
455   While I was roving up and down alone
Seeking I knew not what, I chanced to cross
One of those open fields, which, shaped like ears,
Make green peninsulas on Esthwaite's Lake.
Twilight was coming on, yet through the gloom
460   I saw distinctly on the opposite shore
A heap of garments, left as I supposed
By one who there was bathing. Long I watched,
But no one owned them; meanwhile the calm lake
Grew dark, with all the shadows on its breast,
465   And now and then a fish up-leaping snapped
The breathless stillness. The succeeding day—
Those unclaimed garments telling a plain tale—
Went there a company, and in their boat
Sounded with grappling-irons and long poles:
470   At length, the dead man, 'mid that beauteous scene
Of trees and hills and water, bolt upright
Rose with his ghastly face, a spectre shape—
Of tenor even. And yet no vulgar fear,
Young as I was, a child not nine years old,
475   Possessed me, for my inner eye had seen
Such sights before among the shining streams
Of fairyland, the forests of romance—
Thence came a spirit hallowing what I saw
With decoration and ideal grace,
480   A dignity, a smoothness, like the works
Of Grecian art and purest poesy.

* * *

---

1. At age nine Wordsworth was sent away from home to attend school at Hawkshead in the Esthwaite valley.

From Book Sixth.

Cambridge and the Alps

["HUMAN NATURE SEEMING BORN AGAIN"]

* * *

When the third summer brought its liberty[1]
A fellow student and myself, he too
340   A mountaineer, together sallied forth,
And, staff in hand on foot pursued our way
Towards the distant Alps. An open slight
Of college cares and study was the scheme,[2]
Nor entertained without concern for those
345   To whom my worldly interests were dear,
But Nature then was sovereign in my heart,
And mighty forms seizing a youthful fancy
Had given a charter[3] to irregular hopes.
In any age, without an impulse sent
350   From work of nations and their goings-on,
I should have been possessed by like desire;
But 'twas a time when Europe was rejoiced,
France standing on the top of golden hours,
And human nature seeming born again.
355   Bound, as I said, to the Alps, it was our lot
To land at Calais on the very eve
Of that great federal day;[4] and there we saw,
In a mean° city and among a few,   *lowly*
How bright a face is worn when joy of one
Is joy of tens of millions.

* * *

[CROSSING SIMPLON PASS]

'Tis not my present purpose to retrace
That variegated journey step by step;
A march it was of military speed,
And earth did change her images and forms
430   Before us fast as clouds are changed in heaven.
Day after day, up early and down late,
From vale to vale, from hill to hill we went,
From province on to province did we pass,
Keen hunters in a chace of fourteen weeks—

1. Wordsworth was a student at St. John's College, Cambridge University, from 1787 to 1791. Books 3 and 4 describe his first year there and the succeeding summer vacation. In this book, after reviewing briefly his second and third years at university, Wordsworth describes his trip through France and Switzerland with a college friend, Robert Jones, during the summer vacation of 1790. France was then in the "golden hours" of the early period of the Revolution; the fall of the Bastille had occurred on July 14 of the preceding year.
2. Undergraduates were expected to spend their third summer preparing for the final examinations that would determine their rank upon graduation and shape their career prospects.
3. Privileged freedom.
4. Wordsworth and Jones landed at the port of Calais in northeast France on July 13, 1790, just before the Festival of Federation, the ceremony, also marking the anniversary of the fall of the Bastille, in which King Louis XVI swore to be faithful to the nation's new, democratic constitution.

435 Eager as birds of prey, or as a ship
Upon the stretch when winds are blowing fair.
Sweet coverts did we cross of pastoral life,
Enticing vallies—greeted them, and left
Too soon, while yet the very flash and gleam
440 Of salutation were not passed away.
Oh, sorrow for the youth who could have seen
Unchastened, unsubdued, unawed, unraised
To patriarchal dignity of mind
And pure simplicity of wish and will,
445 Those sanctified abodes of peaceful man.
My heart leaped up when first I did look down
On that which was first seen of those deep haunts,
A green recess, an aboriginal° vale,   primitive, untouched
Quiet, and lorded over and possessed
450 By naked huts, wood-built, and sown like tents
Or Indian cabins over the fresh lawns
And by the river-side.

That day we first
Beheld the summit of Mount Blanc, and grieved
To have a soulless image on the eye
455 Which had usurped upon a living thought
That never more could be.[5] The wondrous Vale
Of Chamouny[6] did, on the following dawn,
With its dumb° cataracts and streams of ice—   silent
A motionless array of mighty waves,
460 Five rivers broad and vast—make rich amends,
And reconciled us to realities.
There small birds warble from the leafy trees,
The eagle soareth in the element,
There doth the reaper bind the yellow sheaf,
465 The maiden spread the haycock in the sun,
While Winter like a tamèd lion walks,
Descending from the mountain to make sport
Among the cottages by beds of flowers.

Whate'er in this wide circuit we beheld
470 Or heard was fitted to our unripe state
Of intellect and heart. By simple strains
Of feeling, the pure breath of real life,
We were not left untouched. With such a book
Before our eyes we could not chuse but read
475 A frequent lesson of sound tenderness,
The universal reason of mankind,
The truth of young and old. Nor, side by side
Pacing, two brother pilgrims, or alone
Each with his humour,° could we fail to abound—   temperament
480 Craft this which hath been hinted at before—
In dreams and fictions pensively composed:

---

5. The "image" is the actual sight of Mont Blanc,
as contrasted with what the poet has imagined
the famous Swiss mountain to be.

6. Chamonix, a valley in eastern France, north
of Mont Blanc.

Dejection taken up for pleasure's sake,
And gilded sympathies, the willow wreath,[7]
Even among those solitudes sublime,
485 And sober posies of funereal flowers,
Culled from the gardens of the Lady Sorrow,
Did sweeten many a meditative hour.

Yet still in me, mingling with these delights,
Was something of stern mood, an under-thirst
490 Of vigour, never utterly asleep.
Far different dejection once was mine—
A deep and genuine sadness then I felt—
The circumstances I will here relate
Even as they were. Upturning with a band
495 Of travellers, from the Valais we had clomb°   climbed
Along the road that leads to Italy;[8]
A length of hours, making of these our guides,
Did we advance, and, having reached an inn
Among the mountains, we together ate
500 Our noon's repast, from which the travellers rose
Leaving us at the board. Erelong we followed,
Descending by the beaten road that led
Right to a rivulet's edge, and there broke off;
The only track now visible was one
505 Upon the further side, right opposite,
And up a lofty mountain. This we took,
After a little scruple° and short pause,   hesitation
And climbed with eagerness—though not, at length,
Without surprize and some anxiety
510 On finding that we did not overtake
Our comrades gone before. By fortunate chance,
While every moment now encreased our doubts,
A peasant met us, and from him we learned
That to the place which had perplexed us first
515 We must descend, and there should find the road
Which in the stony channel of the stream
Lay a few steps, and then along its banks—
And further, that thenceforward all our course
Was downwards with the current of that stream.
520 Hard of belief, we questioned him again,
And all the answers which the man returned
To our inquiries, in their sense and substance
Translated by the feelings which we had,
Ended in this—that we had crossed the Alps.[9]

525   Imagination!—lifting up itself
Before the eye and progress of my song°   The Prelude itself
Like an unfathered vapour,[1] here that power,

7. The mention of the "willow wreath" suggests that the poetry the two travelers composed to while away their time was conventionally sentimental. "Gilded": laid on like gilt—i.e., superficial.
8. Simplon Pass.
9. As Dorothy Wordsworth baldly put it later on, "The ambition of youth was disappointed at these tidings." The visionary experience that follows (lines 525–48) did not occur in the Alps; Wordsworth celebrates the creative power that he experiences at the time of writing this passage, fourteen years after the disappointment at Simplon Pass.
1. Vapor appearing suddenly from no apparent source.

In all the might of its endowments, came
Athwart me. I was lost as in a cloud,
530 Halted without a struggle to break through,
And now, recovering, to my soul I say
'I recognise thy glory'. In such strength
Of usurpation, in such visitings
Of awful° promise, when the light of sense   *awe-inspiring*
535 Goes out in flashes that have shewn to us
The invisible world, doth greatness make abode,
There harbours whether we be young or old.
Our destiny, our nature, and our home,
Is with infinitude—and only there;
540 With hope it is, hope that can never die,
Effort, and expectation, and desire,
And something evermore about to be.
The mind beneath such banners militant
Thinks not of spoils or trophies, nor of aught
545 That may attest its prowess, blest in thoughts
That are their own perfection and reward—
Strong in itself, and in the access of joy
Which hides it like the overflowing Nile.

The dull and heavy slackening which ensued
550 Upon those tidings by the peasant given
Was soon dislodged; downwards we hurried fast,
And entered with the road which we had missed
Into a narrow chasm. The brook and road
Were fellow-travellers in this gloomy pass,
555 And with them did we journey several hours
At a slow step. The immeasurable height
Of woods decaying, never to be decayed,
The stationary blasts of waterfalls,
And everywhere along the hollow rent
560 Winds thwarting winds, bewildered and forlorn,
The torrents shooting from the clear blue sky,
The rocks that muttered close upon our ears—
Black drizzling crags that spake by the wayside
As if a voice were in them—the sick sight
565 And giddy prospect of the raving stream,
The unfettered clouds and region of the heavens,
Tumult and peace, the darkness and the light,
Were all like workings of one mind, the features
Of the same face, blossoms upon one tree,
570 Characters of the great apocalypse,
The types and symbols of eternity,[2]
Of first, and last, and midst, and without end.[3]

*   *   *

2. The objects in this natural scene are like the written words ("characters") of the Apocalypse—i.e., of the Book of Revelation, concluding book of the New Testament. "Types": signs foreshadowing eternity.
3. See Revelation 1.8: "I am Alpha and Omega [the first and last letters of the Greek alphabet], the beginning and the ending, saith the Lord." In *Paradise Lost* 5.153–65 Milton says that all God's works declare their Creator, and call on all to extol "him first, him last, him midst, and without end."

From Book Tenth.

Residence in France and French Revolution

* * *

[RETROSPECT: FIRST IMPRESSION OF THE REVOLUTION;
THE OUTBREAK OF WAR BETWEEN FRANCE AND BRITAIN][1]

* * *

   O pleasant exercise of hope and joy,
690 For great were the auxiliars° which then stood   *allies*
   Upon our side, we who were strong in love.
   Bliss was it in that dawn to be alive,
   But to be young was very heaven! O times,
   In which the meagre, stale, forbidding ways
695 Of custom, law, and statute took at once
   The attraction of a country in romance—
   When Reason seemed the most to assert her rights
   When most intent on making of herself
   A prime enchanter to assist the work
700 Which then was going forwards in her name.
   Not favored spots alone, but the whole earth,
   The beauty wore of promise, that which sets
   (To take an image which was felt, no doubt,
   Among the bowers of Paradise itself)
705 The budding rose above the rose full-blown.
   What temper° at the prospect did not wake   *temperament*
   To happiness unthought of? The inert
   Were rouzed, and lively natures rapt away.°   *enraptured*
   They who had fed their childhood upon dreams—
710 The playfellows of fancy, who had made
   All powers of swiftness, subtlety, and strength
   Their ministers, used to stir in lordly wise
   Among the grandest objects of the sense,
   And deal with whatsoever they found there
715 As if they had within some lurking right
   To wield it—they too, who, of gentle mood,
   Had watched all gentle motions, and to these
   Had fitted their own thoughts (schemers more mild,
   And in the region of their peaceful selves),
720 Did now find helpers to their hearts' desire
   And stuff at hand plastic° as they could wish,   *malleable*
   Were called upon to exercise their skill
   Not in Utopia—subterraneous fields,
   Or some secreted island, heaven knows where—

1. Wordsworth visited France for the second time in 1791–92 and, as he explains in this book, became, initially, a passionate partisan of the Revolution. His lack of money forced him to return to England late in 1792. From there he looked on despairingly as the radicals, led by Robespierre, who ascended to power in France in the summer of 1793, undertook a campaign of mass arrests and executions in order to purge the new Republic of its enemies. Wordsworth follows his account of Robespierre's rise and fall with a retrospect, a backward glance at the high hopes that the Revolution had raised at its start. He published lines 689–727 as a separate poem, first in Coleridge's journal *The Friend* in 1809, then in his own *Poems* of 1815, with the title "French Revolution as It Appeared to Enthusiasts at Its Commencement."

725　But in the very world which is the world
　　　Of all of us, the place in which, in the end,
　　　We find our happiness, or not at all.

　　　　Why should I not confess that earth was then
　　　To me what an inheritance new-fallen
730　Seems, when the first time visited, to one
　　　Who thither comes to find in it his home?
　　　He walks about and looks upon the place
　　　With cordial transport—moulds it and remoulds—
　　　And is half pleased with things that are amiss,
735　'Twill be such joy to see them disappear.

*　*　*

[CRISIS, BREAKDOWN, AND RECOVERY]

After what hath been
　　　Already said of patriotic love,
865　And hinted at in other sentiments,
　　　We need not linger long upon this theme,
　　　This only may be said, that from the first
　　　Having two natures in me (joy the one
　　　The other melancholy), and withal°　　　　　　　　　*nevertheless*
870　A happy man, and therefore bold to look
　　　On painful things—slow, somewhat, too, and stern
　　　In temperament—I took the knife in hand,
　　　And, stopping not at parts less sensitive,
　　　Endeavoured with my best of skill to probe
875　The living body of society
　　　Even to the heart. I pushed without remorse
　　　My speculations forward, yea, set foot
　　　On Nature's holiest places.

Time may come
　　　When some dramatic story may afford
880　Shapes livelier to convey to thee, my friend,°　　　*i.e., Coleridge*
　　　What then I learned—or think I learned—of truth,
　　　And the errors into which I was betrayed
　　　By present objects, and by reasonings false
　　　From the beginning, inasmuch as drawn
885　Out of a heart which had been turned aside
　　　From Nature by external accidents,
　　　And which was thus confounded more and more,
　　　Misguiding and misguided. Thus I fared,
　　　Dragging all passions, notions, shapes of faith,
890　Like culprits to the bar,° suspiciously　　　　　　*courtroom*
　　　Calling the mind to establish in plain day
　　　Her titles° and her honours, now believing,　　*legal entitlements*
　　　Now disbelieving, endlessly perplexed
　　　With impulse, motive, right and wrong, the ground
895　Of moral obligation—what the rule,
　　　And what the sanction—till, demanding proof,
　　　And seeking it in every thing, I lost

All feeling of conviction, and, in fine,°   *in the end*
Sick, wearied out with contrarieties,
900   Yielded up moral questions in despair,
And for my future studies, as the sole
Employment of the inquiring faculty,
Turned towards mathematics, and their clear
And solid evidence.
                                Ah, then it was
905   That thou, most precious friend, about this time
First known to me, didst lend a living help
To regulate my soul. And then it was
That the belovèd woman in whose sight
Those days were passed—now speaking in a voice
910   Of sudden admonition like a brook
That does but cross a lonely road; and now
Seen, heard and felt, and caught at every turn,
Companion never lost through many a league—
Maintained for me a saving intercourse°   *communion*
915   With my true self (for, though impaired, and changed
Much, as it seemed, I was no further changed
Than as a clouded, not a waning moon);
She, in the midst of all, preserved me still
A poet, made me seek beneath that name
920   My office° upon earth, and nowhere else.[2]   *duty*
And lastly, Nature's self, by human love
Assisted, through the weary labyrinth
Conducted me again to open day,
Revived the feelings of my earlier life,
925   Gave me that strength and knowledge full of peace,
Enlarged, and never more to be disturbed,
Which through the steps of our degeneracy,
All degradation of this age, hath still
Upheld me, and upholds me at this day
930   In the catastrophe° (for so they dream,   *dramatic climax*
And nothing less), when, finally to close
And rivet up the gains of France, a Pope
Is summoned in to crown an Emperor[3]—
This last opprobrium,° when we see the dog   *disgrace*
935   Returning to his vomit,[4] when the sun
That rose in splendour, was alive, and moved
In exultation among living clouds,
Hath put his function and his glory off,
And, turned into a gewgaw,° a machine,   *toy*
940   Sets like an opera phantom.[5]

* * *

2. After a long separation Dorothy Wordsworth came to live with her brother at Racedown in 1795.
3. The ultimate blow to liberal hopes for France occurred when on December 2, 1804, Napoleon summoned the pope to officiate at the ceremony elevating him to emperor. At the last moment Napoleon grabbed the crown from the pope and donned it himself.
4. Allusion to Proverbs 26.11: "As a dog returneth to his vomit, a fool returneth to his folly."
5. Stage machinery used for theatrical effect.

From Book Eleventh.

Imagination, How Impaired and Restored

[SPOTS OF TIME]¹

* * *

  There are in our existence spots of time,
  Which with distinct preeminence retain
  A renovating virtue,° whence, depressed   *power of renewal*
260 By false opinion and contentious thought,
  Or aught of heavier or more deadly weight
  In trivial occupations and the round
  Of ordinary intercourse, our minds
  Are nourished and invisibly repaired—
265 A virtue, by which pleasure is enhanced,
  That penetrates, enables us to mount
  When high, more high, and lifts us up when fallen.
  This efficacious spirit chiefly lurks
  Among those passages of life in which
270 We have had deepest feeling that the mind
  Is lord and master, and that outward sense²
  Is but the obedient servant of her will.
  Such moments, worthy of all gratitude,
  Are scattered everywhere, taking their date
275 From our first childhood—in our childhood even
  Perhaps are most conspicuous. Life with me,
  As far as memory can look back, is full
  Of this beneficent influence.
           At a time
  When scarcely (I was then not six years old)
280 My hand could hold a bridle, with proud hopes
  I mounted, and we rode towards the hills:
  We were a pair of horsemen—honest James
  Was with me, my encourager and guide.³
  We had not travelled long ere some mischance
285 Disjoined me from my comrade, and, through fear
  Dismounting, down the rough and stony moor
  I led my horse, and stumbling on, at length
  Came to a bottom° where in former times   *valley*
  A murderer had been hung in iron chains.
290 The gibbet-mast⁴ was mouldered down, the bones
  And iron case were gone, but on the turf
  Hard by, soon after that fell deed was wrought,
  Some unknown hand had carved the murderer's name.
  The monumental writing was engraven
295 In times long past, and still from year to year

---

1. Wordsworth's account in the lines that follow of two memories from childhood was originally drafted for the first book of the two-book *Prelude* of 1798. By transferring these early memories close to the end of his completed autobiography, rather than presenting them in its opening books alongside his other boyhood memories, he enacts his own theory about how remembrance of things past nourishes the imagination.
2. Perception of the external world.
3. The 1850 *Prelude* refers to "an ancient Servant of my Father's house" (12.229).
4. The post with a projecting arm used for hanging criminals.

By superstition of the neighbourhood
The grass is cleared away; and to this hour
The letters are all fresh and visible.
Faltering, and ignorant where I was, at length
300   I chanced to espy those characters° inscribed   *letters*
On the green sod: forthwith I left the spot,
And, reascending the bare common, saw
A naked pool that lay beneath the hills,
The beacon on the summit,[5] and more near,
305   A girl who bore a pitcher on her head
And seemed with difficult steps to force her way
Against the blowing wind. It was, in truth,
An ordinary sight, but I should need
Colours and words that are unknown to man
310   To paint the visionary dreariness
Which, while I looked all round for my lost guide,
Did at that time invest the naked pool,
The beacon on the lonely eminence,
The woman, and her garments vexed and tossed
315   By the strong wind. When, in blessèd season,
With those two dear ones[6]—to my heart so dear—
When, in the blessèd time of early love,
Long afterwards I roamed about
In daily presence of this very scene,
320   Upon the naked pool and dreary crags,
And on the melancholy beacon, fell
The spirit of pleasure and youth's golden gleam—
And think ye not with radiance more divine
From these remembrances, and from the power
325   They left behind? So feeling comes in aid
Of feeling, and diversity of strength
Attends us, if but once we have been strong,

        Oh mystery of man, from what a depth
Proceed thy honours! I am lost, but see
330   In simple childhood something of the base
On which thy greatness stands—but this I feel,
That from thyself it is that thou must give,
Else never canst receive. The days gone by
Come back upon me from the dawn almost
335   Of life; the hiding-places of my power
Seem open, I approach, and then they close;
I see by glimpses now, when age comes on
May scarcely see at all; and I would give
While yet we may, as far as words can give,
340   A substance and a life to what I feel:
I would enshrine the spirit of the past
For future restoration. Yet another
Of these to me affecting incidents,
With which we will conclude.

5. A signal beacon on a hill above Penrith.
6. His future wife, Mary Hutchinson, and his sister, Dorothy.

One Christmas-time,[7]

345 The day before the holidays began,
Feverish, and tired, and restless, I went forth
Into the fields, impatient for the sight
Of those two horses which should bear us home,
My brothers and myself. There was a crag,

350 An eminence,° which from the meeting-point   *elevated ground*
Of two highways ascending overlooked
At least a long half-mile of those two roads,
By each of which the expected steeds might come—
The choice uncertain. Thither I repaired

355 Up to the highest summit. 'Twas a day
Stormy, and rough, and wild, and on the grass
I sate half sheltered by a naked wall.
Upon my right hand was a single sheep,
A whistling hawthorn on my left, and there,

360 With those companions at my side, I watched,
Straining my eyes intensely as the mist
Gave intermitting prospect of the wood
And plain beneath. Ere I to school returned
That dreary time, ere I had been ten days

365 A dweller in my father's house, he died,
And I and my two brothers, orphans then,
Followed his body to the grave.[8] The event,
With all the sorrow which it brought, appeared
A chastisement; and when I called to mind

370 That day so lately past, when from the crag
I looked in such anxiety of hope,
With trite reflections of morality,
Yet in the deepest passion, I bowed low
To God who thus corrected my desires.

375 And afterwards the wind and sleety rain,
And all the business[9] of the elements,
The single sheep, and the one blasted tree,
And the bleak music of that old stone wall,
The noise of wood and water, and the mist

380 Which on the line of each of those two roads
Advanced in such indisputable shapes[1]—
All these were spectacles and sounds to which
I often would repair, and thence would drink
As at a fountain. And I do not doubt

385 That in this later time, when storm and rain
Beat on my roof at midnight, or by day
When I am in the woods, unknown to me
The workings of my spirit thence are brought.

*   *   *

7. In 1783. Wordsworth, aged thirteen, was at
Hawkshead School with two of his brothers.
8. John Wordsworth died on December 30, 1783.
William's mother had died five years earlier.
9. Busy-ness, motions.

1. I.e., shapes one did not dare question. Cf.
Hamlet's declaration to the ghost of his father:
"Thou com'st in such questionable shape / That I
will speak to thee" (*Hamlet* 1.4.24–25).

From Book Thirteenth.

Conclusion

[VISION ON MOUNT SNOWDON]

In one of these excursions, travelling then
Through Wales on foot and with a youthful friend,
I left Bethkelet's huts at couching-time,
And westward took my way to see the sun
5   Rise from the top of Snowdon.[1] Having reached
The cottage at the mountain's foot, we there
Rouzed up the shepherd who by ancient right
Of office is the stranger's usual guide,
And after short refreshment sallied forth.

10   It was a summer's night, a close warm night,
Wan, dull, and glaring,[2] with a dripping mist
Low-hung and thick that covered all the sky,
Half threatening storm and rain; but on we went
Unchecked, being full of heart and having faith
15   In our tried pilot. Little could we see,
Hemmed round on every side with fog and damp,
And, after ordinary travellers' chat
With our conductor, silently we sunk
Each into commerce with his private thoughts.
20   Thus did we breast the ascent, and by myself
Was nothing either seen or heard the while
Which took me from my musings, save that once
The shepherd's cur did to his own great joy
Unearth a hedgehog in the mountain-crags,
25   Round which he made a barking turbulent.
This small adventure—for even such it seemed
In that wild place and at the dead of night—
Being over and forgotten, on we wound
In silence as before. With forehead bent
30   Earthward, as if in opposition set
Against an enemy, I panted up
With eager pace, and no less eager thoughts,
Thus might we wear perhaps an hour away,
Ascending at loose distance each from each,
35   And I, as chanced, the foremost of the band—
When at my feet the ground appeared to brighten,
And with a step or two seemed brighter still;
Nor had I time to ask the cause of this,
For instantly a light upon the turf
40   Fell like a flash. I looked about, and lo,

1. Wordsworth climbed Mount Snowdon—the highest peak in Wales, some ten miles from the sea—with Robert Jones, the friend with whom he had also hiked through the Alps (book 6). The climb started from the village of Beddgelert ("Bethkelet") at "couching-time" (line 3), the time of night when the sheep lie down to sleep. This event took place in 1791 or possibly 1793; Words- worth presents it out of its chronological order so as to introduce at this point "the perfect image" (line 69) for the mind, and especially for the activ- ity of the imagination, whose "restoration" the previous books have described.
2. In the dialect of northern England, *glairie*, applied to the weather, means dull or rainy.

The moon stood naked in the heavens at height
Immense above my head, and on the shore
I found myself of a huge sea of mist,
Which meek and silent rested at my feet.
45 A hundred hills their dusky backs upheaved
All over this still ocean,[3] and beyond,
Far, far beyond, the vapours shot themselves
In headlands, tongues, and promontory shapes,
Into the sea, the real sea, that seemed
50 To dwindle and give up its majesty,
Usurped upon as far as sight could reach.
Meanwhile, the moon looked down upon this shew
In single glory, and we stood, the mist
Touching our very feet; and from the shore
55 At distance not the third part of a mile
Was a blue chasm, a fracture in the vapour,
A deep and gloomy breathing-place, through which
Mounted the roar of waters, torrents, streams
Innumerable, roaring with one voice.
60 The universal spectacle throughout
Was shaped for admiration and delight,
Grand in itself alone, but in that breach
Through which the homeless voice of waters rose,
That dark deep thoroughfare, had Nature lodged
65 The soul, the imagination of the whole.

A meditation rose in me that night
Upon the lonely mountain when the scene
Had passed away, and it appeared to me
The perfect image of a mighty mind,
70 Of one that feeds upon infinity,
That is exalted by an under-presence,
The sense of God, or whatsoe'er is dim
Or vast in its own being—above all,
One function of such mind had Nature there
75 Exhibited by putting forth, and that
With circumstance most awful° and sublime: *awe-inspiring*
That domination which she oftentimes
Exerts upon the outward face of things,
So moulds them, and endues, abstracts, combines,
80 Or by abrupt and unhabitual influence
Doth make one object so impress itself
Upon all others, and pervades them so,
That even the grossest° minds must see and hear,   *dullest*
And cannot chuse but feel. The power which these
85 Acknowledge when thus moved, which Nature thus
Thrusts forth upon the senses, is the express
Resemblance—in the fullness of its strength
Made visible—a genuine counterpart
And brother of the glorious faculty

3. In Milton's description of God's creation of land from the waters, "the mountains huge appear / Emergent, and their broad bare backs upheave / Into the clouds" (*Paradise Lost* 7.285–87).

90　Which higher minds bear with them as their own.[4]
　　This is the very spirit in which they deal
　　With all the objects of the universe:
　　They from their native selves can send abroad
　　Like transformation, for themselves create
95　A like existence, and, when'er it is
　　Created for them, catch it by an instinct.
　　Them the enduring and the transient both
　　Serve to exalt. They build up greatest things
　　From least suggestions, ever on the watch,
100　Willing to work and to be wrought upon.
　　They need not extraordinary calls
　　To rouze them—in a world of life they live,
　　By sensible° impressions not enthralled,　　　　　　*sensory*
　　But quickened, rouzed, and made thereby more fit
105　To hold communion with the invisible world.
　　Such minds are truly from the Deity,
　　For they are powers; and hence the highest bliss
　　That can be known is theirs—the consciousness
　　Of whom they are, habitually infused
110　Through every image,[5] and through every thought,
　　And all impressions; hence religion, faith,
　　And endless occupation for the soul,
　　Whether discursive or intuitive;[6]
　　Hence sovereignty within and peace at will,
115　Emotion which best foresight need not fear,
　　Most worthy then of trust when most intense;
　　Hence chearfulness in every act of life;
　　Hence truth in moral judgements; and delight
　　That fails not, in the external universe.

120　　　Oh, who is he that hath his whole life long
　　Preserved, enlarged, this freedom in himself?—
　　For this alone is genuine liberty.
　　Witness, ye solitudes, where I received
　　My earliest visitations (careless then
125　Of what was given me), and where now I roam,
　　A meditative, oft a suffering man,
　　And yet I trust with undiminished powers;
　　Witness—whatever falls my better mind,
　　Revolving with the accidents of life,
130　May have sustained—that, howsoe'er misled,
　　I never in the quest of right and wrong
　　Did tamper with myself° from private aims;　　　*my conscience*
　　Nor was in any of my hopes the dupe
　　Of selfish passions; nor did wilfully

4. The "glorious faculty" is the imagination, which transfigures and re-creates what is given to it, much as, in Wordsworth's account of the night on Snowdon, the moonlit mist, layering a metaphoric sea atop a "real sea," transfigures the familiar landscape.
5. I.e., through all they see.

6. An echo of Archangel Raphael's account to Adam of the soul's powers of reason (*Paradise Lost* 5.488–89). Discursive reason, mainly a human quality according to Raphael, undertakes to reach truths through a logical sequence of premises, observations, and conclusions; "intuitive" reason, mainly angelic, comprehends truth immediately.

135　Yield ever to mean cares and low pursuits;
　　But rather did with jealousy° shrink back　　　　　　　　*vigilance*
　　From every combination that might aid
　　The tendency, too potent in itself,
　　Of habit to enslave the mind—I mean
140　Oppress it by the laws of vulgar° sense,　　　　　　　*commonplace*
　　And substitute a universe of death,
　　The falsest of all worlds, in place of that
　　Which is divine and true.[7]

* * *

[FINAL PROPHECY]

　　Oh, yet a few short years of useful life,
　　And all will be complete—thy race be run,
430　Thy monument of glory will be raised.[8]
　　Then, though too weak to tread the ways of truth,
　　This age fall back to old idolatry,
　　Though men return to servitude as fast
　　As the tide ebbs, to ignominy and shame
435　By nations sink together,[9] we shall still
　　Find solace in the knowledge which we have,
　　Blessed with true happiness if we may be
　　United helpers forward of a day
　　Of firmer trust, joint labourers in the work—
440　Should Providence such grace to us vouchsafe°—　　　*grant*
　　Of their° redemption, surely yet to come.　　　　　　*men's*
　　Prophets of Nature, we to them will speak
　　A lasting inspiration, sanctified
　　By reason and by truth; what we have loved
445　Others will love, and we may teach them how:
　　Instruct them how the mind of man becomes
　　A thousand times more beautiful than the earth
　　On which he dwells, above this frame of things
　　(Which, 'mid all revolutions in the hopes
450　And fears of men, doth still remain unchanged)
　　In beauty exalted, as it is itself
　　Of substance and of fabric more divine.

1805　　　　　　　　　　　　　　　　　　　　　　　1926

---

7. In *Paradise Lost* 2.622, the phrase "universe of death" is used to describe Hell. Wordsworth's Hell is a place in which individuals are enslaved by an unimaginative reliance on the senses and habitual perceptions.

8. In his conclusion, Wordsworth once again addresses Coleridge.
9. I.e., though men—whole nations of them together—sink to ignominy (disgrace) and shame.

DOROTHY WORDSWORTH
1771–1855

D orothy Wordsworth has an enduring place in English literature even though she wrote almost no word for publication. Not until long after her death did scholars gradually retrieve and print her letters, a few poems, and a series of journals that she kept sporadically between 1798 and 1828 because, she wrote, "I shall give William Pleasure by it." It has always been known, from tributes to her by her brother and Coleridge, that she exerted an important influence on the lives and writings of both these men. It is now apparent that she also possessed a power surpassing that of the two poets for precise observation of people and the natural world, together with a genius for terse, luminous, and delicately nuanced description in prose.

Dorothy was born on Christmas Day 1771, twenty-one months after William; she was the only girl of five Wordsworth children. From her seventh year, when her mother died, she lived with various relatives—some of them tolerant and affectionate, others rigid and tyrannical—and saw William and her other brothers only occasionally, during the boys' summer vacations from school. In 1795, when she was twenty-four, an inheritance that William received enabled her to carry out a long-held plan to join her brother in a house at Racedown, and the two spent the rest of their long lives together, first in Dorsetshire and Somersetshire, in the southwest of England, then in their beloved Lake District. She uncomplainingly subordinated her own talents to looking after her brother and his household. She also became William's secretary, tirelessly copying and recopying the manuscripts of his poems to ready them for publication. Despite the scolding of a great-aunt, who deemed "rambling about . . . on foot" ladylike, she accompanied her brother, too, in vigorous cross-country walks in which they sometimes covered as much as thirty-three miles in a day.

All her adult life she was overworked; after a severe illness in 1835, she suffered a physical and mental collapse. She spent the rest of her existence as an invalid. Hardest for her family to endure was the drastic change in her temperament: from a high-spirited and compassionate woman she became (save for brief intervals of lucidity) bad-tempered, demanding, and at times violent. In this half-life she lingered for twenty years, attended devotedly by William until his death five years before her own in 1855.

Our principal selections are from the journal Dorothy kept in 1798 at Alfoxden, Somersetshire, where the Wordsworths had moved from Racedown to be near Coleridge at Nether Stowey, as well as from her journals while at Grasmere (1800–1803), with Coleridge residing some thirteen miles away at Greta Hall, Keswick. Her records cover the period when both men emerged as major poets, and in their achievements Dorothy played an indispensable role. In book 10 of the 1805 *Prelude*, William says that in the time of his spiritual crisis, Dorothy "maintained for me a saving intercourse / With my true self" and "preserved me still / A Poet"; in a letter of 1797, Coleridge stressed the delicacy and tact in the responses of William's "exquisite sister" to the world of sense: "Her manners are simple, ardent, impressive. . . . Her information various—her eye watchful in minutest observation of nature—and her taste a perfect electrometer—it bends, protrudes, and draws in, at subtlest beauties & most recondite faults."

The verbal sketches of natural scenes given in the journal passages that we reprint are often echoed in Wordsworth's and Coleridge's poems. Of at least equal importance for Wordsworth was her chronicling of the busy wayfaring life of rural England. These were exceedingly hard times for country people, when the suffering caused by the displacement of small farms and of household crafts by large-scale farms and industries was aggravated by the economic distress caused by protracted Continental wars (see Wordsworth's comment in *The Ruined Cottage*, lines 133ff., p. 155). Peddlers, maimed war veterans, leech gatherers, adult and infant beggars, ousted farm families, fugitives, and women abandoned by husbands or lovers streamed along the rural roads and into William's brooding poetic imagination—often by way of Dorothy's prose records.

The journals also show the intensity of Dorothy's love for her brother. Inevitably in our era, the mutual devotion of the orphaned brother and sister has evoked psychoanalytic speculation. It is important to note that Mary Hutchinson, a gentle and openhearted young woman, had been Dorothy's closest friend since childhood, and that Dorothy encouraged William's courtship and marriage, even though she realized that it entailed her own displacement as a focus of her brother's life. All the evidence indicates that their lives in a single household never strained the affectionate relationship between the two women; indeed Dorothy, until she became an invalid, added to her former functions as William's chief support, housekeeper, and scribe a loving ministration to her brother's children.

In 1897 William Wordsworth's biographer William Knight published the first transcripts of Dorothy Wordsworth's Alfoxden and Grasmere journals, and those transcripts are the basis for the excerpts printed here. The exception is the entry from autumn 1802, in which Dorothy describes her distress on her brother's wedding day: since Knight excluded it from his edition, we rely there on Pamela Woof's edition of the Grasmere journals (Oxford University Press, 1991). Dorothy Wordsworth's poems, many of them originally written for the children in her brother's household, survived through the nineteenth and most of the twentieth centuries mainly as manuscripts in various family commonplace books. (William Wordsworth did, however, include three in his *Poems* of 1815, ascribing them to a "Female Friend.") Her poems were not collected until 1987, when Susan M. Levin edited thirty of them in an appendix ("The Collected Poems of Dorothy Wordsworth") to her *Dorothy Wordsworth and Romanticism*. The two poems included here are reprinted from that source.

From The Alfoxden Journal

Jan. 31, 1798. Set forward to Stowey[1] at half-past five. A violent storm in the wood; sheltered under the hollies. When we left home the moon immensely large, the sky scattered over with clouds. These soon closed in, contracting the dimensions of the moon without concealing her.[2] The sound of the pattering shower, and the gusts of wind, very grand. Left the wood when nothing remained of the storm but the driving wind, and a few scattering drops of rain. Presently all clear, Venus first showing herself between the struggling clouds; afterwards Jupiter appeared. The hawthorn hedges, black and pointed, glittering with millions of diamond drops; the hollies shining with broader patches of light. The road to the village of Holford glittered like another stream. On our return, the wind high—a violent storm of hail and rain at the Castle of Comfort.[3] All the Heavens seemed in one perpetual motion when the rain ceased; the moon appearing, now half veiled, and now retired behind heavy clouds, the stars still moving, the roads very dirty.

1. I.e., to Coleridge's cottage at Nether Stowey, three miles from Alfoxden.
2. Compare Coleridge's *Christabel*, lines 16–19

(p. 276).
3. A tavern halfway between Holford and Nether Stowey

* * *

Feb. 3. A mild morning, the windows open at breakfast, the redbreasts singing in the garden. Walked with Coleridge over the hills. The sea at first obscured by vapour; that vapour afterwards slid in one mighty mass along the sea-shore; the islands and one point of land clear beyond it. The distant country (which was purple in the clear dull air), overhung by straggling clouds that sailed over it, appeared like the darker clouds, which are often seen at a great distance apparently motionless, while the nearer ones pass quickly over them, driven by the lower winds. I never saw such a union of earth, sky, and sea. The clouds beneath our feet spread themselves to the water, and the clouds of the sky almost joined them. Gathered sticks in the wood; a perfect stillness. The redbreasts sang upon the leafless boughs. Of a great number of sheep in the field, only one standing. Returned to dinner at five o'clock. The moonlight still and warm as a summer's night at nine o'clock.

Feb. 4. Walked a great part of the way to Stowey with Coleridge. The morning warm and sunny. The young lasses seen on the hill-tops, in the villages and roads, in their summer holiday clothes—pink petticoats and blue. Mothers with their children in arms, and the little ones that could just walk, tottering by their side. Midges or small flies spinning in the sunshine; the songs of the lark and redbreast; daisies upon the turf; the hazels in blossom; honeysuckles budding. I saw one solitary strawberry flower under a hedge. The furze gay with blossom. The moss rubbed from the pailings by the sheep, that leave locks of wool, and the red marks with which they are spotted, upon the wood.[4]

* * *

Feb. 8. Went up the Park, and over the tops of the hills, till we came to a new and very delicious pathway, which conducted us to the Coombe.[5] Sat a considerable time upon the heath. Its surface restless and glittering with the motion of the scattered piles of withered grass, and the waving of the spiders' threads.[6] On our return the mist still hanging over the sea, but the opposite coast clear, and the rocky cliffs distinguishable. In the deep Coombe, as we stood upon the sunless hill, we saw miles of grass, light and glittering, and the insects passing.

Feb. 9. William gathered sticks.

Feb. 10. Walked to Woodlands, and to the waterfall. The adder's-tongue and the ferns green in the low damp dell. These plants now in perpetual motion from the current of the air; in summer only moved by the drippings of the rocks. A cloudy day.[7]

* * *

Mar. 7. William and I drank tea at Coleridge's. A cloudy sky. Observed nothing particularly interesting—the distant prospect obscured. One only leaf upon the top of a tree—the sole remaining leaf—danced round and round like a rag blown by the wind.[8]

4. Compare Wordsworth's *The Ruined Cottage*, lines 330–36 (p. 159).
5. Hodder's Coombe is in the Quantock Hills, near Alfoxden. A coombe is a deep valley.
6. Compare Coleridge's *The Rime of the Ancient Mariner*, line 189 (p. 261).
7. Compare the description of the dell in Coleridge's "This Lime-Tree Bower My Prison," lines 13–20 (p. 254).
8. Compare *Christabel*, lines 49ff. (p. 277).

Mar. 8. Walked in the Park in the morning. I sate under the fir trees. Coleridge came after dinner, so we did not walk again. A foggy morning, but a clear sunny day.

Mar. 9. A clear sunny morning, went to meet Mr. and Mrs. Coleridge. The day very warm.

Mar. 10. Coleridge, Wm., and I walked in the evening to the top of the hill. We all passed the morning in sauntering about the park and gardens, the children playing about, the old man at the top of the hill gathering furze; interesting groups of human creatures, the young frisking and dancing in the sun, the elder quietly drinking in the life and soul of the sun and air.

Mar. 11. A cold day. The children went down towards the sea. William and I walked to the top of the hills above Holford. Met the blacksmith. Pleasant to see the labourer on Sunday jump with the friskiness of a cow upon a sunny day.

* * *

1798   1897

From The Grasmere Journals

1800

May 14, 1800.—Wm. and John set off into Yorkshire[1] after dinner at half-past two o'clock, cold pork in their pockets. I left them at the turning of the Lowwood bay under the trees. My heart was so full that I could hardly speak to W. when I gave him a farewell kiss. I sate a long time upon a stone at the margin of the lake, and after a flood of tears my heart was easier. The lake looked to me, I knew not why, dull and melancholy, and the weltering on the shores seemed a heavy sound. I walked as long as I could amongst the stones of the shore. The wood rich in flowers; a beautiful yellow (palish yellow) flower, that looked thick, round, and double—the smell very sweet (I supposed it was a ranunculus), crowfoot, the grassy-leaved rabbit-looking white flower, strawberries, geraniums, scentless violets, anemones, two kinds of orchises, primroses, the hackberry very beautiful, the crab coming out as a low shrub. Met an old man, driving a very large beautiful bull, and a cow. He walked with two sticks. Came home by Clappersgate. The valley very green; many sweet views up to Rydale, when I could juggle away the fine houses; but they disturbed me, even more than when I have been happier; one beautiful view of the bridge, without Sir Michael's.[2] Sate down very often, though it was cold. I resolved to write a journal of the time, till W. and J. return, and I set about keeping my resolve, because I will not quarrel with myself, and because I shall give William pleasure by it when he comes home again. At Rydale, a woman of the village, stout and well dressed, begged a half-penny. She had never she said done it before, but these hard times! Arrived at home, set some slips of privet, the evening cold, had a fire, my face now flame-coloured. It is nine o'clock. I shall now go to bed.

1. William and his younger brother John, on the way to visit Mary Hutchinson, whom William was to marry two and a half years later.

2. Sir Michael le Fleming's estate, Rydal Hall. "Without": outside or beyond.

* * *

Friday, 3rd October. Very rainy all the morning. Wm. walked to Ambleside after dinner. I went with him part of the way. He talked much about the object of his essay for the second volume of "L. B."[3] * * *

N.B.—When William and I returned from accompanying Jones, we met an old man almost double.[4] He had on a coat, thrown over his shoulders, above his waistcoat and coat. Under this he carried a bundle, and had an apron on and a night-cap. His face was interesting. He had dark eyes and a long nose. John, who afterwards met him at Wytheburn, took him for a Jew. He was of Scotch parents, but had been born in the army. He had had a wife, and "she was a good woman, and it pleased God to bless us with ten children." All these were dead but one, of whom he had not heard for many years, a sailor. His trade was to gather leeches, but now leeches were scarce, and he had not strength for it. He lived by begging, and was making his way to Carlisle, where he should buy a few godly books to sell. He said leeches were very scarce, partly owing to this dry season, but many years they have been scarce. He supposed it owing to their being much sought after, that they did not breed fast, and were of slow growth. Leeches were formerly 2s. 6d.[5] per 100; they are now 30s. He had been hurt in driving a cart, his leg broken, his body driven over, his skull fractured. He felt no pain till he recovered from his first insensibility. It was then late in the evening, when the light was just going away.

* * *

Saturday, [Oct.] 11th. A fine October morning. Sat in the house working all the morning. William composing. * * * After dinner we walked up Greenhead Gill in search of a sheepfold.[6] We went by Mr. Olliff's, and through his woods. It was a delightful day, and the views looked excessively cheerful and beautiful, chiefly that from Mr. Olliff's field, where our own house is to be built. The colours of the mountains soft, and rich with orange fern; the cattle pasturing upon the hilltops; kites sailing in the sky above our heads; sheep bleating, and feeding in the water courses, scattered over the mountains. They come down and feed, on the little green islands in the beds of the torrents, and so may be swept away. The sheepfold is falling away. It is built nearly in the form of a heart unequally divided. Looked down the brook, and saw the drops rise upwards and sparkle in the air at the little falls. The higher sparkled the tallest. We walked along the turf of the mountain till we came to a track, made by the cattle which come upon the hills.

* * *

Sunday, October 12th. Sate in the house writing in the morning while Wm. went into the wood to compose. Wrote to John in the morning; copied poems for the L. B. In the evening wrote to Mrs. Rawson. Mary Jameson and Sally Ashburner dined. We pulled apples after dinner, a large basket full. We walked

3. The Preface to the second edition of *Lyrical Ballads*, 1800.
4. William's "Resolution and Independence," composed one and a half years later, incorporated various details of Dorothy's description of the leech gatherer. See May 4 and 7, 1802 (pp. 243 and 244), for William working on the poem he originally called "The Leech Gatherer."
5. Two shillings, six pence.
6. The sheepfold (pen for sheep) in William's "Michael." Lines 1–7 of the poem describe the walk up Greenhead Gill.

before tea by Bainriggs to observe the many-coloured foliage. The oaks dark green with yellow leaves, the birches generally still green, some near the water yellowish, the sycamore crimson and crimson-tufted, the mountain ash a deep orange, the common ash lemon-colour, but many ashes still fresh in their peculiar green, those that were discoloured chiefly near the water. Wm. composing in the evening. Went to bed at 12 o'clock.

1801

Tuesday, [*Nov.*] *24th* * * * It was very windy, and we heard the wind everywhere about us as we went along the lane, but the walls sheltered us. John Green's house looked pretty under Silver How. As we were going along we were stopped at once, at the distance perhaps of 50 yards from our favourite birch tree. It was yielding to the gusty wind with all its tender twigs. The sun shone upon it, and it glanced in the wind like a flying sun-shiny shower. It was a tree in shape, with stem and branches, but it was like a spirit of water. The sun went in, and it resumed its purplish appearance, the twigs still yielding to the wind, but not so visibly to us. The other birch trees that were near it looked bright and cheerful, but it was a creature by its own self among them. . . . We went through the wood. It became fair. There was a rainbow which spanned the lake from the island-house to the foot of Bainriggs. The village looked populous and beautiful. Catkins are coming out; palm trees budding; the alder, with its plum-coloured buds. We came home over the stepping-stones. The lake was foamy with white waves. I saw a solitary butter-flower in the wood. * * * Reached home at dinner time. Sent Peggy Ashburner some goose. She sent me some honey, with a thousand thanks. "Alas! the gratitude of men has," etc.[7] I went in to set her right about this, and sate a while with her. She talked about Thomas's having sold his land. "I," says she, "said many a time he's not come fra London to buy our land, however." Then she told me with what pains and industry they had made up their taxes, interest, etc. etc., how they all got up at 5 o'clock in the morning to spin and Thomas carded, and that they had paid off a hundred pounds of the interest. She said she used to take much pleasure in the cattle and sheep. "O how pleased I used to be when they fetched them down, and when I had been a bit poorly I would gang out upon a hill and look over 't fields and see them, and it used to do me so much good you cannot think." Molly said to me when I came in, "Poor body! she's very ill, but one does not know how long she may last. Many a fair face may gang before her." We sate by the fire without work for some time, then Mary read a poem of Daniel.[8] * * * Wm. read Spenser, now and then, a little aloud to us. We were making his waistcoat. We had a note from Mrs. C., with bad news from poor C.—very ill. William went to John's Grove. I went to find him. Moonlight, but it rained. * * * He had been surprised, and terrified, by a sudden rushing of winds, which seemed to bring earth, sky, and lake together, as if the whole were going to enclose him in. He was glad he was in a high road.

In speaking of our walk on Sunday evening, the 22nd November, I forgot to notice one most impressive sight. It was the moon and the moonlight seen through hurrying driving clouds immediately behind the Stone-Man

---

7. A quotation from William's "Simon Lee." "Alas! the gratitude of men / Has oft'ner left me mourning."

8. Identified as Samuel Daniel's poem *Muso-philes: Containing a General Defence of Learning* (1599).

upon the top of the hill, on the forest side. Every tooth and every edge of rock was visible, and the Man stood like a giant watching from the roof of a lofty castle. The hill seemed perpendicular from the darkness below it. It was a sight that I could call to mind at any time, it was so distinct.

1802

Thursday [*Mar. 4*]. Before we had quite finished breakfast Calvert's man brought the horses for Wm.[9] We had a deal to do, pens to make, poems to put in order for writing, to settle for the press, pack up; and the man came before the pens were made, and he was obliged to leave me with only two. Since he left me at half-past 11 (it is now 2) I have been putting the drawers into order, laid by his clothes which he had thrown here and there and everywhere, filed two months' newspapers and got my dinner, 2 boiled eggs and 2 apple tarts. I have set Molly on to clean the garden a little, and I myself have walked. I transplanted some snowdrops—the Bees are busy. Wm. has a nice bright day. It was hard frost in the night. The Robins are singing sweetly. Now for my walk. I *will* be busy. I *will* look well, and be well when he comes back to me. O the Darling! Here is one of his bitten apples. I can hardly find it in my heart to throw it into the fire. * * * I walked round the two Lakes, crossed the stepping-stones at Rydale foot. Sate down where we always sit. I was full of thought about my darling. Blessings on him. I came home at the foot of our own hill under Loughrigg. They are making sad ravages in the woods. Benson's wood is going, and the woods above the River. The wind has blown down a small fir tree on the Rock, that terminates John's path. I suppose the wind of Wednesday night. I read German after tea. I worked and read the L. B., enchanted with the *Idiot Boy*. Wrote to Wm. and then went to bed. It snowed when I went to bed.

* * *

Monday [*Mar. 22*]. A rainy day. William very poorly. 2 letters from Sara, and one from poor Annette. Wrote to my brother Richard. We talked a good deal about C. and other interesting things. We resolved to see Annette, and that Wm. should go to Mary.[1] Wm. wrote to Coleridge not to expect us till Thursday or Friday.

Tuesday.—A mild morning. William worked at *The Cuckoo* poem.[2] I sewed beside him. After dinner he slept. I read German, and, at the closing-in of day, went to sit in the orchard. William came to me, and walked backwards and forwards. We talked about C. Wm. repeated the poem to me. I left him there, and in 20 minutes he came in, rather tired with attempting to write. He is now reading Ben Jonson. I am going to read German. It is about 10 o'clock, a quiet night. The fire flickers, and the watch ticks. I hear nothing save the breathing of my Beloved as he now and then pushes his book forward, and turns over a leaf. * * *

* * *

9. For a journey to Keswick to visit Coleridge.
1. It had been arranged several months earlier that William was to marry Mary Hutchinson (Sara is Mary's sister, with whom Coleridge had fallen in love). Now the Wordsworths resolve to go to France to settle affairs with Annette Vallon, mother of William's daughter, Caroline. William did not conceal the facts of his early love affair from his family, or from Mary Hutchinson.
2. "To the Cuckoo."

Thursday, [*Apr.*] 15*th* It was a threatening, misty morning, but mild. We set off after dinner from Eusemere. Mrs. Clarkson went a short way with us, but turned back.[3] The wind was furious, and we thought we must have returned. We first rested in the large boathouse, then under a furze bush opposite Mr. Clarkson's. Saw the plough going in the field. The wind seized our breath. The lake was rough. There was a boat by itself floating in the middle of the bay below Water Millock. We rested again in the Water Millock Lane. The hawthorns are black and green, the birches here and there greenish, but there is yet more of purple to be seen on the twigs. We got over into a field to avoid some cows—people working. A few primroses by the roadside—woodsorrel flower, the anemone, scentless violets, strawberries, and that starry, yellow flower which Mrs. C. calls pile wort. When we were in the woods beyond Gowbarrow Park we saw a few daffodils close to the water-side.[4] We fancied that the sea had floated the seeds ashore, and that the little colony had so sprung up. But as we went along there were more and yet more; and at last, under the boughs of the trees, we saw that there was a long belt of them along the shore, about the breadth of a country turnpike road. I never saw daffodils so beautiful. They grew among the mossy stones about and above them; some rested their heads upon these stones, as on a pillow, for weariness; and the rest tossed and reeled and danced, and seemed as if they verily laughed with the wind, that blew upon them over the lake; they looked so gay, ever glancing, ever changing. This wind blew directly over the lake to them. There was here and there a little knot, and a few stragglers higher up; but they were so few as not to disturb the simplicity, unity, and life of that one busy highway. We rested again and again. The bays were stormy, and we heard the waves at different distances, and in the middle of the water, like the sea. Rain came on. * * * William was sitting by a good fire when I came downstairs. He soon made his way to the library, piled up in a corner of the window. He brought out a volume of Enfield's *Speaker,*[5] another miscellany, and an odd volume of Congreve's plays. We had a glass of warm rum and water. We enjoyed ourselves, and wished for Mary. It rained and blew, when we went to bed. * * *

Friday, 16*th April* (*Good Friday*).—When I undrew curtains in the morning, I was much affected by the beauty of the prospect, and the change. The sun shone, the wind had passed away, the hills looked cheerful, the river was very bright as it flowed into the lake. The church rises up behind a little knot of rocks, the steeple not so high as an ordinary three-story house. Trees in a row in the garden under the wall. The valley is at first broken by little woody knolls that make retiring places, fairy valleys in the vale, the river winds along under these hills, travelling, not in a bustle but not slowly, to the lake. We saw a fisherman in the flat meadow on the other side of the water. He came towards us, and threw his line over the two-arched bridge. It is a bridge of a heavy construction, almost bending inwards in the middle, but it is grey, and there is a look of ancientry in the architecture of it that pleased

3. Catherine Clarkson, the wife of the anti-slave-trade campaigner Thomas Clarkson, was a neighbor and became one of Dorothy Wordsworth's closest friends.
4. William did not compose his poem on the daffodils, "I wandered lonely as a cloud," until two years later. Comparison with the poem will show how extensive was his use of Dorothy's prose description (p. 177).
5. William Enfield's *The Speaker* (1774), a volume of selections suitable for elocution.

me. As we go on the vale opens out more into one vale, with somewhat of a cradle bed. Cottages, with groups of trees, on the side of the hills. We passed a pair of twin children, two years old. Sate on the next bridge which we crossed—a single arch. We rested again upon the turf, and looked at the same bridge. We observed arches in the water, occasioned by the large stones sending it down in two streams. A sheep came plunging through the river, stumbled up the bank, and passed close to us. It had been frightened by an insignificant little dog on the other side. Its fleece dropped a glittering shower under its belly. Primroses by the road-side, pile wort that shone like stars of gold in the sun, violets, strawberries, retired and half-buried among the grass. When we came to the foot of Brothers Water, I left William sitting on the bridge, and went along the path on the right side of the lake through the wood. I was delighted with what I saw. The water under the boughs of the bare old trees, the simplicity of the mountains, and the exquisite beauty of the path. There was one grey cottage. I repeated *The Glow-worm*,[6] as I walked along. I hung over the gate, and thought I could have stayed for ever. When I returned, I found William writing a poem descriptive of the sights and sounds we saw and heard. There was the gentle flowing of the stream, the glittering, lively lake, green fields without a living creature to be seen on them; behind us, a flat pasture with forty-two cattle feeding; to our left, the road leading to the hamlet. No smoke there, the sun shone on the bare roofs. The people were at work ploughing, harrowing, and sowing; . . . a dog barking now and then, cocks crowing, birds twittering, the snow in patches at the top of the highest hills, yellow palms, purple and green twigs on the birches, ashes with their glittering stems quite bare. The hawthorn a bright green, with black stems under the oak. The moss of the oak glossy. We went on. Passed two sisters at work (they first passed us), one with two pitchforks in her hand, the other had a spade. We had come to talk with them. They laughed long after we were gone, perhaps half in wantonness, half boldness. William finished his poem.[7] Before we got to the foot of Kirkstone, there were hundreds of cattle in the vale. * * *

Thursday, [*Apr.*] 29*th*. * * * After I had written down *The Tinker*, which William finished this morning,[8] Luff called. He was very lame, limped into the kitchen. He came on a little pony. We then went to John's Grove, sate a while at first; afterwards William lay, and I lay, in the trench under the fence—he with his eyes shut, and listening to the waterfalls and the birds. There was no one waterfall above another—it was a sound of waters in the air—the voice of the air. William heard me breathing, and rustling now and then, but we both lay still, and unseen by one another. He thought that it would be so sweet thus to lie in the grave, to hear the peaceful sounds of the earth, and just to know that our dear friends were near. The lake was still; there was a boat out. Silver How reflected with delicate purple and yellowish hues, as I have seen spar; lambs on the island, and running races together by the half-dozen, in the round field near us. The copses greenish, hawthorns green, . . . cottages smoking. As I lay down on the grass, I observed the glittering silver line on the ridge of the backs of the sheep, owing to their situation respecting the sun, which made them look beautiful, but with something

---

6. William's poem beginning "Among all lovely things my Love had been," composed four days earlier; "my Love" in this line is Dorothy.

7. The short lyric "Written in March."
8. William never published his comic poem "The Tinkers." It was first printed in 1897.

of strangeness, like animals of another kind, as if belonging to a more splendid world.* * *

* * *

Tuesday, May 4th. Though William went to bed nervous, and jaded in the extreme, he rose refreshed, wrote out *The Leech Gatherer*[9] for him, which he had begun the night before and of which he wrote several stanzas in bed this Monday morning. It was very hot. * * * We rested several times by the way,—read, and repeated *The Leech Gatherer.* * * * We saw Coleridge on the Wytheburn side of the water; he crossed the beck to us. Mr. Simpson was fishing there. William and I ate luncheon and then went on towards the waterfall. It is a glorious wild solitude under that lofty purple crag. It stood upright by itself; its own self, and its shadow below, one mass; all else was sunshine. We went on further. A bird at the top of the crag was flying round and round, and looked in thinness and transparency, shape and motion like a moth. We climbed the hill, but looked in vain for a shade, except at the foot of the great waterfall. We came down, and rested upon a moss-covered rock rising out of the bed of the river. There we lay, ate our dinner, and stayed there till about four o'clock or later. William and Coleridge repeated and read verses. I drank a little brandy and water, and was in heaven. The stag's horn is very beautiful and fresh, springing upon the fells; mountain ashes, green. We drank tea at a farm house. * * * We parted from Coleridge at Sara's crag, after having looked for the letters which C. carved in the morning. I missed them all. William deepened the T. with C.'s pen-knive.[1] We sate afterwards on the wall, seeing the sun go down, and the reflections in the still water. C. looked well, and parted from us cheerfully, hopping upon the side stones. On the Raise we met a woman with two little girls, one in her arms, the other, about four years old, walking by her side, a pretty little thing, but half-starved. * * * The mother, when we accosted her, told us how her husband had left her, and gone off with another woman, and how she *"pursued"* them. Then her fury kindled, and her eyes rolled about. She changed again to tears. She was a Cockermouth woman, thirty years of age—a child at Cockermouth when I was. I was moved, and gave her a shilling. . . . We had the crescent moon with the "auld moon in her arms."[2] We rested often, always upon the bridges. Reached home at about ten o'clock. * * * We went soon to bed. I repeated verses to William while he was in bed; he was soothed, and I left him. "This is the spot"[3] over and over again.

* * *

Thursday, 6th May.—A sweet morning. We have put the finishing stroke to our bower, and here we are sitting in the orchard. It is one o'clock. We are sitting upon a seat under the wall, which I found my brother building up, when I came to him.—He had intended that it should have been done before I came. It is a nice, cool, shady spot. The small birds are singing, lambs bleating, cuckoos calling, the thrush sings by fits, Thomas Ashburner's axe

9. The poem that was published as "Resolution and Independence." For its origin see the entry for October 3, 1800 (p. 238).
1. The rock, which has since been blasted away to make room for a new road, contained the carved letters W. W., M. H., D. W., S. T. C., J. W., S. M. C. M. H. and S. H. are Mary and Sara Hutchinson; J. W. is John Wordsworth.
2. From the "Ballad of Sir Patrick Spens." See p. 292.
3. William never completed this poem.

is going quietly (without passion) in the orchard, hens are cackling, flies humming, the women talking together at their doors, plum and pear trees are in blossom—apple trees greenish—the opposite woods green, the crows are cawing, we have heard ravens, the ash trees are in blossom, birds flying all about us, the stitchwort is coming out, there is one budding lychnis, the primroses are passing their prime, celandine, violets, and wood sorrel for ever more, little geraniums and pansies on the wall. We walked in the evening to Tail End, to inquire about hurdles for the orchard shed. * * * When we came in we found a magazine, and review, and a letter from Coleridge, verses to Hartley, and Sara H. We read the review,[4] etc. The moon was a perfect boat, a silver boat, when we were out in the evening. The birch tree is all over green in *small* leaf, more light and elegant than when it is full out. It bent to the breezes, as if for the love of its own delightful motions. Sloethorns and hawthorns in the hedges.

Friday, 7th May.—William had slept uncommonly well, so, feeling himself strong, he fell to work at *The Leech Gatherer*; he wrote hard at it till dinner time, then he gave over, tired to death—he had finished the poem.[5] I was making Derwent's frocks. After dinner we sate in the orchard. It was a thick, hazy, dull air. The thrush sang almost continually; the little birds were more than usually busy with their voices. The sparrows are now full fledged. The nest is so full that they lie upon one another; they sit quietly in their nest with closed mouths. I walked to Rydale after tea, which we drank by the kitchen fire. The evening very dull; a terrible kind of threatening brightness at sunset above Easedale. The sloe-thorn beautiful in the hedges, and in the wild spots higher up among the hawthorns. No letters. William met me. He had been digging in my absence, and cleaning the well. We walked up beyond Lewthwaites. A very dull sky; coolish; crescent moon now and then. I had a letter brought me from Mrs. Clarkson while we were walking in the orchard. I observed the sorrel leaves opening at about nine o'clock. William went to bed tired with thinking about a poem.

* * *

[*July.*] On Thursday morning, 29th, we arrived in London.[6] Wm. left me at the Sun. * * * After various troubles and disasters, we left London on Saturday morning at half-past five or six, the 31st of July. We mounted the Dover coach at Charing Cross. It was a beautiful morning. The city, St. Paul's, with the river, and a multitude of little boats, made a most beautiful sight as we crossed Westminster Bridge. The houses were not overhung by their cloud of smoke, and they were spread out endlessly, yet the sun shone so brightly, with such a fierce light, that there was even something like the purity of one of nature's own grand spectacles.[7]

We rode on cheerfully, now with the Paris diligence before us, now behind. We walked up the steep hills, a beautiful prospect everywhere, till we even reached Dover. * * * We arrived at Calais at four o'clock on Sunday morning, the 31st of July.[8] We stayed in the vessel till half-past seven; then William went for letters at about half-past eight or nine. We found out Annette and

---

4. The *Monthly Review* for March 1802.
5. Later entries show, however, that William kept working on the manuscript until July 4.
6. On the way to France to visit Annette Vallon and Caroline (see the entry for March 22, 1802, p. 240).

7. Compare William's sonnet "Composed upon Westminster Bridge" (p. 184).
8. The actual date was August 1. One of the walks by the sea that Dorothy goes on to describe was the occasion for William's sonnet "It is a beauteous evening."

C. chez Madame Avril dans la Rue de la Tête d'or. We lodged opposite two ladies, in tolerably decent-sized rooms, but badly furnished. * * * The weather was very hot. We walked by the sea-shore almost every evening with Annette and Caroline, or William and I alone. I had a bad cold, and could not bathe at first, but William did. It was a pretty sight to see as we walked upon the sands when the tide was low, perhaps a hundred people bathing about a quarter of a mile distant from us. And we had delightful walks after the heat of the day was passed—seeing far off in the west the coast of England like a cloud crested with Dover castle, which was but like the summit of the cloud—the evening star and the glory of the sky, the reflections in the water were more beautiful than the sky itself, purple waves brighter than precious stones, for ever melting away upon the sands.

* * *

[*Sept. 24 and following.*] Mary first met us in the avenue. She looked so fat and well that we were made very happy by the sight of her—then came Sara, & last of all Joanna.[9] Tom was forking corn standing upon the corn cart. We dressed ourselves immediately & got tea—the garden looked gay with asters & sweet peas—I looked at everything with tranquillity & happiness but I was ill both on Saturday & Sunday & continued to be poorly most of the time of our stay. Jack & George came on Friday Evening 1st October. On Saturday 2nd we rode to Hackness, William Jack George & Sara single, I behind Tom. On Sunday 3rd Mary & Sara were busy packing. On Monday 4th October 1802, my Brother William was married to Mary Hutchinson. I slept a good deal of the night & rose fresh & well in the morning—at a little after 8 o'clock I saw them go down the avenue towards the Church. William had parted from me up stairs. I gave him the wedding ring—with how deep a blessing! I took it from my forefinger where I had worn it the whole of the night before—he slipped it again onto my finger and blessed me fervently. When they were absent my dear little Sara prepared the breakfast. I kept myself as quiet as I could, but when I saw the two men running up the walk, coming to tell us it was over, I could stand it no longer & threw myself on the bed where I lay in stillness, neither hearing or seeing any thing, till Sara came upstairs to me & said "They are coming." This forced me from the bed where I lay & I moved I knew not how straight forward, faster than my strength could carry me till I met my beloved William & fell upon his bosom. He & John Hutchinson led me to the house & there I stayed to welcome my dear Mary. As soon as we had breakfasted we departed.[1] It rained when we set off. Poor Mary was much agitated when she parted from her Brothers & Sisters & her home. Nothing particular occurred till we reached Kirby. We had sunshine & showers, pleasant talk, love & chearfulness. * * * It rained very hard when we reached Windermere. We sate in the rain at Wilcock's to change horses, & arrived at Grasmere at about 6 o'clock on Wednesday Evening, the 6th of October 1802. Molly was overjoyed to see us,—for my part I cannot describe what I felt, & our dear Mary's feelings would I dare say not be easy to speak of. We went by candle light into the

<hr>

9. The Wordsworths have come to Gallow Hill, Yorkshire, for the marriage of William and Mary. The people mentioned are Mary's sisters and brothers (Sara, Joanna, Tom, Jack, and George Hutchinson). Out of consideration for Dorothy's overwrought feelings, only Joanna, Jack, and Tom attended the ceremony at Brampton Church.
1. Dorothy accompanied William and Mary on the three-day journey back to their cottage at Grasmere.

garden & were astonished at the growth of the Brooms, Portugal Laurels, &c &c &—The next day, Thursday, we unpacked the Boxes. On Friday 8th we baked Bread, & Mary & I walked, first upon the Hill side, & then in John's Grove, then in view of Rydale, the first walk that I had taken with my Sister.

* * *

24th December.—Christmas Eve. William is now sitting by me, at half-past ten o'clock. I have been * * * repeating some of his sonnets to him, listening to his own repeating, reading some of Milton's, and the *Allegro* and *Penseroso*. It is a quick, keen frost. * * * Coleridge came this morning with Wedgwood. We all turned out * * * one by one, to meet him. He looked well. We had to tell him of the birth of his little girl, born yesterday morning at six o'clock. William went with them to Wytheburn in the chaise, and M. and I met W. on the Raise. It was not an unpleasant morning. * * * The sun shone now and then, and there was no wind, but all things looked cheerless and distinct; no meltings of sky into mountains, the mountains like stone work wrought up with huge hammers. Last Sunday was as mild a day as I ever remember. * * * Mary and I went round the lakes. There were flowers of various kinds—the topmost bell of a foxglove, geraniums, daisies, a buttercup in the water (but this I saw two or three days before), small yellow flowers (I do not know their name) in the turf. A large bunch of strawberry blossoms. * * * It is Christmas Day, Saturday, 25th December 1802. I am thirty-one years of age. It is a dull, frosty day.

* * *

Grasmere—A Fragment

Peaceful our valley, fair and green,
And beautiful her cottages,
Each in its nook, its sheltered hold,
Or underneath its tuft of trees.

5   Many and beautiful they are;
But there is *one* that I love best,
A lowly shed, in truth, it is,
A brother of the rest.

Yet when I sit on rock or hill,
10 Down looking on the valley fair,
That Cottage with its clustering trees
Summons my heart; it settles there.

Others there are whose small domain
Of fertile fields and hedgerows green
15 Might more seduce a wanderer's mind
To wish that *there* his home had been.

Such wish be his! I blame him not,
My fancies they perchance are wild

—I love that house because it is
20 The very Mountains' child.

Fields hath it of its own, green fields,
But they are rocky steep and bare;
Their fence is of the mountain stone,
And moss and lichen flourish there.

25 And when the storm comes from the North
It lingers near that pastoral spot,
And, piping through the mossy walls,
It seems delighted with its lot.

And let it take its own delight;
30 And let it range the pastures bare;
Until it reach that group of trees,
—It may not enter there!

A green unfading grove it is,
Skirted with many a lesser tree,
35 Hazel and holly, beech and oak,
A bright and flourishing company.

Precious the shelter of those trees;
They screen the cottage that I love;
The sunshine pierces to the roof,
40 And the tall pine-trees tower above.

When first I saw that dear abode,
It was a lovely winter's day:
After a night of perilous storm
The west wind ruled with gentle sway;

45 A day so mild, it might have been
The first day of the gladsome spring;
The robins warbled, and I heard
One solitary throstle sing.

A Stranger, Grasmere, in thy Vale,
50 All faces then to me unknown,
I left my sole companion-friend
To wander out alone.

Lured by a little winding path,
I quitted soon the public road,
55 A smooth and tempting path it was,
By sheep and shepherds trod.

Eastward, toward the lofty hills,
This pathway led me on
Until I reached a stately Rock,
60 With velvet moss o'ergrown.

With russet oak and tufts of fern
Its top was richly garlanded;
Its sides adorned with eglantine
Bedropp'd with hips of glossy red.

65 There, too, in many a sheltered chink
The foxglove's broad leaves flourished fair,
And silver birch whose purple twigs
Bend to the softest breathing air.

Beneath that Rock my course I stayed,
70 And, looking to its summit high,
"Thou wear'st," said I, "a splendid garb,
Here winter keeps his revelry.

"Full long a dweller on the Plains,
I griev'd when summer days were gone;
75 No more I'll grieve; for Winter here
Hath pleasure gardens of his own.

"What need of flowers? The splendid moss
Is gayer than an April mead;
More rich its hues of various green,
80 Orange, and gold, & glittering red."

—Beside that gay and lovely Rock
There came with merry voice
A foaming streamlet glancing by;
It seemed to say "Rejoice!"

85 My youthful wishes all fulfill'd,
Wishes matured by thoughtful choice,
I stood an Inmate of this vale
How *could* I but rejoice?

ca. 1802–1805   1892

Thoughts on My Sick-Bed[1]

And has the remnant of my life
Been pilfered of this sunny Spring?
And have its own prelusive sounds
Touched in my heart no echoing string?

5 Ah! say not so—the hidden life
Couchant° within this feeble frame   *lying*
Hath been enriched by kindred gifts,
That, undesired, unsought-for, came

1. In a letter of May 25, 1832, William Wordsworth's daughter Dora mentions this as "an
affecting poem which she [her aunt Dorothy] has
written on the pleasure she received from the first
spring flowers that were carried up to her when

confined to her sick room." The lines refer to half
a dozen or more poems by William, including "I
wandered lonely as a cloud" (in line 18) and "Tintern Abbey" (lines 45–52).

With joyful heart in youthful days
10 When fresh each season in its Round
I welcomed the earliest Celandine
Glittering upon the mossy ground;

With busy eyes I pierced the lane
In quest of known and *un*known things,
15 —The primrose a lamp on its fortress rock,
The silent butterfly spreading its wings,

The violet betrayed by its noiseless breath,
The daffodil dancing in the breeze,
The carolling thrush, on his naked perch,
20 Towering above the budding trees.

Our cottage-hearth no longer our home,
Companions of Nature were we,
The Stirring, the Still, the Loquacious, the Mute—
To all we gave our sympathy.

25 Yet never in those careless days
When spring-time in rock, field, or bower
Was but a fountain of earthly hope
A promise of fruits & the *splendid* flower.

No! then I never felt a bliss
30 That might with *that* compare
Which, piercing to my couch of rest,
Came on the vernal air.

When loving Friends an offering brought,
The first flowers of the year,
35 Culled from the precincts of our home,
From nooks to Memory dear.

With some sad thoughts the work was done,
Unprompted and unbidden,
But joy it brought to my *hidden* life,
40 To consciousness no longer hidden.

I felt a Power unfelt before,
Controlling weakness, languor, pain;
It bore me to the Terrace walk
I trod the Hills again;—

45 No prisoner in this lonely room,
I *saw* the green Banks of the Wye,
Recalling thy prophetic words,
Bard, Brother, Friend from infancy!

No need of motion, or of strength,
50 Or even the breathing air:
—I thought of Nature's loveliest scenes;
And with Memory I was there.

May 1832   1978

SAMUEL TAYLOR COLERIDGE
1772–1834

In *The Prelude* Wordsworth, recording his gratitude to the mountains, lakes, and winds "that dwell among the hills where I was born," commiserates with Coleridge because "thou, my Friend! wert reared / In the great City, 'mid far other scenes." Samuel Taylor Coleridge had in fact been born in the small town of Ottery St. Mary, in rural Devonshire, but on the death of his father he had been sent to school at Christ's Hospital in London. He was a dreamy, enthusiastic, and extraordinarily precocious schoolboy. Charles Lamb, his schoolmate and lifelong friend, in an essay on Christ's Hospital gave a vivid sketch of Coleridge's loneliness, his learning, and his eloquence. When in 1791 Coleridge entered Jesus College, Cambridge, he was an accomplished scholar; but he found little intellectual stimulation at the university, fell into idleness, dissoluteness, and debt, then in despair fled to London and enlisted in the Light Dragoons under the alias of Silas Tomkyn Comberbache—one of the most inept cavalrymen in the long history of the British army. Although rescued by his brothers and sent back to Cambridge, he left in 1794 without a degree.

In June 1794 Coleridge met Robert Southey, then a student at Oxford who, like himself, had poetic aspirations, was a radical in religion and politics, and sympathized with the republican experiment in France. Together the two young men planned to establish an ideal democratic community in America for which Coleridge coined the name "Pantisocracy," signifying an equal rule by all. A plausible American real-estate agent persuaded them that the ideal location would be on the banks of the Susquehanna in Pennsylvania. Twelve men undertook to go; and because perpetuation of the scheme required offspring, hence wives, Coleridge dutifully became engaged to Sara Fricker, conveniently at hand as the sister of Southey's fiancée. The Pantisocracy scheme collapsed, but at Southey's insistence Coleridge went through with the marriage, "resolved," as he said, "but wretched." Later Coleridge's radicalism waned, and he became a conservative in politics—a highly philosophical one—and a staunch Anglican in religion.

In 1795 Coleridge met Wordsworth and at once judged him to be "the best poet of the age." When in 1797 Wordsworth brought his sister, Dorothy, to settle at Alfoxden, only three miles from the Coleridges at Nether Stowey, the period of intimate communication and poetic collaboration began that was the golden time of Coleridge's life. An annual allowance of £150, granted to Coleridge by Thomas and Josiah Wedgwood, sons of the founder of the famous pottery firm, came just in time to deflect him from assuming a post as a Unitarian minister. After their joint publication of *Lyrical Ballads* in 1798, Coleridge and the Wordsworths spent a winter in Germany, where Coleridge attended the University of Göttingen and began the lifelong study of German philosophers and critics—Kant, Schiller, Schelling, and Fichte—that helped alter profoundly his thinking about philosophy, religion, and aesthetics.

Back in England, Coleridge in 1800 followed the Wordsworths to the Lake District, settling at Greta Hall, Keswick. He had become gradually disaffected from his wife, and now he fell helplessly and hopelessly in love with Sara Hutchinson, whose sister, Mary, Wordsworth married in 1802. In accord with the medical prescription of that time, Coleridge had been taking laudanum (opium dissolved in alcohol) to ease the painful physical ailments from which he had suffered from an early age. In 1800–1801 heavy dosages during attacks of rheumatism made opium a necessity to him, and Coleridge soon recognized that the drug was a greater evil than the diseases it did not cure. "Dejection: An Ode," published in 1802, was Coleridge's despairing farewell to health, happiness, and poetic creativity. A two-year sojourn on the Mediterranean island of Malta, intended to restore his health, instead completed his decline. When he returned to England in the late summer of 1806, he was a broken man, a drug addict, estranged from his wife, suffering from agonies of remorse, and subject to terrifying nightmares of guilt and despair from which his own shrieks awakened him. By 1810, when he and Wordsworth quarreled bitterly, it must have seemed that he could not fall any lower.

Under these conditions Coleridge's literary efforts, however sporadic and fragmentary, were little short of heroic. In 1808 he debuted as a speaker at one of the new lecturing institutions that sprang up in British cities in the early nineteenth century. His lectures on poetry, like his later series on Shakespeare, became part of the social calendar for fashionable Londoners—women, excluded still from universities, particularly. He wrote for newspapers and single-handedly undertook to write, publish, and distribute a periodical, *The Friend*, which lasted for some ten months beginning in June 1809. A tragedy, *Remorse*, had in 1813 a successful run of twenty performances at the Drury Lane theater. In 1816 he took up residence at Highgate, a northern suburb of London, under the supervision of the excellent and endlessly forbearing physician James Gillman, who managed to control, although not to eliminate, Coleridge's consumption of opium. The next three years were Coleridge's most sustained period of literary activity. While continuing to lecture and to write for the newspapers on a variety of subjects, he published *Biographia Literaria, Zapolya* (a drama), a book consisting of the essays in *The Friend* (revised and greatly enlarged), two collections of poems, and several important treatises on philosophical and religious subjects. In these treatises and those that followed over the next fifteen years, he emerged as the heir to the conservatism of Edmund Burke, an opponent to secularism and a defender of the Anglican Church, and an unapologetic intellectual elitist with an ambitious account of the role elites might play in modern states, outlined in his discussions of national culture and of the "clerisy" who would take responsibility for preserving it.

The remaining years of his life, which he spent with Dr. and Mrs. Gillman, were quieter and happier than any he had known since the turn of the century. He came to a peaceful understanding with his wife and was reconciled with Wordsworth, with whom he toured the Rhineland in 1828. His rooms at Highgate became a center for friends, for the London literati, and for a steady stream of pilgrims from England and America. They came to hear one of the wonders of the age, the Sage of Highgate's conversation—or monologue—for even in his decline, Coleridge's talk never lost the almost hypnotic power that Hazlitt has immortalized in "My First Acquaintance with Poets." Mary Shelley appears to have been haunted by the memory of the evening when, a small child, she hid behind a sofa to listen to Coleridge, one of her father's visitors, recite *The Rime of the Ancient Mariner*, and a stanza from that poem of dark mystery found its way into *Frankenstein*, just as her recollections of that visitor's voice contributed to her depictions of the irresistible hold her novel's storytellers have over their auditors. When he died, Coleridge left his friends with the sense that an incomparable intellect had vanished from the world.

Coleridge's friends, however, abetted by his own merciless self-judgments, set current the opinion, still common, that he was great in promise but not in performance. Even in his buoyant youth he described his own character as "indolence capable of energies"; and it is true that while his mind was incessantly active and fertile, he lacked application and staying power. He also manifested early in life a profound sense of guilt and a need for public expiation. After drug addiction sapped his strength and will, he often adapted (or simply adopted) passages from other writers, with little or no acknowledgment, and sometimes in a context that seems designed to reveal that he relies on sources that he does not credit. Whatever the tangled motives for his procedure, Coleridge has repeatedly been charged with gross plagiarism, from his day to ours. After *The Ancient Mariner*, most of the poems he completed were written, like the first version of "Dejection: An Ode," in a spasm of intense effort. Writings that required sustained planning and application were either left unfinished or, like

Biographia Literaria, made up of brilliant sections padded out with filler, sometimes lifted from other writers, in a desperate effort to meet a deadline. Many of his speculations Coleridge merely confided to his notebooks and the ears of his friends, incorporated in letters, and poured out in the margins of his own and other people's books.

Even so, it is only when measured against his own potentialities that Coleridge's achievements appear limited. In an 1838 essay the philosopher John Stuart Mill hailed the recently deceased Coleridge as one of "the two great seminal minds of England": according to Mill, Coleridge's conservatism had, along with the very different utilitarian philosophy of Jeremy Bentham (the other seminal mind identified in Mill's essay), revolutionized the political thought of the day. Coleridge was also one of the important and influential literary theorists of the nineteenth century. One of his major legacies is the notion that culture, the nation's artistic and spiritual heritage, represents a force with the power to combat the fragmentation of a modern, market-driven society and to restore a common, collective life. This was an idea that he worked out largely in opposition to Bentham's utilitarianism, the newly prestigious discipline of political economy, and the impoverished, soulless account of human nature that these systems of thought offered. And in *Biographia Literaria* and elsewhere, Coleridge raised the stakes for literary criticism, making it into a kind of writing that could address the most difficult and abstract questions—questions about, for instance, the relations between literary language and ordinary language, or between poetry and philosophy, or between perception and imagination. Above all, Coleridge's writings in verse—whether we consider the poetry of Gothic demonism in *Christabel* or the meditative conversation poems like "Frost at Midnight" or "This Lime-Tree Bower My Prison"—are the achievements of a remarkably innovative poet.

The Eolian Harp[1]

Composed at Clevedon, Somersetshire

My pensive Sara! thy soft cheek reclined
Thus on mine arm, most soothing sweet it is
To sit beside our cot, our cot o'ergrown
With white flowered jasmin, and the broad-leaved myrtle,
5   (Meet emblems they of Innocence and Love!)
And watch the clouds, that late were rich with light,
Slow saddening round, and mark the star of eve
Serenely brilliant (such should wisdom be)
Shine opposite! How exquisite the scents
10   Snatched from yon bean-field! and the world so hushed!

---

1. Named for Aeolus, god of the winds, the harp has strings stretched over a rectangular sounding box. When placed in an opened window, the harp (also called "Eolian lute," "Eolian lyre," "wind harp") responds to the altering wind by sequences of musical chords. This instrument, which seems to voice nature's own music, was a favorite household furnishing in the period and was repeatedly alluded to in Romantic poetry. It served also as one of the recurrent Romantic images for the mind—either the mind in poetic inspiration, as in the last stanza of Shelley's "Ode to the West Wind" (p. 388), or else the mind in perception, responding to an intellectual breeze by trembling into consciousness, as in this poem, lines 44–48.

Coleridge wrote this poem to Sara Fricker, whom he married on October 4, 1795, and took to a cottage (the "cot" of lines 3 and 64) at Clevedon, overlooking the Bristol Channel. He later several times expanded and altered the original version; the famous lines 26–29, for example, were not added until 1817. Originally it was titled "Effusion XXXV" and was one of thirty-six such effusions that Coleridge included in a 1796 volume of verse; revised and retitled, it became what he called a "conversation poem"—the designation used since his day for a sustained blank-verse lyric of description and meditation, in the mode of conversation addressed to a silent auditor. This was the form that Coleridge perfected in "Frost at Midnight" and that Wordsworth adopted in "Tintern Abbey."

The stilly murmur of the distant sea
Tells us of silence.

             And that simplest lute,
Placed length-ways in the clasping casement, hark!
How by the desultory breeze caressed,
15   Like some coy maid half yielding to her lover,
It pours such sweet upbraiding,° as must needs   *scolding*
Tempt to repeat the wrong! And now, its strings
Boldlier swept, the long sequacious° notes   *regularly following*
Over delicious surges sink and rise,
20   Such a soft floating witchery of sound
As twilight Elfins make, when they at eve
Voyage on gentle gales from Fairy-Land,
Where Melodies round honey-dropping flowers,
Footless and wild, like birds of Paradise,[2]
25   Nor pause, nor perch, hovering on untamed wing!
O the one life within us and abroad,
Which meets all motion and becomes its soul,
A light in sound, a sound-like power in light,
Rhythm in all thought, and joyance[3] every where—
30   Methinks, it should have been impossible
Not to love all things in a world so filled;
Where the breeze warbles, and the mute still air
Is Music slumbering on her instrument.

       And thus, my love! as on the midway slope
35   Of yonder hill I stretch my limbs at noon,
Whilst through my half-closed eye-lids I behold
The sunbeams dance, like diamonds, on the main,°   *ocean*
And tranquil muse upon tranquillity;
Full many a thought uncalled and undetained,
40   And many idle flitting phantasies,
Traverse my indolent and passive brain,
As wild and various as the random gales
That swell and flutter on this subject lute!

       And what if all of animated nature
45   Be but organic harps diversely framed,
That tremble into thought, as o'er them sweeps
Plastic and vast, one intellectual breeze,
At once the Soul of each, and God of All?

       But thy more serious eye a mild reproof
50   Darts, O beloved woman! nor such thoughts
Dim and unhallowed dost thou not reject,
And biddest me walk humbly with my God.
Meek daughter in the family of Christ!

2. Brilliantly colored birds found in New Guinea and adjacent islands. The native practice of removing the legs when preparing the skin led Europeans to believe that the birds were footless and spent their lives hovering in the air and feeding on nectar.
3. An archaic term for enjoyment, coined in the 16th century by Spenser and reintroduced by Coleridge.

Well hast thou said and holily dispraised
55 These shapings of the unregenerate[4] mind;
Bubbles that glitter as they rise and break
On vain Philosophy's aye-babbling° spring.   *ever babbling*
For never guiltless may I speak of him,
The Incomprehensible! save when with awe
60 I praise him, and with Faith that inly feels;
Who with his saving mercies healed me,
A sinful and most miserable man,
Wildered and dark, and gave me to possess
Peace, and this cot, and thee, heart-honored Maid!

1795   1796

This Lime-Tree Bower My Prison

> In the June of 1797, some long-expected Friends paid a visit to the author's cottage; and on the morning of their arrival, he met with an accident, which disabled him from walking during the whole time of their stay. One evening, when they had left him for a few hours, he composed the following lines in the garden-bower.[1]

Well, they are gone, and here must I remain,
This lime-tree bower my prison! I have lost
Beauties and feelings, such as would have been
Most sweet to my remembrance even when age
5 Had dimmed mine eyes to blindness! They, meanwhile,
Friends, whom I never more may meet again,
On springy[2] heath, along the hill-top edge,
Wander in gladness, and wind down, perchance,
To that still roaring dell, of which I told;
10 The roaring dell, o'erwooded, narrow, deep,
And only speckled by the mid-day sun;
Where its slim trunk the ash from rock to rock
Flings arching like a bridge;—that branchless ash,
Unsunned and damp, whose few poor yellow leaves
15 Ne'er tremble in the gale, yet tremble still,
Fanned by the water-fall! and there my friends
Behold the dark green file of long lank weeds,
That all at once (a most fantastic sight!)
Still nod and drip beneath the dripping edge
Of the blue clay-stone.[3]

20   Now, my friends emerge
Beneath the wide wide Heaven—and view again

4. Spiritually unredeemed; not born again.
1. The time was in fact July 1797; the visiting friends were William and Dorothy Wordsworth and Charles Lamb; the accident was the fault of Mrs. Coleridge—"dear Sara," Coleridge wrote, "accidentally emptied a skillet of boiling milk on my foot"; and the bower consisted of lime (i.e., linden) trees in the garden of Thomas Poole, next door to Coleridge's cottage at Nether Stowey.

Coleridge related these facts in a letter to Robert Southey, July 17, 1797, in which he transcribed the first version of this poem. In the earliest printed text the title is followed by "Addressed to Charles Lamb, of the India-House, London."
2. *Elastic*, I mean [Coleridge's note].
3. Cf. Dorothy Wordsworth's description of the "low damp dell" in her *Alfoxden Journal*, February 10, 1798 (p. 236).

The many-steepled tract magnificent
Of hilly fields and meadows, and the sea,
With some fair bark,° perhaps, whose sails light up   *boat*
25   The slip of smooth clear blue betwixt two Isles
Of purple shadow! Yes! they wander on
In gladness all; but thou, methinks, most glad,
My gentle-hearted Charles! for thou hast pined
And hungered after Nature, many a year,
30   In the great City pent,[4] winning thy way
With sad yet patient soul, through evil and pain
And strange calamity![5] Ah! slowly sink
Behind the western ridge, thou glorious sun!
Shine in the slant beams of the sinking orb,
35   Ye purple heath-flowers! richlier burn, ye clouds!
Live in the yellow light, ye distant groves!
And kindle, thou blue ocean! So my Friend
Struck with deep joy may stand, as I have stood,
Silent with swimming sense; yea, gazing round
40   On the wide landscape, gaze till all doth seem
Less gross than bodily; and of such hues
As veil the Almighty Spirit, when yet he makes
Spirits perceive his presence.

A delight
Comes sudden on my heart, and I am glad
45   As I myself were there! Nor in this bower,
This little lime-tree bower, have I not marked
Much that has soothed me. Pale beneath the blaze
Hung the transparent foliage; and I watched
Some broad and sunny leaf, and loved to see
50   The shadow of the leaf and stem above
Dappling its sunshine! And that walnut-tree
Was richly tinged, and a deep radiance lay
Full on the ancient ivy, which usurps
Those fronting elms, and now, with blackest mass
55   Makes their dark branches gleam a lighter hue
Through the late twilight: and though now the bat
Wheels silent by, and not a swallow twitters,
Yet still the solitary humble bee
Sings in the bean-flower! Henceforth I shall know
60   That Nature ne'er deserts the wise and pure;
No plot so narrow, be but Nature there,
No waste so vacant, but may well employ
Each faculty of sense, and keep the heart
Awake to Love and Beauty! and sometimes
65   'Tis well to be bereft of promised good,
That we may lift the Soul, and contemplate
With lively joy the joys we cannot share.
My gentle-hearted Charles! when the last rook

---

4. Despite Coleridge's claim, Charles Lamb eminently preferred London over what he called
"dead Nature." For Lamb's love of city life, see his
letter to Wordsworth in the supplemental ebook.

5. Some ten months earlier Charles Lamb's sister, Mary, had stabbed their mother to death in a
fit of insanity.

Beat its straight path along the dusky air
70   Homewards, I blessed it! deeming its black wing
(Now a dim speck, now vanishing in light)
Had crossed the mighty orb's dilated glory,
While thou stood'st gazing; or when all was still,
Flew creeking o'er thy head, and had a charm
75   For thee, my gentle-hearted Charles, to whom
No sound is dissonant which tells of Life.

1797   1800

The Rime of the Ancient Mariner[1]

IN SEVEN PARTS

Facile credo, plures esse Naturas invisibiles quam visibiles in rerum universitate. Sed horum [sic] omnium familiam quis nobis enarrabit, et gradus et cognationes et discrimina et singulorum munera? Quid agunt? quae loca habitant? Harum rerum notitiam semper ambivit ingenium humanum, nunquam attigit. Juvat, interea, non diffiteor, quandoque in animo, tanquam in tabulâ, majoris et melioris mundi imaginem contemplari: ne mens assuefacta hodiernae vitae minutiis se contrahat nimis, et tota subsidat in pusillas cogitationes. Sed veritati interea invigilandum est, modusque servandus, ut certa ab incertis, diem a nocte, distinguamus.

T. BURNET, *Archaeol. Phil.* p. 68.[2]

Part 1

An ancient Mariner meeteth three gallants bidden to a wedding-feast, and detaineth one.

It is an ancient Mariner
And he stoppeth one of three.
"By thy long grey beard and glittering eye,
Now wherefore stopp'st thou me?

The Bridegroom's doors are opened wide,   5
And I am next of kin;
The guests are met, the feast is set:
May'st hear the merry din."

1. Coleridge describes the origin of this poem in the opening section of chap. 14 of *Biographia Literaria*. In a comment made to the Reverend Alexander Dyce in 1835 and in a note on "We Are Seven" dictated in 1843, Wordsworth added some details. The poem, based on a dream of Coleridge's friend Cruikshank, was originally planned as a collaboration between Coleridge and Wordsworth, to pay the expense of a walking tour they took with Dorothy Wordsworth in November 1797. Before he dropped out of the enterprise, Wordsworth suggested the shooting of the albatross and the navigation of the ship by the dead men; he also contributed lines 13–16 and 226–27.

When printed in *Lyrical Ballads* (1798), this poem was titled "The Rime of the Ancyent Marinere" and contained many archaic words and spellings, which Wordsworth believed, hurt the sales of their volume. In later editions Coleridge revised the poem, in part by pruning those archaisms. He also added the Latin epigraph and the marginal glosses written in the old-fashioned style of 17th-century learning.

2. "I readily believe that there are more invisible than visible Natures in the universe. But who will explain for us the family of all these beings, and the ranks and relations and distinguishing features and functions of each? What do they do? What places do they inhabit? The human mind has always sought the knowledge of these things, but never attained it. Meanwhile I do not deny that it is helpful sometimes to contemplate in the mind, as on a tablet, the image of a greater and better world, lest the intellect, habituated to the petty things of daily life, narrow itself and sink wholly into trivial thoughts. But at the same time we must be watchful for the truth and keep a sense of proportion, so that we may distinguish the certain from the uncertain, day from night." Adapted by Coleridge from Thomas Burnet, *Archaeologiae Philosophicae* (1692).

He holds him with his skinny hand,
"There was a ship," quoth he.   10
"Hold off! unhand me, grey-beard loon!"
Eftsoons[3] his hand dropt he.

The wedding guest is
spellbound by the eye
of the old sea-faring
man, and con-
strained to hear his
tale.

He holds him with his glittering eye—
The wedding-guest stood still,
And listens like a three years' child: 15
The Mariner hath his will.[4]

The wedding-guest sat on a stone:
He cannot choose but hear;
And thus spake on that ancient man,
The bright-eyed Mariner.   20

"The ship was cheered, the harbor cleared,
Merrily did we drop
Below the kirk,[5] below the hill,
Below the light house top.

The Mariner tells
how the ship sailed
southward with a
good wind and fair
weather, till it
reached the line.

The sun came up upon the left,   25
Out of the sea came he!
And he shone bright, and on the right
Went down into the sea.

Higher and higher every day,
Till over the mast at noon[6]—"   30
The wedding-guest here beat his breast,
For he heard the loud bassoon.

The Wedding Guest
heareth the bridal
music; but the
mariner continueth
his tale.

The bride hath paced into the hall,
Red as a rose is she;
Nodding their heads before her goes   35
The merry minstrelsy.

The wedding-guest he beat his breast,
Yet he cannot choose but hear;
And thus spake on that ancient man,
The bright-eyed Mariner.   40

The ship driven by a
storm toward the
south pole.

"And now the storm-blast came, and he
Was tyrannous and strong:
He struck with his o'ertaking wings,
And chased us south along.

With sloping masts and dipping prow,   45
As who pursued with yell and blow
Still treads the shadow of his foe,
And forward bends his head,

3. At once.
4. I.e., the Mariner has gained control of the will
of the wedding guest by hypnosis—or, as it was

called in Coleridge's time, by "mesmerism."
5. Church.
6. The ship had reached the equator.

The ship drove fast, loud roared the blast,
And southward aye[7] we fled.   50

And now there came both mist and snow,
And it grew wondrous cold:
And ice, mast-high, came floating by,
As green as emerald.

The land of ice, and   And through the drifts the snowy clifts   55
of fearful sounds   Did send a dismal sheen:
where no living thing   Nor shapes of men nor beasts we ken[8]—
was to be seen.   The ice was all between.

The ice was here, the ice was there,
The ice was all around: 60
It cracked and growled, and roared and howled,
Like noises in a swound![9]

Till a great sea-bird,   At length did cross an Albatross,
called the Albatross,   Thorough the fog it came;
came through the   As if it had been a Christian soul,   65
snow-fog, and was   We hailed it in God's name.
received with great
joy and hospitality.

It ate the food it ne'er had eat,
And round and round it flew.
The ice did split with a thunder-fit;
The helmsman steered us through!   70

And lo! the Albatross   And a good south wind sprung up behind;
proveth a bird of   The Albatross did follow,
good omen, and   And every day, for food or play,
followeth the ship as   Came to the mariners' hollo!
it returned north-
ward through fog
and floating ice.

In mist or cloud, on mast or shroud,[1]   75
It perched for vespers nine;
Whiles all the night, through fog-smoke white,
Glimmered the white moon-shine."

The ancient Mariner   "God save thee, ancient Mariner!
inhospitably killeth   From the fiends, that plague thee thus!—   80
the pious bird of   Why look'st thou so?"—With my cross-bow
good omen.   I shot the Albatross.

Part 2

The Sun now rose upon the right:[2]
Out of the sea came he,
Still hid in mist, and on the left   85
Went down into the sea.

---

7. Always.
8. Knew.
9. Swoon.

1. Rope supporting the mast.
2. Having rounded Cape Horn, the ship heads
north into the Pacific.

And the good south wind still blew behind,
But no sweet bird did follow,
Nor any day for food or play
Came to the mariners' hollo! 90

His shipmates cry out against the ancient Mariner, for killing the bird of good luck.

And I had done a hellish thing,
And it would work 'em woe:
For all averred, I had killed the bird
That made the breeze to blow.
Ah wretch! said they, the bird to slay, 95
That made the breeze to blow!

But when the fog cleared off, they justify the same, and thus make themselves accomplices in the crime.

Nor dim nor red, like God's own head,
The glorious Sun uprist:
Then all averred, I had killed the bird
That brought the fog and mist. 100
'Twas right, said they, such birds to slay,
That bring the fog and mist.

The fair breeze continues; the ship enters the Pacific Ocean, and sails northward, even till it reaches the Line.[3]

The fair breeze blew, the white foam flew,
The furrow followed free;
We were the first that ever burst 105
Into that silent sea.

The ship hath been suddenly becalmed.

Down dropt the breeze, the sails dropt down,
'Twas sad as sad could be;
And we did speak only to break
The silence of the sea! 110

All in a hot and copper sky,
The bloody Sun, at noon,
Right up above the mast did stand,
No bigger than the Moon.

Day after day, day after day, 115
We stuck, nor breath nor motion;
As idle as a painted ship
Upon a painted ocean.

And the Albatross begins to be avenged.

Water, water, every where,
And all the boards did shrink; 120
Water, water, every where,
Nor any drop to drink.

The very deep did rot: O Christ!
That ever this should be!
Yea, slimy things did crawl with legs 125
Upon the slimy sea.

---

3. I.e., the equator. Unless it is simply an error (Coleridge misreading his own poem), this gloss anticipates the ship's later arrival at the equator, on its trip north from the region of the South Pole, as described in lines 381–84.

About, about, in reel and rout
The death-fires[4] danced at night;
The water, like a witch's oils,
Burnt green, and blue and white.   130

A spirit had followed them; one of the invisible inhabitants of this planet, neither departed souls nor angels; concerning whom the learned
And some in dreams assured were
Of the spirit that plagued us so;
Nine fathom deep he had followed us
From the land of mist and snow.

Jew, Josephus, and the Platonic Constantinopolitan, Michael Psellus, may be consulted. They are very numerous, and there is no climate or element without one or more.

And every tongue, through utter drought,   135
Was withered at the root;
We could not speak, no more than if
We had been choked with soot.

The shipmates, in their sore distress, would fain throw the whole guilt on the ancient Mariner: in sign whereof they hang the dead sea bird round his neck.
Ah! well-a-day! what evil looks
Had I from old and young!   140
Instead of the cross, the Albatross
About my neck was hung.

Part 3

There passed a weary time. Each throat
Was parched, and glazed each eye.
A weary time! a weary time!   145
How glazed each weary eye,
The ancient Mariner beholdeth a sign in the element afar off.
When looking westward, I beheld
A something in the sky.

At first it seemed a little speck,
And then it seemed a mist;   150
It moved and moved, and took at last
A certain shape, I wist.[5]

A speck, a mist, a shape, I wist!
And still it neared and neared:
As if it dodged a water-sprite,[6]   155
It plunged and tacked and veered.

At its nearer approach, it seemeth him to be a ship; and at a dear ransom he freeth his speech from the bonds of thirst.
With throats unslaked, with black lips baked,
We could nor laugh nor wail;
Through utter drought all dumb we stood!
I bit my arm, I sucked the blood,   160
And cried, A sail! a sail!

With throats unslaked, with black lips baked,
Agape they heard me call:

4. Usually glossed as St. Elmo's fire—an atmospheric electricity on a ship's mast or rigging—believed by superstitious sailors to portend disaster. Possibly the reference is instead to phosphorescence resulting from the decomposition of organic matter in the sea (see line 123).
5. Knew.
6. A supernatural being that supervises the natural elements (but Coleridge may in fact have been using the term to mean water-*spout*).

A flash of joy;

Gramercy![7] they for joy did grin,
And all at once their breath drew in,   165
As they were drinking all.

And horror follows.
For can it be a ship
that comes onward
without wind or tide?

See! see! (I cried) she tacks no more!
Hither to work us weal;[8]
Without a breeze, without a tide,
She steadies with upright keel!   170

The western wave was all a-flame.
The day was well nigh done!
Almost upon the western wave
Rested the broad bright Sun;
When that strange shape drove suddenly   175
Betwixt us and the Sun.

It seemeth him but
the skeleton of a
ship.

And straight the Sun was flecked with bars,
(Heaven's Mother send us grace!)
As if through a dungeon-grate he peered
With broad and burning face.   180

Alas! (thought I, and my heart beat loud)
How fast she nears and nears!
Are those her sails that glance in the Sun,
Like restless gossameres?[9]

And its ribs are seen
as bars on the face of
the setting Sun. The
specter-woman and
her death-mate, and
no other on board
the skeleton-ship.

Are those her ribs through which the Sun   185
Did peer, as through a grate?
And is that Woman all her crew?
Is that a Death? and are there two?
Is Death that woman's mate?

Like vessel, like
crew!

Her lips were red, her looks were free,   190
Her locks were yellow as gold:
Her skin was as white as leprosy,
The Night-mare Life-in-Death was she,
Who thicks man's blood with cold.

Death and Life-in-
death have diced for
the ship's crew, and
she (the latter)
winneth the ancient
Mariner.

The naked hulk[1] alongside came,   195
And the twain were casting dice;
"The game is done! I've won! I've won!"
Quoth she, and whistles thrice.

No twilight within
the courts of the sun.

The Sun's rim dips; the stars rush out:
At one stride comes the dark;   200
With far-heard whisper, o'er the sea,
Off shot the spectre-bark.[2]

At the rising of the
Moon,

We listened and looked sideways up!
Fear at my heart, as at a cup,

7. Great thanks; from the French *grand-merci.*   1. Large ship.
8. Benefit.   2. Ghost ship.
9. Filmy cobwebs floating in the air.

My life-blood seemed to sip!   205
The stars were dim, and thick the night,
The steersman's face by his lamp gleamed white;
From the sails the dew did drip—
Till clomb above the eastern bar
The horned Moon, with one bright star   210
Within the nether tip.[3]

One after another, One after one, by the star-dogged Moon,
Too quick for groan or sigh,
Each turned his face with a ghastly pang,
And cursed me with his eye.   215

His shipmates drop Four times fifty living men,
down dead. (And I heard nor sigh nor groan)
With heavy thump, a lifeless lump,
They dropped down one by one.

But Life-in-Death The souls did from their bodies fly,—   220
begins her work on They fled to bliss or woe!
the ancient And every soul, it passed me by,
Mariner. Like the whizz of my cross-bow!

Part 4

The wedding guest "I fear thee, ancient Mariner!
feareth that a spirit is I fear thy skinny hand!   225
talking to him. And thou art long, and lank, and brown,
As is the ribbed sea-sand.

I fear thee and thy glittering eye,
And thy skinny hand, so brown."—
But the ancient Mar- Fear not, fear not, thou wedding-guest!   230
iner assureth him of This body dropt not down.
his bodily life, and
proceedeth to relate
his horrible penance. Alone, alone, all, all alone,
Alone on a wide wide sea!
And never a saint took pity on
My soul in agony.   235

He despiseth the The many men, so beautiful!
creatures of the And they all dead did lie:
calm, And a thousand thousand slimy things
Lived on; and so did I.

And envieth that I looked upon the rotting sea,   240
they should live, and And drew my eyes away;
so many lie dead. I looked upon the rotting deck,
And there the dead men lay.

3. An omen of impending evil.

I looked to heaven, and tried to pray;
But or ever a prayer had gusht,   245
A wicked whisper came, and made
My heart as dry as dust.

I closed my lids, and kept them close,
And the balls like pulses beat;
For the sky and the sea, and the sea and the sky   250
Lay like a load on my weary eye,
And the dead were at my feet.

But the curse liveth The cold sweat melted from their limbs,
for him in the eye of
the dead men. Nor rot nor reek did they:
The look with which they looked on me   255
Had never passed away.

An orphan's curse would drag to hell
A spirit from on high;
But oh! more horrible than that
Is the curse in a dead man's eye!   260
Seven days, seven nights, I saw that curse,
And yet I could not die.

In his loneliness and The moving Moon went up the sky,
fixedness he yearneth
towards the journeying And no where did abide:
Moon, and the
stars that still Softly she was going up,   265
sojourn, yet still And a star or two beside—
move onward; and
everywhere the blue sky belongs to them, and is their appointed rest, and their native country and their
own natural homes, which they enter unannounced, as lords that are certainly expected and yet there
is a silent joy at their arrival.

Her beams bemocked the sultry main,
Like April hoar-frost spread;
But where the ship's huge shadow lay,
The charmed water burnt alway   270
A still and awful red.

By the light of the Beyond the shadow of the ship,
Moon he beholdeth
God's creatures of I watched the water-snakes:
the great calm. They moved in tracks of shining white,
And when they reared, the elfish light   275
Fell off in hoary flakes.

Within the shadow of the ship
I watched their rich attire:
Blue, glossy green, and velvet black,
They coiled and swam; and every track   280
Was a flash of golden fire.

Their beauty and O happy living things! no tongue
their happiness. Their beauty might declare:
A spring of love gushed from my heart,

He blesseth them in his heart.

And I blessed them unaware:
Sure my kind saint took pity on me,
And I blessed them unaware.   285

The spell begins to break.

The selfsame moment I could pray;
And from my neck so free
The Albatross fell off, and sank   290
Like lead into the sea.

Part 5

Oh sleep! it is a gentle thing,
Beloved from pole to pole!
To Mary Queen the praise be given!
She sent the gentle sleep from Heaven,   295
That slid into my soul.

By grace of the holy Mother, the ancient Mariner is refreshed with rain.

The silly[4] buckets on the deck,
That had so long remained,
I dreamt that they were filled with dew;
And when I awoke, it rained.   300

My lips were wet, my throat was cold,
My garments all were dank;
Sure I had drunken in my dreams,
And still my body drank.

I moved, and could not feel my limbs: 305
I was so light—almost
I thought that I had died in sleep,
And was a blessed ghost.

He heareth sounds and seeth strange sights and commotions in the sky and the element.

And soon I heard a roaring wind:
It did not come anear;   310
But with its sound it shook the sails,
That were so thin and sere.

The upper air burst into life!
And a hundred fire-flags sheen,[5]
To and fro they were hurried about!   315
And to and fro, and in and out,
The wan stars danced between.

And the coming wind did roar more loud,
And the sails did sigh like sedge;[6]
And the rain poured down from one black cloud;   320
The Moon was at its edge.

The thick black cloud was cleft, and still
The Moon was at its side:

---

4. Simple, homely.
5. Shone. These fire-flags are probably St. Elmo's fire (see n. 4, p. 260), but Coleridge may be describing the Aurora Australis, or Southern Lights, and possibly also lightning.
6. A rushlike plant growing in wet soil.

Like waters shot from some high crag,
The lightning fell with never a jag, 325
A river steep and wide.

The bodies of the ship's crew are inspired, and the ship moves on;

The loud wind never reached the ship,
Yet now the ship moved on!
Beneath the lightning and the moon
The dead men gave a groan. 330

They groaned, they stirred, they all uprose,
Nor spake, nor moved their eyes;
It had been strange, even in a dream,
To have seen those dead men rise.

The helmsman steered, the ship moved on; 335
Yet never a breeze up blew;
The mariners all 'gan work the ropes,
Where they were wont to do;
They raised their limbs like lifeless tools—
We were a ghastly crew. 340

The body of my brother's son
Stood by me, knee to knee:
The body and I pulled at one rope,
But he said nought to me.

But not by the souls of the men, nor by dæmons[7] of earth or middle air, but by a blessed troop of angelic spirits, sent down by the invocation of the guardian saint.

"I fear thee, ancient Mariner!" 345
Be calm, thou Wedding-Guest!
'Twas not those souls that fled in pain,
Which to their corses[8] came again,
But a troop of spirits blest:

For when it dawned—they dropped their arms, 350
And clustered round the mast;
Sweet sounds rose slowly through their mouths,
And from their bodies passed.

Around, around, flew each sweet sound,
Then darted to the Sun; 355
Slowly the sounds came back again,
Now mixed, now one by one.

Sometimes a-dropping from the sky
I heard the sky-lark sing;
Sometimes all little birds that are, 360
How they seemed to fill the sea and air
With their sweet jargoning![9]

And now 'twas like all instruments,
Now like a lonely flute;

---

7. Supernatural beings halfway between mortals and gods (the type of spirit that Coleridge describes in the gloss beside lines 131–34).   8. Corpses.
9. Warbling (Middle English).

And now it is an angel's song,   365
That makes the heavens be mute.

It ceased; yet still the sails made on
A pleasant noise till noon,
A noise like of a hidden brook
In the leafy month of June,   370
That to the sleeping woods all night
Singeth a quiet tune.

Till noon we quietly sailed on,
Yet never a breeze did breathe:
Slowly and smoothly went the ship,   375
Moved onward from beneath.

The lonesome spirit
from the south-pole
carries on the ship
as far as the line, in
obedience to the
angelic troop, but
still requireth
vengeance.

Under the keel nine fathom deep,
From the land of mist and snow,
The spirit slid: and it was he
That made the ship to go.   380
The sails at noon left off their tune,
And the ship stood still also.

The Sun, right up above the mast,
Had fixed her to the ocean:
But in a minute she 'gan stir,   385
With a short uneasy motion—
Backwards and forwards half her length
With a short uneasy motion.

Then like a pawing horse let go,
She made a sudden bound: 390
It flung the blood into my head,
And I fell down in a swound.

The Polar Spirit's
fellow dæmons, the
invisible inhabitants
of the element, take
part in his wrong;
and two of them
relate, one to the
other, that penance
long and heavy for
the ancient Mariner
hath been accorded
to the Polar Spirit,
who returneth
southward.

How long in that same fit I lay,
I have not[1] to declare;
But ere my living life returned,   395
I heard and in my soul discerned
Two voices in the air.

"Is it he?" quoth one, "Is this the man?
By him who died on cross,
With his cruel bow he laid full low   400
The harmless Albatross.

The spirit who bideth by himself
In the land of mist and snow,
He loved the bird that loved the man
Who shot him with his bow."   405

The other was a softer voice,
As soft as honey-dew:

---

1. I.e., have not the knowledge.

Quoth he, "The man hath penance done,
And penance more will do."

Part 6

FIRST VOICE

"But tell me, tell me! speak again,   410
Thy soft response renewing—
What makes that ship drive on so fast?
What is the ocean doing?"

SECOND VOICE

"Still as a slave before his lord,
The ocean hath no blast;   415
His great bright eye most silently
Up to the Moon is cast—

If he may know which way to go;
For she guides him smooth or grim.
See, brother, see! how graciously   420
She looketh down on him."

FIRST VOICE

The Mariner hath been cast into a trance; for the angelic power causeth the vessel to drive northward faster than human life could endure.

"But why drives on that ship so fast,
Without or wave or wind?"

SECOND VOICE

"The air is cut away before,
And closes from behind.   425

Fly, brother, fly! more high, more high!
Or we shall be belated:
For slow and slow that ship will go,
When the Mariner's trance is abated."

The supernatural motion is retarded; the Mariner awakes, and his penance begins anew.

I woke, and we were sailing on   430
As in a gentle weather:
'Twas night, calm night, the moon was high;
The dead men stood together.

All stood together on the deck,
For a charnel-dungeon fitter: 435
All fixed on me their stony eyes,
That in the Moon did glitter.

The pang, the curse, with which they died,
Had never passed away:
I could not draw my eyes from theirs,   440
Nor turn them up to pray.

The curse is finally expiated.

And now this spell was snapt: once more
I viewed the ocean green,

And looked far forth, yet little saw
Of what had else been seen—   445

Like one, that on a lonesome road
Doth walk in fear and dread,
And having once turned round walks on,
And turns no more his head;
Because he knows, a frightful fiend   450
Doth close behind him tread.

But soon there breathed a wind on me,
Nor sound nor motion made:
Its path was not upon the sea,
In ripple or in shade.   455

It raised my hair, it fanned my cheek
Like a meadow-gale of spring—
It mingled strangely with my fears,
Yet it felt like a welcoming.

Swiftly, swiftly flew the ship,   460
Yet she sailed softly too:
Sweetly, sweetly blew the breeze—
On me alone it blew.

And the ancient
Mariner beholdeth
his native country.
Oh! dream of joy! is this indeed
The light-house top I see?   465
Is this the hill? is this the kirk?
Is this mine own countree?

We drifted o'er the harbour-bar,
And I with sobs did pray—
O let me be awake, my God!   470
Or let me sleep alway.

The harbour-bay was clear as glass,
So smoothly it was strewn!
And on the bay the moonlight lay,
And the shadow of the moon.   475

The rock shone bright, the kirk no less,
That stands above the rock:
The moonlight steeped in silentness
The steady weathercock.

And the bay was white with silent light,   480
Till rising from the same,
The angelic spirits
leave the dead
bodies,
Full many shapes, that shadows were,
In crimson colours came.

And appear in their
own forms of light.
A little distance from the prow
Those crimson shadows were: 485
I turned my eyes upon the deck—
Oh, Christ! what saw I there!

Each corse lay flat, lifeless and flat,
And, by the holy rood!
A man all light, a seraph-man,[2]   490
On every corse there stood.

This seraph-band, each waved his hand:
It was a heavenly sight!
They stood as signals to the land,
Each one a lovely light;   495

This seraph-band, each waved his hand,
No voice did they impart—
No voice; but oh! the silence sank
Like music on my heart.

But soon I heard the dash of oars,   500
I heard the Pilot's cheer;
My head was turned perforce away,
And I saw a boat appear.

The Pilot and the Pilot's boy,
I heard them coming fast: 505
Dear Lord in Heaven! it was a joy
The dead men could not blast.

I saw a third—I heard his voice:
It is the Hermit good!
He singeth loud his godly hymns   510
That he makes in the wood.
He'll shrieve[3] my soul, he'll wash away
The Albatross's blood.

Part 7

The Hermit of the wood,

This Hermit good lives in that wood
Which slopes down to the sea.   515
How loudly his sweet voice he rears!
He loves to talk with marineres
That come from a far countree.

He kneels at morn, and noon, and eve—
He hath a cushion plump: 520
It is the moss that wholly hides
The rotted old oak-stump.

The skiff-boat neared: I heard them talk,
"Why, this is strange, I trow!
Where are those lights so many and fair,   525
That signal made but now?"

Approacheth the ship with wonder.

"Strange, by my faith!" the Hermit said—
"And they answered not our cheer!

2. A shining celestial being, highest in the ranks   3. Absolve.
of the angels. "Rood": cross.

The planks looked warped! and see those sails,
How thin they are and sere!   530
I never saw aught like to them,
Unless perchance it were

Brown skeletons of leaves that lag
My forest-brook along;
When the ivy-tod[4] is heavy with snow,   535
And the owlet whoops to the wolf below,
That eats the she-wolf's young."

"Dear Lord! it hath a fiendish look"—
(The Pilot made reply)
"I am a-feared"—"Push on, push on!"   540
Said the Hermit cheerily.

The boat came closer to the ship,
But I nor spake nor stirred;
The boat came close beneath the ship,
And straight a sound was heard.   545

*The ship suddenly
sinketh.*

Under the water it rumbled on,
Still louder and more dread:
It reached the ship, it split the bay;
The ship went down like lead.

*The ancient Mariner
is saved in the Pilot's
boat.*

Stunned by that loud and dreadful sound,   550
Which sky and ocean smote,
Like one that hath been seven days drowned
My body lay afloat;
But swift as dreams, myself I found
Within the Pilot's boat.   555

Upon the whirl, where sank the ship,
The boat spun round and round;
And all was still, save that the hill
Was telling of the sound.

I moved my lips—the Pilot shrieked   560
And fell down in a fit;
The holy Hermit raised his eyes,
And prayed where he did sit.

I took the oars: the Pilot's boy,
Who now doth crazy go,   565
Laughed loud and long, and all the while
His eyes went to and fro.
"Ha! ha!" quoth he, "full plain I see,
The Devil knows how to row."

And now, all in my own countree,   570
I stood on the firm land!

4. Clump of ivy.

The Hermit stepped forth from the boat,
And scarcely he could stand.

"O shrieve me, shrieve me, holy man!"
The Hermit crossed his brow.[5]   575
"Say quick," quoth he, "I bid thee say—
What manner of man art thou?"

Forthwith this frame of mine was wrenched
With a woful agony,
Which forced me to begin my tale;   580
And then it left me free.

Since then, at an uncertain hour,
That agony returns:
And till my ghastly tale is told,
This heart within me burns.   585

I pass, like night, from land to land;
I have strange power of speech;
That moment that his face I see,
I know the man that must hear me:
To him my tale I teach.   590

What loud uproar bursts from that door!
The wedding-guests are there:
But in the garden-bower the bride
And bride-maids singing are:
And hark the little vesper bell,   595
Which biddeth me to prayer!

O Wedding-Guest! this soul hath been
Alone on a wide wide sea:
So lonely 'twas, that God himself
Scarce seemed there to be.   600

O sweeter than the marriage-feast,
'Tis sweeter far to me,
To walk together to the kirk
With a goodly company!—

To walk together to the kirk,   605
And all together pray,
While each to his great Father bends,
Old men, and babes, and loving friends,
And youths and maidens gay!

Farewell, farewell! but this I tell   610
To thee, thou Wedding-Guest!
He prayeth well, who loveth well
Both man and bird and beast.

5. Made the sign of the cross on his forehead. "Shrieve me": hear my confession and grant me absolution.

He prayeth best, who loveth best
All things both great and small;   615
For the dear God who loveth us,
He made and loveth all.[6]

The Mariner, whose eye is bright,
Whose beard with age is hoar,
Is gone: and now the Wedding-Guest   620
Turned from the bridegroom's door.

He went like one that hath been stunned,
And is of sense forlorn:[7]
A sadder and a wiser man,
He rose the morrow morn.   625

1797   1798, 1817

Kubla Khan

Or, A Vision in a Dream. A Fragment

In[1] the summer of the year 1797, the Author, then in ill health, had retired to a lonely farm house between Porlock and Linton, on the Exmoor confines of Somerset and Devonshire. In consequence of a slight indisposition, an anodyne had been prescribed, from the effect of which he fell asleep in his chair at the moment that he was reading the following sentence, or words of the same substance, in *Purchas's Pilgrimage*: "Here the Khan Kubla commanded a palace to be built, and a stately garden thereunto: and thus ten miles of fertile ground were inclosed with a wall."[2] The author continued for about three hours in a profound sleep, at least of the external senses,[3] during which time he has the most vivid confidence, that he could not have composed less than from two to three hundred lines; if that indeed can be called composition in which all the images rose up before him as things, with a parallel production of the correspondent expressions, without any sensation or consciousness of effort. On awaking he appeared to himself to have a distinct recollection of the whole, and taking his pen, ink, and paper, instantly and

6. Coleridge said in 1830, answering the objection of the poet Anna Barbauld that the poem "lacked a moral": "I told her that in my own judgment the poem had too much; and that the only, or chief fault, if I might say so, was the obtrusion of the moral sentiment so openly on the reader as a principle or cause of action in a work of pure imagination. It ought to have had no more moral than the *Arabian Nights'* tale of the merchant's sitting down to eat dates by the side of a well and throwing the shells aside, and lo! a genie starts up and says he *must* kill the aforesaid merchant *because* one of the date shells had, it seems, put out the eye of the genie's son."
7. Bereft.
1. In the texts of 1816–29, this note began with an additional short paragraph: "The following fragment is here published at the request of a poet of great and deserved celebrity, and, as far as the Author's own opinions are concerned, rather as a psychological curiosity, than on the ground of any supposed *poetic* merits." The "poet of . . . celebrity" was Lord Byron.
2. "In Xamdu did Cublai Can build a stately Palace, encompassing sixteene miles of plaine ground with a wall, wherein are fertile Meddowes, pleasant Springs, delightfull Streames, and all sorts of beasts of chase and game, and in the middest thereof a sumptuous house of pleasure, which may be removed from place to place." From Samuel Purchas's book of travelers' tales, *Purchas his Pilgrimage* (1613). The historical Kublai Khan founded the Mongol dynasty in China in the 13th century.
3. In a note on a manuscript copy of "Kubla Khan," Coleridge gave a more precise account of the nature of this "sleep": "This fragment with a good deal more, not recoverable, composed, in a sort of reverie brought on by two grains of opium, taken to check a dysentery, at a farmhouse between Porlock and Linton, a quarter of a mile from Culbone Church, in the fall of the year, 1797."

eagerly wrote down the lines that are here preserved. At this moment he was unfortunately called out by a person on business from Porlock, and detained by him above an hour, and on his return to his room, found, to his no small surprise and mortification, that though he still retained some vague and dim recollection of the general purport of the vision, yet, with the exception of some eight or ten scattered lines and images, all the rest had passed away like the images on the surface of a stream into which a stone had been cast, but, alas! without the after restoration of the latter:

> Then all the charm
> Is broken—all that phantom-world so fair
> Vanishes, and a thousand circlets spread,
> And each mis-shape[s] the other. Stay awhile,
> Poor youth! who scarcely dar'st lift up thine eyes—
> The stream will soon renew its smoothness, soon
> The visions will return! And lo! he stays,
> And soon the fragments dim of lovely forms
> Come trembling back, unite, and now once more
> The pool becomes a mirror.
> [From Coleridge's *The Picture; or, the Lover's Resolution*,
> lines 91–100]

Yet from the still surviving recollections in his mind, the Author has frequently purposed to finish for himself what had been originally, as it were, given to him. Αὔριον ἄδιον ἄσω:[4] but the to-morrow is yet to come.

As a contrast to this vision, I have annexed a fragment of a very different character, describing with equal fidelity the dream of pain and disease.[5]—1816.

> In Xanadu did Kubla Khan
> A stately pleasure-dome decree:
> Where Alph,[6] the sacred river, ran
> Through caverns measureless to man
> 5   Down to a sunless sea.
> So twice five miles of fertile ground
> With walls and towers were girdled round:
> And there were gardens bright with sinuous rills
> Where blossomed many an incense-bearing tree;
> 10 And here were forests ancient as the hills,
> Enfolding sunny spots of greenery.
>
> But oh! that deep romantic chasm which slanted
> Down the green hill athwart a cedarn cover!
> A savage place! as holy and enchanted
> 15 As e'er beneath a waning moon was haunted
> By woman wailing for her demon-lover!

4. I shall sing a sweeter song tomorrow (Greek; recalled from Theocritus's *Idyls* 1.145).

A number of Coleridge's assertions in this preface have been debated by critics: whether the poem was written in 1797 or later, whether it was actually composed in a "dream" or opium reverie, even whether it is a fragment or in fact is complete. All critics agree, however, that this visionary poem of demonic inspiration is much more than a mere "psychological curiosity."

5. Coleridge refers to "The Pains of Sleep."

6. Derived probably from the Greek river Alpheus, which flows into the Ionian Sea. Its waters were fabled to rise again in Sicily as the fountain of Arethusa.

And from this chasm, with ceaseless turmoil seething,
As if this earth in fast thick pants were breathing,
A mighty fountain momently was forced:
20 Amid whose swift half-intermitted burst
Huge fragments vaulted like rebounding hail,
Or chaffy grain beneath the thresher's flail:
And 'mid these dancing rocks at once and ever
It flung up momently the sacred river.
25 Five miles meandering with a mazy motion
Through wood and dale the sacred river ran,
Then reached the caverns measureless to man,
And sank in tumult to a lifeless ocean:
And 'mid this tumult Kubla heard from far
30 Ancestral voices prophesying war!

The shadow of the dome of pleasure
Floated midway on the waves;
Where was heard the mingled measure
From the fountain and the caves.
35 It was a miracle of rare device,
A sunny pleasure-dome with caves of ice!

A damsel with a dulcimer
In a vision once I saw:
It was an Abyssinian maid,
40 And on her dulcimer she played,
Singing of Mount Abora.[7]
Could I revive within me
Her symphony and song,
To such a deep delight 'twould win me,
45 That with music loud and long,
I would build that dome in air,
That sunny dome! those caves of ice!
And all who heard should see them there,
And all should cry, Beware! Beware!
50 His flashing eyes, his floating hair!
Weave a circle round him thrice,[8]
And close your eyes with holy dread,
For he on honey-dew hath fed,
And drunk the milk of Paradise.[9]

ca. 1797–98   1816

---

7. Apparently a reminiscence of Milton's *Paradise Lost* 4.280–82: "where Abassin Kings their issue guard / Mount Amara (though this by some supposed / True Paradise) under the Ethiop line."
8. A magic ritual, to protect the inspired poet from intrusion.

9. Lines 50ff. echo in part the description, in Plato's *Ion* 533–34, of inspired poets, who are "like Bacchic maidens who draw milk and honey from the rivers when they are under the influence of Dionysus but not when they are in their right mind."

Christabel[1]

Preface

The first part of the following poem was written in the year 1797, at Stowey, in the county of Somerset. The second part, after my return from Germany, in the year 1800, at Keswick, Cumberland. It is probable, that if the poem had been finished at either of the former periods, or if even the first and second part had been published in the year 1800, the impression of its originality would have been much greater than I dare at present expect. But for this, I have only my own indolence to blame. The dates are mentioned for the exclusive purpose of precluding charges of plagiarism or servile imitation from myself. For there is amongst us a set of critics, who seem to hold, that every possible thought and image is traditional; who have no notion that there are such things as fountains in the world, small as well as great; and who would therefore charitably derive every rill they behold flowing, from a perforation made in some other man's tank. I am confident, however, that as far as the present poem is concerned, the celebrated poets[2] whose writings I might be suspected of having imitated, either in particular passages, or in the tone and the spirit of the whole, would be among the first to vindicate me from the charge, and who, on any striking coincidence, would permit me to address them in this doggerel version of two monkish Latin hexameters.

> Tis mine and it is likewise yours;
> But an if this will not do;
> Let it be mine, good friend! for I
> Am the poorer of the two.

I have only to add, that the metre of the Christabel is not, properly speaking, irregular, though it may seem so from its being founded on a new principle: namely, that of counting in each line the accents, not the syllables.[3] Though the latter may vary from seven to twelve, yet in each line the accents will be found to be only four. Nevertheless this occasional variation in number of syllables is not introduced wantonly, or for the mere ends of convenience, but in correspondence with some transition, in the nature of the imagery or passion.

Part 1

'Tis the middle of night by the castle clock,
And the owls have awakened the crowing cock;

---

1. Coleridge had planned to publish *Christabel* in the 2nd edition of *Lyrical Ballads* (1800) but had not been able to complete the poem. When *Christabel* was finally published in 1816 in its present fragmentary state, he still hoped to finish it, for the Preface contained this sentence (deleted in the edition of 1834): "But as, in my very first conception of the tale, I had the whole present to my mind, with the wholeness, no less than with the liveliness of a vision; I trust that I shall be able to embody in verse the three parts yet to come, in the course of the present year."
2. Sir Walter Scott and Lord Byron, who had read and admired *Christabel* while it circulated in manuscript. Coleridge has in mind Scott's *Lay of the Last Minstrel* (1805) and Byron's *Siege of Corinth* (1816), which showed the influence of *Christabel*, especially in their meter.
3. Much of the older English versification, following the example of Anglo-Saxon poetry, had been based on stress, or "accent," and some of it shows as much freedom in varying the number of syllables as does *Christabel*. The poem, however, is a radical departure from the theory and practice of versification in the 18th century, which had been based on a recurrent number of syllables in each line.

Tu—whit!——Tu—whoo!
And hark, again! the crowing cock,
5   How drowsily it crew.

Sir Leoline, the Baron rich,
Hath a toothless mastiff bitch;
From her kennel beneath the rock
She maketh answer to the clock,
10   Four for the quarters, and twelve for the hour;
Ever and aye,° by shine and shower,   *always*
Sixteen short howls, not over loud;
Some say, she sees my lady's shroud.

Is the night chilly and dark?
15   The night is chilly, but not dark.
The thin gray cloud is spread on high,
It covers but not hides the sky.
The moon is behind, and at the full;
And yet she looks both small and dull.
20   The night is chill, the cloud is gray:
'Tis a month before the month of May,
And the Spring comes slowly up this way.

The lovely lady, Christabel,
Whom her father loves so well,
25   What makes her in the wood so late,
A furlong from the castle gate?
She had dreams all yesternight
Of her own betrothed knight;
And she in the midnight wood will pray
30   For the weal° of her lover that's far away.   *well-being*

She stole along, she nothing spoke,
The sighs she heaved were soft and low,
And naught was green upon the oak,
But moss and rarest mistletoe:[4]
35   She kneels beneath the huge oak tree,
And in silence prayeth she.

The lady sprang up suddenly,
The lovely lady, Christabel!
It moaned as near, as near can be,
40   But what it is, she cannot tell.—
On the other side it seems to be,
Of the huge, broad-breasted, old oak tree.

The night is chill; the forest bare;
Is it the wind that moaneth bleak?
45   There is not wind enough in the air
To move away the ringlet curl

---

4. In Celtic Britain the mistletoe (a parasitic plant) had been held in veneration when it was found growing—as it rarely does—on an oak tree. (Its usual host is the apple tree.)

From the lovely lady's cheek—
There is not wind enough to twirl
The one red leaf, the last of its clan,
50 That dances as often as dance it can,
Hanging so light, and hanging so high,
On the topmost twig that looks up at the sky.

Hush, beating heart of Christabel!
Jesu, Maria, shield her well!
55 She folded her arms beneath her cloak,
And stole to the other side of the oak.
        What sees she there?

There she sees a damsel bright,
Drest in a silken robe of white,
60 That shadowy in the moonlight shone:
The neck that made that white robe wan,
Her stately neck, and arms were bare;
Her blue-veined feet unsandal'd were,
And wildly glittered here and there
65 The gems entangled in her hair.
I guess, 'twas frightful there to see
A lady so richly clad as she—
Beautiful exceedingly!

"Mary mother, save me now!"
70 (Said Christabel,) "And who art thou?"

The lady strange made answer meet,°   *appropriate*
And her voice was faint and sweet:—
"Have pity on my sore distress,
I scarce can speak for weariness:
75 Stretch forth thy hand, and have no fear!"
Said Christabel, "How cam'st thou here?"
And the lady, whose voice was faint and sweet,
Did thus pursue her answer meet:—

"My sire is of a noble line,
80 And my name is Geraldine:
Five warriors seized me yestermorn,
Me, even me, a maid forlorn:
They choked my cries with force and fright,
And tied me on a palfrey white.
85 The palfrey was as fleet as wind,
And they rode furiously behind.
They spurred amain,° their steeds were white: *at top speed*
And once we crossed the shade of night.
As sure as Heaven shall rescue me,
90 I have no thought what men they be;
Nor do I know how long it is
(For I have lain entranced I wis⁵)

---

5. I believe (Coleridge's misinterpretation of the Middle English adverb *ywis*, meaning "certainly").

Since one, the tallest of the five,
Took me from the palfrey's back,
95   A weary woman, scarce alive.
Some muttered words his comrades spoke:
He placed me underneath this oak;
He swore they would return with haste;
Whither they went I cannot tell—
100   I thought I heard, some minutes past,
Sounds as of a castle bell.
Stretch forth thy hand" (thus ended she),
"And help a wretched maid to flee."

Then Christabel stretched forth her hand
105   And comforted fair Geraldine:
"O well, bright dame! may you command
The service of Sir Leoline;
And gladly our stout chivalry
Will he send forth and friends withal
110   To guide and guard you safe and free
Home to your noble father's hall."

She rose: and forth with steps they passed
That strove to be, and were not, fast.
Her gracious stars the lady blest,
115   And thus spake on sweet Christabel:
"All our household are at rest,
The hall as silent as the cell;°   *of a monastery*
Sir Leoline is weak in health,
And may not well awakened be,
120   But we will move as if in stealth,
And I beseech your courtesy,
This night, to share your couch with me."

They crossed the moat, and Christabel
Took the key that fitted well;
125   A little door she opened straight,
All in the middle of the gate;
The gate that was ironed within and without,
Where an army in battle array had marched out.
The lady sank, belike through pain,
130   And Christabel with might and main
Lifted her up, a weary weight,
Over the threshold of the gate:[6]
Then the lady rose again,
And moved, as she were not in pain.

135   So free from danger, free from fear,
They crossed the court: right glad they were.
And Christabel devoutly cried
To the Lady by her side;
"Praise we the Virgin all divine

---

6. According to legend, a witch cannot cross the threshold by her own power because it has been blessed against evil spirits.

140   Who hath rescued thee from thy distress!"
       "Alas, alas!" said Geraldine,
       "I cannot speak for weariness."
       So free from danger, free from fear,
       They crossed the court: right glad they were.

145   Outside her kennel the mastiff old
       Lay fast asleep, in moonshine cold.
       The mastiff old did not awake,
       Yet she an angry moan did make!
       And what can ail the mastiff bitch?
150   Never till now she uttered yell
       Beneath the eye of Christabel.
       Perhaps it is the owlet's scritch:
       For what can ail the mastiff bitch?

       They passed the hall, that echoes still,
155   Pass as lightly as you will!
       The brands were flat, the brands were dying,
       Amid their own white ashes lying;
       But when the lady passed, there came
       A tongue of light, a fit of flame;
160   And Christabel saw the lady's eye,
       And nothing else saw she thereby,
       Save the boss of the shield of Sir Leoline tall,
       Which hung in a murky old niche in the wall.
       "O softly tread," said Christabel,
165   "My father seldom sleepeth well."

       Sweet Christabel her feet doth bare,
       And, jealous of the listening air,
       They steal their way from stair to stair,
       Now in glimmer, and now in gloom,
170   And now they pass the Baron's room,
       As still as death with stifled breath!
       And now have reached her chamber door;
       And now doth Geraldine press down
       The rushes[7] of the chamber floor.

175   The moon shines dim in the open air,
       And not a moonbeam enters here.
       But they without its light can see
       The chamber carved so curiously,
       Carved with figures strange and sweet,
180   All made out of the carver's brain,
       For a lady's chamber meet:
       The lamp with twofold silver chain
       Is fastened to an angel's feet.

       The silver lamp burns dead and dim;
185   But Christabel the lamp will trim.

---

7. Often used as a floor covering in the Middle Ages.

She trimmed the lamp, and made it bright,
And left it swinging to and fro,
While Geraldine, in wretched plight,
Sank down upon the floor below.

190   "O weary lady, Geraldine,
I pray you, drink this cordial wine!
It is a wine of virtuous powers;
My mother made it of wild flowers."

"And will your mother pity me,
195   Who am a maiden most forlorn?"
Christabel answered—"Woe is me!
She died the hour that I was born.
I have heard the grey-haired friar tell,
How on her death-bed she did say,
200   That she should hear the castle-bell
Strike twelve upon my wedding day.
O mother dear! that thou wert here!"
"I would," said Geraldine, "she were!"

But soon with altered voice, said she—
205   "Off, wandering mother!⁸ Peak and pine!
I have power to bid thee flee."
Alas! what ails poor Geraldine?
Why stares she with unsettled eye?
Can she the bodiless dead espy?
210   And why with hollow voice cries she,
"Off, woman, off! this hour is mine—
Though thou her guardian spirit be,
Off, woman, off! 'tis given to me."

Then Christabel knelt by the lady's side,
215   And raised to heaven her eyes so blue—
"Alas!" said she, "this ghastly ride—
Dear lady! it hath wildered you!"
The lady wiped her moist cold brow,
And faintly said, "'tis over now!"

220   Again the wild-flower wine she drank:
Her fair large eyes 'gan glitter bright,
And from the floor whereon she sank,
The lofty lady stood upright;
She was most beautiful to see,
225   Like a lady of a far countrée.

And thus the lofty lady spake—
"All they who live in the upper sky,
Do love you, holy Christabel!
And you love them, and for their sake

---

8. A term that could designate a fit of hysteria. "Peak and pine": Shakespeare's *Macbeth* 1.3.22.

230 And for the good which me befell,
Even I in my degree will try,
Fair maiden, to requite you well.
But now unrobe yourself; for I
Must pray, ere yet in bed I lie."

235 Quoth Christabel, "So let it be!"
And as the lady bade, did she.
Her gentle limbs did she undress,
And lay down in her loveliness.

But through her brain of weal and woe
240 So many thoughts moved to and fro,
That vain it were her lids to close;
So half-way from the bed she rose,
And on her elbow did recline
To look at the lady Geraldine.

245 Beneath the lamp the lady bowed,
And slowly rolled her eyes around;
Then drawing in her breath aloud,
Like one that shuddered, she unbound
The cincture° from beneath her breast: *belt*
250 Her silken robe, and inner vest,
Dropt to her feet, and full in view,
Behold! her bosom and half her side——
A sight to dream of, not to tell!
O shield her! shield sweet Christabel!⁹

255 Yet Geraldine nor speaks nor stirs;
Ah! what a stricken look was hers!
Deep from within she seems half-way
To lift some weight with sick assay,°   *attempt*
And eyes the maid and seeks delay;
260 Then suddenly as one defied
Collects herself in scorn and pride,
And lay down by the maiden's side!—
And in her arms the maid she took,
        Ah well-a-day!
265 And with low voice and doleful look
These words did say:
"In the touch of this bosom there worketh a spell,
Which is lord of thy utterance, Christabel!
Thou knowest to-night, and wilt know to-morrow
270 This mark of my shame, this seal of my sorrow;
        But vainly thou warrest,
            For this is alone in
        Thy power to declare,
            That in the dim forest
275   Thou heard'st a low moaning,

9. In several manuscripts and the first printing, this line reads "And she is to sleep by [or with] Christabel."

And found'st a bright lady, surpassingly fair:
And didst bring her home with thee in love and in charity,
To shield her and shelter her from the damp air."

The Conclusion to Part 1

It was a lovely sight to see
280　The lady Christabel, when she
Was praying at the old oak tree.
　　　Amid the jagged shadows
　　　Of mossy leafless boughs,
　　　Kneeling in the moonlight,
285　　　To make her gentle vows;
Her slender palms together prest,
Heaving sometimes on her breast;
Her face resigned to bliss or bale°—　　　　　　　　　evil, sorrow
Her face, oh call it fair not pale,
290　And both blue eyes more bright than clear,
Each about to have a tear.

With open eyes (ah woe is me!)
Asleep, and dreaming fearfully,
Fearfully dreaming, yet I wis,
295　Dreaming that alone, which is—
O sorrow and shame! Can this be she,
The lady, who knelt at the old oak tree?
And lo! the worker of these harms,
That holds the maiden in her arms,
300　Seems to slumber still and mild,
As a mother with her child.

A star hath set, a star hath risen,
O Geraldine! since arms of thine
Have been the lovely lady's prison.
305　O Geraldine! one hour was thine—
Thou'st had thy will! By tairn[1] and rill,
The night-birds all that hour were still.
But now they are jubilant anew,
From cliff and tower, tu—whoo! tu—whoo!
310　Tu—whoo! tu—whoo! from wood and fell![2]

And see! the lady Christabel
Gathers herself from out her trance;
Her limbs relax, her countenance
Grows sad and soft; the smooth thin lids
315　Close o'er her eyes; and tears she sheds—
Large tears that leave the lashes bright!
And oft the while she seems to smile
As infants at a sudden light!
Yea, she doth smile, and she doth weep,

1. Tarn, a mountain pool.　　　　　　　2. Elevated moor, or hill.

320   Like a youthful hermitess,
      Beauteous in a wilderness,
      Who, praying always, prays in sleep.
      And, if she move unquietly,
      Perchance, 'tis but the blood so free,
325   Comes back and tingles in her feet.
      No doubt, she hath a vision sweet.
      What if her guardian spirit 'twere?
      What if she knew her mother near?
      But this she knows, in joys and woes,
330   That saints will aid if men will call:
      For the blue sky bends over all!

Part 2

      "Each matin bell," the Baron saith,
      "Knells us back to a world of death."
      These words Sir Leoline first said,
335   When he rose and found his lady dead:
      These words Sir Leoline will say,
      Many a morn to his dying day!

      And hence the custom and law began,
      That still at dawn the sacristan,[3]
340   Who duly pulls the heavy bell,
      Five and forty beads must tell[4]
      Between each stroke—a warning knell,
      Which not a soul can choose but hear
      From Bratha Head to Wyndermere.[5]

345   Saith Bracy the bard, "So let it knell!
      And let the drowsy sacristan
      Still count as slowly as he can!
      There is no lack of such, I ween,°   *believe*
      As well fill up the space between.
350   In Langdale Pike° and Witch's Lair,   *Peak*
      And Dungeon-ghyll[6] so foully rent,
      With ropes of rock and bells of air
      Three sinful sextons' ghosts are pent,
      Who all give back, one after t'other,
355   The death-note to their living brother;
      And oft too, by the knell offended,
      Just as their one! two! three! is ended,
      The devil mocks the doleful tale
      With a merry peal from Borodale."

360   The air is still! through mist and cloud
      That merry peal comes ringing loud;
      And Geraldine shakes off her dread,

---

3. Church officer who digs the graves and rings the bells.
4. Pray while "telling" (keeping count on) the beads of a rosary.
5. These and the following names are of localities in the English Lake District.
6. Ravine forming the bed of a stream.

And rises lightly from the bed;
Puts on her silken vestments white,
365   And tricks her hair in lovely plight,°   *plait*
And nothing doubting of her spell
Awakens the lady Christabel.
"Sleep you, sweet lady Christabel?
I trust that you have rested well."

370   And Christabel awoke and spied
The same who lay down by her side—
O rather say, the same whom she
Raised up beneath the old oak tree!
Nay, fairer yet! and yet more fair!
375   For she belike hath drunken deep
Of all the blessedness of sleep!
And while she spake, her looks, her air
Such gentle thankfulness declare,
That (so it seemed) her girded vests
380   Grew tight beneath her heaving breasts.
"Sure I have sinned!" said Christabel,
"Now heaven be praised if all be well!"
And in low faltering tones, yet sweet,
Did she the lofty lady greet
385   With such perplexity of mind
As dreams too lively leave behind.

So quickly she rose, and quickly arrayed
Her maiden limbs, and having prayed
That He, who on the cross did groan,
390   Might wash away her sins unknown,
She forthwith led fair Geraldine
To meet her sire, Sir Leoline.

The lovely maid and the lady tall
Are pacing both into the hall,
395   And pacing on through page and groom,
Enter the Baron's presence room.

The Baron rose, and while he prest
His gentle daughter to his breast,
With cheerful wonder in his eyes
400   The lady Geraldine espies,
And gave such welcome to the same,
As might beseem so bright a dame!

But when he heard the lady's tale,
And when she told her father's name,
405   Why waxed Sir Leoline so pale,
Murmuring o'er the name again,
Lord Roland de Vaux of Tryermaine?

Alas! they had been friends in youth;
But whispering tongues can poison truth;

410 And constancy lives in realms above;
And life is thorny; and youth is vain;
And to be wroth with one we love,
Doth work like madness in the brain.
And thus it chanced, as I divine,
415 With Roland and Sir Leoline.
Each spake words of high disdain
And insult to his heart's best brother:
They parted—ne'er to meet again!
But never either found another
420 To free the hollow heart from paining—
They stood aloof, the scars remaining,
Like cliffs which had been rent asunder;
A dreary sea now flows between;—
But neither heat, nor frost, nor thunder,
425 Shall wholly do away, I ween,
The marks of that which once hath been.

Sir Leoline, a moment's space,
Stood gazing on the damsel's face:
And the youthful Lord of Tryermaine
430 Came back upon his heart again.

O then the Baron forgot his age,
His noble heart swelled high with rage;
He swore by the wounds in Jesu's side,
He would proclaim it far and wide
435 With trump and solemn heraldry,
That they who thus had wronged the dame,
Were base as spotted infamy!
"And if they dare deny the same,
My herald shall appoint a week,
440 And let the recreant traitors seek
My tourney court[7]—that there and then
I may dislodge their reptile souls
From the bodies and forms of men!"
He spake: his eye in lightning rolls!
445 For the lady was ruthlessly seized; and he kenned
In the beautiful lady the child of his friend!

And now the tears were on his face,
And fondly in his arms he took
Fair Geraldine, who met the embrace,
450 Prolonging it with joyous look.
Which when she viewed, a vision fell
Upon the soul of Christabel,
The vision of fear, the touch and pain!
She shrunk and shuddered, and saw again—
455 (Ah, woe is me! Was it for thee,
Thou gentle maid! such sights to see?)
Again she saw that bosom old,

7. Arena for tournaments.

Again she felt that bosom cold,
And drew in her breath with a hissing sound:
460 Whereat the Knight turned wildly round,
And nothing saw, but his own sweet maid
With eyes upraised, as one that prayed.

The touch, the sight, had passed away,
And in its stead that vision blest,
465 Which comforted her after-rest,
While in the lady's arms she lay,
Had put a rapture in her breast,
And on her lips and o'er her eyes
Spread smiles like light!
                                With new surprise,
470 "What ails then my beloved child?"
The Baron said—His daughter mild
Made answer, "All will yet be well!"
I ween, she had no power to tell
Aught else: so mighty was the spell.

475 Yet he, who saw this Geraldine,
Had deemed her sure a thing divine.
Such sorrow with such grace she blended,
As if she feared, she had offended
Sweet Christabel, that gentle maid!
480 And with such lowly tones she prayed,
She might be sent without delay
Home to her father's mansion.
                                        "Nay!
Nay, by my soul!" said Leoline.
"Ho! Bracy, the bard, the charge be thine!
485 Go thou, with music sweet and loud,
And take two steeds with trappings proud,
And take the youth whom thou lov'st best
To bear thy harp, and learn thy song,
And clothe you both in solemn vest,
490 And over the mountains haste along,
Lest wandering folk, that are abroad,
Detain you on the valley road.
And when he has crossed the Irthing flood,
My merry bard! he hastes, he hastes
495 Up Knorren Moor, through Halegarth Wood,
And reaches soon that castle good
Which stands and threatens Scotland's wastes.

"Bard Bracy! bard Bracy! your horses are fleet,
Ye must ride up the hall, your music so sweet,
500 More loud than your horses' echoing feet!
And loud and loud to Lord Roland call,
Thy daughter is safe in Langdale hall!
Thy beautiful daughter is safe and free—
Sir Leoline greets thee thus through me.
505 He bids thee come without delay

With all thy numerous array;
And take thy lovely daughter home:
And he will meet thee on the way
With all his numerous array
510 White with their panting palfreys' foam:
And by mine honour! I will say,
That I repent me of the day
When I spake words of fierce disdain
To Roland de Vaux of Tryermaine!—
515 —For since that evil hour hath flown,
Many a summer's sun hath shone;
Yet ne'er found I a friend again
Like Roland de Vaux of Tryermaine."

The lady fell, and clasped his knees,
520 Her face upraised, her eyes o'erflowing;
And Bracy replied, with faltering voice,
His gracious hail on all bestowing!—
"Thy words, thou sire of Christabel,
Are sweeter than my harp can tell;
525 Yet might I gain a boon of thee,
This day my journey should not be,
So strange a dream hath come to me;
That I had vowed with music loud
To clear yon wood from thing unblest,
530 Warned by a vision in my rest!
For in my sleep I saw that dove,
That gentle bird, whom thou dost love,
And call'st by thy own daughter's name—
Sir Leoline! I saw the same
535 Fluttering, and uttering fearful moan,
Among the green herbs in the forest alone.
Which when I saw and when I heard,
I wonder'd what might ail the bird;
For nothing near it could I see,
540 Save the grass and green herbs underneath the old tree.

"And in my dream methought I went
To search out what might there be found;
And what the sweet bird's trouble meant,
That thus lay fluttering on the ground.
545 I went and peered, and could descry
No cause for her distressful cry;
But yet for her dear lady's sake
I stooped, methought, the dove to take,
When lo! I saw a bright green snake
550 Coiled around its wings and neck,
Green as the herbs on which it couched,
Close by the dove's its head it crouched;
And with the dove it heaves and stirs,
Swelling its neck as she swelled hers!
555 I woke; it was the midnight hour,
The clock was echoing in the tower;

But though my slumber was gone by,
This dream it would not pass away—
It seems to live upon my eye!
560 And thence I vowed this self-same day,
With music strong and saintly song
To wander through the forest bare,
Lest aught unholy loiter there."

Thus Bracy said: the Baron, the while,
565 Half-listening heard him with a smile;
Then turned to Lady Geraldine,
His eyes made up of wonder and love;
And said in courtly accents fine,
"Sweet maid, Lord Roland's beauteous dove,
570 With arms more strong than harp or song,
Thy sire and I will crush the snake!"
He kissed her forehead as he spake,
And Geraldine, in maiden wise,°   manner
Casting down her large bright eyes,
575 With blushing cheek and courtesy fine
She turned her from Sir Leoline;
Softly gathering up her train,
That o'er her right arm fell again;
And folded her arms across her chest,
580 And couched her head upon her breast,
And looked askance at Christabel—
Jesu Maria, shield her well!

A snake's small eye blinks dull and shy,
And the lady's eyes they shrunk in her head,
585 Each shrunk up to a serpent's eye,
And with somewhat of malice, and more of dread,
At Christabel she looked askance!—
One moment—and the sight was fled!
But Christabel in dizzy trance
590 Stumbling on the unsteady ground
Shuddered aloud, with a hissing sound;
And Geraldine again turned round,
And like a thing, that sought relief,
Full of wonder and full of grief,
595 She rolled her large bright eyes divine
Wildly on Sir Leoline.

The maid, alas! her thoughts are gone,
She nothing sees—no sight but one!
The maid, devoid of guile and sin,
600 I know not how, in fearful wise
So deeply had she drunken in
That look, those shrunken serpent eyes,
That all her features were resigned
To this sole image in her mind;
605 And passively did imitate
That look of dull and treacherous hate!

And thus she stood, in dizzy trance,
Still picturing that look askance
With forced unconscious sympathy
610 Full before her father's view——
As far as such a look could be,
In eyes so innocent and blue!
And when the trance was o'er, the maid
Paused awhile, and inly prayed:
615 Then falling at the Baron's feet,
"By my mother's soul do I entreat
That thou this woman send away!"
She said: and more she could not say:
For what she knew she could not tell,
620 O'er-mastered by the mighty spell.

Why is thy cheek so wan and wild,
Sir Leoline? Thy only child
Lies at thy feet, thy joy, thy pride,
So fair, so innocent, so mild;
625 The same, for whom thy lady died!
O by the pangs of her dear mother
Think thou no evil of thy child!
For her, and thee, and for no other,
She prayed the moment ere she died:
630 Prayed that the babe for whom she died,
Might prove her dear lord's joy and pride!
    That prayer her deadly pangs beguiled,
        Sir Leoline!
    And wouldst thou wrong thy only child,
635   Her child and thine?

Within the Baron's heart and brain
If thoughts, like these, had any share,
They only swelled his rage and pain,
And did but work confusion there.
640 His heart was cleft with pain and rage,
His cheeks they quivered, his eyes were wild,
Dishonoured thus in his old age;
Dishonoured by his only child,
And all his hospitality
645 To the wrong'd daughter of his friend
By more than woman's jealousy
Brought thus to a disgraceful end—
He rolled his eye with stern regard
Upon the gentle minstrel bard,
650 And said in tones abrupt, austere—
"Why, Bracy! dost thou loiter here?
I bade thee hence!" The bard obeyed;
And turning from his own sweet maid,
The aged knight, Sir Leoline,
655 Led forth the lady Geraldine!

The Conclusion to Part 2

A little child, a limber elf,
Singing, dancing to itself,
A fairy thing with red round cheeks,
That always finds, and never seeks,
660 Makes such a vision to the sight
As fills a father's eyes with light;
And pleasures flow in so thick and fast
Upon his heart, that he at last
Must needs express his love's excess
665 With words of unmeant bitterness.
Perhaps 'tis pretty to force together
Thoughts so all unlike each other;
To mutter and mock a broken charm,
To dally with wrong that does no harm.
670 Perhaps 'tis tender too and pretty
At each wild word to feel within
A sweet recoil of love and pity.
And what, if in a world of sin
(O sorrow and shame should this be true!)
675 Such giddiness of heart and brain
Comes seldom save from rage and pain,
So talks as it's most used to do.

1798–1800   1816

Frost at Midnight[1]

The frost performs its secret ministry,
Unhelped by any wind. The owlet's cry
Came loud—and hark, again! loud as before.
The inmates of my cottage, all at rest,
5 Have left me to that solitude, which suits
Abstruser musings: save that at my side
My cradled infant slumbers peacefully.
'Tis calm indeed! so calm, that it disturbs
And vexes meditation with its strange
10 And extreme silentness. Sea, hill, and wood,
This populous village! Sea, and hill, and wood,
With all the numberless goings on of life,
Inaudible as dreams! the thin blue flame
Lies on my low burnt fire, and quivers not;
15 Only that film,[2] which fluttered on the grate,

---

1. The scene is Coleridge's cottage at Nether Stowey; the infant in line 7 is his son Hartley, then aged seventeen months.
2. In all parts of the kingdom these films are called *strangers* and supposed to portend the arrival of some absent friend [Coleridge's note]. The "film" is a piece of soot fluttering on the bar of the grate. Cf. Cowper's *The Task* 4.292–95, in which the poet describes how, dreaming before the parlor fire, he watches "The sooty films that play upon the bars, / Pendulous and foreboding, in the view / Of superstition prophesying still, / Though still deceived, some stranger's near approach." Several editions of Cowper's poems were advertised on the verso of the last page of Coleridge's text in the 1798 volume in which "Frost at Midnight" was first published.

Still flutters there, the sole unquiet thing.
Methinks, its motion in this hush of nature
Gives it dim sympathies with me who live,
Making it a companionable form,
20 Whose puny flaps and freaks the idling Spirit
By its own moods interprets, every where
Echo or mirror seeking of itself,
And makes a toy of Thought.

                          But O! how oft,
How oft, at school, with most believing mind,
25 Presageful, have I gazed upon the bars,
To watch that fluttering stranger! and as oft
With unclosed lids, already had I dreamt
Of my sweet birth-place,[3] and the old church-tower,
Whose bells, the poor man's only music, rang
30 From morn to evening, all the hot Fair-day,
So sweetly, that they stirred and haunted me
With a wild pleasure, falling on mine ear
Most like articulate sounds of things to come!
So gazed I, till the soothing things I dreamt
35 Lulled me to sleep, and sleep prolonged my dreams!
And so I brooded all the following morn,
Awed by the stern preceptor's[4] face, mine eye
Fixed with mock study on my swimming book:
Save if the door half opened, and I snatched
40 A hasty glance, and still my heart leaped up,
For still I hoped to see the stranger's face,
Townsman, or aunt, or sister more beloved,
My play-mate when we both were clothed alike![5]

    Dear Babe, that sleepest cradled by my side,
45 Whose gentle breathings, heard in this deep calm,
Fill up the interspersed vacancies
And momentary pauses of the thought!
My babe so beautiful! it thrills my heart
With tender gladness, thus to look at thee,
50 And think that thou shalt learn far other lore
And in far other scenes! For I was reared
In the great city, pent 'mid cloisters dim,
And saw nought lovely but the sky and stars.
But thou, my babe! shalt wander like a breeze
55 By lakes and sandy shores, beneath the crags
Of ancient mountain, and beneath the clouds,
Which image in their bulk both lakes and shores
And mountain crags: so shalt thou see and hear
The lovely shapes and sounds intelligible
60 Of that eternal language, which thy God
Utters, who from eternity doth teach
Himself in all, and all things in himself.

---

3. Coleridge was born at Ottery St. Mary, Devonshire, but went to school in London, beginning at the age of nine.
4. The Reverend James Boyer at Coleridge's school, Christ's Hospital.
5. I.e., when both Coleridge and his sister Ann still wore infant clothes, before he was deemed old enough to be breeched.

Great universal Teacher! he shall mould
Thy spirit, and by giving make it ask.

65   Therefore all seasons shall be sweet to thee,
Whether the summer clothe the general earth
With greenness, or the redbreast sit and sing
Betwixt the tufts of snow on the bare branch
Of mossy apple-tree, while the nigh thatch
70   Smokes in the sun-thaw; whether the eave-drops fall
Heard only in the trances of the blast,
Or if the secret ministry of frost
Shall hang them up in silent icicles,
Quietly shining to the quiet Moon.

Feb. 1798   1798

Dejection: An Ode[1]

> Late, late yestreen I saw the new Moon,
> With the old Moon in her arms;
> And I fear, I fear, my Master dear!
> We shall have a deadly storm.
> *Ballad of Sir Patrick Spence*

I

Well! If the Bard was weather-wise, who made
The grand old ballad of Sir Patrick Spence,
This night, so tranquil now, will not go hence
Unroused by winds, that ply a busier trade
5   Than those which mould yon cloud in lazy flakes,
Or the dull sobbing draft, that moans and rakes
Upon the strings of this Eolian lute,[2]
Which better far were mute.
For lo! the New-moon winter-bright!
10   And overspread with phantom light,
(With swimming phantom light o'erspread
But rimmed and circled by a silver thread)
I see the old Moon in her lap, foretelling
The coming on of rain and squally blast.
15   And oh! that even now the gust were swelling,
And the slant night-shower driving loud and fast!

1. This poem originated in a verse letter of 340 lines, called "A Letter to——," that Coleridge wrote on the night of April 4, 1802, after hearing the opening stanzas of "Ode: Intimations of Immortality," which Wordsworth had just composed. The "Letter" was addressed to Sara Hutchinson (whom Coleridge sometimes called "Asra"), the sister of Wordsworth's fiancée, Mary. It picked up the theme of a loss in the quality of perceptual experience that Wordsworth had presented at the beginning of his "Ode." In his original poem Coleridge lamented at length his unhappy marriage and the hopelessness of his love for Sara Hutchinson. In the next six months Coleridge deleted more than half the original lines, revised and reordered the remaining passages, and so transformed a long verse confession into the compact and dignified "Dejection: An Ode." He published the "Ode," in substantially its present form, on October 4, 1802, Wordsworth's wedding day—and also the seventh anniversary of Coleridge's own disastrous marriage to Sara Flicker.
2. A stringed instrument played upon by the wind (see "The Eolian Harp," n. 1, p. 252).

Those sounds which oft have raised me, whilst they awed,
    And sent my soul abroad,
Might now perhaps their wonted° impulse give,   *customary*
20 Might startle this dull pain, and make it move and live!

2

A grief without a pang, void, dark, and drear,
    A stifled, drowsy, unimpassioned grief,
    Which finds no natural outlet, no relief,
        In word, or sigh, or tear—
25 O Lady![3] in this wan and heartless mood,
To other thoughts by yonder throstle woo'd,
    All this long eve, so balmy and serene,
Have I been gazing on the western sky,
    And its peculiar tint of yellow green:
30 And still I gaze—and with how blank an eye!
And those thin clouds above, in flakes and bars,
That give away their motion to the stars;
Those stars, that glide behind them or between,
Now sparkling, now bedimmed, but always seen:
35 Yon crescent Moon as fixed as if it grew
In its own cloudless, starless lake of blue;
I see them all so excellently fair,
I see, not feel, how beautiful they are!

3

    My genial° spirits fail;   *creative*
40   And what can these avail
To lift the smothering weight from off my breast?
    It were a vain endeavour,
    Though I should gaze for ever
On that green light that lingers in the west:
45 I may not hope from outward forms to win
The passion and the life, whose fountains are within.

4

O Lady! we receive but what we give,
And in our life alone does nature live:
Ours is her wedding-garment, ours her shroud![4]
50   And would we aught° behold, of higher worth,   *anything*
Than that inanimate cold world allowed
To the poor loveless ever-anxious crowd,
    Ah! from the soul itself must issue forth,
A light, a glory,[5] a fair luminous cloud
55   Enveloping the Earth—

---

3. In the original version "Sara"—i.e., Sara Hutchinson. After intervening versions, in which the poem was addressed first to "William" (Wordsworth) and then to "Edmund," Coleridge introduced the noncommittal "Lady" in 1817.
4. I.e., nature's wedding garment and shroud are ours to give to her.
5. A "glory" is a halo. Coleridge often uses the term to identify in particular the phenomenon that occurs in the mountains when a walker sees his or her own figure projected by the sun in the mist, enlarged and with light encircling its head.

And from the soul itself must there be sent
   A sweet and potent voice, of its own birth,
Of all sweet sounds the life and element!

5

    O pure of heart! thou need'st not ask of me
60 What this strong music in the soul may be!
    What, and wherein it doth exist,
    This light, this glory, this fair luminous mist,
    This beautiful and beauty-making power.
      Joy, virtuous Lady! Joy that ne'er was given,
65 Save to the pure, and in their purest hour,
    Life, and Life's effluence, cloud at once and shower,
    Joy, Lady! is the spirit and the power,
    Which wedding Nature to us gives in dower,
      A new Earth and new Heaven,[6]
70 Undreamt of by the sensual and the proud—
    Joy is the sweet voice, Joy the luminous cloud—
      We in ourselves rejoice!
    And thence flows all that charms or ear or sight,
      All melodies the echoes of that voice,
75 All colours a suffusion from that light.

6

There was a time when, though my path was rough,
   This joy within me dallied with distress,
And all misfortunes were but as the stuff
   Whence Fancy made me dreams of happiness:
80 For hope grew round me, like the twining vine,
And fruits, and foliage, not my own, seemed mine.
But now afflictions bow me down to earth:
Nor care I that they rob me of my mirth,
   But oh! each visitation°   *i.e., of affliction*
85 Suspends what nature gave me at my birth,
   My shaping spirit of Imagination.
For not to think of what I needs must feel,
   But to be still and patient, all I can;
And haply by abstruse research to steal
90   From my own nature all the natural man—
   This was my sole resource, my only plan:
Till that which suits a part infects the whole,
And now is almost grown the habit of my soul.

7

Hence, viper thoughts, that coil around my mind,
95   Reality's dark dream!
I turn from you, and listen to the wind,

6. The sense becomes clearer if line 68 is punctuated in the way that Coleridge punctuated it when quoting the passage in one of his essays: "Which, wedding Nature to us, gives in dower." I.e., Joy marries us to Nature and gives us, for our dowry, "a new Earth and a new Heaven," a phrase echoing Revelation 21.1.

Which long has raved unnoticed. What a scream
Of agony by torture lengthened out
That lute sent forth! Thou Wind, that ravest without,
100 Bare crag, or mountain-tairn,[7] or blasted tree,
Or pine-grove whither woodman never clomb,°   *climbed*
Or lonely house, long held the witches' home,
 Methinks were fitter instruments for thee,
Mad Lutanist! who in this month of showers,
105 Of dark brown gardens, and of peeping flowers,
Mak'st Devils' yule,[8] with worse than wintry song,
The blossoms, buds, and timorous leaves among.
 Thou Actor, perfect in all tragic sounds!
Thou mighty Poet, e'en to frenzy bold!
110 What tell'st thou now about?
 'Tis of the rushing of a host in rout,
With groans of trampled men, with smarting wounds—
At once they groan with pain, and shudder with the cold!
But hush! there is a pause of deepest silence!
115 And all that noise, as of a rushing crowd,
With groans, and tremulous shudderings—all is over—
 It tells another tale, with sounds less deep and loud!
  A tale of less affright,
  And tempered with delight,
120 As Otway's[9] self had framed the tender lay,
  'Tis of a little child
  Upon a lonesome wild,
Not far from home, but she hath lost her way:
And now moans low in bitter grief and fear,
125 And now screams loud, and hopes to make her mother hear.

8

'Tis midnight, but small thoughts have I of sleep:
Full seldom may my friend such vigils keep!
Visit her, gentle Sleep! with wings of healing,
 And may this storm be but a mountain-birth,[1]
130 May all the stars hang bright above her dwelling,
 Silent as though they watched the sleeping Earth!
  With light heart may she rise,
  Gay fancy, cheerful eyes,
 Joy lift her spirit, joy attune her voice;
135 To her may all things live, from pole to pole,
Their life the eddying of her living soul!
 O simple spirit, guided from above,
Dear Lady! friend devoutest of my choice,
Thus mayest thou ever, evermore rejoice.

Apr. 4, 1802   1802

7. Tarn, or mountain pool.
8. Christmas as, in a perverted form, it is celebrated by devils.
9. Thomas Otway (1652–1685), a dramatist noted
for the pathos of his tragic passages. The poet
originally named was "William," and the allusion
was probably to Wordsworth's "Lucy Gray."
1. Probably, "May this be a typical mountain
storm, short though violent," although Coleridge
might have intended an allusion to Horace's
phrase "the mountain labored and brought forth
a mouse."

The Pains of Sleep[1]

Ere on my bed my limbs I lay,
It hath not been my use° to pray   *custom*
With moving lips or bended knees;
But silently, by slow degrees,
5   My spirit I to Love compose,
In humble trust mine eye-lids close,
With reverential resignation,
No wish conceived, no thought exprest,
Only a sense of supplication;
10   A sense o'er all my soul imprest
That I am weak, yet not unblest,
Since in me, round me, every where
Eternal strength and wisdom are.

But yester-night I prayed aloud
15   In anguish and in agony,
Up-starting from the fiendish crowd
Of shapes and thoughts that tortured me:
A lurid light, a trampling throng,
Sense of intolerable wrong,
20   And whom I scorned, those only strong!
Thirst of revenge, the powerless will
Still baffled, and yet burning still!
Desire with loathing strangely mixed
On wild or hateful objects fixed.
25   Fantastic passions! maddening brawl!
And shame and terror over all!
Deeds to be hid which were not hid,
Which all confused I could not know,
Whether I suffered, or I did:
30   For all seemed guilt, remorse or woe,
My own or others still the same
Life-stifling fear, soul-stifling shame.

So two nights passed: the night's dismay
Saddened and stunned the coming day.
35   Sleep, the wide blessing, seemed to me
Distemper's worst calamity.
The third night, when my own loud scream
Had waked me from the fiendish dream,
O'ercome with sufferings strange and wild,
40   I wept as I had been a child;
And having thus by tears subdued

---

1. Coleridge included a draft of this poem in a letter to Robert Southey, September 11, 1803, in which he wrote that "my spirits are dreadful, owing entirely to the Horrors of every night—I truly dread to sleep. It is no shadow with me, but substantial Misery foot-thick, that makes me sit by my bedside of a morning, & cry—. I have abandoned all opiates except Ether be one; & that only in *fits*. . . ." The last sentence indicates what Coleridge did not know—that his guilty nightmares were probably withdrawal symptoms from opium. The dreams he describes are very similar to those that De Quincey represents as "The Pains of Opium" in his *Confessions of an English Opium-Eater*.

My anguish to a milder mood,
Such punishments, I said, were due
To natures deepliest stained with sin,—
45 For aye entempesting anew
The unfathomable hell within,
The horror of their deeds to view,
To know and loathe, yet wish and do!
Such griefs with such men well agree,
50 But wherefore, wherefore fall on me?
To be beloved is all I need,
And whom I love, I love indeed.

1803   1816

To William Wordsworth

*Composed on the Night after His Recitation of a Poem on the
Growth of an Individual Mind*[1]

Friend of the wise! and teacher of the good!
Into my heart have I received that lay°   *song*
More than historic, that prophetic lay
Wherein (high theme by thee first sung aright)
5 Of the foundations and the building up
Of a Human Spirit thou hast dared to tell
What may be told, to the understanding mind
Revealable; and what within the mind
By vital breathings secret as the soul
10 Of vernal° growth, oft quickens in the heart   *springtime*
Thoughts all too deep for words![2]—

                        Theme hard as high!
Of smiles spontaneous, and mysterious fears
(The first-born they of Reason and twin birth),
Of tides obedient to external force,
15 And currents self-determined, as might seem,
Or by some inner power; of moments awful,°   *awe-inspiring*
Now in thy inner life, and now abroad,
When power streamed from thee, and thy soul received
The light reflected, as a light bestowed—
20 Of fancies fair, and milder hours of youth,
Hyblean[3] murmurs of poetic thought
Industrious in its joy, in vales and glens
Native or outland, lakes and famous hills!
Or on the lonely high-road, when the stars

1. This was the poem (later called *The Prelude*), addressed to Coleridge, that Wordsworth had completed in 1805. After Coleridge returned from Malta, very low in health and spirits, Wordsworth read the poem aloud to him during the evenings of almost two weeks. Coleridge wrote most of the present response immediately after the reading was completed, on January 7, 1807.

2. Wordsworth had described the effect on his mind of the animating breeze ("vital breathings") in *The Prelude* 1.1–47. "Thoughts . . . words" echoes the last line of Wordsworth's "Intimations" ode. Coleridge goes on to summarize the major themes and events of *The Prelude*.
3. Sweet. Hybla, in ancient Sicily, was famous for its honey.

25 Were rising; or by secret mountain-streams,
The guides and the companions of thy way!

Of more than Fancy, of the Social Sense
Distending wide, and man beloved as man,
Where France in all her towns lay vibrating
30 Like some becalmed bark beneath the burst
Of Heaven's immediate thunder, when no cloud
Is visible, or shadow on the main.
For thou wert there, thine own brows garlanded,
Amid the tremor of a realm aglow,
35 Amid a mighty nation jubilant,
When from the general heart of human kind
Hope sprang forth like a full-born Deity!
——Of that dear Hope afflicted and struck down,
So summoned homeward, thenceforth calm and sure
40 From the dread watch-tower of man's absolute self,
With light unwaning on her eyes, to look
Far on—herself a glory to behold,
The Angel of the vision! Then (last strain)
Of Duty, chosen laws controlling choice,
45 Action and joy!—An Orphic song[4] indeed,
A song divine of high and passionate thoughts
To their own music chanted!

O great Bard!
Ere yet that last strain dying awed the air,
With steadfast eye I viewed thee in the choir
50 Of ever-enduring men. The truly great
Have all one age, and from one visible space
Shed influence! They, both in power and act,
Are permanent, and Time is not with them,
Save as it worketh for them, they in it.
55 Nor less a sacred roll, than those of old,
And to be placed, as they, with gradual fame
Among the archives of mankind, thy work
Makes audible a linked lay of Truth,
Of Truth profound a sweet continuous lay,
60 Not learnt, but native, her own natural notes!
Ah! as I listened with a heart forlorn,
The pulses of my being beat anew:
And even as life returns upon the drowned,
Life's joy rekindling roused a throng of pains—
65 Keen pangs of Love, awakening as a babe
Turbulent, with an outcry in the heart;
And fears self-willed, that shunned the eye of hope;
And hope that scarce would know itself from fear;
Sense of past youth, and manhood come in vain,
70 And genius given, and knowledge won in vain;

4. As enchanting and oracular as the song of the legendary Orpheus. There may also be an allusion to the Orphic mysteries, involving spiritual death and rebirth (see lines 61–66). "The Angel of the vision" (line 43) probably alludes to "the great vision of the guarded mount" in Milton's "Lycidas," line 161.

And all which I had culled in wood-walks wild,
And all which patient toil had reared, and all,
Commune with thee had opened out—but flowers
Strewed on my corse, and borne upon my bier,
75 In the same coffin, for the self-same grave!

   That way no more! and ill beseems it me,
Who came a welcomer in herald's guise,
Singing of glory, and futurity,
To wander back on such unhealthful road,
80 Plucking the poisons of self-harm! And ill
Such intertwine beseems triumphal wreaths
Strewed before thy advancing!

                              Nor do thou,
Sage Bard! impair the memory of that hour
Of thy communion with my nobler mind⁵
85 By pity or grief, already felt too long!
Nor let my words import more blame than needs.
The tumult rose and ceased: for peace is nigh
Where wisdom's voice has found a listening heart.
Amid the howl of more than wintry storms,
90 The halcyon⁶ hears the voice of vernal hours
Already on the wing.

                    Eve following eve,⁷
Dear tranquil time, when the sweet sense of Home
Is sweetest! moments for their own sake hailed
And more desired, more precious for thy song,
95 In silence listening, like a devout child,
My soul lay passive, by thy various strain
Driven as in surges now beneath the stars,
With momentary stars of my own birth,
Fair constellated foam, still darting off
100 Into the darkness; now a tranquil sea,
Outspread and bright, yet swelling to the moon.

   And when—O Friend! my comforter and guide!
Strong in thyself, and powerful to give strength!—
Thy long sustained Song finally closed,
105 And thy deep voice had ceased—yet thou thyself
Wert still before my eyes, and round us both
That happy vision of beloved faces—
Scarce conscious, and yet conscious of its close
I sate, my being blended in one thought
110 (Thought was it? or aspiration? or resolve?)
Absorbed, yet hanging still upon the sound—
And when I rose, I found myself in prayer.

1807   1817

---

5. I.e., during the early association between the two poets (1797–98).
6. A fabled bird, able to calm the sea where it nested in winter.
7. The evenings during which Wordsworth read his poem aloud.

Epitaph[1]

Stop, Christian Passer-by!—Stop, child of God,
And read with gentle breast. Beneath this sod
A poet lies, or that which once seem'd he.—
O, lift one thought in prayer for S. T. C.;
5 That he who many a year with toil of breath
Found death in life, may here find life in death!
Mercy for praise—to be forgiven for[2] fame
He ask'd, and hoped, through Christ. Do thou the same!

1833   1834

Biographia Literaria   In March 1815 Coleridge was preparing a collected edition of his poems and planned to include "a general preface . . . on the principles of philosophic and genial criticism." As was typical for Coleridge, the materials developed as he worked on them until, on July 29, he declared that the preface had expanded to become a book in its own right, an "Autobiographia Literaria." In a characteristic Romantic reinvention of autobiography, the work merged personal experience with philosophical speculation, as well as with what Coleridge identified as "digression and anecdotes." It was to consist of two main parts, "my literary life and opinions, as far as poetry and *poetical* criticism [are] concerned" and a critique of Wordsworth's theory of poetic diction. This work was ready by September 17, 1815, but the *Biographia Literaria*, in two volumes, was not published until July 1817. The delay was caused by a series of miscalculations by his printer, which forced Coleridge to add 150 pages of miscellaneous materials to pad out the length of the second volume.

Coleridge had been planning a detailed critique of Wordsworth's theory of poetic diction ever since 1802, when he had detected "a radical difference in our theoretical opinions respecting poetry." In the selection from chapter 17, Coleridge agrees with Wordsworth's general aim of reforming the artifices of current poetic diction, but he sharply denies Wordsworth's claim that there is no essential difference between the language of poetry and the language spoken by people in real life. The other selections printed here are devoted mainly to the central principle of Coleridge's own critical theory, the distinction between the mechanical "fancy" and the organic imagination, which is tersely summarized in the conclusion to chapter 13. The definition of poetry at the end of chapter 14 develops at greater length the nature of the "synthetic and magical power . . . of imagination," which, for Coleridge, has the capacity to dissolve the divisions (between, for instance, the perceiving human subject and his or her objects of perception) that characterize human beings' fallen state.

For another selection from *Biographic Literaria*, see "'Self-constituted judge of poesy': Reviewer vs. Poet in the Romantic Period" in the supplemental ebook.

---

1. Written by Coleridge the year before he died. One version that he sent in a letter had as a title: "Epitaph on a Poet little known, yet better known by the Initials of his name than by the Name Itself."

2. "For" in the sense of "instead of" [Coleridge's note].

From Biographia Literaria

From *Chapter 4*

[MR. WORDSWORTH'S EARLIER POEMS]

* * * During the last year of my residence at Cambridge, I became acquainted with Mr. Wordsworth's first publication, entitled *Descriptive Sketches*;[1] and seldom, if ever, was the emergence of an original poetic genius above the literary horizon more evidently announced. In the form, style, and manner of the whole poem, and in the structure of the particular lines and periods, there is a harshness and acerbity connected and combined with words and images all a-glow which might recall those products of the vegetable world, where gorgeous blossoms rise out of the hard and thorny rind and shell within which the rich fruit was elaborating. The language was not only peculiar and strong, but at times knotty and contorted, as by its own impatient strength; while the novelty and struggling crowd of images, acting in conjunction with the difficulties of the style, demanded always a greater closeness of attention than poetry (at all events than descriptive poetry) has a right to claim. It not seldom therefore justified the complaint of obscurity. In the following extract I have sometimes fancied that I saw an emblem of the poem itself and of the author's genius as it was then displayed:

> 'Tis storm; and hid in mist from hour to hour,
> All day the floods a deepening murmur pour;
> The sky is veiled, and every cheerful sight:
> Dark is the region as with coming night;
> And yet what frequent bursts of overpowering light!
> Triumphant on the bosom of the storm,
> Glances the fire-clad eagle's wheeling form;
> Eastward, in long perspective glittering, shine
> The wood-crowned cliffs that o'er the lake recline;
> Wide o'er the Alps a hundred streams unfold,
> At once to pillars turned that flame with gold;
> Behind his sail the peasant strives to shun
> The West, that burns like one dilated sun,
> Where in a mighty crucible expire
> The mountains, glowing hot, like coals of fire.[2]

The poetic Psyche, in its process to full development, undergoes as many changes as its Greek namesake, the butterfly.[3] And it is remarkable how soon genius clears and purifies itself from the faults and errors of its earliest products; faults which, in its earliest compositions, are the more obtrusive and confluent because, as heterogeneous elements which had only a temporary use, they constitute the very *ferment* by which themselves are carried off. Or we may compare them to some diseases, which must work on the humors and be thrown out on the surface in order to secure the patient from their future recurrence. I was in my twenty-fourth year when I had the happiness of knowing Mr. Wordsworth personally;[4] and, while memory lasts, I

---

1. Published 1793, the year before Coleridge left Cambridge; a long descriptive-meditative poem in closed couplets, recounting Wordsworth's walking tour in the Alps in 1790. Wordsworth describes the same tour in *The Prelude*, book 6.

2. *Descriptive Sketches* (1815 version), lines 332ff.
3. In Greek, Psyche is the common name for the soul and the butterfly [Coleridge's note].
4. The meeting occurred in September 1795.

shall hardly forget the sudden effect produced on my mind by his recitation of a manuscript poem which still remains unpublished, but of which the stanza and tone of style were the same as those of *The Female Vagrant* as originally printed in the first volume of the *Lyrical Ballads*.[5] There was here no mark of strained thought or forced diction, no crowd or turbulence of imagery, and, as the poet hath himself well described in his lines on revisiting the Wye,[6] manly reflection and human associations had given both variety and an additional interest to natural objects which in the passion and appetite of the first love they had seemed to him neither to need or permit. The occasional obscurities, which had risen from an imperfect control over the resources of his native language, had almost wholly disappeared, together with that worse defect of arbitrary and illogical phrases, at once hackneyed and fantastic, which hold so distinguished a place in the *technique* of ordinary poetry and will, more or less, alloy the earlier poems of the truest genius, unless the attention has been specifically directed to their worthlessness and incongruity. I did not perceive anything particular in the mere style of the poem alluded to during its recitation, except indeed such difference as was not separable from the thought and manner; and the Spenserian stanza which always, more or less, recalls to the reader's mind Spenser's own style, would doubtless have authorized in my then opinion a more frequent descent to the phrases of ordinary life than could, without an ill effect, have been hazarded in the heroic couplet. It was not however the freedom from false taste, whether as to common defects or to those more properly his own, which made so unusual an impression on my feelings immediately, and subsequently on my judgment. It was the union of deep feeling with profound thought; the fine balance of truth in observing with the imaginative faculty in modifying the objects observed; and above all the original gift of spreading the tone, the *atmosphere*, and with it the depth and height of the ideal world, around forms, incidents, and situations of which, for the common view, custom had bedimmed all the luster, had dried up the sparkle and the dewdrops. "To find no contradiction in the union of old and new, to contemplate the Ancient of Days and all his works with feelings as fresh as if all had then sprang forth at the first creative fiat,[7] characterizes the mind that feels the riddle of the world and may help to unravel it. To carry on the feelings of childhood into the powers of manhood; to combine the child's sense of wonder and novelty with the appearances which every day for perhaps forty years had rendered familiar;

> With sun and moon and stars throughout the year,
> And man and woman;[8]

this is the character and privilege of genius, and one of the marks which distinguish genius from talents. And therefore it is the prime merit of genius, and its most unequivocal mode of manifestation, so to represent familiar objects as to awaken in the minds of others a kindred feeling concerning them, and that freshness of sensation which is the constant accompaniment of mental no less than of bodily convalescence. Who has not a thousand times seen snow fall on water? Who has not watched it with a new feeling from the time that he has read Burns' comparison of sensual pleasure

5. *Salisbury Plain* (1793–94), which was left in manuscript until Wordsworth published a revised version in 1842 under the title "Guilt and Sorrow." An excerpt from *Salisbury Plain* was printed as "The Female Vagrant," in *Lyrical Ballads* (1798).

6. Wordsworth's "Tintern Abbey," lines 76ff.
7. The first divine command: "Let there be light."
8. Altered from Milton's sonnet "To Mr. Cyriack Skinner upon His Blindness."

> To snow that falls upon a river
> A moment white—then gone forever![9]

In poems, equally as in philosophic disquisitions, genius produces the strongest impressions of novelty while it rescues the most admitted truths from the impotence caused by the very circumstance of their universal admission. Truths of all others the most awful and mysterious, yet being at the same time of universal interest, are too often considered as *so* true, that they lose all the life and efficiency of truth and lie bedridden in the dormitory of the soul side by side with the most despised and exploded errors." *The Friend*, p. 76, no. 5.[1]

[ON FANCY AND IMAGINATION—THE INVESTIGATION OF THE DISTINCTION IMPORTANT TO THE FINE ARTS]

This excellence, which in all Mr. Wordsworth's writings is more or less predominant and which constitutes the character of his mind, I no sooner felt than I sought to understand. Repeated meditations led me first to suspect (and a more intimate analysis of the human faculties, their appropriate marks, functions, and effects, matured my conjecture into full conviction) that fancy and imagination were two distinct and widely different faculties, instead of being, according to the general belief, either two names with one meaning, or at furthest the lower and higher degree of one and the same power. It is not, I own, easy to conceive a more apposite translation of the Greek *phantasia* than the Latin *imaginatio*; but it is equally true that in all societies there exists an instinct of growth, a certain collective unconscious good sense working progressively to desynonymize those words originally of the same meaning which the conflux of dialects had supplied to the more homogeneous languages, as the Greek and German: and which the same cause, joined with accidents of translation from original works of different countries, occasion in mixed languages like our own. The first and most important point to be proved is, that two conceptions perfectly distinct are confused under one and the same word, and (this done) to appropriate that word exclusively to one meaning, and the synonym (should there be one) to the other. But if (as will be often the case in the arts and sciences) no synonym exists, we must either invent or borrow a word. In the present instance the appropriation had already begun and been legitimated in the derivative adjective: Milton had a highly *imaginative*, Cowley a very *fanciful*, mind. If therefore I should succeed in establishing the actual existence of two faculties generally different, the nomenclature would be at once determined. To the faculty by which I had characterized Milton we should confine the term *imagination*; while the other would be contradistinguished as *fancy*. Now were it once fully ascertained that this division is no less grounded in nature than that of delirium from mania, or Otway's

> Lutes, lobsters, seas of milk, and ships of amber,[2]

from Shakespeare's

> What! have his daughters brought him to this pass?[3]

---

9. Altered from Burns's "Tam o' Shanter," lines 61–62.
1. A periodical published by Coleridge (1809–10).

2. Thomas Otway, in *Venice Preserved* (1682), wrote "laurels" in place of "lobsters" (5.2.151).
3. *King Lear* 3.4.59.

or from the preceding apostrophe to the elements, the theory of the fine arts and of poetry in particular could not, I thought, but derive some additional and important light. It would in its immediate effects furnish a torch of guidance to the philosophical critic, and ultimately to the poet himself. In energetic minds truth soon changes by domestication into power; and from directing in the discrimination and appraisal of the product becomes influencive in the production. To admire on principle is the only way to imitate without loss of originality. * * *

From *Chapter 13*

[ON THE IMAGINATION, OR ESEMPLASTIC[4] POWER]

* * * The IMAGINATION, then, I consider either as primary, or secondary. The primary IMAGINATION I hold to be the living power and prime agent of all human perception, and as a repetition in the finite mind of the eternal act of creation in the infinite I AM. The secondary I consider as an echo of the former, coexisting with the conscious will, yet still as identical with the primary in the *kind* of its agency, and differing only in *degree*, and in the *mode* of its operation. It dissolves, diffuses, dissipates, in order to recreate; or where this process is rendered impossible, yet still, at all events, it struggles to idealize and to unify. It is essentially *vital*, even as all objects (*as* objects) are essentially fixed and dead.

FANCY, on the contrary, has no other counters to play with but fixities and definites. The fancy is indeed no other than a mode of memory emancipated from the order of time and space; and blended with, and modified by that empirical phenomenon of the will which we express by the word CHOICE. But equally with the ordinary memory it must receive all its materials ready made from the law of association.[5] * * *

Chapter 14

OCCASION OF THE *LYRICAL BALLADS*, AND THE OBJECTS ORIGINALLY PROPOSED—PREFACE TO THE SECOND EDITION—THE ENSUING CONTROVERSY, ITS CAUSES AND ACRIMONY—PHILOSOPHIC DEFINITIONS OF A POEM AND POETRY WITH SCHOLIA.[6]

During the first year that Mr. Wordsworth and I were neighbours,[7] our conversations turned frequently on the two cardinal points of poetry, the power of exciting the sympathy of the reader by a faithful adherence to the truth of nature, and the power of giving the interest of novelty by the modifying colors of imagination.[8] The sudden charm which accidents of light and shade, which moonlight or sunset diffused over a known and familiar landscape, appeared

---

4. Coleridge coined this word and used it to mean "molding into unity."
5. Coleridge conceives God's creation to be a continuing process, which has an analogy in the creative perception ("primary imagination") of all human minds. The creative process is repeated, or "echoed," on still a third level, by the "secondary imagination" of the poet, which dissolves the products of primary perception to shape them into a new and unified creation—the imaginative

passage or poem. The "fancy," on the other hand, can only manipulate "fixities and definites" that, linked by association, come to it ready-made from perception.
6. Additional remarks, after a philosophic demonstration.
7. At Nether Stowey and Alfoxden, Somerset, in 1797.
8. Cf. Wordsworth's account in his Preface to *Lyrical Ballads* (p. 136).

to represent the practicability of combining both. These are the poetry of nature. The thought suggested itself (to which of us I do not recollect) that a series of poems might be composed of two sorts. In the one, the incidents and agents were to be, in part at least, supernatural; and the excellence aimed at was to consist in the interesting of the affections by the dramatic truth of such emotions as would naturally accompany such situations, supposing them real. And real in *this* sense they have been to every human being who, from whatever source of delusion, has at any time believed himself under supernatural agency. For the second class, subjects were to be chosen from ordinary life; the characters and incidents were to be such as will be found in every village and its vicinity where there is a meditative and feeling mind to seek after them, or to notice them when they present themselves.

In this idea originated the plan of the *Lyrical Ballads*; in which it was agreed that my endeavours should be directed to persons and characters supernatural, or at least romantic; yet so as to transfer from our inward nature a human interest and a semblance of truth sufficient to procure for these shadows of imagination that willing suspension of disbelief for the moment, which constitutes poetic faith. Mr. Wordsworth, on the other hand, was to propose to himself as his object to give the charm of novelty to things of every day, and to excite a feeling analogous to the supernatural, by awakening the mind's attention from the lethargy of custom and directing it to the loveliness and the wonders of the world before us; an inexhaustible treasure, but for which, in consequence of the film of familiarity and selfish solicitude, we have eyes yet see not, ears that hear not, and hearts that neither feel nor understand.[9]

With this view I wrote *The Ancient Mariner*, and was preparing, among other poems, *The Dark Ladie*, and the *Christabel*, in which I should have more nearly realized my ideal than I had done in my first attempt. But Mr. Wordsworth's industry had proved so much more successful and the number of his poems so much greater, that my compositions, instead of forming a balance, appeared rather an interpolation of heterogeneous matter.[1] Mr. Wordsworth added two or three poems written in his own character, in the impassioned, lofty, and sustained diction which is characteristic of his genius. In this form the *Lyrical Ballads* were published; and were presented by him, as an *experiment*,[2] whether subjects which from their nature rejected the usual ornaments and extra-colloquial style of poems in general might not be so managed in the language of ordinary life as to produce the pleasurable interest which it is the peculiar business of poetry to impart. To the second edition[3] he added a preface of considerable length; in which, notwithstanding some passages of apparently a contrary import, he was understood to contend for the extension of this style to poetry of all kinds, and to reject as vicious and indefensible all phrases and forms of style that were not included in what he (unfortunately, I think, adopting an equivocal expression) called the language of *real* life. From this preface, prefixed to poems in which it was impossible to deny the presence of original genius, however mistaken its direction might be deemed, arose the whole long-continued controversy.[4] For from the

9. Cf. Isaiah 6.9–10.
1. The first edition of *Lyrical Ballads*, published anonymously in 1798, contained nineteen poems by Wordsworth, four by Coleridge.
2. *Experiments* was the word used by Words-

worth in his *Advertisement* to the first edition.
3. Published in 1800.
4. The controversy over Wordsworth's theory and poetical practice in the literary reviews of the day.

conjunction of perceived power with supposed heresy I explain the inveteracy[5] and in some instances, I grieve to say, the acrimonious passions with which the controversy has been conducted by the assailants.

Had Mr. Wordsworth's poems been the silly, the childish things which they were for a long time described as being; had they been really distinguished from the compositions of other poets merely by meanness[6] of language and inanity of thought; had they indeed contained nothing more than what is found in the parodies and pretended imitations of them; they must have sunk at once, a dead weight, into the slough of oblivion, and have dragged the preface along with them. But year after year increased the number of Mr. Wordsworth's admirers. They were found too not in the lower classes of the reading public, but chiefly among young men of strong sensibility and meditative minds; and their admiration (inflamed perhaps in some degree by opposition) was distinguished by its intensity, I might almost say, by its *religious* fervor. These facts, and the intellectual energy of the author, which was more or less consciously felt where it was outwardly and even boisterously denied, meeting with sentiments of aversion to his opinions and of alarm at their consequences, produced an eddy of criticism which would of itself have borne up the poems by the violence with which it whirled them round and round. With many parts of this preface, in the sense attributed to them and which the words undoubtedly seem to authorize, I never concurred; but, on the contrary objected to them as erroneous in principle, and as contradictory (in appearance at least) both to other parts of the same preface and to the author's own practice in the greater number of the poems themselves. Mr. Wordsworth in his recent collection[7] has, I find, degraded this prefatory disquisition to the end of his second volume, to be read or not at the reader's choice. But he has not, as far as I can discover, announced any change in his poetic creed. At all events, considering it as the source of a controversy in which I have been honored more than I deserve by the frequent conjunction of my name with his, I think it expedient to declare once for all in what points I coincide with his opinions, and in what points I altogether differ. But in order to render myself intelligible I must previously, in as few words as possible, explain my ideas, first, of a POEM; and secondly, of POETRY itself, in *kind* and in *essence*.

The office of philosophical *disquisition* consists in just *distinction;* while it is the privilege of the philosopher to preserve himself constantly aware that distinction is not division. In order to obtain adequate notions of any truth, we must intellectually separate its distinguishable parts; and this is the technical of philosophy. But having so done, we must then restore them in our conceptions to the unity in which they actually coexist; and this is the *result* of philosophy. A poem contains the same elements as a prose composition; the difference therefore must consist in a different combination of them, in consequence of a different object proposed. According to the difference of the object will be the difference of the combination. It is possible that the object may be merely to facilitate the recollection of any given facts or observations by artificial arrangement; and the composition will be a poem, merely because it is distinguished from prose by meter, or by rhyme, or by both conjointly. In this, the lowest sense, a man might attribute the name of a poem to the well-known enumeration of the days in the several months:

> Thirty days hath September,
> April, June, and November, etc.

and others of the same class and purpose. And as a particular pleasure is found in anticipating the recurrence of sounds and quantities, all compositions that have this charm superadded, whatever be their contents, *may* be entitled poems.

So much for the superficial *form*. A difference of object and contents supplies an additional ground of distinction. The immediate purpose may be the communication of truths; either of truth absolute and demonstrable, as in works of science; or of facts experienced and recorded, as in history. Pleasure, and that of the highest and most permanent kind, may *result* from the *attainment* of the end; but it is not itself the immediate end. In other works the communication of pleasure may be the immediate purpose; and though truth, either moral or intellectual, ought to be the *ultimate* end, yet this will distinguish the character of the author, not the class to which the work belongs. Blessed indeed is that state of society in which the immediate purpose would be baffled by the perversion of the proper ultimate end; in which no charm of diction or imagery could exempt the Bathyllus even of an Anacreon, or the Alexis of Virgil,[8] from disgust and aversion!

But the communication of pleasure may be the immediate object of a work not metrically composed; and that object may have been in a high degree attained, as in novels and romances. Would then the mere superaddition of meter, with or without rhyme, entitle *these* to the name of poems? The answer is that nothing can permanently please which does not contain in itself the reason why it is so, and not otherwise. If meter be superadded, all other parts must be made consonant with it. They must be such as to justify the perpetual and distinct attention to each part which an exact correspondent recurrence of accent and sound are calculated to excite. The final definition then, so deduced, may be thus worded. A poem is that species of composition which is opposed to works of science by proposing for its *immediate* object pleasure, not truth; and from all other species (having *this* object in common with it) it is discriminated by proposing to itself such delight from the *whole* as is compatible with a distinct gratification from each component *part*.

Controversy is not seldom excited in consequence of the disputants attaching each a different meaning to the same word; and in few instances has this been more striking than in disputes concerning the present subject. If a man chooses to call every composition a poem which is rhyme, or measure, or both, I must leave his opinion uncontroverted. The distinction is at least competent to characterize the writer's intention. If it were subjoined that the whole is likewise entertaining or affecting as a tale or as a series of interesting reflections, I of course admit this as another fit ingredient of a poem and an additional merit. But if the definition sought for be that of a *legitimate* poem, I answer it must be one the parts of which mutually support

---

8. The reference is to poems of homosexual love. Bathyllus was a beautiful boy praised by Anacreon, a Greek lyric poet (ca. 560–475 B.C.E.); Alexis was a young man loved by the shepherd Corydon in Virgil's *Eclogue* 2.

and explain each other; all in their proportion harmonizing with, and supporting the purpose and known influences of metrical arrangement. The philosophic critics of all ages coincide with the ultimate judgment of all countries in equally denying the praises of a just poem on the one hand to a series of striking lines or distichs,[9] each of which absorbing the whole attention of the reader to itself disjoins it from its context and makes it a separate whole, instead of a harmonizing part; and on the other hand, to an unsustained composition, from which the reader collects rapidly the general result unattracted by the component parts. The reader should be carried forward, not merely or chiefly by the mechanical impulse of curiosity, or by a restless desire to arrive at the final solution; but by the pleasurable activity of mind excited by the attractions of the journey itself. Like the motion of a serpent, which the Egyptians made the emblem of intellectual power; or like the path of sound through the air; at every step he pauses and half recedes, and from the retrogressive movement collects the force which again carries him onward. "*Praecipitandus est* liber *spiritus*,"[1] says Petronius Arbiter most happily. The epithet *liber* here balances the preceding verb; and it is not easy to conceive more meaning condensed in fewer words.

But if this should be admitted as a satisfactory character of a poem, we have still to seek for a definition of poetry. The writings of Plato, and Bishop Taylor, and the *Theoria Sacra* of Burnet,[2] furnish undeniable proofs that poetry of the highest kind may exist without meter, and even without the contradistinguishing objects of a poem. The first chapter of Isaiah (indeed a very large proportion of the whole book) is poetry in the most emphatic sense; yet it would be not less irrational than strange to assert that pleasure, and not truth, was the immediate object of the prophet. In short, whatever *specific* import we attach to the word poetry, there will be found involved in it, as a necessary consequence, that a poem of any length neither can be, nor ought to be, all poetry. Yet if a harmonious whole is to be produced, the remaining parts must be preserved in *keeping*[3] with the poetry; and this can be no otherwise effected than by such a studied selection and artificial arrangement as will partake of *one*, though not a *peculiar*, property of poetry. And this again can be no other than the property of exciting a more continuous and equal attention than the language of prose aims at, whether colloquial or written.

My own conclusions on the nature of poetry, in the strictest use of the word, have been in part anticipated in the preceding disquisition on the fancy and imagination. What is poetry? is so nearly the same question with, what is a poet? that the answer to the one is involved in the solution of the other. For it is a distinction resulting from the poetic genius itself, which sustains and modifies the images, thoughts, and emotions of the poet's own mind.

The poet, described in *ideal* perfection, brings the whole soul of man into activity, with the subordination of its faculties to each other, according to their relative worth and dignity. He diffuses a tone and spirit of unity

---

9. Pairs of lines.
1. "The *free* spirit [of the poet] must be hurled onward." From the *Satyricon*, by the Roman satirist Petronius Arbiter (1st century C.E.).
2. Thomas Burnet (1635?–1715), author of *The Sacred Theory of the Earth.* Bishop Jeremy Taylor (1613–1667), author of *Holy Living* and *Holy*

Dying. Coleridge greatly admired the elaborate and sonorous prose of both these writers. He took from a work by Burnet the Latin motto for *The Rime of the Ancient Mariner.*
3. A term from the theory of painting for the maintenance of the harmony of a composition.

that blends and (as it were) *fuses*, each into each, by that synthetic and magical power to which we have exclusively appropriated the name of imagination. This power, first put in action by the will and understanding and retained under their irremissive,[4] though gentle and unnoticed, control (*laxis effertur habenis*)[5] reveals itself in the balance or reconciliation of opposite or discordant qualities:[6] of sameness, with difference; of the general, with the concrete; the idea, with the image; the individual, with the representative; the sense of novelty and freshness, with old and familiar objects; a more than usual state of emotion, with more than usual order; judgment ever awake and steady self-possession, with enthusiasm and feeling profound or vehement; and while it blends and harmonizes the natural and the artificial, still subordinates art to nature; the manner to the matter; and our admiration of the poet to our sympathy with the poetry. "Doubtless," as Sir John Davies observes of the soul (and his words may with slight alteration be applied, and even more appropriately, to the poetic IMAGINATION):

> Doubtless this could not be, but that she turns
>   Bodies to spirit by sublimation strange,
> As fire converts to fire the things it burns,
>   As we our food into our nature change.
>
> From their gross matter she abstracts their forms,
>   And draws a kind of quintessence from things;
> Which to her proper nature she transforms,
>   To bear them light on her celestial wings.
>
> Thus does she, when from individual states
>   She doth abstract the universal kinds;
> Which then reclothed in divers names and fates
>   Steal access through our senses to our minds.[7]

Finally, GOOD SENSE is the BODY of poetic genius, FANCY its DRAPERY,[8] MOTION its LIFE, and IMAGINATION the SOUL that is everywhere, and in each; and forms all into one graceful and intelligent whole.

From *Chapter 17*

[EXAMINATION OF THE TENETS PECULIAR TO MR. WORDSWORTH]

As far then as Mr. Wordsworth in his preface contended, and most ably contended, for a reformation in our poetic diction, as far as he has evinced the truth of passion, and the *dramatic* propriety of those figures and metaphors in the original poets which, stripped of their justifying reasons and converted into mere artifices of connection or ornament, constitute the characteristic falsity in the poetic style of the moderns; and as far as he has, with equal acuteness and clearness, pointed out the process by which this change was effected and the resemblances between that state into which the reader's mind is thrown by the pleasurable confusion of thought from an

---

4. Continuous.
5. Driven with loosened reins (Latin).
6. Here Coleridge introduces the concept, which became central to the American New Critics of the mid-20th century, that the best poetry incorporates and reconciles opposite or discordant elements.
7. Adapted from John Davies's *Nosce Teipsum* ("Know Thyself"), a philosophical poem (1599).
8. Clothing.

unaccustomed train of words and images and that state which is induced by the natural language of impassioned feeling, he undertook a useful task and deserves all praise, both for the attempt and for the execution. The provocations to this remonstrance in behalf of truth and nature were still of perpetual recurrence before and after the publication of this preface. * * *

My own differences from certain supposed parts of Mr. Wordsworth's theory ground themselves on the assumption that his words had been rightly interpreted, as purporting that the proper diction for poetry in general consists altogether in a language taken, with due exceptions, from the mouths of men in real life, a language which actually constitutes the natural conversation of men under the influence of natural feelings.[9] My objection is, first, that in *any* sense this rule is applicable only to *certain* classes of poetry; secondly, that even to these classes it is not applicable, except in such a sense as hath never by anyone (as far as I know or have read) been denied or doubted; and, lastly, that as far as, and in that degree in which it is *practicable*, yet as a *rule* it is useless, if not injurious, and therefore either need not or ought not to be practiced. * * *

[RUSTIC LIFE (ABOVE ALL, *LOW* AND RUSTIC LIFE) ESPECIALLY UNFAVORABLE
TO THE FORMATION OF A HUMAN DICTION—THE BEST PARTS OF LANGUAGE
THE PRODUCTS OF PHILOSOPHERS, NOT CLOWNS[1] OR SHEPHERDS]

As little can I agree with the assertion that from the objects with which the rustic hourly communicates the best part of language is formed. For first, if to communicate with an object implies such an acquaintance with it, as renders it capable of being discriminately reflected on; the distinct knowledge of an uneducated rustic would furnish a very scanty vocabulary. The few things, and modes of action, requisite for his bodily conveniences, would alone be individualized; while all the rest of nature would be expressed by a small number of confused general terms. Secondly, I deny that the words and combinations of words derived from the objects, with which the rustic is familiar, whether with distinct or confused knowledge, can be justly said to form the *best* part of language. It is more than probable that many classes of the brute creation possess discriminating sounds, by which they can convey to each other notices of such objects as concern their food, shelter, or safety. Yet we hesitate to call the aggregate of such sounds a language, otherwise than metaphorically. The best part of human language, properly so called, is derived from reflection on the acts of the mind itself. It is formed by a voluntary appropriation of fixed symbols to internal acts, to processes and results of imagination, the greater part of which have no place in the consciousness of uneducated man; though in civilized society, by imitation and passive remembrance of what they hear from their religious instructors and other superiors, the most uneducated share in the harvest which they neither sowed or reaped. * * *

9. Wordsworth's Preface to *Lyrical Ballads* (1800, 1802): "A selection of the real language of men in a state of vivid sensation. . . . Low and rustic life was generally chosen. . . . The language, too, of these men is adopted."
1. Rustic people.

[THE LANGUAGE OF MILTON AS MUCH THE LANGUAGE OF *REAL* LIFE, YEA,
INCOMPARABLY MORE SO THAN THAT OF THE COTTAGER]

Here let me be permitted to remind the reader that the positions which I
controvert are contained in the sentences—"a selection of the REAL language
of men"; "the language of these men (i.e., men in low and rustic life) I propose
to myself to imitate, and as far as possible to adopt the very language of men."
"Between the language of prose and that of metrical composition there neither is, nor can be any essential difference." It is against these exclusively that
my opposition is directed.

I object, in the very first instance, to an equivocation in the use of the word
"real." Every man's language varies according to the extent of his knowledge,
the activity of his faculties, and the depth or quickness of his feelings. Every
man's language has, first, its *individualities;* secondly, the common properties
of the *class* to which he belongs; and thirdly, words and phrases of *universal*
use. The language of Hooker, Bacon, Bishop Taylor, and Burke[2] differs from
the common language of the learned class only by the superior number and
novelty of the thoughts and relations which they had to convey. The language
of Algernon Sidney[3] differs not at all from that which every well-educated
gentleman would wish to write, and (with due allowances for the undeliber-
ateness and less connected train of thinking natural and proper to conversation) such as he would wish to talk. Neither one nor the other differ half
as much from the general language of cultivated society as the language of
Mr. Wordsworth's homeliest composition differs from that of a common peasant. For "real" therefore we must substitute *ordinary,* or *lingua communis.*[4]
And this, we have proved, is no more to be found in the phraseology of low
and rustic life than in that of any other class. Omit the peculiarities of each,
and the result of course must be common to all. And assuredly the omissions
and changes to be made in the language of rustics before it could be transferred to any species of poem, except the drama or other professed imitation,
are at least as numerous and weighty as would be required in adapting to
the same purpose the ordinary language of tradesmen and manufacturers.
Not to mention that the language so highly extolled by Mr. Wordsworth varies in every county, nay, in every village, according to the accidental character
of the clergyman, the existence or nonexistence of schools; or even, perhaps,
as the exciseman, publican, or barber happen to be, or not to be, zealous politicians and readers of the weekly newspaper *pro bono publico.*[5] Anterior to
cultivation the *lingua communis* of every country, as Dante has well observed,
exists every where in parts and no where as a whole.[6]

Neither is the case rendered at all more tenable by the addition of the
words "in a state of excitement."[7] For the nature of a man's words, when he is
strongly affected by joy, grief, or anger, must necessarily depend on the

2. Richard Hooker (1554–1600), author of *The
Laws of Ecclesiastical Polity;* Francis Bacon
(1561–1626), essayist and philosopher, and Jeremy Taylor were all, together with the late-18th-
century politician and opponent of the French
Revolution Edmund Burke (1729–1797), lauded
for their prose styles.
3. Republican soldier and statesman (1622–
1683), author of *Discourses Concerning Government,* executed for his part in the Rye House Plot

to assassinate Charles II.
4. The common language (Latin).
5. For the public welfare (Latin).
6. In *De Vulgari Eloquentia* ("On the Speech of
the people") Dante discusses—and affirms—the
fitness for poetry of the unlocalized Italian
vernacular.
7. Wordsworth: "the manner in which we associate ideas in a state of excitement."

number and quality of the general truths, conceptions, and images, and of the words expressing them, with which his mind had been previously stored. For the property of passion is not to *create*, but to set in increased activity. At least, whatever new connections of thoughts or images, or (which is equally, if not more than equally, the appropriate effect of strong excitement) whatever generalizations of truth or experience the heat of passion may produce, yet the terms of their conveyance must have pre-existed in his former conversations, and are only collected and crowded together by the unusual stimulation. It is indeed very possible to adopt in a poem the unmeaning repetitions, habitual phrases, and other blank counters which an unfurnished or confused understanding interposes at short intervals in order to keep hold of his subject which is still slipping from him, and to give him time for recollection; or in mere aid of vacancy, as in the scanty companies of a country stage the same player pops backwards and forwards, in order to prevent the appearance of empty spaces, in the procession of *Macbeth* or *Henry VIIIth*. But what assistance to the poet or ornament to the poem these can supply, I am at a loss to conjecture. Nothing assuredly can differ either in origin or in mode more widely from the apparent tautologies of intense and turbulent feeling in which the passion is greater and of longer endurance than to be exhausted or satisfied by a single representation of the image or incident exciting it. Such repetitions I admit to be a beauty of the highest kind; as illustrated by Mr. Wordsworth himself from the song of Deborah. "At her feet he bowed, he fell, he lay down; at her feet he bowed, he fell; where he bowed, there he fell down dead."[8]

1815   1817

8. Judges 5.27. Cited by Wordsworth in a note to *The Thorn* as an example of the natural repetitiousness of "impassioned feelings."

GEORGE GORDON, LORD BYRON
1788–1824

In his *History of English Literature*, written in the late 1850s, the French critic Hippolyte Taine gave only a few condescending pages to Wordsworth, Coleridge, Percy Shelley, and Keats and then devoted a long chapter to Lord Byron, "the greatest and most English of these artists; he is so great and so English that from him alone we shall learn more truths of his country and of his age than from all the rest together." This comment reflects the fact that Byron had achieved an immense European reputation during his own lifetime, while admirers of his English contemporaries were much more limited in number. Through much of the nineteenth century he continued to be rated as one of the greatest of English poets and the very prototype of literary Romanticism. His influence was manifested everywhere, among the major poets and novelists (Balzac and Stendhal in France, Pushkin and Dostoyevsky in Russia, and Melville in America), painters (especially Delacroix), and composers (including Beethoven and Berlioz).

Yet even as poets, painters, and composers across Europe and the Americas struck Byronic attitudes, Byron's place within the canon of English Romantic poetry was becoming insecure. The same Victorian critics who first described the Romantic period *as* a literary period warned readers against the immorality of Byron's poetry, finding in his voluptuous imagination and aristocratic disdain for the commonplace an affront to their own, middle-class values: "Close thy Byron; open thy Goethe," Thomas Carlyle urged in *Sartor Resartus* (1834), meaning to redirect the nation toward healthier reading matter. After getting a glimpse of the scandalous stuff recorded in Byron's journals, Felicia Hemans ceased to wear the brooch in which she had preserved a lock of the poet's hair: she could venerate him no longer. Indeed, Byron would have had qualms about being considered a representative figure of a period that also included Wordsworth (memorialized in Byron's *Don Juan* as "Wordy") or Keats (a shabby Cockney brat, Byron claimed) or scribbling women such as Hemans. These reservations were reciprocated. Of Byron's best-known male contemporaries, only Shelley thought highly of either the man or his work (although there are signs that, among the naysayers, the negative reactions were tinged with some resentment at Byron's success in developing a style that spoke to a popular audience). Byron in fact insisted that, measured against the poetic practice of Alexander Pope, he and his contemporaries were "all in the wrong, one as much as another. . . . We are upon a wrong revolutionary poetical system, or systems, not worth a damn in itself." Pope's Horatian satires, along with Laurence Sterne's novel *Tristram Shandy,* exerted a significant influence on the style that Byron developed for his epic survey of modern folly, *Don Juan.*

Still, even as he had recourse to old-fashioned eighteenth-century models, Byron cultivated a skepticism about established systems of belief that, in its restlessness and defiance, expressed the intellectual and social ferment of his era. And through much of his best poetry, he shared his contemporaries' fascination with the internal dramas of the individual mind (although Byron explored personality in an improvisatory and mercurial manner that could not have been more different from Wordsworth's autobiographical accounts of his psychological development). Readers marveled over the intensity of the feelings his verse communicated—"its force, fire, and thought," said the novelist Lady Sydney Morgan—and the vividness of the sense of self they found in it. Byron's chief claim to be considered an arch-Romantic is that he provided the age with what Taine called its "ruling personage; that is, the model that contemporaries invest with their admiration and sympathy." This personage is the "Byronic hero." He is first sketched in the opening canto of *Childe Harold*, then recurs in various guises in the verse romances and dramas that followed. In his developed form, as we find it in *Manfred*, he is an alien, mysterious, and gloomy spirit, superior in his passions and powers to the common run of humanity, whom he regards with disdain. He harbors the torturing memory of an enormous, nameless guilt that drives him toward an inevitable doom. And he exerts an attraction on other characters that is the more compelling because it involves their terror at his obliviousness to ordinary human concerns and values. This figure, infusing the archrebel in a nonpolitical form with a strong erotic interest, was imitated in life as well as in art and helped shape the intellectual and the cultural history of the later nineteenth century. The literary descendants of the Byronic hero include Heathcliff in *Wuthering Heights*, Captain Ahab in *Moby-Dick*, and the hero of Pushkin's great poem *Eugene Onegin*. Byron also lived on in the guise of the Undead, thanks to the success of a novella by his former friend and traveling companion John Polidori, whose "The Vampyre" (1819) mischievously made Byron its model for the title character. Earlier Byron had in his writings helped introduce the English to the Eastern Mediterranean's legends of bloodsucking evil spirits; it was left to Polidori, however, to portray the vampire as a habitué of England's most fashionable social circles. The fact that, for all their menace, vampires—from Bela Lugosi's Count Dracula to Anne Rice's L'Estat—remain models of well-dressed, aristocratic elegance represents yet another tribute to the staying power of Byron's image.

Byron's contemporaries insisted on identifying the author with his fictional characters, reading his writing as veiled autobiography even when it dealt with supernatural themes. (They also read other people's writing this way: to Polidori's chagrin, authorship of "The Vampyre" was attributed to Byron.) Byron's letters and the testimony of his friends show, however, that, except for recurrent moods of deep depression, his own temperament was in many respects opposite to that of his heroes. While he was passionate and willful, he was also a witty conversationalist capable of taking an ironic attitude toward his own activities as well as those of others. But although Byronism was largely a fiction, produced by a collaboration between Byron's imagination and that of his public, the fiction was historically more important than the actual person.

Byron was descended from two aristocratic families, both of them colorful, violent, and dissolute. His grandfather was an admiral nicknamed "Foulweather Jack"; his great-uncle was the fifth Baron Byron, known to his rural neighbors as the "Wicked Lord," who was tried by his peers for killing his kinsman William Chaworth in a drunken duel; his father, Captain John Byron, was a rake and fortune hunter who rapidly spent his way through the fortunes of two wealthy wives. Byron's mother was a Scotswoman, Catherine Gordon of Gight, the last descendant of a line of lawless Scottish lairds. After her husband died (Byron was then three), she brought up her son in near poverty in Aberdeen, where he was indoctrinated with the Calvinistic morality of Scottish Presbyterianism. Catherine Byron was an ill-educated and extremely irascible woman who nevertheless had an abiding love for her son; they fought violently when together, but corresponded affectionately enough when apart, until her death in 1811.

When Byron was ten the death of his great-uncle, preceded by that of more immediate heirs to the title, made him the sixth Lord Byron. In a fashion suitable to his new status, he was sent to Harrow School, then to Trinity College, Cambridge. He had a deformed foot, made worse by inept surgical treatment, about which he felt acute embarrassment. His lameness made him avid for athletic prowess; he played cricket and made himself an expert boxer, fencer, and horseman and a powerful swimmer. Both at Cambridge and at his ancestral estate of Newstead, he engaged with more than ordinary zeal in the expensive pursuits and fashionable dissipations of a young Regency lord. As a result, despite a sizable and increasing income, he got into financial difficulties from which he did not entirely extricate himself until late in his life. In the course of his schooling, he formed many close and devoted friendships, the most important with John Cam Hobhouse, a sturdy political liberal and commonsense moralist who exerted a steadying influence throughout Byron's turbulent life.

Despite his distractions at the university, Byron found time to try his hand at lyric verse, some of which was published in 1807 in a slim and conventional volume titled *Hours of Idleness*. This was treated so harshly by the *Edinburgh Review* that Byron was provoked to write in reply his first important poem, *English Bards and Scotch Reviewers*, a vigorous satire in which he incorporated brilliant ridicule (whose tactlessness he later came to regret) of important contemporaries, including Scott, Wordsworth, Coleridge, and the *Edinburgh* critics.

After attaining his M.A. degree and his legal independence from his guardians, Byron set out with Hobhouse in 1809 on a tour through Portugal and Spain to Malta, and then to little-known Albania, Greece, and Asia Minor. There, in the classic locale for Greek love, he encountered a culture that accepted sexual relations between older aristocratic men and beautiful boys, and he accumulated materials that, sometimes rather slyly, he incorporated into many of his important poems, including his last work, *Don Juan*. The first literary product was *Childe Harold*; he wrote the opening two cantos while on the tour that the poem describes; published them in 1812 soon after his return to England; and, in his own oft-quoted phrase, "awoke one morning and found myself famous." He became the celebrity of fashionable London, and increased his literary success with a series of highly readable

Eastern tales; in these the Byronic hero, represented against various exotic back-drops as a "Giaour" (an "infidel" within Muslim society), or a "Corsair" (a pirate), or in other forms, flaunts his misanthropy and undergoes violent and romantic adventures that current gossip attributed to the author. In his chronic shortage of money, Byron could well have used the huge income from these publications, but instead maintained his status as an aristocratic amateur by giving the royalties away. Occupying his inherited seat in the House of Lords, he also became briefly active on the liberal side of the Whig party and spoke courageously in defense of the Nottingham weavers who had resorted to smashing the newly invented textile machines that had thrown them out of work. He also supported other liberal measures, including that of Catholic Emancipation.

Byron was extraordinarily handsome—"so beautiful a countenance," Coleridge wrote, "I scarcely ever saw . . . his eyes the open portals of the sun—things of light, and for light." Because of a constitutional tendency to obesity, however, he was able to maintain his looks only by resorting again and again to a starvation diet of biscuits, soda water, and strong purgatives. Often as a result of female initiative rather than his own, Byron entered into a sequence of liaisons with ladies of fashion. One of these, the flamboyant and eccentric young Lady Caroline Lamb, caused him so much distress by her pursuit that Byron turned for relief to marriage with Annabella Milbanke, who was in every way Lady Caroline's opposite, for she was unworldly and intellectual (with a special passion for mathematics) and naively believed that she could reform her husband. This ill-starred marriage produced a daughter (Augusta Ada) and many scenes in which Byron, goaded by financial difficulties, behaved so frantically that his wife suspected his sanity; after only one year the union ended in a legal separation. The final blow came when Lady Byron discovered her husband's incestuous relations with his half-sister, Augusta Leigh. The two had been raised apart, so that they were almost strangers when they met as adults. Byron's affection for his sister, however guilty, was genuine and endured all through his life. This affair, enhanced by rumors about Byron's earlier liaisons with men, proved a delicious morsel even to the jaded palate of a public that was used to eating up stories of aristocratic vice. Byron was ostracized by all but a few friends and was finally forced to leave England forever on April 25, 1816.

Byron now resumed the travels incorporated in the third and fourth cantos of *Childe Harold*. At Geneva he lived for several months in close and intellectually fruitful relation to Percy and Mary Shelley, who were accompanied by Mary's step-sister, Claire Clairmont—a misguided seventeen-year-old who had had an affair with Byron while he was still in England and who in January 1817 bore him a daughter, Allegra. In the fall of 1817, Byron established himself in Venice, where he began a year and a half of debauchery that, he estimated, involved liaisons with more than two hundred women. This period, however, was also one of great literary creativity. Often working through the night, he finished his tragedy *Manfred*; wrote the fourth canto of *Childe Harold*; and then, feeling more and more trapped by the poetic modes that had won him his popularity, tested out an entirely new mode in *Beppo: A Venetian Story*, a comic verse tale about a deceived husband in which he previewed the playful narrative manner and the ottava rima stanzas of *Don Juan*. In December 1818 he began the composition of *Don Juan*.

Exhausted and bored by promiscuity, Byron in 1819 settled into a placid and relatively faithful relationship with Teresa Guiccioli, the young wife of the elderly Count Alessandro Guiccioli; according to the Italian upper-class mores of the times, having contracted a marriage of convenience, she could now with some propriety take Byron as her lover. Through the countess's nationalistic family, the Gambas, Byron became involved with a group of political conspirators seeking to end the Austrian Empire's control over northern Italy. When the Gambas were forced by the authorities to move to Pisa, Byron followed them there and, for the second time, joined the Shelleys. There grew up about them the "Pisan Circle," which in addition to the Gambas included their friends Thomas Medwin and Edward and Jane Williams, as well as the Greek nationalist leader Prince Mavrocordatos, the picturesque Irish Count Taaffe, and the adventurer Edward Trelawny, a great teller of tall tales who seems to have stepped out of one of Byron's romances. Leigh Hunt, the journalist and essayist, joined them, drawing Byron and Percy Shelley into his plan to make Italy the base for a radical political journal, *The Liberal*. This circle was gradually broken up, however, first by the Shelleys' anger over Byron's treatment of his daughter Allegra (Byron had sent the child to be brought up as a Catholic in an Italian convent, where she died of a fever in 1822); then by the expulsion of the Gambas, whom Byron followed to Genoa; and finally by the drowning of Percy Shelley and Edward Williams in July 1822.

Byron meanwhile had been steadily at work on a series of closet tragedies (including *Cain, Sardanapalus*, and *Marino Faliero*) and on his devastating satire on the life and death of George III, *The Vision of Judgment*. But increasingly he devoted himself to the continuation of *Don Juan*. He had always been diffident in his self-judgments and easily swayed by literary advice. But now, confident that he had at last found his true gifts as a poet, he kept on, in spite or persistent objections against the supposed immorality of the poem by the English public, by his publisher John Murray, by his friends and well-wishers, and by his extremely decorous lover, the Countess Guiccioli—by almost everyone, in fact, except the idealist Shelley, who thought *Juan* incomparably better than anything he himself could write and insisted "that every word of it is pregnant with immortality."

Byron finally broke off literature for action when he organized an expedition to assist in the Greek war for independence from the Ottoman Empire. He knew too well the conditions in Greece, and had too skeptical an estimate of human nature, to entertain hope of success; but, in part because his own writings had helped kindle European enthusiasm for the Greek cause, he now felt honor-bound to try what could be done. In the dismal, marshy town of Missolonghi, he lived a Spartan existence, training troops whom he had subsidized and exhibiting practical grasp and a power of leadership amid a chaos of factionalism, intrigue, and military ineptitude. Worn out, he succumbed to a series of feverish attacks and died just after he had reached his thirty-sixth birthday. To this day Byron is revered by the Greek people as a national hero.

Students of Byron still feel, as his friends had felt, the magnetism of his volatile temperament. As Mary Shelley wrote six years after his death, when she read Thomas Moore's edition of his *Letters and Journals*: "The Lord Byron I find there is our Lord Byron—the fascinating—faulty—childish—philosophical being—daring the world—docile to a private circle—impetuous and indolent—gloomy and yet more gay than any other." Of his contradictions Byron was well aware; he told his friend Lady Blessington: "I am so changeable, being everything by turns and nothing long—I am such a strange *mélange* of good and evil, that it would be difficult to describe me." Yet he remained faithful to his code: a determination to tell the truth as he saw it about the world and about himself (his refusal to suppress or conceal any of his moods is in part what made him seem so contradictory) and a dedication to the freedom of nations and individuals. As he went on to say to Lady Blessington: "There are but two sentiments to which I am constant—a strong love of liberty, and a detestation of cant."

The poetry texts printed here are taken from the *Byron's Poetry and Prose: A Norton Critical Edition*, edited by Alice Levine.

Written after Swimming from Sestos to Abydos[1]

May 9, 1810

1

If, in the month of dark December,
   Leander, who was nightly wont
(What maid will not the tale remember?)
   To cross thy stream, broad Hellespont!

2

5 If, when the wintry tempest roar'd,
   He sped to Hero, nothing loth,
And thus of old thy current pour'd,
   Fair Venus! how I pity both!

3

For *me*, degenerate modern wretch,
10   Though in the genial month of May,
My dripping limbs I faintly stretch,
   And think I've done a feat to-day.

4

But since he cross'd the rapid tide,
   According to the doubtful story,
15 To woo,—and—Lord knows what beside,
   And swam for Love, as I for Glory;

5

'Twere hard to say who fared the best:
   Sad mortals! thus the Gods still plague you!
He lost his labour, I my jest:
20   For he was drown'd, and I've the ague.

1810   1812

1. The Hellespont (now called the Dardanelles) is the narrow strait between Europe and Asia. In the ancient story, retold in Christopher Marlowe's *Hero and Leander*, young Leander of Abydos, on the Asian side, swam nightly to visit Hero, a priestess of the goddess Venus at Sestos, until he was drowned when he made the attempt in a storm. Byron and a young Lieutenant Ekenhead swam the Hellespont in the reverse direction on May 3, 1810. Byron alternated between complacency and humor in his many references to the event. In a note to the poem, he mentions that the distance was "upwards of four English miles, though the actual breadth is barely one. The rapidity of the current is such that no boat can row directly across. . . . The water was extremely cold, from the melting of the mountain snows."

She Walks in Beauty[1]

1

She walks in beauty, like the night
  Of cloudless climes and starry skies;
And all that's best of dark and bright
  Meet in her aspect and her eyes:
5 Thus mellow'd to that tender light
  Which heaven to gaudy day denies.

2

One shade the more, one ray the less,
  Had half impair'd the nameless grace
Which waves in every raven tress,
10 Or softly lightens o'er her face;
Where thoughts serenely sweet express
  How pure, how dear their dwelling-place.

3

And on that cheek, and o'er that brow,
  So soft, so calm, yet eloquent,
15 The smiles that win, the tints that glow,
  But tell of days in goodness spent,
A mind at peace with all below,
  A heart whose love is innocent!

June 1814   1815

Stanzas for Music

"Felix qui potuit rerum cognoscere causas."[1]
Virgil.

1

They say that Hope is happiness—
  But genuine Love must prize the past,
And Memory wakes the thoughts that bless:
  They rose the first—they set the last.

---

1. From *Hebrew Melodies* (1815), a collection of lyrics on Old Testament themes that Byron composed to accompany the musician Isaac Nathan's settings of traditional synagogue chants. Byron wrote these lines about his beautiful cousin by marriage, Anne Wilmot, who at the ball where they first met wore a black mourning gown brightened with spangles. In their context as the opening poem of *Hebrew Melodies*, the lines praise any one of a number of Old Testament heroines. Happy is he who has been able to learn the causes of things (Latin; Georgics 2.490).

1. Happy is he who has been able to learn the causes of things (Latin; Georgics 2.490).

2

5 And all that Memory loves the most
　　Was once our only Hope to be,
And all that Hope adored and lost
　　Hath melted into Memory.

3

10 Alas! it is delusion all—
　　The future cheats us from afar:
Nor can we be what we recall.
　　Nor dare we think on what we are.

When We Two Parted

1

When we two parted
　　In silence and tears,
Half broken-hearted
　　To sever for years,
5 Pale grew thy cheek and cold,
　　Colder thy kiss;
Truly that hour foretold
　　Sorrow to this.

2

The dew of the morning
10 　　Sunk chill on my brow—
It felt like the warning
　　Of what I feel now.
Thy vows are all broken,
　　And light is thy fame;
15 I hear thy name spoken,
　　And share in its shame.

3

They name thee before me,
　　A knell to mine ear;
A shudder comes o'er me—
20 　　Why wert thou so dear?
They know not I knew thee,
　　Who knew thee too well:—
Long, long shall I rue thee,
　　Too deeply to tell.

4

25   In secret we met—
      In silence I grieve,
  That thy heart could forget,
      Thy spirit deceive.
  If I should meet thee
30   After long years,
  How should I greet thee?—
     With silence and tears.

Darkness[1]

I had a dream, which was not all a dream.
The bright sun was extinguish'd, and the stars
Did wander darkling° in the eternal space,   *in the dark*
Rayless, and pathless, and the icy earth
5 Swung blind and blackening in the moonless air;
Morn came and went—and came, and brought no day,
And men forgot their passions in the dread
Of this their desolation; and all hearts
Were chill'd into a selfish prayer for light:
10 And they did live by watchfires—and the thrones,
The palaces of crowned kings—the huts,
The habitations of all things which dwell,
Were burnt for beacons; cities were consumed,
And men were gather'd round their blazing homes
15 To look once more into each other's face;
Happy were those who dwelt within the eye
Of the volcanos, and their mountain-torch:
A fearful hope was all the world contain'd;
Forests were set on fire—but hour by hour
20 They fell and faded—and the crackling trunks
Extinguish'd with a crash—and all was black.
The brows of men by the despairing light
Wore an unearthly aspect, as by fits
The flashes fell upon them; some lay down
And hid their eyes and wept; and some did rest
25 Their chins upon their clenched hands, and smiled;
And others hurried to and fro, and fed
Their funeral piles with fuel, and look'd up
With mad disquietude on the dull sky,
The pall of a past world; and then again
30 With curses cast them down upon the dust,
And gnash'd their teeth and howl'd: the wild birds shriek'd,
And, terrified, did flutter on the ground,

1. A powerful blank-verse description of the end of life on earth. New geological sciences and an accompanying interest in what the fossil record indicated about the extinction of species made such speculations hardly less common in Byron's time than in ours. Mary Shelley would later take up the theme in her novel *The Last Man* (1826).

And flap their useless wings; the wildest brutes
35 Came tame and tremulous; and vipers crawl'd
And twined themselves among the multitude,
Hissing, but stingless—they were slain for food:
And War, which for a moment was no more,
Did glut himself again;—a meal was bought
40 With blood, and each sate sullenly apart
Gorging himself in gloom: no love was left;
All earth was but one thought—and that was death,
Immediate and inglorious; and the pang
Of famine fed upon all entrails—men
45 Died, and their bones were tombless as their flesh;
The meagre by the meagre were devour'd,
Even dogs assail'd their masters, all save one,
And he was faithful to a corse, and kept
The birds and beasts and famish'd men at bay,
50 Till hunger clung° them, or the dropping dead   *withered*
Lured their lank jaws; himself sought out no food,
But with a piteous and perpetual moan,
And a quick desolate cry, licking the hand
Which answer'd not with a caress—he died.
55 The crowd was famish'd by degrees; but two
Of an enormous city did survive,
And they were enemies; they met beside
The dying embers of an altar-place
Where had been heap'd a mass of holy things
60 For an unholy usage; they raked up,
And shivering scraped with their cold skeleton hands
The feeble ashes, and their feeble breath
Blew for a little life, and made a flame
Which was a mockery; then they lifted up
65 Their eyes as it grew lighter, and beheld
Each other's aspects—saw, and shriek'd, and died—
Even of their mutual hideousness they died,
Unknowing who he was upon whose brow
Famine had written Fiend. The world was void,
70 The populous and the powerful—was a lump,
Seasonless, herbless,° treeless, manless, lifeless—   *without vegetation*
A lump of death—a chaos of hard clay.
The rivers, lakes, and ocean all stood still,
And nothing stirr'd within their silent depths;
75 Ships sailorless lay rotting on the sea,
And their masts fell down piecemeal; as they dropp'd
They slept on the abyss without a surge—
The waves were dead; the tides were in their grave,
The moon, their mistress, had expired before;
80 The winds were wither'd in the stagnant air,
And the clouds perish'd; Darkness had no need
Of aid from them—She was the Universe.

Diodati, July, 1816

1816   1816

So we'll go no more a roving[1]

So we'll go no more a roving
　　So late into the night,
Though the heart be still as loving,
　　And the moon be still as bright.

5　For the sword outwears its sheath,
　　And the soul wears out the breast,
And the heart must pause to breathe,
　　And Love itself have rest.

Though the night was made for loving,
10　　And the day returns too soon,
Yet we'll go no more a roving
　　By the light of the moon.

1817   1830

From Childe Harold's Pilgrimage: A Romaunt[1]

From Canto the First

["SIN'S LONG LABYRINTH"]

1

Oh, thou! in Hellas° deem'd of heavenly birth,　　　　　*Greece*
Muse! form'd or fabled at the minstrel's will!
Since shamed full oft by later lyres on earth,
Mine dares not call thee from thy sacred hill:
5　Yet there I've wander'd by thy vaunted rill;
Yes! sigh'd o'er Delphi's long-deserted shrine,
Where, save that feeble fountain, all is still;
Nor mote° my shell awake the weary Nine[2]　　　　　　*may*
To grace so plain a tale—this lowly lay° of mine.　　　　*song*

2

10　Whilome[3] in Albion's° isle there dwelt a youth,　　　*England's*
Who ne in virtue's ways did take delight;
But spent his days in riot most uncouth,
And vex'd with mirth the drowsy ear of Night.
Ah, me! in sooth he was a shameless wight,°　　　　　　*creature*
15　Sore given to revel and ungodly glee;

1. Composed in the Lenten aftermath of a period of late-night carousing during the Carnival season in Venice, and included in a letter to Thomas Moore, February 28, 1817. Byron wrote, "I find 'the sword wearing out the scabbard,' though I have but just turned the corner of twenty-nine." The poem is based on the refrain of a bawdy Scottish song, "The Jolly Beggar": "And we'll gang nae mair a roving / Sae late into the nicht."
1. A romance or narrative of adventure.
2. The Muses, whose "vaunted rill" (line 5) was the Castalian spring. "Shell": lyre. Hermes is fabled to have invented the lyre by stretching strings over the hollow of a tortoise shell.
3. Once upon a time; one of the many archaisms that Byron borrowed from Spenser.

Few earthly things found favour in his sight
Save concubines and carnal companie,
And flaunting wassailers⁴ of high and low degree.

3

Childe Harold was he hight:°—but whence his name   *called*
20   And lineage long, it suits me not to say;
Suffice it, that perchance they were of fame,
And had been glorious in another day:
But one sad losel⁵ soils a name for aye,
However mighty in the olden time;
25   Nor all that heralds rake from coffin'd clay,
Nor florid prose, nor honied lies of rhyme,
Can blazon evil deeds, or consecrate a crime.

4

Childe Harold bask'd him in the noontide sun,
Disporting there like any other fly;
30   Nor deem'd before his little day was done
One blast might chill him into misery.
But long ere scarce a third of his pass'd by,
Worse than adversity the Childe befell;
He felt the fulness of satiety:
35   Then loathed he in his native land to dwell,
Which seem'd to him more lone than Eremite's⁶ sad cell.

5

For he through Sin's long labyrinth had run,
Nor made atonement when he did amiss,
Had sigh'd to many though he loved but one,
40   And that loved one, alas! could ne'er be his.
Ah, happy she! to 'scape from him whose kiss
Had been pollution unto aught so chaste;
Who soon had left her charms for vulgar bliss,
And spoil'd her goodly lands to gild his waste,
45   Nor calm domestic peace had ever deign'd to taste.

6

And now Childe Harold was sore sick at heart,
And from his fellow bacchanals⁷ would flee;
'Tis said, at times the sullen tear would start,
But Pride congeal'd the drop within his ee:°   *eye*
50   Apart he stalk'd in joyless reverie,
And from his native land resolved to go,

---

4. Noisy, insolent drinkers (Byron is thought to refer to his own youthful carousing with friends at Newstead Abbey).
5. Rascal. Byron's great-uncle, the fifth Lord Byron, had killed a kinsman in a drunken duel.
6. A religious hermit.
7. Worshipers of Bacchus, ancient Roman god of wine and revelry.

And visit scorching climes beyond the sea;
With pleasure drugg'd, he almost long'd for woe,
And e'en for change of scene would seek the shades below.

From *Canto the Third*

["ONCE MORE UPON THE WATERS"]

1

Is thy face like thy mothers, my fair child!
ADA![1] sole daughter of my house and heart?
When last I saw thy young blue eyes they smiled,
And when we parted,—not as now we part,
5   But with a hope.—
             Awaking with a start,
The waters heave around me; and on high
The winds lift up their voices: I depart,
Whither I know not; but the hour's gone by,
When Albion's lessening shores could grieve or glad mine eye.

2

10   Once more upon the waters! yet once more!
And the waves bound beneath me as a steed
That knows his rider. Welcome, to their roar!
Swift be their guidance, wheresoe'er it lead!
Though the strain'd mast should quiver as a reed,
15   And the rent canvass fluttering strew the gale,
Still must I on; for I am as a weed,
Flung from the rock, on Ocean's foam, to sail
Where'er the surge may sweep, or tempest's breath prevail.

3

In my youth's summer[2] I did sing of One,
20   The wandering outlaw of his own dark mind;
Again I seize the theme, then but begun,
And bear it with me, as the rushing wind
Bears the cloud onwards: in that Tale I find
The furrows of long thought, and dried-up tears,
25   Which, ebbing, leave a sterile track behind,
O'er which all heavily the journeying years
Plod the last sands of life,—where not a flower appears.

4

Since my young days of passion—joy, or pain,
Perchance my heart and harp have lost a string,

---

1. Byron's daughter Augusta Ada, born in December 1815, a month before her parents separated. Byron's "hope" (line 5) had been for a reconciliation, but he was never to see Ada again.
2. Byron wrote canto 1 at age twenty-one; he is now twenty-eight.

30 And both may jar:[3] it may be, that in vain
I would essay as I have sung to sing.
Yet, though a dreary strain, to this I cling;
So that it wean me from the weary dream
Of selfish grief or gladness—so it fling
35 Forgetfulness around me—it shall seem
To me, though to none else, a not ungrateful theme.

5

He, who grown aged in this world of woe,
In deeds, not years, piercing the depths of life,
So that no wonder waits him; nor below
40 Can love, or sorrow, fame, ambition, strife,
Cut to his heart again with the keen knife
Of silent, sharp endurance: he can tell
Why thought seeks refuge in lone caves, yet rife
With airy images, and shapes which dwell
45 Still unimpair'd, though old, in the soul's haunted cell.

6

'Tis to create, and in creating live
A being more intense, that we endow
With form our fancy, gaining as we give
The life we image, even as I do now.
50 What am I? Nothing: but not so art thou,
Soul of my thought![4] with whom I traverse earth,
Invisible but gazing, as I glow
Mix'd with thy spirit, blended with thy birth,
And feeling still with thee in my crush'd feelings' dearth.

7

55 Yet must I think less wildly:—I *have* thought
Too long and darkly, till my brain became,
In its own eddy boiling and o'erwrought,
A whirling gulf of phantasy and flame:
And thus, untaught in youth my heart to tame,
60 My springs of life were poison'd. 'Tis too late!
Yet am I changed; though still enough the same
In strength to bear what time can not abate,
And feed on bitter fruits without accusing Fate.

8

Something too much of this:—but now 'tis past,
65 And the spell closes with its silent seal.[5]
Long absent HAROLD re-appears at last;

3. Sound discordant.
4. I.e., Childe Harold, his literary creation.

5. I.e., he sets the seal of silence on his personal
tale ("spell").

He of the breast which fain no more would feel,
Wrung with the wounds which kill not, but ne'er heal;
Yet Time, who changes all, had alter'd him
70   In soul and aspect as in age: years steal
Fire from the mind as vigour from the limb;
And life's enchanted cup but sparkles near the brim.

9

His had been quaff'd too quickly, and he found
The dregs were wormwood; but he fill'd again,
75   And from a purer fount, on holier ground,
And deem'd its spring perpetual; but in vain!
Still round him clung invisibly a chain
Which gall'd for ever, fettering though unseen,
And heavy though it clank'd not; worn with pain,
80   Which pined although it spoke not, and grew keen,
Entering with every step he took through many a scene.

10

Secure in guarded coldness, he had mix'd
Again in fancied safety with his kind,
And deem'd his spirit now so firmly fix'd
85   And sheathed with an invulnerable mind,
That, if no joy, no sorrow lurk'd behind;
And he, as one, might 'midst the many stand
Unheeded, searching through the crowd to find
Fit speculation; such as in strange land
90 He found in wonder-works of God and Nature's hand.

11

But who can view the ripen'd rose, nor seek
To wear it? who can curiously behold
The smoothness and the sheen of beauty's cheek,
Nor feel the heart can never all grow old?
95   Who can contemplate Fame through clouds unfold
The star which rises o'er her steep, nor climb?
Harold, once more within the vortex, roll'd
On with the giddy circle, chasing Time,
Yet with a nobler aim than in his youth's fond° prime.   *foolish*

12

100   But soon he knew himself the most unfit
Of men to herd with Man; with whom he held
Little in common; untaught to submit
His thoughts to others, though his soul was quell'd
In youth by his own thoughts; still uncompell'd,
105   He would not yield dominion of his mind
To spirits against whom his own rebell'd;

Proud though in desolation; which could find
A life within itself, to breathe without mankind.

13

Where rose the mountains, there to him were friends;
110 Where roll'd the ocean, thereon was his home;
Where a blue sky, and glowing clime, extends,
He had the passion and the power to roam;
The desert, forest, cavern, breaker's foam,
Were unto him companionship; they spake
105 A mutual language, clearer than the tome°   *book*
Of his land's tongue, which he would oft forsake,
For Nature's pages glass'd° by sunbeams on the lake.   *made glassy*

14

Like the Chaldean,[6] he could watch the stars,
Till he had peopled them with beings bright
120 As their own beams; and earth, and earth-born jars,
And human frailties, were forgotten quite:
Could he have kept his spirit to that flight
He had been happy; but this clay will sink
Its spark immortal, envying it the light
125 To which it mounts, as if to break the link
That keeps us from yon heaven which woos us to its brink.

15

But in Man's dwellings he became a thing
Restless and worn, and stern and wearisome,
Droop'd as a wild-born falcon with clipt wing,
130 To whom the boundless air alone were home:
Then came his fit again, which to o'ercome,
As eagerly the barr'd-up bird will beat
His breast and beak against his wiry dome
Till the blood tinge his plumage, so the heat
135 Of his impeded soul would through his bosom eat.

16

Self-exiled Harold wanders forth again,
With nought of hope left, but with less of gloom;
The very knowledge that he lived in vain,
That all was over on this side the tomb,
140 Had made Despair a smilingness assume,
Which, though 'twere wild,—as on the plunder'd wreck
When mariners would madly meet their doom
With draughts intemperate on the sinking deck,—
Did yet inspire a cheer, which he forebore to check.

6. A people of ancient Babylonia, expert in astronomy.

[WATERLOO]

17

145 Stop!—for thy tread is on an Empire's dust!
An Earthquake's spoil is sepulchred below!
Is the spot mark'd with no colossal bust?
Nor column trophied for triumphal show?[7]
None; but the moral's truth tells simpler so,
150 As the ground was before, thus let it be;—
How that red rain hath made the harvest grow!
And is this all the world has gain'd by thee,
Thou first and last of fields! king-making Victory?

18

And Harold stands upon this place of skulls,
155 The grave of France, the deadly Waterloo;[8]
How in an hour the power which gave annuls
Its gifts, transferring fame as fleeting too!
In "pride of place" here last the eagle flew,[9]
Then tore with bloody talon the rent plain,
160 Pierced by the shaft of banded nations[1] through;
Ambitions life and labours all were vain;
He wears the shatter'd links of the world's broken chain.[2]

19

Fit retribution! Gaul[3] may champ the bit
And foam in fetters;—but is Earth more free?
165 Did nations combat to make One submit;
Or league to teach all kings true sovereignty?
What! shall reviving Thraldom again be
The patch'd-up idol of enlighten'd days?
Shall we, who struck the Lion down, shall we
170 Pay the Wolf homage? proffering lowly gaze
And servile knees to thrones? No; prove[4] before ye praise!

20

If not, o'er one fallen despot boast no more!
In vain fair cheeks were furrow'd with hot tears
For Europe's flowers long rooted up before
175 The trampler of her vineyards; in vain years

---

7. Referring to the triumphal arches erected in ancient Rome to honor conquering generals, a custom Napoleon had revived.
8. Napoleon's defeat at Waterloo, near Brussels, had occurred only the year before, on June 18, 1815. The battlefield, where almost fifty thousand English, Prussian, and French soldiers were killed in a single day, quickly became a gruesome tourist attraction. See "Romantic Literature and Wartime" in the supplemental ebook.
9. "Pride of place," is a term of falconry, and

means the highest pitch of flight [Byron's note, which continues by referring to the use of the term in Shakespeare's Macbeth 2.4]. The eagle was the symbol of Napoleon.
1. The Grand Alliance formed in opposition to Napoleon.
2. Napoleon was then a prisoner at St. Helena.
3. France. Byron, like other liberals, saw the defeat of the Napoleonic tyranny as a victory for tyrannical kings and the forces of reaction throughout Europe.
4. Await the test (proof) of experience.

Of death, depopulation, bondage, fears,
Have all been borne, and broken by the accord
Of roused-up millions: all that most endears
Glory, is when the myrtle wreathes a sword
180   Such as Harmodius drew on Athens' tyrant lord.[5]

* * *

1812, 1816

Don Juan   Byron began his masterpiece (pronounced in the English fashion, *Don Joó-un*) in July 1818, published it in installments beginning with cantos 1 and 2 in 1819, and continued working on it almost until his death. Initially he improvised the poem from episode to episode. "I *have* no plan," he said, "I *had* no plan; but I had or have materials." The work was composed with remarkable speed (the 888 lines of canto 13, for example, were dashed off within a week), and it aims at the effect of improvisation rather than of artful compression; it asks to be read rapidly, at a conversational pace.

The poem breaks off with the sixteenth canto, but even in its unfinished state *Don Juan* is the longest satirical poem, and indeed one of the longest poems of any kind, in English. Its hero, the Spanish libertine, had in the original legend been superhuman in his sexual energy and wickedness. Throughout Byron's version the unspoken but persistent joke is that this archetypal lady-killer of European legend is in fact more acted upon than active. Unfailingly amiable and well intentioned, he is guilty largely of youth, charm, and a courteous and compliant spirit. The women do all the rest.

The chief models for the poem were the Italian seriocomic versions of medieval chivalric romances; the genre had been introduced by Pulci in the fifteenth century and was adopted by Ariosto in his *Orlando Furioso* (1532). From these writers Byron caught the mixed moods and violent oscillations between the sublime and the ridiculous as well as the colloquial management of the complex ottava rima—an eight-line stanza in which the initial interlaced rhymes (*ababab*) build up to the comic turn in the final couplet (*cc*). Byron was influenced in the English use of this Italian form by a mildly amusing poem published in 1817, under the pseudonym of "Whistle-craft," by his friend John Hookham Frere. Other recognizable antecedents of *Don Juan* are Jonathan Swift's *Gulliver's Travels* and Samuel Johnson's *Rasselas*, both of which had employed the naive traveler as a satiric device, and Laurence Sterne's novel *Tristram Shandy*, with its comic exploitation of a narrative medium blatantly subject to the whimsy of the author. But even the most original literary works play variations on inherited conventions. Shelley at once recognized his friend's poem as "something wholly new and relative to the age."

Byron's literary advisers thought the poem unacceptably immoral, and John Murray took the precaution of printing the first two installments (cantos 1–2, then 3–5) without identifying Byron as the author or himself as the publisher. The eleven completed cantos that followed were, because of Murray's continuing jitters, brought out in 1823–24 by the radical publisher John Hunt. In those cantos Byron's purpose deepened. He set out to create a comic yet devastatingly critical history of the Europe of his own age, sending the impressionable Juan from West to East and back again, from his native Spain to a Russian court (by way of a primitive Greek island and the 1790 siege of the Turkish town of Ismail) and then into the English gentry's country manors. These journeys, which facilitated Byron's satire on almost all existing forms of political organization, would, according to the scheme that he projected for the

---

5. In 514 B.C.E. Harmodius and Aristogeiton, hiding their daggers in myrtle (symbol of love), killed Hipparchus, tyrant of Athens.

poem as a whole, ultimately have taken Juan to a death by guillotining in Revolution-ary France.

Yet the controlling element of *Don Juan* is not the narrative but the narrator. His running commentary on Juan's misadventures, his reminiscences, and his opinion-ated remarks on the epoch of political reaction in which he is actually telling Juan's story together add another level to the poem's engagement with history. The narra-tor's reflections also at the same time lend unity to *Don Juan*'s effervescent variety. Tellingly, the poem opens with the first-person pronoun and immediately lets us into the storyteller's predicament: "I want a hero. . . ." The voice then goes on, for almost two thousand stanzas, with effortless volubility and shifts of mood. The poet who in his brilliant successful youth created the gloomy Byronic hero, in his later and sadder life created a character (not the hero, but the narrator of *Don Juan*) who is one of the great comic inventions in English literature.

FROM DON JUAN

Fragment[1]

On the back of the Poet's MS. of Canto I

I would to heaven that I were so much clay,
    As I am blood, bone, marrow, passion, feeling—
Because at least the past were pass'd away—
    And for the future—(but I write this reeling,
Having got drunk exceedingly to-day,
    So that I seem to stand upon the ceiling)
I say—the future is a serious matter—
And so—for God's sake—hock[2] and soda-water!

From Canto the First

[JUAN AND DONNA JULIA]

1

I want a hero: an uncommon want,
    When every year and month sends forth a new one,
Till, after cloying the gazettes with cant,
    The age discovers he is not the true one;
5   Of such as these I should not care to vaunt,
    I'll therefore take our ancient friend Don Juan—
We all have seen him, in the pantomime,[1]
Sent to the devil somewhat ere his time.

* * *

---

1. This stanza was written on the back of a page of the manuscript of canto 1. For the author's revi-sions while composing two stanzas of *Don Juan*, see "Poems in Process" in the supplemental ebook.

2. A white Rhine wine, from the German *Hoch-heimer*.
1. The Juan of legend was a popular subject in English pantomime.

5

Brave men were living before Agamemnon[2]
   And since, exceeding valorous and sage,
35 A good deal like him too, though quite the same none;
   But then they shone not on the poet's page,
And so have been forgotten:—I condemn none,
   But can't find any in the present age
Fit for my poem (that is, for my new one);
40 So, as I said, I'll take my friend Don Juan.

6

Most epic poets plunge "in medias res"[3]
   (Horace makes this the heroic turnpike road),[4]
And then your hero tells, whene'er you please,
   What went before—by way of episode,
45 While seated after dinner at his ease,
   Beside his mistress in some soft abode,
Palace, or garden, paradise, or cavern,
Which serves the happy couple for a tavern.

7

That is the usual method, but not mine—
50   My way is to begin with the beginning;
The regularity of my design
   Forbids all wandering as the worst of sinning,
And therefore I shall open with a line
   (Although it cost me half an hour in spinning)
55 Narrating somewhat of Don Juan's father,
And also of his mother, if you'd rather.

8

In Seville was he born, a pleasant city,
   Famous for oranges and women—he
Who has not seen it will be much to pity,
60   So says the proverb—and I quite agree;
Of all the Spanish towns is none more pretty,
   Cadiz perhaps—but that you soon may see:—
Don Juan's parents lived beside the river,
A noble stream, and call'd the Guadalquivir.

9

65 His father's name was Jóse[5]—*Don*, of course,
   A true Hidalgo,° free from every stain   *nobleman*

2. In Homer's *Iliad* the king commanding the Greeks in the siege of Troy. This line is translated from a Latin ode by Horace.
3. Into the middle of things (Latin; Horace's *Art of Poetry* 148).
4. I.e., the smoothest road for heroic poetry.
5. Normally "José"; Byron transferred the accent to keep his meter.

Of Moor or Hebrew blood, he traced his source
   Through the most Gothic gentlemen of Spain;
A better cavalier ne'er mounted horse,
70   Or, being mounted, e'er got down again,
Than Jóse, who begot our hero, who
Begot—but that's to come—Well, to renew:

10

His mother was a learned lady, famed
   For every branch of every science known—
75 In every Christian language ever named,
   With virtues equall'd by her wit alone,
She made the cleverest people quite ashamed,
   And even the good with inward envy groan,
Finding themselves so very much exceeded
80 In their own way by all the things that she did.

11

Her memory was a mine: she knew by heart
   All Calderon and greater part of Lopé,[6]
So that if any actor miss'd his part
   She could have served him for the prompter's copy;
85 For her Feinagle's[7] were an useless art,
   And he himself obliged to shut up shop—he
Could never make a memory so fine as
That which adorn'd the brain of Donna Inez.

12

Her favourite science was the mathematical,
90   Her noblest virtue was her magnanimity,
Her wit (she sometimes tried at wit) was Attic[8] all,
   Her serious sayings darken'd to sublimity;
In short, in all things she was fairly what I call
   A prodigy—her morning dress was dimity,°   *cotton*
95 Her evening silk, or, in the summer, muslin,
And other stuffs, with which I won't stay puzzling.

13

She knew the Latin—that is, "the Lord's prayer,"
   And Greek—the alphabet—I'm nearly sure;
She read some French romances here and there,
100   Although her mode of speaking was not pure;
For native Spanish she had no great care,
   At least her conversation was obscure;

6. Calderón de la Barca and Lope de Vega, the great Spanish dramatists of the early 17th century.
7. Gregor von Feinagle, a German expert on the art of memory who had lectured in England in 1811.
8. Athenian. *Attic salt* is a term for the famed wit of the Athenians.

Her thoughts were theorems, her words a problem,
As if she deem'd that mystery would ennoble 'em.

* * *

22

'Tis pity learned virgins ever wed
170   With persons of no sort of education,
Or gentlemen, who, though well born and bred,
    Grow tired of scientific conversation:
I don't choose to say much upon this head,
    I'm a plain man, and in a single station,
175 But—Oh! ye lords of ladies intellectual,
Inform us truly, have they not hen-peck'd you all?

23

Don Jóse and his lady quarrell'd—*why*,
    Not any of the many could divine,
Though several thousand people chose to try,
180   'Twas surely no concern of theirs nor mine;
I loathe that low vice—curiosity;
    But if there's any thing in which I shine,
'Tis in arranging all my friends' affairs,
Not having, of my own, domestic cares.

24

185 And so I interfered, and with the best
    Intentions, but their treatment was not kind;
I think the foolish people were possess'd,
    For neither of them could I ever find,
Although their porter afterwards confess'd—
190   But that's no matter, and the worst's behind,
For little Juan o'er me threw, down stairs,
A pail of housemaid's water unawares.

25

A little curly-headed, good-for-nothing,
    And mischief-making monkey from his birth;
195 His parents ne'er agreed except in doting
    Upon the most unquiet imp on earth;
Instead of quarrelling, had they been but both in
    Their senses, they'd have sent young master for
To school, or had him soundly whipp'd at home,
200 To teach him manners for the time to come.

26

Don Jóse and the Donna Inez led
    For some time an unhappy sort of life,

Wishing each other, not divorced, but dead;
   They lived respectably as man and wife,
205 Their conduct was exceedingly well-bred,
   And gave no outward signs of inward strife,
Until at length the smother'd fire broke out,
And put the business past all kind of doubt.

27

For Inez call'd some druggists, and physicians,
210   And tried to prove her loving lord was *mad*,[9]
But as he had some lucid intermissions,
   She next decided he was only *bad*;
Yet when they ask'd her for her depositions,
   No sort of explanation could be had,
215 Save that her duty both to man and God
Required this conduct—which seem'd very odd.

28

She kept a joürnal, where his faults were noted,
   And open'd certain trunks of books and letters,
All which might, if occasion served, be quoted;
220   And then she had all Seville for abettors,
Besides her good old grandmother (who doted);
   The hearers of her case became repeaters,
Then advocates, inquisitors, and judges,
Some for amusement, others for old grudges.

29

225 And then this best and meekest woman bore
   With such serenity her husband's woes,
Just as the Spartan ladies did of yore,
   Who saw their spouses kill'd, and nobly chose
Never to say a word about them more——
230   Calmly she heard each calumny that rose,
And saw *his* agonies with such sublimity,
That all the world exclaim'd, "What magnanimity!

       *   *   *

32

Their friends had tried at reconciliation,
   Then their relations, who made matters worse:
('Twere hard to say upon a like occasion
   To whom it may be best to have recourse—
I can't say much for friend or yet relation):

9. Lady Byron had thought her husband might be insane and sought medical advice on the matter. This and other passages obviously allude to his wife, although Byron insisted that Donna Inez was not intended to be a caricature of Lady Byron. In her determination to preserve her son's innocence, Donna Inez also shares traits with Byron's mother.

The lawyers did their utmost for divorce,
255   But scarce a fee was paid on either side
Before, unluckily, Don Jóse died.

33

He died: and most unluckily, because,
    According to all hints I could collect
From counsel learned in those kinds of laws,
260   (Although their talk's obscure and circumspect)
His death contrived to spoil a charming cause;°   *lawsuit*
    A thousand pities also with respect
To public feeling, which on this occasion
Was manifested in a great sensation.

*   *   *

37

Dying intestate,° Juan was sole heir   *without a will*
290   To a chancery suit, and messuages,[1] and lands,
Which, with a long minority and care,
    Promised to turn out well in proper hands:
Inez became sole guardian, which was fair,
    And answer'd but to nature's just demands;
295   An only son left with an only mother
Is brought up much more wisely than another.

38

Sagest of women, even of widows, she
    Resolved that Juan should be quite a paragon,
And worthy of the noblest pedigree:
300   (His sire was of Castile, his dam from Aragon.)
Then for accomplishments of chivalry,
    In case our lord the king should go to war again,
He learn'd the arts of riding, fencing, gunnery,
And how to scale a fortress—or a nunnery.

39

305   But that which Donna Inez most desired,
    And saw into herself each day before all
The learned tutors whom for him she hired,
    Was, that his breeding should be strictly moral:
Much into all his studies she enquired,
310   And so they were submitted first to her, all,
Arts, sciences, no branch was made a mystery
To Juan's eyes, excepting natural history.[2]

---

1. Houses and the adjoining lands. "Chancery suit": a case in what was then the highest English court, notorious for its delays.
2. Includes biology, physiology, and particularly botany, popular in the era in part because study of plants' stamens and pistils offered a form of surreptitious sex education.

40

The languages, especially the dead,
 The sciences, and most of all the abstruse,
315 The arts, at least all such as could be said
 To be the most remote from common use,
In all these he was much and deeply read;
 But not a page of any thing that's loose,
Or hints continuation of the species,
320 Was ever suffer'd, lest he should grow vicious.

41

His classic studies made a little puzzle,
 Because of filthy loves of gods and goddesses,
Who in the earlier ages made a bustle,
 But never put on pantaloons or bodices;
325 His reverend tutors had at times a tussle,
 And for their Aeneids, Iliads, and Odysseys,
Were forced to make an odd sort of apology,
For Donna Inez dreaded the Mythology.

42

Ovid's a rake, as half his verses show him,
330 Anacreon's morals are a still worse sample,
Catullus scarcely has a decent poem,
 I don't think Sappho's Ode a good example,
Although Longinus[3] tells us there is no hymn
 Where the sublime soars forth on wings more ample;
335 But Virgil's songs are pure, except that horrid one
Beginning with "Formosum Pastor Corydon."[4]

43

Lucretius' irreligion[5] is too strong
 For early stomachs, to prove wholesome food;
I can't help thinking Juvenal[6] was wrong,
340 Although no doubt his real intent was good,
For speaking out so plainly in his song,
 So much indeed as to be downright rude;
And then what proper person can be partial
To all those nauseous epigrams of Martial?

---

3. In *On the Sublime* 10, the Greek rhetorician Longinus praises a passage of erotic longing from one of Sappho's odes.
4. Virgil's *Eclogue* 2 begins: "The shepherd, Corydon, burned with love for the handsome Alexis."
5. In *De Rerum Natura* (*On the Nature of Things*), Lucretius argues that the universe can be explained in entirely materialist terms without reference to any god.
6. The Latin satires of Juvenal attacked the corruption of Roman society in the 1st century C.E. and displayed its vices.

44

345   Juan was taught from out the best edition,
     Expurgated by learned men, who place,
Judiciously, from out the schoolboy's vision,
     The grosser parts; but fearful to deface
Too much their modest bard by this omission,
350   And pitying sore his mutilated case,
They only add them all in an appendix,[7]
Which saves, in fact, the trouble of an index;

*   *   *

52

For my part I say nothing—nothing—but
410   *This* I will say—my reasons are my own—
That if I had an only son to put
     To school (as God be praised that I have none),
'Tis not with Donna Inez I would shut
     Him up to learn his catechism alone,
415 No—no—I'd send him out betimes to college,
For there it was I pick'd up my own knowledge.

53

For there one learns—'tis not for me to boast,
     Though I acquired—but I pass over *that,*
As well as all the Greek I since have lost:
420   I say that there's the place—but *"Verbum sat,"*[8]
I think I pick'd up too, as well as most,
     Knowledge of matters—but no matter *what*—
I never married—but, I think, I know
That sons should not be educated so.

54

425   Young Juan now was sixteen years of age,
     Tall, handsome, slender, but well knit: he seem'd
Active, though not so sprightly, as a page;
     And every body but his mother deem'd
Him almost man; but she flew in a rage
430   And bit her lips (for else she might have scream'd)
If any said so, for to be precocious
Was in her eyes a thing the most atrocious.

55

Amongst her numerous acquaintance, all
     Selected for discretion and devotion,
435 There was the Donna Julia, whom to call

---

7. Fact! There is, or was, such an edition, with all the obnoxious epigrams of Martial placed by themselves at the end [Byron's note]. Martial, another Latin poet, was a contemporary of Juvenal.

8. A word [to the wise] is sufficient (Latin).

Pretty were but to give a feeble notion
Of many charms in her as natural
   As sweetness to the flower, or salt to ocean,
Her zone to Venus,[9] or his bow to Cupid,
440   (But this last simile is trite and stupid.)

56

The darkness of her Oriental eye
   Accorded with her Moorish origin;
(Her blood was not all Spanish, by the by;
   In Spain, you know, this is a sort of sin.)
445 When proud Granada fell, and, forced to fly,
   Boabdil wept,[1] of Donna Julia's kin
Some went to Africa, some stay'd in Spain,
Her great great grandmamma chose to remain.

57

She married (I forget the pedigree)
450 With an Hidalgo, who transmitted down
His blood less noble than such blood should be;
   At such alliances his sires would frown,
In that point so precise in each degree
   That they bred *in and in*, as might be shown,
455 Marrying their cousins—nay, their aunts, and nieces,
Which always spoils the breed, if it increases.

58

This heathenish cross restored the breed again,
   Ruin'd its blood, but much improved its flesh;
For from a root the ugliest in Old Spain
460   Sprung up a branch as beautiful as fresh;
The sons no more were short, the daughters plain:
   But there's a rumour which I fain would hush,
'Tis said that Donna Julia's grandmamma
Produced her Don more heirs at love than law.

59

465 However this might be, the race° went on   *family line*
   Improving still through every generation,
Until it centred in an only son,
   Who left an only daughter; my narration
May have suggested that this single one
470   Could be but Julia (whom on this occasion
I shall have much to speak about), and she
Was married, charming, chaste,[2] and twenty-three.

---

9. The belt ("zone") of Venus made its wearer
sexually irresistible.
1. The Moorish king of Granada (the last
Islamic enclave in Spain) wept when his capital
fell and he and his people were forced to emigrate to Africa (1492).
2. I.e., faithful to her husband.

60

Her eye (I'm very fond of handsome eyes)
    Was large and dark, suppressing half its fire
475 Until she spoke, then through its soft disguise
    Flash'd an expression more of pride than ire,
And love than either; and there would arise
    A something in them which was not desire,
But would have been, perhaps, but for the soul
480   Which struggled through and chasten'd down the whole.

61

Her glossy hair was cluster'd o'er a brow
    Bright with intelligence, and fair, and smooth;
Her eyebrow's shape was like th' aërial bow,
    Her cheek all purple with the beam of youth,
485 Mounting, at times, to a transparent glow,
    As if her veins ran lightning; she, in sooth,
Possess'd an air and grace by no means common:
Her stature tall—I hate a dumpy woman.

62

Wedded she was some years, and to a man
490   Of fifty, and such husbands are in plenty;
And yet, I think, instead of such a ONE
    'Twere better to have two of five-and-twenty,
Especially in countries near the sun:
    And now I think on't, "mi vien in mente,"[3]
495 Ladies even of the most uneasy virtue
Prefer a spouse whose age is short of thirty.

63

'Tis a sad thing, I cannot choose but say,
    And all the fault of that indecent sun,
Who cannot leave alone our helpless clay,
500   But will keep baking, broiling, burning on,
That howsoever people fast and pray,
    The flesh is frail, and so the soul undone:
What men call gallantry, and gods adultery,
Is much more common where the climate's sultry.

64

505 Happy the nations of the moral North!
    Where all is virtue, and the winter season
Sends sin, without a rag on, shivering forth
    ('Twas snow that brought St. Francis back to reason);
Where juries cast up what a wife is worth,
510   By laying whate'er sum, in mulct,[4] they please on

---

3. It comes to my mind (Italian).   4. By way of a fine or legal penalty.

The lover, who must pay a handsome price,
Because it is a marketable vice.

65

Alfonso was the name of Julia's lord,
   A man well looking for his years, and who
515 Was neither much beloved nor yet abhorr'd:
   They lived together, as most people do,
Suffering each other's foibles by accord,
   And not exactly either *one* or *two*;
Yet he was jealous, though he did not show it,
520 For jealousy dislikes the world to know it.

*   *   *

69

545 Juan she saw, and, as a pretty child,
   Caress'd him often—such a thing might be
Quite innocently done, and harmless styled,
   When she had twenty years, and thirteen he;
But I am not so sure I should have smiled
550   When he was sixteen, Julia twenty-three;
These few short years make wondrous alterations,
Particularly amongst sun-burnt nations.

70

Whate'er the cause might be, they had become
   Changed; for the dame grew distant, the youth shy,
555 Their looks cast down, their greetings almost dumb,
   And much embarrassment in either eye;
There surely will be little doubt with some
   That Donna Julia knew the reason why,
But as for Juan, he had no more notion
560 Than he who never saw the sea of ocean.

71

Yet Julias very coldness still was kind,
   And tremulously gentle her small hand
Withdrew itself from his, but left behind
   A little pressure, thrilling, and so bland
565 And slight, so very slight, that to the mind
   'Twas but a doubt; but ne'er magician's wand
Wrought change with all Armida's[5] fairy art
Like what this light touch left on Juan's heart.

---

5. The sorceress in Torquato Tasso's *Jerusalem Delivered* (1581) who seduces Rinaldo into forgetting his vows as a crusader.

72

And if she met him, though she smiled no more,
₅₇₀   She look'd a sadness sweeter than her smile,
As if her heart had deeper thoughts in store
     She must not own, but cherish'd more the while
For that compression in its burning core;
     Even innocence itself has many a wile,
₅₇₅ And will not dare to trust itself with truth,
And love is taught hypocrisy from youth.

* * *

75

Poor Julia's heart was in an awkward state;
     She felt it going, and resolved to make
₅₉₅ The noblest efforts for herself and mate,
     For honour's, pride's, religion's, virtue's sake;
Her resolutions were most truly great,
     And almost might have made a Tarquin⁶ quake:
She pray'd the Virgin Mary for her grace,
₆₀₀ As being the best judge of a lady's case.

76

She vow'd she never would see Juan more,
     And next day paid a visit to his mother,
And look'd extremely at the opening door,
     Which, by the Virgin's grace, let in another;
₆₀₅ Grateful she was, and yet a little sore—
     Again it opens, it can be no other,
'Tis surely Juan now—No! I'm afraid
That night the Virgin was no further pray'd.

77

She now determined that a virtuous woman
₆₁₀   Should rather face and overcome temptation,
That flight was base and dastardly, and no man
     Should ever give her heart the least sensation;
That is to say, a thought beyond the common
     Preference, that we must feel upon occasion,
₆₁₅ For people who are pleasanter than others,
But then they only seem so many brothers.

78

And even if by chance—and who can tell?
     The devil's so very sly—she should discover
That all within was not so very well,

---

6. A member of a legendary family of Roman kings noted for tyranny and cruelty; perhaps a reference specifically to Lucius Tarquinus, the villain of Shakespeare's *The Rape of Lucrece*.

620 And, if still free, that such or such a lover
Might please perhaps, a virtuous wife can quell
    Such thoughts, and be the better when they're over;
And if the man should ask, 'tis but denial:
I recommend young ladies to make trial.

79

625 And then there are such things as love divine,
    Bright and immaculate, unmix'd and pure,
Such as the angels think so very fine,
    And matrons, who would be no less secure,
Platonic, perfect, "just such love as mine:"
630   Thus Julia said—and thought so, to be sure;
And so I'd have her think, were I the man
On whom her reveries celestial ran.

*   *   *

86

So much for Julia. Now we'll turn to Juan,
    Poor little fellow! he had no idea
Of his own case, and never hit the true one;
    In feelings quick as Ovid's Miss Medea,[7]
685 He puzzled over what he found a new one,
    But not as yet imagined it could be a
Thing quite in course, and not at all alarming,
Which, with a little patience, might grow charming.

*   *   *

90

Young Juan wander'd by the glassy brooks
    Thinking unutterable things; he threw
715 Himself at length within the leafy nooks
    Where the wild branch of the cork forest grew;
There poets find materials for their books,
    And every now and then we read them through,
So that their plan and prosody are eligible,
720 Unless, like Wordsworth, they prove unintelligible.

91

He, Juan, (and not Wordsworth) so pursued
    His self-communion with his own high soul,
Until his mighty heart, in its great mood,
    Had mitigated part, though not the whole
725 Of its disease; he did the best he could
    With things not very subject to control,

7. In *Metamorphoses* 7 Ovid tells the story of Medea's mad infatuation for Jason.

And turn'd, without perceiving his condition,
Like Coleridge, into a metaphysician.

92

He thought about himself, and the whole earth,
730   Of man the wonderful, and of the stars,
And how the deuce they ever could have birth;
    And then he thought of earthquakes, and of wars,
How many miles the moon might have in girth,
    Of air-balloons, and of the many bars
735   To perfect knowledge of the boundless skies;—
And then he thought of Donna Julia's eyes.

93

In thoughts like these true wisdom may discern
    Longings sublime, and aspirations high,
Which some are born with, but the most part learn
740   To plague themselves withal, they know not why:
'Twas strange that one so young should thus concern
    His brain about the action of the sky;
Do *you* think 'twas philosophy that this did,
I can't help thinking puberty assisted.

94

745   He pored upon the leaves, and on the flowers,
    And heard a voice in all the winds; and then
He thought of wood-nymphs and immortal bowers,
    And how the goddesses came down to men:
He miss'd the pathway, he forgot the hours,
750   And when he look'd upon his watch again,
He found how much old Time had been a winner—
He also found that he had lost his dinner.

* * *

103

'Twas on a summer's day—the sixth of June:—
    I like to be particular in dates,
Not only of the age, and year, but moon;
820   They are a sort of post-house, where the Fates
Change horses, making history change its tune,
    Then spur away o'er empires and o'er states,
Leaving at last not much besides chronology,
Excepting the post-obits[8] of theology.

---

8. I.e., postobit bonds (*post obitum*, "after death" [Latin]): loans to an heir that fall due after the death of the person whose estate he or she is to inherit. Byron's meaning is probably that only theology purports to tell us what rewards are due in heaven.

104

825 'Twas on the sixth of June, about the hour
    Of half-past six—perhaps still nearer seven—
When Julia sate within as pretty a bower
    As e'er held houri in that heathenish heaven
Described by Mahomet, and Anacreon Moore,[9]
830   To whom the lyre and laurels have been given,
With all the trophies of triumphant song—
He won them well, and may he wear them long!

105

She sate, but not alone; I know not well
    How this same interview had taken place,
835 And even if I knew, I should not tell—
    People should hold their tongues in any case;
No matter how or why the thing befell,
    But there were she and Juan, face to face—
When two such faces are so, 'twould be wise,
840 But very difficult, to shut their eyes.

106

How beautiful she look'd! her conscious[1] heart
    Glow'd in her cheek, and yet she felt no wrong.
Oh Love! how perfect is thy mystic art,
    Strengthening the weak, and trampling on the strong,
845 How self-deceitful is the sagest part
    Of mortals whom thy lure hath led along—
The precipice she stood on was immense,
So was her creed° in her own innocence.   *belief*

107

She thought of her own strength, and Juan's youth
850   And of the folly of all prudish fears,
Victorious virtue, and domestic truth,
    And then of Don Alfonso's fifty years:
I wish these last had not occurr'd, in sooth,
    Because that number rarely much endears,
855 And through all climes, the snowy and the sunny,
Sounds ill in love, whate'er it may in money.

*   *   *

---

9. Byron's friend the poet Thomas Moore, who in 1800 had translated the *Odes* of the ancient Greek Anacreon and whose popular Orientalist poem *Lalla Rookh* (1817) had portrayed the "hea-thenish heaven" of Islam as populated by "houris," beautiful maidens who in the afterlife will give heroes their reward.
1. Secretly aware (of her feelings).

113

The sun set, and up rose the yellow moon:
　　The devil's in the moon for mischief; they
Who call'd her CHASTE, methinks, began too soon
900　　Their nomenclature; there is not a day,
The longest, not the twenty-first of June,
　　Sees half the business in a wicked way
On which three single hours of moonshine smile—
And then she looks so modest all the while.

114

905　There is a dangerous silence in that hour,
　　A stillness, which leaves room for the full soul
To open all itself, without the power
　　Of calling wholly back its self-control;
The silver light which, hallowing tree and tower,
910　　Sheds beauty and deep softness o'er the whole,
Breathes also to the heart, and o'er it throws
A loving languor, which is not repose.

115

And Julia sate with Juan, half embraced
　　And half retiring from the glowing arm,
915　Which trembled like the bosom where 'twas placed;
　　Yet still she must have thought there was no harm,
Or else 'twere easy to withdraw her waist;
　　But then the situation had its charm,
And then——God knows what next—I can't go on;
920　I'm almost sorry that I e'er begun.

116

Oh Plato! Plato! you have paved the way,
　　With your confounded fantasies, to more
Immoral conduct by the fancied sway
　　Your system feigns o'er the controulless core
925　Of human hearts, than all the long array
　　Of poets and romancers:—You're a bore,
A charlatan, a coxcomb—and have been,
At best, no better than a go-between.

117

And Julia's voice was lost, except in sighs,
930　　Until too late for useful conversation;
The tears were gushing from her gentle eyes,
　　I wish, indeed, they had not had occasion,
But who, alas! can love, and then be wise?
　　Not that remorse did not oppose temptation,

935 A little still she strove, and much repented,
And whispering "I will ne'er consent"—consented.

* * *

126

'Tis sweet to win, no matter how, one's laurels,
By blood or ink; 'tis sweet to put an end
To strife; 'tis sometimes sweet to have our quarrels,
Particularly with a tiresome friend:
1005 Sweet is old wine in bottles, ale in barrels;
Dear is the helpless creature we defend
Against the world; and dear the schoolboy spot
We ne'er forget, though there we are forgot.

127

But sweeter still than this, than these, than all,
1010 Is first and passionate love—it stands alone,
Like Adam's recollection of his fall;
The tree of knowledge has been pluck'd—all's known—
And life yields nothing further to recall
Worthy of this ambrosial sin, so shown,
1015 No doubt in fable, as the unforgiven
Fire which Prometheus[2] filch'd for us from heaven.

* * *

133

Man's a phenomenon, one knows not what,
And wonderful beyond all wondrous measure;
'Tis pity though, in this sublime world, that
1060 Pleasure's a sin, and sometimes sin's a pleasure;
Few mortals know what end they would be at,
But whether glory, power, or love, or treasure,
The path is through perplexing ways, and when
The goal is gain'd, we die, you know—and then——

134

1065 What then?—I do not know, no more do you—
And so good night.—Return we to our story:
'Twas in November, when fine days are few,
And the far mountains wax a little hoary,
And clap a white cape on their mantles blue;
1070 And the sea dashes round the promontory,
And the loud breaker boils against the rock,
And sober suns must set at five o'clock.

---

2. The Titan Prometheus incurred the wrath of Zeus by stealing fire from heaven for humans.

135

'Twas, as the watchmen say, a cloudy night;
    No moon, no stars, the wind was low or loud
1075 By gusts, and many a sparkling hearth was bright
    With the piled wood, round which the family crowd;
There's something cheerful in that sort of light,
    Even as a summer sky's without a cloud:
I'm fond of fire, and crickets, and all that,
1080 A lobster salad, and champagne, and chat.

136

'Twas midnight—Donna Julia was in bed,
    Sleeping, most probably,—when at her door
Arose a clatter might awake the dead,
    If they had never been awoke before,
1085 And that they have been so we all have read,
    And are to be so, at the least, once more;—
The door was fasten'd, but with voice and fist
First knocks were heard, then "Madam—Madam—hist!

137

"For God's sake, Madam—Madam—here's my master,
1090   With more than half the city at his back—
Was ever heard of such a curst disaster!
    'Tis not my fault—I kept good watch—Alack!
Do pray undo the bolt a little faster—
    They're on the stair just now, and in a crack°   *moment*
1095 Will all be here; perhaps he yet may fly—
Surely the window's not so *very* high!"

138

By this time Don Alfonso was arrived,
    With torches, friends, and servants in great number;
The major part of them had long been wived,
1100   And therefore paused not to disturb the slumber
Of any wicked woman, who contrived
    By stealth her husband's temples to encumber:[3]
Examples of this kind are so contagious.
Were *one* not punish'd, *all* would be outrageous.

139

1105 I can't tell how, or why, or what suspicion
    Could enter into Don Alfonso's head;
But for a cavalier of his condition°   *rank*

3. I.e., with horns that, growing on the forehead, were the traditional emblem of the cuckolded husband.

It surely was exceedingly ill-bred,
Without a word of previous admonition,
1110   To hold a levee[4] round his lady's bed,
And summon lackeys, arm'd with fire and sword,
To prove himself the thing he most abhorr'd.

140

Poor Donna Julia! starting as from sleep,
    (Mind—that I do not say—she had not slept)
1115 Began at once to scream, and yawn, and weep;
    Her maid Antonia, who was an adept,
Contrived to fling the bed-clothes in a heap,
    As if she had just now from out them crept:
I can't tell why she should take all this trouble
1120 To prove her mistress had been sleeping double.

141

But Julia mistress, and Antonia maid,
    Appear'd like two poor harmless women, who
Of goblins, but still more of men afraid,
    Had thought one man might be deterr'd by two,
1125 And therefore side by side were gently laid,
    Until the hours of absence should run through,
And truant husband should return, and say,
"My dear, I was the first who came away."

142

Now Julia found at length a voice, and cried,
1130   "In heaven's name, Don Alfonso, what d' ye mean?
Has madness seized you? would that I had died
    Ere such a monster's victim I had been!
What may this midnight violence betide,
    A sudden fit of drunkenness or spleen?
1135 Dare you suspect me, whom the thought would kill?
Search, then, the room!"—Alfonso said, "I will."

143

He search'd, *they* search'd, and rummaged every where,
    Closet and clothes' press, chest and window-seat,
And found much linen, lace, and several pair
1140   Of stockings, slippers, brushes, combs, complete,
With other articles of ladies fair,
    To keep them beautiful, or leave them neat:
Arras[5] they prick'd and curtains with their swords,
And wounded several shutters, and some boards.

---

4. Morning reception.   5. A tapestry hanging on a wall.

144

1145 Under the bed they search'd, and there they found—[6]
    No matter what—it was not that they sought;
They open'd windows, gazing if the ground
    Had signs or footmarks, but the earth said nought;
And then they stared each others' faces round:
1150   'T is odd, not one of all these seekers thought,
And seems to me almost a sort of blunder,
Of looking *in* the bed as well as under.

145

During this inquisition, Julia's tongue
    Was not asleep—"Yes, search and search," she cried,
1155 "Insult on insult heap, and wrong on wrong!
    It was for this that I became a bride!
For this in silence I have suffer'd long
    A husband like Alfonso at my side;
But now I'll bear no more, nor here remain,
1160 If there be law, or lawyers, in all Spain.

146

"Yes, Don Alfonso! husband now no more,
    If ever you indeed deserved the name,
Is't worthy of your years?—you have threescore—
    Fifty, or sixty, it is all the same—
1165 Is't wise or fitting, causeless to explore
    For facts against a virtuous woman's fame?
Ungrateful, perjured, barbarous Don Alfonso,
How dare you think your lady would go on so?"

*   *   *

159

1265 The Senhor Don Alfonso stood confused;
    Antonia bustled round the ransack'd room,
And, turning up her nose, with looks abused
    Her master, and his myrmidons,[7] of whom
Not one, except the attorney, was amused;
1270   He, like Achates,[8] faithful to the tomb,
So there were quarrels, cared not for the cause,
Knowing they must be settled by the laws.

160

With prying snub-nose, and small eyes, he stood,
    Following Antonia's motions here and there,

---

6. Perhaps a chamber pot.
7. Servants, so named for the followers Achilles led to the Trojan War.
8. The *fidus Achates* ("faithful Achates") of Virgil's *Aeneid*, whose loyalty to Aeneas has become proverbial.

1275 With much suspicion in his attitude;
    For reputations he had little care;
So that a suit or action were made good,
    Small pity had he for the young and fair,
And ne'er believed in negatives, till these
1280 Were proved by competent false witnesses.

161

But Don Alfonso stood with downcast looks,
    And, truth to say, he made a foolish figure;
When, after searching in five hundred nooks,
    And treating a young wife with so much rigour,
1285 He gain'd no point, except some self-rebukes,
    Added to those his lady with such vigour
Had pour'd upon him for the last half-hour,
Quick, thick, and heavy—as a thunder-shower.

162

At first he tried to hammer an excuse,
1290   To which the sole reply was tears, and sobs,
And indications of hysterics, whose
    Prologue is always certain throes, and throbs,
Gasps, and whatever else the owners choose:
    Alfonso saw his wife, and thought of Job's;[9]
1295 He saw too, in perspective, her relations,
And then he tried to muster all his patience.

163

He stood in act to speak, or rather stammer,
    But sage Antonia cut him short before
The anvil of his speech received the hammer,
1300   With "Pray, sir, leave the room, and say no more,
Or madam dies."—Alfonso mutter'd, "D—n her,"
    But nothing else, the time of words was o'er;
He cast a rueful look or two, and did,
He knew not wherefore, that which he was bid.

164

1305 With him retired his *"posse comitatus,"*[1]
    The attorney last, who linger'd near the door,
Reluctantly, still tarrying there as late as
    Antonia let him—not a little sore
At this most strange and unexplain'd *"hiatus"*
1310   In Don Alfonso's facts, which just now wore

---

9. Job's wife advised her afflicted husband to "curse God, and die." He replied, "Thou speakest as one of the foolish women speaketh" (Job 2.9–10).

1. The complete form of the modern word *posse* (*posse comitatus* means literally "power of the county" [Latin], i.e., the body of citizens summoned by a sheriff to preserve order in the county).

An awkward look; as he revolved the case,
The door was fasten'd in his legal face.

165

No sooner was it bolted, than—Oh shame!
    Oh sin! Oh sorrow! and Oh womankind!
1315 How can you do such things and keep your fame,
    Unless this world, and t'other too, be blind?
Nothing so dear as an unfilch'd good name!
    But to proceed—for there is more behind:
With much heartfelt reluctance be it said,
1320 Young Juan slipp'd, half-smother'd, from the bed.

166

He had been hid—I don't pretend to say
    How, nor can I indeed describe the where—
Young, slender, and pack'd easily, he lay,
    No doubt, in little compass, round or square;
1325 But pity him I neither must nor may
    His suffocation by that pretty pair;
'Twere better, sure, to die so, than be shut
With maudlin Clarence in his Malmsey butt.[2]

* * *

169

1345 What's to be done? Alfonso will be back
    The moment he has sent his fools away.
Antonia's skill was put upon the rack,
    But no device could be brought into play—
And how to parry the renew'd attack?
1350   Besides, it wanted but few hours of day:
Antonia puzzled; Julia did not speak,
But press'd her bloodless lip to Juan's cheek.

170

He turn'd his lip to hers, and with his hand
    Call'd back the tangles of her wandering hair;
1355 Even then their love they could not all command,
    And half forgot their danger and despair:
Antonia's patience now was at a stand—
    "Come, come, 'tis no time now for fooling there,"
She whisper'd, in great wrath—"I must deposit
1360 This pretty gentleman within the closet:"

* * *

2. Clarence, brother of Edward IV and of the future Richard III, was reputed to have been assassinated by being drowned in a cask ("butt") of malmsey, a sweet and aromatic wine.

173

Now, Don Alfonso entering, but alone,
   Closed the oration of the trusty maid:
She loiter'd, and he told her to be gone,
1380   An order somewhat sullenly obey'd;
However, present remedy was none,
   And no great good seem'd answer'd if she staid:
Regarding both with slow and sidelong view,
She snuff'd the candle, curtsied, and withdrew.

174

1385 Alfonso paused a minute—then begun
   Some strange excuses for his late proceeding;
He would not justify what he had done,
   To say the best, it was extreme ill-breeding;
But there were ample reasons for it, none
1390   Of which he specified in this his pleading:
His speech was a fine sample, on the whole,
Of rhetoric, which the learn'd call *"rigmarole."*

* * *

180

Alfonso closed his speech, and begg'd her pardon,
   Which Julia half withheld, and then half granted,
1435 And laid conditions, he thought, very hard on,
   Denying several little things he wanted:
He stood like Adam lingering near his garden,
   With useless penitence perplex'd and haunted,
Beseeching she no further would refuse,
1440 When, lo! he stumbled o'er a pair of shoes.

181

A pair of shoes!—what then? not much, if they
   Are such as fit with ladies' feet, but these
(No one can tell how much I grieve to say)
   Were masculine; to see them, and to seize,
1445 Was but a moment's act.—Ah! well-a-day!
   My teeth begin to chatter, my veins freeze—
Alfonso first examined well their fashion,
And then flew out into another passion.

182

He left the room for his relinquish'd sword,
1450   And Julia instant to the closet flew.
"Fly, Juan, fly! for heaven's sake—not a word—
   The door is open—you may yet slip through

The passage you so often have explored—
    Here is the garden-key—Fly—fly—Adieu!
1455   Haste—haste! I hear Alfonso's hurrying feet—
    Day has not broke—there's no one in the street."

183

None can say that this was not good advice,
    The only mischief was, it came too late;
Of all experience 'tis the usual price,
1460   A sort of income-tax laid on by fate:
Juan had reach'd the room-door in a trice,
    And might have done so by the garden-gate,
But met Alfonso in his dressing-gown,
Who threaten'd death—so Juan knock'd him down.

184

1465   Dire was the scuffle, and out went the light;
    Antonia cried out "Rape!" and Julia "Fire!"
But not a servant stirr'd to aid the fight.
    Alfonso, pommell'd to his heart's desire,
Swore lustily he'd be revenged this night;
1470   And Juan, too, blasphemed an octave higher;
His blood was up: though young, he was a Tartar,[3]
And not at all disposed to prove a martyr.

185

Alfonso's sword had dropp'd ere he could draw it,
    And they continued battling hand to hand,
1475   For Juan very luckily ne'er saw it;
    His temper not being under great command,
If at that moment he had chanced to claw it,
    Alfonso's days had not been in the land
Much longer.—Think of husbands', lovers' lives!
1480   And how ye may be doubly widows—wives!

186

Alfonso grappled to detain the foe,
    And Juan throttled him to get away,
And blood ('twas from the nose) began to flow;
    At last, as they more faintly wrestling lay,
1485   Juan contrived to give an awkward blow,
    And then his only garment quite gave way;
He fled, like Joseph,[4] leaving it; but there,
I doubt, all likeness ends between the pair.

---

3. A formidable opponent.
4. In Genesis 39.7ff. the chaste Joseph flees from the advances of Potiphar's wife, leaving "his garment in her hand."

187

Lights came at length, and men, and maids, who found
1490   An awkward spectacle their eyes before;
Antonia in hysterics, Julia swoon'd,
    Alfonso leaning, breathless, by the door;
Some half-torn drapery scatter'd on the ground,
    Some blood, and several footsteps, but no more:
1495 Juan the gate gain'd, turn'd the key about,
And liking not the inside, lock'd the out.

188

Here ends this canto.—Need I sing, or say,
    How Juan, naked, favour'd by the night,
Who favours what she should not, found his way,
1500   And reach'd his home in an unseemly plight?
The pleasant scandal which arose next day,
    The nine days' wonder which was brought to light,
And how Alfonso sued for a divorce,
Were in the English newspapers, of course.

189

1505 If you would like to see the whole proceedings,
    The depositions, and the cause at full,
The names of all the witnesses, the pleadings
    Of counsel to nonsuit,[5] or to annul,
There's more than one edition, and the readings
1510   Are various, but they none of them are dull;
The best is that in short-hand ta'en by Gurney,[6]
Who to Madrid on purpose made a journey.

190

But Donna Inez, to divert the train
    Of one of the most circulating scandals
1515 That had for centuries been known in Spain,
    Since Roderic's Goths, or older Genseric's Vandals,[7]
First vow'd (and never had she vow'd in vain)
    To Virgin Mary several pounds of candles;
And then, by the advice of some old ladies,
1520 She sent her son to be embark'd at Cadiz.

191

She had resolved that he should travel through
    All European climes, by land or sea,

---

5. Judgment against the plaintiff for failure to establish his case.
6. William B. Gurney (1777–1855), official short-hand writer for the houses of Parliament and a famous court reporter.
7. The Germanic tribes that overran Spain and other parts of southern Europe in the 5th through 8th centuries, notorious for rape and violence.

To mend his former morals, or get new,
   Especially in France and Italy
1525 (At least this is the thing most people do).
   Julia was sent into a nunnery
And there, perhaps, her feelings may be better
Shown in the following copy of her letter:—

192

"They tell me 'tis decided; you depart:
1530   'Tis wise—'tis well, but not the less a pain;
I have no further claim on your young heart,
   Mine is the victim, and would be again;
To love too much has been the only art
   I used;—I write in haste, and if a stain
1535 Be on this sheet, 'tis not what it appears;
My eyeballs burn and throb, but have no tears.

193

"I loved, I love you, for that love have lost
   State, station, heaven, mankind's, my own esteem,
And yet can not regret what it hath cost,
1540   So dear is still the memory of that dream;
Yet, if I name my guilt, 'tis not to boast,
   None can deem harshlier of me than I deem:
I trace this scrawl because I cannot rest—
I've nothing to reproach, nor to request.

194

1545 "Man's love is of his life a thing apart,
   'Tis woman's whole existence; man may range
The court, camp, church, the vessel, and the mart,
   Sword, gown, gain, glory, offer in exchange
Pride, fame, ambition, to fill up his heart,
1550   And few there are whom these can not estrange;
Men have all these resources, we but one,
To love again, and be again undone.

195

"My breast has been all weakness, is so yet;
   I struggle, but cannot collect my mind;
1555 My blood still rushes where my spirit's set,
   As roll the waves before the settled wind;
My brain is feminine, nor can forget—
   To all, except your image, madly blind;
As turns the needle[8] trembling to the pole
1560 It ne'er can reach, so turns to you, my soul.

8. Of a compass.

196

"You will proceed in beauty, and in pride,
  Beloved and loving many; all is o'er
For me on earth, except some years to hide
  My shame and sorrow deep in my heart's core;
1565 These I could bear, but cannot cast aside
  The passion which still rages as before,—
And so farewell—forgive me, love me—No,
That word is idle now—but let it go.

197

"I have no more to say, but linger still,
1570   And dare not set my seal upon this sheet,
And yet I may as well the task fulfil,
  My misery can scarce be more complete:
I had not lived till now, could sorrow kill;
  Death flies the wretch who fain the blow would meet,
1575 And I must even survive this last adieu,
And bear with life, to love and pray for you!"

198

This note was written upon gilt-edged paper
  With a neat crow-quill, rather hard, but new;
Her small white fingers scarce could reach the taper,[9]
1580   But trembled as magnetic needles do,
And yet she did not let one tear escape her;
  The seal a sun-flower; *Elle vous suit partout*,"[1]
The motto, cut upon a white cornelian;
The wax was superfine, its hue vermilion.

199

1585 This was Don Juan's earliest scrape; but whether
  I shall proceed with his adventures is
Dependent on the public altogether;
  We'll see, however, what they say to this,
Their favour in an author's cap's a feather,
1590   And no great mischief's done by their caprice;
And if their approbation we experience,
Perhaps they'll have some more about a year hence.

200

My poem's epic, and is meant to be
  Divided in twelve books; each book containing,

---

9. The candle (to melt wax to seal the letter).
1. She follows you everywhere (French). This motto was inscribed on one of Byron's seals and on a jewel he gave to John Edleston, the boy with whom he had a romantic friendship while at Cambridge. Their friendship was memorialized in Byron's 1807 poem "The Cornelian."

1595 With love, and war, a heavy gale at sea,
 A list of ships, and captains, and kings reigning,
New characters; the episodes are three:
 A panoramic view of hell's in training,
After the style of Virgil and of Homer,
1600 So that my name of Epic's no misnomer.

201

All these things will be specified in time,
 With strict regard to Aristotle's rules,
The *Vade Mecum*[2] of the true sublime,
 Which makes so many poets, and some fools:
1605 Prose poets like blank-verse, I'm fond of rhyme,
 Good workmen never quarrel with their tools;
I've got new mythological machinery,[3]
And very handsome supernatural scenery.

202

There's only one slight difference between
1610 Me and my epic brethren gone before,
And here the advantage is my own, I ween;
 (Not that I have not several merits more,
But this will more peculiarly be seen;)
 They so embellish, that 'tis quite a bore
1615 Their labyrinth of fables to thread through,
Whereas this story's actually true.

203

If any person doubt it, I appeal
 To history, tradition, and to facts,
To newspapers, whose truth all know and feel,
1620 To plays in five, and operas in three acts;
All these confirm my statement a good deal,
 But that which more completely faith exacts
Is, that myself, and several now in Seville,
Saw Juan's last elopement with the devil.[4]

204

1625 If ever I should condescend to prose,
 I'll write poetical commandments, which
Shall supersede beyond all doubt all those
 That went before; in these I shall enrich
My text with many things that no one knows,

---

2. Go with me (Latin, literal trans.); handbook.
Byron is deriding the neoclassical view that Aristotle's *Poetics* proposes "rules" for writing epic
and tragedy.
3. The assemblage of supernatural personages
and incidents introduced into a literary work.
4. The usual plays on the Juan legend ended
with Juan in hell; an early 20th-century version
is Bernard Shaw's *Man and Superman*.

1630   And carry precept to the highest pitch:
    I'll call the work "Longinus o'er a Bottle,
    Or, Every Poet his *own* Aristotle."

205

    Thou shalt believe in Milton, Dryden, Pope;[5]
      Thou shalt not set up Wordsworth, Coleridge, Southey;
1635   Because the first is crazed beyond all hope,
      The second drunk, the third so quaint and mouthy:
    With Crabbe it may be difficult to cope,
      And Campbell's Hippocrene[6] is somewhat drouthy:
    Thou shalt not steal from Samuel Rogers, nor
1640   Commit—flirtation with the muse of Moore.

206

    Thou shalt not covet Mr. Sotheby's Muse,
      His Pegasus,[7] nor any thing that's his;
    Thou shalt not bear false witness like "the Blues"[8]—
      (There's one, at least, is very fond of this);
1645   Thou shalt not write, in short, but what I choose:
      This is true criticism, and you may kiss—
    Exactly as you please, or not,—the rod;
    But if you don't, I'll lay it on, by G—d![9]

207

    If any person should presume to assert
1650   This story is not moral, first, I pray,
    That they will not cry out before they're hurt,
      Then that they'll read it o'er again, and say,
    (But, doubtless, nobody will be so pert)
      That this is not a moral tale, though gay;
1655   Besides, in Canto Twelfth, I mean to show
    The very place where wicked people go.

*   *   *

213

    But now at thirty years my hair is grey—
      (I wonder what it will be like at forty?

5. This is one of many passages, in prose and verse, in which Byron vigorously defends Dryden and Pope against his Romantic contemporaries.
6. Fountain on Mount Helicon whose waters supposedly gave inspiration. George Crabbe, whom Byron admired, was the author of *The Village* and other realistic poems of rural life. Thomas Campbell, Samuel Rogers, and Thomas Moore were lesser poets of the Romantic period; the last two were close friends of Byron and members of London's liberal Whig circles.
7. The winged horse symbolizing poetic inspira-

tion. The wealthy William Sotheby, minor poet and translator, is satirized, as Botherby, in Byron's *Beppo*.
8. I.e., Bluestockings, a contemporary term for female intellectuals, among whom Byron numbered his wife (line 1644).
9. Byron's parody of the Ten Commandments seemed blasphemous to some commentators. In 1817 the radical publisher William Hone was put on trial for the ostensible blasphemy of a political satire that had used the form of the Anglican Church's creed and catechism.

I thought of a peruke° the other day—)   *wig*
1700   My heart is not much greener; and, in short, I
Have squander'd my whole summer while 'twas May,
        And feel no more the spirit to retort; I
Have spent my life, both interest and principal,
And deem not, what I deem'd, my soul invincible.

214

1705   No more—no more—Oh! never more on me
        The freshness of the heart can fall like dew,
Which out of all the lovely things we see
        Extracts emotions beautiful and new,
Hived in our bosoms like the bag o' the bee:
1710   Think'st thou the honey with those objects grew?
Alas! 'twas not in them, but in thy power
To double even the sweetness of a flower.

215

No more—no more—Oh! never more, my heart,
        Canst thou be my sole world, my universe!
1715   Once all in all, but now a thing apart,
        Thou canst not be my blessing or my curse:
The illusion's gone for ever, and thou art
        Insensible, I trust, but none the worse,
And in thy stead I've got a deal of judgment,
1720   Though heaven knows how it ever found a lodgement.

216

My days of love are over; me no more
        The charms of maid, wife, and still less of widow,
Can make the fool of which they made before,—
        In short, I must not lead the life I did do;
1725   The credulous hope of mutual minds is o'er,
        The copious use of claret is forbid too,
So for a good old-gentlemanly vice,
I think I must take up with avarice.

217

Ambition was my idol, which was broken
1730   Before the shrines of Sorrow, and of Pleasure;
And the two last have left me many a token
        O'er which reflection may be made at leisure:
Now, like Friar Bacon's brazen head, I've spoken,
        "Time is, Time was, Time's past:"[1]—a chymic treasure[2]

---

1. Spoken by a bronze bust in Robert Greene's *Friar Bacon and Friar Bungay* (1594). This comedy was based on legends about the magical power of Roger Bacon, the 13th-century Francis- can monk who was said to have built with diabolical assistance a brazen head capable of speech.
2. "Chymic": alchemic; i.e., the "treasure" is counterfeit gold.

1735　Is glittering youth, which I have spent betimes—
　　　My heart in passion, and my head on rhymes.

218

　　　What is the end of Fame? 'tis but to fill
　　　　A certain portion of uncertain paper:
　　　Some liken it to climbing up a hill,
1740　　Whose summit, like all hills, is lost in vapour;
　　　For this men write, speak, preach, and heroes kill,
　　　　And bards burn what they call their "midnight taper,"
　　　To have, when the original is dust,
　　　A name, a wretched picture, and worse bust.[3]

219

1745　What are the hopes of man? Old Egypt's King
　　　　Cheops erected the first pyramid
　　　And largest, thinking it was just the thing
　　　　To keep his memory whole, and mummy hid;
　　　But somebody or other rummaging,
1750　　Burglariously broke his coffin's lid:
　　　Let not a monument give you or me hopes,
　　　Since not a pinch of dust remains of Cheops.

220

　　　But I being fond of true philosophy,
　　　　Say very often to myself, "Alas!
1755　All things that have been born were born to die,
　　　　And flesh (which Death mows down to hay) is grass;[4]
　　　You've pass'd your youth not so unpleasantly,
　　　　And if you had it o'er again—'twould pass—
　　　So thank your stars that matters are no worse,
1760　And read your Bible, sir, and mind your purse."

221

　　　But for the present, gentle reader! and
　　　　Still gentler purchaser! the bard—that's I—
　　　Must, with permission, shake you by the hand,
　　　　And so your humble servant, and good-b'ye!
1765　We meet again, if we should understand
　　　　Each other; and if not, I shall not try
　　　Your patience further than by this short sample—
　　　'Twere well if others follow'd my example.

222

　　　"Go, little book, from this my solitude!
1770　　I cast thee on the waters—go thy ways!

---

3. Byron was unhappy with the portrait bust of him recently made by the Danish sculptor Thorwaldsen.

4. An echo of Isaiah 40.6 and 1 Peter 1.24: "All flesh is grass."

And if, as I believe, thy vein be good,
　　The world will find thee after many days."
When Southey's read, and Wordsworth understood,
　　I can't help putting in my claim to praise—
1775　The four first rhymes are Southey's every line:[5]
For God's sake, reader! take them not for mine.

From Canto the Second

[JUAN AND HAIDEE]

111

How long in his damp trance young Juan lay
　　He knew not, for the earth was gone for him,
And Time had nothing more of night nor day
　　For his congealing blood, and senses dim;
885　And how this heavy faintness pass'd away
　　He knew not, till each painful pulse and limb,
And tingling vein, seem'd throbbing back to life,
For Death, though vanquish'd, still retired with strife.

112

His eyes he open'd, shut, again unclosed,
890　　For all was doubt and dizziness; he thought
He still was in the boat, and had but dozed,
　　And felt again with his despair o'erwrought,
And wish'd it death in which he had reposed.
　　And then once more his feelings back were brought,
895　And slowly by his swimming eyes was seen
A lovely female face of seventeen.

113

'Twas bending close o'er his, and the small mouth
　　Seem'd almost prying into his for breath;
And chafing him, the soft warm hand of youth
900　　Recall'd his answering spirits back from death;
And, bathing his chill temples, tried to soothe
　　Each pulse to animation, till beneath
Its gentle touch and trembling care, a sigh
To these kind efforts made a low reply.

114

905　Then was the cordial pour'd, and mantle flung
　　Around his scarce-clad limbs; and the fair arm
Raised higher the faint head which o'er it hung;
　　And her transparent cheek, all pure and warm,

---

5. The lines are part of the last stanza of Southey's "Epilogue to the Lay of the Laureate."

Pillow'd his death-like forehead; then she wrung
910 His dewy curls, long drench'd by every storm;
And watch'd with eagerness each throb that drew
A sigh from his heaved bosom—and hers, too.

115

And lifting him with care into the cave,
  The gentle girl, and her attendant,—one
915 Young, yet her elder, and of brow less grave,
  And more robust of figure,—then begun
To kindle fire, and as the new flames gave
  Light to the rocks that roof'd them, which the sun
Had never seen, the maid, or whatsoe'er
920 She was, appear'd distinct, and tall, and fair.

116

Her brow was overhung with coins of gold,
  That sparkled o'er the auburn of her hair,
Her clustering hair, whose longer locks were roll'd
  In braids behind, and though her stature were
925 Even of the highest for a female mould,
  They nearly reach'd her heel; and in her air
There was a something which bespoke command,
As one who was a lady in the land.

117

Her hair, I said, was auburn; but her eyes
930 Were black as death, their lashes the same hue,
Of downcast length, in whose silk shadow lies
  Deepest attraction, for when to the view
Forth from its raven fringe the full glance flies,
  Ne'er with such force the swiftest arrow flew;
935 'Tis as the snake late coil'd, who pours his length,
And hurls at once his venom and his strength.

*   *   *

123

And these two tended him, and cheer'd him both
  With food and raiment, and those soft attentions,
Which are—(as I must own)—of female growth,
980 And have ten thousand delicate inventions:
They made a most superior mess of broth,
  A thing which poesy but seldom mentions,
But the best dish that e'er was cook'd since Homer's
Achilles order'd dinner for new comers.[1]

---

1. A reference to the lavish feast with which Achilles entertained Ajax, Phoenix, and Ulysses (*Iliad* 9.193ff.).

124

985 I'll tell you who they were, this female pair,
    Lest they should seem princesses in disguise;
Besides, I hate all mystery, and that air
    Of clap-trap, which your recent poets prize;
And so, in short, the girls they really were
990   They shall appear before your curious eyes,
Mistress and maid; the first was only daughter
Of an old man, who lived upon the water.

125

A fisherman he had been in his youth,
    And still a sort of fisherman was he;
995 But other speculations were, in sooth,
    Added to his connection with the sea,
Perhaps not so respectable, in truth:
    A little smuggling, and some piracy,
Left him, at last, the sole of many masters
1000 Of an ill-gotten million of piastres.[2]

126

A fisher, therefore, was he,—though of men,
    Like Peter the Apostle,[3]—and he fish'd
For wandering merchant-vessels, now and then,
    And sometimes caught as many as he wish'd;
1005 The cargoes he confiscated, and gain
    He sought in the slave-market too, and dish'd
Full many a morsel for that Turkish trade,
By which, no doubt, a good deal may be made.

127

He was a Greek, and on his isle had built
1010   (One of the wild and smaller Cyclades)[4]
A very handsome house from out his guilt,
    And there he lived exceedingly at ease;
Heaven knows, what cash he got, or blood he spilt,
    A sad[5] old fellow was he, if you please;
1015 But this I know, it was a spacious building,
Full of barbaric carving, paint, and gilding.

128

He had an only daughter, call'd Haidee,
    The greatest heiress of the Eastern Isles;
Besides, so very beautiful was she,

---

2. Near Eastern coins.
3. Christ's words to Peter and Andrew, both fishermen: "Follow me, and I will make you fish-ers of men" (Matthew 4.19).
4. A group of islands in the Aegean Sea.
5. In the playful sense: wicked.

1020   Her dowry was as nothing to her smiles:
Still in her teens, and like a lovely tree
    She grew to womanhood, and between whiles
Rejected several suitors, just to learn
How to accept a better in his turn.

129

1025 And walking out upon the beach, below
    The cliff, towards sunset, on that day she found,
Insensible,° not dead, but nearly so,—   *unconscious*
    Don Juan, almost famish'd, and half drown'd;
But being naked, she was shock'd, you know,
1030   Yet deem'd herself in common pity bound,
As far as in her lay, "to take him in,
A stranger"[6] dying, with so white a skin.

130

But taking him into her father's house
    Was not exactly the best way to save,
1035 But like conveying to the cat the mouse,
    Or people in a trance into their grave;
Because the good old man had so much "γους,"[7]
    Unlike the honest Arab thieves so brave,
He would have hospitably cured the stranger,
1040 And sold him instantly when out of danger.

131

And therefore, with her maid, she thought it best
    (A virgin always on her maid relies)
To place him in the cave for present rest:
    And when, at last, he open'd his black eyes,
1045 Their charity increased about their guest;
    And their compassion grew to such a size,
It open'd half the turnpike-gates to heaven—
(St. Paul says, 'tis the toll which must be given.)[8]

*   *   *

141

And Haidee met the morning face to face;
    Her own was freshest, though a feverish flush
Had dyed it with the headlong blood, whose race
    From heart to cheek is curb'd into a blush,
1125 Like to a torrent which a mountain's base,
    That overpowers some Alpine river's rush,

---

6. Cf. Matthew 25.35: "I was a stranger, and ye took me in."
7. *Nous,* intelligence (Greek); in England pronounced so as to rhyme with *mouse.*

8. 1 Corinthians 13.13: "And now abideth faith, hope, charity, these three; but the greatest of these is charity."

Checks to a lake, whose waves in circles spread;
Or the Red Sea—but the sea is not red.

142

And down the cliff the island virgin came,
    And near the cave her quick light footsteps drew,
While the sun smiled on her with his first flame,
    And young Aurora° kiss'd her lips with dew,   *dawn*
Taking her for a sister; just the same
    Mistake you would have made on seeing the two,
Although the mortal, quite as fresh and fair,
Had all the advantage, too, of not being air.

143

And when into the cavern Haidee stepp'd
    All timidly, yet rapidly, she saw
That like an infant Juan sweetly slept;
    And then she stopp'd, and stood as if in awe
(For sleep is awful),° and on tiptoe crept   *awe-inspiring*
    And wrapt him closer, lest the air, too raw,
Should reach his blood, then o'er him still as death
Bent, with hush'd lips, that drank his scarce-drawn breath.

*   *   *

148

And she bent o'er him, and he lay beneath,
    Hush'd as the babe upon its mother's breast,
Droop'd as the willow when no winds can breathe,
    Lull'd like the depth of ocean when at rest,
Fair as the crowning rose of the whole wreath,
    Soft as the callow° cygnet° in its nest;   *young / swan*
In short, he was a very pretty fellow,
Although his woes had turn'd him rather yellow.

149

He woke and gazed, and would have slept again,
    But the fair face which met his eyes forbade
Those eyes to close, though weariness and pain
    Had further sleep a further pleasure made;
For woman's face was never form'd in vain
    For Juan, so that even when he pray'd
He turn'd from grisly saints, and martyrs hairy,
To the sweet portraits of the Virgin Mary.

150

And thus upon his elbow he arose,
    And look'd upon the lady, in whose cheek

1195 The pale contended with the purple rose,
    As with an effort she began to speak;
Her eyes were eloquent, her words would pose,
    Although she told him, in good modern Greek,
With an Ionian accent, low and sweet,
1200 That he was faint, and must not talk, but eat.

* * *

168

And every day by daybreak—rather early
    For Juan, who was somewhat fond of rest—
She came into the cave, but it was merely
1340   To see her bird reposing in his nest;
And she would softly stir his locks so curly,
    Without disturbing her yet slumbering guest,
Breathing all gently o'er his cheek and mouth,
As o'er a bed of roses the sweet south.[9]

169

1345 And every morn his colour freshlier came,
    And every day help'd on his convalescence;
'Twas well, because health in the human frame
    Is pleasant, besides being true love's essence,
For health and idleness to passion's flame
1350   Are oil and gunpowder; and some good lessons
Are also learnt from Ceres[1] and from Bacchus,
Without whom Venus will not long attack us.

170

While Venus fills the heart (without heart really
    Love, though good always, is not quite so good,)
1355 Ceres presents a plate of vermicelli,—
    For love must be sustain'd like flesh and blood,—
While Bacchus pours out wine, or hands a jelly:
    Eggs, oysters, too, are amatory food;
But who is their purveyor from above
1360 Heaven knows,—it may be Neptune, Pan, or Jove.

171

When Juan woke he found some good things ready,
    A bath, a breakfast, and the finest eyes
That ever made a youthful heart less steady,
    Besides her maid's, as pretty for their size;
1365 But I have spoken of all this already—
    And repetition's tiresome and unwise,—

---

9. The south wind.
1. Ceres, goddess of the grain; Bacchus, god of wine and revelry.

Well—Juan, after bathing in the sea,
Came always back to coffee and Haidee.

172

Both were so young, and one so innocent,
1370   That bathing pass'd for nothing; Juan seem'd
To her, as 'twere, the kind of being sent,
    Of whom these two years she had nightly dream'd,
A something to be loved, a creature meant
    To be her happiness, and whom she deem'd
1375   To render happy; all who joy would win
Must share it,—Happiness was born a twin.

173

It was such pleasure to behold him, such
    Enlargement of existence to partake
Nature with him, to thrill beneath his touch,
1380   To watch him slumbering, and to see him wake:
To live with him for ever were too much;
    But then the thought of parting made her quake:
He was her own, her ocean-treasure, cast
Like a rich wreck—her first love, and her last.

174

1385 And thus a moon° roll'd on, and fair Haidee   *month*
    Paid daily visits to her boy, and took
Such plentiful precautions, that still he
    Remain'd unknown within his craggy nook;
At last her father's prows put out to sea,
1390   For certain merchantmen upon the look,
Not as of yore to carry off an Io,[2]
But three Ragusan vessels, bound for Scio.[3]

175

Then came her freedom, for she had no mother,
    So that, her father being at sea, she was
1395 Free as a married woman, or such other
    Female, as where she likes may freely pass,
Without even the incumbrance of a brother,
    The freest she that ever gazed on glass:°   *in a mirror*
I speak of Christian lands in this comparison,
1400 Where wives, at least, are seldom kept in garrison.

176

Now she prolong'd her visits and her talk
    (For they must talk), and he had learnt to say

---

2. A mistress of Zeus who was persecuted by his jealous wife, Hera, and kidnapped by Phoenician merchants.

3. The Italian name for Chios, an island near Turkey. "Ragusan": Ragusa (or Dubrovnik) is an Adriatic port located in what is now Croatia.

So much as to propose to take a walk,—
    For little had he wander'd since the day
1405 On which, like a young flower snapp'd from the stalk,
    Drooping and dewy on the beach he lay,—
And thus they walk'd out in the afternoon,
And saw the sun set opposite the moon.

177

It was a wild and breaker-beaten coast,
1410   With cliffs above, and a broad sandy shore,
Guarded by shoals and rocks as by an host,
    With here and there a creek, whose aspect wore
A better welcome to the tempest-tost;
    And rarely ceased the haughty billow's roar,
1415 Save on the dead long summer days, which make
The outstretch'd ocean glitter like a lake.

178

And the small ripple spilt upon the beach
    Scarcely o'erpass'd the cream of your champagne,
When o'er the brim the sparkling bumpers reach,
1420   That spring-dew of the spirit! the heart's rain!
Few things surpass old wine; and they may preach
    Who please,—the more because they preach in vain,—
Let us have wine and women, mirth and laughter,
Sermons and soda-water the day after.

179

1425 Man, being reasonable, must get drunk;
    The best of life is but intoxication:
Glory, the grape, love, gold, in these are sunk
    The hopes of all men, and of every nation;
Without their sap, how branchless were the trunk
1430   Of life's strange tree, so fruitful on occasion:
But to return,—Get very drunk; and when
You wake with headach, you shall see what then.

180

Ring for your valet—bid him quickly bring
    Some hock and soda-water, then you'll know
1435 A pleasure worthy Xerxes[4] the great king;
    For not the blest sherbet, sublimed with snow,
Nor the first sparkle of the desert-spring,
    Nor Burgundy in all its sunset glow,
After long travel, ennui, love, or slaughter,
1440 Vie with that draught of hock and soda-water.

---

4. The 5th-century Persian king was said to have offered a reward to anyone who could discover a new kind of pleasure.

181

The coast—I think it was the coast that I
 Was just describing—Yes, it *was* the coast—
Lay at this period quiet as the sky,
 The sands untumbled, the blue waves untost,
1445 And all was stillness, save the sea-bird's cry,
 And dolphin's leap, and little billow crost
By some low rock or shelve, that made it fret
Against the boundary it scarcely wet.

182

And forth they wander'd, her sire being gone,
1450 As I have said, upon an expedition;
And mother, brother, guardian, she had none,
 Save Zoe, who, although with due precision
She waited on her lady with the sun,
 Thought daily service was her only mission,
1455 Bringing warm water, wreathing her long tresses,
And asking now and then for cast-off dresses.

183

It was the cooling hour, just when the rounded
 Red sun sinks down behind the azure hill,
Which then seems as if the whole earth it bounded,
1460 Circling all nature, hush'd, and dim, and still,
With the far mountain-crescent half surrounded
 On one side, and the deep sea calm and chill
Upon the other, and the rosy sky,
With one star sparkling through it like an eye.

184

1465 And thus they wander'd forth, and hand in hand,
 Over the shining pebbles and the shells,
Glided along the smooth and harden'd sand,
 And in the worn and wild receptacles
Work'd by the storms, yet work'd as it were plann'd,
1470 In hollow halls, with sparry roofs and cells,
They turn'd to rest; and, each clasp'd by an arm,
Yielded to the deep twilight's purple charm.

185

They look'd up to the sky, whose floating glow
 Spread like a rosy ocean, vast and bright;
1475 They gazed upon the glittering sea below,
 Whence the broad moon rose circling into sight;
They heard the wave's splash, and the wind so low,
 And saw each other's dark eyes darting light
Into each other—and, beholding this,
1480 Their lips drew near, and clung into a kiss;

186

A long, long kiss, a kiss of youth and love
 And beauty, all concentrating like rays
Into one focus, kindled from above;
 Such kisses as belong to early days,
1485 Where heart, and soul, and sense, in concert move,
 And the blood's lava, and the pulse a blaze,
Each kiss a heart-quake,—for a kiss's strength,
I think, it must be reckon'd by its length.

187

By length I mean duration; theirs endured
1490 Heaven knows how long—no doubt they never reckon'd;
And if they had, they could not have secured
 The sum of their sensations to a second:
They had not spoken; but they felt allured,
 As if their souls and lips each other beckon'd,
1495 Which, being join'd, like swarming bees they clung—
Their hearts the flowers from whence the honey sprung.

188

They were alone, but not alone as they
 Who shut in chambers think it loneliness;
The silent ocean, and the starlight bay,
1500 The twilight glow, which momently grew less,
The voiceless sands, and dropping caves, that lay
 Around them, made them to each other press,
As if there were no life beneath the sky
Save theirs, and that their life could never die.

189

1505 They fear'd no eyes nor ears on that lone beach,
 They felt no terrors from the night, they were
All in all to each other: though their speech
 Was broken words, they *thought* a language there,—
And all the burning tongues the passions teach
1510 Found in one sigh the best interpreter
Of nature's oracle—first love,—that all
Which Eve has left her daughters since her fall.

190

Haidee[5] spoke not of scruples, ask'd no vows,
 Nor offer'd any; she had never heard
1515 Of plight and promises to be a spouse,
 Or perils by a loving maid incurr'd;

---

5. According to the Countess of Blessington, who published *Conversations with Lord Byron* in 1834, Byron said, with reference to Haidee: "I was, and am, penetrated with the conviction that women only know evil from men, whereas men have no criterion to judge of purity or goodness but woman."

She was all which pure ignorance allows,
    And flew to her young mate like a young bird;
And, never having dreamt of falsehood, she
1520   Had not one word to say of constancy.

191

She loved, and was beloved—she adored,
    And she was worshipp'd; after nature's fashion,
Their intense souls, into each other pour'd,
    If souls could die, had perish'd in that passion,—
1525   But by degrees their senses were restored,
    Again to be o'ercome, again to dash on;
And, beating 'gainst *his* bosom, Haidee's heart
Felt as if never more to beat apart.

192

Alas! they were so young, so beautiful,
1530   So lonely, loving, helpless, and the hour
Was that in which the heart is always full,
    And, having o'er itself no further power,
Prompts deeds eternity can not annul,
    But pays off moments in an endless shower
1535   Of hell-fire—all prepared for people giving
Pleasure or pain to one another living.

193

Alas! for Juan and Haidee! they were
    So loving and so lovely—till then never,
Excepting our first parents, such a pair
1540   Had run the risk of being damn'd for ever;
And Haidee, being devout as well as fair,
    Had, doubtless, heard about the Stygian river,[6]
And hell and purgatory—but forgot
Just in the very crisis she should not.

194

1545   They look upon each other, and their eyes
    Gleam in the moonlight; and her white arm clasps
Round Juan's head, and his around hers lies
    Half buried in the tresses which it grasps;
She sits upon his knee, and drinks his sighs,
1550   He hers, until they end in broken gasps;
And thus they form a group that's quite antique,
Half naked, loving, natural, and Greek.

195

And when those deep and burning moments pass'd,
    And Juan sunk to sleep within her arms,

6. The Styx, which flows through Hades.

1555 She slept not, but all tenderly, though fast,
   Sustain'd his head upon her bosom's charms;
And now and then her eye to heaven is cast,
   And then on the pale cheek her breast now warms,
Pillow'd on her o'erflowing heart, which pants
1560 With all it granted, and with all it grants.

196

An infant when it gazes on a light,
   A child the moment when it drains the breast,
A devotee when soars the Host[7] in sight,
   An Arab with a stranger for a guest,
1565 A sailor when the prize has struck[8] in fight,
   A miser filling his most hoarded chest,
Feel rapture; but not such true joy are reaping
As they who watch o'er what they love while sleeping.

197

For there it lies so tranquil, so beloved,
1570   All that it hath of life with us is living;
So gentle, stirless, helpless, and unmoved,
   And all unconscious of the joy 'tis giving;
All it hath felt, inflicted, pass'd, and proved,
   Hush'd into depths beyond the watcher's diving;
1575 There lies the thing we love with all its errors
And all its charms, like death without its terrors.

198

The lady watch'd her lover—and that hour
   Of Love's, and Night's, and Ocean's solitude,
O'erflow'd her soul with their united power;
1580   Amidst the barren sand and rocks so rude
She and her wave-worn love had made their bower,
   Where nought upon their passion could intrude,
And all the stars that crowded the blue space
Saw nothing happier than her glowing face.

199

1585 Alas! the love of women! it is known
   To be a lovely and a fearful thing;
For all of theirs upon that die is thrown,
   And if 'tis lost, life hath no more to bring
To them but mockeries of the past alone,
1590   And their revenge is as the tiger's spring,
Deadly, and quick, and crushing; yet, as real
Torture is theirs, what they inflict they feel.

7. The bread or wafer that a priest consecrates to celebrate Mass.

8. When a captured vessel (a "prize") lowers its flag in token of surrender.

200

They are right; for man, to man so oft unjust,
   Is always so to women; one sole bond
1595 Awaits them, treachery is all their trust;
   Taught to conceal, their bursting hearts despond
Over their idol, till some wealthier lust
   Buys them in marriage—and what rests beyond?
A thankless husband, next a faithless lover,
1600 Then dressing, nursing, praying, and all's over.

201

Some take a lover, some take drams° or prayers,   *drink*
   Some mind their household, others dissipation,
Some run away, and but exchange their cares,
   Losing the advantage of a virtuous station;
1605 Few changes e'er can better their affairs,
   Theirs being an unnatural situation,
From the dull palace to the dirty hovel:
Some play the devil, and then write a novel.[9]

202

Haidee was Nature's bride, and knew not this;
1610   Haidee was Passion's child, born where the sun
Showers triple light, and scorches even the kiss
   Of his gazelle-eyed daughters; she was one
Made but to love, to feel that she was his
   Who was her chosen: what was said or done
1615 Elsewhere was nothing.—She had nought to fear,
Hope, care, nor love, beyond, her heart beat *here*.

203

And oh! that quickening of the heart, that beat!
   How much it costs us! yet each rising throb
Is in its cause as its effect so sweet,
1620   That Wisdom, ever on the watch to rob
Joy of its alchymy and to repeat
   Fine truths, even Conscience, too, has a tough job
To make us understand each good old maxim,
So good—I wonder Castlereagh[1] don't tax 'em.

204

1625 And now 'twas done—on the lone shore were plighted
     Their hearts; the stars, their nuptial torches, shed

9. The impetuous Lady Caroline Lamb, having thrown herself at Byron and been after a time rejected, incorporated incidents from the affair in her novel *Glenarvon* (1816).
1. Robert Stewart, Viscount Castlereagh, detested by Byron for the ruthlessness he had shown in 1798 as the government's chief secretary for Ireland and for the foreign policy he later pursued as foreign secretary (1812–22). His belligerence with political opponents contributed to his unpopularity. Byron refers to a famously testy speech in which Castlereagh complained of "an ignorant impatience of taxation."

Beauty upon the beautiful they lighted:
    Ocean their witness, and the cave their bed,
By their own feelings hallow'd and united,
1630   Their priest was Solitude, and they were wed:
And they were happy, for to their young eyes
Each was an angel, and earth paradise.[2]

*   *   *

208

But Juan! had he quite forgotten Julia?
    And should he have forgotten her so soon?
I can't but say it seems to me most truly a
1660   Perplexing question; but, no doubt, the moon
Does these things for us, and whenever newly a
    Palpitation rises, 'tis her boon,
Else how the devil is it that fresh features
Have such a charm for us poor human creatures?

209

1665 I hate inconstancy—I loathe, detest,
    Abhor, condemn, abjure the mortal made
Of such quicksilver clay that in his breast
    No permanent foundation can be laid;
Love, constant love, has been my constant guest,
1670   And yet last night, being at a masquerade,
I saw the prettiest creature, fresh from Milan,
Which gave me some sensations like a villain.

210

But soon Philosophy came to my aid,
    And whisper'd, "Think of every sacred tie!"
1675 "I will, my dear Philosophy!" I said,
    "But then her teeth, and then, oh, Heaven! her eye!
I'll just enquire if she be wife or maid,
    Or neither—out of curiosity."
"Stop!" cried Philosophy, with air so Grecian,
1680 (Though she was masqued then as a fair Venetian).

211

"Stop!" so I stopp'd.—But to return: that which
    Men call inconstancy is nothing more
Than admiration due where nature's rich
    Profusion with young beauty covers o'er
1685 Some favour'd object; and as in the niche

2. This episode rewrites *Aeneid* 4, in which, influenced by the malicious goddess Juno's love spells, the hero Aeneas and Dido, queen of Car-thage, consummate their union in the cave in which they have taken refuge from a storm.

A lovely statue we almost adore,
This sort of adoration of the real
Is but a heightening of the "beau ideal."[3]

212

'Tis the perception of the beautiful,
1690   A fine extension of the faculties,
Platonic, universal, wonderful,
    Drawn from the stars, and filter'd through the skies,
Without which life would be extremely dull;
    In short, it is the use of our own eyes,
1695 With one or two small senses added, just
To hint that flesh is form'd of fiery dust.

213

Yet 'tis a painful feeling, and unwilling,
    For surely if we always could perceive
In the same object graces quite as killing
1700   As when she rose upon us like an Eve,
'Twould save us many a heartache, many a shilling
    (For we must get them any how, or grieve),
Whereas if one sole lady pleased for ever,
How pleasant for the heart, as well as liver!

*   *   *

216

In the mean time, without proceeding more
    In this anatomy, I've finish'd now
Two hundred and odd stanzas as before,
    That being about the number I'll allow
1725 Each canto of the twelve, or twenty-four;
    And, laying down my pen, I make my bow,
Leaving Don Juan and Haidee to plead
For them and theirs with all who deign to read.[4]

1818–9   1819

---

3. Ideal beauty (French), a common phrase in discussions of aesthetics.

4. Haidee's and Juan's tryst is brought to an abrupt end by the unexpected return of her pirate father, who erupts in rage when he discovers the two together. Haidee dies of a broken heart, but Juan's adventures continue. Her father's crew wound him in a fight and then ship him off as a slave. In the slave market of Constantinople, he is bought by an enamored sultana, who disguises him as a girl and adds him to her husband's harem for convenience of access. Juan escapes, joins the Russian army that is besieging Ismail, and distinguishes himself so well in the capture of the town that he is sent with dispatches to the Russian capital. (For Byron's account of the siege, see "Romantic Literature and Wartime," in the supplemental ebook.) In Russia, Juan becomes "man-mistress" to the insatiable empress, Catherine the Great. As a result of her attentions, he falls into a physical decline and in the hope that a change of scene will restore his health is sent on a diplomatic mission to England. In canto 16, the last that Byron finished, Juan is in the middle of an amorous adventure while a guest in the haunted mansion of an English nobleman and his beautiful wife, the "fair most fatal Juan ever met."

PERCY BYSSHE SHELLEY
1792–1822

Percy Bysshe Shelley, radical in every aspect of his life and thought, emerged from a solidly conservative background. His ancestors had been Sussex aristocrats since early in the seventeenth century; his grandfather, Sir Bysshe Shelley, made himself the richest man in Horsham, Sussex; his father, Timothy Shelley, was a hardheaded and conventional member of Parliament. Percy Shelley was in line for a baronetcy and, as befitted his station, was sent to be educated at Eton and Oxford. As a youth he was slight of build, eccentric in manner, and unskilled in sports or fighting and, as a consequence, was mercilessly bullied by older and stronger boys. He later said that he saw the petty tyranny of schoolmasters and schoolmates as representative of man's general inhumanity to man, and dedicated his life to a war against injustice and oppression. As he described the experience in the Dedication to *Laon and Cythna*:

> So without shame, I spake:—"I will be wise,
> And just, and free, and mild, if in me lies
> Such power, for I grow weary to behold
> The selfish and the strong still tyrannise
> Without reproach or check." I then controuled
> My tears, my heart grew calm, and I was meek and bold.

At Oxford in the autumn of 1810, Shelley's closest friend was Thomas Jefferson Hogg, a self-centered, self-confident young man who shared Shelley's love of philosophy and scorn of orthodoxy. The two collaborated on a pamphlet, *The Necessity of Atheism,* which claimed that God's existence cannot be proved on empirical grounds, and, provocatively, they mailed it to the bishops and heads of the colleges at Oxford. Shelley refused to repudiate the document and, to his shock and grief, was peremptorily expelled, terminating a university career that had lasted only six months. This event opened a breach between Shelley and his father that widened over the years.

Shelley went to London, where he took up the cause of Harriet Westbrook, the pretty and warmhearted daughter of a well-to-do tavern keeper, whose father, Shelley wrote to Hogg, "has persecuted her in a most horrible way by endeavoring to compel her to go to school." Harriet threw herself on Shelley's protection, and "gratitude and admiration," he wrote, "all demand that I shall love her *forever.*" He eloped with Harriet to Edinburgh and married her, against his conviction that marriage was a tyrannical and degrading social institution. He was then eighteen years of age; his bride, sixteen. The couple moved restlessly from place to place, living on a small allowance granted reluctantly by their families. In February 1812, accompanied by Harriet's sister Eliza, they traveled to Dublin to distribute Shelley's *Address to the Irish People* and otherwise take part in the movement for Catholic emancipation and for the amelioration of that oppressed and poverty-stricken people.

Back in London Shelley eagerly sought the acquaintance of the radical novelist and philosopher William Godwin, author of *Inquiry Concerning Political Justice* (1794), and in 1813 he published his first important work, *Queen Mab, A Philosophical Poem,* which owes much to Godwin's optimistic conviction in *Political Justice* that the regeneration of the human species was at hand and that in these modern times "the phalanx of reason" would prove "invulnerable" in its advance. In

Shelley's long poem, which he printed at his own expense, so as to maneuver around blasphemy and sedition laws, the fairy Queen Mab reveals to a journeying soul visions of the woeful past, a dreadful present, and a utopian future. Queen Mab's denunciations of institutional religion, aristocracy, and monarchy are elaborated at length in the poem's many endnotes. These atheistic and revolutionary sentiments made Shelley infamous for the rest of his life. They also, somewhat to his embarrassment in later life, came to the attention of the radical press, which kept Queen Mab in print, in cheap, pirated editions, for the rest of the century.

In the following spring Shelley, who had drifted away from Harriet, fell in love with Godwin's and the late Mary Wollstonecraft's beautiful and intelligent daughter, Mary. Convinced that cohabitation without love was immoral, he abandoned Harriet, fled to France with Mary (taking along her stepsister, Claire Clairmont), and—in accordance with his belief in nonexclusive love—invited Harriet to come live with them as another sister. Shelley's elopement with Mary outraged her father, even though his own views of marriage had once been, on the testimony of Political Justice, no less radical than Shelley's and even though Shelley, despite his own financial difficulties, had earlier taken over Godwin's substantial debts. When he returned to London Shelley found that the public, his family, and many friends regarded him as not only an atheist and a revolutionist but also a libertine. When two years later Harriet, pregnant by an unknown lover, drowned herself in a fit of despair, the courts denied Shelley the custody of their two children. (His first child with Mary Godwin had died earlier, only twelve days after her birth in February 1815.) Percy and Mary married in December 1816, and in spring 1818 they moved to Italy.

In Italy Shelley resumed his restless way of life, evading the people to whom he owed money by moving from town to town and house to house. His health was usually bad. Although the death of his grandfather in 1815 had provided a substantial income, he dissipated so much of it by his warmhearted but imprudent support of Godwin and other needy acquaintances that he was constantly short of funds. Within nine months of their arrival in Italy, both Clara and William, the children Mary had borne in 1815 and 1817, died. Grief over these deaths destroyed the earlier harmony of the Shelleys' marriage; the birth in November 1819 of another son, Percy Florence (their only child to survive to adulthood), was not enough to mend the rift.

In these circumstances Shelley wrote his greatest works. Exile from England prompted him, on the one hand, to envision himself as an alien and outcast, bereft of an audience, and rejected by the human race to whose welfare he had dedicated his powers. It also prompted him, on the other hand, to imagine and, to a lesser extent, initiate new kinds of intellectual alliances and forms of ethical and political community, ambitions manifested in his friendship with Lord Byron and in the invitations to join him in Italy that he extended to Keats, Leigh Hunt, Thomas Peacock, and others. The poems of 1819–21, so rich and complex in part because they often seek to reconcile these conflicting accounts of the poetic self in relation to community, include (from 1819 alone) Prometheus Unbound, an epic-scale "closet-drama" about the Greek Titan's survival and transcendence of oppression; his Jacobean-style revenge tragedy of incest and parricide, The Cenci; his visionary call for revolution, The Mask of Anarchy; a witty satire on Wordsworth, Peter Bell the Third; a penetrating, proto-Marxist essay, "A Philosophical View of Reform"; and numerous lyric poems. Later came "A Defence of Poetry"; Epipsychidion, a rhapsodic view of love as a spiritual union beyond earthly limits; Adonais, his elegy on Keats, representing the younger poet as a victim of a politicized review culture; and Hellas, a lyrical drama inspired by the Greek war for liberation from the Turks.

These writings are enriched by Shelley's omnivorous reading, in the natural sciences, ancient and modern philosophy, Dante, Milton, the Bible—reading that he carried on, as his friend Hogg said, "in season and out of season, at table, in bed, and especially during a walk" until he became one of the most erudite of the English poets. In particular the late works often evince Shelley's study of Plato (whose Ion and *Symposium* he translated) and of the Neoplatonists. The Platonic division of the cosmos into two worlds—the ordinary world of change, mortality, evil, and suffering, which is contrasted with the ideal world of perfect and eternal forms, of which the world of sense experience is only a distant and illusory reflection—was immensely attractive to Shelley. His *Adonais* set out that contrast memorably: "Life like a dome of many-coloured glass / Stains the white radiance of eternity" (lines 462–63). At the same time, however, the idealism these lines register as they evoke a beauty that is offset by the "stain" of temporal existence was often, within Shelley's late writings, tempered by his enthusiastic study of British empiricist philosophy, which limits knowledge to what is given in sense experience, and tempered, especially, by the affinities he felt for the radical skepticism of David Hume. Works such as "Mont Blanc" are shaped by his sense that there are narrow limits to what human beings can know with certainty. Out of this divided intellectual inheritance, Shelley developed, some critics have proposed, a "skeptical idealism," an attitude that also colors the hopes for radical social and political reform that he retained even at a historical moment that seemed (with the restoration of the old autocratic monarchies after 1815, with the suffering of the poor in the economic depression that followed the end of the war) to have delivered an insurmountable setback to the cause of liberty. For him such hopes were moral obligations, more than they were expressions of intellectual certainty. We must continue to hope because, by keeping open the possibility of a better future, hope releases the imaginative and creative powers that are the only means of achieving that end. Shelley had a motto in Italian inscribed on a ring that he often wore: "Il buon tempo verra" ("the good time will come").

When in 1820 the Shelleys settled finally at Pisa, he came closer to finding contentment than at any other time in his adult life. A group of friends, Shelley's "Pisan Circle," gathered around them, including for a while Byron and the swashbuckling Cornishman Edward Trelawny. Chief in Shelley's affections were Edward Williams, a retired lieutenant of a cavalry regiment serving in India, and his common-law wife Jane, with whom Shelley became infatuated and to whom he addressed some of his best lyrics and verse letters. The end came suddenly, and in a way prefigured uncannily in the last stanza of *Adonais*, in which he had described his spirit as a ship driven by a violent storm out into the dark unknown. On July 8, 1822, Shelley and Edward Williams were sailing their open boat, the *Don Juan*, on the Gulf of Spezia. A violent squall swamped the boat. When several days later the bodies were washed ashore, they were cremated, and Shelley's ashes were buried in the Protestant Cemetery at Rome, near the graves of John Keats and William Shelley, the poet's young son.

Shelley's character has been the subject of heated and contradictory estimates, and commentators have also disagreed, analogously, in their assessments of his success at mixing politics and poetry. The actions that he justified to himself because they were true to his convictions often led to disastrous consequences for those near him, especially women; and even recent scholars, while repudiating the vicious attacks made by Shelley's contemporaries, attribute some of those actions to a self-assured egotism that masked itself as idealism. Yet Byron, who knew Shelley intimately, and did not readily pay compliments, wrote to his publisher John Murray, in response to attacks on Shelley at the time of his death: "You are all brutally mistaken about Shelley, who was, without exception, the *best* and least selfish man I ever knew." Vilified by the Tory press during his lifetime, Shelley's politics recommended his poetry to many later political radicals: the Chartists in the middle of the nineteenth century, Marx and Engels at the end, and at the start of the twentieth century, Mahatma Gandhi and many guiding lights of the British Labour Party. And, despite their ideological differences, Wordsworth recognized early on the extent to which Shelley in that poetry had expanded English versification's metrical and stanzaic resources: "Shelley," Wordsworth said, "is one of the best *artists* of us all."

The texts printed here are those prepared by Donald H. Reiman and Neil Fraistat for *Shelley's Poetry and Prose: A Norton Critical Edition*, 2nd ed. (2001); Reiman has also edited for this anthology a few poems not included in that edition.

Mutability

We are as clouds that veil the midnight moon;
    How restlessly they speed, and gleam, and quiver,
Streaking the darkness radiantly!—yet soon
    Night closes round, and they are lost for ever:

5   Or like forgotten lyres,° whose dissonant strings   *wind harps*
    Give various response to each varying blast,
To whose frail frame no second motion brings
    One mood or modulation like the last.

We rest.—A dream has power to poison sleep;
10   We rise.—One wandering thought pollutes the day;
We feel, conceive or reason, laugh or weep;
    Embrace fond woe, or cast our cares away:

It is the same!—For, be it joy or sorrow,
    The path of its departure still is free:
15   Man's yesterday may ne'er be like his morrow;
    Nought may endure but Mutability.

ca. 1814–15   1816

To Wordsworth[1]

Poet of Nature, thou hast wept to know
That things depart which never may return:
Childhood and youth, friendship and love's first glow,
Have fled like sweet dreams, leaving thee to mourn.
5   These common woes I feel. One loss is mine
Which thou too feel'st, yet I alone deplore.
Thou wert as a lone star, whose light did shine
On some frail bark° in winter's midnight roar: *small ship*
Thou hast like to a rock-built refuge stood
10   Above the blind and battling multitude:
In honoured poverty thy voice did weave
Songs consecrate to truth and liberty,[2]—
Deserting these, thou leavest me to grieve,
Thus having been, that thou shouldst cease to be.

ca. 1814–15   1816

1. Shelley's grieved comment on the poet of nature and of social radicalism after his views had become conservative.
2. Perhaps an allusion to "Sonnets Dedicated to Liberty," the title that Wordsworth gave to the section of sonnets such as "London, 1802" when he republished them in his *Poems* of 1807.

Mont Blanc[1]

Lines Written in the Vale of Chamouni

I

The everlasting universe of things
Flows through the mind, and rolls its rapid waves,
Now dark—now glittering—now reflecting gloom—
Now lending splendour, where from secret springs
5   The source of human thought its tribute brings
Of waters,—with a sound but half its own,
Such as a feeble brook will oft assume
In the wild woods, among the mountains lone,
Where waterfalls around it leap forever,
10 Where woods and winds contend, and a vast river
Over its rocks ceaselessly bursts and raves.

2

Thus thou, Ravine of Arve—dark, deep Ravine—
Thou many-coloured, many-voiced vale,
Over whose pines, and crags, and caverns sail
15 Fast cloud shadows and sunbeams: awful° scene,   *awe-inspiring*
Where Power in likeness of the Arve comes down
From the ice gulphs that gird his secret throne,
Bursting through these dark mountains like the flame
Of lightning through the tempest;—thou dost lie,
20 Thy giant brood of pines around thee clinging,
Children of elder° time, in whose devotion   *earlier, ancient*
The chainless winds still come and ever came
To drink their odours, and their mighty swinging
To hear—an old and solemn harmony;
25 Thine earthly rainbows stretched across the sweep
Of the etherial waterfall, whose veil
Robes some unsculptured[2] image; the strange sleep
Which when the voices of the desart fail

1. "Mont Blanc," in which Shelley both echoes and argues with the poetry of natural description written by Wordsworth and Coleridge, was first published as the conclusion to the *History of a Six Weeks' Tour*. This was a book that Percy and Mary Shelley wrote together detailing the excursion that they and Claire Clairmont took in July 1816 to the valley of Chamonix, in what is now southeastern France. That valley lies at the foot of Mont Blanc, the highest mountain in the Alps and in all Europe.

In the *History* Percy Shelley commented on his poem: "It was composed under the immediate impression of the deep and powerful feelings excited by the objects it attempts to describe; and, as an indisciplined overflowing of the soul rests its claim to approbation on an attempt to imitate the untamable wildness and inaccessible solemnity from which those feelings sprang." He was inspired to write the poem while standing on a bridge spanning the river Arve, which flows through the valley of Chamonix and is fed from above by the meltoff of the glacier, the Mer de Glace.

In a letter to Thomas Love Peacock drafted in the same week as "Mont Blanc," Shelley had recalled that the count de Buffon, a French pioneer of the science we now know as geology, had proposed a "sublime but gloomy theory—that this globe which we inhabit will at some future period be changed to a mass of frost." This sense, which Shelley takes from Buffon, of a Nature that is utterly alien and indifferent to human beings (and whose history takes shape on a timescale of incomprehensible immensity) is counterposed throughout "Mont Blanc" with Shelley's interest, fueled by his reading of 18th-century skeptics such as David Hume, in questions about the human mind, its powers, and the limits of knowledge. "All things exist as they are perceived: at least in relation to the percipient," Shelley would later write in "A Defence of Poetry" (p. 431). In "Mont Blanc" the priority that this statement gives to the mind over the external world is challenged by the sheer destructive power of the mountain.

2. I.e., not formed by humans.

Wraps all in its own deep eternity;—
30 Thy caverns echoing to the Arve's commotion,
A loud, lone sound no other sound can tame;
Thou art pervaded with that ceaseless motion,
Thou art the path of that unresting sound—
Dizzy Ravine! and when I gaze on thee
35 I seem as in a trance sublime and strange
To muse on my own separate phantasy,
My own, my human mind, which passively
Now renders and receives fast influencings,
Holding an unremitting interchange
40 With the clear universe of things around;
One legion of wild thoughts, whose wandering wings
Now float above thy darkness, and now rest
Where that° or thou° art no unbidden guest,   *thy darkness / the Ravine*
In the still cave of the witch Poesy,[3]   .
45 Seeking among the shadows that pass by
Ghosts of all things that are, some shade of thee,
Some phantom, some faint image; till the breast
From which they fled recalls them, thou art there![4]

3

Some say that gleams of a remoter world
50 Visit the soul in sleep,—that death is slumber,
And that its shapes the busy thoughts outnumber
Of those who wake and live.—I look on high;
Has some unknown omnipotence unfurled
The veil of life and death? or do I lie
55 In dream, and does the mightier world of sleep
Spread far around and inaccessibly
Its circles? For the very spirit fails,
Driven like a homeless cloud from steep to steep
That vanishes among the viewless° gales!   *invisible*
60 Far, far above, piercing the infinite sky,
Mont Blanc appears,—still, snowy, and serene—
Its subject mountains their unearthly forms
Pile around it, ice and rock; broad vales between
Of frozen floods, unfathomable deeps,
65 Blue as the overhanging heaven, that spread
And wind among the accumulated steeps;
A desert peopled by the storms alone,
Save° when the eagle brings some hunter's bone,   *except*
And the wolf tracts° her there—how hideously   *tracks*
70 Its shapes are heaped around! rude, bare, and high,

3. I.e., in the part of the mind that creates poetry.
4. In these difficult lines (41–48) Shelley seems to be recalling Plato's allegory in the *Republic* of the mind as cave. Plato describes human beings' sense of reality as if it were based only on the shadows cast by firelight on the walls and we remained ignorant of the light of reality outside the cave. The syntax in the passage blurs the distinction between what is inside the human viewer's mind and outside in the world that he views: the thoughts (line 41) seek in the poet's creative faculty ("the still cave of the witch Poesy") some "shade," "phantom," or "faint image" of the Ravine of the Arve, and when the Ravine is thereby remembered (when "the breast" from which the images has fled "recalls them"), then the Ravine exists.

Ghastly, and scarred, and riven.°—Is this the scene   *split*
Where the old Earthquake-dæmon[5] taught her young
Ruin? Were these their toys? or did a sea
Of fire, envelope once this silent snow?
75 None can reply—all seems eternal now.
The wilderness has a mysterious tongue
Which teaches awful doubt,[6] or faith so mild,
So solemn, so serene, that man may be
But for such faith[7] with nature reconciled;
80 Thou hast a voice, great Mountain, to repeal
Large codes of fraud and woe; not understood
By all, but which[8] the wise, and great, and good
Interpret, or make felt, or deeply feel.

4

The fields, the lakes, the forests, and the streams,
85 Ocean, and all the living things that dwell
Within the dædal[9] earth; lightning, and rain,
Earthquake, and fiery flood, and hurricane,
The torpor of the year when feeble dreams
Visit the hidden buds, or dreamless sleep
90 Holds every future leaf and flower;—the bound
With which from that detested trance they leap;
The works and ways of man, their death and birth,
And that of him and all that his may be;
All things that move and breathe with toil and sound
95 Are born and die; revolve, subside and swell.
Power dwells apart in its tranquillity
Remote, serene, and inaccessible:
And *this*, the naked countenance of earth,
On which I gaze, even these primæval mountains
100 Teach the adverting° mind. The glaciers creep   *observant*
Like snakes that watch their prey, from their far fountains,
Slow rolling on; there, many a precipice,
Frost and the Sun in scorn of mortal power
Have piled: dome, pyramid, and pinnacle,
105 A city of death, distinct with many a tower
And wall impregnable of beaming ice.
Yet not a city, but a flood of ruin
Is there, that from the boundaries of the sky
Rolls its perpetual stream; vast pines are strewing
110 Its destined path, or in the mangled soil
Branchless and shattered stand: the rocks, drawn down
From yon remotest waste, have overthrown
The limits of the dead and living world,
Never to be reclaimed. The dwelling-place

5. A supernatural being, halfway between mortals and the gods. Here it represents the force that makes earthquakes. Shelley views this landscape as the product of violent geological upheavals in the past.
6. Awe-filled open-mindedness.
7. I.e., only through holding such a faith. Drafts of the poem support this reading: Shelley also wrote "In such wise faith with Nature reconciled" and "In such a faith."
8. The reference is to "voice," line 80.
9. Intricately formed; derived from Daedalus, builder of the labyrinth in Crete.

115 Of insects, beasts, and birds, becomes its spoil;
 Their food and their retreat for ever gone,
 So much of life and joy is lost. The race
 Of man, flies far in dread; his work and dwelling
 Vanish, like smoke before the tempest's stream,
120 And their place is not known. Below, vast caves
 Shine in the rushing torrents' restless gleam,
 Which from those secret chasms in tumult welling[1]
 Meet in the vale, and one majestic River,[2]
 The breath and blood of distant lands, for ever
125 Rolls its loud waters to the ocean waves,
 Breathes its swift vapours to the circling air.

5

 Mont Blanc yet gleams on high:—the power is there,
 The still and solemn power of many sights,
 And many sounds, and much of life and death.
130 In the calm darkness of the moonless nights,
 In the lone glare of day, the snows descend
 Upon that Mountain; none beholds them there,
 Nor when the flakes burn in the sinking sun,
 Or the star-beams dart through them:—Winds contend
135 Silently there, and heap the snow with breath
 Rapid and strong, but silently! Its home
 The voiceless lightning in these solitudes
 Keeps innocently, and like vapour broods
 Over the snow. The secret strength of things
140 Which governs thought, and to the infinite dome
 Of heaven is as a law, inhabits thee!
 And what were thou,° and earth, and stars, and sea,   *Mont Blanc*
 If to the human mind's imaginings
 Silence and solitude were vacancy?

1816   1817

Hymn to Intellectual Beauty[1]

1

 The awful shadow of some unseen Power
  Floats though unseen amongst us,—visiting
  This various world with as inconstant wing
 As summer winds that creep from flower to flower.—
5 Like moonbeams that behind some piny mountain shower,[2]

---

1. This description (as well as that in lines 9–11) seems to be an echo of Coleridge's description of the chasm and sacred river in the recently published "Kubla Khan," lines 12–24.
2. The Arve, which flows into Lake Geneva. Nearby the river Rhone flows out of Lake Geneva to begin its course through France and into the Mediterranean.

1. "Intellectual" means nonmaterial, that which is beyond access to the human senses. In this poem intellectual beauty is something postulated to account for occasional states of awareness that lend splendor, grace, and truth both to the natural world and to people's moral consciousness.
2. Used as a verb.

It visits with inconstant glance
Each human heart and countenance;
Like hues and harmonies of evening,—
Like clouds in starlight widely spread,—
10 Like memory of music fled,—
Like aught that for its grace may be
Dear, and yet dearer for its mystery.

2

Spirit of BEAUTY, that dost consecrate
With thine own hues all thou dost shine upon
15 Of human thought or form,—where art thou gone?
Why dost thou pass away and leave our state,
This dim vast vale of tears, vacant and desolate?
Ask why the sunlight not forever
Weaves rainbows o'er yon mountain river,
20 Why aught° should fail and fade that once is shewn,   *anything*
Why fear and dream and death and birth
Cast on the daylight of this earth
Such gloom,—why man has such a scope
For love and hate, despondency and hope?

3

25 No voice from some sublimer world hath ever
To sage or poet these responses given—
Therefore the name of God and ghosts and Heaven,
Remain the records of their vain endeavour,[3]
Frail spells—whose uttered charm might not avail to sever,
30 From all we hear and all we see,
Doubt, chance, and mutability.
Thy light alone—like mist o'er mountains driven,
Or music by the night wind sent
Through strings of some still instrument,
35 Or moonlight on a midnight stream,
Gives grace and truth to life's unquiet dream.

4

Love, Hope, and Self-esteem, like clouds depart
And come, for some uncertain moments lent.
Man were immortal, and omnipotent,
40 Didst thou, unknown and awful as thou art,
Keep with thy glorious train firm state within his heart.[4]
Thou messenger of sympathies,
That wax and wane in lovers' eyes—
Thou—that to human thought art nourishment,
45 Like darkness to a dying flame![5]

3. The names (line 27) represent nothing better than the feeble guesses that philosophers and poets have made in attempting to answer the questions posed in stanza 2, but these guesses also delude us as though they were magic spells.

4. I.e., "man would be immortal . . . if thou didst keep."
5. Darkness may be said to nourish the dying flame by providing the contrast that offsets its light.

Depart not as thy shadow came,
Depart not—lest the grave should be,
Like life and fear, a dark reality.

5

While yet a boy I sought for ghosts, and sped
50   Through many a listening chamber, cave and ruin,
   And starlight wood, with fearful steps pursuing
Hopes of high talk with the departed dead.
I called on poisonous names with which our youth is fed;[6]
   I was not heard—I saw them not—
55   When musing deeply on the lot
Of life, at that sweet time when winds are wooing
   All vital things that wake to bring
   News of buds and blossoming,—
   Sudden, thy shadow fell on me;
60 I shrieked, and clasped my hands in extacy!

6

I vowed that I would dedicate my powers
   To thee and thine—have I not kept the vow?
   With beating heart and streaming eyes, even now
I call the phantoms of a thousand hours
65 Each from his voiceless grave: they have in visioned bowers
   Of studious zeal or love's delight
   Outwatched with me the envious night[7]—
They know that never joy illumed my brow
   Unlinked with hope that thou wouldst free
70   This world from its dark slavery,
   That thou—O awful LOVELINESS,
Wouldst give whate'er these words cannot express.

7

The day becomes more solemn and serene
   When noon is past—there is a harmony
75   In autumn, and a lustre in its sky,
Which through the summer is not heard or seen,
As if it could not be, as if it had not been!
   Thus let thy power, which like the truth
   Of nature on my passive youth
80 Descended, to my onward life supply
   Its calm—to one who worships thee,
   And every form containing thee,
   Whom, SPIRIT fair, thy spells did bind
To fear[8] himself, and love all human kind.

1816   1817

6. Lines 49–52 refer to Shelley's youthful experiments with magic and conjuring. In one manuscript version this line reads "I called on that false name with which our youth is fed"; the next line continues, "He answered not." This version would have clinched Shelley's scandalous reputation for atheism.
7. I.e., stayed up until the night, envious of their delight, had reluctantly departed.
8. Probably in the old sense: "to stand in awe of."

Ozymandias[1]

I met a traveller from an antique land,
Who said—"Two vast and trunkless° legs of stone   *without a torso*
Stand in the desert. . . . Near them, on the sand,
Half sunk a shattered visage lies, whose frown,
5   And wrinkled lip, and sneer of cold command,
Tell that its sculptor well those passions read
Which yet survive,° stamped on these lifeless things,   *outlive*
The hand that mocked them, and the heart that fed;[2]
And on the pedestal, these words appear:
10   My name is Ozymandias, King of Kings,
Look on my Works, ye Mighty, and despair!
Nothing beside remains. Round the decay
Of that colossal Wreck, boundless and bare
The lone and level sands stretch far away."

1817   1818

A Song: "Men of England"[1]

Men of England, wherefore plough
For the lords who lay ye low?
Wherefore weave with toil and care
The rich robes your tyrants wear?

5   Wherefore feed and clothe and save
From the cradle to the grave
Those ungrateful drones who would
Drain your sweat—nay, drink your blood?

Wherefore, Bees of England, forge
10   Many a weapon, chain, and scourge,
That these stingless drones may spoil
The forced produce of your toil?

Have ye leisure, comfort, calm,
Shelter, food, love's gentle balm?
15   Or what is it ye buy so dear
With your pain and with your fear?

---

1. According to Diodorus Siculus, Greek historian of the 1st century B.C.E., the largest statue in Egypt had the inscription "I am Ozymandias, king of kings; if anyone wishes to know what I am and where I lie, let him surpass me in some of my exploits." Ozymandias was the Greek name for Ramses II of Egypt, 13th century B.C.E.
2. "The hand" is the sculptor's, who had "mocked" (both imitated and satirized) the sculptured passions; "the heart" is the king's, which has "fed" his

passions.
1. This and the two following poems were written at a time of turbulent unrest, after the return of troops from the Napoleonic Wars had precipitated a great economic depression. The "Song," expressing Shelley's hope for a proletarian revolution, was originally planned as one of a series for workers. It has become, as the poet wished, a hymn of the British labor movement.

The seed ye sow, another reaps;
The wealth ye find, another keeps;
The robes ye weave, another wears;
20 The arms ye forge, another bears.

Sow seed—but let no tyrant reap:
Find wealth—let no impostor heap:
Weave robes—let not the idle wear:
Forge arms—in your defence to bear.

25 Shrink to your cellars, holes, and cells—
In halls ye deck another dwells.
Why shake the chains ye wrought? Ye see
The steel ye tempered glance on ye.

With plough and spade and hoe and loom
30 Trace your grave and build your tomb
And weave your winding-sheet—till fair
England be your Sepulchre.

1819   1839

England in 1819[1]

An old, mad, blind, despised, and dying King;[2]
Princes, the dregs of their dull race, who flow
Through public scorn,—mud from a muddy spring;
Rulers who neither see nor feel nor know,
5 But leechlike to their fainting country cling
Till they drop, blind in blood, without a blow.
A people starved and stabbed in th' untilled field;[3]
An army, whom liberticide[4] and prey
Makes as a two-edged sword to all who wield;
10 Golden and sanguine laws[5] which tempt and slay;
Religion Christless, Godless—a book sealed;
A senate, Time's worst statute, unrepealed—
Are graves from which a glorious Phantom[6] may
Burst, to illumine our tempestuous day.

1819   1839

1. Knowing full well that this sonnet on a turbulent time of injustice and unrest would read as sedition, Shelley, when he sent it to Leigh Hunt, his friend and the editor of *The Examiner*, wrote, "I don't expect you to publish it, but you may show it to whom you wish." Shelley also planned to include it in a book of political poetry, "a little volume of popular songs . . . destined to awaken and direct the imagination of the reformers," but that plan came to nothing. The sonnet finally appeared as a part of a grouping of "Poems of 1819" in Mary Shelley's 1839 edition of her late husband's work.

2. George III, who had been declared insane in 1811. He died in 1820.
3. Alluding to the Peterloo Massacre on August 16, 1819. In St. Peter's field, near Manchester, a troop of cavalry had charged into a crowd attending a peaceful rally in support of parliamentary reform.
4. The killing of liberty.
5. Laws bought with gold and leading to bloodshed.
6. I.e., a revolution.

Ode to the West Wind[1]

I

O wild West Wind, thou breath of Autumn's being,
Thou, from whose unseen presence the leaves dead
Are driven, like ghosts from an enchanter fleeing,

Yellow, and black, and pale, and hectic[2] red,
5   Pestilence-stricken multitudes: O Thou,
Who chariotest to their dark wintry bed

The winged seeds, where they lie cold and low,
Each like a corpse within its grave, until
Thine azure sister of the Spring[3] shall blow

10   Her clarion[4] o'er the dreaming earth, and fill
(Driving sweet buds like flocks to feed in air)
With living hues and odours plain and hill:

Wild Spirit, which art moving everywhere;
Destroyer and Preserver;[5] hear, O hear!

2

15   Thou on whose stream, 'mid the steep sky's commotion,
Loose clouds like Earth's decaying leaves are shed,
Shook from the tangled boughs of Heaven and Ocean,

Angels[6] of rain and lightning: there are spread
On the blue surface of thine aery surge,
20   Like the bright hair uplifted from the head

Of some fierce Mænad,[7] even from the dim verge
Of the horizon to the zenith's height,
The locks of the approaching storm. Thou Dirge

---

1. This poem was conceived and chiefly written in a wood that skirts the Arno, near Florence, and on a day when that tempestuous wind, whose temperature is at once mild and animating, was collecting the vapours which pour down the autumnal rains [Shelley's note]. As in other major Romantic poems—for example, the opening of Wordsworth's *Prelude*, Coleridge's "Dejection: An Ode," and the conclusion to Shelley's *Adonais*—the rising wind, linked with the cycle of the seasons, is presented as the correspondent in the external world to an inner change, a burst of creative power that is paralleled to the inspiration of prophets. In many languages the words for *wind, breath, soul,* and *inspiration* are identical or related. Thus Shelley's west wind is a "spirit" (the Latin *spiritus:* wind, breath, soul, and the root word for *inspiration*), the "breath of Autumn's being," which on earth, sky, and sea destroys in autumn to revive in the spring. In some philosophical histories written in Shelley's period, the spirit of liberty was said to have deserted Europe for the Americas. In blowing from the west, the wind may carry liberty back again.

Shelley's sonnet-length stanza, developed from the interlaced three-line units of the Italian *terza rima (aba bcb cdc,* etc.), consists of a set of four such tercets, closed by a couplet rhyming with the middle line of the preceding tercet: *aba bcb cdc ded ee.*

2. Referring to the kind of fever that occurs in tuberculosis.

3. The west wind that will blow in the spring.

4. A high, shrill trumpet.

5. Refers to the Hindu gods Siva the Destroyer and Vishnu the Preserver.

6. In the old sense of messengers.

7. A female worshipper who danced frenziedly in the worship of Dionysus (Bacchus), the Greek god of wine and vegetation. As vegetation god he was fabled to die in the fall and to be resurrected in the spring.

Of the dying year, to which this closing night
25 Will be the dome of a vast sepulchre,
Vaulted with all thy congregated might

Of vapours,° from whose solid atmosphere   *clouds*
Black rain and fire and hail will burst: O hear!

3

Thou who didst waken from his summer dreams
30 The blue Mediterranean, where he lay,
Lulled by the coil of his chrystalline streams,[8]

Beside a pumice isle in Baiæ's bay,[9]
And saw in sleep old palaces and towers
Quivering within the wave's intenser day,

35 All overgrown with azure moss and flowers
So sweet, the sense faints picturing them! Thou
For whose path the Atlantic's level powers

Cleave themselves into chasms, while far below
The sea-blooms and the oozy woods which wear
40 The sapless foliage of the ocean, know

Thy voice, and suddenly grow grey with fear,
And tremble and despoil themselves:[1] O hear!

4

If I were a dead leaf thou mightest bear;
If I were a swift cloud to fly with thee;
45 A wave to pant beneath thy power, and share

The impulse of thy strength, only less free
Than thou, O Uncontrollable! If even
I were as in my boyhood, and could be

The comrade of thy wanderings over Heaven,
50 As then, when to outstrip thy skiey speed
Scarce seemed a vision; I would ne'er have striven

As thus with thee in prayer in my sore need.
Oh! lift me as a wave, a leaf, a cloud!
I fall upon the thorns of life! I bleed!

55 A heavy weight of hours has chained and bowed
One too like thee: tameless, and swift, and proud.

---

8. The currents that flow in the Mediterranean Sea, sometimes with a visible difference in color.
9. West of Naples, the locale of imposing villas built in the glory days of imperial Rome. Their ruins are reflected in the waters of the bay, a sight Mary Shelley also describes in the Introduction to *The Last Man.*
1. The vegetation at the bottom of the sea . . . sympathizes with that of the land in the change of seasons, and is consequently influenced by the winds which announce it [Shelley's note].

5

Make me thy lyre,[2] even as the forest is:
What if my leaves are falling like its own!
The tumult of thy mighty harmonies

60 Will take from both a deep, autumnal tone,
Sweet though in sadness. Be thou, Spirit fierce,
My spirit! Be thou me, impetuous one!

Drive my dead thoughts over the universe
Like withered leaves to quicken a new birth![3]
65 And, by the incantation of this verse,

Scatter, as from an unextinguished hearth
Ashes and sparks, my words among mankind!
Be through my lips to unawakened Earth

The trumpet of a prophecy! O Wind,
70 If Winter comes, can Spring be far behind?

1819   1820

Prometheus Unbound Shelley composed this work in Italy between the autumn of 1818 and the close of 1819 and published it the following summer. Upon its completion he wrote in a letter, "It is a drama, with characters and mechanism of a kind yet unattempted; and I think the execution is better than any of my former attempts." It is based on the *Prometheus Bound* of Aeschylus, which dramatizes the sufferings of Prometheus, unrepentant champion of humanity, who, because he had stolen fire from heaven, was condemned by Zeus to be chained to Mount Caucasus and to be tortured by a vulture feeding on his liver; in a lost sequel Aeschylus reconciled Prometheus with his oppressor. Shelley continued Aeschylus's story but transformed it into a symbolic drama about the origin of evil and the possibility of overcoming it. In such early writings as *Queen Mab*, Shelley had expressed his belief that injustice and suffering could be eliminated by an external revolution that would wipe out or radically reform the causes of evil, attributed to existing social, political, and religious institutions. Implicit in *Prometheus Unbound*, on the other hand, is the view that both evil and the possibility of reform are the moral responsibility of men and women. Social chaos and wars are a gigantic projection of human moral disorder and inner division and conflict; tyrants are the outer representatives of the tyranny of our baser over our better elements; hatred for others is a product of self-contempt; and external political reform is impossible unless we have first reformed our own nature at its roots, by substituting selfless love for divisive hatred. Shelley thus incorporates into his secular myth—of universal regeneration by a triumph of humanity's moral imagination—the ethical teaching of Christ on the Mount, together with the classical morality represented in the *Prometheus* of Aeschylus.

---

2. The Eolian lyre, which responds to the wind with rising and falling musical chords.

3. This line may play on the secondary sense of "leaves" as pages in a book.

FROM PROMETHEUS UNBOUND

A Lyrical Drama in Four Acts

Audisne hæc Amphiarae, sub terram abdite?[1]

Preface

The Greek tragic writers, in selecting as their subject any portion of their national history or mythology, employed in their treatment of it a certain arbitrary discretion. They by no means conceived themselves bound to adhere to the common interpretation or to imitate in story as in title their rivals and predecessors. Such a system would have amounted to a resignation of those claims to preference over their competitors which incited the composition. The Agamemnonian story was exhibited on the Athenian theatre with as many variations as dramas.

I have presumed to employ a similar licence.—The *Prometheus Unbound* of Æschylus, supposed the reconciliation of Jupiter with his victim as the price of the disclosure of the danger threatened to his empire by the consummation of his marriage with Thetis. Thetis, according to this view of the subject, was given in marriage to Peleus, and Prometheus by the permission of Jupiter delivered from his captivity by Hercules.[2]—Had I framed my story on this model I should have done no more than have attempted to restore the lost drama of Æschylus; an ambition, which, if my preference to this mode of treating the subject had incited me to cherish, the recollection of the high comparison such an attempt would challenge, might well abate. But in truth I was averse from a catastrophe so feeble as that of reconciling the Champion with the Oppressor of mankind. The moral interest of the fable which is so powerfully sustained by the sufferings and endurance of Prometheus, would be annihilated if we could conceive of him as unsaying his high language, and quailing before his successful and perfidious adversary. The only imaginary being resembling in any degree Prometheus, is Satan; and Prometheus is, in my judgement, a more poetical character than Satan because, in addition to courage and majesty and firm and patient opposition to omnipotent force, he is susceptible of being described as exempt from the taints of ambition, envy, revenge, and a desire for personal aggrandisement, which in the Hero of *Paradise Lost*, interfere with the interest. The character of Satan engenders in the mind a pernicious casuistry[3] which leads us to weigh his faults with his wrongs and to excuse the former because the latter exceed all measure. In the minds of those who consider that magnificent fiction with a religious feeling, it engenders something worse. But Prometheus is, as it were, the type of the highest perfection of moral and

1. Cicero, *Tusculan Disputations* 2.60: "Do you hear this, O Amphiaraus, concealed under the earth?" In Greek myth Amphiaraus was a seer. Fleeing from an unsuccessful assault on Thebes, he was saved from his pursuers by Zeus, who by a thunderbolt opened a cleft in the earth that swallowed him up.

In his *Disputations* Cicero is arguing for the Stoic doctrine of the need to master pain and suffering. He quotes this line (a Latin translation from Aeschylus's lost drama *Epigoni*) in the course of an anecdote about Dionysius of Heraclea, who, tormented by kidney stones, abjures the doctrine of his Stoic teacher Zeno that pain is not an evil. By way of reproof his fellow-Stoic Cleanthes strikes his foot on the ground and utters this line. Cicero interprets it as an appeal to Zeno the Stoic master (under the name of Amphiaraus).

2. Shelley's description of the subject of Aeschylus's lost drama, *Prometheus Unbound*, is a speculation based on surviving fragments.

3. Slippery reasoning.

intellectual nature, impelled by the purest and the truest motives to the best and noblest ends.

This Poem was chiefly written upon the mountainous ruins of the Baths of Caracalla, among the flowery glades, and thickets of odoriferous blossoming trees which are extended in ever winding labyrinths upon its immense platforms and dizzy arches suspended in the air. The bright blue sky of Rome, and the effect of the vigorous awakening of spring in that divinest climate, and the new life with which it drenches the spirits even to intoxication, were the inspiration of this drama.

The imagery which I have employed will be found in many instances to have been drawn from the operations of the human mind, or from those external actions by which they are expressed. This is unusual in modern Poetry; although Dante and Shakespeare are full of instances of the same kind: Dante indeed more than any other poet and with greater success. But the Greek poets, as writers to whom no resource of awakening the sympathy of their contemporaries was unknown, were in the habitual use of this power, and it is the study of their works (since a higher merit would probably be denied me) to which I am willing that my readers should impute this singularity.

One word is due in candour to the degree in which the study of contemporary writings may have tinged my composition, for such has been a topic of censure with regard to poems far more popular, and indeed more deservedly popular than mine. It is impossible that any one who inhabits the same age with such writers as those who stand in the foremost ranks of our own, can conscientiously assure himself, that his language and tone of thought may not have been modified by the study of the productions of those extraordinary intellects. It is true, that, not the spirit of their genius, but the forms in which it has manifested itself, are due, less to the peculiarities of their own minds, than to the peculiarity of the moral and intellectual condition of the minds among which they have been produced. Thus a number of writers possess the form, whilst they want the spirit of those whom, it is alleged, they imitate; because the former is the endowment of the age in which they live, and the latter must be the uncommunicated lightning of their own mind.

The peculiar style of intense and comprehensive imagery which distinguishes the modern literature of England, has not been, as a general power, the product of the imitation of any particular writer. The mass of capabilities remains at every period materially the same; the circumstances which awaken it to action perpetually change. If England were divided into forty republics, each equal in population and extent to Athens, there is no reason to suppose but that, under institutions not more perfect than those of Athens, each would produce philosophers and poets equal to those who (if we except Shakespeare) have never been surpassed. We owe the great writers of the golden age of our literature to that fervid awakening of the public mind which shook to dust the oldest and most oppressive form of the Christian Religion. We owe Milton to the progress and developement of the same spirit; the sacred Milton was, let it ever be remembered, a Republican,[4] and a bold enquirer into morals and religion. The great writers of our own age are, we have reason to suppose, the companions and forerunners of some unimag-

4. I.e., Milton hoped that the overthrow of the monarchy during the Civil War would lead to England's rebirth as a republic.

ined change in our social condition or the opinions which cement it. The cloud of mind is discharging its collected lightning, and the equilibrium between institutions and opinions is now restoring, or is about to be restored.[5]

As to imitation; Poetry is a mimetic art. It creates, but it creates by combination and representation. Poetical abstractions are beautiful and new, not because the portions of which they are composed had no previous existence in the mind of man or in nature, but because the whole produced by their combination has some intelligible and beautiful analogy with those sources of emotion and thought, and with the contemporary condition of them: one great poet is a masterpiece of nature, which another not only ought to study but must study. He might as wisely and as easily determine that his mind should no longer be the mirror of all that is lovely in the visible universe, as exclude from his contemplation the beautiful which exists in the writings of a great contemporary. The pretence of doing it would be a presumption in any but the greatest; the effect, even in him, would be strained, unnatural and ineffectual. A Poet, is the combined product of such internal powers as modify the nature of others, and of such external influences as excite and sustain these powers; he is not one, but both. Every man's mind is in this respect modified by all the objects of nature and art, by every word and every suggestion which he ever admitted to act upon his consciousness; it is the mirror upon which all forms are reflected, and in which they compose one form. Poets, not otherwise than philosophers, painters, sculptors and musicians, are in one sense the creators and in another the creations of their age. From this subjection the loftiest do not escape. There is a similarity between Homer and Hesiod, between Æschylus and Euripides, between Virgil and Horace, between Dante and Petrarch, between Shakespeare and Fletcher, between Dryden and Pope; each has a generic resemblance under which their specific distinctions are arranged. If this similarity be the result of imitation, I am willing to confess that I have imitated.

Let this opportunity be conceded to me of acknowledging that I have, what a Scotch philosopher characteristically terms, "a passion for reforming the world:"[6] what passion incited him to write and publish his book, he omits to explain. For my part I had rather be damned with Plato and Lord Bacon, than go to Heaven with Paley and Malthus.[7] But it is a mistake to suppose that I dedicate my poetical compositions solely to the direct enforcement of reform, or that I consider them in any degree as containing a reasoned system on the theory of human life. Didactic poetry is my abhorrence; nothing can be equally well expressed in prose that is not tedious and supererogatory in verse. My purpose has hitherto been simply to familiarise the highly refined imagination of the more select classes of poetical readers with beautiful idealisms of moral excellence; aware that until the mind can love, and admire, and trust, and hope, and endure, reasoned principles of moral conduct are seeds cast upon the highway of life which the unconscious passenger tramples

5. See Shelley's similar tribute to his great contemporaries in the concluding paragraph of his "Defence of Poetry" (p. 443).
6. This is the title of chap. 16 in *The Principles of Moral Science* (1805), by the Scottish writer Robert Forsyth.
7. Thomas Malthus's *An Essay on the Principle of Population* (1798) argued that the rate of increase in population will soon exceed the rate of increase

in the food supply necessary to sustain it. William Paley wrote *Evidences of Christianity* (1794), which undertakes to prove that the design apparent in natural phenomena, and especially in the human body, entails the existence of God as the great Designer. Shelley ironically expresses his contempt for the doctrines of both these thinkers, which he conceives as arguments for accepting uncomplainingly the present state of the world.

into dust, although they would bear the harvest of his happiness. Should I live to accomplish what I purpose, that is, produce a systematical history of what appear to me to be the genuine elements of human society,[8] let not the advocates of injustice and superstition flatter themselves that I should take Æschylus rather than Plato as my model.

The having spoken of myself with unaffected freedom will need little apology with the candid; and let the uncandid consider that they injure me less than their own hearts and minds by misrepresentation. Whatever talents a person may possess to amuse and instruct others, be they ever so inconsiderable, he is yet bound to exert them: if his attempt be ineffectual, let the punishment of an unaccomplished purpose have been sufficient; let none trouble themselves to heap the dust of oblivion upon his efforts; the pile they raise will betray his grave which might otherwise have been unknown.

Prometheus Unbound

From Act 1

SCENE: *A Ravine of Icy Rocks in the Indian Caucasus.* PROMETHEUS *is discovered bound to the Precipice.* PANTHEA *and* IONE[1] *are seated at his feet. Time, Night. During the Scene, Morning slowly breaks.*

PROMETHEUS   Monarch of Gods and Dæmons, and all Spirits
But One,[2] who throng those bright and rolling Worlds
Which Thou and I alone of living things
Behold with sleepless eyes! regard this Earth
5   Made multitudinous with thy slaves, whom thou
Requitest for knee-worship, prayer and praise,
And toil, and hecatombs[3] of broken hearts,
With fear and self contempt and barren hope;
Whilst me, who am thy foe, eyeless° in hate,   blinded
10   Hast thou made reign and triumph, to thy scorn,
O'er mine own misery and thy vain revenge.—
Three thousand years of sleep-unsheltered hours
And moments—aye° divided by keen pangs   always
Till they seemed years, torture and solitude,
15   Scorn and despair,—these are mine empire:—
More glorious far than that which thou surveyest
From thine unenvied throne, O Mighty God!
Almighty, had I deigned[4] to share the shame
Of thine ill tyranny, and hung not here
20   Nailed to this wall of eagle-baffling mountain,
Black, wintry, dead, unmeasured; without herb,°   vegetation
Insect, or beast, or shape or sound of life.
Ah me, alas, pain, pain ever, forever!

8. Shelley did not live to write this history.
1. Ione, Panthea, and Asia (introduced in the following scene) are sisters and Oceanids—i.e., daughters of Oceanus.
2. Demogorgon (see 2.4). "Daemons": supernatural beings, intermediary between gods and mortals. Prometheus is addressing Jupiter.
3. Large sacrificial offerings.
4. I.e., you would have been all-powerful, if I had deigned.

No change, no pause, no hope!—Yet I endure.
I ask the Earth, have not the mountains felt?
I ask yon Heaven—the all-beholding Sun,
Has it not seen? The Sea, in storm or calm,
Heaven's ever-changing Shadow, spread below—
Have its deaf waves not heard my agony?
Ah me, alas, pain, pain ever, forever!

The crawling glaciers pierce me with the spears
Of their moon-freezing chrystals; the bright chains
Eat with their burning cold into my bones.
Heaven's winged hound, polluting from thy lips
His beak in poison not his own, tears up
My heart;[5] and shapeless sights come wandering by,
The ghastly people of the realm of dream,
Mocking me: and the Earthquake-fiends are charged
To wrench the rivets from my quivering wounds
When the rocks split and close again behind;
While from their loud abysses howling throng
The genii of the storm, urging the rage
Of whirlwind, and afflict me with keen hail.
And yet to me welcome is Day and Night,
Whether one breaks the hoar frost of the morn,
Or starry, dim, and slow, the other climbs
The leaden-coloured East; for then they lead
Their wingless, crawling Hours,[6] one among whom
—As some dark Priest hales° the reluctant victim—   *drags*
Shall drag thee, cruel King, to kiss the blood
From these pale feet,[7] which then might trample thee
If they disdained not such a prostrate slave.
Disdain? Ah no! I pity thee.[8]—What Ruin
Will hunt thee undefended through wide Heaven!
How will thy soul, cloven to its depth with terror,
Gape like a Hell within! I speak in grief,
Not exultation, for I hate no more,
As then, ere misery made me wise.—The Curse
Once breathed on thee I would recall.[9] Ye Mountains,
Whose many-voiced Echoes, through the mist
Of cataracts, flung the thunder of that spell!
Ye icy Springs, stagnant with wrinkling frost,
Which vibrated to hear me, and then crept
Shuddering through India! Thou serenest Air,
Through which the Sun walks burning without beams!
And ye swift Whirlwinds, who on poised wings
Hung mute and moveless o'er yon hushed abyss,
As thunder louder than your own made rock
The orbed world! If then my words had power

---

5. The vulture, tearing daily at Prometheus's heart, was kissed by Jupiter by way of reward.
6. The Hours were represented in Greek myth and art by human figures with wings.
7. One of a number of implied parallels between the agony of Prometheus and the passion of Christ.

8. At this early point occurs the crisis of the action: the beginning of Prometheus's change of heart from hate to compassion, consummated in lines 303–5.
9. I.e., remember. But the word's alternative sense, "revoke," will later become crucial.

70 —Though I am changed so that aught evil wish
Is dead within, although no memory be
Of what is hate—let them not lose it now![1]
What was that curse? for ye all heard me speak.[2]

* * *

PHANTASM

Fiend, I defy thee! with a calm, fixed mind,
    All that thou canst inflict I bid thee do;
Foul Tyrant both of Gods and Humankind,
265   One only being shalt thou not subdue.
        Rain then thy plagues upon me here,
        Ghastly disease and frenzying fear;
        And let alternate frost and fire
        Eat into me, and be thine ire
270 Lightning and cutting hail and legioned forms
Of furies, driving by upon the wounding storms.

Aye, do thy worst. Thou art Omnipotent.
    O'er all things but thyself I gave thee power,
And my own will. Be thy swift mischiefs sent
275   To blast mankind, from yon etherial tower.
        Let thy malignant spirit move
        Its darkness over those I love:
        On me and mine I imprecate°   call down
        The utmost torture of thy hate
280 And thus devote to sleepless agony
This undeclining head while thou must reign on high.

But thou who art the God and Lord—O thou
    Who fillest with thy soul this world of woe,
To whom all things of Earth and Heaven do bow
285   In fear and worship—all-prevailing foe!
        I curse thee! let a sufferer's curse
        Clasp thee, his torturer, like remorse,
        Till thine Infinity shall be
        A robe of envenomed agony;[3]
290 And thine Omnipotence a crown of pain
To cling like burning gold round thy dissolving brain.

Heap on thy soul by virtue of this Curse
    Ill deeds, then be thou damned, beholding good,
Both infinite as is the Universe,
295   And thou, and thy self-torturing solitude.
        An awful Image of calm power
        Though now thou sittest, let the hour

1. Let my words not lose their power now.
2. In the passage here omitted, none dares, for fear of the god's vengeance, to repeat the curse Prometheus had proclaimed against Jupiter. Prometheus is finally forced to call up the Phantasm of Jupiter himself, who, in the next excerpt, repeats the words of Prometheus's curse.
3. Like the poisoned shirt of the centaur Nessus, which consumed Hercules' flesh when he put it on. The next two lines allude to the mock crowning of Christ with a crown of thorns.

Come, when thou must appear to be
That which thou art internally.
300 And after many a false and fruitless crime
Scorn track thy lagging fall through boundless space and time.

　　　　　　　　　　　　　　　　　　[The Phantasm vanishes.]

PROMETHEUS　Were these my words, O Parent?
THE EARTH　　　　　　　　　　　　　　They were thine.
PROMETHEUS　It doth repent me: words are quick and vain;
　　　Grief for awhile is blind, and so was mine.
305 　　I wish no living thing to suffer pain.

　　　　　　　　THE EARTH
　　Misery, O misery to me,
　　That Jove at length should vanquish thee.
　　Wail, howl aloud, Land and Sea,
　　The Earth's rent heart shall answer ye.
310 Howl, Spirits of the living and the dead,
　　Your refuge, your defence lies fallen and vanquished.

　　　　　　　FIRST ECHO
Lies fallen and vanquished?

　　　　　　　SECOND ECHO
　　　　Fallen and vanquished!

　　　　　　　　IONE
　　Fear not—'tis but some passing spasm,
315 　　The Titan is unvanquished still.[4]

　　　　　　　*　*　*

FURY　Behold, an emblem—those who do endure
595 　Deep wrongs for man, and scorn and chains, but heap
　　Thousand-fold torment on themselves and him.
PROMETHEUS　Remit the anguish of that lighted stare—
　　Close those wan lips—let that thorn-wounded brow
　　Stream not with blood—it mingles with thy tears!
600 　Fix, fix those tortured orbs in peace and death
　　So thy sick throes shake not that crucifix,
　　So those pale fingers play not with thy gore.—
　　O horrible! Thy name I will not speak,
　　It hath become a curse.[5] I see, I see
605 　The wise, the mild, the lofty and the just,
　　Whom thy slaves hate for being like to thee,
　　Some hunted by foul lies from their heart's home,
　　An early-chosen, late-lamented home,
　　As hooded ounces[6] cling to the driven hind,°　　　　　　　doe

---

4. In the omitted passage the herald Mercury, at Jupiter's command, brings a group of Furies (in Greek myth, avengers of crimes against the gods) who tempt Prometheus to despair by revealing the loathsome potentialities for evil in humankind's conscious and unconscious mind. In the climactic temptation a Fury tears aside a veil to reveal a representation ("emblem," line 594) of the suffering Christ on the cross.
5. I.e., the name "Christ" has become, literally, a curse word, and metaphorically, a curse to humankind, in that His religion of love is used to justify religious wars and bloody oppression.
6. Cheetahs, or leopards, used in hunting (hoods were sometimes placed over their eyes to make them easier to control).

610　　Some linked to corpses in unwholesome cells:
　　　　Some—hear I not the multitude laugh loud?—
　　　　Impaled in lingering fire: and mighty realms
　　　　Float by my feet like sea-uprooted isles
　　　　Whose sons are kneaded down in common blood
615　　By the red light of their own burning homes.
　　FURY   Blood thou canst see, and fire; and canst hear groans;
　　　　Worse things, unheard, unseen, remain behind.
　　PROMETHEUS   Worse?
　　FURY　　　　　　　　In each human heart terror survives
　　　　The ravin it has gorged:[7] the loftiest fear
620　　All that they would disdain to think were true:
　　　　Hypocrisy and custom make their minds
　　　　The fanes° of many a worship, now outworn.　　　　　　　　　*temples*
　　　　They dare not devise good for man's estate
　　　　And yet they know not that they do not dare.
625　　The good want power, but to weep barren tears.[8]
　　　　The powerful goodness want: worse need for them.
　　　　The wise want love, and those who love want wisdom;
　　　　And all best things are thus confused to ill.
　　　　Many are strong and rich,—and would be just,—
630　　But live among their suffering fellow men
　　　　As if none felt: they know not what they do.[9]
　　PROMETHEUS   Thy words are like a cloud of winged snakes
　　　　And yet, I pity those they torture not.
　　FURY   Thou pitiest them? I speak no more!　　　　　　　　[*Vanishes.*]
　　PROMETHEUS　　　　　　　　　　　　　Ah woe!
635　　Ah woe! Alas! pain, pain ever, forever!
　　　　I close my tearless eyes, but see more clear
　　　　Thy works within my woe-illumed mind,
　　　　Thou subtle Tyrant![1] . . . Peace is in the grave—
　　　　The grave hides all things beautiful and good—
640　　I am a God and cannot find it there,
　　　　Nor would I seek it: for, though dread revenge,
　　　　This is defeat, fierce King, not victory.
　　　　The sights with which thou torturest gird my soul
　　　　With new endurance, till the hour arrives
645　　When they shall be no types of things which are.
　　PANTHEA   Alas! what sawest thou?
　　PROMETHEUS　　　　　　　　　　There are two woes:
　　　　To speak and to behold; thou spare me one.[2]
　　　　Names are there, Nature's sacred watchwords—they
　　　　Were borne aloft in bright emblazonry.[3]
650　　The nations thronged around, and cried aloud
　　　　As with one voice, "Truth, liberty and love!"
　　　　Suddenly fierce confusion fell from Heaven
　　　　Among them—there was strife, deceit and fear;

7. The prey that it has greedily devoured.
8. I.e., the good lack ("want") power except to weep "barren tears."
9. The Fury ironically echoes Christ's plea for forgiveness of his crucifiers: "Father, forgive them: for they know not what they do" (Luke 23.34).

1. Jupiter (also addressed as "fierce King," line 642).
2. I.e., spare me the woe of speaking (about what I have beheld).
3. As in a brilliant display of banners.

Tyrants rushed in, and did divide the spoil.
655 This was the shadow of the truth I saw.
THE EARTH   I felt thy torture, Son, with such mixed joy
As pain and Virtue give.—To cheer thy state
I bid ascend those subtle and fair spirits
Whose homes are the dim caves of human thought
660 And who inhabit, as birds wing the wind,
Its world-surrounding ether;[4] they behold
Beyond that twilight realm, as in a glass,°   *mirror*
The future—may they speak comfort to thee!

* * *

From *Act 2*

SCENE 4—*The Cave of* DEMOGORGON. ASIA *and* PANTHEA.[5]

PANTHEA   What veiled form sits on that ebon throne?
ASIA   The veil has fallen! . . .
PANTHEA   I see a mighty Darkness
Filling the seat of power; and rays of gloom
Dart round, as light from the meridian Sun,
5 Ungazed upon and shapeless—neither limb
Nor form—nor outline;[6] yet we feel it is
A living Spirit.
DEMOGORGON   Ask what thou wouldst know.
ASIA   What canst thou tell?
DEMOGORGON   All things thou dar'st demand.
ASIA   Who made the living world?
DEMOGORGON   God.
ASIA   Who made all
10 That it contains—thought, passion, reason, will,
Imagination?
DEMOGORGON   God, Almighty God.
ASIA   Who made that sense[7] which, when the winds of Spring
In rarest visitation, or the voice
Of one beloved heard in youth alone,
15 Fills the faint eyes with falling tears, which dim
The radiant looks of unbewailing flowers,
And leaves this peopled earth a solitude
When it returns no more?
DEMOGORGON   Merciful God.

4. A medium, weightless and infinitely elastic, once supposed to permeate the universe.
5. Act 2 has opened with Asia—the feminine principle and embodiment of love, who was separated from Prometheus at the moment of his fall into divisive hate—in a lovely Indian valley at the first hour of the dawn of the spring season of redemption. Asia and her sister Panthea have been led, by a sweet and irresistible compulsion, first to the portal and then down into the depths of the cave of Demogorgon—the central enigma of Shelley's poem.
 As the father of all that exists, Demogorgon may represent the ultimate reason for the way things are. As such, Shelley appears to argue, Demogorgon must be a mystery inaccessible to knowledge and must be ignorant of the principle controlling him. In this scene Demogorgon can give only riddling answers to Asia's questions about the "why" of creation, good, and evil.
6. Echoing Milton's description of Death, *Paradise Lost* 2.666–73.
7. Presumably the sense by which one is aware of the "unseen Power" that Shelley calls "Intellectual Beauty" (see "Hymn to Intellectual Beauty," stanza 2, p. 384).

ASIA   And who made terror, madness, crime, remorse,
20   Which from the links of the great chain of things
        To every thought within the mind of man
        Sway and drag heavily—and each one reels
        Under the load towards the pit of death;
        Abandoned hope, and love that turns to hate;
25   And self-contempt, bitterer to drink than blood;
        Pain whose unheeded and familiar speech
        Is howling and keen shrieks, day after day;
        And Hell, or the sharp fear of Hell?[8]

DEMOGORGON   He reigns.

ASIA   Utter his name—a world pining in pain
30   Asks but his name; curses shall drag him down.

DEMOGORGON   He reigns.

ASIA   I feel, I know it—who?

DEMOGORGON   He reigns.

ASIA   Who reigns? There was the Heaven and Earth at first
        And Light and Love;—then Saturn,[9] from whose throne
        Time fell, an envious shadow; such the state
35   Of the earth's primal spirits beneath his sway
        As the calm joy of flowers and living leaves
        Before the wind or sun has withered them
        And semivital worms; but he refused
        The birthright of their being, knowledge, power,
40   The skill which wields the elements, the thought
        Which pierces this dim Universe like light,
        Self-empire and the majesty of love,
        For thirst of which they fainted. Then Prometheus
        Gave wisdom, which is strength, to Jupiter
45   And with this law alone: "Let man be free,"
        Clothed him with the dominion of wide Heaven.
        To know nor faith nor love nor law, to be
        Omnipotent but friendless, is to reign;
        And Jove now reigned; for on the race of man
50   First famine, and then toil, and then disease,
        Strife, wounds, and ghastly death unseen before,
        Fell; and the unseasonable seasons drove,
        With alternating shafts of frost and fire,
        Their shelterless, pale tribes to mountain caves;
55   And in their desart° hearts fierce wants he sent   *empty*
        And mad disquietudes, and shadows idle
        Of unreal good, which levied mutual war,
        So ruining the lair wherein they raged.
        Prometheus saw, and waked the legioned hopes
60   Which sleep within folded Elysian flowers,
        Nepenthe, Moly, Amaranth,[1] fadeless blooms;

---

8. The nouns "hope," "love," etc. (lines 24–28) are all objects of the verb "made" (line 19).
9. In Greek myth Saturn's reign was the golden age. In Shelley's version Saturn refused to grant mortals knowledge and science, so that it was an age of ignorant innocence in which the deepest human needs remained unfulfilled.
1. These are medicinal drugs and flowers in Greek myth. Asia is describing (lines 59–97) the various sciences and arts given to humans by Prometheus, the culture bringer.

That they might hide with thin and rainbow wings
The shape of Death; and Love he sent to bind
The disunited tendrils of that vine
65 Which bears the wine of life, the human heart;
And he tamed fire which, like some beast of prey,
Most terrible, but lovely, played beneath
The frown of man, and tortured to his will
Iron and gold, the slaves and signs of power,
70 And gems and poisons, and all subtlest forms,
Hidden beneath the mountains and the waves.
He gave man speech, and speech created thought,
Which is the measure of the Universe;
And Science struck the thrones of Earth and Heaven
75 Which shook, but fell not; and the harmonious mind
Poured itself forth in all-prophetic song,
And music lifted up the listening spirit
Until it walked, exempt from mortal care,
Godlike, o'er the clear billows of sweet sound;
80 And human hands first mimicked and then mocked[2]
With moulded limbs more lovely than its own
The human form, till marble grew divine,
And mothers, gazing, drank the love men see
Reflected in their race, behold, and perish.[3]—
85 He told the hidden power of herbs and springs,
And Disease drank and slept—Death grew like sleep.—
He taught the implicated° orbits woven   *intertwined*
Of the wide-wandering stars, and how the Sun
Changes his lair, and by what secret spell
90 The pale moon is transformed, when her broad eye
Gazes not on the interlunar[4] sea;
He taught to rule, as life directs the limbs,
The tempest-winged chariots of the Ocean,
And the Celt knew the Indian.[5] Cities then
95 Were built, and through their snow-like columns flowed
The warm winds, and the azure æther shone,
And the blue sea and shadowy hills were seen . . .
Such the alleviations of his state
Prometheus gave to man—for which he hangs
100 Withering in destined pain—but who rains down
Evil, the immedicable plague, which while
Man looks on his creation like a God
And sees that it is glorious, drives him on,
The wreck of his own will, the scorn of Earth,
105 The outcast, the abandoned, the alone?—
Not Jove: while yet his frown shook Heaven, aye when

2. I.e., sculptors first merely reproduced but later improved on and heightened the beauty of the human form, so that the original was inferior to, and hence "mocked" by, the copy.
3. Expectant mothers looked at the beautiful statues so that their children might, by prenatal influence, be born with the beauty that makes beholders die of love.
4. The phase between old and new moons, when the moon is invisible.
5. The reference is to the ships in which the Celtic (here, non-Greco-Roman) races of Europe were able to sail to India.

His adversary from adamantine° chains   *unbreakable*
Cursed him, he trembled like a slave. Declare
Who is his master? Is he too a slave?

110 DEMOGORGON   All spirits are enslaved which serve things evil:
Thou knowest if Jupiter be such or no.

ASIA   Whom calledst thou God?

DEMOGORGON   I spoke but as ye speak—
For Jove is the supreme of living things.

ASIA   Who is the master of the slave?

DEMOGORGON   —If the Abysm
115 Could vomit forth its secrets:—but a voice
Is wanting, the deep truth is imageless;
For what would it avail to bid thee gaze
On the revolving world? what to bid speak
Fate, Time, Occasion, Chance and Change? To these
120 All things are subject but eternal Love.

ASIA   So much I asked before, and my heart gave
The response thou hast given; and of such truths
Each to itself must be the oracle.—
One more demand . . . and do thou answer me
125 As my own soul would answer, did it know
That which I ask.—Prometheus shall arise
Henceforth the Sun of this rejoicing world:
When shall the destined hour arrive?

DEMOGORGON   Behold![6]

ASIA   The rocks are cloven, and through the purple night
130 I see Cars drawn by rainbow-winged steeds
Which trample the dim winds—in each there stands
A wild-eyed charioteer, urging their flight.
Some look behind, as fiends pursued them there
And yet I see no shapes but the keen stars:
135 Others with burning eyes lean forth, and drink
With eager lips the wind of their own speed,
As if the thing they loved fled on before,
And now—even now they clasped it; their bright locks
Stream like a comet's flashing hair: they all
Sweep onward.—

140 DEMOGORGON   These are the immortal Hours
Of whom thou didst demand.—One waits for thee.

ASIA   A Spirit with a dreadful countenance
Checks its dark chariot by the craggy gulph.
Unlike thy brethren, ghastly charioteer,
145 What art thou? whither wouldst thou bear me? Speak!

SPIRIT   I am the shadow of a destiny
More dread than is my aspect—ere yon planet
Has set, the Darkness which ascends with me
Shall wrap in lasting night Heaven's kingless throne.

ASIA   What meanest thou?

150 PANTHEA   That terrible shadow[7] floats

---

6. Demogorgon's answer is a gesture: he points   7. Demogorgon (the "Darkness" of line 148), who
to the approaching chariots ("Cars").   is ascending (lines 150–55) to dethrone Jupiter.

Up from its throne, as may the lurid° smoke   *red-glaring*
Of earthquake-ruined cities o'er the sea.—
Lo! it ascends the Car . . . the coursers fly
Terrified; watch its path among the stars
Blackening the night!

155 ASIA   Thus I am answered—strange!
PANTHEA   See, near the verge° another chariot stays;   *horizon*
An ivory shell inlaid with crimson fire
Which comes and goes within its sculptured rim
Of delicate strange tracery—the young Spirit
160 That guides it, has the dovelike eyes of hope.
How its soft smiles attract the soul!—as light
Lures winged insects[8] through the lampless air.

SPIRIT

My coursers are fed with the lightning,
    They drink of the whirlwind's stream
165 And when the red morning is brightning
    They bathe in the fresh sunbeam;
    They have strength for their swiftness, I deem:
        Then ascend with me, daughter of Ocean.

I desire—and their speed makes night kindle;
170   I fear—they outstrip the Typhoon;
Ere the cloud piled on Atlas[9] can dwindle
    We encircle the earth and the moon:
    We shall rest from long labours at noon:
        Then ascend with me, daughter of Ocean.

SCENE 5—*The Car pauses within a Cloud on the Top of a snowy Mountain.*
ASIA, PANTHEA, *and the* SPIRIT OF THE HOUR.

SPIRIT

On the brink of the night and the morning
    My coursers are wont to respire,[1]
But the Earth has just whispered a warning
    That their flight must be swifter than fire:
5   They shall drink the hot speed of desire!

ASIA   Thou breathest on their nostrils—but my breath
    Would give them swifter speed.
SPIRIT   Alas, it could not.
PANTHEA   O Spirit! pause and tell whence is the light
    Which fills the cloud? the sun is yet unrisen.
10 SPIRIT   The sun will rise not until noon.[2]—Apollo
    Is held in Heaven by wonder—and the light
    Which fills this vapour, as the aerial hue

---

8. The ancient image of the soul, or *psyche*, was a moth. The chariot described here will carry Asia to a reunion with Prometheus.
9. A mountain in North Africa that the Greeks regarded as so high that it supported the heavens.
1. Catch their breath.
2. The time of the reunion of Prometheus and Asia.

Of fountain-gazing roses fills the water,
Flows from thy mighty sister.

PANTHEA   Yes, I feel . . .

15   ASIA   What is it with thee, sister? Thou art pale.

PANTHEA   How thou art changed! I dare not look on thee;
I feel, but see thee not. I scarce endure
The radiance of thy beauty.[3] Some good change
Is working in the elements which suffer
20   Thy presence thus unveiled.—The Nereids tell
That on the day when the clear hyaline°   glassy sea
Was cloven at thy uprise, and thou didst stand
Within a veined shell,[4] which floated on
Over the calm floor of the chrystal sea,
25   Among the Ægean isles, and by the shores
Which bear thy name, love, like the atmosphere
Of the sun's fire filling the living world,
Burst from thee, and illumined Earth and Heaven
And the deep ocean and the sunless caves,
30   And all that dwells within them; till grief cast
Eclipse upon the soul from which it came:
Such art thou now, nor is it I alone,
Thy sister, thy companion, thine own chosen one,
But the whole world which seeks thy sympathy.
35   Hearest thou not sounds i' the air which speak the love
Of all articulate beings? Feelest thou not
The inanimate winds enamoured of thee?—List!   [Music.]

ASIA   Thy words are sweeter than aught else but his
Whose echoes they are—yet all love is sweet,
40   Given or returned; common as light is love
And its familiar voice wearies not ever.
    Like the wide Heaven, the all-sustaining air,
    It makes the reptile equal to the God . . .
    They who inspire it most are fortunate
45   As I am now; but those who feel it most
Are happier still, after long sufferings
As I shall soon become.

PANTHEA   List! Spirits speak.

VOICE (in the air, singing)[5]
    Life of Life! thy lips enkindle
        With their love the breath between them
50   And thy smiles before they dwindle
        Make the cold air fire; then screen them
    In those looks where whoso gazes
    Faints, entangled in their mazes.

---

3. In an earlier scene Panthea had envisioned in a dream the radiant and eternal inner form of Prometheus emerging through his "wound-worn limbs." The corresponding transfiguration of Asia, prepared for by her descent to the underworld to question Demogorgon, now takes place.
4. The story told by the Nereids (sea nymphs) serves to associate Asia with Aphrodite, goddess of love, emerging (as in Botticelli's painting) from the Mediterranean on a seashell.
5. The voice attempts to describe, in a dizzying whirl of optical paradoxes, what it feels like to look on the naked essence of love and beauty.

Child of Light! thy limbs are burning
55   Through the vest which seems to hide them
As the radiant lines of morning
     Through the clouds ere they divide them,
And this atmosphere divinest
Shrouds thee wheresoe'er thou shinest.

60 Fair are others;—none beholds thee
     But thy voice sounds low and tender
Like the fairest, for it folds thee
     From the sight, that liquid splendour,
And all feel, yet see thee never
65 As I feel now, lost forever!

Lamp of Earth! where'er thou movest
     Its dim shapes are clad with brightness
And the souls of whom thou lovest
     Walk upon the winds with lightness
70 Till they fail, as I am failing,
Dizzy, lost . . . yet unbewailing!

ASIA

My soul is an enchanted Boat
     Which, like a sleeping swan, doth float
Upon the silver waves of thy sweet singing,
75   And thine doth like an Angel sit
     Beside the helm conducting it
Whilst all the winds with melody are ringing.
     It seems to float ever—forever—
     Upon that many winding River
80   Between mountains, woods, abysses,
     A Paradise of wildernesses,
Till like one in slumber bound
Borne to the Ocean, I float down, around,
Into a Sea profound, of ever-spreading sound.

85   Meanwhile thy spirit lifts its pinions°   *wings*
     In Music's most serene dominions,
Catching the winds that fan that happy Heaven.
     And we sail on, away, afar,
     Without a course—without a star—
90 But by the instinct of sweet Music driven
     Till, through Elysian garden islets
     By thee, most beautiful of pilots,
     Where never mortal pinnace° glided,   *small boat*
     The boat of my desire is guided—
95 Realms where the air we breathe is Love
Which in the winds and on the waves doth move,
Harmonizing this Earth with what we feel above.

We have past Age's icy caves,
     And Manhood's dark and tossing waves
100 And Youth's smooth ocean, smiling to betray;

Beyond the glassy gulphs we flee
Of shadow-peopled Infancy,
Through Death and Birth to a diviner day,[6]
A Paradise of vaulted bowers
105 Lit by downward-gazing flowers
And watery paths that wind between
Wildernesses calm and green,
Peopled by shapes too bright to see,
And rest, having beheld—somewhat like thee,
110 Which walk upon the sea, and chaunt melodiously!

From *Act 3*

SCENE 1—*Heaven,* JUPITER *on his Throne;* THETIS *and the other Deities assembled.*

JUPITER Ye congregated Powers of Heaven who share
The glory and the strength of him ye serve,
Rejoice! henceforth I am omnipotent.
All else had been subdued to me—alone
5 The soul of man, like unextinguished fire,
Yet burns towards Heaven with fierce reproach and doubt
And lamentation and reluctant prayer,
Hurling up insurrection, which might make
Our antique empire insecure, though built
10 On eldest faith, and Hell's coeval,[7] fear.
And though my curses through the pendulous° air   overhanging
Like snow on herbless peaks, fall flake by flake
And cling to it[8]—though under my wrath's night
It climb the crags of life, step after step,
15 Which wound it, as ice wounds unsandalled feet,
It yet remains supreme o'er misery,
Aspiring . . . unrepressed; yet soon to fall:
Even now have I begotten a strange wonder,
That fatal Child,[9] the terror of the Earth,
20 Who waits but till the destined Hour arrive,
Bearing from Demogorgon's vacant throne
The dreadful might of ever living limbs
Which clothed that awful spirit unbeheld—
To redescend, and trample out the spark[1] . . .

25 Pour forth Heaven's wine, Idæan Ganymede,
And let it fill the dædal[2] cups like fire
And from the flower-inwoven soil divine

---

6. Asia is describing what it feels like to be transfigured—in the image of moving backward in the stream of time, through youth and infancy and birth, in order to die to this life and be born again to a "diviner" existence.
7. Of the same age.
8. "It" (as also in lines 14 and 16) is "the soul of man" (line 5).
9. The son of Jupiter and Thetis. Jupiter believes that he has begotten a child who will assume the bodily form of the conquered Demogorgon and then return to announce his victory and the defeat of the resistance of Prometheus.
1. Of Prometheus's defiance.
2. Skillfully wrought (from the name of the Greek craftsman Daedalus). Ganymede (line 25) had been seized on Mount Ida by an eagle and carried to heaven to be Jupiter's cupbearer.

Ye all triumphant harmonies arise
As dew from Earth under the twilight stars;
30 Drink! be the nectar circling through your veins
The soul of joy, ye everliving Gods,
Till exultation burst in one wide voice
Like music from Elysian winds.—

And thou
Ascend beside me, veiled in the light
35 Of the desire which makes thee one with me,
Thetis, bright Image of Eternity!—
When thou didst cry, "Insufferable might![3]
God! spare me! I sustain not the quick flames,
The penetrating presence; all my being,
40 Like him whom the Numidian seps[4] did thaw
Into a dew with poison, is dissolved,
Sinking through its foundations"—even then
Two mighty spirits, mingling, made a third
Mightier than either—which unbodied now
45 Between us, floats, felt although unbeheld,
Waiting the incarnation, which ascends—
Hear ye the thunder of the fiery wheels
Griding[5] the winds?—from Demogorgon's throne.—
Victory! victory! Feel'st thou not, O World,
50 The Earthquake of his chariot thundering up
Olympus?

[*The Car of the* HOUR *arrives.* DEMOGORGON *descends and moves
toward the Throne of* JUPITER.]

Awful Shape, what art thou? Speak!
DEMOGORGON   Eternity—demand no direr name.
Descend, and follow me down the abyss;
I am thy child,[6] as thou wert Saturn's child,
55 Mightier than thee; and we must dwell together
Henceforth in darkness.—Lift thy lightnings not.
The tyranny of Heaven none may retain,
Or reassume, or hold succeeding thee . . .
Yet if thou wilt—as 'tis the destiny
60 Of trodden worms to writhe till they are dead—
Put forth thy might.
JUPITER   Detested prodigy!
Even thus beneath the deep Titanian prisons[7]
I trample thee! . . . thou lingerest?

Mercy! mercy!
No pity—no release, no respite! . . . Oh,
65 That thou wouldst make mine enemy my judge.
Even where he hangs, seared by my long revenge
On Caucasus—he would not doom me thus.—
Gentle and just and dreadless, is he not

---

3. This description of Jupiter's rape of Thetis is a
grotesque parody of the reunion of Prometheus
and Asia.
4. A serpent of Numidia (North Africa) whose
bite was thought to cause putrefaction.
5. Cutting with a rasping sound.

6. Ironically, and in a figurative sense: Demogorgon's function follows from Jupiter's actions.
7. After they overthrew the Titans, Jupiter and
the Olympian gods imprisoned them in Tartarus,
deep beneath the earth.

The monarch of the world? what then art thou? . . .
No refuge! no appeal— . . .
70   Sink with me then—
We two will sink in the wide waves of ruin
Even as a vulture and a snake outspent
Drop, twisted in inextricable fight,[8]
Into a shoreless sea.—Let Hell unlock
75 Its mounded Oceans of tempestuous fire,
And whelm on them° into the bottomless void   *wash them*
The desolated world and thee and me,
The conqueror and the conquered, and the wreck
Of that for which they combated.
                                  Ai! Ai![9]
80 The elements obey me not . . . I sink . . .
Dizzily down—ever, forever, down—
And, like a cloud, mine enemy above
Darkens my fall with victory!—Ai! Ai!

From SCENE 4—*A Forest. In the Background a Cave.* PROMETHEUS, ASIA, PANTHEA, IONE, *and the* SPIRIT OF THE EARTH.[1]

                              ✻   ✻   ✻

                    [*The* SPIRIT OF THE HOUR *enters.*]
PROMETHEUS   We feel what thou hast heard and seen—yet speak.
SPIRIT OF THE HOUR   Soon as the sound had ceased whose thunder filled
The abysses of the sky, and the wide earth,
100 There was a change . . . the impalpable thin air
And the all-circling sunlight were transformed
As if the sense of love dissolved in them
Had folded itself round the sphered world.
My vision then grew clear and I could see
105 Into the mysteries of the Universe.[2]
Dizzy as with delight I floated down,
Winnowing the lightsome air with languid plumes,
My coursers sought their birthplace in the sun
Where they henceforth will live exempt from toil,
110 Pasturing flowers of vegetable fire—
And where my moonlike car will stand within
A temple, gazed upon by Phidian forms,[3]
Of thee, and Asia and the Earth, and me
And you fair nymphs, looking the love we feel,
115 In memory of the tidings it has borne,
Beneath a dome fretted with graven flowers,
Poised on twelve columns of resplendent stone

---

8. The eagle (or vulture) and the snake locked in equal combat—a favorite Shelleyan image (cf. *Alastor*, lines 227–32).
9. Traditional Greek cry of sorrow.
1. After Jupiter's annihilation (described in scene 2), Hercules unbinds Prometheus, who is reunited with Asia and retires to a cave "where we will sit and talk of time and change / . . . ourselves unchanged." In the speech that concludes the act (included here) the Spirit of the Hour describes

what happened in the human world when he sounded the apocalyptic trumpet.
2. I.e., the earth's atmosphere clarifies, no longer refracting the sunlight, and so allows the Spirit of the Hour to see what is happening on earth.
3. The crescent-shaped ("moonlike") chariot, its apocalyptic mission accomplished, will be frozen to stone and will be surrounded by the sculptured forms of other agents in the drama. Phidias (5th century B.C.E.) was the noblest of Greek sculptors.

And open to the bright and liquid sky.
Yoked to it by an amphisbænic snake[4]
120 The likeness of those winged steeds will mock[5]
The flight from which they find repose.—Alas,
Whither has wandered now my partial[6] tongue
When all remains untold which ye would hear!—
As I have said, I floated to the Earth:
125 It was, as it is still, the pain of bliss
To move, to breathe, to be; I wandering went
Among the haunts and dwellings of mankind
And first was disappointed not to see
Such mighty change as I had felt within
130 Expressed in outward things; but soon I looked,
And behold! thrones were kingless, and men walked
One with the other even as spirits do,
None fawned, none trampled; hate, disdain or fear,
Self-love or self-contempt on human brows
135 No more inscribed, as o'er the gate of hell,
"All hope abandon, ye who enter here";[7]
None frowned, none trembled, none with eager fear
Gazed on another's eye of cold command
Until the subject of a tyrant's will
140 Became, worse fate, the abject of his own[8]
Which spurred him, like an outspent° horse, to death.   exhausted
None wrought his lips in truth-entangling lines
Which smiled the lie his tongue disdained to speak;
None with firm sneer trod out in his own heart
145 The sparks of love, and hope, till there remained
Those bitter ashes, a soul self-consumed,
And the wretch crept, a vampire among men,
Infecting all with his own hideous ill.
None talked that common, false, cold, hollow talk
150 Which makes the heart deny the *yes* it breathes
Yet question that unmeant hypocrisy
With such a self-mistrust as has no name.
And women too, frank, beautiful and kind
As the free Heaven which rains fresh light and dew
155 On the wide earth, past: gentle, radiant forms,
From custom's evil taint exempt and pure;
Speaking the wisdom once they could not think,
Looking emotions once they feared to feel
And changed to all which once they dared not be,
160 Yet being now, made Earth like Heaven—nor pride
Nor jealousy nor envy nor ill shame,
The bitterest of those drops of treasured gall,
Spoilt the sweet taste of the nepenthe,[9] love.

---

4. A mythical snake with a head at each end; it serves here as a symbolic warning that a reversal of the process is always possible.
5. "Imitate" and also, in their immobility, "mock at" the flight they represent.
6. Biased or, possibly, telling only part of the story.

7. The inscription over the gate of hell in Dante's *Inferno* 3.9.
8. I.e., he was so abjectly enslaved that his own will accorded with the tyrant's will.
9. A drug (probably opium) that brings forgetfulness of pain and sorrow.

Thrones, altars, judgement-seats and prisons; wherein
165 And beside which, by wretched men were borne
Sceptres, tiaras, swords and chains, and tomes
Of reasoned wrong glozed on[1] by ignorance,
Were like those monstrous and barbaric shapes,
The ghosts of a no more remembered fame,
170 Which from their unworn obelisks[2] look forth
In triumph o'er the palaces and tombs
Of those who were their conquerors, mouldering round.
Those imaged to the pride of Kings and Priests
A dark yet mighty faith, a power as wide
175 As is the world it wasted, and are now
But an astonishment; even so the tools
And emblems of its last captivity
Amid the dwellings of the peopled Earth,
Stand, not o'erthrown, but unregarded now.
180 And those foul shapes, abhorred by God and man—
Which under many a name and many a form
Strange, savage, ghastly, dark and execrable
Were Jupiter,[3] the tyrant of the world;
And which the nations panic-stricken served
185 With blood, and hearts broken by long hope, and love
Dragged to his altars soiled and garlandless
And slain amid men's unreclaiming tears,
Flattering the thing they feared, which fear was hate—
Frown, mouldering fast, o'er their abandoned shrines.
190 The painted veil, by those who were, called life,[4]
Which mimicked, as with colours idly spread,
All men believed and hoped, is torn aside—
The loathsome mask has fallen, the man remains
Sceptreless, free, uncircumscribed—but man:
195 Equal, unclassed, tribeless, and nationless,
Exempt from awe, worship, degree,—the King
Over himself; just, gentle, wise—but man:
Passionless? no—yet free from guilt or pain
Which were, for his will made, or suffered them,
200 Nor yet exempt, though ruling them like slaves,
From chance and death and mutability,
The clogs of that which else might oversoar
The loftiest star of unascended Heaven
Pinnacled dim in the intense inane.[5]

1. Annotated, explained.
2. The Egyptian obelisks (tapering shafts of stone), brought to Rome by its conquering armies, included hieroglyphs that—because they were still undeciphered in Shelley's time—seemed "monstrous and barbaric shapes" (line 168).
3. The "foul shapes" (line 180) were statues of the gods who, whatever their names, were all really manifestations of Jupiter.
4. I.e., which was thought to be life by humans as they were before their regeneration.
5. I.e., a dim point in the extreme of empty space. The sense of lines 198–204 is if regenerate man were to be released from all earthly and biological impediments ("clogs"), he would become what even the stars are not—a pure ideal.

From *Act 4*[6]

SCENE—*A Part of the Forest near the Cave of* PROMETHEUS.

*   *   *

DEMOGORGON

This is the Day which down the void Abysm
555 At the Earth-born's spell[7] yawns for Heaven's Despotism,
    And Conquest is dragged Captive through the Deep;[8]
Love from its awful° throne of patient power   *awesome*
In the wise heart, from the last giddy hour
    Of dread endurance, from the slippery, steep,
560 And narrow verge of crag-like Agony, springs
And folds over the world its healing wings.

Gentleness, Virtue, Wisdom and Endurance,—
    These are the seals of that most firm assurance
        Which bars the pit over Destruction's strength;
565 And if, with infirm hand, Eternity,
    Mother of many acts and hours, should free
        The serpent that would clasp her with his length[9]—
These are the spells by which to reassume
An empire o'er the disentangled Doom.[1]

570 To suffer woes which Hope thinks infinite;
To forgive wrongs darker than Death or Night;
    To defy Power which seems Omnipotent;
To love, and bear; to hope, till Hope creates
From its own wreck the thing it contemplates;
575   Neither to change nor falter nor repent:
This, like thy glory, Titan! is to be
Good, great and joyous, beautiful and free;
This is alone Life, Joy, Empire and Victory.

1818–19   1820

6. The original drama, completed in the spring of 1819, consisted of three acts. Later that year Shelley added a jubilant fourth act. In Revelation 21 the apocalyptic replacement of the old world by "a new heaven and new earth" had been symbolized by the marriage of the Lamb with the New Jerusalem. Shelley's fourth act, somewhat like the conclusion of Blake's *Jerusalem*, expands this figure into a cosmic epithalamion, representing a union of divided elements that enacts everywhere the reunion of Prometheus and Asia taking place offstage.

Shelley's model is the Renaissance court-masque, which combines song and dance with spectacular displays. Panthea and Ione serve as commentators on the action, which is divided into three episodes. In the first episode the purified "Spirits of the human mind" unite in a ritual dance with the Hours of the glad new day. In the second episode (lines 194–318), there appear emblematic representations of the moon and the earth, each bearing an infant whose hour has come round at last. Shelley based this description in part on Ezekiel 1, the vision of the chariot of divine glory, which had traditionally been interpreted as a portent of apocalypse. The third episode (lines 319–502) is the bacchanalian dance of the love-intoxicated Moon around her brother and paramour, the rejuvenescent Earth.

7. Prometheus's spell—the magically effective words of pity, rather than vengefulness, that he spoke in act 1.

8. Ephesians 4.8: "When [Christ] ascended up on high, he led captivity captive."

9. A final reminder that the serpent incessantly struggles to break loose and start the cycle of humanity's fall all over again.

1. Shelley's four cardinal virtues (line 562), which seal the serpent in the pit, also constitute the magic formulas ("spells") by which to remaster him, should he again break loose.

The Cloud

I bring fresh showers for the thirsting flowers,
  From the seas and streams;
I bear light shade for the leaves when laid
  In their noon-day dreams.
5 From my wings are shaken the dews that waken
  The sweet buds every one,
When rocked to rest on their mother's° breast,   *earth's*
  As she dances about the Sun.
I wield the flail[1] of the lashing hail,
10 And whiten the green plains under,
And then again I dissolve it in rain,
  And laugh as I pass in thunder.

I sift the snow on the mountains below,
  And their great pines groan aghast;
15 And all the night 'tis my pillow white,
  While I sleep in the arms of the blast.
Sublime on the towers of my skiey bowers,
  Lightning my pilot sits;
In a cavern under is fettered the thunder,
20 It struggles and howls at fits;°   *fitfully*
Over Earth and Ocean, with gentle motion,
  This pilot is guiding me,
Lured by the love of the genii that move
  In the depths of the purple sea;[2]
25 Over the rills, and the crags, and the hills,
  Over the lakes and the plains,
Wherever he dream, under mountain or stream,
  The Spirit he loves remains;
And I all the while bask in Heaven's blue smile,[3]
30 Whilst he is dissolving in rains.

The sanguine Sunrise, with his meteor eyes,
  And his burning plumes outspread,[4]
Leaps on the back of my sailing rack,[5]
  When the morning star shines dead;
35 As on the jag of a mountain crag,
  Which an earthquake rocks and swings,
An eagle alit one moment may sit
  In the light of its golden wings.
And when Sunset may breathe, from the lit Sea beneath,
40 Its ardours of rest and of love,
And the crimson pall° of eve may fall   *rich coverlet*
  From the depth of Heaven above,

---

1. Either a weapon fashioned as a ball and chain or a tool for threshing grain.
2. I.e., atmospheric electricity, guiding the cloud (line 18), discharges as lightning when "lured" by the attraction of an opposite charge.
3. The upper part of the cloud remains exposed to the sun.
4. The sun's corona. "Meteor eyes": as bright as a burning meteor.
5. High, broken clouds, driven by the wind.

With wings folded I rest, on mine aëry nest,
    As still as a brooding dove.[6]

45 That orbed maiden with white fire laden
    Whom mortals call the Moon,
Glides glimmering o'er my fleece-like floor,
    By the midnight breezes strewn;
And wherever the beat of her unseen feet,
50   Which only the angels hear,
May have broken the woof,° of my tent's thin roof,   *texture*
    The stars peep behind her, and peer;
And I laugh to see them whirl and flee,
    Like a swarm of golden bees,
55 When I widen the rent in my wind-built tent,
    Till the calm rivers, lakes, and seas,
Like strips of the sky fallen through me on high,
    Are each paved with the moon and these.[7]

I bind the Sun's throne with a burning zone°   *belt, sash*
60   And the Moon's with a girdle of pearl;
The volcanos are dim and the stars reel and swim
    When the whirlwinds my banner unfurl.
From cape to cape, with a bridge-like shape,
    Over a torrent sea,
65 Sunbeam-proof, I hang like a roof—
    The mountains its columns be!
The triumphal arch, through which I march
    With hurricane, fire, and snow,
When the Powers of the Air, are chained to my chair,°   *chariot*
70   Is the million-coloured Bow;
The sphere-fire° above its soft colours wove   *sunlight*
    While the moist Earth was laughing below.

I am the daughter of Earth and Water,
    And the nursling of the Sky;
75 I pass through the pores, of the ocean and shores;
    I change, but I cannot die—
For after the rain, when with never a stain
    The pavilion of Heaven is bare,
And the winds and sunbeams, with their convex gleams,
80   Build up the blue dome of Air[8]—
I silently laugh at my own cenotaph,[9]
    And out of the caverns of rain,
Like a child from the womb, like a ghost from the tomb,
    I arise, and unbuild it again.—

1820   1820

6. An echo of Milton's description of his Muse, identified with the Holy Spirit, who "with mighty wings outspread / Dove-like sat'st brooding on the vast abyss" (*Paradise Lost* 1.20–21).
7. The stars reflected in the water.
8. The blue color of the sky. The phenomenon, as Shelley indicates, results from the way "sunbeams" are filtered by the earth's atmosphere.
9. The memorial monument of the dead cloud is the cloudless blue dome of the sky. (The point is that a cenotaph is a monument that does not contain a corpse.)

To a Sky-Lark[1]

Hail to thee, blithe Spirit!
   Bird thou never wert—
That from Heaven, or near it,
   Pourest thy full heart
5   In profuse strains of unpremeditated art.

   Higher still and higher
   From the earth thou springest
Like a cloud of fire;
   The blue deep thou wingest,
10   And singing still dost soar, and soaring ever singest.

   In the golden lightning
   Of the sunken Sun—
O'er which clouds are brightning,
   Thou dost float and run;
15   Like an unbodied joy whose race is just begun.

   The pale purple even°   *evening*
   Melts around thy flight,
Like a star of Heaven
   In the broad day-light
20   Thou art unseen,—but yet I hear thy shrill delight,

   Keen as are the arrows
   Of that silver sphere,[2]
Whose intense lamp narrows
   In the white dawn clear
25   Until we hardly see—we feel that it is there.

   All the earth and air
   With thy voice is loud,
As when Night is bare
   From one lonely cloud
30   The moon rains out her beams—and Heaven is overflowed.

   What thou art we know not;
   What is most like thee?
From rainbow clouds there flow not
   Drops so bright to see
35   As from thy presence showers a rain of melody.

   Like a Poet hidden
   In the light of thought,
Singing hymns unbidden,
   Till the world is wrought
40   To sympathy with hopes and fears it heeded not:

1. The European skylark is a small bird that sings only in flight, often when it is too high to be visible.

2. The morning star, Venus.

Like a high-born maiden
   In a palace-tower,
Soothing her love-laden
   Soul in secret hour,
45 With music sweet as love—which overflows her bower:

Like a glow-worm golden
   In a dell of dew,
Scattering unbeholden
   Its aerial hue
50 Among the flowers and grass which screen it from the view:

Like a rose embowered
   In its own green leaves—
By warm winds deflowered—
   Till the scent, it gives
55 Makes faint with too much sweet those heavy-winged thieves:[3]

Sound of vernal° showers   *springtime*
   On the twinkling grass,
Rain-awakened flowers,
   All that ever was
60 Joyous, and clear and fresh, thy music doth surpass.

Teach us, Sprite° or Bird,   *spirit*
   What sweet thoughts are thine;
I have never heard
   Praise of love or wine
65 That panted forth a flood of rapture so divine:

Chorus Hymeneal[4]
   Or triumphal chaunt
Matched with thine would be all
   But an empty vaunt,
70 A thing wherein we feel there is some hidden want.

What objects are the fountains
   Of thy happy strain?
What fields or waves or mountains?
   What shapes of sky or plain?
75 What love of thine own kind? what ignorance of pain?

With thy clear keen joyance
   Languor cannot be—
Shadow of annoyance
   Never came near thee;
80 Thou lovest—but ne'er knew love's sad satiety.

Waking or asleep,
   Thou of death must deem
Things more true and deep

3. The "warm winds," line 53.   4. Marital (from Hymen, Greek god of marriage).

Than we mortals dream,
85   Or how could thy notes flow in such a chrystal stream?

We look before and after,
    And pine for what is not—
Our sincerest laughter
    With some pain is fraught—
90   Our sweetest songs are those that tell of saddest thought.

Yet if we could scorn
    Hate and pride and fear;
If we were things born
    Not to shed a tear,
95   I know not how thy joy we ever should come near.

Better than all measures
    Of delightful sound—
Better than all treasures
    That in books are found—
100   Thy skill to poet were, thou Scorner of the ground!

Teach me half the gladness
    That thy brain must know,
Such harmonious madness
    From my lips would flow
105   The world should listen then—as I am listening now.

1820   1820

Adonais.   John Keats died in Rome on February 23, 1821, and was buried there
in the Protestant Cemetery. In the Preface to *Adonais*, his elegy for Keats, Percy Shelley, who had buried his three-year-old son William in that "romantic and lonely cemetery" a year and a half earlier, describes the site as "an open space among the ruins
covered in winter with violets and daisies." "It might make one in love with death," he
adds, "to think that one should be buried in so sweet a place." In fact, after his drowning in 1822, Shelley's ashes would be interred in that sweet place also.

Shelley had met Keats, had invited him to be his guest at Pisa in Italy (an invitation Keats did not live to accept), and had gradually come to realize that Keats was,
as the Preface to *Adonais* states, "among the writers of the highest genius who have
adorned our age." In his elegy, which he began writing in April 1821, almost immediately after hearing of Keats's death, Shelley mourns Keats, honors him, and also
pursues a case against the reviewers of Keats's poems—in particular the anonymous critic for the influential *Quarterly Review* (now known to be the Tory civil
servant John Wilson Croker), who had written a grossly insulting review of Keats's
Endymion. Shelley believed, wrongly, that Keats's disappointment over the review
had caused his illness and death: Keats's "genius," he stated in the Preface, "was not
less delicate and fragile than it was beautiful. . . . The savage criticism . . . produced the most violent effect on his susceptible mind." Shelley's readiness to
believe the exaggerated rumors about Keats's reaction to his bad reviews is the
more understandable when one remembers that he had been savaged by reviewers
on several occasions himself. It is also true that in this period of fierce political
enmities rancorous book reviews were very near being the norm rather than the
exception. (Those antagonisms, which helped define Romantic understandings of
the modern author, are explored at length in "'Self-constituted judge of poesy':
Reviewer vs. Poet in the Romantic Period," found in the supplemental ebook.)

Shelley in a letter described *Adonais* as a "highly wrought piece of art." Its artistry consists in part in the care with which it follows the conventions of the pastoral elegy, the literary form established more than two thousand years earlier by the Greek poets Bion, Moschus, and Theocritus—Shelley had translated into English Bion's *Lament for Adonis* and Moschus's *Lament for Bion*. Those conventions include an invocation to a muse; descriptions of nature's sympathetic participation in the grieving and of the procession of mourners; and, most important, the final turn from despair to consolation, in the discovery that, paradoxically, the grave is the gate to a higher existence. The name that Shelley gives to Keats in this pastoral elegy, "Adonais," likely derives from Adonis, the name of the beautiful mortal who was beloved by the goddess Venus. Slain by a wild boar while hunting, Adonis was restored to life and a kind of immortality on the condition that he spend only part of the year with Venus, and the remaining part with Proserpine in the underworld. This cycle of rebirth and death, symbolic of the alternate return of summer and winter, suggests why Adonis was central to ancient fertility myths. This cycle is also an integral element of *Adonais*.

Published first in Pisa in 1821, *Adonais* was not issued in England until 1829, in an edition sponsored by the so-called Cambridge Apostles, a group including the poets Alfred Tennyson and A. H. Hallam. The appearance of this edition marked the beginning of Keats's posthumous emergence from obscurity.

Adonais

An Elegy on the Death of John Keats, Author of Endymion, Hyperion, etc.

[Thou wert the morning star among the living,
  Ere thy fair light had fled—
Now, having died, thou art as Hesperus, giving
  New splendour to the dead.][1]

I

I weep for Adonais—he is dead!
O, weep for Adonais! though our tears
Thaw not the frost which binds so dear a head!
And thou, sad Hour,[2] selected from all years

5   To mourn our loss, rouse thy obscure compeers,°   companions
And teach them thine own sorrow, say: with me
Died Adonais; till the Future dares
Forget the Past, his fate and fame shall be
  An echo and a light unto eternity!

2

10   Where wert thou mighty Mother,[3] when he lay,
When thy Son lay, pierced by the shaft which flies
In darkness?[4] where was lorn° Urania   forlorn
When Adonais died? With veiled eyes,
  'Mid listening Echoes, in her Paradise

1. Shelley prefixed to *Adonais* a Greek epigraph attributed to Plato; this is Shelley's translation of the Greek. The planet Venus appears both as the morning star, Lucifer, and as the evening star, Hesperus or Vesper. Shelley makes of this phenomenon a key symbol for Adonais's triumph over death, in stanzas 44–46.
2. Shelley follows the classical mode of personifying the hours, which mark the passage of time and turn of the seasons.
3. Urania. She had originally been the Muse of astronomy, but the name was also an epithet for Venus. Shelley converts Venus Urania, who in Greek myth had been the lover of Adonis, into the mother of Adonais.
4. Alludes to the anonymity of the review of *Endymion*.

15 She sate, while one,[5] with soft enamoured breath,
   Rekindled all the fading melodies,
   With which, like flowers that mock the corse° beneath,   *corpse*
   He had adorned and hid the coming bulk of death.

3

O, weep for Adonais—he is dead!
20 Wake, melancholy Mother, wake and weep!
   Yet wherefore? Quench within their burning bed
   Thy fiery tears, and let thy loud heart keep
   Like his, a mute and uncomplaining sleep;
   For he is gone, where all things wise and fair
25 Descend;—oh, dream not that the amorous Deep°   *abyss*
   Will yet restore him to the vital air;
   Death feeds on his mute voice, and laughs at our despair.

4

Most musical of mourners, weep again!
   Lament anew, Urania!—He[6] died,
30 Who was the Sire of an immortal strain,
   Blind, old, and lonely, when his country's pride,
   The priest, the slave, and the liberticide,
   Trampled and mocked with many a loathed rite
   Of lust and blood; he went, unterrified,
35 Into the gulph of death; but his clear Sprite°   *spirit*
   Yet reigns o'er earth; the third among the sons of light.[7]

5

Most musical of mourners, weep anew!
   Not all to that bright station dared to climb;
   And happier they their happiness who knew,
40 Whose tapers° yet burn through that night of time   *candles*
   In which suns perished; others more sublime,
   Struck by the envious wrath of man or God,
   Have sunk, extinct in their refulgent° prime;   *radiant*
   And some yet live, treading the thorny road,
45 Which leads, through toil and hate, to Fame's serene abode.

6

But now, thy youngest, dearest one, has perished—
   The nursling of thy widowhood, who grew,
   Like a pale flower by some sad maiden cherished,
   And fed with true love tears, instead of dew;[8]
50 Most musical of mourners, weep anew!
   Thy extreme[9] hope, the loveliest and the last,

---

5. I.e., one of the Echoes (line 14).
6. Milton, regarded as precursor of the great poetic tradition in which Keats wrote. He had adopted Urania as the muse of *Paradise Lost*. Lines 31–35 describe Milton's life during the restoration of the Stuart monarchy.

7. In "A Defence of Poetry," Shelley says that Milton was the third great epic poet, along with Homer and Dante. The stanza following describes the fate of other poets, up to Shelley's own time.
8. An allusion to an incident in Keats's *Isabella*.
9. Last, as well as highest.

The bloom, whose petals nipt before they blew°   *bloomed*
    Died on the promise of the fruit, is waste;
The broken lily lies—the storm is overpast.

7

55   To that high Capital,° where kingly Death   *Rome*
    Keeps his pale court in beauty and decay,
    He came; and bought, with price of purest breath,
    A grave among the eternal.—Come away!
    Haste, while the vault of blue Italian day
60   Is yet his fitting charnel-roof! while still
    He lies, as if in dewy sleep he lay;
    Awake him not! surely he takes his fill
Of deep and liquid rest, forgetful of all ill.

8

He will awake no more, oh, never more!—
65   Within the twilight chamber spreads apace,
    The shadow of white Death, and at the door
    Invisible Corruption waits to trace
    His extreme way to her dim dwelling-place;
    The eternal Hunger sits, but pity and awe
70   Soothe her pale rage, nor dares she to deface
    So fair a prey, till darkness, and the law
Of change, shall o'er his sleep the mortal curtain draw.

9

O, weep for Adonais!—The quick° Dreams,   *living*
    The passion-winged Ministers of thought,
75   Who were his flocks,[1] whom near the living streams
    Of his young spirit he fed, and whom he taught
    The love which was its music, wander not,—
    Wander no more, from kindling brain to brain,
    But droop there, whence they sprung; and mourn their lot
80   Round the cold heart, where, after their sweet pain,
They ne'er will gather strength, or find a home again.

10

And one[2] with trembling hands clasps his cold head,
    And fans him with her moonlight wings, and cries;
    "Our love, our hope, our sorrow, is not dead;
85   See, on the silken fringe of his faint eyes,
    Like dew upon a sleeping flower, there lies
    A tear some Dream has loosened from his brain."
    Lost Angel of a ruined Paradise!
    She knew not 'twas her own; as with no stain
90   She faded, like a cloud which had outwept its rain.

---

1. The products of Keats's imagination, figuratively represented (according to the conventions
of the pastoral elegy) as his sheep.
2. One of the Dreams (line 73).

11

One from a lucid° urn of starry dew   *luminous*
Washed his light limbs as if embalming them;
Another clipt her profuse locks, and threw
The wreath upon him, like an anadem,°   *rich garland*
95   Which frozen tears instead of pearls begem;
Another in her wilful grief would break
Her bow and winged reeds,° as if to stem   *arrows*
A greater loss with one which was more weak;
And dull the barbed fire against his frozen cheek.

12

100   Another Splendour on his mouth alit,
That mouth, whence it was wont° to draw the breath   *accustomed*
Which gave it strength to pierce the guarded wit,[3]
And pass into the panting heart beneath
With lightning and with music: the damp death
105   Quenched its caress upon his icy lips;
And, as a dying meteor stains a wreath
Of moonlight vapour, which the cold night clips,°   *clasps*
It flushed through his pale limbs, and past to its eclipse.

13

And others came . . . Desires and Adorations,
110   Winged Persuasions and veiled Destinies,
Splendours, and Glooms, and glimmering Incarnations
Of hopes and fears, and twilight Phantasies;
And Sorrow, with her family of Sighs,
And Pleasure, blind with tears, led by the gleam
115   Of her own dying smile instead of eyes,
Came in slow pomp;—the moving pomp might seem
Like pageantry of mist on an autumnal stream.

14

All he had loved, and moulded into thought,
From shape, and hue, and odour, and sweet sound,
120   Lamented Adonais. Morning sought
Her eastern watchtower, and her hair unbound,
Wet with the tears which should adorn the ground,
Dimmed the aerial eyes that kindle day;
Afar the melancholy thunder moaned,
125   Pale Ocean in unquiet slumber lay,
And the wild winds flew round, sobbing in their dismay.

15

Lost Echo sits amid the voiceless mountains,
And feeds her grief with his remembered lay,°   *song*
And will no more reply to winds or fountains,
130   Or amorous birds perched on the young green spray,

3. The cautious intellect (of the listener).

Or herdsman's horn, or bell at closing day;
Since she can mimic not his lips, more dear
Than those for whose disdain she pined away
Into a shadow of all sounds:[4]—a drear
135   Murmur, between their songs, is all the woodmen hear.

                    16

Grief made the young Spring wild, and she threw down
Her kindling buds, as if she Autumn were,
Or they dead leaves; since her delight is flown
For whom should she have waked the sullen year?
140   To Phoebus was not Hyacinth so dear[5]
Nor to himself Narcissus, as to both
Thou Adonais: wan they stand and sere[6]
Amid the faint companions of their youth,
With dew all turned to tears; odour, to sighing ruth.°   *pity*

                    17

145   Thy spirit's sister, the lorn nightingale[7]
Mourns not her mate with such melodious pain;
Not so the eagle, who like thee could scale
Heaven, and could nourish in the sun's domain
Her mighty youth with morning,[8] doth complain,°   *lament*
150   Soaring and screaming round her empty nest,
As Albion° wails for thee: the curse of Cain   *England*
Light on his head[9] who pierced thy innocent breast,
And scared the angel soul that was its earthly guest!

                    18

Ah woe is me! Winter is come and gone,
155   But grief returns with the revolving year;
The airs and streams renew their joyous tone;
The ants, the bees, the swallows reappear;
Fresh leaves and flowers deck the dead Seasons' bier;
The amorous birds now pair in every brake,°   *thicket*
160   And build their mossy homes in field and brere;°   *briar*
And the green lizard, and the golden snake,
Like unimprisoned flames, out of their trance awake.

                    19

Through wood and stream and field and hill and Ocean
A quickening life from the Earth's heart has burst
165   As it has ever done, with change and motion,
From the great morning of the world when first
God dawned on Chaos; in its stream immersed

4. Because of her unrequited love for Narcissus, who was enamored of his own reflection (line 141), the nymph Echo pined away until she was only a reflected sound.
5. Young Hyacinthus was loved by Phoebus Apollo, who accidentally killed him in a game of quoits. Apollo made the hyacinth flower spring from his blood.
6. Dried, withered.
7. To whom Keats had written "Ode to a Nightingale."
8. In the legend the aged eagle, to renew his youth, flies toward the sun until his old plumage is burned off and the film cleared from his eyes.
9. The reviewer of *Endymion*.

The lamps of Heaven flash with a softer light;
All baser things pant with life's sacred thirst;
170   Diffuse themselves; and spend in love's delight,
The beauty and the joy of their renewed might.

20

The leprous corpse touched by this spirit tender
Exhales itself in flowers of gentle breath;
Like incarnations of the stars, when splendour
175   Is changed to fragrance, they illumine death
And mock the merry worm that wakes beneath;
Nought we know, dies. Shall that alone which knows
Be as a sword consumed before the sheath[1]
By sightless° lightning?—th' intense atom glows   *invisible*
180   A moment, then is quenched in a most cold repose.

21

Alas! that all we loved of him should be,
But for our grief, as if it had not been,
And grief itself be mortal! Woe is me!
Whence are we, and why are we? of what scene
185   The actors or spectators? Great and mean°   *low*
Meet massed in death, who lends what life must borrow.
As long as skies are blue, and fields are green,
Evening must usher night, night urge the morrow,
Month follow month with woe, and year wake year to sorrow.

22

190   *He* will awake no more, oh, never more!
"Wake thou," cried Misery, "childless Mother, rise
Out of thy sleep, and slake,° in thy heart's core,   *assuage*
A wound more fierce than his with tears and sighs."
And all the Dreams that watched Urania's eyes,
195   And all the Echoes whom their sister's song[2]
Had held in holy silence, cried: "Arise!"
Swift as a Thought by the snake Memory stung,
From her ambrosial rest the fading Splendour° sprung.   *Urania*

23

She rose like an autumnal Night, that springs
200   Out of the East, and follows wild and drear
The golden Day, which, on eternal wings,
Even as a ghost abandoning a bier,
Had left the Earth a corpse. Sorrow and fear
So struck, so roused, so rapt Urania;
205   So saddened round her like an atmosphere
Of stormy mist; so swept her on her way
Even to the mournful place where Adonais lay.

1. The "sword" is the mind that knows; the   2. I.e., the Echo in line 127.
"sheath" is its vehicle, the material body.

24

Out of her secret Paradise she sped,
Through camps and cities rough with stone, and steel,
210 And human hearts, which to her aery tread
Yielding not, wounded the invisible
Palms of her tender feet where'er they fell:
And barbed tongues, and thoughts more sharp than they
Rent° the soft Form they never could repel,   *tore*
215 Whose sacred blood, like the young tears of May,
    Paved with eternal flowers that undeserving way.

25

In the death chamber for a moment Death
Shamed by the presence of that living Might
Blushed to annihilation, and the breath
220 Revisited those lips, and life's pale light
Flashed through those limbs, so late her dear delight.
"Leave me not wild and drear and comfortless,
As silent lightning leaves the starless night!
Leave me not!" cried Urania: her distress
225 Roused Death: Death rose and smiled, and met her vain caress.

26

"Stay yet awhile! speak to me once again;
Kiss me, so long but as a kiss may live;
And in my heartless[3] breast and burning brain
That word, that kiss shall all thoughts else survive
230 With food of saddest memory kept alive,
Now thou art dead, as if it were a part
Of thee, my Adonais! I would give
All that I am to be as thou now art!
But I am chained to Time, and cannot thence depart!

27

235 "Oh gentle child, beautiful as thou wert,
Why didst thou leave the trodden paths of men
Too soon, and with weak hands though mighty heart
Dare° the unpastured dragon in his den?[4]   *challenge*
Defenceless as thou wert, oh where was then
240 Wisdom the mirrored shield, or scorn the spear?[5]
Or hadst thou waited the full cycle, when
Thy spirit should have filled its crescent sphere,[6]
The monsters of life's waste had fled from thee like deer.

28

"The herded wolves, bold only to pursue;
245 The obscene ravens, clamorous o'er the dead;

3. Because her heart had been given to Adonais.
4. I.e., the hostile reviewers.
5. The allusion is to Perseus, who had cut off
Medusa's head while avoiding the direct sight of
her (which would have turned him to stone) by
looking only at her reflection in his shield.
6. I.e., when thy spirit, like the full moon, should
have reached its maturity.

The vultures to the conqueror's banner true
Who feed where Desolation first has fed,
And whose wings rain contagion;—how they fled,
When like Apollo, from his golden bow,
250   The Pythian of the age[7] one arrow sped
And smiled!—The spoilers tempt no second blow,
They fawn on the proud feet that spurn them lying low.

29

"The sun comes forth, and many reptiles spawn;
He sets, and each ephemeral insect[8] then
255   Is gathered into death without a dawn,
And the immortal stars awake again;
So is it in the world of living men:
A godlike mind soars forth, in its delight
Making earth bare and veiling heaven,[9] and when
260   It sinks, the swarms that dimmed or shared its light
Leave to its kindred lamps[1] the spirit's awful night."

30

Thus ceased she: and the mountain shepherds came,
Their garlands sere, their magic mantles° rent;   *cloaks*
The Pilgrim of Eternity,[2] whose fame
265   Over his living head like Heaven is bent,
An early but enduring monument,
Came, veiling all the lightnings of his song
In sorrow; from her wilds Ierne sent
The sweetest lyrist[3] of her saddest wrong,
270   And love taught grief to fall like music from his tongue.

31

Midst others of less note, came one frail Form,[4]
A phantom among men; companionless
As the last cloud of an expiring storm
Whose thunder is its knell;° he, as I guess,   *funeral bell*
275   Had gazed on Nature's naked loveliness,
Actæon-like, and now he fled astray
With feeble steps o'er the world's wilderness,
And his own thoughts, along that rugged way,
Pursued, like raging hounds, their father and their prey.[5]

---

7. Byron, who had directed against critics of the age his satiric poem *English Bards and Scotch Reviewers* (1809). The allusion is to Apollo, called "the Pythian" because he had slain the dragon Python.
8. Insect that lives and dies in a single day.
9. As the sun reveals the earth but veils the other stars.
1. The other stars (i.e., creative minds), of lesser brilliance than the sun.
2. Byron, who had referred to his Childe Harold

as one of the "wanderers o'er Eternity" (3.669).
3. Thomas Moore (1779–1852), from Ireland ("Ierne"), who had written poems about the oppression of his native land.
4. Shelley, represented in one of his aspects— such as the Poet in *Alastor*, rather than the author of *Prometheus Unbound*.
5. Actaeon, while hunting, came upon the naked Diana bathing and, as a punishment, was turned into a stag and torn to pieces by his own hounds.

32

| 280 | A pardlike° Spirit beautiful and swift— | *leopardlike* |

A pardlike° Spirit beautiful and swift—   *leopardlike*
A Love in desolation masked;—a Power
Girt round with weakness;—it can scarce uplift
The weight of the superincumbent hour;[6]
It is a dying lamp, a falling shower,
A breaking billow;—even whilst we speak
Is it not broken? On the withering flower
The killing sun smiles brightly: on a cheek
The life can burn in blood, even while the heart may break.

33

His head was bound with pansies overblown,
And faded violets, white, and pied, and blue;
And a light spear topped with a cypress cone,
Round whose rude shaft dark ivy tresses grew[7]
Yet dripping with the forest's noonday dew,
Vibrated, as the ever-beating heart
Shook the weak hand that grasped it; of that crew
He came the last, neglected and apart;
A herd-abandoned deer struck by the hunter's dart.

34

All stood aloof, and at his partial moan
Smiled through their tears; well knew that gentle band
Who in another's fate now wept his own;
As in the accents of an unknown land,
He sung new sorrow; sad Urania scanned
The Stranger's mien, and murmured: "who art thou?"
He answered not, but with a sudden hand
Made bare his branded and ensanguined° brow,   *bloodied*
Which was like Cain's or Christ's[8]—Oh! that it should be so!

35

What softer voice is hushed over the dead?
Athwart what brow is that dark mantle thrown?
What form leans sadly o'er the white death-bed,
In mockery of monumental stone,[9]
The heavy heart heaving without a moan?
If it be He,[1] who, gentlest of the wise,
Taught, soothed, loved, honoured the departed one;
Let me not vex, with inharmonious sighs
The silence of that heart's accepted sacrifice.

---

6. The heavy, overhanging hour of Keats's death.
7. Like the thyrsus, the leaf-entwined and cone-topped staff carried by Dionysus, to whom leopards (see line 280) are sacred. The pansies, which are "overblown," i.e., past their bloom, are emblems of sorrowful thought. The cypress is an emblem of mourning.

8. His bloody ("ensanguined") brow bore a mark like that with which God had branded Cain for murdering Abel—or like that left by Christ's crown of thorns.
9. In imitation of a memorial statue.
1. Leigh Hunt, close friend of both Keats and Shelley.

36

Our Adonais has drunk poison—oh!
What deaf and viperous murderer could crown
Life's early cup with such a draught of woe?
The nameless worm[2] would now itself disown:
320 It felt, yet could escape the magic tone
Whose prelude held all envy, hate, and wrong,
But what was howling in one breast alone,
Silent with expectation of the song,[3]
Whose master's hand is cold, whose silver lyre unstrung.

37

325 Live thou, whose infamy is not thy fame!
Live! fear no heavier chastisement from me,
Thou noteless blot on a remembered name!
But be thyself, and know thyself to be!
And ever at thy season be thou free
330 To spill the venom when thy fangs o'erflow:
Remorse and Self-contempt shall cling to thee;
Hot Shame shall burn upon thy secret brow,
And like a beaten hound tremble thou shalt—as now.

38

Nor let us weep that our delight is fled
335 Far from these carrion kites[4] that scream below;
He wakes or sleeps with the enduring dead;
Thou canst not soar where he is sitting now.—
Dust to the dust! but the pure spirit shall flow
Back to the burning fountain whence it came,
340 A portion of the Eternal,[5] which must glow
Through time and change, unquenchably the same,
Whilst thy cold embers choke the sordid hearth of shame.

39

Peace, peace! he is not dead, he doth not sleep—
He hath awakened from the dream of life—
345 'Tis we, who lost in stormy visions, keep
With phantoms an unprofitable strife,
And in mad trance, strike with our spirit's knife
Invulnerable nothings.—We decay
Like corpses in a charnel; fear and grief
350 Convulse us and consume us day by day,
And cold hopes swarm like worms within our living clay.

2. Snake—the anonymous reviewer.
3. The promise of later greatness in Keats's early poems "held . . . silent" the expression of "all envy, hate, and wrong" except the reviewer's.
4. A species of hawk that feeds on dead flesh.
5. Shelley adopts for this poem the Neoplatonic view that all life and all forms emanate from the Absolute, the eternal One. The Absolute is imaged as both a radiant light source and an overflowing fountain, which circulates continuously through the dross of matter (stanza 43) and back to its source.

40

He has outsoared the shadow of our night;[6]
Envy and calumny° and hate and pain,   *slander*
And that unrest which men miscall delight,
355   Can touch him not and torture not again;
From the contagion of the world's slow stain
He is secure, and now can never mourn
A heart grown cold, a head grown grey in vain;
Nor, when the spirit's self has ceased to burn,
360 With sparkless ashes load an unlamented urn.

41

He lives, he wakes—'tis Death is dead, not he;
Mourn not for Adonais.—Thou young Dawn
Turn all thy dew to splendour, for from thee
The spirit thou lamentest is not gone;
365   Ye caverns and ye forests, cease to moan!
Cease ye faint flowers and fountains, and thou Air
Which like a mourning veil thy scarf hadst thrown
O'er the abandoned Earth, now leave it bare
Even to the joyous stars which smile on its despair![7]

42

370   He is made one with Nature: there is heard
His voice in all her music, from the moan
Of thunder, to the song of night's sweet bird;[8]
He is a presence to be felt and known
In darkness and in light, from herb and stone,
375   Spreading itself where'er that Power may move
Which has withdrawn his being to its own;
Which wields the world with never wearied love,
Sustains it from beneath, and kindles it above.

43

He is a portion of the loveliness
380   Which once he made more lovely: he doth bear
His part, while the one Spirit's plastic[9] stress
Sweeps through the dull dense world, compelling there,
All new successions to the forms they wear;
Torturing th' unwilling dross that checks its flight
385   To its own likeness, as each mass may bear;[1]
And bursting in its beauty and its might
From trees and beasts and men into the Heaven's light.

---

6. He has soared beyond the shadow cast by the earth as it intercepts the sun's light.
7. Shelley's science is accurate: it is the envelope of air around the earth that, by diffusing and reflecting sunlight, veils the stars so that they are invisible during the day.
8. The nightingale, in allusion to Keats's "Ode to a Nightingale."
9. Formative, shaping.
1. I.e., to the degree that a particular substance will permit.

44

The splendours of the firmament of time
May be eclipsed, but are extinguished not;
390 Like stars to their appointed height they climb
And death is a low mist which cannot blot
The brightness it may veil.[2] When lofty thought
Lifts a young heart above its mortal lair,
And love and life contend in it, for what°   *whatever*
395 Shall be its earthly doom,° the dead live there[3]   *destiny*
And move like winds of light on dark and stormy air.

45

The inheritors of unfulfilled renown[4]
Rose from their thrones, built beyond mortal thought,
Far in the Unapparent. Chatterton
400 Rose pale, his solemn agony had not
Yet faded from him; Sidney, as he fought
And as he fell and as he lived and loved
Sublimely mild, a Spirit without spot,
Arose; and Lucan, by his death approved:°   *justified*
405 Oblivion as they rose shrank like a thing reproved.

46

And many more, whose names on Earth are dark
But whose transmitted effluence cannot die
So long as fire outlives the parent spark,
Rose, robed in dazzling immortality.
410 "Thou art become as one of us," they cry,
"It was for thee yon kingless sphere has long
Swung blind in unascended majesty,
Silent alone amid an Heaven of song.
Assume thy winged throne, thou Vesper of our throng!"[5]

47

415 Who mourns for Adonais? oh come forth
Fond° wretch! and know thyself and him aright.   *foolish*
Clasp with thy panting soul the pendulous[6] Earth;
As from a centre, dart thy spirit's light
Beyond all worlds, until its spacious might°   *power*
420 Satiate the void circumference: then shrink
Even to a point within our day and night;[7]

2. The radiance of stars (i.e., of poets) persists, even when they are temporarily "eclipsed" by another heavenly body, or obscured by the veil of the earth's atmosphere.
3. I.e., in the thought of the "young heart."
4. Poets who (like Keats) died young, before achieving their full measure of fame: the seventeen-year-old Thomas Chatterton (1752–1770) was believed to have committed suicide out of despair over his poverty and lack of recognition, Sir Philip Sidney (1554–1586) died in battle at thirty-two, and the Roman poet Lucan (39–65 C.E.) killed himself at twenty-six to escape a sentence of death for having plotted against the tyrant Nero.
5. Adonais assumes his place in the sphere of Vesper, the evening star, hitherto unoccupied ("kingless"), hence also "silent" amid the music of the other spheres.
6. Suspended, floating in space.
7. The poet bids the mourner to stretch his imagination so as to reach the poet's own cosmic viewpoint and then allow it to contract ("shrink") back to its ordinary vantage point on Earth—where, unlike Adonais in his heavenly place, we have an alternation of day and night.

And keep thy heart light lest it make thee sink
When hope has kindled hope, and lured thee to the brink.

48

Or go to Rome, which is the sepulchre
O, not of him, but of our joy: 'tis nought
That ages, empires, and religions there
Lie buried in the ravage they have wrought;
For such as he can lend,—they[8] borrow not
Glory from those who made the world their prey;
And he is gathered to the kings of thought
Who waged contention with their time's decay,
And of the past are all that cannot pass away.

49

Go thou to Rome,—at once the Paradise,
The grave, the city, and the wilderness;
And where its wrecks° like shattered mountains rise,   *ruins*
And flowering weeds, and fragrant copses[9] dress
The bones of Desolation's nakedness
Pass, till the Spirit of the spot shall lead
Thy footsteps to a slope of green access[1]
Where, like an infant's smile, over the dead,
A light of laughing flowers along the grass is spread.

50

And grey walls moulder round,[2] on which dull Time
Feeds, like slow fire upon a hoary brand;[3]
And one keen pyramid with wedge sublime,[4]
Pavilioning the dust of him who planned
This refuge for his memory, doth stand
Like flame transformed to marble; and beneath,
A field is spread, on which a newer band
Have pitched in Heaven's smile their camp of death[5]
Welcoming him we lose with scarce extinguished breath.

51

Here pause: these graves are all too young as yet
To have outgrown the sorrow which consigned
Its charge to each; and if the seal is set,
Here, on one fountain of a mourning mind,[6]
Break it not thou! too surely shalt thou find
Thine own well full, if thou returnest home,
Of tears and gall. From the world's bitter wind

425, 430, 435, 440, 445, 450, 455

---

8. Poets such as Keats.
9. Undergrowth. In Shelley's time the ruins of ancient Rome were overgrown with weeds and shrubs, almost as if the ground were returning to its natural state.
1. The Protestant Cemetery, Keats's burial place. The next line is a glancing allusion to Shelley's three-year-old son, William, also buried there.
2. The wall of ancient Rome formed one bound-ary of the cemetery.
3. A burning log, white with ash.
4. The tomb of Caius Cestius, a Roman tribune, just outside the cemetery.
5. A common name for a cemetery in Italy is *camposanto*, "holy camp or ground." Shelley is punning on the Italian word.
6. Shelley's mourning for his son.

Seek shelter in the shadow of the tomb.
What Adonais is, why fear we to become?

52

460   The One remains, the many change and pass;
       Heaven's light forever shines, Earth's shadows fly;
       Life, like a dome of many-coloured glass,
       Stains the white radiance of Eternity,
       Until Death tramples it to fragments.[7]—Die,
465   If thou wouldst be with that which thou dost seek!
       Follow where all is fled!—Rome's azure sky,
       Flowers, ruins, statues, music, words, are weak
    The glory they transfuse with fitting truth to speak.

53

       Why linger, why turn back, why shrink, my Heart?
470   Thy hopes are gone before; from all things here
       They have departed; thou shouldst now depart!
       A light is past° from the revolving year,   *passed*
       And man, and woman; and what still is dear
       Attracts to crush, repels to make thee wither.
475   The soft sky smiles,—the low wind whispers near:
       'Tis Adonais calls! oh, hasten thither,
    No more let Life divide what Death can join together.

54

       That Light whose smile kindles the Universe,
       That Beauty in which all things work and move,
480   That Benediction which the eclipsing Curse
       Of birth can quench not, that sustaining Love
       Which through the web of being blindly wove
       By man and beast and earth and air and sea,
       Burns bright or dim, as each are mirrors of[8]
485   The fire for which all thirst;[9] now beams on me,
    Consuming the last clouds of cold mortality.

55

       The breath whose might I have invoked in song[1]
       Descends on me; my spirit's bark is driven,
       Far from the shore, far from the trembling throng
490   Whose sails were never to the tempest given;
       The massy earth and sphered skies are riven![2]
       I am borne darkly, fearfully, afar;

7. Earthly life colors ("stains") the pure white light of the One, which is the source of all light (see lines 339–40, n. 5). The azure sky, flowers, etc., of lines 466–68 exemplify earthly colors that, however beautiful, fall far short of the "glory" of the pure Light that they transmit but also refract ("transfuse").
8. I.e., according to the degree that each reflects.
9. The "thirst" of the human spirit is to return to the fountain and fire (the "burning fountain," line 339) that are its source.
1. Two years earlier Shelley had "invoked" (prayed to, and also asked for) "the breath of Autumn's being" in his "Ode to the West Wind" (p. 388).
2. In her 1839 edition of her husband's works, Mary Shelley, thinking of the manner of Percy's death, asked: "who but will regard as a prophecy the last stanza of the 'Adonais'?"

> Whilst burning through the inmost veil of Heaven,
> The soul of Adonais, like a star,
495 Beacons from the abode where the Eternal are.

1821   1821

A Defence of Poetry   In 1820 Shelley's good friend Thomas Love Peacock
published an ironic essay, "The Four Ages of Poetry," implicitly directed against the
towering claims for poetry and the poetic imagination made by his Romantic contemporaries. In this essay, which is available in the supplemental ebook, Peacock adopted
the premise of Wordsworth and some other Romantic critics—that poetry in its origin was a primitive use of language and mind—but from this premise he proceeded
to draw the conclusion that poetry had become a useless anachronism in his own Age
of Bronze, a time defined by new sciences (including economics and political theory)
and technologies that had the potential to improve the world. Peacock was a poet as
well as an excellent prose satirist, and Shelley saw the joke; but he also recognized
that the view that Peacock, as a satirist, had assumed was very close to that actually
held in his day by Utilitarian philosophers and the material-minded public, which
either attacked or contemptuously ignored the imaginative faculty and its achievements. He therefore undertook, as he good-humoredly wrote to Peacock, "to break
a lance with you . . . in honor of my mistress Urania" (giving the cause for which he
battled the name that Milton had used for the muse inspiring *Paradise Lost*), even
though he was only "the knight of the shield of shadow and the lance of gossamere."
The result was "A Defence of Poetry," planned to consist of three parts. The last two
parts were never written, and even the existing section, written in 1821, remained
unpublished until 1840, eighteen years after Shelley's death.

Shelley's emphasis in this essay is not on the particularity of individual poems
but on the universal and permanent qualities and values that, he believes, all great
poems, as products of imagination, have in common. Shelley in addition extends
the term *poet* to include all creative minds that break out of the conditions of their
historical time and place in order to envision such values. This category includes
not only writers in prose as well as verse but also artists, legislators, prophets, and
the founders of new social and religious institutions.

The "Defence" is an eloquent and enduring claim for the indispensability of the
visionary and creative imagination in all the great human concerns. Few later social
critics have equaled the cogency of Shelley's attack on our acquisitive society and its
narrowly material concepts of utility and progress. Such a bias has opened the way
to enormous advances in the physical sciences and our material well-being, but
without a proportionate development of our "poetic faculty," the moral imagination.
The result, Shelley says, is that "man, having enslaved the elements, remains himself
a slave."

From A Defence of Poetry

or Remarks Suggested by an Essay Entitled "The Four Ages of Poetry"

According to one mode of regarding those two classes of mental action,
which are called reason and imagination, the former may be considered as
mind contemplating the relations borne by one thought to another, however
produced; and the latter, as mind acting upon those thoughts so as to colour
them with its own light, and composing from them, as from elements, other
thoughts, each containing within itself the principle of its own integrity. The

one[1] is the *to poiein*,[2] or the principle of synthesis, and has for its objects those forms which are common to universal nature and existence itself; the other is the *to logizein*,[3] or principle of analysis, and its action regards the relations of things, simply as relations; considering thoughts, not in their integral unity, but as the algebraical representations which conduct to certain general results. Reason is the enumeration of quantities already known; imagination is the perception of the value of those quantities, both separately and as a whole. Reason respects the differences, and imagination the similitudes of things. Reason is to Imagination as the instrument to the agent, as the body to the spirit, as the shadow to the substance.

Poetry, in a general sense, may be defined to be "the expression of the Imagination": and poetry is connate with the origin of man. Man is an instrument over which a series of external and internal impressions are driven, like the alternations of an ever-changing wind over an Æolian lyre,[4] which move it by their motion to ever-changing melody. But there is a principle within the human being, and perhaps within all sentient beings, which acts otherwise than in the lyre, and produces not melody, alone, but harmony, by an internal adjustment of the sounds or motions thus excited to the impressions which excite them. It is as if the lyre could accommodate its chords to the motions of that which strikes them, in a determined proportion of sound; even as the musician can accommodate his voice to the sound of the lyre. A child at play by itself will express its delight by its voice and motions; and every inflexion of tone and every gesture will bear exact relation to a corresponding antitype in the pleasurable impressions which awakened it; it will be the reflected image of that impression; and as the lyre trembles and sounds after the wind has died away, so the child seeks, by prolonging in its voice and motions the duration of the effect, to prolong also a consciousness of the cause. In relation to the objects which delight a child, these expressions are, what poetry is to higher objects. The savage (for the savage is to ages what the child is to years) expresses the emotions produced in him by surrounding objects in a similar manner; and language and gesture, together with plastic[5] or pictorial imitation, become the image of the combined effect of those objects, and of his apprehension of them. Man in society, with all his passions and his pleasures, next becomes the object of the passions and pleasures of man; an additional class of emotions produces an augmented treasure of expressions; and language, gesture, and the imitative arts, become at once the representation and the medium, the pencil and the picture, the chisel and the statue, the chord and the harmony. The social sympathies, or those laws from which as from its elements society results, begin to develope themselves from the moment that two human beings coexist; the future is contained within the present as the plant within the seed; and equality, diversity, unity, contrast, mutual dependence, become the principles alone capable of affording the motives according to which the will of a social being is determined to action, inasmuch as he is social; and constitute pleasure in sensation, virtue in sentiment, beauty in art, truth

---

1. The imagination. "The other" (later in the sentence) is the reason.
2. Making. The Greek word from which the English term *poet* derives means "maker," and "maker" was often used as equivalent to "poet" by Renaissance critics such as Sir Philip Sidney in

his *Defence of Poesy*, which Shelley had carefully studied.
3. Calculating, reasoning.
4. A wind harp (see Coleridge, "The Eolian Harp," p. 252).
5. Sculptural.

in reasoning, and love in the intercourse of kind. Hence men, even in the infancy of society, observe a certain order in their words and actions, distinct from that of the objects and the impressions represented by them, all expression being subject to the laws of that from which it proceeds. But let us dismiss those more general considerations which might involve an enquiry into the principles of society itself, and restrict our view to the manner in which the imagination is expressed upon its forms.

In the youth of the world, men dance and sing and imitate natural objects, observing[6] in these actions, as in all others, a certain rhythm or order. And, although all men observe a similar, they observe not the same order, in the motions of the dance, in the melody of the song, in the combinations of language, in the series of their imitations of natural objects. For there is a certain order or rhythm belonging to each of these classes of mimetic representation, from which the hearer and the spectator receive an intenser and purer pleasure than from any other: the sense of an approximation to this order has been called taste, by modern writers. Every man in the infancy of art, observes an order which approximates more or less closely to that from which this highest delight results: but the diversity is not sufficiently marked, as that its gradations should be sensible,[7] except in those instances where the predominance of this faculty of approximation to the beautiful (for so we may be permitted to name the relation between this highest pleasure and its cause) is very great. Those in whom it exists in excess are poets, in the most universal sense of the word; and the pleasure resulting from the manner in which they express the influence of society or nature upon their own minds, communicates itself to others, and gathers a sort of reduplication from that community. Their language is vitally metaphorical; that is, it marks the before unapprehended relations of things, and perpetuates their apprehension, until the words which represent them, become through time signs for portions or classes of thoughts[8] instead of pictures of integral thoughts; and then if no new poets should arise to create afresh the associations which have been thus disorganized, language will be dead to all the nobler purposes of human intercourse. These similitudes or relations are finely said by Lord Bacon to be "the same footsteps of nature impressed upon the various subjects of the world"[9]—and he considers the faculty which perceives them as the storehouse of axioms common to all knowledge. In the infancy of society every author is necessarily a poet, because language itself is poetry; and to be a poet is to apprehend the true and the beautiful, in a word the good which exists in the relation, subsisting, first between existence and perception, and secondly between perception and expression. Every original language near to its source is in itself the chaos of a cyclic poem:[1] the copiousness of lexicography and the distinctions of grammar are the works of a later age, and are merely the catalogue and the form of the creations of Poetry.

But Poets, or those who imagine and express this indestructible order, are not only the authors of language and of music, of the dance and architecture and statuary and painting: they are the institutors of laws, and the founders of civil society and the inventors of the arts of life and the teachers, who draw into a certain propinquity with the beautiful and the true that partial

6. Following, obeying.
7. Discernible.
8. I.e., abstract concepts.
9. Francis Bacon's *The Advancement of Learn-*

ing 3.1.
1. A group of poems (e.g., "the Arthurian cycle") that deal with the same subject.

apprehension of the agencies of the invisible world which is called religion.[2] Hence all original religions are allegorical, or susceptible of allegory, and like Janus[3] have a double face of false and true. Poets, according to the circumstances of the age and nation in which they appeared, were called in the earlier epochs of the world legislators or prophets:[4] a poet essentially comprises and unites both these characters. For he not only beholds intensely the present as it is, and discovers those laws according to which present things ought to be ordered, but he beholds the future in the present, and his thoughts are the germs of the flower and the fruit of latest time. Not that I assert poets to be prophets in the gross sense of the word, or that they can foretell the form as surely as they foreknow the spirit of events: such is the pretence of superstition which would make poetry an attribute of prophecy, rather than prophecy an attribute of poetry. A Poet participates in the eternal, the infinite, and the one; as far as relates to his conceptions, time and place and number are not. The grammatical forms which express the moods of time, and the difference of persons and the distinction of place are convertible with respect to the highest poetry without injuring it as poetry, and the choruses of Æschylus, and the book of Job, and Dante's Paradise would afford, more than any other writings, examples of this fact, if the limits of this essay did not forbid citation. The creations of sculpture, painting, and music, are illustrations still more decisive.

Language, colour, form, and religious and civil habits of action are all the instruments and materials of poetry; they may be called poetry by that figure of speech which considers the effect as a synonime of the cause. But poetry in a more restricted sense[5] expresses those arrangements of language, and especially metrical language, which are created by that imperial faculty, whose throne is curtained within the invisible nature of man. And this springs from the nature itself of language, which is a more direct representation of the actions and passions of our internal being, and is susceptible of more various and delicate combinations, than colour, form, or motion, and is more plastic and obedient to the controul of that faculty of which it is the creation. For language is arbitrarily produced by the Imagination and has relation to thoughts alone; but all other materials, instruments and conditions of art, have relations among each other, which limit and interpose between conception and expression. The former[6] is as a mirror which reflects, the latter as a cloud which enfeebles, the light of which both are mediums of communication. Hence the fame of sculptors, painters and musicians, although the intrinsic powers of the great masters of these arts, may yield in no degree to that of those who have employed language as the hieroglyphic of their thoughts, has never equalled that of poets in the restricted sense of the term; as two performers of equal skill will produce unequal effects from a guitar and a harp. The fame of legislators and founders of religions, so long as their institutions last, alone seems to exceed that of poets in the restricted sense; but it can scarcely be a question whether,

2. Here Shelley enlarges the scope of the term *poetry* to denote all the creative achievements, or imaginative breakthroughs, of humankind, including noninstitutional religious insights.
3. Roman god of beginnings and endings, often represented by two heads facing opposite directions.
4. Sir Philip Sidney had pointed out, in his

Defence of Poesy, that *vates*, the Roman term for "poet," signifies "a diviner, fore-seer, or Prophet."
5. I.e., restricted to specifically verbal poetry, as against the inclusive sense in which Shelley has been applying the term.
6. I.e., language, as opposed to the media of sculpture, painting, and music.

if we deduct the celebrity which their flattery of the gross opinions of the vulgar usually conciliates, together with that which belonged to them in their higher character of poets, any excess will remain.

We have thus circumscribed the meaning of the word Poetry within the limits of that art which is the most familiar and the most perfect expression of the faculty itself. It is necessary however to make the circle still narrower, and to determine the distinction between measured and unmeasured language;[7] for the popular division into prose and verse is inadmissible in accurate philosophy.

Sounds as well as thoughts have relation both between each other and towards that which they represent, and a perception of the order of those relations has always been found connected with a perception of the order of the relations of thoughts. Hence the language of poets has ever affected a certain uniform and harmonious recurrence of sound, without which it were not poetry, and which is scarcely less indispensable to the communication of its influence, than the words themselves, without reference to that peculiar order. Hence the vanity of translation; it were as wise to cast a violet into a crucible that you might discover the formal principle of its colour and odour, as seek to transfuse from one language into another the creations of a poet. The plant must spring again from its seed or it will bear no flower—and this is the burthen of the curse of Babel.[8]

An observation of the regular mode of the recurrence of this harmony in the language of poetical minds, together with its relation to music, produced metre, or a certain system of traditional forms of harmony of language. Yet it is by no means essential that a poet should accommodate his language to this traditional form, so that the harmony which is its spirit, be observed. The practise is indeed convenient and popular, and to be preferred, especially in such composition as includes much form and action: but every great poet must inevitably innovate upon the example of his predecessors in the exact structure of his peculiar versification. The distinction between poets and prose writers is a vulgar error. The distinction between philosophers and poets has been anticipated.[9] Plato was essentially a poet—the truth and splendour of his imagery and the melody of his language is the most intense that it is possible to conceive. He rejected the measure of the epic, dramatic, and lyrical forms, because he sought to kindle a harmony in thoughts divested of shape and action, and he forbore to invent any regular plan of rhythm which would include, under determinate forms, the varied pauses of his style. Cicero[1] sought to imitate the cadence of his periods but with little success. Lord Bacon was a poet.[2] His language has a sweet and majestic rhythm, which satisfies the sense, no less than the almost superhuman wisdom of his philosophy satisfies the intellect; it is a strain which distends, and then bursts the circumference of the hearer's mind, and pours itself forth together with it into the universal element with which it has perpetual sympathy. All the authors of revolutions in opinion are not only necessarily poets as they are inventors, nor even as their words unveil the permanent

---

7. I.e., in meter versus in prose.
8. When the descendants of Noah, who spoke a single language, undertook to build the Tower of Babel, which would reach heaven, God cut short the attempt by multiplying languages so that the builders could no longer communicate (see Genesis 11.1–9).
9. I.e., in what Shelley has already said.
1. Marcus Tullius Cicero, the great Roman orator of the 1st century B.C.E.
2. See the *Filium Labyrinthi* and the *Essay on Death* particularly [Shelley's note].

analogy of things by images which participate in the life of truth; but as their periods are harmonious and rhythmical and contain in themselves the elements of verse; being the echo of the eternal music. Nor are those supreme poets, who have employed traditional forms of rhythm on account of the form and action of their subjects, less capable of perceiving and teaching the truth of things, than those who have omitted that form. Shakespeare, Dante, and Milton (to confine ourselves to modern writers) are philosophers of the very loftiest power.

A poem is the very image of life expressed in its eternal truth. There is this difference between a story and a poem, that a story is a catalogue of detached facts, which have no other bond of connexion than time, place, circumstance, cause and effect; the other is the creation of actions according to the unchangeable forms of human nature, as existing in the mind of the creator, which is itself the image of all other minds. The one is partial, and applies only to a definite period of time, and a certain combination of events which can never again recur; the other is universal, and contains within itself the germ of a relation to whatever motives or actions have place in the possible varieties of human nature. Time, which destroys the beauty and the use of the story of particular facts, stript of the poetry which should invest them, augments that of Poetry, and for ever develops new and wonderful applications of the eternal truth which it contains. Hence epitomes[3] have been called the moths of just history;[4] they eat out the poetry of it. The story of particular facts is as a mirror which obscures and distorts that which should be beautiful: Poetry is a mirror which makes beautiful that which is distorted.

The parts of a composition may be poetical, without the composition as a whole being a poem. A single sentence may be considered as a whole though it be found in a series of unassimilated portions; a single word even may be a spark of inextinguishable thought. And thus all the great historians, Herodotus, Plutarch, Livy,[5] were poets; and although the plan of these writers, especially that of Livy, restrained them from developing this faculty in its highest degree, they make copious and ample amends for their subjection, by filling all the interstices of their subjects with living images.

Having determined what is poetry, and who are poets, let us proceed to estimate its effects upon society.

Poetry is ever accompanied with pleasure: all spirits on which it falls, open themselves to receive the wisdom which is mingled with its delight. In the infancy of the world, neither poets themselves nor their auditors are fully aware of the excellence of poetry: for it acts in a divine and unapprehended manner, beyond and above consciousness; and it is reserved for future generations to contemplate and measure the mighty cause and effect in all the strength and splendour of their union. Even in modern times, no living poet ever arrived at the fulness of his fame; the jury which sits in judgement upon a poet, belonging as he does to all time, must be composed of his peers: it must be impanelled by Time from the selectest of the wise of many generations. A Poet is a nightingale, who sits in darkness and sings to cheer its own solitude with sweet sounds: his auditors are as men entranced by the melody

3. Abstracts, summaries.
4. By Bacon in *The Advancement of Learning* 2.2.4.
5. Titus Livius (59 B.C.E.–17 C.E.) wrote an immense history of Rome. Herodotus (ca. 480–ca. 425 B.C.E.) wrote the first systematic history of Greece. Plutarch (ca. 46–ca. 120 C.E.) wrote *Parallel Lives* (of eminent Greeks and Romans).

of an unseen musician, who feel that they are moved and softened, yet know not whence or why. The poems of Homer and his contemporaries were the delight of infant Greece; they were the elements of that social system which is the column upon which all succeeding civilization has reposed. Homer embodied the ideal perfection of his age in human character; nor can we doubt that those who read his verses were awakened to an ambition of becoming like to Achilles, Hector and Ulysses: the truth and beauty of friendship, patriotism and persevering devotion to an object, were unveiled to the depths in these immortal creations: the sentiments of the auditors must have been refined and enlarged by a sympathy with such great and lovely impersonations, until from admiring they imitated, and from imitation they identified themselves with the objects of their admiration. Nor let it be objected, that these characters are remote from moral perfection, and that they can by no means be considered as edifying patterns for general imitation. Every epoch under names more or less specious has deified its peculiar errors; Revenge is the naked Idol of the worship of a semi-barbarous age; and Self-deceit is the veiled Image of unknown evil before which luxury and satiety lie prostrate. But a poet considers the vices of his contemporaries as the temporary dress in which his creations must be arrayed, and which cover without concealing the eternal proportions of their beauty. An epic or dramatic personage is understood to wear them around his soul, as he may the antient armour or the modern uniform around his body; whilst it is easy to conceive a dress more graceful than either. The beauty of the internal nature cannot be so far concealed by its accidental vesture, but that the spirit of its form shall communicate itself to the very disguise, and indicate the shape it hides from the manner in which it is worn. A majestic form and graceful motions will express themselves through the most barbarous and tasteless costume. Few poets of the highest class have chosen to exhibit the beauty of their conceptions in its naked truth and splendour; and it is doubtful whether the alloy of costume, habit, etc., be not necessary to temper this planetary music[6] for mortal ears.

The whole objection, however, of the immorality of poetry[7] rests upon a misconception of the manner in which poetry acts to produce the moral improvement of man. Ethical science[8] arranges the elements which poetry has created, and propounds schemes and proposes examples of civil and domestic life: nor is it for want of admirable doctrines that men hate, and despise, and censure, and deceive, and subjugate one another. But Poetry acts in another and diviner manner. It awakens and enlarges the mind itself by rendering it the receptacle of a thousand unapprehended combinations of thought. Poetry lifts the veil from the hidden beauty of the world, and makes familiar objects be as if they were not familiar; it reproduces[9] all that it represents, and the impersonations clothed in its Elysian light stand thenceforward in the minds of those who have once contemplated them, as memorials of that gentle and exalted content[1] which extends itself over all thoughts and actions with which it coexists. The great secret of morals is Love; or a going out of our own nature, and an identification of ourselves with the beautiful

6. The music made by the revolving crystalline spheres of the planets, inaudible to human ears.
7. In the preceding paragraph Shelley has been implicitly dealing with the charge, voiced by Plato in his *Republic*, that poetry is immoral because it represents evil characters acting evilly.
8. Moral philosophy.
9. Produces anew, re-creates.
1. Contentment.

which exists in thought, action, or person, not our own. A man, to be greatly good, must imagine intensely and comprehensively; he must put himself in the place of another and of many others; the pains and pleasures of his species must become his own. The great instrument of moral good is the imagination;[2] and poetry administers to the effect by acting upon the cause. Poetry enlarges the circumference of the imagination by replenishing it with thoughts of ever new delight, which have the power of attracting and assimilating to their own nature all other thoughts, and which form new intervals and interstices whose void for ever craves fresh food. Poetry strengthens that faculty which is the organ of the moral nature of man, in the same manner as exercise strengthens a limb. A Poet therefore would do ill to embody his own conceptions of right and wrong, which are usually those of his place and time, in his poetical creations, which participate in neither. By this assumption of the inferior office of interpreting the effect, in which perhaps after all he might acquit himself but imperfectly, he would resign the glory in a participation in the cause.[3] There was little danger that Homer, or any of the eternal Poets, should have so far misunderstood themselves as to have abdicated this throne of their widest dominion. Those in whom the poetical faculty, though great, is less intense, as Euripides, Lucan, Tasso,[4] Spenser, have frequently affected[5] a moral aim, and the effect of their poetry is diminished in exact proportion to the degree in which they compel us to advert to this purpose.[6]

* * *

It is difficult to define pleasure in its highest sense; the definition involving a number of apparent paradoxes. For, from an inexplicable defect of harmony in the constitution of human nature, the pain of the inferior is frequently connected with the pleasures of the superior portions of our being. Sorrow, terror, anguish, despair itself are often the chosen expressions of an approximation to the highest good. Our sympathy in tragic fiction depends on this principle; tragedy delights by affording a shadow of the pleasure which exists in pain. This is the source also of the melancholy which is inseparable from the sweetest melody. The pleasure that is in sorrow is sweeter than the pleasure of pleasure itself. And hence the saying, "It is better to go to the house of mourning, than to the house of mirth."[7] Not that this highest species of pleasure is necessarily linked with pain. The delight of love and friendship, the ecstasy of the admiration of nature, the joy of the perception and still more of the creation of poetry is often wholly unalloyed.

The production and assurance of pleasure in this highest sense is true utility. Those who produce and preserve this pleasure are Poets or poetical philosophers.

---

2. Central to Shelley's theory is the concept (developed by 18th-century philosophers) of the sympathetic imagination—the faculty by which an individual is enabled to identify with the thoughts and feelings of others. Shelley insists that the faculty in poetry that enables us to share the joys and sufferings of invented characters is also the basis of all morality, for it compels us to feel for others as we feel for ourselves.
3. The "effect," or the explicit moral standards into which imaginative insights are translated at a particular time or place, is contrasted to the "cause" of all morality, the imagination itself.
4. Tasso Torquato (1544–1595), Italian poet, author of *Jerusalem Delivered*, an epic poem about a crusade. Euripides (ca. 484–406 B.C.E.), Greek writer of tragedies. Lucan (39–65 C.E.), Roman poet, author of the *Pharsalia*.
5. Assumed, adopted.
6. In the following, omitted passage, Shelley reviews the history of drama and poetry in relation to civilization and morality and proceeds to refute the charge that poets are less useful than "reasoners and merchants." He begins by defining *utility* in terms of pleasure and then distinguishes between the lower (physical and material) and the higher (imaginative) pleasures.
7. Ecclesiastes 7.2.

The exertions of Locke, Hume, Gibbon, Voltaire, Rousseau,[8] and their disciples, in favour of oppressed and deluded humanity, are entitled to the gratitude of mankind. Yet it is easy to calculate the degree of moral and intellectual improvement which the world would have exhibited, had they never lived. A little more nonsense would have been talked for a century or two; and perhaps a few more men, women, and children, burnt as heretics. We might not at this moment have been congratulating each other on the abolition of the Inquisition in Spain.[9] But it exceeds all imagination to conceive what would have been the moral condition of the world if neither Dante, Petrarch, Boccaccio, Chaucer, Shakespeare, Calderon, Lord Bacon, nor Milton, had ever existed; if Raphael and Michael Angelo had never been born; if the Hebrew poetry had never been translated; if a revival of the study of Greek literature had never taken place; if no monuments of antient sculpture had been handed down to us; and if the poetry of the religion of the antient world had been extinguished together with its belief. The human mind could never, except by the intervention of these excitements, have been awakened to the invention of the grosser sciences, and that application of analytical reasoning to the aberrations of society, which it is now attempted to exalt over the direct expression of the inventive and creative faculty itself.

We have more moral, political and historical wisdom, than we know how to reduce into practice; we have more scientific and economical knowledge than can be accommodated to the just distribution of the produce which it multiplies. The poetry in these systems of thought, is concealed by the accumulation of facts and calculating processes. There is no want of knowledge respecting what is wisest and best in morals, government, and political economy, or at least, what is wiser and better than what men now practise and endure. But we let "I dare not wait upon I would, like the poor cat i' the adage."[1] We want[2] the creative faculty to imagine that which we know; we want the generous impulse to act that which we imagine; we want the poetry of life: our calculations have outrun conception; we have eaten more than we can digest. The cultivation of those sciences which have enlarged the limits of the empire of man over the external world, has, for want of the poetical faculty, proportionally circumscribed those of the internal world; and man, having enslaved the elements, remains himself a slave. To what but a cultivation of the mechanical arts in a degree disproportioned to the presence of the creative faculty, which is the basis of all knowledge, is to be attributed the abuse of all invention for abridging and combining labour, to the exasperation of the inequality of mankind? From what other cause has it arisen that these inventions which should have lightened, have added a weight to the curse imposed on Adam?[3] Poetry, and the principle of Self, of which money is the visible incarnation, are the God and Mammon of the world.[4]

The functions of the poetical faculty are two-fold; by one it creates new materials of knowledge, and power and pleasure; by the other it engenders

8. I follow the classification adopted by the author of Four Ages of Poetry. But Rousseau was essentially a poet. The others, even Voltaire, were mere reasoners [Shelley's note].
9. The Inquisition had been suspended following the Spanish Revolution of 1820, the year before Shelley wrote this essay; it was not abolished permanently until 1834.
1. The words with which Lady Macbeth encourages her husband's ambition (Shakespeare, Mac-

beth 1.7.44–45).
2. Lack.
3. God says to Adam: "cursed is the ground for thy sake. . . . Thorns also and thistles shall it bring forth. . . . In the sweat of thy face shalt thou eat bread, till thou return unto the ground" (Genesis 3.17–19).
4. Matthew 6.24: "Ye cannot serve God and Mammon."

in the mind a desire to reproduce and arrange them according to a certain rhythm and order which may be called the beautiful and the good. The cultivation of poetry is never more to be desired than at periods when, from an excess of the selfish and calculating principle, the accumulation of the materials of external life exceed the quantity of the power of assimilating them to the internal laws of human nature. The body has then become too unwieldy for that which animates it.

Poetry is indeed something divine. It is at once the centre and circumference of knowledge; it is that which comprehends all science, and that to which all science must be referred. It is at the same time the root and blossom of all other systems of thought; it is that from which all spring, and that which adorns all; and that which, if blighted, denies the fruit and the seed, and withholds from the barren world the nourishment and the succession of the scions of the tree of life. It is the perfect and consummate surface and bloom of things; it is as the odour and the colour of the rose to the texture of the elements which compose it, as the form and the splendour of unfaded beauty to the secrets of anatomy and corruption. What were Virtue, Love, Patriotism, Friendship etc.—what were the scenery of this beautiful Universe which we inhabit—what were our consolations on this side of the grave—and what were our aspirations beyond it—if Poetry did not ascend to bring light and fire from those eternal regions where the owl-winged faculty of calculation dare not ever soar? Poetry is not like reasoning, a power to be exerted according to the determination of the will. A man cannot say, "I will compose poetry." The greatest poet even cannot say it: for the mind in creation is as a fading coal which some invisible influence, like an inconstant wind, awakens to transitory brightness: this power arises from within, like the colour of a flower which fades and changes as it is developed, and the conscious portions of our natures are unprophetic either of its approach or its departure. Could this influence be durable in its original purity and force, it is impossible to predict the greatness of the results; but when composition begins, inspiration is already on the decline, and the most glorious poetry that has ever been communicated to the world is probably a feeble shadow of the original conception of the poet. I appeal to the greatest Poets of the present day, whether it be not an error to assert that the finest passages of poetry are produced by labour and study. The toil and the delay recommended by critics can be justly interpreted to mean no more than a careful observation of the inspired moments, and an artificial connexion of the spaces between their suggestions by the intertexture of conventional expressions; a necessity only imposed by the limitedness of the poetical faculty itself. For Milton conceived the Paradise Lost as a whole before he executed it in portions. We have his own authority also for the Muse having "dictated" to him the "unpremeditated song,"[5] and let this be an answer to those who would allege the fifty-six various readings of the first line of the Orlando Furioso.[6] Compositions so produced are to poetry what mosaic is to painting. This instinct and intuition of the poetical faculty is still more observable in the plastic and pictorial arts: a great statue or picture grows under the power of the artist as a child in the mother's womb; and the very

5. *Paradise Lost* 9.21–24.
6. The epic poem by the 16th-century Italian poet Ariosto, noted for his care in composition.

mind which directs the hands in formation is incapable of accounting to itself for the origin, the gradations, or the media of the process.

Poetry is the record of the best and happiest[7] moments of the happiest and best minds. We are aware of evanescent visitations of thought and feeling sometimes associated with place or person, sometimes regarding our own mind alone, and always arising unforeseen and departing unbidden, but elevating and delightful beyond all expression: so that even in the desire and the regret they leave, there cannot but be pleasure, participating as it does in the nature of its object. It is as it were the interpenetration of a diviner nature through our own; but its footsteps are like those of a wind over a sea, where the coming calm erases, and whose traces remain only as on the wrinkled sand which paves it. These and corresponding conditions of being are experienced principally by those of the most delicate sensibility[8] and the most enlarged imagination; and the state of mind produced by them is at war with every base desire. The enthusiasm of virtue, love, patriotism, and friendship is essentially linked with these emotions; and whilst they last, self appears as what it is, an atom to a Universe. Poets are not only subject to these experiences as spirits of the most refined organization, but they can colour all that they combine with the evanescent hues of this etherial world; a word, or a trait in the representation of a scene or a passion, will touch the enchanted chord, and reanimate, in those who have ever experienced these emotions, the sleeping, the cold, the buried image of the past. Poetry thus makes immortal all that is best and most beautiful in the world; it arrests the vanishing apparitions which haunt the interlunations[9] of life, and veiling them or in language or in form sends them forth among mankind, bearing sweet news of kindred joy to those with whom their sisters abide—abide, because there is no portal of expression from the caverns of the spirit which they inhabit into the universe of things. Poetry redeems from decay the visitations of the divinity in man.

Poetry turns all things to loveliness; it exalts the beauty of that which is most beautiful, and it adds beauty to that which is most deformed; it marries exultation and horror, grief and pleasure, eternity and change; it subdues to union under its light yoke all irreconcilable things. It transmutes all that it touches, and every form moving within the radiance of its presence is changed by wondrous sympathy to an incarnation of the spirit which it breathes; its secret alchemy turns to potable gold[1] the poisonous waters which flow from death through life; it strips the veil of familiarity from the world, and lays bare the naked and sleeping beauty which is the spirit of its forms.

All things exist as they are perceived: at least in relation to the percipient. "The mind is its own place, and of itself can make a heaven of hell, a hell of heaven."[2] But poetry defeats the curse which binds us to be subjected to the accident of surrounding impressions. And whether it spreads its own figured curtain or withdraws life's dark veil from before the scene of things, it equally creates for us a being within our being. It makes us the inhabitants of a world to which the familiar world is a chaos. It reproduces the common universe of

7. In the double sense of "most joyous" and "most apt or felicitous in invention."
8. Sensitivity, capacity for sympathetic feeling.
9. The dark intervals between the old and new moons.

1. Alchemists aimed to produce a drinkable ("potable") form of gold that would be an elixir of life, curing all diseases.
2. Satan's speech, *Paradise Lost* 1.254–55.

which we are portions and percipients, and it purges from our inward sight the film of familiarity which obscures from us the wonder of our being. It compels us to feel that which we perceive, and to imagine that which we know. It creates anew the universe after it has been annihilated in our minds by the recurrence of impressions blunted by reiteration.[3] It justifies that bold and true word of Tasso: *Non merita nome di creatore, se non Iddio ed il Poeta.*[4]

A Poet, as he is the author to others of the highest wisdom, pleasure, virtue and glory, so he ought personally to be the happiest, the best, the wisest, and the most illustrious of men. As to his glory, let Time be challenged to declare whether the fame of any other institutor of human life be comparable to that of a poet. That he is the wisest, the happiest, and the best, inasmuch as he is a poet, is equally incontrovertible: the greatest poets have been men of the most spotless virtue, of the most consummate prudence, and, if we could look into the interior of their lives, the most fortunate of men: and the exceptions, as they regard those who possessed the poetic faculty in a high yet inferior degree, will be found on consideration to confirm rather than destroy the rule. Let us for a moment stoop to the arbitration of popular breath, and usurping and uniting in our own persons the incompatible characters of accuser, witness, judge and executioner, let us decide without trial, testimony, or form that certain motives of those who are "there sitting where we dare not soar"[5] are reprehensible. Let us assume that Homer was a drunkard, that Virgil was a flatterer, that Horace was a coward, that Tasso was a madman, that Lord Bacon was a peculator, that Raphael was a libertine, that Spenser was a poet laureate.[6] It is inconsistent with this division of our subject to cite living poets, but Posterity has done ample justice to the great names now referred to. Their errors have been weighed and found to have been dust in the balance; if their sins "were as scarlet, they are now white as snow";[7] they have been washed in the blood of the mediator and the redeemer Time. Observe in what a ludicrous chaos the imputations of real or fictitious crime have been confused in the contemporary calumnies against poetry and poets;[8] consider how little is, as it appears—or appears, as it is; look to your own motives, and judge not, lest ye be judged.[9]

Poetry, as has been said, in this respect differs from logic, that it is not subject to the controul of the active powers of the mind, and that its birth and recurrence has no necessary connexion with consciousness or will. It is presumptuous to determine that these[1] are the necessary conditions of all mental causation, when mental effects are experienced insusceptible of

---

3. Shelley's version of a widespread Romantic doctrine that the poetic imagination transforms the familiar into the miraculous and re-creates the old world into a new world. See, e.g., Coleridge's *Biographia Literaria*, chap. 4: "To carry on the feelings of childhood into the powers of manhood; to combine the child's sense of wonder and novelty with the appearances which every day for perhaps forty years has rendered familiar; . . . this is the character and privilege of genius" (p. 301).
4. "No one merits the name of Creator except God and the Poet." Quoted by Pierantonio Serassi in his *Life of Torquato Tasso* (1785).
5. Satan's scornful words to the angels who discover him after he has surreptitiously entered Eden: "Ye knew me once no mate / For you, sitting

where ye durst not soar" (*Paradise Lost* 4.828–29).
6. Charges that had in fact been made against these men. The use of "poet laureate" as a derogatory term was a dig at Robert Southey, who held that honor at the time Shelley was writing. "Peculator": an embezzler of public money. Raphael is the 16th-century Italian painter.
7. Isaiah 1.18.
8. Shelley alludes especially to the charges of immorality by contemporary reviewers against Lord Byron and himself.
9. Christ's warning in Matthew 7.1.
1. I.e., consciousness or will. Shelley again proposes that some mental processes are unconscious—outside our control or awareness.

being referred to them. The frequent recurrence of the poetical power, it is obvious to suppose, may produce in the mind an habit of order and harmony correlative with its own nature and with its effects upon other minds. But in the intervals of inspiration, and they may be frequent without being durable, a poet becomes a man, and is abandoned to the sudden reflux of the influences under which others habitually live. But as he is more delicately organized than other men, and sensible[2] to pain and pleasure, both his own and that of others, in a degree unknown to them, he will avoid the one and pursue the other with an ardour proportioned to this difference. And he renders himself obnoxious to calumny,[3] when he neglects to observe the circumstances under which these objects of universal pursuit and flight have disguised themselves in one another's garments.

But there is nothing necessarily evil in this error, and thus cruelty, envy, revenge, avarice, and the passions purely evil, have never formed any portion of the popular imputations on the lives of poets.

I have thought it most favourable to the cause of truth to set down these remarks according to the order in which they were suggested to my mind, by a consideration of the subject itself, instead of following that of the treatise that excited me to make them public.[4] Thus although devoid of the formality of a polemical reply; if the view they contain be just, they will be found to involve a refutation of the doctrines of the Four Ages of Poetry, so far at least as regards the first division of the subject. I can readily conjecture what should have moved the gall of the learned and intelligent author of that paper; I confess myself, like him, unwilling to be stunned by the Theseids of the hoarse Codri of the day. Bavius and Maevius[5] undoubtedly are, as they ever were, insufferable persons. But it belongs to a philosophical critic to distinguish rather than confound.

The first part of these remarks has related to Poetry in its elements and principles; and it has been shewn, as well as the narrow limits assigned them would permit, that what is called poetry, in a restricted sense, has a common source with all other forms of order and of beauty according to which the materials of human life are susceptible of being arranged, and which is poetry in an universal sense.

The second part[6] will have for its object an application of these principles to the present state of the cultivation of Poetry, and a defence of the attempt to idealize the modern forms of manners and opinions, and compel them into a subordination to the imaginative and creative faculty. For the literature of England, an energetic developement of which has ever preceded or accompanied a great and free developement of the national will, has arisen as it were from a new birth. In spite of the low-thoughted envy which would undervalue contemporary merit, our own will be a memorable age in intellectual achievements, and we live among such philosophers and poets as surpass beyond

2. I.e., sensitive to, conscious of. Cf. Wordsworth's Preface to *Lyrical Ballads* (p. 136): "What is a poet? . . . He is a man speaking to men: a man, it is true, endued with more lively sensibility, more enthusiasm, and tenderness, who has a greater knowledge of human nature, and a more comprehensive soul, than are supposed to be common among mankind."
3. Exposed to slander.
4. Peacock's "Four Ages of Poetry."

5. Would-be poets satirized by Virgil and Horace. "Theseids": epic poems about Theseus. Codrus (plural "Codri") was the Roman author of a long, dull *Theseid* attacked by Juvenal and others. In 1794 and 1795 the conservative critic William Gifford had borrowed from Virgil and Horace and published the *Baviad* and the *Maeviad*, hard-hitting and highly influential satires on popular poetry and drama.
6. Shelley, however, completed only the first part.

comparison any who have appeared since the last national struggle for civil and religious liberty.[7] The most unfailing herald, companion, and follower of the awakening of a great people to work a beneficial change in opinion or institution, is Poetry. At such periods there is an accumulation of the power of communicating and receiving intense and impassioned conceptions respecting man and nature. The persons in whom this power resides, may often, as far as regards many portions of their nature, have little apparent correspondence with that spirit of good of which they are the ministers. But even whilst they deny and abjure, they are yet compelled to serve, the Power which is seated upon the throne of their own soul. It is impossible to read the compositions of the most celebrated writers of the present day without being startled with the electric life which burns within their words. They measure the circumference and sound the depths of human nature with a comprehensive and all-penetrating spirit, and they are themselves perhaps the most sincerely astonished at its manifestations, for it is less their spirit than the spirit of the age. Poets are the hierophants[8] of an unapprehended inspiration, the mirrors of the gigantic shadows which futurity casts upon the present, the words which express what they understand not; the trumpets which sing to battle, and feel not what they inspire: the influence which is moved not, but moves.[9] Poets are the unacknowledged legislators of the World.

1821   1840

7. In the age of Milton and the English Civil Wars.
8. Priests who are expositors of sacred mysteries.
9. Aristotle had said that God is the "Unmoved Mover" of the universe.

JOHN CLARE
1793–1864

Since the mid-eighteenth century, when critics had begun to worry that the authentic vigor of poetry was being undermined in their age of modern learning and refinement, they had looked for untaught primitive geniuses among the nation's peasantry. In the early-nineteenth-century literary scene, John Clare was the nearest thing to a "natural poet" there was. An earlier peasant poet, Robert Burns, had managed to acquire a solid liberal education. Clare, however, was born at Helpston, a Northamptonshire village, the son of a field laborer and a mother who was entirely illiterate, and he obtained only enough schooling to enable him to read and write. Although he was a sickly and fearful child, he had to work hard in the field, where he found himself composing verse "for downright pleasure in giving vent to my feelings." The fragments of an autobiography that he wrote later in life describe movingly, and with humor, the stratagems that as a young man he devised in order to find the time and the materials for writing. A blank notebook could cost him a week's wages. In 1820 publication of his *Poems Descriptive of Rural Life and Scenery* attracted critical attention, and on a trip to London, he was made much of by leading writers of the day. But his celebrity soon dimmed, and his three later books of verse were financial failures. Under these and other disappointments his mind gave way in 1837, and he spent almost all the rest of his life in an asylum. The place was for him a refuge as well as a confinement, for he was treated kindly, allowed to wander about the countryside, and encouraged to go on writing his verses. Some of his best achievements are the poems composed during his madness.

Clare did not, of course, write independently of literary influences, for he had studied the poetry of James Thomson, William Cowper, Burns, Milton, Wordsworth, and Coleridge. But he stayed true to his own experience of everyday country sights and customs. His nightingale poem, written in a long-established literary tradition, has many more particulars of nature than any of those by his predecessors, and his homely mouse, in the fourth poem printed below, is a bit of pure rustic impressionism in a way that even Burns's moralized mouse is not (see "To a Mouse," p. 85). Some of Clare's introspective asylum poems achieve so haunting a poignancy and are spoken in so quietly distinctive a voice that they have made the great mass of manuscripts he left at his death an exciting place of discovery for recent scholars.

Those same manuscripts are, however, currently a site of contention among Clare critics. Words are spelled erratically, and there is almost no punctuation: the pages are cluttered with revisions and erasures. In his own day Clare was respelled, punctuated, and generally tidied up by his publisher, John Taylor. (Taylor had done the same for John Keats, another of his poets who took a casual view of such matters.) Clare had mixed feelings about the transformation his writings underwent as they became printed books. Sometimes it felt like meddling. Critics and editors who propose that Clare's works should now be published without such emendation often cite a letter he sent to Taylor in 1822. "Grammer in learning is like Tyranny in government," Clare wrote: "confound the bitch, I'll never be her slave." As the analogy suggests, the standardization of his language that Taylor promoted, as he tried to broaden the poems' appeal and bring them into line with the expectations of a middle-class readership, could to the poet feel like an instance of class oppression. (Clare's aristocratic patrons in Northamptonshire certainly felt free to warn their protégé away from vulgarity and rebelliousness.) On the other hand, Clare actively sought assistance in preparing his work for the press and often acknowledged that the work was better for that assistance: "If I cannot hear from John Taylor now and then I cannot rhyme." And Taylor took to print himself to dispute readers' objections to Clare's unconventional diction and their wish (as he put it) that Clare "would *thresh* and not *thump* the corn."

Eric Robinson, David Powell, and P. M. S. Dawson, who number among those modern critics who believe that Clare's work should be presented without editors' emendations, have recently completed the monumental task of transcribing Clare's three and a half thousand manuscript poems for their nine-volume edition for Oxford University Press. This edition aims for the utmost fidelity to Clare's work, thereby correcting previous editions' misrepresentations. But in that form, however authentic, the poems can be difficult reading for an audience that is not already familiar with Clare's voice. Though based on their edition, the texts printed below are therefore presented as "reading" versions of Clare's lines and employ modern punctuation and spelling.

The Nightingale's Nest

Up this green woodland ride° let's softly rove,   *riding path*
And list° the nightingale—she dwelleth here.   *listen to*
Hush! let the wood gate softly clap, for fear
The noise may drive her from her home of love;
5   For here I've heard her many a merry year—
At morn and eve, nay, all the livelong day,
As though she lived on song. This very spot,
Just where that old man's beard[1] all wildly trails
Rude arbours o'er the road and stops the way—

1. *Clematis vitalba*, a vine.

10 And where that child its blue-bell flowers hath got,
Laughing and creeping through the mossy rails°—   *fence rails*
There have I hunted like a very boy,
Creeping on hands and knees through matted thorns
To find her nest and see her feed her young.
15 And vainly did I many hours employ:
All seemed as hidden as a thought unborn.
And where these crimping° fern leaves ramp° among   *curling / shoot up*
The hazel's under-boughs, I've nestled down
And watched her while she sung; and her renown
20 Hath made me marvel that so famed a bird[2]
Should have no better dress than russet brown.
Her wings would tremble in her ecstasy,
And feathers stand on end, as 'twere with joy,
And mouth wide open to release her heart
25 Of its out-sobbing songs. The happiest part
Of summer's fame she shared, for so to me
Did happy fancies shapen her employ;[3]
But if I touched a bush or scarcely stirred,
All in a moment stopt. I watched in vain:
30 The timid bird had left the hazel bush,
And at a distance hid to sing again.
Lost in a wilderness of listening leaves,
Rich ecstasy would pour its luscious strain,
Till envy spurred the emulating thrush
35 To start less wild and scarce inferior songs;
For cares with him for half the year remain,
To damp the ardour of his speckled breast,
While nightingales to summer's life belongs,
And naked trees and winter's nipping wrongs
40 Are strangers to her music and her rest.
Her joys are evergreen, her world is wide—
Hark! there she is as usual—let's be hush—
For in this black-thorn clump, if rightly guessed,
Her curious house is hidden. Part aside
45 These hazel branches in a gentle way,
And stoop right cautious 'neath the rustling boughs,
For we will have another search to-day,
And hunt this fern-strewn thorn clump round and round;
And where this seeded wood grass idly bows,
50 We'll wade right through, it is a likely nook:
In such like spots, and often on the ground,
They'll build where rude boys never think to look—
Aye, as I live! her secret nest is here,
Upon this whitethorn stulp°—I've searched about   *stump*
55 For hours in vain. There! put that bramble by—
Nay, trample on its branches and get near.
How subtle is the bird! she started out

2. The nightingale had been celebrated by, among others, Chaucer, Spenser, Shakespeare, Milton, and, closer to Clare's time, William Cowper, Charlotte Smith, Mary Robinson, Coleridge, Wordsworth, and Keats. In lines 22, 24–25, and 33, Clare echoes lines 57–58 of Keats's "Ode to a Nightingale."
3. Give shape to her (the nightingale's) regular activities.

And raised a plaintive note of danger nigh,
Ere we were past the brambles; and now, near
60 Her nest, she sudden stops—as° choking fear   *as if*
That might betray her home. So even now
We'll leave it as we found it: safety's guard
Of pathless solitude shall keep it still.
See, there she's sitting on the old oak bough,
65 Mute in her fears; our presence doth retard
Her joys, and doubt turns all her rapture chill.

   Sing on, sweet bird! may no worse hap° befall   *fate*
Thy visions, than the fear that now deceives.
We will not plunder music of its dower,°   *dowry, gift*
70 Nor turn this spot of happiness to thrall;°   *misery*
For melody seems hid in every flower,
That blossoms near thy home. These harebells all
Seem bowing with the beautiful in song;
And gaping cuckoo° with its spotted leaves   *a spring flower*
75 Seems blushing of the singing it has heard.
How curious is the nest; no other bird
Uses such loose materials, or weaves
Their dwellings in such spots: dead oaken leaves
Are placed without, and velvet moss within,
80 And little scraps of grass, and, scant and spare,
Of what seems scarce materials, down and hair;
For from man's haunts she seemeth nought to win.
Yet nature is the builder and contrives
Homes for her children's comfort even here;
85 Where solitude's disciples spend their lives
Unseen save when a wanderer passes near
That loves such pleasant places. Deep adown,
The nest is made an hermit's mossy cell.
Snug lie her curious eggs, in number five,
90 Of deadened green, or rather olive brown;
And the old prickly thorn-bush guards them well.
And here we'll leave them, still unknown to wrong,
As the old woodland's legacy of song.

1825–30   1835

Pastoral Poesy

True poesy is not in words,
But images that thoughts express,
By which the simplest hearts are stirred
To elevated happiness.

5   Mere books would be but useless things
Where none had taste or mind to read,
Like unknown lands where beauty springs
And none are there to heed.

But poesy is a language meet,°   *suitable, proper*
10 And fields are every one's employ;°   *concern*
The wild flower 'neath the shepherd's feet
Looks up and gives him joy;

A language that is ever green,
That feelings unto all impart,
15 As hawthorn blossoms, soon as seen,
Give May to every heart.

The pictures that our summer minds
In summer's dwellings meet;
The fancies that the shepherd finds
20 To make his leisure sweet;

The dust mills that the cowboy delves
In banks for dust to run,[1]
Creates a summer in ourselves—
He does as we have done.

25 An image to the mind is brought,
Where happiness enjoys
An easy thoughtlessness of thought
And meets excess of joys.

The world is in that little spot
30 With him—and all beside
Is nothing, all a life forgot,
In feelings satisfied.

And such is poesy; its power
May varied lights employ,
35 Yet to all minds it gives the dower
Of self-creating joy.

And whether it be hill or moor,
I feel where'er I go
A silence that discourses more
40 That any tongue can do.

Unruffled quietness hath made
A peace in every place,
And woods are resting in their shade
Of social loneliness.

45 The storm, from which the shepherd turns
To pull his beaver° down,   *beaver hat*
While he upon the heath sojourns,
Which autumn bleaches brown,

Is music, aye, and more indeed
50 To those of musing mind

---

1. The boy tending the cows has (as an amusement) dug miniature millstreams in the dirt.

Who through the yellow woods proceed
And listen to the wind.

The poet in his fitful glee
And fancy's many moods
55 Meets it as some strange melody,
And poem of the woods.

It sings and whistles in his mind,
And then it talks aloud,
While by some leaning tree reclined
60 He shuns a coming cloud,

That sails its bulk against the sun,
A mountain in the light—
He heeds not for the storm begun
But dallies with delight.

65 And now a harp that flings around
The music of the wind,
The poet often hears the sound
When beauty fills the mind.

The morn with saffron° strips and gray,   *orange-yellow*
70 Or blushing to the view,
Like summer fields when run away
In weeds of crimson hue,

Will simple shepherds' hearts imbue
With nature's poesy,
75 Who inly fancy while they view
How grand must heaven be.

With every musing mind she steals
Attendance² on their way;
The simplest thing her heart reveals
80 Is seldom thrown away.

The old man, full of leisure hours,
Sits cutting at his door
Rude fancy sticks to tie his flowers
—They're sticks and nothing more

85 With many passing by his door—
But pleasure has its bent;°   *inclination*
With him 'tis happiness and more,
Heart satisfied content.

Those box-edged borders that impart
90 Their fragrance near his door
Hath been the comfort of his heart
For sixty years and more.

2. She (nature) demands attention (to her beauties).

That mossy thatch above his head
In winter's drifting showers
95 To him and his old partner made
A music many hours.

It patted to their hearts a joy[3]
That humble comfort made—
A little fire to keep them dry
100 And shelter over head.

And such no matter what they call
Each all are nothing less
Than poesy's power that gives to all
A cheerful blessedness.

105 So would I my own mind employ,
And my own heart impress,
That poesy's self's a dwelling joy
Of humble quietness.

So would I for the biding° joy   _abiding, lasting_
110 That to such thoughts belong,
That I life's errand may employ
As harmless as a song.

1824–32   1935

[The Lament of Swordy Well][1]

Petitioners are full of prayers
To fall in pity's way,
But if her hand the gift forbears
They'll sooner swear than pray.
5 They're not the worst to want who lurch
On plenty with complaints,
No more than those who go to church
Are e'er the better saints.

I hold no hat to beg a mite
10 Nor pick it up when thrown,
Nor limping leg I hold in sight
But pray to keep me own.
Where profit gets his clutches in

---

3. The patter of the rain on the thatch (lines 93–94) enhanced the comfort of the fire and shelter indoors.

1. Located near Clare's native village, Helpston, Swordy Well, also known as Swaddywell, was an ancient stone quarry first used by the Romans. During Clare's youth, waste grounds like these, formerly places where poor families gathered fuel or found pasturage for their cows or horses, were, through Acts of Parliament, enclosed—converted to private property and fenced off from the community. As part of this enclosures movement, Swordy Well was handed over to overseers of the parish roads to be used for mending-stone. Clare's poem, unpublished and untitled during his lifetime, gives this piece of land a voice with which to lament its misfortunes. Swordy Well speaks in the tones of a laboring man who hates how enclosure has made him a charity case.

There's little he will leave;
15　Gain stooping for a single pin
Will stick it on his sleeve.

For passers-by I never pin
No troubles to my breast,
Nor carry round some names to win,
20　More money from the rest.
I'm Swordy Well, a piece of land
That's fell upon the town,
Who worked me till I couldn't stand
And crush me now I'm down.

25　In parish bonds I well may wail,
Reduced to every shift;
Pity may grieve at trouble's tale,
But cunning shares the gift.
Harvests with plenty on his brow
30　Leaves losses' taunts with me,
Yet gain comes yearly with the plough
And will not let me be.

Alas, dependence thou'rt a brute
Want° only understands;　　　　　　　　　　　*poverty*
35　His feelings wither branch and root
That falls in parish hands.
The muck that clouts the ploughman's shoe,
The moss that hides the stone,
Now I'm become the parish due
40　Is more than I can own.

Though I'm no man yet any wrong
Some sort of right may seek;
And I am glad if e'en a song
Gives me the room to speak.
45　I've got among such grubbling gear[2]
And such a hungry pack,
If I brought harvests twice a year,
They'd bring me nothing back.

When war their tyrant prices got,
50　I trembled with alarms;
They fell and saved my little spot,
Or towns had turned to farms.
Let profit keep an humble place
That gentry may be known;
55　Let pedigrees their honours trace
And toil enjoy its own.

The silver springs grown naked dykes
Scarce own a bunch of rushes;

2. I.e., people digging for wealth, money-grubbers.

When grain got high the tasteless tykes°   *country bumpkins*
60   Grubbed up trees, banks, and bushes,
And me, they turned me inside out
For sand and grit and stones
And turned my old green hills about
And picked my very bones.

65   These things that claim my own as theirs
Were born but yesterday,
But ere I fell to town affairs
I were as proud as they.
I kept my horses, cows, and sheep
70   And built the town below
Ere they had cat or dog to keep—
And then to use me so.

Parish allowance, gaunt and dread,
Had it the earth to keep
75   Would even pine° the bees to dead   *torment*
To save an extra keep.
Pride's workhouse[3] is a place that yields
From poverty its gains
And mine's a workhouse for the fields
80   A-starving the remains.

The bees fly round in feeble rings
And find no blossom by,
Then thrum° their almost weary wings   *beat*
Upon the moss and die.
85   Rabbits that find my hills turned o'er
Forsake my poor abode;
They dread a workhouse like the poor
And nibble on the road.

If with a clover bottle now
90   Spring dares to lift her head,
The next day brings the hasty plough
And makes me misery's bed.
The butterflies may whir and come,
I cannot keep 'em now,
95   Nor can they bear my parish home
That withers on my brow.

No, now not e'en a stone can lie,
I'm just what e'er they like;
My hedges like the winter fly
100   And leave me but the dyke;
My gates are thrown from off the hooks,
The parish thoroughfare:
Lord, he that's in the parish books
Has little wealth to spare.

3. An institution where the able-bodied poor who sought help from the parish were confined and set to work.

105 I couldn't keep a dust of grit
Nor scarce a grain of sand,
But bags and carts claimed every bit,
And now they've got the land.
I used to bring the summer's life
110 To many a butterfly,
But in oppression's iron strife
Dead tussocks° bow and sigh.   *tufts of grass*

I've scarce a nook to call my own
For things that creep or fly;
115 The beetle hiding 'neath a stone
Does well to hurry by;
Stock[4] eats my struggles every day
As bare as any road;
He's sure to be in something's way
120 If e'er he stirs abroad.

I am no man to whine and beg,
But fond of freedom still,
I hing° no lies on pity's peg   *hang*
To bring a grist to mill;
125 On pity's back I needn't jump,
My looks speak loud alone:
My only tree they've left a stump
And nought remains my own.

My mossy hills gain's greedy hand,
130 And more than greedy mind,
Levels into a russet land,
Nor leaves a bent° behind.   *blade of grass*
In summers gone I bloomed in pride,
Folks came for miles to prize
135 My flowers that bloomed nowhere beside
And scarce believed their eyes.

Yet worried with a greedy pack,
They rend and delve and tear
The very grass from off my back—
140 I've scarce a rag to wear.
Gain takes my freedom all away
Since its dull suit I wore,
And yet scorn vows I never pay
And hurts me more and more.

145 And should the price of grain get high—
Lord help and keep it low—
I shan't possess a single fly
Or get a weed to grow;
I shan't possess a yard of ground
150 To bid a mouse to thrive,

4. Generic term for a stupid person.

For gain has put me in a pound,
I scarce can keep alive.

I own I'm poor like many more,
But then the poor mun° live,   *must*
155 And many came for miles before
For what I had to give;
But since I fell upon the town
They pass me with a sigh;
I've scarce the room to say sit down
160 And so they wander by.

Though now I seem so full of clack,°   *chatter*
Yet when yer' riding by
The very birds upon my back
Are not more fain to fly.
165 I feel so lorn° in this disgrace,   *forlorn*
God send the grain to fall;
I am the oldest in the place
And the worst served of all.

Lord bless ye, I was kind to all,
170 And poverty in me
Could always find a humble stall,
A rest and lodging free.
Poor bodies with an hungry ass
I welcomed many a day,
175 And gave him tether, room, and grass,
And never said him nay.

There was a time my bit of ground
Made freemen of the slave;
The ass no pindar'd⁵ dare to pound
180 When I his supper gave.
The gypsies' camp was not afraid,
I made his dwelling free,
Till vile enclosure came and made
A parish slave of me.

185 The gypsies further on sojourn,
No parish bounds they like.
No sticks I own, and would earth burn,
I shouldn't own a dyke.
I am no friend to lawless work,
190 Nor would a rebel be,
And why I call a Christian Turk⁶
Is they are Turks to me.

And if I could but find a friend
With no deceit to sham,

---

5. Pindar: person in charge of impounding stray animals.

6. Common designation for a cruel and barbaric person.

195 Who'd send me some few sheep to tend,
And leave me as I am,
To keep my hills from cart and plough
And strife of mongrel men,
And as spring found me find me now,
200 I should look up again.

And save his Lordship's woods that past
The day of danger dwell,
Of all the fields I am the last
That my own face can tell.
205 Yet what with stone pits' delving holes
And strife to buy and sell,
My name will quickly be the whole,
That's left of Swordy Well.

1832–37   1935

[Mouse's Nest]

I found a ball of grass among the hay
And progged° it as I passed and went away;   *prodded*
And when I looked I fancied something stirred,
And turned again and hoped to catch the bird—
5 When out an old mouse bolted in the wheat
With all her young ones hanging at her teats;
She looked so odd and so grotesque to me,
I ran and wondered what the thing could be,
And pushed the knapweed[1] bunches where I stood,
10 When the mouse hurried from the crawling brood.
The young ones squeaked, and when I went away
She found her nest again among the hay.
The water o'er the pebbles scarce could run
And broad old cesspools[2] glittered in the sun.

1835–37   1935

A Vision

I

I lost the love of heaven above;
I spurn'd the lust of earth below;
I felt the sweets of fancied love,—
And hell itself my only foe.

---

1. A plant with knobs of purple flowers.
2. Rainwater pools on the surface of a peat bog (a "cess"). In the manuscript Clare in fact spelled this word "sexpools," perhaps deliberately testing readers' tolerance.

2

5   I lost earth's joys but felt the glow
Of heaven's flame abound in me:
Till loveliness and I did grow
The bard of immortality.

3

I loved, but woman fell away;
10   I hid me from her faded fame:
I snatch'd the sun's eternal ray,—
And wrote till earth was but a name.

4

In every language upon earth,
On every shore, o'er every sea,
15   I gave my name immortal birth,
And kept my spirit with the free.

Aug. 2, 1844   1924

I Am

1

I am—yet what I am, none cares or knows;
    My friends forsake me like a memory lost:—
I am the self-consumer of my woes;—
    They rise and vanish in oblivion's host,
5   Like shadows in love's frenzied stifled throes:—
And yet I am, and live—like vapours tossed

2

Into the nothingness of scorn and noise,—
    Into the living sea of waking dreams,
Where there is neither sense of life or joys,
10   But the vast shipwreck of my life's esteems;
Even the dearest that I love the best
Are strange—nay, rather, stranger than the rest.

3

I long for scenes where man hath never trod,
    A place where woman never smiled or wept,
15   There to abide with my Creator, God,
    And sleep as I in childhood sweetly slept,
Untroubling and untroubled where I lie,
The grass below—above, the vaulted sky.

1842–46   1848

FELICIA DOROTHEA HEMANS
1793–1835

Born in Liverpool and brought up in Wales, Felicia Hemans published her first two volumes—*Poems* and *England and Spain, or Valour and Patriotism*—when she was fifteen. She followed these four years later with *The Domestic Affections and Other Poems* (1812) and from 1816 on into the 1830s produced new books of poetry almost annually: short sentimental lyrics, tales and "historic scenes," translations, songs for music, sketches of women, hymns for children. She also published literary criticism in magazines and wrote three plays. Her work was widely read, anthologized, memorized, and set to music throughout the nineteenth century and was especially popular and influential in the United States, where the first of many collected editions of her poems appeared in 1825. When she died she was eulogized by many poets, including William Wordsworth, Letitia Landon, and Elizabeth Barrett—a sign of the high regard in which she was held by her contemporaries.

A tablet erected by her brothers in the cathedral of St. Asaph, in north Wales, reads in part, "In memory of Felicia Hemans, whose character is best pourtrayed in her writings." But there are several characters in her poems, and some of them seem not entirely compatible with some of the others. She is frequently thought of as the poet (in the nineteenth century as "the poetess") of domestic affections, at the center of a cult of domesticity in which the home is conceptualized as a haven apart from the stresses of the public world, to which only men are suited. Her poems have been viewed as celebrations of a feminine ethic founded on women's—especially mothers'—capacities for forbearance, piety, and long suffering. Among her most popular pieces in this vein, "Evening Prayer, at a Girls' School" depicts the happy ignorance of schoolgirls whose enjoyment of life will end when they reach womanhood, and "Indian Woman's Death-Song" is the lament of a Native American woman whose husband has abandoned her, sung as she plunges in her canoe over a cataract to suicide with an infant in her arms.

Many of Hemans's longer narratives, by contrast, recount the exploits of women warriors who, to avenge personal, family, or national injustice or insult, destroy enemies in a manner not conventionally associated with female behavior. In *The Widow of Crescentius*, Stephania stalks and poisons the German emperor Otho, the murderer of her husband; in "The Wife of Asdrubal," a mother publicly kills her own children and herself to show contempt for her husband, a betrayer of the Carthaginians whom he governed; the heroine of "The Bride of the Greek Isle," boarding the ship of the pirates who have killed her husband, annihilates them (and herself) in a conflagration rivaling the monumental explosion described in "Casabianca." Among the numerous themes of her work, patriotism and military action recur frequently; there may be a biographical basis for these motifs, given that her two oldest brothers distinguished themselves in the Peninsular War and her military husband (who deserted her and their five sons in 1818) had also served in Spain. But some of her most famous patriotic and military poems are now being viewed as critiques of the virtues and ideologies they had been thought by earlier readers to inculcate. "The Homes of England," for example, has been read as both asserting and undermining the idea that all homes are equal, ancestral estates and cottages alike; and in "Casabianca," the boy's automatic steadfastness has been interpreted as empty obedience rather than admirable loyalty.

Hemans was the highest paid writer in *Blackwood's Magazine* during her day. Her books sold more copies than those of any other contemporary poet except Byron and Walter Scott. She was a shrewd calculator of the literary marketplace and a genius in her negotiations with publishers (which she carried on entirely through the mails). Her self-abasing women of the domestic affections and her scimitar-wielding superwomen of the revenge narratives exist side by side throughout her works. These and other seeming dissonances clearly enhanced the strong appeal of her poems to a wide range of readers, men as well as women.

England's Dead

Son of the ocean isle!
Where sleep your mighty dead?
Show me what high and stately pile
   Is rear'd o'er Glory's bed.

5   Go, stranger! track the deep,
Free, free the white sail spread!
Wave may not foam, nor wild wind sweep,
   Where rest not England's dead.

On Egypt's burning plains,
10   By the pyramid o'ersway'd,
With fearful power the noonday reigns,
   And the palm trees yield no shade.[1]

But let the angry sun
From heaven look fiercely red,
15 Unfelt by those whose task is done!—
   There slumber England's dead.

The hurricane hath might
Along the Indian shore,
And far by Ganges' banks at night,
20   Is heard the tiger's roar.

But let the sound roll on!
It hath no tone of dread,
For those that from their toils are gone;—
   There slumber England's dead.

25   Loud rush the torrent floods
   The western wilds among,
And free, in green Columbia's woods,
   The hunter's bow is strung.

But let the floods rush on!
30   Let the arrow's flight be sped!
Why should *they* reck whose task is done?—
   There slumber England's dead!

1. English forces defeated the French at Alexandria in the spring of 1801. The rest of the references—to 18th- and early-19th-century battles in India (lines 17–24), America (lines 25–32), Spain (lines 33–40), and on the sea (lines 41–48)—are more general.

The mountain storms rise high
    In the snowy Pyrenees,
35 And toss the pine boughs through the sky,
    Like rose leaves on the breeze.

But let the storm rage on!
    Let the fresh wreaths be shed!
For the Roncesvalles' field[2] is won,—
40   *There* slumber England's dead.

On the frozen deep's repose
    'Tis a dark and dreadful hour,
When round the ship the ice-fields close,
    And the northern night clouds lower.

45   But let the ice drift on!
    Let the cold-blue desert spread!
Their course with mast and flag is done,—
    Even there sleep England's dead.

The warlike of the isles,
50   The men of field and wave!
Are not the rocks their funeral piles,
    The seas and shores their grave?

Go, stranger! track the deep,
    Free, free the white sail spread!
55 Wave may not foam, nor wild wind sweep,
    Where rest not England's dead.

1822

Casabianca[1]

The boy stood on the burning deck
    Whence all but he had fled;
The flame that lit the battle's wreck
    Shone round him o'er the dead.

5 Yet beautiful and bright he stood,
    As born to rule the storm;
A creature of heroic blood,
    A proud, though childlike form.

2. Roncesvalles, the mountain pass in the Pyrenees between France and Spain, was a scene of action during the Peninsular War (1808–14).

1. Young Casabianca, a boy about thirteen years old, son to the Admiral of the *Orient*, remained at his post (in the Battle of the Nile) after the ship had taken fire, and all the guns had been abandoned; and perished in the explosion of the vessel, when the flames had reached the powder [Hemans's note]. The Battle of the Nile, in which Nelson captured and destroyed the French fleet in Aboukir Bay, took place on August 1, 1798. Admiral Casabianca and his son (who was in fact only ten) were among those killed by the British forces.

The flames roll'd on—he would not go
10   Without his Father's word;
That Father, faint in death below,
    His voice no longer heard.

He call'd aloud:—"Say, Father, say
    If yet my task is done?"
15   He knew not that the chieftain lay
    Unconscious of his son.

"Speak, Father!" once again he cried,
    "If I may yet be gone!
And"—but the booming shots replied,
20   And fast the flames roll'd on.

Upon his brow he felt their breath,
    And in his waving hair,
And look'd from that lone post of death
    In still, yet brave despair.

25   And shouted but once more aloud,
    "My Father! must I stay?"
While o'er him fast, through sail and shroud,
    The wreathing fires made way.

They wrapt the ship in splendour wild,
30   They caught the flag on high,
And stream'd above the gallant child,
    Like banners in the sky.

There came a burst of thunder sound—
    The boy—oh! where was he?
35   Ask of the winds that far around
    With fragments strew'd the sea!—

With mast, and helm, and pennon fair,
    That well had borne their part,
But the noblest thing which perish'd there
40   Was that young faithful heart!

1826

The Homes of England

Where's the coward that would not dare
To fight for such a land?
        —*Marmion*[1]

The stately Homes of England,
    How beautiful they stand!

1. From Sir Walter Scott's long poem *Marmion* (1808), 4.633–34, a tale of betrayal and bloody conflict between the English and the Scots. When she first published the poem, in *Blackwood's*, April 1827, Hemans used as epigraph a passage from the work of another Scottish author, Joanna Baillie's *Ethwald: A Tragedy*, part 2 (1802), 1.2. 76–82.

Amidst their tall ancestral trees,
    O'er all the pleasant land.
5 The deer across their greensward bound
    Through shade and sunny gleam,
And the swan glides past them with the sound
    Of some rejoicing stream.

The merry Homes of England!
10   Around their hearths by night,
What gladsome looks of household love
    Meet in the ruddy light!
There woman's voice flows forth in song,
    Or childhood's tale is told,
15 Or lips move tunefully along
    Some glorious page of old.

The blessed Homes of England!
    How softly on their bowers
Is laid the holy quietness
20   That breathes from Sabbath-hours!
Solemn, yet sweet, the church-bell's chime
    Floats through their woods at morn;
All other sounds, in that still time,
    Of breeze and leaf are born.

25 The Cottage Homes of England!
    By thousands on her plains,
They are smiling o'er the silvery brooks,
    And round the hamlet-fanes.°   *village churches*
Through glowing orchards forth they peep,
30   Each from its nook of leaves,
And fearless there the lowly sleep,
    As the bird beneath their eaves.

The free, fair Homes of England!
    Long, long, in hut and hall,
35 May hearts of native proof be rear'd
    To guard each hallow'd wall!
And green for ever be the groves,
    And bright the flowery sod,
Where first the child's glad spirit loves
40   Its country and its God!

1827

Properzia Rossi

Properzia Rossi, a celebrated female sculptor of Bologna, possessed also of talents for poetry and music, died in consequence of an unrequited attachment.—A painting by Ducis represents her showing her last work, a basso-relievo of Ariadne, to a Roman Knight, the object of her affection, who regards it with indifference.[1]

1. Establishing her poem's connection to a tradition of ecphrastic verse, Hemans's initial note refers to two visual artists: Properzia de Rossi (ca. 1490–1530), the female sculptor active in early-16th-century Italy, whose life was recounted in Giorgio Vasari's *Lives of the Artists* (1550; 2nd ed.,

——Tell me no more, no more
Of my soul's lofty gifts! Are they not vain
To quench its haunting thirst for happiness?
Have I not lov'd, and striven, and fail'd to bind
One true heart unto me, whereon my own
Might find a resting-place, a home for all
Its burden of affections? I depart,
Unknown, tho' Fame goes with me; I must leave
The earth unknown. Yet it may be that death
Shall give my name a power to win such tears
As would have made life precious.[2]

I

One dream of passion and of beauty more!
And in its bright fulfilment let me pour
My soul away! Let earth retain a trace
Of that which lit my being, tho' its race
5 Might have been loftier far.—Yet one more dream!
From my deep spirit one victorious gleam
Ere I depart! For thee alone, for thee!
May this last work, this farewell triumph be,
Thou, lov'd so vainly! I would leave enshrined
10 Something immortal of my heart and mind,
That yet may speak to thee when I am gone,
Shaking thine inmost bosom with a tone
Of lost affection;—something that may prove
What she hath been, whose melancholy love
15 On thee was lavish'd; silent pang and tear,
And fervent song, that gush'd when none were near,
And dream by night, and weary thought by day,
Stealing the brightness from her life away,—
While thou——Awake! not yet within me die.
20 Under the burden and the agony
Of this vain tenderness,—my spirit, wake!
Ev'n for thy sorrowful affection's sake,
Live! in thy work breathe out!—that he may yet,
Feeling sad mastery there, perchance regret
25 Thine unrequited gift.

II

It comes,—the power
Within me born, flows back; my fruitless dower°   *gift*
That could not win me love. Yet once again
I greet it proudly, with its rushing train
30 Of glorious images:—they throng—they press—
A sudden joy lights up my loneliness,—
I shall not perish all!
        The bright work grows

1568); and Louis Ducis (1775–1847), the French painter who between 1818 and 1822 had exhibited at the Louvre a series of allegorical paintings representing the various arts "under the influence of love." The painting that Ducis devotes to the art of sculpture depicts Properzia de Rossi as she unveils her bas-relief sculpture of Ariadne to a man in Renaissance dress. He has that man regard her work, or perhaps Properzia herself, with evident admiration, however. The "indifference" that Hemans mentions in this note is her addition.

2. The blank verse epigraph is by Hemans.

Beneath my hand, unfolding, as a rose,
35   Leaf after leaf, to beauty; line by line,
I fix my thought, heart, soul, to burn, to shine,
Thro' the pale marble's veins. It grows—and now
I give my own life's history to thy brow,
Forsaken Ariadne![3] thou shalt wear
40   My form, my lineaments; but oh! more fair,
Touch'd into lovelier being by the glow
    Which in me dwells, as by the summer-light
All things are glorified. From thee my woe
    Shall yet look beautiful to meet his sight,
45   When I am pass'd away. Thou art the mould
Wherein I pour the fervent thoughts, th' untold,
The self-consuming! Speak to him of me,
Thou, the deserted by the lonely sea,
With the soft sadness of thine earnest eye,
50   Speak to him, lorn° one, deeply, mournfully,   *forlorn*
Of all my love and grief! Oh! could I throw
Into thy frame a voice, a sweet, and low,
And thrilling voice of song! when he came nigh,
To send the passion of its melody
55   Thro' his pierced bosom—on its tones to bear
My life's deep feeling, as the southern air
Wafts the faint myrtle's breath,—to rise, to swell,
To sink away in accents of farewell,
Winning but one, *one* gush of tears, whose flow
60   Surely my parted spirit yet might know,
If love be strong as death!

III

      Now fair thou art,
Thou form, whose life is of my burning heart!
Yet all the vision that within me wrought,
65   I cannot make thee! Oh! I might have given
Birth to creations of far nobler thought,
    I might have kindled, with the fire of heaven,
Things not of such as die! But I have been
Too much alone; a heart, whereon to lean,
70   With all these deep affections that o'erflow
My aching soul, and find no shore below;
An eye to be my star, a voice to bring
Hope o'er my path, like sounds that breathe of spring,
These are denied me—dreamt of still in vain,—
75   Therefore my brief aspirings from the chain,
Are ever but as some wild fitful song,
Rising triumphantly, to die ere long
In dirge-like echoes.

3. In Greek mythology, Ariadne, daughter of King Minos of Crete, in love with the Greek prince Theseus, helped Theseus defeat the monstrous Minotaur by teaching him how to find his way out of the labyrinth in which he had been imprisoned as a sacrifice to the monster. Theseus married Ariadne, but then deserted her on the island of Naxos, where, in some versions of the myth, she pined away.

IV

Yet the world will see

80   Little of this, my parting work, in thee,
    Thou shalt have fame! Oh, mockery! give the reed
   From storms a shelter,—give the drooping vine
   Something round which its tendrils may entwine,—
    Give the parch'd flower a rain-drop, and the meed°   *reward*
85   Of love's kind words to woman! Worthless fame!
   That in *his* bosom wins not for my name
   Th' abiding place it asked! Yet how my heart,
   In its own fairy world of song and art,
   Once beat for praise!—Are those high longings o'er?
90   That which I have been can I be no more?—
   Never, oh! never more; tho' still thy sky
   Be blue as then, my glorious Italy!
   And tho' the music, whose rich breathings fill
   Thine air with soul, be wandering past me still,
95   And tho' the mantle of thy sunlight streams
   Unchang'd on forms instinct with° poet-dreams;   *animated by*
   Never, oh! never more! Where'er I move,
   The shadow of this broken-hearted love
   Is on me and around! Too well *they* know,
100   Whose life is all within, too soon and well,
   When there the blight hath settled;—but I go
    Under the silent wings of Peace to dwell;
   From the slow wasting, from the lonely pain,
   The inward burning of those words—*"in vain,"*
105   Sear'd on the heart—I go. 'Twill soon be past.
   Sunshine, and song, and bright Italian heaven,
    And thou, oh! thou, on whom my spirit cast
   Unvalued wealth,—who know'st not what was given
   In that devotedness,—the sad, and deep,
110   And unrepaid—farewell! If I could weep
   Once, only once, belov'd one! on thy breast,
   Pouring my heart forth ere I sink to rest!
   But that were happiness, and unto me
   Earth's gift is *fame.* Yet I was form'd to be
115   So richly blest! With thee to watch the sky,
   Speaking not, feeling but that thou wert nigh;
   With thee to listen, while the tones of song
   Swept ev'n as part of our sweet air along,
   To listen silently;—with thee to gaze
120   On forms, the deified of olden days,—
   This had been joy enough;—and hour by hour,
   From its glad well-springs drinking life and power,
   How had my spirit soar'd, and made its fame
    A glory for thy brow!—Dreams, dreams!—the fire
125   Burns faint within me. Yet I leave my name—
    As a deep thrill° may linger on the lyre   *vibration*
   When its full chords are hush'd—awhile to live,
   And one day haply in thy heart revive
   Sad thoughts of me:—I leave it, with a sound,

130 A spell o'er memory, mournfully profound,
I leave it, on my country's air to dwell,—
Say proudly yet—"'Twas hers who lov'd me well!"

1828

Indian Woman's Death Song

An Indian woman, driven to despair by her husband's desertion of her for another wife, entered a canoe with her children, and rowed it down the Mississippi towards a cataract. Her voice was heard from the shore singing a mournful death-song, until overpowered by the sound of the waters in which she perished. The tale is related in Long's *Expedition to the Source of St Peter's River*.[1]

> *Non, je ne puis vivre avec un coeur brisé. Il faut que je retrouve la joie, et que je m'unisse aux esprits libres de l'air.*
> *Bride of Messina,*
> Translated by Madame de Staël[2]

> *Let not my child be a girl, for very sad is the life of a woman.*
> *The Prairie*[3]

Down a broad river of the western wilds,
Piercing thick forest glooms, a light canoe
Swept with the current: fearful was the speed
5 Of the frail bark, as by a tempest's wing
Borne leaf-like on to where the mist of spray
Rose with the cataract's thunder.—Yet within,
Proudly, and dauntlessly, and all alone,
Save that a babe lay sleeping at her breast,
A woman stood: upon her Indian brow
10 Sat a strange gladness, and her dark hair wav'd
As if triumphantly. She press'd her child,
In its bright slumber, to her beating heart,
And lifted her sweet voice, that rose awhile
Above the sound of waters, high and clear,
15 Wafting a wild proud strain, her song of death.

Roll swiftly to the Spirit's land, thou mighty stream and free!
Father of ancient waters,[4] roll! and bear our lives with thee!
The weary bird that storms have toss'd, would seek the sunshine's calm,
And the deer that hath the arrow's hurt, flies to the woods of balm.

20 Roll on!—my warrior's eye hath look'd upon another's face,
And mine hath faded from his soul, as fades a moonbeam's trace;

---

1. William Hippolytus Keating, *Narrative of an Expedition to the Source of St. Peter's River* (1824), which compiles notes taken by Stephen Harriman Long and other members of an 1823 expedition that traveled up the Minnesota River (then called St. Peter's River) to the northern Great Plains.
2. "No, I cannot live with a broken heart. I must regain joy and join the free spirits of the air":

Staël cites Friedrich Schiller's tragedy *The Bride of Messina*, which she discusses in her book on German culture, *Germany* (1810).
3. From the last of James Fenimore Cooper's series of Leatherstocking novels, *The Prairie* (1827), spoken by a Sioux woman.
4. "Father of waters," the Indian name for the Mississippi [Hemans's note].

My shadow comes not o'er his path, my whisper to his dream,
He flings away the broken reed—roll swifter yet, thou stream!

The voice that spoke of other days is hush'd within *his* breast,
25 But *mine* its lonely music haunts, and will not let me rest;
It sings a low and mournful song of gladness that is gone,
I cannot live without that light—Father of waves! roll on!

Will he not miss the bounding step that met him from the chase?°   hunt
The heart of love that made his home an ever sunny place?
30 The hand that spread the hunter's board, and deck'd his couch of yore?—
He will not!—roll, dark foaming stream, on to the better shore!

Some blessed fount amidst the woods of that bright land must flow,
Whose waters from my soul may lave the memory of this woe;
35 Some gentle wind must whisper there, whose breath may waft away
The burden of the heavy night, the sadness of the day.

And thou, my babe! tho' born, like me, for woman's weary lot,
Smile!—to that wasting of the heart, my own! I leave thee not;
Too bright a thing art *thou* to pine in aching love away,
Thy mother bears thee far, young Fawn! from sorrow and decay.

40 She bears thee to the glorious bowers where none are heard to weep,
And where th' unkind one hath no power again to trouble sleep;
And where the soul shall find its youth, as wakening from a dream,—
One moment, and that realm is ours—On, on, dark rolling stream!

1828

JOHN KEATS
1795–1821

John Keats's father was head stableman at a London livery stable; he married his employer's daughter and inherited the business. The poet's mother, by all reports, was an affectionate but negligent parent to her children; remarrying almost immediately after a fall from a horse killed her first husband, she left the eight-year-old John (her firstborn), his brothers, and a sister with their grandmother and did not reenter their lives for four years. The year before his father's death, Keats had been sent to the Reverend John Clarke's private school at Enfield, famous for its progressive curriculum, where he was a noisy, high-spirited boy; despite his small stature (when full-grown, he was barely over five feet in height), he distinguished himself in sports and fistfights. Here he had the good fortune to have as a mentor Charles Cowden Clarke, son of the headmaster, who later became a writer and an editor; he encouraged Keats's passion for reading and, both at school and in the course of their later friendship, introduced him to Spenser and other poets, to music, and to the theater.

When Keats's mother returned to her children, she was already ill, and in 1810 she died of tuberculosis. Although the livery stable had prospered, and £8,000 had been left in trust to the children by Keats's grandmother, the estate remained tied up in the law courts for all of Keats's lifetime. The children's guardian, Richard Abbey, an unimaginative and practical-minded businessman, took Keats out of school at the age of fifteen and bound him apprentice to Thomas Hammond, a surgeon and apothecary at Edmonton. In 1815 Keats carried on his medical studies at Guy's Hospital, London, and the next year qualified to practice as an apothecary-surgeon— but almost immediately, over his guardian's protests, he abandoned medicine for poetry.

This decision was influenced by Keats's friendship with Leigh Hunt, then editor of the *Examiner* and a leading political radical, poet, and prolific writer of criticism and periodical essays. Hunt, the first successful author of Keats's acquaintance, added his enthusiastic encouragement of Keats's poetic efforts to that of Clarke. More important, he introduced him to writers greater than Hunt himself—William Hazlitt, Charles Lamb, and Percy Shelley—as well as to Benjamin Robert Haydon, painter of grandiose historical and religious canvases. Through Hunt, Keats also met John Hamilton Reynolds and then Charles Wentworth Dilke and Charles Brown, who became his intimate friends and provided him with an essential circumstance for a fledgling poet: a sympathetic and appreciative audience.

The rapidity and sureness of Keats's development has no match. Although he did not begin writing poetry until his eighteenth year, by 1816 in the bold sonnet "On First Looking into Chapman's Homer" he had found his voice. Later that same year he wrote "Sleep and Poetry," in which he laid out for himself a program deliberately modeled on the careers of the greatest poets, asking only

> for ten years, that I may overwhelm
> Myself in poesy; so I may do the deed
> That my own soul has to itself decreed.

For even while his health was good, Keats felt a foreboding of early death and applied himself to his art with a desperate urgency. In 1817 he went on to compose *Endymion*, an ambitious undertaking of more than four thousand lines. It is a rich allegory of a mortal's quest for an ideal feminine counterpart and a flawless happiness beyond earthly possibility; in a number of passages, it already exhibits the sure movement and phrasing of his mature poetic style. But Keats's critical judgment and aspiration exceeded his achievement: long before he completed it, he declared impatiently that he carried on with the "slipshod" *Endymion* only as a "trial of invention" and began to block out *Hyperion*, conceived on the model of Milton's *Paradise Lost* in that most demanding of forms, the epic poem. His success in achieving the Miltonic manner is one of the reasons why Keats abandoned *Hyperion* before it was finished, for he recognized that he was uncommonly susceptible to poetic influences and regarded this as a threat to his individuality. "I will write independently," he insisted. "The Genius of Poetry must work out its own salvation in a man." He had refused the chance of intimacy with Shelley "that I might have my own unfettered scope"; he had broken away from Leigh Hunt's influence lest he get "the reputation of Hunt's *élève* [pupil]"; now he shied away from domination by Milton's powerfully infectious style.

In sentimental, later nineteenth-century accounts of "poor Keats," 1818 was cast as the year in which this rising genius, already frail and sensitive, was mortally crushed by vicious reviews. Percy Shelley helped initiate this myth in *Adonais*, which describes Keats as "a pale flower." Byron, who did not like Keats's verse, put it unsentimentally: Keats, he wrote, was "snuffed out by an article." It is true that the critics were brutal to Keats, those associated with the Tory journals especially. (On the new power and hostility of the reviewers in Keats's day, see "'Self-constituted judge of poesy': Reviewer vs. Poet in the Romantic Period" in the supplemental ebook.) For these critics his poetry proved an irresistible target precisely because it had been promoted by the radical Hunt. *Endymion* was mauled in the *Quarterly Review*, and one of the articles on "the Cockney School of Poetry" that appeared in *Blackwood's Magazine* condemned Keats as hopelessly vulgar, a writer who wanted to be a poet of nature but thought, as a social-climbing, undereducated Londoner would, that nature was "flowers seen in window-pots." "It is a better and wiser thing to be a starved apothecary than a starved poet," the reviewer scolded: "so back to the shop Mr John." Keats had for his own part the good sense to recognize that the attacks were motivated by political prejudice and class snobbery, and he had already passed his own severe judgment on *Endymion*: "My own domestic criticism," he said, "has given me pain without comparison beyond what *Blackwood* or the *Quarterly* could possibly inflict." More important was the financial distress of his brother George and his young bride, who emigrated to Kentucky and lost their money in an ill-advised investment. Keats, short of funds and needing to supplement the family income, had now to find ways to make money from his writing: he turned to journalism and began planning plays. His brother Tom contracted tuberculosis, and the poet, in devoted attendance, helplessly watched him waste away until his death that December. In the summer of that year, Keats had taken a strenuous walking tour in the English Lake District, Scotland, and Ireland. It was a glorious adventure but a totally exhausting one in wet, cold weather, and he returned in August with a chronically ulcerated throat made increasingly ominous by the shadow of the tuberculosis that had killed his mother and brother. And in the late fall of that same year, Keats fell unwillingly but deeply in love with Fanny Brawne, the eighteen-year-old girl next door. They became engaged, knowing, though, that Keats's poverty and worsening health might well make their marriage impossible.

In this period of turmoil, Keats achieved the culmination of his brief poetic career. Between January and September of 1819, masterpiece followed masterpiece in astonishing succession: *The Eve of St. Agnes*, "La Belle Dame sans Merci," all of the "great odes," *Lamia*, and a sufficient number of fine sonnets to make him, with Wordsworth, the major Romantic craftsman in that form. All of these poems possess the distinctive qualities of the work of Keats's maturity: a slow-paced, gracious movement; a concreteness of description in which all the senses—tactile, gustatory, kinetic, visceral, as well as visual and auditory—combine to give the total apprehension of an experience; a delight at the sheer existence of things outside himself, the poet seeming to lose his own identity in a total identification with the object he contemplates; and a concentrated felicity of phrasing that reminded his friends, as it has many critics since, of the language of Shakespeare. Under the richly sensuous surface, we find Keats's characteristic presentation of all experience as a tangle of inseparable but irreconcilable opposites. He finds melancholy in delight and pleasure in pain; he feels the highest intensity of love as an approximation to death; he inclines equally toward a life of indolence and "sensation" and toward a life of thought; he is aware both of the attraction of an imaginative dream world without "disagreeables" and the remorseless pressure of the actual; he aspires at the same time to aesthetic detachment and to social responsibility.

His letters, hardly less remarkable than his poetry, show that Keats felt on his pulses the conflicts he dramatized in his major poems. Above all, they reveal him wrestling with the problem of evil and suffering—what to make of our lives in the discovery that "the world is full of misery and heartbreak, pain, sickness and oppression." To the end of his life, he refused to seek solace for the complexity and contradictions of experience either in the abstractions of inherited philosophical doctrines or in the absolutes of a religious creed. At the close of his poetic career, in the latter part of 1819, Keats began to rework the epic *Hyperion* into the form of a dream vision that he called *The Fall of Hyperion*. In the introductory section of this fragment the poet is told by the prophetess Moneta that he has hitherto been merely a dreamer; he must know that

> The poet and the dreamer are distinct,
> Diverse, sheer opposite, antipodes,

and that the height of poetry can be reached only by

> those to whom the miseries of the world
> Are misery, and will not let them rest.

He was seemingly planning to undertake a new direction and subject matter, when illness and death intervened.

On the night of February 3, 1820, he coughed up blood. As a physician he refused to evade the truth: "I cannot be deceived in that colour; that drop of blood is my death warrant. I must die." That spring and summer a series of hemorrhages rapidly weakened him. In the autumn he allowed himself to be persuaded to seek the milder climate of Italy in the company of Joseph Severn, a young painter, but these last months were only what he called "a posthumous existence." He died in Rome on February 23, 1821, and was buried in the Protestant Cemetery, where Mary and Percy Shelley had already interred their little son William, and where Percy's ashes, too, would be deposited in 1822. At times the agony of his disease, the seeming frustration of his hopes for great poetic achievement, and the despair of his passion for Fanny Brawne compelled even Keats's brave spirit to bitterness and jealousy, but he always recovered his gallantry. His last letter, written to Charles Brown, concludes: "I can scarcely bid you good bye even in a letter. I always made an awkward bow. God bless you! John Keats."

No one can read Keats's poems and letters without sensing the tragic waste of an extraordinary intellect and genius cut off so early. What he might have done is beyond conjecture; what we do know is that his poetry, when he stopped writing at the age of twenty-four, exceeds the accomplishment at the same age of Chaucer, Shakespeare, and Milton.

The texts here are taken from Jack Stillinger's edition, *The Poems of John Keats* (Cambridge, Mass., 1978).

On First Looking into Chapman's Homer[1]

> Much have I travell'd in the realms of gold,
>   And many goodly states and kingdoms seen;
>   Round many western islands have I been
> Which bards in fealty to Apollo hold.
> 5 Oft of one wide expanse had I been told
>   That deep-brow'd Homer ruled as his demesne;[2]
>   Yet did I never breathe its pure serene[3]
> Till I heard Chapman speak out loud and bold:
> Then felt I like some watcher of the skies
> 10   When a new planet swims into his ken;°   view
> Or like stout Cortez when with eagle eyes
>   He star'd at the Pacific—and all his men
> Look'd at each other with a wild surmise—
>   Silent, upon a peak in Darien.

Oct. 1816   1816

1. It was the gold-hunter Balboa, not Cortez, the Spanish conqueror of Mexico, who caught his first sight of the Pacific from the heights of Darien, in Panama, but none of Keats's contemporaries noticed the supposed error, and modern scholarship (KEATS-SHELLEY JOURNAL 2002) has strongly argued that Keats knew exactly what he was doing.
2. Realm, feudal possession.
3. Clear expanse of air.

From Sleep and Poetry[1]

[O FOR TEN YEARS]

O for ten years, that I may overwhelm
Myself in poesy; so I may do the deed
That my own soul has to itself decreed.
Then will I pass the countries that I see
100 In long perspective, and continually
Taste their pure fountains. First the realm I'll pass
Of Flora, and old Pan:[2] sleep in the grass,
Feed upon apples red, and strawberries,
And choose each pleasure that my fancy sees;
105 Catch the white-handed nymphs in shady places,
To woo sweet kisses from averted faces,—
Play with their fingers, touch their shoulders white
Into a pretty shrinking with a bite
As hard as lips can make it: till agreed,
110 A lovely tale of human life we'll read.
And one will teach a tame dove how it best
May fan the cool air gently o'er my rest;
Another, bending o'er her nimble tread,
Will set a green robe floating round her head,
115 And still will dance with ever varied ease,
Smiling upon the flowers and the trees:
Another will entice me on, and on
Through almond blossoms and rich cinnamon;
Till in the bosom of a leafy world
120 We rest in silence, like two gems upcurl'd
In the recesses of a pearly shell.

And can I ever bid these joys farewell?
Yes, I must pass them for a nobler life,
Where I may find the agonies, the strife
125 Of human hearts: for lo! I see afar,
O'er sailing the blue cragginess, a car[3]
And steeds with streamy manes—the charioteer
Looks out upon the winds with glorious fear:
And now the numerous tramplings quiver lightly
130 Along a huge cloud's ridge; and now with sprightly
Wheel downward come they into fresher skies,
Tipt round with silver from the sun's bright eyes.

1. At the age of twenty-one, Keats set himself a regimen of poetic training modeled on the course followed by the greatest poets. Virgil had established the pattern of beginning with pastoral writing and proceeding gradually to the point at which he was ready to undertake the epic, and this pattern had been deliberately followed by Spenser and Milton. Keats's version of this program, as he describes it here, is to begin with the realm "of Flora, and old Pan" (line 102) and, within ten years, to climb up to the level of poetry dealing with "the agonies, the strife / Of human hearts" (lines 124–25). The program Keats set himself is illuminated by his analysis of Wordsworth's progress in his letter to J. H. Reynolds of May 3, 1818 (p. 519).
2. I.e., the carefree pastoral world. Flora was the Roman goddess of flowers. Pan was the Greek god of pastures, woods, and animal life.
3. Chariot. The description that follows recalls the traditional portrayal of Apollo, god of the sun and poetry, and represents the higher poetic imagination, which bodies forth the matters "of delight, of mystery, and fear" (line 138) that characterize the grander poetic genres.

Still downward with capacious whirl they glide;
And now I see them on a green-hill's side
135 In breezy rest among the nodding stalks.
The charioteer with wond'rous gesture talks
To the trees and mountains; and there soon appear
Shapes of delight, of mystery, and fear,
Passing along before a dusky space
140 Made by some mighty oaks: as they would chase
Some ever-fleeting music on they sweep.
Lo! how they murmur, laugh, and smile, and weep:
Some with upholden hand and mouth severe;
Some with their faces muffled to the ear
145 Between their arms; some, clear in youthful bloom,
Go glad and smilingly athwart° the gloom;   *against*
Some looking back, and some with upward gaze;
Yes, thousands in a thousand different ways
Flit onward—now a lovely wreath of girls
150 Dancing their sleek hair into tangled curls;
And now broad wings. Most awfully intent,
The driver of those steeds is forward bent,
And seems to listen: O that I might know
All that he writes with such a hurrying glow.

155 The visions all are fled—the car is fled
Into the light of heaven, and in their stead
A sense of real things comes doubly strong,
And, like a muddy stream, would bear along
My soul to nothingness: but I will strive
160 Against all doubtings, and will keep alive
The thought of that same chariot, and the strange
Journey it went.

        *   *   *

Oct.–Dec. 1816   1817

On Seeing the Elgin Marbles[1]

My spirit is too weak—mortality
 Weighs heavily on me like unwilling sleep,
 And each imagined pinnacle and steep
Of godlike hardship tells me I must die
5 Like a sick eagle looking at the sky.
 Yet 'tis a gentle luxury to weep
 That I have not the cloudy winds to keep
Fresh for the opening of the morning's eye.

1. Lord Elgin had brought to England in 1806 many of the marble statues and friezes that adorned the Parthenon at Athens. In 1817 Keats, along with his artist friend Haydon, viewed the marbles at the British Museum, which had just purchased them, an acqusition that was and remains controversial. Keats's sonnet first appeared on the same day in both Leigh Hunt's *Examiner* and, through Keats's friend Reynolds, *The Champion*, and then was reprinted in Haydon's magazine *Annals of the Fine Arts*.

Such dim-conceived glories of the brain
10   Bring round the heart an undescribable feud;
So do these wonders a most dizzy pain,
   That mingles Grecian grandeur with the rude
Wasting of old time—with a billowy main°—   *ocean*
A sun—a shadow of a magnitude.

Mar. 1 or 2, 1817   1817

From Endymion: A Poetic Romance[1]

"The stretched metre of an antique song"

INSCRIBED TO THE MEMORY OF THOMAS CHATTERTON

Preface

Knowing within myself the manner in which this Poem has been produced, it is not without a feeling of regret that I make it public.

What manner I mean, will be quite clear to the reader, who must soon perceive great inexperience, immaturity, and every error denoting a feverish attempt, rather than a deed accomplished. The two first books, and indeed the two last, I feel sensible are not of such completion as to warrant their passing the press; nor should they if I thought a year's castigation would do them any good;—it will not: the foundations are too sandy. It is just that this youngster should die away: a sad thought for me, if I had not some hope that while it is dwindling I may be plotting, and fitting myself for verses fit to live.

This may be speaking too presumptuously, and may deserve a punishment: but no feeling man will be forward to inflict it: he will leave me alone, with the conviction that there is not a fiercer hell than the failure in a great object. This is not written with the least atom of purpose to forestall criticisms of course, but from the desire I have to conciliate men who are competent to look, and who do look with a zealous eye, to the honour of English literature.

The imagination of a boy is healthy, and the mature imagination of a man is healthy; but there is a space of life between, in which the soul is in a ferment, the character undecided, the way of life uncertain, the ambition thick-sighted: thence proceeds mawkishness, and all the thousand bitters which those men I speak of must necessarily taste in going over the following pages.

---

1. This poem of more than four thousand lines (based on the classical myth of a mortal beloved by the goddess of the moon) tells of Endymion's long and agonized search for an immortal goddess whom he had seen in several visions. In the course of his wanderings, he comes upon an Indian maid who had been abandoned by the followers of Bacchus, god of wine and revelry. To his utter despair, he succumbs to a sensual passion for her, in apparent betrayal of his love for his heavenly ideal. The conclusion to Keats's "romance" offers a way of resolving this opposition, which runs throughout the poem, between the inevitably mortal pleasures of this world and the possibility of delights that would be eternal: the Indian maid reveals that she is herself Cynthia (Diana), goddess of the moon, the celestial subject of his earlier visions.

The verse epigraph is adapted from Shakespeare's Sonnet 17, line 12: "And stretchèd metre of an antique song." Thomas Chatterton (1752–1770), to whom *Endymion* is dedicated, and who is the "marvellous Boy" of Wordsworth's "Resolution and Independence," wrote a number of brilliant pseudoarchaic poems that he attributed to an imaginary 15th-century poet, Thomas Rowley. Keats described him as "the most English of poets except Shakespeare."

I hope I have not in too late a day touched the beautiful mythology of Greece,[2] and dulled its brightness: for I wish to try once more,[3] before I bid it farewell.

Teignmouth, April 10, 1818

From *Book 1*

[A THING OF BEAUTY]

A thing of beauty is a joy for ever:
Its loveliness increases; it will never
Pass into nothingness; but still will keep
A bower quiet for us, and a sleep
5   Full of sweet dreams, and health, and quiet breathing.
Therefore, on every morrow, are we wreathing
A flowery band to bind us to the earth,
Spite° of despondence, of the inhuman dearth   *despite*
Of noble natures, of the gloomy days,
10   Of all the unhealthy and o'er-darkened ways
Made for our searching: yes, in spite of all,
Some shape of beauty moves away the pall
From our dark spirits. Such the sun, the moon,
Trees old, and young sprouting a shady boon
15   For simple sheep; and such are daffodils
With the green world they live in; and clear rills°   *small streams*
That for themselves a cooling covert make
'Gainst the hot season; the mid forest brake,°   *thicket*
Rich with a sprinkling of fair musk-rose blooms:
20   And such too is the grandeur of the dooms°   *judgments*
We have imagined for the mighty dead;
All lovely tales that we have heard or read:
An endless fountain of immortal drink,
Pouring unto us from the heaven's brink.

25   Nor do we merely feel these essences
For one short hour; no, even as the trees
That whisper round a temple become soon
Dear as the temple's self, so does the moon,
The passion poesy, glories infinite,
30   Haunt us till they become a cheering light
Unto our souls, and bound to us so fast,
That, whether there be shine, or gloom o'ercast,
They alway must be with us, or we die.

      Therefore, 'tis with full happiness that I
35   Will trace the story of Endymion.

---

2. In 1820 an anonymous reviewer of Keats's final volume of poems cited this phrase and, in a complaint that suggests the political charge that the poetic use of classical mythology could carry at this time, wrote disparagingly of "the nonsense that Mr. Keats . . . and Mr. Percy Bysshe Shelley, and some of the poets about town, have been talk-ing of 'the beautiful mythology of Greece'"; "To some persons . . . that mythology comes recom-mended chiefly by its grossness—its alliance to the sensitive pleasures which belong to the ani-mal."
3. In *Hyperion*, which Keats was already plan-ning.

The very music of the name has gone
Into my being, and each pleasant scene
Is growing fresh before me as the green
Of our own vallies. * * *

[THE "PLEASURE THERMOMETER"]

"Peona!⁴ ever have I long'd to slake
770　My thirst for the world's praises: nothing base,
No merely slumberous phantasm, could unlace
The stubborn canvas for my voyage prepar'd—
Though now 'tis tatter'd; leaving my bark bar'd
And sullenly drifting: yet my higher hope
775　Is of too wide, too rainbow-large a scope,
To fret at myriads of earthly wrecks.
Wherein lies happiness? In that which becks°　　　　　　beckons
Our ready minds to fellowship divine,
A fellowship with essence; till we shine,
780　Full alchemiz'd,⁵ and free of space. Behold
The clear religion of heaven! Fold
A rose leaf round thy finger's taperness,
And soothe thy lips: hist,° when the airy stress　　　　listen
Of music's kiss impregnates the free winds,
785　And with a sympathetic touch unbinds
Eolian⁶ magic from their lucid wombs:
Then old songs waken from enclouded tombs;
Old ditties sigh above their father's grave;
Ghosts of melodious prophecyings rave
790　Round every spot where trod Apollo's foot;
Bronze clarions awake, and faintly bruit,⁷
Where long ago a giant battle was;
And, from the turf, a lullaby doth pass
In every place where infant Orpheus⁸ slept.
795　Feel we these things?—that moment have we stept
Into a sort of oneness, and our state
Is like a floating spirit's. But there are
Richer entanglements, enthralments far
More self-destroying, leading, by degrees,
800　To the chief intensity: the crown of these
Is made of love and friendship, and sits high
Upon the forehead of humanity.
All its more ponderous and bulky worth
Is friendship, whence there ever issues forth

4. The sister to whom Endymion confides his troubles. Of lines 769–857 Keats said to his publisher, John Taylor: "When I wrote it, it was the regular stepping of the Imagination towards a Truth. My having written that Argument will perhaps be of the greatest Service to me of anything I ever did—It set before me at once the gradations of Happiness even like a kind of Pleasure Thermometer, and is my first step towards the chief attempt in the Drama—the playing of different Natures with Joy and Sorrow." The gradations on this "Pleasure Thermometer" mark the stages on the way to what Keats calls "happiness" (line 777)—his secular version of the religious concept of "felicity" that, in the orthodox view, is to be achieved by a surrender of oneself to God. For Keats the way to happiness lies through a fusion of ourselves, first sensuously, with the lovely objects of nature and art (lines 781–97), then on a higher level, with other human beings through "love and friendship" (line 801) and, ultimately, sexual love.
5. Transformed by alchemy from a base to a precious metal.
6. From Aeolus, god of winds.
7. Make a sound.
8. The musician of Greek legend, whose beautiful music could move even inanimate things.

805 A steady splendour; but at the tip-top
There hangs by unseen film, an orbed drop
Of light, and that is love: its influence,
Thrown in our eyes, genders° a novel sense,   *engenders*
At which we start and fret; till in the end,
810 Melting into its radiance, we blend,
Mingle, and so become a part of it,—
Nor with aught else can our souls interknit
So wingedly: when we combine therewith,
Life's self is nourish'd by its proper pith,[9]
815 And we are nurtured like a pelican brood.[1]
Aye, so delicious is the unsating food,[2]
That men, who might have tower'd in the van°   *forefront*
Of all the congregated world, to fan
And winnow from the coming step of time
820 All chaff of custom, wipe away all slime
Left by men-slugs and human serpentry,
Have been content to let occasion die,
Whilst they did sleep in love's elysium.°   *heaven*
And, truly, I would rather be struck dumb,
825 Than speak against this ardent listlessness:
For I have ever thought that it might bless
The world with benefits unknowingly;
As does the nightingale, upperched high,
And cloister'd among cool and bunched leaves—
830 She sings but to her love, nor e'er conceives
How tiptoe Night holds back her dark-grey hood.[3]
Just so may love, although 'tis understood
The mere commingling of passionate breath,
Produce more than our searching witnesseth:
835 What I know not: but who, of men, can tell
That flowers would bloom, or that green fruit would swell
To melting pulp, that fish would have bright mail,
The earth its dower of river, wood, and vale,
The meadows runnels, runnels pebble-stones,
840 The seed its harvest, or the lute its tones,
Tones ravishment, or ravishment its sweet,
If human souls did never kiss and greet?

    "Now, if this earthly love has power to make
Men's being mortal, immortal; to shake
845 Ambition from their memories, and brim
Their measure of content; what merest whim,
Seems all this poor endeavour after fame,
To one, who keeps within his stedfast aim
A love immortal, an immortal too.
850 Look not so wilder'd; for these things are true,
And never can be born of atomies°   *mites*
That buzz about our slumbers, like brain-flies,
Leaving us fancy-sick. No, no, I'm sure,

---

9. Its own elemental substance.
1. Young pelicans were once thought to feed on their mother's flesh. In a parallel way our life is nourished by another's life, with which it fuses in love.
2. Food that never satiates, that never ceases to satisfy.
3. I.e., in order to hear better.

My restless spirit never could endure
855 To brood so long upon one luxury,
Unless it did, though fearfully, espy
A hope beyond the shadow of a dream."

Apr.–Nov. 1817   1818

On Sitting Down to Read King Lear Once Again[1]

O golden-tongued Romance, with serene lute!
    Fair plumed syren,[2] queen of far-away!
    Leave melodizing on this wintry day,
Shut up thine olden pages, and be mute.
5 Adieu! for, once again, the fierce dispute
    Betwixt damnation and impassion'd clay
    Must I burn through; once more humbly assay°   test
The bitter-sweet of this Shakespearean fruit.
Chief Poet! and ye clouds of Albion,[3]
10   Begetters of our deep eternal theme!
When through the old oak forest I am gone,
    Let me not wander in a barren dream:
But, when I am consumed in the fire,
Give me new phoenix[4] wings to fly at my desire.

Jan. 22, 1818   1838

When I have fears that I may cease to be[1]

When I have fears that I may cease to be
    Before my pen has glean'd my teeming brain,
Before high piled books, in charactry,[2]
    Hold like rich garners the full ripen'd grain;
5 When I behold, upon the night's starr'd face,
    Huge cloudy symbols of a high romance,
And think that I may never live to trace
    Their shadows, with the magic hand of chance;
And when I feel, fair creature of an hour,
10   That I shall never look upon thee more,
Never have relish in the fairy power
    Of unreflecting love;—then on the shore
Of the wide world I stand alone, and think
Till love and fame to nothingness do sink.

Jan. 1818   1848

---

1. Keats pauses, while revising *Endymion: A Poetic Romance*, to read again Shakespeare's great tragedy. The word "syren" (line 2) indicates Keats's feeling that "Romance" was enticing him from the poet's prime duty, to deal with "the agonies, the strife / Of human hearts" (*Sleep and Poetry*, lines 124–25).
2. Syrens (sirens) were sea nymphs whose singing lured listeners to their deaths.

3. Old name for England. *King Lear* is set in Celtic Britain.
4. The fabulous bird that periodically burns itself to death to rise anew from the ashes.
1. The first, and one of the most successful, of Keats's attempts at the sonnet in the Shakespearean rhyme scheme.
2. Characters; printed letters of the alphabet.

To Homer

Standing aloof in giant ignorance,
  Of thee I hear and of the Cyclades,[1]
As one who sits ashore and longs perchance
  To visit dolphin-coral in deep seas.
5 So wast thou blind;—but then the veil was rent,
  For Jove uncurtain'd heaven to let thee live,
And Neptune made for thee a spumy tent,
  And Pan made sing for thee his forest-hive;
Aye on the shores of darkness there is light,
10   And precipices show untrodden green,
There is a budding morrow in midnight,
  There is a triple sight in blindness keen;
Such seeing hadst thou, as it once befel
To Dian, Queen of Earth, and Heaven, and Hell.[2]

1818   1848

The Eve of St. Agnes[1]

I

St. Agnes' Eve—Ah, bitter chill it was!
The owl, for all his feathers, was a-cold;
The hare limp'd trembling through the frozen grass,
And silent was the flock in woolly fold:
5 Numb were the Beadsman's[2] fingers, while he told
His rosary, and while his frosted breath,
Like pious incense from a censer old,
Seem'd taking flight for heaven, without a death,
Past the sweet Virgin's picture, while his prayer he saith.

2

10 His prayer he saith, this patient, holy man;
Then takes his lamp, and riseth from his knees,
And back returneth, meagre,° barefoot, wan,   lean
Along the chapel aisle by slow degrees:
The sculptur'd dead, on each side, seem to freeze,
15 Emprison'd in black, purgatorial rails:

1. A group of islands in the Aegean Sea, off Greece. Keats's allusion is to his ignorance of the Greek language. Schooling in Greek was a badge of gentlemanly identity in the period.
2. In late pagan cults Diana was worshiped as a three-figured goddess, the deity of nature and of the moon as well as the queen of hell. The "triple sight" that blind Homer paradoxically commands is of these three regions and also of heaven, sea, and earth (the realms of Jove, Neptune, and Pan, lines 6–8).
1. St. Agnes, martyred ca. 303 at the age of thirteen, is the patron saint of virgins. Legend has it that if a chaste young woman performs the proper ritual, she will dream of her future husband on the evening before St. Agnes's Day, January 21. Keats combines this superstition with the Romeo and Juliet theme of young love thwarted by feuding families and tells the story in a sequence of evolving Spenserian stanzas. The poem is Keats's first complete success in sustained narrative romance. For the author's revisions while composing stanzas 26 and 30 of The Eve of St. Agnes, see "Poems in Process," in the supplemental ebook.
2. One who is paid to pray for his benefactor. He "tells" (counts) the beads of his rosary to keep track of his prayers.

Knights, ladies, praying in dumb° orat'ries,°   *silent / chapels*
He passeth by; and his weak spirit fails
To think[3] how they may ache in icy hoods and mails.

3

Northward he turneth through a little door,
20   And scarce three steps, ere Music's golden tongue
Flatter'd° to tears this aged man and poor;   *charmed*
But no—already had his deathbell rung;
The joys of all his life were said and sung:
His was harsh penance on St. Agnes' Eve:
25   Another way he went, and soon among
Rough ashes sat he for his soul's reprieve,°   *salvation*
And all night kept awake, for sinners' sake to grieve.

4

That ancient Beadsman heard the prelude soft;
And so it chanc'd, for many a door was wide,
30   From hurry to and fro. Soon, up aloft,
The silver, snarling trumpets 'gan to chide:
The level chambers, ready with their pride,°   *ostentation*
Were glowing to receive a thousand guests:
The carved angels, ever eager-eyed,
35   Star'd, where upon their heads the cornice rests,
With hair blown back, and wings put cross-wise on their breasts.

5

At length burst in the argent revelry,[4]
With plume, tiara, and all rich array,
Numerous as shadows haunting fairily
40   The brain, new stuff'd, in youth, with triumphs gay
Of old romance.° These let us wish away,   *stories*
And turn, sole-thoughted, to one Lady there,
Whose heart had brooded, all that wintry day,
On love, and wing'd St. Agnes' saintly care,
45 As she had heard old dames full many times declare.

6

They told her how, upon St. Agnes' Eve,
Young virgins might have visions of delight,
And soft adorings from their loves receive
Upon the honey'd middle of the night,
50   If ceremonies due they did aright;
As, supperless to bed they must retire,
And couch supine their beauties, lily white;
Nor look behind, nor sideways, but require
Of heaven with upward eyes for all that they desire.

---

3. I.e., when he thinks.   4. Silver-adorned revelers.

7

Full of this whim was thoughtful Madeline:
The music, yearning like a god in pain,
She scarcely heard: her maiden eyes divine,
Fix'd on the floor, saw many a sweeping train[5]
Pass by—she heeded not at all: in vain
Came many a tiptoe, amorous cavalier,
And back retir'd, not cool'd by high disdain;
But she saw not: her heart was otherwhere:
She sigh'd for Agnes' dreams, the sweetest of the year.

8

She danc'd along with vague, regardless eyes,
Anxious her lips, her breathing quick and short:
The hallow'd hour was near at hand: she sighs
Amid the timbrels,° and the throng'd resort   *tambourines*
Of whisperers in anger, or in sport;
'Mid looks of love, defiance, hate, and scorn,
Hoodwink'd with faery fancy; all amort,[6]
Save to St. Agnes[6] and her lambs unshorn,[7]
And all the bliss to be before to-morrow morn.

9

So, purposing each moment to retire,
She linger'd still. Meantime, across the moors,
Had come young Porphyro, with heart on fire
For Madeline. Beside the portal doors,
Buttress'd from moonlight,[8] stands he, and implores
All saints to give him sight of Madeline,
But for one moment in the tedious hours,
That he might gaze and worship all unseen;
Perchance speak, kneel, touch, kiss—in sooth such things have been.

10

He ventures in: let no buzz'd whisper tell:
All eyes be muffled, or a hundred swords
Will storm his heart, Love's fev'rous citadel:
For him, those chambers held barbarian hordes,
Hyena foemen, and hot-blooded lords,
Whose very dogs would execrations howl
Against his lineage: not one breast affords
Him any mercy, in that mansion foul,
Save one old beldame,[9] weak in body and in soul.

---

5. Skirts sweeping along the ground.
6. Entirely oblivious or dead ("amort") to everything except St. Agnes. "Hoodwinked": covered by a hood or blindfolded.
7. On St. Agnes's Day it was the custom to offer lambs' wool at the altar, to be made into cloth by nuns.
8. Sheltered from the moonlight by the buttresses (the supports projecting from the wall).
9. Old (and, usually, homely) woman; an ironic development in English from the French meaning, "lovely lady."

11

Ah, happy chance! the aged creature came,
Shuffling along with ivory-headed wand,°   *staff*
To where he stood, hid from the torch's flame,
Behind a broad hall-pillar, far beyond
95   The sound of merriment and chorus bland:°   *soft*
He startled her; but soon she knew his face,
And grasp'd his fingers in her palsied hand,
    Saying, "Mercy, Porphyro! hie thee from this place;
They are all here to-night, the whole blood-thirsty race!

12

100   "Get hence! get hence! there's dwarfish Hildebrand;
He had a fever late, and in the fit
He cursed thee and thine, both house and land:
Then there's that old Lord Maurice, not a whit
More tame for his gray hairs—Alas me! flit!
105   Flit like a ghost away."—"Ah, Gossip¹ dear,
We're safe enough; here in this arm-chair sit,
    And tell me how"—"Good Saints! not here, not here;
Follow me, child, or else these stones will be thy bier."°   *tomb*

13

He follow'd through a lowly arched way,
110   Brushing the cobwebs with his lofty plume,
And as she mutter'd "Well-a—well-a-day!"
He found him in a little moonlight room,
Pale, lattic'd, chill, and silent as a tomb.
"Now tell me where is Madeline," said he,
115   "O tell me, Angela, by the holy loom
    Which none but secret sisterhood may see,
When they St. Agnes' wool are weaving piously."

14

"St. Agnes! Ah! it is St. Agnes' Eve—
Yet men will murder upon holy days:
120   Thou must hold water in a witch's sieve,²
And be liege-lord of all the Elves and Fays,
To venture so: it fills me with amaze
To see thee, Porphyro!—St. Agnes' Eve!
God's help! my lady fair the conjuror plays³
125   This very night: good angels her deceive!
    But let me laugh awhile, I've mickle° time to grieve."   *much*

15

Feebly she laugheth in the languid moon,
While Porphyro upon her face doth look,

---

1. In the old sense: godmother or old friend.
2. A sieve made to hold water by witchcraft.

3. I.e., uses magic in her attempt to evoke the
vision of her lover.

Like puzzled urchin on an aged crone
130 Who keepeth clos'd a wond'rous riddle-book,
As spectacled she sits in chimney nook.
But soon his eyes grew brilliant, when she told
His lady's purpose; and he scarce could brook°   restrain
Tears, at the thought of those enchantments cold,
135 And Madeline asleep in lap of legends old.

16

Sudden a thought came like a full-blown rose,
Flushing his brow, and in his pained heart
Made purple riot: then doth he propose
A stratagem, that makes the beldame start:
140 "A cruel man and impious thou art:
Sweet lady, let her pray, and sleep, and dream
Alone with her good angels, far apart
From wicked men like thee. Go, go!—I deem
Thou canst not surely be the same that thou didst seem."

17

145 "I will not harm her, by all saints I swear,"
Quoth Porphyro: "O may I ne'er find grace
When my weak voice shall whisper its last prayer,
If one of her soft ringlets I displace,
Or look with ruffian passion in her face:
150 Good Angela, believe me by these tears;
Or I will, even in a moment's space,
Awake, with horrid shout, my foemen's ears,
And beard° them, though they be more fang'd than wolves and   confront
    bears."

18

"Ah! why wilt thou affright a feeble soul?
155 A poor, weak, palsy-stricken, churchyard thing,
Whose passing-bell° may ere the midnight toll;   death knell
Whose prayers for thee, each morn and evening,
Were never miss'd."—Thus plaining,° doth she bring   complaining
A gentler speech from burning Porphyro;
160 So woful, and of such deep sorrowing,
That Angela gives promise she will do
Whatever he shall wish, betide her weal or woe.[4]

19

Which was, to lead him, in close secrecy,
Even to Madeline's chamber, and there hide
165 Him in a closet, of such privacy
That he might see her beauty unespied,
And win perhaps that night a peerless bride,

4. I.e., whether good or ill befalls her.

While legion'd fairies pac'd the coverlet,
And pale enchantment held her sleepy-eyed.
170 Never on such a night have lovers met,
Since Merlin paid his Demon all the monstrous debt.[5]

20

"It shall be as thou wishest," said the Dame:
"All cates° and dainties shall be stored there   *delicacies*
Quickly on this feast-night: by the tambour frame[6]
175 Her own lute thou wilt see: no time to spare,
For I am slow and feeble, and scarce dare
On such a catering trust my dizzy head.
Wait here, my child, with patience; kneel in prayer
The while: Ah! thou must needs the lady wed,
180 Or may I never leave my grave among the dead."

21

So saying, she hobbled off with busy fear.
The lover's endless minutes slowly pass'd;
The dame return'd, and whisper'd in his ear
To follow her; with aged eyes aghast
185 From fright of dim espial. Safe at last,
Through many a dusky gallery, they gain°   *arrive at*
The maiden's chamber, silken, hush'd, and chaste;
Where Porphyro took covert, pleas'd amain.°   *mightily*
His poor guide hurried back with agues° in her brain.   *shivering*

22

190 Her falt'ring hand upon the balustrade,
Old Angela was feeling for the stair,
When Madeline, St. Agnes' charmed maid,
Rose, like a mission'd spirit,[7] unaware:
With silver taper's light, and pious care,
195 She turn'd, and down the aged gossip led
To a safe level matting. Now prepare,
Young Porphyro, for gazing on that bed;
She comes, she comes again, like ring-dove fray'd° and fled.   *frightened*

23

Out went the taper as she hurried in;
200 Its little smoke, in pallid moonshine, died:
She clos'd the door, she panted, all akin
To spirits of the air, and visions wide:
No uttered syllable, or, woe betide!
But to her heart, her heart was voluble,
205 Paining with eloquence her balmy side;

---

5. Probably the episode in the Arthurian legends in which Merlin, the magician, lost his life when the wily Vivien turned one of his own spells against him.
6. A drum-shaped embroidery frame.
7. I.e., like an angel sent on a mission.

As though a tongueless nightingale[8] should swell
Her throat in vain, and die, heart-stifled, in her dell.

24

A casement° high and triple-arch'd there was,   *window*
All garlanded with carven imag'ries
210 Of fruits, and flowers, and bunches of knot-grass,
And diamonded with panes of quaint device,
Innumerable of stains and splendid dyes,
As are the tiger-moth's deep-damask'd wings;
And in the midst, 'mong thousand heraldries,
215 And twilight saints, and dim emblazonings,
A shielded scutcheon blush'd with blood of queens and kings.[9]

25

Full on this casement shone the wintry moon,
And threw warm gules[1] on Madeline's fair breast,
As down she knelt for heaven's grace and boon;°   *gift, blessing*
220 Rose-bloom fell on her hands, together prest,
And on her silver cross soft amethyst,
And on her hair a glory,° like a saint: *halo*
She seem'd a splendid angel, newly drest,
Save wings, for heaven:—Porphyro grew faint:
225 She knelt, so pure a thing, so free from mortal taint.

26

Anon his heart revives: her vespers done,
Of all its wreathed pearls her hair she frees;[2]
Unclasps her warmed jewels one by one;
Loosens her fragrant boddice; by degrees
230 Her rich attire creeps rustling to her knees:
Half-hidden, like a mermaid in sea-weed,
Pensive awhile she dreams awake, and sees,
In fancy, fair St. Agnes in her bed,
But dares not look behind, or all the charm is fled.

27

235 Soon, trembling in her soft and chilly nest,
In sort of wakeful swoon, perplex'd[3] she lay,
Until the poppied warmth of sleep oppress'd
Her soothed limbs, and soul fatigued away;
Flown, like a thought, until the morrow-day;

8. An allusion to Ovid's story, in the *Metamorphoses*, of Philomel, who was raped by Tereus, her sister's husband. He cut out Philomel's tongue to prevent her from speaking of his crime, but she managed to weave her story and make herself understood to her sister, Procne. Just as Tereus was about to kill both women, Philomel and Procne were metamorphosed into a nightingale and a swallow.
9. I.e., among the genealogical emblems ("heraldries") and other devices ("emblazonings"), a heraldic shield signified by its colors that the family was of royal blood.
1. Red (heraldry).
2. The Pre-Raphaelite-inspired painter Daniel Maclise represented this moment in Keats's romance in his painting of 1868, *Madeline after Prayer*.
3. In a confused state between waking and sleeping.

240   Blissfully haven'd both from joy and pain;
       Clasp'd like a missal where swart Paynims pray;[4]
       Blinded alike from sunshine and from rain,
    As though a rose should shut, and be a bud again.

28

       Stol'n to this paradise, and so entranced,
245   Porphyro gazed upon her empty dress,
       And listen'd to her breathing, if it chanced
       To wake into a slumberous tenderness;
       Which when he heard, that minute did he bless,
       And breath'd himself: then from the closet crept,
250   Noiseless as fear in a wide wilderness,
       And over the hush'd carpet, silent, stept,
    And 'tween the curtains peep'd, where, lo!—how fast she slept.

29

       Then by the bed-side, where the faded moon
       Made a dim, silver twilight, soft he set
255   A table, and, half anguish'd, threw thereon
       A cloth of woven crimson, gold, and jet:—
       O for some drowsy Morphean amulet![5]
       The boisterous, midnight, festive clarion,[6]
       The kettle-drum, and far-heard clarionet,
260   Affray° his ears, though but in dying tone:—   *frighten*
    The hall door shuts again, and all the noise is gone.

30

       And still she slept an azure-lidded sleep,
       In blanched linen, smooth, and lavender'd,
       While he from forth the closet brought a heap
265   Of candied apple, quince, and plum, and gourd;°   *melon*
       With jellies soother than the creamy curd,
       And lucent syrops, tinct with cinnamon;
       Manna and dates, in argosy transferr'd
       From Fez,[7] and spiced dainties, every one,
270   From silken Samarcand to cedar'd Lebanon.

31

       These delicates he heap'd with glowing hand
       On golden dishes and in baskets bright
       Of wreathed silver: sumptuous they stand
       In the retired quiet of the night,
275   Filling the chilly room with perfume light.—

---

4. Variously interpreted; perhaps: held tightly, cherished (or else kept shut, fastened with a clasp), like a Christian prayer book ("missal") in a land where the religion is that of dark-skinned pagans ("swart Paynims").
5. Sleep-producing charm.
6. High-pitched trumpet.
7. I.e., jellies softer ("soother") than the curds of cream, clear ("lucent") syrups tinged with cinnamon, and sweet gums ("manna") and dates transported in a great merchant ship ("argosy") from Fez, in Morocco.

"And now, my love, my seraph[8] fair, awake!
Thou art my heaven, and I thine eremite:[9]
Open thine eyes, for meek St. Agnes' sake,
Or I shall drowse beside thee, so my soul doth ache."

32

280 Thus whispering, his warm, unnerved° arm   *unmanned, weak*
Sank in her pillow. Shaded was her dream
By the dusk curtains:—'twas a midnight charm
Impossible to melt as iced stream:
The lustrous salvers° in the moonlight gleam;   *trays*
285 Broad golden fringe upon the carpet lies:
It seem'd he never, never could redeem
From such a stedfast spell his lady's eyes;
So mus'd awhile, entoil'd in woofed phantasies.[1]

33

Awakening up, he took her hollow lute,—
290 Tumultuous,—and, in chords that tenderest be,
He play'd an ancient ditty, long since mute,
In Provence call'd, "La belle dame sans mercy":[2]
Close to her ear touching the melody;—
Wherewith disturb'd, she utter'd a soft moan:
295 He ceased—she panted quick—and suddenly
Her blue affrayed eyes wide open shone:
Upon his knees he sank, pale as smooth-sculptured stone.

34

Her eyes were open, but she still beheld,
Now wide awake, the vision of her sleep:
300 There was a painful change, that nigh° expell'd   *nearly*
The blisses of her dream so pure and deep:
At which fair Madeline began to weep,
And moan forth witless words with many a sigh;
While still her gaze on Porphyro would keep;
305 Who knelt, with joined hands and piteous eye,
Fearing to move or speak, she look'd so dreamingly.

35

"Ah, Porphyro!" said she, "but even now
Thy voice was at sweet tremble in mine ear,
Made tuneable with every sweetest vow;
310 And those sad eyes were spiritual and clear:
How chang'd thou art! how pallid, chill, and drear!
Give me that voice again, my Porphyro,
Those looks immortal, those complainings dear!

---

8. One of the highest orders of angels.
9. Hermit, religious solitary.
1. Entangled in a weave of fantasies.

2. "The Lovely Lady without Pity," title of a work
by the medieval poet Alain Chartier. Keats later
adopted the title for his own ballad.

Oh leave me not in this eternal woe,
315 For if thou diest, my love, I know not where to go."

36

Beyond a mortal man impassion'd far
At these voluptuous accents, he arose,
Ethereal, flush'd, and like a throbbing star
Seen mid the sapphire heaven's deep repose;
320 Into her dream he melted, as the rose
Blendeth its odour with the violet,—
Solution° sweet: meantime the frost-wind blows   *fusion*
Like Love's alarum pattering the sharp sleet
Against the window-panes; St. Agnes' moon hath set.

37

325 'Tis dark: quick pattereth the flaw-blown° sleet: *gust-blown*
"This is no dream, my bride, my Madeline!"
'Tis dark: the iced gusts still rave and beat:
"No dream, alas! alas! and woe is mine!
Porphyro will leave me here to fade and pine.—
330 Cruel! what traitor could thee hither bring?
I curse not, for my heart is lost in thine,
Though thou forsakest a deceived thing;—
A dove forlorn and lost with sick unpruned wing."

38

"My Madeline! sweet dreamer! lovely bride!
335 Say, may I be for aye thy vassal blest?
Thy beauty's shield, heart-shap'd and vermeil° dyed?   *vermilion, bright red*
Ah, silver shrine, here will I take my rest
After so many hours of toil and quest,
A famish'd pilgrim,—saved by miracle.
340 Though I have found, I will not rob thy nest
Saving of thy sweet self; if thou think'st well
To trust, fair Madeline, to no rude infidel.

39

"Hark! 'tis an elfin-storm from faery land,
Of haggard[3] seeming, but a boon indeed:
345 Arise—arise! the morning is at hand;—
The bloated wassaillers[4] will never heed:—
Let us away, my love, with happy speed;
There are no ears to hear, or eyes to see,—
Drown'd all in Rhenish and the sleepy mead:[5]
350 Awake! arise! my love, and fearless be,
For o'er the southern moors I have a home for thee."

---

3. Wild, untamed (originally, a wild hawk).
4. Drunken carousers.

5. Rhine wine and the sleep-producing mead (a heavy fermented drink made with honey).

40

She hurried at his words, beset with fears,
For there were sleeping dragons all around,
At glaring watch, perhaps, with ready spears—
355 Down the wide stairs a darkling[6] way they found.—
In all the house was heard no human sound.
A chain-droop'd lamp was flickering by each door;
The arras,° rich with horseman, hawk, and hound,   *tapestry*
Flutter'd in the besieging wind's uproar;
360 And the long carpets rose along the gusty floor.

41

They glide, like phantoms, into the wide hall;
Like phantoms, to the iron porch, they glide;
Where lay the Porter, in uneasy sprawl,
With a huge empty flaggon by his side:
365 The wakeful bloodhound rose, and shook his hide,
But his sagacious eye an inmate owns:[7]
By one, and one, the bolts full easy slide:—
The chains lie silent on the footworn stones;—
The key turns, and the door upon its hinges groans.

42

370 And they are gone: ay, ages long ago
These lovers fled away into the storm.
That night the Baron dreamt of many a woe,
And all his warrior-guests, with shade and form
Of witch, and demon, and large coffin-worm,
375 Were long be-nightmar'd. Angela the old
Died palsy-twitch'd, with meagre face deform;
The Beadsman, after thousand aves[8] told,
For aye° unsought for slept among his ashes cold.   *ever*

Jan.–Feb. 1819   1820

Bright star, would I were stedfast as thou art[1]

Bright star, would I were stedfast as thou art—
Not in lone splendor hung aloft the night,
And watching, with eternal lids apart,
Like nature's patient, sleepless eremite,[2]
5 The moving waters at their priestlike task

---

6. In the dark.
7. Acknowledges a member of the household.
8. The prayers beginning *Ave Maria* ("Hail Mary").
1. While on a tour of the Lake District in 1818, Keats had said that the austere scenes "refine one's sensual vision into a sort of north star which can never cease to be open lidded and steadfast over the wonders of the great Power." The thought developed into this sonnet, which Keats drafted in 1819, then copied into his volume of Shakespeare's poems at the end of September or the beginning of October 1820, while on his way to Italy, where he died.
2. Hermit, religious solitary.

Of pure ablution[3] round earth's human shores,
Or gazing on the new soft-fallen mask
Of snow upon the mountains and the moors;
No—yet still stedfast, still unchangeable,
10   Pillow'd upon my fair love's ripening breast,
To feel for ever its soft swell and fall,
Awake for ever in a sweet unrest,
Still, still to hear her tender-taken breath,
And so live ever—or else swoon to death.[4]

1819   1838

La Belle Dame sans Merci: A Ballad[1]

1

O what can ail thee, knight at arms,
Alone and palely loitering?
The sedge° has wither'd from the lake,   rushes
And no birds sing.

2

5   O what can ail thee, knight at arms,
So haggard and so woe-begone?
The squirrel's granary is full,
And the harvest's done.

3

I see a lily on thy brow
10   With anguish moist and fever dew,
And on thy cheeks a fading rose
Fast withereth too.

4

I met a lady in the meads,
Full beautiful, a fairy's child;
15   Her hair was long, her foot was light,
And her eyes were wild.

5

I made a garland for her head,
And bracelets too, and fragrant zone;[2]

3. Washing, as part of a religious rite.
4. In the earlier version: "Half passionless, and so swoon on to death."
1. The title, though not the subject, was taken from a medieval poem by Alain Chartier and means "The Lovely Lady without Pity." The story of a mortal destroyed by his love for a supernatural femme fatale has been told repeatedly in myth, fairy tale, and ballad. The text printed here is Keats's earlier version of the poem, as transcribed by Charles Brown. The version published in 1820 begins, "Ah, what can ail thee, wretched wight."

Keats imitates a frequent procedure of folk ballads by casting the poem into the dialogue form. The first three stanzas are addressed to the knight, and the rest of the poem is his reply.
2. Belt (of flowers).

She look'd at me as she did love,
20   And made sweet moan.

6

I set her on my pacing steed,
    And nothing else saw all day long,
For sidelong would she bend, and sing
    A fairy's song.

7

25 She found me roots of relish° sweet,   *flavor*
    And honey wild, and manna dew,
And sure in language strange she said—
    I love thee true.

8

She took me to her elfin grot°   *cave*
30   And there she wept, and sigh'd full sore,
And there I shut her wild wild eyes
    With kisses four.[3]

9

And there she lulled me asleep,
    And there I dream'd—Ah! woe betide!
35 The latest° dream I ever dream'd   *last*
    On the cold hill's side.

10

I saw pale kings, and princes too,
    Pale warriors, death pale were they all;
They cried—"La belle dame sans merci
40   Hath thee in thrall!"

11

I saw their starv'd lips in the gloom°   *twilight*
    With horrid warning gaped wide,
And I awoke and found me here
    On the cold hill's side.

12

45 And this is why I sojourn here,
    Alone and palely loitering,
Though the sedge is wither'd from the lake,
    And no birds sing.

Apr. 1819   1820

3. Keats commented in a letter to his brother and
sister-in-law, "Why four kisses—you will say—
why four because I wish to restrain the headlong
impetuosity of my Muse—she would have fain
said 'score' without hurting the rhyme—but we
must temper the Imagination as the Critics say
with Judgment. I was obliged to choose an even
number that both eyes might have fair play."

Sonnet to Sleep

    O soft embalmer of the still midnight,
      Shutting with careful fingers and benign
    Our gloom-pleas'd eyes, embower'd from the light,
      Enshaded in forgetfulness divine:
5   O soothest° Sleep! if so it please thee, close,   *softest*
      In midst of this thine hymn, my willing eyes,
    Or wait the Amen ere thy poppy[1] throws
      Around my bed its lulling charities.
    Then save me or the passed day will shine
10   Upon my pillow, breeding many woes:
    Save me from curious° conscience, that still hoards   *scrupulous*
      Its strength for darkness, burrowing like the mole;
    Turn the key deftly in the oiled wards,[2]
    And seal the hushed casket of my soul.

Apr. 1819   1838

Ode to Psyche[1]

    O Goddess! hear these tuneless numbers,° wrung   *verses*
      By sweet enforcement and remembrance dear,
    And pardon that thy secrets should be sung
      Even into thine own soft-conched[2] ear:
5   Surely I dreamt to-day, or did I see
      The winged Psyche with awaken'd eyes?
    I wander'd in a forest thoughtlessly,
      And, on the sudden, fainting with surprise,
    Saw two fair creatures, couched side by side
10   In deepest grass, beneath the whisp'ring roof
      Of leaves and trembled blossoms, where there ran
        A brooklet, scarce espied:
    'Mid hush'd, cool-rooted flowers, fragrant-eyed,
      Blue, silver-white, and budded Tyrian,[3]
15   They lay calm-breathing on the bedded grass;

---

1. Opium is made from the dried juice of the opium poppy.
2. The ridges in a lock that correspond to the notches of the key.
1. This poem initiated the sequence of great odes that Keats wrote in the spring of 1819. It is copied into the same journal-letter that included the "Sonnet to Sleep" and several other sonnets as well as a comment about "endeavoring to discover a better sonnet stanza than we have." It is therefore likely that Keats's experiments with sonnet schemes led to the development of the intricate and varied stanzas of his odes and also that he abandoned the sonnet on discovering the richer possibilities of the more spacious form.
  Psyche, which gives us our modern term *psychology*, means mind or soul (and also butterfly)

in Greek. In the story told by the Roman author Apuleius in the 2nd century, Psyche was a lovely mortal beloved by Cupid, the "winged boy" (line 21), son of Venus. To keep their love a secret from his mother, who envied Psyche's beauty, he visited his lover only in the dark of night, and had her promise never to try to discover his identity. After Psyche broke the promise, she endured various tribulations as a penance and then was finally wedded to Cupid and translated to heaven as an immortal. To this goddess, added to the pantheon of pagan gods too late to have been the center of a cult, Keats in the last two stanzas promises to establish a place of worship within his own mind, with himself as poet-priest and prophet.
2. Soft and shaped like a seashell.
3. The purple dye once made in ancient Tyre.

Their arms embraced, and their pinions° too;   *wings*
Their lips touch'd not, but had not bade adieu,
As if disjoined by soft-handed slumber,
And ready still past kisses to outnumber
20   At tender eye-dawn of aurorean love:[4]
            The winged boy I knew;
But who wast thou, O happy, happy dove?
            His Psyche true!

O latest born and loveliest vision far
25   Of all Olympus' faded hierarchy![5]
Fairer than Phoebe's sapphire-region'd star,[6]
            Or Vesper,° amorous glow-worm of the sky;   *evening star*
Fairer than these, though temple thou hast none,
            Nor altar heap'd with flowers;
30   Nor virgin-choir to make delicious moan
            Upon the midnight hours;
No voice, no lute, no pipe, no incense sweet
            From chain-swung censer teeming;
No shrine, no grove, no oracle, no heat
35   Of pale-mouth'd prophet dreaming.

O brightest! though too late for antique vows,[7]
            Too, too late for the fond believing lyre,
When holy were the haunted° forest boughs,   *spirit-filled*
            Holy the air, the water, and the fire;
40   Yet even in these days so far retir'd
            From happy pieties, thy lucent fans,°   *shining wings*
Fluttering among the faint Olympians,
            I see, and sing, by my own eyes inspired.
So let me be thy choir, and make a moan
45   Upon the midnight hours;
Thy voice, thy lute, thy pipe, thy incense sweet
            From swinged censer teeming;
Thy shrine, thy grove, thy oracle, thy heat
            Of pale-mouth'd prophet dreaming.

50   Yes, I will be thy priest, and build a fane°   *temple*
            In some untrodden region of my mind,
Where branched thoughts, new grown with pleasant pain,
            Instead of pines shall murmur in the wind:
Far, far around shall those dark-cluster'd trees
55   Fledge the wild-ridged mountains steep by steep;[8]
And there by zephyrs,° streams, and birds, and bees,   *breezes*

4. Aurora was the goddess of the dawn.
5. The ranks of the gods who lived on Mount Olympus, according to the classical mythology now eclipsed (made "faded") by Christianity. "You must recollect that Psyche was not embodied as a goddess before the time of Apuleius the Platonist who lived after the Augustan age, and consequently the Goddess was never worshiped or sacrificed to with any of the ancient fervour—and perhaps never thought of in the old religion—I am more orthodox tha[n] to let a hethen Goddess be so neglected" (Keats, in a long letter written over several months to George and Georgiana Keats in America, April 30, 1819).
6. The moon, supervised by the goddess Phoebe (Diana).
7. I.e., of worshipers.
8. I.e., the trees shall stand, rank against rank, like layers of feathers.

The moss-lain Dryads° shall be lull'd to sleep;   *wood nymphs*
And in the midst of this wide quietness
A rosy sanctuary will I dress
60   With the wreath'd trellis of a working brain,
With buds, and bells, and stars without a name,
With all the gardener Fancy e'er could feign,
Who breeding flowers, will never breed the same:
And there shall be for thee all soft delight
65   That shadowy thought can win,
A bright torch, and a casement ope at night,
To let the warm Love[9] in!

Apr. 1819   1820

Ode to a Nightingale[1]

1

My heart aches, and a drowsy numbness pains
My sense, as though of hemlock[2] I had drunk,
Or emptied some dull opiate to the drains
One minute past, and Lethe[3]-wards had sunk:
5   'Tis not through envy of thy happy lot,
But being too happy in thine happiness,—
That thou, light-winged Dryad of the trees,
In some melodious plot
Of beechen green, and shadows numberless,
10   Singest of summer in full-throated ease.

2

O, for a draught of vintage!° that hath been   *wine*
Cool'd a long age in the deep-delved earth,
Tasting of Flora[4] and the country green,
Dance, and Provençal song,[5] and sunburnt mirth!
15   O for a beaker full of the warm South,
Full of the true, the blushful Hippocrene,[6]
With beaded bubbles winking at the brim,
And purple-stained mouth;
That I might drink, and leave the world unseen,
20   And with thee fade away into the forest dim:

---

9. I.e., Cupid, god of love.
1. Charles Brown, with whom Keats was then living in Hampstead, wrote: "In the spring of 1819 a nightingale had built her nest near my house. Keats felt a tranquil and continual joy in her song; and one morning he took his chair from the breakfast table to the grass plot under a plum tree, where he sat for two or three hours. When he came into the house, I perceived he had some scraps of paper in his hand, and these he was quietly thrusting behind the books. On inquiry, I found those scraps, four or five in number, contained his poetic feeling on the song of our night-

ingale."
2. A poisonous herb, not the North American evergreen tree; a sedative if taken in small doses.
3. River in Hades whose waters cause forgetfulness.
4. The Roman goddess of flowers or the flowers themselves.
5. Provence, in southern France, was in the late Middle Ages renowned for its troubadours—writers and singers of love songs.
6. Fountain of the Muses on Mount Helicon, hence the waters of inspiration, here applied metaphorically to a beaker of wine.

3

Fade far away, dissolve, and quite forget
   What thou among the leaves hast never known,
The weariness, the fever, and the fret
   Here, where men sit and hear each other groan;
25 Where palsy shakes a few, sad, last gray hairs,
    Where youth grows pale, and spectre-thin, and dies;[7]
      Where but to think is to be full of sorrow
        And leaden-eyed despairs,
    Where Beauty cannot keep her lustrous eyes,
30   Or new Love pine at them beyond to-morrow.

4

Away! away! for I will fly to thee,
   Not charioted by Bacchus and his pards,
But on the viewless wings of Poesy,[8]
   Though the dull brain perplexes and retards:
35 Already with thee! tender is the night,
    And haply the Queen-Moon is on her throne,
      Cluster'd around by all her starry Fays;°   *fairies*
        But here there is no light,
    Save what from heaven is with the breezes blown
40   Through verdurous° glooms and winding mossy   *green-foliaged*
      ways.

5

I cannot see what flowers are at my feet,
   Nor what soft incense hangs upon the boughs,
But, in embalmed° darkness, guess each sweet   *perfumed*
   Wherewith the seasonable month endows
45 The grass, the thicket, and the fruit-tree wild;
    White hawthorn, and the pastoral eglantine;[9]
      Fast fading violets cover'd up in leaves;
        And mid-May's eldest child,
    The coming musk-rose, full of dewy wine,
50   The murmurous haunt of flies on summer eves.

6

Darkling° I listen; and, for many a time   *in darkness*
   I have been half in love with easeful Death,
Call'd him soft names in many a mused° rhyme,   *meditated*
   To take into the air my quiet breath;
55 Now more than ever seems it rich to die,
    To cease upon the midnight with no pain,
      While thou art pouring forth thy soul abroad
        In such an ecstasy!

---

7. Keats's brother Tom, wasted by tuberculosis, had died the preceding winter.
8. I.e., by getting drunk not on wine (the "vintage" of stanza 2) but on the invisible ("viewless") wings of the poetic imagination. (Bacchus, god of wine, was sometimes represented in a chariot drawn by "pards"—leopards.)
9. Sweetbrier or honeysuckle.

Still wouldst thou sing, and I have ears in vain—
60   To thy high requiem° become a sod.   mass for the dead

7

Thou wast not born for death, immortal Bird!
    No hungry generations tread thee down;
The voice I hear this passing night was heard
    In ancient days by emperor and clown:°   peasant
65   Perhaps the self-same song that found a path
    Through the sad heart of Ruth,[1] when, sick for home,
        She stood in tears amid the alien corn;°   wheat
        The same that oft-times hath
    Charm'd magic casements,° opening on the foam   windows
70   Of perilous seas, in faery lands forlorn.

8

Forlorn! the very word is like a bell
    To toll me back from thee to my sole self!
Adieu! the fancy[2] cannot cheat so well
    As she is fam'd to do, deceiving elf.
75   Adieu! adieu! thy plaintive anthem° fades   hymn
    Past the near meadows, over the still stream,
        Up the hill-side; and now 'tis buried deep
        In the next valley-glades:
    Was it a vision, or a waking dream?
80   Fled is that music:—Do I wake or sleep?

May 1819   1819

Ode on a Grecian Urn[1]

I

Thou still unravish'd bride of quietness,
    Thou foster-child of silence and slow time,
Sylvan[2] historian, who canst thus express
    A flowery tale more sweetly than our rhyme:
5   What leaf-fring'd legend haunts about thy shape
    Of deities or mortals, or of both,
        In Tempe or the dales of Arcady?[3]

1. The young widow in the biblical Book of Ruth.
2. I.e., imagination, "the viewless wings of Poesy" of line 33.
1. Another poem that Keats published in Haydon's *Annals of the Fine Arts*. This urn, with its sculptured reliefs of revelry and panting young lovers in chase and in flight, of a pastoral piper under spring foliage, and of the quiet procession of priest and townspeople, resembles parts of various vases, sculptures, and paintings, but it existed in all its particulars only in Keats's imagination. In the urn—which captures moments of intense experience in attitudes of grace and immobilizes them in marble—Keats found the perfect correlative for his concern with the longing for permanence in a world of change. The interpretation of the details with which he develops this concept, however, is hotly disputed. The disputes begin with the opening phrase: is "still" an adverb ("as yet"), or is it an adjective ("motionless"), as the punctuation of the *Annals* version, which adds a comma after "still," suggests?
2. Rustic, representing a woodland scene.
3. The valleys of Arcadia, a state in ancient Greece often used as a symbol of the pastoral ideal. "Tempe": a beautiful valley in Greece that has come to represent rural beauty.

What men or gods are these? What maidens loth?
What mad pursuit? What struggle to escape?
10   What pipes and timbrels? What wild ecstasy?

2

Heard melodies are sweet, but those unheard
    Are sweeter; therefore, ye soft pipes, play on;
Not to the sensual ear,[4] but, more endear'd,
    Pipe to the spirit ditties of no tone:
15 Fair youth, beneath the trees, thou canst not leave
    Thy song, nor ever can those trees be bare;
        Bold lover, never, never canst thou kiss,
Though winning near the goal—yet, do not grieve;
    She cannot fade, though thou hast not thy bliss,
20   For ever wilt thou love, and she be fair!

3

Ah, happy, happy boughs! that cannot shed
    Your leaves, nor ever bid the spring adieu;
And, happy melodist, unwearied,
    For ever piping songs for ever new;
25 More happy love! more happy, happy love!
    For ever warm and still to be enjoy'd,
        For ever panting, and for ever young;
All breathing human passion far above,
    That leaves a heart high-sorrowful and cloy'd,
30   A burning forehead, and a parching tongue.

4

Who are these coming to the sacrifice?
    To what green altar, O mysterious priest,
Lead'st thou that heifer lowing at the skies,
    And all her silken flanks with garlands drest?
35 What little town by river or sea shore,
    Or mountain-built with peaceful citadel,
        Is emptied of this folk, this pious morn?
And, little town, thy streets for evermore
    Will silent be; and not a soul to tell
40   Why thou art desolate, can e'er return.

5

O Attic[5] shape! Fair attitude![6] with brede
    Of marble men and maidens overwrought,[7]
With forest branches and the trodden weed;
    Thou, silent form, dost tease us out of thought

---

4. The ear of sense (as opposed to that of the "spirit," or imagination).
5. Greek. Attica was the region of Greece in which Athens was located.
6. Probably used in its early, technical sense: the pose struck by a figure in statuary or painting.

7. Ornamented all over ("overwrought") with an interwoven pattern ("brede"). The adjective "overwrought" might also modify "maidens" and even "men" and so hint at the emotional anguish of the figures portrayed on the urn.

45   As doth eternity: Cold Pastoral!
      When old age shall this generation waste,
      Thou shalt remain, in midst of other woe
      Than ours, a friend to man, to whom thou say'st,
      "Beauty is truth, truth beauty,"[8]—that is all
50   Ye know on earth, and all ye need to know.

1819   1820

Ode on Melancholy   This is Keats's best-known statement of his recurrent theme of the mingled contrarieties of life. The remarkable last stanza, in which Melancholy becomes a veiled goddess worshiped in secret religious rites, implies that it is the tragic human destiny that beauty, joy, and life itself owe not only their quality but their value to the fact that they are transitory and turn into their opposites. Melancholy—a synonym for depression, involving a paralyzing self-consciousness engendered by an excess of thought—is a highly literary and even bookish ailment, as Keats knew. Shakespeare's Hamlet and Milton's speaker in "Il Penseroso" are the disorder's most famous sufferers. Keats was also an admirer of Robert Burton's encyclopedic *Anatomy of Melancholy* (1621).

The poem once had the following initial stanza, which Keats canceled in manuscript:

> Though you should build a bark of dead men's bones,
>   And rear a phantom gibbet for a mast,
> Stitch creeds together for a sail, with groans
>   To fill it out, bloodstained and aghast;
> Although your rudder be a Dragon's tail,
>   Long sever'd, yet still hard with agony,
>   Your cordage large uprootings from the skull
> Of bald Medusa: certes you would fail
>   To find the Melancholy, whether she
>   Dreameth in any isle of Lethe dull.

Ode on Melancholy

I

No, no, go not to Lethe,[1] neither twist
   Wolf's-bane, tight-rooted, for its poisonous wine;
Nor suffer thy pale forehead to be kiss'd
   By nightshade, ruby grape of Proserpine;[2]
5   Make not your rosary of yew-berries,[3]
   Nor let the beetle, nor the death-moth be

8. The quotation marks around this phrase are found in the volume of poems Keats published in 1820, but there are no quotation marks in the version printed in *Annals of the Fine Arts* that same year or in the transcripts of the poem made by Keats's friends. This discrepancy has multiplied the diversity of critical interpretations of the last two lines. Critics disagree whether the whole of these lines is said by the urn, or "Beauty is truth, truth beauty" by the urn and the rest by the lyric speaker; whether the "ye" in the last line is addressed to the lyric speaker, to the readers, to the urn, or to the figures on the urn; whether "all ye know" is that beauty is truth, or this plus the statement in lines 46–48; and whether "beauty is truth" is a profound metaphysical proposition or an overstatement representing the limited point of view of the urn.

1. The waters of forgetfulness in Hades.
2. The wife of Pluto and queen of the underworld. "Nightshade" and "wolf's-bane" (line 2) are poisonous plants.
3. A symbol of death.

Your mournful Psyche,[4] nor the downy owl
A partner in your sorrow's mysteries;[5]
For shade to shade will come too drowsily,
10   And drown the wakeful anguish of the soul.[6]

2

But when the melancholy fit shall fall
    Sudden from heaven like a weeping cloud,
That fosters the droop-headed flowers all,
    And hides the green hill in an April shroud;
15 Then glut thy sorrow on a morning rose,
    Or on the rainbow of the salt sand-wave,
        Or on the wealth of globed peonies;
Or if thy mistress some rich anger shows,
    Emprison her soft hand, and let her rave,
20   And feed deep, deep upon her peerless eyes.

3

She[7] dwells with Beauty—Beauty that must die;
    And Joy, whose hand is ever at his lips
Bidding adieu; and aching Pleasure nigh,
    Turning to poison while the bee-mouth sips:
25 Ay, in the very temple of Delight
    Veil'd Melancholy has her sovran shrine,
        Though seen of none save him whose strenuous tongue
    Can burst Joy's grape against his palate fine;[8]
His soul shall taste the sadness of her might,
30   And be among her cloudy trophies hung.[9]

1819   1820

Ode on Indolence[1]

"They toil not, neither do they spin."[2]

I

One morn before me were three figures seen,
    With bowed necks, and joined hands, side-faced;

4. In ancient times Psyche (the soul) was sometimes represented as a butterfly or moth, fluttering out of the mouth of a dying man. The allusion may also be to the death's-head moth, which has skull-like markings on its back. The "beetle" of line 6 refers to replicas of the large black beetle, the scarab, which were often placed by Egyptians in their tombs as a symbol of resurrection.
5. Secret rituals.
6. I.e., sorrow needs contrast to sustain its intensity.
7. Usually taken to refer to Melancholy rather than to "thy mistress" in line 18.
8. Sensitive, refined.
9. A reference to the Greek and Roman practice of hanging trophies in the temples of the gods.

1. On March 19, 1819, Keats wrote to George and Georgiana Keats: "This morning I am in a sort of temper indolent and supremely careless. . . . Neither Poetry, nor Ambition, nor Love have any alertness of countenance as they pass by me: they seem rather like three figures on a greek vase—a Man and two women—whom no one but myself could distinguish in their disguisement. This is the only happiness; and is a rare instance of advantage in the body overpowering the Mind." The ode was probably written soon after this time, but was not published until 1848, long after the poet's death.
2. Matthew 6.28. Christ's comment on the lilies of the field—a parable justifying those who trust to God rather than worry about how they will feed or clothe themselves.

And one behind the other stepp'd serene,
     In placid sandals, and in white robes graced:
5   They pass'd, like figures on a marble urn,
          When shifted round to see the other side;
              They came again: as when the urn once more
     Is shifted round, the first seen shades return;
          And they were strange to me, as may betide
10   With vases, to one deep in Phidian[3] lore.

2

How is it, shadows, that I knew ye not?
     How came ye muffled in so hush a masque?
Was it a silent deep-disguised plot
     To steal away, and leave without a task
15 My idle days? Ripe was the drowsy hour;
          The blissful cloud of summer-indolence
              Benumb'd my eyes; my pulse grew less and less;
Pain had no sting, and pleasure's wreath no flower.
          O, why did ye not melt, and leave my sense
20   Unhaunted quite of all but—nothingness?

3

A third time pass'd they by, and, passing, turn'd
     Each one the face a moment whiles to me;
Then faded, and to follow them I burn'd
     And ached for wings, because I knew the three:
25 The first was a fair maid, and Love her name;
          The second was Ambition, pale of cheek,
              And ever watchful with fatigued eye;
The last, whom I love more, the more of blame
     Is heap'd upon her, maiden most unmeek,—
30   I knew to be my demon[4] Poesy.

4

They faded, and, forsooth! I wanted wings:
     O folly! What is Love? and where is it?
And for that poor Ambition—it springs
     From a man's little heart's short fever-fit;
35 For Poesy!—no,—she has not a joy,—
          At least for me,—so sweet as drowsy noons,
              And evenings steep'd in honied indolence;
O, for an age so shelter'd from annoy,
     That I may never know how change the moons,
40   Or hear the voice of busy common-sense!

5

A third time came they by;—alas! wherefore?
     My sleep had been embroider'd with dim dreams;

3. Phidias was the great Athenian sculptor of the 5th century B.C.E. who designed the marble sculptures for the Parthenon.

4. Meaning both devil and, as in Greek myth, the spirit that attends constantly on the human individual.

My soul had been a lawn besprinkled o'er
   With flowers, and stirring shades, and baffled beams:
45 The morn was clouded, but no shower fell,
   Though in her lids hung the sweet tears of May;
    The open casement° press'd a new-leaved vine,   *window*
   Let in the budding warmth and throstle's lay;°   *thrush's song*
   O shadows! 'twas a time to bid farewell!
50   Upon your skirts had fallen no tears of mine.

6

So, ye three ghosts, adieu! Ye cannot raise
   My head cool-bedded in the flowery grass;
For I would not be dieted with praise,
   A pet-lamb in a sentimental farce![5]
55 Fade softly from my eyes, and be once more
   In masque-like figures on the dreamy urn;
    Farewell! I yet have visions for the night,
   And for the day faint visions there is store;
    Vanish, ye phantoms, from my idle spright,°   *spirit*
60   Into the clouds, and never more return!

Spring 1819   1848

Lamia   In a note printed at the end of the poem, Keats cited as his source the following story in Robert Burton's *Anatomy of Melancholy* (1621):

> One Menippus Lycius, a young man twenty-five years of age, that going betwixt Cenchreas and Corinth, met such a phantasm in the habit of a fair gentlewoman, which, taking him by the hand, carried him home to her house, in the suburbs of Corinth. . . . The young man, a philosopher, otherwise staid and discreet, able to moderate his passions, though not this of love, tarried with her a while to his great content, and at last married her, to whose wedding, amongst other guests, came Apollonius; who, by some probable conjectures, found her out to be a serpent, a lamia; and that all her furniture was, like Tantalus's gold, described by Homer, no substance but mere illusions. When she saw herself descried, she wept, and desired Apollonius to be silent, but he would not be moved, and thereupon she, plate, house, and all that was in it, vanished in an instant: many thousands took notice of this fact, for it was done in the midst of Greece.

In ancient demonology a "lamia" was a monster in woman's form who preyed on human beings. There are various clues that Keats invested the ancient legend with allegorical significance (see especially 2.229–38). Its interpretation, however, and even the inclination of Keats's sympathies in the contest between Lamia and Apollonius, have been disputed. Perhaps Keats simply failed to make up his mind or wavered in the course of composition. In any case the poem presents an inevitably fatal situation, in which no one is entirely blameless or blameworthy and no character monopolizes either our sympathy or our antipathy.

5. In a letter of June 9, 1819, Keats wrote: "I have been very idle lately, very averse to writing; both from the overpowering idea of our dead poets and from abatement of my love of fame. I hope I am a little more of a Philosopher than I was, consequently a little less of a versifying Pet-lamb. . . . You will judge of my 1819 temper when I tell you that the thing I have most enjoyed this year has been writing an ode to Indolence."

The poem, written between late June and early September 1819, is a return, after the Spenserian stanzas of *The Eve of St. Agnes*, to the pentameter couplets Keats had used in *Endymion* and other early poems. But Keats had in the meantime been studying John Dryden's closed and strong-paced couplets. The initial lines of Dryden's version of Boccaccio's story *Cymon and Iphigenia* demonstrate the kind of narrative model that helped Keats make the technical transition from the fluent but sprawling gracefulness of the opening of *Endymion* to the vigor and economy of the opening of *Lamia*:

> In that sweet isle where Venus keeps her court,
> And every grace, and all the loves, resort;
> Where either sex is formed of softer earth,
> And takes the bent of pleasure from their birth;
> There lived a Cyprian lord, above the rest
> Wise, wealthy, with a numerous issue blessed. . . .

Lamia

Part 1

Upon a time, before the faery broods
Drove Nymph and Satyr[1] from the prosperous woods,
Before King Oberon's bright diadem,
Sceptre, and mantle, clasp'd with dewy gem,
5   Frighted away the Dryads and the Fauns
From rushes green, and brakes,° and cowslip'd lawns,   *thickets*
The ever-smitten Hermes[2] empty left
His golden throne, bent warm on amorous theft:
From high Olympus had he stolen light,
10 On this side of Jove's clouds, to escape the sight
Of his great summoner, and made retreat
Into a forest on the shores of Crete.
For somewhere in that sacred island dwelt
A nymph, to whom all hoofed Satyrs knelt;
15 At whose white feet the languid Tritons[3] poured
Pearls, while on land they wither'd and adored.
Fast by the springs where she to bathe was wont,°   *accustomed*
And in those meads where sometime she might haunt,
Were strewn rich gifts, unknown to any Muse,
20 Though Fancy's casket were unlock'd to choose.
Ah, what a world of love was at her feet!
So Hermes thought, and a celestial heat
Burnt from his winged heels to either ear,
That from a whiteness, as the lily clear,
25 Blush'd into roses 'mid his golden hair,
Fallen in jealous curls about his shoulders bare.[4]

1. Nymphs and satyrs—like the dryads and fauns in line 5—were minor classical deities of the woods and fields, said here to have been driven off by Oberon, king of the fairies, who were supernatural beings of the postclassical era.
2. Or Mercury; wing-footed messenger at the summons of Jove (line 11), Hermes was notoriously amorous.
3. Minor sea gods.
4. I.e., the curls clung jealously to his bare shoulders. This line is the first of a number of Alexandrines, a six-foot line, used to vary the metrical movement—a device that Keats learned from Dryden. Another such device is the triplet, occurring first in lines 61–63.

From vale to vale, from wood to wood, he flew,
Breathing upon the flowers his passion new,
And wound with many a river to its head,
30   To find where this sweet nymph prepar'd her secret bed:
In vain; the sweet nymph might nowhere be found,
And so he rested, on the lonely ground,
Pensive, and full of painful jealousies
Of the Wood-Gods, and even the very trees.
35   There as he stood, he heard a mournful voice,
Such as once heard, in gentle heart, destroys
All pain but pity: thus the lone voice spake:
"When from this wreathed tomb shall I awake!
When move in a sweet body fit for life,
40   And love, and pleasure, and the ruddy strife
Of hearts and lips! Ah, miserable me!"
The God, dove-footed,⁵ glided silently
Round bush and tree, soft-brushing, in his speed,
The taller grasses and full-flowering weed,
45   Until he found a palpitating snake,
Bright, and cirque-couchant⁶ in a dusky brake.

She was a gordian⁷ shape of dazzling hue,
Vermilion-spotted, golden, green, and blue;
Striped like a zebra, freckled like a pard,°   *leopard*
50   Eyed like a peacock,⁸ and all crimson barr'd;
And full of silver moons, that, as she breathed,
Dissolv'd, or brighter shone, or interwreathed
Their lustres with the gloomier tapestries—
So rainbow-sided, touch'd with miseries,
55   She seem'd, at once, some penanced lady elf,
Some demon's mistress, or the demon's self.
Upon her crest she wore a wannish⁹ fire
Sprinkled with stars, like Ariadne's tiar:¹
Her head was serpent, but ah, bitter-sweet!
60   She had a woman's mouth with all its pearls² complete:
And for her eyes: what could such eyes do there
But weep, and weep, that they were born so fair?
As Proserpine still weeps for her Sicilian air.³
Her throat was serpent, but the words she spake
65   Came, as through bubbling honey, for Love's sake,
And thus; while Hermes on his pinions° lay,   *wings*
Like a stoop'd falcon⁴ ere he takes his prey.

5. I.e., quietly as a dove.
6. Lying in a circular coil. Keats borrows the language of heraldry.
7. Intricately twisted, like the knot tied by King Gordius, which no one could undo.
8. Having multicolored spots, like the "eyes" in a peacock's tail.
9. Rather dark.
1. Ariadne's jeweled wedding crown, or tiara ("tiar"), was given to her by the god Bacchus, who took her as his wife after she was abandoned by her faithless mortal lover Theseus. The crown, transformed into a constellation of stars

in the sky, is represented in Titian's *Bacchus and Ariadne,* which Keats had seen when the painting was exhibited in London in 1816. Keats's memories of this painting may also inform his reference to Bacchus's chariot and leopards in "Ode to a Nightingale," line 32.
2. "Pearls" had become almost a synonym for teeth in Elizabethan love poems.
3. Proserpine had been carried off to Hades by Pluto from the field of Enna, in Sicily.
4. *Stoop* is the term for the plunge of a falcon on his prey.

"Fair Hermes, crown'd with feathers, fluttering light,
I had a splendid dream of thee last night:
70   I saw thee sitting, on a throne of gold,
Among the Gods, upon Olympus old,
The only sad one; for thou didst not hear
The soft, lute-finger'd Muses chaunting clear,
Nor even Apollo when he sang alone,
75   Deaf to his throbbing throat's long, long melodious moan.
I dreamt I saw thee, robed in purple flakes,
Break amorous through the clouds, as morning breaks,
And, swiftly as a bright Phœbean dart,[5]
Strike for the Cretan isle; and here thou art!
80   Too gentle Hermes, hast thou found the maid?"
Whereat the star of Lethe[6] not delay'd
His rosy eloquence, and thus inquired:
"Thou smooth-lipp'd serpent, surely high inspired!
Thou beauteous wreath, with melancholy eyes,
85   Possess whatever bliss thou canst devise,
Telling me only where my nymph is fled,—
Where she doth breathe!" "Bright planet, thou hast said,"
Return'd the snake, "but seal with oaths, fair God!"
"I swear," said Hermes, "by my serpent rod,
90   And by thine eyes, and by thy starry crown!"
Light flew his earnest words, among the blossoms blown.
Then thus again the brilliance feminine:
"Too frail of heart! for this lost nymph of thine,
Free as the air, invisibly, she strays
95   About these thornless wilds; her pleasant days
She tastes unseen; unseen her nimble feet
Leave traces in the grass and flowers sweet;
From weary tendrils, and bow'd branches green,
She plucks the fruit unseen, she bathes unseen:
100   And by my power is her beauty veil'd
To keep it unaffronted, unassail'd
By the love-glances of unlovely eyes,
Of Satyrs, Fauns, and blear'd Silenus'[7] sighs.
Pale grew her immortality, for woe
105   Of all these lovers, and she grieved so
I took compassion on her, bade her steep
Her hair in weïrd° syrops, that would keep   *magical*
Her loveliness invisible, yet free
To wander as she loves, in liberty.
110   Thou shalt behold her, Hermes, thou alone,
If thou wilt, as thou swearest, grant my boon!"
Then, once again, the charmed God began
An oath, and through the serpent's ears it ran
Warm, tremulous, devout, psalterian.[8]
115   Ravish'd, she lifted her Circean head,

---

5. A ray of Phoebus Apollo, god of the sun.
6. Hermes, when he appeared like a star on the banks of Lethe, in the darkness of Hades. (One of Hermes' offices was to guide the souls of the dead to the lower regions.)
7. Satyr, a tutor of Bacchus, usually represented as a fat, jolly drunkard.
8. Either "like a psalm" or "like the sound of the psaltery" (an ancient stringed instrument).

Blush'd a live damask,[9] and swift-lisping said,
"I was a woman, let me have once more
A woman's shape, and charming as before.
I love a youth of Corinth—O the bliss!
120 Give me my woman's form, and place me where he is.
Stoop, Hermes, let me breathe upon thy brow,
And thou shalt see thy sweet nymph even now."
The God on half-shut feathers sank serene,
She breath'd upon his eyes, and swift was seen
125 Of both the guarded nymph near-smiling on the green.
It was no dream; or say a dream it was,
Real are the dreams of Gods, and smoothly pass
Their pleasures in a long immortal dream.
One warm, flush'd moment, hovering, it might seem
130 Dash'd by the wood-nymph's beauty, so he burn'd;
Then, lighting on the printless verdure, turn'd
To the swoon'd serpent, and with languid arm,
Delicate, put to proof the lythe Caducean charm.[1]
So done, upon the nymph his eyes he bent
135 Full of adoring tears and blandishment,
And towards her stept: she, like a moon in wane,
Faded before him, cower'd, nor could restrain
Her fearful sobs, self-folding like a flower
That faints into itself at evening hour:
140 But the God fostering her chilled hand,
She felt the warmth, her eyelids open'd bland,°   softly
And, like new flowers at morning song of bees,
Bloom'd, and gave up her honey to the lees.°   dregs
Into the green-recessed woods they flew;
145 Nor grew they pale, as mortal lovers do.

Left to herself, the serpent now began
To change; her elfin blood in madness ran,
Her mouth foam'd, and the grass, therewith besprent,°   sprinkled
Wither'd at dew so sweet and virulent;
150 Her eyes in torture fix'd, and anguish drear,
Hot, glaz'd, and wide, with lid-lashes all sear,
Flash'd phosphor and sharp sparks, without one cooling tear.
The colours all inflam'd throughout her train,
She writh'd about, convuls'd with scarlet pain:
155 A deep volcanian yellow took the place
Of all her milder-mooned body's grace;[2]
And, as the lava ravishes the mead,
Spoilt all her silver mail, and golden brede;[3]
Made gloom of all her frecklings, streaks and bars,
160 Eclips'd her crescents, and lick'd up her stars:
So that, in moments few, she was undrest
Of all her sapphires, greens, and amethyst,

---

9. The color of a damask rose (large and fragrant pink rose). "Circean": like that of Circe, the enchantress in the *Odyssey*.
1. I.e., put to the test the magic of the flexible Caduceus (the name given to Hermes' wand).

2. I.e., the yellow of sulfur (thrown up by a volcano) replaced her former silvery moon color.
3. Embroidery, interwoven pattern. "Mail": interlinked rings, as in a coat of armor.

    And rubious-argent:° of all these bereft,   *silvery red*
    Nothing but pain and ugliness were left.
165   Still shone her crown; that vanish'd, also she
    Melted and disappear'd as suddenly;
    And in the air, her new voice luting soft,
    Cried, "Lycius! gentle Lycius!"—Borne aloft
    With the bright mists about the mountains hoar°   *white*
170   These words dissolv'd: Crete's forests heard no more.

      Whither fled Lamia, now a lady bright,
    A full-born beauty new and exquisite?
    She fled into that valley they pass o'er
    Who go to Corinth from Cenchreas' shore;[4]
175   And rested at the foot of those wild hills,
    The rugged founts of the Peæran rills,
    And of that other ridge whose barren back
    Stretches, with all its mist and cloudy rack,
    South-westward to Cleone. There she stood
180   About a young bird's flutter from a wood,
    Fair, on a sloping green of mossy tread,
    By a clear pool, wherein she passioned[5]
    To see herself escap'd from so sore ills,
    While her robes flaunted with the daffodils.

185   Ah, happy Lycius!—for she was a maid
    More beautiful than ever twisted braid,
    Or sigh'd, or blush'd, or on spring-flowered lea°   *meadow*
    Spread a green kirtle° to the minstrelsy: *gown*
    A virgin purest lipp'd, yet in the lore
190   Of love deep learned to the red heart's core:
    Not one hour old, yet of sciential brain
    To unperplex bliss from its neighbour pain;
    Define their pettish limits, and estrange
    Their points of contact, and swift counterchange;[6]
195   Intrigue with the specious chaos,[7] and dispart
    Its most ambiguous atoms with sure art;
    As though in Cupid's college she had spent
    Sweet days a lovely graduate, still unshent,°   *unspoiled*
    And kept his rosy terms[8] in idle languishment.

200   Why this fair creature chose so fairily
    By the wayside to linger, we shall see;
    But first 'tis fit to tell how she could muse
    And dream, when in the serpent prison-house,
    Of all she list,° strange or magnificent: *wished*
205   How, ever, where she will'd, her spirit went;
    Whether to faint Elysium,[9] or where

---

4. Cenchrea (Keats's "Cenchreas") was a harbor of Corinth, in southern Greece.
5. Felt intense excitement.
6. I.e., of knowledgeable ("sciential") brain to disentangle ("unperplex") bliss from its closely related pain, to define their quarreled-over ("pettish") limits, and to separate out ("estrange") their points of contact and the swift changes of each condition into its opposite. Cf. Keats's "Ode on Melancholy," lines 21–26 (pp. 497).
7. I.e., turn to her own artful purpose the seeming ("specious") chaos.
8. The terms spent studying in "Cupid's college."
9. Region inhabited by the virtuous after death.

Down through tress-lifting waves the Nereids[1] fair
Wind into Thetis' bower by many a pearly stair;
Or where God Bacchus drains his cups divine,
210   Stretch'd out, at ease, beneath a glutinous pine;
Or where in Pluto's gardens palatine°   *palatial*
Mulciber's columns gleam in far piazzian line.[2]
And sometimes into cities she would send
Her dream, with feast and rioting to blend;
215   And once, while among mortals dreaming thus,
She saw the young Corinthian Lycius
Charioting foremost in the envious race,
Like a young Jove with calm uneager face,
And fell into a swooning love of him.
220   Now on the moth-time of that evening dim
He would return that way, as well she knew,
To Corinth from the shore; for freshly blew
The eastern soft wind, and his galley now
Grated the quaystones with her brazen prow
225   In port Cenchreas, from Egina isle
Fresh anchor'd; whither he had been awhile
To sacrifice to Jove, whose temple there
Waits with high marble doors for blood and incense rare.
Jove heard his vows, and better'd his desire;
230   For by some freakful chance he made retire
From his companions, and set forth to walk,
Perhaps grown wearied of their Corinth talk:
Over the solitary hills he fared,
Thoughtless at first, but ere eve's star appeared
235   His phantasy was lost, where reason fades,
In the calm'd twilight of Platonic shades.[3]
Lamia beheld him coming, near, more near—
Close to her passing, in indifference drear,
His silent sandals swept the mossy green;
240   So neighbour'd to him, and yet so unseen
She stood: he pass'd, shut up in mysteries,
His mind wrapp'd like his mantle, while her eyes
Follow'd his steps, and her neck regal white
Turn'd—syllabling thus, "Ah, Lycius bright,
245   And will you leave me on the hills alone?
Lycius, look back! and be some pity shown."
He did; not with cold wonder fearingly,
But Orpheus-like at an Eurydice;[4]
For so delicious were the words she sung,
250   It seem'd he had lov'd them a whole summer long:
And soon his eyes had drunk her beauty up,
Leaving no drop in the bewildering cup,
And still the cup was full,—while he, afraid

---

1. Sea nymphs, of whom Thetis (line 208, the mother of Achilles) was one.
2. I.e., columns made by Mulciber (Vulcan, god of fire and metalworking) gleam in long lines around open courts (piazzas).
3. I.e., he was absorbed in musing about the obscurities of Plato's philosophy.
4. As Orpheus looked at Eurydice in Hades. Orpheus was allowed by Pluto to lead Eurydice back to Earth on condition that he not look back at her, but he could not resist doing so and hence lost her once more.

Lest she should vanish ere his lip had paid
255 Due adoration, thus began to adore;
Her soft look growing coy, she saw his chain so sure:
"Leave thee alone! Look back! Ah, Goddess, see
Whether my eyes can ever turn from thee!
For pity do not this sad heart belie[5]—
260 Even as thou vanishest so I shall die.
Stay! though a Naiad of the rivers, stay!
To thy far wishes will thy streams obey:
Stay! though the greenest woods be thy domain,
Alone they can drink up the morning rain:
265 Though a descended Pleiad,[6] will not one
Of thine harmonious sisters keep in tune
Thy spheres, and as thy silver proxy shine?
So sweetly to these ravish'd ears of mine
Came thy sweet greeting, that if thou shouldst fade
270 Thy memory will waste me to a shade:—
For pity do not melt!"—"If I should stay,"
Said Lamia, "here, upon this floor of clay,
And pain my steps upon these flowers too rough,
What canst thou say or do of charm enough
275 To dull the nice[7] remembrance of my home?
Thou canst not ask me with thee here to roam
Over these hills and vales, where no joy is,—
Empty of immortality and bliss!
Thou art a scholar, Lycius, and must know
280 That finer spirits cannot breathe below
In human climes, and live: Alas! poor youth,
What taste of purer air hast thou to soothe
My essence? What serener palaces,
Where I may all my many senses please,
285 And by mysterious sleights a hundred thirsts appease?
It cannot be—Adieu!" So said, she rose
Tiptoe with white arms spread. He, sick to lose
The amorous promise of her lone complain,
Swoon'd, murmuring of love, and pale with pain.
290 The cruel lady, without any show
Of sorrow for her tender favourite's woe,
But rather, if her eyes could brighter be,
With brighter eyes and slow amenity,°   pleasure
Put her new lips to his, and gave afresh
295 The life she had so tangled in her mesh:
And as he from one trance was wakening
Into another, she began to sing,
Happy in beauty, life, and love, and every thing,
A song of love, too sweet for earthly lyres,
300 While, like held breath, the stars drew in their panting fires.
And then she whisper'd in such trembling tone,
As those who, safe together met alone
For the first time through many anguish'd days,

---

5. Be false to.
6. One of the seven sisters composing the constellation Pleiades. The lines that follow allude to the ancient belief that the planets traveled
inside crystalline spheres whose movements produced heavenly music.
7. Detailed, minutely accurate.

Use other speech than looks; bidding him raise
305 His drooping head, and clear his soul of doubt,
For that she was a woman, and without
Any more subtle fluid in her veins
Than throbbing blood, and that the self-same pains
Inhabited her frail-strung heart as his.
310 And next she wonder'd how his eyes could miss
Her face so long in Corinth, where, she said,
She dwelt but half retir'd, and there had led
Days happy as the gold coin could invent
Without the aid of love; yet in content
315 Till she saw him, as once she pass'd him by,
Where 'gainst a column he leant thoughtfully
At Venus' temple porch, 'mid baskets heap'd
Of amorous herbs and flowers, newly reap'd
Late on that eve, as 'twas the night before
320 The Adonian feast;[8] whereof she saw no more,
But wept alone those days, for why should she adore?
Lycius from death awoke into amaze,
To see her still, and singing so sweet lays;
Then from amaze into delight he fell
325 To hear her whisper woman's lore so well;
And every word she spake entic'd him on
To unperplex'd delight[9] and pleasure known.
Let the mad poets say whate'er they please
Of the sweets of Fairies, Peris,[1] Goddesses,
330 There is not such a treat among them all,
Haunters of cavern, lake, and waterfall,
As a real woman, lineal indeed
From Pyrrha's pebbles[2] or old Adam's seed.
Thus gentle Lamia judg'd, and judg'd aright,
335 That Lycius could not love in half a fright,
So threw the goddess off, and won his heart
More pleasantly by playing woman's part,
With no more awe than what her beauty gave,
That, while it smote, still guaranteed to save.
340 Lycius to all made eloquent reply,
Marrying to every word a twinborn sigh;
And last, pointing to Corinth, ask'd her sweet,
If 'twas too far that night for her soft feet.
The way was short, for Lamia's eagerness
345 Made, by a spell, the triple league decrease
To a few paces; not at all surmised
By blinded Lycius, so in her comprized.[3]
They pass'd the city gates, he knew not how,
So noiseless, and he never thought to know.

350   As men talk in a dream, so Corinth all,
Throughout her palaces imperial,

---

8. The feast of Adonis, beloved by Venus.
9. I.e., delight not mixed with its neighbor, pain
(see line 192).
1. Fairylike creatures in Persian mythology.

2. Descended from the pebbles with which, in
Greek myth, Pyrrha and Deucalion repeopled
the earth after the flood.
3. Bound up, absorbed.

And all her populous streets and temples lewd,[4]
Mutter'd, like tempest in the distance brew'd,
To the wide-spreaded night above her towers.
355 Men, women, rich and poor, in the cool hours,
Shuffled their sandals o'er the pavement white,
Companion'd or alone; while many a light
Flared, here and there, from wealthy festivals,
And threw their moving shadows on the walls,
360 Or found them cluster'd in the corniced shade
Of some arch'd temple door, or dusky colonnade.

Muffling his face, of greeting friends in fear,
Her fingers he press'd hard, as one came near
With curl'd gray beard, sharp eyes, and smooth bald crown,
365 Slow-stepp'd, and robed in philosophic gown:
Lycius shrank closer, as they met and past,
Into his mantle, adding wings to haste,
While hurried Lamia trembled: "Ah," said he,
"Why do you shudder, love, so ruefully?
370 Why does your tender palm dissolve in dew?"—
"I'm wearied," said fair Lamia: "tell me who
Is that old man? I cannot bring to mind
His features:—Lycius! wherefore did you blind
Yourself from his quick eyes?" Lycius replied,
375 "'Tis Apollonius sage, my trusty guide
And good instructor; but to-night he seems
The ghost of folly haunting my sweet dreams."

While yet he spake they had arrived before
A pillar'd porch, with lofty portal door,
380 Where hung a silver lamp, whose phosphor glow
Reflected in the slabbed steps below,
Mild as a star in water; for so new,
And so unsullied was the marble hue,
So through the crystal polish, liquid fine,
385 Ran the dark veins, that none but feet divine
Could e'er have touch'd there. Sounds Æolian[5]
Breath'd from the hinges, as the ample span
Of the wide doors disclos'd a place unknown
Some time to any, but those two alone,
390 And a few Persian mutes, who that same year
Were seen about the markets: none knew where
They could inhabit; the most curious
Were foil'd, who watch'd to trace them to their house:
And but the flitter-winged verse must tell,
395 For truth's sake, what woe afterwards befel,
'Twould humour many a heart to leave them thus,
Shut from the busy world of more incredulous.

4. Temples of Venus, whose worship sometimes involved ritual prostitution. The city of Corinth was notorious in antiquity as a site of commerce and prostitution.

5. Like sounds from the wind harp (Aeolus is god of winds), which responds musically to a current of air.

Part 2

Love in a hut, with water and a crust,
Is—Love, forgive us!—cinders, ashes, dust;
Love in a palace is perhaps at last
More grievous torment than a hermit's fast:—
5   That is a doubtful tale from faery land,
Hard for the non-elect to understand.
Had Lycius liv'd to hand his story down,
He might have given the moral a fresh frown,
Or clench'd it quite: but too short was their bliss
10   To breed distrust and hate, that make the soft voice hiss.
Besides, there, nightly, with terrific glare,
Love, jealous grown of so complete a pair,
Hover'd and buzz'd his wings, with fearful roar,
Above the lintel of their chamber door,
15   And down the passage cast a glow upon the floor.

    For all this came a ruin: side by side
They were enthroned, in the even tide,
Upon a couch, near to a curtaining
Whose airy texture, from a golden string,
20   Floated into the room, and let appear
Unveil'd the summer heaven, blue and clear,
Betwixt two marble shafts:—there they reposed,
Where use had made it sweet, with eyelids closed,
Saving a tythe which love still open kept,
25   That they might see each other while they almost slept;
When from the slope side of a suburb hill,
Deafening the swallow's twitter, came a thrill
Of trumpets—Lycius started—the sounds fled,
But left a thought, a buzzing in his head.
30   For the first time, since first he harbour'd in
That purple-lined palace of sweet sin,
His spirit pass'd beyond its golden bourn°   *boundary*
Into the noisy world almost forsworn.
The lady, ever watchful, penetrant,
35   Saw this with pain, so arguing a want
Of something more, more than her empery°   *empire*
Of joys; and she began to moan and sigh
Because he mused beyond her, knowing well
That but a moment's thought is passion's passing bell.°   *death knell*
40   "Why do you sigh, fair creature?" whisper'd he:
"Why do you think?" return'd she tenderly:
"You have deserted me;—where am I now?
Not in your heart while care weighs on your brow:
No, no, you have dismiss'd me; and I go
45   From your breast houseless: ay, it must be so."
He answer'd, bending to her open eyes,
Where he was mirror'd small in paradise,
"My silver planet, both of eve and morn!⁶

---

6. The planet Venus, which is both the morning and the evening star.

Why will you plead yourself so sad forlorn,
50   While I am striving how to fill my heart
With deeper crimson, and a double smart?
How to entangle, trammel up and snare
Your soul in mine, and labyrinth you there
Like the hid scent in an unbudded rose?
55   Ay, a sweet kiss—you see your mighty woes.[7]
My thoughts! shall I unveil them? Listen then!
What mortal hath a prize, that other men
May be confounded and abash'd withal,
But lets it sometimes pace abroad majestical,
60   And triumph, as in thee I should rejoice
Amid the hoarse alarm of Corinth's voice.
Let my foes choke, and my friends shout afar,
While through the thronged streets your bridal car°   chariot
Wheels round its dazzling spokes."—The lady's cheek
65   Trembled; she nothing said, but, pale and meek,
Arose and knelt before him, wept a rain
Of sorrows at his words; at last with pain
Beseeching him, the while his hand she wrung,
To change his purpose. He thereat was stung,
70   Perverse, with stronger fancy to reclaim
Her wild and timid nature to his aim:
Besides, for all his love, in self despite,
Against his better self, he took delight
Luxurious in her sorrows, soft and new.
75   His passion, cruel grown, took on a hue
Fierce and sanguineous as 'twas possible
In one whose brow had no dark veins to swell.
Fine was the mitigated fury, like
Apollo's presence when in act to strike
80   The serpent—Ha, the serpent! certes, she
Was none. She burnt, she lov'd the tyranny,
And, all subdued, consented to the hour
When to the bridal he should lead his paramour.
Whispering in midnight silence, said the youth,
85   "Sure some sweet name thou hast, though, by my truth,
I have not ask'd it, ever thinking thee
Not mortal, but of heavenly progeny,
As still I do. Hast any mortal name,
Fit appellation for this dazzling frame?
90   Or friends or kinsfolk on the citied earth,
To share our marriage feast and nuptial mirth?"
"I have no friends," said Lamia, "no, not one;
My presence in wide Corinth hardly known:
My parents' bones are in their dusty urns
95   Sepulchred, where no kindled incense burns,
Seeing all their luckless race are dead, save me,
And I neglect the holy rite for thee.
Even as you list° invite your many guests;   choose
But if, as now it seems, your vision rests
100   With any pleasure on me, do not bid

7. Playfully: "You see how great your troubles were!"

Old Apollonius—from him keep me hid."
Lycius, perplex'd at words so blind and blank,
Made close inquiry; from whose touch she shrank,
Feigning a sleep; and he to the dull shade
105 Of deep sleep in a moment was betray'd.

It was the custom then to bring away,
The bride from home at blushing shut of day,
Veil'd, in a chariot, heralded along
By strewn flowers, torches, and a marriage song,
110 With other pageants: but this fair unknown
Had not a friend. So being left alone,
(Lycius was gone to summon all his kin)
And knowing surely she could never win
His foolish heart from its mad pompousness,
115 She set herself, high-thoughted, how to dress
The misery in fit magnificence.
She did so, but 'tis doubtful how and whence
Came, and who were her subtle servitors.
About the halls, and to and from the doors,
120 There was a noise of wings, till in short space
The glowing banquet-room shone with wide-arched grace.
A haunting music, sole perhaps and lone
Supportress of the faery-roof, made moan
Throughout, as fearful the whole charm might fade.
125 Fresh carved cedar, mimicking a glade
Of palm and plantain, met from either side,
High in the midst, in honour of the bride:
Two palms and then two plantains, and so on,
From either side their stems branch'd one to one
130 All down the aisled place; and beneath all
There ran a stream of lamps straight on from wall to wall.
So canopied, lay an untasted feast
Teeming with odours. Lamia, regal drest,
Silently paced about, and as she went,
135 In pale contented sort of discontent,
Mission'd her viewless° servants to enrich   *invisible*
The fretted[8] splendour of each nook and niche.
Between the tree-stems, marbled plain at first,
Came jasper pannels; then, anon, there burst
140 Forth creeping imagery of slighter trees,
And with the larger wove in small intricacies.
Approving all, she faded at self-will,
And shut the chamber up, close, hush'd and still,
Complete and ready for the revels rude,
145 When dreadful° guests would come to spoil her solitude.   *terrifying*

The day appeared, and all the gossip rout.
O senseless Lycius! Madman! wherefore flout
The silent-blessing fate, warm cloister'd hours,
And show to common eyes these secret bowers?
150 The herd approach'd; each guest, with busy brain,

---

8. Adorned with fretwork (interlaced patterns).

Arriving at the portal, gaz'd amain,°   *intently*
And enter'd marveling: for they knew the street,
Remember'd it from childhood all complete
Without a gap, yet ne'er before had seen
155 That royal porch, that high-built fair demesne;°   *estate*
So in they hurried all, maz'd, curious and keen:
Save one, who look'd thereon with eye severe,
And with calm-planted steps walk'd in austere;
'Twas Apollonius: something too he laugh'd,
160 As though some knotty problem, that had daft°   *baffled*
His patient thought, had now begun to thaw,
And solve and melt:—'twas just as he foresaw.

He met within the murmurous vestibule
His young disciple. "'Tis no common rule,
165 Lycius," said he, "for uninvited guest
To force himself upon you, and infest
With an unbidden presence the bright throng
Of younger friends; yet must I do this wrong,
And you forgive me." Lycius blush'd, and led
170 The old man through the inner doors broad-spread;
With reconciling words and courteous mien°   *appearance*
Turning into sweet milk the sophist's° spleen.   *scholar's*

Of wealthy lustre was the banquet-room,
Fill'd with pervading brilliance and perfume:
175 Before each lucid pannel fuming stood
A censer fed with myrrh and spiced wood,
Each by a sacred tripod held aloft,
Whose slender feet wide-swerv'd upon the soft
Wool-woofed° carpets: fifty wreaths of smoke   *woven*
180 From fifty censers their light voyage took
To the high roof, still mimick'd as they rose
Along the mirror'd walls by twin-clouds odorous.
Twelve sphered tables, by silk seats insphered,
High as the level of a man's breast rear'd
185 On libbard's° paws, upheld the heavy gold   *leopard's*
Of cups and goblets, and the store thrice told
Of Ceres' horn,[9] and, in huge vessels, wine
Come from the gloomy tun with merry shine.
Thus loaded with a feast the tables stood,
190 Each shrining in the midst the image of a God.

When in an antichamber every guest
Had felt the cold full sponge to pleasure press'd,
By minist'ring slaves, upon his hands and feet,
And fragrant oils with ceremony meet°   *suitable*
195 Pour'd on his hair, they all mov'd to the feast
In white robes, and themselves in order placed
Around the silken couches, wondering
Whence all this mighty cost and blaze of wealth could spring.

9. The horn of plenty, overflowing with the products of Ceres, goddess of grain.

Soft went the music the soft air along,
200 While fluent Greek a vowel'd undersong
Kept up among the guests, discoursing low
At first, for scarcely was the wine at flow;
But when the happy vintage touch'd their brains,
Louder they talk, and louder come the strains
205 Of powerful instruments:—the gorgeous dyes,
The space, the splendour of the draperies,
The roof of awful richness, nectarous cheer,
Beautiful slaves, and Lamia's self, appear,
Now, when the wine has done its rosy deed,
210 And every soul from human trammels freed,
No more so strange; for merry wine, sweet wine,
Will make Elysian shades not too fair, too divine.

Soon was God Bacchus at meridian height;
Flush'd were their cheeks, and bright eyes double bright:
215 Garlands of every green, and every scent
From vales deflower'd, or forest-trees branch-rent,
In baskets of bright osier'd[1] gold were brought
High as the handles heap'd, to suit the thought
Of every guest; that each, as he did please,
220 Might fancy-fit his brows, silk-pillow'd at his ease.

What wreath for Lamia? What for Lycius?
What for the sage, old Apollonius?
Upon her aching forehead be there hung
The leaves of willow and of adder's tongue;[2]
225 And for the youth, quick, let us strip for him
The thyrsus,[3] that his watching eyes may swim
Into forgetfulness; and, for the sage,
Let spear-grass and the spiteful thistle wage
War on his temples. Do not all charms fly
230 At the mere touch of cold philosophy?[4]
There was an awful° rainbow once in heaven: awe-inspiring
We know her woof, her texture; she is given
In the dull catalogue of common things.
Philosophy will clip an Angel's wings,
235 Conquer all mysteries by rule and line,
Empty the haunted air, and gnomed mine[5]—
Unweave a rainbow, as it erewhile made
The tender-person'd Lamia melt into a shade.

By her glad Lycius sitting, in chief place,
240 Scarce saw in all the room another face,
Till, checking his love trance, a cup he took
Full brimm'd, and opposite sent forth a look

1. Plaited. An "osier" is a strip of willow used in weaving baskets.
2. A fern whose spikes resemble a serpent's tongue.
3. The vine-covered staff of Bacchus, used to signify drunkenness.
4. In the sense of "natural philosophy," or sci-
ence. Benjamin Haydon tells in his *Autobiography* how, at a hard-drinking and high-spirited dinner party, Keats had agreed with Charles Lamb (to what extent jokingly, it is not clear) that Newton's *Optics* "had destroyed all the poetry of the rainbow by reducing it to the prismatic colors."
5. Gnomes were guardians of mines.

'Cross the broad table, to beseech a glance
From his old teacher's wrinkled countenance,
245 And pledge[6] him. The bald-head philosopher
Had fix'd his eye, without a twinkle or stir
Full on the alarmed beauty of the bride,
Brow-beating her fair form, and troubling her sweet pride.
Lycius then press'd her hand, with devout touch,
250 As pale it lay upon the rosy couch:
'Twas icy, and the cold ran through his veins;
Then sudden it grew hot, and all the pains
Of an unnatural heat shot to his heart.
"Lamia, what means this? Wherefore dost thou start?
255 Know'st thou that man?" Poor Lamia answer'd not.
He gaz'd into her eyes, and not a jot
Own'd° they the lovelorn piteous appeal: *acknowledged*
More, more he gaz'd: his human senses reel:
Some hungry spell that loveliness absorbs;
260 There was no recognition in those orbs.
"Lamia!" he cried—and no soft-toned reply.
The many heard, and the loud revelry
Grew hush; the stately music no more breathes;
The myrtle[7] sicken'd in a thousand wreaths.
265 By faint degrees, voice, lute, and pleasure ceased;
A deadly silence step by step increased,
Until it seem'd a horrid presence there,
And not a man but felt the terror in his hair.
"Lamia!" he shriek'd; and nothing but the shriek
270 With its sad echo did the silence break.
"Begone, foul dream!" he cried, gazing again
In the bride's face, where now no azure vein
Wander'd on fair-spaced temples; no soft bloom
Misted the cheek; no passion to illume
275 The deep-recessed vision:—all was blight;
Lamia, no longer fair, there sat a deadly white.
"Shut, shut those juggling[8] eyes, thou ruthless man!
Turn them aside, wretch! or the righteous ban
Of all the Gods, whose dreadful images
280 Here represent their shadowy presences,
May pierce them on the sudden with the thorn
Of painful blindness; leaving thee forlorn,
In trembling dotage to the feeblest fright
Of conscience, for their long offended might,
285 For all thine impious proud-heart sophistries,
Unlawful magic, and enticing lies.
Corinthians! look upon that gray-beard wretch!
Mark how, possess'd, his lashless eyelids stretch
Around his demon eyes! Corinthians, see!
290 My sweet bride withers at their potency."
"Fool!" said the sophist, in an under-tone
Gruff with contempt; which a death-nighing moan
From Lycius answer'd, as heart-struck and lost,
He sank supine beside the aching ghost.

6. Drink a toast to.   8. Deceiving, full of trickery.
7. Sacred to Venus, hence an emblem of love.

295   "Fool! Fool!" repeated he, while his eyes still
      Relented not, nor mov'd; "from every ill
      Of life have I preserv'd thee to this day,
      And shall I see thee made a serpent's prey?"
      Then Lamia breath'd death breath; the sophist's eye,
300   Like a sharp spear, went through her utterly,
      Keen, cruel, perceant,° stinging: she, as well   *piercing*
      As her weak hand could any meaning tell,
      Motion'd him to be silent; vainly so,
      He look'd and look'd again a level—No!
305   "A Serpent!" echoed he; no sooner said,
      Than with a frightful scream she vanished:
      And Lycius' arms were empty of delight,
      As were his limbs of life, from that same night.
      On the high couch he lay!—his friends came round—
310   Supported him—no pulse, or breath they found,
      And, in its marriage robe, the heavy body wound.

July–Aug. 1819   1820

To Autumn[1]

1

    Season of mists and mellow fruitfulness,
      Close bosom-friend of the maturing sun;
    Conspiring with him how to load and bless
      With fruit the vines that round the thatch-eves run;
5   To bend with apples the moss'd cottage-trees,
      And fill all fruit with ripeness to the core;
        To swell the gourd, and plump the hazel shells
      With a sweet kernel; to set budding more,
    And still more, later flowers for the bees,
10   Until they think warm days will never cease,
        For summer has o'er-brimm'd their clammy cells.

2

    Who hath not seen thee oft amid thy store?
      Sometimes whoever seeks abroad may find
    Thee sitting careless on a granary floor,
15   Thy hair soft-lifted by the winnowing[2] wind;
    Or on a half-reap'd furrow sound asleep,
      Drows'd with the fume of poppies, while thy hook°   *scythe*
        Spares the next swath and all its twined flowers:
    And sometimes like a gleaner thou dost keep
20   Steady thy laden head across a brook;
      Or by a cyder-press, with patient look,
        Thou watchest the last oozings hours by hours.

1. Two days after this ode was composed, Keats wrote to J. H. Reynolds: "I never liked stubble fields so much as now—Aye, better than the chilly green of the spring. Somehow a stubble plain looks warm—this struck me so much in my Sunday's walk that I composed upon it." For the author's revisions while composing "To Autumn," see "Poems in Process," in the supplementary ebook.
2. To "winnow" is to fan the chaff from the grain.

3

Where are the songs of spring? Ay, where are they?
    Think not of them, thou hast thy music too,—
25 While barred clouds bloom the soft-dying day,
    And touch the stubble-plains with rosy hue;
Then in a wailful choir the small gnats mourn
    Among the river sallows,° borne aloft   *willows*
    Or sinking as the light wind lives or dies;
30 And full-grown lambs loud bleat from hilly bourn;°   *region*
    Hedge-crickets sing; and now with treble soft
The red-breast whistles from a garden-croft;[3]
    And gathering swallows twitter in the skies.

Sept. 19, 1819   1820

Letters   Keats's letters serve as a running commentary on his life, reading, thinking, and writing. They are, in his career, the equivalent of the essays, prefaces, and defenses of poetry produced by his contemporaries. His early reputation as a poet of pure luxury, sensation, and art for art's sake has undergone a radical change since, in the twentieth century, critics began to pay close attention to the letters. For Keats thought hard and persistently about life and art, and any seed of an ethical or critical idea that he picked up from his contemporaries (in particular, Hazlitt, Coleridge, Wordsworth) instantly germinated and flourished in the rich soil of his imagination. What T. S. Eliot said about the Metaphysical poets applies to Keats in his letters: his "mode of feeling was directly and freshly altered by [his] reading and thought." And like Donne, he looked not only into the heart but, literally, "into the cerebral cortex, the nervous system, and the digestive tract." A number of Keats's casual comments on the poet and on poetry included here—especially those dealing with "negative capability" and the kind of imaginative identification with someone or something outside ourselves that we now call empathy—have become standard points of reference in aesthetic theory. But Keats regarded nothing that he said as final; each statement constituted only a stage in his continuing exploration into what he called "the mystery."

    The text printed here is that of the edition of the *Letters* by Hyder E. Rollins (1958), which reproduces the original manuscripts precisely.

LETTERS

To Benjamin Bailey[1]

["THE AUTHENTICITY OF THE IMAGINATION"]

[November 22, 1817]

My dear Bailey,

    * * * O I wish I was as certain of the end of all your troubles as that of your momentary start about the authenticity of the Imagination. I am certain of

---

3. An enclosed plot of farmland.
1. One of Keats's closest friends. Keats had

stayed with him the month before at Oxford, where Bailey was an undergraduate.

nothing but of the holiness of the Heart's affections and the truth of Imagination—What the imagination seizes as Beauty must be truth[2]— whether it existed before or not—for I have the same Idea of all our Passions as of Love they are all in their sublime, creative of essential Beauty—In a Word, you may know my favorite Speculation by my first Book and the little song[3] I sent in my last—which is a representation from the fancy of the probable mode of operating in these Matters—The Imagination may be compared to Adam's dream[4]—he awoke and found it truth. I am the more zealous in this affair, because I have never yet been able to perceive how any thing can be known for truth by consequitive reasoning[5]—and yet it must be—Can it be that even the greatest Philosopher ever ~~when~~ arrived at his goal without putting aside numerous objections—However it may be, O for a Life of Sensations[6] rather than of Thoughts! It is "a Vision in the form of Youth" a Shadow of reality to come—and this consideration has further conv[i]nced me for it has come as auxiliary to another favorite Speculation of mine, that we shall enjoy ourselves here after by having what we called happiness on Earth repeated in a finer tone and so repeated[7]—And yet such a fate can only befall those who delight in sensation rather than hunger as you do after Truth—Adam's dream will do here and seems to be a conviction that Imagination and its empyreal[8] reflection is the same as human Life and its spiritual repetition. But as I was saying—the simple imaginative Mind may have its rewards in the repeti[ti]on of its own silent Working coming continually on the spirit with a fine suddenness—to compare great things with small—have you never by being surprised with an old Melody—in a delicious place—by a delicious voice, fe[l]t over again your very speculations and surmises at the time it first operated on your soul—do you not remember forming to yourself the singer's face more beautiful [than] it was possible and yet with the elevation of the Moment you did not think so—even then you were mounted on the Wings of Imagination so high—that the Prototype must be here after—that delicious face you will see—What a time! I am continually running away from the subject—sure this cannot be exactly the case with a complex Mind—one that is imaginative and at the same time careful of its fruits—who would exist partly on sensation partly on thought—to whom it is necessary that years should bring the philosophic Mind[9]—such an one I consider your's and therefore it is necessary to your eternal Happiness that you not only drink this old Wine of Heaven which I shall call the redigestion of our most ethereal Musings on Earth; but also increase in knowledge and know all things. I am glad to hear you are in a fair Way for Easter—you will soon get through your unpleasant reading and then!—but the world is full of troubles and I have not much reason to think myself pesterd with many—I think Jane or Marianne has a better opinion of me than I deserve—for really and truly I do not think my Brothers illness connected with mine—you know

2. At the close of "Ode on a Grecian Urn," Keats also grapples with these categories. Where Keats uses "truth" we might substitute the words *real* or *reality*.
3. The song was "O Sorrow," from book 4 of *Endymion*.
4. In Milton's *Paradise Lost* 8.452–90 Adam dreams that Eve has been created and awakes to find her real. Adam also describes an earlier prefigurative dream in the same work, 8.283–311.

5. Consecutive reasoning—reasoning that moves by logical steps.
6. Probably not only sense experiences but also the intuitive perceptions of truths, as opposed to truth achieved by consecutive reasoning.
7. Cf. the "Pleasure Thermometer" in *Endymion* 1.777ff. (p. 474).
8. Heavenly.
9. An echo of Wordsworth, "Ode: Intimations of Immortality," line 187.

more of the real Cause than they do—nor have I any chance of being rack'd as you have been[1]—you perhaps at one time thought there was such a thing as Worldly Happiness to be arrived at, at certain periods of time marked out—you have of necessity from your disposition been thus led away—I scarcely remember counting upon any Happiness—I look not for it if it be not in the present hour—nothing startles me beyond the Moment. The setting sun will always set me to rights—or if a Sparrow come before my Window I take part in its existence and pick about the Gravel. The first thing that strikes me on hea[r]ing a Misfortune having befalled another is this. "Well it cannot be helped.—he will have the pleasure of trying the resourses of his spirit, and I beg now my dear Bailey that hereafter should you observe any thing cold in me not to [put] it to the account of heartlessness but abstraction— for I assure you I sometimes feel not the influence of a Passion or Affection during a whole week—and so long this sometimes continues I begin to suspect myself and the genuiness of my feelings at other times—thinking them a few barren Tragedy-tears. * * *

Your affectionate friend
John Keats—

To George and Thomas Keats

["NEGATIVE CAPABILITY"]

[December 21, 27 (?), 1817]

My dear Brothers

I must crave your pardon for not having written ere this. * * * I spent Friday evening with Wells[1] & went the next morning to see *Death on the Pale horse*. It is a wonderful picture, when West's[2] age is considered; But there is nothing to be intense upon; no women one feels mad to kiss; no face swelling into reality. the excellence of every Art is its intensity, capable of making all disagreeables evaporate, from their being in close relationship with Beauty & Truth[3]—Examine King Lear & you will find this examplified throughout; but in this picture we have unpleasantness without any momentous depth of speculation excited, in which to bury its repulsiveness—The picture is larger than Christ rejected—I dined with Haydon[4] the sunday after you left, & had a very pleasant day, I dined too (for I have been out too much lately) with Horace Smith & met his two Brothers with Hill & Kingston & one Du Bois,[5] they only served to convince me, how superior humour is to wit in respect to enjoyment—These men say things which make one start, without making one feel, they are all alike; their manners are alike; they all know fashionables; they have a mannerism in their very eating &

1. Keats's friends Jane and Mariane Reynolds feared that his ill health at this time threatened tuberculosis, from which his brother Tom was suffering. Bailey had recently experienced pain (been "racked") because of an unsuccessful love affair.
1. Charles Wells, a former schoolmate of Tom Keats.
2. Benjamin West (1738–1820), painter of historical pictures, was an American who moved to England and became president of the Royal Academy. The *Christ Rejected* mentioned a few

sentences farther on is also by West.
3. Keats's solution to a problem at least as old as Aristotle's *Poetics*: why do we take pleasure in the aesthetic representation of a subject that in life would be ugly or painful?
4. Keats's close friend Benjamin Haydon, painter of large-scale historical and religious pictures.
5. Smith was one of the best-known literary wits of the day; the others mentioned were men of letters or of literary interests.

drinking, in their mere handling a Decanter—They talked of Kean[6] & his low company—Would I were with that company instead of yours said I to myself! I know such like acquaintance will never do for me & yet I am going to Reynolds, on Wednesday—Brown & Dilke[7] walked with me & back from the Christmas pantomime.[8] I had not a dispute but a disquisition with Dilke, on various subjects; several things dovetailed in my mind, & at once it struck me, what quality went to form a Man of Achievement especially in Literature & which Shakespeare possessed so enormously—I mean *Negative Capability*,[9] that is when man is capable of being in uncertainties, Mysteries, doubts, without any irritable reaching after fact & reason—Coleridge, for instance, would let go by a fine isolated verisimilitude caught from the Penetralium[1] of mystery, from being incapable of remaining content with half knowledge. This pursued through Volumes would perhaps take us no further than this, that with a great poet the sense of Beauty overcomes every other consideration, or rather obliterates all consideration.

Shelley's poem[2] is out & there are words about its being objected too, as much as Queen Mab was. Poor Shelley I think he has his Quota of good qualities, in sooth la!! Write soon to your most sincere friend & affectionate Brother

John

To John Hamilton Reynolds[1]

[WORDSWORTH'S POETRY]

[February 3, 1818]

My dear Reynolds,

* * * It may be said that we ought to read our Contemporaries, that Wordsworth &c should have their due from us but for the sake of a few fine imaginative or domestic passages, are we to be bullied into a certain Philosophy engendered in the whims of an Egotist—Every man has his speculations, but every man does not brood and peacock over them till he makes a false coinage and deceives himself—Many a man can travel to the very bourne[2] of Heaven, and yet want confidence to put down his halfseeing. Sancho[3] will invent a Journey heavenward as well as any body. We hate poetry that has a

---

6. Edmund Kean, noted Shakespearean actor. His popularity in the early 19th century was contentious because he made no secret of his humble class origins. Keats had written an article on Kean for the *Champion*.
7. Charles Armitage Brown, John Hamilton Reynolds, and Charles Wentworth Dilke were all writers and friends of Keats. Keats interrupted the writing of this letter after the dash; beginning with "Brown & Dilke" he is writing several days after the preceding sentences.
8. Christmas pantomimes were performed each year at Drury Lane and Covent Garden theaters.
9. This famous and elusive phrase has been much discussed. Keats coins it so as to distinguish between, on the one hand, a poetry that is evidently shaped by the writer's personal interests and beliefs and, on the other hand, a poetry of impersonality that records the writer's receptivity to the "uncertainties" of experience. This second kind of poetry, in which a sense of beauty overcomes considerations of truth versus falsehood, is that produced by the poet of "negative capability." Cf. Keats's dislike, in his letter to John Hamilton Reynolds, February 3, 1818, of "poetry that has a palpable design upon us."
1. The Latin *penetralia* signified the innermost and most secret parts of a temple.
2. *Laon and Cythna* (1817), whose treatment of incest created scandal and which had to be withdrawn by the author. Shelley revised and republished it as *The Revolt of Islam* (1818). In *Queen Mab* (1813) Shelley had presented a radical program for the achievement of a millennial earthly state through the elimination of "kings, priests, and statesmen."
1. A close friend who was at this time an insurance clerk and also an able poet and man of letters.
2. Boundary.
3. Sancho Panza, the earthy squire in Cervantes's *Don Quixote*.

palpable design upon us—and if we do not agree, seems to put its hand in its breeches pocket.[4] Poetry should be great & unobtrusive, a thing which enters into one's soul, and does not startle it or amaze it with itself but with its subject.—How beautiful are the retired flowers! how would they lose their beauty were they to throng into the highway crying out, "admire me I am a violet! dote upon me I am a primrose! Modern poets differ from the Elizabethans in this. Each of the moderns like an Elector of Hanover governs his petty state, & knows how many straws are swept daily from the Causeways in all his dominions & has a continual itching that all the Housewives should have their coppers well scoured: the antients were ~~Emperors of large~~ Emperors of vast Provinces, they had only heard of the remote ones and scarcely cared to visit them.—I will cut all this—I will have no more of Wordsworth or Hunt[5] in particular—Why should we be of the tribe of Manasseh, when we can wander with Esau?[6] why should we kick against the Pricks, when we can walk on Roses? Why should we be owls, when we can be Eagles? Why be teased with "nice Eyed wagtails," when we have in sight "the Cherub Contemplation"?[7]—Why with Wordsworths "Matthew with a bough of wilding in his hand" when we can have Jacques "under an oak &c"[8]—The secret of the Bough of Wilding will run through your head faster than I can write it—Old Matthew spoke to him some years ago on some nothing, & because he happens in an Evening Walk to imagine the figure of the old man—he must stamp it down in black & white, and it is henceforth sacred—I don't mean to deny Wordsworth's grandeur & Hunt's merit, but I mean to say we need not be teazed with grandeur & merit—when we can have them uncontaminated & unobtrusive. Let us have the old Poets, & robin Hood[9] Your letter and its sonnets gave me more pleasure than will the 4th Book of Childe Harold[1] & the whole of any body's life & opinions. * * *

Y^r sincere friend and Coscribbler

John Keats.

To John Taylor[1]

[KEATS'S AXIOMS IN POETRY]

[February 27, 1818]

My dear Taylor,

Your alteration strikes me as being a great improvement—the page, looks much better. * * * It is a sorry thing for me that any one should have to overcome Prejudices in reading my Verses—that affects me more than any hypercriticism on any particular Passage. In *Endymion* I have most likely but moved into the Go-cart from the leading strings.[2] In Poetry I have a few

---

4. I.e., sulks and refuses to interact with us.
5. Leigh Hunt, a poet who earlier had strongly influenced Keats's style.
6. I.e., why should we carry on a conventional way of life (as did the tribe of Manasseh in Old Testament history) when we can become adventurers (like Esau, who sold his birthright in Genesis 25.29–34 and became an outlaw).
7. Milton, "Il Penseroso," line 54. "Nice Eyed wagtails": from Hunt's *Nymphs.*
8. Shakespeare's *As You Like It* 2.1.31. The Wordsworth phrase is from his poem "The Two

April Mornings." A "wilding" is a wild apple tree.
9. A reference to two sonnets on Robin Hood, written by Reynolds, which he had sent to Keats.
1. Canto 4 of Byron's *Childe Harold's Pilgrimage* was being eagerly awaited by English readers.
1. Partner in the publishing firm of Taylor and Hessey, to whom Keats wrote this letter while *Endymion* was being put through the press.
2. Go-carts were the wheeled walkers in which 19th-century toddlers learned to walk. Leading-strings were the harnesses with which they were guided and supported while they learned. Keats's

Axioms, and you will see how far I am from their Centre. 1st I think Poetry should surprise by a fine excess and not by Singularity—it should strike the Reader as a wording of his own highest thoughts, and appear almost a Remembrance—2nd Its touches of Beauty should never be half way therby making the reader breathless instead of content: the rise, the progress, the setting of imagery should like the Sun come natural natural too him—shine over him and set soberly although in magnificence leaving him in the Luxury of twilight—but it is easier to think what Poetry should be than to write it—and this leads me on to another axiom. That if Poetry comes not as naturally as the Leaves to a tree it had better not come at all. However it may be with me I cannot help looking into new countries with "O for a Muse of fire to ascend!"[3]—If Endymion serves me as a Pioneer perhaps I ought to be content. I have great reason to be content, for thank God I can read and perhaps understand Shakspeare to his depths, and I have I am sure many friends, who, if I fail, will attribute any change in my Life and Temper to Humbleness rather than to Pride—to a cowering under the Wings of great Poets rather than to a Bitterness that I am not appreciated. I am anxious to get Endymion printed that I may forget it and proceed. * * *

Your sincere and oblig[d] friend
John Keats—

P.S. You shall have a sho[r]t *Preface* in good time—

To John Hamilton Reynolds

[MILTON, WORDSWORTH, AND THE CHAMBERS OF HUMAN LIFE]

[May 3, 1818]

My dear Reynolds.

* * * Were I to study physic or rather Medicine again,—I feel it would not make the least difference in my Poetry; when the Mind is in its infancy a Bias is in reality a Bias, but when we have acquired more strength, a Bias becomes no Bias. Every department of knowledge we see excellent and calculated towards a great whole. I am so convinced of this, that I am glad at not having given away my medical Books, which I shall again look over to keep alive the little I know thitherwards; and moreover intend through you and Rice to become a sort of Pip-civilian.[1] An extensive knowledge is needful to thinking people—it takes away the heat and fever; and helps, by widening speculation, to ease the Burden of the Mystery:[2] a thing I begin to understand a little, and which weighed upon you in the most gloomy and true sentence in your Letter. The difference of high Sensations with and without knowledge appears to me this—in the latter case we are falling continually ten thousand fathoms deep and being blown up again without wings[3] and with all [the] horror of a ~~Case~~ bare shoulderd Creature—in the former case, our shoulders are fledged[4] and we go thro' the same ~~Fir~~ air and space without fear. * * *

point appears to be that as a poet he has not advanced and may even have regressed in *Endymion.*
3. Altered from Shakespeare's *Henry V,* Prologue, line 1.
1. Apparently "a small-scale layman." James Rice,

a lawyer, was one of Keats's favorite friends.
2. Wordsworth, "Tintern Abbey," line 38.
3. Recalls the description of Satan's flight through Chaos (Milton, *Paradise Lost* 2.933–34).
4. Grow wings.

You say "I fear there is little chance of any thing else in this life." You seem by that to have been going through with a more painful and acute ~~test~~ zest the same labyrinth that I have—I have come to the same conclusion thus far. My Branchings out therefrom have been numerous: one of them is the consideration of Wordsworth's genius and as a help, in the manner of gold being the meridian Line of worldly wealth,—how he differs from Milton.[5]— And here I have nothing but surmises, from an uncertainty whether Miltons apparently less anxiety for Humanity proceeds from his seeing further or no than Wordsworth: And whether Wordsworth has in truth epic passions, and martyrs himself to the human heart, the main region of his song[6]—In regard to his genius alone—we find what he says true as far as we have experienced and we can judge no further but by larger experience—for axioms in philosophy are not axioms until they are proved upon our pulses: We read fine——things but never feel them to [the] full until we have gone the same steps as the Author.—I know this is not plain; you will know exactly my meaning when I say, that now I shall relish Hamlet more than I ever have done—Or, better—You are sensible no man can set down Venery[7] as a bestial or joyless thing until he is sick of it and therefore all philosophizing on it would be mere wording. Until we are sick, we understand not;—in fine, as Byron says, "Knowledge is Sorrow";[8] and I go on to say that "Sorrow is Wisdom"—and further for aught we can know for certainty! "Wisdom is folly." * * *

I will return to Wordsworth—whether or no he has an extended vision or a circumscribed grandeur—whether he is an eagle in his nest, or on the wing—And to be more explicit and to show you how tall I stand by the giant, I will put down a simile of human life as far as I now perceive it; that is, to the point to which I say we both have arrived at—Well—I compare human life to a large Mansion of Many Apartments, two of which I can only describe, the doors of the rest being as yet shut upon me—The first we step into we call the infant or thoughtless Chamber, in which we remain as long as we do not think—We remain there a long while, and notwithstanding the doors of the second Chamber remain wide open, showing a bright appearance, we care not to hasten to it; but are at length imperceptibly impelled by the awakening of the thinking principle—within us—we no sooner get into the second Chamber, which I shall call the Chamber of Maiden-Thought,[9] than we become intoxicated with the light and the atmosphere, we see nothing but pleasant wonders, and think of delaying there for ever in delight: However among the effects this breathing is father of is that tremendous one of sharpening one's vision into the ~~head~~ heart and nature of Man—of convincing ones nerves that the World is full of Misery and Heartbreak, Pain, Sickness and oppression—whereby This Chamber of Maiden Thought becomes gradually darken'd and at the same time on all sides of it many doors are set open—but all dark—all leading to dark passages—We see not the ballance of good and evil. We are in a Mist—*We* are now in that state—We feel the "burden of the Mystery," To this point was Wordsworth come, as far as I can conceive when he wrote "Tintern Abbey" and it seems to me that his Genius

---

5. I.e., as gold is the standard of material wealth (in the way that the meridian line of Greenwich Observatory, England, is the reference for measuring degrees of longitude), so Milton is the standard of poetic value, by which we may measure Wordsworth.

6. In the Prospectus to *The Recluse*, Wordsworth,

laying out his poetic program, had identified "the Mind of Man" as "My haunt, and the main region of my song" (lines 40–41).

7. Sexual indulgence.

8. *Manfred* 1.1.10: "Sorrow is knowledge."

9. I.e., innocent thought, with the implication (as in "maiden voyage") of a first undertaking.

is explorative of those dark Passages. Now if we live, and go on thinking, we too shall explore them. he is a Genius and superior [to] us, in so far as he can, more than we, make discoveries, and shed a light in them—Here I must think Wordsworth is deeper than Milton—though I think it has depended more upon the general and gregarious advance of intellect, than individual greatness of Mind—From the Paradise Lost and the other Works of Milton, I hope it is not too presuming, even between ourselves to say, his Philosophy, human and divine, may be tolerably understood by one not much advanced in years, In his time englishmen were just emancipated from a great superstition—and Men had got hold of certain points and resting places in reasoning which were too newly born to be doubted, and too much ~~oppressed~~ opposed by the Mass of Europe not to be thought etherial and authentically divine—who could gainsay his ideas on virtue, vice, and Chastity in Comus, just at the time of the dismissal of Codpieces[1] and a hundred other disgraces? who would not rest satisfied with his hintings at good and evil in the Paradise Lost, when just free from the inquisition and burrning in Smithfield?[2] The Reformation produced such immediate and great benefits, that Protestantism was considered under the immediate eye of heaven, and its own remaining Dogmas and superstitions, then, as it were, regenerated, constituted those resting places and seeming sure points of Reasoning—from that I have mentioned, Milton, whatever he may have thought in the sequel,[3] appears to have been content with these by his writings—He did not think into the human heart, as Wordsworth has done—Yet Milton as a Philosop[h]er, had sure as great powers as Wordsworth—What is then to be inferr'd? O many things—It proves there is really a grand march of intellect—, It proves that a mighty providence subdues the mightiest Minds to the service of the time being, whether it be in human Knowledge or Religion— * * * Tom[4] has spit a leetle blood this afternoon, and that is rather a damper—but I know—the truth is there is something real in the World Your third Chamber of Life shall be a lucky and a gentle one—stored with the wine of love—and the Bread of friendship— * * *

Your affectionate friend
John Keats.

To Richard Woodhouse[1]

["A POET HAS NO IDENTITY"]

[October 27, 1818]

My dear Woodhouse,

Your Letter gave me a great satisfaction; more on account of its friendliness, than any relish of that matter in it which is accounted so acceptable in

---

1. In the 15th and 16th centuries, the codpiece was a flap, often ornamental, that covered an opening in the front of men's breeches. In Milton's masque the chastity of a young lady is put to the proof by the evil enchanter Comus.
2. An open place northwest of the walls of the City of London where, in the 16th century, heretics were burned.

3. Later on.
4. Keats's younger brother, then eighteen, who was dying of tuberculosis.
1. A young lawyer with literary interests who early recognized Keats's talents and prepared, or preserved, manuscript copies of many of his poems and letters.

the "genus irritabile"[2] The best answer I can give you is in a clerklike manner to make some observations on two principle points, which seem to point like indices into the midst of the whole pro and con, about genius, and views and atchievements and ambition and cœtera. 1st As to the poetical Character itself, (I mean that sort of which, if I am any thing, I am a Member; that sort distinguished from the wordsworthian or egotistical sublime; which is a thing per se and stands alone) it is not itself—it has no self—it is every thing and nothing—It has no character—it enjoys light and shade; it lives in gusto,[3] be it foul or fair, high or low, rich or poor, mean or elevated—It has as much delight in conceiving an Iago as an Imogen.[4] What shocks the virtuous philosop[h]er, delights the camelion[5] Poet. It does no harm from its relish of the dark side of things any more than from its taste for the bright one; because they both end in speculation.[6] A Poet is the most unpoetical of any thing in existence; because he has no Identity—he is continually in for[7]— and filling some other Body—The Sun, the Moon, the Sea and Men and Women who are creatures of impulse are poetical and have about them an unchangeable attribute—the poet has none; no identity—he is certainly the most unpoetical of all God's Creatures. If then he has no self, and if I am a Poet, where is the Wonder that I should say I would write no more? Might I not at that very instant [have] been cogitating on the Characters of saturn and Ops?[8] It is a wretched thing to confess; but is a very fact that not one word I ever utter can be taken for granted as an opinion growing out of my identical nature—how can it, when I have no nature? When I am in a room with People if I ever am free from speculating on creations of my own brain, then not myself goes home to myself: but the identity of every one in the room begins to to press upon me[9] that, I am in a very little time an[ni]hilated—not only among Men; it would be the same in a Nursery of children: I know not whether I make myself wholly understood: I hope enough so to let you see that no dependence is to be placed on what I said that day.

In the second place I will speak of my views, and of the life I purpose to myself—I am ambitious of doing the world some good: if I should be spared that may be the work of maturer years—in the interval I will assay to reach to as high a summit in Poetry as the nerve bestowed upon me will suffer. The faint conceptions I have of Poems to come brings the blood frequently into my forehead—All I hope is that I may not lose all interest in human affairs—that the solitary indifference I feel for applause even from the finest Spirits, will not blunt any acuteness of vision I may have. I do not think it will—I feel assured I should write from the mere yearning and fondness I have for the Beautiful even if my night's labours should be burnt every morning and no eye ever shine upon them. But even now I am perhaps not speaking from myself; but from some character in whose soul I now live. I

2. "The irritable race," a phrase Horace had applied to poets (*Epistles* 2.2.102).
3. Hazlitt had defined gusto in an 1816 essay as "power or passion."
4. Iago is the villain in Shakespeare's *Othello* and Imogen the virtuous heroine in his *Cymbeline*.
5. The chameleon is a lizard that camouflages itself by changing its color to match its surroundings.
6. I.e., without affecting our practical judgment or actions. Cf. Keats's discussion of the poet of "negative capability" in his letter to George and Thomas Keats begun on December 21, 1817 (p. 518).
7. Instead of "in for," Keats may have intended to write "informing."
8. Characters in Keats's *Hyperion*. Woodhouse had recently written Keats to express concern at a remark by the poet that, because former writers had preempted the best poetic materials and styles, there was nothing new left for the modern poet.
9. Perhaps "*so* to press upon me."

am sure however that this next sentence is from myself. I feel your anxiety, good opinion and friendliness in the highest degree, and am

Your's most sincerely
John Keats

To George and Georgiana Keats[1]

[["THE VALE OF SOUL-MAKING"]]

[February 14–May 3, 1819]

My dear Brother & Sister—

* * * I have this moment received a note from Haslam[2] in which he expects the death of his Father who has been for some time in a state of insensibility—his mother bears up he says very well—I shall go to [town] tommorow to see him. This is the world—thus we cannot expect to give way many hours to pleasure—Circumstances are like Clouds continually gathering and bursting—While we are laughing the seed of some trouble is put into ~~he~~ the wide arable land of events—while we are laughing it sprouts [it] grows and suddenly bears a poison fruit which we must pluck—Even so we have leisure to reason on the misfortunes of our friends; our own touch us too nearly for words. Very few men have ever arrived at a complete disinterestedness[3] of Mind: very few have been influenced by a pure desire of the benefit of others—in the greater part of the Benefactors ~~of~~ & to Humanity some meretricious motive has sullied their greatness—some melodramatic scenery has facinated them—From the manner in which I feel Haslam's misfortune I perceive how far I am from any humble standard of disinterestedness—Yet this feeling ought to be carried to its highest pitch, as there is no fear of its ever injuring society—which it would do I fear pushed to an extremity—For in wild nature the Hawk would loose his Breakfast of Robins and the Robin his of Worms The Lion must starve as well as the swallow—The greater part of Men make their way with the same instinctiveness, the same unwandering eye from their purposes, the same animal eagerness as the Hawk—The Hawk wants a Mate, so does the Man—look at them both they set about it and procure on[e] in the same manner—They want both a nest and they both set about one in the same manner—they get their food in the same manner—The noble animal Man for his amusement smokes his pipe—the Hawk balances about the Clouds—that is the only difference of their leisures. This it is that makes the Amusement of Life—to a speculative Mind. I go among the Feilds and catch a glimpse of a stoat[4] or a fieldmouse peeping out of the withered grass—the creature hath a purpose and its eyes are bright with it—I go amongst the buildings of a city and I see a Man hurrying along—to what? The Creature has a purpose and his eyes are bright with it. But then as Wordsworth says, "we have all one human heart"[5]—there is an ellectric fire in human nature

---

1. Keats's brother and his wife, who had emigrated to Louisville, Kentucky, in 1818. This is part of a long letter that Keats wrote over a period of several months, and into which he transcribed several of his poems, including "Ode to Psyche." The date of this first extract is March 19.

2. William Haslam, a young businessman and close friend.
3. Transcendence of self-interest, of one's selfish instincts.
4. A weasel.
5. "The Old Cumberland Beggar," line 153.

tending to purify—so that among these human creature[s] there is continually some birth of new heroism—The pity is that we must wonder at it: as we should at finding a pearl in rubbish—I have no doubt that thousands of people never heard of have had hearts completely disinterested: I can remember but two—Socrates and Jesus—their Histories evince it—What I heard a little time ago, Taylor observe with respect to Socrates, may be said of Jesus—That he was so great as man that though he transmitted no writing of his own to posterity, we have his Mind and his sayings and his greatness handed to us by others. It is to be lamented that the history of the latter was written and revised by Men interested in the pious frauds of Religion. Yet through all this I see his splendour. Even here though I myself am pursueing the same instinctive course as the veriest human animal you can think of—I am however young writing at random—straining at particles of light in the midst of a great darkness—without knowing the bearing of any one assertion of any one opinion. Yet may I not in this be free from sin? May there not be superior beings amused with any graceful, though instinctive attitude my mind [may] fall into, as I am entertained with the alertness of a Stoat or the anxiety of a Deer? Though a quarrel in the streets is a thing to be hated, the energies displayed in it are fine; the commonest Man shows a grace in his quarrel—By a superior being our reasoning[s] may take the same tone—though erroneous they may be fine—This is the very thing in which consists poetry; and if so it is not so fine a thing as philosophy—For the same reason that an eagle is not so fine a thing as a truth—Give me this credit—Do you not think I strive—to know myself? Give me this credit—and you will not think that on my own accou[n]t I repeat Milton's lines

> "How charming is divine Philosophy
> Not harsh and crabbed as dull fools suppose
> But musical as is Apollo's lute"—[6]

No—no for myself—feeling grateful as I do to have got into a state of mind to relish them properly—Nothing ever becomes real till it is experienced—Even a Proverb is no proverb to you till your Life has illustrated it— * * *

    * * * I have been reading lately two very different books Robertson's America and Voltaire's Siecle De Louis xiv[7] It is like walking arm and arm between Pizarro and the great-little Monarch.[8] In How lementabl[e] a case do we see the great body of the people in both instances: in the first, where Men might seem to inherit quiet of Mind from unsophisticated senses; from uncontamination of civilisation; and especially from their being as it were estranged from the mutual helps of Society and its mutual injuries—and thereby more immediately under the Protection of Providence—even there they had mortal pains to bear as bad; or even worse than Baliffs,[9] Debts and Poverties of civilised Life—The whole appears to resolve into this—that Man is originally "a poor forked creature"[1] subject to the same mischances as the beasts of the forest, destined to hardships and disquietude of some kind or other. If he improves by degrees his bodily accommodations and comforts—at each stage, at each accent there are waiting for him a fresh set of annoyances—he is mor-

6. *Comus*, lines 475–77.
7. Two books of history, Voltaire's *Le Siècle de Louis XIV* (1751) and William Robertson's *The History of America* (1777). In this second extract from the journal-letter, Keats is writing toward the end of April (on the 21st or 28th).
8. Francisco Pizarro, the Spanish explorer whose exploits are described in Robertson's *America*. The "Monarch" is Louis XIV of France.
9. Bailiffs: officers of the law whose duties included making arrests for bad debts.
1. Shakespeare's *King Lear* 3.4.95–97. Lear says of "Poor Tom," "Unaccommodated man is no more but such a poor, bare, forked animal as thou art."

tal and there is still a heaven with its Stars abov[e] his head. The most interesting question that can come before us is, How far by the persevering endeavours of a seldom appearing Socrates Mankind may be made happy—I can imagine such happiness carried to an extreme—but what must it end in?—Death—and who could in such a case bear with death—the whole troubles of life which are now frittered away in a series of years, would the[n] be accumulated for the last days of a being who instead of hailing its approach, would leave this world as Eve left Paradise—But in truth I do not at all believe in this sort of perfectibility—the nature of the world will not admit of it—the inhabitants of the world will correspond to itself—Let the fish philosophise the ice away from the Rivers in winter time and they shall be at continual play in the tepid delight of summer. Look at the Poles and at the sands of Africa, Whirlpools and volcanoes—Let men exterminate them and I will say that they may arrive at earthly Happiness—The point at which Man may arrive is as far as the paralel state in inanimate nature and no further—For instance suppose a rose to have sensation, it blooms on a beautiful morning it enjoys itself—but there comes a cold wind, a hot sun—it can not escape it, it cannot destroy its annoyances—they are as native to the world as itself: no more can man be happy in spite, the world[l]y elements will prey upon his nature—The common cognomen of this world among the misguided and superstitious is "a vale of tears" from which we are to be redeemed by a certain arbitrary interposition of God and taken to Heaven—What a little circumscribe[d] straightened notion! Call the world if you Please "The vale of Soul-making" Then you will find out the use of the world (I am speaking now in the highest terms for human nature admitting it to be immortal which I will here take for granted for the purpose of showing a thought which has struck me concerning it) I say "*Soul making*" Soul as distinguished from an Intelligence—There may be intelligences or sparks of the divinity in millions—but they are not Souls the till they acquire identities, till each one is personally itself. I[n]telligences are atoms of perception—they know and they see and they are pure, in short they are God—how then are Souls to be made? How then are these sparks which are God to have identity given them—so as ever to possess a bliss peculiar to each ones individual existence? How, but by the medium of a world like this? This point I sincerely wish to consider because I think it a grander system of salvation than the chrystean religion—or rather it is a system of Spirit-creation[2]—This is effected by three grand materials acting the one upon the other for a series of years—These three Materials are the *Intelligence*—the *human heart* (as distinguished from intelligence or Mind) and the *World* or *Elemental space* suited for the proper action of *Mind and Heart* on each other for the purpose of forming the *Soul* or *Intelligence destined to possess the sense of Identity.* I can scarcely express what I but dimly perceive—and yet I think I perceive it—that you may judge the more clearly I will put it in the most homely form possible—I will call the *world* a School instituted for the purpose of teaching little children to read—I will call the *human heart* the *horn Book*[3] used in that School—and I will call the *Child able to read, the Soul* made from

2. Keats is struggling for an analogy that will embody his solution to the ancient riddle of evil, as an alternative to what he understands to be the Christian view: that evil exists as a test of the individual's worthiness of salvation in heaven, and this world is only a proving ground for a later and better life. Keats proposes that the function of the human experience of sorrow and pain is to feed and discipline the formless and unstocked "intelligence" that we possess at birth and thus to shape it into a rich and coherent "identity," or "soul." This result provides a justification ("salvation") for our suffering in terms of our earthly life: i.e., experience is its own reward.

3. A child's primer, which used to consist of a sheet of paper mounted on thin wood, protected by a sheet of transparent horn.

that *school* and its *hornbook*. Do you not see how necessary a World of Pains and troubles is to school an Intelligence and make it a soul? A Place where the heart must feel and suffer in a thousand diverse ways! Not merely is the Heart a Hornbook, It is the Minds Bible, it is the Minds experience, it is the teat from which the Mind or intelligence sucks its identity—As various as the Lives of Men are—so various become their souls, and thus does God make individual beings, Souls, Identical Souls of the sparks of his own essence— This appears to me a faint sketch of a system of Salvation which does not affront our reason and humanity—I am convinced that many difficulties which christians labour under would vanish before it—There is one wh[i]ch even now Strikes me—the Salvation of Children—In them the Spark or intelligence returns to God without any identity—it having had no time to learn of, and be altered by, the heart—or seat of the human Passions—It is pretty generally suspected that the chr[i]stian scheme has been coppied from the ancient persian and greek Philosophers. Why may they not have made this simple thing even more simple for common apprehension by introducing Mediators and Personages in the same manner as in the hethen mythology abstractions are personified—Seriously I think it probable that this System of Soul-making—may have been the Parent of all the more palpable and personal Schemes of Redemption, among the Zoroastrians the Christians and the Hindoos. For as one part of the human species must have their carved Jupiter; so another part must have the palpable and named Mediatior and saviour, their Christ their Oromanes and their Vishnu[4]—If what I have said should not be plain enough, as I fear it may not be, I will [put] you in the place where I began in this series of thoughts—I mean, I began by seeing how man was formed by circumstances—and what are circumstances?—but touchstones of his heart—? and what are touch stones?—but proovings of his hearrt?[5]—and what are proovings of his heart but fortifiers or alterers of his nature? and what is his altered nature but his soul?—and what was his soul before it came into the world and had These provings and alterations and perfectionings?—An intelligences—without Identity—and how is this Identity to be made? Through the medium of the Heart? And how is the heart to become this Medium but in a world of Circumstances?—There now I think what with Poetry and Theology you may thank your Stars that my pen is not very long winded— * * *

This is the 3d of May & every thing is in delightful forwardness; the violets are not withered, before the peeping of the first rose; You must let me know every thing, how parcels go & come, what papers you have, & what Newspapers you want, & other things—God bless you my dear Brother & Sister
Your ever Affectionate Brother
John Keats—

---

4. The deity who creates and preserves the world, in Hindu belief. Oromanes (Ahriman) was the principle of evil, locked in a persisting struggle with Ormazd, the principle of good, in the Zoroastrian religion of ancient Persia.

5. I.e., experiences by which the human heart is put to the test.

To Fanny Brawne

[FANNY BRAWNE AS KEATS'S "FAIR STAR"]

[July 25, 1819]

My sweet Girl,

I hope you did not blame me much for not obeying your request of a Letter on Saturday: we have had four in our small room playing at cards night and morning leaving me no undisturb'd opportunity to write. Now Rice and Martin are gone I am at liberty. Brown to my sorrow confirms the account you give of your ill health. You cannot conceive how I ache to be with you: how I would die for one hour——for what is in the world? I say you cannot conceive; it is impossible you should look with such eyes upon me as I have upon you: it cannot be. Forgive me if I wander a little this evening, for I have been all day employ'd in a very abstr[a]ct Poem[1] and I am in deep love with you—two things which must excuse me. I have, believe me, not been an age in letting you take possession of me; the very first week I knew you I wrote myself your vassal; but burnt the Letter as the very next time I saw you I thought you manifested some dislike to me. If you should ever feel for Man at the first sight what I did for you, I am lost. Yet I should not quarrel with you, but hate myself if such a thing were to happen—only I should burst if the thing were not as fine as a Man as you are as a Woman. Perhaps I am too vehement, then fancy me on my knees, especially when I mention a part of your Letter which hurt me; you say speaking of Mr. Severn[2] "but you must be satisfied in knowing that I admired you much more than your friend." My dear love, I cannot believe there ever was or ever could be any thing to admire in me especially as far as sight goes—I cannot be admired, I am not a thing to be admired. You are, I love you; all I can bring you is a swooning admiration of your Beauty. I hold that place among Men which snub-nos'd brunettes with meeting eyebrows do among women—they are trash to me—unless I should find one among them with a fire in her heart like the one that burns in mine. You absorb me in spite of myself—you alone: for I look not forward with any pleasure to what is call'd being settled in the world; I tremble at domestic cares—yet for you I would meet them, though if it would leave you the happier I would rather die than do so. I have two luxuries to brood over in my walks, your Loveliness and the hour of my death. O that I could have possession of them both in the same minute. I hate the world: it batters too much the wings of my self-will, and would I could take a sweet poison from your lips to send me out of it. From no others would I take it. I am indeed astonish'd to find myself so careless of all cha[r]ms but yours—remembring as I do the time when even a bit of ribband was a matter of interest with me. What softer words can I find for you after this—what it is I will not read. Nor will I say more here, but in a Postscript answer any thing else you may have mentioned in your Letter in so many words—for I am distracted with a thousand thoughts. I will imagine you Venus tonight and pray, pray, pray to your star like a Hethen.[3]

Your's ever, fair Star,

John Keats.

---

1. Probably *The Fall of Hyperion*.
2. Joseph Severn, who later looked after Keats in Rome during his final illness.

3. See Keats's sonnet "Bright star" (p. 487) for parallels to this and other remarks in the present letter.

To Percy Bysshe Shelley[1]

["LOAD EVERY RIFT WITH ORE"]

[August 16, 1820]

My dear Shelley,

I am very much gratified that you, in a foreign country, and with a mind almost over occupied, should write to me in the strain of the Letter beside me. If I do not take advantage of your invitation it will be prevented by a circumstance I have very much at heart to prophesy[2]—There is no doubt that an english winter would put an end to me, and do so in a lingering hateful manner, therefore I must either voyage or journey to Italy as a soldier marches up to a battery. My nerves at present are the worst part of me, yet they feel soothed when I think that come what extreme may, I shall not be destined to remain in one spot long enough to take a hatred of any four particular bedposts. I am glad you take any pleasure in my poor Poem;[3]— which I would willingly take the trouble to unwrite, if possible, did I care so much as I have done about Reputation. I received a copy of the Cenci,[4] as from yourself from Hunt. There is only one part of it I am judge of; the Poetry, and dramatic effect, which by many spirits now a days is considered the mammon. A modern work it is said must have a purpose,[5] which may be the God—*an artist* must serve Mammon—he must have "self concentration" selfishness perhaps. You I am sure will forgive me for sincerely remarking that you might curb your magnanimity and be more of an artist, and "load every rift"[6] of your subject with ore. The thought of such discipline must fall like cold chains upon you, who perhaps never sat with your wings furl'd for six Months together. And is not this extraordinary talk for the writer of Endymion? whose mind was like a pack of scattered cards—I am pick'd up and sorted to a pip.[7] My Imagination is a Monastry and I am its Monk—you must explain my metap^{cs}[8] to yourself. I am in expectation of Prometheus[9] every day. Could I have my own wish for its interest effected you would have it still in manuscript—or be but now putting an end to the second act. I remember you advising me not to publish my first-blights, on Hampstead heath—I am returning advice upon your hands. Most of the Poems in the volume I send you[1] have been written above two years, and would never have been publish'd but from a hope of gain; so you see I am inclined enough to take your advice now. I must exp[r]ess once more my deep sense of your kindness, adding my sincere thanks and respects for Mrs Shelley. In the hope of soon seeing you I remain

most sincerely yours,
John Keats—

1. Written in reply to a letter urging Keats (who was ill) to spend the winter with the Shelleys in Pisa.
2. His own death.
3. Keats's *Endymion*, Shelley had written, contains treasures, "though treasures poured forth, with indistinct profusion." Keats here responds with advice in kind.
4. Shelley's blank-verse tragedy, *The Cenci*, had been published in the spring of 1820.
5. Wordsworth had said this in his Preface to *Lyrical Ballads*. For "Mammon" see Matthew 6.24 and Luke 16.13: "Ye cannot serve God and mammon."
6. From Spenser's description of the Cave of Mammon in *The Faerie Queene* 2.7.28: "With rich metall loaded every rifte."
7. Perfectly ordered; all the suits in the deck matched up ("pips" are the conventional spots on playing cards).
8. Metaphysics.
9. *Prometheus Unbound*, of which Shelley had promised Keats a copy.
1. Keats's volume of 1820, including *Lamia, The Eve of St. Agnes*, and the odes. When Shelley drowned he had this small book in his pocket.

To Charles Brown[1]

[KEATS'S LAST LETTER]

Rome. 30 November 1820.

My dear Brown,

'Tis the most difficult thing in the world to me to write a letter. My stomach continues so bad, that I feel it worse on opening any book,—yet I am much better than I was in Quarantine.[2] Then I am afraid to encounter the proing and conning of any thing interesting to me in England. I have an habitual feeling of my real life having past, and that I am leading a posthumous existence. God knows how it would have been—but it appears to me—however, I will not speak of that subject. I must have been at Bedhampton nearly at the time you were writing to me from Chichester[3]—how unfortunate—and to pass on the river too! There was my star predominant![4] I cannot answer any thing in your letter, which followed me from Naples to Rome, because I am afraid to look it over again. I am so weak (in mind) that I cannot bear the sight of any hand writing of a friend I love so much as I do you. Yet I ride the little horse,—and, at my worst, even in Quarantine, summoned up more puns, in a sort of desperation, in one week than in any year of my life. There is one thought enough to kill me—I have been well, healthy, alert &c, walking with her[5]—and now—the knowledge of contrast, feeling for light and shade, all that information (primitive sense) necessary for a poem are great enemies to the recovery of the stomach. There, you rogue, I put you to the torture,—but you must bring your philosophy to bear—as I do mine, really—or how should I be able to live? D[r] Clarke is very attentive to me; he says, there is very little the matter with my lungs, but my stomach, he says, is very bad. I am well disappointed in hearing good news from George,—for it runs in my head we shall all die young. I have not written to x x x x x yet,[6] which he must think very neglectful; being anxious to send him a good account of my health, I have delayed it from week to week. If I recover, I will do all in my power to correct the mistakes made during sickness; and if I should not, all my faults will be forgiven. I shall write to x x x to-morrow, or next day. I will write to x x x x x in the middle of next week. Severn is very well, though he leads so dull a life with me. Remember me to all friends, and tell x x x x I should not have left London without taking leave of him, but from being so low in body and mind. Write to George as soon as you receive this, and tell him how I am, as far as you can guess;—and also a note to my sister— who walks about my imagination like a ghost—she is so like Tom.[7] I can scarcely bid you good bye even in a letter. I always made an awkward bow.

God bless you!
John Keats.

1. Written to Keats's friend Charles Armitage Brown from the house on the Spanish Steps, in the Piazza di Spagna, where Keats was being tended in his mortal illness by the devoted Joseph Severn.
2. When it landed at Naples, Keats's ship had been quarantined for ten miserably hot days.
3. Bedhampton and Chichester are both near the harbor town of Portsmouth, where Keats had embarked for Naples two months before.
4. I.e., that was my usual luck. Cf. Shakespeare's The Winter's Tale 1.2.202–3: "It is a bawdy planet, that will strike / Where 'tis predominant."
5. Fanny Brawne.
6. Charles Brown, whose manuscript transcription is the only text for this letter, substituted crosses for the names of Keats's friends to conceal their identities.
7. Keats's youngest brother, whom Fanny, his only sister, closely resembled, had died of tuberculosis on December 1, 1818. George was John Keats's younger brother.

The Victorian Age
1830–1901

In 1897 Mark Twain was visiting London during the Diamond Jubilee celebrations honoring the sixtieth anniversary of Queen Victoria's coming to the throne. "British history is two thousand years old," Twain observed, "and yet in a good many ways the world has moved farther ahead since the Queen was born than it moved in all the rest of the two thousand put together." And if the whole world had "moved" during that long lifetime and reign of Victoria's, it was in her own country itself that the change was most marked and dramatic, a change that brought England to its highest point of development as a world power.

In the eighteenth century the pivotal city of Western civilization had been Paris; by the second half of the nineteenth century this center of influence had shifted to London, a city that expanded from about two million inhabitants when Victoria came to the throne to six and a half million at the time of her death. The rapid growth of London is one of the many indications of the most important development of the age: the shift from a way of life based on the ownership of land to a modern urban economy based on trade and manufacturing. "We have been living, as it were, the life of three hundred years in thirty" was the impression formed by Dr. Thomas Arnold during the early stages of

---

Work (detail), Ford Madox Brown, 1852. For more information about this image, see the color insert in this volume.

England's industrialization. By the end of the century—after the resources of steam power had been more fully exploited for fast railways and iron ships, looms, printing presses, and farmers' combines, and after the introduction of the telegraph, intercontinental cable, photography, anesthetics, and universal compulsory education—a late Victorian could look back with astonishment on these developments during his or her lifetime. Walter Besant, one of these late Victorians, observed that so completely transformed were "the mind and habits of the ordinary Englishman" by 1897, "that he would not, could he see him, recognize his own grandfather."

Because England was the first country to become industrialized, its transformation was an especially painful one: it experienced a host of social and economic problems consequent to rapid and unregulated industrialization. England also experienced an enormous increase in wealth. An early start enabled England to capture markets all over the globe. Cotton and other manufactured products were exported in English ships, a merchant fleet whose size was without parallel in other countries. The profits gained from trade led also to extensive capital investments in all continents. After England had become the world's workshop, London became, from 1870 on, the world's banker. England gained particular profit from the development of its own colonies, which, by 1890, comprised more than a quarter of all the territory on the surface of the earth; one in four people was a subject of Queen Victoria. By the end of the century England was the world's foremost imperial power.

The reactions of Victorian writers to the fast-paced expansion of England were various. Thomas Babington Macaulay (1800–1859) relished the spectacle with enthusiasm. During the prosperous 1850s Macaulay's essays and histories, with their recitations of the statistics of industrial growth, constituted a Hymn to Progress as well as a celebration of the superior qualities of the English people—"the greatest and most highly civilized people that ever the world saw." Other writers felt that leadership in commerce and industry was being paid for at a terrible price in human happiness, that a so-called progress had been gained only by abandoning traditional rhythms of life and traditional patterns of human relationships. The melancholy poetry of Matthew Arnold often strikes this note:

> For what wears out the life of mortal men?
> 'Tis that from change to change their being rolls;
> 'Tis that repeated shocks, again, again,
> Exhaust the energy of strongest souls.

Although many Victorians shared a sense of satisfaction in the industrial and political preeminence of England during the period, they also suffered from an anxious sense of something lost, a sense too of being displaced persons in a world made alien by technological changes that had been exploited too quickly for the adaptive powers of the human psyche. In concert with the era's profound challenges to the security of traditional religious beliefs, these changes tempered the triumphalism of the Victorian spirit with, at times, an anxious and self-questioning melancholy.

QUEEN VICTORIA AND THE VICTORIAN TEMPER

Queen Victoria's long reign, from 1837 to 1901, defines the historical period that bears her name. The question naturally arises whether the distinctive character of those years justifies the adjective *Victorian*. In part Victoria herself encouraged her own identification with the qualities we associate with the adjective—earnestness, moral responsibility, domestic propriety. As a young wife, as the mother of nine children, and as the black-garbed Widow of Windsor in the forty years after her husband's death in 1861, Victoria represented the domestic fidelities her citizens embraced. After her death Henry James wrote, "I mourn the safe and motherly old middle-class queen, who held the nation warm under the fold of her big, hideous Scotch-plaid shawl." Changes in the reproduction of visual images aided in making her the icon she became. She is the first British monarch of whom we have photographs. These pictures, and the ease and cheapness with which they were reproduced, facilitated her representing her country's sense of itself during her reign.

Victoria came to the throne in a decade that does seem to mark a different historical consciousness among Britain's writers. In 1831 John Stuart Mill asserts, "we are living in an age of transition." In the same year Thomas Carlyle writes, "The Old has passed away, but alas, the New appears not in its stead; the Time is still in pangs of travail with the New." Although the historical changes that created the England of the 1830s had been in progress for many decades, writers of the thirties shared a sharp new sense of modernity, of a break with the past, of historical self-consciousness. They responded to

The Royal Family, Francis Xavier Winterhalter, 1846.

their sense of the historical moment with a call to action that they self-consciously distinguished from the attitude of the previous generation.

In 1834 Carlyle urged his contemporaries, "Close thy *Byron*; open thy *Goethe*." He was saying, in effect, to abandon the introspection of the Romantics and to turn to the higher moral purpose that he found in Goethe. The popular novelist Edward Bulwer-Lytton in his *England and the English* (1833) made a similar judgment. "When Byron passed away," he wrote, ". . . we turned to the actual and practical career of life: we awoke from the morbid, the dreaming, 'the moonlight and dimness of the mind,' and by a natural reaction addressed ourselves to the active and daily objects which lay before us." This sense of historical self-consciousness, of strenuous social enterprise, and of growing national achievement led writers as early as the 1850s and 1860s to define their age as Victorian. The very fact that Victoria reigned for so long sustained the concept of a distinctive historical period that writers defined even as they lived it.

When Queen Victoria died, a reaction developed against many of the achievements of the previous century; this reinforced the sense that the Victorian age was a distinct period. In the earlier decades of the twentieth century, writers took pains to separate themselves from the Victorians. It was then the fashion for most literary critics to treat their Victorian predecessors as somewhat absurd creatures, stuffily complacent prigs with whose way of life they had little in common. Writers of the Georgian period (1911–36) took great delight in puncturing overinflated Victorian balloons, as Lytton Strachey, a member of Virginia Woolf's circle, did in *Eminent Victorians* (1918). A subtler example occurs in Woolf's *Orlando* (1928), a fictionalized survey of English literature from Elizabethan times to 1928, in which the Victorians are presented in terms of dampness, rain, and proliferating vegetation:

> Ivy grew in unparalleled profusion. Houses that had been of bare stone were smothered in greenery. . . . And just as the ivy and the evergreen rioted in the damp earth outside, so did the same fertility show itself within. The life of the average woman was a succession of childbirths. . . . Giant cauliflowers towered deck above deck till they rivaled . . . the elm trees themselves. Hens laid incessantly eggs of no special tint. . . . The whole sky itself as it spread wide above the British Isles was nothing but a vast feather bed.

This witty description not only identifies a distinguishing quality of Victorian life and literature—a superabundant energy—but reveals the author's distaste for its smothering profusion. Woolf was the daughter of Sir Leslie Stephen (1832–1904), an eminent Victorian. In her later life, when assessing her father's powerful personality, Woolf recorded in her diary that she could never have become a writer if he had not died when he did. Growing up under such towering shadows, she and her generation mocked their predecessors to make them less intimidating. In his reminiscences *Portraits from Life* (1937), the novelist Ford Madox Ford recalled his feelings of terror when he confronted the works of Carlyle and Ruskin, which he likened to an overpowering range of high mountains. The mid-Victorians, he wrote, were "a childish nightmare to me."

The Georgian reaction against the Victorians is now only a matter of the history of taste, but its aftereffects still sometimes crop up when the term *Victorian* is employed in an exclusively pejorative sense, as prudish or old-fashioned. Contemporary historians and critics find the Victorian period a richly complex example of a society struggling with the issues and problems we identify with modernism. But to give the period the single designation *Victorian* reduces its complexity. Since it is a period of almost seventy years, we can hardly expect generalizations to be uniformly applicable. It is, therefore, helpful to subdivide the age into three phases: early Victorian (1830–48), mid-Victorian (1848–70), and late Victorian (1870–1901). It is also helpful to consider the final decade, the nineties, as a bridge between two centuries.

THE EARLY PERIOD (1830–48): A TIME OF TROUBLES

In the early 1830s two historical events occurred of momentous consequence for England. In 1830 the Liverpool and Manchester Railway opened, becoming the first steam-powered, public railway line in the world. A burst of railway construction followed. By 1850 6,621 miles of railway line connected all of England's major cities. By 1900 England had 15,195 lines of track and an underground railway system beneath London. The train transformed England's landscape, supported the growth of its commerce, and shrank the distances between its cities. The opening of England's first railway coincided with the opening of the country's Reform Parliament. The railway had increased the pressure for parliamentary reform. "Parliamentary reform must follow soon after the opening of this road," a Manchester man observed in 1830. "A million of persons will pass over it in the course of this year, and see that hitherto unseen village of Newton; and they must be convinced of the absurdity of its sending two members to Parliament while Manchester sends none." Despite the growth of manufacturing cities consequent to the Industrial Revolution, England was still governed by an archaic electoral system whereby some of the new industrial cities were unrepresented in Parliament while "rotten boroughs" (communities that had become depopulated) elected the nominees of the local squire to Parliament.

By 1830 a time of economic distress had brought England close to revolution. Manufacturing interests, who refused to tolerate their exclusion from the political process any longer, led working men in agitating for reform. Fearing the kind of revolution it had seen in Europe, Parliament passed a Reform Bill in 1832 that transformed England's class structure. The Reform Bill of 1832 extended the right to vote to all males owning property worth £10 or more in annual rent. In effect the voting public thereafter included the lower middle classes but not the working classes, who did not obtain the vote until 1867, when a second Reform Bill was passed. Even more important than the extension of the franchise was the virtual abolition of the rotten boroughs and the redistribution of parliamentary representation. Because it broke up the monopoly of power that the conservative landowners had so long enjoyed (the Tory party had been in office almost continuously from 1783 to 1830), the Reform Bill represents the beginning of a new age, in which middle-class economic interests gained increasing power.

Yet even the newly constituted Parliament was unable to find legislative solutions to the problems facing the nation. The economic and social difficulties attendant on industrialization were so severe that the 1830s and 1840s became known as the Time of Troubles. After a period of prosperity from 1832 to 1836, a crash in 1837, followed by a series of bad harvests, produced a period of unemployment, desperate poverty, and rioting. Conditions in the new industrial and coal-mining areas were terrible. Workers and their families in the slums of such cities as Manchester lived in horribly crowded, unsanitary housing; and the conditions under which men, women, and children toiled in mines and factories were unimaginably brutal. Elizabeth Barrett's poem "The Cry of the Children" (1843) expresses her horrified response to an official report on child labor that described five-year-olds sitting alone in darkness to open and close ventilation doors, and twelve-year-olds dragging heavy tubs of coal through low-ceilinged mine passages for sixteen hours a day.

The owners of mines and factories regarded themselves as innocent of blame for such conditions, for they were wedded to an economic theory of laissez-faire, which assumed that unregulated working conditions would ultimately benefit everyone. A sense of the seemingly hopeless complexity of the situation during the Hungry Forties is provided by an entry for 1842 in the diary of the statesman Charles Greville, an entry written at the same time that Carlyle was making his contribution to the "Condition of England Question," *Past and Present*. Conditions in the north of England, Greville reports, were "appalling."

> There is an immense and continually increasing population, no adequate demand for labor, . . . no confidence, but a universal alarm, disquietude, and discontent. Nobody can sell anything. . . . Certainly I have never seen . . . so serious a state of things as that which now stares us in the face; and this after thirty years of uninterrupted peace, and the most ample scope afforded for the development of all our resources. . . . One remarkable feature in the present condition of affairs is that nobody can account for it, and nobody pretends to be able to point out any remedy.

In reality many remedies were proposed. One of the most striking was put forward by the Chartists, a large organization of workers. In 1838 the organization drew up a "People's Charter" advocating the extension of the right to vote, the use of secret balloting, and other legislative reforms. For ten years the Chartist leaders engaged in agitation to have their program adopted by Parliament. Their fiery speeches, delivered at conventions designed to collect signatures for petitions to Parliament, created fears of revolution. In "Locksley Hall" (1842), Alfred, Lord Tennyson seems to have had the Chartist demonstrations in mind when he wrote: "Slowly comes a hungry people, as a lion, creeping nigher, / Glares at one that nods and winks behind a slowly-dying fire." Although the Chartist movement had fallen apart by 1848, it succeeded in creating an atmosphere open to reform. One of the most important reforms was the abolition of the high tariffs on imported grains, tariffs known as the Corn Laws (the word *corn* in England refers to wheat and other grains). These high tariffs had been established to protect English farm products from having to compete with low-priced products imported from abroad. Landowners and farmers fought to keep these tariffs in force so that high prices for their wheat would be ensured; but the rest of the population suffered severely from the exorbitant price of bread or, in years of bad crops, from scarcity of food. In 1845 serious crop failures in England and the outbreak of potato blight in Ireland convinced Sir Robert Peel, the Tory prime minister, that traditional protectionism must be abandoned. In 1846 the Corn Laws were repealed by Parliament, and the way was paved for the introduction of a system of free trade whereby goods could be imported

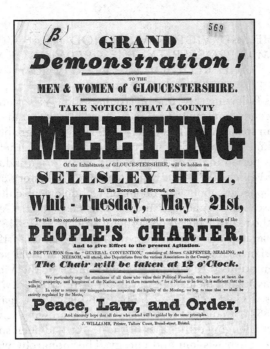

Chartism. Announcement of a Chartist meeting in Gloucestershire, 1839.

with the payment of only minimal tariff duties. Although free trade did not eradicate the slums of Manchester, it worked well for many years and helped relieve the major crisis of the Victorian economy. In 1848, when revolutions were breaking out all over Europe, England was relatively unaffected. A large Chartist demonstration in London seemed to threaten violence, but it came to nothing. The next two decades were relatively calm and prosperous.

This Time of Troubles left its mark on some early Victorian literature. "Insurrection is a most sad necessity," Carlyle writes in his *Past and Present*, "and governors who wait for that to instruct them are surely getting into the fatalest courses." A similar refrain runs through Carlyle's history *The French Revolution* (1837). Memories of the French Reign of Terror lasted longer than memories of British victories over Napoleon at Trafalgar and Waterloo, memories freshened by later outbreaks of civil strife, "the red fool-fury of the Seine" as Tennyson described one of the violent overturnings of government in France. The most marked response to the industrial and political scene, however, comes in the "Condition of England" novels of the 1840s and early 1850s. Vivid records of these times are to be found in the fiction of Charles Kingsley (1819–1875); Elizabeth Gaskell (1810–1865); and Benjamin Disraeli (1804–1881), a novelist who became prime minister. For his novel *Sybil* (1845), Disraeli chose an appropriate subtitle, *The Two Nations*—a phrase that pointed out the line dividing the England of the rich from the other nation, the England of the poor.

THE MID-VICTORIAN PERIOD (1848–70):
ECONOMIC PROSPERITY, THE GROWTH OF EMPIRE,
AND RELIGIOUS CONTROVERSY

In the decades following the Time of Troubles some Victorian writers, such as Charles Dickens, continued to make critical attacks on the shortcomings of the Victorian social scene. Even more critical and indignant than Dickens was John Ruskin, who turned from a purely moral and aesthetic criticism of art during this period to denounce the evils of Victorian industry, as in his *The Stones of Venice* (1851–53), which combines a history of architecture with stern prophecies about the doom of technological culture, or in his attacks on laissez-faire economics in *Unto This Last* (1862). Generally speaking, however, the realistic novels of Anthony Trollope (1815–1882), with their comfortable tolerance and equanimity, are a more characteristic reflection of the mid-Victorian attitude toward the social and political scene than are Ruskin's lamentations. Overall, this second phase of the Victorian period had many harassing problems, but it was a time of prosperity. On the whole its institutions worked well. Even the badly bungled war against Russia in the Crimea (1854–56) did not seriously affect the growing sense of satisfaction that the challenging difficulties of the 1840s had been solved or would be solved by English wisdom and energy. The monarchy was proving its worth in a modern setting. The queen and her husband, Prince Albert, were models of middle-class domesticity and devotion to duty. The aristocracy was discovering that free trade was enriching rather than impoverishing their estates; agriculture flourished together with trade and industry. And through a succession of Factory Acts in Parliament, which restricted child labor and limited hours of employment, the condition of the working classes was also being gradually improved. When we speak of Victorian complacency or stability or optimism, we are usually referring to this mid-Victorian phase—"The Age of Improvement," as the historian Asa Briggs has called it. "Of all the decades in our history," writes G. M. Young, "a wise man would choose the eighteen-fifties to be young in."

In 1851 Prince Albert opened the Great Exhibition in Hyde Park, where a gigantic glass greenhouse, the Crystal Palace, had been erected to display the exhibits of modern industry and science. The Crystal Palace was one of the first buildings constructed according to modern architectural principles in which materials such as glass and iron are employed for purely functional ends (much late Victorian furniture, on the other hand, with its fantastic and irrelevant ornamentation, was constructed according to the opposite principle). The building, as well as the exhibits, symbolized the triumphant feats of Victorian technology. As Benjamin Disraeli wrote to a friend in 1862: "It is a privilege to live in this age of rapid and brilliant events. What an error to consider it a utilitarian age. It is one of infinite romance."

England's technological progress, together with its prosperity, led to an enormous expansion of its influence around the globe. Its annual export of goods nearly trebled in value between 1850 and 1870. Not only the export of goods but that of people and capital increased. Between 1853 and 1880 2,466,000 emigrants left Britain, many bound for British colonies. By 1870 British capitalists had invested £800 million abroad; in 1850 the total had been only £300 million. This investment, of people, money, and technology,

The Medieval Court, Joseph Nash (1809–1878), from *Dickinson's Comprehensive Pictures of the Great Exhibition of 1851* (1854).

created the British Empire. Important building blocks of the empire were put in place in the mid-Victorian period. In the 1850s and 1860s there was large-scale immigration to Australia; in 1867 Parliament unified the Canadian provinces into the Dominion of Canada. In 1857 Parliament took over the government of India from the private East India Company, which had controlled the country, and started to put in place its civil service government. In 1876 Queen Victoria was named empress of India. Although the competitive scramble for African colonies did not take place until the final decades of the century, the model of empire was created earlier, made possible by technological revolution in communication and transportation. Much as Rome had built roads through Europe in the years of the Roman Empire, Britain built railways and strung telegraph wires. It also put in place a framework for education and government that preserves British influence in former colonies even today. Britain's motives, in creating its empire, were many. It sought wealth, markets for manufactured goods, sources for raw materials, and world power and influence. Many English people also saw the expansion of empire as a moral responsibility—what Rudyard Kipling, in another context, termed "the White Man's burden." Queen Victoria stated that the imperial mission was "to protect the poor natives and advance civilization." Missionary societies flourished, spreading Christianity in India, Asia, and Africa.

At the same time that the British missionary enterprise was expanding, there was increasing debate about religious belief. By the mid-Victorian period the Church of England had evolved into three major divisions: Evangelical, or Low Church; Broad Church; and High Church. The Evangelicals emphasized spiritual transformation of the individual by conversion and a strictly moral Christian life. Zealously dedicated to good causes (they were responsible for the emancipation of all slaves in the British Empire as early as 1833), advocates of a strict Puritan code of morality, and righteously censorious of worldliness in others, the Evangelicals became a powerful and active minority in the early part of the nineteenth century. Much of the power of the Evangelicals depended on the fact that their view of life and religion was virtually identical with that of a much larger group external to the Church of England: the Nonconformists, or Dissenters—that is, Baptists, Methodists, Congregationalists, and other Protestant denominations. The High Church was also associated with a group external to the Church of England; it was the "Catholic" side of the Church, emphasizing the importance of tradition, ritual, and authority. In the 1830s a High Church movement took shape, known both as "the Oxford movement," because it originated at Oxford University, and as "Tractarianism," because its leaders developed their arguments in a series of pamphlets or tracts. Led by John Henry Newman, who later converted to Roman Catholicism, Tractarians argued that the Church could maintain its power and authority only by resisting liberal tendencies and holding to its original traditions. The Broad Church resisted the doctrinal and ecclesiastical controversies that separated the High Church and Evangelical divisions. Open to modern advances in thought, its adherents emphasized the broadly inclusive nature of the Church.

Some rationalist challenges to religious belief that developed before the Victorian period maintained their influence. The most significant was Utilitarianism, also known as Benthamism or Philosophical Radicalism. Utilitarianism derived from the thought of Jeremy Bentham (1748–1832) and his disciple James Mill (1773–1836), the father of John Stuart Mill. Bentham believed that all human beings seek to maximize pleasure and minimize pain. The criterion by which we should judge a morally correct action, therefore, is the extent to which it provides the greatest pleasure to the greatest number. Measuring religion by this moral arithmetic, Benthamites concluded that it was an outmoded superstition; it did not meet the rationalist test of value. Utilitarianism was widely influential in providing a philosophical basis for political and social reforms, but it aroused considerable opposition on the part of those who felt it failed to recognize people's spiritual needs. Raised according to strict utilitarian principles by his father, John Stuart Mill came to be critical of them. In the mental and spiritual crisis portrayed in his *Autobiography* (1873), Mill describes his realization that his utilitarian upbringing had left him no power to feel. In *Sartor Resartus* (1833–34) Carlyle describes a similar spiritual crisis in which he struggles to rediscover the springs of religious feeling in the face of his despair at the specter of a universe governed only by utilitarian principles. Later both Dickens, in his portrayal of Thomas Gradgrind in *Hard Times* (1854), "a man of facts and calculations" who is "ready to weigh and measure any parcel of human nature," and Ruskin, in his *Unto This Last*, attack utilitarianism.

In mid-Victorian England, however, the challenge to religious belief gradually shifted from the Utilitarians to some of the leaders of science, in particular to Thomas Henry Huxley, who popularized the theories of Charles Darwin. Although many English scientists were themselves individuals of strong religious convictions, the impact of their scientific discoveries seemed consistently damaging to established faiths. Complaining in 1851 about the "flimsiness" of his own religious faith, Ruskin exclaimed:

"If only the Geologists would let me alone, I could do very well, but those dreadful hammers! I hear the clink of them at the end of every cadence of the Bible verses."

The damage lamented by Ruskin was effected in two ways. First the scientific attitude of mind was applied toward a study of the Bible. This kind of investigation, developed especially in Germany, was known as the "Higher Criticism." Instead of treating the Bible as a sacredly infallible document, scientifically minded scholars examined it as a mere text of history and presented evidence about its composition that believers, especially in Protestant countries, found disconcerting, to say the least. A noteworthy example of such Higher Criticism studies was David Friedrich Strauss's *Das Leben Jesu*, which was translated by George Eliot in 1846 as *The Life of Jesus*. The second kind of damage was effected by the view of humanity implicit in the discoveries of geology and astronomy, the new and "Terrible Muses" of literature, as Tennyson called them in a late poem. Geology, by extending the history of the earth backward millions of years, reduced the stature of the human species in time. John Tyndall, an eminent physicist, said in an address at Belfast in 1874 that in the eighteenth century people had an "unwavering trust" in the "chronology of the Old Testament" but in Victorian times they had to become accustomed to

> the idea that not for six thousand, nor for sixty thousand, nor for six thousand thousand, but for aeons embracing untold millions of years, this earth has been the theater of life and death. The riddle of the rocks has been read by the geologist and paleontologist, from sub-Cambrian depths to the deposits thickening over the sea bottoms of today. And upon the leaves of that stone book are . . . stamped the characters, plainer and surer than those formed by the ink of history, which carry the mind back into abysses of past time.

The discoveries of astronomers, by extending a knowledge of stellar distances to dizzying expanses, were likewise disconcerting. Carlyle's friend John Sterling remarked in a letter of 1837 how geology "gives one the same sort of bewildering view of the abysmal extent of Time that Astronomy does of Space." To Tennyson's speaker in *Maud* (1855) the stars are "innumerable" tyrants of "iron skies." They are "Cold fires, yet with power to burn and brand / His nothingness into man."

In the mid-Victorian period biology reduced humankind even further into "nothingness." Darwin's great treatise *The Origin of Species* (1859) was interpreted by the nonscientific public in a variety of ways. Some chose to assume that evolution was synonymous with progress, but most readers recognized that Darwin's theory of natural selection conflicted not only with the concept of creation derived from the Bible but also with long-established assumptions of the values attached to humanity's special role in the world. Darwin's later treatise *The Descent of Man* (1871) raised more explicitly the haunting question of our identification with the animal kingdom. If the principle of survival of the fittest was accepted as the key to conduct, there remained the inquiry: fittest for what? As John Fowles writes in his 1968 novel about Victorian England, *The French Lieutenant's Woman*, Darwin's theories made the Victorians feel "infinitely isolated." "By the 1860s the great iron structures of their philosophies, religions, and social stratifications were already beginning to look dangerously corroded to the more perspicacious."

Disputes about evolutionary science, like the disputes about religion, are a reminder that beneath the placidly prosperous surface of the mid-Victorian age there were serious conflicts and anxieties. In the same year as the Great Exhibition, with its celebration of the triumphs of trade and industry, Charles Kingsley wrote, "The young men and women of our day are fast parting from their parents and each other; the more thoughtful are wandering either towards Rome, towards sheer materialism, or towards an unchristian and unphilosophic spiritualism."

THE LATE PERIOD (1870–1901): DECAY OF VICTORIAN VALUES

The third phase of the Victorian age is more difficult to categorize. At first glance its point of view seems merely an extension of mid-Victorianism, whose golden glow lingered on through the Jubilee years of 1887 and 1897 (years celebrating the fiftieth and sixtieth anniversaries of the queen's accession) down to 1914. For many affluent Victorians, this final phase of the century was a time of serenity and security, the age of house parties and long week-ends in the country. In the amber of Henry James's prose is immortalized a sense of the comfortable pace of these pleasant, food-filled gatherings. Life in London, too, was for many an exhilarating heyday. In *My Life and Loves* the Irish-American Frank Harris (1854–1931), often a severe critic of the English scene, records his recollections of the gaiety of London in the 1880s: "London: who would give even an idea of its varied delights: London, the center of civilization, the queen city of the world without a peer in the multitude of its attractions, as superior to Paris as Paris is to New York." The exhilarating sense of London's delights reflects in part the proliferation of things: commodities, inventions, products that were changing the texture of modern life.

Piccadilly Circus, ca. 1893, in the center of London.

England had become committed not only to continuing technological change but also to a culture of consumerism, generating new products for sale.

The wealth of England's empire provided the foundation on which its economy was built. The final decades of the century saw the apex of British imperialism, yet the cost of the empire became increasingly apparent in rebellions, massacres, and bungled wars, such as the Indian Mutiny in 1857; the Jamaica Rebellion in 1865; the massacre of General Gordon and his troops at Khartoum, in the Sudan, in 1885, where he had been sent to evacuate the British in the face of a religiously inspired revolt; and the Anglo-Boer War, at the end of the century, in which England engaged in a long, bloody, and unpopular struggle to annex two independent republics in the south of Africa controlled by Dutch settlers called Boers. In addition the "Irish Question," as it was called, grew especially divisive in the 1880s, when home rule for Ireland became a topic of heated debate—a proposed reform that was unsuccessfully advocated by Prime Minister Gladstone and other leaders. And outside the British Empire, other developments challenged Victorian stability and security. The sudden emergence of Bismarck's Germany after the defeat of France in 1871 was progressively to confront England with powerful threats to its naval and military position and also to its preeminence in trade and industry. The recovery of the United States after the Civil War likewise provided new and serious competition not only in industry but also in agriculture. As the westward expansion of railroads in the United States and Canada opened up the vast, grain-rich prairies, the typical English farmer had to confront lower grain prices and a dramatically different scale of productivity, which England could not match. In 1873 and 1874 such severe economic depressions occurred that the rate of emigratio rose to an alarming degree. Another change in the mid-Victorian balance o power was the growth of labor as a political and economic force. In 1867, under Disraeli's guidance, a second Reform Bill had been passed that extended the right to vote to sections of the working classes; the increasing educational opportunities that opened up for the poor over the course of the century also served to heighten political awareness and activity. These factors, together with the subsequent development of trade unions, made labor a powerful political force that included a wide variety of kinds of socialism. Some labor leaders were disciples of the Tory-socialism of John Ruskin and shared his idealistic conviction that the middle-class economic and political system, with its distrust of state interference, was irresponsible and immoral. Other labor leaders had been influenced instead by the revolutionary theories of Karl Marx and Friedrich Engels as expounded in their *Communist Manifesto* of 1847 and in Marx's *Das Kapital* (1867, 1885, 1895). The first English author of note to embrace Marxism was the poet and painter William Morris, who shared with Marx a conviction that utopia could be achieved only after the working classes had, by revolution, taken control of government and industry.

In much of the literature of this final phase of Victorianism we can sense an overall change of attitudes. Some of the late Victorian writers expressed the change openly by simply attacking the major mid-Victorian idols. Samuel Butler, for example, set about demolishing Darwin, Tennyson, and Prime Minister Gladstone, figures whose aura of authority reminded him of his own father. For the more worldly and casual-mannered Prime Minister Disraeli, on the other hand, Butler could express considerable admiration: "Earnestness was his greatest danger, but if he did not quite overcome it (as who indeed can? it is the last enemy that shall be subdued), he managed to veil it with a fair amount of success." In his novel *The Way of All Flesh* (1903), much of which was written in the 1870s, Butler satirized family life, in particular the tyrannical self-righteousness of a Victorian father, his own father (a clergyman) serving as his model. In a different vein Walter Pater and his followers concluded that the striving of their predecessors was ultimately pointless, that the answers to our problems are not to be found, and that our role is to enjoy the fleeting moments of beauty in "this short day of frost and sun."

THE NINETIES

The changes in attitude that had begun cropping up in the 1870s became much more conspicuous in the final decade of the century and give the nineties a special aura of notoriety. Of course the changes were not in evidence everywhere. At the empire's outposts in India and Africa, the English were building railways and administering governments with the same strenuous energy as in the mid-Victorian period. The stories of Kipling and Joseph Conrad variously record the struggles of such people. Also embodying the task of sustaining an empire were the soldiers and sailors who fought in various colonial wars, most notably in the war against the Boers in South Africa (1899–1902). But back in England, Victorian standards were breaking down on several fronts. One colorful embodiment of changing values was Victoria's son and heir, Edward, Prince of Wales, who was entering his fiftieth year as the nineties began. A pleasure-seeking easygoing person, Edward was the antithesis of his father, Prince Albert, an earnest-minded intellectual who had devoted his life to hard work and to administrative responsibilities. Edward's carryings-on were a favorite topic for newspaper articles, one of which noted how this father of five children "openly maintained scandalous relations with ballet dancers and chorus singers."

Much of the writing of the decade illustrates a breakdown of a different sort. Melancholy, not gaiety, is characteristic of its spirit. Artists of the nineties, representing the aesthetic movement, were very much aware of living at the end of a great century and often cultivated a deliberately fin de siècle ("end-of-century") pose. A studied languor, a weary sophistication, a search for new ways of titillating jaded palates can be found in both the poetry and the prose of the period. *The Yellow Book,* a periodical that ran from 1894 to 1897, is generally taken to represent the aestheticism of the nineties. The startling black-and-white drawings and designs of its art editor, Aubrey Beardsley, the prose of George Moore and Max Beerbohm, and the poetry of Ernest Dowson illustrate different aspects of the movement. Writings of the era that embraced other values and attracted broader readerships nevertheless shared aestheticism's perspective that a distinctly new spirit was at large, at least in the metropolis. Sir Arthur Conan Doyle's hugely popular Sherlock Holmes stories, for instance, present both a hero who simultaneously embodies and polices the city's cosmopolitan decadence and his bluff sidekick Dr. Watson, to whom London is "that great cesspool into which all the loungers and idlers of the Empire are irresistibly drained." In 1893 the Austrian critic Max Nordau summed up what seemed to him to be happening, in a book that was as sensational as its title: *Degeneration.*

Oscar Wilde. One of the photographic portraits of Wilde taken by Napoleon Sarony (1821–1896) in 1882.

From our perspective, however, it is easy to see in the nineties the beginning of the modernist movement in literature; a number of the great writers of the twentieth century—Yeats, Hardy, Conrad, Shaw—were already publishing.

In Dickens's *David Copperfield* (1850) the hero affirms: "I have always been thoroughly in earnest." Forty-five years later Oscar Wilde's comedy *The Importance of Being Earnest* (1895) turns the typical mid-Victorian word *earnest* into a pun, a key joke in this comic spectacle of earlier Victorian values being turned upside down. As Richard Le Gallienne (a novelist of the nineties) remarked in *The Romantic Nineties* (1926): "Wilde made dying Victorianism laugh at itself, and it may be said to have died of the laughter."

THE ROLE OF WOMEN

Political and legal reforms in the course of the Victorian period had given citizens many rights. In 1844 Friedrich Engels observed: "England is unquestionably the freest—that is the least unfree—country in the world, North America not excepted." England had indeed done much to extend its citizens' liberties, but women did not share in these freedoms. They could not vote or hold political office. (Although petitions to Parliament advocating women's suffrage were introduced as early as the 1840s, women did not get the vote until 1918.) Until the passage of the Married Women's Property Acts (1870–1908), married women could not own or handle their own property. While men could divorce their wives for adultery, wives could divorce their husbands only if adultery were combined with cruelty, bigamy, incest, or bestiality. Educational and employment opportunities for women were limited. These inequities stimulated a spirited debate about women's roles known as the "Woman Question." Some of the social changes that such discussion helped foster eventually affected the lives of all, or many, of the country's female population; nevertheless, it is important to recognize that this Victorian debate, despite the inclusive claims of its title was, with a few exceptions, conducted by the middle classes about middle-class women.

Arguments for women's rights were based on the same libertarian principles that had formed the basis of extended rights for men. In Hardy's last novel, *Jude the Obscure* (1895), his heroine justifies leaving her husband by quoting a passage from Mill's *On Liberty* (1859). She might have quoted another work by Mill, *The Subjection of Women* (1869), which, like Mary Wollstonecraft's *A Vindication of the Rights of Woman* (1792), challenges long-established assumptions about women's role in society. Legislative measures over the course of the nineteenth century gradually brought about changes in a number of areas.

The Custody Act of 1839 gave a mother the right to petition the court for access to her minor children and custody of children under seven (raised to sixteen in 1878). The Divorce and Matrimonial Causes Act of 1857 established a civil divorce court (divorce previously could be granted only by an ecclesiastical court) and provided a deserted wife the right to apply for a protection order that would allow her rights to her property. Although divorce remained so expensive as to be available only to the very rich, these changes in marriage and divorce laws, together with the Married Women's Property Acts, began to establish a basis for the rights of women in marriage.

In addition to pressuring Parliament for legal reform, feminists worked to enlarge female educational opportunities. In 1837 none of England's three universities was open to women. Tennyson's long poem *The Princess* (1847), with its fantasy of a women's college from whose precincts all males are excluded, was inspired by contemporary discussions of the need for women to obtain an education more advanced than that provided by the popular finishing schools ("Miss Pinkerton's Academy" in William Makepeace Thackeray's *Vanity Fair* [1847–48] is a good parody of one of these institutions). Although by the end of the poem Princess Ida has repented of her Amazonian scheme, she and the prince look forward to a future in which man will be "more of woman, she of man." The poem reflects a climate of opinion that led in 1848 to the establishment of the first women's college in London, an example later recommended by Thomas Henry Huxley, a strong advocate of advanced education for women. By the end of Victoria's reign, women could take degrees at twelve universities or university colleges and could study, although not earn a degree, at Oxford and Cambridge.

There was also agitation for improved employment opportunities for women. Writers as diverse as Charlotte Brontë, Elizabeth Barrett Browning, and Florence Nightingale complained that women from middle- and upper-class homes were taught trivial accomplishments to fill up days in which there was nothing important to do. Had they been aware of such complaints, women from the majority lower-class population might have found it hard to show sympathy: the working lives of poor English women had always been strenuous, inside and outside the house, but industrial society brought unprecedented pressures. Although the largest proportion of working women labored as servants in the homes of the more affluent, the explosive growth of mechanized industries, especially in the textile trade, created new and grueling forms of paid employment. Hundreds of thousands of lower-class women worked at factory jobs under appalling conditions, while the need for coal to fuel England's industrial development brought women into the mines for the first time. A series of Factory Acts (1802–78) gradually regulated the conditions of labor in mines and factories, eventually reducing the sixteen-hour day and banning women from mine work altogether; but even with such changes, the lot of the country's poorest women, whether factory operatives or housemaids, seamstresses or field laborers, was undoubtedly hard. Bad working conditions and underemployment drove thousands of women into prostitution, which in the nineteenth century became increasingly professionalized—and the subject of an almost obsessive public concern, whose manifestations included frequent literary and artistic representation.

For the most part, prostitution was a trade for working-class women, but there was considerable anxiety about the possible fates of what contemporary journalists called the "surplus" or "redundant" women of the middle classes—that is, women who remained unmarried because of the imbalance in numbers between the sexes. Such women (of whom there were approximately half a million in mid-Victorian England) had few employment opportunities, none of them attractive or profitable. Emigration was frequently proposed as a solution to the problem, but the number of single female emigrants was never high enough to affect the population imbalance significantly. The only occupation at which an unmarried middle-class woman could earn a living and maintain some claim to gentility was that of a governess, but a governess could expect no security of employment, only minimal wages, and an ambiguous status, somewhere between servant and family member, that isolated her within the household. Perhaps because the governess so clearly indicated the precariousness of the unmarried middle-class woman's status in Victorian England, the governess novel, of which the most famous examples are *Jane Eyre* (1847) and *Vanity Fair*, became a popular genre through which to explore women's roles in society.

As such novels indicate, Victorian society was preoccupied not only with legal and economic limitations on women's lives but with the very nature of woman. In *The Subjection of Women,* John Stuart Mill argues that "what is now called the nature of women is eminently an artificial thing—the result of forced repression in some directions, unnatural stimulation in others." In Tennyson's *The Princess* the king voices a more traditional view of male and female roles, a view that has come to be known as the doctrine of "separate spheres":

> Man for the field and woman for the hearth:
> Man for the sword and for the needle she:
> Man with the head and woman with the heart:
> Man to command and woman to obey.

The king's relegation of women to the hearth and heart reflects an ideology that claimed that woman had a special nature peculiarly fit for her domestic role. Most aptly epitomized by the title of Coventry Patmore's immensely popular poem *The Angel in the House* (1854–62), this concept of womanhood stressed woman's purity and selflessness. Protected and enshrined within the home, her role was to create a place of peace where man could take refuge from the difficulties of modern life. In "Of Queens' Gardens" (1865), John Ruskin writes:

> This is the true nature of home—it is the place of Peace; the shelter, not only from all injury, but from all terror, doubt, and division. In so far as it is not this, it is not home; so far as the anxieties of the outer life penetrate into it, and the inconsistently-minded, unknown, unloved, or hostile society of the outer world is allowed either by husband or wife to cross the threshold, it ceases to be home; it is then only a part of that outer world which you have roofed over, and lighted fire in. But so far as it is a sacred place, a vestal temple, a temple of the hearth watched over by Household Gods, . . . so far it vindicates the name, and fulfills the praise, of home.

Such an exalted conception of home placed great pressure on the woman who ran it to be, in Ruskin's words, "enduringly, incorruptibly good; instinctively, infallibly wise—wise, not for self-development, but for self-renunciation." It is easy to recognize the oppressive aspects of this domestic ideology. Paradoxically, however, it was used not only by antifeminists, eager to keep woman in her place, but by some feminists as well, in justifying the special contribution that woman could make to public life.

In his preface to *The Portrait of a Lady* (1881) Henry James writes: "Millions of presumptuous girls, intelligent or not intelligent, daily affront their destiny, and what is it open to their destiny to *be*, at the most, that we should make an ado about it?" Every major Victorian novelist makes the "ado" that James describes in addressing the question of woman's vocation; by the 1890s the "New Woman," an emerging form of emancipated womanhood, was endlessly debated in a wave of fiction and magazine articles. Ultimately, as Victorian texts illustrate, the basic problem was not only political, economic, and educational. It was how women were regarded, and regarded themselves, as members of a society.

LITERACY, PUBLICATION, AND READING

Literacy increased significantly during the Victorian period, although precise figures are difficult to calculate. In 1837 about half of the adult male population could read and write to some extent; by the end of the century, basic literacy was almost universal, the product in part of compulsory national education, required by 1880 to the age of ten. There was also an explosion of things to read. Because of technological changes in printing—presses powered by steam, paper made from wood pulp rather than rags, and, toward the end of the century, typesetting machines—publishers could bring out more printed material more cheaply than ever before. The number of newspapers, periodicals, and books increased exponentially during the Victorian period. Books remained fairly expensive, and most readers borrowed them from commercial lending libraries. (There were few public libraries until the final decades of the century.) After the repeal of the stamp tax and duties on advertisements just after midcentury, an extensive popular press developed.

The most significant development in publishing from the point of view of literary culture was the growth of the periodical. In the first thirty years of the Victorian period, 170 new periodicals were started in London alone. There were magazines for every taste: cheap and popular magazines, like the "penny dreadfuls" that published sensational tales; religious monthlies; weekly newspapers; satiric periodicals noted for their political cartoons (the most famous of these was *Punch*); women's magazines; monthly miscellanies publishing fiction, poetry, and articles on current affairs; and reviews and quarterlies, ostensibly reviewing new books but using the reviews, which were always unsigned, as occasions for essays on the subjects in question. The chief reviews and monthly magazines had a great deal of power and influence; they defined issues in public affairs, and they made and broke literary reputations. They also published the major writers of the period: the fiction of Dickens, Thackeray, Eliot, Trollope, Gaskell, and Hardy; the essays of Carlyle, Mill, Arnold, and Ruskin; and the poetry of Tennyson and the Brownings all appeared in monthly magazines.

The circumstances of periodical publication exerted a shaping force on literature. Novels and long works of nonfiction prose were published in serial form. Although serial publication of works began in the late eighteenth century, it was the publication of Dickens's *Pickwick Papers* (1836–37) in individual numbers that established its popularity. All of Dickens's novels and many of those of his contemporaries were published in serial form. Readers therefore read these works in relatively short, discrete installments over a period that could extend more than a year, with time for reflection and interpretation in between. Serial publication encouraged a certain kind of plotting and pacing and allowed writers to take account of their readers' reactions as they constructed subsequent installments. Writers created a continuing world, punctuated by the ends of installments, which served to stimulate the curiosity that would keep readers buying subsequent issues. Serial publication also created a distinctive sense of a community of readers, a sense encouraged by the practice of reading aloud in family gatherings.

As the family reading of novels suggests, the middle-class reading public enjoyed a common reading culture. Poets such as Tennyson and Elizabeth Barrett Browning and anthologies such as Palgrave's *Golden Treasury* (1861) appealed to a large body of readers; prose writers such as Carlyle, Arnold, and Ruskin achieved a status as sages; and the major Victorian novelists were popular writers. Readers shared the expectation that literature would not only delight but instruct, that it would be continuous with the lived world, and that it would illuminate social problems. "Tennyson," one of his college friends warned him, "we cannot live in Art." These expectations weighed more heavily on some writers than others. Tennyson wore his public mantle with considerable ambivalence; Arnold abandoned the private mode of lyric poetry in order to speak about public issues in lectures and essays.

By the 1870s the sense of a broad readership, with a shared set of social concerns, had begun to dissolve. Some writers had begun to define themselves in opposition to a general public; poets like the Pre-Raphaelites pursued art for art's sake, doing exactly what Tennyson's friend had warned against; other writers consciously catered to the new and diverse markets springing up within the increasing ranks of the literate. By the end of Victoria's reign, writers could no longer assume a unified reading public.

SHORT FICTION AND THE NOVEL

Fiction flourished in a variety of forms in the Victorian period. A staple of the era's thriving periodical culture, short works were extremely popular and demonstrated considerable ingenuity in genre; the series of Christmas stories

Dickens wrote in the wake of the huge success he enjoyed with *A Christmas Carol* (1843) offers a good case in point. The last two decades of the century saw some of the most celebrated achievements in short fiction, such as Stevenson's thrilling novella *The Strange Case of Dr. Jekyll and Mr. Hyde,* Kipling's colonial tales, and the detective adventures of Sherlock Holmes, but there is a rich archive for the entire period. It is, however, the novel that has come to be seen as the era's pre-eminent literary triumph. Initially published, for the most part, in serial form, novels subsequently appeared in three-volume editions, or "three-deckers." "Large loose baggy monsters," Henry James called them, reflecting his dissatisfaction with their sprawling panoramic expanse. As their size suggests, Victorian novels seek to represent a large and comprehensive social world, with the variety of classes and social settings that constitute a community. They contain a multitude of characters and a number of plots, setting in motion the kinds of patterns that reveal the author's vision of the deep structures of the social world—how, in George Eliot's words, "the mysterious mixture behaves under the varying experiments of Time." They present themselves as realistic, that is, as representing a social world that shares the features of the one we inhabit. The French novelist Stendhal (1783–1842) called the novel "a mirror wandering down a road," but the metaphor of the mirror is somewhat deceptive, since it implies that writers exert no shaping force on their material. It would be more accurate to speak not of realism but of realisms, since each novelist presents a specific vision of reality whose representational force he or she seeks to persuade us to acknowledge through a variety of techniques and conventions. The worlds of Dickens, of Trollope, of Eliot, of the Brontës hardly seem continuous with each other, but their authors share the attempt to convince us that the characters and events they imagine resemble those we experience in actual life.

The experience that Victorian novelists most frequently depict is the set of social relationships in the middle-class society developing around them. It is a society where the material conditions of life indicate social position, where money defines opportunity, where social class enforces a powerful sense of stratification, yet where chances for class mobility exist. Pip can aspire to the great expectations that provide the title for Dickens's novel; Jane Eyre can marry her employer, a landed gentleman. Most Victorian novels focus on a protagonist whose effort to define his or her place in society is the main concern of the plot. The novel thus constructs a tension between surrounding social conditions and the aspiration of the hero or heroine, whether it be for love, social position, or a life adequate to his or her imagination. This tension makes the novel the natural form to use in portraying woman's struggle for self-realization in the context of the constraints imposed upon her. For both men and women writers, the heroine is often, therefore, the representative protagonist whose search for fulfillment emblematizes the human condition. The great heroines of Victorian fiction—Jane Eyre, Maggie Tulliver, Dorothea Brooke, Isabel Archer, Tess of the d'Urbervilles, even Becky Sharp—all seem in some way to illustrate George Eliot's judgment, voiced in the Prelude to *Middlemarch* (1871–72), of "a certain spiritual grandeur ill-matched with meanness of opportunity."

From the beginning of the nineteenth century, the novel was more than a fertile medium for the portrayal of women; women writers were, for the first time, not figures on the margins but major authors. Jane Austen, the Brontës, Elizabeth Gaskell, George Eliot—all helped define the genre. When Charlotte Brontë screwed up her courage to write to the poet laureate, Robert

Southey, to ask his advice about a career as a writer, he warned her, "Literature cannot be the business of a woman's life, and it ought not to be." Charlotte Brontë put this letter, with one other from Southey, in an envelope, with the inscription "Southey's advice to be kept forever. My twenty-first birthday." Brontë's ability ultimately to depart from this advice derived in part from how amenable the novel was to women writers. It concerned the domestic life that women knew well—courtship, family relationships, marriage. It was a popular form whose market women could enter easily. It did not carry the burden of an august tradition as poetry did, nor did it build on the learning of a university education. In his essay "The Lady Novelists" (1852) George Henry Lewes declared, "The advent of female literature promises woman's view of life, woman's experience." His common-law wife, George Eliot, together with many of her sister novelists, fulfilled his prophecy.

Whether written by women or men, the Victorian novel was extraordinarily various. It encompassed a wealth of styles and genres from the extravagant comedy of Dickens to the Gothic romances of the Brontë sisters; from the satire of Thackeray to the probing psychological fiction of Eliot; from the social and political realism of Trollope to the sensation novels of Wilkie Collins; and from the grim naturalism of Gissing to the rural tragedies of Hardy. For the Victorians the novel was both a principal form of entertainment and a spur to social sympathy. There was not a social topic that the novel did not address. Dickens, Gaskell, and many lesser novelists tried to stimulate efforts for social reform through their depiction of social problems. Writing at the beginning of the twentieth century, Joseph Conrad defined the novel in a way that could speak for the Victorians: "What is a novel if not a conviction of our fellow-men's existence strong enough to take upon itself a form of imagined life clearer than reality and whose accumulated verisimilitude of selected episodes puts to shame the pride of documentary history?"

POETRY

Although today we generally consider the novel as not only the most distinctive, but also the most important, literary form of the Victorian era, nineteenth-century readers would have disagreed; for them, poetry represented literature's highest pinnacle. Some made even loftier claims. The most famous of these appeared in Matthew Arnold's book *The Study of Poetry* (1880):

> More and more mankind will discover that we have to turn to poetry to interpret life for us, to console us, to sustain us. Without poetry, our science will appear incomplete; and most of what now passes with us for religion and philosophy will be replaced by poetry.

Arnold, whose lifetime activities encompassed the composition of poetry, the writing of influential books and articles on poetry, and, as part of his duties as a governmental official and inspector of schools, the institutionalization of poetry within the nation's elementary curriculum, did all a man could do to bring about such a state of affairs. And demographically speaking, poetry became part of the lives of more people than ever before in the Victorian period, inasmuch as poems were printed in the pages of every kind of newspaper and periodical, regularly heard in domestic and public settings alike, and, from the late 1870s onward, repeatedly recited in the nation's growing network of schools for the masses. But this pervasive presence and democratization of poetry proved in many ways to be its downfall, at least from the point of view of the influential criticism of the first half of the twentieth century, from which literary studies in later years inherited certain engrained opinions. Long deemed sentimental and anti-intellectual, popular poetry reading in the Victorian period is however now beginning to receive serious attention.

To a degree, this denigration of the era's poetic culture extended itself not only to how people read poems in the Victorian period, but also to how they wrote them; Victorian poetry has often been treated as if it languishes in an uninspired dip between the twin peaks of Romantic and Modernist achievement. Yet this is a perspective that requires careful examination so that we can better understand the special qualities of Victorian poetry. Influenced by the vibrancy and formal advances of the novel in this period, poets devised new ways of telling stories in verse; examples include Tennyson's *Maud*, Elizabeth Barrett Browning's *Aurora Leigh* (1857), Robert Browning's *The Ring and the Book* (1868–69), and Arthur Hugh Clough's *Amours de Voyage* (1857–58). Poets and critics debated what the appropriate subjects of such long narrative poems should be. Some, like Matthew Arnold, held that poets should use the heroic materials of the past; others, like Elizabeth Barrett Browning, felt that poets should represent "their age, not Charlemagne's." Poets also experimented with character and perspective. *Amours de Voyage* is a long epistolary poem that tells the story of a failed romance through letters written by its various characters; *The Ring and the Book* presents its plot—an old Italian murder story—through ten different perspectives.

Undeniably innovative, Victorian poetry was nevertheless deeply affected by the shadow of Romanticism. By 1837, when Victoria ascended the throne, all the major Romantic poets, save William Wordsworth, were dead, but they had died young, and many readers consequently still regarded them as their contemporaries. Not even twenty years separated the birth dates of Tennyson and Browning from that of John Keats, but they lived more than three times as long as he did. All the Victorian poets show the strong influence of the Romantics, but they cannot sustain the confidence that the Romantics felt in the power of the imagination. The Victorians often rewrite Romantic poems with a sense of belatedness and distance. When, in his poem "Resignation," Arnold addresses his sister upon revisiting a landscape, much as Wordsworth had addressed his sister in "Tintern Abbey," he tells her the rocks and sky "seem to bear rather than rejoice." Tennyson frequently represents his muse as an embowered woman, cut off from the world and doomed to death. The speakers of Browning's poems who embrace the visions that their imaginations present are madmen. When Hardy writes "The Darkling Thrush," in December 1900, Keats's nightingale has become "an aged thrush, frail, gaunt, and small."

Victorian poets build upon this sense of belated Romanticism in a number of different ways. Some poets writing in the second half of the century, like Dante Gabriel Rossetti and Algernon Charles Swinburne, embrace an attenuated Romanticism, art pursued for its own sake. Reacting against what he sees as the insufficiency of an allegory of the state of one's own mind as the basis of poetry, Arnold seeks an objective basis for poetic emotion and finally gives up writing poems altogether when he decides that the present age lacks the culture necessary to support great poetry. The more fruitful reaction to the subjectivity of Romantic poetry, however, was not Arnold's but Browning's. Turning from the mode of his early poetry, modeled on Percy Bysshe Shelley, Browning began writing dramatic monologues—poems, he said, that are "Lyric in expression" but "Dramatic in principle, and so many utterances of so many imaginary persons, not mine." Tennyson simultaneously developed a more lyric form of the dramatic monologue. The idea of creating a lyric poem in the voice of a speaker ironically distinct from the poet is the great achievement of Victorian poetry, one developed extensively in the twentieth century. In *Poetry and the Age* (1953), the modernist poet and critic Randall Jarrell acknowledges this fact: "The dramatic monologue, which once had depended for its effect upon being a departure from the norm of poetry, now became in one form or other the norm."

The formal experimentation of Victorian poetry, both in long narrative and in the dramatic monologue, may make it seem eclectic, but Victorian poetry shares a number of characteristics. It tends to be pictorial, using detail to construct visual images that represent the emotion or situation the poem concerns. In his review of Tennyson's first volume of poetry, Arthur Henry Hallam defines this kind of poetry as "picturesque," as combining visual impressions in such a way that they create a picture that carries the dominant emotion of the poem. This aesthetic brings poets and painters close together. Contemporary artists frequently illustrated Victorian poems, and poems themselves often present paintings. Victorian poetry also uses sound in a distinctive way. Whether it be the mellifluousness of Tennyson or Swinburne, with its emphasis on beautiful cadences, alliteration, and vowel sounds, or the roughness of Browning or Gerard Manley Hopkins, a roughness adopted in part in reaction against Tennyson, the sound of Victorian poetry reflects an attempt to use poetry as a medium with a presence almost independent of sense. The resulting style can become so syntactically elaborate that it is easy to parody, as in Hopkins's description of Browning as a man "bouncing up from table with his mouth full of bread and cheese" or T. S. Eliot's criticism of Swinburne's poetry, where "meaning is merely the hallucination of meaning." Yet it is important to recognize that these poets use sound to convey meaning, to quote Hallam's review of Tennyson once more, "where words would not." "The tone becomes the sign of the feeling." In all of these developments—the experimentation with narrative and perspective, the dramatic monologue, the use of visual detail and sound—Victorian poets seek to represent psychology in a different way. Their most distinctive achievement is a poetry of mood and character. They therefore sat in uneasy relationship to the public expectation that poets be sages with something to teach. Tennyson, Browning, and Arnold showed varying discomfort with this public role; poets beginning to write in the second half of the century distanced themselves from their public by embracing an identity as bohemian rebels. Women poets encountered a different set of difficulties in developing their poetic voice. When, in Barrett Browning's epic about the growth of a woman poet, Aurora Leigh's cousin Romney discourages her poetic ambitions by telling her that women are "weak for art" but "strong for life and duty," he articulates the prejudice of an age. Women poets view their vocation in the context of the constraints and expectations upon their sex. Perhaps because of this, their poems are less complicated by the experiments in perspective than those of their male contemporaries.

PROSE

Although Victorian poets felt ambivalent about the didactic mission the public expected of the man of letters, writers of nonfictional prose aimed specifically to instruct. Although the term *nonfictional prose* is clumsy and not quite exact (the Victorians themselves referred instead to history, biography, theology, criticism, political economy, and so forth), it has its uses not only to distinguish these prose writers from the novelists but also to indicate the centrality of argument and persuasion to Victorian intellectual life. The growth of the periodical press, described earlier, provided the vehicle and marketplace for nonfictional prose. It reflects a vigorous sense of shared intellectual life and the public urgency of social and moral issues. On a wide range of controversial topics—religious, political, and aesthetic—writers seek to convince their readers to share their convictions and values. Such writers seem at times almost secular priests. Indeed, in the fifth lecture of *On Heroes, Hero-Worship, and the Heroic in History* (1841), Carlyle defines the writer precisely in these terms: "Men of Letters are a perpetual Priesthood, from age to age, teaching all Men that God is still present in their life. . . . In the true Literary Man, there is thus ever, acknowledged or not by the world, a sacredness." The modern man of letters, Carlyle argues, differs from his earlier counterpart in that he writes for money. "Never, till about a hundred years ago, was there seen any figure of a Great Soul living apart in that anomalous manner; endeavouring to speak forth the inspiration that was in him by Printed Books, and find place and subsistence by what the world would please him for doing that." This combination, of a new market position for nonfictional writing and an exalted sense of the didactic function of the writer, produces a quintessential Victorian form.

On behalf of nonfictional prose, Walter Pater argued in his essay "Style" (1889) that it was "the special and opportune art of the modern world." He believed not that it was superior to verse but that it more readily conveys the "chaotic variety and complexity" of modern life, the "incalculable" intellectual diversity of the "master currents of the present time." Pater's characterization of prose helps us understand what its writers were attempting to do. Despite the diversity of styles and subjects, Victorian prose writers were engaged in shaping belief in a bewilderingly complex and changing world. Their modes of persuasion differ. Mill and Huxley rely on clear reasoning, logical argument, and the kind of lucid style favored by essayists of the eighteenth century. Carlyle and Ruskin write a prose that is more Romantic in character, that seeks to move readers as well as convince them. Whatever the differences in their rhetorical techniques, however, they share an urgency of exposition. Not only by what they said but by how they said it, Victorian prose writers were claiming a place for literature in a scientific and materialistic culture. Arnold and Pater share this as an explicit aim. Each in his own way argues that culture—the intensely serious appreciation of great works of literature—provides the kind of immanence and meaning that people once found in religion. For Arnold this is an intensely moral experience; for Pater it is aesthetic. Together they develop the basis for the claims of modern literary criticism.

DRAMA AND THEATER

The plays written and performed in the Victorian age, apart from those in the final decade of the century, have to date received relatively little scholarly attention. Yet the theater, throughout the period, was a flourishing and popular institution, which staged not merely conventional dramas but a rich variety of theatrical entertainments, many with lavish spectacular effects—burlesques, extravaganzas, highly scenic and altered versions of Shakespeare's plays, melodramas, pantomimes, and musicals. Robert Corrigan gives figures that suggest the extent of the popularity of such entertainment: "In the decade between 1850 and 1860 the number of theaters built throughout the country was doubled, and in the middle of the sixties, in London alone, 150,000 would be attending the theater on any given day." The popularity of theatrical entertainment made it a powerful influence on other genres. Dickens was devoted to the theater and composed many of the scenes of his novels with theatrical techniques. Thackeray represents himself as the puppet master of his characters in *Vanity Fair* and employs the stock gestures and expressions of melodramatic acting in his illustrations for the novel. Tennyson, Browning, and Henry James tried their hands at writing plays, though with no commercial success. Successful plays on stage were written by such figures as Dion Boucicault (1820–1890) and Henry Arthur Jones (1851–1921), prolific dramatists of the period. The comic operas of W. S. Gilbert (1836–1911) and Arthur Sullivan (1842–1900) were also hugely popular. Their satire of Victorian values and institutions, what Gilbert called their "topsyturvydom," and their grave and quasi-respectful treatment of the ridiculous not only make them delightful in themselves but anticipate the techniques of two great figures of British theater from this period, the Irishmen George Bernard Shaw and Oscar Wilde. Around 1890, when the socially controversial plays of the Norwegian dramatist Henrik Ibsen (1828–1906) became known in England, Arthur Pinero (1855–1934) and Shaw began writing "problem plays," which addressed difficult social issues. In the 1890s Shaw and Wilde transformed British theater with their comic masterpieces. Although they did not like each other's work, they both created a kind of comedy that took aim at Victorian pretense and hypocrisy.

The Victorian Age

TEXTS	CONTEXTS
1830 Alfred Lord Tennyson, *Poems, Chiefly Lyrical*	1830 Opening of Liverpool and Manchester Railway
1832 Sir Charles Lyell, *Principles of Geology*	1832 First Reform Bill
1833 Thomas Carlyle, *Sartor Resartus*	1833 Factory Act. Abolition of Slavery Act. Beginning of Oxford Movement
1836 Charles Dickens, *Pickwick Papers*	1836 First train in London
1837 Carlyle, *The French Revolution*	1837 Victoria becomes queen
	1838 "People's Charter" issued by Chartist Movement
	1840 Queen marries Prince Albert
1842 Tennyson, *Poems*. Robert Browning, *Dramatic Lyrics*	1842 Chartist Riots. Copyright Act. Mudie's Circulating Library
1843 John Ruskin, *Modern Painters* (vol. 1)	
	1845–46 Potato famine in Ireland. Mass emigration to North America
1846 George Eliot, *The Life of Jesus* (translation)	1846 Repeal of Corn Laws. Robert Browning marries Elizabeth Barrett
1847 Charlotte Brontë, *Jane Eyre*. Emily Brontë, *Wuthering Heights*	1847 Ten Hours Factory Act
1848 Elizabeth Gaskell, *Mary Barton*. William Makepeace Thackeray, *Vanity Fair*	1848 Revolution on the Continent. Second Republic established in France. Founding of Pre-Raphaelite Brotherhood
1850 Tennyson, *In Memoriam*. William Wordsworth, *The Prelude* (posthumous publication)	1850 Tennyson succeeds Wordsworth as Poet Laureate
1851 Ruskin, *Stones of Venice*	1851 Great Exhibition of science and industry at the Crystal Palace
1853 Matthew Arnold, *Poems*	
1854 Dickens, *Hard Times*	1854 Crimean War. Florence Nightingale organizes nurses to care for sick and wounded
1855 Robert Browning, *Men and Women*	
1857 Elizabeth Barrett Browning, *Aurora Leigh*	1857 Indian Mutiny. Matrimonial Causes Act
1859 Charles Darwin, *Origin of Species*. John Stuart Mill, *On Liberty*. Tennyson, *Idylls of the King* (books 1–4)	
1860 Dickens, *Great Expectations*. Eliot, *The Mill on the Floss*	1860 Italian unification
	1861 Death of Prince Albert
	1861–65 American Civil War
1862 Christina Rossetti, *Goblin Market*	
1864 R. Browning, *Dramatis Personae*	
1865 Lewis Carroll, *Alice's Adventures in Wonderland*	1865 Jamaica Rebellion

TEXTS	CONTEXTS
1866 Algernon Charles Swinburne, *Poems and Ballads*	
1867 Karl Marx, *Das Kapital*	1867 Second Reform Bill
	1868 Opening of Suez Canal
1869 Arnold, *Culture and Anarchy*. Mill, *The Subjection of Women*	
	1870 Married Women's Property Act. Victory in Franco-Prussian War makes Germany a world power. Elementary Education Act
1871 Darwin, *Descent of Man*	1871 Newnham College (first women's Oxbridge college) founded at Cambridge
1872 Eliot, *Middlemarch*	
1873 Walter Pater, *Studies in the History of the Renaissance*	
	1877 Queen Victoria made empress of India. Gerard Manley Hopkins joins Jesuit order
	1878 Electric street lighting in London
1885 W. S. Gilbert and Arthur Sullivan, *The Mikado*	1885 Massacre of General Gordon and his forces and fall of Khartoum
1886 Robert Louis Stevenson, *Doctor Jekyll and Mr. Hyde*	
1888 Rudyard Kipling, *Plain Tales from the Hills*	
1889 William Butler Yeats, *Crossways*	
	1890 First subway line in London
1891 Thomas Hardy, *Tess of the D'Urbervilles*. Bernard Shaw, *The Quintessence of Ibsenism*. Oscar Wilde, *The Picture of Dorian Grey*. Arthur Conan Doyle, *Adventures of Sherlock Holmes*	1891 Free elementary education
1893 Shaw, *Mrs. Warren's Profession*	1893 Independent Labour Party
1895 Wilde, *The Importance of Being Earnest*. Hardy, *Jude the Obscure*	1895 Oscar Wilde arrested and imprisoned for homosexuality
1896 A. E. Housman, *A Shropshire Lad*	
1898 Hardy, *Wessex Poems*	1898 Discovery of radium
	1899 Irish Literary Theatre founded in Dublin
	1899–1902 Anglo-Boer War
1900 Joseph Conrad, *Lord Jim*	
	1901 Death of Queen Victoria; succession of Edward VII

THOMAS CARLYLE
1795–1881

W. B. Yeats once asked William Morris which writers had inspired the socialist movement of the 1880s, and Morris replied: "Oh, Ruskin and Carlyle, but somebody should have been beside Carlyle and punched his head every five minutes." Morris's mixed feelings of admiration and exasperation are typical of the response Thomas Carlyle evokes in many readers. Anyone approaching his prose for the first time should expect to be sometimes bewildered. Like Bernard Shaw, Carlyle discovered, early in life, that exaggeration can be a highly effective way of gaining the attention of an audience. But it can also be a way of distracting an audience unfamiliar with the idiosyncrasies of his rhetoric and unprepared for the distinctive enjoyments his writings can provide.

One of the idiosyncrasies of his prose is that it is meant to be read aloud. "His paragraphs," as Ralph Waldo Emerson observes, "are all a sort of splendid conversation." As a talker Carlyle was as famous in his day as Samuel Johnson in his. Charles Darwin testified that he was "the best worth listening to of any man I know." No Boswell has adequately recorded this talk, but no Boswell was needed, for Carlyle's prose adopts the rhythm, idiosyncrasy, and spontaneity of the spoken voice. It is a noisy and emphatic voice, startling on a first reading.

Carlyle was forty-one years old when Victoria became queen of England. He had been born in the same year as John Keats, yet he is rarely grouped with his contemporaries among the Romantic writers. Instead his name is linked with younger men such as Charles Dickens, Robert Browning, and John Ruskin, the early generation of Victorian writers, for whom he became (according to Elizabeth Barrett Browning) "the great teacher of the age." The classification is fitting, for it was Carlyle's role to foresee the problems that were to preoccupy the Victorians and to report on his experiences in confronting these problems. After 1837 his loud voice began to attract an audience; and he soon became one of the most influential figures of the age, affecting the attitudes of scientists, statesmen, and especially of writers. His wife once complained that Emerson had no ideas (except mad ones) that he had not derived from Carlyle. "'But pray, Mrs. Carlyle,' replied a friend, 'who has?'"

Carlyle was born in Ecclefechan, a village in Scotland, the eldest child of a large family. His mother, at the time of her marriage, was illiterate. His father, James Carlyle, a stonemason and later a farmer, was proudly characterized by his son as a peasant. The key to the character of James Carlyle was the Scottish Calvinism that he instilled into the members of his household. Frugality, hard work, a tender but undemonstrative family loyalty, and a peculiar blend of self-denial and self-righteousness were characteristic features of Carlyle's childhood home.

With his father's aid the young Carlyle was educated at Annan Academy and at Edinburgh University, the subject of his special interest being mathematics; he left without taking a degree. It was his parents' hope that their son would become a clergyman, but in this respect Thomas made a severe break with his ancestry. He was a prodigious reader; and his exposure to such skeptical writers as David Hume, Voltaire, and Edward Gibbon had undermined his faith. Gibbon's *Decline and Fall of the Roman Empire* (1776–88), he told Emerson, was "the splendid bridge from the old world to the new." By the time he was twenty-three Carlyle had crossed the bridge and had abandoned his Christian faith and his proposed career as a clergyman. During the period in which he was thinking through his religious position, he supported himself by teaching school in Scotland and, later, by tutoring private pupils;

but from 1824 to the end of his life he relied exclusively on his writings for his livelihood. His early writings consisted of translations, biographies, and critical studies of Johann Wolfgang von Goethe and other German authors, to whose view of life he was deeply attracted. The German Romantics (loosely grouped by Carlyle under the label "Mystics") were the second most important influence on his life and character, exceeded only by his early family experiences. Aided by the writings of these German poets and philosophers, he arrived finally at a faith in life that served as a substitute for the Christian faith he had lost.

His most significant early essay, "Characteristics," appeared in *The Edinburgh Review* in 1831. A year earlier he had begun writing *Sartor Resartus,* an account of the life and opinions of an imaginary philosopher, Professor Diogenes Teufelsdröckh, a work that he had great difficulty in persuading anyone to publish. In book form *Sartor* first appeared in America in 1836, where Carlyle's follower Emerson had prepared an enthusiastic audience for this unusual work. His American following (which was later to become a vast one) did little at first, however, to relieve the poverty in which he still found himself after fifteen years of writing. In 1837 the tide at last turned when he published *The French Revolution.* "O it has been a great success, dear," his wife assured him; but her husband, embittered by the long struggle, was incredulous that the sought-for recognition had at last come to him.

It was in character for his wife, Jane Welsh Carlyle, to be less surprised by his success than he was. That Thomas Carlyle was a genius had been an article of faith to her from her first meeting with him in 1821. A witty, intelligent, and intellectually ambitious young woman, the daughter of a doctor of good family, Jane Welsh had many suitors. When in 1826 she finally accepted Carlyle, her family and friends were shocked. This peasant's son, of no fixed employment, seemed a preposterous choice. Subsequent events seemed to confirm her family's verdict. Not long after marriage Carlyle insisted on their retiring to a remote farm at Craigenputtock, where for six years (1828–34) this sociable woman was obliged to live in isolation and loneliness. After they moved to London in 1834 and settled in a house on Cheyne Walk in Chelsea, Jane Carlyle was considerably happier and enjoyed her role at the center of the intellectual and artistic circle that surrounded her husband. Her husband, however, remained a difficult man to live with. His stomach ailments, irascible nerves, and preoccupation with his writings, as well as the lionizing to which he was subjected, left him with little inclination for domestic amenities or for encouraging his wife's considerable intellectual talents. As a young girl she had wanted to be a writer; her letters, some of the most remarkable of the century, show that she had considerable literary talent.

This marriage of the Carlyles has aroused almost as much interest as that of the Brownings. Their friend the Reverend W. H. Brookfield (whose marriage was an unhappy one) once said cynically that marrying is "dipping into a pitcher of snakes for the chance of an eel," and some biographers have argued that Jane Welsh Carlyle drew a snake instead of an eel. Yet if we study her letters, it is evident that she wanted to marry a man of genius who would change the world. Despite the years she endured of comparative poverty, poor health, and loneliness, she had the satisfaction of recognizing her husband's triumph when the peasant's son she had chosen returned to Scotland to deliver his inaugural address as lord rector of Edinburgh University. While he was away, to Carlyle's great grief, she died.

During the first thirty years of his residence in London Carlyle wrote extensive historical works and many pamphlets concerning contemporary issues. After *The French Revolution* he edited, in 1845, the *Letters and Speeches of Oliver Cromwell,* a Puritan leader of heroic dimensions in Carlyle's eyes, and later wrote a full-length biography, *The History of Friedrich II of Prussia, Called Frederick the Great* (1858–65). Carlyle's pamphleteering is seen at its best in *Past and Present* (1843) and in its most violent phase in his *Latter-Day Pamphlets* (1850). Following the death of his wife, he wrote very little. For the remaining fifteen years of his life, he confined himself to reading or to talking to the stream of visitors who called at Cheyne Walk to listen to the "Sage of Chelsea," as he came to be called. In 1874 he accepted the Prussian Order of Merit from Bismarck but declined an English baronetcy offered by Disraeli. In 1881 he died and was buried near his family in Ecclefechan churchyard.

To understand Carlyle's role as historian, biographer, and social critic, it is essential to understand his attitude toward religion. Like many Victorians, Carlyle underwent a crisis of religious belief. By the time he was twenty-three, he had been shorn of his faith in Christianity. At this stage, as Carlyle observed with dismay, many people seemed content simply to stop or, worse, to adopt antispiritual ideas. A Utilitarian such as James Mill or some of his commonsensical professors at the University of Edinburgh regarded society and the universe as machines. To such thinkers the machines might sometimes seem complex, but they were not mysterious, for machines are subject to humankind's control and understanding through reason and observation. To Carlyle, and to many others, life without a sense of the divine was a meaningless nightmare. In the first part of "The Everlasting No," a chapter of *Sartor Resartus*, he memorably depicts the horrors of such a soulless world that drove him in 1822 to thoughts of suicide. The eighteenth-century Enlightenment had left him not in light but in darkness.

In developing his views of religion, Carlyle used the metaphor of the "Clothes Philosophy." The naked individual seeks clothing for protection. One solution, represented by Coleridge and his followers, was to repudiate the skepticism of Voltaire and Hume and to return to the protective beliefs and rituals of the Christian Church. To Carlyle such a return was pointless. The traditional Christian coverings were worn out—"Hebrew Old Clothes," he called them. His own solution, described in "The Everlasting Yea," was to tailor a new suit of beliefs from German philosophy, shreds of Scottish Calvinism, and his own observations. The following summarizes his basic religious attitude: "Gods die with the men who have conceived them. But the god-stuff roars eternally, like the sea. . . . Even the gods must be born again. We must be born again." Although this passage is from *The Plumed Serpent* (1926) by D. H. Lawrence (a writer who resembles Carlyle at many points), it might have come from any one of Carlyle's own books—most especially from *Sartor Resartus*, in which he describes his being born again—his "Fire-baptism"—into a new secular faith. Carlyle was thus in many ways the quintessential nineteenth-century mystic; yet at the same time, many contemporary critics note, his writings also gesture toward postmodernism. Certainly his self-aware, genre-defying, and often contradictory prose exposes the inherent difficulty of assuming that literature or philosophy can ever achieve a unified, foundational truth.

Nevertheless, Carlyle often talked like a *vitalist*; that is, as though the presence of energy in the world was, in itself, a sign of the godhead. Carlyle therefore judges everything in terms of the presence or absence of some vital spark. The minds of people, books, societies, Churches, or even landscapes are rated as alive or dead, dynamic or merely mechanical. The government of Louis XVI, for example, was obviously moribund, doomed to be swept away by the dynamic forces of the French Revolution. The government of Victorian England seemed likewise to be doomed unless infused with vital energies of leadership and an awareness of the real needs of humankind. When an editor complained that his essay "Characteristics" was "inscrutable," Carlyle remarked: "My own fear was that it might be too *scrutable*; for it indicates decisively enough that Society (in my view) is utterly condemned to destruction, and even now beginning its long travail-throes of Newbirth."

In his inquiry into the principles of government and social order, Carlyle, like many of his contemporaries, is seeking to understand a world of great social unrest and historical change. This preoccupation with revolution and the destruction of the old orders suggests that Carlyle's politics were radical, but his position is bewilderingly difficult to classify. During the Hungry Forties he was one of the most outspoken critics of middle-class bunglings and of the economic theory of laissez-faire that, in his opinion, was ultimately responsible for those bunglings. He worked strenuously on behalf of the millions of people suffering from the miseries attendant on a major breakdown of industry and agriculture. At other times, because of his insistence on strong and heroic leadership, Carlyle appears to be a violent conservative or, as some have argued, virtually a fascist. He had no confidence that democratic institutions could work efficiently. A few individuals in every age are, in his view, leaders; the rest are followers and are happy only as followers. Society should be organized so that these gifted leaders can have scope to govern effectively. Such leaders are, for Carlyle, heroes. Bernard Shaw, who learned much from Carlyle, would call them "supermen." Liberals and democrats, however, might call them dictators. Although Carlyle was aware that the Western world was committed to a faith in a system of balloting and of legislative debate, he was confident that the system would eventually break down. The democratic assumption that all voters are equally capable of choice and the assumption that people value liberty more than they value order seemed to him nonsense. Carlyle's authoritarianism intensified as he grew older. When the governor of Jamaica violently repressed a rebellion of black plantation workers, Carlyle served as chair of his defense fund, arguing that England owed the governor honor and thanks for his defense of civilization.

Carlyle's prose style reflects the intensity of his views. At the time he began to write, the essayists of the eighteenth century, Samuel Johnson in particular, were the models of good prose. Carlyle recognized that their style, however admirable an instrument for reasoning, analysis, and generalized exposition, did not suit his purposes. Like a poet, he wanted to convey the sense of experience itself. Like a preacher or prophet, he wanted to exhort or inspire his readers rather than to develop a chain of logical argument. Like a psychoanalyst, he wanted to explore the unconscious and irrational levels of human life, the hidden nine-tenths of the iceberg rather than the conscious and rational fraction above the surface. To this end he developed his highly individual manner of writing, with its vivid imagery of fire and barnyard and zoo, its mixture of biblical rhythms and explosive talk, and its inverted and unorthodox syntax. Classicists may complain, as Walter Savage Landor did, that the result is not English. Carlyle would reply that it is not eighteenth-century English, but that his style was appropriate for a Victorian who reports of revolutions in society and in thought. In reply to a friend who had protested about his stylistic experiments, Carlyle exclaimed: "Do you reckon this really a time for Purism of Style? I do not: with whole ragged battalions of Scott's Novel Scotch, with Irish, German, French, and even Newspaper Cockney . . . storming in on us, and the whole structure of our Johnsonian English breaking up from its foundations—revolution *there* as visible as anywhere else?" George Eliot wrote (in an essay of 1855) that Carlyle was "more of an artist than a philosopher." As she said: "No novelist has made his creations live for us more thoroughly." Carlyle is best regarded, that is, as a man of letters, the inventor of a distinctive and extremely effective prose medium, and one who strove tirelessly to create a new spiritual and political philosophy adequate to the age.

Sartor Resartus

Sartor Resartus is a combination of novel, autobiography, and essay. To present some of his own experiences, Carlyle invented a hero, Professor Diogenes Teufelsdröckh of Germany, whose name (meaning "God-Begotten Devil's Dreck") suggests the grotesque humor that Carlyle uses to expound a serious treatise. Teufelsdröckh tells the story of his unhappiness in love and of his difficulties in religion. He also airs his opinions on a variety of subjects. Interspersed between the professor's words (which are in quotation marks) are the remarks of an editor, also imaginary, who has the task of putting together the story from assorted documents written by Teufelsdröckh. The title, meaning "The Tailor Retailored," refers to the editor's role of patching the story together. The title also refers to Carlyle's so-called Clothes Philosophy, which is expounded by the hero in many chapters of *Sartor*. In effect this Clothes Philosophy is an attempt to demonstrate the difference between the appearances of things and their reality. The appearance of an individual depends on the costume he or she wears; the reality of that individual is the body underneath the costume. By analogy Carlyle suggests that institutions, such as churches or governments, are like clothes. They may be useful "visible emblems" of the spiritual forces that they cover, but they wear out and have to be replaced by new clothes. The Christian Church, for example, which once expressed humanity's permanent religious desires, is, in Carlyle's terms, worn out and must be discarded. But the underlying religious spirit must be recognized and kept alive at all costs. Carlyle also uses the clothes analogy to describe the relationship between the material and spiritual worlds. Clothes hide the body just as the world of nature cloaks the reality of God and as the body itself cloaks the reality of the soul. The discovery of these realities behind the appearances is, for Carlyle and for his hero, the initial stage of a solution to the dilemmas of life. As contemporary critics have pointed out, the Clothes Philosophy, as well as the unusual form of the book, suggests that Carlyle is also concerned with fundamental problems of language and representation. Implicitly, and sometimes explicitly, his text often questions whether a biographer or autobiographer can ever capture the "essence" of his or her subject.

These selections are chapters 7 and 9 of book 2.

From Sartor Resartus

The Everlasting No

Under the strange nebulous envelopment, wherein our Professor has now shrouded himself, no doubt but his spiritual nature is nevertheless progressive, and growing: for how can the "Son of Time," in any case, stand still? We behold him, through those dim years, in a state of crisis, of transition: his mad Pilgrimings, and general solution[1] into aimless Discontinuity, what is all this but a mad Fermentation; wherefrom, the fiercer it is, the clearer product will one day evolve itself?

Such transitions are ever full of pain: thus the Eagle when he moults is sickly; and, to attain his new beak, must harshly dash-off the old one upon rocks. What Stoicism soever our Wanderer, in his individual acts and motions, may affect, it is clear that there is a hot fever of anarchy and misery raging within; coruscations of which flash out: as, indeed, how could there be other? Have we not seen him disappointed, bemocked of Destiny, through long years? All that the young heart might desire and pray for has been denied; nay, as in the last worst instance, offered and then snatched away. Ever an "excellent Passivity"; but of useful, reasonable Activity, essential to the former as Food to Hunger, nothing granted: till at length, in this wild Pilgrimage, he must forcibly seize for himself an Activity, though useless, unreasonable. Alas, his cup of bitterness, which had been filling drop by drop, ever since that first "ruddy morning" in the Hinterschlag Gymnasium, was at the very lip; and then with that poison-drop, of the Towgood-and-Blumine[2] business, it runs over, and even hisses over in a deluge of foam.

He himself says once, with more justice than originality: "Man is, properly speaking, based upon Hope, he has no other possession but Hope; this world of his is emphatically the Place of Hope." What, then, was our Professor's possession? We see him, for the present, quite shut-out from Hope; looking not into the golden orient, but vaguely all round into a dim copper firmament, pregnant with earthquake and tornado.

1. Dissolution.
2. A woman loved by Teufelsdröckh who had married his friend Towgood. His distress is pictured in the preceding chapter, titled "Sorrows of Teufelsdröckh." "Hinterschlag Gymnasium": "Smack-bottom" high school, a fake German name invented by Carlyle.

Alas, shut-out from Hope, in a deeper sense than we yet dream of! For, as he wanders wearisomely through this world, he has now lost all tidings of another and higher. Full of religion, or at least of religiosity, as our Friend has since exhibited himself, he hides not that, in those days, he was wholly irreligious: "Doubt had darkened into Unbelief," says he; "shade after shade goes grimly over your soul, till you have the fixed, starless, Tartarean[3] black." To such readers as have reflected, what can be called reflecting, on man's life, and happily discovered, in contradiction to much Profit-and-loss Philosophy, speculative and practical, that Soul is *not* synonymous with Stomach; who understand, therefore, in our Friend's words, "that, for man's well-being, Faith is properly the one thing needful;[4] how, with it, Martyrs, otherwise weak, can cheerfully endure the shame and the cross; and without it, World-lings puke-up their sick existence, by suicide, in the midst of luxury": to such it will be clear that, for a pure moral nature, the loss of his religious Belief was the loss of everything. Unhappy young man! All wounds, the crush of long-continued Destitution, the stab of false Friendship and of false Love, all wounds in thy so genial heart, would have healed again, had not its life-warmth been withdrawn. Well might he exclaim, in his wild way: "Is there no God, then; but at best an absentee God, sitting idle, ever since the first Sabbath, at the outside of his Universe, and *see*ing it go? Has the word Duty no meaning; is what we call Duty no divine Messenger and Guide, but a false earthly Fantasm, made-up of Desire and Fear, of emanations from the Gallows and from Dr. Graham's Celestial-Bed?[5] Happiness of an approving Conscience! Did not Paul of Tarsus, whom admiring men have since named Saint, feel that *he* was 'the chief of sinners';[6] and Nero of Rome, jocund in spirit (*wohlgemuth*), spend much of his time in fiddling?[7] Foolish Word-monger and Motive-grinder, who in thy Logic-mill hast an earthly mechanism for the Godlike itself, and wouldst fain grind me out Virtue from the husks of Pleasure,[8]—I tell thee, Nay! To the unregenerate Prometheus Vinctus[9] of a man, it is ever the bitterest aggravation of his wretchedness that he is conscious of Virtue, that he feels himself the victim not of suffering only, but of injustice. What then? Is the heroic inspiration we name Virtue but some Passion; some bubble of the blood, bubbling in the direction others *profit* by? I know not; only this I know, If what thou namest Happiness be our true aim, then are we all astray. With Stupidity and sound Digestion man may front much. But what, in these dull unimaginative days, are the terrors of Conscience to the diseases of the Liver! Not on Morality, but on Cookery, let us build our stronghold: there brandishing our frying-pan, as censer, let us offer sweet incense to the Devil, and live at ease on the fat things *he* has provided for his Elect!"

Thus has the bewildered Wanderer to stand, as so many have done, shouting question after question into the Sibyl-cave of Destiny,[1] and receive no

---

3. Of Tartarus, the lowest region of the classical underworld, where the wicked were punished.
4. Luke 10.42.
5. James Graham (1745–1794), a quack doctor, had invented an elaborate bed that was supposed to cure sterility in couples using it. In this passage, the bed is apparently a symbol of sexual desires.
6. Paraphrase of 1 Timothy 1.15.
7. Nero (37–68 C.E.; Roman emperor, 54–68) was rumored to have recited his poems and played his lyre during a great fire in 64 C.E. that destroyed much of Rome; thus the familiar saying "Nero fiddled while Rome burned."

8. Here, as in his earlier reference to "Profit-and-loss Philosophy," Carlyle attacks the Utilitarian concepts of Jeremy Bentham (1748–1832), who argued that the Good is whatever brings the greatest happiness (or pleasure) to the greatest number of people.
9. I.e., Prometheus Bound; this is also the title of a play by Aeschylus depicting the sufferings of a hero who defied Zeus.
1. An allusion to Virgil's *Aeneid* 6.36ff.; there Aeneas questions the Cumaean Sibyl, who foretells the future.

Answer but an Echo. It is all a grim Desert, this once-fair world of his; wherein is heard only the howling of wild-beasts, or the shrieks of despairing, hate-filled men; and no Pillar of Cloud by day, and no Pillar of Fire by night,[2] any longer guides the Pilgrim. To such length has the spirit of Inquiry carried him. "But what boots it (was thut's)?" cries he: "it is but the common lot in this era. Not having come to spiritual majority prior to the Siècle de Louis Quinze,[3] and not being born purely a Loghead (Dummkopf), thou hast no other outlook. The whole world is, like thee, sold to Unbelief, their old Temples of the Godhead, which for long have not been rainproof, crumble down; and men ask now: Where is the Godhead; our eyes never saw him?"

Pitiful enough were it, for all these wild utterances, to call our Diogenes wicked. Unprofitable servants as we all are,[4] perhaps at no era of his life was he more decisively the Servant of Goodness, the Servant of God, than even now when doubting God's existence. "One circumstance I note," says he: "after all the nameless woe that Inquiry, which for me, what it is not always, was genuine Love of Truth, had wrought me, I nevertheless still loved Truth, and would bate no jot[5] of my allegiance to her. 'Truth!' I cried, 'though the Heavens crush me for following her: no Falsehood! though a whole celestial Lubberland[6] were the price of Apostasy.' In conduct it was the same. Had a divine Messenger from the clouds, or miraculous Handwriting on the wall, convincingly proclaimed to me *This thou shalt do,* with what passionate readiness, as I often thought, would I have done it, had it been leaping into the infernal Fire. Thus, in spite of all Motive-grinders, and Mechanical Profit-and-Loss Philosophies, with the sick ophthalmia and hallucination they had brought on, was the Infinite nature of Duty still dimly present to me: living without God in the world, of God's light I was not utterly bereft; if my as yet sealed eyes, with their unspeakable longing, could nowhere see Him, nevertheless in my heart He was present, and His heaven-written Law still stood legible and sacred there."

Meanwhile, under all these tribulations, and temporal and spiritual destitutions, what must the Wanderer, in his silent soul, have endured! "The painfullest feeling," writes he, "is that of your own Feebleness (*Unkraft*); ever, as the English Milton says, to be weak is the true misery.[7] And yet of your Strength there is and can be no clear feeling, save by what you have prospered in, by what you have done. Between vague wavering Capability and fixed indubitable Performance, what a difference! A certain inarticulate Self-consciousness dwells dimly in us; which only our Works can render articulate and decisively discernible. Our Works are the mirror wherein the spirit first sees its natural lineaments. Hence, too, the folly of that impossible Precept, *Know thyself;*[8] till it be translated into this partially possible one, *Know what thou canst work at.*

"But for me, so strangely unprosperous had I been, the net-result of my Workings amounted as yet simply to—Nothing. How then could I believe in

2. Exodus 13.21.
3. The Century of Louis XV (French), allusion to *Précis du Siècle de Louis XV* (1768), Voltaire's history of the skeptical and inquiring spirit of 18th-century France during the reign of Louis XV (1715–74).
4. An allusion to Matthew 25.20 and Luke 17.7–10.
5. Would hold back no part.
6. Land of Plenty.
7. *Paradise Lost* 1.157: "Fallen cherub, to be weak is miserable."
8. This maxim was inscribed in the temple of Apollo at Delphi.

my Strength, when there was as yet no mirror to see it in? Ever did this agitating, yet, as I now perceive, quite frivolous question, remain to me insoluble: Hast thou a certain Faculty, a certain Worth, such even as the most have not; or art thou the completest Dullard of these modern times? Alas! the fearful Unbelief is unbelief in yourself; and how could I believe? Had not my first, last Faith in myself, when even to me the Heavens seemed laid open, and I dared to love, been all-too cruelly belied? The speculative Mystery of Life grew ever more mysterious to me: neither in the practical Mystery[9] had I made the slightest progress, but been everywhere buffeted, foiled, and contemptuously cast-out. A feeble unit in the middle of a threatening Infinitude, I seemed to have nothing given me but eyes, whereby to discern my own wretchedness. Invisible yet impenetrable walls, as of Enchantment, divided me from all living: was there, in the wide world, any true bosom I could press trustfully to mine? O Heaven, No, there was none! I kept a lock upon my lips: why should I speak much with that shifting variety of so-called Friends, in whose withered, vain and too-hungry souls Friendship was but an incredible tradition? In such cases, your resource is to talk little, and that little mostly from the Newspapers. Now when I look back, it was a strange isolation I then lived in. The men and women around me, even speaking with me, were but Figures; I had, practically, forgotten that they were alive, that they were not merely automatic. In midst of their crowded streets and assemblages, I walked solitary; and (except as it was my own heart, not another's, that I kept devouring) savage also, as the tiger in his jungle. Some comfort it would have been, could I, like a Faust,[1] have fancied myself tempted and tormented of the Devil; for a Hell, as I imagine, without Life, though only diabolic Life, were more frightful: but in our age of Downpulling and Disbelief, the very Devil has been pulled down, you cannot so much as believe in a Devil. To me the Universe was all void of Life, of Purpose, of Volition, even of Hostility: it was one huge, dead, immeasurable Steamengine, rolling on, in its dead indifference, to grind me limb from limb. O, the vast, gloomy, solitary Golgotha,[2] and Mill of Death! Why was the Living banished thither companionless, conscious? Why, if there is no Devil; nay, unless the Devil is your God?"

A prey incessantly to such corrosions, might not, moreover, as the worst aggravation to them, the iron constitution even of a Teufelsdröckh threaten to fail? We conjecture that he has known sickness; and, in spite of his locomotive habits, perhaps sickness of the chronic sort. Hear this, for example: "How beautiful to die of broken-heart, on Paper! Quite another thing in practice; every window of your Feeling, even of your Intellect, as it were, begrimed and mud-bespattered, so that no pure ray can enter; a whole Drugshop in your inwards; the fordone soul drowning slowly in quagmires of Disgust!"

Putting all which external and internal miseries together, may we not find in the following sentences, quite in our Professor's still vein, significance enough? "From Suicide a certain aftershine (Nachschein) of Christianity withheld me: perhaps also a certain indolence of character; for, was not that a remedy I had at any time within reach? Often, however, was there a question present to me: Should some one now, at the turning of that corner, blow thee suddenly out of Space, into the other World, or other No-World, by pistol-shot,—how were it? On which ground, too, I have often, in sea-storms and sieged cities and other death-scenes, exhibited an imperturbability, which passed, falsely enough, for courage.

"So had it lasted," concludes the Wanderer, "so had it lasted, as in bitter protracted Death-agony, through long years. The heart within me, unvisited by any heavenly dewdrop, was smouldering in sulphurous, slow-consuming fire. Almost since earliest memory I had shed no tear; or once only when I, murmuring half-audibly, recited Faust's Deathsong, that wild *Selig der den er im Siegesglanze findet* (Happy whom *he* finds in Battle's splendour),[3] and thought that of this last Friend even I was not forsaken, that Destiny itself could not doom me not to die. Having no hope, neither had I any definite fear, were it of Man or of Devil: nay, I often felt as if it might be solacing, could the Arch-Devil himself, though in Tartarean terrors, but rise to me, that I might tell him a little of my mind. And yet, strangely enough, I lived in a continual, indefinite, pining fear; tremulous, pusillanimous, apprehensive of I knew not what: it seemed as if all things in the Heavens above and the Earth beneath would hurt me; as if the Heavens and the Earth were but boundless jaws of a devouring monster, wherein I, palpitating, waited to be devoured.

"Full of such humour,[4] and perhaps the miserablest man in the whole French Capital or Suburbs, was I, one sultry Dogday, after much perambulation, toiling along the dirty little *Rue Saint-Thomas de l'Enfer*,[5] among civic rubbish enough, in a close atmosphere, and over pavements hot as Nebuchadnezzar's Furnace;[6] whereby doubtless my spirits were little cheered; when, all at once, there rose a Thought in me, and I asked myself: 'What *art* thou afraid of? Wherefore, like a coward, dost thou forever pip and whimper, and go cowering and trembling? Despicable biped! what is the sum-total of the worst that lies before thee? Death? Well, Death; and say the pangs of Tophet[7] too, and all that the Devil and Man may, will or can do against thee! Hast thou not a heart; canst thou not suffer whatsoever it be; and, as a Child of Freedom, though outcast, trample Tophet itself under thy feet, while it consumes thee? Let it come, then; I will meet it and defy it!' And as I so thought, there rushed like a stream of fire over my whole soul; and I shook base Fear away from me forever. I was strong, of unknown strength; a spirit, almost a god. Ever from that time, the temper of my misery was changed: not Fear or whining Sorrow was it, but Indignation and grim fire-eyed Defiance.

"Thus had the EVERLASTING NO[8] (*das ewige Nein*) pealed authoritatively through all the recesses of my Being, of my ME; and then was it that my whole ME stood up, in native God-created majesty, and with emphasis recorded its

---

3. Adapted from Goethe's *Faust* (1808) 1.4.1573–76.
4. State of mind.
5. St. Thomas-of-Hell Street (French). In later life Carlyle admitted that this incident was based on his own experience during a walk in Edinburgh (rather than in Paris). "Dogday": i.e., in the dog days, a hot and unwholesome summer period coinciding with the prominence of Sirius, the Dog Star.
6. Cf. Daniel 3: the Babylonian king Nebuchad-

nezzar erected a golden idol and threw those who refused to fall down and worship it into a fiery furnace.
7. Hell.
8. This phrase does not signify the hero's protest; it represents the sum of all the forces that had denied meaning to life. These negative forces, which had hitherto held the hero in bondage, are repudiated by his saying no to the "Everlasting No."

Protest. Such a Protest, the most important transaction in Life, may that same Indignation and Defiance, in a psychological point of view, be fitly called. The Everlasting No had said: 'Behold, thou art fatherless, outcast, and the Universe is mine (the Devil's)'; to which my whole Me now made answer: '*I am not thine, but Free, and forever hate thee!*'

"It is from this hour that I incline to date my Spiritual Newbirth, or Baphometic Fire-baptism,[9] perhaps I directly thereupon began to be a Man."

The Everlasting Yea

"Temptations in the Wilderness!"[1] exclaims Teufelsdröckh: "Have we not all to be tried with such? Not so easily can the old Adam, lodged in us by birth, be dispossessed. Our Life is compassed round with Necessity; yet is the meaning of Life itself no other than Freedom, than Voluntary Force: thus have we a warfare; in the beginning, especially, a hard-fought battle. For the God-given mandate, *Work thou in Welldoing*, lies mysteriously written, in Promethean[2] Prophetic Characters, in our hearts; and leaves us no rest, night or day, till it be deciphered and obeyed; till it burn forth, in our conduct, a visible, acted Gospel of Freedom. And as the clay-given mandate, *Eat thou and be filled*, at the same time persuasively proclaims itself through every nerve,—must not there be a confusion, a contest, before the better Influence can become the upper?

"To me nothing seems more natural than that the Son of Man, when such God-given mandate first prophetically stirs within him, and the Clay must now be vanquished, or vanquish,—should be carried of the spirit into grim Solitudes, and there fronting the Tempter do grimmest battle with him; defiantly setting him at naught, till he yield and fly. Name it as we choose: with or without visible Devil, whether in the natural Desert of rocks and sands, or in the populous moral Desert of selfishness and baseness,—to such Temptation are we all called. Unhappy if we are not! Unhappy if we are but Half-men, in whom that divine handwriting has never blazed forth, all-subduing, in true sun-splendour; but quivers dubiously amid meaner lights: or smoulders, in dull pain, in darkness, under earthly vapours!—Our Wilderness is the wide World in an Atheistic Century; our Forty Days[3] are long years of suffering and fasting: nevertheless, to these also comes an end. Yes, to me also was given, if not Victory, yet the consciousness of Battle, and the resolve to persevere therein while life or faculty is left. To me also, entangled in the enchanted forests, demon-peopled, doleful of sight and of sound, it was given, after weariest wanderings, to work out my way into the higher sunlit slopes—of that Mountain which has no summit, or whose summit is in Heaven only!"

He says elsewhere, under a less ambitious figure; as figures are, once for all, natural to him: "Has not thy Life been that of most sufficient men (*tüchtigen Männer*) thou hast known in this generation? An outflush of foolish young Enthusiasm, like the first fallow-crop, wherein are as many weeds as

---

9. A transformation by a flash of spiritual illumination. The term may derive from Baphomet, an idol that the Knights Templar in the 14th century were accused of worshipping as part of their initiation ceremony.
1. Paraphrase of Matthew 4.1.

2. Fiery or fiery-spirited, an allusion to Prometheus, the defiant Titan who brought the secret of fire-making to humanity.
3. The length of time that Jesus spent fasting in the wilderness (Matthew 4.2).

valuable herbs: this all parched away, under the Droughts of practical and spiritual Unbelief, as Disappointment, in thought and act, often-repeated gave rise to Doubt, and Doubt gradually settled into Denial! If I have had a second-crop, and now see the perennial greensward, and sit under umbrageous[4] cedars, which defy all Drought (and Doubt); herein too, be the Heavens praised, I am not without examples, and even exemplars."

So that, for Teufelsdröckh also, there has been a "glorious revolution":[5] these mad shadow-hunting and shadow-hunted Pilgrimings of his were but some purifying "Temptation in the Wilderness," before his Apostolic work (such as it was) could begin; which Temptation is now happily over, and the Devil once more worsted! Was "that high moment in the *Rue de l'Enfer*," then, properly the turning-point of the battle; when the Fiend said, *Worship me or be torn in shreds*; and was answered valiantly with an *Apage Satana?*[6]— Singular Teufelsdröckh, would thou hadst told thy singular story in plain words! But it is fruitless to look there, in those Paper-bags,[7] for such. Nothing but innuendoes, figurative crotchets:[8] a typical Shadow, fitfully wavering, prophetic-satiric; no clear logical Picture. "How paint to the sensual eye," asks he once, "what passes in the Holy-of-Holies of Man's Soul; in what words, known to these profane times, speak even afar-off of the unspeakable?" We ask in turn: Why perplex these times, profane as they are, with needless obscurity, by omission and by commission? Not mystical only is our Professor, but whimsical; and involves himself, now more than ever, in eye-bewildering *chiaroscuro.*[9] Successive glimpses, here faithfully imparted, our more gifted readers must endeavour to combine for their own behoof.

He says: "The hot Harmattan wind[1] had raged itself out; its howl went silent within me; and the long-deafened soul could now hear. I paused in my wild wanderings; and sat me down to wait, and consider; for it was as if the hour of change drew nigh. I seemed to surrender, to renounce utterly, and say: Fly, then, false shadows of Hope; I will chase you no more, I will believe you no more. And ye too, haggard spectres of Fear, I care not for you; ye too are all shadows and a lie. Let me rest here: for I am way-weary and life-weary; I will rest here, were it but to die: to die or to live is alike to me; alike insignificant."—And again: "Here, then, as I lay in that CENTRE OF INDIFFERENCE; cast, doubtless by benignant upper Influence, into a healing sleep, the heavy dreams rolled gradually away, and I awoke to a new Heaven and a new Earth.[2] The first preliminary moral Act, Annihilation of Self (*Selbsttödtung*), had been happily accomplished; and my mind's eyes were now unsealed, and its hands ungyved."[3]

Might we not also conjecture that the following passage refers to his Locality, during this same "healing sleep"; that his Pilgrim-staff lies cast aside here, on "the high table-land"; and indeed that the repose is already taking wholesome effect on him? If it were not that the tone, in some parts, has more of riancy,[4] even of levity, than we could have expected! However, in Teufelsdröckh, there is always the strangest Dualism: light dancing, with guitar-music, will be going on in the fore-court, while by fits from within comes the faint whimpering of woe and wail. We transcribe the piece entire:

4. Shady.
5. The overthrow of James II of England in 1688.
6. Get thee hence, Satan (Greek; Matthew 4.10).
7. Bags containing documents and writings by Teufelsdröckh.
8. Perverse notions.

9. Light and shade (Italian).
1. A hot and dry wind in Africa.
2. Revelation 21.1.
3. Unfettered.
4. Gaiety.

"Beautiful it was to sit there, as in my skyey Tent, musing and meditating; on the high table-land, in front of the Mountains; over me, as roof, the azure Dome, and around me, for walls, four azure-flowing curtains,—namely, of the Four azure winds, on whose bottom-fringes also I have seen gilding. And then to fancy the fair Castles that stood sheltered in these Mountain hollows; with their green flower-lawns, and white dames and damosels, lovely enough: or better still, the straw-roofed Cottages, wherein stood many a Mother baking bread, with her children round her:—all hidden and protectingly folded-up in the valley-folds; yet there and alive, as sure as if I beheld them. Or to see, as well as fancy, the nine Towns and Villages, that lay round my mountain-seat, which, in still weather, were wont to speak to me (by their steeple-bells) with metal tongue; and, in almost all weather, proclaimed their vitality by repeated Smoke-clouds; whereon, as on a culinary horologe,[5] I might read the hour of the day. For it was the smoke of cookery, as kind housewives at morning, midday, eventide, were boiling their husband's kettles; and ever a blue pillar rose up into the air, successively or simultaneously, from each of the nine, saying, as plainly as smoke could say: Such and such a meal is getting ready here. Not uninteresting! For you have the whole Borough, with all its love-makings and scandal-mongeries, contentions and contentments, as in miniature, and could cover it all with your hat.—If, in my wide Wayfarings, I had learned to look into the business of the World in its details, here perhaps was the place for combining it into general propositions, and deducing inferences therefrom.

"Often also could I see the black Tempest marching in anger through the Distance: round some Schreckhorn,[6] as yet grim-blue, would the eddying vapour gather, and there tumultuously eddy, and flow down like a mad witch's hair; till, after a space, it vanished, and, in the clear sunbeam, your Schreckhorn stood smiling grim-white, for the vapour had held snow. How thou fermentest and elaboratest, in thy great fermenting-vat and laboratory of an Atmosphere, of a World, O Nature!—Or what is Nature? Ha! why do I not name thee GOD? Art not thou the 'Living Garment of God'?[7] O Heavens, is it, in very deed, HE, then, that ever speaks through thee; that lives and loves in thee, that lives and loves in me?

"Fore-shadows, call them rather fore-splendours, of that Truth, and Beginning of Truths, fell mysteriously over my soul. Sweeter than Dayspring to the Shipwrecked in Nova Zembla;[8] ah, like the mother's voice to her little child that strays bewildered, weeping, in unknown tumults; like soft streamings of celestial music to my too-exasperated heart, came that Evangel. The Universe is not dead and demoniacal, a charnel-house with spectres; but godlike, and my Father's!

"With other eyes, too, could I now look upon my fellow man; with an infinite Love, an infinite Pity. Poor, wandering, wayward man! Art thou not tired, and beaten with stripes, even as I am? Ever, whether thou bear the royal mantle or the beggar's gabardine, art thou not so weary, so heavy-laden; and thy Bed of Rest is but a Grave. O my Brother, my Brother, why cannot I shelter thee in my bosom, and wipe away all tears from thy eyes! Truly, the din of many-voiced Life, which, in this solitude, with the mind's organ, I

---

5. Clock.
6. Peak of Terror (German); a mountain in Switzerland.
7. Goethe, *Faust* 1.509.

8. A Dutch sea captain, whose ship was wrecked off the island of Nova Zembla in the Arctic in 1596, recorded in his journal his thankfulness at the coming of daylight.

could hear, was no longer a maddening discord, but a melting one; like inarticulate cries, and sobbings of a dumb creature, which in the ear of Heaven are prayers. The poor Earth, with her poor joys, was now my needy Mother, not my cruel Stepdame; man, with his so mad Wants and so mean Endeavours, had become the dearer to me; and even for his sufferings and his sins, I now first named him Brother. Thus I was standing in the porch of that 'Sanctuary of Sorrow';[9] by strange, steep ways had I too been guided thither; and ere long its sacred gates would open, and the 'Divine Depth of Sorrow' lie disclosed to me."

The Professor says, he here first got eye on the Knot that had been strangling him, and straightway could unfasten it, and was free. "A vain interminable controversy," writes he, "touching what is at present called Origin of Evil, or some such thing, arises in every soul, since the beginning of the world; and in every soul, that would pass from idle Suffering into actual Endeavouring, must first be put an end to. The most, in our time, have to go content with a simple, incomplete enough Suppression of this controversy; to a few some Solution of it is indispensable. In every new era, too, such Solution comes-out in different terms; and ever the Solution of the last era has become obsolete, and is found unserviceable. For it is man's nature to change his Dialect from century to century; he cannot help it though he would. The authentic Church-Catechism of our present century has not yet fallen into my hands: meanwhile, for my own private behoof, I attempt to elucidate the matter so. Man's Unhappiness, as I construe, comes of his Greatness; it is because there is an Infinite in him, which with all his cunning[1] he cannot quite bury under the Finite. Will the whole Finance Ministers and Upholsterers and Confections of modern Europe undertake, in joint-stock company, to make one Shoeblack HAPPY? They cannot accomplish it, above an hour or two; for the Shoeblack also has a Soul quite other than his Stomach; and would require, if you consider it, for his permanent satisfaction and saturation, simply this allotment, no more, and no less: *God's infinite Universe altogether to himself,* therein to enjoy infinitely, and fill every wish as fast as it rose. Oceans of Hochheimer, a Throat like that of Ophiuchus:[2] speak not of them; to the infinite Shoeblack they are as nothing. No sooner is your ocean filled, than he grumbles that it might have been of better vintage. Try him with half of a Universe, of an Omnipotence, he sets to quarrelling with the proprietor of the other half, and declares himself the most maltreated of men.—Always there is a black spot in our sunshine: it is even as I said, the *Shadow of Ourselves.*

"But the whim we have of Happiness is somewhat thus. By certain valuations, and averages, of our own striking, we come upon some sort of average terrestrial lot; this we fancy belongs to us by nature, and of indefeasible right. It is simple payment of our wages, of our deserts; requires neither thanks nor complaint; only such *overplus* as there may be do we account Happiness; any *deficit* again is Misery. Now consider that we have the valuation of our own deserts ourselves, and what a fund of Self-conceit there is in each of us,—do you wonder that the balance should so often dip the wrong way, and many a Blockhead cry: See there, what a payment; was ever worthy gentleman so

9. Adapted from Goethe's *Wilhelm Meister* (1821–29).
1. Skill.

2. The constellation also known as the Serpent Holder. "Hochheimer": Rhine wine or hock from Hochheim.

used!—I tell thee, Blockhead, it all comes of thy Vanity; of what thou *fanciest* those same deserts of thine to be. Fancy that thou deservest to be hanged (as is most likely), thou wilt feel it happiness to be only shot: fancy that thou deservest to be hanged in a hair-halter, it will be a luxury to die in hemp.

"So true is it, what I then say, that *the Fraction of Life can be increased in value not so much by increasing your Numerator as by lessening your Denominator.* Nay, unless my Algebra deceive me, *Unity* itself divided by *Zero* will give *Infinity.* Make thy claim of wages a zero, then; thou hast the world under thy feet. Well did the Wisest of our time write: 'It is only with Renunciation (*Entsagen*) that Life, properly speaking, can be said to begin.'[3]

"I asked myself: What is this that, ever since earliest years, thou hast been fretting and fuming, and lamenting and self-tormenting, on account of? Say it in a word: is it not because thou art not HAPPY? Because the THOU (sweet gentleman) is not sufficiently honoured, nourished, soft-bedded, and lovingly cared for? Foolish soul! What Act of Legislature was there that *thou* shouldst be Happy? A little while ago thou hadst no right to *be* at all. What if thou wert born and predestined not to be Happy, but to be Unhappy! Art thou nothing other than a Vulture, then, that fliest through the Universe seeking after somewhat to *eat*; and shrieking dolefully because carrion enough is not given thee? Close thy *Byron*; open thy *Goethe*."

"*Es leuchtet mir ein,*[4] I see a glimpse of it!" cries he elsewhere: "there is in man a HIGHER than Love of Happiness: he can do without Happiness, and instead thereof find Blessedness! Was it not to preach-forth this same HIGHER that sages and martyrs, the Poet and the Priest, in all times, have spoken and suffered; bearing testimony, through life and through death, of the Godlike that is in Man, and how in the Godlike only has he Strength and Freedom? Which God-inspired Doctrine art thou also honoured to be taught; O Heavens! and broken with manifold merciful Afflictions, even till thou become contrite, and learn it! O, thank thy Destiny for these; thankfully bear what yet remain: thou hadst need of them; the Self in thee needed to be annihilated. By benignant fever-paroxysms is Life rooting out the deep-seated chronic Diseases, and triumphs over Death. On the roaring billows of Time, thou art not engulfed, but borne aloft into the azure of Eternity. Love not Pleasure; love God.[5] This is the EVERLASTING YEA wherein all contradiction is solved: wherein whoso walks and works, it is well with him."

And again: "Small is it that thou canst trample the Earth with its injuries under thy feet, as old Greek Zeno[6] trained thee: thou canst love the Earth while it injures thee, and even because it injures thee; for this a Greater than Zeno was needed, and he too was sent. Knowest thou that 'Worship of Sorrow'?[7] the Temple thereof, founded some eighteen centuries ago, now lies in ruins, overgrown with jungle, the habitation of doleful creatures:[8] nevertheless, venture forward; in a low crypt, arched out of falling fragments, thou findest the Altar still there, and its sacred Lamp perennially burning."

Without pretending to comment on which strange utterances, the Editor will only remark, that there lies beside them much of a still more questionable

---

3. Adapted from *Wilhelm Meister* by Goethe ("wisest of our time").
4. An exclamation of Wilhelm Meister's (German).
5. Adapted from 2 Timothy 3.4.
6. Stoic philosopher (3rd century B.C.E.), who, after being injured in a fall, is reputed to have

struck the earth with his hand as if the earth were responsible for his injury. Afterward he committed suicide. Hence he is said to "trample the Earth."
7. Christianity.
8. Isaiah 34.13–15.

character; unsuited to the general apprehension; nay wherein he himself does not see his way. Nebulous disquisitions on Religion, yet not without bursts of splendour; on the "perennial continuance of Inspiration"; on Prophecy; that there are "true Priests, as well as Baal-Priests,[9] in our own day": with more of the like sort. We select some fractions, by way of finish to this farrago.

"Cease, my much-respected Herr von Voltaire,"[1] thus apostrophises the Professor: "shut thy sweet voice; for the task appointed thee seems finished. Sufficiently has thou demonstrated this proposition, considerable or otherwise: That the Mythus of the Christian Religion looks not in the eighteenth century as it did in the eighth. Alas, were thy six-and-thirty quartos, and the six-and-thirty thousand other quartos and folios, and flying sheets or reams, printed before and since on the same subject, all needed to convince us of so little! But what next? Wilt thou help us to embody the divine Spirit of that Religion in a new Mythus, in a new vehicle and vesture, that our Souls, otherwise too like perishing, may live? What! thou hast no faculty in that kind? Only a torch for burning, no hammer for building? Take our thanks, then, and—thyself away.

"Meanwhile what are antiquated Mythuses to me? Or is the God present, felt in my own heart, a thing which Herr von Voltaire will dispute out of me; or dispute into me? To the 'Worship of Sorrow' ascribe what origin and genesis thou pleasest, *has* not that Worship originated, and been generated; is it not *here*? Feel it in thy heart, and then say whether it is of God! This is Belief; all else is Opinion,—for which latter whoso will let him worry and be worried."

"Neither," observes he elsewhere, "shall ye tear-out one another's eyes, struggling over 'Plenary Inspiration,'[2] and suchlike: try rather to get a little even Partial Inspiration, each of you for himself. One BIBLE I know, of whose Plenary Inspiration doubt is not so much as possible; nay with my own eyes I saw God's-Hand writing it: thereof all other Bibles are but leaves,—say, in Picture-Writing to assist the weaker faculty."

Or, to give the wearied reader relief, and bring it to an end, let him take the following perhaps more intelligible passage:

"To me, in this our life," says the Professor, "which is an internecine warfare with the Time-spirit, other warfare seems questionable. Hast thou in any way a Contention with thy brother, I advise thee, think well what the meaning thereof is. If thou gauge it to the bottom, it is simply this: 'Fellow, see! thou art taking more than thy share of Happiness in the world, something from *my* share: which, by the Heavens, thou shalt not; nay I will fight thee rather.'—Alas, and the whole lot to be divided is such a beggarly matter, truly a 'feast of shells,'[3] for the substance has been spilled out: not enough to quench one Appetite; and the collective human species clutching at them!— Can we not, in all such cases, rather say: 'Take it, thou too-ravenous individual; take that pitiful additional fraction of a share, which I reckoned mine, but which thou so wantest; take it with a blessing: would to Heaven I had enough for thee!'—If Fichte's *Wissenschaftslehre*[4] be, 'to a certain extent,

9. False priests, mentioned in 1 Kings 18.17–40.
1. French philosopher, satirist, and encyclopedist (1694–1778), famously hostile to superstition, injustice, and organized religion.
2. Doctrine that all statements in the Bible are supernaturally inspired and authoritative. Voltaire had sought to demonstrate that this doctrine was absurd.

3. Empty eggshells. The phrase appears in both James Macpherson's *Fingal* (1761) and Byron's imitation of it, "The Death of Calmer and Orla" (1806).
4. The doctrine of knowledge (German); the shortened title of the 1798 work by Johann Gottlieb Fichte (1762–1814), German philosopher.

Applied Christianity,' surely to a still greater extent, so is this. We have here not a Whole Duty of Man,[5] yet a Half Duty, namely the Passive half: could we but do it, as we can demonstrate it!

"But indeed Conviction, were it never so excellent, is worthless till it convert itself into Conduct. Nay properly Conviction is not possible till then; inasmuch as all Speculation is by nature endless, formless, a vortex amid vortices: only by a felt indubitable certainty of Experience does it find any centre to revolve round, and so fashion itself into a system. Most true is it, as a wise man teaches us, that 'Doubt of any sort cannot be removed except by Action.' On which ground, too, let him who gropes painfully in darkness or uncertain light, and prays vehemently that the dawn may ripen into day, lay this other precept well to heart, which to me was of invaluable service: '*Do the Duty which lies nearest thee,*'[6] which thou knowest to be a Duty! Thy second Duty will already have become clearer.

"May we not say, however, that the hour of Spiritual Enfranchisement is even this: When your Ideal World, wherein the whole man has been dimly struggling and inexpressibly languishing to work, becomes revealed, and thrown open; and you discover, with amazement enough, like the Lothario in *Wilhelm Meister*, that your 'America is here or nowhere'? The Situation that has not its Duty, its Ideal, was never yet occupied by man. Yes here, in this poor, miserable, hampered, despicable Actual, wherein thou even now standest, here or nowhere is thy Ideal: work it out therefrom; and working, believe, live, be free. Fool! the Ideal is in thyself, the impediment too is in thyself: thy Condition is but the stuff thou art to shape that same Ideal out of: what matters whether such stuff be of this sort or that, so the Form thou give it be heroic, be poetic? O thou that pinest in the imprisonment of the Actual, and criest bitterly to the gods for a kingdom wherein to rule and create, know this of a truth: the thing thou seekest is already with thee, 'here or nowhere,' couldst thou only see!

"But it is with man's Soul as it was with Nature: the beginning of Creation is—Light.[7] Till the eye have vision, the whole members are in bonds.[8] Divine moment, when over the tempest-tost Soul, as once over the wild-weltering Chaos, it is spoken: Let there be Light! Ever to the greatest that has felt such moment, is it not miraculous and God-announcing; even as, under simpler figures, to the simplest and least. The mad primeval Discord is hushed; the rudely-jumbled conflicting elements bind themselves into separate Firmaments: deep silent rock-foundations are built beneath; and the skyey vault with its everlasting Luminaries above: instead of a dark wasteful Chaos, we have a blooming, fertile, heaven-encompassed World.

"I too could now say to myself: Be no longer a Chaos, but a World, or even Worldkin.[9] Produce! Produce! Were it but the pitifullest infinitesimal fraction of a Product, produce it, in God's name! 'Tis the utmost thou hast in thee: out with it, then. Up, up! Whatsoever thy hand findeth to do, do it with thy whole might. Work while it is called Today; for the Night cometh, wherein no man can work."[1]

1830–31   1833–34

5. Title of an anonymous book of religious instruction first published in 1659. The phrase is from Ecclesiastes 12.13.
6. This and the previous quotation are from Goethe's *Wilhelm Meister*.
7. Cf. Genesis 1.3: "And God said, Let there be light: and there was light."
8. Cf. Matthew 6.22: "The light of the body is the eye."
9. A little world, a microcosm.
1. Adapted from Ecclesiastes 9.10 and John 9.4.

From Past and Present[1]

From *Democracy*

If the Serene Highnesses and Majesties do not take note of that,[2] then, as I perceive, *that* will take note of itself! The time for levity, insincerity, and idle babble and play-acting, in all kinds, is gone by; it is a serious, grave time. Old long-vexed questions, not yet solved in logical words or parliamentary laws, are fast solving themselves in facts, somewhat unblessed to behold! This largest of questions, this question of Work and Wages, which ought, had we heeded Heaven's voice, to have begun two generations ago or more, cannot be delayed longer without hearing Earth's voice. "Labour" will verily need to be somewhat "organized," as they say,—God knows with what difficulty. Man will actually need to have his debts and earnings a little better paid by man; which, let Parliaments speak of them, or be silent of them, are eternally his due from man, and cannot, without penalty and at length not without death-penalty,[3] be withheld. How much ought to cease among us straightway; how much ought to begin straightway, while the hours yet are!

Truly they are strange results to which this of leaving all to "Cash"; of quietly shutting up the God's Temple, and gradually opening wide-open the Mammon's Temple, with "Laissez-faire, and Every man for himself,"[4]—have led us in these days! We have Upper, speaking Classes, who indeed do "speak" as never man spake before;[5] the withered flimsiness, godless baseness and barrenness of whose Speech might of itself indicate what kind of Doing and practical Governing went on under it! For Speech is the gaseous element out of which most kinds of Practice and Performance, especially all kinds of moral Performance, condense themselves, and take shape; as the one is, so will the other be. Descending, accordingly, into the Dumb Class in its Stockport Cellars and Poor-Law Bastilles,[6] have we not to announce that they are hitherto unexampled in the History of Adam's Posterity?

Life was never a May-game for men: in all times the lot of the dumb millions born to toil was defaced with manifold sufferings, injustices, heavy burdens, avoidable and unavoidable; not play at all, but hard work

---

1. In 1843 there were reputedly one and a half million unemployed in England (out of a population of eighteen million). The closing of factories and the reduction of wages led to severe rioting in the manufacturing districts. Bread-hungry protesters (as well as the Chartist demonstrators who demanded political reforms) caused many observers to dread that a large-scale revolution was imminent. Carlyle was so appalled by the plight of the industrial workers that he postponed his research into the life and times of Cromwell to air his views on the contemporary crisis. *Past and Present*, a book written in seven weeks, was a call for heroic leadership. Cromwell and other historic leaders are cited, but the principal example from the past is Abbot Samson, a medieval monk who established order in the monasteries under his charge. Carlyle hoped that the "Captains of Industry" might provide a comparable leadership in 1843. He was aware that the spread of democracy was inevitable, but he had little confidence in it as a method of producing leaders. Nor did he have any confidence, at this time, in the landed aristocracy, who seemed to him preoccupied with foxhunting, preserving their game, and upholding the tariffs on grain (Corn Laws). In place of a "Do nothing Aristocracy" there was need for a "Working Aristocracy." This first selection is from book 3, chap. 13.

2. The previous chapter, "Reward," had urged that English manufacturers needed the help of everyone and that Parliament should remove the tariffs (Corn Laws) restricting the growth of trade and industry.

3. I.e., by the outbreak of a revolution, as in France.

4. The pursuit of wealth (Mammon is the devil of covetousness) under a noninterventionist economic policy. *Laissez-faire* literally means "let it be" (French).

5. John 7.46.

6. I.e., workhouses for the unemployed. "Stockport Cellars": in a cellar in the slum district of Stockport, an industrial town near Manchester, three children were poisoned by their starving parents, who wanted to collect insurance benefits from a burial society.

that made the sinews sore and the heart sore. As bond-slaves, *villani, bordarii, sochemanni*, nay indeed as dukes, earls and kings, men were oftentimes made weary of their life; and had to say, in the sweat of their brow[7] and of their soul, Behold, it is not sport, it is grim earnest, and our back can bear no more! Who knows not what massacrings and harryings there have been; grinding, long-continuing, unbearable injustices,—till the heart had to rise in madness, and some "*Eu Sachsen, nimith euer sachses*, You Saxons, out with your gully-knives, then!" You Saxons, some "arrestment," partial "arrestment of the Knaves and Dastards" has become indispensable!—The page of Dryasdust[8] is heavy with such details.

And yet I well venture to believe that in no time, since the beginnings of Society, was the lot of those same dumb millions of toilers so entirely unbearable as it is even in the days now passing over us. It is not to die, or even to die of hunger, that makes a man wretched; many men have died; all men must die,—the last exit of us all is in a Fire-Chariot of Pain.[9] But it is to live miserable we know not why; to work sore and yet gain nothing; to be heartworn, weary, yet isolated, unrelated, girt-in with a cold universal Laissez-faire: it is to die slowly all our life long, imprisoned in a deaf, dead, Infinite Injustice, as in the accursed iron belly of a Phalaris' Bull![1] This is and remains for ever intolerable to all men whom God has made. Do we wonder at French Revolutions, Chartisms, Revolts of Three Days?[2] The times, if we will consider them, are really unexampled.

Never before did I hear of an Irish Widow reduced to "prove her sisterhood by dying of typhus-fever and infecting seventeen persons,"—saying in such undeniable way, "You *see*, I was your sister!"[3] Sisterhood, brotherhood, was often forgotten; but not till the rise of these ultimate Mammon and Shotbelt Gospels[4] did I ever see it so expressly denied. If no pious Lord or *Lawward* would remember it, always some pious Lady ("*Hlaf-dig*," Benefactress, "*Loaf-giveress*," they say she is,—blessings on her beautiful heart!) was there, with mild mother-voice and hand, to remember it; some pious thoughtful *Elder*, what we now call "Prester," *Presbyter* or "Priest," was there to put all men in mind of it, in the name of the God who had made all.

Not even in Black Dahomey[5] was it ever, I think, forgotten to the typhus-fever length. Mungo Park,[6] resourceless, had sunk down to die under the Negro Village-Tree, a horrible White object in the eyes of all. But in the poor Black Woman, and her daughter who stood aghast at him, whose earthly wealth and funded capital consisted of one small calabash of rice, there lived a heart richer than "*Laissez-faire*": they, with a royal munificence, boiled their rice for him; they sang all night to him, spinning assiduous on their cotton distaffs, as he lay to sleep: "Let us pity the poor white man; no mother has he to fetch him milk, no sister to grind him corn!" Thou poor black Noble One,—thou *Lady* too: did not a God make thee too; was there not in thee too something of a God!—

7. Genesis 3.19.
8. An imaginary author of dull histories.
9. 2 Kings 2.11.
1. Phalaris was a Sicilian tyrant (6th century B.C.E.) whose victims were roasted alive by being confined inside the brass figure of a bull under which a fire was lit.
2. The 1830 revolution in France (July 27–29).
3. An incident referred to several times in *Past and Present*. Dickens in *Bleak House* (1851) also showed how indifference to the lack of sanitation in London slums led to the spread of disease to other parts of the city.
4. The attitudes of land-owning aristocracy who were committed to preserving their exclusive right to shoot game birds and animals.
5. A state in west Africa where human sacrifice and cannibalism persisted.
6. Explorer and author (1771–1806); he was killed by Africans.

Gurth,[7] born thrall of Cedric the Saxon, has been greatly pitied by Dry-asdust and others. Gurth, with the brass collar round his neck, tending Cedric's pigs in the glades of the wood, is not what I call an exemplar of human felicity: but Gurth, with the sky above him, with the free air and tinted boscage and umbrage round him, and in him at least the certainty of supper and social lodging when he came home; Gurth to me seems happy, in comparison with many a Lancashire and Buckinghamshire man, of these days, not born thrall of anybody! Gurth's brass collar did not gall him: Cedric *deserved* to be his Master. The pigs were Cedric's, but Gurth too would get his parings of them. Gurth had the inexpressible satisfaction of feeling himself related indissolubly, though in a rude brass-collar way, to his fellow-mortals in this Earth. He had superiors, inferiors, equals.—Gurth is now "emancipated" long since; has what we call "Liberty." Liberty, I am told, is a Divine thing. Liberty when it becomes the "Liberty to die by starvation" is not so divine!

Liberty? The true liberty of a man, you would say, consisted in his finding out, or being forced to find out, the right path, and to walk thereon. To learn, or to be taught, what work he actually was able for; and then by permission, persuasion, and even compulsion, to set about doing of the same! That is his true blessedness, honour, "liberty" and maximum of wellbeing: if liberty be not that, I for one have small care about liberty. You do not allow a palpable madman to leap over precipices; you violate his liberty, you that are wise; and keep him, were it in strait-waistcoats, away from the precipices! Every stupid, every cowardly and foolish man is but a less palpable madman: his true liberty were that a wiser man, that any and every wiser man, could, by brass collars, or in whatever milder or sharper way, lay hold of him when he was going wrong, and order and compel him to go a little righter. O, if thou really art my *Senior*, Seigneur, my *Elder*, Presbyter or Priest,—if thou art in very deed my *Wiser*, may a beneficent instinct lead and impel thee to "conquer" me, to command me! If thou do know better than I what is good and right, I conjure[8] thee in the name of God, force me to do it; were it by never such brass collars, whips and handcuffs, leave me not to walk over precipices! That I have been called, by all the Newspapers, a "free man" will avail me little, if my pilgrimage have ended in death and wreck. O that the Newspapers had called me slave, coward, fool, or what it pleased their sweet voices to name me, and I had attained not death, but life!—Liberty requires new definitions.

A conscious abhorrence and intolerance of Folly, of Baseness, Stupidity, Poltroonery and all that brood of things, dwells deep in some men: still deeper in others an *un*conscious abhorrence and intolerance, clothed moreover by the beneficent Supreme Powers in what stout appetites, energies, egoisms so-called, are suitable to it;—these latter are your Conquerors, Romans, Normans, Russians, Indo-English; Founders of what we call Aristocracies. Which indeed have they not the most "divine right" to found;—being themselves very truly *Aristoi*, Bravest, Best; and conquering generally a confused rabble of Worst, or at lowest, clearly enough, of Worse? I think their divine right, tried, with affirmatory verdict, in the greatest Law-Court known to me, was good! A class of men who are dreadfully exclaimed against

---

7. A swineherd described in Scott's *Ivanhoe* (1819).
8. Solemnly charge.

by Dryasdust; of whom nevertheless beneficent Nature has oftentimes had need; and may, alas, again have need.

When, across the hundredfold poor scepticisms, trivialisms, and constitutional cobwebberies of Dryasdust, you catch any glimpse of a William the Conqueror, a Tancred of Hauteville[9] or such like,—do you not discern veritably some rude outline of a true God-made King; whom not the Champion of England[1] cased in tin, but all Nature and the Universe were calling to the throne? It is absolutely necessary that he get thither. Nature does not mean her poor Saxon children to perish, of obesity, stupor or other malady, as yet: a stern Ruler and Line of Rulers therefore is called in,—a stern but most beneficent *perpetual House-Surgeon* is by Nature herself called in, and even the appropriate *fees* are provided for him! Dryasdust talks lamentably about Hereward and the Fen Counties; fate of earl Waltheof;[2] Yorkshire and the North reduced to ashes; all of which is undoubtedly lamentable. But even Dryasdust apprises me of one fact: "A child, in this William's reign, might have carried a purse of gold from end to end of England." My erudite friend, it is a fact which outweighs a thousand! Sweep away thy constitutional, sentimental, and other cobwebberies; look eye to eye, if thou still have any eye, in the face of this big burly William Bastard: thou wilt see a fellow of most flashing discernment, of most strong lion-heart;—in whom, as it were, within a frame of oak and iron, the gods have planted the soul of "a man of genius"! Dost thou call that nothing? I call it an immense thing!—Rage enough was in this Willelmus Conquaestor, rage enough for his occasions;—and yet the essential element of him, as of all such men, is not scorching *fire*, but shining illuminative *light*. Fire and light are strangely interchangeable; nay, at bottom, I have found them different forms of the same most godlike "elementary substance" in our world: a thing worth stating in these days. The essential element of this Conquaestor is, first of all, the most sun-eyed perception of what *is* really what on this God's-Earth;—which, thou wilt find, does mean at bottom "Justice," and "Virtues" not a few: *Conformity* to what the Maker has seen good to make; that, I suppose, will mean Justice and a Virtue or two?—

Dost thou think Willelmus Conquaestor would have tolerated ten years' jargon, one hour's jargon, on the propriety of killing Cotton-manufactures by partridge Corn-Laws?[3] I fancy, this was not the man to knock out of his night's-rest with nothing but a noisy bedlamism in your mouth![4] "Assist us still better to bush the partridges; strangle Plugson who spins the shirts?"— *"Par la Splendeur de Dieu!"*[5]—Dost thou think Willelmus Conquaestor, in

9. Norman hero of the First Crusade (1095–99). King William I of England (ca. 1028–1087; reigned 1066–87), surnamed *the Conqueror* after the Battle of Hastings in 1066. Being an illegitimate son, he also bore the surname of William the Bastard. Although some historians condemn William as a ruthless ruler, he is ranked by Carlyle as a hero because of his strong and efficient government. William fulfilled the requirements of the kingly hero described by Carlyle in his lectures *On Heroes:* a man fittest "to *command* over us . . . to tell us what we are to *do*."
1. An official who goes through a formality, at coronation ceremonies, of demanding whether anyone challenges the right of the monarch to ascend the throne. He wears full armor ("cased in tin") and is a symbol of outworn feudal customs.
2. His execution in 1075, on a supposedly

trumped-up charge, is cited as a blot on William's record as king. Hereward the Wake was an outlaw whose exploits against William the Conqueror made him seem a romantic figure like Robin Hood.
3. See nn. 1, 2, p. 576.
4. I.e., not the man to disturb with your mad ravings. Bedlam, the hospital of St. Mary in Bethlehem, was London's most famous lunatic asylum.
5. By the splendor of God! (French): one of William's oaths. Plugson of Undershot was Carlyle's fictive representative of the new class of industrial leaders. This imaginary speech ("Assist us . . .") sums up the pleas of the High Tariff lobby in Parliament. "Keep the Corn Laws intact so that the aristocratic landlords may continue to enjoy shooting partridges on their estates; subdue the manufacturing leaders by preventing trade."

this new time, with Steam-engine Captains of Industry on one hand of him, and Joe-Manton Captains of Idleness[6] on the other, would have doubted which *was* really the BEST; which did deserve strangling, and which not?

I have a certain indestructible regard for Willelmus Conquaestor. A resident House-Surgeon, provided by Nature for her beloved English People, and even furnished with the requisite fees, as I said; for he by no means felt himself doing Nature's work, this Willelmus, but his own work exclusively! And his own work withal it was; informed *"par la Splendeur de Dieu."*—I say, it is necessary to get the work out of such a man, however harsh that be! When a world, not yet doomed for death, is rushing down to ever-deeper Baseness and Confusion, it is a dire necessity of Nature's to bring in her ARISTOCRACIES, her BEST, even by forcible methods. When their descendants or representatives cease entirely to *be* the Best, Nature's poor world will very soon rush down again to Baseness; and it becomes a dire necessity of Nature's to cast them out. Hence French Revolutions, Five-point Charters,[7] Democracies, and a mournful list of *Etceteras*, in these our afflicted times.

* * *

Democracy, the chase of Liberty in that direction, shall go its full course; unrestrained by him of Pferdefuss-Quacksalber,[8] or any of *his* household. The Toiling Millions of Mankind, in most vital need and passionate instinctive desire of Guidance, shall cast away False-Guidance; and hope, for an hour, that No-Guidance will suffice them: but it can be for an hour only. The smallest item of human Slavery is the oppression of man by his Mock-Superiors; the palpablest, but I say at bottom the smallest. Let him shake off such oppression, trample it indignantly under his feet; I blame him not, I pity and commend him. But oppression by your Mock-Superiors well shaken off, the grand problem yet remains to solve: That of finding government by your Real-Superiors! Alas, how shall we ever learn the solution of that, benighted, bewildered, sniffing, sneering, godforgetting unfortunates as we are? It is a work for centuries; to be taught us by tribulations, confusions, insurrections, obstructions; who knows if not by conflagration and despair! It is a lesson inclusive of all other lessons; the hardest of all lessons to learn.

Captains of Industry[9]

If I believed that Mammonism with its adjuncts was to continue henceforth the one serious principle of our existence, I should reckon it idle to solicit remedial measures from any Government, the disease being insusceptible of remedy. Government can do much, but it can in no wise do all. Government, as the most conspicuous object in Society, is called upon to give signal of what shall be done; and, in many ways, to preside over further, and command the doing of it. But the Government cannot do, by all its signalling and commanding, what the Society is radically indisposed to do. In the long-run every Government is the exact symbol of its People, with their wisdom and unwisdom; we have to say, Like People like Government.—The main sub-

6. The idle aristocracy who wasted time shooting partridges with guns made by Joseph Manton, a London gunsmith.
7. The Chartist movement for political reform called first for six, then for five major changes to the existing system of parliamentary democracy.
8. Horse foot quack doctor (a fake German name invented by Carlyle).
9. From book 4, chap. 4.

stance of this immense Problem of Organizing Labour, and first of all of Managing the Working Classes, will, it is very clear, have to be solved by those who stand practically in the middle of it; by those who themselves work and preside over work. Of all that can be enacted by any Parliament in regard to it, the germs must already lie potentially extant in those two Classes, who are to obey such enactment. A Human Chaos *in* which there is no light, you vainly attempt to irradiate by light shed *on* it: order never can arise there.

But it is my firm conviction that the "Hell of England" will *cease* to be that of "not making money"; that we shall get a nobler Hell and a nobler Heaven! I anticipate light *in* the Human Chaos, glimmering, shining more and more; under manifold true signals from without That light shall shine. Our deity no longer being Mammon,—O Heavens, each man will then say to himself: "Why such deadly haste to make money? I shall not go to Hell, even if I do not make money! There is another Hell, I am told!" Competition, at railway-speed, in all branches of commerce and work will then abate:—good felt-hats for the head, in every sense, instead of seven-feet lath-and-plaster hats on wheels,[1] will then be discoverable! Bubble-periods,[2] with their panics and commercial crises, will again become infrequent; steady modest industry will take the place of gambling speculation. To be a noble Master, among noble Workers, will again be the first ambition with some few; to be a rich Master only the second. How the Inventive Genius of England, with the whirr of its bobbins and billy-rollers[3] shoved somewhat into the backgrounds of the brain, will contrive and devise, not cheaper produce exclusively, but fairer distribution of the produce at its present cheapness! By degrees, we shall again have a Society with something of Heroism in it, something of Heaven's Blessing on it; we shall again have, as my German friend[4] asserts, "instead of Mammon-Feudalism with unsold cotton-shirts and Preservation of the Game, noble just Industrialism and Government by the Wisest!"

It is with the hope of awakening here and there a British man to know himself for a man and divine soul, that a few words of parting admonition, to all persons to whom the Heavenly Powers have lent power of any kind in this land, may now be addressed. And first to those same Master-Workers, Leaders of Industry; who stand nearest, and in fact powerfullest, though not most prominent, being as yet in too many senses a Virtuality rather than an Actuality.

The Leaders of Industry, if Industry is ever to be led, are virtually the Captains of the World; if there be no nobleness in them, there will never be an Aristocracy more. But let the Captains of Industry consider: once again, are they born of other clay than the old Captains of Slaughter; doomed for ever to be not Chivalry, but a mere gold-plated *Doggery*,—what the French well name *Canaille*, "Doggery" with more or less gold carrion at its disposal? Captains of Industry are the true Fighters, henceforth recognizable as the only true ones: Fighters against Chaos, Necessity and the Devils and Jötuns;[5] and lead on Mankind in that great, and alone true, and universal warfare; the stars in their courses fighting for them, and all Heaven and all Earth

---

1. A London hatter's mode of advertising.
2. Periods of violent fluctuation in the stock market caused by unsound speculating.
3. Machines used to prepare cotton or wool for spinning.
4. Teufelsdröckh, the hero of *Sartor Resartus* (1833–34).
5. Giants of Scandinavian mythology.

saying audibly, Well done! Let the Captains of Industry retire into their own hearts, and ask solemnly, If there is nothing but vulturous hunger for fine wines, valet reputation and gilt carriages, discoverable there? Of hearts made by the Almighty God I will not believe such a thing. Deep-hidden under wretchedest god-forgetting Cants, Epicurisms, Dead-Sea Apisms;[6] forgotten as under foullest fat Lethe[7] mud and weeds, there is yet, in all hearts born into this God's-World, a spark of the Godlike slumbering. Awake, O nightmare sleepers; awake, arise, or be for ever fallen![8] This is not playhouse poetry; it is sober fact. Our England, our world cannot live as it is. It will connect itself with a God again, or go down with nameless throes and fire-consummation to the Devils. Thou who feelest aught of such a Godlike stirring in thee, any faintest intimation of it as through heavy-laden dreams, follow *it*, I conjure thee. Arise, save thyself, be one of those that save thy country.

Bucaniers,[9] Chactaw Indians, whose supreme aim in fighting is that they may get the scalps, the money, that they may amass scalps and money; out of such came no Chivalry, and never will! Out of such came only gore and wreck, infernal rage and misery; desperation quenched in annihilation. Behold it, I bid thee, behold there, and consider! What is it that thou have a hundred thousand-pound bills laid up in thy strong-room, a hundred scalps hung up in thy wigwam? I value not them or thee. Thy scalps and thy thousand-pound bills are as yet nothing, if no nobleness from within irradiate them; if no Chivalry, in action, or in embryo ever struggling towards birth and action, be there.

Love of men cannot be bought by cash-payment; and without love, men cannot endure to be together. You cannot lead a Fighting World without having it regimented, chivalried: the thing, in a day, becomes impossible; all men in it, the highest at first, the very lowest at last, discern consciously, or by a noble instinct, this necessity. And can you any more continue to lead a Working World unregimented, anarchic? I answer, and the Heavens and Earth are now answering, No! The thing becomes not "in a day" impossible; but in some two generations it does. Yes, when fathers and mothers, in Stockport hunger-cellars, begin to eat their children, and Irish widows have to prove their relationship by dying of typhus-fever; and amid Governing "Corporations of the Best and Bravest," busy to preserve their game by "bushing," dark millions of God's human creatures start up in mad Chartisms, impracticable Sacred-Months, and Manchester Insurrections;[1]—and there is a virtual Industrial Aristocracy as yet only half-alive, spell-bound amid money-bags and ledgers; and an actual Idle Aristocracy seemingly near dead in somnolent delusions, in trespasses and double-barrels,[2] "sliding," as on inclined-planes, which every new year they *soap* with new Hansard's-jargon under God's sky, and so are "sliding" ever faster, towards a "scale"[3] and

---

6. A reference to a Muslim story in which members of a tribe living near the Dead Sea were transformed into apes because they had ignored the prophecies of Moses.
7. The river of forgetfulness in the classical underworld.
8. Satan's appeal to the devils in Milton's *Paradise Lost* 1.330.
9. Buccaneers.
1. In 1819 a large open-air labor meeting in Manchester was broken up by charging cavalry. Thirteen men and women were massacred, and many

others were wounded. "Bushing": protecting game from poachers who use nets, by positioning bushes or branches on the grounds.
2. I.e., the only concern of the landed aristocrats is to keep trespassers off their game preserves and reserve shooting rights to themselves.
3. The "sliding scale" refers to the system of variable tariffs within the Corn Laws that benefited the aristocratic landlords. "Hansard's-jargon": parliamentary oratory, as in Hansard's printed record of debates in the Houses of Parliament.

balance-scale whereon is written *Thou art found Wanting;*[4]—in such days, after a generation or two, I say, it does become, even to the low and simple, very palpably impossible! No Working World, any more than a Fighting World, can be led on without a noble Chivalry of Work, and laws and fixed rules which follow out of that,—far nobler than any Chivalry of Fighting was. As an anarchic multitude on mere Supply-and-demand, it is becoming inevitable that we dwindle in horrid suicidal convulsion, and self-abrasion, frightful to the imagination, into *Chactaw* Workers. With wigwams and scalps,—with palaces and thousand-pound bills; with savagery, depopulation, chaotic desolation! Good Heavens, will not one French Revolution and Reign of Terror suffice us, but must there be two? There will be two if needed; there will be twenty if needed; there will be precisely as many as needed. The Laws of Nature will have themselves fulfilled. That is a thing certain to me.

Your gallant battle-hosts and work-hosts, as the others did, will need to be made loyally yours; they must and will be regulated, methodically secured in their just share of conquest under you;—joined with you in veritable brotherhood, sonhood, by quite other and deeper ties than those of temporary day's wages! How would mere redcoated regiments, to say nothing of chivalries, fight for you, if you could discharge them on the evening of the battle, on payment of the stipulated shillings,—and they discharge you on the morning of it! Chelsea Hospitals,[5] pensions, promotions, rigorous lasting covenant on the one side and on the other, are indispensable even for a hired fighter. The Feudal Baron, much more,—how could he subsist with mere temporary mercenaries round him, at sixpence a day; ready to go over to the other side, if sevenpence were offered? He could not have subsisted;—and his noble instinct saved him from the necessity of even trying! The Feudal Baron had a Man's Soul in him; to which anarchy, mutiny, and the other fruits of temporary mercenaries, were intolerable: he had never been a Baron otherwise, but had continued a Chactaw and Bucanier. He felt it precious, and at last it became habitual, and his fruitful enlarged existence included it as a necessity, to have men round him who in heart loved him; whose life he watched over with rigour yet with love; who were prepared to give their life for him, if need came. It was beautiful; it was human! Man lives not otherwise, nor can live contented, anywhere or anywhen. Isolation is the sum-total of wretchedness to man. To be cut off, to be left solitary: to have a world alien, not your world; all a hostile camp for you; not a home at all, of hearts and faces who are yours, whose you are! It is the frightfullest enchantment; too truly a work of the Evil One. To have neither superior, nor inferior, nor equal, united manlike to you. Without father, without child, without brother. Man knows no sadder destiny. "How is each of us," exclaims Jean Paul,[6] "so lonely in the wide bosom of the All!" Encased each as in his transparent "ice-palace"; our brother visible in his, making signals and gesticulations to us;—visible, but for ever unattainable: on his bosom we shall never rest, nor he on ours. It was not a God that did this; no!

Awake, ye noble Workers, warriors in the one true war: all this must be remedied. It is you who are already half-alive, whom I will welcome into life; whom I will conjure in God's name to shake off your enchanted sleep, and live wholly! Cease to count scalps, goldpurses; not in these lies your or

4. The message of the miraculous writing on the wall in Daniel 5.
5. Homes for disabled veterans.

6. Jean Paul Richter (1763–1825), German humorist.

our salvation. Even these, if you count only these, will not be left. Let bucaniering be put far from you; alter, speedily abrogate all laws of the bucaniers, if you would gain any victory that shall endure. Let God's justice, let pity, nobleness and manly valour, with more gold-purses or with fewer, testify themselves in this your brief Life-transit to all the Eternities, the Gods and Silences. It is to you I call; for ye are not dead, ye are already half-alive: there is in you a sleepless dauntless energy, the prime-matter of all nobleness in man. Honour to you in your kind. It is to you I call: ye know at least this, That the mandate of God to His creature man is: Work! The future Epic of the World rests not with those that are near dead, but with those that are alive, and those that are coming into life.

Look around you. Your world-hosts are all in mutiny, in confusion, destitution; on the eve of fiery wreck and madness! They will not march farther for you, on the sixpence a day and supply-and-demand principle; they will not; nor ought they, nor can they. Ye shall reduce them to order, begin reducing them. To order, to just subordination; noble loyalty in return for noble guidance. Their souls are driven nigh mad; let yours be sane and ever saner. Not as a bewildered bewildering mob; but as a firm regimented mass, with real captains over them, will these men march any more. All human interests, combined human endeavours, and social growths in this world, have, at a certain stage of their development, required organizing: and Work, the grandest of human interests, does now require it.

God knows, the task will be hard: but no noble task was ever easy. This task will wear away your lives, and the lives of your sons and grandsons: but for what purpose, if not for tasks like this, were lives given to men? Ye shall cease to count your thousand-pound scalps, the noble of you shall cease! Nay, the very scalps, as I say, will not long be left if you count on these. Ye shall cease wholly to be barbarous vulturous Chactaws, and become noble European Nineteenth-Century Men. Ye shall know that Mammon, in never such gigs[7] and flunkey "respectabilities," is not the alone God; that of himself he is but a Devil, and even a Brute-god.

Difficult? Yes, it will be difficult. The short-fibre cotton; that too was difficult. The waste cotton-shrub, long useless, disobedient, as the thistle by the wayside,—have ye not conquered it; made it into beautiful bandana webs; white woven shirts for men; bright-tinted air-garments wherein flit goddesses? Ye have shivered mountains asunder, made the hard iron pliant to you as soft putty: the Forest-giants, Marsh-jötuns bear sheaves of golden grain; Aegir the Seademon[8] himself stretches his back for a sleek highway to you, and on Firehorses and Windhorses ye career. Ye are most strong. Thor red-bearded, with his blue sun-eyes, with his cheery heart and strong thunder-hammer, he and you have prevailed. Ye are most strong, ye Sons of the icy North, of the far East,—far marching from your rugged Eastern Wildernesses, hitherward from the grey Dawn of Time! Ye are Sons of the *Jötun-land*; the land of Difficulties Conquered. Difficult? You must try this thing. Once try it with the understanding that it will and shall have to be done. Try it as ye try the paltrier thing, making of money! I will bet on you once more, against all Jötuns, Tailor-gods,[9] Double-barrelled Law-wards, and Denizens of Chaos whatsoever.

1843   1843

---

7. Light carriages; to own one was a sign of respectability.

8. From Scandinavian mythology.
9. False gods.

ELIZABETH BARRETT BROWNING
1806–1861

During her lifetime Elizabeth Barrett Browning was one of England's most famous poets. Passionately admired by contemporaries as diverse as John Ruskin, Algernon Charles Swinburne, and Emily Dickinson for her moral and emotional ardor and her energetic engagement with the issues of her day, she was better known than her husband, Robert Browning, at the time of her death. Her work fell into disrepute with the modernist reaction against what was seen as the inappropriate didacticism and rhetorical excess of Victorian poetry; but recently scholars interested in her exploration of what it means to be a woman poet and in her response to social and political events have restored her status as a major writer.

Barrett Browning received an unusual education for a woman of her time. Availing herself of her brother's tutor, she studied Latin and Greek. She read voraciously in history, philosophy, and literature and began to write poetry from an early age—her first volume of poetry was published when she was thirteen. But as her intellectual and literary powers matured, her personal life became increasingly circumscribed both by ill health and by a tyrannically protective father, who had forbidden any of his eleven children to marry. By the age of thirty-nine, Elizabeth Barrett was a prominent woman of letters who lived in semiseclusion as an invalid in her father's house, where she occasionally received visitors in her room. One of these visitors was Robert Browning, who, moved by his admiration of her poetry, wrote to tell her "I do as I say, love these books with all my heart—and I love you too." He thereby initiated a courtship that culminated in 1846 in their secret marriage and elopement to Italy, for which her father never forgave her. In Italy Barrett Browning regained much health and strength, bearing and raising a son, Pen, to whom she was ardently devoted, and becoming deeply involved in Italian nationalist politics. She and her husband made their home in Florence, at the house called Casa Guidi, where she died in 1861.

Barrett Browning's poetry is characterized by a fervent moral sensibility. In her early work she tended to use the visionary modes of Romantic narrative poetry, but she turned increasingly to contemporary topics, particularly to liberal causes of her day. For example, in 1843, when government investigations exposed the exploitation of children employed in coal mines and factories, she wrote "The Cry of the Children," a powerful indictment of the appalling use of child labor. Like Harriet Beecher Stowe in *Uncle Tom's Cabin* (1851–52), Barrett Browning uses literature as a tool of social protest and reform, lending her voice, for example, to the cause of American abolitionism in "The Runaway Slave at Pilgrim's Point." In later poems she took up the cause of the *risorgimento,* the movement to unify Italy as a nation-state, in which Italy's struggle for freedom and identity found resonance with her own.

For many years Elizabeth Barrett Browning was best-known for her *Sonnets from the Portuguese* (1850), a sequence of forty-four sonnets presented under the guise of a translation from the Portuguese language, in which she recorded the stages of her love for Robert Browning. But increasingly, her verse novel *Aurora Leigh* (1857) has attracted critical attention. The poem depicts the growth of a woman poet and is thus, as Cora Kaplan observes, the first work in English by a woman writer in which the heroine herself is an author. When Barrett Browning first envisioned the poem, she wrote, "My chief *intention* just now is the writing of a sort of novel-poem . . . running into the midst of our conventions, and rushing into drawing-rooms and the like 'where angels fear to tread'; and so, meeting face to face and without mask the Humanity of the age, and speaking the truth as I conceive of it out plainly." The poem is a portrait of the artist as a young woman committed to a socially inclusive realist art. It is a daring work both in its presentation of social issues concerning women and in its claims for Aurora's poetic vocation; on her twentieth birthday, to pursue her career as a poet, Aurora refuses a proposal of marriage from her cousin Romney, who wants her to be his helpmate in the liberal causes he has embraced. Later in the poem, she rescues a fallen woman and takes her to Italy, where they settle together and confront a chastened Romney.

Immensely popular in its own day, *Aurora Leigh* had extravagant admirers (like Ruskin, who asserted that it was the greatest poem written in English) and critics who found fault with both its poetry and its morality. With its crowded canvas and melodramatic plot, it seems closer to the novel than to poetry, but it is important to view the poem in the context of the debate about appropriate poetic subject matter that engaged other Victorian poets. Unlike Matthew Arnold, who believed that the present age had not produced actions heroic enough to be the subject of great poetry, and unlike Alfred, Lord Tennyson, who used Arthurian legend to represent contemporary concerns, Barrett Browning felt that the present age contained the materials for an epic poetry. Virginia Woolf writes that "Elizabeth Barrett was inspired by a flash of true genius when she rushed into the drawing-room and said that here, where we live and work, is the true place for the poet." *Aurora Leigh* succeeds in giving us what Woolf describes as "a sense of life in general, of people who are unmistakably

"Hurrier." An illustration of a "hurrier" in a Yorkshire coalmine, from the 1842–43 Children's Employment Commission report, which informed Barrett Browning's "The Cry of the Children."

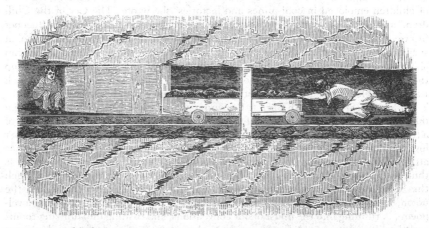

"Trapper" and "Thruster." An illustration of a "trapper" and a "thruster" in a Lancashire coalmine, from the 1842–43 Children's Employment Commission report.

Victorian, wrestling with the problems of their own time, all brightened, intensified, and compacted by the fire of poetry. . . . Aurora Leigh, with her passionate interest in social questions, her conflict as artist and woman, her longing for knowledge and freedom, is the true daughter of her age."

The Cry of the Children[1]

"*Φεῦ, φεῦ, τί προσδέρκεσθέ μ' ὄμμασιν, τέκνα;*"
—*Medea*[2]

Do ye hear the children weeping, O my brothers,
    Ere the sorrow comes with years?
They are leaning their young heads against their mothers,
    And *that* cannot stop their tears.
5   The young lambs are bleating in the meadows,
    The young birds are chirping in the nest,
The young fawns are playing with the shadows,
    The young flowers are blowing toward the west—
But the young, young children, O my brothers,
10   They are weeping bitterly!
They are weeping in the playtime of the others,
    In the country of the free.

Do you question the young children in the sorrow
    Why their tears are falling so?
15 The old man may weep for his to-morrow
      Which is lost in Long Ago;
The old tree is leafless in the forest,
    The old year is ending in the frost,
The old wound, if stricken, is the sorest,
20   The old hope is hardest to be lost:
But the young, young children, O my brothers,
      Do you ask them why they stand
Weeping sore° before the bosoms of their mothers,   *bitterly*
    In our happy Fatherland?
25 They look up with their pale and sunken faces,
    And their looks are sad to see,
For the man's hoary anguish draws and presses
      Down the cheeks of infancy;
"Your old earth," they say, "is very dreary,"
30   "Our young feet," they say, "are very weak;
Few paces have we taken, yet are weary—
    Our grave-rest is very far to seek:
Ask the aged why they weep, and not the children,
    For the outside earth is cold,

---

1. Barrett Browning wrote "The Cry of the Children" in response to the report of a parliamentary commission, to which her friend R. H. Horne contributed, on the labor of children in mines and factories. Many of the details of Barrett Browning's poem derive from the report. Illustrations from this report appear on the facing page.

2. Alas, my children, why do you look at me? (Greek), from Euripides' tragedy *Medea*. Medea speaks these lines before killing her children in vengeance against her husband, who has taken a new wife. (The poem's title is spoken by the chorus.)

35   And we young ones stand without, in our bewildering,
            And the graves are for the old."

        "True," say the children, "it may happen
            That we die before our time:
        Little Alice died last year, her grave is shapen
40   Like a snowball, in the rime.°   *frost*
        We looked into the pit prepared to take her:
            Was no room for any work in the close clay!
        From the sleep wherein she lieth none will wake her,
            Crying, 'Get up, little Alice! it is day.'
45   If you listen by that grave, in sun and shower,
            With your ear down, little Alice never cries;
        Could we see her face, be sure we should not know her,
            For the smile has time for growing in her eyes:
        And merry go her moments, lulled and stilled in
50   The shroud by the kirk° chime.   *church*
        It is good when it happens," say the children,
            "That we die before our time."

        Alas, alas, the children! they are seeking
            Death in life, as best to have:
55   They are binding up their hearts away from breaking,
            With a ceremen° from the grave.   *shroud*
        Go out, children, from the mine and from the city,
            Sing out, children, as the little thrushes do;
        Pluck your handfuls of the meadow-cowslips pretty,
60   Laugh aloud, to feel your fingers let them through!
        But they answer, "Are your cowslips of the meadows
            Like our weeds anear the mine?[3]
        Leave us quiet in the dark of the coal-shadows,
            From your pleasures fair and fine!

65   "For oh," say the children, "we are weary,
            And we cannot run or leap;
        If we cared for any meadows, it were merely
            To drop down in them and sleep.
        Our knees tremble sorely in the stooping,
70   We fall upon our faces, trying to go;
        And, underneath our heavy eyelids drooping,
            The reddest flower would look as pale as snow.
        For, all day, we drag our burden tiring
            Through the coal-dark, underground;
75   Or, all day, we drive the wheels of iron
            In the factories, round and round.

        "For, all day, the wheels are droning, turning;
            Their wind comes in our faces,
        Till our hearts turn, our heads with pulses burning,
80   And the walls turn in their places:

---

3. A commissioner mentions the fact of weeds being thus confounded with the idea of flowers [Barrett Browning's note].

Turns the sky in the high window blank and reeling,
    Turns the long light that drops adown the wall,
Turn the black flies that crawl along the ceiling,
    All are turning, all the day, and we with all.
85   And all day, the iron wheels are droning,
       And sometimes we could pray,
'O ye wheels,' (breaking out in a mad moaning)
       'Stop! be silent for to-day!' "

Ay, be silent! Let them hear each other breathing
90   For a moment, mouth to mouth!
Let them touch each other's hands, in a fresh wreathing
       Of their tender human youth!
Let them feel that this cold metallic motion
       Is not all the life God fashions or reveals:
95   Let them prove their living souls against the notion
       That they live in you, or under you, O wheels!
Still, all day, the iron wheels go onward,
       Grinding life down from its mark;
And the children's souls, which God is calling sunward,
100   Spin on blindly in the dark.

Now tell the poor young children; O my brothers,
       To look up to Him and pray;
So the blessed One who blesseth all the others,
       Will bless them another day.
105 They answer, "Who is God that He should hear us,
       While the rushing of the iron wheels is stirred?
When we sob aloud, the human creatures near us
       Pass by, hearing not, or answer not a word.
And *we* hear not (for the wheels in their resounding)
110   Strangers speaking at the door:
Is it likely God, with angels singing round Him,
       Hears our weeping any more?

Two words, indeed, of praying we remember,
       And at midnight's hour of harm,
115 'Our Father,' looking upward in the chamber,
       We say softly for a charm.
We know no other words except 'Our Father.'
       And we think that, in some pause of angels' song,
God may pluck them with the silence sweet to gather,
120   And hold both within His right hand which is strong.
'Our Father!' If He heard us, He would surely
       (For they call Him good and mild)
Answer, smiling down the steep world very purely,
       'Come and rest with me, my child.'

125 "But, no!" say the children, weeping faster,
       "He is speechless as a stone:
And they tell us, of His image is the master
       Who commands us to work on.
Go to!" say the children,—"up in Heaven,

130   Dark, wheel-like, turning clouds are all we find.
       Do not mock us; grief has made us unbelieving:
       We look up for God, but tears have made us blind."
       Do you hear the children weeping and disproving,
           O my brothers, what ye preach?
135   For God's possible is taught by His world's loving,[4]
           And the children doubt of each.

       And well may the children weep before you!
           They are weary ere they run;
       They have never seen the sunshine, nor the glory
140   Which is brighter than the sun.
       They know the grief of man, without its wisdom;
         They sink in man's despair, without its calm;
       Are slaves, without the liberty in Christdom,
         Are martyrs, by the pang without the palm:[5]
145   Are worn as if with age, yet unretrievingly
           The harvest of its memories cannot reap,—
       Are orphans of the earthly love and heavenly.
           Let them weep! let them weep!

       They look up with their pale and sunken faces,
150   And their look is dread to see,
       For they mind you of their angels in high places,
           With eyes turned on Deity.
       "How long," they say, "how long, O cruel nation,
         Will you stand, to move the world, on a child's heart,—
155   Stifle down with a mailed heel its palpitation,
         And tread onward to your throne amid the mart?
       Our blood splashes upward, O gold-heaper,
           And your purple[6] shows your path!
       But the child's sob in the silence curses deeper
160   Than the strong man in his wrath."

                          1843

From Sonnets from the Portuguese

21

     Say over again, and yet once over again,
     That thou dost love me. Though the word repeated
     Should seem "a cuckoo song,"[1] as thou dost treat it,
     Remember, never to the hill or plain,
5   Valley and wood, without her cuckoo strain
     Comes the fresh Spring in all her green completed.
     Belovèd, I, amid the darkness greeted
     By a doubtful spirit voice, in that doubt's pain

---

4. I.e., we gain our sense of the possibilities of God's love from our experience of love in the world.
5. Palm branch, symbol of victory.

6. Color associated with royalty and (in poetry) with blood.
1. The cuckoo has a repeating call.

Cry, "Speak once more—thou lovest!" Who can fear
10 Too many stars, though each in heaven shall roll,
Too many flowers, though each shall crown the year?
Say thou dost love me, love me, love me—toll
The silver iterance!°—only minding, Dear,   *repetition*
To love me also in silence with thy soul.

22

When our two souls stand up erect and strong,
Face to face, silent, drawing nigh and nigher,
Until the lengthening wings break into fire
At either curvèd point—what bitter wrong
5 Can the earth do to us, that we should not long
Be here contented? Think. In mounting higher,
The angels would press on us and aspire
To drop some golden orb of perfect song
Into our deep, dear silence. Let us stay
10 Rather on earth, Belovèd,—where the unfit
Contrarious moods of men recoil away
And isolate pure spirits, and permit
A place to stand and love in for a day,
With darkness and the death-hour rounding it.

32

The first time that the sun rose on thine oath
To love me, I looked forward to the moon
To slacken all those bonds which seemed too soon
And quickly tied to make a lasting troth.
5 Quick-loving hearts, I thought, may quickly loathe;
And, looking on myself, I seemed not one
For such man's love!—more like an out-of-tune
Worn viol, a good singer would be wroth
To spoil his song with, and which, snatched in haste,
10 Is laid down at the first ill-sounding note.
I did not wrong myself so, but I placed
A wrong on *thee*. For perfect strains may float
'Neath master-hands, from instruments defaced—
And great souls, at one stroke, may do and dote.

43

How do I love thee? Let me count the ways.
I love thee to the depth and breadth and height
My soul can reach, when feeling out of sight
For the ends of Being and ideal Grace.
5 I love thee to the level of everyday's
Most quiet need, by sun and candlelight.
I love thee freely, as men strive for Right;
I love thee purely, as they turn from Praise.
I love thee with the passion put to use
10 In my old griefs, and with my childhood's faith.

I love thee with a love I seemed to lose
With my lost saints—I love thee with the breath,
Smiles, tears, of all my life!—and, if God choose,
I shall but love thee better after death.

1845–47   1850

The Runaway Slave at Pilgrim's Point[1]

I

I stand on the mark beside the shore
    Of the first white pilgrim's bended knee,
Where exile turned to ancestor,
    And God was thanked for liberty.
5   I have run through the night, my skin is as dark,
    I bend my knee down on this mark:
        I look on the sky and the sea.

II

O pilgrim-souls, I speak to you!
    I see you come proud and slow
10   From the land of the spirits pale as dew
    And round me and round me ye go.
O pilgrims, I have gasped and run
All night long from the whips of one
    Who in your names works sin and woe!

III

15   And thus I thought that I would come
    And kneel here where ye knelt before,
And feel your souls around me hum
    In undertone to the ocean's roar;
And lift my black face, my black hand,
20   Here, in your names, to curse this land
    Ye blessed in freedom's, evermore.

IV

I am black, I am black,
    And yet God made me, they say:
But if He did so, smiling back
25   He must have cast his work away
Under the feet of his white creatures,
With a look of scorn, that the dusky features
    Might be trodden again to clay.

V

And yet He has made dark things
30   To be glad and merry as light:

1. Plymouth Rock, Massachusetts, where the Pilgrims landed in November 1620.

There's a little dark bird sits and sings,
   There's a dark stream ripples out of sight,
And the dark frogs chant in the safe morass,°   *marsh*
And the sweetest stars are made to pass
35   O'er the face of the darkest night.

VI

But *we* who are dark, we are dark!
   Ah God, we have no stars!
About our souls in care and cark°   *anxiety*
   Our blackness shuts like prison-bars:
40 The poor souls crouch so far behind
That never a comfort can they find
   By reaching through the prison-bars.

VII

Indeed we live beneath the sky,
   That great smooth Hand of God stretched out
45 On all His children fatherly,
   To save them from the dread and doubt
Which would be if, from this low place,
All opened straight up to His face
   Into the grand eternity.

VIII

50 And still God's sunshine and His frost,
   They make us hot, they make us cold,
As if we were not black and lost;
   And the beasts and birds, in wood and fold,
Do fear and take us for very men:
55 Could the whip-poor-will or the cat of the glen°   *bobcat*
   Look into my eyes and be bold?

IX

I am black, I am black!
   But, once, I laughed in girlish glee,
For one of my colour stood in the track
60   Where the drivers drove, and looked at me,
And tender and full was the look he gave—
Could a slave look *so* at another slave?—
   I look at the sky and the sea.

X

And from that hour our spirits grew
65   As free as if unsold, unbought:
Oh, strong enough, since we were two,
   To conquer the world, we thought.
The drivers drove us day by day;
We did not mind, we went one way,
70   And no better a freedom sought.

XI

In the sunny ground between the canes,°   *sugar canes*
  He said "I love you" as he passed;
When the shingle-roof rang sharp with the rains,
  I heard how he vowed it fast:
75 While others shook he smiled in the hut,
As he carved me a bowl of the cocoa-nut
  Through the roar of the hurricanes.

XII

I sang his name instead of a song,
  Over and over I sang his name,
80 Upward and downward I drew it along
  My various notes,—the same, the same!
I sang it low, that the slave-girls near
Might never guess, from aught they could hear,
  It was only a name—a name.

XIII

85 I look on the sky and the sea.
  We were two to love, and two to pray:
Yes, two, O God, who cried to Thee,
  Though nothing didst Thou say!
Coldly Thou sat'st behind the sun:
90 And now I cry who am but one,
  Thou wilt not speak to-day.

XIV

We were black, we were black,
  We had no claim to love and bliss,
What marvel if each went to wrack?°   *ruin*
95 They wrung my cold hands out of his,
They dragged him—where? I crawled to touch
His blood's mark in the dust . . . not much,
  Ye pilgrim-souls, though plain as *this!*

XV

Wrong, followed by a deeper wrong!
100 Mere grief's too good for such as I:
So the white men brought the shame ere long
  To strangle the sob of my agony.
They would not leave me for my dull
Wet eyes!—it was too merciful
105 To let me weep pure tears and die.

XVI

I am black, I am black!
  I wore a child upon my breast,
An amulet that hung too slack,

And, in my unrest, could not rest:
110 Thus we went moaning, child and mother,
One to another, one to another,
    Until all ended for the best.

XVII

For hark! I will tell you low, low,
    I am black, you see,—
115 And the babe who lay on my bosom so,
    Was far too white, too white for me;
As white as the ladies who scorned to pray
Beside me at church but yesterday,
    Though my tears had washed a place for my knee.

XVIII

120 My own, own child! I could not bear
    To look in his face, it was so white;
I covered him up with a kerchief there,
    I covered his face in close and tight:
And he moaned and struggled, as well might be,
125 For the white child wanted his liberty—
    Ha, ha! he wanted the master-right.

XIX

He moaned and beat with his head and feet,
    His little feet that never grew;
He struck them out, as it was meet,
130   Against my heart to break it through:
I might have sung and made him mild,
But I dared not sing to the white-faced child
    The only song I knew.

XX

I pulled the kerchief very close:
135   He could not see the sun, I swear,
More, then, alive, than now he does
    From between the roots of the mango . . . where?
I know where. Close! A child and mother
Do wrong to look at one another
140   When one is black and one is fair.

XXI

Why, in that single glance I had
    Of my child's face, . . . I tell you all,
I saw a look that made me mad!
    The *master's* look, that used to fall
145 On my soul like his lash . . . or worse!
And so, to save it from my curse,
    I twisted it round in my shawl.

XXII

And he moaned and trembled from foot to head,
   He shivered from head to foot;
150 Till after a time, he lay instead
   Too suddenly still and mute.
I felt, beside, a stiffening cold:
I dared to lift up just a fold,
   As in lifting a leaf of the mango-fruit.

XXIII

155 But *my* fruit . . . ha, ha!—there, had been
   (I laugh to think on 't at this hour!)
Your fine white angels (who have seen
   Nearest the secret of God's power)
And plucked my fruit to make them wine,
160 And sucked the soul of that child of mine
   As the humming-bird sucks the soul of the flower.

XXIV

Ha, ha, the trick of the angels white!
   They freed the white child's spirit so.
I said not a word, but day and night
165   I carried the body to and fro,
And it lay on my heart like a stone, as chill.
—The sun may shine out as much as he will:
   I am cold, though it happened a month ago.

XXV

From the white man's house, and the black man's hut,
170   I carried the little body on;
The forest's arms did round us shut,
   And silence through the trees did run:
They asked no question as I went,
They stood too high for astonishment,
175   They could see God sit on His throne.

XXVI

My little body, kerchiefed fast,
   I bore it on through the forest, on;
And when I felt it was tired at last,
   I scooped a hole beneath the moon:
180 Through the forest-tops the angels far,
With a white sharp finger from every star,
   Did point and mock at what was done.

XXVII

Yet when it was all done aright,—
   Earth, 'twixt me and my baby, strewed,—
185 All, changed to black earth,—nothing white,—
   A dark child in the dark!—ensued

Some comfort, and my heart grew young;
I sate down smiling there and sung
   The song I learnt in my maidenhood.

XXVIII

190 And thus we two were reconciled,
   The white child and black mother, thus;
For as I sang it soft and wild,
   The same song, more melodious,
Rose from the grave whereon I sate:
195 It was the dead child singing that,
   To join the souls of both of us.

XXIX

I look on the sea and the sky.
   Where the pilgrims' ships first anchored lay
The free sun rideth gloriously,
200   But the pilgrim-ghosts have slid away
Through the earliest streaks of the morn:
My face is black, but it glares with a scorn
   Which they dare not meet by day.

XXX

Ha!—in their stead, their hunter sons!
205   Ha, ha! they are on me—they hunt in a ring!
Keep off! I brave you all at once,
   I throw off your eyes like snakes that sting!
You have killed the black eagle at nest, I think:
Did you ever stand still in your triumph, and shrink
210   From the stroke of her wounded wing?

XXXI

(Man, drop that stone you dared to lift!—)
   I wish you who stand there five abreast,
Each, for his own wife's joy and gift,
   A little corpse as safely at rest
215 As mine in the mangoes! Yes, but *she*
May keep live babies on her knee,
   And sing the song she likes the best.

XXXII

I am not mad: I am black.
   I see you staring in my face—
220 I know you staring, shrinking back,
   Ye are born of the Washington-race,[2]
And this land is the free America,
And this mark on my wrist—(I prove° what I say)   *demonstrate*
   Ropes tied me up here to the flogging-place.

---

2. I.e., the white race (the race of George Washington, the first president of the United States).

XXXIII

225 You think I shrieked then? Not a sound!
    I hung, as a gourd hangs in the sun;
I only cursed them all around
    As softly as I might have done
My very own child: from these sands
230 Up to the mountains, lift your hands,
    O slaves, and end what I begun!

XXXIV

Whips, curses; these must answer those!
    For in this UNION you have set
Two kinds of men in adverse rows,
235   Each loathing each; and all forget
The seven wounds in Christ's body fair,
While HE sees gaping everywhere
    Our countless wounds that pay no debt.

XXXV

Our wounds are different. Your white men
240   Are, after all, not gods indeed,
Nor able to make Christs again
    Do good with bleeding. *We* who bleed
(Stand off!) we help not in our loss!
We are too heavy for our cross,
245   And fall and crush you and your seed.

XXXVI

I fall, I swoon! I look at the sky.
    The clouds are breaking on my brain;
I am floated along, as if I should die
    Of liberty's exquisite pain.
250 In the name of the white child waiting for me
In the death-dark where we may kiss and agree,
White men, I leave you all curse-free
    In my broken heart's disdain!

1846   1848, 1850

From Aurora Leigh

From *Book 1*

[THE EDUCATION OF AURORA LEIGH][1]

Then, land!—then, England! oh, the frosty cliffs[2]
Looked cold upon me. Could I find a home

---

1. Aurora Leigh, the only child of an Italian mother and an English father, is raised in Italy by her father after her mother's death when Aurora is four years old. When she is thirteen her father also dies, and the orphaned girl is sent to live in England with her father's sister, who is to be responsible for the girl's education.
2. The white chalk cliffs at Dover.

Among those mean red houses through the fog?
And when I heard my father's language first
255 From alien lips which had no kiss for mine
I wept aloud, then laughed, then wept, then wept,
And some one near me said the child was mad
Through much sea-sickness. The train swept us on:
Was this my father's England? the great isle?
260 The ground seemed cut up from the fellowship
Of verdure, field from field,[3] as man from man;
The skies themselves looked low and positive,
As almost you could touch them with a hand,
And dared to do it they were so far off
265 From God's celestial crystals;[4] all things blurred
And dull and vague. Did Shakespeare and his mates
Absorb the light here?—not a hill or stone
With heart to strike a radiant colour up
Or active outline on the indifferent air.

270 I think I see my father's sister stand
Upon the hall-step of her country-house
To give me welcome. She stood straight and calm,
Her somewhat narrow forehead braided tight
As if for taming accidental thoughts
275 From possible pulses;[5] brown hair pricked with gray
By frigid use of life (she was not old,
Although my father's elder by a year),
A nose drawn sharply, yet in delicate lines;
A close mild mouth, a little soured about
280 The ends, through speaking unrequited loves
Or peradventure niggardly° half-truths;   *miserly*
Eyes of no colour,—once they might have smiled,
But never, never have forgot themselves
In smiling; cheeks, in which was yet a rose
285 Of perished summers, like a rose in a book,
Kept more for ruth° than pleasure,—if past bloom,   *remorse*
Past fading also.
     She had lived, we'll say,
A harmless life, she called a virtuous life,
A quiet life, which was not life at all
290 (But that, she had not lived enough to know),
Between the vicar and the county squires,
The lord-lieutenant[6] looking down sometimes
From the empyrean° to assure their souls   *highest heaven*
Against chance vulgarisms, and, in the abyss,
295 The apothecary,[7] looked on once a year
To prove their soundness of humility.
The poor-club[8] exercised her Christian gifts
Of knitting stockings, stitching petticoats,
Because we are of one flesh, after all,

---

3. English fields were separated from each other by hedgerows.
4. Perhaps a reference to the ancient notion that the sky was composed of several crystalline spheres orbiting the earth.
5. I.e., pulsation in her temples from excitement.
6. Governor of the county.
7. Pharmacist, who in England at the time could prescribe as well as sell medicine.
8. Club devoted to making things for the poor.

300   And need one flannel[9] (with a proper sense
    Of difference in the quality)—and still
    The book-club, guarded from your modern trick
    Of shaking dangerous questions from the crease,[1]
    Preserved her intellectual.° She had lived   *intellectual gifts*
305   A sort of cage-bird life, born in a cage,
    Accounting that to leap from perch to perch
    Was act and joy enough for any bird.
    Dear heaven, how silly are the things that live
    In thickets, and eat berries!
                      I, alas,
310   A wild bird scarcely fledged, was brought to her cage,
    And she was there to meet me. Very kind.
    Bring the clean water, give out the fresh seed.

    She stood upon the steps to welcome me,
    Calm, in black garb. I clung about her neck,—
315   Young babes, who catch at every shred of wool
    To draw the new light closer, catch and cling
    Less blindly. In my ears my father's word
    Hummed ignorantly, as the sea in shells,
    "Love, love, my child." She, black there with my grief,
320   Might feel my love—she was his sister once—
    I clung to her. A moment she seemed moved,
    Kissed me with cold lips, suffered me to cling,
    And drew me feebly through the hall into
    The room she sat in.
                  There, with some strange spasm
325   Of pain and passion, she wrung loose my hands
    Imperiously, and held me at arm's length,
    And with two grey-steel naked-bladed eyes
    Searched through my face,—ay, stabbed it through and through,
    Through brows and cheeks and chin, as if to find
330   A wicked murderer in my innocent face,
    If not here, there perhaps. Then, drawing breath,
    She struggled for her ordinary calm—
    And missed it rather,—told me not to shrink,
    As if she had told me not to lie or swear,—
335   "She loved my father and would love me too
    As long as I deserved it." Very kind.

    I understood her meaning afterward;
    She thought to find my mother in my face,
    And questioned it for that. For she, my aunt,
340   Had loved my father truly, as she could,
    And hated, with the gall of gentle souls,
    My Tuscan[2] mother who had fooled away
    A wise man from wise courses, a good man
    From obvious duties, and, depriving her,

---

9. I.e., flannel petticoat.
1. The fold between two pages of a book, which had to be cut to open the pages. Presumably, modern books were more apt to reveal dangerous material when the crease was cut.
2. From Tuscany, a region in central Italy.

345 His sister, of the household precedence,
Had wronged his tenants, robbed his native land,
And made him mad, alike by life and death,
In love and sorrow. She had pored° for years   *pored over*
What sort of woman could be suitable
350 To her sort of hate, to entertain it with,
And so, her very curiosity
Became hate too, and all the idealism
She ever used in life was used for hate,
Till hate, so nourished, did exceed at last
355 The love from which it grew, in strength and heat,
And wrinkled her smooth conscience with a sense
Of disputable virtue (say not, sin)
When Christian doctrine was enforced at church.

And thus my father's sister was to me
360 My mother's hater. From that day she did
Her duty to me (I appreciate it
In her own word as spoken to herself),
Her duty, in large measure, well pressed out
But measured always. She was generous, bland,
365 More courteous than was tender, gave me still
The first place,—as if fearful that God's saints
Would look down suddenly and say "Herein
You missed a point, I think, through lack of love."
Alas, a mother never is afraid
370 Of speaking angerly to any child,
Since love, she knows, is justified of love.
And I, I was a good child on the whole,
A meek and manageable child. Why not?
I did not live, to have the faults of life:
375 There seemed more true life in my father's grave
Than in all England. Since *that* threw me off
Who fain would cleave (his latest will, they say,
Consigned me to his land), I only thought
Of lying quiet there where I was thrown
380 Like sea-weed on the rocks, and suffering her
To prick me to a pattern with her pin,[3]
Fibre from fibre, delicate leaf from leaf,
And dry out from my drowned anatomy
The last sea-salt left in me.
                    So it was.
385 I broke the copious curls upon my head
In braids, because she liked smooth-ordered hair.
I left off saying my sweet Tuscan words
Which still at any stirring of the heart
Came up to float across the English phrase
390 As lilies (*Bene* or *Che che*[4]), because
She liked my father's child to speak his tongue.
I learnt the collects[5] and the catechism,

3. As in embroidery.
4. No, no, indeed (Italian). *"Bene"*: it is well
(Italian).

5. Seasonal opening prayers in the Anglican
Church service.

The creeds, from Athanasius back to Nice,[6]
The Articles, the Tracts *against* the times[7]
395 (By no means Buonaventure's "Prick of Love"[8]),
And various popular synopses of
Inhuman doctrines never taught by John,[9]
Because she liked instructed piety.
I learnt my complement of classic French
400 (Kept pure of Balzac and neologism[1])
And German also, since she liked a range
Of liberal education,—tongues,° not books.   languages
I learnt a little algebra, a little
Of the mathematics,—brushed with extreme flounce[2]
405 The circle of the sciences, because
She misliked women who are frivolous.
I learnt the royal genealogies
Of Oviedo,[3] the internal laws
Of the Burmese empire,—by how many feet
410 Mount Chimborazo outsoars Teneriffe,
What navigable river joins itself
To Lara,[4] and what census of the year five
Was taken at Klagenfurt,[5]—because she liked
A general insight into useful facts.
415 I learnt much music,—such as would have been
As quite impossible in Johnson's day[6]
As still it might be wished—fine sleights of hand
And unimagined fingering, shuffling off
The hearer's soul through hurricanes of notes
420 To a noisy Tophet;° and I drew . . . costumes   hell
From French engravings, nereids° neatly draped   sea nymphs
(With smirks of simmering godship): I washed in[7]
Landscapes from nature (rather say, washed out).
I danced the polka and Cellarius,[8]
425 Spun glass, stuffed birds, and modeled flowers in wax,
Because she liked accomplishments in girls.
I read a score of books on womanhood
To prove, if women do not think at all,
They may teach thinking (to a maiden aunt
430 Or else the author),—books that boldly assert
Their right of comprehending husband's talk

---

6. Articles of Christian faith such as those proclaimed by Athanasius, an Egyptian theologian of the 4th century c.e., and at the early Church council held at Nicaea in the same era.
7. In the 1830s leaders of the conservative High Church party, such as John Henry Newman, had published *Tracts for the Times*, which expounded arguments against efforts by liberals to modernize the Anglican Church. Aurora's version of the title is hence ironic. "Articles": the thirty-nine articles are the principles of faith of the Church of England.
8. St. Bonaventure's doctrine that the power of the heart to love leads to higher illumination than the power of the mind to reason.
9. I.e., the author of the Gospel.
1. A new word or expression. Honoré de Balzac (1799–1850), a French novelist whose realism

made him improper reading for a young English lady of the 19th century.
2. An ornamental edge to a skirt. "Extreme": outermost.
3. Spanish historian (16th century), who wrote a book on the genealogies of Spanish noblemen.
4. A town in Spain on the river Arlanza. Mount Chimborazo is one of the highest peaks of the Andes. Teneriffe is a mountain in the Canary Islands.
5. A town in Austria.
6. Allusion to the story about Samuel Johnson (1709–1784), who, when informed of the difficulty of a piece of music a young lady was playing, replied, "I would it had been impossible."
7. As in painting with watercolors.
8. A kind of waltz.

When not too deep, and even of answering
With pretty "may it please you," or "so it is,"—
Their rapid insight and fine aptitude,
435 Particular worth and general missionariness,
As long as they keep quiet by the fire
And never say "no" when the world says "ay,"
For that is fatal,—their angelic reach
Of virtue, chiefly used to sit and darn,
440 And fatten household sinners,—their, in brief,
Potential faculty in everything
Of abdicating power in it: she owned
She liked a woman to be womanly,
And English women, she thanked God and sighed
445 (Some people always sigh in thanking God),
Were models to the universe. And last
I learnt cross-stitch,[9] because she did not like
To see me wear the night with empty hands
A-doing nothing. So, my shepherdess
450 Was something after all (the pastoral saints
Be praised for't), leaning lovelorn with pink eyes
To match her shoes, when I mistook the silks;
Her head uncrushed by that round weight of hat
So strangely similar to the tortoise shell
Which slew the tragic poet.[1]
455   By the way,
The works of women are symbolical.
We sew, sew, prick our fingers, dull our sight,
Producing what? A pair of slippers, sir,
To put on when you're weary—or a stool
460 To stumble over and vex you . . . "curse that stool!"
Or else at best, a cushion, where you lean
And sleep, and dream of something we are not
But would be for your sake. Alas, alas!
This hurts most, this—that, after all, we are paid
The worth of our work, perhaps.
465   In looking down
Those years of education (to return)
I wonder if Brinvilliers suffered more
In the water-torture[2] . . . flood succeeding flood
To drench the incapable throat and split the veins . . .
470 Than I did. Certain of your feebler souls
Go out° in such a process; many pine   *die*
To a sick, inodorous light; my own endured:
I had relations in the Unseen, and drew
The elemental nutriment and heat
475 From nature, as earth feels the sun at nights,
Or as a babe sucks surely in the dark.
I kept the life thrust on me, on the outside

9. I.e., embroidery.
1. According to tradition, the Greek playwright Aeschylus was killed by an eagle who, mistaking his bald head for a stone, dropped a tortoise on it to break the shell.

2. Marie Marguerite, Marquise de Brinvilliers, a celebrated criminal who was beheaded in 1676, was tortured by having water forced down her throat.

Of the inner life with all its ample room
For heart and lungs, for will and intellect,
480 Inviolable by conventions. God,
I thank thee for that grace of thine!
                                    At first
I felt no life which was not patience,—did
The thing she bade me, without heed to a thing
Beyond it, sat in just the chair she placed,
485 With back against the window, to exclude
The sight of the great lime-tree on the lawn,[3]
Which seemed to have come on purpose from the woods
To bring the house a message,—ay, and walked
Demurely in her carpeted low rooms,
490 As if I should not, harkening my own steps,
Misdoubt° I was alive. I read her books,   doubt
Was civil to her cousin, Romney Leigh,
Gave ear to her vicar, tea to her visitors,
And heard them whisper, when I changed a cup
495 (I blushed for joy at that),—"The Italian child,
For all her blue eyes and her quiet ways,
Thrives ill in England: she is paler yet
Than when we came the last time; she will die."

From *Book 2*

[AURORA'S ASPIRATIONS][4]

Times followed one another. Came a morn
I stood upon the brink of twenty years,
And looked before and after, as I stood
Woman and artist,—either incomplete,
5 Both credulous of completion. There I held
The whole creation in my little cup,
And smiled with thirsty lips before I drank
"Good health to you and me, sweet neighbour mine,
And all these peoples."
                          I was glad, that day;
10 The June was in me, with its multitudes
Of nightingales all singing in the dark,
And rosebuds reddening where the calyx[5] split.
I felt so young, so strong, so sure of God!
So glad, I could not choose be very wise!
15 And, old at twenty, was inclined to pull
My childhood backward in a childish jest
To see the face of't once more, and farewell!
In which fantastic mood I bounded forth
At early morning,—would not wait so long

3. Cf. Coleridge's "This Lime-Tree Bower My Prison" (1800), in which the lime tree becomes the vehicle of a realization that Nature never deserts the wise and pure even when they seem to be cut off from her most beautiful vistas.
4. Stifled by her aunt's oppressive conventionality, Aurora has found three sources of comfort and inspiration: poetic aspirations, fostered by the discovery of her father's library; the beauty of the natural world; and the intellectual companionship of her cousin Romney Leigh, an idealistic young man troubled by the misery of the poor and inspired by contemporary notions of social reform.
5. The protective outer leaves covering a flower or bud.

20 As even to snatch my bonnet by the strings,
    But, brushing a green trail across the lawn
    With my gown in the dew, took will and away
    Among the acacias of the shrubberies,
    To fly my fancies in the open air
25 And keep° my birthday, till my aunt awoke   *observe*
    To stop good dreams. Meanwhile I murmured on
    As honeyed bees keep humming to themselves,
    "The worthiest poets have remained uncrowned
    Till death has bleached their foreheads to the bone;
30 And so with me it must be unless I prove
    Unworthy of the grand adversity,
    And certainly I would not fail so much.
    What, therefore, if I crown myself to-day
    In sport, not pride, to learn the feel of it,
35 Before my brows be numbed as Dante's own
    To all the tender pricking of such leaves?
    Such leaves! what leaves?"
                                        I pulled the branches down
    To choose from.
                    "Not the bay!⁶ I choose no bay
    (The fates deny us if we are overbold),
40 Nor myrtle—which means chiefly love; and love
    Is something awful which one dares not touch
    So early o' mornings. This verbena strains
    The point of passionate fragrance; and hard by,
    This guelder-rose,° at far too slight a beck   *cranberry bush*
45 Of the wind, will toss about her flower-apples.
    Ah—there's my choice,—that ivy on the wall,
    That headlong ivy! not a leaf will grow
    But thinking of a wreath. Large leaves, smooth leaves,
    Serrated like my vines, and half as green.
50 I like such ivy, bold to leap a height
    'Twas strong to climb; as good to grow on graves
    As twist about a thyrsus;⁷ pretty too
    (And that's not ill) when twisted round a comb."
    Thus speaking to myself, half singing it,
55 Because some thoughts are fashioned like a bell
    To ring with once being touched, I drew a wreath
    Drenched, blinding me with dew, across my brow,
    And fastening it behind so, turning faced
    . . . My public!—cousin Romney—with a mouth
    Twice graver than his eyes.
60   I stood there fixed,—
    My arms up, like the caryatid,⁸ sole
    Of some abolished temple, helplessly
    Persistent in a gesture which derides
    A former purpose. Yet my blush was flame,
    As if from flax, not stone.

6. Laurel, associated with poetry and prophecy by the ancient Greeks, who also crowned the athletic victors in the Pythian games with a laurel wreath.
7. Staff twined with ivy that was carried, accord-ing to Greek myth, by Dionysus, god of wine and fertility.
8. Classical column in the form of a draped female figure.

65   "Aurora Leigh,
The earliest of Auroras!"[9]
               Hand stretched out
I clasped, as shipwrecked men will clasp a hand,
Indifferent to the sort of palm. The tide
Had caught me at my pastime, writing down
70 My foolish name too near upon the sea
Which drowned me with a blush as foolish. "You,
My cousin!"
         The smile died out in his eyes
And dropped upon his lips, a cold dead weight,
For just a moment, "Here's a book I found!
75 No name writ on it—poems, by the form;
Some Greek upon the margin,—lady's Greek
Without the accents.[1] Read it? Not a word.
I saw at once the thing had witchcraft in't,
Whereof the reading calls up dangerous spirits:
I rather bring it to the witch."
80   "My book.
You found it" . . .
         "In the hollow by the stream
That beech leans down into—of which you said
The Oread in it has a Naiad's[2] heart
And pines for waters."
          "Thank you."
                "Thanks to *you*
85 My cousin! that I have seen you not too much
Witch, scholar, poet, dreamer, and the rest,
To be a woman also."
          With a glance
The smile rose in his eyes again and touched
The ivy on my forehead, light as air.
90 I answered gravely "Poets needs must be
Or° men or women—more's the pity."   *either*
             "Ah,
But men, and still less women, happily,
Scarce need be poets. Keep to the green wreath,
Since even dreaming of the stone and bronze
95 Brings headaches, pretty cousin, and defiles
The clean white morning dresses."
             "So you judge!
Because I love the beautiful I must
Love pleasure chiefly, and be overcharged
For ease and whiteness! well, you know the world,
100 And only miss your cousin, 'tis not much.
But learn this; I would rather take my part
With God's Dead, who afford to walk in white
Yet spread His glory, than keep quiet here
And gather up my feet from even a step
105 For fear to soil my gown in so much dust.
I choose to walk at all risks.—Here, if heads

---

9. Dawns; from Aurora, Roman goddess of the dawn.

1. Romney is gently mocking Aurora for her apparent ignorance of the complex rules of classical Greek accentuation.

2. Water nymph's. "Oread": tree nymph.

That hold a rhythmic thought, must ache perforce,
For my part I choose headaches,—and to-day's
My birthday,"
     "Dear Aurora, choose instead
To cure them. You have balsams."°   *soothing cures*
110   "I perceive.
The headache is too noble for my sex.
You think the heartache would sound decenter,
Since that's the woman's special, proper ache,
And altogether tolerable, except
115 To a woman."

[AURORA'S REJECTION OF ROMNEY]³

       There he glowed on me
With all his face and eyes. "No other help?"
Said he—"no more than so?"
345   "What help?" I asked.
"You'd scorn my help,—as Nature's self, you say,
Has scorned to put her music in my mouth
Because a woman's. Do you now turn round
And ask for what a woman cannot give?"

350 "For what she only can, I turn and ask,"
He answered, catching up my hands in his,
And dropping on me from his high-eaved brow
The full weight of his soul,—"I ask for love,
And that, she can; for life in fellowship
355 Through bitter duties—that, I know she can;
For wifehood—will she?"
      "Now," I said, "may God
Be witness 'twixt us two!" and with the word,
Meeseemed⁴ I floated into a sudden light
Above his stature,—"am I proved too weak
360 To stand alone, yet strong enough to bear
Such leaners on my shoulder? poor to think,
Yet rich enough to sympathise with thought?
Incompetent to sing, as blackbirds can,
Yet competent to love, like HIM?"
         I paused;
365 Perhaps I darkened, as the lighthouse will
That turns upon the sea. "It's always so.
Anything does for a wife."
       "Aurora, dear,
And dearly honoured,"—he pressed in at once
With eager utterance,—"you translate me ill.
370 I do not contradict my thought of you
Which is most reverent, with another thought

---

3. Romney and Aurora have been arguing about whether art, particularly a young woman's poetry, is useful in a world that, according to Romney, is full of human suffering. Romney claims that women have no ability to generalize from their personal experiences and are, therefore, doomed to be trivial poets and ineffectual social reformers. Aurora is quick to agree that to be merely an inferior poet would be intolerable to her, but while she admires Romney's lofty concern for humanity, she remains untempted to join forces with him.
4. It seemed to me.

Found less so. If your sex is weak for art
(And I, who said so, did but honour you
By using truth in courtship), it is strong
375 For life and duty. Place your fecund heart
In mine, and let us blossom for the world
That wants love's colour in the grey of time.
My talk, meanwhile, is arid to you, ay,
Since all my talk can only set you where
380 You look down coldly on the arena-heaps
Of headless bodies, shapeless, indistinct!
The Judgment-Angel scarce would find his way
Through such a heap of generalised distress
To the individual man with lips and eyes,
385 Much less Aurora. Ah, my sweet, come down,
And hand in hand we'll go where yours shall touch
These victims, one by one! till, one by one,
The formless, nameless trunk of every man
Shall seem to wear a head with hair you know,
390 And every woman catch your mother's face
To melt you into passion."
                              "I am a girl,"
I answered slowly; "you do well to name
My mother's face. Though far too early, alas,
God's hand did interpose 'twixt it and me,
395 I know so much of love as used to shine
In that face and another. Just so much;
No more indeed at all. I have not seen
So much love since, I pray you pardon me,
As answers even to make a marriage with
400 In this cold land of England. What you love
Is not a woman, Romney, but a cause:
You want a helpmate, not a mistress, sir,
A wife to help your ends,—in her no end.
Your cause is noble, your ends excellent,
405 But I, being most unworthy of these and that,
Do otherwise conceive of love. Farewell."

"Farewell, Aurora? you reject me thus?"
He said.
            "Sir, you were married long ago.
You have a wife already whom you love,
410 Your social theory. Bless you both, I say.
For my part, I am scarcely meek enough
To be the handmaid of a lawful spouse.
Do I look a Hagar,[5] think you?"
                                    "So you jest."

"Nay, so, I speak in earnest," I replied.
415 "You treat of° marriage too much like, at least,   *talk about*
A chief apostle: you would bear with you
A wife . . . a sister . . . shall we speak it out?

---

5. In Genesis 16 Sarah's maidservant, who bore a child, Ishmael, by Sarah's husband, Abraham.

A sister of charity."
　　　　　"Then, must it be
Indeed farewell? And was I so far wrong
420 In hope and in illusion, when I took
The woman to be nobler than the man,
Yourself the noblest woman, in the use
And comprehension of what love is,—love,
That generates the likeness of itself
425 Through all heroic duties? so far wrong,
In saying bluntly, venturing truth on love,
'Come, human creature, love and work with me,'—
Instead of 'Lady, thou art wondrous fair,
'And, where the Graces[6] walk before, the Muse
430 'Will follow at the lightning of their eyes,
'And where the Muse walks, lovers need to creep:
'Turn round and love me, or I die of love.'"

With quiet indignation I broke in.
"You misconceive the question like a man,
435 Who sees a woman as the complement
Of his sex merely. You forget too much
That every creature, female as the male,
Stands single in responsible act and thought
As also in birth and death. Whoever says
440 To a loyal woman, 'Love and work with me,'
Will get fair answers if the work and love,
Being good themselves, are good for her—the best
She was born for. Women of a softer mood,
Surprised by men when scarcely awake to life,
445 Will sometimes only hear the first word, love,
And catch up with it any kind of work,
Indifferent, so that dear love go with it.
I do not blame such women, though, for love,
They pick much oakum;[7] earth's fanatics make
450 Too frequently heaven's saints. But *me* your work
Is not the best for,—nor your love the best,
Nor able to commend the kind of work
For love's sake merely. Ah, you force me, sir,
To be overbold in speaking of myself:
455 I too have my vocation,—work to do,
The heavens and earth have set me since I changed
My father's face for theirs, and, though your world
Were twice as wretched as you represent,
Most serious work, most necessary work
460 As any of the economists'. Reform,
Make trade a Christian possibility,
And individual right no general wrong;
Wipe out earth's furrows of the Thine and Mine,
And leave one green for men to play at bowls,[8]

6. In classical mythology goddesses who personified beauty and charm.
7. Fiber derived by untwisting (picking) old rope,
a task frequently assigned to workhouse inmates.
8. A game of skill played on a smooth lawn with weighted wooden balls.

465   With innings for them all! . . . What then, indeed,
       If mortals are not greater by the head
       Than any of their prosperities? what then,
       Unless the artist keep up open roads
       Betwixt the seen and unseen,—bursting through
470   The best of your conventions with his best,
       The speakable, imaginable best
       God bids him speak, to prove what lies beyond
       Both speech and imagination? A starved man
       Exceeds a fat beast: we'll not barter, sir,
475   The beautiful for barley.—And, even so,
       I hold you will not compass your poor ends
       Of barley-feeding and material ease,
       Without a poet's individualism
       To work your universal. It takes a soul,
480   To move a body: it takes a high-souled man,
       To move the masses, even to a cleaner stye:
       It takes the ideal, to blow a hair's-breadth off
       The dust of the actual.—Ah, your Fouriers[9] failed,
       Because not poets enough to understand
485   That life develops from within.——For me,
       Perhaps I am not worthy, as you say,
       Of work like this: perhaps a woman's soul
       Aspires, and not creates: yet we aspire,
       And yet I'll try out your perhapses, sir,
490   And if I fail . . . why, burn me up my straw[1]
       Like other false works—I'll not ask for grace;
       Your scorn is better, cousin Romney. I
       Who love my art, would never wish it lower
       To suit my stature. I may love my art.
495   You'll grant that even a woman may love art,
       Seeing that to waste true love on anything
       Is womanly, past question."

From *Book 5*

[POETS AND THE PRESENT AGE]

       The critics say that epics have died out
140   With Agamemnon and the goat-nursed gods;[2]
       I'll not believe it. I could never deem,
       As Payne Knight[3] did (the mythic mountaineer
       Who travelled higher than he was born to live,
       And showed sometimes the goitre[4] in his throat
145   Discoursing of an image seen through fog),

---

9. I.e., Utopian thinkers; François-Marie-Charles Fourier (1772–1837), a French political theorist who advocated communal property as a basis for social harmony.
1. I.e., destroy my poetry. See 1 Corinthians 3.12–15.
2. Zeus, the ruler of the ancient Greek gods, was nursed by a goat. Agamemnon: the commander of the Greeks in the Trojan War.

3. Richard Payne Knight (1750–1824), a classical philologist who claimed that Lord Elgin had wasted his labor taking the marble friezes from the Parthenon in Greece to England because the marbles were not all Greek.
4. A disease often contracted in high mountain areas because of the low iodine content of the water.

That Homer's heroes measured twelve feet high.
They were but men:—his Helen's hair turned grey
Like any plain Miss Smith's who wears a front;[5]
And Hector's infant whimpered at a plume[6]
150 As yours last Friday at a turkey-cock.
All actual heroes are essential men,
And all men possible heroes: every age,
Heroic in proportions, double-faced,
Looks backward and before, expects a morn
And claims an epos.°   *epic poem*
155   Ay, but every age
Appears to souls who live in't (ask Carlyle)[7]
Most unheroic. Ours, for instance, ours:
The thinkers scout it,° and the poets abound   *dismiss it scornfully*
Who scorn to touch it with a finger-tip:
160 A pewter age,[8]—mixed metal, silver-washed;
An age of scum, spooned off the richer past,
An age of patches for old gaberdines,°   *coats*
An age of mere transition,[9] meaning nought
Except that what succeeds° must shame it quite   *fallows*
165 If God please. That's wrong thinking, to my mind,
And wrong thoughts make poor poems.
                            Every age,
Through being beheld too close, is ill-discerned
By those who have not lived past it. We'll suppose
Mount Athos carved, as Alexander schemed,
170 To some colossal statue of a man.[1]
The peasants, gathering brushwood in his ear,
Had guessed as little as the browsing goats
Of form or feature of humanity
Up there,—in fact, had travelled five miles off
175 Or ere the giant image broke on them,
Full human profile, nose and chin distinct,
Mouth, muttering rhythms of silence up the sky
And fed at evening with the blood of suns;
Grand torso,—hand, that flung perpetually
180 The largesse of a silver river down
To all the country pastures. 'Tis even thus
With times we live in,—evermore too great
To be apprehended near.
                    But poets should
Exert a double vision; should have eyes
185 To see near things as comprehensively

---

5. A piece of false hair worn over the forehead by women.
6. In the *Iliad*, book 6, the Trojan hero Hector reaches for his infant son, but the child clings to his nurse, frightened of his father's helmet and crest.
7. In *Heroes, Hero-Worship, and the Heroic in History* (1841), Carlyle argues that the present age needs a renewed perception of the heroic.
8. Allusion to the convention, which originates in Hesiod (Greek poet, ca. 8th century B.C.E), of describing civilization's decline through a suc-

cession of ages named for increasingly less precious materials: i.e., the Golden Age, the Silver Age, the Bronze Age.
9. In *The Spirit of the Age* (1831), John Stuart Mill calls the present age "an age of transition."
1. Deinocrates, a Macedonian architect (4th century B.C.E.), is said to have suggested to Alexander the Great that Mount Athos be carved into the statue of a conqueror with a city in his left hand and a basin in his right, where all the waters of the region could be collected and used to water the pasture lands below.

As if afar they took their point of sight,
And distant things as intimately deep
As if they touched them. Let us strive for this.
I do distrust the poet who discerns
190 No character or glory in his times,
And trundles back his soul five hundred years,
Past moat and drawbridge, into a castle-court,
To sing—oh, not of lizard or of toad
Alive i' the ditch there,—'twere excusable,
195 But of some black chief, half knight, half sheep-lifter,°   *sheep stealer*
Some beauteous dame, half chattel and half queen,
As dead as must be, for the greater part,
The poems made on their chivalric bones;
And that's no wonder: death inherits death.
200 Nay, if there's room for poets in this world
A little overgrown (I think there is),
Their sole work is to represent the age,
Their age, not Charlemagne's,[2]—this live, throbbing age,
That brawls, cheats, maddens, calculates, aspires,
205 And spends more passion, more heroic heat,
Betwixt the mirrors of its drawing-rooms,
Than Roland[3] with his knights at Roncesvalles.
To flinch from modern varnish, coat or flounce,
Cry out for togas and the picturesque,
210 Is fatal,—foolish too. King Arthur's self
Was commonplace to Lady Guenever;
And Camelot to minstrels seemed as flat
As Fleet Street[4] to our poets.
                                    Never flinch,
But still, unscrupulously epic, catch
215 Upon the burning lava of a song
The full-veined, heaving, double-breasted Age:
That, when the next shall come, the men of that
May touch the impress° with reverent hand, and say   *impression*
"Behold,—behold the paps° we all have sucked!   *breasts*
220 This bosom seems to beat still, or at least
It sets ours beating: this is living art,
Which thus presents and thus records true life."

1853–56   1857

---

2. Frankish conqueror (742–814), who created a European empire.
3. Legendary medieval hero, whose adventures are told in the epic poem *Chanson de Roland*

(11th century); his last battle is fought at Roncesvalles, a Spanish village.
4. A center for book shops and newspaper and publishing offices in London.

ALFRED, LORD TENNYSON
1809–1892

In his own lifetime Tennyson was the most popular of poets; his works, from 1850 onward, occupied a significant space on the bookshelves of almost every family of readers in England and the United States. Such popularity inevitably provoked a reaction in the decades following his death. In the course of repudiating their Victorian predecessors, the Edwardians and Georgians established the fashion of making fun of Tennyson's achievements. Samuel Butler (1835–1902), who anticipated early-twentieth-century tastes, has a characteristic entry in his *Notebooks:* "Talking it over, we agreed that Blake was no good because he learnt Italian at sixty in order to study Dante, and we knew Dante was no good because he was so fond of Virgil, and Virgil was no good because Tennyson ran [followed] him, and as for Tennyson— well, Tennyson goes without saying." Butler's flippant dismissal expresses an attitude that is no longer fashionable: Tennyson's stature as one of the major poets of the English language seems uncontroversial today.

Like his poetry, Tennyson's life and character have been reassessed in recent times. To many of his contemporaries he seemed a remote wizard secure in his laureate's robes, a man whose life had been sheltered, marred only by the loss of his best friend in youth. During much of his career Tennyson may have been isolated, but his was not a sheltered life in the real sense of the word. His childhood home, a parsonage, was a household dominated by frictions and loyalties and broodings over ancestral inheritances, in which the children showed marked strains of instability and eccentricity.

Alfred Tennyson was the fourth son in a family of twelve children. One of his brothers had to be confined to an insane asylum for life; another was long addicted to opium; another had violent quarrels with his father, the Reverend Dr. George Tennyson. This father, a man of considerable learning, had been born the eldest son of a wealthy landowner and had, therefore, expected to be heir to his family's estates. Instead he was disinherited in favor of his younger brother and had to make his own livelihood by joining the clergy, a profession that he disliked. After George Tennyson had settled in a small rectory in Somersby, his brooding sense of dissatisfaction led to increasingly violent bouts of drunkenness; he was nevertheless able to act as his sons' tutor in classical and modern languages to prepare them for entering the university.

Before leaving this strange household for Cambridge, Tennyson had already demonstrated a flair for writing verse—precocious exercises in the manner of John Milton or Byron or the Elizabethan dramatists. He had even published a volume in 1827, in collaboration with his brother Charles, *Poems by Two Brothers.* This feat drew him to the attention of a group of gifted undergraduates at Cambridge, "the Apostles," who encouraged him to devote his life to poetry. Up until that time the young man had known scarcely anyone outside the circle of his own family. Despite his massive frame and powerful physique, he was painfully shy, and the friendships he found at Cambridge as well as the intellectual and political discussions in which he participated gave him confidence and widened his horizons as a poet. The most important of these friendships was with Arthur Hallam, a leader of the Apostles, who later became engaged to Tennyson's sister Emily. Hallam's sudden death, in 1833, seemed an overwhelming calamity to his friend. Not only the long elegy *In Memoriam* (1850) but many of Tennyson's other poems are tributes to this early friendship.

Tennyson's career at Cambridge was interrupted and finally broken off in 1831 by family dissensions and financial need, and he returned home to study and practice the craft of poetry. His early volumes (1830 and 1832) were attacked as "obscure" or "affected" by some of the reviewers. Tennyson suffered acutely under hostile criticism, but he also profited from it. His 1842 volume demonstrated a remarkable leap forward, and in 1850 he at last attained fame and full critical recognition with *In Memoriam*. In the same year he became poet laureate in succession to William Wordsworth. The struggle during the previous twenty years had been made especially painful by the long postponement of his marriage to Emily Sellwood, whom he had loved since 1836 but could not marry, because of poverty, until 1850.

His life thereafter was a comfortable one. He was as popular as Byron had been, and the earnings from his poetry (sometimes exceeding £10,000 a year) enabled him to purchase a house in the country and to enjoy the kind of seclusion he liked. His notoriety was enhanced, like that of Bernard Shaw and Walt Whitman, by his colorful appearance. Huge and shaggy in cloak and broad-brimmed hat, gruff in manner, he impressed everyone as what is called a "character." The pioneering photographer Julia Cameron, who took magnificent portraits of him, called him "the most beautiful old man on earth." Like Dylan Thomas in the twentieth century, Tennyson had a booming voice that electrified listeners when he read his poetry, "mouthing out his hollow o's and a's, / Deep-chested music," as he would covertly describe himself in an early version of his Arthurian epic. Moreover, for many Victorian readers, he seemed not only a great poetical phrase maker and a striking individual but also a wise man whose occasional pronouncements on politics or world affairs represented the national voice itself. In 1884 he accepted a peerage. In 1892 he died and was buried in Westminster Abbey.

It is often said that success was bad for Tennyson and that after *In Memoriam* his poetic power seriously declined. That in his last forty-two years certain of his mannerisms became accentuated is true. One of the difficulties of his dignified blank verse was, as he said himself, that it is hard to describe commonplace objects and "at the same time to retain poetical elevation." This difficulty is evident, for example, in *Enoch Arden* (1864), a long blank verse narrative of everyday life in a fishing village, in which a basketful of fish is ornately described as "Enoch's ocean spoil / In ocean-smelling osier." In his later poems dealing with national affairs, there is also an increased shrillness of tone—a mannerism accentuated by Tennyson's realizing that he, like Charles Dickens, had a vast public behind him to back up his pronouncements.

It would be unwise, however, to ignore all of Tennyson's later productions. In 1855 he published his experimental monologue *Maud*, in which he presents an alienated hero who feels great bitterness toward society. In 1859 appeared four books of his *Idylls of the King*, a large-scale epic that occupied most of his energies in the second half of his career. The *Idylls* uses the body of Arthurian legend to construct a vision of civilization's rise and fall. In this civilization women both inspire men's highest efforts and sow the seeds of those efforts' destruction. The *Idylls* provides Tennyson's most extensive social vision, one that typifies much social thought of the age in its concern with medieval ideals of social community, heroism, and courtly love and in its despairing sense of the cycles of historical change.

W. H. Auden stated that Tennyson had "the finest ear, perhaps, of any English poet." The interesting point is that Tennyson did not "have" such an ear: he developed it. Studies of the original versions of his poems in the 1830 and 1832 volumes demonstrate how hard he worked at his craftsmanship. Like Geoffrey Chaucer or Alexander Pope or John Keats, Tennyson studied his predecessors assiduously to perfect his technique. Anyone wanting to learn the traditional craft of English verse can study profitably the various stages of revision that poems such as "The Lotos-Eaters" were subjected to by this painstaking and artful poet.

Tennyson's early poetry shows other skills as well. One of these was a capacity for linking scenery to states of mind. As early as 1835 J. S. Mill identified the special kind of scene painting to be found in poems such as "Mariana" (1830): "not the power of producing that rather vapid species of composition usually termed descriptive poetry . . . but the power of *creating* scenery, in keeping with some state of human feeling so fitted to it as to be the embodied symbol of it, and to summon up the state of feeling itself, with a force not to be surpassed by anything but reality."

The state of feeling to which Tennyson was most intensely drawn was a melancholy isolation, often portrayed through the consciousness of an abandoned woman, as in "Mariana." Tennyson's absorption with such emotions in his early poetry evoked considerable criticism. His friend R. C. Trench warned him, "Tennyson, we cannot live in Art," and Mill urged him to "cultivate, and with no half devotion, philosophy as well as poetry." Advice of this kind Tennyson was already predisposed to heed. The death of Hallam and the religious uncertainties that he had himself experienced, together with his own extensive study of writings by geologists, astronomers, and biologists, led him to confront many of the religious issues that bewildered his and later generations. The result was *In Memoriam*, a long elegy written over a period of seventeen years, embodying the poet's reflections on the relation of human beings to God and to nature.

Tennyson's exploration of these vast subjects prompted some readers, such as T. H. Huxley, to consider him an intellectual giant, a thinker who had mastered the scientific thought of his century and fully confronted the issues it raised. Others dismissed Tennyson, in this phase, as a lightweight. Auden went so far as to call him the "stupidest" of English poets. He added, "There was little about melancholia that he didn't know; there was little else that he did." Perhaps T. S. Eliot's evaluation of *In Memoriam* is the more thought-provoking: the poem, he wrote, is remarkable not "because of the quality of its faith but because of the quality of its doubt." Tennyson's mind was slow, ponderous, brooding; for the composition of *In Memoriam* such qualities of mind were assets, not liabilities. Very different are the poems Tennyson writes of events of the moment over which his thoughts and feelings have had no time to brood. Several of these are what he himself called "newspaper verse." They are letters to the editor in effect, with the heat we expect of such productions. "The Charge of the Light Brigade" (1854), inspired by a report in the London *Times* of a cavalry charge at Balaclava during the Crimean War, is one of the most fascinating of his productions in this category.

Tennyson's poems of contemporary events were inevitably popular in his own day. So too were those poems in which, as in "Locksley Hall" (1842), he dipped into the future. The technological changes wrought by Victorian inventors and engineers fascinated him, sometimes giving him an exultant assurance of human progress. At other times the horrors of industrialism's by-products in the slums, the persistence of barbarity and bloodshed, and the greed of the newly rich destroyed his hopes that humanity was evolving upward. In the final book of *Idylls of the King* (1869), Arthur laments that his "realm / Reels back into the beast": Tennyson was similarly haunted by the possibility of retrogression.

For despite Tennyson's fascination with technological developments, he was essentially a poet of the countryside, a man whose whole being was conditioned by the recurring rhythms of rural rather than urban life. He had the country dweller's awareness of traditional roots and sense of the past. It is appropriate that so many of his poems are about the past, not about the present or future. Tennyson said that "the words 'far, far away' had always a strange charm" for him, even in his childhood; he was haunted by what he called "the passion of the past." The past became his great theme, whether it be his own past (such as the times he shared with Hallam), his country's past (as in *Idylls of the King*), or the past of the world itself.

Though Tennyson more often is inspired by the recorded past of humankind, he is the first major writer to express this awareness of the vast extent of geological time that has haunted human consciousness since Victorian scientists exposed the history of the earth's crust.

Mariana[1]

"Mariana in the moated grange."
—*Measure for Measure*

With blackest moss the flower-plots
    Were thickly crusted, one and all;
The rusted nails fell from the knots
    That held the pear to the gable wall.
5   The broken sheds looked sad and strange:
    Unlifted was the clinking latch;
    Weeded°and worn the ancient thatch   *full of weeds*
Upon the lonely moated grange.
      She only said, "My life is dreary,
10   He cometh not," she said;
      She said, "I am aweary, aweary,
        I would that I were dead!"

Her tears fell with the dews at even;
    Her tears fell ere the dews were dried;
15   She could not look on the sweet heaven,
    Either at morn or eventide.
After the flitting of the bats,
    When thickest dark did trance° the sky,   *cross*
    She drew her casement curtain by,
20   And glanced athwart° the glooming flats.   *across*
      She only said, "The night is dreary,
        He cometh not," she said;
      She said, "I am aweary, aweary,
        I would that I were dead!"

25   Upon the middle of the night,
    Waking she heard the nightfowl crow;
The cock sung out an hour ere light;
    From the dark fen° the oxen's low   *marshland*
Came to her; without hope of change,
30   In sleep she seemed to walk forlorn,
    Till cold winds woke the gray-eyed morn
About the lonely moated grange.
      She only said, "The day is dreary,
        He cometh not," she said;
35   She said, "I am aweary, aweary,
        I would that I were dead!"

About a stonecast° from the wall   *stone's throw*
    A sluice with blackened waters slept,
And o'er it many, round and small,
40   The clustered marish-mosses[2] crept.
Hard° by a poplar shook alway,   *close*

---

1. Mariana, in Shakespeare's *Measure for Measure* 3.1.255, waits in a grange (an outlying farmhouse) for her lover, who has deserted her.

2. The little marsh-moss lumps that float on the surface of water [Tennyson's note].

All silver-green with gnarlèd bark:
For leagues no other tree did mark
The level waste, the rounding gray.
45 She only said, "My life is dreary,
He cometh not," she said;
She said, "I am aweary, aweary,
I would that I were dead!"

And ever when the moon was low,
50 And the shrill winds were up and away,
In the white curtain, to and fro,
She saw the gusty shadow sway.
But when the moon was very low,
And wild winds bound within their cell,[3]
55 The shadow of the poplar fell
Upon her bed, across her brow.
She only said, "The night is dreary,
He cometh not," she said;
She said, "I am aweary, aweary,
60 I would that I were dead!"

All day within the dreamy house,
The doors upon their hinges creaked;
The blue fly sung in the pane; the mouse
Behind the moldering wainscot° shrieked, *wooden paneling*
65 Or from the crevice peered about.
Old faces glimmered through the doors,
Old footsteps trod the upper floors,
Old voices called her from without.
She only said, "My life is dreary,
70 He cometh not," she said;
She said, "I am aweary, aweary,
I would that I were dead!"

The sparrow's chirrup on the roof,
The slow clock ticking, and the sound
75 Which to the wooing wind aloof
The poplar made, did all confound
Her sense; but most she loathed the hour
When the thick-moted sunbeam lay
Athwart the chambers, and the day
80 Was sloping toward his western bower.
Then, said she, "I am very dreary,
He will not come," she said;
She wept, "I am aweary, aweary,
Oh God, that I were dead!"

1830

---

3. According to Virgil, Aeolus, god of winds, kept the winds imprisoned in a cave (*Aeneid* 1.50–59).

The Lady of Shalott[1]

Part 1

On either side the river lie
Long fields of barley and of rye,
That clothe the wold° and meet the sky;   *rolling plain*
And through the field the road runs by
5 To many-towered Camelot;
And up and down the people go,
Gazing where the lilies blow°   *bloom*
Round an island there below,
  The island of Shalott.

10 Willows whiten, aspens quiver,
Little breezes dusk and shiver
Through the wave that runs forever
By the island in the river
  Flowing down to Camelot.
15 Four gray walls, and four gray towers,
Overlook a space of flowers,
And the silent isle imbowers
  The Lady of Shalott.

By the margin, willow-veiled,
20 Slide the heavy barges trailed
By slow horses; and unhailed
The shallop° flitteth silken-sailed   *light open boat*
  Skimming down to Camelot:
But who hath seen her wave her hand?
25 Or at the casement seen her stand?
Or is she known in all the land,
  The Lady of Shalott?

Only reapers, reaping early
In among the bearded barley,
30 Hear a song that echoes cheerly
From the river winding clearly,
  Down to towered Camelot;
And by the moon the reaper weary,
Piling sheaves in uplands airy,
35 Listening, whispers " 'Tis the fairy
  Lady of Shalott."

Part 2

There she weaves by night and day
A magic web with colors gay.

---

1. The story of the Lady of Shalott is a version of
the tale of "Elaine the fair maid of Astolat," which
appears in book 18 of *Morte Darthur* (1470) by Sir
Thomas Malory (ca. 1405–1471). Tennyson, however, claimed he did not know Malory's version
when he wrote his draft in 1832, identifying his
source as a 14th-century tale about "la Damigella

di Scalot": "I met the story first in some Italian
novelle: but the web, mirror, island, etc., were my
own. Indeed, I doubt whether I should ever have
put it in that shape if I had been aware of the
Maid of Astolat in *Morte d'Arthur.*" Tennyson subjected this poem to numerous revisions over the
years.

She has heard a whisper say,
40 A curse is on her if she stay°   *pause*
     To look down to Camelot.
She knows not what the curse may be,
And so she weaveth steadily,
And little other care hath she,
45   The Lady of Shalott.

And moving through a mirror clear²
That hangs before her all the year,
Shadows of the world appear.
There she sees the highway near
50   Winding down to Camelot;
There the river eddy whirls,
And there the surly village churls,°   *peasants*
And the red cloaks of market girls,
     Pass onward from Shalott.

55 Sometimes a troop of damsels glad,
An abbot on an ambling pad,°   *easy-paced horse*
Sometimes a curly shepherd lad,
Or long-haired page in crimson clad,
     Goes by to towered Camelot;
60 And sometimes through the mirror blue
The knights come riding two and two:
She hath no loyal knight and true,
     The Lady of Shalott.

But in her web she still delights
65 To weave the mirror's magic sights,
For often through the silent nights
A funeral, with plumes and lights
     And music, went to Camelot;
Or when the moon was overhead,
70 Came two young lovers lately wed:
"I am half sick of shadows," said
     The Lady of Shalott.

Part 3

A bowshot from her bower eaves,
He rode between the barley sheaves,
75 The sun came dazzling through the leaves,
And flamed upon the brazen greaves³
     Of bold Sir Lancelot.
A red-cross knight forever kneeled
To a lady in his shield,
80 That sparkled on the yellow field,
     Beside remote Shalott.

The gemmy bridle glittered free,
Like to some branch of stars we see

---

2. Weavers used mirrors, placed facing their looms, to see the progress of their work.   3. Armor protecting the leg below the knee.

Hung in the golden Galaxy.
85   The bridle bells rang merrily
      As he rode down to Camelot;
  And from his blazoned baldric[4] slung
  A mighty silver bugle hung,
  And as he rode his armor rung,
90   Beside remote Shalott.

  All in the blue unclouded weather
  Thick-jeweled shone the saddle leather,
  The helmet and the helmet-feather
  Burned like one burning flame together,
95   As he rode down to Camelot;
  As often through the purple night,
  Below the starry clusters bright,
  Some bearded meteor, trailing light,
      Moves over still Shalott.

100   His broad clear brow in sunlight glowed;
  On burnished hooves his war horse trode;
  From underneath his helmet flowed
  His coal-black curls as on he rode,
      As he rode down to Camelot.
105   From the bank and from the river
  He flashed into the crystal mirror,
  "Tirra lirra,"[5] by the river
      Sang Sir Lancelot.

  She left the web, she left the loom,
110   She made three paces through the room,
  She saw the water lily bloom,
  She saw the helmet and the plume,
      She looked down to Camelot.
  Out flew the web and floated wide;
115   The mirror cracked from side to side;
  "The curse is come upon me," cried
      The Lady of Shalott.

Part 4

  In the stormy east wind straining,
  The pale yellow woods were waning,
120   The broad stream in his banks complaining,
  Heavily the low sky raining
      Over towered Camelot;
  Down she came and found a boat
  Beneath a willow left afloat,
125   And round about the prow she wrote
      The Lady of Shalott.

---

4. A belt worn diagonally from one shoulder to the opposite hip, supporting a sword or bugle. "Blazoned": painted with a heraldic device.

5. Cf. Autolycus's song in Shakespeare's *The Winter's Tale* 4.3.9: "The lark, that tirra-lirra chants."

And down the river's dim expanse
Like some bold seër in a trance,
Seeing all his own mischance—
130　With a glassy countenance
　　　　Did she look to Camelot.
And at the closing of the day
She loosed the chain, and down she lay;
The broad stream bore her far away,
135　　　　The Lady of Shalott.

Lying, robed in snowy white
That loosely flew to left and right—
The leaves upon her falling light—
Through the noises of the night
140　　　　She floated down to Camelot;
And as the boat-head wound along
The willowy hills and fields among,
They heard her singing her last song,
　　　　The Lady of Shalott.

145　Heard a carol, mournful, holy,
Chanted loudly, chanted lowly,
Till her blood was frozen slowly,
And her eyes were darkened wholly,[6]
　　　　Turned to towered Camelot.
150　For ere she reached upon the tide
The first house by the waterside,
Singing in her song she died,
　　　　The Lady of Shalott.

Under tower and balcony,
155　By garden wall and gallery,
A gleaming shape she floated by,
Dead-pale between the houses high,
　　　　Silent into Camelot.
Out upon the wharfs they came,
160　Knight and burgher, lord and dame,
And round the prow they read her name,
　　　　The Lady of Shalott.

Who is this? and what is here?
And in the lighted palace near
165　Died the sound of royal cheer;
And they crossed themselves for fear,
　　　　All the knights at Camelot:
But Lancelot mused a little space;
He said, "She has a lovely face;
170　God in his mercy lend her grace,
　　　　The Lady of Shalott."

1831–32　　　　　　　　　　　　　　　　　　　　　　　　　1832, 1842

6. In the 1832 version this line read: "And her smooth face sharpened slowly." George Eliot informed Tennyson that she preferred the earlier version.

The Lotos-Eaters[1]

"Courage!" he[2] said, and pointed toward the land,
"This mounting wave will roll us shoreward soon."
In the afternoon they came unto a land[3]
In which it seemèd always afternoon.
5   All round the coast the languid air did swoon,
Breathing like one that hath a weary dream.
Full-faced above the valley stood the moon;
And, like a downward smoke, the slender stream
Along the cliff to fall and pause and fall did seem.

10   A land of streams! some, like a downward smoke,
Slow-dropping veils of thinnest lawn,° did go;   *fine thin linen*
And some through wavering lights and shadows broke,
Rolling a slumbrous sheet of foam below.
They saw the gleaming river seaward flow
15   From the inner land; far off, three mountaintops
Three silent pinnacles of aged snow,
Stood sunset-flushed; and, dewed with showery drops,
Up-clomb° the shadowy pine above the woven copse.   *climbed up*

The charmèd sunset lingered low adown
20   In the red West; through mountain clefts the dale
Was seen far inland, and the yellow down[4]
Bordered with palm, and many a winding vale
And meadow, set with slender galingale;[5]
A land where all things always seemed the same!
25   And round about the keel with faces pale,
Dark faces pale against that rosy flame,
The mild-eyed melancholy Lotos-eaters came.

Branches they bore of that enchanted stem,
Laden with flower and fruit, whereof they gave
30   To each, but whoso did receive of them
And taste, to him the gushing of the wave
Far far away did seem to mourn and rave
On alien shores; and if his fellow spake,
His voice was thin, as voices from the grave;
35   And deep-asleep he seemed, yet all awake,
And music in his ears his beating heart did make.

1. Based on a short episode from the *Odyssey* (9.82–97) in which the weary Greek veterans of the Trojan War are tempted by a desire to abandon their long voyage homeward. As Odysseus later reported: "On the tenth day we set foot on the land of the lotos-eaters who eat a flowering food. . . . I sent forth certain of my company [who] . . . mixed with the men of the lotos-eaters who gave . . . them of the lotos to taste. Now whosoever of them did eat the honey-sweet fruit of the lotos had no more wish to bring tidings nor to come back, but there he chose to abide . . . forgetful of his homeward way."
   Tennyson expands Homer's brief account into an elaborate picture of weariness and the desire

for rest and death. The descriptions in the first stanzas are similar to Spenser's *The Faerie Queene* (1590) 2.6 and employ the same stanza form. The final section derives, in part, from Lucretius's conception of the gods in *De Rerum Natura* (ca. 55 B.C.E.).
2. Odysseus (or Ulysses).
3. The repetition of "land" from line 1 was deliberate; Tennyson said that this "no rhyme" was "lazier" in its effect. This technique of repeating words, phrases, and sounds continues; cf. "afternoon" (lines 3–4) and the rhyming of "adown" and "down" (lines 19 and 21).
4. An open plain on high ground.
5. A plant resembling tall coarse grass.

They sat them down upon the yellow sand,
Between the sun and moon upon the shore;
And sweet it was to dream of Fatherland,
40 Of child, and wife, and slave; but evermore
Most weary seemed the sea, weary the oar,
Weary the wandering fields of barren foam,
Then some one said, "We will return no more";
And all at once they sang, "Our island home°   *Ithaca*
45 Is far beyond the wave; we will no longer roam."

Choric Song[6]

1

There is sweet music here that softer falls
Than petals from blown roses on the grass,
Or night-dews on still waters between walls
Of shadowy granite, in a gleaming pass;
50 Music that gentlier on the spirit lies,
Than tired[7] eyelids upon tired eyes;
Music that brings sweet sleep down from the blissful skies.
Here are cool mosses deep,
And through the moss the ivies creep,
55 And in the stream the long-leaved flowers weep,
And from the craggy ledge the poppy hangs in sleep.

2

Why are we weighed upon with heaviness,
And utterly consumed with sharp distress,
While all things else have rest from weariness?
60 All things have rest: why should we toil alone,
We only toil, who are the first of things,
And make perpetual moan,
Still from one sorrow to another thrown;
Nor ever fold our wings,
65 And cease from wanderings,
Nor steep our brows in slumber's holy balm;
Nor harken what the inner spirit sings,
"There is no joy but calm!"—
Why should we only toil, the roof and crown of things?[8]

3

70 Lo! in the middle of the wood,
The folded leaf is wooed from out the bud
With winds upon the branch, and there
Grows green and broad, and takes no care,
Sun-steeped at noon, and in the moon
75 Nightly dew-fed; and turning yellow
Falls, and floats adown the air.

---

6. Sung by the mariners.
7. Tennyson wanted the word to be pronounced as *tie-yerd* rather than *tier'd* or *tire-èd*, thus "making the word neither monosyllable or disyllabic, but a dreamy child of the two."

8. Cf. *The Faerie Queene* 2.6.17: "Why then dost thou, O man, that of them all / Art Lord, and eke of nature Sovereaine, / Wilfully . . . wast thy joyous houres in needlesse paine?"

Lo! sweetened with summer light,
The full-juiced apple, waxing over-mellow,
Drops in a silent autumn night.
80 All its allotted length of days
The flower ripens in its place,
Ripens and fades, and falls, and hath no toil,
Fast-rooted in the fruitful soil.

4

Hateful is the dark blue sky,
85 Vaulted o'er the dark blue sea.
Death is the end of life; ah, why
Should life all labor be?
Let us alone. Time driveth onward fast,
And in a little while our lips are dumb.
90 Let us alone. What is it that will last?
All things are taken from us, and become
Portions and parcels of the dreadful past.
Let us alone. What pleasure can we have
To war with evil? Is there any peace
95 In ever climbing up the climbing wave?
All things have rest, and ripen toward the grave
In silence—ripen, fall, and cease:
Give us long rest or death, dark death, or dreamful ease.[9]

5

How sweet it were, hearing the downward stream,
100 With half-shut eyes ever to seem
Falling asleep in a half-dream!
To dream and dream, like yonder amber light,
Which will not leave the myrrh-bush[1] on the height;
To hear each other's whispered speech;
105 Eating the Lotos day by day,
To watch the crisping° ripples on the beach,   *curling*
And tender curving lines of creamy spray;
To lend our hearts and spirits wholly
To the influence of mild-minded melancholy;
110 To muse and brood and live again in memory,
With those old faces of our infancy
Heaped over with a mound of grass,
Two handfuls of white dust, shut in an urn of brass!

6

Dear is the memory of our wedded lives,
115 And dear the last embraces of our wives
And their warm tears; but all hath suffered change;
For surely now our household hearths are cold,
Our sons inherit us,° our looks are strange,   *succeed us as our heirs*
And we should come like ghosts to trouble joy.

9. Cf. *The Faerie Queen* 1.9.40: "Sleepe after toyle, port after stormie seas, / Ease after warre, death after life does greatly please."

1. Myrrh, a resin used in perfume and incense, is associated with sweetness and comfort.

120 Or else the island princes[2] overbold
Have eat our substance, and the minstrel sings
Before them of the ten years' war in Troy,
And our great deeds, as half-forgotten things.
Is there confusion in the little isle?
125 Let what is broken so remain.
The Gods are hard to reconcile;
'Tis hard to settle order once again.
There *is* confusion worse than death,
Trouble on trouble, pain on pain,
130 Long labor unto aged breath,
Sore tasks to hearts worn out by many wars
And eyes grown dim with gazing on the pilot-stars.

7

But, propped on beds of amaranth and moly,[3]
How sweet—while warm airs lull us, blowing lowly—
135 With half-dropped eyelid still,
Beneath a heaven dark and holy,
To watch the long bright river drawing slowly
His waters from the purple hill—
To hear the dewy echoes calling
140 From cave to cave through the thick-twined vine—
To watch the emerald-colored water falling
Through many a woven acanthus[4] wreath divine!
Only to hear and see the far-off sparkling brine,
Only to hear were sweet, stretched out beneath the pine.

8

145 The Lotos blooms below the barren peak,
The Lotos blows by every winding creek;
All day the wind breathes low with mellower tone;
Through every hollow cave and alley lone
Round and round the spicy downs the yellow Lotos dust is blown.
150 We have had enough of action, and of motion we,
Rolled to starboard, rolled to larboard, when the surge was seething free,
Where the wallowing monster spouted his foam-fountains in the sea.
Let us swear an oath, and keep it with an equal mind,
In the hollow Lotos land to live and lie reclined
155 On the hills like Gods together, careless of mankind.
For they lie beside their nectar, and the bolts° are hurled   *thunderbolts*
Far below them in the valleys, and the clouds are lightly curled
Round their golden houses, girdled with the gleaming world;
Where they smile in secret, looking over wasted lands,
160 Blight and famine, plague and earthquake, roaring deeps and fiery sands,
Clanging fights, and flaming towns, and sinking ships, and praying hands.
But they smile, they find a music centred in a doleful song
Steaming up, a lamentation and an ancient tale of wrong,
Like a tale of little meaning though the words are strong;

2. The suitors of Penelope, Odysseus's wife; during his long absence they have settled themselves as guests in his hall as they pressure her to remarry. 3. A flower with magical properties mentioned by Homer. "Amaranth": a legendary unfading flower. 4. A plant resembling a thistle. Its leaves were the model for ornaments on Corinthian columns.

165   Chanted from an ill-used race of men that cleave the soil,
     Sow the seed, and reap the harvest with enduring toil,
     Storing yearly little dues of wheat, and wine and oil;
     Till they perish and they suffer—some, 'tis whispered—down in hell
     Suffer endless anguish, others in Elysian valleys dwell,
170   Resting weary limbs at last on beds of asphodel.[5]
     Surely, surely, slumber is more sweet than toil, the shore
     Than labor in the deep mid-ocean, wind and wave and oar;
     O, rest ye, brother mariners, we will not wander more.

1832, 1842

Ulysses[1]

    It little profits that an idle king,
    By this still hearth, among these barren crags,
    Matched with an aged wife, I mete and dole
    Unequal laws[2] unto a savage race,
5   That hoard, and sleep, and feed,[3] and know not me.
      I cannot rest from travel; I will drink
    Life to the lees. All times I have enjoyed
    Greatly, have suffered greatly, both with those
    That loved me, and alone; on shore, and when
10 Through scudding drifts the rainy Hyades[4]
    Vexed the dim sea. I am become a name;
    For always roaming with a hungry heart
    Much have I seen and known—cities of men
    And manners, climates, councils, governments,
15 Myself not least, but honored of them all—
    And drunk delight of battle with my peers,
    Far on the ringing plains of windy Troy,
    I am a part of all that I have met;
    Yet all experience is an arch wherethrough
20 Gleams that untraveled world whose margin fades
    Forever and forever when I move.
    How dull it is to pause, to make an end,
    To rust unburnished, not to shine in use![5]
    As though to breathe were life! Life piled on life
25 Were all too little, and of one to me

---

5. A yellow lilylike flower supposed to grow in Elysium—in classical mythology a paradise for heroes favored by the gods.

1. According to Dante, after the fall of Troy, Ulysses never returned to his island home of Ithaca. Instead he persuaded some of his followers to seek new experiences by a voyage of exploration westward out beyond the Strait of Gibraltar. In his inspiring speech to his aging crew he said: "Consider your origin: you were not made to live as brutes, but to pursue virtue and knowledge" (*Inferno* 26). Tennyson modified Dante's 14th-century version by combining it with Homer's account (*Odyssey* 19–24). Thus Tennyson has Ulysses make his speech in Ithaca some time after he has returned home; reunited with his wife, Penelope, and his son, Telemachus; and, presumably, resumed his administrative responsi-

bilities involved in governing his kingdom.

Tennyson stated that this poem expressed his own "need of going forward and braving the struggle of life" after the death of Arthur Hallam.

2. Measure out rewards and punishments.

3. Cf. Shakespeare's *Hamlet* 4.4.9.23–25: "What is a man / If his chief good . . . Be but to sleep and feed?—a beast, no more."

4. A group of stars (literally, "rainy ones") in the constellation Taurus; their heliacal rising and setting generally coincided with the season of heavy rains. "Scudding drifts": driving showers of spray and rain.

5. Cf. Ulysses' speech in Shakespeare's *Troilus and Cressida* 3.3.144–47: "Perseverance, dear my lord, / Keeps honour bright. To have done is to hang / Quite out of fashion, like a rusty mail / In monumental mock'ry."

Little remains; but every hour is saved
From that eternal silence, something more,
A bringer of new things; and vile it were
For some three suns to store and hoard myself,
30 And this gray spirit yearning in desire
To follow knowledge like a sinking star,
Beyond the utmost bound of human thought.

This is my son, mine own Telemachus,
To whom I leave the scepter and the isle—
35 Well-loved of me, discerning to fulfill
This labor, by slow prudence to make mild
A rugged people, and through soft degrees
Subdue them to the useful and the good.
Most blameless is he, centered in the sphere
40 Of common duties, decent not to fail
In offices of tenderness, and pay
Meet° adoration to my household gods,   suitable, fitting
When I am gone. He works his work, I mine.

There lies the port; the vessel puffs her sail;
45 There gloom the dark, broad seas. My mariners,
Souls that have toiled, and wrought, and thought with me—
That ever with a frolic welcome took
The thunder and the sunshine,[6] and opposed
Free hearts, free foreheads[7]—you and I are old;
50 Old age hath yet his honor and his toil.
Death closes all; but something ere the end,
Some work of noble note, may yet be done,
Not unbecoming men that strove with Gods.
The lights begin to twinkle from the rocks;
55 The long day wanes; the slow moon climbs; the deep
Moans round with many voices. Come, my friends,
'Tis not too late to seek a newer world.
Push off, and sitting well in order smite
The sounding furrows; for my purpose holds
60 To sail beyond the sunset, and the baths[8]
Of all the western stars, until I die.
It may be that the gulfs will wash us down;
It may be we shall touch the Happy Isles,[9]
And see the great Achilles,[1] whom we knew.
65 Though much is taken, much abides; and though
We are not now that strength which in old days
Moved earth and heaven, that which we are, we are—
One equal temper of heroic hearts,
Made weak by time and fate, but strong in will
70 To strive, to seek, to find, and not to yield.

1833   1842

6. I.e., varying fortunes.
7. Confidence.
8. The outer ocean or river that the Greeks believed surrounded the flat circle of the earth; the stars descended into it.
9. In Greek myth the Islands of the Blessed, a

paradise of perpetual summer in the far-western ocean, where the virtuous and heroes dwell forever after death (often identified with Elysium).
1. The greatest of the Greek warriors at Troy, where he was killed.

Tithonus[1]

The woods decay, the woods decay and fall,
The vapors weep their burthen to the ground,
Man comes and tills the field and lies beneath,
And after many a summer dies the swan.[2]
5 Me only cruel immortality
Consumes; I wither slowly in thine arms,[3]
Here at the quiet limit of the world,
A white-haired shadow roaming like a dream
The ever-silent spaces of the East,
10 Far-folded mists, and gleaming halls of morn.
    Alas! for this gray shadow, once a man—
So glorious in his beauty and thy choice,
Who madest him thy chosen, that he seemed
To his great heart none other than a God!
15 I asked thee, "Give me immortality."
Then didst thou grant mine asking with a smile,
Like wealthy men who care not how they give.
But thy strong Hours indignant worked their wills,
And beat me down and marred and wasted me,
20 And though they could not end me, left me maimed
To dwell in presence of immortal youth,
Immortal age beside immortal youth,
And all I was in ashes. Can thy love,
Thy beauty, make amends, though even now,
25 Close over us, the silver star,[4] thy guide,
Shines in those tremulous eyes that fill with tears
To hear me? Let me go; take back thy gift.
Why should a man desire in any way
To vary from the kindly race of men,
30 Or pass beyond the goal of ordinance[5]
Where all should pause, as is most meet for all?
    A soft air fans the cloud apart; there comes
A glimpse of that dark world where I was born.
Once more the old mysterious glimmer steals
35 From thy pure brows, and from thy shoulders pure,
And bosom beating with a heart renewed.
Thy cheek begins to redden through the gloom,
Thy sweet eyes brighten slowly close to mine,
Ere yet they blind the stars, and the wild team[6]
40 Which love thee, yearning for thy yoke, arise,
And shake the darkness from their loosened manes,
And beat the twilight into flakes of fire.
    Lo! ever thus thou growest beautiful
In silence, then before thine answer given

---

1. A Trojan prince loved by the goddess of the dawn, Eos or Aurora, who obtained for him the gift of living forever but neglected to ask for the gift of everlasting youth.
2. Some species of swans live for at least fifty years.

3. Aurora's arms.
4. The morning star that precedes the dawn.
5. What is decreed or ordained as human destiny.
6. The horses that draw Aurora's chariot into the sky at daybreak.

45   Departest, and thy tears are on my cheek.
         Why wilt thou ever scare me with thy tears,
     And make me tremble lest a saying learnt,
     In days far-off, on that dark earth, be true?
     "The Gods themselves cannot recall their gifts."
50   Ay me! ay me! with what another heart
     In days far-off, and with what other eyes
     I used to watch—if I be he that watched—
     The lucid outline forming round thee; saw
     The dim curls kindle into sunny rings;
55   Changed with thy mystic change, and felt my blood
     Glow with the glow that slowly crimsoned all
     Thy presence and thy portals, while I lay,
     Mouth, forehead, eyelids, growing dewy-warm
     With kisses balmier than half-opening buds
60   Of April, and could hear the lips that kissed
     Whispering I knew not what of wild and sweet,
     Like that strange song I heard Apollo sing,
     While Ilion like a mist rose into towers.[7]
         Yet hold me not forever in thine East;
65   How can my nature longer mix with thine?
     Coldly thy rosy shadows bathe me, cold
     Are all thy lights, and cold my wrinkled feet
     Upon thy glimmering thresholds, when the steam
     Floats up from those dim fields about the homes
70   Of happy men that have the power to die,
     And grassy barrows° of the happier dead.   *burial mounds*
     Release me, and restore me to the ground.
     Thou seest all things, thou wilt see my grave;
     Thou wilt renew thy beauty morn by morn,
75   I earth in earth forget these empty courts,
     And thee returning on thy silver wheels.

1833, 1859   1860

Break, Break, Break

     Break, break, break,
         On thy cold gray stones, O Sea!
     And I would that my tongue could utter
         The thoughts that arise in me.

5   O, well for the fisherman's boy,
         That he shouts with his sister at play!
     O, well for the sailor lad,
         That he sings in his boat on the bay!

     And the stately ships go on
10   To their haven under the hill;
     But O for the touch of a vanished hand,
         And the sound of a voice that is still!

---

7. The walls of Troy ("Ilion") were supposed to have been built to the strains of the god Apollo's music.

Break, break, break,
    At the foot of thy crags, O Sea!
15 But the tender grace of a day that is dead
    Will never come back to me.

1834   1842

Locksley Hall[1]

Comrades, leave me here a little, while as yet 'tis early morn;
Leave me here, and when you want me, sound upon the bugle horn.

'Tis the place, and all around it, as of old, the curlews call,
Dreary gleams[2] about the moorland flying over Locksley Hall;

5   Locksley Hall, that in the distance overlooks the sandy tracts,
And the hollow ocean-ridges roaring into cataracts.

Many a night from yonder ivied casement, ere I went to rest,
Did I look on great Orion sloping slowly to the west.

Many a night I saw the Pleiads,[3] rising through the mellow shade,
10 Glitter like a swarm of fireflies tangled in a silver braid.

Here about the beach I wandered, nourishing a youth sublime
With the fairy tales of science, and the long result of time;

When the centuries behind me like a fruitful land reposed;
When I clung to all the present for the promise that it closed°   *enclosed*

15 When I dipped into the future far as human eye could see,
Saw the vision of the world and all the wonder that would be.—

In the spring a fuller crimson comes upon the robin's breast;
In the spring the wanton lapwing gets himself another crest;

In the spring a livelier iris changes on the burnished dove;[4]
20 In the spring a young man's fancy lightly turns to thoughts of love.

Then her cheek was pale and thinner than should be for one so young,
And her eyes on all my motions with a mute observance hung.

---

1. The situation in this poem—of a young man's being jilted by a woman who chose to marry a wealthy landowner—may have been suggested to Tennyson by the experience of his brother Frederick, a hot-tempered man who had fallen in love with his cousin Julia Tennyson and who was similarly unsuccessful. It may also have been inspired by Tennyson's own frustrated courtship of Rosa Baring, who rejected the young poet in favor of a wealthy suitor. Concerning the ranting tone of the speaker (a tone accentuated by the heavily marked trochaic meter), Tennyson said: "The whole poem represents young life, its good side, its deficiencies, and its yearnings."
2. Tennyson stated that the noun "gleams" refers not to "curlews" flying but to streaks of light.
3. Or the Pleiades, seven stars in the constellation Taurus.
4. The rainbowlike colors of a dove's throat plumage are intensified in the mating season.

And I said, "My cousin Amy, speak, and speak the truth to me,
Trust me, cousin, all the current of my being sets to thee."

25   On her pallid cheek and forehead came a color and a light,
As I have seen the rosy red flushing in the northern night.

And she turned—her bosom shaken with a sudden storm of sighs—
All the spirit deeply dawning in the dark of hazel eyes—

Saying, "I have hid my feelings, fearing they should do me wrong";
30   Saying, "Dost thou love me, cousin?" weeping, "I have loved thee long."

Love took up the glass of Time, and turned it in his glowing hands;
Every moment, lightly shaken, ran itself in golden sands.

Love took up the harp of Life, and smote on all the chords with might;
Smote the chord of Self, that, trembling, passed in music out of sight.

35   Many a morning on the moorland did we hear the copses ring,
And her whisper thronged my pulses with the fullness of the spring.

Many an evening by the waters did we watch the stately ships,
And our spirits rushed together at the touching of the lips.

O my cousin, shallow-hearted! O my Amy, mine no more!
40   O the dreary, dreary moorland! O the barren, barren shore!

Falser than all fancy fathoms, falser than all songs have sung,
Puppet to a father's threat, and servile to a shrewish tongue!

Is it well to wish thee happy?—having known me—to decline
On a range of lower feelings and a narrower heart than mine!

45   Yet it shall be; thou shalt lower to his level day by day,
What is fine within thee growing coarse to sympathize with clay.

As the husband is, the wife is; thou art mated with a clown,°   *boor*
And the grossness of his nature will have weight to drag thee down.

He will hold thee, when his passion shall have spent its novel force,
50   Something better than his dog, a little dearer than his horse.

What is this? his eyes are heavy; think not they are glazed with wine.
Go to him, it is thy duty; kiss him, take his hand in thine.

It may be my lord is weary, that his brain is overwrought;
Soothe him with thy finer fancies, touch him with thy lighter thought.

55   He will answer to the purpose, easy things to understand—
Better thou wert dead before me, though I slew thee with my hand!

Better thou and I were lying, hidden from the heart's disgrace,
Rolled in one another's arms, and silent in a last embrace.

Cursed be the social wants that sin against the strength of youth!
60 Cursed be the social lies that warp us from the living truth!

Cursed be the sickly forms that err from honest Nature's rule!
Cursed be the gold that gilds the straitened° forehead of the fool!   narrowed

Well—'tis well that I should bluster!—Hadst thou less unworthy proved—
Would to God—for I had loved thee more than ever wife was loved.

65 Am I mad, that I should cherish that which bears but bitter fruit?
I will pluck it from my bosom, though my heart be at the root.

Never, though my mortal summers to such length of years should come
As the many-wintered crow[5] that leads the clanging rookery home.

Where is comfort? in division of the records of the mind?
70 Can I part her from herself, and love her, as I knew her, kind?

I remember one that perished; sweetly did she speak and move;
Such a one do I remember, whom to look at was to love.

Can I think of her as dead, and love her for the love she bore?
No—she never loved me truly; love is love for evermore.

75 Comfort? comfort scorned of devils! this is truth the poet[6] sings,
That a sorrow's crown of sorrow is remembering happier things.

Drug thy memories, lest thou learn it, lest thy heart be put to proof,
In the dead unhappy night, and when the rain is on the roof.

Like a dog, he hunts in dreams, and thou art staring at the wall,
80 Where the dying night-lamp flickers, and the shadows rise and fall.

Then a hand shall pass before thee, pointing to his drunken sleep,
To thy widowed[7] marriage-pillows, to the tears that thou wilt weep.

Thou shalt hear the "Never, never," whispered by the phantom years.
And a song from out the distance in the ringing of thine ears;

85 And an eye shall vex thee, looking ancient kindness on thy pain.
Turn thee, turn thee on thy pillow; get thee to thy rest again.

Nay, but Nature brings thee solace; for a tender voice will cry.
'Tis a purer life than thine, a lip to drain thy trouble dry.

Baby lips will laugh me down; my latest rival brings thee rest.
90 Baby fingers, waxen touches, press me from the mother's breast.

O, the child too clothes the father with a dearness not his due.
Half is thine and half is his; it will be worthy of the two.

5. A rook, a long-lived bird.
6. Dante; see *Inferno* 5.121–23: "There is no greater sorrow / Than to be mindful of the happy time in misery" [Longfellow's translation].
7. Presumably figurative. Her marriage having become a mockery, she is widowed.

O, I see thee old and formal, fitted to thy petty part,
With a little hoard of maxims preaching down a daughter's heart.

95 "They were dangerous guides the feelings—she herself was not
    exempt—
Truly, she herself had suffered"—Perish in thy self-contempt!

Overlive it—lower yet—be happy! wherefore should I care?
I myself must mix with action, lest I wither by despair.

What is that which I should turn to, lighting upon days like these?
100 Every door is barred with gold, and opens but to golden keys.

Every gate is thronged with suitors, all the markets overflow.
I have but an angry fancy; what is that which I should do?

I had been content to perish, falling on the foeman's ground,
When the ranks are rolled in vapor, and the winds are laid with
    sound.[8]

105 But the jingling of the guinea helps the hurt that Honor feels,
And the nations do but murmur, snarling at each other's heels.

Can I but relive in sadness? I will turn that earlier page.
Hide me from my deep emotion, O thou wondrous Mother-Age![9]

Make me feel the wild pulsation that I felt before the strife,
110 When I heard my days before me, and the tumult of my life;

Yearning for the large excitement that the coming years would yield,
Eager-hearted as a boy when first he leaves his father's field,

And at night along the dusky highway near and nearer drawn,
Sees in heaven the light of London flaring like a dreary dawn;

115 And his spirit leaps within him to be gone before him then,
Underneath the light he looks at, in among the throngs of men;

Men, my brothers, men the workers, ever reaping something new;
That which they have done but earnest° of the things that they   *pledge*
    shall do.

For I dipped into the future, far as human eye could see,
120 Saw the Vision of the world, and all the wonder that would be;

Saw the heavens fill with commerce, argosies of magic sails,[1]
Pilots of the purple twilight, dropping down with costly bales;

Heard the heavens fill with shouting, and there rained a ghastly dew
From the nations' airy navies grappling in the central blue;

---

8. It was once believed that the firing of artillery stilled the winds.
9. A happier past at life's beginning, which generated a more confident anticipation of the future (see also line 185).
1. Probably airships, such as balloons. "Argosies": merchant vessels.

125 Far along the world-wide whisper of the south wind rushing warm,
With the standards of the peoples plunging through the thunderstorm;

Till the war drum throbbed no longer, and the battle flags were furled
In the Parliament of man, the Federation of the world.

There the common sense of most shall hold a fretful realm in awe,
130 And the kindly earth shall slumber, lapped in° universal law.   *encompassed by*

So I triumphed ere my passion sweeping through me left me dry,
Left me with the palsied heart, and left me with the jaundiced eye;

Eye, to which all order festers, all things here are out of joint.
Science moves, but slowly, slowly, creeping on from point to point;

135 Slowly comes a hungry people, as a lion, creeping nigher,
Glares at one that nods and winks behind a slowly-dying fire.

Yet I doubt not through the ages one increasing purpose runs,
And the thoughts of men are widened with the process of the suns.

What is that to him that reaps not harvest of his youthful joys,
140 Though the deep heart of existence beat forever like a boy's?

Knowledge comes, but wisdom lingers, and I linger on the shore,
And the individual withers, and the world is more and more.

Knowledge comes, but wisdom lingers, and he bears a laden breast,
Full of sad experience, moving toward the stillness of his rest.

145 Hark, my merry comrades call me, sounding on the bugle horn,
They to whom my foolish passion were a target for their scorn.

Shall it not be scorn to me to harp on such a moldered string?
I am shamed through all my nature to have loved so slight a thing.

Weakness to be wroth with weakness! woman's pleasure, woman's pain—
150 Nature made them blinder motions bounded in a shallower brain.

Woman is the lesser man, and all thy passions, matched with mine,
Are as moonlight unto sunlight, and as water unto wine—

Here at least, where nature sickens, nothing. Ah, for some retreat
Deep in yonder shining Orient, where my life began to beat.

155 Where in wild Mahratta-battle[2] fell my father evil-starred—
I was left a trampled orphan, and a selfish uncle's ward.

Or to burst all links of habit—there to wander far away,
On from island unto island at the gateways of the day.

---

2. Reference to wars waged by a Hindu people against the British forces in India (1803 and 1817).

Larger constellations burning, mellow moons and happy skies,
160 Breadths of tropic shade and palms in cluster, knots of Paradise.

Never comes the trader, never floats an European flag,
Slides the bird o'er lustrous woodland, swings the trailer° from the   *vine*
     crag;

Droops the heavy-blossomed bower, hangs the heavy-fruited tree—
Summer isles of Eden lying in dark purple spheres of sea.

165 There methinks would be enjoyment more than in this march of mind,
In the steamship, in the railway, in the thoughts that shake mankind.

There the passions cramped no longer shall have scope and breathing
     space;
I will take some savage woman, she shall rear my dusky race.

Iron-jointed, supple-sinewed, they shall dive, and they shall run,
170 Catch the wild goat by the hair, and hurl their lances in the sun;

Whistle back the parrot's call, and leap the rainbows of the brooks,
Not with blinded eyesight poring over miserable books—

Fool, again the dream, the fancy! but I *know* my words are wild,
But I count the gray barbarian lower than the Christian child.

175 I, to herd with narrow foreheads, vacant of our glorious gains,
Like a beast with lower pleasures, like a beast with lower pains!

Mated with a squalid savage—what to me were sun or clime?
I the heir of all the ages, in the foremost files of time—

I that rather held it better men should perish one by one,
180 Than that earth should stand at gaze like Joshua's moon in Ajalon![3]

Not in vain the distance beacons. Forward, forward let us range,
Let the great world spin forever down the ringing grooves[4] of change.

Through the shadow of the globe we sweep into the younger day;
Better fifty years of Europe than a cycle of Cathay.[5]

185 Mother-Age—for mine I knew not—help me as when life begun;
Rift the hills, and roll the waters, flash the lightnings, weigh the sun.

O, I see the crescent promise of my spirit hath not set.
Ancient founts of inspiration well through all my fancy yet.

Howsoever these things be, a long farewell to Locksley Hall!
190 Now for me the woods may wither, now for me the roof-tree fall.

3. At Joshua's command the sun and moon stood
still while the Israelites completed the slaughter
of their enemies in the valley of Ajalon (Joshua
10.12–13).

4. Railroad tracks. Tennyson at one time had the
impression that train wheels ran in grooved rails.
5. China, regarded in the 19th century as a
static, unprogressive country

Comes a vapor from the margin,° blackening over heath and   *riverbank*
   holt,°   *wood*
Cramming all the blast before it, in its breast a thunderbolt.

Let it fall on Locksley Hall, with rain or hail, or fire or snow;
For the mighty wind arises, roaring seaward, and I go.

1837–38   1842

In Memoriam A. H. H. When Arthur Hallam died suddenly at the age of twenty-two, probably of a stroke, Tennyson felt that his life had been shattered. Hallam was not only Tennyson's closest friend, and his sister's fiancé, but a critic and champion of his poetry. Widely regarded as the most promising young man of his generation, Hallam had written a review of Tennyson's first book of poetry that is still one of the best assessments of it. When Tennyson lost Hallam's love and support, he was overwhelmed with doubts about his own life and vocation and about the meaning of the universe and humankind's place in it, doubts reinforced by his study of geology and other sciences. To express the variety of his feelings and reflections, he began to compose a series of lyrics. Tennyson later arranged these "short swallow-flights of song," as he called them, written over a period of seventeen years, into one long elegy. Although the resulting poem has many affinities with traditional elegies like Milton's "Lycidas" (1638) and Shelley's *Adonais* (1821), its structure is strikingly different. It is made up of individual lyric units that are seemingly self-contained but take their full meaning from their place in the whole. As T. S. Eliot has written, "It is unique: it is a long poem made by putting together lyrics, which have only the unity and continuity of a diary, the concentrated diary of a man confessing himself." Though intensely personal, the elegy expresses the religious doubts of Tennyson's age. It is also a love poem. Like Shakespeare's sonnets, to which the poem alludes, *In Memoriam* vests its most intense emotion in male relationships.

The sections of the poem record a progressive development from despair to some sort of hope. Some of the early sections of the poem resemble traditional pastoral elegies, including those portraying the voyage during which Hallam's body was brought to England for burial (sections 9 to 15 and 19). Other early sections portraying the speaker's loneliness, in which even Christmas festivities seem joyless (sections 28 to 30), are more distinctive. The poem's internal chronology covers a span of around three years, and with the passage of time, indicated by anniversaries and by recurring changes of the seasons, the speaker comes to accept the loss and to assert his belief in life and in an afterlife. In particular the recurring Christmases (sections 28, 78, 104) indicate the stages of his development, yet the pattern of progress in the poem is not a simple unimpeded movement upward. Dramatic conflicts recur throughout. Thus the most intense expression of doubt occurs not at the beginning of *In Memoriam* but as late as sections 54, 55, and 56.

The quatrain form in which the whole poem is written is usually called the "*In Memoriam* stanza," although it had been occasionally used by earlier poets. So rigid a form taxed Tennyson's ingenuity in achieving variety, but is is one of several means by which the diverse parts of the poem are knitted together.

The introductory section, consisting of eleven stanzas, is commonly referred to as the "Prologue," although Tennyson did not assign a title to it. It was written in 1849 after the rest of the poem was complete.

From In Memoriam A. H. H.

OBIIT MDCCCXXXIII[1]

Strong Son of God, immortal Love,
  Whom we, that have not seen thy face,
  By faith, and faith alone, embrace,
Believing where we cannot prove;[2]

5 Thine are these orbs[3] of light and shade;
  Thou madest Life in man and brute;
  Thou madest Death; and lo, thy foot
Is on the skull which thou hast made.

Thou wilt not leave us in the dust:
10 Thou madest man, he knows not why,
  He thinks he was not made to die;
And thou hast made him: thou art just.

Thou seemest human and divine,
  The highest, holiest manhood, thou.
15 Our wills are ours, we know not how;
Our wills are ours, to make them thine.

Our little systems[4] have their day;
  They have their day and cease to be;
  They are but broken lights of thee,
20 And thou, O Lord, art more than they.

We have but faith: we cannot know,
  For knowledge is of things we see;
  And yet we trust it comes from thee,
A beam in darkness: let it grow.

25 Let knowledge grow from more to more,
  But more of reverence in us dwell;
  That mind and soul, according well,
May make one music as before,[5]

But vaster. We are fools and slight;
30 We mock thee when we do not fear:
  But help thy foolish ones to bear;
Help thy vain worlds to bear thy light.

Forgive what seemed my sin in me,
  What seemed my worth since I began;
35 For merit lives from man to man,
And not from man, O Lord, to thee.

---

1. He died 1833 (Latin).
2. Cf. John 20.24–29, in which Jesus rebukes Thomas for his doubts concerning the Resurrection: "Blessed are they that have not seen, and yet have believed."

3. The sun and moon (according to Tennyson's note).
4. Of religion and philosophy.
5. As in the days of fixed religious faith.

Forgive my grief for one removed,
    Thy creature, whom I found so fair.
    I trust he lives in thee, and there
40   I find him worthier to be loved.

Forgive these wild and wandering cries,
    Confusions of a wasted° youth;   *desolated*
    Forgive them where they fail in truth,
And in thy wisdom make me wise.

1849

1

I held it truth, with him who sings
    To one clear harp in divers tones,[6]
    That men may rise on stepping stones
Of their dead selves to higher things.

5   But who shall so forecast the years
    And find in loss a gain to match?
    Or reach a hand through time to catch
The far-off interest of tears?

Let Love clasp Grief lest both be drowned,
10   Let darkness keep her raven gloss.
    Ah, sweeter to be drunk with loss,
To dance with Death, to beat the ground,

Than that the victor Hours should scorn
    The long result of love, and boast,
15   "Behold the man that loved and lost,
But all he was is overworn."

2

Old yew, which graspest at the stones
    That name the underlying dead,
    Thy fibres net the dreamless head,
Thy roots are wrapped about the bones.

5   The seasons bring the flower again,
    And bring the firstling to the flock;
    And in the dusk of thee the clock
Beats out the little lives of men.

O, not for thee the glow, the bloom,
10   Who changest not in any gale,
    Nor branding summer suns avail
To touch thy thousand years of gloom[7]

---

6. Identified by Tennyson as the German poet Johann Wolfgang von Goethe (1749–1832).
7. The ancient yew tree, growing in the grounds near the clock tower and church where Hallam was to be buried, seems neither to blossom in spring nor to change from its dark mournful color in summer. "Thousand years": cf. Book of Common Prayer, Psalm 90: "For a thousand years in Thy sight are but as yesterday when it is past, and as a watch in the night."

And gazing on thee, sullen tree,
    Sick for° thy stubborn hardihood,   *envying*
15   I seem to fail from out my blood
And grow incorporate into thee.

3

O Sorrow, cruel fellowship,
    O Priestess in the vaults of Death,
    O sweet and bitter in a breath,
What whispers from thy lying lip?

5   "The stars," she whispers, "blindly run;
    A web is woven across the sky;
    From out waste places comes a cry,
And murmurs from the dying sun;

"And all the phantom, Nature, stands—
10   With all the music in her tone,
    A hollow echo of my own—
A hollow form with empty hands."

And shall I take a thing so blind,
    Embrace her° as my natural good;   *Sorrow*
15   Or crush her, like a vice of blood,
Upon the threshold of the mind?

4

To Sleep I give my powers away;
    My will is bondsman to the dark;
    I sit within a helmless bark,
And with my heart I muse and say:

5   O heart, how fares it with thee now,
    That thou should fail from thy desire,
    Who scarcely darest to inquire,
"What is it makes me beat so low?"

Something it is which thou hast lost,
10   Some pleasure from thine early years.
    Break thou deep vase of chilling tears,
That grief hath shaken into frost!⁸

Such clouds of nameless trouble cross
    All night below the darkened eyes;
15   With morning wakes the will, and cries,
"Thou shalt not be the fool of loss."

---

8. Water can be brought below freezing-point and not turn into ice—if it be kept still; but if it be moved suddenly it turns into ice and may break a vase [Tennyson's note].

5

I sometimes hold it half a sin
   To put in words the grief I feel;
   For words, like Nature, half reveal
And half conceal the Soul within.

5 But, for the unquiet heart and brain,
   A use in measured language lies;
   The sad mechanic exercise,
Like dull narcotics, numbing pain.

In words, like weeds,° I'll wrap me o'er,   *mourning garments*
10   Like coarsest clothes against the cold;
   But that large grief which these enfold
Is given in outline and no more.

6

One writes, that "Other friends remain,"
   That "Loss is common to the race"—
   And common is the commonplace,
And vacant chaff° well meant for grain.   *husks*

5 That loss is common would not make
   My own less bitter, rather more:
   Too common! Never morning wore
To evening, but some heart did break.

O father, wheresoe'er thou be,
10   Who pledgest° now thy gallant son;   *toasts*
   A shot, ere half thy draft be done,
Hath stilled the life that beat from thee.

O mother, praying God will save
   Thy sailor—while thy head is bowed,
15   His heavy-shotted hammock-shroud
Drops in his vast and wandering grave.[9]

Ye know no more than I who wrought
   At that last hour to please him well;[1]
   Who mused on all I had to tell,
20 And something written, something thought;

Expecting still his advent home;
   And ever met him on his way
   With wishes, thinking, "here today,"
Or "here tomorrow will he come."

25 O somewhere, meek, the unconscious dove,
   That sittest ranging° golden hair;   *arranging*

---

9. Sailors buried at sea were often wrapped in their own hammocks. "Heavy-shotted": heavily weighted.

1. According to his son, Tennyson discovered that he had been writing a letter to Hallam during the very hour in which his friend died.

And glad to find thyself so fair,
Poor child, that waitest for thy love!

For now her father's chimney glows
30   In expectation of a guest;
And thinking "this will please him best,"
She takes a riband or a rose;

For he will see them on tonight;
And with the thought her color burns;
35   And, having left the glass, she turns
Once more to set a ringlet right;

And, even when she turned, the curse
Had fallen, and her future Lord
Was drowned in passing through the ford,
40 Or killed in falling from his horse.

O what to her shall be the end?
And what to me remains of good?
To her, perpetual maidenhood,
And unto me no second friend.

7

Dark house,[2] by which once more I stand
Here in the long unlovely street,
Doors, where my heart was used to beat
So quickly, waiting for a hand,

5   A hand that can be clasped no more—
Behold me, for I cannot sleep,
And like a guilty thing I creep
At earliest morning to the door.

He is not here; but far away
10   The noise of life begins again,
And ghastly through the drizzling rain
On the bald street breaks the blank day.

8

A happy lover who has come
To look on her that loves him well,
Who 'lights° and rings the gateway bell,   *alights*
And learns her gone and far from home;

5   He saddens, all the magic light
Dies off at once from bower and hall,
And all the place is dark, and all
The chambers emptied of delight:

2. The house on Wimpole Street, in London, where Hallam had lived.

So find I every pleasant spot
10   In which we two were wont to meet,
        The field, the chamber, and the street,
For all is dark where thou art not.

Yet as that other, wandering there
        In those deserted walks, may find
15   A flower beat with rain and wind,
Which once she fostered up with care;

So seems it in my deep regret,
        O my forsaken heart, with thee
        And this poor flower of poesy
20   Which little cared for fades not yet.

But since it pleased a vanished eye,[3]
        I go to plant it on his tomb,
        That if it can it there may bloom,
Or dying, there at least may die.

9

Fair ship, that from the Italian shore[4]
        Sailest the placid ocean-plains
        With my lost Arthur's loved remains,
Spread thy full wings, and waft him o'er.

5   So draw him home to those that mourn
        In vain; a favorable speed
        Ruffle thy mirrored mast, and lead
Through prosperous floods his holy urn.

All night no ruder air perplex
10   Thy sliding keel, till Phosphor,° bright   *morning star*
        As our pure love, through early light
Shall glimmer on the dewy decks.

Sphere all your lights around, above;
        Sleep, gentle heavens, before the prow;
15   Sleep, gentle winds, as he sleeps now,
My friend, the brother of my love;

My Arthur, whom I shall not see
        Till all my widowed race be run;
        Dear as the mother to the son,
20   More than my brothers are to me.

10

I hear the noise about thy keel;
        I hear the bell struck in the night;

---

3. Hallam expressed enthusiasm for Tennyson's early poetry in a review written in 1831.

4. Hallam's body was conveyed back to England by ship from Trieste, Italy.

I see the cabin window bright;
I see the sailor at the wheel.

5   Thou bring'st the sailor to his wife,
     And traveled men from foreign lands;
     And letters unto trembling hands;
And, thy dark freight, a vanished life.

So bring him; we have idle dreams;
10   This look of quiet flatters thus
     Our home-bred fancies. O, to us,
The fools of habit, sweeter seems

To rest beneath the clover sod,
     That takes the sunshine and the rains,
15   Or where the kneeling hamlet drains
The chalice of the grapes of God;[5]

Than if with thee the roaring wells
     Should gulf him fathom-deep in brine,
     And hands so often clasped in mine,
20   Should toss with tangle° and with shells.   *seaweed*

11

Calm is the morn without a sound,
     Calm as to suit a calmer grief,
     And only through the faded leaf
The chestnut pattering to the ground;

5   Calm and deep peace on this high wold,°   *open countryside*
     And on these dews that drench the furze,
     And all the silvery gossamers
That twinkle into green and gold;

Calm and still light on yon great plain
10   That sweeps with all its autumn bowers,
     And crowded farms and lessening towers,
To mingle with the bounding main;

Calm and deep peace in this wide air,
     These leaves that redden to the fall,
15   And in my heart, if calm at all,
If any calm, a calm despair;

Calm on the seas, and silver sleep,
     And waves that sway themselves in rest,
     And dead calm in that noble breast
20   Which heaves but with the heaving deep.

---

5. Reference to a burial inside a church building rather than in the churchyard.

12

Lo, as a dove when up she springs
　　To bear through Heaven a tale of woe,
　　Some dolorous message knit below
The wild pulsation of her wings;

5　Like her I go; I cannot stay;
　　I leave this mortal ark behind,
　　A weight of nerves without a mind,
And leave the cliffs, and haste away

O'er ocean-mirrors rounded large,
10　And reach the glow of southern skies,
　　And see the sails at distance rise,
And linger weeping on the marge,°　　　　　　　　　　　*shore*

And saying; "Comes he thus, my friend?
　　Is this the end of all my care?"
15　And circle moaning in the air:
"Is this the end? Is this the end?"

And forward dart again, and play
　　About the prow, and back return
　　To where the body sits, and learn
20　That I have been an hour away.

13

Tears of the widower, when he sees
　　A late-lost form that sleep reveals,
　　And moves his doubtful arms, and feels
Her place is empty, fall like these;

5　Which weep a loss forever new,
　　A void where heart on heart reposed;
　　And, where warm hands have pressed and closed,
Silence, till I be silent too;

Which weep the comrade of my choice,
10　An awful thought, a life removed,
　　The human-hearted man I loved,
A Spirit, not a breathing voice.

Come, Time, and teach me, many years,
　　I do not suffer in a dream;
15　For now so strange do these things seem,
Mine eyes have leisure for their tears,

My fancies time to rise on wing,
　　And glance about the approaching sails,
　　As though they brought but merchants' bales,
20　And not the burthen that they bring.

14

If one should bring me this report,
    That thou° hadst touched the land today,   *the ship*
    And I went down unto the quay;[6]
And found thee lying in the port;

5 And standing, muffled round with woe,
    Should see thy passengers in rank
    Come stepping lightly down the plank
And beckoning unto those they know;

And if along with these should come
10   The man I held as half divine,
    Should strike a sudden hand in mine,
And ask a thousand things of home;

And I should tell him all my pain,
    And how my life had drooped of late,
15   And he should sorrow o'er my state
And marvel what possessed my brain;

And I perceived no touch of change,
    No hint of death in all his frame,
    But found him all in all the same,
20 I should not feel it to be strange.

15

Tonight the winds begin to rise
    And roar from yonder dropping day;
    The last red leaf is whirled away,
The rooks are blown about the skies;

5 The forest cracked, the waters curled,
    The cattle huddled on the lea;
    And wildly dashed on tower and tree
The sunbeam strikes along the world:

And but for fancies, which aver
10   That all thy motions gently pass
    Athwart a plane of molten glass,[7]
I scarce could brook the strain and stir

That makes the barren branches loud;
    And but for fear it is not so,
15   The wild unrest that lives in woe
Would dote and pore on yonder cloud

That rises upward always higher,
    And onward drags a laboring breast,

---

6. By 1850 the accepted pronunciation of "quay" would rhyme with *key*, but Tennyson reverts to an earlier pronunciation, *kay*.
7. I.e., a calm sea.

And topples round the dreary west,
20   A looming bastion fringed with fire.

* * *

19

The Danube to the Severn[8] gave
    The darkened heart that beat no more;
    They laid him by the pleasant shore,
And in the hearing of the wave.

5   There twice a day the Severn fills;
    The salt sea water passes by,
    And hushes half the babbling Wye,[9]
And makes a silence in the hills.

The Wye is hushed nor moved along,
10   And hushed my deepest grief of all,
    When filled with tears that cannot fall,
I brim with sorrow drowning song.

The tide flows down, the wave again
    Is vocal in its wooded walls;[1]
15   My deeper anguish also falls,
And I can speak a little then.

* * *

21

I sing to him that rests below
    And, since the grasses round me wave,
    I take the grasses of the grave,[2]
And make them pipes whereon to blow.

5   The traveler hears me now and then,
    And sometimes harshly will he speak:
    "This fellow would make weakness weak,
And melt the waxen hearts of men."

Another answers: "Let him be,
10   He loves to make parade of pain,
    That with his piping he may gain
The praise that comes to constancy."

A third is wroth: "Is this an hour
    For private sorrow's barren song,

8. Hallam died at Vienna on the river Danube. His burial place is on the banks of the Severn, a tidal river in the southwest of England.
9. A tributary of the Severn.
1. The water of the Wye River is dammed up as the tide flows in, and its sound is silenced until, with the turn of the tide, its "wave" once more becomes "vocal"; these stanzas were written at Tintern Abbey in the Wye valley.
2. The poet assumes that the burial was in the churchyard; in fact, on January 3, 1834, at St. Andrews in Clevedon, Somersetshire, Hallam's body was interred in a vault inside the church.

15   When more and more the people throng
       The chairs and thrones of civil power?

       "A time to sicken and to swoon,
           When Science reaches forth her arms[3]
           To feel from world to world, and charms
20   Her secret from the latest moon?"[4]

       Behold, ye speak an idle thing;
           Ye never knew the sacred dust.
           I do but sing because I must,
       And pipe but as the linnets sing:

25   And one is glad; her note is gay,
           For now her little ones have ranged;
           And one is sad; her note is changed,
       Because her brood is stolen away.

22

       The path by which we twain did go,
           Which led by tracts that pleased us well,
           Through four sweet years arose and fell,
       From flower to flower, from snow to snow;

5   And we with singing cheered the way,
           And, crowned with all the season lent,
           From April on to April went,
       And glad at heart from May to May.

       But where the path we walked began
10   To slant the fifth autumnal slope,[5]
           As we descended following Hope,
       There sat the Shadow feared of man;

       Who broke our fair companionship,
           And spread his mantle dark and cold,
15   And wrapped thee formless in the fold,
       And dulled the murmur on thy lip,

       And bore thee where I could not see
           Nor follow, though I walk in haste,
           And think that somewhere in the waste
20   The Shadow sits and waits for me.

23

       Now, sometimes in my sorrow shut,
           Or breaking into song by fits,
           Alone, alone, to where he sits,
       The Shadow cloaked from head to foot,

3. Astronomical instruments, such as telescopes.
4. Probably alluding to the discovery in 1846 of the planet Neptune and one of its moons.

5. Hallam died just before the beginning of autumn (September 15, 1833) in the fifth year of the friendship.

⁵ Who keeps the keys of all the creeds,
    I wander, often falling lame,
    And looking back to whence I came,
Or on to where the pathway leads;

And crying, How changed from where it ran
¹⁰   Through lands where not a leaf was dumb,
    But all the lavish hills would hum
The murmur of a happy Pan;[6]

When each by turns was guide to each,
    And Fancy light from Fancy caught,
¹⁵   And Thought leapt out to wed with Thought
Ere Thought could wed itself with Speech;

And all we met was fair and good,
    And all was good that Time could bring,
    And all the secret of the Spring
²⁰ Moved in the chambers of the blood;

And many an old philosophy
    On Argive[7] heights divinely sang,
    And round us all the thicket rang
To many a flute of Arcady.[8]

24

And was the day of my delight
    As pure and perfect as I say?
    The very source and fount of day
Is dashed with wandering isles of night.[9]

⁵ If all was good and fair we met,
    This earth had been the Paradise
    It never looked to human eyes
Since our first sun arose and set.

And is it that the haze of grief
¹⁰   Makes former gladness loom so great?
    The lowness of the present state,
That sets the past in this relief?

Or that the past will always win
    A glory from its being far,
¹⁵   And orb into the perfect star
We saw not when we moved therein?[1]

6. In Greek mythology the god of woods and pastures.
7. Of Argos, an ancient city-state in the north-eastern Peloponnesus; more generally, Greek.
8. A sheep-raising region in Greece associated with pastoral poetry.
9. Moving spots on the sun.
1. The poet wonders whether Earth would have the deceptive appearance of being a perfect orb if viewed from afar, on another planet.

25

I know that this was Life—the track
 Whereon with equal feet we fared;
 And then, as now, the day prepared
The daily burden for the back.

5 But this it was that made me move
 As light as carrier birds in air;
 I loved the weight I had to bear,
Because it needed help of Love;

Nor could I weary, heart or limb,
10 When mighty Love would cleave in twain
 The lading° of a single pain,   *burden*
And part it, giving half to him.

26

Still onward winds the dreary way;
 I with it, for I long to prove
 No lapse of moons can canker Love,
Whatever fickle tongues may say.

5 And if that eye which watches guilt
 And goodness, and hath power to see
 Within the green the mouldered tree,
And towers fallen as soon as built—

O, if indeed that eye foresee
10 Or see—in Him is no before—
 In more of life true life no more
And Love the indifference to be,

Then might I find, ere yet the morn
 Breaks hither over Indian seas,
15 That Shadow waiting with the keys,
To shroud me from my proper scorn.[2]

27

I envy not in any moods
 The captive void of noble rage,
 The linnet born within the cage,
That never knew the summer woods;

5 I envy not the beast that takes
 His license in the field of time,
 Unfettered by the sense of crime,
To whom a conscience never wakes;

2. The Deity, being outside time, sees (rather than foresees) whether or not the rest of life ("more of life," line 11) will be pointless. If pointless, then the way for the speaker to deal with his self-scorn ("proper scorn") might be to seek death.

Nor, what may count itself as blest,
10   The heart that never plighted troth
    But stagnates in the weeds of sloth;
Nor any want-begotten rest.[3]

I hold it true, whate'er befall;
    I feel it, when I sorrow most;
15   'Tis better to have loved and lost
Than never to have loved at all.

28

The time draws near the birth of Christ.[4]
    The moon is hid, the night is still;
    The Christmas bells from hill to hill
Answer each other in the mist.

5   Four voices of four hamlets round,
    From far and near, on mead and moor,
    Swell out and fail, as if a door
Were shut between me and the sound;

Each voice four changes[5] on the wind,
10   That now dilate, and now decrease,
    Peace and goodwill, goodwill and peace,
Peace and goodwill, to all mankind.

This year I slept and woke with pain,
    I almost wished no more to wake,
15   And that my hold on life would break
Before I heard those bells again;

But they my troubled spirit rule,
    For they controlled me when a boy;
    They bring me sorrow touched with joy,
20   The merry, merry bells of Yule.

29

With such compelling cause to grieve
    As daily vexes household peace,
    And chains regret to his decease,
How dare we keep our Christmas eve;

5   Which brings no more a welcome guest
    To enrich the threshold of the night
    With showered largess of delight
In dance and song and game and jest?

Yet go, and while the holly boughs
10   Entwine the cold baptismal font,

3. Complacency resulting from some deficiency ("want").
4. The first Christmas after Hallam's death (1833); the setting is Tennyson's family home in Lincolnshire.
5. Different sequences in which church bells are pealed.

Make one wreath more for Use and Wont,[6]
That guard the portals of the house;

Old sisters of a day gone by,
   Gray nurses, loving nothing new;
15   Why should they miss their yearly due
Before their time? They too will die.

30

With trembling fingers did we weave
   The holly round the Christmas hearth;
   A rainy cloud possessed the earth,
And sadly fell our Christmas eve.

5 At our old pastimes in the hall
   We gamboled, making vain pretense
   Of gladness, with an awful sense
Of one mute Shadow watching all.

We paused: the winds were in the beech;
10   We heard them sweep the winter land;
   And in a circle hand-in-hand
Sat silent, looking each at each.

Then echo-like our voices rang;
   We sung, though every eye was dim,
15   A merry song we sang with him
Last year; impetuously we sang.

We ceased; a gentler feeling crept
   Upon us: surely rest is meet.°   *proper, appropriate*
   "They rest," we said, "their sleep is sweet,"
20 And silence followed, and we wept.

Our voices took a higher range;
   Once more we sang: "They do not die
   Nor lose their mortal sympathy,
Nor change to us, although they change;

25 "Rapt from[7] the fickle and the frail
   With gathered power, yet the same,
   Pierces the keen seraphic flame
From orb to orb, from veil[8] to veil."

Rise, happy morn, rise, holy morn,
30   Draw forth the cheerful day from night:
   O Father, touch the east, and light
The light that shone when Hope was born.

*   *   *

6. Personifying the spirits who expect customary observances of the Christmas season to be
followed.
7. Carried away from.
8. An image representing the boundary between
different worlds, especially that between Earth
and heaven (cf. section 56, line 28). "From orb to
orb": the angelic spirit ("flame") of the dead moves
from star to star.

34

My own dim life should teach me this,
 That life shall live forevermore,
 Else earth is darkness at the core,
And dust and ashes all that is;

5 This round of green, this orb of flame,
 Fantastic beauty; such as lurks
 In some wild poet, when he works
Without a conscience or an aim.

What then were God to such as I?
10 'Twere hardly worth my while to choose
 Of things all mortal, or to use
A little patience ere I die;

'Twere best at once to sink to peace,
 Like birds the charming serpent[9] draws,
15 To drop head-foremost in the jaws
Of vacant darkness and to cease.

35

Yet if some voice that man could trust
 Should murmur from the narrow house,
 "The cheeks drop in, the body bows;
Man dies, nor is there hope in dust";

5 Might I not say? "Yet even here,
 But for one hour, O Love, I strive
 To keep so sweet a thing alive."
But I should turn mine ears and hear

The moanings of the homeless sea,
10 The sound of streams that swift or slow
 Draw down Aeonian[1] hills, and sow
The dust of continents to be;

And Love would answer with a sigh,
 "The sound of that forgetful shore[2]
15 Will change my sweetness more and more,
Half-dead to know that I shall die."

O me, what profits it to put
 An idle case? If Death were seen
 At first as Death, Love had not been,
20 Or been in narrowest working shut,

Mere fellowship of sluggish moods,
 Or in his coarsest Satyr-shape[3]

---

9. Some snakes are reputed to capture their prey by hypnotizing it.
1. Eons old, seemingly everlasting.
2. I.e., of Lethe, the river in the classical under-world whose water caused forgetfulness.
3. In Greek mythology satyrs were half-man, half-beast (goat or horse) in appearance, desires, and behavior.

Had bruised the herb and crushed the grape,
And basked and battened° in the woods.[4]   *grown fat*

* * *

39

Old warder of these buried bones,
　　And answering now my random stroke
　　With fruitful cloud and living smoke,
Dark yew, that graspest at the stones

5　　And dippest toward the dreamless head,
　　To thee too comes the golden hour
　　When flower is feeling after flower;[5]
But Sorrow—fixed upon the dead,

And darkening the dark graves of men—
10　　What whispered from her lying lips?
　　Thy gloom is kindled at the tips,[6]
And passes into gloom again.

* * *

47

That each, who seems a separate whole,
　　Should move his rounds,[7] and fusing all
　　The skirts[8] of self again, should fall
Remerging in the general Soul,

5　　Is faith as vague as all unsweet.
　　Eternal form shall still divide
　　The eternal soul from all beside;
And I shall know him when we meet;

And we shall sit at endless feast,
10　　Enjoying each the other's good.
　　What vaster dream can hit the mood
Of Love on earth? He seeks at least

Upon the last and sharpest height,
　　Before the spirits fade away,
15　　Some landing place, to clasp and say,
"Farewell! We lose ourselves in light."[9]

---

4. Lines 18–24 may be paraphrased: if we knew death to be final and that no afterlife were possible, love could not exist except on a primitive or bestial level.
5. The ancient yew tree in the graveyard was described in section 2 as never changing. Now the poet discovers that in the flowering season, if the tree is struck ("my random stroke"), it gives off a cloud of golden pollen.

6. Only the tips of the yew branches are in flower.
7. I.e., go through the customary circuit of life.
8. Outer edges or fringes.
9. These lines express the hope that, as Tennyson wrote, "individuality lasts after death, and we are not utterly absorbed into the Godhead. If we are to be finally merged into the Universal Soul, Love asks to have at least one more parting before we lose ourselves."

48

If these brief lays, of Sorrow born,
    Were taken to be such as closed
    Grave doubts and answers here proposed,
Then these were such as men might scorn.

5   Her° care is not to part and prove;   *Sorrow's*
    She takes, when harsher moods remit,
    What slender shade of doubt may flit,
And makes it vassal unto love;

And hence, indeed, she sports with words,
10   But better serves a wholesome law,
    And holds it sin and shame to draw
The deepest measure from the chords;

Nor dare she trust a larger lay,°   *song*
    But rather loosens from the lip
15   Short swallow-flights of song, that dip
Their wings in tears, and skim away.

*   *   *

50

Be near me when my light is low,
    When the blood creeps, and the nerves prick
    And tingle; and the heart is sick,
And all the wheels of being slow.

5   Be near me when the sensuous frame
    Is racked with pangs that conquer trust;
    And Time, a maniac scattering dust,
And Life, a Fury slinging flame.

Be near me when my faith is dry,
10   And men the flies of latter spring,
    That lay their eggs, and sting and sing
And weave their petty cells and die.

Be near me when I fade away,
    To point the term of human strife,
15   And on the low dark verge of life
The twilight of eternal day.

*   *   *

54

O, yet we trust that somehow good
    Will be the final goal of ill,
    To pangs of nature, sins of will,
Defects of doubt, and taints of blood;

5   That nothing walks with aimless feet;
     That not one life shall be destroyed,
     Or cast as rubbish to the void,
When God hath made the pile complete;

That not a worm is cloven in vain;
10   That not a moth with vain desire
     Is shriveled in a fruitless fire,
Or but° subserves another's gain.   *only*

Behold, we know not anything;
     I can but trust that good shall fall
15   At last—far off—at last, to all,
And every winter change to spring.

So runs my dream; but what am I?
     An infant crying in the night;
     An infant crying for the light,
20   And with no language but a cry.

55

The wish, that of the living whole
     No life may fail beyond the grave,
     Derives it not from what we have
The likest God within the soul?[1]

5   Are God and Nature then at strife,
     That Nature lends such evil dreams?
     So careful of the type she seems,
So careless of the single life,

That I, considering everywhere
10   Her secret meaning in her deeds,
     And finding that of fifty seeds
She often brings but one to bear,

I falter where I firmly trod,
     And falling with my weight of cares
15   Upon the great world's altar-stairs
That slope through darkness up to God,

I stretch lame hands of faith, and grope,
     And gather dust and chaff, and call
     To what I feel is Lord of all,
20   And faintly trust the larger hope.[2]

56

"So careful of the type?" but no.
     From scarpèd[3] cliff and quarried stone

---

1. According to Tennyson, the "inner conscience—the divine in man."
2. As expressed in lines 1 and 2.
3. Cut away so that the strata are exposed.

She° cries, "A thousand types are gone;   *Nature*
 I care for nothing, all shall go.

5 "Thou makest thine appeal to me:
 I bring to life, I bring to death;
 The spirit does but mean the breath:
I know no more." And he, shall he,

Man, her last work, who seemed so fair,
10 Such splendid purpose in his eyes,
 Who rolled the psalm to wintry skies,
Who built him fanes° of fruitless prayer,   *temples*

Who trusted God was love indeed
 And love Creation's final law—
15 Though Nature, red in tooth and claw
With ravine, shrieked against his creed—

Who loved, who suffered countless ills,
 Who battled for the True, the Just,
 Be blown about the desert dust,
20 Or sealed within the iron hills?[4]

No more? A monster then, a dream,
 A discord. Dragons of the prime,°   *primeval age*
 That tare° each other in their slime,   *tore (archaic)*
Were mellow music matched with° him.   *compared to*

25 O life as futile, then, as frail!
 O for thy voice to soothe and bless!
 What hope of answer, or redress?
Behind the veil, behind the veil.

57

Peace; come away: the song of woe
 Is after all an earthly song.
 Peace; come away: we do him wrong
To sing so wildly: let us go.

5 Come; let us go: your cheeks are pale;
 Methinks my friend is richly shrined;
 But half my life I leave behind.
But I shall pass, my work will fail.

Yet in these ears, till hearing dies,
10 One set slow bell will seem to toll
 The passing of the sweetest soul
That ever looked with human eyes.

I hear it now, and o'er and o'er,
 Eternal greetings to the dead;

4. Preserved like fossils in rock.

15   And "Ave,[5] Ave, Ave," said,
    "Adieu, adieu," forevermore.

58

In those sad words I took farewell.
    Like echoes in sepulchral halls,
    As drop by drop the water falls
In vaults and catacombs, they fell;

5   And, falling, idly broke the peace
    Of hearts that beat from day to day,
    Half-conscious of their dying clay,
And those cold crypts where they shall cease.

The high Muse answered: "Wherefore grieve
10   Thy brethren with a fruitless tear?
    Abide a little longer here,
And thou shalt take a nobler leave."

59

O Sorrow, wilt thou live with me
    No casual mistress, but a wife,
    My bosom friend and half of life;
As I confess it needs must be?

5   O Sorrow, wilt thou rule my blood,
    Be sometimes lovely like a bride,
    And put thy harsher moods aside,
If thou wilt have me wise and good?

My centered passion cannot move,
10   Nor will it lessen from today;
    But I'll have leave at times to play
As with the creature of my love;

And set thee forth, for thou art mine,
    With so much hope for years to come,
15   That, howsoe'er I know thee, some
Could hardly tell what name were thine.

*   *   *

67

When on my bed the moonlight falls,
    I know that in thy place of rest
    By that broad water[6] of the west
There comes a glory on the walls:

5   Thy marble bright in dark appears,
    As slowly steals a silver flame

5. Hail (Latin).
6. The Severn River.

Along the letters of thy name,
And o'er the number of thy years.

The mystic glory swims away,
10   From off my bed the moonlight dies;
And closing eaves of wearied eyes
I sleep till dusk is dipped in gray;

And then I know the mist is drawn
A lucid veil from coast to coast,
15   And in the dark church like a ghost
Thy tablet glimmers to the dawn.

*   *   *

70

I cannot see the features right,
When on the gloom I strive to paint
The face I know; the hues are faint
And mix with hollow masks of night;

5   Cloud-towers by ghostly masons wrought,
A gulf that ever shuts and gapes,
A hand that points, and pallèd shapes
In shadowy thoroughfares of thought;

And crowds that stream from yawning doors,
10   And shoals of puckered faces drive;
Dark bulks that tumble half alive,
And lazy lengths on boundless shores;

Till all at once beyond the will
I hear a wizard music roll,
15   And through a lattice on the soul
Looks thy fair face and makes it still.

71

Sleep, kinsman thou to death and trance
And madness, thou has forged at last
A night-long present of the past
In which we went through summer France.[7]

5   Hadst thou such credit with the soul?
Then bring an opiate trebly strong,
Drug down the blindfold sense of wrong,
That so my pleasure may be whole;

While now we talk as once we talked
10   Of men and minds, the dust of change,
The days that grow to something strange,
In walking as of old we walked

---

7. In the summer of 1830 Hallam and Tennyson went through southern France en route to Spain.

Beside the river's wooded reach,
 The fortress, and the mountain ridge,
15 The cataract flashing from the bridge,
The breaker breaking on the beach.

72

Risest thou thus, dim dawn, again,[8]
 And howlest, issuing out of night,
 With blasts that blow the poplar white,
And lash with storm the streaming pane?

5 Day, when my crowned estate[9] begun
 To pine in that reverse of doom,[1]
 Which sickened every living bloom,
And blurred the splendor of the sun;

Who usherest in the dolorous hour
10 With thy quick tears that make the rose
 Pull sideways, and the daisy close
Her crimson fringes to the shower;

Who mightst have heaved a windless flame
 Up the deep East, or, whispering, played
15 A checker-work of beam and shade
Along the hills, yet looked the same,

As wan, as chill, as wild as now;
 Day, marked as with some hideous crime,
 When the dark hand struck down through time,
20 And canceled nature's best: but thou,

Lift as thou mayst thy burthened brows
 Through clouds that drench the morning star,
 And whirl the ungarnered sheaf afar,
And sow the sky with flying boughs,

25 And up thy vault with roaring sound
 Climb thy thick noon, disastrous day;
 Touch thy dull goal of joyless gray,
And hide thy shame beneath the ground.

*   *   *

78

Again at Christmas[2] did we weave
 The holly round the Christmas hearth;
 The silent snow possessed the earth,
And calmly fell our Christmas eve.

8. September 15, 1834, the first anniversary of Hallam's death.
9. State of happiness.
1. The reversal or disaster that doom brought upon him when Hallam died.
2. The second Christmas (1834) after Hallam's death.

5   The yule clog° sparkled keen with frost,   *log*
        No wing of wind the region swept,
        But over all things brooding slept
    The quiet sense of something lost.

    As in the winters left behind,
10   Again our ancient games had place,
        The mimic picture's[3] breathing grace,
    And dance and song and hoodman-blind.[4]

    Who showed a token of distress?
        No single tear, no mark of pain—
15   O sorrow, then can sorrow wane?
    O grief, can grief be changed to less?

    O last regret, regret can die!
        No—mixed with all this mystic frame,
        Her deep relations are the same,
20   But with long use her tears are dry.

*   *   *

<h2 style="text-align:center">82</h2>

    I wage not any feud with Death
        For changes wrought on form and face;
        No lower life that earth's embrace
    May breed with him can fright my faith.

5   Eternal process moving on,
        From state to state the spirit walks;
        And these are but the shattered stalks,
    Or ruined chrysalis of one.

    Nor blame I Death, because he bare
10   The use of virtue out of earth;
        I know transplanted human worth
    Will bloom to profit, otherwhere.

    For this alone on Death I wreak
        The wrath that garners in my heart:
15   He put our lives so far apart
    We cannot hear each other speak.

<h2 style="text-align:center">83</h2>

    Dip down upon the northern shore,
        O sweet new-year° delaying long;   *spring 1835*
        Thou doest expectant Nature wrong;
    Delaying long, delay no more.

---

3. A game in which the participants pose in the manner of some famous statue or painting and the spectators try to guess what work of art is being portrayed.
4. The player in the game of blindman's buff who wears a blindfold or hood.

5   What stays thee from the clouded noons,
      Thy sweetness from its proper place?
      Can trouble live with April days,
Or sadness in the summer moons?

Bring orchis, bring the foxglove spire,
10   The little speedwell's° darling blue,   *spring flower*
      Deep tulips dashed with fiery dew,
Laburnums, dropping-wells of fire.

O thou, new-year, delaying long,
      Delayest the sorrow in my blood,
15   That longs to burst a frozen bud
And flood a fresher throat with song.

84

When I contemplate all alone
      The life that had been thine below,
      And fix my thoughts on all the glow
To which thy crescent would have grown,

5   I see thee sitting crowned with good,
      A central warmth diffusing bliss
      In glance and smile, and clasp and kiss,
On all the branches of thy blood;

Thy blood, my friend, and partly mine;
10   For now the day was drawing on,
      When thou shouldst link thy life with one
Of mine own house, and boys of thine

Had babbled "Uncle" on my knee;
      But that remorseless iron hour
15   Made cypress of her orange flower,[5]
Despair of hope, and earth of thee.

I seem to meet their least desire,
      To clap their cheeks, to call them mine.
      I see their unborn faces shine
20   Beside the never-lighted fire.

I see myself an honored guest,
      Thy partner in the flowery walk
      Of letters, genial table talk,
Or deep dispute, and graceful jest;

25   While now thy prosperous labor fills
      The lips of men with honest praise,
      And sun by sun the happy days
Descend below the golden hills

---

5. Orange blossoms are associated with brides—here the poet's sister Emily Tennyson, to whom Hallam had been engaged. Cypress branches are associated with funerals.

With promise of a morn as fair;
30   And all the train of bounteous hours
  Conduct, by paths of growing powers,
To reverence and the silver hair;

Till slowly worn her earthly robe,
  Her lavish mission richly wrought,
35   Leaving great legacies of thought,
Thy spirit should fail from off the globe;

What time mine own might also flee,
  As linked with thine in love and fate,
  And, hovering o'er the dolorous strait
40 To the other shore, involved in thee,

Arrive at last the blessed goal,
  And He that died in Holy Land
  Would reach us out the shining hand,
And take us as a single soul.

45 What reed was that on which I leant?
  Ah, backward fancy, wherefore wake
  The old bitterness again, and break
The low beginnings of content?

*   *   *

86

Sweet after showers, ambrosial air,
  That rollest from the gorgeous gloom
  Of evening over brake° and bloom   *thicket*
And meadow, slowly breathing bare

5 The round of space,[6] and rapt below
  Through all the dewy-tasseled wood,
  And shadowing down the hornèd flood[7]
In ripples, fan my brows and blow

The fever from my cheek, and sigh
10   The full new life that feeds thy breath
  Throughout my frame, till Doubt and Death,
Ill brethren, let the fancy fly

From belt to belt of crimson seas
  On leagues of odor streaming far,
15   To where in yonder orient star
A hundred spirits whisper "Peace."

6. The "ambrosial air" is slowly clearing the clouds from the sky.
7. Between two promontories [Tennyson's note].

87

I passed beside the reverend walls[8]
   In which of old I wore the gown;
   I roved at random through the town,
And saw the tumult of the halls;

5   And heard once more in college fanes°   *chapels*
   The storm their high-built organs make,
   And thunder-music, rolling, shake
The prophet blazoned on the panes;

And caught once more the distant shout,
10   The measured pulse of racing oars
   Among the willows; paced the shores
And many a bridge, and all about

The same gray flats again, and felt
   The same, but not the same; and last
15   Up that long walk of limes I passed
To see the rooms in which he dwelt.

Another name was on the door.
   I lingered; all within was noise
   Of songs, and clapping hands, and boys
20   That crashed the glass and beat the floor;

Where once we held debate, a band
   Of youthful friends,[9] on mind and art,
   And labor, and the changing mart,
And all the framework of the land;

25   When one would aim an arrow fair,
   But send it slackly from the string;
   And one would pierce an outer ring,
And one an inner, here and there;

And last the master bowman, he,
30   Would cleave the mark. A willing ear
   We lent him. Who but hung to hear
The rapt oration flowing free

From point to point, with power and grace
   And music in the bounds of law,
35   To those conclusions when we saw
The God within him light his face,

And seem to lift the form, and glow
   In azure orbits heavenly-wise;

8. Of Trinity College, Cambridge University.
9. The Apostles, an undergraduate club to which Tennyson and Hallam had belonged.

And over those ethereal eyes
40 The bar of Michael Angelo?[1]

88

Wild bird,[2] whose warble, liquid sweet,
 Rings Eden through the budded quicks,[3]
 O tell me where the senses mix,
O tell me where the passions meet,

5 Whence radiate: fierce extremes employ
 Thy spirits in the darkening leaf,
 And in the midmost heart of grief
Thy passion clasps a secret joy;

And I—my harp would prelude woe—
10 I cannot all command the strings;
 The glory of the sum of things
Will flash along the chords and go.

89

Witch elms that counterchange the floor
 Of this flat lawn with dusk and bright;[4]
 And thou, with all thy breadth and height
Of foliage, towering sycamore;

5 How often, hither wandering down,
 My Arthur found your shadows fair,
 And shook to all the liberal air
The dust and din and steam of town!

He brought an eye for all he saw;
10 He mixed in all our simple sports;
 They pleased him, fresh from brawling courts
And dusty purlieus° of the law.[5]   *regions*

O joy to him in this retreat,
 Immantled in ambrosial dark,
15 To drink the cooler air, and mark
The landscape winking through the heat!

O sound to rout the brood of cares,
 The sweep of scythe in morning dew,
 The gust that round the garden flew,
20 And tumbled half the mellowing pears!

O bliss, when all in circle drawn
 About him, heart and ear were fed

---

1. Hallam, like the Italian artist Michelangelo (1475–1564), had a prominent ridge of bone above his eyes.
2. Probably a nightingale.
3. Hawthorn hedges.

4. Shadows of the elm tree checker the lawn at Somersby, the Tennysons' country home.
5. Hallam became a law student in London after leaving Cambridge.

To hear him, as he lay and read
The Tuscan poets[6] on the lawn!

25 Or in the all-golden afternoon
    A guest, or happy sister, sung,
    Or here she brought the harp and flung
A ballad to the brightening moon.

Nor less it pleased in livelier moods,
30   Beyond the bounding hill to stray,
    And break the livelong summer day
With banquet in the distant woods;

Whereat we glanced from theme to theme,
    Discussed the books to love or hate,
35   Or touched the changes of the state,
Or threaded some Socratic dream;[7]

But if I praised the busy town,
    He loved to rail against it still,
    For "ground in yonder social mill
40 We rub each other's angles down,

"And merge," he said, "in form and gloss
    The picturesque of man and man."
    We talked: the stream beneath us ran,
The wine-flask lying couched in moss,

45 Or cooled within the glooming wave;
    And last, returning from afar,
    Before the crimson-circled star[8]
Had fallen into her father's[9] grave,

And brushing ankle-deep in flowers,
50   We heard behind the woodbine veil
    The milk that bubbled in° the pail,   *into*
And buzzings of the honeyed hours.

                    ✷   ✷   ✷

                    91

When rosy plumelets tuft the larch,
    And rarely° pipes the mounted thrush,   *exquisitely*
    Or underneath the barren bush
Flits by the sea-blue bird° of March;   *kingfisher*

5 Come, wear the form by which I know
    Thy spirit in time among thy peers;

---

6. A group of 13th- and 14th-century poets in central Italy (Tuscany); the best-known of them are Dante and Petrarch.
7. I.e., worked our way through some discourse of Socrates (as recorded by Plato).

8. Venus, which will sink into the west as the Sun has done.
9. According to the nebular hypothesis, planets condensed out of the sun's atmosphere; in this sense the Sun is the "father" of planets.

The hope of unaccomplished years
Be large and lucid round thy brow.

When summer's hourly-mellowing change
10   May breathe, with many roses sweet,
Upon the thousand waves of wheat
That ripple round the lowly grange,°   *outlying farmhouse*

Come; not in watches of the night,
But where the sunbeam broodeth warm,
15   Come, beauteous in thine after form,
And like a finer light in light.

*   *   *

93

I shall not see thee. Dare I say
No spirit ever brake the band
That stays him from the native land
Where first he walked when clasped in clay?[1]

5 No visual shade of someone lost,
But he, the Spirit himself, may come
Where all the nerve of sense is numb,
Spirit to Spirit, Ghost to Ghost.

Oh, therefore from thy sightless° range   *invisible*
10   With gods in unconjectured bliss,
Oh, from the distance of the abyss
Of tenfold-complicated change,

Descend, and touch, and enter; hear
The wish too strong for words to name,
15   That in this blindness of the frame°   *human body*
My Ghost may feel that thine is near.

94

How pure at heart and sound in head,
With what divine affections bold
Should be the man whose thought would hold
An hour's communion with the dead.

5 In vain shalt thou, or any, call
The spirits from their golden day,
Except, like them, thou too canst say,
My spirit is at peace with all.

They haunt the silence of the breast,
10   Imaginations calm and fair,

---

1. I.e., when he was alive and in fleshly form.

The memory like a cloudless air,
The conscience as a sea at rest;

But when the heart is full of din,
   And doubt beside the portal waits,
15   They can but listen at the gates,
And hear the household jar° within.   *noise*

95

By night we lingered on the lawn,
   For underfoot the herb was dry;
   And genial warmth; and o'er the sky
The silvery haze of summer drawn;

5   And calm that let the tapers burn
    Unwavering: not a cricket chirred;
    The brook alone far off was heard,
And on the board the fluttering urn.²

And, bats went round in fragrant skies,
10   And wheeled or lit the filmy shapes³
    That haunt the dusk, with ermine capes
And woolly breasts and beaded eyes;

While now we sang old songs that pealed
   From knoll to knoll, where, couched at ease,
15   The white kine° glimmered, and the trees   *cows*
Laid their dark arms⁴ about the field.

But when those others, one by one,
   Withdrew themselves from me and night,
   And in the house light after light
20   Went out, and I was all alone,

A hunger seized my heart; I read
   Of that glad year which once had been,
   In those fallen leaves which kept their green,
The noble letters of the dead.

25   And strangely on the silence broke
    The silent-speaking words, and strange
    Was love's dumb cry defying change
To test his worth; and strangely spoke

The faith, the vigor, bold to dwell
30   On doubts that drive the coward back,
    And keen through wordy snares to track
Suggestion to her inmost cell.

So word by word, and line by line,
   The dead man touched me from the past,

---

2. Vessel for boiling water for tea or coffee, heated by a fluttering flame.
3. The white-winged night moths called ermine moths.
4. Cast the shadows of their branches.

35 And all at once it seemed at last
The[5] living soul was flashed on mine.

And mine in this was wound, and whirled
About empyreal° heights of thought,   *heavenly*
And came on that which is, and caught
40 The deep pulsations of the world,

Aeonian music[6] measuring out
The steps of Time—the shocks of Chance—
The blows of Death. At length my trance
Was canceled, stricken through with doubt.[7]

45 Vague words! but ah, how hard to frame
In matter-molded forms of speech,
Or even for intellect to reach
Through memory that which I became.

Till now the doubtful dusk revealed
50 The knolls once more where, couched at ease,
The white kine glimmered, and the trees
Laid their dark arms about the field;

And sucked from out the distant gloom
A breeze began to tremble o'er
55 The large leaves of the sycamore,
And fluctuate all the still perfume,

And gathering freshlier overhead,
Rocked the full-foliaged elms, and swung
The heavy-folded rose, and flung
60 The lilies to and fro, and said,

"The dawn, the dawn," and died away;
And East and West, without a breath,
Mixed their dim lights, like life and death,
To broaden into boundless day.

96

You say, but with no touch of scorn,
Sweet-hearted, you,[8] whose light blue eyes

5. "His" in the 1st edition. Also in the 1st edition, line 37 read: "And mine in his was wound."
6. Music of the universe, which has pulsated for eons.
7. In a letter of 1874, replying to an inquiry about his experience of mystical trances, Tennyson wrote: "A kind of waking trance I have frequently had, quite up from boyhood, when I have been all alone. This has generally come upon me through repeating my own name two or three times to myself silently, till all at once, as it were out of the intensity of the consciousness of individuality, the individuality itself seemed to dissolve and fade away into boundless being, and this not a confused state, but the clearest of the clearest, the surest of the surest, the weirdest of the weirdest, utterly beyond words, where death was an almost laughable impossibility, the loss of personality (if so it were) seeming no extinction but the only true life. . . . This might . . . be the state which St. Paul describes, 'Whether in the body I cannot tell, or whether out of the body I cannot tell.' . . . I am ashamed of my feeble description. Have I not said the state is utterly beyond words? But in a moment, when I come back to my normal state of 'sanity,' I am ready to fight for *mein liebes Ich* [my dear self], and hold that it will last for aeons of aeons" (*Alfred Lord Tennyson, A Memoir,* 1897, vol. 1, 320).
8. A woman of simple faith.

Are tender over drowning flies,
You tell me, doubt is Devil-born.

5   I know not: one indeed I knew
    In many a subtle question versed,
    Who touched a jarring lyre at first,
But ever strove to make it true;

Perplexed in faith, but pure in deeds,
10   At last he beat his music out.
    There lives more faith in honest doubt,
Believe me, than in half the creeds.

He fought his doubts and gathered strength,
    He would not make his judgment blind,
15   He faced the specters of the mind
And laid them; thus he came at length

To find a stronger faith his own,
    And Power was with him in the night,
    Which makes the darkness and the light,
20 And dwells not in the light alone,

But in the darkness and the cloud,
    As over Sinaï's peaks of old,
    While Israel made their gods of gold,
Although the trumpet blew so loud.[9]

*   *   *

99

Risest thou thus, dim dawn, again,[1]
    So loud with voices of the birds,
    So thick with lowings of the herds,
Day, when I lost the flower of men;

5   Who tremblest through thy darkling red
    On yon swollen brook that bubbles fast[2]
    By meadows breathing of the past,
And woodlands holy to the dead;

Who murmurest in the foliage eaves
10   A song that slights the coming care,[3]
    And Autumn laying here and there
A fiery finger on the leaves;

Who wakenest with thy balmy breath
    To myriads on the genial° earth,   *generative*

9. After veiling Mount Sinai in a "thick cloud" and signifying the divine presence by "the voice of the trumpet" (Exodus 19.16), God addresses Moses from the "thick darkness" (20.21). Meanwhile Aaron made, and the Israelites worshipped, a golden calf (32.1–6).

1. September 15, 1835, the second anniversary of Hallam's death.
2. I.e., reflections of the clouded red light of dawn quiver on the surface of the fast-moving water.
3. I.e., that disregards future events such as death or the coming of autumn.

15   Memories of bridal, or of birth,
      And unto myriads more, of death.

    Oh, wheresoever those[4] may be,
      Betwixt the slumber of the poles,
      Today they count as kindred souls;
20   They know me not, but mourn with me.

*   *   *

103

On that last night before we went
    From out the doors where I was bred,[5]
    I dreamed a vision of the dead,
Which left my after-morn content.

5   Methought I dwelt within a hall,
      And maidens with me; distant hills
      From hidden summits fed with rills
A river sliding by the wall.

The hall with harp and carol rang.
10   They sang of what is wise and good
      And graceful. In the center stood
A statue veiled, to which they sang;

And which, though veiled, was known to me,
    The shape of him I loved, and love
15   Forever. Then flew in a dove
And brought a summons from the sea;

And when they learnt that I must go,
    They wept and wailed, but led the way
    To where the little shallop° lay   *light open boat*
20   At anchor in the flood below;

And on by many a level mead,°   *meadow*
    And shadowing bluff that made the banks,
    We glided winding under ranks
Of iris and the golden reed;

25   And still as vaster grew the shore
      And rolled the floods in grander space,
      The maidens gathered strength and grace
And presence, lordlier than before;

And I myself, who sat apart
30   And watched them, waxed° in every limb;   *grown*

---

4. I.e., the many who remember death.
5. In 1837 Tennyson and his family moved away from their home in Lincolnshire, which had been closely associated with his friendship with Hal-lam. In section 104 the move seems to occur in 1835, the year of the third Christmas after Hal-lam's death.

I felt the thews of Anakim,[6]
  The pulses of a Titan's[7] heart;

As one would sing the death of war,
  And one would chant the history
35   Of that great race which is to be,[8]
And one the shaping of a star;

Until the forward-creeping tides
  Began to foam, and we to draw
  From deep to deep, to where we saw
40 A great ship lift her shining sides.[9]

The man we loved was there on deck,
  But thrice as large as man he bent
  To greet us. Up the side I went,
And fell in silence on his neck;

45 Whereat those maidens with one mind
  Bewailed their lot; I did them wrong:
  "We served thee here," they said, "so long,
And wilt thou leave us now behind?"

So rapt° I was, they could not win   *entranced*
50 An answer from my lips, but he
  Replying, "Enter likewise ye
And go with us:" they entered in.

And while the wind began to sweep
  A music out of sheet and shroud,
55 We steered her toward a crimson cloud
That landlike slept along the deep.

104

The time draws near the birth of Christ;[1]
  The moon is hid, the night is still;
  A single church below the hill
Is pealing, folded in the mist.

5 A single peal of bells below,
  That wakens at this hour of rest
  A single murmur in the breast,
That these are not the bells I know.

Like strangers' voices here they sound,
10 In lands where not a memory strays,

---

6. Plural of *Anak*; a reference to the giant sons of Anak (see Numbers 13.33).
7. Giant of Greek mythology.
8. See the account of the "crowning race" in "Epilogue," lines 128–44.
9. Cf. *The Passing of Arthur*, lines 361–469, in which Bedivere is left behind as Arthur's barge, the ship of death, sails away. In the present dream vision the speaker is taken aboard, as are his companions, who represent the creative arts of this world—"all the human powers and talents that do not pass with life but go along with it," as Tennyson said of this passage.
1. The third Christmas (1835) after Hallam's death.

Nor landmark breathes of other days,
But all is new unhallowed ground.

105

Tonight ungathered let us leave
　This laurel, let this holly stand:[2]
　We live within the stranger's land,
And strangely falls our Christmas eve.

5　Our father's dust is left alone
　And silent under other snows:
　There in due time the woodbine blows,°　　　　*blooms*
The violet comes, but we are gone.

No more shall wayward grief abuse
10　The genial hour with mask and mime;
　For change of place, like growth of time,
Has broke the bond of dying use.

Let cares that petty shadows cast,
　By which our lives are chiefly proved,
15　A little spare the night I loved,
And hold it solemn to the past.

But let no footstep beat the floor,
　Nor bowl of wassail mantle warm;[3]
　For who would keep an ancient form
20　Through which the spirit breathes no more?

Be neither song, nor game, nor feast;
　Nor harp be touched, nor flute be blown;
　No dance, no motion, save alone
What lightens in the lucid east

25　Of rising worlds[4] by yonder wood.
　Long sleeps the summer in the seed;
　Run out your measured arcs, and lead
The closing cycle rich in good.

106

Ring out, wild bells, to the wild sky,
　The flying cloud, the frosty light:
　The year is dying in the night;
Ring out, wild bells, and let him die.

5　Ring out the old, ring in the new,
　Ring, happy bells, across the snow:

---

2. Cf. section 29, in which the family in their former home still continued to gather holly. In the new home the customary observances lapse.
3. I.e., let no bowl of hot punch warm the man-
telpiece.
4. The scintillating motion of the stars that rise [Tennyson's note].

The year is going, let him go;
Ring out the false, ring in the true.

Ring out the grief that saps the mind,
For those that here we see no more;
Ring out the feud of rich and poor,
Ring in redress to all mankind.

Ring out a slowly dying cause,
And ancient forms of party strife;
Ring in the nobler modes of life,
With sweeter manners, purer laws.

Ring out the want, the care, the sin,
The faithless coldness of the times:
Ring out, ring out my mournful rhymes,
But ring the fuller minstrel in.

Ring out false pride in place and blood,
The civic slander and the spite;
Ring in the love of truth and right,
Ring in the common love of good.

Ring out old shapes of foul disease;
Ring out the narrowing lust of gold;
Ring out the thousand wars of old,
Ring in the thousand years of peace.

Ring in the valiant man and free,
The larger heart, the kindlier hand;
Ring out the darkness of the land,
Ring in the Christ that is to be.[5]

107

It is the day when he was born.°   *February 1*
A bitter day that early sank
Behind a purple-frosty bank
Of vapor, leaving night forlorn.

The time admits not flowers or leaves
To deck the banquet. Fiercely flies
The blast of North and East, and ice
Makes daggers at the sharpened eaves,

And bristles all the brakes° and thorns   *thickets*
To yon hard crescent, as she hangs
Above the wood which grides[6] and clangs
Its leafless ribs and iron horns

5. These allusions to the second coming of Christ and to the millennium are derived from Revelation 20, but Tennyson has interpreted the biblical account in his own way. He once told his son of his conviction that "the forms of Christian religion would alter; but that the spirit of Christ would still grow from more to more."
6. Clashes with a strident noise.

Together, in the drifts⁷ that pass
To darken on the rolling brine
15   That breaks the coast. But fetch the wine,
Arrange the board and brim the glass;

Bring in great logs and let them lie,
To make a solid core of heat;
Be cheerful-minded, talk and treat
20   Of all things even as he were by;

We keep the day. With festal cheer,
With books and music, surely we
Will drink to him, whate'er he be,
And sing the songs he loved to hear.

108

I will not shut me from my kind,
And, lest I stiffen into stone,
I will not eat my heart alone,
Nor feed with sighs a passing wind:

5   What profit lies in barren faith,
And vacant yearning, though with might
To scale the heaven's highest height,
Or dive below the wells of Death?

What find I in the highest place,
10   But mine own phantom chanting hymns?
And on the depths of death there swims
The reflex of a human face.°   *his own face*

I'll rather take what fruit may be
Of sorrow under human skies:
15   'Tis held that sorrow makes us wise,
Whatever wisdom sleep with thee.°   *Hallam*

109

Heart-affluence in discursive talk
From household fountains never dry;
The critic clearness of an eye
That saw through all the Muses' walk;⁸

5   Seraphic intellect and force
To seize and throw the doubts of man;
Impassioned logic, which outran
The hearer in its fiery course;

---

7. Either cloud drifts or clouds of snow.   8. The realm of art and literature.

High nature amorous of the good,
10   But touched with no ascetic gloom;
    And passion pure in snowy bloom
Through all the years of April blood;

A love of freedom rarely felt,
    Of freedom in her regal seat
15   Of England; not the schoolboy heat,
The blind hysterics of the Celt;[9]

And manhood fused with female grace
    In such a sort, the child would twine
    A trustful hand, unasked, in thine,
20   And find his comfort in thy face;

All these have been, and thee mine eyes
    Have looked on: if they looked in vain,
    My shame is greater who remain,
Nor let thy wisdom make me wise.

* * *

115

Now fades the last long streak of snow,
    Now burgeons every maze of quick°   *hawthorn hedge*
    About the flowering squares,° and thick   *fields*
By ashen roots the violets blow.

5   Now rings the woodland loud and long,
    The distance takes a lovelier hue,
    And drowned in yonder living blue
The lark becomes a sightless song.

Now dance the lights on lawn and lea,
10   The flocks are whiter down the vale,
    And milkier every milky sail
On winding stream or distant sea;

Where now the seamew° pipes, or dives   *seabird*
    In yonder greening gleam, and fly
15   The happy birds, that change their sky
To build and brood, that live their lives

From land to land; and in my breast
    Spring wakens too, and my regret
    Becomes an April violet,
20   And buds and blossoms like the rest.

* * *

9. A member or descendant of one of the groups of peoples populating ancient Britain; cf. Arnold's description of the Irish temperament in *On the Study of Celtic Literature*

118

Contèmplate all this work of Time,
   The giant laboring in his youth;
   Nor dream of human love and truth,
As dying Nature's earth and lime;[1]

5   But trust that those we call the dead
   Are breathers of an ampler day
   For ever nobler ends. They° say,   *Scientists*
The solid earth whereon we tread

In tracts of fluent heat began,
10   And grew to seeming-random forms,
   The seeming prey of cyclic storms,
Till at the last arose the man;

Who throve and branched from clime to clime,
   The herald of a higher race,
15   And of himself in higher place
If so he type[2] this work of time

Within himself, from more to more;
   Or, crowned with attributes of woe
   Like glories, move his course, and show
20   That life is not as idle ore,

But iron dug from central gloom,
   And heated hot with burning fears,
   And dipped in baths of hissing tears,
And battered with the shocks of doom

25   To shape and use. Arise and fly
   The reeling Faun,[3] the sensual feast;
   Move upward, working out the beast,
And let the ape and tiger die.

119

Doors,[4] where my heart was used to beat
   So quickly, not as one that weeps
   I come once more; the city sleeps;
I smell the meadow in the street;

5   I hear a chirp of birds; I see
   Betwixt the black fronts long-withdrawn
   A light blue lane of early dawn,
And think of early days and thee,

---

1. Two of the perishable organic ingredients of the human body.
2. Emulate, prefigure as a type.
3. In Roman mythology a half-human, half-beast deity of the woods and mountains.
4. The doors of Hallam's house on London's Wimpole Street. Cf. section 7.

And bless thee, for thy lips are bland,°   *gentle*
10   And bright the friendship of thine eye;
    And in my thoughts with scarce a sigh
I take the pressure of thine hand.

120

I trust I have not wasted breath:
    I think we are not wholly brain,
    Magnetic mockeries;[5] not in vain,
Like Paul[6] with beasts, I fought with Death;

5 Not only cunning° casts in clay: *skillful*
    Let Science prove we are, and then
    What matters Science unto men,
At least to me? I would not stay.

Let him, the wiser man who springs
10   Hereafter, up from childhood shape
    His action like the greater ape,
But I was *born* to other things.

121

Sad Hesper° o'er the buried sun   *evening star*
    And ready, thou, to die with him,
    Thou watchest all things ever dim
And dimmer, and a glory done.

5 The team is loosened from the wain,°   *hay wagon*
    The boat is drawn upon the shore;
    Thou listenest to the closing door,
And life is darkened in the brain.

Bright Phosphor,° fresher for the night,   *morning star*
10   By thee the world's great work is heard
    Beginning, and the wakeful bird;
Behind thee comes the greater light.[7]

The market boat is on the stream,
    And voices hail it from the brink;
15   Thou hear'st the village hammer clink,
And see'st the moving of the team.

Sweet Hesper-Phosphor, double name[8]
    For what is one, the first, the last,

---

5. Mechanisms operated by responses to electrical forces.
6. 1 Corinthians 15.32.
7. Cf. Genesis 1.16: "the greater light to rule the day."

8. The planet Venus, named for the Roman goddess of love, is both the evening star and the morning star (visible at different times in different seasons).

Thou, like my present and my past,
20   Thy place is changed; thou art the same.

*   *   *

123

There rolls the deep where grew the tree.
    O earth, what changes hast thou seen!
    There where the long street roars hath been
The stillness of the central sea.[9]

5   The hills are shadows, and they flow
        From form to form, and nothing stands;
        They melt like mist, the solid lands,
    Like clouds they shape themselves and go.

But in my spirit will I dwell,
10   And dream my dream, and hold it true;
        For though my lips may breathe adieu,
    I cannot think the thing farewell.

124

That which we dare invoke to bless;
    Our dearest faith; our ghastliest doubt;
    He, They, One, All; within, without;
The Power in darkness whom we guess—

5   I found Him not in world or sun,
        Or eagle's wing, or insect's eye,[1]
        Nor through the questions men may try,
    The petty cobwebs we have spun.

If e'er when faith had fallen asleep,
10   I heard a voice, "believe no more,"
        And heard an ever-breaking shore
    That tumbled in the Godless deep,

A warmth within the breast would melt
    The freezing reason's colder part,
15   And like a man in wrath the heart
Stood up and answered, "I have felt."[2]

No, like a child in doubt and fear:
    But that blind clamor made me wise;

9. In a passage from *The Principles of Geology* (1832), a book well known to Tennyson, Sir Charles Lyell discusses the "interchange of sea and land" that has occurred "on the surface of our globe": "In the Mediterranean alone, many flourishing inland towns and a still greater number of ports now stand where the sea rolled its waves since the era when civilized nations first grew in Europe."

1. He does not discover satisfactory proof of God's existence in the 18th-century argument that because objects in nature are designed there must exist a designer.
2. Cf. Carlyle's *Sartor Resartus* (1833–34), "The Everlasting No" (p. 564).

Then was I as a child that cries,
20   But, crying, knows his father near;

And what I am beheld again
    What is, and no man understands;
    And out of darkness came the hands
That reach through nature, molding men.

*   *   *

126

Love is and was my lord and king,
    And in his presence I attend
    To hear the tidings of my friend,
Which every hour his couriers bring.

5   Love is and was my king and lord,
    And will be, though as yet I keep
    Within the court on earth, and sleep
Encompassed by his faithful guard,

And hear at times a sentinel
10   Who moves about from place to place,
    And whispers to the worlds of space,
In the deep night, that all is well.

127

And all is well, though faith and form[3]
    Be sundered in the night of fear;
    Well roars the storm to those that hear
A deeper voice across the storm,

5   Proclaiming social truth shall spread,
    And justice, even though thrice again
    The red fool-fury of the Seine
Should pile her barricades with dead.[4]

But ill for him that wears a crown,
10   And him, the lazar,[5] in his rags!
    They tremble, the sustaining crags;
The spires of ice are toppled down,

And molten up, and roar in flood;
    The fortress crashes from on high,
15   The brute earth lightens[6] to the sky,
And the great Aeon[7] sinks in blood,

3. Traditional institutions through which faith was formerly expressed, such as the Church.
4. Reference to revolutionary uprisings in France, in each of which a king lost his throne (line 9): in 1789 against Louis XVI, in 1830 against Charles X, and in 1848 against Louis-Philippe. If, as Tennyson recollected, section 127 was finished at a date earlier than 1848, the reference to three revolutions (line 6) was prophetic. Seine: the river that runs through Paris.
5. Pauper suffering from disease.
6. Is lit up by fire.
7. A vast tract of time, here perhaps modern Western civilization.

And compassed by the fires of hell,
   While thou, dear spirit, happy star,
   O'erlook'st the tumult from afar,
20 And smilest, knowing all is well.

          *   *   *

129

Dear friend, far off, my lost desire,
   So far, so near in woe and weal,°   *happiness*
   O loved the most, when most I feel
There is a lower and a higher;

5 Known and unknown, human, divine;
   Sweet human hand and lips and eye;
   Dear heavenly friend that canst not die,
Mine, mine, forever, ever mine;

Strange friend, past, present, and to be;
10   Loved deeplier, darklier understood;
   Behold, I dream a dream of good,
And mingle all the world with thee.

130

Thy voice is on the rolling air
   I hear thee where the waters run;
   Thou standest in the rising sun,
And in the setting thou art fair.

5 What art thou then? I cannot guess;
   But though I seem in star and flower
   To feel thee some diffusive power,
I do not therefore love thee less.

My love involves the love before;
10   My love is vaster passion now;
   Tho' mix'd with God and Nature thou,
I seem to love thee more and more.

Far off thou art, but ever nigh;
   I have thee still, and I rejoice;
15   I prosper, circled with thy voice;
I shall not lose thee tho' I die.

131

O living will[8] that shalt endure
   When all that seems shall suffer shock,
   Rise in the spiritual rock,[9]
Flow through our deeds and make them pure,

---

8. Tennyson later commented that he meant here the moral will of humankind.
9. Christ. Cf. 1 Corinthians 10.4: "And did all drink the same spiritual drink; for they drank of that spiritual Rock that followed them: and that Rock was Christ."

5   That we may lift from out of dust
    A voice as unto him that hears,
    A cry above the conquered years
  To one that with us works, and trust,

  With faith that comes of self-control,
10   The truths that never can be proved
    Until we close with all we loved,
  And all we flow from, soul in soul.

The Charge of the Light Brigade[1]

1

  Half a league,[2] half a league,
  Half a league onward,
  All in the valley of Death
    Rode the six hundred.
5   "Forward the Light Brigade!
  Charge for the guns!" he said.
  Into the valley of Death
    Rode the six hundred.[3]

2

  "Forward, the Light Brigade!"
10   Was there a man dismayed?
  Not though the soldier knew
    Someone had blundered.
  Theirs not to make reply,
  Theirs not to reason why,
15   Theirs but to do and die.
  Into the valley of Death
    Rode the six hundred.

3

  Cannon to right of them,
  Cannon to left of them,
20   Cannon in front of them
    Volleyed and thundered;
  Stormed at with shot and shell,
  Boldly they rode and well,
  Into the jaws of Death,

1. During the Crimean War (1854–56), owing to confusion of orders, a brigade of British cavalry charged some entrenched batteries of Russian artillery. This blunder cost the lives of three-quarters of the six hundred horsemen engaged (see Cecil Woodham-Smith, *The Reason Why*, 1954). Tennyson rapidly composed his "ballad" (as he called the poem) after reading an account of the battle in a newspaper.
2. About a mile and a half.
3. In the recording Tennyson made of this poem, "hundred" sounds like "hunderd"—a Lincolnshire pronunciation that reinforces the rhyme with "thundered," etc. "Valley of Death": see Psalms 23.4 ("Yea, though I walk through the valley of the shadow of death").

25 Into the mouth of hell
  Rode the six hundred.

4

Flashed all their sabers bare,
Flashed as they turned in air
Sab'ring the gunners there,
30 Charging an army, while
  All the world wondered.
Plunged in the battery smoke
Right through the line they broke;
Cossack and Russian
35 Reeled from the saber stroke
  Shattered and sundered.
Then they rode back, but not,
  Not the six hundred.

5

Cannon to right of them,
40 Cannon to left of them,
Cannon behind them
  Volleyed and thundered;
Stormed at with shot and shell,
While horse and hero fell.
45 They that had fought so well
Came through the jaws of Death,
Back from the mouth of hell,
All that was left of them,
  Left of six hundred.

6

50 When can their glory fade?
O the wild charge they made!
  All the world wondered.
Honor the charge they made!
Honor the Light Brigade,
55   Noble six hundred!

1854   1854

Idylls of the King

When John Milton was considering subjects suitable for an epic poem, one of those he entertained was the story of the British king Arthur, a semilegendary leader of about 500 C.E. who fought off the Saxon invaders who had swarmed into Britain after the withdrawal of the Roman legions. Tennyson likewise saw that the Arthurian story had epic potential and selected it for his lifework as "the greatest of all poetical subjects." At intervals, during a period of fifty years, he labored over the twelve books that make up his *Idylls of the King*, completing the work in 1888.

The principal source of Tennyson's stories of Arthur and his knights was Sir Thomas Malory's *Morte Darthur*, a version that Malory translated into English prose from French sources in 1470. As Talbot Donaldson suggested, one basis of the appeal of the Arthurian stories, like the legends of Robin Hood and stories of the American West, is that they represent the struggle of individuals to restore order when chaos and anarchy are ascendant, a task performed in the face of seemingly overwhelming odds. The individual stories in Tennyson's *Idylls* have the same basic appeal, but the overall design of the whole poem is more ambitious and impressive. The epic represents the rise and fall of a civilization, and its underlying theme is that after two thousand years of Christianity, Western civilization may be going through a cycle in which it must confront the possibilities of a renewal in the future or an apocalyptic extinction. The first book, *The Coming of Arthur*, introduces the basic myth of a springtime hero transforming a wasteland and inspiring faith and hope in the highest values of civilized life among his devoted followers, the knights of his Round Table. Succeeding books move through summer and autumn and culminate in the bleak wintry scene of Arthur's last battle in which his order perishes in a civil war; the leader of the enemy forces is his own nephew, Sir Modred.

Throughout the later books of the *Idylls* the forces of opposition grow in strength, and discontent and resentment infect leading figures of the Round Table itself. The most glaring example is the adulterous relationship between Guinevere, Arthur's "sumptuous" queen (as Tennyson once described her), and the king's chief lieutenant and friend, Sir Lancelot. Many other fallings away subsequently come to light, such as the deceitful betrayal by Sir Gawain in the ninth book, *Pelleas and Ettarre*, and the cynical conduct of Sir Tristram, whose story is told in the bitter tenth book, *The Last Tournament*. Even Merlin, Arthur's trusted magician and counselor, becomes corrupted and can perform no further offices for the king (*Merlin and Vivien*). *The Passing of Arthur* depicts the apocalyptic end of this long process of disintegration and decay.

From Idylls of the King

The Passing of Arthur[1]

That story which the bold Sir Bedivere,[2]
First made and latest left of all the knights,
Told, when the man was no more than a voice
In the white winter of his age, to those
5   With whom he dwelt, new faces, other minds.

For on their march to westward, Bedivere,
Who slowly paced among the slumbering host,
Heard in his tent the moanings of the King:

"I found Him in the shining of the stars,
10   I marked Him in the flowering of His fields,
But in His ways with men I find Him not.
I waged His wars, and now I pass and die.
O me! for why is all around us here

---

1. The principal source is Malory's *Morte Dar-thur* 21.4–5. Preceding the action of this idyll, Arthur has been in France with his nephew Gawain, fighting against the forces of Lancelot. Learning at that time of the gathering of an army against him in England, under the leadership of his nephew, Modred, Arthur returns there to engage in his last battle. Upon landing at Dover, Gawain is slain.

2. A knight who has long been close to the king, described in *The Coming of Arthur*, lines 173–74: "Bedivere, the first of all his knights / Knighted by Arthur at his crowning."

As if some lesser god had made the world,
15   But had not force to shape it as he would,
Till the High God behold it from beyond,
And enter it, and make it beautiful?
Or else as if the world were wholly fair,
But that these eyes of men are dense and dim,
20   And have not power to see it as it is:
Perchance, because we see not to the close;—
For I, being simple, thought to work His will,
And have but stricken with the sword in vain;
And all whereon I leaned in wife and friend
25   Is traitor to my peace, and all my realm
Reels back into the beast, and is no more.
My God, thou hast forgotten me in my death:[3]
Nay—God my Christ—I pass but shall not die."

Then, ere that last weird battle in the west,
30   There came on Arthur sleeping, Gawain killed
In Lancelot's war, the ghost of Gawain blown
Along a wandering wind, and past his ear
Went shrilling. "Hollow, hollow all delight!
Hail, King! tomorrow thou shalt pass away.
35   Farewell! there is an isle of rest for thee.
And I am blown along a wandering wind,
And hollow, hollow, hollow all delight."
And fainter onward, like wild birds that change
Their season in the night and wail their way
40   From cloud to cloud, down the long wind the dream
Shrilled; but in going mingled with dim cries
Far in the moonlit haze among the hills,
As of some lonely city sacked by night,
When all is lost, and wife and child with wail
45   Pass to new lords; and Arthur woke and called,
"Who spake? A dream. O light upon the wind,
Thine, Gawain, was the voice—are these dim cries
Thine? or doth all that haunts the waste and wild
Mourn, knowing it will go along with me?"

50   This heard the bold Sir Bedivere and spake:
"O me, my King, let pass whatever will,
Elves, and the harmless glamour of the field;[4]
But in their stead thy name and glory cling
To all high places like a golden cloud
55   Forever: but as yet thou shalt not pass.
Light was Gawain in life, and light in death
Is Gawain, for the ghost is as the man;
And care not thou for dreams from him, but rise—
I hear the steps of Modred in the west,
60   And with him many of thy people, and knights
Once thine, whom thou hast loved, but grosser grown

3. Cf. Jesus' cry in Matthew 27.46: "My God, my
God, why hast thou forsaken me?"
4. Tennyson said the reference is to "the legends
which cluster round the King's name." One legend told of the elves' bestowing gifts on Arthur
as a child.

Than heathen, spitting at their vows and thee.
Right well in heart they know thee for the King.
Arise, go forth and conquer as of old."

65   Then spake King Arthur to Sir Bedivere:
"Far other is this battle in the west
Whereto we move, than when we strove in youth,
And brake the petty kings, and fought with Rome,
Or thrust the heathen from the Roman wall,[5]
70   And shook him through the north. Ill doom° is mine   *destiny*
To war against my people and my knights.
The king who fights his people fights himself.
And they my knights, who loved me once, the stroke
That strikes them dead is as my death to me.
75   Yet let us hence, and find or feel a way
Through this blind haze, which ever since I saw
One lying in the dust at Almesbury,[6]
Hath folded in the passes of the world."

        Then rose the King and moved his host by night,
80   And ever pushed Sir Modred, league by league,
Back to the sunset bound of Lyonnesse[7]—
A land of old upheaven from the abyss
By fire, to sink into the abyss again;
Where fragments of forgotten peoples dwelled,
85   And the long mountains ended in a coast
Of ever-shifting sand, and far away
The phantom circle of a moaning sea.
There the pursuer could pursue no more,
And he that fled no further fly the King;
90   And there, that day when the great light of heaven
Burned at his lowest in the rolling year,
On the waste sand by the waste sea they closed.
Nor ever yet had Arthur fought a fight
Like this last, dim, weird battle of the west.
95   A deathwhite mist slept over sand and sea:
Whereof the chill, to him who breathed it, drew
Down with his blood, till all his heart was cold
With formless fear; and even on Arthur fell
Confusion, since he saw not whom he fought.
100   For friend and foe were shadows in the mist,
And friend slew friend not knowing whom he slew;[8]
And some had visions out of golden youth,
And some beheld the faces of old ghosts
Look in upon the battle; and in the mist
105   Was many a noble deed, many a base,

5. Hadrian's Wall, built in northern Britain, by the 2nd-century Roman emperor Hadrian as a defense against invaders from the north.
6. The convent to which Guinevere withdraws in the eleventh idyll; during the king's farewell visit to her there, she lies in the dust at his feet.
7. Legendary land, extending west from Cornwall, that sank into the sea.

8. Cf. the description of a battle by the Greek writer Thucydides (ca. 455–ca. 400 B.C.E.) in his *History of the Peloponnesian War* (7.44), in which the invaders become confused by darkness and slaughter many of their own men, and Matthew Arnold's 1851 reworking of this scene in "Dover Beach," lines 35–37 (p. 765).

And chance and craft and strength in single fights,
And ever and anon with host to host
Shocks, and the splintering spear, the hard mail hewn,
Shield-breakings, and the clash of brands,° the crash   *swords*
110 Of battleaxes on shattered helms, and shrieks
After the Christ, of those who falling down
Looked up for heaven, and only saw the mist;
And shouts of heathen and the traitor knights,
Oaths, insult, filth, and monstrous blasphemies,
115 Sweat, writhings, anguish, laboring of the lungs
In that close mist, and cryings for the light,
Moans of the dying, and voices of the dead.

    Last, as by some one deathbed after wail
Of suffering, silence follows, or through death
120 Or deathlike swoon, thus over all that shore,
Save for some whisper of the seething seas,
A dead hush fell; but when the dolorous day
Grew drearier toward twilight falling, came
A bitter wind, clear from the North, and blew
125 The mist aside, and with that wind the tide
Rose, and the pale King glanced across the field
Of battle: but no man was moving there;
Nor any cry of Christian heard thereon,
Nor yet of heathen; only the wan wave
130 Brake in among dead faces, to and fro
Swaying the helpless hands, and up and down
Tumbling the hollow helmets of the fallen,
And shivered brands that once had fought with Rome,
And rolling far along the gloomy shores
135 The voice of days of old and days to be.

    Then spake King Arthur to Sir Bedivere,
And whiter than the mist that all day long
Had held the field of battle was the King:

    "Hearest thou this great voice that shakes the world,
140 And wastes the narrow realm whereon we move,
And beats upon the faces of the dead,
My dead, as though they had not died for me?—
O Bedivere, for on my heart hath fallen
Confusion, till I know not what I am,
145 Nor whence I am, nor whether I be King.
Behold, I seem but King among the dead."

    Then spake the bold Sir Bedivere: "My King,
King everywhere! and so the dead have kings,
There also will I worship thee as King.
150 Yet still thy life is whole, and still I live
Who love thee; but who hates thee, he that brought
The heathen back among us, yonder stands,
Modred, unharmed, the traitor of thine house."

    Then spake the King: "My house hath been my doom.
155 But call not thou this traitor of my house
Who hath but dwelled beneath one roof with me.
My house are rather they who sware my vows,
Yea, even while they brake them, owned° me King.   *acknowledged*
And well for thee, saying in my dark hour,
160 When all the purport of my throne hath failed,
That quick or dead thou holdest me for King.
King am I, whatsoever be their cry;
And one last act of kinghood shalt thou see
Yet, ere I pass." And uttering this the King
165 Made at the man: then Modred smote his liege
Hard on that helm which many a heathen sword
Had beaten thin; while Arthur at one blow,
Striking the last stroke with Excalibur,
Slew him, and all but slain himself, he fell.

170   So all day long the noise of battle rolled
Among the mountains by the winter sea;
Until King Arthur's Table, man by man,
Had fallen in Lyonnesse about their lord,
King Arthur. Then, because his wound was deep,
175 The bold Sir Bedivere uplifted him,
And bore him to a chapel nigh the field,
A broken chancel with a broken cross,
That stood on a dark strait of barren land:
On one side lay the Ocean, and on one
180 Lay a great water, and the moon was full.

    Then spake King Arthur to Sir Bedivere:
"The sequel of today unsolders all
The goodliest fellowship of famous knights
Whereof this world holds record. Such a sleep
185 They sleep—the men I loved. I think that we
Shall never more, at any future time,
Delight our souls with talk of knightly deeds,
Walking about the gardens and the halls
Of Camelot, as in the days that were.
190 I perish by this people which I made,—
Though Merlin sware that I should come again
To rule once more;[9] but, let what will be, be,
I am so deeply smitten through the helm
That without help I cannot last til morn.
195 Thou therefore take my brand Excalibur,
Which was my pride: for thou rememberest how
In those old days, one summer noon, an arm
Rose up from out the bosom of the lake,
Clothed in white samite,[1] mystic, wonderful,
200 Holding the sword—and how I rowed across

---

9. Cf. Malory, *Morte Darthur* 21.7: "Some men yet say in many parts of England that King Arthur is not dead, but by the will of our Lord in another place. And men say that he will come again." 1. A rich silk fabric.

And took it, and have worn it, like a king;
And, wheresoever I am sung or told
In aftertime, this also shall be known:
But now delay not: take Excalibur,
205   And fling him far into the middle mere:°   *middle of the lake*
Watch what thou seëst, and lightly° bring me word."   *quickly*

    To him replied the bold Sir Bedivere:
"It is not meet,° Sir King, to leave thee thus,   *fitting*
Aidless, alone, and smitten through the helm—
210   A little thing may harm a wounded man;
Yet I thy hest° will all perform at full,   *command*
Watch what I see, and lightly bring thee word."

    So saying, from the ruined shrine he stepped,
And in the moon athwart° the place of tombs,   *across*
215   Where lay the mighty bones of ancient men,
Old knights, and over them the sea-wind sang
Shrill, chill, with flakes of foam. He, stepping down
By zigzag paths, and juts of pointed rock,
Came on the shining levels of the lake.

220   There drew he forth the brand Excalibur,
And o'er him, drawing it, the winter moon,
Brightening the skirts of a long cloud, ran forth
And sparkled keen with frost against the hilt:
For all the haft° twinkled with diamond sparks,   *hilt*
225   Myriads of topaz-lights, and jacinth°-work   *red gem*
Of subtlest jewelry. He gazed so long
That both his eyes were dazzled as he stood,
This way and that dividing the swift mind,
In act to throw: but at the last it seemed
230   Better to leave Excalibur concealed
There in the many-knotted waterflags,
That whistled stiff and dry about the marge.°   *shore*
So strode he back slow to the wounded King.

    Then spake King Arthur to Sir Bedivere:
235   "Hast thou performed my mission which I gave?
What is it thou hast seen? or what hast heard?"

    And answer made the bold Sir Bedivere:
"I heard the ripple washing in the reeds,
And the wild water lapping on the crag."

240   To whom replied King Arthur, faint and pale:
"Thou hast betrayed thy nature and thy name.
Not rendering true answer, as beseemed
Thy fëalty, nor like a noble knight:
For surer sign had followed, either hand,
245   Or voice, or else a motion of the mere.
This is a shameful thing for men to lie.
Yet now, I charge thee, quickly go again,

As thou art lief° and dear, and do the thing   *beloved*
I bade thee, watch, and lightly bring me word."

250   Then went Sir Bedivere the second time
Across the ridge, and paced beside the mere,
Counting the dewy pebbles, fixed in thought;
But when he saw the wonder of the hilt,
How curiously and strangely chased,[2] he smote
255   His palms together, and he cried aloud:

    "And if indeed I cast the brand away,
Surely a precious thing, one worthy note,
Should thus be lost forever from the earth,
Which might have pleased the eyes of many men.
260   What good should follow this, if this were done?
What harm, undone? Deep harm to disobey,
Seeing obedience is the bond of rule.
Were it well to obey then, if a king demand
An act unprofitable, against himself?
265   The King is sick, and knows not what he does.
What record, or what relic of my lord
Should be to aftertime, but empty breath
And rumors of a doubt? But were this kept,
Stored in some treasure-house of mighty kings,
270   Some one might show it at a joust of arms,
Saying, 'King Arthur's sword, Excalibur,
Wrought by the lonely maiden of the Lake.
Nine years she wrought it, sitting in the deeps
Upon the hidden bases of the hills.'
275   So might some old man speak in the aftertime
To all the people, winning reverence.
But now much honor and much fame were lost."

    So spake he, clouded with his own conceit,[3]
And hid Excalibur the second time,
280   And so strode back slow to the wounded king.

    Then spoke King Arthur, breathing heavily:
"What is it thou hast seen? or what hast heard?"

    And answer made the bold Sir Bedivere:
"I heard the water lapping on the crag,
285   And the long ripple washing in the reeds."

    To whom replied King Arthur, much in wrath:
"Ah, miserable and unkind, untrue,
Unknightly, traitor-hearted! Woe is me!
Authority forgets a dying king,
290   Laid widowed of the power in his eye
That bowed the will. I see thee what thou art,
For thou, the latest-left of all my knights,
In whom should meet the offices of all,

2. Decorated. "Curiously": skillfully.   3. Vain and foolish fancies.

Thou wouldst betray me for the precious hilt;
295   Either from lust of gold, or like a girl
Valuing the giddy pleasure of the eyes.
Yet, for a man may fail in duty twice,
And the third time may prosper, get thee hence:
But, if thou spare to fling Excalibur,
300   I will arise and slay thee with my hands."

Then quickly rose Sir Bedivere, and ran,
And, leaping down the ridges lightly, plunged
Among the bullrush beds, and clutched the sword,
And strongly wheeled and threw it. The great brand
305   Made lightnings in the splendor of the moon,
And flashing round and round and whirled in an arch,
Shot like a streamer of the northern morn,[4]
Seen where the moving isles of winter shock[5]
By night, with noises of the Northern Sea.
310   So flashed and fell the brand Excalibur:
But ere he dipped the surface, rose an arm
Clothed in white samite, mystic, wonderful,
And caught him by the hilt, and brandished him
Three times, and drew him under in the mere.
315   And lightly went the other to the King.

Then spoke King Arthur, drawing thicker breath:
"Now see I by thine eyes that this is done.
Speak out: what is it thou hast heard, or seen?"

And answer made the bold Sir Bedivere:
320   "Sir King, I closed mine eyelids, lest the gems
Should blind my purpose, for I never saw,
Nor shall see, here or elsewhere, till I die,
Not though I live three lives of mortal men,
So great a miracle as yonder hilt.
325   Then with both hands I flung him, wheeling him;
But when I looked again, behold an arm,
Clothed in white samite, mystic, wonderful,
That caught him by the hilt, and brandished him
Three times, and drew him under in the mere."

330   And answer made King Arthur, breathing hard:
"My end draws nigh; 'tis time that I were gone.
Make broad thy shoulders to receive my weight,
And bear me to the margin; yet I fear
My wound hath taken cold, and I shall die."

335   So saying, from the pavement he half rose,
Slowly, with pain, reclining on his arm,
And looking wistfully with wide blue eyes
As in a picture. Him Sir Bedivere
Remorsefully regarded through his tears,

4. The northern lights.   5. Where the icebergs collide.

340 And would have spoken, but he found not words;
Then took with care, and kneeling on one knee,
O'er both his shoulders drew the languid hands,
And rising bore him through the place of tombs.

But, as he walked, King Arthur panted hard,
345 Like one that feels a nightmare on his bed
When all the house is mute. So sighed the King,
Muttering and murmuring at his ear, "Quick, quick!
I fear it is too late, and I shall die."
But the other swiftly strode from ridge to ridge,
350 Clothed with his breath, and looking, as he walked,
Larger than human on the frozen hills.
He heard the deep behind him, and a cry
Before. His own thought drove him like a goad.
Dry clashed his harness in the icy caves
355 And barren chasms, and all to left and right
The bare black cliff clanged round him, as he based
His feet on juts of slippery crag that rang
Sharp-smitten with the dint of armèd heels—
And on a sudden, lo! the level lake,
360 And the long glories of the winter moon.

Then saw they how there hove a dusky barge,
Dark as a funeral scarf from stem to stern,
Beneath them; and descending they were ware°   *aware*
That all the decks were dense with stately forms,
365 Black-stoled, black-hooded, like a dream—by these
Three Queens with crowns of gold: and from them rose
A cry that shivered to the tingling stars,
And, as it were one voice, an agony
Of lamentation, like a wind that shrills
370 All night in a waste land, where no one comes,
Or hath come, since the making of the world.

Then murmured Arthur, "Place me in the barge."
So to the barge they came. There those three Queens
Put forth their hands, and took the King, and wept.
375 But she, that rose the tallest of them all
And fairest, laid his head upon her lap,
And loosed the shattered casque,° and chafed his hands,   *helmet*
And called him by his name, complaining loud,
And dropping bitter tears against a brow
380 Striped with dark blood: for all his face was white
And colorless, and like the withered moon
Smote by the fresh beam of the springing east;
And all his greaves and cuisses[6] dashed with drops
Of onset;[7] and the light and lustrous curls—
385 That made his forehead like a rising sun
High from the daïs-throne—were parched with dust;
Or, clotted into points and hanging loose,

---

6. Armor to protect the front of the thighs. "Greaves": armor to protect the leg below the knee.
7. Blood from battle.

Mixed with the knightly growth that fringed his lips.
So like a shattered column lay the King;
390 Not like that Arthur who, with lance in rest,
From spur to plume a star of tournament,
Shot through the lists at Camelot, and charged
Before the eyes of ladies and of kings.

Then loudly cried the bold Sir Bedivere:
395 "Ah! my Lord Arthur, whither shall I go?
Where shall I hide my forehead and my eyes?
For now I see the true old times are dead,
When every morning brought a noble chance,
And every chance brought out a noble knight.
400 Such times have been not since the light[8] that led
The holy Elders with the gift of myrrh.
But now the whole Round Table is dissolved
Which was an image of the mighty world,
And I, the last, go forth companionless,
405 And the days darken round me, and the years,
Among new men, strange faces, other minds."

And slowly answered Arthur from the barge:
"The old order changeth, yielding place to new,
And God fulfills himself in many ways,
410 Lest one good custom should corrupt the world.
Comfort thyself: what comfort is in me?
I have lived my life, and that which I have done
May He within himself make pure! but thou,
If thou shouldst never see my face again,
415 Pray for my soul. More things are wrought by prayer
Than this world dreams of. Wherefore, let thy voice
Rise like a fountain for me night and day.
For what are men better than sheep or goats
That nourish a blind life within the brain,
420 If, knowing God, they lift not hands of prayer
Both for themselves and those who call them friend?
For so the whole round earth is every way
Bound by gold chains about the feet of God.
But now farewell. I am going a long way
425 With these thou seëst—if indeed I go
(For all my mind is clouded with a doubt)—
To the island-valley of Avilion;[9]
Where falls not hail, or rain, or any snow,
Nor ever wind blows loudly: but it lies
430 Deep-meadowed, happy, fair with orchard lawns
And bowery hollows crowned with summer sea,
Where I will heal me of my grievous wound."

So said he, and the barge with oar and sail
Moved from the brink, like some full-breasted swan

8. I.e., the star that guided the three kings ("Elders") to the infant Jesus at Bethlehem. See Matthew 2.1–12.

9. Or Avalon; in Celtic mythology and medieval romance, the Vale of the Blessed where heroes enjoyed life after death.

435   That, fluting a wild carol ere her death,
      Ruffles her pure cold plume, and takes the flood
      With swarthy webs.° Long stood Sir Bedivere   *webbed feet*
      Revolving many memories, till the hull
      Looked one black dot against the verge of dawn,
440   And on the mere the wailing died away.

      But when that moan had passed for evermore,
      The stillness of the dead world's winter dawn
      Amazed him, and he groaned, "The King is gone."
      And therewithal came on him the weird rhyme,[1]
445   "From the great deep to the great deep he goes."

      Whereat he slowly turned and slowly clomb
      The last hard footstep of that iron crag;
      Thence marked the black hull moving yet, and cried,
      "He passes to be King among the dead,
450   And after healing of his grievous wound
      He comes again; but—if he come no more—
      O me, be yon dark Queens in yon black boat,
      Who shrieked and wailed, the three whereat we gazed
      On that high day, when, clothed with living light,
455   They stood before his throne in silence, friends
      Of Arthur, who should help him at his need?"[2]

      Then from the dawn it seemed there came, but faint
      As from beyond the limit of the world,
      Like the last echo born of a great cry,
460   Sounds, as if some fair city were one voice
      Around a king returning from his wars.

      Thereat once more he moved about, and clomb
      Even to the highest he could climb, and saw,
      Straining his eyes beneath an arch of hand,
465   Or thought he saw, the speck that bare the King,
      Down that long water opening on the deep
      Somewhere far off, pass on and on, and go
      From less to less and vanish into light.
      And the new sun rose bringing the new year.

1833–69   1869

Crossing the Bar[1]

      Sunset and evening star,
        And one clear call for me!
      And may there be no moaning of the bar,[2]
        When I put out to sea,

1. In *The Coming of Arthur*, lines 402–10, Merlin speaks a mysterious prophecy, in verse, concerning Arthur's birth.
2. In *The Coming of Arthur*, lines 275–78, Arthur's half-sister Bellicent describes his coronation.

1. Although not the last poem written by Tennyson, "Crossing the Bar" appears, at his request, as the final poem in all collections of his work.
2. Mournful sound of the ocean beating on a sand bar at the mouth of a harbor.

5 But such a tide as moving seems asleep,
  Too full for sound and foam,
When that which drew from out the boundless deep
  Turns again home.

  Twilight and evening bell,
10   And after that the dark!
And may there be no sadness of farewell,
  When I embark;

For though from out our bourne° of Time and Place   *boundary*
  The flood may bear me far,
15 I hope to see my Pilot face to face
  When I have crossed the bar.

1889   1889

ELIZABETH GASKELL
1810–1865

It is ironic that the writer whom contemporaries and future generations knew as "Mrs. Gaskell" once instructed her sister-in-law that it was "a silly piece of bride-like affectation not to sign yourself by your proper name." Despite the wifely identity that the name Mrs. Gaskell connotes, Elizabeth Gaskell, as she always signed herself, wrote fiction on contemporary social topics that stimulated considerable controversy. Her first novel, *Mary Barton* (1848), presents a sympathetic picture of the hardships and the grievances of the working class. Another early novel, *Ruth* (1853), portrays the seduction and rehabilitation of an unmarried mother.

Elizabeth Cleghorn Gaskell was born in 1810 in Chelsea, on the outskirts of London, to a family that followed Unitarianism, a Christian movement that rejected the doctrine of the Trinity and advocated religious tolerance. Her mother died when Gaskell was one, and the girl was sent to rural Knutsford, in Cheshire, to be raised by her aunt. At the age of twenty-one, she met and married William Gaskell, a Unitarian minister whose chapel was in the industrial city of Manchester. For the first ten years of her marriage, she led the life of a minister's wife, bearing five children, keeping a house, and helping her husband serve his congregation. When her fourth child and only son, William, died at the age of one year, Gaskell became depressed. Her husband encouraged her to write as a way of allaying her grief, and so she produced *Mary Barton*, subtitled *A Tale of Manchester Life*. In the preface to the novel, she wrote that she was inspired by thinking "how deep might be the romance in the lives of some of those who elbowed me daily in the busy streets of the town in which I resided. I had always felt a deep sympathy with the careworn men, who looked as if doomed to struggle through their lives in strange alternations between work and want." Observing the mutual distrust of the rich and the poor, and their accompanying resentments, Gaskell hoped that her novel would help create within her middle-class readership understanding and sympathy for the working classes.

Anonymously published, the novel was widely reviewed and discussed. Gaskell was soon identified as the author; she subsequently developed a wide acquaintance in literary circles. She wrote five more novels and about thirty short stories, many of which were published in Charles Dickens's journal *Household Words* and its successor, *All the Year Round*. The contrasting experiences Gaskell's existence had given her of two ways of life, of rural Knutsford and industrial Manchester, defined the poles of her fiction. Her second novel, *Cranford* (1853), presents a delicate picture of the small events of country village life, a subject to which she returns with greater range and psychological depth in her last novel, *Wives and Daughters* (1866). In *North and South* (1855), Gaskell brings together the two worlds of her fiction in the story of Margaret Hale, a young woman from a village in the south of England who moves to a factory town in the north.

One of the writers Gaskell's literary fame led her to know was Charlotte Brontë, with whom she became friends. When Brontë died in 1855, Gaskell was approached by Patrick Brontë to write the story of his daughter's life. Gaskell's *Life of Charlotte Brontë* (1857) is a masterpiece of English biography and one of her finest portrayals of character. Her focus in the *Life* on the relationship between Brontë's identity as a writer and her role as daughter, sister, and wife reflects the balance Gaskell herself sought between the stories she wove and the people she cared for. Referred to by Dickens as "my dear Scheherazade," Gaskell wrote not just to entertain but also to critique society and to promote social reform.

The Old Nurse's Story[1]

You know, my dears, that your mother was an orphan, and an only child; and I dare say you have heard that your grandfather was a clergyman up in Westmoreland, where I come from. I was just a girl in the village school, when, one day, your grandmother came in to ask the mistress if there was any scholar there who would do for a nurse-maid; and mighty proud I was, I can tell ye, when the mistress called me up, and spoke to my being a good girl at my needle, and a steady honest girl, and one whose parents were very respectable, though they might be poor. I thought I should like nothing better than to serve the pretty young lady, who was blushing as deep as I was, as she spoke of the coming baby, and what I should have to do with it. However, I see you don't care so much for this part of my story, as for what you think is to come, so I'll tell you at once I was engaged,[2] and settled at the parsonage before Miss Rosamond (that was the baby, who is now your mother) was born. To be sure, I had little enough to do with her when she came, for she was never out of her mother's arms, and slept by her all night long; and proud enough was I sometimes when missis trusted her to me. There never was such a baby before or since, though you've all of you been fine enough in your turns; but for sweet winning ways, you've none of you come up to your mother. She took after her mother, who was a real lady born; a Miss Furnivall, a granddaughter of Lord Furnivall's in Northumberland. I believe she had neither brother nor sister, and had been brought up in my lord's family till she had married your grandfather, who was just a curate, son to a shopkeeper in Carlisle—but a clever fine gentleman as ever was—and one who

---

1. Originally published anonymously in the 1852 Christmas number of Dickens's journal *Household Words*; it was later republished in Gaskell's   *Lizzie Leigh, and Other Tales* (1855).
2. Hired.

was a right-down hard worker in his parish, which was very wide, and scattered all abroad over the Westmoreland Fells. When your mother, little Miss Rosamond, was about four or five years old, both her parents died in a fortnight—one after the other. Ah! that was a sad time. My pretty young mistress and me was looking for another baby, when my master came home from one of his long rides, wet and tired, and took the fever he died of; and then she never held up her head again, but just lived to see her dead baby, and have it laid on her breast before she sighed away her life. My mistress had asked me, on her death-bed, never to leave Miss Rosamond; but if she had never spoken a word, I would have gone with the little child to the end of the world.

The next thing, and before we had well stilled our sobs, the executors and guardians came to settle the affairs. They were my poor young mistress's own cousin, Lord Furnivall, and Mr. Esthwaite, my master's brother, a shopkeeper in Manchester; not so well to do then, as he was afterwards, and with a large family rising about him. Well! I don't know if it were their settling, or because of a letter my mistress wrote on her death-bed to her cousin, my lord; but somehow it was settled that Miss Rosamond and me were to go to Furnivall Manor House, in Northumberland, and my lord spoke as if it had been her mother's wish that she should live with his family, and as if he had no objections, for that one or two more or less could make no difference in so grand a household. So, though that was not the way in which I should have wished the coming of my bright and pretty pet to have been looked at—who was like a sunbeam in any family, be it never so grand—I was well pleased that all the folks in the Dale should stare and admire, when they heard I was going to be young lady's maid at my Lord Furnivall's at Furnivall Manor.

But I made a mistake in thinking we were to go and live where my lord did. It turned out that the family had left Furnivall Manor House fifty years or more. I could not hear that my poor young mistress had ever been there, though she had been brought up in the family; and I was sorry for that, for I should have liked Miss Rosamond's youth to have passed where her mother's had been.

My lord's gentleman, from whom I asked as many questions as I durst, said that the Manor House was at the foot of the Cumberland Fells, and a very grand place; that an old Miss Furnivall, a great-aunt of my lord's, lived there, with only a few servants; but that it was a very healthy place, and my lord had thought that it would suit Miss Rosamond very well for a few years, and that her being there might perhaps amuse his old aunt.

I was bidden by my lord to have Miss Rosamond's things ready by a certain day. He was a stern, proud man, as they say all the Lord Furnivalls were; and he never spoke a word more than was necessary. Folk did say he had loved my young mistress; but that, because she knew that his father would object, she would never listen to him, and married Mr. Esthwaite; but I don't know. He never married at any rate. But he never took much notice of Miss Rosamond; which I thought he might have done if he had cared for her dead mother. He sent his gentleman with us to the Manor House, telling him to join him at Newcastle that same evening; so there was no great length of time for him to make us known to all the strangers before he, too, shook us off; and we were left, two lonely young things (I was not eighteen), in the great old Manor House. It seems like yesterday that we drove there.

We had left our own dear parsonage very early, and we had both cried as if our hearts would break, though we were travelling in my lord's carriage, which I had thought so much of once. And now it was long past noon on a September day, and we stopped to change horses for the last time at a little smoky town, all full of colliers and miners. Miss Rosamond had fallen asleep, but Mr. Henry told me to waken her, that she might see the park and the Manor House as we drove up. I thought it rather a pity; but I did what he bade me, for fear he should complain of me to my lord. We had left all signs of a town or even a village, and were then inside the gates of a large wild park—not like the parks here in the south, but with rocks, and the noise of running water, and gnarled thorn-trees, and old oaks, all white and peeled with age.

The road went up about two miles, and then we saw a great and stately house, with many trees close around it, so close that in some places their branches dragged against the walls when the wind blew; and some hung broken down; for no one seemed to take much charge of the place;—to lop the wood, or to keep the moss-covered carriage-way in order. Only in front of the house all was clear. The great oval drive was without a weed; and neither tree nor creeper was allowed to grow over the long, many-windowed front; at both sides of which a wing projected, which were each the ends of other side fronts; for the house, although it was so desolate, was even grander than I expected. Behind it rose the Fells, which seemed unenclosed and bare enough; and on the left hand of the house as you stood facing it, was a little old-fashioned flower-garden, as I found out afterwards. A door opened out upon it from the west front; it had been scooped out of the thick dark wood for some old Lady Furnivall; but the branches of the great forest trees had grown and overshadowed it again, and there were very few flowers that would live there at that time.

When we drove up to the great front entrance, and went into the hall I thought we should be lost—it was so large, and vast, and grand. There was a chandelier all of bronze, hung down from the middle of the ceiling; and I had never seen one before, and looked at it all in amaze. Then, at one end of the hall, was a great fire-place, as large as the sides of the houses in my country, with massy andirons and dogs[3] to hold the wood; and by it were heavy old-fashioned sofas. At the opposite end of the hall, to the left as you went in—on the western side—was an organ built into the wall, and so large that it filled up the best part of that end. Beyond it, on the same side, was a door; and opposite, on each side of the fire-place, were also doors leading to the east front; but those I never went through as long as I stayed in the house, so I can't tell you what lay beyond.

The afternoon was closing in, and the hall, which had no fire lighted in it, looked dark and gloomy; but we did not stay there a moment. The old servant who had opened the door for us bowed to Mr. Henry, and took us in through the door at the further side of the great organ, and led us through several smaller halls and passages into the west drawing-room, where he said that Miss Furnivall was sitting. Poor little Miss Rosamond held very tight to me, as if she were scared and lost in that great place, and, as for myself, I was not much better. The west drawing-room was very cheerful-looking, with

3. Large decorative fireplace supports.

a warm fire in it, and plenty of good comfortable furniture about. Miss Furnivall was an old lady not far from eighty, I should think, but I do not know. She was thin and tall, and had a face as full of fine wrinkles as if they had been drawn all over it with a needle's point. Her eyes were very watchful, to make up, I suppose, for her being so deaf as to be obliged to use a trumpet.[4] Sitting with her, working at the same great piece of tapestry, was Mrs. Stark, her maid and companion, and almost as old as she was. She had lived with Miss Furnivall ever since they both were young, and now she seemed more like a friend than a servant; she looked so cold and grey, and stony, as if she had never loved or cared for any one; and I don't suppose she did care for any one, except her mistress; and, owing to the great deafness of the latter, Mrs. Stark treated her very much as if she were a child. Mr. Henry gave some message from my lord, and then he bowed good-bye to us all,—taking no notice of my sweet little Miss Rosamond's out-stretched hand—and left us standing there, being looked at by the two old ladies through their spectacles.

I was right glad when they rung for the old footman who had shown us in at first, and told him to take us to our rooms. So we went out of that great drawing-room, and into another sitting-room, and out of that, and then up a great flight of stairs, and along a broad gallery—which was something like a library, having books all down one side, and windows and writing-tables all down the other—till we came to our rooms, which I was not sorry to hear were just over the kitchens; for I began to think I should be lost in that wilderness of a house. There was an old nursery, that had been used for all the little lords and ladies long ago, with a pleasant fire burning in the grate, and the kettle boiling on the hob, and tea things spread out on the table; and out of that room was the night-nursery, with a little crib for Miss Rosamond close to my bed. And old James called up Dorothy, his wife, to bid us welcome; and both he and she were so hospitable and kind, that by-and-by Miss Rosamond and me felt quite at home; and by the time tea was over, she was sitting on Dorothy's knee, and chattering away as fast as her little tongue could go. I soon found out that Dorothy was from Westmoreland, and that bound her and me together, as it were; and I would never wish to meet with kinder people than were old James and his wife. James had lived pretty nearly all his life in my lord's family, and thought there was no one so grand as they. He even looked down a little on his wife; because, till he had married her, she had never lived in any but a farmer's household. But he was very fond of her, as well he might be. They had one servant under them, to do all the rough work. Agnes they called her; and she and me, and James and Dorothy, with Miss Furnivall and Mrs. Stark, made up the family; always remembering my sweet little Miss Rosamond! I used to wonder what they had done before she came, they thought so much of her now. Kitchen and drawing-room, it was all the same. The hard, sad Miss Furnivall, and the cold Mrs. Stark, looked pleased when she came fluttering in like a bird, playing and pranking hither and thither, with a continual murmur, and pretty prattle of gladness. I am sure, they were sorry many a time when she flitted away into the kitchen, though they were too proud to ask her to stay with them, and were a little surprised at her taste; though, to be sure, as Mrs. Stark said, it was not to be wondered at, remembering what stock her father had come of.

4. A horn-shaped device used by the hard of hearing to amplify sound.

The great, old rambling house, was a famous[5] place for little Miss Rosamond. She made expeditions all over it, with me at her heels; all, except the east wing, which was never opened, and whither we never thought of going. But in the western and northern part was many a pleasant room; full of things that were curiosities to us, though they might not have been to people who had seen more. The windows were darkened by the sweeping boughs of the trees, and the ivy which had overgrown them: but, in the green gloom, we could manage to see old China jars and carved ivory boxes, and great heavy books, and, above all, the old pictures!

Once, I remember, my darling would have Dorothy go with us to tell us who they all were; for they were all portraits of some of my lord's family, though Dorothy could not tell us the names of every one. We had gone through most of the rooms, when we came to the old state drawing-room over the hall, and there was a picture of Miss Furnivall; or, as she was called in those days, Miss Grace, for she was the younger sister. Such a beauty she must have been! but with such a set, proud look, and such scorn looking out of her handsome eyes, with her eyebrows just a little raised, as if she wondered how any one could have the impertinence to look at her; and her lip curled at us, as we stood there gazing. She had a dress on, the like of which I had never seen before, but it was all the fashion when she was young; a hat of some soft white stuff like beaver, pulled a little over her brows, and a beautiful plume of feathers sweeping round it on one side; and her gown of blue satin was open in front to a quilted white stomacher.[6]

"Well, to be sure!" said I, when I had gazed my fill. "Flesh is grass,[7] they do say; but who would have thought that Miss Furnivall had been such an out-and-out beauty, to see her now?"

"Yes," said Dorothy. "Folks change sadly. But if what my master's father used to say was true, Miss Furnivall, the elder sister, was handsomer than Miss Grace. Her picture is here somewhere; but, if I show it you, you must never let on, even to James, that you have seen it. Can the little lady hold her tongue, think you?" asked she.

I was not so sure, for she was such a little sweet, bold, open-spoken child, so I set her to hide herself; and then I helped Dorothy to turn a great picture, that leaned with its face towards the wall, and was not hung up as the others were. To be sure, it beat Miss Grace for beauty; and, I think, for scornful pride, too, though in that matter it might be hard to choose. I could have looked at it an hour, but Dorothy seemed half frightened of having shown it to me, and hurried it back again, and bade me run and find Miss Rosamond, for that there were some ugly places about the house, where she should like ill for the child to go. I was a brave, high-spirited girl, and thought little of what the old woman said, for I liked hide-and-seek as well as any child in the parish; so off I ran to find my little one.

As winter drew on, and the days grew shorter, I was sometimes almost certain that I heard a noise as if some one was playing on the great organ in the hall. I did not hear it every evening; but, certainly, I did very often; usually when I was sitting with Miss Rosamond, after I had put her to bed, and keeping quite still and silent in the bedroom. Then I used to hear it booming

5. Exciting, wonderful.
6. Ornamental covering for the front of the body. "Beaver": felted wool.
7. Cf. 1 Peter 1.24 ("For all flesh is as grass, and all the glory of men as the flower of grass. The grass withereth, and the flower thereof falleth away").

and swelling away in the distance. The first night, when I went down to my supper, I asked Dorothy who had been playing music, and James said very shortly that I was a gowk to take the wind soughing[8] among the trees for music; but I saw Dorothy look at him very fearfully, and Bessy, the kitchen-maid, said something beneath her breath, and went quite white. I saw they did not like my question, so I held my peace till I was with Dorothy alone, when I knew I could get a good deal out of her. So, the next day, I watched my time, and I coaxed and asked her who it was that played the organ; for I knew that it was the organ and not the wind well enough, for all I had kept silence before James. But Dorothy had had her lesson, I'll warrant, and never a word could I get from her. So then I tried Bessy, though I had always held my head rather above her, as I was evened[9] to James and Dorothy, and she was little better than their servant. So she said I must never, never tell; and, if I ever told, I was never to say *she* had told me; but it was a very strange noise, and she had heard it many a time, but most of all on winter nights, and before storms; and folks did say, it was the old lord playing on the great organ in the hall, just as he used to do when he was alive; but who the old lord was, or why he played, and why he played on stormy winter evenings in particular, she either could not or would not tell me. Well! I told you I had a brave heart; and I thought it was rather pleasant to have that grand music rolling about the house, let who would be the player; for now it rose above the great gusts of wind, and wailed and triumphed just like a living creature, and then it fell to a softness most complete; only it was always music and tunes, so it was nonsense to call it the wind. I thought, at first, it might be Miss Furnivall who played, unknown to Bessy; but, one day when I was in the hall by myself, I opened the organ and peeped all about it, and around it, as I had done to the organ in Crosthwaite Church once before, and I saw it was all broken and destroyed inside, though it looked so brave[1] and fine; and then, though it was noon-day, my flesh began to creep a little, and I shut it up, and ran away pretty quickly to my own bright nursery; and I did not like hearing the music for some time after that, any more than James and Dorothy did. All this time Miss Rosamond was making herself more and more beloved. The old ladies liked her to dine with them at their early dinner; James stood behind Miss Furnivall's chair, and I behind Miss Rosamond's, all in state; and, after dinner, she would play about in a corner of the great drawing-room, as still as any mouse, while Miss Furnivall slept, and I had my dinner in the kitchen. But she was glad enough to come to me in the nursery afterwards; for, as she said, Miss Furnivall was so sad, and Mrs. Stark so dull; but she and I were merry enough; and, by-and-by, I got not to care for that weird rolling music, which did one no harm, if we did not know where it came from.

That winter was very cold. In the middle of October the frosts began, and lasted many, many weeks. I remember, one day at dinner, Miss Furnivall lifted up her sad, heavy eyes, and said to Mrs. Stark, "I am afraid we shall have a terrible winter," in a strange kind of meaning way. But Mrs. Stark pretended not to hear, and talked very loud of something else. My little lady and I did not care for the frost;—not we! As long as it was dry we climbed up the steep brows, behind the house, and went up on the Fells, which were bleak and bare enough, and there we ran races in the fresh, sharp air; and once we

8. Moaning. "Shortly": curtly. "Gowk": fool. 1. Excellent.
9. Of equal status.

came down by a new path that took us past the two old gnarled holly-trees, which grew about half-way down by the east side of the house. But the days grew shorter and shorter; and the old lord, if it was he, played away more and more stormily and sadly on the great organ. One Sunday afternoon,—it must have been towards the end of November—I asked Dorothy to take charge of little Missey when she came out of the drawing-room, after Miss Furnivall had had her nap; for it was too cold to take her with me to church, and yet I wanted to go. And Dorothy was glad enough to promise, and was so fond of the child that all seemed well; and Bessy and I set off very briskly, though the sky hung heavy and black over the white earth, as if the night had never fully gone away; and the air, though still, was very biting and keen.

"We shall have a fall of snow," said Bessy to me. And sure enough, even while we were in church, it came down thick, in great large flakes, so thick it almost darkened the windows. It had stopped snowing before we came out, but it lay soft, thick and deep beneath our feet, as we tramped home. Before we got to the hall the moon rose, and I think it was lighter then,—what with the moon, and what with the white dazzling snow—than it had been when we went to church, between two and three o'clock. I have not told you that Miss Furnivall and Mrs. Stark never went to church: they used to read the prayers together, in their quiet gloomy way; they seemed to feel the Sunday very long without their tapestry-work to be busy at. So when I went to Dorothy in the kitchen, to fetch Miss Rosamond and take her up-stairs with me, I did not much wonder when the old woman told me that the ladies had kept the child with them, and that she had never come to the kitchen, as I had bidden her, when she was tired of behaving pretty in the drawing-room. So I took off my things and went to find her, and bring her to her supper in the nursery. But when I went into the best drawing-room, there sat the two old ladies, very still and quiet, dropping out a word now and then, but looking as if nothing so bright and merry as Miss Rosamond had ever been near them. Still I thought she might be hiding from me; it was one of her pretty ways; and that she had persuaded them to look as if they knew nothing about her; so I went softly peeping under this sofa, and behind that chair, making believe I was sadly frightened at not finding her.

"What's the matter, Hester?" said Mrs. Stark sharply. I don't know if Miss Furnivall had seen me, for, as I told you, she was very deaf, and she sat quite still, idly staring into the fire, with her hopeless face. "I'm only looking for my little Rosy-Posy," replied I, still thinking that the child was there, and near me, though I could not see her.

"Miss Rosamond is not here," said Mrs. Stark. "She went away more than an hour ago to find Dorothy." And she too turned and went on looking into the fire.

My heart sank at this, and I began to wish I had never left my darling. I went back to Dorothy and told her. James was gone out for the day, but she and me and Bessy took lights, and went up into the nursery first and then we roamed over the great large house, calling and entreating Miss Rosamond to come out of her hiding place, and not frighten us to death in that way. But there was no answer; no sound.

"Oh!" said I at last, "Can she have got into the east wing and hidden there?"

But Dorothy said it was not possible, for that she herself had never been in there; that the doors were always locked, and my lord's steward had the keys, she believed; at any rate, neither she nor James had ever seen them: so, I said I would go back and see if, after all, she was not hidden in the drawing-room, unknown to the old ladies; and if I found her there, I said, I would whip her well for the fright she had given me; but I never meant to do it. Well, I went back to the west drawing-room, and I told Mrs. Stark we could not find her anywhere, and asked for leave to look all about the furniture there, for I thought now, that she might have fallen asleep in some warm hidden corner; but no! we looked, Miss Furnivall got up and looked, trembling all over, and she was no where there; then we set off again, every one in the house, and looked in all the places we had searched before, but we could not find her. Miss Furnivall shivered and shook so much, that Mrs. Stark took her back into the warm drawing-room; but not before they had made me promise to bring her to them when she was found. Well-a-day! I began to think she never would be found, when I bethought me to look out into the great front court, all covered with snow. I was up-stairs when I looked out; but, it was such clear moonlight, I could see quite plain two little footprints, which might be traced from the hall door, and round the corner of the east wing. I don't know how I got down, but I tugged open the great, stiff hall door; and, throwing the skirt of my gown over my head for a cloak, I ran out. I turned the east corner, and there a black shadow fell on the snow; but when I came again into the moonlight, there were the little footmarks going up— up to the Fells. It was bitter cold; so cold that the air almost took the skin off my face as I ran, but I ran on, crying to think how my poor little darling must be perished[2] and frightened. I was within sight of the holly-trees, when I saw a shepherd coming down the hill, bearing something in his arms wrapped in his maud. He shouted to me, and asked me if I had lost a bairn;[3] and, when I could not speak for crying, he bore towards me, and I saw my wee bairnie lying still, and white, and stiff, in his arms, as if she had been dead. He told me he had been up the Fells to gather in his sheep, before the deep cold of night came on, and that under the holly-trees (black marks on the hill-side, where no other bush was for miles around) he had found my little lady—my lamb—my queen—my darling—stiff and cold, in the terrible sleep which is frost-begotten. Oh! the joy, and the tears of having her in my arms once again! for I would not let him carry her; but took her, maud and all, into my own arms, and held her near my own warm neck and heart, and felt the life stealing slowly back again into her little gentle limbs. But she was still insensible when we reached the hall, and I had no breath for speech. We went in by the kitchen door.

"Bring the warming-pan," said I; and I carried her up-stairs and began undressing her by the nursery fire, which Bessy had kept up. I called my little lammie all the sweet and playful names I could think of,—even while my eyes were blinded by my tears; and at last, oh! at length she opened her large blue eyes. Then I put her into her warm bed, and sent Dorothy down to tell Miss Furnivall that all was well; and I made up my mind to sit by my darling's bedside the live-long night. She fell away into a soft sleep as soon as her pretty head had touched the pillow, and I watched by her till morning light; when she wakened up bright and clear—or so I thought at first—and, my dears, so I think now.

2. Extremely cold.
3. Child. "Maud": shawl of gray plaid used by shepherds in the region.

She said, that she had fancied that she should like to go to Dorothy, for that both the old ladies were asleep, and it was very dull in the drawing-room; and that, as she was going through the west lobby, she saw the snow through the high window falling—falling—soft and steady; but she wanted to see it lying pretty and white on the ground; so she made her way into the great hall; and then, going to the window, she saw it bright and soft upon the drive; but while she stood there, she saw a little girl, not so old as she was, "but so pretty," said my darling, "and this little girl beckoned to me to come out; and oh, she was so pretty and so sweet, I could not choose but go." And then this other little girl had taken her by the hand, and side by side the two had gone round the east corner.

"Now you are a naughty little girl, and telling stories," said I. "What would your good mamma, that is in heaven, and never told a story in her life, say to her little Rosamond, if she heard her—and I dare say she does—telling stories!"

"Indeed, Hester," sobbed out my child; "I'm telling you true. Indeed I am."

"Don't tell me!" said I, very stern. "I tracked you by your foot-marks through the snow; there were only yours to be seen: and if you had had a little girl to go hand-in-hand with you up the hill, don't you think the foot-prints would have gone along with yours?"

"I can't help it, dear, dear Hester," said she, crying, "if they did not; I never looked at her feet, but she held my hand fast and tight in her little one, and it was very, very cold. She took me up the Fell-path, up to the holly trees; and there I saw a lady weeping and crying; but when she saw me, she hushed her weeping, and smiled very proud and grand, and took me on her knees, and began to lull me to sleep; and that's all, Hester—but that is true; and my dear mamma knows it is," said she, crying. So I thought the child was in a fever, and pretended to believe her, as she went over her story—over and over again, and always the same. At last Dorothy knocked at the door with Miss Rosamond's breakfast; and she told me the old ladies were down in the eating-parlour, and that they wanted to speak to me. They had both been into the night-nursery the evening before, but it was after Miss Rosamond was asleep; so they had only looked at her—not asked me any questions.

"I shall catch it," thought I to myself, as I went along the north gallery. "And yet," I thought, taking courage, "it was in their charge I left her; and it's they that's to blame for letting her steal away unknown and unwatched." So I went in boldly, and told my story. I told it all to Miss Furnivall, shouting it close to her ear; but when I came to the mention of the other little girl out in the snow, coaxing and tempting her out, and willing her up to the grand and beautiful lady by the Holly-tree, she threw her arms up—her old and withered arms—and cried aloud, "Oh! Heaven, forgive! Have mercy!"

Mrs. Stark took hold of her; roughly enough, I thought; but she was past Mrs. Stark's management, and spoke to me, in a kind of wild warning and authority.

"Hester! keep her from that child! It will lure her to her death! That evil child! Tell her it is a wicked, naughty child." Then, Mrs. Stark hurried me out of the room; where, indeed, I was glad enough to go; but Miss Furnivall kept shrieking out, "Oh! have mercy! Wilt Thou never forgive! It is many a long year ago——"

I was very uneasy in my mind after that. I durst never leave Miss Rosamond, night or day, for fear lest she might slip off again, after some fancy or

other; and all the more, because I thought I could make out that Miss Furnivall was crazy, from their odd ways about her; and I was afraid lest something
of the same kind (which might be in the family, you know) hung over my
darling. And the great frost never ceased all this time; and, whenever it was
a more stormy night than usual, between the gusts, and through the wind,
we heard the old lord playing on the great organ. But, old lord, or not, wherever Miss Rosamond went, there I followed; for my love for her, pretty helpless
orphan, was stronger than my fear for the grand and terrible sound. Besides,
it rested with me to keep her cheerful and merry, as beseemed her age. So we
played together, and wandered together, here and there, and everywhere; for
I never dared to lose sight of her again in that large and rambling house. And
so it happened, that one afternoon, not long before Christmas day, we were
playing together on the billiard-table in the great hall (not that we knew the
right way of playing, but she liked to roll the smooth ivory balls with her
pretty hands, and I liked to do whatever she did); and, by-and-bye, without
our noticing it, it grew dusk indoors, though it was still light in the open air,
and I was thinking of taking her back into the nursery, when, all of a sudden,
she cried out:

"Look, Hester! look! there is my poor little girl out in the snow!"

I turned towards the long narrow windows, and there, sure enough, I saw
a little girl, less than my Miss Rosamond—dressed all unfit to be out-of-doors
such a bitter night—crying, and beating against the window-panes, as if, she
wanted to be let in. She seemed to sob and wail, till Miss Rosamond could
bear it no longer, and was flying to the door to open it, when, all of a sudden,
and close upon us, the great organ pealed out so loud and thundering, it
fairly made me tremble; and all the more, when I remembered me that, even
in the stillness of that dead-cold weather, I had heard no sound of little
battering hands upon the window-glass, although the Phantom Child had
seemed to put forth all its force; and, although I had seen it wail and cry, no
faintest touch of sound had fallen upon my ears. Whether I remembered all
this at the very moment, I do not know; the great organ sound had so stunned
me into terror; but this I know, I caught up Miss Rosamond before she got
the hall-door opened, and clutched her, and carried her away, kicking and
screaming, into the large bright kitchen, where Dorothy and Agnes were busy
with their mince-pies.

"What is the matter with my sweet one?" cried Dorothy, as I bore in Miss
Rosamond, who was sobbing as if her heart would break.

"She won't let me open the door for my little girl to come in; and she'll die
if she is out on the Fells all night. Cruel, naughty Hester," she said, slapping
me; but she might have struck harder, for I had seen a look of ghastly terror
on Dorothy's face, which made my very blood run cold.

"Shut the back kitchen door fast, and bolt it well," said she to Agnes. She
said no more; she gave me raisins and almonds to quiet Miss Rosamond: but
she sobbed about the little girl in the snow, and would not touch any of the
good things. I was thankful when she cried herself to sleep in bed. Then I
stole down to the kitchen, and told Dorothy I had made up my mind. I would
carry my darling back to my father's house in Applethwaite; where, if we lived
humbly, we lived at peace. I said I had been frightened enough with the old
lord's organ-playing; but now, that I had seen for myself this little moaning
child, all decked out as no child in the neighborhood could be, beating and
battering to get in, yet always without any sound or noise—with the dark

wound on its right shoulder; and that Miss Rosamond had known it again for the phantom that had nearly lured her to her death (which Dorothy knew was true); I would stand it no longer.

I saw Dorothy change color once or twice. When I had done, she told me she did not think I could take Miss Rosamond with me, for that she was my lord's ward, and I had no right over her; and she asked me, would I leave the child that I was so fond of, just for sounds and sights that could do me no harm; and that they had all had to get used to in their turns? I was all in a hot, trembling passion; and I said it was very well for her to talk, that knew what these sights and noises betokened, and that had, perhaps, had something to do with the Spectre-child while it was alive. And I taunted her so, that she told me all she knew, at last; and then I wished I had never been told, for it only made me more afraid than ever.

She said she had heard the tale from old neighbors, that were alive when she was first married; when folks used to come to the hall sometimes, before it had got such a bad name on the country side: it might not be true, or it might, what she had been told.

The old lord was Miss Furnivall's father—Miss Grace, as Dorothy called her, for Miss Maude was the elder, and Miss Furnivall by rights. The old lord was eaten up with pride. Such a proud man was never seen or heard of; and his daughters were like him. No one was good enough to wed them, although they had choice enough; for they were the great beauties of their day, as I had seen by their portraits, where they hung in the state drawing-room. But, as the old saying is, "Pride will have a fall;" and these two haughty beauties fell in love with the same man, and he no better than a foreign musician, whom their father had down from London to play music with him at the Manor House. For, above all things, next to his pride, the old lord loved music. He could play on nearly every instrument that ever was heard of; and it was a strange thing it did not soften him; but he was a fierce dour old man, and had broken his poor wife's heart with his cruelty, they said. He was mad after music, and would pay any money for it. So he got this foreigner to come; who made such beautiful music, that they said the very birds on the trees stopped their singing to listen. And, by degrees, this foreign gentleman got such a hold over the old lord, that nothing would serve him but that he must come every year; and it was he that had the great organ brought from Holland and built up in the hall, where it stood now. He taught the old lord to play on it; but many and many a time, when Lord Furnivall was thinking of nothing but his fine organ, and his finer music, the dark foreigner was walking abroad in the woods with one of the young ladies; now Miss Maude, and then Miss Grace.

Miss Maude won the day and carried off the prize, such as it was; and he and she were married, all unknown to any one; and before he made his next yearly visit, she had been confined of[4] a little girl at a farm-house on the Moors, while her father and Miss Grace thought she was away at Doncaster Races. But though she was a wife and a mother, she was not a bit softened, but as haughty and as passionate as ever; and perhaps more so, for she was jealous of Miss Grace, to whom her foreign husband paid a deal of court—by way of blinding her—as he told his wife. But Miss Grace triumphed over Miss Maude, and Miss Maude grew fiercer and fiercer, both with her husband and

4. Given birth to.

with her sister; and the former—who could easily shake off what was disagreeable, and hide himself in foreign countries—went away a month before his usual time that summer, and half threatened that he would never come back again. Meanwhile, the little girl was left at the farm-house, and her mother used to have her horse saddled and gallop wildly over the hills to see her once every week, at the very least—for where she loved, she loved; and where she hated, she hated. And the old lord went on playing—playing on his organ; and the servants thought the sweet music he made had soothed down his awful temper, of which (Dorothy said) some terrible tales could be told. He grew infirm too, and had to walk with a crutch; and his son—that was the present Lord Furnivall's father—was with the army in America, and the other son at sea; so Miss Maude had it pretty much her own way, and she and Miss Grace grew colder and bitterer to each other every day; till at last they hardly ever spoke, except when the old lord was by. The foreign musician came again the next summer, but it was for the last time; for they led him such a life with their jealousy and their passions, that he grew weary, and went away, and never was heard of again. And Miss Maude, who had always meant to have her marriage acknowledged when her father should be dead, was left now a deserted wife—whom nobody knew to have been married—with a child that she dared not own, although she loved it to distraction; living with a father whom she feared, and a sister whom she hated. When the next summer passed over and the dark foreigner never came, both Miss Maude and Miss Grace grew gloomy and sad; they had a haggard look about them, though they looked handsome as ever. But by and by Miss Maude brightened; for her father grew more and more infirm, and more than ever carried away by his music; and she and Miss Grace lived almost entirely apart, having separate rooms, the one on the west side—Miss Maude on the east— those very rooms which were now shut up. So she thought she might have her little girl with her, and no one need ever know except those who dared not speak about it, and were bound to believe that it was, as she said, a cottager's child she had taken a fancy to. All this, Dorothy said, was pretty well known; but what came afterwards no one knew, except Miss Grace, and Mrs. Stark, who was even then her maid, and much more of a friend to her than ever her sister had been. But the servants supposed, from words that were dropped, that Miss Maude had triumphed over Miss Grace, and told her that all the time the dark foreigner had been mocking her with pretended love—he was her own husband; the colour left Miss Grace's cheek and lips that very day for ever, and she was heard to say many a time that sooner or later she would have her revenge; and Mrs. Stark was for ever spying about the east rooms.

One fearful night, just after the New Year had come in, when the snow was lying thick and deep, and the flakes were still falling—fast enough to blind any one who might be out and abroad—there was a great and violent noise heard, and the old lord's voice above all, cursing and swearing awfully,—and the cries of a little child,—and the proud defiance of a fierce woman,—and the sound of a blow,—and a dead stillness,—and moans and wailings dying away on the hill-side! Then the old lord summoned all his servants, and told them, with terrible oaths, and words more terrible, that his daughter had disgraced herself, and that he had turned her out of doors,—her, and her child,—and that if ever they gave her help,—or food—or shelter,—he prayed that they might never enter Heaven. And, all the while, Miss Grace stood by him, white and still as any stone; and when he had ended she heaved a great sigh, as much as to say her work was done, and her end was accomplished. But the old lord never touched his organ again, and died within the year; and no wonder! for, on the morrow of that wild and fearful night, the shepherds, coming down the Fell side, found Miss Maude sitting, all crazy and smiling, under the holly-trees, nursing a dead child,—with a terrible mark on its right shoulder. "But that was not what killed it," said Dorothy; "it was the frost and the cold—every wild creature was in its hole, and every beast in its fold,— while the child and its mother were turned out to wander on the Fells! And now you know all! and I wonder if you are less frightened now?"

I was more frightened than ever; but I said I was not. I wished Miss Rosamond and myself well out of that dreadful house for ever; but I would not leave her, and I dared not take her away. But oh! how I watched her, and guarded her! We bolted the doors, and shut the window-shutters fast, an hour or more before dark, rather than leave them open five minutes too late. But my little lady still heard the weird child crying and mourning; and not all we could do or say, could keep her from wanting to go to her, and let her in from the cruel wind and the snow. All this time, I kept away from Miss Furnivall and Mrs. Stark, as much as ever I could; for I feared them—I knew no good could be about them, with their grey hard faces, and their dreamy eyes, looking back into the ghastly years that were gone. But, even in my fear, I had a kind of pity—for Miss Furnivall, at least. Those gone down to the pit[5] can hardly have a more hopeless look than that which was ever on her face. At last I even got so sorry for her—who never said a word but what was quite forced from her—that I prayed for her; and I taught Miss Rosamond to pray for one who had done a deadly sin; but often when she came to those words, she would listen, and start up from her knees, and say, "I hear my little girl plaining[6] and crying very sad—Oh! let her in, or she will die!"

One night—just after New Year's Day had come at last, and the long winter had taken a turn as I hoped—I heard the west drawing-room bell ring three times, which was the signal for me. I would not leave Miss Rosamond alone, for all she was asleep—for the old lord had been playing wilder than ever—and I feared lest my darling should waken to hear the spectre child; see her I knew she could not, I had fastened the windows too well for that. So, I took her out of her bed and wrapped her up in such outer clothes as were most handy, and carried her down to the drawing-room, where the old ladies sat at their tapestry work as usual. They looked up when I came in, and Mrs. Stark asked, quite astounded, "Why did I bring Miss Rosamond there, out of her warm bed?" I had begun to whisper, "Because I was afraid of her being tempted out while I was away, by the wild child in the snow," when she stopped me short (with a glance at Miss Furnivall) and said Miss Furnivall wanted me to undo some work she had done wrong, and which neither of them could see to unpick. So, I laid my pretty dear on the sofa, and sat down on a stool by them, and hardened my heart against them as I heard the wind rising and howling.

Miss Rosamond slept on sound, for all the wind blew so; and Miss Furnivall said never a word, nor looked round when the gusts shook the windows. All at once she started up to her full height, and put up one hand as if to bid us listen.

5. Hell. 6. Lamenting.

"I hear voices!" said she. "I hear terrible screams—I hear my father's voice!"

Just at that moment, my darling wakened with a sudden start: "My little girl is crying, oh, how she is crying!" and she tried to get up and go to her, but she got her feet entangled in the blanket, and I caught her up; for my flesh had begun to creep at these noises, which they heard while we could catch no sound. In a minute or two the noises came, and gathered fast, and filled our ears; we, too, heard voices and screams, and no longer heard the winter's wind that raged abroad. Mrs. Stark looked at me, and I at her, but we dared not speak. Suddenly Miss Furnivall went towards the door, out into the ante-room, through the west lobby, and opened the door into the great hall. Mrs. Stark followed, and I durst not be left, though my heart almost stopped beating for fear. I wrapped my darling tight in my arms, and went out with them. In the hall the screams were louder than ever; they sounded to come from the east wing—nearer and nearer—close on the other side of the locked-up doors—close behind them. Then I noticed that the great bronze chandelier seemed all alight, though the hall was dim, and that a fire was blazing in the vast hearth-place, though it gave no heat; and I shuddered up with terror, and folded my darling closer to me. But as I did so, the east door shook, and she, suddenly struggling to get free from me, cried, "Hester! I must go! My little girl is there; I hear her; she is coming! Hester, I must go!"

I held her tight with all my strength; with a set will, I held her. If I had died, my hands would have grasped her still; I was so resolved in my mind. Miss Furnivall stood listening, and paid no regard to my darling, who had got down to the ground, and whom I, upon my knees now, was holding with both my arms clasped round her neck; she still striving and crying to get free.

All at once, the east door gave way with a thundering crash, as if torn open in a violent passion, and there came into that broad and mysterious light, the figure of a tall old man, with grey hair and gleaming eyes. He drove before him, with many a relentless gesture of abhorrence, a stern and beautiful woman, with a little child clinging to her dress.

"Oh Hester! Hester!" cried Miss Rosamond. "It's the lady! the lady below the holly-trees; and my little girl is with her. Hester! Hester! let me go to her; they are drawing me to them. I feel them—I feel them. I must go!"

Again she was almost convulsed by her efforts to get away; but I held her tighter and tighter; till I feared I should do her a hurt; but rather that than let her go towards those terrible phantoms. They passed along towards the great hall-door, where the winds howled and ravened for their prey; but before they reached that, the lady turned; and I could see that she defied the old man with a fierce and proud defiance; but then she quailed—and then she threw up her arms wildly and piteously to save her child—her little child—from a blow from his uplifted crutch.

And Miss Rosamond was torn as by a power stronger than mine, and writhed in my arms, and sobbed (for by this time the poor darling was growing faint).

"They want me to go with them on to the Fells—they are drawing me to them. Oh, my little girl! I would come, but cruel, wicked Hester holds me very tight." But when she saw the uplifted crutch she swooned away, and I thanked God for it. Just at this moment—when the tall old man, his hair streaming as in the blast of a furnace, was going to strike the little shrinking child—Miss Furnivall, the old woman by my side, cried out, "Oh, father!

father! spare the little innocent child!" But just then I saw—we all saw—another phantom shape itself, and grow clear out of the blue and misty light that filled the hall; we had not seen her till now, for it was another lady who stood by the old man, with a look of relentless hate and triumphant scorn. That figure was very beautiful to look upon, with a soft white hat drawn down over the proud brows, and a red and curling lip. It was dressed in an open robe of blue satin. I had seen that figure before. It was the likeness of Miss Furnivall in her youth; and the terrible phantoms moved on, regardless of old Miss Furnivall's wild entreaty,—and the uplifted crutch fell on the right shoulder of the little child, and the younger sister looked on, stony and deadly serene. But at that moment, the dim lights, and the fire that gave no heat, went out of themselves, and Miss Furnivall lay at our feet stricken down by the palsy—death-stricken.

Yes! she was carried to her bed that night never to rise again. She lay with her face to the wall, muttering low but muttering alway: "Alas! alas! what is done in youth can never be undone in age! What is done in youth can never be undone in age!"

1852

ROBERT BROWNING
1812–1889

During the years of his marriage, Robert Browning was sometimes referred to as "Mrs. Browning's husband." Elizabeth Barrett was at that time a famous poet, whereas her husband was a relatively unknown experimenter whose poems were greeted with misunderstanding or indifference. Not until the 1860s did he at last gain a public and become recognized as the rival or equal of Alfred, Lord Tennyson. In the twentieth century his reputation persisted but in an unusual way: his poetry was admired by two groups of readers widely different in tastes. To one group, among whom were the Browning societies that flourished in England and America, Browning was a wise philosopher and religious teacher who resolved the doubts that troubled Matthew Arnold and Tennyson. The second group of readers enjoyed Browning less for his attempt to solve problems of religious doubt than for his attempt to solve the problems of how poetry should be written. Poets such as Ezra Pound and Robert Lowell argued that more than any other nineteenth-century poet, it was Browning who energetically hacked through a trail that subsequently became the main road of twentieth-century poetry. In *Poetry and the Age* (1953) Randall Jarrell remarked that "the dramatic monologue, which once had depended for its effect upon being a departure from the norm of poetry, now became in one form or another the norm."

The dramatic monologue, as Browning uses it, separates the speaker from the poet in such a way that the reader must work through the words of the speaker to discover the meaning of the poet. For example, in the well-known early monologue "My Last Duchess" (1842), we listen to the duke as he speaks of his dead wife. From his one-sided conversation we piece together the situation, both past and present, and we infer what sort of woman the duchess really was and what sort of man the duke is.

Ultimately, we may also infer what the poet himself thinks of the speaker he has created. In this instance it is fairly easy to reach such a judgment; the pleasure of the poem results from our reconstruction of a story quite different from the one the duke thinks he is telling. Many of Browning's poems are far less stable, and it is difficult to discern the relationship of the poet to his speaker. In "'Childe Roland to the Dark Tower Came'" (1855), for example, is the speaker describing a phantasmagoric landscape of his own paranoid imagining, or is the poem a fable of courage and defiance in a modern wasteland?

In addition to his experiments with the dramatic monologue, Browning also experimented with language and syntax. The grotesque rhymes and jaw-breaking diction that he often employs have been repugnant to some critics; George Santayana, for instance, dismissed him as a clumsy barbarian. But to those who appreciate Browning, the incongruities of language are a humorous and appropriate counterpart to an imperfect world. Ezra Pound's tribute to "Old Hippety-Hop o' the accents," as he addresses Browning, is both affectionate and memorable:

> Heart that was big as the bowels of Vesuvius
> Words that were winged as her sparks in eruption,
> Eagled and thundered as Jupiter Pluvius
> Sound in your wind past all signs o' corruption.

Robert Browning was born in Camberwell, a London suburb. His father, a bank clerk, was a learned man with an extensive library. His mother was a kindly, religious-minded woman, interested in music, whose love for her brilliant son was warmly reciprocated. Until the time of his marriage, at the age of thirty-four, Browning was rarely absent from his parents' home. He attended a boarding school near Camberwell, traveled a little (to Russia and Italy), and was a student at the University of London for a short period, but he preferred to pursue his education at home, where he was tutored in foreign languages, music, boxing, and horsemanship and where he read omnivorously. From this unusual education he acquired a store of knowledge on which to draw for the background of his poems.

The "obscurity" of which his contemporaries complained in his earlier poetry may be partly accounted for by the circumstances of Browning's education, but it also reflects his anxious desire to avoid exposing himself too explicitly before his readers. His first poem, *Pauline* (1833), published when he was twenty-one, had been modeled on the example of Percy Bysshe Shelley, the most personal of poets. When an otherwise admiring review by John Stuart Mill noted that the young author was afflicted with an "intense and morbid self-consciousness," Browning was overwhelmed with embarrassment. He resolved to avoid confessional writings thereafter.

One way of reducing the personal element in his poetry was to write plays instead of soul-searching narratives or lyrics. In 1836, encouraged by the actor W. C. Macready, Browning began work on his first play, *Strafford*, a historical tragedy that lasted only four nights when it was produced in London in 1837. For ten years the young writer struggled to write for the theater, but all his stage productions remained failures. Nevertheless, writing dialogue for actors led him to explore another form more congenial to his genius—the dramatic monologue, a form that enabled him through imaginary speakers to avoid explicit autobiography. His first collection of such monologues, *Dramatic Lyrics*, appeared in 1842; but it received no more critical enthusiasm than did his plays.

Browning's resolution to avoid the subjective manner of Shelley did not preclude his being influenced by the earlier poet in other ways. At fourteen, when he first discovered Shelley's works, he became an atheist and liberal. Although he grew away from the atheism, after a struggle, and also the extreme phases of his liberalism, he retained from Shelley's influence something permanent and more difficult to define: an ardent dedication to ideals (often undefined ideals) and an energetic striving toward goals (often undefined goals).

Browning's ardent romanticism also found expression in his love affair with Elizabeth Barrett, which had the dramatic ingredients of Browning's own favorite story of

St. George rescuing the maiden from the dragon. Few would have forecast the outcome when Browning met Elizabeth Barrett in 1845. She was six years older than he was, and a semi-invalid, jealously guarded by her possessively tyrannical father. But love, as the poet was to say later, is best; and love swept aside all obstacles. After their elopement to Italy, the former semi-invalid was soon enjoying far better health and a full life. The husband likewise seemed to thrive during the years of this remarkable marriage. His most memorable volume of poems, *Men and Women* (1855), reflects his enjoyment of Italy: its picturesque landscapes and lively street scenes as well as its monuments from the past—its Renaissance past in particular.

The happy fifteen-year sojourn in Italy ended in 1861 with Elizabeth's death. The widower returned to London with his son. During the twenty-eight years remaining to him, he continued to produce large quantities of verse. *Dramatis Personae* (1864) is a volume containing some of his most intriguing monologues, such as "Caliban upon Setebos." And in 1868 he published his longest and most significant single poem, *The Ring and the Book*, which was inspired by his discovery of an old book of legal records concerning a murder trial in seventeenth-century Rome. His poem tells the story of a brutally sadistic husband, Count Guido Franceschini. The middle-aged Guido grows dissatisfied with his young wife, Pompilia, and accuses her of having adulterous relations with a handsome priest who, like St. George, had tried to rescue her from the appalling situation in which her husband confined her. Eventually Guido stabs his wife to death and is himself executed. In a series of twelve books, Browning retells this tale of violence, presenting it from the contrasting points of view of participants and spectators. Because of its vast scale, *The Ring and the Book* is like a Victorian novel, but in its experiments with multiple points of view it anticipates later works such as Joseph Conrad's novel *Lord Jim* (1900) and Akira Kurosawa's film *Rashōmon* (1950).

After *The Ring and the Book* several more volumes appeared. In general, Browning's writings during the last two decades of his life exhibit a certain mechanical repetition of mannerism and an excess of argumentation—tendencies into which he may have been led by the unqualified enthusiasm of his admirers, for it was during this period that he gained his great following. When he died, in 1889, he was buried in Westminster Abbey.

During the London years Browning became extremely fond of social life. He dined at the homes of friends and at clubs, where he enjoyed port wine and conversation. He would talk loudly and emphatically about many topics—except his own poetry, about which he was usually reticent. Despite his bursts of outspokenness, Browning's character seemed, in Thomas Hardy's words, "*the* literary puzzle of the nineteenth century." Like William Butler Yeats, he was a poet preoccupied with masks. On the occasion of his burial, his friend Henry James reflected that many oddities and many great writers have been buried in Westminster Abbey, "but none of the odd ones have been so great and none of the great ones been so odd."

Just as Browning's character is hard to identify so also are his poems difficult to relate to the age in which they were written. Bishops and painters of the Renaissance, an inmate of a Spanish monastery, Shakespeare's "man-monster" on a distant isle—as we explore this gallery of talking portraits we seem to be in remote times or places, far from the world of steam engines and disputes about human beings' descent from the ape. Yet our first impression is misleading. Many of these portraits explore problems that confronted Browning's contemporaries, especially problems of faith and doubt, of good and evil, and of the function of the artist in modern life. "Caliban upon Setebos," for example, is a highly topical critique of Darwinism and of natural (as opposed to supernatural) religions. Browning's own attitude toward these topics is partially concealed because of his use of speakers and of settings from earlier ages, yet we do encounter certain recurrent religious assumptions that we can safely assign to the poet himself. The most recurrent is that God has created an imperfect world as a kind of testing ground, a "vale of soul-making," as John Keats had said. It followed, for Browning's purposes, that the human soul must be immortal and that heaven itself be perfect. Armed with such a faith, Browning sometimes gives the impression that he was himself untroubled by the doubts that gnawed at the hearts of

Tennyson, Arnold, and other figures in the mid-Victorian period. Yet Browning's apparent optimism is consistently being tested by his bringing to light the evils of human nature. His gallery of villains—murderers, sadistic husbands, mean and petty manipulators—is an extraordinary one. Few writers, in fact, seem to have been more aware of the existence of evil.

A second aspect of Browning's poetry that separates it from the Victorian age is its style. The most representative Victorian poets such as Tennyson and Dante Gabriel Rossetti write in the manner of Keats, John Milton, and Edmund Spenser, and of classical poets such as Virgil. Theirs is the central stylistic tradition in English poetry, one that favors smoothly polished texture, elevated diction and subjects, and pleasing liquidity of sound. Browning draws from a different tradition, more colloquial and discordant, a tradition that includes the poetry of John Donne, the soliloquies of William Shakespeare, and certain features of the narrative style of Geoffrey Chaucer. Of most significance are Browning's affinities with Donne. Both poets sacrifice, on occasion, the pleasures of harmony and of a consistent elevation of tone by using a harshly discordant style and unexpected juxtapositions that startle us into an awareness of a world of everyday realities and trivialities. Readers who dislike this kind of poetry in Browning or in Donne argue that it suffers from prosiness. Oscar Wilde once described the novelist George Meredith as "a prose Browning." And so, he added, was Browning. Wilde's joke may help us to understand Browning's relationship to the writers of his era. For if Browning seems out of step with other Victorian poets, he is by no means out of step with his contemporaries in prose. The grotesque, which plays such a prominent role in the style and subject matter of Carlyle and Dickens and in the aesthetic theories of John Ruskin, is equally prominent in Browning's verse:

> Fee, faw, fum! bubble and squeak!
> Blessedest Thursday's the fat of the week.
> Rumble and tumble, sleek and rough,
> Stinking and savory, smug and gruff.

Like Thomas Carlyle's *Sartor Resartus* (1833–34), these lines from "Holy-Cross Day" (1855) present a situation of grave seriousness with noisy jocularity. It was fitting that Browning and Carlyle remained good friends, even though the elder writer kept urging Browning to give up verse in favor of prose.

The link between Browning and the Victorian prose writers is not limited to style. With the later generation of Victorian novelists, George Eliot, George Meredith, and Henry James, Browning shares a central preoccupation. Like Eliot in particular, he was interested in exposing the devious ways in which our minds work and the complexity of our motives. "My stress lay on incidents in the development of a human soul," he wrote; "little else is worth study." His psychological insights can be readily detected in poems such as "The Bishop Orders His Tomb" (1845) and "Andrea del Sarto" (1855). Although these are spoken monologues, not inner monologues in the manner of James Joyce, the insight into the workings of the mind is similarly acute. As in reading Joyce, we must follow the rapid shifts of the speaker's mental processes as jumps are made from one cluster of associations to another. A further challenge for the reader of Browning is to identify what has been left out. As was remarked in a letter by the 1890s poet Ernest Dowson, Browning's "masterpieces in verse" demonstrate both "subtlety" and "the tact of omission." "My Last Duchess," he added, "is pure Henry James."

But Browning's role as a forerunner of twentieth-century literature should not blind us to his essential Victorianism. Energy is the most characteristic aspect of his writing and of the man (Ivan Turgenev compared Browning's handshake to an electric shock). Gerard Manley Hopkins described Browning as "a man bouncing up from table with his mouth full of bread and cheese and saying that he meant to stand no blasted nonsense." This buoyancy imparts a creative vitality to all of Browning's writings.

Porphyria's Lover[1]

The rain set early in tonight,
    The sullen wind was soon awake,
It tore the elm-tops down for spite,
    And did its worst to vex the lake:
5   I listened with heart fit to break.
When glided in Porphyria; straight
    She shut the cold out and the storm,
And kneeled and made the cheerless grate
    Blaze up, and all the cottage warm;
10   Which done, she rose, and from her form
Withdrew the dripping cloak and shawl,
    And laid her soiled gloves by, untied
Her hat and let the damp hair fall,
    And, last, she sat down by my side
15   And called me. When no voice replied,
She put my arm about her waist,
    And made her smooth white shoulder bare,
And all her yellow hair displaced,
    And, stooping, made my cheek lie there,
20   And spread, o'er all, her yellow hair,
Murmuring how she loved me—she
    Too weak, for all her heart's endeavor,
To set its struggling passion free
    From pride, and vainer ties dissever,
25   And give herself to me forever.
But passion sometimes would prevail,
    Nor could tonight's gay feast restrain
A sudden thought of one so pale
    For love of her, and all in vain:
30   So, she was come through wind and rain.
Be sure I looked up at her eyes
    Happy and proud; at last I knew
Porphyria worshiped me: surprise
    Made my heart swell, and still it grew
35   While I debated what to do.
That moment she was mine, mine, fair,
    Perfectly pure and good: I found
A thing to do, and all her hair
    In one long yellow string I wound
40   Three times her little throat around,
And strangled her. No pain felt she;
    I am quite sure she felt no pain.
As a shut bud that holds a bee,
    I warily oped her lids: again
45   Laughed the blue eyes without a stain.
And I untightened next the tress
    About her neck; her cheek once more

1. One of a pair of monologues originally published as "Madhouse Cells," a title that emphasized the speaker's abnormal state of mind.

Blushed bright beneath my burning kiss:
  I propped her head up as before,
50   Only, this time my shoulder bore
Her head, which droops upon it still:
  The smiling rosy little head,
So glad it has its utmost will,
  That all it scorned at once is fled,
55   And I, its love, am gained instead!
Porphyria's love: she guessed not how
  Her darling one wish would be heard.
And thus we sit together now,
  And all night long we have not stirred,
60   And yet God has not said a word!

1834   1836, 1842

Soliloquy of the Spanish Cloister

1

Gr-r-r—there go, my heart's abhorrence!
  Water your damned flowerpots, do!
If hate killed men, Brother Lawrence,
  God's blood,[1] would not mine kill you!
5 What? your myrtle bush wants trimming?
  Oh, that rose has prior claims—
Needs its leaden vase filled brimming?
  Hell dry you up with its flames!

2

At the meal we sit together:
10   *Salve tibi!*[2] I must hear
Wise talk of the kind of weather,
  Sort of season, time of year:
Not a plenteous cork crop: scarcely
  Dare we hope oak-galls,[3] *I doubt:*
15 *What's the Latin name for "parsley"?*
  What's the Greek name for Swine's Snout?[4]

3

Whew! We'll have our platter burnished,
  Laid with care on our own shelf!
With a fire-new spoon we're furnished,
20   And a goblet for ourself,
Rinsed like something sacrificial

---

1. An oath (archaic).
2. Hail to thee! (Latin); i.e., "your health!" This and other speeches in italics in this stanza are the words of Brother Lawrence.
3. Abnormal outgrowths on oak trees, used for tanning.
4. Dandelion (19th-century use).

Ere 'tis fit to touch our chaps°   *jaws*
Marked with L. for our initial!
(He-he! There his lily snaps!)

4

25 *Saint*, forsooth! While brown Dolores
    Squats outside the Convent bank
With Sanchicha, telling stories,
    Steeping tresses in the tank,
Blue-black, lustrous, thick like horsehairs,
30   —Can't I see his dead eye glow,
Bright as 'twere a Barbary corsair's?[5]
    (That is, if he'd let it show!)

5

When he finishes refection,°   *dinner*
    Knife and fork he never lays
35 Cross-wise, to my recollection,
    As do I, in Jesu's praise.
I the Trinity illustrate,
    Drinking watered orange pulp—
In three sips the Arian[6] frustrate;
40   While he drains his at one gulp.

6

Oh, those melons? If he's able
    We're to have a feast! so nice!
One goes to the Abbot's table,
    All of us get each a slice.
45 How go on your flowers? None double?
    Not one fruit-sort can you spy?
Strange!—And I, too, at such trouble,
    Keep them close-nipped on the sly!

7

There's a great text in Galatians,[7]
50   Once you trip on it, entails
Twenty-nine distinct damnations,
    One sure, if another fails:
If I trip him just a-dying,
    Sure of heaven as sure can be,
55 Spin him round and send him flying
    Off to hell, a Manichee?[8]

5. Pirate of the Barbary Coast of northern Africa, renowned for fierceness and lechery.
6. Heretical follower of Arius (256–336 C.E.), who denied the doctrine of the Trinity.
7. The speaker hopes to obtain Lawrence's damnation by luring him into a heresy when he may prove unable to interpret "Galatians" in an unswervingly orthodox way. In Galatians 5.15–23 St. Paul specifies an assortment of "works of the flesh" that lead to damnation, which could make up a total of "twenty-nine" (line 51).
8. A heretic, a follower of Mani (3rd century), Persian religious leader.

8

Or, my scrofulous French novel
    On gray paper with blunt type!
Simply glance at it, you grovel
60   Hand and foot in Belial's° gripe: *the devil's*
If I double down its pages
    At the woeful sixteenth print,
When he gathers his greengages,
    Ope a sieve and slip it in't?

9

65 Or, there's Satan!—one might venture
    Pledge one's soul to him, yet leave
Such a flaw in the indenture
    As he'd miss till, past retrieve,
Blasted lay that rose-acacia[9]
70   We're so proud of! *Hy, Zy, Hine*[1]
'St, there's Vespers![2] *Plena gratiâ*
    Ave, Virgo![3] Gr-r-r—you swine!

ca. 1839   1842

My Last Duchess[1]

Ferrara

That's my last Duchess painted on the wall,
Looking as if she were alive. I call
That piece a wonder, now: Frà Pandolf's[2] hands
Worked busily a day, and there she stands.
5 Will't please you sit and look at her? I said
"Frà Pandolf" by design, for never read
Strangers like you that pictured countenance,
The depth and passion of its earnest glance,
But to myself they turned (since none puts by
10 The curtain I have drawn for you, but I)
And seemed as they would ask me, if they durst,
How such a glance came there; so, not the first
Are you to turn and ask thus. Sir, 'twas not
Her husband's presence only, called that spot

---

9. The speaker would pledge his own soul to Satan in return for blasting Lawrence and his "rose-acacia," but the pledge would be so cleverly worded that the speaker would not have to pay his debt to Satan. There would be an escape clause ("flaw in the indenture") for himself.
1. Perhaps the opening of a mysterious curse against Lawrence.
2. Evening prayers.
3. Full of grace, Hail, Virgin! (Latin). The speaker's twisted state of mind may be reflected in his mixed-up version of the prayer to Mary: "Ave, Maria, gratia plena."
1. The poem is based on incidents in the life of Alfonso II, Duke of Ferrara in Italy, whose first wife, Lucrezia, a young woman, died in 1561 after three years of marriage. Following her death, the duke negotiated through an agent to marry a niece of the Count of Tyrol. Browning represents the duke as addressing this agent.
2. Friar Pandolf, an imaginary painter.

15   Of joy into the Duchess' cheek: perhaps
     Frà Pandolf chanced to say "Her mantle laps
     Over my lady's wrist too much," or "Paint
     Must never hope to reproduce the faint
     Half-flush that dies along her throat": such stuff
20   Was courtesy, she thought, and cause enough
     For calling up that spot of joy. She had
     A heart—how shall I say?—too soon made glad,
     Too easily impressed; she liked whate'er
     She looked on, and her looks went everywhere.
25   Sir, 'twas all one! My favor at her breast,
     The dropping of the daylight in the West,
     The bough of cherries some officious fool
     Broke in the orchard for her, the white mule
     She rode with round the terrace—all and each
30   Would draw from her alike the approving speech,
     Or blush, at least. She thanked men—good! but thanked
     Somehow—I know not how—as if she ranked
     My gift of a nine-hundred-years-old name
     With anybody's gift. Who'd stoop to blame
35   This sort of trifling? Even had you skill
     In speech—(which I have not)—to make your will
     Quite clear to such an one, and say, "Just this
     Or that in you disgusts me; here you miss,
     Or there exceed the mark"—and if she let
40   Herself be lessoned so, nor plainly set
     Her wits to yours, forsooth, and made excuse
     —E'en then would be some stooping; and I choose
     Never to stoop. Oh sir, she smiled, no doubt,
     Whene'er I passed her; but who passed without
45   Much the same smile? This grew; I gave commands;
     Then all smiles stopped together. There she stands
     As if alive. Will 't please you rise? We'll meet
     The company below, then. I repeat,
     The Count your master's known munificence
50   Is ample warrant that no just pretense
     Of mine for dowry will be disallowed;
     Though his fair daughter's self, as I avowed
     At starting, is my object. Nay, we'll go
     Together down, sir. Notice Neptune, though,
55   Taming a sea horse, thought a rarity,
     Which Claus of Innsbruck[3] cast in bronze for me!

1842   1842

3. An unidentified or imaginary sculptor. The Count of Tyrol had his capital at Innsbruck.

The Bishop Orders His Tomb at
Saint Praxed's Church[1]

Rome, 15—

Vanity, saith the preacher, vanity![2]
Draw round my bed: is Anselm keeping back?
Nephews—sons mine . . . ah God, I know not! Well—
She, men would have to be your mother once,
5   Old Gandolf envied me, so fair she was!
What's done is done, and she is dead beside,
Dead long ago, and I am Bishop since,
And as she died so must we die ourselves,
And thence ye may perceive the world's a dream.
10   ife, how and what is it? As here I lie
In this state chamber, dying by degrees,
Hours and long hours in the dead night, I ask
"Do I live, am I dead?" Peace, peace seems all.
Saint Praxed's ever was the church for peace;
15   And so, about this tomb of mine. I fought
With tooth and nail to save my niche, ye know:
—Old Gandolf cozened° me, despite my care;   *cheated*
Shrewd was that snatch from out the corner south
He graced his carrion with,[3] God curse the same!
20   Yet still my niche is not so cramped but thence
One sees the pulpit o' the epistle side,[4]
And somewhat of the choir, those silent seats,
And up into the aery dome where live
The angels, and a sunbeam's sure to lurk:
25   And I shall fill my slab of basalt[5] there,
And 'neath my tabernacle[6] take my rest,
With those nine columns round me, two and two,
The odd one at my feet where Anselm stands:
Peach-blossom marble all, the rare, the ripe
30   As fresh-poured red wine of a mighty pulse.[7]

---

1. In "Fra Lippo Lippi" (p. 729), Browning represents the dawn of the Renaissance in Italy, with its fresh zest for human experiences in this world. In this monologue he portrays a later stage of the Renaissance when such worldliness, full-blown, had infected some of the leading clergy of Italy. Browning's portrait of the dying bishop is, however, not primarily a satire against corruption in the church. It is a brilliant exposition of the workings of a mind, a mind that has been conditioned by special historical circumstances. The Victorian historian of art John Ruskin said of this poem:

> I know of no other piece of modern English, prose or poetry, in which there is so much told, as in these lines, of the Renaissance spirit—its worldliness, inconsistency, pride, hypocrisy, ignorance of itself, love of art, of luxury, and of good Latin. It is nearly all that I have said of the central Renaissance in thirty pages of the *Stones of Venice*, put into as many lines, Browning's also being the antecedent work.

St. Praxed's Church was named in honor of St. Praxedes, a Roman virgin of the 2nd century who gave her riches to poor Christians. Both the bishop and his predecessor, Gandolf, are imaginary persons.
2. Cf. Ecclesiastes 1.2: "Vanity of vanities; all is vanity."
3. Bishop Gandolf shrewdly chose a prize spot in the southern corner of the church for his burial place. The tomb that the speaker is ordering will also be inside the church, as was common for important people in this era.
4. The Epistles of the New Testament are read from the right-hand side of the altar (as one faces it).
5. Dark-colored igneous rock.
6. Stone canopy or tentlike roof, presumably supported by the "nine columns" under which the sculptured effigy of the bishop would lie on the "slab of basalt."
7. A pulpy mash of fermented grapes from which a strong wine might be poured off.

—Old Gandolf with his paltry onion-stone,[8]
Put me where I may look at him! True peach,
Rosy and flawless: how I earned the prize!
Draw close: that conflagration of my church
35 —What then? So much was saved if aught were missed!
My sons, ye would not be my death? Go dig
The white-grape vineyard where the oil-press stood,
Drop water gently till the surface sink,
And if ye find . . . Ah God, I know not, I! . . .
40 Bedded in store of rotten fig leaves soft,
And corded up in a tight olive-frail,[9]
Some lump, ah God, of *lapis lazuli*,[1]
Big as a jew's head cut off at the nape,[2]
Blue as a vein o'er the Madonna's breast . . .
45 Sons, all have I bequeathed you, villas, all,
That brave Frascati[3] villa with its bath,
So, let the blue lump poise between my knees,
Like God the Father's globe on both his hands
Ye worship in the Jesu Church[4] so gay,
50 For Gandolf shall not choose but see and burst!
Swift as a weaver's shuttle fleet our years:[5]
Man goeth to the grave, and where is he?
Did I say basalt for my slab, sons? Black[6]—
'Twas ever antique-black I meant! How else
55 Shall ye contrast my frieze[7] to come beneath?
The bas-relief[8] in bronze ye promised me,
Those Pans and Nymphs ye wot° of, and perchance   *know*
Some tripod, thyrsus, with a vase or so,
The Saviour at his sermon on the mount,
60 Saint Praxed in a glory, and one Pan
Ready to twitch the Nymph's last garment off,
And Moses with the tables[9] . . . but I know
Ye mark° me not! What do they whisper thee,   *heed*
Child of my bowels, Anselm? Ah, ye hope
65 To revel down my villas while I gasp
Bricked o'er with beggar's moldy travertine°   *Italian limestone*
Which Gandolf from his tomb-top chuckles at!
Nay, boys, ye love me—all of jasper, then!
'Tis jasper ye stand pledged to, lest I grieve
70 My bath must needs be left behind, alas!
One block, pure green as a pistachio nut,

8. An inferior marble that peels in layers.
9. Basket for holding olives.
1. Valuable bright blue stone.
2. Perhaps a reference to the head of John the Baptist, cut off at Salomé's request (Matthew 14.6–11).
3. Suburb of Rome, used as a resort by wealthy Italians.
4. Il Gesù, a Jesuit church in Rome. In a chapel in this church the figure of an angel (rather than God) holds a huge lump of lapis lazuli in his hands.
5. Cf. Job 7.6: "My days are swifter than a weaver's shuttle."
6. I.e., black marble.

7. Continuous band of sculpture.
8. Sculpture in which the figures do not project far from the background surface.
9. The sculpture would consist of a mixture of pagan and Christian iconography. "Tripod": seat on which the Oracle of Delphi made prophecies. "Thyrsus": a staff twined with ivy that was carried, according to Greek mythology, by Dionysus, god of wine and fertility. "Glory": halo. "Tables": the stone tablets on which the Ten Commandments were written. Such intermingling of pagan and Christian traditions, characteristic of the Renaissance, had been attacked in 1841 in *Contrasts*, a book on architecture by A. W. Pugin, a Roman Catholic.

There's plenty jasper somewhere in the world—
And have I not Saint Praxed's ear to pray
Horses for ye, and brown Greek manuscripts,
75 And mistresses with great smooth marbly limbs?
—That's if ye carve my epitaph aright,
Choice Latin, picked phrase, Tully's[1] every word,
No gaudy ware like Gandolf's second line—
Tully, my masters? Ulpian[2] serves his need!
80 And then how I shall lie through centuries,
And hear the blessed mutter of the mass,
And see God made and eaten all day long,[3]
And feel the steady candle flame, and taste
Good strong thick stupefying incense-smoke!
85 For as I lie here, hours of the dead night,
Dying in state and by such slow degrees,
I fold my arms as if they clasped a crook,°   *bishop's staff*
And stretch my feet forth straight as stone can point,
And let the bedclothes, for a mortcloth,[4] drop
90 Into great laps and folds of sculptor's-work:
And as yon tapers dwindle, and strange thoughts
Grow, with a certain humming in my ears,
About the life before I lived this life,
And this life too, popes, cardinals, and priests,
95 Saint Praxed at his sermon on the mount,[5]
Your tall pale mother with her talking eyes,
And new-found agate urns as fresh as day,
And marble's language, Latin pure, discreet
—Aha, ELUCESCEBAT[6] quoth our friend?
100 No Tully, said I, Ulpian at the best!
Evil and brief hath been my pilgrimage.[7]
All *lapis*, all, sons! Else I give the Pope
My villas! Will ye ever eat my heart?
Ever your eyes were as a lizard's quick,
105 They glitter like your mother's for my soul,
Or ye would heighten my impoverished frieze,
Piece out its starved design, and fill my vase
With grapes, and add a vizor and a Term,[8]
And to the tripod ye would tie a lynx[9]
110 That in his struggle throws the thyrsus down,
To comfort me on my entablature[1]
Whereon I am to lie till I must ask
"Do I live, am I dead?" There, leave me, there!
For ye have stabbed me with ingratitude

1. I.e., Marcus Tullius Cicero (106–43 B.C.E.), orator and statesman who was one of the great stylists of classical Latin prose.
2. Late Latin author of legal commentaries (d. 228 C.E.); not a model of good style.
3. Reference to the doctrine of transubstantiation.
4. Rich cloth spread over a dead body or coffin.
5. The bishop is confusing St. Praxed (a woman) with Jesus—an indication that his mind is wandering.
6. He was illustrious (Latin); word from Gandolf's epitaph. The bishop considers the form of

the verb to be in "gaudy" bad taste (line 78). If the epitaph had been copied from Cicero instead of from Ulpian, the word would have been *elucebat*.
7. Cf. Genesis 47.9: "few and evil have the days of the years of my life been."
8. Statue of Terminus, the Roman god of boundaries, usually represented without arms. "Vizor": part of a helmet, often represented in sculpture.
9. An animal that traditionally accompanied Bacchus.
1. Horizontal platform supporting a statue or effigy.

115 To death—ye wish it—God, ye wish it! Stone—
   Gritstone,[2] a-crumble! Clammy squares which sweat
   As if the corpse they keep were oozing through—
   And no more *lapis* to delight the world!
   Well go! I bless ye. Fewer tapers there,
120 But in a row: and, going, turn your backs
   —Aye, like departing altar-ministrants,
   And leave me in my church, the church for peace,
   That I may watch at leisure if he leers—
   Old Gandolf, at me, from his onion-stone,
125 As still he envied me, so fair she was!

1844   1845

Love among the Ruins

1

Where the quiet-colored end of evening smiles,
         Miles and miles
On the solitary pastures where our sheep
         Half-asleep
5   Tinkle homeward through the twilight, stray or stop
         As they crop—
Was the site once of a city great and gay
         (So they say),
Of our country's very capital, its prince
10   Ages since
Held his court in, gathered councils, wielding far
         Peace or war.

2

Now—the country does not even boast a tree,
         As you see,
15   To distinguish slopes of verdure, certain rills
         From the hills
Intersect and give a name to (else they run
         Into one),
Where the domed and daring palace shot its spires
20   Up like fires
O'er the hundred-gated circuit of a wall
         Bounding all,
Made of marble, men might march on nor be pressed,
         Twelve abreast.

3

25   And such plenty and perfection, see, of grass
         Never was!

2. Coarse sandstone.

Such a carpet as, this summertime, o'erspreads
    And embeds
Every vestige of the city, guessed alone,
30   Stock or stone—
Where a multitude of men breathed joy and woe
    Long ago;
Lust of glory pricked their hearts up, dread of shame
    Struck them tame;
35 And that glory and that shame alike, the gold
    Bought and sold.

4

Now—the single little turret that remains
    On the plains,
By the caper overrooted, by the gourd
40   Overscored,
While the patching houseleek's[1] head of blossom winks
    Through the chinks—
Marks the basement whence a tower in ancient time
    Sprang sublime,
45 And a burning ring, all round, the chariots traced
    As they raced,
And the monarch and his minions and his dames
    Viewed the games.

5

And I know, while thus the quiet-colored eve
50   Smiles to leave
To their folding, all our many-tinkling fleece
    In such peace,
And the slopes and rills in undistinguished gray
    Melt away—
55 That a girl with eager eyes and yellow hair
    Waits me there
In the turret whence the charioteers caught soul
    For the goal,
When the king looked, where she looks now, breathless, dumb
60   Till I come.

6

But he looked upon the city, every side,
    Far and wide,
All the mountains topped with temples, all the glades'
    Colonnades,
65 All the causeys,[2] bridges, aqueducts—and then,
    All the men!
When I do come, she will speak not, she will stand,
    Either hand

---

1. Common European plant with petals clustered in the shape of rosettes.   2. Causeways or roads raised above low ground.

On my shoulder, give her eyes the first embrace
      Of my face,
Ere we rush, ere we extinguish sight and speech
      Each on each.

70

7

In one year they sent a million fighters forth
      South and north,
And they built their gods a brazen° pillar high   *brass*
      As the sky,
Yet reserved a thousand chariots in full force—
      Gold, of course.
Oh heart! oh blood that freezes, blood that burns!
      Earth's returns
For whole centuries of folly, noise, and sin!
      Shut them in,
With their triumphs and their glories and the rest!
      Love is best.

75

80

1853   1855

"Childe Roland to the Dark Tower Came"[1]

(*See Edgar's Song in "Lear"*)

1

My first thought was, he lied in every word,
      That hoary cripple, with malicious eye
      Askance° to watch the working of his lie   *squinting sideways*
On mine, arid mouth scarce able to afford
Suppression of the glee, that pursed and scored
      Its edge, at one more victim gained thereby.

5

2

What else should he be set for, with his staff?
      What, save to waylay with his lies, ensnare
      All travelers who might find him posted there,
And ask the road? I guessed what skull-like laugh
Would break, what crutch 'gin° write my epitaph   *would begin to*
      For pastime in the dusty thoroughfare,

10

1. Browning stated that this poem "came upon me as a kind of dream," and that it was written in one day. Although the poem was among those of his own writings that pleased him most, he was reluctant to explain what the dream (or nightmare) signified. He once agreed with a friend's suggestion that the meaning might be expressed in the statement: "He that endureth to the end shall be saved" (cf. Matthew 24.13). Most readers have responded to the poem in this way, finding in the story of Roland's quest an inspiring expression of defiance and courage. Other readers find that the poem expresses despair more than enduring hope, and it is at least true that the landscape is as grim and nightmarelike as in 20th-century writings such as T. S. Eliot's "The Hollow Men" (1925) or Franz Kafka's "In the Penal Colony" (1919).

    The lines from Shakespeare's *King Lear* 3.4 (lines 158–60), from which the title is taken, are spoken when Lear is about to enter a hovel on the heath, and Edgar, feigning madness, chants the fragment of a song reminiscent of quests and challenges in fairy tales: "Child Roland to the dark tower come, / His word was still, 'Fie, fo, and fum; / I smell the blood of a British man." "Childe": a youth of noble birth, usually a candidate for knighthood.

3

If at his counsel I should turn aside
    Into that ominous tract which, all agree,
15   Hides the Dark Tower. Yet acquiescingly
I did turn as he pointed: neither pride
Nor hope rekindling at the end descried,
    So much as gladness that some end might be.

4

For, what with my whole world-wide wandering,
20   What with my search drawn out through years, my hope
    Dwindled into a ghost not fit to cope
With that obstreperous joy success would bring,
I hardly tried now to rebuke the spring
    My heart made, finding failure in its scope.

5

25 As when a sick man very near to death
    Seems dead indeed, and feels begin and end
    The tears and takes the farewell of each friend,
And hears one bid the other go, draw breath
Freelier outside ("since all is o'er," he saith,
30   "And the blow fallen no grieving can amend"),

6

While some discuss if near the other graves
    Be room enough for this, and when a day
    Suits best for carrying the corpse away,
With care about the banners, scarves and staves:[2]
35 And still the man hears all, and only craves
    He may not shame such tender love and stay.

7

Thus, I had so long suffered in this quest,
    Heard failure prophesied so oft, been writ
    So many times among "The Band"—to wit,
40 The knights who to the Dark Tower's search addressed
Their steps—that just to fail as they, seemed best,
    And all the doubt was now—should I be fit?

8

So, quiet as despair, I turned from him,
    That hateful cripple, out of his highway
45   Into the path he pointed. All the day
Had been a dreary one at best, and dim
Was settling to its close, yet shot one grim
    Red leer to see the plain catch its estray.[3]

---

2. The trappings of an imagined funeral.
3. Literally, a domestic animal that has strayed away from its home.

9

For mark! no sooner was I fairly found
50   Pledged to the plain, after a pace or two,
      Than, pausing to throw backward a last view
O'er the safe road, 'twas gone; gray plain all round:
Nothing but plain to the horizon's bound.
      I might go on; naught else remained to do.

10

55 So, on I went. I think I never saw
      Such starved ignoble nature; nothing throve:
      For flowers—as well expect a cedar grove!
But, cockle, spurge,[4] according to their law
Might propagate their kind, with none to awe,
60   You'd think; a burr had been a treasure trove.

11

No! penury, inertness and grimace,
      In some strange sort, were the land's portion. "See
      Or shut your eyes," said Nature peevishly,
"It nothing skills:[5] I cannot help my case;
65 'Tis the Last Judgment's fire must cure this place,
      Calcine[6] its clods and set my prisoners free."

12

If there pushed any ragged thistle stalk
      Above its mates, the head was chopped; the bents[7]
      Were jealous else. What made those holes and rents
70 In the dock's° harsh swarth leaves, bruised as to balk   *coarse plant*
All hope of greenness? 'tis a brute must walk
      Pashing° their life out, with a brute's intents.   *smashing*

13

As for the grass, it grew as scant as hair
      In leprosy; thin dry blades pricked the mud
75   Which underneath looked kneaded up with blood.
One stiff blind horse, his every bone a-stare,
Stood stupefied, however he came there:
      Thrust out past service from the devil's stud!

14

Alive? he might be dead for aught I know,
80   With that red gaunt and colloped° neck a-strain,   *ridged*
      And shut eyes underneath the rusty mane;
Seldom went such grotesqueness with such woe;
I never saw a brute I hated so;
      He must be wicked to deserve such pain.

---

4. A bitter-juiced weed. "Cockle": a weed that
bears burrs.
5. I.e., it is no use.

6. Turn to powder by heat.
7. Coarse stiff grasses.

15

85   I shut my eyes and turned them on my heart.
      As a man calls for wine before he fights,
      I asked one draught of earlier, happier sights,
  Ere fitly I could hope to play my part.
  Think first, fight afterwards—the soldier's art:
90   One taste of the old time sets all to rights.

16

  Not it! I fancied Cuthbert's reddening face
      Beneath its garniture of curly gold,
      Dear fellow, till I almost felt him fold
  An arm in mine to fix me to the place,
95   That way he used. Alas, one night's disgrace!
      Out went my heart's new fire and left it cold.

17

  Giles then, the soul of honor—there he stands
      Frank as ten years ago when knighted first.
      What honest man should dare (he said) he durst.
100   Good—but the scene shifts—faugh! what hangman hands
  Pin to his breast a parchment? His own bands
      Read it. Poor traitor, spit upon and cursed!

18

  Better this present than a past like that;
      Back therefore to my darkening path again!
105   No sound, no sight as far as eye could strain.
  Will the night send a howlet° or a bat?   *owl*
  I asked: when something on the dismal flat
      Came to arrest my thoughts and change their train.

19

  A sudden little river crossed my path
110   As unexpected as a serpent comes.
      No sluggish tide congenial to the glooms;
  This, as it frothed by, might have been a bath
  For the fiend's glowing hoof—to see the wrath
      Of its black eddy bespate° with flakes and spumes.   *bespattered*

20

115   So petty yet so spiteful! All along,
      Low scrubby alders kneeled down over it;
      Drenched willows flung them headlong in a fit
  Of mute despair, a suicidal throng:
  The river which had done them all the wrong,
120   Whate'er that was, rolled by, deterred no whit.

21

Which, while I forded—good saints, how I feared
    To set my foot upon a dead man's cheek,
    Each step, or feel the spear I thrust to seek
For hollows, tangled in his hair or beard!
125   —It may have been a water rat I speared,
    But, ugh! it sounded like a baby's shriek.

22

Glad was I when I reached the other bank.
    Now for a better country. Vain presage!
    Who were the strugglers, what war did they wage,
130 Whose savage trample thus could pad the dank
Soil to a plash?° Toads in a poisoned tank,   *puddle*
    Or wild cats in a red-hot iron cage—

23

The fight must so have seemed in that fell cirque.°   *dreadful arena*
    What penned them there, with all the plain to choose?
135   No footprint leading to that horrid mews,[8]
None out of it. Mad brewage set to work
    Their brains, no doubt, like galley slaves the Turk
    Pits for his pastime, Christians against Jews.

24

And more than that—a furlong on—why, there!
140   What bad use was that engine for, that wheel,
    Or brake,[9] not wheel—that harrow fit to reel
Men's bodies out like silk? with all the air
Of Tophet's° tool, on earth left unaware,   *hell's*
    Or brought to sharpen its rusty teeth of steel.

25

145 Then came a bit of stubbed ground, once a wood,
    Next a marsh, it would seem, and now mere earth
    Desperate and done with; (so a fool finds mirth,
Makes a thing and then mars it, till his mood
Changes and off he goes!) within a rood[1]
150   Bog, clay and rubble, sand and stark black dearth.

26

Now blotches rankling, colored gay and grim,
    Now patches where some leanness of the soil's
    Broke into moss or substances like boils;
Then came some palsied oak, a cleft in him

8. Enclosed stable yard.
9. A toothed machine used for separating the fibers of flax or hemp; here an instrument of torture.
1. I.e., a short distance (6–8 yards).

155 Like a distorted mouth that splits its rim
    Gaping at death, and dies while it recoils.

27

And just as far as ever from the end!
    Naught in the distance but the evening, naught
    To point my footstep further! At the thought,
160 A great black bird, Apollyon's[2] bosom friend,
    Sailed past, nor beat his wide wing dragon-penned[3]
    That brushed my cap—perchance the guide I sought.

28

For, looking up, aware I somehow grew,
    'Spite of the dusk, the plain had given place
165   All round to mountains—with such name to grace
Mere ugly heights and heaps now stolen in view.
    How thus they had surprised me—solve it, you!
    How to get from them was no clearer case.

29

Yet half I seemed to recognize some trick
170   Of mischief happened to me, God knows when—
    In a bad dream perhaps. Here ended, then,
Progress this way. When, in the very nick
Of giving up, one time more, came a click
    As when a trap shuts—you're inside the den!

30

175 Burningly it came on me all at once,
    This was the place! those two hills on the right,
    Crouched like two bulls locked horn in horn in fight;
While to the left, a tall scalped mountain . . . Dunce,
Dotard, a-dozing at the very nonce,°   *moment*
180   After a life spent training for the sight!

31

What in the midst lay but the Tower itself?
    The round squat turret, blind as the fool's heart,[4]
    Built of brown stone, without a counterpart
In the whole world. The tempest's mocking elf
185   Points to the shipman thus the unseen shelf
    He strikes on, only when the timbers start.°   *separate; come loose*

32

Not see? because of night perhaps?—why, day
    Came back again for that! before it left,

2. In Revelation 9.11 Apollyon is "the angel of the bottomless pit." In *The Pilgrim's Progress* (1678) by John Bunyan (1628–1688) he is a hideous "monster"; "he had wings like a dragon."

3. With wings or pinions like those of a dragon.
4. Cf. Psalm 14.1: "The fool hath said in his heart, There is no God."

The dying sunset kindled through a cleft:
190   The hills, like giants at a hunting, lay,
       Chin upon hand, to see the game at bay—
       "Now stab and end the creature—to the heft!"[5]

33

Not hear? when noise was everywhere! it tolled
    Increasing like a bell. Names in my ears
195   Of all the lost adventurers my peers—
How such a one was strong, and such was bold,
And such was fortunate, yet each of old
    Lost, lost! one moment knelled the woe of years.

34

There they stood, ranged along the hillsides, met
200   To view the last of me, a living frame
    For one more picture! in a sheet of flame
I saw them and I knew them all. And yet
Dauntless the slug-horn[6] to my lips I set,
    And blew. *"Childe Roland to the Dark Tower came."*

1852   1855

Fra Lippo Lippi[1]

I am poor brother Lippo, by your leave!
You need not clap your torches to my face.
Zooks,[2] what's to blame? you think you see a monk!
What, 'tis past midnight, and you go the rounds,
5   And here you catch me at an alley's end
Where sportive ladies leave their doors ajar?
The Carmine's[3] my cloister: hunt it up,
Do—harry out, if you must show your zeal,
Whatever rat, there, haps on his wrong hole,
10   And nip each softling of a wee white mouse,
Weke, weke, that's crept to keep him company!
Aha, you know your betters! Then, you'll take
Your hand away that's fiddling on my throat,
And please to know me likewise. Who am I?
15   Why, one, sir, who is lodging with a friend

5. Handle of dagger or sword.
6. The war cry or slogan of a clan about to engage in battle (Scottish). In 1770, however, the poet Thomas Chatterton was misled into using it to mean a kind of trumpet or horn. Browning followed Chatterton's example, although the original meaning would also be relevant here.
1. This monologue portrays the dawn of the Renaissance in Italy at a point when the medieval attitude toward life and art was about to be displaced by a fresh appreciation of earthly pleasures. It was from Giorgio Vasari's *Lives of the*

Painters (1550) that Browning derived most of his information about the life of the Florentine painter and friar Lippo Lippi (1406–1469), but the theory of art propounded by Lippi in the poem was developed by the poet.
2. A shortened version of *Gadzooks,* a mild oath now obscure in meaning but perhaps resembling a phrase still in use: "God's truth."
3. Santa Maria del Carmine, a church and cloister of the Carmelite order of friars to which Lippi belonged.

Three streets off—he's a certain . . . how d'ye call?
Master—a . . . Cosimo of the Medici,[4]
I' the house that caps the corner. Boh! you were best!
Remember and tell me, the day you're hanged,
20 How you affected such a gullet's gripe![5]
But you,[6] sir, it concerns you that your knaves
Pick up a manner nor discredit you:
Zooks, are we pilchards,° that they sweep the streets   small fish
And count fair prize what comes into this net?
25 He's Judas to a tittle, that man is![7]
Just such a face! Why, sir, you make amends.
Lord, I'm not angry! Bid your hangdogs go
Drink out this quarter-florin[8] to the health
Of the munificent House that harbors me
30 (And many more beside, lads! more beside!)
And all's come square again. I'd like his face—
His, elbowing on his comrade in the door
With the pike and lantern—for the slave that holds
John Baptist's head a-dangle by the hair
35 With one hand ("Look you, now," as who should say)
And his weapon in the other, yet unwiped!
It's not your chance to have a bit of chalk,
A wood-coal° or the like? or you should see!   piece of charcoal
Yes, I'm the painter, since you style me so.
40 What, brother Lippo's doings, up and down,
You know them and they take you? like enough!
I saw the proper twinkle in your eye—
'Tell you, I liked your looks at very first.
Let's sit and set things straight now, hip to haunch.
45 Here's spring come, and the nights one makes up bands
To roam the town and sing out carnival,[9]
And I've been three weeks shut within my mew,°   private den
A-painting for the great man, saints and saints
And saints again. I could not paint all night—
50 Ouf! I leaned out of window for fresh air.
There came a hurry of feet and little feet,
A sweep of lute-strings, laughs, and whifts of song—
Flower o' the broom,
Take away love, and our earth is a tomb!
55 *Flower o' the quince,*
I let Lisa go, and what good in life since?[1]
Flower o' the thyme—and so on. Round they went.
Scarce had they turned the corner when a titter
Like the skipping of rabbits by moonlight—three slim shapes,
60 And a face that looked up . . . zooks, sir, flesh and blood,
That's all I'm made of! Into shreds it went,

4. Lippi's patron, a banker and virtual ruler of Florence (1389–1464).
5. I.e., how you had the arrogance to choke the gullet of someone with my connections.
6. The officer in charge of the patrol of policemen or watchmen.
7. I.e., one of the watchmen has a face that would serve as a model for a painting of Judas. "To a tittle": to a tee; absolutely.
8. I.e., buy a drink worth a quarter of a florin (the florin was a gold coin first minted in Florence).
9. Season of revelry before the commencement of Lent.
1. This and other interspersed flower songs are called *stornelli* in Italy.

Curtain and counterpane and coverlet,
All the bed-furniture—a dozen knots,
There was a ladder! Down I let myself,
65 Hands and feet, scrambling somehow, and so dropped,
And after them. I came up with the fun
Hard by Saint Laurence,[2] hail fellow, well met—
Flower o' the rose,
If I've been merry, what matter who knows!
70 And so as I was stealing back again
To get to bed and have a bit of sleep
Ere I rise up tomorrow and go work
On Jerome knocking at his poor old breast
With his great round stone to subdue the flesh,[3]
75 You snap me of the sudden. Ah, I see!
Though your eye twinkles still, you shake your head—
Mine's shaved—a monk, you say—the sting's in that!
If Master Cosimo announced himself,
Mum's the word naturally; but a monk!
80 Come, what am I a beast for? tell us, now!
I was a baby when my mother died
And father died and left me in the street.
I starved there, God knows how, a year or two
On fig skins, melon parings, rinds and shucks,
85 Refuse and rubbish. One fine frosty day,
My stomach being empty as your hat,
The wind doubled me up and down I went.
Old Aunt Lapaccia trussed me with one hand
(Its fellow° was a stinger as I knew),   *i.e., her other hand*
90 And so along the wall, over the bridge,
By the straight cut to the convent. Six words there,
While I stood munching my first bread that month:
"So, boy, you're minded," quoth the good fat father
Wiping his own mouth, 'twas refection time°—   *mealtime*
95 "To quit this very miserable world?
Will you renounce" . . . "the mouthful of bread?" thought I;
By no means! Brief, they made a monk of me;
I did renounce the world, its pride and greed,
Palace, farm, villa, shop, and banking house,
100 Trash, such as these poor devils of Medici
Have given their hearts to—all at eight years old.
Well, sir, I found in time, you may be sure,
'Twas not for nothing—the good bellyful,
The warm serge and the rope that goes all round,[4]
105 And day-long blessed idleness beside!
"Let's see what the urchin's fit for"—that came next.
Not overmuch their way, I must confess.
Such a to-do! They tried me with their books:
Lord, they'd have taught me Latin in pure waste!
110 *Flower o' the clove,*

2. San Lorenzo, a church in Florence. "Hard
by": next to.
3. A picture of Saint Jerome (ca. 340–420),
whose ascetic observances were hardly a congenial subject for a painter such as Lippi.
4. The material ("serge") and belt ("rope") of a
monk's clothing.

All the Latin I construe is "amo," I love!
But, mind you, when a boy starves in the streets
Eight years together, as my fortune was,
Watching folk's faces to know who will fling
115 The bit of half-stripped grape bunch he desires,
And who will curse or kick him for his pains—
Which gentleman processional and fine,
Holding a candle to the Sacrament,
Will wink and let him lift a plate and catch
120 The droppings of the wax to sell again,
Or holla for the Eight° and have him whipped—   *Florentine magistrates*
How say I?—nay, which dog bites, which lets drop
His bone from the heap of offal in the street—
Why, soul and sense of him grow sharp alike,
125 He learns the look of things, and none the less
For admonition from the hunger-pinch.
I had a store of such remarks, be sure,
Which, after I found leisure, turned to use.
I drew men's faces on my copybooks,
130 Scrawled them within the antiphonary's marge,[5]
Joined legs and arms to the long music-notes,
Found eyes and nose and chin for A's and B's,
And made a string of pictures of the world
Betwixt the ins and outs of verb and noun,
135 On the wall, the bench, the door. The monks looked black.
"Nay," quoth the Prior,[6] "turn him out, d' ye say?
In no wise. Lose a crow and catch a lark.
What if at last we get our man of parts,°   *skill, genius*
We Carmelites, like those Camaldolese
140 And Preaching Friars,[7] to do our church up fine
And put the front on it that ought to be!"
And hereupon he bade me daub away.
Thank you! my head being crammed, the walls a blank,
Never was such prompt disemburdening.
145 First, every sort of monk, the black and white,
I drew them, fat and lean: then, folk at church,
From good old gossips waiting to confess
Their cribs° of barrel droppings, candle ends—   *petty thefts*
To the breathless fellow at the altar-foot,
150 Fresh from his murder, safe[8] and sitting there
With the little children round him in a row
Of admiration, half for his beard and half
For that white anger of his victim's son
Shaking a fist at him with one fierce arm,
155 Signing himself with the other because of Christ
(Whose sad face on the cross sees only this
After the passion° of a thousand years)   *sufferings*
Till some poor girl, her apron o'er her head
(Which the intense eyes looked through), came at eve
160 On tiptoe, said a word, dropped in a loaf,
Her pair of earrings and a bunch of flowers

---

5. Margin of a music book used for choral singing.
6. Head of a Carmelite convent.

7. Benedictine and Dominican religious orders,
respectively.
8. Having claimed sanctuary in the church.

(The brute took growling), prayed, and so was gone.
I painted all, then cried "'Tis ask and have;
Choose, for more's ready!"—laid the ladder flat,
165 And showed my covered bit of cloister wall.
The monks closed in a circle and praised loud
Till checked, taught what to see and not to see,
Being simple bodies—"That's the very man!
Look at the boy who stoops to pat the dog!
170 That woman's like the Prior's niece who comes
To care about his asthma: it's the life!"
But there my triumph's straw-fire flared and funked;[9]
Their betters took their turn to see and say:
The Prior and the learned pulled a face
175 And stopped all that in no time. "How? what's here?
Quite from the mark of painting, bless us all!
Faces, arms, legs and bodies like the true
As much as pea and pea! it's devil's game!
Your business is not to catch men with show,
180 With homage to the perishable clay,
But lift them over it, ignore it all,
Make them forget there's such a thing as flesh.
Your business is to paint the souls of men—
Man's soul, and it's a fire, smoke . . . no, it's not . . .
185 It's vapor done up like a newborn babe—
(In that shape when you die it leaves your mouth)
It's . . . well, what matters talking, it's the soul!
Give us no more of body than shows soul!
Here's Giotto,[1] with his Saint a-praising God,
190 That sets us praising—why not stop with him?
Why put all thoughts of praise out of our head
With wonder at lines, colors, and what not?
Paint the soul, never mind the legs and arms!
Rub all out, try at it a second time.
195 Oh, that white smallish female with the breasts,
She's just° my niece . . . Herodias,[2] I would say—   *exactly like*
Who went and danced and got men's heads cut off!
Have it all out!" Now, is this sense, I ask?
A fine way to paint soul, by painting body
200 So ill, the eye can't stop there, must go further
And can't fare worse! Thus, yellow does for white
When what you put for yellow's simply black,
And any sort of meaning looks intense
When all beside itself means and looks naught.
205 Why can't a painter lift each foot in turn,
Left foot and right foot, go a double step,
Make his flesh liker and his soul more like,
Both in their order? Take the prettiest face,
The Prior's niece . . . patron-saint—is it so pretty
210 You can't discover if it means hope, fear,

9. Went up in smoke.
1. Great Florentine painter (1276–1337) whose stylized pictures of religious subjects were admired as models of pre-Renaissance art.
2. I.e., Salomé (her mother was Herodias, the sister-in-law of King Herod). Because John the Baptist had aroused her mother's displeasure, Salomé asked for his head on a platter after she danced (Matthew 14.6–11).

Sorrow or joy? won't beauty go with these?
Suppose I've made her eyes all right and blue,
Can't I take breath and try to add life's flash,
And then add soul and heighten them threefold?
215 Or say there's beauty with no soul at all—
(I never saw it—put the case the same—)
If you get simple beauty and naught else,
You get about the best thing God invents:
That's somewhat: and you'll find the soul you have missed,
220 Within yourself, when you return him thanks.
"Rub all out!" Well, well, there's my life, in short,
And so the thing has gone on ever since.
I'm grown a man no doubt, I've broken bounds:
You should not take a fellow eight years old
225 And make him swear to never kiss the girls.
I'm my own master, paint now as I please—
Having a friend, you see, in the Corner-house!³
Lord, it's fast holding by the rings in front—
Those great rings serve more purposes than just
230 To plant a flag in, or tie up a horse!
And yet the old schooling sticks, the old grave eyes
Are peeping o'er my shoulder as I work,
The heads shake still—"It's art's decline, my son!
You're not of the true painters, great and old;
235 Brother Angelico's the man, you'll find;
Brother Lorenzo⁴ stands his single peer:
Fag on° at flesh, you'll never make the third!"   work hard
Flower o' the pine,
You keep your mistr . . . manners, and I'll stick to mine!
240 I'm not the third, then: bless us, they must know!
Don't you think they're the likeliest to know,
They with their Latin? So, I swallow my rage,
Clench my teeth, suck my lips in tight, and paint
To please them—sometimes do and sometimes don't;
245 For, doing most, there's pretty sure to come
A turn, some warm eve finds me at my saints—
A laugh, a cry, the business of the world—
(*Flower o' the peach,*
Death for us all, and his own life for each!)
250 And my whole soul revolves, the cup runs over,
The world and life's too big to pass for a dream,
And I do these wild things in sheer despite,
And play the fooleries you catch me at,
In pure rage! The old mill-horse, out at grass
255 After hard years, throws up his stiff heels so,
Although the miller does not preach to him
The only good of grass is to make chaff.°   straw
What would men have? Do they like grass or no⁵—

3. The Medici palace.
4. Fra Angelico (1387–1455) and Lorenzo Monaco (1370–1425), whose paintings were in the approved traditional manner.
5. I.e., while horses are allowed to enjoy playing in the grass, human beings are taught by the Church that physical experience is valuable only in its relation to their future condition in the afterlife. The biblical text "all flesh is as grass" (1 Peter 1.24) lurks within Lippi's question.

May they or mayn't they? all I want's the thing
260   Settled forever one way. As it is,
You tell too many lies and hurt yourself:
You don't like what you only like too much,
You do like what, if given you at your word,
You find abundantly detestable.
265   For me, I think I speak as I was taught;
I always see the garden[6] and God there
A-making man's wife: and, my lesson learned,
The value and significance of flesh,
I can't unlearn ten minutes afterwards.

270   You understand me: I'm a beast, I know.
But see, now—why, I see as certainly
As that the morning star's about to shine,
What will hap some day. We've a youngster here
Comes to our convent, studies what I do,
275   Slouches and stares and lets no atom drop:
His name is Guidi[7]—he'll not mind the monks—
They call him Hulking Tom, he lets them talk—
He picks my practice up—he'll paint apace,
I hope so—though I never live so long,
280   I know what's sure to follow. You be judge!
You speak no Latin more than I, belike;
However, you're my man, you've seen the world
—The beauty and the wonder and the power,
The shapes of things, their colors, lights and shades,
285   Changes, surprises—and God made it all!
—For what? Do you feel thankful, aye or no,
For this fair town's face, yonder river's line,
The mountain round it and the sky above,
Much more the figures of man, woman, child,
290   These are the frame to? What's it all about?
To be passed over, despised? or dwelt upon,
Wondered at? oh, this last of course!—you say.
But why not do as well as say—paint these
Just as they are, careless what comes of it?
295   God's works—paint any one, and count it crime
To let a truth slip. Don't object, "His works
Are here already; nature is complete:
Suppose you reproduce her—(which you can't)
There's no advantage! You must beat her, then."
300   For, don't you mark?° we're made so that we love   *observe*
First when we see them painted, things we have passed
Perhaps a hundred times nor cared to see;
And so they are better, painted—better to us,
Which is the same thing. Art was given for that;

6. I.e., Eden.
7. Guidi or Masaccio (1401–1428), a painter who
may have been Lippi's master rather than his
pupil, although Browning, in a letter to the press
in 1870, argued that Lippi had been born earlier.

Like Lippi, Masaccio was in revolt against the
medieval theory of art. His frescoes in the chapel
of Santa Maria del Carmine are considered his
masterpiece.

305 God uses us to help each other so,
Lending our minds out. Have you noticed, now,
Your cullion's° hanging face? A bit of chalk,   *rascal's*
And trust me but you should, though! How much more,
If I drew higher things with the same truth!
310 That were to take the Prior's pulpit-place,
Interpret God to all of you! Oh, oh,
It makes me mad to see what men shall do
And we in our graves! This world's no blot for us,
Nor blank; it means intensely, and means good:
315 To find its meaning is my meat and drink.
"Aye, but you don't so instigate to prayer!"
Strikes in the Prior: "when your meaning's plain
It does not say to folk—remember matins,
Or, mind you fast next Friday!" Why, for this
320 What need of art at all? A skull and bones,
Two bits of stick nailed crosswise, or, what's best,
A bell to chime the hour with, does as well.
I painted a Saint Laurence[8] six months since
At Prato, splashed the fresco[9] in fine style:
325 "How looks my painting, now the scaffold's down?"
I ask a brother: "Hugely," he returns—
"Already not one phiz° of your three slaves   *face*
Who turn the Deacon off his toasted side,
But it's scratched and prodded to our heart's content,
330 The pious people have so eased their own
With coming to say prayers there in a rage:
We get on fast to see the bricks beneath.
Expect another job this time next year,
For pity and religion grow i' the crowd—
335 Your painting serves its purpose!" Hang the fools!

        —That is—you'll not mistake an idle word
Spoke in a huff by a poor monk, God wot,°   *knows*
Tasting the air this spicy night which turns
The unaccustomed head like Chianti wine!
340 Oh, the church knows! don't misreport me, now!
It's natural a poor monk out of bounds
Should have his apt word to excuse himself:
And hearken how I plot to make amends.
I have bethought me: I shall paint a piece
345 . . . There's for you! Give me six months, then go, see
Something in Sant' Ambrogio's![1] Bless the nuns!
They want a cast o' my office.[2] I shall paint
God in the midst, Madonna and her babe,
Ringed by a bowery flowery angel brood,
350 Lilies and vestments and white faces, sweet

8. A scene representing the fiery martyrdom of
Saint Laurence.
9. Painted on a freshly plastered surface. It must
be painted quickly before the plaster dries. Prato
is a town near Florence.

1. A convent church in Florence.
2. Sample of my work. The completed painting,
which Browning saw in Florence, is Lippi's *Coronation of the Virgin* (1441).

As puff on puff of grated orris-root[3]
When ladies crowd to Church at midsummer.
And then i' the front, of course a saint or two—
Saint John, because he saves the Florentines,
355 Saint Ambrose, who puts down in black and white
The convent's friends and gives them a long day,
And Job,[4] I must have him there past mistake,
The man of Uz (and Us without the z,
Painters who need his patience). Well, all these
360 Secured at their devotion, up shall come
Out of a corner when you least expect,
As one by a dark stair into a great light,
Music and talking, who but Lippo! I!—
Mazed,° motionless and moonstruck—I'm the man!   *confused*
365 Back I shrink—what is this I see and hear?
I, caught up with my monk's things by mistake,
My old serge gown and rope that goes all round,
I, in this presence, this pure company!
Where's a hole, where's a corner for escape?
370 Then steps a sweet angelic slip of a thing
Forward, puts out a soft palm—"Not so fast!"
—Addresses the celestial presence, "nay—
He made you and devised you, after all,
Though he's none of you! Could Saint John there draw—
375 His camel-hair[5] make up a painting-brush?
We come to brother Lippo for all that,
Iste perfecit opus!"[6] So, all smile—
I shuffle sideways with my blushing face
Under the cover of a hundred wings
380 Thrown like a spread of kirtles° when you're gay   *skirts*
And play hot cockles,[7] all the doors being shut,
Till, wholly unexpected, in there pops
The hothead husband! Thus I scuttle off
To some safe bench behind, not letting go
385 The palm of her, the little lily thing
That spoke the good word for me in the nick,
Like the Prior's niece . . . Saint Lucy, I would say.
And so all's saved for me, and for the church
A pretty picture gained. Go, six months hence!
390 Your hand, sir, and good-by: no lights, no lights!
The street's hushed, and I know my own way back,
Don't fear me! There's the gray beginning. Zooks!

ca. 1853   1855

3. A powder (like talcum) made from sweet-smelling roots of a flower.
4. The prosperous man who endured immense suffering without once questioning God's will (see the book of Job).
5. Cf. Mark 1.6: "And John was clothed with camel's hair."
6. This man made the work! (Latin). In this painting, as later completed, these words appear beside a figure that Browning took to be Lippi's self-portrait.
7. A game in which a player wears a blindfold.

Andrea del Sarto[1]

(called "The Faultless Painter")

But do not let us quarrel any more,
No, my Lucrezia; bear with me for once:
Sit down and all shall happen as you wish.
You turn your face, but does it bring your heart?
5   I'll work then for your friend's friend, never fear,
Treat his own subject after his own way,
Fix his own time, accept too his own price,
And shut the money into this small hand
When next it takes mine. Will it? tenderly?
10 Oh, I'll content him—but tomorrow, Love!
I often am much wearier than you think,
This evening more than usual, and it seems
As if—forgive now—should you let me sit
Here by the window with your hand in mine
15 And look a half-hour forth on Fiesole,[2]
Both of one mind, as married people use,°   *usually are*
Quietly, quietly the evening through,
I might get up tomorrow to my work
Cheerful and fresh as ever. Let us try.
20 Tomorrow, how you shall be glad for this!
Your soft hand is a woman of itself,
And mine the man's bared breast she curls inside.
Don't count the time lost, neither; you must serve
For each of the five pictures we require:
25 It saves° a model. So! keep looking so—   *saves the expense of*
My serpentining beauty, rounds on rounds![3]
—How could you ever prick those perfect ears,
Even to put the pearl there! oh, so sweet—
My face, my moon, my everybody's moon,
30 Which everybody looks on and calls his,
And, I suppose, is looked on by in turn,
While she looks—no one's: very dear, no less.[4]
You smile? why, there's my picture ready made,
There's what we painters call our harmony!
35 A common grayness silvers everything[5]—
All in a twilight, you and I alike
—You, at the point of your first pride in me

---

1. This portrait of Andrea del Sarto (1486–1531) was derived from a biography written by his pupil Giorgio Vasari, author of *The Lives of the Painters* (1550). Vasari's account seeks to explain why his Florentine master, one of the most skillful painters of the Renaissance, never altogether fulfilled the promise he had shown early in his career and why he had never arrived (in Vasari's opinion) at the level of such artists as Raphael. Vasari noted that Andrea suffered from "a certain timidity of mind . . . which rendered it impossible that those evidences of ardor and animation, which are proper to the more exalted character, should ever appear in him."
   Browning also follows Vasari's account of Andrea's marriage to a beautiful widow, Lucrezia, "an artful woman who made him do as she pleased in all things." Vasari reports that Andrea's "immoderate love for her soon caused him to neglect the studies demanded by his art" and that this infatuation had "more influence over him than the glory and honor towards which he had begun to make such hopeful advances."
2. A suburb on the hills overlooking Florence.
3. Coils of hair like the coils of a serpent.
4. Her affections are centered on no one person, not even on her husband, yet she is nevertheless dear to him.
5. The predominant color in many of Andrea's paintings is silver gray.

(That's gone you know)—but I, at every point;
My youth, my hope, my art, being all toned down
40 To yonder sober pleasant Fiesole.
There's the bell clinking from the chapel top;
That length of convent wall across the way
Holds the trees safer, huddled more inside;
The last monk leaves the garden; days decrease,
45 And autumn grows, autumn in everything.
Eh? the whole seems to fall into a shape
As if I saw alike my work and self
And all that I was born to be and do,
A twilight-piece. Love, we are in God's hand.
50 How strange now, looks the life he makes us lead;
So free we seem, so fettered fast we are!
I feel he laid the fetter: let it lie!
This chamber for example—turn your head—
All that's behind us! You don't understand
55 Nor care to understand about my art,
But you can hear at least when people speak:
And that cartoon,° the second from the door   drawing
—It is the thing, Love! so such things should be—
Behold Madonna!—I am bold to say.
60 I can do with my pencil what I know,
What I see, what at bottom of my heart
I wish for, if I ever wish so deep—
Do easily, too—when I say, perfectly,
I do not boast, perhaps: yourself are judge,
65 Who listened to the Legate's[6] talk last week,
And just as much they used to say in France.
At any rate 'tis easy, all of it!
No sketches first, no studies, that's long past:
I do what many dream of, all their lives,
70 —Dream? strive to do, and agonize to do,
And fail in doing. I could count twenty such
On twice your fingers, and not leave this town,
Who strive—you don't know how the others strive
To paint a little thing like that you smeared
75 Carelessly passing with your robes afloat—
Yet do much less, so much less, Someone[7] says
(I know his name, no matter)—so much less!
Well, less is more, Lucrezia: I am judged.
There burns a truer light of God in them,
80 In their vexed beating stuffed and stopped-up brain,
Heart, or whate'er else, than goes on to prompt
This low-pulsed forthright craftsman's hand of mine.
Their works drop groundward, but themselves, I know,
Reach many a time a heaven that's shut to me,
85 Enter and take their place there sure enough,
Though they come back and cannot tell the world.
My works are nearer heaven, but I sit here.

6. A deputy of the pope.
7. Probably the artist Michelangelo (1475–1564).

The sudden blood of these men! at a word—
Praise them, it boils, or blame them, it boils too.
90 I, painting from myself and to myself,
Know what I do, am unmoved by men's blame
Or their praise either. Somebody remarks
Morello's[8] outline there is wrongly traced,
His hue mistaken; what of that? or else,
95 Rightly traced and well ordered; what of that?
Speak as they please, what does the mountain care?
Ah, but a man's reach should exceed his grasp,
Or what's a heaven for? All is silver-gray
Placid and perfect with my art: the worse!
100 I know both what I want and what might gain,
And yet how profitless to know, to sigh
"Had I been two, another and myself,
Our head would have o'erlooked the world!" No doubt.
Yonder's a work now, of that famous youth
105 The Urbinate[9] who died five years ago.
('Tis copied,[1] George Vasari sent it me.)
Well, I can fancy how he did it all,
Pouring his soul, with kings and popes to see,
Reaching, that heaven might so replenish him,
110 Above and through his art—for it gives way;
That arm is wrongly put—and there again—
A fault to pardon in the drawing's lines,
Its body, so to speak: its soul is right,
He means right—that, a child may understand.
115 Still, what an arm! and I could alter it:
But all the play, the insight and the stretch—
Out of me, out of me! And wherefore out?
Had you enjoined them on me, given me soul,
We might have risen to Rafael, I and you!
120 Nay, Love, you did give all I asked, I think—
More than I merit, yes, by many times.
But had you—oh, with the same perfect brow,
And perfect eyes, and more than perfect mouth,
And the low voice my soul hears, as a bird
125 The fowler's pipe,[2] and follows to the snare—
Had you, with these the same, but brought a mind!
Some women do so. Had the mouth there urged
"God and the glory! never care for gain.
The present by the future, what is that?
130 Live for fame, side by side with Agnolo!°   *Michelangelo*
Rafael is waiting: up to God, all three!"
I might have done it for you. So it seems:
Perhaps not. All is as God overrules.
Beside, incentives come from the soul's self;
135 The rest avail not. Why do I need you?
What wife had Rafael, or has Agnolo?

8. A mountain peak outside Florence.
9. Raphael (1483–1520), or Raffaello Sanzio, born at Urbino.
1. In saying that the painting is a copy, Andrea may perhaps be concerned to prevent Lucrezia from selling it.
2. Whistle or call used by hunters to lure wild fowl into range.

In this world, who can do a thing, will not;
And who would do it, cannot, I perceive:
Yet the will's somewhat°—somewhat, too, the power—   *of some importance*
140   And thus we half-men struggle. At the end,
God, I conclude, compensates, punishes.
'Tis safer for me, if the award be strict,
That I am something underrated here.
Poor this long while, despised, to speak the truth.
145   I dared not, do you know, leave home all day,
For fear of chancing on the Paris lords.
The best is when they pass and look aside;
But they speak sometimes; I must bear it all.
Well may they speak! That Francis,[3] that first time,
150   And that long festal year at Fontainebleau!
I surely then could sometimes leave the ground,
Put on the glory, Rafael's daily wear,
In that humane great monarch's golden look—
One finger in his beard or twisted curl
155   Over his mouth's good mark that made the smile,
One arm about my shoulder, round my neck,
The jingle of his gold chain in my ear,
I painting proudly with his breath on me,
All his court round him, seeing with his eyes,
160   Such frank French eyes, and such a fire of souls
Profuse, my hand kept plying by those hearts—
And, best of all, this, this, this face beyond,
This in the background, waiting on my work,
To crown the issue with a last reward!
165   A good time, was it not, my kingly days?
And had you not grown restless . . . but I know—
'Tis done and past; 'twas right, my instinct said;
Too live the life grew, golden and not gray,
And I'm the weak-eyed bat no sun should tempt
170   Out of the grange° whose four walls make his world.   *farmhouse*
How could it end in any other way?
You called me, and I came home to your heart.
The triumph was—to reach and stay there; since
I reached it ere the triumph, what is lost?
175   Let my hands frame your face in your hair's gold,
You beautiful Lucrezia that are mine!
"Rafael did this, Andrea painted that;
The Roman's is the better when you pray,
But still the other's Virgin was his wife—"
180   Men will excuse me. I am glad to judge
Both pictures in your presence; clearer grows
My better fortune, I resolve to think.
For, do you know, Lucrezia, as God lives,
Said one day Agnolo, his very self,

3. King Francis I of France (1494–1547; reigned 1515–47) had invited Andrea to his court at Fontainebleau and warmly encouraged him in his painting. On returning to Florence, however, Andrea is reputed to have stolen some funds entrusted to him by Francis; and to please Lucrezia he built a house with the money. Now he is afraid of being insulted by "Paris lords" on the streets.

185   To Rafael . . . I have known it all these years . . .
     (When the young man was flaming out his thoughts
     Upon a palace wall for Rome to see,
     Too lifted up in heart because of it)
     "Friend, there's a certain sorry little scrub
190   Goes up and down our Florence, none cares how,
     Who, were he set to plan and execute
     As you are, pricked on by your popes and kings,
     Would bring the sweat into that brow of yours!"
     To Rafael's—And indeed the arm is wrong.
195   I hardly dare . . . yet, only you to see,
     Give the chalk here—quick, thus the line should go!
     Aye, but the soul! he's Rafael! rub it out!
     Still, all I care for, if he spoke the truth,
     (What he? why, who but Michel Agnolo?
200   Do you forget already words like those?)
     If really there was such a chance, so lost—
     Is, whether you're—not grateful—but more pleased.
     Well, let me think so. And you smile indeed!
     This hour has been an hour! Another smile?
205   If you would sit thus by me every night
     I should work better, do you comprehend?
     I mean that I should earn more, give you more.
     See, it is settled dusk now; there's a star;
     Morello's gone, the watch-lights show the wall,
210   The cue-owls[4] speak the name we call them by.
     Come from the window, love—come in, at last,
     Inside the melancholy little house
     We built to be so gay with. God is just.
     King Francis may forgive me: oft at nights
215   When I look up from painting, eyes tired out,
     The walls become illumined, brick from brick
     Distinct, instead of mortar, fierce bright gold,
     That gold of his I did cement them with!
     Let us but love each other. Must you go?
220   That Cousin here again? he waits outside?
     Must see you—you, and not with me? Those loans?
     More gaming debts to pay?[5] you smiled for that?
     Well, let smiles buy me! have you more to spend?
     While hand and eye and something of a heart
225   Are left me, work's my ware, and what's it worth?
     I'll pay my fancy. Only let me sit
     The gray remainder of the evening out,
     Idle, you call it, and muse perfectly
     How I could paint, were I but back in France,
230   One picture, just one more—the Virgin's face,
     Not yours this time! I want you at my side
     To hear them—that is, Michel Agnolo—

4. Scops owls; the term is Browning's coinage from the Italian *chiù* or *ciù*, a name that imitates their cry.
5. Lucrezia's "Cousin" (or lover or friend) owes gambling debts to a creditor. Andrea has already contracted (lines 5–10) to pay off these debts by painting some pictures according to the creditor's specifications. Now he agrees to pay off further debts.

Judge all I do and tell you of its worth.
Will you? Tomorrow, satisfy your friend.
235 I take the subjects for his corridor,
Finish the portrait out of hand—there, there,
And throw him in another thing or two
If he demurs; the whole should prove enough
To pay for this same Cousin's freak.° Beside,   *whim*
240 What's better and what's all I care about,
Get you the thirteen scudi° for the ruff!   *Italian coins*
Love, does that please you? Ah, but what does he,
The Cousin! What does he to please you more?

      I am grown peaceful as old age tonight.
245 I regret little, I would change still less.
Since there my past life lies, why alter it?
The very wrong to Francis!—it is true
I took his coin, was tempted and complied,
And built this house and sinned, and all is said.
250 My father and my mother died of want.[6]
Well, had I riches of my own? you see
How one gets rich! Let each one bear his lot.
They were born poor, lived poor, and poor they died:
And I have labored somewhat in my time
255 And not been paid profusely. Some good son
Paint my two hundred pictures—let him try!
No doubt, there's something strikes a balance. Yes,
You loved me quite enough, it seems tonight.
This must suffice me here. What would one have?
260 In heaven, perhaps, new chances, one more chance—
Four great walls in the New Jerusalem,[7]
Meted on each side by the angel's reed,°   *measuring rod*
For Leonard,[8] Rafael, Agnolo and me
To cover—the three first without a wife,
265 While I have mine! So—still they overcome
Because there's still Lucrezia—as I choose.

Again the Cousin's whistle! Go, my Love.

ca. 1853   1855

Caliban upon Setebos

Caliban upon Setebos Shakespeare's *Tempest* provided Browning with the idea for his speaker (Caliban is Prospero's brutish slave, half-man, half-beast) and the subject of his musings (Setebos is briefly referred to in the play as the god of Caliban's mother, the witch Sycorax). From these beginnings Browning wrote a poem that reflects on two closely related controversies of the Victorian period. The first concerned the nature of God and God's responsibility for the existence of pain in the world. The second debate, stimulated by the publication of Darwin's *Origin of Species* (1859), focused on humanity's origins and our relation to other beings.

6. According to Vasari, Andrea's infatuation for Lucrezia prompted him to stop supporting his poverty-stricken parents.

7. Cf. Revelation 21.10–21, which gives a description of "that great city, the holy Jerusalem."
8. Leonardo da Vinci (1452–1519).

As the poem's epigraph reveals, Browning is interested in the idea that the human conception of the divine is conditioned by our own limitations, or by our understanding of ourselves. Caliban, a lower being, draws his notion of the god who he believes dictates his fortunes from three main sources: his observations of life on the island, his own character, and his experiences with Prospero, his master. The first of these, his knowledge of the behavior and sufferings of animal life, gives rise to his "natural theology": that is, his tendency to understand the character of his god from evidences provided by nature rather than from the evidence of supernatural revelation. From his perceptions of his own motivations and the conduct of his earthly ruler comes Caliban's conception of Setebos's willful power. Caliban admires power and thinks of his god as a being who selects at random some creatures who are to be saved and others who are condemned to suffer. His musings thus connect in complex ways with key and pressing issues for the religious and scientific communities of the Victorian era: through the lens of this most unlikely philosopher, Browning raises the topics both of eternal salvation and of natural selection. Significantly, Caliban feels the need to posit a higher divine being, or presence, that exists "over Setebos": puzzling about this other deity, "the Quiet," Browning's speaker delves into fundamental questions of origin and the construction of myth.

An obstacle for the reader is Caliban's use of the third-person pronoun to refer to himself. Thus "'Will sprawl" means "Caliban will sprawl" (an apostrophe before the verb usually indicates that Caliban is the implied subject). Setebos is also referred to in the third person but with an initial capital letter ("He").

Caliban upon Setebos

Or Natural Theology in the Island

"Thou thoughtest that I was altogether such a one as thyself."[1]

['Will sprawl, now that the heat of day is best,
Flat on his belly in the pit's much mire,
With elbows wide, fists clenched to prop his chin.
And, while he kicks both feet in the cool slush,
5   And feels about his spine small eft-things°   *water lizards*
Run in and out each arm, and make him laugh:
And while above his head a pompion° plant,   *pumpkin*
Coating the cave-top as a brow its eye,
Creeps down to touch and tickle hair and beard,
10   And now a flower drops with a bee inside,
And now a fruit to snap at, catch and crunch—
He looks out o'er yon sea which sunbeams cross
And recross till they weave a spider web
(Meshes of fire, some great fish breaks at times)
15   And talks to his own self, howe'er he please,
Touching that other, whom his dam° called God.   *mother*
Because to talk about Him, vexes—ha,
Could He but know! and time to vex is now,
When talk is safer than in wintertime.
20   Moreover Prosper and Miranda[2] sleep
In confidence he drudges at their task,

---

1. Psalm 50.21. The speaker is God.   2. Prospero's daughter.

And it is good to cheat the pair, and gibe,°   *insult them*
Letting the rank tongue blossom into speech.]

Setebos, Setebos, and Setebos!
25 'Thinketh, He dwelleth i' the cold o' the moon.

'Thinketh He made it, with the sun to match,
But not the stars; the stars came otherwise;
Only made clouds, winds, meteors, such as that:
Also this isle, what lives and grows thereon,
30 And snaky sea which rounds and ends the same.

'Thinketh, it came of being ill at ease:
He hated that He cannot change His cold,
Nor cure its ache. 'Hath spied an icy fish
That longed to 'scape the rock-stream where she lived,
35 And thaw herself within the lukewarm brine
O' the lazy sea her stream thrusts far amid,
A crystal spike 'twixt two warm walls of wave;[3]
Only, she ever sickened, found repulse
At the other kind of water, not her life,
40 (Green-dense and dim-delicious, bred o' the sun)
Flounced back from bliss she was not born to breathe,
And in her old bounds buried her despair,
Hating and loving warmth alike: so He.

'Thinketh, He made thereat the sun, this isle,
45 Trees and the fowls here, beast and creeping thing.
Yon otter, sleek-wet, black, lithe as a leech;
Yon auk,° one fire-eye in a ball of foam,   *seabird*
That floats and feeds; a certain badger brown
He hath watched hunt with that slant white-wedge eye
50 By moonlight; and the pie° with the long tongue   *magpie*
That pricks deep into oakwarts for a worm,
And says a plain word when she finds her prize,
But will not eat the ants; the ants themselves
That build a wall of seeds and settled stalks
55 About their hole—He made all these and more,
Made all we see, and us, in spite: how else?
He could not, Himself, make a second self
To be His mate; as well have made Himself:
He would not make what he mislikes or slights,
60 An eyesore to Him, or not worth His pains:
But did, in envy, listlessness, or sport,
Make what Himself would fain,° in a manner, be—   *gladly*
Weaker in most points, stronger in a few,
Worthy, and yet mere playthings all the while,
65 Things He admires and mocks too—that is it.
Because, so brave, so better though they be,
It nothing skills if He begin to plague.[4]
Look now, I melt a gourd-fruit into mash,
Add honeycomb and pods, I have perceived,

3. I.e., the thin stream of cold water that is driven
into the warm ocean like a spike between walls.

4. I.e., the superior virtues of Setebos's creatures
are no help to them if he decides to torture them.

70 Which bite like finches when they bill and kiss—
  Then, when froth rises bladdery,° drink up all,   *bubbly*
  Quick, quick, till maggots scamper through my brain;
  Last, throw me on my back i' the seeded thyme,
  And wanton, wishing I were born a bird.
75 Put case, unable to be what I wish,
  I yet could make a live bird out of clay:
  Would not I take clay, pinch my Caliban
  Able to fly?—for, there, see, he hath wings,
  And great comb like the hoopoe's[5] to admire,
80 And there, a sting to do his foes offense,
  There, and I will that he begin to live,
  Fly to yon rock-top, nip me off the horns
  Of griggs° high up that make the merry din,   *grasshoppers*
  Saucy through their veined wings, and mind me not.
85 In which feat, if his leg snapped, brittle clay,
  And he lay stupid-like—why, I should laugh;
  And if he, spying me, should fall to weep,
  Beseech me to be good, repair his wrong,
  Bid his poor leg smart less or grow again—
90 Well, as the chance were, this might take or else
  Not take my fancy: I might hear his cry,
  And give the mankin° three sound legs for one,   *little man*
  Or pluck the other off, leave him like an egg,
  And lessoned° he was mine and merely clay.   *thus taught*
95 Were this no pleasure, lying in the thyme,
  Drinking the mash, with brain become alive,
  Making and marring clay at will? So He.
  'Thinketh, such shows nor right nor wrong in Him,
  Nor kind, nor cruel: He is strong and Lord.
100 'Am strong myself compared to yonder crabs
  That march now from the mountain to the sea;
  'Let twenty pass, and stone the twenty-first,
  Loving not, hating not, just choosing so.
  'Say, the first straggler that boasts purple spots
105 Shall join the file, one pincer twisted off;
  'Say, this bruised fellow shall receive a worm,
  And two worms he whose nippers end in red;
  As it likes me each time, I do: so He.

  Well then, 'supposeth He is good i' the main,
110 Placable if His mind and ways were guessed,
  But rougher than His handiwork, be sure!
  Oh, He hath made things worthier than Himself,
  And envieth that, so helped, such things do more
  Than He who made them! What consoles but this?
115 That they, unless through Him, do naught at all,
  And must submit: what other use in things?
  'Hath cut a pipe of pithless elder-joint
  That, blown through, gives exact the scream o' the jay
  When from her wing you twitch the feathers blue:
120 Sound this, and little birds that hate the jay

5. Bird with bright plumage.

Flock within stone's throw, glad their foe is hurt:
Put case such pipe could prattle and boast forsooth,
"I catch the birds, I am the crafty thing,
I make the cry my maker cannot make
125 With his great round mouth; he must blow through mine!"
Would not I smash it with my foot? So He.

But wherefore rough, why cold and ill at ease?
Aha, that is a question! Ask, for that,
What knows—the something over Setebos
130 That made Him, or He, may be, found and fought,
Worsted, drove off and did to nothing,° perchance.   *completely*
There may be something quiet o'er His head,   *overcame*
Out of His reach, that feels nor° joy nor grief,   *neither*
Since both derive from weakness in some way.
135 I joy because the quails come; would not joy
Could I bring quails here when I have a mind:
This Quiet, all it hath a mind to, doth.
'Esteemeth° stars the outposts of its couch,   *he believes*
But never spends much thought nor care that way.
140 It may look up, work up—the worse for those
It works on! 'Careth but for Setebos[6]
The many-handed as a cuttlefish,
Who, making Himself feared through what He does,
Looks up, first, and perceives he cannot soar
145 To what is quiet and hath happy life;
Next looks down here, and out of very spite
Makes this a bauble-world to ape yon real,
These good things to match those as hips[7] do grapes.
'Tis solace making baubles, aye, and sport.
150 Himself peeped late, eyed Prosper at his books
Careless and lofty, lord now of the isle:
Vexed, 'stitched a book of broad leaves, arrow-shaped,
Wrote thereon, he knows what, prodigious words;
Has peeled a wand and called it by a name;
155 Weareth at whiles for an enchanter's robe
The eyed skin of a supple oncelot;[8]
And hath an ounce[9] sleeker than youngling mole,
A four-legged serpent he makes cower and couch,
Now snarl, now hold its breath and mind his eye,
160 And saith she is Miranda and my wife:
'Keeps for his Ariel[1] a tall pouch-bill crane
He bids go wade for fish and straight° disgorge;   *immediately*
Also a sea beast, lumpish, which he snared,
Blinded the eyes of, and brought somewhat tame,
165 And split its toe-webs, and now pens the drudge
In a hole o' the rock and calls him Caliban;
A bitter heart that bides its time and bites.
'Plays thus at being Prosper in a way,

6. Caliban's concern is to appease only Setebos, not the other deity—the Quiet.
7. Hard fruits produced by wild roses.
8. Browning may have invented this term from the Spanish *oncela* or from the French *ocelot* (i.e., a leopard or spotted wildcat).
9. A lynx or other wild feline of moderate size or a snow leopard.
1. In *The Tempest* a spirit who serves Prospero.

Taketh his mirth with make-believes: so He.
170 His dam held that the Quiet made all things
Which Setebos vexed only: 'holds not so.
Who made them weak, meant weakness He might vex.
Had He meant other, while His hand was in,
Why not make horny eyes no thorn could prick,
175 Or plate my scalp with bone against the snow,
Or overscale my flesh 'neath joint and joint,
Like an orc's° armor? Aye—so spoil His sport!   *sea monster's*
He is the One now: only He doth all.

'Saith, He may like, perchance, what profits Him.
180 Aye, himself loves what does him good; but why?
'Gets good no otherwise. This blinded beast
Loves whoso places flesh-meat on his nose,
But, had he eyes, would want no help, but hate
Or love, just as it liked him: He hath eyes.
185 Also it pleaseth Setebos to work,
Use all His hands, and exercise much craft,
By no means for the love of what is worked.
'Tasteth, himself, no finer good i' the world
When all goes right, in this safe summertime,
190 And he wants little, hungers, aches not much,
Than trying what to do with wit and strength.
'Falls to make something: 'piled yon pile of turfs,
And squared and stuck there squares of soft white chalk,
And, with a fish-tooth, scratched a moon on each,
195 And set up endwise certain spikes of tree,
And crowned the whole with a sloth's skull a-top,
Found dead i' the woods, too hard for one to kill.
No use at all i' the work, for work's sole sake;
'Shall some day knock it down again: so He.

200 'Saith He is terrible: watch His feats in proof!
One hurricane will spoil six good months' hope.
He hath a spite against me, that I know,
Just as He favors Prosper, who knows why?
So it is, all the same, as well I find.
205 'Wove wattles half the winter, fenced them firm
With stone and stake to stop she-tortoises
Crawling to lay their eggs here: well, one wave,
Feeling the foot of Him upon its neck,
Gaped as a snake does, lolled out its large tongue,
210 And licked the whole labor flat; so much for spite.
'Saw a ball° flame down late (yonder it lies)   *meteorite*
Where, half an hour before, I slept i' the shade:
Often they scatter sparkles: there is force!
'Dug up a newt He may have envied once
215 And turned to stone, shut up inside a stone.
Please Him and hinder this?—What Prosper does?[2]
Aha, if He would tell me how! Not He!

2. I.e., shall I please Setebos, as Prospero does, and thus prevent my being punished as the newt was punished?

There is the sport: discover how or die!
All need not die, for of the things o' the isle
220 Some flee afar, some dive, some run up trees;
Those at His mercy—why, they please Him most
When . . . when . . . well, never try the same way twice!
Repeat what act has pleased, He may grow wroth.
You must not know His ways, and play Him off,
225 Sure of the issue.° 'Doth the like himself: outcome
'Spareth a squirrel that it nothing fears
But steals³ the nut from underneath my thumb,
And when I threat, bites stoutly in defense:
'Spareth an urchin° that contrariwise   hedgehog
230 Curls up into a ball, pretending death
For fright at my approach: the two ways please.
But what would move my choler more than this,
That either creature counted on its life
Tomorrow and next day and all days to come,
235 Saying, forsooth, in the inmost of its heart,
"Because he did so yesterday with me,
And otherwise with such another brute,
So must he do henceforth and always."—Aye?
Would teach the reasoning couple what "must" means!
240 'Doth as he likes, or wherefore Lord? So He.

'Conceiveth all things will continue thus,
And we shall have to live in fear of Him
So long as He lives, keeps His strength: no change,
If He have done His best, make no new world
245 To please Him more, so leave off watching this—
If He surprise not even the Quiet's self
Some strange day—or, suppose, grow into it
As grubs grow butterflies: else, here are we,
And there is He, and nowhere help at all.
250 'Believeth with the life, the pain shall stop.
His dam held different, that after death
He both plagued enemies and feasted friends:
Idly!⁴ He doth His worst in this our life,
Giving just respite lest we die through pain,
255 Saving last pain for worst—with which, an end.
Meanwhile, the best way to escape His ire
Is, not to seem too happy. 'Sees, himself,
Yonder two flies, with purple films and pink,
Bask on the pompion-bell above: kills both.
260 'Sees two black painful beetles roll their ball
On head and tail as if to save their lives:
Moves them the stick away they strive to clear.

Even so, 'would have Him misconceive, suppose
This Caliban strives hard and ails no less,
265 And always, above all else, envies Him;
Wherefore he mainly dances on dark nights,

3. I.e., that is fearless enough to steal.
4. I.e., Caliban thinks his mother's opinion was
wrong or idle. Setebos's sport with his creatures
is confined to this world: there is no afterlife.

Moans in the sun, gets under holes to laugh,
And never speaks his mind save housed as now:
Outside, 'groans, curses. If He caught me here,
270 O'erheard this speech, and asked "What chucklest at?"
'Would, to appease Him, cut a finger off,
Or of my three kid yearlings burn the best,
Or let the toothsome apples rot on tree,
Or push my tame beast for the orc to taste:
275 While myself lit a fire, and made a song
And sung it, *"What I hate, be consecrate*
To celebrate Thee and Thy state, no mate
For Thee; what see for envy in poor me?"
Hoping the while, since evils sometimes mend,
280 Warts rub away and sores are cured with slime,
That some strange day, will either the Quiet catch
And conquer Setebos, or likelier He
Decrepit may doze, doze, as good as die.

_____

[What, what? A curtain o'er the world at once!
285 Crickets stop hissing; not a bird—or, yes,
There scuds His raven[5] that has told Him all!
It was fool's play this prattling! Ha! The wind
Shoulders the pillared dust, death's house o' the move,[6]
And fast invading fires begin! White blaze—
290 A tree's head snaps—and there, there, there, there, there,
His thunder follows! Fool to gibe at Him!
Lo! 'Lieth flat and loveth Setebos!
'Maketh his teeth meet through his upper lip,
Will let those quails fly, will not eat this month
295 One little mess of whelks,° so he may 'scape!]   *shellfish*

ca. 1860   1864

5. In Norse mythology ravens brought the daily
news to Odin, the most powerful god.

6. The whirlwind stirs up a column of dust that
Caliban associates with a house of death.

MATTHEW ARNOLD
1822–1888

How is a full and enjoyable life to be lived in a modern industrial society? This was the recurrent topic in the poetry and prose of Matthew Arnold. In his poetry the question itself is raised; in his prose some answers are attempted. "The misapprehensiveness [wrongheadedness] of his age is exactly what a poet is sent to remedy," wrote Robert Browning, and yet it is to Arnold's work, not Browning's, that the statement seems more applicable. In response to rapid and potentially dislocating social changes, Arnold strove to help his contemporaries achieve a richer intellectual and emotional existence.

Matthew Arnold was born in Laleham, a village in the valley of the Thames. It seems appropriate that his childhood was spent near a river, for clear-flowing streams were later to appear in his poems as symbols of serenity. At the age of six, Arnold was moved to Rugby School, where his father, Dr. Thomas Arnold, had become headmaster. As a clergyman Dr. Arnold was a leader of the liberal or Broad Church and hence one of the principal opponents of John Henry Newman. As a headmaster he became famous as an educational reformer, a teacher who instilled in his pupils an earnest preoccupation with moral and social issues and also an awareness of the connection between liberal studies and modern life. At Rugby his eldest son, Matthew, was directly exposed to the powerful force of the father's mind and character. The son's attitude toward this force was a mixture of attraction and repulsion. That he was permanently influenced by his father is evident in his poems and in his writings on religion, education, and politics; but like many sons of clergymen, he made a determined effort in his youth to be different. As a student at Oxford he behaved like a dandy. Elegantly and colorfully dressed, alternately languid or merry in manner, he refused to be serious and irritated more solemn undergraduate friends and acquaintances with his irreverent jokes. "His manner displeases, from its seeming foppery," wrote Charlotte Brontë after talking with the young man in later years. "The shade of Dr. Arnold," she added, "seemed to me to frown on his young representative." The son of Dr. Arnold thus appeared to have no connection with Rugby School's standards of earnestness. Even his studies did not seem to occupy him seriously. By a session of cramming, he managed to earn second-class honors in his final examinations, a near disaster that was redeemed by his election to a fellowship at Oriel College.

Arnold's biographers usually dismiss his youthful frivolity of spirit as only a temporary pose or mask, but it permanently colored his prose style, brightening his most serious criticism with geniality and wit. For most readers the jauntiness of his prose is a virtue, though others find it offensive. Anyone suspicious of urbanity and irony would applaud Walt Whitman's sour comment that Arnold is "one of the dudes [dandies, or city slickers] of literature." A more appropriate estimate of his manner is provided by Arnold's own description of the French writer Charles-Augustin Sainte-Beuve: "a critic of measure, not exuberant; of the centre, not provincial . . . with gay and amiable temper, his manner as good as his matter—the 'critique souriant' [smiling critic]."

Unlike authors such as Alfred, Lord Tennyson and Thomas Carlyle who committed themselves solely to their literary pursuits, Arnold confined his writing and reading to his spare time. In 1847 he took the post of private secretary to Lord Lansdowne; and in 1851, the year of his marriage, he became an inspector of schools, a demanding and time-consuming position that he held for thirty-five years. Although his work as an inspector may have reduced his output as a writer, it had several advantages. His extensive traveling in England took him to the homes of the more ardently Protestant middle classes, and when he criticized the dullness of middle-class life (as he often did), his scorn was based on intimate knowledge. His position also led to travel on the Continent to study the schools of Europe. As a critic of English education, he was thus able to make helpful comparisons and to draw on a stock of fresh ideas in the same way as in his literary criticism he used his familiarity with French, German, Italian, and classical literatures to talk knowledgeably about the distinctive qualities of English writers. Despite the monotony of much of his work as an inspector, Arnold became convinced of its importance. It contributed to what he regarded as his century's most important need: the development of a satisfactory national system of education.

In 1849 Arnold published *The Strayed Reveler*, his first volume of poetry. Eight years later, as a tribute to his poetic achievement, he was elected to the professorship of poetry at Oxford, a part-time position that he held for ten years. Later, like Charles Dickens and William Makepeace Thackeray before him, Arnold toured America to make money by lecturing. His lectures could leave audiences indifferent, but sometimes they were highly acclaimed: thus the *Washington Post* reported that, following a two-hour address in the U.S. capital, the African American leader Frederick Douglass "moved that a tremendous vote of thanks be tendered to the speaker." A further inducement for his two visits (in 1883 and 1886) was the opportunity of seeing his daughter Lucy, who had married an American. In 1888 Arnold died of a sudden heart attack.

Arnold's career as a writer can be roughly divided into four periods. In the 1850s most of his poems appeared; in the 1860s, literary criticism and social criticism; in the 1870s, his religious and educational writings; and in the 1880s, his second set of essays in literary criticism.

Today Arnold is perhaps better known as a writer of prose than as a poet, although individual poems such as "Dover Beach" (1867) continue to be widely popular. In his own era his decision to spend hardly any time composing poetry after 1860 was considered wrongheaded by some: "Tell Mat not to write any more of those prose things like *Literature and Dogma*," Tennyson wrote in a letter, wishing that Arnold would instead "give us something like his Thyrsis,' 'Scholar Gypsy,' or 'Forsaken Merman.'" Others have felt that he made the right move: Arnold's poetry has been criticized, in both the nineteenth and the twentieth centuries, on numerous grounds. Some have disliked its excessive reliance on italics instead of on meter to emphasize the meaning of a line, while others object to the prosy flatness of certain passages or, conversely, to overelaborated similes in others. Yet despite these cavils, many readers find much to cherish and admire. Given Arnold's sophistication as a writer, it is perhaps surprising that his evocations of nature function so memorably in his poetry: rather than simply providing a picturesque backdrop, the setting—seashore or river or mountaintop— draws the poem's meaning together. In this respect, as in many others, Arnold displays a debt to William Wordsworth, whose poetry he greatly admired; but he also draws on his own bond with particular landscapes, especially those associated with his youth and early adulthood. The stanzas of "The Scholar Gypsy" (1853), for instance—suffused in a deep familiarity with the changing patterns of the rural scene, from the "frail-leafed, white anemone" and "dark bluebells drenched with dews" of May to the "scarlet poppies" and "pale pink convolvulus" of August—record with sensuous care the distinct seasons of the English countryside and Arnold's nostalgic memories of the rambles of his Oxford days.

Arnold's own verdict on the qualities of his poetry is interesting. In an 1869 letter to his mother, he writes:

> My poems represent, on the whole, the main movement of mind of the last quarter of a century, and thus they will probably have their day as people become conscious to themselves of what that movement of mind is, and interested in the literary productions which reflect it. It might be fairly urged that I have less poetical sentiment than Tennyson, and less intellectual vigour and abundance than Browning; yet, because I have perhaps more of a fusion of the two than either of them, and have more regularly applied that fusion to the main line of modern development, I am likely enough to have my turn, as they have had theirs.

The emphasis in the letter on "movement of mind" suggests that Arnold's poetry and prose should be studied together. Such an approach can be fruitful provided that it does not obscure the important difference between Arnold the poet and Arnold the critic. T. S. Eliot once said of his own writings that "in one's prose reflections one may be legitimately occupied with ideals, whereas in the writing of verse, one can deal only with actuality." Arnold's writings offer a nice verification of Eliot's seeming paradox. As a poet he usually records his own experiences, his own feelings of loneliness and isolation as a lover, his longing for a serenity that he cannot find, his melancholy sense of the passing of youth (more than for many men, Arnold's thirtieth birthday was an awe-inspiring landmark after which he felt, he said, "three parts iced over"). Above all he records his despair in a universe in which humanity's role seemed an incongruous as it was later to seem to Thomas Hardy. In a memorable passage of his "Stanzas from the Grande Chartreuse" (1855), he describes himself as "Wandering between two worlds, one dead, / The other powerless to be born." And addressing the representatives of a faith that seems to him dead, he cries: "Take me, cowled forms, and fence me round, / Till I possess my soul again." As a poet, then, like T. S. Eliot and W. H. Auden, Arnold provides a record of a troubled individual in a troubled society. This was "actuality" as he experienced it—an actuality, like Eliot's and Auden's, representative of his era. As a prose writer, a formulator of "ideals," he seeks a different role—to be what Auden calls the "healer" of a diseased society, or as he himself called Goethe, the "Physician of the iron age." And in this difference we have a clue to answering the question of why Arnold virtually abandoned the writing of poetry to move into criticism. One reason was his dissatisfaction with the kind of poetry he was writing.

In one of his fascinating letters to his friend Arthur Hugh Clough in the 1850s (letters that provide the best insight we have into Arnold's mind and tastes), this note of dissatisfaction is struck: "I am glad you like the *Gypsy Scholar*—but what does it *do* for you? Homer *animates*—Shakespeare *animates*—in its poor way I think *Sohrab and Rustum animates*—the *Gypsy Scholar* at best awakens a pleasing melancholy. But this is not what we want." It is evident that early in his career Arnold had evolved a theory of what poetry should do for its readers, a theory based, in part, on his impression of what classical poetry had achieved. To help make life bearable, poetry, in Arnold's view, must bring joy. As he says in the 1853 preface to his *Poems*, it must "inspirit and rejoice the reader"; it must "convey a charm, and infuse delight." Such a demand does not exclude tragic poetry but does exclude works "in which suffering finds no vent in action; in which a continual state of mental distress is prolonged." Of Charlotte Brontë's novel *Villette* (1853) he says witheringly: "The writer's mind contains nothing but hunger, rebellion, and rage . . . No fine writing can hide this thoroughly, and it will be fatal to her in the long run." Judged by such a standard, most nineteenth-century poems, including his own long poem *Empedocles on Etna* (1852), were unsatisfactory. And when Arnold tried to write poems that would meet his own requirements—*Sohrab and Rustum* (1853) or *Balder Dead* (1855)—he felt that something was lacking. By the late 1850s he thus found himself at a dead end. Turning aside to literary criticism enabled him partially to escape the dilemma. In his prose his melancholy and "morbid" personality was subordinated to the resolutely cheerful and purposeful character he had created for himself by an effort of will.

Arnold's two volumes of *Essays in Criticism* (1865, 1888) repeatedly show how authors as different as Marcus Aurelius, Leo Tolstoy, Homer, and Wordsworth provide the virtues he sought in his reading. Among these virtues was plainness of style. Although he could on occasion recommend the richness of language of such poets as John Keats or Tennyson—their "natural magic," as he called it—Arnold usually preferred literature that was unadorned. And beyond stylistic excellences, the principal virtue he admired as a critic was the quality of "high seriousness." In a world in which the role of formal religion appeared to be shrinking, Arnold increasingly emphasized that the poet must be a serious thinker who could offer guidance to his readers. This belief perhaps caused him to undervalue other qualities in literature: in "The Study of Poetry" (1880), for instance, he displays little appreciation for Chaucer's humor and chooses instead to castigate him for his lack of high seriousness.

In "The Function of Criticism at the Present Time" (1864), Arnold makes clear that he regarded good literary criticism, like literature itself, as a potent force in producing what he conceived as a civilized society. From a close study of this essay one could forecast the third stage of his career: his excursion into the criticism of society that was to culminate in *Culture and Anarchy* (1869) and *Friendship's Garland* (1871).

Arnold's starting point as a critic of society is different from that of Carlyle and John Ruskin. The older prophets attacked the Victorian middle classes on the grounds of their materialism, their selfish indifference to the sufferings of the poor—their immorality, in effect. Arnold argued instead that the "Philistines," as he called them, were not so much wicked as ignorant, narrow-minded, and suffering from the dullness of their private lives. This novel analysis was reinforced by

Arnold's conviction that the world of the future, both in England and in America, would be a middle-class world and therefore would be dominated by a class inadequately equipped either to lead or to enjoy civilized living.

To establish this point Arnold employed cajolery, satire, and even quotations from current newspapers with considerable effect. He also used memorable catch phrases (such as "sweetness and light") that sometimes pose an obstacle to understanding the complexities of his position. His view of civilization, for example, was pared down to a four-point formula of the four "powers": conduct, intellect and knowledge, beauty, and social life and manners. Applying this simple formula to a range of civilizations, Arnold had a scale by which to judge the virtues as well as the inadequacies of different countries. When he turned this instrument on his own country, he usually awarded the Victorian middle classes an A in the first category (i.e., conduct) but a failing grade in the other three categories. Unsurprisingly, he also had pronounced opinions on what he viewed as the distinct national characters of different peoples: a sample of this strain in Arnold's writing appears in the extract from his lectures *On the Study of Celtic Literature* (1867).

Arnold's relentless exposure of middle-class narrow-mindedness in his own country eventually led him into the arena of religious controversy. As a critic of religious institutions he was arguing, in effect, that just as the middle classes did not know how to lead full lives, neither did they know how to read the Bible intelligently or attend church intelligently. Of the Christian religion he remarked that there are two things "that surely must be clear to anybody with eyes in his head. One is, that men cannot do without it; the other that they cannot do with it as it is." His three full-length studies of the Bible, including *Literature and Dogma* (1873), are thus best considered a postscript to his social criticism. The Bible, to Arnold, was a great work of literature like the *Odyssey*, and the Church of England was a great national institution like Parliament. Both Bible and Church must be preserved not because historical Christianity was credible but because both, when properly understood, were agents of what he called "culture"—they contributed to making humanity more civilized.

Culture is perhaps Arnold's most familiar catchword, although what he meant by it has sometimes been misunderstood. He used the term to capture the qualities of an open-minded intelligence (as described in "The Function of Criticism")—a refusal to take things on authority. In this respect Arnold appears close to T. H. Huxley and J. S. Mill. But the word also connotes a full awareness of humanity's past and a capacity to enjoy the best works of art, literature, history, and philosophy that have come down to us from that past. As a way of viewing life in all its aspects, including the social, political, and religious, culture represents for Arnold the most effective cure for the ills of a sick society. It is his principal prescription.

The attempt to define culture brings us to a final aspect of Arnold's career as a critic: his writings on education, in which he sought to make cultural values, as he said, "prevail." Most obviously these writings comprise his reply to Huxley (his admirably reasoned essay "Literature and Science," 1882) and his volumes of official reports written as an inspector of schools. Less obviously, they comprise all his prose. At their core is his belief that good education is *the* crucial need. Arnold was essentially a great teacher. He has the faults of a teacher—a tendency to repeat himself, to lean too hard on formulaic phrases—and he displays something of the lectern manner at times. He also has the great teacher's virtues, in particular the ability to skillfully convey to us the conviction on which all his arguments are based. This conviction is that the humanist tradition of which he is the expositor can enable the individual man or woman to live life more fully and to change the course of society. He believes that a democratic society can thrive only if its citizens become educated in what he saw as the great Western tradition, "the best that is known and thought." These values, which some readers find elitist, make Arnold both timely and controversial. Arnold fought for these values with the gloves on—kid gloves, his opponents used to say—and he provided a lively exhibition of footwork that is a pleasure to observe. Yet the gracefulness of the display should not obscure the fact that he lands hard blows squarely on his opponents.

Although his lifelong attacks upon the inadequacies of Puritanism make Arnold one of the most anti-Victorian figures of his age, behind his attacks is a characteristically Victorian assumption: that the Puritan middle classes *can* be changed, that they are, as we would more clumsily say, educable. In 1852, writing to Clough on the subject of equality (a political objective in which he believed by conviction if not by instinct), Arnold observed: "I am more and more convinced that the world tends to become more comfortable for the mass, and more uncomfortable for those of any natural gift or distinction—and it is as well perhaps that it should be so—for hitherto the gifted have astonished and delighted the world, but not trained or inspired or in any real way changed it." Arnold's gifts as a poet and critic enabled him to do both: to delight the world and to change it.

To Marguerite—Continued

Yes! in the sea of life enisled,°   *encircled*
With echoing straits between us thrown,
Dotting the shoreless watery wild,
We mortal millions live *alone*.
5 The islands feel the enclasping flow,
And then their endless bounds they know.

But when the moon their hollows lights,
And they are swept by balms of spring,
And in their glens, on starry nights,
10 The nightingales divinely sing;
And lovely notes, from shore to shore,
Across the sounds and channels pour—

Oh! then a longing like despair
Is to their farthest caverns sent;
15 For surely once, they feel, we were
Parts of a single continent!
Now round us spreads the watery plain—
Oh might our marges meet again!

Who ordered that their longing's fire
20 Should be, as soon as kindled, cooled?
Who renders vain their deep desire?—
A God, a God their severance ruled!
And bade betwixt their shores to be
The unplumbed, salt, estranging sea.

1849   1852

The Buried Life

Light flows our war of mocking words, and yet,
Behold, with tears mine eyes are wet!

I feel a nameless sadness o'er me roll.
Yes, yes, we know that we can jest,
5   We know, we know that we can smile!
But there's a something in this breast,
To which thy light words bring no rest,
And thy gay smiles no anodyne.
Give me thy hand, and hush awhile,
10   And turn those limpid eyes on mine,
And let me read there, love! thy inmost soul.

Alas! is even love too weak
To unlock the heart, and let it speak?
Are even lovers powerless to reveal
15   To one another what indeed they feel?
I knew the mass of men concealed
Their thoughts, for fear that if revealed
They would by other men be met
With blank indifference, or with blame reproved;
20   I knew they lived and moved
Tricked° in disguises, alien to the rest   *dressed up*
Of men, and alien to themselves—and yet
The same heart beats in every human breast!

But we, my love!—doth a like spell benumb
25   Our hearts, our voices?—must we too be dumb?
Ah! well for us, if even we,
Even for a moment, can get free
Our heart, and have our lips unchained;
For that which seals them hath been deep-ordained!

30   Fate, which foresaw
How frivolous a baby man would be—
By what distractions he would be possessed,
How he would pour himself in every strife,
And well-nigh change his own identity—
35   That it might keep from his capricious play
His genuine self, and force him to obey
Even in his own despite his being's law,
Bade through the deep recesses of our breast
The unregarded river of our life
40   Pursue with indiscernible flow its way;
And that we should not see
The buried stream, and seem to be
Eddying at large in blind uncertainty,
Though driving on with it eternally.

45   But often, in the world's most crowded streets,[1]
But often, in the din of strife,
There rises an unspeakable desire

---

1. This passage, like many others in Arnold's poetry, illustrates William Wordsworth's effect on his writings. In this instance cf. Wordsworth's "Tintern Abbey (1798), lines 25–27: "But oft, in lonely rooms, and 'mid the din / Of towns and cities, I have owed to them, / In hours of weariness, sensations sweet." Cf. also *The Prelude* (1850) 7.626: "How oft amid those overflowing streets . . ."

After the knowledge of our buried life;
A thirst to spend our fire and restless force
In tracking out our true, original course;
A longing to inquire
Into the mystery of this heart which beats
So wild, so deep in us—to know
Whence our lives come and where they go.
And many a man in his own breast then delves,
But deep enough, alas! none ever mines.
And we have been on many thousand lines,
And we have shown, on each, spirit and power;
But hardly have we, for one little hour,
Been on our own line, have we been ourselves—
Hardly had skill to utter one of all
The nameless feelings that course through our breast,
But they course on forever unexpressed.
And long we try in vain to speak and act
Our hidden self, and what we say and do
Is eloquent, is well—but 'tis not true!
And then we will no more be racked
With inward striving, and demand
Of all the thousand nothings of the hour
Their stupefying power;
Ah yes, and they benumb us at our call!
Yet still, from time to time, vague and forlorn,
From the soul's subterranean depth upborne
As from an infinitely distant land,
Come airs, and floating echoes, and convey
A melancholy into all our day.[2]

Only—but this is rare—
When a beloved hand is laid in ours,
When, jaded with the rush and glare
Of the interminable hours,
Our eyes can in another's eyes read clear,
When our world-deafened ear
Is by the tones of a loved voice caressed—
A bolt is shot back somewhere in our breast,
And a lost pulse of feeling stirs again.
The eye sinks inward, and the heart lies plain,
And what we mean, we say, and what we would, we know.
A man becomes aware of his life's flow,
And hears its winding murmur; and he sees
The meadows where it glides, the sun, the breeze.

And there arrives a lull in the hot race
Wherein he doth forever chase
That flying and elusive shadow, rest.
An air of coolness plays upon his face,
And an unwonted calm pervades his breast.

2. Cf. Wordsworth's "Ode: Intimations of Immortality" (1807), lines 149–51: "Those shadowy recollections, / Which, be they what they may, / Are yet the fountain light of all our day."

And then he thinks he knows
The hills where his life rose,
And the sea where it goes.

1852

The Scholar Gypsy

The story of a seventeenth-century student who left Oxford and joined a band of gypsies had made a strong impression on Arnold. In the poem he wistfully imagines that the spirit of this scholar is still to be encountered in the Cumner countryside near Oxford, having achieved immortality by a serene pursuit of the secret of human existence. Like Keats's nightingale, the scholar has escaped "the weariness, the fever, and the fret" of modern life.

At the outset the poet addresses a shepherd who has been helping him in his search for traces of the scholar. The shepherd is addressed as *you*. After line 61, with the shift to *thou* and *thy*, the person addressed is the scholar, and the poet thereafter sometimes uses the pronoun *we* to indicate he is speaking for all humanity of later generations.

About the setting Arnold wrote to his brother Tom on May 15, 1857: "You alone of my brothers are associated with that life at Oxford, the *freest* and most delightful part, perhaps, of my life, when with you and Clough and Walrond I shook off all the bonds and formalities of the place, and enjoyed the spring of life and that unforgotten Oxfordshire and Berkshire country. Do you remember a poem of mine called 'The Scholar Gipsy'? It was meant to fix the remembrance of those delightful wanderings of ours in the Cumner Hills."

The passage from Joseph Glanvill's *Vanity of Dogmatizing* (1661) that inspired the poem was included by Arnold as a note:

> There was very lately a lad in the University of Oxford, who was by his poverty forced to leave his studies there; and at last to join himself to a company of vagabond gypsies. Among these extravagant people, by the insinuating subtilty of his carriage, he quickly got so much of their love and esteem as that they discovered to him their mystery. After he had been a pretty while exercised in the trade, there chanced to ride by a couple of scholars, who had formerly been of his acquaintance. They quickly spied out their old friend among the gypsies; and he gave them an account of the necessity which drove him to that kind of life, and told them that the people he went with were not such imposters as they were taken for, but that they had a traditional kind of learning among them, and could do wonders by the power of imagination, their fancy binding that of others: that himself had learned much of their art, and when he had compassed the whole secret, he intended, he said, to leave their company, and give the world an account of what he had learned.

The Scholar Gypsy

Go, for they call you, shepherd, from the hill;
   Go, shepherd, and untie the wattled cotes![1]
     No longer leave thy wistful flock unfed,
    Nor let thy bawling fellows rack their throats,
5   Nor the cropped herbage shoot another head.

1. Sheepfolds woven from sticks.

But when the fields are still,
And the tired men and dogs all gone to rest,
And only the white sheep are sometimes seen
Cross and recross the strips of moon-blanched green,
10   Come, shepherd, and again begin the quest!

Here, where the reaper was at work of late—
In this high field's dark corner, where he leaves
His coat, his basket, and his earthen cruse,[2]
And in the sun all morning binds the sheaves,
15   Then here, at noon, comes back his stores to use—
Here will I sit and wait,
While to my ear from uplands far away
The bleating of the folded° flocks is borne,   *penned up*
With distant cries of reapers in the corn[3]—
20   All the live murmur of a summer's day.

Screened is this nook o'er the high, half-reaped field,
And here till sundown, shepherd! will I be.
Through the thick corn the scarlet poppies peep,
And round green roots and yellowing stalks I see
25   Pale pink convolvulus in tendrils creep;
And air-swept lindens yield
Their scent, and rustle down their perfumed showers
Of bloom on the bent grass where I am laid,
And bower me from the August sun with shade;
30   And the eye travels down to Oxford's towers.

And near me on the grass lies Glanvill's book—
Come, let me read the oft-read tale again!
The story of the Oxford scholar poor,
Of pregnant parts[4] and quick inventive brain,
35   Who, tired of knocking at preferment's door,
One summer morn forsook
His friends, and went to learn the gypsy lore,
And roamed the world with that wild brotherhood,
And came, as most men deemed, to little good,
40   But came to Oxford and his friends no more.

But once, years after, in the country lanes,
Two scholars, whom at college erst° he knew,   *long ago*
Met him, and of his way of life inquired;
Whereat he answered, that the gypsy crew,
45   His mates, had arts to rule as they desired
The workings of men's brains,
And they can bind them to what thoughts they will.
"And I," he said, "the secret of their art,
When fully learned, will to the world impart;
50   But it needs heaven-sent moments for this skill."

This said, he left them, and returned no more.—
But rumors hung about the countryside,

---

2. Pot or jug for carrying his drink.   4. Of rich conception, many ideas.
3. Grain or wheat.

That the lost Scholar long was seen to stray,
Seen by rare glimpses, pensive and tongue-tied,
55   In hat of antique shape, and cloak of grey,
The same the gypsies wore.
Shepherds had met him on the Hurst[5] in spring;
At some lone alehouse in the Berkshire moors,
On the warm ingle-bench, the smock-frocked boors[6]
60   Had found him seated at their entering,

But, 'mid their drink and clatter, he would fly.
And I myself seem half to know thy looks,
And put the shepherds, wanderer! on thy trace;
And boys who in lone wheatfields scare the rooks[7]
65   I ask if thou hast passed their quiet place;
Or in my boat I lie
Moored to the cool bank in the summer heats,
'Mid wide grass meadows which the sunshine fills,
And watch the warm, green-muffled Cumner hills,
70   And wonder if thou haunt'st their shy retreats.

For most, I know, thou lov'st retired ground!
Thee at the ferry Oxford riders blithe,
Returning home on summer nights, have met
Crossing the stripling Thames at Bab-lock-hithe,[8]
75   Trailing in the cool stream thy fingers wet,
As the punt's rope chops round;[9]
And leaning backward in a pensive dream,
And fostering in thy lap a heap of flowers
Plucked in shy fields and distant Wychwood bowers,
80   And thine eyes resting on the moonlit stream.

And then they land, and thou art seen no more!—
Maidens, who from the distant hamlets come
To dance around the Fyfield elm in May,
Oft through the darkening fields have seen thee roam,
85   Or cross a stile into the public way.
Oft thou hast given them store
Of flowers—the frail-leafed, white anemone,
Dark bluebells drenched with dews of summer eves,
And purple orchises with spotted leaves—
90   But none hath words she can report of thee.

And, above Godstow Bridge, when hay time's here
In June, and many a scythe in sunshine flames,
Men who through those wide fields of breezy grass
Where black-winged swallows haunt the glittering Thames,

5. A hill near Oxford. All the place-names in the poem (except those in the final two stanzas) refer to the countryside near Oxford.
6. Rustics. "Ingle-bench": fireside bench.
7. Crows.
8. Or Bablock Hythe (a *hithe* or *hythe* is a landing place on a river). "The stripling Thames": the narrow upper reaches of the river before it broadens out to its full width.
9. The scholar's flat-bottomed boat ("punt") is tied up by a rope at the riverbank near the ferry crossing (in the previous stanza), which was "moored to the cool bank." The motion of the boat as it is stirred by the current of the river causes the chopping sound of the rope in the water.

95   To bathe in the abandoned lasher[1] pass,
            Have often passed thee near
        Sitting upon the river bank o'ergrown;
            Marked thine outlandish garb, thy figure spare,
            Thy dark vague eyes, and soft abstracted air—
100   But, when they came from bathing, thou wast gone!

        At some lone homestead in the Cumner hills,
            Where at her open door the housewife darns,
                Thou hast been seen, or hanging on a gate
            To watch the threshers in the mossy barns.
105   Children, who early range these slopes and late
                For cresses from the rills,
            Have known thee eying, all an April day,
                The springing pastures and the feeding kine;°   *cattle*
                And marked thee, when the stars come out and shine,
110   Through the long dewy grass move slow away.

        In autumn, on the skirts of Bagley Wood—
            Where most the gypsies by the turf-edged way
                Pitch their smoked tents, and every bush you see
            With scarlet patches tagged and shreds of grey,
115   Above the forest ground called Thessaly—
                The blackbird, picking food,
            Sees thee, nor stops his meal, nor fears at all;
                So often has he known thee past him stray,
                Rapt, twirling in thy hand a withered spray,
120   And waiting for the spark from heaven to fall.

        And once, in winter, on the causeway chill
            Where home through flooded fields foot-travelers go,
                Have I not passed thee on the wooden bridge,
            Wrapped in thy cloak and battling with the snow,
125   Thy face tow'rd Hinksey and its wintry ridge?
                And thou hast climbed the hill,
            And gained the white brow of the Cumner range;
                Turned once to watch, while thick the snowflakes fall,
                The line of festal light in Christ Church hall[2]—
130   Then sought thy straw in some sequestered grange.°   *farmhouse*

        But what—I dream! Two hundred years are flown
            Since first thy story ran through Oxford halls,
                And the grave Glanvill did the tale inscribe
            That thou wert wandered from the studious walls
135   To learn strange arts, and join a gypsy tribe;
                And thou from earth art gone
            Long since, and in some quiet churchyard laid—
                Some country nook, where o'er thy unknown grave
                Tall grasses and white flowering nettles wave,
140   Under a dark, red-fruited yew tree's shade.

---

1. Water that spills over a dam or weir.   2. The dining hall of this Oxford college.

—No, no, thou hast not felt the lapse of hours!
 For what wears out the life of mortal men?
  'Tis that from change to change their being rolls;
  'Tis that repeated shocks, again, again,
145   Exhaust the energy of strongest souls
   And numb the elastic powers.
 Till having used our nerves with bliss and teen,°   *vexation*
  And tired upon a thousand schemes our wit,
  To the just-pausing Genius³ we remit
150 Our worn-out life, and are—what we have been.

Thou hast not lived, why should'st thou perish, so?
 Thou hadst *one* aim, *one* business, *one* desire;
  Else wert thou long since numbered with the dead!
  Else hadst thou spent, like other men, thy fire!
155   The generations of thy peers are fled,
   And we ourselves shall go;
 But thou possessest an immortal lot,
  And we imagine thee exempt from age
  And living as thou liv'st on Glanvill's page,
160 Because thou hadst—what we, alas! have not.

For early didst thou leave the world, with powers
 Fresh, undiverted to the world without,
  Firm to their mark, not spent on other things;
  Free from the sick fatigue, the languid doubt,
165   Which much to have tried, in much been baffled, brings.
   O life unlike to ours!
 Who fluctuate idly without term or scope,
  Of whom each strives, nor knows for what he strives,
  And each half⁴ lives a hundred different lives;
170 Who wait like thee, but not, like thee, in hope.

Thou waitest for the spark from heaven! and we,
 Light half-believers of our casual creeds,
  Who never deeply felt, nor clearly willed,
  Whose insight never has borne fruit in deeds,
175   Whose vague resolves never have been fulfilled;
   For whom each year we see
 Breeds new beginnings, disappointments new;
  Who hesitate and falter life away,
  And lose tomorrow the ground won today—
180 Ah! do not we, wanderer! await it too?

Yes, we await it!—but it still delays,
 And then we suffer! and amongst us one,⁵
  Who most has suffered, takes dejectedly
  His seat upon the intellectual throne;
185   And all his store of sad experience he

3. Perhaps the spirit of the universe, which pauses briefly to receive back the life given to us. (In Roman mythology a *genius* was an attendant spirit.)

4. An adverb modifying "lives."
5. Probably Goethe, although possibly referring to Tennyson, whose *In Memoriam* had appeared in 1850.

Lays bare of wretched days;
Tells us his misery's birth and growth and signs,
 And how the dying spark of hope was fed,
 And how the breast was soothed, and how the head,
190 And all his hourly varied anodynes.

This for our wisest! and we others pine,
 And wish the long unhappy dream would end,
  And waive all claim to bliss, and try to bear;
 With close-lipped patience for our only friend,
195   Sad patience, too near neighbor to despair—
   But none has hope like thine!
Thou through the fields and through the woods dost stray,
  Roaming the countryside, a truant boy,
  Nursing thy project in unclouded joy,
200 And every doubt long blown by time away.

O born in days when wits were fresh and clear,
 And life ran gaily as the sparkling Thames;
  Before this strange disease of modern life,
 With its sick hurry, its divided aims,
205   Its heads o'ertaxed, its palsied hearts, was rife—
   Fly hence, our contact fear!
Still fly, plunge deeper in the bowering wood!
  Averse, as Dido did with gesture stern
  From her false friend's approach in Hades turn,[6]
210 Wave us away, and keep thy solitude!

Still nursing the unconquerable hope,
 Still clutching the inviolable shade,
  With a free, onward impulse brushing through,
 By night, the silvered branches of the glade—
215   Far on the forest skirts, where none pursue.
   On some mild pastoral slope
  Emerge, and resting on the moonlit pales
  Freshen thy flowers as in former years
  With dew, or listen with enchanted ears,
220 From the dark dingles,° to the nightingales!   *small deep valleys*

But fly our paths, our feverish contact fly!
 For strong the infection of our mental strife,
  Which, though it gives no bliss, yet spoils for rest;
 And we should win thee from thy own fair life,
225   Like us distracted, and like us unblest.
   Soon, soon thy cheer would die,
  Thy hopes grow timorous, and unfixed thy powers,
  And thy clear aims be cross and shifting made;
  And then thy glad perennial youth would fade,
230 Fade, and grow old at last, and die like ours.

---

6. Dido committed suicide after her lover, Aeneas, deserted her. When he later encountered her in Hades, she silently turned away from him (see Virgil's *Aeneid*, book 6).

Then fly our greetings, fly our speech and smiles!
  —As some grave Tyrian trader, from the sea,
    Descried at sunrise an emerging prow
  Lifting the cool-haired creepers stealthily,
235   The fringes of a southward-facing brow
      Among the Aegean isles;
  And saw the merry Grecian coaster come,
    Freighted with amber grapes, and Chian wine,
    Green, bursting figs, and tunnies° steeped in brine—   *tuna fish*
240   And knew the intruders on his ancient home,

The young lighthearted masters of the waves—
  And snatched his rudder, and shook out more sail;
    And day and night held on indignantly
  O'er the blue Midland waters with the gale,
245   Betwixt the Syrtes[7] and soft Sicily,
      To where the Atlantic raves
  Outside the western straits; and unbent sails
    There, where down cloudy cliffs, through sheets of foam,
    Shy traffickers, the dark Iberians[8] come;
250   And on the beach undid his corded bales.[9]

1853

Dover Beach

  The sea is calm tonight.
  The tide is full, the moon lies fair
  Upon the straits—on the French coast the light
  Gleams and is gone; the cliffs of England stand,
5 Glimmering and vast, out in the tranquil bay.
  Come to the window, sweet is the night air!
  Only, from the long line of spray
  Where the sea meets the moon-blanched land,

  Listen! you hear the grating roar
10 Of pebbles which the waves draw back, and fling,

7. Shoals off the coast of North Africa.
8. Dark inhabitants of Spain and Portugal—perhaps associated with gypsies.
9. The elaborate simile of the final two stanzas has been variously interpreted. The trader from Tyre (a Phoenician city, on the coast of what is now Lebanon) is disconcerted to see a new business rival, "the merry Grecian coaster," emerging from one of his habitual trading ports in the Greek islands. Like the Scholar Gypsy, when similarly intruded on by hearty extroverts, he resolves to flee and seek a less competitive sphere of life.

  The reference (line 249) to the Iberians as "*shy traffickers*" (traders) is explained by Kenneth Allott as having been derived from Herodotus's *History* (4.196). Herodotus describes a distinctive method of selling goods established by merchants from Carthage who used to sail through the Strait of Gibraltar to trade with the inhabitants of the coast of West Africa. The Carthaginians would leave bales of their merchandise on display along the beaches and, without having seen their prospective customers, would return to their ships. The shy natives would then come down from their inland hiding places and set gold beside the bales they wished to buy. When the natives withdrew in their turn, the Carthaginians would return to the beach and decide whether payments were adequate, a process repeated until agreement was reached. On the Atlantic coasts this method of bargaining persisted into the 19th century. As William Beloe, a translator of the ancient Greek historian, noted in 1844: "In this manner they transact their exchange without seeing one another, or without the least instance of dishonesty . . . on either side." For the solitary Tyrian trader such a procedure, with its avoidance of "contact" (line 221), would have been especially appropriate.

At their return, up the high strand,
Begin, and cease, and then again begin,
With tremulous cadence slow, and bring
The eternal note of sadness in.

15 Sophocles long ago
Heard it on the Aegean, and it brought
Into his mind the turbid ebb and flow
Of human misery;[1] we
Find also in the sound a thought,
20 Hearing it by this distant northern sea.

The Sea of Faith
Was once, too, at the full, and round earth's shore
Lay like the folds of a bright girdle furled.[2]
But now I only hear
25 Its melancholy, long, withdrawing roar,
Retreating, to the breath
Of the night wind, down the vast edges drear
And naked shingles[3] of the world.

Ah, love, let us be true
30 To one another! for the world, which seems
To lie before us like a land of dreams,
So various, so beautiful, so new,
Hath really neither joy, nor love, nor light,
Nor certitude, nor peace, nor help for pain;
35 And we are here as on a darkling plain
Swept with confused alarms of struggle and flight,
Where ignorant armies[4] clash by night.

ca. 1851   1867

Stanzas from the Grande Chartreuse[1]

Through Alpine meadows soft-suffused
With rain, where thick the crocus blows,
Past the dark forges long disused,

---

1. A reference to a chorus in *Antigone* that compares human sorrow to the sound of the waves moving the sand beneath them (lines 585–91).
2. This difficult line means, in general, that at high tide the sea envelops the land closely. Its forces are "gathered" up (to use William Wordsworth's term) like the "folds" of bright clothing ("girdle") that have been compressed ("furled"). At ebb tide, as the sea retreats, it is unfurled and spread out. It still surrounds the shoreline but not as an "enclasping flow" (as in "To Marguerite—Continued").
3. Beaches covered with pebbles.
4. Perhaps alluding to conflicts in Arnold's own time such as occurred during the revolutions of 1848 in Europe, or at the Siege of Rome by the French in 1849 (the poem's date of composition is unknown, although generally assumed to be 1851). But the passage also refers back to another battle, one that occurred more than two thousand years earlier when an Athenian army was attempting an invasion of Sicily at nighttime. As this "night battle" was described by the ancient Greek historian Thucydides in his *History of the Peloponnesian War* (7.44), the invaders became confused by darkness and slaughtered many of their own men. Hence "ignorant armies."
1. A monastery situated high in the French Alps. It was established in 1084 by Saint Bruno, founder of the Carthusians (line 30), whose austere regimen of solitary contemplation, fasting, and religious exercises (lines 37–44) had remained virtually unchanged for centuries. Arnold visited the site on September 7, 1851, accompanied by his bride. His account may be compared with that by William Wordsworth (*Prelude* [1850] 6.414–88), who had made a similar visit in 1790.

The mule track from Saint Laurent goes.
5   The bridge is crossed, and slow we ride,
Through forest, up the mountainside.

The autumnal evening darkens round,
The wind is up, and drives the rain;
While, hark! far down, with strangled sound
10   Doth the Dead Guier's[2] stream complain,
Where that wet smoke, among the woods,
Over his boiling cauldron broods.

Swift rush the spectral vapors white
Past limestone scars° with ragged pines,   cliffs
15   Showing—then blotting from our sight!—
Halt—through the cloud-drift something shines!
High in the valley, wet and drear,
The huts of Courrerie appear.

Strike leftward! cries our guide; and higher
20   Mounts up the stony forest way.
At last the encircling trees retire;
Look! through the showery twilight grey
What pointed roofs are these advance?—
A palace of the Kings of France?

25   Approach, for what we seek is here!
Alight, and sparely sup, and wait
For rest in this outbuilding near;
Then cross the sward and reach that gate.
Knock; pass the wicket!° Thou art come   gate
30   To the Carthusians' world-famed home.

The silent courts, where night and day
Into their stone-carved basins cold
The splashing icy fountains play—
The humid corridors behold!
35   Where, ghostlike in the deepening night,
Cowled forms brush by in gleaming white.

The chapel, where no organ's peal
Invests the stern and naked prayer—
With penitential cries they kneel
40   And wrestle; rising then, with bare
And white uplifted faces stand,
Passing the Host from hand to hand;[3]

Each takes, and then his visage wan
Is buried in his cowl once more.

2. The Guiers Mort River flows down from the monastery and joins the Guiers Vif in the valley below; in French, Mort and Vif mean "dead" and "alive," respectively. Wordsworth speaks of the two rivers as "the sister streams of Life and Death."

3. Arnold, during his short visit, may not actu-ally have witnessed Mass in the monastery. Dur-ing the service the consecrated wafer ("the Host") is not passed from the hand of the offici-ating priest to the hands of the communicant (as is the practice in Arnold's own Anglican Church) but is placed directly on the tongue of the com-municant (who kneels rather than stands).

45   The cells!—the suffering Son of Man
Upon the wall—the knee-worn floor—
And where they sleep, that wooden bed,
Which shall their coffin be, when dead![4]

The library, where tract and tome
50   Not to feed priestly pride are there,
To hymn the conquering march of Rome,
Nor yet to amuse, as ours are!
They paint of souls the inner strife,
Their drops of blood, their death in life.

55   The garden, overgrown—yet mild,
See, fragrant herbs[5] are flowering there!
Strong children of the Alpine wild
Whose culture is the brethren's care;
Of human tasks their only one,
60   And cheerful works beneath the sun.

Those halls, too, destined to contain
Each its own pilgrim-host of old,
From England, Germany, or Spain—
All are before me! I behold
65   The House, the Brotherhood austere!
—And what am I, that I am here?

For rigorous teachers seized my youth,
And purged its faith, and trimmed its fire,
Showed me the high, white star of Truth,
70   There bade me gaze, and there aspire.
Even now their whispers pierce the gloom:
What dost thou in this living tomb?

Forgive me, masters of the mind![6]
At whose behest I long ago
75   So much unlearnt, so much resigned—
I come not here to be your foe!
I seek these anchorites, not in ruth,[7]
To curse and to deny your truth;

Not as their friend, or child, I speak!
80   But as, on some far northern strand,
Thinking of his own Gods, a Greek
In pity and mournful awe might stand
Before some fallen Runic stone[8]—
For both were faiths, and both are gone.

4. A Carthusian is buried on a wooden plank but does not sleep in a coffin.
5. From which the liqueur Chartreuse is manufactured. Sales of this liqueur provide the principal revenues for the monastery's upkeep.
6. Writers whose insistence on testing religious beliefs in the light of fact and reason persuaded Arnold that faith in Christianity (especially in the Roman Catholic or Anglo-Catholic forms) was no longer tenable in the modern world.
7. Remorse for having adopted the rationalist view of Christianity.
8. A monument inscribed in Teutonic letters (runes), emblematic of a Nordic religion that has become extinct. The relic reminds the Greek that his own religion is likewise dying and will soon be extinct.

85 Wandering between two worlds, one dead,
The other powerless to be born,
With nowhere yet to rest my head,
Like these, on earth I wait forlorn.
Their faith, my tears, the world deride—
90 I come to shed them at their side.

Oh, hide me in your gloom profound,
Ye solemn seats of holy pain!
Take me, cowled forms, and fence me round,
Till I possess my soul again;
95 Till free my thoughts before me roll,
Not chafed by hourly false control!

For the world cries your faith is now
But a dead time's exploded dream;
My melancholy, sciolists[9] say,
100 Is a passed mode, an outworn theme—
As if the world had ever had
A faith, or sciolists been sad!

Ah, if it *be* passed, take away,
At least, the restlessness, the pain;
105 Be man henceforth no more a prey
To these out-dated stings again!
The nobleness of grief is gone—
Ah, leave us not the fret alone!

But—if you[1] cannot give us ease—
110 Last of the race of them who grieve
Here leave us to die out with these
Last of the people who believe!
Silent, while years engrave the brow;
Silent—the best are silent now.

115 Achilles[2] ponders in his tent,
The kings of modern thought[3] are dumb;
Silent they are, though not content,
And wait to see the future come.
They have the grief men had of yore,
120 But they contend and cry no more.

Our fathers[4] watered with their tears
This sea of time whereon we sail,
Their voices were in all men's ears

9. Superficial-minded persons who pretend to know the answers to all questions.
1. It is not clear whether the speaker has resumed addressing his "rigorous teachers" (line 67) or (as would seem more likely) a combination of the sciolists, who scorn the speaker's melancholy, and the worldly, who scorn the faith of the monks. See his address to the "sons of the world" (lines 161–68).
2. Until the death of Patroclus, he refused to participate in the Trojan War; hence he is simi-

lar to modern intellectual leaders who refuse to speak out about their frustrated sense of alienation.
3. Variously but never satisfactorily identified as John Henry Newman or Thomas Carlyle (the latter was said to have preached the gospel of silence in forty volumes). Another advocate of stoical silence was the French poet Alfred de Vigny (1797–1863).
4. Predecessors among the Romantic writers such as Byron.

Who passed within their puissant hail.
125 Still the same ocean round us raves,
But we stand mute, and watch the waves.

For what availed it, all the noise
And outcry of the former men?—
Say, have their sons achieved more joys,
130 Say, is life lighter now than then?
The sufferers died, they left their pain—
The pangs which tortured them remain.

What helps it now, that Byron bore,
With haughty scorn which mocked the smart,
135 Through Europe to the Aetolian shore[5]
The pageant of his bleeding heart?
That thousands counted every groan,
And Europe made his woe her own?

What boots° it, Shelley! that the breeze   *avails*
140 Carried thy lovely wail away,
Musical through Italian trees
Which fringe thy soft blue Spezzian bay?[6]
Inheritors of thy distress
Have restless hearts one throb the less?

145 Or are we easier, to have read,
O Obermann![7] the sad, stern page,
Which tells us how thou hidd'st thy head
From the fierce tempest of thine age
In the lone brakes° of Fontainebleau,   *thickets*
150 Or chalets near the Alpine snow?

Ye slumber in your silent grave!
The world, which for an idle day
Grace to your mood of sadness gave,
Long since hath flung her weeds° away.   *mourning clothes*
155 The eternal trifler[8] breaks your spell;
But we—we learnt your lore too well!

Years hence, perhaps, may dawn an age,
More fortunate, alas! than we,
Which without hardness will be sage,
160 And gay without frivolity.
Sons of the world, oh, speed those years;
But, while we wait, allow our tears!

Allow them! We admire with awe
The exulting thunder of your race;
165 You give the universe your law,

---

5. Region in Greece where Byron died.
6. The Gulf of Spezia in Italy, where Percy Bysshe Shelley was drowned.
7. Melancholy hero of *Obermann* (1804), a
novel by the French writer Éitienne Sénancour
(1770–1846).
8. The sciolist, as in line 99.

You triumph over time and space!
Your pride of life, your tireless powers,
We laud them, but they are not ours.

We are like children reared in shade
170 Beneath some old-world abbey wall,
Forgotten in a forest glade,
And secret from the eyes of all.
Deep, deep the greenwood round them waves,
Their abbey, and its close° of graves!   *enclosure*

175 But, where the road runs near the stream,
Oft through the trees they catch a glance
Of passing troops in the sun's beam—
Pennon, and plume, and flashing lance!
Forth to the world those soldiers fare,
180 To life, to cities, and to war!

And through the wood, another way,
Faint bugle notes from far are borne,
Where hunters gather, staghounds bay,
Round some fair forest-lodge at morn.
185 Gay dames are there, in sylvan green;
Laughter and cries—those notes between!

The banners flashing through the trees
Make their blood dance and chain their eyes;
That bugle music on the breeze
190 Arrests them with a charmed surprise.
Banner by turns and bugle woo:
Ye shy recluses, follow too!

O children, what do ye reply?—
"Action and pleasure, will ye roam
195 Through these secluded dells to cry
And call us?—but too late ye come!
Too late for us your call ye blow,
Whose bent° was taken long ago.   *natural inclination*

"Long since we pace this shadowed nave;
200 We watch those yellow tapers shine,
Emblems of hope over the grave,
In the high altar's depth divine;
The organ carries to our ear
Its accents of another sphere.[9]

205 "Fenced early in this cloistral round
Of reverie, of shade, of prayer,
How should we grow in other ground?

---

9. The organ music is from the abbey in the greenwood (line 174), as contrasted with the monastery on the mountaintop in which there is no organ (line 37).

How can we flower in foreign air?
—Pass, banners, pass, and bugles, cease;
210   And leave our desert to its peace!"

1852(?)   1855

From The Function of Criticism at the Present Time[1]

Many objections have been made to a proposition which, in some remarks of mine on translating Homer,[2] I ventured to put forth; a proposition about criticism, and its importance at the present day. I said: "Of the literature of France and Germany, as of the intellect of Europe in general, the main effort, for now many years, has been a critical effort; the endeavor, in all branches of knowledge, theology, philosophy, history, art, science, to see the object as in itself it really is." I added, that owing to the operation in English literature of certain causes, "almost the last thing for which one would come to English literature is just that very thing which now Europe most desires— criticism"; and that the power and value of English literature was thereby impaired. More than one rejoinder declared that the importance I here assigned to criticism was excessive, and asserted the inherent superiority of the creative effort of the human spirit over its critical effort. And the other day, having been led by a Mr. Shairp's excellent notice of Wordsworth[3] to turn again to his biography, I found, in the words of this great man, whom I, for one, must always listen to with the profoundest respect, a sentence passed on the critic's business, which seems to justify every possible disparagement of it. Wordsworth says in one of his letters:

> The writers in these publications (the Reviews), while they prosecute their inglorious employment, cannot be supposed to be in a state of mind very favorable for being affected by the finer influences of a thing so pure as genuine poetry.

And a trustworthy reporter[4] of his conversation quotes a more elaborate judgment to the same effect:

> Wordsworth holds the critical power very low, infinitely lower than the inventive; and he said today that if the quantity of time consumed in writing critiques on the works of others were given to original composition, of whatever kind it might be, it would be much better employed; it would make a man find out sooner his own level, and it would do infinitely less mischief. A false or malicious criticism may do much injury

---

1. This essay served as an introduction to *Essays in Criticism* (1865).
2. *On Translating Homer* (1861).
3. J. C. Shairp's essay "Wordsworth: The Man and the Poet" was published in 1864. Arnold comments in a footnote:

> I cannot help thinking that a practice, common in England during the last century, and still followed in France, of printing a notice of this kind—a notice by a competent critic—to serve as an introduction to an eminent author's works, might be revived among us with advan-

tage. To introduce all succeeding editions of Wordsworth, Mr. Shairp's notice might, it seems to me, excellently serve; it is written from the point of view of an admirer, nay, of a disciple, and that is right; but then the disciple must be also, as in this case he is, a critic, a man of letters, not, as too often happens, some relation or friend with no qualification for his task except affection for his author.

4. Christopher Wordsworth, *Memoirs of William Wordsworth* (1851).

to the minds of others; a stupid invention, either in prose or verse, is quite harmless.

It is almost too much to expect of poor human nature, that a man capable of producing some effect in one line of literature, should, for the greater good of society, voluntarily doom himself to impotence and obscurity in another. Still less is this to be expected from men addicted to the composition of the "false or malicious criticism" of which Wordsworth speaks. However, everybody would admit that a false or malicious criticism had better never have been written. Everybody, too, would be willing to admit, as a general proposition, that the critical faculty is lower than the inventive. But is it true that criticism is really, in itself, a baneful and injurious employment; is it true that all time given to writing critiques on the works of others would be much better employed if it were given to original composition, of whatever kind this may be? Is it true that Johnson had better have gone on producing more *Irenes*[5] instead of writing his *Lives of the Poets;* nay, is it certain that Wordsworth himself was better employed in making his Ecclesiastical Sonnets than when he made his celebrated Preface[6] so full of criticism, and criticism of the works of others? Wordsworth was himself a great critic, and it is to be sincerely regretted that he has not left us more criticism; Goethe was one of the greatest of critics, and we may sincerely congratulate ourselves that he has left us so much criticism. Without wasting time over the exaggeration which Wordsworth's judgment on criticism clearly contains, or over an attempt to trace the causes—not difficult, I think, to be traced—which may have led Wordsworth to this exaggeration, a critic may with advantage seize an occasion for trying his own conscience, and for asking himself of what real service, at any given moment, the practice of criticism either is or may be made to his own mind and spirit, and to the minds and spirits of others.

The critical power is of lower rank than the creative. True; but in assenting to this proposition, one or two things are to be kept in mind. It is undeniable that the exercise of a creative power, that a free creative activity, is the highest function of man; it is proved to be so by man's finding in it his true happiness. But it is undeniable, also, that men may have the sense of exercising this free creative activity in other ways than in producing great works of literature or art; if it were not so, all but a very few men would be shut out from the true happiness of all men. They may have it in well-doing, they may have it in learning, they may have it even in criticizing. This is one thing to be kept in mind. Another is, that the exercise of the creative power in the production of great works of literature or art, however high this exercise of it may rank, is not at all epochs and under all conditions possible; and that therefore labor may be vainly spent in attempting it, which might with more fruit be used in preparing for it, in rendering it possible. This creative power works with elements, with materials; what if it has not those materials, those elements, ready for its use? In that case it must surely wait till they are ready. Now, in literature—I will limit myself to literature, for it is about literature that the question arises—the elements with which the creative power works are ideas; the best ideas on every matter which literature touches, current at the time. At any rate we may lay it down as certain that in modern literature

5. *Irene* (1749) is a clumsy play by Samuel Johnson (1709–1784), whose *Lives of the Poets* (1779–81) is a major work of criticism.

6. To *Lyrical Ballads* (1800). "Ecclesiastical Sonnets": a sonnet sequence (1821–22) by Wordsworth, usually regarded as minor verse.

no manifestation of the creative power not working with these can be very important or fruitful. And I say *current* at the time, not merely accessible at the time; for creative literary genius does not principally show itself in discovering new ideas, that is rather the business of the philosopher. The grand work of literary genius is a work of synthesis and exposition, not of analysis and discovery; its gift lies in the faculty of being happily inspired by a certain intellectual and spiritual atmosphere, by a certain order of ideas, when it finds itself in them; of dealing divinely with these ideas, presenting them in the most effective and attractive combinations—making beautiful works with them, in short. But it must have the atmosphere, it must find itself amidst the order of ideas, in order to work freely; and these it is not so easy to command. This is why great creative epochs in literature are so rare, this is why there is so much that is unsatisfactory in the productions of many men of real genius; because, for the creation of a masterwork of literature two powers must concur, the power of the man and the power of the moment, and the man is not enough without the moment; the creative power has, for its happy exercise, appointed elements, and those elements are not in its own control.

Nay, they are more within the control of the critical power. It is the business of the critical power, as I said in the words already quoted, "in all branches of knowledge, theology, philosophy, history, art, science, to see the object as in itself it really is." Thus it tends, at last, to make an intellectual situation of which the creative power can profitably avail itself. It tends to establish an order of ideas, if not absolutely true, yet true by comparison with that which it displaces; to make the best ideas prevail. Presently these new ideas reach society, the touch of truth is the touch of life, and there is a stir and growth everywhere; out of this stir and growth come the creative epochs of literature.

Or, to narrow our range, and quit these considerations of the general march of genius and of society—considerations which are apt to become too abstract and impalpable—everyone can see that a poet, for instance, ought to know life and the world before dealing with them in poetry; and life and the world being in modern times very complex things, the creation of a modern poet, to be worth much, implies a great critical effort behind it; else it must be a comparatively poor, barren, and short-lived affair. This is why Byron's poetry had so little endurance in it, and Goethe's so much; both Byron and Goethe had a great productive power, but Goethe's was nourished by a great critical effort providing the true materials for it, and Byron's was not; Goethe knew life and the world, the poet's necessary subjects, much more comprehensively and thoroughly than Byron. He knew a great deal more of them, and he knew them much more as they really are.

It has long seemed to me that the burst of creative activity in our literature, through the first quarter of this century, had about it in fact something premature; and that from this cause its productions are doomed, most of them, in spite of the sanguine hopes which accompanied and do still accompany them, to prove hardly more lasting than the productions of far less splendid epochs. And this prematureness comes from its having proceeded without having its proper data, without sufficient materials to work with. In other words, the English poetry of the first quarter of this century, with plenty of energy, plenty of creative force, did not know enough. This makes Byron so empty of matter, Shelley so incoherent, Wordsworth even, profound as he is, yet so wanting in completeness and variety. Wordsworth cared little for books, and disparaged Goethe. I admire Wordsworth, as he is, so much that I cannot wish him different; and it is vain, no doubt, to imagine such a man different from what he is, to suppose that he *could* have been different. But surely the one thing wanting to make Wordsworth an even greater poet than he is—his thought richer, and his influence of wider application—was that he should have read more books, among them, no doubt, those of that Goethe whom he disparaged without reading him.

But to speak of books and reading may easily lead to a misunderstanding here. It was not really books and reading that lacked to our poetry at this epoch: Shelley had plenty of reading, Coleridge had immense reading. Pindar and Sophocles[7]—as we all say so glibly, and often with so little discernment of the real import of what we are saying—had not many books; Shakespeare was no deep reader. True; but in the Greece of Pindar and Sophocles, in the England of Shakespeare, the poet lived in a current of ideas in the highest degree animating and nourishing to the creative power; society was, in the fullest measure, permeated by fresh thought, intelligent and alive. And this state of things is the true basis for the creative power's exercise, in this it finds its data, its materials, truly ready for its hand; all the books and reading in the world are only valuable as they are helps to this. Even when this does not actually exist, books and reading may enable a man to construct a kind of semblance of it in his own mind, a world of knowledge and intelligence in which he may live and work. This is by no means an equivalent to the artist for the nationally diffused life and thought of the epochs of Sophocles or Shakespeare; but, besides that it may be a means of preparation for such epochs, it does really constitute, if many share in it, a quickening and sustaining atmosphere of great value. Such an atmosphere the many-sided learning and the long and widely combined critical effort of Germany formed for Goethe, when he lived and worked. There was no national glow of life and thought there as in the Athens of Pericles or the England of Elizabeth.[8] That was the poet's weakness. But there was a sort of equivalent for it in the complete culture and unfettered thinking of a large body of Germans. That was his strength. In the England of the first quarter of this century there was neither a national glow of life and thought, such as we had in the age of Elizabeth, nor yet a culture and a force of learning and criticism such as were to be found in Germany. Therefore the creative power of poetry wanted, for success in the highest sense, materials and a basis; a thorough interpretation of the world was necessarily denied to it.

At first sight it seems strange that out of the immense stir of the French Revolution and its age should not have come a crop of works of genius equal to that which came out of the stir of the great productive time of Greece, or out of that of the Renascence, with its powerful episode the Reformation. But the truth is that the stir of the French Revolution took a character which essentially distinguished it from such movements as these. These were, in the main, disinterestedly intellectual and spiritual movements; movements in which the human spirit looked for its satisfaction in itself and in the increased

7. Greek tragedian (ca. 496–406 B.C.E.). Pindar (518–438 B.C.E.), Greek lyric poet.
8. Elizabeth I (1533–1603; reigned 1558–1603). Pericles (ca. 495–429 B.C.E.), the leading states-man of Athens during the period of the city's most outstanding achievements in art, literature, and politics.

play of its own activity. The French Revolution took a political, practical character. The movement, which went on in France under the old *régime,* from 1700 to 1789, was far more really akin than that of the Revolution itself to the movement of the Renascence; the France of Voltaire and Rousseau[9] told far more powerfully upon the mind of Europe than the France of the Revolution. Goethe reproached this last expressly with having "thrown quiet culture back."[1] Nay, and the true key to how much in our Byron, even in our Wordsworth, is this!—that they had their source in a great movement of feeling, not in a great movement of mind. The French Revolution, however—that object of so much blind love and so much blind hatred—found undoubtedly its motive power in the intelligence of men, and not in their practical sense; this is what distinguishes it from the English Revolution of Charles the First's time.[2] This is what makes it a more spiritual event than our Revolution, an event of much more powerful and worldwide interest, though practically less successful; it appeals to an order of ideas which are universal, certain, permanent. 1789 asked of a thing, Is it rational? 1642 asked of a thing, Is it legal? or, when it went furthest, Is it according to conscience? This is the English fashion, a fashion to be treated, within its own sphere, with the highest respect; for its success, within its own sphere, has been prodigious. But what is law in one place is not law in another; what is law here today is not law even here tomorrow; and as for conscience, what is binding on one man's conscience is not binding on another's. The old woman who threw her stool at the head of the surpliced minister in St. Giles's Church at Edinburgh[3] obeyed an impulse to which millions of the human race may be permitted to remain strangers. But the prescriptions of reason are absolute, unchanging, of universal validity; *to count by tens is the easiest way of counting*—that is a proposition of which everyone, from here to the Antipodes, feels the force; at least I should say so if we did not live in a country where it is not impossible that any morning we may find a letter in the *Times* declaring that a decimal coinage is an absurdity.[4] That a whole nation should have been penetrated with an enthusiasm for pure reason, and with an ardent zeal for making its prescriptions triumph, is a very remarkable thing, when we consider how little of mind, or anything so worthy and quickening as mind, comes into the motives which alone, in general, impel great masses of men. In spite of the extravagant direction given to this enthusiasm, in spite of the crimes and follies in which it lost itself, the French Revolution derives from the force, truth, and universality of the ideas which it took for its law, and from the passion with which it could inspire a multitude for these ideas, a unique and still living power; it is—it will probably long remain—the greatest, the most animating event in history. And as no sincere passion for the things of the mind, even though it turn out in many respects an unfortunate passion, is ever quite thrown away and quite barren of good, France has

---

9. Jean-Jacques Rousseau (1712–1778), Swiss-born French philosopher and political theorist. Voltaire (1694–1778), pen name of the French writer François Marie Arouet.
1. See "Vier Jahreszeiten Herbst" (1796) in his *Werke* (1887) 1.354.
2. Disputes between Charles I (1600–1649; reigned 1625–49) and Parliament led in 1642 to civil war and ultimately to the king's beheading. (Eleven years later his son, Charles II, was recalled from exile and proclaimed king.)

3. In 1637 rioting broke out in Scotland against a new kind of church service that was prescribed by Charles I. The riot was started by an old woman hurling a stool at a clergyman, whom she accused of saying Mass.
4. In 1863 a proposal in Parliament to introduce the French decimal system for weights and measures had provoked articles in the London *Times* defending the English system (of ounces and pounds or inches and feet) as more practical. Decimal coinage was finally instituted in 1971.

reaped from hers one fruit—the natural and legitimate fruit though not precisely the grand fruit she expected: she is the country in Europe where *the people* is most alive.

But the mania for giving an immediate political and practical application to all these fine ideas of the reason was fatal. Here an Englishman is in his element: on this theme we can all go on for hours. And all we are in the habit of saying on it has undoubtedly a great deal of truth. Ideas cannot be too much prized in and for themselves, cannot be too much lived with; but to transport them abruptly into the world of politics and practice, violently to revolutionize this world to their bidding—that is quite another thing. There is the world of ideas and there is the world of practice; the French are often for suppressing the one and the English the other; but neither is to be suppressed. A member of the House of Commons said to me the other day: "That a thing is an anomaly, I consider to be no objection to it whatever." I venture to think he was wrong; that a thing is an anomaly *is* an objection to it, but absolutely and in the sphere of ideas: it is not necessarily, under such and such circumstances, or at such and such a moment, an objection to it in the sphere of politics and practice. Joubert[5] has said beautifully: *"C'est la force et le droit qui règlent toutes choses dans le monde; la force en attendant le droit."*—"Force and right are the governors of this world; force till right is ready." *Force till right is ready;* and till right is ready, force, the existing order of things, is justified, is the legitimate ruler. But right is something moral, and implies inward recognition, free assent of the will; we are not ready for right—*right,* so far as we are concerned, is *not ready*—until we have attained this sense of seeing it and willing it. The way in which for us it may change and transform force, the existing order of things, and become, in its turn, the legitimate ruler of the world, should depend on the way in which, when our time comes, we see it and will it. Therefore for other people enamored of their own newly discerned right, to attempt to impose it upon us as ours, and violently to substitute their right for our force, is an act of tyranny, and to be resisted. It sets at nought the second great half of our maxim, *force till right is ready.* This was the grand error of the French Revolution; and its movement of ideas, by quitting the intellectual sphere and rushing furiously into the political sphere, ran, indeed a prodigious and memorable course, but produced no such intellectual fruit as the movement of ideas of the Renascence, and created, in opposition to itself, what I may call an *epoch of concentration.* The great force of that epoch of concentration was England; and the great voice of that epoch of concentration was Burke.[6] It is the fashion to treat Burke's writings on the French Revolution as superannuated and conquered by the event; as the eloquent but unphilosophical tirades of bigotry and prejudice. I will not deny that they are often disfigured by the violence and passion of the moment, and that in some directions Burke's view was bounded, and his observation therefore at fault. But on the whole, and for those who can make the needful corrections, what distinguishes these writings is their profound, permanent, fruitful, philosophical truth, They contain the true philosophy of an epoch of concentra-

5. Joseph Joubert (1754–1824), French moralist about whom Arnold wrote in his *Essays in Criticism.*
6. Edmund Burke (1729–1797), prominent statesman and author of *Reflections on the French Revolution* (1790), which expressed the conservative opposition to revolutionary theories.

tion, dissipate the heavy atmosphere which its own nature is apt to engender round it, and make its resistance rational instead of mechanical.

But Burke is so great because, almost alone in England, he brings thought to bear upon politics, he saturates politics with thought. It is his accident[7] that his ideas were at the service of an epoch of concentration, not of an epoch of expansion; it is his characteristic that he so lived by ideas, and had such a source of them welling up within him, that he could float even an epoch of concentration and English Tory politics with them. It does not hurt him that Dr. Price[8] and the Liberals were enraged with him; it does not even hurt him that George the Third and the Tories were enchanted with him. His greatness is that he lived in a world which neither English Liberalism nor English Toryism is apt to enter—the world of ideas, not the world of catch-words and party habits. So far is it from being really true of him that he "to party gave up what was meant for mankind,"[9] that at the very end of his fierce struggle with the French Revolution, after all his invectives against its false pretensions, hollowness, and madness, with his sincere convictions of its mischievousness, he can close a memorandum on the best means of combating it, some of the last pages he ever wrote[1]—the *Thoughts on French Affairs*, in December 1791—with these striking words:

> The evil is stated, in my opinion, as it exists. The remedy must be where power, wisdom, and information, I hope, are more united with good intentions than they can be with me. I have done with this subject, I believe, forever. It has given me many anxious moments for the last two years. *If a great change is to be made in human affairs, the minds of men will be fitted to it; the general opinions and feelings will draw that way. Every fear, every hope will forward it; and then they who persist in opposing this mighty current in human affairs, will appear rather to resist the decrees of Providence itself, than the mere designs of men. They will not be resolute and firm, but perverse and obstinate.*

That return of Burke upon himself has always seemed to me one of the finest things in English literature, or indeed in any literature. That is what I call living by ideas: when one side of a question has long had your earnest support, when all your feelings are engaged, when you hear all round you no language but one, when your party talks this language like a steam engine and can imagine no other—still to be able to think, still to be irresistibly carried, if so it be, by the current of thought to the opposite side of the question, and, like Balaam, to be unable to speak anything *but what the Lord has put in your mouth.*[2] I know nothing more striking, and I must add that I know nothing more un-English.

For the Englishman in general is like my friend the Member of Parliament, and believes, point-blank, that for a thing to be an anomaly is absolutely no objection to it whatever. He is like the Lord Auckland[3] of Burke's day, who, in a memorandum on the French Revolution, talks of certain "miscreants,

7. Fortune.
8. Richard Price (1723–1791), a prorevolutionary clergyman who was an opponent of Burke's.
9. From the poem "Retaliation" (1774) by Oliver Goldsmith (1728–1774).
1. Arnold was mistaken; Burke continued to write for another six years after 1791. According to Arnold's editor, R. H. Super, the mistake was caused by misunderstanding a passage in one of Burke's letters.
2. Balaam, a false and worldly prophet, pronounced a blessing on the Israelites instead of the curse he had intended (Numbers 22.38).
3. William Eden, first Baron Auckland (1744–1814), statesman and diplomat.

assuming the name of philosophers, who have presumed themselves capable of establishing a new system of society." The Englishman has been called a political animal, and he values what is political and practical so much that ideas easily become objects of dislike in his eyes, and thinkers, "miscreants," because ideas and thinkers have rashly meddled with politics and practice. This would be all very well if the dislike and neglect confined themselves to ideas transported out of their own sphere, and meddling rashly with practice; but they are inevitably extended to ideas as such, and to the whole life of intelligence; practice is everything, a free play of the mind is nothing. The notion of the free play of the mind upon all subjects being a pleasure in itself, being an object of desire, being an essential provider of elements without which a nation's spirit, whatever compensations it may have for them, must, in the long run, die of inanition, hardly enters into an Englishman's thoughts. It is noticeable that the word *curiosity*, which in other languages is used in a good sense, to mean, as a high and fine quality of man's nature, just this disinterested love of a free play of the mind on all subjects, for its own sake—it is noticeable, I say, that this word has in our language no sense of the kind, no sense but a rather bad and disparaging one. But criticism, real criticism, is essentially the exercise of this very quality. It obeys an instinct prompting it to try to know the best that is known and thought in the world, irrespectively of practice, politics, and everything of the kind; and to value knowledge and thought as they approach this best, without the intrusion of any other considerations whatever. This is an instinct for which there is, I think, little original sympathy in the practical English nature, and what there was of it has undergone a long benumbing period of blight and suppression in the epoch of concentration which followed the French Revolution.

But epochs of concentration cannot well endure forever; epochs of expansion, in the due course of things, follow them. Such an epoch of expansion seems to be opening in this country. In the first place all danger of a hostile forcible pressure of foreign ideas upon our practice has long disappeared; like the traveler in the fable, therefore, we begin to wear our cloak a little more loosely.[4] Then, with a long peace, the ideas of Europe steal gradually and amicably in, and mingle, though in infinitesimally small quantities at a time, with our own notions. Then, too, in spite of all that is said about the absorbing and brutalizing influence of our passionate material progress, it seems to me indisputable that this progress is likely, though not certain, to lead in the end to an apparition of intellectual life; and that man, after he has made himself perfectly comfortable and has now to determine what to do with himself next, may begin to remember that he has a mind, and that the mind may be made the source of great pleasure. I grant it is mainly the privilege of faith, at present, to discern this end to our railways, our business, and our fortune-making; but we shall see if, here as elsewhere, faith is not in the end the true prophet. Our ease, our traveling, and our unbounded liberty to hold just as hard and securely as we please to the practice to which our notions have given birth, all tend to beget an inclination to deal a little more freely with these notions themselves, to canvass them a little, to penetrate a little into their real nature. Flutterings of curiosity, in the foreign sense of the word, appear amongst us, and it is in these that criticism must

4. In Aesop's fable of the wind and the sun, the two compete to see who is more powerful. The sun wins by causing the traveler to take off his coat (the goal of both), whereas the wind can only make him hold it closely.

look to find its account. Criticism first; a time of true creative activity, perhaps—which, as I have said, must inevitably be preceded amongst us by a time of criticism—hereafter, when criticism has done its work.

It is of the last importance that English criticism should clearly discern what rule for its course, in order to avail itself of the field now opening to it, and to produce fruit for the future, it ought to take. The rule may be summed up in one word—*disinterestedness*.[5] And how is criticism to show disinterestedness? By keeping aloof from what is called "the practical view of things"; by resolutely following the law of its own nature, which is to be a free play of the mind on all subjects which it touches. By steadily refusing to lend itself to any of those ulterior, political, practical considerations about ideas, which plenty of people will be sure to attach to them, which perhaps ought often to be attached to them, which in this country at any rate are certain to be attached to them quite sufficiently, but which criticism has really nothing to do with. Its business is, as I have said, simply to know the best that is known and thought in the world, and by in its turn making this known, to create a current of true and fresh ideas. Its business is to do this with inflexible honesty, with due ability; but its business is to do no more, and to leave alone all questions of practical consequences and applications, questions which will never fail to have due prominence given to them. Else criticism, besides being really false to its own nature, merely continues in the old rut which it has hitherto followed in this country, and will certainly miss the chance now given to it. For what is at present the bane of criticism in this country? It is that practical considerations cling to it and stifle it. It subserves interests not its own. Our organs of criticism are organs of men and parties having practical ends to serve, and with them those practical ends are the first thing and the play of mind the second; so much play of mind as is compatible with the prosecution of those practical ends is all that is wanted. An organ like the *Revue des Deux Mondes*,[6] having for its main function to understand and utter the best that is known and thought in the world, existing, it may be said, as just an organ for a free play of the mind, we have not. But we have the *Edinburgh Review*, existing as an organ of the old Whigs, and for as much play of mind as may suit its being that; we have the *Quarterly Review*, existing as an organ of the Tories, and for as much play of mind as may suit its being that; we have the *British Quarterly Review*, existing as an organ of the political Dissenters, and for as much play of mind as may suit its being that; we have the *Times*, existing as an organ of the common, satisfied, well-to-do Englishman, and for as much play of mind as may suit its being that. And so on through all the various fractions, political and religious, of our society; every fraction has, as such, its organ of criticism, but the notion of combining all fractions in the common pleasure of a free disinterested play of mind meets with no favor. Directly this play of mind wants to have more scope, and to forget the pressure of practical considerations a little, it is checked, it is made to feel the chain. We saw this the other day in the extinction, so much to be regretted, of the *Home and Foreign Review*.[7] Perhaps in no organ of criticism in this country was there so much knowledge, so much play of mind; but these could not save it. The *Dublin Review* subordinates play of

5. This key word in Arnold's argument connotes independence and objectivity of mind. It means not having an interest, in the sense of an ax to grind. It does not mean lack of interest.

6. An international magazine of exceptionally high quality, founded in Paris in 1829.
7. A liberal Catholic periodical, founded in 1862, which ceased publication in 1864.

mind to the practical business of English and Irish Catholicism, and lives. It must needs be that men should act in sects and parties, that each of these sects and parties should have its organ, and should make this organ subserve the interests of its action; but it would be well, too, that there should be a criticism, not the minister of these interests, not their enemy, but absolutely and entirely independent of them. No other criticism will ever attain any real authority or make any real way towards its end—the creating a current of true and fresh ideas.

It is because criticism has so little kept in the pure intellectual sphere, has so little detached itself from practice, has been so directly polemical and controversial, that it has so ill accomplished, in this country, its best spiritual work, which is to keep man from a self-satisfaction which is retarding and vulgarizing, to lead him towards perfection, by making his mind dwell upon what is excellent in itself, and the absolute beauty and fitness of things. A polemical practical criticism makes men blind even to the ideal imperfection of their practice, makes them willingly assert its ideal perfection, in order the better to secure it against attack; and clearly this is narrowing and baneful for them. If they were reassured on the practical side, speculative considerations of ideal perfection they might be brought to entertain, and their spiritual horizon would thus gradually widen. Sir Charles Adderley[8] says to the Warwickshire farmers:

> Talk of the improvement of breed! Why, the race we ourselves represent, the men and women, the old Anglo-Saxon race, are the best breed in the whole world. . . . The absence of a too enervating climate, too unclouded skies, and a too luxurious nature, has produced so vigorous a race of people, and has rendered us so superior to all the world.

Mr. Roebuck says to the Sheffield cutlers:[9]

> I look around me and ask what is the state of England? Is not property safe? Is not every man able to say what he likes? Can you not walk from one end of England to the other in perfect security? I ask you whether, the world over or in past history, there is anything like it? Nothing. I pray that our unrivaled happiness may last.

Now obviously there is a peril for poor human nature in words and thoughts of such exuberant self-satisfaction, until we find ourselves safe in the streets of the Celestial City.

> *Das wenige verschwindet leicht dem Blicke*
> *Der vorwärts sieht, wie viel noch übrig bleibt*—[1]

says Goethe; "the little that is done seems nothing when we look forward and see how much we have yet to do." Clearly this is a better line of reflection for weak humanity, so long as it remains on this earthly field of labor and trial.

But neither Sir Charles Adderley nor Mr. Roebuck is by nature inaccessible to considerations of this sort. They only lose sight of them owing to the controversial life we all lead, and the practical form which all speculation takes with us. They have in view opponents whose aim is not ideal, but

8. Conservative politician and wealthy landowner (1814–1905).
9. Makers of knives and forks. John Arthur Roebuck (1801–1879), radical politician and representative in Parliament for the industrial city of Sheffield, famous for its metalworking trades.
1. Goethe's *Iphigenie auf Tauris* (1787) 1.2.91–92.

practical; and in their zeal to uphold their own practice against these innovators, they go so far as even to attribute to this practice an ideal perfection. Somebody has been wanting to introduce a six-pound franchise, or to abolish church-rates,[2] or to collect agricultural statistics by force, or to diminish local self-government. How natural, in reply to such proposals, very likely improper or ill-timed, to go a little beyond the mark and to say stoutly, "Such a race of people as we stand, so superior to all the world! The old Anglo-Saxon race, the best breed in the whole world! I pray that our unrivaled happiness may last! I ask you whether, the world over or in past history, there is anything like it?" And so long as criticism answers this dithyramb by insisting that the old Anglo-Saxon race would be still more superior to all others if it had no church-rates, or that our unrivaled happiness would last yet longer with a six-pound franchise, so long will the strain, "The best breed in the whole world!" swell louder and louder, everything ideal and refining will be lost out of sight, and both the assailed and their critics will remain in a sphere, to say the truth, perfectly unvital, a sphere in which spiritual progression is impossible. But let criticism leave church-rates and the franchise alone, and in the most candid spirit, without a single lurking thought of practical innovation, confront with our dithyramb this paragraph on which I stumbled in a newspaper immediately after reading Mr. Roebuck:

> A shocking child murder has just been committed at Nottingham.[3] A girl named Wragg left the workhouse there on Saturday morning with her young illegitimate child. The child was soon afterwards found dead on Mapperly Hills, having been strangled. Wragg is in custody.

Nothing but that; but, in juxtaposition with the absolute eulogies of Sir Charles Adderley and Mr. Roebuck, how eloquent, how suggestive are those few lines! "Our old Anglo-Saxon breed, the best in the whole world!"—how much that is harsh and ill-favored there is in this best! *Wragg!* If we are to talk of ideal perfection, of "the best in the whole world," has anyone reflected what a touch of grossness in our race, what an original shortcoming in the more delicate spiritual perceptions, is shown by the natural growth amongst us of such hideous names—Higginbottom, Stiggins, Bugg! In Ionia and Attica[4] they were luckier in this respect than "the best race in the world"; by the Ilissus[5] there was no Wragg, poor thing! And "our unrivaled happiness"— what an element of grimness, bareness, and hideousness mixes with it and blurs it; the workhouse, the dismal Mapperly Hills[6]—how dismal those who have seen them will remember—the gloom, the smoke, the cold, the strangled illegitimate child! "I ask you whether, the world over or in past history, there is anything like it?" Perhaps not, one is inclined to answer; but at any rate, in that case, the world is very much to be pitied. And the final touch— short, bleak and inhuman: *Wragg is in custody.* The sex lost in the confusion of our unrivaled happiness; or (shall I say?) the superfluous Christian name lopped off by the straightforward vigor of our old Anglo-Saxon breed! There is profit for the spirit in such contrasts as this; criticism serves the cause of perfection by establishing them. By eluding sterile conflict, by refusing to

---

2. Taxes supporting the Church of England. "Six-pound franchise": a radical proposal to extend the right to vote to anyone owning land worth £6 annual rent.
3. It occurred on September 10, 1864.
4. The district in Greece that includes Athens.

Ionia: area of the west coast of Asia Minor where Homer was believed to have lived.
5. A stream south of Athens.
6. Adjacent to the coal-mining and industrial area of Nottingham (later associated with the writings of D. H. Lawrence).

remain in the sphere where alone narrow and relative conceptions have any worth and validity, criticism may diminish its momentary importance, but only in this way has it a chance of gaining admittance for those wider and more perfect conceptions to which all its duty is really owed. Mr. Roebuck will have a poor opinion of an adversary who replies to his defiant songs of triumph only by murmuring under his breath, *Wragg is in custody*; but in no other way will these songs of triumph be induced gradually to moderate themselves, to get rid of what in them is excessive and offensive, and to fall into a softer and truer key.

It will be said that it is a very subtle and indirect action which I am thus prescribing for criticism, and that, by embracing in this manner the Indian[7] virtue of detachment and abandoning the sphere of practical life, it condemns itself to a slow and obscure work. Slow and obscure it may be, but it is the only proper work of criticism. The mass of mankind will never have any ardent zeal for seeing things as they are; very inadequate ideas will always satisfy them. On these inadequate ideas reposes, and must repose, the general practice of the world. That is as much as saying that whoever sets himself to see things as they are will find himself one of a very small circle; but it is only by this small circle resolutely doing its own work that adequate ideas will ever get current at all. The rush and roar of practical life will always have a dizzying and attracting effect upon the most collected spectator, and tend to draw him into its vortex; most of all will this be the case where that life is so powerful as it is in England. But it is only by remaining collected, and refusing to lend himself to the point of view of the practical man, that the critic can do the practical man any service, and it is only by the greatest sincerity in pursuing his own course, and by at last convincing even the practical man of his sincerity, that he can escape misunderstandings which perpetually threaten him.

For the practical man is not apt for fine distinctions, and yet in these distinctions truth and the highest culture greatly find their account. But it is not easy to lead a practical man—unless you reassure him as to your practical intentions, you have no chance of leading him—to see that a thing which he has always been used to look at from one side only, which he greatly values, and which, looked at from that side, quite deserves, perhaps, all the prizing and admiring which he bestows upon it—that this thing, looked at from another side, may appear much less beneficent and beautiful, and yet retain all its claims to our practical allegiance. Where shall we find language innocent enough, how shall we make the spotless purity of our intentions evident enough, to enable us to say to the political Englishman that the British Constitution itself, which, seen from the practical side, looks such a magnificent organ of progress and virtue, seen from the speculative side— with its compromises, its love of facts, its horror of theory, its studied avoidance of clear thoughts—that, seen from this side, our august Constitution sometimes looks—forgive me, shade of Lord Somers!—a colossal machine for the manufacture of Philistines?[8] How is Cobbett[9] to say this and not be misunderstood, blackened as he is with the smoke of a lifelong conflict in

7. I.e., Hindu.
8. The unenlightened middle classes, whose opposition to the defenders of culture is akin to that of the biblical tribe that fought against the people of Israel, "the children of light." Arnold's repeated use of this parallel has established the term in our language. John Somers (1651–1716), statesman responsible for formulating the Declaration of Rights.
9. William Cobbett (1762–1835), vehement reformer and champion of the poor and oppressed.

the field of political practice? how is Mr. Carlyle to say it and not be misunderstood, after his furious raid into this field with his *Latter-day Pamphlets*? how is Mr. Ruskin, after his pugnacious political economy?[1] I say, the critic must keep out of the region of immediate practice in the political, social, humanitarian sphere if he wants to make a beginning for that more free speculative treatment of things, which may perhaps one day make its benefits felt even in this sphere, but in a natural and thence irresistible manner.

* * *

If I have insisted so much on the course which criticism must take where politics and religion are concerned, it is because, where these burning matters are in question, it is most likely to go astray. I have wished, above all, to insist on the attitude which criticism should adopt towards things in general; on its right tone and temper of mind. But then comes another question as to the subject matter which literary criticism should most seek. Here, in general, its course is determined for it by the idea which is the law of its being; the idea of a disinterested endeavour to learn and propagate the best that is known and thought in the world, and thus to establish a current of fresh and true ideas. By the very nature of things, as England is not all the world, much of the best that is known and thought in the world cannot be of English growth, must be foreign; by the nature of things, again, it is just this that we are least likely to know, while English thought is streaming in upon us from all sides, and takes excellent care that we shall not be ignorant of its existence. The English critic of literature, therefore, must dwell much on foreign thought, and with particular heed on any part of it, which, while significant and fruitful in itself, is for any reason specially likely to escape him. Again, judging is often spoken of as the critic's one business, and so in some sense it is; but the judgment which almost insensibly forms itself in a fair and clear mind, along with fresh knowledge, is the valuable one; and thus knowledge, and ever fresh knowledge, must be the critic's great concern for himself. And it is by communicating fresh knowledge, and letting his own judgment pass along with it—but insensibly, and in the second place, not the first, as a sort of companion and clue, not as an abstract lawgiver—that the critic will generally do most good to his readers. Sometimes, no doubt, for the sake of establishing an author's place in literature, and his relation to a central standard (and if this is not done, how are we to get at our *best in the world*?) criticism may have to deal with a subject matter so familiar that fresh knowledge is out of the question, and then it must be all judgment; an enunciation and detailed application of principles. Here the great safeguard is never to let oneself become abstract, always to retain an intimate and lively consciousness of the truth of what one is saying, and, the moment this fails us, to be sure that something is wrong. Still under all circumstances, this mere judgment and application of principles is, in itself, not the most satisfactory work to the critic; like mathematics, it is tautological, and cannot well give us, like fresh learning, the sense of creative activity.

But stop, some one will say; all this talk is of no practical use to us whatever; this criticism of yours is not what we have in our minds when we speak of criticism; when we speak of critics and criticism, we mean critics and

---

1. Reference to *Unto This Last* (1862), in which John Ruskin shifted from art criticism to an attack on traditional theories of economics. In *Latter-* *Day Pamphlets* (1850), Thomas Carlyle expressed bitter antidemocratic views.

criticism of the current English literature of the day; when you offer to tell criticism its function, it is to this criticism that we expect you to address yourself. I am sorry for it, for I am afraid I must disappoint these expectations. I am bound by my own definition of criticism: *a disinterested endeavour to learn and propagate the best that is known and thought in the world.* How much of current English literature comes into this "best that is known and thought in the world"? Not very much I fear; certainly less, at this moment, than of the current literature of France or Germany. Well, then, am I to alter my definition of criticism, in order to meet the requirements of a number of practicing English critics, who, after all, are free in their choice of a business? That would be making criticism lend itself just to one of those alien practical considerations, which, I have said, are so fatal to it. One may say, indeed, to those who have to deal with the mass—so much better disregarded—of current English literature, that they may at all events endeavour, in dealing with this, to try it, so far as they can, by the standard of the best that is known and thought in the world; one may say, that to get anywhere near this standard, every critic should try and possess one great literature, at least, besides his own; and the more unlike his own, the better. But, after all, the criticism I am really concerned with—the criticism which alone can much help us for the future, the criticism which, throughout Europe, is at the present day meant, when so much stress is laid on the importance of criticism and the critical spirit—is a criticism which regards Europe as being, for intellectual and spiritual purposes, one great confederation, bound to a joint action and working to a common result, and whose members have, for their proper outfit, a knowledge of Greek, Roman, and Eastern antiquity, and of one another. Special, local, and temporary advantages being put out of account, that modern nation will in the intellectual and spiritual sphere make most progress, which most thoroughly carries out this program. And what is that but saying that we too, all of us, as individuals, the more thoroughly we carry it out, shall make the more progress?

There is so much inviting us!—what are we to take? what will nourish us in growth towards perfection? That is the question which, with the immense field of life and of literature lying before him, the critic has to answer; for himself first, and afterwards for others. In this idea of the critic's business the essays brought together in the following pages have had their origin; in this idea, widely different as are their subjects, they have, perhaps, their unity.

I conclude with what I said at the beginning: to have the sense of creative activity is the great happiness and the great proof of being alive, and it is not denied to criticism to have it; but then criticism must be sincere, simple, flexible, ardent, ever widening its knowledge. Then it may have, in no contemptible measure, a joyful sense of creative activity; a sense which a man of insight and conscience will prefer to what he might derive from a poor, starved, fragmentary, inadequate creation. And at some epochs no other creation is possible.

Still, in full measure, the sense of creative activity belongs only to genuine creation; in literature we must never forget that. But what true man of letters ever can forget it? It is no such common matter for a gifted nature to come into possession of a current of true and living ideas, and to produce amidst the inspiration of them, that we are likely to underrate it. The epochs of Aeschylus[2]

2. Greek tragedian (525–456 B.C.E.).

and Shakespeare make us feel their pre-eminence. In an epoch like those is, no doubt, the true life of literature; there is the promised land, towards which criticism can only beckon. That promised land it will not be ours to enter, and we shall die in the wilderness:[3] but to have desired to enter it, to have saluted it from afar, is already, perhaps, the best distinction among contemporaries; it will certainly be the best title to esteem with posterity.

1864, 1865

From Culture and Anarchy[1]

From Chapter 1. Sweetness and Light

The impulse of the English race towards moral development and self-conquest has nowhere so powerfully manifested itself as in Puritanism. Nowhere has Puritanism found so adequate an expression as in the religious organization of the Independents.[2] The modern Independents have a newspaper, the *Nonconformist*, written with great sincerity and ability. The motto, the standard, the profession of faith which this organ of theirs carries aloft, is: "The Dissidence of Dissent and the Protestantism of the Protestant religion." There is sweetness and light, and an ideal of complete harmonious human perfection! One need not go to culture and poetry to find language to judge it. Religion, with its instinct for perfection, supplies language to judge it, language, too, which is in our mouths every day. "Finally, be of one mind, united in feeling," says St. Peter.[3] There is an ideal which judges the Puritan ideal: "The Dissidence of Dissent and the Protestantism of the Protestant religion!" And religious organizations like this are what people believe in, rest in, would give their lives for! Such, I say, is the wonderful virtue of even the beginnings of perfection, of having conquered even the plain faults of our animality, that the religious organization which has helped us to do it can seem to us something precious, salutary, and to be propagated, even when it wears such a brand of imperfection on its forehead as this. And men have got such a habit of giving to the language of religion a special application, of making it a mere jargon, that for the condemnation which religion itself passes on the shortcomings of their religious organizations they have no ear; they are sure to cheat themselves and to explain this condemnation away. They can only be reached by the criticism which culture, like poetry, speaking of language not to be sophisticated, and reso-

3. An allusion to the fate of rebellious Israelites (Numbers 14.26–35).
1. Arnold began *Culture and Anarchy* in the context of the turbulent political debate that preceded the passage of the second Reform Bill in 1867. The political climate seemed to some to threaten anarchy, to which Arnold opposed culture. A characteristic quality of the cultured state of mind is summed up, for his purposes, in his formula "sweetness and light," a phrase suggesting reasonableness of temper and intellectual insight. Arnold derived the phrase from a fable contrasting the spider with the bee in Jonathan Swift's *The Battle of the Books* (1704). The spider (representing a narrow, self-centered, and uncultured mind) spins out of itself "nothing at all but

flybane and cobweb." The bee (representing a cultured mind that has drawn nourishment from the humanist tradition) ranges far and wide and makes in its hive honey and also wax out of which candles may be made. Therefore, the bee, Swift says, furnishes humankind "with the two noblest of things, which are sweetness and light."
The selection illustrates aspects of Arnold's indictment of the middle classes for their lack of sweetness and light, exposing the narrowness and dullness of middleclass Puritan religious institutions in both the 17th and 19th centuries.
2. A 17th-century Puritan group (of which Oliver Cromwell was an adherent), allied with the Congregationalists.
3. Cf. 1 Peter 3.8.

lutely testing these organizations by the ideal of a human perfection complete on all sides, applies to them.

But men of culture and poetry, it will be said, are again and again failing, and failing conspicuously, in the necessary first stage to a harmonious perfection, in the subduing of the great obvious faults of our animality, which it is the glory of these religious organizations to have helped us to subdue. True, they do often so fail. They have often been without the virtues as well as the faults of the Puritan; it has been one of their dangers that they so felt the Puritan's faults that they too much neglected the practice of his virtues. I will not, however, exculpate them at the Puritan's expense. They have often failed in morality, and morality is indispensable. And they have been punished for their failure, as the Puritan has been rewarded for his performance. They have been punished wherein they erred; but their ideal of beauty, of sweetness and light, and a human nature complete on all its sides, remains the true ideal of perfection still; just as the Puritan's ideal of perfection remains narrow and inadequate, although for what he did well he has been richly rewarded. Notwithstanding the mighty results of the Pilgrim Fathers' voyage, they and their standard of perfection are rightly judged when we figure to ourselves Shakespeare or Virgil[4]—souls in whom sweetness and light, and all that in human nature is most humane, were eminent—accompanying them on their voyage, and think what intolerable company Shakespeare and Virgil would have found them! In the same way let us judge the religious organizations which we see all around us. Do not let us deny the good and the happiness which they have accomplished; but do not let us fail to see clearly that their idea of human perfection is narrow and inadequate, and that the Dissidence of Dissent and the Protestantism of the Protestant religion will never bring humanity to its true goal. As I said with regard to wealth: Let us look at the life of those who live in and for it—so I say with regard to the religious organizations. Look at the life imaged in such a newspaper as the *Nonconformist*—a life of jealousy of the Establishment,[5] disputes, tea-meetings, openings of chapels, sermons; and then think of it as an ideal of a human life completing itself on all sides, and aspiring with all its organs after sweetness, light, and perfection!

From The Study of Poetry[1]

"The future of poetry is immense, because in poetry, where it is worthy of its high destinies, our race, as time goes on, will find an ever surer and surer stay. There is not a creed which is not shaken, not an

4. Roman poet (70–19 B.C.E.).
5. The Church of England or the Established Church.
1. Aside from its vindication of the importance of literature, this essay is an interesting example of the variety of Arnold's reading. To know literature in only one language seemed to him not to know literature. His personal *Notebooks* show that throughout his active life he continued to read books in French, German, Italian, Latin, and Greek. His favorite authors in these languages are used by him as a means of testing English poetry. The testing is sometimes a severe one. Readers

may also protest that despite Arnold's wit, his essay is limited by an incomplete recognition of the values of comic literature, a shortcoming abundantly evident in the discussion of Chaucer. Nevertheless, whether we agree or disagree with some of Arnold's verdicts, we can be attracted by the combination of traditionalism and impressionism on which these verdicts are based, and we can enjoy the memorable phrasemaking in which the verdicts are expressed. "The Study of Poetry" has been extraordinarily potent in shaping literary tastes in England and in America.

accredited dogma which is not shown to be questionable, not a received tradition which does not threaten to dissolve. Our religion has materialized itself in the fact, in the supposed fact; it has attached its emotion to the fact, and now the fact is failing it. But for poetry the idea is everything; the rest is a world of illusion, of divine illusion. Poetry attaches its emotion to the idea; the idea *is* the fact. The strongest part of our religion today is its unconscious poetry."

Let me be permitted to quote these words of my own, as uttering the thought which should, in my opinion, go with us and govern us in all our study of poetry. In the present work[2] it is the course of one great contributory stream to the world-river of poetry that we are invited to follow. We are here invited to trace the stream of English poetry. But whether we set ourselves, as here, to follow only one of the several streams that make the mighty river of poetry, or whether we seek to know them all, our governing thought should be the same. We should conceive of poetry worthily, and more highly than it has been the custom to conceive of it. We should conceive of it as capable of higher uses, and called to higher destinies, than those which in general men have assigned to it hitherto. More and more mankind will discover that we have to turn to poetry to interpret life for us, to console us, to sustain us. Without poetry, our science will appear incomplete; and most of what now passes with us for religion and philosophy will be replaced by poetry. Science, I say, will appear incomplete without it. For finely and truly does Wordsworth call poetry "the impassioned expression which is in the countenance of all science";[3] and what is a countenance without its expression? Again, Wordsworth finely and truly calls poetry "the breath and finer spirit of all knowledge": our religion, parading evidences such as those on which the popular mind relies now; our philosophy, pluming itself on its reasonings about causation and finite and infinite being; what are they but the shadows and dreams and false shows of knowledge? The day will come when we shall wonder at ourselves for having trusted to them, for having taken them seriously; and the more we perceive their hollowness, the more we shall prize "the breath and finer spirit of knowledge" offered to us by poetry.

But if we conceive thus highly of the destinies of poetry, we must also set our standard for poetry high, since poetry, to be capable of fulfilling such high destinies, must be poetry of a high order of excellence. We must accustom ourselves to a high standard and to a strict judgment. * * *

The best poetry is what we want; the best poetry will be found to have a power of forming, sustaining, and delighting us, as nothing else can. A clearer, deeper sense of the best in poetry, and of the strength and joy to be drawn from it, is the most precious benefit which we can gather from a poetical collection such as the present. And yet in the very nature and conduct of such a collection there is inevitably something which tends to obscure in us the consciousness of what our benefit should be, and to distract us from the pursuit of it. We should therefore steadily set it before our minds at the outset, and should compel ourselves to revert constantly to the thought of it as we proceed.

Yes; constantly in reading poetry, a sense for the best, the really excellent, and of the strength and joy to be drawn from it, should be present in our

---

2. An anthology of English poetry for which this essay served as the introduction.

3. Preface to *Lyrical Ballads* (1800).

minds and should govern our estimate of what we read. But this real estimate, the only true one, is liable to be superseded, if we are not watchful, by
two other kinds of estimate, the historic estimate and the personal estimate,
both of which are fallacious. A poet or a poem may count to us historically,
they may count to us on grounds personal to ourselves, and they may count
to us really. They may count to us historically. The course of development of
a nation's language, thought, and poetry, is profoundly interesting; and by
regarding a poet's work as a stage in this course of development we may easily bring ourselves to make it of more importance as poetry than in itself it
really is, we may come to use a language of quite exaggerated praise in criticizing it; in short, to overrate it. So arises in our poetic judgments the fallacy
caused by the estimate which we may call historic. Then, again, a poet or
a poem may count to us on grounds personal to ourselves. Our personal
affinities, likings, and circumstances, have great power to sway our estimate
of this or that poet's work, and to make us attach more importance to it as
poetry than in itself it really possesses, because to us it is, or has been, of
high importance. Here also we overrate the object of our interest, and apply
to it a language of praise which is quite exaggerated. And thus we get the
source of a second fallacy in our poetic judgments—the fallacy caused by
an estimate which we may call personal.

* * *

The historic estimate is likely in especial to affect our judgment and our
language when we are dealing with ancient poets; the personal estimate
when we are dealing with poets our contemporaries, or at any rate modern.
The exaggerations due to the historic estimate are not in themselves, perhaps, of very much gravity. Their report hardly enters the general ear; probably they do not always impose even on the literary men who adopt them. But
they lead to a dangerous abuse of language. So we hear Caedmon,[4] amongst
our own poets, compared to Milton. I have already noticed the enthusiasm
of one accomplished French critic for "historic origins."[5] Another eminent
French critic, M. Vitet, comments upon that famous document of the early
poetry of his nation, the *Chanson de Roland.*[6] It is indeed a most interesting
document. The *joculator* or *jongleur*[7] Taillefer, who was with William the
Conqueror's army at Hastings,[8] marched before the Norman troops, so said
the tradition, singing "of Charlemagne and of Roland and of Oliver, and of
the vassals who died at Roncevaux"; and it is suggested that in the *Chanson
de Roland* by one Turoldus or Theroulde, a poem preserved in a manuscript
of the twelfth century in the Bodleian Library at Oxford, we have certainly
the matter, perhaps even some of the words, of the chant which Taillefer
sang. The poem has vigor and freshness; it is not without pathos. But M.
Vitet is not satisfied with seeing in it a document of some poetic value, and
of very high historic and linguistic value; he sees in it a grand and beautiful
work, a monument of epic genius. In its general design he finds the grandiose

4. A 7th-century Old English poet.
5. Charles d'Héricault (1823–1899), a French
critic cited earlier in a passage omitted here.
Arnold had mildly reprimanded him for his "historical" bias in praising a 15th-century poet,
Clément Marot, at the expense of classical 17th-
century poets such as Racine.
6. An 11th-century epic poem in Old French that

tells of the 8th-century wars of Charlemagne
against the Moors in Spain and of the bravery of
the French leaders Roland and Oliver. Ludovic
Vitet (1802–1873) wrote of it in his *Essais Histo-
riques et Littéraires* (1862).
7. Jester or minstrel (French).
8. The battle in 1066 in which Harold II was
killed and the English army defeated.

conception, in its details he finds the constant union of simplicity with greatness, which are the marks, he truly says, of the genuine epic, and distinguish
it from the artificial epic of literary ages. One thinks of Homer; this is the
sort of praise which is given to Homer, and justly given. Higher praise there
cannot well be, and it is the praise due to epic poetry of the highest order
only, and to no other. Let us try, then, the *Chanson de Roland* at its best.
Roland, mortally wounded, lays himself down under a pine tree, with his face
turned towards Spain and the enemy—

> *De plusurs choses à remembrer li prist,*
> *De tantes teres cume li bers cunquist,*
> *De dulce France, des humes de sun lign,*
> *De Carlemagne sun seignor ki l'nurrit.*[9]

That is primitive work, I repeat, with an undeniable poetic quality of its own. It
deserves such praise, and such praise is sufficient for it. But now turn to Homer—

> Ὣς φάτο τοὺς δ᾽ ἤδη κάτεχεν φυσίζοος αἶα
> ἐν Λακεδαίμονι αὖθι, φίλῃ ἐν πατρίδι γαίῃ.[1]

We are here in another world, another order of poetry altogether; here is
rightly due such supreme praise as that which M. Vitet gives to the *Chanson de Roland*. If our words are to have any meaning, if our judgments are
to have any solidity, we must not heap that supreme praise upon poetry of
an order immeasurably inferior.

Indeed there can be no more useful help for discovering what poetry
belongs to the class of the truly excellent, and can therefore do us most good,
than to have always in one's mind lines and expressions of the great masters,
and to apply them as a touchstone to other poetry. Of course we are not to
require this other poetry to resemble them; it may be very dissimilar. But if
we have any tact we shall find them, when we have lodged them well in our
minds, an infallible touchstone for detecting the presence or absence of high
poetic quality, and also the degree of this quality, in all other poetry which
we may place beside them. Short passages, even single lines, will serve our
turn quite sufficiently. Take the two lines which I have just quoted from
Homer, the poet's comment on Helen's mention of her brothers—or take his

> Ἆ δειλώ, τί σφῶϊ δόμεν Πηλῆϊ ἄνακτι
> θνητῷ; ὑμεῖς δ᾽ἐστὸν ἀγήρω τ᾽ἀθανάτω τε.
> ἦ ἵνα δυστήνοισι μετ᾽ ἀνδράσιν ἄλγε᾽ ἔχητον;[2]

the address of Zeus to the horses of Peleus—or take finally his

> Καὶ σέ, γέρον, τὸ πρὶν μὲν ἀκούομεν ὄλβιον εἶναι.[3]

the words of Achilles to Priam, a suppliant before him. Take that incomparable line and a half of Dante, Ugolino's tremendous words—

9. "Then began he to call many things to
remembrance—all the lands which his valor
conquered and pleasant France, and the men of
his lineage, and Charlemagne his liege lord who
nourished him." *Chanson de Roland* 3.939–42
[Arnold's note].
1. "So said she; they long since in Earth's soft
arms were reposing, / There, in their own dear
land, their fatherland, Lacedaemon." *Iliad* 3.243–
44 (translated by Dr. Hawtrey) [Arnold's note].

2. "Ah, unhappy pair, why gave we you to King
Peleus, to a mortal? but ye are without old age,
and immortal. Was it that with men born to
misery ye might have sorrow?" *Iliad* 17.443–45
[Arnold's note].
3. "Nay, and thou too, old man, in former days
wast, as we hear, happy." *Iliad* 24.543 [Arnold's
note]. Priam, king of Troy, has begged Achilles
to return the body of his son Hector, whom the
Greek warrior had killed.

> *Io no piangeva; sì dentro impietrai.*
> *Piangevan elli . . .* [4]

take the lovely words of Beatrice to Virgil—

> *Io son fatta da Dio, sua mercè, tale,*
> *Che la vostra miseria non mi tange,*
> *Nè fiamma d'esto incendio non m'assale . . .* [5]

take the simple, but perfect, single line—

> *In la sua volontade è nostra pace.* [6]

Take of Shakespeare a line or two of Henry the Fourth's expostulation with sleep—

> Wilt thou upon the high and giddy mast
> Seal up the shipboy's eyes, and rock his brains
> In cradle of the rude imperious surge . . . [7]

and take, as well, Hamlet's dying request to Horatio—

> If thou didst ever hold me in thy heart,
> Absent thee from felicity awhile,
> And in this harsh world draw thy breath in pain,
> To tell my story . . . [8]

Take of Milton that Miltonic passage—

> Darkened so, yet shone
> Above them all the archangel; but his face
> Deep scars of thunder had intrenched, and care
> Sat on his faded cheek . . . [9]

add two such lines as—

> And courage never to submit or yield
> And what is else not to be overcome . . . [1]

and finish with the exquisite close to the loss of Proserpine, the loss

> . . . which cost Ceres all that pain
> To seek her through the world. [2]

These few lines, if we have tact and can use them, are enough even of themselves to keep clear and sound our judgments about poetry, to save us from fallacious estimates of it, to conduct us to a real estimate.

The specimens I have quoted differ widely from one another, but they have in common this: the possession of the very highest poetical quality. If we are thoroughly penetrated by their power, we shall find that we have acquired a sense enabling us, whatever poetry may be laid before us, to feel the degree in which a high poetical quality is present or wanting there. Critics

---

4. "I wailed not, so of stone I grew within; *they* wailed." *Inferno* 33.49–50 [Arnold's note].
5. "Of such sort hath God, thanked be His mercy, made me, that your misery toucheth me not, neither doth the flame of this fire strike me." *Inferno* 2.91–93 [Arnold's note]. The Roman poet Virgil is Dante's guide.
6. "In His will is our peace." *Paradiso* 3.85 [Arnold's note].

7. *2 Henry IV* 3.1.18–20.
8. *Hamlet* 5.2.288–91.
9. *Paradise Lost* 1.599–602.
1. *Paradise Lost* 1.108–9.
2. *Paradise Lost* 4.271–72. Ceres, the Roman goddess of grain, searched for her daughter Proserpina, not knowing that she had been abducted by Pluto, the god of the underworld.

give themselves great labour to draw out what in the abstract constitutes the characters of a high quality of poetry. It is much better simply to have recourse to concrete examples—to take specimens of poetry of the high, the very highest quality, and to say: The characters of a high quality of poetry are what is expressed *there*. They are far better recognized by being felt in the verse of the master, than by being perused in the prose of the critic. Nevertheless if we are urgently pressed to give some critical account of them, we may safely, perhaps, venture on laying down, not indeed how and why the characters arise, but where and in what they arise. They are in the matter and substance of the poetry, and they are in its manner and style. Both of these, the substance and matter on the one hand, the style and manner on the other, have a mark, an accent, of high beauty, worth, and power. But if we are asked to define this mark and accent in the abstract, our answer must be: No, for we should thereby be darkening the question, not clearing it. The mark and accent are as given by the substance and matter of that poetry, by the style and manner of that poetry, and of all other poetry which is akin to it in quality.

Only one thing we may add as to the substance and matter of poetry, guiding ourselves by Aristotle's profound observation that the superiority of poetry over history consists in its possessing a higher truth and a higher seriousness ($\phi\iota\lambda\sigma\sigma\sigma\phi\omega\tau\epsilon\rho\sigma\nu$ $\kappa\alpha\iota$ $\sigma\pi\sigma\upsilon\delta\alpha\iota\delta\tau\epsilon\rho\sigma\nu$).[3] Let us add, therefore, to what we have said, this: that the substance and matter of the best poetry acquire their special character from possessing, in an eminent degree, truth and seriousness. We may add yet further, what is in itself evident, that to the style and manner of the best poetry their special character, their accent, is given by their diction, and, even yet more, by their movement. And though we distinguish between the two characters, the two accents, of superiority, yet they are nevertheless vitally connected one with the other. The superior character of truth and seriousness, in the matter and substance of the best poetry, is inseparable from the superiority of diction and movement marking its style and manner. The two superiorities are closely related, and are in steadfast proportion one to the other. So far as high poetic truth and seriousness are wanting to a poet's matter and substance, so far also, we may be sure, will a high poetic stamp of diction and movement be wanting to his style and manner. In proportion as this high stamp of diction and movement, again, is absent from a poet's style and manner, we shall find, also, that high poetic truth and seriousness are absent from his substance and matter.

So stated, these are but dry generalities; their whole force lies in their application. And I could wish every student of poetry to make the application of them for himself. Made by himself, the application would impress itself upon his mind far more deeply than made by me. Neither will my limits allow me to make any full application of the generalities above propounded; but in the hope of bringing out, at any rate, some significance in them, and of establishing an important principle more firmly by their means, I will, in the space which remains to me, follow rapidly from the commencement the course of our English poetry with them in my view.

* * *

Chaucer's * * * poetical importance does not need the assistance of the historic estimate; it is real. He is a genuine source of joy and strength, which is flowing still for us and will flow always. He will be read, as time goes on, far

3. Aristotle's *Poetics* 9.

more generally than he is read now. His language is a cause of difficulty for us; but so also, and I think in quite as great a degree, is the language of Burns.[4] In Chaucer's case, as in that of Burns, it is a difficulty to be unhesitatingly accepted and overcome.

If we ask ourselves wherein consists the immense superiority of Chaucer's poetry over the romance poetry—why it is that in passing from this to Chaucer we suddenly feel ourselves to be in another world, we shall find that his superiority is both in the substance of his poetry and in the style of his poetry. His superiority in substance is given by his large, free, simple, clear yet kindly view of human life—so unlike the total want, in the romance poets, of all intelligent command of it. Chaucer has not their helplessness; he has gained the power to survey the world from a central, a truly human point of view. We have only to call to mind the Prologue to *The Canterbury Tales*. The right comment upon it is Dryden's: "It is sufficient to say, according to the proverb, that *here is God's plenty*." And again: "He is a perpetual fountain of good sense."[5] It is by a large, free, sound representation of things, that poetry, this high criticism of life, has truth of substance; and Chaucer's poetry has truth of substance.

Of his style and manner, if we think first of the romance poetry and then of Chaucer's divine liquidness of diction, his divine fluidity of movement, it is difficult to speak temperately. They are irresistible, and justify all the rapture with which his successors speak of his "gold dewdrops of speech."[6] Johnson misses the point entirely when he finds fault with Dryden for ascribing to Chaucer the first refinement of our numbers, and says that Gower[7] also can show smooth numbers and easy rhymes. The refinement of our numbers means something far more than this. A nation may have versifiers with smooth numbers and easy rhymes, and yet may have no real poetry at all. Chaucer is the father of our splendid English poetry; he is our "well of English undefiled,"[8] because by the lovely charm of his diction, the lovely charm of his movement, he makes an epoch and founds a tradition. In Spenser, Shakespeare, Milton, Keats, we can follow the tradition of the liquid diction, the fluid movement, of Chaucer; at one time it is his liquid diction of which in these poets we feel the virtue, and at another time it is his fluid movement. And the virtue is irresistible.

Bounded as is my space, I must yet find room for an example of Chaucer's virtue, as I have given examples to show the virtue of the great classics. I feel disposed to say that a single line is enough to show the charm of Chaucer's verse; that merely one line like this—

O martyr souded[9] in virginitee!

has a virtue of manner and movement such as we shall not find in all the verse of romance poetry—but this is saying nothing. The virtue is such as we shall not find, perhaps, in all English poetry, outside the poets whom I have named as the special inheritors of Chaucer's tradition. A single line,

4. Robert Burns (1759–1796), whose language is difficult because he frequently uses Scottish dialect.
5. Both quotations are from John Dryden's (1631–1700) preface to his *Fables Ancient and Modern* (1700).
6. "The Life of Our Lady," a poem by John Lydgate (ca. 1370–ca.1451).
7. John Gower (ca. 1325–1408), friend of Chaucer and author of the *Confessio Amantis*, a long poem in octosyllabic couplets. Samuel Johnson (1709–1784), critic, essayist, and poet.
8. Said of Chaucer by Edmund Spenser (1552–1599) in *The Faerie Queene* (1590) 4.2.32.
9. The French *soudé*: soldered, fixed fast [Arnold's note]. From *The Canterbury Tales*, *The Prioress's Tale* (line 127); Chaucer wrote "souded to" rather than "souded in."

however, is too little if we have not the strain of Chaucer's verse well in our memory; let us take a stanza. It is from *The Prioress's Tale*, the story of the Christian child murdered in a Jewry—[1]

> My throte is cut unto my nekke-bone
> Saidè this child, and as by way of kinde
> I should have deyd, yea, longè time agone;
> But Jesu Christ, as ye in bookès finde,
> Will that his glory last and be in minde,
> And for the worship of his mother dere
> Yet may I sing *O Alma* loud and clere.

Wordsworth has modernized this Tale, and to feel how delicate and evanescent is the charm of verse, we have only to read Wordsworth's first three lines of this stanza after Chaucer's—

> My throat is cut unto the bone, I trow,
> Said this young child, and by the law of kind
> I should have died, yea, many hours ago.

The charm is departed. It is often said that the power of liquidness and fluidity in Chaucer's verse was dependent upon a free, a licentious dealing with language, such as is now impossible; upon a liberty, such as Burns too enjoyed, of making words like *neck, bird,* into a dissyllable by adding to them, and words like *cause, rhyme,* into a dissyllable by sounding the *e* mute. It is true that Chaucer's fluidity is conjoined with this liberty, and is admirably served by it; but we ought not to say that it was dependent upon it. It was dependent upon his talent. Other poets with a like liberty do not attain to the fluidity of Chaucer; Burns himself does not attain to it. Poets, again, who have a talent akin to Chaucer's, such as Shakespeare or Keats, have known how to attain to his fluidity without the like liberty.

And yet Chaucer is not one of the great classics. His poetry transcends and effaces, easily and without effort, all the romance poetry of Catholic Christendom; it transcends and effaces all the English poetry contemporary with it, it transcends and effaces all the English poetry subsequent to it down to the age of Elizabeth. Of such avail is poetic truth of substance, in its natural and necessary union with poetic truth of style. And yet, I say, Chaucer is not one of the great classics. He has not their accent. What is wanting to him is suggested by the mere mention of the name of the first great classic of Christendom, the immortal poet who died eighty years before Chaucer—Dante. The accent of such verse as

> *In la sua volontade è nostra pace . . .*

is altogether beyond Chaucer's reach; we praise him, but we feel that this accent is out of the question for him. It may be said that it was necessarily out of the reach of any poet in the England of that stage of growth. Possibly; but we are to adopt a real, not a historic, estimate of poetry. However we may account for its absence, something is wanting, then, to the poetry of Chaucer, which poetry must have before it can be placed in the glorious class of the best. And there is no doubt what that something is. It is the

1. Jewish ghetto.

σπουδαιότης, the high and excellent seriousness, which Aristotle assigns as one of the grand virtues of poetry. The substance of Chaucer's poetry, his view of things and his criticism of life, has largeness, freedom, shrewdness, benignity; but it has not this high seriousness. Homer's criticism of life has it, Dante's has it, Shakespeare's has it. It is this chiefly which gives to our spirits what they can rest upon; and with the increasing demands of our modern ages upon poetry, this virtue of giving us what we can rest upon will be more and more highly esteemed. A voice from the slums of Paris, fifty or sixty years after Chaucer, the voice of poor Villon out of his life of riot and crime, has at its happy moments (as, for instance, in the last stanza of *La Belle Heaulmière*)[2] more of this important poetic virtue of seriousness than all the productions of Chaucer. But its apparition[3] in Villon, and in men like Villon, is fitful; the greatness of the great poets, the power of their criticism of life, is that their virtue is sustained.

To our praise, therefore, of Chaucer as a poet there must be this limitation: he lacks the high seriousness of the great classics, and therewith an important part of their virtue. Still, the main fact for us to bear in mind about Chaucer is his sterling value according to that real estimate which we firmly adopt for all poets. He has poetic truth of substance, though he has not high poetic seriousness, and corresponding to his truth of substance he has an exquisite virtue of style and manner. With him is born our real poetry.

For my present purpose I need not dwell on our Elizabethan poetry, or on the continuation and close of this poetry in Milton. We all of us profess to be agreed in the estimate of this poetry; we all of us recognize it as great poetry, our greatest, and Shakespeare and Milton as our poetical classics. The real estimate, here, has universal currency. With the next age of our poetry divergency and difficulty begin. An historic estimate of that poetry has established itself; and the question is, whether it will be found to coincide with the real estimate.

The age of Dryden, together with our whole eighteenth century which followed it, sincerely believed itself to have produced poetical classics of its own, and even to have made advance, in poetry, beyond all its predecessors. Dryden regards as not seriously disputable the opinion "that the sweetness of English verse was never understood or practiced by our fathers."[4] Cowley[5] could see nothing at all in Chaucer's poetry. Dryden heartily admired it, and, as we have seen, praised its matter admirably; but of its exquisite manner and movement all he can find to say is that "there is the rude sweetness of a Scotch tune in it, which is natural and pleasing, though not perfect."[6] Addison,[7] wishing to praise Chaucer's numbers, compares them with Dryden's own. And all through the eighteenth century, and down even into our own times, the stereotyped phrase of approbation for good verse found

---

2. The name *Heaulmière* is said to be derived from a headdress (helm) worn as a mask by courtesans. In Villon's ballad a poor old creature of this class laments her days of youth and beauty. The last stanza of the ballad runs thus—"*Ainsi le bon temps regretons / Entrenous, pauvres vieilles sottes, / Assises bas, à croppetons, / Tout en ung tas comme pelottes, / A petit feu de chenevottes / Tost allumeé's, tost estaincles, / Et jadis fusmes si mignottes! / Ainsi en prend à maintz et maintes.*" [It may be translated:] "Thus amongst ourselves we regret the good time, poor silly old things, low-

seated on our heels, all in a heap like so many balls; by a little fire of hemp stalks, soon lighted, soon spent. And once we were such darlings! So fares it with many and many a one" [Arnold's note]. François Villon (1431–1484), French poet and vagabond.

3. Appearance.

4. *Essay on Dramatic Poesy* (1668).

5. Abraham Cowley (1618–1667), English poet.

6. Preface to his *Fables*.

7. Joseph Addison (1672–1719), essayist and poet.

in our early poetry has been, that it even approached the verse of Dryden, Addison, Pope, and Johnson.

Are Dryden and Pope poetical classics? Is the historic estimate, which represents them as such, and which has been so long established that it cannot easily give way, the real estimate? Wordsworth and Coleridge, as is well known, denied it; but the authority of Wordsworth and Coleridge does not weigh much with the young generation, and there are many signs to show that the eighteenth century and its judgments are coming into favor again. Are the favorite poets of the eighteenth century classics?

It is impossible within my present limits to discuss the question fully. And what man of letters would not shrink from seeming to dispose dictatorially of the claims of two men who are, at any rate, such masters in letters as Dryden and Pope; two men of such admirable talent, both of them, and one of them, Dryden, a man, on all sides, of such energetic and genial power? And yet, if we are to gain the full benefit from poetry, we must have the real estimate of it. I cast about for some mode of arriving, in the present case, at such an estimate without offense. And perhaps the best way is to begin, as it is easy to begin, with cordial praise.

When we find Chapman,[8] the Elizabethan translator of Homer, expressing himself in his preface thus: "Though truth in her very nakedness sits in so deep a pit, that from Gades to Aurora and Ganges few eyes can sound her, I hope yet those few here will so discover and confirm that, the date being out of her darkness in this morning of our poet, he shall now gird his temples with the sun," we pronounce that such a prose is intolerable. When we find Milton writing: "And long it was not after, when I was confirmed in this opinion, that he, who would not be frustrate of his hope to write well hereafter in laudable things, ought himself to be a true poem"[9]—we pronounce that such a prose has its own grandeur, but that it is obsolete and inconvenient. But when we find Dryden telling us: "What Virgil wrote in the vigor of his age, in plenty and at ease, I have undertaken to translate in my declining years; struggling with wants, oppressed with sickness, curbed in my genius, liable to be misconstrued in all I write"[1]—then we exclaim that here at last we have the true English prose, a prose such as we would all gladly use if we only knew how. Yet Dryden was Milton's contemporary.

But after the Restoration the time had come when our nation felt the imperious need of a fit prose. So, too, the time had likewise come when our nation felt the imperious need of freeing itself from the absorbing preoccupation which religion in the Puritan age had exercised. It was impossible that this freedom should be brought about without some negative excess, without some neglect and impairment of the religious life of the soul; and the spiritual history of the eighteenth century shows us that the freedom was not achieved without them. Still, the freedom was achieved; the preoccupation, an undoubtedly baneful and retarding one if it had continued, was got rid of. And as with religion amongst us at that period, so it was also with letters. A fit prose was a necessity; but it was impossible that a fit prose should establish itself amongst us without some touch of frost to the imaginative life of the soul. The needful qualities for a fit prose are regularity, uniformity, precision,

8. George Chapman (ca. 1559–1634), poet and dramatist; the quotation is from his translation (1598–1611) of the *Iliad*.

9. "Apology for Smectymnuus" (1642).
1. "Postscript to the Reader" (1698) in his translation of Virgil.

balance. The men of letters, whose destiny it may be to bring their nation to the attainment of a fit prose, must of necessity, whether they work in prose or in verse, give a predominating, an almost exclusive attention to the qualities of regularity, uniformity, precision, balance. But an almost exclusive attention to these qualities involves some repression and silencing of poetry.

We are to regard Dryden as the puissant and glorious founder, Pope as the splendid high priest, of our age of prose and reason, of our excellent and indispensable eighteenth century. For the purposes of their mission and destiny their poetry, like their prose, is admirable. Do you ask me whether Dryden's verse, take it almost where you will, is not good?

> A milk-white Hind, immortal and unchanged,
> Fed on the lawns and in the forest ranged.[2]

I answer: Admirable for the purposes of the inaugurator of an age of prose and reason. Do you ask me whether Pope's verse, take it almost where you will, is not good?

> To Hounslow Heath I point, and Banstead Down;
> Thence comes your mutton, and these chicks my own.[3]

I answer: Admirable for the purposes of the high priest of an age of prose and reason. But do you ask me whether such verse proceeds from men with an adequate poetic criticism of life, from men whose criticism of life has a high seriousness, or even, without that high seriousness, has poetic largeness, freedom, insight, benignity? Do you ask me whether the application of ideas to life in the verse of these men, often a powerful application, no doubt, is a powerful *poetic* application? Do you ask me whether the poetry of these men has either the matter or the inseparable manner of such an adequate poetic criticism; whether it has the accent of

> Absent thee from felicity awhile . . .

or of

> And what is else not to be overcome . . .

or of

> O martyr souded in virginitee!

I answer: It has not and cannot have them; it is the poetry of the builders of an age of prose and reason. Though they may write in verse, though they may in a certain sense be masters of the art of versification, Dryden and Pope are not classics of our poetry, they are classics of our prose.

Gray[4] is our poetical classic of that literature and age; the position of Gray is singular, and demands a word of notice here. He has not the volume or the power of poets who, coming in times more favorable, have attained to an independent criticism of life. But he lived with the great poets, he lived, above all, with the Greeks, through perpetually studying and enjoying them; and he caught their poetic point of view for regarding life, caught their poetic manner. The point of view and the manner are not self-sprung in him, he caught them of others; and he had not the free and abundant use of them.

---

2. *The Hind and the Panther* (1687) 1.1–2.   4. Thomas Gray (1716–1771), British poet.
3. *Imitations of Horace* (1737), Satire 2.2.143–44.

But whereas Addison and Pope never had the use of them, Gray had the use of them at times. He is the scantiest and frailest of classics in our poetry, but he is a classic.[5]

*　*　*

At any rate the end to which the method and the estimate are designed to lead, and from leading to which, if they do lead to it, they get their whole value—the benefit of being able clearly to feel and deeply to enjoy the best, the truly classic, in poetry—is an end, let me say it once more at parting, of supreme importance. We are often told that an era is opening in which we are to see multitudes of a common sort of readers, and masses of a common sort of literature; that such readers do not want and could not relish anything better than such literature, and that to provide it is becoming a vast and profitable industry. Even if good literature entirely lost currency with the world, it would still be abundantly worth while to continue to enjoy it by oneself. But it never will lose currency with the world, in spite of momentary appearances; it never will lose supremacy. Currency and supremacy are insured to it, not indeed by the world's deliberate and conscious choice, but by something far deeper—by the instinct of self-preservation in humanity.

1880

5. After Gray, the only other poet discussed by Arnold is Burns (not printed here). Arnold concludes that "Burns, like Chaucer, comes short of the high seriousness of the great classics."

CHRISTINA ROSSETTI
1830–1894

Referring to the title of George Gissing's 1893 novel about women who choose not to marry, the critic Jerome McGann calls Christina Rossetti "one of nineteenth-century England's greatest 'Odd Women.'" Her life had little apparent incident. She was the youngest child in the Rossetti family. Her father was an exiled Italian patriot who wrote poetry and commentaries on Dante that tried to find evidence in his poems of mysterious ancient conspiracies; her mother was an Anglo-Italian who had worked as a governess. Their household was a lively gathering place for Italian exiles, full of conversation of politics and culture; and Christina, like her brothers Dante Gabriel and William Michael, was encouraged to develop an early love for art and literature and to draw and write poetry from a very early age. When she was an adolescent, her life changed dramatically: her father became a permanent invalid, the family's economic situation worsened, and her own health deteriorated. Subsequently she, her mother, and her sister became intensely involved with the Anglo-Catholic movement within the Church of England. For the rest of her life, Rossetti governed herself by strict religious principles, giving up theater, opera, and chess; on two occasions she canceled plans for marriage because of religious scruples, breaking her first engagement when her fiancé reverted to Roman Catholicism and ultimately refusing to marry a second suitor because he seemed insufficiently concerned with religion. She lived a quiet life, occupying herself with charitable work—including ten years of volunteer service at a penitentiary for fallen women—with caring for her family, and with writing poetry.

Rossetti's first volume of poetry, *Goblin Market and Other Poems* (1862), contains all the different poetic modes that mark her achievement—pure lyric, narrative fable, ballad, and the devotional verse to which she increasingly turned in her later years. The most remarkable poem in the book is the title piece, which early established its popularity as a seemingly simple moral fable for children. Later readers have likened it to S. T. Coleridge's *The Rime of the Ancient Mariner* (1798) and have detected in it a complex representation of the religious themes of temptation and sin, and of redemption by vicarious suffering; the fruit that tempts Laura, however, clearly is not from the tree of knowledge but from the orchard of sensual delights. In its deceptively simple style *Goblin Market,* like many of Rossetti's poems, demonstrates her affinity with the early aims of the Pre-Raphaelite group, though her work as a whole resists this classification. A consciousness of gender often leads her to criticize the conventional representation of women in Pre-Raphaelite art, as in her sonnet "In an Artist's Studio" (1896), and a stern religious vision controls the sensuous impulses typical of Pre-Raphaelite poetry and painting. Virginia Woolf has described the distinctive combination of sensuousness and religious severity in Rossetti's work:

> Your poems are full of gold dust and "sweet geraniums' varied brightness"; your eye noted incessantly how rushes are "velvet headed," and lizards have a "strange metallic mail"—your eye, indeed, observed with a sensual pre-Raphaelite intensity that must have surprised Christina the Anglo-Catholic. But to her you owed perhaps the fixity and sadness of your muse. . . . No sooner have you feasted on beauty with your eyes than your mind tells you that beauty is vain and beauty passes. Death, oblivion, and rest lap round your songs with their dark wave.

William Michael Rossetti wrote of his sister, "She was replete with the spirit of self-postponement." Christina Rossetti was a poet who created, in Sandra M. Gilbert and Susan Gubar's phrase, "an aesthetics of renunciation." She writes a poetry of deferral, of deflection, of negation, whose very denials and constraints give her a powerful way to articulate a poetic self in critical relationship to the little that the world offers. Like Emily Dickinson, she often, as in "Winter: My Secret" (1862), uses a coy playfulness and sardonic wit to reduce the self but at the same time to preserve for it a secret inner space. And like Dickinson, she wrote many poems of an extraordinarily pure lyric beauty that made Virginia Woolf compare Rossetti's work to that of classical composers: "Your instinct was so sure, so direct, so intense that it produced poems that sing like music in one's ears—like a melody by Mozart or an air by Gluck."

Song

She sat and sang alway
   By the green margin of a stream,
Watching the fishes leap and play
   Beneath the glad sunbeam.

5   I sat and wept alway
   Beneath the moon's most shadowy beam,
Watching the blossoms of the May
   Weep leaves into the stream.

I wept for memory;
10   She sang for hope that is so fair:
My tears were swallowed by the sea;
    Her songs died on the air.

1848   1862

Song

When I am dead, my dearest,
    Sing no sad songs for me;
Plant thou no roses at my head,
    Nor shady cypress tree:[1]
5   Be the green grass above me
        With showers and dewdrops wet;
    And if thou wilt, remember,
        And if thou wilt, forget.

I shall not see the shadows,
10   I shall not feel the rain;
I shall not hear the nightingale
    Sing on, as if in pain:
And dreaming through the twilight
    That doth not rise nor set,
15   Haply° I may remember,   *perhaps*
    And haply may forget.

1848   1862

After Death

The curtains were half drawn, the floor was swept
    And strewn with rushes, rosemary and may[1]
Lay thick upon the bed on which I lay,
Where thro' the lattice ivy-shadows crept.
5   He leaned above me, thinking that I slept
    And could not hear him; but I heard him say:
    "Poor child, poor child": and as he turned away
Came a deep silence, and I knew he wept.
He did not touch the shroud, or raise the fold
10   That hid my face, or take my hand in his,
        Or ruffle the smooth pillows for my head:
        He did not love me living; but once dead
    He pitied me; and very sweet it is
To know he still is warm tho' I am cold.

1849   1862

---

1. The cypress tree is associated with mourning.   1. Flowers associated with death.

Dead before Death

Ah! changed and cold, how changed and very cold!
   With stiffened smiling lips and cold calm eyes:
   Changed, yet the same; much knowing, little wise;
This was the promise of the days of old!
5 Grown hard and stubborn in the ancient mould,
   Grown rigid in the sham of lifelong lies:
   We hoped for better things as years would rise,
But it is over as a tale once told.
All fallen the blossom that no fruitage bore,
10   All lost the present and the future time,
All lost, all lost, the lapse that went before:
So lost till death shut-to the opened door,
   So lost from chime to everlasting chime,
So cold and lost for ever evermore.

1854   1862

Cobwebs

It is a land with neither night nor day,
   Nor heat nor cold, nor any wind, nor rain,
   Nor hills nor valleys; but one even plain
Stretches thro' long unbroken miles away:
5 While thro' the sluggish air a twilight grey
   Broodeth; no moons or seasons wax and wane,
   No ebb and flow are there along the main,°   *ocean*
No bud-time no leaf-falling, there for aye:°—   *forever*
No ripple on the sea, no shifting sand,
10   No beat of wings to stir the stagnant space,
No pulse of life thro' all the loveless land:
And loveless sea; no trace of days before,
   No guarded home, no toil-won resting place,
No future hope no fear for evermore.

1855   1896

A Triad

Three sang of love together: one with lips
   Crimson, with cheeks and bosom in a glow,
Flushed to the yellow hair and finger tips;
   And one there sang who soft and smooth as snow
5 Bloomed like a tinted hyacinth at a show;
And one was blue with famine after love,
   Who like a harpstring snapped rang harsh and low
The burden of what those were singing of.

One shamed herself in love; one temperately
10   Grew gross in soulless love, a sluggish wife;
One famished died for love. Thus two of three
        Took death for love and won him after strife;
One droned in sweetness like a fattened bee:
        All on the threshold, yet all short of life.

1856   1862

In an Artist's Studio[1]

One face looks out from all his canvases,
        One selfsame figure sits or walks or leans;
        We found her hidden just behind those screens,
That mirror gave back all her loveliness.
5 A queen in opal or in ruby dress,
        A nameless girl in freshest summer-greens,
        A saint, an angel;—every canvas means
The same one meaning, neither more nor less.
He feeds upon her face by day and night,
10   And she with true kind eyes looks back on him
Fair as the moon and joyful as the light:
        Not wan with waiting, not with sorrow dim;
Not as she is, but was when hope shone bright;
        Not as she is, but as she fills his dream.

1856   1896

A Birthday

My heart is like a singing bird
        Whose nest is in a watered shoot;°   *slim branch*
My heart is like an apple tree
        Whose boughs are bent with thickset fruit;
5 My heart is like a rainbow shell
        That paddles in a halcyon° sea;   *tranquil*
My heart is gladder than all these
        Because my love is come to me.

Raise me a dais of silk and down;
10   Hang it with vair° and purple dyes;   *squirrel fur*
Carve it in doves and pomegranates,
        And peacocks with a hundred eyes;
Work it in gold and silver grapes,
        In leaves and silver fleurs-de-lys;

---

1. According to Christina's brother William Michael, this poem focuses on the work of their older brother, Dante Gabriel: "The reference is apparently to our brother's studio, and to his constantly repeated heads of the lady whom he afterwards married, Miss Siddal."

₁₅ Because the birthday of my life
Is come, my love is come to me.

1857   1862

An Apple-Gathering

I plucked pink blossoms from mine apple tree
And wore them all that evening in my hair:
Then in due season when I went to see
I found no apples there.

₅ With dangling basket all along the grass
As I had come I went the selfsame track:
My neighbours mocked me while they saw me pass
So empty-handed back.

Lilian and Lilias smiled in trudging by,
₁₀ Their heaped-up basket teazed me like a jeer;
Sweet-voiced they sang beneath the sunset sky,
Their mother's home was near.

Plump Gertrude passed me with her basket full,
A stronger hand than hers helped it along;
₁₅ A voice talked with her thro' the shadows cool
More sweet to me than song.

Ah Willie, Willie, was my love less worth
Than apples with their green leaves piled above?
I counted rosiest apples on the earth
₂₀ Of far less worth than love.

So once it was with me you stooped to talk
Laughing and listening in this very lane:
To think that by this way we used to walk
We shall not walk again!

₂₅ I let my neighbours pass me, ones and twos
And groups; the latest said the night grew chill,
And hastened: but I loitered, while the dews
Fell fast I loitered still.

1857   1862

Up-Hill

Does the road wind up-hill all the way?
Yes, to the very end.
Will the day's journey take the whole long day?
From morn to night, my friend.

The Romantic Period
(1785–1832)

Sir Brooke Boothby, Joseph Wright of Derby, 1781

Many details combine here to portray Boothby, a Derbyshire landowner and intellectual, as a progressive man of his times: the soberly colored wool suit, one cuff casually unbuttoned, that he wears instead of the bright silks of court dress; the fact that he has taken philosophical contemplation outdoors, into an untamed woodland scene. Boothby's left hand caresses a book by Jean-Jacques Rousseau, the French philosopher whom Boothby had recently edited: the portrait seems an endorsement of Rousseau's argument for a return to nature. Offsetting Boothby's modern guise, in the reclining attitude Wright has chosen for his depiction there is a recollection of statuary depicting classical river gods. Tate Collection.

Le triomphe de la Liberté en l'élargissement de la Bastille, engraving by James Gillray after a painting by James Northcote, 1790

Gillray's engraving, which reproduces a no longer extant painting, was published in time to commemorate the first anniversary of the Parisian people's capture of the Bastille, an event retrospectively recognized as the beginning of the French Revolution. Descending into the prison's dark depths, a rescue party has found a site out of gothic fiction, a place of unburied bodies and ghastly instruments of torture. The revolutionists lead a manacled figure grown old in captivity into the light of freedom. BRITISH MUSEUM, LONDON.

Glad Day, or *The Dance of Albion,* William Blake, ca. 1793

Blake kept returning to this image of liberation. He first designed it in 1780, shortly after finishing his apprenticeship as an engraver, when the vision of a rising sun and a radiant human body may have expressed his own youthful sense of freedom. But later, in an age of revolution, he identified the figure as Albion—"Albion rose from where he labourd at the Mill with Slaves." For Blake the giant Albion represents the ancient form of Britain, a universal man who has fallen on evil, repressive times but is destined to awake and to unite all people in a dance of liberty, both political and spiritual. Eventually, in *Jerusalem* (ca. 1820), Blake's last great prophetic work, the figure of Albion merged with Jesus, risen from the tomb as an embodiment of "the human form divine"—immortal and perpetually creative. BRITISH MUSEUM, LONDON / BRIDGEMAN ART LIBRARY.

Plate 1, Copy D, of *The Marriage of Heaven and Hell,* William Blake, 1790–93

This title page of a work composed in the early years of the French Revolution (p. 153) juxtaposes lighthearted activities (birds and humans soaring, strolling, playing music, dancing, embracing) with bleak and ominous surroundings (the leaflessness of the trees, the intensity of the flames). The larger reclining figures at the bottom of the page, sexy but genderless, are usually read as a devil and an angel whose embrace symbolizes the union ("marriage") of contraries running throughout the work. LIBRARY OF CONGRESS, WASHINGTON DC / BRIDGEMAN ART LIBRARY.

The Sick Rose, William Blake, 1794

Blake's "illumination" (plate 39, copy C, of *Songs of Innocence and of Experience*; see p. 133) further complicates an already highly ambiguous poetic text. In the picture are two worms—one eating a leaf in the upper left corner, the other coming out of the fallen blossom at the bottom—and three female figures, two of which, situated on the thorny stems above the engraved text, appear to be in postures of despair. The third female figure, emerging from the blossom, has arms flung forward in an expression of either ecstasy or terror. LIBRARY OF CONGRESS, WASHINGTON DC / BRIDGEMAN ART LIBRARY.

Interior of Tintern Abbey,
J. M. W. Turner, 1794

Turner painted this watercolor at the age of nineteen, a year after Wordsworth made his first visit to the abbey (1793) and four years before the poet returned for a second visit (1798), as recorded in the famous "Lines" pondering the changes that have taken place in both the speaker and the scene (p. 297). In Turner's version—as, in a different way, in Wordsworth's—the ruined symbol of religion, towering above two tiny human figures, presumably tourists, in the lower left, is in the process of being taken over (allegorically superseded) by the more powerful force of nature.
VICTORIA & ALBERT MUSEUM, LONDON / ART RESOURCE, NY.

Gordale Scar, James Ward, ca. 1812–14

Eroded over millennia by the River Aire, runoff of an ancient glacier, these limestone cliffs were a popular destination for nineteenth-century sightseers in search of the sublime. One such visitor, William Wordsworth, wrote a sonnet about this wild landscape's capacity to overwhelm the viewer. Ward's enigmatic and vast painting—it measures twelve by fourteen feet—manipulates the viewer's perspective so as to further emphasize the height of the overhanging cliffs, which, along with the thunderclouds, dwarf the cattle and deer huddled on the ground below. TATE COLLECTION.

The Nightmare, Henry Fuseli, ca. 1783–91

The first version of this painting created a sensation when the Swiss-born artist Fuseli exhibited it at London's Royal Academy in 1781. Even Horace Walpole, who had used his own nightmare of "a gigantic hand in armour" when composing his Gothic novel, *The Castle of Otranto,* found Fuseli's trademark blend of violence, eroticism, and the irrational excessively disturbing: "shockingly mad, madder than ever; quite mad" was Walpole's verdict on the witchcraft scene that Fuseli exhibited four years later. It is no surprise to learn that during the 1920s Sigmund Freud kept an engraving of *The Nightmare* on display. SNARK / ART RESOURCE, NY.

A Philosopher in a Moonlit Churchyard, Phillipe de Loutherbourg, 1790

When, twenty years before this painting, de Loutherbourg first came to England from France, he assumed the job of scene designer for Drury Lane Theater. The atmospheric effects that he created for the theater's extravaganzas are recalled in this painting. The philosopher, looking up from his book, contemplates a painting of the risen Christ, while a grave housing the remains of a Norman knight lies at his feet. De Loutherbourg both gestures toward gothic mysteries and registers contemporary antiquarians' researches into the material remnants of medieval culture. The ruins are modeled on Tintern Abbey's. TATE COLLECTION.

The Sleep of Endymion, Anne-Louis Girodet, 1791

For this otherworldly love scene, the French painter Girodet draws on Greek mythology's legends of the love the goddess of the moon bore for a mortal, the shepherd Endymion, whom she visited while he slept. Girodet adds to the story a figure sometimes identified as Eros, sometimes as Zephyr, the personification of the breeze, who is shown on the left half-smiling as he parts the surrounding foliage, the better to enable the moonbeams to embrace the sleeper. The unconscious Endymion is, by contrast, a gorgeously passive figure, though he does appear to stir in his sleep (dreaming perhaps) and turn his face toward the silvery light. In some versions of the legend, the goddess arranges for Endymion to sleep eternally, preserving his physical perfection and making him immortal. "A thing of beauty is a joy for ever": in 1818, in his first long poem, which opens with this line, John Keats would also represent Endymion's story and, like Girodet, use it to think about pleasure, love, dream, arrested time, and their relations. Louvre.

Lord Byron, Thomas Phillips, 1835
(after an original of 1813)

Garbed theatrically in an Albanian soldier's dress that he had purchased while on his travels, Byron appears in this portrait as one of his own exotic heroes. The profits from his "Eastern" tales *Lara* and *The Corsair* in fact helped pay the painter's fees for the portrait, which Byron commissioned in 1813, choosing to be pictured not as a member of the British establishment but as an outsider. The archives of London's National Portrait Gallery record more than forty portraits of Byron done during his lifetime, as well as a waxwork model from life made by Madame Tussaud in 1816: a statistic that suggests the poet's keen awareness of the magnetism and marketability of his image. NATIONAL PORTRAIT GALLERY, LONDON / BRIDGEMAN ART LIBRARY.

A Scene from Byron's "Manfred," Thomas Cole, 1833

Visualizing Byron's "dramatic poem" of 1817 was a challenge several nineteenth-century painters and set designers found irresistible. Here the American painter Thomas Cole evokes the beautiful horror of the dizzy heights and toppling crags of ice that Byron had evoked in words. The painting likely represents Act 2, Scene 2 of *Manfred*, in which the hero conjures up the Witch of the Alps, an apparition that rises, Byron wrote in his stage direction, "beneath the arch of the sunbow of the torrent." Cole's Witch is a figure of light and mist, hovering on the verge of substantiality. WIKIMEDIA COMMONS.

Disappointed Love, Francis Danby, 1821

In this, the first work he exhibited at the Royal Academy, the Anglo-Irish, Bristol-based painter Francis Danby adopted an unprecedented approach to the combination of figure and landscape that was increasingly central to nineteenth-century painting. *Disappointed Love* owes its power to its fusion of the general and the particularized. The depiction of the young woman, her face and individuality concealed from the viewer, allies her with allegorical representations of melancholy, mourning figures placed atop mortuary monuments, or even some of the female figures in Blake's illuminated books. The scene in which she is placed, by contrast, based on Danby's study of scenery along the River Frome on Bristol's outskirts, is rendered in minute, naturalistic detail. He depicts the plants around her with a botanist's eye. VICTORIA & ALBERT MUSEUM, THE SHEEPSHANKS COLLECTION AND THE ACADEMY.

The Victorian Age
(1830–1901)

Slave Ship (Slavers Throwing Overboard the Dead and Dying—Typhoon Coming On),
J. M. W. Turner, 1840

The subject of Turner's painting—slaves thrown overboard, still in chains, as a storm
approaches—is the occasion for apocalyptic use of light and color. For several years John
Ruskin owned this painting, a gift from his father; but he later sold it, finding the subject "too
painful to live with." While many contemporaries criticized the painting for what they saw as
its extravagance, Ruskin praised it as Turner's noblest work, in a passage from *Modern
Painters* that is one of Ruskin's own finest passages of prose painting (p. 1339). Burstein
Collection / Corbis.

Christic in the Carpenter's Shop
(Christ in the House of His
Parents), John Everett Millais,
1849–50

This scene, from the boyhood of
Christ, shows Joseph in his
carpenter's shop, with Mary in the
center, kneeling by her son, who,
in prefiguration of his death, has
cut himself on a nail. John the
Baptist brings water to wash the
wound; Mary's mother, Anne, is in
the background. The painting
combines scrupulous fidelity to
natural detail (Millais set up his
easel in a carpenter's shop and
used a carpenter to model Joseph
to get the musculature just right)
and dense symbolism. The picture
elicited intensely negative criticism,
including Dickens's response
in "Old Lamps for New Ones"
(p. 1465). Tate Britain, London.

Ophelia, John Everett Millais, 1851–52

Millais's painting illustrates the lines from *Hamlet* (4.7.137–54) in which Gertrude describes Ophelia's drowning herself. Many of the individual plants and flowers—the pansies on her dress, the violets around her neck—derive from the queen's speech and Ophelia's mad scene (4.5.163–94). Like much Pre-Raphaelite art, the painting sets an erotic subject in the midst of photographically precise, symbolic detail. The model for the painting was Elizabeth Siddal (later to become Dante Gabriel Rossetti's wife), who posed for the picture in a warm bath. ERICH LESSING / ART RESOURCE, NY.

Work, Ford Madox Brown, 1852, 1856–63

Brown's painting constructs a comprehensive picture of Victorian society through the relationships of various classes of the population to work. The excavators at the center represent work in its essential, physical form; the leisured gentry on horseback at the top of the painting have no need to work; the ragged girl in the foreground cares for her orphaned brothers and sisters. Under the trees are vagrants and distressed haymakers. Thomas Carlyle and F. D. Maurice, "brain workers" whose social ideas influenced the painting, stand on the right. MANCHESTER CITY ART GALLERY, MANCHESTER, UK.

The Awakening Conscience, William Holman Hunt, 1853–54

As John Ruskin's letter to the *Times* (p. 1466) points out, every detail of Hunt's painting of a fallen woman, hearing the voice of conscience while in the arms of her lover, has symbolic resonance—the soiled glove on the carpet, the bird that has escaped the cat, the songs on the piano ("Oft in the Stilly Night") and on the floor ("Tears, Idle Tears"), the window through which the woman gazes, reflected in the mirror behind the couple. Like Millais's *Ophelia,* the painting surrounds and interprets its subject with a crowded canvas of discrete, photographically rendered objects. TATE GALLERY, LONDON / ART RESOURCE, NY.

Soul's Beauty, Dante Gabriel Rossetti, 1864–70

Also titled *Sibylla Palmifera* (the palm-bearing sibyl), *Soul's Beauty* represents the unattainable ideal that inspires the artist. Painted as a companion to the sonnet of the same name, the picture strives to represent and evoke the erotic and aesthetic absorption the poem allegorizes. Rossetti devoted the last fifteen years of his painting career to these looming frontal portraits with richly decorated backgrounds, the details of which carry symbolic significance (in this painting, the arch of life, the cupid, the poppies, the skull, the butterflies).

Body's Beauty, Dante Gabriel Rossetti, 1864–73

Also titled *Lady Lilith* (after Adam's first wife, who ran away to become a witch), *Body's Beauty* represents sensual absorption. Paired with the sonnet of the same name, the painting associates the sexual allure of the woman at the center with the golden hair that represents her value, and her narcissistic contemplation of herself with the art that she embodies. Like the Lady of Shalott, Lady Lilith is a weaver but a deadly one—the poppies and roses surrounding her link death and sexuality.

The Beguiling of Merlin, Edward Burne-Jones, 1870–74

Burne-Jones draws on a medieval version of the Arthurian legend for this painting, in which Merlin's pupil, Nimuë (also called Nimiane, Vivian, or Vivien), uses one of Merlin's own spells to imprison him in a hawthorn tree. The winding branches of the tree, echoed in the Medusa-like snakes of Nimuë's hair, create a flat decorative surface. Although the Nimuë of the story is a femme fatale enchanting the helpless Merlin, her posture and expression and the similarity of the two faces make the painting ambiguous. THE BOARD OF TRUSTEES OF THE NATIONAL MUSEUMS AND GALLERIES ON MERSEYSIDE, LADY LEVER ART GALLERY, LIVERPOOL, ENGLAND.

The Passing of Arthur, Julia Margaret Cameron, 1875

Using photography in the way that earlier artists had used engravings to illustrate literary texts, Cameron produced a set of tableaux vivants for Tennyson's *Idylls of the King*, posing family and friends in costume, in a combination of reality and fantasy that recalls the Pre-Raphaelites. This photograph illustrates lines 361–93 of *The Passing of Arthur* (pp. 1256–57), where the three queens attend the dying king in the barge that takes him to Avalon. HULTON-DEUTSCH COLLECTION / CORBIS.

Nocturne in Black and Gold, the Falling Rocket, James A. M. Whistler, 1875

Whistler's impressionist painting of fireworks approaches the abstraction suggested in his title. He emphatically rejected the precise depiction of objects in earlier Victorian painting. When the critic John Ruskin saw the painting in Grosvenor Gallery, he wrote in *Fors Clavigera* that he "never expected to hear a coxcomb ask two hundred guineas for flinging a pot of paint in the public's face." Whistler sued Ruskin for libel and won; but he was awarded damages of only one farthing, and the trial left him financially ruined. THE DETROIT INSTITUTE OF ARTS, USA / BRIDGEMAN ART LIBRARY. GIFT OF DEXTER M. FERRY, JR.

Les Demoiselles d'Avignon, Pablo Picasso, 1907

This masterpiece by Spanish expatriate painter Pablo Picasso helped unleash the experimental energies of modern art. The painting breaks with formal traditions of one-point perspective and human modeling, violently fracturing space in jagged planes. At the same time it defies conventions of sexual decorum in the visual arts, confronting the viewer with five naked prostitutes in a brothel. The masklike faces, particularly of the women to the right, echo African art; they suggest the crucial role non-Western art will play in the development of modernism. The abstract faces, angular forms, and formally fragmented bodies intimate the revolutionary techniques of analytic cubism that Picasso and his French collaborator Georges Braque would develop in Paris from 1907 to 1914.
THE MUSEUM OF MODERN ART / LICENSED BY SCALA / ART RESOURCE, NY.

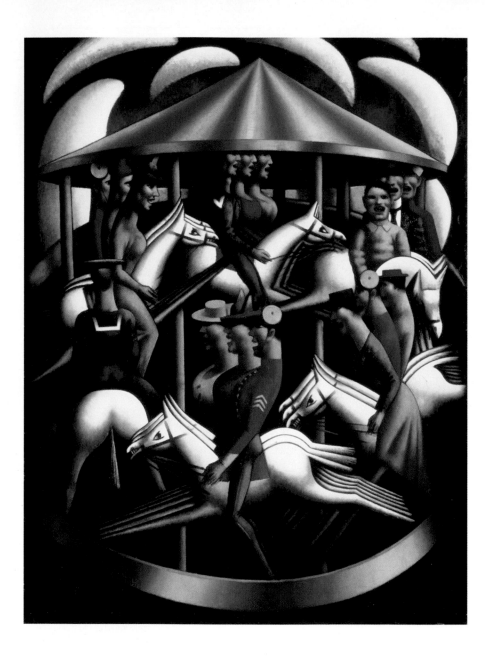

The Merry-Go-Round, Mark Gertler, 1916

Painted in the midst of World War I, *The Merry-Go-Round* explores the insufferable condition of life on the home front and on the battlefields. Its circularity describes the frustration of the deadlock on the Western Front, while its mingling of automatized soldiers and women conveys the sense of psychological menace pervading civilian society. The grinning puppetlike figures and the fun-fair setting convey an atmosphere of ghastly levity, in which war becomes a game. Glaring artificial colors contribute to the impression of a violent and confined world, where even nature is mechanical. TATE GALLERY, LONDON / ART RESOURCE, NY.

Over the Top, 1st Artists' Rifles at Marcoing, 30th December 1917,
John Northcote Nash, 1918

John Nash enlisted in the Artists' Rifles in 1916 and survived several attempts at going "over the top" before his appointment as a War Artist two years later. In this painting he powerfully recollects the futile danger of an attack near Cambrai in 1917. A line of soldiers clambers out of a crude, wound-red trench to trudge through snow toward an unseen enemy. Several men are killed immediately, then fall prostrate or fall back into the ready-made grave of their recent refuge. Years later Nash recalled that the advance had from the outset been doomed, "was in fact pure murder," designed to divert attention from a bombing raid elsewhere. Of the eighty men who set out, only twelve, including Nash, returned.
IMPERIAL WAR MUSEUM, LONDON, UK / BRIDGEMAN ART LIBRARY.

Tube Shelter Perspective, 1941, and *Family Group,* 1947, Henry Moore

In their disparate treatments of space and community, these works powerfully demonstrate the antithetic atmospheres of war and peace. Moore took up sketching during World War I because of a scarcity of sculpting material. His impression of crowds sheltering in the London Underground during an air raid, ranged in parallel lines down a seemingly endless tunnel, evokes the involuntary intimacy of strangers—forced into proximity, yet still isolated and anonymous. *Family Group,* by contrast, expresses a postwar moment of relative security, when the birth of Moore's only daughter coincided with the government's promotion of traditional family values, and Moore's return to sculpture found a ready market for large-scale public art. Two parents, infants on their knees, sit in a cozy circle, their bodies merging in a physical expression of unity. The holes within the sculpture recall the wartime tunnel, transforming it from a void that swallows masses of people to a harmonious space controlled by the bodies. *Family Group*: Christie's Images/Corbis; *Tube Shelter Perspective*: Henry Moore Foundation; Tate Gallery, London / Art Resource, NY.

Painting, Francis Bacon, 1946

Bacon's nightmarish association of the slaughterhouse with the emblems of political and religious power conjures both the suffering and the hypocrisy of the twentieth century. The bust of a man, his face overshadowed by an open umbrella, surrounded by microphones, the whole superimposed upon a butcher's display, evokes the discrepancy between rhetoric and means of power. While the umbrella offers a ludicrous symbol of respectability, the visual parallels between man and meat draw attention to the brutal foundations of political influence. The man's broad shoulders resemble the squared outline of the carcass behind him. The red and white of his face, and his exposed teeth, suggest the flesh and bone of the beef. Incongruous religious references, in the cruciform spread of the carcass and the churchlike decorations on the walls, augment the painting's insinuations of corruption. The Estate of Francis Bacon / ARS, NY / DACS, London; Digital Image; The Museum of Modern Art / Licensed by Scala / Art Resource, NY.

Model with Unfinished Self-Portrait, David Hockney, 1977

In *Model with Unfinished Self-Portrait* layers of illusion, realism undermined by artifice, and pictures within pictures draw our attention to the deceptive nature of painting. At first we seem to see in mirror image a model (Gregory Evans, Hockney's lover) sleeping while the artist paints; but as the title implies, the figure in fact lies in front of *Self-Portrait with Blue Guitar*, a painting developed concurrently with *Model*, depicting Hockney as Picasso, drawing a guitar. Hockney used the relationship between the canvases to reinforce his persona: *Model* invokes Picasso's technique of combining naturalistic with stylized or unfinished elements; while *Self-Portrait*, which eventually incorporated a bust of Dora Maar, Picasso's mistress, encourages an analogy between Picasso, Hockney, and their respective muses.

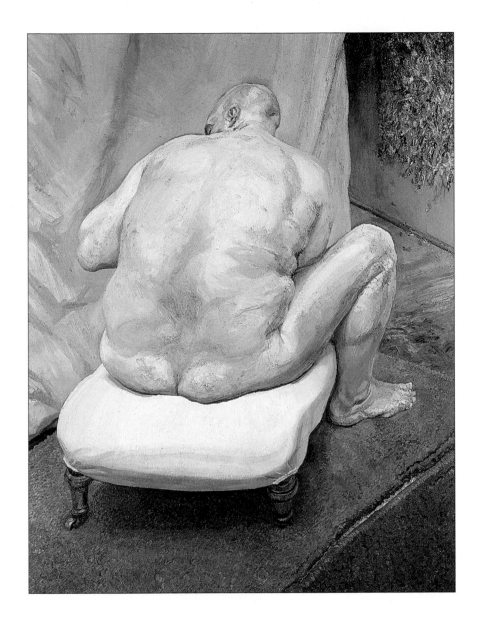

Naked Man, Back View, Lucian Freud, 1993

Freud's nudes study the details of the human body with an unflinching fascination that is modern in its refusal to censor or sentimentalize. Bowery, Freud's model, was a two-hundred-pound nightclub performer, famous for the gorgeous and outrageous costumes he used to reinvent himself in public. Yet Freud, recalling their first encounter, remembered the shape of his lower limbs rather than his outfit, observing that "his calves went right down to his feet, almost avoiding the whole business of ankles altogether." His depiction of Bowery in the nude strongly evokes the magnificence and the vulnerability of a body better known for its sartorial transformations. Courtesy of Acquavella Galleries, Inc. © 1993 The Metropolitan Museum of Art, Purchase Lila Acheson Wallace Gift (1993.71).

Yinka Shonibare, *Nelson's Ship in a Bottle,* May 24, 2010–December 31, 2011

Commissioned as a temporary addition to London's Trafalgar Square, Anglo-Nigerian artist Yinka Shonibare's work is a scaled replica of the ship that carried Admiral Horatio Nelson (whose statue ascends nearby) to victory over Napoleon at the Battle of Trafalgar in 1805—except that Shonibare playfully corks the ship in a massive, dreamy bottle and refashions the sails out of brightly colored cloth. This textile, frequently seen in his work, is often considered authentically African. But in the cross-cultural irony he relishes, its designs were originally Indonesian, its production English and Dutch, for sale to West Africans. Nelson's victory enabled the British colonization of Africa but also ultimately the reverse colonization of Britain's cultural landscape by people like Shonibare, a self-described "postcolonial hybrid." GETTY IMAGES.

5   But is there for the night a resting-place?
        A roof for when the slow dark hours begin.
    May not the darkness hide it from my face?
        You cannot miss that inn.

    Shall I meet other wayfarers at night?
10   Those who have gone before.
    Then must I knock, or call when just in sight?
        They will not keep you standing at that door.

    Shall I find comfort, travel-sore and weak?
        Of labour you shall find the sum.
15 Will there be beds for me and all who seek?
        Yea, beds for all who come.

1858   1862

Goblin Market

    Morning and evening
    Maids heard the goblins cry:
    "Come buy our orchard fruits,
    Come buy, come buy:
5   Apples and quinces,
    Lemons and oranges,
    Plump unpecked cherries,
    Melons and raspberries,
    Bloom-down-cheeked peaches,
10 Swart-headed mulberries,
    Wild free-born cranberries,
    Crab-apples, dewberries,
    Pine-apples, blackberries,
    Apricots, strawberries;—
15 All ripe together
    In summer weather,—
    Morns that pass by,
    Fair eves that fly;
    Come buy, come buy:
20 Our grapes fresh from the vine,
    Pomegranates full and fine,
    Dates and sharp bullaces,
    Rare pears and greengages,
    Damsons¹ and bilberries,
25 Taste them and try:
    Currants and gooseberries,
    Bright-fire-like barberries,
    Figs to fill your mouth,
    Citrons from the South,
30 Sweet to tongue and sound to eye;
    Come buy, come buy."

---

1. Bullaces, greengages, and damsons are varieties of plums.

Evening by evening
Among the brookside rushes,
Laura bowed her head to hear,
35 Lizzie veiled her blushes:
Crouching close together
In the cooling weather,
With clasping arms and cautioning lips,
With tingling cheeks and finger tips.
40 "Lie close," Laura said,
Pricking up her golden head:
"We must not look at goblin men,
We must not buy their fruits:
Who knows upon what soil they fed
45 Their hungry thirsty roots?"
"Come buy," call the goblins
Hobbling down the glen.
"Oh," cried Lizzie, "Laura, Laura,
You should not peep at goblin men."
50 Lizzie covered up her eyes,
Covered close lest they should look;
Laura reared her glossy head,
And whispered like the restless brook:
"Look, Lizzie, look, Lizzie,
55 Down the glen tramp little men.
One hauls a basket,
One bears a plate,
One lugs a golden dish
Of many pounds weight.
60 How fair the vine must grow
Whose grapes are so luscious;
How warm the wind must blow
Thro' those fruit bushes."
"No," said Lizzie: "No, no, no;
65 Their offers should not charm us,
Their evil gifts would harm us."
She thrust a dimpled finger
In each ear, shut eyes and ran:
Curious Laura chose to linger
70 Wondering at each merchant man.
One had a cat's face,
One whisked a tail,
One tramped at a rat's pace,
One crawled like a snail,
75 One like a wombat prowled obtuse and furry,
One like a ratel[2] tumbled hurry skurry.
She heard a voice like voice of doves
Cooing all together:
They sounded kind and full of loves
80 In the pleasant weather.

Laura stretched her gleaming neck
Like a rush-imbedded swan,

---

2. South African mammal resembling a badger (pronounced *ray-tell*).

Like a lily from the beck,°   *small brook*
Like a moonlit poplar branch,
85   Like a vessel at the launch
When its last restraint is gone.

Backwards up the mossy glen
Turned and trooped the goblin men,
With their shrill repeated cry,
90   "Come buy, come buy."
When they reached where Laura was
They stood stock still upon the moss,
Leering at each other,
Brother with queer brother;
95   Signalling each other,
Brother with sly brother.
One set his basket down,
One reared° his plate;   *raised*
One began to weave a crown
100   Of tendrils, leaves and rough nuts brown
(Men sell not such in any town);
One heaved the golden weight
Of dish and fruit to offer her:
"Come buy, come buy," was still their cry.
105   Laura stared but did not stir,
Longed but had no money:
The whisk-tailed merchant bade her taste
In tones as smooth as honey,
The cat-faced purr'd,
110   The rat-paced spoke a word
Of welcome, and the snail-paced even was heard;
One parrot-voiced and jolly
Cried "Pretty Goblin" still° for "Pretty Polly;"—   *always*
One whistled like a bird.

115   But sweet-tooth Laura spoke in haste:
"Good folk, I have no coin;
To take were to purloin:
I have no copper in my purse,
I have no silver either,
120   And all my gold is on the furze
That shakes in windy weather
Above the rusty heather."
"You have much gold upon your head,"
They answered all together:
125   "Buy from us with a golden curl."
She clipped a precious golden lock,
She dropped a tear more rare than pearl,
Then sucked their fruit globes fair or red:
Sweeter than honey from the rock.
130   Stronger than man-rejoicing wine,[3]
Clearer than water flowed that juice;

3. Psalm 104.15. "Sweeter . . . rock": Psalm 81.16.

She never tasted such before,
How should it cloy with length of use?
She sucked and sucked and sucked the more
135 Fruits which that unknown orchard bore;
She sucked until her lips were sore;
Then flung the emptied rinds away
But gathered up one kernel-stone,
And knew not was it night or day
140 As she turned home alone.

Lizzie met her at the gate
Full of wise upbraidings:
"Dear, you should not stay so late,
Twilight is not good for maidens;
145 Should not loiter in the glen
In the haunts of goblin men.
Do you not remember Jeanie,
How she met them in the moonlight,
Took their gifts both choice and many,
150 Ate their fruits and wore their flowers
Plucked from bowers
Where summer ripens at all hours?
But ever in the noonlight
She pined and pined away;
155 Sought them by night and day,
Found them no more but dwindled and grew grey;
Then fell with the first snow,
While to this day no grass will grow
Where she lies low:
160 I planted daisies there a year ago
That never blow.°   *bloom*
You should not loiter so."
"Nay, hush," said Laura:
"Nay, hush, my sister:
165 I ate and ate my fill,
Yet my mouth waters still;
Tomorrow night I will
Buy more:" and kissed her:
"Have done with sorrow;
170 I'll bring you plums tomorrow
Fresh on their mother twigs,
Cherries worth getting;
You cannot think what figs
My teeth have met in,
175 What melons icy-cold
Piled on a dish of gold
Too huge for me to hold,
What peaches with a velvet nap,
Pellucid grapes without one seed:
180 Odorous indeed must be the mead
Whereon they grow, and pure the wave they drink
With lilies at the brink,
And sugar-sweet their sap."

Golden head by golden head,
185 Like two pigeons in one nest
Folded in each other's wings,
They lay down in their curtained bed:
Like two blossoms on one stem,
Like two flakes of new-fall'n snow,
190 Like two wands of ivory
Tipped with gold for awful° kings.   *awe-inspiring*
Moon and stars gazed in at them,
Wind sang to them lullaby,
Lumbering owls forbore to fly,
195 Not a bat flapped to and fro
Round their rest:
Cheek to cheek and breast to breast
Locked together in one nest.

Early in the morning
200 When the first cock crowed his warning,
Neat like bees, as sweet and busy,
Laura rose with Lizzie:
Fetched in honey, milked the cows,
Aired and set to rights the house,
205 Kneaded cakes of whitest wheat,
Cakes for dainty mouths to eat,
Next churned butter, whipped up cream,
Fed their poultry, sat and sewed;
Talked as modest maidens should:
210 Lizzie with an open heart,
Laura in an absent dream,
One content, one sick in part;
One warbling for the mere bright day's delight,
One longing for the night.

215 At length slow evening came:
They went with pitchers to the reedy brook;
Lizzie most placid in her look,
Laura most like a leaping flame.
They drew the gurgling water from its deep;
220 Lizzie plucked purple and rich golden flags,°   *irises*
Then turning homewards said: "The sunset flushes
Those furthest loftiest crags;
Come, Laura, not another maiden lags,
No wilful squirrel wags,
225 The beasts and birds are fast asleep."
But Laura loitered still among the rushes
And said the bank was steep.

And said the hour was early still,
The dew not fall'n, the wind not chill:
230 Listening ever, but not catching
The customary cry,

"Come buy, come buy,"
With its iterated jingle
Of sugar-baited words:
235 Not for all her watching
Once discerning even one goblin
Racing, whisking, tumbling, hobbling;
Let alone the herds
That used to tramp along the glen,
240 In groups or single,
Of brisk fruit-merchant men.

Till Lizzie urged, "O Laura, come;
I hear the fruit-call but I dare not look:
You should not loiter longer at this brook:
245 Come with me home.
The stars rise, the moon bends her arc,
Each glowworm winks her spark,
Let us get home before the night grows dark:
For clouds may gather
250 Tho' this is summer weather,
Put out the lights and drench us thro';
Then if we lost our way what should we do?"

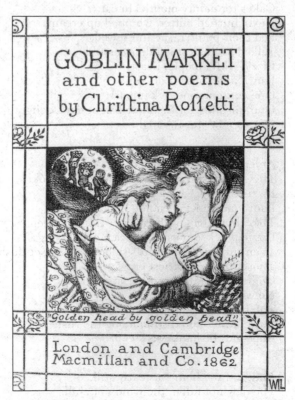

Goblin Market. This frontispiece is one of the two illustrations that Dante Gabriel Rossetti provided for his sister's first volume of poetry in 1862.

Laura turned cold as stone
To find her sister heard that cry alone,
255 That goblin cry,
"Come buy our fruits, come buy."
Must she then buy no more such dainty fruit?
Must she no more such succous° pasture find, *juicy, succulent*
Gone deaf and blind?
260 Her tree of life drooped from the root:
She said not one word in her heart's sore ache;
But peering thro' the dimness, nought discerning,
Trudged home, her pitcher dripping all the way;
So crept to bed, and lay
265 Silent till Lizzie slept;
Then sat up in a passionate yearning,
And gnashed her teeth for baulked desire, and wept
As if her heart would break.

Day after day, night after night,
270 Laura kept watch in vain
In sullen silence of exceeding pain.
She never caught again the goblin cry:
"Come buy, come buy;"—
She never spied the goblin men
275 Hawking their fruits along the glen:
But when the noon waxed bright
Her hair grew thin and gray;
She dwindled, as the fair full moon doth turn
To swift decay and burn
280 Her fire away.

One day remembering her kernel-stone
She set it by a wall that faced the south;
Dewed it with tears, hoped for a root,
Watched for a waxing shoot,
285 But there came none;
It never saw the sun,
It never felt the trickling moisture run:
While with sunk eyes and faded mouth
She dreamed of melons, as a traveller sees
290 False waves in desert drouth
With shade of leaf-crowned trees,
And burns the thirstier in the sandful breeze.

She no more swept the house,
Tended the fowls or cows,
295 Fetched honey, kneaded cakes of wheat,
Brought water from the brook:
But sat down listless in the chimney-nook
And would not eat.

Tender Lizzie could not bear
300 To watch her sister's cankerous care
Yet not to share.
She night and morning

Caught the goblins' cry:
"Come buy our orchard fruits,
305 Come buy, come buy:"—
Beside the brook, along the glen,
She heard the tramp of goblin men,
The voice and stir
Poor Laura could not hear;
310 Longed to buy fruit to comfort her,
But feared to pay too dear.
She thought of Jeanie in her grave,
Who should have been a bride;
But who for joys brides hope to have
315 Fell sick and died
In her gay prime,
In earliest Winter time,
With the first glazing rime,
With the first snow-fall of crisp Winter time.

320 Till Laura dwindling
Seemed knocking at Death's door:
Then Lizzie weighed° no more   *evaluated, considered*
Better and worse;
But put a silver penny in her purse,
325 Kissed Laura, crossed the heath with clumps of furze
At twilight, halted by the brook:
And for the first time in her life
Began to listen and look.

Laughed every goblin
330 When they spied her peeping:
Came towards her hobbling,
Flying, running, leaping,
Puffing and blowing,
Chuckling, clapping, crowing,
335 Clucking and gobbling,
Mopping and mowing,[4]
Full of airs and graces,
Pulling wry faces,
Demure grimaces,
340 Cat-like and rat-like,
Ratel-and wombat-like,
Snail-paced in a hurry,
Parrot-voiced and whistler,
Helter skelter, hurry skurry,
345 Chattering like magpies,
Fluttering like pigeons,
Gliding like fishes,—
Hugged her and kissed her,
Squeezed and caressed her:
350 Stretched up their dishes,
Panniers, and plates:
"Look at our apples

4. Grimacing, making faces.

Russet and dun,
Bob at our cherries,
355   Bite at our peaches,
Citrons and dates,
Grapes for the asking,
Pears red with basking
Out in the sun,
360   Plums on their twigs;
Pluck them and suck them,
Pomegranates, figs."—

"Good folk," said Lizzie,
Mindful of Jeanie:
365   "Give me much and many:"—
Held out her apron,
Tossed them her penny.
"Nay, take a seat with us,
Honour and eat with us,"
370   They answered grinning:
"Our feast is but beginning.
Night yet is early,
Warm and dew-pearly,
Wakeful and starry:
375   Such fruits as these
No man can carry;
Half their bloom would fly,
Half their dew would dry,
Half their flavour would pass by.
380   Sit down and feast with us,
Be welcome guest with us,
Cheer you and rest with us."—
"Thank you," said Lizzie: "But one waits
At home alone for me:
385   So without further parleying,
If you will not sell me any
Of your fruits tho' much and many,
Give me back my silver penny
I tossed you for a fee."—

390   They began to scratch their pates,
No longer wagging, purring,
But visibly demurring,
Grunting and snarling.
One called her proud,
395   Cross-grained, uncivil;
Their tones waxed loud,
Their looks were evil.
Lashing their tails
They trod and hustled her,
400   Elbowed and jostled her,
Clawed with their nails,
Barking, mewing, hissing, mocking,
Tore her gown and soiled her stocking,
Twitched her hair out by the roots,

405   Stamped upon her tender feet,
       Held her hands and squeezed their fruits
       Against her mouth to make her eat.

       White and golden Lizzie stood,
       Like a lily in a flood,—
410   Like a rock of blue-veined stone
       Lashed by tides obstreperously,—
       Like a beacon left alone
       In a hoary roaring sea,
       Sending up a golden fire,—
415   Like a fruit-crowned orange-tree
       White with blossoms honey-sweet
       Sore beset by wasp and bee,—
       Like a royal virgin town
       Topped with gilded dome and spire
420   Close beleaguered by a fleet
       Mad to tug her standard down.

       One may lead a horse to water,
       Twenty cannot make him drink.
       Tho' the goblins cuffed and caught her,
425   Coaxed and fought her,
       Bullied and besought her,
       Scratched her, pinched her black as ink,
       Kicked and knocked her,
       Mauled and mocked her,
430   Lizzie uttered not a word;
       Would not open lip from lip
       Lest they should cram a mouthful in:
       But laughed in heart to feel the drip
       Of juice that syruped all her face,
435   And lodged in dimples of her chin,
       And streaked her neck which quaked like curd.
       At last the evil people
       Worn out by her resistance
       Flung back her penny, kicked their fruit
440   Along whichever road they took,
       Not leaving root or stone or shoot;
       Some writhed into the ground,
       Some dived into the brook
       With ring and ripple,
445   Some scudded on the gale without a sound,
       Some vanished in the distance.

       In a smart, ache, tingle,
       Lizzie went her way;
       Knew not was it night or day;
450   Sprang up the bank, tore thro' the furze,
       Threaded copse and dingle,
       And heard her penny jingle
       Bouncing in her purse,
       Its bounce was music to her ear.
455   She ran and ran

As if she feared some goblin man
Dogged her with gibe or curse
Or something worse:
But not one goblin skurried after,
460   Nor was she pricked by fear;
The kind heart made her windy-paced
That urged her home quite out of breath with haste
And inward laughter.

She cried "Laura," up the garden,
465   "Did you miss me?
Come and kiss me.
Never mind my bruises,
Hug me, kiss me, suck my juices
Squeezed from goblin fruits for you,
470   Goblin pulp and goblin dew.
Eat me, drink me, love me;
Laura, make much of me:
For your sake I have braved the glen
And had to do with goblin merchant men."

475   Laura started from her chair,
Flung her arms up in the air,
Clutched her hair:
"Lizzie, Lizzie, have you tasted
For my sake the fruit forbidden?
480   Must your light like mine be hidden,
Your young life like mine be wasted,
Undone in mine undoing
And ruined in my ruin,
Thirsty, cankered, goblin-ridden?"—
485   She clung about her sister,
Kissed and kissed and kissed her:
Tears once again
Refreshed her shrunken eyes,
Dropping like rain
490   After long sultry drouth;
Shaking with aguish° fear, and pain,   *feverish*
She kissed and kissed her with a hungry mouth.

Her lips began to scorch,
That juice was wormwood to her tongue,
495   She loathed the feast:
Writhing as one possessed she leaped and sung,
Rent all her robe, and wrung
Her hands in lamentable haste,
And beat her breast.
500   Her locks streamed like the torch
Borne by a racer at full speed,
Or like the mane of horses in their flight,
Or like an eagle when she stems⁵ the light

5. Makes headway against.

Straight toward the sun,
505 Or like a caged thing freed,
Or like a flying flag when armies run.

Swift fire spread thro' her veins, knocked at her heart,
Met the fire smouldering there
And overbore its lesser flame;
510 She gorged on bitterness without a name:
Ah! fool, to choose such part
Of soul-consuming care!
Sense failed in the mortal strife:
Like the watch-tower of a town
515 Which an earthquake shatters down,
Like a lightning-stricken mast,
Like a wind-uprooted tree
Spun about,
Like a foam-topped waterspout
520 Cast down headlong in the sea,
She fell at last;
Pleasure past and anguish past,
Is it death or is it life?

Life out of death.
525 That night long Lizzie watched by her,
Counted her pulse's flagging stir,
Felt for her breath,
Held water to her lips, and cooled her face
With tears and fanning leaves:
530 But when the first birds chirped about their eaves,
And early reapers plodded to the place
Of golden sheaves,
And dew-wet grass
Bowed in the morning winds so brisk to pass,
535 And new buds with new day
Opened of cup-like lilies on the stream,
Laura awoke as from a dream,
Laughed in the innocent old way,
Hugged Lizzie but not° twice or thrice;   *not only*
540 Her gleaming locks showed not one thread of grey,
Her breath was sweet as May
And light danced in her eyes.

Days, weeks, months, years
Afterwards, when both were wives
545 With children of their own;
Their mother-hearts beset with fears,
Their lives bound up in tender lives;
Laura would call the little ones
And tell them of her early prime,
550 Those pleasant days long gone
Of not-returning time:
Would talk about the haunted glen,
The wicked, quaint° fruit-merchant men,   *strange*

Their fruits like honey to the throat
555 But poison in the blood;
(Men sell not such in any town:)
Would tell them how her sister stood
In deadly peril to do her good,
And win the fiery antidote:
560 Then joining hands to little hands
Would bid them cling together,
"For there is no friend like a sister
In calm or stormy weather;
To cheer one on the tedious way,
565 To fetch one if one goes astray,
To lift one if one totters down,
To strengthen whilst one stands."

1859   1862

"No, Thank You, John"

I never said I loved you, John:
    Why will you teaze me day by day,
And wax a weariness to think upon
    With always "do" and "pray"?

5 You know I never loved you, John;
    No fault of mine made me your toast:
Why will you haunt me with a face as wan
    As shows an hour-old ghost?

I dare say Meg or Moll would take
10   Pity upon you, if you'd ask:
And pray don't remain single for my sake
    Who can't perform that task.

I have no heart?—Perhaps I have not;
    But then you're mad to take offence
15 That I don't give you what I have not got:
    Use your own common sense.

Let bygones be bygones:
    Don't call me false, who owed not to be true:
I'd rather answer "No" to fifty Johns
20   Than answer "Yes" to you.

Let's mar our pleasant days no more,
    Song-birds of passage, days of youth:
Catch at today, forget the days before:
    I'll wink° at your untruth.   close (both) eyes

25 Let us strike hands as hearty friends;
    No more, no less; and friendship's good:
Only don't keep in view ulterior ends,
    And points not understood

In open treaty. Rise above
30   Quibbles and shuffling off and on:
Here's friendship for you if you like; but love,—
No, thank you, John.

1860   1862

Promises Like Pie-Crust

Promise me no promises,
    So will I not promise you:
Keep we both our liberties,
    Never false and never true:
5   Let us hold the die uncast,
    Free to come as free to go:
For I cannot know your past,
    And of mine what can you know?

You, so warm, may once have been
10   Warmer towards another one:
I, so cold, may once have seen
    Sunlight, once have felt the sun:
Who shall show us if it was
    Thus indeed in time of old?
15   Fades the image from the glass,
    And the fortune is not told.

If you promised, you might grieve
    For lost liberty again:
If I promised, I believe
20   I should fret to break the chain.
Let us be the friends we were,
    Nothing more but nothing less:
Many thrive on frugal fare
    Who would perish of excess.

1861   1896

Cardinal Newman[1]

In the grave, whither thou goest[2]

O weary Champion of the Cross, lie still:
    Sleep thou at length the all-embracing sleep:
    Long was thy sowing-day, rest now and reap:
Thy fast was long, feast now thy spirit's fill.
5   Yea, take thy fill of love, because thy will

---

1. Written on the occasion of the death of John   2. Ecclesiastes 9.10.
Henry Newman (1801–1890).

Chose love not in the shallows but the deep:
Thy tides were springtides, set against the neap[3]
Of calmer souls: thy flood rebuked their rill.°   *small stream*
Now night has come to thee—please God, of rest:
10   So some time must it come to every man;
To first and last, where many last are first.[4]
Now fixed and finished thine eternal plan,
Thy best has done its best, thy worst its worst:
Thy best its best, Please God, thy best its best.

1890

Sleeping at Last

Sleeping at last, the trouble & tumult over,
Sleeping at last, the struggle & horror past,
Cold & white out of sight of friend & of lover
Sleeping at last.

5   No more a tired heart downcast or overcast,
No more pangs that wring or shifting fears that hover,
Sleeping at last in a dreamless sleep locked fast.

Fast asleep. Singing birds in their leafy cover
Cannot wake her, nor shake her the gusty blast.
10   Under the purple thyme and the purple clover
Sleeping at last.

1896

3. Tides that do not rise to the high-water mark of the spring tides.
4. Rossetti alludes to the parable of the vine-yard, in which "the last shall be first." See Matthew 20.16, Luke 13.30.

GERARD MANLEY HOPKINS
1844–1889

It has been said that the most important date in Gerard Manley Hopkins's career was 1918, twenty-nine years after his death, for it was then that the first publication of his poems made them accessible to the world of readers. During his lifetime these remarkable poems, most of them celebrating the wonders of God's creation, had been known only to a small circle of friends, including his literary executor, the poet Robert Bridges, who waited until 1918 before releasing them to a publisher. Partly because his work was first made public in a twentieth-century volume, but especially because of his striking experiments in meter and diction, Hopkins was widely hailed as a pioneering figure of "modern" literature, miraculously unconnected with his fellow Victorian poets (who during the 1920s and 1930s were largely out of fashion among critical readers). And this way of classifying and evaluating his writings has long persisted. In 1936 a substantial selection of his poems led off *The Faber Book of Modern Verse*, one of the most influential anthologies of the century, featuring poets such as W. H. Auden, Dylan Thomas, and T. S. Eliot (the only one whose selections occupy more pages than those allotted to Hopkins). And the first four editions of *The Norton Anthology of English Literature* (1962–79) grouped Hopkins with these twentieth-century poets. To reclassify him is not to repudiate his earlier reputation as a "modern" but rather to suggest that his work can be better understood and appreciated if it is restored to the Victorian world out of which it developed.

Hopkins was born near London into a large and cultivated family in comfortable circumstances. After a brilliant career at Highgate School, he entered Oxford in 1863, where he was exposed to a variety of Victorian ways of thinking, both secular and religious. Among the influential leaders at Oxford was Matthew Arnold, professor of poetry; but more important for Hopkins was his tutor, Walter Pater, an aesthetician whose emphasis on the intense apprehension of sensuous beauty struck a responsive chord in Hopkins. At Oxford he was also exposed to the Broad Church theology of one of the tutors at his college (Balliol), Benjamin Jowett. But Hopkins became increasingly attracted first to the High Church movement represented at Oxford by Edward Pusey, and then to Roman Catholicism. Profoundly influenced by John Henry Newman's conversion to Rome and by subsequent conversations with Newman, Hopkins entered the Roman Catholic Church in 1866. The estrangement from his family that resulted from his conversion was very painful for him; his parents' letters to him were so "terrible" (he reported to Newman) that he could not bear to "read them twice." And this alienation was heightened by his decision not only to become a Roman Catholic but to become a priest and, in particular, a Jesuit priest, for many Victorian Protestants regarded the Jesuit order with a special distrust. For the rest of his life, Hopkins served as a priest and teacher in various places, among them Oxford, Liverpool, and Lancashire. In 1884 he was appointed professor of classics at University College in Dublin.

At school and at Oxford in the early 1860s, Hopkins had written poems in the vein of John Keats. He burned most of these early writings after his conversion (although drafts survive), for he believed that his vocation must require renouncing such personal satisfactions as the writing of poems. Only after his superiors in the church encouraged him to do so did he resume writing poetry. Yet during the seven years of silence, as his letters show, he had been thinking about experimenting with what he called a "new rhythm." The result, in 1876, was his rhapsodic lyric-narrative, "The Wreck of the Deutschland," a long ode about the wreck of a ship in which five Franciscan nuns were drowned. The style of the poem was so distinctive that the editor of the Jesuit magazine to which he had submitted it "dared not print it," as Hopkins reported. During the remaining fourteen years of his life, Hopkins wrote poems but seldom submitted them for publication, partly because he was convinced that poetic fame was incompatible with his religious vocation but also because of a fear that readers would be discouraged by the eccentricity of his work.

Hopkins's sense of his own uniqueness is in accord with the larger philosophy that informs his poetry. Drawing on the theology of Duns Scotus, a medieval philosopher, he felt that everything in the universe was characterized by what he called *inscape*, the distinctive design that constitutes individual identity. This identity is not static but dynamic. Each being in the universe "selves," that is, enacts its identity. And the human being, the most highly selved, the most individually distinctive being in the universe, recognizes the inscape of other beings in an act that Hopkins calls *instress*, the apprehension of an object in an intense thrust of energy toward it that enables one to realize its specific distinctiveness. Ultimately, the instress of inscape leads one to Christ, for the individual identity of any object is the stamp of divine creation on it. In the act of instress, therefore, the human being becomes a celebrant of the divine, at once recognizing God's creation and enacting his or her own God-given identity within it.

Poetry for Hopkins enacts this celebration. It is instress, and it realizes the inscape of its subject in its own distinctive design. Hopkins wrote, "But as air, melody, is what strikes me most of all in music and design in painting, so design, pattern or what I am in the habit of calling 'inscape' is what I above all aim at in poetry." To create inscape, Hopkins seeks to give each poem a unique design that captures the initial inspiration when he is "caught" by his subject. Many of the characteristics of Hopkins's style—his disruption of conventional syntax, his coining and compounding of words, his use of ellipsis and repetition—can be understood as ways of representing the stress and action of the brain in moments of inspiration. He creates compounds to represent the unique interlocking of the characteristics of an object—"piece-bright," "dapple-dawn-drawn," "blue-bleak." He omits syntactical connections to fuse qualities more intensely—"the dearest freshness deep down things." He creates puns to suggest how God's creation rhymes and chimes in a divine patterning. He violates conventional syntactic order to represent the shape of mental experience. In the act of imaginative apprehension, a language particular to the moment generates itself.

Hopkins also uses a new rhythm to give each poem its distinctive design. In the new metric system he created, which he called *sprung rhythm,* lines have a given number of stresses, but the number and placement of unstressed syllables is highly variable. Hopkins rarely marks all the intended stresses, only those that readers might not anticipate. To indicate stressed syllables, Hopkins often uses both the stress (´) and the "great stress" (˝). A curved line marks an "outride"—one or more syllables added to a foot but not counted in the scansion of the line; they indicate a stronger stress on the preceding syllable and a short pause after the outride. Here, for example, is the scansion for the first three lines of "The Windhover":

> I caúght this mórning mórning's mínion, kíng-
> > dom of dáylight's daúphin, dapple-dáwn-drawn Fálcon, in his ríding
> > Of the rólling level underneáth him steady aír, and stríding

Hopkins argued that sprung rhythm was the natural rhythm of common speech and written prose, as well as of music. He found a model for it in Old English poetry and in nursery rhymes, but he claimed that it had not been used in English poetry since the Elizabethan age.

The density and difficulty that result from Hopkins's unconventional rhythm and syntax make his poetry seem modern, but his concern with the imagination's shaping of the natural world puts him very much in the Romantic tradition; and his creation of a rough and difficult style, designed to capture the mind's own motion, resembles the style of Robert Browning. "A horrible thing has happened to me," Hopkins wrote in 1864, "I have begun to *doubt* Tennyson." He criticizes Tennyson for using the grand style as a smooth and habitual poetic speech. Like Algernon Charles Swinburne, Walter Pater, and Henry James as well as Browning, Hopkins displays a new mannerism, characteristic of the latter part of the nineteenth century, which paradoxically combines an elaborate aestheticism with a more complex representation of consciousness.

In Hopkins's early poetry his singular apprehension of the beauty of individual objects always brings him to an ecstatic illumination of the presence of God. But in his late poems, the so-called terrible sonnets, his distinctive individuality comes to isolate him from the God who made him thus. Hopkins wrote, "To me there is no resemblance: searching nature, I taste *self* but at one tankard, that of my own being." In the terrible sonnets Hopkins confronts the solipsism to which his own stress on individuality seems to lead him. Like the mad speakers of so many Victorian dramatic monologues, he cannot escape a world solely of his own imagining. Yet even these

poems of despair, which simultaneously echo the bleaker side of the Romantic tradition and anticipate more modern attitudes, reflect a traditional religious vision: the
dark night of the soul as described by the Spanish mystic Saint John of the Cross.

In his introduction to *The Oxford Book of Modern Verse*, Yeats calls Hopkins's
poetry "a last development of poetical diction." Yeats's remark indicates the anomaly
that Hopkins's work poses. Perhaps it is only appropriate for a writer who stressed
the uniqueness of inscape to strike us with the individuality of his achievement.

God's Grandeur

The world is charged with the grandeur of God.
  It will flame out, like shining from shook foil;[1]
  It gathers to a greatness, like the ooze of oil
Crushed.[2] Why do men then now not reck his rod?
5 Generations have trod, have trod, have trod;
  And all is seared with trade; bleared, smeared with toil;
  And wears man's smudge and shares man's smell: the soil
Is bare now, nor can foot feel, being shod.

And for° all this, nature is never spent;   *despite*
10 There lives the dearest freshness deep down things;
And though the last lights off the black West went
  Oh, morning, at the brown brink eastward, springs—
Because the Holy Ghost over the bent
  World broods with warm breast and with ah! bright wings.

1877   1918

The Starlight Night

Look at the stars! look, look up at the skies!
  O look at all the fire-folk sitting in the air!
  The bright boroughs, the circle-citadels there!
Down in dim woods the diamond delves!° the elves'-eyes! *quarries*
5 The grey lawns cold where gold, where quickgold;[1] lies!
  Wind-beat whitebeam! airy abeles° set on a flare! *white poplars*
  Flake-doves sent floating forth at a farmyard scare!—
Ah well! it is all a purchase, all is a prize.

Buy then! bid then!—What?—Prayer, patience, alms, vows.
10 Look, look: a May-mess,[2] like on orchard boughs!
  Look! March-bloom, like on mealed-with-yellow sallows![3]
These are indeed the barn; withindoors house

1. Hopkins explained this image in a letter: "I
mean foil in its sense of leaf or tinsel. . . . Shaken
goldfoil gives off broad glares like sheet lightning
and also, and this is true of nothing else, owing to
its zigzag dints and creasings and network of small
many cornered facets, a sort of fork lightning too."
2. I.e., from the crushing of olives.

1. Coined by analogy with quicksilver. The starlight night resembles the lawns below it, where
the dew, reflecting the starlight, looks like gold.
2. A profusion of growing things such as May
blossoms.
3. Willows, here with yellow spots like meal.

The shocks. This piece-bright paling[4] shuts the spouse
    Christ home, Christ and his mother and all his hallows.°   *saints*

1877   1918

As Kingfishers Catch Fire

As kingfishers catch fire, dragonflies draw flame;
    As tumbled over rim in roundy wells
    Stones ring; like each tucked° string tells, each hung bell's   *plucked*
Bow swung finds tongue to fling out broad its name;
5 Each mortal thing does one thing and the same:
    Deals out that being indoors° each one dwells;   *within*
    Selves[1]—goes itself; *myself* it speaks and spells,
Crying *What I do is me: for that I came.*

I say more: the just man justices;[2]
10   Keeps gráce: thát keeps all his goings graces;
Acts in God's eye what in God's eye he is—
    Chríst. For Christ plays in ten thousand places,
Lovely in limbs, and lovely in eyes not his
    To the Father through the features of men's faces.

1877   1918

Spring

Nothing is so beautiful as Spring—
    When weeds, in wheels, shoot long and lovely and lush;
    Thrush's eggs look little low heavens, and thrush
Through the echoing timber does so rinse and wring
5 The ear, it strikes like lightnings to hear him sing;
    The glassy peartree leaves and blooms, they brush
    The descending blue; that blue is all in a rush
With richness; the racing lambs too have fair their fling.

What is all this juice and all this joy?
10   A strain of the earth's sweet being in the beginning
In Eden garden.—Have, get, before it cloy,
    Before it cloud, Christ, lord, and sour with sinning,
Innocent mind and Mayday in girl and boy,
    Most, O maid's child,[1] thy choice and worthy the winning.

1877   1918

---

4. This word choice connects the upright siding of the barn's walls to the planks (or "pales") of a fence. "Shocks": sheaves of grain.

1. Fulfills its individuality.
2. Acts in a just manner.
1. Jesus, son of the Virgin Mary.

The Windhover[1]

To Christ our Lord

I caught this morning morning's minion,° king-   darling
   dom of daylight's dauphin,[2] dapple-dawn-drawn Falcon, in his riding
   Of the rolling level underneath him steady air, and striding
High there, how he rung upon the rein of a wimpling[3] wing
5   In his ecstasy! then off, off forth on swing,
   As a skate's heel sweeps smooth on a bow-bend: the hurl and gliding
   Rebuffed the big wind. My heart in hiding
Stirred for a bird,—the achieve of, the mastery of the thing!

Brute beauty and valour and act, oh, air, pride, plume, here
10   Buckle![4] AND the fire that breaks from thee then, a billion
Times told lovelier, more dangerous, O my chevalier!°   knight

No wonder of it: shéer plód makes plough down sillion[5]
Shine, and blue-bleak embers, ah my dear,
   Fall, gall[6] themselves, and gash gold-vermilion.

1877   1918

Pied[1] Beauty

Glory be to God for dappled things—
   For skies of couple-colour as a brinded[2] cow;
      For rose-moles all in stipple upon trout that swim;
Fresh-firecoal chestnut-falls,[3] finches' wings;
5   Landscape plotted and pieced—fold, fallow, and plough;[4]
      And áll trádes, their gear and tackle and trim.°   equipment

All things counter, original, spare,[5] strange;
   Whatever is fickle, freckled (who knows how?)
      With swift, slow; sweet, sour; adazzle, dim;
10 He fathers-forth whose beauty is past change:
             Praise him.

1877   1918

1. Kestrel, a small falcon noted for hovering in the air.
2. A prince who is heir to the French throne.
3. Rippling. "Rung upon the rein": circled at the end of a rein.
4. The verb can be read as imperative or indicative. All three meanings are relevant: to prepare for action, to fasten together, to collapse.
5. The ridge between two furrows of a plowed field.

6. Break the surface of.
1. Of two or more colors in blotches, variegated.
2. Brownish orange in color with streaks of gray.
3. I.e., freshly fallen chestnuts, bright as coals.
4. Divided into fields used as pastures ("fold"), lying fallow, or plowed for cultivation. The landscape thus appears like patches of different colors.
5. Rare. "Counter": contrary.

Hurrahing in Harvest

Summer ends now; now, barbarous in beauty, the stooks[1] rise
Around; up above, what wind-walks! what lovely behaviour
Of silk-sack clouds! has wilder, wilful-wavier
Meal-drift moulded ever and melted across skies?

5   I walk, I lift up, I lift up heart, eyes,
Down all that glory in the heavens to glean our Saviour;
And, éyes, heárt, what looks, what lips yet gave you a
Rapturous love's greeting of realer, of rounder replies?

And the azurous hung hills are his world-wielding shoulder
10 Majestic—as a stallion stalwart, very-violet-sweet!—
These things, these things were here and but the beholder
Wanting; which two when they once meet,
The heart rears wings bold and bolder
And hurls for him, O half hurls earth for him off under his feet.

1877   1918

Binsey Poplars

felled 1879

My aspens dear, whose airy cages quelled,
Quelled or quenched in leaves the leaping sun,
All felled, felled, are all felled;
   Of a fresh and following folded rank
5   Not spared, not one
          That dandled a sandalled
        Shadow that swam or sank
On meadow and river and wind-wandering
      weed-winding bank.

10   O if we but knew what we do
          When we delve° or hew—   *dig*
     Hack and rack° the growing green!   *torture*
         Since country is so tender
      To touch, her being só slender,
15   That, like this sleek and seeing ball°   *the eye*
      But a prick will make no eye at all,

      Where we, even where we mean
         To mend her we end her,
        When we hew or delve:
20   After-comers cannot guess the beauty been.
       Ten or twelve, only ten or twelve
       Strokes of havoc únselve°   *rob of self*

1. Sheaves of grain.

The sweet especial scene,
Rural scene, a rural scene,
25   Sweet especial rural scene.

1879   1918

Duns Scotus's Oxford[1]

Towery city and branchy between towers;
Cuckoo-echoing, bell-swarmèd, lark-charmèd, rook-racked, river-rounded;
The dapple-eared lily below thee; that country and town did
Once encounter in, here coped and poisèd powers;

5   Thou hast a base and brickish skirt there, sours
That neighbour-nature thy grey beauty is grounded
Best in;[2] graceless growth, thou hast confounded
Rural rural keeping—folk, flocks, and flowers.

Yet ah! this air I gather and I release
10   He lived on; these weeds and waters, these walls are what
He haunted who of all men most sways my spirits to peace;

Of realty° the rarest-veinèd unraveller; a not   *reality*
Rivalled insight, be rival Italy or Greece;
Who fired France for Mary without spot.[3]

1879   1918

Felix Randal

Felix Randal the farrier,° O is he dead then? my duty   *blacksmith*
    all ended,
Who have watched his mould of man, big-boned and hardy-handsome
Pining, pining, till time when reason rambled in it and some
Fatal four disorders, fleshed there, all contended?

5   Sickness broke him. Impatient, he cursed at first, but mended
Being anointed[1] and all; though a heavenlier heart began some
Months earlier, since I had our sweet reprieve and ransom[2]

---

1. Duns Scotus, the medieval theologian, lectured at Oxford about 1301. His idea that individuality is the final perfection of any creature influenced Hopkins's conception of inscape. When Hopkins came on two of Scotus's commentaries in 1872, he wrote that he was immediately "flush with a new stroke of enthusiasm . . . when I took in any inscape of the sky or sea I thought of Scotus."
2. Hopkins contrasts the "here" of the "grey beauty" of the medieval city of Oxford, where country and town are both protected ("coped," as within a priest's cloak) and in equilibrium ("poisèd powers"), with the "there" of its new surburban "brickish skirt": housing developments and industrial complexes that were built around the perimeter of the city in the 19th century.
3. In Paris, Scotus was influential in defending the doctrine of the Immaculate Conception—i.e., that Mary was born without original sin.
1. In Extreme Unction (the sacrament for the dying.)
2. Holy Communion preceded by confession and absolution.

Tendered to him. Ah well, God rest him all road ever[3] he offended!
This seeing the sick endears them to us, us too it endears.
10 My tongue had taught thee comfort, touch had quenched thy tears,
Thy tears that touched my heart, child, Felix, poor Felix Randal;
How far from then forethought of, all thy more boisterous years,
When thou at the random[4] grim forge, powerful amidst peers,
Didst fettle° for the great grey drayhorse his bright and   *prepare*
    battering sandal!

1880   1918

Spring and Fall:[1]

to a young child

Márgarét, áre you gríeving
Over Goldengrove unleaving?
Leáves, líke the things of man, you
With your fresh thoughts care for, can you?
5 Áh! ás the heart grows older
It will come to such sights colder
By and by, nor spare a sigh
Though worlds of wanwood leafmeal[2] lie;
And yet you *will* weep and know why.
10 Now no matter, child, the name:
Sórrow's spríngs áre the same.
Nor mouth had, no nor mind, expressed
What heart heard of, ghost° guessed: *spirit*
It ís the blight man was born for,
15 It is Margaret you mourn for.

1880   1918

[Carrion Comfort][1]

Not, I'll not, carrion comfort, Despair, not feast on thee,[2]
Not untwist—slack they may be—these last strands of man
In me ór, most weary, cry *I can no more*. I can;
Can something, hope, wish day come, not choose not to be.

5 But ah, but O thou terrible, why wouldst thou rude on me
Thy wring-world right foot rock?[3] lay a lionlimb against me?
    scan

---

3. In whatever way.
4. Built with stones of irregular size and shape.
1. This deceptively simple poem is deeply informed by Christian theology: according to Catholic doctrine, the fall of Adam and Eve brought into the world both mortality and the legacy of Original Sin for all human beings ("the blight man was born for").
2. Coined by analogy with piecemeal. "Wanwood": pale or dim; the forest may be pale because

of light-colored autumn leaves or dim because light is filtered through the leaves.
1. This title was supplied by Bridges. The poem is one of the "terrible sonnets," as are the three following poems.
2. The satisfaction of giving in to despair as a kind of "comfort" is implicitly likened to a vulture's satisfaction in feasting on dead flesh.
3. I.e., why would you roughly rock me with your world-wringing right foot?

With darksome devouring eyes my bruisèd bones? and fan,
O in turns of tempest, me heaped there; me frantic to avoid
    thee and flee?

Why? That my chaff might fly; my grain lie,[4] sheer and clear.
10 Nay in all that toil, that coil,° since (seems) I kissed the rod,   *tumult*
Hand rather,[5] my heart lo! lapped strength, stole joy, would
    laugh, chéer.
Cheer whom though? The Hero whose heaven-handling
    flung me, fóot tród
Me? or me that fought him? O which one? is it each one?
    That night, that year
Of now done darkness I wretch lay wrestling with (my God!)
    my God.

1885   1918

No worst, there is none

No worst, there is none. Pitched past pitch of grief,
More pangs will, schooled at forepangs, wilder wring.
Comforter, where, where is your comforting?
Mary, mother of us, where is your relief?

5 My cries heave, herds-long;[1] huddle in a main, a chief-
woe, world-sorrow; on an age-old anvil wince and sing—
Then lull, then leave off. Fury had shrieked "No ling-
ering! Let me be fell: force[2] I must be brief."
O the mind, mind has mountains; cliffs of fall
10 Frightful, sheer, no-man-fathomed. Hold them cheap
May who ne'er hung there. Nor does long our small
Durance° deal with that steep or deep. Here! creep,   *endurance*
Wretch, under a comfort serves in a whirlwind: all
Life death does end and each day dies with sleep.

1885   1918

I wake and feel the fell of dark, not day

I wake and feel the fell° of dark, not day.   *cruelty*
What hours, O what black hoürs we have spent
This night! what sights you, heart, saw; ways you went!
And more must, in yet longer light's delay.

5 With witness I speak this. But where I say
Hours I mean years, mean life. And my lament

---

4. Metaphors of winnowing, or removing the empty husks ("chaff") that are blown away from the valuable grain that remains, appear frequently in the Bible to represent the separation of virtue from wickedness. See, e.g., Psalm 1.4,

Luke 3.16–17.
5. I.e., the hand that wields the rod.
1. Like the succession of cries made by cattle that have been following one another in a long line.
2. Necessarily, inevitably. "Fell": fierce or cruel.

Is cries countless, cries like dead letters[1] sent
To dearest him that lives alas! away.

I am gall, I am heartburn. God's most deep decree
10   Bitter would have me taste: my taste was me;
Bones built in me, flesh filled, blood brimmed the curse.

Selfyeast of spirit a dull dough sours. I see
The lost are like this, and their scourge to be
As I am mine, their sweating selves; but worse.

1885   1918

That Nature Is a Heraclitean Fire[1] and of the Comfort of the Resurrection

Cloud-puffball, torn tufts, tossed pillows | flaunt forth, then chevy°   *race*
    on an air-
built thoroughfare: heaven-roysterers,° in gay-gangs | they   *swaggerers*
    throng; they glitter in marches.
Down roughcast, down dazzling whitewash, | wherever an elm arches.
Shivelights and shadowtackle[2] in long | lashes lace, lance, and pair.
5 Delightfully the bright wind boisterous | ropes, wrestles, beats earth bare
Of yestertempest's creases; in pool and rut peel parches[3]
Squandering ooze to squeezed | dough, crust, dust; stanches, starches
Squadroned masks and manmarks[4] | treadmire toil there
Footfretted in it. Million-fuelèd, | nature's bonfire burns on.
10 But quench her bonniest, dearest | to her, her clearest-selvèd° *most individual*
    spark
Man, how fast his firedint | his mark on mind, is gone!
Both are in an unfathomable, all is in an enormous dark
Drowned. O pity and indig | nation! Manshape, that shone
Sheer off, disseveral,° a star, | death blots black out; nor mark   *separate*
15   Is any of him at all so stark
But vastness blurs and time | beats level. Enough! the Resurrection,
A heart's-clarion! Away grief's gasping, | joyless days, dejection.
          Across my foundering deck shone
A beacon, an eternal beam. | Flesh fade, and mortal trash
20 Fall to the residuary worm; | world's wildfire, leave but ash:
          In a flash, at a trumpet crash,
I am all at once what Christ is, | since he was what I am, and
This Jack, joke, poor potsherd, | patch, matchwood,[5] immortal diamond,
          Is immortal diamond.

1888   1918

---

1. Letters undelivered or returned to the sender by the post office.
1. The Greek philosopher Heraclitus (fl. ca. 500 B.C.E.) taught that all things are in flux and that they ultimately return to the basic principle of fire.
2. Branches imagined as the shadows of a ship's rigging. "Shivelights": strips of light.
3. Ruts described as peeled places. "Parches" is a verb whose subject is *wind*.
4. The marks that people have made on the earth by walking ("footfretted") on it.
5. Kindling. "Jack": ordinary man.

Thou art indeed just, Lord

Justus quidem tu es, Domine, si disputem tecum; verumtamen justa
loquar ad te: Quare via impiorum prosperatur? &c.[1]

Thou art indeed just, Lord, if I contend
With thee; but, sir, so what I plead is just.
Why do sinners' ways prosper? and why must
Disappointment all I endeavour end?

5   Wert thou my enemy, O thou my friend,
How wouldst thou worse, I wonder, than thou dost
Defeat, thwart me? Oh, the sots and thralls of lust
Do in spare hours more thrive than I that spend,

Sir, life upon thy cause. See, banks and brakes°   *thickets*
10   Now, leavèd how thick! lacèd they are again
With fretty chervil,[2] look, and fresh wind shakes

Them; birds build—but not I build; no, but strain,
Time's eunuch, and not breed one work that wakes.
Mine, O thou lord of life, send my roots rain.

1889   1918

From Journal[1]

May 3 [1866]. Cold. Morning raw and wet, afternoon fine. Walked then with Addis, crossing Bablock Hythe, round by Skinner's Weir[2] through many fields into the Witney road. Sky sleepy blue without liquidity. From Cumnor Hill saw St. Philip's and the other spires through blue haze rising pale in a pink light. On further side of the Witney road hills, just fleeced with grain or other green growth, by their dips and waves foreshortened here and there and so differenced in brightness and opacity the green on them, with delicate effect. On left, brow of the near hill glistening with very bright newly turned sods and a scarf of vivid green slanting away beyond the skyline, against which the clouds shewed the slightest tinge of rose or purple. Copses in grey-red or grey-yellow—the tinges immediately forerunning the opening of full leaf. Meadows skirting Seven-bridge road voluptuous green. Some oaks are out in small leaf. Ashes not out, only tufted with their fringy blooms. Hedges springing richly. Elms in small leaf, with more or less opacity. White poplars most beautiful in small grey crisp spray-like leaf.

---

1. "Righteous art thou, O Lord, when I plead with thee: yet let me talk with thee of thy judgments: Wherefore doth the way of the wicked prosper?" (Jeremiah 12.1). The Latin was Hopkins's title.
2. A kind of herb, related to parsley.
1. With the exception of one year, Hopkins kept a journal from May 1866 to Feb. 1875. Its most interesting entries are minutely observed descriptions of natural phenomena, which reveal the character of his imagination. The brackets and abbreviations are Hopkins's.
2. Dam. William E. Addis (1844–1917), friend of Hopkins at Oxford; like him he became a Catholic convert and priest. The places mentioned are around Oxford. Compare Matthew Arnold's evocation of this same landscape in "The Scholar Gypsy" (p. 758).

Cowslips capriciously colouring meadows in creamy drifts. Bluebells, purple orchis. Over the green water of the river passing the slums of the town and under its bridges swallows shooting, blue and purple above and shewing their amber-tinged breasts reflected in the water, their flight unsteady with wagging wings and leaning first to one side then the other. Peewits flying. Towards sunset the sky partly swept, as often, with moist white cloud, tailing off across which are morsels of grey-black woolly clouds. Sun seemed to make a bright liquid hole in this, its texture had an upward northerly sweep or drift from the W, marked softly in grey. Dog violets. Eastward after sunset range of clouds rising in bulky heads moulded softly in tufts or bunches of snow—so it looks—and membered somewhat elaborately, rose-coloured. Notice often imperfect fairy rings. Apple and other fruit trees blossomed beautifully.

* * *

Feb.—1870. One day in the Long Retreat (which ended on Xmas Day) they were reading in the refectory Sister Emmerich's account[3] of the Agony in the Garden[4] and I suddenly began to cry and sob and could not stop. I put it down for this reason, that if I had been asked a minute beforehand I should have said that nothing of the sort was going to happen and even when it did I stood in a manner wondering at myself not seeing in my reason the traces of an adequate cause for such strong emotion—the traces of it I say because of course the cause in itself is adequate for the sorrow of a lifetime. I remember much the same thing on Maundy Thursday when the presanctified Host[5] was carried to the sacristy. But neither the weight nor the stress of sorrow, that is to say of the thing which should cause sorrow, by themselves move us or bring the tears as a sharp knife does not cut for being pressed as long as it is pressed without any shaking of the hand but there is always one touch, something striking sideways and unlooked for, which in both cases undoes resistance and pierces, and this may be so delicate that the pathos seems to have gone directly to the body and cleared the understanding in its passage. On the other hand the pathetic touch by itself, as in dramatic pathos, will only draw slight tears if its matter is not important or not of import to us, the strong emotion coming from a force which was gathered before it was discharged: in this way a knife may pierce the flesh which it had happened only to graze and only grazing will go no deeper.

* * *

May 18 [1870].—Great brilliancy and projection: the eye seemed to fall perpendicular from level to level along our trees, the nearer and further Park; all things hitting the sense with double but direct instress. * * *

This was later. One day when the bluebells were in bloom I wrote the following. I do not think I have ever seen anything more beautiful than the bluebell I have been looking at. I know the beauty of our Lord by it. It[s inscape] is [mixed of] strength and grace, like an ash [tree]. The head is strongly drawn over [backwards] and arched down like a cutwater[6] [drawing

---

3. *The Dolorous Passion of Our Lord Jesus Christ; from the Meditations of Anne Catherine Emmerich,* an Augustinian nun (1774–1824).
4. Luke 22.39–44.

5. The bread wafer sanctified for Holy Communion. "Maundy Thursday": the Thursday before Easter, day of the Last Supper.
6. The forward edge of a ship's prow.

itself back from the line of the keel.] The lines of the bells strike and overlie this, rayed but not symmetrically, some lie parallel. They look steely against [the] paper, the shades lying between the bells and behind the cockled petal-ends and nursing up the precision of their distinctness, the petal-ends themselves being delicately lit. Then there is the straightness of the trumpets in the bells softened by the slight entasis[7] and [by] the square splay of the mouth. One bell, the lowest, some way detached and carried on a longer footstalk, touched out with the tips of the petals on oval / not like the rest in a plane perpendicular of the axis of the bell but a little atilt, and so with [the] square-in-rounding turns of the petals.

✻ ✻ ✻

Aug. 10 [1872].—I was looking at high waves. The breakers always are parallel to the coast and shape themselves to it except where the curve is sharp however the wind blows. They are rolled out by the shallowing shore just as a piece of putty between the palms whatever its shape runs into a long roll. The slant ruck[8] or crease one sees in them shows the way of the wind. The regularity of the barrels surprised and charmed the eye; the edge behind the comb or crest was as smooth and bright as glass. It may be noticed to be green behind and silver white in front: the silver marks where the air begins, the pure white is foam, the green / solid water. Then looked at to the right or left they are scrolled over like mouldboards[9] or feathers or jibsails seen by the edge. It is pretty to see the hollow of the barrel disappearing as the white combs on each side run along the wave gaining ground till the two meet at a pitch and crush and overlap each other.

About all the turns of the scaping from the break and flooding of wave to its run out again I have not yet satisfied myself. The shores are swimming and the eyes have before them a region of milky surf but it is hard for them to unpack the huddling and gnarls of the water and law out the shapes and the sequence of the running: I catch however the looped or forked wisp made by every big pebble the backwater runs over—if it were clear and smooth there would be a network from their overlapping, such as can in fact be seen on smooth sand after the tide is out—; then I saw it run browner, the foam dwindling and twitched into long chains of suds, while the strength of the back-draught shrugged the stones together and clocked them one against another.

1959

---

7. Outward curvature.
8. Fold or crease.

9. Curved iron plates attached to plowshares.

ROBERT LOUIS STEVENSON
1850–1894

R obert Louis (originally Lewis) Balfour Stevenson was born in Edinburgh on
November 13, 1850, the only child of Margaret Balfour and Thomas Stevenson, a
well-known marine engineer and designer of lighthouses. His family was part of the
respectable Scottish middle classes, a membership that would both benefit
Stevenson—although there were difficult stretches in his relationship with his father,
he generally did not have to worry about money—and leave him with a restlessness
for adventure and excitement. Driven at the same time by a quest for a climate that
would ease his chronically diseased lungs, Stevenson traveled more broadly than any
other prominent Victorian writer. And yet it could be argued that although he was
constantly on the move in far-flung lands, Stevenson returned again and again in his
creative fiction, explicitly or implicitly, to the tensions of his own personal and
national heritage—to the pronounced conflicts of his upbringing and of Scotland's
somber, religiously oppressive society.

An awkward sensitive boy, Stevenson was subjected to the disciplinary strictures
of his stern Presbyterian father and to the more affectionate, although also deeply
devout, care of his mother and his nurse. Plagued by night terrors and bouts of sickness, the young Stevenson seemed "in body . . . assuredly badly set up," as a schoolmate said in later years; "his limbs were long, lean, and spidery, and his chest flat, so
as almost to suggest some malnutrition." This constitutional weakness was to afflict
Stevenson throughout his life, and he enjoyed only short periods of reasonable
health. As a student at Edinburgh University, Stevenson soon began to avoid the
engineering classes that would have enabled him to follow in his father's footsteps,
and embarked instead on a course of reading—"an extensive and highly rational
system of truancy," as he called it—to learn how to become a writer. In time, as a
compromise to placate his father, he switched to the study of law; although he never
practiced as a lawyer, he did pass the Scottish bar examination in 1875. But Stevenson's interests clearly lay elsewhere; in this period he began reading scandalous
French poetry and hanging around brothels, where the prostitutes nicknamed him
"Velvet Jacket." His appearance and wit attracted attention: describing their first
encounter in 1873, Stevenson's friend the folklorist and writer Andrew Lang later
recalled that he "wore a wide blue cloak, with a grace that hovered between that of an
Italian poet and an early pirate. It was impossible not to discover, in a short conversation, that he was very clever."

At the age of twenty-two, Stevenson further distanced himself from his father by
confessing that he had turned both socialist and agnostic; he subsequently began to
spend increasingly longer periods in France, partly because of respiratory troubles
but also to be in the company of painters and writers. Back in Britain he developed
important and useful friendships with artistic and literary figures, including Sidney
Colvin, a professor of art, and the poet and editor W. E. Henley; with their support
Stevenson started to publish essays and books of travel writing. As if to complete his
breach with bourgeois Scottish respectability, Stevenson then fell in love with Fanny
Osbourne, an American woman ten years his senior, who was estranged from her husband but not yet divorced.

In 1879 Stevenson's global wanderings began in earnest, starting with a trip to
California to marry the newly divorced Fanny. Despite constant travel and recurrent
illness, Stevenson found the time and energy to write. *Treasure Island*, begun as an
amusement for his stepson, was his first popular success: serialized in 1881 and

published in book form in 1883, the story of the cabin boy Jim Hawkins's adventures includes a covert portrait of Stevenson's one-legged friend Henley in the figure of the pirate Long John Silver. Soon thereafter he published another children's classic: *A Child's Garden of Verses* (1885), a collection of poems dedicated to his former nurse. In the years to come, Stevenson worked in numerous genres, including short fiction, swashbuckling romances, historical adventures (*Kidnapped*, 1886, a story set in Scotland just after the Jacobite rebellion of 1745, and its sequel, *Catriona*, 1893), and more gothic undertakings, such as the bleak and brooding novel *The Master of Ballantrae* (1889).

The work that first established Stevenson's critical reputation, however, was a horror story that prefigured *The Master of Ballantrae*'s fascination with the darker side of human nature and reflected his long-standing interest in the idea of a double life: *The Strange Case of Dr. Jekyll and Mr. Hyde*, written in 1885 and published the following year. The novella rapidly became a best-seller in both Britain and America, and like Mary Shelley's *Frankenstein* of 1818 (to which *Jekyll and Hyde* pays homage at various moments) and Bram Stoker's *Dracula* (1897), the story has enjoyed a continuous and lively presence in popular culture up to the present day. Yet our familiarity with the outline of the tale may not prepare us for the psychological and ethical complexity of the original. Certainly the novelist's friends found *Jekyll and Hyde* genuinely unnerving: the writer and historian J. A. Symonds wrote to Stevenson that the story "has left such a deeply painful impression on my heart that I do not know how I am ever to turn to it again," while Lang commented that "we would welcome a spectre, a ghoul, or even a vampire, rather than meet Mr. Edward Hyde." For some, many aspects of the novella have seemed markedly Scottish in flavor: the novelist G. K. Chesterton insisted that its London is really Edinburgh, its Englishmen actually Scotsmen—"No modern English lawyer," he protested of the character Mr. Utterson, "ever read a book of dry divinity in the evening, merely because it was Sunday." Nevertheless, the distinctive tone and theme of *Jekyll and Hyde* have led many critics to characterize it—often together with another work that shares its preoccupation with the divided self, Oscar Wilde's *Picture of Dorian Gray* (1891)—as an expression of quintessentially fin de siècle anxieties.

From 1888 onward the Stevensons embarked upon a series of journeys in the South Seas, once again in the hope that the climate would benefit the writer's health. They eventually settled in Samoa, where Stevenson became a favorite with the locals (who called him Tusitala, or "teller of tales") before he died of a cerebral hemorrhage in 1894. At the time of his death, Stevenson was only forty-four years old and still furiously at work, this time on a historical novel titled *Weir of Hermiston*.

The Strange Case of Dr. Jekyll and Mr. Hyde

Story of the Door

Mr. Utterson the lawyer was a man of a rugged countenance, that was never lighted by a smile; cold, scanty and embarrassed in discourse; backward in sentiment; lean, long, dusty, dreary and yet somehow lovable. At friendly meetings, and when the wine was to his taste, something eminently human beaconed from his eye; something indeed which never found its way into his talk, but which spoke not only in these silent symbols of the after-dinner face, but more often and loudly in the acts of his life. He was austere with himself; drank gin when he was alone, to mortify a taste for vintages; and though he enjoyed the theatre, had not crossed the doors of one for twenty years. But he had an approved[1] tolerance for others; sometimes wondering, almost with envy, at the high pressure of spirits involved in their misdeeds; and in any extremity inclined to help rather than to reprove. "I incline to Cain's heresy,"[2] he used to say quaintly: "I let my brother go to the devil in his own way." In this character, it was frequently his fortune to be the last reputable acquaintance and the last good influence in the lives of down-going men. And to such as these, so long as they came about his chambers, he never marked a shade of change in his demeanour.

No doubt the feat was easy to Mr. Utterson; for he was undemonstrative at the best, and even his friendship seemed to be founded in a similar catholicity[3] of good-nature. It is the mark of a modest man to accept his friendly circle ready-made from the hands of opportunity; and that was the lawyer's way. His friends were those of his own blood or those whom he had known the longest; his affections, like ivy, were the growth of time, they implied no aptness in the object. Hence, no doubt, the bond that united him to Mr. Richard Enfield, his distant kinsman, the well-known man about town. It was a nut to crack for many, what these two could see in each other, or what subject they could find in common. It was reported by those who encountered them in their Sunday walks, that they said nothing, looked singularly dull, and would hail with obvious relief the appearance of a friend. For all that, the two men put the greatest store by these excursions, counted them the chief jewel of each week, and not only set aside occasions of pleasure, but even resisted the calls of business, that they might enjoy them uninterrupted.

It chanced on one of these rambles that their way led them down a bystreet in a busy quarter of London. The street was small and what is called quiet, but it drove a thriving trade on the week-days. The inhabitants were all doing well, it seemed, and all emulously hoping to do better still, and laying out the surplus of their gains in coquetry;[4] so that the shop fronts stood along that thoroughfare with an air of invitation, like rows of smiling saleswomen. Even on Sunday, when it veiled its more florid charms and lay comparatively empty of passage, the street shone out in contrast to its dingy neighbourhood, like a fire in a forest; and with its freshly painted shutters, well-polished brasses, and general cleanliness and gaiety of note, instantly caught and pleased the eye of the passenger.[5]

Two doors from one corner, on the left hand going east, the line was broken by the entry of a court; and just at that point, a certain sinister block of building thrust forward its gable on the street. It was two storeys high; showed no window, nothing but a door on the lower storey and a blind forehead of discoloured wall on the upper; and bore in every feature, the marks of prolonged and sordid negligence. The door, which was equipped with neither bell nor knocker, was blistered and distained.[6] Tramps slouched into the recess and struck matches on the panels; children kept shop upon the steps; the schoolboy had tried his knife on the mouldings; and for close on a generation, no one had appeared to drive away these random visitors or to repair their ravages.

---

1. Proved.
2. Refusal of responsibility for one's fellow human beings. After Cain kills his brother, Abel, and God asks where Abel is, Cain responds, "Am I my brother's keeper?" (Genesis 4.9).
3. Universality.
4. Attractive display.
5. Passerby.
6. Discolored.

Mr. Enfield and the lawyer were on the other side of the by-street; but when they came abreast of the entry, the former lifted up his cane and pointed.

"Did you ever remark that door?" he asked; and when his companion had replied in the affirmative, "It is connected in my mind," added he, "with a very odd story."

"Indeed?" said Mr. Utterson, with a slight change of voice, "and what was that?"

"Well, it was this way," returned Mr. Enfield: "I was coming home from some place at the end of the world, about three o'clock of a black winter morning, and my way lay through a part of town where there was literally nothing to be seen but lamps. Street after street, and all the folks asleep— street after street, all lighted up as if for a procession and all as empty as a church—till at last I got into that state of mind when a man listens and listens and begins to long for the sight of a policeman. All at once, I saw two figures: one a little man who was stumping along eastward at a good walk, and the other a girl of maybe eight or ten who was running as hard as she was able down a cross street. Well, sir, the two ran into one another naturally enough at the corner; and then came the horrible part of the thing; for the man trampled calmly over the child's body and left her screaming on the ground. It sounds nothing to hear, but it was hellish to see. It wasn't like a man; it was like some damned Juggernaut.[7] I gave a view halloa,[8] took to my heels, collared my gentleman, and brought him back to where there was already quite a group about the screaming child. He was perfectly cool and made no resistance, but gave me one look, so ugly that it brought out the sweat on me like running. The people who had turned out were the girl's own family; and pretty soon, the doctor, for whom she had been sent, put in his appearance. Well, the child was not much the worse, more frightened, according to the Sawbones;[9] and there you might have supposed would be an end to it. But there was one curious circumstance. I had taken a loathing to my gentleman at first sight. So had the child's family, which was only natural. But the doctor's case was what struck me. He was the usual cut and dry apothecary, of no particular age and colour, with a strong Edinburgh accent, and about as emotional as a bagpipe. Well, sir, he was like the rest of us; every time he looked at my prisoner, I saw that Sawbones turn sick and white with the desire to kill him. I knew what was in his mind, just as he knew what was in mine; and killing being out of the question, we did the next best. We told the man we could and would make such a scandal out of this, as should make his name stink from one end of London to the other. If he had any friends or any credit,[1] we undertook that he should lose them. And all the time, as we were pitching it in red hot, we were keeping the women off him as best we could, for they were as wild as harpies.[2] I never saw a circle of such hateful faces; and there was the man in the middle, with a kind of black, sneering coolness—frightened too, I could see that—but carrying it off, sir, really like Satan. 'If you choose to make capital out of this

---

7. A relentless force that crushes individuals in its path. Originally a title of Krishna (an avatar of the Hindu god Vishnu); at an annual festival his statue was drawn on an enormous cart, under whose wheels many worshippers threw themselves to be crushed.

8. Shout.
9. Doctor (slang).
1. Good name.
2. In classical mythology monsters with women's faces and bodies and birds' wings and claws.

accident,' said he, 'I am naturally helpless. No gentleman but wishes to avoid a scene,' says he. 'Name your figure.' Well, we screwed him up to a hundred pounds for the child's family; he would have clearly liked to stick out; but there was something about the lot of us that meant mischief, and at last he struck.[3] The next thing was to get the money; and where do you think he carried us but to that place with the door?—whipped out a key, went in, and presently came back with the matter of ten pounds in gold and a cheque for the balance on Coutts's,[4] drawn payable to bearer and signed with a name that I can't mention, though it's one of the points of my story, but it was a name at least very well known and often printed. The figure was stiff; but the signature was good for more than that, if it was only genuine. I took the liberty of pointing out to my gentleman that the whole business looked apocryphal, and that a man does not, in real life, walk into a cellar door at four in the morning and come out of it with another man's cheque for close upon a hundred pounds. But he was quite easy and sneering. 'Set your mind at rest,' says he, 'I will stay with you till the banks open and cash the cheque myself.' So we all set off, the doctor, and the child's father, and our friend and myself, and passed the rest of the night in my chambers; and next day, when we had breakfasted, went in a body to the bank. I gave in the check myself, and said I had every reason to believe it was a forgery. Not a bit of it. The cheque was genuine."

"Tut-tut," said Mr. Utterson.

"I see you feel as I do," said Mr. Enfield. "Yes, it's a bad story. For my man was a fellow that nobody could have to do with, a really damnable man; and the person that drew the cheque is the very pink of the proprieties, celebrated too, and (what makes it worse) one of your fellows who do what they call good. Black mail, I suppose; an honest man paying through the nose for some of the capers of his youth. Black Mail House is what I call that place with the door, in consequence. Though even that, you know, is far from explaining all," he added, and with the words fell into a vein of musing.

From this he was recalled by Mr. Utterson asking rather suddenly: "And you don't know if the drawer of the cheque lives there?"

"A likely place, isn't it?" returned Mr. Enfield. "But I happen to have noticed his address; he lives in some square or other."

"And you never asked about the—place with the door?" said Mr. Utterson.

"No, sir: I had a delicacy," was the reply. "I feel very strongly about putting questions; it partakes too much of the style of the day of judgment. You start a question, and it's like starting a stone. You sit quietly on the top of a hill; and away the stone goes, starting others; and presently some bland old bird (the last you would have thought of) is knocked on the head in his own back garden and the family have to change their name. No, sir, I make it a rule of mine: the more it looks like Queer Street,[5] the less I ask."

"A very good rule, too," said the lawyer.

"But I have studied the place for myself," continued Mr. Enfield. "It seems scarcely a house. There is no other door, and nobody goes in or out of that one but, once in a great while, the gentleman of my adventure. There are three windows looking on the court on the first floor;[6] none below; the win-

3. Gave in.
4. A prestigious London bank.
5. I.e., looks like someone is in trouble or a bad

fix (slang).
6. I.e., the first floor above the ground floor (what Americans call the second floor).

dows are always shut but they're clean. And then there is a chimney which is generally smoking; so somebody must live there. And yet it's not so sure; for the buildings are so packed together about that court, that it's hard to say where one ends and another begins."

The pair walked on again for a while in silence; and then "Enfield," said Mr. Utterson, "that's a good rule of yours."

"Yes, I think it is," returned Enfield.

"But for all that," continued the lawyer, "there's one point I want to ask: I want to ask the name of that man who walked over the child."

"Well," said Mr. Enfield, "I can't see what harm it would do. It was a man of the name of Hyde."

"H'm," said Mr. Utterson. "What sort of a man is he to see?"

"He is not easy to describe. There is something wrong with his appearance; something displeasing, something downright detestable. I never saw a man I so disliked, and yet I scarce know why. He must be deformed somewhere; he gives a strong feeling of deformity, although I couldn't specify the point. He's an extraordinary looking man, and yet I really can name nothing out of the way. No, sir; I can make no hand of it; I can't describe him. And it's not want of memory; for I declare I can see him this moment."

Mr. Utterson again walked some way in silence and obviously under a weight of consideration. "You are sure he used a key?" he inquired at last.

"My dear sir . . ." began Enfield, surprised out of himself.

"Yes, I know," said Utterson; "I know it must seem strange. The fact is, if I do not ask you the name of the other party, it is because I know it already. You see, Richard, your tale has gone home. If you have been inexact in any point, you had better correct it."

"I think you might have warned me," returned the other with a touch of sullenness. "But I have been pedantically exact, as you call it. The fellow had a key; and what's more, he has it still. I saw him use it, not a week ago."

Mr. Utterson sighed deeply but said never a word; and the young man presently resumed. "Here is another lesson to say nothing," said he. "I am ashamed of my long tongue. Let us make a bargain never to refer to this again."

"With all my heart," said the lawyer. "I shake hands on that, Richard."

Search for Mr. Hyde

That evening Mr. Utterson came home to his bachelor house in sombre spirits and sat down to dinner without relish. It was his custom of a Sunday, when this meal was over, to sit close by the fire, a volume of some dry divinity[7] on his reading desk, until the clock of the neighbouring church rang out the hour of twelve, when he would go soberly and gratefully to bed. On this night, however, as soon as the cloth was taken away, he took up a candle and went into his business room. There he opened his safe, took from the most private part of it a document endorsed on the envelope as Dr. Jekyll's Will, and sat down with a clouded brow to study its contents. The will was holograph,[8] for Mr. Utterson, though he took charge of it now that it was made, had refused to lend the least assistance in the making of it; it provided not only that, in case of the decease of Henry Jekyll, M.D., D.C.L., LL.D.,

---

7. Theology.   8. In the author's handwriting.

F.R.S.,[9] etc., all his possessions were to pass into the hands of his "friend and benefactor Edward Hyde," but that in case of Dr. Jekyll's "disappearance or unexplained absence for any period exceeding three calendar months," the said Edward Hyde should step into the said Henry Jekyll's shoes without further delay and free from any burthen or obligation, beyond the payment of a few small sums to the members of the doctor's household. This document had long been the lawyer's eyesore. It offended him both as a lawyer and as a lover of the sane and customary sides of life, to whom the fanciful was the immodest. And hitherto it was his ignorance of Mr. Hyde that had swelled his indignation; now, by a sudden turn, it was his knowledge. It was already bad enough when the name was but a name of which he could learn no more. It was worse when it began to be clothed upon with detestable attributes; and out of the shifting, insubstantial mists that had so long baffled his eye, there leaped up the sudden, definite presentment[1] of a fiend.

"I thought it was madness," he said, as he replaced the obnoxious paper in the safe, "and now I begin to fear it is disgrace."

With that he blew out his candle, put on a greatcoat, and set forth in the direction of Cavendish Square, that citadel of medicine,[2] where his friend, the great Dr. Lanyon, had his house and received his crowding patients. "If anyone knows, it will be Lanyon," he had thought.

The solemn butler knew and welcomed him; he was subjected to no stage of delay, but ushered direct from the door to the dining-room where Dr. Lanyon sat alone over his wine. This was a hearty, healthy, dapper, red-faced gentleman, with a shock of hair prematurely white, and a boisterous and decided manner. At sight of Mr. Utterson, he sprang up from his chair and welcomed him with both hands. The geniality, as was the way of the man, was somewhat theatrical to the eye; but it reposed on genuine feeling. For these two were old friends, old mates both at school and college, both thorough respecters of themselves and of each other, and, what does not always follow, men who thoroughly enjoyed each other's company.

After a little rambling talk, the lawyer led up to the subject which so disagreeably preoccupied his mind.

"I suppose, Lanyon," said he, "you and I must be the two oldest friends that Henry Jekyll has?"

"I wish the friends were younger," chuckled Dr. Lanyon. "But I suppose we are. And what of that? I see little of him now."

"Indeed?" said Utterson. "I thought you had a bond of common interest."

"We had," was the reply. "But it is more than ten years since Henry Jekyll became too fanciful for me. He began to go wrong, wrong in mind; and though of course I continue to take an interest in him for old sake's sake, as they say, I see and I have seen devilish little of the man. Such unscientific balderdash," added the doctor, flushing suddenly purple, "would have estranged Damon and Pythias."[3]

This little spirit of temper was somewhat of a relief to Mr. Utterson. "They have only differed on some point of science," he thought; and being a man of no scientific passions (except in the matter of conveyancing,[4]) he even added:

9. Doctor of Medicine, Doctor of Civil Law, Doctor of Laws, and Fellow of the Royal Society.
1. Image.
2. A once-aristocratic neighborhood where fashionable doctors had their offices.

3. Two inseparable youths in Greek legend whose willingness to die for each other symbolizes true friendship.
4. Legal transfer of property by writing deeds.

"It is nothing worse than that!" He gave his friend a few seconds to recover his composure, and then approached the question he had come to put. "Did you ever come across a protégé of his—one Hyde?" he asked.

"Hyde?" repeated Lanyon. "No. Never heard of him. Since my time."

That was the amount of information that the lawyer carried back with him to the great, dark bed on which he tossed to and fro, until the small hours of the morning began to grow large. It was a night of little ease to his toiling mind, toiling in mere[5] darkness and besieged by questions.

Six o'clock struck on the bells of the church that was so conveniently near to Mr. Utterson's dwelling, and still he was digging at the problem. Hitherto it had touched him on the intellectual side alone; but now his imagination also was engaged, or rather enslaved; and as he lay and tossed in the gross darkness of the night and the curtained room, Mr. Enfield's tale went by before his mind in a scroll of lighted pictures. He would be aware of the great field of lamps of a nocturnal city; then of the figure of a man walking swiftly; then of a child running from the doctor's; and then these met, and that human Juggernaut trod the child down and passed on regardless of her screams. Or else he would see a room in a rich house, where his friend lay asleep, dreaming and smiling at his dreams; and then the door of that room would be opened, the curtains of the bed plucked apart, and the sleeper recalled,[6] and lo! there would stand by his side a figure to whom power was given, and even at that dead hour, he must rise and do its bidding. The figure in these two phases haunted the lawyer all night; and if at any time he dozed over, it was but to see it glide more stealthily through sleeping houses, or move the more swiftly and still the more swiftly, even to dizziness, through wider labyrinths of lamp-lighted city, and at every street corner crush a child and leave her screaming. And still the figure had no face by which he might know it; even in his dreams, it had no face, or one that baffled him and melted before his eyes; and thus it was that there sprang up and grew apace in the lawyer's mind a singularly strong, almost an inordinate, curiosity to behold the features of the real Mr. Hyde. If he could but once set eyes on him, he thought the mystery would lighten and perhaps roll altogether away, as was the habit of mysterious things when well examined. He might see a reason for his friend's strange preference or bondage (call it which you please) and even for the startling clause of the will. At least it would be a face worth seeing: the face of a man who was without bowels of mercy:[7] a face which had but to show itself to raise up, in the mind of the unimpressionable Enfield, a spirit of enduring hatred.

From that time forward, Mr. Utterson began to haunt the door in the bystreet of shops. In the morning before office hours, at noon when business was plenty, and time scarce, at night under the face of the fogged city moon, by all lights and at all hours of solitude or concourse, the lawyer was to be found on his chosen post.

"If he be Mr. Hyde," he had thought, "I shall be Mr. Seek."

And at last his patience was rewarded. It was a fine dry night; frost in the air; the streets as clean as a ballroom floor; the lamps, unshaken by any wind, drawing a regular pattern of light and shadow. By ten o'clock, when the shops were closed, the by-street was very solitary and, in spite of the low growl

---

5. Pure.
6. Revived, awakened.

7. Compassion.

of London from all round, very silent. Small sounds carried far; domestic sounds out of the houses were clearly audible on either side of the roadway; and the rumour[8] of the approach of any passenger preceded him by a long time. Mr. Utterson had been some minutes at his post, when he was aware of an odd, light footstep drawing near. In the course of his nightly patrols, he had long grown accustomed to the quaint effect with which the footfalls of a single person, while he is still a great way off, suddenly spring out distinct from the vast hum and clatter of the city. Yet his attention had never before been so sharply and decisively arrested; and it was with a strong, superstitious prevision of success that he withdrew into the entry of the court.

The steps drew swiftly nearer, and swelled out suddenly louder as they turned the end of the street. The lawyer, looking forth from the entry, could soon see what manner of man he had to deal with. He was small and very plainly dressed, and the look of him, even at that distance, went somehow strongly against the watcher's inclination. But he made straight for the door, crossing the roadway to save time; and as he came, he drew a key from his pocket like one approaching home.

Mr. Utterson stepped out and touched him on the shoulder as he passed. "Mr. Hyde, I think?"

Mr. Hyde shrank back with a hissing intake of the breath. But his fear was only momentary; and though he did not look the lawyer in the face, he answered coolly enough: "That is my name. What do you want?"

"I see you are going in," returned the lawyer. "I am an old friend of Dr. Jekyll's—Mr. Utterson of Gaunt Street—you must have heard my name; and meeting you so conveniently, I thought you might admit me."

"You will not find Dr. Jekyll; he is from home," replied Mr. Hyde, blowing in the key. And then suddenly, but still without looking up, "How did you know me?" he asked.

"On your side," said Mr. Utterson, "will you do me a favour?"

"With pleasure," replied the other. "What shall it be?"

"Will you let me see your face?" asked the lawyer.

Mr. Hyde appeared to hesitate, and then, as if upon some sudden reflection, fronted about with an air of defiance; and the pair stared at each other pretty fixedly for a few seconds. "Now I shall know you again," said Mr. Utterson. "It may be useful."

"Yes," returned Mr. Hyde, "it is as well we have met; and à propos, you should have my address." And he gave a number of a street in Soho.[9]

"Good God!" thought Mr. Utterson, "can he, too, have been thinking of the will?" But he kept his feelings to himself and only grunted in acknowledgment of the address.

"And now," said the other, "how did you know me?"

"By description," was the reply.

"Whose description?"

"We have common friends," said Mr. Utterson.

"Common friends?" echoed Mr. Hyde, a little hoarsely. "Who are they?"

"Jekyll, for instance," said the lawyer.

"He never told you," cried Mr. Hyde, with a flush of anger. "I did not think you would have lied."

---

8. Noise.
9. Seedy district in central London. "À propos": by the way (French).

"Come," said Mr. Utterson, "that is not fitting language."

The other snarled aloud into a savage laugh; and the next moment, with extraordinary quickness, he had unlocked the door and disappeared into the house.

The lawyer stood awhile when Mr. Hyde had left him, the picture of disquietude. Then he began slowly to mount the street, pausing every step or two and putting his hand to his brow like a man in mental perplexity. The problem he was thus debating as he walked, was one of a class that is rarely solved. Mr. Hyde was pale and dwarfish, he gave an impression of deformity without any nameable malformation, he had a displeasing smile, he had borne himself to the lawyer with a sort of murderous mixture of timidity and boldness, and he spoke with a husky, whispering and somewhat broken voice; all these were points against him, but not all of these together could explain the hitherto unknown disgust, loathing and fear with which Mr. Utterson regarded him. "There must be something else," said the perplexed gentleman. "There *is* something more, if I could find a name for it. God bless me, the man seems hardly human! Something troglodytic, shall we say? or can it be the old story of Dr. Fell? or is it the mere radiance of a foul soul that thus transpires through, and transfigures, its clay continent?[1] The last, I think; for, O my poor old Harry Jekyll, if ever I read Satan's signature upon a face, it is on that of your new friend."

Round the corner from the by-street, there was a square of ancient, handsome houses, now for the most part decayed from their high estate and let in flats and chambers to all sorts and conditions of men: map-engravers, architects, shady lawyers and the agents of obscure enterprises. One house, however, second from the corner, was still occupied entire; and at the door of this, which wore a great air of wealth and comfort, though it was now plunged in darkness except for the fanlight, Mr. Utterson stopped and knocked. A well-dressed, elderly servant opened the door.

"Is Dr. Jekyll at home, Poole?" asked the lawyer.

"I will see, Mr. Utterson," said Poole, admitting the visitor, as he spoke, into a large, low-roofed, comfortable hall, paved with flags,[2] warmed (after the fashion of a country house) by a bright, open fire, and furnished with costly cabinets of oak. "Will you wait here by the fire, sir? or shall I give you a light in the dining-room?"

"Here, thank you," said the lawyer, and he drew near and leaned on the tall fender.[3] This hall, in which he was now left alone, was a pet fancy of his friend the doctor's; and Utterson himself was wont to speak of it as the pleasantest room in London. But to-night there was a shudder in his blood; the face of Hyde sat heavy on his memory; he felt (what was rare with him) a nausea and distaste of life; and in the gloom of his spirits, he seemed to read a menace in the flickering of the firelight on the polished cabinets and the uneasy starting of the shadow on the roof. He was ashamed of his relief, when Poole presently returned to announce that Dr. Jekyll was gone out.

"I saw Mr. Hyde go in by the old dissecting-room door, Poole," he said. "Is that right, when Dr. Jekyll is from home?"

"Quite right, Mr. Utterson, sir," replied the servant. "Mr. Hyde has a key."

1. Container. "Troglodytic": like a prehistoric cave dweller or apelike. Dr. Fell: figure from the nursery rhyme "I do not like thee Dr. Fell; / The reason why I cannot tell."
2. Flagstones.
3. Metal frame in front of a fireplace.

"Your master seems to repose a great deal of trust in that young man, Poole," resumed the other musingly.

"Yes, sir, he do indeed," said Poole. "We have all orders to obey him."

"I do not think I ever met Mr. Hyde?" asked Utterson.

"O, dear no, sir. He never *dines* here," replied the butler. "Indeed we see very little of him on this side of the house; he mostly comes and goes by the laboratory."

"Well, good-night, Poole."

"Good-night, Mr. Utterson."

And the lawyer set out homeward with a very heavy heart. "Poor Harry Jekyll," he thought, "my mind misgives me he is in deep waters! He was wild when he was young; a long while ago to be sure; but in the law of God, there is no statute of limitations. Ay, it must be that; the ghost of some old sin, the cancer of some concealed disgrace: punishment coming, *pede claudo*,[4] years after memory has forgotten and self-love condoned the fault." And the lawyer, scared by the thought, brooded awhile on his own past, groping in all the corners of memory, lest by chance some Jack-in-the-Box of an old iniquity should leap to light there. His past was fairly blameless; few men could read the rolls of their life with less apprehension; yet he was humbled to the dust by the many ill things he had done, and raised up again into a sober and fearful gratitude by the many that he had come so near to doing, yet avoided. And then by a return on his former subject, he conceived a spark of hope. "This Master Hyde, if he were studied," thought he, "must have secrets of his own; black secrets, by the look of him; secrets compared to which poor Jekyll's worst would be like sunshine. Things cannot continue as they are. It turns me cold to think of this creature stealing like a thief to Harry's bedside; poor Harry, what a wakening! And the danger of it; for if this Hyde suspects the existence of the will, he may grow impatient to inherit. Ay, I must put my shoulder to the wheel—if Jekyll will but let me," he added, "if Jekyll will only let me." For once more he saw before his mind's eye, as clear as a transparency, the strange clauses of the will.

Dr. Jekyll Was Quite at Ease

A fortnight later, by excellent good fortune, the doctor gave one of his pleasant dinners to some five or six old cronies, all intelligent, reputable men and all judges of good wine; and Mr. Utterson so contrived that he remained behind after the others had departed. This was no new arrangement, but a thing that had befallen many scores of times. Where Utterson was liked, he was liked well. Hosts loved to detain the dry lawyer, when the light-hearted and the loose-tongued had already their foot on the threshold; they liked to sit awhile in his unobtrusive company, practising for solitude, sobering their minds in the man's rich silence after the expense and strain of gaiety. To this rule, Dr. Jekyll was no exception; and as he now sat on the opposite side of the fire—a large, well-made, smooth-faced man of fifty, with something of a slyish cast perhaps, but every mark of capacity and kindness—you could see by his looks that he cherished for Mr. Utterson a sincere and warm affection.

4. With lame foot (Latin). From the Roman poet Horace's *Odes* 3.2.32: "Rarely has Vengeance with her lame foot abandoned the wicked man with a head start on her."

"I have been wanting to speak to you, Jekyll," began the latter. "You know that will of yours?"

A close observer might have gathered that the topic was distasteful; but the doctor carried it off gaily. "My poor Utterson," said he, "you are unfortunate in such a client. I never saw a man so distressed as you were by my will; unless it were that hide-bound pedant, Lanyon, at what he called my scientific heresies. O, I know he's a good fellow—you needn't frown—an excellent fellow, and I always mean to see more of him; but a hide-bound pedant for all that; an ignorant, blatant pedant. I was never more disappointed in any man than Lanyon."

"You know I never approved of it," pursued Utterson, ruthlessly disregarding the fresh topic.

"My will? Yes, certainly, I know that," said the doctor, a trifle sharply. "You have told me so."

"Well, I tell you so again," continued the lawyer. "I have been learning something of young Hyde."

The large handsome face of Dr. Jekyll grew pale to the very lips, and there came a blackness about his eyes. "I do not care to hear more," said he. "This is a matter I thought we had agreed to drop."

"What I heard was abominable," said Utterson.

"It can make no change. You do not understand my position," returned the doctor, with a certain incoherency of manner. "I am painfully situated, Utterson; my position is a very strange—a very strange one. It is one of those affairs that cannot be mended by talking."

"Jekyll," said Utterson, "you know me: I am a man to be trusted. Make a clean breast of this in confidence; and I make no doubt I can get you out of it."

"My good Utterson," said the doctor, "this is very good of you, this is downright good of you, and I cannot find words to thank you in. I believe you fully; I would trust you before any man alive, ay, before myself, if I could make the choice; but indeed it isn't what you fancy; it is not so bad as that; and just to put your good heart at rest, I will tell you one thing: the moment I choose, I can be rid of Mr. Hyde. I give you my hand upon that; and I thank you again and again; and I will just add one little word, Utterson, that I'm sure you'll take in good part: this is a private matter, and I beg of you to let it sleep."

Utterson reflected a little, looking in the fire.

"I have no doubt you are perfectly right," he said at last, getting to his feet.

"Well, but since we have touched upon this business, and for the last time I hope," continued the doctor, "there is one point I should like you to understand. I have really a very great interest in poor Hyde. I know you have seen him; he told me so; and I fear he was rude. But I do sincerely take a great, a very great interest in that young man; and if I am taken away, Utterson, I wish you to promise me that you will bear with him and get his rights for him. I think you would, if you knew all; and it would be a weight off my mind if you would promise."

"I can't pretend that I shall ever like him," said the lawyer.

"I don't ask that," pleaded Jekyll, laying his hand upon the other's arm; "I only ask for justice; I only ask you to help him for my sake, when I am no longer here."

Utterson heaved an irrepressible sigh. "Well," said he, "I promise."

The Carew Murder Case

Nearly a year later, in the month of October, 18—, London was startled by a crime of singular ferocity and rendered all the more notable by the high position of the victim. The details were few and startling. A maid servant living alone in a house not far from the river, had gone upstairs to bed about eleven. Although a fog rolled over the city in the small hours, the early part of the night was cloudless, and the lane, which the maid's window overlooked, was brilliantly lit by the full moon. It seems she was romantically given, for she sat down upon her box, which stood immediately under the window, and fell into a dream of musing. Never (she used to say, with streaming tears, when she narrated that experience), never had she felt more at peace with all men or thought more kindly of the world. And as she so sat she became aware of an aged and beautiful gentleman with white hair, drawing near along the lane; and advancing to meet him, another and very small gentleman, to whom at first she paid less attention. When they had come within speech (which was just under the maid's eyes) the older man bowed and accosted the other with a very pretty manner of politeness. It did not seem as if the subject of his address were of great importance; indeed, from his pointing, it sometimes appeared as if he were only inquiring his way; but the moon shone on his face as he spoke, and the girl was pleased to watch it, it seemed to breathe such an innocent and old-world kindness of disposition, yet with something high too, as of a well-founded self-content. Presently her eye wandered to the other, and she was surprised to recognise in him a certain Mr. Hyde, who had once visited her master and for whom she had conceived a dislike. He had in his hand a heavy cane, with which he was trifling; but he answered never a word, and seemed to listen with an ill-contained impatience. And then all of a sudden he broke out in a great flame of anger, stamping with his foot, brandishing the cane, and carrying on (as the maid described it) like a madman. The old gentleman took a step back, with the air of one very much surprised and a trifle hurt; and at that Mr. Hyde broke out of all bounds and clubbed him to the earth. And next moment, with ape-like fury, he was trampling his victim under foot and hailing down a storm of blows, under which the bones were audibly shattered and the body jumped upon the roadway. At the horror of these sights and sounds, the maid fainted.

It was two o'clock when she came to herself and called for the police. The murderer was gone long ago; but there lay his victim in the middle of the lane, incredibly mangled. The stick with which the deed had been done, although it was of some rare and very tough and heavy wood, had broken in the middle under the stress of this insensate cruelty; and one splintered half had rolled in the neighbouring gutter—the other, without doubt, had been carried away by the murderer. A purse and a gold watch were found upon the victim; but no cards or papers, except a sealed and stamped envelope, which he had been probably carrying to the post,[5] and which bore the name and address of Mr. Utterson.

This was brought to the lawyer the next morning, before he was out of bed; and he had no sooner seen it and been told the circumstances, than he shot out a solemn lip. "I shall say nothing till I have seen the body," said he; "this may be very serious. Have the kindness to wait while I dress." And with the

5. I.e., postal letter box.

same grave countenance he hurried through his breakfast and drove to the police station, whither the body had been carried. As soon as he came into the cell, he nodded.

"Yes," said he, "I recognise him. I am sorry to say that this is Sir Danvers Carew."

"Good God, sir," exclaimed the officer, "is it possible?" And the next moment his eye lighted up with professional ambition. "This will make a deal of noise," he said. "And perhaps you can help us to the man." And he briefly narrated what the maid had seen, and showed the broken stick.

Mr. Utterson had already quailed at the name of Hyde; but when the stick was laid before him, he could doubt no longer; broken and battered as it was, he recognised it for one that he had himself presented many years before to Henry Jekyll.

"Is this Mr. Hyde a person of small stature?" he inquired.

"Particularly small and particularly wicked-looking, is what the maid calls him," said the officer.

Mr. Utterson reflected; and then, raising his head, "If you will come with me in my cab," he said, "I think I can take you to his house."

It was by this time about nine in the morning, and the first fog of the season. A great chocolate-coloured pall lowered[6] over heaven, but the wind was continually charging and routing these embattled vapours; so that as the cab crawled from street to street, Mr. Utterson beheld a marvellous number of degrees and hues of twilight; for here it would be dark like the back-end of evening; and there would be a glow of a rich, lurid brown, like the light of some strange conflagration; and here, for a moment, the fog would be quite broken up, and a haggard shaft of daylight would glance in between the swirling wreaths. The dismal quarter of Soho seen under these changing glimpses, with its muddy ways, and slatternly passengers, and its lamps, which had never been extinguished or had been kindled afresh to combat this mournful reinvasion of darkness, seemed, in the lawyer's eyes, like a district of some city in a nightmare. The thoughts of his mind, besides, were of the gloomiest dye; and when he glanced at the companion of his drive, he was conscious of some touch of that terror of the law and the law's officers, which may at times assail the most honest.

As the cab drew up before the address indicated, the fog lifted a little and showed him a dingy street, a gin palace, a low French eating house, a shop for the retail of penny numbers[7] and twopenny salads, many ragged children huddled in the doorways, and many women of many different nationalities passing out, key in hand, to have a morning glass; and the next moment the fog settled down again upon that part, as brown as umber, and cut him off from his blackguardly surroundings. This was the home of Henry Jekyll's favourite; of a man who was heir to quarter of a million sterling.[8]

An ivory-faced and silvery-haired old woman opened the door. She had an evil face, smoothed by hypocrisy; but her manners were excellent. Yes, she said, this was Mr. Hyde's, but he was not at home; he had been in that night very late, but had gone away again in less than an hour; there was nothing strange in that; his habits were very irregular, and he was often absent; for instance, it was nearly two months since she had seen him till yesterday.

---

6. Was gloomy and threatening.
7. Cheap serial installments of popular fiction.

"Gin palace": cheap bar.
8. I.e., pounds sterling.

"Very well, then, we wish to see his rooms," said the lawyer; and when the woman began to declare it was impossible, "I had better tell you who this person is," he added. "This is Inspector Newcomen of Scotland Yard."

A flash of odious joy appeared upon the woman's face. "Ah!" said she, "he is in trouble! What has he done?"

Mr. Utterson and the inspector exchanged glances. "He don't seem a very popular character," observed the latter. "And now, my good woman, just let me and this gentleman have a look about us."

In the whole extent of the house, which but for the old woman remained otherwise empty, Mr. Hyde had only used a couple of rooms; but these were furnished with luxury and good taste. A closet was filled with wine; the plate was of silver, the napery[9] elegant; a good picture hung upon the walls, a gift (as Utterson supposed) from Henry Jekyll, who was much of a connoisseur; and the carpets were of many piles and agreeable in colour. At this moment, however, the rooms bore every mark of having been recently and hurriedly ransacked; clothes lay about the floor, with their pockets inside out; lock-fast drawers stood open; and on the hearth there lay a pile of gray ashes, as though many papers had been burned. From these embers the inspector disinterred the butt end of a green cheque book, which had resisted the action of the fire; the other half of the stick was found behind the door; and as this clinched his suspicions, the officer declared himself delighted. A visit to the bank, where several thousand pounds were found to be lying to the murderer's credit, completed his gratification.

"You may depend upon it, sir," he told Mr. Utterson: "I have him in my hand. He must have lost his head, or he never would have left the stick or, above all, burned the cheque book. Why, money's life to the man. We have nothing to do but wait for him at the bank, and get out the handbills."

This last, however, was not so easy of accomplishment; for Mr. Hyde had numbered few familiars—even the master of the servant maid had only seen him twice; his family could nowhere be traced; he had never been photographed; and the few who could describe him differed widely, as common observers will. Only on one point, were they agreed; and that was the haunting sense of unexpressed deformity with which the fugitive impressed his beholders.

Incident of the Letter

It was late in the afternoon, when Mr. Utterson found his way to Dr. Jekyll's door, where he was at once admitted by Poole, and carried down by the kitchen offices and across a yard which had once been a garden, to the building which was indifferently[1] known as the laboratory or the dissecting rooms. The doctor had bought the house from the heirs of a celebrated surgeon; and his own tastes being rather chemical than anatomical, had changed the destination[2] of the block at the bottom of the garden. It was the first time that the lawyer had been received in that part of his friend's quarters; and he eyed the dingy, windowless structure with curiosity, and gazed round with a distasteful sense of strangeness as he crossed the theatre,[3] once crowded

9. Table linen.
1. Without distinction.
2. Purpose.

3. Room with tiers of rising seats surrounding a central platform, used for lectures and medical demonstrations.

with eager students and now lying gaunt and silent, the tables laden with chemical apparatus, the floor strewn with crates and littered with packing straw, and the light falling dimly through the foggy cupola. At the further end, a flight of stairs mounted to a door covered with red baize; and through this, Mr. Utterson was at last received into the doctor's cabinet.[4] It was a large room, fitted round with glass presses, furnished, among other things, with a cheval-glass[5] and a business table, and looking out upon the court by three dusty windows barred with iron. A fire burned in the grate; a lamp was set lighted on the chimney shelf, for even in the houses the fog began to lie thickly; and there, close up to the warmth, sat Dr. Jekyll, looking deadly sick. He did not rise to meet his visitor, but held out a cold hand and bade him welcome in a changed voice.

"And now," said Mr. Utterson, as soon as Poole had left them, "you have heard the news?"

The doctor shuddered. "They were crying it in the square," he said. "I heard them in my dining-room."

"One word," said the lawyer. "Carew was my client, but so are you, and I want to know what I am doing. You have not been mad enough to hide this fellow?"

"Utterson, I swear to God," cried the doctor, "I swear to God I will never set eyes on him again. I bind my honour to you that I am done with him in this world. It is all at an end. And indeed he does not want my help; you do not know him as I do; he is safe, he is quite safe; mark my words, he will never more be heard of."

The lawyer listened gloomily; he did not like his friend's feverish manner. "You seem pretty sure of him," said he; "and for your sake, I hope you may be right. If it came to a trial, your name might appear."

"I am quite sure of him," replied Jekyll; "I have grounds for certainty that I cannot share with anyone. But there is one thing on which you may advise me. I have—I have received a letter; and I am at a loss whether I should show it to the police. I should like to leave it in your hands, Utterson; you would judge wisely, I am sure; I have so great a trust in you."

"You fear, I suppose, that it might lead to his detection?" asked the lawyer.

"No," said the other. "I cannot say that I care what becomes of Hyde; I am quite done with him. I was thinking of my own character, which this hateful business has rather exposed."

Utterson ruminated awhile; he was surprised at his friend's selfishness, and yet relieved by it. "Well," said he, at last, "let me see the letter."

The letter was written in an odd, upright hand and signed "Edward Hyde": and it signified, briefly enough, that the writer's benefactor, Dr. Jekyll, whom he had long so unworthily repaid for a thousand generosities, need labour under no alarm for his safety, as he had means of escape on which he placed a sure dependence. The lawyer liked this letter well enough; it put a better colour on the intimacy than he had looked for; and he blamed himself for some of his past suspicions.

"Have you the envelope?" he asked.

"I burned it," replied Jekyll, "before I thought what I was about. But it bore no postmark. The note was handed in."

---

4. Small private room. "Baize": coarse woolen material.

5. Large freestanding mirror, hinged on a frame. "Presses": cupboards with glass doors.

"Shall I keep this and sleep upon it?" asked Utterson.

"I wish you to judge for me entirely," was the reply. "I have lost confidence in myself."

"Well, I shall consider," returned the lawyer. "And now one word more: it was Hyde who dictated the terms in your will about that disappearance?"

The doctor seemed seized with a qualm of faintness; he shut his mouth tight and nodded.

"I knew it," said Utterson. "He meant to murder you. You have had a fine escape."

"I have had what is far more to the purpose," returned the doctor solemnly: "I have had a lesson—O God, Utterson, what a lesson I have had!" And he covered his face for a moment with his hands.

On his way out, the lawyer stopped and had a word or two with Poole. "By the bye," said he, "there was a letter handed in to-day: what was the messenger like?" But Poole was positive nothing had come except by post; "and only circulars by that," he added.

This news sent off the visitor with his fears renewed. Plainly the letter had come by the laboratory door; possibly, indeed, it had been written in the cabinet; and if that were so, it must be differently judged, and handled with the more caution. The newsboys, as he went, were crying themselves hoarse along the footways: "Special edition. Shocking murder of an M.P."[6] That was the funeral oration of one friend and client; and he could not help a certain apprehension lest the good name of another should be sucked down in the eddy of the scandal. It was, at least, a ticklish decision that he had to make; and self-reliant as he was by habit, he began to cherish a longing for advice. It was not to be had directly; but perhaps, he thought, it might be fished for.

Presently after, he sat on one side of his own hearth, with Mr. Guest, his head clerk, upon the other, and midway between, at a nicely calculated distance from the fire, a bottle of a particular old wine that had long dwelt unsunned in the foundations of his house. The fog still slept on the wing above the drowned city, where the lamps glimmered like carbuncles;[7] and through the muffle and smother of these fallen clouds, the procession of the town's life was still rolling in through the great arteries with a sound as of a mighty wind. But the room was gay with firelight. In the bottle the acids were long ago resolved; the imperial dye[8] had softened with time, as the colour grows richer in stained windows; and the glow of hot autumn afternoons on hillside vineyards, was ready to be set free and to disperse the fogs of London. Insensibly the lawyer melted. There was no man from whom he kept fewer secrets than Mr. Guest; and he was not always sure that he kept as many as he meant. Guest had often been on business to the doctor's; he knew Poole; he could scarce have failed to hear of Mr. Hyde's familiarity about the house; he might draw conclusions: was it not as well, then, that he should see a letter which put that mystery to rights? and above all since Guest, being a great student and critic of handwriting, would consider the step natural and obliging? The clerk, besides, was a man of counsel; he would scarce read so strange a document without dropping a remark; and by that remark Mr. Utterson might shape his future course.

6. Member of Parliament.
7. Precious fiery-red stones.
8. Purple.

"This is a sad business about Sir Danvers," he said.

"Yes, sir, indeed. It has elicited a great deal of public feeling," returned Guest. "The man, of course, was mad."

"I should like to hear your views on that," replied Utterson. "I have a document here in his handwriting; it is between ourselves, for I scarce know what to do about it; it is an ugly business at the best. But there it is; quite in your way: a murderer's autograph."

Guest's eyes brightened, and he sat down at once and studied it with passion. "No, sir," he said: "not mad; but it is an odd hand."

"And by all accounts a very odd writer," added the lawyer.

Just then the servant entered with a note.

"Is that from Dr. Jekyll, sir?" inquired the clerk. "I thought I knew the writing. Anything private, Mr. Utterson?"

"Only an invitation to dinner. Why? Do you want to see it?"

"One moment. I thank you, sir;" and the clerk laid the two sheets of paper alongside and sedulously compared their contents. "Thank you, sir," he said at last, returning both; "it's a very interesting autograph."

There was a pause, during which Mr. Utterson struggled with himself. "Why did you compare them, Guest?" he inquired suddenly.

"Well, sir," returned the clerk, "there's a rather singular resemblance; the two hands are in many points identical: only differently sloped."

"Rather quaint,"[9] said Utterson.

"It is, as you say, rather quaint," returned Guest.

"I wouldn't speak of this note, you know," said the master.

"No, sir," said the clerk. "I understand."

But no sooner was Mr. Utterson alone that night than he locked the note into his safe, where it reposed from that time forward. "What!" he thought. "Henry Jekyll forge for a murderer!" And his blood ran cold in his veins.

Remarkable Incident of Dr. Lanyon

Time ran on; thousands of pounds were offered in reward, for the death of Sir Danvers was resented as a public injury; but Mr. Hyde had disappeared out of the ken of the police as though he had never existed. Much of his past was unearthed, indeed, and all disreputable: tales came out of the man's cruelty, at once so callous and violent; of his vile life, of his strange associates, of the hatred that seemed to have surrounded his career; but of his present whereabouts, not a whisper. From the time he had left the house in Soho on the morning of the murder, he was simply blotted out; and gradually, as time drew on, Mr. Utterson began to recover from the hotness of his alarm, and to grow more at quiet with himself. The death of Sir Danvers was, to his way of thinking, more than paid for by the disappearance of Mr. Hyde. Now that that evil influence had been withdrawn, a new life began for Dr. Jekyll. He came out of his seclusion, renewed relations with his friends, became once more their familiar guest and entertainer; and whilst he had always been known for charities, he was now no less distinguished for religion. He was busy, he was much in the open air, he did good; his face seemed to open and brighten, as if with an inward consciousness of service; and for more than two months, the doctor was at peace.

9. Odd, unusual.

On the 8th of January Utterson had dined at the doctor's with a small party; Lanyon had been there; and the face of the host had looked from one to the other as in the old days when the trio were inseparable friends. On the 12th, and again on the 14th, the door was shut against the lawyer. "The doctor was confined to the house," Poole said, "and saw no one." On the 15th, he tried again, and was again refused; and having now been used for the last two months to see his friend almost daily, he found this return of solitude to weigh upon his spirits. The fifth night he had in Guest to dine with him; and the sixth he betook himself to Dr. Lanyon's.

There at least he was not denied admittance; but when he came in, he was shocked at the change which had taken place in the doctor's appearance. He had his death-warrant written legibly upon his face. The rosy man had grown pale; his flesh had fallen away; he was visibly balder and older; and yet it was not so much these tokens of a swift physical decay that arrested the lawyer's notice, as a look in the eye and quality of manner that seemed to testify to some deep-seated terror of the mind. It was unlikely that the doctor should fear death; and yet that was what Utterson was tempted to suspect. "Yes," he thought; "he is a doctor, he must know his own state and that his days are counted; and the knowledge is more than he can bear." And yet when Utterson remarked on his ill-looks, it was with an air of great firmness that Lanyon declared himself a doomed man.

"I have had a shock," he said, "and I shall never recover. It is a question of weeks. Well, life has been pleasant; I liked it; yes, sir, I used to like it. I sometimes think if we knew all, we should be more glad to get away."

"Jekyll is ill, too," observed Utterson. "Have you seen him?"

But Lanyon's face changed, and he held up a trembling hand. "I wish to see or hear no more of Dr. Jekyll," he said in a loud, unsteady voice. "I am quite done with that person; and I beg that you will spare me any allusion to one whom I regard as dead."

"Tut-tut," said Mr. Utterson; and then after a considerable pause, "Can't I do anything?" he inquired. "We are three very old friends, Lanyon; we shall not live to make others."

"Nothing can be done," returned Lanyon; "ask himself."

"He will not see me," said the lawyer.

"I am not surprised at that," was the reply. "Some day, Utterson, after I am dead, you may perhaps come to learn the right and wrong of this. I cannot tell you. And in the meantime, if you can sit and talk with me of other things, for God's sake, stay and do so; but if you cannot keep clear of this accursed topic, then, in God's name, go, for I cannot bear it."

As soon as he got home, Utterson sat down and wrote to Jekyll, complaining of his exclusion from the house, and asking the cause of this unhappy break with Lanyon; and the next day brought him a long answer, often very pathetically worded, and sometimes darkly mysterious in drift. The quarrel with Lanyon was incurable. "I do not blame our old friend," Jekyll wrote, "but I share his view that we must never meet. I mean from henceforth to lead a life of extreme seclusion; you must not be surprised, nor must you doubt my friendship, if my door is often shut even to you. You must suffer me to go my own dark way. I have brought on myself a punishment and a danger that I cannot name. If I am the chief of sinners, I am the chief of sufferers also. I could not think that this earth contained a place for sufferings and terrors so unmanning; and you can do but one thing, Utterson, to lighten this destiny, and that is to respect my silence." Utterson was amazed; the dark influence of Hyde had been withdrawn, the doctor had returned to his old tasks and amities; a week ago, the prospect had smiled with every promise of a cheerful and an honoured age; and now in a moment, friendship, and peace of mind, and the whole tenor of his life were wrecked. So great and unprepared a change pointed to madness; but in view of Lanyon's manner and words, there must lie for it some deeper ground.

A week afterwards Dr. Lanyon took to his bed, and in something less than a fortnight he was dead. The night after the funeral, at which he had been sadly affected, Utterson locked the door of his business room, and sitting there by the light of a melancholy candle, drew out and set before him an envelope addressed by the hand and sealed with the seal of his dead friend. "PRIVATE: for the hands of G. J. Utterson ALONE, and in case of his predecease *to be destroyed unread*," so it was emphatically superscribed; and the lawyer dreaded to behold the contents. "I have buried one friend today," he thought: "what if this should cost me another?" And then he condemned the fear as a disloyalty, and broke the seal. Within there was another enclosure, likewise sealed, and marked upon the cover as "not to be opened till the death or disappearance of Dr. Henry Jekyll." Utterson could not trust his eyes. Yes, it was disappearance; here again, as in the mad will which he had long ago restored to its author, here again were the idea of a disappearance and the name of Henry Jekyll bracketted. But in the will, that idea had sprung from the sinister suggestion of the man Hyde; it was set there with a purpose all too plain and horrible. Written by the hand of Lanyon, what should it mean? A great curiosity came on the trustee, to disregard the prohibition and dive at once to the bottom of these mysteries; but professional honour and faith to his dead friend were stringent obligations; and the packet slept in the inmost corner of his private safe.

It is one thing to mortify curiosity, another to conquer it; and it may be doubted if, from that day forth, Utterson desired the society of his surviving friend with the same eagerness. He thought of him kindly; but his thoughts were disquieted and fearful. He went to call indeed; but he was perhaps relieved to be denied admittance; perhaps, in his heart, he preferred to speak with Poole upon the doorstep and surrounded by the air and sounds of the open city, rather than to be admitted into that house of voluntary bondage, and to sit and speak with its inscrutable recluse. Poole had, indeed, no very pleasant news to communicate. The doctor, it appeared, now more than ever confined himself to the cabinet over the laboratory, where he would sometimes even sleep; he was out of spirits, he had grown very silent, he did not read; it seemed as if he had something on his mind. Utterson became so used to the unvarying character of these reports, that he fell off little by little in the frequency of his visits.

Incident at the Window

It chanced on Sunday, when Mr. Utterson was on his usual walk with Mr. Enfield, that their way lay once again through the by-street; and that when they came in front of the door, both stopped to gaze on it.

"Well," said Enfield, "that story's at an end at least. We shall never see more of Mr. Hyde."

"I hope not," said Utterson. "Did I ever tell you that I once saw him, and shared your feeling of repulsion?"

"It was impossible to do the one without the other," returned Enfield. "And by the way, what an ass you must have thought me, not to know that this was a back way to Dr. Jekyll's! It was partly your own fault that I found it out, even when I did."

"So you found it out, did you?" said Utterson. "But if that be so, we may step into the court and take a look at the windows. To tell you the truth, I am uneasy about poor Jekyll; and even outside, I feel as if the presence of a friend might do him good."

The court was very cool and a little damp, and full of premature twilight, although the sky, high up overhead, was still bright with sunset. The middle one of the three windows was half way open; and sitting close beside it, taking the air with an infinite sadness of mien, like some disconsolate prisoner, Utterson saw Dr. Jekyll.

"What! Jekyll!" he cried. "I trust you are better."

"I am very low, Utterson," replied the doctor, drearily, "very low. It will not last long, thank God."

"You stay too much indoors," said the lawyer. "You should be out, whipping up the circulation like Mr. Enfield and me. (This is my cousin—Mr. Enfield—Dr. Jekyll.) Come now; get your hat and take a quick turn with us."

"You are very good," sighed the other. "I should like to very much; but no, no, no, it is quite impossible; I dare not. But indeed, Utterson, I am very glad to see you; this is really a great pleasure; I would ask you and Mr. Enfield up, but the place is really not fit."

"Why then," said the lawyer, good-naturedly, "the best thing we can do is to stay down here and speak with you from where we are."

"That is just what I was about to venture to propose," returned the doctor with a smile. But the words were hardly uttered, before the smile was struck out of his face and succeeded by an expression of such abject terror and despair, as froze the very blood of the two gentlemen below. They saw it but for a glimpse, for the window was instantly thrust down; but that glimpse had been sufficient, and they turned and left the court without a word. In silence, too, they traversed the by-street; and it was not until they had come into a neighbouring thoroughfare, where even upon a Sunday there were still some stirrings of life, that Mr. Utterson at last turned and looked at his companion. They were both pale; and there was an answering horror in their eyes.

"God forgive us, God forgive us," said Mr. Utterson.

But Mr. Enfield only nodded his head very seriously, and walked on once more in silence.

The Last Night

Mr. Utterson was sitting by his fireside one evening after dinner, when he was surprised to receive a visit from Poole.

"Bless me, Poole, what brings you here?" he cried; and then taking a second look at him, "What ails you?" he added; "is the doctor ill?"

"Mr. Utterson," said the man, "there is something wrong."

"Take a seat, and here is a glass of wine for you," said the lawyer. "Now, take your time, and tell me plainly what you want."

"You know the doctor's ways, sir," replied Poole, "and how he shuts himself up. Well, he's shut up again in the cabinet; and I don't like it, sir—I wish I may die if I like it. Mr. Utterson, sir, I'm afraid."

"Now, my good man," said the lawyer, "be explicit. What are you afraid of?"

"I've been afraid for about a week," returned Poole, doggedly disregarding the question, "and I can bear it no more."

The man's appearance amply bore out his words; his manner was altered for the worse; and except for the moment when he had first announced his terror, he had not once looked the lawyer in the face. Even now, he sat with the glass of wine untasted on his knee, and his eyes directed to a corner of the floor. "I can bear it no more," he repeated.

"Come," said the lawyer, "I see you have some good reason, Poole; I see there is something seriously amiss. Try to tell me what it is."

"I think there's been foul play," said Poole, hoarsely.

"Foul play!" cried the lawyer, a good deal frightened and rather inclined to be irritated in consequence. "What foul play? What does the man mean?"

"I daren't say, sir," was the answer; "but will you come along with me and see for yourself?"

Mr. Utterson's only answer was to rise and get his hat and great coat; but he observed with wonder the greatness of the relief that appeared upon the butler's face, and perhaps with no less, that the wine was still untasted when he set it down to follow.

It was a wild, cold, seasonable night of March, with a pale moon, lying on her back as though the wind had tilted her, and a flying wrack of the most diaphanous and lawny[1] texture. The wind made talking difficult, and flecked the blood into the face. It seemed to have swept the streets unusually bare of passengers, besides; for Mr. Utterson thought he had never seen that part of London so deserted. He could have wished it otherwise; never in his life had he been conscious of so sharp a wish to see and touch his fellow-creatures; for struggle as he might, there was born in upon his mind a crushing anticipation of calamity. The square, when they got there, was all full of wind and dust, and the thin trees in the garden were lashing themselves along the railing. Poole, who had kept all the way a pace or two ahead, now pulled up in the middle of the pavement, and in spite of the biting weather, took off his hat and mopped his brow with a red pocket-handkerchief. But for all the hurry of his coming, these were not the dews of exertion that he wiped away, but the moisture of some strangling anguish; for his face was white and his voice, when he spoke, harsh and broken.

"Well, sir," he said, "here we are, and God grant there be nothing wrong."

"Amen, Poole," said the lawyer.

Thereupon the servant knocked in a very guarded manner; the door was opened on the chain; and a voice asked from within, "Is that you, Poole?"

"It's all right," said Poole. "Open the door."

The hall, when they entered it, was brightly lighted up; the fire was built high; and about the hearth the whole of the servants, men and women, stood huddled together like a flock of sheep. At the sight of Mr. Utterson, the housemaid broke into hysterical whimpering; and the cook, crying out "Bless God! it's Mr. Utterson," ran forward as if to take him in her arms.

---

1. Of fine linen. "Wrack": i.e., rack, a mass of high clouds driven by the wind.

"What, what? Are you all here?" said the lawyer peevishly. "Very irregular, very unseemly; your master would be far from pleased."

"They're all afraid," said Poole.

Blank silence followed, no one protesting; only the maid lifted up her voice and now wept loudly.

"Hold your tongue!" Poole said to her, with a ferocity of accent that testified to his own jangled nerves; and indeed, when the girl had so suddenly raised the note of her lamentation, they had all started and turned towards the inner door with faces of dreadful expectation. "And now," continued the butler, addressing the knife-boy, "reach me a candle, and we'll get this through hands² at once." And then he begged Mr. Utterson to follow him, and led the way to the back garden.

"Now, sir," said he, "you come as gently as you can. I want you to hear, and I don't want you to be heard. And see here, sir, if by any chance he was to ask you in, don't go."

Mr. Utterson's nerves, at this unlooked-for termination, gave a jerk that nearly threw him from his balance; but he recollected his courage and followed the butler into the laboratory building and through the surgical theatre, with its lumber³ of crates and bottles, to the foot of the stair. Here Poole motioned him to stand on one side and listen; while he himself, setting down the candle and making a great and obvious call on his resolution, mounted the steps and knocked with a somewhat uncertain hand on the red baize of the cabinet door.

"Mr. Utterson, sir, asking to see you," he called; and even as he did so, once more violently signed to the lawyer to give ear.

A voice answered from within: "Tell him I cannot see anyone," it said complainingly.

"Thank you, sir," said Poole, with a note of something like triumph in his voice; and taking up his candle, he led Mr. Utterson back across the yard and into the great kitchen, where the fire was out and the beetles were leaping on the floor.

"Sir," he said, looking Mr. Utterson in the eyes, "was that my master's voice?"

"It seems much changed," replied the lawyer, very pale, but giving look for look.

"Changed? Well, yes, I think so," said the butler. "Have I been twenty years in this man's house, to be deceived about his voice? No, sir; master's made away with; he was made away with, eight days ago, when we heard him cry out upon the name of God; and *who's* in there instead of him, and *why* it stays there, is a thing that cries to Heaven, Mr. Utterson!"

"This is a very strange tale, Poole; this is rather a wild tale, my man," said Mr. Utterson, biting his finger. "Suppose it were as you suppose, supposing Dr. Jekyll to have been—well, murdered, what could induce the murderer to stay? That won't hold water; it doesn't commend itself to reason."

"Well, Mr. Utterson, you are a hard man to satisfy, but I'll do it yet," said Poole. "All this last week (you must know) him, or it, or whatever it is that lives in that cabinet, has been crying night and day for some sort of medicine and cannot get it to his mind. It was sometimes his way—the master's, that is—to write his orders on a sheet of paper and throw it on the stair. We've had

2. We'll deal with this.   3. Stored accumulation.

nothing else this week back; nothing but papers, and a closed door, and the very meals left there to be smuggled in when nobody was looking. Well, sir, every day, ay, and twice and thrice in the same day, there have been orders and complaints, and I have been sent flying to all the wholesale chemists in town. Every time I brought the stuff back, there would be another paper telling me to return it, because it was not pure, and another order to a different firm. This drug is wanted bitter bad, sir, whatever for."

"Have you any of these papers?" asked Mr. Utterson.

Poole felt in his pocket and handed out a crumpled note, which the lawyer, bending nearer to the candle, carefully examined. Its contents ran thus: "Dr. Jekyll presents his compliments to Messrs. Maw. He assures them that their last sample is impure and quite useless for his present purpose. In the year 18—, Dr. J. purchased a somewhat large quantity from Messrs. M. He now begs them to search with the most sedulous care, and should any of the same quality be left, to forward it to him at once. Expense is no consideration. The importance of this to Dr. J. can hardly be exaggerated." So far the letter had run composedly enough, but here with a sudden splutter of the pen, the writer's emotion had broken loose. "For God's sake," he had added, "find me some of the old."

"This is a strange note," said Mr. Utterson; and then sharply, "How do you come to have it open?"

"The man at Maw's was main angry, sir, and he threw it back to me like so much dirt," returned Poole.

"This is unquestionably the doctor's hand, do you know?" resumed the lawyer.

"I thought it looked like it," said the servant rather sulkily; and then, with another voice, "But what matters hand of write?" he said. "I've seen him!"

"Seen him?" repeated Mr. Utterson. "Well?"

"That's it!" said Poole. "It was this way. I came suddenly into the theatre from the garden. It seems he had slipped out to look for this drug or whatever it is; for the cabinet door was open, and there he was at the far end of the room digging among the crates. He looked up when I came in, gave a kind of cry, and whipped upstairs into the cabinet. It was but for one minute that I saw him, but the hair stood upon my head like quills. Sir, if that was my master, why had he a mask upon his face? If it was my master, why did he cry out like a rat, and run from me? I have served him long enough. And then . . ." The man paused and passed his hand over his face.

"These are all very strange circumstances," said Mr. Utterson, "but I think I begin to see daylight. Your master, Poole, is plainly seized with one of those maladies that both torture and deform the sufferer; hence, for aught I know, the alteration of his voice; hence the mask and the avoidance of his friends; hence his eagerness to find this drug, by means of which the poor soul retains some hope of ultimate recovery—God grant that he be not deceived! There is my explanation; it is sad enough, Poole, ay, and appalling to consider; but it is plain and natural, hangs well together, and delivers us from all exorbitant alarms."

"Sir," said the butler, turning to a sort of mottled pallor, "that thing was not my master, and there's the truth. My master"—here he looked round him and began to whisper—"is a tall, fine build of a man, and this was more of a dwarf." Utterson attempted to protest. "O, sir," cried Poole, "do you think I do not know my master after twenty years? Do you think I do not know

where his head comes to in the cabinet door, where I saw him every morning of my life? No, sir, that thing in the mask was never Dr. Jekyll—God
knows what it was, but it was never Dr. Jekyll; and it is the belief of my heart
that there was murder done."

"Poole," replied the lawyer, "if you say that, it will become my duty to make
certain. Much as I desire to spare your master's feelings, much as I am puzzled by this note which seems to prove him to be still alive, I shall consider it
my duty to break in that door."

"Ah, Mr. Utterson, that's talking!" cried the butler.

"And now comes the second question," resumed Utterson: "Who is going
to do it?"

"Why, you and me," was the undaunted reply.

"That's very well said," returned the lawyer; "and whatever comes of it,
I shall make it my business to see you are no loser."

"There is an axe in the theatre," continued Poole; "and you might take the
kitchen poker for yourself."

The lawyer took that rude but weighty instrument into his hand, and balanced it. "Do you know, Poole," he said, looking up, "that you and I are about
to place ourselves in a position of some peril?"

"You may say so, sir, indeed," returned the butler.

"It is well, then, that we should be frank," said the other. "We both think
more than we have said; let us make a clean breast. This masked figure that
you saw, did you recognise it?"

"Well, sir, it went so quick, and the creature was so doubled up, that I
could hardly swear to that," was the answer. "But if you mean, was it Mr.
Hyde?—why, yes, I think it was! You see, it was much of the same bigness;
and it had the same quick, light way with it; and then who else could have got
in by the laboratory door? You have not forgot, sir, that at the time of the
murder he had still the key with him? But that's not all. I don't know, Mr.
Utterson, if ever you met this Mr. Hyde?"

"Yes," said the lawyer, "I once spoke with him."

"Then you must know as well as the rest of us that there was something
queer about that gentleman—something that gave a man a turn—I don't
know rightly how to say it, sir, beyond this: that you felt it in your marrow
kind of cold and thin."

"I own I felt something of what you describe," said Mr. Utterson.

"Quite so, sir," returned Poole. "Well, when that masked thing like a monkey jumped from among the chemicals and whipped into the cabinet, it went
down my spine like ice. O, I know it's not evidence, Mr. Utterson; I'm book-
learned enough for that; but a man has his feelings, and I give you my bible-
word it was Mr. Hyde!"

"Ay, ay," said the lawyer. "My fears incline to the same point. Evil, I fear,
founded—evil was sure to come—of that connection. Ay, truly, I believe you;
I believe poor Harry is killed; and I believe his murderer (for what purpose,
God alone can tell) is still lurking in his victim's room. Well, let our name
be vengeance. Call Bradshaw."

The footman came at the summons, very white and nervous.

"Pull yourself together, Bradshaw," said the lawyer. "This suspense, I know,
is telling upon all of you; but it is now our intention to make an end of it.
Poole, here, and I are going to force our way into the cabinet. If all is well, my
shoulders are broad enough to bear the blame. Meanwhile, lest anything

should really be amiss, or any malefactor seek to escape by the back, you and the boy must go round the corner with a pair of good sticks and take your post at the laboratory door. We give you ten minutes, to get to your stations."

As Bradshaw left, the lawyer looked at his watch. "And now, Poole, let us get to ours," he said; and taking the poker under his arm, led the way into the yard. The scud[4] had banked over the moon, and it was now quite dark. The wind, which only broke in puffs and draughts into that deep well of building, tossed the light of the candle to and fro about their steps, until they came into the shelter of the theatre, where they sat down silently to wait. London hummed solemnly all around; but nearer at hand, the stillness was only broken by the sounds of a footfall moving to and fro along the cabinet floor.

"So it will walk all day, sir," whispered Poole; "ay, and the better part of the night. Only when a new sample comes from the chemist, there's a bit of a break. Ah, it's an ill-conscience that's such an enemy to rest! Ah, sir, there's blood foully shed in every step of it! But hark again, a little closer—put your heart in your ears, Mr. Utterson, and tell me, is that the doctor's foot?"

The steps fell lightly and oddly, with a certain swing, for all they went so slowly; it was different indeed from the heavy creaking tread of Henry Jekyll. Utterson sighed. "Is there never anything else?" he asked.

Poole nodded. "Once," he said. "Once I heard it weeping!"

"Weeping? how that?" said the lawyer, conscious of a sudden chill of horror.

"Weeping like a woman or a lost soul," said the butler. "I came away with that upon my heart, that I could have wept too."

But now the ten minutes drew to an end. Poole disinterred the axe from under a stack of packing straw; the candle was set upon the nearest table to light them to the attack; and they drew near with bated breath to where that patient foot was still going up and down, up and down, in the quiet of the night.

"Jekyll," cried Utterson, with a loud voice, "I demand to see you." He paused a moment, but there came no reply. "I give you fair warning, our suspicions are aroused, and I must and shall see you," he resumed; "if not by fair means, then by foul—if not of your consent, then by brute force!"

"Utterson," said the voice, "for God's sake, have mercy!"

"Ah, that's not Jekyll's voice—it's Hyde's!" cried Utterson. "Down with the door, Poole!"

Poole swung the axe over his shoulder; the blow shook the building, and the red baize door leaped against the lock and hinges. A dismal screech, as of mere animal terror, rang from the cabinet. Up went the axe again, and again the panels crashed and the frame bounded; four times the blow fell; but the wood was tough and the fittings were of excellent workmanship; and it was not until the fifth, that the lock burst in sunder and the wreck of the door fell inwards on the carpet.

The besiegers, appalled by their own riot and the stillness that had succeeded, stood back a little and peered in. There lay the cabinet before their eyes in the quiet lamplight, a good fire glowing and chattering on the hearth, the kettle singing its thin strain, a drawer or two open, papers neatly set forth on the business table, and nearer the fire, the things laid out for tea: the

---

4. Loose clouds driven rapidly before the wind.

quietest room, you would have said, and, but for the glazed presses full of chemicals, the most commonplace that night in London.

Right in the midst there lay the body of a man sorely contorted and still twitching. They drew near on tip-toe, turned it on its back and beheld the face of Edward Hyde. He was dressed in clothes far too large for him, clothes of the doctor's bigness; the cords of his face still moved with a semblance of life, but life was quite gone: and by the crushed phial in the hand and the strong smell of kernels[5] that hung upon the air, Utterson knew that he was looking on the body of a self-destroyer.

"We have come too late," he said sternly, "whether to save or punish. Hyde is gone to his account; and it only remains for us to find the body of your master."

The far greater proportion of the building was occupied by the theatre, which filled almost the whole ground story and was lighted from above, and by the cabinet, which formed an upper story at one end and looked upon the court. A corridor joined the theatre to the door on the by-street; and with this the cabinet communicated separately by a second flight of stairs. There were besides a few dark closets and a spacious cellar. All these they now thoroughly examined. Each closet needed but a glance, for all were empty, and all, by the dust that fell from their doors, had stood long unopened. The cellar, indeed, was filled with crazy lumber, mostly dating from the times of the surgeon who was Jekyll's predecessor; but even as they opened the door they were advertised of the uselessness of further search, by the fall of a perfect mat of cobweb which had for years sealed up the entrance. Nowhere was there any trace of Henry Jekyll, dead or alive.

Poole stamped on the flags of the corridor. "He must be buried here," he said, hearkening to the sound.

"Or he may have fled," said Utterson, and he turned to examine the door in the by-street. It was locked; and lying near by on the flags, they found the key, already stained with rust.

"This does not look like use," observed the lawyer.

"Use!" echoed Poole. "Do you not see, sir, it is broken? much as if a man had stamped on it."

"Ay," continued Utterson, "and the fractures, too, are rusty." The two men looked at each other with a scare. "This is beyond me, Poole," said the lawyer. "Let us go back to the cabinet."

They mounted the stair in silence, and still with an occasional awestruck glance at the dead body, proceeded more thoroughly to examine the contents of the cabinet. At one table, there were traces of chemical work, various measured heaps of some white salt being laid on glass saucers, as though for an experiment in which the unhappy man had been prevented.

"That is the same drug that I was always bringing him," said Poole; and even as he spoke, the kettle with a startling noise boiled over.

This brought them to the fireside, where the easy-chair was drawn cosily up, and the tea things stood ready to the sitter's elbow, the very sugar in the cup. There were several books on a shelf; one lay beside the tea things open, and Utterson was amazed to find it a copy of a pious work, for which Jekyll had several times expressed a great esteem, annotated, in his own hand, with startling blasphemies.

---

5. I.e., pits: cyanide smells of bitter almond or of peach pits.

Next, in the course of their review of the chamber, the searchers came to the cheval glass, into whose depths they looked with an involuntary horror. But it was so turned as to show them nothing but the rosy glow playing on the roof, the fire sparkling in a hundred repetitions along the glazed front of the presses, and their own pale and fearful countenances stooping to look in.

"This glass have seen some strange things, sir," whispered Poole.

"And surely none stranger than itself," echoed the lawyer in the same tones. "For what did Jekyll"—he caught himself up at the word with a start, and then conquering the weakness—"what could Jekyll want with it?" he said.

"You may say that!" said Poole.

Next they turned to the business table. On the desk, among the neat array of papers, a large envelope was uppermost, and bore, in the doctor's hand, the name of Mr. Utterson. The lawyer unsealed it, and several enclosures fell to the floor. The first was a will, drawn in the same eccentric terms as the one which he had returned six months before, to serve as a testament in case of death and as a deed of gift in case of disappearance; but in place of the name of Edward Hyde, the lawyer, with indescribable amazement, read the name of Gabriel John Utterson. He looked at Poole, and then back at the paper, and last of all at the dead malefactor stretched upon the carpet.

"My head goes round," he said. "He has been all these days in possession; he had no cause to like me; he must have raged to see himself displaced; and he has not destroyed this document."

He caught up the next paper; it was a brief note in the doctor's hand and dated at the top. "O Poole!" the lawyer cried, "he was alive and here this day. He cannot have been disposed of in so short a space; he must be still alive, he must have fled! And then, why fled? and how? and in that case, can we venture to declare this suicide? O, we must be careful. I foresee that we may yet involve your master in some dire catastrophe."

"Why don't you read it, sir?" asked Poole.

"Because I fear," replied the lawyer solemnly. "God grant I have no cause for it!" And with that he brought the paper to his eyes and read as follows:

"MY DEAR UTTERSON,—When this shall fall into your hands, I shall have disappeared, under what circumstances I have not the penetration to foresee, but my instinct and all the circumstances of my nameless situation tell me that the end is sure and must be early. Go then, and first read the narrative which Lanyon warned me he was to place in your hands; and if you care to hear more, turn to the confession of

"Your unworthy and unhappy friend,
"HENRY JEKYLL."

"There was a third enclosure?" asked Utterson.

"Here, sir," said Poole, and gave into his hands a considerable packet sealed in several places.

The lawyer put it in his pocket. "I would say nothing of this paper. If your master has fled or is dead, we may at least save his credit. It is now ten; I must go home and read these documents in quiet; but I shall be back before midnight, when we shall send for the police."

They went out, locking the door of the theatre behind them; and Utterson, once more leaving the servants gathered about the fire in the hall, trudged back to his office to read the two narratives in which this mystery was now to be explained.

Dr. Lanyon's Narrative

On the ninth of January, now four days ago, I received by the evening delivery a registered envelope, addressed in the hand of my colleague and old school-companion, Henry Jekyll. I was a good deal surprised by this; for we were by no means in the habit of correspondence; I had seen the man, dined with him, indeed, the night before; and I could imagine nothing in our intercourse that should justify formality of registration. The contents increased my wonder; for this is how the letter ran:

"10th December, 18—[6]

"DEAR LANYON,—You are one of my oldest friends; and although we may have differed at times on scientific questions, I cannot remember, at least on my side, any break in our affection. There was never a day when, if you had said to me, 'Jekyll, my life, my honour, my reason, depend upon you,' I would not have sacrificed my left hand to help you. Lanyon, my life, my honour, my reason, are all at your mercy; if you fail me tonight I am lost. You might suppose, after this preface, that I am going to ask you for something dishonourable to grant. Judge for yourself.

"I want you to postpone all other engagements for to-night—ay, even if you were summoned to the bedside of an emperor; to take a cab, unless your carriage should be actually at the door; and with this letter in your hand for consultation, to drive straight to my house. Poole, my butler, has his orders; you will find him waiting your arrival with a locksmith. The door of my cabinet is then to be forced: and you are to go in alone; to open the glazed press (letter E) on the left hand, breaking the lock if it be shut; and to draw out, *with all its contents as they stand*, the fourth drawer from the top or (which is the same thing) the third from the bottom. In my extreme distress of mind, I have a morbid fear of misdirecting you; but even if I am in error, you may know the right drawer by its contents: some powders, a phial and a paper book. This drawer I beg of you to carry back with you to Cavendish Square exactly as it stands.

"That is the first part of the service: now for the second. You should be back, if you set out at once on the receipt of this, long before midnight; but I will leave you that amount of margin, not only in the fear of one of those obstacles that can neither be prevented nor foreseen, but because an hour when your servants are in bed is to be preferred for what will then remain to do. At midnight, then, I have to ask you to be alone in your consulting room, to admit with your own hand into the house a man who will present himself in my name, and to place in his hands the drawer that you will have brought with you from my cabinet.

6. Stevenson's own error; the first sentence of *Dr. Lanyon's Narrative* makes it clear that the letter should be dated "9th January." Literary critic Richard Dury attributes the slip to the following circumstances: Stevenson had originally wanted to publish his story in time for the Christmas market and align Lanyon's witnessing of Hyde's transformation with December, a time for mysterious events. Later he forgot to change this detail.

Then you will have played your part and earned my gratitude completely. Five minutes afterwards, if you insist upon an explanation, you will have understood that these arrangements are of capital importance; and that by the neglect of one of them, fantastic as they must appear, you might have charged your conscience with my death or the shipwreck of my reason.

"Confident as I am that you will not trifle with this appeal, my heart sinks and my hand trembles at the bare thought of such a possibility. Think of me at this hour, in a strange place, labouring under a blackness of distress that no fancy can exaggerate, and yet well aware that, if you will but punctually serve me, my troubles will roll away like a story that is told. Serve me, my dear Lanyon, and save

"Your friend,

H. J."

"P. S.—I had already sealed this up when a fresh terror struck upon my soul. It is possible that the post-office may fail me, and this letter not come into your hands until to-morrow morning. In that case, dear Lanyon, do my errand when it shall be most convenient for you in the course of the day; and once more expect my messenger at midnight. It may then already be too late; and if that night passes without event, you will know that you have seen the last of Henry Jekyll."

Upon the reading of this letter, I made sure my colleague was insane; but till that was proved beyond the possibility of doubt, I felt bound to do as he requested. The less I understood of this farrago[7] the less I was in a position to judge of its importance; and an appeal so worded could not be set aside without a grave responsibility. I rose accordingly from table, got into a hansom, and drove straight to Jekyll's house. The butler was awaiting my arrival; he had received by the same post as mine a registered letter of instruction, and had sent at once for a locksmith and a carpenter. The tradesmen came while we were yet speaking; and we moved in a body to old Dr. Denman's surgical theatre, from which (as you are doubtless aware) Jekyll's private cabinet is most conveniently entered. The door was very strong, the lock excellent; the carpenter avowed he would have great trouble and have to do much damage, if force were to be used; and the locksmith was near despair. But this last was a handy fellow, and after two hours' work, the door stood open. The press marked E was unlocked; and I took out the drawer, had it filled up with straw and tied in a sheet, and returned with it to Cavendish Square.

Here I proceeded to examine its contents. The powders were neatly enough made up, but not with the nicety of the dispensing chemist; so that it was plain they were of Jekyll's private manufacture: and when I opened one of the wrappers I found what seemed to me a simple crystalline salt of a white colour. The phial, to which I next turned my attention, might have been about half full of a blood-red liquor, which was highly pungent to the sense of smell and seemed to me to contain phosphorus and some volatile ether. At the other ingredients I could make no guess. The book was an ordinary version book[8] and contained little but a series of dates. These covered a

---

7. Mixture.

8. School notebook used to record translations.

period of many years, but I observed that the entries ceased nearly a year ago and quite abruptly. Here and there a brief remark was appended to a date, usually no more than a single word: "double" occurring perhaps six times in a total of several hundred entries; and once very early in the list and followed by several marks of exclamation, "total failure!!!" All this, though it whetted my curiosity, told me little that was definite. Here were a phial of some tincture, a paper of some salt, and the record of a series of experiments that had led (like too many of Jekyll's investigations) to no end of practical usefulness. How could the presence of these articles in my house affect either the honour, the sanity, or the life of my flighty colleague? If his messenger could go to one place, why could he not go to another? And even granting some impediment, why was this gentleman to be received by me in secret? The more I reflected the more convinced I grew that I was dealing with a case of cerebral disease; and though I dismissed my servants to bed, I loaded an old revolver, that I might be found in some posture of self-defence.

Twelve o'clock had scarce rung out over London, ere the knocker sounded very gently on the door. I went myself at the summons, and found a small man crouching against the pillars of the portico.

"Are you come from Dr. Jekyll?" I asked.

He told me "yes" by a constrained gesture; and when I had bidden him enter, he did not obey me without a searching backward glance into the darkness of the square. There was a policeman not far off, advancing with his bull's eye[9] open; and at the sight, I thought my visitor started and made greater haste.

These particulars struck me, I confess, disagreeably; and as I followed him into the bright light of the consulting room, I kept my hand ready on my weapon. Here, at last, I had a chance of clearly seeing him. I had never set eyes on him before, so much was certain. He was small, as I have said; I was struck besides with the shocking expression of his face, with his remarkable combination of great muscular activity and great apparent debility of constitution, and—last but not least—with the odd, subjective disturbance caused by his neighbourhood. This bore some resemblance to incipient rigour,[1] and was accompanied by a marked sinking of the pulse. At the time, I set it down to some idiosyncratic, personal distaste, and merely wondered at the acuteness of the symptoms; but I have since had reason to believe the cause to lie much deeper in the nature of man, and to turn on some nobler hinge than the principle of hatred.

This person (who had thus, from the first moment of his entrance, struck in me what I can only describe as a disgustful curiosity) was dressed in a fashion that would have made an ordinary person laughable; his clothes, that is to say, although they were of rich and sober fabric, were enormously too large for him in every measurement—the trousers hanging on his legs and rolled up to keep them from the ground, the waist of the coat below his haunches, and the collar sprawling wide upon his shoulders. Strange to relate, this ludicrous accoutrement was far from moving me to laughter. Rather, as there was something abnormal and misbegotten in the very essence of the creature that now faced me—something seizing,[2] surpris-

---

9. Sliding door of his lantern.
1. Sudden chill.

2. Powerfully impressive.

ing and revolting—this fresh disparity seemed but to fit in with and to reinforce it; so that to my interest in the man's nature and character, there was added a curiosity as to his origin, his life, his fortune and status in the world.

These observations, though they have taken so great a space to be set down in, were yet the work of a few seconds. My visitor was, indeed, on fire with sombre excitement.

"Have you got it?" he cried. "Have you got it?" And so lively was his impatience that he even laid his hand upon my arm and sought to shake me.

I put him back, conscious at his touch of a certain icy pang along my blood. "Come, sir," said I. "You forget that I have not yet the pleasure of your acquaintance. Be seated, if you please." And I showed him an example, and sat down myself in my customary seat and with as fair an imitation of my ordinary manner to a patient, as the lateness of the hour, the nature of my preoccupations, and the horror I had of my visitor, would suffer me to muster.

"I beg your pardon, Dr. Lanyon," he replied civilly enough. "What you say is very well founded; and my impatience has shown its heels to my politeness. I come here at the instance[3] of your colleague, Dr. Henry Jekyll, on a piece of business of some moment; and I understood . . ." He paused and put his hand to his throat, and I could see, in spite of his collected manner, that he was wrestling against the approaches of the hysteria—"I understood, a drawer . . ."

But here I took pity on my visitor's suspense, and some perhaps on my own growing curiosity.

"There it is, sir," said I, pointing to the drawer, where it lay on the floor behind a table and still covered with the sheet.

He sprang to it, and then paused, and laid his hand upon his heart: I could hear his teeth grate with the convulsive action of his jaws; and his face was so ghastly to see that I grew alarmed both for his life and reason.

"Compose yourself," said I.

He turned a dreadful smile to me, and as if with the decision of despair, plucked away the sheet. At sight of the contents, he uttered one loud sob of such immense relief that I sat petrified. And the next moment, in a voice that was already fairly well under control, "Have you a graduated[4] glass?" he asked.

I rose from my place with something of an effort and gave him what he asked.

He thanked me with a smiling nod, measured out a few minims[5] of the red tincture and added one of the powders. The mixture, which was at first of a reddish hue, began, in proportion as the crystals melted, to brighten in colour, to effervesce audibly, and to throw off small fumes of vapour. Suddenly and at the same moment, the ebullition[6] ceased and the compound changed to a dark purple, which faded again more slowly to a watery green. My visitor, who had watched these metamorphoses with a keen eye, smiled, set down the glass upon the table, and then turned and looked upon me with an air of scrutiny.

"And now," said he, "to settle what remains. Will you be wise? will you be guided? will you suffer me to take this glass in my hand and to go forth from

---

3. Request.
4. Marked with lines to indicate quantities.
5. Drops (a minim is a liquid measure equal to

1/480th of an ounce).
6. Bubbling.

your house without further parley? or has the greed of curiosity too much command of you? Think before you answer, for it shall be done as you decide. As you decide, you shall be left as you were before, and neither richer nor wiser, unless the sense of service rendered to a man in mortal distress may be counted as a kind of riches of the soul. Or, if you shall so prefer to choose, a new province of knowledge and new avenues to fame and power shall be laid open to you, here, in this room, upon the instant; and your sight shall be blasted by a prodigy to stagger the unbelief of Satan."

"Sir," said I, affecting a coolness that I was far from truly possessing, "you speak enigmas, and you will perhaps not wonder that I hear you with no very strong impression of belief. But I have gone too far in the way of inexplicable services to pause before I see the end."

"It is well," replied my visitor. "Lanyon, you remember your vows: what follows is under the seal of our profession. And now, you who have so long been bound to the most narrow and material views, you who have denied the virtue of transcendental medicine, you who have derided your superiors—behold!"

He put the glass to his lips and drank at one gulp. A cry followed; he reeled, staggered, clutched at the table and held on, staring with injected[7] eyes, gasping with open mouth; and as I looked there came, I thought, a change—he seemed to swell—his face became suddenly black and the features seemed to melt and alter—and the next moment, I had sprung to my feet and leaped back against the wall, my arm raised to shield me from that prodigy, my mind submerged in terror.

"O God!" I screamed, and "O God!" again and again; for there before my eyes—pale and shaken, and half fainting, and groping before him with his hands, like a man restored from death—there stood Henry Jekyll!

What he told me in the next hour, I cannot bring my mind to set on paper. I saw what I saw, I heard what I heard, and my soul sickened at it; and yet now when that sight has faded from my eyes, I ask myself if I believe it, and I cannot answer. My life is shaken to its roots; sleep has left me; the deadliest terror sits by me at all hours of the day and night; I feel that my days are numbered, and that I must die; and yet I shall die incredulous. As for the moral turpitude that man unveiled to me, even with tears of penitence, I cannot, even in memory, dwell on it without a start of horror. I will say but one thing, Utterson, and that (if you can bring your mind to credit it) will be more than enough. The creature who crept into my house that night was, on Jekyll's own confession, known by the name of Hyde and hunted for in every corner of the land as the murderer of Carew.

HASTIE LANYON.

Henry Jekyll's Full Statement of the Case

I was born in the year 18—to a large fortune, endowed besides with excellent parts,[8] inclined by nature to industry, fond of the respect of the wise and good among my fellow-men, and thus, as might have been supposed, with every guarantee of an honourable and distinguished future. And indeed the worst of my faults was a certain impatient gaiety of disposition, such as

7. Swollen.   8. Abilities.

has made the happiness of many, but such as I found it hard to reconcile with my imperious desire to carry my head high, and wear a more than commonly grave countenance before the public. Hence it came about that I concealed my pleasures; and that when I reached years of reflection, and began to look round me and take stock of my progress and position in the world, I stood already committed to a profound duplicity of life. Many a man would have even blazoned such irregularities as I was guilty of; but from the high views that I had set before me, I regarded and hid them with an almost morbid sense of shame. It was thus rather the exacting nature of my aspirations than any particular degradation in my faults, that made me what I was, and, with even a deeper trench than in the majority of men, severed in me those provinces of good and ill which divide and compound man's dual nature. In this case, I was driven to reflect deeply and inveterately on that hard law of life, which lies at the root of religion and is one of the most plentiful springs of distress. Though so profound a double-dealer, I was in no sense a hypocrite; both sides of me were in dead earnest; I was no more myself when I laid aside restraint and plunged in shame, than when I laboured, in the eye of day, at the furtherance of knowledge or the relief of sorrow and suffering. And it chanced that the direction of my scientific studies, which led wholly towards the mystic and the transcendental, reacted and shed a strong light on this consciousness of the perennial war among my members. With every day, and from both sides of my intelligence, the moral and the intellectual, I thus drew steadily nearer to that truth, by whose partial discovery I have been doomed to such a dreadful shipwreck: that man is not truly one, but truly two. I say two, because the state of my own knowledge does not pass beyond that point. Others will follow, others will outstrip me on the same lines; and I hazard the guess that man will be ultimately known for a mere polity of multifarious, incongruous and independent denizens. I for my part, from the nature of my life, advanced infallibly in one direction and in one direction only. It was on the moral side, and in my own person, that I learned to recognise the thorough and primitive duality of man; I saw that, of the two natures that contended in the field of my consciousness, even if I could rightly be said to be either, it was only because I was radically both; and from an early date, even before the course of my scientific discoveries had begun to suggest the most naked possibility of such a miracle, I had learned to dwell with pleasure, as a beloved day-dream, on the thought of the separation of these elements. If each, I told myself, could but be housed in separate identities, life would be relieved of all that was unbearable; the unjust might go his way, delivered from the aspirations and remorse of his more upright twin; and the just could walk steadfastly and securely on his upward path, doing the good things in which he found his pleasure, and no longer exposed to disgrace and penitence by the hands of this extraneous evil. It was the curse of mankind that these incongruous faggots[9] were thus bound together—that in the agonised womb of consciousness, these polar twins should be continuously struggling. How, then, were they dissociated?

I was so far in my reflections when, as I have said, a side light began to shine upon the subject from the laboratory table. I began to perceive more deeply than it has ever yet been stated, the trembling immateriality, the mist-

---

9. Bundles of sticks used for fuel.

like transience, of this seemingly so solid body in which we walk attired. Certain agents I found to have the power to shake and to pluck back that fleshly vestment, even as a wind might toss the curtains of a pavilion. For two good reasons, I will not enter deeply into this scientific branch of my confession. First, because I have been made to learn that the doom and burthen of our life is bound forever on man's shoulders, and when the attempt is made to cast it off, it but returns upon us with more unfamiliar and more awful pressure. Second, because, as my narrative will make, alas! too evident, my discoveries were incomplete. Enough, then, that I not only recognised my natural body for the mere aura and effulgence of certain of the powers that made up my spirit, but managed to compound a drug by which these powers should be dethroned from their supremacy, and a second form and countenance substituted, none the less natural to me because they were the expression, and bore the stamp, of lower elements in my soul.

I hesitated long before I put this theory to the test of practice. I knew well that I risked death; for any drug that so potently controlled and shook the very fortress of identity, might by the least scruple[1] of an overdose or at the least inopportunity in the moment of exhibition, utterly blot out that immaterial tabernacle which I looked to it to change. But the temptation of a discovery so singular and profound, at last overcame the suggestions of alarm. I had long since prepared my tincture; I purchased at once, from a firm of wholesale chemists, a large quantity of a particular salt which I knew, from my experiments, to be the last ingredient required; and late one accursed night, I compounded the elements, watched them boil and smoke together in the glass, and when the ebullition had subsided, with a strong glow of courage, drank off the potion.

The most racking pangs succeeded: a grinding in the bones, deadly nausea, and a horror of the spirit that cannot be exceeded at the hour of birth or death. Then these agonies began swiftly to subside, and I came to myself as if out of a great sickness. There was something strange in my sensations, something indescribably new and, from its very novelty, incredibly sweet. I felt younger, lighter, happier in body; within I was conscious of a heady recklessness, a current of disordered sensual images running like a mill race[2] in my fancy, a solution of the bonds of obligation, an unknown but not an innocent freedom of the soul. I knew myself, at the first breath of this new life, to be more wicked, tenfold more wicked, sold a slave to my original evil; and the thought, in that moment, braced and delighted me like wine. I stretched out my hands, exulting in the freshness of these sensations; and in the act, I was suddenly aware that I had lost in stature.

There was no mirror, at that date, in my room; that which stands beside me as I write, was brought there later on and for the very purpose of these transformations. The night, however, was far gone into the morning—the morning, black as it was, was nearly ripe for the conception of the day—the inmates of my house were locked in the most rigorous hours of slumber; and I determined, flushed as I was with hope and triumph, to venture in my new shape as far as to my bedroom. I crossed the yard, wherein the constellations looked down upon me, I could have thought, with wonder, the first creature of that sort that their unsleeping vigilance had yet disclosed to them; I stole

1. A minute amount (literally, an apothecaries' weight equal to about 1.3 grams). 2. Water current that drives a mill wheel.

through the corridors, a stranger in my own house; and coming to my room, I saw for the first time the appearance of Edward Hyde.

I must here speak by theory alone, saying not that which I know, but that which I suppose to be most probable. The evil side of my nature, to which I had now transferred the stamping efficacy, was less robust and less developed than the good which I had just deposed. Again, in the course of my life, which had been, after all, nine-tenths a life of effort, virtue and control, it had been much less exercised and much less exhausted. And hence, as I think, it came about that Edward Hyde was so much smaller, slighter and younger than Henry Jekyll. Even as good shone upon the countenance of the one, evil was written broadly and plainly on the face of the other. Evil besides (which I must still believe to be the lethal side of man) had left on that body an imprint of deformity and decay. And yet when I looked upon that ugly idol in the glass, I was conscious of no repugnance, rather of a leap of welcome. This, too, was myself. It seemed natural and human. In my eyes it bore a livelier image of the spirit, it seemed more express and single, than the imperfect and divided countenance I had been hitherto accustomed to call mine. And in so far I was doubtless right. I have observed that when I wore the semblance of Edward Hyde, none could come near to me at first without a visible misgiving of the flesh. This, as I take it, was because all human beings, as we meet them, are commingled out of good and evil: and Edward Hyde, alone in the ranks of mankind, was pure evil.

I lingered but a moment at the mirror: the second and conclusive experiment had yet to be attempted; it yet remained to be seen if I had lost my identity beyond redemption and must flee before daylight from a house that was no longer mine; and hurrying back to my cabinet, I once more prepared and drank the cup, once more suffered the pangs of dissolution, and came to myself once more with the character, the stature and the face of Henry Jekyll.

That night I had come to the fatal cross roads. Had I approached my discovery in a more noble spirit, had I risked the experiment while under the empire of generous or pious aspirations, all must have been otherwise, and from these agonies of death and birth, I had come forth an angel instead of a fiend. The drug had no discriminating action; it was neither diabolical nor divine; it but shook the doors of the prison-house of my disposition; and like the captives of Philippi, that which stood within ran forth.[3] At that time my virtue slumbered; my evil, kept awake by ambition, was alert and swift to seize the occasion; and the thing that was projected was Edward Hyde. Hence, although I had now two characters as well as two appearances, one was wholly evil, and the other was still the old Henry Jekyll, that incongruous compound of whose reformation and improvement I had already learned to despair. The movement was thus wholly towards the worse.

Even at that time, I had not yet conquered my aversion to the dryness of a life of study. I would still be merrily disposed at times; and as my pleasures were (to say the least) undignified, and I was not only well known and highly considered, but growing towards the elderly man, this incoherency of my life was daily growing more unwelcome. It was on this side that my new power tempted me until I fell in slavery. I had but to drink the cup, to doff at once

3. Cf. Acts 16.26: when the apostle Paul and his friend Silas were imprisoned at Philippi, a city in eastern Macedonia, an earthquake freed all the prisoners (none of whom fled).

the body of the noted professor, and to assume, like a thick cloak, that of Edward Hyde. I smiled at the notion; it seemed to me at the time to be humorous; and I made my preparations with the most studious care. I took and furnished that house in Soho, to which Hyde was tracked by the police; and engaged as housekeeper a creature whom I well knew to be silent and unscrupulous. On the other side, I announced to my servants that a Mr. Hyde (whom I described) was to have full liberty and power about my house in the square; and to parry mishaps, I even called and made myself a familiar object, in my second character. I next drew up that will to which you so much objected; so that if anything befell me in the person of Dr. Jekyll, I could enter on that of Edward Hyde without pecuniary loss. And thus fortified, as I supposed, on every side, I began to profit by the strange immunities of my position.

Men have before hired bravos[4] to transact their crimes, while their own person and reputation sat under shelter. I was the first that ever did so for his pleasures. I was the first that could thus plod in the public eye with a load of genial respectability, and in a moment, like a schoolboy, strip off these lendings[5] and spring headlong into the sea of liberty. But for me, in my impenetrable mantle, the safety was complete. Think of it—I did not even exist! Let me but escape into my laboratory door, give me but a second or two to mix and swallow the draught that I had always standing ready; and whatever he had done, Edward Hyde would pass away like the stain of breath upon a mirror; and there in his stead, quietly at home, trimming the midnight lamp in his study, a man who could afford to laugh at suspicion, would be Henry Jekyll.

The pleasures which I made haste to seek in my disguise were, as I have said, undignified; I would scarce use a harder term. But in the hands of Edward Hyde, they soon began to turn towards the monstrous. When I would come back from these excursions, I was often plunged into a kind of wonder at my vicarious depravity. This familiar[6] that I called out of my own soul, and sent forth alone to do his good pleasure, was a being inherently malign and villainous; his every act and thought centered on self; drinking pleasure with bestial avidity from any degree of torture to another; relentless like a man of stone. Henry Jekyll stood at times aghast before the acts of Edward Hyde; but the situation was apart from ordinary laws, and insidiously relaxed the grasp of conscience. It was Hyde, after all, and Hyde alone, that was guilty. Jekyll was no worse; he woke again to his good qualities seemingly unimpaired; he would even make haste, where it was possible, to undo the evil done by Hyde. And thus his conscience slumbered.

Into the details of the infamy at which I thus connived (for even now I can scarce grant that I committed it) I have no design of entering; I mean but to point out the warnings and the successive steps with which my chastisement approached. I met with one accident which, as it brought on no consequence, I shall no more than mention. An act of cruelty to a child aroused against me the anger of a passer-by, whom I recognised the other day in the person of your kinsman; the doctor and the child's family joined him; there were moments when I feared for my life; and at last, in order to pacify

---

4. Thugs.
5. Borrowed clothing; a reference to King Lear's cry on the heath, "Off, off you lendings!" (Shakespeare, *King Lear* 3.4.97).
6. Spirit or demon.

their too just resentment, Edward Hyde had to bring them to the door, and pay them in a cheque drawn in the name of Henry Jekyll. But this danger was easily eliminated from the future, by opening an account at another bank in the name of Edward Hyde himself; and when, by sloping my own hand backward, I had supplied my double with a signature, I thought I sat beyond the reach of fate.

Some two months before the murder of Sir Danvers, I had been out for one of my adventures, had returned at a late hour, and woke the next day in bed with somewhat odd sensations. It was in vain I looked about me; in vain I saw the decent furniture and tall proportions of my room in the square; in vain that I recognised the pattern of the bed curtains and the design of the mahogany frame; something still kept insisting that I was not where I was, that I had not wakened where I seemed to be, but in the little room in Soho where I was accustomed to sleep in the body of Edward Hyde. I smiled to myself, and, in my psychological way began lazily to inquire into the elements of this illusion, occasionally, even as I did so, dropping back into a comfortable morning doze. I was still so engaged when, in one of my more wakeful moments, my eyes fell upon my hand. Now the hand of Henry Jekyll (as you have often remarked) was professional in shape and size: it was large, firm, white and comely. But the hand which I now saw, clearly enough, in the yellow light of a mid-London morning, lying half shut on the bed clothes, was lean, corded, knuckly, of a dusky pallor and thickly shaded with a swart[7] growth of hair. It was the hand of Edward Hyde.

I must have stared upon it for near half a minute, sunk as I was in the mere stupidity of wonder, before terror woke up in my breast as sudden and startling as the crash of cymbals; and bounding from my bed, I rushed to the mirror. At the sight that met my eyes, my blood was changed into something exquisitely thin and icy. Yes, I had gone to bed Henry Jekyll, I had awakened Edward Hyde. How was this to be explained? I asked myself; and then, with another bound of terror—how was it to be remedied? It was well on in the morning; the servants were up; all my drugs were in the cabinet—a long journey down two pair of stairs, through the back passage, across the open court and through the anatomical theatre, from where I was then standing horror-struck. It might indeed be possible to cover my face; but of what use was that, when I was unable to conceal the alteration in my stature? And then with an overpowering sweetness of relief, it came back upon my mind that the servants were already used to the coming and going of my second self. I had soon dressed, as well as I was able, in clothes of my own size: had soon passed through the house, where Bradshaw stared and drew back at seeing Mr. Hyde at such an hour and in such a strange array; and ten minutes later, Dr. Jekyll had returned to his own shape and was sitting down, with a darkened brow, to make a feint of breakfasting.

Small indeed was my appetite. This inexplicable incident, this reversal of my previous experience, seemed, like the Babylonian finger on the wall,[8] to be spelling out the letters of my judgment; and I began to reflect more seriously than ever before on the issues and possibilities of my double existence. That part of me which I had the power of projecting, had lately been much exercised and nourished; it had seemed to me of late as though the

---

7. Dark.
8. In Daniel 5.5–31; the writing foretold the overthrow of Belshazzar, the Babylonian king, because of his transgressions against the Lord.

body of Edward Hyde had grown in stature, as though (when I wore that form) I were conscious of a more generous tide of blood; and I began to spy a danger that, if this were much prolonged, the balance of my nature might be permanently overthrown, the power of voluntary change be forfeited, and the character of Edward Hyde become irrevocably mine. The power of the drug had not been always equally displayed. Once, very early in my career, it had totally failed me; since then I had been obliged on more than one occasion to double, and once, with infinite risk of death, to treble the amount; and these rare uncertainties had cast hitherto the sole shadow on my contentment. Now, however, and in the light of that morning's accident, I was led to remark that whereas, in the beginning, the difficulty had been to throw off the body of Jekyll, it had of late gradually but decidedly transferred itself to the other side. All things therefore seemed to point to this: that I was slowly losing hold of my original and better self, and becoming slowly incorporated with my second and worse.

Between these two, I now felt I had to choose. My two natures had memory in common, but all other faculties were most unequally shared between them. Jekyll (who was composite) now with the most sensitive apprehensions, now with a greedy gusto, projected and shared in the pleasures and adventures of Hyde; but Hyde was indifferent to Jekyll, or but remembered him as the mountain bandit remembers the cavern in which he conceals himself from pursuit. Jekyll had more than a father's interest; Hyde had more than a son's indifference. To cast in my lot with Jekyll, was to die to those appetites which I had long secretly indulged and had of late begun to pamper. To cast it in with Hyde, was to die to a thousand interests and aspirations, and to become, at a blow and forever, despised and friendless. The bargain might appear unequal; but there was still another consideration in the scales; for while Jekyll would suffer smartingly in the fires of abstinence, Hyde would be not even conscious of all that he had lost. Strange as my circumstances were, the terms of this debate are as old and commonplace as man; much the same inducements and alarms cast the die for any tempted and trembling sinner; and it fell out with me, as it falls with so vast a majority of my fellows, that I chose the better part and was found wanting in the strength to keep to it.

Yes, I preferred the elderly and discontented doctor, surrounded by friends and cherishing honest hopes; and bade a resolute farewell to the liberty, the comparative youth, the light step, leaping impulses and secret pleasures, that I had enjoyed in the disguise of Hyde. I made this choice perhaps with some unconscious reservation, for I neither gave up the house in Soho, nor destroyed the clothes of Edward Hyde, which still lay ready in my cabinet. For two months, however, I was true to my determination; for two months I led a life of such severity as I had never before attained to, and enjoyed the compensations of an approving conscience. But time began at last to obliterate the freshness of my alarm; the praises of conscience began to grow into a thing of course; I began to be tortured with throes and longings, as of Hyde struggling after freedom; and at last, in an hour of moral weakness, I once again compounded and swallowed the transforming draught.

I do not suppose that, when a drunkard reasons with himself upon his vice, he is once out of five hundred times affected by the dangers that he runs through his brutish, physical insensibility; neither had I, long as I had considered my position, made enough allowance for the complete moral insensibility and insensate readiness to evil, which were the leading characters of Edward Hyde. Yet it was by these that I was punished. My devil had been long caged, he came out roaring. I was conscious, even when I took the draught, of a more unbridled, a more furious propensity to ill. It must have been this, I suppose, that stirred in my soul that tempest of impatience with which I listened to the civilities of my unhappy victim; I declare, at least, before God, no man morally sane could have been guilty of that crime upon so pitiful a provocation; and that I struck in no more reasonable spirit than that in which a sick child may break a plaything. But I had voluntarily stripped myself of all those balancing instincts by which even the worst of us continues to walk with some degree of steadiness among temptations; and in my case, to be tempted, however slightly, was to fall.

Instantly the spirit of hell awoke in me and raged. With a transport of glee, I mauled the unresisting body, tasting delight from every blow; and it was not till weariness had begun to succeed, that I was suddenly, in the top fit of my delirium, struck through the heart by a cold thrill of terror. A mist dispersed; I saw my life to be forfeit; and fled from the scene of these excesses, at once glorifying and trembling, my lust of evil gratified and stimulated, my love of life screwed to the topmost peg.[9] I ran to the house in Soho, and (to make assurance doubly sure) destroyed my papers; thence I set out through the lamplit streets, in the same divided ecstasy of mind, gloating on my crime, light-headedly devising others in the future, and yet still hastening and still hearkening in my wake for the steps of the avenger. Hyde had a song upon his lips as he compounded the draught, and as he drank it, pledged[1] the dead man. The pangs of transformation had not done tearing him, before Henry Jekyll, with streaming tears of gratitude and remorse, had fallen upon his knees and lifted his clasped hands to God. The veil of self-indulgence was rent from head to foot.[2] I saw my life as a whole: I followed it up from the days of childhood, when I had walked with my father's hand, and through the self-denying toils of my professional life, to arrive again and again, with the same sense of unreality, at the damned horrors of the evening. I could have screamed aloud; I sought with tears and prayers to smother down the crowd of hideous images and sounds with which my memory swarmed against me; and still, between the petitions, the ugly face of my iniquity stared into my soul. As the acuteness of this remorse began to die away, it was succeeded by a sense of joy. The problem of my conduct was solved. Hyde was thenceforth impossible; whether I would or not, I was now confined to the better part of my existence; and O, how I rejoiced to think it! with what willing humility, I embraced anew the restrictions of natural life! with what sincere renunciation, I locked the door by which I had so often gone and come, and ground the key under my heel!

The next day, came the news that the murder had been overlooked,[3] that the guilt of Hyde was patent to the world, and that the victim was a man high in public estimation. It was not only a crime, it had been a tragic folly. I think I was glad to know it; I think I was glad to have my better impulses thus buttressed and guarded by the terrors of the scaffold. Jekyll was now my city

9. Strained to the highest point.
1. Drank a toast to.
2. See Matthew 27.51: "the veil of the temple was rent in twain, from the top to the bottom."
3. Seen from above.

of refuge; let but Hyde peep out an instant, and the hands of all men would be raised to take and slay him.

I resolved in my future conduct to redeem the past; and I can say with honesty that my resolve was fruitful of some good. You know yourself how earnestly in the last months of last year, I laboured to relieve suffering; you know that much was done for others, and that the days passed quietly, almost happily for myself. Nor can I truly say that I wearied of this beneficent and innocent life; I think instead that I daily enjoyed it more completely; but I was still cursed with my duality of purpose; and as the first edge of my penitence wore off, the lower side of me, so long indulged, so recently chained down, began to growl for license. Not that I dreamed of resuscitating Hyde; the bare idea of that would startle me to frenzy: no, it was in my own person, that I was once more tempted to trifle with my conscience; and it was as an ordinary secret sinner, that I at last fell before the assaults of temptation.

There comes an end to all things; the most capacious measure is filled at last; and this brief condescension to my evil finally destroyed the balance of my soul. And yet I was not alarmed; the fall seemed natural, like a return to the old days before I had made my discovery. It was a fine, clear, January day, wet under foot where the frost had melted, but cloudless overhead; and the Regent's Park[4] was full of winter chirrupings and sweet with spring odours. I sat in the sun on a bench; the animal within me licking the chops of memory; the spiritual side a little drowsed, promising subsequent penitence, but not yet moved to begin. After all, I reflected, I was like my neighbours; and then I smiled, comparing myself with other men, comparing my active goodwill with the lazy cruelty of their neglect. And at the very moment of that vain-glorious thought, a qualm came over me, a horrid nausea and the most deadly shuddering. These passed away, and left me faint; and then as in its turn the faintness subsided, I began to be aware of a change in the temper of my thoughts, a greater boldness, a contempt of danger, a solution of the bonds of obligation. I looked down; my clothes hung formlessly on my shrunken limbs; the hand that lay on my knee was corded and hairy. I was once more Edward Hyde. A moment before I had been safe of all men's respect, wealthy, beloved—the cloth laying for me in the dining-room at home; and now I was the common quarry of mankind, hunted, houseless, a known murderer, thrall to the gallows.

My reason wavered, but it did not fail me utterly. I have more than once observed that, in my second character, my faculties seemed sharpened to a point and my spirits more tensely elastic; thus it came about that, where Jekyll perhaps might have succumbed, Hyde rose to the importance of the moment. My drugs were in one of the presses of my cabinet; how was I to reach them? That was the problem that (crushing my temples in my hands) I set myself to solve. The laboratory door I had closed. If I sought to enter by the house, my own servants would consign me to the gallows. I saw I must employ another hand, and thought of Lanyon. How was he to be reached? how persuaded? Supposing that I escaped capture in the streets, how was I to make my way into his presence? and how should I, an unknown and displeasing visitor, prevail on the famous physician to rifle the study of his colleague, Dr. Jekyll? Then I remembered that of my original character, one

4. A large park in northwest London.

part remained to me: I could write my own hand; and once I had conceived that kindling spark, the way that I must follow became lighted up from end to end.

Thereupon, I arranged my clothes as best I could, and summoning a passing hansom, drove to an hotel in Portland Street, the name of which I chanced to remember. At my appearance (which was indeed comical enough, however tragic a fate these garments covered) the driver could not conceal his mirth. I gnashed my teeth upon him with a gust of devilish fury; and the smile withered from his face—happily for him—yet more happily for myself, for in another instant I had certainly dragged him from his perch. At the inn, as I entered, I looked about me with so black a countenance as made the attendants tremble; not a look did they exchange in my presence; but obsequiously took my orders, led me to a private room, and brought me wherewithal to write. Hyde in danger of his life was a creature new to me; shaken with inordinate anger, strung to the pitch of murder, lusting to inflict pain. Yet the creature was astute; mastered his fury with a great effort of the will; composed his two important letters, one to Lanyon and one to Poole; and that he might receive actual evidence of their being posted, sent them out with directions that they should be registered.

Thenceforward, he sat all day over the fire in the private room, gnawing his nails; there he dined, sitting alone with his fears, the waiter visibly quailing before his eye; and thence, when the night was fully come, he set forth in the corner of a closed cab, and was driven to and fro about the streets of the city. He, I say—I cannot say, I. That child of Hell had nothing human; nothing lived in him but fear and hatred. And when at last, thinking the driver had begun to grow suspicious, he discharged the cab and ventured on foot, attired in his misfitting clothes, an object marked out for observation, into the midst of the nocturnal passengers, these two base passions raged within him like a tempest. He walked fast, hunted by his fears, chattering to himself, skulking through the less frequented thoroughfares, counting the minutes that still divided him from midnight. Once a woman spoke to him, offering, I think, a box of lights.[5] He smote her in the face, and she fled.

When I came to myself at Lanyon's, the horror of my old friend perhaps affected me somewhat: I do not know; it was at least but a drop in the sea to the abhorrence with which I looked back upon these hours. A change had come over me. It was no longer the fear of the gallows, it was the horror of being Hyde that racked me. I received Lanyon's condemnation partly in a dream; it was partly in a dream that I came home to my own house and got into bed. I slept after the prostration of the day, with a stringent and profound slumber which not even the nightmares that wrung me could avail to break. I awoke in the morning shaken, weakened, but refreshed. I still hated and feared the thought of the brute that slept within me, and I had not of course forgotten the appalling dangers of the day before; but I was once more at home, in my own house and close to my drugs; and gratitude for my escape shone so strong in my soul that it almost rivalled the brightness of hope.

I was stepping leisurely across the court after breakfast, drinking the chill of the air with pleasure, when I was seized again with those indescribable sensations that heralded the change; and I had but the time to gain the shelter of my cabinet, before I was once again raging and freezing with

5. Matches.

the passions of Hyde. It took on this occasion a double dose to recall me to myself; and alas! six hours after, as I sat looking sadly in the fire, the pangs returned, and the drug had to be re-administered. In short, from that day forth it seemed only by a great effort as of gymnastics, and only under the immediate stimulation of the drug, that I was able to wear the countenance of Jekyll. At all hours of the day and night, I would be taken with the premonitory shudder; above all, if I slept, or even dozed for a moment in my chair, it was always as Hyde that I awakened. Under the strain of this continually impending doom and by the sleeplessness to which I now condemned myself, ay, even beyond what I had thought possible to man, I became, in my own person, a creature eaten up and emptied by fever, languidly weak both in body and mind, and solely occupied by one thought: the horror of my other self. But when I slept, or when the virtue of the medicine wore off, I would leap almost without transition (for the pangs of transformation grew daily less marked) into the possession of a fancy brimming with images of terror, a soul boiling with causeless hatreds, and a body that seemed not strong enough to contain the raging energies of life. The powers of Hyde seemed to have grown with the sickliness of Jekyll. And certainly the hate that now divided them was equal on each side. With Jekyll, it was a thing of vital instinct. He had now seen the full deformity of that creature that shared with him some of the phenomena of consciousness, and was co-heir with him to death: and beyond these links of community, which in themselves made the most poignant part of his distress, he thought of Hyde, for all his energy of life, as of something not only hellish but inorganic. This was the shocking thing; that the slime of the pit seemed to utter cries and voices; that the amorphous dust gesticulated and sinned; that what was dead, and had no shape, should usurp the offices of life. And this again, that that insurgent horror was knit to him closer than a wife, closer than an eye; lay caged in his flesh, where he heard it mutter and felt it struggle to be born; and at every hour of weakness, and in the confidence of slumber, prevailed against him, and deposed him out of life. The hatred of Hyde for Jekyll, was of a different order. His terror of the gallows drove him continually to commit temporary suicide, and return to his subordinate station of a part instead of a person; but he loathed the necessity, he loathed the despondency into which Jekyll was now fallen, and he resented the dislike with which he was himself regarded. Hence the apelike tricks that he would play me, scrawling in my own hand blasphemies on the pages of my books, burning the letters and destroying the portrait of my father; and indeed, had it not been for his fear of death, he would long ago have ruined himself in order to involve me in the ruin. But his love of life is wonderful; I go further: I, who sicken and freeze at the mere thought of him, when I recall the abjection and passion of this attachment, and when I know how he fears my power to cut him off by suicide, I find it in my heart to pity him.

It is useless, and the time awfully fails me, to prolong this description; no one has ever suffered such torments, let that suffice; and yet even to these, habit brought—no, not alleviation—but a certain callousness of soul, a certain acquiescence of despair; and my punishment might have gone on for years, but for the last calamity which has now fallen, and which has finally severed me from my own face and nature. My provision of the salt, which had never been renewed since the date of the first experiment, began to run low. I sent out for a fresh supply, and mixed the draught; the ebullition followed, and the first change of colour, not the second; I drank it and it was without efficiency. You will learn from Poole how I have had London ransacked; it was in vain; and I am now persuaded that my first supply was impure, and that it was that unknown impurity which lent efficacy to the draught.

About a week has passed, and I am now finishing this statement under the influence of the last of the old powders. This, then, is the last time, short of a miracle, that Henry Jekyll can think his own thoughts or see his own face (now how sadly altered!) in the glass. Nor must I delay too long to bring my writing to an end; for if my narrative has hitherto escaped destruction, it has been by a combination of great prudence and great good luck. Should the throes of change take me in the act of writing it, Hyde will tear it in pieces; but if some time shall have elapsed after I have laid it by, his wonderful self-ishness and circumscription to the moment will probably save it once again from the action of his apelike spite. And indeed the doom that is closing on us both, has already changed and crushed him. Half an hour from now, when I shall again and forever reindue[6] that hated personality, I know how I shall sit shuddering and weeping in my chair, or continue, with the most strained and fearstruck ecstasy of listening, to pace up and down this room (my last earthly refuge) and give ear to every sound of menace. Will Hyde die upon the scaffold? or will he find courage to release himself at the last moment? God knows; I am careless;[7] this is my true hour of death, and what is to follow concerns another than myself. Here then, as I lay down the pen and proceed to seal up my confession, I bring the life of that unhappy Henry Jekyll to an end.

1885   1886

6. Put on again.   7. Indifferent.

OSCAR WILDE
1854–1900

In Oscar Wilde's comedy *The Importance of Being Earnest* (1895) Jack Worthing claims to have received a telegram about the death of his (imaginary) rakish brother Ernest in a Paris hotel. Five years later Wilde died in a hotel in Paris, where he was living in exile. The coincidence seems a curious paradigm of Wilde's career, for the connections between his life and his art were unusually close. Indeed, in his last years he told André Gide that he seemed to have put his genius into his life and only his talent into his writings.

His father, Sir William, was a distinguished surgeon in Dublin, where Wilde was born and grew up. After studying classics at Trinity College, Dublin, he won a scholarship to Oxford and there established a brilliant academic record. At Oxford he came under the influence of the aesthetic theories of John Ruskin (who was at the time professor of fine arts) and, more important, of Walter Pater. With characteristic hyperbole Wilde affirmed of Pater's *Studies in the History of the Renaissance* (1873):

Salome. Oscar Wilde asked Aubrey Beardsley (1872–1898) to illustrate the English translation of his play *Salome* (1894; the original version of the play [1891] was in French); this image is entitled "Climax."

"It is my golden book; I never travel anywhere without it. But it is the very flower of decadence; the last trumpet should have sounded the moment it was written."

After graduating in 1878, Wilde moved to London, where his fellow Irishmen Bernard Shaw and William Butler Yeats were also to settle. Here Wilde quickly established himself both as a writer and as a spokesperson for the school of "art for art's sake." In Wilde's view this school included not only French poets and critics but also a line of English poets going back through Dante Gabriel Rossetti and the Pre-Raphaelites to John Keats. In 1882 he visited America for a long (and successful) lecture tour, during which he startled audiences by airing the gospel of the "aesthetic movement." In one of these lectures, he asserted that "to disagree with three fourths of all England on all points of view is one of the first elements of sanity."

For his role as a spokesperson for aestheticism, Wilde had many gifts. From all accounts he was a dazzling conversationalist. Yeats reported, after first listening to him: "I never before heard a man talking with perfect sentences, as if he had written them all overnight with labour and yet all spontaneous." Wilde delighted his listeners not only by his polished wordplay but also by uttering opinions that were both outrageous and incongruous—for example, his solemn affirmation that Queen Victoria was one of the three women he most admired and whom he would have married "with pleasure" (the other two were the actress Sarah Bernhardt and Lillie Langtry, reputedly a mistress of Victoria's son Edward, Prince of Wales).

In addition to his mastery of witty conversation, Wilde had the gifts of an actor who delights in gaining attention. Pater had been a very shy and reticent man, but there was nothing reticent about his disciple, who had early discovered that a flamboyant style of dress was one of the most effective means of gaining attention. Like the dandies of the earlier decades of the nineteenth century (including Benjamin Disraeli and Charles Dickens), Wilde favored colorful costumes in marked contrast to the sober black suits of the late-Victorian middle classes. A green carnation in his buttonhole and velvet knee breeches became for Wilde badges of his youthful iconoclasm; and even when he approached middle age, he continued to emphasize the gap between generations. In a letter written when he was forty-two years old, he remarks: "The opinions of the old on matters of Art are, of course, of no value whatever."

Wilde's campaign quickly gained an amused response from middle-class quarters. In 1881 W. S. Gilbert and Sir Arthur Sullivan staged their comic opera *Patience*, which mocked the affectations of the aesthetes in the character of Bunthorne, especially in his song "If You're Anxious for to Shine in the High Aesthetic Line."

Wilde's successes for seventeen years in England and America were, of course, not limited to his self-advertising stunts as a dandy. In his writings he excelled in a variety of genres: as a critic of literature and of society (*The Decay of Lying*, 1889, and *The Soul of Man under Socialism*, 1891) and also as a novelist, poet, and dramatist. Much of his prose, including *The Critic as Artist* (1890), develops Pater's aestheticism, particularly its sense of the superiority of art to life and its lack of obligation to any standards of mimesis. His novel *The Picture of Dorian Gray*, which created a sensation when it was published in 1891, takes a somewhat different perspective. The novel is a strikingly ingenious story of a handsome young man and his selfish pursuit of sensual pleasures. Until the end of the book he remains fresh and healthy in appearance while his portrait mysteriously changes into a horrible image of his corrupted soul. Although the preface to the novel (reprinted here) emphasizes that art and morality are totally separate, in the novel, at least in its later chapters, Wilde seems to be portraying the evils of self-regarding hedonism.

As a poet Wilde felt overshadowed by the Victorian predecessors whom he admired—Robert Browning, D. G. Rossetti, and Algernon Charles Swinburne—and had trouble finding his own voice. Many of the poems in his first volume (1881) are highly derivative, but pieces such as "Impression du Matin" (1885) and "The Harlot's House" (1881) offer a distinctive perspective on city streets that seems to anticipate early poems by T. S. Eliot. His most outstanding success, however, was as a writer of comedies; staged in London and New York from 1892 through 1895, these included *Lady Windermere's Fan, A Woman of No Importance, An Ideal Husband,* and *The Importance of Being Earnest.*

In the spring of 1895 this triumphant success suddenly crumbled when Wilde was arrested and sentenced to prison, with hard labor, for two years. Although Wilde was married and the father of two children, he did not hide his relationships with men, and in fact ended up shaping, to his personal cost, a long-standing public image of "the homosexual." When he began a romance (in 1891) with the handsome young poet Lord Alfred Douglas, he set in motion the events that brought about his ruin. In 1895 Lord Alfred's father, the marquess of Queensberry, accused Wilde of homosexuality; Wilde recklessly sued for libel, lost the case, and was thereupon arrested and convicted for what had only recently come onto the statute books as a serious offense. (A late addition to the Criminal Law Amendment Act of 1885, known as the Labouchère Amendment after the member of Parliament who had proposed it, effectively criminalized all forms of sexual relations between men.) The revulsion of feeling against him in Britain and America was violent, and the aesthetic movement suffered a severe setback not only with the public but among writers as well.

His two years in jail led Wilde to write two sober and emotionally high-pitched works, his poem *The Ballad of Reading Gaol* (1898) and his prose confession *De Profundis* (1905). After leaving prison, Wilde, a ruined man, emigrated to France, where he lived out the last three years of his life under an assumed name. Before his departure from England he had been divorced and declared a bankrupt, and in France he had to rely on friends for financial support. Wilde is buried in Paris in the Père Lachaise cemetery.

From The Critic as Artist[1]

[CRITICISM ITSELF AN ART]

ERNEST   Gilbert, you sound too harsh a note. Let us go back to the more gracious fields of literature. What was it you said? That it was more difficult to talk about a thing than to do it?

GILBERT [*After a pause.*]   Yes: I believe I ventured upon that simple truth. Surely you see now that I am right? When man acts he is a puppet. When he describes he is a poet. The whole secret lies in that. It was easy enough on the sandy plains by windy Ilion[2] to send the notched arrow from the painted bow, or to hurl against the shield of hide and flamelike brass the long ash-handled spear. It was easy for the adulterous queen to spread the Tyrian carpets for her lord,[3] and then, as he lay couched in the marble bath, to throw over his head the purple net, and call to her smooth-faced lover to stab through the meshes at the heart that should have broken at Aulis.[4] For Antigone[5] even, with Death waiting for her as her bridegroom, it was easy to pass through the tainted air at noon, and climb the hill, and strew with kindly earth the wretched naked corse that had no tomb. But what of those who wrote about these things? What of those who gave them reality, and made them live forever? Are they not greater than the men and women they sing of? "Hector that sweet knight is dead."[6] And Lucian[7] tells us how in the dim underworld Menippus saw the bleaching skull of Helen, and marveled that it was for so grim a favour that all those horned ships were launched, those beautiful mailed men laid low, those towered cities brought to dust. Yet, every day the

1. In "the library of a house in Piccadilly," Gilbert and Ernest, two sophisticated young men, are talking about the use and function of criticism. Earlier in the dialogue Ernest had complained that criticism is officious and useless: "Why should the artist be troubled by the shrill clamour of criticism? Why should those who cannot create take upon themselves to estimate the value of creative work?" Gilbert, in his reply, argues that criticism is creative in its own right. He digresses to compare the life of action unfavorably with the life of art: actions are dangerous and their results unpredictable; "if we lived long enough to see the results of our actions it may be that those who call themselves good would be sickened by a dull remorse, and those whom the world calls evil stirred by a noble joy." The excerpt printed here begins immediately following this digression.
2. Troy. Gilbert is referring to Homer's *Iliad*.
3. Agamemnon, king of Mycenae. Aeschylus's tragedy of that name tells how his wife, Clytem-

nestra ("the adulterous queen"), and his cousin Aegisthus ("her smooth-faced lover") conspired to murder him. He hubristically walked on carpets dyed purple, a color derived from shellfish off Tyre (a city located in what is today Lebanon).
4. Where Agamemnon sacrificed his daughter Iphigenia (so that the Greek fleet could sail for Troy), thus incurring Clytemnestra's wrath.
5. Antigone defied Creon, king of Thebes, by sprinkling earth on the body of her brother whose burial Creon had forbidden, and was punished by death; see Sophocles' play *Antigone* (ca. 441 B.C.E.).
6. Cf. Shakespeare's *Love's Labour's Lost* 5.2.647: "The sweet war-man [Hector] is dead and rotten."
7. Greek satirist (b. ca. 120 C.E.), one of whose main influences was Menippus (early 3rd century B.C.E.), a Greek philosopher who was the first to express his views in a seriocomic style. The reference is to Lucian's *Dialogues of the Dead*.

swanlike daughter of Leda comes out on the battlements, and looks down at the tide of war. The greybeards wonder at her loveliness, and she stands by the side of the king.[8] In his chamber of stained ivory lies her leman.[9] He is polishing his dainty armour, and combing the scarlet plume. With squire and page, her husband passes from tent to tent. She can see his bright hair, and hears, or fancies that she hears, that clear cold voice. In the courtyard below, the son of Priam is buckling on his brazen cuirass. The white arms of Andromache[1] are around his neck. He sets his helmet on the ground, lest their babe should be frightened. Behind the embroidered curtains of his pavilion sits Achilles,[2] in perfumed raiment, while in harness of gilt and silver the friend of his soul[3] arrays himself to go forth to fight. From a curiously carven chest that his mother Thetis had brought to his shipside, the Lord of the Myrmidons[4] takes out that mystic chalice that the lip of man had never touched, and cleanses it with brimstone, and with fresh water cools it, and, having washed his hands, fills with black wine its burnished hollow, and spills the thick grape-blood upon the ground in honor of Him whom at Dodona[5] barefooted prophets worshipped, and prays to Him, and knows not that he prays in vain, and that by the hands of two knights from Troy, Panthous' son, Euphorbus, whose love-locks were looped with gold, and the Priamid,[6] the lion-hearted, Patroclus, the comrade of comrades, must meet his doom. Phantoms, are they? Heroes of mist and mountain? Shadows in a song? No: they are real. Action! What is action? It dies at the moment of its energy. It is a base concession to fact. The world is made by the singer for the dreamer.

ERNEST While you talk it seems to me to be so.

GILBERT It is so in truth. On the mouldering citadel of Troy lies the lizard like a thing of green bronze. The owl has built her nest in the palace of Priam. Over the empty plain wander shepherd and goatherd with their flocks, and where, on the wine-surfaced, oily sea, οἶνοψ πόντος,[7] as Homer calls it, copper-prowed and streaked with vermilion, the great galleys of the Danaoi[8] came in their gleaming crescent, the lonely tunny-fisher[9] sits in his little boat and watches the bobbing corks of his net. Yet, every morning the doors of the city are thrown open, and on foot, or in horse-drawn chariot, the warriors go forth to battle, and mock their enemies from behind their iron masks. All day long the fight rages, and when night comes the torches gleam by the tents, and the cresset[1] burns in the hall. Those who live in marble or on painted panel know of life but a single exquisite instant, eternal indeed in its beauty, but limited to one note of passion or one mood of calm. Those whom the poet makes live have their myriad emotions of joy and terror, of courage and despair, of pleasure and of suffering. The seasons come and go in glad or saddening

8. Priam. Homer in *Iliad* 3.156–58 describes the old men of Troy admiring the beauty of Helen, daughter of Leda and of Zeus (who came to Leda in the form of a swan).
9. Lover (i.e., Paris).
1. Wife of Hector, one of the sons of Priam and the finest Trojan warrior.
2. Son of Peleus and of the sea nymph Thetis; Achilles was the greatest Greek warrior fighting in the Trojan War. The scene set here is a tissue of recollections from the *Iliad*.

3. I.e., Patroclus.
4. Warriors who accompanied Achilles to Troy.
5. Seat of a very ancient oracle of Zeus.
6. The son of Priam, i.e., Hector. With Euphorbus's help he killed Patroclus, and in turn he was slain by Achilles.
7. Wine-dark sea (Greek).
8. Greeks.
9. Tuna-fishers.
1. Metal basket holding fuel burned for illumination, often hung from the ceiling.

pageant, and with winged or leaden feet the years pass by before them. They have their youth and their manhood, they are children, and they grow old. It is always dawn for St. Helena, as Veronese saw her at the window.[2] Through the still morning air the angels bring her the symbol of God's pain.[3] The cool breezes of the morning lift the gilt threads from her brow. On that little hill by the city of Florence, where the lovers of Giorgione[4] are lying, it is always the solstice of noon, made so languorous by summer suns that hardly can the slim naked girl dip into the marble tank the round bubble of clear glass, and the long fingers of the lute player rest idly upon the chords. It is twilight always for the dancing nymphs whom Corot[5] set free among the silver poplars of France. In eternal twilight they move, those frail diaphanous figures, whose tremulous white feet seem not to touch the dew-drenched grass they tread on. But those who walk in epos,[6] drama, or romance, see through the labouring months the young moons wax and wane, and watch the night from evening unto morning star, and from sunrise unto sunsetting can note the shifting day with all its gold and shadow. For them, as for us, the flowers bloom and wither, and the Earth, that Green-tressed Goddess as Coleridge calls her,[7] alters her raiment for their pleasure. The statue is concentrated to one moment of perfection. The image stained upon the canvas possesses no spiritual element of growth or change. If they know nothing of death, it is because they know little of life, for the secrets of life and death belong to those, and those only, whom the sequence of time affects, and who possess not merely the present but the future, and can rise or fall from a past of glory or of shame. Movement, that problem of the visible arts, can be truly realized by Literature alone. It is Literature that shows us the body in its swiftness and the soul in its unrest.

ERNEST   Yes; I see now what you mean. But, surely, the higher you place the creative artist, the lower must the critic rank.

GILBERT   Why so?

ERNEST   Because the best that he can give us will be but an echo of rich music, a dim shadow of clear-outlined form. It may, indeed, be that life is chaos, as you tell me that it is; that its martyrdoms are mean and its heroisms ignoble; and that it is the function of Literature to create, from the rough material of actual existence, a new world that will be more marvellous, more enduring, and more true than the world that common eyes look upon, and through which common natures seek to realize their perfection. But surely, if this new world has been made by the spirit and touch of a great artist, it will be a thing so complete and perfect that there will be nothing left for the critic to do. I quite understand now, and indeed admit most readily, that it is far more difficult to talk about a thing than to do it. But it seems to me that this sound and sensible maxim, which is really extremely soothing to one's feelings, and should be adopted as its motto by every Academy of Literature all over the world, applies only to the relations that exist between Art and Life, and not to any relations that there may be between Art and Criticism.

---

2. One of the best-known works of the Italian painter Paolo Veronese (Paolo Caliari, 1528–1588) is *Helena's Vision*.
3. I.e., the cross.
4. Italian painter (ca. 1477–1511), the most brilliant colorist of his time. The painting is *The Concert*.

5. Jean-Baptiste-Camille Corot (1796–1875), French painter best-known for his shimmering trees.
6. Epic poetry.
7. Cf. S. T. Coleridge's "Hymn to the Earth" (1834), line 10, where Earth is called "Green-haired Goddess."

GILBERT But, surely, Criticism is itself an art. And just as artistic creation implies the working of the critical faculty, and, indeed, without it
cannot be said to exist at all, so Criticism is really creative in the highest
sense of the word. Criticism is, in fact, both creative and independent.

ERNEST Independent?

GILBERT Yes; independent. Criticism is no more to be judged by any low
standard of imitation or resemblance than is the work of poet or sculptor. The critic occupies the same relation to the work of art that he criticizes as the artist does to the visible world of form and colour, or the
unseen world of passion and of thought. He does not even require for the
perfection of his art the finest materials. Anything will serve his purpose. And just as out of the sordid and sentimental amours of the silly
wife of a small country doctor in the squalid village of Yonville-l'Abbaye,
near Rouen, Gustave Flaubert[8] was able to create a classic, and make a
masterpiece of style, so, from subjects of little or of no importance, such
as the pictures in this year's Royal Academy,[9] or in any year's Royal
Academy for that matter, Mr. Lewis Morris's poems, M. Ohnet's novels,
or the plays of Mr. Henry Arthur Jones,[1] the true critic can, if it be his
pleasure so to direct or waste his faculty of contemplation, produce work
that will be flawless in beauty and instinct with intellectual subtlety.
Why not? Dullness is always an irresistible temptation for brilliancy, and
stupidity is the permanent *Bestia Trionfans*[2] that calls wisdom from its
cave. To an artist so creative as the critic, what does subject matter signify? No more and no less than it does to the novelist and the painter.
Like them, he can find his motives everywhere. Treatment is the test.
There is nothing that has not in it suggestion or challenge.

ERNEST But is Criticism really a creative art?

GILBERT Why should it not be? It works with materials, and puts them
into a form that is at once new and delightful. What more can one say of
poetry? Indeed, I would call criticism a creation within a creation. For
just as the great artists, from Homer and Aeschylus, down to Shakespeare and Keats, did not go directly to life for their subject matter, but
sought for it in myth, and legend, and ancient tale, so the critic deals
with materials that others have, as it were, purified for him, and to
which imaginative form and colour have been already added. Nay, more,
I would say that the highest Criticism, being the purest form of personal
impression, is in its way more creative than creation, as it has least reference to any standard external to itself, and is, in fact, its own reason for
existing, and, as the Greeks would put it, in itself, and to itself, an end.
Certainly, it is never trammeled by any shackles of verisimilitude. No
ignoble considerations of probability, that cowardly concession to the
tedious repetitions of domestic or public life, affect it ever. One may
appeal from fiction unto fact. But from the soul there is no appeal.

ERNEST From the soul?

---

8. French novelist (1821–1880); the reference is
to his novel *Madame Bovary* (1857).
9. The Royal Academy of Arts, founded in 1768,
holds an annual summer exhibition of new work.
1. Wilde is mischievously suggesting his low
opinion of the contemporary writers just named.
Morris (1833–1907) was a popular Welsh poet
and essayist often ridiculed by the critics; Georges

Ohnet (1848–1918) was a French novelist and
dramatist; and Jones (1851–1929) was one of the
leading English playwrights of his time.
2. Triumphant beast (Wilde's mixture of Italian
and Latin); a reference to *Spaccio della Bestia
Trionfante* (*Expulsion of the Triumphant Beast*,
1584), a philosophical allegory by the Italian
philosopher Giordano Bruno.

GILBERT   Yes, from the soul. That is what the highest criticism really is, the record of one's own soul. It is more fascinating than history, as it is concerned simply with oneself. It is more delightful than philosophy, as its subject is concrete and not abstract, real and not vague. It is the only civilized form of autobiography, as it deals not with the events, but with the thoughts of one's life, not with life's physical accidents of deed or circumstance, but with the spiritual moods and imaginative passions of the mind. I am always amused by the silly vanity of those writers and artists of our day who seem to imagine that the primary function of the critic is to chatter about their second-rate work. The best that one can say of most modern creative art is that it is just a little less vulgar than reality, and so the critic, with his fine sense of distinction and sure instinct of delicate refinement, will prefer to look into the silver mirror or through the woven veil, and will turn his eyes away from the chaos and clamour of actual existence, though the mirror be tarnished and the veil be torn. His sole aim is to chronicle his own impressions. It is for him that pictures are painted, books written, and marble hewn into form.

ERNEST   I seem to have heard another theory of Criticism.

GILBERT   Yes: it has been said by one whose gracious memory we all revere,[3] and the music of whose pipe once lured Proserpina from her Sicilian fields, and made those white feet stir, and not in vain, the Cumnor cowslips, that the proper aim of Criticism is to see the object as in itself it really is. But this is a very serious error, and takes no cognizance of Criticism's most perfect form, which is in its essence purely subjective, and seeks to reveal its own secret and not the secret of another. For the highest Criticism deals with art not as expressive but as impressive purely.

ERNEST   But is that really so?

GILBERT   Of course it is. Who cares whether Mr. Ruskin's views on Turner[4] are sound or not? What does it matter? That mighty and majestic prose of his, so fervid and so fiery-colored in its noble eloquence, so rich in its elaborate symphonic music, so sure and certain, at its best, in subtle choice of word and epithet, is at least as great a work of art as any of those wonderful sunsets that bleach or rot on their corrupted canvases in England's Gallery; greater indeed, one is apt to think at times, not merely because its equal beauty is more enduring, but on account of the fuller variety of its appeal, soul speaking to soul in those long-cadenced lines, not through form and colour alone, though through these, indeed, completely and without loss, but with intellectual and emotional utterance, with lofty passion and with loftier thought, with imaginative insight, and with poetic aim; greater, I always think, even as Literature is the greater art. Who, again, cares whether Mr. Pater has put into the portrait of Mona Lisa[5] something that Leonardo never dreamed of? The painter may have been merely the slave of an archaic smile, as some have fancied,

3. I.e., Matthew Arnold, whose poem "Thyrsis" (1866; lines 91–100) evokes the legend of Proserpina, a goddess associated with the pastoral landscapes of Sicily. Arnold believed that it would be "in vain" to summon Proserpina to visit the Cumnor hills landscape (near Oxford), but Wilde's speaker here flatters Arnold that the summons was so beautiful that it was "not in vain." For the prose passage about the "aim of Criticism," see

Arnold's "The Function of Criticism at the Present Time" (1864; p. 771).
4. For John Ruskin's defense of the paintings of J. M. W. Turner, see *Modern Painters* (1843), especially his praise of Turner's *The Slave Ship*.
5. All remaining references in this paragraph and the first in the next are to Walter Pater's *Studies in the History of the Renaissance*.

but whenever I pass into the cool galleries of the Palace of the Louvre, and stand before that strange figure "set in its marble chair in that cirque of fantastic rocks, as in some faint light under sea," I murmur to myself, "She is older than the rocks among which she sits; like the vampire, she has been dead many times, and learned the secrets of the grave; and has been a diver in deep seas, and keeps their fallen day about her: and trafficked for strange webs with Eastern merchants; and, as Leda, was the mother of Helen of Troy, and, as St. Anne, the mother of Mary; and all this has been to her but as the sound of lyres and flutes, and lives only in the delicacy with which it has moulded the changing lineaments, and tinged the eyelids and the hands." And I say to my friend, "The presence that thus so strangely rose beside the waters is expressive of what in the ways of a thousand years man had come to desire"; and he answers me, "Hers is the head upon which all 'the ends of the world are come,' and the eyelids are a little weary."

And so the picture becomes more wonderful to us than it really is, and reveals to us a secret of which, in truth, it knows nothing, and the music of the mystical prose is as sweet in our ears as was that flute-player's music that lent to the lips of La Gioconda[6] those subtle and poisonous curves. Do you ask me what Leonardo would have said had any one told him of this picture that "all the thoughts and experience of the world had etched and moulded therein that which they had of power to refine and make expressive the outward form, the animalism of Greece, the lust of Rome, the reverie of the Middle Age with its spiritual ambition and imaginative loves, the return of the Pagan world, the sins of the Borgias?" He would probably have answered that he had contemplated none of these things, but had concerned himself simply with certain arrangements of lines and masses, and with new and curious colour-harmonies of blue and green. And it is for this very reason that the criticism which I have quoted is criticism of the highest kind. It treats the work of art simply as a starting point for a new creation. It does not confine itself—let us at least suppose so for the moment—to discovering the real intention of the artist and accepting that as final. And in this it is right, for the meaning of any beautiful created thing is, at least, as much in the soul of him who looks at it, as it was in his soul who wrought it. Nay, it is rather the beholder who lends to the beautiful thing its myriad meanings, and makes it marvelous for us, and sets it in some new relation to the age, so that it becomes a vital portion of our lives, and symbol of what we pray for, or perhaps of what, having prayed for, we fear that we may receive. The longer I study, Ernest, the more clearly I see that the beauty of the visible arts is, as the beauty of music, impressive[7] primarily, and that it may be marred, and indeed often is so, by any excess of intellectual intention on the part of the artist. For when the work is finished it has, as it were, an independent life of its own, and may deliver a message far other than that which was put into its lips to say. Sometimes, when I listen to the overture to *Tannhäuser*,[8] I seem indeed to see that comely

6. I.e., the *Mona Lisa* (the portrait was of the wife of Francesco del Gioconda—hence "La Gioconda").
7. I.e., designed to create an impression of the senses.

8. The 1845 opera by Richard Wagner, based on the legend of a 14th-century German poet who fell under the spell of Venus and lived with her in a mountain, Hörselberg.

knight treading delicately on the flower-strewn grass, and to hear the voice of Venus calling to him from the caverned hill. But at other times it speaks to me of a thousand different things, of myself, it may be, and my own life, or of the lives of others whom one has loved and grown weary of loving, or of the passions that man has known, or of the passions that man has not known, and so has sought for. Tonight it may fill one with that ΕΡΩΣ ΤΩΝ ΑΔΥΝΑΤΩΝ, that *amour de l'impossible*,[9] which falls like a madness on many who think they live securely and out of reach of harm, so that they sicken suddenly with the poison of unlimited desire, and, in the infinite pursuit of what they may not obtain, grow faint and swoon or stumble. Tomorrow, like the music of which Aristotle and Plato tell us, the noble Dorian music of the Greek,[1] it may perform the office of a physician, and give us an anodyne against pain, and heal the spirit that is wounded, and "bring the soul into harmony with all right things." And what is true about music is true about all the arts. Beauty has as many meanings as man has moods. Beauty is the symbol of symbols. Beauty reveals everything, because it expresses nothing. When it shows us itself, it shows us the whole fiery-coloured world.

ERNEST   But is such work as you have talked about really criticism?

GILBERT   It is the highest Criticism, for it criticizes not merely the individual work of art, but Beauty itself, and fills with wonder a form which the artist may have left void, or not understood, or understood incompletely.

ERNEST   The highest Criticism, then, is more creative than creation, and the primary aim of the critic is to see the object as in itself it really is not; that is your theory, I believe?

GILBERT   Yes, that is my theory. To the critic the work of art is simply a suggestion for a new work of his own, that need not necessarily bear any obvious resemblance to the thing it criticizes. The one characteristic of a beautiful form is that one can put into it whatever one wishes, and see in it whatever one chooses to see; and the Beauty, that gives to creation its universal and aesthetic element, makes the critic a creator in his turn, and whispers of a thousand different things which were not present in the mind of him who carved the statue or painted the panel or graved the gem.

It is sometimes said by those who understand neither the nature of the highest Criticism nor the charm of the highest Art, that the pictures that the critic loves most to write about are those that belong to the anecdotage of painting, and that deal with scenes taken out of literature or history. But this is not so. Indeed, pictures of this kind are far too intelligible. As a class, they rank with illustrations, and even considered from this point of view are failures, as they do not stir the imagination, but set definite bounds to it. For the domain of the painter is, as I suggested before, widely different from that of the poet. To the latter belongs life in its full and absolute entirety; not merely the beauty that men look at, but the beauty that men listen to also; not merely the momentary grace of form or the transient gladness of colour, but the whole sphere of feeling,

---

9. Love of the impossible, in Greek (in capital letters, perhaps to give the effect of an inscription) and in French.
1. Both Plato (*Republic* 3) and Aristotle (*Politics* 8) praise the educational appropriateness of the

Dorian mode (Aristotle calls it especially steady and manly), as opposed to eastern music; the Dorians were a people of ancient Greece, the last of the northern invaders (ca. 1100–950 B.C.E.).

the perfect cycle of thought. The painter is so far limited that it is only through the mask of the body that he can show us the mystery of the soul; only through conventional images that he can handle ideas; only through its physical equivalents that he can deal with psychology. And how inadequately does he do it then, asking us to accept the torn turban of the Moor for the noble rage of Othello, or a dotard in a storm for the wild madness of Lear! Yet it seems as if nothing could stop him. Most of our elderly English painters spend their wicked and wasted lives in poaching upon the domain of the poets, marring their motives by clumsy treatment, and striving to render, by visible form or colour, the marvel of what is invisible, the splendour of what is not seen. Their pictures are, as a natural consequence, insufferably tedious. They have degraded the invisible arts into the obvious arts, and the one thing not worth looking at is the obvious. I do not say that poet and painter may not treat of the same subject. They have always done so, and will always do so. But while the poet can be pictorial or not, as he chooses, the painter must be pictorial always. For a painter is limited, not to what he sees in nature, but to what upon canvas may be seen.

And so, my dear Ernest, pictures of this kind will not really fascinate the critic. He will turn from them to such works as make him brood and dream and fancy, to works that possess the subtle quality of suggestion, and seem to tell one that even from them there is an escape into a wider world. It is sometimes said that the tragedy of an artist's life is that he cannot realize his ideal. But the true tragedy that dogs the steps of most artists is that they realize their ideal too absolutely. For, when the ideal is realized, it is robbed of its wonder and its mystery, and becomes simply a new starting point for an ideal that is other than itself. This is the reason why music is the perfect type of art. Music can never reveal its ultimate secret. This, also, is the explanation of the value of limitations in art. The sculptor gladly surrenders imitative colour, and the painter the actual dimensions of form, because by such renunciations they are able to avoid too definite a presentation of the Real, which would be mere imitation, and too definite a realization of the Ideal, which would be too purely intellectual. It is through its very incompleteness that Art becomes complete in beauty, and so addresses itself, not to the faculty of recognition nor to the faculty of reason, but to the aesthetic sense alone, which, while accepting both reason and recognition as stages of apprehension, subordinates them both to a pure synthetic impression of the work of art as a whole, and, taking whatever alien emotional elements the work may possess, uses their very complexity as a means by which a richer unity may be added to the ultimate impression itself. You see, then, how it is that the aesthetic critic rejects these obvious modes of art that have but one message to deliver, and having delivered it become dumb and sterile, and seeks rather for such modes as suggest reverie and mood, and by their imaginative beauty make all interpretations true, and no interpretation final. Some resemblance, no doubt, the creative work of the critic will have to the work that has stirred him to creation, but it will be such resemblance as exists, not between Nature and the mirror that the painter of landscape or figure may be supposed to hold up to her, but between Nature and the work of the decorative artist. Just as on the flowerless carpets of Persia, tulip and rose blossom indeed and are lovely to look on, though they are not reproduced in visible shape or line; just as the pearl and purple of the sea shell is echoed in the church of St. Mark at Venice; just as the vaulted ceiling of the wondrous chapel at Ravenna is made gorgeous by the gold and green and sapphire of the peacock's tail, though the birds of Juno[2] fly not across it; so the critic reproduces the work that he criticizes in a mode that is never imitative, and part of whose charm may really consist in the rejection of resemblance, and shows us in this way not merely the meaning but also the mystery of Beauty, and, by transforming each art into literature, solves once for all the problem of Art's unity.

But I see it is time for supper. After we have discussed some Chambertin and a few ortolans,[3] we will pass on to the question of the critic considered in the light of the interpreter.

ERNEST Ah! you admit, then, that the critic may occasionally be allowed to see the object as in itself it really is.

GILBERT I am not quite sure. Perhaps I may admit it after supper. There is a subtle influence in supper.

1890, 1891

Preface to *The Picture of Dorian Gray*

The artist is the creator of beautiful things.
To reveal art and conceal the artist is art's aim.
The critic is he who can translate into another manner or a new
material his impression of beautiful things.
> The highest, as the lowest, form of criticism is a mode of
> autobiography.
Those who find ugly meanings in beautiful things are corrupt without being
charming. This is a fault.
> Those who find beautiful meanings in beautiful things are
> the cultivated. For these there is hope.
They are the elect to whom beautiful things mean only Beauty.
> There is no such thing as a moral or an immoral book.
> Books are well written, or badly written. That is all.
The nineteenth-century dislike of Realism is the rage of Caliban[1] seeing his
own face in a glass.
> The nineteenth-century dislike of Romanticism is the rage of
> Caliban not seeing his own face in a glass.
> The moral life of man forms part of the subject matter of the artist,
> but the morality of art consists in the perfect use of an imperfect
> medium. No artist desires to prove anything. Even things that are
> true can be proved.
> > No artist has ethical sympathies. An ethical sympathy in an
> > artist is an unpardonable mannerism of style.

2. Peacocks, associated in classical mythology with the goddess Juno (in Greek, Hera) because she is said to have set in the bird's tail the eyes of hundred-eyed Argus, who died in her service.
3. Small birds esteemed by epicures for their delicate flavor. "Chambertin": one of the finest wines of Burgundy.
1. The character in Shakespeare's *The Tempest* who is half-human, half-monster.

No artist is ever morbid. The artist can express everything.

Thought and language are to the artist instruments of an art.

Vice and Virtue are to the artist materials for an art.

From the point of view of form, the type of all the arts is the art of the musician.

From the point of view of feeling, the actor's craft is the type.

All art is at once surface and symbol.

Those who go beneath the surface do so at their peril.

Those who read the symbol do so at their peril.

It is the spectator, and not life, that art really mirrors.

Diversity of opinion about a work of art shows that the work is new, complex, and vital.

When critics disagree the artist is in accord with himself. We can forgive a man for making a useful thing as long as he does not admire it. The only excuse for making a useless thing is that one admires it intensely.

All art is quite useless.

1891

The Importance of Being Earnest

Of the four stage comedies by Wilde, his last, *The Importance of Being Earnest*, is generally regarded as his masterpiece. It was first staged in February 1895 and was an immediate hit. Only one critic failed to find it delightful; curiously, this was Wilde's fellow playwright from Ireland, Bernard Shaw, who, though amused, found Wilde's wit "hateful" and "sinister," and thought the play exhibited "real degeneracy." Despite Shaw's complaints, the first London production ran for eighty-six performances; but when Wilde was sentenced to prison, production ceased for several years. Shortly before his death it was revived in London and New York, and it has subsequently become a classic.

In its original version the play was in four acts. At the request of the stage producer, Wilde reduced it to three acts—the version almost always used in performances and the version reprinted here. A few of the notes in the text cite passages from the four-act version.

The play was first published in 1899. Earlier, in an interview, Wilde had described his overall aim in writing it: "It has as its philosophy . . . that we should treat all the trivial things of life seriously, and all the serious things of life with sincere and studied triviality." Just before his death he remarked that although he was pleased with the "bright and happy" tone and temper of his play, he wished it might have had a "higher seriousness of intent." Later critics have found this seriousness of intent in the play's deconstruction of Victorian moral and social values. Like another Victorian masterpiece of the absurd, *Alice's Adventures in Wonderland* (1865), *The Importance of Being Earnest* empties manners and morals of their underlying sense to create a nominalist world where earnest is not a quality of character but a name, where words, to paraphrase Humpty Dumpty in *Through the Looking-Glass* (1871), mean what you choose them to mean, neither more nor less.

The literary ancestry of Wilde's play has been variously identified. In its witty wordplay and worldly attitudes it has been likened to comedies of the Restoration period such as William Congreve's *Love for Love* (1695). In its genial and lighthearted tone, it has some affinities with the festive comedies of Shakespeare, such as *Twelfth Night* (ca. 1601), and with Oliver Goldsmith's *She Stoops to Conquer* (1773). A more immediate predecessor was *Engaged* (1877), a comic play by W. S. Gilbert that anticipated some of the burlesque effects exploited by Wilde, such as the inviolable imperturbability of the speakers and the interrupting of sentimental scenes by the consumption of food. Gilbert's advice to the actors who were putting on his *Engaged* is worth citing as a clue to how *The Importance of Being Earnest* may be most effectively imagined as a stage representation:

> It is absolutely essential to the success of this piece that it should be played with the most perfect earnestness and gravity throughout. . . . Directly the actors show that they are conscious of the absurdity of their utterances the piece begins to drag.

The Importance of Being Earnest

First Act

SCENE—*Morning room in* ALGERNON's *flat in Half-Moon Street.*[1]

The room is luxuriously and artistically furnished. The sound of a piano is heard in the adjoining room.

[LANE *is arranging afternoon tea on the table, and after the music has ceased,* ALGERNON *enters.*]

ALGERNON   Did you hear what I was playing, Lane?

LANE   I didn't think it polite to listen, sir.

ALGERNON   I'm sorry for that, for your sake. I don't play accurately— anyone can play accurately—but I play with wonderful expression. As far as the piano is concerned, sentiment is my forte. I keep science for Life.

LANE   Yes, sir.

ALGERNON   And, speaking of the science of Life, have you got the cucumber sandwiches cut for Lady Bracknell?[2]

LANE   Yes, sir. [*Hands them on a salver.*]

ALGERNON [*Inspects them, takes two, and sits down on the sofa.*]   Oh! . . . by the way, Lane, I see from your book[3] that on Thursday night, when Lord Shoreham and Mr. Worthing were dining with me, eight bottles of champagne are entered as having been consumed.

LANE   Yes, sir; eight bottles and a pint.

ALGERNON   Why is it that at a bachelor's establishment the servants invariably drink the champagne? I ask merely for information.

LANE   I attribute it to the superior quality of the wine, sir. I have often observed that in married households the champagne is rarely of a first-rate brand.

ALGERNON   Good Heavens! Is marriage so demoralizing as that?

LANE   I believe it *is* a very pleasant state, sir. I have had very little experience of it myself up to the present. I have only been married once. That was in consequence of a misunderstanding between myself and a young person.

ALGERNON [*Languidly.*]   I don't know that I am much interested in your family life, Lane.

LANE   No, sir; it is not a very interesting subject. I never think of it myself.

ALGERNON   Very natural, I am sure. That will do, Lane, thank you.

---

1. A highly fashionable location (at the time of the play) in the West End of London.
2. Bracknell is the name of a place in Berkshire where the mother of Lord Alfred Douglas had her summer home, which Wilde had visited.
3. Cellar book, in which records were kept of wines.

LANE Thank you, sir. [LANE *goes out.*]

ALGERNON Lane's views on marriage seem somewhat lax. Really, if the lower orders don't set us a good example, what on earth is the use of them? They seem, as a class, to have absolutely no sense of moral responsibility.

[*Enter* LANE.]

LANE Mr. Ernest Worthing.

[*Enter* JACK.] [LANE *goes out.*]

ALGERNON How are you, my dear Ernest? What brings you up to town?

JACK Oh, pleasure, pleasure! What else should bring one anywhere? Eating as usual, I see, Algy!

ALGERNON [*Stiffly.*] I believe it is customary in good society to take some slight refreshment at five o'clock. Where have you been since last Thursday?

JACK [*Sitting down on the sofa.*] In the country.

ALGERNON What on earth do you do there?

JACK [*Pulling off his gloves.*] When one is in town one amuses oneself. When one is in the country one amuses other people. It is excessively boring.

ALGERNON And who are the people you amuse?

JACK [*Airily.*] Oh, neighbours, neighbours.

ALGERNON Got nice neighbours in your part of Shropshire?

JACK Perfectly horrid! Never speak to one of them.

ALGERNON How immensely you must amuse them! [*Goes over and takes sandwich.*] By the way, Shropshire is your county, is it not?

JACK Eh? Shropshire?[4] Yes, of course. Hallo! Why all these cups? Why cucumber sandwiches? Why such reckless extravagance in one so young? Who is coming to tea?

ALGERNON Oh! merely Aunt Augusta and Gwendolen.

JACK How perfectly delightful!

ALGERNON Yes, that is all very well; but I am afraid Aunt Augusta won't quite approve of your being here.

JACK May I ask why?

ALGERNON My dear fellow, the way you flirt with Gwendolen is perfectly disgraceful. It is almost as bad as the way Gwendolen flirts with you.

JACK I am in love with Gwendolen. I have come up to town expressly to propose to her.

ALGERNON I thought you had come up for pleasure? . . . I call that business.

JACK How utterly unromantic you are!

ALGERNON I really don't see anything romantic in proposing. It is very romantic to be in love. But there is nothing romantic about a definite proposal. Why, one may be accepted. One usually is, I believe. Then the excitement is all over. The very essence of romance is uncertainty. If ever I get married, I'll certainly try to forget the fact.

---

4. As we learn later, the estate is in Hertfordshire, a long distance from Shropshire. In the four-act version of the play, when this discrepancy is pointed out by Algernon, Jack replies: "My dear fellow! Surely you don't expect me to be accurate about geography? No gentleman is accurate about geography. Why, I got a prize for geography when I was at school. I can't be expected to know anything about it now."

JACK   I have no doubt about that, dear Algy. The Divorce Court was specially invented for people whose memories are so curiously constituted.

ALGERNON   Oh! there is no use speculating on that subject. Divorces are
made in Heaven—[JACK *puts out his hand to take a sandwich.* ALGERNON
at once interferes.] Please don't touch the cucumber sandwiches. They
are ordered specially for Aunt Augusta. [*Takes one and eats it.*]

JACK   Well, you have been eating them all the time.

ALGERNON   That is quite a different matter. She is my aunt. [*Takes plate
from below.*] Have some bread and butter. The bread and butter is for
Gwendolen. Gwendolen is devoted to bread and butter.

JACK [*Advancing to table and helping himself.*]   And very good bread and
butter it is too.

ALGERNON   Well, my dear fellow, you need not eat as if you were going to
eat it all. You behave as if you were married to her already. You are not
married to her already, and I don't think you ever will be.

JACK   Why on earth do you say that?

ALGERNON   Well, in the first place, girls never marry the men they flirt
with. Girls don't think it right.

JACK   Oh, that is nonsense!

ALGERNON   It isn't. It is a great truth. It accounts for the extraordinary
number of bachelors that one sees all over the place. In the second
place, I don't give my consent.

JACK   Your consent!

ALGERNON   My dear fellow, Gwendolen is my first cousin. And before I
allow you to marry her, you will have to clear up the whole question of
Cecily. [*Rings bell.*]

JACK   Cecily! What on earth do you mean? What do you mean, Algy, by
Cecily? I don't know anyone of the name of Cecily.
        [*Enter* LANE.]

ALGERNON   Bring me that cigarette case Mr. Worthing left in the
smoking-room the last time he dined here.

LANE   Yes, sir.   [LANE *goes out.*]

JACK   Do you mean to say you have had my cigarette case all this time? I
wish to goodness you had let me know. I have been writing frantic letters to Scotland Yard[5] about it. I was very nearly offering a large reward.

ALGERNON   Well, I wish you would offer one. I happen to be more than
usually hard up.[6]

JACK   There is no good offering a large reward now that the thing is found.
        [*Enter* LANE *with the cigarette case on a salver.* ALGERNON *takes it at
        once.* LANE *goes out.*]

ALGERNON   I think that is rather mean of you, Ernest, I must say. [*Opens
case and examines it.*] However, it makes no matter, for, now that I look
at the inscription inside, I find that the thing isn't yours after all.

JACK   Of course it's mine. [*Moving to him.*] You have seen me with it a
hundred times, and you have no right whatsoever to read what is written
inside. It is a very ungentlemanly thing to read a private cigarette case.

ALGERNON   Oh! it is absurd to have a hard-and-fast rule about what one
should read and what one shouldn't. More than half of modern culture
depends on what one shouldn't read.

5. Police headquarters in London.   6. Short of money.

JACK   I am quite aware of the fact, and I don't propose to discuss modern culture. It isn't the sort of thing one should talk of in private. I simply want my cigarette case back.

ALGERNON   Yes; but this isn't your cigarette case. This cigarette case is a present from someone of the name of Cecily, and you said you didn't know anyone of that name.

JACK   Well, if you want to know, Cecily happens to be my aunt.

ALGERNON   Your aunt!

JACK   Yes. Charming old lady she is, too. Lives at Tunbridge Wells.[7] Just give it back to me, Algy.

ALGERNON [*Retreating to back of sofa.*]   But why does she call herself little Cecily if she is your aunt and lives at Tunbridge Wells? [*Reading.*] "From little Cecily with her fondest love."

JACK [*Moving to sofa and kneeling upon it.*]   My dear fellow, what on earth is there in that? Some aunts are tall, some aunts are not tall. That is a matter that surely an aunt may be allowed to decide for herself. You seem to think that every aunt should be exactly like your aunt! That is absurd! For Heaven's sake give me back my cigarette case. [*Follows Algy round the room.*]

ALGERNON   Yes. But why does your aunt call you her uncle? "From little Cecily, with her fondest love to her dear Uncle Jack." There is no objection, I admit, to an aunt being a small aunt, but why an aunt, no matter what her size may be, should call her own nephew her uncle, I can't quite make out. Besides, your name isn't Jack at all; it is Ernest.

JACK   It isn't Ernest; it's Jack.

ALGERNON   You have always told me it was Ernest. I have introduced you to everyone as Ernest. You answer to the name of Ernest. You look as if your name was Ernest. You are the most earnest looking person I ever saw in my life. It is perfectly absurd your saying that your name isn't Ernest. It's on your cards. Here is one of them. [*Taking it from case.*] "Mr. Ernest Worthing, B. 4, The Albany."[8] I'll keep this as a proof that your name is Ernest if ever you attempt to deny it to me, or to Gwendolen, or to anyone else. [*Puts the card in his pocket.*]

JACK   Well, my name is Ernest in town and Jack in the country, and the cigarette case was given to me in the country.

ALGERNON   Yes, but that does not account for the fact that your small Aunt Cecily, who lives at Tunbridge Wells, calls you her dear uncle. Come, old boy, you had much better have the thing out at once.

JACK   My dear Algy, you talk exactly as if you were a dentist. It is very vulgar to talk like a dentist when one isn't a dentist. It produces a false impression.

ALGERNON   Well, that is exactly what dentists always do. Now, go on! Tell me the whole thing. I may mention that I have always suspected you of being a confirmed and secret Bunburyist; and I am quite sure of it now.

JACK   Bunburyist? What on earth do you mean by a Bunburyist?

ALGERNON   I'll reveal to you the meaning of that incomparable expression as soon as you are kind enough to inform me why you are Ernest in town and Jack in the country.

7. A fashionable resort town south of London.
8. A former residence of the duke of Albany (brother of George IV) near Piccadilly that had been converted to elegant apartments.

JACK   Well, produce my cigarette case first.

ALGERNON   Here it is. [*Hands cigarette case.*] Now produce your explanation, and pray make it improbable. [*Sits on sofa.*]

JACK   My dear fellow, there is nothing improbable about my explanation at all. In fact it's perfectly ordinary. Old Mr. Thomas Cardew, who adopted me when I was a little boy, made me in his will guardian to his grand-daughter, Miss Cecily Cardew. Cecily, who addresses me as her uncle from motives of respect that you could not possibly appreciate, lives at my place in the country under the charge of her admirable governess, Miss Prism.

ALGERNON   Where is that place in the country, by the way?

JACK   That is nothing to you, dear boy. You are not going to be invited. . . . I may tell you candidly that the place is not in Shropshire.

ALGERNON   I suspected that, my dear fellow! I have Bunburyed all over Shropshire on two separate occasions. Now, go on. Why are you Ernest in town and Jack in the country?

JACK   My dear Algy, I don't know whether you will be able to understand my real motives. You are hardly serious enough. When one is placed in the position of guardian, one has to adopt a very high moral tone on all subjects. It's one's duty to do so. And as a high moral tone can hardly be said to conduce very much to either one's health or one's happiness, in order to get up to town I have always pretended to have a younger brother of the name of Ernest, who lives in the Albany, and gets into the most dreadful scrapes. That, my dear Algy, is the whole truth pure and simple.

ALGERNON   The truth is rarely pure and never simple. Modern life would be very tedious if it were either, and modern literature a complete impossibility!

JACK   That wouldn't be at all a bad thing.

ALGERNON   Literary criticism is not your forte, my dear fellow. Don't try it. You should leave that to people who haven't been at a University. They do it so well in the daily papers. What you really are is a Bunburyist. I was quite right in saying you were a Bunburyist. You are one of the most advanced Bunburyists I know.

JACK   What on earth do you mean?

ALGERNON   You have invented a very useful young brother called Ernest, in order that you may be able to come up to town as often as you like. I have invented an invaluable permanent invalid called Bunbury, in order that I may be able to go down into the country whenever I choose. Bunbury is perfectly invaluable. If it wasn't for Bunbury's extraordinary bad health, for instance, I wouldn't be able to dine with you at Willis's tonight, for I have been really engaged[9] to Aunt Augusta for more than a week.

JACK   I haven't asked you to dine with me anywhere tonight.

ALGERNON   I know. You are absurdly careless about sending out invitations. It is very foolish of you. Nothing annoys people so much as not receiving invitations.

JACK   You had much better dine with your Aunt Augusta.

ALGERNON   I haven't the smallest intention of doing anything of the kind. To begin with, I dined there on Monday, and once a week is quite enough to dine with one's own relations. In the second place, whenever

9. I.e., committed to attend her dinner party. "Willis's": a first-class restaurant in the vicinity of St. James's Street, in the center of London.

I do dine there I am always treated as a member of the family, and sent down with[1] either no woman at all, or two. In the third place, I know perfectly well whom she will place me next to, tonight. She will place me next Mary Farquhar, who always flirts with her own husband across the dinner table. That is not very pleasant. Indeed, it is not even decent . . . and that sort of thing is enormously on the increase. The amount of women in London who flirt with their own husbands is perfectly scandalous. It looks so bad. It is simply washing one's clean linen in public. Besides, now that I know you to be a confirmed Bunburyist, I naturally want to talk to you about Bunburying. I want to tell you the rules.

JACK   I'm not a Bunburyist at all. If Gwendolen accepts me, I am going to kill my brother, indeed I think I'll kill him in any case. Cecily is a little too much interested in him. It is rather a bore. So I am going to get rid of Ernest. And I strongly advise you to do the same with Mr. . . . with your invalid friend who has the absurd name.

ALGERNON   Nothing will induce me to part with Bunbury, and if you ever get married, which seems to me extremely problematic, you will be very glad to know Bunbury. A man who marries without knowing Bunbury has a very tedious time of it.

JACK   That is nonsense. If I marry a charming girl like Gwendolen, and she is the only girl I ever saw in my life that I would marry, I certainly won't want to know Bunbury.

ALGERNON   Then your wife will. You don't seem to realize, that in married life three is company and two is none.

JACK [*Sententiously*.]   That, my dear young friend, is the theory that the corrupt French Drama has been propounding for the last fifty years.[2]

ALGERNON   Yes; and that the happy English home has proved in half the time.

JACK   For heaven's sake, don't try to be cynical. It's perfectly easy to be cynical.

ALGERNON   My dear fellow, it isn't easy to be anything nowadays. There's such a lot of beastly competition about. [*The sound of an electric bell is heard.*] Ah! that must be Aunt Augusta. Only relatives, or creditors, ever ring in that Wagnerian manner.[3] Now, if I get her out of the way for ten minutes, so that you can have an opportunity for proposing to Gwendolen, may I dine with you tonight at Willis's?

JACK   I suppose so, if you want to.

ALGERNON   Yes, but you must be serious about it. I hate people who are not serious about meals. It is so shallow of them.

[*Enter* LANE.]

LANE   Lady Bracknell and Miss Fairfax.

[ALGERNON *goes forward to meet them. Enter* LADY BRACKNELL *and* GWENDOLEN.]

LADY BRACKNELL   Good afternoon, dear Algernon, I hope you are behaving very well.

ALGERNON   I'm feeling very well, Aunt Augusta.

---

1. I.e., required to escort, as a dinner partner.
2. Almost all the plays by the leading French playwrights of the second half of the 19th century (Alexandre Dumas *fils*, Émile Augier, and Victorien Sardou) focus on marital infidelity. As Brander Matthews, an American critic, noted in 1882, "the trio—husband, wife, and lover" had become "almost universal" in the French theater.
3. Insistently loud, like some of the music in the large-scale operas of Richard Wagner (1813–1883).

LADY BRACKNELL   That's not quite the same thing. In fact the two things rarely go together. [*Sees* JACK *and bows to him with icy coldness.*]

ALGERNON [*To* GWENDOLEN.]   Dear me, you are smart![4]

GWENDOLEN   I am always smart! Aren't I, Mr. Worthing?

JACK   You're quite perfect, Miss Fairfax.

GWENDOLEN   Oh! I hope I am not that. It would leave no room for developments, and I intend to develop in many directions. [GWENDOLEN *and* JACK *sit down together in the corner.*]

LADY BRACKNELL   I'm sorry if we are a little late, Algernon, but I was obliged to call on dear Lady Harbury. I hadn't been there since her poor husband's death. I never saw a woman so altered; she looks quite twenty years younger. And now I'll have a cup of tea, and one of those nice cucumber sandwiches you promised me.

ALGERNON   Certainly, Aunt Augusta. [*Goes over to tea-table.*]

LADY BRACKNELL   Won't you come and sit here, Gwendolen?

GWENDOLEN   Thanks, mamma,[5] I'm quite comfortable where I am.

ALGERNON [*Picking up empty plate in horror.*]   Good heavens! Lane! Why are there no cucumber sandwiches? I ordered them specially.

LANE [*Gravely.*]   There were no cucumbers in the market this morning, sir. I went down twice.

ALGERNON   No cucumbers!

LANE   No, sir. Not even for ready money.[6]

ALGERNON   That will do, Lane, thank you.

LANE   Thank you, sir.

ALGERNON   I am greatly distressed, Aunt Augusta, about there being no cucumbers, not even for ready money.

LADY BRACKNELL   It really makes no matter, Algernon. I had some crumpets[7] with Lady Harbury, who seems to me to be living entirely for pleasure now.

ALGERNON   I hear her hair has turned quite gold from grief.

LADY BRACKNELL   It certainly has changed its colour. From what cause I, of course, cannot say. [ALGERNON *crosses and hands tea.*] Thank you. I've quite a treat for you tonight, Algernon. I am going to send you down with Mary Farquhar. She is such a nice woman, and so attentive to her husband. It's delightful to watch them.

ALGERNON   I am afraid, Aunt Augusta, I shall have to give up the pleasure of dining with you tonight after all.

LADY BRACKNELL [*Frowning.*]   I hope not, Algernon. It would put my table completely out. Your uncle would have to dine upstairs.[8] Fortunately he is accustomed to that.

ALGERNON   It is a great bore, and, I need hardly say, a terrible disappointment to me, but the fact is I have just had a telegram to say that my poor friend Bunbury is very ill again. [*Exchanges glances with* JACK.] They seem to think I should be with him.

LADY BRACKNELL   It is very strange. This Mr. Bunbury seems to suffer from curiously bad health.

ALGERNON   Yes; poor Bunbury is a dreadful invalid.

4. Elegantly fashionable.
5. Pronounced with the accent on the second syllable.
6. Immediate payment in cash (rather than on credit).
7. Round griddle breads, served toasted.
8. Because otherwise she would have more women than men at the table.

LADY BRACKNELL   Well, I must say, Algernon, that I think it is high time that Mr. Bunbury made up his mind whether he was going to live or to die. This shilly-shallying with the question is absurd. Nor do I in any way approve of the modern sympathy with invalids. I consider it morbid. Illness of any kind is hardly a thing to be encouraged in others. Health is the primary duty of life. I am always telling that to your poor uncle, but he never seems to take much notice . . . as far as any improvement in his ailments goes. I should be obliged if you would ask Mr. Bunbury, from me, to be kind enough not to have a relapse on Saturday, for I rely on you to arrange my music for me. It is my last reception, and one wants something that will encourage conversation, particularly at the end of the season[9] when everyone has practically said whatever they had to say, which, in most cases, was probably not much.

ALGERNON   I'll speak to Bunbury, Aunt Augusta, if he is still conscious, and I think I can promise you he'll be all right by Saturday. Of course the music is a great difficulty. You see, if one plays good music, people don't listen, and if one plays bad music, people don't talk. But I'll run over the program I've drawn out, if you will kindly come into the next room for a moment.

LADY BRACKNELL   Thank you, Algernon. It is very thoughtful of you. [*Rising, and following* ALGERNON.] I'm sure the program will be delightful, after a few expurgations. French songs I cannot possibly allow. People always seem to think that they are improper, and either look shocked, which is vulgar, or laugh, which is worse. But German sounds a thoroughly respectable language, and indeed, I believe is so. Gwendolen, you will accompany me.

GWENDOLEN   Certainly, mamma.

    [LADY BRACKNELL *and* ALGERNON *go into the music room,* GWENDOLEN *remains behind.*]

JACK   Charming day it has been, Miss Fairfax.

GWENDOLEN   Pray don't talk to me about the weather, Mr. Worthing. Whenever people talk to me about the weather, I always feel quite certain that they mean something else. And that makes me so nervous.

JACK   I do mean something else.

GWENDOLEN   I thought so. In fact, I am never wrong.

JACK   And I would like to be allowed to take advantage of Lady Bracknell's temporary absence . . .

GWENDOLEN   I would certainly advise you to do so. Mamma has a way of coming back suddenly into a room that I have often had to speak to her about.

JACK [*Nervously.*]   Miss Fairfax, ever since I met you I have admired you more than any girl . . . I have ever met since . . . I met you.

GWENDOLEN   Yes, I am quite aware of the fact. And I often wish that in public, at any rate, you had been more demonstrative. For me you have always had an irresistible fascination. Even before I met you I was far from indifferent to you. [JACK *looks at her in amazement.*] We live, as I hope you know, Mr. Worthing, in an age of ideals. The fact is constantly mentioned in the more expensive monthly magazines, and has reached

---

9. The social season, extending from May through July, when people of fashion came into London from their country estates for entertainments and parties.

the provincial pulpits, I am told: and my ideal has always been to love someone of the name of Ernest. There is something in that name that inspires absolute confidence. The moment Algernon first mentioned to me that he had a friend called Ernest, I knew I was destined to love you.

JACK   You really love me, Gwendolen?

GWENDOLEN   Passionately!

JACK   Darling! You don't know how happy you've made me.

GWENDOLEN   My own Ernest!

JACK   But you don't really mean to say that you couldn't love me if my name wasn't Ernest?

GWENDOLEN   But your name is Ernest.

JACK   Yes, I know it is. But supposing it was something else? Do you mean to say you couldn't love me then?

GWENDOLEN   [Glibly.]   Ah! that is clearly a metaphysical speculation, and like most metaphysical speculations has very little reference at all to the actual facts of real life, as we know them.

JACK   Personally, darling, to speak quite candidly, I don't much care about the name of Ernest . . . I don't think the name suits me at all.

GWENDOLEN   It suits you perfectly. It is a divine name. It has a music of its own. It produces vibrations.

JACK   Well, really, Gwendolen, I must say that I think there are lots of other much nicer names. I think Jack, for instance, a charming name.

GWENDOLEN   Jack? . . . No, there is very little music in the name Jack, if any at all, indeed. It does not thrill. It produces absolutely no vibrations. . . . I have known several Jacks, and they all, without exception, were more than usually plain. Besides, Jack is a notorious domesticity for John! And I pity any woman who is married to a man called John. She would probably never be allowed to know the entrancing pleasure of a single moment's solitude. The only really safe name is Ernest.

JACK   Gwendolen, I must get christened at once—I mean we must get married at once. There is no time to be lost.

GWENDOLEN   Married, Mr. Worthing?

JACK   [Astounded.]   Well . . . surely. You know that I love you, and you led me to believe, Miss Fairfax, that you were not absolutely indifferent to me.

GWENDOLEN   I adore you. But you haven't proposed to me yet. Nothing has been said at all about marriage. The subject has not even been touched on.

JACK   Well . . . may I propose to you now?

GWENDOLEN   I think it would be an admirable opportunity. And to spare you any possible disappointment, Mr. Worthing, I think it only fair to tell you quite frankly beforehand that I am fully determined to accept you.

JACK   Gwendolen!

GWENDOLEN   Yes, Mr. Worthing, what have you got to say to me?

JACK   You know what I have got to say to you.

GWENDOLEN   Yes, but you don't say it.

JACK   Gwendolen, will you marry me? [Goes on his knees.]

GWENDOLEN   Of course I will, darling. How long you have been about it! I am afraid you have had very little experience in how to propose.

JACK   My own one, I have never loved anyone in the world but you.

GWENDOLEN   Yes, but men often propose for practice. I know my brother Gerald does. All my girlfriends tell me so. What wonderfully blue eyes you have, Ernest! They are quite, quite blue. I hope you will always look at me just like that, especially when there are other people present.

[*Enter* LADY BRACKNELL.]

LADY BRACKNELL   Mr. Worthing! Rise, sir, from this semi-recumbent posture. It is most indecorous.

GWENDOLEN   Mamma! [*He tries to rise; she restrains him.*] I must beg you to retire. This is no place for you. Besides, Mr. Worthing has not quite finished yet.

LADY BRACKNELL   Finished what, may I ask?

GWENDOLEN   I am engaged to Mr. Worthing, mamma.

[*They rise together.*]

LADY BRACKNELL   Pardon me, you are not engaged to anyone. When you do become engaged to someone, I, or your father, should his health permit him, will inform you of the fact. An engagement should come on a young girl as a surprise, pleasant or unpleasant, as the case may be. It is hardly a matter that she could be allowed to arrange for herself. . . . And now I have a few questions to put to you, Mr. Worthing. While I am making these inquiries, you, Gwendolen, will wait for me below in the carriage.

GWENDOLEN [*Reproachfully.*]   Mamma!

LADY BRACKNELL   In the carriage, Gwendolen! [GWENDOLEN *goes to the door. She and* JACK *blow kisses to each other behind* LADY BRACKNELL's *back.* LADY BRACKNELL *looks vaguely about as if she could not understand what the noise was. Finally turns round.*] Gwendolen, the carriage!

GWENDOLEN   Yes, mamma. [*Goes out, looking back at* JACK.]

LADY BRACKNELL [*Sitting down.*]   You can take a seat, Mr. Worthing.

[*Looks in her pocket for notebook and pencil.*]

JACK   Thank you, Lady Bracknell, I prefer standing.

LADY BRACKNELL [*Pencil and notebook in hand.*]   I feel bound to tell you that you are not down on my list of eligible young men, although I have the same list as the dear Duchess of Bolton has. We work together, in fact. However, I am quite ready to enter your name, should your answers be what a really affectionate mother requires. Do you smoke?

JACK   Well, yes, I must admit I smoke.

LADY BRACKNELL   I am glad to hear it. A man should always have an occupation of some kind. There are far too many idle men in London as it is. How old are you?

JACK   Twenty-nine.

LADY BRACKNELL   A very good age to be married at. I have always been of opinion that a man who desires to get married should know either everything or nothing. Which do you know?

JACK [*After some hesitation.*]   I know nothing, Lady Bracknell.

LADY BRACKNELL   I am pleased to hear it. I do not approve of anything that tampers with natural ignorance. Ignorance is like a delicate exotic fruit; touch it and the bloom is gone. The whole theory of modern education is radically unsound. Fortunately in England, at any rate, education produces no effect whatsoever. If it did, it would prove a serious danger to the upper classes, and probably lead to acts of violence in Grosvenor Square.[1] What is your income?

---

1. A fashionable residential area in the West End of London.

JACK   Between seven and eight thousand a year.

LADY BRACKNELL [*Makes a note in her book.*]   In land, or in investments?

JACK   In investments, chiefly.

LADY BRACKNELL   That is satisfactory. What between the duties expected of one during one's lifetime, and the duties exacted from one after one's death,[2] land has ceased to be either a profit or a pleasure. It gives one position, and prevents one from keeping it up. That's all that can be said about land.

JACK   I have a country house with some land, of course, attached to it, about fifteen hundred acres, I believe; but I don't depend on that for my real income. In fact, as far as I can make out, the poachers are the only people who make anything out of it.

LADY BRACKNELL   A country house! How many bedrooms? Well, that point can be cleared up afterwards. You have a town house, I hope? A girl with a simple, unspoiled nature, like Gwendolen, could hardly be expected to reside in the country.

JACK   Well, I own a house in Belgrave Square,[3] but it is let by the year to Lady Bloxham. Of course, I can get it back whenever I like, at six months' notice.

LADY BRACKNELL   Lady Bloxham? I don't know her.

JACK   Oh, she goes about very little. She is a lady considerably advanced in years.

LADY BRACKNELL   Ah, nowadays that is no guarantee of respectability of character. What number in Belgrave Square?

JACK   149.

LADY BRACKNELL [*Shaking her head.*]   The unfashionable side. I thought there was something. However, that could easily be altered.

JACK   Do you mean the fashion, or the side?

LADY BRACKNELL [*Sternly.*]   Both, if necessary, I presume. What are your politics?

JACK   Well, I am afraid I really have none. I am a Liberal Unionist.[4]

LADY BRACKNELL   Oh, they count as Tories. They dine with us. Or come in the evening, at any rate. Now to minor matters. Are your parents living?

JACK   I have lost both my parents.

LADY BRACKNELL   Both? To lose one parent may be regarded as a misfortune—to lose *both* seems like carelessness. Who was your father? He was evidently a man of some wealth. Was he born in what the Radical papers call the purple of commerce, or did he rise from the ranks of aristocracy?

JACK   I am afraid I really don't know. The fact is, Lady Bracknell, I said I had lost my parents. It would be nearer the truth to say that my parents seem to have lost me. . . . I don't actually know who I am by birth. I was . . . well, I was found.

LADY BRACKNELL   Found!

JACK   The late Mr. Thomas Cardew, an old gentleman of a very charitable and kindly disposition, found me, and gave me the name of Worthing,

---

2. The wordplay is on "death duties"—i.e., inheritance taxes.
3. Another fashionable residential area in the West End.

4. A splinter group of members of the Liberal Party who in 1886, led by Joseph Chamberlain, joined forces with the Conservative Party (the "Tories") in opposing home rule for Ireland.

because he happened to have a first-class ticket for Worthing in his pocket at the time. Worthing is a place in Sussex. It is a seaside resort.

LADY BRACKNELL   Where did the charitable gentleman who had a first-class ticket for this seaside resort find you?

JACK [*Gravely.*]   In a handbag.

LADY BRACKNELL   A handbag?

JACK [*Very seriously.*]   Yes, Lady Bracknell. I was in a handbag—a somewhat large, black leather handbag, with handles to it—an ordinary handbag, in fact.

LADY BRACKNELL   In what locality did this Mr. James, or Thomas, Cardew come across this ordinary handbag?

JACK   In the cloak room at Victoria Station. It was given to him in mistake for his own.[5]

LADY BRACKNELL   The cloak room at Victoria Station?

JACK   Yes. The Brighton line.

LADY BRACKNELL   The line is immaterial. Mr. Worthing, I confess I feel somewhat bewildered by what you have just told me. To be born, or at any rate, bred in a handbag, whether it had handles or not, seems to me to display a contempt for the ordinary decencies of family life that reminds one of the worst excesses of the French Revolution. And I presume you know what that unfortunate movement led to? As for the particular locality in which the handbag was found, a cloak room at a railway station might serve to conceal a social indiscretion—has probably, indeed, been used for that purpose before now—but it could hardly be regarded as an assured basis for a recognized position in good society.

JACK   May I ask you then what you would advise me to do? I need hardly say I would do anything in the world to ensure Gwendolen's happiness.

LADY BRACKNELL   I would strongly advise you, Mr. Worthing, to try and acquire some relations as soon as possible, and to make a definite effort to produce at any rate one parent, of either sex, before the season is quite over.[6]

JACK   Well, I don't see how I could possibly manage to do that. I can produce the handbag at any moment, it is in my dressing room at home. I really think that should satisfy you, Lady Bracknell.

LADY BRACKNELL   Me, sir! What has it to do with me? You can hardly imagine that I and Lord Bracknell would dream of allowing our only daughter—a girl brought up with the utmost care—to marry into a cloak room, and form an alliance with a parcel? Good morning, Mr. Worthing!

[LADY BRACKNELL *sweeps out in majestic indignation.*]

JACK   Good morning! [ALGERNON, *from the other room, strikes up the Wedding March.* JACK *looks perfectly furious, and goes to the door.*] For goodness' sake don't play that ghastly tune, Algy! How idiotic you are!

[*The music stops, and* ALGERNON *enters cheerily.*]

---

5. In the four-act version of the play, Jack explains further what happened to Mr. Cardew: "He did not discover the error till he arrived at his own house. All subsequent efforts to ascertain who I was were unavailing."

6. In the four-act version of the play, Jack later comments to Algernon about Lady Bracknell's demands about locating parents: "After all what does it matter whether a man has ever had a father and mother or not? Mothers, of course, are all right. They pay a chap's bills and don't bother him. But fathers bother a chap and never pay his bills. I don't know a single chap at the club who speaks to his father." And Algernon remarks: "Yes. Fathers are certainly not popular just at present. . . . They are like these chaps, the minor poets. They are never quoted."

ALGERNON Didn't it go off all right, old boy? You don't mean to say Gwendolen refused you? I know it is a way she has. She is always refusing people. I think it is most ill-natured of her.

JACK Oh, Gwendolen is as right as a trivet.[7] As far as she is concerned, we are engaged. Her mother is perfectly unbearable. Never met such a Gorgon[8] . . . I don't really know what a Gorgon is like, but I am quite sure that Lady Bracknell is one. In any case, she is a monster, without being a myth, which is rather unfair . . . I beg your pardon, Algy, I suppose I shouldn't talk about your own aunt in that way before you.

ALGERNON My dear boy, I love hearing my relations abused. It is the only thing that makes me put up with them at all. Relations are simply a tedious pack of people who haven't got the remotest knowledge of how to live, nor the smallest instinct about when to die.

JACK Oh, that is nonsense!

ALGERNON It isn't!

JACK Well, I won't argue about the matter. You always want to argue about things.

ALGERNON That is exactly what things were originally made for.

JACK Upon my word, if I thought that, I'd shoot myself . . . [A pause.] You don't think there is any chance of Gwendolen becoming like her mother in about a hundred and fifty years, do you, Algy?

ALGERNON All women become like their mothers. That is their tragedy. No man does. That's his.

JACK Is that clever?

ALGERNON It is perfectly phrased! and quite as true as any observation in civilized life should be.

JACK I am sick to death of cleverness. Everybody is clever nowadays. You can't go anywhere without meeting clever people. The thing has become an absolute public nuisance. I wish to goodness we had a few fools left.

ALGERNON We have.

JACK I should extremely like to meet them. What do they talk about?

ALGERNON The fools? Oh! about the clever people, of course.

JACK What fools!

ALGERNON By the way, did you tell Gwendolen the truth about your being Ernest in town, and Jack in the country?

JACK [In a very patronizing manner.] My dear fellow, the truth isn't quite the sort of thing one tells to a nice sweet refined girl. What extraordinary ideas you have about the way to behave to a woman!

ALGERNON The only way to behave to a woman is to make love to[9] her, if she is pretty, and to someone else if she is plain.

JACK Oh, that is nonsense.

ALGERNON What about your brother? What about the profligate Ernest?

JACK Oh, before the end of the week I shall have got rid of him. I'll say he died in Paris of apoplexy. Lots of people die of apoplexy, quite suddenly, don't they?

ALGERNON Yes, but it's hereditary, my dear fellow. It's a sort of thing that runs in families. You had much better say a severe chill.

---

7. Proverbial expression meaning reliably steady, like a tripod ("trivet") used to support pots over a fire.
8. In classical mythology a snake-haired female monster; at the sight of her, other creatures turned to stone.
9. Woo, court.

JACK You are sure a severe chill isn't hereditary, or anything of that kind?

ALGERNON Of course it isn't!

JACK Very well, then. My poor brother Ernest is carried off suddenly in Paris, by a severe chill. That gets rid of him.[1]

ALGERNON But I thought you said that . . . Miss Cardew was a little too much interested in your poor brother Ernest? Won't she feel his loss a good deal?

JACK Oh, that is all right. Cecily is not a silly romantic girl, I am glad to say. She has got a capital appetite, goes on long walks, and pays no attention at all to her lessons.

ALGERNON I would rather like to see Cecily.

JACK I will take very good care you never do. She is excessively pretty, and she is only just eighteen.

ALGERNON Have you told Gwendolen yet that you have an excessively pretty ward who is only just eighteen?

JACK Oh! one doesn't blurt these things out to people. Cecily and Gwendolen are perfectly certain to be extremely great friends. I'll bet you anything you like that half an hour after they have met, they will be calling each other sister.

ALGERNON Women only do that when they have called each other a lot of other things first. Now, my dear boy, if we want to get a good table at Willis's, we really must go and dress. Do you know it is nearly seven?

JACK [Irritably.] Oh! it always is nearly seven.

ALGERNON Well, I'm hungry.

JACK I never knew you when you weren't. . . .

ALGERNON What shall we do after dinner? Go to the theatre?

JACK Oh no! I loathe listening.

ALGERNON Well, let us go to the club?

JACK Oh, no! I hate talking.

ALGERNON Well, we might trot around to the Empire[2] at ten?

JACK Oh no! I can't bear looking at things. It is so silly.

ALGERNON Well, what shall we do?

JACK Nothing!

ALGERNON It is awfully hard work doing nothing. However, I don't mind hard work where there is no definite object of any kind.

[Enter LANE.]

LANE Miss Fairfax.

[Enter GWENDOLEN. LANE goes out.]

ALGERNON Gwendolen, upon my word!

GWENDOLEN Algy, kindly turn your back. I have something very particular to say to Mr. Worthing.

ALGERNON Really, Gwendolen, I don't think I can allow this at all.

GWENDOLEN Algy, you always adopt a strictly immoral attitude towards life. You are not quite old enough to do that. [ALGERNON retires to the fireplace.]

JACK My own darling!

---

1. In the four-act version of the play, Jack explains further: "I'll wear mourning for him, of course; that would be only decent. I don't at all mind wearing mourning. I think that all black, with a good pearl pin, rather smart. Then I'll go down home and break the news to my household."
2. A music hall in Leicester Square that featured light entertainment.

GWENDOLEN   Ernest, we may never be married. From the expression on mamma's face I fear we never shall. Few parents nowadays pay any regard to what their children say to them. The old-fashioned respect for the young is fast dying out. Whatever influence I ever had over mamma, I lost at the age of three. But although she may prevent us from becoming man and wife, and I may marry someone else, and marry often, nothing that she can possibly do can alter my eternal devotion to you.

JACK   Dear Gwendolen!

GWENDOLEN   The story of your romantic origin, as related to me by mamma, with unpleasing comments, has naturally stirred the deeper fibres of my nature. Your Christian name has an irresistible fascination. The simplicity of your character makes you exquisitely incomprehensible to me. Your town address at the Albany I have. What is your address in the country?

JACK   The Manor House, Woolton, Hertfordshire.

[ALGERNON, who has been carefully listening, smiles to himself, and writes the address on his shirt-cuff.³ Then picks up the Railway Guide.]

GWENDOLEN   There is a good postal service, I suppose? It may be necessary to do something desperate. That of course will require serious consideration. I will communicate with you daily.

JACK   My own one!

GWENDOLEN   How long do you remain in town?

JACK   Till Monday.

GWENDOLEN   Good! Algy, you may turn round now.

ALGERNON   Thanks, I've turned round already.

GWENDOLEN   You may also ring the bell.

JACK   You will let me see you to your carriage, my own darling?

GWENDOLEN   Certainly.

JACK [To LANE, who now enters.]   I will see Miss Fairfax out.

LANE   Yes, sir. [JACK and GWENDOLEN go off.]

[LANE presents several letters on a salver to ALGERNON. It is to be surmised that they are bills, as ALGERNON after looking at the envelopes, tears them up.]

ALGERNON   A glass of sherry, Lane.

LANE   Yes, sir.

ALGERNON   Tomorrow, Lane, I'm going Bunburying.

LANE   Yes, sir.

ALGERNON   I shall probably not be back till Monday. You can put up my dress clothes, my smoking jacket,⁴ and all the Bunbury suits . . .

LANE   Yes, sir. [Handing sherry.]

ALGERNON   I hope tomorrow will be a fine day, Lane.

LANE   It never is, sir.

ALGERNON   Lane, you're a perfect pessimist.

LANE   I do my best to give satisfaction, sir.

[Enter JACK. LANE goes off.]

JACK   There's a sensible, intellectual girl! the only girl I ever cared for in my life. [ALGERNON is laughing immoderately.] What on earth are you so amused at?

3. Because shirt cuffs were heavily starched they provided a good surface on which to make notes.
4. Coat worn when gentlemen assembled in a room designated for smoking. The object was to avoid contaminating their regular clothing with the smell of cigars or pipes, which was considered offensive to ladies. "Put up": pack up.

ALGERNON   Oh, I'm a little anxious about poor Bunbury, that is all.

JACK   If you don't take care, your friend Bunbury will get you into a serious scrape some day.

ALGERNON   I love scrapes. They are the only things that are never serious.

JACK   Oh, that's nonsense, Algy. You never talk anything but nonsense.

ALGERNON   Nobody ever does.

> [JACK *looks indignantly at him, and leaves the room.* ALGERNON *lights a cigarette, reads his shirt-cuff, and smiles.*]

ACT-DROP[5]

Second Act

> SCENE—*Garden at the Manor House. A flight of grey stone steps leads up to the house. The garden, an old-fashioned one, full of roses. Time of year, July. Basket chairs, and a table covered with books, are set under a large yew tree.*

> [MISS PRISM[6] *discovered seated at the table.* CECILY *is at the back watering flowers.*]

MISS PRISM [*Calling.*]   Cecily, Cecily! Surely such a utilitarian occupation as the watering of flowers is rather Moulton's duty than yours? Especially at a moment when intellectual pleasures await you. Your German grammar is on the table. Pray open it at page fifteen. We will repeat yesterday's lesson.

CECILY [*Coming over very slowly.*]   But I don't like German. It isn't at all a becoming language. I know perfectly well that I look quite plain after my German lesson.

MISS PRISM   Child, you know how anxious your guardian is that you should improve yourself in every way. He laid particular stress on your German, as he was leaving for town yesterday. Indeed, he always lays stress on your German when he is leaving for town.

CECILY   Dear Uncle Jack is so very serious! Sometime he is so serious that I think he cannot be quite well.

MISS PRISM [*Drawing herself up.*]   Your guardian enjoys the best of health, and his gravity of demeanour is especially to be commended in one so comparatively young as he is. I know no one who has a higher sense of duty and responsibility.

CECILY   I suppose that is why he often looks a little bored when we three are together.

MISS PRISM   Cecily! I am surprised at you. Mr. Worthing has many troubles in his life. Idle merriment and triviality would be out of place in his conversation. You must remember his constant anxiety about that unfortunate young man his brother.

CECILY   I wish Uncle Jack would allow that unfortunate young man, his brother, to come down here sometimes. We might have a good influence over him, Miss Prism. I am sure you certainly would. You know German, and geology, and things of that kind influence a man very much. [CECILY *begins to write in her diary.*]

---

5. A special curtain lowered during theatrical performances to denote intervals between acts or scenes.

6. The name recalls Charles Dickens's *Little Dor-* *rit* (1855–57), in which Mrs. General, a prim and proper teacher of manners for young ladies, trains them to repeat "prunes and prism" aloud because this exercise "gives a pretty form to the lips."

MISS PRISM [*Shaking her head.*]   I do not think that even I could produce any effect on a character that according to his own brother's admission is irretrievably weak and vacillating. Indeed I am not sure that I would desire to reclaim him. I am not in favor of this modern mania for turning bad people into good people at a moment's notice. As a man sows so let him reap.[7] You must put away your diary, Cecily. I really don't see why you should keep a diary at all.

CECILY   I keep a diary in order to enter the wonderful secrets of my life. If I didn't write them down I should probably forget all about them.

MISS PRISM   Memory, my dear Cecily, is the diary that we all carry about with us.

CECILY   Yes, but it usually chronicles the things that have never happened, and couldn't possibly have happened. I believe that Memory is responsible for nearly all the three-volume novels that Mudie[8] sends us.

MISS PRISM   Do not speak slightingly of the three-volume novel, Cecily. I wrote one myself in earlier days.

CECILY   Did you really, Miss Prism? How wonderfully clever you are! I hope it did not end happily? I don't like novels that end happily. They depress me so much.

MISS PRISM   The good ended happily, and the bad unhappily. That is what Fiction means.

CECILY   I suppose so. But it seems very unfair. And was your novel ever published?

MISS PRISM   Alas! no. The manuscript unfortunately was abandoned. I use the word in the sense of lost or mislaid. To your work, child, these speculations are profitless.

CECILY [*Smiling.*]   But I see dear Dr. Chasuble[9] coming up through the garden.

MISS PRISM [*Rising and advancing.*]   Dr. Chasuble! This is indeed a pleasure.

[*Enter* CANON CHASUBLE.]

CHASUBLE   And how are we this morning? Miss Prism, you are, I trust, well?

CECILY   Miss Prism has just been complaining of a slight headache. I think it would do her so much good to have a short stroll with you in the Park, Dr. Chasuble.

MISS PRISM   Cecily, I have not mentioned anything about a headache.

CECILY   No, dear Miss Prism, I know that, but I felt instinctively that you had a headache. Indeed I was thinking about that, and not about my German lesson, when the Rector came in.

CHASUBLE   I hope, Cecily, you are not inattentive.

CECILY   Oh, I am afraid I am.

CHASUBLE   That is strange. Were I fortunate enough to be Miss Prism's pupil, I would hang upon her lips. [MISS PRISM *glares.*] I spoke metaphorically.—My metaphor was drawn from bees. Ahem! Mr. Worthing, I suppose, has not returned from town yet?

MISS PRISM   We do not expect him till Monday afternoon.

---

7. Cf. Galatians 6.7: "whatsoever a man soweth, that shall he also reap."
8. Mudie's Circulating Library, which lent copies of new three-volume novels (usually sentimental tales) to subscribers for a moderate fee. Mudie's

power in controlling the book market, especially for novels, was on the wane by 1895.
9. A chasuble is an ornate garment worn by a priest.

CHASUBLE Ah yes, he usually likes to spend his Sunday in London. He is not one of those whose sole aim is enjoyment, as, by all accounts, that unfortunate young man his brother seems to be. But I must not disturb Egeria[1] and her pupil any longer.

MISS PRISM Egeria? My name is Laetitia, Doctor.

CHASUBLE [*Bowing.*] A classical allusion merely, drawn from the Pagan authors. I shall see you both no doubt at Evensong?[2]

MISS PRISM I think, dear Doctor, I will have a stroll with you. I find I have a headache after all, and a walk might do it good.

CHASUBLE With pleasure, Miss Prism, with pleasure. We might go as far as the schools and back.

MISS PRISM That would be delightful. Cecily, you will read your Political Economy[3] in my absence. The chapter on the Fall of the Rupee[4] you may omit. It is somewhat too sensational. Even these metallic problems have their melodramatic side. [*Goes down the garden with* DR. CHASUBLE.]

CECILY [*Picks up books and throws them back on table.*] Horrid Political Economy! Horrid Geography! Horrid, horrid German!

[*Enter* MERRIMAN *with a card on a salver.*]

MERRIMAN Mr. Ernest Worthing has just driven over from the station. He has brought his luggage with him.

CECILY [*Takes the card and reads it.*] "Mr. Ernest Worthing, B. 4, The Albany, W." Uncle Jack's brother! Did you tell him Mr. Worthing was in town?

MERRIMAN Yes, Miss. He seemed very much disappointed. I mentioned that you and Miss Prism were in the garden. He said he was anxious to speak to you privately for a moment.

CECILY. Ask Mr. Ernest Worthing to come here. I suppose you had better talk to the housekeeper about a room for him.

MERRIMAN Yes, Miss.   [MERRIMAN *goes off.*]

CECILY I have never met any really wicked person before. I feel rather frightened. I am so afraid he will look just like everyone else. [*Enter* ALGERNON, *very gay and debonair.*] He does!

ALGERNON [*Raising his hat.*] You are my little cousin Cecily, I'm sure.

CECILY You are under some strange mistake. I am not little. In fact, I believe I am more than usually tall for my age. [ALGERNON *is rather taken aback.*] But I am your cousin Cecily. You, I see from your card, are Uncle Jack's brother, my cousin Ernest, my wicked cousin Ernest.

ALGERNON Oh! I am not really wicked at all, cousin Cecily. You mustn't think that I am wicked.

CECILY If you are not, then you have certainly been deceiving us all in a very inexcusable manner. I hope you have not been leading a double life, pretending to be wicked and being really good all the time. That would be hypocrisy.

ALGERNON [*Looks at her in amazement*] Oh! Of course I have been rather reckless.

CECILY I am glad to hear it.

---

1. In Roman legend a nymph who gave counsel to the second king of Rome. Her name was therefore also used as an epithet for a woman who provides guidance.
2. Evening church services.
3. I.e., book about economics.
4. The basic unit of currency in India. British civil servants who worked in India were paid in rupees and would suffer from its fall in value.

ALGERNON   In fact, now you mention the subject, I have been very bad in my own small way.

CECILY   I don't think you should be so proud of that, though I am sure it must have been very pleasant.

ALGERNON   It is much pleasanter being here with you.

CECILY   I can't understand how you are here at all. Uncle Jack won't be back till Monday afternoon.

ALGERNON   That is a great disappointment. I am obliged to go up by the first train on Monday morning. I have a business appointment that I am anxious . . . to miss.

CECILY   Couldn't you miss it anywhere but in London?

ALGERNON   No: the appointment is in London.

CECILY   Well, I know, of course, how important it is not to keep a business engagement, if one wants to retain any sense of the beauty of life, but still I think you had better wait till Uncle Jack arrives. I know he wants to speak to you about your emigrating.

ALGERNON   About my what?

CECILY   Your emigrating. He has gone up to buy your outfit.

ALGERNON   I certainly wouldn't let Jack buy my outfit. He has no taste in neckties at all.

CECILY   I don't think you will require neckties. Uncle Jack is sending you to Australia.[5]

ALGERNON   Australia? I'd sooner die.

CECILY   Well, he said at dinner on Wednesday night, that you would have to choose between this world, the next world, and Australia.

ALGERNON   Oh, well! The accounts I have received of Australia and the next world are not particularly encouraging. This world is good enough for me, cousin Cecily.

CECILY   Yes, but are you good enough for it?

ALGERNON   I'm afraid I'm not that. That is why I want you to reform me. You might make that your mission, if you don't mind, cousin Cecily.

CECILY   I'm afraid I've no time, this afternoon.

ALGERNON   Well, would you mind my reforming myself this afternoon?

CECILY   It is rather Quixotic of you. But I think you should try.

ALGERNON   I will. I feel better already.

CECILY   You are looking a little worse.

ALGERNON   That is because I am hungry.

CECILY   How thoughtless of me. I should have remembered that when one is going to lead an entirely new life, one requires regular and wholesome meals. Won't you come in?

ALGERNON   Thank you. Might I have a buttonhole[6] first? I never have any appetite unless I have a buttonhole first.

CECILY   A Maréchal Niel?[7] [Picks up scissors.]

ALGERNON   No, I'd sooner have a pink rose.

CECILY   Why? [Cuts a flower.]

---

5. The British had originally viewed Australia as a place to which they banished their criminals. By this time, however, it was perceived in some quarters as a place, like Canada, to which families might send harmless but useless members, who would be paid an allowance to remain abroad.

6. I.e., a flower to wear in the buttonhole of his coat lapel.

7. A chrome-yellow variety of rose named after Adolphe Niel (1802–1869), one of the generals of Napoleon III.

ALGERNON   Because you are like a pink rose, cousin Cecily.

CECILY   I don't think it can be right for you to talk to me like that. Miss Prism never says such things to me.

ALGERNON   Then Miss Prism is a shortsighted old lady. [CECILY *puts the rose in his buttonhole.*] You are the prettiest girl I ever saw.

CECILY   Miss Prism says that all good looks are a snare.

ALGERNON   They are a snare that every sensible man would like to be caught in.

CECILY   Oh! I don't think I would care to catch a sensible man. I shouldn't know what to talk to him about.

    [*They pass into the house.* MISS PRISM *and* DR. CHASUBLE *return.*]

MISS PRISM   You are too much alone, dear Dr. Chasuble. You should get married. A misanthrope I can understand—a womanthrope, never!

CHASUBLE [*With a scholar's shudder.*][8]   Believe me, I do not deserve so neologistic a phrase. The precept as well as the practice of the Primitive Church[9] was distinctly against matrimony.

MISS PRISM [*Sententiously.*]   That is obviously the reason why the Primitive Church has not lasted up to the present day. And you do not seem to realize, dear Doctor, that by persistently remaining single, a man converts himself into a permanent public temptation. Men should be more careful; this very celibacy leads weaker vessels astray.

CHASUBLE   But is a man not equally attractive when married?

MISS PRISM   No married man is ever attractive except to his wife.

CHASUBLE   And often, I've been told, not even to her.

MISS PRISM   That depends on the intellectual sympathies of the woman. Maturity can always be depended on. Ripeness can be trusted. Young women are green. [DR. CHASUBLE *starts.*] I spoke horticulturally. My metaphor was drawn from fruits. But where is Cecily?

CHASUBLE   Perhaps she followed us to the schools.

    [*Enter* JACK *slowly from the back of the garden. He is dressed in the deepest mourning, with crape hat-band and black gloves.*]

MISS PRISM   Mr. Worthing!

CHASUBLE   Mr. Worthing?

MISS PRISM   This is indeed a surprise. We did not look for you till Monday afternoon.

JACK [*Shakes* MISS PRISM*'s hand in a tragic manner.*]   I have returned sooner than I expected. Dr. Chasuble, I hope you are well?

CHASUBLE   Dear Mr. Worthing, I trust this garb of woe does not betoken some terrible calamity?

JACK   My brother.

MISS PRISM   More shameful debts and extravagance?

CHASUBLE   Still leading his life of pleasure?

JACK [*Shaking his head.*]   Dead!

CHASUBLE   Your brother Ernest dead?

JACK   Quite dead.

MISS PRISM   What a lesson for him! I trust he will profit by it.

CHASUBLE   Mr. Worthing, I offer you my sincere condolence. You have at least the consolation of knowing that you were always the most generous and forgiving of brothers.

---

8. He shudders because instead of using the correct word for woman hater, *misogynist*, she has coined her own term, one that is etymologically nonsensical.

9. The early Christian Church, of the 1st to 4th centuries.

JACK   Poor Ernest! He had many faults, but it is a sad, sad blow.

CHASUBLE   Very sad indeed. Were you with him at the end?

JACK   No. He died abroad; in Paris, in fact. I had a telegram last night from the manager of the Grand Hotel.

CHASUBLE   Was the cause of death mentioned?

JACK   A severe chill, it seems.

MISS PRISM   As a man sows, so shall he reap.

CHASUBLE [*Raising his hand.*]   Charity, dear Miss Prism, charity! None of us are perfect. I myself am peculiarly susceptible to drafts. Will the interment take place here?

JACK   No. He seemed to have expressed a desire to be buried in Paris.

CHASUBLE   In Paris! [*Shakes his head.*] I fear that hardly points to any very serious state of mind at the last. You would no doubt wish me to make some slight allusion to this tragic domestic affliction next Sunday. [JACK *presses his hand convulsively.*] My sermon on the meaning of the manna in the wilderness can be adapted to almost any occasion, joyful, or, as in the present case, distressing. [*All sigh.*] I have preached it at harvest celebrations, christenings, confirmations, on days of humiliation and festal days. The last time I delivered it was in the Cathedral, as a charity sermon on behalf of the Society for the Prevention of Discontent among the Upper Orders. The Bishop, who was present, was much struck by some of the analogies I drew.

JACK   Ah! That reminds me, you mentioned christenings, I think, Dr. Chasuble? I suppose you know how to christen all right? [DR. CHASUBLE *looks astounded.*] I mean, of course, you are continually christening, aren't you?

MISS PRISM   It is, I regret to say, one of the Rector's most constant duties in this parish. I have often spoken to the poorer classes on the subject. But they don't seem to know what thrift is.

CHASUBLE   But is there any particular infant in whom you are interested, Mr. Worthing? Your brother was, I believe, unmarried, was he not?

JACK   Oh yes.

MISS PRISM [*Bitterly.*]   People who live entirely for pleasure usually are.

JACK   But it is not for any child, dear Doctor. I am very fond of children. No! the fact is, I would like to be christened myself, this afternoon, if you have nothing better to do.

CHASUBLE   But surely, Mr. Worthing, you have been christened already?

JACK   I don't remember anything about it.

CHASUBLE   But have you any grave doubts on the subject?

JACK   I certainly intend to have. Of course I don't know if the thing would bother you in any way, or if you think I am a little too old now.

CHASUBLE   Not at all. The sprinkling, and, indeed, the immersion of adults is a perfectly canonical practice.

JACK   Immersion!

CHASUBLE   You need have no apprehensions. Sprinkling is all that is necessary, or indeed I think advisable. Our weather is so changeable. At what hour would you wish the ceremony performed?

JACK   Oh, I might trot round about five if that would suit you.

CHASUBLE   Perfectly, perfectly! In fact I have two similar ceremonies to perform at that time. A case of twins that occurred recently in one of the outlying cottages on your own estate. Poor Jenkins the carter, a most hardworking man.

JACK   Oh! I don't see much fun in being christened along with other babies. It would be childish. Would half-past five do?

CHASUBLE   Admirably! Admirably! [*Takes out watch.*] And now, dear Mr. Worthing, I will not intrude any longer into a house of sorrow. I would merely beg you not to be too much bowed down by grief. What seem to us bitter trials are often blessings in disguise.

MISS PRISM   This seems to me a blessing of an extremely obvious kind.

[*Enter* CECILY *from the house.*]

CECILY   Uncle Jack! Oh, I am pleased to see you back. But what horrid clothes you have got on! Do go and change them.

MISS PRISM   Cecily!

CHASUBLE   My child! my child! [CECILY *goes towards* JACK; *he kisses her brow in a melancholy manner.*]

CECILY   What is the matter, Uncle Jack? Do look happy! You look as if you had toothache, and I have got such a surprise for you. Who do you think is in the dining room? Your brother!

JACK   Who?

CECILY   Your brother Ernest. He arrived about half an hour ago.

JACK   What nonsense! I haven't got a brother!

CECILY   Oh, don't say that. However badly he may have behaved to you in the past he is still your brother. You couldn't be so heartless as to disown him. I'll tell him to come out. And you will shake hands with him, won't you, Uncle Jack? [*Runs back into the house.*]

CHASUBLE   These are very joyful tidings.

MISS PRISM   After we had all been resigned to his loss, his sudden return seems to me peculiarly distressing.

JACK   My brother is in the dining room? I don't know what it all means. I think it is perfectly absurd.

[*Enter* ALGERNON *and* CECILY *hand in hand. They come slowly up to* JACK.]

JACK   Good heavens! [*Motions* ALGERNON *away.*]

ALGERNON   Brother John, I have come down from town to tell you that I am very sorry for all the trouble I have given you, and that I intend to lead a better life in the future. [JACK *glares at him and does not take his hand.*]

CECILY   Uncle Jack, you are not going to refuse your own brother's hand?

JACK   Nothing will induce me to take his hand. I think his coming down here disgraceful. He knows perfectly well why.

CECILY   Uncle Jack, do be nice. There is some good in everyone. Ernest has just been telling me about his poor invalid friend Mr. Bunbury whom he goes to visit so often. And surely there must be much good in one who is kind to an invalid, and leaves the pleasures of London to sit by a bed of pain.

JACK   Oh! he has been talking about Bunbury, has he?

CECILY   Yes, he has told me all about poor Mr. Bunbury, and his terrible state of health.

JACK   Bunbury! Well, I won't have him talk to you about Bunbury or about anything else. It is enough to drive one perfectly frantic.

ALGERNON   Of course I admit that the faults were all on my side. But I must say that I think that Brother John's coldness to me is peculiarly painful. I expected a more enthusiastic welcome, especially considering it is the first time I have come here.

CECILY   Uncle Jack, if you don't shake hands with Ernest, I will never forgive you.

JACK   Never forgive me?

CECILY   Never, never, never!

JACK   Well, this is the last time I shall ever do it. [*Shakes hands with* ALGERNON *and glares.*]

CHASUBLE   It's pleasant, is it not, to see so perfect a reconciliation? I think we might leave the two brothers together.

MISS PRISM   Cecily, you will come with us.

CECILY   Certainly, Miss Prism. My little task of reconciliation is over.

CHASUBLE   You have done a beautiful action today, dear child.

MISS PRISM   We must not be premature in our judgments.

CECILY   I feel very happy. [*They all go off.*]

JACK   You young scoundrel, Algy, you must get out of this place as soon as possible. I don't allow any Bunburying here.

[*Enter* MERRIMAN.]

MERRIMAN   I have put Mr. Ernest's things in the room next to yours, sir. I suppose that is all right?

JACK   What?

MERRIMAN   Mr. Ernest's luggage, sir. I have unpacked it and put it in the room next to your own.

JACK   His luggage?

MERRIMAN   Yes, sir. Three portmanteaus, a dressing case, two hat-boxes, and a large luncheon basket.[1]

ALGERNON   I am afraid I can't stay more than a week this time.

JACK   Merriman, order the dogcart[2] at once. Mr. Ernest has been suddenly called back to town.

MERRIMAN   Yes, sir.   [*Goes back into the house.*]

ALGERNON   What a fearful liar you are, Jack. I have not been called back to town at all.

JACK   Yes, you have.

ALGERNON   I haven't heard anyone call me.

JACK   Your duty as a gentleman calls you back.

ALGERNON   My duty as a gentleman has never interfered with my pleasures in the smallest degree.

JACK   I can quite understand that.

ALGERNON   Well, Cecily is a darling.

JACK   You are not to talk of Miss Cardew like that. I don't like it.

ALGERNON   Well, I don't like your clothes. You look perfectly ridiculous in them. Why on earth don't you go up and change? It is perfectly childish to be in deep mourning for a man who is actually staying for a whole week with you in your house as a guest. I call it grotesque.

JACK   You are certainly not staying with me for a whole week as a guest or anything else. You have got to leave . . . by the four-five train.

---

1. According to *Cassell's Domestic Dictionary* (1877–79), "a convenient little receptacle in which gentlemen who are going out shooting for the day, or artists who wish to sketch, can carry their luncheon with them." "Portmanteaus": large leather suitcases. A "dressing case" (also according to *Cassell's*) was "ordinarily made of rosewood, mahogany or coromandel wood." It was supposed to include "scent bottles, jars for pomade and tooth-powders, hair brushes and combs, shaving, nail and tooth brushes, razors and strop, nail scissors, button-hook, tweezer, nail file and penknife" [noted by Russell Jackson].

2. A horse-drawn cart with seats, originally designed to carry hunters and their hunting dogs.

ALGERNON   I certainly won't leave you so long as you are in mourning. It would be most unfriendly. If I were in mourning you would stay with me, I suppose. I should think it very unkind if you didn't.

JACK   Well, will you go if I change my clothes?

ALGERNON   Yes, if you are not too long. I never saw anybody take so long to dress, and with such little result.

JACK   Well, at any rate, that is better than being always overdressed as you are.

ALGERNON   If I am occasionally a little overdressed, I make up for it by being always immensely overeducated.

JACK   Your vanity is ridiculous, your conduct an outrage, and your presence in my garden utterly absurd. However, you have got to catch the four-five, and I hope you will have a pleasant journey back to town. This Bunburying, as you call it, has not been a great success for you. [*Goes into the house.*]

ALGERNON   I think it has been a great success. I'm in love with Cecily, and that is everything.

   [*Enter* CECILY *at the back of the garden. She picks up the can and begins to water the flowers.*]

But I must see her before I go, and make arrangements for another Bunbury. Ah, there she is.

CECILY   Oh, I merely came back to water the roses. I thought you were with Uncle Jack.

ALGERNON   He's gone to order the dogcart for me.

CECILY   Oh, is he going to take you for a nice drive?

ALGERNON   He's going to send me away.

CECILY   Then have we got to part?

ALGERNON   I am afraid so. It's very painful parting.

CECILY   It is always painful to part from people whom one has known for a very brief space of time. The absence of old friends one can endure with equanimity. But even a momentary separation from anyone to whom one has just been introduced is almost unbearable.

ALGERNON   Thank you.

   [*Enter* MERRIMAN.]

MERRIMAN   The dogcart is at the door, sir. [ALGERNON *looks appealingly at* CECILY.]

CECILY   It can wait, Merriman . . . for . . . five minutes.

MERRIMAN   Yes, Miss.   [*Exit* MERRIMAN.]

ALGERNON   I hope, Cecily, I shall not offend you if I state quite frankly and openly that you seem to me to be in every way the visible personification of absolute perfection.

CECILY   I think your frankness does you great credit, Ernest. If you will allow me I will copy your remarks into my diary. [*Goes over to table and begins writing in diary.*]

ALGERNON   Do you really keep a diary? I'd give anything to look at it. May I?

CECILY   Oh no. [*Puts her hand over it.*] You see, it is simply a very young girl's record of her own thoughts and impressions, and consequently meant for publication. When it appears in volume form I hope you will order a copy. But pray, Ernest, don't stop. I delight in taking down from dictation. I have reached "absolute perfection." You can go on. I am quite ready for more.

ALGERNON [*Somewhat taken aback.*]   Ahem! Ahem!

CECILY   Oh, don't cough, Ernest. When one is dictating one should speak fluently and not cough. Besides, I don't know how to spell a cough. [*Writes as* ALGERNON *speaks.*]

ALGERNON [*Speaking very rapidly.*]   Cecily, ever since I first looked upon your wonderful and incomparable beauty, I have dared to love you wildly, passionately, devotedly, hopelessly.

CECILY   I don't think that you should tell me that you love me wildly, passionately, devotedly, hopelessly. Hopelessly doesn't seem to make much sense, does it?

ALGERNON   Cecily!

      [*Enter* MERRIMAN.]

MERRIMAN   The dogcart is waiting, sir.

ALGERNON   Tell it to come round next week, at the same hour.

MERRIMAN [*Looks at* CECILY, *who makes no sign.*]   Yes, sir.

      [MERRIMAN *retires.*]

CECILY   Uncle Jack would be very much annoyed if he knew you were staying on till next week, at the same hour.

ALGERNON   Oh, I don't care about Jack. I don't care for anybody in the whole world but you. I love you, Cecily. You will marry me, won't you?

CECILY   You silly boy! Of course. Why, we have been engaged for the last three months.

ALGERNON   For the last three months?

CECILY   Yes, it will be exactly three months on Thursday.

ALGERNON   But how did we become engaged?

CECILY   Well, ever since dear Uncle Jack first confessed to us that he had a younger brother who was very wicked and bad, you of course have formed the chief topic of conversation between myself and Miss Prism. And of course a man who is much talked about is always very attractive. One feels there must be something in him after all. I daresay it was foolish of me, but I fell in love with you, Ernest.

ALGERNON   Darling! And when was the engagement actually settled?

CECILY   On the 14th of February last. Worn out by your entire ignorance of my existence, I determined to end the matter one way or the other, and after a long struggle with myself I accepted you under this dear old tree here. The next day I bought this little ring in your name, and this is the little bangle with the true lovers' knot I promised you always to wear.

ALGERNON   Did I give you this? It's very pretty, isn't it?

CECILY   Yes, you've wonderfully good taste, Ernest. It's the excuse I've always given for your leading such a bad life. And this is the box in which I keep all your dear letters. [*Kneels at table, opens box, and produces letters tied up with blue ribbon.*]

ALGERNON   My letters! But my own sweet Cecily, I have never written you any letters.

CECILY   You need hardly remind me of that, Ernest. I remember only too well that I was forced to write your letters for you. I always wrote three times a week, and sometimes oftener.

ALGERNON   Oh, do let me read them, Cecily?

CECILY   Oh, I couldn't possibly. They would make you far too conceited. [*Replaces box.*] The three you wrote me after I had broken off the engagement are so beautiful, and so badly spelled, that even now I can hardly read them without crying a little.

ALGERNON   But was our engagement ever broken off?

CECILY   Of course it was. On the 22nd of last March. You can see the entry if you like. [*Shows diary.*] "Today I broke off my engagement with Ernest. I feel it is better to do so. The weather still continues charming."

ALGERNON   But why on earth did you break it off? What had I done? I had done nothing at all. Cecily, I am very much hurt indeed to hear you broke it off. Particularly when the weather was so charming.

CECILY   It would hardly have been a really serious engagement if it hadn't been broken off at least once. But I forgave you before the week was out.

ALGERNON   [*Crossing to her, and kneeling.*]   What a perfect angel you are, Cecily.

CECILY   You dear romantic boy. [*He kisses her, she puts her fingers through his hair.*] I hope your hair curls naturally, does it?

ALGERNON   Yes, darling, with a little help from others.

CECILY   I am so glad.

ALGERNON   You'll never break off our engagement again, Cecily?

CECILY   I don't think I could break it off now that I have actually met you. Besides, of course, there is the question of your name.

ALGERNON   Yes, of course. [*Nervously.*]

CECILY   You must not laugh at me, darling, but it had always been a girlish dream of mine to love someone whose name was Ernest. [ALGERNON *rises,* CECILY *also.*] There is something in that name that seems to inspire absolute confidence. I pity any poor married woman whose husband is not called Ernest.

ALGERNON   But, my dear child, do you mean to say you could not love me if I had some other name?

CECILY   But what name?

ALGERNON   Oh, any name you like—Algernon—for instance . . .

CECILY   But I don't like the name of Algernon.

ALGERNON   Well, my own dear, sweet, loving little darling, I really can't see why you should object to the name of Algernon. It is not at all a bad name. In fact, it is rather an aristocratic name. Half of the chaps who get into the Bankruptcy Court are called Algernon. But seriously, Cecily . . . [*Moving to her.*] . . . if my name was Algy, couldn't you love me?

CECILY [*Rising.*]   I might respect you, Ernest, I might admire your character, but I fear that I should not be able to give you my undivided attention.

ALGERNON   Ahem! Cecily! [*Picking up hat.*] Your Rector here is, I suppose, thoroughly experienced in the practice of all the rites and ceremonials of the Church?

CECILY   Oh, yes. Dr. Chasuble is a most learned man. He has never written a single book, so you can imagine how much he knows.

ALGERNON   I must see him at once on a most important christening—I mean on most important business.

CECILY   Oh!

ALGERNON   I shan't be away more than half an hour.

CECILY   Considering that we have been engaged since February the 14th, and that I only met you today for the first time, I think it is rather hard that you should leave me for so long a period as half an hour. Couldn't you make it twenty minutes?

ALGERNON I'll be back in no time. [*Kisses her and rushes down the garden.*]

CECILY What an impetuous boy he is! I like his hair so much. I must enter his proposal in my diary.

[*Enter* MERRIMAN.]

MERRIMAN A Miss Fairfax has just called to see Mr. Worthing. On very important business, Miss Fairfax states.

CECILY Isn't Mr. Worthing in his library?

MERRIMAN Mr. Worthing went over in the direction of the Rectory some time ago.

CECILY Pray ask the lady to come out here; Mr. Worthing is sure to be back soon. And you can bring tea.

MERRIMAN Yes, Miss. [*Goes out.*]

CECILY Miss Fairfax! I suppose one of the many good elderly women who are associated with Uncle Jack in some of his philanthropic work in London. I don't quite like women who are interested in philanthropic work. I think it is so forward of them.

[*Enter* MERRIMAN.]

MERRIMAN Miss Fairfax.

[*Enter* GWENDOLEN.] [*Exit* MERRIMAN.]

CECILY [*Advancing to meet her.*] Pray let me introduce myself to you. My name is Cecily Cardew.

GWENDOLEN Cecily Cardew? [*Moving to her and shaking hands.*] What a very sweet name! Something tells me that we are going to be great friends. I like you already more than I can say. My first impressions of people are never wrong.

CECILY How nice of you to like me so much after we have known each other such a comparatively short time. Pray sit down.

GWENDOLEN [*Still standing up.*] I may call you Cecily, may I not?

CECILY With pleasure!

GWENDOLEN And you will always call me Gwendolen, won't you?

CECILY If you wish.

GWENDOLEN Then that is all quite settled, is it not?

CECILY I hope so. [*A pause. They both sit down together.*]

GWENDOLEN Perhaps this might be a favourable opportunity for my mentioning who I am. My father is Lord Bracknell. You have never heard of papa, I suppose?

CECILY I don't think so.

GWENDOLEN Outside the family circle, papa, I am glad to say, is entirely unknown. I think that is quite as it should be. The home seems to me to be the proper sphere for the man. And certainly once a man begins to neglect his domestic duties he becomes painfully effeminate, does he not? And I don't like that. It makes men so very attractive. Cecily, mamma, whose views on education are remarkably strict, has brought me up to be extremely shortsighted; it is part of her system; so do you mind my looking at you through my glasses?

CECILY Oh! not at all, Gwendolen. I am very fond of being looked at.

GWENDOLEN [*After examining* CECILY *carefully through a lorgnette.*] You are here on a short visit, I suppose.

CECILY Oh no! I live here.

GWENDOLEN [*Severely.*] Really? Your mother, no doubt, or some female relative of advanced years, resides here also?

CECILY Oh no! I have no mother, nor, in fact, any relations.

GWENDOLEN Indeed?

CECILY My dear guardian, with the assistance of Miss Prism, has the arduous task of looking after me.

GWENDOLEN Your guardian?

CECILY Yes, I am Mr. Worthing's ward.

GWENDOLEN Oh! It is strange he never mentioned to me that he had a ward. How secretive of him! He grows more interesting hourly. I am not sure, however, that the news inspires me with feelings of unmixed delight. [*Rising and going to her.*] I am very fond of you, Cecily; I have liked you ever since I met you! But I am bound to state that now that I know that you are Mr. Worthing's ward, I cannot help expressing a wish you were—well just a little older than you seem to be—and not quite so very alluring in appearance. In fact, if I may speak candidly——

CECILY Pray do! I think that whenever one has anything unpleasant to say, one should always be quite candid.

GWENDOLEN Well, to speak with perfect candour, Cecily, I wish that you were fully forty-two, and more than usually plain for your age. Ernest has a strong upright nature. He is the very soul of truth and honour. Disloyalty would be as impossible to him as deception. But even men of the noblest possible moral character are extremely susceptible to the influence of the physical charms of others. Modern, no less than Ancient History, supplies us with many most painful examples of what I refer to. If it were not so, indeed, History would be quite unreadable.

CECILY I beg your pardon, Gwendolen, did you say Ernest?

GWENDOLEN Yes.

CECILY Oh, but it is not Mr. Ernest Worthing who is my guardian. It is his brother—his elder brother.

GWENDOLEN [*Sitting down again.*] Ernest never mentioned to me that he had a brother.

CECILY I am sorry to say they have not been on good terms for a long time.

GWENDOLEN Ah! that accounts for it. And now that I think of it I have never heard any man mention his brother. The subject seems distasteful to most men. Cecily, you have lifted a load from my mind. I was growing almost anxious. It would have been terrible if any cloud had come across a friendship like ours, would it not? Of course you are quite, quite sure that it is not Mr. Ernest Worthing who is your guardian?

CECILY Quite sure. [*A pause.*] In fact, I am going to be his.

GWENDOLEN [*Inquiringly.*] I beg your pardon?

CECILY [*Rather shy and confidingly.*] Dearest Gwendolen, there is no reason why I should make a secret of it to you. Our little county newspaper is sure to chronicle the fact next week. Mr. Ernest Worthing and I are engaged to be married.

GWENDOLEN [*Quite politely, rising.*] My darling Cecily, I think there must be some slight error. Mr. Ernest Worthing is engaged to me. The announcement will appear in the *Morning Post*[3] on Saturday at the latest.

CECILY [*Very politely, rising.*] I am afraid you must be under some misconception. Ernest proposed to me exactly ten minutes ago. [*Shows diary.*]

GWENDOLEN [*Examines diary through her lorgnette carefully.*] It is certainly very curious, for he asked me to be his wife yesterday afternoon

3. A popular journal featuring society gossip and also announcements of engagements and marriages.

at 5:30. If you would care to verify the incident, pray do so. [*Produces diary of her own.*] I never travel without my diary. One should always have something sensational to read in the train. I am so sorry, dear Cecily, if it is any disappointment to you, but I am afraid *I* have the prior claim.

CECILY   It would distress me more than I can tell you, dear Gwendolen, if it caused you any mental or physical anguish, but I feel bound to point out that since Ernest proposed to you he clearly has changed his mind.

GWENDOLEN [*Meditatively.*]   If the poor fellow has been entrapped into any foolish promise I shall consider it my duty to rescue him at once, and with a firm hand.

CECILY [*Thoughtfully and sadly.*]   Whatever unfortunate entanglement my dear boy may have got into, I will never reproach him with it after we are married.

GWENDOLEN   Do you allude to me, Miss Cardew, as an entanglement? You are presumptuous. On an occasion of this kind it becomes more than a moral duty to speak one's mind. It becomes a pleasure.

CECILY   Do you suggest, Miss Fairfax, that I entrapped Ernest into an engagement? How dare you? This is no time for wearing the shallow mask of manners. When I see a spade I call it a spade.

GWENDOLEN [*Satirically.*]   I am glad to say that I have never seen a spade. It is obvious that our social spheres have been widely different.

> [*Enter* MERRIMAN, *followed by the footman. He carries a salver, table-cloth, and plate stand.* CECILY *is about to retort. The presence of the servants exercises a restraining influence, under which both girls chafe.*]

MERRIMAN   Shall I lay tea here as usual, Miss?

CECILY [*Sternly, in a calm voice.*]   Yes, as usual.

> [MERRIMAN *begins to clear table and lay cloth. A long pause.* CECILY *and* GWENDOLEN *glare at each other.*]

GWENDOLEN   Are there many interesting walks in the vicinity, Miss Cardew?

CECILY   Oh! yes! a great many. From the top of one of the hills quite close one can see five counties.

GWENDOLEN   Five counties! I don't think I should like that. I hate crowds.

CECILY [*Sweetly.*]   I suppose that is why you live in town?

> [GWENDOLEN *bites her lip, and beats her foot nervously with her parasol.*]

GWENDOLEN [*Looking round.*]   Quite a well-kept garden this is, Miss Cardew.

CECILY   So glad you like it, Miss Fairfax.

GWENDOLEN   I had no idea there were any flowers in the country.

CECILY   Oh, flowers are as common here, Miss Fairfax, as people are in London.

GWENDOLEN   Personally I cannot understand how anybody manages to exist in the country, if anybody who is anybody does. The country always bores me to death.

CECILY   Ah! This is what the newspapers call agricultural depression, is it not? I believe the aristocracy are suffering very much from it just at present.[4] It is almost an epidemic amongst them, I have been told. May I offer you some tea, Miss Fairfax?

GWENDOLEN [*With elaborate politeness.*]   Thank you. [*Aside.*] Detestable girl! But I require tea!

---

4. From the 1870s on, landowners (including aristocrats) had been suffering severe losses because of adverse economic conditions.

CECILY [*Sweetly.*] Sugar?

GWENDOLEN [*Superciliously.*] No, thank you. Sugar is not fashionable any more, [CECILY *looks angrily at her, takes up the tongs and puts four lumps of sugar into the cup.*]

CECILY [*Severely.*] Cake or bread and butter?

GWENDOLEN [*In a bored manner.*] Bread and butter, please. Cake is rarely seen at the best houses nowadays.

CECILY [*Cuts a very large slice of cake, and puts it on the tray.*] Hand that to Miss Fairfax.

> [MERRIMAN *does so, and goes out with footman.* GWENDOLEN *drinks the tea and makes a grimace. Puts down cup at once, reaches out her hand to the bread and butter, looks at it, and finds it is cake. Rises in indignation.*]

GWENDOLEN You have filled my tea with lumps of sugar, and though I asked most distinctly for bread and butter, you have given me cake. I am known for the gentleness of my disposition, and the extraordinary sweetness of my nature, but I warn you, Miss Cardew, you may go too far.

CECILY [*Rising.*] To save my poor, innocent, trusting boy from the machinations of any other girl there are no lengths to which I would not go.

GWENDOLEN From the moment I saw you I distrusted you. I felt that you were false and deceitful. I am never deceived in such matters. My first impressions of people are invariably right.

CECILY It seems to me, Miss Fairfax, that I am trespassing on your valuable time. No doubt you have many other calls of a similar character to make in the neighborhood.

> [*Enter* JACK.]

GWENDOLEN [*Catching sight of him.*] Ernest! My own Ernest!

JACK Gwendolen! Darling! [*Offers to kiss her.*]

GWENDOLEN [*Drawing hack.*] A moment! May I ask if you are engaged to be married to this young lady? [*Points to* CECILY.]

JACK [*Laughing.*] To dear little Cecily! Of course not! What could have put such an idea into your pretty little head?

GWENDOLEN Thank you. You may! [*Offers her cheek.*]

CECILY [*Very sweetly.*] I knew there must be some misunderstanding, Miss Fairfax. The gentleman whose arm is at present round your waist is my dear guardian, Mr. John Worthing.

GWENDOLEN I beg your pardon?

CECILY This is Uncle Jack.

GWENDOLEN [*Receding.*] Jack! Oh!

> [*Enter* ALGERNON.]

CECILY Here is Ernest.

ALGERNON [*Goes straight over to* CECILY *without noticing anyone else.*] My own love! [*Offers to kiss her.*]

CECILY [*Drawing back.*] A moment, Ernest! May I ask you—are you engaged to be married to this young lady?

ALGERNON [*Looking round.*] To what young lady? Good heavens! Gwendolen!

CECILY Yes! to good heavens, Gwendolen, I mean to Gwendolen.

ALGERNON [*Laughing.*] Of course not! What could have put such an idea into your pretty little head?

CECILY Thank you. [*Presenting her cheek to be kissed.*] You may. [ALGERNON *kisses her.*]

GWENDOLEN I felt there was some slight error, Miss Cardew. The gentleman who is now embracing you is my cousin, Mr. Algernon Moncrieff.

CECILY. [*Breaking away from* ALGERNON,] Algernon Moncrieff! Oh! [*The two girls move towards each other and put their arms round each other's waists as if for protection.*]

CECILY Are you called Algernon?

ALGERNON I cannot deny it.

CECILY Oh!

GWENDOLEN Is your name really John?

JACK [*Standing rather proudly.*] I could deny it if I liked, I could deny anything if I liked. But my name certainly is John. It has been John for years.

CECILY [*To* GWENDOLEN.] A gross deception has been practiced on both of us.

GWENDOLEN My poor wounded Cecily!

CECILY My sweet wronged Gwendolen!

GWENDOLEN [*Slowly and seriously.*] You will call me sister, will you not? [*They embrace.* JACK *and* ALGERNON *groan and walk up and down.*]

CECILY [*Rather brightly.*] There is just one question I would like to be allowed to ask my guardian.

GWENDOLEN An admirable idea! Mr. Worthing, there is just one question I would like to be permitted to put to you. Where is your brother Ernest? We are both engaged to be married to your brother Ernest, so it is a matter of some importance to us to know where your brother Ernest is at present.

JACK [*Slowly and hesitatingly.*] Gwendolen—Cecily—it is very painful for me to be forced to speak the truth. It is the first time in my life that I have ever been reduced to such a painful position, and I am really quite inexperienced in doing anything of the kind. However I will tell you quite frankly that I have no brother Ernest. I have no brother at all. I never had a brother in my life, and I certainly have not the smallest intention of ever having one in the future.

CECILY [*Surprised.*] No brother at all?

JACK [*Cheerily.*] None!

GWENDOLEN [*Severely.*] Had you never a brother of any kind?

JACK [*Pleasantly.*] Never. Not even of any kind.

GWENDOLEN I am afraid it is quite clear, Cecily, that neither of us is engaged to be married to anyone.

CECILY It is not a very pleasant position for a young girl suddenly to find herself in. Is it?

GWENDOLEN Let us go into the house. They will hardly venture to come after us there.

CECILY No, men are so cowardly, aren't they?
      [*They retire into the house with scornful looks.*]

JACK This ghastly state of things is what you call Bunburying, I suppose?

ALGERNON Yes, and a perfectly wonderful Bunbury it is. The most wonderful Bunbury I have ever had in my life.

JACK Well, you've no right whatsoever to Bunbury here.

ALGERNON That is absurd. One has a right to Bunbury anywhere one chooses. Every serious Bunburyist knows that.

JACK Serious Bunburyist! Good heavens!

ALGERNON Well, one must be serious about something, if one wants to have any amusement in life. I happen to be serious about Bunburying. What on earth you are serious about I haven't got the remotest idea. About everything, I should fancy. You have such an absolutely trivial nature.

JACK Well, the only small satisfaction I have in the whole of this wretched business is that your friend Bunbury is quite exploded. You won't be able to run down to the country quite so often as you used to do, dear Algy. And a very good thing too.

ALGERNON Your brother is a little off-colour, isn't he, dear Jack? You won't be able to disappear to London quite so frequently as your wicked custom was. And not a bad thing either.

JACK As for your conduct towards Miss Cardew, I must say that your taking in a sweet, simple, innocent girl like that is quite inexcusable. To say nothing of the fact that she is my ward.

ALGERNON I can see no possible defence at all for your deceiving a brilliant, clever, thoroughly experienced young lady like Miss Fairfax. To say nothing of the fact that she is my cousin.

JACK I wanted to be engaged to Gwendolen, that is all. I love her.

ALGERNON Well, I simply wanted to be engaged to Cecily. I adore her.

JACK There is certainly no chance of your marrying Miss Cardew.

ALGERNON I don't think there is much likelihood, Jack, of you and Miss Fairfax being united.

JACK Well, that is no business of yours.

ALGERNON If it was my business, I wouldn't talk about it. [*Begins to eat muffins.*] It is very vulgar to talk about one's business. Only people like stockbrokers do that, and then merely at dinner parties.

JACK How can you sit there, calmly eating muffins when we are in this horrible trouble, I can't make out. You seem to me to be perfectly heartless.

ALGERNON Well, I can't eat muffins in an agitated manner. The butter would probably get on my cuffs. One should always eat muffins quite calmly. It is the only way to eat them.

JACK I say it's perfectly heartless your eating muffins at all, under the circumstances.

ALGERNON When I am in trouble, eating is the only thing that consoles me. Indeed, when I am in really great trouble, as anyone who knows me intimately will tell you, I refuse everything except food and drink. At the present moment I am eating muffins because I am unhappy. Besides, I am particularly fond of muffins. [*Rising.*]

JACK [*Rising.*] Well, that is no reason why you should eat them all in that greedy way. [*Takes muffins from* ALGERNON.]

ALGERNON [*Offering tea cake.*] I wish you would have tea cake instead. I don't like tea cake.

JACK Good heavens! I suppose a man may eat his own muffins in his own garden.

ALGERNON But you have just said it was perfectly heartless to eat muffins.

JACK I said it was perfectly heartless of you, under the circumstances. That is a very different thing.

ALGERNON That may be. But the muffins are the same. [*He seizes the muffin dish from* JACK.]

JACK Algy, I wish to goodness you would go.

ALGERNON   You can't possibly ask me to go without having some dinner. It's absurd. I never go without my dinner. No one ever does, except vegetarians and people like that. Besides I have just made arrangements with Dr. Chasuble to be christened at a quarter to six under the name of Ernest.

JACK   My dear fellow, the sooner you give up that nonsense the better. I made arrangements this morning with Dr. Chasuble to be christened myself at 5:30, and I naturally will take the name of Ernest. Gwendolen would wish it. We can't both be christened Ernest. It's absurd. Besides, I have a perfect right to be christened if I like. There is no evidence at all that I ever have been christened by anybody. I should think it extremely probable I never was, and so does Dr. Chasuble. It is entirely different in your case. You have been christened already.

ALGERNON   Yes, but I have not been christened for years.

JACK   Yes, but you have been christened. That is the important thing.

ALGERNON   Quite so. So I know my constitution can stand it. If you are not quite sure about your ever having been christened, I must say I think it rather dangerous your venturing on it now. It might make you very unwell. You can hardly have forgotten that someone very closely connected with you was very nearly carried off this week in Paris by a severe chill.

JACK   Yes, but you said yourself that a severe chill was not hereditary.

ALGERNON   It usen't to be, I know—but I daresay it is now. Science is always making wonderful improvements in things.

JACK   [*Picking up the muffin dish.*]   Oh, that is nonsense; you are always talking nonsense.

ALGERNON   Jack, you are at the muffins again! I wish you wouldn't. There are only two left. [*Takes them.*] I told you I was particularly fond of muffins.

JACK   But I hate tea cake.

ALGERNON   Why on earth then do you allow tea cake to be served up for your guests? What ideas you have of hospitality!

JACK   Algernon! I have already told you to go. I don't want you here. Why don't you go!

ALGERNON   I haven't quite finished my tea yet! and there is still one muffin left. [*Jack groans, and sinks into a chair.* ALGERNON *still continues eating.*]

ACT-DROP

Third Act

SCENE—*Morning room*[5] *at the Manor House.*

[GWENDOLEN *and* CECILY *are at the window, looking out into the garden.*]

GWENDOLEN   The fact that they did not follow us at once into the house, as anyone else would have done, seems to me to show that they have some sense of shame left.

---

5. A relatively informally furnished room for receiving visitors making morning calls (usually close friends of the host or hostess). Afternoon visitors, on the other hand, would be received in the drawing room, a much more formal and elegant setting.

CECILY   They have been eating muffins. That looks like repentance.

GWENDOLEN [*After a pause.*]   They don't seem to notice us at all. Couldn't you cough?

CECILY   But I haven't got a cough.

GWENDOLEN   They're looking at us. What effrontery!

CECILY   They're approaching. That's very forward of them.

GWENDOLEN   Let us preserve a dignified silence.

CECILY   Certainly. It's the only thing to do now.

[*Enter* JACK *followed by* ALGERNON. *They whistle some dreadful popular air from a British Opera.*[6]]

GWENDOLEN   This dignified silence seems to produce an unpleasant effect.

CECILY   A most distasteful one.

GWENDOLEN   But we will not be the first to speak.

CECILY   Certainly not.

GWENDOLEN   Mr. Worthing, I have something very particular to ask you. Much depends on your reply.

CECILY   Gwendolen, your common sense is invaluable. Mr. Moncrieff, kindly answer me the following question. Why did you pretend to be my guardian's brother?

ALGERNON   In order that I might have an opportunity of meeting you.

CECILY [*To* GWENDOLEN.]   That certainly seems a satisfactory explanation, does it not?

GWENDOLEN   Yes, dear, if you can believe him.

CECILY   I don't. But that does not affect the wonderful beauty of his answer.

GWENDOLEN   True. In matters of grave importance, style, not sincerity is the vital thing. Mr. Worthing, what explanation can you offer to me for pretending to have a brother? Was it in order that you might have an opportunity of coming up to town to see me as often as possible?

JACK   Can you doubt it, Miss Fairfax?

GWENDOLEN   I have the gravest doubts upon the subject. But I intend to crush them. This is not the moment for German scepticism.[7] [*Moving to* CECILY.] Their explanations appear to be quite satisfactory, especially Mr. Worthing's. That seems to me to have the stamp of truth upon it.

CECILY   I am more than content with what Mr. Moncrieff said. His voice alone inspires one with absolute credulity.

GWENDOLEN   Then you think we should forgive them?

CECILY   Yes. I mean no.

GWENDOLEN   True! I had forgotten. There are principles at stake that one cannot surrender. Which of us should tell them? The task is not a pleasant one.

CECILY   Could we not both speak at the same time?

GWENDOLEN   An excellent idea! I nearly always speak at the same time as other people. Will you take the time from me?

---

6. Probably a reference to one of the operas of W. S. Gilbert and Sir Arthur Sullivan.
7. Many 19th-century German scholars (e.g., D. F. Strauss) were notorious among the British for being skeptical in their analyses of religious texts.

CECILY   Certainly. [GWENDOLEN *beats time with uplifted finger.*]

GWENDOLEN AND CECILY [*Speaking together.*]   Your Christian names are still an insuperable barrier. That is all!

JACK AND ALGERNON [*Speaking together.*]   Our Christian names! Is that all? But we are going to be christened this afternoon.

GWENDOLEN [*To* JACK.]   For my sake you are prepared to do this terrible thing?

JACK   I am.

CECILY [*To* ALGERNON.]   To please me you are ready to face this fearful ordeal?

ALGERNON   I am!

GWENDOLEN   How absurd to talk of the equality of the sexes! Where questions of self-sacrifice are concerned, men are infinitely beyond us.

JACK   We are. [*Clasps hands with* ALGERNON.]

CECILY   They have moments of physical courage of which we women know absolutely nothing.

GWENDOLEN [*To* JACK.]   Darling!

ALGERNON [*To* CECILY.]   Darling. [*They fall into each other's arms.*]
    [*Enter* MERRIMAN. *When he enters he coughs loudly, seeing the situation.*]

MERRIMAN   Ahem! Ahem! Lady Bracknell!

JACK   Good heavens!
    [*Enter* LADY BRACKNELL. *The couples separate in alarm. Exit* MERRIMAN.]

LADY BRACKNELL   Gwendolen! What does this mean?

GWENDOLEN   Merely that I am engaged to be married to Mr. Worthing, mamma.

LADY BRACKNELL   Come here. Sit down. Sit down immediately. Hesitation of any kind is a sign of mental decay in the young, of physical weakness in the old. [*Turns to* JACK.] Apprised, sir, of my daughter's sudden flight by her trusty maid, whose confidence I purchased by means of a small coin, I followed her at once by a luggage train.[8] Her unhappy father is, I am glad to say, under the impression that she is attending a more than usually lengthy lecture by the University Extension Scheme on the Influence of a Permanent Income on Thought. I do not propose to undeceive him. Indeed I have never undeceived him on any question. I would consider it wrong. But of course, you will clearly understand that all communication between yourself and my daughter must cease immediately from this moment. On this point, as indeed on all points, I am firm.

JACK   I am engaged to be married to Gwendolen, Lady Bracknell!

LADY BRACKNELL   You are nothing of the kind, sir. And now, as regards Algernon! . . . Algernon!

ALGERNON   Yes, Aunt Augusta.

LADY BRACKNELL   May I ask if it is in this house that your invalid friend Mr. Bunbury resides?

ALGERNON [*Stammering.*]   Oh! No! Bunbury doesn't live here. Bunbury is somewhere else at present. In fact, Bunbury is dead.

LADY BRACKNELL   Dead! When did Mr. Bunbury die? His death must have been extremely sudden.

8. Freight train.

ALGERNON [*Airily.*] Oh! I killed Bunbury this afternoon. I mean poor Bunbury died this afternoon.

LADY BRACKNELL What did he die of?

ALGERNON Bunbury? Oh, he was quite exploded.

LADY BRACKNELL Exploded! Was he the victim of a revolutionary outrage? I was not aware that Mr. Bunbury was interested in social legislation. If so, he is well punished for his morbidity.

ALGERNON My dear Aunt Augusta, I mean he was found out! The doctors found out that Bunbury could not live, that is what I mean—so Bunbury died.

LADY BRACKNELL He seems to have had great confidence in the opinion of his physicians. I am glad, however, that he made up his mind at the last to some definite course of action, and acted under proper medical advice. And now that we have finally got rid of this Mr. Bunbury, may I ask, Mr. Worthing, who is that young person whose hand my nephew Algernon is now holding in what seems to me a peculiarly unnecessary manner?

JACK That lady is Miss Cecily Cardew, my ward.
[LADY BRACKNELL *bows coldly to* CECILY.]

ALGERNON I am engaged to be married to Cecily, Aunt Augusta.

LADY BRACKNELL I beg your pardon?

CECILY Mr. Moncrieff and I are engaged to be married, Lady Bracknell.

LADY BRACKNELL [*With a shiver, crossing to the sofa and sitting down.*] I do not know whether there is anything peculiarly exciting in the air of this particular part of Hertfordshire, but the number of engagements that go on seems to me considerably above the proper average that statistics have laid down for our guidance. I think some preliminary inquiry on my part would not be out of place. Mr. Worthing, is Miss Cardew at all connected with any of the larger railway stations in London? I merely desire information. Until yesterday I had no idea that there were any families or persons whose origin was a Terminus.[9] [JACK *looks perfectly furious, but restrains himself.*]

JACK [*In a clear, cold voice.*] Miss Cardew is the granddaughter of the late Mr. Thomas Cardew of 149, Belgrave Square, S.W.; Gervase Park, Dorking, Surrey; and the Sporran, Fifeshire, N.B.[1]

LADY BRACKNELL That sounds not unsatisfactory. Three addresses always inspire confidence, even in tradesmen. But what proof have I of their authenticity?

JACK I have carefully preserved the Court Guides[2] of the period. They are open to your inspection, Lady Bracknell.

LADY BRACKNELL [*Grimly.*] I have known strange errors in that publication.

JACK Miss Cardew's family solicitors are Messrs. Markby, Markby, and Markby.

LADY BRACKNELL Markby, Markby, and Markby? A firm of the very highest position in their profession. Indeed I am told that one of the Mr. Markbys is occasionally to be seen at dinner parties. So far I am satisfied.

JACK [*Very irritably.*] How extremely kind of you, Lady Bracknell! I have also in my possession, you will be pleased to hear, certificates of Miss

---

9. Station at the end of a railway line.
1. Presumably North Britain, i.e., Scotland.

2. Directories commonly used in this era.

Cardew's birth, baptism, whooping cough, registration, vaccination, confirmation, and the measles; both the German and the English variety.

LADY BRACKNELL Ah! A life crowded with incident, I see; though perhaps somewhat too exciting for a young girl. I am not myself in favor of premature experiences. [*Rises, looks at her watch.*] Gwendolen! the time approaches for our departure. We have not a moment to lose. As a matter of form, Mr. Worthing, I had better ask you if Miss Cardew has any little fortune?

JACK Oh! about a hundred and thirty thousand pounds in the Funds.[3] That is all. Good-bye, Lady Bracknell. So pleased to have seen you.

LADY BRACKNELL [*Sitting down again.*]   A moment, Mr. Worthing. A hundred and thirty thousand pounds! And in the Funds! Miss Cardew seems to me a most attractive young lady, now that I look at her. Few girls of the present day have any really solid qualities, any of the qualities that last, and improve with time. We live, I regret to say, in an age of surfaces. [*To* CECILY.] Come over here, dear, [CECILY *goes across.*] Pretty child! your dress is sadly simple, and your hair seems almost as Nature might have left it. But we can soon alter all that. A thoroughly experienced French maid produces a really marvellous result in a very brief space of time. I remember recommending one to young Lady Lancing, and after three months her own husband did not know her.

JACK [*Aside.*]   And after six months nobody knew her.[4]

LADY BRACKNELL [*Glares at* JACK *for a few moments. Then bends, with a practiced smile, to* CECILY.]   Kindly turn round, sweet child. [CECILY *turns completely round.*] No, the side view is what I want, [CECILY *presents her profile.*] Yes, quite as I expected. There are distinct social possibilities in your profile. The two weak points in our age are its want of principle and its want of profile. The chin a little higher, dear. Style largely depends on the way the chin is worn. They are worn very high, just at present. Algernon!

ALGERNON Yes, Aunt Augusta!

LADY BRACKNELL There are distinct social possibilities in Miss Cardew's profile.

ALGERNON Cecily is the sweetest, dearest, prettiest girl in the whole world. And I don't care twopence about social possibilities.

LADY BRACKNELL Never speak disrespectfully of Society, Algernon. Only people who can't get into it do that. [*To* CECILY.] Dear child, of course you know that Algernon has nothing but his debts to depend upon. But I do not approve of mercenary marriages. When I married Lord Bracknell I had no fortune of any kind. But I never dreamed for a moment of allowing that to stand in my way. Well, I suppose I must give my consent.

ALGERNON Thank you, Aunt Augusta.

LADY BRACKNELL Cecily, you may kiss me!

CECILY [*Kisses her.*]   Thank you, Lady Bracknell.

LADY BRACKNELL You may also address me as Aunt Augusta for the future.

CECILY Thank you, Aunt Augusta.

LADY BRACKNELL The marriage, I think, had better take place quite soon.

ALGERNON Thank you, Aunt Augusta.

CECILY Thank you, Aunt Augusta.

---

3. Interest-bearing government bonds.
4. I.e., she became socially unacceptable
because of her scandalous behavior.

LADY BRACKNELL To speak frankly, I am not in favour of long engagements. They give people the opportunity of finding out each other's character before marriage, which I think is never advisable.

JACK I beg your pardon for interrupting you, Lady Bracknell, but this engagement is quite out of the question. I am Miss Cardew's guardian, and she cannot marry without my consent until she comes of age. That consent I absolutely decline to give.

LADY BRACKNELL Upon what grounds may I ask? Algernon is an extremely, I may almost say an ostentatiously, eligible young man. He has nothing, but he looks everything. What more can one desire?

JACK It pains me very much to have to speak frankly to you, Lady Bracknell, about your nephew, but the fact is that I do not approve at all of his moral character. I suspect him of being untruthful. [ALGERNON and CECILY *look at him in indignant amazement.*]

LADY BRACKNELL Untruthful! My nephew Algernon? Impossible! He is an Oxonian.[5]

JACK I fear there can be no possible doubt about the matter. This afternoon, during my temporary absence in London on an important question of romance, he obtained admission to my house by means of the false pretence of being my brother. Under an assumed name he drank, I've just been informed by my butler, an entire pint bottle of my Perrier-Jouet, Brut, '89;[6] a wine I was specially reserving for myself. Continuing his disgraceful deception, he succeeded in the course of the afternoon in alienating the affections of my only ward. He subsequently stayed to tea, and devoured every single muffin. And what makes his conduct all the more heartless is, that he was perfectly well aware from the first that I have no brother, that I never had a brother, and that I don't intend to have a brother, not even of any kind. I distinctly told him so myself yesterday afternoon.

LADY BRACKNELL Ahem! Mr. Worthing, after careful consideration I have decided entirely to overlook my nephew's conduct to you.

JACK That is very generous of you, Lady Bracknell. My own decision, however, is unalterable. I decline to give my consent.

LADY BRACKNELL [*To* CECILY.] Come here, sweet child, [CECILY *goes over.*] How old are you, dear?

CECILY Well, I am really only eighteen, but I always admit to twenty when I go to evening parties.

LADY BRACKNELL You are perfectly right in making some slight alteration. Indeed, no woman should ever be quite accurate about her age. It looks so calculating. . . . [*In a meditative manner.*] Eighteen, but admitting to twenty at evening parties. Well, it will not be very long before you are of age and free from the restraints of tutelage. So I don't think your guardian's consent is, after all, a matter of any importance.

JACK Pray excuse me, Lady Bracknell, for interrupting you again, but it is only fair to tell you that according to the terms of her grandfather's will Miss Cardew does not come legally of age till she is thirty-five.

LADY BRACKNELL That does not seem to me to be a grave objection. Thirty-five is a very attractive age. London society is full of women of the very highest birth who have, of their own free choice, remained thirty-five for years. Lady Dumbleton is an instance in point. To my

---

5. I.e., he had been a student at Oxford (in medieval Latin, *Oxonia*).

6. An outstanding brand and year of dry champagne.

own knowledge she has been thirty-five ever since she arrived at the age of forty, which was many years ago now. I see no reason why our dear Cecily should not be even still more attractive at the age you mention than she is at present. There will be a large accumulation of property.

CECILY Algy, could you wait for me till I was thirty-five?

ALGERNON Of course I could, Cecily. You know I could.

CECILY Yes, I felt it instinctively, but I couldn't wait all that time. I hate waiting even five minutes for anybody. It always makes me rather cross. I am not punctual myself, I know, but I do like punctuality in others, and waiting, even to be married, is quite out of the question.

ALGERNON Then what is to be done, Cecily?

CECILY I don't know, Mr. Moncrieff.

LADY BRACKNELL My dear Mr. Worthing, as Miss Cardew states positively that she cannot wait till she is thirty-five—a remark which I am bound to say seems to me to show a somewhat impatient nature—I would beg of you to reconsider your decision.

JACK But my dear Lady Bracknell, the matter is entirely in your own hands. The moment you consent to my marriage with Gwendolen, I will most gladly allow your nephew to form an alliance with my ward.

LADY BRACKNELL [*Rising and drawing herself up.*] You must be quite aware that what you propose is out of the question.

JACK Then a passionate celibacy is all that any of us can look forward to.

LADY BRACKNELL This is not the destiny I propose for Gwendolen. Algernon, of course, can choose for himself. [*Pulls out her watch.*] Come, dear; [GWENDOLEN *rises.*] we have already missed five, if not six, trains. To miss any more might expose us to comment on the platform.

    [*Enter* DR. CHASUBLE.]

CHASUBLE Everything is quite ready for the christenings.

LADY BRACKNELL The christenings, sir! Is not that somewhat premature!

CHASUBLE [*Looking rather puzzled, and pointing to* JACK *and* ALGERNON.] Both these gentlemen have expressed a desire for immediate baptism.

LADY BRACKNELL At their age? The idea is grotesque and irreligious! Algernon, I forbid you to be baptized. I will not hear of such excesses. Lord Bracknell would be highly displeased if he learned that that was the way in which you wasted your time and money.

CHASUBLE Am I to understand then that there are to be no christenings at all this afternoon?

JACK I don't think that, as things are now, it would be of much practical value to either of us, Dr. Chasuble.

CHASUBLE I am grieved to hear such sentiments from you, Mr. Worthing. They savour of the heretical views of the Anabaptists,[7] views that I have completely refuted in four of my unpublished sermons. However, as your present mood seems to be one peculiarly secular, I will return to the church at once. Indeed, I have just been informed by the pew-opener[8] that for the last hour and a half Miss Prism has been waiting for me in the vestry.

LADY BRACKNELL [*Starting.*] Miss Prism! Did I hear you mention a Miss Prism?

CHASUBLE Yes, Lady Bracknell. I am on my way to join her.

---

7. A radical Protestant sect of the 17th century, whose repudiation of infant baptism was regarded as heretical by Anglicans.

8. A person employed at church services to usher worshippers to their pews and open the doors for them.

LADY BRACKNELL   Pray allow me to detain you for a moment. This matter may prove to be one of vital importance to Lord Bracknell and myself. Is this Miss Prism a female of repellent aspect, remotely connected with education?

CHASUBLE [*Somewhat indignantly.*]   She is the most cultivated of ladies, and the very picture of respectability.

LADY BRACKNELL   It is obviously the same person. May I ask what position she holds in your household?

CHASUBLE [*Severely.*]   I am a celibate, madam.

JACK [*Interposing.*]   Miss Prism, Lady Bracknell, has been for the last three years Miss Cardew's esteemed governess and valued companion.

LADY BRACKNELL   In spite of what I hear of her, I must see her at once. Let her be sent for.

CHASUBLE [*Looking off.*]   She approaches; she is nigh.

[*Enter* MISS PRISM *hurriedly.*]

MISS PRISM   I was told you expected me in the vestry, dear Canon. I have been waiting for you there for an hour and three quarters. [*Catches sight of* LADY BRACKNELL *who has fixed her with a stony glare.* MISS PRISM *grows pale and quails. She looks anxiously round as if desirous to escape.*]

LADY BRACKNELL [*In a severe, judicial voice.*]   Prism! [MISS PRISM *bows her head in shame.*] Come here, Prism! [MISS PRISM *approaches in a humble manner.*] Prism! Where is that baby? [*General consternation.* THE CANON *starts back in horror.* ALGERNON *and* JACK *pretend to be anxious to shield* CECILY *and* GWENDOLEN *from hearing the details of a terrible public scandal.*] Twenty-eight years ago, Prism, you left Lord Bracknell's house, Number 104, Upper Grosvenor Street, in charge of a perambulator that contained a baby, of the male sex. You never returned. A few weeks later, through the elaborate investigations of the Metropolitan police, the perambulator was discovered at midnight, standing by itself in a remote corner of Bayswater.[9] It contained the manuscript of a three-volume novel of more than usually revolting sentimentality, [MISS PRISM *starts in involuntary indignation.*] But the baby was not there! [*Everyone looks at* MISS PRISM.] Prism! Where is that baby? [*A pause.*]

MISS PRISM   Lady Bracknell, I admit with shame that I do not know. I only wish I did. The plain facts of the case are these. On the morning of the day you mention, a day that is forever branded on my memory, I prepared as usual to take the baby out in its perambulator. I had also with me a somewhat old, but capacious handbag, in which I had intended to place the manuscript of a work of fiction that I had written during my few unoccupied hours. In a moment of mental abstraction, for which I never can forgive myself, I deposited the manuscript in the bassinette, and placed the baby in the handbag.

JACK [*Who has been listening attentively.*]   But where did you deposit the handbag?

MISS PRISM   Do not ask me, Mr. Worthing.

JACK   Miss Prism, this is a matter of no small importance to me. I insist on knowing where you deposited the handbag that contained that infant.

MISS PRISM   I left it in the cloak room of one of the larger railway stations in London.

---

9. A once fashionable locality in the West End near Kensington Gardens.

JACK What railway station?

MISS PRISM [*Quite crushed.*] Victoria. The Brighton line. [*Sinks into a chair.*]

JACK I must retire to my room for a moment. Gwendolen, wait here for me.

GWENDOLEN If you are not too long, I will wait here for you all my life.

[*Exit* JACK *in great excitement.*]

CHASUBLE What do you think this means, Lady Bracknell?

LADY BRACKNELL I dare not even suspect, Dr. Chasuble. I need hardly tell you that in families of high position strange coincidences are not supposed to occur. They are hardly considered the thing.

[*Noises heard overhead as if someone was throwing trunks about. Everyone looks up.*]

CECILY Uncle Jack seems strangely agitated.

CHASUBLE Your guardian has a very emotional nature.

LADY BRACKNELL This noise is extremely unpleasant. It sounds as if he was having an argument. I dislike arguments of any kind. They are always vulgar, and often convincing.

CHASUBLE [*Looking up.*] It has stopped now. [*The noise is redoubled.*]

LADY BRACKNELL I wish he would arrive at some conclusion.

GWENDOLEN This suspense is terrible. I hope it will last.

[*Enter* JACK *with a handbag of black leather in his hand.*]

JACK [*Rushing over to* MISS PRISM.] Is this the handbag, Miss Prism? Examine it carefully before you speak. The happiness of more than one life depends on your answer.

MISS PRISM [*Calmly.*] It seems to be mine. Yes, here is the injury it received through the upsetting of a Gower Street omnibus in younger and happier days. Here is the stain on the lining caused by the explosion of a temperance beverage, an incident that occurred at Leamington. And here, on the lock, are my initials. I had forgotten that in an extravagant mood I had had them placed there. The bag is undoubtedly mine. I am delighted to have it so unexpectedly restored to me. It has been a great inconvenience being without it all these years.

JACK [*In a pathetic voice.*] Miss Prism, more is restored to you than this handbag. I was the baby you placed in it.

MISS PRISM [*Amazed.*] You!

JACK [*Embracing her.*] Yes . . . mother!

MISS PRISM [*Recoiling in indignant astonishment*] Mr. Worthing! I am unmarried!

JACK Unmarried! I do not deny that is a serious blow. But after all, who has the right to cast a stone[1] against one who has suffered? Cannot repentance wipe out an act of folly? Why should there be one law for men, and another for women? Mother, I forgive you. [*Tries to embrace her again.*]

MISS PRISM [*Still more indignant.*] Mr. Worthing, there is some error. [*Pointing to* LADY BRACKNELL.] There is the lady who can tell you who you really are.

JACK [*After a pause.*] Lady Bracknell, I hate to seem inquisitive, but would you kindly inform me who I am?

---

1. When the scribes and Pharisees brought to Jesus an adulterous woman with the reminder that the law of Moses required her to be stoned, he answered: "He that is without sin among you, let him first cast a stone at her" (John 8.7).

LADY BRACKNELL   I am afraid that the news I have to give you will not altogether please you. You are the son of my poor sister, Mrs. Moncrieff, and consequently Algernon's elder brother.

JACK   Algy's elder brother! Then I have a brother after all. I knew I had a brother! I always said I had a brother! Cecily—how could you have ever doubted that I had a brother? [*Seizes hold of* ALGERNON.] Dr. Chasuble, my unfortunate brother. Miss Prism, my unfortunate brother. Gwendolen, my unfortunate brother. Algy, you young scoundrel, you will have to treat me with more respect in the future. You have never behaved to me like a brother in all your life.

ALGERNON   Well, not till today, old boy, I admit. I did my best, however, though I was out of practice. [*Shakes hands.*]

GWENDOLEN [*To* JACK.]   My own! But what own are you? What is your Christian name, now that you have become someone else?

JACK   Good heavens! . . . I had quite forgotten that point. Your decision on the subject of my name is irrevocable, I suppose?

GWENDOLEN   I never change, except in my affections.

CECILY   What a noble nature you have, Gwendolen!

JACK   Then the question had better be cleared up at once. Aunt Augusta, a moment. At the time when Miss Prism left me in the handbag, had I been christened already?

LADY BRACKNELL   Every luxury that money could buy, including christening, had been lavished on you by your fond and doting parents.

JACK   Then I was christened! That is settled. Now, what name was I given? Let me know the worst.

LADY BRACKNELL   Being the eldest son you were naturally christened after your father.

JACK [*Irritably.*]   Yes, but what was my father's Christian name?

LADY BRACKNELL [*Meditatively.*]   I cannot at the present moment recall what the General's Christian name was. But I have no doubt he had one. He was eccentric, I admit. But only in later years. And that was the result of the Indian climate, and marriage, and indigestion, and other things of that kind.

JACK   Algy! Can't you recollect what our father's Christian name was?

ALGERNON   My dear boy, we were never even on speaking terms. He died before I was a year old.

JACK   His name would appear in the Army Lists of the period, I suppose, Aunt Augusta?

LADY BRACKNELL   The General was essentially a man of peace, except in his domestic life. But I have no doubt his name would appear in any military directory.

JACK   The Army Lists of the last forty years are here. These delightful records should have been my constant study. [*Rushes to bookcase and tears the books out.*] M. Generals . . . Mallam, Maxbohm,[2] Magley, what ghastly names they have—Markby, Migsby, Mobbs, Moncrieff! Lieutenant 1840, Captain, Lieutenant Colonel, Colonel, General 1869, Christian names, Ernest John. [*Puts book very quietly down and speaks quite calmly.*] I always told you, Gwendolen, my name was Ernest, didn't I? Well it is Ernest after all. I mean it naturally is Ernest.

---

2. A play on the name of Max Beerbohm (1872–1956), English essayist, caricaturist, and parodist.

LADY BRACKNELL Yes, I remember now that the General was called Ernest. I knew I had some particular reason for disliking the name.

GWENDOLEN Ernest! My own Ernest! I felt from the first that you could have no other name!

JACK Gwendolen, it is a terrible thing for a man to find out suddenly that all his life he has been speaking nothing but the truth. Can you forgive me?

GWENDOLEN I can. For I feel that you are sure to change.

JACK My own one!

CHASUBLE [*To* MISS PRISM.] Laetitia! [*Embraces her.*]

MISS PRISM [*Enthusiastically.*] Frederick! At last!

ALGERNON Cecily! [*Embraces her.*] At last!

JACK Gwendolen! [*Embraces her.*] At last!

LADY BRACKNELL My nephew, you seem to be displaying signs of triviality.

JACK On the contrary, Aunt Augusta, I've now realized for the first time in my life the vital Importance of Being Earnest.

CURTAIN

performed 1895   1899

RUDYARD KIPLING
1865–1936

Like many children born to upper- or middle-class Britons living in India in the Victorian era, Rudyard Kipling was sent to Great Britain at the age of six to begin his education. For the next six years in England, he was desperately unhappy; his parents had chosen to board him in a rigidly Calvinistic foster home, and he was treated with considerable cruelty. His parents finally removed him when he was twelve and sent him to a private school, where his experience was far better. His views in later life were deeply affected by the English schoolboy code of honor and duty, especially when it involved loyalty to a group or team. At seventeen he rejoined his parents in India, where his father taught sculpture at the Bombay School of Art. By the time he returned to England seven years later, the poems and stories he had written while working as a newspaper reporter in India had brought him early fame. In 1892 he married an American woman; they lived in Brattleboro, Vermont, until a fierce quarrel with his brother-in-law drove him back to England in 1896. Kipling settled on a country estate and purchased, at the turn of the century, an expensive early-model automobile. He seems to have been the first English author to own an automobile—an appropriate distinction, because he was intrigued by all kinds of machinery and feats of engineering. In this keen interest, as in many tastes, he differed markedly from his contemporaries in the nineties, the aesthetes. Kipling was also the first English author to receive the Nobel Prize for Literature (1907).

In the final decades of the nineteenth century, India was the most important colony of Britain's empire—the "Jewel in the Crown," as Prime Minister Benjamin Disraeli had dubbed it. The English were consequently curious about the world of

India, a world that Kipling's stories and poems helped them envision. Indeed, Leonard Woolf, Virginia Woolf's husband, wrote of his own experience in India in the early years of the twentieth century: "I could never make up my mind whether Kipling had moulded his characters accurately in the image of Anglo-Indian society or whether we were moulding our characters accurately in the image of a Kipling story." During his seven years in India in the 1880s, Kipling gained a rich experience of colonial life, which he presented in his stories and poems. His first volume of stories, *Plain Tales from the Hills* (1888), explores some of the psychological and moral problems of the Anglo-Indians and their relationship with the people they had colonized. In his two volumes of the *Jungle Book* (1894, 1895) he draws on the Indian scene to create a world of jungle animals. Capable, on occasion, of constructing offensive stereotypes, Kipling at other times demonstrates a remarkably detailed and intelligent interest in Indian culture, as in his complex novel *Kim* (1901): amid a welter of representations of different modes of existence, the contemplative and religious way of life of the Indian *lama*, or monk, is treated with no less respect and sympathy than the active and worldly way of life of the Victorian English governing classes.

In his poems Kipling also draws on the Indian scene, most commonly as it is viewed through the eyes of the men sent out from England to garrison the country and fight off invaders on the northwest frontiers. Kipling is usually thought of as the poet of British imperialism, as indeed he often was; but these poems about ordinary British soldiers in India contain little by way of flag-waving celebrations of the triumph of empire. The soldier who speaks in "The Widow at Windsor" (1892) is simply bewildered by the events in which he has taken part. As one of the soldiers of the queen (one of "Missis Victorier's sons"), he has done his duty, but he does not see the empire as a divine design to which he has contributed. Kipling develops a new subject in the working-class imperial soldier (a subject, we should note, who frequently gives voice to deeply racist attitudes), and thus a new way to portray modern social experience.

The common man's perspective, expressed in the accent of the London cockney, was one of the qualities that gained Kipling an immediate audience for his *Barrack-Room Ballads* (1890, 1892). For many years Kipling was extremely popular. What attracted his vast audience was not just the novelty of his subjects but also his mastery of swinging verse rhythms. To some degree Kipling's literary ancestry helps explain his success. In part he learned his craft as a poet from traditional sources. His own family had connections with the Pre-Raphaelites, and he was considerably influenced by such immediate literary predecessors as Robert Browning and Algernon Charles Swinburne. But two of the forces strongly influencing his style and rhythms were not traditional. One of these was the Protestant hymn. Both his parents were children of Methodist clergymen, and chapel singing, as well as preaching, affected him profoundly. "Three generations of Wesleyan ministers . . . lie behind me," he noted; the family tradition can be heard in such secular sermons as "If" (1910) and the elegiac hymn "Recessional" (1897). The second influence came from what seems an antithetical secular quarter: the songs of the music hall. As a teenager in London, Kipling had enjoyed music hall entertainments, which were to reach their peak of popularity in the 1890s. Like Tennyson, Kipling knew how to make poems that call to be set to music, verses such as "Mandalay" (1890) or "Gentlemen-Rankers" (1892), with its memorable refrain: "We're poor little lambs who've lost our way, / Baa! Baa! Baa!" Much of Kipling's poetry is best appreciated with the melodies and ambience of the music hall in mind.

In recent years Kipling's stories have received more attention than his poems. By portraying the British community in India and its relationship with the people it ruled, Kipling created a rich and various fictional world that reflects on England's imperialism as lived by the officers of the empire in all their peculiar social relationships. "The Man Who Would Be King" (1888) presents an intriguing approach to the topic. The narrator, a newspaper editor, tells us of his dealings with a couple of "Loafers." Peachey Carnehan and Daniel Dravot have no official positions in

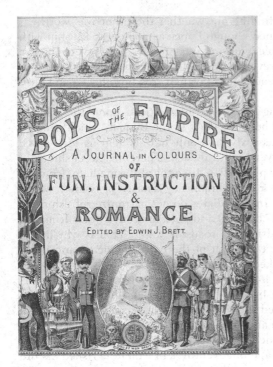

Boys of the Empire. Brett published numerous popular weekly magazines for boys from 1866 onward; this cover dates from 1882.

India but are quick to exploit any opportunities their European status may afford them; this pair of rogues heads out to the mountainous region of Kafiristan, intent on establishing their own dynasty. An action-packed tale of adventure in faraway places with strange-sounding names, the story also invites us to think critically about the general project of empire—about the assumptions it holds, the methods it employs, and the human cost of its endeavors.

After leaving India, Kipling gradually turned to English subjects in his fiction, but the cataclysm of World War I did much to diminish his output. As chair of the Imperial War Graves Commission, he played a difficult and important public role, responsible for (among other things) choosing the words to be inscribed on count-less monuments and memorials across the globe. Kipling's task was all the more poignant because the body of his only son, who had died in the battle of Loos (1915), was never found. A deeply melancholy autobiography, *Something of Myself*, was published in 1937, the year after Kipling's death.

The Man Who Would Be King[1]

"Brother to a Prince and fellow to a beggar if he be found worthy."[2]

The law, as quoted, lays down a fair conduct of life, and one not easy to fol-low. I have been fellow to a beggar again and again under circumstances

---

1. Kipling based his story on the true-life exploits of an American adventurer, Josiah Harlan, who awarded himself the title of prince after occupy-ing a region in the Hindu Kush in the late 1830s.
2. Meant to suggest the principles of Freema-sonry, a secret fraternal society that developed

from the masons' guild in medieval Britain. By Victorian times it had grown to a prominent organization, whose members were bound to help each other in times of distress. Kipling was a member.

which prevented either of us finding out whether the other was worthy. I have still to be brother to a Prince, though I once came near to kinship with what might have been a veritable King and was promised the reversion of[3] a Kingdom—army, law-courts, revenue and policy all complete. But, to-day, I greatly fear that my King is dead, and if I want a crown I must go and hunt it for myself.

The beginning of everything was in a railway train upon the road to Mhow from Ajmir.[4] There had been a Deficit in the Budget, which necessitated traveling, not Second-class, which is only half as dear as First-class, but by Intermediate, which is very awful indeed. There are no cushions in the Intermediate class, and the population are either Intermediate, which is Eurasian, or native, which for a long night journey is nasty, or Loafer,[5] which is amusing though intoxicated. Intermediates do not patronize refreshment-rooms. They carry their food in bundles and pots, and buy sweets from the native sweetmeat-sellers, and drink the roadside water. That is why in the hot weather Intermediates are taken out of the carriages dead, and in all weathers are most properly looked down upon.

My particular Intermediate happened to be empty till I reached Nasir-abad, when a huge gentleman in shirt-sleeves entered, and, following the custom of Intermediates, passed the time of day. He was a wanderer and a vagabond like myself, but with an educated taste for whiskey. He told tales of things he had seen and done, of out-of-the-way corners of the Empire into which he had penetrated, and of adventures in which he risked his life for a few days' food. "If India was filled with men like you and me, not knowing more than the crows where they'd get their next day's rations, it isn't seventy millions of revenue the land would be paying—it's seven hundred millions," said he; and as I looked at his mouth and chin I was disposed to agree with him. We talked politics—the politics of Loaferdom that sees things from the underside where the lath and plaster is not smoothed off[6]—and we talked postal arrangements because my friend wanted to send a telegram back from the next station to Ajmir, which is the turning-off place from the Bombay to the Mhow line as you travel westward. My friend had no money beyond eight annas which he wanted[7] for dinner, and I had no money at all, owing to the hitch in the Budget before mentioned. Further, I was going into a wilderness where, though I should resume touch with the Treasury, there were no telegraph offices. I was, therefore, unable to help him in any way.

"We might threaten a Station-master, and make him send a wire on tick,"[8] said my friend, "but that'd mean inquiries for you and for me, and I've got my hands full these days. Did you say you are traveling back along this line within any days?"

"Within ten," I said.

"Can't you make it eight?" said he. "Mine is rather urgent business."

"I can send your telegram within ten days if that will serve you," I said.

"I couldn't trust the wire to fetch him now I think of it. It's this way. He leaves Delhi on the 23d for Bombay. That means he'll be running through Ajmir about the night of the 23d."

3. Right to inherit.
4. These, and the other places mentioned at the beginning of the story, are in northern India.
5. A European in India with no official attachment or position.

6. I.e., the unfinished side of a wall.
7. Needed. "Annas": there are sixteen annas in a rupee, the basic monetary unit of India.
8. On credit.

"But I'm going into the Indian Desert," I explained.

"Well *and* good," said he. "You'll be changing at Marwar Junction to get into Jodhpore territory—you must do that—and he'll be coming through Marwar Junction in the early morning of the 24th by the Bombay Mail. Can you be at Marwar Junction on that time? 'Twon't be inconveniencing you because I know that there's precious few pickings to be got out of these Central India States—even though you pretend to be correspondent of the *Backwoodsman*."[9]

"Have you ever tried that trick?" I asked.

"Again and again, but the Residents[1] find you out, and then you get escorted to the Border before you've time to get your knife into them. But about my friend here. I *must* give him a word o' mouth to tell him what's come to me or else he won't know where to go. I would take it more than kind of you if you was to come out of Central India in time to catch him at Marwar Junction, and say to him:—'He has gone South for the week.' He'll know what that means. He's a big man with a red beard, and a great swell[2] he is. You'll find him sleeping like a gentleman with all his luggage round him in a Second-class compartment. But don't you be afraid. Slip down the window, and say:—'He has gone South for the week,' and he'll tumble.[3] It's only cutting your time of stay in those parts by two days. I ask you as a stranger—going to the West,"[4] he said, with emphasis.

"Where have *you* come from?" said I.

"From the East," said he, "and I am hoping that you will give him the message on the Square[5]—for the sake of my Mother as well as your own."

Englishmen are not usually softened by appeals to the memory of their mothers, but for certain reasons, which will be fully apparent, I saw fit to agree.

"It's more than a little matter," said he, "and that's why I ask you to do it—and now I know that I can depend on you doing it. A Second-class carriage at Marwar Junction, and a red-haired man asleep in it. You'll be sure to remember. I get out at the next station, and I must hold on there till he comes or sends me what I want."

"I'll give the message if I catch him," I said, "and for the sake of your Mother as well as mine I'll give you a word of advice. Don't try to run the Central India States just now as the correspondent of the *Backwoodsman*. There's a real one knocking about here, and it might lead to trouble."

"Thank you," said he, simply, "and when will the swine be gone? I can't starve because he's ruining my work. I wanted to get hold of the Degumber Rajah down here about his father's widow, and give him a jump."

"What did he do to his father's widow, then?"

"Filled her up with red pepper and slippered her to death as she hung from a beam. I found that out myself, and I'm the only man that would dare going into the State to get hush-money for it. They'll try to poison me, same as they did in Chortumna when I went on the loot there. But you'll give the man at Marwar Junction my message?"

---

9. This fictitious newspaper appears to be based on the Allahabad *Pioneer*, for which Kipling worked as a roving correspondent. "Central India States": quasi-independent "Native States," as they were also known, presided over by Indian royalty.
1. British political officers appointed to oversee affairs at the courts of Indian rulers.
2. Fashionable fellow.
3. Catch on, understand.
4. This phrase and the following one are from the code of the Freemasons.
5. Honestly.

He got out at a little roadside station, and I reflected. I had heard, more than once, of men personating correspondents of newspapers and bleeding small Native States with threats of exposure, but I had never met any of the caste before. They lead a hard life, and generally die with great suddenness. The Native States have a wholesome horror of English newspapers, which may throw light on their peculiar methods of government, and do their best to choke correspondents with champagne, or drive them out of their mind with four-in-hand barouches.[6] They do not understand that nobody cares a straw for the internal administration of Native States so long as oppression and crime are kept within decent limits, and the ruler is not drugged, drunk, or diseased from one end of the year to the other. Native States were created by Providence in order to supply picturesque scenery, tigers, and tall-writing.[7] They are the dark places of the earth, full of unimaginable cruelty, touching the Railway and the Telegraph on one side, and, on the other, the days of Harun-al-Raschid.[8] When I left the train I did business with divers Kings, and in eight days passed through many changes of life. Sometimes I wore dress-clothes and consorted with Princes and Politicals,[9] drinking from crystal and eating from silver. Sometimes I lay out upon the ground and devoured what I could get, from a plate made of a flapjack, and drank the running water, and slept under the same rug as my servant. It was all in the day's work.

Then I headed for the Great Indian Desert upon the proper date, as I had promised, and the night Mail set me down at Marwar Junction, where a funny little, happy-go-lucky, native-managed railway runs to Jodhpore. The Bombay Mail from Delhi makes a short halt at Marwar. She arrived as I got in, and I had just time to hurry to her platform and go down the carriages. There was only one Second-class on the train. I slipped the window, and looked down upon a flaming red beard, half covered by a railway rug. That was my man, fast asleep, and I dug him gently in the ribs. He woke with a grunt, and I saw his face in the light of the lamps. It was a great and shining face.

"Tickets again?" said he.

"No," said I. "I am to tell you that he is gone South for the week. He is gone South for the week!"

The train had begun to move out. The red man rubbed his eyes. "He has gone South for the week," he repeated. "Now that's just like his impidence. Did he say that I was to give you anything?—'Cause I won't."

"He didn't," I said, and dropped away, and watched the red lights die out in the dark. It was horribly cold, because the wind was blowing off the sands. I climbed into my own train—not an Intermediate Carriage this time—and went to sleep.

If the man with the beard had given me a rupee I should have kept it as a memento of a rather curious affair. But the consciousness of having done my duty was my only reward.

Later on I reflected that two gentlemen like my friends could not do any good if they foregathered and personated correspondents of newspapers, and might, if they "stuck up"[1] one of the little rat-trap states of Central India or Southern Rajputana, get themselves into serious difficulties. I therefore

---

6. Fashionable four-wheeled carriages.
7. Tall tales.
8. The caliph of Baghdad (763–809), who figures in many tales of the *Arabian Nights*.

9. I.e., Residents.
1. Fraudulently extorted money from. "Foregathered": met.

took some trouble to describe them as accurately as I could remember to people who would be interested in deporting them; and succeeded, so I was later informed, in having them headed back from Degumber borders.

Then I became respectable, and returned to an Office where there were no Kings and no incidents except the daily manufacture of a newspaper. A newspaper office seems to attract every conceivable sort of person, to the prejudice of discipline. Zenana-mission ladies[2] arrive, and beg that the Editor will instantly abandon all his duties to describe a Christian prize-giving in a back-slum of a perfectly inaccessible village; Colonels who have been overpassed for commands sit down and sketch the outline of a series of ten, twelve, or twenty-four leading articles on Seniority *versus* Selection; missionaries wish to know why they have not been permitted to escape from their regular vehicles of abuse and swear at a brother missionary under special patronage of the editorial We; stranded theatrical companies troop up to explain that they cannot pay for their advertisements, but on their return from New Zealand or Tahiti will do so with interest; inventors of patent punkah[3]-pulling machines, carriage couplings and unbreakable swords and axle-trees call with specifications in their pockets and hours at their disposal; tea-companies enter and elaborate their prospectuses with the office pens; secretaries of ball-committees clamour to have the glories of their last dance more fully expounded; strange ladies rustle in and say:—"I want a hundred lady's cards printed *at once*, please," which is manifestly part of an Editor's duty; and every dissolute ruffian that ever tramped the Grand Trunk Road[4] makes it his business to ask for employment as a proof-reader. And, all the time, the telephone-bell is ringing madly, and Kings are being killed on the Continent, and Empires are saying—"You're another," and Mister Gladstone is calling down brimstone upon the British Dominions,[5] and the little black copy-boys are whining, *"kaapi chay-ha-yeh"* (copy wanted) like tired bees, and most of the paper is as blank as Modred's shield.[6]

But that is the amusing part of the year. There are other six months wherein none ever come to call, and the thermometer walks inch by inch up to the top of the glass, and the office is darkened to just above reading-light, and the press machines are red-hot of touch, and nobody writes anything but accounts of amusements in the Hill-stations[7] or obituary notices. Then the telephone becomes a tinkling terror, because it tells you of the sudden deaths of men and women that you knew intimately, and the prickly-heat covers you as with a garment, and you sit down and write:—"A slight increase of sickness is reported from the Khuda Janta Khan[8] District. The outbreak is purely sporadic in its nature, and, thanks to the energetic efforts of the District authorities, is now almost at an end. It is, however, with deep regret we record the death, etc."

Then the sickness really breaks out, and the less recording and reporting the better for the peace of the subscribers. But the Empires and the Kings continue to divert themselves as selfishly as before, and the Foreman thinks

---

2. Female missionaries doing work among Indian women, who were customarily confined to a part of the house called the *Zenana*.
3. Large swinging fan, usually worked by hand.
4. Major road connecting Calcutta and Delhi.
5. Places under British control. William Ewart Gladstone (1809–1898), leader of the Liberal Party from 1868 to 1875 and 1880 to 1894, and four times prime minister; he strongly opposed

overseas expansion. "Brimstone": i.e., fire and brimstone, the supposed torments of hell.
6. In British legend the shield of King Arthur's traitorous nephew was blank because he had done no deeds of valor.
7. Official outposts in the northern hills, to which many British people in India would retire during the hottest months.
8. "God Knows Town": i.e., Nowheresville.

that a daily paper really ought to come out once in twenty-four hours, and all the people at the Hill-stations in the middle of their amusements say:— "Good gracious! Why can't the paper be sparkling? I'm sure there's plenty going on up here."

That is the dark half of the moon, and, as the advertisements say, "must be experienced to be appreciated."

It was in that season, and a remarkably evil season, that the paper began running the last issue of the week on Saturday night, which is to say, Sunday morning, after the custom of a London paper. This was a great convenience, for immediately after the paper was put to bed,[9] the dawn would lower the thermometer from 96° to almost 84° for half an hour, and in that chill—you have no idea how cold is 84° on the grass until you begin to pray for it—a very tired man could set off to sleep ere the heat roused him.

One Saturday night it was my pleasant duty to put the paper to bed alone. A King or courtier or a courtesan or a community was going to die or get a new Constitution, or do something that was important on the other side of the world, and the paper was to be held open till the latest possible minute in order to catch the telegram. It was a pitchy black night, as stifling as a June night can be, and the *loo*, the red-hot wind from the westward, was booming among the tinder-dry trees and pretending that the rain was on its heels. Now and again a spot of almost boiling water would fall on the dust with the flop of a frog, but all our weary world knew that was only pretence. It was a shade cooler in the press-room than the office, so I sat there, while the type clicked and clicked and the night-jars hooted at the windows, and the all but naked compositors wiped the sweat from their foreheads and called for water. The thing that was keeping us back, whatever it was, would not come off, though the *loo* dropped and the last type was set, and the whole round earth stood still in the choking heat, with its finger on its lip, to wait the event. I drowsed, and wondered whether the telegraph was a blessing, and whether this dying man, or struggling people, was aware of the inconvenience the delay was causing. There was no special reason beyond the heat and worry to make tension, but, as the clock hands crept up to three o'clock and the machines spun their fly-wheels two and three times to see that all was in order, before I said the word that would set them off, I could have shrieked aloud.

Then the roar and rattle of the wheels shivered the quiet into little bits. I rose to go away, but two men in white clothes stood in front of me. The first one said:—"It's him!" The second said:—"So it is!" And they both laughed almost as loudly as the machinery roared, and mopped their foreheads. "We see there was a light burning across the road and we were sleeping in that ditch there for coolness, and I said to my friend here, 'The office is open. Let's come along and speak to him as turned us back from the Degumber State,'" said the smaller of the two. He was the man I had met in the Mhow train, and his fellow was the red-bearded man of Marwar Junction. There was no mistaking the eyebrows of the one or the beard of the other.

I was not pleased, because I wished to go to sleep, not to squabble with loafers. "What do you want?" I asked.

"Half an hour's talk with you cool and comfortable, in the office," said the red-bearded man. "We'd *like* some drink—the Contrack doesn't begin

___
9. The final preparations were made for printing the newspaper.

yet, Peachey, so you needn't look—but what we really want is advice. We don't want money. We ask you as a favour, because you did us a bad turn about Degumber."

I led from the press-room to the stifling office with the maps on the walls, and the red-haired man rubbed his hands. "That's something like," said he. "This was the proper shop to come to. Now, Sir, let me introduce to you Brother[1] Peachey Carnehan, that's him, and Brother Daniel Dravot, that is *me*, and the less said about our professions the better, for we have been most things in our time. Soldier, sailor, compositor, photographer, proof-reader, street-preacher, and correspondents of the *Backwoodsman* when we thought the paper wanted one. Carnehan is sober, and so am I. Look at us first and see that's sure. It will save you cutting into my talk. We'll take one of your cigars apiece, and you shall see us light."

I watched the test. The men were absolutely sober, so I gave them each a tepid peg.[2]

"Well *and* good," said Carnehan of the eyebrows, wiping the froth from his moustache. "Let me talk now, Dan. We have been all over India, mostly on foot. We have been boiler-fitters, engine-drivers, petty contractors, and all that, and we have decided that India isn't big enough for such as us."

They certainly were too big for the office. Dravot's beard seemed to fill half the room and Carnehan's shoulders the other half, as they sat on the big table. Carnehan continued: "The country isn't half worked out because they that governs it won't let you touch it. They spend all their blessed time in governing it, and you can't lift a spade, nor chip a rock, nor look for oil, nor anything like that without all the Government saying—'Leave it alone and let us govern.' Therefore, such as it is, we will let it alone, and go away to some other place where a man isn't crowded and can come to his own. We are not little men, and there is nothing that we are afraid of except Drink, and we have signed a Contrack on that. *Therefore*, we are going away to be Kings."

"Kings in our own right," muttered Dravot.

"Yes, of course," I said. "You've been tramping in the sun, and it's a very warm night, and hadn't you better sleep over the notion? Come to-morrow."

"Neither drunk nor sunstruck," said Dravot. "We have slept over the notion half a year, and require to see Books and Atlases, and we have decided that there is only one place now in the world that two strong men can Sar-a-*whack*.[3] They call it Kafiristan.[4] By my reckoning it's the top right-hand corner of Afghanistan, not more than three hundred miles from Pesha-wur. They have two and thirty heathen idols there, and we'll be the thirty-third. It's a mountainous country, and the women of those parts are very beautiful."

"But that is provided against in the Contrack," said Carnehan. "Neither Women nor Liquor, Daniel."

"And that's all we know, except that no one has gone there, and they fight, and in any place where they fight, a man who knows how to drill men can always be a King. We shall go to those parts and say to any King we find—'D'you want to vanquish your foes?' and we will show him how to drill

1. A title meant to recall the Freemason connection.
2. A drink.
3. A reference to Sir James Brooke (1803–1868), "the White Rajah of Sarawak," who, in return for helping the rajah of Sarawak, in Borneo, put down a rebellion, succeeded him after his death, and established a dynasty.
4. A real place, in the Hindu Kush.

men; for that we know better than anything else. Then we will subvert that King and seize his Throne and establish a Dy-nasty."

"You'll be cut to pieces before you're fifty miles across the Border," I said. "You have to travel through Afghanistan to get to that country. It's one mass of mountains and peaks and glaciers, and no Englishman has been through it. The people are utter brutes, and even if you reached them you couldn't do anything."

"That's more like," said Carnehan: "If you could think us a little more mad we would be more pleased. We have come to you to know about this country, to read a book about it, and to be shown maps. We want you to tell us that we are fools and to show us your books." He turned to the bookcases.

"Are you at all in earnest?" I said.

"A little," said Dravot, sweetly. "As big a map as you have got, even if it's all blank where Kafiristan is, and any books you've got. We can read, though we aren't very educated."

I uncased the big thirty-two-miles-to-the-inch map of India, and two smaller Frontier maps, hauled down volume INF-KAN of the *Encyclopaedia Britannica*, and the men consulted them.

"See here!" said Dravot, his thumb on the map. "Up to Jagdallak, Peachey and me know the road. We was there with Roberts's Army.[5] We'll have to turn off to the right at Jagdallak through Laghmann territory. Then we get among the hills—fourteen thousand feet—fifteen thousand—it will be cold work there, but it don't look very far on the map."

I handed him Wood on the *Sources of the Oxus*.[6] Carnehan was deep in the *Encyclopaedia*.

"They're a mixed lot," said Dravot, reflectively; "and it won't help us to know the names of their tribes. The more tribes the more they'll fight, and the better for us. From Jagdallak to Ashang. H'mm!"

"But all the information about the country is as sketchy and inaccurate as can be," I protested. "No one knows anything about it really. Here's the file of the *United Services' Institute*. Read what Bellew says."

"Blow Bellew!" said Carnehan. "Dan, they're an all-fired lot of heathens, but this book here says they think they're related to us English."

I smoked while the men pored over Raverty, Wood, the maps, and the *Encyclopaedia*.

"There is no use your waiting," said Dravot, politely. "It's about four o'clock now. We'll go before six o'clock if you want to sleep, and we won't steal any of the papers. Don't you sit up. We're two harmless lunatics and if you come, to-morrow evening, down to the Serai[7] we'll say good-bye to you."

"You *are* two fools," I answered. "You'll be turned back at the Frontier or cut up the minute you set foot in Afghanistan. Do you want any money or a recommendation downcountry? I can help you to the chance of work next week."

"Next week we shall be hard at work ourselves, thank you," said Dravot. "It isn't so easy being a King as it looks. When we've got our Kingdom in going order we'll let you know, and you can come up and help us to govern it."

"Would two lunatics make a Contrack like that?" said Carnehan, with subdued pride, showing me a greasy half-sheet of note-paper on which was written the following. I copied it, then and there, as a curiosity:

5. In the Second Afghan War (1878–80), a force under the command of General Frederick Roberts made a three-hundred-mile forced march through the area.

6. The Oxus is a river whose sources are in the area.

7. Place or building for the accommodation of travelers and their pack animals.

This Contract between me and you persuing witnesseth in the name of God—Amen and so forth.

(One) *That me and you will settle this matter together: i.e., to be Kings of Kafiristan.*

(Two) *That you and me will not, while this matter is being settled, look at any Liquor, nor any Woman, black, white or brown, so as to get mixed up with one or the other harmful.*

(Three) *That we conduct ourselves with dignity and discretion and if one of us gets into trouble the other will stay by him.*

Signed by you and me this day.

Peachey Taliaferro Carnehan.

Daniel Dravot.

Both Gentlemen at Large.

"There was no need for the last article," said Carnehan, blushing modestly; "but it looks regular. Now you know the sort of men that loafers are—we *are* loafers, Dan, until we get out of India—and *do* you think that we would sign a Contrack like that unless we was in earnest? We have kept away from the two things that make life worth having."

"You won't enjoy your lives much longer if you are going to try this idiotic adventure. Don't set the office on fire," I said, "and go away before nine o'clock."

I left them still poring over the maps and making notes on the back of the "Contrack." "Be sure to come down to the Serai to-morrow," were their parting words.

The Kumharsen Serai is the great foursquare sink of humanity where the strings of camels and horses from the North load and unload. All the nationalities of Central Asia may be found there, and most of the folk of India proper. Balkh and Bokhara there meet Bengal and Bombay, and try to draw eye-teeth. You can buy ponies, turquoises, Persian pussy-cats, saddle-bags, fat-tailed sheep and musk in the Kumharsen Serai, and get many strange things for nothing. In the afternoon I went down there to see whether my friends intended to keep their word or were lying about drunk.

A priest attired in fragments of ribbons and rags stalked up to me, gravely twisting a child's paper whirligig.[8] Behind was his servant bending under the load of a crate of mud toys. The two were loading up two camels, and the inhabitants of the Serai watched them with shrieks of laughter.

"The priest is mad," said a horse-dealer to me. "He is going up to Kabul to sell toys to the Amir.[9] He will either be raised to honor or have his head cut off. He came in here this morning and has been behaving madly ever since."

"The witless are under the protection of God," stammered a flat-cheeked Usbeg[1] in broken Hindi. "They foretell future events."

"Would they could have foretold that my caravan would have been cut up by the Shinwaris almost within shadow of the Pass!"[2] grunted the Eusufzai agent of a Rajputana trading-house whose goods had been feloniously diverted into the hands of other robbers just across the Border, and whose misfortunes were the laughing-stock of the bazar. "Ohé, priest, whence come you and whither do you go?"

8. Pinwheel.
9. The ruler of Afghanistan, based in the city of Kabul.
1. Person from Uzbekistan.

2. The Khyber or Khaiber Pass, running thirty-three miles through the mountains. Then on the northwest frontier of British India, it now links Afghanistan and Pakistan.

"From Roum[3] have I come," shouted the priest, waving his whirligig; "from Roum, blown by the breath of a hundred devils across the sea! O thieves, robbers, liars, the blessing of Pir Khan on pigs, dogs, and perjurers! Who will take the Protected of God to the North to sell charms that are never still to the Amir? The camels shall not gall,[4] the sons shall not fall sick, and the wives shall remain faithful while they are away, of the men who give me place in their caravan. Who will assist me to slipper the King of the Roos[5] with a golden slipper with a silver heel? The protection of Pir Khan be upon his labors!" He spread out the skirts of his gaberdine and pirouetted between the lines of tethered horses.

"There starts a caravan from Peshawur to Kabul in twenty days, *Huzrut*,"[6] said the Eusufzai trader. "My camels go therewith. Do thou also go and bring us good-luck."

"I will go even now!" shouted the priest. "I will depart upon my winged camels, and be at Peshawur in a day! Ho! Hazar[7] Mir Khan," he yelled to his servant, "drive out the camels, but let me first mount my own."

He leaped on the back of his beast as it knelt, and, turning round to me, cried:—"Come thou also, Sahib, a little along the road, and I will sell thee a charm—an amulet that shall make thee King of Kafiristan."

Then the light broke upon me, and I followed the two camels out of the Serai till we reached open road and the priest halted.

"What d' you think o' that?" said he in English. "Carnehan can't talk their patter, so I've made him my servant. He makes a handsome servant. 'Tisn't for nothing that I've been knocking about the country for fourteen years. Didn't I do that talk neat? We'll hitch on to a caravan at Peshawur till we get to Jagdallak, and then we'll see if we can get donkeys for our camels, and strike into Kafiristan. Whirligigs for the Amir, O Lor! Put your hand under the camel-bags and tell me what you feel."

I felt the butt of a Martini,[8] and another and another.

"Twenty of 'em," said Dravot, placidly. "Twenty of 'em, and ammunition to correspond, under the whirligigs and the mud dolls."

"Heaven help you if you are caught with those things!" I said. "A Martini is worth her weight in silver among the Pathans."[9]

"Fifteen hundred rupees of capital—every rupee we could beg, borrow, or steal—are invested on these two camels," said Dravot. "We won't get caught. We're going through the Khaiber with a regular caravan. Who'd touch a poor mad priest?"

"Have you got everything you want?" I asked, overcome with astonishment.

"Not yet, but we shall soon. Give us a memento of your kindness, *Brother*. You did me a service yesterday, and that time in Marwar. Half my Kingdom shall you have, as the saying is." I slipped a small charm compass from my watch-chain and handed it up to the priest.

"Good-bye," said Dravot, giving me hand cautiously. "It's the last time we'll shake hands with an Englishman these many days. Shake hands with him, Carnehan," he cried, as the second camel passed me.

Carnehan leaned down and shook hands. Then the camels passed away along the dusty road, and I was left alone to wonder. My eye could detect no

---

3. Turkey.
4. Become sore.
5. Czar of Russia.
6. Presence (an honorary form of address).
7. Get ready.
8. Rifle issued to British infantry.
9. The principal tribe in Afghanistan.

failure in the disguises. The scene in Serai attested that they were complete to the native mind. There was just the chance, therefore, that Carnehan and Dravot would be able to wander through Afghanistan without detection. But, beyond, they would find death, certain and awful death.

Ten days later a native friend of mine, giving me the news of the day from Peshawur, wound up his letter with:—"There has been much laughter here on account of a certain mad priest who is going in his estimation to sell petty gauds and insignificant trinkets which he ascribes as great charms to H. H.[1] the Amir of Bokhara. He passed through Peshawur and associated himself to the Second Summer caravan that goes to Kabul. The merchants are pleased, because through superstition they imagine that such mad fellows bring good-fortune."

The two, then, were beyond the Border. I would have prayed for them, but, that night, a real King died in Europe, and demanded an obituary notice.

The wheel of the world swings through the same phases again and again. Summer passed and winter thereafter, and came and passed again. The daily paper continued and I with it, and upon the third summer there fell a hot night, a night-issue, and a strained waiting for something to be telegraphed from the other side of the world, exactly as had happened before. A few great men had died in the past two years, the machines worked with more clatter, and some of the trees in the Office garden were a few feet taller. But that was all the difference.

I passed over to the press-room, and went through just such a scene as I have already described. The nervous tension was stronger than it had been two years before, and I felt the heat more acutely. At three o'clock I cried, "Print off," and turned to go, when there crept to my chair what was left of a man. He was bent into a circle, his head was sunk between his shoulders, and he moved his feet one over the other like a bear. I could hardly see whether he walked or crawled—this rag-wrapped, whining cripple who addressed me by name, crying that he was come back. "Can you give me a drink?" he whimpered. "For the Lord's sake, give me a drink!"

I went back to the office, the man following with groans of pain, and I turned up the lamp.

"Don't you know me?" he gasped, dropping into a chair, and he turned his drawn face, surmounted by a shock of grey hair, to the light.

I looked at him intently. Once before had I seen eyebrows that met over the nose in an inch-broad black band, but for the life of me I could not tell where.

"I don't know you," I said, handing him the whiskey. "What can I do for you?"

He took a gulp of the spirit raw, and shivered in spite of the suffocating heat.

"I've come back," he repeated; "and I was the King of Kafiristan—me and Dravot—crowned Kings we was! In this office we settled it—you setting there and giving us the books. I am Peachey—Peachey Taliaferro Carnehan, and you've been setting here ever since—O Lord!"

I was more than a little astonished, and expressed my feelings accordingly.

"It's true," said Carnehan, with a dry cackle, nursing his feet, which were wrapped in rags. "True as gospel. Kings we were, with crowns upon our heads—me and Dravot—poor Dan—oh, poor, poor Dan, that would never take advice, not though I begged of him!"

"Take the whiskey," I said, "and take your own time. Tell me all you can recollect of everything from beginning to end. You got across the border on your camels, Dravot dressed as a mad priest and you his servant. Do you remember that?"

"I ain't mad—yet, but I shall be that way soon. Of course I remember. Keep looking at me, or maybe my words will go all to pieces. Keep looking at me in my eyes and don't say anything."

I leaned forward and looked into his face as steadily as I could. He dropped one hand upon the table and I grasped it by the wrist. It was twisted like a bird's claw, and upon the back was a ragged, red, diamond-shaped scar.

"No, don't look there. Look at *me*," said Carnehan.

"That comes afterward, but for the Lord's sake don't distrack me. We left with that caravan, me and Dravot playing all sorts of antics to amuse the people we were with. Dravot used to make us laugh in the evenings when all the people was cooking their dinners—cooking their dinners, and . . . what did they do then? They lit little fires with sparks that went into Dravot's beard, and we all laughed—fit to die. Little red fires they was, going into Dravot's big red beard—so funny." His eyes left mine and he smiled foolishly.

"You went as far as Jagdallak with that caravan," I said, at a venture, "after you had lit those fires. To Jagdallak, where you turned off to try to get into Kafiristan."

"No, we didn't neither. What are you talking about? We turned off before Jagdallak, because we heard the roads was good. But they wasn't good enough for our two camels—mine and Dravot's. When we left the caravan, Dravot took off all his clothes and mine too, and said we would be heathen, because the Kafirs[2] didn't allow Mohammedans to talk to them. So we dressed betwixt and between, and such a sight as Daniel Dravot I never saw yet nor expect to see again. He burned half his beard, and slung a sheep-skin over his shoulder, and shaved his head into patterns. He shaved mine, too, and made me wear outrageous things to look like a heathen. That was in a most mountaineous country, and our camels couldn't go along any more because of the mountains. They were tall and black, and coming home I saw them fight like wild goats—there are lots of goats in Kafiristan. And these mountains, they never keep still, no more than goats. Always fighting they are, and don't let you sleep at night."

"Take some more whiskey," I said, very slowly. "What did you and Daniel Dravot do when the camels could go no further because of the rough roads that led into Kafiristan?"

"What did which do? There was a party called Peachey Taliaferro Carnehan that was with Dravot. Shall I tell you about him? He died out there in the cold. Slap from the bridge fell old Peachey, turning and twisting in the air like a penny whirligig that you can sell to the Amir—No; they was two for three ha'pence, those whirligigs, or I am much mistaken and woful sore. And then these camels were no use, and Peachey said to Dravot—'For the Lord's sake, let's get out of this before out heads are chopped off,' and with that they killed the camels all among the mountains, not having anything in particular to eat, but first they took off the boxes with the guns and the ammunition, till

2. Non-Muslims.

two men came along driving four mules. Dravot up and dances in front of them, singing,—'Sell me four mules.' Says the first man,—'If you are rich enough to buy, you are rich enough to rob;' but before ever he could put his hand to his knife, Dravot breaks his neck over his knee, and the other party runs away. So Carnehan loaded the mules with the rifles that was taken off the camels, and together we starts forward into those bitter cold mountaineous parts, and never a road broader than the back of your hand."

He paused for a moment, while I asked him if he could remember the nature of the country through which he had journeyed.

"I am telling you as straight as I can, but my head isn't as good as it might be. They drove nails through it to make me hear better how Dravot died. The country was mountaineous and the mules were most contrary, and the inhabitants was dispersed and solitary. They went up and up, and down and down, and that other party, Carnehan, was imploring of Dravot not to sing and whistle so loud, for fear of bringing down the tremenjus avalanches. But Dravot says that if a King couldn't sing it wasn't worth being King, and whacked the mules over the rump, and never took no heed for ten cold days. We came to a big level valley all among the mountains, and the mules were near dead, so we killed them, not having anything in special for them or us to eat. We sat upon the boxes, and played odd and even[3] with the cartridges that was jolted out.

"Then ten men with bows and arrows ran down that valley, chasing twenty men with bows and arrows, and the row was tremenjus. They was fair men—fairer than you or me—with yellow hair and remarkable well built.[4] Says Dravot, unpacking the guns—'This is the beginning of the business. We'll fight for the ten men,' and with that he fires two rifles at the twenty men, and drops one of them at two hundred yards from the rock where we was sitting. The other men began to run, but Carnehan and Dravot sits on the boxes picking them off at all ranges, up and down the valley. Then we goes up to the ten men that had run across the snow too, and they fires a footy[5] little arrow at us. Dravot he shoots above their heads and they all falls down flat. Then he walks over and kicks them, and then he lifts them up and shakes hands all round to make them friendly like. He calls them and gives them the boxes to carry, and waves his hand for all the world as though he was King already. They takes the boxes and him across the valley and up the hill into a pine wood on the top, where there was half a dozen big stone idols. Dravot he goes to the biggest—a fellow they call Imbra—and lays a rifle and a cartridge at his feet, rubbing his nose respectful with his own nose, patting him on the head, and saluting in front of it. He turns round to the men and nods his head, and says,—'That's all right. I'm in the know too, and all these old jim-jams[6] are my friends.' Then he opens his mouth and points down it, and when the first man brings him food, he says—'No;' and when the second man brings him food, he says—'No;' but when one of the old priests and the boss of the village brings him food, he says—'Yes;' very haughty, and eats it slow. That was how we came to our first village, without any trouble, just as though we had tumbled from the skies. But we tumbled from one of those damned rope-bridges, you see, and you couldn't expect a man to laugh much after that."

3. A game in which a player guesses the number of objects that another player is holding.
4. There was a legend that Alexander the Great had left a Greek colony in the area in the 4th century B.C.E.
5. Paltry, insignificant.
6. Knickknacks.

"Take some more whiskey and go on," I said. "That was the first village you came into. How did you get to be King?"

"I wasn't King," said Carnehan. "Dravot he was the King, and a handsome man he looked with the gold crown on his head and all. Him and the other party stayed in that village, and every morning Dravot sat by the side of old Imbra, and the people came and worshipped. That was Dravot's order. Then a lot of men came into the valley, and Carnehan and Dravot picks them off with the rifles before they knew where they was, and runs down into the valley and up again the other side, and finds another village, same as the first one, and the people all falls down flat on their faces, and Dravot says,— 'Now what is the trouble between you two villages?' and the people points to a woman, as fair as you or me, that was carried off, and Dravot takes her back to the first village and counts up the dead—eight there was. For each dead man Dravot pours a little milk on the ground and waves his arms like a whirligig and 'That's all right,' says he. Then he and Carnehan takes the big boss of each village by the arm and walks them down into the valley, and shows them how to scratch a line with a spear right down the valley, and gives each a sod of turf from both sides o' the line. Then all the people comes down and shouts like the devil and all, and Dravot says,—'Go and dig the land, and be fruitful and multiply,'[7] which they did, though they didn't understand. Then we asks the names of things in their lingo—bread and water and fire and idols and such, and Dravot leads the priest of each village up to the idol, and says he must sit there and judge the people, and if anything goes wrong he is to be shot.

"Next week they was all turning up the land in the valley as quiet as bees and much prettier, and the priests heard all the complaints and told Dravot in dumb show what it was about. 'That's just the beginning,' says Dravot. 'They think we're Gods.' He and Carnehan picks out twenty good men and shows them how to click off a rifle, and form fours, and advance in line, and they was very pleased to do so, and clever to see the hang of it. Then he takes out his pipe and his baccy-pouch and leaves one at one village and one at the other, and off we two goes to see what was to be done in the next valley. That was all rock, and there was a little village there, and Carnehan says,—'Send 'em to the old valley to plant,' and takes 'em there and gives 'em some land that wasn't took before. They were a poor lot, and we blooded 'em with a kid[8] before letting 'em into the new Kingdom. That was to impress the people, and then they settled down quiet, and Carnehan went back to Dravot, who had got into another valley, all snow and ice and most mountaineous. There was no people there, and the Army got afraid, so Dravot shoots one of them, and goes on till he finds some people in a village, and the Army explains that unless the people wants to be killed they had better not shoot their little matchlocks;[9] for they had matchlocks. We makes friends with the priest and I stays there alone with two of the Army, teaching the men how to drill, and a thundering big Chief comes across the snow with kettle-drums and horns twanging, because he heard there was a new God kicking about. Carnehan sights for the brown[1] of the men half a mile across the snow and wings one of them. Then he sends a message to the Chief that, unless he wished to be

7. God's command to Adam and Eve (Genesis 1.28).
8. I.e., a kid goat, a fake religious ritual.
9. Primitive muskets.

1. A hunting term, meaning to fire into the middle of a group of game birds rather than aiming at a particular one.

killed, he must come and shake hands with me and leave his arms behind. The Chief comes alone first, and Carnehan shakes hands with him and whirls his arms about, same as Dravot used, and very much surprised that Chief was, and strokes my eyebrows. Then Carnehan goes alone to the Chief, and asks him in dumb show if he had an enemy he hated. 'I have,' says the Chief. So Carnehan weeds out the pick of his men, and sets the two of the Army to show them drill, and at the end of two weeks the men can manoeuvre about as well as Volunteers. So he marches with the Chief to a great big plain on the top of a mountain, and the Chief's men rushes into a village and takes it; we three Martinis firing into the brown of the enemy. So we took that village too, and I gives the Chief a rag from my coat and says, 'Occupy till I come;'[2] which was scriptural. By way of a reminder, when me and the Army was eighteen hundred yards away, I drops a bullet near him standing on the snow, and all the people falls flat on their faces. Then I sends a letter to Dravot, wherever he be by land or by sea."

At the risk of throwing the creature out of train I interrupted,—"How could you write a letter up yonder?"

"The letter?—Oh!—The letter! Keep looking at me between the eyes, please. It was a string-talk letter, that we'd learned the way of it from a blind beggar in the Punjab."

I remember that there had once come to the office a blind man with a knotted twig and a piece of string which he wound round the twig according to some cipher of his own. He could, after the lapse of days or hours, repeat the sentence which he had reeled up. He had reduced the alphabet to eleven primitive sounds; and tried to teach me his method, but failed.

"I sent that letter to Dravot," said Carnehan; "and told him to come back because this Kingdom was growing too big for me to handle, and then I struck for the first valley, to see how the priests were working. They called the village we took along with the Chief, Bashkai, and the first village we took, Er-Heb. The priests at Er-Heb was doing all right, but they had a lot of pending cases about land to show me, and some men from another village had been firing arrows at night. I went out and looked for that village and fired four rounds at it from a thousand yards. That used all the cartridges I cared to spend, and I waited for Dravot, who had been away two or three months, and I kept my people quiet.

"One morning I heard the devil's own noise of drums and horns, and Dan Dravot marches down the hill with his Army and a tail of hundreds of men, and, which was the most amazing—a great gold crown on his head. 'My Gord, Carnehan,' says Daniel, 'this is a tremenjus business, and we've got the whole country as far as it's worth having. I am the son of Alexander by Queen Semiramis,[3] and you're my younger brother and a God too! It's the biggest thing we've ever seen. I've been marching and fighting for six weeks with the Army, and every footy[4] little village for fifty miles has come in rejoiceful; and more than that, I've got the key of the whole show, as you'll see, and I've got a crown for you! I told 'em to make two of 'em at a place called Shu, where the gold lies in the rock like suet in mutton. Gold I've seen, and turquoise I've kicked out of the cliffs, and there's garnets in the

---

2. In Jesus' parable of the talents, a nobleman gives each of his servants a coin to invest with those instructions (Luke 19.13).

3. Legendary Assyrian queen.

4. Worthless.

sands of the river, and here's a chunk of amber that a man brought me. Call up all the priests and, here, take your crown.'

"One of the men opens a black hair bag and I slips the crown on. It was too small and too heavy, but I wore it for the glory. Hammered gold it was— five pound weight, like a hoop of a barrel.

"'Peachey,' says Dravot, 'we don't want to fight no more. The Craft's[5] the trick, so help me!' and he brings forward that same Chief that I left at Bashkai—Billy Fish we called him afterward, because he was so like Billy Fish that drove the big tank-engine at Mach on the Bolan[6] in the old days. 'Shake hands with him,' says Dravot, and I shook hands and nearly dropped, for Billy Fish gave me the Grip.[7] I said nothing, but tried him with the Fellow Craft Grip. He answers, all right, and I tried the Master's Grip, but that was a slip. 'A Fellow Craft he is!' I says to Dan. 'Does he know the word?' 'He does,' says Dan, 'and all the priests know. It's a miracle! The Chiefs and the priests can work a Fellow Craft Lodge in a way that's very like ours, and they've cut the marks on the rocks, but they don't know the Third Degree, and they've come to find out. It's Gord's Truth. I've known these long years that the Afghans knew up to the Fellow Craft Degree, but this is a miracle. A God and a Grand-Master of the Craft am I, and a Lodge in the Third Degree I will open, and we'll raise the head priests and the Chiefs of the villages.'

"'It's against all the law,' I says, 'holding a Lodge without warrant from any one; and we never held office in any Lodge.'

"'It's a master-stroke of policy,' says Dravot. 'It means running the country as easy as a four-wheeled bogy[8] on a down grade. We can't stop to inquire now, or they'll turn against us. I've forty Chiefs at my heel, and passed and raised according to their merit they shall be. Billet these men on the villages and see that we run up a Lodge of some kind. The temple of Imbra will do for the Lodge-room. The women must make aprons as you show them. I'll hold a levee[9] of Chiefs to-night and Lodge to-morrow.'

"I was fair run off my legs, but I wasn't such a fool as not to see what a pull this Craft business gave us. I showed the priests' families how to make aprons of the degrees, but for Dravot's apron the blue border and marks was made of turquoise lumps on white hide, not cloth. We took a great square stone in the temple for the Master's chair, and little stones for the officers' chairs, and painted the black pavement with white squares, and did what we could to make things regular.

"At the levee which was held that night on the hillside with big bonfires, Dravot gives out that him and me were Gods and sons of Alexander, and Past Grand-Masters in the Craft, and was come to make Kafiristan a country where every man should eat in peace and drink in quiet, and specially obey us. Then the Chiefs come round to shake hands, and they was so hairy and white and fair it was just shaking hands with old friends. We gave them names according as they was like men we had known in India—Billy Fish, Holly Wilworth, Pikky Kergan that was Bazar-master when I was at Mhow, and so on and so on.

"*The* most amazing miracle was at Lodge next night. One of the old priests was watching us continuous, and I felt uneasy, for I knew we'd have to fudge the Ritual, and I didn't know what the men knew. The old priest was a stranger

---

5. Freemasonry.
6. The Bolan Pass, which was brought under British control in 1879 during the Second Afghan War.
7. Freemason handshake.
8. Railway truck.
9. Gathering.

come in from beyond the village of Bashkai. The minute Dravot puts on the Master's apron that the girls had made for him, the priest fetches a whoop and a howl, and tries to overturn the stone that Dravot was sitting on. 'It's all up now,' I says. 'That comes of meddling with the Craft without warrant!' Dravot never winked an eye, not when ten priests took and tilted over the Grand-Master's chair—which was to say the stone of Imbra. The priest begins rubbing the bottom end of it to clear away the black dirt, and presently he shows all the other priests the Master's Mark, same as was on Dravot's apron, cut into the stone. Not even the priests of the temple of Imbra knew it was there. The old chap falls flat on his face at Dravot's feet and kisses 'em. 'Luck again,' says Dravot, across the Lodge to me, 'they say it's the missing Mark that no one could understand the why of. We're more than safe now.' Then he bangs the butt of his gun for a gavel and says:—'By virtue of the authority vested in me by my own right hand and the help of Peachey, I declare myself Grand-Master of all Freemasonry in Kafiristan in this the Mother Lodge o' the country, and King of Kafiristan equally with Peachey!' At that he puts on his crown and I puts on mine—I was doing Senior Warden—and we opens the Lodge in most ample form. It was a amazing miracle! The priests moved in Lodge through the first two degrees almost without telling, as if the memory was coming back to them. After that, Peachey and Dravot raised such as was worthy—high priests and Chiefs of far-off villages. Billy Fish was the first, and I can tell you we scared the soul out of him. It was not in any way according to Ritual, but it served our turn. We didn't raise more than ten of the biggest men, because we didn't want to make the Degree common. And they was clamoring to be raised.

"'In another six months,' says Dravot, 'we'll hold another Communication[1] and see how you are working.' Then he asks them about their villages, and learns that they was fighting one against the other and were fair sick and tired of it. And when they wasn't doing that they was fighting with the Mohammedans. 'You can fight those when they come into our country,' says Dravot. 'Tell off[2] every tenth man of your tribes for a Frontier guard, and send two hundred at a time to this valley to be drilled. Nobody is going to be shot or speared any more so long as he does well, and I know that you won't cheat me because you're white people—sons of Alexander—and not like common, black Mohammedans. You are *my* people and by God,' says he, running off into English at the end—'I'll make a damned fine Nation of you, or I'll die in the making!'

"I can't tell all we did for the next six months because Dravot did a lot I couldn't see the hang off, and he learned their lingo in a way I never could. My work was to help the people plough, and now and again go out with some of the Army and see what the other villages were doing, and make 'em throw rope-bridges across the ravines which cut up the country horrid. Dravot was very kind to me, but when he walked up and down in the pine wood pulling that bloody red beard of his with both fists I knew he was thinking plans I could not advise him about, and I just waited for orders.

"But Dravot never showed me disrespect before the people. They were afraid of me and the Army, but they loved Dan. He was the best of friends with the priests and the Chiefs; but any one could come across the hills with a complaint and Dravot would hear him out fair, and call four priests

---

1. In Freemasonry an official Lodge meeting, in which all members have a part. 2. Count off.

together and say what was to be done. He used to call in Billy Fish from Bashkai, and Pikky Kergan from Shu, and an old Chief we called Kafuzelum—it was like enough to his real name—and hold councils with 'em when there was any fighting to be done in small villages. That was his Council of War, and the four priests of Bashkai, Shu, Khawak, and Madora was his Privy Council. Between the lot of 'em they sent me, with forty men and twenty rifles, and sixty men carrying turquoises, into the Ghorband country to buy those hand-made Martini rifles, that come out of the Amir's workshops at Kabul, from one of the Amir's Herati regiments that would have sold the very teeth out of their mouths for turquoises.

"I stayed in Ghorband a month, and gave the Governor there the pick of my baskets for hush-money, and bribed the Colonel of the regiment some more, and, between the two and the tribes-people, we got more than a hundred handmade Martinis, a hundred good Kohat Jezails[3] that'll throw to six hundred yards, and forty man-loads of very bad ammunition for the rifles. I came back with what I had, and distributed 'em among the men that the Chiefs sent to me to drill. Dravot was too busy to attend to those things, but the old Army that we first made helped me, and we turned out five hundred men that could drill, and two hundred that knew how to hold arms pretty straight. Even those cork-screwed, hand-made guns was a miracle to them. Dravot talked big about powder-shops and factories, walking up and down in the pine wood when the winter was coming on.

"'I won't make a Nation,' says he. 'I'll make an Empire! These men aren't niggers; they're English! Look at their eyes—look at their mouths. Look at the way they stand up. They sit, on chairs in their own houses. They're the Lost Tribes,[4] or something like it, and they've grown to be English. I'll take a census in the spring if the priests don't get frightened. There must be a fair two million of 'em in these hills. The villages are full o' little children. Two million people—two hundred and fifty thousand fighting men—and all English! They only want the rifles and a little drilling. Two hundred and fifty thousand men, ready to cut in on Russia's right flank when she tries for India! Peachey, man,' he says, chewing his beard in great hunks, 'we shall be Emperors—Emperors of the Earth! Rajah Brooke will be a suckling to us. I'll treat with the Viceroy[5] on equal terms. I'll ask him to send me twelve picked English—twelve that I know of—to help us govern a bit. There's Mackray, Sergeant-pensioner at Segowli—many's the good dinner he's given me, and his wife a pair of trousers. There's Donldn, the Warder of Tounghoo Jail; there's hundreds that I could lay my hand on if I was in India. The Viceroy shall do it for me. I'll send a man through in the spring for those men, and I'll write for a dispensation from the Grand-Lodge for what I've done as Grand-Master. That—and all the Sniders[6] that'll be thrown out when the native troops in India take up the Martini. They'll be worn smooth, but they'll do for fighting in these hills. Twelve English, a hundred thousand Sniders run through the Amir's country in driblets—I'd be content with twenty thousand in one year—and we'd be an Empire. When everything was shipshape, I'd hand over the crown—this crown I'm wearing now—to Queen Victoria on my knees, and she'd say: "Rise up, Sir

---

3. Afghan muskets.
4. Of the twelve original Hebrew tribes mentioned in the Bible, ten were lost by assimilating with neighboring peoples.

5. Head of the British administration in India. Rajah Brooke: see n. 3, p. 937. "Suckling": infant.
6. Older rifles being replaced by Martinis.

Daniel Dravot." Oh, it's big! It's big, I tell you! But there's so much to be done in every place—Bashkai, Khawak, Shu, and everywhere else.'

"'What is it?' I says. There are no more men coming in to be drilled this autumn. Look at those fat, black clouds. They're bringing the snow.'

"'It isn't that,' says Daniel, putting his hand very hard on my shoulder; 'and I don't wish to say anything that's against you, for no other living man would have followed me and made me what I am as you have done. You're a first-class Commander-in-Chief, and the people know you; but—it's a big country, and somehow you can't help me, Peachey, in the way I want to be helped.'

"'Go to your blasted priests, then!' I said, and I was sorry when I made that remark, but it did hurt me sore to find Daniel talking so superior when I'd drilled all the men, and done all he told me.

"'Don't let's quarrel, Peachey,' says Daniel, without cursing. 'You're a King, too, and the half of this Kingdom is yours; but can't you see, Peachey, we want cleverer men than us now—three or four of 'em, that we can scatter about for our Deputies. It's a hugeous great State, and I can't always tell the right thing to do, and I haven't time for all I want to do, and here's the winter coming on and all.' He put half his beard into his mouth, and it was as red as the gold of his crown.

"'I'm sorry, Daniel,' says I. 'I've done all I could. I've drilled the men and shown the people how to stack their oats better; and I've brought in those tinware rifles from Ghorband—but I know what you're driving at. I take it Kings always feel oppressed that way.'

"'There's another thing too,' says Dravot, walking up and down. 'The winter's coming and these people won't be giving much trouble and if they do we can't move about. I want a wife.'

"'For Gord's sake leave the women alone!' I says. 'We've both got all the work we can, though I *am* a fool. Remember the Contrack, and keep clear o' women.'

"'The Contrack only lasted till such time as we was Kings; and Kings we have been these months past,' says Dravot, weighing his crown in his hand. 'You go get a wife too, Peachey—a nice, strappin', plump girl that'll keep you warm in the winter. They're prettier than English girls, and we can take the pick of 'em. Boil 'em once or twice in hot water, and they'll come as fair as chicken and ham.'

"'Don't tempt me!' I says. 'I will not have any dealings with a woman not till we are a dam' side more settled than we are now. I've been doing the work o' two men, and you've been doing the work o' three. Let's lie off a bit, and see if we can get some better tobacco from Afghan country and run in some good liquor; but no women.'

"'Who's talking o' *women*?' says Dravot. 'I said *wife*—a Queen to breed a King's son for the King. A Queen out of the strongest tribe, that'll make them your blood-brothers, and that'll lie by your side and tell you all the people thinks about you and their own affairs. That's what I want.'

"'Do you remember that Bengali woman I kept at Mogul Serai when I was a plate-layer?'[7] says I. 'A fat lot o' good she was to me. She taught me the lingo and one or two other things; but what happened? She ran away with the Station-master's servant and half my month's pay. Then she turned up at

7. Layer of railway track.

Dadur Junction in tow of a half-caste, and had the impidence to say I was her husband—all among the drivers in the running-shed!'

"'We've done with that,' says Dravot. 'These women are whiter than you or me, and a Queen I will have for the winter months.'

"'For the last time o' asking, Dan, do *not*,' I says. 'It'll only bring us harm. The Bible says that Kings ain't to waste their strength on women,[8] 'specially when they've got a new raw Kingdom to work over.'

"'For the last time of answering, I will,' said Dravot, and he went away through the pine-trees looking like a big red devil. The low sun hit his crown and beard on one side and the two blazed like hot coals.

"But getting a wife was not as easy as Dan thought. He put it before the Council, and there was no answer till Billy Fish said that he'd better ask the girls. Dravot damned them all round. 'What's wrong with me?' he shouts, standing by the idol Imbra. 'Am I a dog or am I not enough of a man for your wenches? Haven't I put the shadow of my hand over this country? Who stopped the last Afghan raid?' It was me really, but Dravot was too angry to remember. 'Who brought your guns? Who repaired the bridges? Who's the Grand-Master of the sign cut in the stone?' and he thumped his hand on the block that he used to sit on in Lodge, and at Council, which opened like Lodge always. Billy Fish said nothing, and no more did the others. 'Keep your hair on, Dan,' said I; 'and ask the girls. That's how it's done at Home, and these people are quite English.'

"'The marriage of the King is a matter of State,' says Dan, in a white-hot rage, for he could feel, I hope, that he was going against his better mind. He walked out of the Council-room, and the others sat still, looking at the ground.

"'Billy Fish,' says I to the Chief of Bashkai, 'what's the difficulty here? A straight answer to a true friend,' 'You know,' says Billy Fish. 'How should a man tell you who know everything? How can daughters of men marry Gods or Devils? It's not proper.'

"I remembered something like that in the Bible;[9] but if, after seeing us as long as they had, they still believed we were Gods, it wasn't for me to undeceive them.

"'A God can do anything,' says I. 'If the King is fond of a girl he'll not let her die.' 'She'll have to,' said Billy Fish. 'There are all sorts of Gods and Devils in these mountains, and now and again a girl marries one of them and isn't seen any more. Besides, you two know the Mark cut in the stone. Only the Gods know that. We thought you were men till you showed the sign of the Master.'

"I wished then that we had explained about the loss of the genuine secrets of a Master-Mason at the first go-off; but I said nothing. All that night there was a blowing of horns in a little dark temple half-way down the hill, and I heard a girl crying fit to die. One of the priests told us that she was being prepared to marry the King.

"'I'll have no nonsense of that kind,' says Dan. 'I don't want to interfere with your customs, but I'll take my own wife.' 'The girl's a little bit afraid,' says the priest. 'She thinks she's going to die, and they are a-heartening of her up down in the temple.'

---

8. "Give not thy strength unto women, nor thy ways to that which destroyeth kings" (Proverbs 31.3).

9. "That the sons of God saw the daughters of men that they were fair; and they took them wives of all which they chose" (Genesis 6.2).

"'Hearten her very tender, then,' says Dravot, 'or I'll hearten you with the butt of a gun so that you'll never want to be heartened again.' He licked his lips, did Dan, and stayed up walking about more than half the night, thinking of the wife that he was going to get in the morning. I wasn't any means comfortable, for I knew that dealings with a woman in foreign parts, though you was a crowned King twenty times over, could not but be risky. I got up very early in the morning while Dravot was asleep, and I saw the priests talking together in whispers, and the Chiefs talking together too, and they looked at me out of the corners of their eyes.

"'What is up, Fish?' I says to the Bashkai man, who was wrapped up in his furs and looking splendid to behold.

"'I can't rightly say,' says he; 'but if you can induce the King to drop all this nonsense about marriage, you'll be doing him and me and yourself a great service.'

"'That I do believe,' says I. 'But sure, you know, Billy, as well as me, having fought against and for us, that the King and me are nothing more than two of the finest men that God Almighty ever made. Nothing more, I do assure you.'

"'That may be,' says Billy Fish, 'and yet I should be sorry if it was.' He sinks his head upon his great fur cloak for a minute and thinks. 'King,' says he, 'be you man or God or Devil, I'll stick by you to-day. I have twenty of my men with me, and they will follow me. We'll go to Bashkai until the storm blows over.'

"A little snow had fallen in the night, and everything was white except the greasy fat clouds that blew down and down from the north. Dravot came out with his crown on his head, swinging his arms and stamping his feet, and looking more pleased than Punch.[1]

"'For the last time, drop it, Dan,' says I, in a whisper. 'Billy Fish here says that there will be a row.'

"'A row among my people!' says Dravot. 'Not much. Peachey, you're a fool not to get a wife too. Where's the girl?' says he, with a voice as loud as the braying of a jackass. 'Call up all the Chiefs and priests, and let the Emperor see if his wife suits him.'

"There was no need to call any one. They were all there leaning on their guns and spears round the clearing in the centre of the pine wood. A deputation of priests went down to the little temple to bring up the girl, and the horns blew up fit to wake the dead. Billy Fish saunters round and gets as close to Daniel as he could, and behind him stood his twenty men with matchlocks. Not a man of them under six feet. I was next to Dravot, and behind me was twenty men of the regular Army. Up comes the girl, and a strapping wench she was, covered with silver and turquoises, but white as death, and looking back every minute at the priests.

"'She'll do,' said Dan, looking her over. 'What's to be afraid of, lass? Come and kiss me.' He puts his arm round her. She shuts her eyes, gives a bit of a squeak, and down goes her face in the side of Dan's flaming red beard.

"'The slut's bitten me!' says he, clapping his hand to his neck, and, sure enough, his hand was red with blood. Billy Fish and two of his matchlockmen catches hold of Dan by the shoulders and drags him into the Bashkai lot, while the priests howl in their lingo,—'Neither God nor Devil, but a

1. Common expression: the character in the Punch-and-Judy puppet show has a fixed grin and is delighted with his evil deeds.

man!' I was all taken aback, for a priest cut at me in front, and the Army behind began firing into the Bashkai men.

"'God A-mighty!' says Dan. 'What is the meaning o' this?'

"'Come back! Come away!' says Billy Fish. 'Ruin and Mutiny is the matter. We'll break for Bashkai if we can.'

"I tried to give some sort of orders to my men—the men o' the regular Army—but it was no use, so I fired into the brown of 'em with an English Martini and drilled three beggars in a line. The valley was full of shouting, howling creatures, and every soul was shrieking, 'Not a God nor a Devil, but only a man!' The Bashkai troops stuck to Billy Fish all they were worth, but their matchlocks wasn't half as good as the Kabul breech-loaders, and four of them dropped. Dan was bellowing like a bull, for he was very wrathy; and Billy Fish had a hard job to prevent him running out at the crowd.

"'We can't stand,' says Billy Fish. 'Make a run for it down the valley! The whole place is against us.' The matchlock-men ran, and we went down the valley in spite of Dravot's protestations. He was swearing horribly and crying out that he was a King. The priests rolled great stones on us, and the regular Army fired hard, and there wasn't more than six men, not counting Dan, Billy Fish, and Me, that came down to the bottom of the valley alive.

"Then they stopped firing and the horns in the temple blew again. 'Come away—for Gord's sake come away!' says Billy Fish. 'They'll send runners out to all the villages before ever we get to Bashkai. I can protect you there, but I can't do anything now.'

"My own notion is that Dan began to go mad in his head from that hour. He stared up and down like a stuck pig. Then he was all for walking back alone and killing the priests with his bare hands; which he could have done. 'An Emperor am I,' says Daniel, 'and next year I shall be a Knight of the Queen.'

"'All right, Dan,' says I; 'but come along now while there's time.'

"'It's your fault,' says he, 'for not looking after your Army better. There was mutiny in the midst and you didn't know—you damned engine-driving, plate-laying, missionary's-pass-hunting hound!' He sat upon a rock and called me every foul name he could lay tongue to. I was too heart-sick to care, though it was all his foolishness that brought the smash.

"'I'm sorry, Dan,' says I, 'but there's no accounting for natives. This business is our Fifty-Seven.[2] Maybe we'll make something out of it yet, when we've got to Bashkai.'

"'Let's get to Bashkai, then,' says Dan, 'and, by God, when I come back here again I'll sweep the valley so there isn't a bug in a blanket left!'

"We walked all that day, and all that night Dan was stumping up and down on the snow, chewing his beard and muttering to himself.

"'There's no hope o' getting clear,' said Billy Fish. 'The priests will have sent runners to the villages to say that you are only men. Why didn't you stick on as Gods till things was more settled? I'm a dead man,' says Billy Fish, and he throws himself down on the snow and begins to pray to his Gods.

"Next morning we was in a cruel bad country—all up and down, no level ground at all, and no food either. The six Bashkai men looked at Billy Fish hungry-wise as if they wanted to ask something, but they said never a word.

---

2. Mutiny of 1857, when regiments of the Bengal army rebelled against their British officers.

At noon we came to the top of a flat mountain all covered with snow, and when we climbed up into it, behold, there was an Army in position waiting in the middle!

"'The runners have been very quick,' says Billy Fish, with a little bit of a laugh. 'They are waiting for us.'

"Three or four men began to fire from the enemy's side, and a chance shot took Daniel in the calf of the leg. That brought him to his senses. He looks across the snow at the Army, and sees the rifles that we had brought into the country.

"'We're done for,' says he. 'They are Englishmen, these people,—and it's my blasted nonsense that has brought you to this. Get back, Billy Fish, and take your men away; you've done what you could, and now cut for it. Carnehan,' says he, 'shake hands with me and go along with Billy. Maybe they won't kill you. I'll go and meet 'em alone. It's me that did it. Me, the King!'

"'Go!' says I. 'Go to Hell, Dan. I'm with you here. Billy Fish, you clear out, and we two will meet those folk.'

"'I'm a Chief,' says Billy Fish, quite quiet. 'I stay with you. My men can go.'

"The Bashkai fellows didn't wait for a second word, but ran off, and Dan and me and Billy Fish walked across to where the drums were drumming and the horns were horning. It was cold—awful cold. I've got that cold in the back of my head now. There's a lump of it there."

The punkah-coolies[3] had gone to sleep. Two kerosene lamps were blazing in the office, and the perspiration poured down my face and splashed on the blotter as I leaned forward. Carnehan was shivering, and I feared that his mind might go. I wiped my face, took a fresh grip of the piteously mangled hands, and said: "What happened after that?"

The momentary shift of my eyes had broken the clear current.

"What was you pleased to say?" whined Carnehan. "They took them without any sound. Not a little whisper all along the snow, not though the King knocked down the first man that set hand on him—not though old Peachey fired his last cartridge into the brown of 'em. Not a single solitary sound did those swines make. They just closed up tight, and I tell you their furs stunk. There was a man called Billy Fish, a good friend of us all, and they cut his throat, Sir, then and there, like a pig; and the King kicks up the bloody snow and says:—'We've had a dashed fine run for our money. What's coming next?' But Peachey, Peachey Taliaferro, I tell you, Sir, in confidence as betwixt two friends, he lost his head, Sir. No, he didn't neither. The King lost his head, so he did, all along o' one of those cunning rope-bridges. Kindly let me have the paper-cutter, Sir. It tilted this way. They marched him a mile across that snow to a rope-bridge over a ravine with a river at the bottom. You may have seen such. They prodded him behind like an ox. 'Damn your eyes!' says the King. 'D'you suppose I can't die like a gentleman?' He turns to Peachey—Peachey that was crying like a child. 'I've brought you to this, Peachey,' says he. 'Brought you out of your happy life to be killed in Kafiristan, where you was late Commander-in-Chief of the Emperor's forces. Say you forgive me, Peachey.' 'I do,' says Peachey. 'Fully and freely do I forgive you, Dan.' 'Shake hands, Peachey,' says he. 'I'm going now. Out he goes, looking neither right nor left, and when he was plumb in the middle of those dizzy dancing ropes,

---

3. Servants who operate punkahs, or fans.

'Cut, you beggars,' he shouts; and they cut, and old Dan fell, turning round and round and round twenty thousand miles, for he took half an hour to fall till he struck the water, and I could see his body caught on a rock with the gold crown close beside.

"But do you know what they did to Peachey between two pine trees? They crucified him, Sir, as Peachey's hand will show. They used wooden pegs for his hands and his feet; and he didn't die. He hung there and screamed, and they took him down next day, and said it was a miracle that he wasn't dead. They took him down—poor old Peachey that hadn't done them any harm—that hadn't done them any . . ."

He rocked to and fro and wept bitterly, wiping his eyes with the back of his scarred hands and moaning like a child for some ten minutes.

"They was cruel enough to feed him up in the temple, because they said he was more of a God than old Daniel that was a man. Then they turned him out on the snow, and told him to go home, and Peachey came home in about a year, begging along the roads quite safe; for Daniel Dravot he walked before and said:—'Come along, Peachey. It's a big thing we're doing.' The mountains they danced at night, and the mountains they tried to fall on Peachey's head, but Dan he held up his hand, and Peachey came along bent double. He never let go of Dan's hand, and he never let go of Dan's head. They gave it to him as a present in the temple, to remind him not to come again, and though the crown was pure gold, and Peachey was starving, never would Peachey sell the same. You knew Dravot, Sir! You knew Right Worshipful Brother Dravot! Look at him now!"

He fumbled in the mass of rags round his bent waist; brought out a black horsehair bag embroidered with silver thread; and shook therefrom on to my table—the dried, withered head of Daniel Dravot! The morning sun that had long been paling the lamps struck the red beard and blind, sunken eyes; struck, too, a heavy circlet of gold studded with raw turquoises, that Carnehan placed tenderly on the battered temples.

"You behold now," said Carnehan, "the Emperor in his habit as he lived[4]—the King of Kafiristan with his crown upon his head. Poor old Daniel that was a monarch once!"

I shuddered, for, in spite of defacements manifold, I recognized the head of the man of Marwar Junction. Carnehan rose to go. I attempted to stop him. He was not fit to walk abroad. "Let me take away the whiskey, and give me a little money," he gasped. "I was a King once. I'll go to the Deputy Commissioner and ask to set in the Poorhouse till I get my health. No, thank you, I can't wait till you get a carriage for me. I've urgent private affairs—in the south—at Marwar."

He shambled out of the office and departed in the direction of the Deputy Commissioner's house. That day at noon I had occasion to go down the blinding hot Mall, and I saw a crooked man crawling along the white dust of the roadside, his hat in his hand, quavering dolorously after the fashion of street-singers at Home. There was not a soul in sight, and he was out of all possible earshot of the houses. And he sang through his nose, turning his head from right to left:

4. Allusion to Hamlet's description of his father's ghost: "My father, in his habit as he lived" (Shakespeare, *Hamlet* 3.4.126).

"The Son of Man goes forth to war,
  A golden crown to gain;
His blood-red banner streams afar—
  Who follows in his train?"[5]

I waited to hear no more, but put the poor wretch into my carriage and drove him off to the nearest missionary for eventual transfer to the Asylum. He repeated the hymn twice while he was with me, whom he did not in the least recognize, and I left him singing it to the missionary.

Two days later I inquired after his welfare of the Superintendent of the Asylum.

"He was admitted suffering from sunstroke. He died early yesterday morning," said the Superintendent. "Is it true that he was half an hour bareheaded in the sun at midday?"

"Yes," said I, "but do you happen to know if he had anything upon him by any chance when he died?"

"Not to my knowledge," said the Superintendent.

And there the matter rests.

1888

The White Man's Burden[1]

Take up the White Man's burden—
  Send forth the best ye breed—
Go bind your sons to exile
  To serve your captives' need;
5 To wait in heavy harness,
    On fluttered folk and wild—
Your new-caught, sullen peoples,
  Half-devil and half-child.

Take up the White Man's burden—
10   In patience to abide,
To veil the threat of terror
  And check the show of pride;
By open speech and simple,
  An hundred times made plain,
15 To seek another's profit,
  And work another's gain.

Take up the White Man's burden—
  The savage wars of peace—
Fill full the mouth of Famine

---

5. A well-known hymn, by Reginald Heber (1783–1826), corrected in later editions to the actual words of the first line: "The Son of God goes forth to war."
1. This poem was conceived for Queen Victoria's Jubilee in 1897, but Kipling abandoned it in favor of "Recessional." He returned to the poem when disagreements between Spain and the United States over Spanish colonial rule in Cuba and elsewhere sparked the Spanish-American War in 1898. In its revised form the poem reacts to resistance in the Philippines to the United States' assumption of colonial power.

20 And bid the sickness cease;
    And when your goal is nearest
    The end for others sought,
    Watch Sloth and heathen Folly
    Bring all your hope to nought.

25 Take up the White Man's burden—
    No tawdry rule of kings,
    But toil of serf and sweeper[2]—
    The tale of common things.
    The ports ye shall not enter,
30 The roads ye shall not tread,
    Go make them with your living,
    And mark them with your dead.

    Take up the White Man's burden—
    And reap his old reward:
35 The blame of those ye better,
    The hate of those ye guard—
    The cry of hosts ye humour
    (Ah, slowly!) toward the light:—
    'Why brought ye us from bondage,
40 Our loved Egyptian night?'[3]

    Take up the White Man's burden—
    Ye dare not stoop to less—
    Nor call too loud on Freedom
    To cloak your weariness;
45 By all ye cry or whisper,
    By all ye leave or do,
    The silent, sullen peoples
    Shall weigh your Gods and you.

    Take up the White Man's burden—
50 Have done with childish days—
    The lightly proffered laurel,[4]
    The easy, ungrudged praise.
    Comes now, to search your manhood
    Through all the thankless years,
55 Cold, edged with dear-bought wisdom,
    The judgment of your peers!

1899

---

2. Street sweeper, who in India would belong to the lowest caste.
3. Cf. Exodus 16.2–3. When the Israelites were suffering from hunger in the wilderness, they criticized Moses and Aaron for taking them from what they saw as the relative comfort of Egyptian slavery.
4. A symbol of military distinction in the triumphs celebrated by victorious Roman generals (later, Roman emperors wore a laurel crown as part of their official regalia).

If—

If you can keep your head when all about you
    Are losing theirs and blaming it on you;
If you can trust yourself when all men doubt you,
    But make allowance for their doubting too;
5 If you can wait and not be tired by waiting,
    Or being lied about, don't deal in lies,
Or being hated don't give way to hating,
    And yet don't look too good, nor talk too wise:

If you can dream—and not make dreams your master;
10   If you can think—and not make thoughts your aim,
If you can meet with Triumph and Disaster
    And treat those two impostors just the same;
If you can bear to hear the truth you've spoken
    Twisted by knaves to make a trap for fools,
15 Or watch the things you gave your life to, broken,
    And stoop and build 'em up with worn-out tools:

If you can make one heap of all your winnings
    And risk it on one turn of pitch-and-toss,[1]
      And lose, and start again at your beginnings
20   And never breathe a word about your loss;
If you can force your heart and nerve and sinew
    To serve your turn long after they are gone,
And so hold on when there is nothing in you
    Except the Will which says to them: 'Hold on!'

25 If you can talk with crowds and keep your virtue,
    Or walk with Kings—nor° lose the common touch,   *and not*
If neither foes nor loving friends can hurt you,
    If all men count with you, but none too much;
If you can fill the unforgiving minute
30   With sixty seconds' worth of distance run,
Yours is the Earth and everything that's in it,
    And—which is more—you'll be a Man, my son!

1910

1. A game, played with coins, that combines skill (tossing a coin as close as possible to a fixed mark) and luck (flipping coins and keeping those that come up heads).

The Twentieth Century and After

1914–18:   World War I
1922:   James Joyce's *Ulysses*; T. S. Eliot's *The Waste
             Land*
1929:   Stock market crash; Great Depression begins
1939–45:   World War II
1947:   India and Pakistan become independent
             nations
1953:   Premiere of Samuel Beckett's *Waiting for
             Godot*
1957–62:   Ghana, Nigeria, Uganda, Jamaica, and
             Trinidad and Tobago become independent
             nations
1981:   Salman Rushdie's *Midnight's Children*
1991:   Collapse of the Soviet Union
2001:   Attacks destroy World Trade Center

HISTORICAL BACKGROUND

The roots of modern literature are in the late nineteenth century. The aesthetic movement, with its insistence on "art for art's sake," assaulted middle-class assumptions about the nature and function of art. Rejecting Victorian notions of the artist's moral and educational duties, aestheticism helped widen the breach between writers and the general public, resulting in the "alienation" of the modern artist from society. This alienation is evident in the lives and work of the French symbolists and other late nineteenth-century bohemians who repudiated conventional notions of respectability, and it underlies key works of modern literature, such as James Joyce's *Portrait of the Artist as a Young Man* and T. S. Eliot's *The Waste Land*.

The growth of public education in England as a result of the Education Act of 1870, which finally made elementary schooling compulsory and universal, led

---

The Merry-Go-Round (detail), 1916, Mark Gertler. For more information about this image, see the color insert in this volume.

Ascot Race Track. Spectators segregated by class at the track, England, June 1, 1907. Top hats and dress distinguish the upper class in the top rows. Working-class men are barred from the stands and wear cloth caps. Middle-class men wear bowlers and straw hats. Virginia Woolf critically inspects the British class system in *Mrs. Dalloway*, a novel that mentions Ascot, among other London athletic and social venues (pp. 1109).

to the rapid emergence of a mass literate population, at whom a new mass-produced popular literature and new cheap journalism (the "yellow press") were directed. The audience for literature split up into "highbrows," "middle-brows," and "lowbrows," and the segmentation of the reading public, developing with unprecedented speed and to an unprecedented degree, helped widen the gap between popular art and art esteemed only by the sophisticated and the expert. This breach yawned ever wider with the twentieth-century emergence of modernist iconoclasm and avant-garde experiment in literature, music, and the visual arts.

To Queen Victoria's contemporaries her Jubilee in 1887 and, even more, her Diamond Jubilee in 1897 marked the end of an era. The reaction against middle-class Victorian attitudes that is central to modernism was already under way in the two decades before the queen's death in 1901. Samuel Butler attacked the Victorian conceptions of the family, education, and religion in his novel *The Way of All Flesh* (completed in 1884, posthumously published in 1903), the bitterest indictment in English literature of Victorian conventions. And the high tide of anti-Victorianism was marked by the publication in 1918 of a classic of ironic debunking, Lytton Strachey's collection of biographical essays, *Eminent Victorians*.

A pivotal figure between Victorianism and modernism, Thomas Hardy marked the end of the Victorian period and the dawn of the new age in "The Darkling Thrush," a poem originally titled "By the Century's Deathbed" and postdated December 31, 1900, the last day of the nineteenth century. The poem marks the demise of a century of relative conviction and optimism, and it intimates the beginnings of a new era in its skeptical irresolution, its bleak sense of the modern world as "hard and dry"—favorite adjectives of later writers such as Ezra Pound and T. E. Hulme:

> The land's sharp features seemed to be
> The Century's corpse outleant,
> His crypt the cloudy canopy,
> The wind his death-lament.
> The ancient pulse of germ and birth
> Was shrunken hard and dry,
> And every spirit upon earth
> Seemed fervourless as I.

This poem and other works by Hardy, A. E. Housman, and Joseph Conrad exemplify the pessimism of imaginative writing in the last decade of the nineteenth century and the first decade of the twentieth. Stoicism—a stiff-upper-lip determination to endure whatever fate may bring—also character-izes the literature written in the transitional period between the Victorian era and modernism, including the work of minor authors such as Robert Louis Stevenson and Rudyard Kipling.

By the dawn of the twentieth century, traditional stabilities of society, religion, and culture seemed to have weakened, the pace of change to be accelerating. The unsettling force of modernity profoundly challenged tra-ditional ways of structuring and making sense of human experience. Because of the rapid pace of social and technological change; because of the mass dislocation of populations by war, empire, and economic migra-tion; and because of the mixing in close quarters of cultures and classes in rapidly expanding cities, modernity disrupted the old order, upended ethi-cal and social codes, cast into doubt previously stable assumptions about self, community, the world, and the divine.

Early-twentieth-century writers were keenly aware that powerful concepts and vocabularies were emerging in anthropology, psychology, philosophy, and the visual arts that reimagined human identity in radically new ways. Sigmund Freud's seminal *Interpretation of Dreams* was published in 1900, and soon psychoanalysis was changing how people saw and described ratio-nality, the self, and personal development. In his prose and poetry D. H. Lawrence adapted the Oedipus complex to interpret and present his relation-ships with his parents, though rejecting Freud's negative definition of the unconscious. By the time of his death in 1939, Freud had become, as W. H. Auden wrote in an elegy for him, "a whole climate of opinion // under whom we conduct our different lives." Also in the early twentieth century, Sir James Frazer's *Golden Bough* (1890–1915) and other works of anthropology were altering basic conceptions of culture, religion, and myth. Eliot observed that Frazer's work "influenced our generation profoundly," and the critic Lionel Trilling suggested that "perhaps no book has had so decisive an effect upon modern literature as Frazer's." For both anthropologists and modern writers, Western religion was now decentered by being placed in a comparative con-text as one of numerous related mythologies, with Jesus Christ linked to "primitive" fertility gods thought to die and revive in concert with the seasons. Furthering this challenge to religious doctrine were the writings of Friedrich Nietzsche, the nineteenth-century German philosopher who declared the death of God, repudiated Christianity, and offered instead a harshly tragic conception of life: people look "deeply into the true nature of things" and real-ize "that no action of theirs can work any change," but they nevertheless laugh and stoically affirm their fate. W. B. Yeats, who remarks in a 1902 letter that his eyes are exhausted from reading "that strong enchanter," greets death and destruction in a Nietzschean spirit of tragic exultation.

These profound changes in modern intellectual history coincided with changes of a more mundane sort, for everyday life was also undergoing rapid transformation during the first years of the twentieth century. Electricity was spreading, cinema and radio were proliferating, and new pharmaceuticals such as aspirin were being developed. As labor was increasingly managed and rationalized, as more and more people crowded into cities, as communica-tions and transportation compressed global space and accelerated time, literature could not stand still, and modern writers sought to create forms that could register these profound alterations in human experience. This was a period of scientific revolution, as exemplified in German physics by Max Planck's quantum theory (1900) and Albert Einstein's theory of relativity (1905), and T. S. Eliot reflects the increasing dominance of science when he argues that the poet surrenders to tradition and thus extinguishes rather than expresses personality: "It is in this depersonalization that art may be said to approach the condition of science," he claims, adding that "the mind of the poet is the shred of platinum" that catalyzes change but itself remains "inert, neutral, and unchanged" ("Tradition and the Individual Talent").

The early twentieth century also brought countless advances in technology: the first wireless communication across the Atlantic occurred in 1901, the Wright Brothers flew the first airplane in 1903, and Henry Ford introduced the first mass-produced car, the Model T or "Tin Lizzie," in 1913. Not that modern writers univocally embraced such changes. Although some were more sanguine, many modern writers were paradoxically repulsed by aspects of modernization. Mass-produced appliances and products, such as the "gramophone" and canned goods ("tins"), are objects of revulsion in Eliot's *Waste Land*, for example. Because scientific materialism and positivism, according to which empirical explanations could be found for everything, were weakening the influence of organized religion, many writers looked to literature as an alternative. His "simple-minded" Protestantism spoiled by science, Yeats says in his autobiography, he "made a new religion, almost an infallible church of poetic tradition." Whether or not they welcomed the demise of tradition, habit, and certitude in favor of the new, modern writers articulated the effects of modernity's relentless change, loss, and destabilization. "Things fall apart," Yeats wrote, "the centre cannot hold." Eliot describes in *Four Quartets* his quest for the "still point of the turning world." The modernist drive to "make it new"—in Ezra Pound's famous slogan—thus arises in part out of an often ambivalent consciousness of the relentless mutations brought by modernization.

The position of women, too, was rapidly changing during this period. The Married Woman's Property Act of 1882 allowed wives to own property in their own right, and women were admitted to universities at different times during the latter part of the century. Since the days of Mary Wollstonecraft, women in Great Britain had been arguing and lobbying for the right to vote, but in the first decades of the twentieth century, Emmeline Pankhurst and her daughter Christabel encouraged suffragettes, as they were known, to take a more militant approach, which included boycotts, bombings, and hunger strikes. The long fight for women's suffrage was finally won in 1918 for women thirty and over, and in 1928 for women twenty-one and over. These shifts in attitudes toward women, in the roles women played in the national life, and in the relations between the sexes are reflected in a variety of ways in the literature of the period.

Britain's modern political history begins with the Anglo-Boer War (1899–1902), fought by the British to establish political and economic control over the Boer republics (self-governing states) of South Africa. It was an imperial war against which many British intellectuals protested and one that the British in the end were slightly ashamed of having won. The war spanned the reign of Queen Victoria, who died in 1901, and Edward VII, who held the throne from 1901 to 1910. This latter decade is known as the Edwardian period, and the king stamped his extrovert and self-indulgent character upon it. The wealthy made it a vulgar age of conspicuous enjoyment, but most writers and artists kept well away from involvement in high society: in general this period had no equivalent to Queen Victoria's friendship with Tennyson. The alienation of artists and intellectuals from political rulers and middle-class society was proceeding apace. From 1910 (when George V came to the throne) until World War I broke out in August 1914, Britain achieved a temporary equilibrium between Victorian earnestness and Edwardian flashiness; in retrospect the Georgian period seems peculiarly golden, the last phase of assurance and stability before the old order

Women's Suffrage. Emmeline Pankhurst being arrested at a demonstration outside Buckingham Palace, London, January 5, 1914. A leader in Britain of the movement for women's right to vote, she and other militant "suffragettes" were repeatedly jailed. During their hunger strikes they were force-fed.

throughout Europe broke up in violence. Yet even then, under the surface, there was restlessness and experimentation. The age of Rupert Brooke's idyllic sonnets on the English countryside was also the age of T. S. Eliot's first experiments in a radically new kind of poetry, James Joyce's and Virginia Woolf's in radically new forms of fiction.

Edwardian as a term applied to English cultural history suggests a period in which the social and economic stabilities of the Victorian age—country houses with numerous servants, a flourishing and confident middle class, a strict hierarchy of social classes—remained unimpaired, though on the level of ideas a sense of change and liberation existed. *Georgian* refers largely to the lull before the storm of World War I. That war, as the bitterly skeptical and antiheroic work of Wilfred Owen, Siegfried Sassoon, Isaac Rosenberg, and other war poets makes clear, produced major shifts in attitude toward Western myths of progress and civilization. The postwar disillusion of the 1920s resulted, in part, from the sense of utter social and political collapse during a war in which unprecedented millions were killed.

By the beginning of World War I, nearly a quarter of the earth's surface and more than a quarter of the world's population were under British dominion, including the vast African territories acquired in the preceding hundred years. Some of the colonies in the empire were settler nations with large European populations, such as Canada, Australia, and New Zealand, and in 1907 the empire granted them the new status of dominions, recognizing their relative control over internal affairs. Over time these largely independent nations came to be known as the British Commonwealth, an association of self-governing countries. The twentieth century witnessed the emergence of internationally acclaimed literary voices from these dominions, from the

The Easter Rising. Dublin buildings destroyed during the Easter Rising of 1916. In revolt against British rule of Ireland, rebels took over key positions on April 24 until the British crushed the insurrection a week later and then executed fifteen leaders. (See Yeats's "Easter, 1916," p. 1068.)

early-century New Zealander Katherine Mansfield to the late-century Australian Les Murray and Canadians Alice Munro and Margaret Atwood. The rest of the colonies in the British Empire consisted primarily of indigenous populations that had little or no political power, but nationalist movements were gaining strength in the early years of the century—as when, in 1906, the Congress movement in India first demanded *swaraj* ("self-rule") soon to become the mantra of Indian nationalism. In Britain imperialist and anti-imperialist sentiments often met head on in Parliament and the press, the debate involving writers as far apart as Rudyard Kipling and E. M. Forster.

A steadily rising Irish nationalism resulted in increasingly violent protests against the cultural, economic, and political subordination of Ireland to the British Crown and government. During the Easter Rising of 1916, Irish rebels in Dublin staged a revolt against British rule, and by executing fifteen Irish leaders, the British inadvertently intensified the drive for independence, finally achieved in 1921–22 when the southern counties were declared the Irish Free State. (The six counties of Northern Ireland remained, however, part of Great Britain.) No one can fully understand Yeats or Joyce without some awareness of the Irish struggle for independence and the way in which the Irish literary revival of the late nineteenth and early twentieth centuries (with Yeats at the forefront) reflected a determination to achieve a vigorous national life culturally even if the road seemed blocked politically.

Depression and unemployment in the early 1930s, followed by the rise of Hitler and the shadow of fascism and Nazism over Europe, with its threat of another war, deeply affected the emerging poets and novelists of the time. Feminism, pacifism, and liberal attitudes on sexuality and gender relations were espoused by some members of the Bloomsbury Group, named after the London district where its adherents congregated, including the writers Virginia Woolf and E. M. Forster, as well as the economist John Maynard Keynes. But many other prominent literary figures of this older generation, such as Eliot, Lawrence, Wyndham Lewis, Yeats, and Pound, turned to the political right. The impotence of capitalist governments in the face of fascism combined with economic dislocation to turn the majority of young intellectuals (and not only intellectuals) in the 1930s to the political left. The 1930s were the so-called red decade, because only the left seemed to offer any solution in various forms of socialism, communism, and liberalism. The early poetry of W. H. Auden and his contemporaries cried out for "the death of the old gang" (in Auden's phrase) and a clean sweep politically and economically, while the right-wing army's rebellion against the left-wing republican government in Spain, which started in the summer of 1936 and soon led to full-scale civil war, was regarded as a rehearsal for an inevitable second international conflict and thus further emphasized the inadequacy of politicians. Yet though the younger writers of the period expressed the up-to-date, radical political views of the left, they were less technically inventive than the first-generation modernists, such as Eliot, Joyce, and Woolf. The outbreak of World War II in September 1939—following shortly on Hitler's pact with the Soviet Union, which so shocked and disillusioned many of the young left-wing writers that they subsequently moved politically to the center—marked the sudden end of the red decade. What was from the beginning expected to be a long and costly war brought inevitable exhaustion. The diminution of British political power, its secondary status in relation to the United States as a player in the Cold War, led to a painful reappraisal of Britain's place in the world, even as countries that had lost the war—West Germany and Japan—were, in economic terms, winning the peace that followed.

In winning a war, Great Britain lost an empire. The largest, most powerful, best organized of the modern European empires, it had expropriated enormous quantities of land, raw materials, and labor from its widely scattered overseas territories. India, long the jewel in the imperial Crown, won its independence in 1947, along with the newly formed Muslim state of Pakistan. The postwar wave of decolonization that began in South Asia spread to Africa and the Caribbean: in 1957 Ghana was the first nation in sub-Saharan Africa to become independent, unleashing an unstoppable wave of liberation from British rule that freed Nigeria in 1960, Sierra Leone in 1961, Uganda in 1962, Kenya in 1963; in the Caribbean, Jamaica and Trinidad and Tobago

Decolonization. Dancers celebrate on the eve of Ghana's creation and independence, in March 1957. After India and Pakistan won independence from Britain in 1947, Ghana was the first sub-Saharan nation to gain its freedom, beginning a wave of decolonization that swept through most of Britain's remaining colonies.

in 1962, Barbados and Guyana in 1966, and Saint Lucia in 1979. India and Pakistan elected to remain within a newly expanded and reconceived British Commonwealth, but other former colonies did not. The Irish Republic withdrew from the Commonwealth in 1949; the Republic of South Africa, in 1961. Postwar decolonization coincided with and encouraged the efflorescence of postcolonial writing that would bring about the most dramatic geographic shift in literature in English since its inception. Writers from Britain's former colonies published influential and innovative novels, plays, and poems, hybridizing their local traditions and varieties of English with those of the empire. The names of the Nobel Prize winners Wole Soyinka, Nadine Gordimer, Derek Walcott, V. S. Naipaul, J. M. Coetzee, and Doris Lessing were added to the annals of literature in English.

While Britain was decolonizing its empire, the former empire was colonizing Britain, as Louise Bennett wryly suggests in her poem "Colonization in Reverse." Encouraged by the postwar labor shortage in England and the scarcity of work at home, waves of Caribbean migrants journeyed to and settled in "the motherland," the first group on the *Empire Windrush* that sailed from Jamaica to Tilbury Docks, near London, in 1948. Migrants followed from India, Pakistan, Bangladesh, Africa, and other regions of the "New Commonwealth." Even as immigration laws became more restrictive in the late 1960s, relatives of earlier migrants and refugees from these and other nations continued to arrive, transforming Britain into an increasingly multiracial society and infusing energy into British arts and literature. But people of Caribbean, African, and South Asian origin, who brought distinc-

Immigration. Caribbean immigrants arriving by ship in Southampton, England, July 1, 1962. The waves of largely economic immigrants from the British Empire and the Commonwealth in the 1950s and 1960s created a multiracial Britain, which included substantial Caribbean, African, and Asian minorities.

tive vernaculars and cultural traditions with them, painfully discovered that their official status as British subjects often did not translate into their being welcomed as full-fledged members of British society. Many of them experienced racial discrimination in jobs and housing, and bigotry sometimes erupted into violent attacks on them, such as race riots in Nottingham and London's Notting Hill in 1958. Conservative Member of Parliament Enoch Powell delivered his infamous "Rivers of Blood" speech in 1968, foreseeing deadly interracial strife and warning against further immigration. The collision between the Anglo-Saxon conception of Englishness and the emerging multiracial reality of English society prompted a large-scale, ongoing rethinking of national identity in Britain. Among the arrivals in England were many who journeyed there to study in the late 1940s and 1950s and eventually became prominent writers, such as Bennett, Soyinka, Kamau (then Edward) Brathwaite, and Chinua Achebe. In the 1970s and 1980s a younger generation of black and Asian British writers emerged—some born in the U.K., some in the ex-empire—including Salman Rushdie, Hanif Kureishi, Grace Nichols and Caryl Phillips, and in the 1990s and the first decade of the new millennium, still younger writers including Jackie Kay and Zadie Smith.

London, as the capital of the empire, had long dominated the culture as well as the politics and the economy of the British Isles. London spoke for Britain in the impeccable southern English intonations of the radio announcers, of the state-owned British Broadcasting Corporation (known as the BBC), but from the end of World War II this changed. Regional dialects and multicultural accents were admitted to the airwaves. Regional radio and television stations sprang up. In the 1940s and 1950s the BBC produced a weekly program called "Caribbean Voices," which proved an important stimulus to anglophone writing in the West Indies. The Arts Council, which had subsidized the nation's drama, literature, music, painting, and plastic arts from London, delegated much of its grant-giving responsibility to regional arts councils. This gave a new confidence to writers and artists outside London— the Beatles were launched from Liverpool—and has since contributed to a notable renaissance of regional literature.

From the 1960s London ceased to be essentially the sole cultural stage of the United Kingdom, and though its Parliament remained the sole political stage until 1999, successive governments came under increasing pressure from the regions and the wider world. After decades of predominantly Labour governments, Margaret Thatcher led the Conservatives to power in the general election of 1979, becoming thereby the country's first woman to hold the office of prime minister, an office she was to occupy for an unprecedented twelve years. Pursuing a vision of a "new," more productive Britain, she curbed the power of the unions and began to dismantle the "welfare state," privatizing nationalized industries and utilities in the interests of an aggressive free-market economy. Initially her policies seemed to have a bracing effect on a nation still sunk in postwar, postimperial torpor, but writers such as Ian McEwan, Hanif Kureishi, and Caryl Churchill and filmmakers such as Derek Jarman protested that Conservative reforms widened the gap between rich and poor, black and white, north and south, and between the constituent parts of the United Kingdom.

From the late 1960s, the Irish Republican Army waged a bloody campaign for a united Ireland and against British rule. The IRA was met by violent suppression by the British Army and reprisals by Protestant Unionists, who

Boys in Belfast, Northern Ireland, May 16, 1976. They run toward a British armed vehicle to throw bottles and rocks as part of a campaign against British rule. From the late 1960s to the 1990s, members of the Irish Catholic minority in Northern Ireland protested discrimination by the Protestant Unionist majority, backed by the British military.

sought to keep Northern Ireland a part of the United Kingdom. In the 1990s, politics finally took precedence over armed struggle in the Republican movement. In 1998 the Good Friday Agreement, also known as the Belfast Agreement, led to elections to a Northern Ireland Assembly, which convened for the first time in 1999, and the leaders of the main Roman Catholic and Protestant parties were jointly awarded the Nobel Peace Prize.

Thatcher was deposed by her own party in 1990, and the Conservatives were routed in the election of 1997. The electorate's message was clear, and Tony Blair, the new Labour prime minister, moved to restore the run-down Health Service and system of state education. Honoring other of his campaign pledges, he offered Scotland its own parliament and Wales its own assembly, each with tax-raising powers and a substantial budget for the operation of its social services, and each holding its first elections in 1999. Blair and his Labour Party successor Gordon Brown faced increasing skepticism over their justification for joining forces with the U.S.-led invasion and occupation of Iraq in 2003 and over their handling of the economy. In 2010, David Cameron, the first Conservative Party prime minister in thirteen years, headed a coalition government with the Liberal Democrats, the first formal coalition government since World War II.

POETRY

The years leading up to World War I saw the start of a poetic revolution. The imagist movement, influenced by the philosopher poet T. E. Hulme's insistence on hard, clear, precise images, arose in reaction to what it saw as Romantic fuzziness and facile emotionalism in poetry. (Like other modernists, the imagists somewhat oversimplified the nineteenth-century aesthetic against which they defined their own artistic ideal, while scanting underlying continuities.) The movement developed initially in London, where the modernist American poet Ezra Pound was living, and quickly migrated across the Atlantic, and its early members included Hulme, Pound, H. D. (Hilda Doolittle), Amy Lowell, Richard Aldington, John Gould Fletcher, and F. S. Flint. As Flint explained in an article in March 1913, partly dictated by Pound, imagists insisted on "direct treatment of the 'thing,' whether subjective or objective," on the avoidance of all words "that did not contribute to the presentation," and on a freer metrical movement than a strict adherence to the "sequence of a metronome" could allow. Inveighing in manifestos against Victorian discursiveness, the imagists wrote short, sharply etched, descriptive lyrics, but they lacked a technique for the production of longer and more complex poems.

Other new ideas about poetry helped provide this technique, many of them associated with another American in London, T. S. Eliot. Sir Herbert Grierson's 1912 edition of John Donne's poems both reflected and encouraged a new enthusiasm for seventeenth-century Metaphysical poetry. The revived interest in Metaphysical "wit" brought with it a desire on the part of pioneering poets to introduce into their work a much higher degree of intellectual complexity than had been found among the Victorians or the Georgians. The full subtlety of French symbolist poetry also now came to be appreciated; it had been admired in the 1890s, but more for its dreamy suggestiveness than for its imagistic precision and complexity. At the same time, modernist writers wanted to bring poetic language and rhythms closer to those of conversation, or at least to spice the formalities of poetic utterance with echoes of the colloquial and even the slangy. Irony, which made possible several levels of discourse simultaneously, and wit, with the use of puns (banished from serious poetry for more than two hundred years), helped achieve that union of thought and passion that Eliot, in his review of Grierson's anthology of Metaphysical poetry (1921), saw as characteristic of the Metaphysicals and wished to bring back into poetry. A new critical movement and a new creative movement in poetry went hand in hand, with Eliot the high priest of both. He extended the scope of imagism by bringing the English Metaphysicals and the French symbolists (as well as the English Jacobean dramatists) to the rescue, thus adding new criteria of complexity and allusiveness to the criteria of concreteness and precision stressed by the imagists. Eliot also introduced into modern English and American poetry the kind of irony achieved by shifting suddenly from the formal to the colloquial, or by oblique allusions to objects or ideas that contrasted sharply with the surface meaning of the poem. Nor were Eliot and the imagists alone in their efforts to reinvent poetry. From 1912 D. H. Lawrence began writing poems freer in form and emotion, wanting to unshackle verse from the constraints of the "gem-like" lyric and to approach even the "insurgent naked throb of the instant moment." From 1915 the self-declared "Anglo-Mongrel" Mina Loy "mongrelized" the diction of English-language poetry and desentimentalized Anglo-American love poetry. Thus between, say, 1911 (the first year covered by Edward Marsh's anthologies of Georgian poetry) and 1922 (the year of the publication of *The Waste Land*), a major revolution occurred in English—and for that matter American—poetic theory and practice, one that determined the way in which many poets now think about their art.

This modernist revolution was by no means an isolated literary phenomenon. Writers on both sides of the English Channel were influenced by the French impressionist, postimpressionist, and cubist painters' radical reexamination of the nature of reality. The influence of Italian futurism was likewise strong on the painter and writer Wyndham Lewis, whose short-lived journal *Blast* was meant to be as shocking in its visual design as in its violent rhetoric. Mina Loy shared the futurist fascination with modernity and speed, while repudiating its misogyny and jingoism, as evidenced by her "Feminist Manifesto." Pound wrote books about the French sculptor Henri Gaudier-Brzeska and the American composer George Antheil, and indeed the jagged rhythms and wrenching dissonances of modern music influenced a range of writers. Wilfred Owen wrote in 1918: "I suppose I am doing in poetry what the advanced composers are doing in music"; and Eliot, while writing *The Waste Land* three years later, was so impressed by a performance of the composer Igor Stravinsky's *Le Sacre du Printemps* (*The Rite of Spring*) that he stood up at the end and cheered.

The posthumous 1918 publication by Robert Bridges of Gerard Manley Hopkins's poetry encouraged experimentation in language and rhythms, as evidenced by the verse's influence on Eliot, Auden, and the Welshman Dylan Thomas. Hopkins combined precision of the individual image with a complex ordering of images and a new kind of metrical patterning he named "sprung rhythm," in which the stresses of a line could be more freely distributed.

Meanwhile Yeats's remarkable oeuvre, stretching across the whole modern period, reflected varying developments of the age yet maintained an unmistakably individual accent. Beginning with the ideas of the aesthetes, turning to a tougher and sparer ironic language without losing its characteristic verbal magic, working out its author's idiosyncratic notions of symbolism, developing in its full maturity into a rich symbolic and Metaphysical poetry with its own curiously haunting cadences and with imagery both shockingly realistic and movingly suggestive, Yeats's work encapsulates a history of English poetry between 1890 and 1939.

In his poem "Remembering the 'Thirties," Donald Davie declared: "A neutral tone is nowadays preferred." That tone—Auden's coolly clinical tone—dominated the poetry of the decade. The young poets of the early 1930s—Auden, Stephen Spender, C. Day Lewis, Louis MacNeice—were the first generation to grow up in the shadow of the first-generation modern poets. Hopkins's attention to sonorities, Hardy's experiments in stanzaic patterns, Yeats's ambivalent meditations on public themes, Eliot's satiric treatment of a mechanized and urbanized world, and Owen's pararhymed enactments of pity influenced Auden and the other poets in his circle. But these younger poets also had to distinguish themselves from the still-living eminences in poetry, and they did so by writing poems more low-pitched and ironic than Yeats's, for example, or more individually responsive to and active in the social world than Eliot's. Stevie Smith's poetry, though largely independent of the period style, shared its progressive politics, conversational idiom, and ironic (if often whimsical) tone, as well as an interest in adapting oral forms, such as ballads, folk songs, and even nursery rhymes.

As World War II began, the Auden group's neutral tone gave way to an increasingly direct and humane voice, as in Auden's work, and to the vehemence of what came to be known as the New Apocalypse. The poets of this movement, most notably Dylan Thomas, owed something of their imagistic audacity and rhetorical violence to the French surrealists, whose poetry was introduced to English readers in translations and in *A Short Survey of Surrealism* (1936) by David Gascoyne, one of the New Apocalypse poets. Many of the surrealists, such as Salvador Dalí and André Breton, were both poets and painters, and in their verbal as well as their visual art they sought to express, often by free association, the operation of the unconscious mind.

With the coming of the 1950s, however, the pendulum swung back. A new generation of poets, including Donald Davie, Thom Gunn, and Philip Larkin, reacted against what seemed to them the verbal excesses and extravagances of Dylan Thomas and Edith Sitwell, as well as the arcane myths and knotty allusiveness of Yeats, Eliot, and Pound. "The Movement," as this new group came to be called, aimed once again for a neutral tone, a purity of diction, in which to render an unpretentious fidelity to mundane experience. Larkin, its most notable exponent, rejected the intimidating gestures of an imported modernism in favor of a more civil and accessible "native" tradition that went back to Hardy, Housman, and the Georgian pastoralists of the 1910s.

Not everyone in England followed the lead of Larkin and the Movement, some rejecting the Movement's notion of a limited, rationalist, polished poetics. In the late 1950s and the 1960s Ted Hughes began to write poems in which predators and victims in the natural world suggest the violence and irrationality of modern history, including the carnage of World War I, in which his father had fought. Geoffrey Hill also saw a rationalist humanism as inadequate to the ethical and religious challenges of twentieth-century war, genocide, and atrocity, which he evoked in a strenuous language built on the traditions of high modernism and Metaphysical poetry.

Since the 1980s the spectrum of Britain's poets has become more diverse in class, ethnicity, gender, and region than ever before, introducing a range of voices into the English literary tradition. Born in the northern English region of Yorkshire Tony Harrison and Simon Armitage brought the local vernacular rhythms into contact with traditional English and classical verse. The daughter of an Irish mother and raised in Scotland in a left-wing, working-class Catholic family, Carol Ann Duffy grew up amid Irish, Scottish, and Standard varieties of English, and this youthful experience helped equip her to speak in different voices in her feminist monologues.

Post–World War II Ireland—both North and South—was among the most productive spaces for poetry in the second half of the twentieth century. Born just two and a half weeks after Yeats died, Seamus Heaney, his most celebrated successor, responds to the horrors of sectarian bloodshed in Northern Ireland with subtlety and acute ethical sensitivity in poems that draw on both Irish genres and sonorities and the English literary tradition of Wordsworth, Hopkins, and Ted Hughes. Paul Muldoon, one of Heaney's former students in Belfast, also writes about the Troubles in Northern Ireland but through eerily distorted fixed forms and multiple screens of irony, combining experimental zaniness with formal reserve. A native of the Irish Republic, Eavan Boland has made a space within the largely male tradition of Irish verse—with its standard, mythical emblems of femininity—for Irish women's historical experiences of suffering and survival.

The massive postwar change in the geographical contours of poetry written in English involved, in part, the emergence of new voices and styles from the

"Old Commonwealth," or dominions, such as Canada and Australia. Self-conscious about being at the margins of the former empire, Les Murray fashions a brash, playful, overbrimming poetry that mines the British and classical traditions while remaking them in what he styles his "redneck" Australian manner. Deliberately Canadian and feminist, Margaret Atwood writes out of the "inescapable doubleness," isolation, and alienation she ascribes to Canadian writing: "We are all immigrants to this place," she says, "even if we were born here."

From the former colonies of the British Empire in the so-called Third World came some of the most important innovations in the language and thematic reach of poetry in English. Born under British rule, students of colonial educations that repressed or denigrated native languages and traditions, these postcolonial poets grew up with an acute awareness of the riches of their own cultural inheritances, as well as a deep knowledge of the British literary canon. They expanded the range of possibilities in English-language poetry by hybridizing traditions of the British Isles with their indigenous images and speech rhythms, creoles, and genres. Some of these writers, such as the Nobel laureate Derek Walcott, the most eminent West Indian poet, have drawn largely on British, American, and classical European models, though Walcott creolizes the rhythms, diction, and sensibility of English-language poetry. "I have Dutch, nigger, and English in me," declares the mulatto hero of "The Schooner *Flight*, "and either I'm nobody, or I'm a nation." Other poets have emphasized even more strongly African Caribbean inheritances in speech and culture. When colonial prejudices still branded West Indian English, or Creole, a backward language, a "corruption" of English, the African Jamaican poets Claude McKay and Louise Bennett claimed its wit, vibrancy, and proverbial richness for poetry. In the late 1960s the Barbadian Kamau (then Edward) Brathwaite revalued the linguistic, musical, and mythic survivals of Africa in the Caribbean—resources long repressed because of colonial attitudes. In poetry as well as fiction, Nigeria was the most prolific anglophone African nation around the time of independence, said to be the "golden age" of letters in sub-Saharan Africa. Wole Soyinka, later the first black African to win the Nobel Prize, stretched English syntax and figurative language in poems dense with Yoruba-inspired wordplay and myth. At the same time poets from India were bringing its great variety of indigenous cultures into English-language poetry. A. K. Ramanujan's sharply etched poems interfuse Anglo-modernist principles with the south Indian legacies of Tamil and Kannada poetry. All of these poets respond with emotional ambivalence and linguistic versatility to the experience of living after colonialism, between non-Western traditions and modernity, in a period of explosive change in the relation between Western and "native" cultures.

A century that began with a springtime of poetic innovation drew to its close with the full flowering of older poets such as Walcott, Hill, and Heaney, and the twenty-first century opened with welcome signs of fresh growth in English-language poetry, including new books by Paul Muldoon, elected Oxford Professor of Poetry from 1999 to 2004, and Carol Ann Duffy, appointed poet laureate from 2009 to 2019, the first woman and first Scot to hold the position.

FICTION

Novels—"loose baggy monsters," in Henry James's phrase—can be, can do, can include anything at all. The form defies prescriptions and limits. Yet its variety converges on persistent issues such as the construction of the self within society, the reproduction of the real world, and the temporality of human experience and of narrative. The novel's flexibility and porousness, its omnivorousness and multivoicedness have enabled writers to take advantage of modernity's global dislocation and mixture of peoples, while meeting the challenges to the imagination of mass death and world war, of the relentless and rapid mutations in modern cultures and societies, in evolving knowledge and belief.

The twentieth century's novels may be divided roughly into three main subperiods: high modernism through the 1920s, celebrating personal and textual inwardness, complexity, and difficulty; the reaction against modernism, involving a return to social realism, moralism, and assorted documentary endeavors, in the 1930s, 1940s, and 1950s; and the period after the collapse of the British Empire (especially from the time of the countercultural revolution of the 1960s), in which the fictional claims of various realisms—urban, proletarian, provincial English (e.g., northern), regional (e.g., Scottish and Irish), immigrant, postcolonial, feminist, gay—are asserted alongside, but also through, a continuing self-consciousness about language and form and meaning that is, in effect, the enduring legacy of modernism. By the end of the century, modernism had given way to the striking pluralism of postmodernism and postcolonialism. Yet the roots of the late-century panoramic mix of voices and styles lay in the early part of the century, when writers on the margins of "Englishness"—a Pole, Joseph Conrad; an Irishman, James Joyce; an American, Henry James; an Englishwoman, Virginia Woolf; and a working-class Englishman, D. H. Lawrence—were the most instrumental inventors of the modernist "English" novel.

The high modernists wrote in the wake of the shattering of confidence in the old certainties about the deity and the Christian faith, about the person, knowledge, materialism, history, the old grand narratives, which had, more or less, sustained the Western novel through the nineteenth century. They boldly ventured into this general shaking of belief in the novel's founding assumptions—that the world, things, and selves were knowable, that language was a reliably revelatory instrument, that the author's story gave history meaning and moral shape, that narratives should fall into ethically instructive beginnings, middles, and endings. Trying to be true to the new skepticisms and hesitations, the modernists also attempted to construct credible new alternatives to the old belief systems.

The once-prevailing nineteenth-century notions of ordinary reality came under serious attack. In her famous essay "Modern Fiction" (1919, revised 1925), Virginia Woolf explicitly assaulted the "materialism" of the realistic Edwardian heirs of Victorian naturalist confidence, Arnold Bennett, H. G. Wells, and John Galsworthy. For Woolf, as for other modernists, what was knowable, and thus representable, could not be thought of as some given, fixed, transcribable essence. Reality existed, rather, only as it was perceived. Hence the introduction of the impressionistic, flawed, even utterly unreliable narrator—a substitute for the classic nineteenth-century authoritative narrating voice, usually the voice of the author or some close substitute. Even a relatively reliable narrator, such as Conrad's Marlow, the main narrating voice of *Heart of Darkness*, as of *Lord Jim*, dramatized the struggle to know, penetrate, and interpret reality, with his large rhetoric of the invisible, inaudible, impossible, unintelligible, and so unsayable. The real was offered, thus, as refracted and reflected in the novel's representative consciousness. "Look within," Woolf urged the novelist. Reality and its truth had gone inward.

Woolf's subject would be "an ordinary mind on an ordinary day." The life that mattered most would now be mental life. And so the modernist novel turned resolutely inward, its concern being now with consciousness—a flow of reflections, momentary impressions, disjunctive bits of recall and half-memory, simultaneously revealing both the past and the way the past is repressed. Psychoanalysis partly enabled this concentration: to narrate the reality of persons as the life of the mind in all its complexity and inner tumult—consciousness, unconsciousness, id, libido, and so on. And the apparent truths of this inward life were, of course, utterly tricky, scattered, fragmentary, spotty, now illuminated, now twilit, now quite occluded. For Woolf, Joyce's *Ulysses* was a prime expression of this desired impressionistic agenda: "he is concerned at all costs to reveal the flickerings of that innermost flame which flashes its messages through the brain."

The characters of Joyce and Woolf are caught, then, as they are immersed in the so-called stream of consciousness; and some version of an interior flow of thought becomes the main modernist access to "character." The reader overhears the characters speaking, so to say, from within their particular consciousnesses, but not always directly. The modernists felt free also to enter their characters' minds, to speak as it were on their behalf, in the technique known as "free indirect style" (*style indirect libre* in French).

A marked feature of the new fictional selfhood was a fraught condition of existential loneliness. Conrad's Lord Jim, Joyce's Leopold Bloom and Stephen Dedalus, Lawrence's Paul Morel and Birkin, and Woolf's Mrs. Dalloway were people on their own, individuals bereft of the old props, Church, Bible, ideological consensus, and so doomed to make their own puzzled way through life's labyrinths without much confidence in belief, in the knowable solidity of the world, above all in language as a tool of knowledge about self and other. Jacob of Woolf's *Jacob's Room* remains stubbornly unknowable to his closest friends and loved ones, above all to his novelist. The walls and cupboards of Rhoda's room in *The Waves*, also by Woolf, bend disconcertingly around her bed; she tries in vain to restore her sense of the solidity of things by touching the bottom bed rail with her toes; her mind "pours" out of her; the very boundaries of her self soften, slip, dissolve. The old conclusive plots—everything resolved on the novel's last page, on the model of the detective story—gave place to irresolute open endings: the unending vista of the last paragraph in Lawrence's *Sons and Lovers*; the jump from third-person narration to a fragmentary diary at the conclusion of Joyce's *Portrait of the Artist as a Young Man*; the melancholy of regret and unfulfilled desire at the end of Woolf's *Mrs. Dalloway*.

Novelists built modern myths on the dry bones of the old Christian ones. In his review of *Ulysses* ("*Ulysses*, Order, and Myth," 1923), T. S. Eliot famously praised the novel for replacing the old "narrative method" by a new "mythical method": Joyce's Irish Jew, Bloom, is mythicized as a modern Ulysses, his day's odyssey often ironically reviving episodes in Homer's

Odyssey. This manipulation of "a continuous parallel between contemporaneity and antiquity" was, Eliot thought, "a step toward making the modern world possible for art," much in keeping with the new anthropology and psychology as well as with what Yeats was doing in verse. In Joyce's *Portrait of the Artist*, Stephen Dedalus's last name sets up (sometimes ironic) parallels between the mythical Greek past and the aspirations of a contemporary young Irishman. Modernism's private mythmaking could, of course, take worrying turns. The "religion of the blood" that D. H. Lawrence celebrated led directly to the fascist sympathies of his *Aaron's Rod* and the revived Aztec blood cult of *The Plumed Serpent*.

Language and textuality, reading and writing were now central to these highly metafictional novels, which are often about writers and artists, and surrogates for artists, such as Woolf's Mrs. Ramsay with her dinners and Mrs. Dalloway with her party, producers of what Woolf called the "unpublished works of women." But this self-reflexivity was not necessarily consoling—Mrs. Flanders's vision blurs and an inkblot spreads across the postcard we find her writing in the opening page of *Jacob's Room*. Perhaps the greatest modernist example of language gone rampant, *Finnegans Wake* taxes even its most dedicated readers and verges on unreadability for others.

The skeptical modernist linguistic turn, the rejection of materialist externality and of the Victorians' realist project, left ineradicable traces on later fiction, but modernism's revolutions were not absolute or permanent. *Ulysses* and *Finnegans Wake* were influential but unrepeatable. And even within the greatest modernist fictions the worldly and the material, political and moral questions never dried up. Woolf and Joyce, for example, celebrate the perplexities of urban life in London and Dublin, and, indeed, modernist fiction is largely an art of the great city. Lawrence was preoccupied with the condition of England, industrialism, provincial life. Satire was one of modernism's recurrent notes. So it was not odd for the right-wing novelists who came through in the 1920s, such as Wyndham Lewis and Evelyn Waugh, to resort to the social subject and the satiric stance, nor for their left-leaning contemporaries—who came to be seen as even more characteristic of the red decade of the 1930s—such as Graham Greene and George Orwell, to engage with the human condition in ways that Dickens or Balzac, let alone Bennett-Wells-Galsworthy, would have recognized as not all that distant from their own spirit.

Despite the turn to documentary realism in the 1930s, the modernist emphasis on linguistic self-consciousness did not disappear. Instead the new writers politicized the modern novel's linguistic self-consciousness: they deployed the discourse of the unemployed or of the West Midlands' proletariat, for example, for political ends. The comically chaotic meeting of English and German languages in Christopher Isherwood's *Berlin Stories* is central to the fiction's dire warning about Anglo-German politics; Newspeak in George Orwell's *Nineteen Eighty-Four* is the culmination of the author's nearly two decades of politically motivated engagement with the ways of English speakers at home and abroad. In this politicized aftermath of the modernist experiment, novelists such as Aldous Huxley in *Brave New World* satirically engage the socio-politico-moral matter of the 1930s in part through reflections on the corruptions of language.

Where World War I was a great engine of modernism, endorsing the chaos of shattered belief, the fragility of language and of the human subject, the Spanish Civil War and then World War II confirmed the English novel in its return to registering the social scene and the historical event. World War II provoked whole series of more or less realist fictions, including Evelyn Waugh's *Sword of Honour* trilogy, as well as powerful singletons such as Graham Greene's *Ministry of Fear* and Waugh's *Brideshead Revisited*. The new fictions of the post–World War II period speak with the satirical energies of the young demobilized officer class (Kingsley Amis's *Lucky Jim* set the disgruntled tone), and of the ordinary provincial citizen finding a fictional voice yet again in the new Welfare State atmosphere of the 1950s, as in Alan Sillitoe's proletarian Nottingham novel *Saturday Night and Sunday Morning.*

Questing for new moral bases for the post-Holocaust nuclear age, William Golding published the first of many intense post-Christian moral fables with *The Lord of the Flies*, and Iris Murdoch released the first of many novels of moral philosophy with *Under the Net*, both in 1954. Murdoch espoused the "sovereignty of good" and the importance of the novel's loving devotion to "the otherness of the other person." Murdoch and Golding were consciously retrospective (as were the contemporary Roman Catholic novelists Greene, Waugh, and Muriel Spark) in their investment in moral form. But even such firmly grounded determinations could not calm the anxieties of belatedness. As the century drew on, British fiction struggled with a disconcertingly pervasive sense of posteriority—postwar flatness, postimperial diminutions of power and influence, and the sense of the grand narratives now losing their force as never before.

Some younger novelists, such as Ian McEwan and Martin Amis (son of Kingsley), became obsessed with Germany (the now accusingly prosperous old foe) and with the still haunting ghosts of the *Hitlerzeit*—and not least after 1989, when the Berlin Wall came down and wartime European horrors stirred into vivid focus. The dereliction of the once-grand imperial center, London, became a main topic for McEwan and for Amis, as well as for the later Kingsley Amis and the ex-Rhodesian Doris Lessing. Whereas Conrad, E. M. Forster (*A Passage to India*), and Jean Rhys (*Wide Sargasso Sea*) had been harshly accusatory about Britain's overseas behavior, now nostalgia for old imperial days shrouded the pages of Lawrence Durrell's *Alexandria Quartet* and Paul Scott's *Raj Quartet* and *Staying On*. Observers of English fiction worried that the only tasks left for it were to ruminate over past history and rehash old stories. The modernist Joycean strategy of resurrecting ancient narratives to revitalize present consciousness had given way to a fear that the postmodern novelist was condemned to a disabled career of parroting old stuff. *On est parlé*, "one is spoken," rather than speaking for oneself, thinks the main character of Julian Barnes's *Flaubert's Parrot*, reflecting in some dismay on this dilemma. Ventriloquial reproduction of old voices became Peter Ackroyd's trademark. Worries about being merely possessed by the past came to seem central to late-twentieth-century English fiction, as in A. S. Byatt's *Possession*, which is about the magnetism of past (Victorian) writers and writings.

Yet this was also a time for the spectacular emergence of many robust voices, particularly from assorted margins—writers for whom the enervation at the English center represented an opportunity for telling their untold stories. After a sensational trial in 1960, the ban on D. H. Lawrence's erotically explicit *Lady Chatterley's Lover* was finally lifted, ensuring greater freedom in the narrative exploration of sexuality. Relaxing views on gender roles, the influx of women into the workplace, and the collapse of the grand patriarchal narratives also gave impetus to feminist revisionary narratives of history, and the remaking of narrative technique as more fluid and free. In the 1980s and 1990s prominent and inventive women's voices included those of Jeanette Winterson, celebrator of women's arts and bodiliness, and Angela Carter, feminist neomythographer, reviser of fairy tales, rewriter of the Marquis de Sade, espouser of raucous and rebellious heroines. Among the chorus of voices seeking to express with new intimacy and vividness experiences once held taboo were those of uncloseted gay writers, such as Alan Hollinghurst, pioneer of the openly male-homosexual literary novel of the post–World War II period, and Adam Mars-Jones, short-story chronicler of the HIV/AIDS crisis. The literary counterpart for political decolonization and devolution within the British Isles was the emergence of a multitude of regional and national voices outside the south of England, many deploying a vigorously local idiom, such as the Scottish novelist Irvine Welsh and the Irish writer Roddy Doyle, who reached mass international audiences through 1990s film versions of their novels *Trainspotting* (Welsh) and *The Commitments* (Doyle).

While postimperial anxieties and exhaustion seemed to beset many postwar English writers, postcolonial novelists were energetically claiming for literature in English untold histories, hybrid identities, and vibrantly creolized vocabularies. A major phase in the huge geographic shift in the center of gravity of English-language fiction occurred during the postwar decolonization of much of South Asia, Africa, and the Caribbean, when Chinua Achebe's *Things Fall Apart* (1958) was published, just two years before Nigerian independence. Retelling the story of colonial incursion from an indigenous viewpoint, Achebe's influential novel intricately represents an African community before and after the arrival of whites, in a language made up of English and Igbo words, encompassed by a narrative that enmeshes African proverbs and oral tales with English realism and modernist reflexivity. A few years later and on the eve of his natal island's independence, the Trinidad-born writer V. S. Naipaul published his first major novel, *A House for Mr. Biswas* (1961), one of many works that brilliantly develop the potential of a translucent realist fiction to explore issues such as migrant identities, cross-cultural mimicry, and the spaces of colonialism. The Indian-born Salman Rushdie, more restive than Naipaul in relation to Englishness and English literary traditions, has exuberantly championed hybrid narrative forms made out of the fresh convergence of modern European fiction and "Third World" orality, magical realism, and polyglossia. His novels, such as *Midnight's Children* (1981) and *The Satanic Verses* (1988), wryly offer a "chutnification of history" in South Asia and in an Asianized England. The colonies where English literature had once been used in imposing imperial models of "civilization" now gave rise to novelists who, ironically, outstripped in lively imagination, cultural energy, and narrative inventiveness their counterparts from the seat of the empire.

White fiction writers from the colonies and dominions, many of them women, and many of them resident in England, such as Katherine Mansfield, Doris Lessing, and Jean Rhys, had long brought fresh perspectives to the novel from the outposts of empire, each of these eminent writers sharply etching a feminist critique of women's lives diminished by subordination to the colonial order. South Africa, not least because of its fraught racial and political history, can count among its progeny some of the most celebrated fiction writers of the late twentieth century. Nadine Gordimer has extended the potential of an ethical narrative realism to probe the fierce moral challenges of apartheid and its aftermath, whereas J. M. Coetzee has used self-reflexively postmodern and allegorical forms to inquire into the tangled complexities and vexed complicities of white South African experience.

Late twentieth-century and early twenty-first-century "English" fiction would have looked startlingly thin and poverty-stricken were it not for the large presence in Britain of writers of non-European origin. Like the first modern novelists, many of the writers who have most enriched English-language fiction in recent decades are migrants, émigrés, and expatriates, such as Naipaul and Rushdie, and such as the delicately ironic realist Kazuo Ishiguro, from Japan, and the postsurreal fabulist Wilson Harris, from Guyana. Still others are the sons and daughters of non-European immigrants to Britain, including two of the most visible exemplars of the often comically cross-cultural fiction of a new multiracial England, Hanif Kureishi and Zadie Smith, both born on the peripheries of London, Kureishi to a Pakistani father and English mother, Smith to a Jamaican mother and English father. Their first novels, both set in London—Kureishi's *The Buddha of Suburbia* (1990) and Smith's *White Teeth* (2000)—helped establish a paradigm for the vibrantly cross-cultural and interethnic novel. These and other "British" novelists of color, giving voice to new and emergent experiences of immigration, hybridization, and cross-racial encounter, take advantage of the novel's fecund polymorphousness with little anxiety about belatedness, no fright over parroting, and no neomodernist worries about attempting realistic encounters with the world.

DRAMA

Late Victorians from one perspective, Oscar Wilde and Bernard Shaw can also be seen as early moderns, forerunners of the twentieth century's renovators of dramatic form. The wit of Wilde's drawing-room comedies is combative and generative of paradoxes, but beneath the glitter of his verbal play are serious—if heavily coded—reflections on social, political, and feminist issues. Shaw brought still another kind of wit into drama—not Wilde's lighthearted sparkle but the provocative paradox that was meant to tease and disturb, to challenge the complacency of the audience. Over time the desire to unsettle, to shock, even to alienate the audience became one hallmark of modern drama.

Wilde and Shaw were both born in Ireland, and it was in Dublin that the century's first major theatrical movement originated. To nourish Irish poetic drama and foster the Irish literary renaissance, Yeats and Lady Augusta Gregory founded the Irish Literary Theatre in 1899, with Yeats's early nationalist play *The Countess Cathleen* as its first production. In 1902 the Irish Literary Theatre was able to maintain a permanent all-Irish company and changed its name to the Irish National Theatre, which moved in 1904 to the Abbey Theatre, by which name it has been known ever since. J. M. Synge brought the speech and imagination of Irish country people into theater, but the Abbey's 1907 staging of his play *The Playboy of the Western World* so offended orthodox religious and nationalist sentiment that the audience rioted. While defending Synge and other pioneers of Irish drama, Yeats continued to write his own plays, which drew themes from old Irish legend and which, after 1913, stylized and ritualized theatrical performance on the model of Japanese Noh drama. In the 1920s, Sean O'Casey brought new vitality to the Abbey Theatre, using the Easter Rising and Irish civil war as a background for controversial plays (one of which again sparked riots) that combined tragic melodrama, humor of character, and irony of circumstance. In England T. S. Eliot attempted with considerable success to revive a ritual poetic drama with his *Murder in the Cathedral* (1935), though his later attempts to combine religious symbolism with the chatter of entertaining society comedy, as in *The Cocktail Party* (1950), were uneven.

Despite the achievements of Yeats, Synge, O'Casey, and Eliot, it cannot be said of Irish and British drama, as it can of poetry and fiction in the first half of the century, that a technical revolution changed the whole course of literary history. The major innovations in the first half of the twentieth century were on the Continent. German expressionist drama developed out of the dark, psychological focus of the later plays of the Swedish dramatist August Strindberg (1849–1912). Another worldwide influence was the "epic" drama of the leftist German dramatist Bertolt Brecht (1898–1956): to foster ideological awareness, he rejected the idea that the audience should identify with a play's characters and become engrossed in its plot; the playwright should break the illusion of reality through the alienation effect (*Verfremdungseffekt*) and foreground the play's theatrical constructedness and historical specificity. The French dramatist Antonin Artaud (1896–1948) also defied realism and rationalism, but unlike Brecht, his theory of the theater of cruelty sought a transformative, mystical communion with the audience through incantations and sounds, physical gestures and strange scenery. Another French dramatist, the Romanian-born Eugène Ionesco (1909–1994), helped inaugurate the theater of the absurd just after World War II, in plays that enact people's hopeless efforts to communicate and that comically intimate a tragic vision of life devoid of meaning or purpose. In such Continental drama the influences of symbolism (on the later Strindberg), Marxism (on Brecht), and surrealism (on Artaud and Ionesco) contributed to the shattering of naturalistic convention in drama, making the theater a space where linear plot gave way to fractured scenes and circular action, transparent conversation was displaced by misunderstanding and verbal opacity, a predictable and knowable universe was unsettled by eruptions of the irrational and the absurd.

In Britain the impact of these Continental innovations was delayed by a conservative theater establishment until the late 1950s and 1960s, when they converged with the countercultural revolution to transform the nature of English-language theater. Meanwhile the person who played the most significant role in the anglophone absorption of modernist experiment was the Irishman Samuel Beckett. He changed the history of drama with his first produced play, written in French in 1948 and translated by the author as *Waiting for Godot* (premiered in Paris in 1953, in London in 1955). The play astonishingly did away with plot ("Nothing happens—twice," as one critic put it), as did *Endgame* (1958) and Beckett's later plays, such as *Not I* (1973) and *That Time* (1976). In the shadow of the mass death of World War II, the plotlessness, the minimal characterization and setting, the absurdist intimation of an existential darkness without redemption, the tragicomic melding of anxiety, circular wordplay, and slapstick action in Beckett's plays gave impetus to a seismic shift in British writing for the theater.

The epicenter of the new developments in British drama was the Royal Court Theatre, symbolically located a little away from London's West End "theater land" (the rough equivalent of Broadway in New York). From 1956 the Royal Court was the home of the English Stage Company. Together they provided a venue and a vision that provoked and enabled a new wave of writers. John Osborne's *Look Back in Anger* (1956), the hit of the ESC's first season (significantly helped by the play's television broadcast), offered the audience "lessons in feeling" through a searing depiction of class-based indignation, emotional cruelty, and directionless angst, all in a surprisingly nonmetropolitan setting. At the Royal Court the working-class naturalism of the so-called kitchen-sink dramatists and other "angry young men" of the 1950s, such as Arnold Wesker, author of the trilogy *Chicken Soup with Barley* (1958), also broke with the genteel proprieties and narrowly upper-class set designs that, in one unadventurous drawing-room comedy after another, had dominated the British stage for decades. The political consciousness of the new theater was still more evident in John Arden's plays produced for the Royal Court, such as *Sergeant Musgrave's Dance* (1959), which explores colonial oppression, communal guilt for wartime atrocities, and pacifism in the stylized setting of an isolated mining town. By the later 1960s the influence of the counterculture on British theater was unavoidable. Joe Orton challenged bourgeois sentiment in a series of classically precise, blackly comic, and sexually ambiguous parodies—for example, his farce *What the Butler Saw* (1969).

While plays of social and political critique were one response to the postwar period, Beckett and the theater of the absurd inspired another group of Royal Court writers to refocus theater on language, symbolism, and existential realities. Informed by kitchen-sink naturalism and absurdism, Harold Pinter's "comedies of menace" map out a social trajectory from his early study of working-class stress and inarticulate anxiety, *The Room* (1957), through the film-noirish black farce of *The Dumb Waiter* (1960) and the emotional power plays of *The Caretaker* (1960), to the savagely comic study of middle-class escape from working-class mores in *The Homecoming* (1965). Later plays reflect on patrician suspicion and betrayal, though in the 1980s his work acquired a more overtly political voice. Though less bleak than Pinter, Tom Stoppard is no less indebted to Beckett's wordplay, skewed conversations, and theatrical technique, as evidenced by *Rosencrantz and Guildenstern Are Dead* (1967) and other plays, many of which embed within themselves earlier literary works (such as *Godot* and *Hamlet*) and thus offer virtuoso postmodernist reflections on art, language, and performance. This enjoyment and exploitation of self-conscious theatricality arises partly out of the desire to show theater as different from film and television and is also apparent in the 1970s productions of another playwright: the liturgical stylization of Peter Shaffer's *Equus* (1973) and the bleak mental landscape of his Antonio Salieri in *Amadeus* (1979) emphasize the stage as battleground and site of struggle (an effect lost in their naturalistic film versions). Stoppard's time shifts and memory lapses in *Travesties* (1974) allow a nonnaturalistic study of the role of memory and imagination in the creative process, a theme he returns to in *Arcadia* (1993), a stunning double-exposure account of a Romantic poet and his modern critical commentators occupying the same physical space but never reaching intellectual common ground.

Legal reform intensified the postwar ferment in British theater. Since the Theatres Act of 1843, writers for the public stage had been required to submit their playscripts to the Lord Chamberlain's office for state censorship, but in 1968 a new Theatres Act abolished that office. With this new freedom from conservative mores and taste, Howard Brenton, Howard Barker, Edward Bond, and David Hare were able to write challenging studies of violence, social deprivation, and political and sexual aggression, often using mythical settings and epic stories to construct austere tableaux of power and oppression. Bond's *Lear* (1971) typifies his ambitious combination of soaring lyrical language and alienatingly realistic violence. Directors such as Peter Brook took advantage of the new freedom in plays that emphasized, as had Artaud's theater of cruelty, physical gesture, bodily movement, and ritualized spectacle. The post-1968 liberalization also encouraged the emergence of new theater groups addressing specific political agendas, many of them inspired by Brecht's "epic" theater's distancing, discontinuous, and socially critical style. Companies such as Monstrous Regiment, Gay Sweatshop, Joint Stock, and John McGrath's 7: 84 worked collaboratively with dramatists who were invited to help devise and develop shows. Increasingly in the 1970s published plays were either transcriptions of the first production or "blueprints for the alchemy of live performance" (Micheline Wandor). In Ireland the founding of the Field Day Theatre Company in 1980 by the well-established playwright Brian Friel and actor Stephen Rea had similar motives of collaborative cultural catalysis. Their first production, Friel's *Translations* (1980), exploring linguistic colonialism and the fragility of cultural identity in nineteenth-century Ireland, achieved huge international success.

This ethos of collaboration and group development helped foster the first major cohort of women dramatists to break through onto mainstream stages. Working with Joint Stock and Monstrous Regiment in the late 1970s on plays such as the gender-bending anticolonial *Cloud Nine* (1979), Caryl Churchill developed plays out of workshops exploring gender, class, and colonialism. She carefully transcribes and overlaps the speech of her characters to create a seamlessly interlocking web of discourse, a streamlined version of the ebb and flow of normal speech. In *Top Girls* (1982) and *Serious Money* (1987), plays that anatomize the market-driven ethos of the 1980s, she explores modern society with the wit and detachment of Restoration comedy. Pam Gems studies the social and sexual politics of misogyny and feminism in her campy theatrical explorations of strong women—*Queen Cristina* (1977), *Piaf* (1978), *Camille* (1984)—while Sarah Daniels reinterprets the naturalism of kitchen-sink drama by adding to it the linguistic stylization of Churchill.

Massive strides in the diversification of English-language theater occurred during the era of decolonization, when two eminent poets, Derek Walcott and Wole Soyinka, helped breathe new life into anglophone drama. As early as the 1950s Derek Walcott was writing and directing plays about Caribbean history and experience, re-creating in his drama a West Indian "oral culture, of chants, jokes, folk-songs, and fables," at a time when theater in the Caribbean tended to imitate European themes and styles. After moving to Trinidad in 1958, he founded what came to be known as the Trinidad Theatre Workshop, and for much of the next twenty years devoted himself to directing and writing plays that included *Dream on Monkey*

Mountain, first produced in 1967, in which Eurocentric and Afrocentric visions of Caribbean identity collide. Since then, a notable breakthrough in Caribbean theater has been the collaborative work of the Sistren Theatre Collective in Jamaica, which, following the lead of Louise Bennett and other West Indian poets, draws on women's personal histories in dramatic performances that make vivid use of Jamaican speech, expression, and rhythm. Meanwhile in Africa, Wole Soyinka, who had been involved with the Royal Court Theatre in the late 1950s when Brecht's influence was first being absorbed, returned to Nigeria in the year of its independence to write and direct plays that fused Euromodernist dramatic techniques with conventions from Yoruba popular and traditional drama. His play *Death and the King's Horseman*, premiered in Nigeria in 1976, represents a tragic confrontation between colonial officials and the guardians of Yoruba rituals and beliefs. While Soyinka has been a towering presence in sub-Saharan Africa, other playwrights, such as the fellow Nigerian Femi Osofisan and the South African Athol Fugard, have used the stage to probe issues of class, race, and the often violent legacy of colonialism. In England playwrights of Caribbean, African, and Asian origin or descent, such as Mustapha Matura, Caryl Phillips, and Hanif Kureishi, the latter of whom is best-known internationally for his screenplays for *My Beautiful Laundrette* (1985), *Sammy and Rosie Get Laid* (1988), *My Son the Fanatic* (1998), *The Mother* (2004), *Venus* (2006), and *Weddings and Beheadings* (2007), have revitalized British drama with a host of new vocabularies, new techniques, new visions of identity in an increasingly cross-ethnic and transnational world. The century that began with its first great dramatic movement in Ireland was followed by a century that began with English-language drama more diverse in its accents and styles, more international in its bearings and vision than ever before.

The Twentieth Century and After

TEXTS	CONTEXTS
1899, 1902 Joseph Conrad, *Heart of Darkness*	
	1900 Max Planck, quantum theory
	1901 First wireless communication across the Atlantic
	1901–10 Reign of Edward VII
	1902 End of the Anglo-Boer War
	1903 Henry Ford introduces the first mass-produced car. Wright Brothers make the first successful airplane flight
	1905 Albert Einstein, theory of special relativity. Impressionist exhibition, London
1910 Bernard Shaw, *Pygmalion*	**1910** Postimpressionist exhibition, London
	1910–36 Reign of George V
1913 Ezra Pound, "A Few Don'ts by an Imagiste"	
1914 James Joyce, *Dubliners.* Thomas Hardy, *Satires of Circumstance*	**1914–18** World War I
1914–15 *Blast*	
1916 Joyce, *A Portrait of the Artist as a Young Man*	**1916** Easter Rising in Dublin
1917 T. S. Eliot, "The Love Song of J. Alfred Prufrock"	
1918 Gerard Manley Hopkins, *Poems*	**1918** Armistice. Franchise Act grants vote to women thirty and over
1920 D. H. Lawrence, *Women in Love.* Wilfred Owen, *Poems*	**1920** Treaty of Versailles. League of Nations formed
1921 William Butler Yeats, *Michael Robartes and the Dancer*	**1921–22** Formation of Irish Free State with Northern Ireland (Ulster) remaining part of Great Britain
1922 Katherine Mansfield, *The Garden Party and Other Stories.* Joyce, *Ulysses.* Eliot, *The Waste Land*	
1924 E. M. Forster, *A Passage to India*	
1927 Virginia Woolf, *To the Lighthouse*	
1928 Yeats, *The Tower*	**1928** Women twenty-one and over granted voting rights
1929 Woolf, *A Room of One's Own.* Robert Graves, *Goodbye to All That*	**1929** Stock market crash; Great Depression begins
	1933 Hitler comes to power in Germany
1935 Eliot, *Murder in the Cathedral*	
	1936 Edward VIII succeeds George V, but abdicates in favor of his brother, crowned as George VI
	1936–39 Spanish Civil War
1937 David Jones, *In Parenthesis*	

TEXTS	CONTEXTS
1939 Joyce, *Finnegans Wake*. Yeats, *Last Poems and Two Plays*	1939–45 World War II
1940 W. H. Auden, *Another Time*	1940 Fall of France. Battle of Britain
	1941–45 The Holocaust
1943 Eliot, *Four Quartets*	
1945 Auden, *Collected Poems*. George Orwell, *Animal Farm*	1945 First atomic bombs dropped, on Japan
1946 Dylan Thomas, *Deaths and Entrances*	
	1947 India and Pakistan become independent nations
	1948 *Empire Windrush* brings West Indians to U.K.
1949 Orwell, *Nineteen Eighty-Four*	
	1950 Apartheid laws passed in South Africa
1953 Premiere of Samuel Beckett's *Waiting for Godot*	
	1956 Suez crisis
	1957 Ghana becomes independent
1958 Chinua Achebe, *Things Fall Apart*	
	1960 Nigeria becomes independent
	1961 Berlin Wall erected
1962 Doris Lessing, *The Golden Notebook*	1962 Cuban missile crisis. Uganda, Jamaica, Trinidad and Tobago become independent
1964 Philip Larkin, *The Whitsun Weddings*	
	1965 U.S. troops land in South Vietnam
1966 Nadine Gordimer, *The Late Bourgeois World*. Tom Stoppard, *Rosencrantz and Guildenstern Are Dead*. Jean Rhys, *Wide Sargasso Sea*	1966 Barbados and Guyana become independent
	1969 *Apollo* moon landing
1971 V. S. Naipaul, *In a Free State*	1971 Indo-Pakistan War, leading to creation of Bangladesh
	1972 Britain enters European Common Market
	1973 U.S. troops leave Vietnam
1975 Seamus Heaney, *North*	
1979 Caryl Churchill, *Cloud 9*	1979 Islamic Revolution in Iran; the shah flees. Soviets invade Afghanistan
	1979–90 Margaret Thatcher is British prime minister
1980 J. M. Coetzee, *Waiting for the Barbarians*	1980–88 Iran-Iraq War

TEXTS	CONTEXTS
1981 Salman Rushdie, *Midnight's Children*. Brian Friel, *Translations*	
	1982 Falklands War
1985 Production of Hanif Kureishi's *My Beautiful Laundrette*. Margaret Atwood, *The Handmaid's Tale*	
1988 Rushdie, *The Satanic Verses*	
1989 Kazuo Ishiguro, *The Remains of the Day*	**1989** Fall of the Berlin Wall. Tiananmen Square, Beijing, demonstration and massacre
1990 Derek Walcott, *Omeros*	
	1991 Collapse of the Soviet Union
1992 Thom Gunn, *The Man with Night Sweats*	
1993 Tom Stoppard, *Arcadia*	
	1994 Democracy comes to South Africa
1997 Arundhati Roy, *The God of Small Things*	**1997** Labour Party victory in the U.K. ends eighteen years of Conservative government
	1998 British handover of Hong Kong to China. Northern Ireland Assembly established
1999 Carol Ann Duffy, *The World's Wife*	
2000 Zadie Smith, *White Teeth*	
2001 Ian McEwan, *Atonement*	**2001** September 11 attacks destroy World Trade Center
2002 Paul Muldoon, *Moy Sand and Gravel*	**2002** Euro becomes sole currency in most of European Union
	2003 Invasion of Iraq led by U.S. and U.K.
	2005 Bombings of London transport system
2006 Kiran Desai, *The Inheritance of Loss*	
	2010 David Cameron is first Conservative Party prime minister in 13 years

THOMAS HARDY
1840–1928

Thomas Hardy was born in the Dorset hamlet of Higher Bockhampton, in that area of southwest England that he was to make the "Wessex" of his fiction and poetry. The son of a stonemason, the young Hardy was kept mostly at home, where he closely observed and came to love the surrounding countryside, the rhythms of the seasons and the songs, stories, and folk beliefs of a still predominantly oral culture. He attended local schools until the age of sixteen, when he was apprenticed to a Dorchester architect in whose office he remained for six years. In 1862 he moved to London and found a position as a draftsman in the office of Arthur Blomfield, a leading architect of Gothic-style buildings. Meanwhile, as Hardy was completing his general education informally through his eclectic reading, he began to study and write poetry. His first novel, seen as an attack on upper-class pretensions, was rejected by publishers in 1868, though one of the readers, George Meredith, advised Hardy to write another work of fiction, with a more complicated plot. The result was the sensational novel *Desperate Remedies* (1871), which was followed by a tale of rural life, *Under the Greenwood Tree* (1872). The serialization of his next two novels, *A Pair of Blue Eyes* (1872–73) and *Far from the Madding Crowd* (1874), provided him with sufficient income to abandon architecture for literature. He continued to write novels until the sexual frankness and irreligiousness of his last novel, *Jude the Obscure* (1895), resulted in a hostile critical reception, including reviews headed "Jude the Obscene" and "Hardy the Degenerate." Financial security finally enabled Hardy to make his long-desired return to poetry. Straddling the Victorian and modern periods, he published all his novels in the nineteenth century, and all but the first of his poetry collections, *Wessex Poems and Other Verses* (1898), in the twentieth. His remarkable epic drama of the Napoleonic Wars, *The Dynasts*, came out in three parts between 1903 and 1908, and he continued to write verse until his death, at age 87.

In Hardy's fiction, set in the predominantly rural "Wessex," acutely observed and richly detailed, the forces of nature outside and inside individuals combine to shape human destiny. Against a background of immemorial agricultural labor, with ancient monuments such as Stonehenge or a Roman amphitheater reminding us of the past, he presents characters at the mercy of elements beyond their control: their emotions or sexual impulses, and the barriers of social class and restrictions of social mores. Men and women in Hardy's fiction are rarely masters of their fates; walking long distances across a landscape that dwarfs them, they may be subjected to the indifferent forces that manipulate their behavior and their relations with others. They can achieve dignity, however, through endurance, heroism, or simple strength of character. Most of his fiction is tragic or at least tragicomic, observing humanity with a mixture of cold detachment and searching empathy, and exploring the bitter ironies of life with an almost malevolent staging of coincidence to emphasize the disparity between human desire and ambition, on the one hand, and, on the other, what fate—often determined by the character's very nature—has in store. One of the darkest of Hardy's novels, *Tess of the d'Urbervilles* (1891), is the story of an intelligent and sensitive young woman, daughter of a poor family, who is driven to murder, and thus to death by hanging, by a painfully ironic concatenation of events and circumstances. Published in the same year as *Tess*, the story anthologized here, "On the Western Circuit," similarly has at its center a young country woman deceived by a sophisticated city man; her "ruin" (see also Hardy's poem

"The Ruined Maid") leads—contrary to the good intentions of the three protagonists, and again as the result of bitter irony—to *his* ruin and a lifetime of misery for all concerned.

Hardy denied that he was a pessimist, calling himself a "meliorist"—that is, one who believes that the world can be made better by human effort. But there is little sign of meliorism in either his fiction or his poetry. A number of his poems, such as the one he wrote about the *Titanic* disaster, "The Convergence of the Twain," illustrate the perversity of fate, the disastrous or ironic coincidence of events. Other poems go beyond this mood to present, with quiet gravity and a carefully controlled elegiac feeling, some aspect of human sorrow, loss, frustration, or regret, always grounded in a particular, fully realized situation. "Hap" shows Hardy in the characteristic mood of complaining about the irony of human destiny in a universe ruled by chance, while "The Walk" (one of a group of poems written after the death of his first wife in 1912) gives, with remarkable power, concrete embodiment to a sense of loss.

Hardy's verse, like his prose, often has a self-taught air about it; both can seem, on first reading, roughly hewn. He said he wanted to avoid "the jewelled line," and like many modern and contemporary poets, he sought instead what he called "dissonances, and other irregularities" in his art, because they convey more authenticity and spontaneity. "Art is a disproportioning . . . of realities," he declared. While adhering to the metered line, Hardy roughens prosody and contorts syntax, and he creates irregular and complex stanza forms. His diction includes archaisms and deliberately awkward coinages (e.g., "Powerfuller" and "unblooms" in "Hap"). He distorts, vigorously revises, and sometimes forces together conventions of traditional genres such as the sonnet, the ballad, the love poem, the war poem, and the elegy. Though rooted in the Victorian period, Hardy thus looks ahead to the dislocations of poetic form carried out by subsequent poets of the twentieth century.

The sadness in Hardy—his skepticism about the existence of a benevolent God, his sense of the waste and frustration involved in human life, his insistent irony when faced with moral or metaphysical questions—is part of the late Victorian mood, found also, say, in A. E. Housman's poetry and, earlier, in Edward FitzGerald's *Rubáiyát of Omar Khayyám*, published when Hardy was eighteen. Although his attitudes toward the sacred remained tangled and vexed, what has been termed "the disappearance of God" affected him more deeply than it did many of his contemporaries, not least because as a young man he seriously considered becoming a Church of England priest. Yet his characteristic themes and attitudes cannot be viewed simply as the reaction to the scientific and philosophical developments (Darwin's theory of evolution, for example) that we see in many forms in late nineteenth-century literature. The favorite poetic mood of both Tennyson and Matthew Arnold was also elegiac (e.g., in Tennyson's "Break, Break, Break" and Arnold's "Dover Beach"), but the mood of Hardy's poetry differs from Victorian sorrow; it is sterner, more skeptical, as though braced by a long look at the worst. It is this sternness, this ruggedness of his poetry, together with its verbal and emotional integrity, its formal variety and tonal complexity, its quietly searching individual accent and even occasional playfulness, that helped bring about the steady rise in Hardy's reputation as a poet. Ezra Pound remarked in a 1934 letter: "Nobody has taught me anything about writing since Thomas Hardy died." W. H. Auden begins an essay with this testament to the effect of Hardy's verse: "I cannot write objectively about Thomas Hardy because I was once in love with him." And Hardy appears as the major figure—with more poems than either Yeats or Eliot—in Philip Larkin's influential *Oxford Book of Twentieth-Century English Verse* (1973).

Hap[1]

If but some vengeful god would call to me
From up the sky, and laugh: 'Thou suffering thing,
Know that thy sorrow is my ecstasy,
That thy love's loss is my hate's profiting!'

5 Then would I bear it, clench myself, and die,
Steeled by the sense of ire° unmerited;   *anger*
Half-eased in that a Powerfuller than I
Had willed and meted° me the tears I shed.   *allotted, given*

But not so. How arrives it joy lies slain,
10 And why unblooms the best hope ever sown?
—Crass Casualty obstructs the sun and rain,
And dicing Time for gladness casts a moan. . . .
These purblind Doomsters[2] had as readily strown
Blisses about my pilgrimage as pain.

1866   1898

Neutral Tones

We stood by a pond that winter day,
And the sun was white, as though chidden of° God,   *rebuked by*
And a few leaves lay on the starving sod;°   *turf*
  —They had fallen from an ash, and were gray.

5 Your eyes on me were as eyes that rove
Over tedious riddles of years ago;
And some words played between us to and fro
  On which lost the more by our love.

The smile on your mouth was the deadest thing
10 Alive enough to have strength to die;
And a grin of bitterness swept thereby
  Like an ominous bird a-wing . . .

Since then, keen lessons that love deceives,
And wrings with wrong, have shaped to me
15 Your face, and the God-curst sun, and a tree,
  And a pond edged with grayish leaves.

1867   1898

---

1. I.e., chance (as also "Casualty," line 11).   2. Half-blind judges.

Drummer Hodge

1

They throw in Drummer Hodge, to rest
    Uncoffined—just as found:
His landmark is a kopje-crest
    That breaks the veldt[1] around;
5   And foreign constellations[2] west°   *set*
    Each night above his mound.

2

Young Hodge the Drummer never knew—
    Fresh from his Wessex home—
The meaning of the broad Karoo,[3]
10   The Bush,[4] the dusty loam,
And why uprose to nightly view
    Strange stars amid the gloam.

3

Yet portion of that unknown plain
    Will Hodge for ever be;
15   His homely Northern breast and brain
    Grow to some Southern tree,
And strange-eyed constellations reign
    His stars eternally.

1899, 1901

The Darkling[1] Thrush

I leant upon a coppice gate[2]
    When Frost was spectre-gray,
And Winter's dregs made desolate
    The weakening eye of day.
5   The tangled bine-stems[3] scored the sky
    Like strings of broken lyres,
And all mankind that haunted nigh°   *near*
    Had sought their household fires.

The land's sharp features seemed to be
10   The Century's corpse outleant,[4]
His crypt the cloudy canopy,
    The wind his death-lament.

1. South African Dutch (Afrikaans) word for a plain or prairie. "Kopje-crest": Afrikaans for a small hill. The poem is a lament for an English soldier killed in the Anglo-Boer War (1899–1902).
2. Those visible only in the Southern Hemisphere.
3. A dry tableland region in South Africa (usually spelled "Karroo").

4. British colonial word for an uncleared area of land.
1. In the dark.
2. Gate leading to a small wood or thicket.
3. Twining stems of shrubs.
4. Leaning out (of its coffin); i.e., the 19th century was dead. This poem was dated December 31, 1900.

The ancient pulse of germ and birth
  Was shrunken hard and dry,
15 And every spirit upon earth
  Seemed fervourless as I.

At once a voice arose among
  The bleak twigs overhead
In a full-hearted evensong
20   Of joy illimited;
An aged thrush, frail, gaunt, and small,
  In blast-beruffled plume,
Had chosen thus to fling his soul
  Upon the growing gloom.

25 So little cause for carolings
  Of such ecstatic sound
Was written on terrestrial things
  Afar or nigh around,
That I could think there trembled through
30   His happy good-night air
Some blessed Hope, whereof he knew
  And I was unaware.

            1900, 1901

The Ruined Maid

'O 'Melia,[1] my dear, this does everything crown!
Who could have supposed I should meet you in Town?
And whence such fair garments, such prosperi-ty?'—
'O didn't you know I'd been ruined?' said she.

5 —'You left us in tatters, without shoes or socks,
Tired of digging potatoes, and spudding up docks;[2]
And now you've gay bracelets and bright feathers three!'—
'Yes: that's how we dress when we're ruined,' said she.

—'At home in the barton° you said "thee" and "thou",   *farmyard*
10 And "thik oon", and "theäs oon", and "t'other"; but now
Your talking quite fits 'ee for high compa-ny!'—
'Some polish is gained with one's ruin,' said she.

—'Your hands were like paws then, your face blue and bleak
But now I'm bewitched by your delicate cheek,
15 And your little gloves fit as on any la-dy!'—
'We never do work when we're ruined,' said she.

—'You used to call home-life a hag-ridden dream,
And you'd sigh, and you'd sock;° but at present you seem   *sigh*

---

1. Diminutive form of Amelia.   2. Digging up a species of thick-rooted weed.

To know not of megrims° or melancho-ly!'—   *low spirits*
20 'True. One's pretty lively when ruined,' said she.

—'I wish I had feathers, a fine sweeping gown,
And a delicate face, and could strut about Town!'—
'My dear—a raw country girl, such as you be,
Cannot quite expect that. You ain't ruined,' said she.

1866   1901

Channel Firing[1]

That night your great guns, unawares,
Shook all our coffins as we lay,
And broke the chancel[2] window-squares,
We thought it was the Judgement-day

5   And sat upright. While drearisome
Arose the howl of wakened hounds:
The mouse let fall the altar-crumb,
The worms drew back into the mounds,

The glebe cow[3] drooled. Till God called, 'No;
10 It's gunnery practise out at sea
Just as before you went below;
The world is as it used to be:

'All nations striving strong to make
Red war yet redder. Mad as hatters[4]
15 They do no more for Christès[5] sake
Than you who are helpless in such matters.

'That this is not the judgement-hour
For some of them's a blessed thing,
For if it were they'd have to scour
20 Hell's floor for so much threatening. . . .

'Ha, ha. It will be warmer when
I blow the trumpet (if indeed
I ever do; for you are men,
And rest eternal sorely need).'

25 So down we lay again. 'I wonder,
Will the world ever saner be,'
Said one, 'than when He sent us under
In our indifferent century!'

1. Written in April 1914, when Anglo-German naval rivalry was growing steadily more acute; the title refers to gunnery practice in the English Channel. Four months later (August 4), World War I broke out.
2. Part of church nearest to the altar.
3. I.e., cow on a small plot of land belonging to a church (a "glebe" is a small field).
4. Cf. the Mad Hatter in Lewis Carroll's *Alice's Adventures in Wonderland* (1865).
5. The archaic spelling and pronunciation suggest a ballad note of doom.

And many a skeleton shook his head.
30 'Instead of preaching forty year,'
My neighbour Parson Thirdly said,
'I wish I had stuck to pipes and beer.'

Again the guns disturbed the hour,
Roaring their readiness to avenge,
35 As far inland as Stourton Tower,
And Camelot, and starlit Stonehenge.[6]

1914   1914

The Convergence of the Twain

(*Lines on the loss of the* Titanic)[1]

I

In a solitude of the sea
Deep from human vanity,
And the Pride of Life that planned her, stilly couches she.

2

Steel chambers, late the pyres
5 Of her salamandrine[2] fires,
Cold currents thrid,[3] and turn to rhythmic tidal lyres.

3

Over the mirrors meant
To glass the opulent
The sea-worm crawls—grotesque, slimed, dumb, indifferent.

4

10 Jewels in joy designed
To ravish the sensuous mind
Lie lightless, all their sparkles bleared and black and blind.

5

Dim moon-eyed fishes near
Gaze at the gilded gear
15 And query: 'What does this vaingloriousness down here?' . . .

---

6. The sound of guns preparing for war across the Channel reaches Alfred's ("Stourton") Tower (near Stourton in Dorset), commemorating King Alfred's defeat of a Danish invasion in 878; also the site of King Arthur's court at Camelot (supposedly near Glastonbury) and the famous prehistoric stone circle of Stonehenge on Salisbury Plain.
1. The *Titanic* was the largest and most luxurious ocean liner of the day. Considered unsinkable, it sank with great loss of life on April 15, 1912, on the ship's maiden voyage, from Southampton to the United States, after colliding with an iceberg. "Twain": two.
2. I.e., destructive. The salamander was supposed to be able to survive fire.
3. A variant form of the verb *thread*.

6

Well: while was fashioning
This creature of cleaving wing,
The Immanent Will[4] that stirs and urges everything

7

Prepared a sinister mate
20   For her—so gaily great—
A Shape of Ice, for the time far and dissociate.

8

And as the smart ship grew
In stature, grace, and hue,
In shadowy silent distance grew the Iceberg too.

9

25   Alien they seemed to be:
No mortal eye could see
The intimate welding of their later history,

10

Or sign that they were bent
By paths coincident
30 On being anon° twin halves of one august° event,   soon / important

11

Till the Spinner of the Years
Said 'Now!' And each one hears,
And consummation comes, and jars two hemispheres.

1912   1912, 1914

Ah, Are You Digging on My Grave?

'Ah, are you digging on my grave
My loved one?—planting rue?'[1]
—'No: yesterday he went to wed
One of the brightest wealth has bred.
5   'It cannot hurt her now,' he said,
"That I should not be true."'

4. The force (blind, but slowly gaining consciousness throughout history) that drives the
world, according to Hardy's philosophy.

1. A yellow-flowered herb, traditionally an
emblem of sorrow (rue is also an archaic word for
"sorrow").

'Then who is digging on my grave?
    My nearest dearest kin?'
—'Ah, no; they sit and think, "What use!
10 What good will planting flowers produce?
No tendance of her mound can loose
    Her spirit from Death's gin." '°   *trap*

'But some one digs upon my grave?
    My enemy?—prodding sly?'
15 —'Nay: when she heard you had passed the Gate
That shuts on all flesh soon or late,
She thought you no more worth her hate,
    And cares not where you lie.'

'Then, who is digging on my grave?
20   Say—since I have not guessed!'
—'O it is I, my mistress dear,
Your little dog, who still lives near,
And much I hope my movements here
    Have not disturbed your rest?'

25 'Ah, yes! *You* dig upon my grave . . .
    Why flashed it not on me
That one true heart was left behind!
What feeling do we ever find
To equal among human kind
30   A dog's fidelity!'

'Mistress, I dug upon your grave
    To bury a bone, in case
I should be hungry near this spot
When passing on my daily trot.
35 I am sorry, but I quite forgot
    It was your resting-place.'

1914

In Time of 'The Breaking of Nations'[1]

1

Only a man harrowing clods
    In a slow silent walk
With an old horse that stumbles and nods
    Half asleep as they stalk.

2

5   Only thin smoke without flame
    From the heaps of couch-grass;

1. Cf. "Thou art my battle axe and weapon of war: for with thee will I break in pieces the nations" (Jeremiah 51.20). The poem was written during World War I.

Yet this will go onward the same
    Though Dynasties pass.

3

Yonder a maid and her wight°   *man*
10   Come whispering by:
War's annals will cloud into night
    Ere their story die.

1915   1916, 1917

He Never Expected Much

[or]

A CONSIDERATION

(A reflection) On my Eighty-Sixth Birthday

Well, World, you have kept faith with me,
    Kept faith with me;
Upon the whole you have proved to be
    Much as you said you were.
5   Since as a child I used to lie
Upon the leaze° and watch the sky,   *pasture*
Never, I own, expected I
    That life would all be fair.

'Twas then you said, and since have said,
10   Times since have said,
In that mysterious voice you shed
    From clouds and hills around:
'Many have loved me desperately,
Many with smooth serenity,
15   While some have shown contempt of me
    Till they dropped underground.

'I do not promise overmuch,
    Child; overmuch;
Just neutral-tinted haps° and such,'   *happenings*
20   You said to minds like mine.
Wise warning for your credit's sake!
Which I for one failed not to take,
And hence could stem such strain and ache
    As each year might assign.

1926   1928

JOSEPH CONRAD
1857–1924

Joseph Conrad was born Józef Teodor Konrad Korzeniowski in Poland (then under Russian rule), son of a Polish patriot who suffered exile in Russia for his Polish nationalist activities and died in 1869, leaving Conrad to be brought up by a maternal uncle. At the age of fifteen he amazed his family and friends by announcing his passionate desire to go to sea; he was eventually allowed to go to Marseilles, France, in 1874, and from there he made a number of voyages on French merchant ships to Martinique and other islands in the Caribbean. In 1878 he signed on an English ship that brought him to the east coast English port of Lowestoft, where (still as an ordinary seaman) he joined the crew of a small coasting vessel plying between Lowestoft and Newcastle. In six voyages between these two ports he learned English. Thus launched on a career in the British merchant service, Conrad sailed on a variety of British ships to East Asia, Australia, India, South America, and Africa, eventually gaining his master's certificate in 1886, the year he became a naturalized British subject. He received his first command in 1888, and in 1890 took a steamboat up the Congo River in nightmarish circumstances (described in *Heart of Darkness*, 1899) that permanently afflicted his health and his imagination.

In the early 1890s he was already thinking of turning some of his Malayan experiences into English fiction, and in 1892–93, when serving as first mate on the *Torrens* sailing from London to Adelaide, he revealed to a sympathetic passenger that he had begun a novel (*Almayer's Folly*), while on the return journey he impressed the young novelist John Galsworthy, who was on board, with his conversation. Conrad found it difficult to obtain a command, and this disappointment, together with the interest aroused by *Almayer's Folly* when it was published in 1895, helped turn him away from the sea to a career as a writer. He settled in London and in 1896 married an Englishwoman. This son of a Polish patriot turned merchant seaman turned writer was henceforth—after twenty years at sea—an English novelist.

In his travels through Asian, African, and Caribbean landscapes that eventually made their way into his fiction, Conrad witnessed at close range the workings of European empires, including the British, French, Belgian, Dutch, and German, that at the time controlled most of the earth's surface and were extracting from it vast quantities of raw materials and profiting from forced or cheap labor. In the essay "Geography and Some Explorers," Conrad describes the imperial exploitation he observed in Africa as "the vilest scramble for loot that ever disfigured the history of human conscience and geographical exploration." What he saw of the uses and abuses of imperial power helped make him deeply skeptical. Marlow, the intermediate narrator of *Heart of Darkness*, reflects: "The conquest of the earth, which mostly means the taking it away from those who have a different complexion or slightly flatter noses than ourselves, is not a pretty thing when you look into it too much. What redeems it is the idea only. An idea at the back of it. . . ." And yet in this novella, the ideas at the back of colonialism's ruthless greed and violence are hardly shown to redeem anything at all.

Conrad's questioning of the ethics of empire, perhaps harkening back to his childhood experience as a Pole under Russian occupation, is part of his many-faceted exploration of the ethical ambiguities in human experience. In his great novel *Lord Jim* (1900), which like *Heart of Darkness* uses the device of an intermediate narrator, he probes the meaning of a gross failure of duty on the part of a romantic and idealistic young sailor, and by presenting the hero's history from a series of different points of view, he sustains the ethical questioning to the end. By deploying intermediate narrators and multiple points of view in his fiction, Conrad suggests the complexity of experience and the difficulty of judging human actions.

Although Conrad's plots and exotic settings recall imperial romance and Victorian tales of adventure, he helped develop modern narrative strategies—frame narration, fragmented perspective, flashbacks and flash-forwards, psychologically laden symbolism—that disrupt chronology, render meaning indeterminate, reveal unconscious drives, blur boundaries between civilization and barbarism, and radically cast in doubt epistemological and ethical certainties. Another indication of Conrad's modernist proclivities is the alienation of his characters. Many of his works expose the difficulty of true communion, while also paradoxically exposing how communication is sometimes unexpectedly forced on us, often with someone who may be on the surface our moral opposite, so that we are compelled into a mysterious recognition of our opposite as our true self. Other stories and novels—and Conrad wrote prolifically despite his late start—explore the ways in which the codes we live by are tested in moments of crisis, revealing either their inadequacy or our own. Imagination can corrupt (as with Lord Jim) or save (as in The Shadow-Line, 1917), and a total lack of it can either see a person through (Captain MacWhirr in Typhoon, 1902) or render a person comically ridiculous (Captain Mitchell in Nostromo, 1904). Set in an imaginary Latin American republic, Nostromo subtly studies the corrupting effects of politics and "material interests" on personal relationships. Conrad wrote two other political novels—The Secret Agent (1906) and Under Western Eyes (1911). The latter is a story of Dostoyevskian power about a Russian student who becomes involuntarily associated with anti-government violence in czarist Russia and is maneuvered by circumstances into a position where, although a government spy, he has to pretend to be a revolutionary among revolutionaries. Having to pretend consistently to be the opposite of what he is, this character, like others in Conrad's fiction, is alienated, trapped, unable to communicate. Conrad was as much a pessimist as Hardy, but Conrad aesthetically embodied his pessimism in subtler ways.

He was also a great master of English prose, an astonishing fact given that English was his third language, after Polish and French; that he was twenty-one before he learned English; and that to the end of his life he spoke English with a strong foreign accent. He approached English's linguistic and literary conventions aslant, but the seeming handicap of his foreignness helped him bring to the English novel a fresh geopolitical understanding, a formal seriousness, and a psychological depth, all of which opened up new possibilities for imaginative literature in English, as indicated by his profound, if vexed, influence on later writers as different from himself as the Nigerian Chinua Achebe and the Anglo-Trinidadian V. S. Naipaul.

Heart of Darkness

This story is derived from Conrad's experience in the Congo in 1890. Like Marlow, the narrator of the story, Conrad had as a child determined one day to visit the heart of Africa. "It was in 1868, when nine years old or thereabouts, that while looking at a map of Africa at the time and putting my finger on the blank space then representing the unsolved mystery of that continent, I said to myself with absolute assurance and an amazing audacity which are no longer in my character now: 'When I grow up I shall go there'" (A Personal Record, 1912).

Conrad was promised a job as a Congo River pilot through the influence of his distant cousin Marguerite Poradowska, who lived in Brussels and knew important officials of the Belgian company that exploited the Congo. At this time the Congo, although nominally an independent state, the Congo Free State (État Indépendent du Congo), was virtually the personal property of Leopold II, king of Belgium, who made a fortune out of it. Later, the appalling abuses involved in the naked colonial exploitation that went on in the Congo were exposed to public view, and international

The Congo Free State. Indigenous inhabitants of a village on the Kasai River, a tributary of the Congo, in 1888. They are visiting the *Roi des Belges,* the steamship on which Conrad served two years later as second-in-command. Under King Leopold II's rule of the Congo Free State, the local people suffered violent abuse and exploitation.

criticism compelled the setting up of a committee of inquiry in 1904. From 1885 to 1908, masses of Congolese men were worked to death, women were raped, hands were cut off, villages were looted and burned. What Conrad saw in 1890 shocked him profoundly and shook his view of the moral basis of colonialism, of exploration and trade in newly discovered countries, indeed of civilization in general. "*Heart of Darkness* is experience, too," Conrad wrote in his 1917 "Author's Note," "but it is experience pushed a little (and only very little) beyond the actual facts of the case for the perfectly legitimate, I believe, purpose of bringing it home to the minds and bosoms of the readers." And later he told Edward Garnett: "Before the Congo I was just a mere animal."

Conrad arrived in Africa in May 1890 and made his way up the Congo River very much as described in *Heart of Darkness.* At Kinshasa (which Conrad spells Kinchassa) on Stanley Pool, which he reached after an exhausting two-hundred-mile trek from Matadi, near the mouth of the river, Conrad was taken aback to learn that the steamer of which he was to be captain had been damaged and was undergoing repairs. He was sent as supernumerary on another steamer to learn the river. This steamer was sent to Stanley Falls to collect and bring back to Kinshasa one Georges Antoine Klein, an agent of the company who had fallen so gravely ill that he died on board. Conrad then fell seriously ill and eventually returned to London in January 1891 without ever having served as a Congo River pilot. The Congo experience permanently impaired his health; it also permanently haunted his imagination. The nightmare atmosphere of *Heart of Darkness* is an accurate reflection of Conrad's response to his traumatic experience.

The theme of the story is partly the "choice of nightmares" facing whites in the Congo—either to become like the commercially minded manager, who sees Africa, its people, and its resources solely as instruments of financial gain, or to become like Kurtz, the self-tortured and corrupted idealist (inspired by Klein). The manager is a "hollow man" (T. S. Eliot used a quotation from this story as one epigraph for his poem "The Hollow Men"); his only objections to Kurtz are commercial, not moral: Kurtz's methods are "unsound" and would therefore lose the company money. At the last Kurtz seems to recognize the moral horror of his having succumbed to the dark temptations that African life posed for the European. "He had summed up—he had judged." But the story also has other levels of meaning, and the counterpointing of Western civilization in Europe with what that civilization has done in Africa (see the concluding interview between Marlow and Kurtz's "intended"—based on an interview between Conrad and the dead Klein's fiancée) illuminates several of these. The story first appeared in *Blackwood's Magazine* in 1899 and was revised for book publication in 1902 as part of *Youth: A Narrative, and Two Other Stories.*

Heart of Darkness

1

The *Nellie*, a cruising yawl,[1] swung to her anchor without a flutter of the sails, and was at rest. The flood had made, the wind was nearly calm, and being bound down the river, the only thing for it was to come to and wait for the turn of the tide.

The sea-reach of the Thames stretched before us like the beginning of an interminable waterway. In the offing the sea and the sky were welded together without a joint, and in the luminous space the tanned sails of the barges drifting up with the tide seemed to stand still in red clusters of canvas sharply peaked, with gleams of varnished sprits. A haze rested on the low shores that ran out to sea in vanishing flatness. The air was dark above Gravesend,[2] and farther back still seemed condensed into a mournful gloom, brooding motionless over the biggest, and the greatest, town on earth.

The Director of Companies was our captain and our host. We four affectionately watched his back as he stood in the bows looking to seaward. On the whole river there was nothing that looked half so nautical. He resembled a pilot, which to a seaman is trustworthiness personified. It was difficult to realise his work was not out there in the luminous estuary, but behind him, within the brooding gloom.

Between us there was, as I have already said somewhere, the bond of the sea. Besides holding our hearts together through long periods of separation, it had the effect of making us tolerant of each other's yarns—and even convictions. The Lawyer—the best of old fellows—had, because of his many years and many virtues, the only cushion on deck, and was lying on the only rug. The Accountant had brought out already a box of dominoes, and was toying architecturally with the bones. Marlow sat cross-legged right aft, leaning against the mizzenmast. He had sunken cheeks, a yellow complexion, a straight back, an ascetic aspect, and, with his arms dropped, the palms of hands outwards, resembled an idol. The Director, satisfied the anchor had good hold, made his way aft and sat down amongst us. We exchanged a few words lazily. Afterwards there was silence on board the yacht. For some reason or other we did not begin that game of dominoes. We felt meditative, and fit for nothing but placid staring. The day was ending in a serenity of still and exquisite brilliance. The water shone pacifically;

1. Two-masted boat.
2. River port on the south bank of the Thames twenty-four miles east (downriver) of London.

the sky, without a speck, was a benign immensity of unstained light; the very mist on the Essex marshes was like a gauzy and radiant fabric, hung from the wooded rises inland, and draping the low shores in diaphanous folds. Only the gloom to the west, brooding over the upper reaches, became more sombre every minute, as if angered by the approach of the sun.

And at last, in its curved and imperceptible fall, the sun sank low, and from glowing white changed to a dull red without rays and without heat, as if about to go out suddenly, stricken to death by the touch of that gloom brooding over a crowd of men.

Forthwith a change came over the waters, and the serenity became less brilliant but more profound. The old river in its broad reach rested unruffled at the decline of day, after ages of good service done to the race that peopled its banks, spread out in the tranquil dignity of a waterway leading to the uttermost ends of the earth. We looked at the venerable stream not in the vivid flush of a short day that comes and departs for ever, but in the august light of abiding memories. And indeed nothing is easier for a man who has, as the phrase goes, "followed the sea" with reverence and affection, than to evoke the great spirit of the past upon the lower reaches of the Thames. The tidal current runs to and fro in its unceasing service, crowded with memories of men and ships it has borne to the rest of home or to the battles of the sea. It had known and served all the men of whom the nation is proud, from Sir Francis Drake to Sir John Franklin,[3] knights all, titled and untitled—the great knights-errant of the sea. It had borne all the ships whose names are like jewels flashing in the night of time, from the *Golden Hind* returning with her round flanks full of treasure, to be visited by the Queen's Highness and thus pass out of the gigantic tale, to the *Erebus* and *Terror*, bound on other conquests—and that never returned. It had known the ships and the men. They had sailed from Deptford, from Greenwich, from Erith—the adventurers and the settlers; kings' ships and the ships of men on 'Change; captains, admirals, the dark "interlopers"[4] of the Eastern trade, and the commissioned "generals" of East India fleets. Hunters for gold or pursuers of fame, they all had gone out on that stream, bearing the sword, and often the torch, messengers of the might within the land, bearers of a spark from the sacred fire. What greatness had not floated on the ebb of that river into the mystery of an unknown earth! . . . The dreams of men, the seed of commonwealths, the germs of empires.

The sun set; the dusk fell on the stream, and lights began to appear along the shore. The Chapman lighthouse, a three-legged thing erect on a mudflat, shone strongly. Lights of ships moved in the fairway[5]—a great stir of lights going up and going down. And farther west on the upper reaches the place of the monstrous town was still marked ominously on the sky, a brooding gloom in sunshine, a lurid glare under the stars.

---

3. Sir John Franklin (1786–1847), Arctic explorer who in 1845 commanded an expedition consisting of the ships *Erebus* and *Terror* in search of the Northwest Passage. The ships never returned. Sir Francis Drake (ca. 1540–1596), Elizabethan naval hero and explorer, sailed around the world on his ship *The Golden Hind*. Queen Elizabeth knighted Drake aboard his ship, loaded with captured Spanish treasure, on his return.
4. Private ships muscling in on the monopoly of the East India Company, which was founded in

1600, lost its trading monopoly in 1813, and transferred its governmental functions to the Crown in 1858. Deptford, on the south bank of the Thames, on the eastern edge of London, was once an important dockyard. Greenwich is on the south bank of the Thames immediately east of Deptford. Erith is eight miles farther east.
"'Change": the Stock Exchange.
5. Navigable part of a river, through which ships enter and depart.

"And this also," said Marlow suddenly, "has been one of the dark places of the earth."

He was the only man of us who still "followed the sea." The worst that could be said of him was that he did not represent his class. He was a seaman, but he was a wanderer too, while most seamen lead, if one may so express it, a sedentary life. Their minds are of the stay-at-home order, and their home is always with them—the ship; and so is their country—the sea. One ship is very much like another, and the sea is always the same. In the immutability of their surroundings the foreign shores, the foreign faces, the changing immensity of life, glide past, veiled not by a sense of mystery but by a slightly disdainful ignorance; for there is nothing mysterious to a seaman unless it be the sea itself, which is the mistress of his existence and as inscrutable as Destiny. For the rest, after his hours of work, a casual stroll or a casual spree on shore suffices to unfold for him the secret of a whole continent, and generally he finds the secret not worth knowing. The yarns of seamen have a direct simplicity, the whole meaning of which lies within the shell of a cracked nut. But Marlow was not typical (if his propensity to spin yarns be excepted), and to him the meaning of an episode was not inside like a kernel but outside, enveloping the tale which brought it out only as a glow brings out a haze, in the likeness of one of these misty halos that sometimes are made visible by the spectral illumination of moonshine.

His remark did not seem at all surprising. It was just like Marlow. It was accepted in silence. No one took the trouble to grunt even; and presently he said, very slow:

"I was thinking of very old times, when the Romans first came here, nineteen hundred years ago—the other day. . . . Light came out of this river since—you say Knights? Yes; but it is like a running blaze on a plain, like a flash of lightning in the clouds. We live in the flicker—may it last as long as the old earth keeps rolling! But darkness was here yesterday. Imagine the feelings of a commander of a fine—what d'ye call 'em?—trireme[6] in the Mediterranean, ordered suddenly to the north; run overland across the Gauls in a hurry; put in charge of one of these craft the legionaries—a wonderful lot of handy men they must have been too—used to build, apparently by the hundred, in a month or two, if we may believe what we read. Imagine him here—the very end of the world, a sea the colour of lead, a sky the colour of smoke, a kind of ship about as rigid as a concertina—and going up this river with stores, or orders, or what you like. Sandbanks, marshes, forests, savages—precious little to eat fit for a civilised man, nothing but Thames water to drink. No Falernian wine[7] here, no going ashore. Here and there a military camp lost in a wilderness, like a needle in a bundle of hay—cold, fog, tempests, disease, exile, and death—death skulking in the air, in the water, in the bush. They must have been dying like flies here. Oh yes—he did it. Did it very well, too, no doubt, and without thinking much about it either, except afterwards to brag of what he had gone through in his time, perhaps. They were men enough to face the darkness. And perhaps he was cheered by keeping his eye on a chance of promotion to the fleet at Ravenna[8] by and by, if he

---

6. Ancient Greek and Roman galley with three ranks of oars.
7. Wine from a famed wine-making district in Campania (Italy).

8. A city in northern Italy once directly on the Adriatic Sea and an important naval station in Roman times. It is now about six miles from the sea, connected with it by a canal.

had good friends in Rome and survived the awful climate. Or think of a decent young citizen in a toga—perhaps too much dice, you know—coming out here in the train of some prefect, or tax-gatherer, or trader, even, to mend his fortunes. Land in a swamp, march through the woods, and in some inland post feel the savagery, the utter savagery, had closed round him—all that mysterious life of the wilderness that stirs in the forest, in the jungles, in the hearts of wild men. There's no initiation either into such mysteries. He has to live in the midst of the incomprehensible, which is also detestable. And it has a fascination, too, that goes to work upon him. The fascination of the abomination—you know. Imagine the growing regrets, the longing to escape, the powerless disgust, the surrender, the hate."

He paused.

"Mind," he began again, lifting one arm from the elbow, the palm of the hand outwards, so that, with his legs folded before him, he had the pose of a Buddha preaching in European clothes and without a lotus-flower—"Mind, none of us would feel exactly like this. What saves us is efficiency—the devotion to efficiency. But these chaps were not much account, really. They were no colonists; their administration was merely a squeeze, and nothing more, I suspect. They were conquerors, and for that you want only brute force— nothing to boast of, when you have it, since your strength is just an accident arising from the weakness of others. They grabbed what they could get for the sake of what was to be got. It was just robbery with violence, aggravated murder on a great scale, and men going at it blind—as is very proper for those who tackle a darkness. The conquest of the earth, which mostly means the taking it away from those who have a different complexion or slightly flatter noses than ourselves, is not a pretty thing when you look into it too much. What redeems it is the idea only. An idea at the back of it; not a sentimental pretence but an idea; and an unselfish belief in the idea—something you can set up, and bow down before, and offer a sacrifice to. . . ."

He broke off. Flames glided in the river, small green flames, red flames, white flames, pursuing, overtaking, joining, crossing each other—then separating slowly or hastily. The traffic of the great city went on in the deepening night upon the sleepless river. We looked on, waiting patiently— there was nothing else to do till the end of the flood; but it was only after a long silence, when he said, in a hesitating voice, "I suppose you fellows remember I did once turn fresh-water sailor for a bit," that we knew we were fated, before the ebb began to run, to hear about one of Marlow's inconclusive experiences.

"I don't want to bother you much with what happened to me personally," he began, showing in this remark the weakness of many tellers of tales who seem so often unaware of what their audience would best like to hear; "yet to understand the effect of it on me you ought to know how I got out there, what I saw, how I went up that river to the place where I first met the poor chap. It was the farthest point of navigation and the culminating point of my experience. It seemed somehow to throw a kind of light on everything about me—and into my thoughts. It was sombre enough too—and pitiful— not extraordinary in any way—not very clear either. No, not very clear. And yet it seemed to throw a kind of light.

"I had then, as you remember, just returned to London after a lot of Indian Ocean, Pacific, China Seas—a regular dose of the East—six years or so, and I was loafing about, hindering you fellows in your work and invading your homes, just as though I had got a heavenly mission to civilise you. It was very fine for a time, but after a bit I did get tired of resting. Then I began to look for a ship—I should think the hardest work on earth. But the ships wouldn't even look at me. And I got tired of that game too.

"Now when I was a little chap I had a passion for maps. I would look for hours at South America, or Africa, or Australia, and lose myself in all the glories of exploration. At that time there were many blank spaces on the earth, and when I saw one that looked particularly inviting on a map (but they all look that) I would put my finger on it and say, When I grow up I will go there. The North Pole was one of these places, I remember. Well, I haven't been there yet, and shall not try now. The glamour's off. Other places were scattered about the Equator, and in every sort of latitude all over the two hemispheres. I have been in some of them, and . . . well, we won't talk about that. But there was one yet—the biggest, the most blank, so to speak—that I had a hankering after.

"True, by this time it was not a blank space any more. It had got filled since my boyhood with rivers and lakes and names. It had ceased to be a blank space of delightful mystery—a white patch for a boy to dream gloriously over. It had become a place of darkness. But there was in it one river especially, a mighty big river, that you could see on the map, resembling an immense snake uncoiled, with its head in the sea, its body at rest curving afar over a vast country, and its tail lost in the depths of the land. And as I looked at the map of it in a shop-window, it fascinated me as a snake would a bird—a silly little bird. Then I remembered there was a big concern, a Company for trade on that river. Dash it all! I thought to myself, they can't trade without using some kind of craft on that lot of fresh water— steamboats! Why shouldn't I try to get charge of one? I went on along Fleet Street,[9] but could not shake off the idea. The snake had charmed me.

"You understand it was a Continental concern, that Trading Society; but I have a lot of relations living on the Continent, because it's cheap and not so nasty as it looks, they say.

"I am sorry to own I began to worry them. This was already a fresh departure for me. I was not used to get things that way, you know. I always went my own road and on my own legs where I had a mind to go. I wouldn't have believed it of myself; but, then—you see—I felt somehow I must get there by hook or by crook. So I worried them. The men said, 'My dear fellow,' and did nothing. Then—would you believe it?—I tried the women. I, Charlie Marlow, set the women to work—to get a job. Heavens! Well, you see, the notion drove me. I had an aunt, a dear enthusiastic soul. She wrote: 'It will be delightful. I am ready to do anything, anything for you. It is a glorious idea. I know the wife of a very high personage in the Administration, and also a man who has lots of influence with,' etc. etc. She was determined to make no end of fuss to get me appointed skipper of a river steamboat, if such was my fancy.

"I got my appointment—of course; and I got it very quick. It appears the Company had received news that one of their captains had been killed in a scuffle with the natives. This was my chance, and it made me the more anxious to go. It was only months and months afterwards, when I made the attempt to recover what was left of the body, that I heard the original quarrel

9. Street in central London.

arose from a misunderstanding about some hens. Yes, two black hens. Fresleven—that was the fellow's name, a Dane—thought himself wronged somehow in the bargain, so he went ashore and started to hammer the chief of the village with a stick. Oh, it didn't surprise me in the least to hear this, and at the same time to be told that Fresleven was the gentlest, quietest creature that ever walked on two legs. No doubt he was; but he had been a couple of years already out there engaged in the noble cause, you know, and he probably felt the need at last of asserting his self-respect in some way. Therefore he whacked the old nigger mercilessly, while a big crowd of his people watched him, thunderstruck, till some man—I was told the chief's son—in desperation at hearing the old chap yell, made a tentative jab with a spear at the white man—and of course it went quite easy between the shoulder-blades. Then the whole population cleared into the forest, expecting all kinds of calamities to happen, while, on the other hand, the steamer Fresleven commanded left also in a bad panic, in charge of the engineer, I believe. Afterwards nobody seemed to trouble much about Fresleven's remains, till I got out and stepped into his shoes. I couldn't let it rest, though; but when an opportunity offered at last to meet my predecessor, the grass growing through his ribs was tall enough to hide his bones. They were all there. The supernatural being had not been touched after he fell. And the village was deserted, the huts gaped black, rotting, all askew within the fallen enclosures. A calamity had come to it, sure enough. The people had vanished. Mad terror had scattered them, men, women, and children, through the bush, and they had never returned. What became of the hens I don't know either. I should think the cause of progress got them, anyhow. However, through this glorious affair I got my appointment, before I had fairly begun to hope for it.

"I flew around like mad to get ready, and before forty-eight hours I was crossing the Channel to show myself to my employers, and sign the contract. In a very few hours I arrived in a city that always makes me think of a whited sepulchre. Prejudice no doubt. I had no difficulty in finding the Company's offices. It was the biggest thing in the town, and everybody I met was full of it. They were going to run an over-sea empire, and make no end of coin by trade.

"A narrow and deserted street in deep shadow, high houses, innumerable windows with Venetian blinds, a dead silence, grass sprouting between the stones, imposing carriage archways right and left, immense double doors standing ponderously ajar. I slipped through one of these cracks, went up a swept and ungarnished staircase, as arid as a desert, and opened the first door I came to. Two women, one fat and the other slim, sat on straw-bottomed chairs, knitting black wool. The slim one got up and walked straight at me—still knitting with downcast eyes—and only just as I began to think of getting out of her way, as you would for a somnambulist, stood still, and looked up. Her dress was as plain as an umbrella-cover, and she turned round without a word and preceded me into a waiting-room. I gave my name, and looked about. Deal table in the middle, plain chairs all round the walls, on one end a large shining map, marked with all the colours of a rainbow. There was a vast amount of red—good to see at any time, because one knows that some real work is done in there, a deuce of a lot of blue, a little green, smears of orange, and, on the East Coast, a purple patch, to show where the jolly pioneers of progress drink the jolly lager-beer. However, I wasn't going into any of these. I was going into the yellow. Dead in the centre. And the river was there—fascinating—deadly—like a snake. Ough! A door opened, a white-haired secretarial head, but wearing a compassionate expression, appeared, and a skinny forefinger beckoned me into the sanctuary. Its light was dim, and a heavy writing desk squatted in the middle. From behind that structure came out an impression of pale plumpness in a frockcoat. The great man himself. He was five feet six, I should judge, and had his grip on the handle-end of ever so many millions. He shook hands, I fancy, murmured vaguely, was satisfied with my French. *Bon voyage.*

"In about forty-five seconds I found myself again in the waiting-room with the compassionate secretary, who, full of desolation and sympathy, made me sign some document. I believe I undertook amongst other things not to disclose any trade secrets. Well, I am not going to.

"I began to feel slightly uneasy. You know I am not used to such ceremonies, and there was something ominous in the atmosphere. It was just as though I had been let into some conspiracy—I don't know—something not quite right; and I was glad to get out. In the outer room the two women knitted black wool feverishly. People were arriving, and the younger one was walking back and forth introducing them. The old one sat on her chair. Her flat cloth slippers were propped up on a foot-warmer, and a cat reposed on her lap. She wore a starched white affair on her head, had a wart on one cheek, and silver-rimmed spectacles hung on the tip of her nose. She glanced at me above the glasses. The swift and indifferent placidity of that look troubled me. Two youths with foolish and cheery countenances were being piloted over, and she threw at them the same quick glance of unconcerned wisdom. She seemed to know all about them and about me too. An eerie feeling came over me. She seemed uncanny and fateful. Often far away there I thought of these two, guarding the door of Darkness, knitting black wool as for a warm pall, one introducing, introducing continuously to the unknown, the other scrutinising the cheery and foolish faces with unconcerned old eyes. *Ave!* Old knitter of black wool. *Morituri te salutant.*[1] Not many of those she looked at ever saw her again—not half, by a long way.

"There was yet a visit to the doctor. 'A simple formality,' assured me the secretary, with an air of taking an immense part in all my sorrows. Accordingly a young chap wearing his hat over the left eyebrow, some clerk I suppose—there must have been clerks in the business, though the house was as still as a house in a city of the dead—came from somewhere upstairs, and led me forth. He was shabby and careless, with ink-stains on the sleeves of his jacket, and his cravat was large and billowy, under a chin shaped like the toe of an old boot. It was a little too early for the doctor, so I proposed a drink, and thereupon he developed a vein of joviality. As we sat over our vermuths he glorified the Company's business, and by and by I expressed casually my surprise at him not going out there. He became very cool and collected all at once. 'I am not such a fool as I look, quoth Plato to his disciples,' he said sententiously, emptied his glass with great resolution, and we rose.

"The old doctor felt my pulse, evidently thinking of something else the while. 'Good, good for there,' he mumbled, and then with a certain eagerness asked me whether I would let him measure my head. Rather surprised,

---

1. "Hail! . . . Those who are about to die salute you" (Latin). The Roman gladiators' salute to the emperor on entering the arena.

I said Yes, when he produced a thing like callipers and got the dimensions back and front and every way, taking notes carefully. He was an unshaven little man in a threadbare coat like a gaberdine, with his feet in slippers, and I thought him a harmless fool. 'I always ask leave, in the interests of science, to measure the crania of those going out there,' he said. 'And when they come back too?' I asked. 'Oh, I never see them,' he remarked; 'and, moreover, the changes take place inside, you know.' He smiled, as if at some quiet joke. 'So you are going out there. Famous. Interesting too.' He gave me a search-ing glance, and made another note. 'Ever any madness in your family?' he asked, in a matter-of-fact tone. I felt very annoyed. 'Is that question in the interests of science too?' 'It would be,' he said, without taking notice of my irritation, 'interesting for science to watch the mental changes of individu-als, on the spot, but . . .' 'Are you an alienist?'[2] I interrupted. 'Every doctor should be—a little,' answered that original[3] imperturbably. 'I have a little theory which you Messieurs who go out there must help me to prove. This is my share in the advantages my country shall reap from the possession of such a magnificent dependency. The mere wealth I leave to others. Pardon my questions, but you are the first Englishman coming under my observa-tion . . .' I hastened to assure him I was not in the least typical. 'If I were,' said I, 'I wouldn't be talking like this with you.' 'What you say is rather pro-found, and probably erroneous,' he said, with a laugh. 'Avoid irritation more than exposure to the sun. Adieu. How do you English say, eh? Good-bye. Ah! Good-bye. Adieu. In the tropics one must before everything keep calm.' . . . He lifted a warning forefinger. . . . *'Du calme, du calme. Adieu.'*

"One thing more remained to do—say good-bye to my excellent aunt. I found her triumphant. I had a cup of tea—the last decent cup of tea for many days—and in a room that most soothingly looked just as you would expect a lady's drawing-room to look, we had a long quiet chat by the fire-side. In the course of these confidences it became quite plain to me I had been represented to the wife of the high dignitary, and goodness knows to how many more people besides, as an exceptional and gifted creature—a piece of good fortune for the Company—a man you don't get hold of every day. Good heavens! and I was going to take charge of a two-penny-halfpenny river-steamboat with a penny whistle attached! It appeared, however, I was also one of the Workers, with a capital—you know. Something like an emis-sary of light, something like a lower sort of apostle. There had been a lot of such rot let loose in print and talk just about that time, and the excellent woman, living right in the rush of all that humbug, got carried off her feet. She talked about 'weaning those ignorant millions from their horrid ways,' till, upon my word, she made me quite uncomfortable. I ventured to hint that the Company was run for profit.

"'You forget, dear Charlie, that the labourer is worthy of his hire,' she said brightly. It's queer how out of touch with truth women are. They live in a world of their own, and there had never been anything like it, and never can be. It is too beautiful altogether, and if they were to set it up it would go to pieces before the first sunset. Some confounded fact we men have been living contentedly with ever since the day of creation would start up and knock the whole thing over.

---

2. Doctor who treats mental diseases. (The term   3. Eccentric person.
has now been replaced by *psychiatrist*.)

"After this I got embraced, told to wear flannel, be sure to write often, and so on—and I left. In the street—I don't know why—a queer feeling came to me that I was an impostor. Odd thing that I, who used to clear out for any part of the world at twenty-four hours' notice, with less thought than most men give to the crossing of a street, had a moment—I won't say of hesitation, but of startled pause, before this commonplace affair. The best way I can explain it to you is by saying that, for a second or two, I felt as though, instead of going to the centre of a continent, I were about to set off for the centre of the earth.

"I left in a French steamer, and she called in every blamed port they have out there, for, as far as I could see, the sole purpose of landing soldiers and custom-house officers. I watched the coast. Watching a coast as it slips by the ship is like thinking about an enigma. There it is before you—smiling, frowning, inviting, grand, mean, insipid, or savage, and always mute with an air of whispering, Come and find out. This one was almost featureless, as if still in the making, with an aspect of monotonous grimness. The edge of a colossal jungle, so dark green as to be almost black, fringed with white surf, ran straight, like a ruled line, far, far away along a blue sea whose glitter was blurred by a creeping mist. The sun was fierce, the land seemed to glisten and drip with steam. Here and there greyish-whitish specks showed up clustered inside the white surf, with a flag flying above them perhaps—settlements some centuries old, and still no bigger than pin-heads on the untouched expanse of their background. We pounded along, stopped, landed soldiers; went on, landed custom-house clerks to levy toll in what looked like a God-forsaken wilderness, with a tin shed and a flag-pole lost in it; landed more soldiers—to take care of the custom-house clerks presumably. Some, I heard, got drowned in the surf; but whether they did or not, nobody seemed particularly to care. They were just flung out there, and on we went. Every day the coast looked the same, as though we had not moved; but we passed various places—trading places—with names like Gran' Bassam, Little Popo; names that seemed to belong to some sordid farce acted in front of a sinister back-cloth. The idleness of a passenger, my isolation amongst all these men with whom I had no point of contact, the oily and languid sea, the uniform sombreness of the coast, seemed to keep me away from the truth of things, within the toil of a mournful and senseless delusion. The voice of the surf heard now and then was a positive pleasure, like the speech of a brother. It was something natural, that had its reason, that had a meaning. Now and then a boat from the shore gave one a momentary contact with reality. It was paddled by black fellows. You could see from afar the white of their eyeballs glistening. They shouted, sang; their bodies streamed with perspiration; they had faces like grotesque masks—these chaps; but they had bone, muscle, a wild vitality, an intense energy of movement, that was as natural and true as the surf along their coast. They wanted no excuse for being there. They were a great comfort to look at. For a time I would feel I belonged still to a world of straightforward facts; but the feeling would not last long. Something would turn up to scare it away. Once, I remember, we came upon a man-of-war anchored off the coast. There wasn't even a shed there, and she was shelling the bush. It appears the French had one of their wars going on thereabouts. Her ensign dropped limp like a rag; the muzzles of the long six-inch guns stuck out all over the low hull; the greasy, slimy swell swung her up lazily and let her down, swaying her thin masts. In the empty immensity of earth, sky, and water, there she was, incomprehensible, firing into a continent. Pop, would go one of the six-inch guns; a small flame would dart and vanish, a little white smoke would disappear, a tiny projectile would give a feeble screech—and nothing happened. Nothing could happen. There was a touch of insanity in the proceeding, a sense of lugubrious drollery in the sight; and it was not dissipated by somebody on board assuring me earnestly there was a camp of natives—he called them enemies!—hidden out of sight somewhere.

"We gave her her letters (I heard the men in that lonely ship were dying of fever at the rate of three a day) and went on. We called at some more places with farcical names, where the merry dance of death and trade goes on in a still and earthy atmosphere as of an overheated catacomb; all along the formless coast bordered by dangerous surf, as if Nature herself had tried to ward off intruders; in and out of rivers, streams of death in life, whose banks were rotting into mud, whose waters, thickened into slime, invaded the contorted mangroves,[4] that seemed to writhe at us in the extremity of an impotent despair. Nowhere did we stop long enough to get a particularised impression, but the general sense of vague and oppressive wonder grew upon me. It was like a weary pilgrimage amongst hints for nightmares.

"It was upward of thirty days before I saw the mouth of the big river. We anchored off the seat of the government. But my work would not begin till some two hundred miles farther on. So as soon as I could I made a start for a place thirty miles higher up.

"I had my passage on a little sea-going steamer. Her captain was a Swede, and knowing me for a seaman, invited me on the bridge. He was a young man, lean, fair, and morose, with lanky hair and a shuffling gait. As we left the miserable little wharf, he tossed his head contemptuously at the shore. 'Been living there?' he asked. I said, 'Yes.' 'Fine lot these government chaps—are they not?' he went on, speaking English with great precision and considerable bitterness. 'It is funny what some people will do for a few francs a month. I wonder what becomes of that kind when it goes up country?' I said to him I expected to see that soon. 'So-o-o!' he exclaimed. He shuffled athwart, keeping one eye ahead vigilantly. 'Don't be too sure,' he continued. 'The other day I took up a man who hanged himself on the road. He was a Swede, too.' 'Hanged himself! Why, in God's name?' I cried. He kept on looking out watchfully. 'Who knows? The sun too much for him, or the country perhaps.'

"At last we opened a reach. A rocky cliff appeared, mounds of turned-up earth by the shore, houses on a hill, others with iron roofs, amongst a waste of excavations, or hanging to the declivity. A continuous noise of the rapids above hovered over this scene of inhabited devastation. A lot of people, mostly black and naked, moved about like ants. A jetty[5] projected into the river. A blinding sunlight drowned all this at times in a sudden recrudescence of glare. "There's your Company's station,' said the Swede, pointing to three wooden barrack-like structures on the rocky slope. 'I will send your things up. Four boxes did you say? So. Farewell.'

"I came upon a boiler wallowing in the grass, then found a path leading up the hill. It turned aside for the boulders, and also for an undersized railway truck lying there on its back with its wheels in the air. One was off. The

---

4. Tropical evergreen trees or shrubs with roots and stems forming dense thickets.   5. Wharf or pier.

thing looked as dead as the carcass of some animal. I came upon more pieces of decaying machinery, a stack of rusty nails. To the left a clump of trees made a shady spot, where dark things seemed to stir feebly. I blinked, the path was steep. A horn tooted to the right, and I saw the black people run. A heavy and dull detonation shook the ground, a puff of smoke came out of the cliff, and that was all. No change appeared on the face of the rock. They were building a railway. The cliff was not in the way or anything; but this objectless blasting was all the work going on.

"A slight clinking behind me made me turn my head. Six black men advanced in a file, toiling up the path. They walked erect and slow, balancing small baskets full of earth on their heads, and the clink kept time with their footsteps. Black rags were wound round their loins, and the short ends behind waggled to and fro like tails. I could see every rib, the joints of their limbs were like knots in a rope; each had an iron collar on his neck, and all were connected together with a chain whose bights swung between them, rhythmically clinking. Another report from the cliff made me think suddenly of that ship of war I had seen firing into a continent. It was the same kind of ominous voice; but these men could by no stretch of imagination be called enemies. They were called criminals, and the outraged law, like the bursting shells, had come to them, an insoluble mystery from the sea. All their meagre breasts panted together, the violently dilated nostrils quivered, the eyes stared stonily uphill. They passed me within six inches, without a glance, with that complete, deathlike indifference of unhappy savages. Behind this raw matter one of the reclaimed, the product of the new forces at work, strolled despondently, carrying a rifle by its middle. He had a uniform jacket with one button off, and seeing a white man on the path, hoisted his weapon to his shoulder with alacrity. This was simple prudence, white men being so much alike at a distance that he could not tell who I might be. He was speedily reassured, and with a large, white, rascally grin, and a glance at his charge, seemed to take me into partnership in his exalted trust. After all, I also was a part of the great cause of these high and just proceedings.

"Instead of going up, I turned and descended to the left. My idea was to let that chain-gang get out of sight before I climbed the hill. You know I am not particularly tender; I've had to strike and to fend off. I've had to resist and to attack sometimes—that's only one way of resisting—without counting the exact cost, according to the demands of such sort of life as I had blundered into. I've seen the devil of violence, and the devil of greed, and the devil of hot desire; but, by all the stars! these were strong, lusty, red-eyed devils, that swayed and drove men—men, I tell you. But as I stood on this hillside, I foresaw that in the blinding sunshine of that land I would become acquainted with a flabby, pretending, weak-eyed devil of a rapacious and pitiless folly. How insidious he could be, too, I was only to find out several months later and a thousand miles farther. For a moment I stood appalled, as though by a warning. Finally I descended the hill, obliquely, towards the trees I had seen.

"I avoided a vast artificial hole somebody had been digging on the slope, the purpose of which I found it impossible to divine. It wasn't a quarry or a sandpit, anyhow. It was just a hole. It might have been connected with the philanthropic desire of giving the criminals something to do. I don't know. Then I nearly fell into a very narrow ravine, almost no more than a scar in the hillside. I discovered that a lot of imported drainage-pipes for the settlement had been tumbled in there. There wasn't one that was not broken. It was a wanton smash-up. At last I got under the trees. My purpose was to stroll into the shade for a moment; but no sooner within than it seemed to me I had stepped into the gloomy circle of some Inferno. The rapids were near, and an uninterrupted, uniform, headlong, rushing noise filled the mournful stillness of the grove, where not a breath stirred, not a leaf moved, with a mysterious sound—as though the tearing pace of the launched earth had suddenly become audible.

"Black shapes crouched, lay, sat between the trees, leaning against the trunks, clinging to the earth, half coming out, half effaced within the dim light, in all the attitudes of pain, abandonment, and despair. Another mine on the cliff went off, followed by a slight shudder of the soil under my feet. The work was going on. The work! And this was the place where some of the helpers had withdrawn to die.

"They were dying slowly—it was very clear. They were not enemies, they were not criminals, they were nothing earthly now—nothing but black shadows of disease and starvation, lying confusedly in the greenish gloom. Brought from all the recesses of the coast in all the legality of time contracts, lost in uncongenial surroundings, fed on unfamiliar food, they sickened, became inefficient, and were then allowed to crawl away and rest. These moribund shapes were free as air—and nearly as thin. I began to distinguish the gleam of eyes under the trees. Then, glancing down, I saw a face near my hand. The black bones reclined at full length with one shoulder against the tree, and slowly the eyelids rose and the sunken eyes looked up at me, enormous and vacant, a kind of blind, white flicker in the depths of the orbs, which died out slowly. The man seemed young—almost a boy—but you know with them it's hard to tell. I found nothing else to do but to offer him one of my good Swede's ship's biscuits I had in my pocket. The fingers closed slowly on it and held—there was no other movement and no other glance. He had tied a bit of white worsted[6] round his neck—Why? Where did he get it? Was it a badge—an ornament—a charm—a propitiatory act? Was there any idea at all connected with it? It looked startling round his black neck, this bit of white thread from beyond the seas.

"Near the same tree two more bundles of acute angles sat with their legs drawn up. One, with his chin propped on his knees, stared at nothing, in an intolerable and appalling manner: his brother phantom rested its forehead, as if overcome with a great weariness; and all about others were scattered in every pose of contorted collapse, as in some picture of a massacre or a pestilence. While I stood horror-struck, one of these creatures rose to his hands and knees, and went off on all-fours towards the river to drink. He lapped out of his hand, then sat up in the sunlight, crossing his shins in front of him, and after a time let his woolly head fall on his breastbone.

"I didn't want any more loitering in the shade, and I made haste towards the station. When near the buildings I met a white man, in such an unexpected elegance of get-up that in the first moment I took him for a sort of vision. I saw a high starched collar, white cuffs, a light alpaca[7] jacket, snowy trousers, a clear necktie, and varnished boots. No hat. Hair parted, brushed, oiled, under a green-lined parasol held in a big white hand. He was amazing, and had a penholder behind his ear.

6. Fine wool fabric.
7. Made from the wool of a South American animal by that name.

"I shook hands with this miracle, and I learned he was the Company's chief accountant, and that all the book-keeping was done at this station. He had come out for a moment, he said, 'to get a breath of fresh air.' The expression sounded wonderfully odd, with its suggestion of sedentary desk-life. I wouldn't have mentioned the fellow to you at all, only it was from his lips that I first heard the name of the man who is so indissolubly connected with the memories of that time. Moreover, I respected the fellow. Yes; I respected his collars, his vast cuffs, his brushed hair. His appearance was certainly that of a hairdresser's dummy; but in the great demoralisation of the land he kept up his appearance. That's backbone. His starched collars and got-up shirt-fronts were achievements of character. He had been out nearly three years; and, later, I could not help asking him how he managed to sport such linen. He had just the faintest blush, and said modestly, 'I've been teaching one of the native women about the station. It was difficult. She had a distaste for the work.' Thus this man had verily accomplished something. And he was devoted to his books, which were in apple-pie order.

"Everything else in the station was in a muddle,—heads, things, buildings. Strings of dusty niggers with splay feet arrived and departed; a stream of manufactured goods, rubbishy cottons, beads, and brass-wire set into the depths of darkness, and in return came a precious trickle of ivory.

"I had to wait in the station for ten days—an eternity. I lived in a hut in the yard, but to be out of the chaos I would sometimes get into the accountant's office. It was built of horizontal planks, and so badly put together that, as he bent over his high desk, he was barred from neck to heels with narrow strips of sunlight. There was no need to open the big shutter to see. It was hot there too; big flies buzzed fiendishly, and did not sting, but stabbed. I sat generally on the floor, while, of faultless appearance (and even slightly scented), perching on a high stool, he wrote, he wrote. Sometimes he stood up for exercise. When a truckle-bed with a sick man (some invalided agent from up country) was put in there, he exhibited a gentle annoyance. 'The groans of this sick person' he said, 'distract my attention. And without that it is extremely difficult to guard against clerical errors in this climate.'

"One day he remarked, without lifting his head, 'In the interior you will no doubt meet Mr Kurtz.' On my asking who Mr Kurtz was, he said he was a first-class agent; and seeing my disappointment at this information, he added slowly, laying down his pen, 'He is a very remarkable person.' Further questions elicited from him that Mr Kurtz was at present in charge of a trading-post, a very important one, in the true ivory-country, at 'the very bottom of there. Sends in as much ivory as all the others put together . . .' He began to write again. The sick man was too ill to groan. The flies buzzed in a great peace.

"Suddenly there was a growing murmur of voices and a great tramping of feet. A caravan had come in. A violent babble of uncouth sounds burst out on the other side of the planks. All the carriers were speaking together, and in the midst of the uproar the lamentable voice of the chief agent was heard 'giving it up' tearfully for the twentieth time that day. . . . He rose slowly. 'What a frightful row,' he said. He crossed the room gently to look at the sick man, and returning, said to me, 'He does not hear.' 'What! Dead?' I asked, startled. 'No, not yet,' he answered, with great composure. Then, alluding with a toss of the head to the tumult in the station-yard, 'When one has got to make correct entries, one comes to hate those savages—hate them to the death.' He remained thoughtful for a moment. 'When you see Mr Kurtz,' he went on, 'tell him from me that everything here'—he glanced at the desk—'is very satisfactory. I don't like to write to him—with those messengers of ours you never know who may get hold of your letter—at that Central Station.' He stared at me for a moment with his mild, bulging eyes. 'Oh, he will go far, very far,' he began again. 'He will be a somebody in the Administration before long. They, above—the Council in Europe, you know—mean him to be.'

"He turned to his work. The noise outside had ceased, and presently in going out I stopped at the door. In the steady buzz of flies the homeward-bound agent was lying flushed and insensible; the other, bent over his books, was making correct entries of perfectly correct transactions; and fifty feet below the doorstep I could see the still tree-tops of the grove of death.

"Next day I left that station at last, with a caravan of sixty men, for a two-hundred-mile tramp.

"No use telling you much about that. Paths, paths, everywhere; a stamped-in network of paths spreading over the empty land, through long grass, through burnt grass, through thickets, down and up chilly ravines, up and down stony hills ablaze with heat; and a solitude, a solitude, nobody, not a hut. The population had cleared out a long time ago. Well, if a lot of mysterious niggers armed with all kinds of fearful weapons suddenly took to travelling on the road between Deal and Gravesend, catching the yokels right and left to carry heavy loads for them, I fancy every farm and cottage thereabouts would get empty very soon. Only here the dwellings were gone too. Still, I passed through several abandoned villages. There's something pathetically childish in the ruins of grass walls. Day after day, with the stamp and shuffle of sixty pair of bare feet behind me, each pair under a 60-lb. load. Camp, cook, sleep, strike camp, march. Now and then a carrier dead in harness, at rest in the long grass near the path, with an empty water-gourd and his long staff lying by his side. A great silence around and above. Perhaps on some quiet night the tremor of far-off drums, sinking, swelling, a tremor vast, faint; a sound weird, appealing, suggestive, and wild—and perhaps with as profound a meaning as the sound of bells in a Christian country. Once a white man in an unbuttoned uniform, camping on the path with an armed escort of lank Zanzibaris,[8] very hospitable and festive—not to say drunk. Was looking after the upkeep of the road, he declared. Can't say I saw any road or any upkeep, unless the body of a middle-aged negro, with a bullet-hole in the forehead, upon which I absolutely stumbled three miles farther on, may be considered as a permanent improvement. I had a white companion too, not a bad chap, but rather too fleshy and with the exasperating habit of fainting on the hot hillsides, miles away from the least bit of shade and water. Annoying, you know, to hold your own coat like a parasol over a man's head while he is coming-to. I couldn't help asking him once what he meant by coming there at all. 'To make money, of course. What do you think?' he said scornfully. Then he got fever, and had to be carried in a hammock slung under a pole. As he weighed sixteen stone[9] I had no end of rows with the carriers. They jibbed,

8. Natives of Zanzibar, an island off the east coast of Africa, once part of the sultanate of Zanzibar and a British protectorate, now part of the independent state of Tanzania. Zanzibaris were used as mercenaries throughout Africa.

9. One stone equals 14 pounds. The man weighed 224 pounds.

ran away, sneaked off with their loads in the night—quite a mutiny. So, one evening, I made a speech in English with gestures, not one of which was lost to the sixty pairs of eyes before me, and the next morning I started the hammock off in front all right. An hour afterwards I came upon the whole concern wrecked in a bush—man, hammock, groans, blankets, horrors. The heavy pole had skinned his poor nose. He was very anxious for me to kill somebody, but there wasn't the shadow of a carrier near. I remembered the old doctor—'It would be interesting for science to watch the mental changes of individuals, on the spot.' I felt I was becoming scientifically interesting. However, all that is to no purpose. On the fifteenth day I came in sight of the big river again, and hobbled into the Central Station. It was on a back water surrounded by scrub and forest, with a pretty border of smelly mud on one side, and on the three others enclosed by a crazy fence of rushes. A neglected gap was all the gate it had, and the first glance at the place was enough to let you see the flabby devil was running that show. White men with long staves in their hands appeared languidly from amongst the buildings, strolling up to take a look at me, and then retired out of sight somewhere. One of them, a stout, excitable chap with black moustaches, informed me with great volubility and many digressions, as soon as I told him who I was, that my steamer was at the bottom of the river. I was thunderstruck. What, how, why? Oh, it was 'all right.' The 'manager himself was there. All quite correct. 'Everybody had behaved splendidly! splendidly!'—'You must,' he said in agitation, 'go and see the general manager at once. He is waiting!'

"I did not see the real significance of that wreck at once. I fancy I see it now, but I am not sure—not at all. Certainly the affair was too stupid—when I think of it—to be altogether natural. Still . . . But at the moment it presented itself simply as a confounded nuisance. The steamer was sunk. They had started two days before in a sudden hurry up the river with the manager on board, in charge of some volunteer skipper, and before they had been out three hours they tore the bottom out of her on stones, and she sank near the south bank. I asked myself what I was to do there, now my boat was lost. As a matter of fact, I had plenty to do in fishing my command out of the river. I had to set about it the very next day. That, and the repairs when I brought the pieces to the station, took some months.

"My first interview with the manager was curious. He did not ask me to sit down after my twenty-mile walk that morning. He was commonplace in complexion, in feature, in manners, and in voice. He was of middle size and of ordinary build. His eyes, of the usual blue, were perhaps remarkably cold, and he certainly could make his glance fall on one as trenchant and heavy as an axe. But even at these times the rest of his person seemed to disclaim the intention. Otherwise there was only an indefinable, faint expression of his lips, something stealthy—a smile—not a smile—I remember it, but I can't explain. It was unconscious, this smile was, though just after he had said something it got intensified for an instant. It came at the end of his speeches like a seal applied on the words to make the meaning of the commonest phrase appear absolutely inscrutable. He was a common trader, from his youth up employed in these parts—nothing more. He was obeyed, yet he inspired neither love nor fear, nor even respect. He inspired uneasiness. That was it! Uneasiness. Not a definite mistrust—just uneasiness—nothing more. You have no idea how effective such a . . . a . . . faculty can be. He had no genius for organising, for initiative, or for order even. That was evident in such things as the deplorable state of the station. He had no learning, and no intelligence. His position had come to him—why? Perhaps because he was never ill . . . He had served three terms of three years out there . . . Because triumphant health in the general rout of constitutions is a kind of power in itself. When he went home on leave he rioted on a large scale—pompously. Jack ashore—with a difference—in externals only. This one could gather from his casual talk. He originated nothing, he could keep the routine going—that's all. But he was great. He was great by this little thing that it was impossible to tell what could control such a man. He never gave that secret away. Perhaps there was nothing within him. Such a suspicion made one pause—for out there there were no external checks. Once when various tropical diseases had laid low almost every 'agent' in the station, he was heard to say, 'Men who come out here should have no entrails.' He sealed the utterance with that smile of his, as though it had been a door opening into a darkness he had in his keeping. You fancied you had seen things—but the seal was on. When annoyed at meal-times by the constant quarrels of the white men about precedence, he ordered an immense round table to be made, for which a special house had to be built. This was the station's mess-room. Where he sat was the first place—the rest were nowhere. One felt this to be his unalterable conviction. He was neither civil nor uncivil. He was quiet. He allowed his 'boy'—an overfed young negro from the coast—to treat the white men, under his very eyes, with provoking insolence.

"He began to speak as soon as he saw me. I had been very long on the road. He could not wait. Had to start without me. The up-river stations had to be relieved. There had been so many delays already that he did not know who was dead and who was alive, and how they got on—and so on, and so on. He paid no attention to my explanations, and, playing with a stick of sealing-wax, repeated several times that the situation was 'very grave, very grave.' There were rumours that a very important station was in jeopardy, and its chief, Mr Kurtz, was ill. Hoped it was not true. Mr Kurtz was . . . I felt weary and irritable. Hang Kurtz, I thought. I interrupted him by saying I had heard of Mr Kurtz on the coast. 'Ah! So they talk of him down there,' he murmured to himself. Then he began again, assuring me Mr Kurtz was the best agent he had, an exceptional man, of the greatest importance to the Company; therefore I could understand his anxiety. He was, he said, 'very, very uneasy.' Certainly he fidgeted on his chair a good deal, exclaimed, 'Ah, Mr Kurtz!' broke the stick of sealing-wax and seemed dumbfounded by the accident. Next thing he wanted to know 'how long it would take to' . . . I interrupted him again. Being hungry, you know, and kept on my feet too, I was getting savage. 'How can I tell?' I said, 'I haven't even seen the wreck yet—some months, no doubt.' All this talk seemed to me so futile. 'Some months,' he said. 'Well, let us say three months before we can make a start. Yes. That ought to do the affair.' I flung out of his hut (he lived all alone in a clay hut with a sort of verandah) muttering to myself my opinion of him. He was a chattering idiot. Afterwards I took it back when it was borne in upon me startlingly with what extreme nicety he had estimated the time requisite for the 'affair.'

"I went to work the next day, turning, so to speak, my back on that station. In that way only it seemed to me I could keep my hold on the redeeming facts of life. Still, one must look about sometimes; and then I saw this station, these men strolling aimlessly about in the sunshine of the yard. I asked myself sometimes what it all meant. They wandered here and there with their absurd long staves in their hands, like a lot of faithless pilgrims bewitched inside a rotten fence. The word 'ivory' rang in the air, was whispered, was sighed. You would think they were praying to it. A taint of imbecile rapacity blew through it all, like a whiff from some corpse. By Jove! I've never seen anything so unreal in my life. And outside, the silent wilderness surrounding this cleared speck on the earth struck me as something great and invincible, like evil or truth, waiting patiently for the passing away of this fantastic invasion.

"Oh, these months! Well, never mind. Various things happened. One evening a grass shed full of calico, cotton prints, beads, and I don't know what else, burst into a blaze so suddenly that you would have thought the earth had opened to let an avenging fire consume all that trash. I was smoking my pipe quietly by my dismantled steamer, and saw them all cutting capers in the light, with their arms lifted high, when the stout man with moustaches came tearing down to the river, a tin pail in his hand, assured me that everybody was 'behaving splendidly, splendidly,' dipped about a quart of water and tore back again. I noticed there was a hole in the bottom of his pail.

"I strolled up. There was no hurry. You see the thing had gone off like a box of matches. It had been hopeless from the very first. The flame had leaped high, driven everybody back, lighted up everything—and collapsed. The shed was already a heap of embers glowing fiercely. A nigger was being beaten near by. They said he had caused the fire in some way; be that as it may, he was screeching most horribly. I saw him, later, for several days, sitting in a bit of shade looking very sick and trying to recover himself: afterwards he arose and went out—and the wilderness without a sound took him into its bosom again. As I approached the glow from the dark I found myself at the back of two men, talking. I heard the name of Kurtz pronounced, then the words, 'take advantage of this unfortunate accident.' One of the men was the manager. I wished him a good evening. 'Did you ever see anything like it—eh? it is incredible,' he said, and walked off. The other man remained. He was a first-class agent, young, gentlemanly, a bit reserved, with a forked little beard and a hooked nose. He was standoffish with the other agents, and they on their side said he was the manager's spy upon them. As to me, I had hardly ever spoken to him before. We got into talk, and by and by we strolled away from the hissing ruins. Then he asked me to his room, which was in the main building of the station. He struck a match, and I perceived that this young aristocrat had not only a silver-mounted dressing-case but also a whole candle all to himself. Just at that time the manager was the only man supposed to have any right to candles. Native mats covered the clay walls; a collection of spears, assegais,[1] shields, knives, was hung up in trophies. The business entrusted to this fellow was the making of bricks—so I had been informed; but there wasn't a fragment of a brick anywhere in the station, and he had been there more than a year—waiting. It seems he could not make bricks without something, I don't know what—straw maybe. Anyway, it could not be found there, and as it was not likely to be sent from Europe, it did not appear clear to me what he was waiting for. An act of special creation perhaps. However, they were all waiting—all the sixteen or

1. Slender iron-tipped spears.

twenty pilgrims of them—for something; and upon my word it did not seem an uncongenial occupation, from the way they took it, though the only thing that ever came to them was disease—as far as I could see. They beguiled the time by backbiting and intriguing against each other in a foolish kind of way. There was an air of plotting about that station, but nothing came of it, of course. It was as unreal as everything else—as the philanthropic pretence of the whole concern, as their talk, as their government, as their show of work. The only real feeling was a desire to get appointed to a trading-post where ivory was to be had, so that they could earn percentages. They intrigued and slandered and hated each other only on that account—but as to effectually lifting a little finger—oh no. By heavens! there is something after all in the world allowing one man to steal a horse while another must not look at a halter. Steal a horse straight out. Very well. He has done it. Perhaps he can ride. But there is a way of looking at a halter that would provoke the most charitable of saints into a kick.

"I had no idea why he wanted to be sociable, but as we chatted in there it suddenly occurred to me the fellow was trying to get at something—in fact, pumping me. He alluded constantly to Europe, to the people I was supposed to know there—putting leading questions as to my acquaintances in the sepulchral city, and so on. His little eyes glittered like mica[2] discs—with curiosity—though he tried to keep up a bit of superciliousness. At first I was astonished, but very soon I became awfully curious to see what he would find out from me. I couldn't possibly imagine what I had in me to make it worth his while. It was very pretty to see how he baffled himself, for in truth my body was full only of chills, and my head had nothing in it but that wretched steamboat business. It was evident he took me for a perfectly shameless pre-varicator. At last he got angry, and, to conceal a movement of furious annoyance, he yawned. I rose. Then I noticed a small sketch in oils, on a panel, representing a woman, draped and blindfolded, carrying a lighted torch. The background was sombre—almost black. The movement of the woman was stately, and the effect of the torchlight on the face was sinister.

"It arrested me, and he stood by civilly, holding an empty half-pint champagne bottle (medical comforts) with the candle stuck in it. To my question he said Mr Kurtz had painted this—in this very station more than a year ago—while waiting for means to go to his trading-post. 'Tell me, pray,' said I, 'who is this Mr Kurtz?'

"'The chief of the Inner Station,' he answered in a short tone, looking away. 'Much obliged,' I said, laughing. 'And you are the brickmaker of the Central Station. Every one knows that.' He was silent for a while. 'He is a prodigy,' he said at last. 'He is an emissary of pity, and science, and progress, and devil knows what else. We want,' he began to declaim suddenly, 'for the guidance of the cause entrusted to us by Europe, so to speak, higher intelligence, wide sympathies, a singleness of purpose.' 'Who says that?' I asked. 'Lots of them,' he replied. 'Some even write that; and so *he* comes here, a special being, as you ought to know.' 'Why ought I to know?' I interrupted, really surprised. He paid no attention. 'Yes. To-day he is chief of the best station, next year he will be assistant-manager, two years more and . . . but I daresay you know what he will be in two years' time. You are of the new gang—the gang of virtue. The same people who sent him spe-

2. Glassy mineral.

cially also recommended you. Oh, don't say no. I've my own eyes to trust.'
Light dawned upon me. My dear aunt's influential acquaintances were
producing an unexpected effect upon that young man. I nearly burst into a
laugh. 'Do you read the Company's confidential correspondence?' I asked.
He hadn't a word to say. It was great fun. 'When Mr Kurtz,' I continued
severely, 'is General Manager, you won't have the opportunity.'

"He blew the candle out suddenly, and we went outside. The moon had
risen. Black figures strolled about listlessly, pouring water on the glow,
whence proceeded a sound of hissing; steam ascended in the moonlight;
the beaten nigger groaned somewhere. 'What a row the brute makes!' said
the indefatigable man with the moustaches, appearing near us. 'Serve him
right. Transgression—punishment—bang! Pitiless, pitiless. That's the only
way. This will prevent all conflagrations for the future. I was just telling the
manager . . .' He noticed my companion, and became crestfallen all at
once. 'Not in bed yet,' he said, with a kind of servile heartiness; 'it's so natural. Ha! Danger—agitation.' He vanished. I went on to the river-side, and
the other followed me. I heard a scathing murmur at my ear, 'Heap of
muffs—go to.' The pilgrims could be seen in knots gesticulating, discussing. Several had still their staves in their hands. I verily believe they took
these sticks to bed with them. Beyond the fence the forest stood up spec-
trally in the moonlight, and through the dim stir, through the faint sounds
of that lamentable courtyard, the silence of the land went home to one's
very heart—its mystery, its greatness, the amazing reality of its concealed
life. The hurt nigger moaned feebly somewhere near by, and then fetched a
deep sigh that made me mend my pace away from there. I felt a hand introducing itself under my arm. 'My dear sir,' said the fellow, 'I don't want to be
misunderstood, and especially by you, who will see Mr Kurtz long before I
can have that pleasure. I wouldn't like him to get a false idea of my
disposition. . . .'

"I let him run on, this papier-mâché Mephistopheles, and it seemed to me
that if I tried I could poke my forefinger through him, and would find nothing inside but a little loose dirt, maybe. He, don't you see, had been planning
to be assistant-manager by and by under the present man, and I could see
that the coming of that Kurtz had upset them both not a little. He talked
precipitately, and I did not try to stop him. I had my shoulders against the
wreck of my steamer, hauled up on the slope like a carcass of some big river
animal. The smell of mud, of primeval mud, by Jove! was in my nostrils, the
high stillness of primeval forest was before my eyes; there were shiny patches
on the black creek. The moon had spread over everything a thin layer of
silver—over the rank grass, over the mud, upon the wall of matted vegetation standing higher than the wall of a temple, over the great river I could
see through a sombre gap glittering, glittering, as it flowed broadly by without a murmur. All this was great, expectant, mute, while the man jabbered
about himself. I wondered whether the stillness on the face of the immensity
looking at us two were meant as an appeal or as a menace. What were we
who had strayed in here? Could we handle that dumb thing, or would it
handle us? I felt how big, how confoundedly big, was that thing that couldn't
talk and perhaps was deaf as well. What was in there? I could see a little
ivory coming out from there, and I had heard Mr Kurtz was in there. I had
heard enough about it too—God knows! Yet somehow it didn't bring any
image with it—no more than if I had been told an angel or a fiend was in

there. I believed it in the same way one of you might believe there are inhabitants in the planet Mars. I knew once a Scotch sailmaker who was certain,
dead sure, there were people in Mars. If you asked him for some idea how
they looked and behaved, he would get shy and mutter something about
'walking on all-fours.' If you as much as smiled, he would—though a man of
sixty—offer to fight you. I would not have gone so far as to fight for Kurtz,
but I went for him near enough to a lie. You know I hate, detest, and can't
bear a lie, not because I am straighter than the rest of us, but simply because
it appals me. There is a taint of death, a flavour of mortality in lies—which
is exactly what I hate and detest in the world—what I want to forget. It
makes me miserable and sick, like biting something rotten would do. Temperament, I suppose. Well, I went near enough to it by letting the young fool
there believe anything he liked to imagine as to my influence in Europe. I
became in an instant as much of a pretence as the rest of the bewitched
pilgrims. This simply because I had a notion it somehow would be of help to
that Kurtz whom at the time I did not see—you understand. He was just
a word for me. I did not see the man in the name any more than you do. Do
you see him? Do you see the story? Do you see anything? It seems to me I am
trying to tell you a dream—making a vain attempt, because no relation of a
dream can convey the dream-sensation, that commingling of absurdity, surprise, and bewilderment in a tremor of struggling revolt, that notion of being
captured by the incredible which is of the very essence of dreams. . . ."

He was silent for a while.

". . . No, it is impossible; it is impossible to convey the life-sensation of
any given epoch of one's existence—that which makes its truth, its
meaning—its subtle and penetrating essence. It is impossible. We live, as
we dream—alone. . . ."

He paused again as if reflecting, then added:

"Of course in this you fellows see more than I could then. You see me,
whom you know. . . ."

It had become so pitch dark that we listeners could hardly see one
another. For a long time already he, sitting apart, had been no more to us
than a voice. There was not a word from anybody. The others might have
been asleep, but I was awake. I listened, I listened on the watch for the
sentence, for the word, that would give me the clue to the faint uneasiness
inspired by this narrative that seemed to shape itself without human lips in
the heavy night-air of the river.

". . . Yes—I let him run on," Marlow began again, "and think what he
pleased about the powers that were behind me. I did! And there was nothing behind me! There was nothing but that wretched, old, mangled steamboat I was leaning against, while he talked fluently about 'the necessity for
every man to get on.' 'And when one comes out here, you conceive, it is not
to gaze at the moon.' Mr Kurtz was a 'universal genius,' but even a genius
would find it easier to work with 'adequate tools—intelligent men.' He did
not make bricks—why, there was a physical impossibility in the way—as I
was well aware; and if he did secretarial work for the manager, it was
because 'no sensible man rejects wantonly the confidence of his superiors.'
Did I see it? I saw it. What more did I want? What I really wanted was rivets, by heaven! Rivets. To get on with the work—to stop the hole. Rivets I
wanted. There were cases of them down at the coast—cases—piled up—
burst—split! You kicked a loose rivet at every second step in that station

yard on the hillside. Rivets had rolled into the grove of death. You could fill your pockets with rivets for the trouble of stooping down—and there wasn't one rivet to be found where it was wanted. We had plates that would do, but nothing to fasten them with. And every week the messenger, a lone negro, letter-bag on shoulder and staff in hand, left our station for the coast. And several times a week a coast caravan came in with trade goods—ghastly glazed calico that made you shudder only to look at it, glass beads value about a penny a quart, confounded spotted cotton handkerchiefs. And no rivets. Three carriers could have brought all that was wanted to set that steamboat afloat.

"He was becoming confidential now, but I fancy my unresponsive attitude must have exasperated him at last, for he judged it necessary to inform me he feared neither God nor devil, let alone any mere man. I said I could see that very well, but what I wanted was a certain quantity of rivets—and rivets were what really Mr Kurtz wanted, if he had only known it. Now letters went to the coast every week. . . . 'My dear sir,' he cried, 'I write from dictation.' I demanded rivets. There was a way—for an intelligent man. He changed his manner; became very cold, and suddenly began to talk about a hippopotamus; wondered whether sleeping on board the steamer (I stuck to my salvage night and day) I wasn't disturbed. There was an old hippo that had the bad habit of getting out on the bank and roaming at night over the station grounds. The pilgrims used to turn out in a body and empty every rifle they could lay hands on at him. Some even had sat up o' nights for him. All this energy was wasted, though. 'That animal has a charmed life,' he said; 'but you can say this only of brutes in this country. No man—you apprehend me?—no man here bears a charmed life.' He stood there for a moment in the moonlight with his delicate hooked nose set a little askew, and his mica eyes glittering without a wink, then, with a curt Good-night, he strode off. I could see he was disturbed and considerably puzzled, which made me feel more hopeful than I had been for days. It was a great comfort to turn from that chap to my influential friend, the battered, twisted, ruined, tinpot steamboat. I clambered on board. She rang under my feet like an empty Huntley & Palmer biscuit-tin kicked along a gutter; she was nothing so solid in make, and rather less pretty in shape, but I had expended enough hard work on her to make me love her. No influential friend would have served me better. She had given me a chance to come out a bit—to find out what I could do. No, I don't like work. I had rather laze about and think of all the fine things that can be done. I don't like work—no man does—but I like what is in the work—the chance to find yourself. Your own reality—for yourself, not for others—what no other man can ever know. They can only see the mere show, and never can tell what it really means.

"I was not surprised to see somebody sitting aft, on the deck, with his legs dangling over the mud. You see I rather chummed with the few mechanics there were in that station, whom the other pilgrims naturally despised—on account of their imperfect manners, I suppose. This was the foreman—a boiler-maker by trade—a good worker. He was a lank, bony, yellow-faced man, with big intense eyes. His aspect was worried, and his head was as bald as the palm of my hand; but his hair in falling seemed to have stuck to his chin, and had prospered in the new locality, for his beard hung down to his waist. He was a widower with six young children (he had left them in charge of a sister of his to come out there), and the passion of his life was pigeon-flying. He was an enthusiast and a connoisseur. He would rave about pigeons. After work hours he used sometimes to come over from his hut for a talk about his children and his pigeons; at work, when he had to crawl in the mud under the bottom of the steamboat, he would tie up that beard of his in a kind of white serviette[3] he brought for the purpose. It had loops to go over his ears. In the evening he could be seen squatted on the bank rinsing that wrapper in the creek with great care, then spreading it solemnly on a bush to dry.

"I slapped him on the back and shouted 'We shall have rivets!' He scrambled to his feet exclaiming 'No! Rivets!' as though he couldn't believe his ears. Then in a low voice, 'You . . . eh?' I don't know why we behaved like lunatics. I put my finger to the side of my nose and nodded mysteriously. 'Good for you!' he cried, snapped his fingers above his head, lifting one foot. I tried a jig. We capered on the iron deck. A frightful clatter came but of that hulk, and the virgin forest on the other bank of the creek sent it back in a thundering roll upon the sleeping station. It must have made some of the pilgrims sit up in their hovels. A dark figure obscured the lighted doorway of the manager's hut, vanished, then, a second or so after, the doorway itself vanished too. We stopped, and the silence driven away by the stamping of our feet flowed back again from the recesses of the land. The great wall of vegetation, an exuberant and entangled mass of trunks, branches, leaves, boughs, festoons, motionless in the moonlight, was like a rioting invasion of soundless life, a rolling wave of plants, piled up, crested, ready to topple over the creek, to sweep every little man of us out of his little existence. And it moved not. A deadened burst of mighty splashes and snorts reached us from afar, as though an ichthyosaurus[4] had been taking a bath of glitter in the great river. 'After all,' said the boiler-maker in a reasonable tone, 'why shouldn't we get the rivets?' Why not, indeed! I did not know of any reason why we shouldn't. 'They'll come in three weeks,' I said confidently.

"But they didn't. Instead of rivets there came an invasion, an infliction, a visitation. It came in sections during the next three weeks, each section headed by a donkey carrying a white man in new clothes and tan shoes, bowing from that elevation right and left to the impressed pilgrims. A quarrelsome band of footsore sulky niggers trod on the heels of the donkey; a lot of tents, campstools, tin boxes, white cases, brown bales would be shot down in the courtyard, and the air of mystery would deepen a little over the muddle of the station. Five such instalments came, with their absurd air of disorderly flight with the loot of innumerable outfit shops and provision stores, that, one would think, they were lugging, after a raid, into the wilderness for equitable division. It was an inextricable mess of things decent in themselves but that human folly made look like the spoils of thieving.

"This devoted band called itself the Eldorado[5] Exploring Expedition, and I believe they were sworn to secrecy. Their talk, however, was the talk of sordid buccaneers: it was reckless without hardihood, greedy without audacity, and cruel without courage; there was not an atom of foresight or of serious intention in the whole batch of them, and they did not seem aware these things are wanted for the work of the world. To tear treasure out of the bowels of the

---

3. Table napkin.
4. Large prehistoric marine creature.
5. Fabled land of gold (el dorado, Spanish for

"the gilded") imagined by the Spanish conquistadors to exist in South America.

land was their desire, with no more moral purpose at the back of it than there is in burglars breaking into a safe. Who paid the expenses of the noble enterprise I don't know; but the uncle of our manager was leader of that lot.

"In exterior he resembled a butcher in a poor neighbourhood, and his eyes had a look of sleepy cunning. He carried his fat paunch with ostentation on his short legs, and during the time his gang infested the station spoke to no one but his nephew. You could see these two roaming about all day long with their heads close together in an everlasting confab.[6]

"I had given up worrying myself about the rivets. One's capacity for that kind of folly is more limited than you would suppose. I said Hang!—and let things slide. I had plenty of time for meditation, and now and then I would give some thought to Kurtz. I wasn't very interested in him. No. Still, I was curious to see whether this man, who had come out equipped with moral ideas of some sort, would climb to the top after all, and how he would set about his work when there."

2

"One evening as I was lying flat on the deck of my steamboat, I heard voices approaching—and there were the nephew and the uncle strolling along the bank. I laid my head on my arm again, and had nearly lost myself in a doze, when somebody said in my ear, as it were: 'I am as harmless as a little child, but I don't like to be dictated to. Am I the manager—or am I not? I was ordered to send him there. It's incredible.' . . . I became aware that the two were standing on the shore alongside the forepart of the steamboat, just below my head. I did not move; it did not occur to me to move: I was sleepy. 'It *is* unpleasant,' grunted the uncle. 'He has asked the Administration to be sent there,' said the other, 'with the idea of showing what he could do; and I was instructed accordingly. Look at the influence that man must have. Is it not frightful?' They both agreed it was frightful, then made several bizarre remarks: 'Make rain and fine weather—one man—the Council—by the nose'—bits of absurd sentences that got the better of my drowsiness, so that I had pretty near the whole of my wits about me when the uncle said, 'The climate may do away with this difficulty for you. Is he alone there?' 'Yes,' answered the manager; 'he sent his assistant down the river with a note to me in these terms: "Clear this poor devil out of the country, and don't bother sending more of that sort. I had rather be alone than have the kind of men you can dispose of with me." It was more than a year ago. Can you imagine such impudence?' 'Anything since then?' asked the other hoarsely. 'Ivory,' jerked the nephew; 'lots of it—prime sort—lots—most annoying, from him.' 'And with that?' questioned the heavy rumble. 'Invoice,' was the reply fired out, so to speak. Then silence. They had been talking about Kurtz.

"I was broad awake by this time, but, lying perfectly at ease, remained still, having no inducement to change my position. 'How did that ivory come all this way?' growled the elder man, who seemed very vexed. The other explained that it had come with a fleet of canoes in charge of an English half-caste clerk Kurtz had with him; that Kurtz had apparently intended to return himself, the station being by that time bare of goods and stores, but

6. Confabulation, talk.

after coming three hundred miles, had suddenly decided to go back, which he started to do alone in a small dugout with four paddlers, leaving the half-caste to continue down the river with the ivory. The two fellows there seemed astounded at anybody attempting such a thing. They were at a loss for an adequate motive. As for me, I seemed to see Kurtz for the first time. It was a distinct glimpse: the dugout, four paddling savages, and the lone white man turning his back suddenly on the headquarters, on relief, on thoughts of home—perhaps; setting his face towards the depths of the wilderness, towards his empty and desolate station. I did not know the motive. Perhaps he was just simply a fine fellow who stuck to his work for its own sake. His name, you understand, had not been pronounced once. He was 'that man.' The half-caste, who, as far as I could see, had conducted a difficult trip with great prudence and pluck, was invariably alluded to as 'that scoundrel.' The 'scoundrel' had reported that the 'man' had been very ill— had recovered imperfectly. . . . The two below me moved away then a few paces, and stroked back and forth at some little distance. I heard: 'Military post—doctor—two hundred miles—quite alone now—unavoidable delays— nine months—no news—strange rumours.' They approached again, just as the manager was saying, 'No one, as far as I know, unless a species of wan-dering trader—a pestilential fellow, snapping ivory from the natives.' Who was it they were talking about now? I gathered in snatches that this was some man supposed to be in Kurtz's district, and of whom the manager did not approve. 'We will not be free from unfair competition till one of these fellows is hanged for an example,' he said. 'Certainly,' grunted the other; 'get him hanged! Why not? Anything—anything can be done in this country. That's what I say; nobody here, you understand, here, can endanger your position. And why? You stand the climate—you outlast them all. The danger is in Europe; but there before I left I took care to—' They moved off and whispered, then their voices rose again. 'The extraordinary series of delays is not my fault. I did my possible.'[7] The fat man sighed, 'Very sad.' 'And the pestiferous absurdity of his talk,' continued the other; 'he bothered me enough when he was here. "Each station should be like a beacon on the road towards better things, a centre for trade of course, but also for humanising, improving, instructing." Conceive you—that ass! And he wants to be man-ager! No, it's—' Here he got choked by excessive indignation, and I lifted my head the least bit. I was surprised to see how near they were—right under me. I could have spat upon their hats. They were looking on the ground, absorbed in thought. The manager was switching his leg with a slender twig: his sagacious relative lifted his head. 'You have been well since you came out this time?' he asked. The other gave a start. 'Who? I? Oh! Like a charm— like a charm. But the rest—oh, my goodness! All sick. They die so quick, too, that I haven't the time to send them out of the country—it's incredible!' 'H'm. Just so,' grunted the uncle. 'Ah! my boy, trust to this—I say, trust to this.' I saw him extend his short flipper of an arm for a gesture that took in the forest, the creek, the mud, the river—seemed to beckon with a dishon-ouring flourish before the sunlit face of the land a treacherous appeal to the lurking death, to the hidden evil, to the profound darkness of its heart. It

---

7. Literal rendering of the French *J'ai fait mon possible* (I have done all I could). Conrad sprin-kles the conversation of his Belgian characters with Gallicisms to remind us that their words, though reported in English, were spoken in French. Other examples are "a species of wander-ing trader" (above), "Conceive you" (below), "I would be desolated" (p. 1029).

was so startling that I leaped to my feet and looked back at the edge of the forest, as though I had expected an answer of some sort to that black display of confidence. You know the foolish notions that come to one sometimes. The high stillness confronted these two figures with its ominous patience, waiting for the passing away of a fantastic invasion.

"They swore aloud together—out of sheer fright, I believe—then, pretending not to know anything of my existence, turned back to the station. The sun was low; and leaning forward side by side, they seemed to be tugging painfully uphill their two ridiculous shadows of unequal length, that trailed behind them slowly over the tall grass without bending a single blade.

"In a few days the Eldorado Expedition went into the patient wilderness, that closed upon it as the sea closes over a diver. Long afterwards the news came that all the donkeys were dead. I know nothing as to the fate of the less valuable animals. They, no doubt, like the rest of us, found what they deserved. I did not inquire. I was then rather excited at the prospect of meeting Kurtz very soon. When I say very soon I mean it comparatively. It was just two months from the day we left the creek when we came to the bank below Kurtz's station.

"Going up that river was like travelling back to the earliest beginnings of the world, when vegetation rioted on the earth and the big trees were kings. An empty stream, a great silence, an impenetrable forest. The air was warm, thick, heavy, sluggish. There was no joy in the brilliance of sunshine. The long stretches of the waterway ran on, deserted, into the gloom of overshadowed distances. On silvery sandbanks hippos and alligators sunned themselves side by side. The broadening waters flowed through a mob of wooded islands; you lost your way on that river as you would in a desert, and butted all day long against shoals, trying to find the channel, till you thought yourself bewitched and cut off for ever from everything you had known once—somewhere—far away—in another existence perhaps. There were moments when one's past came back to one, as it will sometimes when you have not a moment to spare to yourself; but it came in the shape of an unrestful and noisy dream, remembered with wonder amongst the overwhelming realities of this strange world of plants, and water, and silence. And this stillness of life did not in the least resemble a peace. It was the stillness of an implacable force brooding over an inscrutable intention. It looked at you with a vengeful aspect. I got used to it afterwards; I did not see it any more; I had no time. I had to keep guessing at the channel; I had to discern, mostly by inspiration, the signs of hidden banks; I watched for sunken stones; I was learning to clap my teeth smartly before my heart flew out, when I shaved by a fluke some infernal sly old snag that would have ripped the life out of the tin-pot steamboat and drowned all the pilgrims; I had to keep a look-out for the signs of dead wood we could cut up in the night for next day's steaming. When you have to attend to things of that sort, to the mere incidents of the surface, the reality—the reality, I tell you—fades. The inner truth is hidden—luckily, luckily. But I felt it all the same; I felt often its mysterious stillness watching me at my monkey tricks, just as it watches you fellows performing on your respective tight-ropes for—what is it? half a crown a tumble—"

"Try to be civil, Marlow," growled a voice, and I knew there was at least one listener awake besides myself.

"I beg your pardon. I forgot the heartache which makes up the rest of the price. And indeed what does the price matter, if the trick be well done? You do your tricks very well. And I didn't do badly either, since I managed not to sink that steamboat on my first trip. It's a wonder to me yet. Imagine a blindfolded man set to drive a van over a bad road. I sweated and shivered over that business considerably, I can tell you. After all, for a seaman, to scrape the bottom of the thing that's supposed to float all the time under his care is the unpardonable sin. No one may know of it, but you never forget the thump—eh? A blow on the very heart. You remember it, you dream of it, you wake up at night and think of it—years after—and go hot and cold all over. I don't pretend to say that steamboat floated all the time. More than once she had to wade for a bit, with twenty cannibals splashing around and pushing. We had enlisted some of these chaps on the way for a crew. Fine fellows—cannibals—in their place. They were men one could work with, and I am grateful to them. And, after all, they did not eat each other before my face: they had brought along a provision of hippo-meat which went rotten, and made the mystery of the wilderness stink in my nostrils. Phoo! I can sniff it now. I had the manager on board and three or four pilgrims with their staves—all complete. Sometimes we came upon a station close by the bank, clinging to the skirts of the unknown, and the white men rushing out of a tumble-down hovel, with great gestures of joy and surprise and welcome, seemed very strange—had the appearance of being held there captive by a spell. The word 'ivory' would ring in the air for a while—and on we went again into the silence, along empty reaches, round the still bends, between the high walls of our winding way, reverberating in hollow claps the ponderous beat of the stern-wheel. Trees, trees, millions of trees, massive, immense, running up high; and at their foot, hugging the bank against the stream, crept the little begrimed steamboat, like a sluggish beetle crawling on the floor of a lofty portico. It made you feel very small, very lost, and yet it was not altogether depressing, that feeling. After all, if you were small, the grimy beetle crawled on—which was just what you wanted it to do. Where the pilgrims imagined it crawled to I don't know. To some place where they expected to get something, I bet! For me it crawled towards Kurtz—exclusively; but when the steam-pipes started leaking we crawled very slow. The reaches opened before us and closed behind, as if the forest had stepped leisurely across the water to bar the way for our return. We penetrated deeper and deeper into the heart of darkness. It was very quiet there. At night sometimes the roll of drums behind the curtain of trees would run up the river and remain sustained faintly, as if hovering in the air high over our heads, till the first break of day. Whether it meant war, peace, or prayer we could not tell. The dawns were heralded by the descent of a chill stillness; the woodcutters slept, their fires burned low; the snapping of a twig would make you start. We were wanderers on a prehistoric earth, on an earth that wore the aspect of an unknown planet. We could have fancied ourselves the first of men taking possession of an accursed inheritance, to be subdued at the cost of profound anguish and of excessive toil. But suddenly, as we struggled round a bend, there would be a glimpse of rush walls, of peaked grass-roofs, a burst of yells, a whirl of black limbs, a mass of hands clapping, of feet stamping, of bodies swaying, of eyes rolling, under the droop of heavy and motionless foliage. The steamer toiled along slowly on the edge of a black and incomprehensible frenzy. The prehistoric man was cursing us, praying to us, welcoming us—who could tell? We were cut off from the comprehension of our surroundings; we glided past like phantoms, wondering and secretly appalled, as sane men would be before an enthusiastic outbreak in a madhouse. We could not understand because we were too far and could not remember, because we were travelling in the night of first ages, of those ages that are gone, leaving hardly a sign—and no memories.

"The earth seemed unearthly. We are accustomed to look upon the shackled form of a conquered monster, but there—there you could look at a thing monstrous and free. It was unearthly, and the men were—No, they were not inhuman. Well, you know, that was the worst of it—this suspicion of their not being inhuman. It would come slowly to one. They howled and leaped, and spun, and made horrid faces; but what thrilled you was just the thought of their humanity—like yours—the thought of your remote kinship with this wild and passionate uproar. Ugly. Yes, it was ugly enough; but if you were man enough you would admit to yourself that there was in you just the faintest trace of a response to the terrible frankness of that noise, a dim suspicion of there being a meaning in it which you—you so remote from the night of first ages—could comprehend. And why not? The mind of man is capable of anything—because everything is in it, all the past as well as all the future. What was there after all? Joy, fear, sorrow, devotion, valour, rage—who can tell?—but truth—truth stripped of its cloak of time. Let the fool gape and shudder—the man knows, and can look on without a wink. But he must at least be as much of a man as these on the shore. He must meet that truth with his own true stuff—with his own inborn strength. Principles? Principles won't do. Acquisitions, clothes, pretty rags—rags that would fly off at the first good shake. No; you want a deliberate belief. An appeal to me in this fiendish row—is there? Very well; I hear; I admit, but I have a voice too, and for good or evil mine is the speech that cannot be silenced. Of course, a fool, what with sheer fright and fine sentiments, is always safe. Who's that grunting? You wonder I didn't go ashore for a howl and a dance? Well, no—I didn't. Fine sentiments, you say? Fine sentiments be hanged! I had no time. I had to mess about with white-lead and strips of woollen blanket helping to put bandages on those leaky steam-pipes—I tell you. I had to watch the steering, and circumvent those snags, and get the tin-pot along by hook or by crook. There was surface-truth enough in these things to save a wiser man. And between whiles I had to look after the savage who was fireman. He was an improved specimen; he could fire up a vertical boiler. He was there below me, and, upon my word, to look at him was as edifying as seeing a dog in a parody of breeches and a feather hat, walking on his hind legs. A few months of training had done for that really fine chap. He squinted at the steam-gauge and at the water-gauge with an evident effort of intrepidity—and he had filed teeth too, the poor devil, and the wool of his pate shaved into queer patterns, and three ornamental scars on each of his cheeks. He ought to have been clapping his hands and stamping his feet on the bank, instead of which he was hard at work, a thrall to strange witchcraft, full of improving knowledge. He was useful because he had been instructed; and what he knew was this—that should the water in that transparent thing disappear, the evil spirit inside the boiler would get angry through the greatness of his thirst, and take a terrible vengeance. So he sweated and fired up and watched the glass fearfully (with an impromptu charm, made of rags, tied to his arm, and a piece of polished bone, as big as a watch, stuck flatways through his lower lip), while the wooded banks slipped past us slowly, the short noise was left behind, the interminable miles of silence—and we crept on, towards Kurtz. But the snags were thick, the water was treacherous and shallow, the boiler seemed indeed to have a sulky devil in it, and thus neither that fireman nor I had any time to peer into our creepy thoughts.

"Some fifty miles below the Inner Station we came upon a hut of reeds, an inclined and melancholy pole, with the unrecognisable tatters of what had been a flag of some sort flying from it, and a neatly stacked wood-pile. This was unexpected. We came to the bank, and on the stack of firewood found a flat piece of board with some faded pencil-writing on it. When deciphered it said: 'Wood for you. Hurry up. Approach cautiously.' There was a signature, but it was illegible—not Kurtz—a much longer word. Hurry up. Where? Up the river? 'Approach cautiously.' We had not done so. But the warning could not have been meant for the place where it could be only found after approach. Something was wrong above. But what—and how much? That was the question. We commented adversely upon the imbecility of that telegraphic style. The bush around said nothing, and would not let us look very far, either. A torn curtain of red twill hung in the doorway of the hut, and flapped sadly in our faces. The dwelling was dismantled; but we could see a white man had lived there not very long ago. There remained a rude table—a plank on two posts; a heap of rubbish reposed in a dark corner, and by the door I picked up a book. It had lost its covers, and the pages had been thumbed into a state of extremely dirty softness; but the back had been lovingly stitched afresh with white cotton thread, which looked clean yet. It was an extraordinary find. Its title was, *An Inquiry into some Points of Seamanship*, by a man Towser, Towson—some such name— Master in His Majesty's Navy. The matter looked dreary reading enough, with illustrative diagrams and repulsive tables of figures, and the copy was sixty years old. I handled this amazing antiquity with the greatest possible tenderness, lest it should dissolve in my hands. Within, Towson or Towser was inquiring earnestly into the breaking strain of ships' chains and tackle, and other such matters. Not a very enthralling book; but at the first glance you could see there a singleness of intention, an honest concern for the right way of going to work, which made these humble pages, thought out so many years ago, luminous with another than a professional light. The simple old sailor, with his talk of chains and purchases, made me forget the jungle and the pilgrims in a delicious sensation of having come upon something unmistakably real. Such a book being there was wonderful enough; but still more astounding were the notes pencilled in the margin, and plainly referring to the text. I couldn't believe my eyes! They were in cipher! Yes, it looked like cipher. Fancy a man lugging with him a book of that description into this nowhere and studying it—and making notes—in cipher at that! It was an extravagant mystery.

"I had been dimly aware for some time of a worrying noise, and when I lifted my eyes I saw the wood-pile was gone, and the manager, aided by all the pilgrims, was shouting at me from the river-side. I slipped the book into my pocket. I assure you to leave off reading was like tearing myself away from the shelter of an old and solid friendship.

"I started the lame engine ahead. 'It must be this miserable trader—this intruder,' exclaimed the manager, looking back malevolently at the place we had left. 'He must be English,' I said. 'It will not save him from getting into trouble if he is not careful,' muttered the manager darkly. I observed with assumed innocence that no man was safe from trouble in this world.

"The current was more rapid now, the steamer seemed at her last gasp, the stern-wheel flopped languidly, and I caught myself listening on tiptoe for the next beat of the float,[8] for in sober truth I expected the wretched thing to give up every moment. It was like watching the last flickers of a life. But still we crawled. Sometimes I would pick out a tree a little way ahead to measure our progress towards Kurtz by, but I lost it invariably before we got abreast. To keep the eyes so long on one thing was too much for human patience. The manager displayed a beautiful resignation. I fretted and fumed and took to arguing with myself whether or no I would talk openly with Kurtz; but before I could come to any conclusion it occurred to me that my speech or my silence, indeed any action of mine, would be a mere futility. What did it matter what any one knew or ignored? What did it matter who was manager? One gets sometimes such a flash of insight. The essentials of this affair lay deep under the surface, beyond my reach, and beyond my power of meddling.

"Towards the evening of the second day we judged ourselves about eight miles from Kurtz's station. I wanted to push on; but the manager looked grave, and told me the navigation up there was so dangerous that it would be advisable, the sun being very low already, to wait where we were till next morning. Moreover, he pointed out that if the warning to approach cautiously were to be followed, we must approach in daylight—not at dusk, or in the dark. This was sensible enough. Eight miles meant nearly three hours' steaming for us, and I could also see suspicious ripples at the upper end of the reach. Nevertheless, I was annoyed beyond expression at the delay, and most unreasonably too, since one night more could not matter much after so many months. As we had plenty of wood, and caution was the word, I brought up in the middle of the stream. The reach was narrow, straight, with high sides like a railway cutting. The dusk came gliding into it long before the sun had set. The current ran smooth and swift, but a dumb immobility sat on the banks. The living trees, lashed together by the creepers and every living bush of the undergrowth, might have been changed into stone, even to the slenderest twig, to the lightest leaf. It was not sleep—it seemed unnatural, like a state of trance. Not the faintest sound of any kind could be heard. You looked on amazed, and began to suspect yourself of being deaf—then the night came suddenly, and struck you blind as well. About three in the morning some large fish leaped, and the loud splash made me jump as though a gun had been fired. When the sun rose there was a white fog, very warm and clammy, and more blinding than the night. It did not shift or drive; it was just there, standing all round you like something solid. At eight or nine, perhaps, it lifted as a shutter lifts. We had a glimpse of the towering multitude of trees, of the immense matted jungle, with the blazing little ball of the sun hanging over it—all perfectly still—and then the white shutter came down again, smoothly, as if sliding in greased grooves. I ordered the chain, which we had begun to heave in, to be paid out again. Before it stopped running with a muffled rattle, a cry, a very loud cry, as of infinite desolation, soared slowly in the opaque air. It ceased. A

8. Automatic water-level regulator opening and closing a water-supply valve.

complaining clamour, modulated in savage discords, filled our ears. The sheer unexpectedness of it made my hair stir under my cap. I don't know how it struck the others: to me it seemed as though the mist itself had screamed, so suddenly, and apparently from all sides at once, did this tumultuous and mournful uproar arise. It culminated in a hurried outbreak of almost intolerably excessive shrieking, which stopped short, leaving us stiffened in a variety of silly attitudes, and obstinately listening to the nearly as appalling and excessive silence. 'Good God! What is the meaning—?' stammered at my elbow one of the pilgrims—a little fat man, with sandy hair and red whiskers, who wore side-spring boots, and pink pyjamas tucked into his socks. Two others remained open-mouthed a whole minute, then dashed into the little cabin, to rush out incontinently and stand darting scared glances, with Winchesters at 'ready' in their hands. What we could see was just the steamer we were on, her outlines blurred as though she had been on the point of dissolving, and a misty strip of water, perhaps two feet broad, around her—and that was all. The rest of the world was nowhere, as far as our eyes and ears were concerned. Just nowhere. Gone, disappeared; swept off without leaving a whisper or a shadow behind.

"I went forward, and ordered the chain to be hauled in short, so as to be ready to trip the anchor and move the steamboat at once if necessary. 'Will they attack?' whispered an awed voice. 'We will all be butchered in this fog,' murmured another. The faces twitched with the strain, the hands trembled slightly, the eyes forgot to wink. It was very curious to see the contrast of expressions of the white men and of the black fellows of our crew, who were as much strangers to that part of the river as we, though their homes were only eight hundred miles away. The whites, of course greatly discomposed, had besides a curious look of being painfully shocked by such an outrageous row. The others had an alert, naturally interested expression; but their faces were essentially quiet, even those of the one or two who grinned as they hauled at the chain. Several exchanged short, grunting phrases, which seemed to settle the matter to their satisfaction. Their headman, a young, broad-chested black, severely draped in dark-blue fringed cloths, with fierce nostrils and his hair all done up artfully in oily ringlets, stood near me. 'Aha!' I said, just for good fellowship's sake. 'Catch 'im,' he snapped, with a bloodshot widening of his eyes and a flash of sharp teeth—'catch 'im. Give 'im to us.' 'To you, eh?' I asked; 'what would you do with them?' 'Eat 'im!' he said curtly, and, leaning his elbow on the rail, looked out into the fog in a dignified and profoundly pensive attitude. I would no doubt have been properly horrified, had it not occurred to me that he and his chaps must be very hungry: that they must have been growing increasingly hungry for at least this month past. They had been engaged for six months (I don't think a single one of them had any clear idea of time, as we at the end of countless ages have. They still belonged to the beginnings of time—had no inherited experience to teach them, as it were), and of course, as long as there was a piece of paper written over in accordance with some farcical law or other made down the river, it didn't enter anybody's head to trouble how they would live. Certainly they had brought with them some rotten hippo-meat, which couldn't have lasted very long, anyway, even if the pilgrims hadn't, in the midst of a shocking hullabaloo, thrown a considerable quantity of it overboard. It looked like a high-handed proceeding; but it was really a case of legitimate self-defence. You can't breathe dead hippo waking, sleeping, and eating, and at the same time keep your precarious grip on existence. Besides that, they had given them every week three pieces of brass wire, each about nine inches long; and the theory was they were to buy their provisions with that currency in river-side villages. You can see how *that* worked. There were either no villages, or the people were hostile, or the director, who like the rest of us fed out of tins, with an occasional old he-goat thrown in, didn't want to stop the steamer for some more or less recondite reasons. So, unless they swallowed the wire itself, or made loops of it to snare the fishes with, I don't see what good their extravagant salary could be to them. I must say it was paid with a regularity worthy of a large and honourable trading company. For the rest, the only thing to eat—though it didn't look eatable in the least—I saw in their possession was a few lumps of some stuff like half-cooked dough, of a dirty lavender colour, they kept wrapped in leaves, and now and then swallowed a piece of, but so small that it seemed done more for the look of the thing than for any serious purpose of sustenance. Why in the name of all the gnawing devils of hunger they didn't go for us—they were thirty to five—and have a good tuck-in for once, amazes me now when I think of it. They were big powerful men, with not much capacity to weigh the consequences, with courage, with strength, even yet, though their skins were no longer glossy and their muscles no longer hard. And I saw that something restraining, one of those human secrets that baffle probability, had come into play there. I looked at them with a swift quickening of interest—not because it occurred to me I might be eaten by them before very long, though I own to you that just then I perceived—in a new light, as it were—how unwholesome the pilgrims looked, and I hoped, yes, I positively hoped, that my aspect was not so—what shall I say?—so—unappetising: a touch of fantastic vanity which fitted well with the dream-sensation that pervaded all my days at that time. Perhaps I had a little fever too. One can't live with one's finger everlastingly on one's pulse. I had often 'a little fever,' or a little touch of other things—the playful paw-strokes of the wilderness, the preliminary trifling before the more serious onslaught which came in due course. Yes; I looked at them as you would on any human being, with a curiosity of their impulses, motives, capacities, weaknesses, when brought to the test of an inexorable physical necessity. Restraint! What possible restraint? Was it superstition, disgust, patience, fear—or some kind of primitive honour? No fear can stand up to hunger, no patience can wear it out, disgust simply does not exist where hunger is; and as to superstition, beliefs, and what you may call principles, they are less than chaff in a breeze. Don't you know the devilry of lingering starvation, its exasperating torment, its black thoughts, its sombre and brooding ferocity? Well, I do. It takes a man all his inborn strength to fight hunger properly. It's really easier to face bereavement, dishonour, and the perdition of one's soul—than this kind of prolonged hunger. Sad, but true. And these chaps too had no earthly reason for any kind of scruple. Restraint! I would just as soon have expected restraint from a hyena prowling amongst the corpses of a battlefield. But there was the fact facing me—the fact dazzling, to be seen, like the foam on the depths of the sea, like a ripple on an unfathomable enigma, a mystery greater—when I thought of it—than the curious, inexplicable note of desperate grief in this savage clamour that had swept by us on the river-bank, behind the blind whiteness of the fog.

"Two pilgrims were quarrelling in hurried whispers as to which bank. 'Left.' 'No, no; how can you? Right, right, of course.' 'It is very serious,' said the manager's voice behind me; 'I would be desolated if anything should happen to Mr Kurtz before we came up.' I looked at him, and had not the slightest doubt he was sincere. He was just the kind of man who would wish to preserve appearances. That was his restraint. But when he muttered something about going on at once, I did not even take the trouble to answer him. I knew, and he knew, that it was impossible. Were we to let go our hold of the bottom, we would be absolutely in the air—in space. We wouldn't be able to tell where we were going to—whether up or down stream, or across— till we fetched against one bank or the other—and then we wouldn't know at first which it was. Of course I made no move. I had no mind for a smash-up. You couldn't imagine a more deadly place for a shipwreck. Whether drowned at once or not, we were sure to perish speedily in one way or another. 'I authorise you to take all the risks,' he said, after a short silence. 'I refuse to take any,' I said shortly; which was just the answer he expected, though its tone might have surprised him. 'Well, I must defer to your judgment. You are captain,' he said, with marked civility. I turned my shoulder to him in sign of my appreciation, and looked into the fog. How long would it last? It was the most hopeless lookout. The approach to this Kurtz grubbing for ivory in the wretched bush was beset by as many dangers as though he had been an enchanted princess sleeping in a fabulous castle. 'Will they attack, do you think?' asked the manager, in a confidential tone.

"I did not think they would attack, for several obvious reasons. The thick fog was one. If they left the bank in their canoes they would get lost in it, as we would be if we attempted to move. Still, I had also judged the jungle of both banks quite impenetrable—and yet eyes were in it, eyes that had seen us. The river-side bushes were certainly very thick; but the undergrowth behind was evidently penetrable. However, during the short lift I had seen no canoes anywhere in the reach—certainly not abreast of the steamer. But what made the idea of attack inconceivable to me was the nature of the noise—of the cries we had heard. They had not the fierce character boding of immediate hostile intention. Unexpected, wild, and violent as they had been, they had given me an irresistible impression of sorrow. The glimpse of the steamboat had for some reason filled those savages with unrestrained grief. The danger, if any, I expounded, was from our proximity to a great human passion let loose. Even extreme grief may ultimately vent itself in violence—but more generally takes the form of apathy. . . .

"You should have seen the pilgrims stare! They had no heart to grin, or even to revile me; but I believe they thought me gone mad—with fright, maybe. I delivered a regular lecture. My dear boys, it was no good bothering. Keep a look-out? Well, you may guess I watched the fog for the signs of lifting as a cat watches a mouse; but for anything else our eyes were of no more use to us than if we had been buried miles deep in a heap of cotton-wool. It felt like it too—choking, warm, stifling. Besides, all I said, though it sounded extravagant, was absolutely true to fact. What we afterwards alluded to as an attack was really an attempt at repulse. The action was very far from being aggressive—it was not even defensive, in the usual sense: it was undertaken under the stress of desperation, and in its essence was purely protective.

"It developed itself, I should say, two hours after the fog lifted, and its commencement was at a spot, roughly speaking, about a mile and a half below Kurtz's station. We had just floundered and flopped round a bend, when I saw an islet, a mere grassy hummock of bright green, in the middle of the stream. It was the only thing of the kind; but as we opened the reach more, I perceived it was the head of a long sandbank, or rather of a chain of shallow patches stretching down the middle of the river. They were discoloured, just awash, and the whole lot was seen just under the water, exactly as a man's backbone is seen running down the middle of his back under the skin. Now, as far as I did see, I could go to the right or to the left of this. I didn't know either channel, of course. The banks looked pretty well alike, the depth appeared the same; but as I had been informed the station was on the west side, I naturally headed for the western passage.

"No sooner had we fairly entered it than I became aware it was much narrower than I had supposed. To the left of us there was the long uninterrupted shoal,[9] and to the right a high steep bank heavily overgrown with bushes. Above the bush the trees stood in serried ranks. The twigs overhung the current thickly, and from distance to distance a large limb of some tree projected rigidly over the stream. It was then well on in the afternoon, the face of the forest was gloomy, and a broad strip of shadow had already fallen on the water. In this shadow we steamed up—very slowly, as you may imagine. I sheered her well inshore—the water being deepest near the bank, as the sounding-pole informed me.

"One of my hungry and forbearing friends was sounding in the bows just below me. This steamboat was exactly like a decked scow. On the deck there were two little teak-wood houses, with doors and windows. The boiler was in the fore-end, and the machinery right astern. Over the whole there was a light roof, supported on stanchions. The funnel projected through that roof, and in front of the funnel a small cabin built of light planks served for a pilot-house. It contained a couch, two camp-stools, a loaded Martini-Henry[1] leaning in one corner, a tiny table, and the steering-wheel. It had a wide door in front and a broad shutter at each side. All these were always thrown open, of course. I spent my days perched up there on the extreme fore-end of that roof, before the door. At night I slept, or tried to, on the couch. An athletic black belonging to some coast tribe, and educated by my poor predecessor, was the helmsman. He sported a pair of brass earrings, wore a blue cloth wrapper from the waist to the ankles, and thought all the world of himself. He was the most unstable kind of fool I had ever seen. He steered with no end of a swagger while you were by; but if he lost sight of you, he became instantly the prey of an abject funk, and would let that cripple of a steamboat get the upper hand of him in a minute.

"I was looking down at the sounding-pole, and feeling much annoyed to see at each try a little more of it stick out of that river, when I saw my poleman give up the business suddenly, and stretch himself flat on the deck, without even taking the trouble to haul his pole in. He kept hold on it though, and it trailed in the water. At the same time the fireman, whom I could also see below me, sat down abruptly before his furnace and ducked his head. I was amazed. Then I had to look at the river mighty quick, because there was a snag in the fairway. Sticks, little sticks, were flying about—thick; they were whizzing before my nose, dropping below me, striking behind me against my pilot-house. All this time the river, the shore, the

9. Sandbank.
1. Rifle combining the seven-grooved barrel of the Scottish gun maker A. Henry with the block- action breech mechanism introduced by the Swiss inventor F. Martini.

woods, were very quiet—perfectly quiet. I could only hear the heavy splashing thump of the stern-wheel and the patter of these things. We cleared the snag clumsily. Arrows, by Jove! We were being shot at! I stepped in quickly to close the shutter on the landside. That fool-helmsman, his hands on the spokes, was lifting his knees high, stamping his feet, champing his mouth, like a reined-in horse. Confound him! And we were staggering within ten feet of the bank. I had to lean right out to swing the heavy shutter, and I saw a face amongst the leaves on the level with my own, looking at me very fierce and steady; and then suddenly, as though a veil had been removed from my eyes, I made out, deep in the tangled gloom, naked breasts, arms, legs, glaring eyes—the bush was swarming with human limbs in movement, glistening, of bronze colour. The twigs shook, swayed, and rustled, the arrows flew out of them, and then the shutter came to. 'Steer her straight,' I said to the helmsman. He held his head rigid, face forward; but his eyes rolled, he kept on lifting and setting down his feet gently, his mouth foamed a little. 'Keep quiet!' I said in a fury. I might just as well have ordered a tree not to sway in the wind. I darted out. Below me there was a great scuffle of feet on the iron deck; confused exclamations; a voice screamed, 'Can you turn back?' I caught sight of a V-shaped ripple on the water ahead. What? Another snag! A fusillade burst out under my feet. The pilgrims had opened with their Winchesters, and were simply squirting lead into that bush. A deuce of a lot of smoke came up and drove slowly forward. I swore at it. Now I couldn't see the ripple or the snag either. I stood in the doorway, peering, and the arrows came in swarms. They might have been poisoned, but they looked as though they wouldn't kill a cat. The bush began to howl. Our wood-cutters raised a warlike whoop; the report of a rifle just at my back deafened me. I glanced over my shoulder, and the pilot-house was yet full of noise and smoke when I made a dash at the wheel. The fool-nigger had dropped everything, to throw the shutter open and let off that Martini-Henry. He stood before the wide opening, glaring, and I yelled at him to come back, while I straightened the sudden twist out of that steamboat. There was no room to turn even if I had wanted to, the snag was somewhere very near ahead in that confounded smoke, there was no time to lose, so I just crowded her into the bank—right into the bank, where I knew the water was deep.

"We tore slowly along the overhanging bushes in a whirl of broken twigs and flying leaves. The fusillade below stopped short, as I had foreseen it would when the squirts got empty. I threw my head back to a glinting whizz that traversed the pilot-house, in at one shutter-hole and out at the other. Looking past that mad helmsman, who was shaking the empty rifle and yelling at the shore, I saw vague forms of men running bent double, leaping, gliding, distinct, incomplete, evanescent. Something big appeared in the air before the shutter, the rifle went overboard, and the man stepped back swiftly, looked at me over his shoulder in an extraordinary, profound, familiar manner, and fell upon my feet. The side of his head hit the wheel twice, and the end of what appeared a long cane clattered round and knocked over a little camp-stool. It looked as though after wrenching that thing from somebody ashore he had lost his balance in the effort. The thin smoke had blown away, we were clear of the snag, and looking ahead I could see that in another hundred yards or so I would be free to sheer off, away from the bank; but my feet felt so very warm and wet that I had to look down. The man had rolled on his back and stared straight up at me; both his hands clutched that cane. It was the shaft of a spear that, either thrown or lunged through the opening, had caught him in the side just below the ribs; the blade had gone in out of sight, after making a frightful gash; my shoes were full; a pool of blood lay very still, gleaming dark-red under the wheel; his eyes shone with an amazing lustre. The fusillade burst out again. He looked at me anxiously, gripping the spear like something precious, with an air of being afraid I would try to take it away from him. I had to make an effort to free my eyes from his gaze and attend to the steering. With one hand I felt above my head for the line of the steam whistle, and jerked out screech after screech hurriedly. The tumult of angry and warlike yells was checked instantly, and then from the depths of the woods went out such a tremulous and prolonged wail of mournful fear and utter despair as may be imagined to follow the flight of the last hope from the earth. There was a great commotion in the bush; the shower of arrows stopped, a few dropping shots rang out sharply—then silence, in which the languid beat of the stern-wheel came plainly to my ears. I put the helm hard a-starboard at the moment when the pilgrim in pink pyjamas, very hot and agitated, appeared in the doorway. 'The manager sends me—' he began in an official tone, and stopped short. 'Good God!' he said, glaring at the wounded man.

"We two whites stood over him, and his lustrous and inquiring glance enveloped us both. I declare it looked as though he would presently put to us some question in an understandable language; but he died without uttering a sound, without moving a limb, without twitching a muscle. Only in the very last moment, as though in response to some sign we could not see, to some whisper we could not hear, he frowned heavily, and that frown gave to his black death-mask an inconceivably sombre, brooding, and menacing expression. The lustre of inquiring glance faded swiftly into vacant glassiness. 'Can you steer?' I asked the agent eagerly. He looked very dubious; but I made a grab at his arm, and he understood at once I meant him to steer whether or no. To tell you the truth, I was morbidly anxious to change my shoes and socks. 'He is dead,' murmured the fellow, immensely impressed. 'No doubt about it,' said I, tugging like mad at the shoe-laces. 'And by the way, I suppose Mr Kurtz is dead as well by this time.'

"For the moment that was the dominant thought. There was a sense of extreme disappointment, as though I had found out I had been striving after something altogether without a substance. I couldn't have been more disgusted if I had travelled all this way for the sole purpose of talking with Mr Kurtz. Talking with . . . I flung one shoe overboard, and became aware that that was exactly what I had been looking forward to—a talk with Kurtz. I made the strange discovery that I had never imagined him as doing, you know, but as discoursing. I didn't say to myself, 'Now I will never see him,' or 'Now I will never shake him by the hand,' but, 'Now I will never hear him.' The man presented himself as a voice. Not of course that I did not connect him with some sort of action. Hadn't I been told in all the tones of jealousy and admiration that he had collected, bartered, swindled, or stolen more ivory than all the other agents together? That was not the point. The point was in his being a gifted creature, and that of all his gifts the one that stood out pre-eminently, that carried with it a sense of real presence, was his ability to talk, his words—the gift of expression, the bewildering, the illuminating, the most exalted and the most contemptible, the pulsating stream of light, or the deceitful flow from the heart of an impenetrable darkness.

"The other shoe went flying unto the devil-god of that river. I thought, By Jove! it's all over. We are too late; he has vanished—the gift has vanished, by means of some spear, arrow, or club. I will never hear that chap speak after all—and my sorrow had a startling extravagance of emotion, even such as I had noticed in the howling sorrow of these savages in the bush. I couldn't have felt more of lonely desolation somehow, had I been robbed of a belief or had missed my destiny in life. . . . Why do you sigh in this beastly way, somebody? Absurd? Well, absurd. Good Lord! mustn't a man ever— Here, give me some tobacco." . . .

There was a pause of profound stillness, then a match flared, and Marlow's lean face appeared, worn, hollow, with downward folds and dropped eyelids, with an aspect of concentrated attention; and as he took vigorous draws at his pipe, it seemed to retreat and advance out of the night in the regular flicker of the tiny flame. The match went out.

"Absurd!" he cried. "This is the worst of trying to tell . . . Here you all are, each moored with two good addresses, like a hulk with two anchors, a butcher round one corner, a policeman round another, excellent appetites, and temperature normal—you hear—normal from year's end to year's end. And you say, Absurd! Absurd be—exploded! Absurd! My dear boys, what can you expect from a man who out of sheer nervousness had just flung overboard a pair of new shoes? Now I think of it, it is amazing I did not shed tears. I am, upon the whole, proud of my fortitude. I was cut to the quick at the idea of having lost the inestimable privilege of listening to the gifted Kurtz. Of course I was wrong. The privilege was waiting for me. Oh yes, I heard more than enough. And I was right, too. A voice. He was very little more than a voice. And I heard—him—it—this voice—other voices—all of them were so little more than voices—and the memory of that time itself lingers around me, impalpable, like a dying vibration of one immense jabber, silly, atrocious, sordid, savage, or simply mean, without any kind of sense. Voices, voices— even the girl herself—now—"

He was silent for a long time.

"I laid the ghost of his gifts at last with a lie," he began suddenly. "Girl! What? Did I mention a girl? Oh, she is out of it—completely. They—the women I mean—are out of it—should be out of it. We must help them to stay in that beautiful world of their own, lest ours gets worse. Oh, she had to be out of it. You should have heard the disinterred body of Mr Kurtz saying, 'My Intended.' You would have perceived directly then how completely she was out of it. And the lofty frontal bone of Mr Kurtz! They say the hair goes on growing sometimes, but this—ah—specimen was impressively bald. The wilderness had patted him on the head, and, behold, it was like a ball—an ivory ball; it had caressed him, and—lo!—he had withered; it had taken him, loved him, embraced him, got into his veins, consumed his flesh, and sealed his soul to its own by the inconceivable ceremonies of some devilish initiation. He was its spoiled and pampered favourite. Ivory? I should think so. Heaps of it, stacks of it. The old mud shanty was bursting with it. You would think there was not a single tusk left either above or below the ground in the whole country. 'Mostly fossil,' the manager had remarked disparagingly. It was no more fossil than I am; but they call it fossil when it is dug up. It appears these niggers do bury the tusks sometimes—but evidently they couldn't bury this parcel deep enough to save the gifted Mr Kurtz from his fate. We filled the steamboat with it, and had to pile a lot on the deck. Thus he could see and enjoy as long as he could see, because the appreciation of this favour had remained with him to the last. You should have heard him say, 'My ivory.' Oh yes, I heard him. 'My Intended, my ivory, my station, my river, my—' everything belonged to him. It made me hold my breath in expectation of hearing the wilderness burst into a prodigious peal of laughter that would shake the fixed stars in their places. Everything belonged to him—but that was a trifle. The thing was to know what he belonged to, how many powers of darkness claimed him for their own. That was the reflection that made you creepy all over. It was impossible—it was not good for one either—trying to imagine. He had taken a high seat amongst the devils of the land—I mean literally. You can't understand. How could you?—with solid pavement under your feet, surrounded by kind neighbours ready to cheer you or to fall on you, stepping delicately between the butcher and the policeman, in the holy terror of scandal and gallows and lunatic asylums—how can you imagine what particular region of the first ages a man's untrammelled feet may take him into by the way of solitude—utter solitude without a policeman—by the way of silence—utter silence, where no warning voice of a kind neighbour can be heard whispering of public opinion? These little things make all the great difference. When they are gone you must fall back upon your own innate strength, upon your own capacity for faithfulness. Of course you may be too much of a fool to go wrong—too dull even to know you are being assaulted by the powers of darkness. I take it, no fool ever made a bargain for his soul with the devil: the fool is too much of a fool, or the devil too much of a devil—I don't know which. Or you may be such a thunderingly exalted creature as to be altogether deaf and blind to anything but heavenly sights and sounds. Then the earth for you is only a standing place—and whether to be like this is your loss or your gain I won't pretend to say. But most of us are neither one nor the other. The earth for us is a place to live in, where we must put up with sights, with sounds, with smells, too, by Jove!—breathe dead hippo, so to speak, and not be contaminated. And there, don't you see? your strength comes in, the faith in your ability for the digging of unostentatious holes to bury the stuff in—your power of devotion, not to yourself, but to an obscure, back-breaking business. And that's difficult enough. Mind, I am not trying to excuse or even explain—I am trying to account to myself for—for—Mr Kurtz—for the shade of Mr Kurtz. This initiated wraith from the back of Nowhere honoured me with its amazing confidence before it vanished altogether. This was because it could speak English to me. The original Kurtz had been educated partly in England, and—as he was good enough to say himself—his sympathies were in the right place. His mother was half-English, his father was half-French. All Europe contributed to the making of Kurtz; and by and by I learned that, most appropriately, the International Society for the Suppression of Savage Customs had entrusted him with the making of a report, for its future guidance. And he had written it too. I've seen it. I've read it. It was eloquent, vibrating with eloquence, but too high-strung, I think. Seventeen pages of close writing he had found time for! But this must have been before his—let us say—nerves went wrong, and caused him to preside at certain midnight dances ending with unspeakable rites, which—as far as I reluctantly gathered from what I heard at various times—were offered up to him—do you understand?—to Mr Kurtz himself. But it was a beautiful piece of writing. The opening paragraph, however, in the light of later information, strikes me now as ominous. He began with the argument that we whites, from the point of development we had arrived at, 'must necessarily appear to them [savages] in the nature of supernatural beings—we approach them with the might as of a deity,' and so on, and so on. 'By the simple exercise of our will we can exert a power for good practically unbounded,' etc. etc. From that point he soared and took me with him. The peroration was magnificent, though difficult to remember, you know. It gave me the notion of an exotic Immensity ruled by an august Benevolence. It made me tingle with enthusiasm. This was the unbounded power of eloquence—of words—of burning noble words. There were no practical hints to interrupt the magic current of phrases, unless a kind of note at the foot of the last page, scrawled evidently much later, in an unsteady hand, may be regarded as the exposition of a method. It was very simple, and at the end of that moving appeal to every altruistic sentiment it blazed at you, luminous and terrifying, like a flash of lightning in a serene sky: 'Exterminate all the brutes!' The curious part was that he had apparently forgotten all about that valuable postscriptum, because, later on, when he in a sense came to himself, he repeatedly entreated me to take good care of 'my pamphlet' (he called it), as it was sure to have in the future a good influence upon his career. I had full information about all these things, and, besides, as it turned out, I was to have the care of his memory. I've done enough for it to give me the indisputable right to lay it, if I choose, for an everlasting rest in the dust-bin of progress, amongst all the sweepings and, figuratively speaking, all the dead cats of civilisation. But then, you see, I can't choose. He won't be forgotten. Whatever he was, he was not common. He had the power to charm or frighten rudimentary souls into an aggravated witchdance in his honour; he could also fill the small souls of the pilgrims with bitter misgivings: he had one devoted friend at least, and he had conquered one soul in the world that was neither rudimentary nor tainted with self-seeking. No; I can't forget him, though I am not prepared to affirm the fellow was exactly worth the life we lost in getting to him. I missed my late helmsman awfully—I missed him even while his body was still lying in the pilot-house. Perhaps you will think it passing strange this regret for a savage who was no more account than a grain of sand in a black Sahara. Well, don't you see, he had done something, he had steered; for months I had him at my back—a help—an instrument. It was a kind of partnership. He steered for me—I had to look after him, I worried about his deficiencies, and thus a subtle bond had been created, of which I only became aware when it was suddenly broken. And the intimate profundity of that look he gave me when he received his hurt remains to this day in my memory—like a claim of distant kinship affirmed in a supreme moment.

"Poor fool! If he had only left that shutter alone. He had no restraint, no restraint—just like Kurtz—a tree swayed by the wind. As soon as I had put on a dry pair of slippers, I dragged him out, after first jerking the spear out of his side, which operation I confess I performed with my eyes shut tight. His heels leaped together over the little doorstep; his shoulders were pressed to my breast; I hugged him from behind desperately. Oh! he was heavy, heavy; heavier than any man on earth, I should imagine. Then without more ado I tipped him overboard. The current snatched him as though he had been a wisp of grass, and I saw the body roll over twice before I lost sight of it for ever. All the pilgrims and the manager were then congregated on the awning-deck about the pilot-house, chattering at each other like a flock of excited magpies, and there was a scandalised murmur at my heart-less promptitude. What they wanted to keep that body hanging about for I can't guess. Embalm it, maybe. But I had also heard another, and a very ominous, murmur on the deck below. My friends the wood-cutters were likewise scandalised, and with a better show of reason—though I admit that the reason itself was quite inadmissible. Oh, quite! I had made up my mind that if my late helmsman was to be eaten, the fishes alone should have him. He had been a very second-rate helmsman while alive, but now he was dead he might have become a first-class temptation, and possibly cause some startling trouble. Besides, I was anxious to take the wheel, the man in pink pyjamas showing himself a hopeless duffer at the business.

"This I did directly the simple funeral was over. We were going half-speed, keeping right in the middle of the stream, and I listened to the talk about me. They had given up Kurtz, they had given up the station; Kurtz was dead, and the station had been burnt—and so on—and so on. The red-haired pilgrim was beside himself with the thought that at least this poor Kurtz had been properly revenged. 'Say! We must have made a glorious slaughter of them in the bush. Eh? What do you think? Say?' He positively danced, the bloodthirsty little gingery beggar.[2] And he had nearly fainted when he saw the wounded man! I could not help saying, 'You made a glorious lot of smoke, anyhow.' I had seen, from the way the tops of the bushes rustled and flew, that almost all the shots had gone too high. You can't hit anything unless you take aim and fire from the shoulder; but these chaps fired from the hip with their eyes shut. The retreat, I maintained—and I was right—was caused by the screeching of the steam-whistle. Upon this they forgot Kurtz, and began to howl at me with indignant protests.

"The manager stood by the wheel murmuring confidentially about the necessity of getting well away down the river before dark at all events, when I saw in the distance a clearing on the river-side and the outlines of some sort of building. 'What's this?' I asked. He clapped his hands in wonder. 'The station!' he cried. I edged in at once, still going half-speed.

"Through my glasses I saw the slope of a hill interspersed with rare trees and perfectly free from undergrowth. A long decaying building on the summit was half buried in the high grass; the large holes in the peaked roof gaped black from afar; the jungle and the woods made a background. There was no enclosure or fence of any kind; but there had been one apparently, for near the house half a dozen slim posts remained in a row, roughly trimmed, and with their upper ends ornamented with round carved balls. The rails, or whatever there had been between, had disappeared. Of course the forest surrounded all that. The river-bank was clear, and on the water side I saw a white man under a hat like a cart-wheel beckoning persistently with his whole arm. Examining the edge of the forest above and below, I was almost certain I could see movements—human forms gliding here and there. I steamed past prudently, then stopped the engines and let her drift down. The man on the shore began to shout, urging us to land. 'We have been attacked,' screamed the manager. 'I know—I know. It's all right,' yelled back the other, as cheerful as you please. 'Come along. It's all right. I am glad.'

"His aspect reminded me of something I had seen—something funny I had seen somewhere. As I manœuvred to get alongside, I was asking myself,

2. Little redheaded rascal.

'What does this fellow look like?' Suddenly I got it. He looked like a harlequin.[3] His clothes had been made of some stuff that was brown holland[4] probably, but it was covered with patches all over, with bright patches, blue, red, and yellow—patches on the back, patches on the front, patches on elbows, on knees; coloured binding round his jacket, scarlet edging at the bottom of his trousers; and the sunshine made him look extremely gay and wonderfully neat withal, because you could see how beautifully all this patching had been done. A beardless, boyish face, very fair, no features to speak of, nose peeling, little blue eyes, smiles and frowns chasing each other over that open countenance like sunshine and shadow on a wind-swept plain. 'Look out, captain!' he cried; 'there's a snag lodged in here last night.' What! Another snag? I confess I swore shamefully. I had nearly holed my cripple, to finish off that charming trip. The harlequin on the bank turned his little pug nose up to me. 'You English?' he asked, all smiles. 'Are you?' I shouted from the wheel. The smiles vanished, and he shook his head as if sorry for my disappointment. Then he brightened up. 'Never mind!' he cried encouragingly. 'Are we in time?' I asked. 'He is up there,' he replied, with a toss of the head up the hill, and becoming gloomy all of a sudden. His face was like the autumn sky, overcast one moment and bright the next.

"When the manager, escorted by the pilgrims, all of them armed to the teeth, had gone to the house, this chap came on board. 'I say, I don't like this. These natives are in the bush,' I said. He assured me earnestly it was all right. 'They are simple people,' he added; 'well, I am glad you came. It took me all my time to keep them off.' 'But you said it was all right,' I cried. 'Oh, they meant no harm,' he said; and as I stared he corrected himself, 'Not exactly.' Then vivaciously, 'My faith, your pilot-house wants a clean up!' In the next breath he advised me to keep enough steam on the boiler to blow the whistle in case of any trouble. 'One good screech will do more for you than all your rifles. They are simple people,' he repeated. He rattled away at such a rate he quite overwhelmed me. He seemed to be trying to make up for lots of silence, and actually hinted, laughing, that such was the case. 'Don't you talk with Mr Kurtz?' I said. 'You don't talk with that man—you listen to him,' he exclaimed with severe exaltation. 'But now—' He waved his arm, and in the twinkling of an eye was in the uttermost depths of despondency. In a moment he came up again with a jump, possessed himself of both my hands, shook them continuously, while he gabbled: 'Brother sailor . . . honour . . . pleasure . . . delight . . . introduce myself . . . Russian . . . son of an arch-priest . . . Government of Tambov . . . What? Tobacco! English tobacco; the excellent English tobacco! Now, that's brotherly. Smoke? Where's a sailor that does not smoke?'

"The pipe soothed him, and gradually I made out he had run away from school, had gone to sea in a Russian ship; ran away again; served some time in English ships; was now reconciled with the arch-priest. He made a point of that. 'But when one is young one must see things, gather experience, ideas; enlarge the mind.' 'Here!' I interrupted. 'You can never tell! Here I met Mr Kurtz,' he said, youthfully solemn and reproachful. I held my tongue after that. It appears he had persuaded a Dutch trading-house on the coast to fit him out with stores and goods, and had started for the interior with a

---

3. Character from Italian comedy traditionally dressed in multicolored clothes.

4. Coarse linen fabric.

light heart, and no more idea of what would happen to him than a baby. He had been wandering about that river for nearly two years alone, cut off from everybody and everything. 'I am not so young as I look. I am twenty-five,' he said. 'At first old Van Shuyten would tell me to go to the devil,' he narrated with keen enjoyment; 'but I stuck to him, and talked and talked, till at last he got afraid I would talk the hind-leg off his favourite dog, so he gave me some cheap things and a few guns, and told me he hoped he would never see my face again. Good old Dutchman, Van Shuyten. I sent him one small lot of ivory a year ago, so that he can't call me a little thief when I get back. I hope he got it. And for the rest I don't care. I had some wood stacked for you. That was my old house. Did you see?'

"I gave him Towson's book. He made as though he would kiss me, but restrained himself. 'The only book I had left, and I thought I had lost it,' he said, looking at it ecstatically. 'So many accidents happen to a man going about alone, you know. Canoes get upset sometimes—and sometimes you've got to clear out so quick when the people get angry.' He thumbed the pages. 'You made notes in Russian?' I asked. He nodded. 'I thought they were written in cipher,' I said. He laughed, then became serious. 'I had lots of trouble to keep these people off,' he said. 'Did they want to kill you?' I asked. 'Oh no!' he cried, and checked himself. 'Why did they attack us?' I pursued. He hesitated, then said shamefacedly, 'They don't want him to go.' 'Don't they?' I said curiously. He nodded a nod full of mystery and wisdom. 'I tell you,' he cried, 'this man has enlarged my mind.' He opened his arms wide, staring at me with his little blue eyes that were perfectly round."

3

"I looked at him, lost in astonishment. There he was before me, in motley, as though he had absconded from a troupe of mimes, enthusiastic, fabulous. His very existence was improbable, inexplicable, and altogether bewildering. He was an insoluble problem. It was inconceivable how he had existed, how he had succeeded in getting so far, how he had managed to remain—why he did not instantly disappear. 'I went a little farther,' he said, 'then still a little farther—till I had gone so far that I don't know how I'll ever get back. Never mind. Plenty time. I can manage. You take Kurtz away quick—quick—I tell you.' The glamour of youth enveloped his particoloured rags, his destitution, his loneliness, the essential desolation of his futile wanderings. For months—for years—his life hadn't been worth a day's purchase; and there he was gallantly, thoughtlessly alive, to all appearance indestructible solely by the virtue of his few years and of his unreflecting audacity. I was seduced into something like admiration—like envy. Glamour urged him on, glamour kept him unscathed. He surely wanted nothing from the wilderness but space to breathe in and to push on through. His need was to exist, and to move onwards at the greatest possible risk, and with a maximum of privation. If the absolutely pure, uncalculating, unpractical spirit of adventure had ever ruled a human being, it ruled this be-patched youth. I almost envied him the possession of this modest and clear flame. It seemed to have consumed all thought of self so completely, that, even while he was talking to you, you forgot that it was he—the man before your eyes—who had gone through these things. I did not envy him his devotion to Kurtz, though. He had not meditated over it. It came to him, and he accepted it with a sort of eager fatalism. I must say that to me it appeared about the most dangerous thing in every way he had come upon so far.

"They had come together unavoidably, like two ships becalmed near each other, and lay rubbing sides at last. I suppose Kurtz wanted an audience, because on a certain occasion, when encamped in the forest, they had talked all night, or more probably Kurtz had talked. 'We talked of everything,' he said, quite transported at the recollection. 'I forgot there was such a thing as sleep. The night did not seem to last an hour. Everything! Everything! . . . Of love too.' 'Ah, he talked to you of love!' I said, much amused. 'It isn't what you think,' he cried, almost passionately. 'It was in general. He made me see things—things.'

"He threw his arms up. We were on deck at the time, and the head-man of my wood-cutters, lounging near by, turned upon him his heavy and glittering eyes. I looked around, and I don't know why, but I assure you that never, never before, did this land, this river, this jungle, the very arch of this blazing sky, appear to me so hopeless and so dark, so impenetrable to human thought, so pitiless to human weakness. 'And, ever since, you have been with him, of course?' I said.

"On the contrary. It appears their intercourse had been very much broken by various causes. He had, as he informed me proudly, managed to nurse Kurtz through two illnesses (he alluded to it as you would to some risky feat), but as a rule Kurtz wandered alone, far in the depths of the forest. 'Very often coming to this station, I had to wait days and days before he would turn up,' he said. 'Ah, it was worth waiting for!—sometimes.' 'What was he doing? exploring or what?' I asked. 'Oh yes, of course'; he had discovered lots of villages, a lake too—he did not know exactly in what direction; it was dangerous to inquire too much—but mostly his expeditions had been for ivory. 'But he had no goods to trade with by that time,' I objected. 'There's a good lot of cartridges left even yet,' he answered, looking away. 'To speak plainly, he raided the country,' I said. He nodded. 'Not alone, surely!' He muttered something about the villages round that lake. 'Kurtz got the tribe to follow him, did he?' I suggested. He fidgeted a little. 'They adored him,' he said. The tone of these words was so extraordinary that I looked at him searchingly. It was curious to see his mingled eagerness and reluctance to speak of Kurtz. The man filled his life, occupied his thoughts, swayed his emotions. 'What can you expect?' he burst out; 'he came to them with thunder and lightning, you know—and they had never seen anything like it—and very terrible. He could be very terrible. You can't judge Mr Kurtz as you would an ordinary man. No, no, no! Now—just to give you an idea—I don't mind telling you, he wanted to shoot me too one day—but I don't judge him.' 'Shoot you!' I cried. 'What for?' 'Well, I had a small lot of ivory the chief of that village near my house gave me. You see I used to shoot game for them. Well, he wanted it, and wouldn't hear reason. He declared he would shoot me unless I gave him the ivory and then cleared out of the country, because he could do so, and had a fancy for it, and there was nothing on earth to prevent him killing whom he jolly well pleased. And it was true too. I gave him the ivory. What did I care! But I didn't clear out. No, no. I couldn't leave him. I had to be careful, of course, till we got friendly again for a time. He had his second illness then. Afterwards I had to keep out of the way; but I didn't mind. He was living for the most part in those villages on the lake. When he came down to the river, sometimes he would take to me, and sometimes it was better for me to be careful. This man suffered too much. He hated all this, and somehow he couldn't get away. When I had a chance I begged him to try and leave while there was time; I offered to go back with him. And he would say yes, and then he would remain; go off on another ivory hunt; disappear for weeks; forget himself amongst these people— forget himself—you know.' 'Why! he's mad,' I said. He protested indignantly. Mr Kurtz couldn't be mad. If I had heard him talk, only two days ago, I wouldn't dare hint at such a thing. . . . I had taken up my binoculars while we talked, and was looking at the shore, sweeping the limit of the forest at each side and at the back of the house. The consciousness of there being people in that bush, so silent, so quiet—as silent and quiet as the ruined house on the hill—made me uneasy. There was no sign on the face of nature of this amazing tale that was not so much told as suggested to me in desolate exclamations, completed by shrugs, in interrupted phrases, in hints ending in deep sighs. The woods were unmoved, like a mask—heavy, like the closed door of a prison—they looked with their air of hidden knowledge, of patient expectation, of unapproachable silence. The Russian was explaining to me that it was only lately that Mr Kurtz had come down to the river, bringing along with him all the fighting men of that lake tribe. He had been absent for several months—getting himself adored, I suppose—and had come down unexpectedly, with the intention to all appearance of making a raid either across the river or down stream. Evidently the appetite for more ivory had got the better of the—what shall I say?—less material aspirations. However, he had got much worse suddenly. 'I heard he was lying helpless, and so I came up—took my chance,' said the Russian. 'Oh, he is bad, very bad.' I directed my glass to the house. There were no signs of life, but there was the ruined roof, the long mud wall peeping above the grass, with three little square window-holes, no two of the same size; all this brought within reach of my hand, as it were. And then I made a brusque movement, and one of the remaining posts of that vanished fence leaped up in the field of my glass. You remember I told you I had been struck at the distance by certain attempts at ornamentation, rather remarkable in the ruinous aspect of the place. Now I had suddenly a nearer view, and its first result was to make me throw my head back as if before a blow. Then I went carefully from post to post with my glass, and I saw my mistake. These round knobs were not ornamental but symbolic; they were expressive and puzzling, striking and disturbing—food for thought and also for the vultures if there had been any looking down from the sky; but at all events for such ants as were industri- ous enough to ascend the pole. They would have been even more impressive, those heads on the stakes, if their faces had not been turned to the house. Only one, the first I had made out, was facing my way. I was not so shocked as you may think. The start back I had given was really nothing but a move- ment of surprise. I had expected to see a knob of wood there, you know. I returned deliberately to the first I had seen—and there it was, black, dried, sunken, with closed eyelids—a head that seemed to sleep at the top of that pole, and, with the shrunken dry lips showing a narrow white line of the teeth, was smiling too, smiling continuously at some endless and jocose dream of that eternal slumber.

"I am not disclosing any trade secrets. In fact the manager said after- wards that Mr Kurtz's methods had ruined the district. I have no opinion on that point, but I want you clearly to understand that there was nothing exactly profitable in these heads being there. They only show that Mr Kurtz lacked restraint in the gratification of his various lusts, that there was something wanting in him—some small matter which, when the pressing need arose, could not be found under his magnificent eloquence. Whether he knew of this deficiency himself I can't say. I think the knowledge came to him at last—only at the very last. But the wilderness had found him out early, and had taken on him a terrible vengeance for the fantastic invasion. I think it had whispered to him things about himself which he did not know, things of which he had no conception till he took counsel with this great solitude—and the whisper had proved irresistibly fascinating. It echoed loudly within him because he was hollow at the core. . . . I put down the glass, and the head that had appeared near enough to be spoken to seemed at once to have leaped away from me into inaccessible distance.

"The admirer of Mr Kurtz was a bit crestfallen. In a hurried, indistinct voice he began to assure me he had not dared to take these—say, symbols—down. He was not afraid of the natives; they would not stir till Mr Kurtz gave the word. His ascendancy was extraordinary. The camps of these people surrounded the place, and the chiefs came every day to see him. They would crawl . . . 'I don't want to know anything of the ceremonies used when approaching Mr Kurtz,' I shouted. Curious, this feeling that came over me that such details would be more intolerable than those heads drying on the stakes under Mr Kurtz's windows. After all, that was only a savage sight, while I seemed at one bound to have been transported into some lightless region of subtle horrors, where pure, uncomplicated savagery was a positive relief, being something that had a right to exist—obviously—in the sunshine. The young man looked at me with surprise. I suppose it did not occur to him that Mr Kurtz was no idol of mine. He forgot I hadn't heard any of these splendid monologues on, what was it? on love, justice, conduct of life—or what not. If it had come to crawling before Mr Kurtz, he crawled as much as the veriest savage of them all. I had no idea of the conditions, he said: these heads were the heads of rebels. I shocked him excessively by laughing. Rebels! What would be the next definition I was to hear? There had been enemies, criminals, workers—and these were rebels. Those rebellious heads looked very subdued to me on their sticks. 'You don't know how such a life tries a man like Kurtz,' cried Kurtz's last disciple. 'Well, and you?' I said. 'I! I! I am a simple man. I have no great thoughts. I want nothing from anybody. How can you compare me to . . . ?' His feelings were too much for speech, and suddenly he broke down. 'I don't understand,' he groaned. 'I've been doing my best to keep him alive, and that's enough. I had no hand in all this. I have no abilities. There hasn't been a drop of medicine or a mouthful of invalid food for months here. He was shamefully abandoned. A man like this, with such ideas. Shamefully! Shamefully! I—I—haven't slept for the last ten nights. . . .'

"His voice lost itself in the calm of the evening. The long shadows of the forest had slipped down hill while we talked, had gone far beyond the ruined hovel, beyond the symbolic row of stakes. All this was in the gloom, while we down there were yet in the sunshine, and the stretch of the river abreast of the clearing glittered in a still and dazzling splendour, with a murky and overshadowed bend above and below. Not a living soul was seen on the shore. The bushes did not rustle.

"Suddenly round the corner of the house a group of men appeared, as though they had come up from the ground. They waded waist-deep in the grass, in a compact body, bearing an improvised stretcher in their midst.

Instantly, in the emptiness of the landscape, a cry arose whose shrillness pierced the still air like a sharp arrow flying straight to the very heart of the land; and, as if by enchantment, streams of human beings—of naked human beings—with spears in their hands, with bows, with shields, with wild glances and savage movements, were poured into the clearing by the dark-faced and pensive forest. The bushes shook, the grass swayed for a time, and then everything stood still in attentive immobility.

"'Now, if he does not say the right thing to them we are all done for,' said the Russian at my elbow. The knot of men with the stretcher had stopped too, half-way to the steamer, as if petrified. I saw the man on the stretcher sit up, lank and with an uplifted arm, above the shoulders of the bearers. 'Let us hope that the man who can talk so well of love in general will find some particular reason to spare us this time,' I said. I resented bitterly the absurd danger of our situation, as if to be at the mercy of that atrocious phantom had been a dishonouring necessity. I could not hear a sound, but through my glasses I saw the thin arm extended commandingly, the lower jaw moving, the eyes of that apparition shining darkly far in its bony head that nodded with grotesque jerks. Kurtz—Kurtz—that means 'short' in German—don't it? Well, the name was as true as everything else in his life—and death. He looked at least seven feet long. His covering had fallen off, and his body emerged from it pitiful and appalling as from a winding-sheet. I could see the cage of his ribs all astir, the bones of his arm waving. It was as though an animated image of death carved out of old ivory had been shaking its hand with menaces at a motionless crowd of men made of dark and glittering bronze. I saw him open his mouth wide—it gave him a weirdly voracious aspect, as though he had wanted to swallow all the air, all the earth, all the men before him. A deep voice reached me faintly. He must have been shouting. He fell back suddenly. The stretcher shook as the bearers staggered forward again, and almost at the same time I noticed that the crowd of savages was vanishing without any perceptible movement of retreat, as if the forest that had ejected these beings so suddenly had drawn them in again as the breath is drawn in a long aspiration.

"Some of the pilgrims behind the stretcher carried his arms—two shotguns, a heavy rifle, and a light revolver-carbine—the thunderbolts of that pitiful Jupiter. The manager bent over him murmuring as he walked beside his head. They laid him down in one of the little cabins—just a room for a bedplace and a camp-stool or two, you know. We had brought his belated correspondence, and a lot of torn envelopes and open letters littered his bed. His hand roamed feebly amongst these papers. I was struck by the fire of his eyes and the composed languor of his expression. It was not so much the exhaustion of disease. He did not seem in pain. This shadow looked satiated and calm, as though for the moment it had had its fill of all the emotions.

"He rustled one of the letters, and looking straight in my face said, 'I am glad.' Somebody had been writing to him about me. These special recommendations were turning up again. The volume of tone he emitted without effort, almost without the trouble of moving his lips, amazed me. A voice! a voice! It was grave, profound, vibrating, while the man did not seem capable of a whisper. However, he had enough strength in him—factitious no doubt—to very nearly make an end of us, as you shall hear directly.

"The manager appeared silently in the doorway; I stepped out at once and he drew the curtain after me. The Russian, eyed curiously by the pilgrims, was staring at the shore. I followed the direction of his glance.

"Dark human shapes could be made out in the distance, flitting indistinctly against the gloomy border of the forest, and near the river two bronze figures, leaning on tall spears, stood in the sunlight under fantastic head-dresses of spotted skins, warlike and still in statuesque repose. And from right to left along the lighted shore moved a wild and gorgeous apparition of a woman.

"She walked with measured steps, draped in striped and fringed cloths, treading the earth proudly, with a slight jingle and flash of barbarous ornaments. She carried her head high; her hair was done in the shape of a helmet; she had brass leggings to the knee, brass wire gauntlets to the elbow, a crimson spot on her tawny cheek, innumerable necklaces of glass beads on her neck; bizarre things, charms, gifts of witch-men, that hung about her, glittered and trembled at every step. She must have had the value of several elephant tusks upon her. She was savage and superb, wild-eyed and magnificent; there was something ominous and stately in her deliberate progress. And in the hush that had fallen suddenly upon the whole sorrowful land, the immense wilderness, the colossal body of the fecund and mysterious life seemed to look at her, pensive, as though it had been looking at the image of its own tenebrous and passionate soul.

"She came abreast of the steamer, stood still, and faced us. Her long shadow fell to the water's edge. Her face had a tragic and fierce aspect of wild sorrow and of dumb pain mingled with the fear of some struggling, half-shaped resolve. She stood looking at us without a stir, and like the wilderness itself, with an air of brooding over an inscrutable purpose. A whole minute passed, and then she made a step forward. There was a low jingle, a glint of yellow metal, a sway of fringed draperies, and she stopped as if her heart had failed her. The young fellow by my side growled. The pilgrims murmured at my back. She looked at us all as if her life had depended upon the unswerving steadiness of her glance. Suddenly she opened her bared arms and threw them up rigid above her head, as though in an uncontrollable desire to touch the sky, and at the same time the swift shadows darted out on the earth, swept around on the river, gathering the steamer into a shadowy embrace. A formidable silence hung over the scene.

"She turned away slowly, walked on, following the bank, and passed into the bushes to the left. Once only her eyes gleamed back at us in the dusk of the thickets before she disappeared.

"'If she had offered to come aboard I really think I would have tried to shoot her,' said the man of patches nervously. 'I had been risking my life every day for the last fortnight to keep her out of the house. She got in one day and kicked up a row about those miserable rags I picked up in the storeroom to mend my clothes with. I wasn't decent. At least it must have been that, for she talked like a fury to Kurtz for an hour, pointing at me now and then. I don't understand the dialect of this tribe. Luckily for me, I fancy Kurtz felt too ill that day to care, or there would have been mischief. I don't understand. . . . No—it's too much for me. Ah, well, it's all over now.'

"At this moment I heard Kurtz's deep voice behind the curtain: 'Save me!—save the ivory, you mean. Don't tell me. Save *me*! Why, I've had to save you. You are interrupting my plans now. Sick! Sick! Not so sick as you would like to believe. Never mind. I'll carry my ideas out yet—I will return. I'll show you what can be done. You with your little peddling notions—you are interfering with me. I will return. I . . .'

"The manager came out. He did me the honour to take me under the arm and lead me aside. 'He is very low, very low,' he said. He considered it necessary to sigh, but neglected to be consistently sorrowful. 'We have done all we could for him—haven't we? But there is no disguising the fact, Mr Kurtz has done more harm than good to the Company. He did not see the time was not ripe for vigorous action. Cautiously, cautiously—that's my principle. We must be cautious yet. The district is closed to us for a time. Deplorable! Upon the whole, the trade will suffer. I don't deny there is a remarkable quantity of ivory—mostly fossil. We must save it, at all events—but look how precarious the position is—and why? Because the method is unsound.' 'Do you,' said I, looking at the shore, 'call it "unsound method"?' 'Without doubt,' he exclaimed hotly, 'Don't you?' . . . 'No method at all,' I murmured after a while. 'Exactly,' he exulted. 'I anticipated this. Shows a complete want of judgment. It is my duty to point it out in the proper quarter.' 'Oh,' said I, 'that fellow—what's his name?—the brickmaker, will make a readable report for you.' He appeared confounded for a moment. It seemed to me I had never breathed an atmosphere so vile, and I turned mentally to Kurtz for relief—positively for relief. 'Nevertheless, I think Mr Kurtz is a remarkable man,' I said with emphasis. He started, dropped on me a cold heavy glance, said very quietly, 'He *was*,' and turned his back on me. My hour of favour was over; I found myself lumped along with Kurtz as a partisan of methods for which the time was not ripe: I was unsound! Ah! but it was something to have at least a choice of nightmares.

"I had turned to the wilderness really, not to Mr Kurtz, who, I was ready to admit, was as good as buried. And for a moment it seemed to me as if I also were buried in a vast grave full of unspeakable secrets. I felt an intolerable weight oppressing my breast, the smell of the damp earth, the unseen presence of victorious corruption, the darkness of an impenetrable night. . . . The Russian tapped me on the shoulder. I heard him mumbling and stammering something about 'brother seaman—couldn't conceal—knowledge of matters that would affect Mr Kurtz's reputation.' I waited. For him evidently Mr Kurtz was not in his grave; I suspect that for him Mr Kurtz was one of the immortals. 'Well!' said I at last, 'speak out. As it happens, I am Mr Kurtz's friend—in a way.'

"He stated with a good deal of formality that had we not been 'of the same profession,' he would have kept the matter to himself without regard to consequences. He suspected 'there was an active ill-will towards him on the part of these white men that—' 'You are right,' I said, remembering a certain conversation I had overheard. 'The manager thinks you ought to be hanged.' He showed a concern at this intelligence which amused me at first. 'I had better get out of the way quietly,' he said earnestly. 'I can do no more for Kurtz now, and they would soon find some excuse. What's to stop them? There's a military post three hundred miles from here.' 'Well, upon my word,' said I, 'perhaps you had better go if you have any friends amongst the savages near by.' 'Plenty,' he said. 'They are simple people—and I want nothing, you know.' He stood biting his lip, then: 'I don't want any harm to happen to these whites here, but of course I was thinking of Mr Kurtz's reputation—but you are a brother seaman and—' 'All right,' said I, after a time. 'Mr Kurtz's reputation is safe with me.' I did not know how truly I spoke.

"He informed me, lowering his voice, that it was Kurtz who had ordered the attack to be made on the steamer. 'He hated sometimes the idea of being taken away—and then again . . . But I don't understand these matters. I am a simple man. He thought it would scare you away—that you would give it up, thinking him dead. I could not stop him. Oh, I had an awful time of it this last month.' 'Very well,' I said. 'He is all right now.' 'Ye-e-es,' he muttered, not very convinced apparently. 'Thanks,' said I; 'I shall keep my eyes open.' 'But quiet—eh?' he urged anxiously. 'It would be awful for his reputation if anybody here—' I promised a complete discretion with great gravity. 'I have a canoe and three black fellows waiting not very far. I am off. Could you give me a few Martini-Henry cartridges?' I could, and did, with proper secrecy. He helped himself, with a wink at me, to a handful of my tobacco. 'Between sailors—you know—good English tobacco.' At the door of the pilot-house he turned round—'I say, haven't you a pair of shoes you could spare?' He raised one leg. 'Look.' The soles were tied with knotted strings sandal-wise under his bare feet. I rooted out an old pair, at which he looked with admiration before tucking it under his left arm. One of his pockets (bright red) was bulging with cartridges, from the other (dark blue) peeped 'Towson's Inquiry,' etc. etc. He seemed to think himself excellently well equipped for a renewed encounter with the wilderness. 'Ah! I'll never, never meet such a man again. You ought to have heard him recite poetry—his own too it was, he told me. Poetry!' He rolled his eyes at the recollection of these delights. 'Oh, he enlarged my mind!' 'Good-bye,' said I. He shook hands and vanished in the night. Sometimes I ask myself whether I had ever really seen him—whether it was possible to meet such a phenomenon! . . .

"When I woke up shortly after midnight his warning came to my mind with its hint of danger that seemed, in the starred darkness, real enough to make me get up for the purpose of having a look round. On the hill a big fire burned, illuminating fitfully a crooked corner of the station-house. One of the agents with a picket of a few of our blacks, armed for the purpose, was keeping guard over the ivory; but deep within the forest, red gleams that wavered, that seemed to sink and rise from the ground amongst confused columnar shapes of intense blackness, showed the exact position of the camp where Mr Kurtz's adorers were keeping their uneasy vigil. The monotonous beating of a big drum filled the air with muffled shocks and a lingering vibration. A steady droning sound of many men chanting each to himself some weird incantation came out from the black, flat wall of the woods as the humming of bees comes out of a hive, and had a strange narcotic effect upon my half-awake senses. I believe I dozed off leaning over the rail, till an abrupt burst of yells, an overwhelming outbreak of a pent-up and mysterious frenzy, woke me up in a bewildered wonder. It was cut short all at once, and the low droning went on with an effect of audible and soothing silence. I glanced casually into the little cabin. A light was burning within, but Mr Kurtz was not there.

"I think I would have raised an outcry if I had believed my eyes. But I didn't believe them at first—the thing seemed so impossible. The fact is I was completely unnerved by a sheer blank fright, pure abstract terror, unconnected with any distinct shape of physical danger. What made this emotion so overpowering was—how shall I define it?—the moral shock I received, as if something altogether monstrous, intolerable to thought and odious to the soul, had been thrust upon me unexpectedly. This lasted of course the merest fraction of a second, and then the usual sense of commonplace, deadly danger, the possibility of a sudden onslaught and massacre, or something of the kind, which I saw impending, was positively welcome and composing. It pacified me, in fact, so much, that I did not raise an alarm.

"There was an agent buttoned up inside an ulster[5] and sleeping on a chair on deck within three feet of me. The yells had not awakened him; he snored very slightly; I left him to his slumbers and leaped ashore. I did not betray Mr Kurtz—it was ordered I should never betray him—it was written I should be loyal to the nightmare of my choice. I was anxious to deal with this shadow by myself alone—and to this day I don't know why I was so jealous of sharing with any one the peculiar blackness of that experience.

"As soon as I got on the bank I saw a trail—a broad trail through the grass. I remember the exultation with which I said to myself, 'He can't walk—he is crawling on all-fours—I've got him.' The grass was wet with dew. I strode rapidly with clenched fists. I fancy I had some vague notion of falling upon him and giving him a drubbing. I don't know. I had some imbecile thoughts. The knitting old woman with the cat obtruded herself upon my memory as a most improper person to be sitting at the other end of such an affair. I saw a row of pilgrims squirting lead in the air out of Winchesters held to the hip. I thought I would never get back to the steamer, and imagined myself living alone and unarmed in the woods to an advanced age. Such silly things—you know. And I remember I confounded the beat of the drum with the beating of my heart, and was pleased at its calm regularity.

"I kept to the track though—then stopped to listen. The night was very clear; a dark blue space, sparkling with dew and starlight, in which black things stood very still. I thought I could see a kind of motion ahead of me. I was strangely cocksure of everything that night. I actually left the track and ran in a wide semicircle (I verily believe chuckling to myself) so as to get in front of that stir, of that motion I had seen—if indeed I had seen anything. I was circumventing Kurtz as though it had been a boyish game.

"I came upon him, and, if he had not heard me coming, I would have fallen over him too, but he got up in time. He rose, unsteady, long, pale, indistinct, like a vapour exhaled by the earth, and swayed slightly, misty and silent before me; while at my back the fires loomed between the trees, and the murmur of many voices issued from the forest. I had cut him off cleverly; but when actually confronting him I seemed to come to my senses, I saw the danger in its right proportion. It was by no means over yet. Suppose he began to shout? Though he could hardly stand, there was still plenty of vigour in his voice. 'Go away—hide yourself,' he said, in that profound tone. It was very awful. I glanced back. We were within thirty yards of the nearest fire. A black figure stood up, strode on long black legs, waving long black arms, across the glow. It had horns—antelope horns, I think—on its head. Some sorcerer, some witch-man no doubt: it looked fiend-like enough. 'Do you know what you are doing?' I whispered. 'Perfectly,' he answered, raising his voice for that single word: it sounded to me far off and yet loud, like a hail through a speaking-trumpet. If he makes a row we are lost, I thought to myself. This clearly was not a case for fisticuffs, even apart from the very natural aversion I had to beat that Shadow— this wandering and tormented thing. 'You will be lost,' I said—'utterly lost.' One gets sometimes such a flash of inspiration, you know. I did say the

5. Long overcoat.

right thing, though indeed he could not have been more irretrievably lost than he was at this very moment, when the foundations of our intimacy were being laid—to endure—to endure—even to the end—even beyond.

"'I had immense plans,' he muttered irresolutely. 'Yes,' said I; 'but if you try to shout I'll smash your head with—' There was not a stick or a stone near. 'I will throttle you for good,' I corrected myself. 'I was on the threshold of great things,' he pleaded, in a voice of longing, with a wistfulness of tone that made my blood run cold. 'And now for this stupid scoundrel—' 'Your success in Europe is assured in any case,' I affirmed steadily. I did not want to have the throttling of him, you understand—and indeed it would have been very little use for any practical purpose. I tried to break the spell—the heavy, mute spell of the wilderness—that seemed to draw him to its pitiless breast by the awakening of forgotten and brutal instincts, by the memory of gratified and monstrous passions. This alone, I was convinced, had driven him out to the edge of the forest, to the bush, towards the gleam of fires, the throb of drums, the drone of weird incantations; this alone had beguiled his unlawful soul beyond the bounds of permitted aspirations. And, don't you see, the terror of the position was not in being knocked on the head—though I had a very lively sense of that danger too—but in this, that I had to deal with a being to whom I could not appeal in the name of anything high or low. I had, even like the niggers, to invoke him—himself— his own exalted and incredible degradation. There was nothing either above or below him, and I knew it. He had kicked himself loose of the earth. Confound the man! he had kicked the very earth to pieces. He was alone, and I before him did not know whether I stood on the ground or floated in the air. I've been telling you what we said—repeating the phrases we pronounced— but what's the good? They were common everyday words—the familiar, vague sounds exchanged on every waking day of life. But what of that? They had behind them, to my mind, the terrific suggestiveness of words heard in dreams, of phrases spoken in nightmares. Soul! If anybody had ever struggled with a soul, I am the man. And I wasn't arguing with a lunatic either. Believe me or not, his intelligence was perfectly clear—concentrated, it is true, upon himself with horrible intensity, yet clear; and therein was my only chance—barring, of course, the killing him there and then, which wasn't so good, on account of unavoidable noise. But his soul was mad. Being alone in the wilderness, it had looked within itself, and, by heavens! I tell you, it had gone mad. I had—for my sins, I suppose, to go through the ordeal of looking into it myself. No eloquence could have been so withering to one's belief in mankind as his final burst of sincerity. He struggled with himself too. I saw it—I heard it. I saw the inconceivable mystery of a soul that knew no restraint, no faith, and no fear, yet struggling blindly with itself. I kept my head pretty well; but when I had him at last stretched on the couch, I wiped my forehead, while my legs shook under me as though I had carried half a ton on my back down that hill. And yet I had only supported him, his bony arm clasped round my neck—and he was not much heavier than a child.

"When next day we left at noon, the crowd, of whose presence behind the curtain of trees I had been acutely conscious all the time, flowed out of the woods again, filled the clearing, covered the slope with a mass of naked, breathing, quivering, bronze bodies. I steamed up a bit, then swung downstream, and two thousand eyes followed the evolutions of the splashing, thumping, fierce river-demon beating the water with its terrible tail and breathing black smoke into the air. In front of the first rank, along the river, three men, plastered with bright red earth from head to foot, strutted to and fro restlessly. When we came abreast again, they faced the river, stamped their feet, nodded their horned heads, swayed their scarlet bodies; they shook towards the fierce river-demon a bunch of black feathers, a mangy skin with a pendent tail—something that looked like a dried gourd; they shouted periodically together strings of amazing words that resembled no sounds of human language; and the deep murmurs of the crowd, interrupted suddenly, were like the responses of some satanic litany.

"We had carried Kurtz into the pilot-house: there was more air there. Lying on the couch, he stared through the open shutter. There was an eddy in the mass of human bodies, and the woman with helmeted head and tawny cheeks rushed out to the very brink of the stream. She put out her hands, shouted something, and all that wild mob took up the shout in a roaring chorus of articulated, rapid, breathless utterance.

"'Do you understand this?' I asked.

"He kept on looking out past me with fiery, longing eyes, with a mingled expression of wistfulness and hate. He made no answer, but I saw a smile, a smile of indefinable meaning, appear on his colourless lips that a moment after twitched convulsively. 'Do I not?' he said slowly, gasping, as if the words had been torn out of him by a supernatural power.

"I pulled the string of the whistle, and I did this because I saw the pilgrims on deck getting out their rifles with an air of anticipating a jolly lark. At the sudden screech there was a movement of abject terror through that wedged mass of bodies. 'Don't! don't you frighten them away,' cried some one on deck disconsolately. I pulled the string time after time. They broke and ran, they leaped, they crouched, they swerved, they dodged the flying terror of the sound. The three red chaps had fallen flat, face down on the shore, as though they had been shot dead. Only the barbarous and superb woman did not so much as flinch, and stretched tragically her bare arms after us over the sombre and glittering river.

"And then that imbecile crowd down on the deck started their little fun, and I could see nothing more for smoke.

"The brown current ran swiftly out of the heart of darkness, bearing us down towards the sea with twice the speed of our upward progress; and Kurtz's life was running swiftly too, ebbing, ebbing out of his heart into the sea of inexorable time. The manager was very placid, he had no vital anxieties now, he took us both in with a comprehensive and satisfied glance: the 'affair' had come off as well as could be wished. I saw the time approaching when I would be left alone of the party of 'unsound method.' The pilgrims looked upon me with disfavour. I was, so to speak, numbered with the dead. It is strange how I accepted this unforeseen partnership, this choice of nightmares forced upon me in the tenebrous land invaded by these mean and greedy phantoms.

"Kurtz discoursed. A voice! a voice! It rang deep to the very last. It survived his strength to hide in the magnificent folds of eloquence the barren darkness of his heart. Oh, he struggled! he struggled! The wastes of his weary brain were haunted by shadowy images now—images of wealth and fame revolving obsequiously round his unextinguishable gift of noble and lofty expression. My Intended, my station, my career, my ideas—these were the subjects for the occasional utterances of elevated sentiments. The shade of the original Kurtz frequented the bedside of the hollow sham, whose fate it was to be buried presently in the mould of primeval earth. But both the diabolic love and the unearthly hate of the mysteries it had penetrated fought for the possession of that soul satiated with primitive emotions, avid of lying fame, of sham distinction, of all the appearances of success and power.

"Sometimes he was contemptibly childish. He desired to have kings meet him at railway stations on his return from some ghastly Nowhere, where he intended to accomplish great things. 'You show them you have in you something that is really profitable, and then there will be no limits to the recognition of your ability,' he would say. 'Of course you must take care of the motives—right motives—always.' The long reaches that were like one and the same reach, monotonous bends that were exactly alike, slipped past the steamer with their multitude of secular[6] trees looking patiently after this grimy fragment of another world, the forerunner of change, of conquest, of trade, of massacres, of blessings. I looked ahead—piloting. 'Close the shutter,' said Kurtz suddenly one day; 'I can't bear to look at this.' I did so. There was a silence. 'Oh, but I will wring your heart yet!' he cried at the invisible wilderness.

"We broke down—as I had expected—and had to lie up for repairs at the head of an island. This delay was the first thing that shook Kurtz's confidence. One morning he gave me a packet of papers and a photograph—the lot tied together with a shoe-string. 'Keep this for me,' he said. 'This noxious fool' (meaning the manager) 'is capable of prying into my boxes when I am not looking.' In the afternoon I saw him. He was lying on his back with closed eyes, and I withdrew quietly, but I heard him mutter, 'Live rightly, die, die . . .' I listened. There was nothing more. Was he rehearsing some speech in his sleep, or was it a fragment of a phrase from some newspaper article? He had been writing for the papers and meant to do so again, 'for the furthering of my ideas. It's a duty.'

"His was an impenetrable darkness. I looked at him as you peer down at a man who is lying at the bottom of a precipice where the sun never shines. But I had not much time to give him, because I was helping the engine-driver to take to pieces the leaky cylinders, to straighten a bent connecting-rod, and in other such matters. I lived in an infernal mess of rust, filings, nuts, bolts, spanners, hammers, ratchet-drills—things I abominate, because I don't get on with them. I tended the little forge we fortunately had aboard; I toiled wearily in a wretched scrap-heap—unless I had the shakes too bad to stand.

"One evening coming in with a candle I was startled to hear him say a little tremulously, 'I am lying here in the dark waiting for death.' The light was within a foot of his eyes. I forced myself to murmur, 'Oh, nonsense!' and stood over him as if transfixed.

"Anything approaching the change that came over his features I have never seen before, and hope never to see again. Oh, I wasn't touched. I was fascinated. It was as though a veil had been rent. I saw on that ivory face the expression of sombre pride, of ruthless power, of craven terror—of an intense and hopeless despair. Did he live his life again in every detail of desire, temptation, and surrender during that supreme moment of complete knowledge? He cried in a whisper at some image, at some vision—he cried out twice, a cry that was no more than a breath:

6. Centuries old.

"'The horror! The horror!'

"I blew the candle out and left the cabin. The pilgrims were dining in the mess-room, and I took my place opposite the manager, who lifted his eyes to give me a questioning glance, which I successfully ignored. He leaned back, serene, with that peculiar smile of his sealing the unexpressed depths of his meanness. A continuous shower of small flies streamed upon the lamp, upon the cloth, upon our hands and faces. Suddenly the manager's boy put his insolent black head in the doorway, and said in a tone of scathing contempt:

"'Mistah Kurtz—he dead.'

"All the pilgrims rushed out to see. I remained, and went on with my dinner. I believe I was considered brutally callous. However, I did not eat much. There was a lamp in there—light, don't you know—and outside it was so beastly, beastly dark. I went no more near the remarkable man who had pronounced a judgement upon the adventures of his soul on this earth. The voice was gone. What else had been there? But I am of course aware that next day the pilgrims buried something in a muddy hole.

"And then they very nearly buried me.

"However, as you see, I did not go to join Kurtz there and then. I did not. I remained to dream the nightmare out to the end, and to show my loyalty to Kurtz once more. Destiny. My destiny! Droll thing life is—that mysterious arrangement of merciless logic for a futile purpose. The most you can hope from it is some knowledge of yourself—that comes too late—a crop of unextinguishable regrets. I have wrestled with death. It is the most unexciting contest you can imagine. It takes place in an impalpable greyness, with nothing underfoot, with nothing around, without spectators, without clamour, without glory, without the great desire of victory, without the great fear of defeat, in a sickly atmosphere of tepid scepticism, without much belief in your own right, and still less in that of your adversary. If such is the form of ultimate wisdom, then life is a greater riddle than some of us think it to be. I was within a hair's-breadth of the last opportunity for pronouncement, and I found with humiliation that probably I would have nothing to say. This is the reason why I affirm that Kurtz was a remarkable man. He had something to say. He said it. Since I had peeped over the edge myself, I understand better the meaning of his stare, that could not see the flame of the candle, but was wide enough to embrace the whole universe, piercing enough to penetrate all the hearts that beat in the darkness. He had summed up—he had judged. 'The horror!' He was a remarkable man. After all, this was the expression of some sort of belief; it had candour, it had conviction, it had a vibrating note of revolt in its whisper, it had the appalling face of a glimpsed truth—the strange commingling of desire and hate. And it is not my own extremity I remember best—a vision of greyness without form filled with physical pain, and a careless contempt for the evanescence of all things—even of this pain itself. No! It is his extremity that I seem to have lived through. True, he had made that last stride, he had stepped over the edge, while I had been permitted to draw back my hesitating foot. And perhaps in this is the whole difference; perhaps all the wisdom, and all truth, and all sincerity, are just compressed into that inappreciable moment of time in which we step over the threshold of the invisible. Perhaps! I like to think my summing-up would not have been a word of careless contempt. Better his cry—much better. It was an affirmation, a moral victory paid for by innumerable defeats, by abominable terrors, by abominable satisfactions. But it was a victory! That is why I have remained loyal to Kurtz to the last, and even beyond, when a long time after I heard once more, not his own voice, but the echo of his magnificent eloquence thrown to me from a soul as translucently pure as a cliff of crystal.

"No, they did not bury me, though there is a period of time which I remember mistily, with a shuddering wonder, like a passage through some inconceivable world that had no hope in it and no desire. I found myself back in the sepulchral city resenting the sight of people hurrying through the streets to filch a little money from each other, to devour their infamous cookery, to gulp their unwholesome beer, to dream their insignificant and silly dreams. They trespassed upon my thoughts. They were intruders whose knowledge of life was to me an irritating pretence, because I felt so sure they could not possibly know the things I knew. Their bearing, which was simply the bearing of commonplace individuals going about their business in the assurance of perfect safety, was offensive to me like the outrageous flauntings of folly in the face of a danger it is unable to comprehend. I had no particular desire to enlighten them, but I had some difficulty in restraining myself from laughing in their faces, so full of stupid importance. I daresay I was not very well at that time. I tottered about the streets—there were various affairs to settle—grinning bitterly at perfectly respectable persons. I admit my behaviour was inexcusable, but then my temperature was seldom normal in these days. My dear aunt's endeavours to 'nurse up my strength' seemed altogether beside the mark. It was not my strength that wanted nursing, it was my imagination that wanted soothing. I kept the bundle of papers given me by Kurtz, not knowing exactly what to do with it. His mother had died lately, watched over, as I was told, by his Intended. A clean-shaven man, with an official manner and wearing gold-rimmed spectacles, called on me one day and made inquiries, at first circuitous, afterwards suavely pressing, about what he was pleased to denominate certain 'documents.' I was not surprised, because I had had two rows with the manager on the subject out there. I had refused to give up the smallest scrap out of that package, and I took the same attitude with the spectacled man. He became darkly menacing at last, and with much heat argued that the Company had the right to every bit of information about its 'territories.' And, said he, 'Mr Kurtz's knowledge of unexplored regions must have been necessarily extensive and peculiar—owing to his great abilities and to the deplorable circumstances in which he had been placed: therefore—' I assured him Mr Kurtz's knowledge, however extensive, did not bear upon the problems of commerce or administration. He invoked then the name of science. 'It would be an incalculable loss if,' etc. etc. I offered him the report on the 'Suppression of Savage Customs,' with the postscriptum torn off. He took it up eagerly, but ended by sniffing at it with an air of contempt. 'This is not what we had a right to expect,' he remarked. 'Expect nothing else,' I said. 'There are only private letters.' He withdrew upon some threat of legal proceedings, and I saw him no more; but another fellow, calling himself Kurtz's cousin, appeared two days later, and was anxious to hear all the details about his dear relative's last moments. Incidentally he gave me to understand that Kurtz had been essentially a great musician. 'There was the making of an immense success,' said the man, who was an organist, I believe, with lank grey hair flowing over a greasy coat-collar. I had no reason to doubt his statement; and to this day I am unable to say what was Kurtz's profession, whether he ever had any—which was the greatest of his talents. I had taken him for a painter who wrote for the papers, or else for a journalist who could paint—but even the cousin (who took snuff during the interview) could not tell me what he had been—exactly. He was a universal genius—on that point I agreed with the old chap, who thereupon blew his nose noisily into a large cotton handkerchief and withdrew in senile agitation, bearing off some family letters and memoranda without importance. Ultimately a journalist anxious to know something of the fate of his 'dear colleague' turned up. This visitor informed me Kurtz's proper sphere ought to have been politics 'on the popular side.' He had furry straight eyebrows, bristly hair cropped short, an eyeglass on a broad ribbon, and, becoming expansive, confessed his opinion that Kurtz really couldn't write a bit—'but heavens! how that man could talk! He electrified large meetings. He had faith—don't you see?—he had the faith. He could get himself to believe anything—anything. He would have been a splendid leader of an extreme party.' 'What party?' I asked. 'Any party,' answered the other. 'He was an— an—extremist.' Did I not think so? I assented. Did I know, he asked, with a sudden flash of curiosity, 'what it was that had induced him to go out there?' 'Yes,' said I, and forthwith handed him the famous Report for publication, if he thought fit. He glanced through it hurriedly, mumbling all the time, judged 'it would do,' and took himself off with this plunder.

"Thus I was left at last with a slim packet of letters and the girl's portrait. She struck me as beautiful—I mean she had a beautiful expression. I know that the sunlight can be made to lie too, yet one felt that no manipulation of light and pose could have conveyed the delicate shade of truthfulness upon those features. She seemed ready to listen without mental reservation, without suspicion, without a thought for herself. I concluded I would go and give her back her portrait and those letters myself. Curiosity? Yes; and also some other feeling perhaps. All that had been Kurtz's had passed out of my hands: his soul, his body, his station, his plans, his ivory, his career. There remained only his memory and his Intended—and I wanted to give that up too to the past, in a way—to surrender personally all that remained of him with me to that oblivion which is the last word of our common fate. I don't defend myself. I had no clear perception of what it was I really wanted. Perhaps it was an impulse of unconscious loyalty, or the fulfilment of one of those ironic necessities that lurk in the facts of human existence. I don't know. I can't tell. But I went.

"I thought his memory was like the other memories of the dead that accumulate in every man's life—a vague impress on the brain of shadows that had fallen on it in their swift and final passage; but before the high and ponderous door, between the tall houses of a street as still and decorous as a well-kept alley in a cemetery, I had a vision of him on the stretcher, opening his mouth voraciously, as if to devour all the earth with all its mankind. He lived then before me; he lived as much as he had ever lived—a shadow insatiable of splendid appearances, of frightful realities; a shadow darker than the shadow of the night, and draped nobly in the folds of a gorgeous eloquence. The vision seemed to enter the house with me—the stretcher, the phantom-bearers, the wild crowd of obedient worshippers, the gloom of the forests, the glitter of the reach between the murky bends, the beat of the drum, regular and muffled like the beating of a heart—the heart of a conquering darkness. It was a moment of triumph for the wilderness, an invading and vengeful rush which, it seemed to me, I would have to keep back alone for the salvation of another soul. And the memory of what I had heard him say afar there, with the horned shapes stirring at my back, in the glow of fires, within the patient woods, those broken phrases came back to me, were heard again in their ominous and terrifying simplicity. I remembered his abject pleading, his abject threats, the colossal scale of his vile desires, the meanness, the torment, the tempestuous anguish of his soul. And later an I seemed to see his collected languid manner, when he said one day, 'This lot of ivory now is really mine. The Company did not pay for it. I collected it myself at a very great personal risk. I am afraid they will try to claim it as theirs though. H'm. It is a difficult case. What do you think I ought to do—resist? Eh? I want no more than justice.' . . . He wanted no more than justice—no more than justice. I rang the bell before a mahogany door on the first floor, and while I waited he seemed to stare at me out of the glossy panel—stare with that wide and immense stare embracing, condemning, loathing all the universe. I seemed to hear the whispered cry, "The horror! The horror!"

"The dusk was falling. I had to wait in a lofty drawing-room with three long windows from floor to ceiling that were like three luminous and bedraped columns. The bent gilt legs and backs of the furniture shone in indistinct curves. The tall marble fireplace had a cold and monumental whiteness. A grand piano stood massively in a corner; with dark gleams on the flat surfaces like a sombre and polished sarcophagus. A high door opened—closed. I rose.

"She came forward, all in black, with a pale head, floating towards me in the dusk. She was in mourning. It was more than a year since his death, more than a year since the news came; she seemed as though she would remember and mourn for ever. She took both my hands in hers and murmured, 'I had heard you were coming.' I noticed she was not very young—I mean not girlish. She had a mature capacity for fidelity, for belief, for suffering. The room seemed to have grown darker, as if all the sad light of the cloudy evening had taken refuge on her forehead. This fair hair, this pale visage, this pure brow, seemed surrounded by an ashy halo from which the dark eyes looked out at me. Their glance was guileless, profound, confident, and trustful. She carried her sorrowful head as though she were proud of that sorrow, as though she would say, I—I alone know how to mourn for him as he deserves. But while we were still shaking hands, such a look of awful desolation came upon her face that I perceived she was one of those creatures that are not the playthings of Time. For her he had died only yesterday. And, by Jove! the impression was so powerful that for me too he seemed to have died only yesterday—nay, this very minute. I saw her and him in the same instant of time—his death and her sorrow—I saw her sorrow in the very moment of his death. Do you understand? I saw them together—I heard them together. She had said, with a deep catch of the breath, 'I have survived'; while my strained ears seemed to hear distinctly, mingled with her tone of despairing regret, the summing-up whisper of his eternal condemnation. I asked myself what I was doing there, with a sensation of panic in my heart as though I had blundered into a place of cruel and absurd mysteries not fit for a human being to behold. She motioned me to a chair. We sat down. I laid the packet gently on the little table, and she put her hand over it. . . . 'You knew him well,' she murmured, after a moment of mourning silence.

"'Intimacy grows quickly out there,' I said. 'I knew him as well as it is possible for one man to know another.'

"'And you admired him,' she said. 'It was impossible to know him and not to admire him. Was it?'

"'He was a remarkable man,' I said unsteadily. Then before the appealing fixity of her gaze, that seemed to watch for more words on my lips, I went on, 'It was impossible not to—'

"'Love him,' she finished eagerly, silencing me into an appalled dumbness. 'How true! how true! But when you think that no one knew him so well as I! I had all his noble confidence. I knew him best.'

"'You knew him best,' I repeated. And perhaps she did. But with every word spoken the room was growing darker, and only her forehead, smooth and white, remained illumined by the unextinguishable light of belief and love.

"'You were his friend,' she went on. 'His friend,' she repeated, a little louder. 'You must have been, if he had given you this, and sent you to me. I feel I can speak to you—and oh! I must speak. I want you—you who have heard his last words—to know I have been worthy of him. . . . It is not pride. . . . Yes! I am proud to know I understood him better than any one on earth—he told me so himself. And since his mother died I have had no one—no one—to—to—'

"I listened. The darkness deepened. I was not even sure whether he had given me the right bundle. I rather suspect he wanted me to take care of another batch of his papers which, after his death, I saw the manager examining under the lamp. And the girl talked, easing her pain in the certitude of my sympathy; she talked as thirsty men drink. I had heard that her engagement with Kurtz had been disapproved by her people. He wasn't rich enough or something. And indeed I don't know whether he had not been a pauper all his life. He had given me some reason to infer that it was his impatience of comparative poverty that drove him out there.

"'. . . Who was not his friend who had heard him speak once?' she was saying. 'He drew men towards him by what was best in them.' She looked at me with intensity. 'It is the gift of the great,' she went on, and the sound of her low voice seemed to have the accompaniment of all the other sounds, full of mystery, desolation, and sorrow, I had ever heard—the ripple of the river, the soughing of the trees swayed by the wind, the murmurs of the crowds, the faint ring of incomprehensible words cried from afar, the whisper of a voice speaking from beyond the threshold of an eternal darkness. 'But you have heard him! You know!' she cried.

"'Yes, I know,' I said with something like despair in my heart, but bowing my head before the faith that was in her, before that great and saving illusion that shone with an unearthly glow in the darkness, in the triumphant darkness from which I could not have defended her—from which I could not even defend myself.

"'What a loss to me—to us!'—she corrected herself with beautiful generosity; then added in a murmur, 'To the world.' By the last gleams of twilight I could see the glitter of her eyes, full of tears—of tears that would not fall.

"'I have been very happy—very fortunate—very proud,' she went on. 'Too fortunate. Too happy for a little while. And now I am unhappy for—for life.'

"She stood up; her fair hair seemed to catch all the remaining light in a glimmer of gold. I rose too.

"'And of all this,' she went on mournfully, 'of all his promise, and of all his greatness, of his generous mind, of his noble heart, nothing remains—nothing but a memory. You and I—'

"'We shall always remember him,' I said hastily.

"'No!' she cried. 'It is impossible that all this should be lost—that such a life should be sacrificed to leave nothing—but sorrow. You know what vast plans he had. I knew of them too—I could not perhaps understand—but others knew of them. Something must remain. His words, at least, have not died.'

"'His words will remain,' I said.

"'And his example,' she whispered to herself. 'Men looked up to him—his goodness shone in every act. His example—'

"'True,' I said; 'his example too. Yes, his example. I forgot that.'

"'But I do not. I cannot—I cannot believe—not yet. I cannot believe that I shall never see him again, that nobody will see him again, never, never, never.'

"She put out her arms as if after a retreating figure, stretching them black and with clasped pale hands across the fading and narrow sheen of the window. Never see him! I saw him clearly enough then. I shall see this eloquent phantom as long as I live, and I shall see her too, a tragic and familiar Shade, resembling in this gesture another one, tragic also, and bedecked with powerless charms, stretching bare brown arms over the glitter of the infernal stream, the stream of darkness. She said suddenly very low, 'He died as he lived.'

"'His end,' said I, with dull anger stirring in me, 'was in every way worthy of his life.'

"'And I was not with him,' she murmured. My anger subsided before a feeling of infinite pity.

"'Everything that could be done—' I mumbled.

"'Ah, but I believed in him more than any one on earth—more than his own mother, more than—himself. He needed me! Me! I would have treasured every sigh, every word, every sign, every glance.'

"I felt like a chill grip on my chest. 'Don't,' I said, in a muffled voice.

"'Forgive me. I—I—have mourned so long in silence—in silence. . . . You were with him—to the last? I think of his loneliness. Nobody near to understand him as I would have understood. Perhaps no one to hear. . . .'

"'To the very end,' I said shakily. 'I heard his very last words. . . .' I stopped in a fright.

"'Repeat them,' she murmured in a heart-broken tone. 'I want—I want—something—something—to—to live with.'

"I was on the point of crying at her, 'Don't you hear them?' The dusk was repeating them in a persistent whisper all around us, in a whisper that seemed to swell menacingly like the first whisper of a rising wind. 'The horror! The horror!'

"'His last word—to live with,' she insisted. 'Don't you understand I loved him—I loved him—I loved him!'

"I pulled myself together and spoke slowly.

"'The last word he pronounced was—your name.'

"I heard a light sigh and then my heart stood still, stopped dead short by an exulting and terrible cry, by the cry of inconceivable triumph and of unspeakable pain. 'I knew it—I was sure!' . . . She knew. She was sure. I heard her weeping; she had hidden her face in her hands. It seemed to me that the house would collapse before I could escape, that the heavens would fall upon my head. But nothing happened. The heavens do not fall for such a trifle. Would they have fallen, I wonder, if I had rendered Kurtz that justice which was his due? Hadn't he said he wanted only justice? But I couldn't. I could not tell her. It would have been too dark—too dark altogether. . . ."[7]

Marlow ceased, and sat apart, indistinct and silent, in the pose of a meditating Buddha. Nobody moved for a time. "We have lost the first of the ebb," said the Director suddenly. I raised my head. The offing was barred by a black bank of clouds, and the tranquil waterway leading to the uttermost ends of the earth flowed sombre under an overcast sky—seemed to lead into the heart of an immense darkness.

1898–99   1899, 1902

7. Writing to William Blackwood (editor of *Blackwood's Magazine*, where the story first appeared) in May 1902, Conrad referred to "the last pages of Heart of Darkness where the interview of the man and the girl locks in—as it were—the whole 30,000 words of narrative description into one suggestive view of a whole phase of life, and makes of that story something quite on another plane than an anecdote of a man who went mad in the Centre of Africa" (Joseph Conrad, *Letters to William Blackwood and David S. Meldrum*, ed. William Blackburn, 1958).

WILLIAM BUTLER YEATS
1865–1939

William Butler Yeats was born to an Anglo-Irish family in Dublin. His father, J. B. Yeats, had abandoned law to take up painting, at which he made a somewhat precarious living. His mother came from the Pollexfen family that lived near Sligo, in the west of Ireland, where Yeats spent much of his childhood. The Yeatses moved to London in 1874, then returned to Dublin in 1880. Yeats attended first high school and then art school, which he soon left to concentrate on poetry.

Yeats's father was a religious skeptic, but he believed in the "religion of art." Yeats, religious by temperament but unable to believe in Christian orthodoxy, sought all his life to compensate for his lost religion. This search led him to various kinds of mysticism, to folklore, theosophy, spiritualism, and neoplatonism. He said he "made a new religion, almost an infallible church of poetic tradition."

Yeats's childhood and young manhood were spent between Dublin, London, and Sligo, and each of these places contributed something to his poetic development. In London in the 1890s he met the important poets of the day, founded the Irish Literary Society, and acquired late-Romantic, Pre-Raphaelite ideas of poetry: he believed, in this early stage of his career, that a poet's language should be dreamy, evocative, and ethereal. From the countryside around Sligo he gained a knowledge of the life of the peasantry and of their folklore. In Dublin, where he founded the National Literary Society, he was influenced by Irish nationalism and, although often disagreeing with those who wished to use literature for political ends, he nevertheless came to see his poetry as contributing to the rejuvenation of Irish culture.

Yeats's poetry began in the tradition of self-conscious Romanticism, strongly influenced by the English poets Edmund Spenser, Percy Shelley, and, a little later, William Blake, whose works he edited. About the same time, he was writing poems (e.g., "The Stolen Child") deriving from his Sligo experience, with quietly precise nature imagery, Irish place-names, and themes from Irish folklore. A little later he drew on the great stories of the heroic age of Irish history and translations of Gaelic poetry into "that dialect which gets from Gaelic its syntax and keeps its still partly Tudor vocabulary." The heroic legends of ancient Ireland and the folk traditions of the modern Irish countryside helped brace his early dreamlike imagery. "The Lake Isle of Innisfree"—"my first lyric with anything in its rhythm of my own music," said Yeats—is both a Romantic evocation of escape into dream, art, and the imagination, and a specifically Irish reverie on freedom and self-reliance.

Yeats vigorously hybridizes Irish and English traditions, and eventually draws into this potent intercultural mix East and South Asian cultural resources, including Japanese Noh theater and Indian meditative practices. Resolutely Irish, he imaginatively reclaims a land colonized by the British; imposes Irish rhythms, images, genres, and syntax on English-language poetry; and revives native myths, place-names, and consciousness. Yet he is also cosmopolitan, insisting on the transnationalism of the collective storehouse of images he calls "Spiritus Mundi" or "Anima Mundi," spending much of his life in England, and cross-pollinating forms, ideas, and images from Ireland and England, Europe and Asia.

Irish nationalism first sent Yeats in search of a consistently simpler and more popular style, to express the elemental facts about Irish life and aspirations. This led him to the concrete image, as did translations from Gaelic folk songs, in which "nothing . . . was abstract, nothing worn-out." But other forces were also working on him. In 1902 a friend gave him the works of the German philosopher Friedrich Nietzsche, to which he responded with great excitement, and it would seem that, in persuading the passive love poet to get off his knees, Nietzsche's books intensified his search for a more active stance, a more vigorous style. At the start of the twentieth century, Yeats wearied of his early languid aesthetic, declaring his intentions, in a 1901 letter, to make "everything hard and clear" and, in another of 1904, to leave behind "sentiment and sentimental sadness." He wished for poems that did not reach for disembodied beauty but that could "carry the normal, passionate, reasoning self, the personality as a whole." In poems of his middle period, such as "Adam's Curse" and "A Coat," Yeats combines the colloquial with the formal, enacting in his more austere diction, casual rhythms, and passionate syntax his will to leave behind the poetic "embroideries" of his youth and walk "naked." The American poet Ezra Pound, who spent winters from 1913 to 1916 with Yeats in a stone cottage in Sussex, strengthened Yeats's resolve to develop a less mannered, more stripped down style.

In 1889 Yeats had met the beautiful actor and Irish nationalist Maud Gonne, with whom he was desperately in love for many years, but who persistently refused to marry him. She became the subject of many of his early love poems, and in later poems, such as "No Second Troy" and "A Prayer for My Daughter," he expresses anger over her self-sacrifice to political activism. He had also met Lady Gregory, Anglo-Irish writer and promoter of Irish literature, in 1896, and Yeats spent many holidays at her aristocratic country house, Coole Park. Disliking the moneygrubbing and prudery of the middle classes, as indicated in "September 1913," he looked for his ideal characters either below them, to peasants and beggars, or above them, to the aristocracy, for each of these had their own traditions and lived according to them. Under Lady Gregory's influence, Yeats began to organize the Irish dramatic movement in 1899 and, with her help, founded the Abbey Theatre in 1904. His active participation in theatrical production—confronting political censorship, economic problems of paying carpenters and actors, and other aspects of "theatre business, management of men"—also helped toughen his style, as he demonstrates in "The Fascination of What's Difficult." Yeats's long-cherished hope had been to "bring the halves together"—Protestant and Catholic—through a literature infused with Ireland's ancient myths and cultural riches before the divisions between rival Christianities. But in a string of national controversies, he ran afoul of both the Roman Catholic middle class and the Anglo-Irish Protestant ascendancy, and at last, bitterly turning his back on Ireland, moved to England.

Then came the Easter Rising of 1916, led by men and women he had long known, some of whom were executed or imprisoned by the British. Persuaded by Gonne (whose estranged husband was one of the executed leaders) that "tragic dignity had returned to Ireland," Yeats returned. His culturally nationalist work had helped inspire the poet revolutionaries, and so he asked himself, as he put it in the late poem "Man and the Echo," did his work "send out / Certain men the English shot?" Yeats's nationalism and antinationalism, his divided loyalties to Ireland and to England, find powerfully ambivalent expression in "Easter, 1916" and other poems. Throughout his poetry he brilliantly mediates between contending aspects of himself—late-Romantic visionary and astringent modern skeptic, Irish patriot and irreverent antinationalist, shrewd man of action and esoteric dreamer. As he said: "We make out of the quarrel with others, rhetoric, but of the quarrel with ourselves, poetry." Conceiving consciousness as conflict, he fashioned a kind of poetry that could embody the contradictory feelings and ideas of his endless inner debate.

To mark his recommitment to Ireland, Yeats refurbished and renamed Thoor (Castle) Ballylee, the Norman tower on Lady Gregory's land, in which he lived off and on, and which became, along with its inner winding stair, a central symbol in his later poetry. In 1922 he was appointed a senator of the recently established Irish Free State, and he served until 1928, playing an active part not only in promoting the arts but also in mediating general political affairs, in which he supported the views of the minority Protestant landed class. At the same time, he was continuing his esoteric studies. He married Georgie (changed by Yeats to George) Hyde Lees in 1917, when he was fifty-two, and she proved so sympathetic to his imaginative needs that the automatic writing she produced for several years (believed by Yeats to have been dictated by spirits) gave him the elements of a symbolic system that he later worked out in his book *A Vision* (1925, 1937). The system was a theory of the movements of history and of the different types of personality, each movement and type being related to a different phase of the moon. At the center of the symbolic system were the interpenetrating cones, or "gyres," that represented the movement through major cycles of history and across antitheses of human personality.

He compressed and embodied his personal mythology in visionary poems of great scope, linguistic force, and incantatory power, such as "The Second Coming" and "Leda and the Swan." In poems of the 1920s and 1930s, winding stairs, spinning tops, "gyres," spirals of all kinds, are important symbols, serving as a means of resolving some of the contraries that had arrested him from the beginning—paradoxes of time and eternity, change and continuity, spirit and the body, life and art. If his earliest poetry was sometimes static, a beautifully stitched tapestry laden with symbols of inner states, his late poetry became more dynamic, its propulsive syntax and muscular rhythms more suited to his themes of lust, rage, and the body. He had once screened these out of his verse as unpoetic, along with war, violence, "the mire of human veins." Now he embraced the mortal world intensely. In "A Dialogue of Self and Soul," the self defies the soul's injunction to leave the world behind: "I am content to live it all again / And yet again, if it be life to pitch / Into the frog-spawn of a blind man's ditch." Yeats no longer sought transcendence of the human, but instead aimed for the active interpenetration of the corporeal and the visionary. In his Nietzsche-inspired poems of "tragic joy," such as "Lapis Lazuli," he affirmed ruin and destruction as necessary to imaginative creation.

One key to Yeats's greatness is that there are many different Yeatses: a hard nosed skeptic and an esoteric idealist, a nativist and a cosmopolitan, an Irish nationalist and an Ironic antinationalist, a Romantic brooding on loss and unrequited desire and a modernist mocking idealism, nostalgia, and contemporary society. Similarly, in his poetic innovations and consolidations, he is both a conservative and a radical. That is, he is a literary traditionalist, working within such inherited genres as love poetry, the elegy, the self-elegy, the sonnet, and the occasional poem on public themes. But he is also a restless innovator who disrupts generic conventions, breaking up the coherence of the sonnet, de-idealizing the dead mourned in elegies, and bringing into public poems an intense personal ambivalence. In matters of form, too, he rhymes but often in off-rhyme, uses standard meters but bunches or scatters their stresses, employs an elegant syntax that nevertheless has the passionate urgency of colloquial speech; his diction, tone, enjambments, and stanzas intermix ceremony with contortion, controlled artifice with wayward unpredictability. A difficulty in reading Yeats—but also one of the great rewards—is comprehending his many-sidedness.

Like Pound, T. S. Eliot, and Windham Lewis, Yeats was attracted to right-wing politics, and in the 1930s he was briefly drawn to fascism. His late interest in authoritarian politics arose in part from his desire for a feudal, aristocratic society that, unlike middle-class culture, in his view, might allow the imagination to flourish, and in part from his anticolonialism, since he thought a fascist Spain, for example, would "weaken the British Empire." But eventually he was appalled by all political ideologies, and the grim prophecy of "The Second Coming" seemed to him increasingly apt.

Written in a rugged, colloquial, and concrete language, Yeats's last poems have a controlled yet startling wildness. His return to life, to "the foul rag-and-bone shop of the heart," is one of the most impressive final phases of any poet's career. In one of his last letters he wrote: "When I try to put all into a phrase I say, 'Man can embody truth but he cannot know it.' . . . The abstract is not life and everywhere draws out its contradictions. You can refute Hegel but not the Saint or the Song of Sixpence." He died in southern France just before the beginning of World War II. His grave is, as his poem directed, near Sligo, "under Ben Bulben." He left behind a body of verse that, in variety and power, has been an enduring influence for English-language poets around the globe, from W. H. Auden and Seamus Heaney to Derek Walcott and A. K. Ramanujan.

The Stolen Child[1]

Where dips the rocky highland
Of Sleuth Wood[2] in the lake,
There lies a leafy island
Where flapping herons wake
5   The drowsy water-rats;
There we've hid our faery vats,
Full of berries
And of reddest stolen cherries.
Come away, O human child!
10 *To the waters and the wild*
With a faery, hand in hand,
For the world's more full of weeping than you can understand.

Where the wave of moonlight glosses
The dim grey sands with light,
15 Far off by furthest Rosses
We foot it all the night,
Weaving olden dances,
Mingling hands and mingling glances
Till the moon has taken flight;
20 To and fro we leap
And chase the frothy bubbles,
While the world is full of troubles
And is anxious in its sleep.
Come away, O human child!

---

1. I.e., a child stolen by fairies to be their companion, as in Irish folklore.
2. This and other places mentioned in the poem are in County Sligo, in the west of Ireland, where Yeats spent much of his childhood.

25   *To the waters and the wild*
    With a faery, hand in hand,
    For the world's more full of weeping than you can understand.

    Where the wandering water gushes
    From the hills above Glen-Car,
30   In pools among the rushes
    That scarce could bathe a star,
    We seek for slumbering trout
    And whispering in their ears
    Give them unquiet dreams;
35   Leaning softly out
    From ferns that drop their tears
    Over the young streams.
    Come away, O human child!
    To the waters and the wild
40   *With a faery, hand in hand,*
    For the world's more full of weeping than you can understand.

    Away with us he's going,
    The solemn-eyed:
    He'll hear no more the lowing
45   Of the calves on the warm hillside
    Or the kettle on the hob
    Sing peace into his breast,
    Or see the brown mice bob
    Round and round the oatmeal-chest.
50   *For he comes, the human child,*
    To the waters and the wild
    With a faery, hand in hand,
    From a world more full of weeping than he can understand.

                       1886, 1889

The Rose of the World[1]

    Who dreamed that beauty passes like a dream?
    For these red lips, with all their mournful pride,
    Mournful that no new wonder may betide,
    Troy[2] passed away in one high funeral gleam,
5   And Usna's children died.[3]

    We and the labouring world are passing by:
    Amid men's souls, that waver and give place

1. The Platonic idea of eternal beauty. "I notice upon reading these poems for the first time for several years that the quality symbolized as The Rose differs from the Intellectual Beauty of Shelley and of Spenser in that I have imagined it as suffering with man and not as something pursued and seen from afar" [Yeats, in 1925]. Yeats wrote this poem to Maud Gonne.
2. Ancient city destroyed by the Greeks, according to legend, after the abduction of the beautiful Helen.
3. In Old Irish legend the Ulster warrior Naoise, son of Usna or Usnach (pronounced *Úskna*), eloped with the beautiful Deirdre, whom King Conchubar of Ulster had intended to marry, and with his two brothers took her to Scotland. Eventually Conchubar lured the four of them back to Ireland and killed the three brothers.

Like the pale waters in their wintry race,
Under the passing stars, foam of the sky,
10 Lives on this lonely face.

Bow down, archangels, in your dim abode:
Before you were, or any hearts to beat,
Weary and kind one lingered by His seat;
He made the world to be a grassy road
15 Before her wandering feet.

                                        1892, 1895

The Lake Isle of Innisfree[1]

I will arise and go now, and go to Innisfree,
And a small cabin build there, of clay and wattles[2] made:
Nine bean-rows will I have there, a hive for the honey-bee,
And live alone in the bee-loud glade.

5   And I shall have some peace there, for peace comes dropping slow,
Dropping from the veils of the morning to where the cricket sings;
There midnight's all a glimmer, and noon a purple glow,
And evening full of the linnet's wings.

I will arise and go now, for always night and day
10 I hear lake water lapping with low sounds by the shore;
While I stand on the roadway, or on the pavements grey,
I hear it in the deep heart's core.

1890   1890, 1892

The Sorrow of Love[1]

The brawling of a sparrow in the eaves,
The brilliant moon and all the milky sky,
And all that famous harmony of leaves,
Had blotted out man's image and his cry.

5   A girl arose that had red mournful lips
And seemed the greatness of the world in tears,
Doomed like Odysseus and the labouring ships
And proud as Priam murdered with his peers;[2]

---

1. Inis Fraoigh (Heather Island) is a small island in Lough Gill, near Sligo, in the west of Ireland. In his autobiography Yeats writes: "I had still the ambition, formed in Sligo in my teens, of living in imitation of Thoreau on Innisfree . . . and when walking through Fleet Street [in London] very homesick I heard a little tinkle of water and saw a fountain in a shop-window which balanced a little ball upon its jet, and began to remember lake water. From the sudden remembrance came my poem *Innisfree*, my first lyric with anything in its

rhythm of my own music."
2. Stakes interwoven with twigs or branches.
1. For earlier versions of this poem, see "Poems in Process," in the supplemental ebook.
2. Odysseus (whom the Romans called Ulysses) is the hero of Homer's *Odyssey*, which describes how, after having fought in the siege of Troy, he wandered for ten years before reaching his home, the Greek island of Ithaca. Priam was king of Troy at the time of the siege and was killed when the Greeks captured the city.

Arose, and on the instant clamorous eaves,
10 A climbing moon upon an empty sky,
And all that lamentation of the leaves,
Could but compose man's image and his cry.

1891   1892, 1925

When You Are Old[1]

When you are old and grey and full of sleep,
And nodding by the fire, take down this book,
And slowly read, and dream of the soft look
Your eyes had once, and of their shadows deep;

5   How many loved your moments of glad grace,
And loved your beauty with love false or true,
But one man loved the pilgrim soul in you,
And loved the sorrows of your changing face;

And bending down beside the glowing bars,[2]
10 Murmur, a little sadly, how Love fled
And paced upon the mountains overhead
And hid his face amid a crowd of stars.

1891   1892, 1899

Who Goes with Fergus?[1]

Who will go drive with Fergus now,
And pierce the deep wood's woven shade,
And dance upon the level shore?
Young man, lift up your russet brow,
5   And lift your tender eyelids, maid,
And brood on hopes and fear no more.

And no more turn aside and brood
Upon love's bitter mystery;
For Fergus rules the brazen cars,°   *bronze chariots*
10 And rules the shadows of the wood,
And the white breast of the dim sea
And all dishevelled wandering stars.

1893

1. A poem suggested by a sonnet by the French poet Pierre de Ronsard (1524–1585); it begins: "Quand vous serez bien vieille, au soir, à la chandelle" (When you are quite old, in the evening by candlelight).
2. I.e., of the grate.

1. In a late version of this Irish heroic legend, Fergus, "king of the proud Red Branch Kings," gave up his throne voluntarily to King Conchubar of Ulster to learn by dreaming and meditating the bitter wisdom of the poet and philosopher.

The Man Who Dreamed of Faeryland

He stood among a crowd at Drumahair;[1]
His heart hung all upon a silken dress,
And he had known at last some tenderness,
Before earth took him to her stony care;
5   But when a man poured fish into a pile,
It seemed they raised their little silver heads,
And sang what gold morning or evening sheds
Upon a woven world-forgotten isle
Where people love beside the ravelled[2] seas;
10 That Time can never mar a lover's vows
Under that woven changeless roof of boughs:
The singing shook him out of his new ease.

He wandered by the sands of Lissadell;
His mind ran all on money cares and fears,
15 And he had known at last some prudent years
Before they heaped his grave under the hill;
But while he passed before a plashy place,
A lug-worm with its grey and muddy mouth
Sang that somewhere to north or west or south
20 There dwelt a gay, exulting, gentle race
Under the golden or the silver skies;
That if a dancer stayed his hungry foot
It seemed the sun and moon were in the fruit:
And at that singing he was no more wise.

25 He mused beside the well of Scanavin,
He mused upon his mockers: without fail
His sudden vengeance were a country tale,
When earthy night had drunk his body in;
But one small knot-grass growing by the pool
30 Sang where—unnecessary cruel voice—
Old silence bids its chosen race rejoice,
Whatever ravelled waters rise and fall
Or stormy silver fret the gold of day,
And midnight there enfold them like a fleece
35 And lover there by lover be at peace.
The tale drove his fine angry mood away.

He slept under the hill of Lugnagall;
And might have known at last unhaunted sleep
Under that cold and vapour-turbaned steep,
40 Now that the earth had taken man and all:
Did not the worms that spired about his bones
Proclaim with that unwearied, reedy cry
That God has laid His fingers on the sky,
That from those fingers glittering summer runs

1. This and other place-names in the poem refer   2. Tangled; here, turbulent.
to locations in County Sligo.

45   Upon the dancer by the dreamless wave.
       Why should those lovers that no lovers miss
       Dream, until God burn Nature with a kiss?
       The man has found no comfort in the grave.

                                                    1891, 1930

Adam's Curse[1]

       We sat together at one summer's end,
       That beautiful mild woman, your close friend,
       And you and I,[2] and talked of poetry.
       I said, "A line will take us hours maybe;
5   Yet if it does not seem a moment's thought,
       Our stitching and unstitching has been naught.
       Better go down upon your marrow-bones
       And scrub a kitchen pavement, or break stones
       Like an old pauper, in all kinds of weather;
10   For to articulate sweet sounds together
       Is to work harder than all these, and yet
       Be thought an idler by the noisy set
       Of bankers, schoolmasters, and clergymen
       The martyrs call the world."

                                  And thereupon
15   That beautiful mild woman for whose sake
       There's many a one shall find out all heartache
       On finding that her voice is sweet and low
       Replied, "To be born woman is to know—
       Although they do not talk of it at school—
20   That we must labour to be beautiful."

       I said, "It's certain there is no fine thing
       Since Adam's fall but needs much labouring.
       There have been lovers who thought love should be
       So much compounded of high courtesy
25   That they would sigh and quote with learned looks
       Precedents out of beautiful old books;
       Yet now it seems an idle trade enough."

       We sat grown quiet at the name of love;
       We saw the last embers of daylight die,
30   And in the trembling blue-green of the sky
       A moon, worn as if it had been a shell
       Washed by time's waters as they rose and fell
       About the stars and broke in days and years.

1. When Adam was evicted from the Garden of Eden, God cursed him with a life of toil and labor (Genesis 3.17–19).

2. The two women in the poem are modeled on Maud Gonne and her sister, Kathleen Pilcher (1868–1919).

I had a thought for no one's but your ears:
35 That you were beautiful, and that I strove
To love you in the old high way of love;
That it had all seemed happy, and yet we'd grown
As weary-hearted as that hollow moon.

Nov. 1902   1902, 1922

No Second Troy

Why should I blame her[1] that she filled my days
With misery, or that she would of late
Have taught to ignorant men most violent ways,
Or hurled the little streets upon the great,
5 Had they but courage equal to desire?
What could have made her peaceful with a mind
That nobleness made simple as a fire,
With beauty like a tightened bow, a kind
That is not natural in an age like this,
10 Being high and solitary and most stern?
Why, what could she have done, being what she is?
Was there another Troy for her to burn?[2]

Dec. 1908   1910

The Fascination of What's Difficult[1]

The fascination of what's difficult
Has dried the sap out of my veins, and rent
Spontaneous joy and natural content
Out of my heart. There's something ails our colt[2]
5 That must, as if it had not holy blood
Nor on Olympus[3] leaped from cloud to cloud,
Shiver under the lash, strain, sweat and jolt
As though it dragged road metal. My curse on plays
That have to be set up in fifty ways,
10 On the day's war with every knave and dolt,
Theatre business, management of men.
I swear before the dawn comes round again
I'll find the stable and pull out the bolt.

Sept. 1909–Mar. 1910   1910

---

1. Maud Gonne, whose revolutionary activities are at issue in the poem.
2. Helen of Troy was the legendary cause of the Trojan War and thus of Troy's destruction.
1. Written when Yeats was director-manager of the Abbey Theatre. "Subject. To complain of the fascination of what's difficult. It spoils spontane-

ity and pleasure, and wastes time. Repeat the line ending difficult three times and rhyme on bolt, exalt, colt, jolt" [Yeats's diary for September 1909].
2. Pegasus, in Greek mythology a winged horse associated with poetry.
3. A mountain in Greece; the home of the gods.

A Coat

I made my song a coat
Covered with embroideries
Out of old mythologies
From heel to throat;
5 But the fools caught it,
Wore it in the world's eyes
As though they'd wrought it.
Song, let them take it,
For there's more enterprise
10 In walking naked.

1912   1914

September 1913

What need you,[1] being come to sense,
But fumble in a greasy till°   *cash register*
And add the halfpence to the pence
And prayer to shivering prayer, until
5 You have dried the marrow from the bone;
For men were born to pray and save:
Romantic Ireland's dead and gone,
It's with O'Leary[2] in the grave.

Yet they were of a different kind,
10 The names that stilled your childish play,
They have gone about the world like wind,
But little time had they to pray
For whom the hangman's rope was spun,
And what, God help us, could they save?
15 Romantic Ireland's dead and gone,
It's with O'Leary in the grave.

Was it for this the wild geese[3] spread
The grey wing upon every tide,
For this that all that blood was shed,
20 For this Edward Fitzgerald died,
And Robert Emmet and Wolfe Tone,[4]
All that delirium of the brave?

1. Members of the new, largely Roman Catholic middle class. When the art dealer Hugh Lane (d. 1915) offered to give his collection of French impressionist paintings to the city of Dublin, provided they were permanently housed in a suitable gallery, Yeats became angry over fierce public opposition to funding the project.
2. John O'Leary (1830–1907), Irish nationalist, who, after five years' imprisonment and fifteen years' exile, returned to Dublin in 1885; he rallied the young Yeats to the cause of literary nationalism.
3. Popular name for the Irish who, because of the penal laws against Catholics (1695–1727), were forced to flee to the Continent.
4. Theobald Wolfe Tone (1763–1798), one of the chief founders of the United Irishmen (an Irish nationalist organization) and leader of the 1798 Irish Rising, committed suicide in prison. Lord Edward Fitzgerald (1763–1798), British officer who, after being dismissed from the army for disloyal, activities, joined the United Irishmen, helped lead the 1798 Irish Rising, and died in prison. Robert Emmet (1778–1803), a leader of the abortive 1803 Irish Nationalist Revolt, was hanged for treason.

Romantic Ireland's dead and gone,
It's with O'Leary in the grave.

25 Yet could we turn the years again,
And call those exiles as they were
In all their loneliness and pain,
You'd cry, "Some woman's yellow hair
Has maddened every mother's son":
30 They weighed so lightly what they gave.
But let them be, they're dead and gone,
They're with O'Leary in the grave.

Sept. 1913   1913

Easter, 1916[1]

I have met them at close of day
Coming with vivid faces
From counter or desk among grey
Eighteenth-century houses.
5 I have passed with a nod of the head
Or polite meaningless words,
Or have lingered awhile and said
Polite meaningless words,
And thought before I had done
10 Of a mocking tale or a gibe
To please a companion
Around the fire at the club,
Being certain that they and I
But lived where motley[2] is worn:
15 All changed, changed utterly:
A terrible beauty is born.

That woman's days were spent
In ignorant good-will,
Her nights in argument
20 Until her voice grew shrill.
What voice more sweet than hers
When, young and beautiful,
She rode to harriers?[3]
This man had kept a school
25 And rode our wingèd horse;[4]
This other his helper and friend[5]

1. During the Easter Rising of 1916, Irish nationalists revolted against the British government and proclaimed an Irish Republic. Nearly sixteen hundred Irish Volunteers and two hundred members of the Citizen Army seized buildings and a park in Dublin. The rebellion began on Easter Monday, April 24, 1916, and was crushed in six days. Over the next two weeks fifteen of the leaders were executed by firing squad. Yeats knew the chief nationalist leaders personally. For more on the Easter Rising, see "Imagining Ireland" in the supplemental ebook.

2. The multicolored clothes of a jester.
3. Constance Gore-Booth (1868–1927), afterward Countess Markievicz, took a prominent role in the uprising. Her death sentence was reduced to imprisonment. The other rebel leaders to whom Yeats refers were executed.
4. Padraic Pearse (1879–1916), founder of a boys' school in Dublin and poet—hence the "winged horse," or Pegasus, the horse of the Muses.
5. Thomas MacDonagh (1878–1916), poet and dramatist.

Was coming into his force;
He might have won fame in the end,
So sensitive his nature seemed,
30   So daring and sweet his thought.
This other man I had dreamed
A drunken, vainglorious lout.[6]
He had done most bitter wrong
To some who are near my heart,
35   Yet I number him in the song;
He, too, has resigned his part
In the casual comedy;
He, too, has been changed in his turn,
Transformed utterly:
40   A terrible beauty is born.

Hearts with one purpose alone
Through summer and winter seem
Enchanted to a stone
To trouble the living stream.
45   The horse that comes from the road,
The rider, the birds that range
From cloud to tumbling cloud,
Minute by minute they change;
A shadow of cloud on the stream
50   Changes minute by minute;
A horse-hoof slides on the brim,
And a horse plashes within it;
The long-legged moor-hens dive,
And hens to moor-cocks call;
55   Minute by minute they live:
The stone's in the midst of all.

Too long a sacrifice
Can make a stone of the heart.
O when may it suffice?
60   That is Heaven's part, our part
To murmur name upon name,
As a mother names her child
When sleep at last has come
On limbs that had run wild.
65   What is it but nightfall?
No, no, not night but death;
Was it needless death after all?
For England may keep faith
For all that is done and said.[7]
70   We know their dream; enough
To know they dreamed and are dead;
And what if excess of love
Bewildered them till they died?
I write it out in a verse—
75   MacDonagh and MacBride

6. Major John MacBride (1865–1916), Irish revolutionary and estranged husband of Maud Gonne.
7. In 1914 the English government had passed
Home Rule for Ireland into law, but because of
World War I had suspended it, promising to
implement it later.

And Connolly[8] and Pearse
Now and in time to be,
Wherever green is worn,
Are changed, changed utterly:
80   A terrible beauty is born.

May–Sept. 1916   1916, 1920

The Wild Swans at Coole[1]

The trees are in their autumn beauty,
The woodland paths are dry,
Under the October twilight the water
Mirrors a still sky;
5   Upon the brimming water among the stones
Are nine-and-fifty swans.

The nineteenth autumn has come upon me
Since I first made my count[2]
I saw, before I had well finished,
10   All suddenly mount
And scatter wheeling in great broken rings
Upon their clamorous wings.

I have looked upon those brilliant creatures,
And now my heart is sore.
15   All's changed since I, hearing at twilight,
The first time on this shore,
The bell-beat of their wings above my head,
Trod with a lighter tread.

Unwearied still, lover by lover,
20   They paddle in the cold
Companionable streams or climb the air;
Their hearts have not grown old;
Passion or conquest, wander where they will,
Attend upon them still.

25   But now they drift on the still water,
Mysterious, beautiful;
Among what rushes will they build,
By what lake's edge or pool
Delight men's eyes when I awake some day
30   To find they have flown away?

Oct. 1916   1917

---

8. James Connolly (1870–1916), a trade-union
organizer and military commander of the
rebellion.
1. Coole Park, in County Galway, was the estate
of the Irish playwright Lady Augusta Gregory

(1852–1932).
2. Yeats made his first long visit to Coole in
1897; from then on he spent summers there,
often staying into the fall.

In Memory of Major Robert Gregory[1]

1

Now that we're almost settled in our house
I'll name the friends that cannot sup with us
Beside a fire of turf° in th' ancient tower,[2]   *peat*
And having talked to some late hour
5   Climb up the narrow winding stair to bed:
Discoverers of forgotten truth
Or mere companions of my youth,
All, all are in my thoughts to-night being dead.

2

Always we'd have the new friend meet the old
10   And we are hurt if either friend seem cold,
And there is salt to lengthen out the smart
In the affections of our heart,
And quarrels are blown up upon that head;
But not a friend that I would bring
15   This night can set us quarrelling,
For all that come into my mind are dead.

3

Lionel Johnson[3] comes the first to mind,
That loved his learning better than mankind,
Though courteous to the worst; much falling he
20   Brooded upon sanctity
Till all his Greek and Latin learning seemed
A long blast upon the horn that brought
A little nearer to his thought
A measureless consummation that he dreamed.

4

25   And that enquiring man John Synge[4] comes next,
That dying chose the living world for text
And never could have rested in the tomb
But that, long travelling, he had come
Towards nightfall upon certain set apart
30   In a most desolate stony place,
Towards nightfall upon a race
Passionate and simple like his heart.

---

1. Robert Gregory (1881–1918) was the only child of Lady Augusta Gregory. The first printing of this elegy included the following note: "(Major Robert Gregory, R.F.C. [Royal Flying Corps], M.C. [Military Cross], Legion of Honour, was killed in action on the Italian Front, January 23, 1918)." For another of Yeats's poems on Gregory's death, see "Representing the Great War" in the supplemental ebook.
2. In 1917 Yeats purchased the Norman tower Thoor Ballylee, near Lady Gregory's home in Coole Park. While that residence was being renovated, Yeats and his wife were living in a house that Lady Gregory had lent them.
3. English poet and scholar (1867–1902); he was "much falling" (line 19) because of his drinking.
4. Irish playwright (1871–1909), associated with the Irish literary renaissance and the Abbey Theatre. When Yeats first met Synge, in 1896, he encouraged him to travel to the Aran Islands ("a most desolate and stony place") and write about its rural residents.

5

And then I think of old George Pollexfen,[5]
In muscular youth well known to Mayo[6] men
35   For horsemanship at meets or at racecourses,
That could have shown how pure-bred horses
And solid men, for all their passion, live
But as the outrageous stars incline
By opposition, square and trine;[7]
40   Having grown sluggish and contemplative.

6

They were my close companions many a year,
A portion of my mind and life, as it were,
And now their breathless faces seem to look
Out of some old picture-book;
45   I am accustomed to their lack of breath,
But not that my dear friend's dear son,
Our Sidney[8] and our perfect man,
Could share in that discourtesy of death.

7

For all things the delighted eye now sees
50   Were loved by him:[9] the old storm-broken trees
That cast their shadows upon road and bridge;
The tower set on the stream's edge;
The ford where drinking cattle make a stir
Nightly, and startled by that sound
55   The water-hen must change her ground;
He might have been your heartiest welcomer.

8

When with the Galway foxhounds he would ride
From Castle Taylor to the Roxborough side[1]
Or Esserkelly plain, few kept his pace;
60   At Mooneen he had leaped a place
So perilous that half the astonished meet
Had shut their eyes; and where was it
He rode a race without a bit?
And yet his mind outran the horses' feet.

9

65   We dreamed that a great painter had been born[2]
To cold Clare[3] rock and Galway rock and thorn,
To that stern colour and that delicate line

5. Yeats's maternal uncle (1839–1910), with whom he had spent holidays in Sligo as a young man.
6. County in western Ireland.
7. Terms from astrology, in which both Yeats and his uncle were interested.
8. Sir Philip Sidney (1554–1586), English poet and exemplar of the "Renaissance man"; like Gregory, he was killed in battle.
9. Robert Gregory encouraged Yeats to buy the tower.
1. Big country houses in County Galway. Roxborough was Lady Gregory's childhood home.
2. "Robert Gregory painted the Burren Hills and thereby found what promised to grow into a great style, but he had hardly found it before he was killed" (Yeats, "Ireland and the Arts").
3. County south of Galway.

That are our secret discipline
Wherein the gazing heart doubles her might.
70   Soldier, scholar, horseman, he,
And yet he had the intensity
To have published all to be a world's delight.

10

What other could so well have counselled us
In all lovely intricacies of a house
75   As he that practised or that understood
All work in metal or in wood,
In moulded plaster or in carven stone?
Soldier, scholar, horseman, he,
And all he did done perfectly
80   As though he had but that one trade alone.

11

Some burn damp faggots,[4] others may consume
The entire combustible world in one small room
As though dried straw, and if we turn about
The bare chimney is gone black out
85   Because the work had finished in that flare.
Soldier, scholar, horseman, he,
As 'twere all life's epitome,
What made us dream that he could comb grey hair?

12

I had thought, seeing how bitter is that wind
90   That shakes the shutter, to have brought to mind
All those that manhood tried, or childhood loved
Or boyish intellect approved,
With some appropriate commentary on each;
Until imagination brought
95   A fitter welcome; but a thought
Of that late death took all my heart for speech.

June 1918   1918

The Second Coming

Turning and turning in the widening gyre[1]
The falcon cannot hear the falconer;
Things fall apart; the centre cannot hold;
Mere anarchy is loosed upon the world,
5   The blood-dimmed tide is loosed, and everywhere

---

4. Bundles of sticks.
1. Yeats's term (pronounced with a hard g) for a spiraling motion in the shape of a cone. He envisions the two-thousand-year cycle of the Christian age as spiraling toward its end and the next historical cycle as beginning after a violent rever-

sal: "the end of an age, which always receives the revelation of the character of the next age, is represented by the coming of one gyre to its place of greatest expansion and of the other to that of its greatest contraction" [Yeats's note].

The ceremony of innocence is drowned;
The best lack all conviction, while the worst
Are full of passionate intensity.[2]

Surely some revelation is at hand;
10   Surely the Second Coming is at hand.
The Second Coming![3] Hardly are those words out
When a vast image out of *Spiritus Mundi*[4]
Troubles my sight: somewhere in sands of the desert
A shape with lion body and the head of a man,
15   A gaze blank and pitiless as the sun,
Is moving its slow thighs, while all about it
Reel shadows of the indignant desert birds.
The darkness drops again; but now I know
That twenty centuries of stony sleep
20   Were vexed to nightmare by a rocking cradle,
And what rough beast, its hour come round at last,
Slouches towards Bethlehem[5] to be born?

Jan. 1919   1920, 1921

A Prayer for My Daughter

Once more the storm is howling, and half hid
Under this cradle-hood and coverlid
My child sleeps on[1] There is no obstacle
But Gregory's wood[2] and one bare hill
5   Whereby the haystack- and roof-levelling wind,
Bred on the Atlantic, can be stayed;
And for an hour I have walked and prayed
Because of the great gloom that is in my mind.

I have walked and prayed for this young child an hour
10   And heard the sea-wind scream upon the tower,
And under the arches of the bridge, and scream
In the elms above the flooded stream;
Imagining in excited reverie
That the future years had come,
15   Dancing to a frenzied drum,
Out of the murderous innocence of the sea.

May she be granted beauty and yet not
Beauty to make a stranger's eye distraught,

2. The poem was written in January 1919, in the aftermath of World War I and the Russian Revolution and on the eve of the Anglo-Irish War.
3. Christ's second coming is heralded by the coming of the Beast of the Apocalypse, or Antichrist (1 John 2.18).
4. The spirit of the universe (Latin); i.e., Yeats said, "a general storehouse of images," a collective unconscious or memory, in which the human race preserves its past memories.
5. Jesus' birthplace.
1. Yeats's daughter and first child, Anne Butler Yeats, was born on February 26, 1919, in Dublin and brought home to Yeats's refitted Norman tower of Thoor Ballylee in Galway.
2. Lady Gregory's wood at Coole, only a few miles from Thoor Ballylee.

Or hers before a looking-glass, for such,
20 Being made beautiful overmuch,
Consider beauty a sufficient end,
Lose natural kindness and maybe
The heart-revealing intimacy
That chooses right, and never find a friend.

25 Helen being chosen found life flat and dull
And later had much trouble from a fool[3]
While that great Queen, that rose out or the spray,[4]
Being fatherless could have her way
Yet chose a bandy-leggèd smith for man.
30 It's certain that fine women eat
A crazy salad with their meat
Whereby the Horn of Plenty[5] is undone.

In courtesy I'd have her chiefly learned;
Hearts are not had as a gift but hearts are earned
35 By those that are not entirely beautiful;
Yet many, that have played the fool
For beauty's very self, has charm made wise,
And many a poor man that has roved,
Loved and thought himself beloved,
40 From a glad kindness cannot take his eyes.

May she become a flourishing hidden tree
That all her thoughts may like the linnet° be,   *small songbird*
And have no business but dispensing round
Their magnanimities of sound,
45 Not but in merriment begin a chase,
Nor but in merriment a quarrel.
O may she live like some green laurel
Rooted in one dear perpetual place.

My mind, because the minds that I have loved,
50 The sort of beauty that I have approved,
Prosper but little, has dried up of late,
Yet knows that to be choked with hate
May well be of all evil chances chief.
If there's no hatred in a mind
55 Assault and battery of the wind
Can never tear the linnet from the leaf.

An intellectual hatred is the worst,
So let her think opinions are accursed.
Have I not seen the loveliest woman[6] born
60 Out of the mouth of Plenty's horn,

3. Menelaus, Helen's husband. Her abduction by Paris precipitated the Trojan War.
4. Venus, born from the sea, was the Roman goddess of love; her husband, Vulcan, was the lame god of fire and metalwork (line 29).

5. In Greek mythology the goat's horn that suckled the god Zeus flowed with nectar and ambrosia; the cornucopia thus became a symbol of plenty.
6. Maud Gonne.

Because of her opinionated mind
Barter that horn and every good
By quiet natures understood
For an old bellows full of angry wind?

65 Considering that, all hatred driven hence,
The soul recovers radical innocence
And learns at last that it is self-delighting,
Self-appeasing, self-affrighting,
And that its own sweet will is Heaven's will;
70 She can, though every face should scowl
And every windy quarter howl
Or every bellows burst, be happy still.

And may her bridegroom bring her to a house
Where all's accustomed, ceremonious;
75 For arrogance and hatred are the wares
Peddled in the thoroughfares.
How but in custom and in ceremony
Are innocence and beauty born?
Ceremony's a name for the rich horn,
80 And custom for the spreading laurel tree.

Feb.–June 1919   1919, 1921

Leda and the Swan[1]

A sudden blow: the great wings beating still
Above the staggering girl, her thighs caressed
By the dark webs, her nape caught in his bill,
He holds her helpless breast upon his breast.

5 How can those terrified vague fingers push
The feathered glory from her loosening thighs?
And how can body, laid in that white rush,
But feel the strange heart beating where it lies?

A shudder in the loins engenders there
10 The broken wall, the burning roof and tower[2]
And Agamemnon dead.
                              Being so caught up,
So mastered by the brute blood of the air,

---

1. In Greek mythology the god Zeus, in the form of a swan, raped Leda, a mortal. Helen, Clytemnestra, Castor, and Pollux were the children of this union. Yeats saw Leda's rape as the beginning of a new age, analogous with the dove's annunciation to Mary of Jesus' conception: "I imagine the annunciation that founded Greece as made to Leda, remembering that they showed in a Spartan temple, strung up to the roof as a holy relic, an unhatched egg of hers, and that from one of her eggs came love and from the other war" (A Vision). For the author's revisions while composing the poem, see "Poems in Process," in the supplemental ebook.

2. I.e., the destruction of Troy, caused by Helen's abduction by Paris. Agamemnon, the leader of the Greek army that besieged Troy, was murdered by his wife, Clytemnestra, the other daughter of Leda and the swan.

Did she put on his knowledge with his power
Before the indifferent beak could let her drop?

Sept. 1923   1924, 1928

Sailing to Byzantium[1]

1

That is no country for old men. The young
In one another's arms, birds in the trees,
—Those dying generations—at their song,
The salmon-falls, the mackerel-crowded seas,
5   Fish, flesh, or fowl, commend all summer long
Whatever is begotten, born, and dies.
Caught in that sensual music all neglect
Monuments of unageing intellect.

2

An aged man is but a paltry thing,
10   A tattered coat upon a stick, unless
Soul clap its hands and sing,[2] and louder sing
For every tatter in its mortal dress,
Nor is there singing school but studying
Monuments of its own magnificence;
15   And therefore I have sailed the seas and come
To the holy city of Byzantium.

3

O sages standing in God's holy fire
As in the gold mosaic of a wall,[3]
Come from the holy fire, perne in a gyre,[4]
20   And be the singing-masters of my soul.
Consume my heart away; sick with desire
And fastened to a dying animal
It knows not what it is; and gather me
Into the artifice of eternity.

4

25   Once out of nature I shall never take
My bodily form from any natural thing,
But such a form as Grecian goldsmiths make

1. Yeats wrote in *A Vision:* "I think that if I could be given a month of Antiquity and leave to spend it where I chose, I would spend it in Byzantium [now Istanbul] a little before Justinian opened St. Sophia and closed the Academy of Plato [in the 6th century C.E.]. . . . I think that in early Byzantium, maybe never before or since in recorded history, religious, aesthetic and practical life were one, that architect and artificers . . . spoke to the multitude and the few alike. The painter, the mosaic worker, the worker in gold and silver, the illuminator of sacred books, were almost impersonal, almost perhaps without the consciousness of individual design, absorbed in their subject-matter and that the vision of a whole people."
2. The poet William Blake (1757–1827) saw the soul of his dead brother rising to heaven, "clapping his hands for joy."
3. The mosaics in San Apollinaire Nuovo, in Ravenna, Italy, depict rows of Christian saints on a gold background; Yeats saw them in 1907.
4. I.e., whirl in a spiral.

Of hammered gold and gold enamelling
To keep a drowsy Emperor awake;[5]
30   Or set upon a golden bough to sing
To lords and ladies of Byzantium
Of what is past, or passing, or to come.

Sept. 1926   1927

Among School Children

1

I walk through the long schoolroom questioning;
A kind old nun in a white hood replies;
The children learn to cipher° and to sing,   *do arithmetic*
To study reading-books and history,
5   To cut and sew, be neat in everything
In the best modern way—the children's eyes
In momentary wonder stare upon
A sixty-year-old smiling public man.[1]

2

I dream of a Ledaean[2] body, bent
10   Above a sinking fire, a tale that she
Told of a harsh reproof, or trivial event
That changed some childish day to tragedy—
Told, and it seemed that our two natures blent
Into a sphere from youthful sympathy,
15   Or else, to alter Plato's parable,
Into the yolk and white of the one shell.[3]

3

And thinking of that fit of grief or rage
I look upon one child or t'other there
And wonder if she stood so at that age—
20   For even daughters of the swan can share
Something of every paddler's heritage—
And had that colour upon cheek or hair,
And thereupon my heart is driven wild:
She stands before me as a living child.

4

25   Her present image floats into the mind—
Did Quattrocento[4] finger fashion it
Hollow of cheek as though it drank the wind
And took a mess of shadows for its meat?

---

5. I have read somewhere that in the Emperor's palace at Byzantium was a tree made of gold and silver, and artificial birds that sang [Yeats's note].
1. Yeats, as part of his work in the Irish Senate, visited a Montessori school in Waterford in 1926.
2. A body like Leda's. Yeats associated her daughter, Helen of Troy, with Maud Gonne.

3. In the *Symposium*, by the Greek philosopher Plato (ca. 428–ca. 348 B.C.E.), Aristophanes argues that "the primeval man" was both male and female but was divided (like an egg separated into yoke and white); the resulting two beings come together in love to become one again.
4. I.e., the skill of a 15th-century Italian painter.

And I though never of Ledaean kind
30   Had pretty plumage once—enough of that,
Better to smile on all that smile, and show
There is a comfortable kind of old scarecrow.

5

What youthful mother, a shape upon her lap
Honey of generation had betrayed,
35   And that must sleep, shriek, struggle to escape
As recollection or the drug decide,[5]
Would think her son, did she but see that shape
With sixty or more winters on its head,
A compensation for the pang of his birth,
40   Or the uncertainty of his setting forth?

6

Plato thought nature but a spume that plays
Upon a ghostly paradigm of things;[6]
Solider Aristotle played the taws
Upon the bottom of a king of kings;[7]
45   World-famous golden-thighed Pythagoras[8]
Fingered upon a fiddle-stick or strings
What a star sang and careless Muses heard:
Old clothes upon old sticks to scare a bird.

7

Both nuns and mothers worship images,
50   But those the candles light are not as those
That animate a mother's reveries,
But keep a marble or a bronze repose.
And yet they too break hearts—O Presences
That passion, piety or affection knows,
55   And that all heavenly glory symbolise—
O self-born mockers of man's enterprise;

8

Labour is blossoming or dancing where
The body is not bruised to pleasure soul,
Nor beauty born out of its own despair,
60   Nor blear-eyed wisdom out of midnight oil.
O chestnut tree, great-rooted blossomer,
Are you the leaf, the blossom or the bole?°   *trunk*
O body swayed to music, O brightening glance,
How can we know the dancer from the dance?

June 1926   1927

5. I have taken the "honey of generation" from Porphyry's essay on "The Cave of Nymphs" [Yeats's note]. Porphyry (ca. 234–ca. 305 C.E.) was a Neo-platonic philosopher.
6. Plato thought nature merely an image of an ideal world that exists elsewhere.
7. Plato's student Aristotle (384–322 B.C.E.) was "solider" because he regarded this world as the authentic one. He tutored Alexander the Great (356–323 B.C.E.), the "king of kings," and disciplined him with the "taws," or leather strap.
8. Greek philosopher (ca. 580–500 B.C.E), known for his doctrine of the harmony of the spheres and his discovery of the mathematical basis of musical intervals. His disciples, the Pythagoreans, venerated their master as a god with a golden thigh.

A Dialogue of Self and Soul[1]

I

My Soul. I summon to the winding ancient stair;
    Set all your mind upon the steep ascent,
    Upon the broken, crumbling battlement,
    Upon the breathless starlit air,
5   Upon the star that marks the hidden pole;
    Fix every wandering thought upon
    That quarter where all thought is done:
    Who can distinguish darkness from the soul?

My Self. The consecrated blade upon my knees
10   Is Sato's ancient blade, still as it was,
    Still razor-keen, still like a looking-glass
    Unspotted by the centuries;
    That flowering, silken, old embroidery, torn
    From some court-lady's dress and round
15   The wooden scabbard bound and wound,
    Can, tattered, still protect, faded adorn.

My Soul. Why should the imagination of a man
    Long past his prime remember things that are
    Emblematical of love and war?
20   Think of ancestral night that can,
    If but imagination scorn the earth
    And intellect its wandering
    To this and that and t'other thing,
    Deliver from the crime of death and birth.

25 *My Self.* Montashigi, third of his family, fashioned it
    Five hundred years ago, about it lie
    Flowers from I know not what embroidery—
    Heart's purple—and all these I set
    For emblems of the day against the tower
30   Emblematical of the night,
    And claim as by a soldier's right
    A charter to commit the crime once more.

My Soul. Such fullness in that quarter overflows
    And falls into the basin of the mind
35   That man is stricken deaf and dumb and blind,
    For intellect no longer knows
    Is from the *Ought*, or *Knower* from the *Known*—
    That is to say, ascends to Heaven;
    Only the dead can be forgiven;
40   But when I think of that my tongue's a stone.

---

1. In a letter of October 2, 1923, Yeats wrote: "I am writing a new tower poem 'Sword and Tower,' which is a choice of rebirth rather than deliverance from birth. I make my Japanese sword and its silk covering my symbol of life." Junzo Sato, a friend, had given him the ceremonial sword in 1920.

2

My Self. A living man is blind and drinks his drop.
　　　　What matter if the ditches are impure?
　　　　What matter if I live it all once more?
　　　　Endure that toil of growing up;
45　　　The ignominy of boyhood; the distress
　　　　Of boyhood changing into man;
　　　　The unfinished man and his pain
　　　　Brought face to face with his own clumsiness;

　　　　The finished man among his enemies?—
50　　　How in the name of Heaven can he escape
　　　　That defiling and disfigured shape
　　　　The mirror of malicious eyes
　　　　Casts upon his eyes until at last
　　　　He thinks that shape must be his shape?
55　　　And what's the good of an escape
　　　　If honour find him in the wintry blast?

　　　　I am content to live it all again
　　　　And yet again, if it be life to pitch
　　　　Into the frog-spawn of a blind man's ditch,
60　　　A blind man battering blind men;
　　　　Or into that most fecund ditch of all,
　　　　The folly that man does
　　　　Or must suffer, if he woos
　　　　A proud woman not kindred of his soul.

65　　　I am content to follow to its source
　　　　Every event in action or in thought;
　　　　Measure the lot; forgive myself the lot!
　　　　When such as I cast out remorse
　　　　So great a sweetness flows into the breast
70　　　We must laugh and we must sing,
　　　　We are blest by everything,
　　　　Everything we look upon is blest.

July–Dec. 1927　　　　　　　　　　　　　　　　　　1929

Byzantium[1]

　　　　The unpurged images of day recede;
　　　　The Emperor's drunken soldiery are abed;

1. On October 4, 1930, Yeats sent his friend Sturge Moore a copy of this poem, saying: "The poem originates from a criticism of yours. You objected to the last verse of 'Sailing to Byzantium' because a bird made by a goldsmith was just as natural as anything else. That showed me that the idea needed exposition." The previous April, Yeats had noted in his diary: "Subject for a poem": "Describe Byzantium as it is in the system towards the end of the first Christian millennium. A walking mummy. Flames at the street corners where the soul is purified, birds of hammered gold singing in the golden trees, in the harbour [dolphins] offering their backs to the wailing dead that they may carry them to Paradise."

Night resonance recedes, night-walkers' song
After great cathedral gong;
5　A starlit or a moonlit dome² disdains
All that man is,
All mere complexities,
The fury and the mire° of human veins.　　　　　*deep mud*

Before me floats an image, man or shade,
10　Shade more than man, more image than a shade;
For Hades' bobbin³ bound in mummy-cloth
May unwind the winding path;⁴
A mouth that has no moisture and no breath
Breathless mouths may summon;
15　I hail the superhuman;
I call it death-in-life and life-in-death.⁵

Miracle, bird or golden handiwork,
More miracle than bird or handiwork,
Planted on the starlit golden bough,
20　Can like the cocks of Hades crow,
Or, by the moon embittered, scorn aloud
In glory of changeless metal
Common bird or petal
And all complexities of mire or blood.

25　At midnight on the Emperor's pavement flit
Flames that no faggot° feeds, nor steel has lit,　　*bundle of sticks*
Nor storm disturbs, flames begotten of flame,
Where blood-begotten spirits come
And all complexities of fury leave,
30　Dying into a dance,
An agony of trance,
An agony of flame that cannot singe a sleeve.

Astraddle on the dolphin's mire and blood,⁶
Spirit after spirit! The smithies break the flood,
35　The golden smithies of the Emperor!
Marbles of the dancing floor
Break bitter furies of complexity,
Those images that yet
Fresh images beget,
40　That dolphin-torn, that gong-tormented sea.

Sept. 1930　　　　　　　　　　　　　　　　　　　　　　　1932

---

2. Of the great church of St. Sophia.
3. Spool. Hades was the Greek god of the under-world, the realm of the dead.
4. I.e., the spool of people's fate, which spins their destiny and which is wound like a mummy, may be unwound and lead to the timeless world of pure spirit.
5. On Roman tombstones the cock is a herald of rebirth, thus of the continuing cycle of human life.
6. In ancient mythology dolphins were thought to carry the souls of the dead to the Isles of the Blessed.

Crazy Jane Talks with the Bishop[1]

I met the Bishop on the road
And much said he and I.
"Those breasts are flat and fallen now
Those veins must soon be dry;
5   Live in a heavenly mansion,
Not in some foul sty."

"Fair and foul are near of kin,
And fair needs foul," I cried.
"My friends are gone, but that's a truth
10 Nor grave nor bed denied,
Learned in bodily lowliness
And in the heart's pride.

"A woman can be proud and stiff
When on love intent;
15 But Love has pitched his mansion in
The place of excrement;
For nothing can be sole or whole
That has not been rent."

Nov. 1931   1932

Lapis Lazuli

(For Harry Clifton)[1]

I have heard that hysterical women say
They are sick of the palette and fiddle-bow,
Of poets that are always gay,
For everybody knows or else should know
5   That if nothing drastic is done[2]
Aeroplane and Zeppelin[3] will come out,
Pitch like King Billy[4] bomb-balls in
Until the town lie beaten flat.

All perform their tragic play,
10 There struts Hamlet, there is Lear,
That's Ophelia, that Cordelia;
Yet they, should the last scene be there,

1. One of a series of poems about an old woman partly modeled on Cracked Mary, an old woman who lived near Lady Gregory.
1. The English writer Harry Clifton (1908–1978) gave Yeats for his seventieth birthday a piece of lapis lazuli, a deep blue stone, "carved by some Chinese sculptor into the semblance of a mountain with temple, trees, paths, and an ascetic and pupil about to climb the mountain. Ascetic, pupil, hard stone, eternal theme of the sensual east. The heroic cry in the midst of despair. But no, I am wrong, the east has its solutions always and therefore knows nothing of tragedy. It is we, not the east, that must raise the heroic cry" [Yeats to Dorothy Wellesley, July 6, 1935].
2. Because Europe was (in 1936) close to war.
3. German zeppelins, or airships, bombed London during World War I.
4. King William III (William of Orange), who defeated the army of King James II at the Battle of the Boyne, in Ireland, in 1690. In a popular ballad, "King William he threw his bomb-balls in, / And set them on fire."

The great stage curtain about to drop,
If worthy their prominent part in the play,
15 Do not break up their lines to weep.
They know that Hamlet and Lear are gay;
Gaiety transfiguring all that dread.
All men have aimed at, found and lost;
Black out; Heaven blazing into the head:
20 Tragedy wrought to its uttermost.
Though Hamlet rambles and Lear rages,
And all the drop scenes drop at once
Upon a hundred thousand stages,
It cannot grow by an inch or an ounce.

25 On their own feet they came, or on shipboard,
Camel-back, horse-back, ass-back, mule-back,
Old civilisations put to the sword.
Then they and their wisdom went to rack:
No handiwork of Callimachus[5]
30 Who handled marble as if it were bronze,
Made draperies that seemed to rise
When sea-wind swept the corner, stands;
His long lamp chimney shaped like the stem
Of a slender palm, stood but a day;
35 All things fall and are built again
And those that build them again are gay.

Two Chinamen, behind them a third,
Are carved in Lapis Lazuli,
Over them flies a long-legged bird
40 A symbol of longevity;
The third, doubtless a serving-man,
Carries a musical instrument.

Every discolouration of the stone,
Every accidental crack or dent
45 Seems a water-course or an avalanche,
Or lofty slope where it still snows
Though doubtless plum or cherry-branch
Sweetens the little half-way house
Those Chinamen climb towards, and I
50 Delight to imagine them seated there;
There, on the mountain and the sky,
On all the tragic scene they stare.
One asks for mournful melodies;
Accomplished fingers begin to play.
55 Their eyes mid many wrinkles, their eyes,
Their ancient, glittering eyes, are gay.

July 1936   1938

---

5. Athenian sculptor (5th century B.C.E.), supposedly the originator of the Corinthian column
and of the use of the running drill to imitate
folds in drapery in statues. Yeats wrote of him:
"With Callimachus pure Ionic revives again . . .
and upon the only example of his work known to
us, a marble chair, a Persian is represented, and
may one not discover a Persian symbol in that
bronze lamp, shaped like a palm . . . ? But he was
an archaistic workman, and those who set him to
work brought back public life to an older form"
(A Vision).

Under Ben Bulben[1]

1

Swear by what the Sages spoke
Round the Mareotic Lake[2]
That the Witch of Atlas knew,
Spoke and set the cocks a-crow.
5 Swear by those horsemen, by those women,
Complexion and form prove superhuman,[3]
That pale, long visaged company
That airs an immortality
Completeness of their passions won;
10 Now they ride the wintry dawn
Where Ben Bulben sets the scene.

Here's the gist of what they mean.

2

Many times man lives and dies
Between his two eternities,
15 That of race and that of soul,
And ancient Ireland knew it all.
Whether man dies in his bed
Or the rifle knocks him dead,
A brief parting from those dear
20 Is the worst man has to fear.
Though grave-diggers' toil is long,
Sharp their spades, their muscle strong,
They but thrust their buried men
Back in the human mind again.

3

25 You that Mitchel's prayer have heard
"Send war in our time, O Lord!"[4]
Know that when all words are said
And a man is fighting mad,
Something drops from eyes long blind
30 He completes his partial mind,
For an instant stands at ease,
Laughs aloud, his heart at peace,
Even the wisest man grows tense
With some sort of violence
35 Before he can accomplish fate
Know his work or choose his mate.

1. A mountain near Sligo; Yeats's grave is in sight of it, in Drumcliff churchyard.
2. Lake Mareotis, near Alexandria, Egypt, was an ancient center of Christian Neoplatonism and of neo-Pythagorean philosophy. The lake is mentioned in Percy Bysshe Shelley's poem "The Witch of Atlas." In an essay on Shelley, Yeats interprets the witch as a symbol of timeless, absolute beauty; passing in a boat by this and another lake, she "sees all human life shadowed upon its waters . . . and because she can see the reality of things she is described as journeying 'in the calm depths' of 'the wide lake' we journey over unpiloted."
3. Superhuman beings or fairies, like the Sidhe, believed to ride through the countryside near Ben Bulben.
4. From *Jail Journal*, by the Irish nationalist John Mitchel (1815–1875).

4

Poet and sculptor do the work
Nor let the modish painter shirk
What his great forefathers did,
40   Bring the soul of man to God,
Make him fill the cradles right.
Measurement began our might:
Forms a stark Egyptian thought,
Forms that gentler Phidias[5] wrought.

45   Michael Angelo left a proof
On the Sistine Chapel roof,
Where but half-awakened Adam
Can disturb globe-trotting Madam
Till her bowels are in heat,
50   Proof that there's a purpose set
Before the secret working mind:
Profane perfection of mankind.

Quattrocento[6] put in paint,
On backgrounds for a God or Saint,
55   Gardens where a soul's at ease;
Where everything that meets the eye
Flowers and grass and cloudless sky
Resemble forms that are, or seem
When sleepers wake and yet still dream,
60   And when it's vanished still declare,
With only bed and bedstead there,
That Heavens had opened.

               Gyres[7] run on;
When that greater dream had gone
Calvert and Wilson, Blake and Claude[8]
65   Prepared a rest for the people of God,
Palmer's[9] Phrase, but after that
Confusion fell upon our thought.

5

Irish poets learn your trade
Sing whatever is well made,
70   Scorn the sort now growing up
All out of shape from toe to top,
Their unremembering hearts and heads
Base-born products of base beds.
Sing the peasantry, and then
75   Hard-riding country gentlemen,
The holiness of monks, and after

---

5. Greek sculptor (fl. ca. 490–430 B.C.E.).
6. 15th-century Italian art.
7. Yeats's term for conelike spirals or cycles of history.
8. Edward Calvert (1799–1883), English visionary artist and follower of William Blake (1757–

1827), English mystical poet and artist. Richard Wilson (1714–1782), English landscape painter and disciple of Claude Lorraine (1600–1682), French artist.
9. Samuel Palmer (1805–1881), English landscape painter who admired Blake.

Yeats's grave under Ben Bulben, in Drumcliff Churchyard, County Sligo, Ireland. In his late poem "Under Ben Bulben," Yeats imagines himself buried in this setting: "In Drumcliff churchyard Yeats is laid." He commands that there be no "conventional" marble tombstone but a three-line epitaph cut into local limestone. He died in southern France in 1939 but his remains were not moved to Ireland until 1948.

> Porter-drinkers'[1] randy laughter;
> Sing the lords and ladies gay
> That were beaten into the clay
> 80 Through seven heroic centuries;[2]
> Cast your mind on other days
> That we in coming days may be
> Still the indomitable Irishry.

6

> Under bare Ben Bulben's head
> 85 In Drumcliff churchyard Yeats is laid,
> An ancestor was rector there[3]
> Long years ago; a church stands near,
> By the road an ancient Cross.
> No marble, no conventional phrase,
> On limestone quarried near the spot
> By his command these words are cut:

> Cast a cold eye
> On life, on death.
> Horseman, pass by!

Sept. 1938   1939

1. Drinkers of dark brown bitter beer.
2. Since the Norman conquest of Ireland, in the 12th century.

3. Yeats's great-grandfather, the Reverend John Yeats (1774–1846), was rector of Drumcliff Church, Sligo.

The Circus Animals' Desertion

1

I sought a theme and sought for it in vain,
I sought it daily for six weeks or so.
Maybe at last being but a broken man,
I must be satisfied with my heart, although
5   Winter and summer till old age began
My circus animals were all on show,
Those stilted boys, that burnished chariot,
Lion and woman and the Lord knows what.[1]

2

What can I but enumerate old themes,
10   First that sea-rider Oisin[2] led by the nose
Through three enchanted islands, allegorical dreams,
Vain gaiety, vain battle, vain repose,
Themes of the embittered heart, or so it seems,
That might adorn old songs or courtly shows;
15   But what cared I that set him on to ride,
I, starved for the bosom of his fairy bride.

And then a counter-truth filled out its play,
"The Countess Cathleen"[3] was the name I gave it,
She, pity-crazed, had given her soul away,
20   But masterful Heaven had intervened to save it.
I thought my dear must her own soul destroy
So did fanaticism and hate enslave it,
And this brought forth a dream and soon enough
This dream itself had all my thought and love.

25   And when the Fool and Blind Man stole the bread
Cuchulain fought the ungovernable sea;[4]
Heart mysteries there, and yet when all is said
It was the dream itself enchanted me:
Character isolated by a deed
30   To engross the present and dominate memory.
Players and painted stage took all my love
And not those things that they were emblems of.

1. Yeats refers to the ancient Irish heroes of his early work ("Those stilted boys"), the gilded carriage of his play *The Unicorn from the Stars* (1908), and the lion in several of his poems, including "The Second Coming."
2. In the long title poem of Yeats's first successful book, *The Wanderings of Oisin and Other Poems* (1889), the legendary poet warrior Oisin (pronounced *Ushēēn*) is enchanted by the beautiful fairy woman Niamh (pronounced *Neeve*), who leads him to the Islands of Delight, of Many Fears, and of Forgetfulness.
3. A play (published in 1892) about an Irish countess (an idealized version of Maud Gonne) who sells her soul to the devil to buy food for the starving Irish poor but is taken up to heaven (for God "Looks always on the motive, not the deed").
4. In Yeats's play *On Baile's Strand* (1904), the legendary warrior Cuchulain (pronounced *CuHOOlin* by Yeats, *KooHULLin* in Irish), crazed by his discovery that he has killed his son, fights with the sea.

3

Those masterful images because complete
Grew in pure mind but out of what began?
35   A mound of refuse or the sweepings of a street,
Old kettles, old bottles, and a broken can,
Old iron, old bones, old rags, that raving slut
Who keeps the till. Now that my ladder's gone
I must lie down where all the ladders start
40   In the foul rag and bone shop of the heart.

1939

From Introduction
[A General Introduction for My Work][1]
I. The First Principle

A poet writes always of his personal life, in his finest work out of its tragedies, whatever it be, remorse, lost love or mere loneliness; he never speaks directly as to someone at the breakfast table, there is always a phantasmagoria. Dante and Milton had mythologies, Shakespeare the characters of English history, of traditional romance; even when the poet seems most himself, when Raleigh and gives potentates the lie,[2] or Shelley 'a nerve o'er which do creep the else unfelt oppressions of mankind',[3] or Byron when 'the heart wears out the breast as the sword wears out the sheath',[4] he is never the bundle of accident and incoherence that sits down to breakfast; he has been re-born as an idea, something intended, complete. A novelist might describe his accidence, his incoherence, he must not, he is more type than man, more passion than type. He is Lear, Romeo, Oedipus, Tiresias; he has stepped out of a play and even the woman he loves is Rosalind, Cleopatra, never The Dark Lady.[5] He is part of his own phantasmagoria and we adore him because nature has grown intelligible, and by so doing a part of our creative power. 'When mind is lost in the light of the Self', says the Prashna Upanishad,[6] 'it dreams no more; still in the body it is lost in happiness.' 'A wise man seeks in Self', says the Chāndôgya Upanishad, 'those that are alive and those that are dead and gets what the world cannot give.' The world knows nothing because it has made nothing, we know everything because we have made everything.

1. Written in 1937 and originally printed as "A General Introduction for My Work" in *Essays and Introductions* (1961), the text is excerpted from *Later Essays*, ed. William H. O'Donnell (1994), vol. 5 of *The Collected Works of W. B. Yeats*.
2. From "The Lie," by the English writer and explorer Sir Walter Ralegh (1552–1618): "Tell potentates, they live / Acting by others' action; / Not loved unless they give, / Not strong but by a faction: / If potentates' reply, / Give potentates the lie."
3. From "Julian and Maddalo," by the English poet Percy Bysshe Shelley (1792–1822).
4. Cf. "So, we'll go no more a roving," by the English poet George Gordon, Lord Byron.
5. The woman to whom many of Shakespeare's de-idealizing sonnets are addressed. The rest of the names refer to characters in Shakespeare's plays and in Sophocles' ancient Greek drama *Oedipus the King*.
6. One of a series of ancient philosophical dialogues in Sanskrit. From *Ten Principal Upanishads* (1937), translated by Yeats and the Indian monk Shri Purohit Swami (1882–1941).

II. Subject-Matter

* * *

I am convinced that in two or three generations it will become generally known that the mechanical theory[7] has no reality, that the natural and supernatural are knit together, that to escape a dangerous fanaticism we must study a new science; at that moment Europeans may find something attractive in a Christ posed against a background not of Judaism but of Druidism, not shut off in dead history, but flowing, concrete, phenomenal.

I was born into this faith, have lived in it, and shall die in it; my Christ, a legitimate deduction from the Creed of St Patrick[8] as I think, is that Unity of Being Dante compared to a perfectly proportioned human body, Blake's 'Imagination',[9] what the Upanishads have named 'Self': nor is this unity distant and therefore intellectually understandable, but imminent,[1] differing from man to man and age to age, taking upon itself pain and ugliness, 'eye of newt, and leg of frog'.[2]

Subconscious preoccupation with this theme brought me *A Vision*,[3] its harsh geometry an incomplete interpretation. The 'Irishry' have preserved their ancient 'deposit' through wars which, during the sixteenth and seventeenth centuries, became wars of extermination; no people, Lecky said at the opening of his *Ireland in the Eighteenth Century*,[4] have undergone greater persecution, nor did that persecution altogether cease up to our own day. No people hate as we do in whom that past is always alive; there are moments when hatred poisons my life and I accuse myself of effeminacy because I have not given it adequate expression. It is not enough to have put it into the mouth of a rambling peasant poet. Then I remind myself that, though mine is the first English marriage I know of in the direct line, all my family names are English and that I owe my soul to Shakespeare, to Spenser and to Blake, perhaps to William Morris,[5] and to the English language in which I think, speak and write, that everything I love has come to me through English; my hatred tortures me with love, my love with hate. I am like the Tibetan monk who dreams at his initiation that he is eaten by a wild beast and learns on waking that he himself is eater and eaten. This is Irish hatred and solitude, the hatred of human life that made Swift write *Gulliver*[6] and the epitaph upon his tomb, that can still make us wag between extremes and doubt our sanity.

Again and again I am asked why I do not write in Gaelic; some four or five years ago I was invited to dinner by a London society and found myself among

---

7. Theory explaining the universe in strictly naturalistic, Newtonian terms.

8. From the second paragraph of "The Confession of St. Patrick, or His Epistle to the Irish," by the 5th-century saint, the apostle of Ireland.

9. In *Jerusalem* the English poet William Blake (1757–1827) describes imagination as the "Divine body of the lord Jesus." Yeats's ideas about the Unity of Being are drawn from his reading of Dante's *Il Convito*.

1. In manuscript Yeats wrote "imanent" (a misspelling of "immanent"), but he allowed "imminent" to stand in the typescript.

2. Yeats's paraphrase of the ingredients of the witches' cauldron in Shakespeare's *Macbeth* 4.1.

3. Yeats's mystical writings (1925, 1937), in which he sketches out and schematizes many of his theories.

4. *A History of Ireland in the Eighteenth Century*; by the Irish historian William Edward Hartpole Lecky (1838–1903).

5. English poet and designer (1834–1896). Edmund Spenser (1552–1599), English poet who, in addition to poetic works such as *The Faerie Queene*, wrote a treatise proposing the extermination of the Irish.

6. *Gulliver's Travels*, by the Irish satirist Jonathan Swift (1667–1745). Yeats's poem "Swift's Epitaph," a loose translation of the Latin on Swift's tomb, claims that "Swift has sailed into his rest; / Savage indignation there / Cannot lacerate his breast."

London journalists, Indian students and foreign political refugees. An Indian paper says it was a dinner in my honour, I hope not; I have forgotten though I have a clear memory of my own angry mind. I should have spoken as men are expected to speak at public dinners; I should have paid and been paid conventional compliments; then they would speak of the refugees, from that on all would be lively and topical, foreign tyranny would be arraigned, England seem even to those confused Indians the protector of liberty; I grew angrier and angrier; Wordsworth, that typical Englishman, had published his famous sonnet to François Dominique Toussaint, a Santo Domingo negro:

> There's not a breathing of the common wind
> That will forget thee[7]

in the year when Emmet conspired and died, and he remembered that rebellion as little as the half hanging and the pitch cap that preceded it by half a dozen years.[8] That there might be no topical speeches I denounced the oppression of the people of India; being a man of letters, not a politician, I told how they had been forced to learn everything, even their own Sanscrit, through the vehicle of English till the first discoverers of wisdom had become bywords for vague abstract facility. I begged the Indian writers present to remember that no man can think or write with music and vigour except in his mother tongue. I turned a friendly audience hostile, yet when I think of that scene I am unrepentant and angry.

I could no more have written in Gaelic than can those Indians write in English; Gaelic is my national language, but it is not my mother tongue.

III. Style and Attitude

Style is almost unconscious. I know what I have tried to do, little what I have done. Contemporary lyric poems, even those that moved me—'The Stream's Secret', 'Dolores'[9]—seemed too long, but an Irish preference for a swift current might be mere indolence, yet Burns may have felt the same when he read Thomson and Cowper.[1] The English mind is meditative, rich, deliberate; it may remember the Thames[2] valley. I planned to write short lyrics or poetic drama where every speech [would] be short and concentrated, knit by dramatic tension, and I did so with more confidence because young English poets were at that time writing out of emotion at the moment of crisis, though their old slow-moving meditation returned almost at once. Then, and in this English poetry has followed my lead, I tried to make the language of poetry coincide with that of passionate, normal speech. I wanted to write in whatever language comes most naturally when we soliloquise, as I do all day long, upon the events of our own lives or of any life where we can see ourselves for the moment. I sometimes compare myself with the mad old slum women I hear denouncing and remembering; 'how dare you,' I heard

7. From "To Toussaint L'Ouverture," by the English poet William Wordsworth (1770–1850). L'Ouverture (1743–1803) died in prison after rebelling against France's rule in Haiti.
8. Paper caps filled with burning pitch were used for torture during the martial law preceding and following the Irish Rising of 1798. Robert Emmet (1778–1803), Irish nationalist executed after the Irish rebellion of 1803.

9. Long poems by Dante Gabriel Rossetti (1828–1882) and Algernon Charles Swinburne (1837–1909), respectively.
1. James Thomson (1700–1748) and William Cowper (1731–1800), poets most famous for their long poems. Robert Burns (1759–1796), Scottish poet of short lyrics.
2. River that runs through London.

one say of some imaginary suitor, 'and you without health or a home'. If I spoke my thoughts aloud they might be as angry and as wild. It was a long time before I had made a language to my liking; I began to make it when I discovered some twenty years ago that I must seek, not as Wordsworth thought words in common use,[3] but a powerful and passionate syntax, and a complete coincidence between period and stanza. Because I need a passionate syntax for passionate subject-matter I compel myself to accept those traditional metres that have developed with the language. Ezra Pound, Turner, Lawrence, wrote admirable free verse, I could not.[4] I would lose myself, become joyless like those mad old women. The translators of the Bible, Sir Thomas Browne,[5] certain translators from the Greek when translators still bothered about rhythm, created a form midway between prose and verse that seems natural to impersonal meditation; but all that is personal soon rots; it must be packed in ice or salt. Once when I was in delirium from pneumonia I dictated a letter to George Moore[6] telling him to eat salt because it was a symbol of eternity; the delirium passed, I had no memory of that letter, but I must have meant what I now mean. If I wrote of personal love or sorrow in free verse, or in any rhythm that left it unchanged, amid all its accident, I would be full of self-contempt because of my egotism and indiscretion, and I foresee the boredom of my reader. I must choose a traditional stanza, even what I alter must seem traditional. I commit my emotion to shepherds, herdsmen, camel-drivers, learned men, Milton's or Shelley's Platonist, that tower Palmer drew.[7] Talk to me of originality and I will turn on you with rage. I am a crowd, I am a lonely man, I am nothing. Ancient salt is best packing. The heroes of Shakespeare convey to us through their looks, or through the metaphorical patterns of their speech, the sudden enlargement of their vision, their ecstasy at the approach of death, 'She should have died hereafter', 'Of many million kisses, the poor last', 'Absent thee from felicity awhile'; they have become God or Mother Goddess, the pelican, 'My baby at my breast',[8] but all must be cold; no actress has ever sobbed when she played Cleopatra, even the shallow brain of a producer has never thought of such a thing. The supernatural is present, cold winds blow across our hands, upon our faces, the thermometer falls, and because of that cold we are hated by journalists and groundlings. There may be in this or that detail painful tragedy, but in the whole work none. I have heard Lady Gregory say, rejecting some play in the modern manner sent to the Abbey Theatre, 'Tragedy must be a joy to the man who dies.' Nor is it any different with lyrics, songs, narrative poems; neither scholars nor the populace have sung or read anything generation after generation because of its pain. The maid of honour whose tragedy they sing must be lifted out of history with timeless pattern, she is one of the four Maries,[9] the rhythm is old

---

3. In the preface to *Lyrical Ballads* (1800), Wordsworth says that poetry should be written in "language really used by men."
4. In his *Oxford Book of Modern Verse* (1936), Yeats included free verse by the American poet Ezra Pound (1885–1972), the English poet Walter Turner (1889–1946), and the English poet and novelist D. H. Lawrence (1885–1930).
5. English physician and author (1605–1682) with an elaborate prose style.
6. Irish novelist (1852–1933).
7. The English artist Samuel Palmer (1805–1881)

drew "The Lonely Tower" (1879) as an illustration of Milton's poem about the pensive man, "Il Penseroso" (1645), in which a scholar in a "high lonely tower" is dedicated to uncovering Plato's insights; in Shelley's "Prince Athanase," the idealistic hero searches for love.
8. From *Macbeth* 5.4, *Anthony and Cleopatra* 4.15, *Hamlet* 5.2, respectively. "Pelican": thought to feed its babies with its blood and thus often a symbol of self-sacrifice.
9. Mary, Queen of Scots (1542–1587) was served by four women named Mary.

and familiar, imagination must dance, must be carried beyond feeling into the aboriginal ice. Is ice the correct word? I once boasted, copying the phrase from a letter of my father's, that I would write a poem 'cold and passionate as the dawn'.[1]

When I wrote in blank verse I was dissatisfied; my vaguely mediaeval *Countess Cathleen* fitted the measure, but our Heroic Age went better, or so I fancied, in the ballad metre of *The Green Helmet*.[2] There was something in what I felt about Deirdre, about Cuchulain,[3] that rejected the Renaissance and its characteristic metres, and this was a principal reason why I created in dance plays the form that varies blank verse with lyric metres. When I speak blank verse and analyse my feelings I stand at a moment of history when instinct, its traditional songs and dances, its general agreement, is of the past. I have been cast up out of the whale's belly though I still remember the sound and sway that came from beyond its ribs,[4] and, like the Queen in Paul Fort's ballad,[5] I smell of the fish of the sea. The contrapuntal structure of the verse, to employ a term adopted by Robert Bridges,[6] combines the past and present. If I repeat the first line of *Paradise Lost* so as to emphasise its five feet I am among the folk singers, 'Of mán's first dísobédience ánd the frúit', but speak it as I should I cross it with another emphasis, that of passionate prose, 'Of mán's first disobédience and the frúit', or 'Of mán's fírst dísobedience and the frúit', the folk song is still there, but a ghostly voice, an unvariable possibility, an unconscious norm. What moves me and my hearer is a vivid speech that has no laws except that it must not exorcise the ghostly voice. I am awake and asleep, at my moment of revelation, self-possessed in self-surrender; there is no rhyme, no echo of the beaten drum, the dancing foot, that would overset my balance. When I was a boy I wrote a poem upon dancing that had one good line: 'They snatch with their hands at the sleep of the skies.' If I sat down and thought for a year I would discover that but for certain syllabic limitations, a rejection or acceptance of certain elisions, I must wake or sleep.

The Countess Cathleen could speak a blank verse which I had loosened, almost put out of joint, for her need, because I thought of her as mediaeval and thereby connected her with the general European movement. For Deirdre and Cuchulain and all the other figures of Irish legend are still in the whale's belly.

IV. Whither?

The young English poets reject dream and personal emotion; they have thought out opinions that join them to this or that political party; they employ an intricate psychology, action in character, not as in the ballads

---

1. From "The Fisherman" (1916): "Before I am old / I shall have written him one / Poem maybe as cold / And passionate as the dawn."
2. *The Countess Cathleen* (1892, later revised) is written in blank verse; *The Green Helmet* (1910), in iambic heptameter, which resembles the meter of a ballad (alternating between four- and three-stress lines).
3. The warrior hero of the Irish mythological Ulster Cycle; he also appears in Yeats's "dance" plays, derived from Japanese Noh drama. "Deirdre": in the Ulster Cycle, woman chosen to be queen of Ulster before she elopes with Naoise (pronounced *Neesha*).
4. Cf. Jonah 2.10: "And the Lord spake unto the fish, and it vomited out Jonah upon the dry land."
5. "La Reine à la Mer" ("The Queen of the Sea," 1894–96), by the French poet Paul Fort (1872–1960).
6. English poet (1844–1930), who stressed the poetic tension of the counterpoint between regular meters and the rhythm of poetry as actually spoken.

character in action, and all consider that they have a right to the same close attention that men pay to the mathematician and the metaphysician. One of the more distinguished has just explained that man has hitherto slept but must now awake.[7] They are determined to express the factory, the metropolis, that they may be modern. Young men teaching school in some picturesque cathedral town, or settled for life in Capri or in Sicily, defend their type of metaphor by saying that it comes naturally to a man who travels to his work by Tube.[8] I am indebted to a man of this school who went through my work at my request, crossing out all conventional metaphors,[9] but they seem to me to have rejected also those dream associations which were the whole art of Mallarmé.[1] He had topped a previous wave. As they express not what the Upanishads call 'that ancient Self' but individual intellect, they have the right to choose the man in the Tube because of his objective importance. They attempt to kill the whale, push the Renaissance higher yet, out-think Leonardo;[2] their verse kills the folk ghost and yet would remain verse. I am joined to the 'Irishry' and I expect a counter-Renaissance. No doubt it is part of the game to push that Renaissance; I make no complaint; I am accustomed to the geometrical arrangement of history in *A Vision*, but I go deeper than 'custom' for my convictions. When I stand upon O'Connell Bridge[3] in the half-light and notice that discordant architecture, all those electric signs, where modern heterogeneity has taken physical form, a vague hatred comes up out of my own dark and I am certain that wherever in Europe there are minds strong enough to lead others the same vague hatred rises; in four or five or in less generations this hatred will have issued in violence and imposed some kind of rule of kindred. I cannot know the nature of that rule, for its opposite fills the light; all I can do to bring it nearer is to intensify my hatred. I am no Nationalist, except in Ireland for passing reasons; State and Nation are the work of intellect, and when you consider what comes before and after them they are, as Victor Hugo said of something or other, not worth the blade of grass God gives for the nest of the linnet.[4]

1937   1961

---

7. Perhaps W. H. Auden (1907–1973) or C. Day Lewis (1904–1972).
8. London's underground railway. Lewis taught in the spa town of Cheltenham in the early 1930s. D. H. Lawrence lived in Capri and Sicily in the early 1920s.
9. Ezra Pound did this circa 1910.

1. Stéphane Mallarmé (1842–1898), French poet.
2. Leonardo da Vinci (1452–1519), Italian artist and inventor.
3. Over Dublin's river Liffey.
4. Small finch. Victor Hugo (1802–1885), French writer.

VIRGINIA WOOLF
1882–1941

Virginia Woolf was born in London, daughter of Julia Jackson Duckworth, a member of the Duckworth publishing family, and Leslie (later Sir Leslie) Stephen, the Victorian critic, philosopher, biographer, and scholar. She grew up within a large and talented family, educating herself in her father's magnificent library, meeting in childhood many eminent Victorians, and learning Greek from the essayist and critic Walter Pater's sister. Writing and the intellectual life thus came naturally to her. But her youth was shadowed by suffering: her older half-brother sexually abused her; her mother died in 1895, precipitating the first of her mental breakdowns; a beloved half-sister died in childbirth two years later; her father died of cancer in 1904; and a brother died of typhoid in 1906.

After her father's death she settled with her sister and two brothers in Bloomsbury, the district of London that later became associated with the group among whom she moved. The Bloomsbury Group was an intellectual coterie frequented at various times by the biographer Lytton Strachey, the economist John Maynard Keynes, the art critic Roger Fry, and the novelist E. M. Forster. When her sister, Vanessa, a notable painter, married Clive Bell, an art critic, in 1907, Woolf and her brother Adrian took another house in Bloomsbury, and there they entertained their literary and artistic friends at evening gatherings, where the conversation sparkled. The Bloomsbury Group thrived at the center of the middle-class and upper-middle-class London intelligentsia. Their intelligence was equaled by their frankness, notably on sexual topics, and the sexual life of Bloomsbury provided ample material for discussion and contributed to Woolf's freedom of thinking about gender relations. The painter Duncan Grant, for example, was at different times the lover of Keynes, Woolf's brother Adrian, and her sister, whose daughter, Angelica, he fathered. Woolf too was bisexual; and thirteen years after her marriage to the journalist and essayist Leonard Woolf, she fell passionately in love with the poet Vita [Victoria] Sackville-West, wife of the bisexual diplomat and author Harold Nicolson. Woolf's relationship with this aristocratic lesbian inspired the most lighthearted and scintillating of her books, *Orlando* (1928), a novel about a transhistorical androgynous protagonist, whose identity shifts from masculine to feminine over centuries.

Underneath Woolf's liveliness and wit—qualities so well known among the Bloomsbury Group—lay psychological tensions created partly by her childhood wounds and partly by her perfectionism, she being her own most exacting critic. The public was unaware until her death that she had been subject to periods of severe depression, particularly after finishing a book. In March 1941 she drowned herself in a river, an act influenced by her dread of World War II (she and Leonard would have been arrested by the

Virginia Woolf (1882–1941).

Gestapo had the Nazis invaded England) and her fear that she was about to lose her mind and become a burden on her husband, who had supported her emotionally and intellectually. (In 1917 the Woolfs had founded the Hogarth Press, which published some of the most interesting literature of their time, including T. S. Eliot's *Poems* [1919], fiction by Maxim Gorky, Katherine Mansfield, and E. M. Forster, the English translations of Freud, and Virginia's novels.)

As a fiction writer Woolf rebelled against what she called the "materialism" of novelists such as her contemporaries Arnold Bennett and John Galsworthy, who depicted suffering and social injustice through gritty realism, and she sought to render more intricately those aspects of consciousness in which she felt the truth of human experience lay. In her essay "Modern Fiction" she defines the task of the novelist as looking within, as conveying the mind receiving "a myriad impressions," as representing the "luminous halo" or "semi-transparent envelope surrounding us from the beginning of consciousness to the end." In her novels she abandoned linear narratives, in favor of interior monologues and stream of consciousness narration, exploring with great subtlety problems of personal identity and personal relationships as well as the significance of time, change, loss, and memory for human personality. After two conventionally realistic novels, *The Voyage Out* (1915) and *Night and Day* (1919), she developed her own style, a carefully modulated flow that brought into prose fiction something of the rhythms and imagery of lyric poetry. While intensely psychological and interior, her novels also found inspiration and material in the physical realities of the body and in the heavily trafficked and populated streets of London. In *Monday or Tuesday* (1921), a series of sketches, she explored the possibilities of moving between action and contemplation, between retrospection and anticipation, between specific external events and delicate tracings of the flow of consciousness. These technical experiments made possible those later novels in which her characteristic method is fully developed—the elegiac *Jacob's Room* (1922); *Mrs. Dalloway* (1925), the first completely successful realization of her style; *To the Lighthouse* (1927), which in part memorializes her parents; *The Waves* (1931), the most experimental and difficult of her novels; and *Between the Acts* (1941), which includes a discontinuous pageant of English history and was published after her death.

Woolf was also a prodigious reviewer and essayist. She began to write criticism in 1905 for the *Times Literary Supplement* and published some five hundred reviews and essays for it and other periodicals, collected in *The Common Reader* (1925) and *The Second Common Reader* (1932); her prose presents itself as suggestive rather than authoritative and has an engaging air of spontaneity. In marked contrast to the formal language of the lecture hall or philosophical treatise, arenas and forms of learning from which women were historically barred, she writes in an informal, personal, playfully polemical tone, which is implicitly linked to her identity as a female writer. In her essays she is equally concerned with her own craft as a writer and with what it was like to be a quite different person living in a different age. At once more informal and more revealing are the six volumes of her *Letters* (1975–80) and five volumes of her *Diary* (1977–84), which she began to write in 1917. These, with their running commentary on her life and work, resemble a painter's sketchbooks and serve as a reminder that her writings, for all their variety, have the coherence found only in the work of the greatest literary artists.

Over the course of her career, Woolf grew increasingly concerned with the position of women, especially professional women, and the constrictions under which they suffered. She wrote several cogent essays on the subject, and women's social subjection also arises in her fiction. Her novel *The Years* (1937) was originally to have reflections on the position of women interspersed amid the action, but she later decided to publish them as a separate book, *Three Guineas* (1938), which also includes an incisive meditation on war. In *A Room of One's Own* (1929), an essay based on two lectures on "Women and Fiction" delivered to female students at Cambridge, Woolf discusses various male institutions that historically either were denied to or oppressed women. Refused access to education, wealth, and property ownership, women such as Shakespeare's imaginary sister lacked the conditions necessary to write and were unable to develop a literature of their own. Woolf advocated the creation of a literature that would include women's experience and ways of thinking, but instead of encouraging an exclusively female perspective, she proposed literature that would be "androgynous in mind" and resonate equally with men and women.

The Mark on the Wall

Perhaps it was the middle of January in the present year that I first looked up and saw the mark on the wall. In order to fix a date it is necessary to remember what one saw. So now I think of the fire; the steady film of yellow light upon the page of my book; the three chrysanthemums in the round glass bowl on the mantelpiece. Yes, it must have been the winter time, and we had just finished our tea, for I remember that I was smoking a cigarette when I looked up and saw the mark on the wall for the first time. I looked up through the smoke of my cigarette and my eye lodged for a moment upon the burning coals, and that old fancy of the crimson flag flapping from the castle tower came into my mind, and I thought of the cavalcade of red knights riding up the side of the black rock. Rather to my relief the sight of the mark interrupted the fancy, for it is an old fancy, an automatic fancy, made as a child perhaps. The mark was a small round mark, black upon the white wall, about six or seven inches above the mantelpiece.

How readily our thoughts swarm upon a new object, lifting it a little way, as ants carry a blade of straw so feverishly, and then leave it. . . . If that mark was made by a nail, it can't have been for a picture, it must have been for a miniature—the miniature of a lady with white powdered curls, powder-dusted cheeks, and lips like red carnations. A fraud of course, for the people who had this house before us would have chosen pictures in that way—an old picture for an old room. That is the sort of people they were—very interesting people, and I think of them so often, in such queer places, because one will never see them again, never know what happened next. They wanted to leave this house because they wanted to change their style of furniture, so he said, and he was in process of saying that in his opinion art should have ideas behind it when we were torn asunder, as one is torn from the old lady about to pour out tea and the young man about to hit the tennis ball in the back garden of the suburban villa as one rushes past in the train.

But for that mark, I'm not sure about it; I don't believe it was made by a nail after all; it's too big, too round, for that. I might get up, but if I got up and looked at it, ten to one I shouldn't be able to say for certain; because once a thing's done, no one ever knows how it happened. Oh! dear me, the mystery of life; the inaccuracy of thought! The ignorance of humanity! To show how very little control of our possessions we have—what an accidental affair this living is after all our civilisation—let me just count over a few of the things lost in one lifetime, beginning, for that seems always the most mysterious of losses—what cat would gnaw, what rat would nibble—three pale blue canisters of book-binding tools? Then there were the bird cages, the iron hoops, the steel skates, the Queen Anne coal-scuttle, the bagatelle[1] board, the hand organ—all gone, and jewels, too. Opals and emeralds, they lie about the roots of turnips. What a scraping paring affair it is to be sure! The wonder is that I've any clothes on my back, that I sit surrounded by solid furniture at this moment. Why, if one wants to compare life to anything, one must liken it to being blown through the Tube[2] at fifty miles an hour—landing at the other end without a single hairpin in one's hair! Shot out at the feet of God entirely naked! Tumbling head over heels in the asphodel meadows[3] like brown paper parcels pitched down a shoot in the post office! With one's hair flying back like the tail of a race-horse. Yes, that seems to express the rapidity of life, the perpetual waste and repair; all so casual, all so haphazard. . . .

But after life. The slow pulling down of thick green stalks so that the cup of the flower, as it turns over, deluges one with purple and red light. Why, after all, should one not be born there as one is born here, helpless, speechless, unable to focus one's eyesight, groping at the roots of the grass, at the toes of the Giants? As for saying which are trees, and which are men and women, or whether there are such things, that one won't be in a condition to do for fifty years or so. There will be nothing but spaces of light and dark, intersected by thick stalks, and rather higher up perhaps, rose-shaped blots of an indistinct colour—dim pinks and blues—which will, as time goes on, become more definite, become—I don't know what. . . .

And yet that mark on the wall is not a hole at all. It may even be caused by some round black substance, such as a small rose leaf, left over from the summer, and I, not being a very vigilant housekeeper—look at the dust on the mantelpiece, for example, the dust which, so they say, buried Troy[4] three times over, only fragments of pots utterly refusing annihilation, as one can believe.

The tree outside the window taps very gently on the pane. . . . I want to think quietly, calmly, spaciously, never to be interrupted, never to have to rise from my chair, to slip easily from one thing to another, without any sense of hostility, or obstacle. I want to sink deeper and deeper, away from the surface, with its hard separate facts. To steady myself, let me catch hold of the first idea that passes . . . Shakespeare. . . . Well, he will do as well as another. A man who sat himself solidly in an arm-chair, and looked into the fire, so— A shower of ideas fell perpetually from some very high Heaven down through his mind. He leant his forehead on his hand, and people, looking in through the open door—for this scene is supposed to take place on a summer's evening— But how dull this is, this historical fiction! It doesn't interest me at all. I wish I could hit upon a pleasant track of thought, a track indirectly reflecting credit upon myself, for those are the pleasantest thoughts, and very frequent even in the minds of modest mouse-coloured people, who believe genuinely that they dislike to hear their own praises. They are not thoughts directly praising oneself; that is the beauty of them; they are thoughts like this:

1. Game played on oblong table with cue and balls. "Coal-scuttle": metal pail for carrying coal.
2. The London underground railway, or subway.
3. I.e., heaven, the next world (in Greek mythology asphodel flowers grow in the Elysian fields).
4. Legendary site of ancient war chronicled in Homer's Greek epic *The Iliad*.

"And then I came into the room. They were discussing botany. I said how I'd seen a flower growing on a dust heap on the site of an old house in Kingsway.[5] The seed, I said, must have been sown in the reign of Charles the First. What flowers grew in the reign of Charles the First?" I asked—(but I don't remember the answer). Tall flowers with purple tassels to them perhaps. And so it goes on. All the time I'm dressing up the figure of myself in my own mind, lovingly, stealthily, not openly adoring it, for if I did that, I should catch myself out, and stretch my hand at once for a book in self-protection. Indeed, it is curious how instinctively one protects the image of oneself from idolatry or any other handling that could make it ridiculous, or too unlike the original to be believed in any longer. Or is it not so very curious after all? It is a matter of great importance. Suppose the looking-glass smashes, the image disappears, and the romantic figure with the green of forest depths all about it is there no longer, but only that shell of a person which is seen by other people—what an airless, shallow, bald, prominent world it becomes! A world not to be lived in. As we face each other in omnibuses and underground railways we are looking into the mirror; that accounts for the vagueness, the gleam of glassiness, in our eyes. And the novelists in future will realise more and more the importance of these reflections, for of course there is not one reflection but an almost infinite number; those are the depths they will explore, those the phantoms they will pursue, leaving the description of reality more and more out of their stories, taking a knowledge of it for granted, as the Greeks did and Shakespeare perhaps—but these generalisations are very worthless. The military sound of the word is enough. It recalls leading articles, cabinet ministers—a whole class of things indeed which, as a child, one thought the thing itself, the standard thing, the real thing, from which one could not depart save at the risk of nameless damnation. Generalisations bring back somehow Sunday in London, Sunday afternoon walks, Sunday luncheons, and also ways of speaking of the dead, clothes, and habits—like the habit of sitting all together in one room until a certain hour, although nobody liked it. There was a rule for everything. The rule for tablecloths at that particular period was that they should be made of tapestry with little yellow compartments marked upon them, such as you may see in photographs of the carpets in the corridors of the royal palaces. Tablecloths of a different kind were not real tablecloths. How shocking, and yet how wonderful it was to discover that these real things, Sunday luncheons, Sunday walks, country houses, and tablecloths were not entirely real, were indeed half phantoms, and the damnation which visited the disbeliever in them was only a sense of illegitimate freedom. What now takes the place of those things I wonder, those real standard things? Men perhaps, should you be a woman; the masculine point of view which governs our lives, which sets the standard, which establishes Whitaker's Table of Precedency,[6] which has become, I suppose, since the war, half a phantom to many men and women, which soon, one may hope, will be laughed into the dustbin where the phantoms go, the mahogany sideboards and the Landseer[7] prints, Gods and Devils, Hell and so forth,

5. Street in London.
6. *Whitaker's Almanack*, an annual compendium of information, prints a "Table of Precedency," which shows the order in which the various ranks in public life and society proceed on formal

occasions.
7. Sir Edwin Henry Landseer (1802–1873), English painter, reproductions of whose *Stag at Bay, Monarch of the Glen*, and similar animal paintings were often found in Victorian homes.

leaving us all with an intoxicating sense of illegitimate freedom—if freedom exists. . . .

In certain lights that mark on the wall seems actually to project from the wall. Nor is it entirely circular. I cannot be sure, but it seems to cast a perceptible shadow, suggesting that if I ran my finger down that strip of the wall it would, at a certain point, mount and descend a small tumulus, a smooth tumulus like those barrows on the South Downs[8] which are, they say, either tombs or camps. Of the two I should prefer them to be tombs, desiring melancholy like most English people, and finding it natural at the end of a walk to think of the bones stretched beneath the turf. . . . There must be some book about it. Some antiquary must have dug up those bones and given them a name. . . . What sort of a man is an antiquary, I wonder? Retired Colonels for the most part, I daresay, leading parties of aged labourers to the top here, examining clods of earth and stone, and getting into correspondence with the neighbouring clergy, which, being opened at breakfast time, gives them a feeling of importance, and the comparison of arrow-heads necessitates cross-country journeys to the country towns, an agreeable necessity both to them and to their elderly wives, who wish to make plum jam or to clean out the study, and have every reason for keeping that great question of the camp or the tomb in perpetual suspension, while the Colonel himself feels agreeably philosophic in accumulating evidence on both sides of the question. It is true that he does finally incline to believe in the camp; and, being opposed, indites a pamphlet which he is about to read at the quarterly meeting of the local society when a stroke lays him low, and his last conscious thoughts are not of wife or child, but of the camp and that arrowhead there, which is now in the case at the local museum, together with the foot of a Chinese murderess, a handful of Elizabethan nails, a great many Tudor clay pipes, a piece of Roman pottery, and the wineglass that Nelson[9] drank out of—proving I really don't know what.

No, no, nothing is proved, nothing is known. And if I were to get up at this very moment and ascertain that the mark on the wall is really—what shall we say?—the head of a gigantic old nail, driven in two hundred years ago, which has now, owing to the patient attrition of many generations of housemaids, revealed its head above the coat of paint, and is taking its first view of modern life in the sight of a white-walled fire-lit room, what should I gain?— Knowledge? Matter for further speculation? I can think sitting still as well as standing up. And what is knowledge? What are our learned men save the descendants of witches and hermits who crouched in caves and in woods brewing herbs, interrogating shrew-mice and writing down the language of the stars? And the less we honour them as our superstitions dwindle and our respect for beauty and health of mind increases. . . . Yes, one could imagine a very pleasant world. A quiet, spacious world, with the flowers so red and blue in the open fields. A world without professors or specialists or house-keepers with the profiles of policemen, a world which one could slice with one's thought as a fish slices the water with his fin, grazing the stems of the water-lilies, hanging suspended over nests of white sea eggs. . . . How peaceful it is down here, rooted in the centre of the

---

8. A range of low hills in southeastern England. "Barrows": mounds of earth or stones erected by prehistoric peoples, usually as burial places.

9. Horatio Nelson (1758–1805), British admiral. "Tudor": 15th-century English.

world and gazing up through the grey waters, with their sudden gleams of light, and their reflections—if it were not for Whitaker's Almanack—if it were not for the Table of Precedency!

I must jump up and see for myself what that mark on the wall really is—a nail, a rose-leaf, a crack in the wood?

Here is Nature once more at her old game of self-preservation. This train of thought, she perceives, is threatening mere waste of energy, even some collision with reality, for who will ever be able to lift a finger against Whitaker's Table of Precedency? The Archbishop of Canterbury is followed by the Lord High Chancellor; the Lord High Chancellor is followed by the Archbishop of York. Everybody follows somebody, such is the philosophy of Whitaker; and the great thing is to know who follows whom. Whitaker knows, and let that, so Nature counsels, comfort you, instead of enraging you; and if you can't be comforted, if you must shatter this hour of peace, think of the mark on the wall.

I understand Nature's game—her prompting to take action as a way of ending any thought that threatens to excite or to pain. Hence, I suppose, comes our slight contempt for men of action—men, we assume, who don't think. Still, there's no harm in putting a full stop to one's disagreeable thoughts by looking at a mark on the wall.

Indeed, now that I have fixed my eyes upon it, I feel that I have grasped a plank in the sea; I feel a satisfying sense of reality which at once turns the two Archbishops and the Lord High Chancellor to the shadows of shades. Here is something definite, something real. Thus, waking from a midnight dream of horror, one hastily turns on the light and lies quiescent, worshipping the chest of drawers, worshipping solidity, worshipping reality, worshipping the impersonal world which is a proof of some existence other than ours. That is what one wants to be sure of. . . . Wood is a pleasant thing to think about. It comes from a tree; and trees grow, and we don't know how they grow. For years and years they grow, without paying any attention to us, in meadows, in forests, and by the side of rivers—all things one likes to think about. The cows swish their tails beneath them on hot afternoons; they paint rivers so green that when a moorhen dives one expects to see its feathers all green when it comes up again. I like to think of the fish balanced against the stream like flags blown out; and of water-beetles slowly raising domes of mud upon the bed of the river. I like to think of the tree itself: first of the close dry sensation of being wood; then the grinding of the storm; then the slow, delicious ooze of sap; I like to think of it, too, on winter's nights standing in the empty field with all leaves close-furled, nothing tender exposed to the iron bullets of the moon, a naked mast upon an earth that goes tumbling, tumbling, all night long. The song of birds must sound very loud and strange in June; and how cold the feet of insects must feel upon it, as they make laborious progresses up the creases of the bark, or sun themselves upon the thin green awning of the leaves, and look straight in front of them with diamond-cut red eyes. . . . One by one the fibres snap beneath the immense cold pressure of the earth, then the last storm comes and, falling, the highest branches drive deep into the ground again. Even so, life isn't done with; there are a million patient, watchful lives still for a tree, all over the world, in bedrooms, in ships, on the pavement, living rooms, where men and women sit after tea, smoking cigarettes. It is full of peaceful thoughts, happy thoughts, this tree. I should like to take each one separately—but something is getting in the way. . . . Where was I? What has it all been about? A tree? A river? The Downs?[1] Whitaker's Almanack? The fields of asphodel? I can't remember a thing. Everything's moving, falling, slipping, vanishing. . . . There is a vast upheaval of matter. Someone is standing over me and saying:

"I'm going out to buy a newspaper."

"Yes?"

"Though it's no good buying newspapers. . . . Nothing ever happens. Curse this war; God damn this war! . . . All the same, I don't see why we should have a snail on our wall."

Ah, the mark on the wall! It was a snail.

1921

Modern Fiction

In making any survey, even the freest and loosest, of modern fiction, it is difficult not to take it for granted that the modern practice of the art is somehow an improvement upon the old. With their simple tools and primitive materials, it might be said, Fielding[1] did well and Jane Austen even better, but compare their opportunities with ours! Their masterpieces certainly have a strange air of simplicity. And yet the analogy between literature and the process, to choose an example, of making motor cars scarcely holds good beyond the first glance. It is doubtful whether in the course of the centuries, though we have learnt much about making machines, we have learnt anything about making literature. We do not come to write better; all that we can be said to do is to keep moving, now a little in this direction, now in that, but with a circular tendency should the whole course of the track be viewed from a sufficiently lofty pinnacle. It need scarcely be said that we make no claim to stand, even momentarily, upon that vantage-ground. On the flat, in the crowd, half blind with dust, we look back with envy to those happier warriors, whose battle is won and whose achievements wear so serene an air of accomplishment that we can scarcely refrain from whispering that the fight was not so fierce for them as for us. It is for the historian of literature to decide; for him to say if we are now beginning or ending or standing in the middle of a great period of prose fiction, for down in the plain little is visible. We only know that certain gratitudes and hostilities inspire us; that certain paths seem to lead to fertile land, others to the dust and the desert; and of this perhaps it may be worth while to attempt some account.

Our quarrel, then, is not with the classics, and if we speak of quarrelling with Mr Wells, Mr Bennett, and Mr Galsworthy;[2] it is partly that by the mere fact of their existence in the flesh their work has a living, breathing, everyday imperfection which bids us take what liberties with it we choose. But it is also true, that, while we thank them for a thousand gifts, we reserve

---

1. Part of the sea off the east coast of Kent.

1. Henry Fielding (1707–1754), English novelist.

2. H. G. Wells (1866–1946), Arnold Bennett (1867–1931), John Galsworthy (1867–1933), English novelists.

our unconditional gratitude for Mr Hardy, for Mr Conrad, and in much lesser degree for the Mr Hudson of *The Purple Land, Green Mansions*, and *Far Away and Long Ago*.[3] Mr Wells, Mr Bennett, and Mr Galsworthy have excited so many hopes and disappointed them so persistently that our gratitude largely takes the form of thanking them for having shown us what they might have done but have not done; what we certainly could not do, but as certainly, perhaps, do not wish to do. No single phrase will sum up the charge or grievance which we have to bring against a mass of work so large in its volume and embodying so many qualities, both admirable and the reverse. If we tried to formulate our meaning in one word we should say that these three writers are materialists. It is because they are concerned not with the spirit but with the body that they have disappointed us, and left us with the feeling that the sooner English fiction turns its back upon them, as politely as may be, and marches, if only into the desert, the better for its soul. Naturally, no single word reaches the centre of three separate targets. In the case of Mr Wells it falls notably wide of the mark. And yet even with him it indicates to our thinking the fatal alloy in his genius, the great clod of clay that has got itself mixed up with the purity of his inspiration. But Mr Bennett is perhaps the worst culprit of the three, inasmuch as he is by far the best workman. He can make a book so well constructed and solid in its craftsmanship that it is difficult for the most exacting of critics to see through what chink or crevice decay can creep in. There is not so much as a draught between the frames of the windows, or a crack in the boards. And yet—if life should refuse to live there? That is a risk which the creator of *The Old Wives' Tale*, George Cannon, Edwin Clayhanger,[4] and hosts of other figures, may well claim to have surmounted. His characters live abundantly, even unexpectedly, but it remains to ask how do they live, and what do they live for? More and more they seem to us, deserting even the well-built villa in the Five Towns,[5] to spend their time in some softly padded first-class railway carriage, pressing bells and buttons innumerable; and the destiny to which they travel so luxuriously becomes more and more unquestionably an eternity of bliss spent in the very best hotel in Brighton.[6] It can scarcely be said of Mr Wells that he is a materialist in the sense that he takes too much delight in the solidity of his fabric. His mind is too generous in its sympathies to allow him to spend much time in making things shipshape and substantial. He is a materialist from sheer goodness of heart, taking upon his shoulders the work that ought to have been discharged by Government officials, and in the plethora of his ideas and facts scarcely having leisure to realize, or forgetting to think important, the crudity and coarseness of his human beings. Yet what more damaging criticism can there be both of his earth and of his Heaven than that they are to be inhabited here and hereafter by his Joans and his Peters?[7] Does not the inferiority of their natures tarnish whatever institutions and ideals may be provided for them by the generosity of their creator? Nor, profoundly though we respect the

---

3. W. H. Hudson (1841–1922), naturalist and writer, was born in Argentina, although he later lived in London. *The Purple Land* (1885) is about South America; *Green Mansions* (1904), a novel set in South America, was his first real success.
4. Characters in Arnold Bennett's novels; *The Old Wives' Tale* (1908) is the best-known.

5. The pottery towns of Staffordshire in which much of Bennett's fiction was set.
6. Once-fashionable seaside resort on the southwest coast of England.
7. In his novel *Joan and Peter: The Story of an Education* (1918), Wells advocates education to address social problems.

integrity and humanity of Mr Galsworthy, shall we find what we seek in his pages.

If we fasten, then, one label on all these books, on which is one word, materialists, we mean by it that they write of unimportant things; that they spend immense skill and immense industry making the trivial and the transitory appear the true and the enduring.

We have to admit that we are exacting, and, further, that we find it difficult to justify our discontent by explaining what it is that we exact. We frame our question differently at different times. But it reappears most persistently as we drop the finished novel on the crest of a sigh—Is it worth while? What is the point of it all? Can it be that, owing to one of those little deviations which the human spirit seems to make from time to time, Mr Bennett has come down with his magnificent apparatus for catching life just an inch or two on the wrong side? Life escapes; and perhaps without life nothing else is worth while. It is a confession of vagueness to have to make use of such a figure as this, but we scarcely better the matter by speaking, as critics are prone to do, of reality. Admitting the vagueness which afflicts all criticism of novels, let us hazard the opinion that for us at this moment the form of fiction most in vogue more often misses than secures the thing we seek. Whether we call it life or spirit, truth or reality, this, the essential thing, has moved off, or on, and refuses to be contained any longer in such ill-fitting vestments as we provide. Nevertheless, we go on perseveringly, conscientiously, constructing our two and thirty chapters after a design which more and more ceases to resemble the vision in our minds. So much of the enormous labour of proving the solidity, the likeness to life, of the story is not merely labour thrown away but labour misplaced to the extent of obscuring and blotting out the light of the conception. The writer seems constrained, not by his own free will but by some powerful and unscrupulous tyrant who has him in thrall, to provide a plot, to provide comedy, tragedy, love interest, and an air of probability embalming the whole so impeccable that if all his figures were to come to life they would find themselves dressed down to the last button of their coats in the fashion of the hour. The tyrant is obeyed; the novel is done to a turn. But sometimes, more and more often as time goes by, we suspect a momentary doubt, a spasm of rebellion, as the pages fill themselves in the customary way. Is life like this? Must novels be like this?

Look within and life, it seems, is very far from being "like this." Examine for a moment an ordinary mind on an ordinary day. The mind receives a myriad impressions—trivial, fantastic, evanescent, or engraved with the sharpness of steel. From all sides they come, an incessant shower of innumerable atoms; and as they fall, as they shape themselves into the life of Monday or Tuesday,[8] the accent falls differently from of old; the moment of importance came not here but there; so that, if a writer were a free man and not a slave, if he could write what he chose, not what he must, if he could base his work upon his own feeling and not upon convention, there would be no plot, no comedy, no tragedy, no love interest or catastrophe in the accepted style, and perhaps not a single button sewn on as the Bond Street[9] tailors would have it. Life is not a series of gig-lamps[1] symmetrically arranged; life is a luminous halo, a semi-transparent envelope surrounding us from the begin-

---

8. *Monday or Tuesday* was Woolf's 1921 collection of experimental stories and sketches.

9. Fashionable shopping street in London.
1. Carriage lamps.

ning of consciousness to the end. Is it not the task of the novelist to convey this varying, this unknown and uncircumscribed spirit, whatever aberration or complexity it may display, with as little mixture of the alien and external as possible? We are not pleading merely for courage and sincerity; we are suggesting that the proper stuff of fiction is a little other than custom would have us believe it.

It is, at any rate, in some such fashion as this that we seek to define the quality which distinguishes the work of several young writers, among whom Mr James Joyce is the most notable, from that of their predecessors. They attempt to come closer to life, and to preserve more sincerely and exactly what interests and moves them, even if to do so they must discard most of the conventions which are commonly observed by the novelist. Let us record the atoms as they fall upon the mind in the order in which they fall, let us trace the pattern, however disconnected and incoherent in appearance, which each sight or incident scores upon the consciousness. Let us not take it for granted that life exists more fully in what is commonly thought big than in what is commonly thought small. Anyone who has read *The Portrait of the Artist as a Young Man* or, what promises to be a far more interesting work, *Ulysses*,[2] now appearing in the *Little Review*, will have hazarded some theory of this nature as to Mr Joyce's intention. On our part, with such a fragment before us, it is hazarded rather than affirmed; but whatever the intention of the whole, there can be no question but that it is of the utmost sincerity and that the result, difficult or unpleasant as we may judge it, is undeniably important. In contrast with those whom we have called materialists, Mr Joyce is spiritual; he is concerned at all costs to reveal the flickerings of that innermost flame which flashes its messages through the brain, and in order to preserve it he disregards with complete courage whatever seems to him adventitious, whether it be probability, or coherence, or any other of these signposts which for generations have served to support the imagination of a reader when called upon to imagine what he can neither touch nor see. The scene in the cemetery,[3] for instance, with its brilliancy, its sordidity, its incoherence, its sudden lightning flashes of significance, does undoubtedly come so close to the quick of the mind that, on a first reading at any rate, it is difficult not to acclaim a masterpiece. If we want life itself, here surely we have it. Indeed, we find ourselves fumbling rather awkwardly if we try to say what else we wish, and for what reason a work of such originality yet fails to compare, for we must take high examples, with *Youth* or *The Mayor of Casterbridge*.[4] It fails because of the comparative poverty of the writer's mind, we might say simply and have done with it. But it is possible to press a little further and wonder whether we may not refer our sense of being in a bright yet narrow room, confined and shut in, rather than enlarged and set free, to some limitation imposed by the method as well as by the mind. Is it the method that inhibits the creative power? Is it due to the method that we feel neither jovial nor magnanimous, but centred in a self which, in spite of its tremor of susceptibility, never embraces or creates what is outside itself and beyond? Does the emphasis laid, perhaps didactically, upon indecency contribute to the effect of something angular and isolated? Or is it merely that in

2. Written April, 1919 [Woolf's note].
3. The sixth episode ("Hades") of *Ulysses*, where Bloom goes to Paddy Dignam's funeral.

4. A story and a novel by, respectively, Joseph Conrad and Thomas Hardy.

any effort of such originality it is much easier, for contemporaries especially, to feel what it lacks than to name what it gives? In any case it is a mistake to stand outside examining "methods". Any method is right, every method is right, that expresses what we wish to express, if we are writers; that brings us closer to the novelist's intention if we are readers. This method has the merit of bringing us closer to what we were prepared to call life itself; did not the reading of *Ulysses* suggest how much of life is excluded or ignored, and did it not come with a shock to open *Tristram Shandy* or even *Pendennis*[5] and be by them convinced that there are not only other aspects of life, but more important ones into the bargain.

However this may be, the problem before the novelist at present, as we suppose it to have been in the past, is to contrive means of being free to set down what he chooses. He has to have the courage to say that what interests him is no longer "this" but "that": out of "that" alone must he construct his work. For the moderns "that", the point of interest, lies very likely in the dark places of psychology. At once, therefore, the accent falls a little differently; the emphasis is upon something hitherto ignored; at once a different outline of form becomes necessary, difficult for us to grasp, incomprehensible to our predecessors. No one but a modern, no one perhaps but a Russian, would have felt the interest of the situation which Tchekov has made into the short story which he calls "Gusev."[6] Some Russian soldiers lie ill on board a ship which is taking them back to Russia. We are given a few scraps of their talk and some of their thoughts; then one of them dies and is carried away; the talk goes on among the others for a time, until Gusev himself dies, and looking "like a carrot or a radish" is thrown overboard. The emphasis is laid upon such unexpected places that at first it seems as if there were no emphasis at all; and then, as the eyes accustom themselves to twilight and discern the shapes of things in a room we see how complete the story is, how profound, and how truly in obedience to his vision Tchekov has chosen this, that, and the other, and placed them together to compose something new. But it is impossible to say "this is comic," or "that is tragic," nor are we certain, since short stories, we have been taught, should be brief and conclusive, whether this, which is vague and inconclusive, should be called a short story at all.

The most elementary remarks upon modern English fiction can hardly avoid some mention of the Russian influence, and if the Russians are mentioned one runs the risk of feeling that to write of any fiction save theirs is waste of time. If we want understanding of the soul and heart where else shall we find it of comparable profundity? If we are sick of our own materialism the least considerable of their novelists has by right of birth a natural reverence for the human spirit. "Learn to make yourself akin to people. . . . But let this sympathy be not with the mind—for it is easy with the mind—but with the heart, with love towards them." In every great Russian writer we seem to discern the features of a saint, if sympathy for the sufferings of others, love towards them, endeavour to reach some goal worthy of the most exacting demands of the spirit constitute saintliness. It is the saint in them which confounds us with a feeling of our own irreligious triviality, and turns

5. Novels by, respectively, the English writers Laurence Sterne (1713–1768) and William Makepeace Thackeray (1811–1863).

6. 1890 story by the Russian writer Anton Pavlovich Chekhov (1860–1904).

so many of our famous novels to tinsel and trickery. The conclusions of the Russian mind, thus comprehensive and compassionate, are inevitably, perhaps, of the utmost sadness. More accurately indeed we might speak of the inconclusiveness of the Russian mind. It is the sense that there is no answer, that if honestly examined life presents question after question which must be left to sound on and on after the story is over in hopeless interrogation that fills us with a deep, and finally it may be with a resentful, despair. They are right perhaps; unquestionably they see further than we do and without our gross impediments of vision. But perhaps we see something that escapes them, or why should this voice of protest mix itself with our gloom? The voice of protest is the voice of another and an ancient civilisation which seems to have bred in us the instinct to enjoy and fight rather than to suffer and understand. English fiction from Sterne to Meredith[7] bears witness to our natural delight in humour and comedy, in the beauty of earth, in the activities of the intellect, and in the splendour of the body. But any deductions that we may draw from the comparison of two fictions so immeasurably far apart are futile save indeed as they flood us with a view of the infinite possibilities of the art and remind us that there is no limit to the horizon, and that nothing—no "method," no experiment, even of the wildest—is forbidden, but only falsity and pretence. "The proper stuff of fiction" does not exist; everything is the proper stuff of fiction, every feeling, every thought; every quality of brain and spirit is drawn upon; no perception comes amiss. And if we can imagine the art of fiction come alive and standing in our midst, she would undoubtedly bid us break her and bully her, as well as honour and love her, for so her youth is renewed and her sovereignty assured.

1925

Mrs. Dalloway

"Look within," Virginia Woolf urges in her essay "Modern Fiction" (1919, revised 1925): "Examine for a moment an ordinary mind on an ordinary day. The mind receives a myriad impressions—trivial, fantastic, evanescent, or engraved with the sharpness of steel." Her 1925 novel *Mrs. Dalloway* looks deep within the consciousness of a middle-aged woman planning an evening party on a fine London day in the middle of June 1923. In exploring the events of a single day, Woolf's novel recalls James Joyce's day-long narrative in *Ulysses* (1922), which, despite her reservations about its form and "indecency," she admired for revealing "the flickering of that innermost flame which flashes its messages through the brain."

In Woolf's more intimately scaled novel, Clarissa Dalloway's "ordinary mind on an ordinary day" is revealed to contain extraordinary riches, and so too, Woolf suggests, might any mind on any day, at least for the sufficiently attentive novelist. As Clarissa walks through London's streets, reacting to the flood of sights and sounds around her, her exhilarated if fleeting impressions of the present often give way to steel-engraved memories of her young adulthood in an idyllic countryside home in Bourton. Following her there through thoughts conveyed in rich metaphors, precise rhythms, and finely spun syntax, we learn of her disappointed suitor Peter Walsh, alluring but too demanding, now a civil servant in India, though he has made a surprising return; the predictable but victorious suitor Richard Dalloway, still her husband and a Conservative member of Parliament; her independent-minded socialist friend Sally Seton,

7. George Meredith (1828–1909), English novelist.

who once planted a burning kiss on her lips, and many years later will unexpectedly appear at Clarissa's party. Thoughts of more recent events surge just below the surface, such as her daughter Elizabeth's disturbing infatuation with her zealous history tutor. Dismissing more realist novelists' preoccupation with the externalities of plot, Woolf wrote in her diary: "I dig out beautiful caves behind my characters: I think that gives exactly what I want; humanity, humour, depth."

However isolated in its cavelike interiority, each mind in *Mrs. Dalloway* intersects with many others. "The idea is that the caves shall connect," said Woolf, elaborating her metaphor, "and each comes to daylight at the present moment." When a car loudly backfires, the shock of the sound and the mystery of the opulent car's occupants form a hinge between Clarissa Dalloway's consciousness and that of her double, Septimus Warren Smith, a veteran traumatized by his experience on the Western Front in World War I. The two characters never directly meet in the novel, but the narrative weaves back and forth between their minds—"the world seen by the sane and the insane side by side," in Woolf's words. Showing Septimus to be a casualty of modern warfare, class stratification, and the mental health profession, her novel questions the solidity of the dividing line between the sane and the insane. Like many thousands of young men, such as the war poets included in the section "Voices of World War I," Septimus had volunteered to fight for a Britain idealized as Shakespeare and English culture; but the carnage of the war, including the irrepressible memory of his dear friend Evans's death, has demolished all hope for, and faith in, English civilization.

In plumbing the depths of her characters' minds, Woolf's narrative subtly glides from one character to another, and from one narrative method to another, including direct speech, interior monologue, and free indirect speech. The events of the day are refracted from an almost cubistic array of angles, as when bystanders speculate on who is in that mysterious car. When an airplane writes a brand name in the sky, observers arrive at different readings of the airy inscription. The passage of time, as hauntingly and insistently signaled by Big Ben's chimes, assumes various forms in the minds of Woolf's characters.

But for all her interest in focusing on what Woolf called the "radiant halo" of consciousness, things happen in *Mrs. Dalloway*—sometimes violent things. Woolf wrote of her intentions for her novel, "I want to criticise the social system, & to show it at work, at its most intense." She observes Clarissa's class position both sympathetically and critically, a society hostess arranging her all-important party with the labor of less privileged household workers. The British class system is shown to perpetuate the wealth and power of royalty, politicians, and doctors, while putting enormous pressure on people like Septimus Smith and Elizabeth's ill-fated history tutor of German descent. Medical professionals, such as Septimus Smith's doctors, seem to advance themselves above all and to miss the reflection, in some psychiatric illnesses, of a deeply flawed social order. The British Empire demands obeisance to nationalistic symbols of itself and crushes people like Septimus who are summoned to fulfill its will. Barriers along gender lines block the social advancement of women, as well as same-sex sexual fulfillment.

Woolf's ability to "dig out" both the human mind and the social structures and strictures that shape it has helped to make *Mrs. Dalloway* one of the most influential novels of the twentieth century; the work has been rewritten in various novels, including Michael Cunningham's *The Hours* (1998), and adapted for film. In conveying, as part of a larger social mix, the intricacies of Clarissa Dalloway's thoughts and feelings on a summer's day—her exultation in flowers, her longings and regrets in friendship and love, her anxieties about the hovering threat of despondency and death—Woolf fulfills her aspiration to portray life as "a luminous halo, a semi-transparent envelope surrounding us from the beginning of consciousness to the end."

Mrs. Dalloway

Mrs. Dalloway said she would buy the flowers herself.

For Lucy[1] had her work cut out for her. The doors would be taken off their hinges; Rumpelmayer's men[2] were coming. And then, thought Clarissa Dalloway, what a morning—fresh as if issued to children on a beach.

What a lark! What a plunge! For so it had always seemed to her, when, with a little squeak of the hinges, which she could hear now, she had burst open the French windows and plunged at Bourton[3] into the open air. How fresh, how calm, stiller than this of course, the air was in the early morning; like the flap of a wave; the kiss of a wave; chill and sharp and yet (for a girl of eighteen as she then was) solemn, feeling as she did, standing there at the open window, that something awful was about to happen; looking at the flowers, at the trees with the smoke winding off them and the rooks rising, falling; standing and looking until Peter Walsh said, "Musing among the vegetables?"—was that it?—"I prefer men to cauliflowers"—was that it? He must have said it at breakfast one morning when she had gone out on to the terrace—Peter Walsh. He would be back from India one of these days, June or July, she forgot which, for his letters were awfully dull; it was his sayings one remembered; his eyes, his pocket-knife, his smile, his grumpiness and, when millions of things had utterly vanished—how strange it was!—a few sayings like this about cabbages.

She stiffened a little on the kerb, waiting for Durtnall's van[4] to pass. A charming woman, Scrope Purvis thought her (knowing her as one does know people who live next door to one in Westminster[5]); a touch of the bird about her, of the jay, blue-green, light, vivacious, though she was over fifty, and grown very white since her illness. There she perched, never seeing him, waiting to cross, very upright.

For having lived in Westminster—how many years now? over twenty,— one feels even in the midst of the traffic, or waking at night, Clarissa was positive, a particular hush, or solemnity; an indescribable pause; a suspense (but that might be her heart, affected, they said, by influenza[6]) before Big Ben strikes. There! Out it boomed. First a warning, musical; then the hour, irrevocable. The leaden circles dissolved in the air. Such fools we are, she thought, crossing Victoria Street.[7] For Heaven only knows why one loves it so, how one sees it so, making it up, building it round one, tumbling it, creating it every moment afresh; but the veriest frumps,[8] the most dejected of miseries sitting on doorsteps (drink their downfall) do the same; can't be dealt with, she felt positive, by Acts of Parliament for that very reason: they love life. In people's eyes, in the swing, tramp, and trudge; in the bellow and the uproar; the carriages, motor cars, omnibuses, vans, sandwich men shuffling and swinging; brass bands; barrel organs; in the triumph and the jingle and the

---

1. Clarissa Dalloway's maid.
2. Caterers.
3. Village in western England and Mrs. Dalloway's childhood home.
4. A warehouse van.
5. London borough that includes Buckingham Palace, the Houses of Parliament, and Westminster Abbey.

6. The 1918–19 worldwide influenza pandemic had killed over 20 million people.
7. Clarissa is walking north. Her walk and others can be traced on the London map in the appendices to this volume. "Big Ben": the name for the clock tower above the Houses of Parliament.
8. Grumpy, shabbily dressed people.

strange high singing of some aeroplane overhead was what she loved; life; London; this moment of June.

For it was the middle of June. The War[9] was over, except for some one like Mrs. Foxcroft at the Embassy last night eating her heart out because that nice boy was killed and now the old Manor House must go to a cousin; or Lady Bexborough who opened a bazaar[1] they said, with the telegram in her hand, John, her favourite, killed; but it was over; thank Heaven—over. It was June. The King and Queen were at the Palace.[2] And everywhere, though it was still so early, there was a beating, a stirring of galloping ponies, tapping of cricket bats; Lords, Ascot, Ranelagh[3] and all the rest of it; wrapped in the soft mesh of the grey-blue morning air, which, as the day wore on, would unwind them, and set down on their lawns and pitches the bouncing ponies whose forefeet just struck the ground and up they sprung, the whirling young men, and laughing girls in their transparent muslins who, even now, after dancing all night, were taking their absurd woolly dogs for a run; and even now, at this hour, discreet old dowagers were shooting out in their motor cars on errands of mystery; and the shopkeepers were fidgeting in their windows with their paste and diamonds, their lovely old sea-green brooches in eighteenth-century settings to tempt Americans (but one must economise, not buy things rashly for Elizabeth), and she, too, loving it as she did with an absurd and faithful passion, being part of it, since her people were courtiers once in the time of the Georges,[4] she, too, was going that very night to kindle and illuminate; to give her party. But how strange, on entering the Park,[5] the silence; the mist; the hum; the slow-swimming happy ducks; the pouched birds waddling; and who should be coming along with his back against the Government buildings, most appropriately, carrying a despatch box stamped with the Royal Arms,[6] who but Hugh Whitbread; her old friend Hugh—the admirable Hugh!

"Good-morning to you, Clarissa!" said Hugh, rather extravagantly, for they had known each other as children. "Where are you off to?"

"I love walking in London," said Mrs. Dalloway. "Really it's better than walking in the country."

They had just come up—unfortunately—to see doctors. Other people came to see pictures; go to the opera; take their daughters out; the Whitbreads came "to see doctors." Times without number Clarissa had visited Evelyn Whitbread in a nursing home. Was Evelyn ill again? Evelyn was a good deal out of sorts, said Hugh, intimating by a kind of pout or swell of his very well-covered, manly, extremely handsome, perfectly upholstered body (he was almost too well dressed always, but presumably had to be, with his little job at Court) that his wife had some internal ailment, nothing serious, which, as an old friend, Clarissa Dalloway would quite understand without requiring him to specify. Ah yes, she did of course; what a nuisance; and felt

9. World War I (1914–18).
1. Street fair with many stalls selling a variety of goods to benefit a charitable organization.
2. Buckingham Palace, where King George V (1865–1936) and Queen Mary (1867–1953) resided.
3. The Hurlingham Club in Ranelagh Gardens in southwest London, where polo is played. "Lords": the cricket ground at St John's Wood in north London. "Ascot": a town west of London with an annual horse race. Summer sporting events at all three locations have been fixtures of the London social season.
4. Era of the combined reigns of the Kings George I–IV (1714–1830).
5. St James's Park, home to many kinds of water birds and a frequent haunt of politicians.
6. Sign indicating that the box contains papers to or from the royal family.

very sisterly and oddly conscious at the same time of her hat. Not the right hat for the early morning, was that it? For Hugh always made her feel, as he bustled on, raising his hat rather extravagantly and assuring her that she might be a girl of eighteen, and of course he was coming to her party to-night, Evelyn absolutely insisted, only a little late he might be after the party at the Palace to which he had to take one of Jim's boys,—she always felt a little skimpy beside Hugh; schoolgirlish; but attached to him, partly from having known him always, but she did think him a good sort in his own way, though Richard was nearly driven mad by him, and as for Peter Walsh, he had never to this day forgiven her for liking him.

She could remember scene after scene at Bourton—Peter furious; Hugh not, of course, his match in any way, but still not a positive imbecile as Peter made out; not a mere barber's block. When his old mother wanted him to give up shooting or to take her to Bath[7] he did it, without a word; he was really unselfish, and as for saying, as Peter did, that he had no heart, no brain, nothing but the manners and breeding of an English gentleman, that was only her dear Peter at his worst; and he could be intolerable; he could be impossible; but adorable to walk with on a morning like this.

(June had drawn out every leaf on the trees. The mothers of Pimlico[8] gave suck to their young. Messages were passing from the Fleet to the Admiralty.[9] Arlington Street and Piccadilly[1] seemed to chafe the very air in the Park and lift its leaves hotly, brilliantly, on waves of that divine vitality which Clarissa loved. To dance, to ride, she had adored all that.)

For they might be parted for hundreds of years, she and Peter; she never wrote a letter and his were dry sticks; but suddenly it would come over her, If he were with me now what would he say?—some days, some sights bringing him back to her calmly, without the old bitterness; which perhaps was the reward of having cared for people; they came back in the middle of St. James's Park on a fine morning—indeed they did. But Peter—however beautiful the day might be, and the trees and the grass, and the little girl in pink—Peter never saw a thing of all that. He would put on his spectacles, if she told him to; he would look. It was the state of the world that interested him; Wagner, Pope's poetry,[2] people's characters eternally, and the defects of her own soul. How he scolded her! How they argued! She would marry a Prime Minister and stand at the top of a staircase; the perfect hostess he called her (she had cried over it in her bedroom), she had the makings of the perfect hostess, he said.

So she would still find herself arguing in St. James's Park, still making out that she had been right—and she had too—not to marry him. For in marriage a little licence, a little independence there must be between people living together day in day out in the same house; which Richard gave her, and she him. (Where was he this morning for instance? Some committee, she never asked what.) But with Peter everything had to be shared; everything gone into. And it was intolerable, and when it came to that scene in the little

<hr>

7. Spa town in southwest England.
8. Modest London borough southwest of Westminster.
9. Since 1909 a wireless antenna on the Admiralty building in Whitehall had enabled communication by telegraph with British ships at sea.
1. Intersection at the northeast corner of Green Park, marking a luxurious district containing the Ritz Hotel.
2. Works by English poet Alexander Pope (1688–1744). "Wagner": Richard Wilhelm Wagner (1813–1883), German composer famous for his operas.

garden by the fountain, she had to break with him or they would have been destroyed, both of them ruined, she was convinced; though she had borne about with her for years like an arrow sticking in her heart the grief, the anguish; and then the horror of the moment when some one told her at a concert that he had married a woman met on the boat going to India! Never should she forget all that! Cold, heartless, a prude, he called her. Never could she understand how he cared. But those Indian women did presumably— silly, pretty, flimsy nincompoops. And she wasted her pity. For he was quite happy, he assured her—perfectly happy, though he had never done a thing that they talked of; his whole life had been a failure. It made her angry still.

She had reached the Park gates.[3] She stood for a moment, looking at the omnibuses in Piccadilly.

She would not say of any one in the world now that they were this or were that. She felt very young; at the same time unspeakably aged. She sliced like a knife through everything; at the same time was outside, looking on. She had a perpetual sense, as she watched the taxi cabs, of being out, out, far out to sea and alone; she always had the feeling that it was very, very dangerous to live even one day. Not that she thought herself clever, or much out of the ordinary. How she had got through life on the few twigs of knowledge Fräulein Daniels[4] gave them she could not think. She knew nothing; no language, no history; she scarcely read a book now, except memoirs in bed; and yet to her it was absolutely absorbing; all this; the cabs passing; and she would not say of Peter, she would not say of herself, I am this, I am that.

Her only gift was knowing people almost by instinct, she thought, walking on. If you put her in a room with some one, up went her back like a cat's; or she purred. Devonshire House, Bath House, the house with the china cockatoo,[5] she had seen them all lit up once; and remembered Sylvia, Fred, Sally Seton—such hosts of people; and dancing all night; and the waggons plodding past to market; and driving home across the Park. She remembered once throwing a shilling into the Serpentine.[6] But every one remembered; what she loved was this, here, now, in front of her; the fat lady in the cab. Did it matter then, she asked herself, walking towards Bond Street,[7] did it matter that she must inevitably cease completely; all this must go on without her; did she resent it; or did it not become consoling to believe that death ended absolutely? but that somehow in the streets of London, on the ebb and flow of things, here, there, she survived, Peter survived, lived in each other, she being part, she was positive, of the trees at home; of the house there, ugly, rambling all to bits and pieces as it was; part of people she had never met; being laid out like a mist between the people she knew best, who lifted her on their branches as she had seen the trees lift the mist, but it spread ever so far, her life, herself. But what was she dreaming as she looked into Hatchards'[8] shop window? What was she trying to recover? What image of white dawn in the country, as she read in the book spread open:

> Fear no more the heat o' the sun
> Nor the furious winter's rages.[9]

3. Green Park's northeast gate on Piccadilly.
4. Her governess.
5. Private homes near Piccadilly.
6. A large, winding pond in Hyde Park.
7. Important shopping street in northwest London.
8. A bookstore.
9. From a song bidding farewell to the supposedly dead heroine of Shakespeare's *Cymbeline* (4.2.258–81).

This late age of the world's experience had bred in them all, all men and women, a well of tears. Tears and sorrows; courage and endurance; a perfectly upright and stoical bearing. Think, for example, of the woman she admired most, Lady Bexborough, opening the bazaar.

There were Jorrocks' *Jaunts and Jollities*; there were *Soapy Sponge* and Mrs. Asquith's *Memoirs* and *Big Game Shooting in Nigeria*,[1] all spread open. Ever so many books there were; but none that seemed exactly right to take to Evelyn Whitbread in her nursing home. Nothing that would serve to amuse her and make that indescribably dried-up little woman look, as Clarissa came in, just for a moment cordial; before they settled down for the usual interminable talk of women's ailments. How much she wanted it—that people should look pleased as she came in, Clarissa thought and turned and walked back towards Bond Street, annoyed, because it was silly to have other reasons for doing things. Much rather would she have been one of those people like Richard who did things for themselves, whereas, she thought, waiting to cross, half the time she did things not simply, not for themselves; but to make people think this or that; perfect idiocy she knew (and now the policeman held up his hand) for no one was ever for a second taken in. Oh if she could have had her life over again! she thought, stepping on to the pavement, could have looked even differently!

She would have been, in the first place, dark like Lady Bexborough, with a skin of crumpled leather and beautiful eyes. She would have been, like Lady Bexborough, slow and stately; rather large; interested in politics like a man; with a country house; very dignified, very sincere. Instead of which she had a narrow pea-stick figure; a ridiculous little face, beaked like a bird's. That she held herself well was true; and had nice hands and feet; and dressed well, considering that she spent little. But often now this body she wore (she stopped to look at a Dutch picture), this body, with all its capacities, seemed nothing—nothing at all. She had the oddest sense of being herself invisible, unseen; unknown; there being no more marrying, no more having of children now, but only this astonishing and rather solemn progress with the rest of them, up Bond Street, this being Mrs. Dalloway; not even Clarissa any more; this being Mrs. Richard Dalloway.

Bond Street fascinated her; Bond Street early in the morning in the season; its flags flying; its shops; no splash; no glitter; one roll of tweed in the shop where her father had bought his suits for fifty years; a few pearls; salmon on an iceblock.

"That is all," she said, looking at the fishmonger's. "That is all," she repeated, pausing for a moment at the window of a glove shop where, before the War, you could buy almost perfect gloves. And her old Uncle William used to say a lady is known by her shoes and her gloves. He had turned on his bed one morning in the middle of the War. He had said, "I have had enough." Gloves and shoes; she had a passion for gloves; but her own daughter, her Elizabeth, cared not a straw for either of them.

Not a straw, she thought, going on up Bond Street to a shop where they kept flowers for her when she gave a party. Elizabeth really cared for her

---

1. Book invented by Woolf. "Jorrocks' *Jaunts and Jollities*": 1838 collection of stories about a Cockney grocer named Jorrocks by English sporting novelist Robert Smith Surtees (1805–1864). "*Soapy Sponge*": character in another novel by Surtees, *Mr. Sponge's Sporting Tour* (1853). Mrs. Asquith's *Memoirs*: two-volume autobiography (1920–1922) of Emma Alice Margaret (Margot) Asquith (1864–1945), wife of Prime Minister Herbert Henry Asquith (1908–1916).

dog most of all. The whole house this morning smelt of tar. Still, better poor Grizzle than Miss Kilman; better distemper and tar[2] and all the rest of it than sitting mewed in a stuffy bedroom with a prayer book! Better anything, she was inclined to say. But it might be only a phase, as Richard said, such as all girls go through. It might be falling in love. But why with Miss Kilman? who had been badly treated of course; one must make allowances for that, and Richard said she was very able, had a really historical mind. Anyhow they were inseparable, and Elizabeth, her own daughter, went to Communion; and how she dressed, how she treated people who came to lunch she did not care a bit, it being her experience that the religious ecstasy made people callous (so did causes); dulled their feelings, for Miss Kilman would do anything for the Russians, starved herself for the Austrians,[3] but in private inflicted positive torture, so insensitive was she, dressed in a green mackintosh coat.[4] Year in year out she wore that coat; she perspired; she was never in the room five minutes without making you feel her superiority, your inferiority; how poor she was; how rich you were; how she lived in a slum without a cushion or a bed or a rug or whatever it might be, all her soul rusted with that grievance sticking in it, her dismissal from school during the War—poor embittered unfortunate creature! For it was not her one hated but the idea of her, which undoubtedly had gathered in to itself a great deal that was not Miss Kilman; had become one of those spectres with which one battles in the night; one of those spectres who stand astride us and suck up half our life-blood, dominators and tyrants; for no doubt with another throw of the dice, had the black been uppermost and not the white, she would have loved Miss Kilman! But not in this world. No.

It rasped her, though, to have stirring about in her this brutal monster! to hear twigs cracking and feel hooves planted down in the depths of that leaf-encumbered forest, the soul; never to be content quite, or quite secure, for at any moment the brute would be stirring, this hatred, which, especially since her illness, had power to make her feel scraped, hurt in her spine; gave her physical pain, and made all pleasure in beauty, in friendship, in being well, in being loved and making her home delightful rock, quiver, and bend as if indeed there were a monster grubbing at the roots, as if the whole panoply of content were nothing but self love! this hatred!

Nonsense, nonsense! she cried to herself, pushing through the swing doors of Mulberry's the florists.

She advanced, light, tall, very upright, to be greeted at once by button-faced Miss Pym, whose hands were always bright red, as if they had been stood in cold water with the flowers.

There were flowers: delphiniums, sweet peas, bunches of lilac; and carnations, masses of carnations. There were roses; there were irises. Ah yes—so she breathed in the earthy garden sweet smell as she stood talking to Miss Pym who owed her help, and thought her kind, for kind she had been years ago; very kind, but she looked older, this year, turning her head from side to side among the irises and roses and nodding tufts of lilac with her eyes half closed, snuffing in, after the street uproar, the delicious scent, the exquisite coolness. And then, opening her eyes, how fresh like frilled

---

2. Used for dog grooming. "Distemper": an animal disease characterized by cough, loss of strength, and a discharge from the nose or eyes.

3. Peoples suffering poor economies after World War I and the Russian Revolution.
4. Raincoat.

linen clean from a laundry laid in wicker trays the roses looked; and dark
and prim the red carnations, holding their heads up; and all the sweet peas
spreading in their bowls, tinged violet, snow white, pale—as if it were the
evening and girls in muslin frocks came out to pick sweet peas and roses
after the superb summer's day, with its almost blue-black sky, its delphiniums, its carnations, its arum lilies was over; and it was the moment between
six and seven when every flower—roses, carnations, irises, lilac—glows;
white, violet, red, deep orange; every flower seems to burn by itself, softly,
purely in the misty beds; and how she loved the grey-white moths spinning
in and out, over the cherry pie,[5] over the evening primroses!

And as she began to go with Miss Pym from jar to jar, choosing, nonsense,
nonsense, she said to herself, more and more gently, as if this beauty, this
scent, this colour, and Miss Pym liking her, trusting her, were a wave which
she let flow over her and surmount that hatred, that monster, surmount it
all; and it lifted her up and up when—oh! a pistol shot in the street outside!

"Dear, those motor cars,"[6] said Miss Pym, going to the window to look, and
coming back and smiling apologetically with her hands full of sweet peas, as
if those motor cars, those tyres of motor cars, were all *her* fault.

The violent explosion which made Mrs. Dalloway jump and Miss Pym go to
the window and apologise came from a motor car which had drawn to the
side of the pavement precisely opposite Mulberry's shop window. Passers-by
who, of course, stopped and stared, had just time to see a face of the very
greatest importance against the dove-grey upholstery, before a male hand
drew the blind and there was nothing to be seen except a square of dove grey.

Yet rumours were at once in circulation from the middle of Bond Street
to Oxford Street on one side, to Atkinson's scent[7] shop on the other, passing
invisibly, inaudibly, like a cloud, swift, veil-like upon hills, falling indeed with
something of a cloud's sudden sobriety and stillness upon faces which a second before had been utterly disorderly. But now mystery had brushed them
with her wing; they had heard the voice of authority; the spirit of religion was
abroad with her eyes bandaged tight and her lips gaping wide. But nobody
knew whose face had been seen. Was it the Prince of Wales's, the Queen's,
the Prime Minister's? Whose face was it? Nobody knew.

Edgar J. Watkiss, with his roll of lead piping round his arm, said audibly,
humorously of course: "The Proime Minister's kyar."

Septimus Warren Smith, who found himself unable to pass, heard him.

Septimus Warren Smith, aged about thirty, pale-faced, beak-nosed, wearing brown shoes and a shabby overcoat, with hazel eyes which had that look
of apprehension in them which makes complete strangers apprehensive too.
The world has raised its whip; where will it descend?

Everything had come to a standstill. The throb of the motor engines
sounded like a pulse irregularly drumming through an entire body. The sun
became extraordinarily hot because the motor car had stopped outside Mulberry's shop window; old ladies on the tops of omnibuses spread their black
parasols; here a green, here a red parasol opened with a little pop. Mrs. Dalloway, coming to the window with her arms full of sweet peas, looked out
with her little pink face pursed in enquiry. Every one looked at the motor

---

5. Nickname for valerian, an herb with white or
pink flowers.
6. A car has backfired.
7. I.e., perfume.

car. Septimus looked. Boys on bicycles sprang off. Traffic accumulated. And there the motor car stood, with drawn blinds, and upon them a curious pattern like a tree, Septimus thought, and this gradual drawing together of everything to one centre before his eyes, as if some horror had come almost to the surface and was about to burst into flames, terrified him. The world wavered and quivered and threatened to burst into flames. It is I who am blocking the way, he thought. Was he not being looked at and pointed at; was he not weighted there, rooted to the pavement, for a purpose? But for what purpose?

"Let us go on, Septimus," said his wife, a little woman, with large eyes in a sallow pointed face; an Italian girl.

But Lucrezia herself could not help looking at the motor car and the tree pattern on the blinds. Was it the Queen in there—the Queen going shopping?

The chauffeur, who had been opening something, turning something, shutting something, got on to the box.[8]

"Come on," said Lucrezia.

But her husband, for they had been married four, five years now, jumped, started, and said, "All right!" angrily, as if she had interrupted him.

People must notice; people must see. People, she thought, looking at the crowd staring at the motor car; the English people, with their children and their horses and their clothes, which she admired in a way; but they were "people" now, because Septimus had said, "I will kill myself"; an awful thing to say. Suppose they had heard him? She looked at the crowd. Help, help! she wanted to cry out to butchers' boys and women. Help! Only last autumn she and Septimus had stood on the Embankment[9] wrapped in the same cloak and, Septimus reading a paper instead of talking, she had snatched it from him and laughed in the old man's face who saw them! But failure one conceals. She must take him away into some park.

"Now we will cross," she said.

She had a right to his arm, though it was without feeling. He would give her, who was so simple, so impulsive, only twenty-four, without friends in England, who had left Italy for his sake, a piece of bone.

The motor car with its blinds drawn and an air of inscrutable reserve proceeded towards Piccadilly, still gazed at, still ruffling the faces on both sides of the street with the same dark breath of veneration whether for Queen, Prince, or Prime Minister nobody knew. The face itself had been seen only once by three people for a few seconds. Even the sex was now in dispute. But there could be no doubt that greatness was seated within; greatness was passing, hidden, down Bond Street, removed only by a hand's-breadth from ordinary people who might now, for the first and last time, be within speaking distance of the majesty of England, of the enduring symbol of the state which will be known to curious antiquaries, sifting the ruins of time, when London is a grass-grown path and all those hurrying along the pavement this Wednesday morning are but bones with a few wedding rings mixed up in their dust and the gold stoppings of innumerable decayed teeth. The face in the motor car will then be known.

---

8. Because the car stalled, the driver has to crank its starting handle before returning to his seat and continuing to drive.

9. Road running along the Thames River between Westminster and Blackfriars Bridges.

It is probably the Queen, thought Mrs. Dalloway, coming out of Mulberry's with her flowers; the Queen. And for a second she wore a look of extreme dignity standing by the flower shop in the sunlight while the car passed at a foot's pace, with its blinds drawn. The Queen going to some hospital; the Queen opening some bazaar, thought Clarissa.

The crush was terrific for the time of day. Lords, Ascot, Hurlingham,[1] what was it? she wondered, for the street was blocked. The British middle classes sitting sideways on the tops of omnibuses with parcels and umbrellas, yes, even furs on a day like this, were, she thought, more ridiculous, more unlike anything there has ever been than one could conceive; and the Queen herself held up; the Queen herself unable to pass. Clarissa was suspended on one side of Brook Street;[2] Sir John Buckhurst, the old Judge on the other, with the car between them (Sir John had laid down the law for years and liked a well-dressed woman) when the chauffeur, leaning ever so slightly, said or showed something to the policeman, who saluted and raised his arm and jerked his head and moved the omnibus to the side and the car passed through. Slowly and very silently it took its way.

Clarissa guessed; Clarissa knew of course; she had seen something white, magical, circular, in the footman's hand, a disc inscribed with a name,—the Queen's, the Prince of Wales's, the Prime Minister's?—which, by force of its own lustre, burnt its way through (Clarissa saw the car diminishing, disappearing), to blaze among candelabras, glittering stars, breasts stiff with oak leaves,[3] Hugh Whitbread and all his colleagues, the gentlemen of England, that night in Buckingham Palace. And Clarissa, too, gave a party. She stiffened a little; so she would stand at the top of her stairs.

The car had gone, but it had left a slight ripple which flowed through glove shops and hat shops and tailors' shops on both sides of Bond Street. For thirty seconds all heads were inclined the same way—to the window. Choosing a pair of gloves—should they be to the elbow or above it, lemon or pale grey?—ladies stopped; when the sentence was finished something had happened. Something so trifling in single instances that no mathematical instrument, though capable of transmitting shocks in China, could register the vibration; yet in its fulness rather formidable and in its common appeal emotional; for in all the hat shops and tailors' shops strangers looked at each other and thought of the dead; of the flag; of Empire. In a public house[4] in a back street a Colonial[5] insulted the House of Windsor[6] which led to words, broken beer glasses, and a general shindy,[7] which echoed strangely across the way in the ears of girls buying white underlinen threaded with pure white ribbon for their weddings. For the surface agitation of the passing car as it sunk grazed something very profound.

Gliding across Piccadilly, the car turned down St. James's Street. Tall men, men of robust physique, well-dressed men with their tail-coats and their white slips[8] and their hair raked back who, for reasons difficult to discriminate, were standing in the bow window of Brooks's[9] with their hands behind the tails of their coats, looking out, perceived instinctively that great-

1. Club referred to earlier as Ranelagh.
2. Street in Mayfair that crosses Bond Street. From here, Clarissa turns south again and walks home to Westminster.
3. Worn on King Charles II's birthday (May 29) to commemorate his restoration in 1660.
4. Pub.

5. Someone from one of the colonies of the British Empire.
6. An English royal house, or family lineage.
7. A row.
8. Light garment showing under a waistcoat.
9. Aristocratic gentlemen's club on St. James's Street.

ness was passing, and the pale light of the immortal presence fell upon them as it had fallen upon Clarissa Dalloway. At once they stood even straighter, and removed their hands, and seemed ready to attend their Sovereign, if need be, to the cannon's mouth, as their ancestors had done before them. The white busts and the little tables in the background covered with copies of the *Tatler*[1] and syphons of soda water seemed to approve; seemed to indicate the flowing corn and the manor houses of England; and to return the frail hum of the motor wheels as the walls of a whispering gallery return a single voice expanded and made sonorous by the might of a whole cathedral.[2] Shawled Moll Pratt with her flowers on the pavement wished the dear boy well (it was the Prince of Wales for certain) and would have tossed the price of a pot of beer—a bunch of roses—into St. James's Street out of sheer light-heartedness and contempt of poverty had she not seen the constable's eye upon her, discouraging an old Irishwoman's loyalty. The sentries at St. James's saluted; Queen Alexandra's policeman[3] approved.

A small crowd meanwhile had gathered at the gates of Buckingham Palace. Listlessly, yet confidently, poor people all of them, they waited; looked at the Palace itself with the flag flying; at Victoria, billowing on her mound,[4] admired her shelves of running water, her geraniums; singled out from the motor cars in the Mall[5] first this one, then that; bestowed emotion, vainly, upon commoners out for a drive; recalled their tribute to keep it unspent while this car passed and that; and all the time let rumour accumulate in their veins and thrill the nerves in their thighs at the thought of Royalty looking at them; the Queen bowing; the Prince saluting; at the thought of the heavenly life divinely bestowed upon Kings; of the equerries[6] and deep curtsies; of the Queen's old doll's house;[7] of Princess Mary married to an Englishman, and the Prince—ah! the Prince! who took wonderfully, they said, after old King Edward,[8] but was ever so much slimmer. The Prince lived at St. James's; but he might come along in the morning to visit his mother.

So Sarah Bletchley said with her baby in her arms, tipping her foot up and down as though she were by her own fender in Pimlico, but keeping her eyes on the Mall, while Emily Coates ranged over the Palace windows and thought of the housemaids, the innumerable housemaids, the bedrooms, the innumerable bedrooms. Joined by an elderly gentleman with an Aberdeen terrier, by men without occupation, the crowd increased. Little Mr. Bowley, who had rooms in the Albany[9] and was sealed with wax over the deeper sources of life but could be unsealed suddenly, inappropriately, sentimentally, by this sort of thing—poor women waiting to see the Queen go past—poor women, nice little children, orphans, widows, the War—tut-tut—actually had tears in his eyes. A breeze flaunting ever so warmly down the Mall

---

1. Journal reporting high society news.
2. Acoustical effect whereby a curved wall carries a soft sound, such as the whispering gallery in the dome of St. Paul's Cathedral.
3. Guard on duty at Marlborough House, the residence of Queen Alexandra (1844–1925), the widow of King Edward VII. "Sentries at St. James's": guards at St. James's Palace. Both the palace and the house are within view of the car's route down St. James's Street.
4. Queen Victoria's statue outside the entrance to Buckingham Palace.
5. Wide avenue that leads from the Admiralty Arch along St. James's Park to Buckingham Palace.
6. Officers of the royal household.
7. Doll house designed by British architect Sir Edwin Lutyens (1869–1944) in 1923 for Queen Mary.
8. The Prince of Wales, the future Edward VIII (1894–1972), is compared to his grandfather, King Edward VII (1841–1910). Princess Mary (1897–1965), the only daughter of King George V and Queen Mary, married Viscount Lascelles (1882–1947) in 1922.
9. Apartment complex in Piccadilly housing politicians.

through the thin trees, past the bronze heroes,[1] lifted some flag flying in the British breast of Mr. Bowley and he raised his hat as the car turned into the Mall and held it high as the car approached; and let the poor mothers of Pimlico press close to him, and stood very upright. The car came on.

Suddenly Mrs. Coates looked up into the sky. The sound of an aeroplane bored ominously into the ears of the crowd. There it was coming over the trees, letting out white smoke from behind, which curled and twisted, actually writing something! making letters in the sky![2] Every one looked up.

Dropping dead down the aeroplane soared straight up, curved in a loop, raced, sank, rose, and whatever it did, wherever it went, out fluttered behind it a thick ruffled bar of white smoke which curled and wreathed upon the sky in letters. But what letters? A C was it? an E, then an L? Only for a moment did they lie still; then they moved and melted and were rubbed out up in the sky, and the aeroplane shot further away and again, in a fresh space of sky, began writing a K, an E, a Y perhaps?

"Glaxo,"[3] said Mrs. Coates in a strained, awe-stricken voice, gazing straight up, and her baby, lying stiff and white in her arms, gazed straight up.

"Kreemo," murmured Mrs. Bletchley, like a sleepwalker. With his hat held out perfectly still in his hand, Mr. Bowley gazed straight up. All down the Mall people were standing and looking up into the sky. As they looked the whole world became perfectly silent, and a flight of gulls crossed the sky, first one gull leading, then another, and in this extraordinary silence and peace, in this pallor, in this purity, bells struck eleven times, the sound fading up there among the gulls.

The aeroplane turned and raced and swooped exactly where it liked, swiftly, freely, like a skater—

"That's an E," said Mrs. Bletchley—or a dancer—

"It's toffee," murmured Mr. Bowley—(and the car went in at the gates and nobody looked at it), and shutting off the smoke, away and away it rushed, and the smoke faded and assembled itself round the broad white shapes of the clouds.

It had gone; it was behind the clouds. There was no sound. The clouds to which the letters E, G, or L had attached themselves moved freely, as if destined to cross from West to East on a mission of the greatest importance which would never be revealed, and yet certainly so it was—a mission of the greatest importance. Then suddenly, as a train comes out of a tunnel, the aeroplane rushed out of the clouds again, the sound boring into the ears of all people in the Mall, in the Green Park,[4] in Piccadilly, in Regent Street, in Regent's Park, and the bar of smoke curved behind and it dropped down, and it soared up and wrote one letter after another—but what word was it writing?

Lucrezia Warren Smith, sitting by her husband's side on a seat in Regent's Park in the Broad Walk,[5] looked up.

1. The Royal Marines Memorial, completed in 1903 in memory of those who served in artillery and light infantry regiments and died in wars in South Africa and China (1889–1902). The memorial is located in St. James's Park near the Admiralty Arch.
2. The first demonstration of skywriting for advertising, in which Major Cyril Turner wrote the words "Daily Mail," occurred over Epsom Downs, a racecourse southwest of London, in 1922.
3. Name of a baby formula and the firm that produced it.
4. Royal park north of St. James's Park.
5. North–south pedestrian avenue in Regent's Park in north London.

"Look, look, Septimus!" she cried. For Dr. Holmes had told her to make her husband (who had nothing whatever seriously the matter with him but was a little out of sorts) take an interest in things outside himself.

So, thought Septimus, looking up, they are signalling to me. Not indeed in actual words; that is, he could not read the language yet; but it was plain enough, this beauty, this exquisite beauty, and tears filled his eyes as he looked at the smoke words languishing and melting in the sky and bestowing upon him in their inexhaustible charity and laughing goodness one shape after another of unimaginable beauty and signalling their intention to provide him, for nothing, for ever, for looking merely, with beauty, more beauty! Tears ran down his cheeks.

It was toffee; they were advertising toffee, a nursemaid told Rezia. Together they began to spell t . . . o . . . f . . .

"K . . . R . . ." said the nursemaid, and Septimus heard her say "Kay Arr" close to his ear, deeply, softly, like a mellow organ, but with a roughness in her voice like a grasshopper's, which rasped his spine deliciously and sent running up into his brain waves of sound which, concussing, broke. A marvellous discovery indeed—that the human voice in certain atmospheric conditions (for one must be scientific, above all scientific) can quicken trees into life! Happily Rezia put her hand with a tremendous weight on his knee so that he was weighted down, transfixed, or the excitement of the elm trees rising and falling, rising and falling with all their leaves alight and the colour thinning and thickening from blue to the green of a hollow wave, like plumes on horses' heads, feathers on ladies', so proudly they rose and fell, so superbly, would have sent him mad. But he would not go mad. He would shut his eyes; he would see no more.

But they beckoned; leaves were alive; trees were alive. And the leaves being connected by millions of fibres with his own body, there on the seat, fanned it up and down; when the branch stretched he, too, made that statement. The sparrows fluttering, rising, and falling in jagged fountains were part of the pattern; the white and blue, barred with black branches. Sounds made harmonies with premeditation; the spaces between them were as significant as the sounds. A child cried. Rightly far away a horn sounded. All taken together meant the birth of a new religion—

"Septimus!" said Rezia. He started violently. People must notice.

"I am going to walk to the fountain and back," she said.

For she could stand it no longer. Dr. Holmes might say there was nothing the matter. Far rather would she that he were dead! She could not sit beside him when he stared so and did not see her and made everything terrible; sky and tree, children playing, dragging carts, blowing whistles, falling down; all were terrible. And he would not kill himself; and she could tell no one. "Septimus has been working too hard"—that was all she could say to her own mother. To love makes one solitary, she thought. She could tell nobody, not even Septimus now, and looking back, she saw him sitting in his shabby overcoat alone on the seat, hunched up, staring. And it was cowardly for a man to say he would kill himself, but Septimus had fought;[6] he was brave; he was not Septimus now. She put on her lace collar. She put on her new hat and he never noticed; and he was happy without her. Nothing could make her happy without him! Nothing! He was selfish. So men are. For he was not

_____

6. In World War I.

ill. Dr. Holmes said there was nothing the matter with him. She spread her hand before her. Look! Her wedding ring slipped—she had grown so thin. It was she who suffered—but she had nobody to tell.

Far was Italy and the white houses and the room where her sisters sat making hats, and the streets crowded every evening with people walking, laughing out loud, not half alive like people here, huddled up in Bath chairs,[7] looking at a few ugly flowers stuck in pots!

"For you should see the Milan gardens,"[8] she said aloud. But to whom?

There was nobody. Her words faded. So a rocket fades. Its sparks, having grazed their way into the night, surrender to it, dark descends, pours over the outlines of houses and towers; bleak hillsides soften and fall in. But though they are gone, the night is full of them; robbed of colour, blank of windows, they exist more ponderously, give out what the frank daylight fails to transmit—the trouble and suspense of things conglomerated there in the darkness; huddled together in the darkness; reft of the relief which dawn brings when, washing the walls white and grey, spotting each windowpane, lifting the mist from the fields, showing the red brown cows peacefully grazing, all is once more decked out to the eye; exists again. I am alone; I am alone! she cried, by the fountain in Regent's Park (staring at the Indian and his cross[9]), as perhaps at midnight, when all boundaries are lost, the country reverts to its ancient shape, as the Romans[1] saw it, lying cloudy, when they landed, and the hills had no names and rivers wound they knew not where— such was her darkness; when suddenly, as if a shelf were shot forth and she stood on it, she said how she was his wife, married years ago in Milan, his wife, and would never, never tell that he was mad! Turning, the shelf fell; down, down she dropped. For he was gone, she thought—gone, as he threatened, to kill himself—to throw himself under a cart! But no; there he was; still sitting alone on the seat, in his shabby overcoat, his legs crossed, staring, talking aloud.

Men must not cut down trees. There is a God. (He noted such revelations on the backs of envelopes.) Change the world. No one kills from hatred. Make it known (he wrote it down). He waited. He listened. A sparrow perched on the railing opposite chirped Septimus, Septimus, four or five times over and went on, drawing its notes out, to sing freshly and piercingly in Greek words how there is no crime and, joined by another sparrow, they sang in voices prolonged and piercing in Greek words,[2] from trees in the meadow of life beyond a river where the dead walk,[3] how there is no death.

There was his hand; there the dead. White things were assembling behind the railings opposite. But he dared not look. Evans was behind the railings!

"What are you saying?" said Rezia suddenly, sitting down by him.

Interrupted again! She was always interrupting.

Away from people—they must get away from people, he said (jumping up), right away over there, where there were chairs beneath a tree and the long slope of the park dipped like a length of green stuff with a ceiling cloth of blue and pink smoke high above, and there was a rampart of far irregular

---

7. Wheeled chairs for invalids.
8. In Italy.
9. Drinking fountain resembling a cross at the north end of the Broad Walk and commemorating the protection of Parsis, Indian Zoroastrians, under British colonial rule in India.
1. The Roman Empire included most of Britain

from 43 to 410 C.E.
2. Woolf wrote of having a similar experience during a 1904 breakdown, in her 1922 memoir "Old Bloomsbury."
3. Cf. the River Styx, separating the living from the realm of the dead in the mythical Greek underworld.

houses hazed in smoke, the traffic hummed in a circle, and on the right, duncoloured animals stretched long necks over the Zoo[4] palings, barking, howling. There they sat down under a tree.

"Look," she implored him, pointing at a little troop of boys carrying cricket stumps,[5] and one shuffled, spun round on his heel and shuffled, as if he were acting a clown at the music hall.

"Look," she implored him, for Dr. Holmes had told her to make him notice real things, go to a music hall, play cricket—that was the very game, Dr. Holmes said, a nice out-of-door game, the very game for her husband.

"Look," she repeated.

Look the unseen bade him, the voice which now communicated with him who was the greatest of mankind, Septimus, lately taken from life to death, the Lord who had come to renew society, who lay like a coverlet, a snow blanket smitten only by the sun, for ever unwasted, suffering for ever, the scapegoat, the eternal sufferer, but he did not want it, he moaned, putting from him with a wave of his hand that eternal suffering, that eternal loneliness.

"Look," she repeated, for he must not talk aloud to himself out of doors.

"Oh look," she implored him. But what was there to look at? A few sheep. That was all.

The way to Regent's Park Tube[6] station—could they tell her the way to Regent's Park Tube station—Maisie Johnson wanted to know. She was only up from Edinburgh[7] two days ago.

"Not this way—over there!" Rezia exclaimed, waving her aside, lest she should see Septimus.

Both seemed queer, Maisie Johnson thought. Everything seemed very queer. In London for the first time, come to take up a post at her uncle's in Leadenhall Street,[8] and now walking through Regent's Park in the morning, this couple on the chairs gave her quite a turn; the young woman seeming foreign, the man looking queer; so that should she be very old she would still remember and make it jangle again among her memories how she had walked through Regent's Park on a fine summer's morning fifty years ago. For she was only nineteen and had got her way at last, to come to London; and now how queer it was, this couple she had asked the way of, and the girl started and jerked her hand, and the man—he seemed awfully odd; quarrelling, perhaps; parting for ever, perhaps; something was up, she knew; and now all these people (for she returned to the Broad Walk), the stone basins, the prim flowers, the old men and women, invalids most of them in Bath chairs—all seemed, after Edinburgh, so queer. And Maisie Johnson, as she joined that gently trudging, vaguely gazing, breeze-kissed company— squirrels perching and preening, sparrow fountains fluttering for crumbs, dogs busy with the railings, busy with each other, while the soft warm air washed over them and lent to the fixed unsurprised gaze with which they received life something whimsical and mollified—Maisie Johnson positively felt she must cry Oh! (for that young man on the seat had given her quite a turn. Something was up, she knew.)

---

4. In Regent's Park.
5. Upright sticks that, with cross-pieces called bails, form the wicket defended by the batsman in cricket.
6. Underground.

7. Colloquially, one travels "up" to London even if, as in this case, one is actually traveling south from Scotland's capital.
8. Street in east London.

Horror! horror! she wanted to cry. (She had left her people; they had warned her what would happen.)

Why hadn't she stayed at home? she cried, twisting the knob of the iron railing.

That girl, thought Mrs. Dempster (who saved crusts for the squirrels and often ate her lunch in Regent's Park), don't know a thing yet; and really it seemed to her better to be a little stout, a little slack, a little moderate in one's expectations. Percy drank. Well, better to have a son, thought Mrs. Dempster. She had had a hard time of it, and couldn't help smiling at a girl like that. You'll get married, for you're pretty enough, thought Mrs. Dempster. Get married, she thought, and then you'll know. Oh, the cooks, and so on. Every man has his ways. But whether I'd have chosen quite like that if I could have known, thought Mrs. Dempster, and could not help wishing to whisper a word to Maisie Johnson; to feel on the creased pouch of her worn old face the kiss of pity. For it's been a hard life, thought Mrs. Dempster. What hadn't she given to it? Roses; figure; her feet too. (She drew the knobbed lumps beneath her skirt.)

Roses, she thought sardonically. All trash, m'dear. For really, what with eating, drinking, and mating, the bad days and good, life had been no mere matter of roses, and what was more, let me tell you, Carrie Dempster had no wish to change her lot with any woman's in Kentish Town![9] But, she implored, pity. Pity, for the loss of roses. Pity she asked of Maisie Johnson, standing by the hyacinth beds.

Ah, but that aeroplane! Hadn't Mrs. Dempster always longed to see foreign parts? She had a nephew, a missionary. It soared and shot. She always went on the sea at Margate,[1] not out o' sight of land, but she had no patience with women who were afraid of water. It swept and fell. Her stomach was in her mouth. Up again. There's a fine young feller aboard of it, Mrs. Dempster wagered, and away and away it went, fast and fading, away and away the aeroplane shot; soaring over Greenwich[2] and all the masts; over the little island of grey churches, St. Paul's[3] and the rest till, on either side of London, fields spread out and dark brown woods where adventurous thrushes hopping boldly, glancing quickly, snatched the snail and tapped him on a stone, once, twice, thrice.

Away and away the aeroplane shot, till it was nothing but a bright spark; an aspiration; a concentration; a symbol (so it seemed to Mr. Bentley, vigorously rolling his strip of turf at Greenwich) of man's soul; of his determination, thought Mr. Bentley, sweeping round the cedar tree, to get outside his body, beyond his house, by means of thought, Einstein,[4] speculation,[5] mathematics, the Mendelian theory[6]—away the aeroplane shot.

Then, while a seedy-looking nondescript man carrying a leather bag stood on the steps of St. Paul's Cathedral, and hesitated, for within was what balm, how great a welcome, how many tombs with banners waving over them, tokens of victories not over armies, but over, he thought, that plaguy spirit of truth seeking which leaves me at present without a situation, and more than

---

9. Working-class neighborhood in north London near Hampstead Heath.
1. Seaside town in the county of Kent, west of London.
2. London borough south of the Thames.
3. St. Paul's Cathedral, the tallest building in London in 1923.

4. German-born theoretical physicist Albert Einstein (1879–1955) won the 1921 Nobel Prize in Physics.
5. Risky buying and selling for profit.
6. Laws of genetics studied by Austrian monk Gregor Mendel (1822–1884) in his work with pea plants.

that, the cathedral offers company, he thought, invites you to membership of a society; great men belong to it; martyrs have died for it; why not enter in, he thought, put this leather bag stuffed with pamphlets before an altar, a cross, the symbol of something which has soared beyond seeking and questing and knocking of words together and has become all spirit, disembodied, ghostly— why not enter in? he thought and while he hesitated out flew the aeroplane over Ludgate Circus.[7]

It was strange; it was still. Not a sound was to be heard above the traffic. Unguided it seemed; sped of its own free will. And now, curving up and up, straight up, like something mounting in ecstasy, in pure delight, out from behind poured white smoke looping, writing a T, an O, an F.

"What are they looking at?" said Clarissa Dalloway to the maid who opened her door.

The hall of the house was cool as a vault. Mrs. Dalloway raised her hand to her eyes, and, as the maid shut the door to, and she heard the swish of Lucy's skirts, she felt like a nun who has left the world and feels fold round her the familiar veils and the response to old devotions. The cook whistled in the kitchen. She heard the click of the typewriter. It was her life, and, bending her head over the hall table, she bowed beneath the influence, felt blessed and purified, saying to herself, as she took the pad with the telephone message on it, how moments like this are buds on the tree of life, flowers of darkness they are, she thought (as if some lovely rose had blossomed for her eyes only); not for a moment did she believe in God; but all the more, she thought, taking up the pad, must one repay in daily life to servants, yes, to dogs and canaries, above all to Richard her husband, who was the foundation of it—of the gay sounds, of the green lights, of the cook even whistling, for Mrs. Walker was Irish and whistled all day long—one must pay back from this secret deposit of exquisite moments, she thought, lifting the pad, while Lucy stood by her, trying to explain how

"Mr. Dalloway, ma'am"—

Clarissa read on the telephone pad, "Lady Bruton wishes to know if Mr. Dalloway will lunch with her to-day."

"Mr. Dalloway, ma'am, told me to tell you he would be lunching out."

"Dear!" said Clarissa, and Lucy shared as she meant her to her disappointment (but not the pang); felt the concord between them; took the hint; thought how the gentry love; gilded her own future with calm; and, taking Mrs. Dalloway's parasol, handled it like a sacred weapon which a Goddess, having acquitted herself honourably in the field of battle, sheds, and placed it in the umbrella stand.

"Fear no more," said Clarissa. Fear no more the heat o' the sun;[8] for the shock of Lady Bruton asking Richard to lunch without her made the moment in which she had stood shiver, as a plant on the river-bed feels the shock of a passing oar and shivers: so she rocked: so she shivered.

Millicent Bruton, whose lunch parties were said to be extraordinarily amusing, had not asked her. No vulgar jealousy could separate her from Richard. But she feared time itself, and read on Lady Bruton's face, as if it had been a dial cut in impassive stone, the dwindling of life; how year by

7. London intersection west of St. Paul's Cathedral.
8. See p. 1112 and n. 9.

year her share was sliced; how little the margin that remained was capable any longer of stretching, of absorbing, as in the youthful years, the colours, salts, tones of existence, so that she filled the room she entered, and felt often as she stood hesitating one moment on the threshold of her drawing-room, an exquisite suspense, such as might stay a diver before plunging while the sea darkens and brightens beneath him, and the waves which threaten to break, but only gently split their surface, roll and conceal and encrust as they just turn over the weeds with pearl.

She put the pad on the hall table. She began to go slowly upstairs, with her hand on the bannisters, as if she had left a party, where now this friend now that had flashed back her face, her voice; had shut the door and gone out and stood alone, a single figure against the appalling night, or rather, to be accurate, against the stare of this matter-of-fact June morning; soft with the glow of rose petals for some, she knew, and felt it, as she paused by the open staircase window which let in blinds flapping, dogs barking, let in, she thought, feeling herself suddenly shrivelled, aged, breastless, the grinding, blowing, flowering of the day, out of doors, out of the window, out of her body and brain which now failed, since Lady Bruton, whose lunch parties were said to be extraordinarily amusing, had not asked her.

Like a nun withdrawing, or a child exploring a tower, she went upstairs, paused at the window, came to the bathroom. There was the green linoleum and a tap dripping. There was an emptiness about the heart of life; an attic room. Women must put off their rich apparel. At midday they must disrobe. She pierced the pincushion and laid her feathered yellow hat on the bed. The sheets were clean, tight stretched in a broad white band from side to side. Narrower and narrower would her bed be. The candle was half burnt down and she had read deep in Baron Marbot's *Memoirs*.[9] She had read late at night of the retreat from Moscow. For the House sat so long that Richard insisted, after her illness, that she must sleep undisturbed. And really she preferred to read of the retreat from Moscow. He knew it. So the room was an attic; the bed narrow; and lying there reading, for she slept badly, she could not dispel a virginity preserved through childbirth which clung to her like a sheet. Lovely in girlhood, suddenly there came a moment—for example on the river beneath the woods at Clieveden—when, through some contraction of this cold spirit, she had failed him. And then at Constantinople,[1] and again and again. She could see what she lacked. It was not beauty; it was not mind. It was something central which permeated; something warm which broke up surfaces and rippled the cold contact of man and woman, or of women together. For *that* she could dimly perceive. She resented it, had a scruple picked up Heaven knows where, or, as she felt, sent by Nature (who is invariably wise); yet she could not resist sometimes yielding to the charm of a woman, not a girl, of a woman confessing, as to her they often did, some scrape, some folly. And whether it was pity, or their beauty, or that she was older, or some accident—like a faint scent, or a violin next door (so strange is the power of sounds at certain moments), she did undoubtedly then feel what men felt. Only for a moment; but it was

9. Memoirs by French general Jean-Baptiste Antoine Marcellin, baron de Marbot (1782–1854), describe the disastrous Russian campaign undertaken in winter 1812 by Napoleon Bonaparte (1769–1821).
1. Now Istanbul, Turkey. "Clieveden": forest on the banks of the Thames.

enough. It was a sudden revelation, a tinge like a blush which one tried to check and then, as it spread, one yielded to its expansion, and rushed to the farthest verge and there quivered and felt the world come closer, swollen with some astonishing significance, some pressure of rapture, which split its thin skin and gushed and poured with an extraordinary alleviation over the cracks and sores! Then, for that moment, she had seen an illumination; a match burning in a crocus; an inner meaning almost expressed. But the close withdrew; the hard softened. It was over—the moment. Against such moments (with women too) there contrasted (as she laid her hat down) the bed and Baron Marbot and the candle half-burnt. Lying awake, the floor creaked; the lit house was suddenly darkened, and if she raised her head she could just hear the click of the handle released as gently as possible by Richard, who slipped upstairs in his socks and then, as often as not, dropped his hot-water bottle and swore! How she laughed!

But this question of love (she thought, putting her coat away), this falling in love with women. Take Sally Seton; her relation in the old days with Sally Seton. Had not that, after all, been love?

She sat on the floor—that was her first impression of Sally—she sat on the floor with her arms round her knees, smoking a cigarette. Where could it have been? The Mannings? The Kinloch-Jones's? At some party (where, she could not be certain), for she had a distinct recollection of saying to the man she was with, "Who is *that*?" And he had told her, and said that Sally's parents did not get on (how that shocked her—that one's parents should quarrel!). But all that evening she could not take her eyes off Sally. It was an extraordinary beauty of the kind she most admired, dark, large-eyed, with that quality which, since she hadn't got it herself, she always envied—a sort of abandonment, as if she could say anything, do anything; a quality much commoner in foreigners than in Englishwomen. Sally always said she had French blood in her veins, an ancestor had been with Marie Antoinette,[2] had his head cut off, left a ruby ring. Perhaps that summer she came to stay at Bourton, walking in quite unexpectedly without a penny in her pocket, one night after dinner, and upsetting poor Aunt Helena to such an extent that she never forgave her. There had been some quarrel at home. She literally hadn't a penny that night when she came to them—had pawned a brooch to come down. She had rushed off in a passion. They sat up till all hours of the night talking. Sally it was who made her feel, for the first time, how sheltered the life at Bourton was. She knew nothing about sex—nothing about social problems. She had once seen an old man who had dropped dead in a field—she had seen cows just after their calves were born. But Aunt Helena never liked discussion of anything (when Sally gave her William Morris,[3] it had to be wrapped in brown paper). There they sat, hour after hour, talking in her bedroom at the top of the house, talking about life, how they were to reform the world. They meant to found a society to abolish private property, and actually had a letter written, though not sent out. The ideas were Sally's, of course—but very soon she was just as excited—read Plato in bed before breakfast; read Morris; read Shelley[4] by the hour.

Sally's power was amazing, her gift, her personality. There was her way with flowers, for instance. At Bourton they always had stiff little vases all

2. Queen of France and wife of Louis XVI (1755–1793), guillotined during the French Revolution.
3. English designer, writer, and socialist (1834–1896).
4. Percy Bysshe Shelley (1792–1822), English Romantic poet. Plato (ca. 429–347 B.C.E.), Greek philosopher.

the way down the table. Sally went out, picked hollyhocks, dahlias—all sorts of flowers that had never been seen together—cut their heads off, and made them swim on the top of water in bowls. The effect was extraordinary— coming in to dinner in the sunset (Of course Aunt Helena thought it wicked to treat flowers like that.) Then she forgot her sponge, and ran along the passage naked. That grim old housemaid, Ellen Atkins, went about grumbling—"Suppose any of the gentlemen had seen?" Indeed she did shock people. She was untidy, Papa said.

The strange thing, on looking back, was the purity, the integrity, of her feeling for Sally. It was not like one's feeling for a man. It was completely disinterested, and besides, it had a quality which could only exist between women, between women just grown up. It was protective, on her side; sprang from a sense of being in league together, a presentiment of something that was bound to part them (they spoke of marriage always as a catastrophe), which led to this chivalry, this protective feeling which was much more on her side than Sally's. For in those days she was completely reckless; did the most idiotic things out of bravado; bicycled round the parapet on the terrace; smoked cigars. Absurd, she was—very absurd. But the charm was overpowering, to her at least, so that she could remember standing in her bedroom at the top of the house holding the hot-water can in her hands and saying aloud, "She is beneath this roof. . . . She is beneath this roof!"

No, the words meant absolutely nothing to her now. She could not even get an echo of her old emotion. But she could remember going cold with excitement, and doing her hair in a kind of ecstasy (now the old feeling began to come back to her, as she took out her hairpins, laid them on the dressing-table, began to do her hair), with the rooks flaunting up and down in the pink evening light, and dressing, and going downstairs, and feeling as she crossed the hall "if it were now to die 'twere now to be most happy." That was her feeling—Othello's feeling,[5] and she felt it, she was convinced, as strongly as Shakespeare meant Othello to feel it, all because she was coming down to dinner in a white frock to meet Sally Seton!

She was wearing pink gauze—was that possible? She *seemed*, anyhow, all light, glowing, like some bird or air ball[6] that has flown in, attached itself for a moment to a bramble. But nothing is so strange when one is in love (and what was this except being in love?) as the complete indifference of other people. Aunt Helena just wandered off after dinner; Papa read the paper. Peter Walsh might have been there, and old Miss Cummings; Joseph Breitkopf certainly was, for he came every summer, poor old man, for weeks and weeks, and pretended to read German with her, but really played the piano and sang Brahms[7] without any voice.

All this was only a background for Sally. She stood by the fireplace talking, in that beautiful voice which made everything she said sound like a caress, to Papa, who had begun to be attracted rather against his will (he never got over lending her one of his books and finding it soaked on the terrace), when suddenly she said, "What a shame to sit indoors!" and they all went out on to the terrace and walked up and down. Peter Walsh and Joseph Breitkopf went on about Wagner. She and Sally fell a little behind. Then came the most exquisite moment of her whole life passing a stone urn

<hr>

5. From Shakespeare's *Othello* 2.1.87–88.
6. Toy balloon.

7. Johannes Brahms (1837–1897), German Romantic composer.

with flowers in it. Sally stopped; picked a flower; kissed her on the lips. The whole world might have turned upside down! The others disappeared; there she was alone with Sally. And she felt that she had been given a present, wrapped up, and told just to keep it, not to look at it—a diamond, something infinitely precious, wrapped up, which, as they walked (up and down, up and down), she uncovered, or the radiance burnt through, the revelation, the religious feeling!—when old Joseph and Peter faced them:

"Star-gazing?" said Peter.

It was like running one's face against a granite wall in the darkness! It was shocking; it was horrible!

Not for herself. She felt only how Sally was being mauled already, maltreated; she felt his hostility; his jealousy; his determination to break into their companionship. All this she saw as one sees a landscape in a flash of lightning—and Sally (never had she admired her so much!) gallantly taking her way unvanquished. She laughed. She made old Joseph tell her the names of the stars, which he liked doing very seriously. She stood there: she listened. She heard the names of the stars.

"Oh this horror!" she said to herself, as if she had known all along that something would interrupt, would embitter her moment of happiness.

Yet, after all, how much she owed to him later. Always when she thought of him she thought of their quarrels for some reason—because she wanted his good opinion so much, perhaps. She owed him words: "sentimental," "civilised"; they started up every day of her life as if he guarded her. A book was sentimental; an attitude to life sentimental. "Sentimental," perhaps she was to be thinking of the past. What would he think, she wondered, when he came back?

That she had grown older? Would he say that, or would she see him thinking when he came back, that she had grown older? It was true. Since her illness she had turned almost white.

Laying her brooch on the table, she had a sudden spasm, as if, while she mused, the icy claws had had the chance to fix in her. She was not old yet. She had just broken into her fifty-second year. Months and months of it were still untouched. June, July, August! Each still remained almost whole, and, as if to catch the falling drop, Clarissa (crossing to the dressing-table) plunged into the very heart of the moment, transfixed it, there—the moment of this June morning on which was the pressure of all the other mornings, seeing the glass, the dressing-table, and all the bottles afresh, collecting the whole of her at one point (as she looked into the glass), seeing the delicate pink face of the woman who was that very night to give a party; of Clarissa Dalloway; of herself.

How many million times she had seen her face, and always with the same imperceptible contraction! She pursed her lips when she looked in the glass. It was to give her face point. That was her self—pointed; dartlike; definite. That was her self when some effort, some call on her to be her self, drew the parts together, she alone knew how different, how incompatible and composed so for the world only into one centre, one diamond, one woman who sat in her drawing-room and made a meeting-point, a radiancy no doubt in some dull lives, a refuge for the lonely to come to, perhaps; she had helped young people, who were grateful to her; had tried to be the same always, never showing a sign of all the other sides of her—faults, jealousies, vanities, suspicions, like this of Lady Bruton not asking her to lunch; which, she thought (combing her hair finally), is utterly base! Now, where was her dress?

Her evening dresses hung in the cupboard. Clarissa, plunging her hand into the softness, gently detached the green dress and carried it to the window. She had torn it. Some one had trod on the skirt. She had felt it give at the Embassy party at the top among the folds. By artificial light the green shone, but lost its colour now in the sun. She would mend it. Her maids had too much to do. She would wear it to-night. She would take her silks, her scissors, her—what was it?—her thimble, of course, down into the drawing-room, for she must also write, and see that things generally were more or less in order.

Strange, she thought, pausing on the landing, and assembling that diamond shape, that single person, strange how a mistress knows the very moment, the very temper of her house! Faint sounds rose in spirals up the well of the stairs; the swish of a mop; tapping; knocking; a loudness when the front door opened; a voice repeating a message in the basement; the chink of silver on a tray, clean silver for the party. All was for the party.

(And Lucy, coming into the drawing-room with her tray held out, put the giant candlesticks on the mantelpiece, the silver casket[8] in the middle, turned the crystal dolphin towards the clock. They would come; they would stand; they would talk in the mincing tones which she could imitate, ladies and gentlemen. Of all, her mistress was loveliest—mistress of silver, of linen, of china, for the sun, the silver, doors off their hinges, Rumpelmayer's men, gave her a sense, as she laid the paper-knife[9] on the inlaid table, of something achieved. Behold! Behold! she said, speaking to her old friends in the baker's shop, where she had first seen service at Caterham,[1] prying into the glass. She was Lady Angela, attending Princess Mary, when in came Mrs. Dalloway.)

"Oh Lucy," she said, "the silver does look nice!"

"And how," she said, turning the crystal dolphin to stand straight, "how did you enjoy the play last night?" "Oh, they had to go before the end!" she said. "They had to be back at ten!" she said. "So they don't know what happened," she said. "That does seem hard luck," she said (for her servants stayed later, if they asked her). "That does seem rather a shame," she said, taking the old bald-looking cushion in the middle of the sofa and putting it in Lucy's arms, and giving her a little push, and crying:

"Take it away! Give it to Mrs. Walker with my compliments! Take it away!" she cried.

And Lucy stopped at the drawing-room door, holding the cushion, and said, very shyly, turning a little pink, Couldn't she help to mend that dress?

But, said Mrs. Dalloway, she had enough on her hands already, quite enough of her own to do without that.

"But, thank you, Lucy, oh, thank you," said Mrs. Dalloway, and thank you, thank you, she went on saying (sitting down on the sofa with her dress over her knees, her scissors, her silks), thank you, thank you, she went on saying in gratitude to her servants generally for helping her to be like this, to be what she wanted, gentle, generous-hearted. Her servants liked her. And then this dress of hers—where was the tear? and now her needle to be

---

8. Small box.
9. A slim knife used, e.g., for slitting open letters.

1. Town south of London in the county of Surrey.

threaded. This was a favourite dress, one of Sally Parker's, the last almost she ever made, alas, for Sally had now retired, living at Ealing,[2] and if ever I have a moment, thought Clarissa (but never would she have a moment any more), I shall go and see her at Ealing. For she was a character, thought Clarissa, a real artist. She thought of little out-of-the-way things; yet her dresses were never queer. You could wear them at Hatfield;[3] at Buckingham Palace. She had worn them at Hatfield; at Buckingham Palace.

Quiet descended on her, calm, content, as her needle, drawing the silk smoothly to its gentle pause, collected the green folds together and attached them, very lightly, to the belt. So on a summer's day waves collect, overbalance, and fall; collect and fall; and the whole world seems to be saying "that is all" more and more ponderously, until even the heart in the body which lies in the sun on the beach says too, That is all. Fear no more, says the heart. Fear no more, says the heart, committing its burden to some sea, which sighs collectively for all sorrows, and renews, begins, collects, lets fall. And the body alone listens to the passing bee; the wave breaking; the dog barking, far away barking and barking.

"Heavens, the front-door bell!" exclaimed Clarissa, staying her needle. Roused, she listened.

"Mrs. Dalloway will see me," said the elderly man in the hall. "Oh yes, she will see *me*," he repeated, putting Lucy aside very benevolently, and running upstairs ever so quickly. "Yes, yes, yes," he muttered as he ran upstairs. "She will see me. After five years in India,[4] Clarissa will see me."

"Who can—what can," asked Mrs. Dalloway (thinking it was outrageous to be interrupted at eleven o'clock on the morning of the day she was giving a party), hearing a step on the stairs. She heard a hand upon the door. She made to hide her dress, like a virgin protecting chastity, respecting privacy. Now the brass knob slipped. Now the door opened, and in came—for a single second she could not remember what he was called! so surprised she was to see him, so glad, so shy, so utterly taken aback to have Peter Walsh come to her unexpectedly in the morning! (She had not read his letter.)

"And how are you?" said Peter Walsh, positively trembling; taking both her hands; kissing both her hands. She's grown older, he thought, sitting down. I shan't tell her anything about it, he thought, for she's grown older. She's looking at me, he thought, a sudden embarrassment coming over him, though he had kissed her hands. Putting his hand into his pocket, he took out a large pocket-knife and half opened the blade.

Exactly the same, thought Clarissa; the same queer look; the same check suit; a little out of the straight his face is, a little thinner, dryer, perhaps, but he looks awfully well, and just the same.

"How heavenly it is to see you again!" she exclaimed. He had his knife out. That's so like him, she thought.

He had only reached town last night, he said; would have to go down into the country at once; and how was everything, how was everybody—Richard? Elizabeth?

"And what's all this?" he said, tilting his pen-knife towards her green dress.

2. District in west London.
3. Hertfordshire estate.
4. I.e., after five years working in India as a colonial administrator. Peter Walsh's position there would have become more complicated following the 1919 Amritsar Massacre. It created strong anti-British sentiment and led to the Government of India Act, which established a national parliament, and the beginning of Mohandas Gandhi's campaign of civil disobedience (1920).

He's very well dressed, thought Clarissa; yet he always criticises *me*.

Here she is mending her dress; mending her dress as usual, he thought; here she's been sitting all the time I've been in India; mending her dress; playing about; going to parties; running to the House and back and all that, he thought, growing more and more irritated, more and more agitated, for there's nothing in the world so bad for some women as marriage, he thought; and politics; and having a Conservative husband, like the admirable Richard. So it is, so it is, he thought, shutting his knife with a snap.

"Richard's very well. Richard's at a Committee,"[5] said Clarissa.

And she opened her scissors, and said, did he mind her just finishing what she was doing to her dress, for they had a party that night?

"Which I shan't ask you to," she said. "My dear Peter!" she said.

But it was delicious to hear her say that—my dear Peter! Indeed, it was all so delicious—the silver, the chairs; all so delicious!

Why wouldn't she ask him to her party? he asked.

Now of course, thought Clarissa, he's enchanting! perfectly enchanting! Now I remember how impossible it was ever to make up my mind—and why did I make up my mind—not to marry him? she wondered, that awful summer?

"But it's so extraordinary that you should have come this morning!" she cried, putting her hands, one on top of another, down on her dress.

"Do you remember," she said, "how the blinds used to flap at Bourton?"

"They did," he said; and he remembered breakfasting alone, very awkwardly, with her father; who had died; and he had not written to Clarissa. But he had never got on well with old Parry, that querulous, weak-kneed old man, Clarissa's father, Justin Parry.

"I often wish I'd got on better with your father," he said.

"But he never liked any one who—our friends," said Clarissa; and could have bitten her tongue for thus reminding Peter that he had wanted to marry her.

Of course I did, thought Peter; it almost broke my heart too, he thought; and was overcome with his own grief, which rose like a moon looked at from a terrace, ghastly beautiful with light from the sunken day. I was more unhappy than I've ever been since, he thought. And as if in truth he were sitting there on the terrace he edged a little towards Clarissa; put his hand out; raised it; let it fall. There above them it hung, that moon. She too seemed to be sitting with him on the terrace, in the moonlight.

"Herbert has it now," she said. "I never go there now," she said.

Then, just as happens on a terrace in the moonlight, when one person begins to feel ashamed that he is already bored, and yet as the other sits silent, very quiet, sadly looking at the moon, does not like to speak, moves his foot, clears his throat, notices some iron scroll on a table leg, stirs a leaf, but says nothing—so Peter Walsh did now. For why go back like this to the past? he thought. Why make him think of it again? Why make him suffer, when she had tortured him so infernally? Why?

"Do you remember the lake?" she said, in an abrupt voice, under the pressure of an emotion which caught her heart, made the muscles of her throat

<hr />

5. Group of members of Parliament charged with overseeing a particular issue. "The House": the House of Commons, the lower house of Parliament. "Conservative": member of the Conservative Party, the less reforming of the (usually) two major political parties.

stiff, and contracted her lips in a spasm as she said "lake." For she was a child, throwing bread to the ducks, between her parents, and at the same time a grown woman coming to her parents who stood by the lake, holding her life in her arms which, as she neared them, grew larger and larger in her arms, until it became a whole life, a complete life, which she put down by them and said, "This is what I have made of it! This!" And what had she made of it? What, indeed? sitting there sewing this morning with Peter.

She looked at Peter Walsh; her look, passing through all that time and that emotion, reached him doubtfully; settled on him tearfully; and rose and fluttered away, as a bird touches a branch and rises and flutters away. Quite simply she wiped her eyes.

"Yes," said Peter. "Yes, yes, yes," he said, as if she drew up to the surface something which positively hurt him as it rose. Stop! Stop! he wanted to cry. For he was not old; his life was not over; not by any means. He was only just past fifty. Shall I tell her, he thought, or not? He would like to make a clean breast of it all. But she is too cold, he thought; sewing, with her scissors; Daisy would look ordinary beside Clarissa. And she would think me a failure, which I am in their sense, he thought; in the Dalloways' sense. Oh yes, he had no doubt about that; he was a failure, compared with all this—the inlaid table, the mounted paper-knife, the dolphin and the candlesticks, the chair-covers and the old valuable English tinted prints—he was a failure! I detest the smugness of the whole affair, he thought; Richard's doing, not Clarissa's; save that she married him. (Here Lucy came into the room, carrying silver, more silver, but charming, slender, graceful she looked, he thought, as she stooped to put it down.) And this has been going on all the time! he thought; week after week; Clarissa's life; while I—he thought; and at once everything seemed to radiate from him; journeys; rides; quarrels; adventures; bridge parties; love affairs; work; work, work! and he took out his knife quite openly—his old horn-handled knife which Clarissa could swear he had had these thirty years—and clenched his fist upon it.

What an extraordinary habit that was, Clarissa thought; always playing with a knife. Always making one feel, too, frivolous; empty-minded; a mere silly chatterbox, as he used. But I too, she thought, and, taking up her needle, summoned, like a Queen whose guards have fallen asleep and left her unprotected (she had been quite taken aback by this visit—it had upset her) so that any one can stroll in and have a look at her where she lies with the brambles curving over her, summoned to her help the things she did; the things she liked; her husband; Elizabeth; her self, in short, which Peter hardly knew now, all to come about her and beat off the enemy.

"Well, and what's happened to you?" she said. So before a battle begins, the horses paw the ground; toss their heads; the light shines on their flanks; their necks curve. So Peter Walsh and Clarissa, sitting side by side on the blue sofa, challenged each other. His powers chafed and tossed in him. He assembled from different quarters all sorts of things; praise; his career at Oxford; his marriage, which she knew nothing whatever about; how he had loved; and altogether done his job.

"Millions of things!" he exclaimed, and, urged by the assembly of powers which were now charging this way and that and giving him the feeling at once frightening and extremely exhilarating of being rushed through the air on the shoulders of people he could no longer see, he raised his hands to his forehead.

Clarissa sat very upright; drew in her breath.

"I am in love," he said, not to her however, but to some one raised up in the dark so that you could not touch her but must lay your garland down on the grass in the dark.

"In love," he repeated, now speaking rather dryly to Clarissa Dalloway; "in love with a girl in India." He had deposited his garland. Clarissa could make what she would of it.

"In love!" she said. That he at his age should be sucked under in his little bow-tie by that monster! And there's no flesh on his neck; his hands are red; and he's six months older than I am! her eye flashed back to her; but in her heart she felt, all the same, he is in love. He has that, she felt; he is in love.

But the indomitable egotism which for ever rides down the hosts opposed to it, the river which says on, on, on; even though, it admits, there may be no goal for us whatever, still on, on; this indomitable egotism charged her cheeks with colour; made her look very young; very pink; very bright-eyed as she sat with her dress upon her knee, and her needle held to the end of green silk, trembling a little. He was in love! Not with her. With some younger woman, of course.

"And who is she?" she asked.

Now this statue must be brought from its height and set down between them.

"A married woman, unfortunately," he said; "the wife of a Major in the Indian Army."

And with a curious ironical sweetness he smiled as he placed her in this ridiculous way before Clarissa.

(All the same, he is in love, thought Clarissa.)

"She has," he continued, very reasonably, "two small children; a boy and a girl; and I have come over to see my lawyers about the divorce."

There they are! he thought. Do what you like with them, Clarissa! There they are! And second by second it seemed to him that the wife of the Major in the Indian Army[6] (his Daisy) and her two small children became more and more lovely as Clarissa looked at them; as if he had set light to a grey pellet on a plate and there had risen up a lovely tree in the brisk sea-salted air of their intimacy (for in some ways no one understood him, felt with him, as Clarissa did)—their exquisite intimacy.

She flattered him; she fooled him, thought Clarissa; shaping the woman, the wife of the Major in the Indian Army, with three strokes of a knife. What a waste! What a folly! All his life long Peter had been fooled like that; first getting sent down from Oxford;[7] next marrying the girl on the boat going out to India; now the wife of a Major in the Indian Army—thank Heaven she had refused to marry him! Still, he was in love; her old friend, her dear Peter, he was in love.

"But what are you going to do?" she asked him. Oh the lawyers and solicitors, Messrs. Hooper and Grateley of Lincoln's Inn,[8] they were going to do it, he said. And he actually pared his nails with his pocket-knife.

For Heaven's sake, leave your knife alone! she cried to herself in irrepressible irritation; it was his silly unconventionality, his weakness; his lack

6. British Army stationed in India.
7. Compelled to leave the university as a punishment.

8. One of the Inns of Court, or legal societies, that admitted people to the bar to practice law.

of the ghost of a notion what any one else was feeling that annoyed her, had always annoyed her; and now at his age, how silly!

I know all that, Peter thought; I know what I'm up against, he thought, running his finger along the blade of his knife, Clarissa and Dalloway and all the rest of them; but I'll show Clarissa—and then to his utter surprise, suddenly thrown by those uncontrollable forces thrown through the air, he burst into tears; wept; wept without the least shame, sitting on the sofa, the tears running down his cheeks.

And Clarissa had leant forward, taken his hand, drawn him to her, kissed him,—actually had felt his face on hers before she could down the brandishing of silver flashing—plumes like pampas grass in a tropic gale in her breast, which, subsiding, left her holding his hand, patting his knee and, feeling as she sat back extraordinarily at her ease with him and light-hearted, all in a clap it came over her, If I had married him, this gaiety would have been mine all day!

It was all over for her. The sheet was stretched and the bed narrow. She had gone up into the tower alone and left them blackberrying in the sun. The door had shut, and there among the dust of fallen plaster and the litter of birds' nests how distant the view had looked, and the sounds came thin and chill (once on Leith Hill,[9] she remembered), and Richard, Richard! she cried, as a sleeper in the night starts and stretches a hand in the dark for help. Lunching with Lady Bruton, it came back to her. He has left me; I am alone for ever, she thought, folding her hands upon her knee.

Peter Walsh had got up and crossed to the window and stood with his back to her, flicking a bandanna handkerchief from side to side. Masterly and dry and desolate he looked, his thin shoulder-blades lifting his coat slightly; blowing his nose violently. Take me with you, Clarissa thought impulsively, as if he were starting directly upon some great voyage; and then, next moment, it was as if the five acts of a play that had been very exciting and moving were now over and she had lived a lifetime in them and had run away, had lived with Peter, and it was now over.

Now it was time to move, and, as a woman gathers her things together, her cloak, her gloves, her opera-glasses, and gets up to go out of the theatre into the street, she rose from the sofa and went to Peter.

And it was awfully strange, he thought, how she still had the power, as she came tinkling, rustling, still had the power as she came across the room, to make the moon, which he detested, rise at Bourton on the terrace in the summer sky.

"Tell me," he said, seizing her by the shoulders. "Are you happy, Clarissa? Does Richard—"

The door opened.

"Here is my Elizabeth," said Clarissa, emotionally, histrionically, perhaps.

"How d'y do?" said Elizabeth coming forward.

The sound of Big Ben striking the half-hour struck out between them with extraordinary vigour, as if a young man, strong, indifferent, inconsiderate, were swinging dumb-bells this way and that.

"Hullo, Elizabeth!" cried Peter, stuffing his handkerchief into his pocket, going quickly to her, saying "Good-bye, Clarissa" without looking

---

9. The highest point in southeast England, in the county of Surrey, famous for its early summer flowers.

at her, leaving the room quickly, and running downstairs and opening the hall door.

"Peter! Peter!" cried Clarissa, following him out on to the landing. "My party to-night! Remember my party to-night!" she cried, having to raise her voice against the roar of the open air, and, overwhelmed by the traffic and the sound of all the clocks striking, her voice crying "Remember my party to-night!" sounded frail and thin and very far away as Peter Walsh shut the door.

Remember my party, remember my party, said Peter Walsh as he stepped down the street, speaking to himself rhythmically, in time with the flow of the sound, the direct downright sound of Big Ben striking the half-hour. (The leaden circles dissolved in the air.) Oh these parties, he thought; Clarissa's parties. Why does she give these parties, he thought. Not that he blamed her or this effigy of a man in a tail-coat with a carnation in his button-hole coming towards him. Only one person in the world could be as he was, in love. And there he was, this fortunate man, himself, reflected in the plate-glass window of a motor-car manufacturer in Victoria Street. All India lay behind him; plains, mountains; epidemics of cholera; a district twice as big as Ireland; decisions he had come to alone—he, Peter Walsh; who was now really for the first time in his life, in love. Clarissa had grown hard, he thought; and a trifle sentimental into the bargain, he suspected, looking at the great motor-cars capable of doing—how many miles on how many gallons? For he had a turn for mechanics; had invented a plough in his district, had ordered wheel-barrows from England, but the coolies[1] wouldn't use them, all of which Clarissa knew nothing whatever about.

The way she said "Here is my Elizabeth!"—that annoyed him. Why not "Here's Elizabeth" simply? It was insincere. And Elizabeth didn't like it either. (Still the last tremors of the great booming voice shook the air round him; the half-hour; still early; only half-past eleven still.) For he understood young people; he liked them. There was always something cold in Clarissa, he thought. She had always, even as a girl, a sort of timidity, which in middle age becomes conventionality, and then it's all up, it's all up, he thought, looking rather drearily into the glassy depths, and wondering whether by calling at that hour he had annoyed her; overcome with shame suddenly at having been a fool; wept; been emotional; told her everything, as usual, as usual.

As a cloud crosses the sun, silence falls on London; and falls on the mind. Effort ceases. Time flaps on the mast. There we stop; there we stand. Rigid, the skeleton of habit alone upholds the human frame. Where there is nothing, Peter Walsh said to himself; feeling hollowed out, utterly empty within. Clarissa refused me, he thought. He stood there thinking, Clarissa refused me.

Ah, said St. Margaret's,[2] like a hostess who comes into her drawing-room on the very stroke of the hour and finds her guests there already. I am not late. No, it is precisely half-past eleven, she says. Yet, though she is perfectly right, her voice, being the voice of the hostess, is reluctant to inflict its individuality. Some grief for the past holds it back; some concern for the present. It is half-past eleven, she says, and the sound of St. Margaret's glides into the recesses

1. Manual laborers in British colonies, usually from the lower classes.
2. Bells of the parish church for the Houses of Parliament, situated on the grounds of Westminster Abbey.

of the heart and buries itself in ring after ring of sound, like something alive which wants to confide itself, to disperse itself, to be, with a tremor of delight, at rest—like Clarissa herself, thought Peter Walsh, coming down the stairs on the stroke of the hour in white. It is Clarissa herself, he thought, with a deep emotion, and an extraordinarily clear, yet puzzling, recollection of her, as if this bell had come into the room years ago, where they sat at some moment of great intimacy, and had gone from one to the other and had left, like a bee with honey, laden with the moment. But what room? What moment? And why had he been so profoundly happy when the clock was striking? Then, as the sound of St. Margaret's languished, he thought, She has been ill, and the sound expressed languor and suffering. It was her heart, he remembered; and the sudden loudness of the final stroke tolled for death that surprised in the midst of life, Clarissa falling where she stood, in her drawing room. No! No! he cried. She is not dead! I am not old, he cried, and marched up Whitehall,[3] as if there rolled down to him, vigorous, unending, his future.

He was not old, or set, or dried in the least. As for caring what they said of him—the Dalloways, the Whitbreads, and their set, he cared not a straw—not a straw (though it was true he would have, some time or other, to see whether Richard couldn't help him to some job). Striding, staring, he glared at the statue of the Duke of Cambridge.[4] He had been sent down from Oxford—true. He had been a Socialist, in some sense a failure—true. Still the future of civilisation lies, he thought, in the hands of young men like that; of young men such as he was, thirty years ago; with their love of abstract principles; getting books sent out to them all the way from London to a peak in the Himalayas; reading science; reading philosophy. The future lies in the hands of young men like that, he thought.

A patter like the patter of leaves in a wood came from behind, and with it a rustling, regular thudding sound, which as it overtook him drummed his thoughts, strict in step, up Whitehall, without his doing. Boys in uniform, carrying guns, marched with their eyes ahead of them, marched, their arms stiff, and on their faces an expression like the letters of a legend written round the base of a statue praising duty, gratitude, fidelity, love of England.

It is, thought Peter Walsh, beginning to keep step with them, a very fine training. But they did not look robust. They were weedy for the most part, boys of sixteen, who might, tomorrow, stand behind bowls of rice, cakes of soap on counters. Now they wore on them unmixed with sensual pleasure or daily preoccupations the solemnity of the wreath which they had fetched from Finsbury Pavement to the empty tomb.[5] They had taken their vow. The traffic respected it; vans were stopped.

I can't keep up with them, Peter Walsh thought, as they marched up Whitehall, and sure enough, on they marched, past him, past every one, in their steady way, as if one will worked legs and arms uniformly, and life, with its varieties, its irreticences, had been laid under a pavement of monuments and wreaths and drugged into a stiff yet staring corpse by discipline. One had to respect it; one might laugh; but one had to respect it, he thought. There they go, thought Peter Walsh, pausing at the edge of the

---

3. Street in Westminster and site of government buildings.
4. Equestrian statue of Prince George, duke of Cambridge (1819–1904), commander in chief of the army and grandson of King George III.

5. The boys, probably members of the London Cadets, have come from east London, near the Armoury House, to place a wreath at the Cenotaph, a World War I memorial.

pavement; and all the exalted statues, Nelson, Gordon, Havelock, the black, the spectacular images of great soldiers[6] stood looking ahead of them, as if they too had made the same renunciation (Peter Walsh felt he too had made it, the great renunciation), trampled under the same temptations, and achieved at length a marble stare. But the stare Peter Walsh did not want for himself in the least; though he could respect it in others. He could respect it in boys. They don't know the troubles of the flesh yet, he thought, as the marching boys disappeared in the direction of the Strand[7]—all that I've been through, he thought, crossing the road, and standing under Gordon's statue, Gordon whom as a boy he had worshipped; Gordon standing lonely with one leg raised and his arms crossed,—poor Gordon, he thought.

And just because nobody yet knew he was in London, except Clarissa, and the earth, after the voyage, still seemed an island to him, the strangeness of standing alone, alive, unknown, at half-past eleven in Trafalgar Square overcame him. What is it? Where am I? And why, after all, does one do it? he thought, the divorce seeming all moonshine. And down his mind went flat as a marsh, and three great emotions bowled over him; understanding; a vast philanthropy; and finally, as if the result of the others, an irrepressible, exquisite delight; as if inside his brain by another hand strings were pulled, shutters moved, and he, having nothing to do with it, yet stood at the opening of endless avenues, down which if he chose he might wander. He had not felt so young for years.

He had escaped! was utterly free—as happens in the downfall of habit when the mind, like an unguarded flame, bows and bends and seems about to blow from its holding. I haven't felt so young for years! thought Peter, escaping (only of course for an hour or so) from being precisely what he was, and feeling like a child who runs out of doors, and sees, as he runs, his old nurse waving at the wrong window. But she's extraordinarily attractive, he thought, as, walking across Trafalgar Square in the direction of the Haymarket,[8] came a young woman who, as she passed Gordon's statue, seemed, Peter Walsh thought (susceptible as he was), to shed veil after veil, until she became the very woman he had always had in mind; young, but stately; merry, but discreet, black,[9] but enchanting.

Straightening himself and stealthily fingering his pocket-knife he started after her to follow this woman, this excitement, which seemed even with its back turned to shed on him a light which connected them, which singled him out, as if the random uproar of the traffic had whispered through hollowed hands his name, not Peter, but his private name which he called himself in his own thoughts. "You," she said, only "you," saying it with her white gloves and her shoulders. Then the thin long cloak which the wind stirred as she walked past Dent's shop in Cockspur Street[1] blew out with an

6. Monumental statues in Trafalgar Square commemorating the 1805 battle in which the British defeated Napoleon's navy. The statue of the hero of the battle, Horatio Nelson (1758–1805), appears on top of Nelson's Column. The statue of Henry Havelock (1795–1857), killed while serving in India, stands on the southeast plinth of the square. The statue of army officer Charles George Gordon (1833–1885), killed while serving in the Sudan, would be removed in 1943. The silhouetted statues all appear black.
7. Street running east from Trafalgar Square.

8. Street to the west of Trafalgar Square, running northwest toward Piccadilly Circus.
9. With a dark complexion or black hair, i.e., not of African descent.
1. Street connecting Trafalgar Square with Haymarket. Instead of turning here, Walsh follows the young woman up Regent Street (which runs parallel to Haymarket), crosses Piccadilly, and continues north toward Regent's Park. "Dent's shop": headquarters of the company that constructed Big Ben.

enveloping kindness, a mournful tenderness, as of arms that would open and take the tired—

But she's not married; she's young; quite young, thought Peter, the red carnation he had seen her wear as she came across Trafalgar Square burning again in his eyes and making her lips red. But she waited at the kerbstone. There was a dignity about her. She was not worldly, like Clarissa; not rich, like Clarissa. Was she, he wondered as she moved, respectable? Witty, with a lizard's flickering tongue, he thought (for one must invent, must allow oneself a little diversion), a cool waiting wit, a darting wit; not noisy.

She moved; she crossed; he followed her. To embarrass her was the last thing he wished. Still if she stopped he would say "Come and have an ice," he would say, and she would answer, perfectly simply, "Oh yes."

But other people got between them in the street, obstructing him, blotting her out. He pursued; she changed. There was colour in her cheeks; mockery in her eyes; he was an adventurer, reckless, he thought, swift, daring, indeed (landed as he was last night from India) a romantic buccaneer, careless of all these damned proprieties, yellow dressing-gowns, pipes, fishing-rods, in the shop windows; and respectability and evening parties and spruce old men wearing white slips beneath their waistcoats. He was a buccaneer.[2] On and on she went, across Piccadilly, and up Regent Street, ahead of him, her cloak, her gloves, her shoulders combining with the fringes and the laces and the feather boas in the windows to make the spirit of finery and whimsy which dwindled out of the shops on to the pavement, as the light of a lamp goes wavering at night over hedges in the darkness.

Laughing and delightful, she had crossed Oxford Street and Great Portland Street[3] and turned down one of the little streets, and now, and now, the great moment was approaching, for now she slackened, opened her bag, and with one look in his direction, but not at him, one look that bade farewell, summed up the whole situation and dismissed it triumphantly, for ever, had fitted her key, opened the door, and gone! Clarissa's voice saying, Remember my party, Remember my party, sang in his ears. The house was one of those flat red houses with hanging flower-baskets of vague impropriety. It was over.

Well, I've had my fun; I've had it, he thought, looking up at the swinging baskets of pale geraniums. And it was smashed to atoms—his fun, for it was half made up, as he knew very well; invented, this escapade with the girl; made up, as one makes up the better part of life, he thought—making oneself up; making her up; creating an exquisite amusement, and something more. But odd it was, and quite true; all this one could never share—it smashed to atoms.

He turned; went up the street, thinking to find somewhere to sit, till it was time for Lincoln's Inn—for Messrs. Hooper and Grateley. Where should he go? No matter. Up the street, then, towards Regent's Park. His boots on the pavement struck out "no matter"; for it was early, still very early.

It was a splendid morning too. Like the pulse of a perfect heart, life struck straight through the streets. There was no fumbling—no hesitation. Sweeping and swerving, accurately, punctually, noiselessly, there, precisely at the right instant, the motor-car stopped at the door. The girl, silk-stockinged,

2. Pirate.
3. Walsh follows north along Regent Street, crosses Oxford Street, and then turns into a street near Great Portland Street, which leads into Regent's Park.

feathered, evanescent, but not to him particularly attractive (for he had had his fling), alighted. Admirable butlers, tawny chow dogs, halls laid in black and white lozenges[4] with white blinds blowing, Peter saw through the opened door and approved of. A splendid achievement in its own way, after all, London; the season; civilisation. Coming as he did from a respectable Anglo-Indian family[5] which for at least three generations had administered the affairs of a continent (it's strange, he thought, what a sentiment I have about that, disliking India, and empire, and army as he did), there were moments when civilisation, even of this sort, seemed dear to him as a personal possession; moments of pride in England; in butlers; chow dogs; girls in their security. Ridiculous enough, still there it is, he thought. And the doctors and men of business and capable women all going about their business, punctual, alert, robust, seemed to him wholly admirable, good fellows, to whom one would entrust one's life, companions in the art of living, who would see one through. What with one thing and another, the show was really very tolerable; and he would sit down in the shade and smoke.

There was Regent's Park. Yes. As a child he had walked in Regent's Park—odd, he thought, how the thought of childhood keeps coming back to me—the result of seeing Clarissa, perhaps; for women live much more in the past than we do, he thought. They attach themselves to places; and their fathers—a woman's always proud of her father. Bourton was a nice place, a very nice place, but I could never get on with the old man, he thought. There was quite a scene one night—an argument about something or other, what, he could not remember. Politics presumably.

Yes, he remembered Regent's Park; the long straight walk; the little house where one bought air-balls to the left; an absurd statue with an inscription[6] somewhere or other. He looked for an empty seat. He did not want to be bothered (feeling a little drowsy as he did) by people asking him the time. An elderly grey nurse, with a baby asleep in its perambulator—that was the best he could do for himself; sit down at the far end of the seat by that nurse.

She's a queer-looking girl, he thought, suddenly remembering Elizabeth as she came into the room and stood by her mother. Grown big; quite grown-up, not exactly pretty; handsome rather; and she can't be more than eighteen. Probably she doesn't get on with Clarissa. "There's my Elizabeth"—that sort of thing—why not "Here's Elizabeth" simply?—trying to make out, like most mothers, that things are what they're not. She trusts to her charm too much, he thought. She overdoes it.

The rich benignant cigar smoke eddied coolly down his throat; he puffed it out again in rings which breasted the air bravely for a moment; blue, circular—I shall try and get a word alone with Elizabeth to-night, he thought—then began to wobble into hour-glass shapes and taper away; odd shapes they take, he thought. Suddenly he closed his eyes, raised his hand with an effort, and threw away the heavy end of his cigar. A great brush swept smooth across his mind, sweeping across it moving branches, children's voices, the shuffle of feet, and people passing, and humming traffic, rising and falling traffic. Down, down he sank into the plumes and feathers of sleep, sank, and was muffled over.

---

4. Diamondlike shapes.
5. A person of British heritage born in India.

6. Possibly the Matilda drinking fountain, with a statue of a milkmaid.

The grey nurse resumed her knitting as Peter Walsh, on the hot seat beside her, began snoring. In her grey dress, moving her hands indefatigably yet quietly, she seemed like the champion of the rights of sleepers, like one of those spectral presences which rise in twilight in woods made of sky and branches. The solitary traveller, haunter of lanes, disturber of ferns, and devastator of great hemlock plants, looking up, suddenly sees the giant figure at the end of the ride.

By conviction an atheist perhaps, he is taken by surprise with moments of extraordinary exaltation. Nothing exists outside us except a state of mind, he thinks; a desire for solace, for relief, for something outside these miserable pigmies, these feeble, these ugly, these craven men and women. But if he can conceive of her, then in some sort she exists, he thinks, and advancing down the path with his eyes upon sky and branches he rapidly endows them with womanhood; sees with amazement how grave they become; how majestically, as the breeze stirs them, they dispense with a dark flutter of the leaves charity, comprehension, absolution, and then, flinging themselves suddenly aloft, confound the piety of their aspect with a wild carouse.

Such are the visions which proffer great cornucopias full of fruit to the solitary traveller, or murmur in his ear like sirens lolloping away on the green sea waves, or are dashed in his face like bunches of roses, or rise to the surface like pale faces which fishermen flounder through floods to embrace.

Such are the visions which ceaselessly float up, pace beside, put their faces in front of, the actual thing; often overpowering the solitary traveller and taking away from him the sense of the earth, the wish to return, and giving him for substitute a general peace, as if (so he thinks as he advances down the forest ride) all this fever of living were simplicity itself; and myriads of things merged in one thing; and this figure, made of sky and branches as it is, had risen from the troubled sea (he is elderly, past fifty now) as a shape might be sucked up out of the waves to shower down from her magnificent hands compassion, comprehension, absolution. So, he thinks, may I never go back to the lamplight; to the sitting-room; never finish my book; never knock out my pipe; never ring for Mrs. Turner to clear away; rather let me walk straight on to this great figure, who will, with a toss of her head, mount me on her streamers and let me blow to nothingness with the rest.

Such are the visions. The solitary traveller is soon beyond the wood; and there, coming to the door with shaded eyes, possibly to look for his return, with hands raised, with white apron blowing, is an elderly woman who seems (so powerful is this infirmity) to seek, over a desert, a lost son; to search for a rider destroyed; to be the figure of the mother whose sons have been killed in the battles of the world. So, as the solitary traveller advances down the village street where the women stand knitting and the men dig in the garden, the evening seems ominous; the figures still; as if some august fate, known to them, awaited without fear, were about to sweep them into complete annihilation.

Indoors among ordinary things, the cupboard, the table, the window-sill with its geraniums, suddenly the outline of the landlady, bending to remove the cloth, becomes soft with light, an adorable emblem which only the recollection of cold human contacts forbids us to embrace. She takes the marmalade; she shuts it in the cupboard.

"There is nothing more to-night, sir?"

But to whom does the solitary traveller make reply?

So the elderly nurse knitted over the sleeping baby in Regent's Park. So Peter Walsh snored.

He woke with extreme suddenness, saying to himself, "The death of the soul."

"Lord, Lord!" he said to himself out loud, stretching and opening his eyes. "The death of the soul." The words attached themselves to some scene, to some room, to some past he had been dreaming of. It became clearer; the scene, the room, the past he had been dreaming of.

It was at Bourton that summer, early in the 'nineties, when he was so passionately in love with Clarissa. There were a great many people there, laughing and talking, sitting round a table after tea and the room was bathed in yellow light and full of cigarette smoke. They were talking about a man who had married his housemaid, one of the neighbouring squires, he had forgotten his name. He had married his housemaid, and she had been brought to Bourton to call—an awful visit it had been. She was absurdly over-dressed, "like a cockatoo," Clarissa had said, imitating her, and she never stopped talking. On and on she went, on and on. Clarissa imitated her. Then somebody said— Sally Seton it was—did it make any real difference to one's feelings to know that before they'd married she had had a baby? (In those days, in mixed company, it was a bold thing to say.) He could see Clarissa now, turning bright pink; somehow contracting; and saying, "Oh, I shall never be able to speak to her again!" Whereupon the whole party sitting round the tea-table seemed to wobble. It was very uncomfortable.

He hadn't blamed her for minding the fact, since in those days a girl brought up as she was, knew nothing, but it was her manner that annoyed him; timid; hard; something arrogant; unimaginative; prudish. "The death of the soul." He had said that instinctively, ticketing the moment as he used to do—the death of her soul.

Every one wobbled; every one seemed to bow, as she spoke, and then to stand up different. He could see Sally Seton, like a child who has been in mischief, leaning forward, rather flushed, wanting to talk, but afraid, and Clarissa did frighten people. (She was Clarissa's greatest friend, always about the place, totally unlike her, an attractive creature, handsome, dark, with the reputation in those days of great daring and he used to give her cigars, which she smoked in her bedroom. She had either been engaged to somebody or quarrelled with her family and old Parry disliked them both equally, which was a great bond.) Then Clarissa, still with an air of being offended with them all, got up, made some excuse, and went off, alone. As she opened the door, in came that great shaggy dog which ran after sheep. She flung herself upon him, went into raptures. It was as if she said to Peter—it was all aimed at him, he knew—"I know you thought me absurd about that woman just now; but see how extraordinarily sympathetic I am; see how I love my Rob!"

They had always this queer power of communicating without words. She knew directly he criticised her. Then she would do something quite obvious to defend herself, like this fuss with the dog—but it never took him in, he always saw through Clarissa. Not that he said anything, of course; just sat looking glum. It was the way their quarrels often began.

She shut the door. At once he became extremely depressed. It all seemed useless—going on being in love; going on quarrelling; going on making it up, and he wandered off alone, among outhouses, stables, looking at the horses. (The place was quite a humble one; the Parrys were never very well off; but there were always grooms and stable-boys about—Clarissa loved riding—and an old coachman—what was his name?—an old nurse, old Moody, old Goody, some such name they called her, whom one was taken to visit in a little room with lots of photographs, lots of bird-cages.)

It was an awful evening! He grew more and more gloomy, not about that only; about everything. And he couldn't see her; couldn't explain to her; couldn't have it out. There were always people about—she'd go on as if nothing had happened. That was the devilish part of her—this coldness, this woodenness, something very profound in her, which he had felt again this morning talking to her; an impenetrability. Yet Heaven knows he loved her. She had some queer power of fiddling on one's nerves, turning one's nerves to fiddle-strings, yes.

He had gone in to dinner rather late, from some idiotic idea of making himself felt, and had sat down by old Miss Parry—Aunt Helena—Mr. Parry's sister, who was supposed to preside. There she sat in her white Cashmere shawl, with her head against the window—a formidable old lady, but kind to him, for he had found her some rare flower, and she was a great botanist, marching off in thick boots with a black collecting-box slung between her shoulders. He sat down beside her, and couldn't speak. Everything seemed to race past him; he just sat there, eating. And then half-way through dinner he made himself look across at Clarissa for the first time. She was talking to a young man on her right. He had a sudden revelation. "She will marry that man," he said to himself. He didn't even know his name.

For of course it was that afternoon, that very afternoon, that Dalloway had come over; and Clarissa called him "Wickham"; that was the beginning of it all. Somebody had brought him over; and Clarissa got his name wrong. She introduced him to everybody as Wickham.[7] At last he said "My name is Dalloway!"—that was his first view of Richard—a fair young man, rather awkward, sitting on a deck-chair, and blurting out "My name is Dalloway!" Sally got hold of it; always after that she called him "My name is Dalloway!"

He was a prey to revelations at that time. This one—that she would marry Dalloway—was blinding—overwhelming at the moment. There was a sort of—how could he put it?—a sort of ease in her manner to him; something maternal; something gentle. They were talking about politics. All through dinner he tried to hear what they were saying.

Afterwards he could remember standing by old Miss Parry's chair in the drawing-room. Clarissa came up, with her perfect manners, like a real hostess, and wanted to introduce him to some one—spoke as if they had never met before, which enraged him. Yet even then he admired her for it. He admired her courage; her social instinct; he admired her power of carrying things through. "The perfect hostess," he said to her, whereupon she winced all over. But he meant her to feel it. He would have done anything to hurt her after seeing her with Dalloway. So she left him. And he had a feeling that they were all gathered together in a conspiracy against him—laughing

---

7. Cf. George Wickham, the villainous suitor in *Pride and Prejudice* (1813) by English novelist Jane Austen (1775–1817).

and talking—behind his back. There he stood by Miss Parry's chair as though he had been cut out of wood, he talking about wild flowers. Never, never had he suffered so infernally! He must have forgotten even to pretend to listen; at last he woke up; he saw Miss Parry looking rather disturbed, rather indignant, with her prominent eyes fixed. He almost cried out that he couldn't attend because he was in Hell! People began going out of the room. He heard them talking about fetching cloaks; about its being cold on the water, and so on. They were going boating on the lake by moonlight— one of Sally's mad ideas. He could hear her describing the moon. And they all went out. He was left quite alone.

"Don't you want to go with them?" said Aunt Helena—old Miss Parry!— she had guessed. And he turned round and there was Clarissa again. She had come back to fetch him. He was overcome by her generosity—her goodness.

"Come along," she said. "They're waiting."

He had never felt so happy in the whole of his life! Without a word they made it up. They walked down to the lake. He had twenty minutes of perfect happiness. Her voice, her laugh, her dress (something floating, white, crimson), her spirit, her adventurousness; she made them all disembark and explore the island; she startled a hen; she laughed; she sang. And all the time, he knew perfectly well, Dalloway was falling in love with her; she was falling in love with Dalloway; but it didn't seem to matter. Nothing mattered. They sat on the ground and talked—he and Clarissa. They went in and out of each other's minds without any effort. And then in a second it was over. He said to himself as they were getting into the boat, "She will marry that man," dully, without any resentment; but it was an obvious thing. Dalloway would marry Clarissa.

Dalloway rowed them in. He said nothing. But somehow as they watched him start, jumping on to his bicycle to ride twenty miles through the woods, wobbling off down the drive, waving his hand and disappearing, he obviously did feel, instinctively, tremendously, strongly, all that; the night; the romance; Clarissa. He deserved to have her.

For himself, he was absurd. His demands upon Clarissa (he could see it now) were absurd. He asked impossible things. He made terrible scenes. She would have accepted him still, perhaps, if he had been less absurd. Sally thought so. She wrote him all that summer long letters; how they had talked of him; how she had praised him, how Clarissa burst into tears! It was an extraordinary summer—all letters, scenes, telegrams—arriving at Bourton early in the morning, hanging about till the servants were up; appalling *tête-à-têtes* with old Mr. Parry at breakfast; Aunt Helena formidable but kind; Sally sweeping him off for talks in the vegetable garden; Clarissa in bed with headaches.

The final scene, the terrible scene which he believed had mattered more than anything in the whole of his life (it might be an exaggeration—but still so it did seem now) happened at three o'clock in the afternoon of a very hot day. It was a trifle that led up to it—Sally at lunch saying something about Dalloway, and calling him "My name is Dalloway"; whereupon Clarissa suddenly stiffened, coloured, in a way she had, and rapped out sharply, "We've had enough of that feeble joke." That was all; but for him it was precisely as if she had said, "I'm only amusing myself with you; I've an understanding with Richard Dalloway." So he took it. He had not slept for nights. "It's got to be finished one way or the other," he said to himself. He sent a note to her by Sally asking her to meet him by the fountain at three. "Something very important has happened," he scribbled at the end of it.

The fountain was in the middle of a little shrubbery, far from the house, with shrubs and trees all round it. There she came, even before the time, and they stood with the fountain between them, the spout (it was broken) dribbling water incessantly. How sights fix themselves upon the mind! For example, the vivid green moss.

She did not move. "Tell me the truth, tell me the truth," he kept on saying. He felt as if his forehead would burst. She seemed contracted, petrified. She did not move. "Tell me the truth," he repeated, when suddenly that old man Breitkopf popped his head in carrying the *Times*, stared at them; gaped; and went away. They neither of them moved. "Tell me the truth," he repeated. He felt that he was grinding against something physically hard; she was unyielding. She was like iron, like flint, rigid up the backbone. And when she said, "It's no use. It's no use. This is the end"—after he had spoken for hours, it seemed, with the tears running down his cheeks—it was as if she had hit him in the face. She turned, she left him, went away.

"Clarissa!" he cried. "Clarissa!" But she never came back. It was over. He went away that night. He never saw her again.

It was awful, he cried, awful, awful!

Still, the sun was hot. Still, one got over things. Still, life had a way of adding day to day. Still, he thought, yawning and beginning to take notice—Regent's Park had changed very little since he was a boy, except for the squirrels—still, presumably there were compensations—when little Elise Mitchell, who had been picking up pebbles to add to the pebble collection which she and her brother were making on the nursery mantelpiece, plumped her handful down on the nurse's knee and scudded off again full tilt into a lady's legs. Peter Walsh laughed out.

But Lucrezia Warren Smith was saying to herself, It's wicked; why should I suffer? she was asking, as she walked down the broad path. No; I can't stand it any longer, she was saying, having left Septimus, who wasn't Septimus any longer, to say hard, cruel, wicked things, to talk to himself, to talk to a dead man, on the seat over there; when the child ran full tilt into her, fell flat, and burst out crying.

That was comforting rather. She stood her upright, dusted her frock, kissed her.

But for herself she had done nothing wrong; she had loved Septimus; she had been happy; she had had a beautiful home, and there her sisters lived still, making hats. Why should *she* suffer?

The child ran straight back to its nurse, and Rezia saw her scolded, comforted, taken up by the nurse who put down her knitting, and the kind-looking man gave her his watch to blow open[8] to comfort her—but why should *she* be exposed? Why not left in Milan? Why tortured? Why?

Slightly waved by tears the broad path, the nurse, the man in grey, the perambulator, rose and fell before her eyes. To be rocked by this malignant torturer was her lot. But why? She was like a bird sheltering under the thin hollow of a leaf, who blinks at the sun when the leaf moves; starts at the crack of a dry twig. She was exposed; she was surrounded by the enormous

8. Perhaps Walsh opens the cover on his pocket watch and pretends that the child has blown it open.

trees, vast clouds of an indifferent world, exposed; tortured; and why should she suffer? Why?

She frowned; she stamped her foot. She must go back again to Septimus since it was almost time for them to be going to Sir William Bradshaw. She must go back and tell him, go back to him sitting there on the green chair under the tree, talking to himself, or to that dead man Evans, whom she had only seen once for a moment in the shop. He had seemed a nice quiet man; a great friend of Septimus's, and he had been killed in the War. But such things happen to every one. Every one has friends who were killed in the War. Every one gives up something when they marry. She had given up her home. She had come to live here, in this awful city. But Septimus let himself think about horrible things, as she could too, if she tried. He had grown stranger and stranger. He said people were talking behind the bedroom walls. Mrs. Filmer thought it odd. He saw things too—he had seen an old woman's head in the middle of a fern. Yet he could be happy when he chose. They went to Hampton Court[9] on top of a bus, and they were perfectly happy. All the little red and yellow flowers were out on the grass, like floating lamps he said, and talked and chattered and laughed, making up stories. Suddenly he said, "Now we will kill ourselves," when they were standing by the river, and he looked at it with a look which she had seen in his eyes when a train went by, or an omnibus—a look as if something fascinated him; and she felt he was going from her and she caught him by the arm. But going home he was perfectly quiet—perfectly reasonable. He would argue with her about killing themselves; and explain how wicked people were; how he could see them making up lies as they passed in the street. He knew all their thoughts, he said; he knew everything. He knew the meaning of the world, he said. Then when they got back he could hardly walk. He lay on the sofa and made her hold his hand to prevent him from falling down, down, he cried, into the flames! and saw faces laughing at him, calling him horrible disgusting names, from the walls, and hands pointing round the screen. Yet they were quite alone. But he began to talk aloud, answering people, arguing, laughing, crying, getting very excited and making her write things down. Perfect nonsense it was; about death; about Miss Isabel Pole. She could stand it no longer. She would go back.

She was close to him now, could see him staring at the sky, muttering, clasping his hands. Yet Dr. Holmes said there was nothing the matter with him. What then had happened—why had he gone, then, why, when she sat by him, did he start, frown at her, move away, and point at her hand, take her hand, look at it terrified?

Was it that she had taken off her wedding ring? "My hand has grown so thin," she said. "I have put it in my purse," she told him.

He dropped her hand. Their marriage was over, he thought, with agony, with relief. The rope was cut; he mounted; he was free, as it was decreed that he, Septimus, the lord of men, should be free; alone (since his wife had thrown away her wedding ring; since she had left him), he, Septimus, was alone, called forth in advance of the mass of men to hear the truth, to learn the meaning, which now at last, after all the toils of civilisation—Greeks, Romans, Shakespeare, Darwin,[1] and now himself—was to be given whole

---

9. Royal palace on the Thames in western London, near Richmond.
1. Charles Darwin (1809–1882), English scientist whose writings laid the foundation for the study of evolution.

to. . . . "To whom?" he asked aloud. "To the Prime Minister," the voices which rustled above his head replied. The supreme secret must be told to the Cabinet; first that trees are alive; next there is no crime; next love, universal love, he muttered, gasping, trembling, painfully drawing out these profound truths which needed, so deep were they, so difficult, an immense effort to speak out, but the world was entirely changed by them for ever.

No crime; love; he repeated, fumbling for his card and pencil, when a Skye terrier snuffed his trousers and he started in an agony of fear. It was turning into a man! He could not watch it happen! It was horrible, terrible to see a dog become a man! At once the dog trotted away.

Heaven was divinely merciful, infinitely benignant. It spared him, pardoned his weakness. But what was the scientific explanation (for one must be scientific above all things)? Why could he see through bodies, see into the future, when dogs will become men? It was the heat wave presumably, operating upon a brain made sensitive by eons of evolution. Scientifically speaking, the flesh was melted off the world. His body was macerated until only the nerve fibres were left. It was spread like a veil upon a rock.

He lay back in his chair, exhausted but upheld. He lay resting, waiting, before he again interpreted, with effort, with agony, to mankind. He lay very high, on the back of the world. The earth thrilled beneath him. Red flowers grew through his flesh; their stiff leaves rustled by his head. Music began clanging against the rocks up here. It is a motor horn down in the street, he muttered; but up here it cannoned from rock to rock, divided, met in shocks of sound which rose in smooth columns (that music should be visible was a discovery) and became an anthem, an anthem twined round now by a shepherd boy's piping (That's an old man playing a penny whistle by the public-house, he muttered) which, as the boy stood still came bubbling from his pipe, and then, as he climbed higher, made its exquisite plaint while the traffic passed beneath. This boy's elegy is played among the traffic, thought Septimus. Now he withdraws up into the snows, and roses hang about him—the thick red roses which grow on my bedroom wall, he reminded himself. The music stopped. He has his penny, he reasoned it out, and has gone on to the next public-house.

But he himself remained high on his rock, like a drowned sailor on a rock. I leant over the edge of the boat and fell down, he thought I went under the sea. I have been dead, and yet am now alive, but let me rest still; he begged (he was talking to himself again—it was awful, awful!); and as, before waking, the voices of birds and the sound of wheels chime and chatter in a queer harmony, grow louder and louder and the sleeper feels himself drawing to the shores of life, so he felt himself drawing towards life, the sun growing hotter, cries sounding louder, something tremendous about to happen.

He had only to open his eyes; but a weight was on them; a fear. He strained; he pushed; he looked; he saw Regent's Park before him. Long streamers of sunlight fawned at his feet. The trees waved, brandished. We welcome, the world seemed to say; we accept; we create. Beauty, the world seemed to say. And as if to prove it (scientifically) wherever he looked at the houses, at the railings, at the antelopes stretching over the palings, beauty sprang instantly. To watch a leaf quivering in the rush of air was an exquisite joy. Up in the sky swallows swooping, swerving, flinging themselves in and out, round and round, yet always with perfect control as if elastics held them; and the flies rising and falling; and the sun spotting now this leaf, now that, in mockery, dazzling it with soft gold in pure good temper; and now and again some chime (it might be a motor horn) tinkling divinely on the grass stalks—all of this, calm and reasonable as it was, made out of ordinary things as it was, was the truth now; beauty, that was the truth now. Beauty was everywhere.

"It is time," said Rezia.

The word "time" split its husk; poured its riches over him; and from his lips fell like shells, like shavings from a plane, without his making them, hard, white, imperishable words, and flew to attach themselves to their places in an ode to Time; an immortal ode to Time. He sang. Evans answered from behind the tree. The dead were in Thessaly,[2] Evans sang, among the orchids. There they waited till the War was over, and now the dead, now Evans himself—

"For God's sake don't come!" Septimus cried out. For he could not look upon the dead.

But the branches parted. A man in grey was actually walking towards them. It was Evans! But no mud was on him; no wounds; he was not changed. I must tell the whole world, Septimus cried, raising his hand (as the dead man in the grey suit came nearer), raising his hand like some colossal figure who has lamented the fate of man for ages in the desert alone with his hands pressed to his forehead, furrows of despair on his cheeks, and now sees light on the desert's edge which broadens and strikes the iron-black figure (and Septimus half rose from his chair), and with legions of men prostrate behind him he, the giant mourner, receives for one moment on his face the whole—

"But I am so unhappy, Septimus," said Rezia trying to make him sit down.

The millions lamented; for ages they had sorrowed. He would turn round, he would tell them in a few moments, only a few moments more, of this relief, of this joy, of this astonishing revelation—

"The time, Septimus," Rezia repeated. "What is the time?"

He was talking, he was starting, this man must notice him. He was looking at them.

"I will tell you the time," said Septimus, very slowly, very drowsily, smiling mysteriously. As he sat smiling at the dead man in the grey suit the quarter struck—the quarter to twelve.

And that is being young, Peter Walsh thought as he passed them. To be having an awful scene—the poor girl looked absolutely desperate—in the middle of the morning. But what was it about, he wondered, what had the young man in the overcoat been saying to her to make her look like that; what awful fix had they got themselves into, both to look so desperate as that on a fine summer morning? The amusing thing about coming back to England, after five years, was the way it made, anyhow the first days, things stand out as if one had never seen them before; lovers squabbling under a tree; the domestic family life of the parks. Never had he seen London look so enchanting—the softness of the distances; the richness; the greenness; the civilisation, after India, he thought, strolling across the grass.

This susceptibility to impressions had been his undoing no doubt. Still at his age he had, like a boy or a girl even, these alternations of mood; good days, bad days, for no reason whatever, happiness from a pretty face, downright misery at the sight of a frump. After India of course one fell in love with every woman one met. There was a freshness about them; even the poorest dressed better

2. Region of Greece also known as Aeolia.

than five years ago surely; and to his eye the fashions had never been so becoming; the long black cloaks; the slimness; the elegance; and then the delicious and apparently universal habit of paint. Every woman, even the most respectable, had roses blooming under glass; lips cut with a knife; curls of Indian ink; there was design, art, everywhere; a change of some sort had undoubtedly taken place. What did the young people think about? Peter Walsh asked himself.

Those five years—1918 to 1923—had been, he suspected, somehow very important. People looked different. Newspapers seemed different. Now for instance there was a man writing quite openly in one of the respectable weeklies about water-closets. That you couldn't have done ten years ago— written quite openly about water-closets[3] in a respectable weekly. And then this taking out a stick of rouge, or a powder-puff and making up in public. On board ship coming home there were lots of young men and girls—Betty and Bertie he remembered in particular—carrying on quite openly; the old mother sitting and watching them with her knitting, cool as a cucumber. The girl would stand still and powder her nose in front of every one. And they weren't engaged; just having a good time; no feelings hurt on either side. As hard as nails she was—Betty What'shername—; but a thorough good sort. She would make a very good wife at thirty—she would marry when it suited her to marry; marry some rich man and live in a large house near Manchester.[4]

Who was it now who had done that? Peter Walsh asked himself, turning into the Broad Walk,—married a rich man and lived in a large house near Manchester? Somebody who had written him a long, gushing letter quite lately about "blue hydrangeas." It was seeing blue hydrangeas that made her think of him and the old days—Sally Seton, of course! It was Sally Seton—the last person in the world one would have expected to marry a rich man and live in a large house near Manchester, the wild, the daring, the romantic Sally!

But of all that ancient lot, Clarissa's friends—Whitbreads, Kinderleys, Cunninghams, Kinloch-Jones's—Sally was probably the best. She tried to get hold of things by the right end anyhow. She saw through Hugh Whitbread anyhow—the admirable Hugh—when Clarissa and the rest were at his feet.

"The Whitbreads?" he could hear her saying. "Who are the Whitbreads? Coal merchants. Respectable tradespeople."

Hugh she detested for some reason. He thought of nothing but his own appearance, she said. He ought to have been a Duke. He would be certain to marry one of the Royal Princesses. And of course Hugh had the most extraordinary, the most natural, the most sublime respect for the British aristocracy of any human being he had ever come across. Even Clarissa had to own that. Oh, but he was such a dear, so unselfish, gave up shooting to please his old mother—remembered his aunts' birthdays, and so on.

Sally, to do her justice, saw through all that. One of the things he remembered best was an argument one Sunday morning at Bourton about women's rights[5] (that antediluvian topic), when Sally suddenly lost her temper, flared up, and told Hugh that he represented all that was most detestable in British middle-class life. She told him that she considered him responsible for the

---

3. Toilets.
4. Large industrial city in northern England.
5. Campaigns by suffragists led to the right to vote for British women thirty and older in 1918

and, in 1928, for women twenty-one and older. Thus the topic was hardly "antediluvian," i.e., antiquated or outdated.

state of "those poor girls in Piccadilly"[6]—Hugh, the perfect gentleman, poor Hugh!—never did a man look more horrified! She did it on purpose she said afterwards (for they used to get together in the vegetable garden and compare notes). "He's read nothing, thought nothing, felt nothing," he could hear her saying in that very emphatic voice which carried so much farther than she knew. The stable-boys had more life in them than Hugh, she said. He was a perfect specimen of the public school[7] type, she said. No country but England could have produced him. She was really spiteful, for some reason; had some grudge against him. Something had happened—he forgot what—in the smoking-room. He had insulted her—kissed her? Incredible! Nobody believed a word against Hugh of course. Who could? Kissing Sally in the smoking-room! If it had been some Honourable Edith or Lady Violet, perhaps; but not that ragamuffin Sally without a penny to her name, and a father or a mother gambling at Monte Carlo.[8] For of all the people he had ever met Hugh was the greatest snob—the most obsequious—no, he didn't cringe exactly. He was too much of a prig for that. A first-rate valet was the obvious comparison—somebody who walked behind carrying suit cases; could be trusted to send telegrams—indispensable to hostesses. And he'd found his job—married his Honourable Evelyn; got some little post at Court, looked after the King's cellars, polished the Imperial shoe-buckles, went about in knee-breeches and lace ruffles. How remorseless life is! A little job at Court!

He had married this lady, the Honourable Evelyn, and they lived hereabouts, so he thought (looking at the pompous houses overlooking the Park), for he had lunched there once in a house which had, like all Hugh's possessions, something that no other house could possibly have—linen cupboards it might have been. You had to go and look at them—you had to spend a great deal of time always admiring whatever it was—linen cupboards, pillow-cases, old oak furniture, pictures, which Hugh had picked up for an old song. But Mrs. Hugh sometimes gave the show away. She was one of those obscure mouse-like little women who admire big men. She was almost negligible. Then suddenly she would say something quite unexpected—something sharp. She had the relics of the grand manner perhaps. The steam coal was a little too strong for her—it made the atmosphere thick. And so there they lived, with their linen cupboards and their old masters and their pillow-cases fringed with real lace at the rate of five or ten thousand a year presumably, while he, who was two years older than Hugh, cadged for a job.[9]

At fifty-three he had to come and ask them to put him into some secretary's office, to find him some usher's job teaching little boys Latin, at the beck and call of some mandarin[1] in an office, something that brought in five hundred a year; for if he married Daisy, even with his pension, they could never do on less. Whitbread could do it presumably; or Dalloway. He didn't mind what he asked Dalloway. He was a thorough good sort; a bit limited; a bit thick in the head; yes; but a thorough good sort Whatever he took up he did in the same matter-of-fact sensible way; without a touch of imagination, without a spark of brilliancy, but with the inexplicable niceness of his type. He ought to have been a country gentleman—he was wasted on politics. He was at his best out of doors, with horses and dogs—how good he was, for

6. Prostitutes.
7. Fee-paying secondary school (British).
8. City in Monaco with a famous casino.

9. Begged for employment.
1. Powerful, sometimes secretive or corrupt, civil servant.

instance, when that great shaggy dog of Clarissa's got caught in a trap and had its paw half torn off, and Clarissa turned faint and Dalloway did the whole thing; bandaged, made splints; told Clarissa not to be a fool. That was what she liked him for perhaps—that was what she needed. "Now, my dear, don't be a fool. Hold this—fetch that," all the time talking to the dog as if it were a human being.

But how could she swallow all that stuff about poetry? How could she let him hold forth about Shakespeare? Seriously and solemnly Richard Dalloway got on his hind legs and said that no decent man ought to read Shakespeare's sonnets because it was like listening at keyholes (besides the relationship was not one that he approved). No decent man ought to let his wife visit a deceased wife's sister. Incredible! The only thing to do was to pelt him with sugared almonds—it was at dinner. But Clarissa sucked it all in; thought it so honest of him; so independent of him; Heaven knows if she didn't think him the most original mind she'd ever met!

That was one of the bonds between Sally, and himself. There was a garden where they used to walk, a walled-in place, with rose-bushes and giant cauliflowers—he could remember Sally tearing off a rose, stopping to exclaim at the beauty of the cabbage leaves in the moonlight (it was extraordinary how vividly it all came back to him, things he hadn't thought of for years), while she implored him, half laughing of course, to carry off Clarissa, to save her from the Hughs and the Dalloways and all the other "perfect gentlemen" who would "stifle her soul" (she wrote reams of poetry in those days), make a mere hostess of her, encourage her worldliness. But one must do Clarissa justice. She wasn't going to marry Hugh anyhow. She had a perfectly clear notion of what she wanted. Her emotions were all on the surface. Beneath, she was very shrewd—a far better judge of character than Sally, for instance, and with it all, purely feminine; with that extraordinary gift, that woman's gift, of making a world of her own wherever she happened to be. She came into a room; she stood, as he had often seen her, in a doorway with lots of people round her. But it was Clarissa one remembered. Not that she was striking; not beautiful at all; there was nothing picturesque about her; she never said anything specially clever; there she was, however; there she was.

No, no, no! He was not in love with her any more! He only felt, after seeing her that morning, among her scissors and silks, making ready for the party, unable to get away from the thought of her; she kept coming back and back like a sleeper jolting against him in a railway carriage; which was not being in love, of course; it was thinking of her, criticising her, starting again, after thirty years, trying to explain her. The obvious thing to say of her was that she was worldly; cared too much for rank and society and getting on in the world—which was true in a sense; she had admitted it to him. (You could always get her to own up if you took the trouble; she was honest.) What she would say was that she hated frumps, fogies, failures, like himself presumably; thought people had no right to slouch about with their hands in their pockets; must do something, be something; and these great swells, these Duchesses, these hoary old Countesses one met in her drawing-room, unspeakably remote as he felt them to be from anything that mattered a straw, stood for something real to her. Lady Bexborough, she said once, held herself upright (so did Clarissa herself; she never lounged in any sense of the word; she was straight as a dart, a little rigid in fact). She said they had a kind of courage which the older she grew the more she respected. In all this there was a great deal of Dalloway, of course; a great deal of the public-spirited, British Empire, tariff-reform, governing-class spirit,[2] which had grown on her, as it tends to do. With twice his wits, she had to see things through his eyes—one of the tragedies of married life. With a mind of her own, she must always be quoting Richard—as if one couldn't know to a tittle what Richard thought by reading the *Morning Post*[3] of a morning! These parties for example were all for him, or for her idea of him (to do Richard justice he would have been happier farming in Norfolk). She made her drawing-room a sort of meeting-place; she had a genius for it. Over and over again he had seen her take some raw youth, twist him, turn him, wake him up; set him going. Infinite numbers of dull people conglomerated round her of course. But odd unexpected people turned up; an artist sometimes; sometimes a writer; queer fish in that atmosphere. And behind it all was that network of visiting, leaving cards, being kind to people; running about with bunches of flowers, little presents; So-and-so was going to France—must have an air-cushion; a real drain on her strength; all that interminable traffic that women of her sort keep up; but she did it genuinely, from a natural instinct.

Oddly enough, she was one of the most thorough-going sceptics he had ever met, and possibly (this was a theory he used to make up to account for her, so transparent in some ways, so inscrutable in others), possibly she said to herself, As we are a doomed race, chained to a sinking ship (her favourite reading as a girl was Huxley and Tyndall,[4] and they were fond of these nautical metaphors), as the whole thing is a bad joke, let us, at any rate, do our part; mitigate the sufferings of our fellow-prisoners (Huxley again); decorate the dungeon with flowers and air-cushions; be as decent as we possibly can. Those ruffians, the Gods, shan't have it all their own way,—her notion being that the Gods, who never lost a chance of hurting, thwarting and spoiling human lives were seriously put out if, all the same, you behaved like a lady. That phase came directly after Sylvia's death—that horrible affair. To see your own sister killed by a falling tree (all Justin Parry's fault—all his carelessness) before your very eyes, a girl too on the verge of life, the most gifted of them, Clarissa always said, was enough to turn one bitter. Later she wasn't so positive perhaps; she thought there were no Gods; no one was to blame; and so she evolved this atheist's religion of doing good for the sake of goodness.

And of course she enjoyed life immensely. It was her nature to enjoy (though goodness only knows, she had her reserves; it was a mere sketch, he often felt, that even he, after all these years, could make of Clarissa). Anyhow there was no bitterness in her; none of that sense of moral virtue which is so repulsive in good women. She enjoyed practically everything. If you walked with her in Hyde Park now it was a bed of tulips, now a child in a perambulator, now some absurd little drama she made up on the spur of the moment. (Very likely, she would have talked to those lovers, if she had thought them unhappy.) She had a sense of comedy that was really exquisite, but she needed people, always people, to bring it out, with the inevitable result that she frittered her time away, lunching, dining, giving these incessant parties

---

2. Richard's views are typical of the Conservative Party. Tariff reform would have been intended to protect British goods.
3. Conservative daily newspaper.

4. Thomas Henry Huxley (1825–1895), English biologist, and John Tyndall (1820–1893), English physicist. The work of both scientists challenged Victorians' religious worldviews.

of hers, talking nonsense, saying things she didn't mean, blunting the edge of her mind, losing her discrimination. There she would sit at the head of the table taking infinite pains with some old buffer who might be useful to Dalloway—they knew the most appalling bores in Europe—or in came Elizabeth and everything must give way to *her*. She was at a High School,[5] at the inarticulate stage last time he was over, a round-eyed, pale-faced girl, with nothing of her mother in her, a silent stolid creature, who took it all as a matter of course, let her mother make a fuss of her, and then said "May I go now?" like a child of four; going off, Clarissa explained, with that mixture of amusement and pride which Dalloway himself seemed to rouse in her, to play hockey. And now Elizabeth was "out,"[6] presumably; thought him an old fogy, laughed at her mother's friends. Ah well, so be it. The compensation of growing old, Peter Walsh thought, coming out of Regent's Park, and holding his hat in hand, was simply this; that the passions remain as strong as ever, but one has gained—at last!—the power which adds the supreme flavour to existence,—the power of taking hold of experience, of turning it round, slowly, in the light.

A terrible confession it was (he put his hat on again), but now, at the age of fifty-three one scarcely needed people any more. Life itself, every moment of it, every drop of it, here, this instant, now, in the sun, in Regent's Park, was enough. Too much indeed. A whole lifetime was too short to bring out, now that one had acquired the power, the full flavour; to extract every ounce of pleasure, every shade of meaning; which both were so much more solid than they used to be, so much less personal. It was impossible that he should ever suffer again as Clarissa had made him suffer. For hours at a time (pray God that one might say these things without being overheard!), for hours and days he never thought of Daisy.

Could it be that he was in love with her then, remembering the misery, the torture, the extraordinary passion of those days? It was a different thing altogether—a much pleasanter thing—the truth being, of course, that now *she* was in love with *him*. And that perhaps was the reason why, when the ship actually sailed, he felt an extraordinary relief, wanted nothing so much as to be alone; was annoyed to find all her little attentions—cigars, notes, a rug for the voyage—in his cabin. Every one if they were honest would say the same; one doesn't want people after fifty; one doesn't want to go on telling women they are pretty; that's what most men of fifty would say, Peter Walsh thought, if they were honest.

But then these astonishing accesses of emotion—bursting into tears this morning, what was all that about? What could Clarissa have thought of him? thought him a fool presumably, not for the first time. It was jealousy that was at the bottom of it—jealousy which survives every other passion of mankind, Peter Walsh thought, holding his pocket-knife at arm's length. She had been meeting Major Orde, Daisy said in her last letter; said it on purpose he knew; said it to make him jealous; he could see her wrinkling her forehead as she wrote, wondering what she could say to hurt him; and yet it made no difference; he was furious! All this pother of coming to England and seeing lawyers wasn't to marry her, but to prevent her from marrying anybody else. That was what tortured him, that was what came over him when he saw Clarissa so

5. A fee-paying girls' day school.
6. Introduced to society, presented at Court, and participating in the social life of a debutante.

calm, so cold, so intent on her dress or whatever it was; realising what she
might have spared him, what she had reduced him to—a whimpering, snivel-
ling old ass. But women, he thought, shutting his pocketknife, don't know
what passion is. They don't know the meaning of it to men. Clarissa was as
cold as an icicle. There she would sit on the sofa by his side, let him take her
hand, give him one kiss—Here he was at the crossing.

A sound interrupted him; a frail quivering sound, a voice bubbling up
without direction, vigour, beginning or end, running weakly and shrilly and
with an absence of all human meaning into

> ee um fah um so
> foo swee too eem oo—

the voice of no age or sex, the voice of an ancient spring spouting from the
earth; which issued, just opposite Regent's Park Tube station from a tall
quivering shape, like a funnel, like a rusty pump, like a wind-beaten tree for
ever barren of leaves which lets the wind run up and down its branches
singing

> ee um fah um so
> foo swee too eem oo

and rocks and creaks and moans in the eternal breeze.

Through all ages—when the pavement was grass, when it was swamp,
through the age of tusk and mammoth, through the age of silent sunrise, the
battered woman—for she wore a skirt—with her right hand exposed, her
left clutching at her side, stood singing of love—love which has lasted
a million years, she sang, love which prevails, and millions of years ago, her
lover, who had been dead these centuries, had walked, she crooned, with
her in May; but in the course of ages, long as summer days, and flaming,
she remembered, with nothing but red asters, he had gone; death's enormous sickle had swept those tremendous hills, and when at last she laid her
hoary and immensely aged head on the earth, now become a mere cinder
of ice, she implored the Gods to lay by her side a bunch of purple heather,
there on her high burial place which the last rays of the last sun caressed;
for then the pageant of the universe would be over.

As the ancient song bubbled up opposite Regent's Park Tube station still
the earth seemed green and flowery; still, though it issued from so rude a
mouth, a mere hole in the earth, muddy too, matted with root fibres and
tangled grasses, still the old bubbling burbling song, soaking through the
knotted roots of infinite ages, and skeletons and treasure, streamed away in
rivulets over the pavement and all along the Marylebone Road, and down
towards Euston,[7] fertilising, leaving a damp stain.

Still remembering how once in some primeval May she had walked with
her lover, this rusty pump, this battered old woman with one hand exposed
for coppers the other clutching her side, would still be there in ten million
years, remembering how once she had walked in May, where the sea flows
now, with whom it did not matter—he was a man, oh yes, a man who had
loved her. But the passage of ages had blurred the clarity of that ancient
May day, the bright petalled flowers were hoar and silver frosted; and she

---

7. Area in London east of Regent's Park, accessible by walking east along the Marylebone Road, which
lies to the south of the park.

no longer saw, when she implored him (as she did now quite clearly) "look in my eyes with thy sweet eyes intently," she no longer saw brown eyes, black whiskers or sunburnt face but only a looming shape, a shadow shape, to which, with the bird-like freshness of the very aged she still twittered "give me your hand and let me press it gently" (Peter Walsh couldn't help giving the poor creature a coin as he stepped into his taxi), "and if some one should see, what matter they?" she demanded; and her fist clutched at her side, and she smiled, pocketing her shilling, and all peering inquisitive eyes seemed blotted out, and the passing generations—the pavement was crowded with bustling middleclass people—vanished, like leaves, to be trodden under, to be soaked and steeped and made mould of by that eternal spring—

> ee um fah um so
> foo swee too eem oo

"Poor old woman," said Rezia Warren Smith, waiting to cross.

Oh poor old wretch!

Suppose it was a wet night? Suppose one's father, or somebody who had known one in better days had happened to pass, and saw one standing there in the gutter? And where did she sleep at night?

Cheerfully, almost gaily, the invincible thread of sound wound up into the air like the smoke from a cottage chimney, winding up clean beech trees and issuing in a tuft of blue smoke among the topmost leaves. "And if some one should see, what matter they?"

Since she was so unhappy, for weeks and weeks now, Rezia had given meanings to things that happened, almost felt sometimes that she must stop people in the street, if they looked good, kind people, just to say to them "I am unhappy"; and this old woman singing in the street "if some one should see, what matter they?" made her suddenly quite sure that everything was going to be right. They were going to Sir William Bradshaw; she thought his name sounded nice; he would cure Septimus at once. And then there was a brewer's cart, and the grey horses had upright bristles of straw in their tails; there were newspaper placards. It was a silly, silly dream, being unhappy.

So they crossed, Mr. and Mrs. Septimus Warren Smith, and was there, after all, anything to draw attention to them, anything to make a passer-by suspect here is a young man who carries in him the greatest message in the world, and is, moreover, the happiest man in the world, and the most miserable? Perhaps they walked more slowly than other people, and there was something hesitating, trailing, in the man's walk, but what more natural for a clerk, who has not been in the West End[8] on a weekday at this hour for years, than to keep looking at the sky, looking at this, that and the other, as if Portland Place were a room he had come into when the family are away, the chandeliers being hung in holland bags,[9] and the caretaker, as she lets in long shafts of dusty light upon deserted, queer-looking armchairs, lifting one corner of the long blinds, explains to the visitors what a wonderful place it is; how wonderful, but at the same time, he thinks, as he looks at chairs and tables, how strange.

To look at, he might have been a clerk, but of the better sort; for he wore brown boots; his hands were educated; so, too, his profile—his angular,

---

8. Entertainment and shopping district to the west of Portland Place, a street running south from the Regent's Park Tube station toward Oxford Street.
9. Bags made from smooth linen fabric often used as furniture covering.

big-nosed, intelligent, sensitive profile; but not his lips altogether, for they were loose; and his eyes (as eyes tend to be), eyes merely; hazel, large; so that he was, on the whole, a border case, neither one thing nor the other, might end with a house at Purley[1] and a motor car, or continue renting apartments in back streets all his life; one of those half-educated, self-educated men whose education is all learnt from books borrowed from public libraries, read in the evening after the day's work, on the advice of well-known authors consulted by letter.

As for the other experiences, the solitary ones, which people go through alone, in their bedrooms, in their offices, walking the fields and the streets of London, he had them; had left home, a mere boy, because of his mother; she lied; because he came down to tea for the fiftieth time with his hands unwashed; because he could see no future for a poet in Stroud;[2] and so, making a confidant of his little sister, had gone to London leaving an absurd note behind him, such as great men have written, and the world has read later when the story of their struggles has become famous.

London has swallowed up many millions of young men called Smith; thought nothing of fantastic Christian names like Septimus with which their parents have thought to distinguish them. Lodging off the Euston Road,[3] there were experiences, again experiences, such as change a face in two years from a pink innocent oval to a face lean, contracted, hostile. But of all this what could the most observant of friends have said except what a gardener says when he opens the conservatory door in the morning and finds a new blossom on his plant:—It has flowered; flowered from vanity, ambition, idealism, passion, loneliness, courage, laziness, the usual seeds, which all muddled up (in a room off the Euston Road), made him shy, and stammering, made him anxious to improve himself, made him fall in love with Miss Isabel Pole, lecturing in the Waterloo Road[4] upon Shakespeare.

Was he not like Keats?[5] she asked; and reflected how she might give him a taste of *Antony and Cleopatra*[6] and the rest; lent him books; wrote him scraps of letters; and lit in him such a fire as burns only once in a lifetime, without heat, flickering a red gold flame infinitely ethereal and insubstantial over Miss Pole; *Antony and Cleopatra*; and the Waterloo Road. He thought her beautiful, believed her impeccably wise; dreamed of her, wrote poems to her, which, ignoring the subject, she corrected in red ink; he saw her, one summer evening, walking in a green dress in a square. "It has flowered," the gardener might have said, had he opened the door; had he come in, that is to say, any night about this time, and found him writing; found him tearing up his writing; found him finishing a masterpiece at three o'clock in the morning and running out to pace the streets, and visiting churches, and fasting one day, drinking another, devouring Shakespeare, Darwin, *The History of Civilisation*, and Bernard Shaw.[7]

1. Town south of London.
2. Town in Gloucestershire, west of London.
3. Road running east from the Regent's Park Tube station toward King's Cross, a busy train station.
4. Road running south from the Thames. Miss Pole likely teaches classes for Morley College in the Old Vic Theater.
5. John Keats (1795–1821), English Romantic poet.
6. Tragedy by Shakespeare.
7. George Bernard Shaw (1856–1950), Irish playwright, journalist, and Fabian Socialist. "*The History of Civilisation*" (1857–61): two-volume study of human interaction with nature, by English writer Henry Thomas Buckle (1821–1862).

Something was up, Mr. Brewer knew; Mr. Brewer, managing clerk at Sibleys and Arrowsmiths,[8] auctioneers, valuers, land and estate agents; something was up, he thought, and, being paternal with his young men, and thinking very highly of Smith's abilities, and prophesying that he would, in ten or fifteen years, succeed to the leather arm-chair in the inner room under the skylight with the deed-boxes round him, "if he keeps his health," said Mr. Brewer, and that was the danger—he looked weakly; advised football, invited him to supper and was seeing his way to consider recommending a rise of salary, when something happened which threw out many of Mr. Brewer's calculations, took away his ablest young fellows, and eventually, so prying and insidious were the fingers of the European War, smashed a plaster cast of Ceres,[9] ploughed a hole in the geranium beds, and utterly ruined the cook's nerves at Mr. Brewer's establishment at Muswell Hill.[1]

Septimus was one of the first to volunteer. He went to France to save an England which consisted almost entirely of Shakespeare's plays and Miss Isabel Pole in a green dress walking in a square. There in the trenches the change which Mr. Brewer desired when he advised football was produced instantly; he developed manliness; he was promoted; he drew the attention, indeed the affection of his officer, Evans by name. It was a case of two dogs playing on a hearth-rug; one worrying a paper screw, snarling, snapping, giving a pinch, now and then, at the old dog's ear; the other lying somnolent, blinking at the fire, raising a paw, turning and growling good-temperedly. They had to be together, share with each other, fight with each other, quarrel with each other. But when Evans (Rezia who had only seen him once called him "a quiet man," a sturdy red-haired man, undemonstrative in the company of women), when Evans was killed, just before the Armistice,[2] in Italy, Septimus, far from showing any emotion or recognising that here was the end of a friendship, congratulated himself upon feeling very little and very reasonably. The War had taught him. It was sublime. He had gone through the whole show, friendship, European War, death, had won promotion, was still under thirty and was bound to survive. He was right there. The last shells missed him. He watched them explode with indifference. When peace came he was in Milan, billeted in the house of an innkeeper with a courtyard, flowers in tubs, little tables in the open, daughters making hats, and to Lucrezia, the younger daughter, he became engaged one evening when the panic was on him—that he could not feel.

For now that it was all over, truce signed, and the dead buried, he had, especially in the evening, these sudden thunderclaps of fear. He could not feel. As he opened the door of the room where the Italian girls sat making hats, he could see them; could hear them; they were rubbing wires among coloured beads in saucers; they were turning buckram[3] shapes this way and that; the table was all strewn with feathers, spangles, silks, ribbons; scissors were rapping on the table; but something failed him; he could not feel. Still, scissors rapping, girls laughing, hats being made protected him; he was assured of safety; he had a refuge. But he could not sit there all night. There were moments of waking in the early morning. The bed was falling; he was falling. Oh for the scissors and the lamplight and the buckram

8. Fictional real estate company.
9. Roman goddess of agriculture.
1. Residential district in north London.

2. Agreement ending World War I, November 11, 1918.
3. Linen or cotton fabric.

shapes! He asked Lucrezia to marry him, the younger of the two, the gay, the frivolous, with those little artist's fingers that she would hold up and say "It is all in them." Silk, feathers, what not were alive to them.

"It is the hat that matters most," she would say, when they walked out together. Every hat that passed, she would examine; and the cloak and the dress and the way the woman held herself. Ill-dressing, over-dressing she stigmatised, not savagely, rather with impatient movements of the hands, like those of a painter who puts from him some obvious well-meant glaring imposture; and then, generously, but always critically, she would welcome a shopgirl who had turned her little bit of stuff gallantly, or praise, wholly, with enthusiastic and professional understanding, a French lady descending from her carriage, in chinchilla,[4] robes, pearls.

"Beautiful!" she would murmur, nudging Septimus, that he might see. But beauty was behind a pane of glass. Even taste (Rezia liked ices, chocolates, sweet things) had no relish to him. He put down his cup on the little marble table. He looked at people outside; happy they seemed, collecting in the middle of the street, shouting, laughing, squabbling over nothing. But he could not taste, he could not feel. In the teashop among the tables and the chattering waiters the appalling fear came over him—he could not feel. He could reason; he could read, Dante for example, quite easily ("Septimus, do put down your book," said Rezia, gently shutting the *Inferno*[5]), he could add up his bill; his brain was perfect; it must be the fault of the world then—that he could not feel.

"The English are so silent," Rezia said. She liked it, she said. She respected these Englishmen, and wanted to see London, and the English horses, and the tailor-made suits, and could remember hearing how wonderful the shops were, from an Aunt who had married and lived in Soho.[6]

It might be possible, Septimus thought, looking at England from the train window, as they left Newhaven;[7] it might be possible that the world itself is without meaning.

At the office they advanced him to a post of considerable responsibility. They were proud of him; he had won crosses. "You have done your duty; it is up to us—" began Mr. Brewer; and could not finish, so pleasurable was his emotion. They took admirable lodgings off the Tottenham Court Road.[8]

Here he opened Shakespeare once more. That boy's business of the intoxication of language—*Antony and Cleopatra*—had shrivelled utterly. How Shakespeare loathed humanity—the putting on of clothes, the getting of children, the sordidity of the mouth and the belly! This was now revealed to Septimus; the message hidden in the beauty of words. The secret signal which one generation passes, under disguise, to the next is loathing, hatred, despair. Dante the same. Aeschylus[9] (translated) the same. There Rezia sat at the table trimming hats. She trimmed hats for Mrs. Filmer's friends; she trimmed hats by the hour. She looked pale, mysterious, like a lily, drowned, under water, he thought.

4. Soft gray fur from rodents native to South America.
5. Description of hell in one of three parts of *The Divine Comedy*, by Italian poet Dante Alighieri (1265–1321).
6. London district known for its cosmopolitanism, entertainment, and sex industries.
7. Port city on the English Channel south of London.
8. Major London road running north through Bloomsbury, home to Woolf and her friends, toward the Euston Road.
9. Greek dramatist (ca. 525–426 B.C.E.).

"The English are so serious," she would say, putting her arms round Septimus, her cheek against his.

Love between man and woman was repulsive to Shakespeare. The business of copulation was filth to him before the end. But, Rezia said, she must have children. They had been married five years.

They went to the Tower together; to the Victoria and Albert Museum; stood in the crowd to see the King open Parliament.[1] And there were the shops—hat shops, dress shops, shops with leather bags in the window, where she would stand staring. But she must have a boy.

She must have a son like Septimus, she said. But nobody could be like Septimus; so gentle; so serious; so clever. Could she not read Shakespeare too? Was Shakespeare a difficult author? she asked.

One cannot bring children into a world like this. One cannot perpetuate suffering, or increase the breed of these lustful animals, who have no lasting emotions, but only whims and vanities, eddying them now this way, now that.

He watched her snip, shape, as one watches a bird hop, flit in the grass, without daring to move a finger. For the truth is (let her ignore it) that human beings have neither kindness, nor faith, nor charity beyond what serves to increase the pleasure of the moment. They hunt in packs. Their packs scour the desert and vanish screaming into the wilderness. They desert the fallen. They are plastered over with grimaces. There was Brewer at the office, with his waxed moustache, coral tie-pin, white slip, and pleasurable emotions—all coldness and clamminess within,—his geraniums ruined in the War—his cook's nerves destroyed; or Amelia What'shername, handing round cups of tea punctually at five—a leering, sneering obscene little harpy; and the Toms and Berties[2] in their starched shirt fronts oozing thick drops of vice. They never saw him drawing pictures of them naked at their antics in his notebook. In the street, vans roared past him; brutality blared out on placards; men were trapped in mines; women burnt alive; and once a maimed file of lunatics being exercised or displayed for the diversion of the populace (who laughed aloud), ambled and nodded and grinned past him, in the Tottenham Court Road, each half apologetically, yet triumphantly, inflicting his hopeless woe. And would *he* go mad?

At tea Rezia told him that Mrs. Filmer's daughter was expecting a baby. *She* could not grow old and have no children! She was very lonely, she was very unhappy! She cried for the first time since they were married. Far away he heard her sobbing; he heard it accurately, he noticed it distinctly; he compared it to a piston thumping. But he felt nothing.

His wife was crying, and he felt nothing; only each time she sobbed in this profound, this silent, this hopeless way, he descended another step into the pit.

At last, with a melodramatic gesture which he assumed mechanically and with complete consciousness of its insincerity, he dropped his head on his hands. Now he had surrendered; now other people must help him. People must be sent for. He gave in.

1. The monarch traditionally gives a speech to begin the annual session of Parliament. "The Tower": the Tower of London, fortress and royal palace on the Thames, begun in 1078. "Victoria and Albert Museum": exhibition of applied arts opened in 1909.
2. Diminutives of Thomas and Albert, common British names.

Nothing could rouse him. Rezia put him to bed. She sent for a doctor— Mrs. Filmer's Dr. Holmes. Dr. Holmes examined him. There was nothing whatever the matter, said Dr. Holmes. Oh, what a relief! What a kind man, what a good man! thought Rezia. When he felt like that he went to the Music Hall, said Dr. Holmes. He took a day off with his wife and played golf. Why not try two tabloids of bromide[3] dissolved in a glass of water at bedtime? These old Bloomsbury houses, said Dr. Holmes, tapping the wall, are often full of very fine panelling, which the landlords have the folly to paper over. Only the other day, visiting a patient, Sir Somebody Something in Bedford Square[4]—

So there was no excuse; nothing whatever the matter, except the sin for which human nature had condemned him to death; that he did not feel. He had not cared when Evans was killed; that was worst; but all the other crimes raised their heads and shook their fingers and jeered and sneered over the rail of the bed in the early hours of the morning at the prostrate body which lay realising its degradation; how he had married his wife without loving her; had lied to her; seduced her; outraged Miss Isabel Pole, and was so pocked and marked with vice that women shuddered when they saw him in the street. The verdict of human nature on such a wretch was death.

Dr. Holmes came again. Large, fresh coloured, handsome, flicking his boots, looking in the glass, he brushed it all aside—headaches, sleeplessness, fears, dreams—nerve symptoms and nothing more, he said. If Dr. Holmes found himself even half a pound below eleven stone six, he asked his wife for another plate of porridge at breakfast. (Rezia would learn to cook porridge.) But, he continued, health is largely a matter in our own control. Throw yourself into outside interests; take up some hobby. He opened Shakespeare— *Antony and Cleopatra*; pushed Shakespeare aside. Some hobby, said Dr. Holmes, for did he not owe his own excellent health (and he worked as hard as any man in London) to the fact that he could always switch off from his patients on to old furniture? And what a very pretty comb, if he might say so, Mrs. Warren Smith was wearing!

When the damned fool came again, Septimus refused to see him. Did he indeed? said Dr. Holmes, smiling agreeably. Really he had to give that charming little lady, Mrs. Smith, a friendly push before he could get past her into her husband's bedroom.

"So you're in a funk," he said agreeably, sitting down by his patient's side. He had actually talked of killing himself to his wife, quite a girl, a foreigner, wasn't she? Didn't that give her a very odd idea of English husbands? Didn't one owe perhaps a duty to one's wife? Wouldn't it be better to do something instead of lying in bed? For he had had forty years' experience behind him; and Septimus could take Dr. Holmes's word for it—there was nothing whatever the matter with him. And next time Dr. Holmes came he hoped to find Smith out of bed and not making that charming little lady his wife anxious about him.

Human nature, in short, was on him—the repulsive brute, with the blood-red nostrils. Holmes was on him. Dr. Holmes came quite regularly every day. Once you stumble, Septimus wrote on the back of a postcard, human nature is on you. Holmes is on you. Their only chance was to escape, without letting Holmes know; to Italy—anywhere, anywhere, away from Dr. Holmes.

---

3. Potassium bromide, likely taken as a sedative.   4. Residential area in Bloomsbury.

But Rezia could not understand him. Dr. Holmes was such a kind man. He was so interested in Septimus. He only wanted to help them, he said. He had four little children and he had asked her to tea, she told Septimus.

So he was deserted. The whole world was clamouring: Kill yourself, kill yourself, for our sakes. But why should he kill himself for their sakes? Food was pleasant; the sun hot; and this killing oneself, how does one set about it, with a table knife, uglily, with floods of blood,—by sucking a gaspipe? He was too weak; he could scarcely raise his hand. Besides, now that he was quite alone, condemned, deserted, as those who are about to die are alone, there was a luxury in it, an isolation full of sublimity; a freedom which the attached can never know. Holmes had won of course; the brute with the red nostrils had won. But even Holmes himself could not touch this last relic straying on the edge of the world, this outcast, who gazed back at the inhabited regions, who lay, like a drowned sailor, on the shore of the world.

It was at that moment (Rezia gone shopping) that the great revelation took place. A voice spoke from behind the screen. Evans was speaking. The dead were with him.

"Evans, Evans!" he cried.

Mr. Smith was talking aloud to himself, Agnes the servant girl cried to Mrs. Filmer in the kitchen. "Evans, Evans," he had said as she brought in the tray. She jumped, she did. She scuttled downstairs.

And Rezia came in, with her flowers, and walked across the room, and put the roses in a vase, upon which the sun struck directly, and it went laughing, leaping round the room.

She had had to buy the roses, Rezia said, from a poor man in the street. But they were almost dead already, she said, arranging the roses.

So there was a man outside; Evans presumably; and the roses, which Rezia said were half dead, had been picked by him in the fields of Greece. "Communication is health; communication is happiness, communication—" he muttered.

"What are you saying, Septimus?" Rezia asked, wild with terror, for he was talking to himself.

She sent Agnes running for Dr. Holmes. Her husband, she said, was mad. He scarcely knew her.

"You brute! You brute!" cried Septimus, seeing human nature, that is Dr. Holmes, enter the room.

"Now what's all this about?" said Dr. Holmes in the most amiable way in the world. "Talking nonsense to frighten your wife?" But he would give him something to make him sleep. And if they were rich people, said Dr. Holmes, looking ironically round the room, by all means let them go to Harley Street;[5] if they had no confidence in him, said Dr. Holmes, looking not quite so kind.

It was precisely twelve o'clock; twelve by Big Ben; whose stroke was wafted over the northern part of London; blent with that of other clocks, mixed in a thin ethereal way with the clouds and wisps of smoke, and died up there among the seagulls—twelve o'clock struck as Clarissa Dalloway laid her green dress on her bed, and the Warren Smiths walked down Harley Street. Twelve was the hour of their appointment. Probably, Rezia thought, that was Sir William Bradshaw's house with the grey motor car in front of it. The leaden circles dissolved in the air.

---

5. A popular street for doctors, running south from the Marylebone Road.

Indeed it was—Sir William Bradshaw's motor car; low, powerful, grey with plain initials interlocked on the panel, as if the pomps of heraldry were incongruous, this man being the ghostly helper, the priest of science; and, as the motor car was grey, so to match its sober suavity, grey furs, silver grey rugs were heaped in it, to keep her ladyship warm while she waited. For often Sir William would travel sixty miles or more down into the country to visit the rich, the afflicted, who could afford the very large fee which Sir William very properly charged for his advice. Her ladyship waited with the rugs about her knees an hour or more, leaning back, thinking sometimes of the patient, sometimes, excusably, of the wall of gold, mounting minute by minute while she waited; the wall of gold that was mounting between them and all shifts and anxieties (she had borne them bravely; they had had their struggles) until she felt wedged on a calm ocean, where only spice winds blow; respected, admired, envied, with scarcely anything left to wish for, though she regretted her stoutness; large dinner-parties every Thursday night to the profession; an occasional bazaar to be opened; Royalty greeted; too little time, alas, with her husband, whose work grew and grew; a boy doing well at Eton;[6] she would have liked a daughter too; interests she had, however, in plenty; child welfare; the after-care of the epileptic, and photography, so that if there was a church building, or a church decaying, she bribed the sexton,[7] got the key and took photographs, which were scarcely to be distinguished from the work of professionals, while she waited.

Sir William himself was no longer young. He had worked very hard; he had won his position by sheer ability (being the son of a shopkeeper); loved his profession; made a fine figurehead at ceremonies and spoke well—all of which had by the time he was knighted given him a heavy look, a weary look (the stream of patients being so incessant, the responsibilities and privileges of his profession so onerous), which weariness, together with his grey hairs, increased the extraordinary distinction of his presence and gave him the reputation (of the utmost importance in dealing with nerve cases) not merely of lightning skill, and almost infallible accuracy in diagnosis but of sympathy; tact; understanding of the human soul. He could see the first moment they came into the room (the Warren Smiths they were called); he was certain directly he saw the man; it was a case of extreme gravity. It was a case of complete breakdown—complete physical and nervous breakdown, with every symptom in an advanced stage, he ascertained in two or three minutes (writing answers to questions, murmured discreetly, on a pink card).

How long had Dr. Holmes been attending him?

Six weeks.

Prescribed a little bromide? Said there was nothing the matter? Ah yes (those general practitioners! thought Sir William. It took half his time to undo their blunders. Some were irreparable).

"You served with great distinction in the War?"

The patient repeated the word "war" interrogatively.

He was attaching meanings to words of a symbolical kind. A serious symptom, to be noted on the card.

"The War?" the patient asked. The European War—that little shindy of schoolboys with gunpowder? Had he served with distinction? He really forgot. In the War itself he had failed.

---

6. Eton College, aristocratic boys' school in southwest England.

7. Church officer responsible for its property and grounds.

"Yes, he served with the greatest distinction," Rezia assured the doctor; "he was promoted."

"And they have the very highest opinion of you at your office?" Sir William murmured, glancing at Mr. Brewer's very generously worded letter. "So that you have nothing to worry you, no financial anxiety, nothing?"

He had committed an appalling crime and been condemned to death by human nature.

"I have—I have," he began, "committed a crime—"

"He has done nothing wrong whatever," Rezia assured the doctor. If Mr. Smith would wait, said Sir William, he would speak to Mrs. Smith in the next room. Her husband was very seriously ill, Sir William said. Did he threaten to kill himself?

Oh, he did, she cried. But he did not mean it, she said. Of course not. It was merely a question of rest,[8] said Sir William; of rest, rest, rest; a long rest in bed. There was a delightful home down in the country where her husband would be perfectly looked after. Away from her? she asked. Unfortunately, yes; the people we care for most are not good for us when we are ill. But he was not mad, was he? Sir William said he never spoke of "madness"; he called it not having a sense of proportion. But her husband did not like doctors. He would refuse to go there. Shortly and kindly Sir William explained to her the state of the case. He had threatened to kill himself. There was no alternative. It was a question of law.[9] He would lie in bed in a beautiful house in the country. The nurses were admirable. Sir William would visit him once a week. If Mrs. Warren Smith was quite sure she had no more questions to ask—he never hurried his patients—they would return to her husband. She had nothing more to ask—not of Sir William.

So they returned to the most exalted of mankind; the criminal who faced his judges; the victim exposed on the heights; the fugitive; the drowned sailor; the poet of the immortal ode; the Lord who had gone from life to death; to Septimus Warren Smith, who sat in the arm-chair under the skylight staring at a photograph of Lady Bradshaw in Court dress, muttering messages about beauty.

"We have had our little talk," said Sir William.

"He says you are very, very ill," Rezia cried.

"We have been arranging that you should go into a home," said Sir William.

"One of Holmes's homes?" sneered Septimus.

The fellow made a distasteful impression. For there was in Sir William, whose father had been a tradesman, a natural respect for breeding and clothing, which shabbiness nettled; again, more profoundly, there was in Sir William, who had never had time for reading, a grudge, deeply buried, against cultivated people who came into his room and intimated that doctors, whose profession is a constant strain upon all the highest faculties, are not educated men.

"One of *my* homes, Mr. Warren Smith," he said, "where we will teach you to rest."

And there was just one thing more.

He was quite certain that when Mr. Warren Smith was well he was the last man in the world to frighten his wife. But he had talked of killing himself.

8. A period of inactivity was commonly prescribed to treat mental illness.

9. Suicide was illegal in Britain until 1961.

"We all have our moments of depression," said Sir William.

Once you fall, Septimus repeated to himself, human nature is on you. Holmes and Bradshaw are on you. They scour the desert. They fly screaming into the wilderness. The rack and the thumbscrew[1] are applied. Human nature is remorseless.

"Impulses came upon him sometimes?" Sir William asked, with his pencil on a pink card.

That was his own affair, said Septimus.

"Nobody lives for himself alone," said Sir William, glancing at the photograph of his wife in Court dress.

"And you have a brilliant career before you," said Sir William. There was Mr. Brewer's letter on the table. "An exceptionally brilliant career."

But if he confessed? If he communicated? Would they let him off then, his torturers?

"I—I—" he stammered.

But what was his crime? He could not remember it.

"Yes?" Sir William encouraged him. (But it was growing late.)

Love, trees, there is no crime—what was his message?

He could not remember it.

"I—I—" Septimus stammered.

"Try to think as little about yourself as possible," said Sir William kindly. Really, he was not fit to be about.

Was there anything else they wished to ask him? Sir William would make all arrangements (he murmured to Rezia) and he would let her know between five and six that evening he murmured.

"Trust everything to me," he said, and dismissed them.

Never, never had Rezia felt such agony in her life! She had asked for help and been deserted! He had failed them! Sir William Bradshaw was not a nice man.

The upkeep of that motor car alone must cost him quite a lot, said Septimus, when they got out into the street.

She clung to his arm. They had been deserted.

But what more did she want?

To his patients he gave three-quarters of an hour; and if in this exacting science which has to do with what, after all, we know nothing about—the nervous system, the human brain—a doctor loses his sense of proportion, as a doctor he fails. Health we must have; and health is proportion; so that when a man comes into your room and says he is Christ (a common delusion), and has a message, as they mostly have, and threatens, as they often do, to kill himself, you invoke proportion; order rest in bed; rest in solitude; silence and rest; rest without friends, without books, without messages; six months' rest; until a man who went in weighing seven stone six comes out weighing twelve.[2]

Proportion, divine proportion, Sir William's goddess, was acquired by Sir William walking hospitals, catching salmon, begetting one son in Harley Street by Lady Bradshaw, who caught salmon herself and took photographs scarcely to be distinguished from the work of professionals. Worshipping proportion, Sir William not only prospered himself but made England

1. Instruments of torture.
2. A stone is a measure of weight equal to four-teen pounds, hence an increase from 104 to 168 pounds.

prosper, secluded her lunatics, forbade childbirth, penalised despair; made it impossible for the unfit to propagate their views until they, too, shared his sense of proportion—his, if they were men, Lady Bradshaw's if they were women (she embroidered, knitted, spent four nights out of seven at home with her son), so that not only did his colleagues respect him, his subordinates fear him, but the friends and relations of his patients felt for him the keenest gratitude for insisting that these prophetic Christs and Christesses, who prophesied the end of the world, or the advent of God, should drink milk in bed, as Sir William ordered; Sir William with his thirty years' experience of these kinds of cases, and his infallible instinct, this is madness, this sense; in fact, his sense of proportion.

But Proportion has a sister, less smiling, more formidable, a Goddess even now engaged—in the heat and sands of India, the mud and swamp of Africa, the purlieus[3] of London, wherever in short the climate or the devil tempts men to fall from the true belief which is her own—is even now engaged in dashing down shrines, smashing idols, and setting up in their place her own stern countenance. Conversion is her name and she feasts on the wills of the weakly, loving to impress, to impose, adoring her own features stamped on the face of the populace. At Hyde Park Corner[4] on a tub she stands preaching; shrouds herself in white and walks penitentially disguised as brotherly love through factories and parliaments; offers help, but desires power; smites out of her way roughly the dissentient, or dissatisfied; bestows her blessing on those who, looking upward, catch submissively from her eyes the light of their own. This lady too (Rezia Warren Smith divined it) had her dwelling in Sir William's heart, though concealed, as she mostly is, under some plausible disguise; some venerable name; love, duty, self sacrifice. How he would work—how toil to raise funds, propagate reforms, initiate institutions! But conversion, fastidious Goddess, loves blood better than brick, and feasts most subtly on the human will. For example, Lady Bradshaw. Fifteen years ago she had gone under. It was nothing you could put your finger on; there had been no scene, no snap; only the slow sinking, water-logged, of her will into his. Sweet was her smile, swift her submission; dinner in Harley Street, numbering eight or nine courses, feeding ten or fifteen guests of the professional classes, was smooth and urbane. Only as the evening wore on a very slight dulness, or uneasiness perhaps, a nervous twitch, fumble, stumble and confusion indicated, what it was really painful to believe—that the poor lady lied. Once, long ago, she had caught salmon freely: now, quick to minister to the craving which lit her husband's eye so oilily for dominion, for power, she cramped, squeezed, pared, pruned, drew back, peeped through; so that without knowing precisely what made the evening disagreeable, and caused this pressure on the top of the head (which might well be imputed to the professional conversation, or the fatigue of a great doctor whose life, Lady Bradshaw said, "is not his own but his patients'") disagreeable it was: so that guests, when the clock struck ten, breathed in the air of Harley Street even with rapture; which relief, however, was denied to his patients.

There in the grey room, with the pictures on the wall, and the valuable furniture, under the ground glass skylight, they learnt the extent of their transgressions; huddled up in armchairs, they watched him go through, for

3. Outskirts, borders, or slums.
4. Speaker's Corner, at the northeast corner of

Hyde Park, where anyone may stand and talk on any subject.

their benefit, a curious exercise with the arms, which he shot out, brought sharply back to his hip, to prove (if the patient was obstinate) that Sir William was master of his own actions, which the patient was not. There some weakly broke down; sobbed, submitted; others, inspired by Heaven knows what intemperate madness, called Sir William to his face a damnable humbug; questioned, even more impiously, life itself. Why live? they demanded. Sir William replied that life was good. Certainly Lady Bradshaw in ostrich feathers hung over the mantelpiece, and as for his income it was quite twelve thousand a year. But to us, they protested, life has given no such bounty. He acquiesced. They lacked a sense of proportion. And perhaps, after all, there is no God? He shrugged his shoulders. In short, this living or not living is an affair of our own? But there they were mistaken. Sir William had a friend in Surrey where they taught, what Sir William frankly admitted was a difficult art—a sense of proportion. There were, moreover, family affection; honour; courage; and a brilliant career. All of these had in Sir William a resolute champion. If they failed him, he had to support police and the good of society, which, he remarked very quietly, would take care, down in Surrey,[5] that these unsocial impulses, bred more than anything by the lack of good blood, were held in control. And then stole out from her hiding-place and mounted her throne that Goddess whose lust is to override opposition, to stamp indelibly in the sanctuaries of others the image of herself. Naked, defenceless, the exhausted, the friendless received the impress of Sir William's will. He swooped; he devoured. He shut people up. It was this combination of decision and humanity that endeared Sir William so greatly to the relations of his victims.

But Rezia Warren Smith cried, walking down Harley Street, that she did not like that man.

Shredding and slicing, dividing and subdividing, the clocks of Harley Street nibbled at the June day, counselled submission, upheld authority, and pointed out in chorus the supreme advantages of a sense of proportion, until the mound of time was so far diminished that a commercial clock, suspended above a shop in Oxford Street, announced, genially and fraternally, as if it were a pleasure to Messrs. Rigby and Lowndes to give the information gratis, that it was half-past one.

Looking up, it appeared that each letter of their names stood for one of the hours; subconsciously one was grateful to Rigby and Lowndes for giving one time ratified by Greenwich;[6] and this gratitude (so Hugh Whitbread ruminated, dallying there in front of the shop window), naturally took the form later of buying off Rigby and Lowndes socks or shoes. So he ruminated. It was his habit. He did not go deeply. He brushed surfaces; the dead languages, the living, life in Constantinople, Paris, Rome; riding, shooting, tennis, it had been once. The malicious asserted that he now kept guard at Buckingham Palace, dressed in silk stockings and knee-breeches, over what nobody knew. But he did it extremely efficiently. He had been afloat on the cream of English society for fifty-five years. He had known Prime Ministers. His affections were understood to be deep. And if it were true that he had not taken part in any of the great movements of the time or held important office, one

5. English county south of London.
6. Greenwich Mean Time, international standard for deriving time since 1884, is calculated by the Royal Observatory, located on the prime meridian in the London borough of Greenwich. "Messrs. Rigby and Lowndes": fictional department store with a clock.

or two humble reforms stood to his credit; an improvement in public shelters was one; the protection of owls in Norfolk[7] another; servant girls had reason to be grateful to him; and his name at the end of letters to the *Times*,[8] asking for funds, appealing to the public to protect, to preserve, to clear up litter, to abate smoke, and stamp out immorality in parks, commanded respect.

A magnificent figure he cut too, pausing for a moment (as the sound of the half hour died away) to look critically, magisterially, at socks and shoes; impeccable, substantial, as if he beheld the world from a certain eminence, and dressed to match; but realised the obligations which size, wealth, health, entail, and observed punctiliously even when not absolutely necessary, little courtesies, old-fashioned ceremonies which gave a quality to his manner, something to imitate, something to remember him by, for he would never lunch, for example, with Lady Bruton, whom he had known these twenty years, without bringing her in his outstretched hand a bunch of carnations and asking Miss Brush, Lady Bruton's secretary, after her brother in South Africa, which, for some reason, Miss Brush, deficient though she was in every attribute of female charm, so much resented that she said "Thank you, he's doing very well in South Africa," when, for half a dozen years, he had been doing badly in Portsmouth.[9]

Lady Bruton herself preferred Richard Dalloway, who arrived at the next moment. Indeed they met on the doorstep.

Lady Bruton preferred Richard Dalloway of course. He was made of much finer material. But she wouldn't let them run down her poor dear Hugh. She could never forget his kindness—he had been really remarkably kind—she forgot precisely upon what occasion. But he had been—remarkably kind. Anyhow, the difference between one man and another does not amount to much. She had never seen the sense of cutting people up, as Clarissa Dalloway did—cutting them up and sticking them together again; not at any rate when one was sixty-two. She took Hugh's carnations with her angular grim smile. There was nobody else coming, she said. She had got them there on false pretences, to help her out of a difficulty—

"But let us eat first," she said.

And so there began a soundless and exquisite passing to and fro through swing doors of aproned white-capped maids, handmaidens not of necessity, but adepts in a mystery or grand deception practised by hostesses in Mayfair[1] from one-thirty to two, when, with a wave of the hand, the traffic ceases, and there rises instead this profound illusion in the first place about the food—how it is not paid for; and then that the table spreads itself voluntarily with glass and silver, little mats, saucers of red fruit; films of brown cream mask turbot;[2] in casseroles severed chickens swim; coloured, undomestic, the fire burns; and with the wine and the coffee (not paid for) rise jocund visions before musing eyes; gently speculative eyes; eyes to whom life appears musical, mysterious; eyes now kindled to observe genially the beauty of the red carnations which Lady Bruton (whose movements were always angular) had laid beside her plate, so that Hugh Whitbread, feeling at peace with the entire universe and at the same time completely sure of his standing, said, resting his fork,

---

7. English county northeast of London.
8. Major London newspaper since the 1780s.
9. City on the English Channel with a naval base.

1. Posh neighborhood east of Hyde Park.
2. Large flat fish.

"Wouldn't they look charming against your lace?"

Miss Brush resented this familiarity intensely. She thought him an underbred fellow. She made Lady Bruton laugh.

Lady Bruton raised the carnations, holding them rather stiffly with much the same attitude with which the General held the scroll in the picture behind her; she remained fixed, tranced. Which was she now, the General's great-grand-daughter? great-great-grand-daughter? Richard Dalloway asked himself. Sir Roderick, Sir Miles, Sir Talbot—that was it. It was remarkable how in that family the likeness persisted in the women. She should have been a general of dragoons[3] herself. And Richard would have served under her, cheerfully; he had the greatest respect for her; he cherished these romantic views about well-set-up old women of pedigree, and would have liked, in his good-humoured way, to bring some young hot-heads of his acquaintance to lunch with her; as if a type like hers could be bred of amiable tea-drinking enthusiasts! He knew her country. He knew her people. There was a vine, still bearing, which either Lovelace or Herrick[4]—she never read a word of poetry herself, but so the story ran—had sat under. Better wait to put before them the question that bothered her (about making an appeal to the public; if so, in what terms and so on), better wait until they have had their coffee, Lady Bruton thought; and so laid the carnations down beside her plate.

"How's Clarissa?" she asked abruptly.

Clarissa always said that Lady Bruton did not like her. Indeed, Lady Bruton had the reputation of being more interested in politics than people; of talking like a man; of having had a finger in some notorious intrigue of the eighties, which was now beginning to be mentioned in memoirs. Certainly there was an alcove in her drawing-room, and a table in that alcove, and a photograph upon that table of General Sir Talbot Moore, now deceased, who had written there (one evening in the eighties) in Lady Bruton's presence, with her cognisance, perhaps advice, a telegram ordering the British troops to advance upon an historical occasion. (She kept the pen and told the story.) Thus, when she said in her offhand way "How's Clarissa?" husbands had difficulty in persuading their wives and indeed, however devoted, were secretly doubtful themselves, of her interest in women who often got in their husbands' way, prevented them from accepting posts abroad, and had to be taken to the seaside in the middle of the session to recover from influenza. Nevertheless her inquiry, "How's Clarissa?" was known by women infallibly, to be a signal from a well-wisher, from an almost silent companion, whose utterances (half a dozen perhaps in the course of a lifetime) signified recognition of some feminine comradeship which went beneath masculine lunch parties and united Lady Bruton and Mrs. Dalloway, who seldom met, and appeared when they did meet indifferent and even hostile, in a singular bond.

"I met Clarissa in the Park this morning," said Hugh Whitbread, diving into the casserole, anxious to pay himself this little tribute, for he had only to come to London and he met everybody at once; but greedy, one of the greediest men she had ever known, Milly Brush thought, who observed men with unflinching rectitude, and was capable of everlasting devotion, to

---

3. Cavalry soldiers.
4. English lyric poets Richard Lovelace (1617–1657) and Robert Herrick (1591–1674), noted for their love poems and known as Cavalier poets because of their support for Charles I (1600–1649) in the English Civil War.

her own sex in particular, being knobbed, scraped, angular, and entirely without feminine charm.

"D'you know who's in town?" said Lady Bruton suddenly bethinking her. "Our old friend, Peter Walsh."

They all smiled. Peter Walsh! And Mr. Dalloway was genuinely glad, Milly Brush thought; and Mr. Whitbread thought only of his chicken.

Peter Walsh! All three, Lady Bruton, Hugh Whitbread, and Richard Dalloway, remembered the same thing—how passionately Peter had been in love; been rejected; gone to India; come a cropper;[5] made a mess of things; and Richard Dalloway had a very great liking for the dear old fellow too. Milly Brush saw that; saw a depth in the brown of his eyes; saw him hesitate; consider; which interested her, as Mr. Dalloway always interested her, for what was he thinking, she wondered, about Peter Walsh?

That Peter Walsh had been in love with Clarissa; that he would go back directly after lunch and find Clarissa; that he would tell her, in so many words, that he loved her. Yes, he would say that.

Milly Brush once might almost have fallen in love with these silences; and Mr. Dalloway was always so dependable; such a gentleman too. Now, being forty, Lady Bruton had only to nod, or turn her head a little abruptly, and Milly Brush took the signal, however deeply she might be sunk in these reflections of a detached spirit, of an uncorrupted soul whom life could not bamboozle, because life had not offered her a trinket of the slightest value; not a curl, smile, lip, cheek, nose; nothing whatever; Lady Bruton had only to nod, and Perkins was instructed to quicken the coffee.

"Yes; Peter Walsh has come back," said Lady Bruton. It was vaguely flattering to them all. He had come back, battered, unsuccessful, to their secure shores. But to help him, they reflected, was impossible; there was some flaw in his character. Hugh Whitbread said one might of course mention his name to So-and-so. He wrinkled lugubriously, consequentially, at the thought of the letters he would write to the heads of Government offices about "my old friend, Peter Walsh," and so on. But it wouldn't lead to anything—not to anything permanent, because of his character.

"In trouble with some woman," said Lady Bruton. They had all guessed that *that* was at the bottom of it.

"However," said Lady Bruton, anxious to leave the subject, "we shall hear the whole story from Peter himself."

(The coffee was very slow in coming.)

"The address?" murmured Hugh Whitbread; and there was at once a ripple in the grey tide of service which washed round Lady Bruton day in, day out, collecting, intercepting, enveloping her in a fine tissue which broke concussions, mitigated interruptions, and spread round the house in Brook Street[6] a fine net where things lodged and were picked out accurately, instantly, by grey-haired Perkins, who had been with Lady Bruton these thirty years and now wrote down the address; handed it to Mr. Whitbread, who took out his pocketbook, raised his eyebrows, and slipping it in among documents of the highest importance, said that he would get Evelyn to ask him to lunch.

(They were waiting to bring the coffee until Mr. Whitbread had finished.)

5. Failed badly.　　　　　　　　6. In Mayfair.

Hugh was very slow, Lady Bruton thought. He was getting fat, she noticed. Richard always kept himself in the pink of condition.[7] She was getting impatient; the whole of her being was setting positively, undeniably, domineeringly brushing aside all this unnecessary trifling (Peter Walsh and his affairs) upon that subject which engaged her attention, and not merely her attention, but that fibre which was the ramrod of her soul, that essential part of her without which Millicent Bruton would not have been Millicent Bruton; that project for emigrating young people of both sexes born of respectable parents and setting them up with a fair prospect of doing well in Canada.[8] She exaggerated. She had perhaps lost her sense of proportion. Emigration was not to others the obvious remedy, the sublime conception. It was not to them (not to Hugh, or Richard, or even to devoted Miss Brush) the liberator of the pent[9] egotism, which a strong martial woman, well nourished, well descended, of direct impulses, downright feelings, and little introspective power (broad and simple—why could not every one be broad and simple? she asked) feels rise within her, once youth is past, and must eject upon some object—it may be Emigration, it may be Emancipation; but whatever it be, this object round which the essence of her soul is daily secreted, becomes inevitably prismatic, lustrous, half looking-glass, half precious stone; now carefully hidden in case people should sneer at it; now proudly displayed. Emigration had become, in short, largely Lady Bruton.

But she had to write. And one letter to the *Times*, she used to say to Miss Brush, cost her more than to organise an expedition to South Africa (which she had done in the war). After a morning's battle beginning, tearing up, beginning again, she used to feel the futility of her own womanhood as she felt it on no other occasion, and would turn gratefully to the thought of Hugh Whitbread who possessed—no one could doubt it—the art of writing letters to the *Times*.

A being so differently constituted from herself, with such a command of language; able to put things as editors like them put; had passions which one could not call simply greed. Lady Bruton often suspended judgement upon men in deference to the mysterious accord in which they, but no woman, stood to the laws of the universe; knew how to put things; knew what was said; so that if Richard advised her, and Hugh wrote for her, she was sure of being somehow right. So she let Hugh eat his soufflé; asked after poor Evelyn; waited until they were smoking, and then said,

"Milly, would you fetch the papers?"

And Miss Brush went out, came back; laid papers on the table; and Hugh produced his fountain pen; his silver fountain pen, which had done twenty years' service, he said, unscrewing the cap. It was still in perfect order; he had shown it to the makers; there was no reason, they said, why it should ever wear out; which was somehow to Hugh's credit, and to the credit of the sentiments which his pen expressed (so Richard Dalloway felt) as Hugh began carefully writing capital letters with rings round them in the margin, and thus marvellously reduced Lady Bruton's tangles to sense, to grammar such as the editor of the *Times*, Lady Bruton felt, watching the marvellous transformation, must respect. Hugh was slow. Hugh was pertinacious.

---

7. In excellent health.
8. In response to Britain's supposedly "surplus" population and resultant worries about employment, Lady Bruton favors a project encouraging young people to emigrate to Canada, which had suffered great losses in World War I.
9. Unspoken or repressed.

Richard said one must take risks. Hugh proposed modifications in deference to people's feelings, which, he said rather tartly when Richard laughed,
"had to be considered," and read out "how, therefore, we are of opinion
that the times are ripe . . . the superfluous youth of our ever-increasing
population . . . what we owe to the dead . . ." which Richard thought all stuffing and bunkum, but no harm in it, of course, and Hugh went on drafting
sentiments in alphabetical order of the highest nobility, brushing the cigar
ash from his waistcoat, and summing up now and then the progress they had
made until, finally, he read out the draft of a letter which Lady Bruton felt
certain was a masterpiece. Could her own meaning sound like that?

Hugh could not guarantee that the editor would put it in; but he would
be meeting somebody at luncheon.

Whereupon Lady Bruton, who seldom did a graceful thing, stuffed all
Hugh's carnations into the front of her dress, and flinging her hands out
called him "My Prime Minister!" What she would have done without them
both she did not know. They rose. And Richard Dalloway strolled off as
usual to have a look at the General's portrait, because he meant, whenever
he had a moment of leisure, to write a history of Lady Bruton's family.

And Millicent Bruton was very proud of her family. But they could wait,
they could wait, she said, looking at the picture; meaning that her family, of
military men, administrators, admirals, had been men of action, who had
done their duty; and Richard's first duty was to his country, but it was a fine
face, she said; and all the papers were ready for Richard down at Aldmixton
whenever the time came; the Labour Government[1] she meant. "Ah, the
news from India!" she cried.

And then, as they stood in the hall taking yellow gloves from the bowl on
the malachite[2] table and Hugh was offering Miss Brush with quite unnecessary courtesy some discarded ticket or other compliment, which she
loathed from the depths of her heart and blushed brick red, Richard turned
to Lady Bruton, with his hat in his hand, and said,

"We shall see you at our party to-night?" whereupon Lady Bruton resumed
the magnificence which letter-writing had shattered. She might come; or she
might not come. Clarissa had wonderful energy. Parties terrified Lady Bruton. But then, she was getting old. So she intimated, standing at her doorway; handsome; very erect; while her chow stretched behind her, and Miss
Brush disappeared into the background with her hands full of papers.

And Lady Bruton went ponderously, majestically, up to her room, lay, one
arm extended, on the sofa. She sighed, she snored, not that she was asleep,
only drowsy and heavy, drowsy and heavy, like a field of clover in the sunshine this hot June day, with the bees going round and about and the yellow
butterflies. Always she went back to those fields down in Devonshire,[3] where
she had jumped the brooks on Patty, her pony, with Mortimer and Tom, her
brothers. And there were the dogs; there were the rats; there were her father
and mother on the lawn under the trees, with the tea-things out, and the
beds of dahlias, the hollyhocks, the pampas grass; and they, little wretches,
always up to some mischief! stealing back through the shrubbery, so as not to
be seen, all bedraggled from some roguery. What old nurse used to say about
her frocks!

1. I.e., whenever a Labour Government comes
to power, Richard, a Conservative, might be
voted out of office and thus become free to write
her family history.
2. Deep green stone.
3. County in southwest England.

Ah dear, she remembered—it was Wednesday in Brook Street. Those kind good fellows, Richard Dalloway, Hugh Whitbread, had gone this hot day through the streets whose growl came up to her lying on the sofa. Power was hers, position, income. She had lived in the forefront of her time. She had had good friends; known the ablest men of her day. Murmuring London flowed up to her, and her hand, lying on the sofa back, curled upon some imaginary baton such as her grandfathers might have held, holding which she seemed, drowsy and heavy, to be commanding battalions marching to Canada, and those good fellows walking across London, that territory of theirs, that little bit of carpet, Mayfair.

And they went further and further from her, being attached to her by a thin thread (since they had lunched with her) which would stretch and stretch, get thinner and thinner as they walked across London; as if one's friends were attached to one's body, after lunching with them, by a thin thread, which (as she dozed there) became hazy with the sound of bells, striking the hour or ringing to service, as a single spider's thread is blotted with rain-drops, and, burdened, sags down. So she slept.

And Richard Dalloway and Hugh Whitbread hesitated at the corner of Conduit Street[4] at the very moment that Millicent Bruton, lying on the sofa, let the thread snap; snored. Contrary winds buffeted at the street corner. They looked in at a shop window; they did not wish to buy or to talk but to part, only with contrary winds buffeting the street corner, with some sort of lapse in the tides of the body, two forces meeting in a swirl, morning and afternoon, they paused. Some newspaper placard went up in the air, gallantly, like a kite at first, then paused, swooped, fluttered; and a lady's veil hung. Yellow awnings trembled. The speed of the morning traffic slackened, and single carts rattled carelessly down half-empty streets. In Norfolk, of which Richard Dalloway was half thinking, a soft warm wind blew back the petals; confused the waters; ruffled the flowering grasses. Haymakers, who had pitched beneath hedges to sleep away the morning toil, parted curtains of green blades; moved trembling globes of cow parsley to see the sky, the blue, the steadfast, the blazing summer sky.

Aware that he was looking at a silver two-handled Jacobean mug,[5] and that Hugh Whitbread admired condescendingly with airs of connoisseurship a Spanish necklace which he thought of asking the price of in case Evelyn might like it—still Richard was torpid; could not think or move. Life had thrown up this wreckage; shop windows full of coloured paste, and one stood stark with the lethargy of the old, stiff with the rigidity of the old, looking in. Evelyn Whitbread might like to buy this Spanish necklace—so she might. Yawn he must. Hugh was going into the shop.

"Right you are!" said Richard, following.

Goodness knows he didn't want to go buying necklaces with Hugh. But there are tides in the body. Morning meets afternoon. Borne like a frail shallop[6] on deep, deep floods, Lady Bruton's great-grandfather and his memoir and his campaigns in North America were whelmed and sunk. And Millicent Bruton too. She went under. Richard didn't care a straw what became of Emigration; about that letter, whether the editor put it in or not.

4. Street in Mayfair. Richard and Hugh appear to have walked east on Brook Street and then south on Bond Street to this intersection.

5. In the style of, or dating from, the reign of King James I (1603–25).

6. Small boat; dinghy.

The necklace hung stretched between Hugh's admirable fingers. Let him give it to a girl, if he must buy jewels—any girl, any girl in the street. For the worthlessness of this life did strike Richard pretty forcibly—buying necklaces for Evelyn. If he'd had a boy he'd have said, Work, work. But he had his Elizabeth; he adored his Elizabeth.

"I should like to see Mr. Dubonnet," said Hugh in his curt worldly way. It appeared that this Dubonnet had the measurements of Mrs. Whitbread's neck, or, more strangely still, knew her views upon Spanish jewellery and the extent of her possessions in that line (which Hugh could not remember). All of which seemed to Richard Dalloway awfully odd. For he never gave Clarissa presents, except a bracelet two or three years ago, which had not been a success. She never wore it. It pained him to remember that she never wore it. And as a single spider's thread after wavering here and there attaches itself to the point of a leaf, so Richard's mind, recovering from its lethargy, set now on his wife, Clarissa, whom Peter Walsh had loved so passionately; and Richard had had a sudden vision of her there at luncheon; of himself and Clarissa; of their life together; and he drew the tray of old jewels towards him, and taking up first this brooch then that ring, "How much is that?" he asked, but doubted his own taste. He wanted to open the drawing-room door and come in holding out something; a present for Clarissa. Only what? But Hugh was on his legs again. He was unspeakably pompous. Really, after dealing here for thirty-five years he was not going to be put off by a mere boy who did not know his business. For Dubonnet, it seemed, was out, and Hugh would not buy anything until Mr. Dubonnet chose to be in; at which the youth flushed and bowed his correct little bow. It was all perfectly correct. And yet Richard couldn't have said that to save his life! Why these people stood that damned insolence he could not conceive. Hugh was becoming an intolerable ass. Richard Dalloway could not stand more than an hour of his society. And, flicking his bowler hat by way of farewell, Richard turned at the corner of Conduit Street eager, yes, very eager, to travel that spider's thread of attachment between himself and Clarissa; he would go straight to her, in Westminster.

But he wanted to come in holding something. Flowers? Yes, flowers, since he did not trust his taste in gold; any number of flowers, roses, orchids, to celebrate what was, reckoning things as you will, an event; this feeling about her when they spoke of Peter Walsh at luncheon; and they never spoke of it; not for years had they spoken of it; which, he thought, grasping his red and white roses together (a vast bunch in tissue paper), is the greatest mistake in the world. The time comes when it can't be said; one's too shy to say it, he thought, pocketing his sixpence or two of change, setting off with his great bunch held against his body to Westminster to say straight out in so many words (whatever she might think of him), holding out his flowers, "I love you." Why not? Really it was a miracle thinking of the war, and thousands of poor chaps, with all their lives before them, shovelled together, already half forgotten; it was a miracle. Here he was walking across London to say to Clarissa in so many words that he loved her. Which one never does say, he thought. Partly one's lazy; partly one's shy. And Clarissa—it was difficult to think of her; except in starts, as at luncheon, when he saw her quite distinctly; their whole life. He stopped at the crossing; and repeated—being simple by nature, and undebauched, because he had tramped, and shot; being pertinacious and dogged, having championed the downtrodden and

followed his instincts in the House of Commons; being preserved in his simplicity yet at the same time grown rather speechless, rather stiff—he
repeated that it was a miracle that he should have married Clarissa; a
miracle—his life had been a miracle, he thought; hesitating to cross. But it
did make his blood boil to see little creatures of five or six crossing Piccadilly
alone. The police ought to have stopped the traffic at once. He had no illusions about the London police. Indeed, he was collecting evidence of their
malpractices; and those costermongers,[7] not allowed to stand their barrows
in the streets; and prostitutes, good Lord, the fault wasn't in them, nor in
young men either, but in our detestable social system and so forth; all of
which he considered, could be seen considering, grey, dogged, dapper, clean,
as he walked across the Park to tell his wife that he loved her.

For he would say it in so many words, when he came into the room.
Because it is a thousand pities never to say what one feels, he thought, crossing the Green Park and observing with pleasure how in the shade of the
trees whole families, poor families, were sprawling; children kicking up
their legs; sucking milk; paper bags thrown about, which could easily be
picked up (if people objected) by one of those fat gentlemen in livery;[8] for he
was of opinion that every park, and every square, during the summer months
should be open to children (the grass of the park flushed and faded, lighting
up the poor mothers of Westminster and their crawling babies, as if a yellow
lamp were moved beneath). But what could be done for female vagrants like
that poor creature, stretched on her elbow (as if she had flung herself on the
earth, rid of all ties, to observe curiously, to speculate boldly, to consider the
whys and the wherefores, impudent, loose-lipped, humorous), he did not
know. Bearing his flowers like a weapon, Richard Dalloway approached her;
intent he passed her; still there was time for a spark between them—she
laughed at the sight of him, he smiled good-humouredly, considering the
problem of the female vagrant; not that they would ever speak. But he would
tell Clarissa that he loved her, in so many words. He had, once upon a time,
been jealous of Peter Walsh; jealous of him and Clarissa. But she had often
said to him that she had been right not to marry Peter Walsh; which, knowing Clarissa, was obviously true; she wanted support. Not that she was weak;
but she wanted support.

As for Buckingham Palace (like an old prima donna facing the audience all
in white) you can't deny it a certain dignity, he considered, nor despise what
does, after all, stand to millions of people (a little crowd was waiting at the
gate to see the King drive out) for a symbol, absurd though it is; a child with
a box of bricks could have done better, he thought; looking at the memorial
to Queen Victoria (whom he could remember in her horn spectacles driving
through Kensington), its white mound, its billowing motherliness; but he
liked being ruled by the descendant of Horsa;[9] he liked continuity; and the
sense of handing on the traditions of the past. It was a great age in which to
have lived. Indeed, his own life was a miracle; let him make no mistake about
it; here he was, in the prime of life, walking to his house in Westminster to
tell Clarissa that he loved her. Happiness is this, he thought.

---

7. Street vendors who sell fruit from open carts.
8. In uniform, presumably that of park officials.
9. Of Saxon heritage. The brothers Horsa and
Hengist were said to have begun the Anglo-
Saxon invasion of Britain in the fifth century
c.e. "Kensington": London borough west of Hyde
Park, where Kensington Gardens and Kensington Palace are located.

It is this, he said, as he entered Dean's Yard.[1] Big Ben was beginning to strike, first the warning, musical; then the hour, irrevocable. Lunch parties waste the entire afternoon, he thought, approaching his door.

The sound of Big Ben flooded Clarissa's drawing-room, where she sat, ever so annoyed, at her writing-table; worried; annoyed. It was perfectly true that she had not asked Ellie Henderson to her party; but she had done it on purpose. Now Mrs. Marsham wrote "she had told Ellie Henderson she would ask Clarissa—Ellie so much wanted to come."

But why should she invite all the dull women in London to her parties? Why should Mrs. Marsham interfere? And there was Elizabeth closeted all this time with Doris Kilman. Anything more nauseating she could not conceive. Prayer at this hour with that woman. And the sound of the bell flooded the room with its melancholy wave; which receded, and gathered itself together to fall once more, when she heard, distractingly, something fumbling, something scratching at the door. Who at this hour? Three, good Heavens! Three already! For with overpowering directness and dignity the clock struck three; and she heard nothing else; but the door handle slipped round and in came Richard! What a surprise! In came Richard, holding out flowers. She had failed him, once at Constantinople; and Lady Bruton, whose lunch parties were said to be extraordinarily amusing, had not asked her. He was holding out flowers—roses, red and white roses. (But he could not bring himself to say he loved her; not in so many words.)

But how lovely, she said, taking his flowers. She understood; she understood without his speaking; his Clarissa. She put them in vases on the mantelpiece. How lovely they looked! she said. And was it amusing, she asked? Had Lady Bruton asked after her? Peter Walsh was back. Mrs. Marsham had written. Must she ask Ellie Henderson? That woman Kilman was upstairs.

"But let us sit down for five minutes," said Richard.

It all looked so empty. All the chairs were against the wall. What had they been doing? Oh, it was for the party; no, he had not forgotten, the party. Peter Walsh was back. Oh yes; she had had him. And he was going to get a divorce; and he was in love with some woman out there. And he hadn't changed in the slightest. There she was, mending her dress. . . .

"Thinking of Bourton," she said.

"Hugh was at lunch," said Richard. She had met him too! Well, he was getting absolutely intolerable. Buying Evelyn necklaces; fatter than ever; an intolerable ass.

"And it came over me 'I might have married you,'" she said, thinking of Peter sitting there in his little bow-tie; with that knife, opening it, shutting it. "Just as he always was, you know."

They were talking about him at lunch, said Richard. (But he could not tell her he loved her. He held her hand. Happiness is this, he thought.) They had been writing a letter to the *Times* for Millicent Bruton. That was about all Hugh was fit for.

"And our dear Miss Kilman?" he asked. Clarissa thought the roses absolutely lovely, first bunched together; now of their own accord starting apart.

"Kilman arrives just as we've done lunch," she said. "Elizabeth turns pink. They shut themselves up. I suppose they're praying."

---

1. Residential area that was once part of the gardens of Westminster Abbey belonging to its dean.

Lord! He didn't like it; but these things pass over if you let them.

"In a mackintosh with an umbrella," said Clarissa.

He had not said "I love you"; but he held her hand. Happiness is this, is this, he thought.

"But why should I ask all the dull women in London to my parties?" said Clarissa. And if Mrs. Marsham gave a party, did *she* invite her guests?

"Poor Ellie Henderson," said Richard—it was a very odd thing how much Clarissa minded about her parties, he thought.

But Richard had no notion of the look of a room. However—what was he going to say?

If she worried about these parties he would not let her give them. Did she wish she had married Peter? But he must go.

He must be off, he said, getting up. But he stood for a moment as if he were about to say something; and she wondered what? Why? There were the roses.

"Some Committee?" she asked, as he opened the door.

"Armenians," he said; or perhaps it was "Albanians."[2]

And there is a dignity in people; a solitude; even between husband and wife a gulf; and that one must respect, thought Clarissa, watching him open the door; for one would not part with it oneself, or take it, against his will, from one's husband, without losing one's independence, one's self-respect—something, after all, priceless.

He returned with a pillow and a quilt.

"An hour's complete rest after luncheon," he said. And he went.

How like him! He would go on saying "An hour's complete rest after luncheon" to the end of time, because a doctor had ordered it once. It was like him to take what doctors said literally; part of his adorable, divine simplicity, which no one had to the same extent; which made him go and do the thing while she and Peter frittered their time away bickering. He was already halfway to the House of Commons, to his Armenians, his Albanians, having settled her on the sofa, looking at his roses. And people would say, "Clarissa Dalloway is spoilt." She cared much more for her roses than for the Armenians. Hunted out of existence, maimed, frozen, the victims of cruelty and injustice (she had heard Richard say so over and over again)—no, she could feel nothing for the Albanians, or was it the Armenians? but she loved her roses (didn't that help the Armenians?)—the only flowers she could bear to see cut. But Richard was already at the House of Commons; at his Committee, having settled all her difficulties. But no; alas, that was not true. He did not see the reasons against asking Ellie Henderson. She would do it, of course, as he wished it. Since he had brought the pillows, she would lie down. . . . But—but—why did she suddenly feel, for no reason that she could discover, desperately unhappy? As a person who has dropped some grain of pearl or diamond into the grass and parts the tall blades very carefully, this way and that, and searches here and there vainly, and at last spies it there at the roots, so she went through one thing and another; no, it was not Sally Seton saying that Richard would never be in the Cabinet because he had a second-class brain (it came back to her); no, she did not

2. Armenians, a Christian minority in Turkey, were persecuted; 1.75 million were forced to emigrate between 1915 and 1921. Their plight is more likely to be the subject of Richard's meeting than that of the Albanians, who, after a period of unrest (1908–21), had their territorial security guaranteed by the League of Nations.

mind that; nor was it to do with Elizabeth either and Doris Kilman; those were facts. It was a feeling, some unpleasant feeling, earlier in the day perhaps; something that Peter had said, combined with some depression of her own, in her bedroom, taking off her hat; and what Richard had said had added to it, but what had he said? There were his roses. Her parties! That was it! Her parties! Both of them criticised her very unfairly, laughed at her very unjustly, for her parties. That was it! That was it!

Well, how was she going to defend herself? Now that she knew what it was, she felt perfectly happy. They thought, or Peter at any rate thought, that she enjoyed imposing herself; liked to have famous people about her; great names; was simply a snob in short. Well, Peter might think so. Richard merely thought it foolish of her to like excitement when she knew it was bad for her heart. It was childish, he thought. And both were quite wrong. What she liked was simply life.

"That's what I do it for," she said, speaking aloud, to life.

Since she was lying on the sofa, cloistered, exempt, the presence of this thing which she felt to be so obvious became physically existent; with robes of sound from the street, sunny, with hot breath, whispering, blowing out the blinds. But suppose Peter said to her, "Yes, yes, but your parties—what's the sense of your parties?" all she could say was (and nobody could be expected to understand): They're an offering; which sounded horribly vague. But who was Peter to make out that life was all plain sailing?—Peter always in love, always in love with the wrong woman? What's your love? she might say to him. And she knew his answer; how it is the most important thing in the world and no woman possibly understood it. Very well. But could any man understand what she meant either? about life? She could not imagine Peter or Richard taking the trouble to give a party for no reason whatever.

But to go deeper, beneath what people said (and these judgements, how superficial, how fragmentary they are!) in her own mind now, what did it mean to her, this thing she called life? Oh, it was very queer. Here was So-and-so in South Kensington; some one up in Bayswater;[3] and somebody else, say, in Mayfair. And she felt quite continuously a sense of their existence; and she felt what a waste; and she felt what a pity; and she felt if only they could be brought together; so she did it. And it was an offering; to combine, to create; but to whom?

An offering for the sake of offering, perhaps. Anyhow, it was her gift. Nothing else had she of the slightest importance; could not think, write, even play the piano. She muddled Armenians and Turks; loved success; hated discomfort; must be liked; talked oceans of nonsense: and to this day, ask her what the Equator was, and she did not know.

All the same, that one day should follow another; Wednesday, Thursday, Friday, Saturday, that one should wake up in the morning; see the sky; walk in the park; meet Hugh Whitbread; then suddenly in came Peter; then these roses; it was enough. After that, how unbelievable death was!—that it must end; and no one in the whole world would know how she had loved it all; how, every instant . . .

The door opened. Elizabeth knew that her mother was resting. She came in very quietly. She stood perfectly still. Was it that some Mongol[4] had been

---

wrecked on the coast of Norfolk (as Mrs. Hilbery said), had mixed with the Dalloway ladies, perhaps, a hundred years ago? For the Dalloways, in general, were fair-haired; blue-eyed; Elizabeth, on the contrary, was dark; had Chinese eyes[5] in a pale face; an Oriental mystery; was gentle, considerate, still. As a child, she had had a perfect sense of humour; but now at seventeen, why, Clarissa could not in the least understand, she had become very serious; like a hyacinth, sheathed in glossy green, with buds just tinted, a hyacinth which has had no sun.

She stood quite still and looked at her mother; but the door was ajar, and outside the door was Miss Kilman, as Clarissa knew; Miss Kilman in her mackintosh, listening to whatever they said.

Yes, Miss Kilman stood on the landing, and wore a mackintosh; but had her reasons. First, it was cheap; second, she was over forty; and did not, after all, dress to please. She was poor, moreover; degradingly poor. Otherwise she would not be taking jobs from people like the Dalloways; from rich people, who liked to be kind. Mr. Dalloway, to do him justice, had been kind. But Mrs. Dalloway had not. She had been merely condescending. She came from the most worthless of all classes—the rich, with a smattering of culture. They had expensive things everywhere; pictures, carpets, lots of servants. She considered that she had a perfect right to anything that the Dalloways did for her.

She had been cheated. Yes, the word was no exaggeration, for surely a girl has a right to some kind of happiness? And she had never been happy, what with being so clumsy and so poor. And then, just as she might have had a chance at Miss Dolby's school, the war came; and she had never been able to tell lies. Miss Dolby thought she would be happier with people who shared her views about the Germans. She had had to go. It was true that the family was of German origin; spelt the name Kiehlman in the eighteenth century; but her brother had been killed. They turned her out because she would not pretend that the Germans were all villains—when she had German friends, when the only happy days of her life had been spent in Germany! And after all, she could read history. She had had to take whatever she could get. Mr. Dalloway had come across her working for the Friends.[6] He had allowed her (and that was really generous of him) to teach his daughter history. Also she did a little Extension lecturing[7] and so on. Then Our Lord had come to her (and here she always bowed her head). She had seen the light two years and three months ago. Now she did not envy women like Clarissa Dalloway; she pitied them.

She pitied and despised them from the bottom of her heart, as she stood on the soft carpet, looking at the old engraving of a little girl with a muff.[8] With all this luxury going on, what hope was there for a better state of things? Instead of lying on a sofa—"My mother is resting," Elizabeth had said—she should have been in a factory; behind a counter; Mrs. Dalloway and all the other fine ladies!

Bitter and burning, Miss Kilman had turned in to a church two years three months ago. She had heard the Rev. Edward Whittaker preach; the boys sing; had seen the solemn lights descend, and whether it was the music, or the

---

5. Almond-shaped, presumably, and suggestive to Britons at this time of an "oriental" mystery.
6. Religious Society of Friends, or Quakers.
7. Teaching students who are not part of a typical degree program.
8. A cylindrical warmer for both hands.

voices (she herself when alone in the evening found comfort in a violin; but the sound was excruciating; she had no ear), the hot and turbulent feelings which boiled and surged in her had been assuaged as she sat there, and she had wept copiously, and gone to call on Mr. Whittaker at his private house in Kensington. It was the hand of God, he said. The Lord had shown her the way. So now, whenever the hot and painful feelings boiled within her, this hatred of Mrs. Dalloway, this grudge against the world, she thought of God. She thought of Mr. Whittaker. Rage was succeeded by calm. A sweet savour filled her veins, her lips parted, and, standing formidable upon the landing in her mackintosh, she looked with steady and sinister serenity at Mrs. Dalloway, who came out with her daughter.

Elizabeth said she had forgotten her gloves. That was because Miss Kilman and her mother hated each other. She could not bear to see them together. She ran upstairs to find her gloves.

But Miss Kilman did not hate Mrs. Dalloway. Turning her large gooseberry-coloured eyes upon Clarissa, observing her small pink face, her delicate body, her air of freshness and fashion, Miss Kilman felt, Fool! Simpleton! You who have known neither sorrow nor pleasure; who have trifled your life away! And there rose in her an overmastering desire to overcome her; to unmask her. If she could have felled her it would have eased her. But it was not the body; it was the soul and its mockery that she wished to subdue; make feel her mastery. If only she could make her weep; could ruin her; humiliate her; bring her to her knees crying, You are right! But this was God's will, not Miss Kilman's. It was to be a religious victory. So she glared; so she glowered.

Clarissa was really shocked. This a Christian—this woman! This woman had taken her daughter from her! She in touch with invisible presences! Heavy, ugly, commonplace, without kindness or grace, she know the meaning of life!

"You are taking Elizabeth to the Stores?"[9] Mrs. Dalloway said.

Miss Kilman said she was. They stood there. Miss Kilman was not going to make herself agreeable. She had always earned her living. Her knowledge of modern history was thorough in the extreme. She did out of her meagre income set aside so much for causes she believed in; whereas this woman did nothing, believed nothing; brought up her daughter—but here was Elizabeth, rather out of breath, the beautiful girl.

So they were going to the Stores. Odd it was, as Miss Kilman stood there (and stand she did, with the power and taciturnity of some prehistoric monster armoured for primeval warfare), how, second by second, the idea of her diminished, how hatred (which was for ideas, not people) crumbled, how she lost her malignity, her size, became second by second merely Miss Kilman, in a mackintosh, whom Heaven knows Clarissa would have liked to help.

At this dwindling of the monster, Clarissa laughed. Saying good-bye, she laughed.

Off they went together, Miss Kilman and Elizabeth, downstairs.

With a sudden impulse, with a violent anguish, for this woman was taking her daughter from her, Clarissa leant over the bannisters and cried out, "Remember the party! Remember our party to-night!"

---

9. The Army and Navy Stores in Victoria Street, founded as a cooperative society to supply cheap goods to military families.

But Elizabeth had already opened the front door; there was a van passing; she did not answer.

Love and religion! thought Clarissa, going back into the drawing-room, tingling all over. How detestable, how detestable they are! For now that the body of Miss Kilman was not before her, it overwhelmed her—the idea. The crudest things in the world, she thought, seeing them clumsy, hot, domineering, hypocritical, eavesdropping, jealous, infinitely cruel and unscrupulous, dressed in a mackintosh coat, on the landing; love and religion. Had she ever tried to convert any one herself? Did she not wish everybody merely to be themselves? And she watched out of the window the old lady opposite climbing upstairs. Let her climb upstairs if she wanted to; let her stop; then let her, as Clarissa had often seen her, gain her bedroom, part her curtains, and disappear again into the background. Somehow one respected that—that old woman looking out of the window, quite unconscious that she was being watched. There was something solemn in it—but love and religion would destroy that, whatever it was, the privacy of the soul. The odious Kilman would destroy it. Yet it was a sight that made her want to cry.

Love destroyed too. Everything that was fine, everything that was true went. Take Peter Walsh now. There was a man, charming, clever, with ideas about everything. If you wanted to know about Pope, say, or Addison,[1] or just to talk nonsense, what people were like, what things meant, Peter knew better than any one. It was Peter who had helped her; Peter who had lent her books. But look at the women he loved—vulgar, trivial, commonplace. Think of Peter in love—he came to see her after all these years, and what did he talk about? Himself. Horrible passion! she thought. Degrading passion! she thought, thinking of Kilman and her Elizabeth walking to the Army and Navy Stores.

Big Ben struck the half-hour.

How extraordinary it was, strange, yes, touching, to see the old lady (they had been neighbours ever so many years) move away from the window, as if she were attached to that sound, that string. Gigantic as it was, it had something to do with her. Down, down, into the midst of ordinary things the finger fell making the moment solemn. She was forced, so Clarissa imagined, by that sound, to move, to go—but where? Clarissa tried to follow her as she turned and disappeared, and could still just see her white cap moving at the back of the bedroom. She was still there moving about at the other end of the room. Why creeds and prayers and mackintoshes? when, thought Clarissa, that's the miracle, that's the mystery; that old lady, she meant, whom she could see going from chest of drawers to dressing-table. She could still see her. And the supreme mystery which Kilman might say she had solved, or Peter might say he had solved, but Clarissa didn't believe either of them had the ghost of an idea of solving, was simply this: here was one room; there another. Did religion solve that, or love?

Love—but here the other clock, the clock which always struck two minutes after Big Ben, came shuffling in with its lap full of odds and ends, which it dumped down as if Big Ben were all very well with his majesty laying down the law, so solemn, so just, but she must remember all sorts of little things besides—Mrs. Marsham, Ellie Henderson, glasses for ices—all sorts of little things came flooding and lapping and dancing in on the wake

---

1. Joseph Addison (1672–1719), English politician and writer.

of that solemn stroke which lay flat like a bar of gold on the sea. Mrs. Marsham, Ellie Henderson, glasses for ices. She must telephone now at once.

Volubly, troublously, the late clock sounded, coming in on the wake of Big Ben, with its lap full of trifles. Beaten up, broken up by the assault of carriages, the brutality of vans, the eager advance of myriads of angular men, of flaunting women, the domes and spires of offices and hospitals, the last relics of this lap full of odds and ends seemed to break, like the spray of an exhausted wave, upon the body of Miss Kilman standing still in the street for a moment to mutter "It is the flesh."

It was the flesh that she must control. Clarissa Dalloway had insulted her. That she expected. But she had not triumphed; she had not mastered the flesh. Ugly, clumsy, Clarissa Dalloway had laughed at her for being that; and had revived the fleshly desires, for she minded looking as she did beside Clarissa. Nor could she talk as she did. But why wish to resemble her? Why? She despised Mrs. Dalloway from the bottom of her heart. She was not serious. She was not good. Her life was a tissue of vanity and deceit. Yet Doris Kilman had been overcome. She had, as a matter of fact, very nearly burst into tears when Clarissa Dalloway laughed at her. "It is the flesh, it is the flesh," she muttered (it being her habit to talk aloud) trying to subdue this turbulent and painful feeling as she walked down Victoria Street. She prayed to God. She could not help being ugly; she could not afford to buy pretty clothes. Clarissa Dalloway had laughed—but she would concentrate her mind upon something else until she had reached the pillar-box.[2] At any rate she had got Elizabeth. But she would think of something else; she would think of Russia; until she reached the pillar-box.

How nice it must be, she said, in the country, struggling, as Mr. Whittaker had told her, with that violent grudge against the world which had scorned her, sneered at her, cast her off, beginning with this indignity—the infliction of her unlovable body which people could not bear to see. Do her hair as she might, her forehead remained like an egg, bald, white. No clothes suited her. She might buy anything. And for a woman, of course, that meant never meeting the opposite sex. Never would she come first with any one. Sometimes lately it had seemed to her that, except for Elizabeth, her food was all that she lived for; her comforts; her dinner, her tea; her hot-water bottle at night. But one must fight; vanquish; have faith in God. Mr. Whittaker had said she was there for a purpose. But no one knew the agony! He said, pointing to the crucifix, that God knew. But why should she have to suffer when other women, like Clarissa Dalloway, escaped? Knowledge comes through suffering, said Mr. Whittaker.

She had passed the pillar-box, and Elizabeth had turned into the cool brown tobacco department of the Army and Navy Stores while she was still muttering to herself what Mr. Whittaker had said about knowledge coming through suffering and the flesh. "The flesh," she muttered.

What department did she want? Elizabeth interrupted her.

"Petticoats," she said abruptly, and stalked straight on to the lift.

Up they went. Elizabeth guided her this way and that; guided her in her abstraction as if she had been a great child, an unwieldy battleship. There were the petticoats, brown, decorous, striped, frivolous, solid, flimsy; and she chose, in her abstraction, portentously, and the girl serving thought her mad.

2. Mailbox shaped like a pillar.

Elizabeth rather wondered, as they did up the parcel, what Miss Kilman was thinking. They must have their tea, said Miss Kilman, rousing, collecting herself. They had their tea.

Elizabeth rather wondered whether Miss Kilman could be hungry. It was her way of eating, eating with intensity, then looking, again and again, at a plate of sugared cakes on the table next them; then, when a lady and a child sat down and the child took the cake, could Miss Kilman really mind it? Yes, Miss Kilman did mind it. She had wanted that cake—the pink one. The pleasure of eating was almost the only pure pleasure left her, and then to be baffled even in that!

When people are happy, they have a reserve, she had told Elizabeth, upon which to draw, whereas she was like a wheel without a tyre (she was fond of such metaphors), jolted by every pebble, so she would say staying on after the lesson standing by the fire-place with her bag of books, her "satchel," she called it, on a Tuesday morning, after the lesson was over. And she talked too about the war. After all, there were people who did not think the English invariably right. There were books. There were meetings. There were other points of view. Would Elizabeth like to come with her to listen to So-and-so (a most extraordinary looking old man)? Then Miss Kilman took her to some church in Kensington and they had tea with a clergyman. She had lent her books. Law, medicine, politics, all professions are open to women of your generation, said Miss Kilman. But for herself, her career was absolutely ruined and was it her fault? Good gracious, said Elizabeth, no.

And her mother would come calling to say that a hamper had come from Bourton and would Miss Kilman like some flowers? To Miss Kilman she was always very, very nice, but Miss Kilman squashed the flowers all in a bunch, and hadn't any small talk, and what interested Miss Kilman bored her mother, and Miss Kilman and she were terrible together; and Miss Kilman swelled and looked very plain. But then Miss Kilman was frightfully clever. Elizabeth had never thought about the poor. They lived with everything they wanted,—her mother had breakfast in bed every day; Lucy carried it up; and she liked old women because they were Duchesses, and being descended from some Lord. But Miss Kilman said (one of those Tuesday mornings when the lesson was over), "My grandfather kept an oil and colour shop[3] in Kensington." Miss Kilman made one feel so small.

Miss Kilman took another cup of tea. Elizabeth, with her oriental bearing, her inscrutable mystery, sat perfectly upright; no, she did not want anything more. She looked for her gloves—her white gloves. They were under the table. Ah, but she must not go! Miss Kilman could not let her go! this youth, that was so beautiful, this girl, whom she genuinely loved! Her large hand opened and shut on the table.

But perhaps it was a little flat somehow, Elizabeth felt. And really she would like to go.

But said Miss Kilman, "I've not quite finished yet."

Of course, then, Elizabeth would wait. But it was rather stuffy in here.

"Are you going to the party to-night?" Miss Kilman said. Elizabeth supposed she was going; her mother wanted her to go. She must not let parties absorb her, Miss Kilman said, fingering the last two inches of a chocolate éclair.

---

3. Store selling oils, paints, and other supplies.

She did not much like parties, Elizabeth said. Miss Kilman opened her mouth, slightly projected her chin, and swallowed down the last inches of the chocolate éclair, then wiped her fingers, and washed the tea round in her cup.

She was about to split asunder, she felt. The agony was so terrific. If she could grasp her, if she could clasp her, if she could make her hers absolutely and forever and then die; that was all she wanted. But to sit here, unable to think of anything to say; to see Elizabeth turning against her; to be felt repulsive even by her—it was too much; she could not stand it. The thick fingers curled inwards.

"I never go to parties," said Miss Kilman, just to keep Elizabeth from going. "People don't ask me to parties"—and she knew as she said it that it was this egotism that was her undoing; Mr. Whittaker had warned her; but she could not help it. She had suffered so horribly. "Why should they ask me?" she said. "I'm plain, I'm unhappy." She knew it was idiotic. But it was all those people passing—people with parcels who despised her, who made her say it. However, she was Doris Kilman. She had her degree. She was a woman who had made her way in the world. Her knowledge of modern history was more than respectable.

"I don't pity myself," she said. "I pity"—she meant to say "your mother" but no, she could not, not to Elizabeth. "I pity other people," she said, "more."

Like some dumb creature who has been brought up to a gate for an unknown purpose, and stands there longing to gallop away, Elizabeth Dalloway sat silent. Was Miss Kilman going to say anything more?

"Don't quite forget me," said Doris Kilman; her voice quivered. Right away to the end of the field the dumb creature galloped in terror.

The great hand opened and shut.

Elizabeth turned her head. The waitress came. One had to pay at the desk, Elizabeth said, and went off, drawing out, so Miss Kilman felt, the very entrails in her body, stretching them as she crossed the room, and then, with a final twist, bowing her head very politely, she went.

She had gone. Miss Kilman sat at the marble table among the éclairs, stricken once, twice, thrice by shocks of suffering. She had gone. Mrs. Dalloway had triumphed. Elizabeth had gone. Beauty had gone, youth had gone.

So she sat. She got up, blundered off among the little tables, rocking slightly from side to side, and somebody came after her with her petticoat, and she lost her way, and was hemmed in by trunks specially prepared for taking to India; next got among the accouchement[4] sets, and baby linen; through all the commodities of the world, perishable and permanent, hams, drugs, flowers, stationery, variously smelling, now sweet, now sour she lurched; saw herself thus lurching with her hat askew, very red in the face, full length in a looking-glass; and at last came out into the street.

The tower of Westminster Cathedral[5] rose in front of her, the habitation of God. In the midst of the traffic, there was the habitation of God. Doggedly she set off with her parcel to that other sanctuary, the Abbey,[6] where, raising her hands in a tent before her face, she sat beside those driven into shelter too; the variously assorted worshippers, now divested of social rank, almost of sex, as they raised their hands before their faces; but once they

4. Childbirth.
5. Roman Catholic cathedral (1903) on Victoria Street, with a high bell tower.

6. Westminster Abbey, Anglican cathedral near Parliament.

removed them, instantly reverent, middle class, English men and women, some of them desirous of seeing the wax works.[7]

But Miss Kilman held her tent before her face. Now she was deserted; now rejoined. New worshippers came in from the street to replace the strollers, and still, as people gazed round and shuffled past the tomb of the Unknown Warrior,[8] still she barred her eyes with her fingers and tried in this double darkness, for the light in the Abbey was bodiless, to aspire above the vanities, the desires, the commodities, to rid herself both of hatred and of love. Her hands twitched. She seemed to struggle. Yet to others God was accessible and the path to Him smooth. Mr. Fletcher, retired, of the Treasury, Mrs. Gorham, widow of the famous K.C.,[9] approached Him simply, and having done their praying, leant back, enjoyed the music (the organ pealed sweetly), and saw Miss Kilman at the end of the row, praying, praying, and, being still on the threshold of their underworld, thought of her sympathetically as a soul haunting the same territory, a soul cut out of immaterial substance; not a woman, a soul.

But Mr. Fletcher had to go. He had to pass her, and being himself neat as a new pin, could not help being a little distressed by the poor lady's disorder; her hair down; her parcel on the floor. She did not at once let him pass. But, as he stood gazing about him, at the white marbles, grey window panes, and accumulated treasures (for he was extremely proud of the Abbey), her largeness, robustness, and power as she sat there shifting her knees from time to time (it was so rough the approach to her God—so tough her desires) impressed him, as they had impressed Mrs. Dalloway (she could not get the thought of her out of her mind that afternoon), the Rev. Edward Whittaker, and Elizabeth too.

And Elizabeth waited in Victoria Street for an omnibus. It was so nice to be out of doors. She thought perhaps she need not go home just yet. It was so nice to be out in the air. So she would get on to an omnibus. And already, even as she stood there, in her very well cut clothes, it was beginning. . . . People were beginning to compare her to poplar trees, early dawn, hyacinths, fawns, running water, and garden lilies, and it made her life a burden to her, for she so much preferred being left alone to do what she liked in the country, but they would compare her to lilies, and she had to go to parties, and London was so dreary compared with being alone in the country with her father and the dogs.

Buses swooped, settled, were off—garish caravans, glistening with red and yellow varnish. But which should she get on to? She had no preferences. Of course, she would not push her way. She inclined to be passive. It was expression she needed, but her eyes were fine, Chinese, oriental, and, as her mother said, with such nice shoulders and holding herself so straight, she was always charming to look at; and lately, in the evening especially, when she was interested, for she never seemed excited, she looked almost beautiful, very stately, very serene. What could she be thinking? Every man fell in love with her, and she was really awfully bored. For it was beginning. Her mother could see that—the compliments were beginning. That she did not care more about it—for instance for her clothes—sometimes worried

7. Effigies of monarchs buried in the Abbey, such as Elizabeth I, located in the Abbey Museum.
8. The Tomb of the Unknown Warrior, in the Abbey's nave, commemorates the dead of World War I; it contains the body of an unidentified soldier, buried there on November 11, 1920.
9. King's Counsel, senior barrister or lawyer.

Clarissa, but perhaps it was as well with all those puppies and guinea pigs about having distemper, and it gave her a charm. And now there was this odd friendship with Miss Kilman. Well, thought Clarissa about three o'clock in the morning, reading Baron Marbot for she could not sleep, it proves she has a heart.

Suddenly Elizabeth stepped forward and most competently boarded the omnibus, in front of everybody. She took a seat on top. The impetuous creature—a pirate—started forward, sprang away; she had to hold the rail to steady herself, for a pirate it was, reckless, unscrupulous, bearing down ruthlessly, circumventing dangerously, boldly snatching a passenger, or ignoring a passenger, squeezing eel-like and arrogant in between, and then rushing insolently all sails spread up Whitehall. And did Elizabeth give one thought to poor Miss Kilman who loved her without jealousy, to whom she had been a fawn in the open, a moon in a glade? She was delighted to be free. The fresh air was so delicious. It had been so stuffy in the Army and Navy Stores. And now it was like riding, to be rushing up Whitehall; and to each movement of the omnibus the beautiful body in the fawn-coloured coat responded freely like a rider, like the figurehead of a ship, for the breeze slightly disarrayed her; the heat gave her cheeks the pallor of white painted wood; and her fine eyes, having no eyes to meet, gazed ahead, blank, bright, with the staring incredible innocence of sculpture.

It was always talking about her own sufferings that made Miss Kilman so difficult. And was she right? If it was being on committees and giving up hours and hours every day (she hardly ever saw him in London) that helped the poor, her father did that, goodness knows,—if that was what Miss Kilman meant about being a Christian; but it was so difficult to say. Oh, she would like to go a little further. Another penny was it to the Strand? Here was another penny then. She would go up the Strand.

She liked people who were ill. And every profession is open to the women of your generation, said Miss Kilman. So she might be a doctor. She might be a farmer. Animals are often ill. She might own a thousand acres and have people under her. She would go and see them in their cottages. This was Somerset House.[1] One might be a very good farmer—and that, strangely enough though Miss Kilman had her share in it, was almost entirely due to Somerset House. It looked so splendid, so serious, that great grey building. And she liked the feeling of people working. She liked those churches, like shapes of grey paper, breasting the stream of the Strand. It was quite different here from Westminster, she thought, getting off at Chancery Lane.[2] It was so serious; it was so busy. In short, she would like to have a profession. She would become a doctor, a farmer, possibly go into Parliament, if she found it necessary, all because of the Strand.

The feet of those people busy about their activities, hands putting stone to stone, minds eternally occupied not with trivial chatterings (comparing women to poplars—which was rather exciting, of course, but very silly), but with thoughts of ships, of business, of law, of administration, and with it all so stately (she was in the Temple), gay (there was the river), pious (there was the Church[3]), made her quite determined, whatever her mother might say, to become either a farmer or a doctor. But she was, of course, rather lazy.

1. Large 18th-century neoclassical building, between the Strand and the Thames Embankment, housing the national registry for births, marriages, and deaths.

2. A center of the legal profession.
3. The Temple Church, shared by two of the Inns of Court, at the foot of Chancery Lane, between Fleet Street and the Thames.

And it was much better to say nothing about it. It seemed so silly. It was the sort of thing that did sometimes happen, when one was alone—buildings without architects' names, crowds of people coming back from the city having more power than single clergymen in Kensington, than any of the books Miss Kilman had lent her, to stimulate what lay slumbrous, clumsy, and shy on the mind's sandy floor to break surface, as a child suddenly stretches its arms; it was just that, perhaps, a sigh, a stretch of the arms, an impulse, a revelation, which has its effects for ever, and then down again it went to the sandy floor. She must go home. She must dress for dinner. But what was the time?—where was a clock?

She looked up Fleet Street.[4] She walked just a little way towards St. Paul's, shyly, like some one penetrating on tiptoe, exploring a strange house by night with a candle, on edge lest the owner should suddenly fling wide his bedroom door and ask her business, nor did she dare wander off into queer alleys, tempting bye-streets, any more than in a strange house open doors which might be bedroom doors, or sitting-room doors, or lead straight to the larder.[5] For no Dalloways came down the Strand daily; she was a pioneer, a stray, venturing, trusting.

In many ways, her mother felt, she was extremely immature, like a child still, attached to dolls, to old slippers; a perfect baby; and that was charming. But then, of course, there was in the Dalloway family the tradition of public service. Abbesses, principals, head mistresses, dignitaries, in the republic of women—without being brilliant, any of them, they were that. She penetrated a little further in the direction of St. Paul's. She liked the geniality, sisterhood, motherhood, brotherhood of this uproar. It seemed to her good. The noise was tremendous; and suddenly there were trumpets (the unemployed) blaring, rattling about in the uproar, military music; as if people were marching; yet had they been dying—had some woman breathed her last and whoever was watching, opening the window of the room where she had just brought off that act of supreme dignity, looked down on Fleet Street, that uproar, that military music would have come triumphing up to him, consolatory, indifferent.

It was not conscious. There was no recognition in it of one's fortune, or fate, and for that very reason even to those dazed with watching for the last shivers of consciousness on the faces of the dying, consoling. Forgetfulness in people might wound, their ingratitude corrode, but this voice, pouring endlessly, year in year out, would take whatever it might be; this vow; this van; this life; this procession, would wrap them all about and carry them on, as in the rough stream of a glacier the ice holds a splinter of bone, a blue petal, some oak trees, and rolls them on.

But it was later than she thought. Her mother would not like her to be wandering off alone like this. She turned back down the Strand.

A puff of wind (in spite of the heat, there was quite a wind) blew a thin black veil over the sun and over the Strand. The faces faded; the omnibuses suddenly lost their glow. For although the clouds were of mountainous white so that one could fancy hacking hard chips off with a hatchet, with broad golden slopes, lawns of celestial pleasure gardens, on their flanks, and had all the appearance of settled habitations assembled for the conference of gods above the world, there was a perpetual movement among them. Signs were interchanged, when, as if to fulfil some scheme arranged

---

4. Center of the newspaper industry.   5. Room for storing provisions, especially meat.

already, now a summit dwindled, now a whole block of pyramidal size which had kept its station inalterably advanced into the midst or gravely led the procession to fresh anchorage. Fixed though they seemed at their posts, at rest in perfect unanimity, nothing could be fresher, freer, more sensitive superficially than the snow-white or gold-kindled surface; to change, to go, to dismantle the solemn assemblage was immediately possible; and in spite of the grave fixity, the accumulated robustness and solidity, now they struck light to the earth, now darkness.

Calmly and competently, Elizabeth Dalloway mounted the Westminster omnibus.

Going and coming, beckoning, signalling, so the light and shadow which now made the wall grey, now the bananas bright yellow, now made the Strand grey, now made the omnibuses bright yellow, seemed to Septimus Warren Smith lying on the sofa in the sitting-room; watching the watery gold glow and fade with the astonishing sensibility of some live creature on the roses, on the wall-paper. Outside the trees dragged their leaves like nets through the depths of the air; the sound of water was in the room and through the waves came the voices of birds singing. Every power poured its treasures on his head, and his hand lay there on the back of the sofa, as he had seen his hand lie when he was bathing, floating, on the top of the waves, while far away on shore he heard dogs barking and barking far away. Fear no more, says the heart in the body; fear no more.

He was not afraid. At every moment Nature signified by some laughing hint like that gold spot which went round the wall—there, there, there—her determination to show, by brandishing her plumes, shaking her tresses, flinging her mantle this way and that, beautifully, always beautifully, and standing close up to breathe through her hollowed hands Shakespeare's words, her meaning.

Rezia, sitting at the table twisting a hat in her hands, watched him; saw him smiling. He was happy then. But she could not bear to see him smiling. It was not marriage; it was not being one's husband to look strange like that, always to be starting, laughing, sitting hour after hour silent, or clutching her and telling her to write. The table drawer was full of those writings; about war, about Shakespeare; about great discoveries; how there is no death. Lately he had become excited suddenly for no reason (and both Dr. Holmes and Sir William Bradshaw said excitement was the worst thing for him), and waved his hands and cried out that he knew the truth! He knew everything! That man, his friend who was killed, Evans, had come, he said. He was singing behind the screen. She wrote it down just as he spoke it. Some things were very beautiful; others sheer nonsense. And he was always stopping in the middle, changing his mind; wanting to add something; hearing something new; listening with his hand up.

But she heard nothing.

And once they found the girl who did the room reading one of these papers in fits of laughter. It was a dreadful pity. For that made Septimus cry out about human cruelty—how they tear each other to pieces. The fallen, he said, they tear to pieces. "Holmes is on us," he would say, and he would invent stories about Holmes; Holmes eating porridge; Holmes reading Shakespeare—making himself roar with laughter or rage, for Dr. Holmes seemed to stand for something horrible to him. "Human nature," he called him. Then there were the visions. He was drowned, he used to say, and lying on a cliff with the gulls screaming over him. He would look over the edge of the sofa down into the sea. Or he was hearing music. Really it was only a barrel organ or some man crying in the street. But "Lovely!" he used to cry, and the tears would run down his cheeks, which was to her the most dreadful thing of all, to see a man like Septimus, who had fought, who was brave, crying. And he would lie listening until suddenly he would cry that he was falling down, down into the flames! Actually she would look for flames, it was so vivid. But there was nothing. They were alone in the room. It was a dream, she would tell him and so quiet him at last, but sometimes she was frightened too. She sighed as she sat sewing.

Her sigh was tender and enchanting, like the wind outside a wood in the evening. Now she put down her scissors; now she turned to take something from the table. A little stir, a little crinkling, a little tapping built up something on the table there, where she sat sewing. Through his eyelashes he could see her blurred outline; her little black body; her face and hands; her turning movements at the table, as she took up a reel, or looked (she was apt to lose things) for her silk. She was making a hat for Mrs. Filmer's married daughter, whose name was—he had forgotten her name.

"What is the name of Mrs. Filmer's married daughter?" he asked.

"Mrs. Peters," said Rezia. She was afraid it was too small, she said, holding it before her. Mrs. Peters was a big woman; but she did not like her. It was only because Mrs. Filmer had been so good to them. "She gave me grapes this morning," she said—that Rezia wanted to do something to show that they were grateful. She had come into the room the other evening and found Mrs. Peters, who thought they were out, playing the gramophone.

"Was it true?" he asked. She was playing the gramophone? Yes; she had told him about it at the time; she had found Mrs. Peters playing the gramophone.

He began, very cautiously, to open his eyes, to see whether a gramophone was really there. But real things—real things were too exciting. He must be cautious. He would not go mad. First he looked at the fashion papers on the lower shelf, then, gradually at the gramophone with the green trumpet. Nothing could be more exact. And so, gathering courage, he looked at the sideboard; the plate of bananas; the engraving of Queen Victoria and the Prince Consort;[6] at the mantelpiece, with the jar of roses. None of these things moved. All were still; all were real.

"She is a woman with a spiteful tongue," said Rezia.

"What does Mr. Peters do?" Septimus asked.

"Ah," said Rezia, trying to remember. She thought Mrs. Filmer had said that he travelled for some company. "Just now he is in Hull,"[7] she said.

"Just now!" She said that with her Italian accent. She said that herself. He shaded his eyes so that he might see only a little of her face at a time, first the chin, then the nose, then the forehead, in case it were deformed, or had some terrible mark on it. But no, there she was, perfectly natural, sewing, with the pursed lips that women have, the set, the melancholy expression, when sewing. But there was nothing terrible about it, he assured himself, looking a second time, a third time at her face, her hands, for what was frightening or disgusting in her as she sat there in broad daylight, sewing? Mrs.

6. Prince Albert of Saxe-Coburg-Gotha (1819–1861), husband of Queen Victoria.

7. Port city on the river Hull, near the North Sea.

Peters had a spiteful tongue. Mr. Peters was in Hull. Why then rage and prophesy? Why fly scourged and outcast? Why be made to tremble and sob by the clouds? Why seek truths and deliver messages when Rezia sat sticking pins into the front of her dress, and Mr. Peters was in Hull? Miracles, revelations, agonies, loneliness, falling through the sea, down, down into the flames, all were burnt out, for he had a sense, as he watched Rezia trimming the straw hat for Mrs. Peters, of a coverlet of flowers.

"It's too small for Mrs. Peters," said Septimus.

For the first time for days he was speaking as he used to do! Of course it was—absurdly small, she said. But Mrs. Peters had chosen it.

He took it out of her hands. He said it was an organ grinder's monkey's hat.

How it rejoiced her that! Not for weeks had they laughed like this together, poking fun privately like married people. What she meant was that if Mrs. Filmer had come in, or Mrs. Peters or anybody they would not have understood what she and Septimus were laughing at.

"There," she said, pinning a rose to one side of the hat. Never had she felt so happy! Never in her life!

But that was still more ridiculous, Septimus said. Now the poor woman looked like a pig at a fair. (Nobody ever made her laugh as Septimus did.)

What had she got in her work-box? She had ribbons and beads, tassels, artificial flowers. She tumbled them out on the table. He began putting odd colours together—for though he had no fingers, could not even do up a parcel, he had a wonderful eye, and often he was right, sometimes absurd, of course, but sometimes wonderfully right.

"She shall have a beautiful hat!" he murmured, taking up this and that, Rezia kneeling by his side, looking over his shoulder. Now it was finished—that is to say the design; she must stitch it together. But she must be very, very careful, he said, to keep it just as he had made it.

So she sewed. When she sewed, he thought, she made a sound like a kettle on the hob;[8] bubbling, murmuring, always busy, her strong little pointed fingers pinching and poking; her needle flashing straight. The sun might go in and out, on the tassels, on the wallpaper, but he would wait, he thought, stretching out his feet, looking at his ringed sock at the end of the sofa; he would wait in this warm place, this pocket of still air, which one comes on at the edge of a wood sometimes in the evening, when, because of a fall in the ground, or some arrangement of the trees (one must be scientific above all, scientific), warmth lingers, and the air buffets the cheek like the wing of a bird.

"There it is," said Rezia, twirling Mrs. Peters' hat on the tips of her fingers. "That'll do for the moment. Later . . ." her sentence bubbled away drip, drip, drip, like a contented tap left running.

It was wonderful. Never had he done anything which made him feel so proud. It was so real, it was so substantial, Mrs. Peters' hat.

"Just look at it," he said.

Yes, it would always make her happy to see that hat. He had become himself then, he had laughed then. They had been alone together. Always she would like that hat.

He told her to try it on.

---

8. Shelf at the back or side of the fireplace.

"But I must look so queer!" she cried, running over to the glass and look-ing first this side then that. Then she snatched it off again, for there was a tap at the door. Could it be Sir William Bradshaw? Had he sent already?

No! it was only the small girl with the evening paper.

What always happened, then happened—what happened every night of their lives. The small girl sucked her thumb at the door; Rezia went down on her knees; Rezia cooed and kissed; Rezia got a bag of sweets out of the table drawer. For so it always happened. First one thing, then another. So she built it up, first one thing and then another. Dancing, skipping, round and round the room they went. He took the paper. Surrey was all out,[9] he read. There was a heat wave. Rezia repeated: Surrey was all out. There was a heat wave, making it part of the game she was playing with Mrs. Filmer's grandchild, both of them laughing, chattering at the same time, at their game. He was very tired. He was very happy. He would sleep. He shut his eyes. But directly he saw nothing the sounds of the game became fainter and stranger and sounded like the cries of people seeking and not finding, and passing further and further away. They had lost him!

He started up in terror. What did he see? The plate of bananas on the sideboard. Nobody was there (Rezia had taken the child to its mother. It was bedtime). That was it: to be alone forever. That was the doom pro-nounced in Milan when he came into the room and saw them cutting out buckram shapes with their scissors; to be alone forever.

He was alone with the sideboard and the bananas. He was alone, exposed on this bleak eminence, stretched out—but not on a hill-top; not on a crag; on Mrs. Filmer's sitting-room sofa. As for the visions, the faces, the voices of the dead, where were they? There was a screen in front of him, with black bulrushes and blue swallows. Where he had once seen mountains, where he had seen faces, where he had seen beauty, there was a screen.

"Evans!" he cried. There was no answer. A mouse had squeaked, or a curtain rustled. Those were the voices of the dead. The screen, the coal-scuttle, the sideboard remained to him. Let him then face the screen, the coal-scuttle and the sideboard . . . but Rezia burst into the room chattering.

Some letter had come. Everybody's plans were changed. Mrs. Filmer would not be able to go to Brighton[1] after all. There was no time to let Mrs. Williams know, and really Rezia thought it very, very annoying, when she caught sight of the hat and thought . . . perhaps . . . she . . . might just make a little. . . . Her voice died out in contented melody.

"Ah, damn!" she cried (it was a joke of theirs, her swearing), the needle had broken. Hat, child, Brighton, needle. She built it up; first one thing, then another, she built it up, sewing.

She wanted him to say whether by moving the rose she had improved the hat. She sat on the end of the sofa.

They were perfectly happy now, she said, suddenly, putting the hat down. For she could say anything to him now. She could say whatever came into her head. That was almost the first thing she had felt about him, that night in the café when he had come in with his English friends. He had come in, rather shyly, looking round him, and his hat had fallen when he hung it up. That she

9. Headline indicating that the Surrey cricket team has ended its first innings in a match.

1. Popular seaside resort town in Sussex.

could remember: She knew he was English, though not one of the large Englishmen her sister admired, for he was always thin; but he had a beautiful fresh colour; and with his big nose, his bright eyes, his way of sitting a little hunched made her think, she had often told him, of a young hawk, that first evening she saw him, when they were playing dominoes, and he had come in—of a young hawk; but with her he was always very gentle. She had never seen him wild or drunk, only suffering sometimes through this terrible war, but even so, when she came in, he would put it all away. Anything, anything in the whole world, any little bother with her work, anything that struck her to say she would tell him, and he understood at once. Her own family even were not the same. Being older than she was and being so clever—how serious he was, wanting her to read Shakespeare before she could even read a child's story in English!—being so much more experienced, he could help her. And she too could help him.

But this hat now. And then (it was getting late) Sir William Bradshaw.

She held her hands to her head, waiting for him to say did he like the hat or not, and as she sat there, waiting, looking down, he could feel her mind, like a bird, falling from branch to branch, and always alighting, quite rightly; he could follow her mind, as she sat there in one of those loose lax poses that came to her naturally and, if he should say anything, at once she smiled, like a bird alighting with all its claws firm upon the bough.

But he remembered Bradshaw said, "The people we are most fond of are not good for us when we are ill." Bradshaw said, he must be taught to rest. Bradshaw said they must be separated.

"Must," "must," why "must"? What power had Bradshaw over him? "What right has Bradshaw to say 'must' to me?" he demanded.

"It is because you talked of killing yourself," said Rezia. (Mercifully, she could now say anything to Septimus.)

So he was in their power! Holmes and Bradshaw were on him! The brute with the red nostrils was snuffing into every secret place! "Must" it could say! Where were his papers? the things he had written?

She brought him his papers, the things he had written, things she had written for him. She tumbled them out on to the sofa. They looked at them together. Diagrams, designs, little men and women brandishing sticks for arms, with wings—were they?—on their backs; circles traced round shillings and sixpences—the suns and stars; zigzagging precipices with mountaineers ascending roped together, exactly like knives and forks; sea pieces with little faces laughing out of what might perhaps be waves: the map of the world. Burn them! he cried. Now for his writings; how the dead sing behind rhododendron bushes; odes to Time; conversations with Shakespeare; Evans, Evans, Evans—his messages from the dead; do not cut down trees; tell the Prime Minister. Universal love: the meaning of the world. Burn them! he cried.

But Rezia laid her hands on them. Some were very beautiful, she thought. She would tie them up (for she had no envelope) with a piece of silk.

Even if they took him, she said, she would go with him. They could not separate them against their wills, she said.

Shuffling the edges straight, she did up the papers, and tied the parcel almost without looking, sitting beside him, he thought, as if all her petals were about her. She was a flowering tree; and through her branches looked out the face of a lawgiver, who had reached a sanctuary where she feared no one; not Holmes; not Bradshaw; a miracle, a triumph, the last and greatest. Staggering he saw her mount the appalling staircase, laden with Holmes and Bradshaw, men who never weighed less than eleven stone six, who sent their wives to Court, men who made ten thousand a year and talked of proportion; who different in their verdicts (for Holmes said one thing, Bradshaw another), yet judges they were; who mixed the vision and the sideboard; saw nothing clear, yet ruled, yet inflicted. "Must" they said. Over them she triumphed.

"There!" she said. The papers were tied up. No one should get at them. She would put them away.

And, she said, nothing should separate them. She sat down beside him and called him by the name of that hawk or crow which being malicious and a great destroyer of crops was precisely like him. No one could separate them, she said.

Then she got up to go into the bedroom to pack their things, but hearing voices downstairs and thinking that Dr. Holmes had perhaps called, ran down to prevent him coming up.

Septimus could hear her talking to Holmes on the staircase.

"My dear lady, I have come as a friend," Holmes was saying.

"No. I will not allow you to see my husband," she said.

He could see her, like a little hen, with her wings spread barring his passage. But Holmes persevered.

"My dear lady, allow me . . ." Holmes said, putting her aside (Holmes was a powerfully built man).

Holmes was coming upstairs. Holmes would burst open the door. Holmes would say "In a funk, eh?" Holmes would get him. But no; not Holmes; not Bradshaw. Getting up rather unsteadily, hopping indeed from foot to foot, he considered Mrs. Filmer's nice clean bread knife with "Bread" carved on the handle. Ah, but one mustn't spoil that. The gas fire? But it was too late now. Holmes was coming. Razors he might have got, but Rezia, who always did that sort of thing, had packed them. There remained only the window, the large Bloomsbury-lodging house window, the tiresome, the troublesome, and rather melodramatic business of opening the window and throwing himself out. It was their idea of tragedy, not his or Rezia's (for she was with him). Holmes and Bradshaw like that sort of thing. (He sat on the sill.) But he would wait till the very last moment. He did not want to die. Life was good. The sun hot. Only human beings—what did *they* want? Coming down the staircase opposite an old man stopped and stared at him. Holmes was at the door. "I'll give it you!" he cried, and flung himself vigorously, violently down on to Mrs. Filmer's area railings.

"The coward!" cried Dr. Holmes, bursting the door open. Rezia ran to the window, she saw; she understood. Dr. Holmes and Mrs. Filmer collided with each other. Mrs. Filmer flapped her apron and made her hide her eyes in the bedroom. There was a great deal of running up and down stairs. Dr. Holmes came in—white as a sheet, shaking all over, with a glass in his hand. She must be brave and drink something, he said (What was it? Something sweet), for her husband was horribly mangled, would not recover consciousness, she must not see him, must be spared as much as possible, would have the inquest to go through, poor young woman. Who could have foretold it? A sudden impulse, no one was in the least to blame (he told Mrs. Filmer). And why the devil he did it, Dr. Holmes could not conceive.

It seemed to her as she drank the sweet stuff that she was opening long windows, stepping out into some garden. But where? The clock was striking—one, two, three: how sensible the sound was; compared with all this thumping and whispering; like Septimus himself. She was falling asleep. But the clock went on striking, four, five, six and Mrs. Filmer waving her apron (they wouldn't bring the body in here, would they?) seemed part of that garden; or a flag. She had once seen a flag slowly rippling out from a mast when she stayed with her aunt at Venice. Men killed in battle were thus saluted, and Septimus had been through the War. Of her memories, most were happy.

She put on her hat, and ran through cornfields—where could it have been?—on to some hill, somewhere near the sea, for there were ships, gulls, butterflies, they sat on a cliff. In London too, there they sat, and, half dreaming, came to her through the bedroom door, rain falling, whisperings, stirrings among dry corn, the caress of the sea, as it seemed to her, hollowing them in its arched shell and murmuring to her laid on shore, strewn she felt, like flying flowers over some tomb.

"He is dead," she said, smiling at the poor old woman who guarded her with her honest light-blue eyes fixed on the door. (They wouldn't bring him in here, would they?) But Mrs. Filmer pooh-poohed. Oh no, oh no! They were carrying him away now. Ought she not to be told? Married people ought to be together, Mrs. Filmer thought. But they must do as the doctor said.

"Let her sleep," said Dr. Holmes, feeling her pulse. She saw the large outline of his body standing dark against the window. So that was Dr. Holmes.

One of the triumphs of civilisation, Peter Walsh thought. It is one of the triumphs of civilisation, as the light high bell of the ambulance sounded. Swiftly, cleanly the ambulance sped to the hospital, having picked up instantly, humanely, some poor devil; some one hit on the head, struck down by disease, knocked over perhaps a minute or so ago at one of these crossings, as might happen to oneself. That was civilisation. It struck him coming back from the East—the efficiency, the organisation, the communal spirit of London. Every cart or carriage of its own accord drew aside to let the ambulance pass. Perhaps it was morbid; or was it not touching rather, the respect which they showed this ambulance with its victim inside—busy men hurrying home yet instantly bethinking them as it passed of some wife; or presumably how easily it might have been them there, stretched on a shelf with a doctor and a nurse. . . . Ah, but thinking became morbid, sentimental, directly one began conjuring up doctors, dead bodies; a little glow of pleasure, a sort of lust too over the visual impression warned one not to go on with that sort of thing any more—fatal to art, fatal to friendship. True. And yet, thought Peter Walsh, as the ambulance turned the corner though the light high bell could be heard down the next street and still farther as it crossed the Tottenham Court Road, chiming constantly, it is the privilege of loneliness; in privacy one may do as one chooses. One might weep if no one saw. It had been his undoing—this susceptibility—in Anglo-Indian society; not weeping at the right time, or laughing either. I have that in me, he thought standing by the pillar-box, which could now dissolve in tears. Why, Heaven knows. Beauty of some sort probably, and the weight of the day, which beginning with that visit to Clarissa had exhausted him with its heat, its intensity, and the drip, drip, of one impression after another down into that cellar where they stood, deep, dark, and no one would ever know.

Partly for that reason, its secrecy, complete and inviolable, he had found life like an unknown garden, full of turns and corners, surprising, yes; really it took one's breath away, these moments; there coming to him by the pillar-box opposite the British Museum[2] one of them, a moment, in which things came together; this ambulance; and life and death. It was as if he were sucked up to some very high roof by that rush of emotion and the rest of him, like a white shell-sprinkled beach, left bare. It had been his undoing in Anglo-Indian society—this susceptibility.

Clarissa once, going on top of an omnibus with him somewhere, Clarissa superficially at least, so easily moved, now in despair, now in the best of spirits, all aquiver in those days and such good company, spotting queer little scenes, names, people from the top of a bus, for they used to explore London and bring back bags full of treasures from the Caledonian market[3]— Clarissa had a theory in those days—they had heaps of theories, always theories, as young people have. It was to explain the feeling they had of dissatisfaction; not knowing people; not being known. For how could they know each other? You met every day, then not for six months, or years. It was unsatisfactory, they agreed, how little one knew people. But she said, sitting on the bus going up Shaftesbury Avenue, she felt herself everywhere; not "here, here, here"; and she tapped the back of the seat; but everywhere. She waved her hand, going up Shaftesbury Avenue.[4] She was all that. So that to know her, or any one, one must seek out the people who completed them; even the places. Odd affinities she had with people she had never spoken to, some woman in the street, some man behind a counter—even trees, or barns. It ended in a transcendental theory which, with her horror of death, allowed her to believe, or say that she believed (for all her scepticism), that since our apparitions, the part of us which appears, are so momentary compared with the other, the unseen part of us, which spreads wide, the unseen might survive, be recovered somehow attached to this person or that, or even haunting certain places after death . . . perhaps—perhaps.

Looking back over that long friendship of almost thirty years her theory worked to this extent. Brief, broken, often painful as their actual meetings had been what with his absences and interruptions (this morning, for instance, in came Elizabeth, like a long-legged colt, handsome, dumb, just as he was beginning to talk to Clarissa) the effect of them on his life was immeasurable. There was a mystery about it. You were given a sharp, acute, uncomfortable grain—the actual meeting; horribly painful as often as not; yet in absence, in the most unlikely places, it would flower out, open, shed its scent, let you touch, taste, look about you, get the whole feel of it and understanding, after years of lying lost. Thus she had come to him; on board ship; in the Himalayas; suggested by the oddest things (so Sally Seton, generous, enthusiastic goose! thought of *him* when she saw blue hydrangeas). She had influenced him more than any person he had ever known. And always in this way coming before him without his wishing it, cool, lady-like, critical; or ravishing, romantic, recalling some field or English harvest. He saw her most often in the country, not in London. One scene after another at Bourton. . . .

He had reached his hotel. He crossed the hall, with its mounds of reddish chairs and sofas, its spike-leaved, withered-looking plants. He got his key off the hook. The young lady handed him some letters. He went upstairs—he saw her most often at Bourton, in the late summer, when he stayed there for a week, or fortnight even, as people did in those days. First on top of some hill there she would stand, hands clapped to her hair, her cloak blowing out, pointing, crying to them—she saw the Severn[5] beneath. Or in a wood, making the kettle boil—very ineffective with her fingers; the smoke curtseying, blowing in their faces; her little pink face showing through; begging water from an old woman in a cottage, who came to the door to watch them go. They walked always; the others drove. She was bored driving, disliked all animals, except that dog. They tramped miles along roads. She would break off to get her bearings, pilot him back across country; and all the time they argued, discussed poetry, discussed people, discussed politics (she was a Radical then); never noticing a thing except when she stopped, cried out at a view or a tree, and made him look with her; and so on again, through stubble fields, she walking ahead, with a flower for her aunt, never tired of walking for all her delicacy; to drop down on Bourton in the dusk. Then, after dinner, old Breitkopf would open the piano and sing without any voice, and they would lie sunk in arm-chairs, trying not to laugh, but always breaking down and laughing, laughing—laughing at nothing. Breitkopf was supposed not to see. And then in the morning, flirting up and down like a wagtail[6] in front of the house. . . .

Oh it was a letter from her! This blue envelope; that was her hand. And he would have to read it. Here was another of those meetings, bound to be painful! To read her letter needed the devil of an effort. "How heavenly it was to see him. She must tell him that." That was all.

But it upset him. It annoyed him. He wished she hadn't written it. Coming on top of his thoughts, it was like a nudge in the ribs. Why couldn't she let him be? After all, she had married Dalloway, and lived with him in perfect happiness all these years.

These hotels are not consoling places. Far from it. Any number of people had hung up their hats on those pegs. Even the flies, if you thought of it, had settled on other people's noses. As for the cleanliness which hit him in the face, it wasn't cleanliness, so much as bareness, frigidity; a thing that had to be. Some arid matron made her rounds at dawn sniffing, peering, causing blue-nosed[7] maids to scour, for all the world as if the next visitor were a joint of meat to be served on a perfectly clean platter. For sleep, one bed; for sitting in, one arm-chair; for cleaning one's teeth and shaving one's chin, one tumbler, one looking-glass. Books, letters, dressing-gown, slipped about on the impersonality of the horsehair like incongruous impertinences. And it was Clarissa's letter that made him see all this. "Heavenly to see you. She must say so!" He folded the paper; pushed it away; nothing would induce him to read it again!

To get that letter[8] to him by six o'clock she must have sat down and written it directly he left her; stamped it; sent somebody to the post. It was, as people

---

5. The river Severn, in Gloucestershire.
6. Small bird with a characteristic tail-wagging motion.
7. Puritanical or prudish.

8. Multiple daily mail deliveries in the 1920s ensure that Clarissa could write a letter and Peter could receive it on the same day.

say, very like her. She was upset by his visit. She had felt a great deal; had for a moment, when she kissed his hand, regretted, envied him even, remembered possibly (for he saw her look it) something he had said—how they would change the world if she married him perhaps; whereas, it was this; it was middle age; it was mediocrity; then forced herself with her indomitable vitality to put all that aside, there being in her a thread of life which for toughness, endurance, power to overcome obstacles, and carry her triumphantly through he had never known the like of. Yes; but there would come a reaction directly he left the room. She would be frightfully sorry for him; she would think what in the world she could do to give him pleasure (short always of the one thing) and he could see her with the tears running down her cheeks going to her writing-table and dashing off that one line which he was to find greeting him. . . . "Heavenly to see you!" And she meant it.

Peter Walsh had now unlaced his boots.

But it would not have been a success, their marriage. The other thing, after all, came so much more naturally.

It was odd; it was true; lots of people felt it. Peter Walsh, who had done just respectably, filled the usual posts adequately, was liked, but thought a little cranky, gave himself airs—it was odd that *he* should have had, especially now that his hair was grey, a contented look; a look of having reserves. It was this that made him attractive to women who liked the sense that he was not altogether manly. There was something unusual about him, or something behind him. It might be that he was bookish—never came to see you without taking up the book on the table (he was now reading, with his bootlaces trailing on the floor); or that he was a gentleman, which showed itself in the way he knocked the ashes out of his pipe, and in his manners of course to women. For it was very charming and quite ridiculous how easily some girl without a grain of sense could twist him round her finger. But at her own risk. That is to say, though he might be ever so easy, and indeed with his gaiety and good-breeding fascinating to be with, it was only up to a point. She said something—no, no; he saw through that. He wouldn't stand that—no, no. Then he could shout and rock and hold his sides together over some joke with men. He was the best judge of cooking in India. He was a man. But not the sort of man one had to respect—which was a mercy; not like Major Simmons, for instance; not in the least like that, Daisy thought, when, in spite of her two small children, she used to compare them.

He pulled off his boots. He emptied his pockets. Out came with his pocket-knife a snapshot of Daisy on the verandah; Daisy all in white, with a fox-terrier on her knee; very charming, very dark; the best he had ever seen of her. It did come, after all so naturally; so much more naturally than Clarissa. No fuss. No bother. No finicking and fidgeting. All plain sailing. And the dark, adorably pretty girl on the verandah exclaimed (he could hear her). Of course, of course she would give him everything! she cried (she had no sense of discretion) everything he wanted! she cried, running to meet him, whoever might be looking. And she was only twenty-four. And she had two children. Well, well!

Well indeed he had got himself into a mess at his age. And it came over him when he woke in the night pretty forcibly. Suppose they did marry? For him it would be all very well, but what about her? Mrs. Burgess, a good sort and no chatterbox, in whom he had confided, thought this absence of his in England, ostensibly to see lawyers might serve to make Daisy reconsider, think what it meant. It was a question of her position, Mrs. Burgess said; the social barrier; giving up her children. She'd be a widow with a past one of these days, draggling about in the suburbs, or more likely, indiscriminate (you know, she said, what such women get like, with too much paint). But Peter Walsh pooh-poohed all that. He didn't mean to die yet. Anyhow she must settle for herself; judge for herself, he thought, padding about the room in his socks, smoothing out his dress-shirt, for he might go to Clarissa's party, or he might go to one of the Halls, or he might settle in and read an absorbing book written by a man he used to know at Oxford. And if he did retire, that's what he'd do—write books. He would go to Oxford and poke about in the Bodleian.[9] Vainly the dark, adorably pretty girl ran to the end of the terrace; vainly waved her hand; vainly cried she didn't care a straw what people said. There he was, the man she thought the world of, the perfect gentleman, the fascinating, the distinguished (and his age made not the least difference to her), padding about a room in an hotel in Blooms-bury, shaving, washing, continuing, as he took up cans, put down razors, to poke about in the Bodleian, and get at the truth about one or two little matters that interested him. And he would have a chat with whoever it might be, and so come to disregard more and more precise hours for lunch, and miss engagements, and when Daisy asked him, as she would, for a kiss, a scene, fail to come up to the scratch[1] (though he was genuinely devoted to her)—in short it might be happier, as Mrs. Burgess said, that she should forget him, or merely remember him as he was in August 1922, like a figure standing at the cross roads at dusk, which grows more and more remote as the dog-cart[2] spins away, carrying her securely fastened to the back seat, though her arms are outstretched, and as she sees the figure dwindle and disappear still she cries out how she would do anything in the world, any-thing, anything, anything. . . .

He never knew what people thought. It became more and more difficult for him to concentrate. He become absorbed; he became busied with his own concerns; now surly, now gay; dependent on women, absent-minded, moody, less and less able (so he thought as he shaved) to understand why Clarissa couldn't simply find them a lodging and be nice to Daisy; introduce her. And then he could just—just do what? just haunt and hover (he was at the moment actually engaged in sorting out various keys, papers), swoop and taste, be alone, in short, sufficient to himself; and yet nobody of course was more dependent upon others (he buttoned his waistcoat); it had been his undoing. He could not keep out of smoking-rooms, liked colonels, liked golf, liked bridge, and above all women's society, and the fineness of their companionship, and their faithfulness and audacity and greatness in loving which though it had its drawbacks seemed to him (and the dark, adorably pretty face was on top of the envelopes) so wholly admirable, so splendid a flower to grow on the crest of human life, and yet he could not come up to the scratch, being always apt to see round things (Clarissa had sapped something in him permanently), and to tire very easily of mute devotion and to want variety in love, though it would make him furious if Daisy loved anybody else, furious! for he was jealous, uncontrollably jealous by tem-

9. Rare-books library at Oxford University.
1. To meet the required standard.
2. An open carriage with two back-to-back seats, one facing forward for the driver and another facing towards the rear for the passenger.

perament. He suffered tortures! But where was his knife; his watch; his seals, his notecase, and Clarissa's letter which he would not read again but liked to think of, and Daisy's photograph? And now for dinner.

They were eating.

Sitting at little tables round vases, dressed or not dressed, with their shawls and bags laid beside them, with their air of false composure, for they were not used to so many courses at dinner, and confidence, for they were able to pay for it, and strain, for they had been running about London all day shopping, sightseeing; and their natural curiosity, for they looked round and up as the nice-looking gentleman in horn-rimmed spectacles came in, and their good nature, for they would have been glad to do any little service, such as lend a time-table or impart useful information, and their desire, pulsing in them, tugging at them subterraneously, somehow to establish connections if it were only a birthplace (Liverpool,[3] for example) in common or friends of the same name; with their furtive glances, odd silences, and sudden withdrawals into family jocularity and isolation; there they sat eating dinner when Mr. Walsh came in and took his seat at a little table by the curtain.

It was not that he said anything, for being solitary he could only address himself to the waiter; it was his way of looking at the menu, of pointing his forefinger to a particular wine, of hitching himself up to the table, of addressing himself seriously, not gluttonously to dinner, that won him their respect; which, having to remain unexpressed for the greater part of the meal, flared up at the table where the Morrises sat when Mr. Walsh was heard to say at the end of the meal, "Bartlett pears." Why he should have spoken so moderately yet firmly, with the air of a disciplinarian well within his rights which are founded upon justice, neither young Charles Morris, nor old Charles, neither Miss Elaine nor Mrs. Morris knew. But when he said, "Bartlett pears," sitting alone at his table, they felt that he counted on their support in some lawful demand; was champion of a cause which immediately became their own, so that their eyes met his eyes sympathetically, and when they all reached the smoking-room simultaneously, a little talk between them became inevitable.

It was not very profound—only to the effect that London was crowded; had changed in thirty years; that Mr. Morris preferred Liverpool; that Mrs. Morris had been to the Westminster flower-show, and that they had all seen the Prince of Wales. Yet, thought Peter Walsh, no family in the world can compare with the Morrises; none whatever; and their relations to each other are perfect, and they don't care a hang for the upper classes, and they like what they like, and Elaine is training for the family business, and the boy has won a scholarship at Leeds, and the old lady (who is about his own age) has three more children at home; and they have two motor cars, but Mr. Morris still mends the boots on Sunday: it is superb, it is absolutely superb, thought Peter Walsh, swaying a little backwards and forwards with his liqueur glass in his hand among the hairy red chairs and ashtrays, feeling very well pleased with himself, for the Morrises liked him. Yes, they liked a man who said, "Bartlett pears." They liked him, he felt.

He would go to Clarissa's party. (The Morrises moved off; but they would meet again.) He would go to Clarissa's party, because he wanted to ask Rich-

3. Major port city in northwest England, on the Irish Sea.

ard what they were doing in India—the conservative duffers.[4] And what's being acted? And music. . . . Oh yes, and mere gossip.

For this is the truth about our soul, he thought, our self, who fish-like inhabits deep seas and plies among obscurities threading her way between the boles of giant weeds, over sun-flickered spaces and on and on into gloom, cold, deep, inscrutable; suddenly she shoots to the surface and sports on the wind-wrinkled waves; that is, has a positive need to brush, scrape, kindle herself, gossiping. What did the Government mean—Richard Dalloway would know—to do about India?

Since it was a very hot night and the paper boys went by with placards proclaiming in huge red letters that there was a heat-wave, wicker chairs were placed on the hotel steps and there, sipping, smoking, detached gentlemen sat. Peter Walsh sat there. One might fancy that day, the London day, was just beginning. Like a woman who had slipped off her print dress and white apron to array herself in blue and pearls, the day changed, put off stuff, took gauze, changed to evening, and with the same sigh of exhilaration that a woman breathes, tumbling petticoats on the floor, it too shed dust, heat, colour; the traffic thinned; motor cars, tinkling, darting, succeeded the lumber of vans; and here and there among the thick foliage of the squares an intense light hung. I resign, the evening seemed to say, as it paled and faded above the battlements and prominences, moulded, pointed, of hotel, flat, and block of shops, I fade, she was beginning, I disappear, but London would have none of it, and rushed her bayonets into the sky, pinioned her, constrained her to partnership in her revelry.

For the great revolution of Mr. Willett's summer time had taken place since Peter Walsh's last visit to England. The prolonged evening was new to him. It was inspiriting, rather. For as the young people went by with their despatch-boxes,[5] awfully glad to be free, proud too, dumbly, of stepping this famous pavement, joy of a kind, cheap, tinselly, if you like, but all the same rapture, flushed their faces. They dressed well too; pink stockings; pretty shoes. They would now have two hours at the pictures. It sharpened, it refined them, the yellow-blue evening light; and on the leaves in the square shone lurid, livid—they looked as if dipped in sea water—the foliage of a submerged city. He was astonished by the beauty; it was encouraging too, for where the returned Anglo-Indian sat by rights (he knew crowds of them) in the Oriental Club[6] biliously summing up the ruin of the world, here was he, as young as ever; envying young people their summer time[7] and the rest of it, and more than suspecting from the words of a girl, from a housemaid's laughter—intangible things you couldn't lay your hands on—that shift in the whole pyramidal accumulation which in his youth had seemed immovable. On top of them it had pressed; weighed them down, the women especially, like those flowers Clarissa's Aunt Helena used to press between sheets of grey blotting-paper with Littré's dictionary[8] on top, sitting under the lamp after dinner. She was dead now. He had heard of her, from Clarissa, losing the sight of one eye. It seemed so fitting—one of nature's masterpieces—

4. Incompetent people, or fools.
5. Boxes for carrying important messages requiring quick delivery.
6. Gentlemen's club for members of the East India Company.

7. Daylight Savings Time, introduced in Britain in 1916.
8. Four-volume French dictionary by Émile Littré (1801–1881).

that old Miss Parry should turn to glass. She would die like some bird in a frost gripping her perch. She belonged to a different age, but being so entire, so complete, would always stand up on the horizon, stone-white, eminent, like a lighthouse marking some past stage on this adventurous, long, long voyage, this interminable (he felt for a copper[9] to buy a paper and read about Surrey and Yorkshire—he had held out that copper millions of times. Surrey was all out once more)—this interminable life. But cricket was no mere game. Cricket was important. He could never help reading about cricket. He read the scores in the stop press first, then how it was a hot day; then about a murder case. Having done things millions of times enriched them, though it might be said to take the surface off. The past enriched, and experience, and having cared for one or two people, and so having acquired the power which the young lack, of cutting short, doing what one likes, not caring a rap what people say and coming and going without any very great expectations (he left his paper on the table and moved off), which however (and he looked for his hat and coat) was not altogether true of him, not to-night, for here he was starting to go to a party, at his age, with the belief upon him that he was about to have an experience. But what?

Beauty anyhow. Not the crude beauty of the eye. It was not beauty pure and simple—Bedford Place leading into Russell Square.[1] It was straightness and emptiness of course; the symmetry of a corridor; but it was also windows lit up, a piano, a gramophone sounding; a sense of pleasure-making hidden, but now and again emerging when, through the uncurtained window, the window left open, one saw parties sitting over tables, young people slowly circling, conversations between men and women, maids idly looking out (a strange comment theirs, when work was done), stockings drying on top ledges, a parrot, a few plants. Absorbing, mysterious, of infinite richness, this life. And in the large square where the cabs shot and swerved so quick, there were loitering couples, dallying, embracing, shrunk up under the shower of a tree; that was moving; so silent, so absorbed, that one passed, discreetly, timidly, as if in the presence of some sacred ceremony to interrupt which would have been impious. That was interesting. And so on into the flare and glare.

His light overcoat blew open, he stepped with indescribable idiosyncrasy, leant a little forward, tripped, with his hands behind his back and his eyes still a little hawklike; he tripped through London, towards Westminster, observing.

Was everybody dining out, then? Doors were being opened here by a footman to let issue a high-stepping old dame, in buckled shoes, with three purple ostrich feathers in her hair. Doors were being opened for ladies wrapped like mummies in shawls with bright flowers on them, ladies with bare heads. And in respectable quarters with stucco pillars through small front gardens lightly swathed with combs in their hair (having run up to see the children), women came; men waited for them, with their coats blowing open, and the motor started. Everybody was going out. What with these doors being opened, and the descent and the start, it seemed as if the whole of London were embarking in little boats moored to the bank, tossing on the waters, as if the whole place were floating off in carnival. And Whitehall was skated over,

9. Penny or halfpenny.   1. In Bloomsbury.

silver beaten as it was, skated over by spiders, and there was a sense of midges[2] round the arc lamps; it was so hot that people stood about talking. And here in Westminster was a retired Judge, presumably, sitting four square at his house door dressed all in white. An Anglo-Indian presumably.

And here a shindy[3] of brawling women, drunken women; here only a policeman and looming houses, high houses, domed houses, churches, parliaments, and the hoot of a steamer on the river, a hollow misty cry. But it was her street, this, Clarissa's; cabs were rushing round the corner, like water round the piers of a bridge, drawn together, it seemed to him because they bore people going to her party, Clarissa's party.

The cold stream of visual impressions failed him now as if the eye were a cup that overflowed and let the rest run down its china walls unrecorded. The brain must wake now. The body must contract now, entering the house, the lighted house, where the door stood open, where the motor cars were standing, and bright women descending: the soul must brave itself to endure. He opened the big blade of his pocket-knife.

Lucy came running full tilt downstairs, having just nipped in to the drawing-room to smooth a cover, to straighten a chair, to pause a moment and feel whoever came in must think how clean, how bright, how beautifully cared for, when they saw the beautiful silver, the brass fire-irons, the new chair-covers, and the curtains of yellow chintz: she appraised each; heard a roar of voices; people already coming up from dinner; she must fly!

The Prime Minister[4] was coming, Agnes said: so she had heard them say in the dining-room, she said, coming in with a tray of glasses. Did it matter, did it matter in the least, one Prime Minister more or less? It made no difference at this hour of the night to Mrs. Walker among the plates, saucepans, cullenders, frying-pans, chicken in aspic,[5] ice-cream freezers, pared crusts of bread, lemons, soup tureens, and pudding basins which, however hard they washed up in the scullery seemed to be all on top of her, on the kitchen table, on chairs, while the fire blared and roared, the electric lights glared, and still supper had to be laid. All she felt was, one Prime Minister more or less made not a scrap of difference to Mrs. Walker.

The ladies were going upstairs already, said Lucy; the ladies were going up, one by one, Mrs. Dalloway walking last and almost always sending back some message to the kitchen, "My love to Mrs. Walker," that was it one night. Next morning they would go over the dishes—the soup, the salmon; the salmon, Mrs. Walker knew, as usual underdone, for she always got nervous about the pudding and left it to Jenny; so it happened, the salmon was always underdone. But some lady with fair hair and silver ornaments had said, Lucy said, about the entrée, was it really made at home? But it was the salmon that bothered Mrs. Walker, as she spun the plates round and round, and pulled in dampers and pulled out dampers;[6] and there came a burst of laughter from the dining-room; a voice speaking; then another burst of laughter—the gentlemen enjoying themselves when the ladies had gone. The tokay, said Lucy running in. Mr. Dalloway had sent for the tokay, from the Emperor's cellars, the Imperial Tokay.[7]

2. Gnatlike insects.
3. Commotion.
4. Stanley Baldwin (1867–1947) was prime minister in 1923.

5. Meat-flavored jelly. "Cullenders": colanders.
6. Metal plates in chimneys that regulate air flow and thus control the intensity of the fire.
7. Sweet Hungarian wine.

It was borne through the kitchen. Over her shoulder Lucy reported how Miss Elizabeth looked quite lovely; she couldn't take her eyes off her; in her pink dress, wearing the necklace Mr. Dalloway had given her. Jenny must remember the dog, Miss Elizabeth's fox-terrier, which, since it bit, had to be shut up and might, Elizabeth thought, want something. Jenny must remember the dog. But Jenny was not going upstairs with all those people about. There was a motor at the door already! There was a ring at the bell—and the gentlemen still in the dining-room, drinking tokay!

There, they were going upstairs; that was the first to come, and now they would come faster and faster, so that Mrs. Parkinson (hired for parties) would leave the hall door ajar, and the hall would be full of gentlemen waiting (they stood waiting, sleeking down their hair) while the ladies took their cloaks off in the room along the passage; where Mrs. Barnet helped them, old Ellen Barnet, who had been with the family for forty years, and came every summer to help the ladies, and remembered mothers when they were girls, and though very unassuming did shake hands; said "milady" very respectfully, yet had a humorous way with her, looking at the young ladies, and ever so tactfully helping Lady Lovejoy, who had some trouble with her underbodice. And they could not help feeling, Lady Lovejoy and Miss Alice, that some little privilege in the matter of brush and comb, was awarded them having known Mrs. Barnet—"thirty years, milady," Mrs. Barnet supplied her. Young ladies did not use to rouge, said Lady Lovejoy, when they stayed at Bourton in the old days. And Miss Alice didn't need rouge, said Mrs. Barnet, looking at her fondly. There Mrs. Barnet would sit, in the cloakroom, patting down the furs, smoothing out the Spanish shawls, tidying the dressing-table, and knowing perfectly well, in spite of the furs and the embroideries, which were nice ladies, which were not. The dear old body, said Lady Lovejoy, mounting the stairs, Clarissa's old nurse.

And then Lady Lovejoy stiffened. "Lady and Miss Lovejoy," she said to Mr. Wilkins (hired for parties). He had an admirable manner, as he bent and straightened himself, bent and straightened himself and announced with perfect impartiality "Lady and Miss Lovejoy . . . Sir John and Lady Needham . . . Miss Weld . . . Mr. Walsh." His manner was admirable; his family life must be irreproachable, except that it seemed impossible that a being with greenish lips and shaven cheeks could ever have blundered into the nuisance of children.

"How delightful to see you!" said Clarissa. She said it to every one. How delightful to see you! She was at her worst—effusive, insincere. It was a great mistake to have come. He should have stayed at home and read his book, thought Peter Walsh; should have gone to a music hall; he should have stayed at home, for he knew no one.

Oh dear, it was going to be a failure; a complete failure, Clarissa felt it in her bones as dear old Lord Lexham stood there apologising for his wife who had caught cold at the Buckingham Palace garden party. She could see Peter out of the tail of her eye, criticising her, there, in that corner. Why, after all, did she do these things? Why seek pinnacles and stand drenched in fire? Might it consume her anyhow! Burn her to cinders! Better anything, better brandish one's torch and hurl it to earth than taper and dwindle away like some Ellie Henderson! It was extraordinary how Peter put her into these states just by coming and standing in a corner. He made her see herself; exaggerate. It was idiotic. But why did he come, then, merely to criticise?

Why always take, never give? Why not risk one's one little point of view? There he was wandering off, and she must speak to him. But she would not get the chance. Life was that—humiliation, renunciation. What Lord Lexham was saying was that his wife would not wear her furs at the garden party because "my dear, you ladies are all alike"—Lady Lexham being seventy-five at least! It was delicious, how they petted each other, that old couple. She did like old Lord Lexham. She did think it mattered, her party, and it made her feel quite sick to know that it was all going wrong, all falling flat. Anything, any explosion, any horror was better than people wandering aimlessly, standing in a bunch at a corner like Ellie Henderson, not even caring to hold themselves upright.

Gently the yellow curtain with all the birds of Paradise[8] blew out and it seemed as if there were a flight of wings into the room, right out, then sucked back. (For the windows were open.) Was it draughty, Ellie Henderson wondered? She was subject to chills. But it did not matter that she should come down sneezing tomorrow; it was the girls with their naked shoulders she thought of, being trained to think of others by an old father, an invalid, late vicar of Bourton, but he was dead now; and her chills never went to her chest, never. It was the girls she thought of, the young girls with their bare shoulders, she herself having always been a wisp of a creature, with her thin hair and meagre profile; though now, past fifty, there was beginning to shine through some mild beam, something purified into distinction by years of self-abnegation but obscured again, perpetually, by her distressing gentility, her panic fear, which arose from three hundred pounds' income, and her weaponless state (she could not earn a penny) and it made her timid, and more and more disqualified year by year to meet well-dressed people who did this sort of thing every night of the season, merely telling their maids "I'll wear so and so," whereas Ellie Henderson ran out nervously and bought cheap pink flowers, half a dozen, and then threw a shawl over her old black dress. For her invitation to Clarissa's party had come at the last moment. She was not quite happy about it. She had a sort of feeling that Clarissa had not meant to ask her this year.

Why should she? There was no reason really, except that they had always known each other. Indeed, they were cousins. But naturally they had rather drifted apart, Clarissa being so sought after. It was an event to her, going to a party. It was quite a treat just to see the lovely clothes. Wasn't that Elizabeth, grown up, with her hair done in the fashionable way, in the pink dress? Yet she could not be more than seventeen. She was very, very handsome. But girls when they first came out didn't seem to wear white as they used. (She must remember everything to tell Edith.) Girls wore straight frocks, perfectly tight, with skirts well above the ankles. It was not becoming, she thought.

So, with her weak eyesight, Ellie Henderson craned rather forward, and it wasn't so much she who minded not having any one to talk to (she hardly knew anybody there), for she felt that they were all such interesting people to watch; politicians presumably; Richard Dalloway's friends; but it was Richard himself who felt that he could not let the poor creature go on standing there all the evening by herself.

8. Birds native to New Guinea, notable for the beautiful plumage of the males.

"Well, Ellie, and how's the world treating *you*?" he said in his genial way, and Ellie Henderson, getting nervous and flushing and feeling that it was extraordinarily nice of him to come and talk to her, said that many people really felt the heat more than the cold.

"Yes, they do," said Richard Dalloway. "Yes."

But what more did one say?

"Hullo, Richard," said somebody, taking him by the elbow, and, good Lord, there was old Peter, old Peter Walsh. He was delighted to see him—ever so pleased to see him! He hadn't changed a bit. And off they went together walking right across the room, giving each other little pats, as if they hadn't met for a long time, Ellie Henderson thought, watching them go, certain she knew that man's face. A tall man, middle aged, rather fine eyes, dark, wearing spectacles, with a look of John Burrows. Edith would be sure to know.

The curtain with its flight of birds of Paradise blew out again. And Clarissa saw—she saw Ralph Lyon beat it back, and go on talking. So it wasn't a failure after all! it was going to be all right now—her party. It had begun. It had started. But it was still touch and go. She must stand there for the present. People seemed to come in a rush.

Colonel and Mrs. Garrod . . . Mr. Hugh Whitbread . . . Mr. Bowley . . . Mrs. Hilbery . . . Lady Mary Maddox . . . Mr. Quin . . . intoned Wilkin. She had six or seven words with each, and they went on, they went into the rooms; into something now, not nothing, since Ralph Lyon had beat back the curtain.

And yet for her own part, it was too much of an effort. She was not enjoying it. It was too much like being—just anybody, standing there; anybody could do it, yet this anybody she did a little admire, couldn't help feeling that she had, anyhow, made this happen, that it marked a stage, this post that she felt herself to have become, for oddly enough she had quite forgotten what she looked like, but felt herself a stake driven in at the top of her stairs. Every time she gave a party she had this feeling of being something not herself, and that every one was unreal in one way; much more real in another. It was, she thought, partly their clothes, partly being taken out of their ordinary ways, partly the background, it was possible to say things you couldn't say anyhow else, things that needed an effort; possible to go much deeper. But not for her; not yet anyhow.

"How delightful to see you!" she said. Dear old Sir Harry! He would know every one.

And what was so odd about it was the sense one had as they came up the stairs one after another, Mrs. Mount and Celia, Herbert Ainsty, Mrs. Dakers—oh and Lady Bruton!

"How awfully good of you to come!" she said, and she meant it—it was odd how standing there one felt them going on, going on, some quite old, some . . .

What name? Lady Rosseter? But who on earth was Lady Rosseter?

"Clarissa!" That voice! It was Sally Seton! Sally Seton! after all these years! She loomed through a mist. For she hadn't looked like *that*, Sally Seton, when Clarissa grasped the hot water can, to think of her under this roof, under this roof! Not like that!

All on top of each other, embarrassed, laughing, words tumbled out—passing through London; heard from Clara Haydon; what a chance of seeing you! So I thrust myself in—without an invitation. . . .

One might put down the hot water can quite composedly. The lustre had gone out of her. Yet it was extraordinary to see her again, older, happier, less lovely. They kissed each other, first this cheek then that, by the drawing-room door, and Clarissa turned, with Sally's hand in hers, and saw her rooms full, heard the roar of voices, saw the candlesticks, the blowing curtains, and the roses which Richard had given her.

"I have five enormous boys," said Sally.

She had the simplest egotism, the most open desire to be thought first always, and Clarissa loved her for being still like that. "I can't believe it!" she cried, kindling all over with pleasure at the thought of the past.

But alas, Wilkins; Wilkins wanted her; Wilkins was emitting in a voice of commanding authority as if the whole company must be admonished and the hostess reclaimed from frivolity, one name:

"The Prime Minister," said Peter Walsh.

The Prime Minister? Was it really? Ellie Henderson marvelled. What a thing to tell Edith!

One couldn't laugh at him. He looked so ordinary. You might have stood him behind a counter and bought biscuits[9]—poor chap, all rigged up in gold lace. And to be fair, as he went his rounds, first with Clarissa then with Richard escorting him, he did it very well. He tried to look somebody. It was amusing to watch. Nobody looked at him. They just went on talking, yet it was perfectly plain that they all knew, felt to the marrow of their bones, this majesty passing; this symbol of what they all stood for, English society. Old Lady Bruton, and she looked very fine too, very stalwart in her lace, swam up, and they withdrew into a little room which at once became spied upon, guarded, and a sort of stir and rustle rippled through every one, openly: the Prime Minister!

Lord, lord, the snobbery of the English! thought Peter Walsh, standing in the corner. How they loved dressing up in gold lace and doing homage! There! That must be, by Jove it was, Hugh Whitbread, snuffing round the precincts of the great, grown rather fatter, rather whiter, the admirable Hugh!

He looked always as if he were on duty, thought Peter, a privileged, but secretive being, hoarding secrets which he would die to defend, though it was only some little piece of tittle-tattle dropped by a court footman, which would be in all the papers to-morrow. Such were his rattles, his baubles, in playing with which he had grown white, come to the verge of old age, enjoying the respect and affection of all who had the privilege of knowing this type of the English public school man.[1] Inevitably one made up things like that about Hugh; that was his style; the style of those admirable letters which Peter had read thousands of miles across the sea in the *Times*, and had thanked God he was out of that pernicious hubble-bubble if it were only to hear baboons chatter and coolies beat their wives. An olive-skinned youth from one of the Universities stood obsequiously by. Him he would patronise, initiate, teach how to get on. For he liked nothing better than doing kindnessses, making the hearts of old ladies palpitate with the joy of being thought of in their age, their affliction, thinking themselves quite forgotten, yet here was dear Hugh driving up and spending an hour talking of the past, remembering trifles, praising the homemade cake, though Hugh might eat cake with a Duchess

9. Thin, dry cookies.
1. With an elite education from a British public school, analogous to an American private school.

any day of his life, and, to look at him, probably did spend a good deal of time in that agreeable occupation. The All-judging, the All-merciful, might excuse. Peter Walsh had no mercy. Villains there must be, and God knows the rascals who get hanged for battering the brains of a girl out in a train do less harm on the whole than Hugh Whitbread and his kindness. Look at him now, on tip-toe, dancing forward, bowing and scraping, as the Prime Minister and Lady Bruton emerged, intimating for all the world to see that he was privileged to say something, something private, to Lady Bruton as she passed. She stopped. She wagged her fine old head. She was thanking him presumably for some piece of servility. She had her toadies, minor officials in Government offices who ran about putting through little jobs on her behalf, in return for which she gave them luncheon. But she derived from the eighteenth century. She was all right.

And now Clarissa escorted her Prime Minister down the room, prancing, sparkling, with the stateliness of her grey hair. She wore ear-rings, and a silver-green mermaid's dress. Lolloping on the waves and braiding her tresses she seemed, having that gift still; to be; to exist; to sum it all up in the moment as she passed; turned, caught her scarf in some other woman's dress, unhitched it, laughed, all with the most perfect ease and air of a creature floating in its element. But age had brushed her; even as a mermaid might behold in her glass the setting sun on some very clear evening over the waves. There was a breath of tenderness; her severity, her prudery, her woodenness were all warmed through now, and she had about her as she said goodbye to the thick gold-laced man who was doing his best, and good luck to him, to look important, an inexpressible dignity; an exquisite cordiality; as if she wished the whole world well, and must now, being on the very verge and rim of things, take her leave. So she made him think. (But he was not in love.)

Indeed, Clarissa felt, the Prime Minister had been good to come. And, walking down the room with him, with Sally there and Peter there and Rich-ard very pleased, with all those people rather inclined, perhaps, to envy, she had felt that intoxication of the moment, that dilatation of the nerves of the heart itself till it seemed to quiver, steeped, upright;—yes, but after all it was what other people felt, that; for, though she loved it and felt it tingle and sting, still these semblances, these triumphs (dear old Peter, for example, thinking her so brilliant), had a hollowness; at arm's length they were, not in the heart; and it might be that she was growing old but they satisfied her no longer as they used; and suddenly, as she saw the Prime Minister go down the stairs, the gilt rim of the Sir Joshua picture[2] of the little girl with a muff brought back Kilman with a rush; Kilman her enemy. That was satisfying; that was real. Ah, how she hated her—hot, hypocritical, corrupt; with all that power; Elizabeth's seducer; the woman who had crept in to steal and defile (Richard would say, What nonsense!). She hated her: she loved her. It was enemies one wanted, not friends—not Mrs. Durrant and Clara, Sir William and Lady Bradshaw, Miss Truelock and Eleanor Gibson (whom she saw coming upstairs). They must find her if they wanted her. She was for the party!

There was her old friend Sir Harry.

"Dear Sir Harry!" she said, going up to the fine old fellow who had pro-duced more bad pictures than any other two Academicians in the whole of

---

2. Painting by English portraitist Sir Joshua Reynolds (1723–1792).

St. John's Wood[3] (they were always of cattle, standing in sunset pools absorbing moisture, or signifying, for he had a certain range of gesture, by the raising of one foreleg and the toss of the antlers, "the Approach of the Stranger"—all his activities, dining out, racing, were founded on cattle standing absorbing moisture in sunset pools).

"What are you laughing at?" she asked him. For Willie Titcomb and Sir Harry and Herbert Ainsty were all laughing. But no. Sir Harry could not tell Clarissa Dalloway (much though he liked her; of her type he thought her perfect, and threatened to paint her) his stories of the music hall stage. He chaffed her about her party. He missed his brandy. These circles, he said, were above him. But he liked her; respected her, in spite of her damnable, difficult upper-class refinement, which made it impossible to ask Clarissa Dalloway to sit on his knee. And up came that wandering will-o'-the-wisp,[4] that vagulous phosphorescence, old Mrs. Hilbery, stretching her hands to the blaze of his laughter (about the Duke and the Lady), which, as she heard it across the room, seemed to reassure her on a point which sometimes bothered her if she woke early in the morning and did not like to call her maid for a cup of tea; how it is certain we must die.

"They won't tell us their stories," said Clarissa.

"Dear Clarissa!" exclaimed Mrs. Hilbery. She looked tonight, she said, so like her mother as she first saw her walking in a garden in a grey hat.

And really Clarissa's eyes filled with tears. Her mother, walking in a garden! But alas, she must go.

For there was Professor Brierly, who lectured on Milton,[5] talking to little Jim Hutton (who was unable even for a party like this to compass both tie and waistcoat or make his hair lie flat), and even at this distance they were quarrelling, she could see. For Professor Brierly was a very queer fish. With all those degrees, honours, lectureships between him and the scribblers he suspected instantly an atmosphere not favourable to his queer compound; his prodigious learning and timidity; his wintry charm without cordiality, his innocence blent with snobbery; he quivered if made conscious by a lady's unkempt hair, a youth's boots, of an underworld, very creditable doubtless, of rebels, of ardent young people; of would-be geniuses, and intimated with a little toss of the head, with a sniff—Humph!—the value of moderation; of some slight training in the classics in order to appreciate Milton. Professor Brierly (Clarissa could see) wasn't hitting it off with little Jim Hutton (who wore red socks, his black being at the laundry) about Milton. She interrupted.

She said she loved Bach.[6] So did Hutton. That was the bond between them, and Hutton (a very bad poet) always felt that Mrs. Dalloway was far the best of the great ladies who took an interest in art. It was odd how strict she was. About music she was purely impersonal. She was rather a prig. But how charming to look at! She made her house so nice if it weren't for her Professors. Clarissa had half a mind to snatch him off and set him down at the piano in the back room. For he played divinely.

"But the noise!" she said. "The noise!"

"The sign of a successful party." Nodding urbanely, the Professor stepped delicately off.

---

3. District in north London near Regent's Park.
4. Flitting phosphorescent light seen at night in marshes; colloquially, something misleading.

5. John Milton (1608–1674), English poet.
6. Johann Sebastian Bach (1685–1750), German composer.

"He knows everything in the whole world about Milton," said Clarissa.

"Does he indeed?" said Hutton, who would imitate the Professor throughout Hampstead;[7] the Professor on Milton; the Professor on moderation; the Professor stepping delicately off.

But she must speak to that couple, said Clarissa, Lord Gayton and Nancy Blow.

Not that *they* added perceptibly to the noise of the party. They were not talking (perceptibly) as they stood side by side by the yellow curtains. They would soon be off elsewhere, together; and never had very much to say in any circumstances. They looked; that was all. That was enough. They looked so clean, so sound, she with an apricot bloom of powder and paint, but he scrubbed, rinsed, with the eyes of a bird, so that no ball could pass him or stroke surprise him. He struck, he leapt, accurately, on the spot. Ponies' mouths quivered at the end of his reins. He had his honours, ancestral monuments, banners hanging in the church at home. He had his duties; his tenants; a mother and sisters; had been all day at Lords, and that was what they were talking about—cricket, cousins, the movies—when Mrs. Dalloway came up. Lord Gayton liked her most awfully. So did Miss Blow. She had such charming manners.

"It is angelic—it is delicious of you to have come!" she said. She loved Lords; she loved youth, and Nancy, dressed at enormous expense by the greatest artists in Paris, stood there looking as if her body had merely put forth, of its own accord, a green frill.

"I had meant to have dancing," said Clarissa.

For the young people could not talk. And why should they? Shout, embrace, swing, be up at dawn; carry sugar to ponies; kiss and caress the snouts of adorable chows; and then all tingling and streaming, plunge and swim. But the enormous resources of the English language, the power it bestows, after all, of communicating feelings (at their age, she and Peter would have been arguing all the evening), was not for them. They would solidify young. They would be good beyond measure to the people on the estate, but alone, perhaps, rather dull.

"What a pity!" she said. "I had hoped to have dancing."

It was so extraordinarily nice of them to have come! But talk of dancing! The rooms were packed.

There was old Aunt Helena in her shawl. Alas, she must leave them— Lord Gayton and Nancy Blow. There was old Miss Parry, her aunt.

For Miss Helena Parry was not dead: Miss Parry was alive. She was past eighty. She ascended staircases slowly with a stick. She was placed in a chair (Richard had seen to it). People who had known Burma in the 'seventies were always led up to her. Where had Peter got to? They used to be such friends. For at the mention of India, or even Ceylon,[8] her eyes (only one was glass) slowly deepened, became blue, beheld, not human beings—she had no tender memories, no proud illusions about Viceroys, Generals, Mutinies[9]—it was orchids she saw, and mountain passes and herself carried on the backs of coolies in the 'sixties over solitary peaks; or descending to uproot orchids

---

7. A preserved open area in north London, popular with artists.
8. British colonial name for Sri Lanka. "Burma in the 'seventies": southeast Asian country now known as Myanmar, formerly part of the British Empire, which fought three wars to annex it, in 1824–26, 1852, and 1885.
9. Cf. the 1857 Indian Rebellion, or Indian Mutiny, of Indian troops against British colonial rule. "Viceroys": British governors of colonial territories.

(startling blossoms, never beheld before) which she painted in water-colour; an indomitable Englishwoman, fretful if disturbed by the War, say, which dropped a bomb at her very door, from her deep meditation over orchids and her own figure journeying in the 'sixties in India—but here was Peter.

"Come and talk to Aunt Helena about Burma," said Clarissa.

And yet he had not had a word with her all the evening!

"We will talk later," said Clarissa, leading him up to Aunt Helena, in her white shawl, with her stick.

"Peter Walsh," said Clarissa.

That meant nothing.

Clarissa had asked her. It was tiring; it was noisy; but Clarissa had asked her. So she had come. It was a pity that they lived in London—Richard and Clarissa. If only for Clarissa's health it would have been better to live in the country. But Clarissa had always been fond of society.

"He has been in Burma," said Clarissa.

Ah. She could not resist recalling what Charles Darwin had said about her little book on the orchids of Burma.

(Clarissa must speak to Lady Bruton.)

No doubt it was forgotten now, her book on the orchids of Burma, but it went into three editions before 1870, she told Peter. She remembered him now. He had been at Bourton (and he had left her, Peter Walsh remembered, without a word in the drawing-room that night when Clarissa had asked him to come boating).

"Richard so much enjoyed his lunch party," said Clarissa to Lady Bruton.

"Richard was the greatest possible help," Lady Bruton replied. "He helped me to write a letter. And how are you?"

"Oh, perfectly well!" said Clarissa. (Lady Bruton detested illness in the wives of politicians.)

"And there's Peter Walsh!" said Lady Bruton (for she could never think of anything to say to Clarissa; though she liked her. She had lots of fine qualities; but they had nothing in common—she and Clarissa. It might have been better if Richard had married a woman with less charm, who would have helped him more in his work. He had lost his chance of the Cabinet). "There's Peter Walsh!" she said, shaking hands with that agreeable sinner, that very able fellow who should have made a name for himself but hadn't (always in difficulties with women), and, of course, old Miss Parry. Wonderful old lady!

Lady Bruton stood by Miss Parry's chair, a spectral grenadier, draped in black, inviting Peter Walsh to lunch; cordial; but without small talk, remembering nothing whatever about the flora or fauna of India. She had been there, of course; had stayed with three Viceroys; thought some of the Indian civilians uncommonly fine fellows; but what a tragedy it was—the state of India! The Prime Minister had just been telling her (old Miss Parry huddled up in her shawl, did not care what the Prime Minister had just been telling her), and Lady Bruton would like to have Peter Walsh's opinion, he being fresh from the centre, and she would get Sir Sampson to meet him, for really it prevented her from sleeping at night, the folly of it, the wickedness she might say, being a soldier's daughter. She was an old woman now, not good for much. But her house, her servants, her good friend Milly Brush—did he remember her?—were all there only asking to be used if—if they could be of help, in short. For she never spoke of England, but this isle of men, this dear,

dear land,[1] was in her blood (without reading Shakespeare), and if ever a woman could have worn the helmet and shot the arrow, could have led troops to attack, ruled with indomitable justice barbarian hordes and lain under a shield noseless in a church, or made a green grass mound on some primeval hillside, that woman was Millicent Bruton. Debarred by her sex and some truancy, too, of the logical faculty (she found it impossible to write a letter to the *Times*), she had the thought of Empire always at hand, and had acquired from her association with that armoured goddess[2] her ramrod bearing, her robustness of demeanour, so that one could not figure her even in death parted from the earth or roaming territories over which, in some spiritual shape, the Union Jack[3] had ceased to fly. To be not English even among the dead—no, no! Impossible!

But was it Lady Bruton (whom she used to know)? Was it Peter Walsh grown grey? Lady Rosseter asked herself (who had been Sally Seton). It was old Miss Parry certainly—the old aunt who used to be so cross when she stayed at Bourton. Never should she forget running along the passage naked, and being sent for by Miss Parry! And Clarissa! oh Clarissa! Sally caught her by the arm.

Clarissa stopped beside them.

"But I can't stay," she said. "I shall come later. Wait," she said, looking at Peter and Sally. They must wait, she meant, until all these people had gone.

"I shall come back," she said, looking at her old friends, Sally and Peter, who were shaking hands, and Sally, remembering the past no doubt, was laughing.

But her voice was wrung of its old ravishing richness; her eyes not aglow as they used to be, when she smoked cigars, when she ran down the passage to fetch her sponge bag, without a stitch of clothing on her, and Ellen Atkins asked, What if the gentlemen had met her? But everybody forgave her. She stole a chicken from the larder because she was hungry in the night; she smoked cigars in her bedroom; she left a priceless book in the punt.[4] But everybody adored her (except perhaps Papa). It was her warmth; her vitality— she would paint, she would write. Old women in the village never to this day forgot to ask after "your friend in the red cloak who seemed so bright." She accused Hugh Whitbread, of all people (and there he was, her old friend Hugh, talking to the Portuguese Ambassador), of kissing her in the smoking-room to punish her for saying that women should have votes. Vulgar men did, she said. And Clarissa remembered having to persuade her not to denounce him at family prayers—which she was capable of doing with her daring, her recklessness, her melodramatic love of being the centre of every-thing and creating scenes, and it was bound, Clarissa used to think, to end in some awful tragedy; her death; her martyrdom; instead of which she had married, quite unexpectedly, a bald man with a large buttonhole who owned, it was said, cotton mills at Manchester. And she had five boys!

She and Peter had settled down together. They were talking: it seemed so familiar—that they should be talking. They would discuss the past. With the two of them (more even than with Richard) she shared her past; the garden; the trees; old Joseph Breitkopf singing Brahms without any voice;

---

1. Cf. Shakespeare's play *Richard II* 2.1.57.
2. Cf. the Greek goddess Athena, often repre-sented with armor.
3. British national flag.
4. Flat-bottomed, shallow boat.

the drawing-room wallpaper; the smell of the mats. A part of this Sally must always be; Peter must always be. But she must leave them. There were the Bradshaws, whom she disliked. She must go up to Lady Bradshaw (in grey and silver, balancing like a sea-lion at the edge of its tank, barking for invitations, Duchesses, the typical successful man's wife), she must go up to Lady Bradshaw and say . . .

But Lady Bradshaw anticipated her.

"We are shockingly late, dear Mrs. Dalloway, we hardly dared to come in," she said.

And Sir William, who looked very distinguished, with his grey hair and blue eyes, said yes; they had not been able to resist the temptation. He was talking to Richard about that Bill probably, which they wanted to get through the Commons. Why did the sight of him, talking to Richard, curl her up? He looked what he was, a great doctor. A man absolutely at the head of his profession, very powerful, rather worn. For think what cases came before him—people in the uttermost depths of misery; people on the verge of insanity; husbands and wives. He had to decide questions of appalling difficulty. Yet—what she felt was, one wouldn't like Sir William to see one unhappy. No; not that man.

"How is your son at Eton?" she asked Lady Bradshaw.

He had just missed his eleven,[5] said Lady Bradshaw, because of the mumps. His father minded even more than he did, she thought "being," she said, "nothing but a great boy himself."

Clarissa looked at Sir William, talking to Richard. He did not look like a boy—not in the least like a boy. She had once gone with some one to ask his advice. He had been perfectly right; extremely sensible. But Heavens—what a relief to get out to the street again! There was some poor wretch sobbing, she remembered, in the waiting-room. But she did not know what it was—about Sir William; what exactly she disliked. Only Richard agreed with her, "didn't like his taste, didn't like his smell." But he was extraordinarily able. They were talking about this Bill. Some case, Sir William was mentioning, lowering his voice. It had its bearing upon what he was saying about the deferred effects of shell shock.[6] There must be some provision in the Bill.

Sinking her voice, drawing Mrs. Dalloway into the shelter of a common femininity, a common pride in the illustrious qualities of husbands and their sad tendency to overwork, Lady Bradshaw (poor goose—one didn't dislike her) murmured how, "just as we were starting, my husband was called up on the telephone, a very sad case. A young man (that is what Sir William is telling Mr. Dalloway) had killed himself. He had been in the army." Oh! thought Clarissa, in the middle of my party, here's death, she thought.

She went on, into the little room where the Prime Minister had gone with Lady Bruton. Perhaps there was somebody there. But there was nobody. The chairs still kept the impress of the Prime Minister and Lady Bruton, she turned deferentially, he sitting four-square, authoritatively. They had been talking about India. There was nobody. The party's splendour fell to the floor, so strange it was to come in alone in her finery.

---

5. His cricket team, made up of eleven players.
6. Psychological disturbance caused by prolonged exposure to combat (at first thought to be a reaction to the sound of exploding bombshells). The War Office undertook an official inquiry into the subject and issued a report, printed in the *Times* in 1922, that recognized the complexity of the illness. The condition today is known as post-traumatic stress disorder.

What business had the Bradshaws to talk of death at her party? A young man had killed himself. And they talked of it at her party—the Bradshaws, talked of death. He had killed himself—but how? Always her body went through it first, when she was told, suddenly, of an accident; her dress flamed, her body burnt. He had thrown himself from a window. Up had flashed the ground; through him, blundering, bruising, went the rusty spikes. There he lay with a thud, thud, thud in his brain, and then a suffocation of blackness. So she saw it. But why had he done it? And the Bradshaws talked of it at her party!

She had once thrown a shilling into the Serpentine, never anything more. But he had flung it away. They went on living (she would have to go back; the rooms were still crowded; people kept on coming). They (all day she had been thinking of Bourton, of Peter, of Sally), they would grow old. A thing there was that mattered; a thing, wreathed about with chatter, defaced, obscured in her own life, let drop every day in corruption, lies, chatter. This he had preserved. Death was defiance. Death was an attempt to communicate; people feeling the impossibility of reaching the centre which, mystically, evaded them; closeness drew apart; rapture faded, one was alone. There was an embrace in death.

But this young man who had killed himself—had he plunged holding his treasure? "If it were now to die, 'twere now to be most happy,"[7] she had said to herself once, coming down in white.

Or there were the poets and thinkers. Suppose he had had that passion, and had gone to Sir William Bradshaw, a great doctor yet to her obscurely evil, without sex or lust, extremely polite to women, but capable of some indescribable outrage—forcing your soul, that was it—if this young man had gone to him, and Sir William had impressed him, like that, with his power, might he not then have said (indeed she felt it now), Life is made intolerable; they make life intolerable, men like that?

Then (she had felt it only this morning) there was the terror; the overwhelming incapacity, one's parents giving it into one's hands, this life, to be lived to the end, to be walked with serenely; there was in the depths of her heart an awful fear. Even now, quite often if Richard had not been there reading the *Times*, so that she could crouch like a bird and gradually revive, send roaring up that immeasurable delight, rubbing stick to stick, one thing with another, she must have perished. But that young man had killed himself.

Somehow it was her disaster—her disgrace. It was her punishment to see sink and disappear here a man, there a woman, in this profound darkness, and she forced to stand here in her evening dress. She had schemed; she had pilfered. She was never wholly admirable. She had wanted success. Lady Bexborough and the rest of it. And once she had walked on the terrace at Bourton.

It was due to Richard; she had never been so happy. Nothing could be slow enough; nothing last too long. No pleasure could equal, she thought, straightening the chairs, pushing in one book on the shelf, this having done with the triumphs of youth, lost herself in the process of living, to find it, with a shock of delight, as the sun rose, as the day sank. Many a time had she gone, at Bourton when they were all talking, to look at the sky, or seen

7. Cf. p. 1127 and n. 5.

it between people's shoulders at dinner; seen it in London when she could not sleep. She walked to the window.

It held, foolish as the idea was, something of her own in it, this country sky, this sky above Westminster. She parted the curtains; she looked. Oh, but how surprising!—in the room opposite the old lady stared straight at her! She was going to bed. And the sky. It will be a solemn sky, she had thought, it will be a dusky sky, turning away its cheek in beauty. But there it was—ashen pale, raced over quickly by tapering vast clouds. It was new to her. The wind must have risen. She was going to bed, in the room opposite. It was fascinating to watch her, moving about, that old lady, crossing the room, coming to the window. Could she see her? It was fascinating, with people still laughing and shouting in the drawing-room, to watch that old woman, quite quietly, going to bed. She pulled the blind now. The clock began striking. The young man had killed himself; but she did not pity him; with the clock striking the hour, one, two, three, she did not pity him, with all this going on. There! the old lady had put out her light! the whole house was dark now with this going on, she repeated, and the words came to her, Fear no more the heat of the sun. She must go back to them. But what an extraordinary night! She felt somehow very like him—the young man who had killed himself. She felt glad that he had done it; thrown it away. The clock was striking. The leaden circles dissolved in the air. He made her feel the beauty; made her feel the fun. But she must go back. She must assemble. She must find Sally and Peter. And she came in from the little room.

"But where is Clarissa?" said Peter. He was sitting on the sofa with Sally. (After all these years he really could not call her "Lady Rosseter.") "Where's the woman gone to?" he asked. "Where's Clarissa?"

Sally supposed, and so did Peter for the matter of that, that there were people of importance, politicians, whom neither of them knew unless by sight in the picture papers, whom Clarissa had to be nice to, had to talk to. She was with them. Yet there was Richard Dalloway not in the Cabinet. He hadn't been a success, Sally supposed? For herself, she scarcely ever read the papers. She sometimes saw his name mentioned. But then—well, she lived a very solitary life, in the wilds, Clarissa would say, among great merchants, great manufacturers, men, after all, who did things. She had done things too!

"I have five sons!" she told him.

Lord, Lord, what a change had come over her! the softness of motherhood; its egotism too. Last time they met, Peter remembered, had been among the cauliflowers in the moonlight, the leaves "like rough bronze" she had said, with her literary turn; and she had picked a rose. She had marched him up and down that awful night, after the scene by the fountain; he was to catch the midnight train. Heavens, he had wept!

That was his old trick, opening a pocket-knife, thought Sally, always opening and shutting a knife when he got excited. They had been very, very intimate, she and Peter Walsh, when he was in love with Clarissa, and there was that dreadful, ridiculous scene over Richard Dalloway at lunch. She had called Richard "Wickham." Why not call Richard "Wickham"? Clarissa had flared up! and indeed they had never seen each other since, she and Clarissa, not more than half a dozen times perhaps in the last ten years. And Peter Walsh had gone off to India, and she had heard vaguely that he had made an unhappy marriage, and she didn't know whether he had any children, and she couldn't ask him, for he had changed. He was rather shrivelled-looking, but kinder, she felt, and she had a real affection for him, for he was connected with her youth, and she still had a little Emily Brontë[8] he had given her, and he was to write, surely? In those days he was to write.

"Have you written?" she asked him, spreading her hand, her firm and shapely hand, on her knee in a way he recalled.

"Not a word!" said Peter Walsh, and she laughed.

She was still attractive, still a personage, Sally Seton. But who was this Rosseter? He wore two camelias on his wedding day—that was all Peter knew of him. "They have myriads of servants, miles of conservatories,"[9] Clarissa wrote; something like that. Sally owned it with a shout of laughter.

"Yes, I have ten thousand a year"—whether before the tax was paid or after, she couldn't remember, for her husband, "whom you must meet," she said, "whom you would like," she said, did all that for her.

And Sally used to be in rags and tatters. She had pawned her grandmother's ring which Marie Antoinette had given her great-grandfather to come to Bourton.

Oh yes, Sally remembered; she had it still, a ruby ring which Marie Antoinette had given her great-grandfather. She never had a penny to her name in those days, and going to Bourton always meant some frightful pinch. But going to Bourton had meant so much to her—had kept her sane, she believed, so unhappy had she been at home. But that was all a thing of the past—all over now, she said. And Mr. Parry was dead; and Miss Parry was still alive. Never had he had such a shock in his life! said Peter. He had been quite certain she was dead. And the marriage had been, Sally supposed, a success? And that very handsome, very self-possessed young woman was Elizabeth, over there, by the curtains, in red.[1]

(She was like a poplar, she was like a river, she was like a hyacinth, Willie Titcomb was thinking. Oh how much nicer to be in the country and do what she liked! She could hear her poor dog howling, Elizabeth was certain.) She was not a bit like Clarissa, Peter Walsh said.

"Oh, Clarissa!" said Sally.

What Sally felt was simply this. She had owed Clarissa an enormous amount. They had been friends, not acquaintances, friends, and she still saw Clarissa all in white going about the house with her hands full of flowers—to this day tobacco plants made her think of Bourton. But—did Peter understand?—she lacked something. Lacked what was it? She had charm; she had extraordinary charm. But to be frank (and she felt that Peter was an old friend, a real friend—did absence matter? did distance matter? She had often wanted to write to him, but torn it up, yet felt he understood, for people understand without things being said, as one realises growing old, and old she was, had been that afternoon to see her sons at Eton, where they had the mumps), to be quite frank then, how could Clarissa have done it?—married Richard Dalloway? a sportsman, a man who cared only for dogs. Literally, when he came into the room he smelt of the stables. And then all this? She waved her hand.

---

8. A book by the English novelist and poet (1818–1848).   9. Greenhouses.
1. Earlier described as pink.

Hugh Whitbread it was, strolling past in his white waistcoat, dim, fat, blind, past everything he looked, except self-esteem and comfort.

"He's not going to recognise *us*," said Sally, and really she hadn't the courage—so that was Hugh! the admirable Hugh!

"And what does he do?" she asked Peter.

He blacked the King's boots or counted bottles at Windsor,[2] Peter told her. Peter kept his sharp tongue still! But Sally must be frank, Peter said. That kiss now, Hugh's.

On the lips, she assured him, in the smoking-room one evening. She went straight to Clarissa in a rage. Hugh didn't do such things! Clarissa said, the admirable Hugh! Hugh's socks were without exception the most beautiful she had ever seen—and now his evening dress. Perfect! And had he children?

"Everybody in the room has six sons at Eton," Peter told her, except himself. He, thank God, had none. No sons, no daughters, no wife. Well, he didn't seem to mind, said Sally. He looked younger, she thought, than any of them.

But it had been a silly thing to do, in many ways, Peter said, to marry like that; "a perfect goose she was," he said, but, he said, "we had a splendid time of it," but how could that be? Sally wondered; what did he mean? and how odd it was to know him and yet not know a single thing that had happened to him. And did he say it out of pride? Very likely, for after all it must be galling for him (though he was an oddity, a sort of sprite, not at all an ordinary man), it must be lonely at his age to have no home, nowhere to go to. But he must stay with them for weeks and weeks. Of course he would; he would love to stay with them, and that was how it came out. All these years the Dalloways had never been once. Time after time they had asked them. Clarissa (for it was Clarissa of course) would not come. For, said Sally, Clarissa was at heart a snob—one had to admit it, a snob. And it was that that was between them, she was convinced. Clarissa thought she had married beneath her, her husband being—she was proud of it—a miner's son. Every penny they had he had earned. As a little boy (her voice trembled) he had carried great sacks.

(And so she would go on, Peter felt, hour after hour; the miner's son; people thought she had married beneath her; her five sons; and what was the other thing—plants, hydrangeas, syringas, very, very rare hibiscus lilies that never grow north of the Suez Canal,[3] but she, with one gardener in a suburb near Manchester, had beds of them, positively beds! Now all that Clarissa had escaped, unmaternal as she was.)

A snob was she? Yes, in many ways. Where was she, all this time? It was getting late.

"Yet," said Sally, "when I heard Clarissa was giving a party, I felt I couldn't *not* come—must see her again (and I'm staying in Victoria Street, practically next door). So I just came without an invitation. But," she whispered, "tell me, do. Who is this?"

It was Mrs. Hilbery, looking for the door. For how late it was getting! And, she murmured, as the night grew later, as people went, one found old friends; quiet nooks and corners; and the loveliest views. Did they know, she asked, that they were surrounded by an enchanted garden? Lights and trees

2. Windsor Castle, a royal residence west of London.

3. Canal in Egypt connecting the Mediterranean and the Red Seas.

and wonderful gleaming lakes and the sky. Just a few fairy lamps,[4] Clarissa Dalloway had said, in the back garden! But she was a magician! It was a park. . . . And she didn't know their names, but friends she knew they were, friends without names, songs without words, always the best. But there were so many doors, such unexpected places, she could not find her way.

"Old Mrs. Hilbery," said Peter; but who was that? that lady standing by the curtain all the evening, without speaking? He knew her face; connected her with Bourton. Surely she used to cut up underclothes at the large table in the window? Davidson, was that her name?

"Oh, that is Ellie Henderson," said Sally. Clarissa was really very hard on her. She was a cousin, very poor. Clarissa *was* hard on people.

She was rather, said Peter. Yet, said Sally, in her emotional way, with a rush of that enthusiasm which Peter used to love her for, yet dreaded a little now, so effusive she might become—how generous to her friends Clarissa was! and what a rare quality one found it, and how sometimes at night or on Christmas Day, when she counted up her blessings, she put that friendship first. They were young; that was it. Clarissa was pure-hearted; that was it. Peter would think her sentimental. So she was. For she had come to feel that it was the only thing worth saying—what one felt. Cleverness was silly. One must say simply what one felt.

"But I do not know," said Peter Walsh, "what I feel."

Poor Peter, thought Sally. Why did not Clarissa come and talk to them? That was what he was longing for. She knew it. All the time he was thinking only of Clarissa, and was fidgeting with his knife.

He had not found life simple, Peter said. His relations with Clarissa had not been simple. It had spoilt his life, he said. (They had been so intimate—he and Sally Seton, it was absurd not to say it.) One could not be in love twice, he said. And what could she say? Still, it is better to have loved (but he would think her sentimental—he used to be so sharp). He must come and stay with them in Manchester. That is all very true, he said. All very true. He would love to come and stay with them, directly he had done what he had to do in London.

And Clarissa had cared for him more than she had ever cared for Richard. Sally was positive of that.

"No, no, no!" said Peter (Sally should not have said that—she went too far). That good fellow—there he was at the end of the room, holding forth, the same as ever, dear old Richard. Who was he talking to? Sally asked, that very distinguished-looking man? Living in the wilds as she did, she had an insatiable curiosity to know who people were. But Peter did not know. He did not like his looks, he said, probably a Cabinet Minister. Of them all, Richard seemed to him the best, he said—the most disinterested.

"But what has he done?" Sally asked. Public work, she supposed. And were they happy together? Sally asked (she herself was extremely happy); for, she admitted, she knew nothing about them, only jumped to conclusions, as one does, for what can one know even of the people one lives with every day? she asked. Are we not all prisoners? She had read a wonderful play about a man who scratched on the wall of his cell,[5] and she had felt that was true of life—one scratched on the wall. Despairing of human relationships (people were so

---

4. Small colored lights often hung in trees for decoration.   5. Cf. Shakespeare's *Richard II* 5.5.19–21.

difficult), she often went into her garden and got from her flowers a peace which men and women never gave her. But no; he did not like cabbages; he preferred human beings, Peter said. Indeed, the young are beautiful, Sally said, watching Elizabeth cross the room. How unlike Clarissa at her age! Could he make anything of her? She would not open her lips. Not much, not yet, Peter admitted. She was like a lily, Sally said, a lily by the side of a pool. But Peter did not agree that we know nothing. We know everything, he said; at least he did.

But these two, Sally whispered, these two coming now (and really she must go, if Clarissa did not come soon), this distinguished-looking man and his rather common-looking wife who had been talking to Richard—what could one know about people like that?

"That they're damnable humbugs," said Peter, looking at them casually. He made Sally laugh.

But Sir William Bradshaw stopped at the door to look at a picture. He looked in the corner for the engraver's name. His wife looked too. Sir William Bradshaw was so interested in art.

When one was young, said Peter, one was too much excited to know people. Now that one was old, fifty-two[6] to be precise (Sally was fifty-five, in body, she said, but her heart was like a girl's of twenty); now that one was mature then, said Peter, one could watch, one could understand, and one did not lose the power of feeling, he said. No, that is true, said Sally. She felt more deeply, more passionately, every year. It increased, he said, alas, perhaps, but one should be glad of it—it went on increasing in his experience. There was some one in India. He would like to tell Sally about her. He would like Sally to know her. She was married, he said. She had two small children. They must all come to Manchester, said Sally—he must promise before they left.

There's Elizabeth, he said, she feels not half what we feel, not yet. But, said Sally, watching Elizabeth go to her father, one can see they are devoted to each other. She could feel it by the way Elizabeth went to her father.

For her father had been looking at her, as he stood talking to the Bradshaws, and he had thought to himself, Who is that lovely girl? And suddenly he realised that it was his Elizabeth, and he had not recognised her, she looked so lovely in her pink frock! Elizabeth had felt him looking at her as she talked to Willie Titcomb. So she went to him and they stood together, now that the party was almost over, looking at the people going, and the rooms getting emptier and emptier, with things scattered on the floor. Even Ellie Henderson was going, nearly last of all, though no one had spoken to her, but she had wanted to see everything, to tell Edith. And Richard and Elizabeth were rather glad it was over, but Richard was proud of his daughter. And he had not meant to tell her, but he could not help telling her. He had looked at her, he said, and he had wondered, Who is that lovely girl? and it was his daughter! That did make her happy. But her poor dog was howling.

"Richard has improved. You are right," said Sally. "I shall go and talk to him. I shall say good-night. What does the brain matter," said Lady Rosseter, getting up, "compared with the heart?"

---

6. Earlier, fifty-three years old.

"I will come," said Peter, but he sat on for a moment. What is this terror? what is this ecstasy? he thought to himself. What is it that fills me with extraordinary excitement?

It is Clarissa, he said.

For there she was.

Professions for Women[1]

When your secretary invited me to come here, she told me that your Society is concerned with the employment of women and she suggested that I might tell you something about my own professional experiences. It is true I am a woman; it is true I am employed; but what professional experiences have I had? It is difficult to say. My profession is literature; and in that profession there are fewer experiences for women than in any other, with the exception of the stage—fewer, I mean, that are peculiar to women. For the road was cut many years ago—by Fanny Burney, by Aphra Behn, by Harriet Martineau,[2] by Jane Austen, by George Eliot—many famous women, and many more unknown and forgotten, have been before me, making the path smooth, and regulating my steps. Thus, when I came to write, there were very few material obstacles in my way. Writing was a reputable and harmless occupation. The family peace was not broken by the scratching of a pen. No demand was made upon the family purse. For ten and sixpence one can buy paper enough to write all the plays of Shakespeare—if one has a mind that way. Pianos and models, Paris, Vienna, and Berlin, masters and mistresses, are not needed by a writer. The cheapness of writing paper is, of course, the reason why women have succeeded as writers before they have succeeded in the other professions.

But to tell you my story—it is a simple one. You have only got to figure to yourselves a girl in a bedroom with a pen in her hand. She had only to move that pen from left to right—from ten o'clock to one. Then it occurred to her to do what is simple and cheap enough after all—to slip a few of those pages into an envelope, fix a penny stamp in the corner, and drop the envelope into the red box at the corner. It was thus that I became a journalist; and my effort was rewarded on the first day of the following month—a very glorious day it was for me—by a letter from an editor containing a cheque for one pound ten shillings and sixpence. But to show you how little I deserve to be called a professional woman, how little I know of the struggles and difficulties of such lives, I have to admit that instead of spending that sum upon bread and butter, rent, shoes and stockings, or butcher's bills, I went out and bought a cat—a beautiful cat, a Persian cat, which very soon involved me in bitter disputes with my neighbours.

What could be easier than to write articles and to buy Persian cats with the profits? But wait a moment. Articles have to be about something. Mine, I seem to remember, was about a novel by a famous man. And while I was

1. A paper read to the Women's Service League [Woolf's note]. Woolf here echoes her points in *A Room of One's Own* about a woman's needing money (specifically, five hundred British pounds) and a room in which to write.

2. Economist, moralist, journalist, and novelist (1802–1876). Burney (1752–1840), author of *Evelina* and other novels. Behn (1640–1689), writer of romances and plays.

writing this review, I discovered that if I were going to review books I should need to do battle with a certain phantom. And the phantom was a woman, and when I came to know her better I called her after the heroine of a famous poem, The Angel in the House.[3] It was she who used to come between me and my paper when I was writing reviews. It was she who bothered and wasted my time and so tormented me that at last I killed her. You who come of a younger and happier generation may not have heard of her—you may not know what I mean by The Angel in the House. I will describe her as shortly as I can. She was intensely sympathetic. She was immensely charming. She was utterly unselfish. She excelled in the difficult arts of family life. She sacrificed herself daily. If there was chicken, she took the leg; if there was a draught she sat in it—in short she was so constituted that she never had a mind or a wish of her own, but preferred to sympathise always with the minds and wishes of others. Above all—I need not say it— she was pure. Her purity was supposed to be her chief beauty—her blushes, her great grace. In those days—the last of Queen Victoria—every house had its Angel. And when I came to write I encountered her with the very first words. The shadow of her wings fell on my page; I heard the rustling of her skirts in the room. Directly, that is to say, I took my pen in my hand to review that novel by a famous man, she slipped behind me and whispered: 'My dear, you are a young woman. You are writing about a book that has been written by a man. Be sympathetic; be tender; flatter; deceive; use all the arts and wiles of our sex. Never let anybody guess that you have a mind of your own. Above all, be pure.' And she made as if to guide my pen. I now record the one act for which I take some credit to myself, though the credit rightly belongs to some excellent ancestors of mine who left me a certain sum of money—shall we say five hundred pounds a year?—so that it was not necessary for me to depend solely on charm for my living. I turned upon her and caught her by the throat. I did my best to kill her. My excuse, if I were to be had up in a court of law, would be that I acted in self-defence. Had I not killed her she would have killed me. She would have plucked the heart out of my writing. For, as I found, directly I put pen to paper, you cannot review even a novel without having a mind of your own, without expressing what you think to be the truth about human relations, morality, sex. And all these questions, according to the Angel of the House, cannot be dealt with freely and openly by women; they must charm, they must conciliate, they must—to put it bluntly—tell lies if they are to succeed. Thus, whenever I felt the shadow of her wing or the radiance of her halo upon my page, I took up the inkpot and flung it at her. She died hard. Her fictitious nature was of great assistance to her. It is far harder to kill a phantom than a reality. She was always creeping back when I thought I had despatched her. Though I flatter myself that I killed her in the end, the struggle was severe; it took much time that had better have been spent upon learning Greek grammar; or in roaming the world in search of adventures. But it was a real experience; it was an experience that was bound to befall all women writers at that time. Killing the Angel in the House was part of the occupation of a woman writer.

But to continue my story. The Angel was dead; what then remained? You may say that what remained was a simple and common object—a young

3. By Coventry Patmore (1823–1896), published 1854–62.

woman in a bedroom with an inkpot. In other words, now that she had rid herself of falsehood, that young woman had only to be herself. Ah, but what is 'herself'? I mean, what is a woman? I assure you, I do not know. I do not believe that you know. I do not believe that anybody can know until she has expressed herself in all the arts and professions open to human skill. That indeed is one of the reasons why I have come here—out of respect for you, who are in process of showing us by your experiments what a woman is, who are in process of providing us, by your failures and successes, with that extremely important piece of information.

But to continue the story of my professional experiences. I made one pound ten and six by my first review; and I bought a Persian cat with the proceeds. Then I grew ambitious. A Persian cat is all very well, I said; but a Persian cat is not enough. I must have a motor-car. And it was thus that I became a novelist—for it is a very strange thing that people will give you a motor-car if you will tell them a story. It is a still stranger thing that there is nothing so delightful in the world as telling stories. It is far pleasanter than writing reviews of famous novels. And yet, if I am to obey your secretary and tell you my professional experiences as a novelist, I must tell you about a very strange experience that befell me as a novelist. And to understand it you must try first to imagine a novelist's state of mind. I hope I am not giving away professional secrets if I say that a novelist's chief desire is to be as unconscious as possible. He has to induce in himself a state of perpetual lethargy. He wants life to proceed with the utmost quiet and regularity. He wants to see the same faces, to read the same books, to do the same things day after day, month after month, while he is writing, so that nothing may break the illusion in which he is living—so that nothing may disturb or disquiet the mysterious nosings about, feelings round, darts, dashes, and sudden discoveries of that very shy and illusive spirit, the imagination. I suspect that this state is the same both for men and women. Be that as it may, I want you to imagine me writing a novel in a state of trance. I want you to figure to yourselves a girl sitting with a pen in her hand, which for minutes, and indeed for hours, she never dips into the inkpot. The image that comes to my mind when I think of this girl is the image of a fisherman lying sunk in dreams on the verge of a deep lake with a rod held out over the water. She was letting her imagination sweep unchecked round every rock and cranny of the world that lies submerged in the depths of our unconscious being. Now came the experience that I believe to be far commoner with women writers than with men. The line raced through the girl's fingers. Her imagination had rushed away. It had sought the pools, the depths, the dark places where the largest fish slumber. And then there was a smash. There was an explosion. There was foam and confusion. The imagination had dashed itself against something hard. The girl was roused from her dream. She was indeed in a state of the most acute and difficult distress. To speak without figure, she had thought of something, something about the body, about the passions which it was unfitting for her as a woman to say. Men, her reason told her, would be shocked. The consciousness of what men will say of a woman who speaks the truth about her passions had roused her from her artist's state of unconsciousness. She could write no more. The trance was over. Her imagination could work no longer. This I believe to be a very common experience with women writers—they are impeded by the extreme conventionality of the other sex. For though men sensibly allow themselves great freedom in these respects, I doubt that they realize or can control the extreme severity with which they condemn such freedom in women.

These then were two very genuine experiences of my own. These were two of the adventures of my professional life. The first—killing the Angel in the House—I think I solved. She died. But the second, telling the truth about my own experiences as a body, I do not think I solved. I doubt that any woman has solved it yet. The obstacles against her are still immensely powerful—and yet they are very difficult to define. Outwardly, what is simpler than to write books? Outwardly, what obstacles are there for a woman rather than for a man? Inwardly, I think, the case is very different; she has still many ghosts to fight, many prejudices to overcome. Indeed it will be a long time still, I think, before a woman can sit down to write a book without finding a phantom to be slain, a rock to be dashed against. And if this is so in literature, the freest of all professions for women, how is it in the new professions which you are now for the first time entering?

Those are the questions that I should like, had I time, to ask you. And indeed, if I have laid stress upon these professional experiences of mine, it is because I believe that they are, though in different forms, yours also. Even when the path is nominally open—when there is nothing to prevent a woman from being a doctor, a lawyer, a civil servant—there are many phantoms and obstacles, as I believe, looming in her way. To discuss and define them is I think of great value and importance; for thus only can the labour be shared, the difficulties be solved. But besides this, it is necessary also to discuss the ends and the aims for which we are fighting, for which we are doing battle with these formidable obstacles. Those aims cannot be taken for granted; they must be perpetually questioned and examined. The whole position, as I see it—here in this hall surrounded by women practising for the first time in history I know not how many different professions—is one of extraordinary interest and importance. You have won rooms of your own in the house hitherto exclusively owned by men. You are able, though not without great labour and effort, to pay the rent. You are earning your five hundred pounds a year. But this freedom is only a beginning; the room is your own, but it is still bare. It has to be furnished; it has to be decorated; it has to be shared. How are you going to furnish it, how are you going to decorate it? With whom are you going to share it, and upon what terms? These, I think are questions of the utmost importance and interest. For the first time in history you are able to ask them; for the first time you are able to decide for yourselves what the answers should be. Willingly would I stay and discuss those questions and answers—but not tonight. My time is up; and I must cease.

1942

JAMES JOYCE
1882–1941

James Joyce was born in Dublin, son of a talented but feckless father, who is accurately described in Joyce's novel *A Portrait of the Artist as a Young Man* (1916) as having been "a medical student, an oarsman, a tenor, an amateur actor, a shouting politician, a small landlord, a small investor, a drinker, a good fellow, a storyteller, somebody's secretary, something in a distillery, a tax-gatherer, a bankrupt, and at present a praiser of his own past." The elder Joyce, like the father in Joyce's novel, drifted steadily down the financial and social scale, his family moving from house to house, each one less genteel and more shabby than the previous. James Joyce's primary education was Catholic, from the age of six to the age of nine at Clongowes Wood College and from eleven to sixteen at Belvedere College, as vividly recalled in *A Portrait of the Artist*. Both were Jesuit institutions and were normal roads to the priesthood. He then studied modern languages at University College, Dublin.

From a comparatively young age Joyce regarded himself as a rebel against the shabbiness and philistinism of Dublin. In his last year of school at Belvedere he began to reject his Catholic faith in favor of a literary mission that he saw as involving rebellion and exile. He refused to play any part in the nationalist or other popular activities of his fellow students, and he created some stir by his outspoken articles, one of which, on the Norwegian playwright Henrik Ibsen, appeared in London's *Fortnightly Review* when Joyce was eighteen. He taught himself Dano-Norwegian in order to read Ibsen and to write to him. When, on instructions of the faculty adviser, an article by Joyce, significantly titled "The Day of the Rabblement," was refused by the student magazine that had commissioned it, he had it printed privately. By 1902, when he received his A.B. degree, the young man was already committed to a career as exile and writer. For Joyce, as for his character Stephen Dedalus in *A Portrait of the Artist* and *Ulysses*, the latter implied the former.

To preserve his integrity, to avoid involvement in popular causes, to devote himself to the life of the artist, he felt that he had to go abroad.

Joyce went to Paris after graduation, was recalled to Dublin by his mother's fatal illness, had a short spell there as a schoolteacher, then returned to the Continent in 1904 to teach English in Trieste and then in Zurich. He took with him Nora Barnacle, a woman from Galway with no interest in literature; her vivacity and wit charmed Joyce, and the two lived in devoted companionship until his death, although they were not married until 1931. In 1920 Joyce and Barnacle set-

A photographic portrait of James Joyce, 1934.

tled in Paris, where they lived until December 1940, when the war forced them to take refuge in Switzerland; he died in Zurich a few weeks later.

Proud, obstinate, absolutely convinced of his genius, given to fits of sudden gaiety and of sudden silence, Joyce was not always an easy person to get along with, yet he never lacked friends, and throughout his thirty-six years on the Continent he was always the center of a literary circle. Life was hard at first. In Trieste he had little money, and he did not improve matters by drinking heavily, a habit checked somewhat by his brother Stanislaus, who came out from Dublin to act (as Stanislaus put it much later) as his "brother's keeper." Joyce also suffered from eye diseases and, blind for brief periods, underwent twenty-five operations. In 1917 Edith Rockefeller McCormick and then the lawyer John Quinn, steered in Joyce's direction by Ezra Pound, helped out financially. A benefactor who would prove to be permanent was the English feminist and editor Harriet Shaw Weaver, who not only subsidized Joyce generously from 1917 to the end of his life but also occupied herself indefatigably with arrangements for publishing his work.

In spite of doing most of his writing in Trieste, Zurich, and Paris, Joyce paradoxically wrote only and always about Dublin. No writer has ever been more soaked in Dublin, its atmosphere, its history, its topography. He devised ways of expanding his accounts of the Irish capital, however, so that they became microcosms of human history, geography, and experience.

Joyce began his career by writing a series of stories that etched, with extraordinary clarity, aspects of Dublin life. These stories—published as *Dubliners* in 1914—are sharp, realistic sketches of what Joyce called the "paralysis" that beset the lives of people in then-provincial Ireland. The language is crisp, lucid, and detached, and the details are chosen and organized so meticulously that their symbolic meanings intensify as the events and images intersect. Some of the stories, such as "Araby," are built around what Joyce called an "epiphany," a dramatic but fleeting moment of revelation about the self or the world. Many end abruptly, without conventional narrative closure, or they lack overt connectives and transitions, leaving multiple possibilities in suspension. The last story in *Dubliners*, "The Dead," was not part of the original draft of the book but was added later, when Joyce was preoccupied with the nature of artistic objectivity. At a festive event, attended by guests whose portraits Joyce draws with precision and economy, a series of jolting events frees the protagonist, Gabriel, from his possessiveness and egotism. The view he attains at the end is the mood of supreme neutrality that Joyce saw as the beginning of artistic awareness. It is the view of art developed by Stephen Dedalus in *A Portrait of the Artist*.

Dubliners represents Joyce's first phase, in which he came to terms with the life he had rejected. Next he had to come to terms with the meaning of his emergence as a man dedicated to imaginative writing; the result was a novel about the youth and development of an artist, *A Portrait of the Artist as a Young Man* (1916). Joyce wove his autobiography into a work of fiction so finely chiseled and arranged, so stripped of anything superfluous, that each word contributes to the presentation of the theme: the parallel movement toward art and toward exile. A part of his first draft was published posthumously under the original title, *Stephen Hero* (1944), and a comparison between it and the final version, *A Portrait of the Artist*, shows the precision with which Joyce reworked and compressed his material for maximum effect.

From the beginning Joyce had trouble getting his writing into print. The release of *Dubliners* was held up for many years while he fought with both English and Irish editors about words and phrases that they wished to eliminate. Censorship cuts were made to *A Portrait of the Artist* when it was first issued, in serial form, and three European publishers rejected it before it was finally accepted by an American firm. Joyce's next novel, *Ulysses* (1922), was banned in Britain and America on publication; its earlier serialization in an American magazine, *The Little Review* (March 1918–December 1920), had been stopped abruptly when the U.S. Post Office brought a charge of obscenity against the work. Fortunately Judge John Woolsey's history-making decision in a federal district court on December 6, 1933, resulted in the lifting of the ban and the free circulation of *Ulysses* first in America and soon afterward in Britain.

Ulysses is an account of one day in the lives of Dubliners; it thus describes a limited number of events involving a limited number of people in a limited environment. Yet Joyce's ambition—which took him seven years to realize—is to give the events the depth and implication that can convey symbolic significance. The episodes in *Ulysses* correspond to incidents in Homer's ancient Greek epic *Odyssey*, although the Homeric names customarily given to the episodes, such as "Proteus," "Circe," and "Penelope," appear not in the book but in Joyce's schematic outline. Joyce regarded Odysseus, or Ulysses, as the most "complete" man in literature, shown in all his aspects—coward and hero, cautious and reckless, weak and strong, husband and philanderer, father and son, dignified and ridiculous; so he makes his hero, Leopold Bloom, an Irish Jew, into a modern Ulysses. The parallels between the Homeric archetypes and the modern-day characters and events create a host of interpretive complexities. They can seem tight or loose, deflating or ennobling, ironic or heroic, epic or mock-epic, depending on their specific application in a particular episode and, to some extent, on the propensities of the reader.

Joyce's final work, *Finnegans Wake* (1939), took more than fourteen years to write, and Joyce considered it his masterpiece, though some readers have found its dense, multilayered language impenetrable. For this work, Joyce invents a dream language, in which words are combined, distorted, created from bits of other words fitted together, several meanings at once, often drawn from several languages, and fused in conveying a variety of ways to achieve whole clusters of meaning simultaneously. In *Ulysses* Joyce had made the symbolic aspect of the novel at least as important as the realistic aspect, but in *Finnegans Wake* he gave up realism altogether. This vast story of a symbolic Irishman's cosmic dream develops, by enormous reverberating puns, a continuous expansion of meaning, the elements in the puns deriving from every conceivable source in history, literature, mythology, and Joyce's personal experience.

Like his other novels, *Finnegans Wake* put Joyce's consummate craftsmanship at the service of a humanely comic vision. His innovations in organization, style, and narrative technique have influenced countless writers, but his works of fiction are unique.

Araby[1]

North Richmond Street, being blind, was a quiet street except at the hour when the Christian Brothers' School[2] set the boys free. An uninhabited house of two storeys stood at the blind end, detached from its neighbours in a square ground. The other houses of the street, conscious of decent lives within them, gazed at one another with brown imperturbable faces.

1. The third of the fifteen stories in *Dubliners*. This tale of the frustrated quest for beauty in the midst of drabness is both meticulously realistic in its handling of details of Dublin life and the Dublin scene and highly symbolic in that almost every image and incident suggests some particular aspect of the theme (e.g., the suggestion of the Holy Grail in the image of the chalice, mentioned in the fifth paragraph). Joyce was drawing on his own childhood recollections, and the uncle in the story is a reminiscence of Joyce's father. But in all the stories in *Dubliners* dealing

with childhood, the child lives not with his parents but with an uncle and aunt—a symbol of that isolation and lack of proper relation between "consubstantial" (in the flesh) parents and children that is a major theme in Joyce's work.

2. The Joyce family moved to 17 North Richmond Street, Dublin, in 1894; and Joyce had earlier briefly attended the Christian Brothers' school a few doors away (the Christian Brothers are a Catholic religious community). The details of the house described here correspond exactly to those of number 17.

The former tenant of our house, a priest, had died in the back drawing-room. Air, musty from having been long enclosed, hung in all the rooms, and the waste room behind the kitchen was littered with old useless papers. Among these I found a few paper-covered books, the pages of which were curled and damp: *The Abbot*, by Walter Scott, *The Devout Communicant* and *The Memoirs of Vidocq*,[3] I liked the last best because its leaves were yellow. The wild garden behind the house contained a central apple-tree and a few straggling bushes under one of which I found the late tenant's rusty bicycle-pump. He had been a very charitable priest; in his will he had left all his money to institutions and the furniture of his house to his sister.

When the short days of winter came dusk fell before we had well eaten our dinners. When we met in the street the houses had grown sombre. The space of sky above us was the colour of ever-changing violet and towards it the lamps of the street lifted their feeble lanterns. The cold air stung us and we played till our bodies glowed. Our shouts echoed in the silent street. The career of our play brought us through the dark muddy lanes behind the houses where we ran the gantlet of the rough tribes from the cottages, to the back doors of the dark dripping gardens where odours arose from the ashpits, to the dark odorous stables where a coachman smoothed and combed the horse or shook music from the buckled harness. When we returned to the street light from the kitchen windows had filled the areas. If my uncle was seen turning the corner we hid in the shadow until we had seen him safely housed. Or if Mangan's sister came out on the doorstep to call her brother in to his tea we watched her from our shadow peer up and down the street. We waited to see whether she would remain or go in and, if she remained, we left our shadow and walked up to Mangan's steps resignedly. She was waiting for us, her figure defined by the light from the half-opened door. Her brother always teased her before he obeyed and I stood by the railings looking at her. Her dress swung as she moved her body and the soft rope of her hair tossed from side to side.

Every morning I lay on the floor in the front parlour watching her door. The blind was pulled down to within an inch of the sash so that I could not be seen. When she came out on the doorstep my heart leaped. I ran to the hall, seized my books and followed her. I kept her brown figure always in my eye and, when we came near the point at which our ways diverged, I quickened my pace and passed her. This happened morning after morning. I had never spoken to her, except for a few casual words, and yet her name was like a summons to all my foolish blood.

Her image accompanied me even in places the most hostile to romance. On Saturday evenings when my aunt went marketing I had to go to carry some of the parcels. We walked through the flaring streets, jostled by drunken men and bargaining women, amid the curses of labourers, the shrill litanies of shop-boys who stood on guard by the barrels of pigs' cheeks, the nasal chanting of street-singers, who sang a *come-all-you*[4] about O'Donovan Rossa, or a ballad about the troubles in our native land. These noises converged in a single sensation of life for me: I imagined that I bore my chalice safely

3. François Eugéne Vidocq (1775–1857) had an extraordinary career as soldier, thief, chief of the French detective force, and private detective. *The Abbot* is a historical novel dealing with Mary, Queen of Scots. *The Devout Communi-cant* is a Catholic religious manual.
4. Street ballad, so called from its opening words. This one was about the 19th-century Irish nationalist Jeremiah Donovan, popularly known as O'Donovan Rossa.

through a throng of foes. Her name sprang to my lips at moments in strange prayers and praises which I myself did not understand. My eyes were often full of tears (I could not tell why) and at times a flood from my heart seemed to pour itself out into my bosom. I thought little of the future. I did not know whether I would ever speak to her or not or, if I spoke to her, how I could tell her of my confused adoration. But my body was like a harp and her words and gestures were like fingers running upon the wires.

One evening I went into the back drawing-room in which the priest had died. It was a dark rainy evening and there was no sound in the house. Through one of the broken panes I heard the rain impinge upon the earth, the fine incessant needles of water playing in the sodden beds. Some distant lamp or lighted window gleamed below me. I was thankful that I could see so little. All my senses seemed to desire to veil themselves and, feeling that I was about to slip from them, I pressed the palms of my hands together until they trembled, murmuring: *O love! O love!* many times.

At last she spoke to me. When she addressed the first words to me I was so confused that I did not know what to answer. She asked me was I going to *Araby*.[5] I forgot whether I answered yes or no. It would be a splendid bazaar, she said; she would love to go.

—And why can't you? I asked.

While she spoke she turned a silver bracelet round and round her wrist. She could not go, she said, because there would be a retreat that week in her convent.[6] Her brother and two other boys were fighting for their caps and I was alone at the railings. She held one of the spikes, bowing her head towards me. The light from the lamp opposite our door caught the white curve of her neck, lit up her hair that rested there and, falling, lit up the hand upon the railing. It fell over one side of her dress and caught the white border of a petticoat, just visible as she stood at ease.

—It's well for you, she said.

—If I go, I said, I will bring you something.

What innumerable follies laid waste my waking and sleeping thoughts after that evening! I wished to annihilate the tedious intervening days. I chafed against the work of school. At night in my bedroom and by day in the classroom her image came between me and the page I strove to read. The syllables of the word *Araby* were called to me through the silence in which my soul luxuriated and cast an Eastern enchantment over me. I asked for leave to go to the bazaar on Saturday night. My aunt was surprised and hoped it was not some Freemason affair.[7] I answered few questions in class. I watched my master's face pass from amiability to sternness; he hoped I was not beginning to idle. I could not call my wandering thoughts together. I had hardly any patience with the serious work of life which, now that it stood between me and my desire, seemed to me child's play, ugly monotonous child's play.

On Saturday morning I reminded my uncle that I wished to go to the bazaar in the evening. He was fussing at the hallstand, looking for the hat-brush, and answered me curtly:

5. The bazaar, described by its "official catalogue" as a "Grand Oriental Fête," was actually held in Dublin on May 14–19, 1894.
6. I.e., her convent school. "Retreat": period of seclusion from ordinary activities devoted to religious exercises.
7. His aunt shares her Church's distrust of the Freemasons, an old European secret society, reputedly anti-Catholic.

—Yes, boy, I know.

As he was in the hall I could not go into the front parlour and lie at the window. I left the house in bad humour and walked slowly towards the school. The air was pitilessly raw and already my heart misgave me.

When I came home to dinner my uncle had not yet been home. Still it was early. I sat staring at the clock for some time and, when its ticking began to irritate me, I left the room. I mounted the staircase and gained the upper part of the house. The high cold empty gloomy rooms liberated me and I went from room to room singing. From the front window I saw my companions playing below in the street. Their cries reached me weakened and indistinct and, leaning my forehead against the cool glass, I looked over at the dark house where she lived. I may have stood there for an hour, seeing nothing but the brown-clad figure cast by my imagination, touched discreetly by the lamplight at the curved neck, at the hand upon the railings and at the border below the dress.

When I came downstairs again I found Mrs Mercer sitting at the fire. She was an old garrulous woman, a pawn-broker's widow, who collected used stamps for some pious purpose. I had to endure the gossip of the tea-table. The meal was prolonged beyond an hour and still my uncle did not come. Mrs Mercer stood up to go: she was sorry she couldn't wait any longer, but it was after eight o'clock and she did not like to be out late, as the night air was bad for her. When she had gone I began to walk up and down the room, clenching my fists. My aunt said:

—I'm afraid you may put off your bazaar for this night of Our Lord.

At nine o'clock I heard my uncle's latchkey in the halldoor. I heard him talking to himself and heard the hallstand rocking when it had received the weight of his overcoat. I could interpret these signs. When he was midway through his dinner I asked him to give me the money to go to the bazaar. He had forgotten.

—The people are in bed and after their first sleep now, he said.

I did not smile. My aunt said to him energetically:

—Can't you give him the money and let him go? You've kept him late enough as it is.

My uncle said he was very sorry he had forgotten. He said he believed in the old saying: *All work and no play makes Jack a dull boy.* He asked me where I was going and, when I had told him a second time he asked me did I know *The Arab's Farewell to his Steed.*[8] When I left the kitchen he was about to recite the opening lines of the piece to my aunt.

I held a florin[9] tightly in my hand as I strode down Buckingham Street towards the station. The sight of the streets thronged with buyers and glaring with gas recalled to me the purpose of my journey. I took my seat in a third-class carriage of a deserted train. After an intolerable delay the train moved out of the station slowly. It crept onward among ruinous houses and over the twinkling river. At Westland Row Station a crowd of people pressed to the carriage doors; but the porters moved them back, saying that it was a special train for the bazaar. I remained alone in the bare carriage. In a few minutes the train drew up beside an improvised wooden platform. I passed out on to the road and saw by the lighted dial of a clock that it was

8. Once-popular sentimental poem by Caroline Norton.

9. A silver coin, now obsolete, worth two shillings.

ten minutes to ten. In front of me was a large building which displayed the magical name.

I could not find any sixpenny entrance and, fearing that the bazaar would be closed, I passed in quickly through a turnstile, handing a shilling to a weary-looking man. I found myself in a big hall girdled at half its height by a gallery. Nearly all the stalls were closed and the greater part of the hall was in darkness. I recognized a silence like that which pervades a church after a service. I walked into the centre of the bazaar timidly. A few people were gathered about the stalls which were still open. Before a curtain, over which the words *Café Chantant*[1] were written in coloured lamps, two men were counting money on a salver. I listened to the fall of the coins.

Remembering with difficulty why I had come I went over to one of the stalls and examined porcelain vases and flowered tea-sets. At the door of the stall a young lady was talking and laughing with two young gentlemen. I remarked their English accents and listened vaguely to their conversation.

—O, I never said such a thing!

—O, but you did!

—O, but I didn't!

—Didn't she say that?

—Yes. I heard her.

—O, there's a . . . fib!

Observing me the young lady came over and asked me did I wish to buy anything. The tone of her voice was not encouraging; she seemed to have spoken to me out of a sense of duty. I looked humbly at the great jars that stood like eastern guards at either side of the dark entrance to the stall and murmured:

—No, thank you.

The young lady changed the position of one of the vases and went back to the two young men. They began to talk of the same subject. Once or twice the young lady glanced at me over her shoulder.

I lingered before her stall, though I knew my stay was useless, to make my interest in her wares seem the more real. Then I turned away slowly and walked down the middle of the bazaar. I allowed the two pennies to fall against the sixpence in my pocket. I heard a voice call from one end of the gallery that the light was out. The upper part of the hall was now completely dark.

Gazing up into the darkness I saw myself as a creature driven and derided by vanity; and my eyes burned with anguish and anger.

1905   1914

The Dead

Lily, the caretaker's daughter, was literally run off her feet. Hardly had she brought one gentleman into the little pantry behind the office on the ground floor and helped him off with his overcoat than the wheezy hall-door bell

---

1. Singing café (French; literal trans.); a café that provided musical entertainment, popular early in the 20th century.

clanged again and she had to scamper along the bare hallway to let in another guest. It was well for her she had not to attend to the ladies also. But Miss Kate and Miss Julia had thought of that and had converted the bathroom upstairs into a ladies' dressing-room. Miss Kate and Miss Julia were there, gossiping and laughing and fussing, walking after each other to the head of the stairs, peering down over the banisters and calling down to Lily to ask her who had come.

It was always a great affair, the Misses Morkan's annual dance. Everybody who knew them came to it, members of the family, old friends of the family, the members of Julia's choir, any of Kate's pupils that were grown up enough and even some of Mary Jane's pupils too. Never once had it fallen flat. For years and years it had gone off in splendid style as long as anyone could remember; ever since Kate and Julia, after the death of their brother Pat, had left the house in Stoney Batter and taken Mary Jane, their only niece, to live with them in the dark gaunt house on Usher's Island, the upper part of which they had rented from Mr Fulham, the cornfactor[1] on the ground floor. That was a good thirty years ago if it was a day. Mary Jane, who was then a little girl in short clothes, was now the main prop of the household for she had the organ in Haddington Road.[2] She had been through the Academy and gave a pupils' concert every year in the upper room of the Antient Concert Rooms.[3] Many of her pupils belonged to better-class families on the Kingstown and Dalkey line. Old as they were, her aunts also did their share. Julia, though she was quite grey, was still the leading soprano in Adam and Eve's, and Kate, being too feeble to go about much, gave music lessons to beginners on the old square piano in the back room. Lily, the caretaker's daughter, did housemaid's work for them. Though their life was modest they believed in eating well; the best of everything: diamond-bone sirloins, three-shilling tea and the best bottled stout.[4] But Lily seldom made a mistake in the orders so that she got on well with her three mistresses. They were fussy, that was all. But the only thing they would not stand was back answers.

Of course they had good reason to be fussy on such a night. And then it was long after ten o'clock and yet there was no sign of Gabriel and his wife. Besides they were dreadfully afraid that Freddy Malins might turn up screwed.[5] They would not wish for worlds that any of Mary Jane's pupils should see him under the influence; and when he was like that it was sometimes very hard to manage him. Freddy Malins always came late but they wondered what could be keeping Gabriel: and that was what brought them every two minutes to the banisters to ask Lily had Gabriel or Freddy come.

—O, Mr Conroy, said Lily to Gabriel when she opened the door for him, Miss Kate and Miss Julia thought you were never coming. Good-night, Mrs Conroy.

—I'll engage[6] they did, said Gabriel, but they forget that my wife here takes three mortal hours to dress herself.

He stood on the mat, scraping the snow from his goloshes, while Lily led his wife to the foot of the stairs and called out:

1. Grain merchant.
2. Haddington Road, like Adam and Eve's below, is a church.
3. Concert hall in Dublin. The academy was the Royal Irish Academy of Music.
4. A dark brown malt liquor, akin to beer.
5. Drunk.
6. Bet.

—Miss Kate, here's Mrs Conroy.

Kate and Julia came toddling down the dark stairs at once. Both of them kissed Gabriel's wife, said she must be perished alive and asked was Gabriel with her.

—Here I am as right as the mail, Aunt Kate! Go on up. I'll follow, called out Gabriel from the dark.

He continued scraping his feet vigorously while the three women went upstairs, laughing, to the ladies' dressing-room. A light fringe of snow lay like a cape on the shoulders of his overcoat and like toecaps on the toes of his goloshes; and, as the buttons of his overcoat slipped with a squeaking noise through the snow-stiffened frieze,[7] a cold fragrant air from out-of-doors escaped from crevices and folds.

—Is it snowing again, Mr Conroy? asked Lily.

She had preceded him into the pantry to help him off with his overcoat. Gabriel smiled at the three syllables she had given his surname and glanced at her. She was a slim, growing girl, pale in complexion and with hay-coloured hair. The gas in the pantry made her look still paler. Gabriel had known her when she was a child and used to sit on the lowest step nursing a rag doll.

—Yes, Lily, he answered, and I think we're in for a night of it.

He looked up at the pantry ceiling, which was shaking with the stamping and shuffling of feet on the floor above, listened for a moment to the piano and then glanced at the girl, who was folding his overcoat carefully at the end of a shelf.

—Tell me, Lily, he said in a friendly tone, do you still go to school?

—O no, sir, she answered. I'm done schooling this year and more.

—O, then, said Gabriel gaily, I suppose we'll be going to your wedding one of these fine days with your young man, eh?

The girl glanced back at him over her shoulder and said with great bitterness:

—The men that is now is only all palaver[8] and what they can get out of you.

Gabriel coloured as if he felt he had made a mistake and, without looking at her, kicked off his goloshes and flicked actively with his muffler at his patent-leather shoes.

He was a stout tallish young man. The high colour of his cheeks pushed upwards even to his forehead where it scattered itself in a few formless patches of pale red; and on his hairless face there scintillated restlessly the polished lenses and the bright gilt rims of the glasses which screened his delicate and restless eyes. His glossy black hair was parted in the middle and brushed in a long curve behind his ears where it curled slightly beneath the groove left by his hat.

When he had flicked lustre into his shoes he stood up and pulled his waistcoat down more tightly on his plump body. Then he took a coin rapidly from his pocket.

—O Lily, he said, thrusting it into her hands, it's Christmas-time, isn't it? Just . . . here's a little. . . .

---

7. A kind of coarse woolen cloth.　　8. Empty and deceptive talk.

He walked rapidly towards the door.

—O no, sir! cried the girl, following him. Really, sir, I wouldn't take it.

—Christmas-time! Christmas-time! said Gabriel, almost trotting to the stairs and waving his hand to her in deprecation.

The girl, seeing that he had gained the stairs, called out after him:

—Well, thank you, sir.

He waited outside the drawing-room door until the waltz should finish, listening to the skirts that swept against it and to the shuffling of feet. He was still discomposed by the girl's bitter and sudden retort. It had cast a gloom over him which he tried to dispel by arranging his cuffs and the bows of his tie. Then he took from his waistcoat pocket a little paper and glanced at the headings he had made for his speech. He was undecided about the lines from Robert Browning for he feared they would be above the heads of his hearers. Some quotation that they could recognise from Shakespeare or from the Melodies[9] would be better. The indelicate clacking of the men's heels and the shuffling of their soles reminded him that their grade of culture differed from his. He would only make himself ridiculous by quoting poetry to them which they could not understand. They would think that he was airing his superior education. He would fail with them just as he had failed with the girl in the pantry. He had taken up a wrong tone. His whole speech was a mistake from first to last, an utter failure.

Just then his aunts and his wife came out of the ladies' dressing-room. His aunts were two small plainly dressed old women. Aunt Julia was an inch or so the taller. Her hair, drawn low over the tops of her ears, was grey; and grey also, with darker shadows, was her large flaccid face. Though she was stout in build and stood erect her slow eyes and parted lips gave her the appearance of a woman who did not know where she was or where she was going. Aunt Kate was more vivacious. Her face, healthier than her sister's, was all puckers and creases, like a shrivelled red apple, and her hair, braided in the same old-fashioned way, had not lost its ripe nut colour.

They both kissed Gabriel frankly. He was their favourite nephew, the son of their dead elder sister, Ellen, who had married T. J. Conroy of the Port and Docks.[1]

—Gretta tells me you're not going to take a cab back to Monkstown tonight, Gabriel, said Aunt Kate.

—No, said Gabriel, turning to his wife, we had quite enough of that last year, hadn't we? Don't you remember, Aunt Kate, what a cold Gretta got out of it? Cab windows rattling all the way, and the east wind blowing in after we passed Mention. Very jolly it was. Gretta caught a dreadful cold.

Aunt Kate frowned severely and nodded her head at every word.

—Quite right, Gabriel, quite right, she said. You can't be too careful.

—But as for Gretta there, said Gabriel, she'd walk home in the snow if she were let.

Mrs Conroy laughed.

—Don't mind him, Aunt Kate, she said. He's really an awful bother, what with green shades for Tom's eyes at night and making him do the dumb-bells,

9. *Irish Melodies* by Dublin-born Thomas Moore (1779–1852), a collection of songs—including one called "O Ye Dead"—that was extremely popular in late 19th- and early 20th-century Ireland.

1. Board managing the Port of Dublin.

and forcing Eva to eat the stirabout.[2] The poor child! And she simply hates the sight of it! . . . O, but you'll never guess what he makes me wear now!

She broke out into a peal of laughter and glanced at her husband, whose admiring and happy eyes had been wandering from her dress to her face and hair. The two aunts laughed heartily too, for Gabriel's solicitude was a standing joke with them.

—Goloshes! said Mrs Conroy. That's the latest. Whenever it's wet underfoot I must put on my goloshes. To-night even he wanted me to put them on, but I wouldn't. The next thing he'll buy me will be a diving suit.

Gabriel laughed nervously and patted his tie reassuringly while Aunt Kate nearly doubled herself, so heartily did she enjoy the joke. The smile soon faded from Aunt Julia's face and her mirthless eyes were directed towards her nephew's face. After a pause she asked:

—And what are goloshes, Gabriel?

—Goloshes, Julia! exclaimed her sister. Goodness me, don't you know what goloshes are? You wear them over your . . . over your boots, Gretta, isn't it?

—Yes, said Mrs Conroy. Guttapercha things. We both have a pair now. Gabriel says everyone wears them on the continent.

—O, on the continent, murmured Aunt Julia, nodding her head slowly.

Gabriel knitted his brows and said, as if he were slightly angered:

—It's nothing very wonderful but Gretta thinks it very funny because she says the word reminds her of Christy Minstrels.[3]

—But tell me, Gabriel, said Aunt Kate, with brisk tact. Of course, you've seen about the room. Gretta was saying . . .

—O, the room is all right, replied Gabriel. I've taken one in the Gresham[4]

—To be sure, said Aunt Kate, by far the best thing to do. And the children, Gretta, you're not anxious about them?

—O, for one night, said Mrs Conroy. Besides, Bessie will look after them.

—To be sure, said Aunt Kate again. What a comfort it is to have a girl like that, one you can depend on! There's that Lily, I'm sure I don't know what has come over her lately. She's not the girl she was at all.

Gabriel was about to ask his aunt some questions on this point but she broke off suddenly to gaze after her sister who had wandered down the stairs and was craning her neck over the banisters.

—Now, I ask you, she said, almost testily, where is Julia going? Julia! Julia! Where are you going?

Julia, who had gone halfway down one flight, came back and announced blandly:

—Here's Freddy.

At the same moment a clapping of hands and a final flourish of the pianist told that the waltz had ended. The drawing-room door was opened from within and some couples came out. Aunt Kate drew Gabriel aside hurriedly and whispered into his ear:

—Slip down, Gabriel, like a good fellow and see if he's all right, and don't let him up if he's screwed. I'm sure he's screwed. I'm sure he is.

2. Porridge made by stirring oatmeal in boiling milk or water.
3. Originally the name of a troupe of entertainers imitating African Americans, founded by George Christy of New York. By Joyce's time the meaning had become extended to any group with blackened faces who sang what were known as Negro melodies to banjo accompaniment, interspersed with jokes.
4. The Gresham Hotel, still one of the best hotels in Dublin.

Gabriel went to the stairs and listened over the banisters. He could hear two persons talking in the pantry. Then he recognised Freddy Malins' laugh. He went down the stairs noisily.

—It's such a relief, said Aunt Kate to Mrs Conroy, that Gabriel is here. I always feel easier in my mind when he's here. . . . Julia, there's Miss Daly and Miss Power will take some refreshment. Thanks for your beautiful waltz, Miss Daly. It made lovely time.

A tall wizen-faced man, with a stiff grizzled moustache and swarthy skin, who was passing out with his partner said:

—And may we have some refreshment, too, Miss Morkan?

—Julia, said Aunt Kate summarily, and here's Mr Browne and Miss Furlong. Take them in, Julia, with Miss Daly and Miss Power.

—I'm the man for the ladies, said Mr Browne, pursing his lips until his moustache bristled and smiling in all his wrinkles. You know, Miss Morkan, the reason they are so fond of me is—

He did not finish his sentence, but, seeing that Aunt Kate was out of earshot, at once led the three young ladies into the back room. The middle of the room was occupied by two square tables placed end to end, and on these Aunt Julia and the caretaker were straightening and smoothing a large cloth. On the sideboard were arrayed dishes and plates, and glasses and bundles of knives and forks and spoons. The top of the closed square piano served also as a sideboard for viands and sweets. At a smaller sideboard in one corner two young men were standing, drinking hop-bitters.

Mr Browne led his charges thither and invited them all, in jest, to some ladies' punch, hot, strong and sweet. As they said they never took anything strong he opened three bottles of lemonade for them. Then he asked one of the young men to move aside, and, taking hold of the decanter, filled out for himself a goodly measure of whisky. The young men eyed him respectfully while he took a trial sip.

—God help me, he said, smiling, it's the doctor's orders.

His wizened face broke into a broader smile, and the three young ladies laughed in musical echo to his pleasantry, swaying their bodies to and fro, with nervous jerks of their shoulders. The boldest said:

—O, now, Mr Browne, I'm sure the doctor never ordered anything of the kind.

Mr Browne took another sip of his whisky and said, with sidling mimicry:

—Well, you see, I'm like the famous Mrs Cassidy, who is reported to have said: *Now, Mary Grimes, if I don't take it, make me take it, for I feel I want it.*

His hot face had leaned forward a little too confidentially and he had assumed a very low Dublin accent so that the young ladies, with one instinct, received his speech in silence. Miss Furlong, who was one of Mary Jane's pupils, asked Miss Daly what was the name of the pretty waltz she had played; and Mr Browne, seeing that he was ignored, turned promptly to the two young men who were more appreciative.

A red-faced young woman, dressed in pansy, came into the room, excitedly clapping her hands and crying:

—Quadrilles.[5] Quadrilles!

Close on her heels came Aunt Kate, crying:

—Two gentlemen and three ladies, Mary Jane!

5. A square dance usually performed by four couples.

—O, here's Mr Bergin and Mr Kerrigan, said Mary Jane. Mr Kerrigan, will you take Miss Power? Miss Furlong, may I get you a partner, Mr Bergin. O, that'll just do now.

—Three ladies, Mary Jane, said Aunt Kate.

The two young gentlemen asked the ladies if they might have the pleasure, and Mary Jane turned to Miss Daly.

—O, Miss Daly, you're really awfully good, after playing for the last two dances, but really we're so short of ladies to-night.

—I don't mind in the least, Miss Morkan.

—But I've a nice partner for you, Mr Bartell D'Arcy, the tenor. I'll get him to sing later on. All Dublin is raving about him.

—Lovely voice, lovely voice! said Aunt Kate.

As the piano had twice begun the prelude to the first figure Mary Jane led her recruits quickly from the room. They had hardly gone when Aunt Julia wandered slowly into the room, looking behind her at something.

—What is the matter, Julia? asked Aunt Kate anxiously. Who is it?

Julia, who was carrying in a column of table-napkins, turned to her sister and said, simply, as if the question had surprised her:

—It's only Freddy, Kate, and Gabriel with him.

In fact right behind her Gabriel could be seen piloting Freddy Malins across the landing. The latter, a young man of about forty, was of Gabriel's size and build, with very round shoulders. His face was fleshy and pallid, touched with colour only at the thick hanging lobes of his ears and at the wide wings of his nose. He had coarse features, a blunt nose, a convex and receding brow, tumid and protruded lips. His heavy-lidded eyes and the disorder of his scanty hair made him look sleepy. He was laughing heartily in a high key at a story which he had been telling Gabriel on the stairs and at the same time rubbing the knuckles of his left fist backwards and forwards into his left eye.

—Good-evening, Freddy, said Aunt Julia.

Freddy Malins bade the Misses Morkan good-evening in what seemed an offhand fashion by reason of the habitual catch in his voice and then, seeing that Mr Browne was grinning at him from the sideboard, crossed the room on rather shaky legs and began to repeat in an undertone the story he had just told to Gabriel.

—He's not so bad, is he? said Aunt Kate to Gabriel.

Gabriel's brows were dark but he raised them quickly and answered:

—O no, hardly noticeable.

—Now, isn't he a terrible fellow! she said. And his poor mother made him take the pledge[6] on New Year's Eve. But come on, Gabriel, into the drawing-room.

Before leaving the room with Gabriel she signalled to Mr Browne by frowning and shaking her forefinger in warning to and fro. Mr Browne nodded in answer and, when she had gone, said to Freddy Malins:

—Now, then, Teddy, I'm going to fill you out a good glass of lemonade just to buck you up.

Freddy Malins, who was nearing the climax of his story, waved the offer aside impatiently but Mr Browne, having first called Freddy Malins' attention

---

6. Sign a solemn promise not to drink alcohol.

to a disarray in his dress, filled out and handed him a full glass of lemonade. Freddy Malins' left hand accepted the glass mechanically, his right hand being engaged in the mechanical readjustment of his dress. Mr Browne, whose face was once more wrinkling with mirth, poured out for himself a glass of whisky while Freddy Malins exploded, before he had well reached the climax of his story, in a kink of high-pitched bronchitic laughter and, setting down his untasted and overflowing glass, began to rub the knuckles of his left fist backwards and forwards into his left eye, repeating words of his last phrase as well as his fit of laughter would allow him.

Gabriel could not listen while Mary Jane was playing her Academy piece, full of runs and difficult passages, to the hushed drawing-room. He liked music but the piece she was playing had no melody for him and he doubted whether it had any melody for the other listeners, though they had begged Mary Jane to play something. Four young men, who had come from the refreshment-room to stand in the door-way at the sound of the piano, had gone away quietly in couples after a few minutes. The only persons who seemed to follow the music were Mary Jane herself, her hands racing along the key-board or lifted from it at the pauses like those of a priestess in momentary imprecation, and Aunt Kate standing at her elbow to turn the page.

Gabriel's eyes, irritated by the floor, which glittered with beeswax under the heavy chandelier, wandered to the wall above the piano. A picture of the balcony scene in *Romeo and Juliet* hung there and beside it was a picture of the two murdered princes in the Tower[7] which Aunt Julia had worked in red, blue and brown wools when she was a girl. Probably in the school they had gone to as girls that kind of work had been taught, for one year his mother had worked for him as a birthday present a waistcoat of purple tabinet,[8] with little foxes' heads upon it, lined with brown satin and having round mulberry buttons. It was strange that his mother had had no musical talent though Aunt Kate used to call her the brains carrier of the Morkan family. Both she and Julia had always seemed a little proud of their serious and matronly sister. Her photograph stood before the pierglass.[9] She held an open book on her knees and was pointing out something in it to Constantine who, dressed in a man-o'-war suit,[1] lay at her feet. It was she who had chosen the names for her sons for she was very sensible of the dignity of family life. Thanks to her, Constantine was now senior curate[2] in Balbriggan and, thanks to her, Gabriel himself had taken his degree in the Royal University. A shadow passed over his face as he remembered her sullen opposition to his marriage. Some slighting phrases she had used still rankled in his memory; she had once spoken of Gretta as being country cute and that was not true of Gretta at all. It was Gretta who had nursed her during all her last long illness in their house at Monkstown.

He knew that Mary Jane must be near the end of her piece for she was playing again the opening melody with runs of scales after every bar and while he waited for the end the resentment died down in his heart. The piece ended with a trill of octaves in the treble and a final deep octave in the bass. Great applause greeted Mary Jane as, blushing and rolling up her music nervously, she escaped from the room. The most vigorous clapping came from

7. Probably Edward V and his brother Richard, duke of York, reputedly murdered in 1483 by their uncle and successor, Richard III.
8. Silk and wool fabric made chiefly in Ireland.

9. Large tall mirror.
1. Sailor suit, favorite wear for children of both sexes early in the 20th century.
2. Clergyman appointed to assist a parish priest.

the four young men in the doorway who had gone away to the refreshment-room at the beginning of the piece but had come back when the piano had stopped.

Lancers[3] were arranged. Gabriel found himself partnered with Miss Ivors. She was a frank-mannered talkative young lady, with a freckled face and prominent brown eyes. She did not wear a low-cut bodice and the large brooch which was fixed in the front of her collar bore on it an Irish device.

When they had taken their places she said abruptly:

—I have a crow to pluck with you.

—With me? said Gabriel.

She nodded her head gravely.

—What is it? asked Gabriel, smiling at her solemn manner.

—Who is G. C.? answered Miss Ivors, turning her eyes upon him.

Gabriel coloured and was about to knit his brows, as if he did not understand, when she said bluntly:

—O, innocent Amy! I have found out that you write for *The Daily Express*. Now, aren't you ashamed of yourself?

—Why should I be ashamed of myself? asked Gabriel, blinking his eyes and trying to smile.

—Well, I'm ashamed of you, said Miss Ivors frankly. To say you'd write for a rag like that. I didn't think you were a West Briton.[4]

A look of perplexity appeared on Gabriel's face. It was true that he wrote a literary column every Wednesday in *The Daily Express*, for which he was paid fifteen shillings. But that did not make him a West Briton surely. The books he received for review were almost more welcome than the paltry cheque. He loved to feel the covers and turn over the pages of newly printed books. Nearly every day when his teaching in the college was ended he used to wander down the quays to the second-hand booksellers, to Hickey's on Bachelor's Walk, to Webb's, or Massey's on Aston's Quay, or to O'Clohissey's in the by-street. He did not know how to meet her charge. He wanted to say that literature was above politics. But they were friends of many years' standing and their careers had been parallel, first at the University and then as teachers: he could not risk a grandiose phrase with her. He continued blinking his eyes and trying to smile and murmured lamely that he saw nothing political in writing reviews of books.

When their turn to cross had come he was still perplexed and inattentive. Miss Ivors promptly took his hand in a warm grasp and said in a soft friendly tone:

—Of course, I was only joking. Come, we cross now.

When they were together again she spoke of the University question[5] and Gabriel felt more at ease. A friend of hers had shown her his review of Browning's poems. That was how she had found out the secret: but she liked the review immensely. Then she said suddenly:

—O, Mr Conroy, will you come for an excursion to the Aran Isles[6] this summer? We're going to stay there a whole month. It will be splendid out in the Atlantic. You ought to come. Mr Clancy is coming, and Mr Kilkelly and

---

3. A square dance for four or more couples.
4. A pejorative term for one who denies a separate Irish nationality and sees Ireland as simply a western extension of Great Britain.

5. Namely, whether Ireland's elite Protestant universities should be open to Catholics.
6. Three small islands lying across the entrance to Galway Bay, on the west coast of Ireland.

Kathleen Kearney. It would be splendid for Gretta too if she'd come. She's from Connach,[7] isn't she?

—Her people are, said Gabriel shortly.

—But you will come, won't you? said Miss Ivors, laying her warm hand eagerly on his arm.

—The fact is, said Gabriel, I have already arranged to go—

—Go where? asked Miss Ivors.

—Well, you know, every year I go for a cycling tour with some fellows and so—

—But where? asked Miss Ivors.

—Well, we usually go to France or Belgium or perhaps Germany, said Gabriel awkwardly.

—And why do you go to France and Belgium, said Miss Ivors, instead of visiting your own land?

—Well, said Gabriel, it's partly to keep in touch with the languages and partly for a change.

—And haven't you your own language to keep in touch with—Irish? asked Miss Ivors.

—Well, said Gabriel, if it comes to that, you know, Irish is not my language.

Their neighbours had turned to listen to the cross-examination. Gabriel glanced right and left nervously and tried to keep his good humour under the ordeal which was making a blush invade his forehead.

—And haven't you your own land to visit, continued Miss Ivors, that you know nothing of, your own people, and your own country?

—O, to tell you the truth, retorted Gabriel suddenly, I'm sick of my own country, sick of it!

—Why? asked Miss Ivors.

Gabriel did not answer for his retort had heated him.

—Why? repeated Miss Ivors.

They had to go visiting together and, as he had not answered her, Miss Ivors said warmly:

—Of course, you've no answer.

Gabriel tried to cover his agitation by taking part in the dance with great energy. He avoided her eyes for he had seen a sour expression on her face. But when they met in the long chain he was surprised to feel his hand firmly pressed. She looked at him from under her brows for a moment quizzically[8] until he smiled. Then, just as the chain was about to start again, she stood on tiptoe and whispered into his ear:

—West Briton!

When the lancers were over Gabriel went away to a remote corner of the room where Freddy Malins' mother was sitting. She was a stout feeble old woman with white hair. Her voice had a catch in it like her son's and she stuttered slightly. She had been told that Freddy had come and that he was nearly all right. Gabriel asked her whether she had had a good crossing. She lived with her married daughter in Glasgow and came to Dublin on a visit once a year. She answered placidly that she had had a beautiful crossing and that the captain had been most attentive to her. She spoke also of the

7. Or Connaught, a rural region on the west coast of Ireland.

8. Teasingly.

beautiful house her daughter kept in Glasgow, and of all the nice friends they had there. While her tongue rambled on Gabriel tried to banish from his mind all memory of the unpleasant incident with Miss Ivors. Of course the girl or woman, or whatever she was, was an enthusiast but there was a time for all things. Perhaps he ought not to have answered her like that. But she had no right to call him a West Briton before people, even in joke. She had tried to make him ridiculous before people, heckling him and staring at him with her rabbit's eyes.

He saw his wife making her way towards him through the waltzing couples. When she reached him she said into his ear:

—Gabriel, Aunt Kate wants to know won't you carve the goose as usual. Miss Daly will carve the ham and I'll do the pudding.

—All right, said Gabriel.

—She's sending in the younger ones first as soon as this waltz is over so that we'll have the table to ourselves.

—Were you dancing? asked Gabriel.

—Of course I was. Didn't you see me? What words had you with Molly Ivors?

—No words. Why? Did she say so?

—Something like that. I'm trying to get that Mr D'Arcy to sing. He's full of conceit, I think.

—There were no words, said Gabriel moodily, only she wanted me to go for a trip to the west of Ireland and I said I wouldn't.

His wife clasped her hands excitedly and gave a little jump.

—O, do go, Gabriel, she cried. I'd love to see Galway again.

—You can go if you like, said Gabriel coldly.

She looked at him for a moment, then turned to Mrs Malins and said:

—There's a nice husband for you, Mrs Malins.

While she was threading her way back across the room Mrs Malins, without adverting to the interruption, went on to tell Gabriel what beautiful places there were in Scotland and beautiful scenery. Her son-in-law brought them every year to the lakes and they used to go fishing. Her son-in-law was a splendid fisher. One day he caught a fish, a beautiful big big fish, and the man in the hotel boiled it for their dinner.

Gabriel hardly heard what she said. Now that supper was coming near he began to think again about his speech and about the quotation. When he saw Freddy Malins coming across the room to visit his mother Gabriel left the chair free for him and retired into the embrasure[9] of the window. The room had already cleared and from the back room came the clatter of plates and knives. Those who still remained in the drawing-room seemed tired of dancing and were conversing quietly in little groups. Gabriel's warm trembling fingers tapped the cold pane of the window. How cool it must be outside! How pleasant it would be to walk out alone, first along by the river and then through the park! The snow would be lying on the branches of the trees and forming a bright cap on the top of the Wellington Monument.[1] How much more pleasant it would be there than at the supper-table!

9. Opening for a window in a thick wall.
1. Tribute to Arthur Wellesley (1769–1852), 1st duke of Wellington, Dublin-born hero of the British army. The obelisk stands in Dublin's Phoenix Park.

He ran over the headings of his speech: Irish hospitality, sad memories, the Three Graces, Paris,[2] the quotation from Browning. He repeated to himself a phrase he had written in his review: *One feels that one is listening to a thought-tormented music.* Miss Ivors had praised the review. Was she sincere? Had she really any life of her own behind all her propagandism? There had never been any ill-feeling between them until that night. It unnerved him to think that she would be at the supper-table, looking up at him while he spoke with her critical quizzing eyes. Perhaps she would not be sorry to see him fail in his speech. An idea came into his mind and gave him courage. He would say, alluding to Aunt Kate and Aunt Julia: *Ladies and Gentlemen, the generation which is now on the wane among us may have had its faults but for my part I think it had certain qualities of hospitality, of humour, of humanity, which the new and very serious and hypereducated generation that is growing up around us seems to me to lack.* Very good: that was one for Miss Ivors. What did he care that his aunts were only two ignorant old women?

A murmur in the room attracted his attention. Mr Browne was advancing from the door, gallantly escorting Aunt Julia, who leaned upon his arm, smiling and hanging her head. An irregular musketry of applause escorted her also as far as the piano and then, as Mary Jane seated herself on the stool, and Aunt Julia, no longer smiling, half turned so as to pitch her voice fairly into the room, gradually ceased. Gabriel recognised the prelude. It was that of an old song of Aunt Julia's—*Arrayed for the Bridal.*[3] Her voice, strong and clear in tone, attacked with great spirit the runs which embellish the air and though she sang very rapidly she did not miss even the smallest of the grace notes. To follow the voice, without looking at the singer's face, was to feel and share the excitement of swift and secure flight. Gabriel applauded loudly with all the others at the close of the song and loud applause was borne in from the invisible supper-table. It sounded so genuine that a little colour struggled into Aunt Julia's face as she bent to replace in the music-stand the old leather-bound song-book that had her initials on the cover. Freddy Malins, who had listened with his head perched sideways to hear her better, was still applauding when everyone else had ceased and talking animatedly to his mother who nodded her head gravely and slowly in acquiescence. At last, when he could clap no more, he stood up suddenly and hurried across the room to Aunt Julia whose hand he seized and held in both his hands, shaking it when words failed him or the catch in his voice proved too much for him.

—I was just telling my mother, he said, I never heard you sing so well, never. No, I never heard your voice so good as it is to-night. Now! Would you believe that now? That's the truth. Upon my word and honour that's the truth. I never heard your voice sound so fresh and so . . . so clear and fresh, never.

Aunt Julia smiled broadly and murmured something about compliments as she released her hand from his grasp. Mr Browne extended his open

---

2. In Greek mythology Paris was selected by Zeus to choose which of three goddesses was the most beautiful. The Graces were three sister-goddesses—Aglaia, splendor; Euphrosyne, festivity; and Thalia, rejoicing—who together represented loveliness and joy. Gabriel is making a mental note to refer to his two aunts and Mary Jane in a complimentary way.

3. This old song (beginning "Arrayed for the bridal, in beauty behold her") "is replete with long and complicated runs, requiring a sophisticated and gifted singer" (Bowen, *Musical Allusions in the Works of James Joyce*, 1974); the suggestion is that Aunt Julia was a really accomplished singer.

hand towards her and said to those who were near him in the manner of a showman introducing a prodigy to an audience:

—Miss Julia Morkan, my latest discovery!

He was laughing very heartily at this himself when Freddy Malins turned to him and said:

—Well, Browne, if you're serious you might make a worse discovery. All I can say is I never heard her sing half so well as long as I am coming here. And that's the honest truth.

—Neither did I, said Mr Browne. I think her voice has greatly improved.

Aunt Julia shrugged her shoulders and said with meek pride:

—Thirty years ago I hadn't a bad voice as voices go.

—I often told Julia, said Aunt Kate emphatically, that she was simply thrown away in that choir. But she never would be said by me.

She turned as if to appeal to the good sense of the others against a refractory child while Aunt Julia gazed in front of her, a vague smile of reminiscence playing on her face.

—No, continued Aunt Kate, she wouldn't be said or led by anyone, slaving there in that choir night and day, night and day. Six o'clock on Christmas morning! And all for what?

—Well, isn't it for the honour of God, Aunt Kate? asked Mary Jane, twisting round on the piano-stool and smiling.

Aunt Kate turned fiercely on her niece and said:

—I know all about the honour of God, Mary Jane, but I think it's not at all honourable for the pope to turn out the women out of the choirs that have slaved there all their lives and put little whipper-snappers of boys over their heads. I suppose it is for the good of the Church if the pope does it. But it's not just, Mary Jane, and it's not right.

She had worked herself into a passion and would have continued in defence of her sister for it was a sore subject with her but Mary Jane, seeing that all the dancers had come back, intervened pacifically:

—Now, Aunt Kate, you're giving scandal to Mr Browne who is of the other persuasion.[4]

Aunt Kate turned to Mr Browne, who was grinning at this allusion to his religion, and said hastily:

—O, I don't question the pope's being right. I'm only a stupid old woman and I wouldn't presume to do such a thing. But there's such a thing as common everyday politeness and gratitude. And if I were in Julia's place I'd tell that Father Healy straight up to his face . . .

—And besides, Aunt Kate, said Mary Jane, we really are all hungry and when we are hungry we are all very quarrelsome.

—And when we are thirsty we are also quarrelsome, added Mr Browne.

—So that we had better go to supper, said Mary Jane, and finish the discussion afterwards.

On the landing outside the drawing-room Gabriel found his wife and Mary Jane trying to persuade Miss Ivors to stay for supper. But Miss Ivors, who had put on her hat and was buttoning her cloak, would not stay. She did not feel in the least hungry and she had already overstayed her time.

—But only for ten minutes, Molly, said Mrs Conroy. That won't delay you.

4. I.e., Protestant.

—To take a pick itself, said Mary Jane, after all your dancing.

—I really couldn't, said Miss Ivors.

—I am afraid you didn't enjoy yourself at all, said Mary Jane hopelessly.

—Ever so much, I assure you, said Miss Ivors, but you really must let me run off now.

—But how can you get home? asked Mrs Conroy.

—O, it's only two steps up the quay.

Gabriel hesitated a moment and said:

—If you will allow me, Miss Ivors, I'll see you home if you really are obliged to go.

But Miss Ivors broke away from them.

—I won't hear of it, she cried. For goodness sake go in to your suppers and don't mind me. I'm quite well able to take care of myself.

—Well, you're the comical girl, Molly, said Mrs Conroy frankly.

—*Beannacht libh*,[5] cried Miss Ivors, with a laugh, as she ran down the staircase.

Mary Jane gazed after her, a moody puzzled expression on her face, while Mrs Conroy leaned over the banisters to listen for the hall-door. Gabriel asked himself was he the cause of her abrupt departure. But she did not seem to be in ill humour: she had gone away laughing. He stared blankly down the staircase.

At that moment Aunt Kate came toddling out of the supper-room, almost wringing her hands in despair.

—Where is Gabriel? she cried. Where on earth is Gabriel? There's everyone waiting in there, stage to let, and nobody to carve the goose!

—Here I am, Aunt Kate! cried Gabriel, with sudden animation, ready to carve a flock of geese, if necessary.

A fat brown goose lay at one end of the table and at the other end, on a bed of creased paper strewn with sprigs of parsley, lay a great ham, stripped of its outer skin and peppered over with crust crumbs, a neat paper frill round its shin and beside this was a round of spiced beef. Between these rival ends ran parallel lines of side-dishes: two little minsters of jelly, red and yellow; a shallow dish full of blocks of blancmange[6] and red jam, a large green leaf-shaped dish with a stalk-shaped handle, on which lay bunches of purple raisins and peeled almonds, a companion dish on which lay a solid rectangle of Smyrna figs, a dish of custard topped with grated nutmeg, a small bowl full of chocolates and sweets wrapped in gold and silver papers and a glass vase in which stood some tall celery stalks. In the centre of the table there stood, as sentries to a fruit-stand which upheld a pyramid of oranges and American apples, two squat old-fashioned decanters of cut glass, one containing port and the other dark sherry. On the closed square piano a pudding in a huge yellow dish lay in waiting and behind it were three squads of bottles of stout and ale and minerals, drawn up according to the colours of their uniforms, the first two black, with brown and red labels, the third and smallest squad white, with transverse green sashes.

Gabriel took his seat boldly at the head of the table and, having looked to the edge of the carver, plunged his fork firmly into the goose. He felt quite at ease now for he was an expert carver and liked nothing better than to find himself at the head of a well-laden table.

---

5. Blessing on you (Gaelic; literal trans.); goodbye.   6. Sweet almond-flavored pudding.

—Miss Furlong, what shall I send you? he asked. A wing or a slice of the breast?

—Just a small slice of the breast.

—Miss Higgins, what for you?

—O, anything at all, Mr Conroy.

While Gabriel and Miss Daly exchanged plates of goose and plates of ham and spiced beef Lily went from guest to guest with a dish of hot floury potatoes wrapped in a white napkin. This was Mary Jane's idea and she had also suggested apple sauce for the goose but Aunt Kate had said that plain roast goose without apple sauce had always been good enough for her and she hoped she might never eat worse. Mary Jane waited on her pupils and saw that they got the best slices and Aunt Kate and Aunt Julia opened and carried across from the piano bottles of stout and ale for the gentlemen and bottles of minerals for the ladies. There was a great deal of confusion and laughter and noise, the noise of orders and counter-orders, of knives and forks, of corks and glass-stoppers. Gabriel began to carve second helpings as soon as he had finished the first round without serving himself. Everyone protested loudly so that he compromised by taking a long draught of stout for he had found the carving hot work. Mary Jane settled down quietly to her supper but Aunt Kate and Aunt Julia were still toddling round the table, walking on each other's heels, getting in each other's way and giving each other unheeded orders. Mr Browne begged of them to sit down and eat their suppers and so did Gabriel but they said there was time enough so that, at last, Freddy Malins stood up and, capturing Aunt Kate, plumped her down on her chair amid general laughter.

When everyone had been well served Gabriel said, smiling:

—Now, if anyone wants a little more of what vulgar people call stuffing let him or her speak.

A chorus of voices invited him to begin his own supper and Lily came forward with three potatoes which she had reserved for him.

—Very well, said Gabriel amiably, as he took another preparatory draught, kindly forget my existence, ladies and gentlemen, for a few minutes.

He set to his supper and took no part in the conversation with which the table covered Lily's removal of the plates. The subject of talk was the opera company which was then at the Theatre Royal. Mr Bartell D'Arcy, the tenor, a dark-complexioned young man with a smart moustache, praised very highly the leading contralto of the company but Miss Furlong thought she had a rather vulgar style of production. Freddy Malins said there was a negro chieftain singing in the second part of the Gaiety pantomime who had one of the finest tenor voices he had every heard.

—Have you heard him? he asked Mr Bartell D'Arcy across the table.

—No, answered Mr Bartell D'Arcy carelessly.

—Because, Freddy Malins explained, now I'd be curious to hear your opinion of him. I think he has a grand voice.

—It takes Teddy to find out the really good things, said Mr Browne familiarly to the table.

—And why couldn't he have a voice too? asked Freddy Malins sharply. Is it because he's only a black?

Nobody answered this question and Mary Jane led the table back to the legitimate opera. One of her pupils had given her a pass for *Mignon.*[7] Of

7. Opera by Ambroise Thomas first produced in Paris in 1866 and in London in 1870.

course it was very fine, she said, but it made her think of poor Georgina Burns. Mr Browne could go back farther still, to the old Italian companies that used to come to Dublin—Tietjens, Ilma de Murzka, Campanini, the great Trebelli, Giuglini, Ravelli, Aramburo. Those were the days, he said, when there was something like singing to be heard in Dublin. He told too of how the top gallery of the old Royal used to be packed night after night, of how one night an Italian tenor had sung five encores to *Let Me Like a Soldier Fall*,[8] introducing a high C every time, and of how the gallery boys would sometimes in their enthusiasm unyoke the horses from the carriage of some great *prima donna* and pull her themselves through the streets to her hotel. Why did they never play the grand old operas now, he asked, *Dinorah, Lucrezia Borgia*?[9] Because they could not get the voices to sing them: that was why.

—O, well, said Mr Bartell D'Arcy, I presume there are as good singers today as there were then.

—Where are they? asked Mr Browne defiantly.

—In London, Paris, Milan, said Mr Bartell d'Arcy warmly. I suppose Caruso[1] for example, is quite as good, if not better than any of the men you have mentioned.

—Maybe so, said Mr Browne. But I may tell you I doubt it strongly.

—O, I'd give anything to hear Caruso sing, said Mary Jane.

—For me, said Aunt Kate, who had been picking a bone, there was only one tenor. To please me, I mean. But I suppose none of you ever heard of him.

—Who was he, Miss Morkan? asked Mr Bartell D'Arcy politely.

—His name, said Aunt Kate, was Parkinson. I heard him when he was in his prime and I think he had then the purest tenor voice that was ever put into a man's throat.

—Strange, said Mr Bartell d'Arcy. I never even heard of him.

—Yes, yes, Miss Morkan is right, said Mr Browne. I remember hearing of old Parkinson but he's too far back for me.

—A beautiful pure sweet mellow English tenor, said Aunt Kate with enthusiasm.

Gabriel having finished, the huge pudding was transferred to the table. The clatter of forks and spoons began again. Gabriel's wife served out spoonfuls of the pudding and passed the plates down the table. Midway down they were held up by Mary Jane, who replenished them with raspberry or orange jelly or with blancmange and jam. The pudding was of Aunt Julia's making and she received praises for it from all quarters. She herself said that it was not quite brown enough.

—Well, I hope, Miss Morkan, said Mr Browne, that I'm brown enough for you because, you know, I'm all brown.

All the gentlemen, except Gabriel, ate some of the pudding out of compliment to Aunt Julia. As Gabriel never ate sweets the celery had been left for him. Freddy Malins also took a stalk of celery and ate it with his pudding.

---

8. This song, from the opera *Montana* by W. Wallace (it actually begins "Yes! let me like a soldier fall"), ends on middle C; it would be a piece of exhibitionism to end on a high C, as Joyce's father, who had a good voice, used to do. Joyce's brother Stanislaus remembered the song as insufferable rubbish. Mr. Browne is not to be taken seriously as a music critic.
9. An opera by Donizetti, first produced at La Scala, Milan, in 1833. *Dinorah* is an opera by Meyerbeer, first produced in Paris in 1859.
1. Enrico Caruso (1873–1921), the great Italian dramatic tenor.

He had been told that celery was a capital thing for the blood and he was just then under doctor's care. Mrs Malins, who had been silent all through the supper, said that her son was going down to Mount Melleray in a week or so. The table then spoke of Mount Melleray, how bracing the air was down there, how hospitable the monks were and how they never asked for a penny-piece from their guests.

—And do you mean to say, asked Mr Browne incredulously, that a chap can go down there and put up there as if it were a hotel and live on the fat of the land and then come away without paying a farthing?

—O, most people give some donation to the monastery when they leave, said Mary Jane.

—I wish we had an institution like that in our Church, said Mr Browne candidly.

He was astonished to hear that the monks never spoke, got up at two in the morning and slept in their coffins. He asked what they did it for.

—That's the rule of the order, said Aunt Kate firmly.

—Yes, but why? asked Mr Browne.

Aunt Kate repeated that it was the rule, that was all. Mr Browne still seemed not to understand. Freddy Malins explained to him, as best he could, that the monks were trying to make up for the sins committed by all the sinners in the outside world. The explanation was not very clear for Mr Browne grinned and said:

—I like that idea very much but wouldn't a comfortable spring bed do them as well as a coffin?

—The coffin, said Mary Jane, is to remind them of their last end.

As the subject had grown lugubrious it was buried in a silence of the table during which Mrs Malins could be heard saying to her neighbour in an indistinct undertone:

—They are very good men, the monks, very pious men.

The raisins and almonds and figs and apples and oranges and chocolates and sweets were now passed about the table and Aunt Julia invited all the guests to have either port or sherry. At first Mr Bartell D'Arcy refused to take either but one of his neighbours nudged him and whispered something to him upon which he allowed his glass to be filled. Gradually as the last glasses were being filled the conversation ceased. A pause followed, broken only by the noise of the wine and by unsettlings of chairs. The Misses Morkan, all three, looked down at the tablecloth. Someone coughed once or twice and then a few gentlemen patted the table gently as a signal for silence. The silence came and Gabriel pushed back his chair and stood up.

The patting at once grew louder in encouragement and then ceased altogether. Gabriel leaned his ten trembling fingers on the tablecloth and smiled nervously at the company. Meeting a row of upturned faces he raised his eyes to the chandelier. The piano was playing a waltz tune and he could hear the skirts sweeping against the drawing-room door. People, perhaps, were standing in the snow on the quay outside, gazing up at the lighted windows and listening to the waltz music. The air was pure there. In the distance lay the park where the trees were weighted with snow. The Wellington Monument wore a gleaming cap of snow that flashed westward over the white field of Fifteen Acres.

He began:

—Ladies and Gentlemen.

—It has fallen to my lot this evening, as in years past, to perform a very pleasing task but a task for which I am afraid my poor powers as a speaker are all too inadequate.

—No, no! said Mr Browne.

—But, however that may be, I can only ask you to-night to take the will for the deed and to lend me your attention for a few moments while I endeavour to express to you in words what my feelings are on this occasion.

—Ladies and Gentlemen. It is not the first time that we have gathered together under this hospitable roof, around this hospitable board. It is not the first time that we have been the recipients—or perhaps, I had better say, the victims—of the hospitality of certain good ladies.

He made a circle in the air with his arm and paused. Everyone laughed or smiled at Aunt Kate and Aunt Julia and Mary Jane who all turned crimson with pleasure. Gabriel went on more boldly:

—I feel more strongly with every recurring year that our country has no tradition which does it so much honour and which it should guard so jealously as that of its hospitality. It is a tradition that is unique as far as my experience goes (and I have visited not a few places abroad) among the modern nations. Some would say, perhaps, that with us it is rather a failing than anything to be boasted of. But granted even that, it is, to my mind, a princely failing, and one that I trust will long be cultivated among us. Of one thing, at least, I am sure. As long as this one roof shelters the good ladies aforesaid—and I wish from my heart it may do so for many and many a long year to come—the tradition of genuine warm-hearted courteous Irish hospitality, which our forefathers have handed down to us and which we in turn must hand down to our descendants, is still alive among us.

A hearty murmur of assent ran round the table. It shot through Gabriel's mind that Miss Ivors was not there and that she had gone away discourteously: and he said with confidence in himself:

—Ladies and Gentlemen.

—A new generation is growing up in our midst, a generation actuated by new ideas and new principles. It is serious and enthusiastic for these new ideas and its enthusiasm, even when it is misdirected, is, I believe, in the main sincere. But we are living in a sceptical and, if I may use the phrase, a thought-tormented age: and sometimes I fear that this new generation, educated or hypereducated as it is, will lack those qualities of humanity, of hospitality, of kindly humour which belonged to an older day. Listening to-night to the names of all those great singers of the past it seemed to me, I must confess, that we were living in a less spacious age. Those days might, without exaggeration, be called spacious days: and if they are gone beyond recall let us hope, at least, that in gatherings such as this we shall still speak of them with pride and affection, still cherish in our hearts the memory of those dead and gone great ones whose fame the world will not willingly let die.

—Hear, hear! said Mr Browne loudly.

—But yet, continued Gabriel, his voice falling into a softer inflection, there are always in gatherings such as this sadder thoughts that will recur to our minds: thoughts of the past, of youth, of changes, of absent faces that we miss here to-night. Our path through life is strewn with many such sad memories: and were we to brood upon them always we could not find the heart to go on bravely with our work among the living. We have all of us living duties and living affections which claim, and rightly claim, our strenuous endeavours.

—Therefore, I will not linger on the past. I will not let any gloomy moralising intrude upon us here to-night. Here we are gathered together for a brief moment from the bustle and rush of our everyday routine. We are met here as friends, in the spirit of good-fellowship, as colleagues, also to a certain extent, in the true spirit of *camaraderie*, and as the guests of—what shall I call them?—the Three Graces of the Dublin musical world.

The table burst into applause and laughter at this sally. Aunt Julia vainly asked each of her neighbours in turn to tell her what Gabriel had said.

—He says we are the Three Graces,[2] Aunt Julia, said Mary Jane.

Aunt Julia did not understand but she looked up, smiling, at Gabriel, who continued in the same vein:

—Ladies and Gentlemen.

—I will not attempt to play to-night the part that Paris played on another occasion. I will not attempt to choose between them. The task would be an invidious one and one beyond my poor powers. For when I view them in turn, whether it be our chief hostess herself, whose good heart, whose too good heart, has become a byword with all who know her, or her sister, who seems to be gifted with perennial youth and whose singing must have been a surprise and a revelation to us all to-night, or, last but not least, when I consider our youngest hostess, talented, cheerful, hard-working and the best of nieces, I confess, Ladies and Gentlemen, that I do not know to which of them I should award the prize.

Gabriel glanced down at his aunts and, seeing the large smile on Aunt Julia's face and the tears which had risen to Aunt Kate's eyes, hastened to his close. He raised his glass of port gallantly, while every member of the company fingered a glass expectantly, and said loudly:

—Let us toast them all three together. Let us drink to their health, wealth, long life, happiness and prosperity and may they long continue to hold the proud and self-won position which they hold in their profession and the position of honour and affection which they hold in our hearts.

All the guests stood up, glass in hand, and, turning towards the three seated ladies, sang in unison, with Mr Browne as leader:

> *For they are jolly gay fellows,*
> *For they are jolly gay fellows,*
> *For they are jolly gay fellows,*
> *Which nobody can deny.*

Aunt Kate was making frank use of her handkerchief and even Aunt Julia seemed moved. Freddy Malins beat time with his pudding-fork and the singers turned towards one another, as if in melodious conference, while they sang, with emphasis:

> *Unless he tells a lie,*
> *Unless he tells a lie.*

Then, turning once more towards their hostesses, they sang:

2. See n. 2, p. 1238.

For they are jolly gay fellows,
For they are jolly gay fellows,
For they are jolly gay fellows,
Which nobody can deny.

The acclamation which followed was taken up beyond the door of the supper-room by many of the other guests and renewed time after time, Freddy Malins acting as officer with his fork on high.

The piercing morning air came into the hall where they were standing so that Aunt Kate said:

—Close the door, somebody. Mrs Malins will get her death of cold.

—Browne is out there, Aunt Kate, said Mary Jane.

—Browne is everywhere, said Aunt Kate, lowering her voice.

Mary Jane laughed at her tone.

—Really, she said archly, he is very attentive.

—He has been laid on here like the gas, said Aunt Kate in the same tone, all during the Christmas.

She laughed herself this time good-humouredly and then added quickly:

—But tell him to come in, Mary Jane, and close the door. I hope to goodness he didn't hear me.

At that moment the hall-door was opened and Mr Browne came in from the doorstep, laughing as if his heart would break. He was dressed in a long green overcoat with mock astrakhan cuffs and collar and wore on his head an oval fur cap. He pointed down the snow-covered quay from where the sound of shrill prolonged whistling was borne in.

—Teddy will have all the cabs in Dublin out, he said.

Gabriel advanced from the little pantry behind the office, struggling into his overcoat and, looking round the hall, said:

—Gretta not down yet?

—She's getting on her things, Gabriel, said Aunt Kate.

—Who's playing up there? asked Gabriel.

—Nobody. They're all gone.

—O no, Aunt Kate, said Mary Jane. Bartell D'Arcy and Miss O'Callaghan aren't gone yet.

—Someone is strumming at the piano, anyhow, said Gabriel.

Mary Jane glanced at Gabriel and Mr Browne and said with a shiver:

—It makes me feel cold to look at you two gentlemen muffled up like that. I wouldn't like to face your journey home at this hour.

—I'd like nothing better this minute, said Mr Browne stoutly, than a rattling fine walk in the country or a fast drive with a good spanking goer between the shafts.

—We used to have a very good horse and trap[3] at home, said Aunt Julia sadly.

—The never-to-be-forgotten Johnny, said Mary Jane, laughing.

Aunt Kate and Gabriel laughed too.

—Why, what was wonderful about Johnny? asked Mr Browne.

—The late lamented Patrick Morkan, our grandfather, that is, explained Gabriel, commonly known in his later years as the old gentleman, was a glue-boiler.[4]

---

3. A two-wheeled horse-drawn carriage on springs.

4. Glue was made by boiling animal hides and hoofs.

—O, now, Gabriel, said Aunt Kate, laughing, he had a starch mill.

—Well, glue or starch, said Gabriel, the old gentleman had a horse by the name of Johnny. And Johnny used to work in the old gentleman's mill, walking round and round in order to drive the mill. That was all very well; but now comes the tragic part about Johnny. One fine day the old gentleman thought he'd like to drive out with the quality[5] to a military review in the park.

—The Lord have mercy on his soul, said Aunt Kate compassionately.

—Amen, said Gabriel. So the old gentleman, as I said, harnessed Johnny and put on his very best tall hat and his very best stock collar and drove out in grand style from his ancestral mansion somewhere near Back Lane, I think.

Everyone laughed, even Mrs Malins, at Gabriel's manner and Aunt Kate said:

—O now, Gabriel, he didn't live in Back Lane, really. Only the mill was there.

—Out from the mansion of his forefathers, continued Gabriel, he drove with Johnny. And everything went on beautifully until Johnny came in sight of King Billy's statue[6] and whether he fell in love with the horse King Billy sits on or whether he thought he was back again in the mill, anyhow he began to walk round the statue.

Gabriel paced in a circle round the hall in his goloshes amid the laughter of the others.

—Round and round he went, said Gabriel, and the old gentleman, who was a very pompous old gentleman, was highly indignant. *Go on, sir! What do you mean, sir? Johnny! Johnny! Most extraordinary conduct! Can't understand the horse!*

The peals of laughter which followed Gabriel's imitation of the incident were interrupted by a resounding knock at the hall-door. Mary Jane ran to open it and let in Freddy Malins. Freddy Malins, with his hat well back on his head and his shoulders humped with cold, was puffing and steaming after his exertions.

—I could only get one cab, he said.

—O, we'll find another along the quay, said Gabriel.

—Yes, said Aunt Kate. Better not keep Mrs Malins standing in the draught.

Mrs Malins was helped down the front steps by her son and Mr Browne and, after many manœuvres, hoisted into the cab. Freddy Malins clambered in after her and spent a long time settling her on the seat, Mr Browne helping him with advice. At last she was settled comfortably and Freddy Malins invited Mr Browne into the cab. There was a good deal of confused talk, and then Mr Browne got into the cab. The cabman settled his rug over his knees, and bent down for the address. The confusion grew greater and the cabman was directed differently by Freddy Malins and Mr Browne, each of whom had his head out through a window of the cab. The difficulty was to know where to drop Mr Browne along the route and Aunt Kate, Aunt Julia and Mary Jane helped the discussion from the doorstep with cross-directions and contradictions and abundance of laughter. As for Freddy Malins he was speechless with laughter. He popped his head in and out of

---

5. People of rank or high social position.
6. Statue of King William III of England in front of Trinity College, Dublin. He defeated predominantly Irish Catholic forces in the 1690 Battle of the Boyne.

the window every moment, to the great danger of his hat, and told his mother how the discussion was progressing till at last Mr Browne shouted to the bewildered cabman above the din of everybody's laughter:

—Do you know Trinity College?

—Yes, sir, said the cabman.

—Well, drive bang up against Trinity College gates, said Mr Browne, and then we'll tell you where to go. You understand now?

—Yes, sir, said the cabman.

—Make like a bird for Trinity College.

—Right, sir, cried the cabman.

The horse was whipped up and the cab rattled off along the quay amid a chorus of laughter and adieus.

Gabriel had not gone to the door with the others. He was in a dark part of the hall gazing up the staircase. A woman was standing near the top of the first flight, in the shadow also. He could not see her face but he could see the terracotta and salmonpink panels of her skirt which the shadow made appear black and white. It was his wife. She was leaning on the banisters, listening to something. Gabriel was surprised at her stillness and strained his ear to listen also. But he could hear little save the noise of laughter and dispute on the front steps, a few chords struck on the piano and a few notes of a man's voice singing.

He stood still in the gloom of the hall, trying to catch the air that the voice was singing and gazing up at his wife. There was grace and mystery in her attitude as if she were a symbol of something. He asked himself what is a woman standing on the stairs in the shadow, listening to distant music, a symbol of. If he were a painter he would paint her in that attitude. Her blue felt hat would show off the bronze of her hair against the darkness and the dark panels of her skirt would show off the light ones. *Distant Music* he would call the picture if he were a painter.

The hall-door was closed; and Aunt Kate, Aunt Julia and Mary Jane came down the hall, still laughing.

—Well, isn't Freddy terrible? said Mary Jane. He's really terrible.

Gabriel said nothing but pointed up the stairs towards where his wife was standing. Now that the hall-door was closed the voice and the piano could be heard more clearly. Gabriel held up his hand for them to be silent. The song seemed to be in the old Irish tonality and the singer seemed uncertain both of his words and of his voice. The voice, made plaintive by distance and by the singer's hoarseness, faintly illuminated the cadence of the air with words expressing grief:

> *O, the rain falls on my heavy locks*
> *And the dew wets my skin,*
> *My babe lies cold . . .*

—O, exclaimed Mary Jane. It's Bartell D'Arcy singing and he wouldn't sing all the night. O, I'll get him to sing a song before he goes.

—O do, Mary Jane, said Aunt Kate.

Mary Jane brushed past the others and ran to the staircase but before she reached it the singing stopped and the piano was closed abruptly.

—O, what a pity! she cried. Is he coming down, Gretta?

Gabriel heard his wife answer yes and saw her come down towards them. A few steps behind her were Mr Bartell D'Arcy and Miss O'Callaghan.

—O, Mr D'Arcy, cried Mary Jane, it's downright mean of you to break off like that when we were all in raptures listening to you.

—I have been at him all the evening, said Miss O'Callaghan, and Mrs Conroy too and he told us he had a dreadful cold and couldn't sing.

—O, Mr D'Arcy, said Aunt Kate, now that was a great fib to tell.

—Can't you see that I'm as hoarse as a crow? said Mr D'Arcy roughly.

He went into the pantry hastily and put on his overcoat. The others, taken aback by his rude speech, could find nothing to say. Aunt Kate wrinkled her brows and made signs to the others to drop the subject. Mr D'Arcy stood swathing his neck carefully and frowning.

—It's the weather, said Aunt Julia, after a pause.

—Yes, everybody has colds, said Aunt Kate readily, everybody.

—They say, said Mary Jane, we haven't had snow like it for thirty years; and I read this morning in the newspapers that the snow is general all over Ireland.

—I love the look of snow, said Aunt Julia sadly.

—So do I, said Miss O'Callaghan. I think Christmas is never really Christmas unless we have the snow on the ground.

—But poor Mr D'Arcy doesn't like the snow, said Aunt Kate, smiling.

Mr D'Arcy came from the pantry, full swathed and buttoned, and in a repentant tone told them the history of his cold. Everyone gave him advice and said it was a great pity and urged him to be very careful of his throat in the night air. Gabriel watched his wife who did not join in the conversation. She was standing right under the dusty fanlight and the flame of the gas lit up the rich bronze of her hair which he had seen her drying at the fire a few days before. She was in the same attitude and seemed unaware of the talk about her. At last she turned towards them and Gabriel saw that there was colour on her cheeks and that her eyes were shining. A sudden tide of joy went leaping out of his heart.

—Mr D'Arcy, she said, what is the name of that song you were singing?

—It's called *The Lass of Aughrim*,[7] said Mr D'Arcy, but I couldn't remember it properly. Why? Do you know it?

—*The Lass of Aughrim*, she repeated. I couldn't think of the name.

—It's a very nice air, said Mary Jane. I'm sorry you were not in voice tonight.

—Now, Mary Jane, said Aunt Kate, don't annoy Mr D'Arcy. I won't have him annoyed.

Seeing that all were ready to start she shepherded them to the door where good-night was said:

—Well, good-night, Aunt Kate, and thanks for the pleasant evening.

—Good-night, Gabriel. Good-night, Gretta!

—Good-night, Aunt Kate, and thanks ever so much. Good-night, Aunt Julia.

—O, good-night, Gretta, I didn't see you.

—Good-night, Mr D'Arcy. Good-night, Miss O'Callaghan.

—Good-night, Miss Morkan.

—Good-night, again.

---

7. An Irish version of a ballad about a girl deserted by her lover, whom she later tries to find, bringing the baby she had by him. Other versions are called "Love Gregory" and "Lord Gregory" (the name of the deserting lover), "The Lass of Lochryan," and "The Lass of Ocram."

—Good-night, all. Safe home.

—Good-night. Good-night.

The morning was still dark. A dull yellow light brooded over the houses and the river; and the sky seemed to be descending. It was slushy underfoot; and only streaks and patches of snow lay on the roofs, on the parapets of the quay and on the area railings. The lamps were still burning redly in the murky air and, across the river, the palace of the Four Courts stood out menacingly against the heavy sky.

She was walking on before him with Mr Bartell D'Arcy, her shoes in a brown parcel tucked under one arm and her hands holding her skirt up from the slush. She had no longer any grace of attitude but Gabriel's eyes were still bright with happiness. The blood went bounding along his veins; and the thoughts went rioting through his brain, proud, joyful, tender, valorous.

She was walking on before him so lightly and so erect that he longed to run after her noiselessly, catch her by the shoulders and say something foolish and affectionate into her ear. She seemed to him so frail that he longed to defend her against something and then to be alone with her. Moments of their secret life together burst like stars upon his memory. A heliotrope[8] envelope was lying beside his breakfast-cup and he was caressing it with his hand. Birds were twittering in the ivy and the sunny web of the curtain was shimmering along the floor: he could not eat for happiness. They were standing on the crowded platform and he was placing a ticket inside the warm palm of her glove. He was standing with her in the cold, looking in through a grated window at a man making bottles in a roaring furnace. It was very cold. Her face, fragrant in the cold air, was quite close to his; and suddenly she called out to the man at the furnace:

—Is the fire hot, sir?

But the man could not hear her with the noise of the furnace. It was just as well. He might have answered rudely.

A wave of yet more tender joy escaped from his heart and went coursing in warm flood along his arteries. Like the tender fires of stars moments of their life together, that no one knew of or would ever know of, broke upon and illumined his memory. He longed to recall to her those moments, to make her forget the years of their dull existence together and remember only their moments of ecstasy. For the years, he felt, had not quenched his soul or hers. Their children, his writing, her household cares had not quenched all their souls' tender fire. In one letter that he had written to her then he had said: *Why is it that words like these seem to me so dull and cold? Is it because there is no word tender enough to be your name?*

Like distant music these words that he had written years before were borne towards him from the past. He longed to be alone with her. When the others had gone away, when he and she were in their room in the hotel, then they would be alone together. He would call her softly:

—Gretta!

Perhaps she would not hear at once: she would be undressing. Then something in his voice would strike her. She would turn and look at him. . . .

At the corner of Winetavern Street they met a cab. He was glad of its rattling noise as it saved him from conversation. She was looking out of the window and seemed tired. The others spoke only a few words, pointing out some

8. Grayish purple.

building or street. The horse galloped along wearily under the murky morning sky, dragging his old rattling box after his heels, and Gabriel was again in a cab with her, galloping to catch the boat, galloping to their honeymoon.

As the cab drove across O'Connell[9] Bridge Miss O'Callaghan said:

—They say you never cross O'Connell Bridge without seeing a white horse.

—I see a white man this time, said Gabriel.

—Where? asked Mr Bartell D'Arcy.

Gabriel pointed to the statue, on which lay patches of snow. Then he nodded familiarly to it and waved his hand.

—Good-night, Dan, he said gaily.

When the cab drew up before the hotel Gabriel jumped out and, in spite of Mr Bartell D'Arcy's protest, paid the driver. He gave the man a shilling over his fare. The man saluted and said:

—A prosperous New Year to you, sir.

—The same to you, said Gabriel cordially.

She leaned for a moment on his arm in getting out of the cab and while standing at the curbstone, bidding the others good-night. She leaned lightly on his arm, as lightly as when she had danced with him a few hours before. He had felt proud and happy then, happy that she was his, proud of her grace and wifely carriage. But now, after the kindling again of so many memories, the first touch of her body, musical and strange and perfumed, sent through him a keen pang of lust. Under cover of her silence he pressed her arm closely to his side; and, as they stood at the hotel door, he felt that they had escaped from their lives and duties, escaped from home and friends and run away together with wild and radiant hearts to a new adventure.

An old man was dozing in a great hooded chair in the hall. He lit a candle in the office and went before them to the stairs. They followed him in silence, their feet falling in soft thuds on the thickly carpeted stairs. She mounted the stairs behind the porter, her head bowed in the ascent, her frail shoulders curved as with a burden, her skirt girt tightly about her. He could have flung his arms about her hips and held her still for his arms were trembling with desire to seize her and only the stress of his nails against the palms of his hands held the wild impulse of his body in check. The porter halted on the stairs to settle his guttering candle. They halted too on the steps below him. In the silence Gabriel could hear the falling of the molten wax into the tray and the thumping of his own heart against his ribs.

The porter led them along a corridor and opened a door. Then he set his unstable candle down on a toilet-table and asked at what hour they were to be called in the morning.

—Eight, said Gabriel.

The porter pointed to the tap of the electric-light and began a muttered apology but Gabriel out him short.

—We don't want any light. We have light enough from the street. And I say, he added, pointing to the candle, you might remove that handsome article, like a good man.

The porter took up his candle again, but slowly for he was surprised by such a novel idea. Then he mumbled good-night and went out. Gabriel shot the lock to.

9. Daniel O'Connell (1775–1847), Irish nationalist, statesman, and orator. His statue stands by O'Connell Bridge in Dublin.

A ghostly light from the street lamp lay in a long shaft from one window to the door. Gabriel threw his overcoat and hat on a couch and crossed the room towards the window. He looked down into the street in order that his emotion might calm a little. Then he turned and leaned against a chest of drawers with his back to the light. She had taken off her hat and cloak and was standing before a large swinging mirror, unhooking her waist.[1] Gabriel paused for a few moments, watching her, and then said:

—Gretta!

She turned away from the mirror slowly and walked along the shaft of light towards him. Her face looked so serious and weary that the words would not pass Gabriel's lips. No, it was not the moment yet.

—You looked tired, he said.

—I am a little, she answered.

—You don't feel ill or weak?

—No, tired: that's all.

She went on to the window and stood there, looking out. Gabriel waited again and then, fearing that diffidence was about to conquer him, he said abruptly:

—By the way, Gretta!

—What is it?

—You know that poor fellow Malins? he said quickly.

—Yes. What about him?

—Well, poor fellow, he's a decent sort of chap after all, continued Gabriel in a false voice. He gave me back that sovereign I lent him and I didn't expect it really. It's a pity he wouldn't keep away from that Browne, because he's not a bad fellow at heart.

He was trembling now with annoyance. Why did she seem so abstracted? He did not know how he could begin. Was she annoyed, too, about something? If she would only turn to him or come to him of her own accord! To take her as she was would be brutal. No, he must see some ardour in her eyes first. He longed to be master of her strange mood.

—When did you lend him the pound? she asked, after a pause.

Gabriel strove to restrain himself from breaking out into brutal language about the sottish Malins and his pound. He longed to cry to her from his soul, to crush her body against his, to overmaster her. But he said:

—O, at Christmas, when he opened that little Christmas-card shop in Henry Street.

He was in such a fever of rage and desire that he did not hear her come from the window. She stood before him for an instant, looking at him strangely. Then, suddenly raising herself on tiptoe and resting her hands lightly on his shoulders, she kissed him.

—You are a very generous person, Gabriel, she said.

Gabriel, trembling with delight at her sudden kiss and at the quaintness of her phrase, put his hands on her hair and began smoothing it back, scarcely touching it with his fingers. The washing had made it fine and brilliant. His heart was brimming over with happiness. Just when he was wishing for it she had come to him of her own accord. Perhaps her thoughts had been running with his. Perhaps she had felt the impetuous desire that was in him and then the yielding mood had come upon her. Now that she had fallen to him so easily he wondered why he had been so diffident.

---

1. Shirtwaist; a tailored blouse.

He stood, holding her head between his hands. Then, slipping one arm swiftly about her body and drawing her towards him, he said softly:

—Gretta dear, what are you thinking about?

She did not answer nor yield wholly to his arm. He said again, softly:

—Tell me what it is, Gretta. I think I know what is the matter. Do I know?

She did not answer at once. Then she said in an outburst of tears:

—O, I am thinking about that song, *The Lass of Aughrim*.

She broke loose from him and ran to the bed and, throwing her arms across the bed-rail, hid her face. Gabriel stood stock-still for a moment in astonishment and then followed her. As he passed in the way of the cheval-glass[2] he caught sight of himself in full length, his broad, well-filled shirt-front, the face whose expression always puzzled him when he saw it in a mirror and his glimmering gilt-rimmed eyeglasses. He halted a few paces from her and said:

—What about the song? Why does that make you cry?

She raised her head from her arms and dried her eyes with the back of her hand like a child. A kinder note than he had intended went into his voice.

—Why, Gretta? he asked.

—I am thinking about a person long ago who used to sing that song.

—And who was the person long ago? asked Gabriel, smiling.

—It was a person I used to know in Galway when I was living with my grandmother, she said.

The smile passed away from Gabriel's face. A dull anger began to gather again at the back of his mind and the dull fires of his lust began to glow angrily in his veins.

—Someone you were in love with? he asked ironically.

—It was a young boy I used to know, she answered, named Michael Furey. He used to sing that song, *The Lass of Aughrim*. He was very delicate.

Gabriel was silent. He did not wish her to think that he was interested in this delicate boy.

—I can see him so plainly, she said after a moment. Such eyes as he had: big dark eyes! And such an expression in them—an expression!

—O then, you were in love with him? said Gabriel.

—I used to go out walking with him, she said, when I was in Galway.

A thought flew across Gabriel's mind.

—Perhaps that was why you wanted to go to Galway with that Ivors girl? he said coldly.

She looked at him and asked in surprise:

—What for?

Her eyes made Gabriel feel awkward. He shrugged his shoulders and said:

—How do I know! To see him perhaps.

She looked away from him along the shaft of light towards the window in silence.

—He is dead, she said at length. He died when he was only seventeen. Isn't it a terrible thing to die so young as that?

—What was he? asked Gabriel, still ironically.

—He was in the gasworks,[3] she said.

Gabriel felt humiliated by the failure of his irony and by the evocation of this figure from the dead, a boy in the gasworks. While he had been full of memories of their secret life together, full of tenderness and joy and desire,

---

2. Full-length mirror that can be tilted.
3. Factory where coal gas for heating and lighting is produced.

she had been comparing him in her mind with another. A shameful consciousness of his own person assailed him. He saw himself as a ludicrous figure, acting as a pennyboy for his aunts, a nervous well-meaning sentimentalist, orating to vulgarians and idealising his own clownish lusts, the pitiable fatuous fellow he had caught a glimpse of in the mirror. Instinctively he turned his back more to the light lest she might see the shame that burned upon his forehead.

He tried to keep up his tone of cold interrogation but his voice when he spoke was humble and indifferent.

—I suppose you were in love with this Michael Furey, Gretta, he said.

—I was great with him at that time, she said.

Her voice was veiled and sad. Gabriel, feeling now how vain it would be to try to lead her whither he had purposed, caressed one of her hands and said, also sadly:

—And what did he die of so young, Gretta? Consumption, was it?

—I think he died for me, she answered.

A vague terror seized Gabriel at this answer as if, at that hour when he had hoped to triumph, some impalpable and vindictive being was coming against him, gathering forces against him in its vague world. But he shook himself free of it with an effort of reason and continued to caress her hand. He did not question her again for he felt that she would tell him of herself. Her hand was warm and moist: it did not respond to his touch but he continued to caress it just as he had caressed her first letter to him that spring morning.

—It was in the winter, she said, about the beginning of the winter when I was going to leave my grandmother's and come up here to the convent. And he was ill at the time in his lodgings in Galway and wouldn't be let out and his people in Oughterard were written to. He was in decline, they said, or something like that. I never knew rightly.

She paused for a moment and sighed.

—Poor fellow, she said. He was very fond of me and he was such a gentle boy. We used to go out together, walking, you know, Gabriel, like the way they do in the country. He was going to study singing only for his health. He had a very good voice, poor Michael Furey.

—Well; and then? asked Gabriel.

—And then when it came to the time for me to leave Galway and come up to the convent he was much worse and I wouldn't be let see him so I wrote a letter saying I was going up to Dublin and would be back in the summer and hoping he would be better then.

She paused for a moment to get her voice under control and then went on:

—Then the night before I left I was in my grandmother's house in Nuns' Island, packing up, and I heard gravel thrown up against the window. The window was so wet I couldn't see so I ran downstairs as I was and slipped out the back into the garden and there was the poor fellow at the end of the garden, shivering.

—And did you not tell him to go back? asked Gabriel.

—I implored him to go home at once and told him he would get his death in the rain. But he said he did not want to live. I can see his eyes as well as well! He was standing at the end of the wall where there was a tree.

—And did he go home? asked Gabriel.

—Yes, he went home. And when I was only a week in the convent he died and he was buried in Oughterard where his people came from. O, the day I heard that, that he was dead!

She stopped, choking with sobs, and overcome by emotion, flung herself face downward on the bed, sobbing in the quilt. Gabriel held her hand for a moment longer, irresolutely, and then, shy of intruding on her grief, let it fall gently and walked quietly to the window.

She was fast asleep.

Gabriel, leaning on his elbow, looked for a few moments unresentfully on her tangled hair and half-open mouth, listening to her deep-drawn breath. So she had had that romance in her life: a man had died for her sake. It hardly pained him now to think how poor a part he, her husband, had played in her life. He watched her while she slept as though he and she had never lived together as man and wife. His curious eyes rested long upon her face and on her hair: and, as he thought of what she must have been then, in that time of her first girlish beauty, a strange friendly pity for her entered his soul. He did not like to say even to himself that her face was no longer beautiful but he knew that it was no longer the face for which Michael Furey had braved death.

Perhaps she had not told him all the story. His eyes moved to the chair over which she had thrown some of her clothes. A petticoat string dangled to the floor. One boot stood upright, its limp upper fallen down: the fellow of it lay upon its side. He wondered at his riot of emotions of an hour before. From what had it proceeded? From his aunt's supper, from his own foolish speech, from the wine and dancing, the merry-making when saying good-night in the hall, the pleasure of the walk along the river in the snow. Poor Aunt Julia! She, too, would soon be a shade with the shade of Patrick Morkan and his horse. He had caught that haggard look upon her face for a moment when she was singing *Arrayed for the Bridal*. Soon, perhaps, he would be sitting in that same drawing-room, dressed in black, his silk hat on his knees. The blinds would be drawn down and Aunt Kate would be sitting beside him, crying and blowing her nose and telling him how Julia had died. He would cast about in his mind for some words that might console her, and would find only lame and useless ones. Yes, yes: that would happen very soon.

The air of the room chilled his shoulders. He stretched himself cautiously along under the sheets and lay down beside his wife. One by one they were all becoming shades. Better pass boldly into that other world, in the full glory of some passion, than fade and wither dismally with age. He thought of how she who lay beside him had locked in her heart for so many years that image of her lover's eyes when he had told her that he did not wish to live.

Generous tears filled Gabriel's eyes. He had never felt like that himself towards any woman but he knew that such a feeling must be love. The tears gathered more thickly in his eyes and in the partial darkness he imagined he saw the form of a young man standing under a dripping tree. Other forms were near. His soul had approached that region where dwell the vast hosts of the dead. He was conscious of, but could not apprehend, their wayward and flickering existence. His own identity was fading out into a grey impalpable world: the solid world itself which these dead had one time reared and lived in was dissolving and dwindling.

A few light taps upon the pane made him turn to the window. It had begun to snow again. He watched sleepily the flakes, silver and dark, falling obliquely against the lamplight. The time had come for him to set out on his journey westward. Yes, the newspapers were right: snow was general all over Ireland. It was falling on every part of the dark central plain, on the treeless hills, falling softly upon the Bog of Allen[4] and, farther westward, softly falling into the dark mutinous Shannon waves. It was falling, too, upon every part of the lonely churchyard on the hill where Michael Furey lay buried. It lay thickly drifted on the crooked crosses and headstones, on the spears of the little gate, on the barren thorns. His soul swooned slowly as he heard the snow falling faintly through the universe and faintly falling, like the descent of their last end, upon all the living and the dead.

1914

Ulysses   From the vantage point of the twenty-first century, *Ulysses* (1922) is often singled out as the greatest novel of the twentieth century, and so it may be hard to understand the scandal it aroused upon publication. After parts of it first appeared serially in the American journal *The Little Review* from 1918 and the English journal *The Egoist* in 1919, coarse language, masturbation, and other sexual content led to legal prosecution and to the banning of *Ulysses* as obscene in both the United States and the United Kingdom until the 1930s. New York district judge John M. Woolsey's 1933 ruling that the book, "in spite of its unusual frankness," was not pornographic but an "amazing *tour de force*" set an important precedent in obscenity law. In his perceptive appraisal of *Ulysses*, Woolsey explained Joyce's sexual frankness by saying that the novelist had attempted "to show exactly how the minds of his characters operate" and "to tell fully what his characters think about," conveying "the screen of consciousness with its ever-shifting kaleidoscopic impressions"—that is, not only each character's observations of the present but also the residue of "past impressions, some recent and some drawn up by association from the domain of the subconscious."

Ulysses opens at eight o'clock in the morning of June 16, 1904. Stephen Dedalus (the same character as in *A Portrait of the Artist as a Young Man*, but two years after the last glimpse of him there) has been summoned back to Dublin by his mother's fatal illness. The first three episodes of *Ulysses* concentrate on Stephen, the aloof, uncompromising artist, but the fourth introduces the novel's central character, Leopold Bloom. A somewhat frustrated and confused Jewish outsider in Irish society, Bloom emerges as a humane champion of kindness and justice. We follow closely his every activity: attending a funeral, transacting business, eating lunch, walking through the Dublin streets, worrying about his wife's infidelity with Blazes Boylan, even defecating and masturbating—and at each point the contents of his mind, including retrospect and anticipation, are revealed. Finally, late at night, Bloom and Stephen, who have been just missing each other all day, get together, Stephen having had too much to drink. Bloom is moved by a paternal feeling toward Stephen, in part because his own son, Rudy, died in infancy, and in a symbolic way Stephen takes Rudy's place; Bloom follows Stephen during subsequent adventures in the role of fatherly protector. The climax of the book comes when Stephen, far gone in drink, and Bloom, worn out with fatigue, succumb to a series of hallucinations, during which their unconscious minds surface in dramatic form and their personalities are disclosed with extraordinary frankness. Then Bloom takes the unresponsive Stephen home and gives him a meal. After Stephen's departure Bloom retires to bed, while his wife, Molly, lying in bed, ends the novel with a long monologue in which she recalls her romantic and other experiences.

On the level of realistic description, *Ulysses* pulses with life and can be enjoyed for its evocation of early twentieth-century Dublin. On the psychological level, it profoundly and movingly reveals the personalities and consciousnesses of Leopold

---

4. The name given to many separate peat bogs between the rivers Liffey (which runs through Dublin) and Shannon (which runs through the central plain of Ireland).

Bloom, Stephen Dedalus, and Molly Bloom. It explores the paradoxes of human loneliness and sociability (Bloom is both Jew and Dubliner, both exile and citizen), and it examines problems in the relations between parent and child, between the generations, and between the sexes. On the level of style, it shimmers with linguistic virtuosity, with many an episode written in a distinctive way that reflects its subject—e.g., headlines intruding in a chapter set in a newspaper office (the "Aeolus" episode); the sentimental language of women's magazines dominating a chapter set on a beach where girls are playing ("Nausicaa"); and the pastiche of styles of English literature from its Anglo-Saxon birth to the twentieth century in a chapter set in a maternity hospital ("Oxen of the Sun"). Through its use of themes from Homer, Dante, Shakespeare, and from other works of literature, and from philosophy and history, the book weaves a subtle pattern of allusion and suggestion.

Those who come to Ulysses with narrative expectations drawn from Victorian novels or even twentieth-century novelists such as Conrad and Lawrence will find much that is at first puzzling. In the novel's stream of consciousness method, also known as interior monologue, Joyce presents the consciousness of his characters directly, often without authorial comment. Past and present mingle in the texture of the prose because they mingle in the texture of consciousness; this interweaving can be indicated by puns, by sudden breaks in style or subject matter, or by other devices for keeping the reader constantly in sight of the shifting, multilayered nature of human awareness.

"Penelope" is the last of the eighteen episodes that make up Ulysses. It is two o'clock in the morning on June 17, 1904, and Bloom has returned home and joined his wife, Molly, in bed. His return both parallels and differs from Odysseus's return after twenty years' absence to Ithaca, in book 23 of Homer's Odyssey, in which he slays all the suitors who have occupied his house and attempted to woo his patient and faithful wife, Penelope. In Joyce's novel, the "Penelope" episode shifts the narrative focus of Ulysses from Stephen's and Bloom's male voices to the female voice of Molly Bloom, whose thoughts appear as an interior monologue, unpunctuated until the very end. In this episode, as also at the diaristic end of A Portrait of the Artist as a Young Man, there is no third-person narrator. The monologue, often called "Molly Bloom's soliloquy," unfolds in eight flowing, run-on sentences, including the final sentence (or paragraph) printed below, which culminates at the book's end in a resonant affirmation, a memory of her response to Bloom's marriage proposal and ultimately to life itself: "and yes I said yes I will Yes."

In this excerpt, Molly, lying head to toe in bed with the sleeping Bloom, contemplates her relationships with men and often shifts from one "he" to another, from past to present, reality to fantasy, without explicitly marking the change in reference. Although she intermittently tries to quiet her mind ("let me see if I can doze off 1 2 3 4 5"), her thoughts often rapidly tumble forward over memories and hopes and worries, sometimes slowing down to linger over a single point. She revisits the details of her adulterous tryst that afternoon with Blazes Boylan, laments an insufficiently appreciative Bloom's shortcomings as a lover, and fantasizes about finding romantic and sexual fulfillment. She worries about Stephen's family life, spinning out both maternal and erotic fantasies about him, and she remembers the conception and death of her son, Rudy, a deeply felt loss ten years earlier that has stymied her and Bloom's sexual relationship. She also recalls her girlhood in the colorful, culturally diverse Gibraltar. Reflecting on men and women, she contemplates the differences in their anatomies, sexual natures, freedoms and constraints, and capacities to bring world peace. She decides to give Bloom one more chance to prove himself sexually, and if he cannot pass her test, she will tell him about her affair with Boylan (in Homer's Odyssey, Penelope also tests the returning Odysseus to prove he is who he claims to be; her final tests involve knowledge of their bed's construction). Finally, Molly returns to the memory of the day she first gave fully of herself to Bloom, when they lay together on Howth Hill and Bloom proposed to her and she agreed to marry him, a memory infiltrated by and layered with memories of other love interests. All these thoughts and remembrances highlight the differences between Molly and the novel's two other main characters, since Molly's thoughts are neither as abstract as Stephen's nor as concrete as Bloom's, but combine elements of the two, as well as a measure of frank sexuality. Joyce provides an exquisitely detailed and textured portrait of the intricate movements of human consciousness, perhaps more so than can be found in any previous literary work, as Molly swings from the imaginative to the mundane from regret and longing to a rhapsodic embrace of the world in all its multifariousness, her vital and passionate voice bringing *Ulysses* to a resounding culmination.

From Ulysses

FROM [PENELOPE]

no thats no way for him[1] has he no manners nor no refinement nor no nothing in his nature slapping us behind like that on my bottom because I didnt call him Hugh the ignoramus that doesnt know poetry from a cabbage thats what you get for not keeping them in their proper place pulling off his shoes and trousers there on the chair before me so barefaced without even asking permission and standing out that vulgar way in the half of a shirt they wear to be admired like a priest or a butcher or those old hypocrites in the time of Julius Caesar[2] of course hes right enough in his way to pass the time as a joke sure you might as well be in bed with what with a lion God Im sure hed have something better to say for himself an old Lion would[3] O well I suppose its because they were so plump and tempting in my short petticoat he couldnt resist they excite myself sometimes its well for men all the amount of pleasure they get off a womans body were so round and white for them always I wished I was one myself for a change just to try with that thing they have swelling upon you so hard and at the same time so soft when you touch it my uncle John has a thing long I heard those cornerboys saying passing the corner of Marrowbone lane my aunt Mary has a thing hairy because it was dark and they knew a girl was passing it didnt make me blush why should it either its only nature and he puts his thing long into my aunt Marys hairy etcetera and turns out to be you put the handle in a sweeping-brush[4] men again all over they can pick and choose what they please a married woman or a fast widow or a girl for their different tastes like those houses round behind Irish street[5] no but were to be always chained up theyre not going to be chaining me up no damn fear once I start I tell you for stupid husbands jealousy why cant we all remain friends over it instead of quarrelling her husband found it out what they did together well naturally and if he did can he undo it hes coronado anyway whatever he does and then he going to the other mad extreme about the wife in Fair Tyrants[6] of

---

1. Blazes Boylan.
2. Perhaps Julius Caesar's assassins. Toga-wearing Marcus Brutus, together with other conspirators, killed his close friend Caesar and then stood before the public professing his love for him, as dramatized in Shakespeare's *Julius Caesar* (3.1–2).
3. Penelope calls Odysseus "my lord, my lion heart" in Homer's *Odyssey*.
4. Molly recalls a dirty riddle about Uncle John putting his "thing long" into Aunt Mary's "thing

hairy," which actually turns out to be about putting a handle in a sweeping brush. "Marrowbone Lane": a street in southeastern Dublin.
5. I.e., Irish Town in Gibraltar, which Molly implies was the location of prostitutes' houses.
6. Supposed title of a novel by James Lovebirch, who published under this pseudonym in the early twentieth century but is not known to have written anything with this title. "Coronado": tonsured (Spanish), but Molly probably means "cornudo," or cuckolded.

course the man never even casts a 2nd thought on the husband or wife either its the woman he wants and he gets her what else were we given all those desires for Id like to know I cant help it if Im young still can I its a wonder Im not an old shrivelled hag before my time living with him[7] so cold never embracing me except sometimes when hes asleep the wrong end of me not knowing I suppose who he has any man thatd kiss a womans bottom Id throw my hat at him after that hed kiss anything unnatural where we havent 1 atom of any kind of expression in us all of us the same 2 lumps of lard before ever Id do that to a man pfooh the dirty brutes the mere thought is enough I kiss the feet of you senorita theres some sense in that didnt he kiss our halldoor[8] yes he did what a madman nobody understands his cracked ideas but me still of course a woman wants to be embraced 20 times a day almost to make her look young no matter by who so long as to be in love or loved by somebody if the fellow you want isnt there sometimes by the Lord God I was thinking would I go around by the quays there some dark evening where nobodyd know me and pick up a sailor off the sea thatd be hot on for it and not care a pin whose I was only to do it off up in a gate somewhere or one of those wildlooking gipsies in Rathfarnham had their camp pitched near the Bloomfield laundry to try and steal our things if they could I only sent mine there a few times for the name model laundry[9] sending me back over and over some old ones odd stockings that blackguardlooking fellow with the fine eyes peeling a switch attack me in the dark and ride me up against the wall without a word or a murderer anybody what they do them-selves the fine gentlemen in their silk hats that K. C. lives up somewhere this way coming out of Hardwicke lane[1] the night he gave us the fish supper on account of winning over the boxing match of course it was for me he gave it I knew him by his gaiters[2] and the walk and when I turned round a minute after just to see there was a woman after coming out of it too some filthy prostitute then he goes home to his wife after that only I suppose the half of those sailors are rotten again with disease O move over your big carcass out of that for the love of Mike listen to him the winds that waft my sighs to thee so well he may sleep and sigh the great Suggester Don Poldo de la Flora[3] if he knew how he came out on the cards this morning hed have something to sigh for a dark man in some perplexity between 2 7s[4] too in prison for Lord knows what he does that I dont know and Im to be slooching around down in the kitchen to get his lordship his breakfast while hes rolled up like a mummy will I indeed did you ever see me running Id just like to see myself at it show them attention and they treat you like dirt I dont care what anybody says itd be much better for the world to be governed by the women

7. Leopold Bloom.
8. Customary Jewish gesture of kissing or touch-ing the mezuzah, a parchment inscribed with reli-gious text and attached to the doorpost of the house. Since there appears to be no parchment affixed to the Blooms' door, it seems that Bloom has secularized the custom. "I kiss the feet of you senorita" [for *señorita*]: translation of a Spanish expression of courtesy or thanks.
9. Model Laundry, Bloomfield Steam Laundry Company, Ltd., in Rathfarnham, a village four miles south of the Dublin city center.
1. A street to the east of the Blooms' house in Dublin. "K. C.": King's Counsel, a senior barris-ter, or lawyer.

2. Coverings of cloth or leather for the ankle and lower leg.
3. Molly once pretended to be engaged to a Span-ish nobleman named Don Miguel de la Flora, and here she combines his name with her husband's first name, Leopold. "Flora," which means flower, also corresponds to Leopold's last name, Bloom. "The winds that waft my sighs to thee": title of a song by lyricist H. W. Challis and composer Wil-liam V. Wallace.
4. Molly has been telling fortunes with cards, and in her reading, Bloom is represented by the king of clubs ("a dark man"), and his position between two sevens indicates perplexity about how he can "benefit by his own integrity."

in it you wouldnt see women going and killing one another and slaughtering when do you ever see women rolling around drunk like they do or gambling every penny they have and losing it on horses yes because a woman whatever she does she knows where to stop sure they wouldnt be in the world at all only for us they dont know what it is to be a woman and a mother how could they where would they all of them be if they hadnt all a mother to look after them what I never had thats why I suppose hes[5] running wild now out at night away from his books and studies and not living at home on account of the usual rowy[6] house I suppose well its a poor case that those that have a fine son like that theyre not satisfied and I none was he[7] not able to make one it wasnt my fault we came together when I was watching the two dogs up in her behind in the middle of the naked street that disheartened me altogether I suppose I oughtnt to have buried him[8] in that little woolly jacket I knitted crying as I was but give it to some poor child but I knew well Id never have another our 1st death too it was we were never the same since O Im not going to think myself into the glooms about that any more I wonder why he[9] wouldnt stay the night I felt all the time it was somebody strange he[1] brought in instead of roving around the city meeting God knows who night-walkers and pickpockets his poor mother wouldnt like that if she was alive ruining himself for life perhaps still its a lovely hour so silent I used to love coming home after dances the air of the night they have friends they can talk to weve none either he wants what he wont get or its some woman ready to stick her knife in you I hate that in women no wonder they treat us the way they do we are a dreadful lot of bitches I suppose its all the troubles we have makes us so snappy Im not like that he could easy have slept in there on the sofa in the other room I suppose he was as shy as a boy he being so young hardly 20 of me in the next room hed have heard me on the chamber arrah[2] what harm Dedalus I wonder its like those names in Gibraltar Dela-paz Delagracia they had the devils queer names there father Vial plana of Santa Maria that gave me the rosary Rosales y O'Reilly in the Calle las Siete Revueltas and Pisimbo and Mrs Opisso in Governor street[3] O what a name Id go and drown myself in the first river if I had a name like her O my and all the bits of streets Paradise ramp and Bedlam ramp and Rodgers ramp and Crutchetts ramp and the devils gap steps[4] well small blame to me if I am a harumscarum[5] I know I am a bit I declare to God I dont feel a day older than then I wonder could I get my tongue round any of the Spanish como esta usted muy bien gracias y usted[6] see I havent forgotten it all I thought I had only for the grammar a noun is the name of any person place or thing pity I never tried to read that novel cantankerous Mrs Rubio lent me

---

5. Stephen Dedalus.
6. Characterized by rows, or arguments.
7. Leopold Bloom.
8. The Blooms' son, Rudy, who was born on December 29, 1893, and died eleven days later.
9. Stephen Dedalus.
1. Leopold Bloom.
2. Well, indeed (Irish). "On the chamber": on the chamber pot.
3. Mrs. Catherine Opisso, dressmaker whose shop was on Governor's Street in Gibraltar. "Dela-paz Delagracia": de la Paz and de Gracia are common Spanish surnames. "Father Vial plana of Santa Maria": according to Don Gifford, the Reverend J. Vilaplana was associated with the Roman

Catholic Cathedral Church of St. Mary the Crowned, but this association does not appear in the directory in Gibraltar until 1912. "Calle las Siete Revueltas": Street of the Seven Turnings (Spanish), known in English-speaking Gibraltar as City Mill Lane. "Pisimbo": reference unknown.
4. Ravine that separates the upper slopes of Gibraltar from the southern plateau. "Paradise ramp and Bedlam ramp and Rodgers ramp and Crutchetts ramp": all stairway streets that slope up the Rock in Gibraltar.
5. A reckless person.
6. Basic Spanish conversation: "How are you?" "Very well, thank you. And you?"

by Valera with the questions in it all upside down[7] the two ways I always knew wed go away in the end I can tell him[8] the Spanish and he tell me the Italian then hell see Im not so ignorant what a pity he didnt stay Im sure the poor fellow was dead tired and wanted a good sleep badly I could have brought him in his breakfast in bed with a bit of toast so long as I didnt do it on the knife for bad luck[9] or if the woman was going her rounds with the watercress and something nice and tasty there are a few olives in the kitchen he might like I never could bear the look of them in Abrines I could do the criada[1] the room looks all right since I changed it the other way you see something was telling me all the time Id have to introduce myself not knowing me from Adam very funny wouldnt it Im his wife or pretend we were in Spain with him half awake without a Gods notion where he is dos huevos estrellados senor[2] Lord the cracked things come into my head sometimes itd be great fun supposing he stayed with us why not theres the room upstairs empty and Millys[3] bed in the back room he could do his writing and studies at the table in there for all the scribbling he does at it and if he wants to read in bed in the morning like me as hes making the breakfast for 1 he can make it for 2 Im sure Im not going to take in lodgers off the street for him if he takes a gesabo[4] of a house like this Id love to have a long talk with an intelligent welleducated person Id have to get a nice pair of red slippers like those Turks with the fez used to sell or yellow and a nice semitransparent morning gown that I badly want or a peachblossom dressing jacket like the one long ago in Walpoles only 8/6 or 18/6[5] I'll just give him one more chance Ill get up early in the morning Im sick of Cohens[6] old bed in any case I might go over to the markets to see all the vegetables and cabbages and tomatoes and carrots and all kinds of splendid fruits all coming in lovely and fresh who knows whod be the 1st man Id meet theyre out looking for it in the morning Mamy Dillon used to say they are and the night too that was her massgoing Id love a big juicy pear now to melt in your mouth like when I used to be in the longing way then Ill throw him up his eggs and tea in the moustachecup[7] she gave him to make his mouth bigger I suppose hed like my nice cream too I know what Ill do Ill go about rather gay not too much singing a bit now and then mi fa pieta Masetto then Ill start dressing myself to go out presto non son più forte[8] Ill put on my best shift and drawers let him have a good eyeful out of that to make his micky stand for him Ill let him know if thats what he wanted that his wife is fucked yes and damn well fucked too up to my neck nearly not by him 5 or 6 times handrunning theres the mark of his spunk on the clean sheet I wouldnt bother to even iron it out that ought to

7. In Spanish, question marks appear upside down at the beginning of the sentence and right side up at the end. "Mrs Rubio": Molly's family's housekeeper in Gibraltar. "Valera": Juan Valera y Alcalá Galiano (1824–1905), Spanish novelist.
8. Stephen Dedalus.
9. Using a knife instead of a spoon was considered bad luck.
1. Servant (Spanish). "Abrines": name of a bakery in Gibraltar.
2. Two fried eggs, sir (Spanish).
3. The Blooms' teenage daughter, who is away learning photography.
4. According to Gifford, "a vaguely pejorative term, as in 'the whole gesabo,' meaning the whole show or mess."

5. Eight shillings, six pence, or eighteen shillings, six pence. "Fez": hat in the form of a flat-topped cone, usually made of wool or felt. Walpole Brothers was a store selling cloth in Dublin.
6. David Cohen, a boot and shoe salesman, from whom Molly's father purchased the bed in Gibraltar before they moved to Dublin.
7. Cup with a partial cover meant to protect a mustache during drinking.
8. Quick, my strength is failing (Italian). "Mi fa pieta Masetto": I'm sorry for Masetto (Italian). Lines from the opera Don Giovanni (1787) by Austrian composer Wolfgang Amadeus Mozart (1756–1791), which Molly practices in her capacity as a professional singer.

satisfy him if you dont believe me feel my belly unless I made him stand
there and put him into me Ive a mind to tell him every scrap and make him
do it in front of me serve him right its all his own fault if I am an adulteress
as the thing in the gallery said O much about it if thats all the harm ever we
did in this vale of tears[9] God knows its not much doesnt everybody only they
hide it I suppose thats what a woman is supposed to be there for or He
wouldn't have made us the way He did so attractive to men then if he wants
to kiss my bottom Ill drag open my drawers and bulge it right out in his face
as large as life he can stick his tongue 7 miles up my hole as hes there my
brown part then Ill tell him I want £ 1 or perhaps 30/[1] Ill tell him I want to
buy underclothes then if he gives me that well he wont be too bad I dont
want to soak it all out of him like other women do I could often have written out a fine cheque for myself and write his name on it for a couple of
pounds a few times he forgot to lock it up besides he wont spend it Ill let him
do it off on me behind provided he doesnt smear all my good drawers O I
suppose that cant be helped Ill do the indifferent 1 or 2 questions Ill know
by the answers when hes like that he cant keep a thing back I know every
turn in him Ill tighten my bottom well and let out a few smutty words smell-
rump or lick my shit or the first mad thing comes into my head then Ill suggest about yes O wait now sonny my turn is coming Ill be quite gay and
friendly over it O but I was forgetting this bloody pest of a thing[2] pfooh you
wouldnt know which to laugh or cry were such a mixture of plum and apple[3]
no Ill have to wear the old things so much the better itll be more pointed hell
never know whether he did it or not there thats good enough for you any old
thing at all then Ill wipe him off me just like a business his omission[4] then
Ill go out Ill have him eying up at the ceiling where is she gone now make
him want me thats the only way a quarter after[5] what an unearthly hour
I suppose theyre just getting up in China now combing out their pigtails for
the day well soon have the nuns ringing the angelus[6] theyve nobody coming
in to spoil their sleep except an odd priest or two for his night office the
alarmclock next door at cockshout clattering the brains out of itself let me
see if I can doze off 1 2 3 4 5 what kind of flowers are those they invented
like the stars the wallpaper in Lombard street[7] was much nicer the apron he
gave me was like that[8] something only I only wore it twice better lower this
lamp and try again so as I can get up early Ill go to Lambes there beside
Findlaters[9] and get them to send us some flowers to put about the place in
case he brings him[1] home tomorrow today I mean no no Fridays an unlucky
day first I want to do the place up someway the dust grows in it I think while
Im asleep then we can have music and cigarettes I can accompany him first

9. Phrase from Psalms 84.6 (or Psalm 83 in the Douay Bible). "As the thing in the gallery said": during a performance of the play *The Wife of Scarli* (1897), which Molly attended and which she recalls earlier in "Penelope," a man sitting in the gallery hissed at the protagonist, calling her "a woman adulteress." The play—an English version by G. A. Greene of an Italian drama, *Tristi amore*, by Giuseppe Giacosa (1847–1906)—appears to condone the title character's adultery by making her husband an unsympathetic character.
1. Thirty shillings; i.e., one pound, ten shillings.
2. Her menstrual period.
3. A mixture of good and bad things. In slang usage, a plum is a desirable thing, and the apple is the apple plucked by Eve that caused the fall of humankind.
4. I.e., Bloom's emission, or ejaculation.
5. A clock rings a quarter after the hour: it is now 2:15 A.M., and Molly ruminates on the activities of various people at this hour.
6. Devotional exercise commemorating the Incarnation, announced by the ringing of a bell.
7. A street in Dublin where the Blooms had their first house, which Molly remembers fondly.
8. The apron Bloom gave her when they lived at Lombard Street.
9. Alexander Findlater and Company, Ltd., the tea, wine, and spirits store on Sackville Street Upper in Dublin. "Lambes": the fruit and flower shop next to Findlater's store.
1. Bloom brings Stephen.

I must clean the keys of the piano with milk whatll I wear shall I wear a white rose or those fairy cakes in Liptons[2] I love the smell of a rich big shop at 7 ½ d a lb or the other ones with the cherries in them and the pinky sugar 11 d a couple of lbs[3] of course a nice plant for the middle of the table Id get that cheaper in wait wheres this I saw them not long ago I love flowers Id love to have the whole place swimming in roses God of heaven theres nothing like nature the wild mountains then the sea and the waves rushing then the beautiful country with fields of oats and wheat and all kinds of things and all the fine cattle going about that would do your heart good to see rivers and lakes and flowers all sorts of shapes and smells and colours springing up even out of the ditches primroses and violets nature it is as for them saying theres no God I wouldnt give a snap of my two fingers for all their learning why dont they go and create something I often asked him atheists or whatever they call themselves go and wash the cobbles[4] off themselves first then they go howling for the priest and they dying and why why because theyre afraid of hell on account of their bad conscience ah yes I know them well who was the first person in the universe before there was anybody that made it all who ah that they dont know neither do I so there you are they might as well try to stop the sun from rising tomorrow the sun shines for you he said the day we were lying among the rhododendrons on Howth head[5] in the grey tweed suit and his straw hat the day I got him to propose to me yes first I gave him the bit of seedcake out of my mouth and it was leapyear like now yes 16 years ago my God after that long kiss I near lost my breath yes he said I was a flower of the mountain yes so we are flowers all a womans body yes that was one true thing he said in his life and the sun shines for you today yes that was why I liked him because I saw he understood or felt what a woman is and I knew I could always get round him and I gave him all the pleasure I could leading him on till he asked me to say yes and I wouldnt answer first only looked out over the sea and the sky I was thinking of so many things he didnt know of Mulvey and Mr Stanhope and Hester and father and old captain Groves and the sailors playing all birds fly and I say stoop[6] and washing up dishes they called it on the pier and the sentry in front of the governors house with the thing round his white helmet poor devil half roasted and the Spanish girls laughing in their shawls and their tall combs and the auctions in the morning[7] the Greeks and the jews and the Arabs and the devil knows who else from all the ends of Europe and Duke street and the fowl market all clucking outside Larby Sharons and the poor donkeys slipping half asleep and the vague fellows in the cloaks asleep in the shade on the steps and the big wheels of the carts of the bulls and the old castle[8]

2. Lipton's Ltd., a grocery store in Dublin. "Shall I wear a white rose": lyrics from the song "Shall I Wear a White Rose or Shall I Wear a Red?" by H. S. Clarke and E. B. Farmer, quoted by Molly earlier in the episode. "Fairy cakes": cupcakes.

3. Eleven pence for two pounds. "7½d a lb": seven and a half pence per pound.

4. Lumps or blemishes (dialect English).

5. Headland on Dublin Bay, about 9 miles northeast of Dublin, where Leopold and Molly were picnicking on September 10, 1888, the day he proposed to her. Bloom recalls the same moment with the seedcake in "Lestrygonians."

6. A game, which probably depends, like "all birds fly," on the players' ability to obey commands. "Mulvey": Lieutenant Jack Mulvey, Molly's first suitor, whom she recalls at length earlier in the episode. "Mr. Stanhope and Hester": a girlhood friend of Molly's and the friend's husband. "Father": Molly's father, Major Brian Cooper Tweedy of the Royal Dublin Fusiliers. "Old captain Groves": a friend of Molly's father.

7. The daily auction in Commercial Square in Gibraltar. "The thing round his white helmet": a band marking the sentry as a military policeman.

8. The Moorish castle on the Rock of Gibraltar, built in 725 C.E. "Poor donkeys": donkeys were used for carrying supplies up the slopes of the Rock. "Carts of the bulls": carts used for transporting animals for bullfighting.

thousands of years old yes and those handsome Moors all in white and tur-
bans like kings asking you to sit down in their little bit of a shop and Ronda
with the old windows of the posadas glancing eyes a lattice hid for her lover
to kiss the iron and the wineshops half open at night and the castanets and
the night we missed the boat at Algeciras[9] the watchman going about serene
with his lamp and O that awful deepdown torrent O and the sea the sea
crimson sometimes like fire and the glorious sunsets and the figtrees in the
Alameda gardens[1] yes and all the queer little streets and pink and blue and
yellow houses and the rosegardens and the jessamine and geraniums and
cactuses and Gibraltar as a girl where I was a Flower of the mountain yes
when I put the rose in my hair like the Andalusian girls used[2] or shall I wear
a red[3] yes and how he kissed me under the Moorish wall[4] and I thought well
as well him[5] as another and then I asked him with my eyes to ask again yes
and then he asked me would I yes to say yes my mountain flower and first I
put my arms around him yes and drew him down to me so he could feel my
breasts all perfume yes and his heart was going like mad and yes I said yes I
will Yes.

Trieste-Zurich-Paris,
  1914–1921.

1922

9. Town in Spain on the opposite side of the Bay
of Algeciras from Gibraltar. "Ronda": a town in
southern Spain about 40 miles northeast of
Gibraltar, with well-preserved Moorish architecture. "Posadas": inns (Spanish). "Eyes a lattice
hid": lyrics from the song "In Old Madrid," with
words by Clifton Bingham (1859–1913) and music
by Henry Trotere (1855–1912). "For her lover to
kiss the iron": according to Gifford, "a Spanish col-
loquialism for a conventional gesture of courtship,
since the ground-floor windows of Spanish town
houses were usually defended by iron grilles."

1. Garden promenade on Gibraltar.
2. Girls from Andalusia, the southern region of
Spain ruled by Muslims, or Moors, in the Middle
Ages but also including Christians and Jews.
3. More lyrics from the song "Shall I Wear a
White Rose or Shall I Wear a Red?"
4. Wall at the center of the plateau on the upper
slopes of the Rock of Gibraltar and the site of
Molly's first kiss from Lieutenant Mulvey, which
she recalls earlier in the episode: "he was the first
man kissed me under the Moorish wall."
5. Leopold Bloom.

· D. H. LAWRENCE ·
1885–1930

David Herbert Lawrence was born in the midland mining village of Eastwood,
Nottinghamshire. His father was a miner; his mother, better educated than her
husband and self-consciously genteel, fought, all her married life, to lift her children
out of the working class. Lawrence was aware from a young age of the struggle
between his parents, and allied himself with his mother's delicacy and refinement,
resenting his father's coarse and sometimes drunken behavior. In his early novel
Sons and Lovers (1913), against a background of paternal coarseness conflicting with
maternal refinement, Lawrence sets the theme of the demanding mother who has
given up the prospect of achieving a true emotional life with her husband and turns
to her sons with a stultifying and possessive love. Many years later Lawrence came

to feel that he had failed to appreciate his father's vitality and wholeness, even if they were distorted by the culture in which he lived.

Spurred on by his mother, Lawrence escaped from the mining world through education. He won a scholarship to Nottingham high school and later, after working first as a clerk and then as an elementary-school teacher, studied for two years at University College, Nottingham, where he obtained his teacher's certificate. Meanwhile he was reading on his own a great deal of literature and some philosophy and was working on his first novel. Publishing a group of poems in 1909, his first short story and his first novel, *The White Peacock*, in 1910, he was regarded in London literary circles as a promising young writer. He taught school from 1908 to 1912 in Croydon, a southern suburb of London, but he gave this up after falling in love with Frieda von Richthofen Weekley, the German wife of a professor at Nottingham. They went to Germany together and married in 1914, after Frieda's divorce.

Abroad with Frieda, Lawrence finished *Sons and Lovers*, at which he had been working off and on for years. The war brought them back to England, where Frieda's German origins and Lawrence's pacifist objection to the war gave him trouble with the authorities. More and more—especially after the almost immediate banning, for indecency, of his next novel, *The Rainbow*, in 1915—Lawrence came to feel that the forces of modern civilization were arrayed against him. As soon as he could leave England after the war, he sought refuge in Italy, Australia, Mexico, then again in Italy, and finally in the south of France, often desperately ill, restlessly searching for an ideal, or at least a tolerable, community in which to live. He died of tuberculosis in the south of France at the age of forty-four.

In his poetry and his fiction, Lawrence seeks to express the deep-rooted, the elemental, the instinctual in people and nature. He is at constant war with the mechanical and artificial, with the constraints and hypocrisies that civilization imposes. Because he had new things to say and a new way of saying them, he was not easily or quickly appreciated. Although his early novels are more conventional in style and treatment, from the publication of *The Rainbow* the critics turned away in bewilderment and condemnation. The rest of his life, during which he produced about a dozen more novels and many poems, short stories, sketches, and miscellaneous articles, was, in his own words, "a savage enough pilgrimage," marked by incessant struggle and by periods of frustration and despair. Phrases such as "supreme impulse" and "quickening spontaneous emotion" were characteristic of Lawrence's belief in intuition, in the dark forces of the inner self, that must not be allowed to be swamped by the rational faculties but must be brought into a harmonious relation with them.

The genteel culture of Lawrence's mother came more and more to represent death for Lawrence. In much of his later work, and especially in some of his short stories, he sets the deadening restrictiveness of middle-class conventional living against the forces of liberation that are often represented by an outsider—a peasant, a gypsy, a worker, a primitive of some kind, someone free by circumstance or personal effort. The recurring theme of his short stories—which contain some of his best work—is the distortion of love by possessiveness or gentility or a false romanticism or a false conception of the life of the artist and the achievement of a living relation between a man and a woman against the pressure of class-feeling or tradition or habit or prejudice.

In his two masterpieces, *The Rainbow* and *Women in Love* (both of which developed out of what was originally conceived as a single novel to be called *The Sisters*), Lawrence probes with both subtlety and power into various aspects of relationship— the relationship between humans and their environment, the relationship between the generations, the relationship between man and woman, the relationship between instinct and intellect, and above all the proper basis for the marriage relationship as he conceived it. Lawrence's view of marriage as a struggle, bound up with the deepest rhythms and most profound instincts, derived from his own relationship with his strong-minded wife. He explores this and other kinds of human relationships with a combination of uncanny psychological precision and intense poetic feeling.

His novels have an acute surface realism, a sharp sense of time and place, and brilliant topographical detail; at the same time their high symbolism, both of the total pattern of action and of incidents and objects within it, establishes a formal and emotional rhythm.

In poetry as in fiction Lawrence sought out new modes of expression. He began writing in traditional verse forms but, especially after 1912, came to feel that poetry had to be unshackled from habit and fixed form, if it is to make contact with what he called the "insurgent naked throb of the instant moment." Harkening back to the experiments of the American poet Walt Whitman and anticipating the more "open" and "organic" forms of the later twentieth century, Lawrence claimed poetry must be spontaneous, flexible, alive, "direct utterance from the instant, whole man," and should express the "pulsating, carnal self" ("The Poetry of the Present," 1919). To convey the dynamism of animals and people, the emotional intensity of human relationships, his poems repeat and develop symbols or layer clauses in ritualistic cadences or unfold parallels with ancient myths. Vehemently autobiographical, the vital and even ecstatic encounters with nature, sex, and raw feeling in his poems assert the primacy of the unconscious and instinctual self, from which he felt the cerebral-intellectual self had alienated the English middle classes.

In the late 1950s the critic A. Alvarez judged: "The only native English poet of any importance to survive the First World War was D. H. Lawrence." Although there are complex reasons for the posthumous critical triumph of this writer who was so much reviled in his lifetime, there is also a simple and striking reason that must not be forgotten. Lawrence had vision; he responded intensely to life; he had a keen ear and a piercing eye for vitality and color and sound, for landscape—be it of England or Italy or New Mexico—for the individuality and concreteness of things in nature, and for the individuality and concreteness of people. His travel sketches are as impressive in their way as his novels and poems; he seizes both on the symbolic incident and on the concrete reality, and each is interpreted in terms of the other. He looked at the world freshly, with his own eyes, avoiding formulas and clichés; and he forged for himself a kind of utterance that, at his best, was able to convey powerfully and vividly what his original vision showed him. A restless pilgrim, he had uncanny perceptions into the depths of physical things and an uncompromising honesty in his view of human beings and the world.

Odour of Chrysanthemums

I

The small locomotive engine, Number 4, came clanking, stumbling down from Selston with seven full wagons. It appeared round the corner with loud threats of speed, but the colt that it startled from among the gorse,[1] which still flickered indistinctly in the raw afternoon, out-distanced it at a canter. A woman, walking up the railway line to Underwood, drew back into the hedge, held her basket aside, and watched the footplate of the engine advancing. The trucks[2] thumped heavily past, one by one, with slow inevitable movement, as she stood insignificantly trapped between the jolting black wagons and the hedge; then they curved away towards the coppice[3] where the withered oak leaves dropped noiselessly, while the birds, pulling at the scarlet hips beside the track, made off into the dusk that had already crept into the

1. Common prickly bush with yellow flowers.   3. A wood of small trees or shrubs.
2. Open freight cars.

spinney.[4] In the open, the smoke from the engine sank and cleaved to the rough grass. The fields were dreary and forsaken, and in the marshy strip that led to the whimsey,[5] a reedy pit-pond, the fowls had already abandoned their run among the alders, to roost in the tarred fowl-house. The pit-bank loomed up beyond the pond, flames like red sores licking its ashy sides, in the afternoon's stagnant light. Just beyond rose the tapering chimneys and the clumsy black headstocks of Brinsley Colliery.[6] The two wheels were spinning fast up against the sky, and the winding engine rapped out its little spasms. The miners were being turned up.

The engine whistled as it came into the wide bay of railway lines beside the colliery, where rows of trucks stood in harbour.

Miners, single, trailing and in groups, passed like shadows diverging home. At the edge of the ribbed level of sidings squat a low cottage, three steps down from the cinder track. A large bony vine clutched at the house, as if to claw down the tiled roof. Round the bricked yard grew a few wintry primroses. Beyond, the long garden sloped down to a bush-covered brook course. There were some twiggy apple trees, winter-crack trees, and ragged cabbages. Beside the path hung disheveled pink chrysanthemums, like pink cloths hung on bushes. A woman came stooping out of the felt-covered fowl-house, half-way down the garden. She closed and padlocked the door, then drew herself erect, having brushed some bits from her white apron.

She was a tall woman of imperious mien, handsome, with definite black eyebrows. Her smooth black hair was parted exactly. For a few moments she stood steadily watching the miners as they passed along the railway: then she turned towards the brook course. Her face was calm and set, her mouth was closed with disillusionment. After a moment she called:

"John!" There was no answer. She waited, and then said distinctly:

"Where are you?"

"Here!" replied a child's sulky voice from among the bushes. The woman looked piercingly through the dusk.

"Are you at that brook?" she asked sternly.

For answer the child showed himself before the raspberry-canes that rose like whips. He was a small, sturdy boy of five. He stood quite still, defiantly.

"Oh!" said the mother, conciliated. "I thought you were down at that wet brook—and you remember what I told you——"

The boy did not move or answer.

"Come, come on in," she said more gently, "it's getting dark. There's your grandfather's engine coming down the line!"

The lad advanced slowly, with resentful, taciturn movement. He was dressed in trousers and waistcoat of cloth that was too thick and hard for the size of the garments. They were evidently cut down from a man's clothes.

As they went slowly towards the house he tore at the ragged wisps of chrysanthemums and dropped the petals in handfuls along the path.

"Don't do that—it does look nasty," said his mother. He refrained, and she, suddenly pitiful, broke off a twig with three or four wan flowers and held them against her face. When mother and son reached the yard her hand hesi-

4. Thicket.
5. Machine for raising ore or water from a mine.

6. Coal mine. "Headstocks" support revolving parts of a machine.

tated, and instead of laying the flower aside, she pushed it in her apron-band. The mother and son stood at the foot of the three steps looking across the bay of lines at the passing home of the miners. The trundle of the small train was imminent. Suddenly the engine loomed past the house and came to a stop opposite the gate.

The engine-driver, a short man with round grey beard, leaned out of the cab high above the woman.

"Have you got a cup of tea?" he said in a cheery, hearty fashion.

It was her father. She went in, saying she would mash.[7] Directly, she returned.

"I didn't come to see you on Sunday," began the little grey-bearded man.

"I didn't expect you," said his daughter.

The engine-driver winced; then, reassuming his cheery, airy manner, he said:

"Oh, have you heard then? Well, and what do you think——?"

"I think it is soon enough," she replied.

At her brief censure the little man made an impatient gesture, and said coaxingly, yet with dangerous coldness:

"Well, what's a man to do? It's no sort of life for a man of my years, to sit at my own hearth like a stranger. And if I'm going to marry again it may as well be soon as late—what does it matter to anybody?"

The woman did not reply, but turned and went into the house. The man in the engine-cab stood assertive, till she returned with a cup of tea and a piece of bread and butter on a plate. She went up the steps and stood near the footplate of the hissing engine.

"You needn't 'a' brought me bread an' butter," said her father. "But a cup of tea"—he sipped appreciatively—"it's very nice." He sipped for a moment or two, then: "I hear as Walter's got another bout[8] on," he said.

"When hasn't he?" said the woman bitterly.

"I heerd tell of him in the 'Lord Nelson' braggin' as he was going to spend that b—— afore he went: half a sovereign[9] that was."

"When?" asked the woman.

"A' Sat'day night—I know that's true."

"Very likely," she laughed bitterly. "He gives me twenty-three shillings."

"Aye, it's a nice thing, when a man can do nothing with his money but make a beast of himself!" said the grey-whiskered man. The woman turned her head away. Her father swallowed the last of his tea and handed her the cup.

"Aye," he sighed, wiping his mouth. "It's a settler,[1] it is——"

He put his hand on the lever. The little engine strained and groaned, and the train rumbled towards the crossing. The woman again looked across the metals. Darkness was settling over the spaces of the railway and trucks: the miners, in grey somber groups, were still passing home. The winding engine pulsed hurriedly, with brief pauses. Elizabeth Bates looked at the dreary flow of men, then she went indoors. Her husband did not come.

The kitchen was small and full of firelight; red coals piled glowing up the chimney mouth. All the life of the room seemed in the white, warm hearth

7. Steep the tea.
8. Session; i.e., bout of drinking.
9. Gold coin worth twenty shillings. Half a sov-

ereign is worth ten. Lord Nelson is the name of a public house (pub).
1. Crushing (or final) blow.

and the steel fender reflecting the red fire. The cloth was laid for tea; cups glinted in the shadows. At the back, where the lowest stairs protruded into the room, the boy sat struggling with a knife and a piece of white wood. He was almost hidden in the shadow. It was half-past four. They had but to await the father's coming to begin tea. As the mother watched her son's sullen little struggle with the wood, she saw herself in his silence and pertinacity; she saw the father in her child's indifference to all but himself. She seemed to be occupied by her husband. He had probably gone past his home, slunk past his own door, to drink before he came in, while his dinner spoiled and wasted in waiting. She glanced at the clock, then took the potatoes to strain them in the yard. The garden and fields beyond the brook were closed in uncertain darkness. When she rose with the saucepan, leaving the drain steaming into the night behind her, she saw the yellow lamps were lit along the high road that went up the hill away beyond the space of the railway lines and the field.

Then again she watched the men trooping home, fewer now and fewer.

Indoors the fire was sinking and the room was dark red. The woman put her saucepan on the hob,[2] and set a batter-pudding near the mouth of the oven. Then she stood unmoving. Directly, gratefully, came quick young steps to the door. Someone hung on the latch a moment, then a little girl entered and began pulling off her outdoor things, dragging a mass of curls, just ripening from gold to brown, over her eyes with her hat.

Her mother chid her for coming late from school, and said she would have to keep her at home the dark winter days.

"Why, mother, it's hardly a bit dark yet. The lamp's not lighted, and my father's not home."

"No, he isn't. But it's a quarter to five! Did you see anything of him?"

The child became serious. She looked at her mother with large, wistful blue eyes.

"No, mother, I've never seen him. Why? Has he come up an' gone past, to Old Brinsley? He hasn't, mother, 'cos I never saw him."

"He'd watch that," said the mother bitterly, "he'd take care as you didn't see him. But you may depend upon it, he's seated in the 'Prince o' Wales.'[3] He wouldn't be this late."

The girl looked at her mother piteously.

"Let's have our teas, mother, should we?" said she.

The mother called John to table. She opened the door once more and looked out across the darkness of the lines. All was deserted: she could not hear the winding-engines.

"Perhaps," she said to herself, "he's stopped to get some ripping[4] done."

They sat down to tea. John, at the end of the table near the door, was almost lost in the darkness. Their faces were hidden from each other. The girl crouched against the fender[5] slowly moving a thick piece of bread before the fire. The lad, his face a dusky mark on the shadow, sat watching her who was transfigured in the red glow.

"I do think it's beautiful to look in the fire," said the child.

"Do you?" said her mother. "Why?"

2. Part of the fireplace.
3. Name of a pub.
4. Taking out or cutting away coal or stone (a

mining and quarrying term).
5. Frame that keeps coals in the fireplace.

"It's so red, and full of little caves—and it feels so nice, and you can fair smell it."

"It'll want mending directly," replied her mother, "and then if your father comes he'll carry on and say there never is a fire when a man comes home sweating from the pit. A public-house is always warm enough."

There was silence till the boy said complainingly: "Make haste, our Annie."

"Well, I am doing! I can't make the fire do it no faster, can I?"

"She keeps wafflin' it about so's to make 'er slow," grumbled the boy.

"Don't have such an evil imagination, child," replied the mother.

Soon the room was busy in the darkness with the crisp sound of crunching. The mother ate very little. She drank her tea determinedly, and sat thinking. When she rose her anger was evident in the stern unbending of her head. She looked at the pudding in the fender, and broke out:

"It is a scandalous thing as a man can't even come home to his dinner! If it's crozzled[6] up to a cinder I don't see why I should care. Past his very door he goes to get to a public-house, and here I sit with his dinner waiting for him——"

She went out. As she dropped piece after piece of coal on the red fire, the shadows fell on the walls, till the room was almost in total darkness.

"I canna see," grumbled the invisible John. In spite of herself, the mother laughed.

"You know the way to your mouth," she said. She set the dust pan outside the door. When she came again like a shadow on the hearth, the lad repeated, complaining sulkily:

"I canna see."

"Good gracious!" cried the mother irritably, "you're as bad as your father if it's a bit dusk!"

Nevertheless, she took a paper spill from a sheaf on the mantelpiece and proceeded to light the lamp that hung from the ceiling in the middle of the room. As she reached up, her figure displayed itself just rounding with maternity.

"Oh, mother——!" exclaimed the girl.

"What?" said the woman, suspended in the act of putting the lamp-glass over the flame. The copper reflector shone handsomely on her, as she stood with uplifted arm, turning to face her daughter.

"You've got a flower in your apron!" said the child, in a little rapture at this unusual event.

"Goodness me!" exclaimed the woman, relieved. "One would think the house was afire." She replaced the glass and waited a moment before turning up the wick. A pale shadow was seen floating vaguely on the floor.

"Let me smell!" said the child, still rapturously, coming forward and putting her face to her mother's waist.

"Go along, silly!" said the mother, turning up the lamp. The light revealed their suspense so that the woman felt it almost unbearable. Annie was still bending at her waist. Irritably, the mother took the flowers out from her apron-band.

"Oh, mother—don't take them out!" Annie cried, catching her hand and trying to replace the sprig.

6. Curled.

"Such nonsense!" said the mother, turning away. The child put the pale chrysanthemums to her lips, murmuring:

"Don't they smell beautiful!"

Her mother gave a short laugh.

"No," she said, "not to me. It was chrysanthemums when I married him, and chrysanthemums when you were born, and the first time they ever brought him home drunk, he'd got brown chrysanthemums in his buttonhole."

She looked at the children. Their eyes and their parted lips were wondering. The mother sat rocking in silence for some time. Then she looked at the clock.

"Twenty minutes to six!" In a tone of fine bitter carelessness she continued: "Eh, he'll not come now till they bring him. There he'll stick! But he needn't come rolling in here in his pit-dirt, for *I* won't wash him. He can lie on the floor——Eh, what a fool I've been, what a fool! And this is what I came here for, to this dirty hole, rats and all, for him to slink past his very door. Twice last week—he's begun now——"

She silenced herself and rose to clear the table.

While for an hour or more the children played, subduedly intent, fertile of imagination, united in fear of the mother's wrath, and in dread of their father's home-coming, Mrs Bates sat in her rocking chair making a "singlet" of thick cream-coloured flannel, which gave a dull wounded sound as she tore off the grey edge. She worked at her sewing with energy, listening to the children, and her anger wearied itself, lay down to rest, opening its eyes from time to time and steadily watching, its ears raised to listen. Sometimes even her anger quailed and shrank, and the mother suspended her sewing, tracing the footsteps that thudded along the sleepers[7] outside; she would lift her head sharply to bid the children "hush," but she recovered herself in time, and the footsteps went past the gate, and the children were not flung out of their play-world.

But at last Annie sighed, and gave in. She glanced at her wagon of slippers, and loathed the game. She turned plaintively to her mother.

"Mother!"—but she was inarticulate.

John crept out like a frog from under the sofa. His mother glanced up.

"Yes," she said, "just look at those shirt-sleeves!"

The boy held them out to survey them, saying nothing. Then somebody called in a hoarse voice away down the line, and suspense bristled in the room, till two people had gone by outside, talking.

"It is time for bed," said the mother.

"My father hasn't come," wailed Annie plaintively. But her mother was primed with courage.

"Never mind. They'll bring him when he does come—like a log." She meant there would be no scene. "And he may sleep on the floor till he wakes himself. I know he'll not go to work to-morrow after this!"

The children had their hands and faces wiped with a flannel. They were very quiet. When they had put on their night-dresses, they said their prayers, the boy mumbling. The mother looked down at them, at the brown silken bush of intertwining curls in the nape of the girl's neck, at the little black

7. Railroad ties.

head of the lad, and her heart burst with anger at their father, who caused all three such distress. The children hid their faces in her skirts for comfort.

When Mrs Bates came down, the room was strangely empty, with a tension of expectancy. She took up her sewing and stitched for some time without raising her head. Meantime her anger was tinged with fear.

II

The clock struck eight and she rose suddenly, dropping her sewing on her chair. She went to the stair-foot door, opened it, listening. Then she went out, locking the door behind her.

Something scuffled in the yard, and she started, though she knew it was only the rats with which the place was over-run. The night was very dark. In the great bay of railway lines, bulked with trucks, there was no trace of light, only away back she could see a few yellow lamps at the pit-top, and the red smear of the burning pit-bank on the night. She hurried along the edge of the track, then, crossing the converging lines, came to the stile by the white gates, whence she emerged on the road. Then the fear which had led her shrank. People were walking up to New Brinsley; she saw the lights in the houses; twenty yards farther on were the broad windows of the "Prince of Wales," very warm and bright, and the loud voices of men could be heard distinctly. What a fool she had been to imagine that anything had happened to him! He was merely drinking over there at the "Prince of Wales." She faltered. She had never yet been to fetch him, and she never would go. So she continued her walk towards the long straggling line of houses, standing back on the highway. She entered a passage between the dwellings.

"Mr Rigley?—Yes! Did you want him? No, he's not in at this minute."

The raw-boned woman leaned forward from her dark scullery[8] and peered at the other, upon whom fell a dim light through the blind of the kitchen window.

"Is it Mrs Bates?" she asked in a tone tinged with respect.

"Yes. I wondered if your Master was at home. Mine hasn't come yet."

"'Asn't 'e! Oh, Jack's been 'ome an' 'ad 'is dinner an' gone out. 'E's just gone for 'alf an hour afore bed-time. Did you call at the 'Prince of Wales'?"

"No——"

"No, you didn't like——! It's not very nice." The other woman was indulgent. There was an awkward pause. "Jack never said nothink about—about your Master," she said.

"No!—I expect he's stuck in there!"

Elizabeth Bates said this bitterly, and with recklessness. She knew that the woman across the yard was standing at her door listening, but she did not care. As she turned:

"Stop a minute! I'll just go an' ask Jack if 'e knows anythink," said Mrs Rigley.

"Oh no—I wouldn't like to put——!"

"Yes, I will, if you'll just step inside an' see as th' childer doesn't come downstairs and set theirselves afire."

8. Back kitchen.

Elizabeth Bates, murmuring a remonstrance, stepped inside. The other woman apologised for the state of the room.

The kitchen needed apology. There were little frocks and trousers and childish undergarments on the squab[9] and on the floor, and a litter of playthings everywhere. On the black American cloth[1] of the table were pieces of bread and cake, crusts, slops, and a teapot with cold tea.

"Eh, ours is just as bad," said Elizabeth Bates, looking at the woman, not at the house. Mrs Rigley put a shawl over her head and hurried out, saying:

"I shanna be a minute."

The other sat, noting with faint disapproval the general untidiness of the room. Then she fell to counting the shoes of various sizes scattered over the floor. There were twelve. She sighed and said to herself: "No wonder!"—glancing at the litter. There came the scratching of two pairs of feet on the yard, and the Rigleys entered. Elizabeth Bates rose. Rigley was a big man, with very large bones. His head looked particularly bony. Across his temple was a blue scar, caused by a wound got in the pit, a wound in which the coal dust remained blue like tattooing.

"'Asna 'e come whoam yit?" asked the man, without any form of greeting, but with deference and sympathy. "I couldna say wheer he is—'e's non ower theer!"—he jerked his head to signify the "Prince of Wales."

"'E's 'appen gone up to th' Yew,"[2] said Mrs Rigley.

There was another pause. Rigley had evidently something to get off his mind:

"Ah left 'im finishin' a stint," he began. "Loose-all[3] 'ad bin gone about ten minutes when we com'n away, an' I shouted: 'Are ter comin', Walt?' an' 'e said: 'Go on, Ah shanna be but a'ef a minnit,' so we com'n ter th' bottom, me an' Bowers, thinkin' as 'e wor just behint, an' 'ud come up i' th' next bantle[4]——"

He stood perplexed, as if answering a charge of deserting his mate. Elizabeth Bates, now again certain of disaster, hastened to reassure him:

"I expect 'e's gone up to th' 'Yew Tree,' as you say. It's not the first time. I've fretted myself into a fever before now. He'll come home when they carry him."

"Ay, isn't it too bad!" deplored the other woman.

"I'll just step up to Dick's an' see if 'e is theer," offered the man, afraid of appearing alarmed, afraid of taking liberties.

"Oh, I wouldn't think of bothering you that far," said Elizabeth Bates, with emphasis, but he knew she was glad of his offer.

As they stumbled up the entry, Elizabeth Bates heard Rigley's wife run across the yard and open her neighbour's door. At this, suddenly all the blood in her body seemed to switch away from her heart.

"Mind!" warned Rigley. "Ah've said many a time as Ah'd fill up them ruts in this entry, sumb'dy 'll be breakin' their legs yit."

She recovered herself and walked quickly along with the miner.

"I don't like leaving the children in bed, and nobody in the house," she said.

9. Couch.
1. Oilcloth.
2. I.e., the Yew Tree (a pub).

3. Signal for end of work.
4. Group.

"No, you dunna!" he replied courteously. They were soon at the gate of the cottage.

"Well, I shanna be many minnits. Dunna you be frettin' now, 'e'll be all right," said the butty.[5]

"Thank you very much, Mr Rigley," she replied.

"You're welcome!" he stammered, moving away. "I shanna be many minnits."

The house was quiet. Elizabeth Bates took off her hat and shawl, and rolled back the rug. When she had finished, she sat down. It was a few minutes past nine. She was startled by the rapid chuff of the winding-engine at the pit, and the sharp whirr of the brakes on the rope as it descended. Again she felt the painful sweep of her blood, and she put her hand to her side, saying aloud: "Good gracious!—it's only the nine o'clock deputy[6] going down," rebuking herself.

She sat still, listening. Half an hour of this, and she was wearied out.

"What am I working myself up like this for?" she said pitiably to herself, "I s'll only be doing myself some damage."

She took out her sewing again.

At a quarter to ten there were footsteps. One person! She watched for the door to open. It was an elderly woman, in a black bonnet and a black woollen shawl—his mother. She was about sixty years old, pale, with blue eyes, and her face all wrinkled and lamentable. She shut the door and turned to her daughter-in-law peevishly.

"Eh, Lizzie, whatever shall we do, whatever shall we do!" she cried.

Elizabeth drew back a little, sharply.

"What is it, mother?" she said.

The elder woman seated herself on the sofa.

"I don't know, child, I can't tell you!"—she shook her head slowly. Elizabeth sat watching her, anxious and vexed.

"I don't know," replied the grandmother, sighing very deeply. "There's no end to my troubles, there isn't. The things I've gone through, I'm sure it's enough——!" She wept without wiping her eyes, the tears running.

"But, mother," interrupted Elizabeth, "what do you mean? What is it?"

The grandmother slowly wiped her eyes. The fountains of her tears were stopped by Elizabeth's directness. She wiped her eyes slowly.

"Poor child! Eh, you poor thing!" she moaned. "I don't know what we're going to do, I don't—and you as you are—it's a thing, it is indeed!"

Elizabeth waited.

"Is he dead?" she asked, and at the words her heart swung violently, though she felt a slight flush of shame at the ultimate extravagance of the question. Her words sufficiently frightened the old lady, almost brought her to herself.

"Don't say so, Elizabeth! We'll hope it's not as bad as that; no, may the Lord spare us that, Elizabeth. Jack Rigley came just as I was sittin' down to a glass afore going to bed, an' 'e said: ''Appen you'll go down th' line, Mrs. Bates. Walt's had an accident. 'Appen you'll go an' sit wi' 'er till we can get him home.' I hadn't time to ask him a word afore he was gone. An' I put my bonnet on an' come straight down, Lizzie. I thought to myself: 'Eh, that

5. Workmate (cf. "buddy"). Among English coal miners it means a supervisor intermediary between the employers and the men.
6. Minor coal-mine official.

poor blessed child, if anybody should come an' tell her of a sudden, there's no knowin' what'll 'appen to 'er.' You mustn't let it upset you, Lizzie—or you know what to expect. How long is it, six months—or is it five, Lizzie? Ay!"— the old woman shook her head—"time slips on, it slips on! Ay!"

Elizabeth's thoughts were busy elsewhere. If he was killed—would she be able to manage on the little pension and what she could earn?—she counted up rapidly. If he was hurt—they wouldn't take him to the hospital—how tiresome he would be to nurse!—but perhaps she'd be able to get him away from the drink and his hateful ways. She would—while he was ill. The tears offered to come to her eyes at the picture. But what sentimental luxury was this she was beginning? She turned to consider the children. At any rate she was absolutely necessary for them. They were her business.

"Ay!" repeated the old woman, "it seems but a week or two since he brought me his first wages. Ay—he was a good lad, Elizabeth, he was, in his way. I don't know why he got to be such a trouble, I don't. He was a happy lad at home, only full of spirits. But there's no mistake he's been a handful of trouble, he has! I hope the Lord'll spare him to mend his ways. I hope so, I hope so. You've had a sight o' trouble with him, Elizabeth, you have indeed. But he was a jolly enough lad wi' me, he was, I can assure you. I don't know how it is. . . ."

The old woman continued to muse aloud, a monotonous irritating sound, while Elizabeth thought concentratedly, startled once, when she heard the winding-engine chuff quickly, and the brakes skirr with a shriek. Then she heard the engine more slowly, and the brakes made no sound. The old woman did not notice. Elizabeth waited in suspense. The mother-in-law talked, with lapses into silence.

"But he wasn't your son, Lizzie, an' it makes a difference. Whatever he was, I remember him when he was little, an' I learned to understand him and to make allowances. You've got to make allowances for them——"

It was half-past ten, and the old woman was saying: "But it's trouble from beginning to end; you're never too old for trouble, never too old for that——" when the gate banged back, and there were heavy feet on the steps.

"I'll go, Lizzie, let me go," cried the old woman, rising. But Elizabeth was at the door. It was a man in pit-clothes.

"They're bringin' 'im, Missis," he said. Elizabeth's heart halted a moment. Then it surged on again, almost suffocating her.

"Is he—is it bad?" she asked.

The man turned away, looking at the darkness:

"The doctor says 'e'd been dead hours. 'E saw 'im i' th' lamp-cabin."

The old woman, who stood just behind Elizabeth, dropped into a chair, and folded her hands, crying: "Oh, my boy, my boy!"

"Hush!" said Elizabeth, with a sharp twitch of a frown. "Be still, mother, don't waken th' children: I wouldn't have them down for anything!"

The old woman moaned softly, rocking herself. The man was drawing away. Elizabeth took a step forward.

"How was it?" she asked.

"Well, I couldn't say for sure," the man replied, very ill at ease. "'E wor fin-ishin' a stint an' th' butties 'ad gone, an' a lot o' stuff come down atop 'n 'im."

"And crushed him?" cried the widow, with a shudder.

"No," said the man, "it fell at th' back of 'im. 'E wor under th' face an' it niver touched 'im. It shut 'im in. It seems 'e wor smothered."

Elizabeth shrank back. She heard the old woman behind her cry:
"What?—what did 'e say it was?"

The man replied, more loudly: "'E wor smothered!"

Then the old woman wailed aloud, and this relieved Elizabeth.

"Oh, mother," she said, putting her hand on the old woman, "don't waken
th' children, don't waken th' children."

She wept a little, unknowing, while the old mother rocked herself and
moaned. Elizabeth remembered that they were bringing him home, and she
must be ready. "They'll lay him in the parlour," she said to herself, standing
a moment pale and perplexed.

Then she lighted a candle and went into the tiny room. The air was cold
and damp, but she could not make a fire, there was no fireplace. She set
down the candle and looked round. The candlelight glittered on the lustre-
glasses, on the two vases that held some of the pink chrysanthemums, and on
the dark mahogany. There was a cold, deathly smell of chrysanthemums in
the room. Elizabeth stood looking at the flowers. She turned away, and calculated whether there would be room to lay him on the floor, between the
couch and the chiffonier. She pushed the chairs aside. There would be room
to lay him down and to step round him. Then she fetched the old red tablecloth, and another old cloth, spreading them down to save her bit of carpet.
She shivered on leaving the parlour; so, from the dresser drawer she took a
clean shirt and put it at the fire to air. All the time her mother-in-law was
rocking herself in the chair and moaning.

"You'll have to move from there, mother," said Elizabeth. "They'll be bringing him in. Come in the rocker."

The old mother rose mechanically, and seated herself by the fire, continuing to lament. Elizabeth went into the pantry for another candle, and there,
in the little pent-house under the naked tiles, she heard them coming. She
stood still in the pantry doorway, listening. She heard them pass the end of
the house, and come awkwardly down the three steps, a jumble of shuffling
footsteps and muttering voices. The old woman was silent. The men were in
the yard.

Then Elizabeth heard Matthews, the manager of the pit, say: "You go in
first, Jim. Mind!"

The door came open, and the two women saw a collier backing into the
room, holding one end of a stretcher, on which they could see the nailed pit-
boots of the dead man. The two carriers halted, the man at the head stooping to the lintel of the door.

"Wheer will you have him?" asked the manager, a short, white-bearded
man.

Elizabeth roused herself and came from the pantry carrying the unlighted
candle.

"In the parlour," she said.

"In there, Jim!" pointed the manager, and the carriers backed round into
the tiny room. The coat with which they had covered the body fell off as they
awkwardly turned through the two doorways, and the women saw their man,
naked to the waist, lying stripped for work. The old woman began to moan in
a low voice of horror.

"Lay th' stretcher at th' side," snapped the manager, "an' put 'im on th'
cloths. Mind now, mind! Look you now——!"

One of the men had knocked off a vase of chrysanthemums. He stared
awkwardly, then they set down the stretcher. Elizabeth did not look at her

husband. As soon as she could get in the room, she went and picked up the broken vase and the flowers.

"Wait a minute!" she said.

The three men waited in silence while she mopped up the water with a duster.

"Eh, what a job, what a job, to be sure!" the manager was saying, rubbing his brow with trouble and perplexity. "Never knew such a thing in my life, never! He'd no business to ha' been left. I never knew such a thing in my life! Fell over him clean as a whistle, an' shut him in. Not four foot of space, there wasn't—yet it scarce bruised him."

He looked down at the dead man, lying prone, half naked, all grimed with coal-dust.

"''Sphyxiated,' the doctor said. It *is* the most terrible job I've ever known. Seems as if it was done o' purpose. Clean over him, an' shut 'im in, like a mouse-trap"—he made a sharp, descending gesture with his hand.

The colliers standing by jerked aside their heads in hopeless comment.

The horror of the thing bristled upon them all.

Then they heard the girl's voice upstairs calling shrilly: "Mother, mother—who is it? Mother, who is it?"

Elizabeth hurried to the foot of the stairs and opened the door:

"Go to sleep!" she commanded sharply. "What are you shouting about? Go to sleep at once—there's nothing——"

Then she began to mount the stairs. They could hear her on the boards, and on the plaster floor of the little bedroom. They could hear her distinctly:

"What's the matter now?—what's the matter with you, silly thing?"—her voice was much agitated, with an unreal gentleness.

"I thought it was some men come," said the plaintive voice of the child. "Has he come?"

"Yes, they've brought him. There's nothing to make a fuss about. Go to sleep now, like a good child."

They could hear her voice in the bedroom, they waited whilst she covered the children under the bedclothes.

"Is he drunk?" asked the girl, timidly, faintly.

"No! No—he's not! He—he's asleep."

"Is he asleep downstairs?"

"Yes—and don't make a noise."

There was silence for a moment, then the men heard the frightened child again:

"What's that noise?"

"It's nothing, I tell you, what are you bothering for?"

The noise was the grandmother moaning. She was oblivious of everything, sitting on her chair rocking and moaning. The manager put his hand on her arm and bade her "Sh—sh!!"

The old woman opened her eyes and looked at him. She was shocked by this interruption, and seemed to wonder.

"What time is it?" the plaintive thin voice of the child, sinking back unhappily into sleep, asked this last question.

"Ten o'clock," answered the mother more softly. Then she must have bent down and kissed the children.

Matthews beckoned to the men to come away. They put on their caps and took up the stretcher. Stepping over the body, they tiptoed out of the house. None of them spoke till they were far from the wakeful children.

When Elizabeth came down she found her mother alone on the parlour floor, leaning over the dead man, the tears dropping on him.

"We must lay him out," the wife said. She put on the kettle, then returning knelt at the feet, and began to unfasten the knotted leather laces. The room was clammy and dim with only one candle, so that she had to bend her face almost to the floor. At last she got off the heavy boots and put them away.

"You must help me now," she whispered to the old woman. Together they stripped the man.

When they arose, saw him lying in the naïve dignity of death, the women stood arrested in fear and respect. For a few moments they remained still, looking down, the old mother whimpering. Elizabeth felt countermanded.[7] She saw him, how utterly inviolable he lay in himself. She had nothing to do with him. She could not accept it. Stooping, she laid her hand on him, in claim. He was still warm, for the mine was hot where he had died. His mother had his face between her hands, and was murmuring incoherently. The old tears fell in succession as drops from wet leaves; the mother was not weeping, merely her tears flowed. Elizabeth embraced the body of her husband, with cheek and lips. She seemed to be listening, inquiring, trying to get some connection. But she could not. She was driven away. He was impregnable.

She rose, went into the kitchen where she poured warm water into a bowl, brought soap and flannel and a soft towel. "I must wash him," she said.

Then the old mother rose stiffly, and watched Elizabeth as she carefully washed his face, carefully brushing his big blond moustache from his mouth with the flannel. She was afraid with a bottomless fear, so she ministered to him. The old woman, jealous, said:

"Let me wipe him!"—and she kneeled on the other side drying slowly as Elizabeth washed, her big black bonnet sometimes brushing the dark head of her daughter-in-law. They worked thus in silence for a long time. They never forgot it was death, and the touch of the man's dead body gave them strange emotions, different in each of the women; a great dread possessed them both, the mother felt the lie was given to her womb, she was denied; the wife felt the utter isolation of the human soul, the child within her was a weight apart from her.

At last it was finished. He was a man of handsome body, and his face showed no traces of drink. He was blond, full-fleshed, with fine limbs. But he was dead.

"Bless him," whispered his mother, looking always at his face, and speaking out of sheer terror. "Dear lad—bless him!" She spoke in a faint, sibilant ecstasy of fear and mother love.

Elizabeth sank down again to the floor, and put her face against his neck, and trembled and shuddered. But she had to draw away again. He was dead, and her living flesh had no place against his. A great dread and weariness held her: she was so unavailing. Her life was gone like this.

"White as milk he is, clear as a twelve-month baby, bless him, the darling!" the old mother murmured to herself. "Not a mark on him, clear and clean and white, beautiful as ever a child was made," she murmured with pride. Elizabeth kept her face hidden.

"He went peaceful, Lizzie—peaceful as sleep. Isn't he beautiful, the lamb? Ay—he must ha' made his peace, Lizzie. 'Appen he made it all right, Lizzie,

7. Contradicted.

shut in there. He'd have time. He wouldn't look like this if he hadn't made his peace. The lamb, the dear lamb. Eh, but he had a hearty laugh. I loved to hear it. He had the heartiest laugh, Lizzie, as a lad——"

Elizabeth looked up. The man's mouth was fallen back, slightly open under the cover of the moustache. The eyes, half shut, did not show glazed in the obscurity. Life with its smoky burning gone from him, had left him apart and utterly alien to her. And she knew what a stranger he was to her. In her womb was ice of fear, because of this separate stranger with whom she had been living as one flesh. Was this what it all meant—utter, intact separateness, obscured by heat of living? In dread she turned her face away. The fact was too deadly. There had been nothing between them, and yet they had come together, exchanging their nakedness repeatedly. Each time he had taken her, they had been two isolated beings, far apart as now. He was no more responsible than she. The child was like ice in her womb. For as she looked at the dead man, her mind, cold and detached, said clearly: "Who am I? What have I been doing? I have been fighting a husband who did not exist. *He* existed all the time. What wrong have I done? What was that I have been living with? There lies the reality, this man." And her soul died in her for fear: she knew she had never seen him, he had never seen her, they had met in the dark and had fought in the dark, not knowing whom they met or whom they fought. And now she saw, and turned silent in seeing. For she had been wrong. She had said he was something he was not; she had felt familiar with him. Whereas he was apart all the while, living as she never lived, feeling as she never felt.

In fear and shame she looked at his naked body, that she had known falsely. And he was the father of her children. Her soul was torn from her body and stood apart. She looked at his naked body and was ashamed, as if she had denied it. After all, it was itself. It seemed awful to her. She looked at his face, and she turned her own face to the wall. For his look was other than hers, his way was not her way. She had denied him what he was—she saw it now. She had refused him as himself. And this had been her life, and his life. She was grateful to death, which restored the truth. And she knew she was not dead.

And all the while her heart was bursting with grief and pity for him. What had he suffered? What stretch of horror for this helpless man! She was rigid with agony. She had not been able to help him. He had been cruelly injured, this naked man, this other being, and she could make no reparation. There were the children—but the children belonged to life. This dead man had nothing to do with them. He and she were only channels through which life had flowed to issue in the children. She was a mother—but how awful she knew it now to have been a wife. And he, dead now, how awful he must have felt it to be a husband. She felt that in the next world he would be a stranger to her. If they met there, in the beyond, they would only be ashamed of what had been before. The children had come, for some mysterious reason, out of both of them. But the children did not unite them. Now he was dead, she knew how eternally he was apart from her, how eternally he had nothing more to do with her. She saw this episode of her life closed. They had denied each other in life. Now he had withdrawn. An anguish came over her. It was finished then: it had become hopeless between them long before he died. Yet he had been her husband. But how little!

"Have you got his shirt, 'Lizabeth?"

Elizabeth turned without answering, though she strove to weep and behave as her mother-in-law expected. But she could not, she was silenced. She went into the kitchen and returned with the garment.

"It is aired," she said, grasping the cotton shirt here and there to try. She was almost ashamed to handle him; what right had she or anyone to lay hands on him; but her touch was humble on his body. It was hard work to clothe him. He was so heavy and inert. A terrible dread gripped her all the while: that he could be so heavy and utterly inert, unresponsive, apart. The horror of the distance between them was almost too much for her—it was so infinite a gap she must look across.

At last it was finished. They covered him with a sheet and left him lying, with his face bound. And she fastened the door of the little parlour, lest the children should see what was lying there. Then, with peace sunk heavy on her heart, she went about making tidy the kitchen. She knew she submitted to life, which was her immediate master. But from death, her ultimate master, she winced with fear and shame.

1911, 1914

The Horse Dealer's Daughter

"Well, Mabel, and what are you going to do with yourself?" asked Joe, with foolish flippancy. He felt quite safe himself. Without listening for an answer, he turned aside, worked a grain of tobacco to the tip of his tongue, and spat it out. He did not care about anything, since he felt safe himself.

The three brothers and the sister sat round the desolate breakfast-table, attempting some sort of desultory consultation. The morning's post had given the final tap to the family fortunes, and all was over. The dreary dining-room itself, with its heavy mahogany furniture, looked as if it were waiting to be done away with.

But the consultation amounted to nothing. There was a strange air of ineffectuality about the three men, as they sprawled at table, smoking and reflecting vaguely on their own condition. The girl was alone, a rather short, sullen-looking young woman of twenty-seven. She did not share the same life as her brothers. She would have been good-looking, save for the impressive fixity of her face, "bull-dog," as her brothers called it.

There was a confused tramping of horses' feet outside. The three men all sprawled round in their chairs to watch. Beyond the dark holly bushes that separated the strip of lawn from the high-road, they could see a cavalcade of shire horses swinging out of their own yard, being taken for exercise. This was the last time. These were the last horses that would go through their hands. The young men watched with critical, callous look. They were all frightened at the collapse of their lives, and the sense of disaster in which they were involved left them no inner freedom.

Yet they were three fine, well-set fellows enough. Joe, the eldest, was a man of thirty-three, broad and handsome in a hot, flushed way. His face was red, he twisted his black moustache over a thick finger, his eyes were shallow and restless. He had a sensual way of uncovering his teeth when he laughed, and his bearing was stupid. Now he watched the horses with a glazed look of helplessness in his eyes, a certain stupor of downfall.

The great draught horses swung past. They were tied head to tail, four of them, and they heaved along to where a lane branched off from the high-road, planting their great hoofs floutingly in the fine black mud, swinging their great rounded haunches sumptuously, and trotting a few sudden steps as they were led into the lane, round the corner. Every movement showed a massive, slumbrous strength, and a stupidity which held them in subjection. The groom at the head looked back, jerking the leading rope. And the caval-cade moved out of sight up the lane, the tail of the last horse, bobbed up tight and stiff, held out taut from the swinging great haunches as they rocked behind the hedges in a motion-like sleep.

Joe watched with glazed hopeless eyes. The horses were almost like his own body to him. He felt he was done for now. Luckily he was engaged to a woman as old as himself, and therefore her father, who was steward of a neighbouring estate, would provide him with a job. He would marry and go into harness. His life was over, he would be a subject animal now.

He turned uneasily aside, the retreating steps of the horses echoing in his ears. Then, with foolish restlessness, he reached for the scraps of bacon-rind from the plates, and making a faint whistling sound, flung them to the terrier that lay against the fender. He watched the dog swallow them, and waited till the creature looked into his eyes. Then a faint grin came on his face, and in a high, foolish voice he said:

"You won't get much more bacon, shall you, you little b——?"

The dog faintly and dismally wagged its tail, then lowered its haunches, circled round, and lay down again.

There was another helpless silence at the table. Joe sprawled uneasily in his seat, not willing to go till the family conclave was dissolved. Fred Henry, the second brother, was erect, clean-limbed, alert. He had watched the pass-ing of the horses with more *sang-froid*.[1] If he was an animal, like Joe, he was an animal which controls, not one which is controlled. He was master of any horse, and he carried himself with a well-tempered air of mastery. But he was not master of the situations of life. He pushed his coarse brown mous-tache upwards, off his lip, and glanced irritably at his sister, who sat impas-sive and inscrutable.

"You'll go and stop with Lucy for a bit, shan't you?" he asked. The girl did not answer.

"I don't see what else you can do," persisted Fred Henry.

"Go as a skivvy,"[2] Joe interpolated laconically.

The girl did not move a muscle.

"If I was her, I should go in for training for a nurse," said Malcolm, the youngest of them all. He was the baby of the family, a young man of twenty-two, with a fresh, jaunty *museau*.[3]

But Mabel did not take any notice of him. They had talked at her and round her for so many years, that she hardly heard them at all.

The marble clock on the mantelpiece softly chimed the half-hour, the dog rose uneasily from the hearth-rug and looked at the party at the breakfast-table. But still they sat in an ineffectual conclave.

"Oh, all right," said Joe suddenly, apropos of nothing. "I'll get a move on."

1. Cold blood (French, literal trans.); here, calm detachment.
2. Servant girl.
3. Muzzle (French); here, face.

He pushed back his chair, straddled his knees with a downward jerk, to get them free, in horsey fashion, and went to the fire. Still he did not go out of the room; he was curious to know what the others would do or say. He began to charge his pipe, looking down at the dog and saying in a high, affected voice:

"Going wi' me? Going wi' me are ter? Tha'rt goin' further than tha counts on just now, dost hear?"

The dog faintly wagged his tail, the man stuck out his jaw and covered his pipe with his hands, and puffed intently, losing himself in the tobacco, looking down all the while at the dog with an absent brown eye. The dog looked up at him in mournful distrust. Joe stood with his knees stuck out, in real horsey fashion.

"Have you had a letter from Lucy?" Fred Henry asked of his sister.

"Last week," came the neutral reply.

"And what does she say?"

There was no answer.

"Does she *ask* you to go and stop there?" persisted Fred Henry.

"She says I can if I like."

"Well, then, you'd better. Tell her you'll come on Monday."

This was received in silence.

"That's what you'll do then, is it?" said Fred Henry, in some exasperation.

But she made no answer. There was a silence of futility and irritation in the room. Malcolm grinned fatuously.

"You'll have to make up your mind between now and next Wednesday," said Joe loudly, "or else find yourself lodgings on the kerbstone."

The face of the young woman darkened, but she sat on immutable.

"Here's Jack Ferguson!" exclaimed Malcolm, who was looking aimlessly out of the window.

"Where?" exclaimed Joe loudly.

"Just gone past."

"Coming in?"

Malcolm craned his neck to see the gate.

"Yes," he said.

There was a silence. Mabel sat on like one condemned, at the head of the table. Then a whistle was heard from the kitchen. The dog got up and barked sharply. Joe opened the door and shouted:

"Come on."

After a moment a young man entered. He was muffled up in overcoat and a purple woollen scarf, and his tweed cap, which he did not remove, was pulled down on his head. He was of medium height, his face was rather long and pale, his eyes looked tired.

"Hello, Jack! Well, Jack!" exclaimed Malcolm and Joe. Fred Henry merely said: "Jack."

"What's doing?" asked the newcomer, evidently addressing Fred Henry.

"Same. We've got to be out by Wednesday. Got a cold?"

"I have—got it bad, too."

"Why don't you stop in?"

"*Me* stop in? When I can't stand on my legs, perhaps I shall have a chance." The young man spoke huskily. He had a slight Scotch accent.

"It's a knock-out, isn't it," said Joe, boisterously, "if a doctor goes round croaking with a cold. Looks bad for the patients, doesn't it?"

The young doctor looked at him slowly.

"Anything the matter with *you*, then?" he asked sarcastically.

"Not as I know of. Damn your eyes, I hope not. Why?"

"I thought you were very concerned about the patients, wondered if you might be one yourself."

"Damn it, no, I've never been patient to no flaming doctor, and hope I never shall be," returned Joe.

At this point Mabel rose from the table, and they all seemed to become aware of her existence. She began putting the dishes together. The young doctor looked at her, but did not address her. He had not greeted her. She went out of the room with the tray, her face impassive and unchanged.

"When are you off then, all of you?" asked the doctor.

"I'm catching the eleven-forty," replied Malcolm. "Are you goin' down wi' th' trap, Joe?"

"Yes, I've told you I'm going down wi' th' trap, haven't I?"

"We'd better be getting her in then. So long Jack, if I don't see you before I go," said Malcolm, shaking hands.

He went out, followed by Joe, who seemed to have his tail between his legs.

"Well, this is the devil's own," exclaimed the doctor, when he was left alone with Fred Henry. "Going before Wednesday, are you?"

"That's the orders," replied the other.

"Where, to Northampton?"

"That's it."

"The devil!" exclaimed Ferguson, with quiet chagrin.

And there was silence between the two.

"All settled up, are you?" asked Ferguson.

"About."

There was another pause.

"Well, I shall miss yer, Freddy, boy," said the young doctor.

"And I shall miss thee, Jack," returned the other.

"Miss you like hell," mused the doctor.

Fred Henry turned aside. There was nothing to say. Mabel came in again, to finish clearing the table.

"What are *you* going to do, then, Miss Pervin?" asked Ferguson. "Going to your sister's, are you?"

Mabel looked at him with her steady, dangerous eyes, that always made him uncomfortable, unsettling his superficial ease.

"No," she said.

"Well, what in the name of fortune *are* you going to do? Say what you mean to do," cried Fred Henry, with futile intensity.

But she only averted her head, and continued her work. She folded the white table-cloth, and put on the chenille cloth.

"The sulkiest bitch that ever trod!" muttered her brother.

But she finished her task with perfectly impassive face, the young doctor watching her interestedly all the while. Then she went out.

Fred Henry stared after her, clenching his lips, his blue eyes fixing in sharp antagonism, as he made a grimace of sour exasperation.

"You could bray[4] her into bits, and that's all you'd get out of her," he said, in a small, narrowed tone.

4. Grind.

The doctor smiled faintly.

"What's she *going* to do, then?" he asked.

"Strike me if *I* know!" returned the other.

There was a pause. Then the doctor stirred.

"I'll be seeing you tonight, shall I?" he said to his friend.

"Ay—where's it to be? Are we going over to Jessdale?"

"I don't know. I've got such a cold on me. I'll come round to the 'Moon and Stars,'[5] anyway."

"Let Lizzie and May miss their night for once, eh?"

"That's it—if I feel as I do now."

"All's one——"

The two young men went through the passage and down to the back door together. The house was large, but it was servantless now, and desolate. At the back was a small bricked house-yard and beyond that a big square, gravelled fine and red, and having stables on two sides. Sloping, dank, winter-dark fields stretched away on the open sides.

But the stables were empty. Joseph Pervin, the father of the family, had been a man of no education, who had become a fairly large horse dealer. The stables had been full of horses, there was a great turmoil and come-and-go of horses and of dealers and grooms. Then the kitchen was full of servants. But of late things had declined. The old man had married a second time, to retrieve his fortunes. Now he was dead and everything was gone to the dogs,[6] there was nothing but debt and threatening.

For months, Mabel had been servantless in the big house, keeping the home together in penury for her ineffectual brothers. She had kept house for ten years. But previously it was with unstinted means. Then, however brutal and coarse everything was, the sense of money had kept her proud, confident. The men might be foul-mouthed, the women in the kitchen might have had reputations, her brothers might have illegitimate children. But so long as there was money, the girl felt herself established, and brutally proud, reserved.

No company came to the house, save dealers and coarse men. Mabel had no associates of her own sex, after her sister went away. But she did not mind. She went regularly to church, she attended to her father. And she lived in the memory of her mother, who had died when she was fourteen, and whom she had loved. She had loved her father, too, in a different way, depending upon him, and feeling secure in him, until at the age of fifty-four, he married again. And then she had set hard against him. Now he had died and left them all hopelessly in debt.

She had suffered badly during the period of poverty. Nothing, however, could shake the curious, sullen, animal pride that dominated each member of the family. Now, for Mabel, the end had come. Still she would not cast about her. She would follow her own way just the same. She would always hold the keys of her own situation. Mindless and persistent, she endured from day to day. Why should she think? Why should she answer anybody? It was enough that this was the end, and there was no way out. She need not pass any more darkly along the main street of the small town, avoiding every eye. She need not demean herself any more, going into the shops and buying

---

5. Name of a public house (pub).   6. Gone wrong (slang).

the cheapest food. This was at an end. She thought of nobody, not even of herself. Mindless and persistent, she seemed in a sort of ecstasy to be coming nearer to her fulfilment, her own glorification, approaching her dead mother, who was glorified.

In the afternoon, she took a little bag, with shears and sponge and a small scrubbing-brush, and went out. It was a grey, wintry day, with saddened, dark green fields and an atmosphere blackened by the smoke of foundries not far off. She went quickly, darkly along the causeway, heeding nobody, through the town to the churchyard.

There she always felt secure, as if no one could see her, although as a matter of fact she was exposed to the stare of everyone who passed along under the churchyard wall. Nevertheless, once under the shadow of the great looming church, among the graves, she felt immune from the world, reserved within the thick churchyard wall as in another country.

Carefully she clipped the grass from the grave, and arranged the pinky-white, small chrysanthemums in the tin cross. When this was done, she took an empty jar from a neighbouring grave, brought water, and carefully, most scrupulously sponged the marble headstone and the coping-stone.

It gave her sincere satisfaction to do this. She felt in immediate contact with the world of her mother. She took minute pains, went through the park in a state bordering on pure happiness, as if in performing this task she came into a subtle, intimate connection with her mother. For the life she followed here in the world was far less real than the world of death she inherited from her mother.

The doctor's house was just by the church. Ferguson, being a mere hired assistant, was slave to the country-side. As he hurried now to attend to the out-patients in the surgery, glancing across the graveyard with his quick eye, he saw the girl at her task at the grave. She seemed so intent and remote, it was like looking into another world. Some mystical element was touched in him. He slowed down as he walked, watching her as if spellbound.

She lifted her eyes, feeling him looking. Their eyes met. And each looked away again at once, each feeling, in some way, found out by the other. He lifted his cap and passed on down the road. There remained distinct in his consciousness, like a vision, the memory of her face, lifted from the tombstone in the churchyard, and looking at him with slow, large, portentous eyes. It *was* portentous, her face. It seemed to mesmerise him. There was a heavy power in her eyes which laid hold of his whole being, as if he had drunk some powerful drug. He had been feeling weak and done before. Now the life came back into him, he felt delivered from his own fretted, daily self.

He finished his duties at the surgery as quickly as might be, hastily filling up the bottles of the waiting people with cheap drugs. Then, in perpetual haste, he set off again to visit several cases in another part of his round, before tea-time. At all times he preferred to walk if he could, but particularly when he was not well. He fancied the motion restored him.

The afternoon was falling. It was grey, deadened, and wintry, with a slow, moist, heavy coldness sinking in and deadening all the faculties. But why should he think or notice? He hastily climbed the hill and turned across the dark green fields, following the black cinder-track. In the distance, across a shallow dip in the country, the small town was clustered like smouldering ash, a tower, a spire, a heap of low, raw, extinct houses. And on the nearest fringe of the town, sloping into the dip, was Oldmeadow, the Pervins' house.

He could see the stables and the outbuildings distinctly, as they lay towards him on the slope. Well, he would not go there many more times! Another resource would be lost to him, another place gone: the only company he cared for in the alien, ugly little town he was losing. Nothing but work, drudgery, constant hastening from dwelling to dwelling among the colliers and the iron-workers. It wore him out, but at the same time he had a craving for it. It was a stimulant to him to be in the homes of the working people, moving, as it were, through the innermost body of their life. His nerves were excited and gratified. He could come so near, into the very lives of the rough, inarticulate, powerfully emotional men and women. He grumbled, he said he hated the hellish hole. But as a matter of fact it excited him, the contact with the rough, strongly-feeling people was a stimulant applied direct to his nerves.

Below Oldmeadow, in the green, shallow, soddened hollow of fields, lay a square, deep pond. Roving across the landscape, the doctor's quick eye detected a figure in black passing through the gate of the field, down towards the pond. He looked again. It would be Mabel Pervin. His mind suddenly became alive and attentive.

Why was she going down there? He pulled up on the path on the slope above, and stood staring. He could just make sure of the small black figure moving in the hollow of the failing day. He seemed to see her in the midst of such obscurity, that he was like a clairvoyant, seeing rather with the mind's eye than with ordinary sight. Yet he could see her positively enough, whilst he kept his eye attentive. He felt, if he looked away from her, in the thick, ugly falling dusk, he would lose her altogether.

He followed her minutely as she moved, direct and intent, like something transmitted rather than stirring in voluntary activity, straight down the field towards the pond. There she stood on the bank for a moment. She never raised her head. Then she waded slowly into the water.

He stood motionless as the small black figure walked slowly and deliberately towards the centre of the pond, very slowly, gradually moving deeper into the motionless water, and still moving forward as the water got up to her breast. Then he could see her no more in the dusk of the dead afternoon.

"There!" he exclaimed. "Would you believe it?"

And he hastened straight down, running over the wet, soddened fields, pushing through the hedges, down into the depression of callous wintry obscurity. It took him several minutes to come to the pond. He stood on the bank, breathing heavily. He could see nothing. His eyes seemed to penetrate the dead water. Yes, perhaps that was the dark shadow of her black clothing beneath the surface of the water.

He slowly ventured into the pond. The bottom was deep, soft clay, he sank in, and the water clasped dead cold round his legs. As he stirred he could smell the cold, rotten clay that fouled up into the water. It was objectionable in his lungs. Still, repelled and yet not heeding, he moved deeper into the pond. The cold water rose over his thighs, over his loins, upon his abdomen. The lower part of his body was all sunk in the hideous cold element. And the bottom was so deeply soft and uncertain, he was afraid of pitching with his mouth underneath. He could not swim, and was afraid.

He crouched a little, spreading his hands under the water and moving them round, trying to feel for her. The dead cold pond swayed upon his chest. He moved again, a little deeper, and again, with his hands underneath, he felt all around under the water. And he touched her clothing. But it evaded his fingers. He made a desperate effort to grasp it.

And so doing he lost his balance and went under, horribly, suffocating in the foul earthy water, struggling madly for a few moments. At last, after what seemed an eternity, he got his footing, rose again into the air and looked around. He gasped, and knew he was in the world. Then he looked at the water. She had risen near him. He grasped her clothing, and drawing her nearer, turned to take his way to land again.

He went very slowly, carefully, absorbed in the slow progress. He rose higher, climbing out of the pond. The water was now only about his legs; he was thankful, full of relief to be out of the clutches of the pond. He lifted her and staggered on to the bank, out of the horror of wet, grey clay.

He laid her down on the bank. She was quite unconscious and running with water. He made the water come from her mouth, he worked to restore her. He did not have to work very long before he could feel the breathing begin again in her; she was breathing naturally. He worked a little longer. He could feel her live beneath his hands; she was coming back. He wiped her face, wrapped her in his overcoat, looked round into the dim, dark grey world, then lifted her and staggered down the bank and across the fields.

It seemed an unthinkably long way, and his burden so heavy he felt he would never get to the house. But at last he was in the stable-yard, and then in the house-yard. He opened the door and went into the house. In the kitchen he laid her down on the hearth-rug and called. The house was empty. But the fire was burning in the grate.

Then again he kneeled to attend to her. She was breathing regularly, her eyes were wide open and as if conscious, but there seemed something missing in her look. She was conscious in herself, but unconscious of her surroundings.

He ran upstairs, took blankets from a bed, and put them before the fire to warm. Then he removed her saturated, earthy-smelling clothing, rubbed her dry with a towel, and wrapped her naked in the blankets. Then he went into the dining room, to look for spirits. There was a little whisky. He drank a gulp himself, and put some into her mouth.

The effect was instantaneous. She looked full into his face, as if she had been seeing him for some time, and yet had only just become conscious of him.

"Dr. Ferguson?" she said.

"What?" he answered.

He was divesting himself of his coat, intending to find some dry clothing upstairs. He could not bear the smell of the dead, clayey water, and he was mortally afraid for his own health.

"What did I do?" she asked.

"Walked into the pond," he replied. He had begun to shudder like one sick, and could hardly attend to her. Her eyes remained full on him, he seemed to be going dark in his mind, looking back at her helplessly. The shuddering became quieter in him, his life came back to him, dark and unknowing, but strong again.

"Was I out of my mind?" she asked, while her eyes were fixed on him all the time.

"Maybe, for the moment," he replied. He felt quiet, because his strength had come back. The strange fretful strain had left him.

"Am I out of my mind now?" she asked.

"Are you?" he reflected a moment. "No," he answered truthfully. "I don't see that you are." He turned his face aside. He was afraid now, because he felt dazed, and felt dimly that her power was stronger than his, in this issue. And she continued to look at him fixedly all the time. "Can you tell me where I shall find some dry things to put on?" he asked.

"Did you dive into the pond for me?" she asked.

"No," he answered. "I walked in. But I went in overhead as well."

There was silence for a moment. He hesitated. He very much wanted to go upstairs to get into dry clothing. But there was another desire in him. And she seemed to hold him. His will seemed to have gone to sleep, and left him, standing there slack before her. But he felt warm inside himself. He did not shudder at all, though his clothes were sodden on him.

"Why did you?" she asked.

"Because I didn't want you to do such a foolish thing," he said.

"It wasn't foolish," she said, still gazing at him as she lay on the floor, with a sofa cushion under her head. "It was the right thing to do. *I* knew best, then."

"I'll go and shift these wet things," he said. But still he had not the power to move out of her presence, until she sent him. It was as if she had the life of his body in her hands, and he could not extricate himself. Or perhaps he did not want to.

Suddenly she sat up. Then she became aware of her own immediate condition. She felt the blankets about her, she knew her own limbs. For a moment it seemed as if her reason were going. She looked round, with wild eye, as if seeking something. He stood still with fear. She saw her clothing lying scattered.

"Who undressed me?" she asked, her eyes resting full and inevitable on his face.

"I did," he replied, "to bring you round."

For some moments she sat and gazed at him awfully, her lips parted.

"Do you love me, then?" she asked.

He only stood and stared at her, fascinated. His soul seemed to melt.

She shuffled forward on her knees, and put her arms round him, round his legs, as he stood there, pressing her breasts against his knees and thighs, clutching him with strange, convulsive certainty, pressing his thighs against her, drawing him to her face, her throat, as she looked up at him with flaring, humble eyes of transfiguration, triumphant in first possession.

"You love me," she murmured, in strange transport, yearning and triumphant and confident. "You love me. I know you love me, I know."

And she was passionately kissing his knees, through the wet clothing, passionately and indiscriminately kissing his knees, his legs, as if unaware of everything.

He looked down at the tangled wet hair, the wild, bare, animal shoulders. He was amazed, bewildered, and afraid. He had never thought of loving her. He had never wanted to love her. When he rescued her and restored her, he was a doctor, and she was a patient. He had had no single personal thought of her. Nay, this introduction of the personal element was very distasteful to him, a violation of his professional honour. It was horrible to have her there embracing his knees. It was horrible. He revolted from it, violently. And yet— and yet—he had not the power to break away.

She looked at him again, with the same supplication of powerful love, and that same transcendent, frightening light of triumph. In view of the delicate flame which seemed to come from her face like a light, he was powerless. And yet he had never intended to love her. He had never intended. And something stubborn in him could not give way.

"You love me," she repeated, in a murmur of deep, rhapsodic assurance. "You love me."

Her hands were drawing him, drawing him down to her. He was afraid, even a little horrified. For he had, really, no intention of loving her. Yet her hands were drawing him towards her. He put out his hand quickly to steady himself, and grasped her bare shoulder. A flame seemed to burn the hand that grasped her soft shoulder. He had no intention of loving her: his whole will was against his yielding. It was horrible. And yet wonderful was the touch of her shoulders, beautiful the shining of her face. Was she perhaps mad? He had a horror of yielding to her. Yet something in him ached also.

He had been staring away at the door, away from her. But his hand remained on her shoulder. She had gone suddenly very still. He looked down at her. Her eyes were now wide with fear, with doubt, the light was dying from her face, a shadow of terrible greyness was returning. He could not bear the touch of her eyes' question upon him, and the look of death behind the question.

With an inward groan he gave way, and let his heart yield towards her. A sudden gentle smile came on his face. And her eyes, which never left his face, slowly, slowly filled with tears. He watched the strange water rise in her eyes, like some slow fountain coming up. And his heart seemed to burn and melt away in his breast.

He could not bear to look at her any more. He dropped on his knees and caught her head with his arms and pressed her face against his throat. She was very still. His heart, which seemed to have broken, was burning with a kind of agony in his breast. And he felt her slow, hot tears wetting his throat. But he could not move.

He felt the hot tears wet his neck and the hollows of his neck, and he remained motionless, suspended through one of man's eternities. Only now it had become indispensable to him to have her face pressed close to him; he could never let her go again. He could never let her head go away from the close clutch of his arm. He wanted to remain like that for ever, with his heart hurting him in a pain that was also life to him. Without knowing, he was looking down on her damp, soft brown hair.

Then, as it were suddenly, he smelt the horrid stagnant smell of that water. And at the same moment she drew away from him and looked at him. Her eyes were wistful and unfathomable. He was afraid of them, and he fell to kissing her, not knowing what he was doing. He wanted her eyes not to have that terrible, wistful, unfathomable look.

When she turned her face to him again, a faint delicate flush was glowing, and there was again dawning that terrible shining of joy in her eyes, which really terrified him, and yet which he now wanted to see, because he feared the look of doubt still more.

"You love me?" she said, rather faltering.

"Yes." The word cost him a painful effort. Not because it wasn't true. But because it was too newly true, the *saying* seemed to tear open again his newly-torn heart. And he hardly wanted it to be true, even now.

She lifted her face to him, and he bent forward and kissed her on the mouth, gently, with the one kiss that is an eternal pledge. And as he kissed her his heart strained again in his breast. He never intended to love her. But now it was over. He had crossed over the gulf to her, and all that he had left behind had shrivelled and become void.

After the kiss, her eyes again slowly filled with tears. She sat still, away from him, with her face drooped aside, and her hands folded in her lap. The tears fell very slowly. There was complete silence. He too sat there motionless and silent on the hearth-rug. The strange pain of his heart that was broken seemed to consume him. That he should love her? That this was love! That he should be ripped open in this way! Him, a doctor! How they would all jeer if they knew! It was agony to him to think they might know.

In the curious naked pain of the thought he looked again to her. She was sitting there drooped into a muse. He saw a tear fall, and his heart flared hot. He saw for the first time that one of her shoulders was quite uncovered, one arm bare, he could see one of her small breasts; dimly, because it had become almost dark in the room.

"Why are you crying?" he asked, in an altered voice.

She looked up at him, and behind her tears the consciousness of her situation for the first time brought a dark look of shame to her eyes.

"I'm not crying, really," she said, watching him, half frightened.

He reached his hand, and softly closed it on her bare arm.

"I love you! I love you!" he said in a soft, low vibrating voice, unlike himself.

She shrank, and dropped her head. The soft, penetrating grip of his hand on her arm distressed her. She looked up at him.

"I want to go," she said. "I want to go and get you some dry things."

"Why?" he said. "I'm all right."

"But I want to go," she said. "And I want you to change your things."

He released her arm, and she wrapped herself in the blanket, looking at him, rather frightened. And still she did not rise.

"Kiss me," she said wistfully.

He kissed her, but briefly, half in anger.

Then, after a second, she rose nervously, all mixed up in the blanket. He watched her in her confusion as she tried to extricate herself and wrap herself up so that she could walk. He watched her relentlessly, as she knew. And as she went, the blanket trailing, and as he saw a glimpse of her feet and her white leg, he tried to remember her as she was when he had wrapped her in the blanket. But then he didn't want to remember, because she had been nothing to him then, and his nature revolted from remembering her as she was when she was nothing to him.

A tumbling muffled noise from within the dark house startled him. Then he heard her voice: "There are clothes." He rose and went to the foot of the stairs, and gathered up the garments she had thrown down. Then he came back to the fire, to rub himself down and dress. He grinned at his own appearance when he had finished.

The fire was sinking, so he put on coal. The house was now quite dark, save for the light of a street-lamp that shone in faintly from beyond the holly trees. He lit the gas with matches he found on the mantelpiece. Then he emptied the pockets of his own clothes, and threw all his wet things in a heap into the scullery. After which he gathered up her sodden clothes, gently, and put them in a separate heap on the copper-top in the scullery.

It was six o'clock on the clock. His own watch had stopped. He ought to go back to the surgery. He waited, and still she did not come down. So he went to the foot of the stairs and called:

"I shall have to go."

Almost immediately he heard her coming down. She had on her best dress of black voile, and her hair was tidy, but still damp. She looked at him—and in spite of herself, smiled.

"I don't like you in those clothes," she said.

"Do I look a sight?" he answered.

They were shy of one another.

"I'll make you some tea," she said.

"No, I must go."

"Must you?" And she looked at him again with the wide, strained, doubtful eyes. And again, from the pain of his breast, he knew how he loved her. He went and bent to kiss her, gently, passionately, with his heart's painful kiss.

"And my hair smells so horrible," she murmured in distraction. "And I'm so awful, I'm so awful! Oh no, I'm too awful." And she broke into bitter, heart-broken sobbing. "You can't want to love me, I'm horrible."

"Don't be silly, don't be silly," he said, trying to comfort her, kissing her, holding her in his arms. "I want you, I want to marry you, we're going to be married, quickly, quickly—to-morrow if I can."

But she only sobbed terribly, and cried:

"I feel awful. I feel awful. I feel I'm horrible to you."

"No, I want you, I want you," was all he answered, blindly, with that terrible intonation which frightened her almost more than her horror lest he should *not* want her.

1922

Why the Novel Matters

We have curious ideas of ourselves. We think of ourselves as a body with a spirit in it, or a body with a soul in it, or a body with a mind in it. *Mens sana in corpore sano.*[1] The years drink up the wine, and at last throw the bottle away, the body, of course, being the bottle.

It is a funny sort of superstition. Why should I look at my hand, as it so cleverly writes these words, and decide that it is a mere nothing compared to the mind that directs it? Is there really any huge difference between my hand and my brain? Or my mind? My hand is alive, it flickers with a life of its own. It meets all the strange universe in touch, and learns a vast number of things, and knows a vast number of things. My hand, as it writes these words, slips gaily along, jumps like a grasshopper to dot an *i*, feels the table rather cold, gets a little bored if I write too long, has its own rudiments of thought, and is just as much *me* as is my brain, my mind, or my soul. Why should I imagine that there is a *me* which is more *me* than my hand is? Since my hand is absolutely alive, me alive.

Whereas, of course, as far as I am concerned, my pen isn't alive at all. My pen *isn't me* alive. Me alive ends at my finger tips.

---

1. A healthy mind in a healthy body (Latin).

Whatever is me alive is me. Every tiny bit of my hands is alive, every little freckle and hair and fold of skin. And whatever is me alive is me. Only my finger-nails, those ten little weapons between me and an inanimate universe, they cross the mysterious Rubicon[2] between me alive and things like my pen, which are not alive, in my own sense.

So, seeing my hand is all alive, and me alive, wherein is it just a bottle, or a jug, or a tin can, or a vessel of clay, or any of the rest of that nonsense? True, if I cut it it will bleed, like a can of cherries. But then the skin that is cut, and the veins that bleed, and the bones that should never be seen, they are all just as alive as the blood that flows. So the tin can business, or vessel of clay, is just bunk.

And that's what you learn, when you're a novelist. And that's what you are very liable *not* to know, if you're a parson, or a philosopher, or a scientist, or a stupid person. If you're a parson, you talk about souls in heaven. If you're a novelist, you know that paradise is in the palm of your hand, and on the end of your nose, because both are alive; and alive, and man alive, which is more than you can say, for certain, of paradise. Paradise is after life, and I for one am not keen on anything that is *after* life. If you are a philosopher, you talk about infinity, and the pure spirit which knows all things. But if you pick up a novel, you realise immediately that infinity is just a handle to this self-same jug of a body of mine; while as for knowing, if I find my finger in the fire, I know that fire burns, with a knowledge so emphatic and vital, it leaves Nirvana[3] merely a conjecture. Oh, yes, my body, me alive, *knows*, and knows intensely. And as for the sum of all knowledge, it can't be anything more than an accumulation of all the things I know in the body, and you, dear reader, know in the body.

These damned philosophers, they talk as if they suddenly went off in steam, and were then much more important than they are when they're in their shirts. It is nonsense. Every man, philosopher included, ends in his own finger-tips. That's the end of his man alive. As for the words and thoughts and sighs and aspirations that fly from him, they are so many tremulations in the ether, and not alive at all. But if the tremulations reach another man alive, he may receive them into his life, and his life may take on a new colour, like a chameleon creeping from a brown rock on to a green leaf. All very well and good. It still doesn't alter the fact that the so-called spirit, the message or teaching of the philosopher or the saint, isn't alive at all, but just a tremulation upon the ether, like a radio message. All this spirit stuff is just tremulations upon the ether. If you, as man alive, quiver from the tremulation of the ether into new life, that is because you are man alive, and you take sustenance and stimulation into your alive man in a myriad ways. But to say that the message, or the spirit which is communicated to you, is more important than your living body, is nonsense. You might as well say that the potato at dinner was more important.

Nothing is important but life. And for myself, I can absolutely see life nowhere but in the living. Life with a capital L is only man alive. Even a cabbage in the rain is cabbage alive. All things that are alive are amazing. And all things that are dead are subsidiary to the living. Better a live dog than a dead lion. But better a live lion than a live dog. *C'est la vie!*

2. When Julius Caesar crossed the river Rubicon (near Rimini, Italy) in 49 B.C.E., in defiance of the Senate, he indicated his intention of advancing against Pompey and thus involving the country in civil war. Hence to "cross the Rubicon" means to take an important and irrevocable decision.
3. In Buddhist theology the extinction of the self and its desires and the attainment of perfect beatitude.

It seems impossible to get a saint, or a philosopher, or a scientist, to stick to this simple truth. They are all, in a sense, renegades. The saint wishes to offer himself up as spiritual food for the multitude. Even Francis of Assisi[4] turns himself into a sort of angel-cake, of which anyone may take a slice. But an angel-cake is rather less than man alive. And poor St Francis might well apologise to his body, when he is dying: "Oh, pardon me, my body, the wrong I did you through the years!" It was no wafer,[5] for others to eat.

The philosopher, on the other hand, because he can think, decides that nothing but thoughts matter. It is as if a rabbit, because he can make little pills, should decide that nothing but little pills matter. As for the scientist, he has absolutely no use for me so long as I am man alive. To the scientist, I am dead. He puts under the microscope a bit of dead me, and calls it me. He takes me to pieces, and says first one piece, and then another piece, is me. My heart, my liver, my stomach have all been scientifically me, according to the scientist; and nowadays I am either a brain, or nerves, or glands, or something more up-to-date in the tissue line.

Now I absolutely flatly deny that I am a soul, or a body, or a mind, or an intelligence, or a brain, or a nervous system, or a bunch of glands, or any of the rest of these bits of me. The whole is greater than the part. And therefore, I, who am man alive, am greater than my soul, or spirit, or body, or mind, or consciousness, or anything else that is merely a part of me. I am a man, and alive. I am man alive, and as long as I can, I intend to go on being man alive.

For this reason I am a novelist. And being a novelist, I consider myself superior to the saint, the scientist, the philosopher, and the poet, who are all great masters of different bits of man alive, but never get the whole hog.

The novel is the one bright book of life. Books are not life. They are only tremulations on the ether. But the novel as a tremulation can make the whole man alive tremble. Which is more than poetry, philosophy, science, or any other book-tremulation can do.

The novel is the book of life. In this sense, the Bible is a great confused novel. You may say, it is about God. But it is really about man alive. Adam, Eve, Sarai, Abraham, Isaac, Jacob, Samuel, David, Bath-Sheba, Ruth, Esther, Solomon, Job, Isaiah, Jesus, Mark, Judas, Paul, Peter: what is it but man alive, from start to finish? Man alive, not mere bits. Even the Lord is another man alive, in a burning bush, throwing the tablets of stone at Moses's head.

I do hope you begin to get my idea, why the novel is supremely important, as a tremulation on the ether. Plato makes the perfect ideal being tremble in me. But that's only a bit of me. Perfection is only a bit, in the strange makeup of man alive. The Sermon on the Mount[6] makes the selfless spirit of me quiver. But that, too, is only a bit of me. The Ten Commandments set the old Adam shivering in me, warning me that I am a thief and a murderer, unless I watch it. But even the old Adam is only a bit of me.

I very much like all these bits of me to be set trembling with life and the wisdom of life. But I do ask that the whole of me shall tremble in its wholeness, some time or other.

And this, of course, must happen in me, living.

4. Roman Catholic saint (1181 or 1182–1226).   lic Communion.
5. Consumed as Christ's body in Roman Catho-   6. See Matthew 5.7.

But as far as it can happen from a communication, it can only happen when a whole novel communicates itself to me. The Bible—but *all* the Bible—and Homer, and Shakespeare: these are the supreme old novels. These are all things to all men. Which means that in their wholeness they affect the whole man alive, which is the man himself, beyond any part of him. They set the whole tree trembling with a new access of life, they do not just stimulate growth in one direction.

I don't want to grow in any one direction any more. And, if I can help it, I don't want to stimulate anybody else into some particular direction. A particular direction ends in a *cul-de-sac*. We're in a *cul-de-sac* at present.

I don't believe in any dazzling revelation, or in any supreme Word. "The grass withereth, the flower fadeth, but the Word of the Lord shall stand for ever."[7] That's the kind of stuff we've drugged ourselves with. As a matter of fact, the grass withereth, but comes up all the greener for that reason, after the rains. The flower fadeth, and therefore the bud opens. But the Word of the Lord, being man-uttered and a mere vibration on the ether, becomes staler and staler, more and more boring, till at last we turn a deaf ear and it ceases to exist, far more finally than any withered grass. It is grass that renews its youth like the eagle, not any Word.

We should ask for no absolutes, or absolute. Once and for all and for ever, let us have done with the ugly imperialism of any absolute. There is no absolute good, there is nothing absolutely right. All things flow and change, and even change is not absolute. The whole is a strange assembly of apparently incongruous parts, slipping past one another.

Me, man alive, I am a very curious assembly of incongruous parts. My yea! of today is oddly different from my yea! of yesterday. My tears of tomorrow will have nothing to do with my tears of a year ago. If the one I love remains unchanged and unchanging, I shall cease to love her. It is only because she changes and startles me into change and defies my inertia, and is herself staggered in her inertia by my changing, that I can continue to love her. If she stayed put, I might as well love the pepper pot.

In all this change, I maintain a certain integrity. But woe betide me if I try to put my finger on it. If I say of myself, I am this, I am that!—then, if I stick to it, I turn into a stupid fixed thing like a lamp-post. I shall never know wherein lies my integrity, my individuality, my me. I *can* never know it. It is useless to talk about my ego. That only means that I have made up an *idea* of myself, and that I am trying to cut myself out to pattern. Which is no good. You can cut your cloth to fit your coat, but you can't clip bits off your living body, to trim it down to your idea. True, you can put yourself into ideal corsets. But even in ideal corsets, fashions change.

Let us learn from the novel. In the novel, the characters can do nothing but *live*. If they keep on being good, according to pattern, or bad, according to pattern, or even volatile, according to pattern, they cease to live, and the novel falls dead. A character in a novel has got to live, or it is nothing.

We, likewise, in life have got to live, or we are nothing.

What we mean by living is, of course, just as indescribable as what we mean by *being*. Men get ideas into their heads, of what they mean by Life, and they proceed to cut life out to pattern. Sometimes they go into the desert to seek God, sometimes they go into the desert to seek cash, sometimes it is

7. Isaiah 40.8.

wine, woman, and song, and again it is water, political reform, and votes. You never know what it will be next: from killing your neighbour with hideous bombs and gas that tears the lungs, to supporting a Foundlings' Home[8] and preaching infinite Love, and being co-respondent in a divorce.

In all this wild welter, we need some sort of guide. It's no good inventing Thou Shalt Nots!

What then? Turn truly, honourably to the novel, and see wherein you are man alive, and wherein you are dead man in life. You may love a woman as man alive, and you may be making love to a woman as sheer dead man in life. You may eat your dinner as man alive, or as a mere masticating corpse. As man alive you may have shot at your enemy. But as a ghastly simulacrum of life you may be firing bombs into men who are neither your enemies nor your friends, but just things you are dead to. Which is criminal, when the things happen to be alive.

To be alive, to be man alive, to be whole man alive: that is the point. And at its best, the novel, and the novel supremely, can help you. It can help you not to be dead man in life. So much of a man walks about dead and a carcass in the street and house, to-day: so much of women is merely dead. Like a pianoforte with half the notes mute.

But the novel you can see, plainly, when the man goes dead, the woman goes inert. You can develop an instinct for life, if you will, instead of a theory of right and wrong, good and bad.

In life, there is right and wrong, good and bad, all the time. But what is right in one case is wrong in another. And in the novel you see one man becoming a corpse, because of his so-called goodness, another going dead because of his so-called wickedness. Right and wrong is an instinct: but an instinct of the whole consciousness in a man, bodily, mental, spiritual at once. And only in the novel are *all* things given full play, or at least, they may be given full play, when we realize that life itself, and not inert safety, is the reason for living. For out of the full play of all things emerges the only thing that is anything, the wholeness of a man, the wholeness of a woman, man live, and live woman.

1936

Piano[1]

Softly, in the dusk, a woman is singing to me;
Taking me back down the vista of years, till I see
A child sitting under the piano, in the boom of the tingling strings
And pressing the small, poised feet of a mother who smiles as she sings.

5   In spite of myself, the insidious mastery of song
Betrays me back, till the heart of me weeps to belong
To the old Sunday evenings at home, with winter outside
And hymns in the cozy parlour, the tinkling piano our guide.

8. Orphanage.
1. For an earlier version of this poem, see "Poems in Process," in the supplemental ebook.

So now it is vain for the singer to burst into clamour
10   With the great black piano appassionato.° The glamour   *played with passion*
Of childish days is upon me, my manhood is cast
Down in the flood of remembrance, I weep like a child for the past.

1918

Snake

A snake came to my water-trough
On a hot, hot day, and I in pyjamas for the heat,
To drink there.

In the deep, strange-scented shade of the great dark
     carob-tree°   *Mediterranean evergreen*
5   I came down the steps with my pitcher
And must wait, must stand and wait, for there he was at the trough before
     me.

He reached down from a fissure in the earth-wall in the gloom
And trailed his yellow-brown slackness soft-bellied down, over the edge of
     the stone trough
And rested his throat upon the stone bottom,
10   And where the water had dripped from the tap, in a small clearness,
He sipped with his straight mouth,
Softly drank through his straight gums, into his slack long body,
Silently.

Someone was before me at my water-trough,
15   And I, like a second comer, waiting.

He lifted his head from his drinking, as cattle do,
And looked at me vaguely, as drinking cattle do,
And flickered his two-forked tongue from his lips, and mused a moment,
And stooped and drank a little more,
20   Being earth-brown, earth-golden from the burning bowels of
      the earth
On the day of Sicilian July, with Etna° smoking.   *the volcano*

The voice of my education said to me
He must be killed,
For in Sicily the black, black snakes are innocent, the gold are venomous.

25   And voices in me said, If you were a man
You would take a stick and break him now, and finish him off.

But must I confess how I liked him,
How glad I was he had come like a guest in quiet, to drink at my
     water-trough
And depart peaceful, pacified, and thankless
30   Into the burning bowels of this earth?

Was it cowardice, that I dared not kill him?
Was it perversity, that I longed to talk to him?
Was it humility, to feel so honoured?
I felt so honoured.

35 And yet those voices:
If you were not afraid, you would kill him!

And truly I was afraid, I was most afraid,
But even so, honoured still more
That he should seek my hospitality
40 From out the dark door of the secret earth.

He drank enough
And lifted his head, dreamily, as one who has drunken,
And flickered his tongue like a forked night on the air, so black;
Seeming to lick his lips,
45 And looked around like a god, unseeing, into the air,
And slowly turned his head,
And slowly, very slowly, as if thrice adream
Proceeded to draw his slow length curving round
And climb the broken bank of my wall-face.

50 And as he put his head into that dreadful hole,
And as he slowly drew up, snake-easing his shoulders, and entered
     farther,
A sort of horror, a sort of protest against his withdrawing into that horrid
     black hole,
Deliberately going into the blackness, and slowly drawing himself after,
Overcame me now his back was turned.

55 I looked round, I put down my pitcher,
I picked up a clumsy log
And threw it at the water-trough with a clatter.

I think it did not hit him;
But suddenly that part of him that was left behind convulsed in undignified
     haste,
60 Writhed like lightning, and was gone
Into the black hole, the earth-lipped fissure in the wall-front
At which, in the intense still noon, I stared with fascination.

And immediately I regretted it.
I thought how paltry, how vulgar, what a mean act!
65 I despised myself and the voices of my accursed human education.

And I thought of the albatross,[1]
And I wished he would come back, my snake.

1. In Coleridge's Rime of the Ancient Mariner.

For he seemed to me again like a king,
Like a king in exile, uncrowned in the underworld,
70 Now due to be crowned again.

And so, I missed my chance with one of the lords
Of life.
And I have something to expiate;
A pettiness.

1923

T. S. ELIOT
1888–1965

Thomas Stearns Eliot was born in St. Louis, Missouri, of New England stock. He entered Harvard in 1906 and was influenced there by the anti-Romanticism of Irving Babbitt and the philosophical and critical interests of George Santayana, as well as by the enthusiastic study of Renaissance literature and of South Asian religions. He wrote his Harvard dissertation on the English idealist philosopher F. H. Bradley, whose emphasis on the private nature of individual experience, "a circle enclosed on the outside," influenced Eliot's poetry considerably. He also studied literature and philosophy in France and Germany, before going to England shortly after the outbreak of World War I in 1914. He studied Greek philosophy at Oxford, taught school in London, and then obtained a position with Lloyds Bank. In 1915 he married an English writer, Vivienne Haigh-Wood, but the marriage was not a success. She suffered from poor emotional and physical health. The strain told on Eliot, too. By November 1921 distress and worry had brought him to the verge of a nervous breakdown, and on medical advice he went to recuperate in a Swiss sanitorium. Two months later he returned, pausing in Paris long enough to give his early supporter and adviser Ezra Pound the manuscript of *The Waste Land*. Eliot left his wife in 1933, and she was eventually committed to a mental home, where she died in 1947. Ten years later he was happily remarried to his secretary, Valerie Fletcher.

Eliot started writing literary and philosophical reviews soon after settling in London and was assistant editor of *The Egoist* magazine from 1917 to 1919. In 1922 he founded the influential quarterly *The Criterion*, which he edited until it ceased publication in 1939. His poetry first appeared in 1915, when, at Pound's urging, "The Love Song of J. Alfred Prufrock" was printed in *Poetry* magazine (Chicago) and a few other short poems were published in the short-lived periodical *Blast*. His first published collection of poems was *Prufrock and Other Observations*, 1917; two other small collections followed in 1919 and 1920; in 1922 *The Waste Land* appeared, first in *The Criterion* in October, then in *The Dial* (in America) in November, and finally in book form. Meanwhile he was also publishing collections of his critical essays. In 1925 he joined the London publishing firm Faber & Gwyer, and he was made a director when the firm was renamed Faber & Faber. He became a British subject and joined the Church of England in 1927.

"Our civilization comprehends great variety and complexity, and this variety and complexity, playing upon a refined sensibility, must produce various and complex results. The poet must become more and more comprehensive, more allusive, more indirect, in order to force, to dislocate if necessary, language into his meaning." This remark, from Eliot's essay "The Metaphysical Poets" (1921), gives one clue to his poetic method from "Prufrock" through *The Waste Land*. When he settled in London he saw poetry in English as exhausted, with no verbal excitement or original craftsmanship. He sought to make poetry more subtle, more suggestive, and at the same time more precise. Like the imagists, he emphasized the necessity of clear and precise images. From the philosopher poet T. E. Hulme and from Pound, he learned to fear what was seen as Romantic self-indulgence and vagueness, and to regard the poetic medium rather than the poet's personality as the important factor. At the same time the "hard, dry" images advocated by Hulme were not

T. S. Eliot is shown seated in his London office, 19 January 1956.

enough for him; he wanted wit, allusiveness, irony. He saw in the Metaphysical poets how wit and passion could be combined, and he saw in the French symbolists, such as Charles Baudelaire, Stéphane Mallarmé, Paul Verlaine, and Arthur Rimbaud, how an image could be both absolutely precise in what it referred to physically and endlessly suggestive in its meanings because of its relationship to other images. The combination of precision, symbolic suggestion, and ironic mockery in the poetry of the late-nineteenth-century French poet Jules Laforgue attracted and influenced him, as did Laforgue's verse technique that Eliot described in an interview as "rhyming lines of irregular length, with the rhymes coming in irregular places." He also found in the Jacobean dramatists, such as Thomas Middleton, Cyril Tourneur, and John Webster, a flexible blank verse with overtones of colloquial movement, a way of counterpointing the accent of conversation and the note of terror. Eliot's fluency in French and German, his study of Western and non-Western literary and religious texts in their original languages, his rigorous knowledge of philosophy, his exacting critical intellect, his keen sensitivity to colloquial rhythm and idiom, his ability to fuse anguished emotional states with sharply etched intellectual satire—all of these contributed to his crafting one of the twentieth century's most distinctive and influential bodies of poetry.

Hulme's protests against the Romantic concept of poetry reinforced what Eliot had learned from Babbitt at Harvard; yet for all his severity with poets such as Percy Shelley and Walt Whitman, for all his cultivation of a classical viewpoint and his insistence on order and discipline rather than on mere self-expression in art, one side of Eliot's poetic genius is Romantic. The symbolist influence on his imagery, his elegiac lamentation over loss and fragmentation, his interest in the evocative and the suggestive, lines such as "And fiddled whisper music on those strings / And bats with baby faces in the violet light / Whistled, and beat their wings," and recurring images such as the hyacinth girl and the rose garden show what could be called a Romantic element in his poetry. But it is combined with a dry ironic allusiveness, a play of wit and satire, and a colloquial element, which are not normally found in poets of the Romantic tradition.

Eliot's real novelty—and the cause of much bewilderment when his poems first appeared—was his deliberate elimination of all merely connective and transitional passages, his building up of the total pattern of meaning through the immediate juxtaposition of images without overt explanation of what they are doing, together with his use of oblique references to other works of literature (some of them quite obscure to most readers of his time). "Prufrock" presents a symbolic landscape where the meaning emerges from the mutual interaction of the images, and that meaning is enlarged by echoes, often ironic, of Hesiod and Dante and Shakespeare. *The Waste Land* is a series of scenes and images with no author's voice intervening to tell us where we are but with the implications developed through multiple contrasts and through analogies with older literary works often referred to in a distorted quotation or half-concealed allusion. Furthermore, the works referred to are not necessarily central in the Western literary tradition: besides Dante and Shakespeare there are pre-Socratic philosophers; major and minor seventeenth-century poets and dramatists; works of anthropology, history, and philosophy; texts of Buddhism and Hinduism; even popular songs and vaudeville. Ancient and modern voices, high and low art, Western and non-Western languages clash, coincide, jostle alongside one another. In a culture where the poet's public might lack a common cultural heritage, a shared knowledge of works of the past, Eliot felt it necessary to accumulate his own body of references. In this his use of earlier literature differs from, say, John Milton's. Both poets are difficult for the modern reader, who needs editorial assistance in recognizing and understanding many of the allusions—but Milton was drawing on a body of knowledge common to educated people in his day. Nevertheless, this aspect of Eliot can be exaggerated; his imagery and the movement of his verse set the tone he requires, establish the area of meaning to be developed, so that even a reader ignorant of most of the literary allusions can often get the feel of the poem and achieve some understanding of what it says.

Eliot's early poetry, until at least the middle 1920s, is mostly concerned in one way or another with the Waste Land, with aspects of cultural decay in the modern Western world. After his formal acceptance of Anglican Christianity, a penitential note appears in much of his verse, a note of quiet searching for spiritual peace, with considerable allusion to biblical, liturgical, and mystical religious literature and to Dante. *Ash Wednesday* (1930), a poem in six parts, much less fiercely concentrated in style than the earlier poetry, explores with gentle insistence a mood both penitential and questioning. The Ariel poems (so called because published in Faber's Ariel pamphlet series) present or explore aspects of religious doubt or discovery or revelation, sometimes, as in "Journey of the Magi," drawing on biblical incident. In *Four Quartets* (of which the first, "Burnt Norton," appeared in the *Collected Poems* of 1936, though all four were not completed until 1943, when they were published together), Eliot further explored essentially religious moods, dealing with the relation between time and eternity and the cultivation of that selfless passivity that can yield the moment of timeless revelation in the midst of time. The mocking irony, the savage humor, the collage of quotations, the deliberately startling juxtaposition of the sordid and the romantic give way in these later poems to a quieter poetic idiom that is less jagged and more abstract, less fragmentary and more formally patterned.

As a critic Eliot worked out in his reading of older literature what he needed as a poet to hold and to admire. He lent the growing weight of his authority to a shift in literary taste that replaced Milton by John Donne as the great seventeenth-century English poet and replaced Alfred, Lord Tennyson in the nineteenth century by Gerard Manley Hopkins. Rewriting English literary history, he saw the late-seventeenth-century "dissociation of sensibility"—the segregation of intellect and emotion—as determining the course of English poetry throughout the eighteenth and nineteenth centuries. This theory also explained what he was aiming at in his own poetry: the reestablishment of that *unified* sensibility he found in Donne and other early seventeenth-century poets and dramatists, who were able, he suggests in "The Metaphysical Poets," to "feel their thought as immediately as the odour of a rose." His view of tradition, his dislike of the poetic exploitation of the author's personality, his advocacy of what he called "orthodoxy," made him suspicious of what he considered eccentric geniuses such as William Blake and D. H. Lawrence. On the other side, his dislike of the grandiloquent and his insistence on complexity and on the mingling of the formal with the conversational made him distrust Milton's influence on English poetry. He considered himself a "classicist in literature, royalist in politics, and Anglo-Catholic in religion" (*For Lancelot Andrewes*, 1928), in favor of order against chaos, tradition against eccentricity, authority against rampant individualism; yet his own poetry is in many respects untraditional and certainly highly individual in tone. His conservative and even authoritarian habit of mind, his anti-Semitic remarks and missionary zeal, alienated some who admire—and some whose own poetry has been much influenced by—his poetry.

Eliot's plays address, directly or indirectly, religious themes. *Murder in the Cathedral* (1935) deals in an appropriately ritual manner with the killing of Archbishop Thomas à Becket, using a chorus and presenting its central speech as a sermon by the archbishop. *The Family Reunion* (1939) deals with the problem of guilt and redemption in a modern upper-class English family; combining choric devices from Greek tragedy with a poetic idiom subdued to the accents of drawing-room conversation. In his three later plays, all written in the 1950s, *The Cocktail Party, The Confidential Clerk,* and *The Elder Statesman,* he achieved popular success by casting a serious religious theme in the form of a sophisticated modern social comedy, using a verse that is so conversational in movement that when spoken in the theater it does not sound like verse at all.

Critics differ on the degree to which Eliot succeeded in his last plays in combining box-office success with dramatic effectiveness. But there is no disagreement on his importance as one of the great renovators of poetry in English, whose influence on a whole generation of poets, critics, and intellectuals was enormous. His range as a poet is limited, and his interest in the great middle ground of human experience (as distinct from the extremes of saint and sinner) deficient; but when in 1948 he was awarded the rare honor of the Order of Merit by King George VI and also gained the Nobel Prize in literature, his positive qualities were widely and fully recognized—his poetic cunning, his fine craftsmanship, his original accent, his historical importance as *the* poet of the modern symbolist-Metaphysical tradition.

The Love Song of J. Alfred Prufrock[1]

> S'io credesse che mia risposta fosse
> a persona che mai tornasse al mondo,
> questa fiamma staria senza più scosse.
> Ma per cio cche giammai di questo fondo
> non torno vivo alcun, s'i'odo il vero,
> senza tema d'infamia ti rispondo.[2]

Let us go then, you and I,
When the evening is spread out against the sky

---

1. The title implies an ironic contrast between the romantic suggestions of "love song" and the dully prosaic name "J. Alfred Prufrock."
2. "If I thought that my reply would be to one who would ever return to the world, this flame would stay without further movement; but since none has ever returned alive from this depth, if what I hear is true, I answer you without fear of infamy" (Dante, *Inferno* 27.61–66). Guido da Montefeltro, shut up in his flame (the punishment given to false counselors), tells the shame of his evil life to Dante because he believes Dante will never return to earth to report it.

Like a patient etherised upon a table;
Let us go, through certain half-deserted streets,
5   The muttering retreats
Of restless nights in one-night cheap hotels
And sawdust restaurants with oyster shells:
Streets that follow like a tedious argument
Of insidious intent
10 To lead you to an overwhelming question . . .
Oh, do not ask, 'What is it?'
Let us go and make our visit.

In the room the women come and go
Talking of Michelangelo.

15 The yellow fog that rubs its back upon the window-panes,
The yellow smoke that rubs its muzzle on the window-panes
Licked its tongue into the corners of the evening,
Lingered upon the pools that stand in drains,
Let fall upon its back the soot that falls from chimneys,
20 Slipped by the terrace, made a sudden leap,
And seeing that it was a soft October night,
Curled once about the house, and fell asleep.

And indeed there will be time[3]
For the yellow smoke that slides along the street,
25 Rubbing its back upon the window-panes;
There will be time, there will be time
To prepare a face to meet the faces that you meet;
There will be time to murder and create,
And time for all the works and days of hands[4]
30 That lift and drop a question on your plate;
Time for you and time for me,
And time yet for a hundred indecisions,
And for a hundred visions and revisions,
Before the taking of a toast and tea.

35 In the room the women come and go
Talking of Michelangelo.

And indeed there will be time
To wonder, 'Do I dare?' and, 'Do I dare?'
Time to turn back and descend the stair,
40 With a bald spot in the middle of my hair—
(They will say: 'How his hair is growing thin!')
My morning coat, my collar mounting firmly to the chin,
My necktie rich and modest, but asserted by a simple pin—
(They will say: 'But how his arms and legs are thin!')
45 Do I dare

3. Cf. Andrew Marvell, "To His Coy Mistress,"
line 1: "Had we but world enough, and time."
4. *Works and Days* is a poem about the farming
year by the Greek poet Hesiod (8th century

B.C.E.). Eliot contrasts useful agricultural labor
with the futile "works and days of hands" engaged
in meaningless social gesturing.

Disturb the universe?
In a minute there is time
For decisions and revisions which a minute will reverse.

For I have known them all already, known them all—
50 Have known the evenings, mornings, afternoons,
I have measured out my life with coffee spoons;
I know the voices dying with a dying fall[5]
Beneath the music from a farther room.
    So how should I presume?

55 And I have known the eyes already, known them all—
The eyes that fix you in a formulated phrase,
And when I am formulated, sprawling on a pin,
When I am pinned and wriggling on the wall,
Then how should I begin
60 To spit out all the butt-ends of my days and ways?
    And how should I presume?

And I have known the arms already, known them all—
Arms that are braceleted and white and bare
(But in the lamplight, downed with light brown hair!)
65 Is it perfume from a dress
That makes me so digress?
Arms that lie along a table, or wrap about a shawl.
    And should I then presume?
    And how should I begin?

                    .   .   .   .   .

70 Shall I say, I have gone at dusk through narrow streets
And watched the smoke that rises from the pipes
Of lonely men in shirt-sleeves, leaning out of windows? . . .
I should have been a pair of ragged claws
Scuttling across the floors of silent seas,[6]

                    .   .   .   .   .

75 And the afternoon, the evening, sleeps so peacefully!
Smoothed by long fingers,
Asleep . . . tired . . . or it malingers,
Stretched on the floor, here beside you and me.
Should I, after tea and cakes and ices,
80 Have the strength to force the moment to its crisis?
But though I have wept and fasted, wept and prayed,
Though I have seen my head (grown slightly bald) brought in upon a
        platter,[7]
I am no prophet—and here's no great matter;
I have seen the moment of my greatness flicker,

5. Cf. Shakespeare's *Twelfth Night* 1.1.4: "That strain again, it had a dying fall."
6. I.e., he would have been better as a crab on the ocean bed. Perhaps, too, the motion of a crab suggests futility and growing old. Cf. Shakespeare's *Hamlet* 2.2.201–02: "for you yourself, sir, should be old as I am—if, like a crab, you could go backward."
7. Like that of John the Baptist. See Mark 6.17–28 and Matthew 14.3–11.

85 And I have seen the eternal Footman hold my coat, and snicker,
And in short, I was afraid.

And would it have been worth it, after all,
After the cups, the marmalade, the tea,
Among the porcelain, among some talk of you and me,
90 Would it have been worth while,
To have bitten off the matter with a smile,
To have squeezed the universe into a ball[8]
To roll it toward some overwhelming question,
To say: 'I am Lazarus,[9] come from the dead,
95 Come back to tell you all, I shall tell you all'—
If one, settling a pillow by her head,
    Should say: 'That is not what I meant at all.
    That is not it, at all.'

And would it have been worth it, after all,
100 Would it have been worth while,
After the sunsets and the dooryards and the sprinkled streets,
After the novels, after the teacups, after the skirts that trail along the
    floor—
And this, and so much more?—
It is impossible to say just what I mean!
105 But as if a magic lantern threw the nerves in patterns on a screen:
Would it have been worth while
If one, settling a pillow or throwing off a shawl,
And turning toward the window, should say:
    'That is not it at all,
110 That is not what I meant, at all.'

• • • • •

No! I am not Prince Hamlet, nor was meant to be;
Am an attendant lord, one that will do
To swell a progress,[1] start a scene or two,
Advise the prince; no doubt, an easy tool,
115 Deferential, glad to be of use,
Politic, cautious, and meticulous;
Full of high sentence,[2] but a bit obtuse;
At times, indeed, almost ridiculous—
Almost, at times, the Fool.

120 I grow old . . . I grow old . . .
I shall wear the bottoms of my trousers rolled.

Shall I part my hair behind? Do I dare to eat a peach?
I shall wear white flannel trousers, and walk upon the beach.
I have heard the mermaids, singing, each to each.

8. Cf. "To His Coy Mistress," lines 41–44: "Let
us roll all our strength and all / Our sweetness
up into one ball, / And tear our pleasures with
rough strife / Thorough the iron gates of life."
9. Raised by Jesus from the dead (Luke 16.19–
31 and John 11.1–44).
1. In the Elizabethan sense of a state journey

made by a royal or noble person. Elizabethan
plays sometimes showed such "progresses" crossing the stage.
2. In its older meanings: "opinions," "senten-
tiousness." Cf. Chaucer's *General Prologue* to
The Canterbury Tales, line 308.

125   I do not think that they will sing to me.

I have seen them riding seaward on the waves
Combing the white hair of the waves blown back
When the wind blows the water white and black.

We have lingered in the chambers of the sea
130   By sea-girls wreathed with seaweed red and brown
Till human voices wake us, and we drown.

1910–11   1915, 1917

The Waste Land

In the essay "*Ulysses*, Order, and Myth" (1923), Eliot hinted at the ambitions of *The Waste Land* when he declared that others would follow James Joyce "in manipulating a continuous parallel between contemporaneity and antiquity. . . . It is simply a way of controlling, of ordering, of giving a shape and a significance to the immense panorama of futility and anarchy which is contemporary history. . . . It is, I seriously believe, a step toward making the modern world possible in art." Eliot labeled this new technique "the mythical method."

He gave another clue to the theme and structure of *The Waste Land* in a general note, in which he stated that "not only the title, but the plan and a good deal of the symbolism of the poem were suggested by Miss Jessie L. Weston's book on the Grail legend: *From Ritual to Romance* [1920]." He further acknowledged a general indebtedness to Sir James Frazer's *Golden Bough* (thirteen volumes, 1890–1915), "especially the . . . volumes *Adonis, Attis, Osiris*," in which Frazer deals with ancient vegetation myths and fertility ceremonies. Drawing on material from Frazer and other anthropologists, Weston traces the relationship of these myths and rituals to Christianity and especially to the legend of the Holy Grail. She finds an archetypal fertility myth in the story of the Fisher King, whose death, infirmity, or impotence (there are many forms of the myth) brought drought and desolation to the land and failure of the power to reproduce themselves among both humans and beasts. This symbolic Waste Land can be revived only if a "questing knight" goes to the Chapel Perilous, situated in the heart of it, and there asks certain ritual questions about the Grail (or Cup) and the Lance—originally fertility symbols, female and male, respectively. The proper asking of these questions revives the king and restores fertility to the land. The relation of this original Grail myth to fertility cults and rituals found in many different civilizations, and represented by stories of a god who dies and is later resurrected (e.g., Tammuz, Adonis, Attis), shows their common origin in a response to the cyclical movement of the seasons, with vegetation dying in winter to be resurrected again in the spring. Christianity, according to Weston, gave its own spiritual meaning to the myth; it "did not hesitate to utilize the already existing medium of instruction, but boldly identified the Deity of Vegetation, regarded as Life Principle, with the God of the Christian Faith." The Fisher King is related to the use of the fish symbol in early Christianity. Weston states "with certainty that the Fish is a Life symbol of immemorial antiquity, and that the title of Fisher has, from the earliest ages, been associated with the Deities who were held to be specially connected with the origin and preservation of Life." Eliot, following Weston, thus uses a great variety of mythological and religious material, both Western and Eastern, to paint a symbolic picture of the modern Waste Land and the need for regeneration. He vividly presents the terror of that desiccated life—its loneliness, emptiness, and irrational apprehensions—as well as its misuse of sexuality, but he paradoxically ends the poem with a benediction. The mass death and social collapse of World War I inform the poem's vision of a Waste Land strewn with corpses, wreckage, and ruin. Another significant general source for the poem is the German composer Richard Wagner's operas *Götterdämmerung* (*Twilight of the Gods*), *Parsifal, Das Rheingold,* and *Tristan und Isolde.*

The poem as published owes a great deal to the severe pruning of Ezra Pound; the original manuscript, with Pound's excisions and comments, provides fascinating information about the genesis and development of the poem, and was reproduced in facsimile in 1971, edited by Eliot's widow, Valerie Eliot. Reprinted below is the text as first published in book form in December 1922, including Eliot's notes, which are supplemented by the present editors' notes.

The Waste Land

"NAM Sibyllam quidem Cumis ego ipse oculis meis vidi in ampulla pendere, et cum illi pueri dicerent: Σίβυλλα τί θέλεις; respondebat illa: ἀποθανεῖν θέλω."[1]

FOR EZRA POUND
il miglior fabbro[2]

I. The Burial of the Dead[3]

April is the cruellest month, breeding
Lilacs out of the dead land, mixing
Memory and desire, stirring
Dull roots with spring rain.
5 Winter kept us warm, covering
Earth in forgetful snow, feeding
A little life with dried tubers.
Summer surprised us, coming over the Starnbergersee[4]
With a shower of rain; we stopped in the colonnade,
10 And went on in sunlight, into the Hofgarten,[5]
And drank coffee, and talked for an hour.
Bin gar keine Russin, stamm' aus Litauen, echt deutsch.[6]
And when we were children, staying at the archduke's,
My cousin's, he took me out on a sled,
15 And I was frightened. He said, Marie,
Marie, hold on tight. And down we went.
In the mountains, there you feel free.
I read, much of the night, and go south in the winter.

---

1. From the *Satyricon* of Petronius (1st century c.e.): "For once I myself saw with my own eyes the Sibyl at Cumae hanging in a cage, and when the boys said to her 'Sibyl, what do you want?' she replied, 'I want to die.'" (The Greek may be transliterated, "Síbylla tí théleis?" and "apothanéin thélo.") The Cumaean Sibyl was the most famous of the Sibyls, the prophetic old women of Greek mythology; she guided Aeneas through Hades in Virgil's *Aeneid*. She had been granted immortality by Apollo, but because she forgot to ask for perpetual youth, she shrank into withered old age and her authority declined.
2. The better craftsman (Italian); a tribute originally paid to the Provençal poet Arnaut Daniel in Dante's *Purgatorio* 26.117. Ezra Pound (1885–1972), American expatriate poet who was a key figure in the modern movement in poetry, helped Eliot massively revise the manuscript.
3. The title comes from the Anglican burial service.
4. Lake a few miles south of Munich, where the "mad" King Ludwig II of Bavaria drowned in 1886 in mysterious circumstances. This romantic, melancholy king passionately admired Richard Wagner and especially Wagner's opera *Tristan und Isolde,* which plays a significant part in *The Waste Land.* Ludwig's suffering of "death by water" in the Starnbergersee thus evokes a cluster of themes central to the poem. Eliot had met King Ludwig's second cousin Countess Marie Larisch and talked with her. Although he had probably not read the countess's book *My Past,* which discusses King Ludwig at length, he got information about her life and times from her in person, and the remarks made in lines 8–18 are hers.
5. A small public park in Munich.
6. I am not Russian at all; I come from Lithuania, a true German (German).

What are the roots that clutch, what branches grow
20 Out of this stony rubbish? Son of man,[7]
You cannot say, or guess, for you know only
A heap of broken images, where the sun beats,
And the dead tree gives no shelter, the cricket no relief,[8]
And the dry stone no sound of water. Only
25 There is shadow under this red rock,[9]
(Come in under the shadow of this red rock),
And I will show you something different from either
Your shadow at morning striding behind you
Or your shadow at evening rising to meet you;
30 I will show you fear in a handful of dust.

> *Frisch weht der Wind*
> *Der Heimat zu,*
> *Mein Irisch Kind,*
> *Wo weilest du?*[1]

35 "You gave me hyacinths first a year ago;
"They called me the hyacinth girl."
—Yet when we came back, late, from the Hyacinth[2] garden,
Yours arms full, and your hair wet, I could not
Speak, and my eyes failed, I was neither
40 Living nor dead, and I knew nothing,
Looking into the heart of light, the silence.
Oed' und leer das Meer.[3]

Madame Sosostris,[4] famous clairvoyante,
Had a bad cold, nevertheless
45 Is known to be the wisest woman in Europe,
With a wicked pack of cards.[5] Here, said she,

---

7. Cf. Ezekiel II, i [Eliot's note]. God, addressing Ezekiel, continues: "stand upon thy feet, and I will speak unto thee."

8. Cf. Ecclesiastes XII, v [Eliot's note]. The verse Eliot cites is part of the preacher's picture of the desolation of old age, "when they shall be afraid of that which is high, and fears shall be in the way and the almond tree shall flourish, and the grasshopper shall be a burden, and desire shall fail."

9. Cf. Isaiah 32.2: the "righteous king" "shall be . . . as rivers of water in a dry place, as the shadow of a great rock in a weary land."

1. V. [see] *Tristan und Isolde*, I, verses 5–8 [Eliot's note]. In Wagner's opera a sailor recalls the girl he has left behind: "Fresh blows the wind to the homeland; my Irish child, where are you waiting?"

2. Name of a young man loved and accidentally killed by Apollo in Greek mythology; from his blood sprang the flower named for him, inscribed with "AI," a cry of grief.

3. Id. [Ibid] III, verse 24 [Eliot's note]. In act 3 of *Tristan und Isolde*, Tristan lies dying. He is waiting for Isolde to come to him from Cornwall, but a shepherd, appointed to watch for her sail, can report only, "Waste and empty is the sea." *Oed'* (or *Öd'*) was originally misspelled *Od'*.

4. A mock Egyptian name (suggested to Eliot by

"Sesostris, the Sorceress of Ecbatana," the name assumed by a character in Aldous Huxley's novel *Crome Yellow* [1921] who dresses up as a gypsy to tell fortunes at a fair).

5. I.e., the deck of Tarot cards. The four suits of the Tarot pack, discussed by Jessie Weston in *From Ritual to Romance*, are the cup, lance, sword, and dish—the life symbols found in the Grail story. Weston noted that "today the Tarot has fallen somewhat into disrepute, being principally used for purposes of divination." Some of the cards mentioned in lines 46–56 are discussed by Eliot in his note to this passage: "I am not familiar with the exact constitution of the Tarot pack of cards, from which I have obviously departed to suit my own convenience. The Hanged Man, a member of the traditional pack, fits my purpose in two ways: because he is associated in my mind with the Hanged God of Frazer, and because I associate him with the hooded figure in the passage of the disciples to Emmaus in part V. The Phoenician Sailor and the Merchant appear later; also the 'crowds of people,' and Death by Water is executed in part IV. The Man with Three Staves (an authentic member of the Tarot pack) I associate, quite arbitrarily, with the Fisher King himself."

Is your card, the drowned Phoenician Sailor,[6]
(Those are pearls that were his eyes. Look!)
Here is Belladonna,[7] the Lady of the Rocks,
50 The lady of situations.
Here is the man with three staves, and here the Wheel,[8]
And here is the one-eyed merchant,[9] and this card,
Which is blank, is something he carries on his back,
Which I am forbidden to see. I do not find
55 The Hanged Man.[1] Fear death by water.
I see crowds of people, walking round in a ring.
Thank you. If you see dear Mrs. Equitone,
Tell her I bring the horoscope myself:
One must be so careful these days.

60 Unreal City.[2]
Under the brown fog of a winter dawn,
A crowd flowed over London Bridge, so many,[3]
I had not thought death had undone so many.
Sighs, short and infrequent, were exhaled,[4]
65 And each man fixed his eyes before his feet.
Flowed up the hill and down King William Street,
To where Saint Mary Woolnoth kept the hours
With a dead sound on the final stroke of nine.[5]
There I saw one I knew, and stopped him, crying: "Stetson![6]
70 "You who were with me in the ships at Mylae![7]
"That corpse you planted last year in your garden,
"Has it begun to sprout?[8] Will it bloom this year?

6. See part IV. Phlebas the Phoenician and Mr. Eugenides, the Smyrna merchant—both of whom appear later in the poem—are different phases of the same symbolic character, here identified as the "Phoenician Sailor." Mr. Eugenides exports "currants" (line 210); the drowned Phlebas floats in the "current" (line 315). Line 48 draws from Ariel's song in Shakespeare's *The Tempest* (1.2.400–08) to the shipwrecked Ferdinand, who was "sitting on a bank / Weeping again the King my father's wrack," when "this music crept by me on the waters." The song is about the supposed drowning of Ferdinand's father, Alonso. *The Waste Land* contains many references to *The Tempest*. Ferdinand is associated with Phlebas and Mr. Eugenides and, therefore, with the "drowned Phoenician Sailor."
7. Beautiful lady (Italian). The word also suggests Madonna (the Virgin Mary) and, therefore, the Madonna of the Rocks (as in Leonardo da Vinci's painting); the rocks symbolize the Church. Belladonna is also an eye cosmetic and a poison—the deadly nightshade.
8. I.e., the wheel of fortune, whose turning represents the reversals of human life.
9. I.e., Mr. Eugenides, "one-eyed" because the figure is in profile on the card. Unlike the man with three staves and the wheel, which are Tarot cards, he is Eliot's creation.
1. On his card in the Tarot pack he is shown hanging by one foot from a T-shaped cross. He symbolizes the self-sacrifice of the fertility god who is killed so that his resurrection may restore fertility to land and people.
2. Cf. Baudelaire: "Fourmillante cité, cité pleine de rêves, / Où le spectre en plein jour raccroche le passant" [Eliot's note]. The lines are quoted from "Les Sept Vieillards" ("The Seven Old Men") of *Les Fleurs du Mal* (*The Flowers of Evil*), by the French poet Charles Baudelaire (1821–1867): "Swarming city, city full of dreams, / Where the specter in broad daylight accosts the passerby." The word *rêve* was originally misspelled *rève*.
3. Cf. Inferno III, 55–57 [Eliot's note]. The note goes on to quote Dante's lines, which may be translated: "So long a train of people, / that I should never have believed / That death had undone so many." Dante, just outside the gate of hell, has seen "the wretched souls of those who lived without disgrace and without praise."
4. Cf. Inferno IV, 25–27 [Eliot's note]. In Limbo, the first circle of hell, Dante has found the virtuous heathens, who lived before Christianity and are, therefore, eternally unable to achieve their desire of seeing God. Dante's lines, cited by Eliot, mean "Here, so far as I could tell by listening, / there was no lamentation except sighs, / which caused the eternal air to tremble."
5. A phenomenon which I have often noticed [Eliot's note]. St. Mary Woolnoth is a church in the City of London (the financial district); the crowd is flowing across London Bridge to work in the City. According to the Bible, Jesus died at the ninth hour.
6. Presumably representing the "average businessman."
7. The Battle of Mylae (260 B.C.E.) in the First Punic War, which, in some measure like World War I, was fought for economic reasons.
8. A distortion of the fertility god's ritual death, which heralded rebirth.

"Or has the sudden frost disturbed its bed?
"Oh keep the Dog far hence, that's friend to men,
75 "Or with his nails he'll dig it up again![9]
"You! hypocrite lecteur!—mon semblable—mon frère!"[1]

II. A Game of Chess[2]

The Chair she sat in, like a burnished throne,[3]
Glowed on the marble, where the glass
Held up by standards wrought with fruited vines
80 From which a golden Cupidon peeped out
(Another hid his eyes behind his wing)
Doubled the flames of sevenbranched candelabra
Reflecting light upon the table as
The glitter of her jewels rose to meet it,
85 From satin cases poured in rich profusion;
In vials of ivory and coloured glass
Unstoppered, lurked her strange synthetic perfumes,
Unguent, powdered, or liquid—troubled, confused
And drowned the sense in odours; stirred by the air
90 That freshened from the window, these ascended
In fattening the prolonged candle-flames,
Flung their smoke into the laquearia,[4]
Stirring the pattern on the coffered ceiling.
Huge sea-wood fed with copper
95 Burned green and orange, framed by the coloured stone,
In which sad light a carved dolphin swam.
Above the antique mantel was displayed
As though a window gave upon the sylvan scene[5]
The change of Philomel,[6] by the barbarous king
100 So rudely forced; yet there the nightingale
Filled all the desert with inviolable voice
And still she cried, and still the world pursues,

9. Cf. the Dirge in Webster's *White Devil* [Eliot's note]. In the play by John Webster (d. 1625), the dirge, sung by Cornelia, has the lines "But keep the wolf far thence, that's foe to men, / For with his nails he'll dig them up again." Eliot makes the "wolf" into a "dog," which is not a foe but a friend to humans.

1. V. Baudelaire, Preface to *Fleurs du Mal* [Eliot's note]. The passage is the last line of the introductory poem "Au Lecteur" ("To the Reader"), in Baudelaire's *Fleurs du Mal*; it may be translated: "Hypocrite reader!—my likeness—my brother!" "Au Lecteur" describes humans as sunk in stupidity, sin, and evil, but the worst in "each man's foul menagerie of sin" is boredom, the *"monstre délicat"*—"You know him; reader."

2. The title suggests two plays by Thomas Middleton (1580–1627): *A Game at Chess* and, more significant, *Women Beware Women*, which has a scene in which a mother-in-law is distracted by a game of chess while her daughter-in-law is seduced: every move in the chess game represents a move in the seduction.

3. Cf. *Antony and Cleopatra*, II, ii, 1. 190 [Eliot's note]. In Shakespeare's play, Enobarbus's famous description of the first meeting of Antony and Cleopatra begins, "The barge she sat in, like a burnish'd throne, / Burn'd on the water." Eliot's language in the opening lines of part 2 echoes ironically Enobarbus's speech.

4. Laquearia. V. *Aeneid*, I, 726 [Eliot's note]. *Laquearia* means "a paneled ceiling," and Eliot's note quotes the passage in the *Aeneid* that was his source for the word. The passage may be translated: "Blazing torches hang from the gold-paneled ceiling [*laquearibus aureis*], and torches conquer the night with flames." Virgil is describing the banquet given by Dido, queen of Carthage, for Aeneas, with whom she fell in love.

5. Sylvan scene. V. Milton, *Paradise Lost*, IV, 140 [Eliot's note]. The phrase is part of the first description of Eden, seen through Satan's eyes.

6. V. Ovid, *Metamorphoses*, VI, Philomela [Eliot's note]. Philomela was raped by "the barbarous king" Tereus, husband of her sister, Procne. Philomela was then transformed into a nightingale. Eliot's note for line 100 refers ahead to his elaboration of the nightingale's song.

"Jug Jug"[7] to dirty ears.
And other withered stumps of time
105 Were told upon the walls; staring forms
Leaned out, leaning, hushing the room enclosed.
Footsteps shuffled on the stair.
Under the firelight, under the brush, her hair
Spread out in fiery points
110 Glowed into words, then would be savagely still.

"My nerves are bad tonight. Yes, bad. Stay with me.
"Speak to me. Why do you never speak. Speak.
"What are you thinking of? What thinking? What?
"I never know what you are thinking. Think."

115 I think we are in rats' alley[8]
Where the dead men lost their bones.

"What is that noise?"
           The wind under the door.[9]
"What is that noise now? What is the wind doing?"
120   Nothing again nothing.
                  "Do

"You know nothing? Do you see nothing? Do you remember
"Nothing?"

      I remember
125 Those are pearls that were his eyes.[1]
"Are you alive, or not? Is there nothing in your head?"
                              But

O O O O that Shakespeherian Rag[2]—
It's so elegant
130 So intelligent

"What shall I do now? What shall I do?"
"I shall rush out as I am, and walk the street
"With my hair down, so. What shall we do tomorrow?
"What shall we ever do?"
135   The hot water at ten.
And if it rains, a closed car at four.
And we shall play a game of chess,[3]
Pressing lidless eyes and waiting for a knock upon the door.

When Lil's husband got demobbed,[4] I said—
140 I didn't mince my words, I said to her myself,

---

7. Conventional representation of nightingale's song in Elizabethan poetry.
8. Cf. Part III, l. 195 [Eliot's note].
9. Cf. Webster: "Is the wind in that door still?" [Eliot's note]. In John Webster's *The Devil's Law Case* (3.2.162), a physician asks this question on finding that the victim of a murderous attack is still breathing, meaning "Is he still alive?"
1. Cf. Part I, l. 37, 48 [Eliot's note].

2. American ragtime song; a hit of Ziegfeld's Follies in 1912. The chorus is "That Shakespearian Rag, most intelligent, very elegant."
3. Cf. the game of chess in Middleton's *Women Beware Women* [Eliot's note]. The significance of this chess game is discussed in the first note to part 2.
4. British slang for "demobilized" (discharged from the army after World War I).

HURRY UP PLEASE ITS TIME[5]
Now Albert's coming back, make yourself a bit smart.
He'll want to know what you done with that money he gave you
To get yourself some teeth. He did, I was there.
145 You have them all out, Lil, and get a nice set,
He said, I swear, I can't bear to look at you.
And no more can't I, I said, and think of poor Albert,
He's been in the army four years, he wants a good time,
And if you dont give it him, there's others will, I said.
150 Oh is there, she said. Something o' that, I said.
Then I'll know who to thank, she said, and give me a straight look.
HURRY UP PLEASE ITS TIME
If you dont like it you can get on with it, I said,
Others can pick and choose if you can't.
155 But if Albert makes off, it wont be for lack of telling.
You ought to be ashamed, I said, to look so antique.
(And her only thirty-one.)
I can't help it, she said, pulling a long face,
It's them pills I took, to bring it off, she said.
160 (She's had five already, and nearly died of young George.)
The chemist[6] said it would be alright, but I've never been the same.
You *are* a proper fool, I said.
Well, if Albert wont leave you alone, there it is, I said,
What you get married for if you dont want children?
165 HURRY UP PLEASE ITS TIME
Well, that Sunday Albert was home, they had a hot gammon,°   ham, bacon
And they asked me in to dinner, to get the beauty of it hot—
HURRY UP PLEASE ITS TIME
HURRY UP PLEASE ITS TIME
170 Goonight Bill. Goonight Lou. Goonight May. Goonight.
Ta ta. Goonight. Goonight.
Good night, ladies, good night, sweet ladies, good night, good night.[7]

III. The Fire Sermon[8]

The river's tent is broken: the last fingers of leaf
Clutch and sink into the wet bank. The wind
175 Crosses the brown land, unheard. The nymphs are departed.
Sweet Thames, run softly, till I end my song,[9]
The river bears no empty bottles, sandwich papers,
Silk handkerchiefs, cardboard boxes, cigarette ends
Or other testimony of summer nights. The nymphs are departed.
180 And their friends, the loitering heirs of city directors;
Departed, have left no addresses.
By the waters of Leman I sat down and wept,[1] . . .

5. The traditional call of the British bartender at
closing time.
6. Pharmacist. "To bring it off": to cause an
abortion.
7. Cf. the mad Ophelia's departing words (Shakespeare, *Hamlet* 4.5.69–70). Ophelia, too, met
"death by water." Cf. also the popular song lyric
"Good night ladies, we're going to leave you now."
8. The Buddha preached the Fire Sermon,
against the fires of lust and other passions that
destroy people and prevent their regeneration.

9. V. Spenser, *Prothalamion* [Eliot's note]. Eliot's
line is the refrain from Edmund Spenser's marriage song, which is also set by the river Thames
in London.
1. Cf. Psalms 137.1, in which the exiled Hebrews
mourn for their homeland: "By the rivers of Bab-
ylon, there we sat down, yea, we wept, when we
remembered Zion." Lake Leman is another name
for Lake Geneva, in Switzerland; Eliot wrote
The Waste Land in Lausanne, by that lake. The
noun *leman* is an archaic word meaning lover.

Sweet Thames, run softly till I end my song,
Sweet Thames, run softly, for I speak not loud or long.
185 But at my back in a cold blast I hear[2]
The rattle of the bones, and chuckle spread from ear to ear.

A rat crept softly through the vegetation
Dragging its slimy belly on the bank
While I was fishing in the dull canal
190 On a winter evening round behind the gashouse
Musing upon the king my brother's wreck
And on the king my father's death before him,[3]
White bodies naked on the low damp ground
And bones cast in a little low dry garret,
195 Rattled by the rat's foot only, year to year.
But at my back from time to time I hear
The sound of horns and motors,[4] which shall bring
Sweeney to Mrs. Porter in the spring.[5]
O the moon shone bright on Mrs. Porter
200 And on her daughter
They wash their feet in soda water[6]
Et O ces voix d'enfants, chantant dans la coupole![7]

Twit twit twit
Jug jug jug jug jug jug
205 So rudely forc'd.
Tereu[8]

Unreal City
Under the brown fog of a winter noon
Mr. Eugenides, the Smyrna[9] merchant
210 Unshaven, with a pocket full of currants
C.i.f.[1] London: documents at sight,
Asked me in demotic° French   *colloquial*

---

2. An ironic distortion of Andrew Marvell's "To His Coy Mistress," lines 21–22: "But at my back I always hear / Time's wingèd chariot hurrying near." Cf. lines 196–97.
3. Cf. *The Tempest*, I, ii [Eliot's note]. See line 48.
4. Cf. Marvell, *To His Coy Mistress* [Eliot's note].
5. Cf. Day, *Parliament of Bees:* "When of the sudden, listening, you shall hear, / A noise of horns and hunting, which shall bring / Actaeon to Diana in the spring, / Where all shall see her naked skin" [Eliot's note]. Actaeon was changed to a stag and hunted to death after he saw Diana, the goddess of chastity, bathing with her nymphs. John Day (1574–ca. 1640), English poet.
6. I do not know the origin of the ballad from which these lines are taken; it was reported to me from Sydney, Australia [Eliot's note]. One of the less bawdy versions of the song, which was popular among Australian troops in World War I, went as follows: "O the moon shines bright on Mrs. Porter / And on the daughter / Of Mrs. Porter. / They wash their feet in soda water / And so they oughter / To keep them clean."

7. V. Verlaine, *Parsifal* [Eliot's note]: "And O those children's voices singing in the dome!" The sonnet by the French poet Paul Verlaine (1844–1896) describes Parsifal, the questing knight, resisting all sensual temptations to keep himself pure for the Grail and heal the Fisher King; Wagner's Parsifal had his feet washed before entering the castle of the Grail.
8. A reference to Tereus, who "rudely forc'd" Philomela; it was also a word for a nightingale's song in Elizabethan poetry. Cf. the song from John Lyly's *Campaspe* (1584): "Oh, 'tis the ravished nightingale. / Jug, jug, jug, jug, tereu! she cries." Cf. also lines 100ff.
9. Now Izmir, a seaport in western Turkey; here associated with Carthage and the ancient Phoenician and Syrian merchants, who spread the old mystery cults.
1. The currants were quoted at a price "carriage and insurance free to London"; and the Bill of Lading etc. were to be handed to the buyer upon payment of the sight draft [Eliot's note]. Another gloss of C.i.f. is "cost, insurance and freight."

To luncheon at the Cannon Street Hotel
Followed by a weekend at the Metropole.[2]

215 At the violet hour, when the eyes and back
Turn upward from the desk, when the human engine waits
Like a taxi throbbing waiting,
I Tiresias,[3] though blind, throbbing between two lives,
Old man with wrinkled female breasts, can see
220 At the violet hour, the evening hour that strives
Homeward, and brings the sailor home from sea,[4]
The typist home at teatime, clears her breakfast, lights
Her stove, and lays out food in tins.
Out of the window perilously spread
225 Her drying combinations° touched by the sun's last rays,   *undergarments*
On the divan are piled (at night her bed)
Stockings, slippers, camisoles, and stays.°   *corset*
I Tiresias, old man with wrinkled dugs
Perceived the scene, and foretold the rest—
230 I too awaited the expected guest.
He, the young man carbuncular,° arrives,   *pimply*
A small house agent's clerk, with one bold stare,
One of the low on whom assurance sits
As a silk hat on a Bradford[5] millionaire.
235 The time is now propitious, as he guesses,
The meal is ended, she is bored and tired,
Endeavours to engage her in caresses
Which still are unreproved, if undesired.
Flushed and decided, he assaults at once;
240 Exploring hands encounter no defence;
His vanity requires no response,
And makes a welcome of indifference.
(And I Tiresias have foresuffered all

2. Luxury hotel in the seaside resort of Brighton. Cannon Street Hotel, near the station that was then chief terminus for travelers to the Continent, was a favorite meeting place for business-people going or coming from abroad; it was also a locale for homosexual liaisons.
3. Tiresias, although a mere spectator and not indeed a "character," is yet the most important personage in the poem, uniting all the rest. Just as the one-eyed merchant, seller of currants, melts into the Phoenician Sailor, and the latter is not wholly distinct from Ferdinand Prince of Naples, so all the women are one woman, and the two sexes meet in Tiresias. What Tiresias *sees*, in fact, is the substance of the poem. The whole passage from Ovid is of great anthropological interest [Eliot's note]. The note then quotes, from the Latin text of Ovid's *Metamorphoses*, the story of Tiresias's change of sex: "[The story goes that once Jove, having drunk a great deal,] jested with Juno. He said, 'Your pleasure in love is really greater than that enjoyed by men.' She denied it; so they decided to seek the opinion of the wise Tiresias, for he knew both aspects of love. For once, with a blow of his staff, he had committed violence on two huge snakes as they copulated in the green forest; and—wonderful to tell—was turned from a man into a woman and thus spent seven years. In

the eighth year he saw the same snakes again and said: 'If a blow struck at you is so powerful that it changes the sex of the giver, I will now strike at you again.' With these words she struck the snakes, and again became a man. So he was appointed arbitrator in the playful quarrel, and supported Jove's statement. It is said that Saturnia [i.e., Juno] was quite disproportionately upset, and condemned the arbitrator to perpetual blindness. But the almighty father (for no god may undo what has been done by another god), in return for the sight that was taken away, gave him the power to know the future and so lightened the penalty paid by the honor."
4. This may not appear as exact as Sappho's lines, but I had in mind the "longshore" or "dory" fisherman, who returns at nightfall [Eliot's note]. Sappho's poem addressed Hesperus, the evening star, as the star that brings everyone home from work to evening rest; her poem is here distorted by Eliot. There is also an echo of the 19th-century Scottish writer Robert Louis Stevenson's "Requiem," line 221: "Home is the sailor, home from sea."
5. Either the Yorkshire woolen manufacturing town, where many fortunes were made in World War I, or the pioneer oil town of Bradford, Pennsylvania, the home of one of Eliot's wealthy Harvard contemporaries, T. E. Hanley.

Enacted on this same divan or bed;
245   I who have sat by Thebes[6] below the wall
And walked among the lowest of the dead.)
Bestows one final patronising kiss,
And gropes his way, finding the stairs unlit . . .

She turns and looks a moment in the glass,
250   Hardly aware of her departed lover;
Her brain allows one half-formed thought to pass:
"Well now that's done: and I'm glad it's over."
When lovely woman stoops to folly and
Paces about her room again, alone,
255   She smoothes her hair with automatic hand,
And puts a record on the gramophone.[7]

"This music crept by me upon the waters"[8]
And along the Strand, up Queen Victoria Street.
O City, City, I can sometimes hear
260   Beside a public bar in Lower Thames Street,
The pleasant whining of a mandoline
And a clatter and a chatter from within
Where fishmen lounge at noon: where the walls
Of Magnus Martyr hold
265   Inexplicable splendour of Ionian white and gold.[9]

The river sweats[1]
Oil and tar
The barges drift
With the turning tide
270   Red sails
Wide
To leeward, swing on the heavy spar.
The barges wash
Drifting logs
275   Down Greenwich reach
Past the Isle of Dogs.[2]
              Weialala leia
              Wallala leialala

6. For many generations, Tiresias lived in Thebes, where he witnessed the tragic fates of Oedipus and Creon; he prophesied in the marketplace by the wall of Thebes.
7. V. Goldsmith, the song in *The Vicar of Wakefield* [Eliot's note]. Olivia, a character in Oliver Goldsmith's 1766 novel, sings the following song when she returns to the place where she was seduced: "When lovely woman stoops to folly / And finds too late that men betray / What charm can soothe her melancholy, / What art can wash her guilt away? / The only art her guilt to cover, / To hide her shame from every eye, / To give repentance to her lover / And wring his bosom—is to die."
8. V. *The Tempest*, as above [Eliot's note]. Cf. line 48. The line is from Ferdinand's speech, continuing after "weeping again the King my father's wrack."
9. The interior of St. Magnus Martyr is to my mind one of the finest among [Sir Christopher]

Wren's interiors. See *The Proposed Demolition of Nineteen City Churches*: (P. S. King & Son, Ltd.) [Eliot's note]. In these lines the "pleasant" music, the "fishmen" resting after labor, and the splendor of the church interior suggest a world of true values, where work and relaxation are both real and take place in a context of religious meaning.
1. The Song of the (three) Thames-daughters begins here. From line 292 to 306 inclusive they speak in turn. V. *Götterdämmerung*, III, i: the Rhinedaughters [Eliot's note]. Eliot parallels the Thames-daughters with the Rhinemaidens in Wagner's opera *Götterdämmerung* (*The Twilight of the Gods*), who lament that, with the gold of the Rhine stolen, the beauty of the river is gone. The refrain in lines 277–78 is borrowed from Wagner.
2. Greenwich is a borough in London on the south side of the Thames; opposite is the Isle of Dogs (a peninsula).

Elizabeth and Leicester[3]
280 Beating oars
The stern was formed
A gilded shell
Red and gold
The brisk swell
285 Rippled both shores
Southwest wind
Carried down stream
The peal of bells
White towers
290   Weialala leia
      Wallala leialala

"Trams and dusty trees.
Highbury bore me. Richmond and Kew
Undid me.[4] By Richmond I raised my knees
295 Supine on the floor of a narrow canoe."

"My feet are at Moorgate,[5] and my heart
Under my feet. After the event
He wept. He promised 'a new start.'
I made no comment. What should I resent?"

300 "On Margate[6] Sands.
I can connect
Nothing with nothing.
The broken fingernails of dirty hands.
My people humble people who expect
305 Nothing."
      la la

To Carthage then I came[7]

Burning burning burning burning[8]

3. The fruitless love of Queen Elizabeth and the earl of Leicester (Robert Dudley) is recalled in Eliot's note: "V. [J. A.] Froude, *Elizabeth*, Vol. I, ch. iv, letter of De Quadra to Philip of Spain: 'In the afternoon we were in a barge, watching the games on the river. (The queen) was alone with Lord Robert and myself on the poop, when they began to talk nonsense, and went so far that Lord Robert at last said, as I was on the spot there was no reason why they should not be married if the queen pleased.'" Queen Elizabeth I was born in the old Greenwich House, by the river, where Greenwich Hospital now stands.
4. Cf. *Purgatorio*, V, 133 [Eliot's note]. The *Purgatorio* lines, which Eliot here parodies, may be translated: "Remember me, who am La Pia. / Siena made me, Maremma undid me." "Highbury": a residential London suburb. "Richmond": a pleasant part of London westward up the Thames, with boating and riverside hotels. "Kew": adjoining Richmond, has the famous Kew Gardens.
5. Underground (i.e., subway) station Eliot used daily while working at Lloyds Bank.
6. Popular seaside resort on the Thames estuary.

7. V. St. Augustine's *Confessions*: "to Carthage then I came, where a caldron of unholy loves sang all about mine ears" [Eliot's note]. The passage from the *Confessions* quoted here occurs in St. Augustine's account of his youthful life of lust. Cf. line 92 and its note.
8. The complete text of the Buddha's Fire Sermon (which corresponds in importance to the Sermon on the Mount) from which these words are taken, will be found translated in the late Henry Clarke Warren's *Buddhism in Translation* (Harvard Oriental Series). Mr. Warren was one of the great pioneers of Buddhist studies in the occident [Eliot's note]. In the sermon, the Buddha instructs his priests that all things "are on fire. . . . The eye . . . is on fire; forms are on fire; eye-consciousness is on fire; impressions received by the eye are on fire; and whatever sensation, pleasant, unpleasant, or indifferent, originates in dependence on impressions received by the eye, that also is on fire. And with what are these on fire? With the fire of passion, say I, with the fire of hatred, with the fire of infatuation." For Jesus' Sermon on the Mount, see Matthew 5–7.

O Lord Thou pluckest me out[9]
310 O Lord Thou pluckest

burning

IV. Death by Water[1]

Phlebas the Phoenician, a fortnight dead,
Forgot the cry of gulls, and the deep sea swell
And the profit and loss.
315   A current under sea
Picked his bones in whispers. As he rose and fell
He passed the stages of his age and youth
Entering the whirlpool.
                              Gentile or Jew
320 O you who turn the wheel and look to windward,
Consider Phlebas, who was once handsome and tall as you.

V. What the Thunder Said[2]

After the torchlight red on sweaty faces
After the frosty silence in the gardens
After the agony in stony places
325 The shouting and the crying
Prison and palace and reverberation
Of thunder of spring over distant mountains
He who was living is now dead[3]
We who were living are now dying
330 With a little patience

Here is no water but only rock
Rock and no water and the sandy road
The road winding above among the mountains
Which are mountains of rock without water
335 If there were water we should stop and drink
Amongst the rock one cannot stop or think
Sweat is dry and feet are in the sand
If there were only water amongst the rock
Dead mountain mouth of carious° teeth that cannot spit   decayed
340 Here one can neither stand nor lie nor sit
There is not even silence in the mountains
But dry sterile thunder without rain
There is not even solitude in the mountains
But red sullen faces sneer and snarl
345 From doors of mudcracked houses
                              If there were water

9. From St. Augustine's *Confessions* again. The collocation of these two representatives of eastern and western asceticism, as the culmination of this part of the poem, is not an accident [Eliot's note].
1. This section has been interpreted as signifying death by water without resurrection or as symbolizing the sacrificial death that precedes rebirth.
2. In the first part of Part V three themes are employed: the journey to Emmaus, the approach to the Chapel Perilous (see Miss Weston's book), and the present decay of eastern Europe [Eliot's note]. On the journey to Emmaus, the resurrected Jesus walks alongside and converses with two disciples, who think he is a stranger until he reveals his identity (Luke 24.13–14).
3. These lines allude to Jesus' agony in the Garden of Gethsemane, his trial, and his crucifixion.

And no rock
If there were rock
And also water
350 And water
A spring
A pool among the rock
If there were the sound of water only
Not the cicada[4]
355 And dry grass singing
But sound of water over a rock
Where the hermit-thrush[5] sings in the pine trees
Drip drop drip drop drop drop drop
But there is no water

360 Who is the third who walks always beside you?[6]
When I count, there are only you and I together
But when I look ahead up the white road
There is always another one walking beside you
Gliding wrapt in a brown mantle, hooded
365 I do not know whether a man or a woman
—But who is that on the other side of you?

What is that sound high in the air[7]
Murmur of maternal lamentation
Who are those hooded hordes swarming
370 Over endless plains, stumbling in cracked earth
Ringed by the flat horizon only
What is the city over the mountains
Cracks and reforms and bursts in the violet air
Falling towers
375 Jerusalem Athens Alexandria
Vienna London
Unreal

A woman drew her long black hair out tight
And fiddled whisper music on those strings
380 And bats with baby faces in the violet light
Whistled, and beat their wings
And crawled head downward down a blackened wall
And upside down in air were towers

4. Cf. Ecclesiastes' prophecy "the grasshopper shall be a burden, and desire shall fail." Cf. also line 23 and its note.
5. This is *Turdus aonalaschkae pallasii*, the hermit-thrush which I have heard in Quebec County. Chapman says (*Handbook of Birds of Eastern North America*) "it is most at home in secluded woodland and thickety retreats. . . . Its notes are not remarkable for variety or volume, but in purity and sweetness of tone and exquisite modulation they are unequaled." Its "water-dripping song" is justly celebrated [Eliot's note].
6. The following lines were stimulated by the account of one of the Antarctic expeditions (I forget which, but I think one of Shackleton's): it was related that the party of explorers, at the extremity of their strength, had the constant delusion that there was *one more member* than could actually be counted [Eliot's note]. This reminiscence is associated with Jesus' unrecognized presence on the way to Emmaus.
7. Eliot's note for lines 367–77 is: "Cf. Herman Hesse, *Blick ins Chaos* ["A Glimpse into Chaos"]." The note then quotes a passage from the German text, which is translated: "Already half of Europe, already at least half of Eastern Europe, on the way to Chaos, drives drunk in sacred infatuation along the edge of the precipice, sings drunkenly, as though hymn singing, as Dmitri Karamazov [in Dostoyevsky's *Brothers Karamazov*] sang. The offended bourgeois laughs at the songs; the saint and the seer hear them with tears."

Tolling reminiscent bells, that kept the hours
385   And voices singing out of empty cisterns and exhausted wells.

In this decayed hole among the mountains
In the faint moonlight, the grass is singing
Over the tumbled graves, about the chapel
There is the empty chapel, only the wind's home.[8]
390   It has no windows, and the door swings,
Dry bones can harm no one.
Only a cock stood on the rooftree
Co co   rico   co co   rico[9]
In a flash of lightning. Then a damp gust
395   Bringing rain

Ganga[1] was sunken, and the limp leaves
Waited for rain, while the black clouds
Gathered far distant, over Himavant.[2]
The jungle crouched, humped in silence.
400   Then spoke the thunder
DA[3]
Datta: what have we given?
My friend, blood shaking my heart
The awful daring of a moment's surrender
405   Which an age of prudence can never retract
By this, and this only, we have existed
Which is not to be found in our obituaries
Or in memories draped by the beneficent spider[4]
Or under seals broken by the lean solicitor°   lawyer
410   In our empty rooms
DA
Dayadhvam: I have heard the key[5]
Turn in the door once and turn once only

8. Suggesting the moment of near despair before the Chapel Perilous, when the questing knight sees nothing there but decay. This illusion of nothingness is the knight's final test.
9. The crowing of the cock signals the departure of ghosts and evil spirits. Cf. Hamlet 1.1.157ff. In Matthew 26, 34 and 74 the cock crows after Peter betrays Jesus three times.
1. Sanskrit name for the major sacred river in India.
2. I.e., snowy mountain (Sanskrit); usually applied to the Himalayas.
3. Datta, dayadhvam, damyata (Give, sympathize, control). The fable of the meaning of the Thunder is found in the Brihadaranyaka—Upanishad, 5, 1. A translation is found in Deussen's Sechzig Upanishads des Veda, p. 489 [Eliot's note]. In the Old Indian fable "The Three Great Disciplines," the Creator God Prajapati utters the enigmatic syllable DA to three groups. Lesser gods, naturally unruly, interpret it as "Control yourselves" (Damyata); humans, naturally greedy, as "Give" (Datta); demons, naturally cruel, as "Be compassionate" (Dayadhvam); "That very thing is repeated even today by the heavenly voice, in the form of thunder as 'DA' 'DA' 'DA,' which means 'Control yourselves,' 'Give,' and 'Have compassion.' Therefore

one should practice these three things: self-control, giving, and mercy." The Upanishads are ancient philosophical dialogues in Sanskrit. They are primary texts for an early form of Hinduism sometimes called Brahminism.
4. Cf. Webster, The White Devil, V, vi: ". . . they'll remarry / Ere the worm pierce your winding-sheet, ere the spider / Make a thin curtain for your epitaphs" [Eliot's note].
5. Cf. Inferno, XXXIII, 46 [Eliot's note]. In this passage from the Inferno Ugolino recalls his imprisonment in the tower with his children, where they starved to death: "And I heard below the door of the horrible tower being nailed shut." Eliot's note for this line goes on to quote F. H. Bradley, Appearance and Reality, p. 346: "'My external sensations are no less private to myself than are my thoughts or my feelings. In either case my experience falls within my own circle, a circle closed on the outside; and, with all its elements alike, every sphere is opaque to the others which surround it. . . . In brief, regarded as an existence which appears in a soul, the whole world for each is peculiar and private to that soul.'" Eliot wrote his doctoral thesis on Bradley's philosophy.

We think of the key, each in his prison
415 Thinking of the key, each confirms a prison
Only at nightfall, æthereal rumours
Revive for a moment a broken Coriolanus[6]
DA
Damyata: The boat responded
420 Gaily, to the hand expert with sail and oar
The sea was calm, your heart would have responded
Gaily, when invited, beating obedient
To controlling hands

                 I sat upon the shore
425 Fishing[7] with the arid plain behind me
Shall I at least set my lands in order?[8]

London Bridge is falling down falling down falling down[9]
Poi s'ascose nel foco che gli affina[1]
Quando fiam uti chelidon[2]—O swallow swallow[3]
430 *Le Prince d'Aquitaine à la tour abolie*[4]
These fragments I have shored against my ruins
Why then Ile fit you. Hieronymo's mad againe.[5]
Datta. Dayadhvam. Damyata.

        Shantih   shantih   shantih[6]

1921   1922

6. Coriolanus, who acted out of pride rather than duty, exemplifies a man locked in the prison of himself. He led the enemy against his native city out of injured pride (cf. Shakespeare's *Coriolanus*).
7. V. Weston: *From Ritual to Romance*; chapter on the Fisher King [Eliot's note].
8. Cf. Isaiah 38.1: "Thus saith the Lord, Set thine house in order, for thou shalt die, and not live."
9. One of the later lines of this nursery rhyme is "Take the key and lock her up, my fair lady."
1. V. *Purgutorio*, XXVI, 148 [Eliot's note]. The note goes on to quote lines 145–148 of the *Purgatorio*, in which the Provençal poet Arnaut Daniel addresses Dante: "'Now I pray you, by that virtue which guides you to the summit of the stairway, be mindful in due time of my pain.'" Then (in the line Eliot quotes here) "he hid himself in the fire which refines them."
2. V. *Pervigilium Veneris*. Cf. Philomela in parts II and III [Eliot's note]. The Latin phrase in the text, originally misquoting *uti* as *ceu*, means, "When shall I be as the swallow?" It comes from the late Latin poem "*Pervigilium Veneris*" ("Vigil of Venus"), "When will my spring come? When shall I be as the swallow that I may cease to be silent?

I have lost the Muse in silence, and Apollo regards me not."
3. Cf. A. C. Swinburne's "Itylus," which begins, "Swallow, my sister, O sister swallow, / How can thine heart be full of spring?" and Tennyson's lyric in *The Princess*: "O Swallow, Swallow, flying, flying south."
4. V. Gerard de Nerval, Sonnet *El Desdichado* [Eliot's note]. The French line may be translated: "The Prince of Aquitaine in the ruined tower." One of the cards in the Tarot pack is "the tower struck by lightning."
5. V. Kyd's *Spanish Tragedy* [Eliot's note]. Subtitled *Hieronymo's Mad Againe*, Kyd's play (1594) is an early example of the Elizabethan tragedy of revenge. Hieronymo, driven mad by the murder of his son, has his revenge when he is asked to write a court entertainment. He replies, "Why then Ile fit you!" (i.e., accommodate you), and assigns the parts in the entertainment so that, in the course of the action, his son's murderers are killed.
6. Shantih. Repeated as here, a formal ending to an Upanishad. "The Peace which passeth understanding" is a feeble translation of the content of this word [Eliot's note]. On the Upanishads see the note to line 401 above.

The Hollow Men

Mistah Kurtz—he dead[1]
A penny for the Old Guy[2]

I

We are the hollow men
We are the stuffed men
Leaning together
Headpiece filed with straw. Alas!
5 Our dried voices, when
We whisper together
Are quiet and meaningless
As wind in dry glass
Or rats' feet over broken glass
10 In our dry cella[3]

Shape without form, shade without colour,
Paralysed force, gesture without motion;

Those who have crossed
With direct eyes, to death's other Kingdom
15 Remember us—if at all—not as lost
Violent souls, but only
As the hollow men
The stuffed men.

II

Eyes I dare not meet in dreams
20 In death's dream kingdom[4]
These do not appear:
There, the eyes are
Sunlight on a broken column
There, is a tree swinging
25 And voices are
In the wind's singing
More distant and more solemn
Than a fading star.

Let me be no nearer
30 In death's dream kingdom
Let me also wear
Such deliberate disguises
Rat's coat, crowskin, crossed staves

---

1. From Joseph Conrad's *Heart of Darkness* (see p. 1051).
2. Every year on Nov. 5, British children build bonfires, on which they burn a scarecrow effigy of the traitor Guido [Guy] Fawkes, who in 1605 attempted to blow up the Parliament buildings. For some days before this, they ask people in the streets for pennies with which to buy fireworks.
3. Cf. *The Waste Land*, lines 115 and 195.
4. At the end of Dante's *Purgatorio* and in *Paradiso* 4, he cannot meet the gaze of Beatrice (see Eliot's 1929 essay "Dante").

In a field[5]
35 Behaving as the wind behaves
No nearer—

Not that final meeting
In the twilight kingdom[6]

III

This is the dead land
40 This is cactus land
Here the stone images[7]
Are raised, here they receive
The supplication of a dead man's hand
Under the twinkle of a fading star.

45 Is it like this
In death's other kingdom
Waking alone
At the hour when we are
Trembling with tenderness
50 Lips that would kiss
Form prayers to broken stone.

IV

The eyes are not here
There are no eyes here
In this valley of dying stars
55 In this hollow valley
This broken jaw of our lost kingdoms

In this last of meeting places
We grope together
And avoid speech
60 Gathered on this beach of the tumid river[8]

Sightless, unless
The eyes reappear
As the perpetual star
Multifoliate rose[9]
65 Of death's twilight kingdom
The hope only
Of empty men.

---

5. The traditional British scarecrow is made from two sticks tied in the form of a cross (the vertical one stuck in the ground), dressed in cast-off clothes, and sometimes draped with dead vermin.
6. Perhaps a reference to Dante's meeting with Beatrice after he has crossed the river Lethe.

There reminded of his sins, he is allowed to proceed to Paradise (*Purgatorio* 30).
7. Cf. *The Waste Land*, line 22.
8. Dante's Acheron, which encircles hell, and the Congo of Conrad's *Heart of Darkness*.
9. The image of heaven in Dante's *Paradiso* 32.

V

Here we go round the prickly pear
Prickly pear prickly pear
70 *Here we go round the prickly pear*
At five o'clock in the morning.[1]

Between the idea
And the reality
Between the motion
75 And the act[2]
Falls the Shadow[3]
      For Thine is the Kingdom[4]

Between the conception
And the creation
80 Between the emotion
And the response
Falls the Shadow
      Life is very long

Between the desire
85 And the spasm
Between the potency
And the existence
Between the essence
And the descent
90 Falls the Shadow
      For Thine is the Kingdom

For Thine is
Life is
For Thine is the

95 *This is the way the world ends*
This is the way the world ends
This is the way the world ends
Not with a bang but a whimper.

1924–25   1925

Journey of the Magi[1]

'A cold coming we had of it,
Just the worst time of the year

---

1. Parodic version of the children's rhyme ending "Here we go round the mulberry bush / On a cold and frosty morning."
2. Cf. Shakespeare's *Julius Caesar* 2.1.63–65: "Between the acting of a dreadful thing / And the first motion, all the interim is / Like a phantasma or a hideous dream."
3. Cf. Ernest Dowson's "*Non sum qualis eram bonae sub regno Cynarae,*" lines 1–2: "Last night, ah, yesternight, betwixt her lips and mine / There fell thy shadow, Cynara!"
4. Cf. The Lord's Prayer.
1. One of the wise men who came from the east to Jerusalem to do homage to the infant Jesus (Matthew 2.1–12) is recalling in old age the meaning of the experience.

For a journey, and such a long journey:
The ways deep and the weather sharp,
5   The very dead of winter.'[2]
And the camels galled, sore-footed, refractory,
Lying down in the melting snow.
There were times we regretted
The summer palaces on slopes, the terraces,
10   And the silken girls bringing sherbet.
Then the camel men cursing and grumbling
And running away, and wanting their liquor and women,
And the night-fires going out, and the lack of shelters,
And the cities hostile and the towns unfriendly
15   And the villages dirty and charging high prices:
A hard time we had of it.
At the end we preferred to travel all night,
Sleeping in snatches,
With the voices singing in our ears, saying
20   That this was all folly.

    Then at dawn we came down to a temperate valley,
Wet, below the snow line, smelling of vegetation;
With a running stream and a water mill beating the darkness,
And three trees on the low sky[3]
25   And an old white horse galloped away in the meadow.
Then we came to a tavern with vine-leaves over the lintel,
Six hands at an open door dicing for pieces of silver,
And feet kicking the empty wine-skins.
But there was no information, and so we continued
30   And arrived at evening, not a moment too soon
Finding the place; it was (you may say) satisfactory.

    All this was a long time ago, I remember,
And I would do it again, but set down
This set down
35   This: were we led all that way for
Birth or Death? There was a Birth, certainly,
We had evidence and no doubt. I had seen birth and death,
But had thought they were different; this Birth was
Hard and bitter agony for us, like Death, our death.
40   We returned to our places, these Kingdoms,
But no longer at ease here, in the old dispensation,
With an alien people clutching their gods.
I should be glad of another death.

1927

---

2. Adapted from a passage in a 1622 Christmas sermon by Bishop Lancelot Andrewes: "A cold coming they had of it at this time of the year, just the worst time of the year to take a journey, and specially a long journey in. The ways deep, the weather sharp, the days short, the sun farthest off, *in solstitio brumali,* 'the very dead of winter.'"

3. The "three trees" suggest the three crosses, with Jesus crucified on the center one; the men "dicing for pieces of silver" (line 27) suggest the soldiers dicing for Jesus' garments and Judas's betrayal of him for thirty pieces of silver; the empty wineskins recall one of Jesus' parables of old and new (Mark 2.22).

From Four Quartets

Little Gidding[1]

I

Midwinter spring is its own season
Sempiternal° though sodden towards sundown,   *eternal, everlasting*
Suspended in time, between pole and tropic,
When the short day is brightest, with frost and fire,
5   The brief sun flames the ice, on pond and ditches,
In windless cold that is the heart's heat,
Reflecting in a watery mirror
A glare that is blindness in the early afternoon.
And glow more intense than blaze of branch, or brazier,
10   Stirs the dumb spirit: no wind, but pentecostal fire[2]
In the dark time of the year. Between melting and freezing
The soul's sap quivers. There is no earth smell
Or smell of living thing. This is the springtime
But not in time's covenant. Now the hedgerow
15   Is blanched for an hour with transitory blossom
Of snow, a bloom more sudden
Than that of summer, neither budding nor fading,
Not in the scheme of generation.
Where is the summer, the unimaginable
Zero summer?

20   If you came this way,
Taking the route you would be likely to take
From the place you would be likely to come from,
If you came this way in may time, you would find the hedges
White again, in May, with voluptuary sweetness.
25   It would be the same at the end of the journey,
If you came at night like a broken king,[3]
If you came by day not knowing what you came for,
It would be the same, when you leave the rough road
And turn behind the pig-sty to the dull façade
30   And the tombstone. And what you thought you came for
Is only a shell, a husk of meaning

---

1. This is the last of Eliot's *Four Quartets*, four related poems each divided into five "movements" in a manner reminiscent of the structure of a quartet or a sonata and each dealing with some aspect of the relation of time and eternity, the meaning of history, the achievement of the moment of timeless insight. Although the *Four Quartets* constitute a unified sequence, they were written separately and can be read as individual poems. "*Little Gidding* can be understood by itself, without reference to the preceding poems, which it yet so beautifully completes" (Helen Gardner, *The Composition of Four Quartets*). Each of the four is named after a place. Little Gidding is a village in Huntingdonshire, where, in 1625, Nicholas Ferrar established an Anglican religious commu-

nity; the community was broken up in 1647, toward the end of the English Civil War, by the victorious Puritans; the chapel, however, was rebuilt in the 19th century and still exists. Eliot wrote the poem in 1942, when he was taking his turn as a nighttime fire watcher during the incendiary bombings of London in World War II.
2. On the Pentecost day after the death and resurrection of Jesus, there appeared to his apostles "cloven tongues like as of fire . . . And they were all filled with the Holy Ghost" (Acts 2).
3. King Charles I visited Ferrar's community more than once and is said to have paid his last visit in secret after his final defeat at the Battle of Naseby in the Civil War.

From which the purpose breaks only when it is fulfilled
If at all. Either you had no purpose
Or the purpose is beyond the end you figured
35 And is altered in fulfilment. There are other places
Which also are the world's end, some at the sea jaws,
Or over a dark lake, in a desert or a city[4]—
But this is the nearest, in place and time,
Now and in England.

                    If you came this way,
40 Taking any route, starting from anywhere,
At any time or at any season,
It would always be the same: you would have to put off
Sense and notion. You are not here to verify,
Instruct yourself, or inform curiosity
45 Or carry report. You are here to kneel
Where prayer has been valid. And prayer is more
Than an order of words, the conscious occupation
Of the praying mind, or the sound of the voice praying.
And what the dead had no speech for, when living,
50 They can tell you, being dead: the communication
Of the dead is tongued with fire beyond the language of the living.
Here, the intersection of the timeless moment
Is England and nowhere. Never and always.

II

Ash on an old man's sleeve
55 Is all the ash the burnt roses leave.
Dust in the air suspended
Marks the place where a story ended.[5]
Dust inbreathed was a house—
The wall, the wainscot, and the mouse.
60 The death of hope and despair,
    This is the death of air.[6]

There are flood and drouth
Over the eyes and in the mouth,
Dead water and dead sand
65 Contending for the upper hand.
The parched eviscerate soil
Gapes at the vanity of toil,
Laughs without mirth.
    This is the death of earth.

4. "The 'sea jaws' [Eliot] associated with Iona and St. Columba and with Lindisfarne and St. Cuthbert: the 'dark lake' with the lake of Glendalough and St Kevin's hermitage in County Wicklow: the desert with the hermits of the Thebaid and St. Antony: the city with Padua and the other St. Antony" (Gardner).
5. Eliot wrote to a friend: "During the Blitz [bombing] the accumulated debris was suspended in the London air for hours after a bomb-

ing. Then it would slowly descend and cover one's sleeves and coat with a fine white ash."
6. "The death of air," like that of "earth" and of "water and fire" in the succeeding stanzas, recalls the theory of the creative strife of the four elements propounded by Heraclitus (Greek philosopher of 4th and 5th centuries B.C.E.): "Fire lives in the death of air; water lives in the death of earth; and earth lives in the death of water."

70 Water and fire succeed
   The town, the pasture, and the weed.
   Water and fire deride
   The sacrifice that we denied.
   Water and fire shall rot
75 The marred foundations we forgot,
   Of sanctuary and choir.
          This is the death of water and fire.

   In the uncertain hour before the morning[7]
          Near the ending of interminable night
80   At the recurrent end of the unending
   After the dark dove with the flickering tongue[8]
          Had passed below the horizon of his homing
          While the dead leaves still rattled on like tin
   Over the asphalt where no other sound was
85   Between three districts whence the smoke arose
          I met one walking, loitering and hurried
   As if blown towards me like the metal leaves
          Before the urban dawn wind unresisting.
          And as I fixed upon the down-turned face
90 That pointed scrutiny with which we challenge
          The first-met stranger in the waning dusk
          I caught the sudden look of some dead master
   Whom I had known, forgotten, half recalled
          Both one and many; in the brown baked features
95   The eyes of a familiar compound ghost[9]
   Both intimate and unidentifiable.
          So I assumed a double part, and cried
          And heard another's voice cry: 'What! are *you* here?'
   Although we were not. I was still the same,
100   Knowing myself yet being someone other—
          And he a face still forming; yet the words sufficed
   To compel the recognition they preceded.
          And so, compliant to the common wind,
          Too strange to each other for misunderstanding,
105 In concord at this intersection time
          Of meeting nowhere, no before and after,
          We trod the pavement in a dead patrol.
   I said: 'The wonder that I feel is easy,
          Yet ease is cause of wonder. Therefore speak:
110   I may not comprehend, may not remember.'
   And he: 'I am not eager to rehearse
          My thought and theory which you have forgotten.
          These things have served their purpose: let them be.
   So with your own, and pray they be forgiven
115   By others, as I pray you to forgive

7. The pattern of indentation in the left margin
of lines 78–149, their movement and elevated
diction, are meant to suggest the terza rima of
Dante's *Divine Comedy*.
8. The German dive bomber.
9. This encounter with a ghost "compounded"

of W. B. Yeats and his fellow Irishman Jonathan
Swift is modeled on Dante's meeting with Brunette
Latini (*Inferno* 15), including a direct translation
(line 98) of Dante's cry of horrified recognition:
"*Siete voi qui, ser Brunetto?*" Cf. also Shakespeare's
sonnet 86, line 9: "that affable familiar ghost."

Both bad and good. Last season's fruit is eaten
And the fullfed beast shall kick the empty pail.
　　For last year's words belong to last year's language
　　And next year's words await another voice.
120 But, as the passage now presents no hindrance
　　To the spirit unappeased and peregrine°   *foreign, wandering*
　　Between two worlds become much like each other,
So I find words I never thought to speak
　　In streets I never thought I should revisit
125 When I left my body on a distant shore.[1]
Since our concern was speech, and speech impelled us
　　To purify the dialect of the tribe[2]
　　And urge the mind to aftersight and foresight,
Let me disclose the gifts reserved for age
130 　　To set a crown upon your lifetime's effort.
　　First, the cold friction of expiring sense
Without enchantment, offering no promise
　　But bitter tastelessness of shadow fruit
　　As body and soul begin to fall asunder.
135 Second, the conscious impotence of rage[3]
　　At human folly, and the laceration
　　Of laughter at what ceases to amuse.[4]
And last, the rending pain of re-enactment
　　Of all that you have done, and been;[5] the shame
140 　　Of motives late revealed, and the awareness
Of things ill done and done to others' harm
　　Which once you took for exercise of virtue.
　　Then fools' approval stings, and honour stains.
From wrong to wrong the exasperated spirit
145 　　Proceeds, unless restored by that refining fire[6]
　　Where you must move in measure, like a dancer.'[7]
The day was breaking. In the disfigured street
　　He left me, with a kind of valediction,
　　And faded on the blowing of the horn.[8]

III

150 There are three conditions which often look alike
　　Yet differ completely, flourish in the same hedgerow:

---

1. Yeats died on Jan. 28, 1939, at Roquebrune in the south of France.
2. A rendering of the line *"Dormer un sens plus pur aux mots de la tribu"* in Stéphane Mallarmé's 1877 sonnet "Le Tombeau d'Edgar Poe" ("The Tomb of Edgar Poe").
3. Cf. Yeats's "The Spur": "You think it horrible that lust and rage / Should dance attention upon my old age."
4. Cf. Yeats's "Swift's Epitaph" (translated from Swift's own Latin): "Savage indignation there / Cannot lacerate his breast."
5. Cf. Yeats's "Man and the Echo": "All that I have said and done, / Now that I am old and ill, / Turns into a question till / I lie awake night after night / And never get the answer right. / Did that play of mine send out / Certain men the English shot?"

6. Cf. *The Waste Land*, line 428 and its note; also the refining fire in Yeats's "Byzantium," lines 25–32.
7. Cf. Yeats's "Among School Children," line 64: "How can we know the dancer from the dance?"
8. Cf. *Hamlet* 1.2.157: "It faded on the crowing of the cock." The horn is the all-clear signal after an air raid (the dialogue has taken place between the dropping of the last bomb and the sounding of the all clear). Eliot called the section that ends with this line "the nearest equivalent to a canto of the *Inferno* or *Purgatorio*" that he could achieve and spoke of his intention to present "a parallel, by means of contrast, between the *Inferno* and the *Purgatorio* . . . and a hallucinated scene after an air raid."

Attachment to self and to things and to persons, detachment
From self and from things and from persons; and, growing between
    them, indifference
Which resembles the others as death resembles life,
155   Being between two lives—unflowering, between
The live and the dead nettle.[9] This is the use of memory:
For liberation—not less of love but expanding
Of love beyond desire, and so liberation
From the future as well as the past. Thus, love of a country
160   Begins as attachment to our own field of action
And comes to find that action of little importance
Though never indifferent. History may be servitude,
History may be freedom. See, now they vanish,
The faces and places, with the self which, as it could, loved them,
165   To become renewed, transfigured, in another pattern.

Sin is Behovely, but
All shall be well, and
All manner of thing shall be well.[1]
If I think, again, of this place,
170   And of people, not wholly commendable,
Of no immediate kin or kindness,
But some of peculiar genius,
All touched by a common genius,
United in the strife which divided them;
175   If I think of a king at nightfall,[2]
Of three men, and more, on the scaffold
And a few who died forgotten
In other places, here and abroad,
And of one who died blind and quiet[3]
180   Why should we celebrate
These dead men more than the dying?
It is not to ring the bell backward
Nor is it an incantation
To summon the spectre of a Rose.
185   We cannot revive old factions
We cannot restore old policies
Or follow an antique drum.
These men, and those who opposed them
And those whom they opposed
190   Accept the constitution of silence
And are folded in a single party.
Whatever we inherit from the fortunate
We have taken from the defeated
What they had to leave us—a symbol:

9. Eliot wrote to a friend: "The dead nettle is the family of flowering plants of which the White Archangel is one of the commonest and closely resembles the stinging nettle and is found in its company."
1. A quotation from the 14th-century English mystic Dame Julian of Norwich: "Sin is behovabil [inevitable and fitting], but all shall be well and all shall be well and all manner of thing shall be well."
2. I.e.; Charles I. He died "on the scaffold" in 1649, while his principal advisers, Archbishop Laud and Thomas Wentworth, earl of Strafford, were both executed earlier by the victorious parliamentary forces.
3. I.e., Milton, who sided with Cromwell against the king.

195   A symbol perfected in death.
And all shall be well and
All manner of thing shall be well
By the purification of the motive
In the ground of our beseeching.[4]

IV

200   The dove[5] descending breaks the air
With flame of incandescent terror
Of which the tongues declare
The one discharge from sin and error.
The only hope, or else despair
205   Lies in the choice of pyre or pyre—
To be redeemed from fire by fire.

Who then devised the torment? Love.
Love is the unfamiliar Name
Behind the hands that wove
210   The intolerable shirt of flame[6]
Which human power cannot remove.
    We only live, only suspire°   *breathe, sigh*
    Consumed by either fire or fire.

V

What we call the beginning is often the end
215   And to make an end is to make a beginning.
The end is where we start from. And every phrase
And sentence that is right (where every word is at home,
Taking its place to support the others,
The word neither diffident nor ostentatious,
220   And easy commerce of the old and the new,
The common word exact without vulgarity,
The formal word precise but not pedantic,
The complete consort[7] dancing together)
Every phrase and every sentence is an end and a beginning,
225   Every poem an epitaph. And any action
Is a step to the block, to the fire, down the sea's throat
Or to an illegible stone: and that is where we start.
We die with the dying:
See, they depart, and we go with them.
230   We are born with the dead:
See, they return, and bring us with them.
The moment of the rose and the moment of the yew-tree[8]
Are of equal duration. A people without history

4. Dame Julian of Norwich was instructed in a vision that "the ground of our beseeching" is love.
5. Both a dive bomber and the Holy Spirit with its Pentecostal tongues of fire.
6. Out of love for her husband, Hercules, Deianira gave him the poisoned shirt of Nessus. She

had been told that it would increase his love for her, but instead it so corroded his flesh that in his agony he mounted a funeral pyre and burned himself to death.
7. Company; also harmony of sounds.
8. Traditional symbol of death and grief.

Is not redeemed from time, for history is a pattern
235 Of timeless moments. So, while the light fails
On a winter's afternoon, in a secluded chapel
History is now and England.

With the drawing of this Love and the voice of this Calling[9]

We shall not cease from exploration
240 And the end of all our exploring
Will be to arrive where we started
And know the place for the first time.
Through the unknown, remembered gate
When the last of earth left to discover
245 Is that which was the beginning;
At the source of the longest river
The voice of the hidden waterfall
And the children in the apple tree
Not known, because not looked for
250 But heard, half-heard, in the stillness
Between two waves of the sea[1]
Quick now, here, now, always—
A condition of complete simplicity
(Costing not less than everything)
255 And all shall be well and
All manner of thing shall be well
When the tongues of flame are in-folded
Into the crowned knot of fire
And the fire and the rose are one.

1942   1942, 1943

Tradition and the Individual Talent[1]

I

In English writing we seldom speak of tradition, though we occasionally apply its name in deploring its absence. We cannot refer to 'the tradition' or to 'a tradition'; at most, we employ the adjective in saying that the poetry of So-and-so is 'traditional' or even 'too traditional.' Seldom, perhaps, does the word appear except in a phrase of censure. If otherwise, it is vaguely approbative, with the implication, as to the work approved, of some pleasing archaeological reconstruction. You can hardly make the word agreeable to English ears without this comfortable reference to the reassuring science of archæology.

Certainly the word is not likely to appear in our appreciations of living or dead writers. Every nation, every race, has not only its own creative, but its

---

9. This line is from the *Cloud of Unknowing*, an anonymous 14th-century mystical work.
1. The voices of the children in the apple tree symbolize the sudden moment of insight. Cf. the conclusion to "Burnt Norton" (the first of the *Four Quartets*), where the laughter of the chil-

dren in the garden has a like meaning: "Sudden in a shaft of sunlight / Even while the dust moves / There rises the hidden laughter / Of children in the foliage / Quick now, here, now, always."
1. First published in *The Egoist* magazine (1919) and later collected in *The Sacred Wood* (1920).

own critical turn of mind; and is even more oblivious of the shortcomings and limitations of its critical habits than of those of its creative genius. We know, or think we know, from the enormous mass of critical writing that has appeared in the French language the critical method or habit of the French; we only conclude (we are such unconscious people) that the French are 'more critical' than we, and sometimes even plume ourselves a little with the fact, as if the French were the less spontaneous. Perhaps they are; but we might remind ourselves that criticism is as inevitable as breathing, and that we should be none the worse for articulating what passes in our minds when we read a book and feel an emotion about it, for criticizing our own minds in their work of criticism. One of the facts that might come to light in this process is our tendency to insist, when we praise a poet, upon those aspects of his work in which he least resembles anyone else. In these aspects or parts of his work we pretend to find what is individual, what is the peculiar essence of the man. We dwell with satisfaction upon the poet's difference from his predecessors, especially his immediate predecessors; we endeavour to find something that can be isolated in order to be enjoyed. Whereas if we approach a poet without this prejudice we shall often find that not only the best, but the most individual parts of his work may be those in which the dead poets, his ancestors, assert their immortality most vigorously. And I do not mean the impressionable period of adolescence, but the period of full maturity.

Yet if the only form of tradition, of handing down, consisted in following the ways of the immediate generation before us in a blind or timid adherence to its successes, 'tradition' should positively be discouraged. We have seen many such simple currents soon lost in the sand; and novelty is better than repetition. Tradition is a matter of much wider significance. It cannot be inherited, and if you want it you must obtain it by great labour. It involves, in the first place, the historical sense, which we may call nearly indispensable to any one who would continue to be a poet beyond his twenty-fifth year; and the historical sense involves a perception, not only of the pastness of the past, but of its presence; the historical sense compels a man to write not merely with his own generation in his bones, but with a feeling that the whole of the literature of Europe from Homer and within it the whole of the literature of his own country has a simultaneous existence and composes a simultaneous order. This historical sense, which is a sense of the timeless as well as of the temporal and of the timeless and of the temporal together, is what makes a writer traditional. And it is at the same time what makes a writer most acutely conscious of his place in time, of his own contemporaneity.

No poet, no artist of any art, has his complete meaning alone. His significance, his appreciation is the appreciation of his relation to the dead poets and artists. You cannot value him alone; you must set him, for contrast and comparison, among the dead. I mean this as a principle of aesthetic, not merely historical, criticism. The necessity that he shall conform, that he shall cohere, is not one-sided; what happens when a new work of art is created is something that happens simultaneously to all the works of art which preceded it. The existing monuments form an ideal order among themselves, which is modified by the introduction of the new (the really new) work of art among them. The existing order is complete before the new work arrives; for order to persist after the supervention of novelty, the *whole* existing order must be, if ever so slightly, altered; and so the relations, proportions, values of each work of art toward the whole are readjusted; and this is conformity between the old and the new. Whoever has approved this idea of order, of the form of European, of English literature will not find it preposterous that the past should be altered by the present as much as the present is directed by the past. And the poet who is aware of this will be aware of great difficulties and responsibilities.

In a peculiar sense he will be aware also that he must inevitably be judged by the standards of the past. I say judged, not amputated, by them; not judged to be as good as, or worse or better than, the dead; and certainly not judged by the canons of dead critics. It is a judgment, a comparison, in which two things are measured by each other. To conform merely would be for the new work not really to conform at all; it would not be new, and would therefore not be a work of art. And we do not quite say that the new is more valuable because it fits in; but its fitting in is a test of its value—a test, it is true, which can only be slowly and cautiously applied, for we are none of us infallible judges of conformity. We say: it appears to conform, and is perhaps individual, or it appears individual, and may conform; but we are hardly likely to find that it is one and not the other.

To proceed to a more intelligible exposition of the relation of the poet to the past: he can neither take the past as a lump, an indiscriminate bolus,[2] nor can he form himself wholly on one or two private admirations, nor can he form himself wholly upon one preferred period. The first course is inadmissible, the second is an important experience of youth, and the third is a pleasant and highly desirable supplement. The poet must be very conscious of the main current, which does not at all flow invariably through the most distinguished reputations. He must be quite aware of the obvious fact that art never improves, but that the material of art is never quite the same. He must be aware that the mind of Europe—the mind of his own country—a mind which he learns in time to be much more important than his own private mind—is a mind which changes, and that this change is a development which abandons nothing en route, which does not superannuate either Shakespeare, or Homer, or the rock drawing of the Magdalenian[3] draftsmen. That this development, refinement perhaps, complication certainly, is not, from the point of view of the artist, any improvement. Perhaps not even an improvement from the point of view of the psychologist or not to the extent which we imagine; perhaps only in the end based upon a complication in economics and machinery. But the difference between the present and the past is that the conscious present is an awareness of the past in a way and to an extent which the past's awareness of itself cannot show.

Someone said: 'The dead writers are remote from us because we know so much more than they did.' Precisely, and they are that which we know.

I am alive to a usual objection to what is clearly part of my programme for the métier[4] poetry. The objection is that the doctrine requires a ridiculous amount of erudition (pedantry), a claim which can be rejected by appeal to the lives of poets in any pantheon. It will even be affirmed that much learning deadens or perverts poetic sensibility. While, however, we

2. A round mass of anything: a large pill.
3. The most advanced culture of the European Paleolithic period (from discoveries at La Made-
leine, France).
4. Vocation (French).

persist in believing that a poet ought to know as much as will not encroach upon his necessary receptivity and necessary laziness, it is not desirable to confine knowledge to whatever can be put into a useful shape for examinations, drawing-rooms, or the still more pretentious modes of publicity. Some can absorb knowledge, the more tardy must sweat for it. Shakespeare acquired more essential history from Plutarch[5] than most men could from the whole British Museum. What is to be insisted upon is that the poet must develop or procure the consciousness of the past and that he should continue to develop this consciousness throughout his career.

What happens is a continual surrender of himself as he is at the moment to something which is more, valuable. The progress of an artist is a continual self-sacrifice, a continual extinction of personality.

There remains to define this process of depersonalisation and its relation to the sense of tradition. It is in this depersonalization that art may be said to approach the condition of science. I, therefore, invite you to consider, as a suggestive analogy, the action which takes place when a bit of finely filiated[6] platinum is introduced into a chamber containing oxygen and sulphur dioxide.

II

Honest criticism and sensitive appreciation are directed not upon the poet but upon the poetry. If we attend to the confused cries of the newspaper critics and the susurrus[7] of popular repetition that follows, we shall hear the names of poets in great numbers; if we seek not Blue-book[8] knowledge but the enjoyment of poetry, and ask for a poem, we shall seldom find it. I have tried to point out the importance of the relation of the poem to other poems by other authors, and suggested the conception of poetry as a living whole of all the poetry that has ever been written. The other aspect of this Impersonal theory of poetry is the relation of the poem to its author. And I hinted, by an analogy, that the mind of the mature poet differs from that of the immature one not precisely in any valuation of 'personality,' not being necessarily more interesting, or having 'more to say,' but rather by being a more finely perfected medium in which special, or very varied, feelings are at liberty to enter into new combinations.

The analogy was that of the catalyst[9] When the two gases previously mentioned are mixed in the presence of a filament of platinum, they form sulphurous acid. This combination takes place only if the platinum is present; nevertheless the newly formed acid contains no trace of platinum, and the platinum itself is apparently unaffected; has remained inert, neutral, and unchanged. The mind of the poet is the shred of platinum. It may partly or exclusively operate upon the experience of the man himself; but, the more perfect the artist, the more completely separate in him will be the man who suffers and the mind which creates; the more perfectly will the mind digest and transmute the passions which are its material.

The experience, you will notice, the elements which enter the presence of the transforming catalyst, are of two lands: emotions and feelings. The effect

---

5. Greek biographer (1st century C.E.) of famous Greeks and Romans; from his work Shakespeare drew the plots of his Roman plays.
6. Drawn out like a thread.

7. Murmuring, buzzing (Latin).
8. British government publication.
9. Substance that triggers a chemical change without being affected by the reaction.

of a work of art upon the person who enjoys it is an experience different in kind from any experience not of art. It may be formed out of one emotion, or may be a combination of several; and various feelings, inhering for the writer in particular words or phrases or images, may be added to compose the final result. Or great poetry may be made without the direct use of any emotion whatever composed out of feelings solely. Canto XV of the *Inferno* (Brunetto Latini)[1] is a working up of the emotion evident in the situation; but the effect, though single as that of any work of art, is obtained by considerable complexity of detail. The last quatrain gives an image, a feeling attaching to an image, which 'came,' which did not develop simply out of what precedes, but which was probably in suspension in the poet's mind until the proper combination arrived for it to add itself to.[2] The poet's mind is in fact a receptacle for seizing and storing up numberless feelings, phrases, images, which remain there until all the particles which can unite to form a new compound are present together.

If you compare several representative passages of the greatest poetry you see how great is the variety of types of combination, and also how completely any semi-ethical criterion of 'sublimity' misses the mark. For it is not the 'greatness,' the intensity, of the emotions, the components, but the intensity of the artistic process, the pressure, so to speak, under which the fusion takes place, that counts. The episode of Paolo and Francesca[3] employs a definite emotion, but the intensity of the poetry is something quite different from whatever intensity in the supposed experience it may give the impression of. It is no more intense, furthermore, than Canto XXVI,[4] the voyage of Ulysses, which has not the direct dependence upon an emotion. Great variety is possible in the process of transmutation of emotion: the murder of Agamemnon, or the agony of Othello,[5] gives an artistic effect apparently closer to a possible original than the scenes from Dante. In the *Agamemnon*, the artistic emotion approximates to the emotion of an actual spectator; in *Othello* to the emotion of the protagonist himself. But the difference between art and the event is always absolute; the combination which is the murder of Agamemnon is probably as complex as that which is the voyage of Ulysses. In either case there has been a fusion of elements. The ode of Keats contains a number of feelings which have nothing particular to do with the nightingale, but which the nightingale, partly, perhaps, because of its attractive name, and partly because of its reputation, served to bring together.

The point of view which I am struggling to attack is perhaps related to the metaphysical theory of the substantial unity of the soul: for my meaning is, that the poet has, not a 'personality' to express, but a particular medium, which is only a medium and not a personality, in which impressions and experiences combine in peculiar and unexpected ways. Impressions and experiences which are important for the man may take no place in the poetry, and

1. Dante meets in hell his old master, Brunetto Latini, suffering eternal punishment for unnatural lust yet still loved and admired by Dante, who addresses him with affectionate courtesy.
2. Dante's strange interview with Brunetto is over, and Brunetto moves off to continue his punishment: "Then he turned round, and seemed like one of those / Who run for the green cloth [in the footrace] at Verona / In the field; and he seemed among them / Not the loser but the winner."

3. Illicit lovers whom Dante meets in the second circle of hell (*Inferno* 5) and at whose punishment and sorrows he swoons with pity.
4. Of the *Inferno*. Ulysses, suffering in hell for "false counseling," tells Dante of his final voyage.
5. Shakespeare's character kills himself after being duped into jealously murdering his wife. In Aeschylus's play *Agamemnon* the title character is murdered by his wife, Clytemnestra.

those which become important in the poetry may play quite a negligible part in the man, the personality.

I will quote a passage which is unfamiliar enough to be regarded with fresh attention in the light—or darkness—of these observations:

> And now methinks I could e'en chide myself
> For doating on her beauty, though her death
> Shall be revenged after no common action.
> Does the silkworm expend her yellow labours
> For thee? For thee does she undo herself?
> Are lordships solid to maintain ladyships
> For the poor benefit of a bewildering minute?
> Why does yon fellow falsify highways,
> And put his life between the judge's lips,
> To refine such a thing—keeps horse and men
> To beat their valours for her? . . . [6]

In this passage (as is evident if it is taken in its context) there is a combination of positive and negative emotions: an intensely strong attraction toward beauty and an equally intense fascination by the ugliness which is contrasted with it and which destroys it. This balance of contrasted emotion is in the dramatic situation to which the speech is pertinent, but that situation alone is inadequate to it. This is, so to speak, the structural emotion, provided by the drama. But the whole effect, the dominant tone, is due to the fact that a number of floating feelings, having an affinity to this emotion by no means superficially evident, have combined with it to give us a new art emotion.

It is not in his personal emotions, the emotions provoked by particular events in his life, that the poet is in any way remarkable or interesting. His particular emotions may be simple, or crude, or flat. The emotion in his poetry will be a very complex thing, but not with the complexity of the emotions of people who have very complex or unusual emotions in life. One error, in fact, of eccentricity in poetry is to seek for new human emotions to express; and in this search for novelty in the wrong place it discovers the perverse. The business of the poet is not to find new emotions, but to use the ordinary ones and, in working them up into poetry, to express feelings which are not in actual emotions at all. And emotions which he has never experienced will serve his turn as well as those familiar to him. Consequently, we must believe that 'emotion recollected in tranquillity'[7] is an inexact formula. For it is neither emotion, nor recollection, nor, without distortion of meaning, tranquility. It is a concentration, and a new thing resulting from the concentration, of a very great number of experiences which to the practical and active person would not seem to be experiences at all; it is a concentration which does not happen consciously or of deliberation. These experiences are not 'recollected,' and they finally unite in an atmosphere which is 'tranquil' only in that it is a passive attending upon the event. Of course this is not quite the whole story. There is a great deal, in the writing of poetry, which must be conscious and deliberate. In fact, the bad poet is usually

---

6. From Cyril Tourneur's *Revenger's Tragedy* 3.4 (1607).
7. In his preface to *Lyrical Ballads* (2nd ed.,
1800), Wordsworth writes that poetry "takes its origin from emotion recollected in tranquility."

unconscious where he ought to be conscious, and conscious where he ought to be unconscious. Both errors tend to make him 'personal.' Poetry is not a turning loose of emotion, but an escape from emotion; it is not the expression of personality, but an escape from personality. But, of course, only those who have personality and emotions know what it means to want to escape from these things.

III

ὁ δέ νοῦζ ἴσωζ θειό τερόν τι καὶ ἀπαθέζ ἐστιν.[8]

This essay proposes to halt at the frontier of metaphysics or mysticism, and confine itself to such practical conclusions as can be applied by the responsible person interested in poetry. To divert interest from the poet to the poetry is a laudable aim: for it would conduce to a juster estimation of actual poetry, good and bad. There are many people who appreciate the expression of sincere emotion in verse, and there is a smaller number of people who can appreciate technical excellence. But very few know when there is an expression of *significant* emotion, emotion which has its life in the poem and not in the history of the poet. The emotion of art is impersonal. And the poet cannot reach this impersonality without surrendering himself wholly to the work to be done. And he is not likely to know what is to be done unless he lives in what is not merely the present, but the present moment of the past, unless he is conscious, not of what is dead, but of what is already living.

1919, 1920

8. Aristotle's "De Anima" ("On the Soul") 1.4: "The mind is doubtless something more divine and unimpressionable."

KATHERINE MANSFIELD
1888–1923

Kathleen Mansfield Beauchamp was born in Wellington, New Zealand, daughter of a respected businessman who was later knighted. In 1903 the family moved to London, where Kathleen and her sisters entered Queen's College, the first institution in England founded expressly for the higher education of women. The family returned to New Zealand, leaving the girls in London, but the Beauchamps brought their daughters home in 1906. By this time Kathleen had written a number of poems, sketches, and stories; and after experimenting with different pen names, she adopted that of Katherine Mansfield. She was restless and ambitious and chafed against the narrowness of middle-class life in New Zealand, at that time still very much a new country in the shadow of the British Empire.

In July 1908 Mansfield left again for London; she never returned to New Zealand. In 1909 she suddenly married G. C. Bowden, a teacher of singing and elocution, but left him the same evening. Shortly afterward she became pregnant by another man and went to Germany to await the birth, but she had a miscarriage there. Her experiences in Germany are told in carefully observed sketches full of ironic detail in her first published book, *In a German Pension* (1911).

In 1910 she briefly resumed life with Bowden, who put her in touch with A. R. Orage, editor of the avant-garde periodical *The New Age*. There she published a number of her stories and sketches. At the end of 1911 she met the critic John Middleton Murry, editor of the modernist magazine *Rhythm*, and eventually married him. She developed intense but conflicted friendships with D. H. Lawrence, Virginia Woolf, and other writers of the day. During all this time Mansfield experimented in technique and refined her art, attempting within the short story to illuminate the ambivalences and complexities of friendship and family, gender and class. The death in World War I, in October 1915, of her much-loved younger brother sent her imagination back to their childhood days in New Zealand and in doing so gave a fresh charge and significance to her writing. Using her newly developed style with an ever greater subtlety and sensitivity, she now produced her best stories, including "Prelude," "Daughters of the Late Colonel," "At the Bay," and "The Garden Party." With the publication of *The Garden Party and Other Stories* in February 1922, Mansfield's place as a master of the modern short story was ensured. But she was gravely ill with tuberculosis and died suddenly at the age of thirty-four in Fontainebleau, France, where she had gone to try to find a cure by adopting the methods of the controversial mystic George Ivanovich Gurdjieff.

Mansfield produced her best and most characteristic work in her last years, when she combined incident, image, symbol, and structure in a way comparable with, yet interestingly different from, James Joyce's method in *Dubliners*, the two writers sharing an influence in the precise and understated art of the Russian writer Anton Chekhov. "Daughters of the Late Colonel," a story of two middle-aged sisters and their devotion to a tyrannical father, shows her working characteristically through suggestion rather than explicit development to illuminate a late-Victorian world, with the subdued elegiac sense of female lives wasted in the service of an outmoded patriarchal order, although the story's ironic surface is restrained comedy. The meaning is achieved most of all through the atmosphere, built up by the accumulation of small strokes, none of which seems more than a shrewdly observed realistic detail. Mansfield also manipulates time masterfully: she makes particularly effective use of the unobtrusive flashback, where we find ourselves in an earlier phase of the action without quite knowing how we got there but fully aware of its relevance to the total action and atmosphere.

The Garden Party[1]

And after all the weather was ideal. They could not have had a more perfect day for a garden party if they had ordered it. Windless, warm, the sky without a cloud. Only the blue was veiled with a haze of light gold, as it is sometimes in early summer. The gardener had been up since dawn, mowing the lawns and sweeping them, until the grass and the dark flat rosettes where the daisy plants had been seemed to shine. As for the roses, you could not help feeling they understood that roses are the only flowers that

---

1. This story draws on an incident from Mansfield's life. In March 1907 her mother gave a garden party in their Wellington house, but a street accident befell a neighbor living in a poor quarter nearby.

impress people at garden parties; the only flowers that everybody is certain of knowing. Hundreds, yes, literally hundreds, had come out in a single night; the green bushes bowed down as though they had been visited by archangels.

Breakfast was not yet over before the men came to put up the marquee.

'Where do you want the marquee put, mother?'

'My dear child, it's no use asking me. I'm determined to leave everything to you children this year. Forget I am your mother. Treat me as an honoured guest.'

But Meg could not possibly go and supervise the men. She had washed her hair before breakfast, and she sat drinking her coffee in a green turban, with a dark wet curl stamped on each cheek. Jose, the butterfly, always came down in a silk petticoat and a kimono jacket.

'You'll have to go, Laura; you're the artistic one.'

Away Laura flew, still holding her piece of bread-and-butter. It's so delicious to have an excuse for eating out of doors, and besides, she loved having to arrange things; she always felt she could do it so much better than anybody else.

Four men in their shirt-sleeves stood grouped together on the garden path. They carried staves covered with rolls of canvas, and they had big tool-bags slung on their backs. They looked impressive. Laura wished now that she had not got the bread-and-butter, but there was nowhere to put it, and she couldn't possibly throw it away. She blushed and tried to look severe and even a little bit short-sighted as she came up to them.

'Good morning,' she said, copying her mother's voice. But that sounded so fearfully affected that she was ashamed, and stammered like a little girl, 'Oh—er—have you come—is it about the marquee?'

'That's right, miss,' said the tallest of the men, a lanky, freckled fellow, and he shifted his tool-bag, knocked back his straw hat and smiled down at her. 'That's about it.'

His smile was so easy, so friendly that Laura recovered. What nice eyes he had, small, but such a dark blue! And now she looked at the others, they were smiling too. 'Cheer up, we won't bite,' their smile seemed to say. How very nice workmen were! And what a beautiful morning! She mustn't mention the morning; she must be business-like. The marquee.

'Well, what about the lily-lawn? Would that do?'

And she pointed to the lily-lawn with the hand that didn't hold the bread-and-butter. They turned, they stared in the direction. A little fat chap thrust out his under-lip, and the tall fellow frowned.

'I don't fancy it,' said he. 'Not conspicuous enough. You see, with a thing like a marquee,' and he turned to Laura in his easy way, 'you want to put it somewhere where it'll give you a bang slap in the eye, if you follow me.'

Laura's upbringing made her wonder for a moment whether it was quite respectful of a workman to talk to her of bangs slap in the eye. But she did quite follow him.

'A corner of the tennis-court,' she suggested. 'But the band's going to be in one corner.'

'H'm, going to have a band, are you?' said another of the workmen. He was pale. He had a haggard look as his dark eyes scanned the tennis-court. What was he thinking?

'Only a very small band,' said Laura gently. Perhaps he wouldn't mind so much if the band was quite small. But the tall fellow interrupted.

'Look here, miss, that's the place. Against those trees. Over there. That'll do fine.'

Against the karakas. Then the karaka-trees would be hidden. And they were so lovely, with their broad, gleaming leaves, and their clusters of yellow fruit. They were like trees you imagined growing on a desert island, proud, solitary, lifting their leaves and fruits to the sun in a kind of silent splendour. Must they be hidden by a marquee?

They must. Already the men had shouldered their staves and were making for the place. Only the tall fellow was left. He bent down, pinched a sprig of lavender, put his thumb and forefinger to his nose and snuffed up the smell. When Laura saw that gesture she forgot all about the karakas in her wonder at him caring for things like that—caring for the smell of lavender. How many men that she knew would have done such a thing? Oh, how extraordinarily nice workmen were, she thought. Why couldn't she have workmen for friends rather than the silly boys she danced with and who came to Sunday night supper? She would get on much better with men like these.

It's all the fault, she decided, as the tall fellow drew something on the back of an envelope, something that was to be looped up or left to hang, of these absurd class distinctions. Well, for her part, she didn't feel them. Not a bit, not an atom . . . And now there came the chock-chock of wooden hammers. Some one whistled, some one sang out, 'Are you right there, matey?' 'Matey!' The friendliness of it, the—the—Just to prove how happy she was, just to show the tall fellow how at home she felt, and how she despised stupid conventions, Laura took a big bite of her bread-and-butter as she stared at the little drawing. She felt just like a work-girl.

'Laura, Laura, where are you? Telephone, Laura!' a voice cried from the house.

'Coming!' Away she skimmed, over the lawn, up the path, up the steps, across the veranda, and into the porch. In the hall her father and Laurie were brushing their hats ready to go to the office.

'I say, Laura,' said Laurie very fast, 'you might just give a squiz[2] at my coat before this afternoon. See if it wants pressing.'

'I will,' said she. Suddenly she couldn't stop herself. She ran at Laurie and gave him a small, quick squeeze. 'Oh, I do love parties, don't you?' gasped Laura.

'Ra-ther,' said Laurie's warm, boyish voice, and he squeezed his sister too, and gave her a gentle push. 'Dash off to the telephone, old girl.'

The telephone. 'Yes, yes; oh yes. Kitty? Good morning, dear. Come to lunch? Do, dear. Delighted of course. It will only be a very scratch meal—just the sandwich crusts and broken meringue-shells and what's left over. Yes, isn't it a perfect morning? Your white? Oh, I certainly should. One moment—hold the line. Mother's calling.' And Laura sat back. 'What, mother? Can't hear.'

Mrs Sheridan's voice floated down the stairs. 'Tell her to wear that sweet hat she had on last Sunday.'

2. Glance.

'Mother says you're to wear that sweet hat you had on last Sunday. Good. One o'clock. Bye-bye.'

Laura put back the receiver, flung her arms over her head, took a deep breath, stretched and let them fall. 'Huh,' she sighed, and the moment after the sigh she sat up quickly. She was still, listening. All the doors in the house seemed to be open. The house was alive with soft, quick steps and running voices. The green baize[3] door that led to the kitchen regions swung open and shut with a muffled thud. And now there came a long, chuckling absurd sound. It was the heavy piano being moved on its stiff castors. But the air! If you stopped to notice, was the air always like this? Little faint winds were playing chase in at the tops of the windows, out at the doors. And there were two tiny spots of sun, one on the inkpot, one on a silver photograph frame, playing too. Darling little spots. Especially the one on the inkpot lid. It was quite warm. A warm little silver star. She could have kissed it.

The front door bell pealed, and there sounded the rustle of Sadie's print skirt on the stairs. A man's voice murmured; Sadie answered, careless, 'I'm sure I don't know. Wait. I'll ask Mrs Sheridan.'

'What is it, Sadie?' Laura came into the hall.

'It's the florist, Miss Laura.'

It was, indeed. There, just inside the door, stood a wide, shallow tray full of pots of pink lilies. No other kind. Nothing but lilies—canna lilies, big pink flowers, wide open, radiant, almost frighteningly alive on bright crimson stems.

'O-oh, Sadie!' said Laura, and the sound was like a little moan. She crouched down as if to warm herself at that blaze of lilies; she felt they were in her fingers, on her lips, growing in her breast.

'It's some mistake,' she said faintly. 'Nobody ever ordered so many. Sadie, go and find mother.'

But at that moment Mrs Sheridan joined them.

'It's quite right,' she said calmly. 'Yes, I ordered them. Aren't they lovely?' She pressed Laura's arm. 'I was passing the shop yesterday, and I saw them in the window. And I suddenly thought for once in my life I shall have enough canna lilies. The garden party will be a good excuse.'

'But I thought you said you didn't mean to interfere,' said Laura. Sadie had gone. The florist's man was still outside at his van. She put her arm round her mother's neck and gently, very gently, she bit her mother's ear.

'My darling child, you wouldn't like a logical mother, would you? Don't do that. Here's the man.'

He carried more lilies still, another whole tray.

'Bank them up, just inside the door, on both sides of the porch, please,' said Mrs Sheridan. 'Don't you agree, Laura?'

'Oh, I *do* mother.'

In the drawing-room Meg, Jose and good little Hans had at last succeeded in moving the piano.

'Now, if we put this chesterfield against the wall and move everything out of the room except the chairs, don't you think?'

'Quite.'

---

3. Coarse woolen.

'Hans, move these tables into the smoking-room, and bring a sweeper to take these marks off the carpet and—one moment, Hans—' Jose loved giving orders to the servants, and they loved obeying her. She always made them feel they were taking part in some drama. 'Tell mother and Miss Laura to come here at once.'

'Very good, Miss Jose.'

She turned to Meg. 'I want to hear what the piano sounds like, just in case I'm asked to sing this afternoon. Let's try over "This Life is Weary."'

Pom! Ta-ta-ta *Tee*-ta! The piano burst out so passionately that Jose's face changed. She clasped her hands. She looked mournfully and enigmatically at her mother and Laura as they came in.

> This Life is *Wee*-ary,
> A Tear—a Sigh.
> A Love that *Chan*-ges,
> This Life is *Wee*-ary,
> A Tear—a Sigh.
> A Love that *Chan*-ges,
> And then . . . Good-bye!

But at the word 'Good-bye,' and although the piano sounded more desperate than ever, her face broke into a brilliant, dreadfully unsympathetic smile.

'Aren't I in good voice, mummy?' she beamed.

> This Life is *Wee*-ary,
> Hope comes to Die.
> A Dream—a *Wa*-kening.

But now Sadie interrupted them. 'What is it, Sadie?'

'If you please, m'm, cook says have you got the flags[4] for the sandwiches?'

'The flags for the sandwiches, Sadie?' echoed Mrs Sheridan dreamily. And the children knew by her face that she hadn't got them. 'Let me see.' And she said to Sadie firmly, 'Tell cook I'll let her have them in ten minutes.'

Sadie went.

'Now, Laura,' said her mother quickly. 'Come with me into the smoking-room. I've got the names[5] somewhere on the back of an envelope. You'll have to write them out for me. Meg, go upstairs this minute and take that wet thing off your head. Jose, run and finish dressing this instant. Do you hear me, children, or shall I have to tell your father when he comes home to-night? And—and, Jose, pacify cook if you do go into the kitchen, will you? I'm terrified of her this morning.'

The envelope was found at last behind the dining-room clock, though how it had got there Mrs Sheridan could not imagine.

'One of you children must have stolen it out of my bag, because I remember vividly—cream cheese and lemon-curd. Have you done that?'

'Yes.'

---

4. Little paper flags stuck in a plate of small triangular sandwiches indicating what is inside the sandwiches on each plate—an English custom adopted by the New Zealand middle class as a sign of gentility.
5. I.e., the names of the sandwich fillings to be written on each flag.

'Egg and—' Mrs Sheridan held the envelope away from her. 'It looks like mice. It can't be mice, can it?'

'Olive, pet,' said Laura, looking over her shoulder.

'Yes, of course, olive. What a horrible combination it sounds. Egg and olive.'

They were finished at last, and Laura took them off to the kitchen. She found Jose there pacifying the cook, who did not look at all terrifying.

'I have never seen such exquisite sandwiches,' said Jose's rapturous voice. 'How many kinds did you say there were, cook? Fifteen?'

'Fifteen, Miss Jose.'

'Well, cook, I congratulate you.'

Cook swept up crusts with the long sandwich knife and smiled broadly.

'Godber's has come,' announced Sadie, issuing out of the pantry. She had seen the man pass the window.

That meant the cream puffs had come. Godber's were famous for their cream puffs. Nobody ever thought of making them at home.

'Bring them in and put them on the table, my girl,' ordered cook.

Sadie brought them in and went back to the door. Of course Laura and Jose were far too grown-up to really care about such things. All the same, they couldn't help agreeing that the puffs looked very attractive. Very. Cook began arranging them, shaking off the extra icing sugar.

'Don't they carry one back to all one's parties?' said Laura.

'I suppose they do,' said practical Jose, who never liked to be carried back. 'They look beautifully light and feathery, I must say.'

'Have one each, my dears,' said cook in her comfortable voice. 'Yer ma won't know.'

Oh, impossible. Fancy cream puffs so soon after breakfast. The very idea made one shudder. All the same, two minutes later Jose and Laura were licking their fingers with that absorbed inward look that only comes from whipped cream.

'Let's go into the garden, out by the back way,' suggested Laura. 'I want to see how the men are getting on with the marquee. They're such awfully nice men.'

But the back door was blocked by cook, Sadie, Godber's man and Hans. Something had happened.

'Tuk-tuk-tuk,' clucked cook like an agitated hen. Sadie had her hand clapped to her cheek as though she had toothache. Hans's face was screwed up in the effort to understand. Only Godber's man seemed to be enjoying himself; it was his story.

'What's the matter? What's happened?'

'There's been a horrible accident,' said cook. 'A man killed.'

'A man killed! Where? How? When?'

But Godber's man wasn't going to have his story snatched from under his very nose.

'Know those little cottages just below here, miss?' Know them? Of course, she knew them. 'Well, there's a young chap living there, name of Scott, a carter. His horse shied at a traction-engine, corner of Hawke Street this morning, and he was thrown out on the back of his head. Killed.'

'Dead!' Laura stared at Godber's man.

'Dead when they picked him up,' said Godber's man with relish. 'They were taking the body home as I come up here.' And he said to the cook, 'He's left a wife and five little ones.'

'Jose, come here.' Laura caught hold of her sister's sleeve and dragged her through the kitchen to the other side of the green baize door. There she paused and leaned against it. 'Jose!' she said, horrified, 'however are we going to stop everything?'

'Stop everything, Laura!' cried Jose in astonishment. 'What do you mean?'

'Stop the garden party, of course.' Why did Jose pretend?

But Jose was still more amazed. 'Stop the garden party? My dear Laura, don't be so absurd. Of course we can't do anything of the kind. Nobody expects us to. Don't be so extravagant.'

'But we can't possibly have a garden party with a man dead just outside the front gate.'

That really was extravagant, for the little cottages were in a lane to themselves at the very bottom of a steep rise that led up to the house. A broad road ran between. True, they were far too near. They were the greatest possible eyesore, and they had no right to be in that neighbourhood at all. They were little mean dwellings painted a chocolate brown. In the garden patches there was nothing but cabbage stalks, sick hens and tomato cans. The very smoke coming out of their chimneys was poverty-stricken. Little rags and shreds of smoke, so unlike the great silvery plumes that uncurled from the Sheridans' chimneys. Washerwomen lived in the lane and sweeps and a cobbler, and a man whose house-front was studded all over with minute bird-cages. Children swarmed. When the Sheridans were little they were forbidden to set foot there because of the revolting language and of what they might catch. But since they were grown up, Laura and Laurie on their prowls sometimes walked through. It was disgusting and sordid. They came out with a shudder. But still one must go everywhere; one must see everything. So through they went.

'And just think of what the band would sound like to that poor woman,' said Laura.

'Oh, Laura!' Jose began to be seriously annoyed. 'If you're going to stop a band playing every time some one has an accident, you'll lead a very strenuous life. I'm every bit as sorry about it as you. I feel just as sympathetic.' Her eyes hardened. She looked at her sister just as she used to when they were little and fighting together. 'You won't bring a drunken workman back to life by being sentimental,' she said softly.

'Drunk! Who said he was drunk?' Laura turned furiously on Jose. She said, just as they had used to say on those occasions, 'I'm going straight up to tell mother.'

'Do, dear,' cooed Jose.

'Mother, can I come into your room?' Laura turned the big glass door-knob.

'Of course, child. Why, what's the matter? What's given you such a colour?' And Mrs Sheridan turned round from her dressing-table. She was trying on a new hat.

'Mother, a man's been killed,' began Laura.

'Not in the garden?' interrupted her mother.

'No, no!'

'Oh, what a fright you gave me!' Mrs Sheridan sighed with relief, and took off the big hat and held it on her knees.

'But listen, mother,' said Laura. Breathless, half-choking, she told the dreadful story. 'Of course, we can't have our party, can we?' she pleaded.

'The band and everybody arriving. They'd hear us, mother; they're nearly neighbours!'

To Laura's astonishment her mother behaved just like Jose; it was harder to bear because she seemed amused. She refused to take Laura seriously.

'But, my dear child, use your common sense. It's only by accident we've heard of it. If some one had died there normally—and I can't understand how they keep alive in those poky little holes—we should still be having our party, shouldn't we?'

Laura had to say 'yes' to that, but she felt it was all wrong. She sat down on her mother's sofa and pinched the cushion frill.

'Mother, isn't it really terribly heartless of us?' she asked.

'Darling!' Mrs Sheridan got up and came over to her, carrying the hat. Before Laura could stop her she had popped it on. 'My child!' said her mother, 'the hat is yours. It's made for you. It's much too young for me. I have never seen you look such a picture. Look at yourself!' And she held up her hand-mirror.

'But, mother,' Laura began again. She couldn't look at herself; she turned aside.

This time Mrs Sheridan lost patience just as Jose had done.

'You are being very absurd, Laura,' she said coldly. 'People like that don't expect sacrifices from us. And it's not very sympathetic to spoil everybody's enjoyment as you're doing now.'

'I don't understand,' said Laura, and she walked quickly out of the room into her own bedroom. There, quite by chance, the first thing she saw was this charming girl in the mirror, in her black hat trimmed with gold daisies, and a long black velvet ribbon. Never had she imagined she could look like that. Is mother right? she thought. And now she hoped her mother was right. Am I being extravagant? Perhaps it was extravagant. Just for a moment she had another glimpse of that poor woman and those little children, and the body being carried into the house. But it all seemed blurred, unreal, like a picture in the newspaper. I'll remember it again after the party's over, she decided. And somehow that seemed quite the best plan . . .

Lunch was over by half past one. By half past two they were all ready for the fray. The green-coated band had arrived and was established in a corner of the tennis-court.

'My dear!' trilled Kitty Maitland, 'aren't they too like frogs for words? You ought to have arranged them round the pond with the conductor in the middle on a leaf.'

Laurie arrived and hailed them on his way to dress. At the sight of him Laura remembered the accident again. She wanted to tell him. If Laurie agreed with the others, then it was bound to be all right. And she followed him into the hall.

'Laurie!'

'Hallo!' He was half-way upstairs, but when he turned round and saw Laura he suddenly puffed out his cheeks and goggled his eyes at her. 'My word, Laura! You do look stunning,' said Laurie. 'What an absolutely topping hat!'

Laura said faintly 'Is it?' and smiled up at Laurie, and didn't tell him after all.

Soon after that people began coming in streams. The band struck up; the hired waiters ran from the house to the marquee. Wherever you looked there were couples strolling, bending to the flowers, greeting, moving on over the lawn. They were like bright birds that had alighted in the Sheridans' garden for this one afternoon, on their way to—where? Ah, what happiness it is to be with people who all are happy, to press hands, press cheeks, smile into eyes.

'Darling Laura, how well you look!'

'What a becoming hat, child!'

'Laura, you look quite Spanish. I've never seen you look so striking.'

And Laura, glowing, answered softly, 'Have you had tea? Won't you have an ice? The passion-fruit ices really are rather special.' She ran to her father and begged him. 'Daddy darling, can't the band have something to drink?'

And the perfect afternoon slowly ripened, slowly faded, slowly its petals closed.

'Never a more delightful garden party . . .' 'The greatest success . . .' 'Quite the most . . .'

Laura helped her mother with the goodbyes. They stood side by side in the porch till it was all over.

'All over, all over, thank heaven,' said Mrs Sheridan. 'Round up the others, Laura. Let's go and have some fresh coffee. I'm exhausted. Yes, it's been very successful. But oh, these parties, these parties! Why will you children insist on giving parties!' And they all of them sat down in the deserted marquee.

'Have a sandwich, daddy dear. I wrote the flag.'

'Thanks.' Mr Sheridan took a bite and the sandwich was gone. He took another. 'I suppose you didn't hear of a beastly accident that happened today?' he said.

'My dear,' said Mrs Sheridan, holding up her hand, 'we did. It nearly ruined the party. Laura insisted we should put it off.'

'Oh, mother!' Laura didn't want to be teased about it.

'It was a horrible affair all the same,' said Mr Sheridan. 'The chap was married too. Lived just below in the lane, and leaves a wife and half a dozen kiddies, so they say.'

An awkward little silence fell. Mrs Sheridan fidgeted with her cup. Really, it was very tactless of father . . .

Suddenly she looked up. There on the table were all those sandwiches, cakes, puffs, all un-eaten, all going to be wasted. She had one of her brilliant ideas.

'I know,' she said. 'Let's make up a basket. Let's send that poor creature some of this perfectly good food. At any rate, it will be the greatest treat for the children. Don't you agree? And she's sure to have neighbours calling in and so on. What a point to have it all ready prepared. Laura!' She jumped up. 'Get me the big basket out of the stairs cupboard.'

'But, mother, do you really think it's a good idea?' said Laura.

Again, how curious, she seemed to be different from them all. To take scraps from their party. Would the poor woman really like that?

'Of course! What's the matter with you today? An hour or two ago you were insisting on us being sympathetic, and now—'

Oh well! Laura ran for the basket. It was filled, it was heaped by her mother.

'Take it yourself, darling,' said she. 'Run down just as you are. No, wait, take the arum lilies too. People of that class are so impressed by arum lilies.'

'The stems will ruin her lace frock,' said practical Jose.

So they would. Just in time. 'Only the basket, then. And, Laura!'—her mother followed her out of the marquee—'don't on any account—'

'What mother?'

No, better not put such ideas into the child's head! 'Nothing! Run along.'

It was just growing dusky as Laura shut their garden gates. A big dog ran by like a shadow. The road gleamed white, and down below in the hollow the little cottages were in deep shade. How quiet it seemed after the afternoon. Here she was going down the hill to somewhere where a man lay dead, and she couldn't realize it. Why couldn't she? She stopped a minute. And it seemed to her that kisses, voices, tinkling spoons, laughter, the smell of crushed grass were somehow inside her. She had no room for anything else. How strange! She looked up at the pale sky, and all she thought was, 'Yes, it was the most successful.'

Now the broad road was crossed. The lane began, smoky and dark. Women in shawls and men's tweed caps hurried by. Men hung over the palings; the children played in the doorways. A low hum came from the mean little cottages. In some of them there was a flicker of light, and a shadow, crab-like, moved across the window. Laura bent her head and hurried on. She wished now she had put on a coat. How her frock shone! And the big hat with the velvet streamer—if only it was another hat! Were the people looking at her? They must be. It was a mistake to have come; she knew all along it was a mistake. Should she go back even now?

No, too late. This was the house. It must be. A dark knot of people stood outside. Beside the gate an old, old woman with a crutch sat in a chair, watching. She had her feet on a newspaper. The voices stopped as Laura drew near. The group parted. It was as though she was expected, as though they had known she was coming here.

Laura was terribly nervous. Tossing the velvet ribbon over her shoulder, she said to a woman standing by, 'Is this Mrs Scott's house?' and the woman, smiling queerly, said, 'It is, my lass.'

Oh, to be away from this! She actually said, 'Help me, God,' as she walked up the tiny path and knocked. To be away from those staring eyes, or to be covered up in anything, one of those women's shawls even. I'll just leave the basket and go, she decided. I shan't even wait for it to be emptied.

Then the door opened. A little woman in black showed in the gloom.

Laura said, 'Are you Mrs Scott?' But to her horror the woman answered, 'Walk in please, miss,' and she was shut in the passage.

'No,' said Laura, 'I don't want to come in. I only want to leave this basket. Mother sent—'

The little woman in the gloomy passage seemed not to have heard her. 'Step this way, please, miss,' she said in an oily voice, and Laura followed her.

She found herself in a wretched little low kitchen, lighted by a smoky lamp. There was a woman sitting before the fire.

'Em,' said the little creature who had let her in. 'Em! It's a young lady.' She turned to Laura. She said meaningly, 'I'm her sister, Miss. You'll excuse 'er, won't you?'

'Oh, but of course!' said Laura. 'Please, please don't disturb her. I—I only want to leave—'

But at that moment the woman at the fire turned round. Her face, puffed up, red, with swollen eyes and swollen lips, looked terrible. She seemed as though she couldn't understand why Laura was there. What did it mean? Why was this stranger standing in the kitchen with a basket? What was it all about? And the poor face puckered up again.

'All right, my dear,' said the other. 'I'll thenk the young lady.'

And again she began, 'You'll excuse her, miss, I'm sure,' and her face, swollen too, tried an oily smile.

Laura only wanted to get out, to get away. She was back in the passage. The door opened. She walked straight through into the bedroom where the dead man was lying.

'You'd like a look at 'im, wouldn't you?' said Em's sister, and she brushed past Laura over to the bed. 'Don't be afraid, my lass,'—and now her voice sounded fond and sly, and fondly she drew down the sheet—''e looks a picture. There's nothing to show. Come along, my dear.'

Laura came.

There lay a young man, fast asleep—sleeping so soundly, so deeply, that he was far, far away from them both. Oh, so remote, so peaceful. He was dreaming. Never wake him up again. His head was sunk in the pillow, his eyes were closed; they were blind under the closed eyelids. He was given up to his dream. What did garden parties and baskets and lace frocks matter to him? He was far from all those things. He was wonderful, beautiful. While they were laughing and while the band was playing, this marvel had come to the lane. Happy . . . happy . . . All is well, said that sleeping face. This is just as it should be. I am content.

But all the same you had to cry, and she couldn't go out of the room without saying something to him. Laura gave a loud childish sob.

'Forgive my hat,' she said.

And this time she didn't wait for Em's sister. She found her way out of the door, down the path, past all those dark people. At the corner of the lane she met Laurie.

He stepped out of the shadow. 'Is that you, Laura?'

'Yes.'

'Mother was getting anxious. Was it all right?'

'Yes, quite. Oh, Laurie!' She took his arm, she pressed up against him.

'I say, you're not crying, are you?' asked her brother.

Laura shook her head. She was.

Laurie put his arm round her shoulder. 'Don't cry,' he said in his warm, loving voice. 'Was it awful?'

'No,' sobbed Laura. 'It was simply marvellous. But, Laurie—' She stopped, she looked at her brother. 'Isn't life,' she stammered, 'isn't life—' But what life was she couldn't explain. No matter. He quite understood.

'*Isn't* it, darling?' said Laurie.

1921   1922

JEAN RHYS
1890–1979

Jean Rhys was born Ella Gwendolen Rees Williams on the small island of Dominica in the West Indies. Her father was a Welsh doctor; her mother, a Creole (that is, a white West Indian) descended from wealthy, slave-holding plantation owners. Rhys was educated at a convent school in Roseau, Dominica, before, at the age of seventeen, leaving the island to attend the Perse School in Cambridge, England; she returned to her birthplace only once, in 1936. Her feelings toward her Caribbean background and childhood were mixed: she deeply appreciated the rich sensations and cross-racial engagements of her tropical experience; haunted by the knowledge of her violent heritage, however, she carried a heavy burden of historical guilt. As a West Indian she felt estranged from mainstream European culture and identified with the suffering of African Caribbeans, yet as a white Creole she grew up feeling out of place amid the predominantly black population of Dominica.

After studying briefly at the Academy of Dramatic Art in London, Rhys worked as a traveling chorus girl, mannequin, film extra, and—during World War I—volunteer cook. In 1919 she left England to marry the first of three husbands, and for many years she lived abroad, mainly in Paris, where she began to write the stories of her first book, *The Left Bank: Sketches and Studies of Present-Day Bohemian Paris* (1927). It was published with an introduction by the established novelist and poet Ford Madox Ford, who was for a time her lover. Ford grasped the link between Rhys's vulnerability as a person and her strength as a writer; he perceived her "terrifying insight . . . and passion for stating the case of the underdog." Rhys declared, "I have only ever written about myself," and indeed much of her writing is semiautobiographical. Her fiction frequently depicts single, economically challenged women, rootless outsiders living in bohemian London or Paris. Her early sketches were followed by her first novel, *Postures* (1928, reprinted as *Quartet* in 1969), in part an account of her affair with Ford; *After Leaving Mr. Mackenzie* (1930), about sexual betrayal; *Voyage in the Dark* (1934), the story of a nineteen-year-old chorus girl in London who has come from Dominica; and *Good Morning, Midnight* (1939), another first-person narrative of a lonely drifter, this time in Paris.

For many years Rhys published nothing more, dropping out of sight and often living in poverty, until, following the enthusiastic reception of a radio adaptation of *Good Morning, Midnight* in 1957, she began to work in earnest on her masterpiece, *Wide Sargasso Sea* (1966). In this novel, set in Jamaica and Dominica in the 1830s and 1840s, Rhys returns to her Caribbean childhood and, in a brilliant act of imaginative sympathy, creates a West Indian prehistory for the first Mrs. Rochester, the madwoman in the attic of Charlotte Brontë's *Jane Eyre*. Altogether Rhys worked on the novel for twenty-one years, amid bouts of depression, loneliness, and alcoholism, but its immediate acclaim gave her the recognition she had so long been denied. She continued to publish works of fiction and autobiography, and in the year before her death received the Commander of the Order of the British Empire.

Like *Wide Sargasso Sea*, some of Rhys's published short stories draw on her Caribbean youth. Books, narratives, and fiction itself figure prominently in some of these stories. In "The Day They Burned the Books," set in the West Indies, a white girl who only partly understands the painful entanglements of class, race, and prejudice tells how a lower-class Englishman has accumulated a trove of books he values for their cultural prestige, while his mulatto wife, embittered by her husband's racism, comes to despise them as emblems of British imperial oppression.

Rhys is one of the great prose stylists of the twentieth century, her language spare yet lyrical, her sentences exactingly written and rewritten to suggest the most in the fewest possible words. Her writing is almost painfully alert to sensory detail, sensitive to the fears and longings of marginalized people, and fierce in its unmasking of the social and psychic consequences of cruelty and injustice.

The Day They Burned the Books

My friend Eddie was a small, thin boy. You could see the blue veins in his wrists and temples. People said that he had consumption[1] and wasn't long for this world. I loved, but sometimes despised him.

His father, Mr Sawyer, was a strange man. Nobody could make out what he was doing in our part of the world at all. He was not a planter or a doctor or a lawyer or a banker. He didn't keep a store. He wasn't a schoolmaster or a government official. He wasn't—that was the point—a gentleman. We had several resident romantics who had fallen in love with the moon on the Caribees[2]—they were all gentlemen and quite unlike Mr Sawyer who hadn't an 'h' in his composition.[3] Besides, he detested the moon and everything else about the Caribbean and he didn't mind telling you so.

He was agent for a small steamship line which in those days linked up Venezuela and Trinidad[4] with the smaller islands, but he couldn't make much out of that. He must have a private income, people decided, but they never decided why he had chosen to settle in a place he didn't like and to marry a coloured woman. Though a decent, respectable, nicely educated coloured woman, mind you.

Mrs Sawyer must have been very pretty once but, what with one thing and another, that was in days gone by.

When Mr Sawyer was drunk—this often happened—he used to be very rude to her. She never answered him.

'Look at the nigger showing off,' he would say; and she would smile as if she knew she ought to see the joke but couldn't. 'You damned, long-eyed, gloomy half-caste,[5] you don't smell right,' he would say; and she never answered, not even to whisper, 'You don't smell right to me, either.'

The story went that once they had ventured to give a dinner party and that when the servant, Mildred, was bringing in coffee, he had pulled Mrs Sawyer's hair. 'Not a wig, you see,' he bawled. Even then, if you can believe it, Mrs Sawyer had laughed and tried to pretend that it was all part of the joke, this mysterious, obscure, sacred English joke.

1. Wasting of the body associated with tuberculosis.
2. Or Caribbees: old term for the group of islands in the southeastern West Indies, now called the Lesser Antilles.

3. His pronunciation marks him as lower-class.
4. Formerly British, Caribbean island off northeast Venezuela.
5. Offensive term for a person of mixed racial descent.

But Mildred told the other servants in the town that her eyes had gone wicked, like a soucriant's[6] eyes, and that afterwards she had picked up some of the hair he pulled out and put it in an envelope, and that Mr Sawyer ought to look out (hair is obeah[7] as well as hands).

Of course, Mrs Sawyer had her compensations. They lived in a very pleasant house in Hill Street. The garden was large and they had a fine mango tree, which bore prolifically. The fruit was small, round, very sweet and juicy—a lovely, red-and-yellow colour when it was ripe. Perhaps it was one of the compensations, I used to think.

Mr Sawyer built a room on to the back of this house. It was unpainted inside and the wood smelt very sweet. Bookshelves lined the walls. Every time the Royal Mail steamer[8] came in it brought a package for him, and gradually the empty shelves filled.

Once I went there with Eddie to borrow *The Arabian Nights*.[9] That was on a Saturday afternoon, one of those hot, still afternoons when you felt that everything had gone to sleep, even the water in the gutters. But Mrs Sawyer was not asleep. She put her head in at the door and looked at us, and I knew that she hated the room and hated the books.

It was Eddie with the pale blue eyes and straw-coloured hair—the living image of his father, though often as silent as his mother—who first infected me with doubts about 'home', meaning England. He would be so quiet when others who had never seen it—none of us had ever seen it—were talking about its delights, gesticulating freely as we talked—London, the beautiful, rosy-cheeked ladies, the theatres, the shops, the fog, the blazing coal fires in winter, the exotic food (whitebait[1] eaten to the sound of violins), strawberries and cream—the word 'strawberries' always spoken with a guttural and throaty sound which we imagined to be the proper English pronunciation.

'I don't like strawberries,' Eddie said on one occasion.

'You *don't like* strawberries?'

'No, and I don't like daffodils either. Dad's always going on about them. He says they lick the flowers here into a cocked hat[2] and I bet that's a lie.'

We were all too shocked to say, 'You don't know a thing about it.' We were so shocked that nobody spoke to him for the rest of the day. But I for one admired him. I also was tired of learning and reciting poems in praise of daffodils, and my relations with the few 'real' English boys and girls I had met were awkward. I had discovered that if I called myself English they would snub me haughtily: 'You're not English; you're a horrid colonial.' 'Well, I don't much want to be English,' I would say. 'It's much more fun to be French or Spanish or something like that—and, as a matter of fact, I am a bit.' Then I was too killingly funny, quite ridiculous. Not only a horrid colonial, but also ridiculous. Heads I win, tails you lose—that was the English. I had thought about all this, and thought hard, but I had never dared to tell anybody what I thought and I realized that Eddie had been very bold.

---

6. Female vampire, in Caribbean legend.
7. A charm or fetish used in Afro-Caribbean witchcraft or sorcery.
8. Ship, owned by the Royal Mail Steam Packet Company, that ferried mail from London to the West Indies beginning in 1841.
9. Also called *The Thousand and One Nights*, a collection of old stories, largely Persian, Ara-

bian, and Indian in origin.
1. Young of a small fish, such as herring, considered a delicacy when cooked whole.
2. From *knocked into a cocked hat*: make them look terrible by comparison. Daffodils are common in English poetry, but do not grow in the West Indies.

But he was bold, and stronger than you would think. For one thing, he never felt the heat; some coldness in his fair skin resisted it. He didn't burn red or brown, he didn't freckle much.

Hot days seemed to make him feel especially energetic. 'Now we'll run twice round the lawn and then you can pretend you're dying of thirst in the desert and that I'm an Arab chieftain bringing you water.'

'You must drink slowly,' he would say, 'for if you're very thirsty and you drink quickly you die.'

So I learnt the voluptuousness of drinking slowly when you are very thirsty—small mouthful by small mouthful, until the glass of pink, iced Coca-Cola was empty.

Just after my twelfth birthday Mr Sawyer died suddenly, and as Eddie's special friend I went to the funeral, wearing a new white dress. My straight hair was damped with sugar and water the night before and plaited into tight little plaits, so that it should be fluffy for the occasion.

When it was all over everybody said how nice Mrs Sawyer had looked, walking like a queen behind the coffin and crying her eyeballs out at the right moment, and wasn't Eddie a funny boy? He hadn't cried at all.

After this Eddie and I took possession of the room with the books. No one else ever entered it, except Mildred to sweep and dust in the mornings, and gradually the ghost of Mr Sawyer pulling Mrs Sawyer's hair faded, though this took a little time. The blinds were always halfway down and going in out of the sun was like stepping into a pool of brown-green water. It was empty except for the bookshelves, a desk with a green baize[3] top and a wicker rocking-chair.

'My room,' Eddie called it. 'My books,' he would say, 'my books.'

I don't know how long this lasted. I don't know whether it was weeks after Mr Sawyer's death or months after, that I see myself and Eddie in the room. But there we are and there, unexpectedly, are Mrs Sawyer and Mildred. Mrs Sawyer's mouth tight, her eyes pleased. She is pulling all the books out of the shelves and piling them into two heaps. The big, fat glossy ones—the good-looking ones, Mildred explains in a whisper—lie in one heap. The *Encyclopaedia Britannica*, *British Flowers, Birds and Beasts*, various histories, books with maps, Froude's *English in the West Indies*[4] and so on—they are going to be sold. The unimportant books, with paper covers or damaged covers or torn pages, lie in another heap. They are going to be burnt—yes, burnt.

Mildred's expression was extraordinary as she said that—half hugely delighted, half shocked, even frightened. And as for Mrs Sawyer—well, I knew bad temper (I had often seen it), I knew rage, but this was hate. I recognized the difference at once and stared at her curiously. I edged closer to her so that I could see the titles of the books she was handling.

It was the poetry shelf. *Poems*, Lord Byron, *Poetical Works*, Milton, and so on. Vlung, vlung, vlung—all thrown into the heap that were to be sold. But a book by Christina Rossetti, though also bound in leather, went into the heap that was to be burnt, and by a flicker in Mrs Sawyer's eyes I knew that worse than men who wrote books were women who wrote books—infinitely worse. Men could be mercifully shot; women must be tortured.

---

3. Feltlike fabric.
4. Published in 1888 by the English historian James Anthony Froude (1818–1894).

Mrs Sawyer did not seem to notice that we were there, but she was breathing free and easy and her hands had got the rhythm of tearing and pitching. She looked beautiful, too—beautiful as the sky outside which was a very dark blue, or the mango tree, long sprays of brown and gold.

When Eddie said 'no', she did not even glance at him.

'No,' he said again in a high voice. 'Not that one. I was reading that one.'

She laughed and he rushed at her, his eyes starting out of his head, shrieking, 'Now I've got to hate you too. Now I hate you too.'

He snatched the book out of her hand and gave her a violent push. She fell into the rocking-chair.

Well, I wasn't going to be left out of all this, so I grabbed a book from the condemned pile and dived under Mildred's outstretched arm.

Then we were both in the garden. We ran along the path, bordered with crotons.[5] We pelted down the path though they did not follow us and we could hear Mildred laughing—kyah, kyah, kyah, kyah. As I ran I put the book I had taken into the loose front of my brown holland dress. It felt warm and alive.

When we got into the street we walked sedately, for we feared the black children's ridicule. I felt very happy, because I had saved this book and it was my book and I would read it from the beginning to the triumphant words 'The End'. But I was uneasy when I thought of Mrs Sawyer.

'What will she do?' I said.

'Nothing,' Eddie said. 'Not to me.'

He was white as a ghost in his sailor suit, a blue-white even in the setting sun, and his father's sneer was clamped on his face.

'But she'll tell your mother all sorts of lies about you,' he said. 'She's an awful liar. She can't make up a story to save her life, but she makes up lies about people all right.'

'My mother won't take any notice of her,' I said. Though I was not at all sure.

'Why not? Because she's . . . because she isn't white?'

Well, I knew the answer to that one. Whenever the subject was brought up—people's relations and whether they had a drop of coloured blood or whether they hadn't—my father would grow impatient and interrupt. 'Who's white?' he would say. 'Damned few.'

So I said, 'Who's white? Damned few.'

'You can go to the devil,' Eddie said. 'She's prettier than your mother. When she's asleep her mouth smiles and she has your curling eyelashes and quantities and quantities and *quantities* of hair.'

'Yes,' I said truthfully. 'She's prettier than my mother.'

It was a red sunset that evening, a huge, sad, frightening sunset.

'Look, let's go back,' I said. 'If you're sure she won't be vexed with you, let's go back. It'll be dark soon.'

At his gate he asked me not to go. 'Don't go yet, don't go yet.'

We sat under the mango tree and I was holding his hand when he began to cry. Drops fell on my hand like the water from the dripstone in the filter[6] in our yard. Then I began to cry too and when I felt my own tears on my hand I thought, 'Now perhaps we're married.'

5. Tropical plants.
6. Dripstone is a sandstone used as a filter to clean water for household use.

'Yes, certainly, now we're married,' I thought. But I didn't say anything. I didn't say a thing until I was sure he had stopped. Then I asked, 'What's your book?'

'It's *Kim*,'[7] he said. 'But it got torn. It starts at page twenty now. What's the one you took?'

'I don't know, it's too dark to see,' I said.

When I got home I rushed into my bedroom and locked the door because I knew that this book was the most important thing that had ever happened to me and I did not want anybody to be there when I looked at it.

But I was very disappointed, because it was in French and seemed dull. *Fort Comme La Mort*,[8] it was called. . . .

1960

---

7. Novel (1901) by the English writer Rudyard Kipling (1865–1936), about an Irish orphan boy growing up in India.

8. *Strong as Death*, 1889 novel by the French writer Guy de Maupassant (1850–1893).

SAMUEL BECKETT
1906–1989

Samuel Beckett was born near Dublin. Like W. B. Yeats, Bernard Shaw, and Oscar Wilde, he came from an Anglo-Irish Protestant family. He received a B.A. from Trinity College, Dublin, and after teaching English at the École Normale Supérieure in Paris for two years, returned to Trinity College to take his M.A. in 1931. A year later he gave up teaching to write, and having produced an insightful essay on the early stages of James Joyce's *Finnegans Wake*, Beckett also worked as Joyce's amanuensis (secretary) and translator. In 1937 he settled permanently in Paris. There, during World War II, he joined an underground group in the anti-Nazi resistance and, after the group was betrayed, barely escaped into unoccupied France. From the mid-1940s he generally wrote in French and subsequently translated some of his work into an eloquent, Irish-inflected English. His early novels— *Murphy* (1938; Eng. trans., 1957); *Watt* (1953); and the trilogy, *Molloy* (1951; 1955), *Malone Dies* (1951; 1956), and *The Unnameable* (1953; 1958)—have been hailed as masterpieces and precursors of postmodern fiction; but he is best-known for his plays, especially *Waiting for Godot* (1952; 1954) and *Endgame* (1957; 1958). He received the Nobel Prize in Literature in 1969.

Not much happens in a Beckett play; there is little characterization, little plot, and little incident. Characters engage in dialogue or dialectical monologues that go nowhere. There is no progression, no development, no resolution. Rambling exchanges and repetitive actions enact the lack of a fixed center, of meaning, of purpose, in the lives depicted. Yet the characters persist in their habitual, almost ritualistic, activities; they go on talking, even if only to themselves. In spite of the reiterated theme of nonexistence, the characters go on existing—if minimally: a stream of discourse, of thought and will, a consciousness questioning its own meaning and purpose. In *Waiting for Godot* the main characters wait for an arrival that is constantly deferred. They inhabit a bleak landscape seemingly confined to

The second act of *Waiting for Godot*. For the 1961 production at the Paris Odeon, the Italian sculptor Alberto Giacometti, Beckett's friend, designed the tree.

one road, one tree; they talk of moving on, yet never leave. In *Endgame* the main characters—irritable and peevish—live inside a room with two small, high windows, outside of which everything may or may not be dead. Two of their parents live inside garbage cans and appear only from the shoulders up. Subsequent plays restrict the acting space to smaller spaces, such as urns or a mound in which the actor is buried; characters are physically confined or disabled, until *Not I* (1973) presents the most minimal embodiment of human consciousness available to theatrical representation: a disembodied mouth.

Beckett focuses his work on fundamental questions of existence and nonexistence, the mind and the body, the self as known from within and as seen from the outside or in retrospect. Joyce's artistic integrity and stream of consciousness technique influenced him, but the minimalism of Beckett's plays and fiction contrast with the maximalism of Joyce's *Ulysses* and *Finnegans Wake*. "I realised that Joyce had gone as far as one could in the direction of knowing more, in control of one's material," he told the biographer James Knowlson. "I realised my own way was in impoverishment, in lack of knowledge and in taking away, in subtracting rather than adding."

The daring minimalism of *Waiting for Godot*—its radically diminished setting, clownish characters, and circular plot—is often seen as having transformed serious theater for the second half of the twentieth century. Because Act II of the play largely repeats Act I, with subtle variations, the Irish critic Vivian Mercier famously called *Waiting for Godot* "a play in which nothing happens, twice." As they wait for an appointment with the mysteriously indeterminate Godot, the play's central characters, Vladimir and Estragon, nicknamed Didi and Gogo, haplessly amuse, comfort, and annoy each other. The play implicitly contrasts their affable, if vexed, friendship with the master-slave relation between another pair of characters who appear twice on the scene: the sometimes brutal Pozzo and the ironically named Lucky, whipped and driven like an animal by his master. As in subsequent Beckett plays, this one juxtaposes vaudeville, slapstick, and other comic traditions with stark insight into the meaningless void beneath our feet, however we may try to cover it up by speech and action. Blinded and humbled by the second act, Pozzo cries out, "one day we were born, one day we shall die," adding, "They give birth astride of a grave, the light gleams an instant, then it's night once more." Combining such bleak pathos with horseplay, banter, pranks, juggling, and crude puns, *Waiting for Godot* shares its tragicomic quality with absurdist drama, which disrupts the conventions of realist drama, draws attention to its own fictionality, and refuses to provide hierarchies of significance. Reduced to bare essentials, desperately seeking ways to pass the time during their seemingly interminable wait, the characters in *Waiting for Godot*—though often behaving as if bumbling protagonists of a farce—raise unsettling questions about meaning and absurdity, power and dependency, time and repetition, language and death.

Waiting for Godot

A Tragicomedy in Two Acts

CHARACTERS

ESTRAGON   POZZO
VLADIMIR   A BOY
LUCKY

Act 1

A country road. A tree.
Evening.

[ESTRAGON, *sitting on a low mound, is trying to take off his boot. He pulls at it with both hands, panting. He gives up, exhausted, rests, tries again. As before.*]

[*Enter* VLADIMIR.]

ESTRAGON [*giving up again*]   Nothing to be done.
VLADIMIR [*advancing with short, stiff strides, legs wide apart*]   I'm beginning to come round to that opinion. All my life I've tried to put it from me, saying, Vladimir, be reasonable, you haven't yet tried everything. And I resumed the struggle. [*He broods, musing on the struggle. Turning to* ESTRAGON.] So there you are again.
ESTRAGON   Am I?
VLADIMIR   I'm glad to see you back. I thought you were gone for ever.
ESTRAGON   Me too.
VLADIMIR   Together again at last! We'll have to celebrate this. But how? [*He reflects.*] Get up till I embrace you.
ESTRAGON [*irritably*]   Not now, not now.
VLADIMIR [*hurt, coldly*]   May one enquire where His Highness spent the night?
ESTRAGON   In a ditch.
VLADIMIR [*admiringly*]   A ditch! Where?
ESTRAGON [*without gesture*]   Over there.
VLADIMIR   And they didn't beat you?

ESTRAGON   Beat me? Certainly they beat me.

VLADIMIR   The same lot as usual?

ESTRAGON   The same? I don't know.

VLADIMIR   When I think of it . . . all these years . . . but for me . . . where would you be . . . [*Decisively.*] You'd be nothing more than a little heap of bones at the present minute, no doubt about it.

ESTRAGON   And what of it?

VLADIMIR [*gloomily*]   It's too much for one man. [*Pause. Cheerfully.*] On the other hand what's the good of losing heart now, that's what I say. We should have thought of it a million years ago, in the nineties.[1]

ESTRAGON   Ah stop blathering and help me off with this bloody thing.

VLADIMIR   Hand in hand from the top of the Eiffel Tower, among the first.[2] We were respectable in those days. Now it's too late. They wouldn't even let us up. [ESTRAGON *tears at his boot.*] What are you doing?

ESTRAGON   Taking off my boot. Did that never happen to you?

VLADIMIR   Boots must be taken off every day, I'm tired telling you that. Why don't you listen to me?

ESTRAGON [*feebly*]   Help me!

VLADIMIR   It hurts?

ESTRAGON [*angrily*]   Hurts! He wants to know if it hurts!

VLADIMIR [*angrily*]   No one ever suffers but you. I don't count. I'd like to hear what you'd say if you had what I have.

ESTRAGON   It hurts?

VLADIMIR [*angrily*]   Hurts! He wants to know if it hurts!

ESTRAGON [*pointing*]   You might button it all the same.

VLADIMIR [*stooping*]   True. [*He buttons his fly.*] Never neglect the little things of life.

ESTRAGON   What do you expect, you always wait till the last moment.

VLADIMIR [*musingly*]   The last moment . . . [*He meditates.*] Hope deferred maketh the something sick, who said that?[3]

ESTRAGON   Why don't you help me?

VLADIMIR   Sometimes I feel it coming all the same. Then I go all queer. [*He takes off his hat, peers inside it, feels about inside it, shakes it, puts it on again.*] How shall I say? Relieved and at the same time . . . [*He searches for the word.*] . . . appalled. [*With emphasis.*] AP-PALLED. [*He takes off his hat again, peers inside it.*] Funny. [*He knocks on the crown as though to dislodge a foreign body, peers into it again, puts it on again.*] Nothing to be done. [ESTRAGON *with a supreme effort succeeds in pulling off his boot. He peers inside it, feels about inside it, turns it upside down, shakes it, looks on the ground to see if anything has fallen out, finds nothing, feels inside it again, staring sightlessly before him.*] Well?

ESTRAGON   Nothing.

VLADIMIR   Show.

ESTRAGON   There's nothing to show.

VLADIMIR   Try and put it on again.

---

1. I.e., the 1890s. "It": suicide.
2. I.e., they should have jumped from the Eiffel Tower, completed in 1889; it was the tallest human-built structure in the world until 1930.

3. "Hope deferred maketh the heart sick: but when the desire cometh, it is a tree of life" (Proverbs 13.12).

ESTRAGON [*examining his foot*]   I'll air it for a bit.

VLADIMIR   There's man all over for you, blaming on his boots the faults of his feet. [*He takes off his hat again, peers inside it, feels about inside it, knocks on the crown, blows into it, puts it on again.*] This is getting alarming. [*Silence. Vladimir deep in thought, Estragon pulling at his toes.*] One of the thieves was saved.[4] [*Pause.*] It's a reasonable percentage. [*Pause.*] Gogo.

ESTRAGON   What?

VLADIMIR   Suppose we repented.

ESTRAGON   Repented what?

VLADIMIR   Oh . . . [*He reflects.*] We wouldn't have to go into the details.

ESTRAGON   Our being born?

[VLADIMIR *breaks into a hearty laugh which he immediately stifles, his hand pressed to his pubis, his face contorted.*]

VLADIMIR   One daren't even laugh any more.

ESTRAGON   Dreadful privation.

VLADIMIR   Merely smile. [*He smiles suddenly from ear to ear, keeps smiling, ceases as suddenly.*] It's not the same thing. Nothing to be done. [*Pause.*] Gogo.

ESTRAGON [*irritably*]   What is it?

VLADIMIR   Did you ever read the Bible?

ESTRAGON   The Bible . . . [*He reflects.*] I must have taken a look at it.

VLADIMIR   Do you remember the Gospels?

ESTRAGON   I remember the maps of the Holy Land. Coloured they were. Very pretty. The Dead Sea[5] was pale blue. The very look of it made me thirsty. That's where we'll go, I used to say, that's where we'll go for our honeymoon. We'll swim. We'll be happy.

VLADIMIR   You should have been a poet.

ESTRAGON   I was. [*Gesture towards his rags.*] Isn't that obvious?

[*Silence.*]

VLADIMIR   Where was I . . . How's your foot?

ESTRAGON   Swelling visibly.

VLADIMIR   Ah yes, the two thieves. Do you remember the story?

ESTRAGON   No.

VLADIMIR   Shall I tell it to you?

ESTRAGON   No.

VLADIMIR   It'll pass the time. [*Pause.*] Two thieves, crucified at the same time as our Saviour. One—

ESTRAGON   Our what?

VLADIMIR   Our Saviour. Two thieves. One is supposed to have been saved and the other . . . [*he searches for the contrary of saved*] . . . damned.

ESTRAGON   Saved from what?

VLADIMIR   Hell.

ESTRAGON   I'm going.

[*He does not move.*]

VLADIMIR   And yet . . . [*pause*] . . . how is it—this is not boring you I hope—how is it that of the four Evangelists only one speaks of a thief

4. I.e., one of the thieves crucified at the same time as Jesus. Cf. Luke 23.32–43.
5. The salt lake, or inland sea, between Israel and Jordan. "Gospels": the four books of the Bible written by the four Evangelists, Matthew, Mark, Luke, and John.

being saved. The four of them were there—or thereabouts—and only one speaks of a thief being saved. [*Pause.*] Come on, Gogo, return the ball, can't you, once in a way?

ESTRAGON [*with exaggerated enthusiasm*]   I find this really most extraordinarily interesting.

VLADIMIR   One out of four. Of the other three two don't mention any thieves at all and the third says that both of them abused him.[6]

ESTRAGON   Who?

VLADIMIR   What?

ESTRAGON   What's all this about? Abused who?

VLADIMIR   The Saviour.

ESTRAGON   Why?

VLADIMIR   Because he wouldn't save them.

ESTRAGON   From hell?

VLADIMIR   Imbecile! From death.

ESTRAGON   I thought you said hell.

VLADIMIR   From death, from death.

ESTRAGON   Well what of it?

VLADIMIR   Then the two of them must have been damned.

ESTRAGON   And why not?

VLADIMIR   But one of the four says that one of the two was saved.

ESTRAGON   Well? They don't agree and that's all there is to it.

VLADIMIR   But all four were there. And only one speaks of a thief being saved. Why believe him rather than the others?

ESTRAGON   Who believes him?

VLADIMIR   Everybody. It's the only version they know.

ESTRAGON   People are bloody ignorant apes.

[*He rises painfully, goes limping to extreme left, halts, gazes into distance off with his hand screening his eyes, turns, goes to extreme right, gazes into distance,* VLADIMIR *watches him, then goes and picks up the boot, peers into it, drops it hastily.*]

VLADIMIR   Pah!

[*He spits.* ESTRAGON *moves to center, halts with his back to auditorium.*]

ESTRAGON   Charming spot. [*He turns, advances to front, halts facing auditorium.*] Inspiring prospects. [*He turns to* VLADIMIR.] Let's go.

VLADIMIR   We can't.

ESTRAGON   Why not?

VLADIMIR   We're waiting for Godot.

ESTRAGON [*despairingly*]   Ah! [*Pause.*] You're sure it was here?

VLADIMIR   What?

ESTRAGON   That we were to wait.

VLADIMIR   He said by the tree. [*They look at the tree.*] Do you see any others?

ESTRAGON   What is it?

VLADIMIR   I don't know. A willow.[7]

ESTRAGON   Where are the leaves?

6. Verbally attacked him, or used foul language toward him. "The other three": Matthew, Mark, and John. In fact, all the Gospels mention the thieves. John calls them "two others," and both Matthew and Mark say that the thieves verbally attacked Jesus. Cf. John 19.18, Matthew 27.38–44, and Mark 15.27–32.

7. A tree often associated with sadness or grief.

VLADIMIR   It must be dead.

ESTRAGON   No more weeping.

VLADIMIR   Or perhaps it's not the season.

ESTRAGON   Looks to me more like a bush.

VLADIMIR   A shrub.

ESTRAGON   A bush.

VLADIMIR   A—. What are you insinuating? That we've come to the wrong place?

ESTRAGON   He should be here.

VLADIMIR   He didn't say for sure he'd come.

ESTRAGON   And if he doesn't come?

VLADIMIR   We'll come back tomorrow.

ESTRAGON   And then the day after tomorrow.

VLADIMIR   Possibly.

ESTRAGON   And so on.

VLADIMIR   The point is—

ESTRAGON   Until he comes.

VLADIMIR   You're merciless.

ESTRAGON   We came here yesterday.

VLADIMIR   Ah no, there you're mistaken.

ESTRAGON   What did we do yesterday?

VLADIMIR   What did we do yesterday?

ESTRAGON   Yes.

VLADIMIR   Why . . . [*Angrily.*] Nothing is certain when you're about.

ESTRAGON   In my opinion we were here.

VLADIMIR [*looking round*]   You recognize the place?

ESTRAGON   I didn't say that.

VLADIMIR   Well?

ESTRAGON   That makes no difference.

VLADIMIR   All the same . . . that tree . . . [*turning towards auditorium*] that bog . . .

ESTRAGON   You're sure it was this evening?

VLADIMIR   What?

ESTRAGON   That we were to wait.

VLADIMIR   He said Saturday. [*Pause.*] I think.

ESTRAGON   You think.

VLADIMIR   I must have made a note of it. [*He fumbles in his pockets, bursting with miscellaneous rubbish.*]

ESTRAGON [*very insidious*]   But what Saturday? And is it Saturday? Is it not rather Sunday? [*Pause.*] Or Monday? [*Pause.*] Or Friday?

VLADIMIR [*looking wildly about him, as though the date was inscribed in the landscape*]   It's not possible!

ESTRAGON   Or Thursday?

VLADIMIR   What'll we do?

ESTRAGON   If he came yesterday and we weren't here you may be sure he won't come again today.

VLADIMIR   But you say we were here yesterday.

ESTRAGON   I may be mistaken. [*Pause.*] Let's stop talking for a minute, do you mind?

VLADIMIR [*feebly*]   All right. [ESTRAGON *sits down on the mound.* VLADI-MIR *paces agitatedly to and fro, halting from time to time to gaze into distance off.* ESTRAGON *falls asleep.* VLADIMIR *halts finally before* ESTRAGON.] Gogo! . . . Gogo! . . . GOGO!

    [ESTRAGON *wakes with a start.*]

ESTRAGON [*restored to the horror of his situation*] I was asleep! [*Despairingly.*] Why will you never let me sleep?

VLADIMIR I felt lonely.

ESTRAGON I had a dream.

VLADIMIR Don't tell me!

ESTRAGON I dreamt that—

VLADIMIR DON'T TELL ME!

ESTRAGON [*gesture towards the universe*] This one is enough for you? [*Silence.*] It's not nice of you, Didi. Who am I to tell my private nightmares to if I can't tell them to you?

VLADIMIR Let them remain private. You know I can't bear that.

ESTRAGON [*coldly*] There are times when I wonder if it wouldn't be better for us to part.

VLADIMIR You wouldn't go far.

ESTRAGON That would be too bad, really too bad. [*Pause.*] Wouldn't it, Didi, be really too bad? [*Pause.*] When you think of the beauty of the way. [*Pause.*] And the goodness of the wayfarers. [*Pause. Wheedling.*] Wouldn't it, Didi?

VLADIMIR Calm yourself.

ESTRAGON [*voluptuously*] Calm . . . calm . . . The English say cawm. [*Pause.*] You know the story of the Englishman in the brothel?

VLADIMIR Yes.

ESTRAGON Tell it to me.

VLADIMIR Ah stop it!

ESTRAGON An Englishman having drunk a little more than usual proceeds to a brothel. The bawd asks him if he wants a fair one, a dark one or a red-haired one.[8] Go on.

VLADIMIR STOP IT!

    [*Exit* VLADIMIR *hurriedly.* ESTRAGON *gets up and follows him as far as the limit of the stage. Gestures of* ESTRAGON *like those of a spectator encouraging a pugilist.*[9] *Enter* VLADIMIR. *He brushes past* ESTRAGON, *crosses the stage with bowed head.* ESTRAGON *takes a step towards him, halts.*]

ESTRAGON [*gently*] You wanted to speak to me? [*Silence.* ESTRAGON *takes a step forward.*] You had something to say to me? [*Silence. Another step forward.*] Didi . . .

VLADIMIR [*without turning*] I've nothing to say to you.

ESTRAGON [*step forward*] You're angry? [*Silence. Step forward.*] Forgive me. [*Silence. Step forward.* ESTRAGON *lays his hand on* VLADIMIR's *shoulder.*] Come, Didi. [*Silence.*] Give me your hand. [VLADIMIR *half turns.*] Embrace me! [VLADIMIR *stiffens.*] Don't be stubborn! [VLADIMIR *softens. They embrace.* ESTRAGON *recoils.*] You stink of garlic!

---

8. In one version of the rest of the bawdy story, the Englishman replies that he wants a boy. Taken aback, the bawd threatens to call a policeman, to which the Englishman replies, "Oh, no, they're too gritty." In another version, he is shown through a series of doors, marked by hair color and size of private parts, and finally selects one marked "Grands Cons" (in French slang, literally, large vaginas; figuratively, big idiots). Confirming him as *con*, or idiot, his choice lands him back on the street.

9. I.e., a boxer.

VLADIMIR   It's for the kidneys. [*Silence.* ESTRAGON *looks attentively at the tree.*] What do we do now?

ESTRAGON   Wait.

VLADIMIR   Yes, but while waiting.

ESTRAGON   What about hanging ourselves?

VLADIMIR   Hmm. It'd give us an erection.

ESTRAGON [*highly excited*]   An erection!

VLADIMIR   With all that follows. Where it falls mandrakes grow. That's why they shriek when you pull them up.[1] Did you not know that?

ESTRAGON   Let's hang ourselves immediately!

VLADIMIR   From a bough? [*They go towards the tree.*] I wouldn't trust it.

ESTRAGON   We can always try.

VLADIMIR   Go ahead.

ESTRAGON   After you.

VLADIMIR   No no, you first.

ESTRAGON   Why me?

VLADIMIR   You're lighter than I am.

ESTRAGON   Just so!

VLADIMIR   I don't understand.

ESTRAGON   Use your intelligence, can't you?
            [VLADIMIR *uses his intelligence.*]

VLADIMIR [*finally*]   I remain in the dark.

ESTRAGON   This is how it is. [*He reflects.*] The bough . . . the bough . . . [*Angrily.*] *Use your head, can't you?*

VLADIMIR   You're my only hope.

ESTRAGON [*with effort*]   Gogo light—bough not break—Gogo dead. Didi heavy—bough break—Didi alone. Whereas—

VLADIMIR   I hadn't thought of that.

ESTRAGON   If it hangs you it'll hang anything.

VLADIMIR   But am I heavier than you?

ESTRAGON   So you tell me. I don't know. There's an even chance. Or nearly.

VLADIMIR   Well? What do we do?

ESTRAGON   Don't let's do anything. It's safer.

VLADIMIR   Let's wait and see what he says.

ESTRAGON   Who?

VLADIMIR   Godot.

ESTRAGON   Good idea.

VLADIMIR   Let's wait till we know exactly how we stand.

ESTRAGON   On the other hand it might be better to strike the iron before it freezes.[2]

VLADIMIR   I'm curious to hear what he has to offer. Then we'll take it or leave it.

ESTRAGON   What exactly did we ask him for?

VLADIMIR   Were you not there?

ESTRAGON   I can't have been listening.

VLADIMIR   Oh . . . Nothing very definite.

---

1. The mandrake is a plant with a forked root that resembles the human body, which, according to medieval European folklore, was said to grow from the semen ejaculated by hanged men and to shriek when uprooted. Hearing the shriek was said to be fatal, or to make the listener go mad.

2. Cf. the proverb "Strike while the iron is hot."

ESTRAGON   A kind of prayer.

VLADIMIR   Precisely.

ESTRAGON   A vague supplication.

VLADIMIR   Exactly.

ESTRAGON   And what did he reply?

VLADIMIR   That he'd see.

ESTRAGON   That he couldn't promise anything.

VLADIMIR   That he'd have to think it over.

ESTRAGON   In the quiet of his home.

VLADIMIR   Consult his family.

ESTRAGON   His friends.

VLADIMIR   His agents.

ESTRAGON   His correspondents.

VLADIMIR   His books.

ESTRAGON   His bank account.

VLADIMIR   Before taking[3] a decision.

ESTRAGON   It's the normal thing.

VLADIMIR   Is it not?

ESTRAGON   I think it is.

VLADIMIR   I think so too.

>   [*Silence.*]

ESTRAGON [*anxious*]   And we?

VLADIMIR   I beg your pardon?

ESTRAGON   I said, And we?

VLADIMIR   I don't understand.

ESTRAGON   Where do we come in?

VLADIMIR   Come in?

ESTRAGON   Take your time.

VLADIMIR   Come in? On our hands and knees.

ESTRAGON   As bad as that?

VLADIMIR   Your Worship wishes to assert his prerogatives?

ESTRAGON   We've no rights any more?

>   [*Laugh of* VLADIMIR, *stifled as before, less the smile.*]

VLADIMIR   You'd make me laugh if it wasn't prohibited.

ESTRAGON   We've lost our rights?

VLADIMIR [*distinctly*]   We got rid of them.

>   [*Silence. They remain motionless, arms dangling, heads sunk, sagging at the knees.*]

ESTRAGON [*feebly*]   We're not tied? [*Pause.*] We're not—

VLADIMIR   Listen!

>   [*They listen, grotesquely rigid.*]

ESTRAGON   I hear nothing.

VLADIMIR   Hsst! [*They listen.* ESTRAGON *loses his balance, almost falls. He clutches the arm of* VLADIMIR, *who totters. They listen, huddled together.*] Nor I.

>   [*Sighs of relief. They relax and separate.*]

ESTRAGON   You gave me a fright.

VLADIMIR   I thought it was he.

ESTRAGON   Who?

---

3. I.e., making.

VLADIMIR Godot.

ESTRAGON Pah! The wind in the reeds.

VLADIMIR I could have sworn I heard shouts.

ESTRAGON And why would he shout?

VLADIMIR At his horse.

[Silence.]

ESTRAGON [violently] I'm hungry!

VLADIMIR Do you want a carrot?

ESTRAGON Is that all there is?

VLADIMIR I might have some turnips.

ESTRAGON Give me a carrot. [VLADIMIR rummages in his pockets, takes out a turnip and gives it to ESTRAGON who takes a bite out of it. Angrily.] It's a turnip!

VLADIMIR Oh pardon! I could have sworn it was a carrot. [He rummages again in his pockets, finds nothing but turnips.] All that's turnips. [He rummages.] You must have eaten the last. [He rummages.] Wait, I have it. [He brings out a carrot and gives it to ESTRAGON.] There, dear fellow, [ESTRAGON wipes the carrot on his sleeve and begins to eat it.] Make it last, that's the end of them.

ESTRAGON [chewing] I asked you a question.

VLADIMIR Ah.

ESTRAGON Did you reply?

VLADIMIR How's the carrot?

ESTRAGON It's a carrot.

VLADIMIR So much the better, so much the better. [Pause.] What was it you wanted to know?

ESTRAGON I've forgotten. [Chews.] That's what annoys me. [He looks at the carrot appreciatively, dangles it between finger and thumb.] I'll never forget this carrot. [He sucks the end of it meditatively.] Ah yes, now I remember.

VLADIMIR Well?

ESTRAGON [his mouth full, vacuously] We're not tied?

VLADIMIR I don't hear a word you're saying.

ESTRAGON [chews, swallows] I'm asking you if we're tied.

VLADIMIR Tied?

ESTRAGON Ti-ed.

VLADIMIR How do you mean tied?

ESTRAGON Down.

VLADIMIR But to whom? By whom?

ESTRAGON To your man.

VLADIMIR To Godot? Tied to Godot! What an idea! No question of it. [Pause.] For the moment.

ESTRAGON His name is Godot?

VLADIMIR I think so.

ESTRAGON Fancy that. [He raises what remains of the carrot by the stub of leaf, twirls it before his eyes.] Funny, the more you eat the worse it gets.

VLADIMIR With me it's just the opposite.

ESTRAGON In other words?

VLADIMIR I get used to the muck as I go along.

ESTRAGON [after prolonged reflection] Is that the opposite?

VLADIMIR Question of temperament.

ESTRAGON   Of character.

VLADIMIR   Nothing you can do about it.

ESTRAGON   No use struggling.

VLADIMIR   One is what one is.

ESTRAGON   No use wriggling.

VLADIMIR   The essential doesn't change.

ESTRAGON   Nothing to be done. [*He proffers the remains of the carrot to* VLADIMIR.] Like to finish it?

> [*A terrible cry, close at hand.* ESTRAGON *drops the carrot. They remain motionless, then together make a sudden rush towards the wings.* ESTRAGON *stops halfway, runs back, picks up the carrot, stuffs it in his pocket, runs to rejoin* VLADIMIR *who is waiting for him, stops again, runs back, picks up his boot, runs to rejoin* VLADIMIR. *Huddled together, shoulders hunched, cringing away from the menace, they wait.*]

> [*Enter* POZZO *and* LUCKY. POZZO *drives* LUCKY *by means of a rope passed round his neck, so that* LUCKY *is the first to enter, followed by the rope which is long enough to let him reach the middle of the stage before* POZZO *appears.* LUCKY *carries a heavy bag, a folding stool, a picnic basket and a greatcoat,[4]* POZZO *a whip.*]

POZZO [*off*]   On! [*Crack of whip.* POZZO *appears. They cross the stage.* LUCKY *passes before* VLADIMIR *and* ESTRAGON *and exit.* POZZO *at the sight of* VLADIMIR *and* ESTRAGON *stops short. The rope tautens.* POZZO *jerks at it violently.*] Back!

> [*Noise of* LUCKY *falling with all his baggage.* VLADIMIR *and* ESTRAGON *turn towards him, half wishing half fearing to go to his assistance.* VLADIMIR *takes a step towards Lucky,* ESTRAGON *holds him back by the sleeve.*]

VLADIMIR   Let me go!

ESTRAGON   Stay where you are!

POZZO   Be careful! He's wicked. [VLADIMIR *and* ESTRAGON *turn towards* POZZO.] With strangers.

ESTRAGON [*undertone*]   Is that him?

VLADIMIR   Who?

ESTRAGON [*trying to remember the name*]   Er . . .

VLADIMIR   Godot?

ESTRAGON   Yes.

POZZO   I present myself: Pozzo.

VLADIMIR [*to* ESTRAGON]   Not at all!

ESTRAGON   He said Godot.

VLADIMIR   Not at all!

ESTRAGON [*timidly, to* POZZO]   You're not Mr. Godot, Sir?

POZZO [*terrifying voice*]   I am Pozzo! [*Silence.*] Pozzo! [*Silence.*] Does that name mean nothing to you? [*Silence.*] I say does that name mean nothing to you?

> [VLADIMIR *and* ESTRAGON *look at each other questioningly.*]

ESTRAGON [*pretending to search*]   Bozzo . . . Bozzo . . .

VLADIMIR [*ditto*]   Pozzo . . . Pozzo . . .

POZZO   PPPOZZZO!

ESTRAGON   Ah! Pozzo . . . let me see . . . Pozzo . . .

4. An overcoat.

VLADIMIR Is it Pozzo or Bozzo?

ESTRAGON Pozzo . . . no . . . I'm afraid I . . . no . . . I don't seem to . . . [POZZO *advances threateningly.*]

VLADIMIR [*conciliating*] I once knew a family called Cozzo. The mother had the clap.[5]

ESTRAGON [*hastily*] We're not from these parts, Sir.

POZZO [*halting*] You are human beings none the less. [*He puts on his glasses.*] As far as one can see. [*He takes off his glasses.*] Of the same species as myself. [*He bursts into an enormous laugh.*] Of the same species as Pozzo! Made in God's image!

VLADIMIR Well you see—

POZZO [*peremptory*] Who is Godot?

ESTRAGON Godot?

POZZO You took me for Godot.

VLADIMIR Oh no, Sir, not for an instant, Sir.

POZZO Who is he?

VLADIMIR Oh he's a . . . he's a kind of acquaintance.

ESTRAGON Nothing of the kind, we hardly know him.

VLADIMIR True . . . we don't know him very well . . . but all the same . . .

ESTRAGON Personally I wouldn't even know him if I saw him.

POZZO You took me for him.

ESTRAGON [*recoiling before* POZZO] That's to say . . . you understand . . . the dusk . . . the strain . . . waiting . . . I confess . . . I imagined . . . for a second . . .

POZZO Waiting? So you were waiting for him?

VLADIMIR Well you see—

POZZO Here? On my land?

VLADIMIR We didn't intend any harm.

ESTRAGON We meant well.

POZZO The road is free to all.

VLADIMIR That's how we looked at it.

POZZO It's a disgrace. But there you are.

ESTRAGON Nothing we can do about it.

POZZO [*with magnanimous gesture*] Let's say no more about it. [*He jerks the rope.*] Up pig! [*Pause.*] Every time he drops he falls asleep. [*Jerks the rope.*] Up hog! [*Noise of* LUCKY *getting up and picking up his baggage.* POZZO *jerks the rope.*] Back! [*Enter* LUCKY *backwards.*] Stop! [LUCKY *stops.*] Turn! [LUCKY *turns. To* VLADIMIR *and* ESTRAGON, *affably.*] Gentlemen, I am happy to have met you. [*Before their incredulous expression.*] Yes yes, sincerely happy. [*He jerks the rope.*] Closer! [LUCKY *advances.*] Stop! [LUCKY *stops.*] Yes, the road seems long when one journeys all alone for . . . [*he consults his watch*] . . . yes . . . [*he calculates*] . . . yes, six hours, that's right, six hours on end, and never a soul in sight. [*To* LUCKY.] Coat! [LUCKY *puts down the bag, advances, gives the coat, goes back to his place, takes up the bag.*] Hold that! [POZZO *holds out the whip.* LUCKY *advances and, both his hands being occupied, takes the whip in his mouth, then goes back to his place.* POZZO *begins to put on his coat, stops.*] Coat! [LUCKY *puts down the bag, basket and stool, helps* POZZO *on with his coat, goes back to his place and takes up bag, basket*

---

5. A venereal disease, usually gonorrhea (slang).

and stool.] Touch of autumn in the air this evening. [POZZO *finishes buttoning his coat, stoops, inspects himself, straightens up.*] Whip! [LUCKY *advances, stoops,* POZZO *snatches the whip from his mouth,* LUCKY *goes back to his place.*] Yes, gentlemen, I cannot go for long without the society of my likes [*he puts on his glasses and looks at the two likes*] even when the likeness is an imperfect one. [*He takes off his glasses.*] Stool! [LUCKY *puts down bag and basket, advances, opens stool, puts it down, goes back to his place, takes up bag and basket.*] Closer! [LUCKY *puts down bag and basket, advances, moves stool, goes back to his place, takes up bag and basket.* POZZO *sits down, places the butt of his whip against* LUCKY'S *chest and pushes.*] Back! [LUCKY *takes a step back.*] Further! [LUCKY *takes another step back.*] Stop! [LUCKY *stops. To* VLADIMIR *and* ESTRAGON.] That is why, with your permission, I propose to dally with you a moment, before I venture any further. Basket! [LUCKY *advances, gives the basket, goes back to his place.*] The fresh air stimulates the jaded appetite. [*He opens the basket, takes out a piece of chicken and a bottle of wine.*] Basket! [LUCKY *advances, picks up the basket and goes back to his place.*] Further! [LUCKY *takes a step back.*] He stinks. Happy days!

> [*He drinks from the bottle, puts it down and begins to eat. Silence.* VLADIMIR *and* ESTRAGON, *cautiously at first, then more boldly, begin to circle about* LUCKY, *inspecting him up and down.* POZZO *eats his chicken voraciously, throwing away the bones after having sucked them.* LUCKY *sags slowly, until bag and basket touch the ground, then straightens up with a start and begins to sag again. Rhythm of one sleeping on his feet.*]

ESTRAGON   What ails him?
VLADIMIR   He looks tired.
ESTRAGON   Why doesn't he put down his bags?
VLADIMIR   How do I know? [*They close in on him.*] Careful!
ESTRAGON   Say something to him.
VLADIMIR   Look!
ESTRAGON   What?
VLADIMIR [*pointing*]   His neck!
ESTRAGON [*looking at the neck*]   I see nothing.
VLADIMIR   Here.

> [ESTRAGON *goes over beside* VLADIMIR.]

ESTRAGON   Oh I say!
VLADIMIR   A running sore![6]
ESTRAGON   It's the rope.
VLADIMIR   It's the rubbing.
ESTRAGON   It's inevitable.
VLADIMIR   It's the knot.
ESTRAGON   It's the chafing.

> [*They resume their inspection, dwell on the face.*]

VLADIMIR [*grudgingly*]   He's not bad looking.
ESTRAGON [*shrugging his shoulders, wry face*]   Would you say so?
VLADIMIR   A trifle effeminate.
ESTRAGON   Look at the slobber.
VLADIMIR   It's inevitable.

---

6. A wound producing a discharge (hence, figuratively, constant irritation).

ESTRAGON   Look at the slaver.[7]

VLADIMIR   Perhaps he's a halfwit.

ESTRAGON   A cretin.

VLADIMIR [*looking closer*]   Looks like a goiter.[8]

ESTRAGON [*ditto*]   It's not certain.

VLADIMIR   He's panting.

ESTRAGON   It's inevitable.

VLADIMIR   And his eyes!

ESTRAGON   What about them?

VLADIMIR   Goggling out of his head.

ESTRAGON   Looks at his last gasp to me.

VLADIMIR   It's not certain. [*Pause.*] Ask him a question.

ESTRAGON   Would that be a good thing?

VLADIMIR   What do we risk?

ESTRAGON [*timidly*]   Mister . . .

VLADIMIR   Louder.

ESTRAGON [*louder*]   Mister . . .

POZZO   Leave him in peace! [*They turn towards* POZZO *who, having finished eating, wipes his mouth with the back of his hand.*] Can't you see he wants to rest? Basket! [*He strikes a match and begins to light his pipe.* ESTRAGON *sees the chicken bones on the ground and stares at them greedily. As* LUCKY *does not move* POZZO *throws the match angrily away and jerks the rope.*] Basket! [LUCKY *starts, almost falls, recovers his senses, advances, puts the bottle in the basket and goes back to his place.* ESTRAGON *stares at the bones.* POZZO *strikes another match and lights his pipe.*] What can you expect, it's not his job. [*He pulls at his pipe, stretches out his legs.*] Ah! That's better.

ESTRAGON [*timidly*]   Please Sir . . .

POZZO   What is it, my good man?

ESTRAGON   Er . . . you've finished with the . . . er . . . you don't need the . . . er . . . bones, Sir?

VLADIMIR [*scandalized*]   You couldn't have waited?

POZZO   No no, he does well to ask. Do I need the bones? [*He turns them over with the end of his whip.*] No, personally I do not need them any more. [ESTRAGON *takes a step towards the bones.*] But . . . [ESTRAGON *stops short.*] . . . but in theory the bones go to the carrier. He is therefore the one to ask. [ESTRAGON *turns towards* LUCKY, *hesitates.*] Go on, go on, don't be afraid, ask him, he'll tell you.

   [ESTRAGON *goes towards* LUCKY, *stops before him.*]

ESTRAGON   Mister . . . excuse me, Mister . . .

POZZO   You're being spoken to, pig! Reply! [*To* ESTRAGON.] Try him again.

ESTRAGON   Excuse me, Mister, the bones, you won't be wanting the bones?

   [LUCKY *looks long at* ESTRAGON.]

POZZO [*in raptures*]   Mister! [LUCKY *bows his head.*] Reply! Do you want them or don't you? [*Silence of* LUCKY. *To* ESTRAGON.] They're yours. [ESTRAGON *makes a dart at the bones, picks them up and begins to gnaw them.*] I don't like it. I've never known him refuse a bone before. [*He looks*

---

7. Saliva running out of the mouth.
8. A swelling of the thyroid gland, in the neck.

anxiously at LUCKY.] Nice business it'd be if he fell sick on me! [*He puffs at his pipe.*]

VLADIMIR [*exploding*] It's a scandal!

[*Silence. Flabbergasted,* ESTRAGON *stops gnawing, looks at pozzo and* VLADIMIR *in turn.* POZZO *outwardly calm.* VLADIMIR *embarrassed.*]

POZZO [*to* VLADIMIR] Are you alluding to anything in particular?

VLADIMIR [*stutteringly resolute*] To treat a man . . . [*Gesture towards* LUCKY] . . . like that . . . I think that . . . no . . . a human being . . . no . . . it's a scandal!

ESTRAGON [*not to be outdone*] A disgrace! [*He resumes his gnawing.*]

POZZO You are severe. [*To* VLADIMIR.] What age are you, if it's not a rude question? [*Silence.*] Sixty? Seventy? [*To* ESTRAGON.] What age would you say he was?

ESTRAGON Eleven.

POZZO I am impertinent. [*He knocks out his pipe against the whip, gets up.*] I must be getting on. Thank you for your society. [*He reflects.*] Unless I smoke another pipe before I go. What do you say? [*They say nothing.*] Oh I'm only a small smoker, a very small smoker, I'm not in the habit of smoking two pipes one on top of the other, it makes [*hand to heart, sighing*] my heart go pit-a-pat. [*Silence.*] It's the nicotine, one absorbs it in spite of one's precautions. [*Sighs.*] You know how it is. [*Silence.*] But perhaps you don't smoke? Yes? No? It's of no importance. [*Silence.*] But how am I to sit down now, without affectation, now that I have risen? Without appearing to— how shall I say—without appearing to falter. [*To* VLADIMIR.] I beg your pardon? [*Silence.*] Perhaps you didn't speak? [*Silence.*] It's of no importance. Let me see . . . [*He reflects.*]

ESTRAGON Ah! That's better. [*He puts the bones in his pocket.*]

VLADIMIR Let's go.

ESTRAGON So soon?

POZZO One moment! [*He jerks the rope.*] Stool! [*He points with his whip.* LUCKY *moves the stool.*] More! There! [*He sits down.* LUCKY *goes back to his place.*] Done it! [*He fills his pipe.*]

VLADIMIR [*vehemently*] Let's go!

POZZO I hope I'm not driving you away. Wait a little longer, you'll never regret it.

ESTRAGON [*scenting charity*] We're in no hurry.

POZZO [*having lit his pipe*] The second is never so sweet . . . [*he takes the pipe out of his mouth, contemplates it*] . . . as the first I mean. [*He puts the pipe back in his mouth.*] But it's sweet just the same.

VLADIMIR I'm going.

POZZO He can no longer endure my presence. I am perhaps not particularly human, but who cares? [*To* VLADIMIR.] Think twice before you do anything rash. Suppose you go now while it is still day, for there is no denying it is still day. [*They all look up at the sky.*] Good. [*They stop looking at the sky.*] What happens in that case—[*he takes the pipe out of his mouth, examines it*]—I'm out—[*he relights his pipe*]—in that case— [*puff*]—in that case—[*puff*]—what happens in that case to your appointment with this . . . Godet . . . Godot . . . Godin . . . anyhow you see who I mean, who has your future in his hands . . . [*pause*] . . . at least your immediate future?

VLADIMIR Who told you?

POZZO   He speaks to me again! If this goes on much longer we'll soon be old friends.

ESTRAGON   Why doesn't he put down his bags?

POZZO   I too would be happy to meet him. The more people I meet the happier I become. From the meanest creature one departs wiser, richer, more conscious of one's blessings. Even you . . . [*he looks at them ostentatiously in turn to make it clear they are both meant*] . . . even you, who knows, will have added to my store.

ESTRAGON   Why doesn't he put down his bags?

POZZO   But that would surprise me.

VLADIMIR   You're being asked a question.

POZZO [*delighted*]   A question! Who? What? A moment ago you were calling me Sir, in fear and trembling. Now you're asking me questions. No good will come of this!

VLADIMIR [*to* ESTRAGON]   I think he's listening.

ESTRAGON [*circling about* LUCKY]   What?

VLADIMIR   You can ask him now. He's on the alert.

ESTRAGON   Ask him what?

VLADIMIR   Why he doesn't put down his bags.

ESTRAGON   I wonder.

VLADIMIR   Ask him, can't you?

POZZO [*who has followed these exchanges with anxious attention, fearing lest the question get lost*]   You want to know why he doesn't put down his bags, as you call them.

VLADIMIR   That's it.

POZZO [*to* ESTRAGON]   You are sure you agree with that?

ESTRAGON   He's puffing like a grampus.[9]

POZZO   The answer is this. [*To* ESTRAGON.] But stay still, I beg of you, you're making me nervous!

VLADIMIR   Here.

ESTRAGON   What is it?

VLADIMIR   He's about to speak.

[ESTRAGON *goes over beside* VLADIMIR. *Motionless, side by side, they wait.*]

POZZO   Good. Is everybody ready? Is everybody looking at me? [*He looks at* LUCKY, *jerks the rope.* LUCKY *raises his head.*] Will you look at me, pig! [LUCKY *looks at him.*] Good. [*He puts the pipe in his pocket, takes out a little vaporizer and sprays his throat, puts back the vaporizer in his pocket, clears his throat, spits, takes out the vaporizer again, sprays his throat again, puts back the vaporizer in his pocket.*] I am ready. Is everybody listening? Is everybody ready? [*He looks at them all in turn, jerks the rope.*] Hog! [LUCKY *raises his head.*] I don't like talking in a vacuum. Good. Let me see. [*He reflects.*]

ESTRAGON   I'm going.

POZZO   What was it exactly you wanted to know?

VLADIMIR   Why he—

POZZO [*angrily*]   Don't interrupt me! [*Pause. Calmer.*] If we all speak at once we'll never get anywhere. [*Pause.*] What was I saying? [*Pause. Louder.*] What was I saying?

9. A dolphin.

[VLADIMIR *mimics one carrying a heavy burden,* POZZO *looks at him, puzzled.*]

ESTRAGON [*forcibly*]   Bags. [*He points at* LUCKY.] Why? Always hold. [*He sags, panting.*] Never put down. [*He opens his hands, straightens up with relief.*] Why?

POZZO   Ah! Why couldn't you say so before? Why he doesn't make himself comfortable? Let's try and get this clear. Has he not the right to? Certainly he has. It follows that he doesn't want to. There's reasoning for you. And why doesn't he want to? [*Pause.*] Gentlemen, the reason is this.

VLADIMIR [*to* ESTRAGON]   Make a note of this.

POZZO   He wants to impress me, so that I'll keep him.

ESTRAGON   What?

POZZO   Perhaps I haven't got it quite right. He wants to mollify me, so that I'll give up the idea of parting with him. No, that's not exactly it either.

VLADIMIR   You want to get rid of him?

POZZO   He wants to cod[1] me, but he won't.

VLADIMIR   You want to get rid of him?

POZZO   He imagines that when I see how well he carries I'll be tempted to keep him on in that capacity.

ESTRAGON   You've had enough of him?

POZZO   In reality he carries like a pig. It's not his job.

VLADIMIR   You want to get rid of him?

POZZO   He imagines that when I see him indefatigable I'll regret my decision. Such is his miserable scheme. As though I were short of slaves! [*All three look at* LUCKY.] Atlas, son of Jupiter![2] [*Silence.*] Well, that's that I think. Anything else?

[*Vaporizer.*]

VLADIMIR   You want to get rid of him?

POZZO   Remark that I might just as well have been in his shoes and he in mine. If chance had not willed otherwise. To each one his due.

VLADIMIR   You waagerrim?

POZZO   I beg your pardon?

VLADIMIR   You want to get rid of him?

POZZO   I do. But instead of driving him away as I might have done, I mean instead of simply kicking him out on his arse, in the goodness of my heart I am bringing him to the fair, where I hope to get a good price for him. The truth is you can't drive such creatures away. The best thing would be to kill them.

[LUCKY *weeps.*]

ESTRAGON   He's crying!

POZZO   Old dogs have more dignity. [*He proffers his handkerchief to* ESTRAGON.] Comfort him, since you pity him. [ESTRAGON *hesitates.*] Come on. [ESTRAGON *takes the handkerchief.*] Wipe away his tears, he'll feel less forsaken.

[ESTRAGON *hesitates.*]

1. To fool (Irish slang).
2. In classical mythology, his father was the Titan Iapetus, not Jupiter, the chief god of the Roman pantheon. Atlas had to hold the heavens on his shoulders.

VLADIMIR   Here, give it to me, I'll do it.

> [ESTRAGON *refuses to give the handkerchief. Childish gestures.*]

POZZO   Make haste, before he stops. [ESTRAGON *approaches* LUCKY *and makes to wipe his eyes.* LUCKY *kicks him violently in the shins.* ESTRAGON *drops the handkerchief, recoils, staggers about the stage howling with pain.*] Hanky!

> > [LUCKY *puts down bag and basket, picks up handkerchief and gives it to* POZZO, *goes back to his place, picks up bag and basket.*]

ESTRAGON   Oh the swine! [*He pulls up the leg of his trousers.*] He's crippled me!

POZZO   I told you he didn't like strangers.

VLADIMIR   [*to* ESTRAGON]   Show. [ESTRAGON *shows his leg. To* POZZO, *angrily*] He's bleeding!

POZZO   It's a good sign.

ESTRAGON   [*on one leg*]   I'll never walk again!

VLADIMIR   [*tenderly*]   I'll carry you. [*Pause.*] If necessary.

POZZO   He's stopped crying. [*To* ESTRAGON.] You have replaced him as it were. [*Lyrically.*] The tears of the world are a constant quantity. For each one who begins to weep, somewhere else another stops. The same is true of the laugh. [*He laughs.*] Let us not then speak ill of our generation, it is not any unhappier than its predecessors. [*Pause.*] Let us not speak well of it either. [*Pause.*] Let us not speak of it at all. [*Pause. Judiciously.*] It is true the population has increased.

VLADIMIR   Try and walk.

> > [ESTRAGON *takes a few limping steps, stops before* LUCKY *and spits on him, then goes and sits down on the mound.*]

POZZO   Guess who taught me all these beautiful things. [*Pause. Pointing to* LUCKY.] My Lucky!

VLADIMIR   [*looking at the sky*]   Will night never come?

POZZO   But for him all my thoughts, all my feelings, would have been of common things. [*Pause. With extraordinary vehemence.*] Professional worries! [*Calmer.*] Beauty, grace, truth of the first water,[3] I knew they were all beyond me. So I took a knook.[4]

VLADIMIR   [*startled from his inspection of the sky*]   A knook?

POZZO   That was nearly sixty years ago . . . [*he consults his watch*] . . . yes, nearly sixty. [*Drawing himself up proudly.*] You wouldn't think it to look at me, would you? Compared to him I look like a young man, no? [*Pause.*] Hat! [LUCKY *puts down the basket and takes off his hat. His long white hair falls about his face. He puts his hat under his arm and picks up the basket.*] Now look. [POZZO *takes off his hat.*[5] *He is completely bald. He puts on his hat again.*] Did you see?

VLADIMIR   And now you turn him away? Such an old and faithful servant!

ESTRAGON   Swine!

> [POZZO *more and more agitated.*]

VLADIMIR   After having sucked all the good out of him you chuck him away like a . . . like a banana skin. Really . . .

3. Of the highest order.
4. Invented word, apparently referring to Lucky's position as servant; it may echo the Russian word *knout,* or "whip."
5. All four wear bowlers [Beckett's note].

POZZO [*groaning, clutching his head*]   I can't bear it . . . any longer . . .
    the way he goes on . . . you've no idea . . . it's terrible . . . he must go . . .
    [*he waves his arms*] . . . I'm going mad . . . [*he collapses, his head in his
    hands*] . . . I can't bear it . . . any longer . . .
            [*Silence. All look at* POZZO.]
VLADIMIR   He can't bear it.
ESTRAGON   Any longer.
VLADIMIR   He's going mad.
ESTRAGON   It's terrible.
VLADIMIR [*to* LUCKY]   How dare you! It's abominable! Such a good master!
    Crucify him like that! After so many years! Really!
POZZO [*sobbing*]   He used to be so kind . . . so helpful . . . and
    entertaining . . . my good angel . . . and now . . . he's killing me.
ESTRAGON [*to* VLADIMIR]   Does he want to replace him?
VLADIMIR   What?
ESTRAGON   Does he want someone to take his place or not?
VLADIMIR   I don't think so.
ESTRAGON   What?
VLADIMIR   I don't know.
ESTRAGON   Ask him.
POZZO [*calmer*]   Gentlemen, I don't know what came over me. Forgive
    me. Forget all I said. [*More and more his old self.*] I don't remember
    exactly what it was, but you may be sure there wasn't a word of truth in
    it. [*Drawing himself up, striking his chest.*] Do I look like a man that can
    be made to suffer? Frankly? [*He rummages in his pockets.*] What have I
    done with my pipe?
VLADIMIR   Charming evening we're having.
ESTRAGON   Unforgettable.
VLADIMIR   And it's not over.
ESTRAGON   Apparently not.
VLADIMIR   It's only beginning.
ESTRAGON   It's awful.
VLADIMIR   Worse than the pantomime.[6]
ESTRAGON   The circus.
VLADIMIR   The music-hall.[7]
ESTRAGON   The circus.
POZZO   What can I have done with that briar?
ESTRAGON   He's a scream. He's lost his dudeen.[8] [*Laughs noisily.*]
VLADIMIR   I'll be back. [*He hastens towards the wings.*]
ESTRAGON   End of the corridor, on the left.
VLADIMIR   Keep my seat. [*Exit* VLADIMIR.]
POZZO [*on the point of tears*]   I've lost my Kapp and Peterson![9]
ESTRAGON [*convulsed with merriment*]   He'll be the death of me!
POZZO   You didn't see by any chance—. [*He misses* VLADIMIR.] Oh! He's
    gone! Without saying goodbye! How could he! He might have waited!
ESTRAGON   He would have burst.

---

6. A kind of theater involving music and slapstick comedy, usually based on fairy tales and
performed for children around Christmastime in
the British Isles, France, and elsewhere.
7. Vaudeville, or popular entertainment includ-

ing comedy, singing, and dancing.
8. A short clay pipe (Irish). "Briar": a pipe made
from briar wood.
9. A brand of pipe from Dublin's most famous
tobacco shop.

POZZO   Oh! [*Pause.*] Oh well then of course in that case . . .

ESTRAGON   Come here.

POZZO   What for?

ESTRAGON   You'll see.

POZZO   You want me to get up?

ESTRAGON   Quick! [POZZO *gets up and goes over beside* ESTRAGON. ESTRAGON *points off.*] Look!

POZZO [*having put on his glasses*]   Oh I say!

ESTRAGON   It's all over.
> [*Enter* VLADIMIR, *somber. He shoulders* LUCKY *out of his way, kicks over the stool, comes and goes agitatedly.*]

POZZO   He's not pleased.

ESTRAGON [*to* VLADIMIR]   You missed a treat. Pity.
> [VLADIMIR *halts, straightens the stool, comes and goes, calmer.*]

POZZO   He subsides. [*Looking round.*] Indeed all subsides. A great calm descends. [*Raising his hand.*] Listen! Pan sleeps.[1]

VLADIMIR   Will night never come?
> [*All three look at the sky.*]

POZZO   You don't feel like going until it does?

ESTRAGON   Well you see—

POZZO   Why it's very natural, very natural. I myself in your situation, if I had an appointment with a Godin . . . Godet . . . Godot . . . anyhow you see who I mean, I'd wait till it was black night before I gave up. [*He looks at the stool.*] I'd very much like to sit down, but I don't quite know how to go about it.

ESTRAGON   Could I be of any help?

POZZO   If you asked me perhaps.

ESTRAGON   What?

POZZO   If you asked me to sit down.

ESTRAGON   Would that be a help?

POZZO   I fancy so.

ESTRAGON   Here we go. Be seated, Sir, I beg of you.

POZZO   No no, I wouldn't think of it! [*Pause. Aside.*] Ask me again.

ESTRAGON   Come come, take a seat I beseech you, you'll get pneumonia.

POZZO   You really think so?

ESTRAGON   Why it's absolutely certain.

POZZO   No doubt you are right. [*He sits down.*] Done it again! [*Pause.*] Thank you, dear fellow. [*He consults his watch.*] But I must really be getting along, if I am to observe my schedule.

VLADIMIR   Time has stopped.

POZZO [*cuddling his watch to his ear*]   Don't you believe it, Sir, don't you believe it. [*He puts his watch back in his pocket.*] Whatever you like, but not that.

ESTRAGON [*to* POZZO]   Everything seems black to him today.

POZZO   Except the firmament.[2] [*He laughs, pleased with this witticism.*] But I see what it is, you are not from these parts, you don't know what our twilights can do. Shall I tell you? [*Silence.* ESTRAGON *is fiddling with his*

---

1. Greek god of shepherds, flocks, fields, and herds. His appearance was said to create terror similar to that of a stampeding herd, and the word "panic" is derived from his name. Thus, his sleep here may connote an absence of panic.
2. The sky or the heavens.

boot again, VLADIMIR *with his hat*.] I can't refuse you. [*Vaporizer*.] A little attention, if you please. [VLADIMIR *and* ESTRAGON *continue their fiddling*, LUCKY *is half asleep*. POZZO *cracks his whip feebly*.] What's the matter with this whip? [*He gets up and cracks it more vigorously, finally with success*. LUCKY *jumps*. VLADIMIR'S *hat*, ESTRAGON'S *boot*, LUCKY'S *hat, fall to the ground*. POZZO *throws down the whip*.] Worn out, this whip. [*He looks at* VLADIMIR *and* ESTRAGON.] What was I saying?

VLADIMIR   Let's go.

ESTRAGON   But take the weight off your feet, I implore you, you'll catch your death.

POZZO   True. [*He sits down. To* ESTRAGON.] What is your name?

ESTRAGON   Adam.

POZZO [*who hasn't listened*]   Ah yes! The night. [*He raises his head*.] But be a little more attentive, for pity's sake, otherwise we'll never get anywhere. [*He looks at the sky*.] Look! [*All look at the sky except* LUCKY *who is dozing off again*. POZZO *jerks the rope*.] Will you look at the sky, pig! [LUCKY *looks at the sky*.] Good, that's enough. [*They stop looking at the sky*.] What is there so extraordinary about it? Qua sky.[3] It is pale and luminous like any sky at this hour of the day. [*Pause*.] In these latitudes. [*Pause*.] When the weather is fine. [*Lyrical*.] An hour ago [*he looks at his watch, prosaic*] roughly [*lyrical*] after having poured forth even since [*he hesitates, prosaic*] say ten o'clock in the morning [*lyrical*] tirelessly torrents of red and white light it begins to lose its effulgence, to grow pale [*gesture of the two hands lapsing by stages*] pale, ever a little paler, a little paler until [*dramatic pause, ample gesture of the two hands flung wide apart*] pppfff! finished! it comes to rest. But—[*hand raised in admonition*]—but behind this veil of gentleness and peace night is charging [*vibrantly*] and will burst upon us [*snaps his fingers*.] pop! like that! [*His inspiration leaves him*.] just when we least expect it. [*Silence. Gloomily*.] That's how it is on this bitch of an earth.

   [*Long silence*.]

ESTRAGON   So long as one knows.

VLADIMIR   One can bide one's time.

ESTRAGON   One knows what to expect.

VLADIMIR   No further need to worry.

ESTRAGON   Simply wait.

VLADIMIR   We're used to it. [*He picks up his hat, peers inside it, shakes it, puts it on*.]

POZZO   How did you find me? [VLADIMIR *and* ESTRAGON *look at him blankly*.] Good? Fair? Middling? Poor? Positively bad?

VLADIMIR [*first to understand*]   Oh very good, very very good.

POZZO [*to* ESTRAGON]   And you, Sir?

ESTRAGON   Oh tray bong, tray tray tray bong.[4]

POZZO [*fervently*]   Bless you, gentlemen, bless you! [*Pause*.] I have such need of encouragement! [*Pause*.] I weakened a little towards the end, you didn't notice?

---

3. As sky—that is, in the capacity of sky.
4. A play on the French phrase *"oui très bon,"* meaning "yes, very good." "Oui! Tray bong!" was also the title of a popular music-hall song performed at the end of the 19th century by Charles Chaplin Sr. (1863–1901).

VLADIMIR   Oh perhaps just a teeny weeny little bit.

ESTRAGON   I thought it was intentional.

POZZO   You see my memory is defective.
    [*Silence.*]

ESTRAGON   In the meantime nothing happens.

POZZO   You find it tedious?

ESTRAGON   Somewhat.

POZZO [*to* VLADIMIR]   And you, Sir?

VLADIMIR   I've been better entertained.
    [*Silence.* POZZO *struggles inwardly.*]

POZZO   Gentlemen, you have been . . . civil to me.

ESTRAGON   Not at all!

VLADIMIR   What an idea!

POZZO   Yes yes, you have been correct. So that I ask myself is there any-
    thing I can do in my turn for these honest fellows who are having such
    a dull, dull time.

ESTRAGON   Even ten francs[5] would be a help.

VLADIMIR   We are not beggars!

POZZO   Is there anything I can do, that's what I ask myself, to cheer them
    up? I have given them bones, I have talked to them about this and that,
    I have explained the twilight, admittedly. But is it enough, that's what
    tortures me, is it enough?

ESTRAGON   Even five.

VLADIMIR [*to* ESTRAGON, *indignantly*]   That's enough!

ESTRAGON   I couldn't accept less.

POZZO   Is it enough? No doubt. But I am liberal. It's my nature. This eve-
    ning. So much the worse for me. [*He jerks the rope.* LUCKY *looks at him.*]
    For I shall suffer, no doubt about that. [*He picks up the whip.*] What do
    you prefer? Shall we have him dance, or sing, or recite, or think, or—

ESTRAGON   Who?

POZZO   Who! You know how to think, you two?

VLADIMIR   He thinks?

POZZO   Certainly. Aloud. He even used to think very prettily once, I could
    listen to him for hours. Now . . . [*He shudders.*] So much the worse for
    me. Well, would you like him to think something for us?

ESTRAGON   I'd rather he'd dance, it'd be more fun.

POZZO   Not necessarily.

ESTRAGON   Wouldn't it, Didi, be more fun?

VLADIMIR   I'd like well to hear him think.

ESTRAGON   Perhaps he could dance first and think afterwards, if it isn't
    too much to ask him.

VLADIMIR [*to* POZZO]   Would that be possible?

POZZO   By all means, nothing simpler. It's the natural order. [*He laughs
    briefly.*]

VLADIMIR   Then let him dance.
    [*Silence.*]

POZZO   Do you hear, hog?

ESTRAGON   He never refuses?

POZZO   He refused once. [*Silence.*] Dance, misery!

5. Ten French francs were then worth about 3 dollars.

[LUCKY *puts down bag and basket, advances towards front, turns to* POZZO. LUCKY *dances. He stops.*]

ESTRAGON   Is that all?

POZZO   Encore!

[LUCKY *executes the same movements, stops.*]

ESTRAGON   Pooh! I'd do as well myself. [*He imitates* LUCKY, *almost falls.*] With a little practice.

POZZO   He used to dance the farandole, the fling, the brawl, the jig, the fandango and even the hornpipe.[6] He capered. For joy. Now that's the best he can do. Do you know what he calls it?

ESTRAGON   The Scapegoat's Agony.

VLADIMIR   The Hard Stool.

POZZO   The Net. He thinks he's entangled in a net.

VLADIMIR [*squirming like an aesthete*]   There's something about it . . .

[LUCKY *makes to return to his burdens.*]

POZZO   Woaa!

[LUCKY *stiffens.*]

ESTRAGON   Tell us about the time he refused.

POZZO   With pleasure, with pleasure. [*He fumbles in his pockets.*] Wait. [*He fumbles.*] What have I done with my spray? [*He fumbles.*] Well now isn't that . . . [*He looks up, consternation on his features. Faintly.*] I can't find my pulverizer![7]

ESTRAGON [*faintly*]   My left lung is very weak! [*He coughs feebly. In ringing tones.*] But my right lung is as sound as a bell!

POZZO [*normal voice*]   No matter! What was I saying. [*He ponders.*] Wait. [*Ponders.*] Well now isn't that . . . [*He raises his head.*] Help me!

ESTRAGON   Wait!

VLADIMIR   Wait!

POZZO   Wait!

[*All three take off their hats simultaneously, press their hands to their foreheads, concentrate.*]

ESTRAGON [*triumphantly*]   Ah!

VLADIMIR   He has it.

POZZO [*impatient*]   Well?

ESTRAGON   Why doesn't he put down his bags?

VLADIMIR   Rubbish!

POZZO   Are you sure?

VLADIMIR   Damn it haven't you already told us?

POZZO   I've already told you?

ESTRAGON   He's already told us?

VLADIMIR   Anyway he has put them down.

ESTRAGON [*glance at* LUCKY]   So he has. And what of it?

VLADIMIR   Since he has put down his bags it is impossible we should have asked why he does not do so.

POZZO   Stoutly reasoned!

ESTRAGON   And why has he put them down?

POZZO   Answer us that.

VLADIMIR   In order to dance.

---

6. All lively dances, associated, respectively, with Provence, the Scottish Highlands, France, Ireland, Spain, and England.
7. I.e., his vaporizer.

ESTRAGON   True!
POZZO   True!
     [*Silence. They put on their hats.*]
ESTRAGON   Nothing happens, nobody comes, nobody goes, it's awful!
VLADIMIR [*to* POZZO]   Tell him to think.
POZZO   Give him his hat.
VLADIMIR   His hat?
POZZO   He can't think without his hat.
VLADIMIR [*to* ESTRAGON]   Give him his hat.
ESTRAGON   Me! After what he did to me! Never!
VLADIMIR   I'll give it to him. [*He does not move.*]
ESTRAGON [*to* POZZO]   Tell him to go and fetch it.
POZZO   It's better to give it to him.
VLADIMIR   I'll give it to him.
     [*He picks up the hat and tenders it at arm's length to* LUCKY, *who
     does not move.*]
POZZO   You must put it on his head.
ESTRAGON [*to* POZZO]   Tell him to take it.
POZZO   It's better to put it on his head.
VLADIMIR   I'll put it on his head.
     [*He goes round behind* LUCKY, *approaches him cautiously, puts the hat
     on his head and recoils smartly.* LUCKY *does not move. Silence.*]
ESTRAGON   What's he waiting for?
POZZO   Stand back! [VLADIMIR *and* ESTRAGON *move away from* LUCKY.
     POZZO *jerks the rope,* LUCKY *looks at* POZZO.] Think, pig! [*Pause.* LUCKY
     begins to dance.] Stop! [LUCKY *stops.*] Forward! [LUCKY *advances.*] Stop!
     [LUCKY *stops.*] Think!
     [*Silence.*]
LUCKY   On the other hand with regard to—
POZZO   Stop! [LUCKY *stops.*] Back! [LUCKY *moves back.*] Stop! [LUCKY
     stops.] Turn! [LUCKY *turns towards auditorium.*] Think!
LUCKY   Given the existence as uttered forth in the public, works of
     Puncher and Wattmann[8] of a personal God quaquaquaqua[9] with white
     beard quaquaquaqua outside time without extension who from the
     heights of divine apathia divine athambia divine aphasia[1] loves us dearly
     with some exceptions for reasons unknown but time will tell and
[VLADIMIR   suffers like the divine Miranda[2] with those who for reasons
     and   unknown but time will tell are plunged in torment plunged
ESTRAGON   in fire whose fire flames if that continues and who can
     all   doubt it will fire the firmament that is to say blast hell to
attention, heaven so blue still and calm so calm with a calm which even
     POZZO   though intermittent is better than nothing but not so fast
dejected   and considering what is more that as a result of the labors
     and   left unfinished crowned by the Acacacacademy of

8. Made-up scholars' names.
9. Repetition of the Latin word "qua," meaning "in the capacity of," or "as being," in philosophy.
1. Partial or total loss of speech. "Apathia": apathy, or the absence of emotion. "Athambia": absence of fear or surprise. All Greek words, of

which only "aphasia" is common in English.
2. The heroine of Shakespeare's *The Tempest* (1611), who empathizes with the victims of a shipwreck: "O, I have suffered / With those that I saw suffer!" (1.2.5–6).

disgusted.] Anthropopopometry of Essy-in-Possy[3] of Testew and

[VLADIMIR
and
ESTRAGON
*begin to
protest,*
POZZO'S
*sufferings
increase.*]

Cunard[4] it is established beyond all doubt all other doubt
than that which clings to the labors of men that as a result
of the labors unfinished of Testew and Cunard it is
established as hereinafter but not so fast for reasons
unknown that as a result of the public works of Puncher
and Wattmann it is established beyond all doubt that in
view of the labors of Fartov and Belcher[5] left unfinished
for reasons unknown of Testew and Cunard left unfinished
it is established what many deny that man in Possy of
Testew and Cunard that man in Essy that man in short that
man in brief in spite of the strides of alimentation[6] and
defecation wastes and pines wastes and pines and

[VLADIMIR
and
ESTRAGON
*attentive
again,*
POZZO
*more and
more
agitated
and
groaning.*]

concurrently simultaneously what is more for reasons
unknown in spite of the strides of physical culture the
practice of sports such as tennis football running cycling
swimming flying floating riding gliding conating camogie[7]
skating tennis of all kinds dying flying sports of all sorts
autumn summer winter winter tennis of all kinds hockey of
all sorts penicillin and succedanea[8] in a word I resume
flying gliding golf over nine and eighteen holes tennis of
all sorts in a word for reasons unknown in Feckham
Peckham Fulham Clapham[9] namely concurrently
simultaneously what is more for reasons unknown but time
will tell fades away I resume Fulham Clapham in a word
the dead loss per head since the death of Bishop Berkeley[1]
being to the tune of one inch four ounce per head
approximately by and large more or less to the nearest

[VLADIMIR
and
ESTRAGON
*protest
violently.*
POZZO
*jumps up,
pulls on
the rope.
General
outcry.*
LUCKY *pulls*

decimal good measure round figures stark naked in the
stockinged feet in Connemara[2] in a word for reasons
unknown no matter what matter the facts are there and
considering what is more much more grave that in the light
of the labors lost of Steinweg and Peterman[3] it appears
what is more much more grave that in the light the light the
light of the labors lost of Steinweg and Peterman that in
the plains in the mountains by the seas by the rivers running
water running fire the air is the same and then the earth
namely the air and then the earth in the great cold the
great dark the air and the earth abode of stones in the
great cold alas alas in the year of their Lord six hundred and

3. A fictitious place, with a name that echoes the Latin words "*esse*" (to be) and "*posse*" (to be able to). "Acacacacademy": a play on the words "academy" and "*caca*," a children's word for excrement in French. "Anthropopopometry": that is, anthropometry, the measurement of the human body.
4. Made-up scholars' names, playing on words for male and female sexual organs.
5. Made-up scholars' names, with puns on bodily functions.
6. Nourishment, or feeding.
7. Women's version of Irish sport of hurling, played with sticks and a ball. "Conating": attempting or desiring (a word created by Beckett from "*conation*").
8. Substitutes.
9. The last three names are neighborhoods in south London, the first a vulgar pun ("fuck 'em").
1. George Berkeley (1685–1753), Irish philosopher and bishop, who theorized that objects exist only insofar as they are perceived.
2. A region in western Ireland.
3. Made-up scholars' names.

on the rope, something the air the earth the sea the earth abode of
staggers, stones in the great deeps the great cold on sea on land and
shouts his in the air I resume for reasons unknown in spite of the
text. All tennis the facts are there but time will tell I resume alas
three throw alas on on in short in fine on on abode of stones who can
themselves doubt it I resume but not so fast I resume the skull fading
on LUCKY fading fading and concurrently simultaneously what is more
who for reasons unknown in spite of the tennis on on the beard
struggles the flames the tears the stones so blue so calm alas alas on
and shouts on the skull the skull the skull the skull in Connemara in
his text.] spite of the tennis the labors abandoned left unfinished
graver still abode of stones in a word I resume alas alas
abandoned unfinished the skull the skull in Connemara in
spite of the tennis the skull alas the stones Cunard [*mêlée,*
final vociferations] tennis . . . the stones . . . so calm . . .
Cunard . . . unfinished . . .

POZZO   His hat!
[VLADIMIR *seizes* LUCKY's *hat. Silence of* LUCKY. *He falls. Silence. Pant-*
ing of the victors.]

ESTRAGON   Avenged!
[VLADIMIR *examines the hat, peers inside it.*]

POZZO   Give me that! [*He snatches the hat from* VLADIMIR, *throws it on the*
ground, tramples on it.] There's an end to his thinking!

VLADIMIR   But will he be able to walk?

POZZO   Walk or crawl! [*He kicks* LUCKY.] Up pig!

ESTRAGON   Perhaps he's dead.

VLADIMIR   You'll kill him.

POZZO   Up scum! [*He jerks the rope.*] Help me!

VLADIMIR   How?

POZZO   Raise him up!
[VLADIMIR *and* ESTRAGON *hoist* LUCKY *to his feet, support him an*
instant, then let him go. He falls.]

ESTRAGON   He's doing it on purpose!

POZZO   You must hold him. [*Pause.*] Come on, come on, raise him up.

ESTRAGON   To hell with him!

VLADIMIR   Come on, once more.

ESTRAGON   What does he take us for?
[*They raise* LUCKY, *hold him up.*]

POZZO   Don't let him go! [VLADIMIR *and* ESTRAGON *totter.*] Don't move!

POZZO [*fetches bag and basket and brings them towards* LUCKY.] Hold him
tight! [*He puts the bag in* LUCKY's *hand.* LUCKY *drops it immediately.*] Don't
let him go! [*He puts back the bag in* LUCKY's *hand. Gradually, at the feel of*
the bag, LUCKY *recovers his senses and his fingers finally close round the*
handle.] Hold him tight! [*As before with basket.*] Now! You can let him go.
[VLADIMIR *and* ESTRAGON *move away from* LUCKY *who totters, reels, sags,*
but succeeds in remaining on his feet, bag and basket in his hands. POZZO
steps back, cracks his whip.] Forward! [LUCKY *totters forward.*] Back!
[LUCKY *totters back.*] Turn! [LUCKY *turns.*] Done it! He can walk. [*Turn-*
ing to VLADIMIR *and* ESTRAGON.] Thank you, gentlemen, and let me . . .
[*he fumbles in his pockets*] . . . let me wish you . . . [*fumbles.*] . . . wish
you . . . [*fumbles.*] . . . what have I done with my watch? [*fumbles.*] A

genuine half-hunter, gentlemen, with deadbeat escapement![4] [*Sobbing.*] Twas my granpa gave it to me! [*He searches on the ground,* VLADIMIR *and* ESTRAGON *likewise.* POZZO *turns over with his foot the remains of* LUCKY's *hat.*] Well now isn't that just—

VLADIMIR   Perhaps it's in your fob.[5]

POZZO   Wait! [*He doubles up in an attempt to apply his ear to his stomach, listens. Silence.*] I hear nothing. [*He beckons them to approach,* VLADIMIR *and* ESTRAGON *go over to him, bend over his stomach.*] Surely one should hear the tick-tick.

VLADIMIR   Silence!
　　　　[*All listen, bent double.*]

ESTRAGON   I hear something.

POZZO   Where?

VLADIMIR   It's the heart.

POZZO [*disappointed*]   Damnation!

VLADIMIR   Silence!

ESTRAGON   Perhaps it has stopped.
　　　　[*They straighten up.*]

POZZO   Which of you smells so bad?

ESTRAGON   He has stinking breath and I have stinking feet.

POZZO   I must go.

ESTRAGON   And your half-hunter?

POZZO   I must have left it at the manor.
　　　　[*Silence.*]

ESTRAGON   Then adieu.

POZZO   Adieu.

VLADIMIR   Adieu.

POZZO   Adieu.
　　　　[*Silence. No one moves.*]

VLADIMIR   Adieu.

POZZO   Adieu.

ESTRAGON   Adieu.
　　　　[*Silence.*]

POZZO   And thank you.

VLADIMIR   Thank *you.*

POZZO   Not at all.

ESTRAGON   Yes yes.

POZZO   No no.

VLADIMIR   Yes yes.

ESTRAGON   No no.
　　　　[*Silence.*]

POZZO   I don't seem to be able . . . [*long hesitation*] . . . to depart.

ESTRAGON   Such is life.
　　　　[POZZO *turns, moves away from* LUCKY *towards the wings, paying out the rope as he goes.*]

VLADIMIR   You're going the wrong way.

POZZO   I need a running start. [*Having come to the end of the rope, i.e. off stage, he stops, turns and cries.*] Stand back! [VLADIMIR *and* ESTRAGON *stand back, look towards* POZZO. *Crack of whip.*] On! On!

---

4. A check-and-release mechanism in watches; here, "deadbeat" because it does not work. "Half-hunter": a kind of pocket watch with a hinged metal cover, in the center of which is a small glass window allowing the hands to be seen.
5. A small front pocket for a watch.

ESTRAGON   On!
VLADIMIR   On!
          [LUCKY *moves off.*]
POZZO   Faster! [*He appears, crosses the stage preceded by* LUCKY. VLADIMIR *and* ESTRAGON *wave their hats. Exit* LUCKY.] On! On! [*On the point of disappearing in his turn he stops and turns. The rope tautens. Noise of* LUCKY *falling off.*] Stool! [VLADIMIR *fetches stool and gives it to* POZZO *who throws it to* LUCKY.] Adieu!
VLADIMIR ⎱
ESTRAGON ⎰ [*waving*]   Adieu! Adieu!
POZZO   Up! Pig! [*Noise of* LUCKY *getting up.*] On! [*Exit* POZZO.] Faster! On! Adieu! Pig! Yip! Adieu!
          [*Long silence.*]
VLADIMIR   That passed the time.
ESTRAGON   It would have passed in any case.
VLADIMIR   Yes, but not so rapidly.
          [*Pause.*]
ESTRAGON   What do we do now?
VLADIMIR   I don't know.
ESTRAGON   Let's go.
VLADIMIR   We can't.
ESTRAGON   Why not?
VLADIMIR   We're waiting for Godot.
ESTRAGON [*despairingly*]   Ah!
          [*Pause.*]
VLADIMIR   How they've changed!
ESTRAGON   Who?
VLADIMIR   Those two.
ESTRAGON   That's the idea, let's make a little conversation.
VLADIMIR   Haven't they?
ESTRAGON   What?
VLADIMIR   Changed.
ESTRAGON   Very likely. They all change. Only we can't.
VLADIMIR   Likely! It's certain. Didn't you see them?
ESTRAGON   I suppose I did. But I don't know them.
VLADIMIR   Yes you do know them.
ESTRAGON   No I don't know them.
VLADIMIR   We know them, I tell you. You forget everything. [*Pause. To himself.*] Unless they're not the same . . .
ESTRAGON   Why didn't they recognize us then?
VLADIMIR   That means nothing. I too pretended not to recognize them. And then nobody ever recognizes us.
ESTRAGON   Forget it. What we need—ow! [VLADIMIR *does not react.*] Ow!
VLADIMIR [*to himself*]   Unless they're not the same . . .
ESTRAGON   Didi! It's the other foot! [*He goes hobbling towards the mound.*]
VLADIMIR   Unless they're not the same . . .
BOY [*off*]   Mister!
          [ESTRAGON *halts. Both look towards the voice.*]
ESTRAGON   Off we go again.
VLADIMIR   Approach, my child.
          [*Enter* BOY, *timidly. He halts.*]
BOY   Mister Albert . . . ?

VLADIMIR   Yes.

ESTRAGON   What do you want?

VLADIMIR   Approach!

[*The* BOY *does not move.*]

ESTRAGON [*forcibly*]   Approach when you're told, can't you?

[*The* BOY *advances timidly, halts.*]

VLADIMIR   What is it?

BOY   Mr. Godot . . .

VLADIMIR   Obviously . . . [*Pause.*] Approach.

ESTRAGON [*violently*]   Will you approach! [*The* BOY *advances timidly.*] What kept you so late?

VLADIMIR   You have a message from Mr. Godot?

BOY   Yes Sir.

VLADIMIR   Well, what is it?

ESTRAGON   What kept you so late?

[*The* BOY *looks at them in turn, not knowing to which he should reply.*]

VLADIMIR [*to* ESTRAGON]   Let him alone.

ESTRAGON [*violently*]   You let me alone. [*Advancing, to the* BOY.] Do you know what time it is?

BOY [*recoiling*]   It's not my fault, Sir.

ESTRAGON   And whose is it? Mine?

BOY   I was afraid, Sir.

ESTRAGON   Afraid of what? Of us? [*Pause.*] Answer me!

VLADIMIR   I know what it is, he was afraid of the others.

ESTRAGON   How long have you been here?

BOY   A good while, Sir.

VLADIMIR   You were afraid of the whip?

BOY   Yes Sir.

VLADIMIR   The roars?

BOY   Yes Sir.

VLADIMIR   The two big men.

BOY   Yes Sir.

VLADIMIR   Do you know them?

BOY   No Sir.

VLADIMIR   Are you a native of these parts? [*Silence.*] Do you belong to these parts?

BOY   Yes Sir.

ESTRAGON   That's all a pack of lies. [*Shaking the* BOY *by the arm.*] Tell us the truth!

BOY [*trembling*]   But it is the truth, Sir!

VLADIMIR   Will you let him alone! What's the matter with you? [ESTRAGON *releases the* BOY, *moves away, covering his face with his hands.* VLADIMIR *and the* BOY *observe him.* ESTRAGON *drops his hands. His face is convulsed.*] What's the matter with you?

ESTRAGON   I'm unhappy.

VLADIMIR   Not really! Since when?

ESTRAGON   I'd forgotten.

VLADIMIR   Extraordinary the tricks that memory plays!

[ESTRAGON *tries to speak, renounces, limps to his place, sits down and begins to take off his boots. To* BOY]

Well?

BOY   Mr. Godot—

VLADIMIR   I've seen you before, haven't I?

BOY   I don't know, Sir.

VLADIMIR   You don't know me?

BOY   No Sir.

VLADIMIR   It wasn't you came yesterday?

BOY   No Sir.

VLADIMIR   This is your first time?

BOY   Yes Sir.
   [*Silence.*]

VLADIMIR   Words words. [*Pause.*] Speak.

BOY [*in a rush*]   Mr. Godot told me to tell you he won't come this evening
   but surely tomorrow.
   [*Silence.*]

VLADIMIR   Is that all?

BOY   Yes Sir.
   [*Silence.*]

VLADIMIR   You work for Mr. Godot?

BOY   Yes Sir.

VLADIMIR   What do you do?

BOY   I mind the goats, Sir.

VLADIMIR   Is he good to you?

BOY   Yes Sir.

VLADIMIR   He doesn't beat you?

BOY   No Sir, not me.

VLADIMIR   Whom does he beat?

BOY   He beats my brother, Sir.

VLADIMIR   Ah, you have a brother?

BOY   Yes Sir.

VLADIMIR   What does he do?

BOY   He minds the sheep, Sir.[6]

VLADIMIR   And why doesn't he beat you?

BOY   I don't know, Sir.

VLADIMIR   He must be fond of you.

BOY   I don't know, Sir.
   [*Silence.*]

VLADIMIR   Does he give you enough to eat? [*The* BOY *hesitates.*] Does he
   feed you well?

BOY   Fairly well, Sir.

VLADIMIR   You're not unhappy? [*The* BOY *hesitates.*] Do you hear me?

BOY   Yes Sir.

VLADIMIR   Well?

BOY   I don't know, Sir.

VLADIMIR   You don't know if you're unhappy or not?

BOY   No Sir.

VLADIMIR   You're as bad as myself. [*Silence.*] Where do you sleep?

BOY   In the loft, Sir.

VLADIMIR   With your brother?

---

6. Cf. the parable in Matthew 25, in which the goats (the damned) are punished and the sheep (the
saved) are blessed.

BOY   Yes Sir.

VLADIMIR   In the hay?

BOY   Yes Sir.

    [*Silence.*]

VLADIMIR   All right, you may go.

BOY   What am I to tell Mr. Godot, Sir?

VLADIMIR   Tell him . . . [*he hesitates.*] . . . tell him you saw us. [*Pause.*] You did see us, didn't you?

BOY   Yes Sir.

    [*He steps back, hesitates, turns and exits running. The light suddenly fails. In a moment it is night. The moon rises at back, mounts in the sky, stands still, shedding a pale light on the scene.*]

VLADIMIR   At last! [ESTRAGON *gets up and goes towards* VLADIMIR, *a boot in each hand. He puts them down at edge of stage, straightens and contemplates the moon.*] What are you doing?

ESTRAGON   Pale for weariness.

VLADIMIR   Eh?

ESTRAGON   Of climbing heaven and gazing on the likes of us.

VLADIMIR   Your boots, what are you doing with your boots?

ESTRAGON   [*turning to look at the boots*]   I'm leaving them there. [*Pause.*] Another will come, just as . . . as . . . as me, but with smaller feet, and they'll make him happy.

VLADIMIR   But you can't go barefoot!

ESTRAGON   Christ did.

VLADIMIR   Christ! What has Christ got to do with it? You're not going to compare yourself to Christ!

ESTRAGON   All my life I've compared myself to him.

VLADIMIR   But where he lived it was warm, it was dry!

ESTRAGON   Yes. And they crucified quick.

    [*Silence.*]

VLADIMIR   We've nothing more to do here.

ESTRAGON   Nor anywhere else.

VLADIMIR   Ah Gogo, don't go on like that. Tomorrow everything will be better.

ESTRAGON   How do you make that out?

VLADIMIR   Did you not hear what the child said?

ESTRAGON   No.

VLADIMIR   He said that Godot was sure to come tomorrow. [*Pause.*] What do you say to that?

ESTRAGON   Then all we have to do is to wait on here.

VLADIMIR   Are you mad? We must take cover. [*He takes* ESTRAGON *by the arm.*] Come on.

    [*He draws* ESTRAGON *after him.* ESTRAGON *yields, then resists. They halt.*]

ESTRAGON   [*looking at the tree*]   Pity we haven't got a bit of rope.

VLADIMIR   Come on. It's cold.

    [*He draws* ESTRAGON *after him. As before.*]

ESTRAGON   Remind me to bring a bit of rope tomorrow.

VLADIMIR   Yes. Come on.

    [*He draws him after him. As before.*]

ESTRAGON   How long have we been together all the time now?

VLADIMIR   I don't know. Fifty years maybe.
ESTRAGON   Do you remember the day I threw myself into the Rhône?[7]
VLADIMIR   We were grape harvesting.
ESTRAGON   You fished me out.
VLADIMIR   That's all dead and buried.
ESTRAGON   My clothes dried in the sun.
VLADIMIR   There's no good harking back on that. Come on.
   [*He draws him after him. As before.*]
ESTRAGON   Wait!
VLADIMIR   I'm cold!
ESTRAGON   Wait! [*He moves away from* VLADIMIR.] I sometimes wonder if
   we wouldn't have been better off alone, each one for himself. [*He crosses
   the stage and sits down on the mound.*] We weren't made for the same road.
VLADIMIR [*without anger*]   It's not certain.
ESTRAGON   No, nothing is certain.
   [VLADIMIR *slowly crosses the stage and sits down beside* ESTRAGON.]
VLADIMIR   We can still part, if you think it would be better.
ESTRAGON   It's not worth while now.
       [*Silence.*]
VLADIMIR   No, it's not worth while now.
       [*Silence.*]
ESTRAGON   Well, shall we go?
VLADIMIR   Yes, let's go.
       [*They do not move.*]
                    Curtain.

                        Act 2

Next day. Same time.
Same place.

   [ESTRAGON's *boots front center, heels together, toes splayed.* LUCKY's *hat at
   same place.*]

   [*The tree has four or five leaves.*]

   [*Enter* VLADIMIR *agitatedly. He halts and looks long at the tree, then
   suddenly begins to move feverishly about the stage. He halts before the
   boots, picks one up, examines it, sniffs it, manifests disgust, puts it
   back carefully. Comes and goes. Halts extreme right and gazes into
   distance off, shading his eyes with his hand. Comes and goes. Halts
   extreme left, as before. Comes and goes. Halts suddenly and begins to
   sing loudly.*]
VLADIMIR   A dog came in—
   [*Having begun too high he stops, clears his throat, resumes:*]
             A dog came in the kitchen
             And stole a crust of bread.
             Then cook up with a ladle[8]
             And beat him till he was dead.

---

7. A major river in southeastern France.
8. I.e., the cook took up a ladle. Vladimir sings a round song.

Then all the dogs came running
And dug the dog a tomb—

[*He stops, broods, resumes:*]
Then all the dogs came running
And dug the dog a tomb
And wrote upon the tombstone
For the eyes of dogs to come:

A dog came in the kitchen
And stole a crust of bread.
Then cook up with a ladle
And beat him till he was dead.

Then all the dogs came running
And dug the dog a tomb—

[*He stops, broods, resumes:*]
Then all the dogs came running
And dug the dog a tomb—

[*He stops, broods. Softly.*]
And dug the dog a tomb . . .

[*He remains a moment silent and motionless, then begins to move fever-ishly about the stage. He halts before the tree, comes and goes, before the boots, comes and goes, halts extreme right, gazes into distance, extreme left, gazes into distance. Enter* ESTRAGON *right, barefoot, head bowed. He slowly crosses the stage.* VLADIMIR *turns and sees him.*]

VLADIMIR You again! [ESTRAGON *halts but does not raise his head.* VLADI-MIR *goes towards him.*] Come here till I embrace you.

ESTRAGON Don't touch me!
[VLADIMIR *holds back, pained.*]

VLADIMIR Do you want me to go away? [*Pause.*] Gogo! [*Pause.* VLADIMIR *observes him attentively.*] Did they beat you? [*Pause.*] Gogo! [ESTRAGON *remains silent, head bowed.*] Where did you spend the night?

ESTRAGON Don't touch me! Don't question me! Don't speak to me! Stay with me!

VLADIMIR Did I ever leave you?

ESTRAGON You let me go.

VLADIMIR Look at me. [ESTRAGON *does not raise his head. Violently.*] Will you look at me!
[ESTRAGON *raises his head. They look long at each other, then suddenly embrace, clapping each other on the back. End of the embrace.* ESTRAGON, *no longer supported, almost falls.*]

ESTRAGON What a day!

VLADIMIR Who beat you? Tell me.

ESTRAGON Another day done with.

VLADIMIR Not yet.

ESTRAGON For me it's over and done with, no matter what happens. [*Silence.*] I heard you singing.

VLADIMIR That's right, I remember.

ESTRAGON   That finished me. I said to myself, He's all alone, he thinks I'm gone for ever, and he sings.

VLADIMIR   One is not master of one's moods. All day I've felt in great form. [*Pause.*] I didn't get up in the night, not once!

ESTRAGON [*sadly*]   You see, you piss better when I'm not there.

VLADIMIR   I missed you . . . and at the same time I was happy. Isn't that a queer thing?

ESTRAGON [*shocked*]   Happy?

VLADIMIR   Perhaps it's not quite the right word.

ESTRAGON   And now?

VLADIMIR   Now? . . . [*Joyous.*] There you are again . . . [*Indifferent.*] There we are again . . . [*Gloomy.*] There I am again.

ESTRAGON   You see, you feel worse when I'm with you. I feel better alone too.

VLADIMIR [*vexed*]   Then why do you always come crawling back?

ESTRAGON   I don't know.

VLADIMIR   No, but I do. It's because you don't know how to defend yourself. I wouldn't have let them beat you.

ESTRAGON   You couldn't have stopped them.

VLADIMIR   Why not?

ESTRAGON   There was ten of them.

VLADIMIR   No, I mean before they beat you. I would have stopped you from doing whatever it was you were doing.

ESTRAGON   I wasn't doing anything.

VLADIMIR   Then why did they beat you?

ESTRAGON   I don't know.

VLADIMIR   Ah no, Gogo, the truth is there are things escape you that don't escape me, you must feel it yourself.

ESTRAGON   I tell you I wasn't doing anything.

VLADIMIR   Perhaps you weren't. But it's the way of doing it that counts, the way of doing it, if you want to go on living.

ESTRAGON   I wasn't doing anything.

VLADIMIR   You must be happy too, deep down, if you only knew it.

ESTRAGON   Happy about what?

VLADIMIR   To be back with me again.

ESTRAGON   Would you say so?

VLADIMIR   Say you are, even if it's not true.

ESTRAGON   What am I to say?

VLADIMIR   Say, I am happy.

ESTRAGON   I am happy.

VLADIMIR   So am I.

ESTRAGON   So am I.

VLADIMIR   We are happy.

ESTRAGON   We are happy. [*Silence.*] What do we do now, now that we are happy?

VLADIMIR   Wait for Godot. [ESTRAGON *groans. Silence.*] Things have changed here since yesterday.

ESTRAGON   And if he doesn't come.

VLADIMIR [*after a moment of bewilderment*]   We'll see when the time comes. [*Pause.*] I was saying that things have changed here since yesterday.

ESTRAGON   Everything oozes.

VLADIMIR   Look at the tree.

ESTRAGON   It's never the same pus from one second to the next.[9]

VLADIMIR   The tree, look at the tree.

[ESTRAGON *looks at the tree.*]

ESTRAGON   Was it not there yesterday?

VLADIMIR   Yes of course it was there. Do you not remember? We nearly hanged ourselves from it. But you wouldn't. Do you not remember?

ESTRAGON   You dreamt it.

VLADIMIR   Is it possible you've forgotten already?

ESTRAGON   That's the way I am. Either I forget immediately or I never forget.

VLADIMIR   And Pozzo and Lucky, have you forgotten them too?

ESTRAGON   Pozzo and Lucky?

VLADIMIR   He's forgotten everything!

ESTRAGON   I remember a lunatic who kicked the shins off me. Then he played the fool.

VLADIMIR   That was Lucky.

ESTRAGON   I remember that. But when was it?

VLADIMIR   And his keeper, do you not remember him?

ESTRAGON   He gave me a bone.

VLADIMIR   That was Pozzo.

ESTRAGON   And all that was yesterday, you say?

VLADIMIR   Yes of course it was yesterday.

ESTRAGON   And here where we are now?

VLADIMIR   Where else do you think? Do you not recognize the place?

ESTRAGON [*suddenly furious*]   Recognize! What is there to recognize? All my lousy life I've crawled about in the mud! And you talk to me about scenery! [*Looking wildly about him.*] Look at this muckheap! I've never stirred from it!

VLADIMIR   Calm yourself, calm yourself.

ESTRAGON   You and your landscapes! Tell me about the worms!

VLADIMIR   All the same, you can't tell me that this [*gesture*] bears any resemblance to . . . [*he hesitates.*] . . . to the Mâcon country[1] for example. You can't deny there's a big difference.

ESTRAGON   The Mâcon country! Who's talking to you about the Mâcon country?

VLADIMIR   But you were there yourself, in the Mâcon country.

ESTRAGON   No I was never in the Mâcon country! I've puked my puke of a life away here, I tell you! Here! In the Cackon country![2]

VLADIMIR   But we were there together, I could swear to it! Picking grapes for a man called . . . [*he snaps his fingers*] . . . can't think of the name of the man, at a place called . . . [*snaps his fingers*] . . . can't think of the name of the place, do you not remember?

ESTRAGON [*a little calmer*]   It's possible. I didn't notice anything.

VLADIMIR   But down there everything is red!

9. Cf. "You can never step into the same river twice," a statement on flux by the ancient Greek philosopher Heraclitus (active ca. 500 B.C.E.).
1. A wine-producing area in the Burgundy region of eastern France.
2. Punning on "caca," children's word in French for excrement.

ESTRAGON [*exasperated*]   I didn't notice anything, I tell you!
    [*Silence.* VLADIMIR *sighs deeply.*]
VLADIMIR   You're a hard man to get on with, Gogo.
ESTRAGON   It'd be better if we parted.
VLADIMIR   You always say that and you always come crawling back.
ESTRAGON   The best thing would be to kill me, like the other.
VLADIMIR   What other? [*Pause.*] What other?
ESTRAGON   Like billions of others.
VLADIMIR [*sententious*]   To every man his little cross. [*He sighs.*] Till he
    dies. [*Afterthought.*] And is forgotten.
ESTRAGON   In the meantime let us try and converse calmly, since we are
    incapable of keeping silent.
VLADIMIR   You're right, we're inexhaustible.
ESTRAGON   It's so we won't think.
VLADIMIR   We have that excuse.
ESTRAGON   It's so we won't hear.
VLADIMIR   We have our reasons.
ESTRAGON   All the dead voices.
VLADIMIR   They make a noise like wings.
ESTRAGON   Like leaves.
VLADIMIR   Like sand.
ESTRAGON   Like leaves.
    [*Silence.*]
VLADIMIR   They all speak at once.
ESTRAGON   Each one to itself.
    [*Silence.*]
VLADIMIR   Rather they whisper.
ESTRAGON   They rustle.
VLADIMIR   They murmur.
ESTRAGON   They rustle.
    [*Silence.*]
VLADIMIR   What do they say?
ESTRAGON   They talk about their lives.
VLADIMIR   To have lived is not enough for them.
ESTRAGON   They have to talk about it.
VLADIMIR   To be dead is not enough for them.
ESTRAGON   It is not sufficient.
    [*Silence.*]
VLADIMIR   They make a noise like feathers.
ESTRAGON   Like leaves.
VLADIMIR   Like ashes.
ESTRAGON   Like leaves.
    [*Long silence.*]
VLADIMIR   Say something!
ESTRAGON   I'm trying.
    [*Long silence.*]
VLADIMIR [*in anguish*]   Say anything at all!
ESTRAGON   What do we do now?
VLADIMIR   Wait for Godot.
ESTRAGON   Ah!
    [*Silence.*]

VLADIMIR   This is awful!

ESTRAGON   Sing something.

VLADIMIR   No no! [*He reflects.*] We could start all over again perhaps.

ESTRAGON   That should be easy.

VLADIMIR   It's the start that's difficult.

ESTRAGON   You can start from anything.

VLADIMIR   Yes, but you have to decide.

ESTRAGON   True.

    [*Silence.*]

VLADIMIR   Help me!

ESTRAGON   I'm trying.

    [*Silence.*]

VLADIMIR   When you seek you hear.

ESTRAGON   You do.

VLADIMIR   That prevents you from finding.

ESTRAGON   It does.

VLADIMIR   That prevents you from thinking.

ESTRAGON   You think all the same.

VLADIMIR   No no, impossible.

ESTRAGON   That's the idea, let's contradict each other.

VLADIMIR   Impossible.

ESTRAGON   You think so?

VLADIMIR   We're in no danger of ever thinking any more.

ESTRAGON   Then what are we complaining about?

VLADIMIR   Thinking is not the worst.

ESTRAGON   Perhaps not. But at least there's that.

VLADIMIR   That what?

ESTRAGON   That's the idea, let's ask each other questions.

VLADIMIR   What do you mean, at least there's that?

ESTRAGON   That much less misery.

VLADIMIR   True.

ESTRAGON   Well? If we gave thanks for our mercies?

VLADIMIR   What is terrible is to *have* thought.

ESTRAGON   But did that ever happen to us?

VLADIMIR   Where are all these corpses from?

ESTRAGON   These skeletons.

VLADIMIR   Tell me that.

ESTRAGON   True.

VLADIMIR   We must have thought a little.

ESTRAGON   At the very beginning.

VLADIMIR   A charnel-house! A charnel-house![3]

ESTRAGON   You don't have to look.

VLADIMIR   You can't help looking.

ESTRAGON   True.

VLADIMIR   Try as one may.

ESTRAGON   I beg your pardon?

VLADIMIR   Try as one may.

ESTRAGON   We should turn resolutely towards Nature.

VLADIMIR   We've tried that.

---

3. A vault for the bodies or bones of the dead.

ESTRAGON True.

VLADIMIR Oh it's not the worst, I know.

ESTRAGON What?

VLADIMIR To have thought.

ESTRAGON Obviously.

VLADIMIR But we could have done without it.

ESTRAGON Que voulez-vous?[4]

VLADIMIR I beg your pardon?

ESTRAGON Que voulez-vous.

VLADIMIR Ah! que voulez-vous. Exactly.
  [*Silence.*]

ESTRAGON That wasn't such a bad little canter.

VLADIMIR Yes, but now we'll have to find something else.

ESTRAGON Let me see. [*He takes off his hat, concentrates.*]

VLADIMIR Let me see. [*He takes off his hat, concentrates. Long silence.*] Ah!
  [*They put on their hats, relax.*]

ESTRAGON Well?

VLADIMIR What was I saying, we could go on from there.

ESTRAGON What were you saying when?

VLADIMIR At the very beginning.

ESTRAGON The very beginning of WHAT?

VLADIMIR This evening . . . I was saying . . . I was saying . . .

ESTRAGON I'm not a historian.

VLADIMIR Wait . . . we embraced . . . we were happy . . . happy . . . what
  do we do now that we're happy . . . go on waiting . . . waiting . . . let me
  think . . . it's coming . . . go on waiting . . . now that we're happy . . . let
  me see . . . ah! The tree!

ESTRAGON The tree?

VLADIMIR Do you not remember?

ESTRAGON I'm tired.

VLADIMIR Look at it.
  [*They look at the tree.*]

ESTRAGON I see nothing.

VLADIMIR But yesterday evening it was all black and bare. And now it's
  covered with leaves.

ESTRAGON Leaves?

VLADIMIR In a single night.

ESTRAGON It must be the Spring.

VLADIMIR But in a single night!

ESTRAGON I tell you we weren't here yesterday. Another of your
  nightmares.

VLADIMIR And where were we yesterday evening according to you?

ESTRAGON How would I know? In another compartment. There's no lack
  of void.

VLADIMIR [*sure of himself*] Good. We weren't here yesterday evening.
  Now what did we do yesterday evening?

ESTRAGON Do?

VLADIMIR Try and remember.

ESTRAGON Do . . . I suppose we blathered.

___

4. What do you want? (formal French).

VLADIMIR [*controlling himself*] About what?

ESTRAGON Oh . . . this and that I suppose, nothing in particular. [*With assurance.*] Yes, now I remember, yesterday evening we spent blathering about nothing in particular. That's been going on now for half a century.

VLADIMIR You don't remember any fact, any circumstance?

ESTRAGON [*weary*] Don't torment me, Didi.

VLADIMIR The sun. The moon. Do you not remember?

ESTRAGON They must have been there, as usual.

VLADIMIR You didn't notice anything out of the ordinary?

ESTRAGON Alas!

VLADIMIR And Pozzo? And Lucky?

ESTRAGON Pozzo?

VLADIMIR The bones.

ESTRAGON They were like fishbones.

VLADIMIR It was Pozzo gave them to you.

ESTRAGON I don't know.

VLADIMIR And the kick.

ESTRAGON That's right, someone gave me a kick.

VLADIMIR It was Lucky gave it to you.

ESTRAGON And all that was yesterday?

VLADIMIR Show your leg.

ESTRAGON Which?

VLADIMIR Both. Pull up your trousers. [ESTRAGON *gives a leg to* VLADIMIR, *staggers.* VLADIMIR *takes the leg. They stagger.*] Pull up your trousers.

ESTRAGON I can't.

> [VLADIMIR *pulls up the trousers, looks at the leg, lets it go.* ESTRAGON *almost falls.*]

VLADIMIR The other. [ESTRAGON *gives the same leg.*] The other, pig! [ESTRAGON *gives the other leg. Triumphantly.*] There's the wound! Beginning to fester!

ESTRAGON And what about it?

VLADIMIR [*letting go the leg*] Where are your boots?

ESTRAGON I must have thrown them away.

VLADIMIR When?

ESTRAGON I don't know.

VLADIMIR Why?

ESTRAGON [*exasperated*] I don't know why I don't know!

VLADIMIR No, I mean why did you throw them away?

ESTRAGON [*exasperated*] Because they were hurting me!

VLADIMIR [*triumphantly, pointing to the boots*] There they are! [ESTRAGON *looks at the boots.*] At the very spot where you left them yesterday!

> [ESTRAGON *goes towards the boots, inspects them closely.*]

ESTRAGON They're not mine.

VLADIMIR [*stupefied*] Not yours!

ESTRAGON Mine were black. These are brown.

VLADIMIR You're sure yours were black?

ESTRAGON Well they were a kind of grey.

VLADIMIR And these are brown. Show.

ESTRAGON [*picking up a boot*] Well they're a kind of green.

VLADIMIR Show. [ESTRAGON *hands him the boot.* VLADIMIR *inspects it, throws it down angrily.*] Well of all the—

ESTRAGON   You see, all that's a lot of bloody—

VLADIMIR   Ah! I see what it is. Yes, I see what's happened.

ESTRAGON   All that's a lot of bloody—

VLADIMIR   It's elementary. Someone came and took yours and left you his.

ESTRAGON   Why?

VLADIMIR   His were too tight for him, so he took yours.

ESTRAGON   But mine were too tight.

VLADIMIR   For you. Not for him.

ESTRAGON   [*having tried in vain to work it out*]   I'm tired! [*Pause.*] Let's go.

VLADIMIR   We can't.

ESTRAGON   Why not?

VLADIMIR   We're waiting for Godot.

ESTRAGON   Ah! [*Pause. Despairing.*] What'll we do, what'll we do!

VLADIMIR   There's nothing we can do.

ESTRAGON   But I can't go on like this!

VLADIMIR   Would you like a radish?

ESTRAGON   Is that all there is?

VLADIMIR   There are radishes and turnips.

ESTRAGON   Are there no carrots?

VLADIMIR   No. Anyway you overdo it with your carrots.

ESTRAGON   Then give me a radish. [VLADIMIR *fumbles in his pockets, finds nothing but turnips, finally brings out a radish and hands it to* ESTRAGON *who examines it, sniffs it.*] It's black!

VLADIMIR   It's a radish.

ESTRAGON   I only like the pink ones, you know that!

VLADIMIR   Then you don't want it?

ESTRAGON   I only like the pink ones!

VLADIMIR   Then give it back to me. [ESTRAGON *gives it back.*]

ESTRAGON   I'll go and get a carrot. [*He does not move.*]

VLADIMIR   This is becoming really insignificant.

ESTRAGON   Not enough.

   [*Silence.*]

VLADIMIR   What about trying them.

ESTRAGON   I've tried everything.

VLADIMIR   No, I mean the boots.

ESTRAGON   Would that be a good thing?

VLADIMIR   It'd pass the time. [ESTRAGON *hesitates.*] I assure you, it'd be an occupation.

ESTRAGON   A relaxation.

VLADIMIR   A recreation.

ESTRAGON   A relaxation.

VLADIMIR   Try.

ESTRAGON   You'll help me?

VLADIMIR   I will of course.

ESTRAGON   We don't manage too badly, eh Didi, between the two of us?

VLADIMIR   Yes yes. Come on, we'll try the left first.

ESTRAGON   We always find something, eh Didi, to give us the impression we exist?

VLADIMIR   [*impatiently*]   Yes yes, we're magicians. But let us persevere in what we have resolved, before we forget. [*He picks up a boot.*] Come on, give me your foot. [ESTRAGON *raises his foot.*] The other, hog! [ESTRAGON *raises the other foot.*] Higher! [*Wreathed together they stagger about the stage.* VLADIMIR *succeeds finally in getting on the boot.*] Try and walk. [ESTRAGON *walks.*] Well?

ESTRAGON   It fits.

VLADIMIR [*taking string from his pocket*]   We'll try and lace it.

ESTRAGON [*vehemently*]   No no, no laces, no laces!

VLADIMIR   You'll be sorry. Let's try the other. [*As before.*] Well?

ESTRAGON [*grudgingly*]   It fits too.

VLADIMIR   They don't hurt you?

ESTRAGON   Not yet.

VLADIMIR   Then you can keep them.

ESTRAGON   They're too big.

VLADIMIR   Perhaps you'll have socks some day.

ESTRAGON   True.

VLADIMIR   Then you'll keep them?

ESTRAGON   That's enough about these boots.

VLADIMIR   Yes, but—

ESTRAGON [*violently*]   Enough! [*Silence.*] I suppose I might as well sit down. [*He looks for a place to sit down, then goes and sits down on the mound.*]

VLADIMIR   That's where you were sitting yesterday evening.

ESTRAGON   If I could only sleep.

VLADIMIR   Yesterday you slept.

ESTRAGON   I'll try. [*He resumes his foetal posture, his head between his knees.*]

VLADIMIR   Wait. [*He goes over and sits down beside* ESTRAGON *and begins to sing in a loud voice.*]

> Bye bye bye bye
> Bye bye—

ESTRAGON [*looking up angrily*]   Not so loud!

VLADIMIR [*softly*]

> Bye bye bye bye
> Bye bye bye bye
> Bye bye bye bye
> Bye bye . . .

[ESTRAGON *sleeps.* VLADIMIR *gets up softly, takes off his coat and lays it across* ESTRAGON'S *shoulders, then starts walking up and down, swinging his arms to keep himself warm.* ESTRAGON *wakes with a start, jumps up, casts*[5] *about wildly.* VLADIMIR *returns to him, puts his arms round him.*]

There . . . there . . . Didi is there . . . don't be afraid . . .

ESTRAGON   Ah!

VLADIMIR   There . . . there . . . it's all over.

ESTRAGON   I was falling—

VLADIMIR   It's all over, it's all over.

---

5. Looks.

ESTRAGON   I was on top of a—
VLADIMIR   Don't tell me! Come, we'll walk it off.
         [*He takes* ESTRAGON *by the arm and walks him up and down until*
         ESTRAGON *refuses to go any further.*]
ESTRAGON   That's enough. I'm tired.
VLADIMIR   You'd rather be stuck there doing nothing?
ESTRAGON   Yes.
VLADIMIR   Please yourself.
         [*He releases* ESTRAGON, *picks up his coat and puts it on.*]
ESTRAGON   Let's go.
VLADIMIR   We can't.
ESTRAGON   Why not?
VLADIMIR   We're waiting for Godot.
ESTRAGON   Ah! [VLADIMIR *walks up and down.*] Can you not stay still?
VLADIMIR   I'm cold.
ESTRAGON   We came too soon.
VLADIMIR   It's always at nightfall.
ESTRAGON   But night doesn't fall.
VLADIMIR   It'll fall all of a sudden, like yesterday.
ESTRAGON   Then it'll be night.
VLADIMIR   And we can go.
ESTRAGON   Then it'll be day again. [*Pause. Despairing.*] What'll we do,
         what'll we do!
VLADIMIR   [*halting, violently*]   Will you stop whining! I've had about my
         bellyful of your lamentations!
ESTRAGON   I'm going.
VLADIMIR   [*seeing* LUCKY's *hat*]   Well!
ESTRAGON   Farewell.
VLADIMIR   Lucky's hat. [*He goes towards it.*] I've been here an hour and
         never saw it. [*Very pleased.*] Fine!
ESTRAGON   You'll never see me again.
VLADIMIR   I knew it was the right place. Now our troubles are over. [*He
         picks up the hat, contemplates it, straightens it.*] Must have been a very
         fine hat. [*He puts it on in place of his own which he hands to* ESTRAGON.]
         Here.
ESTRAGON   What?
VLADIMIR   Hold that.
         [ESTRAGON *takes* VLADIMIR's *hat.* VLADIMIR *adjusts* LUCKY's *hat on his
         head.* ESTRAGON *puts on* VLADIMIR's *hat in place of his own which he
         hands to* VLADIMIR. VLADIMIR *takes* ESTRAGON's *hat.* ESTRAGON *adjusts*
         VLADIMIR's *hat on his head.* VLADIMIR *puts on* ESTRAGON's *hat in place
         of* LUCKY's *which he hands to* ESTRAGON. ESTRAGON *takes* LUCKY's *hat.*
         VLADIMIR *adjusts* ESTRAGON's *hat on his head.* ESTRAGON *puts on*
         LUCKY's *hat in place of* VLADIMIR's *which he hands to* VLADIMIR. VLADI-
         MIR *takes his hat,* ESTRAGON *adjusts* LUCKY's *hat on his head.* VLADIMIR
         puts on his hat in place of ESTRAGON's *which he hands to* ESTRAGON.
         ESTRAGON *takes his hat.* VLADIMIR *adjusts his hat on his head.* ESTRAGON
         puts on his hat in place of LUCKY's *which he hands to* VLADIMIR. VLADI-
         MIR *takes* LUCKY's *hat.* ESTRAGON *adjusts his hat on his head.* VLADIMIR
         puts on LUCKY's *hat in place of his own which he hands to* ESTRAGON.
         ESTRAGON *takes* VLADIMIR's *hat.* VLADIMIR *adjusts* LUCKY's *hat on his
         head.* ESTRAGON *hands* VLADIMIR's *hat back to* VLADIMIR *who takes it*

and hands it back to ESTRAGON *who takes it and hands it back to* VLADIMIR *who takes it and throws it down.*]

How does it fit me?

ESTRAGON   How would I know?

VLADIMIR   No, but how do I look in it? [*He turns his head coquettishly to and fro, minces like a mannequin.*[6]]

ESTRAGON   Hideous.

VLADIMIR   Yes, but not more so than usual?

ESTRAGON   Neither more nor less.

VLADIMIR   Then I can keep it. Mine irked me. [*Pause.*] How shall I say? [*Pause.*] It itched me. [*He takes off* LUCKY's *hat, peers into it, shakes it, knocks on the crown, puts it on again.*]

ESTRAGON   I'm going.
        [*Silence.*]

VLADIMIR   Will you not play?

ESTRAGON   Play at what?

VLADIMIR   We could play at Pozzo and Lucky.

ESTRAGON   Never heard of it.

VLADIMIR   I'll do Lucky, you do Pozzo. [*He imitates* LUCKY *sagging under the weight of his baggage.* ESTRAGON *looks at him with stupefaction.*] Go on.

ESTRAGON   What am I to do?

VLADIMIR   Curse me!

ESTRAGON [*after reflection*]   Naughty!

VLADIMIR   Stronger!

ESTRAGON   Gonococcus! Spirochete![7]
        [VLADIMIR *sways back and forth, doubled in two.*]

VLADIMIR   Tell me to think.

ESTRAGON   What?

VLADIMIR   Say, Think, pig!

ESTRAGON   Think, pig!
        [*Silence.*]

VLADIMIR   I can't!

ESTRAGON   That's enough of that.

VLADIMIR   Tell me to dance.

ESTRAGON   I'm going.

VLADIMIR   Dance, hog! [*He writhes. Exit* ESTRAGON *left, precipitately.*] I can't! [*He looks up, misses* ESTRAGON.] Gogo! [*He moves wildly about the stage. Enter* ESTRAGON *left, panting. He hastens towards* VLADIMIR, *falls into his arms.*] There you are again at last!

ESTRAGON   I'm accursed!

VLADIMIR   Where were you? I thought you were gone for ever.

ESTRAGON   They're coming!

VLADIMIR   Who?

ESTRAGON   I don't know.

VLADIMIR   How many?

ESTRAGON   I don't know.

VLADIMIR [*triumphantly*]   It's Godot! At last! Gogo! It's Godot! We're saved! Let's go and meet him! [*He drags* ESTRAGON *towards the wings.* ESTRAGON

---

6. A person employed to model clothes.
7. One of a group of bacteria, usually the one that causes syphilis. "Gonococcus": the bacterium that causes gonorrhea.

resists, pulls himself free, exits right.] Gogo! Come back! [VLADIMIR *runs to extreme left, scans the horizon. Enter* ESTRAGON *right, he hastens towards* VLADIMIR, *falls into his arms.*] There you are again again!

ESTRAGON   I'm in hell!

VLADIMIR   Where were you?

ESTRAGON   They're coming there too!

VLADIMIR   We're surrounded! [ESTRAGON *makes a rush towards back.*] Imbecile! There's no way out there. [*He takes* ESTRAGON *by the arm and drags him towards front. Gesture towards front.*] There! Not a soul in sight! Off you go! Quick! [*He pushes* ESTRAGON *towards auditorium.* ESTRAGON *recoils in horror.*] You won't? [*He contemplates auditorium.*] Well I can understand that. Wait till I see. [*He reflects.*] Your only hope left is to disappear.

ESTRAGON   Where?

VLADIMIR   Behind the tree. [ESTRAGON *hesitates.*] Quick! Behind the tree. [ESTRAGON *goes and crouches behind the tree, realizes he is not hidden, comes out from behind the tree.*] Decidedly this tree will not have been the slightest use to us.

ESTRAGON [*calmer*]   I lost my head. Forgive me. It won't happen again. Tell me what to do.

VLADIMIR   There's nothing to do.

ESTRAGON   You go and stand there. [*He draws* VLADIMIR *to extreme right and places him with his back to the stage.*] There, don't move, and watch out. [VLADIMIR *scans horizon, screening his eyes with his hand.* ESTRAGON *runs and takes up same position extreme left. They turn their heads and look at each other.*] Back to back like in the good old days. [*They continue to look at each other for a moment, then resume their watch. Long silence.*] Do you see anything coming?

VLADIMIR [*turning his head.*]   What?

ESTRAGON [*louder*]   Do you see anything coming?

VLADIMIR   No.

ESTRAGON   Nor I.
   [*They resume their watch. Silence.*]

VLADIMIR   You must have had a vision.

ESTRAGON [*turning his head*]   What?

VLADIMIR [*louder*]   You must have had a vision.

ESTRAGON   No need to shout!
   [*They resume their watch. Silence.*]

VLADIMIR }
ESTRAGON } [*turning simultaneously*]   Do you—

VLADIMIR   Oh pardon!

ESTRAGON   Carry on.

VLADIMIR   No no, after you.

ESTRAGON   No no, you first.

VLADIMIR   I interrupted you.

ESTRAGON   On the contrary.
   [*They glare at each other angrily.*]

VLADIMIR   Ceremonious ape!

ESTRAGON   Punctilious pig!

VLADIMIR   Finish your phrase, I tell you!

ESTRAGON   Finish your own!
   [*Silence. They draw closer, halt.*]

VLADIMIR   Moron!

ESTRAGON   That's the idea, let's abuse each other.

[*They turn, move apart, turn again and face each other.*]

VLADIMIR   Moron!

ESTRAGON   Vermin!

VLADIMIR   Abortion!

ESTRAGON   Morpion![8]

VLADIMIR   Sewer-rat!

ESTRAGON   Curate!

VLADIMIR   Cretin!

ESTRAGON [*with finality*]   Crritic!

VLADIMIR   Oh! [*He wilts, vanquished, and turns away.*]

ESTRAGON   Now let's make it up.

VLADIMIR   Gogo!

ESTRAGON   Didi!

VLADIMIR   Your hand!

ESTRAGON   Take it!

VLADIMIR   Come to my arms!

ESTRAGON   Your arms?

VLADIMIR   My breast!

ESTRAGON   Off we go!

[*They embrace. They separate. Silence.*]

VLADIMIR   How time flies when one has fun!

[*Silence.*]

ESTRAGON   What do we do now?

VLADIMIR   While waiting.

ESTRAGON   While waiting.

[*Silence.*]

VLADIMIR   We could do our exercises.

ESTRAGON   Our movements.

VLADIMIR   Our elevations.

ESTRAGON   Our relaxations.

VLADIMIR   Our elongations.

ESTRAGON   Our relaxations.

VLADIMIR   To warm us up.

ESTRAGON   To calm us down.

VLADIMIR   Off we go.

[VLADIMIR *hops from one foot to the other.* ESTRAGON *imitates him.*]

ESTRAGON [*stopping*]   That's enough. I'm tired.

VLADIMIR [*stopping*]   We're not in form. What about a little deep breathing?

ESTRAGON   I'm tired breathing.

VLADIMIR   You're right. [*Pause.*] Let's just do the tree, for the balance.

ESTRAGON   The tree?

[VLADIMIR *does the tree, staggering about on one leg.*]

VLADIMIR [*stopping*]   Your turn.

[ESTRAGON *does the tree, staggers.*]

ESTRAGON   Do you think God sees me?

---

8. Crab louse (a common French word, now obsolete in English).

VLADIMIR   You must close your eyes.
[ESTRAGON *closes his eyes, staggers worse.*]
ESTRAGON [*stopping, brandishing his fists, at the top of his voice*]   God
have pity on me!
VLADIMIR [*vexed*]   And me?
ESTRAGON   On me! On me! Pity! On me!
[*Enter pozzo and* LUCKY. POZZO *is blind.* LUCKY *burdened as before.
Rope as before, but much shorter, so that pozzo may follow more easily.*
LUCKY *wearing a different hat. At the sight of* VLADIMIR *and* ESTRAGON
he stops short. POZZO, *continuing on his way, bumps into him.*]
VLADIMIR   Gogo!
POZZO [*clutching on to* LUCKY *who staggers*]   What is it? Who is it?
[LUCKY *falls, drops everything and brings down pozzo with him. They
lie helpless among the scattered baggage.*]
ESTRAGON   Is it Godot?
VLADIMIR   At last! [*He goes towards the heap.*] Reinforcements at last!
POZZO   Help!
ESTRAGON   Is it Godot?
VLADIMIR   We were beginning to weaken. Now we're sure to see the eve-
ning out.
POZZO   Help!
ESTRAGON   Do you hear him?
VLADIMIR   We are no longer alone, waiting for the night, waiting for
Godot, waiting for . . . waiting. All evening we have struggled, unas-
sisted. Now it's over. It's already tomorrow.
POZZO   Help!
VLADIMIR   Time flows again already. The sun will set, the moon rise, and
we away . . . from here.
POZZO   Pity!
VLADIMIR   Poor Pozzo!
ESTRAGON   I knew it was him.
VLADIMIR   Who?
ESTRAGON   Godot.
VLADIMIR   But it's not Godot.
ESTRAGON   It's not Godot?
VLADIMIR   It's not Godot.
ESTRAGON   Then who is it?
VLADIMIR   It's Pozzo.
POZZO   Here! Here! Help me up!
VLADIMIR   He can't get up.
ESTRAGON   Let's go.
VLADIMIR   We can't.
ESTRAGON   Why not?
VLADIMIR   We're waiting for Godot.
ESTRAGON   Ah!
VLADIMIR   Perhaps he has another bone for you.
ESTRAGON   Bone?
VLADIMIR   Chicken. Do you not remember?
ESTRAGON   It was him?
VLADIMIR   Yes.
ESTRAGON   Ask him.

VLADIMIR Perhaps we should help him first.

ESTRAGON To do what?

VLADIMIR To get up.

ESTRAGON He can't get up?

VLADIMIR He wants to get up.

ESTRAGON Then let him get up.

VLADIMIR He can't.

ESTRAGON Why not?

VLADIMIR I don't know.

[*pozzo writhes, groans, beats the ground with his fists.*]

ESTRAGON We should ask him for the bone first. Then if he refuses we'll leave him there.

VLADIMIR You mean we have him at our mercy?

ESTRAGON Yes.

VLADIMIR And that we should subordinate our good offices to certain conditions?

ESTRAGON What?

VLADIMIR That seems intelligent all right. But there's one thing I'm afraid of.

POZZO Help!

ESTRAGON What?

VLADIMIR That Lucky might get going all of a sudden. Then we'd be ballocksed.[9]

ESTRAGON Lucky?

VLADIMIR The one that went for you yesterday.

ESTRAGON I tell you there was ten of them.

VLADIMIR No, before that, the one that kicked you.

ESTRAGON Is he there?

VLADIMIR As large as life. [*Gesture towards* LUCKY.] For the moment he is inert. But he might run amuck any minute.

POZZO Help!

ESTRAGON And suppose we gave him a good beating the two of us?

VLADIMIR You mean if we fell on him in his sleep?

ESTRAGON Yes.

VLADIMIR That seems a good idea all right. But could we do it? Is he really asleep? [*Pause.*] No, the best would be to take advantage of Pozzo's calling for help—

POZZO Help!

VLADIMIR To help him—

ESTRAGON *We* help *him*?

VLADIMIR In anticipation of some tangible return.

ESTRAGON And suppose he—

VLADIMIR Let us not waste our time in idle discourse! [*Pause. Vehemently.*] Let us do something, while we have the chance! It is not every day that we are needed. Not indeed that we personally are needed. Others would meet the case equally well, if not better. To all mankind they were addressed, those cries for help still ringing in our ears! But at this place, at this moment of time, all mankind is us, whether we like it or

---

9. Screwed (slang); from "bollocks," or testicles.

not. Let us make the most of it, before it is too late! Let us represent worthily for once the foul brood to which a cruel fate consigned us! What do you say? [ESTRAGON *says nothing.*] It is true that when with folded arms we weigh the pros and cons we are no less a credit to our species. The tiger bounds to the help of his congeners[1] without the least reflexion, or else he slinks away into the depths of the thickets. But that is not the question. What are we doing here, *that* is the question. And we are blessed in this, that we happen to know the answer. Yes, in this immense confusion one thing alone is clear. We are waiting for Godot to come—

ESTRAGON Ah!

POZZO Help!

VLADIMIR Or for night to fall. [*Pause.*] We have kept our appointment and that's an end to that. We are not saints, but we have kept our appointment. How many people can boast as much?

ESTRAGON Billions.

VLADIMIR You think so?

ESTRAGON I don't know.

VLADIMIR You may be right.

POZZO Help!

VLADIMIR All I know is that the hours are long, under these conditions, and constrain us to beguile them with proceedings which—how shall I say—which may at first sight seem reasonable, until they become a habit. You may say it is to prevent our reason from foundering. No doubt. But has it not long been straying in the night without end of the abyssal depths? That's what I sometimes wonder. You follow my reasoning?

ESTRAGON [*aphoristic for once*] We are all born mad. Some remain so.

POZZO Help! I'll pay you!

ESTRAGON How much?

POZZO One hundred francs![2]

ESTRAGON It's not enough.

VLADIMIR I wouldn't go so far as that.

ESTRAGON You think it's enough?

VLADIMIR No, I mean so far as to assert that I was weak in the head when I came into the world. But that is not the question.

POZZO Two hundred!

VLADIMIR We wait. We are bored. [*He throws up his hand.*] No, don't protest, we are bored to death, there's no denying it. Good. A diversion comes along and what do we do? We let it go to waste. Come, let's get to work! [*He advances towards the heap, stops in his stride.*] In an instant all will vanish and we'll be alone once more, in the midst of nothingness! [*He broods.*]

POZZO Two hundred!

VLADIMIR We're coming!

[*He tries to pull* POZZO *to his feet, fails, tries again, stumbles, falls, tries to get up, fails.*]

ESTRAGON What's the matter with you all?

VLADIMIR Help!

ESTRAGON I'm going.

---

1. Members of his kind.   2. Then worth about 30 dollars.

VLADIMIR   Don't leave me! They'll kill me!

POZZO   Where am I?

VLADIMIR   Gogo!

POZZO   Help!

VLADIMIR   Help!

ESTRAGON   I'm going.

VLADIMIR   Help me up first, then we'll go together.

ESTRAGON   You promise?

VLADIMIR   I swear it!

ESTRAGON   And we'll never come back?

VLADIMIR   Never!

ESTRAGON   We'll go to the Pyrenees.[3]

VLADIMIR   Wherever you like.

ESTRAGON   I've always wanted to wander in the Pyrenees.

VLADIMIR   You'll wander in them.

ESTRAGON [*recoiling*]   Who farted?

VLADIMIR   Pozzo.

POZZO   Here! Here! Pity!

ESTRAGON   It's revolting!

VLADIMIR   Quick! Give me your hand!

ESTRAGON   I'm going. [*Pause. Louder.*] I'm going.

VLADIMIR   Well I suppose in the end I'll get up by myself. [*He tries, fails.*] In the fullness of time.

ESTRAGON   What's the matter with you?

VLADIMIR   Go to hell.

ESTRAGON   Are you staying there?

VLADIMIR   For the time being.

ESTRAGON   Come on, get up, you'll catch a chill.

VLADIMIR   Don't worry about me.

ESTRAGON   Come on, Didi, don't be pig-headed!

[*He stretches out his hand which* VLADIMIR *makes haste to seize.*]

VLADIMIR   Pull!

[ESTRAGON *pulls, stumbles, falls. Long silence.*]

POZZO   Help!

VLADIMIR   We've arrived.

POZZO   Who are you?

VLADIMIR   We are men.

[*Silence.*]

ESTRAGON   Sweet mother earth!

VLADIMIR   Can you get up?

ESTRAGON   I don't know.

VLADIMIR   Try.

ESTRAGON   Not now, not now.

[*Silence.*]

POZZO   What happened?

VLADIMIR [*violently*]   Will you stop it, you! Pest! He can think of nothing but himself!

ESTRAGON   What about a little snooze?

VLADIMIR   Did you hear him? He wants to know what happened!

---

3. Mountain range along the border between France and Spain.

ESTRAGON   Don't mind him. Sleep.
  [*Silence.*]
POZZO   Pity! Pity!
ESTRAGON [*with a start*]   What is it?
VLADIMIR   Were you asleep?
ESTRAGON   I must have been.
VLADIMIR   It's this bastard Pozzo at it again.
ESTRAGON   Make him stop it. Kick him in the crotch.
VLADIMIR [*striking Pozzo*]   Will you stop it! Crablouse! [POZZO *extricates himself with cries of pain and crawls away. He stops, saws the air blindly, calling for help.* VLADIMIR, *propped on his elbow, observes his retreat.*] He's off! [POZZO *collapses.*] He's down!
ESTRAGON   What do we do now?
VLADIMIR   Perhaps I could crawl to him.
ESTRAGON   Don't leave me!
VLADIMIR   Or I could call to him.
ESTRAGON   Yes, call to him.
VLADIMIR   Pozzo! [*Silence.*] Pozzo! [*Silence.*] No reply.
ESTRAGON   Together.
VLADIMIR }
ESTRAGON } Pozzo! Pozzo!
VLADIMIR   He moved.
ESTRAGON   Are you sure his name is Pozzo?
VLADIMIR [*alarmed*]   Mr. Pozzo! Come back! We won't hurt you!
  [*Silence.*]
ESTRAGON   We might try him with other names.
VLADIMIR   I'm afraid he's dying.
ESTRAGON   It'd be amusing.
VLADIMIR   What'd be amusing?
ESTRAGON   To try him with other names, one after the other. It'd pass the time. And we'd be bound to hit on the right one sooner or later.
VLADIMIR   I tell you his name is Pozzo.
ESTRAGON   We'll soon see. [*He reflects.*] Abel! Abel!
POZZO   Help!
ESTRAGON   Got it in one!
VLADIMIR   I begin to weary of this motif.
ESTRAGON   Perhaps the other is called Cain.[4] Cain! Cain!
POZZO   Help!
ESTRAGON   He's all humanity. [*Silence.*] Look at the little cloud.
VLADIMIR [*raising his eyes*]   Where?
ESTRAGON   There. In the zenith.[5]
VLADIMIR   Well? [*Pause.*] What is there so wonderful about it?
  [*Silence.*]
ESTRAGON   Let's pass on now to something else, do you mind?
VLADIMIR   I was just going to suggest it.
ESTRAGON   But to what?
VLADIMIR   Ah!
  [*Silence.*]

4. The older son of Adam and Eve, who mur-   5. The point of the sky directly overhead.
dered his brother, Abel. Cf. Genesis 4.1–15.

ESTRAGON   Suppose we got up to begin with?
VLADIMIR   No harm trying.
            [*They get up.*]
ESTRAGON   Child's play.
VLADIMIR   Simple question of will-power.
ESTRAGON   And now?
POZZO   Help!
ESTRAGON   Let's go.
VLADIMIR   We can't.
ESTRAGON   Why not?
VLADIMIR   We're waiting for Godot.
ESTRAGON   Ah! [*Despairing.*] What'll we do, what'll we do!
POZZO   Help!
VLADIMIR   What about helping him?
ESTRAGON   What does he want?
VLADIMIR   He wants to get up.
ESTRAGON   Then why doesn't he?
VLADIMIR   He wants us to help him to get up.
ESTRAGON   Then why don't we? What are we waiting for?
            [*They help* POZZO *to his feet, let him go. He falls.*]
VLADIMIR   We must hold him. [*They get him up again.* POZZO *sags between
    them, his arms round their necks.*] Feeling better?
POZZO   Who are you?
VLADIMIR   Do you not recognize us?
POZZO   I am blind.
            [*Silence.*]
ESTRAGON   Perhaps he can see into the future.[6]
VLADIMIR   Since when?
POZZO   I used to have wonderful sight—but are you friends?
ESTRAGON [*laughing noisily*]   He wants to know if we are friends!
VLADIMIR   No, he means friends of his.
ESTRAGON   Well?
VLADIMIR   We've proved we are, by helping him.
ESTRAGON   Exactly. Would we have helped him if we weren't his friends?
VLADIMIR   Possibly.
ESTRAGON   True.
VLADIMIR   Don't let's quibble about that now.
POZZO   You are not highwaymen?
ESTRAGON   Highwaymen! Do we look like highwaymen?
VLADIMIR   Damn it can't you see the man is blind!
ESTRAGON   Damn it so he is. [*Pause.*] So he says.
POZZO   Don't leave me!
VLADIMIR   No question of it.
ESTRAGON   For the moment.
POZZO   What time is it?
VLADIMIR [*inspecting the sky*]   Seven o'clock . . . eight o'clock . . .
ESTRAGON   That depends what time of year it is.

---

6. Perhaps a reference to Tiresias, a figure in Greek mythology and literature who, although blind, possessed the gift of prophecy.

POZZO   Is it evening?

[*Silence.* VLADIMIR *and* ESTRAGON *scrutinize the sunset.*]

ESTRAGON   It's rising.

VLADIMIR   Impossible.

ESTRAGON   Perhaps it's the dawn.

VLADIMIR   Don't be a fool. It's the west over there.

ESTRAGON   How do you know?

POZZO [*anguished*]   Is it evening?

VLADIMIR   Anyway it hasn't moved.

ESTRAGON   I tell you it's rising.

POZZO   Why don't you answer me?

ESTRAGON   Give us a chance.

VLADIMIR [*reassuring*]   It's evening, Sir, it's evening, night is drawing nigh. My friend here would have me doubt it and I must confess he shook me for a moment. But it is not for nothing I have lived through this long day and I can assure you it is very near the end of its repertory. [*Pause.*] How do you feel now?

ESTRAGON   How much longer are we to cart him around? [*They half release him, catch him again as he falls.*] We are not caryatids![7]

VLADIMIR   You were saying your sight used to be good, if I heard you right.

POZZO   Wonderful! Wonderful, wonderful sight!

[*Silence.*]

ESTRAGON [*irritably*]   Expand! Expand!

VLADIMIR   Let him alone. Can't you see he's thinking of the days when he was happy. [*Pause.*] *Memoria praeteritorum bonorum*[8]—that must be unpleasant.

ESTRAGON   We wouldn't know.

VLADIMIR   And it came on you all of a sudden?

POZZO   Quite wonderful!

VLADIMIR   I'm asking you if it came on you all of a sudden.

POZZO   I woke up one fine day as blind as Fortune.[9] [*Pause.*] Sometimes I wonder if I'm not still asleep.

VLADIMIR   And when was that?

POZZO   I don't know.

VLADIMIR   But no later than yesterday—

POZZO [*violently*]   Don't question me! The blind have no notion of time. The things of time are hidden from them too.

VLADIMIR   Well just fancy that! I could have sworn it was just the opposite.

ESTRAGON   I'm going.

POZZO   Where are we?

VLADIMIR   I couldn't tell you.

POZZO   It isn't by any chance the place known as the Board?[1]

VLADIMIR   Never heard of it.

POZZO   What is it like?

---

7. Female figures serving as support columns in classical buildings.
8. The memory of past good (Latin, quoting the *Summa Theologica Secunda* 2.2.36.1, by theologian and philosopher Thomas Aquinas [1225–1274]).
9. The Roman goddess of chance or luck, sometimes depicted as blindfolded.
1. The stage, or the profession of acting, is often called "the boards."

VLADIMIR [*looking round*]   It's indescribable. It's like nothing. There's nothing. There's a tree.

POZZO   Then it's not the Board.

ESTRAGON [*sagging*]   Some diversion!

POZZO   Where is my menial?

VLADIMIR   He's about somewhere.

POZZO   Why doesn't he answer when I call?

VLADIMIR   I don't know. He seems to be sleeping. Perhaps he's dead.

POZZO   What happened exactly?

ESTRAGON   Exactly!

VLADIMIR   The two of you slipped. [*Pause.*] And fell.

POZZO   Go and see is he hurt.

VLADIMIR   We can't leave you.

POZZO   You needn't both go.

VLADIMIR [*to* ESTRAGON]   You go.

ESTRAGON   After what he did to me? Never!

POZZO   Yes yes, let your friend go, he stinks so. [*Silence.*] What is he waiting for?

VLADIMIR   What you waiting for?

ESTRAGON   I'm waiting for Godot.
         [*Silence.*]

VLADIMIR   What exactly should he do?

POZZO   Well to begin with he should pull on the rope, as hard as he likes so long as he doesn't strangle him. He usually responds to that. If not he should give him a taste of his boot, in the face and the privates as far as possible.

VLADIMIR [*to* ESTRAGON]   You see, you've nothing to be afraid of. It's even an opportunity to revenge yourself.

ESTRAGON   And if he defends himself?

POZZO   No no, he never defends himself.

VLADIMIR   I'll come flying to the rescue.

ESTRAGON   Don't take your eyes off me. [*He goes towards* LUCKY.]

VLADIMIR   Make sure he's alive before you start. No point in exerting yourself if he's dead.

ESTRAGON [*bending over* LUCKY]   He's breathing.

VLADIMIR   Then let him have it.
         [*With sudden fury* ESTRAGON *starts kicking* LUCKY, *hurling abuse at him as he does so. But he hurts his foot and moves away, limping and groaning.* LUCKY *stirs.*]

ESTRAGON   Oh the brute!
         [*He sits down on the mound and tries to take off his boot. But he soon desists and disposes himself for sleep, his arms on his knees and his head on his arms.*]

POZZO   What's gone wrong now?

VLADIMIR   My friend has hurt himself.

POZZO   And Lucky?

VLADIMIR   So it is he?

POZZO   What?

VLADIMIR   It is Lucky?

POZZO   I don't understand.

VLADIMIR   And you are Pozzo?

POZZO   Certainly I am Pozzo.

VLADIMIR   The same as yesterday?

POZZO   Yesterday?

VLADIMIR   We met yesterday. [*Silence.*] Do you not remember?

POZZO   I don't remember having met anyone yesterday. But tomorrow I won't remember having met anyone today. So don't count on me to enlighten you.

VLADIMIR   But—

POZZO   Enough! Up pig!

VLADIMIR   You were bringing him to the fair to sell him. You spoke to us. He danced. He thought. You had your sight.

POZZO   As you please. Let me go! [VLADIMIR *moves away.*] Up! [LUCKY *gets up, gathers up his burdens.*]

VLADIMIR   Where do you go from here?

POZZO   On. [LUCKY, *laden down, takes his place before* POZZO.] Whip! [LUCKY *puts everything down, looks for whip, finds it, puts it into* POZZO's *hand, takes up everything again.*] Rope!
    [LUCKY *puts everything down, puts end of rope into* POZZO's *hand, takes up everything again.*]

VLADIMIR   What is there in the bag?

POZZO   Sand. [*He jerks the rope.*] On!

VLADIMIR   Don't go yet.

POZZO   I'm going.

VLADIMIR   What do you do when you fall far from help?

POZZO   We wait till we can get up. Then we go on. On!

VLADIMIR   Before you go tell him to sing.

POZZO   Who?

VLADIMIR   Lucky.

POZZO   To sing?

VLADIMIR   Yes. Or to think. Or to recite.

POZZO   But he is dumb.

VLADIMIR   Dumb!

POZZO   Dumb. He can't even groan.

VLADIMIR   Dumb! Since when?

POZZO   [*suddenly furious*]   Have you not done tormenting me with your accursed time! It's abominable! When! When! One day, is that not enough for you, one day he went dumb, one day I went blind, one day we'll go deaf, one day we were born, one day we shall die, the same day, the same second, is that not enough for you? [*Calmer.*] They give birth astride of a grave, the light gleams an instant, then it's night once more. [*He jerks the rope.*] On!
    [*Exeunt*[2] POZZO *and* LUCKY. VLADIMIR *follows them to the edge of the stage, looks after them. The noise of falling, reinforced by mimic of* VLADIMIR, *announces that they are down again. Silence.* VLADIMIR *goes towards* ESTRAGON, *contemplates him a moment, then shakes him awake.*]

ESTRAGON   [*wild gestures, incoherent words. Finally.*]   Why will you never let me sleep?

VLADIMIR   I felt lonely.

---

2. [They] exit (Latin).

ESTRAGON   I was dreaming I was happy.

VLADIMIR   That passed the time.

ESTRAGON   I was dreaming that—

VLADIMIR [*violently*]   Don't tell me! [*Silence.*] I wonder is he really blind.

ESTRAGON   Blind? Who?

VLADIMIR   Pozzo.

ESTRAGON   Blind?

VLADIMIR   He told us he was blind.

ESTRAGON   Well what about it?

VLADIMIR   It seemed to me he saw us.

ESTRAGON   You dreamt it. [*Pause.*] Let's go. We can't. Ah! [*Pause.*] Are you sure it wasn't him?

VLADIMIR   Who?

ESTRAGON   Godot.

VLADIMIR   But who?

ESTRAGON   Pozzo.

VLADIMIR   Not at all! [*Less sure.*] Not at all! [*Still less sure.*] Not at all!

ESTRAGON   I suppose I might as well get up. [*He gets up painfully.*] Ow! Didi!

VLADIMIR   I don't know what to think any more.

ESTRAGON   My feet! [*He sits down again and tries to take off his boots.*] Help me!

VLADIMIR   Was I sleeping, while the others suffered? Am I sleeping now? Tomorrow, when I wake, or think I do, what shall I say of today? That with Estragon my friend, at this place, until the fall of night, I waited for Godot? That Pozzo passed, with his carrier, and that he spoke to us? Probably. But in all that what truth will there be? [ESTRAGON, *having struggled with his boots in vain, is dozing off again.* VLADIMIR *looks at him.*] He'll know nothing. He'll tell me about the blows he received and I'll give him a carrot. [*Pause.*] Astride of a grave and a difficult birth. Down in the hole, lingeringly, the grave-digger puts on the forceps.[3] We have time to grow old. The air is full of our cries. [*He listens.*] But habit is a great deadener. [*He looks again at* ESTRAGON.] At me too someone is looking, of me too someone is saying, He is sleeping, he knows nothing, let him sleep on. [*Pause.*] I can't go on! [*Pause.*] What have I said?

   [*He goes feverishly to and fro, halts finally at extreme left, broods. Enter* BOY *right. He halts. Silence.*]

BOY   Mister . . . [VLADIMIR *turns.*] Mister Albert . . .

VLADIMIR   Off we go again. [*Pause.*] Do you not recognize me?

BOY   No Sir.

VLADIMIR   It wasn't you came yesterday.

BOY   No Sir.

VLADIMIR   This is your first time.

BOY   Yes Sir.

   [*Silence.*]

VLADIMIR   You have a message from Mr. Godot.

BOY   Yes Sir.

VLADIMIR   He won't come this evening.

BOY   No Sir.

---

3. An instrument used in obstetrics to pull the baby out of the birth canal.

VLADIMIR But he'll come tomorrow.
BOY Yes Sir.
VLADIMIR Without fail.
BOY Yes Sir.
    [*Silence.*]
VLADIMIR Did you meet anyone?
BOY No Sir.
VLADIMIR Two other . . . [*he hesitates.*] . . . men?
BOY I didn't see anyone, Sir.
    [*Silence.*]
VLADIMIR What does he do, Mr. Godot? [*Silence.*] Do you hear me?
BOY Yes Sir.
VLADIMIR Well?
BOY He does nothing, Sir.
    [*Silence.*]
VLADIMIR How is your brother?
BOY He's sick, Sir.
VLADIMIR Perhaps it was he came yesterday.
BOY I don't know, Sir.
    [*Silence.*]
VLADIMIR [*softly*] Has he a beard, Mr. Godot?
BOY Yes Sir.
VLADIMIR Fair or . . . [*he hesitates.*] . . . or black?
BOY I think it's white, Sir.
    [*Silence.*]
VLADIMIR Christ have mercy on us!
    [*Silence.*]
BOY What am I to tell Mr. Godot, Sir?
VLADIMIR Tell him . . . [*he hesitates*] . . . tell him you saw me and that . . .
    [*he hesitates*] . . . that you saw me. [*Pause.* VLADIMIR *advances, the* BOY
    recoils. VLADIMIR *halts, the* BOY *halts. With sudden violence.*] You're sure
    you saw me, you won't come and tell me tomorrow that you never saw
    me!
        [*Silence.* VLADIMIR *makes a sudden spring forward, the* BOY *avoids him
        and exits running. Silence. The sun sets, the moon rises. As in Act 1.*
        VLADIMIR *stands motionless and bowed.* ESTRAGON *wakes, takes off his
        boots, gets up with one in each hand and goes and puts them down cen-
        ter front, then goes towards* VLADIMIR.]
ESTRAGON What's wrong with you?
VLADIMIR Nothing.
ESTRAGON I'm going.
VLADIMIR So am I.
ESTRAGON Was I long asleep?
VLADIMIR I don't know.
    [*Silence.*]
ESTRAGON Where shall we go?
VLADIMIR Not far.
ESTRAGON Oh yes, let's go far away from here.
VLADIMIR We can't.
ESTRAGON Why not?
VLADIMIR We have to come back tomorrow.
ESTRAGON What for?

VLADIMIR   To wait for Godot.

ESTRAGON   Ah! [*Silence.*] He didn't come?

VLADIMIR   No.

ESTRAGON   And now it's too late.

VLADIMIR   Yes, now it's night.

ESTRAGON   And if we dropped him? [*Pause.*] If we dropped him?

VLADIMIR   He'd punish us. [*Silence. He looks at the tree.*] Everything's dead but the tree.

ESTRAGON [*looking at the tree*]   What is it?

VLADIMIR   It's the tree.

ESTRAGON   Yes, but what kind?

VLADIMIR   I don't know. A willow.

[ESTRAGON *draws* VLADIMIR *towards the tree. They stand motionless before it. Silence.*]

ESTRAGON   Why don't we hang ourselves?

VLADIMIR   With what?

ESTRAGON   You haven't got a bit of rope?

VLADIMIR   No.

ESTRAGON   Then we can't.

[*Silence.*]

VLADIMIR   Let's go.

ESTRAGON   Wait, there's my belt.

VLADIMIR   It's too short.

ESTRAGON   You could hang onto my legs.

VLADIMIR   And who'd hang on to mine?

ESTRAGON   True.

VLADIMIR   Show all the same. [ESTRAGON *loosens the cord that holds up his trousers which, much too big for him, fall about his ankles. They look at the cord.*] It might do at a pinch. But is it strong enough?

ESTRAGON   We'll soon see. Here.

[*They each take an end of the cord and pull. It breaks. They almost fall.*]

VLADIMIR   Not worth a curse.

[*Silence.*]

ESTRAGON   You say we have to come back tomorrow?

VLADIMIR   Yes.

ESTRAGON   Then we can bring a good bit of rope.

VLADIMIR   Yes.

[*Silence.*]

ESTRAGON   Didi.

VLADIMIR   Yes.

ESTRAGON   I can't go on like this.

VLADIMIR   That's what you think.

ESTRAGON   If we parted? That might be better for us.

VLADIMIR   We'll hang ourselves tomorrow. [*Pause.*] Unless Godot comes.

ESTRAGON   And if he comes?

VLADIMIR   We'll be saved.

[VLADIMIR *takes off his hat* (LUCKY's), *peers inside it, feels about inside it, shakes it, knocks on the crown, puts it on again.*]

ESTRAGON   Well? Shall we go?

VLADIMIR   Pull on your trousers.

ESTRAGON   What?

VLADIMIR   Pull on your trousers.
ESTRAGON   You want me to pull off my trousers?
VLADIMIR   Pull ON your trousers.
ESTRAGON [*realizing his trousers are down*]   True. [*He pulls up his trousers.*]
VLADIMIR   Well? Shall we go?
ESTRAGON   Yes, let's go.
     [*They do not move.*]
                              Curtain.

                                                      1952; 1954

W. H. AUDEN
1907–1973

Wystan Hugh Auden was born in York, England, the son of a doctor and of a former nurse. He was educated at private schools and Christ Church, Oxford. After graduation from Oxford he traveled abroad, taught school in England from 1930 to 1935, and later worked for a government film unit. His sympathies in the 1930s were with the left, like those of most intellectuals of his age, and he went to Spain during its Civil War, intending to serve as an ambulance driver on the left-wing Republican side. To his surprise he felt so disturbed by the sight of the many Roman Catholic churches gutted and looted by the Republicans that he returned to England without fulfilling his ambition. He traveled in Iceland and China before moving to the United States in 1939; in 1946 he became an American citizen. He taught at a number of American colleges and was professor of poetry at Oxford from 1956 to 1960. Most of his later life was shared between residences in New York City and in Europe—first in southern Italy, then in Austria.

Auden was the most prominent of the young English poets who, in the late 1920s and early 1930s, saw themselves bringing new techniques and attitudes to English poetry. Stephen Spender, C. Day Lewis, and Louis MacNeice were other liberal and leftist poets in this loosely affiliated group. Auden learned metrical and verbal techniques from Gerard Manley Hopkins and Wilfred Owen, and from T. S. Eliot he took a conversational and ironic tone, an acute inspection of cultural decay. Thomas Hardy's metrical variety, formal irregularity, and fusion of panoramic and intimate perspectives also proved a useful example, and Auden admired W. B. Yeats's "serious reflective" poems of "personal and public interest," though he later came to disavow Yeats's grand aspirations and rhetoric. Auden's English studies at Oxford familiarized him with the rhythms and long alliterative line of Anglo-Saxon poetry. He learned, too, from popular and folk culture, particularly the songs of the English music hall and, later, American blues singers.

The Depression that hit America in 1929 hit England soon afterward, and Auden and his contemporaries looked out at an England of industrial stagnation and mass unemployment, seeing not Eliot's metaphorical Waste Land but a more literal Waste Land of poverty and "depressed areas." Auden's early poetry diagnoses the ills of his country. This diagnosis, conducted in a verse that combines irreverence with craftsmanship, draws on both Freud and Marx to show England now as a nation of neurotic invalids, now as the victim of an antiquated economic system. The intellectual liveliness and nervous force of this work made a great impression, even though the compressed, elliptical, impersonal style created difficulties of interpretation.

Gradually Auden sought to clarify his imagery and syntax, and in the late 1930s he produced "Lullaby," "Musée des Beaux Arts," "In Memory of W. B. Yeats," and other poems of finely disciplined movement, pellucid clarity, and deep yet unsentimental feeling. Some of the poems he wrote at this time, such as "Spain" and "September 1, 1939," aspire to a visionary perspective on political and social change; but as Auden became increasingly skeptical of poetry in the grand manner, of poetry as revelation or as a tool for political change, he removed these poems from his canon. (He came to see as false his claim in "September 1, 1939" that "We must love one another or die.") "Poetry is not magic," he said in the essay "Writing," but a form of truth telling that should "disenchant and disintoxicate." As he continued to remake his style during World War II, he created a voice that, in contrast not only to Romanticism but also to the authoritarianism devastating Europe, was increasingly flat, ironic, and conversational. He never lost his ear for popular speech or his ability to combine elements from popular art with technical formality. He daringly mixed the grave and the flippant, vivid detail and allegorical abstraction. He always experimented, particularly in ways of bringing together high artifice and a colloquial tone.

The poems of Auden's last phase are increasingly personal in tone and combine an air of offhand informality with remarkable technical skill in versification. He turned out, as if effortlessly, poems in numerous verse forms, including sestinas, sonnets, ballads, canzones, syllabics, haiku, the blues, even limericks. As he became evermore mistrustful of a prophetic role for the poet, he embraced the ordinary—the hours of the day, the rooms of a house, a changeable landscape. He took refuge in love and friendship, particularly the love and friendship he shared with the American writer Chester Kallmann. Like Eliot, Auden became a member of the Church of England, and the emotions of his late poetry—sometimes comic, sometimes solemn—were grounded in an ever deepening but rarely obtrusive religious feeling. In the last year of his life he returned to England to live in Oxford, feeling the need to be part of a university community as a protection against loneliness. Auden is now generally recognized as one of the masters of twentieth-century English poetry, a thoughtful, seriously playful poet, combining extraordinary intelligence and immense craftsmanship.

A note on the texts: Auden heavily revised his poems, sometimes omitting stanzas (as in "In Memory of W. B. Yeats") or even entire poems ("September 1, 1939"). The texts below are reprinted as they first appeared in book form and again in his *Selected Poems: A New Edition*, ed. Edward Mendelson (1989).

Lullaby[1]

Lay your sleeping head, my love,
Human on my faithless arm;
Time and fevers burn away
Individual beauty from
5   Thoughtful children, and the grave
Proves the child ephemeral:
But in my arms till break of day

---

1. Title from Auden's later collections.

Let the living creature lie,
Mortal, guilty, but to me
10 The entirely beautiful.

Soul and body have no bounds:
To lovers as they lie upon
Her tolerant enchanted slope
In their ordinary swoon,
15 Grave the vision Venus° sends   *Roman goddess of love*
Of supernatural sympathy,
Universal love and hope;
While an abstract insight wakes
Among the glaciers and the rocks
20 The hermit's sensual ecstasy.

Certainty, fidelity
On the stroke of midnight pass
Like vibrations of a bell,
And fashionable madmen raise
25 Their pedantic boring cry:
Every farthing[2] of the cost,
All the dreaded cards foretell,
Shall be paid, but from this night
Not a whisper, not a thought,
30 Not a kiss nor look be lost.

Beauty, midnight, vision dies:
Let the winds of dawn that blow
Softly round your dreaming head
Such a day of sweetness show
35 Eye and knocking heart may bless,
Find the mortal world enough;
Noons of dryness see you fed
By the involuntary powers,
Nights of insult let you pass
40 Watched by every human love.

Jan. 1937   1937, 1940

As I Walked Out One Evening[1]

As I walked out one evening,
    Walking down Bristol Street,
The crowds upon the pavement
    Were fields of harvest wheat.

5 And down by the brimming river
    I heard a lover sing

2. At one time the smallest and least valuable British coin.   1. Title from Auden's later collections.

Under an arch of the railway:
"Love has no ending.

"I'll love you, dear, I'll love you
10 Till China and Africa meet
And the river jumps over the mountain
  And the salmon sing in the street.

"I'll love you till the ocean
  Is folded and hung up to dry
15 And the seven stars[2] go squawking
  Like geese about the sky.

"The years shall run like rabbits
  For in my arms I hold
The Flower of the Ages
20 And the first love of the world."

But all the clocks in the city
  Began to whirr and chime:
"O let not Time deceive you,
  You cannot conquer Time.

25 "In the burrows of the Nightmare
  Where Justice naked is,
Time watches from the shadow
  And coughs when you would kiss.

"In headaches and in worry
30 Vaguely life leaks away,
And Time will have his fancy
  To-morrow or to-day.

"Into many a green valley
  Drifts the appalling[3] snow;
35 Time breaks the threaded dances
  And the diver's brilliant bow.

"O plunge your hands in water,
  Plunge them in up to the wrist;
Stare, stare in the basin
40 And wonder what you've missed.

"The glacier knocks in the cupboard,
  The desert sighs in the bed,
And the crack in the tea-cup opens
  A lane to the land of the dead.

45 "Where the beggars raffle the banknotes
  And the Giant is enchanting to Jack,

2. The constellation of the Pleiades, supposed
by the ancients to be seven sisters. 3. Literally, making white.

And the Lily-white Boy is a Roarer
And Jill goes down on her back.[4]

"O look, look in the mirror,
50   O look in your distress;
Life remains a blessing
Although you cannot bless.

"O stand, stand at the window
As the tears scald and start;
55 You shall love your crooked neighbour
With your crooked heart."

It was late, late in the evening,
The lovers they were gone;
The clocks had ceased their chiming
60   And the deep river ran on.

Nov. 1937   1938, 1940

Musée des Beaux Arts[1]

About suffering they were never wrong,
The Old Masters: how well they understood
Its human position; how it takes place
While someone else is eating or opening a window or just walking
        dully along;
5 How, when the aged are reverently, passionately waiting
For the miraculous birth, there always must be
Children who did not specially want it to happen, skating
On a pond at the edge of the wood:
They never forgot
10 That even the dreadful martyrdom must run its course
Anyhow in a corner, some untidy spot
Where the dogs go on with their doggy life and the torturer's horse
Scratches its innocent behind on a tree.

In Brueghel's *Icarus*,[2] for instance: how everything turns away
15 Quite leisurely from the disaster; the ploughman may
Have heard the splash, the forsaken cry,
But for him it was not an important failure; the sun shone
As it had to on the white legs disappearing into the green
Water; and the expensive delicate ship that must have seen
20 Something amazing, a boy falling out of the sky,
Had somewhere to get to and sailed calmly on.

Dec. 1938   1940

4. The giant of "Jack and the Bean Stalk" is trying to seduce Jack; the "lily-white Boy" (presumably pure) becomes a boisterous reveler; Jill, of
"Jack and Jill," is seduced.
1. Museum of Fine Arts (French).
2. *The Fall of Icarus*, by the Flemish painter
Pieter Brueghel (ca. 1525–1569), in the Musées
Royaux des Beaux Arts in Brussels. In one cor-

ner of Brueghel's painting, Icarus's legs are seen
disappearing into the sea, his wings having
melted when he flew too close to the sun. Auden
also alludes to other paintings by Brueghel: the
nativity scene in *The Numbering at Bethlehem*,
skaters in *Winter Landscape with Skaters and a
Bird Trap*, and possibly animals in *The Massacre
of the Innocents*.

Landscape with the Fall of Icarus (ca. 1555), by Flemish painter Pieter Brueghel (ca. 1525–1569), in the Musées Royaux des Beaux Arts in Brussels. W. H. Auden writes about the painting in the second part of his poem "Musée des Beaux Arts" (p. 1415).

In Memory of W. B. Yeats[1]

(d. January 1939)

I

He disappeared in the dead of winter:
The brooks were frozen, the air-ports almost deserted,
And snow disfigured the public statues;
The mercury sank in the mouth of the dying day.
5   O all the instruments agree
The day of his death was a dark cold day.

Far from his illness
The wolves ran on through the evergreen forests,
The peasant river was untempted by the fashionable quays;
10 By mourning tongues
The death of the poet was kept from his poems.

But for him it was his last afternoon as himself,
An afternoon of nurses and rumours;
The provinces of his body revolted,
15 The squares of his mind were empty,
Silence invaded the suburbs,
The current of his feeling failed: he became his admirers.

1. The Irish poet William Butler Yeats, born in 1865, died on January 29, 1939, in Roquebrune (southern France).

Now he is scattered among a hundred cities
And wholly given over to unfamiliar affections;
20 To find his happiness in another kind of wood[2]
And be punished under a foreign code of conscience.
The words of a dead man
Are modified in the guts of the living.

But in the importance and noise of to-morrow
25 When the brokers are roaring like beasts on the floor of the Bourse,[3]
And the poor have the sufferings to which they are fairly accustomed,
And each in the cell of himself is almost convinced of his freedom;
A few thousand will think of this day
As one thinks of a day when one did something slightly unusual.

30 O all the instruments agree
The day of his death was a dark cold day.

II

You were silly like us: your gift survived it all;
The parish of rich women,[4] physical decay,
Yourself; mad Ireland hurt you into poetry.
35 Now Ireland has her madness and her weather still,
For poetry makes nothing happen: it survives
In the valley of its saying where executives
Would never want to tamper; it flows south
From ranches of isolation and the busy griefs,
40 Raw towns that we believe and die in; it survives,
A way of happening, a mouth.

III[5]

Earth, receive an honoured guest;
William Yeats is laid to rest:
Let the Irish vessel lie
45 Emptied of its poetry.

Time that is intolerant
Of the brave and innocent,
And indifferent in a week
To a beautiful physique,

50 Worships language and forgives
Everyone by whom it lives;
Pardons cowardice, conceit,
Lays its honours at their feet.

---

2. Cf. the beginning of Dante's *Inferno:* "In the middle of the journey of our life I came to myself in a dark wood where the straight way was lost" (1.1–3).
3. The French stock exchange.
4. Several wealthy women, including Lady Augusta Gregory (1852–1932), provided financial help to Yeats.
5. The stanza pattern of this section echoes that of Yeats's late poem "Under Ben Bulben." Auden later omitted the section's second, third, and fourth stanzas.

Time that with this strange excuse
55 Pardoned Kipling[6] and his views,
And will pardon Paul Claudel,[7]
Pardons him for writing well.

In the nightmare of the dark
All the dogs of Europe bark,[8]
60 And the living nations wait,
Each sequestered in its hate;

Intellectual disgrace
Stares from every human face,
And the seas of pity lie
65 Locked and frozen in each eye.

Follow, poet, follow right
To the bottom of the night,
With your unconstraining voice
Still persuade us to rejoice;

70 With the farming of a verse
Make a vineyard of the curse,
Sing of human unsuccess
In a rapture of distress;

In the deserts of the heart
75 Let the healing fountain start,
In the prison of his days
Teach the free man how to praise.

Feb. 1939   1939, 1940

The Unknown Citizen

To JS/07/M/378
This Marble Monument is Erected by the State

He was found by the Bureau of Statistics to be
One against whom there was no official complaint,
And all the reports on his conduct agree
That, in the modern sense of an old-fashioned word, he was a saint,
5 For in everything he did he served the Greater Community.
Except for the War till the day he retired
He worked in a factory and never got fired,
But satisfied his employers, Fudge Motors Inc.
Yet he wasn't a scab or odd in his views,
10 For his Union reports that he paid his dues,
(Our report on his Union shows it was sound)

6. The British writer Rudyard Kipling (1865–
1936) championed imperialism.
7. French author (1868–1955) with extremely

conservative politics. Yeats was at times antidemocratic and appeared to favor dictatorship.
8. World War II began in September 1939.

And our Social Psychology workers found
That he was popular with his mates and liked a drink.
The Press are convinced that he bought a paper every day
15   And that his reactions to advertisements were normal in every way.
Policies taken out in his name prove that he was fully insured,
And his Health-card shows he was once in hospital but left it cured.
Both Producers Research and High-Grade Living declare
He was fully sensible to the advantages of the Installment Plan
20   And had everything necessary to the Modern Man;
A gramophone, a radio, a car and a frigidaire.
Our researchers into Public Opinion are content
That he held the proper opinions for the time of year;
When there was peace, he was for peace; when there was war, he went.
25   He was married and added five children to the population,
Which our Eugenist[1] says was the right number for a parent of his
     generation,
And our teachers report that he never interfered with their education.
Was he free? Was he happy? The question is absurd:
Had anything been wrong, we should certainly have heard.

Mar. 1939   1939, 1940

September 1, 1939[1]

I sit in one of the dives
On Fifty-Second Street[2]
Uncertain and afraid
As the clever hopes expire
5   Of a low dishonest decade:
Waves of anger and fear
Circulate over the bright
And darkened lands of the earth,
Obsessing our private lives;
10   The unmentionable odour of death
Offends the September night.

Accurate scholarship can
Unearth the whole offence
From Luther[3] until now
15   That has driven a culture mad,
Find what occurred at Linz,[4]
What huge imago[5] made
A psychopathic god:
I and the public know
20   What all schoolchildren learn,
Those to whom evil is done
Do evil in return.

---

1. An expert in eugenics, a pseudoscience for the genetic "improvement" of humans.
1. The date of Germany's invasion of Poland and the outbreak of World War II.
2. In New York City, where Auden was living.
3. Martin Luther (1483–1546), founder of the Protestant Reformation.
4. Austrian city where Hitler spent his childhood.
5. Psychoanalytic term for the unconscious representation of a parental figure.

Exiled Thucydides[6] knew
All that a speech can say
25 About Democracy,
And what dictators do,
The elderly rubbish they talk
To an apathetic grave;
Analysed all in his book,
30 The enlightenment driven away,
The habit-forming pain,
Mismanagement and grief:
We must suffer them all again.

Into this neutral air
35 Where blind skyscrapers use
Their full height to proclaim
The strength of Collective Man,
Each language pours its vain
Competitive excuse:
40 But who can live for long
In an euphoric dream;
Out of the mirror they stare,
Imperialism's face
And the international wrong.

45 Faces along the bar
Cling to their average day:
The lights must never go out,
The music must always play,
All the conventions conspire
50 To make this fort assume
The furniture of home;
Lest we should see where we are,
Lost in a haunted wood,
Children afraid of the night
55 Who have never been happy or good.

The windiest militant trash
Important Persons shout
Is not so crude as our wish:
What mad Nijinsky wrote
60 About Diaghiley[7]
Is true of the normal heart;
For the error bred in the bone
Of each woman and each man
Craves what it cannot have,
65 Not universal love
But to be loved alone.

---

6. Greek general (d. ca. 401 B.C.E.) and historian of the Peloponnesian War, exiled from Athens because he failed to prevent the Spartans from seizing a colony.
7. The Russian dancer and choreographer Vas-
lav Nijinsky (1890–1950) wrote that his former lover the ballet impresario Sergey Diaghilev (1872–1929) "does not want universal love, but to be loved alone."

From the conservative dark
Into the ethical life
The dense commuters come,
70 Repeating their morning vow,
"I *will* be true to the wife,
I'll concentrate more on my work,"
And helpless governors wake
To resume their compulsory game:
75 Who can release them now,
Who can reach the deaf,
Who can speak for the dumb?[8]

All I have is a voice
To undo the folded lie,
80 The romantic lie in the brain
Of the sensual man-in-the-street
And the lie of Authority
Whose buildings grope the sky:
There is no such thing as the State
85 And no one exists alone;
Hunger allows no choice
To the citizen or the police;
We must love one another or die.[9]

Defenceless under the night
90 Our world in stupor lies;
Yet, dotted everywhere,
Ironic points of light
Flash out wherever the Just
Exchange their messages:
95 May I, composed like them
Of Eros° and of dust,   *Greek god of desire*
Beleaguered by the same
Negation and despair,
Show an affirming flame.

Sept. 1939   1939, 1940

In Praise of Limestone[1]

If it form the one landscape that we the inconstant ones
   Are consistently homesick for, this is chiefly
Because it dissolves in water. Mark these rounded slopes
   With their surface fragrance of thyme and beneath

8. Proverbs 31.8.
9. Auden later revised this line, which struck him as "dishonest." In one version of the poem the line reads "We must love one another and die." Another version leaves out the entire stanza.
1. Inspired by the limestone landscape outside Florence, Italy, where Auden and his longtime companion Chester Kallman (1921–1975) were

staying; the poem also recalls the poet's native Yorkshire. In a letter to Elizabeth Mayer, Auden wrote: "I hadn't realised till I came how like Italy is to my 'Mutterland', the Pennines [hills in the north of England]. Am in fact starting on a poem, 'In Praise of Limestone', the theme of which is that rock creates the only truly human landscape."

5 A secret system of caves and conduits; hear these springs
      That spurt out everywhere with a chuckle
   Each filling a private pool for its fish and carving
      Its own little ravine whose cliffs entertain
   The butterfly and the lizard; examine this region
10   Of short distances and definite places:
   What could be more like Mother or a fitter background
      For her son, for the nude young male who lounges
   Against a rock displaying his dildo,° never doubting   penis
      That for all his faults he is loved, whose works are but
15 Extensions of his power to charm? From weathered outcrop
      To hill-top temple, from appearing waters to
   Conspicuous fountains, from a wild to a formal vineyard,
      Are ingenious but short steps that a child's wish
   To receive more attention than his brothers, whether
20   By pleasing or teasing, can easily take.

   Watch, then, the band of rivals as they climb up and down
      Their steep stone gennels[2] in twos and threes, sometimes
   Arm in arm, but never, thank God, in step; or engaged
      On the shady side of a square at midday in
25 Voluble discourse, knowing each other too well to think
      There are any important secrets, unable
   To conceive a god whose temper-tantrums are moral
      And not to be pacified by a clever line
   Or a good lay: for, accustomed to a stone that responds,
30   They have never had to veil their faces in awe
   Of a crater whose blazing fury could not be fixed;
      Adjusted to the local needs of valleys
   Where everything can be touched or reached by walking,
      Their eyes have never looked into infinite space
35 Through the lattice-work of a nomad's comb; born lucky,
      Their legs have never encountered the fungi
   And insects of the jungle, the monstrous forms and lives
      With which we have nothing, we like to hope, in common.
   So, when one of them goes to the bad, the way his mind works
40   Remains comprehensible: to become a pimp
   Or deal in fake jewelry or ruin a fine tenor voice
      For effects that bring down the house could happen to all
   But the best and the worst of us . . .
                                    That is why, I suppose,
      The best and worst never stayed here long but sought
45 Immoderate soils where the beauty was not so external,
      The light less public and the meaning of life
   Something more than a mad camp. "Come!" cried the granite wastes,
      "How evasive is your humor, how accidental
   Your kindest kiss, how permanent is death." (Saints-to-be
50   Slipped away sighing.) "Come!" purred the clays and gravels
   "On our plains there is room for armies to drill; rivers
      Wait to be tamed and slaves to construct you a tomb

_____

2. Narrow passages between houses (Yorkshire dialect) or, as here, rocks.

In the grand manner: soft as the earth is mankind and both
    Need to be altered." (Intendant Caesars rose and
55 Left, slamming the door.) But the really reckless were fetched
    By an older colder voice, the oceanic whisper:
"I am the solitude that asks and promises nothing;
    That is how I shall set you free. There is no love;
There are only the various envies, all of them sad."

60 They were right, my dear, all those voices were right
    And still are; this land is not the sweet home that it looks,
       Nor its peace the historical calm of a site
Where something was settled once and for all: A backward
    And dilapidated province, connected
65 To the big busy world by a tunnel, with a certain
    Seedy appeal, is that all it is now? Not quite:
It has a worldly duty which in spite of itself
    It does not neglect, but calls into question
All the Great Powers assume; it disturbs our rights. The poet,
70   Admired for his earnest habit of calling
The sun the sun, his mind Puzzle, is made uneasy
    By these solid statues which so obviously doubt
His antimythological myth; and these gamins,°   *urchins*
    Pursuing the scientist down the tiled colonnade
75 With such lively offers, rebuke his concern for Nature's
    Remotest aspects: I, too, am reproached, for what
And how much you know. Not to lose time, not to get caught,
    Not to be left behind, not, please! to resemble
The beasts who repeat themselves, or a thing like water
80   Or stone whose conduct can be predicted, these
Are our Common Prayer³ whose greatest comfort is music
    Which can be made anywhere, is invisible,
And does not smell. In so far as we have to look forward
    To death as a fact, no doubt we are right: But if
85 Sins can be forgiven, if bodies rise from the dead,
    These modifications of matter into
Innocent athletes and gesticulating fountains,
    Made solely for pleasure, make a further point:
The blessed will not care what angle they are regarded from,
90   Having nothing to hide. Dear, I know nothing of
Either, but when I try to imagine a faultless love
    Or the life to come, what I hear is the murmur
Of underground streams, what I see is a limestone landscape.

May 1948   1948, 1951

---

3. *The Book of Common Prayer* is the liturgical book of the Anglican Church.

The Shield of Achilles[1]

She looked over his shoulder
For vines and olive trees,
Marble well-governed cities,
And ships upon untamed seas,
5   But there on the shining metal
His hands had put instead
An artificial wilderness
And a sky like lead.

A plain without a feature, bare and brown,
10   No blade of grass, no sign of neighborhood,
Nothing to eat and nowhere to sit down,
    Yet, congregated on its blankness, stood
    An unintelligible multitude,
A million eyes, a million boots in line,
15   Without expression, waiting for a sign.

Out of the air a voice without a face
Proved by statistics that some cause was just
In tones as dry and level as the place:
    No one was cheered and nothing was discussed;
20   Column by column in a cloud of dust
They marched away enduring a belief
Whose logic brought them, somewhere else, to grief.

She looked over his shoulder
    For ritual pieties,
25   White flower-garlanded heifers,
    Libation and sacrifice,[2]
But there on the shining metal
    Where the altar should have been,
She saw by his flickering forge-light
30   Quite another scene.

Barbed wire enclosed an arbitrary spot
    Where bored officials lounged (one cracked a joke)
And sentries sweated, for the day was hot:
    A crowd of ordinary decent folk
35   Watched from without and neither moved nor spoke
As three pale figures were led forth and bound
To three posts driven upright in the ground.

1. In Homer's *Iliad* Achilles, the chief Greek hero in the war with Troy, lends his armor to his great friend Patroclus and loses it when Patroclus is killed by Hector. While Achilles is mourning the death of his friend, his mother, the goddess Thetis, goes to Mt. Olympus to beg Hephaestos, the god of fire, to forge new armor for Achilles. The splendid shield of Achilles that Hephaestos then makes is described in book 18 (lines 478–608). On it he depicts the earth, the heavens, the sea, and the planets; a city in peace (with a wedding and a trial) and a city at war; scenes from country life, animal life, and the joyful life of young men and women. The ocean, as the outer border, flows around all these scenes.
2. Cf. John Keats's "Ode on a Grecian Urn" (1820): "Who are these coming to the sacrifice? / To what green altar, O mysterious priest, / Lead'st thou that heifer lowing at the skies, / And all her silken flanks with garlands dressed?" "Libation": sacrifice of wine or other liquid.

The mass and majesty of this world, all
   That carries weight and always weighs the same,
40   Lay in the hands of others; they were small
   And could not hope for help and no help came:
   What their foes liked to do was done, their shame
Was all the worst could wish; they lost their pride
And died as men before their bodies died.

55   She looked over his shoulder
         For athletes at their games,
       Men and women in a dance
         Moving their sweet limbs
        Quick, quick, to music,
50   But there on the shining shield
       His hands had set no dancing-floor
         But a weed-choked field.

   A ragged urchin, aimless and alone,
    Loitered about that vacancy; a bird
55   Flew up to safety from his well-aimed stone:
    That girls are raped, that two boys knife a third,
    Were axioms to him, who'd never heard
   Of any world where promises were kept
   Or one could weep because another wept.

60   The thin-lipped armorer,
         Hephaestos, hobbled away;
       Thetis of the shining breasts
         Cried out in dismay
       At what the god had wrought
65   To please her son, the strong
       Iron-hearted man-slaying Achilles
         Who would not live long.

1952   1952, 1955

[Poetry as Memorable Speech][1]

Of the many definitions of poetry, the simplest is still the best: 'memorable speech.' That is to say, it must move our emotions, or excite our intellect, for only that which is moving or exciting is memorable, and the stimulus is the audible spoken word and cadence, to which in all its power of suggestion and incantation we must surrender, as we do when talking to an intimate friend. We must, in fact, make exactly the opposite kind of mental effort to that we make in grasping other verbal uses, for in the case of the latter the aura of suggestion round every word through which, like the atom radiating lines of force through the whole of space and time, it becomes ultimately a sign for the sum of all possible meanings, must be rigorously suppressed and its meaning confined to a single dictionary one. For this reason the exposition of

1. Excerpted from Auden and John Garrett's introduction to their anthology of verse, *The Poet's Tongue*.

a scientific theory is easier to read than to hear. No poetry, on the other hand, which when mastered is not better heard than read is good poetry.

All speech has rhythm, which is the result of the combination of the alternating periods of effort and rest necessary to all living things, and the laying of emphasis on what we consider important; and in all poetry there is a tension between the rhythm due to the poet's personal values, and those due to the experiences of generations crystallised into habits of language such as the English tendency to alternate weak and accented syllables, and conventional verse forms like the hexameter, the heroic pentameter, or the French Alexandrine. Similes, metaphors of image or idea, and auditory metaphors such as rhyme, assonance, and alliteration help further to clarify and strengthen the pattern and internal relations of the experience described.

Poetry, in fact, bears the same kind of relation to Prose, using prose simply in the sense of all those uses of words that are not poetry, that algebra bears to arithmetic. The poet writes of personal or fictitious experiences, but these are not important in themselves until the reader has realised them in his own consciousness.

> Soldier from the war returning,
> Spoiler of the taken town[2]

It is quite unimportant, though it is the kind of question not infrequently asked, who the soldier is, what regiment he belongs to, what war he had been fighting in, etc. The soldier is you or me, or the man next door. Only when it throws light on our own experience, when these lines occur to us as we see, say, the unhappy face of a stockbroker in the suburban train, does poetry convince us of its significance. The test of a poet is the frequency and diversity of the occasions on which we remember his poetry.

Memorable speech then. About what? Birth, death, the Beatific Vision,[3] the abysses of hatred and fear, the awards and miseries of desire, the unjust walking the earth and the just scratching miserably for food like hens, triumphs, earthquakes, deserts of boredom and featureless anxiety, the Golden Age promised or irrevocably past, the gratifications and terrors of childhood, the impact of nature on the adolescent, the despairs and wisdoms of the mature, the sacrificial victim, the descent into Hell, the devouring and the benign mother? Yes, all of these, but not these only. Everything that we remember no matter how trivial: the mark on the wall, the joke at luncheon, word games, these, like the dance of a stoat[4] or the raven's gamble, are equally the subject of poetry.

We shall do poetry a great disservice if we confine it only to the major experiences of life:

> The soldier's pole is fallen,
> Boys and girls are level now with men,
> And there is nothing left remarkable
> Beneath the visiting moon.
>
> They had a royal wedding.
> All his courtiers wished him well.

---

2. Beginning lines of a poem (in which "war" is plural) by the English poet A. E. Housman (1859–1936).

3. A sight of the glories of heaven.
4. Weasel.

> The horses pranced and the dancers danced.
> O Mister it was swell.
>
> And masculine is found to be
> Hadria the Adriatic Sea.[5]

have all their rightful place, and full appreciation of one depends on full appreciation of the others.

A great many people dislike the idea of poetry as they dislike over-earnest people, because they imagine it is always worrying about the eternal verities.

Those, in Mr Spender's[6] words, who try to put poetry on a pedestal only succeed in putting it on the shelf. Poetry is no better and no worse than human nature; it is profound and shallow, sophisticated and naïve, dull and witty, bawdy and chaste in turn.

In spite of the spread of education and the accessibility of printed matter, there is a gap between what is commonly called 'highbrow' and 'lowbrow' taste, wider perhaps than it has ever been.

The industrial revolution broke up the agricultural communities, with their local conservative cultures, and divided the growing population into two classes: those whether employers or employees who worked and had little leisure, and a small class of shareholders who did no work, had leisure but no responsibilities or roots, and were therefore preoccupied with themselves. Literature has tended therefore to divide into two streams, one providing the first with a compensation and escape, the other the second with a religion and a drug. The Art for Art's sake[7] of the London drawing-rooms of the '90's, and towns like Burnley and Rochdale,[8] are complementary.

Nor has the situation been much improved by the increased leisure and educational opportunities which the population to-day as a whole possess. Were leisure all, the unemployed would have created a second Athens.

Artistic creations may be produced by individuals, and because their work is only appreciated by a few it does not necessarily follow that it is not good; but a universal art can only be the product of a community united in sympathy, sense of worth, and aspiration; and it is improbable that the artist can do his best except in such a society.

* * *

The 'average' man says: 'When I get home I want to spend my time with my wife or in the nursery; I want to get out on to the links[9] or go for a spin in the car, not to read poetry. Why should I? I'm quite happy without it.' We must be able to point out to him that whenever, for example, he makes a good joke he is creating poetry, that one of the motives behind poetry is curiosity, the wish to know what we feel and think, and how, as E. M. Forster[1] says, can I know what I think till I see what I say, and that curiosity is the only human passion that can be indulged in for twenty-four hours a day without satiety.

---

5. A mnemonic to help remember that Hadria, Latin for the Adriatic Sea, is masculine, despite its typically feminine ending. The first quotation is a remembered version of Cleopatra's speech after Antony dies in Shakespeare's *Antony and Cleopatra* (4.16.67–70). The middle quotation is from the popular song "King of Borneo" (1929) by American singer and songwriter Frank Cru-

mit (1889–1943).
6. Stephen Spender (1909–1995), English poet.
7. Phrase associated with aestheticism.
8. Once industrial mill towns in Lancashire, England.
9. Ground on which golf is played.
1. English novelist (1879–1970).

The psychologist maintains that poetry is a neurotic symptom, an attempt to compensate by phantasy for a failure to meet reality. We must tell him that phantasy is only the beginning of writing; that, on the contrary, like psychology, poetry is a struggle to reconcile the unwilling subject and object; in fact, that since psychological truth depends so largely on context, poetry, the parabolie[2] approach, is the only adequate medium for psychology.

The propagandist, whether moral or political, complains that the writer should use his powers over words to persuade people to a particular course of action, instead of fiddling while Rome burns.[3] But Poetry is not concerned with telling people what to do, but with extending our knowledge of good and evil, perhaps making the necessity for action more urgent and its nature more clear, but only leading us to the point where it is possible for us to make a rational and moral choice.

* * *

1935

2. I.e., akin to parable.
3. The Roman emperor Nero (37–68) reputedly fiddled while Rome burned.

DYLAN THOMAS
1914–1953

Dylan Thomas was born in Swansea, Wales, and educated at Swansea Grammar School. After working for a time as a newspaper reporter, he was "discovered" as a poet in 1933 through a poetry contest in a popular newspaper. The following year his *Eighteen Poems* caused considerable excitement because of their powerfully suggestive obscurity and the strange violence of their imagery. It looked as though a new kind of visionary Romanticism had been restored to English poetry after the deliberately muted ironic tones of T. S. Eliot and his followers. Over time it became clear that Thomas was also a master of poetic craft, not merely a shouting rhapsodist. His verbal panache played against strict verse forms, such as the villanelle ("Do Not Go Gentle into That Good Night"). "I am a painstaking, conscientious, involved and devious craftsman in words," he wrote in his "Poetic Manifesto." His images were carefully ordered in a patterned sequence, and his major theme was the unity of all life, the continuing *process* of life and death and new life that linked the generations. Thomas saw the workings of biology as a magical transformation producing unity out of diversity, and again and again in his poetry he sought a poetic ritual to celebrate this unity ("The force that through the green fuse drives the flower / Drives my green age"). He saw men and women locked in cycles of growth, love, procreation, new growth, death, and new life again. Hence each image engenders its opposite in what he called "my dialectical method": "Each image holds within it the seed of its own destruction." Thomas derives his closely woven, sometimes self-contradictory images from the Bible, Welsh folklore and preaching, and Freud. In his poems of reminiscence and autobiographical emotion, such as "Poem in October," he communicates more immediately through compelling use of lyrical feeling and simple natural images. His autobiographical work *Portrait of the Artist as a Young Dog* (1940) and his radio play *Under Milk Wood* (1954) reveal a vividness of observation and a combination of violence and tenderness in expression that show he could handle prose as excitingly as verse.

Thomas was a brilliant talker, an alcoholic, a reckless and impulsive man whose short life was packed with emotional ups and downs. His poetry readings in the United States between 1950 and 1953 were enormous successes, in spite of his sometimes reckless antics. He died suddenly in New York of what was diagnosed as "an insult to the brain," precipitated by alcohol. He played the part of the wild bohemian poet, and while some thought this behavior wonderful, others deplored it. He was a stirring reader of his own and others' poems, and many people who do not normally read poetry were drawn to Thomas's by the magic of his own reading. After his premature death a reaction set in: some critics declared that he had been overrated as a poet because of his sensational life. The "Movement" poets, such as Philip Larkin, repudiated his rhetorical extravagance. Even so, Thomas is still considered an original poet of great power and beauty.

The Force That Through the Green Fuse Drives the Flower

The force that through the green fuse drives the flower
Drives my green age; that blasts the roots of trees
Is my destroyer.
And I am dumb to tell the crooked rose
5   My youth is bent by the same wintry fever.

The force that drives the water through the rocks
Drives my red blood; that dries the mouthing streams
Turns mine to wax.
And I am dumb to mouth unto my veins
10   How at the mountain spring the same mouth sucks.

The hand that whirls the water in the pool[1]
Stirs the quicksand; that ropes the blowing wind
Hauls my shroud sail.
And I am dumb to tell the hanging man
15   How of my clay is made the hangman's lime.[2]

The lips of time leech to the fountain head;
Love drips and gathers, but the fallen blood
Shall calm her sores.

And I am dumb to tell a weather's wind
20   How time has ticked a heaven round the stars.

And I am dumb to tell the lover's tomb
How at my sheet goes the same crooked worm.

1933

---

1. The hand of the angel who troubles the water of the pool Bethesda, thus rendering it curative, in John 5.1–4.

2. Quicklime was sometimes poured into the graves of public hangmen's victims to accelerate decomposition.

Poem in October

It was my thirtieth year to heaven
Woke to my hearing from harbour and neighbour wood
    And the mussel pooled and the heron
        Priested shore
5   The morning beckon
With water praying and call of seagull and rook°   *crow*
And the knock of sailing boats on the net webbed wall
        Myself to set foot
        That second
10   In the still sleeping town and set forth.

    My birthday began with the water-
Birds and the birds of the winged trees flying my name
        Above the farms and the white horses
        And I rose
15   In rainy autumn
And walked abroad in a shower of all my days.
High tide and the heron dived when I took the road
        Over the border
        And the gates
20   Of the town closed as the town awoke.

    A springful of larks in a rolling
Cloud and the roadside bushes brimming with whistling
        Blackbirds and the sun of October
        Summery
25   On the hill's shoulder,
Here were fond climates and sweet singers suddenly
Come in the morning where I wandered and listened
        To the rain wringing
        Wind blow cold
30   In the wood faraway under me.

    Pale rain over the dwindling harbour
And over the sea wet church the size of a snail
        With its horns through mist and the castle
        Brown as owls
35   But all the gardens
Of spring and summer were blooming in the tall tales
Beyond the border and under the lark full cloud.
        There could I marvel
        My birthday
40   Away but the weather turned around.

    It turned away from the blithe country
And down the other air and the blue altered sky
        Streamed again a wonder of summer
        With apples
45   Pears and red currants
And I saw in the turning so clearly a child's

Forgotten mornings when he walked with his mother
                    Through the parables
                        Of sun light
50   And the legends of the green chapels

                    And the twice told fields of infancy
            That his tears burned my cheeks and his heart moved in mine.
                    These were the woods the river and sea
                        Where a boy
55   In the listening
            Summertime of the dead whispered the truth of his joy
            To the trees and the stones and the fish in the tide.
                    And the mystery
                        Sang alive
60   Still in the water and singingbirds.

                    And there could I marvel my birthday
            Away but the weather turned around. And the true
                    Joy of the long dead child sang burning
                        In the sun.
65   It was my thirtieth
            Year to heaven stood there then in the summer noon
            Though the town below lay leaved with October blood.
                    O may my heart's truth
                        Still be sung
70   On this high hill in a year's turning.

1944   1946

Fern Hill[1]

Now as I was young and easy under the apple boughs
About the lilting house and happy as the grass was green,
        The night above the dingle[2] starry,
            Time let me hail and climb
5   Golden in the heydays of his eyes,
And honoured among wagons I was prince of the apple towns
And once below a time I lordly had the trees and leaves
        Trail with daisies and barley
        Down the rivers of the windfall light.

10 And as I was green and carefree, famous among the barns
About the happy yard and singing as the farm was home,
        In the sun that is young once only,
            Time let me play and be
        Golden in the mercy of his means,
15 And green and golden I was huntsman and herdsman, the calves

---

1. Name of the Welsh farmhouse, home of his   holidays as a boy.
aunt Ann Jones, where Thomas spent summer   2. Deep dell or hollow, usually wooded.

Sang to my horn, the foxes on the hills barked clear and cold,
      And the sabbath rang slowly
   In the pebbles of the holy streams.

All the sun long it was running, it was lovely, the hay
20 Fields high as the house, the tunes from the chimneys, it was air
      And playing, lovely and watery
         And fire green as grass.
      And nightly under the simple stars
As I rode to sleep the owls were bearing the farm away,
25 All the moon long I heard, blessed among stables, the night-jars[3]
      Flying with the ricks,° and the horses   *haystacks*
         Flashing into the dark.

And then to awake, and the farm, like a wanderer white
With the dew, come back, the cock on his shoulder: it was all
30   Shining, it was Adam and maiden,[4]
         The sky gathered again
      And the sun grew round that very day.
So it must have been after the birth of the simple light
In the first, spinning place, the spellbound horses walking warm
35   Out of the whinnying green stable
         On to the fields of praise.

And honoured among foxes and pheasants by the gay house
Under the new made clouds and happy as the heart was long,
      In the sun born over and over,
40   I ran my heedless ways,
      My wishes raced through the house high hay
And nothing I cared, at my sky blue trades, that time allows
In all his tuneful turning so few and such morning songs
      Before the children green and golden
45   Follow him out of grace,

Nothing I cared, in the lamb white days, that time would take me
Up to the swallow thronged loft by the shadow of my hand,
      In the moon that is always rising,
         Nor that riding to sleep
50   I should hear him fly with the high fields
And wake to the farm forever fled from the childless land.
Oh as I was young and easy in the mercy of his means,
      Time held me green and dying
      Though I sang in my chains like the sea.

1945   1946

---

3. Species of bird.   4. Cf. Genesis 1.

Do Not Go Gentle into That Good Night

Do not go gentle into that good night,
Old age should burn and rave at close of day;
Rage, rage against the dying of the light.

Though wise men at their end know dark is right,
5   Because their words had forked no lightning they
Do not go gentle into that good night.

Good men, the last wave by, crying how bright
Their frail deeds might have danced in a green bay,
Rage, rage against the dying of the light.

10 Wild men who caught and sang the sun in flight,
And learn, too late, they grieved it on its way,
Do not go gentle into that good night.

Grave men, near death, who see with blinding sight
Blind eyes could blaze like meteors and be gay,
15 Rage, rage against the dying of the light.

And you, my father, there on the sad height,
Curse, bless, me now with your fierce tears, I pray.
Do not go gentle into that good night.
Rage, rage against the dying of the light.

1951   1952

PHILIP LARKIN
1922–1985

Philip Larkin was born in Coventry; was educated at its King Henry VIII School and at St. John's College, Oxford; and was for many years librarian of the Hull University Library. He wrote the poems of his first book, *The North Ship* (1945), under W. B. Yeats's strong enchantment. Although this influence persisted in the English poet's formal skill and subdued visionary longings, Larkin began to read Thomas Hardy seriously after World War II, and Hardy's rugged language, local settings, and ironic tone helped counter Yeats's influence. "After that," Larkin said, "Yeats came to seem so artificial—all that crap about masks and Crazy Jane and all the rest. It all rang so completely unreal." Also rejecting the international modernism of Eliot and Pound because of its mythical allusions, polyglot discourse, and fragmentary syntax, Larkin reclaimed a more direct, personal, formally regular model of poetry, supposedly rooted in a native English tradition of Wordsworth, Hardy, A. E. Housman, Wilfred Owen, and W. H. Auden. Even so, his poetry is not so thoroughly antimodernist as are his declarations: witness his imagist precision and alienated personae, his blending of revulsion and attraction toward modernity.

Larkin was the dominant figure in what came to be known as "the Movement," a group of university poets that included Kingsley Amis, Donald Davie, and Thom Gunn, gathered together in Robert Conquest's landmark anthology of 1956, *New Lines*. Their work was seen as counteracting not only the extravagances of modernism but also the influence of Dylan Thomas's high-flown, apocalyptic rhetoric: like Larkin, these poets preferred a civil grammar and rational syntax over prophecy, suburban realities over mythmaking.

No other poet presents the welfare-state world of postimperial Britain so vividly, so unsparingly, and so tenderly. "Poetry is an affair of sanity, of seeing things as they are," Larkin said; "I don't want to transcend the commonplace, I love the commonplace life. Everyday things are lovely to me." Eschewing the grandiose, he writes poetry that, in its everyday diction and melancholy wryness, worldly subjects and regular meters, affirms rather than contravenes the restrictions of ordinary life. Love's failure, the erosion of religious and national abutments, the loneliness of age and death—Larkin does not avert his poetic gaze from these bleak realities. As indicated by the title of his 1955 collection *The Less Deceived*, disillusionment, drabness, and resignation color these poems. Yet Larkin's drearily mundane world often gives way to muted promise, his speakers' alienation to possible communion, his skepticism to encounters even with the sublime. At the end of "High Windows," the characteristically ironic and self-deprecating speaker glimpses both radiant presence and total absence in the sunlit glass: "And beyond it, the deep blue air, that shows / Nothing, and is nowhere, and is endless."

Like Hardy, Larkin wrote novels—*Jill* (1946) and *A Girl in Winter* (1947)—and his poems have a novelist's sense of place and skill in the handling of direct speech. He also edited a controversial anthology, *The Oxford Book of Twentieth-Century English Verse* (1973), which attempted to construct a modern native tradition in England. But his most significant legacy was his poetry, although his output was limited to four volumes. Out of "the commonplace life" he fashioned uncommon poems—some of the most emotionally complex, rhythmically polished, and intricately rhymed poems of the second half of the twentieth century.

Church Going

Once I am sure there's nothing going on
I step inside, letting the door thud shut.
Another church: matting, seats, and stone,
And little books; sprawlings of flowers, cut
5   For Sunday, brownish now; some brass and stuff
Up at the holy end; the small neat organ;
And a tense, musty, unignorable silence,
Brewed God knows how long. Hatless, I take off
My cycle-clips in awkward reverence,

10   Move forward, run my hand around the font.
From where I stand, the roof looks almost new—
Cleaned, or restored? Someone would know: I don't.
Mounting the lectern, I peruse a few
Hectoring large-scale verses,[1] and pronounce

---

1. I.e., Bible verses printed in large type for reading aloud.

15 "Here endeth" much more loudly than I'd meant.
The echoes snigger briefly. Back at the door
I sign the book, donate an Irish sixpence,[2]
Reflect the place was not worth stopping for.

Yet stop I did: in fact I often do,
20 And always end much at a loss like this,
Wondering what to look for; wondering, too,
When churches fall completely out of use
What we shall turn them into, if we shall keep
A few cathedrals chronically on show,
25 Their parchment, plate and pyx[3] in locked cases,
And let the rest rent-free to rain and sheep.
Shall we avoid them as unlucky places?

Or, after dark, will dubious women come
To make their children touch a particular stone;
30 Pick simples° for a cancer; or on some   *medicinal herbs*
Advised night see walking a dead one?
Power of some sort or other will go on
In games, in riddles, seemingly at random;
But superstition, like belief, must die,
35 And what remains when disbelief has gone?
Grass, weedy pavement, brambles, buttress, sky,

A shape less recognisable each week,
A purpose more obscure. I wonder who
Will be the last, the very last, to seek
40 This place for what it was; one of the crew
That tap and jot and know what rood-lofts[4] were?
Some ruin-bibber, randy for antique,
Or Christmas-addict, counting on a whiff
Of gown-and-bands and organ-pipes and myrrh?[5]
45 Or will he be my representative,

Bored, uninformed, knowing the ghostly silt
Dispersed, yet tending to this cross of ground[6]
Through suburb scrub because it held unspilt
So long and equably what since is found
50 Only in separation—marriage, and birth,
And death, and thoughts of these—for which was built
This special shell? For, though I've no idea
What this accoutred frowsty barn is worth,
It pleases me to stand in silence here;

55 A serious house on serious earth it is,
In whose blent air all our compulsions meet,
Are recognised, and robed as destinies.

2. An Irish sixpence has no value in England.
3. Box in which Communion wafers are kept.
4. Galleries on top of carved screens separating the nave of a church from the choir.
5. Gum resin used in the making of incense; one of three presents given by the three wise men to the infant Jesus. "Gown-and-bands": gown and decorative collar worn by clergypeople.
6. Most churches were built in the shape of a cross.

And that much never can be obsolete,
Since someone will forever be surprising
60   A hunger in himself to be more serious,
And gravitating with it to this ground,
Which, he once heard, was proper to grow wise in,
If only that so many dead lie round.

1954   1955

MCMXIV[1]

Those long uneven lines
Standing as patiently
As if they were stretched outside
The Oval or Villa Park,[2]
5   The crowns of hats, the sun
On moustached archaic faces
Grinning as if it were all
An August bank Holiday lark;

And the shut shops, the bleached,
10   Established names on the sunblinds,
The farthings and sovereigns,[3]
And dark-clothed children at play
Called after kings and queens,
The tin advertisements
15   For cocoa and twist,° and the pubs   tobacco
Wide open all day;

And the countryside not caring:
The place-names all hazed over
With flowering grasses, and fields
20   Shadowing Domesday lines[4]
Under wheat's restless silence;
The differently-dressed servants
With tiny rooms in huge houses,
The dust behind limousines;

25   Never such innocence,
Never before or since,
As changed itself to past
Without a word—the men
Leaving the gardens tidy,
30   The thousands of marriages
Lasting a little while longer:
Never such innocence again.

1960   1964

---

1. 1914, in Roman numerals, as incised on stone memorials to the dead of World War I.
2. London cricket ground and Birmingham football ground.
3. At that time the least valuable and the most valuable British coins, respectively.
4. The still-visible boundaries of medieval farmers' long and narrow plots, ownership of which is recorded in William the Conqueror's *Domesday Book* (1085–86).

Talking in Bed

Talking in bed ought to be easiest,
Lying together there goes back so far,
An emblem of two people being honest.

Yet more and more time passes silently.
5   Outside, the wind's incomplete unrest
Builds and disperses clouds about the sky,

And dark towns heap up on the horizon.
None of this cares for us. Nothing shows why
At this unique distance from isolation

10 It becomes still more difficult to find
Words at once true and kind,
Or not untrue and not unkind.

1960   1964

Ambulances

Closed like confessionals,[1] they thread
Loud noons of cities, giving back
None of the glances they absorb.
Light glossy grey, arms on a plaque,
5   They come to rest at any kerb:
All streets in time are visited.

Then children strewn on steps or road,
Or women coming from the shops
Past smells of different dinners, see
10 A wild white face that overtops
Red stretcher-blankets momently
As it is carried in and stowed,

And sense the solving emptiness
That lies just under all we do,
15 And for a second get it whole,
So permanent and blank and true.
The fastened doors recede. *Poor soul,*
They whisper at their own distress;

For borne away in deadened air
20 May go the sudden shut of loss
Round something nearly at an end,
And what cohered in it across

1. Enclosed stalls in Roman Catholic churches in which priests hear confession.

The years, the unique random blend
Of families and fashions, there

25 At last begin to loosen. Far
From the exchange of love to lie
Unreachable inside a room
The traffic parts to let go by
Brings closer what is left to come,
30 And dulls to distance all we are.

1961   1964

High Windows

When I see a couple of kids
And guess he's fucking her and she's
Taking pills or wearing a diaphragm,
I know this is paradise

5 Everyone old has dreamed of all their lives—
Bonds and gestures pushed to one side
Like an outdated combine harvester,[1]
And everyone young going down the long slide

To happiness, endlessly. I wonder if
10 Anyone looked at me, forty years back,
And thought, *That'll be the life;*
No God any more, or sweating in the dark

About hell and that, or having to hide
What you think of the priest. He
15 *And his lot will all go down the long slide*
Like free bloody birds. And immediately

Rather than words comes the thought of high windows:
The sun-comprehending glass,
And beyond it, the deep blue air, that shows
20 Nothing, and is nowhere, and is endless.

1967   1974

Homage to a Government

Next year we are to bring the soldiers home
For lack of money, and it is all right.
Places they guarded, or kept orderly,
Must guard themselves, and keep themselves orderly.

---

1. Farm machine for harvesting grain.

5 We want the money for ourselves at home
   Instead of working. And this is all right.

   It's hard to say who wanted it to happen,
   But now it's been decided nobody minds.
   The places are a long way off, not here,
10 Which is all right, and from what we hear
   The soldiers there only made trouble happen.
   Next year we shall be easier in our minds.

   Next year we shall be living in a country
   That brought its soldiers home for lack of money.
15 The statues will be standing in the same
   Tree-muffled squares, and look nearly the same.
   Our children will not know it's a different country.
   All we can hope to leave them now is money.

Jan. 10, 1969   1974

This Be The Verse[1]

   They fuck you up, your mum and dad.
      They may not mean to, but they do.
   They fill you with the faults they had
      And add some extra, just for you.

5 But they were fucked up in their turn
      By fools in old-style hats and coats,
   Who half the time were soppy-stern
      And half at one another's throats.

   Man hands on misery to man.
10   It deepens like a coastal shelf.[2]
   Get out as early as you can,
      And don't have any kids yourself.

Apr.? 1971   1974

Aubade[1]

   I work all day, and get half-drunk at night.
   Waking at four to soundless dark, I stare.
   In time the curtain-edges will grow light.
   Till then I see what's really always there:
5 Unresting death, a whole day nearer now,

1. Cf. the elegy "Requiem," by Robert Louis Stevenson (1850–1894), of which the final verse
reads, "This be the verse you grave for me: / Here
he lies where he longed to be, / Home is the sailor,
home from sea, / And the hunter home from the
hill."
2. Underwater land off a coast
1. Music or poem announcing dawn.

Making all thought impossible but how
And where and when I shall myself die.
Arid interrogation: yet the dread
Of dying, and being dead,
10 Flashes afresh to hold and horrify.

The mind blanks at the glare. Not in remorse
—The good not done, the love not given, time
Torn off unused—nor wretchedly because
An only life can take so long to climb
15 Clear of its wrong beginnings, and may never;
But at the total emptiness for ever,
The sure extinction that we travel to
And shall be lost in always. Not to be here,
Not to be anywhere,
20 And soon; nothing more terrible, nothing more true.

This is a special way of being afraid
No trick dispels. Religion used to try,
That vast moth-eaten musical brocade
Created to pretend we never die,
25 And specious stuff that says *No rational being
Can fear a thing it will not feel,* not seeing
That this is what we fear—no sight, no sound,
No touch or taste or smell, nothing to think with,
Nothing to love or link with,
30 The anaesthetic from which none come round.

And so it stays just on the edge of vision,
A small unfocused blur, a standing chill
That slows each impulse down to indecision.
Most things may never happen: this one will,
35 And realisation of it rages out
In furnace-fear when we are caught without
People or drink. Courage is no good:
It means not scaring others. Being brave
Lets no one off the grave.
40 Death is no different whined at than withstood.

Slowly light strengthens, and the room takes shape.
It stands plain as a wardrobe, what we know,
Have always known, know that we can't escape,
Yet can't accept. One side will have to go.
45 Meanwhile telephones crouch, getting ready to ring
In locked-up offices, and all the uncaring
Intricate rented world begins to rouse.
The sky is white as clay, with no sun.
Work has to be done.
50 Postmen like doctors go from house to house.

1977   1977

NADINE GORDIMER
1923–2014

Nadine Gordimer's fiction has given imaginative and moral shape to the recent history of South Africa. From the time of the publication of her first book, *The Lying Days* (1953), she charted the changing patterns of response and resistance to apartheid by exploring the place of the European in Africa, selecting representative themes and governing motifs for novels and short stories, and shifting her ideological focus from a liberal to a more radical position. In recognition of this achievement, of having borne untiring and lucid narrative witness, Gordimer was awarded the 1991 Nobel Prize in Literature.

Born to Jewish immigrant parents in the South African mining town of Springs, Gordimer began writing early, from the beginning taking as her subject the pathologies and everyday realities of a racially divided society. Her decision to remain in Johannesburg through the years of political repression reflected her commitment to her subject and to her vision of a postapartheid future. After apartheid was dismantled in 1994, Gordimer continued to live and write in South Africa, and her late novels, such as *The House Gun* (1998), *The Pickup* (2001), and *Get a Life* (2006), retain an uncompromising focus on the inhabitants of a racially fractured culture.

In her nonfiction Gordimer self-consciously places her writing within a tradition of European realism, most notably that defined by the Hungarian philosopher and critic Georg Lukács (1885–1971). Her aim—as shown in her incisive and highly acclaimed novels of the 1970s, *The Conservationist* (1974) and *Burger's Daughter* (1979)—was to evoke by way of the personal and of the precisely observed particular a broader political and historical totality. This method gives her characters, and the stories in which they reside, their representativeness. As Gordimer famously said, "politics is character in South Africa." Yet throughout the long years of political polarization in that country and the banning of three of her own books, Gordimer distanced herself from polemics and retained a firm humanist belief in what she variously described as the objectivity and the inwardness of the writer. Although she referred to an engagement with political reality as imperative and explores permutations of the question of engagement in novels such as *Burger's Daughter* and *July's People* (1981), she nevertheless asserted the autonomy of the writer's perspective, "the last true judgment." Narrative for Gordimer helped define and clarify historical experience. Her keen sense of history as formation, and as demanding a continual rewriting, has ensured that her novels can be read as at once contemporary in their reference and symbolic of broader social and historical patterns, as in the paranoia surrounding the case of the buried black body on a white farm in *The Conservationist*, or in the psychosocial portrait of Rosa Burger in *Burger's Daughter*.

Gordimer drew criticism both for her apparent lack of attention to feminism in favor of race issues and for the wholeness and unfashionable completeness of her novels—their plottedness, meticulous scene paintings, fully realized characters. However, the searching symbolism and complexity of her narratives generally work against such judgments. As the following short story shows, a prominent feature of her writing is to give a number of different perspectives on a situation, in some cases most poignantly those of apartheid's supporters, and in this way to represent the broader anatomy of a diseased politics and, more generally, of the human being in history.

The Moment before the Gun Went Off

Marais Van der Vyver shot one of his farm labourers, dead. An accident, there are accidents with guns every day of the week—children playing a fatal game with a father's revolver in the cities where guns are domestic objects, nowadays, hunting mishaps like this one, in the country—but these won't be reported all over the world. Van der Vyver knows his will be. He knows that the story of the Afrikaner farmer—regional Party leader and Commandant of the local security commando—shooting a black man who worked for him will fit exactly *their* version of South Africa, it's made for them. They'll be able to use it in their boycott and divestment campaigns, it'll be another piece of evidence in their truth about the country. The papers at home will quote the story as it has appeared in the overseas press, and in the back-and-forth he and the black man will become those crudely-drawn figures on anti-apartheid banners, units in statistics of white brutality against the blacks quoted at the United Nations—he, whom they will gleefully be able to call "a leading member" of the ruling Party.

People in the farming community understand how he must feel. Bad enough to have killed a man, without helping the Party's, the government's, the country's enemies, as well. They see the truth of that. They know, reading the Sunday papers, that when Van der Vyver is quoted saying he is "terribly shocked," he will "look after the wife and children," none of those Americans and English, and none of those people at home who want to destroy the white man's power will believe him. And how they will sneer when he even says of the farm boy (according to one paper, if you can trust any of those reporters), "He was my friend, I always took him hunting with me." Those city and overseas people don't know it's true: farmers usually have one particular black boy they like to take along with them in the lands; you could call it a kind of friend, yes, friends are not only your own white people, like yourself, you take into your house, pray with in church and work with on the Party committee. But how can those others know that? They don't want to know it. They think all blacks are like the big-mouth agitators in town. And Van der Vyver's face, in the photographs, strangely opened by distress—everyone in the district remembers Marais Van der Vyver as a little boy who would go away and hide himself if he caught you smiling at him, and everyone knows him now as a man who hides any change of expression round his mouth behind a thick, soft moustache, and in his eyes by always looking at some object in hand, leaf of a crop fingered, pen or stone picked up, while concentrating on what he is saying, or while listening to you. It just goes to show what shock can do; when you look at the newspaper photographs you feel like apologising, as if you had stared in on some room where you should not be.

There will be an inquiry; there had better be, to stop the assumption of yet another case of brutality against farm workers, although there's nothing in doubt—an accident, and all the facts fully admitted by Van der Vyver. He made a statement when he arrived at the police station with the dead man in his bakkie.[1] Captain Beetge knows him well, of course; he gave him brandy. He was shaking, this big, calm, clever son of Willem Van der

---

1. Pickup truck.

Vyver, who inherited the old man's best farm. The black was stone dead, nothing to be done for him. Beetge will not tell anyone that after the brandy Van der Vyver wept. He sobbed, snot running onto his hands, like a dirty kid. The Captain was ashamed, for him, and walked out to give him a chance to recover himself.

Marais Van der Vyver left his house at three in the afternoon to cull a buck from the family of kudu[2] he protects in the bush areas of his farm. He is interested in wildlife and sees it as the farmers' sacred duty to raise game as well as cattle. As usual, he called at his shed workshop to pick up Lucas, a twenty-year-old farmhand who had shown mechanical aptitude and whom Van der Vyver himself had taught to maintain tractors and other farm machinery. He hooted, and Lucas followed the familiar routine, jumping onto the back of the truck. He liked to travel standing up there, spotting game before his employer did. He would lean forward, braced against the cab below him.

Van der Vyver had a rifle and .300 ammunition beside him in the cab. The rifle was one of his father's, because his own was at the gunsmith's in town. Since his father died (Beetge's sergeant wrote "passed on") no one had used the rifle and so when he took it from a cupboard he was sure it was not loaded. His father had never allowed a loaded gun in the house; he himself had been taught since childhood never to ride with a loaded weapon in a vehicle. But this gun was loaded. On a dirt track, Lucas thumped his fist on the cab roof three times to signal: look left. Having seen the white-ripple-marked flank of a kudu, and its fine horns raking through disguising bush, Van der Vyver drove rather fast over a pot-hole. The jolt fired the rifle. Upright, it was pointing straight through the cab roof at the head of Lucas. The bullet pierced the roof and entered Lucas's brain by way of his throat.

That is the statement of what happened. Although a man of such standing in the district, Van der Vyver had to go through the ritual of swearing that it was the truth. It has gone on record, and will be there in the archive of the local police station as long as Van der Vyver lives, and beyond that, through the lives of his children, Magnus, Helena and Karel—unless things in the country get worse, the example of black mobs in the towns spreads to the rural areas and the place is burned down as many urban police stations have been. Because nothing the government can do will appease the agitators and the whites who encourage them. Nothing satisfies them, in the cities: blacks can sit and drink in white hotels, now, the Immorality Act[3] has gone, blacks can sleep with whites. . . . It's not even a crime any more.

Van der Vyver has a high barbed security fence round his farmhouse and garden which his wife, Alida, thinks spoils completely the effect of her artificial stream with its tree-ferns beneath the jacarandas.[4] There is an aerial soaring like a flag-pole in the back yard. All his vehicles, including the truck in which the black man died, have aerials that swing their whips when the driver hits a pot-hole: they are part of the security system the farmers in the district maintain, each farm in touch with every other by radio, twenty-four hours out of twenty-four. It has already happened that infiltrators from over the border have mined remote farm roads, killing white farmers and their

2. Large African antelope. The males have long, spirally twisted horns.
3. South African government act prohibiting

sexual relations between whites and other races.
4. Tropical trees with blue flowers.

families out on their own property for a Sunday picnic. The pot-hole could have set off a land-mine, and Van der Vyver might have died with his farm boy. When neighbours use the communications system to call up and say they are sorry about "that business" with one of Van der Vyver's boys, there goes unsaid: it could have been worse.

It is obvious from the quality and fittings of the coffin that the farmer has provided money for the funeral. And an elaborate funeral means a great deal to blacks; look how they will deprive themselves of the little they have, in their lifetime, keeping up payments to a burial society so they won't go in boxwood to an unmarked grave. The young wife is pregnant (of course) and another little one, wearing red shoes several sizes too large, leans under her jutting belly. He is too young to understand what has happened, what he is witnessing that day, but neither whines nor plays about; he is solemn without knowing why. Blacks expose small children to everything, they don't protect them from the sight of fear and pain the way whites do theirs. It is the young wife who rolls her head and cries like a child, sobbing on the breast of this relative and that.

All present work for Van der Vyver or are the families of those who work; and in the weeding and harvest seasons, the women and children work for him, too, carried—wrapped in their blankets, on a truck, singing—at sunrise to the fields. The dead man's mother is a woman who can't be more than in her late thirties (they start bearing children at puberty) but she is heavily mature in a black dress between her own parents, who were already working for old Van der Vyver when Marais, like their daughter, was a child. The parents hold her as if she were a prisoner or a crazy woman to be restrained. But she says nothing, does nothing. She does not look up; she does not look at Van der Vyver, whose gun went off in the truck, she stares at the grave. Nothing will make her look up; there need be no fear that she will look up; at him. His wife, Alida, is beside him. To show the proper respect, as for any white funeral, she is wearing the navy-blue-and-cream hat she wears to church this summer. She is always supportive, although he doesn't seem to notice it; this coldness and reserve—his mother says he didn't mix well as a child—she accepts for herself but regrets that it has prevented him from being nominated, as he should be, to stand as the Party's parliamentary candidate for the district. He does not let her clothing, or that of anyone else gathered closely, make contact with him. He, too, stares at the grave. The dead man's mother and he stare at the grave in communication like that between the black man outside and the white man inside the cab the moment before the gun went off.

The moment before the gun went off was a moment of high excitement shared through the roof of the cab, as the bullet was to pass, between the young black man outside and the white farmer inside the vehicle. There were such moments, without explanation, between them, although often around the farm the farmer would pass the young man without returning a greeting, as if he did not recognize him. When the bullet went off what Van der Vyver saw was the kudu stumble in fright at the report and gallop away. Then he heard the thud behind him, and past the window saw the young man fall out of the vehicle. He was sure he had leapt up and toppled—in fright, like the buck. The farmer was almost laughing with relief, ready to tease, as he opened his door, it did not seem possible that a bullet passing through the roof could have done harm.

The young man did not laugh with him at his own fright. The farmer carried him in his arms, to the truck. He was sure, sure he could not be dead. But the young black man's blood was all over the farmer's clothes, soaking against his flesh as he drove.

How will they ever know, when they file newspaper clippings, evidence, proof, when they look at the photographs and see his face—guilty! guilty! they are right!—how will they know, when the police stations burn with all the evidence of what has happened now, and what the law made a crime in the past. How could they know that *they do not know*. Anything. The young black callously shot through the negligence of the white man was not the farmer's boy; he was his son.

1991

DEREK WALCOTT
b. 1930

D erek Walcott was born on the island of Saint Lucia in the British West Indies, where he had a Methodist upbringing in a largely Roman Catholic society. He was educated at St. Mary's College in Saint Lucia and the University of the West Indies in Jamaica. He then moved to Trinidad, where he worked as a book reviewer, art critic, playwright, and artistic director of a theater workshop. Since the early 1980s he has also taught at a number of American colleges and universities, especially Boston University; in 1992 he received the Nobel Prize in Literature.

As a black poet writing from within both the English literary tradition and the history of a colonized people, Walcott has self-mockingly referred to his split allegiances to his African Caribbean and his European inheritances as those of a "schizophrenic," a "mongrel," a "mulatto of style." His background is indeed racially and culturally mixed: his grandmothers were of African descent; his grandfathers were white, a Dutchman and an Englishman. Schooled in the Standard English that is the official language of Saint Lucia, Walcott also grew up speaking the predominantly French Creole (or patois) that is the primary language of everyday life (the island had traded hands fourteen times in colonial wars between the British and the French). In his poetry this cross-cultural inheritance is sometimes the source of pain and ambivalence, as when in "A Far Cry from Africa" he refers to himself as being "poisoned with the blood of both." At other times it fuels a celebratory integration of multiple forms, visions, and energies, as in parts of his long poem *Omeros,* which transposes elements of Homeric epic from the Aegean to the Caribbean.

Even as a schoolboy Walcott knew he was not alone in his effort to sort through his vexed postcolonial affiliations. From a young age he felt a special affinity with Irish writers such as W. B. Yeats, James Joyce, and J. M. Synge, whom he saw as fellow colonials—"They were the niggers of Britain"—with the same paradoxical hatred for the British Empire and worship of the English language. He has repeatedly asked how the postcolonial poet can both grieve the agonizing harm of British colonialism and appreciate the empire's literary gift. Walcott has also acknowledged other English and American writers—T. S. Eliot, Ezra Pound, Hart Crane, W. H. Auden, and Robert Lowell—as enabling influences.

Over the course of his prolific career, Walcott has adapted various European literary archetypes (e.g., the Greek character Philoctetes) and forms (epic, quatrains, terza rima, English meters). He has ascribed his rigorous concern with craft to his youthful Protestantism. At once disciplined and flamboyant as a poet, he insists on the specifically Caribbean opulence of his art: "I come from a place that likes grandeur; it likes large gestures; it is not inhibited by flourish; it is a rhetorical society; it is a society of physical performance; it is a society of style." Although much of his poetry is in a rhetorically elevated Standard English, Walcott adapts the calypso rhythms of a lightly creolized English in "The Schooner *Flight*," and he braids together West Indian English, Standard English, and French patois in *Omeros*. He has a great passion for metaphor, by which he deftly weaves imaginative connections across cultural and racial boundaries. His plays, written in an accurate and energetic language, are similarly infused with the spirit of syncretism, vividly conjoining Caribbean and European motifs, images, and idioms.

A Far Cry from Africa

A wind is ruffling the tawny pelt
Of Africa. Kikuyu,[1] quick as flies,
Batten upon the bloodstreams of the veldt.[2]
Corpses are scattered through a paradise.
5 Only the worm, colonel of carrion, cries:
"Waste no compassion on these separate dead!"
Statistics justify and scholars seize
The salients of colonial policy.
What is that to the white child hacked in bed?
10 To savages, expendable as Jews?

Threshed out by beaters,[3] the long rushes break
In a white dust of ibises whose cries
Have wheeled since civilization's dawn
From the parched river or beast-teeming plain.
15 The violence of beast on beast is read
As natural law, but upright man
Seeks his divinity by inflicting pain.
Delirious as these worried beasts, his wars
Dance to the tightened carcass of a drum,
20 While he calls courage still that native dread
Of the white peace contracted by the dead.
Again brutish necessity wipes its hands
Upon the napkin of a dirty cause, again
A waste of our compassion, as with Spain,[4]
25 The gorilla wrestles with the superman.
I who am poisoned with the blood of both,

1. An east African ethnic group whose members, as Mau Mau fighters, conducted an eight-year campaign of violent resistance against British colonial settlers in Kenya in the 1950s.
2. Open country, neither cultivated nor forest (Afrikaans).
3. In big-game hunting, natives are hired to beat the brush, driving birds—such as ibises—and other animals into the open.
4. The Spanish Civil War (1936–39).

Where shall I turn, divided to the vein?
I who have cursed
The drunken officer of British rule, how choose
30   Between this Africa and the English tongue I love?
Betray them both, or give back what they give?
How can I face such slaughter and be cool?
How can I turn from Africa and live?

1956, 1962

From The Schooner Flight

1 *Adios, Carenage*[1]

In idle August, while the sea soft,
and leaves of brown islands stick to the rim
of this Caribbean, I blow out the light
by the dreamless face of Maria Concepcion
5   to ship as a seaman on the schooner *Flight*.
Out in the yard turning grey in the dawn,
I stood like a stone and nothing else move
but the cold sea rippling like galvanize
and the nail holes of stars in the sky roof,
10   till a wind start to interfere with the trees.
I pass me dry neighbour sweeping she yard
as I went downhill, and I nearly said:
"Sweep soft, you witch, 'cause she don't sleep hard,"
but the bitch look through me like I was dead.
15   A route taxi pull up, park-lights still on.
The driver size up my bags with a grin:
"This time, Shabine, like you really gone!"
I ain't answer the ass, I simply pile in
the back seat and watch the sky burn
20   above Laventille[2] pink as the gown
in which the woman I left was sleeping,
and I look in the rearview and see a man
exactly like me, and the man was weeping
for the houses, the streets, the whole fucking island.

25   Christ have mercy on all sleeping things!
From that dog rotting down Wrightson Road
to when I was a dog on these streets;
if loving these islands must be my load,
out of corruption my soul takes wings,
30   But they had started to poison my soul
with their big house, big car, big-time bohbohl,[3]
coolie, nigger, Syrian, and French Creole,
so I leave it for them and their carnival—

1. Waterfront where schooners are cleaned and repaired. "Adios": good-bye (Spanish).
2. Hillside slum outside Port of Spain, Trinidad.

3. Or *bobol*: corrupt practices or fraud, organized by people in positions of power (Eastern Caribbean English).

I taking a sea-bath, I gone down the road.
35 I know these islands from Monos to Nassau,[4]
a rusty head sailor with sea-green eyes
that they nickname Shabine, the patois° for   *spoken dialect*
any red nigger, and I, Shabine, saw
when these slums of empire was paradise.
40 I'm just a red nigger who love the sea,
I had a sound colonial education,
I have Dutch, nigger, and English in me,
and either I'm nobody, or I'm a nation.

But Maria Concepcion was all my thought
45 watching the sea heaving up and down
as the port side of dories, schooners, and yachts
was painted afresh by the strokes of the sun
signing her name with every reflection;
I knew when dark-haired evening put on
50 her bright silk at sunset, and, folding the sea,
sidled under the sheet with her starry laugh,
that there'd be no rest, there'd be no forgetting.
Is like telling mourners round the graveside
about resurrection, they want the dead back,
55 so I smile to myself as the bow rope untied
and the *Flight* swing seaward: "Is no use repeating
that the sea have more fish. I ain't want her
dressed in the sexless light of a seraph,°   *angel*
I want those round brown eyes like a marmoset,[5] and
60 till the day when I can lean back and laugh,
those claws that tickled my back on sweating
Sunday afternoons, like a crab on wet sand."
As I worked, watching the rotting waves come
past the bow that scissor the sea like silk,
65 I swear to you all, by my mother's milk,
by the stars that shall fly from tonight's furnace,
that I loved them, my children, my wife, my home;
I loved them as poets love the poetry
that kills them, as drowned sailors the sea.

70 You ever look up from some lonely beach
and see a far schooner? Well, when I write
this poem, each phrase go be soaked in salt;
I go draw and knot every line as tight
as ropes in this rigging; in simple speech
75 my common language go be the wind,
my pages the sails of the schooner *Flight*.

1979

---

4. Capital of the Bahamas. "Monos": island off   5. South American monkey.
the northwest coast of Trinidad.

The Season of Phantasmal Peace

Then all the nations of birds lifted together
the huge net of the shadows of this earth
in multitudinous dialects, twittering tongues,
stitching and crossing it. They lifted up
5   the shadows of long pines down trackless slopes,
the shadows of glass-faced towers down evening streets,
the shadow of a frail plant on a city sill—
the net rising soundless as night, the birds' cries soundless, until
there was no longer dusk, or season, decline, or weather,
10   only this passage of phantasmal light
that not the narrowest shadow dared to sever.

And men could not see, looking up, what the wild geese drew,
what the ospreys trailed behind them in silvery ropes
that flashed in the icy sunlight; they could not hear
15   battalions of starlings waging peaceful cries,
bearing the net higher, covering this world
like the vines of an orchard, or a mother drawing
the trembling gauze over the trembling eyes
of a child fluttering to sleep;
                      it was the light
20   that you will see at evening on the side of a hill
in yellow October, and no one hearing knew
what change had brought into the raven's cawing,
the killdeer's screech, the ember-circling chough°   *bird in crow family*
such an immense, soundless, and high concern
25   for the fields and cities where the birds belong,
except it was their seasonal passing, Love,
made seasonless, or, from the high privilege of their birth,
something brighter than pity for the wingless ones
below them who shared dark holes in windows and in houses,
30   and higher they lifted the net with soundless voices
above all change, betrayals of falling suns,
and this season lasted one moment, like the pause
between dusk and darkness, between fury and peace,
but, for such as our earth is now, it lasted long.

                                              1981

FROM OMEROS[1]

Book One
Chapter III

III

"*Mais qui ça qui rivait-'ous, Philoctete?*"[2]

                         "*Moin blessé.*"[3]

"But what is wrong wif you, Philoctete?"

                         "I am blest

wif this wound, Ma Kilman[4] *qui pas ka guérir pièce.*

Which will never heal."

                  "Well, you must take it easy.

5   Go home and lie down, give the foot a lickle°   *little (West Indian English)*
     rest."
Philoctete, his trouser-legs rolled, stares out to sea

from the worn rumshop window. The itch in the sore
tingles like the tendrils of the anemone,
and the puffed blister of Portuguese man-o'-war.°   *jellyfish*

10 He believed the swelling came from the chained ankles
of his grandfathers. Or else why was there no cure?
That the cross he carried was not only the anchor's

but that of his race, for a village black and poor
as the pigs that rooted in its burning garbage,
15 then were hooked on the anchors of the abattoir.°   *slaughterhouse*

Ma Kilman was sewing. She looked up and saw his face
squinting from the white of the street. He was waiting
to pass out on the table. This went on for days.

The ice turned to warm water near the self-hating
20 gesture of clenching his head tight in both hands. She
heard the boys in blue uniforms, going to school,

screaming at his elbow: "Pheeloh! Pheelosophee!"
A mummy embalmed in Vaseline and alcohol.
In the Egyptian silence she muttered softly:

---

1. Modern Greek version of the name Homer. Homer's *Iliad* and *Odyssey* are, along with Dante's *Divine Comedy*, from which Walcott adapts the terza rima stanza, and James Joyce's *Ulysses* (1922) major influences on this Caribbean epic, which moves across centuries and geographies, from Saint Lucia to Africa to Ireland.
2. Pronounced *fee-lock-TET*; a name shared with Philoctetes, who, in the *Iliad* and Sophocles' eponymous play, is abandoned on an island on the way to the Trojan War after receiving a snakebite. The wound never heals and continually torments Philoctetes, who moans uncontrollably. Later the gods decide that the war cannot be won without him, and the Greek soldiers have to go back to the island and beg him to return with them to battle.
3. French patois, punningly mistranslated below, since *blessé* actually means "wounded."
4. The owner of the No Pain Café, Ma Kilman serves in the poem as a sibyl (female prophet) and an obeah woman (one practicing a kind of West Indian sorcery).

25   "It have a flower somewhere, a medicine, and ways
     my grandmother would boil it. I used to watch ants
     climbing her white flower-pot. But, God, in which place?"

     Where was this root? What senna,° what tepid   *medicinal herb*
        tisanes,°   *medicinal beverages*
     could clean the branched river of his corrupted blood,
30   whose sap was a wounded cedar's? What did it mean,

     this name that felt like a fever? Well, one good heft
     of his garden-cutlass would slice the damned name clean
     from its rotting yam. He said, *"Merci."*° Then he left.   *Thank you (French)*

Book Six

Chapter XLIX

I

She bathed him in the brew of the root.[1] The basin
was one of those cauldrons from the old sugar-mill,
with its charred pillars, rock pasture, and one grazing

horse, looking like helmets that have tumbled downhill
5   from an infantry charge. Children rang them with stones.
Wildflowers sprung in them when the dirt found a seam.

She had one in her back yard, close to the crotons,°   *tree or shrub*
agape in its crusted, agonized O: the scream
of centuries. She scraped its rusted scabs, she scoured

10   the mouth of the cauldron, then fed a crackling pyre
with palms and banana-trash. In the scream she poured
tin after kerosene tin, its base black from fire,

of seawater and sulphur. Into this she then fed
the bubbling root and leaves. She led Philoctete
15   to the gurgling lava. Trembling, he entered

his bath like a boy. The lime leaves leeched to his wet
knuckled spine like islands that cling to the basin
of the rusted Caribbean. An icy sweat

glazed his scalp, but he could feel the putrescent shin
20   drain in the seethe like sucked marrow, he felt it drag
the slime from his shame. She rammed him back to his place

as he tried climbing out with: *"Not yet!"* With a rag
sogged in a basin of ice she rubbed his squeezed face
the way boys enjoy their mother's ritual rage,

---

1. Ma Kilman is bathing Philoctete to heal his wound.

25 and as he surrendered to her, the foul flower
on his shin whitened and puckered, the corolla
closed its thorns like the sea-egg. What else did it cure?

II

The bow leapt back to the palm of the warrior.
The yoke of the wrong name lifted from his shoulders.
30 His muscles loosened like those of a brown river

that was dammed with silt, and then silkens its boulders
with refreshing strength. His ribs thudded like a horse
cantering on a beach that bursts into full gallop

while a boy yanks at its rein with terrified "Whoas!"
35 The white foam unlocked his coffles, his ribbed shallop
broke from its anchor, and the water, which he swirled

like a child, steered his brow into the right current,
as calm as *In God We Troust*[2] to that other world,
and his flexed palm enclosed an oar with the identi-

40 ical closure of a mouth around its own name,
the way a sea-anemone closes slyly
into a secrecy many mistake for shame.

Centuries weigh down the head of the swamp-lily,
its tribal burden arches the sea-almond's° spine,   *a tree*
45 in barracoon[3] back yards the soul-smoke still passes,

but the wound has found her own cure. The soft days spin
the spittle of the spider in webbed glasses,
as she drenches the burning trash to its last flame,

and the embers steam and hiss to the schoolboys' cries
50 when he'd weep in the window for their tribal shame.
A shame for the loss of words, and a language tired

of accepting that loss, and then all accepted.
That was why the sea stank from the frothing urine
of surf, and fish-guts reeked from the government shed,

55 and why God pissed on the village for months of rain.
But now, quite clearly the tears trickled down his face
like rainwater down a cracked carafe from Choiseul,[4]

as he stood like a boy in his bath with the first clay's
innocent prick! So she threw Adam a towel.
60 And the yard was Eden. And its light the first day's.

1990

---

2. Near the poem's beginning, the character
Achille chisels this misspelled phrase into his
canoe and then decides, "Leave it! Is God' spelling and mine" (1.1.2).
3. Barracks for housing convicts or slaves.
4. A village in Saint Lucia.

CHINUA ACHEBE
1930–2013

The most celebrated African novelist is Chinua Achebe, whose work has transformed the landscape of African fiction, both in his own continent and in the Western imagination. While steadfastly refusing to sentimentalize the people and traditions of Nigeria, his writings effectively challenge many entrenched impressions of African life and culture, replacing simplistic stereotypes with portrayals of a complex society still suffering from the legacy of colonial oppression.

Achebe was born in Ogidi, an Igbo-speaking town in eastern Nigeria, and educated—in English—at church schools and University College, Ibadan, where he subsequently taught (briefly) before joining the Nigerian Broadcasting Corporation in Lagos. He was director of external broadcasting from 1961 to 1966, and then launched a publishing company with Christopher Okigbo, a poet soon to die in the Nigerian Civil War (1967–70). After the war Achebe taught in the United States, before returning for a time to the University of Nigeria at Nsukka. In 1990 Achebe joined the faculty of Bard College and, in 2009, of Brown University.

A volume of Achebe's poems was joint winner of the Commonwealth Poetry Prize in 1972. He also wrote short stories and essays, including an attack on political corruption in his homeland, *The Trouble with Nigeria* (1983), and reflections on growing up in colonial Nigeria, *The Education of a British-Protected Child* (2009). He was best-known for his novels, however, especially *Things Fall Apart* (1958), written with an insider's understanding of the African world and its history and depicting the destruction of an individual, a family, and a culture at the moment of colonial incursion. The British asserted their authority over the Igbo in Nigeria through trade, religion, politics, and military might. In *Things Fall Apart*, Achebe represents the process of colonization from the vantage point of villagers who are puzzled, intrigued, co-opted, enraged, divided against themselves, or killed. The turn-of-the-nineteenth-century imperial onslaught seems all the more bewildering and violent because the novel has immersed the reader in this village's finely calibrated cultural practices in religion and government, athletics and storytelling, agriculture and the family. The Africans in the novel speak a resonantly proverbial language that operates as an image of all the beautiful and traditional structures transformed irrevocably by colonialism. Achebe's other novels include *No Longer at Ease* (1960), *Arrow of God* (1964), *A Man of the People* (1966), and *Anthills of the Savannah* (1987). Helping to rebut Western preconceptions of African primitivism, Achebe's rich portraits of African culture advanced his ambition to help his "society regain belief in itself and put away the complexes of the years of denigration and self-abasement" produced by the distortions of colonialism. He said he wanted his novels to teach his African "readers that their past—with all its imperfections—was not one long night of savagery from which the first Europeans acting on God's behalf delivered them."

Written in the aftermath of the Nigerian Civil War, Achebe's short story printed here, ironically named "Civil Peace," represents a society coming out of the devastation of the continent's first major post-independence civil conflict. Despite his many losses, Jonathan Iwegbu benevolently welcomes the blessings of survival. Through Achebe's meticulous and terse characterization, Jonathan emerges as a man who humbly affirms life, while shrewdly observing and assessing those around him and his future prospects. Achebe builds dramatic tension when robbers threaten Jonathan and his family in a dramatic scene that blends terror with comedy. As one of his characters says of wartime in another of Achebe's stories, "Girls at War": "It was a tight, blockaded and desperate world but none the less a world—with some goodness and some badness and plenty of heroism, which, however happened most times far, far below the eye-level" of self-important people. Achebe's attention to extraordinarily ordinary characters like Jonathan Iwegbu, though they exist far below eye level, helped him fulfill his lifelong ambition of reversing the dehumanizing preconceptions long affixed to Africans. In "Civil Peace," Achebe deftly interweaves Standard English with pidgin dialogue, economically evokes a society at a moment of historic transition, and sharply draws his characters with wit and compassion, thereby demonstrating in miniature some of the gifts that made him one of the most acclaimed fiction writers of the postcolonial world.

Civil Peace

Jonathan Iwegbu counted himself extra-ordinarily lucky. 'Happy survival!' meant so much more to him than just a current fashion of greeting old friends in the first hazy days of peace. It went deep to his heart. He had come out of the war[1] with five inestimable blessings—his head, his wife Maria's head and the heads of three out of their four children. As a bonus he also had his old bicycle—a miracle too but naturally not to be compared to the safety of five human heads.

The bicycle had a little history of its own. One day at the height of the war it was commandeered 'for urgent military action'. Hard as its loss would have been to him he would still have let it go without a thought had he not had some doubts about the genuineness of the officer. It wasn't his disreputable rags, nor the toes peeping out of one blue and one brown canvas shoes, nor yet the two stars of his rank done obviously in a hurry in biro,[2] that troubled Jonathan; many good and heroic soldiers looked the same or worse. It was rather a certain lack of grip and firmness in his manner. So Jonathan, suspecting he might be amenable to influence, rummaged in his raffia[3] bag and produced the two pounds with which he had been going to buy firewood which his wife, Maria, retailed to camp officials for extra stock-fish and corn meal, and got his bicycle back. That night he buried it in the little clearing in the bush where the dead of the camp, including his own youngest son, were buried. When he dug it up again a year later after the surrender all it needed was a little palm-oil[4] greasing. 'Nothing puzzles God,' he said in wonder.

He put it to immediate use as a taxi and accumulated a small pile of Biafran money[5] ferrying camp officials and their families across the four-mile stretch to the nearest tarred road. His standard charge per trip was six pounds and those who had the money were only glad to be rid of some of it

---

1. The Nigerian Civil War, or Biafran War (1967–70), in which the predominantly Igbo (or Ibo) portion of eastern Nigeria declared itself the independent Republic of Biafra and was put down by the federal government, dominated by the Hausa-Fulani and Yoruba ethnic groups and backed by international support. Perhaps as many as one million Igbo people died as a result of the conflict.
2. In ballpoint pen.
3. Soft fiber made from the leaves of an African palm tree.
4. Oil produced from the palm tree.
5. I.e., money from the now-defunct Republic of Biafra.

in this way. At the end of a fortnight he had made a small fortune of one hundred and fifteen pounds.

Then he made the journey to Enugu[6] and found another miracle waiting for him. It was unbelievable. He rubbed his eyes and looked again and it was still standing there before him. But, needless to say, even that monumental blessing must be accounted also totally inferior to the five heads in the family. This newest miracle was his little house in Ogui Overside.[7] Indeed nothing puzzles God! Only two houses away a huge concrete edifice some wealthy contractor had put up just before the war was a mountain of rubble. And here was Jonathan's little zinc house[8] of no regrets built with mud blocks quite intact! Of course the doors and windows were missing and five sheets off the roof. But what was that? And anyhow he had returned to Enugu early enough to pick up bits of old zinc and wood and soggy sheets of cardboard lying around the neighbourhood before thousands more came out of their forest holes looking for the same things. He got a destitute carpenter with one old hammer, a blunt plane and a few bent and rusty nails in his tool bag to turn this assortment of wood, paper and metal into door and window shutters for five Nigerian shillings or fifty Biafran pounds. He paid the pounds, and moved in with his overjoyed family carrying five heads on their shoulders.

His children picked mangoes near the military cemetery and sold them to soldiers' wives for a few pennies—real pennies this time—and his wife started making breakfast akara balls[9] for neighbours in a hurry to start life again. With his family earnings he took his bicycle to the villages around and bought fresh palm-wine[1] which he mixed generously in his rooms with the water which had recently started running again in the public tap down the road, and opened up a bar for soldiers and other lucky people with good money.

At first he went daily, then every other day and finally once a week, to the offices of the Coal Corporation where he used to be a miner, to find out what was what. The only thing he did find out in the end was that that little house of his was even a greater blessing than he had thought. Some of his fellow ex-miners who had nowhere to return at the end of the day's waiting just slept outside the doors of the offices and cooked what meal they could scrounge together in Bournvita tins.[2] As the weeks lengthened and still nobody could say what was what Jonathan discontinued his weekly visits altogether and faced his palm-wine bar.

But nothing puzzles God. Came the day of the windfall when after five days of endless scuffles in queues and counter-queues in the sun outside the Treasury he had twenty pounds counted into his palms as ex-gratia[3] award for the rebel money he had turned in. It was like Christmas for him and for many others like him when the payments began. They called it (since few could manage its proper official name) *egg-rasher*.

As soon as the pound notes were placed in his palm Jonathan simply closed it tight over them and buried fist and money inside his trouser

---

6. An industrial city in southeastern Nigeria and the Biafran capital during the civil war.
7. Area outside the city of Enugu.
8. House made from sheets of zinc, typically used in roofing.
9. Bean cakes or fritters made from black-eyed peas.
1. Wine made by fermenting the sap of palm trees.
2. Cans that had contained powdered mix for a brand of chocolate malted drink.
3. Given as a favor.

pocket. He had to be extra careful because he had seen a man a couple of days earlier collapse into near-madness in an instant before that oceanic crowd because no sooner had he got his twenty pounds than some heartless ruffian picked it off him. Though it was not right that a man in such an extremity of agony should be blamed yet many in the queues that day were able to remark quietly on the victim's carelessness, especially after he pulled out the innards of his pocket and revealed a hole in it big enough to pass a thief's head. But of course he had insisted that the money had been in the other pocket, pulling it out too to show its comparative wholeness. So one had to be careful.

Jonathan soon transferred the money to his left hand and pocket so as to leave his right free for shaking hands should the need arise, though by fixing his gaze at such an elevation as to miss all approaching human faces he made sure that the need did not arise, until he got home.

He was normally a heavy sleeper but that night he heard all the neighbourhood noises die down one after another. Even the night watchman who knocked the hour on some metal somewhere in the distance had fallen silent after knocking one o'clock. That must have been the last thought in Jonathan's mind before he was finally carried away himself. He couldn't have been gone for long, though, when he was violently awakened again.

'Who is knocking?' whispered his wife lying beside him on the floor.

'I don't know,' he whispered back breathlessly.

The second time the knocking came it was so loud and imperious that the rickety old door could have fallen down.

'Who is knocking?' he asked then, his voice parched and trembling.

'Na tief-man[4] and him people,' came the cool reply. 'Make you hopen de door.' This was followed by the heaviest knocking of all.

Maria was the first to raise the alarm, then he followed and all their children.

'Police-o! Thieves-o! Neighbours-o! Police-o! We are lost! We are dead! Neighbours, are you asleep? Wake up! Police-o!'

This went on for a long time and then stopped suddenly. Perhaps they had scared the thief away. There was total silence. But only for a short while.

'You done finish?' asked the voice outside. 'Make we help you small. Oya,[5] everybody!'

'Police-o! Tief-man-o! Neighbours-o! we done loss-o! Police-o! . . .'

There were at least five other voices besides the leader's.

Jonathan and his family were now completely paralysed by terror. Maria and the children sobbed inaudibly like lost souls. Jonathan groaned continuously.

The silence that followed the thieves' alarm vibrated horribly. Jonathan all but begged their leader to speak again and be done with it.

'My frien,' said he at long last, 'we don try our best for call dem but I tink say dem all done sleep-o . . . So wetin[6] we go do now? Sometaim you wan call soja?[7] Or you wan make we call dem for you? Soja better pass[8] police. No be so?'

4. Thief. "Na": it is (Nigerian pidgin, as in the ensuing glosses).
5. Let's get to it.
6. What.
7. Soldier.
8. Than.

'Na so!' replied his men. Jonathan thought he heard even more voices now than before and groaned heavily. His legs were sagging under him and his throat felt like sand-paper.

'My frien, why you no de talk again. I de ask you say you wan make we call soja?'

'No'.

'Awrighto. Now make we talk business. We no be bad tief. We no like for make trouble. Trouble done finish. War done finish and all the katakata wey de for inside.[9] No Civil War again. This time na Civil Peace. No be so?'

'Na so!' answered the horrible chorus.

'What do you want from me? I am a poor man. Everything I had went with this war. Why do you come to me? You know people who have money. We . . .'

'Awright! We know say you no get plenty money. But we sef no get even anini.[1] So derefore make you open dis window and give us one hundred pound and we go commot.[2] Orderwise we de come for inside now to show you guitar-boy like dis . . .'[3]

A volley of automatic fire rang through the sky. Maria and the children began to weep aloud again.

'Ah, missisi de cry again. No need for dat. We done talk say we na good tief. We just take our small money and go nwayorly.[4] No molest. Abi[5] we de molest?'

'At all!' sang the chorus.

'My friends,' began Jonathan hoarsely. 'I hear what you say and I thank you. If I had one hundred pounds . . .'

'Lookia my frien, no be play we come play for your house. If we make mistake and step for inside you no go like am-o.[6] So derefore . . .'

'To God who made me; if you come inside and find one hundred pounds, take it and shoot me and shoot my wife and children. I swear to God. The only money I have in this life is this twenty-pounds *egg-rasher* they gave me today . . .'

'OK. Time de go. Make you open dis window and bring the twenty pound. We go manage am[7] like dat.'

There were now loud murmurs of dissent among the chorus: 'Na lie de man de lie; e get plenty money . . . Make we go inside and search properly well . . . Wetin[8] be twenty pound? . . .'

'Shurrup!' rang the leader's voice like a lone shot in the sky and silenced the murmuring at once. 'Are you dere? Bring the money quick!'

'I am coming,' said Jonathan fumbling in the darkness with the key of the small wooden box he kept by his side on the mat.

At the first sign of light as neighbours and others assembled to commiserate with him he was already strapping his five-gallon demijohn[9] to his bicycle carrier and his wife, sweating in the open fire, was turning over akara balls

---

9. Trouble it brought.
1. A farthing, a disused coin worth less than a penny.
2. Get out of here.
3. I.e., hold (and fire) guns like guitar players.
4. Gently, quietly, without protest.
5. Is it.

6. It ("am" used in place of pronoun, "-o" for emphasis, a dire warning).
7. Him.
8. What.
9. A large bottle with a round body and narrow neck, usually encased in woven wicker.

in a wide clay bowl of boiling oil. In the corner his eldest son was rinsing out dregs of yesterday's palm wine from old beer bottles.

'I count it as nothing,' he told his sympathizers, his eyes on the rope he was tying. 'What is *egg-rasher*? Did I depend on it last week? Or is it greater than other things that went with the war? I say, let *egg-rasher* perish in the flames! Let it go where everything else has gone. Nothing puzzles God.'

1971

ALICE MUNRO
b. 1931

Alice Munro is one of the leading short-story writers of her generation. Her fiction combines spareness and realism—an uncompromising look at a panorama of faltering lives—with magisterial vision and expansiveness. Munro's signature approach to the short story, in which she uses a deceptively simple style to produce complex, layered, and emotionally potent effects, has influenced many of her English-language contemporaries, both within and outside Canada. In addition to one novel, *Lives of Girls and Women* (1972), she has published numerous collections of short stories, including *Dance of the Happy Shades* (1968), *Something I've Been Meaning to Tell You* (1974), *The Moons of Jupiter* (1982), *Friend of My Youth* (1990), *The Love of a Good Woman* (1998), *Hateship, Friendship, Courtship, Loveship, Marriage* (2001), *Runaway* (2004), *Carried Away* (2006), *The View from Castle Rock* (2006), and *Too Much Happiness* (2009). She won the Man Booker International Prize in 2009.

Many of Munro's stories are written in the first person, often from the perspective of women whose voices and experiences suggest the author's history. She was born Alice Anne Laidlaw to a poor family in Wingham, Ontario, and her parents' struggles within a variety of rural occupations continued throughout her childhood. She began writing in her teens and in 1949 enrolled in the University of Western Ontario; she left the university two years later, to marry and raise three daughters. She typically sets her stories in small towns where poverty stamps itself on all facets of life, and where women confront—often in a spirit that combines resignation with stubborn resistance—the triple binds of economic, gender, and cultural confinement. Through a precise and particular emphasis on setting and character, Munro evokes rural Canadian life in the decades following midcentury, when modernity and the promise of the future are often crowded out by a hardening sense of the past.

In an early writing, Munro describes an approach to the outside world that effectively captures her sense of the mystery within the ordinary—the hallmark of her realist style: "It seems as if there are feelings that have to be translated into a next-door language, which might blow them up and burst them altogether; or else they have to be let alone. The truth about them is always suspected, never verified, the light catches but doesn't define them. . . . Yet there is the feeling—I have the feeling—that at some level these things open; fragments, moments, suggestions, open, full of power." This aura of openness and suggestion, conveyed through "next-door language," gives Munro's stories their haunting aspect, their quality of movement, rippling and widening from the small-scale to the magnificent. The story included here, "Walker Brothers Cowboy," exemplifies her ability to imbue "fragments, moments, suggestions" with fullness and power, as we view through a young girl's eyes both the pathos and the degradation of men and women whose lives have fallen into a potentially deadening cycle of promise and decay.

Walker Brothers Cowboy[1]

After supper my father says, "Want to go down and see if the Lake's still there?" We leave my mother sewing under the dining-room light, making clothes for me against[2] the opening of school. She has ripped up for this purpose an old suit and an old plaid wool dress of hers, and she has to cut and match very cleverly and also make me stand and turn for endless fittings, sweaty, itching from the hot wool, ungrateful. We leave my brother in bed in the little screened porch at the end of the front veranda, and sometimes he kneels on his bed and presses his face against the screen and calls mournfully, "Bring me an ice-cream cone!" but I call back, "You will be asleep," and do not even turn my head.

Then my father and I walk gradually down a long, shabby sort of street, with Silverwoods Ice Cream signs standing on the sidewalk, outside tiny, lighted stores. This is in Tuppertown, an old town on Lake Huron,[3] an old grain port. The street is shaded, in some places, by maple trees whose roots have cracked and heaved the sidewalk and spread out like crocodiles into the bare yards. People are sitting out, men in shirtsleeves and undershirts and women in aprons—not people we know but if anybody looks ready to nod and say, "Warm night," my father will nod too and say something the same. Children are still playing. I don't know them either because my mother keeps my brother and me in our own yard, saying he is too young to leave it and I have to mind him. I am not so sad to watch their evening games because the games themselves are ragged, dissolving. Children, of their own will, draw apart, separate into islands of two or one under the heavy trees, occupying themselves in such solitary ways as I do all day, planting pebbles in the dirt or writing in it with a stick.

Presently we leave these yards and houses behind; we pass a factory with boarded-up windows, a lumberyard whose high wooden gates are locked for the night. Then the town falls away in a defeated jumble of sheds and small junkyards, the sidewalk gives up and we are walking on a sandy path with burdocks, plantains, humble nameless weeds all around. We enter a vacant lot, a kind of park really, for it is kept clear of junk and there is one bench with a slat missing on the back, a place to sit and look at the water. Which is generally gray in the evening, under a lightly overcast sky, no sunsets, the horizon dim. A very quiet, washing noise on the stones of the beach. Further along, towards the main part of town, there is a stretch of sand, a water slide, floats bobbing around the safe swimming area, a lifeguard's rickety throne.

1. Refers to a traveling salesman for a Canadian company, which is probably modeled on the American direct marketer Watkins Products.
2. In time for.

3. One of the Great Lakes, bordering on Ontario and eastern Michigan. Place-names are both real and invented.

Also a long dark-green building, like a roofed veranda, called the Pavilion, full of farmers and their wives, in stiff good clothes, on Sundays. That is the part of the town we used to know when we lived at Dungannon and came here three or four times a summer, to the Lake. That, and the docks where we would go and look at the grain boats, ancient, rusty, wallowing, making us wonder how they got past the breakwater let alone to Fort William.

Tramps hang around the docks and occasionally on these evenings wander up the dwindling beach and climb the shifting, precarious path boys have made, hanging on to dry bushes, and say something to my father which, being frightened of tramps, I am too alarmed to catch. My father says he is a bit hard up himself. "I'll roll you a cigarette if it's any use to you," he says, and he shakes tobacco out carefully on one of the thin butterfly papers, flicks it with his tongue, seals it and hands it to the tramp, who takes it and walks away. My father also rolls and lights and smokes one cigarette of his own.

He tells me how the Great Lakes came to be. All where Lake Huron is now, he says, used to be flat land, a wide flat plain. Then came the ice, creeping down from the North, pushing deep into the low places. Like *that*—and he shows me his hand with his spread fingers pressing the rock-hard ground where we are sitting. His fingers make hardly any impression at all and he says, "Well, the old ice cap had a lot more power behind it than this hand has." And then the ice went back, shrank back towards the North Pole where it came from, and left its fingers of ice in the deep places it had gouged, and ice turned to lakes and there they were today. They were *new*, as time went. I try to see that plain before me, dinosaurs walking on it, but I am not able even to imagine the shore of the Lake when the Indians were there, before Tuppertown. The tiny share we have of time appalls me, though my father seems to regard it with tranquillity. Even my father, who sometimes seems to me to have been at home in the world as long as it has lasted, has really lived on this earth only a little longer than I have, in terms of all the time there has been to live in. He has not known a time, any more than I, when automobiles and electric lights did not at least exist. He was not alive when this century started. I will be barely alive—old, old—when it ends. I do not like to think of it. I wish the Lake to be always just a lake, with the safe-swimming floats marking it, and the breakwater and the lights of Tuppertown.

My father has a job, selling for Walker Brothers. This is a firm that sells almost entirely in the country, the back country. Sunshine, Boylesbridge, Turnaround—that is all his territory. Not Dungannon where we used to live, Dungannon is too near town and my mother is grateful for that. He sells cough medicine, iron tonic, corn plasters, laxatives, pills for female disorders, mouthwash, shampoo, liniment, salves, lemon and orange and raspberry concentrate for making refreshing drinks, vanilla, food coloring, black and green tea, ginger, cloves, and other spices, rat poison. He has a song about it, with these two lines:

> And have all liniments and oils,
> For everything from corns to boils. . . .

Not a very funny song, in my mother's opinion. A peddler's song, and that is what he is, a peddler knocking at backwoods kitchens. Up until last winter we had our own business, a fox farm. My father raised silver foxes and sold their pelts to the people who make them into capes and coats and muffs. Prices fell, my father hung on hoping they would get better next year, and they fell again, and he hung on one more year and one more and finally it was not possible to hang on anymore, we owed everything to the feed company. I have heard my mother explain this, several times, to Mrs. Oliphant, who is the only neighbor she talks to. (Mrs. Oliphant also has come down in the world, being a schoolteacher who married the janitor.) We poured all we had into it, my mother says, and we came out with nothing. Many people could say the same thing, these days, but my mother has no time for the national calamity, only ours. Fate has flung us onto a street of poor people (it does not matter that we were poor before; that was a different sort of poverty), and the only way to take this, as she sees it, is with dignity, with bitterness, with no reconciliation. No bathroom with a claw-footed tub and a flush toilet is going to comfort her, nor water on tap and sidewalks past the house and milk in bottles, not even the two movie theatres and the Venus Restaurant and Woolworths so marvellous it has live birds singing in its fan-cooled corners and fish as tiny as fingernails, as bright as moons, swimming in its green tanks. My mother does not care.

In the afternoons she often walks to Simon's Grocery and takes me with her to help carry things. She wears a good dress, navy blue with little flowers, sheer, worn over a navy-blue slip. Also a summer hat of white straw, pushed down on the side of the head, and white shoes I have just whitened on a newspaper on the back steps. I have my hair freshly done in long damp curls which the dry air will fortunately soon loosen, a stiff large hair ribbon on top of my head. This is entirely different from going out after supper with my father. We have not walked past two houses before I feel we have become objects of universal ridicule. Even the dirty words chalked on the sidewalk are laughing at us. My mother does not seem to notice. She walks serenely like a lady shopping, like a *lady* shopping, past the housewives in loose beltless dresses torn under the arms. With me her creation, wretched curls and flaunting hair bow, scrubbed knees and white socks—all I do not want to be. I loathe even my name when she says it in public, in a voice so high, proud, and ringing, deliberately different from the voice of any other mother on the street.

My mother will sometimes carry home, for a treat, a brick of ice cream— pale Neapolitan; and because we have no refrigerator in our house we wake my brother and eat it at once in the dining room, always darkened by the wall of the house next door. I spoon it up tenderly, leaving the chocolate till last, hoping to have some still to eat when my brother's dish is empty. My mother tries then to imitate the conversations we used to have at Dungannon, going back to our earliest, most leisurely days before my brother was born, when she would give me a little tea and a lot of milk in a cup like hers and we would sit out on the step facing the pump, the lilac tree, the fox pens beyond. She is not able to keep from mentioning those days. "Do you remember when we put you in your sled and Major pulled you?" (Major our dog, that we had to leave with neighbors when we moved.) "Do you remember your sandbox outside the kitchen window?" I pretend to remember far less than I do, wary of being trapped into sympathy or any unwanted emotion.

My mother has headaches. She often has to lie down. She lies on my brother's narrow bed in the little screened porch, shaded by heavy branches. "I look up at that tree and I think I am at home," she says.

1462 | ALICE MUNRO

"What you need," my father tells her, "is some fresh air and a drive in the country." He means for her to go with him, on his Walker Brothers route.

That is not my mother's idea of a drive in the country.

"Can I come?"

"Your mother might want you for trying on clothes."

"I'm beyond sewing this afternoon," my mother says.

"I'll take her then. Take both of them, give you a rest."

What is there about us that people need to be given a rest from? Never mind. I am glad enough to find my brother and make him go to the toilet and get us both into the car, our knees unscrubbed, my hair unringleted. My father brings from the house his two heavy brown suitcases, full of bottles, and sets them on the back seat. He wears a white shirt, brilliant in the sunlight, a tie, light trousers belonging to his summer suit (his other suit is black, for funerals, and belonged to my uncle before he died), and a creamy straw hat. His salesman's outfit, with pencils clipped in the shirt pocket. He goes back once again, probably to say goodbye to my mother, to ask her if she is sure she doesn't want to come, and hear her say, "No. No thanks, I'm better just to lie here with my eyes closed." Then we are backing out of the driveway with the rising hope of adventure, just the little hope that takes you over the bump into the street, the hot air starting to move, turning into a breeze, the houses growing less and less familiar as we follow the shortcut my father knows, the quick way out of town. Yet what is there waiting for us all afternoon but hot hours in stricken farmyards, perhaps a stop at a country store and three ice-cream cones or bottles of pop, and my father singing? The one he made up about himself has a title—"The Walker Brothers Cowboy"—and it starts out like this:

> Old Ned Fields, he now is dead,
> So I am ridin' the route instead. . . .

Who is Ned Fields? The man he has replaced, surely, and if so he really is dead; yet my father's voice is mournful-jolly, making his death some kind of nonsense, a comic calamity. "Wisht I was back on the Rio Grande,[4] plungin' through the dusky sand." My father sings most of the time while driving the car. Even now, heading out of town, crossing the bridge and taking the sharp turn onto the highway, he is humming something, mumbling a bit of a song to himself, just tuning up, really, getting ready to improvise, for out along the highway we pass the Baptist Camp, the Vacation Bible Camp, and he lets loose:

> Where are the Baptists, where are the Baptists,
>   where are all the Baptists today?
> They're down in the water, in Lake Huron water,
>   with their sins all a-gittin' washed away.

My brother takes this for straight truth and gets up on his knees trying to see down to the Lake. "I don't see any Baptists," he says accusingly. "Neither do I, son," says my father. "I told you, they're down in the Lake."

No roads paved when we left the highway. We have to roll up the windows because of dust. The land is flat, scorched, empty. Bush lots at the back of

---

4. A large river that begins in Colorado and flows south, becoming the border between Mexico and the United States.

the farms hold shade, black pine-shade like pools nobody can ever get to. We bump up a long lane and at the end of it what could look more unwelcoming, more deserted than the tall unpainted farmhouse with grass growing uncut right up to the front door, green blinds down, and a door upstairs opening on nothing but air? Many houses have this door, and I have never yet been able to find out why. I ask my father and he says they are for walking in your sleep. *What?* Well, if you happen to be walking in your sleep and you want to step outside. I am offended, seeing too late that he is joking, as usual, but my brother says sturdily, "If they did that they would break their necks."

The 1930s. How much this kind of farmhouse, this kind of afternoon seem to me to belong to that one decade in time, just as my father's hat does, his bright flared tie, our car with its wide running board (an Essex, and long past its prime). Cars somewhat like it, many older, none dustier, sit in the farmyards. Some are past running and have their doors pulled off, their seats removed for use on porches. No living things to be seen, chickens or cattle. Except dogs. There are dogs lying in any kind of shade they can find, dreaming, their lean sides rising and sinking rapidly. They get up when my father opens the car door, he has to speak to them. "Nice boy, there's a boy, nice old boy." They quiet down, go back to their shade. He should know how to quiet animals, he has held desperate foxes with tongs around their necks. One gentling voice for the dogs and another, rousing, cheerful, for calling at doors. "Hello there, missus, it's the Walker Brothers man and what are you out of today?" A door opens, he disappears. Forbidden to follow, forbidden even to leave the car, we can just wait and wonder what he says. Sometimes trying to make my mother laugh, he pretends to be himself in a farm kitchen, spreading out his sample case. "Now then, missus, are you troubled with parasitic life? Your children's scalps, I mean. All those crawly little things we're too polite to mention that show up on the heads of the best of families? Soap alone is useless, kerosene is not too nice a perfume, but I have here—" Or else, "Believe me, sitting and driving all day the way I do I *know* the value of these fine pills. Natural relief. A problem common to old folks too, once their days of activity are over—How about you, Grandma?" He would wave the imaginary box of pills under my mother's nose and she would laugh finally, unwillingly. "He doesn't say that really, does he?" I said, and she said no of course not, he was too much of a gentleman.

One yard after another, then, the old cars, the pumps, dogs, views of gray barns and falling-down sheds and unturning windmills. The men, if they are working in the fields, are not in any fields that we can see. The children are far away, following dry creek beds or looking for blackberries, or else they are hidden in the house, spying at us through cracks in the blinds. The car seat has grown slick with our sweat. I dare my brother to sound the horn, wanting to do it myself but not wanting to get the blame. He knows better. We play I Spy, but it is hard to find many colors. Gray for the barns and sheds and toilets and houses, brown for the yard and fields, black or brown for the dogs. The rusting cars show rainbow patches, in which I strain to pick out purple or green; likewise I peer at doors for shreds of old peeling paint, maroon or yellow. We can't play with letters, which would be better, because my brother is too young to spell. The game disintegrates anyway. He claims my colors are not fair, and wants extra turns.

In one house no door opens, though the car is in the yard. My father knocks and whistles, calls, "Hullo there! Walker Brothers man!" but there is not a stir of reply anywhere. This house has no porch, just a bare, slanting slab of cement on which my father stands. He turns around, searching the barnyard, the barn whose mow must be empty because you can see the sky through it, and finally he bends to pick up his suitcases. Just then a window is opened upstairs, a white pot appears on the sill, is tilted over and its contents splash down the outside wall. The window is not directly above my father's head, so only a stray splash would catch him. He picks up his suitcases with no particular hurry and walks, no longer whistling, to the car. "Do you know what that was?" I say to my brother. *"Pee."* He laughs and laughs.

My father rolls and lights a cigarette before he starts the car. The window has been slammed down, the blind drawn, we never did see a hand or face. "Pee, pee," sings my brother ecstatically. "Somebody dumped down pee!" "Just don't tell your mother that," my father says. "She isn't liable to see the joke." "Is it in your song?" my brother wants to know. My father says no but he will see what he can do to work it in.

I notice in a little while that we are not turning in any more lanes, though it does not seem to me that we are headed home. "Is this the way to Sunshine?" I ask my father, and he answers, "No, ma'am, it's not." "Are we still in your territory?" He shakes his head. "We're going *fast*," my brother says approvingly, and in fact we are bouncing along through dry puddle-holes so that all the bottles in the suitcases clink together and gurgle promisingly.

Another lane, a house, also unpainted, dried to silver in the sun.

"I thought we were out of your territory."

"We are."

"Then what are we going in here for?"

"You'll see."

In front of the house a short, sturdy woman is picking up washing, which had been spread on the grass to bleach and dry. When the car stops she stares at it hard for a moment, bends to pick up a couple more towels to add to the bundle under her arm, comes across to us and says in a flat voice, neither welcoming nor unfriendly, "Have you lost your way?"

My father takes his time getting out of the car. "I don't think so," he says. "I'm the Walker Brothers man."

"George Golley is our Walker Brothers man," the woman says, "and he was out here no more than a week ago. Oh, my Lord God," she says harshly, "it's you."

"It was, the last time I looked in the mirror," my father says.

The woman gathers all the towels in front of her and holds on to them tightly, pushing them against her stomach as if it hurt. "Of all the people I never thought to see. And telling me you were the Walker Brothers man."

"I'm sorry if you were looking forward to George Golley," my father says humbly.

"And look at me, I was prepared to clean the henhouse. You'll think that's just an excuse but it's true. I don't go round looking like this every day." She is wearing a farmer's straw hat, through which pricks of sunlight penetrate and float on her face, a loose, dirty print smock, and canvas shoes. "Who are those in the car, Ben? They're not yours?"

"Well, I hope and believe they are," my father says, and tells our names and ages. "Come on, you can get out. This is Nora, Miss Cronin. Nora, you better tell me, is it still Miss, or have you got a husband hiding in the woodshed?"

"If I had a husband that's not where I'd keep him, Ben," she says, and they both laugh, her laugh abrupt and somewhat angry. "You'll think I got no manners, as well as being dressed like a tramp," she says. "Come on in out of the sun. It's cool in the house."

We go across the yard ("Excuse me taking you in this way but I don't think the front door has been opened since Papa's funeral, I'm afraid the hinges might drop off"), up the porch steps, into the kitchen, which really is cool, high-ceilinged, the blinds of course down, a simple, clean, thread-bare room with waxed worn linoleum, potted geraniums, drinking-pail and dipper, a round table with scrubbed oilcloth. In spite of the cleanness, the wiped and swept surfaces, there is a faint sour smell—maybe of the dishrag or the tin dipper or the oilcloth, or the old lady, because there is one, sitting in an easy chair under the clock shelf. She turns her head slightly in our direction and says, "Nora? Is that company?"

"Blind," says Nora in a quick explaining voice to my father. Then, "You won't guess who it is, Momma. Hear his voice."

My father goes to the front of her chair and bends and says hopefully, "Afternoon, Mrs. Cronin."

"Ben Jordan," says the old lady with no surprise. "You haven't been to see us in the longest time. Have you been out of the country?"

My father and Nora look at each other.

"He's married, Momma," says Nora cheerfully and aggressively. "Married and got two children and here they are." She pulls us forward, makes each of us touch the old lady's dry, cool hand while she says our names in turn. Blind! This is the first blind person I have ever seen close up. Her eyes are closed, the eyelids sunk away down, showing no shape of the eyeball, just hollows. From one hollow comes a drop of silver liquid, a medicine, or a miraculous tear.

"Let me get into a decent dress," Nora says. "Talk to Momma. It's a treat for her. We hardly ever see company, do we, Momma?"

"Not many makes it out this road," says the old lady placidly. "And the ones that used to be around here, our old neighbors, some of them have pulled out."

"True everywhere," my father says.

"Where's your wife then?"

"Home. She's not too fond of the hot weather, makes her feel poorly."

"Well." This is a habit of country people, old people, to say "well," mean-ing, "Is that so?" with a little extra politeness and concern.

Nora's dress, when she appears again—stepping heavily on Cuban heels down the stairs in the hall—is flowered more lavishly than anything my mother owns, green and yellow on brown, some sort of floating sheer crêpe, leaving her arms bare. Her arms are heavy, and every bit of her skin you can see is covered with little dark freckles like measles. Her hair is short, black, coarse and curly, her teeth very white and strong. "It's the first time I knew there was such a thing as green poppies," my father says, looking at her dress.

"You would be surprised all the things you never knew," says Nora, send-ing a smell of cologne far and wide when she moves and displaying a change of voice to go with the dress, something more sociable and youthful.

"They're not poppies anyway, they're just flowers. You go and pump me some good cold water and I'll make these children a drink." She gets down from the cupboard a bottle of Walker Brothers Orange syrup.

"You telling me you were the Walker Brothers man!"

"It's the truth, Nora. You go and look at my sample cases in the car if you don't believe me. I got the territory directly south of here."

"Walker Brothers? Is that a fact? You selling for Walker Brothers?"

"Yes, ma'am."

"We always heard you were raising foxes over Dungannon way."

"That's what I was doing, but I kind of run out of luck in that business."

"So where're you living? How long've you been out selling?"

"We moved into Tuppertown. I been at it, oh, two, three months. It keeps the wolf from the door. Keeps him as far away as the back fence."

Nora laughs. "Well, I guess you count yourself lucky to have the work. Isabel's husband in Brantford, he was out of work the longest time. I thought if he didn't find something soon I was going to have them all land in here to feed, and I tell you I was hardly looking forward to it. It's all I can manage with me and Momma."

"Isabel married," my father says. "Muriel married too?"

"No, she's teaching school out West. She hasn't been home for five years. I guess she finds something better to do with her holidays. I would if I was her." She gets some snapshots out of the table drawer and starts showing him. "That's Isabel's oldest boy, starting school. That's the baby sitting in her carriage. Isabel and her husband. Muriel. That's her roommate with her. That's a fellow she used to go around with, and his car. He was working in a bank out there. That's her school, it has eight rooms. She teaches Grade Five." My father shakes his head. "I can't think of her any way but when she was going to school, so shy I used to pick her up on the road—I'd be on my way to see you—and she would not say one word, not even to agree it was a nice day."

"She's got over that."

"Who are you talking about?" says the old lady.

"Muriel. I said she's got over being shy."

"She was here last summer."

"No, Momma, that was Isabel. Isabel and her family were here last summer. Muriel's out West."

"I meant Isabel."

Shortly after this the old lady falls asleep, her head on the side, her mouth open. "Excuse her manners," Nora says. "It's old age." She fixes an afghan over her mother and says we can all go into the front room where our talking won't disturb her.

"You two," my father says. "Do you want to go outside and amuse your-selves?"

Amuse ourselves how? Anyway, I want to stay. The front room is more interesting than the kitchen, though barer. There is a gramophone and a pump organ and a picture on the wall of Mary, Jesus' mother—I know that much—in shades of bright blue and pink with a spiked band of light around her head. I know that such pictures are found only in the homes of Roman Catholics and so Nora must be one. We have never known any Roman Catholics at all well, never well enough to visit in their houses. I think of what my grandmother and my Aunt Tena, over in Dungannon, used to always say to indicate that somebody was a Catholic. *So-and-so digs with the wrong foot,* they would say. *She digs with the wrong foot.* That was what they would say about Nora.[5]

Nora takes a bottle, half full, out of the top of the organ and pours some of what is in it into the two glasses that she and my father have emptied of the orange drink.

"Keep it in case of sickness?" my father says.

"Not on your life," says Nora. "I'm never sick. I just keep it because I keep it. One bottle does me a fair time, though, because I don't care for drinking alone. Here's luck!" She and my father drink and I know what it is. Whisky. One of the things my mother has told me in our talks together is that my father never drinks whisky. But I see he does. He drinks whisky and he talks of people whose names I have never heard before. But after a while he turns to a familiar incident. He tells about the chamberpot that was emptied out the window. "Picture me there," he says, "hollering my heartiest. *Oh, lady, it's your Walker Brothers man, anybody home?*" He does himself hollering, grinning absurdly, waiting, looking up in pleased expectation, and then—oh, ducking, covering his head with his arms, looking as if he begged for mercy (when he never did anything like that, I was watching), and Nora laughs, almost as hard as my brother did at the time.

"That isn't true! That's not a word true!"

"Oh, indeed it is, ma'am. We have our heroes in the ranks of Walker Brothers. I'm glad you think it's funny," he says sombrely.

I ask him shyly, "Sing the song."

"What song? Have you turned into a singer on top of everything else?"

Embarrassed, my father says, "Oh, just this song I made up while I was driving around, it gives me something to do, making up rhymes."

But after some urging he does sing it, looking at Nora with a droll, apologetic expression, and she laughs so much that in places he has to stop and wait for her to get over laughing so he can go on, because he makes him laugh too. Then he does various parts of his salesman's spiel. Nora when she laughs squeezes her large bosom under her folded arms. "You're crazy," she says. "That's all you are." She sees my brother peering into the gramophone and she jumps up and goes over to him. "Here's us sitting enjoying ourselves and not giving you a thought, isn't it terrible?" she says. "You want me to put a record on, don't you? You want to hear a nice record? Can you dance? I bet your sister can, can't she?"

I say no. "A big girl like you and so good-looking and can't dance!" says Nora. "It's high time you learned. I bet you'd make a lovely dancer. Here, I'm going to put on a piece I used to dance to and even your daddy did, in his dancing days. You didn't know your daddy was a dancer, did you? Well, he is a talented man, your daddy!"

She puts down the lid and takes hold of me unexpectedly around the waist, picks up my other hand, and starts making me go backwards. "This is the way, now, this is how they dance. Follow me. This foot, see. One and one-two. One and one-two. That's fine, that's lovely, don't look at your feet! Follow me, that's right, see how easy? You're going to be a lovely dancer! One and one-two. One and one-two. Ben, see your daughter dancing!"

5. Relations between Protestants and Catholics within the Irish population in southern Ontario were often strained.

Whispering while you cuddle near me, Whispering so no one can hear me . . . [6]

Round and round the linoleum, me proud, intent, Nora laughing and moving with great buoyancy, wrapping me in her strange gaiety, her smell of whisky, cologne, and sweat. Under the arms her dress is damp, and little drops form along her upper lip, hang in the soft black hairs at the corners of her mouth. She whirls me around in front of my father—causing me to stumble, for I am by no means so swift a pupil as she pretends—and lets me go, breathless.

"Dance with me, Ben."

"I'm the world's worst dancer, Nora, and you know it."

"I certainly never thought so."

"You would now."

She stands in front of him, arms hanging loose and hopeful, her breasts, which a moment ago embarrassed me with their warmth and bulk, rising and falling under her loose flowered dress, her face shining with the exercise, and delight.

"Ben."

My father drops his head and says quietly, "Not me, Nora."

So she can only go and take the record off. "I can drink alone but I can't dance alone," she says. "Unless I am a whole lot crazier than I think I am."

"Nora," says my father, smiling. "You're not crazy."

"Stay for supper."

"Oh, no. We couldn't put you to the trouble."

"It's no trouble. I'd be glad of it."

"And their mother would worry. She'd think I'd turned us over in a ditch."

"Oh, well. Yes."

"We've taken a lot of your time now."

"Time," says Nora bitterly. "Will you come by ever again?"

"I will if I can," says my father.

"Bring the children. Bring your wife."

"Yes, I will," says my father. "I will if I can."

When she follows us to the car he says, "You come to see us too, Nora. We're right on Grove Street, left-hand side going in, that's north, and two doors this side—east—of Baker Street."

Nora does not repeat these directions. She stands close to the car in her soft, brilliant dress. She touches the fender, making an unintelligible mark in the dust there.

On the way home my father does not buy any ice cream or pop, but he does go into a country store and get a package of licorice, which he shares with us. She digs with the wrong foot, I think, and the words seem sad to me as never before, dark, perverse. My father does not say anything to me about not mentioning things at home, but I know, just from the thoughtfulness, the pause when he passes the licorice, that there are things not to be mentioned. The whisky, maybe the dancing. No worry about my brother, he does not notice enough. At most he might remember the blind lady, the picture of Mary.

---

6. From the popular song "Whispering," whose original 1920 release was one of the first records to sell a million copies.

"Sing," my brother commands my father, but my father says gravely, "I don't know, I seem to be fresh out of songs. You watch the road and let me know if you see any rabbits."

So my father drives and my brother watches the road for rabbits and I feel my father's life flowing back from our car in the last of the afternoon, darkening and turning strange, like a landscape that has an enchantment on it, making it kindly, ordinary and familiar while you are looking at it, but changing it, once your back is turned, into something you will never know, with all kinds of weathers, and distances you cannot imagine.

When we get closer to Tuppertown the sky becomes gently overcast, as always, nearly always, on summer evenings by the Lake.

1968

SEAMUS HEANEY
1939–2013

Seamus Heaney was born into a Roman Catholic family in predominantly Protestant North Ireland (or Ulster), and he grew up on a farm in County Derry bordered on one side by a stream that marked the frontier with the largely Catholic Irish Republic (or Eire) to the south. He won scholarships first to St. Columb's College, a Catholic boarding school, and then to Queen's University in Belfast. There he became one of an extraordinary group of Northern Irish poets from both Protestant and Catholic backgrounds, including Michael Longley and Derek Mahon, who read, discussed, and spurred on one another's work. He taught at Queen's University, before moving in 1972 to the Irish Republic, where he became a citizen and full-time writer. He was Boylston Professor of Rhetoric and Oratory at Harvard and Professor of Poetry at Oxford, and in 1995 won the Nobel Prize in Literature.

With "Digging," placed appropriately as the first poem of his first book, Heaney defined his territory. He dug into his memory, uncovering first his father and then, going deeper, his grandfather. This idea of poetry as an archaeological process of recovery took on a darker cast after the eruption of internecine violence in Northern Ireland in 1969, culminating in the 1972 Bloody Sunday killing of thirteen Catholic civilians by British paratroopers during a civil rights march in Derry. Across several volumes, especially *North* (1975), Heaney wrote a series of grim "bog poems," about well-preserved Iron Age corpses discovered in the peat of Northern Europe and Ireland. In these poems he sees the bog as a "memory bank," or unconscious, that preserves everything thrown into it, including the victims of ritual killings. He views contemporary violence through the lens of ancient myths, sacrifices, and feuds, an oblique approach that gives his poetry about the Troubles an unusual depth and resonance. He had discovered emblems for the violence in Northern Ireland in *The Bog People*, a book by the Danish archaeologist P. V. Glob, published in translation in 1969, "the year the killing started." Heaney wrote of it:

> It was chiefly concerned with preserved bodies of men and women found in the bogs of Jutland, naked, strangled or with their throats cut, disposed under the peat since early Iron Age times. The author . . . argues convincingly that a

number of these, and in particular, the Tollund Man, whose head is now preserved near Aarhus in the museum of Silkeburg, were ritual sacrifices to the
Mother Goddess, the goddess of the ground who needed new bridegrooms
each winter to bed with her in her sacred place, in the spring. Taken in relation
to the tradition of Irish political martyrdom for the cause whose icon is Kathleen Ni Houlihan [mythic figure emblematic of Mother Ireland], this is more
than an archaic barbarous rite: it is an archetypal pattern. And the unforgettable photographs of these victims blended in my mind with photographs of
atrocities, past and present, in the long rites of Irish political and religious
struggles. ("Feeling into Words")

In the bog poems Heaney reflects on the poet's responsibilities to write about the
dead, yet to do so without prettifying or exploiting them. He probes the vexed relations between lyric song and historical suffering, "beauty and atrocity": the need to
be true to his calling as artist, but also to represent the irredeemable carnage of
modern political violence—"the actual weight / of each hooded victim / slashed
and dumped" ("The Grauballe Man"). The result is a tough-minded witnessing, an
ethically scrupulous and self-aware mourning of collective loss and sectarian murder. (For more on the Troubles, see the "Imagining Ireland" topic in the supplemental
ebook.)

From the late 1970s Heaney elegized specific victims of the Troubles, such as his
acquaintance Louis O'Neill, in "Casualty," as well as more personal losses, such as
the natural death of his mother, in "Clearances." He also wrote poems about domestic love, such as "The Skunk" and "The Sharping Stone." Heaney was thus both a
private poet—skillfully kneading grief, love, and wonder into poems about his family
and his humble origins—and a public poet, affirming his affinities with the Catholic civil rights movement, which has struggled against British and Protestant domination. Even in his public poetry he refused slogans, journalistic reportage, and
political pieties, scrutinizing instead the wellsprings of collective identity, the
ambivalences of individual response to history. Responding obliquely to the destruction of the Twin Towers on September 11, 2001, he reworked a two-thousand-year-
old Latin ode by Horace in "Anything Can Happen," and the bombings of the
London underground (subway) on July 7, 2005, reverberate in District and Circle
(2006).

An Irishman writing in the language of the British Empire, he translated Gaelic
poetry and renewed specifically Irish traditions, such as the aisling, or vision poem,
but he was also steeped in the English literary canon, drawing on British poetry
from Beowulf (his prize-winning translation appears earlier in this anthology) to the
works of William Wordsworth, Gerard Manley Hopkins, and Ted Hughes. Straddling a multiplicity of divisions, transubstantiating crisscross feelings into unexpected images and intricate sonorities, Heaney's work has been embraced by
popular audiences for its accessible style and yet also admired by poets and academic
critics for its lyric subtlety and rigorous technique.

Formally, Heaney's poetry ranges from strenuous free verse—the clipped lines
and unrhymed quatrains of the bog poems—to more traditional forms, such as the
modified terza rima of "Station Island" and the sonnet sequence "Clearances." His
poems are earthy and matter-of-fact, saturated with the physical textures, sights,
smells, and sounds of farm life, and they are also visionary, lit up by hope and spirit,
enacting penitential pilgrimages and unbridled imaginings. That Heaney's poetry is
both earthbound and airborne, free and formed, public and private helps explain
why he is seen by many as the most gifted English-language poet of his generation.

Digging

Between my finger and my thumb
The squat pen rests; snug as a gun.

Under my window, a clean rasping sound
When the spade sinks into gravelly ground:
5   My father, digging. I look down

Till his straining rump among the flowerbeds
Bends low, comes up twenty years away
Stooping in rhythm through potato drills[1]
Where he was digging.

10 The coarse boot nestled on the lug, the shaft
Against the inside knee was levered firmly.
He rooted out tall tops, buried the bright edge deep
To scatter new potatoes that we picked
Loving their cool hardness in our hands.

15 By God, the old man could handle a spade.
Just like his old man.

My grandfather cut more turf[2] in a day
Than any other man on Toner's bog.
Once I carried him milk in a bottle
20 Corked sloppily with paper. He straightened up
To drink it, then fell to right away
Nicking and slicing neatly, heaving sods
Over his shoulder, going down and down
For the good turf. Digging.

25 The cold smell of potato mould, the squelch and slap
Of soggy peat, the curt cuts of an edge
Through living roots awaken in my head.
But I've no spade to follow men like them.

Between my finger and my thumb
30 The squat pen rests.
I'll dig with it.

1966

The Forge

All I know is a door into the dark.
Outside, old axles and iron hoops rusting;

---

1. Small furrows in which seeds are sown.
2. Slabs of peat that, when dried, are a common domestic fuel in Ireland.

Inside, the hammered anvil's short-pitched ring,
The unpredictable fantail of sparks
5 Or hiss when a new shoe toughens in water.
The anvil must be somewhere in the centre,
Horned as a unicorn, at one end square,
Set there immoveable: an altar
Where he expends himself in shape and music.
10 Sometimes, leather-aproned, hairs in his nose,
He leans out on the jamb, recalls a clatter
Of hoofs where traffic is flashing in rows;
Then grunts and goes in, with a slam and flick
To beat real iron out, to work the bellows.

1969

The Grauballe Man[1]

As if he had been poured
in tar, he lies
on a pillow of turf
and seems to weep

5 the black river of himself.
The grain of his wrists
is like bog oak,
the ball of his heel

like a basalt egg.
10 His instep has shrunk
cold as a swan's foot
or a wet swamp root.

His hips are the ridge
and purse of a mussel,
15 his spine an eel arrested
under a glisten of mud.

The head lifts,
the chin is a visor
raised above the vent
20 of his slashed throat

that has tanned and toughened.
The cured wound
opens inwards to a dark
elderberry place.

25 Who will say 'corpse'
to his vivid cast?

---

1. A body exhumed from a Danish bog and photographed in P. V. Glob's book *The Bog People*.

Who will say 'body'
to his opaque repose?

And his rusted hair,
30   a mat unlikely
as a foetus's.
I first saw his twisted face

in a photograph,
a head and shoulder
35   out of the peat,
bruised like a forceps baby,

but now he lies
perfected in my memory,
down to the red horn
40   of his nails,

hung in the scales
with beauty and atrocity:
with the Dying Gaul[2]
too strictly compassed

45   on his shield,
with the actual weight
of each hooded victim,
slashed and dumped.

1975

Punishment[1]

I can feel the tug
of the halter at the nape
of her neck, the wind
on her naked front.

2. Roman marble reproduction of a Greek bronze sculpture depicting a wounded soldier of Gaul, whose matted hair identifies him as a Celt, in Rome's Capitoline Museum.

1. In 1951 the peat-stained body apparently of a young girl, who lived in the late 1st century C.E., was recovered from a bog in Windeby, Germany. As P. V. Glob describes her in *The Bog People*, she "lay naked in the hole in the peat, a bandage over the eyes and a collar round the neck. The band across the eyes was drawn tight and had cut into the neck and the base of the nose. We may feel sure that it had been used to close her eyes to this world. There was no mark of strangulation on the neck, so that it had not been used for that purpose." Her hair "had been shaved off with a razor on the left side of the head. . . . When the brain was removed the convolutions and folds of the surface could be clearly seen [Glob reproduces a photograph of her brain]. . . . This girl of only fourteen had had an inadequate winter diet. . . . To keep the young body under, some birch branches and a big stone were laid upon her." According to the Roman historian Tacitus, the Germanic peoples punished adulterous women by shaving off their hair and then scourging them out of the village or killing them. More recently, her "betraying sisters" were sometimes shaved, stripped, tarred, and handcuffed by the Irish Republican Army (IRA) to the railings of Belfast in punishment for keeping company with British soldiers.

5   It blows her nipples
     to amber beads,
     it shakes the frail rigging
     of her ribs.

     I can see her drowned
10   body in the bog,
     the weighing stone,
     the floating rods and boughs.

     Under which at first
     she was a barked sapling
15   that is dug up
     oak-bone, brain-firkin:°   *small cask*

     her shaved head
     like a stubble of black corn,
     her blindfold a soiled bandage,
20   her noose a ring

     to store
     the memories of love.
     Little adultress,
     before they punished you

25   you were flaxen-haired,
     undernourished, and your
     tar-black face was beautiful.
     My poor scapegoat,

     I almost love you
30   but would have cast, I know,
     the stones of silence.
     I am the artful voyeur

     of your brain's exposed
     and darkened combs,°   *valleys*
35   your muscles' webbing
     and all your numbered bones:

     I who have stood dumb
     when your betraying sisters,
     cauled° in tar,   *wrapped, enclosed*
40   wept by the railings,

     who would connive
     in civilized outrage
     yet understand the exact
     and tribal, intimate revenge.

                                                                        1975

Casualty

1

He would drink by himself
And raise a weathered thumb
Towards the high shelf,
Calling another rum
5   And blackcurrant, without
Having to raise his voice,
Or order a quick stout°   *strong dark beer*
By a lifting of the eyes
And a discreet dumb-show
10 Of pulling off the top;
At closing time would go
In waders and peaked cap
Into the showery dark,
A dole-kept[1] breadwinner
15 But a natural for work.
I loved his whole manner,
Sure-footed but too sly,
His deadpan sidling tact,
His fisherman's quick eye
20 And turned observant back.
Incomprehensible
To him, my other life.
Sometimes, on his high stool,
Too busy with his knife
25 At a tobacco plug
And not meeting my eye
In the pause after a slug°   *gulp of liquor*
He mentioned poetry.
We would be on our own
30 And, always politic
And shy of condescension,
I would manage by some trick
To switch the talk to eels
Or lore of the horse and cart
35 Or the Provisionals.[2]

But my tentative art
His turned back watches too:
He was blown to bits
Out drinking in a curfew
40 Others obeyed, three nights
After they shot dead
The thirteen men in Derry.
PARAS THIRTEEN, the walls said,
BOGSIDE NIL.[3] That Wednesday

---

1. I.e., receiving unemployment benefits.
2. The Provisional branch of the IRA.
3. This graffito records—in the form of a soccer match score—that the British Army's Parachute Regiment had killed thirteen people; the Roman Catholic inhabitants of Derry's Bogside district, none. The IRA bombing occurred after the killing of Catholic demonstrators on Bloody Sunday, January 30, 1972.

45   Everybody held
        His breath and trembled.

                        2

        It was a day of cold
        Raw silence, wind-blown
        Surplice and soutane:[4]
50   Rained-on, flower-laden
        Coffin after coffin
        Seemed to float from the door
        Of the packed cathedral
        Like blossoms on slow water.
55   The common funeral
        Unrolled its swaddling band,[5]
        Lapping, tightening
        Till we were braced and bound
        Like brothers in a ring.

60   But he would not be held
        At home by his own crowd
        Whatever threats were phoned,
        Whatever black flags waved.
        I see him as he turned
65   In that bombed offending place,
        Remorse fused with terror
        In his still knowable face,
        His cornered outfaced stare
        Blinding in the flash.

70   He had gone miles away
        For he drank like a fish
        Nightly, naturally
        Swimming towards the lure
        Of warm lit-up places,
75   The blurred mesh and murmur
        Drifting among glasses
        In the gregarious smoke.
        How culpable was he
        That last night when he broke
80   Our tribe's complicity?[6]
        'Now you're supposed to be
        An educated man,'
        I hear him say. 'Puzzle me
        The right answer to that one.'

                        3

85   I missed his funeral,
        Those quiet walkers

---

4. Vestments worn by Roman Catholic priests.
5. Long cloth in which babies were once wrapped
to restrain and warm them.

6. The Roman Catholic community's agreement
to obey the curfew (of lines 39–40).

And sideways talkers
Shoaling out of his lane
To the respectable
90   Purring of the hearse . . .
They move in equal pace
With the habitual
Slow consolation
Of a dawdling engine,
95   The line lifted, hand
Over fist, cold sunshine
On the water, the land
Banked under fog: that morning
I was taken in his boat,
100   The screw° purling, turning   *propellor*
Indolent fathoms white,
I tasted freedom with him.
To get out early, haul
Steadily off the bottom,
105   Dispraise the catch, and smile
As you find a rhythm
Working you, slow mile by mile,
Into your proper haunt
Somewhere, well out, beyond . . .

110   Dawn-sniffing revenant,[7]
Plodder through midnight rain,
Question me again.

1979

The Skunk

Up, black, striped and damasked like the chasuble[1]
At a funeral mass, the skunk's tail
Paraded the skunk. Night after night
I expected her like a visitor.

5   The refrigerator whinnied into silence.
My desk light softened beyond the verandah.
Small oranges loomed in the orange tree.
I began to be tense as a voyeur.

After eleven years I was composing
10   Love-letters again, broaching the word 'wife'
Like a stored cask, as if its slender vowel
Had mutated into the night earth and air

Of California. The beautiful, useless
Tang of eucalyptus spelt your absence.

7. One returned from the dead.
1. Sleeveless vestment worn by the priest celebrating Mass, its color regulated by the feast of the
day. "Damasked": woven with elaborate designs.

15 The aftermath of a mouthful of wine
Was like inhaling you off a cold pillow.

And there she was, the intent and glamorous,
Ordinary, mysterious skunk,
Mythologized, demythologized,
20 Snuffing the boards five feet beyond me.

It all came back to me last night, stirred
By the sootfall of your things at bedtime,
Your head-down, tail-up hunt in a bottom drawer
For the black plunge-line nightdress.

1979

From Station Island[1]

12

Like a convalescent, I took the hand
stretched down from the jetty, sensed again
an alien comfort as I stepped on ground

to find the helping hand still gripping mine,
5 fish-cold and bony, but whether to guide
or to be guided I could not be certain

for the tall man in step at my side
seemed blind, though he walked straight as a rush
upon his ash plant,[2] his eyes fixed straight ahead.

10 Then I knew him in the flesh
out there on the tarmac° among the cars,   blacktop surface
wintered hard and sharp as a blackthorn bush.

His voice eddying with the vowels of all rivers[3]
came back to me, though he did not speak yet,
15 a voice like a prosecutor's or a singer's,

cunning,[4] narcotic, mimic, definite
as a steel nib's downstroke, quick and clean,
and suddenly he hit a litter basket

1. *Station Island* is a sequence of dream encounters with familiar ghosts, set on Station Island on
Lough Derg in Co. Donegal. The island is also
known as St. Patrick's Purgatory because of a
tradition that Patrick was the first to establish the
penitential vigil of fasting and praying which still
constitutes the basis of the three-day pilgrimage.
Each unit of the contemporary pilgrim's exercises
is called a 'station,' and a large part of each station
involves walking barefoot and praying round the
'beds,' stone circles which are said to be the
remains of early medieval monastic cells [Heaney's
note]. In this last section of the poem, the familiar
ghost is that of Heaney's countryman James Joyce.
Cf. the stanza form and encounter with a ghost in
T. S. Eliot's "Little Gidding."
2. Walking stick made of ash, like the one carried by Stephen Dedalus in Joyce's *Portrait of the
Artist as a Young Man* and *Ulysses*. Joyce was
almost blind.
3. The Anna Livia Plurabelle episode of *Finnegans
Wake* resounds with the names of many rivers.
4. "The only arms I allow myself to use—silence,
exile, and cunning" (Joyce, *A Portrait of the Artist
as a Young Man*).

with his stick, saying, "Your obligation
20   is not discharged by any common rite.
What you must do must be done on your own

so get back in harness. The main thing is to write
for the joy of it. Cultivate a work-lust
that imagines its haven like your hands at night

25   dreaming the sun in the sunspot of a breast.
You are fasted now, light-headed, dangerous.
Take off from here. And don't be so earnest,

let others wear the sackcloth and the ashes.[5]
Let go, let fly, forget.
30   You've listened long enough. Now strike your note."

It was as if I had stepped free into space
alone with nothing that I had not known
already. Raindrops blew in my face

as I came to. "Old father, mother's son,
35   there is a moment in Stephen's diary
for April the thirteenth, a revelation

set among my stars—that one entry
has been a sort of password in my ears,
the collect of a new epiphany,[6]

40   the Feast of the Holy Tundish."[7] "Who cares,"
he jeered, "any more? The English language
belongs to us. You are raking at dead fires,

a waste of time for somebody your age.
That subject° people stuff is a cod's° game,   *colonized / fool's*
45   infantile, like your peasant pilgrimage.

You lose more of yourself than you redeem
doing the decent thing. Keep at a tangent.
When they make the circle wide, it's time to swim

out on your own and fill the element
50   with signatures on your own frequency,
echo soundings, searches, probes, allurements,

---

5. As worn by penitents in biblical times and later.
6. Manifestation of a superhuman being, as of the infant Jesus to the Magi (Matthew 2). In the Christian calendar, the Feast of the Epiphany is January 6. "Epiphany" was also Joyce's term for the "sudden revelation of the whatness of a thing." "Collect": short prayer assigned to a particular day.

7. See the end of James Joyce's *Portrait of the Artist as a Young Man* [Heaney's note]: "*13 April:* That tundish [funnel] has been on my mind for a long time. I looked it up and find it English and good old blunt English too. Damn the dean of studies and his funnel! What did he come here for to teach us his own language or to learn it from us? Damn him one way or the other!"

elver-gleams[8] in the dark of the whole sea."
The shower broke in a cloudburst, the tarmac
fumed and sizzled. As he moved off quickly

55   the downpour loosed its screens round his straight walk.

1984

Clearances

in memoriam M.K.H.,[1] 1911–1984

She taught me what her uncle once taught her:
How easily the biggest coal block split
If you got the grain and hammer angled right.

The sound of that relaxed alluring blow,
5   *Its co-opted and obliterated echo,*
Taught me to hit, taught me to loosen,

Taught me between the hammer and the block
To face the music. Teach me now to listen,
To strike it rich behind the linear black.

1

10   A cobble thrown a hundred years ago
Keeps coming at me, the first stone
Aimed at a great-grandmother's turncoat brow.[2]
The pony jerks and the riot's on.
She's crouched low in the trap
15   Running the gauntlet that first Sunday
Down the brae° to Mass at a panicked gallop.   *steep slope*
He whips on through the town to cries of 'Lundy!'[3]

Call her 'The Convert'. 'The Exogamous[4] Bride'.
Anyhow, it is a genre piece
20   Inherited on my mother's side
And mine to dispose with now she's gone.
Instead of silver and Victorian lace,
The exonerating, exonerated stone.

2

Polished linoleum shone there. Brass taps shone.
25   The china cups were very white and big—

8. Gleams as of young eels.
1. Margaret Kathleen Heaney, the poet's mother.
2. Heaney's Protestant great-grandmother married a Catholic.
3. I.e., traitor. In 1688 the Irish colonel Robert

Lundy knew that Derry (or Londonderry) would be invaded by the English, but failed to prepare adequate defenses.
4. Married outside the group.

An unchipped set with sugar bowl and jug.
The kettle whistled. Sandwich and teascone
Were present and correct. In case it run,
The butter must be kept out of the sun.
30   And don't be dropping crumbs. Don't tilt your chair.
Don't reach. Don't point. Don't make noise when you stir.

It is Number 5, New Row, Land of the Dead,
Where grandfather is rising from his place
With spectacles pushed back on a clean bald head
35   To welcome a bewildered homing daughter
Before she even knocks. 'What's this? What's this?'
And they sit down in the shining room together.

3

When all the others were away at Mass
I was all hers as we peeled potatoes.
40   They broke the silence, let fall one by one
Like solder weeping off the soldering iron:
Cold comforts set between us, things to share
Gleaming in a bucket of clean water.
And again let fall. Little pleasant splashes
45   From each other's work would bring us to our senses.

So while the parish priest at her bedside
Went hammer and tongs at the prayers for the dying
And some were responding and some crying
I remembered her head bent towards my head,
50   Her breath in mine, our fluent dipping knives—
Never closer the whole rest of our lives.

4

Fear of affectation made her affect
Inadequacy whenever it came to
Pronouncing words 'beyond her'. *Bertold Brek*.[5]
55   She'd manage something hampered and askew
Every time, as if she might betray
The hampered and inadequate by too
Well-adjusted a vocabulary.
With more challenge than pride, she'd tell me, 'You
60   Know all them things.' So I governed my tongue
In front of her, a genuinely well-
adjusted adequate betrayal
Of what I knew better. I'd *naw* and *aye*
And decently relapse into the wrong
65   Grammar which kept us allied and at bay.

---

5. Bertolt Brecht (1898–1956), German playwright.

5

The cool that came off sheets just off the line
Made me think the damp must still be in them
But when I took my corners of the linen
And pulled against her, first straight down the hem
70   And then diagonally, then flapped and shook
The fabric like a sail in a cross-wind,
They made a dried-out undulating thwack.
So we'd stretch and fold and end up hand to hand
For a split second as if nothing had happened
75   For nothing had that had not always happened
Beforehand, day by day, just touch and go,
Coming close again by holding back
In moves where I was x and she was o
Inscribed in sheets she'd sewn from ripped-out flour sacks.

6

80   In the first flush of the Easter holidays
The ceremonies during Holy Week
Were highpoints of our *Sons and Lovers*[6] phase.
The midnight fire. The paschal candlestick.[7]
Elbow to elbow, glad to be kneeling next
85   To each other up there near the front
Of the packed church, we would follow the text
And rubrics° for the blessing of the font.[8]   rules
As the hind longs for the streams, so my soul . . . [9]
Dippings. Towellings. The water breathed on.
90   The water mixed with chrism[1] and with oil.
Cruet[2] tinkle. Formal incensation
And the psalmist's outcry taken up with pride:
Day and night my tears have been my bread.[3]

7

In the last minutes he said more to her
95   Almost than in all their life together.
'You'll be in New Row on Monday night
And I'll come up for you and you'll be glad
When I walk in the door . . . Isn't that right?'
His head was bent down to her propped-up head.
100   She could not hear but we were overjoyed.
He called her good and girl. Then she was dead,
The searching for a pulsebeat was abandoned
And we all knew one thing by being there.
The space we stood around had been emptied
105   Into us to keep, it penetrated

---

6. Novel (1913) by the English writer D. H. Lawrence (1885–1930) that largely centers on the
oedipal relationship between a mother and son.
7. Large candle lit during a ceremony on Holy
Saturday, which precedes Easter.

8. Receptacle for holy water.
9. Psalms 42.1.
1. Mixture of olive oil and balsam.
2. Small vessel for wine or water.
3. Psalms 42.3.

Clearances that suddenly stood open.
High cries were felled and a pure change happened.

8

I thought of walking round and round a space
Utterly empty, utterly a source
110 Where the decked chestnut tree had lost its place
In our front hedge above the wallflowers.
The white chips jumped and jumped and skited[4] high.
I heard the hatchet's differentiated
Accurate cut, the crack, the sigh
115 And collapse of what luxuriated
Through the shocked tips and wreckage of it all.
Deep planted and long gone, my coeval[5]
Chestnut from a jam jar in a hole,
Its heft and hush become a bright nowhere,
120 A soul ramifying and forever
Silent, beyond silence listened for.

1987

The Sharping Stone[1]

In an apothecary's° chest of drawers,   *pharmacist's*
Sweet cedar that we'd purchased second hand,
In one of its weighty deep-sliding recesses
I found the sharping stone that was to be
5   Our gift to him. Still in its wrapping paper.
Like a baton of black light I'd failed to pass.

•

Airless cinder-depths. But all the same,
The way it lay there, it wakened something too . . .
I thought of us that evening on the logs,
10   Flat on our backs, the pair of us, parallel,
Supported head to heel, arms straight, eyes front,
Listening to the rain drip off the trees
And saying nothing, braced to the damp bark.
What possessed us? The bare, lopped loveliness
15   Of those two winter trunks, the way they seemed
Prepared for launching, at right angles across
A causeway of short fence-posts set like rollers.
Neither of us spoke. The puddles waited.
The workers had gone home, saws fallen silent.
20   And next thing down we lay, babes in the wood,
Gazing up at the flood-face of the sky
Until it seemed a flood was carrying us
Out of the forest park, feet first, eyes front,

4. Shot off obliquely.   1. Whetstone for sharpening metal blades.
5. Of the same age.

Out of November, out of middle age,
25 Together, out, across the Sea of Moyle.[2]

•

Sarcophage des époux.[3] In terra cotta.
Etruscan couple shown side by side,
Recumbent on left elbows, husband pointing
With his right arm and watching where he points,
30 Wife in front, her earrings in, her braids
Down to her waist, taking her sexual ease.
He is all eyes, she is all brow and dream,
Her right forearm and hand held out as if
Some bird she sees in her deep inward gaze
35 Might be about to roost there. Domestic
Love, the artist thought, warm tones and property,
The frangibility of terra cotta . . .
Which is how they figured on the colour postcard
(*Louvre, Département des Antiquités*)[4]
40 That we'd sent him once, then found among his things.

•

He loved inspired mistakes: his Spanish grandson's
English transliteration, thanking him
For a boat trip: 'That was a marvellous
Walk on the water, granddad.' And indeed
45 He walked on air himself, never more so
Than when he had been widowed and the youth
In him, the athlete who had wooed her—
Breasting tapes and clearing the high bars—
Grew lightsome once again. Going at eighty
50 On the bendiest roads, going for broke
At every point-to-point[5] and poker-school,
'He commenced his wild career' a second time
And not a bother on him. Smoked like a train
And took the power mower in his stride.
55 Flirted and vaunted. Set fire to his bed.
Fell from a ladder. Learned to microwave.

•

So set the drawer on freshets° of thaw water   surges
And place the unused sharping stone inside it:
To be found next summer on a riverbank
60 Where scythes once hung all night in alder trees
And mowers played dawn scherzos[6] on the blades,
Their arms like harpists' arms, one drawing towards,
One sweeping the bright rim of the extreme.

1996

---

2. Channel between the northwestern coast of County Antrim in Ireland and the southwestern coast of Scotland.
3. Coffin for a married couple.
4. Department of Antiquities, Louvre Museum, Paris, in which this Etruscan funerary statue, known as *The Cerveteri Couple*, is to be found.
5. Horse race over jumps.
6. Vigorous light and playful musical compositions.

MARGARET ATWOOD
b. 1939

Margaret Atwood was born in Ottawa, Canada, into a family with roots in Nova Scotia, but when she was seven her family moved to Toronto. She did not receive formal schooling until she was eleven, because her family spent a large part of every year in the northern wildernesses of Quebec and Ontario. There, her father, a forest entomologist, pursued his research on insects, while she immersed herself in both the woods and books. The Canadian wilderness is the setting of a number of her poems, novels, and stories, although her work has ranged among a variety of real and fictional locales, including the Caribbean island of *Bodily Harm* (1981) and the dystopian Boston of *The Handmaid's Tale* (1985). Atwood received her B.A. in English from Victoria College, University of Toronto, in 1961. The next year she earned an M.A. at Harvard, later returning for doctoral research she did not complete, but several volumes of her poetry were published during that time. Before 1972, when she became a full-time writer, Atwood taught at Canadian universities in Vancouver, Montreal, Alberta, and Toronto.

Atwood is the author of more than a dozen collections of poetry, more than twenty volumes of imaginative prose—both novels and short fiction—as well as a large number of essays and critical works. Her earliest books include the poems collected in the self-published *Double Persephone* (1961), and then the regularly published *The Circle Game* (1964), a collection that won the Governor General's Literary Award for Poetry. Precisely carved language, doubleness of vision, ironic inversions of expectations—these are among the qualities that have garnered attention for her poetry. A poem such as "Miss July Grows Older" suggests the complexity of Atwood's surprising and witty examinations of gender relations. It opens with an arresting question in the voice of a smart, wryly self-critical beauty queen who, hardly a passive object, has skillfully manipulated men: "How much longer can I get away / with being so fucking cute?" Atwood has said that poetry is "the heart of the language, the activity through which language is renewed and kept alive."

She has also said that, for her, "fiction is the guardian of the moral and ethical sense of the community." Although she continued to publish collections of poetry over several decades, it is Atwood's fiction that has made her perhaps Canada's best-known writer. Her first novel, *The Edible Woman* (1969), explores a woman's eating disorders long before the sexual politics of anorexia and bulimia were widely discussed. Several of her subsequent novels were short-listed for the Booker Prize, including her most famous work, *The Handmaid's Tale* (1985), about a woman's struggle against imprisonment within sharply hierarchical gender roles in a religious fundamentalist dystopia; *Cat's Eye* (1989), about power and cruelty in girlhood friendships; and *Alias Grace* (1996), a fictionalized narrative of a historical nineteenth-century female servant accused of murder. *The Blind Assassin* (2000), which nests various stories within one another, finally won Atwood the Booker Prize.

Since the publication of her early book of essays, *Survival* (1972), Atwood has helped bring attention and shape to Canadian literature. Early in that book, she hazards a sweeping comparison between Canadian literature and "the sense of adventure or danger" in the literature of the United States (its key symbol being "The Frontier"), the "smugness and/or sense of security" in the literature of England ("The Island"). In her view, Canadian literature reflects a distinct experience. "Our stories are likely to be tales not of those who made it but of those who made it back, from the awful experience—the North, the snowstorm, the sinking ship—that killed everyone else.

The survivor has no triumph or victory but the fact of his survival." Some of Atwood's fictional characters are survivors of the Canadian wilderness, including the young female protagonist of *Surfacing*, a novel published in the same year as *Survival*, who journeys deep into the wilderness in search of her lost father. The main character in *Cat's Eye* reviews and relives the psychological damage inflicted on her by female friendships and bullying during her childhood and teenage years in the forest.

In the short story "Death by Landscape," the central character, Lois, is also a survivor of loss and painful memories, of vexed female friendship and power relations lived out in the Canadian wilderness. Reflecting on coming of age at camp, Lois remembers the singing, the stratification, the role playing as American Indians, but her main focus is her friendship with an American girl, Lucy, who imports into Canada her troubled home life. After a defining incident on a canoe trip, "Death by Landscape," like other of Atwood's novels and short fiction, becomes a narrative in part about the power of stories to give meaning, as well as their potential duplicity—about the power of narrative both to condemn and to explore, of language both to cripple and to liberate.

Death by Landscape

Now that the boys are grown up and Rob is dead, Lois has moved to a condominium apartment in one of the newer waterfront developments. She is relieved not to have to worry about the lawn, or about the ivy pushing its muscular little suckers into the brickwork, or the squirrels gnawing their way into the attic and eating the insulation off the wiring, or about strange noises. This building has a security system, and the only plant life is in pots in the solarium.

Lois is glad she's been able to find an apartment big enough for her pictures. They are more crowded together than they were in the house, but this arrangement gives the walls a European look: blocks of pictures, above and beside one another, rather than one over the chesterfield,[1] one over the fireplace, one in the front hall, in the old acceptable manner of sprinkling art around so it does not get too intrusive. This way has more of an impact. You know it's not supposed to be furniture.

None of the pictures is very large, which doesn't mean they aren't valuable. They are paintings, or sketches and drawings, by artists who were not nearly as well known when Lois began to buy them as they are now. Their work later turned up on stamps, or as silk-screen reproductions hung in the principals' offices of high schools, or as jigsaw puzzles, or on beautifully printed calendars sent out by corporations as Christmas gifts, to their less important clients. These artists painted mostly in the twenties and thirties and forties; they painted landscapes. Lois has two Tom Thomsons, three A. Y. Jacksons, a Lawren Harris. She has an Arthur Lismer, she has a J. E. H. MacDonald. She has a David Milne.[2] They are pictures of convoluted tree trunks on an island or pink wave-smoothed stone, with more islands

---

1. Sofa.
2. All Canadian landscape painters. Tom Thomson (1877–1917). A. Y. Jackson (1882–1974). Lawren Harris (1885–1970). Arthur Lismer (1885–1969). J. E. H. MacDonald (1873–1932). David Milne (1882–1953). Jackson, Harris, Lismer, and MacDonald were members of the Group of Seven, the first major national movement in Canadian art, and Thomson was associated with the group. Its work was usually expressionist in style.

behind; of a lake with rough, bright, sparsely wooded cliffs; of a vivid river shore with a tangle of bush and two beached canoes, one red, one grey; of a yellow autumn woods with the ice-blue gleam of a pond half-seen through the interlaced branches.

It was Lois who'd chosen them. Rob had no interest in art, although he could see the necessity of having something on the walls. He left all the decorating decisions to her, while providing the money, of course. Because of this collection of hers, Lois's friends—especially the men—have given her the reputation of having a good nose for art investments.

But this is not why she bought the pictures, way back then. She bought them because she wanted them. She wanted something that was in them, although she could not have said at the time what it was. It was not peace: she does not find them peaceful in the least. Looking at them fills her with a wordless unease. Despite the fact that there are no people in them or even animals, it's as if there is something, or someone, looking back out.

When she was thirteen, Lois went on a canoe trip. She'd only been on over-nights before. This was to be a long one, into the trackless wilderness, as Cappie put it. It was Lois's first canoe trip, and her last.

Cappie was the head of the summer camp to which Lois had been sent ever since she was nine. Camp Manitou, it was called; it was one of the better ones, for girls, though not the best. Girls of her age whose parents could afford it were routinely packed off to such camps, which bore a generic resemblance to one another. They favoured Indian names and had hearty, energetic leaders, who were called Cappie or Skip or Scottie. At these camps you learned to swim well and sail, and paddle a canoe, and perhaps ride a horse or play tennis. When you weren't doing these things you could do Arts and Crafts and turn out dingy, lumpish clay ashtrays for your mother— mothers smoked more, then—or bracelets made of coloured braided string.

Cheerfulness was required at all times, even at breakfast. Loud shouting and the banging of spoons on the tables were allowed, and even encouraged, at ritual intervals. Chocolate bars were rationed, to control tooth decay and pimples. At night, after supper, in the dining hall or outside around a mosquito-infested campfire ring for special treats, there were singsongs. Lois can still remember all the words to "My Darling Clementine," and to "My Bonnie Lies Over the Ocean," with acting-out gestures: a rippling of the hands for "the ocean," two hands together under the cheek for "lies." She will never be able to forget them, which is a sad thought.

Lois thinks she can recognize women who went to these camps, and were good at it. They have a hardness to their handshakes, even now; a way of standing, legs planted firmly and farther apart than usual; a way of sizing you up, to see if you'd be any good in a canoe—the front, not the back. They themselves would be in the back. They would call it the stern.

She knows that such camps still exist, although Camp Manitou does not. They are one of the few things that haven't changed much. They now offer copper enamelling, and functionless pieces of stained glass baked in elec-tric ovens, though judging from the productions of her friends' grandchil-dren the artistic standards have not improved.

To Lois, encountering it in the first year after the war, Camp Manitou seemed ancient. Its log-sided buildings with the white cement in between the half-logs, its flagpole ringed with whitewashed stones, its weathered grey dock jutting out into Lake Prospect, with its woven rope bumpers and its rusty rings for tying up, its prim round flowerbed of petunias near the office door, must surely have been there always. In truth it dated only from the first decade of the century; it had been founded by Cappie's parents, who'd thought of camping as bracing to the character, like cold showers, and had been passed along to her as an inheritance, and an obligation.

Lois realized, later, that it must have been a struggle for Cappie to keep Camp Manitou going, during the Depression and then the war, when money did not flow freely. If it had been a camp for the very rich, instead of the merely well off, there would have been fewer problems. But there must have been enough Old Girls, ones with daughters, to keep the thing in operation, though not entirely shipshape: furniture was battered, painted trim was peeling, roofs leaked. There were dim photographs of these Old Girls dotted around the dining hall, wearing ample woollen bathing suits and showing their fat, dimpled legs, or standing, arms twined, in odd tennis outfits with baggy skirts.

In the dining hall, over the stone fireplace that was never used, there was a huge moulting stuffed moose head, which looked somehow carnivorous. It was a sort of mascot; its name was Monty Manitou. The older campers spread the story that it was haunted, and came to life in the dark, when the feeble and undependable lights had been turned off or, due to yet another generator failure, had gone out. Lois was afraid of it at first, but not after she got used to it.

Cappie was the same: you had to get used to her. Possibly she was forty, or thirty-five, or fifty. She had fawn-coloured hair that looked as if it was cut with a bowl. Her head jutted forward, jigging like a chicken's as she strode around the camp, clutching notebooks and checking things off in them. She was like their minister in church: both of them smiled a lot and were anxious because they wanted things to go well; they both had the same overwashed skins and stringy necks. But all this disappeared when Cappie was leading a singsong, or otherwise leading. Then she was happy, sure of herself, her plain face almost luminous. She wanted to cause joy. At these times she was loved, at others merely trusted.

There were many things Lois didn't like about Camp Manitou, at first. She hated the noisy chaos and spoon-banging of the dining hall, the rowdy singsongs at which you were expected to yell in order to show that you were enjoying yourself. Hers was not a household that encouraged yelling. She hated the necessity of having to write dutiful letters to her parents claiming she was having fun. She could not complain, because camp cost so much money.

She didn't much like having to undress in a roomful of other girls, even in the dim light, although nobody paid any attention, or sleeping in a cabin with seven other girls, some of whom snored because they had adenoids[3] or colds, some of whom had nightmares, or wet their beds and cried about it. Bottom bunks made her feel closed in, and she was afraid of falling out of top ones; she was afraid of heights. She got homesick, and suspected her parents of having a better time when she wasn't there than when she was,

---

3. Enlarged masses of lymphoid tissue at the top of the throat, blocking the nasal passages.

although her mother wrote to her every week saying how much they missed her. All this was when she was nine. By the time she was thirteen she liked it. She was an old hand by then.

Lucy was her best friend at camp. Lois had other friends in winter, when there was school and itchy woollen clothing and darkness in the after-noons, but Lucy was her summer friend.

She turned up the second year, when Lois was ten, and a Bluejay. (Chick-adees, Bluejays, Ravens, and Kingfishers—these were the names Camp Manitou assigned to the different age groups, a sort of totemic clan system. In those days, thinks Lois, it was birds for girls, animals for boys: wolves, and so forth. Though some animals and birds were suitable and some were not. Never vultures, for instance; never skunks, or rats.)

Lois helped Lucy to unpack her tin trunk and place the folded clothes on the wooden shelves, and to make up her bed. She put her in the top bunk right above her, where she could keep an eye on her. Already she knew that Lucy was an exception, to a good many rules; already she felt proprietorial.

Lucy was from the United States, where the comic books came from, and the movies. She wasn't from New York or Hollywood or Buffalo, the only American cities Lois knew the names of, but from Chicago. Her house was on the lake shore and had gates to it, and grounds. They had a maid, all of the time. Lois's family only had a cleaning lady twice a week.

The only reason Lucy was being sent to *this* camp (she cast a look of minor scorn around the cabin, diminishing it and also offending Lois, while at the same time daunting her) was that her mother had been a camper here. Her mother had been a Canadian once, but had married her father, who had a patch over one eye, like a pirate. She showed Lois the picture of him in her wallet. He got the patch in the war. "Shrapnel," said Lucy. Lois, who was unsure about shrapnel, was so impressed she could only grunt. Her own two-eyed, unwounded father was tame by comparison.

"My father plays golf," she ventured at last.

"*Everyone* plays golf," said Lucy. "My *mother* plays golf."

Lois's mother did not. Lois took Lucy to see the outhouses and the swim-ming dock and the dining hall with Monty Manitou's baleful head, know-ing in advance they would not measure up.

This was a bad beginning; but Lucy was good-natured, and accepted Camp Manitou with the same casual shrug with which she seemed to accept every-thing. She would make the best of it, without letting Lois forget that this was what she was doing.

However, there were things Lois knew that Lucy did not. Lucy scratched the tops off all her mosquito bites and had to be taken to the infirmary to be daubed with Ozonol.[4] She took her T-shirt off while sailing, and although the counsellor spotted her after a while and made her put it back on, she burnt spectacularly, bright red, with the X of her bathing-suit straps standing out in alarming white; she let Lois peel the sheets of whispery-thin burned skin off her shoulders. When they sang "Alouette" around the campfire, she did not know any of the French words. The difference was that Lucy did not care about the things she didn't know, whereas Lois did.

4. First-aid ointment.

During the next winter, and subsequent winters, Lucy and Lois wrote to each other. They were both only children, at a time when this was thought to be a disadvantage, so in their letters they pretended to be sisters, or even twins. Lois had to strain a little over this, because Lucy was so blonde, with translucent skin and large blue eyes like a doll's, and Lois was nothing out of the ordinary—just a tallish, thinnish, brownish person with freckles. They signed their letters LL, with the L's entwined together like the monograms on a towel. (Lois and Lucy, thinks Lois. How our names date us. Lois Lane, Superman's girlfriend, enterprising female reporter; "I Love Lucy." Now we are obsolete, and it's little Jennifers, little Emilys, little Alexandras and Carolines and Tiffanys.)

They were more effusive in their letters than they ever were in person. They bordered their pages with X's and O's, but when they met again in the summers it was always a shock. They had changed so much, or Lucy had. It was like watching someone grow up in jolts. At first it would be hard to think up things to say.

But Lucy always had a surprise or two, something to show, some marvel to reveal. The first year she had a picture of herself in a tutu, her hair in a ballerina's knot on the top of her head; she pirouetted around the swimming dock, to show Lois how it was done, and almost fell off. The next year she had given that up and was taking horseback riding. (Camp Manitou did not have horses.) The next year her mother and father had been divorced, and she had a new stepfather, one with both eyes, and a new house, although the maid was the same. The next year, when they had graduated from Bluejays and entered Ravens, she got her period, right in the first week of camp. The two of them snitched some matches from their counsellor, who smoked illegally, and made a small fire out behind the farthest outhouse, at dusk, using their flashlights. They could set all kinds of fires by now; they had learned how in Campcraft. On this fire they burned one of Lucy's used sanitary napkins. Lois is not sure why they did this, or whose idea it was. But she can remember the feeling of deep satisfaction it gave her as the white fluff singed and the blood sizzled, as if some wordless ritual had been fulfilled.

They did not get caught, but then they rarely got caught at any of their camp transgressions. Lucy had such large eyes, and was such an accomplished liar.

This year Lucy is different again: slower, more languorous. She is no longer interested in sneaking around after dark, purloining cigarettes from the counsellor, dealing in black-market candy bars. She is pensive, and hard to wake in the mornings. She doesn't like her stepfather, but she doesn't want to live with her real father either, who has a new wife. She thinks her mother may be having a love affair with a doctor; she doesn't know for sure, but she's seen them smooching in his car, out on the driveway, when her stepfather wasn't there. It serves him right. She hates her private school. She has a boyfriend, who is sixteen and works as a gardener's assistant. This is how she met him: in the garden. She describes to Lois what it is like when he kisses her— rubbery at first, but then your knees go limp. She has been forbidden to see him, and threatened with boarding school. She wants to run away from home.

Lois has little to offer in return. Her own life is placid and satisfactory, but there is nothing much that can be said about happiness. "You're so lucky,"

Lucy tells her, a little smugly. She might as well say *boring* because this is how it makes Lois feel.

Lucy is apathetic about the canoe trip, so Lois has to disguise her own excitement. The evening before they are to leave, she slouches into the campfire ring as if coerced, and sits down with a sigh of endurance, just as Lucy does.

Every canoe trip that went out of camp was given a special send-off by Cappie and the section leader and counsellors, with the whole section in attendance. Cappie painted three streaks of red across each of her cheeks with a lipstick. They looked like three-fingered claw marks. She put a blue circle on her forehead with fountain-pen ink, and tied a twisted bandanna around her head and stuck a row of frazzle-ended feathers around it, and wrapped herself in a red-and-black Hudson's Bay blanket. The counsellors, also in blankets but with only two streaks of red, beat on tom-toms made of round wooden cheese boxes with leather stretched over the top and nailed in place. Cappie was Chief Cappeosota. They all had to say "How!" when she walked into the circle and stood there with one hand raised.

Looking back on this, Lois finds it disquieting. She knows too much about Indians: this is why. She knows, for instance, that they should not even be called Indians, and that they have enough worries without other people taking their names and dressing up as them. It has all been a form of stealing.

But she remembers, too, that she was once ignorant of this. Once she loved the campfire, the flickering of light on the ring of faces, the sound of the fake tom-toms, heavy and fast like a scared heartbeat; she loved Cappie in a red blanket and feathers, solemn, as a chief should be, raising her hand and saying, "Greetings, my Ravens." It was not funny, it was not making fun. She wanted to be an Indian. She wanted to be adventurous and pure, and aboriginal.

"You go on big water," says Cappie. This is her idea—all their ideas—of how Indians talk. "You go where no man has ever trod. You go many moons." This is not true. They are only going for a week, not many moons. The canoe route is clearly marked, they have gone over it on a map, and there are prepared campsites with names which are used year after year. But when Cappie says this—and despite the way Lucy rolls up her eyes—Lois can feel the water stretching out, with the shores twisting away on either side, immense and a little frightening.

"You bring back much wampum,"[5] says Cappie. "Do good in war, my braves, and capture many scalps." This is another of her pretences: that they are boys, and bloodthirsty. But such a game cannot be played by substituting the word "squaw." It would not work at all.

Each of them has to stand up and step forward and have a red line drawn across her cheeks by Cappie. She tells them they must follow in the paths of their ancestors (who most certainly, thinks Lois, looking out the window of her apartment and remembering the family stash of daguerreotypes[6] and sepia-coloured portraits on her mother's dressing table, the stiff-shirted, black-coated, grim-faced men and the beflounced women with their severe

5. Beads made from polished shells and used as money by Native peoples of North America.   6. Early photographs.

hair and their corseted respectability, would never have considered heading off onto an open lake, in a canoe, just for fun).

At the end of the ceremony they all stood and held hands around the circle, and sang taps. This did not sound very Indian, thinks Lois. It sounded like a bugle call at a military post, in a movie. But Cappie was never one to be much concerned with consistency, or with archaeology.

After breakfast the next morning they set out from the main dock, in four canoes, three in each. The lipstick stripes have not come off completely, and still show faintly pink, like healing burns. They wear their white denim sailing hats, because of the sun, and thin-striped T-shirts, and pale baggy shorts with the cuffs rolled up. The middle one kneels, propping her rear end against the rolled sleeping bags. The counsellors going with them are Pat and Kip. Kip is no-nonsense; Pat is easier to wheedle, or fool.

There are white puffy clouds and a small breeze. Glints come from the little waves. Lois is in the bow of Kip's canoe. She still can't do a J-stroke very well, and she will have to be in the bow or the middle for the whole trip. Lucy is behind her; her own J-stroke is even worse. She splashes Lois with her paddle, quite a big splash.

"I'll get you back," says Lois.

"There was a stable fly on your shoulder," Lucy says.

Lois turns to look at her, to see if she's grinning. They're in the habit of splashing each other. Back there, the camp has vanished behind the first long point of rock and rough trees. Lois feels as if an invisible rope has broken. They're floating free, on their own, cut loose. Beneath the canoe the lake goes down, deeper and colder than it was a minute before.

"No horsing around in the canoe," says Kip. She's rolled her T-shirt sleeves up to the shoulder; her arms are brown and sinewy, her jaw determined, her stroke perfect. She looks as if she knows exactly what she is doing.

The four canoes keep close together. They sing, raucously and with defiance; they sing "The Quartermaster's Store," and "Clementine," and "Alouette." It is more like bellowing than singing.

After that the wind grows stronger, blowing slantwise against the bows, and they have to put all their energy into shoving themselves through the water.

Was there anything important, anything that would provide some sort of reason or clue to what happened next? Lois can remember everything, every detail; but it does her no good.

They stopped at noon for a swim and lunch, and went on in the afternoon. At last they reached Little Birch, which was the first campsite for overnight. Lois and Lucy made the fire, while the others pitched the heavy canvas tents. The fireplace was already there, flat stones piled into a U. A burned tin can and a beer bottle had been left in it. Their fire went out, and they had to restart it. "Hustle your bustle," said Kip. "We're starving."

The sun went down, and in the pink sunset light they brushed their teeth and spat the toothpaste froth into the lake. Kip and Pat put all the food that wasn't in cans into a packsack and slung it into a tree, in case of bears.

Lois and Lucy weren't sleeping in a tent. They'd begged to be allowed to sleep out; that way they could talk without the others hearing. If it rained, they told Kip, they promised not to crawl dripping into the tent over everyone's legs: they would get under the canoes. So they were out on the point.

Lois tried to get comfortable inside her sleeping bag, which smelled of musty storage and of earlier campers, a stale salty sweetness. She curled herself up, with her sweater rolled up under her head for a pillow and her flashlight inside her sleeping bag so it wouldn't roll away. The muscles of her sore arms were making small pings, like rubber bands breaking.

Beside her Lucy was rustling around. Lois could see the glimmering oval of her white face.

"I've got a rock poking into my back," said Lucy.

"So do I," said Lois. "You want to go into the tent?" She herself didn't, but it was right to ask.

"No," said Lucy. She subsided into her sleeping bag. After a moment she said, "It would be nice not to go back."

"To camp?" said Lois.

"To Chicago," said Lucy. "I hate it there."

"What about your boyfriend?" said Lois. Lucy didn't answer. She was either asleep or pretending to be.

There was a moon, and a movement of the trees. In the sky there were stars, layers of stars that went down and down. Kip said that when the stars were bright like that instead of hazy it meant bad weather later on. Out on the lake there were two loons, calling to each other in their insane, mournful voices. At the time it did not sound like grief. It was just background.

The lake in the morning was flat calm. They skimmed along over the glassy surface, leaving V-shaped trails behind them; it felt like flying. As the sun rose higher it got hot, almost too hot. There were stable flies in the canoes, landing on a bare arm or leg for a quick sting. Lois hoped for wind.

They stopped for lunch at the next of the named campsites, Lookout Point. It was called this because, although the site itself was down near the water on a flat shelf of rock, there was a sheer cliff nearby and a trail that led up to the top. The top was the lookout, although what you were supposed to see from there was not clear. Kip said it was just a view.

Lois and Lucy decided to make the climb anyway. They didn't want to hang around waiting for lunch. It wasn't their turn to cook, though they hadn't avoided much by not doing it, because cooking lunch was no big deal, it was just unwrapping the cheese and getting out the bread and peanut butter, but Pat and Kip always had to do their woodsy act and boil up a billy tin[7] for their own tea.

They told Kip where they were going. You had to tell Kip where you were going, even if it was only a little way into the woods to get dry twigs for kindling. You could never go anywhere without a buddy.

"Sure," said Kip, who was crouching over the fire, feeding driftwood into it. "Fifteen minutes to lunch."

"Where are they off to?" said Pat. She was bringing their billy tin of water from the lake.

"Lookout," said Kip.

"Be careful," said Pat. She said it as an afterthought, because it was what she always said.

"They're old hands," Kip said.

_____

7. Metal pail with a close-fitting lid and a wire handle, used for cooking over open fires.

Lois looks at her watch: it's ten to twelve. She is the watch-minder; Lucy is careless of time. They walk up the path, which is dry earth and rocks, big rounded pinky-grey boulders or split-open ones with jagged edges. Spindly balsam and spruce trees grow to either side, the lake is blue fragments to the left. The sun is right overhead; there are no shadows anywhere. The heat comes up at them as well as down. The forest is dry and crackly.

It isn't far, but it's a steep climb and they're sweating when they reach the top. They wipe their faces with their bare arms, sit gingerly down on a scorching-hot rock, five feet from the edge but too close for Lois. It's a look-out all right, a sheer drop to the lake and a long view over the water, back the way they've come. It's amazing to Lois that they've travelled so far, over all that water, with nothing to propel them but their own arms. It makes her feel strong. There are all kinds of things she is capable of doing.

"It would be quite a dive off here," says Lucy.

"You'd have to be nuts," says Lois.

"Why?" says Lucy. "It's really deep. It goes straight down." She stands up and takes a step nearer the edge. Lois gets a stab in her midriff, the kind she gets when a car goes too fast over a bump. "Don't," she says.

"Don't what?" says Lucy, glancing around at her mischievously. She knows how Lois feels about heights. But she turns back. "I really have to pee," she says.

"You have toilet paper?" says Lois, who is never without it. She digs in her shorts pocket.

"Thanks," says Lucy.

They are both adept at peeing in the woods: doing it fast so the mosquitoes don't get you, the underwear pulled up between the knees, the squat with the feet apart so you don't wet your legs, facing downhill. The exposed feeling of your bum, as if someone is looking at you from behind. The etiquette when you're with someone else is not to look. Lois stands up and starts to walk back down the path, to be out of sight.

"Wait for me?" says Lucy.

Lois climbed down, over and around the boulders, until she could not see Lucy; she waited. She could hear the voices of the others, talking and laughing, down near the shore. One voice was yelling, "Ants! Ants!" Someone must have sat on an ant hill. Off to the side, in the woods, a raven was croaking, a hoarse single note.

She looked at her watch: it was noon. This is when she heard the shout.

She has gone over and over it in her mind since, so many times that the first, real shout has been obliterated, like a footprint trampled by other footprints. But she is sure (she is almost positive, she is nearly certain) that it was not a shout of fear. Not a scream. More like a cry of surprise, cut off too soon. Short, like a dog's bark.

"Lucy?" Lois said. Then she called "Lucy!" By now she was clambering back up, over the stones of the path. Lucy was not up there. Or she was not in sight.

"Stop fooling around," Lois said. "It's lunch-time." But Lucy did not rise from behind a rock or step out, smiling, from behind a tree. The sunlight was all around; the rocks looked white. "This isn't funny!" Lois said, and it wasn't, panic was rising in her, the panic of a small child who does not know where the bigger ones are hidden. She could hear her own heart. She looked quickly around; she lay down on the ground and looked over the edge of the cliff. It made her feel cold. There was nothing.

She went back down the path, stumbling; she was breathing too quickly; she was too frightened to cry. She felt terrible—guilty and dismayed, as if she had done something very bad, by mistake. Something that could never be repaired. "Lucy's gone," she told Kip.

Kip looked up from her fire, annoyed. The water in the billy can was boiling. "What do you mean, gone?" she said. "Where did she go?"

"I don't know," said Lois. "She's just gone."

No one had heard the shout, but then no one had heard Lois calling, either. They had been talking among themselves, by the water.

Kip and Pat went up to the lookout and searched and called, and blew their whistles. Nothing answered.

Then they came back down, and Lois had to tell exactly what had happened. The other girls all sat in a circle and listened to her. Nobody said anything. They all looked frightened, especially Pat and Kip. They were the leaders. You did not just lose a camper like this, for no reason at all.

"Why did you leave her alone?" said Kip.

"I was just down the path," said Lois. "I told you. She had to go to the bathroom." She did not say *pee* in front of people older than herself.

Kip looked disgusted.

"Maybe she just walked off into the woods and got turned around," said one of the girls.

"Maybe she's doing it on purpose," said another.

Nobody believed either of these theories.

They took the canoes and searched around the base of the cliff, and peered down into the water. But there had been no sound of falling rock; there had been no splash. There was no clue, nothing at all. Lucy had simply vanished.

That was the end of the canoe trip. It took them the same two days to go back that it had taken coming in, even though they were short a paddler. They did not sing.

After that, the police went in a motorboat, with dogs; they were the Mounties[8] and the dogs were German shepherds, trained to follow trails in the woods. But it had rained since, and they could find nothing.

Lois is sitting in Cappie's office. Her face is bloated with crying, she's seen that in the mirror. By now she feels numbed; she feels as if she has drowned. She can't stay here. It has been too much of a shock. Tomorrow her parents are coming to take her away. Several of the other girls who were on the canoe trip are also being collected. The others will have to stay, because their parents are in Europe, or cannot be reached.

Cappie is grim. They've tried to hush it up, but of course everyone in camp knows. Soon the papers will know too. You can't keep it quiet, but what can be said? What can be said that makes any sense? "Girl vanishes in broad daylight, without a trace." It can't be believed. Other things, worse things, will be suspected. Negligence, at the very least. But they have always taken such care. Bad luck will gather around Camp Manitou like a

---

8. Royal Canadian Mounted Police.

fog; parents will avoid it, in favour of other, luckier places. Lois can see Cappie thinking all this, even through her numbness. It's what anyone would think.

Lois sits on the hard wooden chair in Cappie's office, beside the old wooden desk, over which hangs the thumb-tacked bulletin board of normal camp routine, and gazes at Cappie through her puffy eyelids. Cappie is now smiling what is supposed to be a reassuring smile. Her manner is too casual: she's after something. Lois has seen this look on Cappie's face when she's been sniffing out contraband chocolate bars, hunting down those rumoured to have snuck out of their cabins at night.

"Tell me again," says Cappie, "from the beginning."

Lois has told her story so many times by now, to Pat and Kip, to Cappie, to the police, that she knows it word for word. She knows it, but she no longer believes it. It has become a story. "I told you," she said. "She wanted to go to the bathroom. I gave her my toilet paper. I went down the path, I waited for her. I heard this kind of shout . . ."

"Yes," says Cappie, smiling confidingly, "but before that. What did you say to one another?"

Lois thinks. Nobody has asked her this before. "She said you could dive off there. She said it went straight down."

"And what did you say?"

"I said you'd have to be nuts."

"Were you mad at Lucy?" says Cappie, in an encouraging voice.

"No," says Lois. "Why would I be mad at Lucy? I wasn't ever mad at Lucy." She feels like crying again. The times when she has in fact been mad at Lucy have been erased already. Lucy was always perfect.

"Sometimes we're angry when we don't know we're angry," says Cappie, as if to herself. "Sometimes we get really mad and we don't even know it. Sometimes we might do a thing without meaning to, or without knowing what will happen. We lose our tempers."

Lois is only thirteen, but it doesn't take her long to figure out that Cappie is not including herself in any of this. By *we* she means Lois. She is accusing Lois of pushing Lucy off the cliff. The unfairness of this hits her like a slap. "I didn't!" she says.

"Didn't what?" says Cappie softly. "Didn't what, Lois?"

Lois does the worst thing, she begins to cry. Cappie gives her a look like a pounce. She's got what she wanted.

Later, when she was grown up, Lois was able to understand what this interview had been about. She could see Cappie's desperation, her need for a story, a real story with a reason in it; anything but the senseless vacancy Lucy had left for her to deal with. Cappie wanted Lois to supply the reason, to be the reason. It wasn't even for the newspapers or the parents, because she could never make such an accusation without proof. It was for herself: something to explain the loss of Camp Manitou and of all she had worked for, the years of entertaining spoiled children and buttering up parents and making a fool of herself with feathers stuck in her hair. Camp Manitou was in fact lost. It did not survive.

Lois worked all this out, twenty years later. But it was far too late. It was too late even ten minutes afterwards, when she'd left Cappie's office and was walking slowly back to her cabin to pack. Lucy's clothes were still there, folded on the shelves, as if waiting. She felt the other girls in the cabin watching her with speculation in their eyes. *Could she have done it? She must have done it.* For the rest of her life, she has caught people watching her in this way.

Maybe they weren't thinking this. Maybe they were merely sorry for her. But she felt she had been tried and sentenced, and this is what has stayed with her: the knowledge that she had been singled out, condemned for something that was not her fault.

Lois sits in the living room of her apartment, drinking a cup of tea. Through the knee-to-ceiling window she has a wide view of Lake Ontario, with its skin of wrinkled blue-grey light, and of the willows of Centre Island shaken by a wind, which is silent at this distance, and on this side of the glass. When there isn't too much pollution she can see the far shore, the foreign shore; though today it is obscured.

Possibly she could go out, go downstairs, do some shopping; there isn't much in the refrigerator. The boys say she doesn't get out enough. But she isn't hungry, and moving, stirring from this space, is increasingly an effort.

She can hardly remember, now, having her two boys in the hospital, nursing them as babies; she can hardly remember getting married, or what Rob looked like. Even at the time she never felt she was paying full attention. She was tired a lot, as if she was living not one life but two: her own, and another, shadowy life that hovered around her and would not let itself be realized—the life of what would have happened if Lucy had not stepped sideways, and disappeared from time.

She would never go up north, to Rob's family cottage or to any place with wild lakes and wild trees and the calls of loons. She would never go anywhere near. Still, it was as if she was always listening for another voice, the voice of a person who should have been there but was not. An echo.

While Rob was alive, while the boys were growing up, she could pretend she didn't hear it, this empty space in sound. But now there is nothing much left to distract her.

She turns away from the window and looks at her pictures. There is the pinkish island, in the lake, with the intertwisted trees. It's the same landscape they paddled through, that distant summer. She's seen travelogues of this country, aerial photographs; it looks different from above, bigger, more hopeless: lake after lake, random blue puddles in dark green bush, the trees like bristles.

How could you ever find anything there, once it was lost? Maybe if they cut it all down, drained it all away, they might find Lucy's bones, some time, wherever they are hidden. A few bones, some buttons, the buckle from her shorts.

But a dead person is a body; a body occupies space, it exists somewhere. You can see it; you put it in a box and bury it in the ground, and then it's in a box in the ground. But Lucy is not in a box, or in the ground. Because she is nowhere definite, she could be anywhere.

And these paintings are not landscape paintings. Because there aren't any landscapes up there, not in the old, tidy European sense, with a gentle hill, a curving river, a cottage, a mountain in the background, a golden evening sky. Instead there's a tangle, a receding maze, in which you can become lost almost as soon as you step off the path. There are no backgrounds in any of these paintings, no vistas; only a great deal of foreground that goes back and back, endlessly, involving you in its twists and turns of tree and branch and rock. No matter how far back in you go, there will be more. And the trees themselves are hardly trees; they are currents of energy, charged with violent colour.

Who knows how many trees there were on the cliff just before Lucy disappeared? Who counted? Maybe there was one more, afterwards.

Lois sits in her chair and does not move. Her hand with the cup is raised halfway to her mouth. She hears something, almost hears it: a shout of recognition, or of joy.

She looks at the paintings, she looks into them. Every one of them is a picture of Lucy. You can't see her exactly, but she's there, in behind the pink stone island or the one behind that. In the picture of the cliff she is hidden by the clutch of fallen rocks towards the bottom, in the one of the river shore she is crouching beneath the overturned canoe. In the yellow autumn woods she's behind the tree that cannot be seen because of the other trees, over beside the blue sliver of pond; but if you walked into the picture and found the tree, it would be the wrong one, because the right one would be further on.

Everyone has to be somewhere, and this is where Lucy is. She is in Lois's apartment, in the holes that open inwards on the wall, not like windows but like doors. She is here. She is entirely alive.

1991

Miss July Grows Older

How much longer can I get away
with being so fucking cute?
Not much longer.
The shoes with bows, the cunning underwear
5   with slogans on the crotch—*Knock Here,*
and so forth—
will have to go, along with the cat suit.[1]
After a while you forget
what you really look like.
10 You think your mouth is the size it was.
You pretend not to care.

When I was young I went with my hair
hiding one eye, thinking myself daring;
off to the movies in my jaunty pencil
15 skirt and elastic cinch-belt,
chewed gum, left lipstick
imprints the shape of grateful, rubbery
sighs on the cigarettes of men
I hardly knew and didn't want to.
20 Men were a skill, you had to have

1. Close-fitting jumpsuit, typically covering the body from the neck to the feet.

good hands, breathe into
their nostrils, as for horses. It was something I did well,
like playing the flute, although I don't.

In the forests of grey stems there are standing pools,
25   tarn-coloured,[2] choked with brown leaves.
Through them you can see an arm, a shoulder,
when the light is right, with the sky clouded.
The train goes past silos, through meadows,
the winter wheat on the fields like scanty fur.

30   I still get letters, although not many.
A man writes me, requesting true-life stories
about bad sex. He's doing an anthology.
He got my name off an old calendar,
the photo that's mostly bum and daisies,
35   back when my skin had the golden slick
of fresh-spread margarine.
Not rape, he says, but disappointment,
more like a defeat of expectations.
Dear Sir, I reply, I never had any.
40   Bad sex, that is.
It was never the sex, it was the other things,
the absence of flowers, the death threats,
the eating habits at breakfast.
I notice I'm using the past tense.

45   Though the vaporous cloud of chemicals that enveloped you
like a glowing eggshell, an incense,
doesn't disappear: it just gets larger
and takes in more. You grow out
of sex like a shrunk dress
50   into your common senses, those you share
with whatever's listening. The way the sun
moves through the hours becomes important,
the smeared raindrops
on the window, buds
55   on the roadside weeds, the sheen
of spilled oil on a raw ditch
filling with muddy water.

Don't get me wrong: with the lights out
I'd still take on anyone,
60   if I had the energy to spare.
But after a while these flesh arpeggios get boring,
like Bach[3] over and over;
too much of one kind of glory.

When I was all body I was lazy.
65   I had an easy life, and was not grateful.

2. I.e., the color of a small mountain lake.
3. Johann Sebastian Bach (1685–1750), German composer. "Arpeggios": the notes of a musical chord played in rapid succession.

Now there are more of me.
Don't confuse me with my hen-leg elbows:
what you get is no longer
what you see.

1995

J. M. COETZEE
b. 1940

John Maxwell Coetzee was born in Cape Town, South Africa. His mother was a schoolteacher; his father, a lawyer who became a sheepherder after losing his job. When Coetzee was eight, his family left the provinces, and he chronicles this and other parts of his childhood in third-person memoirs, *Boyhood: Scenes from a Provincial Life* (1997) and *Youth: Scenes from a Provincial Life II* (2002), followed up by a novelistic pseudo-biography of his adulthood, *Summertime* (2009). Coetzee was educated in Cape Town and then lived in London for a few years, working as a computer programmer, before earning his Ph.D. from the University of Texas at Austin, where he wrote a dissertation on the fiction of Samuel Beckett—a major influence, along with Kafka and Dostoyevsky, on Coetzee's fiction. He was appointed, first, assistant professor and, subsequently, Butler Professor of English at the State University of New York at Buffalo. In 1984 he returned to South Africa as professor of general literature at the University of Cape Town, and since 2002 he has lived in Australia. Coetzee is the first novelist to win the prestigious Booker Prize twice, and in 2003 he was awarded the Nobel Prize in Literature.

The central concern of Coetzee's fiction—the oppressive nature of colonialism—made its appearance with his first book, *Dusklands* (1974). This consists of two novellas, one set in the U.S. State Department during the Vietnam War, the other in southern Africa two hundred years earlier. The protagonists of these seemingly different stories—Eugene Dawn, an expert in psychological warfare, and Jacobus Coetzee, an explorer and pioneer—are engaged in similar projects, each leading to oppression and murder. Coetzee's subsequent novels include *In the Heart of the Country* (1977), a feminist anticolonial fable in the voice of a mad South African farmwoman; *Life and Times of Michael K* (1983), about a homeless man trying to survive in war-torn Africa; *Foe* (1986), a retelling of Daniel Defoe's *Robinson Crusoe* from the perspective of a female castaway; *The Master of Petersburg* (1994), a fictionalized account of Dostoyevsky's life; *Disgrace* (1999), about sexual harassment, rape, and race relations; and *Elizabeth Costello: Eight Lessons* (2003), which blends essay and fiction. His many essays and works of criticism have concerned censorship, the rights of animals, South African history, and other themes.

Coetzee is at once a passionate political novelist and an intensely literary one, both qualities emerging in his most compelling indictment of colonialism, *Waiting for the Barbarians* (1980). This novel takes its title and theme from a well-known poem by the Greek poet Constantine Cavafy (1863–1933), which ends (in Rae Dalven's translation):

. . . night is here but the barbarians have not come.
Some people arrived from the frontiers,
And they said that there are no longer any barbarians.
And now what shall become of us without any barbarians?
Those people were a kind of solution.

In Coetzee's novel the rulers of the unnamed empire claim it is threatened by barbarians, but the barbarian threat is, at least in part, a fantasy concocted by the empire to hold itself together. The narrator is a magistrate in charge of a frontier post, poised uneasily between the harmless inhabitants of the region and the empire's ruthless officials, and unable to protect either the natives or himself from his brutal colleague, Colonel Joll. Imprisoned and stripped of his duties, the magistrate becomes increasingly skeptical of the empire's motives. When the imperial army arrives to subdue supposed insurgents, its vicious treatment of prisoners calls into question the relation of "civilization" to "barbarism" and demonstrates, in harrowing scenes of abuse and torture, the ethical dangers of one people's dominance over another. In this medley of realist particularism and allegorical parable, Coetzee leaves the landscape and time of the novel hauntingly unspecified, suggesting that colonialism's degradation and coercion, violence, and moral corruption can occur anywhere, at any time.

From Waiting for the Barbarians

First there is the sound of muskets far away, as diminutive as popguns.[1] Then from nearer by, from the ramparts themselves, come volleys of answering shots. There is a stampede of footsteps across the barracks yard. "The barbarians!" someone shouts; but I think he is wrong. Above all the clamour the great bell begins to peal.

Kneeling with an ear to the crack of the door I try to make out what is going on.

The noise from the square mounts from a hubbub to a steady roar in which no single voice can be distinguished. The whole town must be pouring out in welcome, thousands of ecstatic souls. Volleys of musket-shots keep cracking. Then the tenor of the roar changes, rises in pitch and excitement. Faintly above it come the brassy tones of bugles.

The temptation is too great. What have I to lose? I unlock the door. In glare so blinding that I must squint and shade my eyes, I cross the yard, pass through the gate, and join the rear of the crowd. The volleys and the roar of applause continue. The old woman in black beside me takes my arm to steady herself and stands on her toes. "Can you see?" she says. "Yes, I can see men on horseback," I reply; but she is not listening.

I can see a long file of horsemen who, amid flying banners, pass through the gateway and make their way to the centre of the square where they dismount. There is a cloud of dust over the whole square, but I see that they are smiling and laughing: one of them rides with his hands raised high in triumph, another waves a garland of flowers. They progress slowly, for the crowd presses around them, trying to touch them, throwing flowers, clapping their hands above their heads in joy, spinning round and round in private ecstasies. Children dive past me, scrambling through the legs of the

---

1. The magistrate, narrator of the novel, listens from the prison in which the empire has incarcerated him.

grownups to be nearer to their heroes. Fusillade after fusillade comes from the ramparts, which are lined with cheering people.

One part of the cavalcade does not dismount. Headed by a stern-faced young corporal bearing the green and gold banner of the battalion, it passes through the press of bodies to the far end of the square and then begins a circuit of the perimeter, the crowd surging slowly in its wake. The word runs like fire from neighbour to neighbour: *"Barbarians!"*

The standard-bearer's horse is led by a man who brandishes a heavy stick to clear his way. Behind him comes another trooper trailing a rope; and at the end of the rope, tied neck to neck, comes a file of men, barbarians, stark naked, holding their hands up to their faces in an odd way as though one and all are suffering from toothache. For a moment I am puzzled by the posture, by the tiptoeing eagerness with which they follow their leader, till I catch a glint of metal and at once comprehend. A simple loop of wire runs through the flesh of each man's hands and through holes pierced in his cheeks. "It makes them meek as lambs," I remember being told by a soldier who had once seen the trick: "they think of nothing but how to keep very still." My heart grows sick. I know now that I should not have left my cell.

I have to turn my back smartly to avoid being seen by the two who, with their mounted escort, bring up the rear of the procession: the bareheaded young captain whose first triumph this is, and at his shoulder, leaner and darker after his months of campaigning, Colonel of Police Joll.

The circuit is made, everyone has a chance to see the twelve miserable captives, to prove to his children that the barbarians are real. Now the crowd, myself reluctantly in its wake, flows towards the great gate, where a half-moon of soldiers blocks its way until, compressed at front and rear, it cannot budge.

"What is going on?" I ask my neighbour.

"I don't know," he says, "but help me to lift him." I help him to lift the child he carries on his arm on to his shoulders. "Can you see?" he asks the child.

"Yes."

"What are they doing?"

"They are making those barbarians kneel. What are they going to do to them?"

"I don't know. Let's wait and see."

Slowly, titanically, with all my might, I turn and begin to squeeze my body out, "Excuse me . . . excuse me . . ." I say: "the heat—I'm going to be sick." For the first time I see heads turn, fingers point.

I ought to go back to my cell. As a gesture it will have no effect, it will not even be noticed. Nevertheless, for my own sake, as a gesture to myself alone, I ought to return to the cool dark and lock the door and bend the key and stop my ears to the noise of patriotic bloodlust and close my lips and never speak again. Who knows, perhaps I do my fellow-townsmen an injustice, perhaps at this very minute the shoemaker is at home tapping on his last, humming to himself to drown the shouting, perhaps there are housewives shelling peas in their kitchens, telling stories to occupy their restless children, perhaps there are farmers still going calmly about the repair of the ditches. If comrades like these exist, what a pity I do not know them! For me, at this moment, striding away from the crowd, what has become important above all is that I should neither be contaminated by the atrocity that is about to be committed nor poison myself with impotent hatred of its perpetrators. I cannot save the prisoners, therefore let me save myself. Let it at the very least be said, if it ever comes to be said, if there is ever anyone in some remote future interested to know the way we lived, that in this farthest outpost of the Empire of light there existed one man who in his heart was not a barbarian.

I pass through the barracks gate into my prison yard. At the trough in the middle of the yard I pick up an empty bucket and fill it. With the bucket held up before me, slopping water over its sides, I approach the rear of the crowd again. "Excuse me," I say, and push. People curse me, give way, the bucket tilts and splashes, I forge forward till in a minute I am suddenly clear in the frontmost rank of the crowd behind the backs of the soldiers who, holding staves between them, keep an arena clear for the exemplary spectacle.

Four of the prisoners kneel on the ground. The other eight, still roped together, squat in the shade of the wall watching, their hands to their cheeks.

The kneeling prisoners bend side by side over a long heavy pole. A cord runs from the loop of wire through the first man's mouth, under the pole, up to the second man's loop, back under the pole, up to the third loop, under the pole, through the fourth loop. As I watch a soldier slowly pulls the cord tighter and the prisoners bend further till finally they are kneeling with their faces touching the pole. One of them writhes his shoulders in pain and moans. The others are silent, their thoughts wholly concentrated on moving smoothly with the cord, not giving the wire a chance to tear their flesh.

Directing the soldier with little gestures of the hand is Colonel Joll. Though I am only one in a crowd of thousands, though his eyes are shaded as ever, I stare at him so hard with a face so luminous with query that I know at once he sees me.

Behind me I distinctly hear the word *magistrate*. Do I imagine it or are my neighbours inching away from me?

The Colonel steps forward. Stooping over each prisoner in turn he rubs a handful of dust into his naked back and writes a word with a stick of charcoal. I read the words upside down: ENEMY . . . ENEMY . . . ENEMY . . . ENEMY. He steps back and folds his hands. At a distance of no more than twenty paces he and I contemplate each other.

Then the beating begins. The soldiers use the stout green cane staves, bringing them down with the heavy slapping sounds of washing-paddles, raising red welts on the prisoners' backs and buttocks. With slow care the prisoners extend their legs until they lie flat on their bellies, all except the one who had been moaning and who now gasps with each blow.

The black charcoal and ochre dust begin to run with sweat and blood. The game, I see, is to beat them till their backs are washed clean.

I watch the face of a little girl who stands in the front rank of the crowd gripping her mother's clothes. Her eyes are round, her thumb is in her mouth: silent, terrified, curious, she drinks in the sight of these big naked men being beaten. On every face around me, even those that are smiling, I see the same expression: not hatred, not bloodlust, but a curiosity so intense that their bodies are drained by it and only their eyes live, organs of a new and ravening appetite.

The soldiers doing the beating grow tired. One stands with his hands on his hips panting, smiling, gesturing to the crowd. There is a word from the Colonel: all four of them cease their labour and come forward offering their canes to the spectators.

A girl, giggling and hiding her face, is pushed forward by her friends. "Go on, don't be afraid!" they urge her. A soldier puts a cane in her hand and leads her to the place. She stands confused, embarrassed, one hand still over her face. Shouts, jokes, obscene advice are hurled at her. She lifts the cane, brings it down smartly on the prisoner's buttocks, drops it, and scuttles to safety to a roar of applause.

There is a scramble for the canes, the soldiers can barely keep order, I lose sight of the prisoners on the ground as people press forward to take a turn or simply watch the beating from nearer. I stand forgotten with my bucket between my feet.

Then the flogging is over, the soldiers reassert themselves, the crowd scrambles back, the arena is reconstituted, though narrower than before.

Over his head, exhibiting it to the crowd, Colonel Joll holds a hammer, an ordinary four-pound hammer used for knocking in tent-pegs. Again his gaze meets mine. The babble subsides.

"No!" I hear the first word from my throat, rusty, not loud enough. Then again: "No!" This time the word rings like a bell from my chest. The soldier who blocks my way stumbles aside. I am in the arena holding up my hands to still the crowd: "No! No! No!"

When I turn to Colonel Joll he is standing not five paces from me, his arms folded. I point a finger at him. "You!" I shout. Let it all be said. Let him be the one on whom the anger breaks. "You are depraving these people!"

He does not flinch, he does not reply.

"You!" My arm points at him like a gun. My voice fills the square. There is utter silence; or perhaps I am too intoxicated to hear.

Something crashes into me from behind. I sprawl in the dust, gasp, feel the sear of old pain in my back. A stick thuds down on me. Reaching out to ward it off, I take a withering blow on my hand.

It becomes important to stand up, however difficult the pain makes it. I come to my feet and see who it is that is hitting me. It is the stocky man with the sergeant's stripes who helped with the beatings. Crouched at the knees, his nostrils flaring, he stands with his stick raised for the next blow. "Wait!" I gasp, holding out my limp hand. "I think you have broken it!" He strikes, and I take the blow on the forearm. I hide my arm, lower my head, and try to grope towards him and grapple. Blows fall on my head and shoulders. Never mind: all I want is a few moments to finish what I am saying now that I have begun. I grip his tunic and hug him to me. Though he wrestles, he cannot use his stick; over his shoulder I shout again.

"Not with that!" I shout. The hammer lies cradled in the Colonel's folded arms. "You would not use a hammer on a beast, not on a beast!" In a terrible surge of rage I turn on the sergeant and hurl him from me. Godlike strength is mine. In a minute it will pass: let me use it well while it lasts! "Look!" I shout. I point to the four prisoners who lie docilely on the earth, their lips to the pole, their hands clasped to their faces like monkeys' paws, oblivious of the hammer, ignorant of what is going on behind them, relieved that the offending mark has been beaten from their backs, hoping that the punishment is at an end. I raise my broken hand to the sky. "Look!" I shout. "We are the great miracle of creation! But from some blows this miraculous body cannot repair itself! How—!" Words fail me. "Look at these men!" I recommence. "Men!" Those in the crowd who can crane to look at the prisoners, even at the flies that begin to settle on their bleeding welts.

I hear the blow coming and turn to meet it. It catches me full across the face. "I am blind!" I think, staggering back into the blackness that instantly falls. I swallow blood; something blooms across my face, starting as a rosy warmth, turning to fiery agony. I hide my face in my hands and stamp around in a circle trying not to shout, trying not to fall.

What I wanted to say next I cannot remember. A miracle of creation—I pursue the thought but it eludes me like a wisp of smoke. It occurs to me that we crush insects beneath our feet, miracles of creation too, beetles, worms, cockroaches, ants, in their various ways.

I take my fingers from my eyes and a grey world re-emerges swimming in tears. I am so profoundly grateful that I cease to feel pain. As I am hustled, a man at each elbow, back through the murmuring crowd to my cell, I even find myself smiling.

That smile, that flush of joy, leave behind a disturbing residue. I know that they commit an error in treating me so summarily. For I am no orator. What would I have said if they had let me go on? That it is worse to beat a man's feet to pulp than to kill him in combat? That it brings shame on everyone when a girl is permitted to flog a man? That spectacles of cruelty corrupt the hearts of the innocent? The words they stopped me from uttering may have been very paltry indeed, hardly words to rouse the rabble. What, after all, do I stand for besides an archaic code of gentlemanly behaviour towards captured foes, and what do I stand against except the new science of degradation that kills people on their knees, confused and disgraced in their own eyes? Would I have dared to face the crowd to demand justice for these ridiculous barbarian prisoners with their backsides in the air? *Justice:* once that word is uttered, where will it all end? Easier to shout *No!* Easier to be beaten and made a martyr. Easier to lay my head on a block than to defend the cause of justice for the barbarians: for where can that argument lead but to laying down our arms and opening the gates of the town to the people whose land we have raped? The old magistrate, defender of the rule of law, enemy in his own way of the State, assaulted and imprisoned, impregnably virtuous, is not without his own twinges of doubt.

My nose is broken, I know, and perhaps also the cheekbone where the flesh was laid open by the blow of the stick. My left eye is swelling shut.

As the numbness wears off the pain begins to come in spasms a minute or two apart so intense that I can no longer lie still. At the height of the spasm I trot around the room holding my face, whining like a dog; in the blessed valleys between the peaks I breathe deeply, trying to keep control of myself, trying not to make too disgraceful an outcry. I seem to hear surges and lulls in the noise from the mob on the square but cannot be sure that the roar is not simply in my eardrums.

They bring me my evening meal as usual but I cannot eat. I cannot keep still, I have to walk back and forth or rock on my haunches to keep myself from screaming, tearing my clothes, clawing my flesh, doing whatever people do when the limit of their endurance is reached. I weep, and feel the tears stinging the open flesh. I hum the old song about the rider and the juniper bush over and over again, clinging to the remembered words even after they have ceased to make any sense. One, two, three, four . . . I count. It will be a famous victory, I tell myself, if you can last the night.

In the early hours of the morning, when I am so giddy with exhaustion that I reel on my feet, I finally give way and sob from the heart like a child: I sit in a corner against the wall and weep, the tears running from my eyes without stop. I weep and weep while the throbbing comes and goes according to its own cycles. In this position sleep bursts upon me like a thunderbolt. I am amazed to come to myself in the thin grey light of day, slumped in a corner, with not the faintest sense that time has passed. Though the throbbing is still there I find I can endure it if I remain still. Indeed, it has lost its strangeness. Soon, perhaps, it will be as much part of me as breathing.

So I lie quietly against the wall, folding my sore hand under my armpit for comfort, and fall into a second sleep, into a confusion of images among which I search out one in particular, brushing aside the others that fly at me like leaves. It is of the girl. She is kneeling with her back to me before the snow-castle or sandcastle she has built. She wears a dark blue robe. As I approach I see that she is digging away in the bowels of the castle.

She becomes aware of me and turns. I am mistaken, it is not a castle she has built but a clay oven. Smoke curls up from the vent at the back. She holds out her hands to me offering me something, a shapeless lump which I peer at unwillingly through a mist. Though I shake my head my vision will not clear.

She is wearing a round cap embroidered in gold. Her hair is braided in a heavy plait which lies over her shoulder: there is gold thread worked into the braid. "Why are you dressed in your best?" I want to say: "I have never seen you looking so lovely." She smiles at me: what beautiful teeth she has, what clear jet-black eyes! Also now I can see that what she is holding out to me is a loaf of bread, still hot, with a coarse steaming broken crust. A surge of gratitude sweeps through me. "Where did a child like you learn to bake so well in the desert?" I want to say. I open my arms to embrace her, and come to myself with tears stinging the wound on my cheek. Though I scrabble back at once into the burrow of sleep I cannot re-enter the dream or taste the bread that has made my saliva run.

•   •

Colonel Joll sits behind the desk in my office. There are no books or files; the room is starkly empty save for a vase of fresh flowers.

The handsome warrant officer whose name I do not know lifts the cedarwood chest on to the desk and steps back.

Looking down to refer to his papers, the Colonel speaks. "Among the items found in your apartment was this wooden chest. I would like you to consider it. Its contents are unusual. It contains approximately three hundred slips of white poplar-wood, each about eight inches by two inches, many of them wound about with lengths of string.[2] The wood is dry and brittle. Some of the string is new, some so old that it has perished.

"If one loosens the string one finds that the slip splits open revealing two flat inner surfaces. These surfaces are written on in an unfamiliar script.

"I think you will concur with this description."

I stare into the black lenses. He goes on.

"A reasonable inference is that the wooden slips contain messages passed between yourself and other parties, we do not know when. It remains for you to explain what the messages say and who the other parties were."

---

2. Over the years the magistrate has conducted archaeological digs outside the city, unearthing these poplar slips and other artifacts.

He takes a slip from the chest and flicks it across the polished surface of the desk towards me.

I look at the lines of characters written by a stranger long since dead. I do not even know whether to read from right to left or from left to right. In the long evenings I spent poring over my collection I isolated over four hundred different characters in the script, perhaps as many as four hundred and fifty. I have no idea what they stand for. Does each stand for a single thing, a circle for the sun, a triangle for a woman, a wave for a lake; or does a circle merely stand for "circle", a triangle for "triangle", a wave for "wave"? Does each sign represent a different state of the tongue, the lips, the throat, the lungs, as they combine in the uttering of some multifarious unimaginable extinct barbarian language? Or are my four hundred characters nothing but scribal embellishments of an underlying repertory of twenty or thirty whose primitive forms I am too stupid to see?

"He sends greetings to his daughter," I say. I hear with surprise the thick nasal voice that is now mine. My finger runs along the line of characters from right to left. "Whom he says he has not seen for a long time. He hopes she is happy and thriving. He hopes the lambing season has been good. He has a gift for her, he says, which he will keep till he sees her again. He sends his love. It is not easy to read his signature. It could be simply 'Your father' or it could be something else, a name."

I reach over into the chest and pick out a second slip. The warrant officer, who sits behind Joll with a little notebook open on his knee, stares hard at me, his pencil poised above the paper.

"This one reads as follows," I say: "'I am sorry I must send bad news. The soldiers came and took your brother away. I have been to the fort every day to plead for his return. I sit in the dust with my head bare. Yesterday for the first time they sent a man to speak to me. He says your brother is no longer here. He says he has been sent away. "Where?" I asked, but he would not say. Do not tell your mother, but join me in praying for his safety.'

"And now let us see what this next one says.' The pencil is still poised, he has not written anything, he has not stirred. "'We went to fetch your brother yesterday. They showed us into a room where he lay on a table sewn up in a sheet.'" Slowly Joll leans back in his chair. The warrant officer closes his notebook and half-rises; but with a gesture Joll restrains him. "'They wanted me to take him away like that, but I insisted on looking first. "What if it is the wrong body you are giving me?" I said—"You have so many bodies here, bodies of brave young men." So I opened the sheet and saw that it was indeed he. Through each eyelid, I saw that there was a stitch, "Why have you done that?" I said. "It is our custom," he said. I tore the sheet wide open and saw bruises all over his body, and saw that his feet were swollen and broken. "What happened to him?" I said. "I do not know," said the man, "it is not on the paper; if you have questions you must go to the sergeant, but he is very busy." We have had to bury your brother here, outside their fort, because he was beginning to stink. Please tell your mother and try to console her.'

"Now let us see what the next one says. See, there is only a single character. It is the barbarian character *war*, but it has other senses too. It can stand for *vengeance*, and, if you turn it upside down like this, it can be made to read *justice*. There is no knowing which sense is intended. That is part of barbarian cunning.

"It is the same with the rest of these slips." I plunge my good hand into the chest and stir. "They form an allegory. They can be read in many orders. Further, each single slip can be read in many ways. Together they can be read as a domestic journal, or they can be read as a plan of war, or they can be turned on their sides and read as a history of the last years of the Empire—the old Empire, I mean. There is no agreement among scholars about how to interpret these relics of the ancient barbarians. Allegorical sets like this one can be found buried all over the desert. I found this one not three miles from here in the ruins of a public building. Graveyards are another good place to look in, though it is not always easy to tell where barbarian burial sites lie. It is recommended that you simply dig at random: perhaps at the very spot where you stand you will come upon scraps, shards, reminders of the dead. Also the air: the air is full of sighs and cries. These are never lost: if you listen carefully, with a sympathetic ear, you can hear them echoing forever within the second sphere. The night is best: sometimes when you have difficulty in falling asleep it is because your ears have been reached by the cries of the dead which, like their writings, are open to many interpretations.

"Thank you. I have finished translating."

I have not failed to keep an eye on Joll through all this. He has not stirred again, save to lay a hand on his subordinate's sleeve at the moment when I referred to the Empire and he rose, ready to strike me.

If he comes near me I will hit him with all the strength in my body. I will not disappear into the earth without leaving my mark on them.

The Colonel speaks. "You have no idea how tiresome your behaviour is. You are the one and only official we have had to work with on the frontier who has not given us his fullest co-operation. Candidly, I must tell you I am not interested in these sticks." He waves a hand at the slips scattered on the desk. "They are very likely gambling-sticks. I know that other tribes on the border gamble with sticks.

"I ask you to consider soberly: what kind of future do you have here? You cannot be allowed to remain in your post. You have utterly disgraced yourself. Even if you are not eventually prosecuted—"

"I am waiting for you to prosecute me!" I shout. "When are you going to do it? When are you going to bring me to trial? When am I going to have a chance to defend myself?" I am in a fury. None of the speechlessness I felt in front of the crowd afflicts me. If I were to confront these men now, in public, in a fair trial, I would find the words to shame them. It is a matter of health and strength: I feel my hot words swell in my breast. But they will never bring a man to trial while he is healthy and strong enough to confound them. They will shut me away in the dark till I am a muttering idiot, a ghost of myself; then they will haul me before a closed court and in five minutes dispose of the legalities they find so tiresome.

"For the duration of the emergency, as you know," says the Colonel, "the administration of justice is out of the hands of civilians and in the hands of the Bureau." He sighs. "Magistrate, you seem to believe that we do not dare to bring you to trial because we fear you are too popular a figure in this town. I do not think you are aware of how much you forfeited by neglecting your duties, shunning your friends, keeping company with low people. There is no one I have spoken to who has not at some time felt insulted by your behaviour."

"My private life is none of their business!"

"Nevertheless, I may tell you that our decision to relieve you of your duties has been welcomed in most quarters. Personally I have nothing against you. When I arrived back a few days ago, I had decided that all I wanted from you was a clear answer to a simple question, after which you could have returned to your concubines a free man."

It strikes me suddenly that the insult may not be gratuitous, that perhaps for different reasons these two men might welcome it if I lost my temper. Burning with outrage, tense in every muscle, I guard my silence.

"However, you seem to have a new ambition," he goes on. "You seem to want to make a name for yourself as the One Just Man, the man who is prepared to sacrifice his freedom to his principles.

"But let me ask you: do you believe that that is how your fellow-citizens see you after the ridiculous spectacle you created on the square the other day? Believe me, to people in this town you are not the One Just Man, you are simply a clown, a madman. You are dirty, you stink, they can smell you a mile away. You look like an old beggar-man, a refuse-scavenger. They do not want you back in any capacity. You have no future here.

"You want to go down in history as a martyr, I suspect. But who is going to put you in the history books? These border troubles are of no significance. In a while they will pass and the frontier will go to sleep for another twenty years. People are not interested in the history of the back of beyond."

"There were no border troubles before you came," I say.

"That is nonsense," he says. "You are simply ignorant of the facts. You are living in a world of the past. You think we are dealing with small groups of peaceful nomads. In fact we are dealing with a well organized enemy. If you had travelled with the expeditionary force you would have seen that for yourself."

"Those pitiable prisoners you brought in—are *they* the enemy I must fear? Is that what you say? *You* are the enemy, Colonel!" I can restrain myself no longer. I pound the desk with my fist. "*You* are the enemy, *you* have made the war, and *you* have given them all the martyrs they need—starting not now but a year ago when you committed your first filthy barbarities here! History will bear me out!"

"Nonsense. There will be no history, the affair is too trivial." He seems impassive, but I am sure I have shaken him.

"You are an obscene torturer! You deserve to hang!"

"Thus speaks the judge, the One Just Man," he murmurs.

We stare into each other's eyes.

"Now," he says, squaring the papers before him: "I would like a statement on everything that passed between you and the barbarians on your recent and unauthorized visit to them."

"I refuse."

"Very well. Our interview is over." He turns to his subordinate. "He is your responsibility." He stands up, walks out. I face the warrant officer.

•

The wound on my cheek, never washed or dressed, is swollen and inflamed. A crust like a fat caterpillar has formed on it. My left eye is a mere slit, my nose a shapeless throbbing lump. I must breathe through my mouth.

I lie in the reek of old vomit obsessed with the thought of water. I have had nothing to drink for two days.

In my suffering there is nothing ennobling. Little of what I call suffering is even pain. What I am made to undergo is subjection to the most rudimentary needs of my body: to drink, to relieve itself, to find the posture in which it is least sore. When Warrant Officer Mandel and his man first brought me back here and lit the lamp and closed the door, I wondered how much pain a plump comfortable old man would be able to endure in the name of his eccentric notions of how the Empire should conduct itself. But my torturers were not interested in degrees of pain. They were interested only in demonstrating to me what it meant to live in a body, as a body, a body which can entertain notions of justice only as long as it is whole and well, which very soon forgets them when its head is gripped and a pipe is pushed down its gullet and pints of salt water are poured into it till it coughs and retches and flails and voids itself. They did not come to force the story out of me of what I had said to the barbarians and what the barbarians had said to me. So I had no chance to throw the high-sounding words I had ready in their faces. They came to my cell to show me the meaning of humanity, and in the space of an hour they showed me a great deal.

●   ●

Nor is it a question of who endures longest. I used to think to myself, "They are sitting in another room discussing me. They are saying to each other, 'How much longer before he grovels? In an hour we will go back and see.'"

But it is not like that. They have no elaborated system of pain and deprivation to which they subject me. For two days I go without food and water. On the third day I am fed. "I am sorry," says the man who brings my food, "we forgot." It is not malice that makes them forget. My torturers have their own lives to lead. I am not the centre of their universe. Mandel's underling probably spends his days counting bags in the commissary or patrolling the earthworks, grumbling to himself about the heat. Mandel himself, I am sure, spends more time polishing his straps and buckles than he spends on me. When the mood takes him he comes and gives me a lesson in humanity. How long can I withstand the randomness of their attacks? And what will happen if I succumb, weep, grovel, while yet the attacks go on?

●   ●

They call me into the yard. I stand before them hiding my nakedness, nursing my sore hand, a tired old bear made tame by too much baiting. "Run," Mandel says. I run around the yard under the blazing sun. When I slacken he slaps me on the buttocks with his cane and I trot faster. The soldiers leave their siesta and watch from the shade, the scullery maids hang over the kitchen door, children stare through the bars of the gate. "I cannot!" I gasp. "My heart!" I stop, hang my head, clutch my chest. Everyone waits patiently while I recover myself. Then the cane prods me and I shamble on, moving no faster than a man walks.

Or else I do tricks for them. They stretch a rope at knee-height and I jump back and forth over it. They call the cook's little grandson over and give him one end to hold. "Keep it steady," they say, "we don't want him to trip." The child grips his end of the rope with both hands, concentrating on this important task, waiting for me to jump. I baulk. The point of the cane finds its way between my buttocks and prods. "Jump," Mandel murmurs. I run, make a little skip, blunder into the rope, and stand there. I smell of shit. I am not permitted to wash. The flies follow me everywhere, circling around the appetizing sore on my cheek, alighting if I stand still for a moment. The looping movement of my hand before my face to chase them away has become as automatic as the flick of a cow's tail. "Tell him he must do better next time," Mandel says to the boy. The boy smiles and looks away. I sit down in the dust to wait for the next trick. "Do you know how to skip?" he says to the boy. "Give the rope to the man and ask him to show you how to skip." I skip.

It cost me agonies of shame the first time I had to come out of my den and stand naked before these idlers or jerk my body about for their amusement. Now I am past shame. My mind is turned wholly to the menace of the moment when my knees turn to water or my heart grips me like a crab and I have to stand still; and each time I discover with surprise that after a little rest, after the application of a little pain, I can be made to move, to jump or skip or crawl or run a little further. Is there a point at which I will lie down and say, "Kill me—I would rather die than go on"? Sometimes I think I am approaching that point, but I am always mistaken.

There is no consoling grandeur in any of this. When I wake up groaning in the night it is because I am reliving in dreams the pettiest degradations. There is no way of dying allowed me, it seems, except like a dog in a corner.

•   •

Then one day they throw open the door and I step out to face not two men but a squad standing to attention. "Here," says Mandel, and hands me a woman's calico smock. "Put it on."

"Why?"

"Very well, if you want to go naked, go naked."

I slip the smock over my head. It reaches halfway down my thighs. I catch a glimpse of the two youngest maids ducking back into the kitchen, dissolving in giggles.

My wrists are caught behind my back and tied. "The time has come, Magistrate," Mandel whispers in my ear. "Do your best to behave like a man." I am sure I can smell liquor on his breath.

They march me out of the yard. Under the mulberry trees, where the earth is purple with the juice of fallen berries, there is a knot of people waiting. Children are scrambling about on the branches. As I approach everyone falls silent.

A soldier tosses up the end of a new white hemp rope; one of the children in the tree catches it, loops it over a branch, and drops it back.

I know this is only a trick, a new way of passing the afternoon for men bored with the old torments. Nevertheless my bowels turn to water. "Where is the Colonel?" I whisper. No one pays any heed.

"Do you want to say something?" says Mandel. "Say whatever you wish. We give you this opportunity."

I look into his clear blue eyes, as clear as if there were crystal lenses slipped over his eyeballs. He looks back at me. I have no idea what he sees. Thinking of him, I have said the words *torture . . . torturer* to myself, but they are strange words, and the more I repeat them the more strange they grow, till they lie like stones on my tongue. Perhaps this man, and the man he brings along to help him with his work, and their Colonel, are torturers, perhaps that is their designation on three cards in a pay-office somewhere in the capital, though it is more likely that the cards call them security officers. But when I look at him I see simply the clear blue eyes, the rather rigid good looks, the teeth slightly too long where the gums are receding. He deals with my soul: every day he folds the flesh aside and exposes my soul to the light; he has probably seen many souls in the course of his working life; but the care of souls seems to have left no more mark on him than the care of hearts leaves on the surgeon.

"I am trying very hard to understand your feelings towards me," I say. I cannot help mumbling, my voice is unsteady, I am afraid and the sweat is dripping from me. "Much more than an opportunity to address these people, to whom I have nothing to say, would I appreciate a few words from you. So that I can come to understand why you devote yourself to this work. And can hear what you feel towards me, whom you have hurt a great deal and now seem to be proposing to kill."

Amazed I stare at this elaborate utterance as it winds its way out of me. Am I mad enough to intend a provocation?

"Do you see this hand?" he says. He holds his hand an inch from my face. "When I was younger"—he flexes the fingers—"I used to be able to poke this finger"—he holds up the index finger—"through a pumpkin-shell." He puts the tip of his finger against my forehead and presses. I take a step backwards.

They even have a cap ready for me, a salt-bag which they slip over my head and tie around my throat with a string. Through the mesh I watch them bring up the ladder and prop it against the branch. I am guided to it, my foot is set on the lowest rung, the noose is settled under my ear. "Now climb," says Mandel.

I turn my head and see two dim figures holding the end of the rope. "I can't climb with my hands tied," I say. My heart is hammering. "Climb," he says, steadying me by the arm. The rope tightens. "Keep it tight," he orders.

I climb, he climbs behind me, guiding me. I count ten rungs. Leaves brush against me. I stop. He grips my arm tighter. "Do you think we are playing?" he says. He talks through clenched teeth in a fury I do not understand. "Do you think I don't mean what I say?"

My eyes sting with sweat inside the bag. "No," I say, "I do not think you are playing." As long as the rope remains taut I know they are playing. If the rope goes slack, and I slip, I will die.

"Then what do you want to say to me?"

"I want to say that nothing passed between myself and the barbarians concerning military matters. It was a private affair. I went to return the girl to her family. For no other purpose."

"Is that all you want to say to me?"

"I want to say that no one deserves to die." In my absurd frock and bag, with the nausea of cowardice in my mouth, I say: "I want to live. As every man wants to live. To live and live and live. No matter what."

"That isn't enough." He lets my arm go. I teeter on my tenth rung, the rope saving my balance. "Do you see?" he says. He retreats down the ladder, leaving me alone.

Not sweat but tears.

There is a rustling in the leaves near me. A child's voice: "Can you see, uncle?"

"No."

"Hey, monkeys, come down!" calls someone from below. Through the taut rope I can feel the vibration of their movements in the branches.

So I stand for a long while, balancing carefully on the rung, feeling the comfort of the wood in the curve of my sole, trying not to waver, keeping the tension of the rope as constant as possible.

How long will a crowd of idlers be content to watch a man stand on a ladder? I would stand here till the flesh dropped from my bones, through storm and hail and flood, to live.

But now the rope tightens, I can even hear it rasp as it passes over the bark, till I must stretch to keep it from throttling me.

This is not a contest of patience, then: if the crowd is not satisfied the rules are changed. But of what use is it to blame the crowd? A scapegoat is named, a festival is declared, the laws are suspended: who would not flock to see the entertainment? What is it I object to in these spectacles of abasement and suffering and death that our new regime puts on but their lack of decorum? What will my own administration be remembered for besides moving the shambles from the marketplace to the outskirts of the town twenty years ago in the interests of decency? I try to call out something, a word of blind fear, a shriek, but the rope is now so tight that I am strangled, speechless. The blood hammers in my ears. I feel my toes lose their hold. I am swinging gently in the air, bumping against the ladder, flailing with my feet. The drumbeat in my ears becomes slower and louder till it is all I can hear.

I am standing in front of the old man, screwing up my eyes against the wind, waiting for him to speak. The ancient gun still rests between his horse's ears, but it is not aimed at me. I am aware of the vastness of the sky all around us, and of the desert.

I watch his lips. At any moment now he will speak: I must listen carefully to capture every syllable, so that later, repeating them to myself, poring over them, I can discover the answer to a question which for the moment has flown like a bird from my recollection.

I can see every hair of the horse's mane, every wrinkle of the old man's face, every rock and furrow of the hillside.

The girl, with her black hair braided and hanging over her shoulder in barbarian fashion, sits her horse behind him. Her head is bowed, she too is waiting for him to speak.

I sigh. "What a pity," I think. "It is too late now."

I am swinging loose. The breeze lifts my smock and plays with my naked body. I am relaxed, floating. In a woman's clothes.

What must be my feet touch the ground, though they are numb to all feeling. I stretch myself out carefully, at full length, light as a leaf. Whatever it is that has held my head so tightly slackens its grip. From inside me comes a ponderous grating. I breathe. All is well.

Then the hood comes off, the sun dazzles my eyes, I am hauled to my feet, everything swims before me, I go blank.

The word *flying* whispers itself somewhere at the edge of my consciousness. Yes, it is true, I have been flying.

I am looking into the blue eyes of Mandel. His lips move but I hear no words. I shake my head, and having once started find that I cannot stop.

"I was saying," he says, *"now we will show you another form of flying."*

"He can't hear you," someone says. "He can hear," says Mandel. He slips the noose from my neck and knots it around the cord that binds my wrists. "Pull him up."

If I can hold my arms stiff, if I am acrobat enough to swing a foot up and hook it around the rope, I will be able to hang upside down and not be hurt: that is my last thought before they begin to hoist me. But I am as weak as a baby, my arms come up behind my back, and as my feet leave the ground I feel a terrible tearing in my shoulders as though whole sheets of muscle are giving way. From my throat comes the first mournful dry bellow, like the pouring of gravel. Two little boys drop out of the tree and, hand in hand, not looking back, trot off. I bellow again and again, there is nothing I can do to stop it, the noise comes out of a body that knows itself damaged perhaps beyond repair and roars its fright. Even if all the children of the town should hear me I cannot stop myself: let us only pray that they do not imitate their elders' games, or tomorrow there will be a plague of little bodies dangling from the trees. Someone gives me a push and I begin to float back and forth in an arc a foot above the ground like a great old moth with its wings pinched together, roaring, shouting. "He is calling his barbarian friends," someone observes. "That is barbarian language you hear." There is laughter.

1980

SALMAN RUSHDIE
b. 1947

The most influential novelist to have come from South Asia in the last fifty years is Ahmed Salman Rushdie, whose dynamic narratives—stories of magic, suffering, and the vitality of human beings in the grip of history—have helped generate the literary renaissance flowering in India today. "I come from Bombay," Rushdie has said, "and from a Muslim family, too. 'My' India has always been based on ideas of multiplicity, pluralism, hybridity: ideas to which the ideologies of the communalists are diametrically opposed. To my mind, the defining image of India is the crowd, and a crowd is by its very nature superabundant, heterogeneous, many things at once." Rushdie was educated at Cathedral School, Bombay (now Mumbai), and from the age of thirteen, at Rugby School, Warwickshire, and King's College, Cambridge. After living briefly in Pakistan, where his prosperous family had moved, Rushdie eventually settled in England, working as an actor and as a freelance advertising copywriter (1970–80).

His first novel, *Grimus* (1979), passed unnoticed, but his second, *Midnight's Children* (1981), announced the arrival of a major writer. Taking its title from those who were born—two months later than its author—around midnight on August 15, 1947, when the independent state of India was born, *Midnight's Children* is a work of prodigious prodigality, a cornucopia as richly fertile in character, incident, and language as the subcontinent that is its setting. The book's triumphant progress across the world culminated in its being judged "the Booker of Bookers," the best novel to have won Britain's premier fiction prize in its first twenty-five years. Rushdie has said that "we're all radio-active with history," and the books that have followed *Midnight's Children* have again shown a form of "magical realism"—learned from Latin American writers such as Jorge Luis Borges and Gabriel García Márquez—deployed in the service of a powerful political-historical imagination.

In 1988 Rushdie found himself at the perilous center of a real, rather than a magical realist, political-historical storm. His novel *The Satanic Verses* provoked riots in India, Pakistan, and South Africa, and was judged by senior religious figures in Iran to have blasphemed the Prophet Muhammad (called by the offensive name "Mahound" in the novel), founder of the Muslim faith, and a fatwa, or legal decree, calling for his death was pronounced. He was obliged to go into hiding, and for almost a decade lived under round-the-clock protection from British Secret Service agents, while governments argued for and against the lifting of the fatwa, and the author himself became symbolic of the vulnerability of the intellectual in the face of fundamentalism. The lifting of the fatwa in 1998 allowed Rushdie to reappear in public, but it is seen as irrevocable by some religious groups, and so his life remains under constant threat. Al-Qaeda was among the groups that condemned his being knighted by Queen Elizabeth II in 2007. Rushdie has defended *The Satanic Verses* in the essay "In Good Faith" (1990), while defining the irreverently pluralistic vision behind his "mongrel" aesthetic—a vision that has repeatedly resulted in the burning or banning of his books by political nationalists and religious purists in South Asia and other parts of the world:

> If *The Satanic Verses* is anything, it is a migrant's-eye view of the world. It is written from the very experience of uprooting, disjuncture and metamorphosis (slow or rapid, painful or pleasurable) that is the migrant condition, and from which, I believe, can be derived a metaphor for all humanity.
>
> Standing at the centre of the novel is a group of characters most of whom are British Muslims, or not particularly religious persons of Muslim background, struggling with just the sort of great problems of hybridization and ghettoization, of reconciling the old and the new. Those who oppose the novel most vociferously today are of the opinion that intermingling with a different culture will inevitably weaken and ruin their own. I am of the opposite opinion. *The Satanic Verses* celebrates hybridity, impurity, intermingling, the transformation that comes of new and unexpected combinations of human beings, cultures, ideas, politics, movies, songs. It rejoices in mongrelization and fears the absolutism of the Pure. *Mélange*, hotchpotch, a bit of this and a bit of that is *how newness enters the world*. It is the great possibility that mass migration gives the world, and I have tried to embrace it. *The Satanic Verses* is for change-by-fusion, change-by-conjoining. It is a love-song to our mongrel selves.

An earlier story, published the same year as his groundbreaking *Midnight's Children*, had invoked the Prophet uncontroversially. Like *Midnight's Children*, the story "The Prophet's Hair" buoyantly fuses Standard English with an exuberantly Indianized English, peppered with words of Hindi, Persian, Sanskrit, and Arabic origin—among the many languages that have been used in the extraordinarily polyglot Indian subcontinent. Like *The Satanic Verses*, "The Prophet's Hair" risks playfulness, satire, caricature, and whimsy in its treatment of the religion of his youth (though Rushdie has indicated he was brought up not as a believer but within a relaxed Muslim climate, almost secularized by the variety of other religions surrounding it). The story is at once a moral fable in the tradition of *The Thousand and One Nights* and a magical realist extravaganza, packed with incident, poetic detail ("water to which the cold of the night had given the cloudy consistency of wild honey"), and humor, all brilliantly interwoven at breakneck speed.

The Prophet's[1] Hair

Early in the year 19—, when Srinagar[2] was under the spell of a winter so fierce it could crack men's bones as if they were glass, a young man upon whose cold-pinked skin there lay, like a frost, the unmistakable sheen of wealth was to be seen entering the most wretched and disreputable part of the city, where the houses of wood and corrugated iron seemed perpetually on the verge of losing their balance, and asking in low, grave tones where he might go to engage the services of a dependably professional burglar. The young man's name was Atta, and the rogues in that part of town directed him gleefully into ever darker and less public alleys, until in a yard wet with the blood of a slaughtered chicken he was set upon by two men whose faces he never saw, robbed of the substantial bank-roll which he had insanely brought on his solitary excursion, and beaten within an inch of his life.

Night fell. His body was carried by anonymous hands to the edge of the lake, whence it was transported by shikara[3] across the water and deposited, torn and bleeding, on the deserted embankment of the canal which led to the gardens of Shalimar. At dawn the next morning a flower-vendor was rowing his boat through water to which the cold of the night had given the cloudy consistency of wild honey when he saw the prone form of young Atta, who was just beginning to stir and moan, and on whose now deathly pale skin the sheen of wealth could still be made out dimly beneath an actual layer of frost.

The flower-vendor moored his craft and by stooping over the mouth of the injured man was able to learn the poor fellow's address, which was mumbled through lips that could scarcely move; whereupon, hoping for a large tip, the hawker rowed Atta home to a large house on the shores of the lake, where a beautiful but inexplicably bruised young woman and her distraught, but equally handsome mother, neither of whom, it was clear from their eyes, had slept a wink from worrying, screamed at the sight of their Atta—who was the elder brother of the beautiful young woman—lying motionless amidst the funereally stunted winter blooms of the hopeful florist.

The flower-vendor was indeed paid off handsomely, not least to ensure his silence, and plays no further part in our story. Atta himself, suffering terribly from exposure as well as a broken skull, entered a coma which caused the city's finest doctors to shrug helplessly. It was therefore all the more remarkable that on the very next evening the most wretched and disreputable part of the city received a second unexpected visitor. This was Huma, the sister of the unfortunate young man, and her question was the same as her brother's, and asked in the same low, grave tones:
'Where may I hire a thief?'

The story of the rich idiot who had come looking for a burglar was already common knowledge in those insalubrious[4] gullies, but this time the young

---

woman added: 'I should say that I am carrying no money, nor am I wearing any jewellery items. My father has disowned me and will pay no ransom if I am kidnapped; and a letter has been lodged with the Deputy Commissioner of Police, my uncle, to be opened in the event of my not being safe at home by morning. In that letter he will find full details of my journey here, and he will move Heaven and Earth to punish my assailants.'

Her exceptional beauty, which was visible even through the enormous welts and bruises disfiguring her arms and forehead, coupled with the oddity of her inquiries, had attracted a sizable group of curious onlookers, and because her little speech seemed to them to cover just about everything, no one attempted to injure her in any way, although there were some raucous comments to the effect that it was pretty peculiar for someone who was trying to hire a crook to invoke the protection of a high-up policeman uncle.

She was directed into ever darker and less public alleys until finally in a gully as dark as ink an old woman with eyes which stared so piercingly that Huma instantly understood she was blind motioned her through a doorway from which darkness seemed to be pouring like smoke. Clenching her fists, angrily ordering her heart to behave normally, Huma followed the old woman into the gloom-wrapped house.

The faintest conceivable rivulet of candlelight trickled through the darkness; following this unreliable yellow thread (because she could no longer see the old lady), Huma received a sudden sharp blow to the shins and cried out involuntarily, after which she at once bit her lip, angry at having revealed her mounting terror to whoever or whatever waited before her, shrouded in blackness.

She had, in fact, collided with a low table on which a single candle burned and beyond which a mountainous figure could be made out, sitting cross-legged on the floor. 'Sit, sit,' said a man's calm, deep voice, and her legs, needing no more flowery invitation, buckled beneath her at the terse command. Clutching her left hand in her right, she forced her voice to respond evenly:

'And you, sir, will be the thief I have been requesting?'

Shifting its weight very slightly, the shadow-mountain informed Huma that all criminal activity originating in this zone was well organised and also centrally controlled, so that all requests for what might be termed freelance work had to be channelled through this room.

He demanded comprehensive details of the crime to be committed, including a precise inventory of items to be acquired, also a clear statement of all financial inducements being offered with no gratuities excluded, plus, for filing purposes only, a summary of the motives for the application.

At this, Huma, as though remembering something, stiffened both in body and resolve and replied loudly that her motives were entirely a matter for herself; that she would discuss details with no one but the thief himself; but that the rewards she proposed could only be described as 'lavish'.

'All I am willing to disclose to you, sir, since it appears that I am on the premises of some sort of employment agency, is that in return for such lavish rewards I must have the most desperate criminal at your disposal, a man for whom life holds no terrors, not even the fear of God.

'The worst of fellows, I tell you—nothing less will do!'

At this a paraffin storm-lantern was lighted, and Huma saw facing her a grey-haired giant down whose left cheek ran the most sinister of scars, a cicatrice in the shape of the letter *sín* in the Nastaliq[5] script. She was gripped by the insupportably nostalgic notion that the bogeyman of her childhood nursery had risen up to confront her, because her ayah[6] had always forestalled any incipient acts of disobedience by threatening Huma and Atta: 'You don't watch out and I'll send that one to steal you away—that Sheikh[7] Sín, the Thief of Thieves!'

Here, grey-haired but unquestionably scarred, was the notorious criminal himself—and was she out of her mind, were her ears playing tricks, or had he truly just announced that, given the stated circumstances, he himself was the only man for the job?

Struggling hard against the newborn goblins of nostalgia, Huma warned the fearsome volunteer that only a matter of extreme urgency and peril would have brought her unescorted into these ferocious streets.

'Because we can afford no last-minute backings-out,' she continued, 'I am determined to tell you everything, keeping back no secrets whatsoever. If, after hearing me out, you are still prepared to proceed, then we shall do everything in our power to assist you, and to make you rich.'

The old thief shrugged, nodded, spat. Huma began her story.

Six days ago, everything in the household of her father, the wealthy money-lender Hashim, had been as it always was. At breakfast her mother had spooned khichri[8] lovingly on to the moneylender's plate; the conversation had been filled with those expressions of courtesy and solicitude on which the family prided itself.

Hashim was fond of pointing out that while he was not a godly man he set great store by 'living honourably in the world'. In that spacious lakeside residence, all outsiders were greeted with the same formality and respect, even those unfortunates who came to negotiate for small fragments of Hashim's large fortune, and of whom he naturally asked an interest rate of over seventy per cent, partly, as he told his khichri-spooning wife, 'to teach these people the value of money; let them only learn that, and they will be cured of this fever of borrowing borrowing all the time—so you see that if my plans succeed, I shall put myself out of business!'

In their children, Atta and Huma, the moneylender and his wife had successfully sought to inculcate the virtues of thrift, plain dealing and a healthy independence of spirit. On this, too, Hashim was fond of congratulating himself.

Breakfast ended; the family members wished one another a fulfilling day. Within a few hours, however, the glassy contentment of that household, of

---

5. A Persian cursive script, characterized by rounded forms and elongated horizontal strokes. "Cicatrice": scar of a healed wound.
6. Child's nurse (Anglo-Indian, from Portu-

guese).
7. Chief (Arabic).
8. Rice and lentils cooked together (Hindi).

that life of porcelain delicacy and alabaster sensibilities, was to be shattered beyond all hope of repair.

The moneylender summoned his personal shikara and was on the point of stepping into it when, attracted, by a glint of silver, he noticed a small vial floating between the boat and his private quay. On an impulse, he scooped it out of the glutinous water.

It was a cylinder of tinted glass cased in exquisitely wrought silver, and Hashim saw within its walls a silver pendant bearing a single strand of human hair.

Closing his fist around this unique discovery, he muttered to the boatman that he'd changed his plans, and hurried to his sanctum,[9] where, behind closed doors, he feasted his eyes on his find.

There can be no doubt that Hashim the moneylender knew from the first that he was in possession of the famous relic of the Prophet Muhammad, that revered hair whose theft from its shrine at Hazratbal mosque the previous morning had created an unprecedented hue and cry in the valley.

The thieves—no doubt alarmed by the pandemonium, by the procession through the streets of endless ululating[1] crocodiles of lamentation, by the riots, the political ramifications and by the massive police search which was commanded and carried out by men whose entire careers now hung upon the finding of this lost hair—had evidently panicked and hurled the vial into the gelatine bosom of the lake.

Having found it by a stroke of great good fortune, Hashim's duty as a citizen was clear: the hair must be restored to its shrine, and the state to equanimity and peace.

But the moneylender had a different notion.

All around him in his study was the evidence of his collector's mania. There were enormous glass cases full of impaled butterflies from Gulmarg, three dozen scale models in various metals of the legendary cannon Zamzama, innumerable swords, a Naga spear, ninety-four terracotta camels of the sort sold on railway station platforms, many samovars,[2] and a whole zoology of tiny sandalwood animals, which had originally been carved to serve as children's bathtime toys.

'And after all,' Hashim told himself, 'the Prophet would have disapproved mightily of this relic-worship. He abhorred the idea of being deified! So, by keeping this hair from its distracted devotees, I perform—do I not?—a finer service than I would by returning it! Naturally, I don't want it for its religious value . . . I'm a man of the world, of this world. I see it purely as a secular object of great rarity and blinding beauty. In short, it's the silver vial I desire, more than the hair.

'They say there are American millionaires who purchase stolen art masterpieces and hide them away—they would know how I feel. I must, must have it!'

Every collector must share his treasures with one other human being, and Hashim summoned—and told—his only son Atta, who was deeply perturbed

9. Private room.
1. Howling.

2. Apparatuses for making tea (Russian for self-boilers).

but, having been sworn to secrecy, only spilled the beans when the troubles became too terrible to bear.

The youth excused himself and left his father alone in the crowded solitude of his collections. Hashim was sitting erect in a hard, straight-backed chair, gazing intently at the beautiful vial.

It was well known that the moneylender never ate lunch, so it was not until evening that a servant entered the sanctum to summon his master to the dining-table. He found Hashim as Atta had left him. The same, and not the same—for now the moneylender looked swollen, distended. His eyes bulged even more than they always had, they were red-rimmed, and his knuckles were white.

He seemed to be on the point of bursting! As though, under the influence of the misappropriated relic, he had filled up with some spectral fluid which might at any moment ooze uncontrollably from his every bodily opening.

He had to be helped to the table, and then the explosion did indeed take place.

Seemingly careless of the effect of his words on the carefully constructed and fragile constitution of the family's life, Hashim began to gush, to spume long streams of awful truths. In horrified silence, his children heard their father turn upon his wife, and reveal to her that for many years their marriage had been the worst of his afflictions. 'An end to politeness!' he thundered. 'An end to hypocrisy!'

Next, and in the same spirit, he revealed to his family the existence of a mistress; he informed them also of his regular visits to paid women. He told his wife that, far from being the principal beneficiary of his will, she would receive no more than the eighth portion which was her due under Islamic law. Then he turned upon his children, screaming at Atta for his lack of academic ability—'A dope! I have been cursed with a dope!'—and accusing his daughter of lasciviousness, because she went around the city barefaced, which was unseemly for any good Muslim girl to do. She should, he commanded, enter purdah[3] forthwith.

Hashim left the table without having eaten and fell into the deep sleep of a man who has got many things off his chest, leaving his children stunned, in tears, and the dinner going cold on the sideboard under the gaze of an anticipatory bearer.[4]

At five o'clock the next morning the moneylender forced his family to rise, wash and say their prayers. From then on, he began to pray five times daily for the first time in his life, and his wife and children were obliged to do likewise.

Before breakfast, Huma saw the servants, under her father's direction, constructing a great heap of books in the garden and setting fire to it. The only volume left untouched was the Qur'an,[5] which Hashim wrapped in a silken cloth and placed on a table in the hall. He ordered each member of his family to read passages from this book for at least two hours per day. Visits to

---

3. Area of certain traditional Indian houses in which Hindu or Muslim women live secluded from the sight of men outside their family circle.

4. Servant.

5. Or Koran, Muslims' sacred book: collection of the Prophet Muhammad's oral revelations.

the cinema were forbidden. And if Atta invited male friends to the house, Huma was to retire to her room.

By now, the family had entered a state of shock and dismay; but there was worse to come.

That afternoon, a trembling debtor arrived at the house to confess his inability to pay the latest instalment of interest owed, and made the mistake of reminding Hashim, in somewhat blustering fashion, of the Qur'an's strictures against usury. The moneylender flew into a rage and attacked the fellow with one of his large collection of bullwhips.

By mischance, later the same day a second defaulter came to plead for time, and was seen fleeing Hashim's study with a great gash in his arm, because Huma's father had called him a thief of other men's money and had tried to cut off the wretch's right hand with one of the thirty-eight kukri knives[6] hanging on the study walls.

These breaches of the family's unwritten laws of decorum alarmed Atta and Huma, and when, that evening, their mother attempted to calm Hashim down, he struck her on the face with an open hand. Atta leapt to his mother's defence and he, too, was sent flying.

'From now on,' Hashim bellowed, 'there's going to be some discipline around here!'

The moneylender's wife began a fit of hysterics which continued throughout that night and the following day, and which so provoked her husband that he threatened her with divorce, at which she fled to her room, locked the door and subsided into a raga[7] of sniffling. Huma now lost her composure, challenged her father openly, and announced (with that same independence of spirit which he had encouraged in her) that she would wear no cloth over her face; apart from anything else, it was bad for the eyes.

On hearing this, her father disowned her on the spot and gave her one week in which to pack her bags and go.

By the fourth day, the fear in the air of the house had become so thick that it was difficult to walk around. Atta told his shock-numbed sister: 'We are descending to gutter-level—but I know what must be done.'

That afternoon, Hashim left home accompanied by two hired thugs to extract the unpaid dues from his two insolvent clients. Atta went immediately to his father's study. Being the son and heir, he possessed his own key to the moneylender's safe. This he now used, and removing the little vial from its hiding-place, he slipped it into his trouser pocket and re-locked the safe door.

Now he told Huma the secret of what his father had fished out of Lake Dal, and exclaimed: 'Maybe I'm crazy—maybe the awful things that are happening have made me cracked—but I am convinced there will be no peace in our house until this hair is out of it.'

His sister at once agreed that the hair must be returned, and Atta set off in a hired shikara to Hazratbal mosque. Only when the boat had delivered him into the throng of the distraught faithful which was swirling around

---

6. Curved knives broadening toward the point (Hindi).

7. Musical improvisation (Sanskrit).

the desecrated shrine did Atta discover that the relic was no longer in his pocket. There was only a hole, which his mother, usually so attentive to household matters, must have overlooked under the stress of recent events.

Atta's initial surge of chagrin was quickly replaced by a feeling of profound relief.

'Suppose', he imagined, 'that I had already announced to the mullahs[8] that the hair was on my person! They would never have believed me now—and this mob would have lynched me! At any rate, it has gone, and that's a load off my mind.' Feeling more contented than he had for days, the young man returned home.

Here he found his sister bruised and weeping in the hall; upstairs, in her bedroom, his mother wailed like a brand-new widow. He begged Huma to tell him what had happened, and when she replied that their father, returning from his brutal business trip, had once again noticed a glint of silver between boat and quay, had once again scooped up the errant relic, and was consequently in a rage to end all rages, having beaten the truth out of her—then Atta buried his face in his hands and sobbed out his opinion, which was that the hair was persecuting them, and had come back to finish the job.

It was Huma's turn to think of a way out of their troubles.

While her arms turned black and blue and great stains spread across her forehead, she hugged her brother and whispered to him that she was determined to get rid of the hair *at all costs*—she repeated this last phrase several times.

'The hair', she then declared, 'was stolen from the mosque; so it can be stolen from this house. But it must be a genuine robbery, carried out by a bona-fide thief, not by one of us who are under the hair's thrall—by a thief so desperate that he fears neither capture nor curses.'

Unfortunately, she added, the theft would be ten times harder to pull off now that their father, knowing that there had already been one attempt on the relic, was certainly on his guard.

'Can you do it?'

Huma, in a room lit by candle and storm-lantern, ended her account with one further question: 'What assurances can you give that the job holds no terrors for you still?'

The criminal, spitting, stated that he was not in the habit of providing references, as a cook might, or a gardener, but he was not alarmed so easily, certainly not by any children's djinni[9] of a curse. Huma had to be content with this boast, and proceeded to describe the details of the proposed burglary.

'Since my brother's failure to return the hair to the mosque, my father has taken to sleeping with his precious treasure under his pillow. However, he sleeps alone, and very energetically; only enter his room without waking him, and he will certainly have tossed and turned quite enough to make the theft a simple matter. When you have the vial, come to my room,' and here she handed Sheikh Sín a plan of her home, 'and I will hand over all the jewel-

---

8. Muslims learned in Islamic theology and sacred law.

9. In Muslim demonology a spirit (genie) with supernatural powers.

lery owned by my mother and myself. You will find . . . it is worth . . . that is, you will be able to get a fortune for it . . .'

It was evident that her self-control was weakening and that she was on the point of physical collapse.

'Tonight,' she burst out finally. 'You must come tonight!'

No sooner had she left the room than the old criminal's body was convulsed by a fit of coughing: he spat blood into an old vanaspati[1] can. The great Sheikh, the 'Thief of Thieves', had become a sick man, and every day the time drew nearer when some young pretender to his power would stick a dagger in his stomach. A lifelong addiction to gambling had left him almost as poor as he had been when, decades ago, he had started out in this line of work as a mere pickpocket's apprentice; so in the extraordinary commission he had accepted from the moneylender's daughter he saw his opportunity of amassing enough wealth at a stroke to leave the valley for ever, and acquire the luxury of a respectable death which would leave his stomach intact.

As for the Prophet's hair, well, neither he nor his blind wife had ever had much to say for prophets—that was one thing they had in common with the moneylender's thunderstruck clan.

It would not do, however, to reveal the nature of this, his last crime, to his four sons. To his consternation, they had all grown up to be hopelessly devout men, who even spoke of making the pilgrimage to Mecca some day. 'Absurd!' their father would laugh at them. 'Just tell me how you will go?' For, with a parent's absolutist love, he had made sure they were all provided with a lifelong source of high income by crippling them at birth, so that, as they dragged themselves around the city, they earned excellent money in the begging business.

The children, then, could look after themselves.

He and his wife would be off soon with the jewel-boxes of the money-lender's women. It was a timely chance indeed that had brought the beautiful bruised girl into his corner of the town.

That night, the large house on the shore of the lake lay blindly waiting, with silence lapping at its walls. A burglar's night: clouds in the sky and mists on the winter water. Hashim the moneylender was asleep, the only member of his family to whom sleep had come that night. In another room, his son Atta lay deep in the coils of his coma with a blood-clot forming on his brain, watched over by a mother who had let down her long greying hair to show her grief, a mother who placed warm compresses on his head with gestures redolent of impotence. In a third bedroom Huma waited, fully dressed, amidst the jewel-heavy caskets of her desperation.

At last a bulbul[2] sang softly from the garden below her window and, creeping downstairs, she opened a door to the bird, on whose face there was a scar in the shape of the Nastaliq letter *sín*.

Noiselessly, the bird flew up the stairs behind her. At the head of the staircase they parted, moving in opposite directions along the corridor of their conspiracy without a glance at one another.

---

1. Vegetable fat used as butter in India.   2. Asian song thrush.

Entering the moneylender's room with professional ease, the burglar, Sín, discovered that Huma's predictions had been wholly accurate. Hashim lay sprawled diagonally across his bed, the pillow untenanted by his head, the prize easily accessible. Step by padded step, Sín moved towards the goal.

It was at this point that, in the bedroom next door, young Atta sat bolt upright in his bed, giving his mother a great fright, and without any warning—prompted by goodness knows what pressure of the blood-clot upon his brain—began screaming at the top of his voice:

'Thief! Thief! Thief!'

It seems probable that his poor mind had been dwelling, in these last moments, upon his own father; but it is impossible to be certain, because having uttered these three emphatic words the young man fell back upon his pillow and died.

At once his mother set up a screeching and a wailing and a keening and a howling so earsplittingly intense that they completed the work which Atta's cry had begun—that is, her laments penetrated the walls of her husband's bedroom and brought Hashim wide awake.

Sheikh Sín was just deciding whether to dive beneath the bed or brain the moneylender good and proper when Hashim grabbed the tiger-striped sword-stick which always stood propped up in a corner beside his bed, and rushed from the room without so much as noticing the burglar who stood on the opposite side of the bed in the darkness. Sín stooped quickly and removed the vial containing the Prophet's hair from its hiding-place.

Meanwhile Hashim had erupted into the corridor, having unsheathed the sword inside his cane. In his right hand he held the weapon and was waving it about dementedly. His left hand was shaking the stick. A shadow came rushing towards him through the midnight darkness of the passageway and, in his somnolent anger, the moneylender thrust his sword fatally through its heart. Turning up the light, he found that he had murdered his daughter, and under the dire influence of this accident he was so overwhelmed by remorse that he turned the sword upon himself, fell upon it and so extinguished his life. His wife, the sole surviving member of the family, was driven mad by the general carnage and had to be committed to an asylum for the insane by her brother, the city's Deputy Commissioner of Police.

Sheikh Sín had quickly understood that the plan had gone awry.

Abandoning the dream of the jewel-boxes when he was but a few yards from its fulfilment, he climbed out of Hashim's window and made his escape during the appalling events described above. Reaching home before dawn, he woke his wife and confessed his failure. It would be necessary, he whispered, for him to vanish for a while. Her blind eyes never opened until he had gone.

The noise in the Hashim household had roused their servants and even managed to awaken the night-watchman, who had been fast asleep as usual on his charpoy[3] by the street-gate. They alerted the police, and the Deputy

---

3. Light Indian bedstead.

Commissioner himself was informed. When he heard of Huma's death, the mournful officer opened and read the sealed letter which his niece had given him, and instantly led a large detachment of armed men into the light-repellent gullies of the most wretched and disreputable part of the city.

The tongue of a malicious cat-burglar named Huma's fellow-conspirator; the finger of an ambitious bank-robber pointed at the house in which he lay concealed; and although Sín managed to crawl through a hatch in the attic and attempt a roof-top escape, a bullet from the Deputy Commissioner's own rifle penetrated his stomach and brought him crashing messily to the ground at the feet of Huma's enraged uncle.

From the dead thief's pocket rolled a vial of tinted glass, cased in filigree silver.

The recovery of the Prophet's hair was announced at once on All-India Radio. One month later, the valley's holiest men assembled at the Hazratbal mosque and formally authenticated the relic. It sits to this day in a closely guarded vault by the shores of the loveliest of lakes in the heart of the valley which was once closer than any other place on earth to Paradise.

But before our story can properly be concluded, it is necessary to record that when the four sons of the dead Sheikh awoke on the morning of his death, having unwittingly spent a few minutes under the same roof as the famous hair, they found that a miracle had occurred, that they were all sound of limb and strong of wind, as whole as they might have been if their father had not thought to smash their legs in the first hours of their lives. They were, all four of them, very properly furious, because the miracle had reduced their earning powers by 75 per cent, at the most conservative estimate; so they were ruined men.

Only the Sheikh's widow had some reason for feeling grateful, because although her husband was dead she had regained her sight, so that it was possible for her to spend her last days gazing once more upon the beauties of the valley of Kashmir.

1981

IAN MCEWAN
b. 1948

Born in Aldershot, southwest of London, Ian McEwan spent much of his child-hood at military bases in Libya, Singapore, and other countries where his army officer father, a Scotsman, was stationed. He has attributed his early fascination with imaginative literature to his mother, though she, like McEwan's father, had left school when she was fourteen. When he was twelve years old, McEwan returned to Britain to attend a state-run boarding school. He received a B.A. in English at the University of Sussex in 1970, and the next year, an M.A. in creative writing at the University of East Anglia.

McEwan's first three books—the short-story collection *First Love, Last Rites* (1975), which included a number of works he had written for his master's degree; his second book of short fiction, *In Between the Sheets and Other Stories* (1978); and his first novel, *The Cement Garden* (1978)—launched his reputation as a technically brilliant storyteller with masterful command of suspenseful narration, precise imagery, and deft characterization. The salacious details and shocking incidents in these early works—incest between siblings, a penis pickled in a jar, a girl abused and dumped in a canal—also indicated a fascination with sexual perversity and predatory evil. But as McEwan continued to write a prodigious variety of plays, screenplays, and especially novels, the scope of his work widened. Some of his novels are primarily domestic, such as the exploration of a couple's guilt and anger after their three-year-old child has been abducted, in *The Child in Time* (1987), and others chiefly political, such as the Cold War espionage novel *The Innocent* (1990). Some are set in contemporary times, such as the Booker Award–winning *Amsterdam* (1998), about a euthanasia pact, and *Saturday* (2005), whose events unfold in the shadow of September 11, 2001, while others—in particular, the celebrated World War II–era novel *Atonement* (2001), which centers on the disastrous consequences of an overly imaginative girl's false accusation of rape—take place at pivotal historical moments.

Although some of his early works, such as the story "Solid Geometry" (1975), have mystical elements, his later novels, including *Solar* (2010), about the issue of climate change, are permeated with scientific rationalism. McEwan's narrative method—often crystalline in its detachment, clinical in its analysis—aligns with his empiricist and scientific bent, but it is often put in the service of understanding human psychology. McEwan has commented in an interview that "the creation of character and the mapping out of other minds and the invitation to the reader to step into those other minds seems to me very much the central project of exploring our condition." Among the minds explored in the novel *Enduring Love* (1997) are the hyper-rational science writer, Joe Rose, who intricately examines his experience, and the mad stalker, Jed Parry, who falls obsessively in love with Joe during the novel's opening crisis, exemplifying a psychiatric disorder known as de Clérambault's syndrome.

Explaining in a 2007 interview the strongly visual dimension of his work, McEwan remarked that

> forty percent of the brain's processing is given over to the visual, and the visual region projects deep into other parts of the brain, of language and emotion. We are visual creatures and the novel, more than cincture [a liturgical vestment], for me is ultimately a visual medium. . . . I like, myself, to be able to see a scene. And in the opening scene of *Enduring Love*, for example, the most important element of that set piece was to make the details in the relationship, of all the different bits, the people running across a field towards a balloon that was in trouble, to make that clear.

McEwan went on to talk about the genesis of the scene, widely viewed as one of the most compelling in contemporary fiction. He had been looking for an opening that would "have a sense of urgency and visual clarity with something knocking the heart," and a hiking partner

> suddenly remembered he'd read in a paper of a balloon and a father and son who had tried to tether it and dropped to their deaths. I never could find the newspaper piece 'til long afterwards. But as soon as he told me, I thought—now that's it. And I need more than two people, I need six or seven around that balloon. What better enactment of morality? This notion that if we all hang on we can hold it down, but if one breaks rank then there's no point in being good anymore.

In the opening scene of *Enduring Love*, Joe the science writer has taken his wife, Clarissa, a scholar of John Keats's poetry, for a picnic in the English countryside. On seeing a runaway helium hot air balloon that holds a terrified boy, he hastily joins several other men in an attempt to bring it down. As Joe struggles to hang onto the wind-swept balloon, the suspenseful narrative slows down time, minutely exploring the significance of this crisis moment. The balloon incident becomes the meeting ground for tensions between heroism and retreat, self-preservation and communal collaboration, selfless love for others and self-protective self-love, life and death. As in much contemporary fiction, such meanings proliferate without resolution, as the effects of the moment reverberate through the lives of everyone touched by the incident, leaving some shattered, others groping slowly toward self-understanding.

From Enduring Love

One

The beginning is simple to mark. We were in sunlight under a turkey oak, partly protected from a strong, gusty wind. I was kneeling on the grass with a corkscrew in my hand, and Clarissa was passing me the bottle—a 1987 Daumas Gassac. This was the moment, this was the pinprick on the time map: I was stretching out my hand, and as the cool neck and the black foil touched my palm, we heard a man's shout. We turned to look across the field and saw the danger. Next thing, I was running towards it. The transformation was absolute: I don't recall dropping the corkscrew, or getting to my feet, or making a decision, or hearing the caution Clarissa called after me. What idiocy, to be racing into this story and its labyrinths, sprinting away from our happiness among the fresh spring grasses by the oak. There was the shout again, and a child's cry, enfeebled by the wind that roared in the tall trees along the hedgerows. I ran faster. And there, suddenly, from different points around the field, four other men were converging on the scene, running like me.

I see us from three hundred feet up, through the eyes of the buzzard we had watched earlier, soaring, circling and dipping in the tumult of currents: five men running silently towards the centre of a hundred-acre field. I approached from the south-east, with the wind at my back. About two hundred yards to my left two men ran side by side. They were farm labourers who had been repairing the fence along the field's southern edge where it skirts the road. The same distance beyond them was the motorist, John Logan, whose car was banked on the grass verge with its door, or doors, wide open. Knowing what I know now, it's odd to evoke the figure of Jed Parry directly ahead of me, emerging from a line of beeches on the far side of the field a quarter of a mile away, running into the wind. To the buzzard Parry and I were tiny forms, our white shirts brilliant against the green, rushing towards each other like lovers, innocent of the grief this entanglement would bring. The encounter that would unhinge us was minutes away, its enormity disguised from us not only by the barrier of time but by the colossus in the centre of the field that drew us in with the power of a terrible ratio that set fabulous magnitude against the puny human distress at its base.

What was Clarissa doing? She said she walked quickly towards the centre of the field. I don't know how she resisted the urge to run. By the time it happened—the event I am about to describe, the fall—she had almost caught us up and was well placed as an observer, unencumbered by participation, by the ropes and the shouting, and by our fatal lack of co-operation. What I describe is shaped by what Clarissa saw too, by what we told each other in the time of obsessive re-examination that followed: the aftermath, an appropriate term for what happened in a field waiting for its early summer mowing. The aftermath, the second crop, the growth promoted by that first cut in May.

I'm holding back, delaying the information. I'm lingering in the prior moment because it was a time when other outcomes were still possible; the convergence of six figures in a flat green space has a comforting geometry from the buzzard's perspective, the knowable, limited plane of the snooker table.[1] The initial conditions, the force and the direction of the force, define all the consequent pathways, all the angles of collision and return, and the glow of the overhead light bathes the field, the baize[2] and all its moving bodies, in reassuring clarity. I think that while we were still converging, before we made contact, we were in a state of mathematical grace. I linger on our dispositions, the relative distances and the compass point—because as far as these occurrences were concerned, this was the last time I understood anything clearly at all.

What were we running towards? I don't think any of us would ever know fully. But superficially the answer was, a balloon. Not the nominal space that encloses a cartoon character's speech or thought, or, by analogy, the kind that's driven by mere hot air. It was an enormous balloon filled with helium, that elemental gas forged from hydrogen in the nuclear furnace of the stars, first step along the way in the generation of multiplicity and variety of matter in the universe, including our selves and all our thoughts.

We were running towards a catastrophe, which itself was a kind of furnace in whose heat identities and fates would buckle into new shapes. At the base of the balloon was a basket in which there was a boy, and by the basket, clinging to a rope, was a man in need of help.

Even without the balloon the day would have been marked for memory, though in the most pleasurable of ways, for this was a reunion after a separation of six weeks, the longest Clarissa and I had spent apart in our seven years. On the way out to Heathrow I had made a detour into Covent Garden and found a semi legal place to park, close to Carluccio's.[3] I went in and put together a picnic whose centre-piece was a great ball of mozzarella which the assistant fished out of an earthenware vat with a wooden claw. I also bought black olives, mixed salad and focaccia. Then I hurried up Long Acre to Bertram Rota's[4] to take delivery of Clarissa's birthday present. Apart from the flat and our car, it was the most expensive single item I had ever bought. The rarity of this little book seemed to give off a heat I could feel through the thick brown wrapping paper as I walked back up the street.

Forty minutes later I was scanning the screens for arrival information. The Boston flight had only just landed and I guessed I had a half-hour wait.

1. Billiard table.
2. A type of cloth often used to cover tables.
3. Food shop and café in central London. "Heathrow": airport west of London. "Covent Garden": London district.
4. A rare-book store. "Long Acre": a key street in Covent Garden.

If one ever wanted proof of Darwin's contention that the many expressions of emotion in humans are universal, genetically inscribed, then a few minutes by the arrivals gate in Heathrow's Terminal Four should suffice. I saw the same joy, the same uncontrollable smile, in the faces of a Nigerian earth mama, a thin-lipped Scottish granny and a pale, correct Japanese businessman as they wheeled their trolleys in and recognised a figure in the expectant crowd. Observing human variety can give pleasure, but so too can human sameness. I kept hearing the same sighing sound on a downward note, often breathed through a name as two people pressed forward to go into their embrace. Was it a major second, or a minor third, or somewhere in between? Pa-pa! Yolan-ta! Ho-bi! Nz-e! There was also a rising note, crooned into the solemn, wary faces of babies by long-absent fathers or grandparents, cajoling, beseeching an immediate return of love. Hann-ah? Tom-ee? Let me in!

The variety was in the private dramas: a father and teenage son, Turkish perhaps, stood in a long silent clinch, forgiving each other, or mourning a loss, oblivious to the baggage trolleys jamming around them; identical twins, women in their fifties, greeted each other with clear distaste, just touching hands and kissing without making contact; a small American boy, hoisted on to the shoulders of a father he did not recognise, screamed to be put down, provoking a fit of temper in his tired mother.

But mostly it was smiles and hugs, and in thirty-five minutes I experienced more than fifty theatrical happy endings, each one with the appearance of being slightly less well acted than the one before, until I began to feel emotionally exhausted and suspected that even the children were being insincere. I was just wondering how convincing I myself could be now in greeting Clarissa when she tapped me on the shoulder, having missed me in the crowd and circled round. Immediately my detachment vanished, and I called out her name, in tune with all the rest.

Less than an hour later we were parked by a track that ran through beech woods in the Chiltern Hills, near Christmas Common.[5] While Clarissa changed her shoes I loaded a backpack with our picnic. We set off down our path arm in arm, still elated by our reunion; what was familiar about her— the size and feel of her hand, the warmth and tranquillity in her voice, the Celt's pale skin and green eyes—was also novel, gleaming in an alien light, reminding me of our very first meetings and the months we spent falling in love. Or, I imagined, I was another man, my own sexual competitor, come to steal her from me. When I told her she laughed and said I was the world's most complicated simpleton, and it was while we stopped to kiss and wondered aloud whether we should not have driven straight home to bed, that we glimpsed through the fresh foliage the helium balloon drifting dreamily across the wooded valley to our west. Neither the man nor the boy were visible to us. I remember thinking, but not saying, that it was a precarious form of transport when the wind, rather than the pilot, set the course. Then I thought that perhaps this was the very nature of its attraction. And instantly the idea went out of my mind.

We went through College Wood towards Pishill,[6] stopping to admire the new greenery on the beeches. Each leaf seemed to glow with an internal light. We talked about the purity of this colour, the beech leaf in spring,

5. Village in Oxfordshire. "Chiltern Hills": a range of chalk hills to the west of London.

6. Village in Oxfordshire in the Chiltern Hills.

and how looking at it cleared the mind. As we walked into the wood the wind began to get up and the branches creaked like rusted machinery. We knew this route well. This was surely the finest landscape within an hour of central London. I loved the pitch and roll of the fields and their scatterings of chalk and flint, and the paths that dipped across them to sink into the darkness of the beech stands, certain neglected, badly drained valleys where thick iridescent mosses covered the rotting tree trunks and where you occasionally glimpsed a muntjak[7] blundering through the undergrowth.

For much of the time as we walked westwards we were talking about Clarissa's research—John Keats dying in Rome in the house at the foot of the Spanish Steps where he lodged with his friend Joseph Severn. Was it possible there were still three or four unpublished letters of Keats' in existence? Might one of them be addressed to Fanny Brawne?[8] Clarissa had reason to think so and had spent part of a sabbatical term travelling around Spain and Portugal, visiting houses known to Fanny Brawne and to Keats' sister Fanny. Now she was back from Boston where she had been working in the Houghton Library at Harvard, trying to trace correspondence from Severn's remote family connections. Keats' last known letter was written almost three months before he died to his old friend Charles Brown.[9] It's rather stately in tone, and typical in throwing out, almost as a parenthesis, a brilliant description of artistic creation—'the knowledge of contrast, feeling for light and shade, all that information (primitive sense) necessary for a poem are great enemies to the recovery of the stomach.' It's the one with the famous farewell, so piercing in its reticence and courtesy: 'I can scarcely bid you goodbye, even in a letter. I always made an awkward bow. God bless you! John Keats.' But the biographies agreed that Keats was in remission from tuberculosis when he wrote this letter, and remained so for a further ten days. He visited the Villa Borghese, and strolled down the Corso. He listened with pleasure to Severn playing Haydn,[1] he mischievously tipped his dinner out the window in protest at the quality of the cooking, and he even thought about starting a poem. If letters existed from this period why would Severn or, more likely, Brown, have wanted to suppress them? Clarissa thought she had found the answer in a couple of references in correspondence between distant relations of Brown's written in the 1840s, but she needed more evidence, different sources.

'He knew he'd never see Fanny again,' Clarissa said. 'He wrote to Brown and said that to see her name written would be more than he could bear. But he never stopped thinking about her. He was strong enough those days in December, and he loved her so hard. It's easy to imagine him writing a letter he never intended to send.'

I squeezed her hand and said nothing. I knew little about Keats or his poetry, but I thought it possible that in his hopeless situation he would not have wanted to write precisely because he loved her so much. Lately I'd had the idea that Clarissa's interest in these hypothetical letters had something

---

7. Small deer.
8. Frances Brawne (1800–1865), fiancée of John Keats (1795–1821), English Romantic poet, who went to Italy with his friend the English painter Joseph Severn (1793–1879), in September 1820 to recover from tuberculosis. "The Spanish Steps": hillside staircase in Rome.

9. English writer and friend of Keats (1787–1842).
1. Franz Joseph Haydn (1732–1809), Austrian composer. "Villa Borghese": art museum with lavish gardens in Rome. "The Corso": street near the Villa Borghese.

to do with our own situation, and with her conviction that love that did not find its expression in a letter was not perfect. In the months after we met, and before we bought the apartment, she had written me some beauties, passionately abstract in their exploration of the ways our love was different from and superior to any that had ever existed. Perhaps that's the essence of a love letter, to celebrate the unique. I had tried to match hers, but all that sincerity would permit me were the facts, and they seemed miraculous enough to me: a beautiful woman loved and wanted to be loved by a large, clumsy, balding fellow who could hardly believe his luck.

We stopped to watch the buzzard as we were approaching Maidensgrove.[2] The balloon may have re-crossed our path while we were in the woods that cover the valleys around the nature reserve. By the early afternoon we were on the Ridgeway Path walking north along the line of the escarpment.[3] Then we struck out along one of those broad fingers of land that project westwards from the Chilterns into the rich farmland below. Across the Vale of Oxford we could make out the outlines of the Cotswold Hills and beyond them, perhaps, the Brecon Beacons[4] rising in a faint blue mass. Our plan had been to picnic right out on the end where the view was best, but the wind was too strong by now. We went back across the field and sheltered among the oaks along the northern side. And it was because of these trees that we did not see the balloon's descent. Later I wondered why it had not been blown miles away. Later still I discovered that the wind at five hundred feet was not the same that day as the wind at ground level.

The Keats conversation faded as we unpacked our lunch. Clarissa pulled the bottle from the bag and held it by its base as she offered it to me. As I have said, the neck touched my palm as we heard the shout. It was a baritone, on a rising note of fear. It marked the beginning and, of course, an end. At that moment a chapter, no, a whole stage of my life closed. Had I known, and had there been a spare second or two, I might have allowed myself a little nostalgia. We were seven years into a childless marriage of love. Clarissa Mellon was also in love with another man, but with his two hundredth birthday coming up he was little trouble. In fact he helped in the combative exchanges which were part of our equilibrium, our way of talking about work. We lived in an art deco apartment block in north London with a below average share of worries—a money shortage for a year or so, an unsubstantiated cancer scare, the divorces and illnesses of friends, Clarissa's irritation with my occasional and manic bouts of dissatisfaction with my kind of work—but there was nothing that threatened our free and intimate existence.

What we saw when we stood from our picnic was this: a huge grey balloon, the size of a house, the shape of a tear drop, had come down in the field. The pilot must have been half way out of the passenger basket as it touched the ground. His leg had become entangled in a rope that was attached to an anchor. Now, as the wind gusted, and pushed and lifted the balloon towards the escarpment, he was being half dragged, half carried across the field. In the basket was a child, a boy of about ten. In a sudden lull, the man was on

2. Village in Oxfordshire.
3. Abrupt face or cliff. "The Ridgeway Path": British National Trail along the Chiltern Hills.
4. Mountain range in South Wales. "The Vale of Oxford": valley containing Oxford. "Cotswold Hills": range of hills in west-central England to the west of Oxford.

his feet, clutching at the basket, or at the boy. Then there was another gust, and the pilot was on his back, bumping over the rough ground, trying to dig his feet in for purchase, or lunging for the anchor behind him in order to secure it in the earth. Even if he had been able, he would not have dared disentangle himself from the anchor rope. He needed his weight to keep the balloon on the ground, and the wind could have snatched the rope from his hands.

As I ran I heard him shouting at the boy, urging him to leap clear of the basket. But the boy was tossed from one side to another as the balloon lurched across the field. He regained his balance and got a leg over the edge of the basket. The balloon rose and fell, thumping into a hummock, and the boy dropped backwards out of sight. Then he was up again, arms stretched out towards the man and shouting something in return—words or inarticulate fear, I couldn't tell.

I must have been a hundred yards away when the situation came under control. The wind had dropped, the man was on his feet, bending over the anchor as he drove it into the ground. He had unlooped the rope from his leg. For some reason, complacency, exhaustion or simply because he was doing what he was told, the boy remained where he was. The towering balloon wavered and tilted and tugged, but the beast was tamed. I slowed my pace, though I did not stop. As the man straightened, he saw us—or at least the farm workers and me—and he waved us on. He still needed help, but I was glad to slow to a brisk walk. The farm labourers were also walking now. One of them was coughing loudly. But the man with the car, John Logan, knew something we didn't and kept on running. As for Jed Parry, my view of him was blocked by the balloon that lay between us.

The wind renewed its rage in the treetops just before I felt its force on my back. Then it struck the balloon which ceased its innocent comical wagging and was suddenly stilled. Its only motion was a shimmer of strain that rippled out across its ridged surface as the contained energy accumulated. It broke free, the anchor flew up in a spray of dirt, and balloon and basket rose ten feet in the air. The boy was thrown back, out of sight. The pilot had the rope in his hands and was lifted two feet clear off the ground. If Logan had not reached him and taken hold of one of the many dangling lines the balloon would have carried the boy away. Instead, both men were now being pulled across the field, and the farm workers and I were running again.

I got there before them. When I took a rope the basket was above head height. The boy inside it was screaming. Despite the wind, I caught the smell of urine. Jed Parry was on a rope seconds after me, and the two farm workers, Joseph Lacey and Toby Greene, caught hold just after him. Greene was having a coughing fit, but he kept his grip. The pilot was shouting instructions at us, but too frantically, and no one was listening. He had been struggling too long, and now he was exhausted and emotionally out of control. With five of us on the lines the balloon was secured. We simply had to keep steady on our feet and pull hand over hand to bring the basket down, and this, despite whatever the pilot was shouting, was what we began to do.

By this time we were standing on the escarpment. The ground dropped away sharply at a gradient of about twenty-five per cent, and then levelled out into a gentle slope towards the bottom. In winter this is a favourite tobogganing spot for local kids. We were all talking at once. Two of us, myself and the motorist, wanted to walk the balloon away from the edge. Someone thought the priority was to get the boy out. Someone else was calling for the balloon to be pulled down so that we could anchor it firmly. I saw no contradiction, for we could be pulling the balloon down as we moved back into the field. But the second opinion was prevailing. The pilot had a fourth idea, but no one knew or cared what it was.

I should make something clear. There may have been a vague communality of purpose, but we were never a team. There was no chance, no time. Coincidences of time and place, a predisposition to help had brought us together under the balloon. No one was in charge—or everyone was, and we were in a shouting match. The pilot, red-faced, bawling and sweating, we ignored. Incompetence came off him like heat. But we were beginning to bawl our own instructions too. I know that if I had been uncontested leader the tragedy would not have happened. Later I heard some of the others say the same thing about themselves. But there was not time, no opportunity for force of character to show. Any leader, any firm plan would have been preferable to none. No human society, from the hunter-gatherer to the post-industrial, has come to the attention of anthropologists that did not have its leaders and the led; and no emergency was ever dealt with effectively by democratic process.

It was not so difficult to bring the passenger basket down low enough for us to see inside. We had a new problem. The boy was curled up on the floor. His arms covered his face and he was gripping his hair tightly. 'What's his name?' we said to the red-faced man.

'Harry.'

'Harry!' we shouted. 'Come on Harry. Harry! Take my hand, Harry. Get out of there Harry!'

But Harry curled up tighter. He flinched each time we said his name. Our words were like stones thrown down at his body. He was in paralysis of will, a state known as learned helplessness, often noted in laboratory animals subjected to unusual stress; all impulses to problem-solving disappear, all instinct for survival drains away. We pulled the basket down to the ground and managed to keep it there, and we were just leaning in to try and lift the boy out when the pilot shouldered us aside and attempted to climb in. He said later that he told us what he was trying to do. We heard nothing but our own shouting and swearing. What he was doing seemed ridiculous, but his intentions, it turned out, were completely sensible. He wanted to deflate the balloon by pulling a cord that was tangled in the basket.

'Yer great pillock!'[5] Lacey shouted. 'Help us reach the lad out.'

I heard what was coming two seconds before it reached us. It was as though an express train were traversing the treetops, hurtling towards us. An airy, whining, whooshing sound grew to full volume in half a second. At the inquest the Met office[6] figures for wind speeds that day were part of the evidence, and there were some gusts, it was said, of seventy miles an hour. This must have been one, but before I let it reach us, let me freeze the frame— there's a security in stillness—to describe our circle.

To my right the ground dropped away. Immediately to my left was John Logan, a family doctor from Oxford, forty-two years old, married to a historian, with two children. He was not the youngest of our group, but he was the

---

5. Idiot.
6. National Weather Service of the United Kingdom.

fittest. He played tennis to county level, and belonged to a mountaineering club. He had done a stint with a mountain rescue team in the Western Highlands.[7] Logan was a mild, reticent man apparently, otherwise he might have been able to force himself usefully on us as a leader. To his left was Joseph Lacey, sixty-three, farm labourer, odd job man, captain of his local bowls[8] team. He lived with his wife in Watlington, a small town at the foot of the escarpment. On his left was his mate, Toby Greene, fifty-eight, also a farm labourer, unmarried, living with his mother at Russell's Water.[9] Both men worked for the Stonor estate. Greene was the one with the smoker's cough. Next around the circle, trying to get into the basket, was the pilot, James Gadd, fifty-five, an executive in a small advertising company, who lived in Reading[1] with his wife and one of their grown-up children who was mentally handicapped. At the inquest Gadd was found to have breached half a dozen basic safety procedures which the coroner listed tonelessly. Gadd's ballooning licence was withdrawn. The boy in the basket was Harry Gadd, his grandson, ten years old, from Camberwell, London.[2] Facing me, with the ground sloping away to his left, was Jed Parry. He was twenty-eight, unemployed, living on an inheritance in Hampstead.

This was the crew. As far as we were concerned, the pilot had abdicated his authority. We were breathless, excited, determined on our separate plans, while the boy was beyond participating in his own survival. He lay in a heap, blocking out the world with his forearms. Lacey, Greene and I were attempting to fish him out, and now Gadd was climbing over the top of us. Logan and Parry were calling out their own suggestions. Gadd had placed one foot by his grandson's head, and Greene was cussing him when it happened. A mighty fist socked the balloon in two rapid blows, one-two, the second more vicious than the first. And the first was vicious. It jerked Gadd right out of the basket on to the ground, and it lifted the balloon five feet or so, straight into the air. Gadd's considerable weight was removed from the equation. The rope ran through my grip, scorching my palms, but I managed to keep hold, with two feet of line spare. The others kept hold too. The basket was right above our heads now, and we stood with arms upraised like Sunday bell ringers. Into our amazed silence, before the shouting could resume, the second punch came and knocked the balloon up and westwards. Suddenly we were treading the air with all our weight in the grip of our fists.

Those one or two ungrounded seconds occupy as much space in memory as might a long journey up an uncharted river. My first impulse was to hang on in order to keep the balloon weighted down. The child was incapable, and was about to be borne away. Two miles to the west were high-voltage power lines. A child alone and needing help. It was my duty to hang on, and I thought we would all do the same.

Almost simultaneous with the desire to stay on the rope and save the boy, barely a neuronal pulse later, came other thoughts in which fear and instant calculations of logarithmic complexity were fused. We were rising, and the ground was dropping away as the balloon was pushed westwards. I knew I had to get my legs and feet locked round the rope. But the end of the line barely reached below my waist and my grip was slipping. My legs

7. In Scotland.
8. Outdoor bowling game.
9. Oxfordshire hamlet.

1. Town west of London.
2. District in southeast London.

flailed in the empty air. Every fraction of a second that passed increased the drop, and the point must come when to let go would be impossible or fatal. And compared to me Harry was safe curled up in the basket. The balloon might well come down safely at the bottom of the hill. And perhaps my impulse to hang on was nothing more than a continuation of what I had been attempting moments before, simply a failure to adjust quickly.

And again, less than one adrenally incensed heartbeat later, another variable was added to the equation: someone let go, and the balloon and its hangers-on lurched upwards another several feet.

I didn't know, nor have I ever discovered, who let go first. I'm not prepared to accept that it was me. But everyone claims not to have been first. What is certain is that if we had not broken ranks, our collective weight would have brought the balloon to earth a quarter of the way down the slope a few seconds later as the gust subsided. But as I've said, there was no team, there was no plan, no agreement to be broken. No failure. So can we accept that it was right, every man for himself? Were we all happy afterwards that this was a reasonable course? We never had that comfort, for there was a deeper covenant, ancient and automatic, written in our nature. Co-operation—the basis of our earliest hunting successes, the force behind our evolving capacity for language, the glue of our social cohesion. Our misery in the aftermath was proof that we knew we had failed ourselves. But letting go was in our nature too. Selfishness is also written on our hearts. This is our mammalian conflict—what to give to the others, and what to keep for yourself. Treading that line, keeping the others in check, and being kept in check by them, is what we call morality. Hanging a few feet above the Chilterns escarpment, our crew enacted morality's ancient, irresolvable dilemma: us, or me.

Someone said *me*, and then there was nothing to be gained by saying *us*. Mostly, we are good when it makes sense. A good society is one that makes sense of being good. Suddenly, hanging there below the basket, we were a bad society, we were disintegrating. Suddenly the sensible choice was to look out for yourself. The child was not my child, and I was not going to die for it. The moment I glimpsed a body fall away—but whose?—and I felt the balloon lurch upwards, the matter was settled; altruism had no place. Being good made no sense. I let go and fell, I reckon, about twelve feet. I landed heavily on my side and got away with a bruised thigh. Around me—before or after, I'm not so sure—bodies were thumping to the ground. Jed Parry was unhurt. Toby Greene broke his ankle. Joseph Lacey, the oldest, who had done his National Service[3] with a paratroop regiment, did no more than wind himself.

By the time I got to my feet the balloon was fifty yards away, and one man was still dangling by his rope. In John Logan, husband, father, doctor and mountain rescue worker, the flame of altruism must have burned a little stronger. It didn't need much. When four of us let go, the balloon, with six hundred pounds shed, must have surged upwards. A delay of one second would have been enough to close his options. When I stood up and saw him, he was a hundred feet up, and rising, just where the ground itself was falling. He wasn't struggling, he wasn't kicking or trying to claw his way up. He hung perfectly still along the line of the rope, all his energies concentrated in his

---

3. Compulsory service in the armed forces, in effect for young men in Britain between 1939 and 1962.

weakening grip. He was already a tiny figure, almost black against the sky. There was no sight of the boy. The balloon and its basket lifted away and westwards, and the smaller Logan became, the more terrible it was, so terrible it was funny, it was a stunt, a joke, a cartoon, and a frightened laugh heaved out of my chest. For this was preposterous, the kind of thing that happened to Bugs Bunny, or Tom, or Jerry, and for an instant, I thought it wasn't true, and that only I could see right through the joke, and that my utter disbelief would set reality straight and see Dr Logan safely to the ground.

I don't know whether the others were standing, or sprawling. Toby Greene was probably doubled up over his ankle. But I do remember the silence into which I laughed. No exclamations, no shouted instructions as before. Mute helplessness. He was two hundred yards away now, and perhaps three hundred feet above the ground. Our silence was a kind of acceptance, a death warrant. Or it was horrified shame, because the wind had dropped, and barely stirred against our backs. He had been on the rope so long that I began to think he might stay there until the balloon drifted down, or the boy came to his senses and found the valve that released the gas, or until some beam, or god, or some other impossible cartoon thing came and gathered him up. Even as I had that hope we saw him slip down right to the end of the rope. And still he hung there. For two seconds, three, four. And then he let go. Even then, there was a fraction of time when he barely fell, and I still thought there was a chance that a freak physical law, a furious thermal, some phenomenon no more astonishing than the one we were witnessing would intervene and bear him up. We watched him drop. You could see the acceleration. No forgiveness, no special dispensation for flesh, or bravery, or kindness. Only ruthless gravity. And from somewhere, perhaps from him, perhaps from some indifferent crow, a thin squawk cut through the stilled air. He fell as he had hung, a stiff little black stick. I've never seen such a terrible thing as that falling man.

Two

Best to slow down. Let's give the half minute after John Logan's fall careful consideration. What occurred simultaneously or in quick succession, what was said, how we moved or failed to move, what I thought—these elements need to be separated out. So much followed from this incident, so much branching and subdivision began in those early moments, such pathways of love and hatred blazed from this starting position, that a little reflection, even pedantry, can only help me here. The best description of a reality does not need to mimic its velocity. Whole books, whole research departments, are dedicated to the first half minute in the history of the universe. Vertiginous theories of chaos and turbulence are predicated upon the supremacy of initial conditions which need painstaking depiction.

I've already marked my beginning, the explosion of consequences, with the touch of a wine bottle and a shout of distress. But this pinprick is as notional as a point in Euclidean geometry, and though it seems right, I could have proposed the moment Clarissa and I planned to picnic after I had collected her from the airport, or when we decided on our route, or the field in which to have our lunch, and the time we chose to have it. There are always antecedent causes. A beginning is an artifice, and what recommends one over another is how much sense it makes of what follows. The cool touch of glass on skin and James Gadd's cry—these synchronous moments fix a transition, a divergence from the expected: from the wine we didn't taste (we drank it that night to numb ourselves) to the summons, from the delightful existence we shared and expected to continue, to the ordeal we were to endure in the time ahead.

When I let the wine bottle fall to run across the field towards the balloon and its bumping basket, towards Jed Parry and the others, I chose a branching in the paths that foreclosed a certain kind of easeful life. The struggle with the ropes, the breaking of ranks and the bearing away of Logan— these were the obvious, large-scale events that shaped our story. But I see now that in the moments immediately after his fall there were subtler elements exerting powerful sway over the future. The moment Logan hit the ground should have been the end of this story rather than one more beginning I could have chosen. The afternoon could have ended in mere tragedy.

In the second or two it took for Logan to reach the ground I had a sense of *déjà vu*, and I immediately knew its source. What came back to me was a nightmare I had occasionally in my twenties and thirties from which I used to shout myself awake. The setting varied, but the essentials never did. I found myself in a prominent place watching from far off the unfolding of a disaster—an earthquake, a fire in a skyscraper, a sinking ship, an erupting volcano. I could see helpless people, reduced by distance to an undifferentiated mass, scurrying about in panic, certain to die. The horror was in the contrast between their apparent size and the enormity of their suffering. Life was revealed as cheap; thousands of screaming individuals, no bigger than ants, were about to be annihilated and I could do nothing to help. I did not think about the dream then so much as experience its emotional wash—terror, guilt and helplessness were the components—and feel the nausea of a premonition fulfilled.

Down below us, where the escarpment levelled out, was a grassy field used for pasture, bounded by a line of pollarded[4] willows. Beyond them was a larger pasture where sheep and a few lambs were grazing. It was in the centre of this second field, in our full view, that Logan landed. My impression was that at the moment of impact the little stick figure flowed or poured outwards across the ground, like a drop of viscous fluid. But what we saw in the stillness, as though reconstituted, was the compact dot of his huddled figure. The nearest sheep, twenty feet away, barely looked up from its chewing.

Joseph Lacey was attending to his friend Toby Greene who could not stand. Right next to me was Jed Parry. Some way off behind us was James Gadd. He was less interested than we were in Logan. He was shouting about his grandson who was being carried away in the balloon across the Vale of Oxford towards the line of pylons.[5] Gadd pushed past us and went a few paces down the hill, as if intending to go in pursuit. Such is his genetic investment, I remember thinking stupidly. Clarissa came up behind me and looped her arms around my waist and pressed her face into my back. What surprised me was she was already crying (I could feel the wetness on my shirt) whereas to me, sorrow seemed a long way off.

---

4. With upper trunk and branches cut back.   5. Metal towers for overhead electrical lines.

Like a self in a dream I was both first and third persons. I acted, and saw myself act. I had my thoughts, and I saw them drift across a screen. As in a dream, my emotional responses were non-existent or inappropriate. Clarissa's tears were no more than a fact, but I was pleased by the way my feet were anchored to the ground and set well apart, and the way my arms were folded across my chest. I looked out across the fields and the thought scrolled across: *that man is dead.* I felt a warmth spreading through me, a kind of self-love, and my folded arms hugged me tight. The corollary seemed to be: *and I am alive.* It was a random matter, who was alive or dead at any given time. I happened to be alive. This was when I noticed Jed Parry watching me. His long bony face was framed round a pained question. He looked wretched, like a dog about to be punished. In the second or so that this stranger's clear grey-blue eyes held mine I felt I could include him in the self-congratulatory warmth I felt in being alive. It even crossed my mind to touch him comfortingly on the shoulder. My thoughts were up there on the screen: *this man is in shock. He wants me to help him.*

Had I known what this glance meant to him at the time, and how he was to construe it later and build around it a mental life, I would not have been so warm. In his pained, interrogative look was that first bloom of which I was entirely ignorant. The euphoric calm I felt was simply a symptom of my shock. I honoured Parry with a friendly nod and, ignoring Clarissa at my back—I was a busy man, I would deal with them all one at a time—I said to him in what I thought was a deep and reassuring voice, 'It's all right.'

This flagrant untruth reverberated so pleasantly between my ribs that I almost said it again. Perhaps I did. I was the first one to have spoken since Logan hit the ground. I reached into my trouser pocket and withdrew, of all things to have out here at this time, a mobile phone. I read the fractional widening of the young man's eyes as respect. It was what I felt for myself anyway as I held the dense little slab in my palm, and with the thumb of the same hand jabbed three nines. I was in the world, equipped, capable, connected. When the emergency operator came on I asked for police and ambulance and gave a lucid, minimal account of the accident and the balloon drifting away with the boy, and our position and the nearest access by road. It was all I could do to hold my excitement in. I wanted to shout something—commands, exhortations, inarticulate vowel sounds. I was brittle, speedy, perhaps I looked happy.

When I turned off the phone Joseph Lacey said, 'He won't need no ambulance.'

Greene looked up from his ankle. 'They'll need that to take him away.'

I remembered. Of course. This was what I needed—something to do. I was wild by now, ready to fight, run, dance, you name it. 'He might not be dead,' I said. 'There's always a chance. We'll go down and take a look.'

As I was saying this I became aware of a tremor in my legs. I wanted to stride away down the slope, but I did not trust my balance. Uphill would be better. I said to Parry, 'You'll come.' I meant it as a suggestion, but it came out as a request, something I needed from him. He looked at me, unable to speak. Everything, every gesture, every word I spoke was being stored away, gathered and piled, fuel for the long winter of his obsession.

I unclasped Clarissa's arms from my waist and turned. It didn't occur to me that she was trying to hold me steady. 'Let's go down,' I said quietly. 'There may be something we can do.' I heard my softening of tone, the artful lowering of volume. I was in a soap opera. *Now he's talking to his woman.* It was intimacy, a tight two-shot.

Clarissa put her hand on my shoulder. She told me later that it crossed her mind to slap my face. 'Joe,' she whispered. 'You've got to slow down.'

'What's up?' I said in a louder voice. A man lay dying in a field and no one was stirring. Clarissa looked at me, and though her mouth looked set to frame the words, she wouldn't tell me why I should slow down. I turned away and called to the others who stood about on the grass waiting for me, so I thought, to tell them what to do. 'I'm going down to him. Is anyone coming?' I didn't wait for an answer, but set off down the hill, conscious of the watery looseness in my knees and taking short steps. Twenty seconds later I glanced back. No one had moved.

As I carried on down, the mania began to subside and I felt trapped and lonely in my decision. Also there was the fear, not quite in me, but there in the field, spread like a mist, and denser at the core. I was walking into it without choice now, because they were watching me, and to turn back would have meant climbing up the hill, a double humiliation. As the euphoria lifted, so the fear seeped in. The dead man I did not want to meet was waiting for me in the middle of the field. Even worse would be finding him alive and dying. Then I'd have to face him alone with my first aid techniques, like so many silly party tricks. He wouldn't be taken in. He would go ahead and die anyway, and his death would be in and on my hands. I wanted to turn and shout for Clarissa, but they were watching me, I knew, and I had blustered so much up there I was ashamed. This long descent was my punishment.

I reached the line of pollarded willows at the bottom of the hill, crossed a dry ditch and climbed through a barbed wire fence. By now I was out of their sight and I wanted to be sick. Instead, I urinated against a tree trunk. My hand was trembling badly. Afterwards I stood still, delaying the moment when I would have to set out across the field. Being out of view was physical relief, like being shaded from a desert sun. I was conscious of Logan's position, but even at this distance I didn't care to look.

The sheep that had hardly glanced up at the impact, stared and backed away into faltering runs as I strode among them. I was feeling slightly better. I kept Logan at the periphery of vision, but even so, I knew he was not flat on the ground. Something protruded at the centre of the field, some stumpy antenna of his present or previous self. Not until I was twenty yards away did I permit myself to see him. He was sitting upright, his back to me, as though meditating, or gazing in the direction in which the balloon and Harry had drifted. There was calmness in his posture. I came closer, instinctively troubled to be approaching him unseen from behind, but glad I could not yet see his face. I still clung to the possibility that there was a technique, a physical law or process of which I knew nothing, that would permit him to survive. That he should sit there so quietly in the field, as though he were collecting himself after his terrible experience, gave me hope and made me clear my throat stupidly and say, knowing that no one else could hear me, 'Do you need help?' It was not so ridiculous at the time. I could see his hair curling over his shirt collar and sunburned skin along the tops of his ears.

His tweed jacket was unmarked, though it drooped strangely, for his shoulders were narrower than they should have been. They were narrower than any adult's could be. From the base of the neck there was no lateral spread. The skeletal structure had collapsed internally to produce a head on a thickened stick. And seeing that, I became aware that what I had taken for calmness was *absence*. There was no one there. The quietness was that of the inanimate, and I understood again, because I had seen dead bodies before, why a pre-scientific age would have needed to invent the soul. It was no less clear than the illusion of the evening sun sinking through the sky. The closing down of countless interrelated neural and bio-chemical exchanges combined to suggest to a naked eye the illusion of the extinguished spark, or the simple departure of a single necessary element. However scientifically informed we count ourselves to be, fear and awe still surprise us in the presence of the dead. Perhaps it's life we're really wondering at.

* * *

1997

ZADIE SMITH
b. 1975

The London-born daughter of an English father and a Jamaican mother, Zadie Smith was a product of the great postwar demographic change in Britain, the influx of black and Asian immigrants from the empire's former colonies. Her mother had grown up in Jamaica and like many other West Indians settled in Britain in the 1960s. Of her mixed heritage Smith has written, "When your personal multiplicity is printed on your face, in an almost too obviously thematic manner, in your DNA, in your hair and in the neither this nor that beige of your skin—well, anyone can see you come from Dream City," her tongue-in-cheek name for the space of hybridity. "It is a place of many voices, where the unified singular self is an illusion," where "everything is doubled, everything is various. You have no choice but to cross borders and speak in tongues." Springing from the experience of "personal multiplicity," Smith's fiction has vigorously crossed borders and spoken in a cacophony of tongues.

Smith grew up in what she has called "the big, colorful, working-class sea" of the Willesden area of north London that figures in her fiction. When she was studying English literature at the "smaller, posher pond" (her words) of Cambridge University (B.A., 1997), her fiction had already attracted the interest of major publishers. The result was her prize-winning first novel, *White Teeth* (2000). Before its publication, no work had captured with such humor and zest the multicultural jangle of different peoples, dialects, and styles in contemporary Britain. Less riotously comic, her second novel, *The Autograph Man* (2002), tracked the celebrity quest of a Chinese-Jewish Londoner named Alex-Li Tandem, mourning his father's death in a world made shallow by the commodification of culture, the arts, personality, and ethnicity. Her third novel, *On Beauty* (2005), shifted locales from London largely to the Boston environs, where Smith had spent a year, and deliberately echoed English author E. M. Forster's *Howards End* (1910) in telling the story of two entangled families.

Smith is still best known for her first novel, despite her subsequent successes. A year before *White Teeth* came out, she published the short story "The Waiter's Wife," the work given here that includes scenes and characters that also appear in the novel's third and fourth chapters. The story confects many of the formal ingredients that made her novel famous, including her wisecracking humor and rapid-fire dialogue, mimicry of an array of finely distinguished dialects and accents, and vibrant characterization of people from London's South Asian, black, and other communities. This is a world of often surprising interchanges between East and West, raucous debates about secularism and religion and gender, cross-cultural friendships and marriages that blur the dividing lines among Asians, Caribbeans, Jews, the English, and many others.

Zadie Smith (b. 1975) in 2001, a year after the publication of her first novel, *White Teeth*.

Reveling in cultural and human comminglings, *White Teeth* tells the intertwined stories of three London families, the Anglo-Jamaican Joneses, the Bengali Iqbals, and the Anglo-Jewish Chalfens. At the heart of this sprawling novel is the friendship between the white Englishman Archie Jones and the Bengali Muslim Samad Iqbal. Having met during their less than heroic tour of duty in World War II, they renew their odd-couple bond when Samad leaves Bangladesh for London in 1975, and over time their much younger wives, the gap-toothed Jamaican Clara and the fierce Bangladeshi immigrant Alsana, also begin a friendship. Although each character misconceives other cultures, Smith's focus is less on intercultural strife than on fluid if often bumpy relationships across ethnic divisions. The threat of racist attacks on Bangladeshis in 1970s London hovers in the background (right-wing "kids breaking the basement windows with their steel-capped boots"; Asian families "running to the cellars while windows were smashed"). But in the foreground is an irreversibly hybridized and multiracial Britain. In this world, pulsing with energy and humor and surprise, an underemployed Bengali waiter daydreams while listening to tourists mangle the names of curries; an observant Bengali Muslim woman finds herself sewing black plastic erotic costumes; two pregnant women—one African Caribbean and one South Asian—squeeze with a third woman onto a park bench and exchange thoughts on gender, marriage, and baby names.

In a synoptic passage worth quoting from *White Teeth*, Smith uncovers, in names, emblems of Britain's new cultural heterogeneity:

> This has been the century of strangers, brown, yellow, and white. This has been the century of the great immigrant experiment. It is only this late in the day that you can walk into a playground and find Isaac Leung by the fish pond, Danny Rahman in the football cage, Quang O'Rourke bouncing a basketball, and Irie Jones humming a tune. Children with first and last names on a direct collision course. Names that secrete within them mass exodus, cramped boats and planes, cold arrivals, medical checkups. It is only this late in the day, and possibly only in Willesden, that you can find best friends Sita and Sharon, constantly mistaken for each other because Sita is white (her mother liked the name) and Sharon is Pakistani (her mother thought it best—less trouble).

This is an emerging world that needed the sharp ear, ironic eye, and dazzling wit of Zadie Smith to be named, embodied in plot, and given narrative form. Smith teases out the painful histories of postcolonial migration embedded in her characters' names, yet she also discloses the promise of new criss-crossings of identity, new transnational communities coming into being and yet to be born.

The Waiter's Wife

In the spring of 1975, Samad and Alsana Iqbal left Bangladesh and came to live in Whitechapel, London,[1] the other side of town from Archie and Clara Jones. Samad and Archie had a friendship dating back to the Second World War, back to the hot and claustrophobic Churchill tank in which they sat side by side for three months, close enough to smell each other and to recognize those scents thirty years later when Samad emerged from Gate 12, Heathrow,[2] with a young wife and a paisley patterned luggage set in tow. 'Long time no see,' Archie had said, reaching out to grasp his old friend's palm, but Samad converted the handshake into a hug almost immediately, '*Archibald Jones.* Long time no bloody *smell.*'

They fell back into easy conversation, two old boys slipping swiftly into an acquaintance as comfortable as slippers while their wives stood either side of the bags noting they had this thing in common and no more: that they were young, much younger than the men they stood awkwardly beside. They looked an unlikely pair. Alsana was small and rotund, moon-faced and with thick fingers she hid in the folds of her cardigan. Clara was tall, striking, a black girl with a winning smile, wearing red shorts of a shortness that Alsana had never imagined possible, even in this country.

'Hot pants,' said Clara, shyly, in response to Alsana's wide eyes, 'I made dem myself.'

'I sew also,' Alsana replied, and they had a pleasant enough chat about seams and bobbins, materials and prices per yard, in a motorway service station over an indigestible lunch. 'The wives get on like a house on fire,' Archie had said merrily, giving Samad a nudge in the ribs. But this made them nervous, the two young wives, and after the ice-cream sundaes they sat in silence.

So some black people *are* friendly, thought Alsana after that first meeting was over. It was her habit to single one shining exception out of every minority she disliked; certain dentists, certain singers, certain film stars had been granted specialist treatment in the past and now Clara Jones was to be given Alsana's golden reprieve. Their relations were hesitant in the beginning—a few lunch dates here and there, the occasional coffee; neither wished to admit how much time they had on their hands though newly wed, or that Archie and Samad were always together. It wasn't until the Iqbals moved north, two minutes from Archie and his favourite watering hole, that the women truly resigned themselves to their husbands' mutual appreciation society and started something of a rearguard action. Picnics, the movies, museums, swimming pools—just the two of them. But even when they

1. Poor district where people of Bangladeshi descent are the largest demographic group. 2. London airport.

became fairly close, it was impossible to forget what a peculiar couple they made on the bus, in the park.

It took the Iqbals a year to get to Willesden High Road: a year of mercilessly hard graft to make the momentous move from the wrong side of Whitechapel to the wrong side of Willesden.[3] A year's worth of Alsana banging away at the old Singer machine that sat in the kitchen, sewing together pieces of black plastic for a shop called Domination in Soho[4] (many were the nights Alsana would hold up a piece of clothing she had just made—following the plans she was given—and wonder what on earth it was). A year's worth of Samad softly inclining his head at exactly the correct deferential angle, pencil in his right hand, notepad in his left, listening to the appalling pronunciation of the British, Spanish, American, French, Australian:

Go Bye Ello Sag,[5] Please.

Chicken Jail Fret See[6] Wiv Chips, Fanks.

From six in the evening until four in the morning was work and the rest was sleep, sleep without pause, until daylight was as rare as a decent tip. For what is the point, Samad would think, pushing aside two mints and a receipt to find fifteen pence, what is the point of tipping a man the same amount you would throw in a fountain to chase a wish? But before the illegal thought of folding the fifteen pence discreetly in his napkin hand had a chance to give itself form, Mukhul, Ardashir Mukhul, who ran The Palace and whose wiry frame paced the restaurant, one benevolent eye on the customers, one everwatchful eye on the staff—Ardashir Mukhul was upon him.

'Saaamaad,' he said in his cloying, oleaginous way, 'did you kiss the necessary backside this evening, Cousin?'

Samad and Ardashir were distant cousins, Samad the elder by six years. With what joy (pure bliss!) had Ardashir opened the letter last January, to find his older, cleverer, handsomer cousin could get no work as a food inspector in England and could he possibly . . .

'Fifteen pence, Cousin,' said Samad lifting his palm.

'Well, every little helps, every little helps,' said Ardashir, his dead-fish lips stretching into a stringy smile. 'Into the Piss-Pot with it.'

The Piss-Pot was a black cooking pot that sat on a plinth outside the staff toilets into which all tips were pooled and then split at the end of the night. For the younger, good-looking waiters like Shiva this was a great injustice. Shiva was the only Hindu on the staff, a tribute to his waitering skills that had triumphed over religious difference. He could make fifteen pounds in tips in an evening if the blubberous white divorcee in the corner was lonely enough, and he batted his long lashes at her effectively. He also made money from the polo-necked directors and producers (The Palace sat in the centre of London's Theatreland) who flattered the boy, watched his ass wiggle provocatively to the bar and back, and swore that the next time someone put *A Passage to India*[7] on the stage, the casting couch would be his. For Shiva then, the Piss-Pot system was simply daylight robbery. But for men like Samad, in his forties, and for the even older, like the white-haired Mohammed (Ardashir's great-uncle), who was eighty if he was a day, who had

3. A better-off northwest area with a more heterogeneous population.
4. Area of central London with entertainment and sex industries.
5. Gobi aloo saag, curried potatoes and cauliflower with spinach.
6. Jalfrezi, a curry of onions and green chili.
7. Novel (1924) by English author E. M. Forster (1879–1970), set in 1920s British India.

deep pathways dug into the sides of his mouth where he had smiled when he was young—for men like this the Piss-Pot could not be complained about. It was a boon if anything, and it made more sense to join the collective than pocket fifteen pence and risk being caught (and docked a week's tips).

'You're all on my back!' Shiva would snarl, when he had to relinquish five pounds at the end of the night and drop it into the pot. 'You all live off my back! Somebody get these losers off my back! That was my fiver[8] and now it's going to be split sixty-five-fucking-million ways as a hand out to these losers! What is this, communism?'

And the rest would avoid his glare, and busy themselves quietly with other things until one evening, one fifteen-pence evening, Samad said, 'Shut up, boy,' quietly, almost underneath his breath.

'You!' Shiva swung round to where Samad stood crushing a great tub of lentils for tomorrow's dhal.[9] 'You're the worst of them! You're the worst fucking waiter I've ever seen! You couldn't get a tip if you mugged the bastards! I hear you trying to talk to the customer about biology this, politics that—just serve the food, you idiot—you're a waiter, for fuck's sake, you're not Michael Parkinson.[1] *Did I hear you say Delhi*—' Shiva put his apron over his arm and began posturing around the kitchen (he was a pitiful mimic) '—*I was there myself, you know, Delhi University, it was most fascinating, yes—and I fought in the war, for England, yes—yes, yes, charming, charming—*' round and round the kitchen he went, bending his head and rubbing his hands over and over like Uriah Heep,[2] bowing and genuflecting to the head cook, to the old man arranging great hunks of meat in the walk-in freezer, to the young boy scrubbing the inside of the oven. 'Samad, *Samad* . . .' he said with what seemed infinite pity, then stopped abruptly, pulled the apron off and wrapped it round his waist, 'you're a sad bastard.'

Mohammed looked up from his pot-scrubbing and shook his head again and again. To no one in particular he said, 'These young people—what kind of talk? What happened to respect? What kind of talk is this?'

'And you, you can fuck off too—' said Shiva, brandishing a ladle in his direction, '—You old fool! You're not my father.'

'Second cousin of your mother's uncle,' a voice muttered from the back.

'Bollocks,' said Shiva. 'Bollocks[3] to that.'

He grabbed the mop and was heading off for the toilets, when he stopped by Samad and placed the broom inches from Samad's mouth.

'Kiss it,' he sneered: and then impersonating Ardashir's sluggish drawl, 'Who knows, Cousin, you might get a raise!'

And that's what it was like most nights; abuse from Shiva and others; condescension from Ardashir; never seeing Alsana; never seeing the sun; clutching fifteen pence and then releasing it; wanting desperately to be wearing a sign, a large white placard that said:

> I AM NOT A WAITER. THAT IS, I AM A WAITER, BUT NOT JUST A WAITER. I HAVE BEEN A STUDENT, A SCIENTIST, A SOLDIER. MY WIFE IS CALLED ALSANA. WE LIVE IN EAST LONDON BUT WE WOULD LIKE TO MOVE NORTH. I AM A MUSLIM BUT ALLAH HAS FORSAKEN ME OR I HAVE FORSAKEN ALLAH. I'M NOT SURE. I HAVE AN ENGLISH

8. Five-pound note.
9. Long-cooked dish.
1. English host (b. 1935) of the long-running television show *Parkinson* (1971–1982, 1998–2007).

2. Character in *David Copperfield* (1850), by Charles Dickens.
3. Nonsense; literally, testicles.

FRIEND—ARCHIE—AND OTHERS. I AM FORTY-NINE BUT WOMEN STILL TURN IN THE STREET. SOMETIMES.

But no such placard existing, he had instead the urge, the need, to speak to every man, and like the Ancient Mariner[4] to explain, always to explain, to reassert something, anything. Wasn't that important? But then the heartbreaking disappointment—to find out that the inclining of one's head, poising of one's pen, these were important, so important. It was important to be a good waiter, to listen when someone said:

Lamb Dawn Sock[5] and Rice. Please. With Chips. Thank you.

And fifteen pence clinked on china. Thank you Sir. Thank you so very much.

One evening, shortly after he had put the down payment on the Willesden flat, Samad had waited till everyone left and then climbed the loudly carpeted stairs to Ardashir's office, for he had something to ask him.

'Cousin!' said Ardashir with a friendly grimace at the sight of Samad's body curling cautiously round the door. He knew that Samad had come to enquire about a pay increase, and he wanted his cousin to feel that he had at least considered the case in all his friendly judiciousness before he declined.

'Cousin, come in!'

'Good evening, Ardashir Mukhul,' said Samad, stepping fully into the room.

'Sit down, sit down,' said Ardashir warmly. 'No point standing on ceremony now, is there?'

Samad was glad this was so. He said as much. He took a moment to look with the necessary admiration around the room with its relentless flashes of gold, its thick pile carpet, its furnishings in various shades of yellow and green. One had to admire Ardashir's business sense. He had taken the simple idea of an Indian restaurant (small room, pink tablecloth, loud music, atrocious wallpaper, meals) and just made it bigger. He hadn't improved anything; it was the same old crap but bigger in a bigger building in the biggest tourist trap in London. Leicester Square. You had to admire it and admire the man, who now sat like a benign locust, his slender insectile body swamped in a black leather chair, leaning over the desk, all smiles, a parasite disguised as a philanthropist.

'Cousin, what can I do for you?'

Samad took a deep breath. The matter was . . . what was the matter? The house was the matter. Samad was moving out of East London (where one couldn't bring up children, indeed, one couldn't, not if one didn't wish them to come to bodily harm), from East London, with its National Front[6] gangs, to North London, north-west in fact, where things were more . . . more . . . liberal. Ardashir's eyes glazed over a little as Samad explained his situation. His skinny legs twitched beneath the desk, and in his fingers he manipulated a paperclip until it looked reasonably like an *A. A* for Ardashir.

'I need only a small wage increase to help me finance the move. To make things a little easier as we settle in. And Alsana, well, she is pregnant.'

Pregnant. Difficult. Ardashir realized the case called for extreme diplomacy.

4. Long-winded teller of his sad sea story in the ballad "The Rime of the Ancient Mariner" (1798) by English poet Samuel Taylor Coleridge (1772–1834).

5. Dhansak, a sweet and sour curry.
6. Whites-only, anti-immigrant British political party advocating compulsory repatriation of people of non-European descent.

'Don't mistake me, Samad, we are both intelligent, frank men and I think I can speak frankly . . . I know you're not a *fucking* waiter—' he whispered the expletive and smiled indulgently after it, as if it were a naughty, private thing that brought them closer together, 'I see your position . . . of course I do . . . but you must understand mine . . . If I made allowances for every relative I employ I'd be walking around like bloody Mr Gandhi. Without a pot to piss in. Spinning my thread by the light of the moon.[7] An example: at this very moment that wastrel Fat Elvis brother-in-law of mine, Hussein Ishmael—'

'The butcher?'

'The butcher, demands that I should raise the price I pay for his stinking meat! "But Ardashir, we are brothers-in-law!" he is saying to me. And I am saying to him, but Mohammed, this is *retail* . . .'

It was Samad's turn to glaze over. He thought of his wife, Alsana, who was not as meek as he had assumed when they married, to whom he must deliver the bad news: Alsana, who was prone to moments, even fits—yes, fits was not too strong a word—of rage. Cousins, aunts, brothers thought it a bad sign. They wondered if there wasn't some 'funny mental history' in Alsana's family, they sympathized with him the way you sympathize with a man who has bought a stolen car with more mileage on it than first thought. In his naivety Samad had simply assumed a woman so young would be . . . easy. But Alsana was not . . . no, she was not easy. It was, he supposed, the way with young women these days.

Ardashir came to the end of what he felt was his perfectly worded speech, sat back satisfied, and laid the *M* for Mukhul he had moulded next to the *A* for Ardashir that sat on his lap.

'Thank you, Sir,' said Samad. 'Thank you so very much.'

That evening there was an awful row. Alsana slung the sewing machine, with the black studded hot pants she was working on, to the floor.

'Useless! Tell me, Samad Miah, what is the point of moving here—nice house, yes very nice, very nice—but where is the food?'

'It is a nice area, we have friends here . . .'

'Who are they?' she slammed her little fist on to the kitchen table, sending the salt and pepper flying to collide spectacularly with each other in the air. 'I don't know them! You fight in an old, forgotten war with some Englishman . . . married to a black! Whose friends are they? These are the people my child will grow up around? Their children—half blacky-white? But tell me,' she shouted, returning to her favoured topic, 'where is our food?'

Theatrically, she threw open every cupboard in the kitchen, 'Where is it? Can we eat china?'

Two plates smashed to the floor. She patted her stomach to indicate her unborn child and pointed to the pieces, 'Hungry?'

Samad, who had an equally melodramatic nature when prompted, yanked open the freezer and pulled out a mountain of meat which he piled in the middle of the room. His mother worked through the night preparing meals for her family, he said. His mother did not, he said, spend the household

7. The Indian spiritual and political leader Mohandas Karamchand Gandhi (1869–1948) advocated that Indians spin cloth every day in support of the movement for independence from Britain.

money, as Alsana did, on prepared meals, yogurts and tinned[8] spaghetti. Alsana punched him full square in the stomach.

'Samad Iqbal the traditionalist! Why don't I just squat in the street over a bucket and wash clothes? Eh? In fact, what about my clothes? Edible?'

As Samad clutched his winded belly, there in the kitchen she ripped to shreds every stitch she had on and added them to the pile of frozen lamb, spare cuts from the restaurant. She stood naked before him for a moment, the as yet small mound of her pregnancy in full view, then put on a long, brown coat and left the house.

But all the same, she reflected, slamming the door behind her, it was a nice area; she couldn't deny it as she stormed towards the high street, avoiding pavement trees where previously, in Whitechapel, she had avoided flung-out mattresses and the homeless. It would be good for the child. Alsana had a deep-seated belief that living near green spaces was morally beneficial to the young and there to her right was Gladstone Park, a sweeping horizon of green named after the Liberal prime minister[9] (Alsana was from a respected old Bengal family and had read her English History), and in the Liberal[1] tradition it was a park without fences, unlike the more affluent Queen's Park (Victoria's) with its pointed metal railings. Willesden was not as pretty as Queen's Park but it was a nice area. No denying it. No NF[2] kids breaking the basement windows with their steel-capped boots like in Whitechapel. Now she was pregnant she needed a little bit of peace and quiet. Though it was the same here in a way; they all looked at her strangely, this tiny Indian woman stalking the high street in a mackintosh,[3] her plentiful hair flying every which way. *Mali's Kebabs, Mr Cheungs, Raj's, Malkovich Bakeries*—she read the new, unfamiliar signs as she passed. She was shrewd. She saw what this was. 'Liberal? Hosh-kosh nonsense!' No one was more liberal than anyone else anywhere anyway. It was only that here, in Willesden, there wasn't enough of any one thing to gang up against any other thing and send it running to the cellars while windows were smashed.[4]

'Survival is what it is about!' she concluded out loud (she spoke to her baby: she liked to give it one sensible thought a day), making the bell above Crazy Shoes tinkle as she opened the door. Her niece Neena worked here. It was an old-fashioned cobbler's. Neena fixed heels back on to stilettos.

'Alsana, you look like dog shit,' Neena called over in Bengali. 'What is that horrible coat?'

'It's none of your business is what it is,' replied Alsana in English. 'I came to collect my husband's shoes not to chit-chat with Niece-Of-Shame.'

Neena was used to this, and now Alsana had moved to Willesden there would only be more of it. It used to come in longer sentences (such as, 'Niece, you have brought nothing but shame . . .'), but now because Alsana no longer had the time or energy to summon up the necessary shock each time, it had become abridged to Niece-Of-Shame, an all-purpose tag that summed up the general feeling.

---

8. Canned.
9. William Ewart Gladstone (1809–1898).
1. Gladstone's political party.
2. National Front.

3. Waterproof raincoat.
4. There were numerous racist attacks against Asian and black minorities in 1970s London.

'See these soles?' said Neena, taking Samad's shoes off the shelf and handing Alsana the little blue ticket. 'They were so worn through, Aunty Alsi, I had to reconstruct them from the very base. From the base! What does he do in them? Run marathons?'

'He works,' replied Alsana tersely. 'And prays,' she added, for she liked to make a point of her respectability, and besides she was really very traditional, very religious, lacking nothing except the faith.

'And don't call me Aunty, I am only two years older than you.'

Alsana swept the shoes into a plastic carrier bag and turned to leave.

'I thought that praying was done on people's knees,' said Neena, laughing lightly.

'Both, both, asleep, waking, walking,' snapped Alsana, as she passed under the tinkly bell once more. 'We are never out of sight of the Creator.'

'How's the new house, then?' Neena called after her.

But she had gone. Neena shook her head and sighed as she watched her young aunt disappear down the road like a little brown bullet. Alsana. She was young and old at the same time, Neena reflected. She acted so sensible, so straight-down-the-line in her long sensible coat, but you got the feeling—

'Oi! Miss! There's shoes back here that need your attention!' came a voice from the storeroom.

'Keep your tits on,' said Neena.

At the corner of the road, Alsana popped behind the post office and removed her pinchy sandals in favour of Samad's shoes. (It was an oddity about Alsana. She was small but her feet were enormous, as if she had more growing to do.) In seconds she whipped her hair into an efficient bun, and wrapped her coat tighter around her to keep out the wind. Then she set off, past the library and up a long green road she had never walked along before. 'Survival is all, Little Iqbal,' she said to her bump once more. 'Survival.'

Clara was also pregnant. When their bumps became too large and cinema seats no longer accommodated them, the two women began to meet up for lunch in Kilburn Park,[5] often with the Niece-Of-Shame, the three of them squeezed on to a generous bench, Alsana pressing a thermos of PG Tips[6] into Clara's hand, without milk, with lemon. Unwrapping several layers of cling film to reveal today's peculiar delight: savoury dough-like balls, crumbly Indian sweets shot through with the colours of the kaleidoscope, thin pastry with spiced beef inside, salad with onion, she says to Clara: 'Eat up! Stuff yourself silly! They're in there, wallowing around in your belly, waiting for the menu. Woman, don't torture them! You want to starve the bumps?' for, despite appearances, there are six people on that bench (three living, three coming); one girl for Clara, two boys for Alsana.

Alsana says: 'Nobody's complaining, let's get that straight. A boy is good and two boys is bloody good. But I tell you, when I turned my head and saw the ultra-business thingummybob—'

'Ultrasound,' corrects Clara, through a mouthful of rice.

'—Yes, I almost had the heart attack to finish me off! Two! Feeding one is enough!'

5. In northwest London.   6. Tea.

Clara laughs and says she can imagine Samad's face when he saw it.

'No dearie,'—Alsana is reproving, tucking her large feet underneath the folds of her sari, 'he didn't see anything. He wasn't there. I am not letting him see things like that. A woman has to have the private things—a husband needn't be involved in body-business, in a lady's . . . *parts.*'

Niece-Of-Shame, who is sitting between them, sucks her teeth.

'Bloody Hell, Alsi, he must have been involved in your parts sometime, or is this the immaculate bloody conception?'

'So rude,' says Alsana to Clara in a snooty, English way. 'Too old to be so rude and too young to know any better.' And then Clara and Alsana, with the accidental mirroring that happens when two people are sharing the same experience, both lay their hands on their bulges.

Neena, to redeem herself: 'Yeah, well how are you doing on names? Any ideas?'

Alsana is decisive. '*Magid* and *Millat*. Ems are good. Ems are strong. Mahatma,[7] Mohammed, that funny Mr Morecambe, from Morecambe and Wise[8]—letter you can trust.'

But Clara is more cautious, because naming seems to her a fearful responsibility, a godlike task for a mere mortal: 'I tink I like *Irie*. It patois.[9] Means everyting OK, cool, peaceful, you know?'

Alsana is mock-horrified before the sentence is finished, '"OK"? This is a name for a child? You might as well call her "Wouldsirlikeanypopadums-withthat?"[1] or "Niceweatherwearehaving"—'

'. . . and Archie likes *Sarah*. Well, dere not much you can argue wid Sarah, but dere's not much to get happy bout either. I suppose if it was good enough for the wife of Abraham . . .'

'Ibrahim,'[2] Alsana corrects, out of instinct more than Koranic pedantry. 'Popping out babies when she was a hundred years old, by the grace of Allah.'[3]

And then Neena, groaning at the turn the conversation is taking: 'Well I *like* Irie. It's funky. It's different.'

Alsana loves this: 'For pity's sake, what does Archibald know about *funky* and *different*? If I were you, dearie,' she says patting Clara's knee, 'I'd choose Sarah and let that be an end to it. Sometimes you have to let these men have it their way. Anything for a little—how do you say it in the English? For a little—' she puts her finger over tightly pursed lips, like a guard at the gate, '—*shush.*'

But in response Niece-Of-Shame bats her voluminous eyelashes, wraps her college scarf round her head like purdah,[4] and says, 'Oh yes, Auntie, yes, the little submissive Indian woman. You don't talk to him, he talks at you. You scream and shout at each other, but there's no communication. And in the end he wins anyway because he does whatever he likes when he likes. You don't even know where he is, what he does, what he *feels*, half the time. It's 1975, Alsi. You can't conduct relationships like that any more. It's not like back home. There has to be communication between men and women in the

---

7. Honorific used for Gandhi, meaning "great soul."
8. British television comedy duo with their own show (1961–1983).
9. Jamaican English, or Creole.
1. Papadums are a crisp South Asian bread.

2. Alternate versions of the name of the founding patriarch in Judaism, Christianity, and Islam.
3. In the Koran and the Bible, Sarah miraculously gives birth to Isaac when she is old.
4. Covering.

West, they've got to listen to each other, otherwise . . .' Neena mimes a small mushroom cloud going off in her hand.

'What a load of the codswallop,'[5] says Alsana sonorously, closing her eyes, shaking her head. 'It is you who do not listen. By Allah, I will always give as good as I get. But you presume I *care* what he does. You presume I want to *know*. The truth is, for a marriage to survive you don't need all this talk, talk, talk; all this "I am this" and "I am really like this" like on the television, all this *revelation*—especially when your husband is old, when he is wrinkly and falling apart—you do not *want* to know what is slimy underneath the bed and rattling in the wardrobe.'

Neena frowns. Clara cannot raise serious objection, and the rice is handed around once more.

'Moreover,' says Alsana after a pause, folding her dimpled arms underneath her breasts, pleased to be holding forth on a subject close to this formidable bosom, 'when you are from families such as ours you should have learned that *silence*, what is *not* said, is the very *best* recipe for family life.'

'So let me get this straight,' says Neena, derisively. 'You're saying that a good dose of repression keeps a marriage healthy?'

And as if someone had pressed a button, Alsana is outraged: 'Repression! Nonsense silly-billy[6] word! I'm just talking about common sense. What is my husband? What is yours?' she says pointing to Clara. 'Twenty-five years they live before we are even born. What are they? What are they capable of? What blood do they have on their hands? What is sticky and smelly in their private areas? Who knows?' She throws her hands up, releasing the questions into the unhealthy Kilburn air, sending a troupe of sparrows up with them.

'What you don't understand, my Niece-Of-Shame, what none of your generation understand—'

'But Auntie,' begs Neena, raising her voice, because this is what she really wants to argue about—the largest sticking point between the two of them—Alsana's arranged marriage, 'how could you bear to marry someone you didn't know from Adam?'

In response, an infuriating wink. Alsana always likes to appear jovial at the very moment that her interlocutor becomes hot under the collar. 'Because, *Miss Smarty-pants*, it is by far the easier option. It was exactly because Eve did not know Adam from Adam that they got on so A-OK. Let me explain. Yes, I was married to Samad Iqbal the same evening of the very day I met him. Yes, I didn't know him from Adam. But I liked him well enough. We met in the breakfast room on a steaming Dhaka[7] day and he fanned me with *The Times*. I thought he had a good face, a sweet voice, and his backside was high and well formed for a man of his age. Very good. Now every time I learn something more about him *I like him less*. So you see, we were better off the way we were.'

Neena stamps her foot in exasperation at the skewed logic.

'—Besides, I will never know him well. Getting anything out of my husband is like trying to squeeze water out when you're stoned.'

5. Nonsense (British slang).
6. Here, as elsewhere, Alsana mimics the reduplication (repeating words and forms) common in South Asian languages.
7. Capital of Bangladesh.

Neena laughs despite herself, 'Water out of a stone.'

'Yes, yes. You think I'm so stupid. But I am wise about things like men. I tell you,' Alsana prepares to deliver her summation as she has seen it done many years previously by the young Dhaka lawyers with their slick side-partings, 'men are the last mystery. God is easy compared with men. Now, enough of the philosophy. Samosa?'[8]

She peels the lid off the plastic tub and sits fat, pretty and satisfied on her conclusion.

'Shame that you're having them,' says Neena to her aunt, lighting a fag. 'Boys, I mean. Shame that you're going to have boys.'

'What do you mean?'

This is Clara, who has secretly subscribed (a secret from Alsana and Archie) to a lending library of Neena's through which she has read, in a few short months, *The Female Eunuch* by Greer, *Sex, Race and Class* by Selma James and Jong's *Fear of Flying*,[9] all in a clandestine attempt, on Neena's part, to rid Clara of her 'false consciousness'.[1]

'I mean, I just think men have caused enough chaos this century. There's enough bloody men in the world. If I knew I was going to have a boy . . .' she pauses to prepare her two falsely conscious friends for this new concept, 'I'd have to seriously consider abortion.'

Alsana screams, claps her hands over one of her own ears and one of Clara's, and then almost chokes on a piece of aubergine[2] with the physical exertion. For some reason the remark simultaneously strikes Clara as funny: hysterically, desperately funny, miserably funny; and the Niece-Of-Shame sits between them, nonplussed, while the two egg-shaped women bend over themselves, one in laughter, the other in horror and near asphyxiation.

'Are you all right, ladies?' It is Sol Jozefowicz, the park keeper, standing in front of them, ready as always to be of aid.

'We are all going to burn in hell, Mr Jozefowicz, if you call that being all right . . .' explains Alsana, pulling herself together.

Niece-Of-Shame rolls her eyes: 'Speak for yourself.'

But Alsana is faster than any sniper when it comes to firing back: 'I do, I do—thankfully Allah has arranged it that way.'

'Good afternoon, Neena, good afternoon, Mrs Jones,' says Sol, offering a neat bow to each. 'Are you sure you are all right? Mrs Jones?'

Clara cannot stop the tears from squeezing out of the corners of her eyes. She cannot work out, at this moment, whether she is crying or laughing; the two states suddenly seem only a stone's throw from each other.

'I'm fine, fine. Sorry to have worried you, Mr Jozefowicz. Really, I'm fine.'

'I do not see what so very funny-funny,' mutters Alsana. 'The murder of innocents—is this funny?'

'Not in my experience, Mrs Iqbal, no,' says Sol Jozefowicz[3] in the collected manner in which he says everything, passing his handkerchief to Clara. It strikes all three women—the way history will: embarrassingly, without warn-

8. Stuffed pastry.
9. Studies and a novel, published in 1970, 1974, and 1973, that influenced second-wave feminism.
1. Inability to see oppression and exploitation as they really are.
2. Eggplant.
3. Marked as Jewish by his first name (nickname for Solomon), Eastern European by his last.

ing, like a blush—what the park keeper's experience might have been. They fall silent.

'Well, as long as you ladies are fine, I'll be getting on,' says Sol, motioning that Clara can keep the handkerchief and replacing the hat he had removed in the old fashion. He bows his neat little bow once more, and sets off slowly anticlockwise round the park.

Once Sol is out of earshot Neena says: 'OK, Aunty Alsi. I apologize. I apologize . . . What more do you want?'

'Oh, every-bloody-thing,' says Alsana, her voice losing the fight, becoming vulnerable. 'The whole bloody universe made clear—in a little nutshell. I cannot understand a thing any more, and I am just beginning. You understand?'

She sighs, not waiting for an answer, not looking at Neena, but across the way at the hunched, disappearing figure of Sol winding in and out of the yew trees. 'You may be right about Samad . . . about many things . . . maybe there are no good men, not even the two in this belly . . . and maybe I do not talk enough with mine, maybe I have married a stranger . . . you might see the truth better than I . . . what do I know, a barefoot country girl who never went to the universities . . .'

'Oh, Alsi,' Neena keeps saying, weaving her regret in and out of Alsana's words like tapestry, feeling bad, 'you know I didn't mean it like that.'

'But I cannot be worrying-worrying all the time about the truth. I have to worry about the truth that can be lived with. And that is the difference between losing your marbles drinking the salty sea, or swallowing the stuff from the streams. My Niece-Of-Shame believes in the talking cure,[4] eh?' says Alsana, with something of a grin. 'Talk, talk, talk and it will be better. Be honest, slice open your heart and spread the red stuff around. But the past is made of more than words, dearie. We married old men, you see? These bumps,' Alsana pats them both, 'they will always have Daddy-long-legs for fathers. One leg in the present, one in the past. No talking will change this. Their roots will always be tangled.'

Just as he reaches the far gate, Sol Jozefowicz turns round to wave, and the three women wave back. And Clara feels a little theatrical, flying the park keeper's cream handkerchief above her head. As if she is seeing someone off on a train journey which crosses the border of two countries.

1999

---

4. Term from Freudian psychoanalysis.

APPENDIXES

General Bibliography

This bibliography consists of a list of suggested general readings on English literature. Bibliographies for the authors in *The Norton Anthology of English Literature* are available online in the Supplemental Ebook.

Suggested General Readings

Histories of England and of English Literature

Even the most distinguished of the comprehensive general histories written in past generations have come to seem outmoded. Innovative research in social, cultural, and political history has made it difficult to write a single coherent account of England from the Middle Ages to the present, let alone to accommodate in a unified narrative the complex histories of Scotland, Ireland, Wales, and the other nations where writing in English has flourished. Readers who wish to explore the historical matrix out of which the works of literature collected in this anthology emerged are advised to consult the studies of particular periods listed in the appropriate sections of this bibliography. The multivolume *Oxford History of England* and *New Oxford History of England* are useful, as are the three-volume *Peoples of the British Isles: A New History*, ed. Stanford Lehmberg, 1992; the nine-volume *Cambridge Cultural History of Britain*, ed. Boris Ford, 1992; the three-volume *Cambridge Social History of Britain, 1750–1950*, ed. F. M. L. Thompson, 1992; and the multivolume *Penguin History of Britain*, gen. ed. David Cannadine, 1996–. For Britain's imperial history, readers can consult the five-volume *Oxford History of the British Empire*, ed. Roger Louis, 1998–99, as well as *Gender and Empire*, ed. Philippa Levine, 2004. Given the cultural centrality of London, readers may find particular interest in *The London Encyclopaedia*, ed. Ben Weinreb and Christopher Hibbert, rev. ed., 1993; Roy Porter, *London: A Social History*, 1994; and Jerry White, *London in the Nineteenth Century: "A Human Awful Wonder of God,"* 2007, and *London in the Twentieth Century: A City and Its People*, 2001.

Similar observations may be made about literary history. In the light of such initiatives as women's studies, new historicism, and postcolonialism, the range of authors deemed significant has expanded in recent years, along with the geographical and conceptual boundaries of literature in English. Attempts to capture in a unified account the great sweep of literature from *Beowulf* to the early twenty-first century have largely given way to studies of individual genres, carefully delimited time periods, and specific authors. For these more focused accounts, see the listings by period. Among the large-scale literary surveys, *The Cambridge Guide to Literature in English*, 1994, is useful, as is the seven-volume *Penguin History of Literature*, 1993–94. *The Feminist Companion to Literature in English*, ed. Virginia Blain, Isobel Grundy, and Patricia Clements, 1990, is an important resource, and the editorial materials in *The Norton Anthology of Literature by Women*, 3rd ed., 2007, ed. Sandra M. Gilbert and Susan Gubar, constitute a concise history and set of biographies of women authors since the Middle Ages. *Annals of English Literature, 1475–1950*, rev. 1961, lists important publications year by year, together with the significant literary events for each year. Five volumes have been published in the *Oxford English Literary History*, gen. ed. Jonathan Bate, 2002–: James Simpson, *1350–1547: Reform and Cultural Revolution*; Philip Davis, *1830–1880: The Victorians*; Chris Baldick, *1830–*

1880: The Modern Movement; Randall Stevenson, *1960–2000: The Last of England?*; and Bruce King, *1948–2000: The Internationalization of English Literature*. See also *The Cambridge History of Medieval English Literature*, ed. David Wallace, 1999; *The Cambridge History of Early Modern English Literature*, ed. David Loewenstein and Janel Mueller, 2002; *The Cambridge History of English Literature, 1660–1780*, ed. John Richetti, 2005; *The Cambridge History of English Romantic Literature*, ed. James Chandler, 2009; and *The Cambridge History of Twentieth-Century English Literature*, ed. Laura Marcus and Peter Nicholls, 2005.

Helpful treatments and surveys of English meter, rhyme, and stanza forms are Paul Fussell Jr., *Poetic Meter and Poetic Form*, rev. 1979; Donald Wesling, *The Chances of Rhyme: Device and Modernity*, 1980; Charles O. Hartman, *Free Verse: An Essay in Prosody*, 1983; John Hollander, *Rhyme's Reason: A Guide to English Verse*, rev. 1989; Derek Attridge, *Poetic Rhythm: An Introduction*, 1995; Robert Pinsky, *The Sounds of Poetry: A Brief Guide*, 1998; and Mark Strand and Eavan Boland, eds., *The Making of a Poem: A Norton Anthology of Poetic Forms*, 2000.

On the development and functioning of the novel as a form, see Ian Watt, *The Rise of the Novel*, 1957; Gérard Genette, *Narrative Discourse: An Essay in Method*, 1980; Peter Brooks, *Reading for the Plot: Design and Intention in Narrative*, 1984; *The Columbia History of the British Novel*, ed. John Richetti, 1994; Margaret Doody, *The True Story of the Novel*, 1996; *Theory of the Novel: A Historical Approach*, ed. Michael McKeon, 2000; and McKeon, *The Origins of the English Novel, 1600–1740*, 15th anniversary ed., 2002. On women novelists and readers, see Nancy Armstrong, *Desire and Domestic Fiction: A Political History of the Novel*, 1987; and Catherine Gallagher, *Nobody's Story: The Vanishing Acts of Women Writers in the Marketplace, 1670–1820*, 1994.

On the history of playhouse design, see Richard Leacroft, *The Development of the English Playhouse: An Illustrated Survey of Theatre Building in England from Medieval to Modern Times*, 1988. For a survey of the plays that have appeared on these and other stages, see Allardyce Nicoll, *British Drama*, rev. 1962; the eight-volume *Revels History of Drama in English*, gen. eds. Clifford Leech and T. W. Craik, 1975–83; and Alfred Harbage, *Annals of English Drama, 975–1700*, 3rd ed., 1989, rev. S. Schoenbaum and Sylvia Wagonheim.

On some of the key intellectual currents that are at once reflected in and shaped by literature and contemporary literary criticism, Arthur O. Lovejoy's classic studies *The Great Chain of Being*, 1936, and *Essays in the History of Ideas*, 1948, remain valuable, along with such works as Georg Simmel, *The Philosophy of Money*, 1907; Lovejoy and George Boas, *Primitivism and Related Ideas in Antiquity*, 1935; Norbert Elias, *The Civilizing Process*, orig. pub. 1939, English trans. 1969; Ernst Cassirer, *The Philosophy of Symbolic Forms*, 4 vols., 1953–96; Ernst Kantorowicz, *The King's Two Bodies: A Study in Medieval Political Theology*, 1957, new ed. 1997; Richard Popkin, *The History of Skepticism from Erasmus to Descartes*, 1960; M. H. Abrams, *Natural Supernaturalism: Tradition and Revolution in Romantic Literature*, 1971; Michel Foucault, *Madness and Civilization: A History of Insanity in the Age of Reason*, Eng. trans. 1965, and *The Order of Things: An Archaeology of the Human Sciences*, Eng. trans. 1970; Gaston Bachelard, *The Poetics of Space*, Eng. trans. 1969; Martin Jay, *The Dialectical Imagination: A History of the Frankfurt School and the Institute of Social Research, 1923–1950*, 1973, new ed. 1996; Hayden White, *Metahistory*, 1973; Roland Barthes, *The Pleasure of the Text*, Eng. trans. 1975; Jacques Derrida, *Of Grammatology*, Eng. trans. 1976, and *Dissemination*, Eng. trans. 1981; Richard Rorty, *Philosophy and the Mirror of Nature*, 1979; Gilles Deleuze and Félix Guattari, *A Thousand Plateaus* (1980); Raymond Williams, *Keywords: A Vocabulary of Culture and Society*, rev. 1983; Pierre Bourdieu, *Distinction: A Social Critique of the Judgment of Taste*, Eng. trans. 1984; Michel de Certeau, *The Practice of Everyday Life*, Eng. trans. 1984; Hans Blumenberg, *The Legitimacy of the Modern Age*, Eng. trans. 1985; Jürgen Habermas, *The Philosophical Discourse of Moderntiy*, Eng.

trans, 1987; Slavoj Žižek, *The Sublime Object of Ideology*, 1989; and Sigmund Freud, *Writings on Art and Literature*, ed. Neil Hertz, 1997.

Reference Works

The single most important tool for the study of literature in English is the *Oxford English Dictionary*, 2nd ed. 1989, 3rd ed. in process. The most current edition is available online to subscribers. The *OED* is written on historical principles: that is, it attempts not only to describe current word use but also to record the history and development of the language from its origins before the Norman conquest to the present. It thus provides, for familiar as well as archaic and obscure words, the widest possible range of meanings and uses, organized chronologically and illustrated with quotations. The *OED* can be searched as a conventional dictionary arranged a–z and also by subject, usage, region, origin, and timeline (the first appearance of a word). Beyond the *OED* there are many other valuable dictionaries, such as *The American Heritage Dictionary* (4th ed. 2000), *The Oxford Dictionary of Abbreviations, The Concise Oxford Dictionary of English Etymology, The Oxford Dictionary of English Grammar, A New Dictionary of Eponyms, The Oxford Essential Dictionary of Foreign Terms in English, The Oxford Dictionary of Idioms, The Concise Oxford Dictionary of Linguistics, The Oxford Guide to World English,* and *The Concise Oxford Dictionary of Proverbs.* Other valuable reference works include *The Cambridge Encyclopedia of the English Language*, ed. David Crystal, 1995; *The Concise Oxford Companion to the English Language; Pocket Fowler's Modern English Usage;* and the numerous guides to specialized vocabularies, slang, regional dialects, and the like.

There is a steady flow of new editions of most major and many minor writers in English, along with a ceaseless outpouring of critical appraisals and scholarship. James L. Harner's *Literary Research Guide: An Annotated List of Reference Sources in English Literary Studies* (5th ed., 2008; online ed. at www.mla.org/store/PID335) offers thorough, evaluative annotations of a wide range of sources. For the historical record of scholarship and critical discussion, *The New Cambridge Bibliography of English Literature,* ed. George Watson, 5 vols. (1969–77) and *The Cambridge Bibliography of English Literature,* ed. F. W. Bateson, 5 vols. (1941–57) are useful. The *MLA International Bibliography* (also online) is a key resource for following critical discussion of literatures in English. Ranging from 1926 to the present, it includes journal articles, essays, chapters from collections, books, and dissertations, and covers folklore, linguistics, and film. The *Annual Bibliography of English Language and Literature* (*ABELL*), compiled by the Modern Humanities Research Association, lists monographs, periodical articles, critical editions of literary works, book reviews and collections of essays published anywhere in the world; unpublished doctoral dissertations are covered for the period 1920–99 (available online to subscribers and as part of Literature Online http://lion.chadwyck.com/marketing/index.jsp.)

For compact biographies of English authors, see the multivolume *Oxford Dictionary of National Biography* (*DNB*), ed. H. C. G. Matthew and Brian Harrison, 2004; since 2004 the *DNB* has been extended online with three annual updates. Handy reference books of authors, works, and various literary terms and allusions include many volumes in the *Cambridge Companion* and *Oxford Companion* series (e.g., *The Cambridge Companion to Narrative,* ed David Herman, 2007; *The Oxford Companion to English Literature,* ed. Margaret Drabble, rev. 2009; *The Cambridge Companion to Allegory,* ed. Rita Copeland and Peter Struck, 2010; etc.). *The Oxford Companion to the Theatre,* ed. Phyllis Hartnoll, is available online to subscribers via Oxford Reference Online's Performing Arts collection (www.oxfordreference.com/pub/views/home.html). Likewise, *The New Princeton Encyclopedia of Poetry and Poetics,* ed. Alex Preminger and others, is available online to subscribers in Literature Online (http://lion.chadwyck.com/marketing/index.jsp). Handbooks that define and illustrate literary concepts and terms are *The Penguin Dictionary of Literary Terms and Literary Theory*, ed. J. A. Cuddon, 4th ed., 2000; W. F. Thrall and Addison Hibbard, *A Handbook to Literature*, ed. William Harmon and Hugh Holman, 8th ed., 1999 (companion website http://wps.prenhall.com/hss_harmon_handbook_10); *Critical Terms for Literary Study*, ed. Frank Lentricchia and Thomas McLaughlin, rev. 1995; and M. H. Abrams, *A Glossary of Literary Terms*, 9th ed., 2009. Also useful are Richard Lanham, *A Handlist of Rhetorical Terms*, 2nd ed., 1991; Arthur Quinn, *Figures of Speech: 60 Ways to Turn a Phrase*, 1993; and the *Barnhart Concise Dictionary of Etymology*, ed. Robert K. Barnhart, 1995.

On the Greek and Roman backgrounds, see *The Cambridge History of Classical Literature* (vol. 1: *Greek Literature*, 1982; vol. 2: *Latin Literature*, 1989), both available online; *The Oxford Companion to Classical Literature*, ed. M. C. Howatson, 2nd ed., 1989; Gian Biagio Conte, *Latin Literature: A History*, 1994; *The Oxford Classical Dictionary*, 3rd ed., rev. 2003, also available online; Richard Rutherford, *Classical Literature: A Concise History*, 2005; and Mark P. O. Morford, Robert J. Lenardon, and Michael Sham, *Classical Mythology*, 9th ed., 2010.

Digital resources in the humanities have vastly proliferated since the previous edition of *The Norton Anthology of English Literature* and are continuing to grow rapidly. The NAEL StudySpace (wwnorton.com/nael) is the gateway to an extensive array of annotated texts, images, and other materials especially designed for the readers of this anthology. Among other useful electronic resources for the study of English literature are enormous digital archives, available to subscribers: Early English Books Online (EEBO) http://eebo.chadwyck.com/home; Literature Online http://lion.chadwyck.com/marketing/index.jsp; and Eighteenth Century Collections Online (ECCO) http://mlr.com/DigitalCollections/products/ecco/. There are also numerous free sites of variable quality. Many of the best of these are period or author specific and hence are listed in the subsequent sections of this bibliography. Among the general sites, one of the most useful and wide-ranging is Voice of the Shuttle (http://vox.ucsb.edu), which includes in its aggregation links to Bartleby.com and Project Gutenberg.

Literary Criticism and Theory

Eight volumes of the *Cambridge History of Literary Criticism* have been published, 1989– : *Classical Criticism*, ed. George A. Kennedy; *The Middle Ages*, ed. Alastair Minnis and Ian Johnson; *The Renaissance*, ed. Glyn P. Norton; *The Eighteenth Century*, ed. H. B. Nisbet and Claude Rawson; *Romanticism*, ed. Marshall Brown; *Modernism and the New Criticism*, ed. A. Walton Litz, Louis Menand, and Lawrence Rainey; *From Formalism to Poststructuralism*, ed. Raman Selden; and *Twentieth-Century Historical, Philosophical, and Psychological Perspectives*, ed. Christa Knellwolf and Christopher Norris. See also M. H. Abrams, *The Mirror and the Lamp: Romantic Theory and the Critical Tradition*, 1953; William K. Wimsatt and Cleanth Brooks, *Literary Criticism: A Short History*, 1957; René Wellek, *A History of Modern Criticism: 1750–1950*, 9 vols., 1955–93; Frank Lentricchia, *After the New Criticism*, 1980; and J. Hillis Miller, *On Literature*, 2002. Raman Selden, Peter Widdowson, and Peter Brooker have written *A Reader's Guide to Contemporary Literary Theory*, 1997. Other useful resources include *The Johns Hopkins Guide to Literary Theory and Criticism*, ed. Michael Groden and Martin Kreiswirth, 1994 (also online); *Literary Theory, an Anthology*, ed. Julie Rivkin and Michael Ryan, 1998; and *The Norton Anthology of Theory and Criticism*, 2nd ed., gen. ed. Vincent Leitch, 2010.

Modern approaches to English literature and literary theory were shaped by certain landmark works: William Empson, *Seven Types of Ambiguity*, 1930, 3rd ed. 1953, *Some Versions of Pastoral*, 1935, rpt. 1986, and *The Structure of Complex Words*, 1951; F. R. Leavis, *Revaluation*, 1936, and *The Great Tradition*, 1948; Lionel Trilling, *The Liberal Imagination*, 1950; T. S. Eliot, *Selected Essays*, 3rd ed. 1951, and *On Poetry and Poets*, 1957; Erich Auerbach, *Mimesis: The Representation of Reality in Western Literature*, 1953; William K. Wimsatt, *The Verbal Icon*, 1954;

Northrop Frye, *Anatomy of Criticism*, 1957; Wayne C. Booth, *The Rhetoric of Fiction*, 1961, rev. ed. 1983; and W. J. Bate, *The Burden of the Past and the English Poet*, 1970. René Wellek and Austin Warren, *Theory of Literature*, rev. 1970, is a useful introduction to the variety of scholarly and critical approaches to literature up to the time of its publication. Jonathan Culler's *Literary Theory: A Very Short Introduction*, 1997, discusses recurrent issues and debates.

Beginning in the late 1960s, there was a significant intensification of interest in literary theory as a specific field. Certain forms of literary study had already been influenced by the work of the Russian linguist Roman Jakobson and the Russian formalist Viktor Shklovsky and, still more, by conceptions that derived or claimed to derive from Marx and Engels, but the full impact of these theories was not felt until what became known as the "theory revolution" of the 1970s and '80s. For Marxist literary criticism, see Georg Lukacs, *Theory of the Novel*, 1920, trans. 1971; *The Historical Novel*, 1937, trans. 1983; and *Studies in European Realism*, trans. 1964; Walter Benjamin's essays from the 1920s and '30s represented in *Illuminations*, trans. 1986, and *Reflections*, trans. 1986; Mikhail Bakhtin's essays from the 1930s represented in *The Dialogic Imagination*, trans. 1981, and his *Rabelais and His World*, 1941, trans. 1968; *Selections from the Prison Notebooks of Antonio Gramsci*, ed. and trans. Quintin Hoare and Geoffrey Smith, 1971; Raymond Williams, *Marxism and Literature*, 1977; Fredric Jameson, *The Political Unconscious: Narrative as a Socially Symbolic Act*, 1981; and Terry Eagleton, *Literary Theory: An Introduction*, 1983, and *The Ideology of the Aesthetic*, 1990.

Structural linguistics and anthropology gave rise to a flowering of structuralist literary criticism; convenient introductions include Robert Scholes, *Structuralism in Literature: An Introduction*, 1974, and Jonathan Culler, *Structuralist Poetics*, 1975. Poststructuralist challenges to this approach are epitomized in such influential works as Jacques Derrida, *Writing and Difference*, 1967, trans. 1978, and Paul de Man, *Blindness and Insight: Essays in the Rhetoric of Contemporary Criticism*, 1971, 2nd ed., 1983. Poststructuralism is discussed in Jonathan Culler, *On Deconstruction*, 1982; Slavoj Žižek, *The Sublime Object of Ideology*, 1989; Fredric Jameson, *Postmodernism; or the Cultural Logic of Late Capitalism*, 1991; John McGowan, *Postmodernism and Its Critics*, 1991; and *Beyond Structuralism*, ed. Wendell Harris, 1996. A figure who greatly influenced both structuralism and poststructuralism is Roland Barthes, in *Mythologies*, trans. 1972, and *S/Z*, trans. 1974. Among other influential contributions to literary theory are the psychoanalytic approach in Harold Bloom, *The Anxiety of Influence*, 1973; and the reader-response approach in Stanley Fish, *Is There a Text in This Class?: The Authority of Interpretive Communities*, 1980. For a retrospect on the theory decades, see Terry Eagleton, *After Theory*, 2003.

Influenced by these theoretical currents but not restricted to them, modern feminist literary criticism was fashioned by such works as Patricia Meyer Spacks, *The Female Imagination*, 1975; Ellen Moers, *Literary Women*, 1976; Elaine Showalter, *A Literature of Their Own*, 1977; and Sandra Gilbert and Susan Gubar, *The Madwoman in the Attic*, 1979. More recent studies include Jane Gallop, *The Daughter's Seduction: Feminism and Psychoanalysis*, 1982; Luce Irigaray, *This Sex Which Is Not One*, trans. 1985; Gayatri Chakravorty Spivak, *In Other Worlds: Essays in Cultural Politics*, 1987; Sandra Gilbert and Susan Gubar, *No Man's Land: The Place of the Woman Writer in the Twentieth Century*, 3 vols., 1988–94; Barbara Johnson, *A World of Difference*, 1989; Judith Butler, *Gender Trouble*, 1990; and the critical views sampled in Elaine Showalter, *The New Feminist Criticism*, 1985; *The Hélène Cixous Reader*, ed. Susan Sellers, 1994; *Feminist Literary Theory: A Reader*, ed. Mary Eagleton, 2nd ed., 1995; and *Feminisms: An Anthology of Literary Theory and Criticism*, ed. Robyn R. Warhol and Diane Price Herndl, 2nd ed. 1997.

Gay literature and queer studies are represented in *Inside/Out: Lesbian Theories, Gay Theories*, ed. Diana Fuss, 1991; *The Lesbian and Gay Studies Reader*, ed. Henry Abelove, Michele Barale, and David Halperin, 1993; *The Columbia Anthology of Gay*

Literature: Readings from Western Antiquity to the Present Day, ed. Byrne R. S. Fone, 1998; and by such books as Eve Sedgwick, *Between Men: English Literature and Male Homosocial Desire*, 1985, and *Epistemology of the Closet*, 1990; Diana Fuss, *Essentially Speaking: Feminism, Nature, and Difference*, 1989; Terry Castle, *The Apparitional Lesbian: Female Homosexuality and Modern Culture*, 1993; Leo Bersani, *Homos*, 1995; Gregory Woods, *A History of Gay Literature: The Male Tradition*, 1998; David Halperin, *How to Do the History of Homosexuality*, 2002; and Judith Halberstam, *In a Queer Time and Place: Transgender Bodies, Subcultural Lives*, 2005.

New historicism is represented in Stephen Greenblatt, *Learning to Curse*, 1990; in the essays collected in *The New Historicism Reader*, ed. Harold Veeser, 1993, and *New Historical Literary Study: Essays on Reproducing Texts, Representing History*, ed. Jeffrey N. Cox and Larry J. Reynolds, 1993; and in Catherine Gallagher and Stephen Greenblatt, *Practicing New Historicism*, 2000. The related social and historical dimension of texts is discussed in Jerome McGann, *Critique of Modern Textual Criticism*, 1983; and *Scholarly Editing: A Guide to Research*, ed. D. C. Greetham, 1995. Characteristic of new historicism is an expansion of the field of literary interpretation still further in cultural studies; for a broad sampling of the range of interests, see Lawrence Grossberg, Cary Nelson, and Paula Treichler, eds., *Cultural Studies*, 1992; *The Cultural Studies Reader*, ed. Simon During, 1993; and *A Cultural Studies Reader: History, Theory, Practice*, ed. Jessica Munns and Gita Rajan, 1997. This expansion of the field is similarly reflected in postcolonial studies: see Frantz Fanon, *Black Skin, White Masks*, 1952, new trans. 2008, and *The Wretched of the Earth*, 1961, new trans. 2004; Edward Said, *Orientalism*, 1978, and *Culture and Imperialism*, 1993; *The Post-Colonial Studies Reader*, ed. Bill Ashcroft, Gareth Griffiths, and Helen Tiffin, 1995; and such influential books as Ranajit Guha and Gayatri Chakravorty Spivak, *Selected Subaltern Studies*, 1988; Homi Bhabha, ed., *Nation and Narration*, 1990, and *The Location of Culture*, 1994; Anne McClintock, *Imperial Leather: Race, Gender, and Sexuality in the Colonial Contest*, 1995; Robert J. C. Young, *Postcolonialism: An Historical Introduction*, 2001; Bill Ashcroft, Gareth Griffiths, and Helen Tiffin, *The Empire Writes Back: Theory and Practice in Post-Colonial Literatures*, 1989, 2nd ed. 2002; Elleke Boehmer, *Colonial and Postcolonial Literature*, 1995, 2nd ed. 2005; and *The Cambridge History of Postcolonial Literature*, ed. Ato Quayson, 2011.

In the wake of the theory revolution, critics have focused on a wide array of topics, which can only be briefly surveyed here. One current of work, focusing on the history of emotion, is represented in Brian Massumi, *Parables for the Virtual*, 2002; Sianne Ngai, *Ugly Feelings*, 2005; and *The Affect Theory Reader*, eds. Melissa Gregg and Gregory J. Seigworth, 2010. A somewhat related current, examining the special role of traumatic memory in literature, is exemplified in Cathy Caruth, *Trauma: Explorations in Memory*, 1995; and Dominic LaCapra, *Writing History, Writing Trauma*, 2000. Work on the literary implications of cognitive science may be glimpsed in *Introduction to Cognitive Cultural Studies*, ed. Lisa Zunshine, 2010. A growing interest in quantitative approaches to literature has been sparked by Franco Moretti, *Graphs, Maps, Trees: Abstract Models for Literary History*, 2005. There is an ongoing flourishing of ecocriticism, or studies of literature and the environment, including *The Ecocriticism Reader: Landmarks in Literary Ecology*, ed. Cheryll Glotfelty and Harold Fromm, 1996; *Writing the Environment*, eds. Richard Kerridge and Neil Sammells, 1998; and Jonathan Bate, *The Song of the Earth*, 2002. The relationship between literature and law is central to such works as *Interpreting Law and Literature: A Hermeneutic Reader*, ed. Sanford Levinson and Steven Mailloux, 1988; *Law's Stories: Narrative and Rhetoric in the Law*, ed. Peter Brooks and Paul Gerwertz, 1998; and *Literature and Legal Problem Solving: Law and Literature as Ethical Discourse*, Paul J. Heald, 1998. Ethical questions in literature have been usefully explored by, among others, Geoffrey Galt Harpham in *Getting It Right: Language, Literature, and Ethics*, 1997, and Derek Attridge in *The Singularity of Literature*, 2004. Finally, approaches to literature, such as formalism and literary biography, that had seemed superseded in the theoretical ferment of the late twentieth century, have had a powerful resurgence. A renewed interest in form is evident in Susan Stewart, *Poetry and the Fate of the Senses*, 2002, and *Reading for Form*, ed. Susan J. Wolfson and Marshall Brown, 2007. Revitalized interest in the history of the book has been spearheaded by D. F. McKenzie's *Bibliography and the Sociology of Texts*, 1986; and Roger Chartier's *The Order of Books: Readers, Authors, and Libraries in Europe Between the Fourteenth and Eighteenth Centuries*, 1994. See also *The Cambridge History of the Book in Britain*, 6 vols., 1998–2009; and *The Practice and Representation of Reading in England*, ed. James Raven, Helen Small, and Naomi Tadmor, 2007.

Anthologies representing a range of recent approaches include *Modern Criticism and Theory*, ed. David Lodge, 1988; *Contemporary Literary Criticism*, ed. Robert Con Davis and Ronald Schlieffer, rev. ed. 1998; and *The Norton Anthology of Theory and Criticism*, ed. Vincent Leitch, et al., 2nd ed. 2010.

Literary Terminology*

Using simple technical terms can sharpen our understanding and streamline our discussion of literary works. Some terms, such as the ones in section A, help us address the internal style, structure, form, and kind of works. Other terms, such as those in section B, provide insight into the material forms in which literary works have been produced.

In analyzing what they called "rhetoric," ancient Greek and Roman writers determined the elements of what we call "style" and "structure." Our literary terms are derived, via medieval and Renaissance intermediaries, from the Greek and Latin sources. In the definitions that follow, the etymology, or root, of the word is given when it helps illuminate the word's current usage.

Most of the examples are drawn from texts in this anthology.

Words **boldfaced** within definitions are themselves defined in this appendix. Some terms are defined within definitions; such words are *italicized*.

A. Terms of Style, Structure, Form, and Kind

accent (synonym "stress"): a term of **rhythm.** The special force devoted to the voicing of one syllable in a word over others. In the noun "accent," for example, the accent, or stress, is on the first syllable.

act: the major subdivision of a play, usually divided into **scenes.**

aesthetics (from Greek, "to feel, apprehend by the senses"): the philosophy of artistic meaning as a distinct mode of apprehending untranslatable truth, defined as an alternative to rational enquiry, which is purely abstract. Developed in the late eighteenth century by the German philosopher Immanuel Kant especially.

Alexandrine: a term of **meter.** In French verse a line of twelve syllables, and, by analogy, in English verse a line of six stresses. See **hexameter.**

allegory (Greek "saying otherwise"): saying one thing (the "vehicle" of the allegory) and meaning another (the allegory's "tenor"). Allegories may be momentary aspects of a work, as in **metaphor** ("John is a lion"), or, through extended metaphor, may constitute the basis of narrative, as in Bunyan's *Pilgrim's Progress:* this second meaning is the dominant one. See also **symbol** and **type.** Allegory is one of the most significant **figures of thought.**

alliteration (from Latin "litera," alphabetic letter): a **figure of speech.** The repetition of an initial consonant sound or consonant cluster in consecutive or closely positioned words. This pattern is often an inseparable part of the meter in Germanic languages, where the tonic, or accented **syllable,** is usually the first syllable. Thus all Old English poetry and some varieties of Middle English poetry use alliteration as part of their basic metrical practice. *Sir Gawain and the Green Knight,* line 1: "Sithen the sege and the assaut was sesed at Troye" (see vol. 1/A, p. 184). Otherwise used for local effects; Stevie Smith, "Pretty," lines 4–5: "And in the pretty pool the pike stalks / He stalks his prey . . ." (see vol. 2/F, p. 2604).

*This appendix was devised and compiled by James Simpson with the collaboration of all the editors. We especially thank Professor Lara Bovilsky of the University of Oregon at Eugene, who helped us reshape this appendix for this edition.

allusion: Literary allusion is a passing but illuminating reference within a literary text to another, well-known text (often biblical or **classical**). Topical allusions are also, of course, common in certain modes, especially **satire**.

anagnorisis (Greek "recognition"): the moment of **protagonist's** recognition in a narrative, which is also often the moment of moral understanding.

anapest: a term of **rhythm**. A three-syllable foot following the rhythmic pattern, in English verse, of two unstressed (uu) syllables followed by one stressed (/). Thus, for example, "Illinois."

anaphora (Greek "carrying back"): a **figure of speech**. The repetition of words or groups of words at the beginning of consecutive sentences, clauses, or phrases. Blake, "London," lines 5–8: "In every cry of every Man, / In every Infant's cry of fear, / In every voice, in every ban . . ." (see vol. 2/D, p. 132); Louise Bennett, "Jamaica Oman," lines 17–20: "Some backa man a push, some side-a / Man a hole him han, / Some a lick sense eena him head, / Some a guide him pon him plan!" (see vol. 2/F, p. 2729).

animal fable: a **genre**. A short narrative of speaking animals, followed by moralizing comment, written in a low style and gathered into a collection. Robert Henryson, "The Cock and the Fox" (see vol. 1/A, p. 501).

antithesis (Greek "placing against"): a **figure of thought**. The juxtaposition of opposed terms in clauses or sentences that are next to or near each other; Milton, *Paradise Lost* 1.777–80: "They but now who seemed / In bigness to surpass Earth's giant sons / Now less than smallest dwarfs, in narrow room / Throng numberless" (see vol. 1/B, p. 1964).

apostrophe (from Greek "turning away"): a **figure of thought**. An address, often to an absent person, a force, or a quality. For example, a poet makes an apostrophe to a Muse when invoking her for inspiration.

apposition: a term of **syntax**. The repetition of elements serving an identical grammatical function in one sentence. The effect of this repetition is to arrest the flow of the sentence, but in doing so to add extra semantic nuance to repeated elements. This is an especially important feature of Old English poetic style. See, for example, Caedmon's *Hymn* (vol. 1/A, p. 30), where the phrases "heaven-kingdom's Guardian," "the Measurer's might," "his mind-plans," and "the work of the Glory-Father" each serve an identical syntactic function as the direct objects of "praise."

assonance (Latin "sounding to"): a **figure of speech**. The repetition of identical or near identical stressed vowel sounds in words whose final consonants differ, producing half-rhyme. Tennyson, "The Lady of Shalott," line 100: "His broad clear brow in sunlight glowed" (see vol. 2/E, p. 1163).

aubade (originally from Spanish "alba," dawn): a **genre**. A lover's dawn song or lyric bewailing the arrival of the day and the necessary separation of the lovers; Donne, "The Sun Rising" (see vol. 1/B, p. 1376). Larkin recasts the genre in "Aubade" (see vol. 2/F, p. 2789).

autobiography (Greek "self-life writing"): a **genre**. A narrative of a life written by the subject; Wordsworth, *The Prelude* (see vol. 2/D, p. 349). There are subgenres, such as the spiritual autobiography, narrating the author's path to conversion and subsequent spiritual trials, as in Bunyan's *Grace Abounding*.

ballad stanza: a **verse form**. Usually a **quatrain** in alternating **iambic tetrameter** and **iambic trimeter** lines, rhyming abcb. See "Sir Patrick Spens" (vol. 2/D, p. 36); Louise Bennett's poems (vol. 2/F, pp. 2726–27); Eliot, "Sweeney among the Nightingales" (vol. 2/F, p. 2528); Larkin, "This Be the Verse" (vol. 2/F, p. 2789).

ballade: a **verse form**. A form consisting usually of three stanzas followed by a four-line envoi (French, "send off"). The last line of the first stanza establishes a

refrain, which is repeated, or subtly varied, as the last line of each stanza. The form was derived from French medieval poetry; English poets, from the fourteenth to the sixteenth centuries especially, used it with varying stanza forms. Chaucer, "Complaint to His Purse" (see vol. 1/A, p. 345).

bathos (Greek "depth"): a **figure of thought.** A sudden and sometimes ridiculous descent of tone; Pope, *The Rape of the Lock* 3.157–58: "Not louder shrieks to pitying heaven are cast, / When husbands, or when lapdogs breathe their last" (see vol. 1/C, p. 2169).

beast epic: a **genre.** A continuous, unmoralized narrative, in prose or verse, relating the victories of the wholly unscrupulous but brilliant strategist Reynard the Fox over all adversaries. Chaucer arouses, only to deflate, expectations of the genre in *The Nun's Priest's Tale* (see vol. 1/A, p. 326).

biography (Greek "life-writing"): a **genre.** A life as the subject of an extended narrative. Thus Izaak Walton, *The Life of Dr. Donne* (see vol. 1/B, p. 1424).

blank verse: a **verse form.** Unrhymed **iambic pentameter** lines. Blank verse has no stanzas, but is broken up into uneven units (verse paragraphs) determined by sense rather than form. First devised in English by Henry Howard, Earl of Surrey, in his translation of two books of Virgil's *Aeneid* (see vol. 1/B, p. 669), this very flexible verse type became the standard form for dramatic poetry in the seventeenth century, as in most of Shakespeare's plays. Milton and Wordsworth, among many others, also used it to create an English equivalent to **classical epic.**

blazon: strictly, a heraldic shield; in rhetorical usage, a **topos** whereby the individual elements of a beloved's face and body are singled out for **hyperbolic** admiration. Spenser, *Epithalamion*, lines 167–84 (see vol. 1/B, p. 990). For an inversion of the **topos,** see Shakespeare, Sonnet 130 (vol. 1/B, p. 1183).

burlesque (French and Italian "mocking"): a work that adopts the **conventions** of a genre with the aim less of comically mocking the genre than of satirically mocking the society so represented (see **satire**). Thus Pope's *Rape of the Lock* (see vol. 1/C, p. 2157) does not mock **classical epic** so much as contemporary mores.

caesura (Latin "cut") (plural "caesurae"): a term of **meter.** A pause or breathing space within a line of verse, generally occurring between syntactic units; Louise Bennett, "Colonization in Reverse," lines 5–8: "By de hundred, by de tousan, / From country an from town, / By de ship-load, by de plane-load, / Jamaica is Englan boun" (see vol. 2/F, p. 2727), where the caesurae occur in lines 5 and 7.

canon (Greek "rule"): the group of texts regarded as worthy of special respect or attention by a given institution. Also, the group of texts regarded as definitely having been written by a certain author.

catastrophe (Greek "overturning"): the decisive turn in **tragedy** by which the plot is resolved and, usually, the **protagonist** dies.

catharsis (Greek "cleansing"): According to Aristotle, the effect of **tragedy** on its audience, through their experience of pity and terror, was a kind of spiritual cleansing, or catharsis.

character (Greek "stamp, impression"): a person, personified animal, or other figure represented in a literary work, especially in narrative and drama. The more a character seems to generate the action of a narrative, and the less he or she seems merely to serve a preordained narrative pattern, the "fuller," or more "rounded," a character is said to be. A "stock" character, common particularly in many comic genres, will perform a predictable function in different works of a given genre.

chiasmus (Greek "crosswise"): a **figure of speech.** The inversion of an already established sequence. This can involve verbal echoes: Pope, "Eloisa to Abelard," line 104, "The crime was common, common be the pain" (see vol. 1/C, p. 2180); or it can be purely a matter of syntactic inversion: Pope, *Epistle to Dr. Arbuthnot*, line 8: "They pierce my thickets, through my grot they glide" (see vol. 1/C, p. 2195).

classical, classicism, classic: Each term can be widely applied, but in English literary discourse, "classical" primarily describes the works of either Greek or Roman antiquity. "Classicism" denotes the practice of art forms inspired by classical antiquity, in particular the observance of rhetorical norms of **decorum** and balance, as opposed to following the dictates of untutored inspiration, as in Romanticism. "Classic" denotes an especially famous work within a given **canon.**

climax (Greek "ladder"): a moment of great intensity and structural change, especially in drama. Also a **figure of speech** whereby a sequence of verbally linked clauses is made, in which each successive clause is of greater consequence than its predecessor. Bacon, *Of Studies:* "Studies serve for pastimes, for ornaments, and for abilities. Their chief use for pastimes is in privateness and retiring; for ornament, is in discourse; and for ability, is in judgement" (see vol. 1/B, p. 1673).

comedy: a **genre.** A term primarily applied to drama, and derived from ancient drama, in opposition to **tragedy.** Comedy deals with humorously confusing, sometimes ridiculous situations in which the ending is, nevertheless, happy. A comedy often ends in one or more marriages. Shakespeare, *Twelfth Night* (see vol. 1/B, p. 1186).

comic mode: Many genres (e.g., **romance, fabliau, comedy**) involve a happy ending in which justice is done, the ravages of time are arrested, and that which is lost is found. Such genres participate in a comic mode.

connotation: To understand connotation, we need to understand **denotation.** While many words can denote the same concept—that is, have the same basic meaning—those words can evoke different associations, or connotations. Contrast, for example, the clinical-sounding term "depression" and the more colorful, musical, even poetic phrase "the blues."

consonance (Latin "sounding with"): a **figure of speech.** The repetition of final consonants in words or stressed syllables whose vowel sounds are different. Herbert, "Easter," line 13: "Consort, both heart and lute . . ." (see vol. 1/B, p. 1708).

convention: a repeatedly recurring feature (in either form or content) of works, occurring in combination with other recurring formal features, which constitutes a convention of a particular genre.

couplet: a **verse form.** In English verse two consecutive, rhyming lines usually containing the same number of stresses. Chaucer first introduced the **iambic pentameter** couplet into English (*Canterbury Tales*); the form was later used in many types of writing, including drama; imitations and translations of **classical epic** (thus *heroic couplet*); essays; and **satire** (see Dryden and Pope). The *distich* (Greek "two lines") is a couplet usually making complete sense; Aemilia Lanyer, *Salve Deus Rex Judaeorum*, lines 5–6: "Read it fair queen, though it defective be, / Your excellence can grace both it and me" (see vol. 1/B, p. 1431).

dactyl (Greek "finger," because of the finger's three joints): a term of **rhythm.** A three-syllable foot following the rhythmic pattern, in English verse, of one stressed followed by two unstressed syllables. Thus, for example, "Oregon."

decorum (Latin "that which is fitting"): a rhetorical principle whereby each formal aspect of a work should be in keeping with its subject matter and/or audience.

deixis (Greek "pointing"): relevant to **point of view.** Every work has, implicitly or explicitly, a "here" and a "now" from which it is narrated. Words that refer to or imply this point from which the voice of the work is projected (such as "here," "there," "this," "that," "now," "then") are examples of deixis, or "deictics." This technique is especially important in drama, where it is used to create a sense of the events happening as the spectator witnesses them.

denotation: A word has a basic, "prosaic" (factual) meaning prior to the associations it connotes (see **connotation**). The word "steed," for example, might call to mind a horse fitted with battle gear, to be ridden by a warrior, but its denotation is simply "horse."

denouement (French "unknotting"): the point at which a narrative can be resolved and so ended.

dialogue (Greek "conversation"): a **genre.** Dialogue is a feature of many genres, especially in both the **novel** and drama. As a genre itself, dialogue is used in philosophical traditions especially (most famously in Plato's *Dialogues*), as the representation of a conversation in which a philosophical question is pursued among various speakers.

diction, or **"lexis"** (from, respectively, Latin "dictio" and Greek "lexis," each meaning "word"): the actual words used in any utterance—speech, writing, and, for our purposes here, literary works. The choice of words contributes significantly to the style of a given work.

didactic mode (Greek "teaching mode"): **Genres** in a didactic mode are designed to instruct or teach, sometimes explicitly (e.g., sermons, philosophical **discourses, georgic**), and sometimes through the medium of fiction (e.g., **animal fable, parable**).

diegesis (Greek for "narration"): a term that simply means "narration," but is used in literary criticism to distinguish one kind of story from another. In a *mimetic* story, the events are played out before us (see **mimesis**), whereas in diegesis someone recounts the story to us. Drama is for the most part *mimetic,* whereas the novel is for the most part diegetic. In novels the narrator is not, usually, part of the action of the narrative; s/he is therefore extradiegetic.

dimeter (Greek "two measure"): a term of **meter.** A two-stress line, rarely used as the meter of whole poems, though used with great frequency in single poems by Skelton, e.g., "The Tunning of Elinour Rumming" (see vol. 1/B, p. 567). Otherwise used for single lines, as in Herbert, "Discipline," line 3: "O my God" (see vol. 1/B, p. 1724).

discourse (Latin "running to and fro"): broadly, any nonfictional speech or writing; as a more specific genre, a philosophical meditation on a set theme. Thus Newman, *The Idea of a University* (see vol. 2/E, p. 1078).

dramatic irony: a feature of narrative and drama, whereby the audience knows that the outcome of an action will be the opposite of that intended by a **character.**

dramatic monologue (Greek "single speaking"): a **genre.** A poem in which the voice of a historical or fictional **character** speaks, unmediated by any narrator, to an implied though silent audience. See Tennyson, "Ulysses" (vol. 2/E, p. 1170); Browning, "The Bishop Orders His Tomb" (vol. 2/E, p. 1286); Eliot, "The Love Song of J. Alfred Prufrock" (vol. 2/F, p. 2525); Carol Ann Duffy, "Medusa" and "Mrs Lazarus" (vol. 2/F, pp. 3044–45).

ecphrasis (Greek "speaking out"): a **topos** whereby a work of visual art is represented in a literary work. Auden, "Musée des Beaux Arts" (see vol. 2/F, p. 2686).

elegy: a **genre.** In **classical** literature elegy was a form written in elegiac **couplets** (a **hexameter** followed by a **pentameter**) devoted to many possible topics. In Ovidian elegy a lover meditates on the trials of erotic desire (e.g., Ovid's *Amores*). The **sonnet**

sequences of both Sidney and Shakespeare exploit this genre, and, while it was still practiced in classical tradition by Donne ("On His Mistress" [see vol. 1/B, p. 1392]), by the later seventeenth century the term came to denote the poetry of loss, especially through the death of a loved person. See Tennyson, *In Memoriam* (vol. 2/E, p. 1187); Yeats, "In Memory of Major Robert Gregory" (vol. 2/F, p. 2034); Auden, "In Memory of W. B. Yeats" (see vol. 2/F, p. 2686); Heaney, "Clearances" (vol. 2/F, p. 2963).

emblem (Greek "an insertion"): a **figure of thought**. A picture allegorically expressing a moral, or a verbal picture open to such interpretation. Donne, "A Hymn to Christ," lines 1–2: "In what torn ship soever I embark, / That ship shall be my emblem of thy ark" (see vol. 1/B, p. 1416).

end-stopping: the placement of a complete syntactic unit within a complete line, fulfilling the metrical pattern; Auden, "In Memory of W. B. Yeats," line 42: "Earth, receive an honoured guest" (see vol. 2/F, p. 2688). Compare **enjambment.**

enjambment (French "striding," encroaching): The opposite of **end-stopping**, enjambment occurs when the syntactic unit does not end with the end of the line and the fulfillment of the metrical pattern. When the sense of the line overflows its meter and, therefore, the line break, we have enjambment; Auden, "In Memory of W. B. Yeats," lines 44–45: "Let the Irish vessel lie / Emptied of its poetry" (see vol. 2/F, p. 2688).

epic (synonym, *heroic poetry*): a **genre**. An extended narrative poem celebrating martial heroes, invoking divine inspiration, beginning in medias res (see **order**), written in a high style (including the deployment of **epic similes;** on high style, see **register**), and divided into long narrative sequences. Homer's *Iliad* and Virgil's *Aeneid* were the prime models for English writers of epic verse. Thus Milton, *Paradise Lost* (see vol. 1/B, p. 1943); Wordsworth, *The Prelude* (see vol. 2/D, p. 349); and Walcott, *Omeros* (see vol. 2/F, p. 2806). With its precise repertoire of stylistic resources, epic lent itself easily to **parodic** and **burlesque** forms, known as **mock epic;** thus Pope, *The Rape of the Lock* (see vol. 1/C, p. 2157).

epigram: a **genre**. A short, pithy poem wittily expressed, often with wounding intent. See Jonson, *Epigrams* (see vol. 1/B, p. 1539).

epigraph (Greek "inscription"): a **genre**. Any formal statement inscribed on stone; also the brief formulation on a book's title page, or a quotation at the beginning of a poem, introducing the work's themes in the most compressed form possible.

epistle (Latin "letter"): a **genre**. The letter can be shaped as a literary form, involving an intimate address often between equals. The *Epistles* of Horace provided a model for English writers from the sixteenth century. Thus Wyatt, "Mine own John Poins" (see vol. 1/B, p. 659), or Pope, "Epistle to a Lady" (vol. 1/C, p. 2245). Letters can be shaped to form the matter of an extended fiction, as the eighteenth-century epistolary **novel** (e.g., Samuel Richardson's *Pamela*).

epitaph: a **genre**. A pithy formulation to be inscribed on a funeral monument. Thus Ralegh, "The Author's Epitaph, Made by Himself" (see vol. 1/B, p. 1030).

epithalamion (Greek "concerning the bridal chamber"): a **genre**. A wedding poem, celebrating the marriage and wishing the couple good fortune. Thus Spenser, *Epithalamion* (see vol. 1/B, p. 990).

epyllion (plural "epyllia") (Greek: "little epic"): a **genre**. A relatively short poem in the meter of epic poetry. See, for example, Marlowe, *Hero and Leander.*

essay (French "trial, attempt"): a **genre**. An informal philosophical meditation, usually in prose and sometimes in verse. The journalistic periodical essay was developed in the early eighteenth century. Thus Addison and Steele, periodical essays (see vol. 1/C, p. 2113); Pope, *An Essay on Criticism* (see vol. 1/C, p. 2141).

euphemism (Greek "sweet saying"): a **figure of thought.** The figure by which something distasteful is described in alternative, less repugnant terms (e.g., "he passed away").

exegesis (Greek "leading out"): interpretation, traditionally of the biblical text, but, by transference, of any text.

exemplum (Latin "example"): an example inserted into a usually nonfictional writing (e.g., sermon or **essay**) to give extra force to an abstract thesis. Thus Johnson's example of "Sober" in his essay "On Idleness" (see vol. 1/C, p. 2326).

fabliau (French "little story," plural *fabliaux*): a **genre.** A short, funny, often bawdy narrative in low style (see **register**) imitated and developed from French models most subtly by Chaucer; see *The Miller's Prologue and Tale* (vol. 1/A, p. 264).

farce (French "stuffing"): a **genre.** A play designed to provoke laughter through the often humiliating antics of stock **characters.** Congreve's *The Way of the World* (see vol. 1/C, p. 1832) draws on this tradition.

figures of speech: Literary language often employs patterns perceptible to the eye and/or to the ear. Such patterns are called "figures of speech"; in classical rhetoric they were called "schemes" (from Greek "schema," meaning "form, figure").

figures of thought: Language can also be patterned conceptually, even outside the rules that normally govern it. Literary language in particular exploits this licensed linguistic irregularity. Synonyms for figures of thought are "trope" (Greek "twisting," referring to the irregularity of use) and "conceit" (Latin "concept," referring to the fact that these figures are perceptible only to the mind). Be careful not to confuse **trope** with **topos** (a common error).

first-person narration: relevant to **point of view,** a narrative in which the voice narrating refers to itself with forms of the first-person pronoun ("I," "me," "my," etc., or possibly "we," "us," "our"), and in which the narrative is determined by the limitations of that voice. Thus Mary Wollstonecraft Shelley, *Frankenstein*.

frame narrative: Some narratives, particularly collections of narratives, involve a frame narrative that explains the genesis of, and/or gives a perspective on, the main narrative or narratives to follow. Thus Chaucer, *Canterbury Tales*; Mary Wollstonecraft Shelley, *Frankenstein*; or Conrad, *Heart of Darkness*.

free indirect style: relevant to **point of view,** a narratorial voice that manages, without explicit reference, to imply, and often implicitly to comment on, the voice of a **character** in the narrative itself. Virginia Woolf, "A Sketch of the Past," where the voice, although strictly that of the adult narrator, manages to convey the child's manner of perception: "—I begin: the first memory. This was of red and purple flowers on a black background—my mother's dress."

genre and mode: The **style,** structure, and, often, length of a work, when coupled with a certain subject matter, raise expectations that a literary work conforms to a certain **genre** (French "kind"). Good writers might upset these expectations, but they remain aware of the expectations and thwart them purposefully. Works in different genres may nevertheless participate in the same **mode,** a broader category designating the fundamental perspectives governing various genres of writing. For mode, see **tragic, comic, satiric,** and **didactic modes.** Genres are fluid, sometimes very fluid (e.g., the **novel**); the word "usually" should be added to almost every account of the characteristics of a given genre!

georgic (Greek "farming"): a **genre.** Virgil's *Georgics* treat agricultural and occasionally scientific subjects, giving instructions on the proper management of farms. Unlike **pastoral,** which treats the countryside as a place of recreational idleness among shepherds, the georgic treats it as a place of productive labor. For an English poem that critiques both genres, see Crabbe, "The Village" (vol. 1/C, p. 1932).

hermeneutics (from the Greek god Hermes, messenger between the gods and humankind): the science of interpretation, first formulated as such by the German philosophical theologian Friedrich Schleiermacher in the early nineteenth century.

heroic poetry: see **epic**.

hexameter (Greek "six measure"): a term of **meter**. The hexameter line (a six-stress line) is the meter of **classical** Latin **epic**; while not imitated in that form for epic verse in English, some instances of the hexameter exist. See, for example, the last line of a Spenserian stanza, *Faerie Queene* 1.1.2: "O help thou my weake wit, and sharpen my dull tong" (vol. 1/B, p. 781), or Yeats, "The Lake Isle of Innisfree," line 1: "I will arise and go now, and go to Innisfree" (vol. 2/F, p. 2088).

homily (Greek "discourse"): a **genre**. A sermon, to be preached in church; *Book of Homilies* (see vol. 1/B, p. 692). Writers of literary fiction sometimes exploit the homily, or sermon, as in Chaucer, *The Pardoner's Tale* (see vol. 1/A, p. 310).

homophone (Greek "same sound"): a **figure of speech**. A word that sounds identical to another word but has a different meaning ("bear" / "bare").

hyperbaton (Greek "overstepping"): a term of **syntax**. The rearrangement, or inversion, of the expected word order in a sentence or clause. Gray, "Elegy Written in a Country Churchyard," line 38: "If Memory o'er their tomb no trophies raise" (vol. 1/C, p. 2524). Poets can suspend the expected syntax over many lines, as in the first sentences of the *Canterbury Tales* (vol. 1/A, p. 243) and of *Paradise Lost* (vol. 1/B, p. 1943).

hyperbole (Greek "throwing over"): a **figure of thought**. Overstatement, exaggeration; Marvell, "To His Coy Mistress," lines 11–12: "My vegetable love would grow / Vaster than empires, and more slow" (see vol. 1/B, p. 1797); Auden, "As I Walked Out One Evening," lines 9–12: "'I'll love you, dear, I'll love you / Till China and Africa meet / And the river jumps over the mountain / And the salmon sing in the street" (see vol. 2/F, p. 2684).

hypermetrical (adj.; Greek "over measured"): a term of **meter**; the word describes a breaking of the expected metrical pattern by at least one extra syllable.

hypotaxis, or **subordination** (respectively Greek and Latin "ordering under"): a term of **syntax**. The subordination, by the use of subordinate clauses, of different elements of a sentence to a single main verb. Milton, *Paradise Lost* 9.513–15: "As when a ship by skillful steersman wrought / Nigh river's mouth or foreland, where the wind / Veers oft, as oft so steers, and shifts her sail; So varied he" (vol. 1/B, p. 2102). The contrary principle to **parataxis**.

iamb: a term of **rhythm**. The basic foot of English verse; two syllables following the rhythmic pattern of unstressed followed by stressed and producing a rising effect. Thus, for example, "Vermont."

imitation: the practice whereby writers strive ideally to reproduce and yet renew the **conventions** of an older form, often derived from **classical** civilization. Such a practice will be praised in periods of classicism (e.g., the eighteenth century) and repudiated in periods dominated by a model of inspiration (e.g., Romanticism).

irony (Greek "dissimulation"): a **figure of thought**. In broad usage, irony designates the result of inconsistency between a statement and a context that undermines the statement. "It's a beautiful day" is unironic if it's a beautiful day; if, however, the weather is terrible, then the inconsistency between statement and context is ironic. The effect is often amusing; the need to be ironic is sometimes produced by censorship of one kind or another. Strictly, irony is a subset of allegory: whereas allegory says one thing and means another, irony says one thing and means its opposite. For an extended example of irony, see Swift's "Modest Proposal." See also **dramatic irony.**

journal (French "daily"): a **genre.** A diary, or daily record of ephemeral experience, whose perspectives are concentrated on, and limited by, the experiences of single days. Thus Pepys, *Diary* (see vol. 1/C, p. 1732).

lai: a **genre.** A short narrative, often characterized by images of great intensity; a French term, and a form practiced by Marie de France (see vol. 1/A, p. 142).

legend (Latin "requiring to be read"): a **genre.** A narrative of a celebrated, possibly historical, but mortal **protagonist.** To be distinguished from **myth.** Thus the "Arthurian legend" but the "myth of Proserpine."

lexical set: Words that habitually recur together (e.g., January, February, March, etc.; or red, white, and blue) form a lexical set.

litotes (from Greek "smooth"): a **figure of thought.** Strictly, understatement by denying the contrary; More, *Utopia*: "differences of no slight import" (see vol. 1/B, p. 575). More loosely, understatement; Swift, "A Tale of a Tub": "Last week I saw a woman flayed, and you will hardly believe how much it altered her person for the worse" (see vol. 1/C, p. 1956). Stevie Smith, "Sunt Leones," lines 11–12: "And if the Christians felt a little blue— / Well people being eaten often do" (see vol. 2/F, p. 2600).

lullaby: a **genre.** A bedtime, sleep-inducing song for children, in simple and regular meter. Adapted by Auden, "Lullaby" (see vol. 2/F, p. 2680).

lyric (from Greek "lyre"): Initially meaning a song, "lyric" refers to a short poetic form, without restriction of meter, in which the expression of personal emotion, often by a voice in the first person, is given primacy over narrative sequence. Thus "The Wife's Lament" (see vol. 1/A, p. 120); Yeats, "The Wild Swans at Coole" (see vol. 2/F, p. 2096).

masque: a **genre.** Costly entertainments of the Stuart court, involving dance, song, speech, and elaborate stage effects, in which courtiers themselves participated.

metaphor (Greek "carrying across," etymologically parallel to Latin "translation"): One of the most significant **figures of thought,** metaphor designates identification or implicit identification of one thing with another with which it is not literally identifiable. Blake, "London," lines 11–12: "And the hapless Soldier's sigh / Runs in blood down Palace walls" (see vol. 2/D, p. 132).

meter: Verse (from Latin "versus," turned) is distinguished from prose (from Latin "prorsus," straightforward) as a more compressed form of expression, shaped by metrical norms. **Meter** (Greek "measure") refers to the regularly recurring sound pattern of verse lines. The means of producing sound patterns across lines differ in different poetic traditions. Verse may be **quantitative,** or determined by the quantities of syllables (set patterns of long and short syllables), as in Latin and Greek poetry. It may be **syllabic,** determined by fixed numbers of syllables in the line, as in the verse of Romance languages (e.g., French and Italian). It may be **accentual,** determined by the number of accents, or stresses in the line, with variable numbers of syllables, as in Old English and some varieties of Middle English alliterative verse. Or it may be **accentual-syllabic,** determined by the numbers of accents, but possessing a regular pattern of stressed and unstressed syllables, so as to produce regular numbers of syllables per line. Since Chaucer, English verse has worked primarily within the many possibilities of accentual-syllabic meter. The unit of meter is the **foot.** In English verse the number of feet per line corresponds to the number of accents in a line. For the types and examples of different meters, see **monometer,**

dimeter, trimester, tetrameter, pentameter, and **hexameter.** In the definitions below, "u" designates one unstressed syllable, and "/" one stressed syllable.

metonymy (Greek "change of name"): one of the most significant **figures of thought.** Using a word to **denote** another concept or other concepts, by virtue of habitual association. Thus "The Press," designating printed news media. Fictional names often work by associations of this kind. Closely related to **synecdoche.**

mimesis (Greek for "imitation"): A central function of literature and drama has been to provide a plausible imitation of the reality of the world beyond the literary work; mimesis is the representation and imitation of what is taken to be reality.

mise-en-abyme (French for "cast into the abyss"): Some works of art represent themselves in themselves; if they do so effectively, the represented artifact also represents itself, and so ad infinitum. The effect achieved is called "*mise-en-abyme.*" Hoccleve's *Complaint*, for example, represents a depressed man reading about a depressed man. This sequence threatens to become a *mise-en-abyme.*

monometer (Greek "one measure"): a term of **meter.** An entire line with just one stress; *Sir Gawain and the Green Knight,* line 15, "most (u) grand (/)" (see vol. 1/A, p. 186).

myth: a **genre.** The narrative of **protagonists** with, or subject to, superhuman powers. A myth expresses some profound foundational truth, often by accounting for the origin of natural phenomena. To be distinguished from **legend.** Thus the "Arthurian legend" but the "myth of Proserpine."

novel: an extremely flexible **genre** in both form and subject matter. Usually in prose, giving high priority to narration of events, with a certain expectation of length, novels are preponderantly rooted in a specific, and often complex, social world; sensitive to the realities of material life; and often focused on one **character** or a small circle of central characters. By contrast with chivalric **romance** (the main European narrative genre prior to the novel), novels tend to eschew the marvelous in favor of a recognizable social world and credible action. The novel's openness allows it to participate in all modes, and to be co-opted for a huge variety of subgenres. In English literature the novel dates from the late seventeenth century and has been astonishingly successful in appealing to a huge readership, particularly in the nineteenth and twentieth centuries. The English and Irish tradition of the novel includes, for example, Fielding, Austen, the Brontë sisters, Dickens, George Eliot, Conrad, Woolf, Lawrence, Joyce, to name but a few very great exponents of the genre.

novella: a **genre.** A short **novel,** often characterized by imagistic intensity. Conrad, *Heart of Darkness* (see vol. 2/F, p. 1954).

occupatio (Latin "taking possession"): a **figure of thought.** Denying that one will discuss a subject while actually discussing it; also known as "praeteritio" (Latin "passing by"). See Chaucer, *Nun's Priest's Tale,* lines 414–32 (see vol. 1/A, p. 335).

ode (Greek "song"): a **genre.** A **lyric** poem in elevated, or high style (see **register**), often addressed to a natural force, a person, or an abstract quality. The Pindaric ode in English is made up of **stanzas** of unequal length, while the Horatian ode has stanzas of equal length. For examples of both types, see, respectively, Wordsworth, "Ode: Intimations of Immortality" (vol. 2/D, p. 335); and Marvell, "An Horatian Ode" (vol. 1/B, p. 1806), or Keats, "Ode on Melancholy" (vol. 2/D, p. 931). For a fuller discussion, see the headnote to Jonson's "Ode on Cary and Morison" (vol. 1/B, p. 1551).

omniscient narrator (Latin "all-knowing narrator"): relevant to **point of view.** A narrator who, in the fiction of the narrative, has complete access to both the deeds and the thoughts of all **characters** in the narrative. Thus Thomas Hardy, "On the Western Circuit" (see vol. 2/F, p. 1917).

onomatopoeia (Greek "name making"): a **figure of speech.** Verbal sounds that imitate and evoke the sounds they denotate. Hopkins, "Binsey Poplars," lines 10–12 (about some felled trees): "O if we but knew what we do / When we delve [dig] or hew— / Hack and rack the growing green!" (see vol. 2/E, p. 1552).

order: A story may be told in different narrative orders. A narrator might use the sequence of events as they happened, and thereby follow what **classical** rhetoricians called the *natural order;* alternatively, the narrator might reorder the sequence of events, beginning the narration either in the middle or at the end of the sequence of events, thereby following an *artificial order.* If a narrator begins in the middle of events, he or she is said to begin *in medias res* (Latin "in the middle of the matter"). For a brief discussion of these concepts, see Spenser, *Faerie Queene,* "A Letter of the Authors" (vol. 1/B, p. 777). Modern narratology makes a related distinction, between *histoire* (French "story") for the natural order that readers mentally reconstruct, and *discours* (French, here "narration") for the narrative as presented. See also **plot** and **story.**

ottava rima: a **verse form.** An eight-line stanza form, rhyming abababcc, using **iambic pentameter;** Yeats, "Sailing to Byzantium" (see vol. 2/F, p. 2103). Derived from the Italian poet Boccaccio, an eight-line stanza was used by fifteenth-century English poets for inset passages (e.g., Christ's speech from the Cross in Lydgate's *Testament,* lines 754–897). The form in this rhyme scheme was used in English poetry for long narrative by, for example, Byron (*Don Juan;* see vol. 2/D, p. 672).

oxymoron (Greek "sharp blunt"): a **figure of thought.** The conjunction of normally incompatible terms; Milton, *Paradise Lost* 1.63: "darkness visible" (see vol. 1/B, p. 1947).

panegyric: a **genre.** Demonstrative, or epideictic (Greek "showing"), rhetoric was a branch of **classical** rhetoric. Its own two main branches were the rhetoric of praise on the one hand and of vituperation on the other. Panegyric, or eulogy (Greek "sweet speaking"), or encomium (plural *encomia*), is the term used to describe the speeches or writings of praise.

parable: a **genre.** A simple story designed to provoke, and often accompanied by, **allegorical** interpretation, most famously by Christ as reported in the Gospels.

paradox (Greek "contrary to received opinion"): a **figure of thought.** An apparent contradiction that requires thought to reveal an inner consistency. Chaucer, "Troilus's Song," line 12: "O sweete harm so quainte" (see vol. 1/A, p. 344).

parataxis, or **coordination** (respectively Greek and Latin "ordering beside"): a term of **syntax.** The coordination, by the use of coordinating conjunctions, of different main clauses in a single sentence. Malory, "Morte Darthur": "So Sir Lancelot departed and took his sword under his arm, and so he walked in his mantel, that noble knight, and put himself in great jeopardy" (see vol. 1/A, p. 484). The opposite principle to **hypotaxis.**

parody: a work that uses the **conventions** of a particular genre with the aim of comically mocking a **topos,** a genre, or a particular exponent of a genre. Shakespeare parodies the topos of **blazon** in Sonnet 130 (see vol. 1/B, p. 1183).

pastoral (from Latin "pastor," shepherd): a **genre.** Pastoral is set among shepherds, making often refined **allusion** to other apparently unconnected subjects (sometimes politics) from the potentially idyllic world of highly literary if illiterate shepherds. Pastoral is distinguished from **georgic** by representing recreational rural idleness, whereas the georgic offers instruction on how to manage rural labor. English writers had classical models in the *Idylls* of Theocritus in Greek and Virgil's *Eclogues* in

Latin. Pastoral is also called bucolic (from the Greek word for "herdsman"). Thus Spenser, *Shepheardes Calender* (see vol. 1/B, p. 769).

pathetic fallacy: the attribution of sentiment to natural phenomena, as if they were in sympathy with human feelings. Thus Milton, *Lycidas,* lines 146–47: "With cowslips wan that hang the pensive head, / And every flower that sad embroidery wears" (see vol. 1/B, p. 1922). For critique of the practice, see Ruskin (who coined the term), "Of the Pathetic Fallacy" (vol. 2/E, p. 1340).

pentameter (Greek "five measure"): a term of **meter.** In English verse, a five-stress line. Between the late fourteenth and the nineteenth centuries, this meter, frequently employing an iambic rhythm, was the basic line of English verse. Chaucer, Shakespeare, Milton, and Wordsworth each, for example, deployed this very flexible line as their primary resource; Milton, *Paradise Lost* 1.128: "O Prince, O Chief of many thronèd Powers" (see vol. 1/B, p. 1949).

performative: Verbal expressions have many different functions. They can, for example, be descriptive, or constative (if they make an argument), or performative, for example. A performative utterance is one that makes something happen in the world by virtue of its utterance. "I hereby sentence you to ten years in prison," if uttered in the appropriate circumstances, itself performs an action; it makes something happen in the world. By virtue of its performing an action, it is called a "performative." See also **speech act.**

peripeteia (Greek "turning about"): the sudden reversal of fortune (in both directions) in a dramatic work.

periphrasis (Greek "declaring around"): a **figure of thought.** Circumlocution; the use of many words to express what could be expressed in few or one; Sidney, *Astrophil and Stella* 39.1–4 (vol. 1/B, p. 1091).

persona (Latin "sound through"): originally the mask worn in the Roman theater to magnify an actor's voice; in literary discourse persona (plural *personae*) refers to the narrator or speaker of a text, whose voice is coherent and whose person need have no relation to the person of the actual author of a text. Eliot, "The Love Song of J. Alfred Prufrock" (see vol. 2/F, p. 2525).

personification, or **prosopopoeia** (Greek "person making"): a **figure of thought.** The attribution of human qualities to nonhuman forces or objects; Shakespeare, *King Lear* 3.2.1: "Blow winds and crack your cheeks, rage! Blow!" (see vol. 1/B, p. 1295).

plot: the sequence of events in a story as narrated, as distinct from **story,** which refers to the sequence of events as we reconstruct them from the plot. See also **order.**

point of view: All of the many kinds of writing involve a point of view from which a text is, or seems to be, generated. The presence of such a point of view may be powerful and explicit, as in many novels, or deliberately invisible, as in much drama. In some genres, such as the **novel,** the narrator does not necessarily tell the story from a position we can predict; that is, the needs of a particular story, not the **conventions** of the genre, determine the narrator's position. In other genres, the narrator's position is fixed by convention; in certain kinds of love poetry, for example, the narrating voice is always that of a suffering lover. Not only does the point of view significantly inform the style of a work, but it also informs the structure of that work.

protagonist (Greek "first actor"): the hero or heroine of a drama or narrative.

pun: a **figure of thought.** A sometimes irresolvable doubleness of meaning in a single word or expression; Shakespeare, Sonnet 135, line 1: "Whoever hath her wish, thou hast thy *Will*" (see vol. 1/B, p. 1183).

quatrain: a **verse form.** A stanza of four lines, usually rhyming abcb, abab, or abba. Of many possible examples, see Crashaw, "On the Wounds of Our Crucified Lord" (see vol. 1/B, p. 1746).

refrain: usually a single line repeated as the last line of consecutive stanzas, sometimes with subtly different wording and ideally with subtly different meaning as the poem progresses. See, for example, Wyatt, "Blame not my lute" (vol. 1/B, p. 656).

register: The register of a word is its stylistic level, which can be distinguished by degree of technicality but also by degree of formality. We choose our words from different registers according to context, that is, audience and/or environment. Thus a chemist in a laboratory will say "sodium chloride," a cook in a kitchen "salt." A formal register designates the kind of language used in polite society (e.g., "Mr. President"), while an informal or colloquial register is used in less formal or more relaxed social situations (e.g., "the boss"). In **classical** and medieval rhetoric, these registers of formality were called *high style* and *low style*. A *middle style* was defined as the style fit for narrative, not drawing attention to itself.

rhetoric: the art of verbal persuasion. **Classical** rhetoricians distinguished three areas of rhetoric: the forensic, to be used in law courts; the deliberative, to be used in political or philosophical deliberations; and the demonstrative, or epideictic, to be used for the purposes of public praise or blame. Rhetorical manuals covered all the skills required of a speaker, from the management of style and structure to delivery. These manuals powerfully influenced the theory of poetics as a separate branch of verbal practice, particularly in the matter of style.

rhyme: a **figure of speech.** The repetition of identical vowel sounds in stressed syllables whose initial consonants differ ("dead" / "head"). In poetry, rhyme often links the end of one line with another. *Masculine rhyme:* full rhyme on the final syllable of the line ("decays" / "days"). *Feminine rhyme:* full rhyme on syllables that are followed by unaccented syllables ("fountains" / "mountains"). *Internal rhyme:* full rhyme within a single line; Coleridge, *The Rime of the Ancient Mariner,* line 7: "The guests are met, the feast is set" (see vol. 2/D, p. 444). *Rhyme riche:* rhyming on **homophones;** Chaucer, *General Prologue,* lines 17–18: "seeke" / "seke." *Off rhyme* (also known as *half rhyme, near rhyme,* or *slant rhyme*): differs from perfect rhyme in changing the vowel sound and/or the concluding consonants expected of perfect rhyme; Byron, "They say that Hope is Happiness," lines 5–7: "most" / "lost." *Pararhyme:* stressed vowel sounds differ but are flanked by identical or similar consonants; Owen, "Miners," lines 9–11: "simmer" / "summer" (see vol. 2/F, p. 2037).

rhyme royal: a **verse form.** A **stanza** of seven **iambic pentameter** lines, rhyming ababbcc; first introduced by Chaucer and called "royal" because the form was used by James I of Scotland for his *Kingis Quair* in the early fifteenth century. Chaucer, "Troilus's Song" (see vol. 1/A, p. 344).

rhythm: Rhythm is not absolutely distinguishable from **meter.** One way of making a clear distinction between these terms is to say that rhythm (from the Greek "to flow") denotes the patterns of sound within the feet of verse lines and the combination of those feet. Very often a particular meter will raise expectations that a given rhythm will be used regularly through a whole line or a whole poem. Thus in English verse the pentameter regularly uses an iambic rhythm. Rhythm, however, is much more fluid than meter, and many lines within the same poem using a single meter will frequently exploit different rhythmic possibilities. For examples of different rhythms, see **iamb, trochee, anapest, spondee,** and **dactyl.**

romance: a **genre.** From the twelfth to the sixteenth century, the main form of European narrative, in either verse or prose, was that of chivalric romance. Romance, like the later **novel,** is a very fluid genre, but romances are often characterized by (i) a tripartite structure of social integration, followed by disintegration, involving moral tests and often marvelous events, itself the prelude to reintegration in a happy ending, frequently of marriage; and (ii) aristocratic social milieux. Thus *Sir Gawain and the Green Knight* (see vol. 1/A, p. 186); Spenser's (unfinished) *Faerie Queene* (vol. 1/B, p. 775). The immensely popular, fertile genre was absorbed, in both domesticated and undomesticated form, by the novel. For an adaptation of romance, see Chaucer, *Wife of Bath's Tale* (vol. 1/A, p. 282).

sarcasm (Greek "flesh tearing"): a **figure of thought.** A wounding expression, often expressed ironically; Boswell, *Life of Johnson:* Johnson [asked if any man of the modern age could have written the **epic** poem *Fingal*] replied, "Yes, Sir, many men, many women, and many children" (see vol. 1/C, p. 2446).

satire (Latin for "a bowl of mixed fruits"): a **genre.** In Roman literature (e.g., Juvenal), the communication, in the form of a letter between equals, complaining of the ills of contemporary society. The genre in this form is characterized by a first-person narrator exasperated by social ills; the letter form; a high frequency of contemporary reference; and the use of invective in **low-style** language. Pope practices the genre thus in the *Epistle to Dr. Arbuthnot* (see vol. 1/C, p. 2193). Wyatt's "Mine own John Poins" (see vol. 1/B, p. 659) draws ultimately on a gentler, Horatian model of the genre.

satiric mode: Works in a very large variety of genres are devoted to the more or less savage attack on social ills. Thus Swift's travel narrative *Gulliver's Travels* (see vol. 1/C, p. 1959), his **essay** "A Modest Proposal" (vol. 1/C, p. 2105), Pope's mock-**epic** *The Dunciad* (vol. 1/C, p. 2204), and Gay's *Beggar's Opera* (vol. 1/C, p. 2261), to look no further than the eighteenth century, are all within a satiric mode.

scene: a subdivision of an **act,** itself a subdivision of a dramatic performance and/ or text. The action of a scene usually occurs in one place.

sensibility (from Latin, "capable of being perceived by the senses"): as a literary term, an eighteenth-century concept derived from moral philosophy that stressed the social importance of fellow feeling and particularly of sympathy in social relations. The concept generated a literature of "sensibility," such as the sentimental **novel** (the most famous of which was Goethe's *Sorrows of the Young Werther* [1774]), or sentimental poetry, such as Cowper's passage on the stricken deer in *The Task* (see vol. 1/C, p. 2546).

short story: a **genre.** Generically similar to, though shorter and more concentrated than, the **novel;** often published as part of a collection. Thus Mansfield, "The Daughters of the Late Colonel" (see vol. 2/F, p. 2569).

simile (Latin "like"): a **figure of thought.** Comparison, usually using the word "like" or "as," of one thing with another so as to produce sometimes surprising analogies. Donne, "The Storm," lines 29–30: "Sooner than you read this line did the gale, / Like shot, not feared till felt, our sails assail." Frequently used, in extended form, in **epic** poetry; Milton, *Paradise Lost* 1.338–46 (see vol. 1/B, p. 1954).

soliloquy (Latin "single speaking"): a **topos** of drama, in which a **character,** alone or thinking to be alone on stage, speaks so as to give the audience access to his or her private thoughts. Thus Viola's soliloquy in Shakespeare, *Twelfth Night* 2.2.17– 41 (vol. 1/B, p. 1205).

sonnet: a **verse form.** A form combining a variable number of units of rhymed lines to produce a fourteen-line poem, usually in rhyming **iambic pentameter** lines. In English there are two principal varieties: the Petrarchan sonnet, formed by an octave (an eight-line stanza, often broken into two **quatrains** having the same rhyme scheme, typically abba abba) and a sestet (a six-line stanza, typically cdecde or cdcdcd); and the Shakespearean sonnet, formed by three quatrains (abab cdcd efef) and a **couplet** (gg). The declaration of a sonnet can take a sharp turn, or "volta," often at the decisive formal shift from octave to sestet in the Petrarchan sonnet, or in the final couplet of a Shakespearean sonnet, introducing a trenchant counterstatement. Derived from Italian poetry, and especially from the poetry of Petrarch, the sonnet was first introduced to English poetry by Wyatt, and initially used principally for the expression of unrequited erotic love, though later poets used the form for many other purposes. See Wyatt, "Whoso list to hunt" (vol. 1/B, p. 649); Sidney, *Astrophil and Stella* (vol. 1/B, p. 1084); Shakespeare, *Sonnets* (vol. 1/B, p. 1169); Wordsworth, "London, 1802" (vol. 2/D, p. 346); McKay, "If We Must Die" (vol. 2/F, p. 2724); Heaney, "Clearances" (vol. 2/F, p. 2963).

speech act: Words and deeds are often distinguished, but words are often (perhaps always) themselves deeds. Utterances can perform different speech acts, such as promising, declaring, casting a spell, encouraging, persuading, denying, lying, and so on. See also **performative.**

Spenserian stanza: a **verse form.** The stanza developed by Spenser for *The Faerie Queene;* nine **iambic** lines, the first eight of which are **pentameters,** followed by one **hexameter,** rhyming ababbcbcc. See also, for example, Shelley, *Adonais* (vol. 2/D, p. 839), and Keats, *The Eve of St. Agnes* (vol. 2/D, p. 912).

spondee: a term of **meter.** A two-syllable foot following the rhythmic pattern, in English verse, of two stressed syllables. Thus, for example, "Utah."

stanza (Italian "room"): groupings of two or more lines, though "stanza" is usually reserved for groupings of at least four lines. Stanzas are often joined by rhyme, often in sequence, where each group shares the same metrical pattern and, when rhymed, rhyme scheme. Stanzas can themselves be arranged into larger groupings. Poets often invent new **verse forms,** or they may work within established forms.

story: a narrative's sequence of events, which we reconstruct from those events as they have been recounted by the narrator (i.e., the **plot**). See also **order.**

stream of consciousness: usually a **first-person** narrative that seems to give the reader access to the narrator's mind as it perceives or reflects on events, prior to organizing those perceptions into a coherent narrative. Thus (though generated from a **third-person** narrative) Joyce, *Ulysses,* "Penelope" (see vol. 2/F, p. 2475).

style (from Latin for "writing instrument"): In literary works the manner in which something is expressed contributes substantially to its meaning. The expressions "sun," "mass of helium at the center of the solar system," "heaven's golden orb" all designate "sun," but do so in different manners, or styles, which produce different meanings. The manner of a literary work is its "style," the effect of which is its "tone." We often can intuit the tone of a text; from that intuition of tone we can analyze the stylistic resources by which it was produced. We can analyze the style of literary works through consideration of different elements of style; for example, **diction, figures of thought, figures of speech, meter and rhythm, verse form, syntax, point of view.**

sublime: As a concept generating a literary movement, the sublime refers to the realm of experience beyond the measurable, and so beyond the rational, produced especially by the terrors and grandeur of natural phenomena. Derived especially from the first-century Greek treatise *On the Sublime,* sometimes attributed to Longinus, the notion of the sublime was in the later eighteenth century a spur to Romanticism.

syllable: the smallest unit of sound in a pronounced word. The syllable that receives the greatest stress is called the *tonic* syllable.

symbol (Greek "token"): a **figure of thought.** Something that stands for something else, and yet seems necessarily to evoke that other thing. In Neoplatonic, and therefore Romantic, theory, to be distinguished from **allegory** thus: whereas allegory involves connections between vehicle and tenor agreed by convention or made explicit, the meanings of a symbol are supposedly inherent to it. For discussion, see Coleridge, "On Symbol and Allegory" (vol. 2/D, p. 502).

synecdoche (Greek "to take with something else"): a **figure of thought.** Using a part to express the whole, or vice versa; e.g., "all hands on deck." Closely related to **metonymy.**

syntax (Greek "ordering with"): Syntax designates the rules by which sentences are constructed in a given language. Discussion of meter is impossible without some reference to syntax, since the overall effect of a poem is, in part, always the product of a subtle balance of meter and sentence construction. Syntax is also essential to the understanding of prose style, since prose writers, deprived of the full shaping possibilities of meter, rely all the more heavily on syntactic resources. A working command of syntactical practice requires an understanding of the parts of speech (nouns, verbs, adjectives, adverbs, conjunctions, pronouns, prepositions, and inter- jections), since writers exploit syntactic possibilities by using particular combina- tions and concentrations of the parts of speech.

taste (from Italian "touch"): Although medieval monastic traditions used eating and tasting as a metaphor for reading, the concept of taste as a personal ideal to be cultivated by, and applied to, the appreciation and judgment of works of art in gen- eral was developed in the eighteenth century.

tercet: a **verse form.** A stanza or group of three lines, used in larger forms such as **terza rima,** the **Petrarchan sonnet,** and the **villanelle.**

terza rima: a **verse form.** A sequence of rhymed **tercets** linked by rhyme thus: aba bcb cdc, etc. first used extensively by Dante in *The Divine Comedy,* the form was adapted in English **iambic pentameters** by Wyatt and revived in the nineteenth century. See Wyatt, "Mine own John Poins" (vol. 1/B, p. 659); Shelley, "Ode to the West Wind" (vol. 2/D, p. 791); and Morris, "The Defence of Guinevere" (vol. 2/E, p. 1513). For modern adaptations see Eliot, lines 78–149 (though unrhymed) of "Little Gidding" (vol. 2/F, pp. 2548); Heaney, "Station Island" (vol. 2/F, p. 2961); Walcott, *Omeros* (vol. 2/F, p. 2806).

tetrameter (Greek "four measure"): a term of **meter.** A line with four stresses. Coleridge, *Christabel,* line 31: "She stole along, she nothing spoke" (see vol. 2/D, p. 462).

theme (Greek "proposition"): In literary criticism the term designates what the work is about; the theme is the concept that unifies a given work of literature.

third-person narration: relevant to **point of view.** A narration in which the narrator recounts a narrative of **characters** referred to explicitly or implicitly by third-person pronouns ("he," she," etc.), without the limitation of a **first-person narration.** Thus Johnson, *The History of Rasselas.*

topographical poem (Greek "place writing"): a **genre.** A poem devoted to the medita- tive description of particular places. Thus Gray, "Ode on a Distant Prospect of Eton College" (see vol. 1/C, p. 2519).

topos (Greek "place," plural *topoi*): a commonplace in the content of a given kind of literature. Originally, in **classical** rhetoric, the topoi were tried-and-tested stimuli to literary invention: lists of standard headings under which a subject might be investigated. In medieval narrative poems, for example, it was commonplace to begin with a description of spring. Writers did, of course, render the commonplace uncommon, as in Chaucer's spring scene at the opening of *The Canterbury Tales* (see vol. 1/A, p. 243).

tradition (from Latin "passing on"): A literary tradition is whatever is passed on or revived from the past in a single literary culture, or drawn from others to enrich a writer's culture. "Tradition" is fluid in reference, ranging from small to large referents: thus it may refer to a relatively small aspect of texts (e.g., the tradition of **iambic pentameter**), or it may, at the other extreme, refer to the body of texts that constitute a **canon**.

tragedy: a **genre.** A dramatic representation of the fall of kings or nobles, beginning in happiness and ending in catastrophe. Later transferred to other social milieux. The opposite of **comedy,** Shakespeare, *King Lear* (see vol. 1/B, p. 1251).

tragic mode: Many genres (**epic** poetry, **legend**ary chronicles, **tragedy,** the **novel**) either do or can participate in a tragic mode, by representing the fall of noble **protagonists** and the irreparable ravages of human society and history.

tragicomedy: a **genre.** A play in which potentially tragic events turn out to have a happy, or **comic,** ending. Thus Shakespeare, *Measure for Measure.*

translation (Latin "carrying across"): the rendering of a text written in one language into another.

trimeter (Greek "three measure"): a term of **meter.** A line with three stresses. Herbert, "Discipline," line 1: "Throw away thy rod" (see vol. 1/B, p. 1724).

triplet: a **verse form.** A **tercet** rhyming on the same sound. Pope inserts triplets among heroic **couplets** to emphasize a particular thought; see *Essay on Criticism,* 315–17 (vol. 1/C, p. 2148).

trochee: a term of **rhythm.** A two-syllable foot following the pattern, in English verse, of stressed followed by unstressed syllable, producing a falling effect. Thus, for example, "Texas."

type (Greek "impression, figure"): a **figure of thought** In Christian allegorical interpretation of the Old Testament, pre-Christian figures were regarded as "types," or foreshadowings, of Christ or the Christian dispensation. *Typology* has been the source of much visual and literary art in which the parallelisms between old and new are extended to nonbiblical figures; thus the virtuous plowman in *Piers Plowman* becomes a type of Christ.

unities: According to a theory supposedly derived from Aristotle's *Poetics,* the events represented in a play should have unity of time, place, and action: that the play take up no more time than the time of the play, or at most a day; that the space of action should be within a single city; and that there should be no subplot. See Johnson, *The Preface to Shakespeare* (vol. 1/C, p. 2408).

vernacular (from Latin "verna," servant): the language of the people, as distinguished from learned and arcane languages. From the later Middle Ages especially, the "vernacular" languages and literatures of Europe distinguished themselves from the learned languages and literatures of Latin, Greek, and Hebrew.

verse form: The terms related to **meter** and **rhythm** describe the shape of individual lines. Lines of verse are combined to produce larger groupings, called verse forms. These larger groupings are in the first instance **stanzas.** The combination of a certain meter and stanza shape constitutes the verse form, of which there are many standard kinds.

villanelle: a **verse form.** A fixed form of usually five **tercets** and a **quatrain** employing only two rhyme sounds altogether, rhyming aba for the tercets and abaa for the quatrain, with a complex pattern of two **refrains.** Derived from a French fixed form. Thomas, "Do Not Go Gentle into That Good Night" (see vol. 2/F, p. 2704).

wit: Originally a synonym for "reason" in Old and Middle English, "wit" became a literary ideal in the Renaissance as brilliant play of the full range of mental resources. For eighteenth-century writers, the notion necessarily involved pleasing expression, as in Pope's definition of true wit as "Nature to advantage dressed, / What oft was thought, but ne'er so well expressed" (*Essay on Criticism*, lines 297–98; see vol. 1/C, p. 2147). See also Johnson, *Lives of the Poets*, "Cowley," on "metaphysical wit" (see vol. 1/C, p. 2419). Romantic theory of the imagination deprived wit of its full range of apprehension, whence the word came to be restricted to its modern sense, as the clever play of mind that produces laughter.

zeugma (Greek "a yoking"): a **figure of thought.** A figure whereby one word applies to two or more words in a sentence, and in which the applications are surprising, either because one is unusual, or because the applications are made in very different ways; Pope, *Rape of the Lock* 3.7–8, in which the word "take" is used in two senses: "Here thou, great Anna! whom three realms obey, / Dost sometimes counsel take— and sometimes tea" (see vol. 1/C, p. 2166).

B: Publishing History, Censorship

By the time we read texts in published books, they have already been treated—that is, changed by authors, editors, and printers—in many ways. Although there are differences across history, in each period literary works are subject to pressures of many kinds, which apply before, while, and after an author writes. The pressures might be financial, as in the relations of author and patron; commercial, as in the marketing of books; and legal, as in, during some periods, the negotiation through official and unofficial censorship. In addition, texts in all periods undergo technological processes, as they move from the material forms in which an author produced them to the forms in which they are presented to readers. Some of the terms below designate important material forms in which books were produced, disseminated, and surveyed across the historical span of this anthology. Others designate the skills developed to understand these processes. The anthology's introductions to individual periods discuss the particular forms these phenomena took in different eras.

bookseller: In England, and particularly in London, commercial bookmaking and-selling enterprises came into being in the early fourteenth century. These were loose organizations of artisans who usually lived in the same neighborhoods (around St. Paul's Cathedral in London). A bookseller or dealer would coordinate the production of hand-copied books for wealthy patrons (see **patronage**), who would order books to be custom-made. After the introduction of **printing** in the late fifteenth century, authors generally sold the rights to their work to booksellers, without any further **royalties.** Booksellers, who often had their own shops, belonged to the **Stationers' Company.** This system lasted into the eighteenth century. In 1710, however, authors were for the first time granted **copyright,** which tipped the commercial balance in their favor, against booksellers.

censorship: The term applies to any mechanism for restricting what can be published. Historically, the reasons for imposing censorship are heresy, sedition, blasphemy, libel, or obscenity. External censorship is imposed by institutions having legislative sanctions at their disposal. Thus the pre-Reformation Church imposed the Constitutions of Archbishop Arundel of 1409, aimed at repressing the Lollard "heresy." After the Reformation, some key events in the history of censorship are as follows: 1547, when anti-Lollard legislation and legislation made by Henry VIII concerning treason by writing (1534) were abolished; the Licensing Order of 1643, which legislated that works be licensed, through the Stationers' Company, prior to publication; and 1695, when the last such Act stipulating prepublication licensing lapsed. Postpublication censorship continued in different periods for different reasons.

Thus, for example, British publication of D. H. Lawrence's *Lady Chatterley's Lover* (1928) was obstructed (though unsuccessfully) in 1960, under the Obscene Publications Act of 1959. Censorship can also be international: although not published in Iran, Salman Rushdie's *Satanic Verses* (1988) was censored in that country, where the leader, Ayatollah Ruhollah Khomeini, proclaimed a fatwa (religious decree) promising the author's execution. Very often censorship is not imposed externally, however: authors or publishers can censor work in anticipation of what will incur the wrath of readers or the penalties of the law. Victorian and Edwardian publishers of **novels,** for example, urged authors to remove potentially offensive material, especially for serial publication in popular magazines.

codex: the physical format of most modern books and medieval manuscripts, consisting of a series of separate leaves gathered into quires and bound together, often with a cover. In late antiquity, the codex largely replaced the scroll, the standard form of written documents in Roman culture.

copy text: the particular text of a work used by a textual editor as the basis of an edition of that work.

copyright: the legal protection afforded to authors for control of their work's publication, in an attempt to ensure due financial reward. Some key dates in the history of copyright in the United Kingdom are as follows: 1710, when a statute gave authors the exclusive right to publish their work for fourteen years, and fourteen years more if the author were still alive when the first term had expired; 1842, when the period of authorial control was extended to forty-two years; and 1911, when the term was extended yet further, to fifty years after the author's death. In 1995 the period of protection was harmonized with the laws in other European countries to be the life of the author plus seventy years. In the United States no works first published before 1923 are in copyright. Works published since 1978 are, as in the United Kingdom, protected for the life of the author plus seventy years.

folio: the leaf formed by both sides of a single page. Each folio has two sides: a *recto* (the front side of the leaf, on the right side of a double-page spread in an open codex), and a *verso* (the back side of the leaf, on the left side of a double-page spread). Modern book pagination follows the pattern 1, 2, 3, 4, while medieval manuscript pagination follows the pattern 1r, 1v, 2r, 2v. "Folio" can also designate the size of a printed book. Books come in different shapes, depending originally on the number of times a standard sheet of paper is folded. One fold produces a large volume, a *folio* book; two folds produce a *quarto*, four an *octavo*, and six a very small *duodecimo*. Generally speaking, the larger the book, the grander and more expensive. Shakespeare's plays were, for example, first printed in quartos, but were gathered into a folio edition in 1623.

foul papers: versions of a work before an author has produced, if she or he has, a final copy (a "fair copy") with all corrections removed.

incunabulum (plural "incunabula"): any printed book produced in Europe before 1501. Famous incunabula include the Gutenberg Bible, printed in 1455.

manuscript (Latin, "written by hand"): Any text written physically by hand is a manuscript. Before the introduction of **printing** with moveable type in 1476, all texts in England were produced and reproduced by hand, in manuscript. This is an extremely labor-intensive task, using expensive materials (e.g., **vellum,** or **parchment**); the cost of books produced thereby was, accordingly, very high. Even after the introduction of printing, many texts continued to be produced in manuscript. This is obviously true of letters, for example, but until the eighteenth century, poetry written within aristocratic circles was often transmitted in manuscript copies.

paleography (Greek "ancient writing"): the art of deciphering, describing, and dating forms of handwriting.

parchment: animal skin, used as the material for handwritten books before the introduction of paper. See also **vellum.**

patronage, patron (Latin "protector"): Many technological, legal, and commercial supports were necessary before professional authorship became possible. Although some playwrights (e.g., Shakespeare) made a living by writing for the theater, other authors needed, principally, the large-scale reproductive capacities of **printing** and the security of **copyright** to make a living from writing. Before these conditions obtained, many authors had another main occupation, and most authors had to rely on patronage. In different periods, institutions or individuals offered material support, or patronage, to authors. Thus in Anglo-Saxon England, monasteries afforded the conditions of writing to monastic authors. Between the twelfth and the seventeenth centuries, the main source of patronage was the royal court. Authors offered patrons prestige and ideological support in return for financial support. Even as the conditions of professional authorship came into being at the beginning of the eighteenth century, older forms of direct patronage were not altogether displaced until the middle of the century.

periodical: Whereas journalism, strictly, applies to daily writing (from French "jour," day), periodical writing appears at larger, but still frequent, intervals, characteristically in the form of the **essay.** Periodicals were developed especially in the eighteenth century.

printing: Printing, or the mechanical reproduction of books using moveable type, was invented in Germany in the mid-fifteenth century by Johannes Gutenberg; it quickly spread throughout Europe. William Caxton brought printing into England from the Low Countries in 1476. Much greater powers of reproduction at much lower prices transformed every aspect of literary culture.

publisher: the person or company responsible for the commissioning and publicizing of printed matter. In the early period of **printing,** publisher, printer, and bookseller were often the same person. This trend continued in the ascendancy of the **Stationers' Company,** between the middle of the sixteenth and the end of the seventeenth centuries. Toward the end of the seventeenth century, these three functions began to separate, leading to their modern distinctions.

quire: When medieval manuscripts were assembled, a few loose sheets of parchment or paper would first be folded together and sewn along the fold. This formed a quire (also known as a "gathering" or "signature"). Folded in this way, four large sheets of parchment would produce eight smaller manuscript leaves. Multiple quires could then be bound together to form a codex.

royalties: an agreed-upon proportion of the price of each copy of a work sold, paid by the publisher to the author, or an agreed-upon fee paid to the playwright for each performance of a play.

scribe: In **manuscript** culture, the scribe is the copyist who reproduces a text by hand.

scriptorium (plural "scriptoria"): a place for producing written documents and manuscripts.

serial publication: generally referring to the practice, especially common in the nineteenth-century, of publishing novels a few chapters at a time, in periodicals.

Stationers' Company: The Stationers' Company was an English guild incorporating various tradesmen, including printers, publishers, and booksellers, skilled in the production and selling of books. It was formed in 1403, received its royal charter in 1557, and served as a means both of producing and of regulating books. Authors would sell the manuscripts of their books to individual stationers, who incurred the risks and took the profits of producing and selling the books. The stationers entered their rights over given books in the Stationers' Register. They also regulated the book trade and held their monopoly by licensing books and by being empowered to seize unauthorized books and imprison resisters. This system of licensing broke down in the social unrest of the Civil War and Interregnum (1640–60), and it ended in 1695. Even after the end of licensing, the Stationers' Company continued to be an intrinsic part of the **copyright** process, since the 1710 copyright statute directed that copyright had to be registered at Stationers' Hall.

subscription: An eighteenth-century system of bookselling somewhere between direct **patronage** and impersonal sales. A subscriber paid half the cost of a book before publication and half on delivery. The author received these payments directly. The subscriber's name appeared in the prefatory pages.

textual criticism: Works in all periods often exist in many subtly or not so subtly different forms. This is especially true with regard to manuscript textual reproduction, but it also applies to printed texts. Textual criticism is the art, developed from the fifteenth century in Italy but raised to new levels of sophistication from the eighteenth century, of deciphering different historical states of texts. This art involves the analysis of textual **variants,** often with the aim of distinguishing authorial from scribal forms.

variant: differences that appear among different manuscripts or printed editions of the same text.

vellum: animal skin, used as the material for handwritten books before the introduction of paper. See also **parchment.**

watermark: the trademark of a paper manufacturer, impressed into the paper but largely invisible unless held up to light.

Geographic Nomenclature

The British Isles refers to the prominent group of islands off the northwest coast of Europe, especially to the two largest, **Great Britain** and **Ireland**. At present these comprise two sovereign states: **the Republic of Ireland**, or **Éire**, and **the United Kingdom of Great Britain and Northern Ireland**—known for short as the **United Kingdom** or the **U.K.** Most of the smaller islands are part of the **U.K.** but a few, like the **Isle of Man** and the tiny **Channel Islands**, are largely independent. The **U.K.** is often loosely referred to as "**Britain**" or "**Great Britain**" and is sometimes called simply, if inaccurately, "**England.**" For obvious reasons, the latter usage is rarely heard among the inhabitants of the other countries of the **U.K.**—**Scotland, Wales,** and **Northern Ireland** (sometimes called **Ulster**). England is by far the most populous part of the kingdom, as well as the seat of its capital, London.

From the first to the fifth century C.E. most of what is now **England** and **Wales** was a province of the Roman Empire called **Britain** (in Latin, **Britannia**). After the fall of Rome, much of the island was invaded and settled by peoples from northern Germany and Denmark speaking what we now call Old English. These peoples are collectively known as the Anglo-Saxons, and the word **England** is related to the first element of their name. By the time of the Norman Conquest (1066) most of the kingdoms founded by the Anglo-Saxons and subsequent Viking invaders had coalesced into the kingdom of **England,** which, in the latter Middle Ages, conquered and largely absorbed the neighboring Celtic kingdom of **Wales.** In 1603 James VI of **Scotland** inherited the island's other throne as James I of **England,** and for the next hundred years—except for the brief period of Puritan rule—**Scotland** (both its English-speaking **Lowlands** and its Gaelic-speaking **Highlands**) and **England** (with **Wales**) were two kingdoms under a single king. In 1707 the Act of Union welded them together as **the United Kingdom of Great Britain. Ireland,** where English rule had begun in the twelfth century and been tightened in the sixteenth, was incorporated by the 1800–1801 Act of Union into **the United Kingdom of Great Britain and Ireland**. With the division of Ireland and the establishment of **the Irish Free State** after World War I, this name was modified to its present form, and in 1949 **the Irish Free State** became **the Republic of Ireland**. In 1999 **Scotland** elected a separate parliament it had relinquished in 1707, and **Wales** elected an assembly it lost in 1409; neither Scotland nor Wales ceased to be part of the **United Kingdom**.

The **British Isles** are further divided into counties, which in **Great Britain** are also known as shires. This word, with its vowel shortened in pronunciation, forms the suffix in the names of many counties, such as **Yorkshire, Wiltshire, Somersetshire.**

The Latin names **Britannia (Britain), Caledonia (Scotland),** and **Hibernia (Ireland)** are sometimes used in poetic diction; so too is **Britain's** ancient Celtic name, **Albion.** Because of its accidental resemblance to *albus* (Latin for "white"), **Albion** is especially associated with the chalk cliffs that seem to gird much of the English coast like defensive walls.

The British Empire took its name from **the British Isles** because it was created not only by the **English** but also by the **Irish, Scots,** and **Welsh,** as well as by civilians and servicemen from other constituent countries of the empire. Some of the empire's **overseas colonies,** or **crown colonies,** were populated largely by settlers of European origin and their descendants. These predominantly white **settler colonies,** such as **Canada, Australia,** and **New Zealand,** were allowed significant self-government in the nineteenth century and recognized as **dominions** in the early twentieth century. The **white dominions** became members of **the Commonwealth**

of Nations, also called the Commonwealth, the British Commonwealth, and "the Old Commonwealth" at different times, an association of sovereign states under the symbolic leadership of the British monarch.

Other overseas colonies of the empire had mostly indigenous populations (or, in the Caribbean, the descendants of imported slaves, indentured servants, and others). These colonies were granted political independence after World War II, later than the dominions, and have often been referred to since as postcolonial nations. In South and Southeast Asia, India and Pakistan gained independence in 1947, followed by other countries including Sri Lanka (formerly Ceylon), Burma (now Myanmar), Malaya (now Malaysia), and Singapore. In West and East Africa, the Gold Coast was decolonized as Ghana in 1957, Nigeria in 1960, Sierra Leone in 1961, Uganda in 1962, Kenya in 1963, and so forth, while in southern Africa, the white minority government of South Africa was already independent in 1931, though majority rule did not come until 1994. In the Caribbean, Jamaica and Trinidad and Tobago won independence in 1962, followed by Barbados in 1966, and other islands of the British West Indies in the 1970s and '80s. Other regions with nations emerging out of British colonial rule included Central America (British Honduras, now Belize), South America (British Guiana, now Guyana), the Pacific islands (Fiji), and Europe (Cyprus, Malta). After decolonization, many of these nations chose to remain within a newly conceived Commonwealth and are sometimes referred to as "New Commonwealth" countries. Some nations, such as Ireland, Pakistan, and South Africa, withdrew from the Commonwealth, though South Africa and Pakistan eventually rejoined, and others, such as Burma (Myanmar), gained independence outside the Commonwealth. Britain's last major overseas colony, Hong Kong, was returned to Chinese sovereignty in 1997, but while Britain retains only a handful of dependent territories, such as Bermuda and Montserrat, the scope of the Commonwealth remains vast, with 30 percent of the world's population.

British Money

One of the most dramatic changes to the system of British money came in 1971. In the system previously in place, the pound consisted of 20 shillings, each containing 12 pence, making 240 pence to the pound. Since 1971, British money has been calculated on the decimal system, with 100 pence to the pound. Britons' experience of paper money did not change very drastically: as before, 5- and 10-pound notes constitute the majority of bills passing through their hands (in addition, 20- and 50- pound notes have been added). But the shift necessitated a whole new way of thinking about and exchanging coins and marked the demise of the shilling, one of the fundamental units of British monetary history. Many other coins, still frequently encountered in literature, had already passed. These include the groat, worth 4 pence (the word "groat" is often used to signify a trifling sum); the angel (which depicted the archangel Michael triumphing over a dragon), valued at 10 shillings; the mark, worth in its day two-thirds of a pound or 13 shillings 4 pence; and the sovereign, a gold coin initially worth 22 shillings 6 pence, later valued at 1 pound, last circulated in 1932. One prominent older coin, the guinea, was worth a pound and a shilling; though it has not been minted since 1813, a very few quality items or prestige awards (like the purse in a horse race) may still be quoted in guineas. (The table below includes some other well-known, obsolete coins.) Colloquially, a pound was (and is) called a quid; a shilling a bob; sixpence, a tanner; a copper could refer to a penny, a half-penny, or a farthing (¼ penny).

Old Currency	New Currency
1 pound note	1 pound coin (or note in Scotland)
10 shilling (half-pound note)	50 pence
5 shilling (crown)	
2½ shilling (half crown)	20 pence
2 shilling (florin)	10 pence
1 shilling	5 pence
6 pence	
2½ pence	1 penny
2 pence	
1 penny	
½ penny	
¼ penny (farthing)	

In recent years, the British government and people have been contemplating and debating a change even greater than the shift to the decimal system. Britain, a member of the European Union, may adopt the EU's common currency, the Euro, and eventually see the pound itself become obsolete. More than many other EU-member countries, Britain has resisted this change: many people strongly identify

their country with its rich commercial history and tend to view their currency patri-
otically as a national symbol.

Even more challenging than sorting out the values of obsolete coins is calculating
for any given period the purchasing power of money, which fluctuates over time by its
very nature. At the beginning of the twentieth century, 1 pound was worth about 5
American dollars, though those bought three to four times what they now do. Now,
the pound buys anywhere from $1.50 to $1.90. As difficult as it is to generalize, it is
clear that money used to be worth much more than it is currently. In Anglo-Saxon
times, the most valuable circulating coin was the silver penny: four would buy a
sheep. Beyond long-term inflationary trends, prices varied from times of plenty to
those marked by poor harvests; from peacetime to wartime; from the country to the
metropolis (life in London has always been very expensive); and wages varied according to the availability of labor (wages would sharply rise, for instance, during the
devastating Black Death in the fourteenth century). The chart below provides a
glimpse of some actual prices of given periods and their changes across time, though
all the variables mentioned above prevent them from being definitive. Even from one
year to the next, an added tax on gin or tea could drastically raise prices, and a lottery
ticket could cost much more the night before the drawing than just a month earlier.
Still, the prices quoted below do indicate important trends, such as the disparity of
incomes in British society and the costs of basic commodities. In the chart below, the
symbol £ is used for pound, s. for shilling, d. for a penny (from Latin *denarius*); a sum
would normally be written £2.19.3, i.e., 2 pounds, 19 shillings, 3 pence. (This is Leopold Bloom's budget for the day depicted in Joyce's novel *Ulysses* [1922]; in the new
currency, it would be about £2.96.)

circa	1390	1590	1650	1750	1815	1875	1950
food and drink	gallon (8 pints) of ale, 1.5d.	tankard of beer, .5d.	coffee, 1d. a dish	"drunk for a penny, dead drunk for two-pence" (gin shop sign in Hogarth print)	ounce of laudanum, 3d.	pint of beer, 3d.	pint of Guinness stout, 11d.
	gallon (8 pints) of wine, 3 to 4d.	pound of beef, 2s. 5d.	chicken, 1s. 4d.	dinner at a steakhouse, 1s.	ham and potato dinner for two, 7s.	dinner in a good hotel, 5s.	pound of beef, 2s. 2d.
	pound of cinnamon, 1 to 3s.	pound of cinnamon, 10s. 6d.	pound of tea, £3 10s.	pound of tea, 16s.	Prince Regent's dinner party for 2000, £12.000	pound of tea, 2s.	dinner on railway car, 7s. 6d.
entertainment	no cost to watch a cycle play	admission to public theater, 1 to 3d.	falcon, £11s. 5d.	theater tickets, 1 to 5s.	admission to Covent Garden theater, 1 to 7s.	theater tickets, 6d. to 7s.	admission to Old Vic theater, 1s. 6d. to 10s. 6d.
	contributory admission to professional troupe theater	cheap seat in private theater, 6d.	billiard table, £25	admission to Vauxhall Gardens, 1s.	annual subscription to Almack's (exclusive club), 10 guineas	admission to Madam Tussaud's waxworks, 1s.	admission to Odeon cinema, Manchester, 1s 3d.
	maintenance for royal hounds at Windsor, .75d. a day	"to see a dead Indian" (quoted in *The Tempest*), 1.25d. (ten "doits")	three-quarter length portrait painting, £31	lottery ticket, £20 (shares were sold)	Jane Austen's piano, 30 guineas	annual fees at a gentleman's club, 7 to 10 guineas	tropical fish tank, £4 4s.

circa	1390	1590	1650	1750	1815	1875	1950
reading	cheap romance, 1s.	play quarto, 6d.	pamphlet, 1 to 6d.	issue of The Gentleman's Magazine, 6d.	issue of Edinburgh Review, 6s.	copy of The Times, 3d.	copy of The Times, 3d.
	a Latin Bible, 2 to £4	Shakespeare's First Folio (1623), £1	student Bible, 6s.	cheap edition of Milton, 2s.	membership in circulating library (3rd class), £1 4s. a year	illustrated edition of Through the Looking-glass, 6s.	issue of Eagle comics, 4.5d.
	payment for illuminating a liturgical book, £22 9s.	Foxe's Acts and Monuments, 24s.	Hobbes's Leviathan, 8s.	Johnson's Dictionary, folio, 2 vols., £4 10s.	1st edition of Austen's Pride and Prejudice, 18s.	1st edition of Trollope's The Way We Live Now, 2 vols, £1 1s.	Orwell's Nineteen Eighty-Four, paperback, 3s. 6d.
transportation	night's supply of hay for horse, 2d.	wherry (whole boat) across Thames, 1d.	day's journey, coach, 10s.	boat across Thames, 4d.	coach ride, outside, 2 to 3d. a mile; inside, 4 to 5d. a mile	15-minute journey in a London cab, 1s. 6d.	London tube fare, about 2d. a mile
	coach, £8	hiring a horse for a day, 12d.	coach horse, £30	coach fare, London to Edinburgh, £4 10s.	palanquin transport in Madras, 5s. a day	railway, 3rd class, London to Plymouth, 18s.	petrol, 3s. a gallon
						8d. (about 1d. a mile)	
	quality horse, £10	hiring a coach for a day, 10s.	fancy carriage, £170	transport to America, £5	passage, Liverpool to New York, £10	passage to India, 1st class, £50	midsize Austin sedan, £449 plus £188 4s. 2d. tax
clothes	clothing allowance for peasant, 3s. a year	shoes with buckles, 8d.	footman's frieze coat, 15s.	working woman's gown, 6s. 6d.	checked muslin, 7s. per yard	flannel for a cheap petticoat, 1s. 3d. a yard	woman's sun frock, £3 13s. 10d.

labor/incomes							
	shoes for gentry wearer, 4d.	woman's gloves, £1 5s.	falconer's hat, 10s.	gentleman's suit, £8	hiring a dressmaker for a pelisse, 8s.	overcoat for an Eton schoolboy, £1 1s.	tweed sports jacket, £3 16s. 6d.
	hat for gentry wearer, 10d.	fine cloak, £16	black cloth for mourning household of an earl, £100	very fine wig, £30	ladies silk stockings, 12s.	set of false teeth, £2 10s.	"Teddy boy" drape suit, £20
	hiring a skilled building worker, 4d. a day	actor's daily wage during playing season, 1s.	price of boy slave, £32	agricultural laborer, 6s. 5d. a week	lowest-paid sailor on Royal Navy ship, 10s. 9d. a month	seasonal agricultural laborer, 14s. a week	minimum wage, agricultural laborer, £4 14s. per 47-hour week
	wage for professional scribe, £2 3s. 4d. a year + cloak	household servant 2 to £5 a year + food, clothing	tutor to nobleman's children, £30 a year	housemaid's wage, £6 to £8 a year	contributor to Quarterly Review, 10 guineas per sheet	housemaid's wage, £10 to £25 a year	shorthand typist, £367 a year
	minimum income to be called gentleman £10 a year; for knighthood, 40 to £400	minimum income for eligibility for knighthood, £30 a year	Milton's salary as Secretary of Foreign Tongues, £288 a year	Boswell's allowance, £200 a year	minimum income for a "genteel" family, £100 a year	income of the "comfortable" classes, £800 and up a year	middle manager's salary, £1,480 a year
	income from land of richest magnates, £3,500 a year	income from land of average earl, £4000 a year	Earl of Bedford's income, £8,000 a year	Duke of Newcastle's income, £40,000 a year	Mr. Darcy's income, *Pride and Prejudice*, £10,000	Trollope's income, £4,000 a year	barrister's salary, £2,032 a year

The British Baronage

The English monarchy is in principle hereditary, though at times during the Middle Ages the rules were subject to dispute. In general, authority passes from father to eldest surviving son, from daughters in order of seniority if there is no son, to a brother if there are no children, and in default of direct descendants to collateral lines (cousins, nephews, nieces) in order of closeness. There have been breaks in the order of succession (1066, 1399, 1688), but so far as possible the usurpers have always sought to paper over the break with a legitimate, i.e., hereditary, claim. When a queen succeeds to the throne and takes a husband, he does not become king unless he is in the line of blood succession; rather, he is named prince consort, as Albert was to Victoria. He may father kings, but is not one himself.

The original Saxon nobles were the king's thanes, ealdormen, or earls, who provided the king with military service and counsel in return for booty, gifts, or landed estates. William the Conqueror, arriving from France, where feudalism was fully developed, considerably expanded this group. In addition, as the king distributed the lands of his new kingdom, he also distributed dignities to men who became known collectively as "the baronage." "Baron" in its root meaning signifies simply "man," and barons were the king's men. As the title was common, a distinction was early made between greater and lesser barons, the former gradually assuming loftier and more impressive titles. The first English "duke" was created in 1337; the title of "marquess," or "marquis" (pronounced "markwis"), followed in 1385, and "viscount" ("vyekount") in 1440. Though "earl" is the oldest title of all, an earl now comes between a marquess and a viscount in order of dignity and precedence, and the old term "baron" now designates a rank just below viscount. "Baronets" were created in 1611 as a means of raising revenue for the crown (the title could be purchased for about £1000); they are marginal nobility and have never sat in the House of Lords.

Kings and queens are addressed as "Your Majesty," princes and princesses as "Your Highness," the other hereditary nobility as "My Lord" or "Your Lordship." Peers receive their titles either by inheritance (like Lord Byron, the sixth baron of that line) or from the monarch (like Alfred Lord Tennyson, created first Baron Tennyson by Victoria). The children, even of a duke, are commoners unless they are specifically granted some other title or inherit their father's title from him. A peerage can be forfeited by act of attainder, as for example when a lord is convicted of treason; and, when forfeited, or lapsed for lack of a successor, can be bestowed on another family. Thus in 1605 Robert Cecil was made first earl of Salisbury in the third creation, the first creation dating from 1149, the second from 1337, the title having been in abeyance since 1539. Titles descend by right of succession and do not depend on tenure of land; thus, a title does not always indicate where a lord dwells or holds power. Indeed, noble titles do not always refer to a real place at all. At Prince Edward's marriage in 1999, the queen created him earl of Wessex, although the old kingdom of Wessex has had no political existence since the Anglo-Saxon period, and the name was all but forgotten until it was resurrected by Thomas Hardy as the setting of his novels. (This is perhaps but one of many ways in which the world of the aristocracy increasingly resembles the realm of literature.)

Scottish peers sat in the parliament of Scotland, as English peers did in the parliament of England, till at the Act of Union (1707) Scottish peers were granted sixteen

The king and queen	(These are all of the royal line.)
Prince and princess	
Duke and duchess	(These may or may not be of the royal line, but are ordinarily remote from the succession.)
Marquess and marchioness	
Earl and countess	
Viscount and viscountess	
Baron and baroness	
Baronet and lady	

seats in the English House of Lords, to be filled by election. (In 1963, all Scottish lords were allowed to sit.) Similarly, Irish peers, when the Irish parliament was abolished in 1801, were granted the right to elect twenty-eight of their number to the House of Lords in Westminster. (Now that the Republic of Ireland is a separate nation, this no longer applies.) Women members (peeresses) were first allowed to sit in the House as nonhereditary Life Peers in 1958 (when that status was created for members of both genders); women first sat by their own hereditary right in 1963. Today the House of Lords still retains some power to influence or delay legislation, but its future is uncertain. In 1999, the hereditary peers (then amounting to 750) were reduced to 92 temporary members elected by their fellow peers. Holders of Life Peerages remain, as do senior bishops of the Church of England and high-court judges (the "Law Lords").

Below the peerage the chief title of honor is "knight." Knighthood, which is not hereditary, is generally a reward for services rendered. A knight (Sir John Black) is addressed, using his first name, as "Sir John"; his wife, using the last name, is "Lady Black"—unless she is the daughter of an earl or nobleman of higher rank, in which case she will be "Lady Arabella." The female equivalent of a knight bears the title of "Dame." Though the word itself comes from the Anglo-Saxon *cniht*, there is some doubt as to whether knighthood amounted to much before the arrival of the Normans. The feudal system required military service as a condition of land tenure, and a man who came to serve his king at the head of an army of tenants required a title of authority and badges of identity—hence the title of knighthood and the coat of arms. During the Crusades, when men were far removed from their land (or even sold it in order to go on crusade), more elaborate forms of fealty sprang up that soon expanded into orders of knighthood. The Templars, Hospitallers, Knights of the Teutonic Order, Knights of Malta, and Knights of the Golden Fleece were but a few of these companionships; not all of them were available at all times in England.

Gradually, with the rise of centralized government and the decline of feudal tenures, military knighthood became obsolete, and the rank largely honorific; sometimes, as under James I, it degenerated into a scheme of the royal government for making money. For hundreds of years after its establishment in the fourteenth century, the Order of the Garter was the only English order of knighthood, an exclusive courtly companionship. Then, during the late seventeenth, the eighteenth, and the nineteenth centuries, a number of additional orders were created, with names such as the Thistle, Saint Patrick, the Bath, Saint Michael and Saint George, plus a number of special Victorian and Indian orders. They retain the terminology, ceremony, and dignity of knighthood, but the military implications are vestigial.

Although the British Empire now belongs to history, appointments to the Order of the British Empire continue to be conferred for services to that empire at home or abroad. Such honors (commonly referred to as "gongs") are granted by the monarch in her New Year's and Birthday lists, but the decisions are now made by the government in power. In recent years there have been efforts to popularize and democratize the dispensation of honors, with recipients including rock stars and actors. But this does not prevent large sectors of British society from regarding both knighthood and the peerage as largely irrelevant to modern life.

The Royal Lines of England and Great Britain

England

SAXONS AND DANES

Egbert, king of Wessex	802–839
Ethelwulf, son of Egbert	839–858
Ethelbald, second son of Ethelwulf	858–860
Ethelbert, third son of Ethelwulf	860–866
Ethelred I, fourth son of Ethelwulf	866–871
Alfred the Great, fifth son of Ethelwulf	871–899
Edward the Elder, son of Alfred	899–924
Athelstan the Glorious, son of Edward	924–940
Edmund I, third son of Edward	940–946
Edred, fourth son of Edward	946–955
Edwy the Fair, son of Edmund	955–959
Edgar the Peaceful, second son of Edmund	959–975
Edward the Martyr, son of Edgar	975–978 (murdered)
Ethelred II, the Unready, second son of Edgar	978–1016
Edmund II, Ironside, son of Ethelred II	1016–1016
Canute the Dane	1016–1035
Harold I, Harefoot, natural son of Canute	1035–1040
Hardecanute, son of Canute	1040–1042
Edward the Confessor, son of Ethelred II	1042–1066
Harold II, brother-in-law of Edward	1066–1066 (died in battle)

HOUSE OF NORMANDY

William I the Conqueror	1066–1087
William II, Rufus, third son of William I	1087–1100 (shot from ambush)
Henry I, Beauclerc, youngest son of William I	1100–1135

HOUSE OF BLOIS

Stephen, son of Adela, daughter of William I	1135–1154

HOUSE OF PLANTAGENET

Henry II, son of Geoffrey Plantagenet by Matilda, daughter of Henry I	1154–1189
Richard I, Coeur de Lion, son of Henry II	1189–1199
John Lackland, son of Henry II	1199–1216
Henry III, son of John	1216–1272
Edward I, Longshanks, son of Henry III	1272–1307
Edward II, son of Edward I	1307–1327 (deposed)
Edward III of Windsor, son of Edward II	1327–1377
Richard II, grandson of Edward III	1377–1399 (deposed)

HOUSE OF LANCASTER

Henry IV, son of John of Gaunt, son of Edward III	1399–1413
Henry V, Prince Hal, son of Henry IV	1413–1422
Henry VI, son of Henry V	1422–1461 (deposed), 1470–1471 (deposed)

HOUSE OF YORK

Edward IV, great-great-grandson of Edward III	1461–1470 (deposed), 1471–1483
Edward V, son of Edward IV	1483–1483 (murdered)
Richard III, Crookback	1483–1485 (died in battle)

HOUSE OF TUDOR

Henry VII, married daughter of Edward IV	1485–1509
Henry VIII, son of Henry VII	1509–1547
Edward VI, son of Henry VIII	1547–1553
Mary I, "Bloody," daughter of Henry VIII	1553–1558
Elizabeth I, daughter of Henry VIII	1558–1603

HOUSE OF STUART

James I (James VI of Scotland)	1603–1625
Charles I, son of James I	1625–1649 (executed)

COMMONWEALTH & PROTECTORATE

Council of State	1649–1653
Oliver Cromwell, Lord Protector	1653–1658
Richard Cromwell, son of Oliver	1658–1660 (resigned)

HOUSE OF STUART (RESTORED)

Charles II, son of Charles I	1660–1685
James II, second son of Charles I	1685–1688

(INTERREGNUM, 11 DECEMBER 1688 TO 13 FEBRUARY 1689)

William III of Orange, by	
Mary, daughter of Charles I	1689–1701
and Mary II, daughter of James II	–1694
Anne, second daughter of James II	1702–1714

Great Britain

HOUSE OF HANOVER

George I, son of Elector of Hanover and	
Sophia, granddaughter of James I	1714–1727
George II, son of George I	1727–1760
George III, grandson of George II	1760–1820
George IV, son of George III	1820–1830
William IV, third son of George III	1830–1837
Victoria, daughter of Edward, fourth son	
of George III	1837–1901

HOUSE OF SAXE-COBURG AND GOTHA

Edward VII, son of Victoria	1901–1910

HOUSE OF WINDSOR (NAME ADOPTED 17 JULY 1917)

George V, second son of Edward VII	1910–1936
Edward VIII, eldest son of George V	1936–1936 (abdicated)
George VI, second son of George V	1936–1952
Elizabeth II, daughter of George VI	1952–

Religions in England

In the sixth century C.E., missionaries from Ireland and the Continent introduced Christianity to the Anglo-Saxons—actually, reintroduced it, since it had briefly flourished in the southern parts of the British Isles during the Roman occupation, and even after the Roman withdrawal had persisted in the Celtic regions of Scotland and Wales. By the time the earliest poems included in the *Norton Anthology* were composed, therefore, the English people had been Christians for hundreds of years; such Anglo-Saxon poems as "The Dream of the Rood" bear witness to their faith. Our knowledge of the religion of pre-Christian Britain is sketchy, but it is likely that vestiges of paganism assimilated into, or coexisted with, the practice of Christianity: fertility rites were incorporated into the celebration of Easter resurrection, rituals commemorating the dead into All-Hallows Eve and All Saints Day, and elements of winter solstice festivals into the celebration of Christmas. In English literature such "folkloric" elements often elicit romantic nostalgia. Geoffrey Chaucer's Wife of Bath looks back to a magical time before the arrival of Christianity in which the land was "fulfilled of fairye." Hundreds of years later, the seventeenth-century writer Robert Herrick honors the amalgamation of Christian and pagan elements in agrarian British culture in such poems as "Corinna's Gone A-Maying" and "The Hock Cart."

Medieval Christianity was fairly uniform across Western Europe—hence called "catholic," or universally shared—and its rituals and expectations, common to the whole community, permeated everyday life. The Catholic Church was also an international power structure. In its hierarchy of pope, cardinals, archbishops, and bishops, it resembled the feudal state, but the church power structure coexisted alongside a separate hierarchy of lay authorities with a theoretically different sphere of social responsibilities. The sharing out of lay and ecclesiastical authority in medieval England was sometimes a source of conflict. Chaucer's pilgrims are on their way to visit the memorial shrine to one victim of such struggle: Thomas a Becket, Archbishop of Canterbury, who opposed the policies of King Henry III, was assassinated on the king's orders in 1120 and later made a saint. As an international organization, the church conducted its business in the universal language of Latin, and thus although statistically in the period the largest segment of literate persons were monks and priests, the clerical contribution to great writing in English was relatively modest. Yet the lay writers of the period reflect the importance of the church as an institution and the pervasiveness of religion in everyday life.

Beginning in 1517 the German monk Martin Luther, in Wittenberg, Germany, openly challenged many aspects of Catholic practice and by 1520 had completely repudiated the authority of the Pope, setting in train the Protestant Reformation. Luther argued that the Roman Catholic Church had strayed far from the pattern of Christianity laid out in scripture. He rejected Catholic doctrines for which no biblical authority was to be found, such as the belief in Purgatory, and translated the Bible into German, on the grounds that the importance of scripture for all Christians made its translation into the vernacular tongue essential. Luther was not the first to advance such views—followers of the Englishman John Wycliffe had translated the Bible in the fourteenth century. But Luther, protected by powerful German rulers, was able to speak out with impunity and convert others to his views, rather than suffer the persecution usually meted out to heretics. Soon other reformers were following in Luther's footsteps: of these, the Swiss Ulrich Zwingli and the French Jean Calvin would be especially influential for English religious thought.

At first England remained staunchly Catholic. Its king, Henry VIII, was so severe to heretics that the Pope awarded him the title "Defender of the Faith," which British monarchs have retained to this day. In 1534, however, Henry rejected the authority of the Pope to prevent his divorce from his queen, Catherine of Aragon, and his marriage to his mistress, Ann Boleyn. In doing so, Henry appropriated to himself ecclesiastical as well as secular authority. Thomas More, author of *Utopia*, was executed for refusing to endorse Henry's right to govern the English church. Over the following six years, Henry consolidated his grip on the ecclesiastical establishment by dissolving the powerful, populous Catholic monasteries and redistributing their massive landholdings to his own lay followers. Yet Henry's church largely retained Catholic doctrine and liturgy. When Henry died and his young son, Edward, came to the throne in 1547, the English church embarked on a more Protestant path, a direction abruptly reversed when Edward died and his older sister Mary, the daughter of Catherine of Aragon, took the throne in 1553 and attempted to reintroduce Roman Catholicism. Mary's reign was also short, however, and her successor, Elizabeth I, the daughter of Ann Boleyn, was a Protestant. Elizabeth attempted to establish a "middle way" Christianity, compromising between Roman Catholic practices and beliefs and reformed ones.

The Church of England, though it laid claim to a national rather than pan-European authority, aspired like its predecessor to be the universal church of all English subjects. It retained the Catholic structure of parishes and dioceses and the Catholic hierarchy of bishops, though the ecclesiastical authority was now the Archbishop of Canterbury and the Church's "Supreme Governor" was the monarch. Yet disagreement and controversy persisted. Some members of the Church of England wanted to retain many of the ritual and liturgical elements of Catholicism. Others, the Puritans, advocated a more thoroughgoing reformation. Most Puritans remained within the Church of England, but a minority, the "Separatists" or "Congregationalists," split from the established church altogether. These dissenters no longer the ideal church thought of as an organization to which everybody belonged; instead, they conceived it as a more exclusive group of likeminded people, one not necessarily attached to a larger body of believers.

In the seventeenth century, the succession of the Scottish king James to the English throne produced another problem. England and Scotland were separate nations, and in the sixteenth century Scotland had developed its own national Presbyterian church, or "kirk," under the leadership of the reformer John Knox. The kirk retained fewer Catholic liturgical elements than did the Church of England, and its authorities, or "presbyters," were elected by assemblies of their fellow clerics, rather than appointed by the king. James I and his son Charles I, especially the latter, wanted to bring the Scottish kirk into conformity with Church of England practices. The Scots violently resisted these efforts, with the collaboration of many English Puritans, in a conflict that eventually developed into the English Civil War in the mid-seventeenth century. The effect of these disputes is visible in the poetry of such writers as John Milton, Robert Herrick, Henry Vaughan, and Thomas Traherne, and in the prose of Thomas Browne, Lucy Hutchinson, and Dorothy Waugh. Just as in the mid-sixteenth century, when a succession of monarchs with different religious commitments destabilized the church, so the seventeenth century endured spiritual whiplash. King Charles I's highly ritualistic Church of England was violently overturned by the Puritan victors in the Civil War—until 1660, after the death of the Puritan leader, Oliver Cromwell, when the Church of England was restored along with the monarchy.

The religious and political upheavals of the seventeenth century produced Christian sects that de-emphasized the ceremony of the established church and rejected as well its top-down authority structure. Some of these groups were ephemeral, but the Baptists (founded in 1608 in Amsterdam by the English expatriate John Smyth) and Quakers, or Society of Friends (founded by George Fox in the 1640s), flourished outside the established church, sometimes despite cruel persecution. John Bunyan, a Baptist, wrote the Christian allegory *Pilgrim's Progress* while in prison.

Some dissenters, like the Baptists, shared the reformed reverence for the absolute authority of scripture but interpreted the scriptural texts differently from their fellow Protestants. Others, like the Quakers, favored, even over the authority of the Bible, the "inner light" or voice of individual conscience, which they took to be the working of the Holy Spirit in the lives of individuals.

The Protestant dissenters were not England's only religious minorities. Despite crushing fines and the threat of imprisonment, a minority of Catholics under Elizabeth and James openly refused to give their allegiance to the new church, and others remained secret adherents to the old ways. John Donne was brought up in an ardently Catholic family, and several other writers converted to Catholicism as adults—Ben Jonson for a considerable part of his career, Elizabeth Carey and Richard Crashaw permanently, and at profound personal cost. In the eighteenth century, Catholics remained objects of suspicion as possible agents of sedition, especially after the "Glorious Revolution" in 1688 deposed the Catholic James II in favor of the Protestant William and Mary. Anti-Catholic prejudice affected John Dryden, a Catholic convert, as well as the lifelong Catholic Alexander Pope. By contrast, the English colony of Ireland remained overwhelmingly Roman Catholic, the fervor of its religious commitment at least partly inspired by resistance to English occupation. Starting in the reign of Elizabeth, England shored up its own authority in Ireland by encouraging Protestant immigrants from Scotland to settle in northern Ireland, producing a virulent religious divide the effects of which are still playing out today.

A small community of Jews had moved from France to London after 1066, when the Norman William the Conqueror came to the English throne. Although despised and persecuted by many Christians, they were allowed to remain as moneylenders to the Crown, until the thirteenth century, when the king developed alternative sources of credit. At this point, in 1290, the Jews were expelled from England. In 1655 Oliver Cromwell permitted a few to return, and in the late seventeenth and early eighteenth centuries the Jewish population slowly increased, mainly by immigration from Germany. In the mid-eighteenth century some prominent Jews had their children brought up as Christians so as to facilitate their full integration into English society: thus the nineteenth-century writer and politician Benjamin Disraeli, although he and his father were members of the Church of England, was widely considered a Jew insofar as his ancestry was Jewish.

In the late seventeenth century, as the Church of England reasserted itself, Catholics, Jews, and dissenting Protestants found themselves subject to significant legal restrictions. The Corporation Act, passed in 1661, and the Test Act, passed in 1673, excluded all who refused to take communion in the Church of England from voting, attending university, or working in government or in the professions. Members of religious minorities, as well as Church of England communicants, paid mandatory taxes in support of Church of England ministers and buildings. In 1689 the dissenters gained the right to worship in public, but Jews and Catholics were not permitted to do so.

During the eighteenth century, political, intellectual, and religious history remained closely intertwined. The Church of England came to accommodate a good deal of variety. "Low church" services resembled those of the dissenting Protestant churches, minimizing ritual and emphasizing the sermon; the "high church" retained more elaborate ritual elements, yet its prestige was under attack on several fronts. Many Enlightenment thinkers subjected the Bible to rational critique and found it wanting: the philosopher David Hume, for instance, argued that the "miracles" described therein were more probably lies or errors than real breaches of the laws of nature. Within the Church of England, the "broad church" Latitudinarians welcomed this rationalism, advocating theological openness and an emphasis on ethics rather than dogma. More radically, the Unitarian movement rejected the divinity of Christ while professing to accept his ethical teachings. Taking a different tack, the preacher John Wesley, founder of Methodism, responded to the rationalists' challenge with a newly fervent call to evangelism and personal discipline; his movement was particularly successful in Wales. Revolutions in America and France at the end of the century generated considerable millenarian excitement and fostered more new religious ideas, often in conjunction with a radical social agenda. Many important writers of the Romantic period were indebted to traditions of protestant dissent: Unitarian and rationalist protestant ideas influenced William Hazlitt, Anna Barbauld, Mary Wollstonecraft, and the young Samuel Taylor Coleridge. William Blake created a highly idiosyncratic poetic mythology loosely indebted to radical strains of Christian mysticism. Others were even more heterodox: Lord Byron and Robert Burns, brought up as Scots Presbyterians, rebelled fiercely, and Percy Shelley's writing of an atheistic pamphlet resulted in his expulsion from Oxford.

Great Britain never erected an American-style "wall of separation" between church and state, but in practice religion and secular affairs grew more and more distinct during the nineteenth century. In consequence, members of religious minorities no longer seemed to pose a threat to the commonweal. A movement to repeal the Test Act failed in the 1790s, but a renewed effort resulted in the extension of the franchise to dissenting Protestants in 1828 and to Catholics in 1829. The numbers of Roman Catholics in England were swelled by immigration from Ireland, but there were also some prominent English adherents. Among writers, the converts John Newman and Gerard Manley Hopkins are especially important. The political participation and social integration of Jews presented a thornier challenge. Lionel de Rothschild, repeatedly elected to represent London in Parliament during the 1840s and 1850s, was not permitted to take his seat there because he refused to take his oath of office "on the true faith of a Christian"; finally, in 1858, the Jewish Disabilities Act allowed him to omit these words. Only in 1871, however, were Oxford and Cambridge opened to non-Anglicans.

Meanwhile geological discoveries and Charles Darwin's evolutionary theories increasingly cast doubt on the literal truth of the Creation story, and close philological analysis of the biblical text suggested that its origins were human rather than divine. By the end of the nineteenth century, many writers were bearing witness to a world in which Christianity no longer seemed fundamentally plausible. In his poetry and prose, Thomas Hardy depicts a world devoid of benevolent providence. Matthew Arnold's poem "Dover Beach" is in part an elegy to lost spiritual assurance, as the "Sea of Faith" goes out like the tide: "But now I only hear / Its melancholy, long, withdrawing roar / Retreating." For Arnold, literature must replace religion as a source of spiritual truth, and intimacy between individuals substitute for the lost communal solidarity of the universal church.

The work of many twentieth-century writers shows the influence of a religious upbringing or a religious conversion in adulthood. T. S. Eliot and W. S. Auden embrace Anglicanism, William Butler Yeats spiritualism. James Joyce repudiates Irish Catholicism but remains obsessed with it. Yet religion, or lack of it, is a matter of individual choice and conscience, not social or legal mandate. In the past fifty years, church attendance has plummeted in Great Britain. Although 71 percent of the population still identified itself as "Christian" on the 2000 census, only about 7 percent of these regularly attend religious services of any denomination. Meanwhile, immigration from former British colonies has swelled the ranks of religions once alien to the British Isles—Muslim, Sikh, Hindu, Buddhist—though the numbers of adherents remain small relative to the total population.

THE UNIVERSE ACCORDING TO PTOLEMY

Ptolemy was a Roman astronomer of Greek descent, born in Egypt during the second century C.E.; for nearly fifteen hundred years after his death his account of the design of the universe was accepted as standard. During that time, the basic pattern underwent many detailed modifications and was fitted out with many astrological and pseudoscientific trappings. But in essence Ptolemy's followers portrayed the earth as the center of the universe, with the sun, planets, and fixed stars set in transparent spheres orbiting around it. In this scheme of things, as modified for Christian usage, Hell was usually placed under the earth's surface at the center of the cosmic globe, while Heaven, the abode of the blessed spirits, was in the outermost, uppermost circle, the empyrean. But in 1543 the Polish astronomer Copernicus proposed an alternative hypothesis—that the earth rotates around the sun, not vice versa; and despite theological opposition, observations with the new telescope and careful mathematical calculations insured ultimate acceptance of the new view.

The map of the Ptolemaic universe below is a simplified version of a diagram in Peter Apian's *Cosmography* (1584). In such a diagram, the Firmament is the sphere that contained the fixed stars; the Crystalline Sphere, which contained no heavenly bodies, is a late innovation, included to explain certain anomalies in the observed movement of the heavenly bodies; and the Prime Mover is the sphere that, itself put into motion by God, imparts rotation around the earth to all the other spheres.

Milton, writing in the mid-seventeenth century, used two universes. The Copernican universe, though he alludes to it, was too large, formless, and unfamiliar to be the setting for the war between Heaven and Hell in *Paradise Lost*. He therefore used the Ptolemaic cosmos, but placed Heaven well outside this smaller earth-centered universe, Hell far beneath it, and assigned the vast middle space to Chaos.

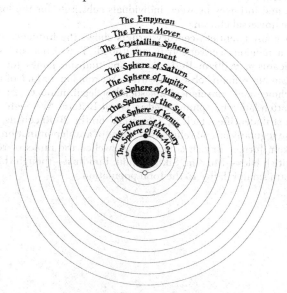

The Empyrean
The Prime Mover
The Crystalline Sphere
The Firmament
The Sphere of Saturn
The Sphere of Jupiter
The Sphere of Mars
The Sphere of the Sun
The Sphere of Venus
The Sphere of Mercury
The Sphere of the Moon

and C. M. Weekley, Executors of the Estate of Frieda Lawrence Ravagli. Used by permission of Viking Penguin, a division of Penguin Group (USA) Inc.

Ian McEwan: From ENDURING LOVE by Ian McEwan, copyright © 1997 by Ian McEwan. published by Vintage Books. Reprinted by permission of The Random House Group Ltd, Knopf Canada, and Doubleday, a division of Random House, Inc.

Alice Munro: "Walker Brothers Cowboy" from DANCE OF THE HAPPY SHADES by Alice Munro. Copyright © 1968 by Alice Munro. Published by Vintage Books. Reprinted by permission of the William Morris Agency, Inc., on behalf of the Author and Random House Group, Ltd. All rights reserved.

Jean Rhys: "The Day They Burned the Books" from TIGERS ARE BETTER-LOOKING: WITH A SELECTION FROM THE LEFT BANK by Jean Rhys (First published by Andre Deutsch 1968, Penguin Books 1972). "The Day They Burned the Books" (First published in The London Magazine) Copyright © Jean Rhys, 1960. Reprinted by permission of Ellen Moerman.

Christina Rossetti: "Cobwebs," "In an Artist's Studio," "Promises Like Piecrust," "In Progress," and "Cardinal Newman" from THE COMPLETE WORKS OF CHRISTINA ROSSETTI edited by R. W. Crump. Copyright © 1990 by Louisiana State University. Reprinted by permission of the Louisiana State University Press.

Salman Rushdie: "The Prophet's Hair" from EAST, WEST: STORIES by Salman Rushdie. Copyright © 1994 by Salman Rushdie. Published by Pantheon Books and Jonathan Cape. Reprinted by permission of Pantheon Books, a division of Random House, Inc., and The Random House Group Ltd.

Percy Bysshe Shelley: Poems from SHELLEY'S POETRY AND PROSE, SECOND EDITION by Percy Bysshe Shelley, edited by Donald H. Reiman & Neil Fraistat. Copyright © 2002 by Donald H. Reiman, Neil Fraistat and Rebecca Thompson. Copyright © 1977 by Donald H. Reiman Sharon B. Powers. Reprinted by permission of W. W. Norton & Company, Inc.

Zadie Smith: "The Waiter's Wife" by Zadie Smith from *Granta*, Vol. 67 (1999). Copyright © 1999 by Zadie Smith. Reproduced by permission of the author c/o Rogers, Coleridge & White Ltd., 20 Powis Mews, London W11 1JN.

Dylan Thomas: "The Force That Through the Green Fuse Drives the Flower" by Dylan Thomas. Copyright © 1939, 1943 by New Directions Publishing Corp. "Poem in October" and "Fern Hill" by Dylan Thomas. Copyright © 1945 by The Trustees for the Copyrights of Dylan Thomas, first published in POETRY. "Do Not Go Gentle into That Good Night" by Dylan Thomas. Copyright © 1952 by Dylan Thomas. All from THE POEMS OF DYLAN THOMAS. Reprinted by permission of New Directions Publishing Corp. and David Higham Associates.

Derek Walcott: "A Far Cry from Africa," Excerpt of 77 lines of *The Schooner Flight* and "The Season of Phantasmal Peace" from THE COLLECTED POEMS 1948–1984 by Derek Walcott. Copyright © 1986 by Derek Walcott. III" and "XLIX" from Books One and Six of OMEROS by Derek Walcott. Copyright © 1990 by Derek Walcott All Reprinted by permission of Faber & Faber and Farrar, Straus & Giroux, Inc.

Mary Wollstonecraft: From A VINDICATION OF THE RIGHTS OF WOMAN: A NORTON CRITICAL EDITION, Second Edition, by Mary Wollstonecraft, edited by Carol H. Poston. Copyright © 1988, 1975 by W. W. Norton & Company, Inc. Reprinted by permission of W. W. Norton & Company, Inc.

Virginia Woolf: "The Mark on the Wall" from A HAUNTED HOUSE AND OTHER SHORT STORIES by Virginia Woolf, copyright © 1944 and renewed 1972 by Harcourt, Inc., reprinted by permission of the publisher. "Modern Fiction" from THE COMMON READER by Virginia Woolf, copyright © 1925 by Harcourt, Inc., and renewed 1953 by Leonard Woolf. reprinted by permission of Houghton Mifflin Harcourt Publishing Company. "Professions for Women" from THE DEATH OF THE MOTH AND OTHER ESSAYS by Virginia Woolf, copyright © 1942 by Harcourt, Inc., and renewed 1970 by Marjorie T. Parsons, Executrix, reprinted by permission of the publisher. MRS. DALLOWAY by Virginia Woolf, copyright © 1925 by Houghton Mifflin Harcourt Publishing Company, and renewed 1953 by Leonard Woolf. Reprinted by permission of Houghton Mifflin Harcourt Publishing Company. All rights reserved.

Dorothy Wordsworth: Letter dated September 24, 1802 from THE GRASMERE JOURNALS, edited by Pamela Woof (1991). Reprinted by permission of Oxford University Press. "Grasmere—A Fragment" and "Thoughts on My Sick Bed" from DOROTHY WORDSWORTH AND ROMANTICISM. Reprinted by permission of The Wordsworth Trust, Dove Cottage, Grasmere.

William Wordsworth: Reprinted from William Wordsworth: THE RUINED COTTAGE AND THE PEDLAR. Edited by James A. Butler. Copyright © 1978 by Cornell University. Used by permission of the publisher, Cornell University Press. From THE PRELUDE 1799, 1805, 1850 by William Wordsworth: A Norton Critical Edition, edited by Jonathan Wordsworth, M. H. Abrams. Copyright © 1979 by W. W. Norton & Company, Inc. Used by permission of W. W. Norton & Company, Inc. "Ode to Duty" reprinted by permission of The Wordsworth Trust, Dover Cottage, Cumbria.

W. B. Yeats: "The Second Coming," reprinted with the permission Scribner, a Division of Simon & Schuster from THE COLLECTED WORKS OF W. B. YEATS, VOLUME I: THE POEMS, revised, edited by W. B. Yeats, edited by Richard J. Finneran. Copyright © 1924 by the Macmillian Company, renewed 1962 by Bertha Georgie Yeats. "Sailing to Byzantium," "Leda and the Swan" and "Among School Children" reprinted with the permission Scribner, a Division of Simon & Schuster from THE COLLECTED WORKS OF W. B. YEATS, VOLUME I: THE POEMS, revised, edited by W. B. Yeats, edited by Richard J. Finneran. Copyright © 1928 by Macmillan Publishing Company; copyright renewed © 1956 by Georgie Yeats. "A Dialogue of Self and Soul," "Crazy Jane Talks with the Bishop," and "Byzantium" reprinted with the permission Scribner, a Division of Simon & Schuster from THE COLLECTED WORKS OF W. B. YEATS, VOLUME I: THE POEMS, revised, edited by W. B. Yeats, edited by Richard J. Finneran. Copyright © 1933 by Macmillan Publishing Company; copyright renewed © 1961 by Bertha Georgie Yeats. "Lapis Lazuli," "The Circus Animals' Desertion," and "Under Ben Bulben" reprinted with the permission Scribner, a Division of Simon & Schuster from THE COLLECTED WORKS OF W. B. YEATS, VOLUME I: THE POEMS, revised, edited by W. B. Yeats, edited by Richard J. Finneran. Copyright © 1940 by Georgie Yeats; copyright renewed © 1968 by Bertha Georgie Yeats, Michael Butler Yeats, and Anne Yeats. From "A General Introduction to My Work," reprinted with the permission of Scribner, a Division of Simon & Schuster, Inc., from ESSAYS AND INTRODUCTIONS by W. B. Yeats. Copyright © 1961 by Mrs. W. B. Yeats. All rights reserved.

IMAGE CREDITS

COLOR INSERT CREDITS

Index